# "TO BE OR NOT TO BE?" MAY BE THE QUESTION. BUT HERE'S WHERE YOU WILL FIND ALL THE ANSWERS.

*How many ghosts appear in Shakespeare's plays?*
More than fourteen, including Caesar's ghost, Banquo's ghost, and the ghost of Hamlet's father. Eleven ghosts haunt Richard III. There are many "ghost characters" who appear in the stage directions but do not appear in the plays.

*In what play does Swinstead Abbey figure?*
A religious establishment in Lincolnshire, it is the setting for *King John* and the site of the death of King John. It is not, however, the site of King John's actual historical death.

*Who first played Lady Macbeth as a sex goddess?*
Dating to Sarah Bernhardt's bold interpretation of the role, this most famous of ambitious wives has been played as a woman who flaunts her charms to entice her husband to murder. And did you know her unlovely first name? It's Gruoch.

FASCINATING, FUN, AND VERY INFORMATIVE,
NO HOME OR SCHOOL LIBRARY SHOULD BE WITHOUT—

## Shakespeare A to Z

# SHAKESPEARE
# A TO Z

## THE ESSENTIAL REFERENCE TO HIS PLAYS, HIS POEMS, HIS LIFE AND TIMES, AND MORE

*Charles Boyce*

*Professor David White, Editorial Consultant*

*Foreword by Terry Hands,*
*Artistic Director,*
*Royal Shakespeare Company*

A Roundtable Press Book

*To Marya*

A LAUREL TRADE PAPERBACK
Published by
Dell Publishing
a division of
Bantam Doubleday Dell Publishing Group, Inc.
666 Fifth Avenue
New York, New York 10103

ISBN: 0-440-50429-5

Reprinted by arrangement with Facts on File, Inc.

Printed in the United States of America

Published simultaneously in Canada

December 1991

10  9  8  7  6  5  4  3  2  1

RRH

# TABLE OF CONTENTS

# FOREWORD

Shakespeare is celebrated the world over for the poetry and passion of his plays. He reformed the English language, enriching the vocabulary and increasing the flexibility of verse and prose. Supremely creative himself, he constantly inspired creativity in others. Above all, his profound humanity has enabled succeeding generations to rediscover within the dramatic intensity of his vision their own individual concerns. To many people, in many nations, Shakespeare is still our greatest living author.

All this we take for granted, but Shakespeare's survival was by no means certain. His plays were not published until 1623, some seven years after his death. The Commonwealth ended performance continuity, and with the Restoration in 1660 control of his work passed to the literate only. They decided what the public would or would not receive as Shakespeare. For fifty years, most of his plays were not performed at all, and the remainder heavily adapted. Scenes were out, characters added or removed, the language rewritten. In this manner the public were treated to John Lacey's *Shrew* not Shakespeare's, Davenant's *Macbeth*, Nabum Tate's *King Lear.* Dryden and Davenant rewrote *The Tempest;* Purcell turned it into a musical.

Sadly the theatre can take little credit for Shakespeare's survival. Occasionally an actor would popularize a play—Betterton's *Pericles* for instance, or Garrick's *Richard III*—but the effects were temporary and the rewriting endemic. Garrick's *Richard III,* for instance, was largely Colley Cibber's, and having promised 'To lose no Drop of that Immortal Man' Garrick proceeded to perform *The Winter's Tale* without three of its five acts.

The seventeenth and eighteenth centuries may have been bad—but they were at least 'lofty' in intention. The nineteenth century made little pretence of presenting Shakespeare for anything other than profit. The plays were 'bowdlerised', rewritten, or if morally irredeemable not performed at all. A famous production of *Henry V* reduced the play to five scenes of which only four appear in the original. Actors pillaged the plays for great roles, great moments, and cut the rest. Managers favoured a few spectacular tableaux. Actor/managers did both. It was not just Kean's acting but Shakespeare himself who was seen only 'by flashes of lightning'.

Paradoxically, throughout this time Shakespeare's reputation continued to grow. The Romantics promoted Shakespeare, but not as a playwright. For them he was a poet to be read rather than seen. Charles Lamb pronounced *King Lear* 'essentially impossible to be represented on a stage'. Considering what the stage was doing to Shakespeare in the nineteenth century, Lamb's assertion was not unreasonable. But where the theatre had failed the publisher was beginning to succeed.

William Poel (1852–1934) first advocated a positive return to Shake-speare's original texts and methods of production. Harley Granville-Barker, in the early twentieth century, took up the theme. But it was not until the post-war years that their principles were generally realised. The key was education. Education and increased literacy created both a new theatre and a new audience. Lilian Baylis's Old Vic and the newly formed RSC re-established the integrity of the plays themselves, while across Europe the principle of state subsidy deferred profit in favour of in-creased audience accessibility. Today the collaboration of critic, scholar, public and profession in the plays of William Shakespeare is probably higher than it has ever been—thanks to the publisher and the general reader.

*Shakespeare A to Z* is a remarkable summation of this new Shakespeare awareness. The focus is rigorously upon the plays themselves, with occa-sional reference to performance, and the tone is at all times individual but rational. It both secures and increases Shakespeare's stature and as such is a brilliant and welcome addition to our knowledge of the man and his works.

—Terry Hands,
Artistic Director and Chief Executive,
Royal Shakespeare Company

# PREFACE

This book is not meant as scholarship; my intention has been to assemble conveniently a body of lore for the information and entertainment of the student and general reader. I have not studded the book with references to the scholarship of others that underlies it, for I have presumed that most readers will have little interest in knowing, say, who first suggested that Brian ANNESLEY was a living model for King LEAR's madness. I make no claim to having discovered this possibility, though I do not name the scholar who did. It is enough that someone did, and that the discovery came to my attention, so that I can bring it to yours.

## A Note on Cross-References

When a name or term that is entered in this book appears in another entry, it is printed in SMALL CAPITALS, except in the case of Shakespeare himself and the titles of his works (see CANON). Each of these is, indeed, treated in its own entry, but this fact seems self-evident and reference to them is so frequent that to cross-refer each time would produce typographical clutter.

## A Note on Citations

Line citations used in this book are taken from the New Arden Shakespeare (Methuen, 1951–1984), except in two instances. For *The Two Noble Kinsmen,* not included in the *New Arden* canon, citations are from the New Penguin edition (Penguin Books, 1977), and for the sonnets, from the exemplary *Shakespeare's Sonnets* of Stephen Booth (Yale, 1977).

**Aaron** Character in *Titus Andronicus*, the chief villain, a vicious criminal who loves evil for its own sake. Aaron, a Moor, is the lover of TAMORA, the Queen of the Goths, and carries out her revenge on TITUS (1) Andronicus, who has permitted her son to be killed. Although Aaron is in the retinue of the captured Queen in Act 1, he is silent. Only in 2.1 does he begin to reveal his character, rejoicing in the advancement of Tamora, who is to marry the Emperor, SATURNINUS, because it will also benefit him. The rich imagery of his first soliloquy (2.1.19–24) suggests that here is a villain who looks forward to catastrophe; it has for him the allure of 'pearl and gold'.

Tamora's two sons lust after LAVINIA, Titus' daughter. Aaron plans their appalling rape and mutilation of the girl that is the centre-piece of the revenge upon her father. Aaron's plots are indeed successful. Not only is Lavinia brutalised, but her new husband, BASSIANUS, is murdered and two of Titus' sons are charged with the crime. Further, Aaron falsely tells Titus that his severed hand is required as ransom for the two sons' lives. Titus submits to the amputation, only to have the sons' heads, and his own hand, delivered to him on a platter. This excessive piece of brutality delights Aaron, and he gloats to himself: 'O, how this villainy / Doth fat me with the very thoughts of it!' (3.1.202–203).

Aaron's blackness was a common symbol of evil in Shakespeare's day (though, as OTHELLO demonstrates, it did not have to have such a connotation). However, even in this early work, Shakespeare doesn't settle for simple conventionality. Later in the play, a NURSE (1) delivers to Aaron Tamora's new-born black infant, his child, calling it 'as loathsome as a toad / Among the fair-faced breeders of our clime' (4.2.67–68). She bears Tamora's orders that Aaron is to kill it to protect her reputation. He refuses and defends the baby at sword's point against Tamora's sons.

The black man's proud defiance of society reflects Shakespeare's awareness that villainy can have ingredients in common with heroism, regardless of race. Although the irony of this extraordinarily evil man cooing over his infant son was probably intended as humorous, it is also a good instance of the play-wright's respect for the full humanity of all his characters, even one intended as a demonstration of cruelty.

Aaron's villainy is certainly still active, for he proceeds to kill the NURSE and send the two sons out to buy a white child for Tamora to claim as her own. Aaron attempts to deliver his infant to friends among the GOTHS, but he is captured, and LUCIUS (1) sentences both father and son to hang. Aaron offers to confess all in exchange for the baby's life. Lucius agrees, and Aaron takes the occasion to boast of his evil, declaring, while detailing his crimes, that in his delight with himself, he 'almost broke my heart with extreme laughter' (5.1.113). Lucius, incredulous, asks whether Aaron is not at all sorry for his 'heinous deeds'. Aaron replies: 'Ay, that I had not done a thousand more' (5.1.124). Lucius has Aaron gagged, and the Moor is taken to Rome. After the grisly banquet scene in which Titus' revenge is accomplished, Aaron is brought forth to be sentenced. He is to be buried to the neck and starved to death. This fate only provokes a last outburst: 'If one good deed in all my life I did, / I do repent it from my very soul' (5.3.189–190).

Aaron is the first of Shakespeare's flamboyantly malevolent villains, foreshadowing the likes of RICHARD III, EDMUND, LADY MACBETH, and, most spectacular of all, IAGO. A less developed personality than the later characters, Aaron more clearly represents the conventional figure from which they all descend, the MACHIAVEL. At the time when Shakespeare was writing *Titus*, *The Jew of Malta*, by Christopher MARLOWE ranked as one of the most successful offerings yet presented in the new world of English theatre, and it featured two very popular Machiavels—Barabas and his assistant Ithamore, racially exotic evil-doers who exult in their criminality. These characters surely influenced the young creator of Aaron. However, some historians of drama see Shakespeare as influenced here by earlier, more purely English theatrical traditions, with Aaron as a descendant of the VICE figure in the medieval MORALITY PLAY. The two propositions are not at all mutually exclusive; the idea of the Machiavel doubtless was influenced by the well-known Vice figure. It is likely that Shakespeare was aware of both and simply used a successful type.

**Abbess, The**  Character in *The Comedy of Errors*. See EMILIA (1).

**Abbot of Westminster, William Colchester (c. 1345–1420)**  Historical figure and character in *Richard II*, a conspirator against BOLINGBROKE (1). After RICHARD II is formally deposed in 4.1, the Abbot conspires with the Bishop of CARLISLE and the Duke of AUMERLE to kill the usurper. The plot is discovered, and the Abbot's death, apparently of a bad conscience, is reported in 5.6.19–21. The historical Abbot was pardoned by Bolingbroke, by then King HENRY IV, after one month in prison, and was permitted to retain his office, which he held until his death. Shakespeare may have confused the Abbot's fate with Carlisle's, as reported (inaccurately) by HOLINSHED. The Bishop is said to have died upon capture, 'more through feare than force of sicknesse'.

**Abergavenny, George Neville, Lord (d. 1535)**  Historical figure and minor character in *Henry VIII*, son-in-law of the Duke of BUCKINGHAM (1). As the play opens, Abergavenny joins Buckingham and the Duke of NORFOLK (3) in their complaints about Cardinal WOLSEY's abuse of power. At the end of 1.1 Abervagenny and Buckingham are arrested for treason, the victims of a plot by Wolsey. Like his father-in-law, Abergavenny calmly accepts his fate, 'The will of Heaven be done, and the king's pleasure / By me obey'd' (1.1.215–216), offering a strong contrast with Wolsey's villainy. Shakespeare took Abergavenny's involvement from HOLINSHED's *Chronicles*, and the lord is merely an echo of Buckingham. At 1.1.211 of the FIRST FOLIO edition of the play, Abergavenny's name is spelled 'Aburgany', indicating its ordinary pronunciation.

**Abhorson**  Character in *Measure for Measure*, an executioner. Abhorson appears in 4.2, where he undertakes to train the pimp POMPEY (1) as his assistant, and in 4.3, where he and Pompey summon the condemned criminal BARNARDINE to be executed, only to be comically frustrated by the victim's refusal to cooperate. Abhorson is part of the comic SUB-PLOT—in 4.2 he drolly claims the status of 'mystery' for his profession—but he serves chiefly to help create the ominous atmosphere of the prison. Abhorson's name, which suggests both the verb 'abhor' and the insulting noun 'whoreson', serves the same two purposes. It conveys clearly the repellent aspects of the man's profession, thereby reinforcing the atmosphere of impending doom that has been established earlier in the play, even as its absurdity helps defuse that tension.

**Abram (Abraham)**  Minor character in *Romeo and Juliet*, a servant of the MONTAGUE (1) family. In 1.1 Abram and BALTHASAR (2) brawl with servants of the CAPULET (1) household. This episode illustrates the extent to which the feud between the two families has upset the civic life of VERONA.

**Academic Drama**  Sixteenth-century literary and theatrical movement, the predecessor of ELIZABETHAN DRAMA. Beginning c. 1540, a body of plays was written and performed, mostly in Latin, by faculty and students of England's two 16th-century universities, Oxford and Cambridge, of its chief graduate school, the INNS OF COURT in LONDON, and of several of England's private secondary schools. The best-known creators of academic drama were Nicholas UDALL and William Gager (c. 1560–1622). Academic plays were secular, but they shared the moralising, allegorical qualities of their medieval religious predecessors (see MORALITY PLAY). They were often intended to improve the Latin and public speech of the students, and compared to the popular theatre of the 1580s they were often quite dull. Nevertheless, they created a generation of theatre-goers and the first important group of English playwrights, the so-called UNIVERSITY WITS.

**Achilles**  Legendary figure and character in *Troilus and Cressida*, a Greek warrior in the TROJAN WAR. Though acknowledged as the greatest Greek warrior, Achilles refuses to fight because he feels he is insufficiently appreciated; he is also motivated by a treasonous desire to please a Trojan lover. Not until Act 5, after his close friend PATROCLUS is killed, does Achilles, enraged with grief, return to the battlefield. Then, he underhandedly has his followers, the MYRMIDONS, kill the chivalrous HECTOR, thereby ensuring the defeat of TROY in the climactic battle. In 5.8 he further discredits himself by declaring that he will mutilate Hector's body by dragging it behind his horse.

Achilles scandalises the Greek camp by ridiculing his superior officers, AGAMEMNON and NESTOR. ULYSSES, in a significant passage, holds Achilles' attitude responsible for the Greek failure to defeat Troy despite seven years of fighting. Societies fail, he says, when hierarchical rankings are not observed. Moreover, Achilles' insubordination has spread, and AJAX is behaving similarly. The prideful warrior thus represents a social defect that is one of the targets of the play's satire—the evil influence of morally deficient leadership. Achilles' selfish, traitorous, and brutally unchivalrous behaviour is the centre-piece of the play's depiction of the ugliness of war and the warrior's life, in principle dedicated to ideals of valour and honour but in fact governed by immorality.

Personally, Achilles is rude and uncivil for the most part, and he falsely claims the honour of having defeated Hector, whom he has merely butchered. His villainy is underlined by the obscene and vicious raillery of his jester, THERSITES, whose remarks include the accurate observation that Achilles has 'too much blood and too little brain' (5.1.47), and the imputation that he keeps Patroclus as a 'masculine whore' (5.1.16).

The Achilles of classical mythology, recorded first in the *Iliad* of HOMER, is an outsider, the son of a sea-nymph and the leader of a semi-civilized tribe in remote Thessaly—what is now north-eastern Greece. He is disliked as the only Greek leader who still makes human sacrifices, and his treatment of Hector's body is associated with his barbarian ways. He is noted for his uncontrollable anger and his merciless rage in battle. He withdraws from combat during a dispute with Agamemnon over a concubine, Briseis (the original of CRESSIDA), returning, as in the play, upon the death of Patroclus. Apparently under the influence of Homer, cults venerating Achilles as a demi-god were established in several distant regions of the classical world. A later tradition, dating only from Roman times, states that Achilles' mother dipped him in the sacred river Styx, rendering him invulnerable except on the heel by which she had held him. He was later killed by an arrow—fired by PARIS (3)—that struck that heel. This legend gives us our name for the tendon attached to the heel: the Achilles tendon.

**Actium** Peninsula on the west coast of Greece, and thus the name given to the naval battle fought near it, which is enacted in 3.7–10 of *Antony and Cleopatra*. The battle of Actium marks the downfall of Mark ANTONY, whose fleet, allied with that of Queen CLEOPATRA, is defeated by the forces of Octavius CAESAR (2). In 3.7 CLEOPATRA insists on participating in the battle despite the objections of ENOBARBUS, and Antony supports her by deciding to fight at sea—for the queen has only naval forces—despite the advice of his followers that Caesar is much weaker on land. In 3.8–9 the leaders deploy their men, and in 3.10 Enobarbus, SCARUS, and CANIDIUS witness the climax of the battle as Cleopatra's ships flee and Antony orders his to follow hers. Canidius declares that he will desert Antony and joins Caesar, and though Enobarbus and Scarus remain loyal, they are severely downcast. We are convinced that Antony's fate has been determined by this battle, and this soon proves to be the case.

Shakespeare followed his source, PLUTARCH's *Lives*, fairly closely, though both he and Plutarch—who used an anti-Antony source—laid more emphasis on Antony's misjudgement than do modern scholars. In the summer of 31 B.C. Antony actually had a larger and better-equipped fleet than Caesar, while his land forces were somewhat undermanned. However, his men had not had much recent experience of naval warfare—conducted largely by ramming and boarding the enemy's ships in what amounted to infantry fighting on seaborne platforms—and Caesar's men had just completed a successful compaign against POMPEY (2). Treachery was to be the most important factor,

however; in the weeks before the battle Antony's followers, including Enobarbus, began to desert. When the fleets met on September 2nd, it appears that most of Antony's men refused to fight, though scholars are in disagreement over the few details that have survived. In any case, Cleopatra's navy fled to Egypt, and Antony followed with a fraction of his own ships. The actual fighting was therefore confined to minor skirmishes though the outcome was decisive, resulting in Caesar's assumption of complete power over the Roman world.

**Adam** Character in *As You Like It*, aged servant of ORLANDO. Adam is a figure of unalloyed goodness, loyalty, and faith. In 2.3 the old man volunteers his life's savings to help Orlando flee the evil intentions of his brother OLIVER (1). Orlando equates Adam's virtue with 'the constant service of the antique world, / When service sweat for duty, not for meed' (2.3.57–58). Their flight to ARDEN (1) nearly kills the old man, and Orlando's attempt to steal food for Adam brings him into contact with the exiled court of DUKE (7) Senior. Adam is a sentimental, melodramatic archetype of the loyal servant, but he also has a credible personality. Verbose and nostalgic in the manner of the aged, he boasts a touching combination of moral strength and physical frailty.

A tradition dating from the 18th century asserts that Shakespeare himself performed the role of Adam in the original production by the CHAMBERLAIN'S MEN. This theory is supported by evidence that the playwright played old men on other occasions, but it cannot be proven. Shakespeare derived the character from his source, Thomas LODGE's *Rosalynde*. Lodge in turn followed a medieval English poem, *The Tale of Gamelyn*, which features a faithful servant named Adam Spencer (meaning 'steward' or 'butler'), and the figure seems to be an ancient staple of English folklore.

**Adams, Joseph Quincy (1881–1946)** American scholar. A longtime professor at Cornell University and director of the FOLGER SHAKESPEARE LIBRARY from 1931 to 1946, Adams wrote a respected biography, *The Life of William Shakespeare* (1923), a volume on Elizabethan theatres, and other works. He was one of the successors to H. H. FURNESS as editor of the *New Variorum* edition of Shakespeare's works (see VARIORUM EDITION).

**Addenbrooke, John (active 1608)** Debtor to Shakespeare. In December 1608 the STRATFORD court ordered Addenbrooke to pay a debt of £6 that he owed to Shakespeare. This was a sizeable amount of money, perhaps equal to a tenth of the playwright's annual income. In March 1609 the court reported that the debtor had moved from Stratford, and Shakespeare was forced to sue Addenbrooke's guarantor, the town blacksmith, Thomas Horneby, from whom he received the debt plus damages and court costs. Nothing more is known of Addenbrooke.

**Adlington, William (active 1566)**   English writer, translator of *The Golden Ass* by APULEIUS, a probable inspiration for *A Midsummer Night's Dream* and a possible minor source for *Cymbeline*. Adlington published his translation—from a French translation of Apuleius' 2nd-century A.D. Latin—in 1566, and his book was popular, being reprinted in 1571, 1582, and 1596. Little is known about Adlington's life beyond an apparent association with Oxford University.

**Admiral's Men**   Acting company of the ELIZABETHAN THEATRE, possible employer of the young Shakespeare and later the chief rivals of his CHAMBERLAIN'S MEN. The company was originally organised in 1576 as Lord Howard's Men, under the patronage of Charles HOWARD, later Lord High Admiral of England. After touring the provinces for several years, they are first recorded in LONDON—as the Admiral's Men—in 1585, when the great actor Edward ALLEYN joined the troupe and became its leader. The company quickly established itself as a rival to the QUEEN'S MEN (1) in the London theatre world. They were especially famed for their presentations of the grandiose tragedies of Christopher MARLOWE (1).

By 1590 the Admiral's Men had a new rival, STRANGE'S MEN, but in that year the two companies joined forces at the THEATRE, owned by James BURBAGE (2). In May 1591 a dispute between Alleyn and Burbage disrupted the link, and Alleyn, along with many players of the combined group, moved to the ROSE THEATRE, owned by Philip HENSLOWE. However, when the theatres of London were closed by plague for much of 1593–1594, Alleyn led a combined Admiral's-Strange's company on tour. When the theatres reopened in 1594, the two troupes separated again, with the Admiral's Men settling at the Rose for the next six years. From then on, the Admiral's and the Chamberlain's Men (as Strange's was now known) were the two leading London theatre companies.

The Admiral's Men continued to revive Marlowe, but they also produced many new plays. Among the playwrights employed by the company were George CHAPMAN, Thomas DEKKER, Michael DRAYTON, Thomas HEYWOOD (2), and Anthony MUNDAY. Besides Alleyn, the principal actors included Thomas DOWNTON, Richard JONES (2), Martin SLATER, and Gabriel SPENCER. The company's name was formally changed to the Earl of Nottingham's Men when Howard was awarded the title in 1597, but they are invariably referred to as the Admiral's Men.

In 1598 the Admiral's Men were somewhat weakened when Spenser was killed (by Ben JONSON) and Alleyn retired from acting, though he continued as a partner in the company. He returned in 1600—at the personal request of Queen ELIZABETH (1), according to rumour—and the troupe moved to the new FORTUNE THEATRE, which it and its successors occupied for a quarter of a century. After the accession of King JAMES I in 1603, Howard was succeeded as patron by the new king's son, Prince HENRY (2), after which the Admiral's Men were known as PRINCE HENRY'S MEN. They later became the PALSGRAVE'S MEN, finally closing in 1625.

Scholars believe that Shakespeare was probably a member of the combined troupe of the Admiral's Men and Strange's Men in 1590 and early 1591. This speculation is supported by the texts of *2* and *3 Henry VI*, which were apparently printed from the author's manuscript and included the names of the actors John HOLLAND (3) and John SINCKLO, known to have been part of the combined company. Thus, it is thought that the young playwright wrote these works for production by the Admiral's-Strange's combine at the Theatre in 1590 or 1591. If this was indeed so, then he was doubtless an actor in the company as well.

**Adrian (1)**   See VOLSCE.

**Adrian (2)**   Minor character in *The Tempest*, a follower of King ALONSO of Naples. Adrian hardly speaks; in 2.1 he briefly supports GONZALO in his optimism, which is mocked by ANTONIO (5) and SEBASTIAN (3), and in 3.3 he speaks only half a line, closing the scene. Adrian, with FRANCISCO (2), has been seen by some scholars as evidence for the existence of an earlier version of *The Tempest*, in which his role was more substantial, for there seems no reason to include him in the play as it stands. He may have been intended for scenes that Shakespeare originally planned but then discarded in the course of composition. In any case, minor attendants help establish the high status of royal figures throughout Shakespeare's plays, and Adrian has this function for Alonso; moreover, his reiteration of Gonzalo's position focusses attention on it and helps maintain our sense of good's survival among villains.

**Adriana**   Character in *The Comedy of Errors*, the jealous but loving wife of ANTIPHOLUS OF EPHESUS. Adriana first appears in 2.1, complaining that Antipholus is late for lunch. She argues with her sister, LUCIANA, about the proper obedience owed a husband, in a standard disputation on marital relations that was common in Shakespeare's day. While Luciana adopts the position that a man is rightly the master of his wife, Adriana asserts, 'There's none but asses will be bridled so' (2.1.14). Later in the scene, she bemoans her husband's attentions to other women, and jealousy is her characteristic trait throughout the play, finally triggering a humorous but acid sermonette by the Abbess, EMILIA, in the final scene (5.1.69–86).

The circumstances of confusion and error that create the atmosphere of the play also stimulate Adriana's jealous streak. In 2.2 she accosts ANTIPHOLUS OF SYRACUSE, thinking him to be her husband, and demands that he come home to eat. Bemused and baffled, he nevertheless goes with her, and there ensues (3.1) the central misidentification of the play; Adriana refuses to admit her real husband to their home, believing him to be an imposter.

In 4.2 Luciana reports to Adriana a declaration of love from the man both believe to be Antipholus of Ephesus; both women thus believe that Adriana's husband is attempting to betray her by courting her own sister. Adriana rails against her husband but concludes: 'Ah, but I think him better than I say, . . . / My heart prays for him, though my tongue do curse' (4.2.25–28).

This note of wifely affection grows stronger as the play hurries to its resolution, for Adriana is truly fond of her husband, irascible and domineering though he may be. She tries to aid him, once she has concluded that he is temporarily insane; the confusions of the plot have led her (and others) to this error. She appears in the final scene just as Antipholus of Syracuse is about to fight a duel, and, thinking him her husband, she implores, 'Hold, hurt him not for God's sake; he is mad' (5.1.33). Antipholus and his servant flee into the PRIORY. Adriana follows her husband there and demands that the Abbess turn Antipholus over to her. The Abbess refuses, however, and Adriana has recourse to the DUKE (8). His investigation triggers the final resolution of the play's confusions, although Adriana plays no great part in that process.

An interesting tradition has it that Adriana was written as a portrait of Anne HATHAWAY, but modern scholarship debunks this idea. Nevertheless, Adriana was clearly an important creation for Shakespeare, for she is a markedly more fully drawn and consequential figure than her predecessor in his source for the play. She is an early example of a Shakespearean character type that recurs often in the plays (e.g., KATHERINA, in *The Taming of the Shrew*, and BEATRICE, in *Much Ado About Nothing*)—an independent woman whose sharp words and sometimes forbidding manner conceal a tender heart. Adriana's dual nature would come to typify Shakespeare's greatest characters. The playwright insisted on presenting multiple points of view about a character or situation, offering his audience varying and often conflicting impressions, and thus re-creating on the stage the inconsistencies of actual life.

**Aedile** Any of several minor characters in CORIOLANUS, subordinates of the Roman tribunes SICINIUS and BRUTUS (3). The Aediles serve chiefly as messengers for the tribunes. They summon the crowds to rally against CORIOLANUS in 3.1; they announce Coriolanus' approach and are instructed in coaching the crowd in 3.3; and an Aedile brings the tribunes the first report of the VOLSCIANS' advance against ROME in 4.6. They demonstrate the institutional power that the tribunes command.

**Aegeon** See EGEON.

**Aemilia** See EMILIA (1).

**Aemilius** Minor character in *Titus Andronicus*. Aemilius delivers messages between SATURNINUS and LUCIUS (1) and helps acclaim Lucius the new Emperor at the end of the play.

**Aeneas** Legendary figure and character in *Troilus and Cressida*, a leader of the Trojan forces in the TROJAN WAR. Aeneas serves as an herald, carrying the challenge of HECTOR in 1.3, accompanying the visiting Greek delegation led by DIOMEDES in 4.1–4, carrying a warning of their arrival to TROILUS in 4.2, and announcing Hector's arrival for his duel with AJAX in 4.5. Aeneas represents the Trojan concern for chivalric honour: he is a stiffly correct model of knightly manners. His exchange with Diomedes in 4.1 of courteous declarations of intent to kill is a bleakly humorous picture of mindless warriors who can reduce the horrors of war to an exercise in etiquette.

In the *Iliad* of HOMER, Aeneas is a more important figure; he is a cousin of King PRIAM who is notably favoured by the gods. The sea-god Poseidon predicts that Aeneas shall be a ruler someday. Later tradition developed this forecast into Aeneas' leadership of the Trojan exiles who wandered the Mediterranean world after the fall of their city, and VIRGIL's *Aeneid* makes him the founder of Rome. Shakespeare and his contemporaries saw Aeneas as an ancestor figure because his great-grandson Brut was thought to have settled England and founded London as New Troy. This is reflected in the anti-Greek bias of the play.

**Africanus, Leo** See LEO AFRICANUS.

**Agamemnon** Legendary figure and character in *Troilus and Cressida*, the leader of the Greek forces in the TROJAN WAR. Although ULYSSES calls him 'Thou great commander, nerves and bone of Greece' (1.3.55), Agamemnon is in fact an ineffectual leader. He preaches ponderously, but ACHILLES can safely ignore his orders; the Greek forces are accordingly stymied in their siege of TROY. Much of what Ulysses calls the absence of 'degree' (1.3.83, 101, 109, etc.)—a dissolution of the hierarchy on which Greek society has been based—can be attributed to Agamemnon's recurrent weakness. At the play's close, Agamemnon still lacks authority; in the last line spoken by a Greek, he sends a messenger to request submissively the presence of Achilles, just as he has had to do all along.

The Agamemnon of classical myth and legend probably derives from a historical king who ruled in the Argive, a region of Greece near Corinth, during the Bronze Age. His post as commander of the Greek forces at Troy is recorded in the *Iliad* of HOMER, as are his lack of resolve and his inability to control Achilles. Homer's *Odyssey* and later plays by Greek dramatists continued his tale after the war: upon his return home, he is killed by his wife, Clytemnestra, and her lover. This murder impels Orestes, his son, to kill his mother in revenge. This event and Orestes' subsequent torment by supernatural spirits constitute the *Oresteia*, the subject of works by all the major Greek dramatists and many other writers, into modern times.

*Age of Kings, An*  British Broadcasting Company production (1960) of Shakespeare's two tetralogies (see TETRALOGY) of HISTORY PLAYS. These eight works, which depict a continuous period from 1399 to 1485, were presented in 15 parts. This extraordinary production, which has been called 'the first mini-series', offered a fresh point of view on several stories and characters. For instance, such episodes as the fall of Humphrey, Duke of GLOUCESTER (4), are lent greater coherence by being isolated from their surroundings, and certain characters—notably Queen MARGARET (1), the Duke of YORK (8), and PRINCE (6) HAL, who becomes HENRY V—demonstrate their growth as individuals over the several plays in which they appear.

**Agincourt**  Town in northern FRANCE (1), battle site in the HUNDRED YEARS WAR and location for Act 4 of *Henry V*. The battle of Agincourt provides the climax of *Henry V* and of the second TETRALOGY of Shakespeare's HISTORY PLAYS. The English army, led by King HENRY V, wins an impressive victory over a much larger French force. Henry attributes the triumph to divine intervention in favour of the English. Soundly defeated, FRANCE (1) signs, in 5.2, a treaty granting Henry the inheritance of the French crown, as well as marriage to the FRENCH KING's daughter, KATHARINE (2). England thus achieves a glorious ascendancy over its traditional enemy.

Shakespeare's presentation of the battle focuses on King Henry. Henry may be seen as a chivalric hero, whose courage and high spirits—reflected particularly in his famous 'St Crispin's Day' speech (4.3.18–67)—and democratic identification with his soldiers, shown in 4.1, give his army the morale necessary to defeat the foe. On the other hand, Henry's assertion in the St Crispin's Day oration that he prefers to be outnumbered in order to garner greater honour smacks of the irrational bravado condemned in HOTSPUR in *1 Henry IV*. Similarly, his order to kill the French prisoners (4.6.37) may indicate a praiseworthy decisiveness at a critical moment, but it can also be interpreted as an act of militaristic savagery.

Historians place much more emphasis on the common soldiers than on Henry. A landmark battle in English and military history, Agincourt—fought on October 25, 1415—was indeed an extraordinary event: a crushing defeat was administered by a weary, sick, and badly damaged English force to a French army three times its size. The English victory was chiefly due to the shrewd use of batteries of longbowmen, who cut down the French cavalrymen before they could approach; it was the first victory of massed infantry over the mounted knights who had dominated medieval battlefields. Shakespeare omits this key feature of the battle in order to direct attention towards his protagonist more effectively. Moreover, despite the impressive English victory, Agincourt did not win France for Henry; it merely staved off defeat. He took his army back to England and reinvaded in 1417. Only three years later, after the conquest of Normandy, were the French prepared to negotiate the treaty of TROYES, presented in 5.2 of the play.

**Agrippa, M. Vipsanius (63–12 B.C.)**  Historical figure and character in *Antony and Cleopatra*, a follower of Octavius CAESAR (2). In 2.2 Agrippa displays considerable influence when he suggests the marriage between ANTONY and OCTAVIA, and in 4.6 and 4.7 he is in command of Caesar's army. For much of the remainder of the play he serves as an opposite to Antony's ENOBARBUS, with whom he exchanges remarks on the principal characters; he displays the demeanour of a gruff veteran soldier.

Shakespeare's character does not reflect the importance of the historical Agrippa, who was probably the most important figure—after Caesar himself—in the defeat of Antony and the subsequent establishment of the Roman Empire. Along with MAECENAS, he was one of Caesar's few close friends and advisers. His origins are entirely obscure; even his contemporaries knew nothing of his family or homeland, although he was believed to have been Caesar's schoolmate in Athens before accompanying the future emperor on his return to Italy after the assassination of Julius CAESAR (1) in 44 B.C. (Agrippa does not appear in Shakespeare's *Julius Caesar.*) He was a prominent general throughout the civil wars. He put down revolts in Italy and Gaul and created and commanded the fleets that defeated POMPEY (2) in Sicily and Antony at Actium. After Antony's defeat, Agrippa was Caesar's right-hand man in governing Rome. In 23 B.C. Caesar nearly died of an illness, and he apparently intended that Agrippa would succeed him as ruler. In 21 B.C. Agrippa married Caesar's daughter. He served as a general and administrator in various parts of the empire until the year of his death.

**Ajax** Legendary figure and character in *Troilus and Cressida*, a Greek warrior in the TROJAN WAR. For the most part, Ajax is a variant on the ancient MILES GLORIOSUS character type: a braggart soldier, a laughable buffoon who is not to be taken seriously. He presents a comic variation on an important theme: the vanity of the warrior's lust for military glory. At the same time, he has notable redeeming features that offer a counterpoint to the play's generally acerbic tone.

Before he appears, Ajax is humorously described by ALEXANDER (1) as a valiant warrior but a beastlike churl with uncontrollable emotions. (Some scholars believe that this passage [1.2.19–31] is a satirical description of Ben JONSON, though the point is extremely disputable.) When he does appear, Ajax is laughably stupid, incapable of responding to THERSITES' teasing except by hitting him. Selected by ULYSSES as a substitute for ACHILLES, Ajax displays ludicrous pride in his undeserved position, especially since he criticises Achilles for *his* pride, and elicits the amused asides of the other Greeks in 2.3.201–224. One of the play's funniest passages is Thersites' imitation of Ajax' ego in 3.3.279–302. Ajax issues a preposterous parody of a chivalric challenge as he directs his trumpeter to summon HECTOR for their duel, saying, 'Now, crack thy lungs, . . . stretch thy chest, and let thy eyes spout blood' (4.5.7–10).

However, Ajax proves a brave soldier who behaves with valour and chivalrous generosity when he actually faces Hector, getting the better of the fight (according to the cries of the spectators in 4.5.113–115) but accepting the truce his opponent desires. Strikingly, when Thersites describes Ajax as 'a very land-fish, languageless, a monster' (3.3.262–263), we see that this brutish fellow resembles a later Shakespearean figure—also sympathetic in spite of his defects—CALIBAN, the fishy monster of *The Tempest*.

Ajax (Latin for the Greek Aias) is the name of two characters in the *Iliad* of HOMER; Shakespeare combines them. The opponent of Hector corresponds to Aias Telamon, described by Homer as the bulwark of the Greek forces, a courageous warrior who is slow of speech but repeatedly a leader in assault and the last to retreat; he successfully duels Hector, as in the play. Otherwise, Shakespeare's character corresponds to Aias Oileus, often called Aias the Lesser, also a fine warrior but notorious for his pride, rudeness, and blasphemy. In the *Odyssey*, he is drowned by the sea-god Poseidon for cursing the gods while escaping a shipwreck. In a later tradition, he raped CASSANDRA on an altar during the sack of TROY, a misdeed whose punishment accounted for a custom by which his descendants were annually required to provide two virgins who ran a gauntlet of the townspeople and, if they survived, served for life in the temple of Athena. The end of this barbaric practice around 100 A.D. was reported by PLUTARCH, who said it had lasted 1,000 years.

**Alarbus** Minor character in *Titus Andronicus*, the eldest son of TAMORA. In 1.1, TITUS (1) Andronicus permits the ritual sacrifice of Alarbus, who is killed despite his mother's pleas for mercy. This sparks the cycle of vengeance that comprises the plot of the play.

**Albany, Duke of** Character in *King Lear*, the virtuous but weak husband of LEAR's villainous daughter, GONERIL. Albany, who does not discover his wife's wickedness until too late, eventually aids the banished Lear and formally restores him to power just before his death. In this way he represents an instance of moral growth in a degraded world. At the play's close he is the ruler of Britain, sharing power with EDGAR and KENT, and intent on repairing the damage to the state that Lear's crisis has produced. In the final lines, Albany offers a possible lesson to be drawn from the tragedy, saying, 'The weight of this sad time we must obey' (5.3.322); he recognises the need to be aware of human susceptibility to catastrophic error, as Lear did not. (Albany's lines here are sometimes given to Edgar, as in the FIRST FOLIO text.)

In his early appearances Albany is ineffectual. He is governed entirely by his wife, who dismisses his question about her rift with Lear by curtly ordering, 'Never afflict yourself to know more of it' (1.4.289). After Act 1 he does not reappear until 4.2, when, having learned of the treacherous blinding of GLOUCESTER (1), he denounces Goneril as an evil-doer. 'You are not worth the dust which the rude wind / Blows in your face', he declares (4.2.30–31). Nevertheless, he goes along with her alliance with EDMUND against CORDELIA's French army, though he privately asserts his intention to revenge Gloucester. Informed by Edgar of Edmund and Goneril's plot against his own life, Albany exposes the villains in 5.3. By this time Albany is clearly intent on rectifying the misdeeds of his wife and her allies, but his earlier weakness has already helped them. His poor judgement in patriotically fighting the French has an unintended and fatal result when Edmund gains control of Lear and Cordelia. Thus, though well-intentioned and finally benevolent, Albany reinforces the play's theme of human fallibility.

**Alcibiades (c. 450–404 B.C.)** Historical figure and character in *Timon of Athens*, an Athenian general and friend of TIMON. Alcibiades is faithful to Timon in adversity and thereby counteracts the play's theme of false friendship. He is most significant as the central figure in a parallel plot in which he is pitted against the cold-hearted, legalistic aristocracy of ATHENS. Like Timon he is the subject of ingratitude and a heartless application of the system and its laws. However, Alcibiades takes action and avenges himself. Thus he is placed in sharp contrast with Timon and his passive withdrawal into misanthropy and madness. Then, at the play's close, his humane nature permits a reconciliation, an ending that offers the central lesson of the play: the superiority of mercy over justice in human affairs.

Unlike Timon, Alcibiades realises that good can exist in a world that is evil, and that mercy is a greater corrective for society than revenge. In his final tribute to 'noble Timon' (5.4.80), Alcibiades extends his mercy to the misanthrope himself. Though Timon, as a suicide, cannot participate in the play's ultimate spirit of reconciliation, his extreme hatred is forgiven and finally countered.

For the first half of the play, Alcibiades is clearly an honest friend amidst a group of obviously insincere and hypocritical courtiers that surround Timon, but he is a minor figure. He assumes importance in 3.5, the pivotal scene of the play, when he pleads with the Athenian rulers (see SENATOR [4]) for mercy on behalf of a veteran soldier sentenced to death for murder. Alcibiades argues that 'pity is the virtue of the law' (3.5.8). This reflects a central concern not only of the play but of Shakespearean drama in general. Banished from Athens because he has questioned authority, he promises revenge, and in 5.1 he threatens to sack the city. Thus, he is clearly in opposition to callous ingratitude while at the same time he threatens disaster for the entire city. Such a catastrophe—though here only potential—demonstrates how immoral behaviour among the ruling class leads to trouble for the entire society, a lesson Shakespeare repeatedly offered in the HISTORY PLAYS, the ROMAN PLAYS, and elsewhere. Alcibiades is both opponent and saviour for the 'coward and lascivious' Athens (5.4.1).

Alcibiades is the only character in *Timon of Athens* who is at all fleshed out. He prefers his profession, soldiering, to the banquets of Timon's world, and his controlled anger in his encounter with the Senate is impressive. He knows himself—'I speak like a captain', he says (3.5.42)—and he can plead for a friend. He also understands the self-exiled Timon—as Timon himself cannot—and sees that 'his wits / Are drown'd and lost in his calamities' (4.3.89–90). In these respects Alcibiades seems somewhat at odds with the rest of the play, which relies heavily on the bold symbolism of allegorical characters. Perhaps this unresolvable contrast contributed to Shakespeare's decision to leave *Timon* unfinished.

The fascinating career of the historical Alcibiades is only faintly reflected in Shakespeare's character. Alcibiades was a brilliant though unstable young aristocrat who led an ostentatiously decadent life but nevertheless became an influential general and leading politician. However, despite his political power, he faced banishment for his part in a sacrilegious mutilation of icons. He fled to avoid trial and joined Athens' enemies, the Spartans. They mistrusted him and he moved on and joined their allies, the Persians, whom he tried to win to an alliance with Athens. From exile, he maintained contact with the turbulent Athenian political world and was thus able to assume command of the Athenian fleet, over the objections of the government.

Shakespeare's source, PLUTARCH's *Lives,* states that Alcibiades refused the navy's demand that he attack the city; this is the germ of Shakespeare's account. Actually, though on his return Alcibiades was supported by a revolutionary government that arose in Athens at that time, there was no question of his attacking the city. He fought the Spartans and Persians with such success that the Athenians gave him total command of the armed forces. However, a minor loss permitted his enemies to revive popular resentment against him, and he again left Athens and took refuge with Spartan allies in Phrygia. There, he was murdered by agents of conservative Athenians who had returned to power and made peace with Sparta. Alcibiades was a byword for treachery in the ancient world, though it was also recognised that the Athenians were foolish to follow political loyalties and discard a military genius when they most needed him.

**Aldridge, Ira (c. 1807–1867)**  American actor. The first highly successful black actor, Aldridge was generally acknowledged to be the most accomplished American on the London stage in the 19th century. Particularly noted for his performances as OTHELLO and AARON, Shakespeare's most prominent black characters, Aldridge was also acclaimed as LEAR, HAMLET, RICHARD III, SHYLOCK, MACBETH, and others. He performed in most of the major capitals of Europe and was universally regarded as among the great actors of his generation.

Born to a New York City minister, Aldridge was intended for the ministry himself, but he was attracted to the stage very early, appearing with a black acting company at the age of 14. Befriended by an English actor, Henry Wallack (1790–1870), Aldridge went to England in 1824 when he recognised that racial prejudice would not permit him an acting career in America. He was immediately popular, and his evident talent and sophistication helped promote the growing movement for the abolition of slavery throughout the British Empire. Aldridge underwent a period of apprenticeship in provincial touring companies before he achieved success in London. He remained at the top of his profession for almost 40 years. He died on tour in Poland while preparing for a home-coming to America.

*Ira Aldridge as Othello. Denied opportunity in the United States because of his race, the actor found great success on the stages of Europe in the 19th century.* (Courtesy of Picture Collection, New York Public Library)

**Alençon, John, Duke of (1409–1476)** Historical figure and character in *1 Henry VI*, one of the French noblemen who lead the forces of CHARLES VII against the English. Like his fellows, the BASTARD (2) OF ORLÉANS, REIGNIER, and Charles himself, Alençon is depicted as a type, a bragging but inept, treacherous, and cowardly warrior. Alençon's father was the French knight whose glove HENRY V of England is said to have taken during the battle of AGINCOURT (*Henry V*, 4.7.159).

**Alexander (1)** Minor character in *Troilus and Cressida*, a servant of CRESSIDA. Alexander appears only in 1.2, where he tells his mistress that the Trojan prince HECTOR is furious because he has been humbled in battle by the Greek warrior AJAX. He describes Ajax in humorous terms as a beastlike man. This brief episode introduces the rivalries of the warriors in a fashion that signals the play's satiric intent.

**Alexander (2), Peter (1894–1969)** British Shakespearean scholar, editor of an edition of Shakespeare's works and author of many works on the playwright and his times. A longtime professor at Glasgow University, Alexander is best known for his *Shakespeare's Life and Art* (1964) and his one-volume edition of the complete works (1951). He also convincingly established Shakespeare's authorship of the *Henry VI* plays in his *Shakespeare's Henry VI and Richard III* (1929).

**Alexandria** City in Egypt located on the Mediterranean coast at the western edge of the Nile River delta, the setting for many scenes in *Antony and Cleopatra*. Alexandria was the capital of the Ptolemaic Empire inherited by CLEOPATRA, and was the site of her palace, where she conducted her affair with Mark ANTONY. It is to this sanctuary that the lovers retreat after being defeated in the battle of ACTIUM, and it is where they die.

The magnificence of the Ptolemaic capital is implicit in the luxurious decadence of Antony and Cleopatra's life, with its servants and banquets—the reputation of 'fine Egyptian cookery' (2.6.63) is several times admired—and in the pomp of their enthronement 'I' the market place' of Alexandria (3.6.3). The richness of Cleopatra's personal adornment, detailed in ENOBARBUS' famed description in 2.2.190–218 (though she was not in Alexandria at the time), confirms the impression. The city's huge and cosmopolitan population is hinted at in Antony's description of when he and the queen would 'wander through the streets, and note / The qualities of people' (1.1.53–54). Cleopatra's recollections of delightful fishing expeditions, in 2.5.10–18, suggest the pleasures of a great city's riverfront.

Alexandria was the chief city of the eastern Mediterranean from its founding by Alexander the Great in 332 B.C. until its conquest by Arab invaders in the 7th century A.D. Until around the time of the play when its population—probably about one million—was surpassed by that of Rome, Alexandria was the largest city of the entire Western world. It remained the major cultural centre of the Roman Empire and, later, the Byzantine Empire. The library at Alexandria was one of the great treasures of the ancient world, containing at one point around 750,000 volumes. Although the library's final destruction when it was torched by the Arabs c. 640 A.D. is regarded as one of the greatest single acts of vandalism known, the Arab conquest merely completed a process that had begun much earlier; in fact, an early installment occurred when Antony's men, burning their vessels as CAESAR (2) approached after the battle of ACTIUM, accidentally set fire to the library and destroyed an unknown quantity of its contents.

**Alexas (Alexas Laodician) (active c. 32 B.C.)** Historical figure and minor character in *Antony and Cleopatra*, an attendant to CLEOPATRA. Alexas is a cheerful fellow who jests with CHARMIAN and IRAS in 1.2. He brings Cleopatra a message from ANTONY in 1.5, and attends her—almost without speaking—in 2.5, 3.3, and 4.2.

However, Alexas' desertion to Octavius CAESAR (2), after the battle of ACTIUM, is reported in 4.6, and he appears to be a more important figure than his earlier role would suggest. ENOBARBUS reflects that Alexas had been sent by Antony to 'Jewry' (4.6.12), where he persuaded the ruler, Herod, to join Caesar. He goes on to remark that Caesar, shocked by this treachery, had executed Alexas. The account elaborates on the important Act 4 theme of Antony's fall as many of his one-time followers are seen to have deserted him.

Shakespeare took his account of Alexas Laodician from his source, PLUTARCH's *Lives*, where the Greek servant's promotion to diplomatic status is said to have resulted from the friendship that developed between him and Antony through his job as Cleopatra's message bearer. His surname—found in Plutarch—suggests that he was from the important ancient city of Laodicia, in Asia Minor, but otherwise Alexas is not found in history.

**Alice**   Minor character in *Henry V,* lady-in-waiting to Princess KATHARINE (2) of France. In 3.4 Alice, said to have been in England, gives her mistress a brief lesson in English, telling her the names for such body parts as the hand, the fingers, and so on, in an exchange marked by comical mispronunciation and unintentional sexual references. This oddly charming episode, conducted entirely in French, appears immediately after King HENRY V's dire threats to sack HARFLEUR and thus subtly contributes to the play's sardonic presentation of Henry's career of conquest, parallel to its glorification of him. The scene also foreshadows Henry's aggressive bilingual courtship of Katharine in 5.2, where Alice is also present.

**Aliena**   In *As You Like It,* the name CELIA takes when she and ROSALIND, banished by DUKE (1) Frederick, travel in disguise to the Forest of ARDEN (1). The name suggests her exiled state.

**Allde, Edward (c. 1583–1624)**   London printer, producer of editions of several of Shakespeare's works. In 1597 Allde printed part of the first, pirated, QUARTO edition of *Romeo and Juliet* when the original printer, John DANTER, was suspended by the STATIONERS' COMPANY for another such piracy. Allde himself underwent suspensions later in the same year, and again in 1599, for printing illicit Catholic materials. However, he was generally successful, printing mostly poetry and plays. In 1611 he printed the third quarto of *Titus Andronicus* for publisher Edward WHITE (1), and the second quarto of The Phoenix and Turtle.

**Alleyn, Edward (1566–1626)**   English actor, the leader of the ADMIRAL'S MEN and the foremost actor of Shakespeare's day. The son of a LONDON innkeeper, Alleyn was a teenage actor in WORCESTER'S MEN, then a provincial company, before joining the Admiral's around 1585 and soon becoming its leader. In 1592 he married the daughter of the theatrical entrepreneur Philip HENSLOWE and formed a partnership with him that lasted until Henslowe's death in 1616. From 1590 to 1594 Alleyn led the combined Admiral's and STRANGE'S MEN companies, which toured the provinces during an outbreak of plague in London. Alleyn's letters from this tour to his wife and father-in-law have survived, and they reveal an amiable and conscientious young man. In the 1590s Alleyn was famous as a great tragedian, especially in the plays of Christopher MARLOWE (1); Thomas NASHE declared him the best actor 'since before Christ was borne' and Ben JONSON was later to declare to him, 'others speak, but only thou dost act'. When he retired briefly, around 1598, it was said that Queen ELIZABETH (1) personally asked him to return to the stage. He did so in 1600 but retired for good in 1604.

He retained a financial interest in PRINCE HENRY'S MEN, as the Admiral's was known after the accession of King JAMES I, along with other investments, theatrical and otherwise. By this time Alleyn was quite a wealthy man. With Henslowe, he was a part-owner of the FORTUNE THEATRE, which they had built, and of the licence to operate the London bear-baiting arena. He also had profitable real estate holdings in and around London, and he later inherited Henslowe's interest in the HOPE THEATRE and the Fortune. In 1605 he bought a manor in Dulwich (now a south London suburb, then a rural hamlet), where he moved in 1613. He founded Dulwich College there, a hospital and school for poor families; it is now the site of a small museum, housing a collection of European paintings along with Alleyn and Henslowe's papers, which provide a rich assemblage of 16th-century theatre lore. Alleyn's wife died in 1623; he remarried in the same year, to the daughter of the poet John Donne (1573–1631).

***All Is True***   Alternative title for *Henry VIII.* The play is called *All Is True* in a contemporary account of its performance the day the GLOBE THEATRE burned down. This was probably a subtitle—perhaps to imply a contrast to another play about HENRY VIII, the blatantly fictitious *When You See Me, You Know Me* (1605) by Samuel ROWLEY (1). Some scholars, however, contend that *All Is True* was Shakespeare's original title, which was altered in the FIRST FOLIO (1623) to go with the other HISTORY PLAYS, all named for kings.

### *All's Well That Ends Well*

#### SYNOPSIS

*Act 1, Scene 1*
The COUNTESS (2) of ROSSILLION's son BERTRAM is leaving for the court of the KING (17) of FRANCE (1). The

Countess and Lord LAFEW discuss the King's poor health; she regrets that the father of her ward, HELENA (2), has died, because he was a great physician. The Countess bids Bertram farewell and departs, and Bertram, after a cursory farewell to Helena, leaves with Lafew. Helena soliloquises on her seemingly hopeless love for Bertram. Bertram's friend PAROLLES arrives and engages Helena in an exchange of witticisms on virginity. Parolles leaves, and Helena decides that she must act if her love is to be rewarded. She sees an opportunity in the King's illness.

*Act 1, Scene 2*
The King discusses the war between Florence and Siena, stating that he has decided to permit French noblemen to fight in the conflict if they wish. Bertram arrives and is welcomed warmly by the King. The King remarks on his ill health and regrets the death of the famed doctor who had served in the court at Rossillion.

*Act 1, Scene 3*
The Countess' jester, the CLOWN (5), requests permission to marry, making obscene jokes and singing songs. The STEWARD (1) wishes to speak about Helena, and the Countess sends the Clown to get her. The Countess remarks on her fondness for Helena, and the Steward confides that he has overheard the young woman musing on her love for Bertram. As the Steward leaves, Helena arrives, and the Countess elicits from her a confession of her love for Bertram and of her intention to go to Paris. Helena asserts that she has secret prescriptions of her father's that she is convinced will cure the King, and the Countess agrees to help her travel to Paris to try them.

*Act 2, Scene 1*
The King bids farewell to the First and Second Lords (see LORD [6]) and other young noblemen leaving to fight in Italy. Bertram regrets that he is commanded to remain at court. Lafew appears and introduces Helena as a young woman who can cure the King's illness. Helena convinces the King to try her medecine, offering to wager her life that it will work within 24 hours. In return, she asks the King to approve her marriage to the man of her choice.

*Act 2, Scene 2*
The Clown jests about life at the King's court, and the Countess gives him a message to take to Helena.

*Act 2, Scene 3*
Lafew, interrupted repeatedly by Parolles, tells of the King's return to health. The King arrives with Helena, who is to choose from among the young gentlemen of the court. She selects Bertram, but he refuses to marry her, saying that her social rank is too low. However, the King orders him to accept, and he acquiesces. Parolles puts on airs, and Lafew disdains him with elaborate insults. Lafew leaves, and Bertram reappears, declaring that he will run away to the wars in Italy before he will consummate his marriage to Helena. He plans to send Helena back to the Countess alone.

*Act 2, Scene 4*
Parolles conveys Bertram's instructions to Helena.

*Act 2, Scene 5*
Lafew warns Bertram not to rely on Parolles. Helena tells Bertram she is ready to leave; he pointedly avoids a farewell kiss. She departs, and Bertram and Parolles leave for Italy.

*Act 3, Scene 1*
The DUKE (4) of FLORENCE receives the First and Second Lords.

*Act 3, Scene 2*
The Countess reads Bertram's letter declaring that he has run away from his new wife, as Helena appears with the First and Second Lords, who are on leave from Florence. She reads aloud a letter from Bertram: he will not acknowledge her as his wife until she wears his ring and bears his child, which, he insists, will never happen. In a soliloquy, Helena decides that she must leave France and become a wanderer so that her husband may live unhindered by an unwanted wife.

*Act 3, Scene 3*
The Duke of Florence makes Bertram his general of cavalry. Bertram rejoices to be engaged in war, not love.

*Act 3, Scene 4*
The Steward reads a letter from Helena stating that she has become a pilgrim. The dismayed Countess orders him to write Bertram, asking him to return, hoping that Helena will eventually come back as well.

*Act 3, Scene 5*
The WIDOW (2) Capilet, a landlady of Florence, her daughter DIANA (1), and their neighbour MARIANA (1) remark that the new French general, Bertram, has attempted to seduce Diana, sending Parolles as his intermediary. Helena appears, identifying herself as a French pilgrim, and she is told about the general, whom the ladies have heard has rejected his wife. Helena agrees to lodge with the Widow.

*Act 3, Scene 6*
The two Lords propose to prove to Bertram that Parolles is a coward. They will kidnap him and make him believe he has been captured by the enemy; they are sure that he will betray his comrades out of fear while Bertram overhears his interrogation. Parolles enters and brags that he will retrieve a captured regimental drum, a prized emblem. He leaves, and the First Lord follows to prepare the plan; Bertram invites the Second Lord to visit Diana with him.

## Act 3, Scene 7

Helena has told the Widow that she is Bertram's wife, and she proposes a plot: if Diana pretends to accept Bertram as a lover, Helena will substitute for the young woman in bed; Bertram will not recognise her in the dark. The Widow agrees.

## Act 4, Scene 1

The First Lord instructs his men to pose as foreign mercenaries, pretending to speak in an exotic language to Parolles. The FIRST SOLDIER volunteers to act as their 'interpreter'. Parolles appears, wondering what excuse he can offer for returning without the drum. He is captured and immediately promises, through the 'interpreter', to reveal military secrets if his life is spared.

## Act 4, Scene 2

Bertram attempts to talk Diana into sleeping with him. She demands that he give her his ring, a family heirloom, and also asks him to promise not to speak to her when they meet later that night. He agrees.

## Act 4, Scene 3

The First and Second Lords discuss Bertram's disgrace for having left his wife, noting also that he has seduced a young woman by giving her his family ring. They have heard that his wife has died, and they regret that he is probably pleased by this. Bertram arrives, and the blindfolded Parolles is brought in to be 'interrogated'. He reveals military secrets, disparaging both Bertram and the Lords as he does so. The blindfold is removed, and Parolles sees who has exposed him. The Lords, Bertram, and the Soldiers bid him a sardonic farewell and leave for France, the war being over. Alone, Parolles declares that having been proven a fool, he will simply have to become a professional FOOL (1), or jester.

## Act 4, Scene 4

Helena intends to take the Widow and Diana to the King's court at MARSEILLES, where she can get an escort to Rossillion and arrive ahead of Bertram.

## Act 4, Scene 5

In Rossillion, Lafew, the Countess, and the Clown mourn Helena. Lafew proposes that Bertram marry his daughter, and the Countess agrees. Lafew has learned that the King will visit Rossillion shortly. The Clown reports Bertram's approach.

## Act 5, Scene 1

In Marseilles, Helena and her companions encounter a GENTLEMAN (4) who informs them that the King has gone on to Rossillion.

## Act 5, Scene 2

In Rossillion, Parolles, now in rags, is teased by the Clown. Lafew appears, and Parolles begs him for assistance. After chastising him for having earned his misfortune through knavery, Lafew promises him a position in his household.

## Act 5, Scene 3

The King pardons Bertram for his part in Helena's death and tells him of his prospective marriage to Lafew's daughter. Bertram offers Lafew a ring to give his daughter. The King recognises it as the one he had given Helena, but Bertram claims that it came from an admirer in Florence. The unbelieving King orders him arrested. Diana arrives and asserts that Bertram cannot deny that he took her virginity. She produces his family ring and says that Parolles can testify to her relationship with him. Bertram insists that she seduced him and then demanded his ring; he equates the gift with payment to a prostitute. Parolles appears and states that Bertram's infatuation with Diana extended to promising marriage. Helena appears and claims Bertram as her husband, reminding him that he had said he would accept her when she wore his ring and bore his child. She says these things are done and tells of her impersonation in Diana's bed. The delighted King promises Diana a dowry if she wants to marry. He speaks an EPILOGUE to the audience, asking for applause.

## COMMENTARY

*All's Well That Ends Well* presents the customary material of COMEDY—the triumph of love over obstacles—in a grotesque and ambivalent light, and this has led most scholars to place it with *Measure for Measure* and *Troilus and Cressida* among the so-called PROBLEM PLAYS. Like its fellows, *All's Well* centres on sex and social relations and offers no sure and convincing resolution at its conclusion, leading its audiences to recognise the inadequacy of humanity to live up to the grand ideals and happy endings of literary romance. Nevertheless, *All's Well* is humorous, and it does in the end offer the traditional comedic resolution, albeit in muted form.

Though love is the play's most prominent subject, there is a marked absence of the mutual joy of earlier Shakespearean lovers—as in, say, *Much Ado About Nothing*. Helena is obsessed with a clearly inferior man whose response to her is wholly negative until his grudging and heavily qualified acceptance at the close, and she wins him only through the rather sordid 'bed trick'. The comments of the Lords, the Clown, and other characters deflate the main plot even further. However, although the play supports negative interpretations, it is clear that Shakespeare did not intend such views to predominate. They are effectively countered by the positive attitudes of the Countess, the King, and Lafew. The playwright is careful to build his lovers up and to minimise the vileness of the bed trick, and he provided the traditional reconciliation scene at the close of the play. Moreover, in Helena's persistent pursuit of Bertram despite his manifest unworthiness, some commentators have seen an allegory of Christian grace, though others disagree. In any case, many critics see an artistic failure in the playwright's attempt to force his naturalistic presentation of Bertram's snobbery and Helena's manipulation into the traditional mould of reconciliation comedy. That *All's Well* is weaker than many other Shakespearean dramas is widely conceded, but it remains of considerable interest precisely because of its conflict between naturalism and romantic fantasy. Though somewhat unsatisfying in its own terms, the play constitutes a step towards the ROMANCES, where a different approach to the same conflict yields more successful results.

*All's Well* centres on Helena. Though she is sometimes seen by critics as a satirical portrait of a possessive woman, this view seems contrary to Shakespeare's intentions, for he presents her in the most flattering of lights. She is the subject of highly complimentary remarks by the Countess and Lafew at the play's outset, and the King also admires her, both before and after the success of her medicine. In restoring a dying monarch to health, she resembles an heroine of age-old legends, and she takes on an appropriate aura of undoubted goodness. Later, the Widow and Diana welcome her into their lives enthusiastically, and upon her return to those who believe her dead, in 5.3, she is received with the awe due a goddess. Moreover, her immediate resolution of all problems seems to justify this reverence; she is a virtual *deus ex machina*.

The only cause for Bertram's rejection of Helena is her non-aristocratic status. In this respect she becomes an emblem of the play's point: true nobility resides in the spirit of an individual, not in his or her rank in the social hierarchy. This idea is expounded by the King when he chastises Bertram's snobbery, observing that 'From lowest place when virtuous things proceed, / The place is dignified by th' doer's deed' (2.3.125–126). Significantly, Helena's inferior social status was invented by Shakespeare for this purpose. In his source, both lovers were aristocrats of equal rank.

Given Helena's highly positive characteristics, the bed trick places her in less disrepute than it otherwise might. It may be seen as a symbol rather than a realistic manoeuvre, a mere plot device that fulfils our expectation that Helena will get her man. In the source, the bed trick results in the presentation of twin sons to the unwary father, but the playwright purposefully muted this outcome to an almost unnoticeable implication that Helena is pregnant in 5.3.307. Moreover, the extreme artificiality of the device, combined with its familiarity to Shakespeare's audience as an element of traditional folklore, help to distance its squalor from Helena's nobility of spirit. Lastly, its importance is further minimised by the prominence given to the exposure of Parolles while it is taking place. Helena is established as an heroine in the first half of the play, and thereafter—when her actions might not seem heroic—she plays a relatively minor role, becoming a central figure again only in the play's last moments.

Bertram, too, is favourably presented in the first half of the play. The Countess and the King both praise him, the Duke of Florence grants him high command despite his youth, and the First and Second Lords, while deploring his morals, recognise his potential worth and hope that their exposure of Parolles will cause the young count to 'take a measure of his own judgements' (4.3.31–32). Though his faults are plainly evident, Shakespeare's unmistakable position is that Bertram has underlying merit. The possibility that the young man will mature and reform is present throughout the play, helping us to accept his folly.

The nearest character to a villain in *All's Well* is Parolles. He is a braggart and a coward, and the depths of his ignobility are exposed when he proves willing to betray his comrades to save his life. Parolles offers another example of the moral that nobility is a matter of spirit, not rank: although a gentleman, apparently on a par with Bertram, he is presented from the outset as an unworthy man. Much of the blame we might otherwise attach to Bertram is placed on Parolles, who encourages his young friend in his errors and who precedes him in suffering humiliation and downfall. However, Parolles' very villainy make him an appropriate object of redemption, and his response to his humiliation is telling, for he is resilient; he accepts his own nature and vows to go on as best he can, espousing the highly sympathetic sentiment that 'There's place and means for every man alive' (4.3. 328). In this spirit, he falls within range of the play's reconciliation, finding a new career as jester to his old enemy, Lafew.

The basic developments of *All's Well* were provided by the play's source material, but Shakespeare inserted some significant details. Several new characters present distinctive slants on the action. As we have seen, Parolles deflects unfavourable attention from Bertram, while Lafew, the Countess, and the King (who appears in the source material but is much less prominent) are entirely wise and generous, in contrast to the more problematic major characters. They are elderly and are concerned with thoughts of death and fond recollections of their own youth, but, unlike the older characters in standard comedies of the day, they are not the opposition who must be defeated for love to triumph. Instead, they are benign figures who offer understanding and support for the lovers, thus establishing a context that muffles the unpleasant aspects of the story.

We have seen that Shakespeare intended his lovers to be well regarded, and the final reconciliation is in no way rendered impossible by the moral defects of the characters, as it seems to be in *Troilus and Cressida*.

Helena is a paragon of virtue, despite the machinations to which she is driven, and Bertram, who is admittedly sinful, is also forgivable. Nevertheless, the ambiguous nature of the lovers' relations puts a strain on the play's conclusion, and Shakespeare tightens this strain to an almost unbearable pitch as he postpones Helena's reappearance. Bertram disgraces himself ever more fully with lies and evasions, and even Diana is duplicitous in not revealing Helena's presence. The emotional tension that this generates is made evident even as it is relaxed, when Lafew admits that his 'eyes smell onions' (5.3.314) and borrows Parolles' handkerchief. This moment also clinches Lafew's acceptance of Parolles, and thus the two most corrupt characters—Parolles and Bertram—are forgiven. The scene's complex emotional tone reflects the reality of its world: as in life, happiness in *All's Well That Ends Well* is unpredictable and emerges, if at all, only through 'The web of our life [which] is of a mingled yarn, good and ill together' (4.3.68–69). Yet in the play's final line, the King fully expresses the spirit of traditional comedic resolution: 'The bitter past, more welcome is the sweet' (5.3.328).

Nonetheless, though the play's title—a proverb used twice by Helena, in 4.4.35 and 5.1.25—refers plainly to the conventionally happy ending of romantic comedy, Helena's happiness is just as clearly precarious. When she finally asks for Bertram's acceptance, he replies only to the King and only conditionally, in 5.3.309–310. Fittingly, the King's remark in the play's next-to-last line—wittily playing on the title—is ambiguous: 'All yet seems well' (5.3.327) is as far as he can go. Bertram and Helena's marital bliss is doubtful.

The naturalism of the play—its well-drawn characters and credible social milieu—leads us to expect a more plausible dénouement, and we emerge dissatisfied. The romance of an adventurous maiden who can cure kings is unsuccessfully integrated with the more realistic tale of sexual intrigue, and the two components of which the play is made—a psychologically real world versus a conventionally comic one—merge at the end only at a considerable cost in dramatic power.

The conclusion of *All's Well* unquestionably lessens its effectiveness, but if the play is considered in light of Shakespeare's development, its failings seem less significant and its ending less arbitrary. The problem plays are similar to the romances in a number of ways: both depend on unrealistic stories, and both emphasise the power of noble spirituality over circumstances. Particularly in their conclusions, both favour symbolism and ritual over psychological realism. However, in *All's Well* (as in *Measure for Measure*, especially), the latter element still has great power, and the balance between the two is uncomfortable, barring a firm sense that spiritual values have indeed triumphed, despite the play's assertion that they have. *Cymbeline* and *The Winter's Tale*, like *All's Well*, have endings that tax belief and that depend on the evocation of supernatural powers while maintaining the underlying assumption that naturalistic causes have in fact been operating. However, whereas the contradictions of *All's Well* generate an atmosphere of conflict and stress, similar polarities in the later plays yield a pleasurable sense of life's many aspects. In *All's Well That Ends Well*, Shakespeare had not yet developed the capacity to sublimate reality without denying it, but his instincts were leading him in that direction.

## SOURCES OF THE PLAY

The main plot of *All's Well That Ends Well*, the story of Bertram and Helena, comes from the *Decameron* (1353) of Giovanni BOCCACCIO, who apparently invented it. Shakespeare used the translation by William PAINTER (2) of Boccaccio's tale in *The Palace of Pleasures* (probably in the 3rd ed., 1575), supplemented by the French translation by Antoine LE MAÇON, which Painter also used. Lord Lafew, the Countess of Rossillion, and the sub-plot concerning Parolles were Shakespeare's inventions, though the last may have been influenced by an episode in *The Unfortunate Traveller* (1594) by Thomas NASHE.

## TEXT OF THE PLAY

*All's Well* was probably written c. 1604. However, no mention of the play prior to its publication in 1623 has survived, and its date of composition has troubled scholars. In the 18th century it was believed to be the mysterious LOVE'S LABOUR'S WON, cited as Shakespearean by Francis MERES in 1598; it was accordingly presumed to have been written before that year. However, *All's Well*'s obvious similarities to *Hamlet, Troilus and Cressida,* and *Measure for Measure* were soon recognised, and Samuel Taylor COLERIDGE introduced another hypothesis: he held that an early version of the play was indeed *Love's Labour's Won* but that Shakespeare rewrote and retitled it between 1604 and 1606. This suggestion was felt to account for perceivable differences in style within the play (as, e.g., the use of a SONNET in 3.4.4–17 and rhymed couplets in several passages). This theory was widely accepted until fairly recently. However, modern scholarship is more inclined to find stylistic variation normal in Shakespeare's plays and to suppose that *All's Well* was a single creation. There is no clear internal evidence to indicate a date for his composition, and estimates have ranged from 1599 to after 1608. However, scholars generally rely on *All's Well*'s close resemblance to the securely datable *Measure for Measure*—in its plot, its heroine, even in its vocabulary—and assign it the same date, 1604.

The play was first published in 1623, in the FIRST FOLIO. The Folio text is believed to have been printed from Shakespeare's own manuscript, or FOUL PAPERS, for several reasons, most notably its vague and inconsistent speech headings and stage directions and the existence of VIOLENTA, a GHOST CHARACTER. The Folio text, though somewhat flawed, is necessarily the basis of all subsequent editions.

THEATRICAL HISTORY OF THE PLAY

No production of *All's Well* is known before a single performance of 1740, although several references suggest that it had been performed in the early 17th century. The play was popular in the 1740s—Theophilus CIBBER (3) was a popular Parolles, and Peg WOFFINGTON played Helena—but was revived only occasionally during the rest of the century. In the early 19th century a 1794 adaptation by John Philip KEMBLE (3), heavily abridged and censored, was performed from time to time, and this version was also put on by other producers, including Samuel PHELPS. However, the play was not frequently staged in any version.

Only in the second half of the 20th century has *All's Well* become more popular. Among noteworthy productions have been those of Robert ATKINS (1949), Tyrone GUTHRIE (1953 and 1959, in Stratford, Ontario and STRATFORD, England) and John BARTON (1967, Stratford, England). Guthrie's presentation—which in 1959 starred Zoë CALDWELL as Helena and Edith EVANS (1) as the Countess—was highly controversial; it freely abridged Shakespeare's text (the Clown was eliminated entirely) and treated the play as a farce, adding much comic stage business involving such modern props as a radio microphone. The scenes in Paris and Rossillion were set in an Edwardian world, while the Italian wars were startlingly represented by modern desert legionnaires. It was extremely popular at both Stratfords. Another production that evoked the punctilious society of the Edwardian era was Trevor NUNN's (1981–1983), which starred Peggy ASHCROFT as the Countess and moved from Stratford to London to Broadway. *All's Well* has also been produced twice for TELEVISION, in 1968 (Guthrie's version) and 1981.

**Alonso, King of Naples** Character in *The Tempest,* father of FERDINAND (2). In 2.1, when Alonso and his followers are shipwrecked on the magician PROSPERO's island, Alonso believes his son has drowned and his grief overwhelms him. In 3.3 Prospero's sprite ARIEL, disguised as a HARPY, declares Alonso, ANTONIO (5), and SEBASTIAN (3) to be 'three men of sin' (3.3.53) and reminds the king that he helped Antonio depose Prospero as Duke of Milan (before the play began). Ariel cites the loss of Ferdinand as Alonso's punishment. The three are made insane by Prospero's magic and must be revived at the play's end, in 5.1. Faced with Prospero, Alonso willingly surrenders Milan to him and begs his pardon. When Prospero reveals the sur-

viving Ferdinand, Alonso is overjoyed; his 'I say, Amen' (5.1.204) offers a religious reference that reinforces the play's point that providence can restore human happiness.

Alonso symbolises several of the play's themes. His story demonstrates the Christian pattern of sin, suffering, repentance, and eventual recompense, thus supporting the play's presentation of moral regeneration and contributing to the final aura of reconciliation and forgiveness. His fall into madness and subsequent revival as a purified man is an instance of another important theme, transfiguration. Finally, his innate goodness—exemplified by his grief for Ferdinand and his admission of guilt—contrasts tellingly with the villainy of those around him, especially Antonio.

**Ambassador (1)** Any of several minor characters in *Henry V,* diplomats representing FRANCE (1) at the court of King HENRY V. In 1.2 one of the Ambassadors conveys the arrogant message of the DAUPHIN (3), including a mocking delivery of tennis balls, implying the king's fitness only for childish games. The insult offers Henry an occasion to declare war.

**Ambassador (2)** Minor character in *Hamlet,* an emissary from England to DENMARK. The Ambassador arrives at the Danish court, in 5.2, after the deaths of the KING (5), the QUEEN (9), LAERTES, and HAMLET. He reports on the execution of ROSENCRANTZ AND GUILDENSTERN, thereby completing an unfinished element in the play's plot. With FORTINBRAS, the Ambassador offers an outsider's shocked view of the bloody collapse of Denmark's monarchy, reinforcing the play's central theme that evil has a corrupting influence that spreads far beyond its immediate consequences.

**Ambassador (3)** Minor character in *Antony and Cleopatra,* a representative of ANTONY. In 3.12 the Ambassador carries his master's formal surrender to Octavius CAESAR (2) after the battle of ACTIUM, and in 3.13, after he has reported that Caesar refuses Antony's request for his life but offers leniency to CLEOPATRA if she will abandon Antony, Antony sends him back to Caesar with a challenge of hand-to-hand combat. Antony identifies the Ambassador as the 'schoolmaster' (3.11.71) of his and CLEOPATRA's children. In 3.12 DOLABELLA observes that the use of the schoolmaster as an emissary indicates the totality of Antony's defeat. This schoolmaster is identified by Shakespeare's source, PLUTARCH, as one Euphronius, presumably a Greek scholar but otherwise unknown in history. Plutarch adds that his diplomatic employment was necessary because of the earlier abandonment of Cleopatra by her attendant, ALEXAS.

**Amiens** Character in *As You Like It,* singer in the court of DUKE (7) Senior. Amiens has no distinct personality of his own and functions primarily to affirm the duke's sentiments about his exile in ARDEN (1). His songs, which he sings in 2.5.1–8, 2.5.35–42, and 2.7. 174–193, insist on the virtues of life in the woods, compared to life at court: 'Here shall [one] see / No enemy, / But winter and rough weather' (2.5.6–8).

Scholars believe that Amiens may have first been played by Robert ARMIN, a singer/comedian who joined Shakespeare's acting company, the CHAMBER-LAIN'S MEN, just before *As You Like It* was written. Armin probably played TOUCHSTONE also, but Amiens' songs may have been created with his abilities in mind.

**Amyot, Jacques (1513–1593)**   French writer and translator of PLUTARCH's *Lives*. Amyot's Plutarch, published in 1559 and now regarded as one of the greatest works of 16th-century French prose, was in turn translated into English by Sir Thomas NORTH and became Shakespeare's primary source for *Antony and Cleopatra, Coriolanus, Julius Caesar,* and *Timon of Athens* and a minor source for other plays. Amyot, born in great poverty, became a leading humanistic churchman and scholar, serving as Bishop of Auxerre and tutor to two French kings-to-be.

**Anderson (1), Judith (b. 1898)**   Australian-born American actress. Anderson came to America in 1918 and began a long and successful career on the New York stage. Perhaps best known for her Medea, she is particularly associated with passionate and ruthless characters. Her Shakespearean roles have included LADY (6) Macbeth—in the 1941 production of Margaret WEBSTER [3] and in a 1960 FILM, both times opposite Maurice EVANS (4)—and Queen GERTRUDE, opposite John GIELGUD's HAMLET, in 1936. Anderson also played Hamlet herself, carrying on a tradition of female Hamlets extending back to the 18th century; she took the part in 1971, at the age of 73.

**Anderson (2), Mary (1859–1940)**   American actress. Anderson, a California native, made her debut as JULIET (1) in Louisville, Kentucky, at 16. She then toured American cities for several years and established herself in New York at 18, in 1877. In 1882 she went to London, where she was successful in a variety of roles, including Juliet and ROSALIND. She returned to New York in 1885 and was regarded as one of the leading lights of the American theatre. In 1887 she was the first actress to play both PERDITA and HERMIONE in *The Winter's Tale.* Two years later she married and retired from the stage. She settled in England, near STRATFORD, where she lived the rest of her life.

**Andrew (1)**   Ship mentioned in *The Merchant of Venice,* a reference that helps scholars to date the play. SALERIO alludes to a shipwreck as an 'Andrew dock'd in sand' (1.1.27); in the original published edition of the

play, the name Andrew was printed in italics, evidently denoting a ship. Shakespeare was referring to an event of 1596 in which an English naval force, commanded by the Earl of ESSEX (2) and Charles HOWARD, captured or sank most of the ships in Cadiz, Spain's greatest Atlantic port, and sacked the town. One of the principal prizes of this expedition was the ship *St Andrew,* which was seized after having run aground during the battle; this vessel became an important British warship over the next few years. The news of the battle at Cadiz reached London on July 30, 1596; therefore, Shakespeare could not have completed *The Merchant of Venice* before then. Shakespeare's audiences doubtless recognised the reference, but its sense was lost to later generations until 20th-century scholarship rediscovered its meaning.

**Andrew (2) Aguecheek, Sir**   Character in *Twelfth Night.* See SIR ANDREW.

**Andromache**   Legendary figure and minor character in *Troilus and Cressida,* the wife of HECTOR. In 5.3, disturbed by dire omens, Andromache unsuccessfully tries to persuade Hector not to fight. The episode humanises the warrior by showing that he has a loving spouse, and it also stresses his fatal destiny. According to classical mythology, Andromache became the slave of ACHILLES' son after the fall of TROY, later marrying HELENUS.

**Andronicus**   See MARCUS ANDRONICUS; TITUS (1).

**Angelo (1)**   Minor character in *The Comedy of Errors,* a goldsmith and friend of ANTIPHOLUS OF EPHESUS. Angelo makes the gold necklace that figures in the confusions and misunderstandings at the play's heart. His effort to have Antipholus arrested for debt, having failed to pay for the necklace, results in ANTIPHOLUS OF SYRACUSE retreating into the sanctuary of the PRIORY (5.1.37). This flight triggers the play's final resolution.

**Angelo (2)**   Character in *Measure for Measure,* deputy to the DUKE (9) of VIENNA and lustful pursuer of ISABELLA. Angelo abuses his office by refusing mercy to CLAUDIO (3) when it is obviously due. Then he attempts to extort sex from Isabella with a promise of a pardon for Claudio. Once he has slept with her (or so he thinks), he goes back on the deal and orders Claudio's execution. Angelo is saved, however, from actually committing these unforgivable deeds by the Duke's machinations—MARIANA (2), whom Angelo had deserted years earlier, replaces Isabella in his bed and, instead of Claudio's head, he is shown that of a criminal who has died naturally. Angelo is himself pardoned at the play's close, as part of its emphasis on forgiveness.

Angelo's criminality is a facet of the play's theme of

good government. His downfall results from an excess of zeal. The Duke is too lax, but Angelo errs in the other extreme. At first a righteous public servant—the Duke calls him 'A man of stricture and firm abstinence' (1.3.12)—he proves to be unreasonably stern. A grievous injustice, Claudio's death sentence, is the result. Angelo's rigid personality is seen to be a cause of evil. He ignores pleas for mercy; he is so confident in his own rightness that he never examines his own humanity—a point made by Isabella in 2.2. Blind to human nature, he is not only a bad ruler, he is also incapable of resisting his sudden lust for Isabella. His initial misdeeds lead him further into evil. He sees this himself and cries, 'Alack, when once our grace we have forgot, / Nothing goes right . . .' (4.4.31–32). It is the Duke who saves him from his own intentions and, after he marries Mariana, he is forgiven by the Duke.

Once Isabella's refusal to meet Angelo's demand has left Claudio facing death, in 3.1, the Duke takes over the play, and Angelo is not seen very much until his conviction and reprieve in 5.1. Because Shakespeare wished to employ the happy ending of traditional COMEDY, he was compelled to abandon the psychological portrait of Angelo, though the fallen deputy remains stern at the close, seeking death rather than marriage and forgiveness. Whether the villain's reduced importance is seen as a flaw in the play or simply as a strategy in the service of a non-realistic end depends on one's view of *Measure for Measure,* but in any case Angelo remains a powerful creation.

**Angiers** City in north-western FRANCE (1), present-day Angers, location for Acts 2 and 3 of *King John* and one scene in *1 Henry VI.* Angiers, capital of ANJOU, the ancient homeland of the PLANTAGENET (1) kings, is presented as a focus of the conflict between FRANCE (1) and England. In 2.1 two armies face each other at the gates of the city, which is acknowledged to be loyal to England. King JOHN (3) of England is opposed by the French ruler, King PHILIP (2), who is backing ARTHUR, whose crown John is said to have usurped. Each side attempts to persuade the town to admit its forces and honour its choice of king. The representative of Angiers—a CITIZEN (4) or HUBERT in various editions—devises a diplomatic solution: John's niece BLANCHE can marry Philip's son LEWIS (1). However, this alliance is quickly dissolved when the papal legate PANDULPH persuades Philip to declare war on John, and Angiers is the scene of a battle in 3.2. England's Queen ELEANOR is almost captured, but John defeats the French and seizes Arthur.

The events of 2.1 are fictitious, devised by Shakespeare to dramatise the disputed succession. He sets the scene in Angiers, the traditional Plantagenet seat, to provide a recognisable symbol of the English holdings in France. Similarly, the events of 3.1 are transferred to Angiers from their historical site at Mira-

beau, a castle elsewhere in Anjou. In 5.3 of *1 Henry VI,* JOAN LA PUCELLE, or Joan of Arc, attempts to summon supernatural FIENDS while at Angiers.

**Angus, Gilchrist, Thane of (active 1056)** Historical figure and minor character in *Macbeth,* a Scottish nobleman. A minor follower of King DUNCAN in Act 1, with ROSSE he brings MACBETH the news that he has been named Thane of CAWDOR, in 1.3.89–116. Angus reappears in 5.2 and 5.4 as one of the Scottish rebels against Macbeth who join the army of Prince MALCOLM. Angus speaks very little, though he does deliver a telling description of the depraved Macbeth, who feels '. . . his title / Hang loose about him, like a giant's robe / Upon a dwarfish thief (5.2.20–22). His mere presence in Malcolm's army is significant, for the rebellion of the nobles demonstrates the extreme disorder in SCOTLAND caused by Macbeth's evil. The historical Thane of Angus, whose surname was Gilchrist, ruled a small territory in eastern Scotland. In 1056, as a reward for his services to Malcolm, he was named Earl of Angus as is anticipated in 5.9.28–30, but little more is known of him; Shakespeare took his name from a list of Malcolm's allies in his source, HOLINSHED's history.

**Anjou** Region in north-western FRANCE (1), a theatre of operations in the HUNDRED YEARS WAR and the location for several scenes in *1 Henry VI.* Three scenes, 5.2–4, are set in Anjou and concern the capture and trial of JOAN LA PUCELLE, or Joan of Arc. In 5.3 Joan attempts to enlist the aid of FIENDS at ANGIERS, present-day Angers, the capital of Anjou. Angiers is also the location of several scenes in *King John.*

**Anne (1) Bullen (Boleyn) (c. 1507–1536)** Historical figure and character in *Henry VIII,* the lover and later the wife of King HENRY VIII, and the mother of ELIZABETH (1). At Cardinal WOLSEY's banquet in 1.4, Anne chats pleasantly with Lord SANDS, before meeting Henry. The king is charmed by Anne when he dances with her, though she does not speak. In 2.3 Anne tolerantly accepts the OLD LADY's bawdy jesting about her potential relationship with the king, but her own mind is on the suffering of the rejected Queen KATHERINE. Thus, Shakespeare disassociates Anne's rise from Katherine's fall, which is blamed on Cardinal WOLSEY. Anne appears but does not speak at her own coronation in 4.1, and she is not present at the christening of her daughter Elizabeth in 5.4. She is depicted as a saintly woman, whose Protestantism is said to be a healthy influence on the king and the country. Her role in the play's events, however, is very understated, probably in order to avoid reminding the audience of her well-known fate: only three years later, after failing to produce sons, she was divorced and executed on trumped-up charges of adultery and treason. Any allusion to this would undermine the play's emphasis on King Henry's growth to wisdom and on the general virtues of the TUDOR DYNASTY, of which Elizabeth was so prominent a member

The historical Anne Boleyn was very different from Shakespeare's Anne, and the course of her affair with the king is only sketchily presented in the play. We are not informed that the king had already had an affair with Anne's older sister, Mary, nor that Anne was pregnant with Elizabeth when the king married her. Anne's personality is hard to discern today, after centuries of accusation and defence, but she was certainly not the high-minded virgin of the play. She appears to have had other affairs before Henry—with the poet Thomas WYATT, at least—and her upbringing was notoriously scandalous. Anne's father, Thomas Boleyn (1477–1539), an ambitious merchant who had married a daughter of the Duke of NORFOLK (3), was a determined participant in the power politics of the king's court. His power and influence increased greatly as a result of his daughters' sexual relationships, and it seems likely that both girls were brought up with such possibilities in mind. Boleyn served Henry as ambassador to FRANCE (1), and from the age of about 12, Anne was a lady-in-waiting at the licentious court of King Francis I, where sexual intrigue was a way of life. King Francis later described Mary Boleyn as 'a great prostitute, infamous above all'—and though Anne is not implicated in such accounts, she was certainly close to the participants. Henry knew Anne slightly at this time: he considered having her marry an Irish nobleman as part of a diplomatic settlement, apparently at her father's suggestion.

Anne returned to England around 1522, when her older sister became Henry's mistress. Anne was soon banished from court for a romantic entanglement that interfered with a proposed political marriage, and it was only after her return in 1526 that Henry fell in love with her. She seems to have resisted his desire for sex for several years, probably in the hope of becoming a wife rather than a mistress, but once sure of her eventual legitimacy, she surrendered. In the meantime she and the king scandalised the court and humiliated Queen Katherine with such behaviour as public caresses and mocking remarks. In marked contrast to Shakespeare's portrait, Anne seems to have taken pains to show her disrespect for the older woman. Such behaviour made Anne widely unpopular with both courtiers and commoners, and her ultimate destiny was welcomed by many.

**Anne (2), Lady (Anne Neville, 1456–1485)**  Historical figure and character in *Richard III*, the wife of King RICHARD III. Courted by Richard—the murderer of her late husband, the PRINCE (4) of Wales, and his father, King HENRY VI—Anne is half-hypnotised by his words and accepts a ring from him in 1.2. When she appears again, in 4.1, she is Richard's wife, and she is called to be crowned following his coup d'état. She predicts that he will murder her, and the play implies that he does so.

The historical Anne is alluded to, although in error, in 3.3.242 of *3 Henry VI*, when the Duke of WARWICK (3) agrees that his eldest daughter shall marry the Prince. Actually, Anne was Warwick's younger daughter, and, although she and the Prince were betrothed, they apparently did not actually marry. In any case, she married Richard in 1474. Historically, she did not attend the funeral of Henry VI, and her dialogue with Richard is entirely fictitious; Shakespeare invented it in order to create a scene that contrasts with Richard's later effort to negotiate a marriage with the daughter of Queen ELIZABETH (2). Also, there has never been any evidence that Anne was murdered; she seems to have died a natural death.

**Anne (3) Page**  Character in *The Merry Wives of Windsor*, a marriageable young woman pursued by SLENDER, Dr CAIUS (2), and FENTON. Anne's father, George PAGE (12), favours Slender because he is rich, although completely vacuous. Her mother, MISTRESS (3) Page, prefers Dr Caius, who is an obnoxious but prestigious physician at Windsor Castle. Anne herself is in love with Fenton. A demure daughter, she urges Fenton to do his utmost to win over her father before they consider elopement. However, she has the good sense to see that the other two suitors are totally unacceptable. After Slender has proposed by observing that it isn't his idea to marry her, but that of his uncle and her father, Anne forthrightly pleads, 'Good mother, do not marry me to yond fool' (3.4.81), and when Mistress Page assures her that Dr Caius is more likely, she cries, 'Alas, I had rather be set quick i' th' earth, and bowl'd to death with turnips!' (3.4.85). When her parents each arrange her abduction by their chosen son-in-law, she rebels and urges Fenton to arrange their secret marriage, which her parents accept in the spirit of conciliation that closes the play.

**Annesley, Brian (d. 1603)**  Contemporary of Shakespeare, a possible model for King LEAR. In 1603 Annesley, a one-time gentleman of the court of Queen ELIZABETH (1), had become insane and was the object of a court case; two of his three daughters sought to have him committed and his estates turned over to them. The third daughter, Cordell (a variant form of CORDELIA), opposed them and wrote to King JAMES I's minister, Robert CECIL (1), asserting that her father's service to the late monarch deserved a better reward than the madhouse. Cecil intervened and Annesley lived his final months in the care of a family friend. He bequeathed his estates to Cordell, and the other sisters went to court again but failed to break the will. This family was known to Shakespeare's patron and friend, the Earl of SOUTHAMPTON (2); in fact, Cordell Annesley married Southampton's stepfather, William HERVEY, not long after her father's death. It is thus quite likely that the playwright—who was writing *King Lear* at the time of or shortly after Brian Annesley's death—knew of this case of madness and filial loyalty and may have incorporated something of it in his play.

**Another Lord**   Character in *Richard II*. See LORD (2).

**Antenor**   Legendary figure and character in *Troilus and Cressida*, a Trojan warrior captured by the Greeks and exchanged for CRESSIDA. This exchange is crucial to the development of the play's love plot, but Antenor's role is otherwise insignificant. He appears in five scenes but never speaks, serving merely to swell the ranks of the Trojan aristocracy.

However, Antenor has a hidden importance, for, in the version of the legend known to Elizabethan England, he later betrayed TROY to the Greeks. Shakespeare does not mention this, presuming that his audience would know it; the knowledge makes evident a striking piece of dramatic irony. When CALCHAS, a Trojan deserter to the Greeks, proposes the prisoner exchange in 3.3, the audience knows, although the characters do not, that he has thus laid the groundwork for two more betrayals beside his own, that of TROILUS by Cressida and, more importantly, that of Antenor against Troy. This irony is signalled by the remarks made about Antenor. He is seen as a very important Trojan—PANDARUS praises him as 'one o'th'soundest judgements in Troy' (1.2.194), and Calchas says that 'Troy holds him very dear . . . their negotiations all must slack, / Wanting his manage' (3.3.19, 24–25).

**Anthony**   Minor character in *Romeo and Juliet*, a SERVING-MAN (2) who helps clear tables in 1.5.

**Antigonus**   Character in *The Winter's Tale*, nobleman at the court of King LEONTES of SICILIA. Antigonus, like his wife, PAULINA, defends Queen HERMIONE against the king's unjust accusation of adultery, and he protests against the cruelty of killing the infant PERDITA, whom the king believes is illegitimate. Leontes threatens him with death for failing to control Paulina's bitter criticism and orders the old man to take the baby and abandon it in the wilderness. Antigonus accepts the king's order and leaves the child on the coast of BOHEMIA, where he is killed and eaten by a BEAR.

Shakespeare has Antigonus die partly so that his knowledge of Perdita's whereabouts will not be available to the repentant Leontes of Act 3. But, more important, the old man's death has a moral point. The bear provides a particularly appalling end for Antigonus, an emblem of the sin of co-operating with evil. Though he is a generally sympathetic figure, hu-

morous when admittedly overwhelmed by Paulina, and courageous in his initial protests to Leontes, he must be compared with his wife, who resists the king's tyranny. Antigonus, though reluctant, is weak; he permits duty to the king to overrule his sense of justice and becomes the agent of Leontes' evil madness. He even comes to believe in Hermione's guilt, as he declares in his soliloquy before abandoning Perdita.

Antigonus' death is part of the workings of providence that underlies the play. At the same time, since he is himself a victim of the king's madness, his death—like that of MAMILLIUS and the MARINER (1)—is an example of the human cost of evil. Antigonus comes to embody the tragic developments of the first half of the play, and his death signals their end, as the drama moves from tragedy to redemption.

Antigonus undergoes a modest redemption himself. The hearty old gentleman who invokes 'the whole dungy earth' (2.1.157) and acknowledges his overwhelming wife with a 'La you now' (2.3.50) is altered by the experiences fate ordains for him. He dares to criticise the king, even if he cannot persist, and he assumes responsibility for Perdita. In his dream of Hermione, he also seems to have a supernatural visitation from the dead. As he leaves Perdita, he recognises his involvement with evil, despairing, 'Weep I cannot, / But my heart bleeds; and most accurs'd am I / To be by oath enjoin'd to this' (3.3.51–53). About to die, he speaks in a poetic diction that elevates him to a nobler level.

**Antioch**   Capital city of the ancient Seleucid Kingdom, located in what is now Turkey, the setting for the first scene of *Pericles*. PERICLES discovers the secret of the incestuous love between King ANTIOCHUS the Great and his DAUGHTER (1), and he must flee the king's anger. Thus, Antioch is the root of the evil that propels Pericles into a wandering exile, the basic premise of the play.

**Antiochus, king of Syria (c. 238–187 B.C.)**   Historical figure and character in *Pericles*, the incestuous father of the DAUGHTER (1) courted by PERICLES. In 1.1 Antiochus proposes a riddle. He who solves it will win the hand of his daughter in marriage, but any who fail will be executed. A row of severed heads attests to many failures. Pericles solves the riddle, but it reveals the king's incest, and, horrified, he withdraws his suit. Antiochus realises that his secret has been uncovered and he decides to kill Pericles, though he attempts to delude his victim by giving him an extra 40 days to answer the riddle. When Pericles flees, Antiochus sends THALIARD in pursuit with orders to murder him. Antiochus appears only in the opening scene and is a conventionally false and vicious villain. In Act 2 the good King SIMONIDES is contrasted with him, and Antiochus' death by 'a fire from heaven' is reported in 2.4.9.

As the play's only historical figure, Antiochus provides us with a date for its action. However, this was unimportant to Shakespeare, who took the name from his sources, which included him because he was one of the most famous rulers of the Greek lands of the eastern Mediterranean. Known as Antiochus the Great, he was a king of the Seleucid dynasty, heirs to a portion of the empire founded by Alexander the Great. Antiochus waged a number of largely unsuccessful wars and is known as 'the Great' because he carried a campaign to 'India' (actually Afghanistan) rather than for any lasting accomplishments. However, he did develop his capital city, and made it one of the great metropolises of its day, after which, as ANTIOCH, it bore his name. No evidence exists that Antiochus was incestuous, though he did have daughters, one of whom, Cleopatra, was married to a ruler of Ptolemaic Egypt and was thus the ancestor of Shakespeare's Egyptian queen. However, the playwright probably did not know of this connection.

**Antipholus of Ephesus; Antipholus of Syracuse**
Characters in *The Comedy of Errors,* long-separated twins who are comically confused with each other and eventually reunited. The twins were parted, each with a different parent, in a shipwreck when they were infants. Twin servants, each called DROMIO, were being brought up with the boys, and they too were separated in the wreck, one going with each master. In 1.1 the twins' father, EGEON, explains their history before they appear, so the audience knows of their relationship, though neither they nor any of the other characters do. In adulthood, the twins have both become merchants, each from a different city, but each bearing the same name.

The two brothers are distinctly different characters. Antipholus of Syracuse arrives in Ephesus, searching the world for his lost brother, for he cannot feel whole until he finds his family. In Ephesus, he is mistaken for his twin, a well-known local merchant, and various strangers startle him by knowing his name and assuming he knows them.

He finds himself dining in his brother's home, and his brother's wife, ADRIANA, believes him to be her husband. Antipholus of Syracuse is so completely mystified by his curious circumstances that he blindly accepts them. Misunderstanding and confusion continue to abound until Antipholus of Syracuse is driven to take refuge in a priory.

Meanwhile, Antipholus of Ephesus has been subjected to similar difficulties, but his responses are characteristically more angry than bemused. For example, when locked out of his house by servants and wife (who believe him an imposter, for the other Antipholus is dining there), he proposes to force his way in with a crow-bar but is dissuaded from this course.

In the end, the brothers are reunited, as the DUKE (3) of Ephesus attempts to resolve the disorders that the confusion has created. The Dromios are brought back together again as well; Antipholus of Ephesus and Adriana are reconciled; Antipholus of Syracuse is free to woo Luciana; and the twins' parents, Egeon and EMILIA (1), rediscover each other, too. The story of the twins presents in an early work a theme that was to be important in Shakespearean COMEDY, the power of providential happenings to defeat potential evil through a general reconciliation. This theme provides the moral ground beneath the farcical atmosphere of *The Comedy of Errors.*

**Antium** Ancient Italian city on the Mediterranean coast south of ROME, the setting for three scenes of *Coriolanus.* Antium is the home of AUFIDIUS, the leader of the VOLSCIANS. When the Roman general CORIOLANUS is expelled from Rome, he seeks revenge and goes to Antium, in 4.4 and 4.5, and offers his services to his country's enemies. Coriolanus' mother dissuades him from sacking Rome with his victorious Volscian troops, and he makes a treaty instead. After this, in 5.6, he reports to the Volscian leaders in Antium, where Aufidius accuses him of treason and kills him. There is no hint, in dialogue or stage directions, as to the character of the city; Shakespeare merely followed his source, PLUTARCH's *Lives,* when he placed the action there. (There is some confusion as to the location of 5.6, which seems to be Antium in 5.6.50, 73, and 80, and CORIOLES in 5.6.90. However, the latter reference is probably rhetorical, though Shakespeare may have carelessly incorporated two settings. This is the sort of error that recurs throughout the plays, and most editors omit a location in the introductory stage directions or place the scene in Antium.)

The historical Antium—the modern Anzio—was an important Volscian stronghold, but it became a Roman colony in 338 B.C. Several centuries later, as part of the Roman Empire, Antium was an aristocratic resort town. It has provided several artistically significant archaeological sites, including the famed villa of the emperor Nero.

**Antonio (1)** Minor character in *The Two Gentlemen of Verona,* the father of PROTEUS. Antonio appears only once, in 1.3, to make the decision that he will send his son to join VALENTINE at court, which results in Proteus' encounter with SILVIA and its subsequent complications.

**Antonio (2)** Title character in *The Merchant of Venice.* Antonio borrows money from SHYLOCK and agrees to let the usurer cut away a pound of his flesh if he defaults on the repayment. Antonio represents the ideal of selfless generosity that the play advocates. He borrows only in order to help his spendthrift friend BASSANIO, who wishes to appear wealthy as he woos PORTIA (1). Antonio's extravagant willingness to risk his money—and his life—stands in opposition to Shylock's calculating greed. Also, his often expressed fondness for Bassanio represents another literary ideal of Shakespeare's day—that of close friendship between males—which the playwright dealt with more extensively in *The Two Gentlemen of Verona*. Although this motif was a common one, some scholars contend that the intensity of Antonio's affection for Bassanio may demonstrate homosexual tendencies in Shakespeare. Whether or not this is the case, Antonio is a passive, melancholy, somewhat colourless man, stoical in the face of death and lonely amid the lovers' happiness at the play's end.

**Antonio (3)** Character in *Much Ado About Nothing*, brother of LEONATO. Antonio is a charming old gentleman, especially when he flirts with URSULA at the MASQUE in 2.1, undismayed when his identity is betrayed by his palsy. He is an unimportant member of Leonato's entourage until 5.1, when, sharing his brother's anger at Don PEDRO and CLAUDIO (1) over their humiliation of HERO, he challenges the two younger men to a duel. His extravagant and blustery rage is somewhat comic, particularly since the audience is aware of the imminent resolution of Hero's dilemma, but it is also touching evidence of Antonio's loyalty to his brother and niece.

**Antonio (4)** Character in *Twelfth Night*, friend of SEBASTIAN (2). After rescuing Sebastian from a shipwreck, Antonio admires the young man so much that he wishes to become his servant. Sebastian rejects this offer, but Antonio follows him to the court of Duke ORSINO of ILLYRIA, although he has many enemies there. In 3.4 he mistakes Sebastian's twin sister, VIOLA, who is disguised as a man, for Sebastian; the episode adds to the play's comic complexities. Antonio's increasing distress—he believes that Sebastian has betrayed him when Viola doesn't acknowledge him, and he is arrested and threatened with death as an old foe of Orsino—contributes to the play's undertone of disquiet and potential violence.

Antonio has had a career at sea, either as a privateer or a naval officer (described in 3.3.26–35 and 5.1.50–61), but otherwise he has little distinctive personality. In addition to participating in minor twists of the plot, he is intended primarily to establish, through his attitude towards Sebastian, the young nobleman's attractive qualities. Indeed, Antonio's references to Sebastian—'I do adore thee so . . .' (2.1.46) and 'how vile an idol proves this god' (3.4.374)—are cited by theorists who believe that Shakespeare intended a religious statement in his portrayal of the young man (see TWELFTH NIGHT, 'Commentary').

**Antonio (5)** Character in *The Tempest*, villainous brother of PROSPERO. Before the play begins, as we learn in 1.2, Antonio deposed Prospero as Duke of MILAN with the help of King ALONSO of Naples. Fearful of Prospero's popularity, he staged a natural death for the duke, abandoning him and his daughter MIRANDA in a small boat at sea. In the play Antonio, along with Alonso and others, is shipwrecked on the island that Prospero rules in exile. He continues to display his villainy in large and small ways, derogating the optimism of GONZALO and encouraging Alonso's brother SEBASTIAN (3) to assassinate the king and assume the throne of Naples. His manipulation of Sebastian in 2.1.197–285 is a striking demonstration of Macchiavellian villainy, and for this Antonio has been compared to Shakespeare's great villains RICHARD III and IAGO.

Antonio, Alonso, and Sebastian are all captured by Prospero, who casts a spell of witless insanity on them; when he releases them from the spell, he takes back his duchy and forgives them their crimes in an atmosphere of reconciliation. Antonio, however, refuses to accept this reconciliation, remaining silent when even the bestial CALIBAN assents. He thereby represents an important qualification to the play's sense of good's triumph: evil cannot be entirely compensated for in a world of human beings, for there are always Antonios who simply will not accept good.

**Antony, Mark (Marcus Antonius) (c. 82–30 B.C.)** Historical figure, character in *Julius Caesar* and title character in *Antony and Cleopatra*. In the former play Antony leads the forces opposing the assassins of Julius CAESAR (1), led by Marcus BRUTUS (4). In the latter, his love for CLEOPATRA leads to his downfall and the triumph of Octavius CAESAR (2).

In *Julius Caesar*, Antony is a courageous but crafty schemer whose political skill brings about a civil war. He helps demonstrate the social harm done by the powerful when they pursue their political ends. On the other hand, Antony, a strong personality, is an emotionally honest man and a much more sympathetic character than the virtuous, but cold and domineering, Brutus. Thus, Antony is both a positive and a negative figure who contributes greatly to the moral uncertainty that is at the heart of the play.

Part of Antony's power in *Julius Caesar* comes from Shakespeare's careful presentation of him. In the first two Acts he is an unimportant figure who speaks only 33 words, but other characters refer to him numerous times and acknowledge his potential greatness. Most significantly, Cassius desires that Antony be killed along with Caesar (2.1.155–161). He calls him a 'shrewd contriver' and accurately predicts that if he lives he will be a difficult opponent.

These references prepare us for Antony's sudden dominance of the play in Act 3. Even before he appears, the message he sends to Caesar's assassins (3.1. 126–137) establishes his strong personal style; a confident and powerful tone, both rhetorical and emotional. He soon arrives in person, and his initial response to the sight of Caesar's corpse is direct, uncalculated, heartfelt grief. Even in the presence of the murderers he does not hide his initial outburst. But he quickly turns to the future and takes control when he arranges to speak at Caesar's funeral.

His boldness and fervour are both powerful and charming, but Antony disqualifies himself for our moral sympathy with the long soliloquy (3.1.254–275) in which he proposes to provoke a ghastly civil war—he describes the bloody slaughter of innocent people in detail—in order to avenge Caesar's death. Antony's fine human qualities—his courage and intelligence—bring about tragic consequences.

Our ambivalence about Antony is furthered by his magnificent funeral oration (3.2.75–254), one of Shakespeare's most renowned passages. The speech's virtues—its bold rhetoric, its manipulative presentation of evidence, its appeal to pathos—seem to be clever but cheap effects intended to exploit the passions of the unthinking multitude. Certainly the speech has this effect, as Antony knew it would. But one realises that Antony does not seek to advance himself personally, and that he does not resort to slander against Brutus, or downright dishonesty. Antony is genuinely grieved by Caesar's death, and his expression of it, while extremely inflammatory, is not false. He actually feels the way he brings his audience to feel. And we, too, are moved to share his emotion, even as we are aware of Brutus' virtues in contrast with the mayhem Antony intends.

In 4.1, in an episode invented by Shakespeare to intensify our response to Antony, he bargains away the life of his nephew PUBLIUS (2). In contrast with Brutus' refusal to kill Antony, this action seems particularly detestable. Moreover, Antony also proposes to loot Caesar's bequest to the people, and his attitude to his ally LEPIDUS, whom he regards as no more than a tool, reinforces a sense that he is a cynical politician. As we approach the play's climax at the battle of PHILIPPI, we are inclined to favour Antony's foes, Brutus and Cassius.

However, at the close of the play when Antony delivers his famous eulogy of Brutus (5.5.68–75), he is very generous, and the balance of our sympathy is somewhat restored. Antony not only acknowledges Brutus' noble motive in killing Caesar, he also observes that Brutus was unable to recognise the true nature of his fellow conspirators. Thus, Antony emphasises once more the play's chief theme: that evil can attend good intentions when established rulers are unseated.

In *Antony and Cleopatra,* written about seven years later, Antony again contributes much to the ambivalence that characterises the work. He is both a major political figure and the protagonist of a love story. As a result of his love, his position in the world undergoes great change. Initially, he wields immense power, ruling half the known world—a status that Shakespeare emphasises with a persistent stream of political affairs. However, he wilfully throws this position away for the sake of his passion—a passion whose self-indulgence is stressed by repeated descriptions of the opulent luxury of Cleopatra's court.

As a soldier, Antony has proven himself a model of Roman military virtues—the Romans are dissatisfied with his conduct in Egypt precisely because they value his earlier record as a 'mate in empire, / Friend and companion in the front of war' (5.1.43–44), whose 'goodly eyes . . . Have glow'd like plated Mars' (1.1. 2–4). His earlier successes enacted in *Julius Caesar* are referred to several times, as in 3.2.54–56. Antony values himself for the same reasons and regrets his 'blemishes in the world's report' (2.3.5), but he is trapped in another role by his intense attraction to Cleopatra. Under her influence he has become a voluptuary; he has abandoned his duty for the 'love of Love, and her soft hours' (1.1.44) in Alexandria.

As a lover, Antony offers us a glimpse of the transcendent nature of passion, a theme that Cleopatra will triumphantly present—in Antony's name—after his death. In 1.1 when Cleopatra, as the wily courtesan, demands that he declare how much he loves her, Antony states that love cannot be totalled, for lovers must 'find out new heaven, new earth' (1.1.17). Thus, it is he who introduces the theme of transcendence through love, and this desire is emphasised by hints of the book of Revelation that frame his story in the play. Indeed, 'new heaven, new earth' is very close to the biblical text (cf. Rev. 21:1)—much more familiar to 17th-century audiences than it is to today's—and the imagery that marks his death confirms the association: 'The star is fall'n. / And time is at his period' (4.14. 106–107 [cf. Rev. 8:10; 10:6]).

Although Cleopatra disrupts Antony's loyalty to Rome, he is not totally committed to her either. Though he only tears himself from her with difficulty, in 1.3, he returns to Rome and makes a political marriage to OCTAVIA. Further, his love for Cleopatra is mingled with distrust—with considerable justification, for the Egyptian queen only transcends the behaviour of a courtesan after Antony's death—and he dies presuming she will strike a bargain with his conqueror, Caesar. Moreover, he dies not as a tragically committed lover, but rather more like a clever Roman politician—albeit a loving one—when he offers Cleopatra advice on the politics of Caesar's court. Antony demonstrates that the ideals of love and power are both insufficient, thus manifesting the duality presented by the play as a whole.

Shakespeare followed his source—PLUTARCH's *Lives*—fairly closely in his account of the historical career of Marcus Antonius, with two exceptions. As already noted, the playwright invented Antony's callous sacrifice of a nephew in *Julius Caesar,* and in *Antony and Cleopatra* he placed Antony's involvement with Cleopatra earlier in the sequence of events; in Plutarch the love affair did not actually begin until after Antony's marriage to Octavia. Thus Shakespeare's Antony seems indecisive about his loyalties, if not actually disloyal to Cleopatra as well as to Octavia. However, the change may simply have been motivated by dramatic strategy, for it is obviously better to begin the play with the love affair than to introduce it in the middle, after the political situation has evolved.

However, in *Antony and Cleopatra* Shakespeare departed from the general impression of Antony left by Plutarch. For the ancient historian, Antony was simply a moral failure, a man who threw away his life because he was unable to control his appetites. Antony's catastrophic moral collapse justified Caesar's war against him, and his defeat was entirely for the good. Shakespeare, however, made certain that we would see that Antony's vices contained germs of virtue, that his passion was firmly bound to a noble, if ill-defined, idea of love.

Plutarch depended on pro-Caesar sources (see, e.g., MESSALA) since the victorious Caesar permitted no others to survive, and thus his account is unfairly biased against Antony in the opinion of modern scholars. The debauchery indulged in by Marcus Antonius was rather ordinary among the powerful Roman aristocrats of the time, and we cannot be certain that the political concessions he made to Cleopatra were in fact made at all, nor that they were as foolish as they seem in the sources. In any case, modern scholars generally agree that it was not his affair with Cleopatra that ruined Antonius, but rather his political and military failings—had he been more clever and ruthless, he might have enforced the maintenance of the joint rule that Caesar upset, or he might have triumphed himself, and ruled Rome.

## Antony and Cleopatra

SYNOPSIS

*Act 1, Scene 1*
In ALEXANDRIA the Roman PHILO laments to DEMETRIUS that their leader, ANTONY, is involved with the Egyptian queen, CLEOPATRA, and neglects his military duties. Cleopatra and Antony appear as news from ROME arrives, and she taunts him and accuses him of subservience to his wife and the Roman senate. He therefore refuses to hear the messages.

*Act 1, Scene 2*
An Egyptian SOOTHSAYER (2) predicts that Cleopatra's waiting-woman CHARMIAN shall outlive her mistress, and adds that she has seen better times in the past than she shall in future. He sees an identical fortune for another waiting-woman, IRAS. The two women laugh over these predictions with their fellow servant ALEXAS. Cleopatra arrives and declares that she will not speak with Antony, who is approaching, and then leaves with her servants. Antony arrives accompanied by a MESSENGER (23) who bears the news that Antony's feuding wife and brother had united to fight against Octavius CAESAR (2), but were defeated. The Messenger also states that a renegade Roman general has led the Parthians in a conquest of Roman territory. Antony is angry with himself, for the conquered lands were lost while he was dallying with Cleopatra. More news arrives: Antony's wife has died. Antony dismisses the messengers and reflects that he had wished his wife dead and now regrets it; he now wishes he could break away from Cleopatra. He summons his lieutenant ENOBARBUS, who makes bawdy jokes about Antony's affair with the queen until Antony sternly orders preparations for a return to Rome where he is needed to aid Caesar against a rebel, POMPEY (2).

*Act 1, Scene 3*
Charmian advises Cleopatra to accommodate Antony in every way if she wants him to love her, but the queen rejects this idea. Antony appears and announces his departure; Cleopatra taunts him, but he remains determined, and she finally wishes him well. He assures her of his love.

*Act 1, Scene 4*
In Rome Caesar disgustedly tells LEPIDUS of Antony's debauchery with Cleopatra. News arrives of the rebel Pompey (2), aided by the pirates MENECRATES and MENAS. Caesar hopes that Antony will return to the soldierly ways he was once famous for.

*Act 1, Scene 5*
In Alexandria Cleopatra grieves over Antony's absence and praises him enthusiastically. Charmian teasingly reminds her that she had once felt the same about Julius CAESAR (1) when he was in Egypt years earlier.

*Act 2, Scene 1*
In MESSINA Pompey confers with Menas and Menecrates. He states that his chances of defeating Caesar and Lepidus are good since Antony, their ally, dallies in Egypt. News arrives that Antony is about to rejoin his friends; Pompey worries but continues to hope for the best.

*Act 2, Scene 2*
Lepidus entreats Enobarbus to encourage in Antony a peaceful attitude towards Caesar, but Enobarbus de-

clares that Antony's honour comes first. Antony and Caesar arrive to negotiate. Antony denies any part in the rebellion of his wife and brother. He apologises for not having assisted Caesar against it and admits that he has been too decadent in Egypt. The two leaders agree to put the issue aside and fight together against Pompey, and to further their alliance Antony shall marry Caesar's sister OCTAVIA. The leaders leave together while their followers remain, and Enobarbus tells MAECENAS and AGRIPPA about the gorgeous Cleopatra. He predicts that Antony will never leave her for good.

*Act 2, Scene 3*
Antony, married to Octavia, promises faithfulness. He consults the Soothsayer who has come to Rome with him. The seer advises him to return to Egypt because Caesar's presence diminishes his prospects for success. Antony decides to follow this advice.

*Act 2, Scene 4*
Lepidus, Maecenas, and Agrippa prepare to leave Rome; they will meet Antony on campaign against Pompey.

*Act 2, Scene 5*
In Alexandria Cleopatra receives word that Antony has married Octavia. Raging, she threatens the MESSENGER (25) with death; calming, she sinks into depression.

*Act 2, Scene 6*
Pompey agrees to a truce with Antony, Caesar, and Lepidus. The leaders leave to attend a celebratory feast aboard Pompey's ship. Enobarbus and Menas stay behind and gossip; they agree that Pompey should have maintained his rebellion while he could. Enobarbus predicts that Antony will abandon Octavia for Cleopatra.

*Act 2, Scene 7*
At the banquet the drunken Lepidus is teased by the other leaders. Menas takes Pompey aside and suggests that they kill all three Roman leaders, leaving Pompey the sole ruler of the empire, but Pompey declares that while he could approve such an action after it was done, he cannot honourably order it ahead of time. To himself, Menas declares that he will desert this foolishly scrupulous master, for Pompey will obviously lose in the political wars. Caesar declares that their drunkenness is wasteful and leaves. The other leaders follow.

*Act 3, Scene 1*
Antony's general VENTIDIUS (1), who has defeated a Parthian army, tells his lieutenant SILIUS that he will not pursue the fleeing enemy. He states that he does not want to succeed too thoroughly lest Antony feel overshadowed and in revenge crush his military ca-

reer. Silius admires Ventidius' political shrewdness. They go to meet Antony in ATHENS.

*Act 3, Scene 2*
Antony and his followers prepare to depart from Rome. Caesar and Octavia are deeply moved at the separation, while he and Antony exchange tense and suspicious farewells.

*Act 3, Scene 3*
Cleopatra interrogates the Messenger about Octavia; he tells her that Antony's new wife is an unattractive woman and details her unappealing features. The queen is greatly relieved.

*Act 3, Scene 4*
In Athens Octavia is upset by the rising enmity between her husband and her brother and begs to be sent as an intermediary between them. Antony agrees, and she prepares to go to Rome.

*Act 3, Scene 5*
EROS informs Enobarbus that Caesar and Lepidus have defeated Pompey, but that Caesar has arrested Lepidus and sentenced him to death. Enobarbus anticipates war between Antony and Caesar.

*Act 3, Scene 6*
In Rome Caesar angrily reports that Antony, now in Egypt, has crowned himself and Cleopatra rulers of the eastern empire—a betrayal of both Octavia and Caesar and a virtual act of war against Rome. Octavia appears to negotiate for Antony, whom she believes is still in Athens.

*Act 3, Scene 7*
At an army camp near ACTIUM Enobarbus tells Cleopatra that her presence is a distraction to Antony, but she insists on remaining. Antony appears and remarks that Caesar has made a very rapid advance. He declares he will accept Caesar's challenge to fight a naval battle, despite the objections of his advisers that they are weakest at sea.

*Act 3, Scene 8*
Caesar warns his general TAURUS not to fight on land until after the sea battle.

*Act 3, Scene 9*
Antony orders Enobarbus to establish a post from which to observe the sea battle.

*Act 3, Scene 10*
Troops from both sides march past; a sea battle is heard. Enobarbus despairs as he sees Antony's flagship retreat. SCARUS reports that just as the battle might have been won by Antony's navy, Cleopatra sailed away from it. Antony followed, and the rest of the fleet followed him. CANIDIUS arrives and confirms the news of defeat. He declares that he will surrender his forces to Caesar.

*Act 3, Scene 11*
Antony tells his attendants to flee, for he no longer deserves their loyalty. He declares to Cleopatra that though he is filled with despair, his love for her still seems worth all that has been lost.

*Act 3, Scene 12*
An AMBASSADOR (3) delivers to Caesar Antony's request that he be permitted to live in Egypt or Athens and that Cleopatra continue to rule Egypt. Caesar sends him back with a rejection of Antony's request and an assurance to Cleopatra that she can have whatever she wants if she will kill Antony or drive him from Egypt. Then he sends THIDIAS to her with the same message, telling him to make her any promises he chooses.

*Act 3, Scene 13*
Thidias arrives and declares to Cleopatra that Caesar believes she had joined Antony out of fear, not love. The queen accepts Caesar's offer of deliverance from Antony. Antony appears as Thidias kisses Cleopatra's hand in acknowledgement of her alliance with Caesar. Antony has his SERVANTS (22) carry Thidias away and whip him, and he accuses Cleopatra bitterly. When the beaten Thidias is returned, Antony sends him back to Caesar with a defiant message. Cleopatra says that despite her surrender to Caesar she still loves Antony. He takes heart and declares that he is prepared to carry on the war against Caesar, who has arrived at Alexandria, with the remnants of his forces. He says that they will have a grand banquet that night, as in the past, and he and Cleopatra leave to prepare for it. Enobarbus reflects on Antony's folly and decides that he will desert him.

*Act 4, Scene 1*
Caesar describes Antony's contemptuous challenges. Maecenas recommends attacking immediately, for Antony's judgement is clearly clouded by anger, and Caesar agrees.

*Act 4, Scene 2*
At the banquet Antony declares that he'll fight to the end and either win or recover his honour in death. When he bids the SERVITORS farewell he suggests that this night might be his last. When the servants and Enobarbus weep, he declares that, on the contrary, they will triumph the next day.

*Act 4, Scene 3*
A group of Antony's sentries hear strange noises that they take to be a bad omen for the forthcoming battle.

*Act 4, Scene 4*
Antony lets Cleopatra help him into his armour, and he leaves for the battle in high spirits.

*Act 4, Scene 5*
Antony learns that Enobarbus has deserted to Caesar but he is not angry. He recognises that his own faults have driven his subordinate to despair. He orders Enobarbus' belongings sent to him.

*Act 4, Scene 6*
At Caesar's headquarters a SOLDIER (10) brings Enobarbus the belongings sent by Antony, and the deserter is stricken by pangs of conscience. He declares that he will die of a broken heart.

*Act 4, Scene 7*
Agrippa and his troops retreat before Antony and Scarus' forces. Scarus is wounded but insists on continuing the pursuit.

*Act 4, Scene 8*
Victorious in the day's fighting, Antony returns to Cleopatra. He praises Scarus for his great bravery and prowess.

*Act 4, Scene 9*
Outside Caesar's camp a SENTRY (2) and his WATCHMEN (4) discover the dying Enobarbus, who regrets his disloyalty and grieves for his lost honour.

*Act 4, Scene 10*
Antony and Scarus prepare for a combined battle on both land and sea.

*Act 4, Scene 11*
Caesar decides to concentrate on fighting at sea.

*Act 4, Scene 12*
Scarus muses on bad omens and on Antony's fretful mood. Antony announces that Cleopatra's navy has deserted to Caesar and that the battle is lost. He sends Scarus to order a general retreat, and he reflects that his desperate condition is the fault of his infatuation with Cleopatra, whom he believes has betrayed him. Cleopatra appears and Antony drives her away with his rage. He declares that he will kill her.

*Act 4, Scene 13*
Cleopatra flees from Antony and takes refuge in a monument. She sends him word that she has committed suicide, speaking his name as she died.

*Act 4, Scene 14*
As Antony contemplates suicide, he is brought word that Cleopatra has killed herself, and he decides to do so, too. He orders Eros to kill him, but Eros kills himself instead. Antony then attempts to fall on his sword, but succeeds only in wounding himself. DECRETAS appears and takes Antony's sword to Caesar to ingratiate himself with the conqueror. DIOMEDES (2) brings word from Cleopatra. Realising that Antony might kill himself, she reveals her lie and summons him. Antony orders himself carried to her on a litter.

*Act 4, Scene 15*
Antony, on his litter, is hoisted up to Cleopatra's hiding place in the monument. He tells Cleopatra that she should trust only PROCULEIUS among Caesar's court.

He proudly states that in killing himself he has prevented Caesar from killing him, and he dies. Cleopatra declares that she too will die in the proud Roman fashion.

## Act 5, Scene 1

Caesar sends DOLABELLA to demand that Antony surrender. Decretas arrives with Antony's sword and word of his suicide. Caesar and his friends mourn the death of a great man even though he was their enemy. An EGYPTIAN appears, sent by Cleopatra to receive Caesar's orders. Caesar sends him back with assurances that he offers mercy to the queen; he sends Proculeius and GALLUS to Cleopatra to confirm the message.

## Act 5, Scene 2

Cleopatra says that she is content to die. Proculeius arrives and assures her that Caesar will give Egypt to her son. Gallus appears with soldiers to guard Cleopatra. When she sees this, she attempts to stab herself but is disarmed by Proculeius. Dolabella arrives to replace Proculeius; moved by Cleopatra's elegy for Antony, he confides that Caesar intends to parade her ignominiously through the streets of Rome. Caesar arrives and generously offers mercy to Cleopatra, who submits, giving him a list of all her possessions. However, her treasurer SELEUCUS asserts that the list is incomplete. Cleopatra rages at him, but Caesar assures her that it does not matter for she can keep whatever she wants. He leaves, and Cleopatra sends Charmian on a secret errand as Dolabella returns to tell the queen that Caesar intends to transport her to Rome in three days. Charmian returns and a CLOWN (7) arrives with poisonous snakes. After he leaves Cleopatra prepares to die. Iras dies, brokenhearted, as Cleopatra applies two asps to herself and dies when they bite her; Charmian does the same. Dolabella and Caesar return, and Caesar declares that Cleopatra shall be buried with Antony after a grand funeral celebrating the nobility of their love.

## COMMENTARY

The opening scenes of *Antony and Cleopatra* establish the basic conflict of the play. Soldierly duty is squarely placed opposite the satisfactions—both physical and emotional—of sexual involvement. The Roman soldiers see Antony as 'a strumpet's fool' (1.1.13), but Antony envisions finding a 'new heaven, new earth' (1.1.17) in the experience of love. Antony refuses to acknowledge the call of duty represented by messages from Rome, and stresses the conflict of the play when he declares, 'Now for the love of Love, and her soft hours, / Let's not confound the time with conference harsh' (1.1.44–45). But when he learns, in 1.2, of a successful revolt against the Roman power he is supposed to be defending, Antony realises that his honour demands that he 'must from this enchanting

queen break off' (1.2.125). He returns to Rome but he can only leave Cleopatra with difficulty. He compromises his sense of duty by telling her he is her 'soldier, servant, making peace or war, / As thou affects' (1.3. 70–71), before he wrenches himself away. In 1.4 a purely Roman view of the situation is presented as Caesar and Lepidus regret Antony's neglect of his duty, even as he is returning to Rome.

Thus Shakespeare efficiently establishes the dramatic action of Acts 1–4 of the play: Antony wavers between his Roman heritage of military rigour and his attraction to the 'soft hours' of indolence and lust. Thus, the emotional centre of the work fluctuates between the too-demanding rigours of Roman power and the too-seductive delights of Egyptian luxury, finally escaping to an immortal world created in the imaginations of the lovers—a paradise 'Where souls do couch on flowers' (4.14.51). In Act 5, after Antony's death, Cleopatra, in a striking transformation that constitutes one of Shakespeare's greatest climaxes, raises the lovers' relationship to the level of transcendent love. But the focus returns to Rome's 'great solemnity' (5.2.364), in the play's final words. Even as love triumphs, the final victory of Rome is affirmed in Caesar's closing speech as he translates the tale into a mundane memorial. Shakespeare does not permit the basic conflict, which extends throughout the play, to be overridden by a clearly stated declaration of values.

The fine balance achieved between the values of Rome and Egypt has led to differing interpretations of Shakespeare's play. *Antony and Cleopatra* has been seen on one hand as a romance on the transcendence over the mundane, and on the other as a lesson against neglect of duty; as an exaltation of love and as a rejection of lust. Antony has been seen as a sordid politician who is transfigured by the love of Cleopatra, a courtesan who is similarly transformed. He has also been seen as a fool who sacrifices his nobility to sensual gratification—in more modern terms, a weak individual who indulges in pleasure to escape reality. The play seems to offer no definite conclusion as to the priority of duty or sensuality. This ambiguity has sometimes led to the classification of *Antony and Cleopatra* among the PROBLEM PLAYS, works with disturbingly unresolved attitudes towards issues of love and sex in public contexts.

However, Shakespeare does provide a resolution; it is simply twofold. Social discipline and order—as seen in the order of Caesar's Rome—is presented as a necessary element for society's health and spiritual development. On the other hand, the lovers' fate—paralleled by that of Enobarbus—brings about an awareness of a different level of fulfilment; for the individual, love is more important than political or material success. When love is opposed by the forces of conventional society, as here, its pursuit can result in an intense realisation of self, which is what happens to Cleopatra in Act 5. Thus, the transfiguration of Cleopatra is not invalidated by Caesar's final triumph because the two climaxes exist in different worlds and point to equally potent but separate resolutions.

After Antony's death in Act 4 the conflict is seen in the opposition of Cleopatra and Caesar—Egypt and Rome, love and duty—and Caesar's victory is stressed in the play's final lines. The virtue of his triumph is made quite plain: Caesar declares as his victory approaches, 'The time of universal peace is near' (4.6.5), a statement that unmistakably refers—though the character is unaware of it—to the imminent coming of Christ. As Shakespeare's original audiences were completely aware, Caesar will found the Roman Empire, which was seen in the 17th century as not only a highlight of history, but as a secular manifestation of the will of God, provided as preparation for the coming of the Messiah.

Although Caesar's victory is thus clearly intended as a genuine resolution and a statement that the tragedy has not been a waste of human potential, his triumph cannot be total. The world of conflicting values that undid the lovers—the world in which Caesar operates—is clearly transcended in Cleopatra's final moments. The lovers, with their jealous quarrels and seeming betrayals, their separations and deceptions, are distinctly of the 'dungy earth' that Antony contrasts to 'the nobleness of life' (1.1.35, 36), but they have the capacity to transcend themselves. Cleopatra's extraordinary vitality leads them beyond death to the 'new heaven, new earth' (1.1.17) that Antony has envisioned. So there are two triumphs: that of Rome, which requires personal sacrifice in the name of the greater good of the world, and that of the lovers, in which individual happiness—particularly as expressed in sexual love—takes precedence over the demands of society.

Cleopatra's ultimate transfiguration cannot be dominated by Caesar's soldiers, and thus the final triumph is that of the individual's aspiration towards transcendence. Cleopatra's vision of reunion with Antony in death is sheer poetry; as such, it can have no effect on the practical, prosaic world of empire building. Her seeming defeat is actually a triumphant assertion of the continuing value of what might have been and what should be. She can, indeed, 'show the cinders of [her] spirits / Through the ashes of [her] chance' (5.2. 172–173). The superiority of the individual imagination over the power of government is stressed, even as the necessities of society maintain their dominance in the real world.

The contrasting elements—power and politics versus pleasure and passion—are mingled and opposed throughout the drama. The political and military developments—first Pompey's rebellion against the Triumvirate and then Caesar's push for sole power—point up the fact that whatever the lovers do has repercussions in the great world, and, conversely, events in the political realm determine their fate. One of the ways in which Shakespeare maintains an even balance between these different worlds is by suppressing the more spectacular aspects of the military situation. The play's two battles occur almost entirely offstage—necessarily so in the case of Actium, a naval battle, but also in Act 4's ground combat—with only glimpses of marching soldiers provided. In fact, the play's only violence is the two suicides. Thus, the love affair is not overwhelmed by the spectacle of clashing powers dividing the known world.

Cleopatra and Antony are not in any sense public figures victimised by the loss of private happiness; their love depends on the political situation that finally destroys them. They value their positions as world figures, and their affection is grounded in this appreciation. Antony promises Cleopatra that he will provide 'Her opulent throne with kingdoms' (1.5.46), and she envisions him as 'an Emperor Antony' (5.2.76). In fact, on his return to Egypt, his gift to her is a political act; as Caesar—who regards the act as a cause of war—observes, Antony 'gave [her] the stablishment of Egypt, made her / Of Lower Syria, Cyprus, Lydia, / Absolute queen' (3.6.9–11). Antony knows that Cleopatra loves power and he delights in giving it to her. But love influences politics as much as politics influences love, and Antony places his power in jeopardy by using it in this way.

The merciless entanglements of power and politics are thus contrasted with the possibility of private withdrawal into sensual pleasure. The aggressive manipulation of society as represented by the armies and ethics of martial Rome has always served an evident social purpose. The nurturing of the individual is an equally pervasive need; it is illustrated extravagantly in the luxuriant court of the Egyptian queen. Antony is absolutely human in his need for both aspects of life; he stands between two principles and he cannot fully reject either. In this lies his grandeur as a tragic hero.

Just as the political world of Rome is both potentially good and a source of tragedy, so love has two aspects, being a manifestation of the life force but also a stimulus towards self-destruction. In the latter mode love demands the renunciation of life, but in the former it glories in life. In this respect, though *Antony and Cleopatra* is unquestionably a TRAGEDY, it displays some of the features of a COMEDY. The structure of the play resembles that of traditional comedy, with Rome and Egypt being similar to the court and the forest of *As You Like It* and *A Midsummer Night's Dream*, or to VENICE and BELMONT in *The Merchant of Venice*. Moreover, comedy traditionally ended in a marriage, typically arranged through the wiles of the leading female character, and *Antony and Cleopatra* closes on a significant reference when Cleopatra, about to die, cries out

'Husband, I come' (5.2.286). Not for nothing are the asps provided by the Clown, a traditional comic rustic.

Further, the comedy of the Clown is only one instance of a feature displayed elsewhere in the play: *Antony and Cleopatra* is often quite funny. In 1.1 Cleopatra's baiting of Antony is humorous, as is her anecdote of dressing her drunken lover in her clothes, in 2.5.19–23. Indeed, in one aspect Antony and Cleopatra embody another ancient comic tradition, that of the infatuated old man enthralled by a scheming young woman. In 1.2 we see an example of the hilarity of Egyptian court pastimes, and in 1.5 the queen jests about the sexlessness of her eunuch, MARDIAN. Cleopatra's mistreatment of the hapless Messenger (2.5. 61–74, 106) may not strike modern audiences as particularly amusing, but such treatment of servants was another traditional comic routine, at least as old as ROMAN DRAMA (compare its use by Shakespeare in *The Comedy of Errors*). The bluff old soldier Enobarbus is at times a quite comical figure, especially when he mocks Lepidus in 2.7 and 3.2. In the former scene Lepidus also assumes a conventional comic role, that of the foolish drunk—a character type in Shakespeare's time that is still seen today. After 3.2 as the political plot comes to fruition and Antony goes down to defeat, the comedy disappears; its re-emergence in 5.2 in the person of the Clown is all the more effective.

The comic aspects of the play point to *Antony and Cleopatra*'s place in the evolution of Shakespeare's work, for the tragic vision of *King Lear, Othello,* and *Macbeth* is here modified by elements from the earlier romantic comedies. The comedies always displayed a potential for tragedy—in the possible success of evil—that was forestalled by the forces of love. In *Antony and Cleopatra* this situation is reversed; tragedy is in the forefront, and the romantic comedy of love amid the Egyptian court remains in a distinctly secondary position. However, the spirit of comedy does recur at the close in support of the final transfiguration of Cleopatra. This treatment foreshadows the magical transcendence that is at the heart of the later ROMANCES.

The mingling of love and politics, lust and strategy, triumph and defeat characterises *Antony and Cleopatra*. In its fusion of the mundane and the exalted—the 'dungy earth' (1.1.35) versus 'fire, and air' (5.2. 288)—*Antony and Cleopatra* is one of the most complex and rewarding of Shakespeare's plays.

## SOURCES OF THE PLAY

By far the most important source for *Antony and Cleopatra* was the 'Life of Marcus Antonius' in Sir Thomas NORTH's *Lives of the Noble Greeks and Romans* (1579), which was a translation of Jacques AMYOT's French version (1559–1565) of PLUTARCH's original Greek (c. 125 A.D.). The playwright followed Plutarch's historical account fairly closely, though he gave different emphasis to its incidents. An earlier play on the subject, Samuel DANIEL's *Cleopatra* (1594), apparently influenced Shakespeare in these variations, especially in his treatment of Cleopatra's suicide. Shakespeare's descriptions of Egypt, particularly in 2.7, probably derive from LEO AFRICANUS as translated by John PORY in *A Geographical History of Africa* (1600).

## TEXT OF THE PLAY

*Antony and Cleopatra* was written before the spring of 1608 when it was registered with the STATIONERS' COMPANY by Edward BLOUNT. Samuel Daniel's *Cleopatra* was altered between its editions of 1605 and 1607 in ways that reflect the influence of *Antony and Cleopatra*, which may therefore have been written as early as 1606. Barnabe BARNES' play *The Devil's Charter* contains an apparent echo of *Antony and Cleopatra;* it was performed in February 1607, then revised and published in October, suggesting that Shakespeare's play had been performed in 1607 or 1606. That it was not written earlier than 1606 is clear in light of the unaltered 1605 version of Daniel's work, as well as on stylistic grounds.

*Antony and Cleopatra* was registered for publication in 1608, but if a printed book was indeed actually produced, no copy of it has survived, and the earliest known text is that published in the FIRST FOLIO (1623). The Folio text was apparently derived from Shakespeare's own manuscript, as is indicated by a number of distinctive mis-spellings and abbreviations, along with elaborate stage directions, often precise yet impractical, unlikely to have been used in a PROMPT-BOOK. As the only authoritative version of the play, the Folio has been the basis for all subsequent editions.

## THEATRICAL HISTORY OF THE PLAY

No early performances of *Antony and Cleopatra* are recorded, but a production of c. 1606—presumably the initial staging—is probable in view of the 1607 alterations made to Samuel Daniel's *Cleopatra.* (see 'Text'). Richard BURBAGE (3) is presumed to have originated the role of Antony. No other production is recorded for a century and a half, though John DRYDEN wrote a play about the lovers—*All for Love, or the World Well Lost* (1678)—that was influenced somewhat by Shakespeare's play. Its popularity was so great that it eclipsed *Antony and Cleopatra* until 1759, when David GARRICK staged a version of Shakespeare's text prepared by the noted scholar Edward CAPELL. Though it featured grandiose sets and elaborate costumes and starred Garrick and Mary Ann YATES, two of the most popular players of the day, the production was a failure, closing after a week; the public preferred *All for Love,* which continued to be revived.

In 1813 J. P. KEMBLE (3) presented *Antony and Cleopatra*—using an abridged text that was amply supplemented with Dryden's lines—that starred Helen FAUCIT. Following the taste of the times, this production featured spectacular effects, including a sea battle and a grand funeral for the title characters, but it was as poorly received as Garrick's. In 1833 William Charles MACREADY starred in his version of the play, likewise spectacular, likewise mixed with Dryden, and likewise unsuccessful. Only in 1849 was Shakespeare's original play produced by Samuel PHELPS, who played Antony opposite Isabel GLYN, though it, too, was a commercial failure.

In the second half of the 19th century *Antony and Cleopatra* increased in popularity, and several productions were ventured, including those of Charles CALVERT (1866), F.B. CHATTERTON (1873), and Ben GREET (1897). Beerbohm TREE's production of 1907 continued the 19th-century tradition of dazzling spectacle requiring many extra players.

In the 20th century *Antony and Cleopatra* has been more widely appreciated, and numerous productions have been staged. The simply staged, textually accurate 1905 presentation of F. R. BENSON (1) was notable for its rejection of the taste for spectacle. This modern tendency was furthered in the 1922 OLD VIC staging by Robert ATKINS, presented on a bare stage. This production starred Edith EVANS (1), who also played Cleopatra in several later productions. In 1936 Theodore KOMISARJEVSKY staged a controversial STRATFORD production starring Donald WOLFIT. Godfrey TEARLE and Katherine CORNELL were acclaimed as the lovers in New York in 1947; Laurence OLIVIER and Vivien LEIGH took the parts in London in 1951; Michael REDGRAVE and Peggy ASHCROFT played them in London and Stratford in a 1953 staging by Glen Byam SHAW (3); and in 1967 Zoë CALDWELL and Christopher PLUMMER triumphed at Stratford, Ontario. In 1972 Trevor NUNN staged all of the ROMAN PLAYS at Stratford, England.

As a FILM, *Antony and Cleopatra* has yielded six movies, three of them silent films. The best-known film version is that directed by and starring Charlton Heston (1972); the fabled flop *Cleopatra* (1962), starring Elizabeth Taylor and Richard Burton, was not derived from Shakespeare's play. An adaptation of *Antony and Cleopatra* was part of SPREAD OF THE EAGLE, a 1963 TELEVISION presentation of the Roman plays, and the play was also produced separately for television in 1981, directed by Jonathan MILLER (2).

**Apemantus**  Character in *Timon of Athens*, an angry, misanthropic philosopher. Apemantus' vulgar insults and remarks offer a strong critique of both the gullible TIMON and the Athenians who sponge off him. In this he resembles a CHORUS (1), and he provides a running commentary on the action of the main plot. Like such similar figures as JAQUES (1) and THERSITES, Apemantus is distinctly unlikeable. This quality ensures his isolation from the other characters and thus assures audiences that his observations are impartial. His cynical attitude, condemned by various characters, proves

to be the one adopted by Timon himself in the end. Apemantus disappears after 2.2, and returns in 4.3 to exchange insults with Timon once the former nobleman has retreated to a life of rage and despair in the woods near ATHENS. Though unlikeable, Apemantus still has right on his side, and when he tells Timon, 'the middle of humanity thou never knewest, but the extremity of both ends' (4.3.301–302), he pinpoints the major defect in Timon's personality. Apemantus refuses to alter his opinions or personality to suit the circumstances of his patron, and this gives him great moral stature compared with Timon's false friends. When this is combined with the honesty of his insults, Apemantus counteracts the play's atmosphere of bleak despair. He helps makes it clear that Timon's misanthropic attitude is not that of the play or the playwright.

**Apocrypha**  Works of dubious authenticity, a term usually associated with certain biblical texts but also useful in literary scholarship. Numerous plays have been attributed to Shakespeare at various times, but it is generally thought that they were written by others and are thus outside the CANON; these comprise the Shakespeare apocrypha. While nearly 50 works, in whole or in part, have been assigned to Shakespeare at some time, only 12 have ever been seriously enough proposed to be included in the apocrypha. Six of these were first attributed to the playwright in the Third FOLIO. They are: LOCRINE; THE LONDON PRODIGAL; THE PURITAN; SIR JOHN OLDCASTLE; THOMAS, LORD CROMWELL, and A YORKSHIRE TRAGEDY. The other six are: ARDEN OF FEVERSHAM; THE BIRTH OF MERLIN; EDWARD III; FAIR EM; THE MERRY DEVIL OF EDMONTON, and MUCEDORUS. In addition, the authorship of *Pericles* and *The Two Noble Kinsmen* remains in sufficient dispute that these two plays, though commonly included in the canon (as they are in this book), are sometimes placed among the apocrypha, as is SIR THOMAS MORE, which contains only a few pages by Shakespeare.

**Apothecary, the**  Minor character in *Romeo and Juliet*, the druggist from whom, in 5.1, ROMEO buys a poison with which to kill himself, believing JULIET (1) to be dead. Romeo believes that the poverty-stricken Apothecary can be bribed to break the law and defy common moral sense by selling him this drug. The young hero veers between contempt for the Apothecary and sympathy for another victim in a world of misery.

**Apparitions**  Minor characters in *Macbeth*, supernatural phenomena shown to MACBETH by the WITCHES, in 4.1. These specters are designated as the First, Second, and Third Apparition; each has a distinctive appearance and message. The First Apparition is described in the stage direction at 4.1.69 as 'an armed head', and it warns Macbeth to beware of MACDUFF. The Second, 'a bloody child' (4.1.76), declares that '. . . none of woman born / Shall harm Macbeth' (4.1. 80–81). The Third Apparition is 'a child crowned, with a tree in his hand' (4.1.86), and it adds that 'Macbeth shall never vanquish'd be, until / Great Birnam wood to high Dunsinane hill / Shall come against him' (4.1.92–94). Macbeth naturally receives these prophecies as 'Sweet bodements!' (4.1.96) and assurances that he will not be killed by his enemies. The tensions of the play tighten with this episode, the first intimation of its climax. Macduff is brought into sharp focus for the first time, yet Macbeth's defeat is made to seem all but impossible. These portents come from the same supernatural agency whose prediction of Macbeth's rise—in the WITCHES' prophecy of 1.3—was gravely accurate.

In Act 5 the prophecies of the Apparitions are borne out, though not as Macbeth anticipates. With hindsight we can see that the Apparitions bear clues as to Macbeth's true fate, for their appearances are symbolically significant. The armoured head that is the First Apparition forecasts the severing of Macbeth's own head after 5.8. The Second Apparition, a bloody child, suggests Macduff 'from his mother's womb / Untimely ripp'd' (5.8.15–16). The Third Apparition, the child crowned, foretells the reign of the young Prince MALCOLM with which the play closes, and the tree it bears refers to his decision to have his soldiers bear boughs cut from Birnam wood as they march on DUNSINANE.

**Apuleius, Lucius (b. c. 123 A.D.)** Roman writer, author of the only surviving Latin novel, a probable inspiration for *A Midsummer Night's Dream* and a possible minor source for *Cymbeline*. Apuleius' *Metamorphoses*, better known as *The Golden Ass*, is a delightful account of a young traveller who dabbles in magic and is accidentally transformed into an ass; in this form he undergoes many adventures before he is restored by the goddess Isis. The transformation of BOTTOM probably comes from this famous tale, still widely read today, and the substitution of a sleeping potion for a poison in *Cymbeline* may reflect Apuleius' use of the same device.

Apuleius specifically identifies his hero—named Lucius—with himself, and his account of an initiation into the sacred mysteries of Isis and Osiris—of great interest to scholars—is presumed to be autobiographical. Apuleius was born in Carthage and in his youth he travelled throughout the Roman Empire. While in Egypt he married and was charged with witchcraft by his bride's disappointed suitor. His defence, which survives as his *Apologia*, offers a tantalising glimpse of provincial life in the ancient world. He returned to his home where he became a noted poet, philosopher, and religious leader. A number of works survive besides *The Golden Ass* and the *Apologia*, mostly miscellaneous philosophical and literary essays, while a great deal more, including his famed poetry, is lost.

**Archbishop (1) of Canterbury, Henry Chichele** Character in *Henry V*. See CANTERBURY (1).

**Archbishop (2) of Canterbury, Thomas Cranmer** Character in *Henry VIII*. See CRANMER.

**Archbishop (3) of York, Richard Scroop (d. 1405)** Historical figure and character in *1* and *2 Henry IV*, a leader of the rebels against King HENRY IV. In *1 Henry IV* the Archbishop appears only briefly, in 4.4, where he confers with his friend Sir MICHAEL (2). He predicts the defeat of HOTSPUR at SHREWSBURY and lays his plans for the rebellions to be enacted in *2 Henry IV*. Shakespeare may have intended the episode as a preparation for the later play, or it may simply have served to remind the audience that the battle of Shrewsbury was not to be the last of Henry's troubles.

In *2 Henry IV* the Archbishop leads the continuing revolt, although his cause is doomed by the treacherous withdrawal of the Earl of NORTHUMBERLAND (1). In 4.1 he states the dilemma of the good man who is provoked into rebellion by poor government but nevertheless believes in the divine right of kings. However, the Earl of WESTMORELAND (1) firmly asserts the point of view of the play: rebellion is a heinous violation of the natural order, and the gravity of the offence is aggravated when the rebel is a clergyman, for a representative of God should not oppose a divinely appointed king. In 4.2 the Archbishop disbands his army, after Prince John of LANCASTER (3) promises that his grievances will be considered, and is then arrested for treason and sentenced to death.

The historical Archbishop had sided with Henry when he deposed RICHARD II, although several members of his family supported Richard, including his brother Stephen SCROOP (3), who appears in *Richard II*. (Later, Stephen's son, Henry SCROOP [1], was executed for treason by HENRY V, as is enacted in *Henry V*.) The Archbishop's cousin William Scroop, Earl of Wiltshire, was one of Richard II's favourites and was executed by Henry in 1399, as is reported in *Richard II* (3.2.142). In 1.3.265 of *1 Henry IV* where Warwick is incorrectly identified as the Archbishop's brother, this execution is said to have sparked the prelate's rebellion against Henry. Although Shakespeare took his information from HOLINSHED, it is not true. The Archbishop supported the new King until 1405, when he and a number of northern barons—among them his brother-in-law Northumberland—joined to oppose the heavy taxes Henry had levied in order to finance his wars against earlier rebels. Once in revolt, the Archbishop was not betrayed by Northumberland; instead, he impetuously began his campaign against the King before his allies were prepared to fight, and he accordingly found himself outnumbered—and then outsmarted—at GAULTREE FOREST.

**Archbishop (4) of York, Thomas Rotherham (1423–1500)**   Historical figure and minor character in *Richard III*, friend of Queen ELIZABETH (2). In 2.4, when news arrives of the imprisonment of the Queen's allies, the Archbishop urges her to seek sanctuary, and he offers her his assistance, even to the illegal extent of giving her the Great Seal of England, with which he has been entrusted. This incident, which Shakespeare took from HALL (2), emphasises the villainy of RICHARD III by presenting opposition to it from a venerable figure.

The historical Rotherham was a powerful clergyman who held a number of secular posts, including that of Chancellor of England, bearer of the Great Seal. He was imprisoned for opposing Richard's accession, but he was soon released. He withdrew from court politics for the remainder of his life, although he remained a prominent churchman.

In some modern editions of the play, the Archbishop of York is eliminated and his lines are given to CARDINAL (2) BOURCHIER, following the 16th-century QUARTO editions. This change was presumably made as an economy for the acting company.

**Archidamus**   Minor character in *The Winter's Tale*, a follower of King POLIXENES of BOHEMIA. In 1.1 Archidamus exchanges diplomatic courtesies with CAMILLO, an adviser of King LEONTES of SICILIA. Their conversation informs the audience of the play's opening situation. Archidamus has no real personality, but his fluent command of courtly language lends the episode a distancing formality, appropriately introducing an extravagant and romantic story. Nevertheless, his last line, 'If the king had no son, they would desire to live on crutches till he had one' (1.1.44–45), closes the scene with a harshness that intimates the misery to come in the play's tragic first half.

**Arcite**   One of the title characters of *The Two Noble Kinsmen*, cousin of PALAMON. In 1.2 Arcite and Palamon are affectionate friends, both nobly concerned with maintaining their honour as chivalrous knights. However, while prisoners of war in ATHENS in 2.1, both fall in love with the beauty of EMILIA (4), sister-in-law of Duke THESEUS (2), and their friendship crumbles as they dispute who may claim her as their loved one. They eventually fight a duel over Emilia, with the stipulation by Theseus that the loser not be killed in the fight, but instead executed. Arcite wins the duel, but he then dies, crushed by a runaway horse, and Palamon gets Emilia.

As the protagonists of a stylised chivalric romance, the two cousins are very similar, and their characterizations tend to blur even more given the unevenness

of the play, a collaboration between Shakespeare and John FLETCHER (2). Nevertheless, some distinctions can be drawn. In 1.1 Arcite is the leader of the two, introducing the idea of fleeing the corrupt court of THEBES and attempting to broaden Palamon's military orientation. When they are obliged to fight for Thebes, Arcite draws the deepest conclusion from their situation. Declaring that they will have to trust 'th'event, / That never-erring arbitrator' (1.1.113–114), he presents an important theme of the play, humanity's helplessness to direct destiny. When their quarrel over Emilia arises, he is the more reasonable of the two, attempting to smooth things over in 2.1, when they meet again in 3.1, and as they prepare to duel in 3.3. He is also more sensible about the approach of Theseus, proposing that Palamon hide and they fight later. Nevertheless, he is perfectly willing to fight it out when Palamon insists, and when the combatants offer petitions to the gods in 5.1, Arcite speaks to Mars, the god of war. At his death, Arcite is simply a pawn of the plot, asking forgiveness with his last breath.

Arcite's personality is still further obscured by the fact that in Acts 2 to 4, Shakespeare probably wrote only one scene (3.1), and Fletcher's Arcite is a somewhat different character from Shakespeare's. A sentimentalist, he laments in 2.1 the fact that imprisonment means the cousins will not find 'The sweet embraces of a loving wife' (2.1.84) or produce children, and he thinks achingly that 'fair-eyed maids shall weep our banishings' (2.1.91). When in 2.2 he decides to enter the wrestling and running competition to gain the attention of the duke's court, he is nothing more than a stereotypical hero-in-disguise. Perhaps in light of this, Shakespeare gives him a beautiful meditation on Emilia at the opening of 3.1. However, Arcite's inconsistencies merely reflect the failings of the play as a whole.

**Arden (1), Forest of**   Anglicisation of the Ardennes, a wooded region on the borders of France, Belgium, and Luxembourg, the setting for most of *As You Like It*. Shakespeare's Forest of Arden, like BELMONT in *The Merchant of Venice* and the island in *The Tempest*, is an artificial world, explicitly removed from society. Here, relatively free from pressures and stress, the characters can find themselves and settle conflicts that escape solution in the real world. Arden is equivalent to Arcadia, the land where amorous shepherds and shepherdesses lead an ideal existence in the PASTORAL literary tradition which *As You Like It* both draws on and lovingly parodies.

We first hear of Arden as the place where the exiled DUKE (7) Senior 'and a many merry men with him . . . live like the old Robin Hood of England . . . and fleet the time carelessly as they did in the golden world' (1.1.114–119), referring to the classical myth of a golden age when an idyllic life was led in the countryside. However, Arden is not a paradise. The duke's praise of his bucolic exile is tempered by his awareness of nature's implacable strength, the 'churlish chiding of the winter's wind' (2.1.7), and his dislike of the need to kill the forest's deer for food. The duke acknowledges that he has 'seen better days' (2.7.120). Moreover, Shakespeare's shepherds are not at all idealised: SILVIUS is a parody of the sentimental Arcadian shepherd, and CORIN is a down-to-earth representative of real rural life. Arden may provide a refuge, but it does not offer a perfect existence. Further, when the duke is restored to power at the close of the play, all of the exiles—except the pessimistic and melancholy JAQUES (1)—are instantly ready to return from Arden to the real world. In the meantime, love has culminated in four marriages, the traditional happy ending in a COMEDY; the artificial world has produced the expected resolutions.

Shakespeare followed his source, Thomas LODGE's *Rosalynde,* in placing his Arcadia in the Ardennes. This forest seemed especially significant in the 16th century because it was a romantic setting in Ludovico ARIOSTO's *Orlando Furioso,* one of the most popular books of its day (from which Shakespeare probably took the name ORLANDO). The name Arden will also have been familiar to the playwright and his audience as that of an ancient wooded area in WARWICKSHIRE—Shakespeare's mother's family took their name from it (see ARDEN [2])—though no forest remained there in Elizabethan times.

**Arden (2), Robert (d. 1556)** Shakespeare's maternal grandfather. A gentleman-farmer, Arden was a minor member of the gentry. He owned land in both Wilmcote and Snitterfield, villages near STRATFORD, most of which he leased to other farmers. One of these was Richard SHAKESPEARE (12), whose son was to marry Arden's youngest daughter, Mary Arden SHAKESPEARE (11), around 1558.

Arden was one of the most prosperous farmers of the Stratford region. He had eight daughters, six of whom married (and were supplied with dowries), and when he died he left Mary several substantial parcels of land. He is traditionally associated with the Ardens of Park Hall, a lordly WARWICKSHIRE family that was among the very few English families whose ancestry could be traced to before the Norman Conquest. In the Domesday Book (1085 A.D.), an Arden held more land than any other Englishman, and the family took its name from a vast forest that it owned (not to be confused with the Forest of ARDEN [1] in *As You Like It*). However, no records substantiate this connection, and while Robert Arden may have had an ancestor who was a younger son of the Park Hall Ardens, his own circumstances were quite modest by comparison.

**Arden of Feversham** Anonymous play formerly attributed to Shakespeare, part of the Shakespeare APOCRYPHA. *Arden of Feversham* was published in 1592, 1599, and 1633. It was not until 1770 that a printer and amateur scholar from Faversham—the modern spelling of the play's setting—published a fourth edition of the play in which he attributed it to Shakespeare and sparked a century of debate. Among many notable commentators, only Algernon SWINBURNE favoured the attribution. Modern scholars generally ascribe the play to Thomas KYD, but in any case, it is unlike any of Shakespeare's known works and thus is an unlikely candidate for inclusion in the CANON.

*Arden of Feversham* is the story of a famous murder that took place in the English town of Faversham in 1551: one Thomas Arden was killed by men hired by his wife, Susan, and her lover, a family servant. The play records Mistress Arden's obsessive intent, through several failures and the withdrawal of several conspirators. She finally succeeds, only to be discovered and sentenced to death with her lover, who romantically declares, 'Faith, I care not, seeing I die with Susan'.

**Argument** Literary device, a plot summary preceding or concluding a long work. Shakespeare used a prose argument as a preface to his narrative poem *The Rape of Lucrece.* The argument was a conventional attribute of long poems in the 16th century; RENAISSANCE writers adopted it from classical tradition and used it to present the reasons why a work was written and to state the points that the author intended to make. Readers were thus provided with a prior awareness of the contents of the work, freeing them to focus on its purely literary values.

In the argument to *Lucrece,* Shakespeare briefly rendered the story of TARQUIN's lust for LUCRECE and its consequences. This account is somewhat fuller than it is in the poem itself. It describes the despotic and warlike ways of the Roman king and relates how his son, Tarquin, was seized with an uncontrollable desire for Lucrece, the wife of COLLATINE, a Roman general. (It is at this point that the poem begins.) The argument goes on to summarise the poem, and its last sentence makes clear what the poem only implies— that the revenge later taken upon Tarquin resulted in the downfall of the monarchy and the establishment of the Roman Republic. The argument thus offers a larger view of the personal tragedy that the poem details, demonstrating the breadth of political and social concern that also informs many of Shakespeare's plays.

**Ariel** Character in *The Tempest,* a sprite, or fairy, who serves the magician PROSPERO. Ariel is invisible to all but Prospero, whom he assists in the schemes that form the plot. He is capable of assuming fantastic disguises and of luring mortals with supernaturally compelling music. He is also something of a theatrical producer, arrangeing the spectacular tableaus that Prospero is fond of, including the magical banquet of 3.3 and the betrothal MASQUE of 4.1. He performs in both, playing a HARPY at the feast and either CERES or IRIS (depending on one's reading of 4.1.167) in the masque. Ariel is eager to please, asking, 'What shall I do? say what; what shall I do?' (1.2.300). To his question 'Do you love me, master?' (4.1.48), Prospero replies, 'Dearly, my delicate Ariel' (4.1.49), and when Prospero returns to MILAN and resumes his role in human society, he regrets departing from the sprite, saying 'my dainty Ariel! I shall miss thee' (5.1.95). A cheerful and intelligent being, Ariel embodies the power of good and is thus an appropriate helper in Prospero's effort to combat the evil represented by ANTONIO (5). In this respect he contrasts strongly with the play's other major non-human figure, CALIBAN, whose innate evil complicates Prospero's task.

Freed by Prospero from a magical imprisonment in a tree trunk, imposed by a witch before the time of the play, Ariel must serve Prospero until the magician releases him. But though he fulfils his tasks cheerfully, he yearns to be free again. Almost as soon as he first appears, he reminds Prospero of his 'worthy service . . . without grudge or grumblings' (1.2.247–249) and requests his liberty. Prospero—more of a grumbler than his supernatural servant—reminds him forcefully of his former torment, and Ariel agrees to continue serving and 'do [his] spriting gently' (1.2.298). He does so, but both he and Prospero frequently mention his coming release. Ariel sings of the future: 'Merrily, merrily shall I live now / Under the blossom that hangs on the bough' (5.1.93–94), and his mingling of nostalgia and fresh spirits is touching. In his last lines before the EPILOGUE, Prospero bids Ariel 'to the elements / Be free, and fare thou well!' (5.1.318). This theme, Ariel's captivity in the human world—along with Caliban's slavery and Antonio's remorselessness—helps maintain a tragic undertone as Prospero's schemes for a final reconciliation are achieved. Shakespeare does not ignore the inexorability of evil, even in a fantasy world, though he can create a charming sprite to combat it.

**Ariosto, Ludovico (1474–1533)** Italian poet whose work became source material for several of Shakespeare's plays. Ariosto's epic poem *Orlando Furioso* (1516, and a longer version in 1532) was one of the most popular literary works of the 16th and 17th centuries. One of the many stories in it contributed an important element to the plot of *Much Ado About Nothing,* the disguising of MARGARET (2) as HERO in order to deceive CLAUDIO (1). Also, Shakespeare gave the

name of Ariosto's title character to the romantic lead in *As You Like It,* knowing that his audience would associate it with the lush enchantment of *Orlando Furioso.* The playwright may have known the work in both an Italian edition (probably that of 1532) and the English translation by Sir John HARINGTON (1591).

Another work by Ariosto contributed to two other Shakespeare plays. His play *I Suppositi* (1509), translated into English as *Supposes* by George GASCOIGNE (performed 1566, published 1575), provided the subplot concerning BIANCA (1) in *The Taming of the Shrew.* Further, *Supposes* provided the device used to fool the PEDANT in the same play, an invented hostility between cities said to endanger the travelling citizen of one of them. A ruse in Ariosto and *The Shrew,* the same situation is real in *A Comedy of Errors,* where EGEON faces the death penalty in consequence.

Italian literature—and the works of Ariosto in particular—was extremely fashionable in Elizabethan England, but behind Ariosto were ancient roots that Shakespeare will also have appreciated. In the original Italian text of *I Suppositi,* a PROLOGUE (1), thought to have been spoken by Ariosto himself at the first performance, expressly refers to *his* sources—the ancient Roman dramatists PLAUTUS and Terence—and also mentions *their* sources in Greek New Comedy. Thus, in deriving his tale of romantic intrigue from Ariosto's work, Shakespeare was adding to a theatrical tradition already almost 2,000 years old.

**Aristotle (384–322 B.C.)** Ancient Greek philosopher, author of a source for *Troilus and Cressida* and possibly *The Tempest.* Aristotle is one of the few Shakespearean sources to be mentioned in a play using his work. HECTOR cites the philosopher's opinion that young men are 'Unfit to hear moral philosophy' (2.2.168) because in their immaturity they form opinions based on their emotions rather than reason. Shakespeare knew this dictum from the *Nicomachean Ethics,* translated into English by John Wilkinson in 1547. Not only does Shakespeare have Hector employ Aristotle's arguments, scholars surmise that the personalities of Hector and TROILUS, and perhaps other characters, were influenced by the psychological types Aristotle proposed in the *Ethics* to illustrate points of morality.

A related aspect of the *Nicomachean Ethics* may have influenced Shakespeare's creation of CALIBAN in *The Tempest.* Aristotle believed in the necessity of civilisation, seeing humanity as naturally incapable of moral behaviour. He saw 'natural man' as morally defective, unable to distinguish good from bad, and thus 'bestial'. He cited 'canibals', reported among the remote barbarians outside the Greek world, as an instance of such people. The animal-like nature of 'the beast Caliban' (4.1.140), as PROSPERO matter-of-factly calls him, is repeatedly referred to, and he is pointedly incapable of understanding wrong, as when he casually acknowl-edges having attempted to rape MIRANDA. His name, moreover, is an anagram of 'canibal', an accepted 17th-century spelling.

Aristotle was the first thinker to analyse the way drama works; his *Poetics* is regarded as the fountain-head of European dramatic criticism. This book on TRAGEDY (a companion work on COMEDY has not sur-vived) assesses the Greek drama of Aristotle's day and concludes that the best tragedies have certain charac-teristics in common. They focus on characters who are essentially good people but who commit a gross moral error through no fault of their own; these plays also deal with family relationships, thereby intensifying the conflict. A well-written work inspires both pity and fear in the audience, so intensely as to elevate our awareness of these emotions. The release from this highly charged response is called *catharsis*—an idea, in various interpretations, that has influenced most criti-cal thought since Aristotle.

However, although Aristotle and his followers were widely studied in universities throughout the Middle Ages, and his ideas were the common coin of literate society (he is mentioned as an object of study in *The Taming of the Shrew* [1.1.32]), his influence on ELIZABE-THAN DRAMA was largely indirect, for the *Poetics* was not translated into English until after Shakespeare's day. The *Nicomachean Ethics* was the only translation of Ar-istotle available in the playwright's lifetime. Though Sir Philip SIDNEY and others wrote about Aristotle's critical theory, it had a greater effect on poetry than the theatre. Shakespeare and his fellow dramatists knew classical drama chiefly through the works of SENECA, which are very different from those Aristotle analysed. Nevertheless, the similarity between the Aristotelian ideal of tragedy and Shakespearean prac-tice indicates that the ancient thinker's opinions had been effectively transmitted.

Aristotle was, with the slightly earlier Plato (c. 429–347 B.C.), one of the Western world's seminal think-ers. Between the two, they formulated most of the categories and concepts—from theology to aesthetic criticism—that have since governed philosophy. The son of a Macedonian physician, Aristotle began to study in ATHENS under Plato at the age of 17. After Plato's death he headed schools of his own in various locations, and for several years he tutored Alexander the Great (356–323 B.C.). He taught again in Athens after 335, establishing a scholarly community that conducted research on a large scale, on subjects rang-ing from politics to botany. After Alexander's death, anti-Macedonian sentiment led to Aristotle's flight from Athens, and he died in exile. Much of his writing has been lost, but the remainder constitutes a major component of the Western intellectual heritage, and his work is still studied intensively by students in a variety of disciplines.

**Armado, Don Adriano de**   Character in *Love's La-bour's Lost,* a comically pedantic and pompous Span-iard who participates in the humorous sub-plot. Armado's language is ludicrous whether he is in-gratiating himself with royalty or wooing his rustic sweetheart, JAQUENETTA. Armado is mocked by his own page, the saucy MOTH (1), and his preposterously rhetorical letters are read aloud as entertainment by the other characters. His pompously inflated lan-guage, like that of the similar characters HOLOFERNES and NATHANIEL (1), is a satirical target of the play.

Armado participates in the pageant put on by the comic characters in 5.2. In its course, it is revealed that Jaquenetta is pregnant by the Spaniard, and at the end of the play he announces that he has taken a vow to his beloved similar to the promises made by the aristo-cratic lovers, thus providing a link between the two plots.

Armado boasts of his acquaintance with the KING (19) of Navarre in a richly comical passage (5.1.87–108) and clearly demonstrates his descent from the comic character type known in ancient Roman drama as the MILES GLORIOSUS, a foolish, bragging soldier. In the Italian COMMEDIA DELL' ARTE, this figure was a Spaniard, an enemy of Italy and also of Shakespeare's England. Armado's very name, attached to so ludi-crous a character, is a derisive reference to the Spanish Armada's grand failure to invade England in 1588.

**Armin, Robert (d. 1615)**   Famed English comic actor, probably the original portrayer of TOUCHSTONE, FESTE, and other comic roles in Shakespeare. Listed in the FIRST FOLIO as among the 26 'Principall Actors' of Shakespeare's plays, Armin joined the CHAMBERLAIN'S MEN in 1599, apparently replacing Will KEMPE as the company's chief comic actor. Shakespeare's comic characters changed significantly at that time to exploit Armin's particular talents. Armin was a small man whose skills were verbal and musical, in contrast to the physical humour of Kempe, and he was accordingly better cast as a clever FOOL (1) than a bumbling CLOWN (1). The dialogue Shakespeare provided for him is filled with wordplay and ingenious arguments, and his characters often sing. Among the Shakespearean parts he is believed to have originated, besides Feste and Touchstone, are THERSITES and the FOOL (2) of *King Lear.* Shakespeare may have intended VIOLA's remark upon meeting Feste—'This fellow is wise enough to play the fool' (*Twelfth Night,* 3.1.61)—as a compliment to Armin.

By all reports a highly competent actor, Armin was capable of playing different sorts of comic parts; he is known to have played DOGBERRY, reviving a part origi-nated by Kempe, and he probably played CLOTEN as well. Moreover, outside his Shakespearean roles, Armin specialised in a character type that he devised himself, a doltish simpleton called John of the Hospital. Armin wrote at least one play, *The Two Maids of Moreclacke* (c. 1598), and two books of comedy routines and jokes, *Foole upon Foole* (1600, reissued as *A Nest of Ninnies* in 1608) and *Quips upon Questions* (1600).

**Arne, Thomas Augustine (1710–1787)** English composer, creator of music for several Shakespearean SONGS. The leading theatrical composer of the mid-18th century, Arne wrote for operas, MASQUES, and plays. He composed incidental music for seven of Shakespeare's plays and set a number of the songs to music, including 'Under the greenwood tree' and 'Blow, blow, thou winter wind' from *As You Like It* (2.5.1–8, 35–42; 2.7.174–193), 'When daisies pied' from *Love's Labour's Lost* (5.2.886–921), and 'Where the bee sucks' from *The Tempest* (5.1.88–94). However, Arne is probably best known today for having written 'Rule Brittania'.

**Arragon (Aragon)** Character in *The Merchant of Venice*, Spanish prince and unsuccessful suitor of PORTIA (1). In selecting among the caskets of silver, gold, and lead to win Portia's hand, Arragon reveals the arrogance that his name suggests. He rejects the lead casket as unworthy and the gold because its inscription promises 'what many men desire' (2.9.24), and he feels himself superior to the 'common spirits' (2.9.32). Although Arragon is a somewhat comic figure—he is a caricature Spaniard of a sort familiar to 16th-century English theatre-goers—his failure to select the correct casket illuminates the thematic values of the play. He is presented as a foil to BASSANIO, who chooses the humble lead casket and wins the lottery and whose victory reflects on the Spaniard's vanity. Further, the villainous SHYLOCK resembles Arragon in his pride, refusing to relinquish an iota of what he feels he deserves. An unselfish sense of community with others is necessary for romantic success, in the play's scheme of things, and Arragon demonstrates its opposite.

**Artemidorus (active 44 B.C.)** Historical figure and minor character in *Julius Caesar*, an ally of CAESAR (1). In 2.3 Artemidorus writes a memorandum detailing the plot against Caesar's life, of which he has learned. However, in 3.1 he is unable to prevail upon the busy general to read it, and moments later Caesar is murdered. According to Shakespeare's source, PLUTARCH's *Lives*, Artemidorus, a professor of rhetoric, knew of the plot through his acquaintance with some of the conspirators, but the playwright ignored this information and simply used the futile warning as an illustration of Caesar's over-confidence.

**Artesius** Minor character in *The Two Noble Kinsmen*, an officer under THESEUS, Duke of ATHENS. When Theseus' wedding is interrupted by the demands of the Three Queens (see QUEEN [1]) for vengeance against King Creon of THEBES, the Duke instructs Artesius to prepare the army for war in 1.1.159–165. He then disappears from the play. His only function is to lend a military air to the preparations.

**Arthur, Prince of England (1187–1203)** Historical figure and character in *King John*, nephew and victim of King JOHN (3). John has usurped Arthur's crown as the play opens. A defenseless boy, Arthur is supported by King PHILIP (2) of FRANCE (1) and the Archduke of AUSTRIA, who go to war with England. Arthur is captured and is taken to England in the custody of HUBERT, who is instructed to kill him. However, Hubert grows fond of his prisoner and cannot bring himself to carry out his orders. First, he decides to blind the boy; then, in 4.1, in response to Arthur's heart-rending pleas for mercy, he spares him altogether. To protect himself, Hubert reports that Arthur has died. Arthur, in the meantime, attempts to escape and perishes jumping from a castle wall. His death provokes a rebellion by John's nobles, whose reservations about the royal succession are now reinforced by revulsion at Arthur's murder, as they believe it to be.

Historically, Arthur had little claim to the English crown, although he was the son of John's older brother, for the rule of primogeniture—succession passing to eldest sons of eldest sons—was not yet accepted in England. John was named heir to the throne in Richard I's will, and he succeeded his brother peacefully, as Shakespeare's sources make clear. Philip's sponsorship of Arthur was intended purely to justify a war and had no legitimacy for Englishmen, but the playwright wished to develop the theme of usurpation.

Further ignoring his sources, Shakespeare made Arthur a young boy, said to be about 3 feet tall (4.2.100), so as to stress the pathos of his treatment. The historical Arthur was an adult by medieval standards. He was a soldier, the nominal leader, at 15 years old, of the force that besieged Queen ELEANOR at Mirabeau, Shakespeare's ANGIERS. Captured in battle there, Arthur was at first in the custody of Hubert but was transferred to an English-held castle at Rouen. He was never taken to England, as in the play.

It is unclear how Arthur died. One contemporary account held that John had proposed blinding and castrating his prisoner to make him unfit for kingship; Hubert dissuaded the King from this course and then falsely announced Arthur's death, intending to discourage his followers. Another source reported that Arthur drowned attempting to escape. Shakespeare combined these two anecdotes. According to a third version of the story, John killed Arthur himself in a fit of drunken rage. The detailed truth cannot be known, but guilt for Arthur's death must ultimately lie with John. The murder did not trigger the barons' revolt, as it does in the play—that event occurred many years later—but it may have contributed to the spate of desertions by various nobles that affected the final year of the war against France, which John lost decisively.

**Arviragus**   Character in *Cymbeline,* one of the two kidnapped sons of King CYMBELINE. Arviragus and his older brother GUIDERIUS have been raised to be woodsmen and hunters in the wilds of WALES (1) by their foster-father BELARIUS, who kidnapped them in infancy when he was unjustly exiled by Cymbeline. When their sister IMOGEN, disguised as a young man, happens onto their cave, the boys immediately love 'him', although they don't know that they are siblings. Like Guiderius, Arviragus is inherently noble and desires to prove himself in the greater world of kingly courts and warfare. When the Romans invade Britain, the brothers have their chance. After they save the British army they are honoured by the king, and then, in the extraordinary sequence of revelations and reconciliations in 5.5, they are reunited with their father.

Both Arviragus and Guiderius are simple fairy-tale figures—lost princes who are eventually discovered and restored to their rightful positions—and they have the princely attributes of courage, sincerity, and high spirits. However, Shakespeare takes care to distinguish them from each other. Arviragus is the more reflective of the two; he also speaks some of the play's best poetry. He responds more strongly to Imogen's beauty, and when Guiderius praises her cooking, the more esthetic Arviragus emphasises her singing. When they believe her dead, Arviragus expresses their grief in a lyrical passage (4.2.218–229) that compares her beauty to the flowers. Arviragus also offers an intellectually grounded, if simple, denunciation of money, in 3.7.26–28. Belarius has given Arviragus the name Cadwal, and this name is occasionally used in dialogue, but he is designated as Arviragus in speech headings and stage directions.

## As You Like It

SYNOPSIS

*Act 1, Scene 1*
ORLANDO reports that his older brother OLIVER (1) has ignored their late father's will, withholding Orlando's inheritance, denying him an education, and treating him like a peasant. Oliver appears and harasses Orlando, finally striking him, at which Orlando seizes his brother and refuses to release him until he vows to reform. Oliver promises and is released, and Orlando leaves. Oliver plots to get rid of Orlando, and the wrestler CHARLES appears with news from the court: DUKE (1) Frederick has usurped his position from DUKE (7) Senior, his older brother; Duke Senior now lives in exile in the Forest of ARDEN (1), although his daughter, ROSALIND, remains at court. Charles goes on to say

that he worries about injuring Orlando in the wrestling competition soon to be held at court. Oliver asserts that Orlando, being proud and evil, intends to kill Charles if he can and suggests that Charles should do the same to him.

*Act 1, Scene 2*
Duke Frederick's daughter, CELIA, attempts to cheer her cousin, Rosalind, who is depressed over her father's banishment, by promising her own friendship and loyalty. TOUCHSTONE, the court jester, or FOOL (1), arrives and jokes on knightly honour. A foppish courtier, LE BEAU, appears and reports that the wrestler Charles has brutally killed several opponents. He says that the matches are to be resumed on the site where they are speaking. The duke's court arrives, accompanied by Charles and Orlando. Rosalind and Celia, taken by Orlando's youth and beauty, attempt to dissuade him from wrestling, but he insists on challenging Charles. They wrestle, and Orlando wins. When Orlando identifies himself, the duke refuses to give him the promised prize because Orlando's father had opposed his usurpation. The duke and his followers leave, but Celia and Rosalind remain and congratulate Orlando. Rosalind is clearly lovestruck, giving Orlando her necklace and attempting to converse further, but the tongue-tied Orlando cannot respond, as he laments once they are gone. Le Beau returns to warn Orlando that the temperamental duke intends evil towards him. Orlando asks him about Rosalind's identity before fleeing.

*Act 1, Scene 3*
Rosalind tells Celia of her love for Orlando. The Duke announces that Rosalind is banished because her father was his enemy. Celia volunteers to share her cousin's exile, and they decide to join Rosalind's father in the Forest of Arden. Rosalind will disguise herself as a young man, take the name GANYMEDE, and pose as Celia's brother; they will ask Touchstone to join them.

*Act 2, Scene 1*
Duke Senior and his noblemen discuss the pleasures of their life in the forest. One LORD (4) describes the amusing sight of the melancholy JAQUES (1) lamenting the death of a shot deer.

*Act 2, Scene 2*
Duke Frederick discovers Celia's absence and mistakenly believes that she and Rosalind are with Orlando. He sends men to arrest Orlando or, if he has fled, Oliver.

*Act 2, Scene 3*
An old family servant, ADAM, meets Orlando to warn him that Oliver intends to kill him. Adam volunteers to flee with Orlando, offering his savings as a means of support.

*Act 2, Scene 4*
Weary with travel, the disguised Rosalind, Celia, and Touchstone arrive in Arden, where they overhear CORIN, an old shepherd, in conversation with SILVIUS, a young man who bewails his unrequited love for a girl named PHEBE. Talking with Corin, they learn that they can buy a house, land, and Corin's sheep, hiring him to tend them.

*Act 2, Scene 5*
AMIENS sings a song of the Spartan virtues of woodland life. Jaques parodies it, mocking the affectation of courtiers who take up rural life.

*Act 2, Scene 6*
Orlando and Adam arrive in Arden, and Adam, exhausted, collapses. Orlando promises to find him something to eat.

*Act 2, Scene 7*
Duke Senior and his men are eating dinner as Jaques reports his encounter in the forest with a FOOL (1), whose comical dissertation on Time has inspired him. He wishes to be a fool himself, licensed to satirise without fear of punishment. Orlando appears, demanding food at swordpoint. The duke offers him a place at the table, and Orlando apologises for his thievish conduct, explaining his desperation. He goes to fetch Adam. Jaques moralises on the stages of human life. Orlando returns with Adam, and the dinner is resumed. Amiens sings of the evils of man and the jolly woodland life, and the duke welcomes Orlando to his court-in-exile.

*Act 3, Scene 1*
Duke Frederick disbelieves Oliver's protestations that he does not know where Orlando is, dispossesses Oliver of his dukedom, and threatens him with death or banishment if he does not find Orlando within a year.

*Act 3, Scene 2*
Orlando hangs a love poem to Rosalind on a tree and wanders off, intending to decorate the forest with such declarations. Touchstone baits Corin on his lack of sophistication, but the old shepherd is confident of the virtues of his simple life. Rosalind appears in her disguise as Ganymede, reading a poem she has found that celebrates herself; Touchstone parodies it. Celia arrives with another poem to Rosalind and informs her that she has seen Orlando sleeping nearby. Orlando and Jaques appear, and the women eavesdrop. Orlando rejects the melancholy Jaques, who mocks his love for Rosalind. Jaques departs, and Rosalind, as Ganymede, approaches Orlando and interrogates him about his love. She proposes to cure him of his lovesickness by posing as Rosalind and spurning his courtship; he agrees to call on Ganymede each day and pretend to woo him as if he were Rosalind.

*Act 3, Scene 3*
Jaques observes Touchstone wooing AUDREY, a goatherd; the fool's comical remarks satirise love, women, and marriage. Nevertheless, he and Audrey have decided to marry, and Sir Oliver MARTEXT, a country parson, arrives to conduct the ceremony. Jaques objects to the irregularity of the rite and escorts the couple away.

*Act 3, Scene 4*
Rosalind is distressed that Orlando is late for his date with Ganymede, and Celia accuses all men of being dishonest breakers of appointments. Corin arrives and offers to show them the courtship of Silvius and Phebe.

*Act 3, Scene 5*
Rosalind, Celia, and Corin overhear Phebe rejecting Silvius. Rosalind steps forward and castigates the thankless young woman for disdaining a good lover, being ugly and unlikely to find better; Phebe instantly falls in love with Ganymede. Left alone with Silvius, she is kinder to him, understanding and pitying his passion, and she agrees to permit him to share her company if he will carry her letters to her new beloved.

*Act 4, Scene 1*
Rosalind berates Jaques for his melancholy and dismisses him. Orlando appears, addressing Ganymede as Rosalind, in accordance with their agreement. She pretends to chastise Orlando for being late and to satirise his talk of love. She asks Celia to perform a mock marriage ceremony between them, after which Orlando announces that he must meet the duke but will return at two o'clock. Rosalind confides to Celia that her passion for Orlando grows more intense.

*Act 4, Scene 2*
Jaques and some of the duke's lords sing a hunting song.

*Act 4, Scene 3*
Orlando is late, to Rosalind's dismay. Silvius arrives with a letter from Phebe to Ganymede, which Rosalind mocks. She sends Silvius back to Phebe with the message that Ganymede rejects her. Oliver appears, seeking Ganymede and his sister. He carries a bloody bandage. He explains that Orlando, walking through the forest, had seen a sleeping man being stalked by a lion. He had recognised the man as his evil elder brother and had contemplated letting the lion kill him. Instead, however, he had mercy, drove the lion away, and was wounded in the process. Oliver confesses that he is the brother, though he has reformed his evil ways, and he goes on to tell that Orlando, recovering from his wound, has asked him to bear a message to Ganymede offering the bloody cloth as excuse for his lateness. He offers the bandage to Rosalind, and she faints. Reviving, she insists that her faint was counterfeit and that Oliver must tell Orlando so.

*Act 5, Scene 1*
Touchstone and Audrey encounter WILLIAM (2), who is also a suitor of Audrey; Touchstone poses as a sophisticate and threateningly drives William away.

*Act 5, Scene 2*
Orlando and Oliver, now reconciled, discuss Oliver's love for Celia, which she has returned; the two are to be married the next day. Oliver asserts that he will surrender all of their father's estate to Orlando and remain with Celia, whom he believes to be a shepherdess. He leaves as Rosalind arrives, still disguised as Ganymede. Orlando declares that his lovesickness for the absent Rosalind is such that he can no longer accept the masquerade of Ganymede as his lover. Ganymede then declares that he knows magic and can summon Rosalind; he promises that Orlando can marry her at Oliver and Celia's wedding the next day. Silvius and Phebe arrive, and Ganymede promises Phebe that, if he will marry any woman, he will marry her, but that if she sees that Ganymede will *not* marry any woman, she must accept Silvius. She agrees.

*Act 5, Scene 3*
Touchstone and Audrey also plan to marry the next day. Two PAGES (7) appear and sing a love song.

*Act 5, Scene 4*
Orlando tells the duke that he is unsure of Ganymede's promised magic. Rosalind, as Ganymede, appears with Silvius and Phebe; she elicits the duke's assurance that he will permit his daughter, Rosalind, to marry Orlando if he can produce her, and he has Phebe reaffirm her promise to marry Silvius if she must refuse Ganymede. Then Ganymede leaves. Touchstone and Audrey arrive; Touchstone satirises duelling and courtly honour. HYMEN (1), the Roman god of marriage, leads a festive MASQUE. Rosalind, appearing as herself, enters and identifies herself as the duke's daughter and Orlando's bride. Phebe sees that she must marry Silvius and agrees with good will, as Hymen sings a wedding hymn. JAQUES (2), a brother of Oliver and Orlando, arrives with the news that Duke Frederick, having come to Arden with the intention of killing Duke Senior, has been reformed by a holy man. He has accordingly restored the duchy to his banished brother and intends to retire to a monastery. The melancholy Jaques decides to join him, preferring a solitary life of contemplation to the festive court. He leaves as the wedding celebration begins with a dance. Rosalind then speaks an EPILOGUE, soliciting applause for the play.

COMMENTARY

*As You Like It,* as its title asserts, has something to offer every taste. On one level it serves as a stock romantic comedy, with disguised princesses, an unjustly deposed ruler, and a handsome leading couple. But the play also offers food for thought on a traditionally entertaining subject, the assets and drawbacks of country life. And the dedicated student of literature can consider the play's relationship to a favourite RENAISSANCE literary mode, the PASTORAL romance, a form of escapist writing with roots in ancient Greece. Further, the play is a sparkling theatrical entertainment, with more SONGS than any other Shakespearean play and several diverting set pieces: an on-stage wrestling match in 1.2, a procession of singing hunters in 4.2 (traditionally carrying a deer's carcass, though a set of antlers has been generally substituted in more modern times), and Hymen's charming masque in 5.4.

These features enliven a work whose plotting is strikingly undramatic. After Act 1 establishes the separate banishments of Duke Senior, Orlando, and Rosalind, Acts 2–4, set in Arden, lack striking change. Adam seems near death in 2.3, but we know that the exiled duke's comfortable establishment is near, and we feel only admiration for Orlando's devotion rather than anxiety for Adam's plight. Orlando invades the Duke's banquet, but we know that he will be graciously received, and we are not chilled by any threat of violence. Oliver's tale of peril and salvation offers no thrilling tension, for we know he survived to tell us about it.

Instead of a plot, the play presents conversations among different combinations of characters. They talk mostly about romantic love, country living, or both. Their remarks weave a shimmering pattern of agreements and contradictions, harmonies and counterpoints, that constitute the substance of Acts 2–4. There emerges from this fabric of ideas an opposition of two points of view: a responsiveness to love and life, represented by Rosalind; and a withdrawal from complexities and commitment, represented by Jaques. The play's climax in Act 5 produces a resolution in favour of the former. Jaques, although no villain, must be defeated if the life-affirming spirit of the lovers is to triumph, for his doctrine of passivity and retreat is ultimately antisocial.

Shakespeare neatly and subtly presents the opposition of Jaques and the lovers by having first Orlando and then Rosalind dismiss the melancholy courtier from the stage with a rebuke, in 3.2.289 and 4.1.36 respectively, before each of the two great wooing scenes. This is a bold instance of the dominant technique in the play; the development of dramatic tension not through plotting, as we have seen, but by juxtaposing encounters among the characters. For the most part, we are not expected to judge the speakers but rather to enjoy their meetings and gradually appreciate their differences.

For instance, the pastoral world of the banished duke in the Forest of Arden is described, even before we see it, as one in which the exiles 'fleet the time carelessly as they did in the golden world' (1.1.118–

119), a reference to the golden age of ancient mythology, analogous to Eden in the Judeo-Christian tradition. However, once the play's action moves to Arden, this proposition is undermined. The duke's praise of his exiled court's woodland life is followed immediately by an account of Jaques' lament for the wounded deer, which critiques human interference with nature. Jaques' comments also present a cynical, distrustful image of human society, as he 'invectively . . . pierceth / The body of country, city, court' (2.1.58–59). In 2.2 Duke Frederick's villainy is once again displayed, supporting Jaques' dark viewpoint but also reaffirming the essential virtue of the exiled Duke Senior's court. Shakespeare establishes Arden as an ideal, pastoral world in which characters criticise the real one, but then other characters criticise *them*, both explicitly and by implication. Further, when Rosalind arrives in Arden with Celia and Touchstone in 2.4, their initial response is humorously unenthusiastic, with Rosalind weary in spirit and Touchstone weary in body; the fool comments that 'at home I was in a better place' (2.4.14). Thus we can ponder several points of view without being diverted from the central situation of the drama.

In 2.5 Amiens sings a song that illustrates the Duke's attitude towards the pastoral life, that those 'who doth ambition shun' (2.5.35) are happy to have no enemies but the weather, but Jaques responds with a comically insulting parody. In 2.7 Jaques' delightfully expressed desire to be a jester like Touchstone, licensed to satirise everyone, provokes a sharp reprimand from the duke for wishing to correct the world's vices when he has sinned himself. Later in the same scene Jaques' position is again rejected. As the melancholy courtier completes his sardonic account of human life with a morbid description of helpless old age, Orlando bears in Adam, whom the duke, who is entirely unaffected by Jaques' speech, treats with reverence. The scene closes with another instance of such subtle contradiction. Amiens sings a song condemning humanity for '. . . ingratitude' and asserting that 'most friendship is feigning, most loving mere folly' (2.7.174–193). Just at that moment, the duke's hospitality is enabling Orlando to express his gratitude for Adam's friendship and loyalty. The bases of the pastoral convention—the idealisation of rustic life and an accompanying cynicism towards sophisticated society—are espoused, but they are just as persistently contradicted and undercut.

Most telling in this respect are the play's comparisons of different lovers. The central figures are Rosalind and Orlando. They are flanked by comic variations: the ridiculously conventional Silvius and Phebe on the one hand, and the equally preposterous yet earthy Touchstone and Audrey (with an assist from William) on the other. The lovesick shepherd and the hard-hearted shepherdess who rejects him were standard figures in pastoral literature, and Silvius and Phebe are absurd manifestations of it. Their exaggeration is emphasised by Rosalind's own overstated realism when she advises Phebe, 'Sell when you can, you are not for all markets' (3.5.60).

Silvius' sentimentality is countered in Touchstone's attitude to Audrey. So far from adoring Audrey, or being in love with love itself, the jester finds only that 'man hath his desires, and as pigeons bill, so wedlock would be nibbling' (3.3.72–73). His detached and resigned submission to human instincts is ironically opposed to the worship of an ideal woman. Touchstone also provides a foil for Rosalind's love for Orlando. When Silvius' plaintive lament reminds the heroine of her seemingly impossible passion (Orlando not yet having arrived in Arden), Touchstone immediately mocks her by saying that his preposterous love for one Jane Smile led him to kiss 'the cow's dugs that her pretty chopt hands had milked' (2.4.46–47).

In another repeated theme, different sorts of rustic characters are contrasted. Silvius and Phebe are essentially stereotypical literary lovers, countrified only vaguely by their occupation as shepherds. Audrey and her hapless swain William are typical rustic buffoons, instances of the Shakespearean CLOWN (1). And Corin is a lifelike peasant, a man who fully understands the realities of extracting a living from the land. In 2.4.73–84 he frankly discusses his poverty and, by implication, the essential falseness and sentimentality of the pastoral convention. At the same time, he does not envy the courtiers their easier but less honest life, and his exchanges with Touchstone in 3.2.11–83 constitute one of the most telling critiques of the pastoral in the play. The country world holds its own against courtly sophistication, yet its hardships and difficulties are clearly stated.

Even the two figures who comment on the activities of the others, Touchstone and Jaques, are pointedly different from each other. They first meet offstage, as we hear in Jaques' enthusiastic report on the 'motley fool' (2.7.13). Touchstone's observations on the human tendency to ripen and then rot appeal greatly to the melancholy courtier. However, the jester ridicules everything and has no philosophy, while Jaques is dedicated to a pessimistic view of life and looks to mockery to 'cleanse the foul body of th'infected world' (2.7.60). His jaded attitude leads him to withdraw from human society at the play's end, whereas Touchstone enters the play's swirl of courtships with enthusiasm, if also with sarcasm. Touchstone eventually joins the 'country copulatives' (5.4.35) and marries, while Jaques departs, declaring himself 'for other than for dancing measures' (5.4.192). The contrast reflects the play's two opposing poles, love and withdrawal.

The play's repeated juxtapositions of ideas and temperaments constitute its overall mood and are perhaps referred to in its title. Each character has an opinion about love and the good life, but then another personality presents a viewpoint that contradicts or modifies it. Each idea is qualified, and each has some merit. In the end, as the multiple marriages in 5.4 suggest, the dominant theme is the unifying power of love.

Rosalind represents this theme throughout, and perhaps the most telling juxtaposition in the play is that of Rosalind to herself in her disguise as Ganymede. Ganymede insists that Orlando's love is a sickness he can cure. The delightful result is the spectacle of Rosalind, while madly in love with Orlando, telling him that 'love is merely a madness' (3.2.388) and then quite hysterically confiding her love to Celia—'O coz, coz, coz . . . that thou didst know how many fathom deep I am in love!' (4.1.195–196). The climax nears in 5.2, when Ganymede's masquerade can no longer suffice. The love between Celia and Oliver is too much for Orlando to witness without pain; he insists that he cannot go on with the pretence that Ganymede is Rosalind. The disguised heroine realises that her lover has outgrown the conventional attitudes she has been teasing him about, and she prepares to resume her true identity. Her turn to magic—reprised in the appearance of the supernatural Hymen in 5.4—is appropriate to the position she has occupied as the prime manipulator of affairs. Disguised as Ganymede, she has been invisible though entirely in control. She returns accompanied by the solemn magic of Hymen's masque, casting a spell of acceptance and reconciliation; even Jaques, despite his withdrawal, blesses the couples with humour and wisdom.

Hymen's nature is problematic, but whether he is a supernatural being or a costumed human recruited by Rosalind is not as important as his role as a symbol of divine approval for the play's happy ending. This suggestion has been prepared for by various religious references. Some are quite touching evocations of traditional religion, such as Adam's touching prayer, 'He that doth the ravens feed, / Yea providently caters for the sparrow, / Be comfort to my age' (2.3.43–45), and Orlando's equation of 'better days' with times when 'bells have knoll'd to church' (2.7.113–114). Others are more prosaic allusions to biblical episodes. Orlando touches on the parable of the prodigal son in describing his lot under Oliver, in 1.1.37–39; In 2.1.5 Duke Senior likens his exile to the expulsion from the Garden of Eden, and Jaques refers to the plagues of Egypt in 2.5.58. Corin assumes that one may 'find the way to heaven / By doing deeds of hospitality' (2.4.79–80). Duke Frederick is converted by 'an old religious man' (5.4.159), and Rosalind invents an 'old religious uncle' (3.2.336) for Ganymede. The entire episode of Sir Oliver Martext, however ridiculous, raises other issues of churchly doctrine. These references subtly suggest the parallels between Christian ideals of pity and loving-kindness and the play's themes of love and reconciliation.

## SOURCES OF THE PLAY

Shakespeare's only important source for *As You Like It* was Thomas LODGE's prose romance, *Rosalynde* (1590, 4th ed. 1598). For the tale of a young heir's mistreatment by his older brother, Lodge drew on a medieval English poem, *The Tale of Gamelyn;* he apparently invented the story of Rosalind and Celia as well as the sub-plot of Corin, Silvius, and Phebe (though Shakespeare changed all of his names except Rosalynde and Phoebe, as Lodge spelled them). Shakespeare added most of the other characters: Jaques, Touchstone, Le Beau, Amiens, Audrey, William, and Martext. Shakespeare also made brothers of the usurped and usurping dukes, providing a parallel to the story of Orlando and Oliver and thus tightening the relationship between the plots. Significantly, the playwright also invented the repentance of Duke Frederick; Lodge's counterpart dies in battle against the denizens of Arden. Shakespeare's atmosphere of reconciliation was to be all-inclusive.

Certain details reflect the playwright's further reading. The name Orlando invokes the hero of ARIOSTO's 16th-century romance *Orlando Furioso*. Another famous romance, Jorge de MONTEMAYOR's *Diana Enamorada*, is actually referred to in 4.1.146, and it may have influenced Shakespeare's creation of a network of lovers here, as it did in *A Midsummer Night's Dream*. Also, *As You Like It* contains echoes of several works by John LYLY, who also influenced Lodge's *Rosalynde*. Finally, the name Corin probably came from an English play of the 1570s, published in 1599, *Syre Clyomon and Clamydes,* as did, perhaps, hints of the characters Audrey and William.

*As You Like It* is both an example and a parody of PASTORAL literary conventions. The pastoral tradition began with the bucolic idylls of the Greek writer Theocritus (c. 308–c. 240 B.C.), six of which appeared in an anonymous English translation in 1588, and was most famously manifested in the *Eclogues* of VIRGIL, which 16th-century English readers knew well. In the English RENAISSANCE the pastoral achieved its greatest popularity in Sir Philip SIDNEY's *Arcadia,* a work that the playwright drew on in other plays. Although Shakespeare did not draw directly on these pastoral works in composing *As You Like It,* they nevertheless underlie its general nature.

## TEXT OF THE PLAY

*As You Like It* was probably written in 1599, though this date is uncertain. The play was in existence by August 1600, when Shakespeare's CHAMBERLAIN'S MEN registered it with the STATIONERS' COMPANY as a play 'to be stayed'—that is, *not* to be published. This was a tactic that theatre companies used as a defence against piracy, and it is believed to have applied only to new plays, suggesting that *As You Like It* was a recent work. This theory is supported by circumstantial evidence. The play is not mentioned in Francis MERES' list of Shakespearean plays, published in 1598. More significantly, for Meres could accidentally have omitted it, the role of Touchstone, Shakespeare's first professional FOOL (1), is thought to have been written for the noted comic Robert ARMIN, who did not join the Chamberlain's Men before early 1599. It is also thought that the company may have intended to profit from a vogue for romantic tales of outlaws, stimulated by two plays about Robin Hood—by Anthony MUNDAY and Henry CHETTLE—presented by the rival ADMIRAL'S MEN in 1598. Duke Senior is compared to the celebrated outlaw in 1.1.116, when his exile is introduced. Further, Jaques' satirical bent and his discussion of humour's purpose in 2.7.45–87 may reflect a dispute on the validity of satire that raged in London in early 1599, culminating in a public book-burning in June of that year.

Another theory holds that the play was originally written much earlier, probably in 1593, and reworked later. The strongest evidence in favour of this hypothesis is a pair of references—one certain, one doubtful—to the killing of Christopher MARLOWE (1) on May 30, 1593. Marlowe's death was among the most notorious news items of the year, and some scholars hold that it is alluded to in Touchstone's remark that 'when a man's verses cannot be understood, . . . it strikes a man more dead than a great reckoning in a little room' (3.3.9–12), which may refer to the fatal dispute—a brawl over a tavern bill, or 'reckoning'—and certainly seems to echo a famous phrase in Marlowe's extremely popular play *The Jew of Malta:* 'infinite riches in a little room'. If this passage indeed refers to Marlowe's death, it does suggest an early date, for it can have had news value for only a season or two. The other instance, in which a line of Marlowe's *Hero and Leander* is quoted and ascribed to a 'dead shepherd' (3.5.81–82) is unquestionably an elegiac reference to Marlowe, though it need not have been made in the wake of his murder. Most scholars still find the earlier dating dubious, and in any case Shakespeare may have cannibalised a lost or unfinished earlier work when writing the surviving text of *As You Like It.*

The play was not published in Shakespeare's lifetime; it first appeared in the FIRST FOLIO (1623). Its text is among the clearest and least disordered in the Folio, and it appears to have been taken from a PROMPT-BOOK, with its brief, imperative stage directions and accurate speech headings. The Folio thus provides the only authoritative text of *As You Like It,* and it has remained the basis of all subsequent editions.

## THEATRICAL HISTORY OF THE PLAY

*As You Like It* may have been written expressly for the first season of the GLOBE THEATRE, in the autumn of 1599, but no certain record of an early performance exists. However, an effort was made to discourage pirate publication, which suggests that the play was popular. Robert ARMIN originated the role of Jaques, and tradition holds that Shakespeare himself played Adam.

The earliest definitely known production of *As You Like It* was LOVE IN A FOREST (1723), by Charles JOHNSON (2), a free adaptation eliminating several characters and incorporating elements from several of Shakespeare's other plays. A reasonably faithful version of Shakespeare's text was staged in 1740, with James QUIN as Jaques, Kitty CLIVE as Celia, and Hannah PRITCHARD as Rosalind. This production was a great success, and the play remained popular throughout the 18th century; the part of Rosalind was taken by most of the leading actresses of the period, including Peg WOFFINGTON, Mary Ann YATES (1), Mary 'Perdita' ROBINSON (2), and Sarah SIDDONS. Dorothy JORDAN was especially successful, playing Rosalind many times between 1787 and 1814. Jaques was played by Colley CIBBER (1) and John HENDERSON, among others. Charles MACKLIN and Richard YATES (2) appeared as Touchstone, but the most famous of the 18th-century jesters was Tom KING (26). From 1776 to 1817 *As You Like It* was the most performed Shakespearean play at London's Drury Lane Theatre.

In the 19th century Rosalind remained in the repertoire of most leading actresses, notably including Helen FAUCIT, Mary ANDERSON (2), and Julia NEILSON (2). J. P. KEMBLE (3) and William Charles MACREADY played Jaques, the latter in his own 1842 production, a careful restoration of Shakespeare's text. In Paris, the French novelist George Sand (1804–1876) staged her adaptation of the play (1856), in which Celia marries Jaques instead of Oliver. Late in the century, two important productions were popular in London: Rosalind was played by Neilson in one and by Ada REHAN in the other. *As You Like It* has been often staged in the 20th century, being particularly popular in outdoor performances. Notable productions have included those of Oscar ASCHE (1907), Glen Byam SHAW (3) (1957), and a controversial 1967 version at England's National Theatre, with an all-male cast headed by Ronald Pickup as Rosalind. Among the other notable Rosalinds of the century have been Edith EVANS (1), and Peggy ASHCROFT.

*As You Like It* was made as a silent FILM three times, but only one modern movie version has appeared, a 1936 film directed by Paul Czinner (1890–1972) and starring Laurence OLIVIER as Orlando. The play has also been produced on TELEVISION several times.

**Asche, Oscar (1871–1936)** English actor, playwright, and producer. Asche is probably best known as the author and director of *Chu-Chin-Chow* (1916), a musical that ran for five years, setting a record that was astonishing for its day. However, he was also a notable Shakespearean director and actor, famous for his portrayals of OTHELLO, KING (5) CLAUDIUS, FALSTAFF, and SHYLOCK. In 1906–1907 he staged a season of acclaimed Shakespearean productions: *Measure for Measure, As You Like It, The Taming of the Shrew,* and *Othello.* Another famous presentation was his modern-dress *Merry Wives of Windsor,* notorious for Falstaff's repeated exit line: 'Taxi!'

**Asnath**   Minor figure in *2 Henry VI,* a supernatural spirit or devil summoned in 1.4 by the witch MARGERY JOURDAIN, with help of spells cast by the sorcerers SOUTHWELL and BOLINGBROKE (2). The spirit is questioned by Bolingbroke; the queries are provided by the DUCHESS (1) of Gloucester, who wishes to examine the prospects for a coup. Asnath displays the traditional reluctance of such spirits to answer, but the laws of magic compel him to obey. He is ambiguous about the future of the King; he forecasts a death by water for the Duke of SUFFOLK (3), and he cautions that the Duke of SOMERSET (1) should avoid castles. Bolingbroke then dismisses him. It is thought that Shakespeare intended his name as an anagram of 'Sathan', a common 16th-century spelling of 'Satan'.

**Aspinall, Alexander (c. 1546–1624)**   Resident of STRATFORD and probable friend of Shakespeare. Aspinall was master of the Stratford grammar school for 42 years, beginning in 1582; however, Shakespeare had probably left the school a few years earlier (his period of attendance is unrecorded). Aspinall and Shakespeare both became prominent figures in Stratford—Aspinall was an alderman and a clerk of the town council—and were neighbours when the playwright lived at NEW PLACE. They were certainly among the most literate and cultured citizens of Stratford, and thus they must have been closely acquainted, at least after Shakespeare retired from London in about 1610.

In 1594 Aspinall was married. In courting his wife, he sent her a pair of gloves, accompanied by the following three-line poem that—according to an account written half a century later—Shakespeare composed: 'The gift is small / The will is all / Alexander Aspinall.' The tradition is highly questionable but it has not been disproved, and, if true, it provides a charming glimpse of the newly successful poet and playwright playfully assisting the romance of an older friend.

**Aspley, William (d. 1640)**   Publisher and bookseller in LONDON. In 1600 Aspley, in partnership with Andrew WISE, published QUARTO editions of both *Much Ado About Nothing* and *2 Henry IV.* He was also a member of the syndicates that published the FIRST FOLIO (1623) and the Second FOLIO (1632), apparently by virtue of his rights in these two plays. He also pub-

lished and sold plays by several other playwrights, including George CHAPMAN and Thomas DEKKER.

**Ashcroft, Peggy (b. 1907)**   English actress. Since achieving stardom at 23 playing DESDEMONA opposite Paul ROBESON, Ashcroft, who was created a Dame of the British Empire in 1956, has played most of Shakespeare's major roles for women. In her youth she was acclaimed as virtually all of Shakespeare's romantic heroines. In 1932 alone, she played IMOGEN, JULIET, MIRANDA, PERDITA, PORTIA, and ROSALIND; remarkably, she could still triumph in these roles many years later—for instance, as BEATRICE in 1950 (opposite John GIELGUD) and as Imogen in 1957. She played the great tragic heroines as well: Desdemona, OPHELIA, CORDELIA, CLEOPATRA. Perhaps her most remarkable role—often cited as one of the great performances of all time—was as Queen MARGARET (1) in the BBC's 'The Wars of the Roses' (1964). She portrayed Margaret as she appears in all four plays of the minor TETRALOGY, growing from the naïve young woman of *1 Henry VI,* to a courageous military leader, to the shrieking and cursing, half-insane ex-queen of *Richard III.*

**Athens**   City in Greece, the setting for *A Midsummer Night's Dream, Timon of Athens, The Two Noble Kinsmen,* and two scenes of *Antony and Cleopatra.* Although references in the dialogue and stage directions of the three full plays set in Athens make it clear where the action is occurring, there is nothing distinctively Athenian in any of them. Shakespeare simply followed his sources in placing his stories in the ancient cultural capital of the Mediterranean world, without troubling to depict the city itself. Only in *Timon* is there any hint of the historical Athens, for the controversial career of ALCIBIADES is sketchily presented.

In *Antony and Cleopatra* Mark ANTONY establishes his headquarters in Athens between the re-establishment of his alliance with Octavius CAESAR (2) and its crumbling into the warfare that results in his final defeat in 3.4 and 3.5. Here Shakespeare simply followed history (as presented in PLUTARCH's *Lives*) in establishing Antony in Athens, and again he makes no effort to delineate the city itself.

**Atkins, Robert (1886–1972)**   English actor and producer. Atkins joined the company at the OLD VIC THEATRE in 1915, and between 1919 and 1925 he directed the Old Vic's complete cycle of Shakespeare's plays. His was the first modern production of *Pericles* (1921), and he startled London with an *Antony and Cleopatra* presented on a bare stage (1922). In 1927–1928 he led a Shakespeare company in Egypt. During the Second World War he ran the Shakespeare Memorial Theatre in STRATFORD, and after the war he produced plays in an outdoor theatre in London. Among his notable later productions was *All's Well That Ends Well* (1949), in which he played LAFEW.

**Attendant (1)** Any of several minor characters in *Antony and Cleopatra,* servants of Mark ANTONY. In 1.1 an Attendant brings word that news has arrived from ROME, though Antony refuses to hear it. In 3.11 a group of Attendants declare their loyalty following Antony's defeat at ACTIUM, though he grandly insists they should flee, his fortunes being obviously on the decline. The Attendants' function is to demonstrate the grandness of Antony's household and the loyalty that his magnanimous leadership inspires. The Attendant in 1.1 is designated a Messenger in some editions.

**Attendant (2)** Any of several minor characters in *Cymbeline,* servants of King CYMBELINE. In 3.5 an Attendant is sent to find IMOGEN and returns to report briefly that her chambers are locked and silent. This informs the court of what the audience already knows—that Imogen has fled. The Attendant serves merely as an instrument of communication. Also, a number of Attendants mutely swell the king's retinue when he is informed of the approaching Roman army, in 4.3; their function is purely decorative.

**Audrey** Character in *As You Like It,* a goatherd loved by TOUCHSTONE. Audrey is a Shakespearean CLOWN (1), a comic caricature of a peasant. She is uneducated to a ridiculous degree—she is unfamiliar with the words 'feature' and 'poetical'—and she says little, being chiefly a butt for Touchstone's humour. She is, however, charming in her simplicity. She acknowledges her homeliness, saying 'and therefore I pray the gods make me honest' (3.3.29–30), and, as her marriage to Touchstone approaches, she rejoices tentatively: 'I do desire it with all my heart; and I hope it is no dishonest desire, to desire to be a woman of the world' (5.3.3–5).

Though she is a minor and somewhat conventional figure, Audrey is a deftly drawn personality who helps fill out the play's satiric presentation of country life and love. Her passivity contrasts tellingly with PHEBE's conventional resistance to SILVIUS; the two couples parody the lovers of the PASTORAL tradition, each in their own ways. Audrey mocks the pretensions of the literary shepherdesses represented by Phebe by being exaggeratedly down to earth.

**Aufidius, Tullus** Legendary figure and character in *Coriolanus,* the leader of the VOLSCIANS and the murderer of CORIOLANUS. Aufidius is the oft-defeated rival of Coriolanus, and he vows that he will overcome him by dishonourable means, since he cannot win in combat. Therefore, when Coriolanus deserts ROME and joins the Volscians, Aufidius schemes to kill him. After

Coriolanus is dissuaded by VOLUMNIA from sacking Rome, Aufidius accuses him of treachery, and the CONSPIRATORS stab the Roman to death in the play's final scene.

Shakespeare found Aufidius in his source, PLUTARCH's *Lives,* but from a single brief mention of their rivalry he constructed the charged relationship of the play. The playwright's villain is a warped mirror image of his protagonist. Aufidius focusses directly on Coriolanus throughout the play, and neither man can forget the other for long. Like Coriolanus—though without his political difficulties—Aufidius is first and foremost a charismatic warrior, motivated by wholly personal, indeed, egotistical drives, and obsessively concerned with his own achievements. When Coriolanus joins the Volscians, the fellowship of warriors leads Aufidius to welcome his rival with the warmth of a lover. 'Let me twine / Mine arms about that body' (4.5.107–108), he says, and compares their encounter with his wedding night. The extraordinary sensuality of this passage offers bizarre evidence of the misplaced emotional thrust engendered by warrior culture.

Frustrated, Aufidius decides to defeat Coriolanus dishonourably, and his grandeur becomes that of a villain rather than a great warrior. He undergoes this change in Act 1, after the siege of CORIOLES, and he admits that his effort 'Hath not that honour in't it had' (1.10.13). In this respect he is a foil to Coriolanus, whose failing is that his pride will not permit him to sacrifice any aspect of his warrior's persona. Also, when compared with the treachery of Aufidius, Coriolanus' betrayal of Rome seems the lesser villainy. However, after he has killed Coriolanus, Aufidius resumes something of his earlier nobility when he acknowledges his enemy's greatness. He grants him a warrior's funeral and declares, 'he shall have a noble memory' (5.6.153), in the play's final statement

**Aumerle, Edward York, Duke of (c. 1373–1415)** Historical figure and character in *Richard II,* a supporter of RICHARD II. Aumerle is a flattering courtier whose loyalty to King Richard is later undercut by his willingness to betray his fellow conspirators, who attempted to restore the deposed king, in order to save his own life. Aumerle displays his hypocrisy with seeming pride in 1.4, when he boasts of having feigned affection for BOLINGBROKE (1). He offers advice to Richard at several points; in 3.2 he suggests firmness in resisting Bolingbroke but then shifts to less honourable stalling tactics (3.3.131–132). After Bolingbroke has triumphed, BAGOT accuses Aumerle of complicity in Richard's murder of the Duke of GLOUCESTER (6); Bolingbroke postpones the question, but we hear in 5.2 that Aumerle has been stripped of his dukedom (though he continues to be designated Aumerle throughout the play). In this scene Aumerle's father, the Duke of YORK (4), discovers his son's involvement in the ABBOT's plot against Bolingbroke and angrily declares that he will inform the new king. Aumerle's mother, the DUCHESS (4), sends him to court to beg for mercy before York can expose him. She follows and successfully pleads for his life. This episode contrasts Aumerle's devious character with his father's forthright patriotism, his mother's maternal passion, and Bolingbroke's generosity.

The historical Aumerle was a favourite of King Richard; when the Duke of Gloucester was killed, before the play opens, Aumerle was awarded much of the dead man's property and was created Duke of Albemarle (corrupted to Aumerle in Elizabethan English). Aumerle accompanied Richard to Ireland, and it was apparently his bad advice that led the King to delay his return to England upon Bolingbroke's arrival and then to dismiss his army when he got there. Further, in an episode probably unknown to Shakespeare, Aumerle abandoned Richard for Bolingbroke at that point; therefore, when he joined the Abbot's conspiracy against Bolingbroke, he was being doubly treacherous, and he was shortly to betray his fellow conspirators as well. His father's part in this action is probably not historical, although it is reported in Shakespeare's chief source, HOLINSHED's *Chronicles*. In any case, Aumerle was pardoned by Bolingbroke, by then HENRY IV, but his mother's involvement is entirely Shakespeare's invention; the Duchess had actually been dead for six years. Moreover, to increase the pathos of her plea, Shakespeare presented Aumerle as an only child; the Duke actually had a younger brother, the Earl of CAMBRIDGE, who is a character in *Henry V*. Aumerle himself reappears as the Duke of YORK (5) in that play.

**Austria, Limoges (Lymoges), Archduke of**  Character in *King John,* ally of ARTHUR and King PHILIP (2) of FRANCE (1). Austria undertakes to fight King JOHN (3) and place Arthur on the throne of England. He claims to have killed the former English king, the famed Richard Coeur-de-Lion, and he wears a lion's skin as a trophy of this act. Austria is boastful, but when he is baited by the BASTARD (1), as in 3.1.56–58 (3.1.131–133, for citation, see KING JOHN, 'Synopsis'), he reveals his cowardice. In 3.2 (3.3) the Bastard displays Austria's head.

Shakespeare confused two historical figures in creating the Archduke. In the 16th century Austria was a major European power, and the playwright treats it as such, but in King John's day it was a minor German state. Leopold of Babenberg, a duke of Austria who died in 1194, five years before the earliest events of the play, had feuded with Richard Coeur-de-Lion when they were both Crusaders in Palestine; he then captured and held Richard for two years, until he received a great ransom. Later, in an unrelated battle,

Richard died while besieging the castle of Waldemar, Viscount of Limoges (d. 1199), who may have been killed in revenge by Richard's illegitimate son (who did not otherwise resemble the fictitious Bastard of the play). Thus Shakespeare makes the territory of one of Richard's foes the first name of another. The playwright apparently took this error from 16th-century popular romances, which recounted Richard's life with little or no regard for accuracy.

**Authorship controversy**  Dispute surrounding the identity of Shakespeare. Despite a wealth of evidence, a modern cult supports the proposition that someone other than Shakespeare—the identification varies—wrote the plays that are attributed to him. Shakespeare, it is contended, was an ignorant, perhaps illiterate, minor actor who was surely incapable of producing such literature. It is further contended that only an aristocratic, learned person could have done so, and that such a person would not have wished to be associated with the theatre. Therefore, it is concluded, the learned man assumed the actor's name as a disguise. A wide range of people have been nominated as the genuine author. Francis Bacon (1561–1626) was the favourite when the craze first developed, in the mid-19th century, though there have been many others since, including Christopher MARLOWE (1), the Earl of ESSEX (2), the Earl of DERBY (3), the Earl of RUTLAND (2), and the Earl of OXFORD (1), and Queen ELIZABETH (1)—to name only some who actually lived during Shakespeare's lifetime. The current trend is towards Oxford, although he was a playwright without benefit of disguise and died midway through Shakespeare's career. Scholars of the period know beyond doubt that Shakespeare wrote Shakespeare, but the authorship controversy remains a minor sideshow of the literary world, and it will doubtless continue to get publicity.

**Autolycus**  Character in *The Winter's Tale,* a vagabond thief who wanders through BOHEMIA. Autolycus appears, singing and bragging about his career as a petty thief, in 4.3. He picks the pocket of the CLOWN (8) and proposes to find further victims at the sheep-shearing festival, making 'the shearers prove sheep' (4.3.117). In 4.4 he attends the festival disguised as a peddler, singing SONGS, selling trinkets, and picking pockets. His songs and patter, his cheerful irresponsibility, and his insouciant delight in life add greatly to our enjoyment of the rustic scene. When King POLIXENES rages against the love of his son FLORIZEL and the shepherdess PERDITA, Autolycus exploits the situation to rob Perdita's foster-father, the SHEPHERD (2), who fears punishment and wants the king to know that Perdita was a foundling. Autolycus terrifies the old man and his son, the Clown, with accounts of the tortures they can expect and then offers, for money, to help them reach the king. However, he actually turns them over to the fleeing Florizel, in the hope of reward. In this way evidence of Perdita's identity gets to SICILIA—she is the long-lost daughter of the Sicilian King LEONTES—resulting in reunions for the play's major characters and the incidental enrichment of the Shepherd and Clown with vast rewards. In 5.2 Autolycus admits that his life has earned no success, and he turns to flattering his former victims, now newly made gentlemen, in the hope of employment.

Autolycus is for the most part a charming rogue. He contributes greatly to the atmosphere of gaiety that surrounds the shepherds' world and thus to the comic tone of the play's second half. His crimes are petty compared with those of Leontes in the tragic first half of the play, but in any case it is part of the virtue of the pastoral world that it has room for this comical villain. The importance of mercy as a moral virtue is emphasised by the fact that Autolycus' depredations are accepted as a part of life. He even has a place in the play's final forgiveness and reconciliation, though the playwright could easily have left him in Bohemia. Autolycus represents the irrepressible mischievousness of human nature; that he selfishly views the world entirely in terms of his own convenience is deplorable, but he compensates through his contagious pleasure in simple things and the delightful songs in which he expresses this pleasure.

Autolycus resembles traditional comic characters, but he is not quite classifiable. He is too sophisticated for a rustic CLOWN (1), nor is he a FOOL (1), for he is not a professional jester. He does, however, resemble a Fool in his mockery, his songs, and his disinterested position relative to the main developments. He resembles FALSTAFF in his anomalous social position, his predatory nature, and his pretensions to an anti-ethic (he boasts of a piece of 'knavery', 'therein am I constant to my profession' [4.4.682–683]). Both characters, though amoral, are admirably independent, and the conflict of our judgements on the two traits yields subtle humour, as our own pretensions and secret predilections are exposed.

Autolycus' nature (like Falstaff's) gradually changes. At first he charms us, and we are inclined to forgive his crimes. However, as the shepherds' festival closes, he seems less pleasant, crying, 'Ha, ha! what a fool Honesty is!' (4.4.596) and gloating over his victims, who are sympathetic characters. When he plots how to profit from the desperate young lovers' situation, he is still funny, but we can no longer ignore his amorality, for it threatens the hero and heroine. His terrorising of the Shepherd with truly horrible descriptions of torture adds to our unease, and Autolycus acquires a darkly satirical cast as he replicates Polixenes' wrath while himself disguised as a courtier. He has changed sides in Shakespeare's opposition of pastoral innocence and sophisticated machinations. It is the Clown who is the comic character in 5.2, while Autolycus is merely another practitioner of the courtier's bowing and scraping to which he at first seemed antithetical.

Autolycus' only real connection to the plot, his role in preventing the Shepherd from revealing Perdita's origins too early, comes from the play's main source, the novella *Pandosto* by Robert GREENE (2), in which a servant of the prince—and Autolycus was once Florizel's servant—performs this function. However, making this figure a vagabond and thief was Shakespeare's invention. The playwright probably took the idea, as well as the name Autolycus, from OVID's description of the god Mercury's son in *The Metamorphoses*. Shakespeare's Autolycus brags of the connection, 'My father named me Autolycus; who, being as I am, littered under Mercury, was likewise a snapper-up of unconsidered trifles' (4.3.24–26).

**Auvergne**   Region in south-central FRANCE (1), where 2.3 of *1 Henry VI* is set. The COUNTESS (1) of Auvergne attempts to capture the English lord TALBOT there.

**Ayscough, Samuel (1745–1804)**   English scholar, the compiler of the first concordance of Shakespeare's works. Ayscough, a librarian at the British Museum, published his *Index, or Concordance of the Works of Shakespeare* in 1790.

# B

**Bad Quarto**  An early edition of a Shakespeare play, usually in QUARTO format, whose text was reconstructed from memory by actors who had performed the play, rather than coming from an authoritative source that accurately reflected what Shakespeare had written, such as his FOUL PAPERS. These texts, which the editors of the FIRST FOLIO described as 'stolen, and surreptitious copies, maimed, and deformed by the frauds and stealthes of iniurious impostors', were presumably made for purposes of piracy. Publishers—or, in some cases, a rival acting company—could profit from a play's popularity even though the script was jealously secreted by the acting company that had produced the play.

The eight undoubted Bad Quarto editions of Shakespeare's plays are: Q1 of *2 Henry VI* (1594); Q1 of *3 Henry VI* (1595); Q1 of *Romeo and Juliet* (1597); Q1 of *Henry V* (1600); Q1 of *The Merry Wives of Windsor* (1602); Q1 of *Hamlet* (1603); Q1 of *King Lear* (1607); and Q of *Pericles* (1609). Q is the only surviving early text of *Pericles;* the other seven Bad Quartos may be compared with the First Folio, and *Romeo and Juliet* and *Hamlet* also appeared as GOOD QUARTOS. In addition, two other plays are often classed as Bad Quartos: THE TAMING OF A SHREW (1594), considered a Bad Quarto of *The Taming of the Shrew*, and THE TROUBLESOME RAIGNE OF KING JOHN (1591), probably a reconstruction of *King John*.

Bad Quartos exhibit certain characteristics that result from errors of memory, including: repetitions and omissions of words; phrases that recollect earlier lines or anticipate later ones; many metrically flawed lines (see METRE); paraphrases and summaries of speeches; stage directions that summarise missing dialogue; and snippets from other plays in which the rememberer had also performed. Also, some passages are less flawed than others. This reflects an actor's firmer recollection of the lines he spoke than of the rest of the play. For instance, the Bad Quarto of *Hamlet* was probably recorded by a man who had played MARCELLUS, since that role is the only one whose dialogue is very accurately rendered.

A Bad Quarto's flaws can be disastrous, as in the notorious misrendering of HAMLET's most famous soliloquy, which in Q1 begins (with modernised spelling): 'To be, or not to be. Aye there's the point, / To die, to sleep, is that all? Aye all: / No, to sleep, to dream, aye marry there it goes . . .' (compare *Hamlet* 3.1.56–65). Although a corrupt text can be replaced by a sound one—except in the case of *Pericles*—a Bad Quarto is nonetheless useful to scholars in establishing a true text, as in another notable instance from *Hamlet* (in 2.2.415). Q1 records 'godly Ballet' (i.e., ballad) for Q2's 'pious chanson' and the First Folio's 'Pons Chanson'; we see that the actors of the day recognised—even if they did not precisely recall—a wry reference to a popular song on a religious subject. The Folio's reading, with its suggestion of the bridges of Paris, is therefore rejected.

**Bagot, Sir John (d. c. 1400)**  Historical figure and character in *Richard II,* a supporter of RICHARD II. Bagot, with his colleagues John BUSHY and Henry GREENE (1), is one of the 'caterpillars' (2.3.165) whose influence on the King is said by BOLINGBROKE (1) to have been disastrous for England. They recognise that their position as favourites of the King is likely to prove dangerous if Bolingbroke defeats him, and in 2.2 they decide to seek safety when Bolingbroke appears. Bushy and Greene are captured and executed, but Bagot joins the King in Ireland and thus lives to appear before the triumphant Bolingbroke at the beginning of 4.1. He brings an accusation against the Duke of AUMERLE, presumably in exchange for clemency, and then disappears from the play.

The historical Bagot was a lesser aristocrat of WARWICKSHIRE and had originally been a supporter of the murdered Duke of GLOUCESTER (6). He was later recruited to Richard's cause and became close to the King; it was at Bagot's residence in COVENTRY that Richard stayed at the time of the trial by combat between Bolingbroke and MOWBRAY (1) that is depicted in 1.3. After the fall of the King, Bagot was imprisoned by Bolingbroke in the TOWER OF LONDON, where he is last known to have been alive.

**Balthasar (1)**  Minor character in *The Comedy of Errors,* a merchant who is a friend of ANTIPHOLUS OF EPHESUS. Balthasar is present when, in 3.1, Antipholus is kept out of his own home by his wife and servants, who believe he is an imposter. Balthasar dissuades Antipholus from breaking down the door, on the grounds that such an action would damage his reputation in the neighbourhood.

**Balthasar (2)** Minor character in *Romeo and Juliet,* servant of ROMEO. In 5.1 Balthasar brings Romeo the erroneous news that JULIET (1) is dead, triggering the last phase of the tragedy. In 5.3 Balthasar accompanies Romeo to Juliet's tomb. Romeo sends him away with a letter to MONTAGUE (1), but, concerned about his master, he stays to observe him. At the end of the play he gives the PRINCE (1) the letter, which helps to explain the tragedy to the lovers' parents.

Balthasar is the only servant of the Montagues in the play except for ABRAM and a nameless companion, who participate in the brawl in 1.1. Accordingly, Balthasar is conventionally designated as the companion, who neither speaks nor is named in early texts of the play.

**Balthasar (3)** Minor character in *The Merchant of Venice,* servant of PORTIA (1). In 3.4 Balthasar is sent with a letter to Portia's cousin, setting in motion her plan to impersonate a lawyer at the hearing of SHYLOCK's suit against ANTONIO (2). Portia later takes Balthasar's name as part of her disguise.

**Balthasar (4)** Minor character in *Much Ado About Nothing,* a musician and singer employed by Don PEDRO. In 2.3 Don Pedro instructs Balthasar to sing the SONG 'Sigh no more, ladies', though Balthasar insists he is not a good singer. In 5.3 he sings the solemn 'Pardon, goddess of the night', as CLAUDIO (1) mourns the supposed death of HERO. Balthasar makes feeble attempts to be witty, especially when he fishes for compliments in 2.3, but he has no real personality. He is part of the play's atmosphere of aristocratic decorum and hospitality, here expressed through courtly music, a standard feature of the great noble households of both RENAISSANCE Italy and Elizabethan England.

In a stage direction in the FIRST FOLIO edition of the play (1623), Balthasar is identified as 'Iacke Wilson', a reference to the actor who played the part. It cannot be known for certain who this was, but scholars frequently propose both Jack WILSON (1) and John WILSON (2).

**Bandello, Matteo (1485–1561)** Italian writer, author of tales that served as sources for several of Shakespeare's works. Bandello's collection of tales, *Novelle* (1554), based loosely on the example of BOCCACCIO's *Decameron* (1353), was adapted in French by François BELLEFOREST and in English by Arthur BROOKE (1), Geoffrey FENTON (2), and William PAINTER (2). Various of these versions and, probably, the Italian original were used by Shakespeare. The creation of AARON in *Titus Andronicus* may have been influenced by a Bandello tale in Belleforest; for *Romeo and Juliet,* the playwright adapted a love story taken from Bandello in versions by Brooke and Painter. The tale of HERO and CLAUDIO (1) in *Much Ado About Nothing* was taken from Bandello's Italian original and *his* source, a tale by ARIOSTO. A single passage in *Twelfth Night* may also have been inspired by Bandello.

Bandello led a highly dramatic life. An aristocrat, he joined the Dominican order as a youth and travelled widely with his uncle, a noted theologian who visited monasteries throughout Europe. However, he soon withdrew from the church to pursue a career as a courtier and man of letters—for instance, for eight years he was court poet to the Duchess of Mantua. Here he began to write the tales that were eventually to make him famous. A political intriguer, Bandello was forced in 1525 to flee hastily from Milan, abandoning all he owned including the manuscripts of many tales. He became an adviser to a pro-French Venetian general, but in 1542 the general was exiled to France, and Bandello followed him.

The French king granted Bandello the income from a bishopric, and he was finally free to assemble the novellas he had been writing for almost half a century. The first edition of *Novelle,* containing some 200 tales, was instantly popular throughout Europe. It consists for the most part of romantic legends retold in a racy, briskly journalistic style. Some stories were virtually pornographic by the standards of the day. Today, Bandello's tales are considered to have very little literary merit, but at the time their influence was widespread in Italy, France, Spain, and England. Besides Shakespeare, other English writers who drew upon Bandello include the English dramatists John WEBSTER (2), Francis BEAUMONT (2) and John FLETCHER (2), and Philip MASSINGER.

**Bandit (Thief)** Any of three minor characters in *Timon of Athens,* thieves who hope to rob TIMON. In 4.3 after Timon has withdrawn from ATHENS to the woods in rage and despair because he has been abandoned by his friends, the Bandits learn that he has found gold and they accost him. They don't know that he intends to give it away in an attempt to corrupt hateful humanity. He ironically praises them for being obvious thieves, and compares them to those who pretend to be good citizens. He gives them gold and encourages them to commit more crimes. 'Cut throats. / All that you meet are thieves. To Athens go . . .' (4.3.448–449), he says. As they leave, the Bandits remark on Timon's misanthropy. Two of the three contemplate giving up thievery since it is advocated by so malicious a man. As the Third Bandit puts it, 'H'as almost charm'd me from my profession, by persuading me to it' (4.3.453–454). Collectively called 'banditti' in the stage direction that introduces them, at 4.3.401, the Bandits are designated as Thieves in many editions.

**Bangor**   Town in WALES (1), possibly the setting for 3.1 of *1 Henry IV*. Some editors of the play, beginning with THEOBALD in the 18th century, have followed Shakespeare's chief source, HOLINSHED, and placed this scene, in which the conspirators against HENRY IV plan to divide the realm among themselves, in the home of the Archdeacon of Bangor. However, Shakespeare made no designation of location, and the host of the meeting appears to be GLENDOWER.

**Banquo**   Character in *Macbeth*, friend and later victim of MACBETH. In 1.3 Banquo and Macbeth encounter the WITCHES, who predict that Macbeth will become Thane of CAWDOR and King of SCOTLAND. They add that Banquo, whom they describe as 'Lesser than Macbeth, and greater' (1.3.65), shall father a line of rulers, though he shall not be one himself. Macbeth, inspired by this encounter to fulfil his ambition, kills King DUNCAN and seizes the throne. He then worries about the possibility that his kingdom will fall to Banquo's heirs, and he orders Banquo and his son FLEANCE murdered. In 3.3 the FIRST MURDERER (3) and his companions kill Banquo, though Fleance escapes. Banquo's GHOST (4) later appears to Macbeth, aggravating his bad conscience. In 4.1 the Ghost confirms the Witches' prediction that his descendants will be KINGS. King JAMES I, England's ruler in Shakespeare's day, was believed to be descended from an historical Lord Banquo.

Banquo is a decent and honourable nobleman who senses that the Witches are evil and thus not to be relied on. He warns Macbeth that 'oftentimes, to win us to our harm, / The instruments of Darkness tell us truths' (1.3.123–124), and his concern contrasts strikingly with Macbeth's susceptibility to the Witches. Banquo's resistance points up Macbeth's failure to resist and stresses his tendency towards evil, the flaw that makes the tragedy possible. When he decides to murder Banquo, Macbeth acknowledges his 'royalty of nature' (3.1.49). He fears that Banquo's righteousness may turn him into an enemy. Thus, we see that Banquo's fate is dictated by his virtue, just as Macbeth's is determined by his villainy.

In Shakespeare's source for *Macbeth*, HOLINSHED's *Chronicles*, Banquo collaborates with Macbeth in the murder of Duncan and is killed because he knows too much. The playwright may have altered Banquo simply to avoid depicting the king's ancestor as a murderer, though Banquo could merely have been omitted to achieve this end. However, Shakespeare probably realised that the play is stronger with only a single villain, and Banquo's supposed ancestry to the king made him an apt choice to stand in opposition to that villain as a pointedly virtuous comrade. That this was Banquo's more important function for Shakespeare is suggested by the playwright's disregard for Fleance's fate or for the question of Banquo's descendants, once Fleance's survival ensures that he could have had some.

Though Holinshed, Shakespeare, and King James himself had no reason to doubt the belief that Banquo was a predecessor of the STUART dynasty, modern scholarship has established that this was not true. Banquo may reflect some ancient chieftain of Scotland, but outside Holinshed's source, the semi-legendary history of Hector BOECE, he has no historical standing.

**Baptista**   Character in *The Taming of the Shrew*, father of KATHERINA and BIANCA (1). Baptista is an ineffectual elderly gentleman, a comic figure in a tradition going back to ancient Roman drama. He is frequently the butt of Katherina's outbursts of temper. He insists on marrying off his elder daughter first, aggravating Katherina's already shrewish nature. In 2.1, once assured that Katherina is betrothed, Baptista literally auctions Bianca to the highest bidder; his calculating behaviour stands in pointed contrast to the infatuation of Bianca's lover, LUCENTIO. These are standard attitudes and actions of a conventional father-of-the-girl figure; otherwise, Baptista has virtually no personality.

**Barbary**   Horse named in *Richard II*. The GROOM (1) who visits RICHARD II in prison in 5.5 tells the deposed King that his successor, BOLINGBROKE (1), has ridden Barbary at his coronation and that the horse carried its new rider 'proudly' (5.5.83). Richard is initially angry with his former steed, but he then berates himself for railing at the animal.

Shakespeare apparently invented this episode, which appears in none of his sources. Barbary is also the name of a highly valued breed of horse exported from North Africa, itself known as Barbary.

**Bardolph (1)**   Character in *1* and *2 Henry IV*, *The Merry Wives of Windsor*, and *Henry V*, a follower of FALSTAFF. In *1 Henry IV* Bardolph participates in the highway robbery of 2.2, and in *2 Henry IV* he assists the fat knight in his illicit recruiting efforts in 3.2, collecting bribes from men who wish to avoid service. When Falstaff is rejected by PRINCE (6) Hal in 5.5, Bardolph goes to prison with him. In *The Merry Wives* Bardolph is only a minor figure who occasionally delivers messages to Falstaff. In *Henry V* he is a soldier in the army of King HENRY V. In 2.1 he defuses the feud between PISTOL and NYM. In 3.2.28–57 the BOY (3) convincingly describes him as a coward and thief. In 3.6 we learn that Bardolph is to be executed for having stolen a sacramental vessel from a French church, and in 4.4 the Boy reports that Bardolph has indeed been hung.

Despite his swaggering, he has little distinctive personality. His peacemaking role in *Henry V* ironically counters King HENRY V's bellicosity in an anti-war reading of the play, but if one interprets Henry as a epic hero, then Bardolph remains a comic soldier, a petty villain whose end helps to demonstrate the King's dedication to justice. Bardolph's most prominent characteristic is his diseased facial complexion, florid and fiery, 'all bubukles, and whelks, and knobs, and flames o' fire' (*Henry V*, 3.6.105–106). He is teased mercilessly about his skin disorder by Falstaff and other characters, finding himself compared to lamps, torches, blushing maids, red wine, red petticoats, hellfire, and even 'Lucifer's privy kitchen' (*2 Henry IV*, 2.4.330).

Bardolph was originally called ROSSILL, but after *2 Henry IV* was written the name was changed, probably to avoid offending a prominent aristocrat, William Russill, Earl of Bedford. The fact that the name Bardolph had already been assigned to another character in *2 Henry IV*, Lord BARDOLPH (2), is only one instance of Shakespeare's tolerance for minor confusions and inconsistencies in his plays.

**Bardolph (2), Lord Thomas (1368–1408)** Historical figure and character in *2 Henry IV*, a follower of the Earl of NORTHUMBERLAND (1) and a rebel against King HENRY IV. He is invariably referred to as Lord Bardolph to distinguish him from BARDOLPH (1), who appears in the same play. Lord Bardolph brings Northumberland a mistaken report of a rebel victory in 1.1, and he helps to encourage the crestfallen Earl after the real news arrives. In 1.3 he urges caution on his fellow rebels, Lord HASTINGS (2) and the ARCHBISHOP (3) of York, who insist on challenging the King. Although he then disappears from the play, the defeat of Lord Bardolph and Northumberland is reported in 4.4; he thus seems associated with Northumberland's betrayal of the rebel cause.

The historical Lord Bardolph, like Northumberland, did not desert the rebellion. He fought with distinction and died in battle several years after GAULTREE FOREST.

A speech prefix in the QUARTO edition of the play (1600) indicates that Lord Bardolph's part in 1.1 was originally written for Sir John UMFREVILE, another follower of Northumberland's, whose part was assigned to Lord Bardolph in order to reduce the number of actors required.

**Barents (Barentz), Willem (c. 1550–1597)** Dutch explorer. Between 1594 and 1597 Barents led several naval expeditions to the Arctic in search of a northeast passage to the Orient; the Barents Sea, north of Scandinavia, is named for him. An account of Barents' voyage of 1596–1597 was published in London in 1598 and was very popular, being reprinted for years. FABIAN is believed to allude to Barents when, in *Twelfth Night*, he tells SIR ANDREW, who has earned OLIVIA's disdain, that he has 'sailed into the north of my lady's opinion, where you will hang like an icicle on a Dutchman's beard' (3.2.25–26).

**Barker, Harley Granville** See GRANVILLE-BARKER.

**Barkloughly Castle** Welsh castle seen in 3.2 of *Richard II*. Shakespeare's source, HOLINSHED's history, incorrectly identified Hertlowli, an ancient name for Harlech Castle, as Barclowlie and thus led the playwright into error. Nevertheless, this name indicates that the scene is in WALES (1) and that Richard has returned to Britain from Ireland.

**Barkstead, William (active 1606–1629)** English poet and dramatist. A very minor figure in English literature, Barkstead is best known for a long poem, *Myrrha, the Mother of Adonis* (1607), in which he modestly (and correctly) referred to Shakespeare as a much greater poet who had dealt with the Adonis story (see VENUS AND ADONIS). He was employed by several minor acting companies, though his only surviving drama is *The Insatiate Countess* (c. 1610), written in collaboration with John MARSTON.

**Barnardine** Minor character in *Measure for Measure*, a condemned criminal whose undeserved pardon epitomises the play's theme of unqualified mercy. Barnardine is a comical brute who is 'drunk many times a day, if not many days entirely drunk' (4.2.147–148). He declares he will not come forward to be executed on the day appointed—when he is to substitute for CLAUDIO (3)—because he has 'been drinking hard all night, and [needs] more time to prepare . . .' (4.3.52–53). The DUKE (9) postpones the execution, saying that under the circumstances it could only send the victim to instant damnation, a responsibility the Duke will not take. In 5.1 the ruler pardons Barnardine and remands him into the custody of the FRIAR (1) as part of the mercy and forgiveness of the play's dénouement.

Barnardine is funny in his stubborn refusal to be killed and helps provide relief from the oppressiveness of the prison, where much of the middle of the play is set. Yet he is a callous murderer 'unfit to live or die' (4.3.63). Although Barnardine is specifically designated as a proper subject for execution, he is pardoned as part of the play's final conciliation; his evilness then highlights the magnanimity of the Duke's mercy.

**Barnardo (Bernardo)** Minor character in *Hamlet*. Barnardo and MARCELLUS are the two sentries who have seen the GHOST (3) of HAMLET's father before the play begins. In 1.1 they introduce Hamlet's friend HORATIO to the phenomenon. When the three tell Hamlet about the spirit in 1.2, Barnardo barely speaks, and when Hamlet accompanies Horatio and Marcellus to encounter the Ghost in 1.4, Barnardo has disappeared from the play.

**Barnes, Barnabe (c. 1569–1609)** English poet and dramatist, author of an influence on *Pericles* and possibly the 'rival poet' of the SONNETS. Barnes' play *The Devil's Charter* (1607) derived from a work by the Italian historian Francesco Guicciardini (1483–1540), and it featured Guicciardini as a CHORUS (1). Shakespeare used this idea in *Pericles*, where the source, the poet John GOWER (3), serves the same function; in fact, some of Gower's speeches echo the words of Barnes' Guicciardini. Because Barnes was a noted SONNET writer who eulogised the Earl of SOUTHAMPTON (2)—Shakespeare's patron—some commentators, following scholar Sidney LEE, consider him a likely nominee for the 'rival poet' of Shakespeare's sonnets.

**Barnet** Location in *3 Henry VI*, a town near London and a battle site of the WARS OF THE ROSES. King EDWARD IV, having taken London and captured HENRY VI, marches north to meet the army of WARWICK (3). In 5.2–3 their forces meet in a conflict that is depicted as a simple rout of Warwick's troops, in which Warwick dies and the other Lancastrian leaders flee to join the army of Queen MARGARET (1). The historical battle of Barnet, which occurred on Easter Sunday, 1471, was very closely fought; it was won for Edward only when one element of Warwick's army mistakenly attacked another in the heavy fog that shrouded the field. However, Shakespeare chose to emphasise the strength of the Yorkist forces, for the dynamic of his play at this point is directed towards their final victory at the battle of TEWKESBURY, which occurs over the next two scenes.

**Barnfield, Richard (1574–1627)** Landed gentleman and amateur poet, an early admirer of Shakespeare. Barnfield published his first work, an imitation of *Venus and Adonis* titled *The Affectionate Shepherd*, at the age of 20; he published three more collections of poems over the next four years, but he then retired to his country estate and apparently stopped writing. He wrote the first published verse in praise of Shakespeare, a stanza in a poem called 'A Remembrance of Some English Poets' (1598). Barnfield was a prominent member of the London literary scene in the 1590s, and Shakespeare was probably acquainted with him. Two of Barnfield's poems were published as Shakespeare's in William JAGGARD's spurious anthology THE PASSIONATE PILGRIM (1599), and it is chiefly for this reason that his work is remembered today.

**Barrett, Lawrence (1838–1891)** American actor. An actor from the age of 14, Barrett established himself in New York in 1857 and became a friend and partner of Edwin BOOTH (2), playing IAGO opposite his OTHELLO, and CASSIUS—the part for which he was best known—opposite Booth's CAESAR (2). He also played RICHARD III, LEAR, and SHYLOCK. Barrett served in the Union army in the Civil War; he then managed a theatre in San Francisco, from 1867 to 1871, before returning to New York to run the Booth's Theatre. In 1884 he took over Henry IRVING's Lyceum Theatre in London, while Irving toured America. Barrett was unusual among actors of his day in taking an intellectual interest in the American theatre; he introduced revivals of several plays and was a theatre historian, the author of *Edwin Forrest* (1881) (see FORREST) and *Edwin Booth and his Contemporaries* (1886).

**Barry (1), Ann (1734–1801)** English actress. Ann Barry's earliest recorded performances were at the Dublin theatre of Spranger BARRY (3), opposite whose LEAR and OTHELLO she was acclaimed as CORDELIA and DESDEMONA. She went with Barry to London and later married him. Though particularly successful in COMEDY, she played all sorts of parts, both new and classical. She was much admired as JULIET (1), ROSALIND, ISABELLA, IMOGEN, and PERDITA. Highly popular, she was regarded as one of the few rivals of Sarah SIDDONS. She died shortly after retiring and was buried in WESTMINSTER (1) ABBEY.

**Barry (2), Elizabeth (1658–1713)** English actress. The leading actress of the late 17th century, Barry is sometimes called the first great English actress. Often playing opposite Thomas BETTERTON, she was especially acclaimed as LADY (6) MACBETH, Queen KATHERINE in *Henry VIII*, and CORDELIA in Nahum TATE's version of *King Lear*. She was said to have garnered her first training as an actress while the mistress of the notorious rake, poet, and aesthete, the Earl of Rochester (1640–1680), with whom she bore a child. Throughout her life, she was named in similar scandals, though at least one man, the playwright Thomas OTWAY, is said to have suffered from her rejection.

**Barry (3), Spranger (1719–1777)** Irish actor. Barry was among the leading Shakespearean actors of the 1750s, especially noted for his portrayal of OTHELLO. His rivalry with David GARRICK was much publicised; the so-called *Romeo and Juliet* war—their simultaneous performances as ROMEO (Barry in the adaptation by Colley CIBBER [1])—was followed by similar match-ups as LEAR and RICHARD III. In 1758 Barry attempted to establish a theatre in Dublin but quickly went bankrupt. He did, however, meet and bring back to London a new leading lady, soon his wife, Ann BARRY (1). Upon his return to London, he joined Garrick's company for the remainder of his career.

**Barrymore, John (1882–1942)** American actor. After establishing himself as a glamorous leading man—a 'matinee idol'—Barrymore stunned the New York theatrical world in 1922 with an electrifying portrayal of HAMLET, repeating the accomplishment in

*John Barrymore as Mercutio (left) in his swordfight with Tybalt (*Romeo and Juliet *3.1). George Cukor's 1936 film also starred Leslie Howard (center) as Romeo and Basil Rathbone (right) as Tybalt.* (Courtesy of Movie Star News)

London in 1925. His Hamlet was regarded as one of the great performances of the day, but Barrymore largely abandoned the stage for film in the remainder of his career. He appeared as MERCUTIO in George Cukor's 1936 film of *Romeo and Juliet.*

John and his siblings, Lionel and Ethel, were regarded as leaders of the American theatre—*The Royal Family,* as the title of a 1927 play about them had it. Both his mother and his father were from long-established theatrical families, and John DREW was his uncle.

**Bartholomew**   Character in *The Taming of the Shrew.* See PAGE (8).

**Bartley, George (c. 1782–1858)**   Nineteenth-century English actor who specialised in playing FALSTAFF. Bartley's success as the fat knight began in 1815 and carried him through to his retirement in 1852. In 1818–1819 he made a triumphal tour of America, although in Hartford, Connecticut, he was arrested by a puritanical official who objected to dramatic readings and enforced a colonial-era 'blue law'.

**Barton (1), John (b. 1928)**   Twentieth-century English theatrical producer. Barton, a long-time director with the Royal Shakespeare Company, has staged many of Shakespeare's plays. Among his most notable productions have been *The Taming of the Shrew* (1960), *Twelfth Night* (1969), *Measure for Measure* (1970), and *Much Ado About Nothing* (1976). With Peter HALL (5), Barton co-directed 'The Wars of the Roses' (1964), the TELEVISION productions that combined the *Henry VI* plays and *Richard III.*

**Barton (2), Richard (active 1584–1601)**   Vicar at STRATFORD. In 1585 Barton baptised Hamnet and Judith SHAKESPEARE (5, 10), the playwright's twin children. Barton, originally from COVENTRY, was vicar in Stratford from 1584–1589. He was apparently a man of Puritan leanings for he was recorded in a Puritan critique of WARWICKSHIRE ministers as a superior cleric. He was much appreciated by the town, which offered him pay raises and miscellaneous gifts in the hope that he would remain, but he accepted a better-paying post elsewhere after five years.

**Bassanio** Character in *The Merchant of Venice*, friend of ANTONIO (2) and suitor of PORTIA (1). In requesting money from Antonio in order to court Portia in style, Bassanio is indirectly responsible for the peril in which the merchant finds himself when he borrows from SHYLOCK and risks his flesh. But Bassanio is also an important figure in his own right. He wins Portia by choosing the correct casket in the lottery required by her father, and, in so doing, he demonstrates a 16th-century ideal of romantic love. He distrusts the rich appearance of the gold and silver caskets (3.2.73–107) and instead selects the casket of lead. Such a choice was a conventional indication of selfless love. Only a true lover would value the maid for herself rather than her 'outward shows' (3.2.73), as Bassanio does. He is a leisured gentleman, presumably able to find a wife elsewhere, but he is willing to risk his chances of matrimony in order to win Portia. Like Antonio, he finds value in reaching for the greatest happiness, and is thus placed in opposition to Shylock's stinginess. Similarly, like Antonio and Portia and unlike Shylock, Bassanio gives what he has. He is a good-hearted spendthrift who cannot refuse a request, as when GRATIANO (1) announces that he has a favour to ask and is immediately told, 'You have obtain'd it' (2.2.169).

Bassanio is sometimes seen in a rather different light. Some critics regard him as an heiress-hunting playboy whose irresponsibility endangers Antonio. However, Bassanio objects to Antonio's acceptance of Shylock's bond (1.3.150–151) and is persuaded only by his friend's assurances that he will certainly be able to repay the loan. And although Bassanio refers to Portia's wealth when he first mentions the idea of marrying her (1.1.161–176), this does not necessarily make him a gold-digger. Such considerations were normal in the 16th century; one would not discuss courtship without bringing up the subject of wealth. For Shakespeare's audience, and for the playwright himself, such behaviour was ordinary, and Bassanio was surely intended as a romantic hero, a personification of good fortune in love.

Bassanio's name—not found in Shakespeare's sources for the play—may have been taken from one of several Bassanios, natives of Venice, who were musicians in the household of Queen ELIZABETH (1) (see LANIER).

**Basse, William** (c. 1583–c. 1653)  English poet. A minor figure in English literature, Basse is best known today for a 20-line EPITAPH on Shakespeare, written c. 1621. This poem was originally published as John DONNE's in 1633; it was credited to 'W. B'. when it appeared in the 1640 edition of Shakespeare's *Poems* (see BENSON [2]). The only other Basse work that is read today is *Angler's Song*, an appreciation of fishing.

**Basset**  Minor character in *1 Henry VI*, a supporter of the Duke of SOMERSET (3). Basset disputes with VERNON (1), a partisan of the Duke of YORK (8), in 3.4 and 4.1. By demonstrating the involvement of lesser figures, these incidents magnify the damage to English morale caused by the dissensions among the noblemen.

**Bassianus**  Character in *Titus Andronicus*, brother of the Emperor, SATURNINUS. In 1.1 Bassianus relinquishes his claim to the throne when TITUS (1) Andronicus declares in favour of his brother, but he will not surrender his fiancée, LAVINIA, to him. The first victim of AARON's plots, Bassianus is killed by CHIRON and DEMETRIUS (1), prior to their rape of Lavinia in 2.3.

**Bastard (1), Philip Faulconbridge, The**  Character in *King John*, illegitimate nephew of King JOHN (3). The Bastard, the most prominent character in the play, is a complicated figure. Early in the play he satirises courtly manners while revealing the self-serving behaviour he mocks. He impulsively insults others and makes humorous asides to himself, yet he is at the same time a calculating social climber. His illegitimacy parallels the king's status as a usurper, and, just as John defies the French challenge to his rule, so the Bastard relies on his strength of character to maintain himself in aristocratic society. Yet while John falls, the Bastard prospers; his rise is concurrent with John's fall, and the contrast lends piquancy to the king's collapse. He begins as a comical figure, but by the end of the play he is clearly the mainstay of the English forces. He has remained true to the king, unlike the other noblemen, and it is he who first acknowledges Prince HENRY (1) as the new king, emphasising the restoration of social order.

The Bastard also functions as a CHORUS (1), commenting on the foibles of society, sometimes contradicting his role in the plot. For instance, he deplores 'commodity', or self-interest, in a famous soliloquy (2.1.561–598), yet he is guilty of commodity himself, as he admits in the last dozen lines of the speech. Shakespeare uses the fictitious Bastard somewhat in the manner of the allegorical figures of a MORALITY PLAY, while at the same time making his spirited courage and loyalty humanly admirable. Most strikingly, while the Bastard bears some resemblance to the ancient dramatic figure of the VICE—in his repeated identification with the devil (e.g., in 2.1.134–

135), and in his presentation of satirical monologues directly to the audience—he is also in some sense the hero of the play, an exemplar of patriotic virtue. He closes the play with a speech (5.7.112–118) that has been a staple of British patriotic literature since it first appeared.

The Bastard is not based on any single historical figure, although elements of his situation are drawn from the lives of several historical bastards. King Richard I did have an illegitimate son named Philip, and, although very little is known of him, he is reputed to have killed the Viscount of Limoges in revenge for his father's death; the Bastard has his first name and kills AUSTRIA, who is identified with Limoges in the play. The name Faulconbridge was borne by another noteworthy bastard, William Neville, Lord FALCONBRIDGE (2), who is mentioned in *3 Henry VI.* An illegitimate Norman nobleman, Faukes de Bréauté (d. c. 1227), led John's armies against the rebellious barons, as the Bastard does in the play, but Shakespeare's character bears no resemblance to this man, a notoriously cruel and oppressive mercenary soldier who finally had to be driven from England by force in 1224. Another famous figure, Jean Dunois, the BASTARD (2) of Orléans, apparently contributed to Shakespeare's character as well. Dunois appears in *1 Henry VI,* but that play does not present this famed general with historical accuracy. However, his proclamation, reported in HOLINSHED's *Chronicles,* that he would rather be the bastard of a great man than the legitimate heir of a humble one, is clearly echoed by the Bastard of *King John* (1.1.164, 259–276).

**Bastard (2) of Orléans, Jean Dunois, The (1403–1468)**   Historical figure and character in *1 Henry VI,* one of the leaders of the French forces. Though the historical Bastard, who was well known by that appellation, was one of the leading soldiers of the 15th century, he is presented in the play as a boastful but cowardly and inept warrior. His personality resembles that of the other French noblemen, whose collective role was simply to demonstrate that France could not have been victorious but for dissensions among the English.

**Bastard (3)**   Character in *Troilus and Cressida.* See MARGARELON.

**Bates, John**   Minor character in *Henry V,* one of the soldiers who encounter the incognito King HENRY V on the eve of the battle of AGINCOURT. Bates is a grumbler who wishes he were elsewhere, even if the King were left alone in FRANCE (1), but he also says, 'yet I determine to fight lustily for him' (4.1.196). He tries to allay the quarrel between WILLIAMS (2) and the stranger (the King), saying, 'Be friends, you English fools, be friends: we have French quarrels enow . . .' (4.1.228–

229). Bates is a typical English soldier, part of the scene's varied presentation of the army's morale before the battle.

**Bavian**   Minor character in *The Two Noble Kinsmen,* a performer dressed as a baboon, or bavian. The Bavian is part of an entertainment performed before THESEUS (2), Duke of ATHENS in 3.5. He speaks only two words, 'Yes, sir' (3.5.37), in response to his director, the SCHOOLMASTER (2), who tells him, 'My friend, carry your tail without offence / Or scandal to the ladies; and be sure / You tumble with audacity and manhood, / And when you bark do it with judgement' (3.5.34–37). This directive casts an amusing light on English rustic entertainments of the 17th century. However, most scholars agree that Shakespeare did not write this scene; the Bavian and his instructions are probably the work of John FLETCHER (2).

**Bawd**   Minor character in *Pericles,* the keeper of a brothel in MYTILENE, who, with her husband the PANDAR, buys the kidnapped MARINA. The Bawd is a hard-boiled madam. She coolly assesses her wenches as 'creatures . . . [who] with continual action are even as good as rotten' (4.2.6–9). She rejects her husband's scruples: 'Other sorts offend as well as we' (4.2.34), she says grumpily. She is prepared to be friendly with the newly-bought Marina, and assures her that she 'shall live in pleasure [and] taste gentlemen of all fashions' (4.2.72–76). When Marina grieves at her plight, however, the Bawd turns nasty, and declares, 'you're a young foolish sapling, and must be bow'd as I would have you' (4.2.83–85). The Bawd jokes cynically with her employee BOULT about the venereal diseases of their clients. This was a traditional subject of humour in Shakespeare's day, but placed in contrast with the virginal Marina it seems shocking. When Marina's virtues begin to encourage moral reform among her customers, the Bawd complains comically, 'Fie, fie upon her! She's able to freeze the god Priapus, and undo a whole generation' (4.6.3–4). In her energetic sinfulness, the Bawd resembles such other Shakespearean ladies of the demi-monde as HOSTESS (2) QUICKLY and MISTRESS (2) OVERDONE, though the underworld of Mytilene is not so developed as those of LONDON and VIENNA. The Bawd contributes to the comic—and realistic—relief from the elevated and melodramatic romance of the main plot.

**Baylis, Lilian (1874–1937)**   English theatrical entrepreneur, director of the OLD VIC and SADLER'S WELLS THEATRES. In 1898 Lilian Baylis, the daughter of professional singers, joined her aunt in the management of the Royal Victoria Coffee Music Hall—a temperance organisation dedicated to liquor-free entertainment—in the theatre building already known as the Old Vic. Baylis added opera performances, and the

Old Vic soon became a leading operatic theatre. In 1914, joined by Ben GREET, she added Shakespearean performances to the schedule, and the Old Vic was soon established as a national centre of Shakespearean production. At her instigation and with her support—though she made a point of leaving all artistic decisions to others—the entire CANON of Shakespeare's plays had been staged by 1923. In 1931 Baylis acquired the Sadler's Wells Theatre as a companion theatre in north London for the Old Vic in south London, and put on Shakespeare there as well, although since 1934 it has been chiefly associated with opera. As a leading light of the Shakespearean theatre, Lilian Baylis was regarded as a British national treasure, and she received many honours including one of the first Oxford honorary degrees given to a woman outside academia.

**Baynard Castle**   London fortress, a setting in *Richard III.* In 3.7 RICHARD III receives the MAYOR (3) of London, accompanied by a number of citizens, in Baynard Castle. Manipulated by the Duke of BUCKINGHAM (2), this group offers Richard the crown, insisting that he take it when he cynically feigns reluctance.

Shakespeare took this historical incident and its setting from his sources. Richard's use of Baynard Castle signalled the strength of his drive for the crown, for it was an important bastion of royalty in London, second in strength and importance only to the TOWER OF LONDON. Like the Tower, it was built by England's Norman conquerors to control the city. Looming across the river from SOUTHWARK, Baynard Castle was a familiar landmark in Shakespeare's day; it was later destroyed in the Great Fire of London in 1666.

**Beadle (1)**   Minor character in *2 Henry VI,* a constable of the village of ST. ALBANS who is assigned to whip the imposter SIMPCOX in 2.1.

**Beadle (2)**   Any of several minor characters in *2 Henry IV,* petty London officials assigned to whip the HOSTESS (2) and DOLL TEARSHEET. In 5.4 the Beadles drag the two women across the stage. One of them speaks, remarking that the punishment has been decreed because the women have been involved in a murder. Both women insult the chief Beadle, referring to his skeletal appearance. In the QUARTO edition of the play, a stage direction identified this Beadle as John SINCKLO, a very thin actor, and it is presumed that Shakespeare wrote this scene with him in mind.

**Bear**   Minor figure in *The Winter's Tale,* wild beast that kills ANTIGONUS as he abandons the infant PERDITA on the coast of BOHEMIA. Antigonus is warned by the MARINER (1) that wild animals are present, and as he completes his task, he is attacked. At 3.3.58 one of Shakespeare's most famous stage directions instructs

Antigonus, 'Exit, pursued by a bear'. Later in the scene, the CLOWN (8) reports that the bear has 'half dined upon the gentleman' (3.3.105). The startling appearance of a bear makes Antigonus' death a vivid event, forcefully elevating it as a symbol of the consequences of tragedy. At the same time Antigonus' appalling end suggests humanity's helplessness in the face of nature and thus reinforces a major theme of the play, our ultimate dependence on providence.

Carnivores of all sorts figure prominently in Shakespeare's imagery, and bears in particular consistently represent fearsome savagery. Sometimes the image is comical, as in the remark of a stubborn bachelor, 'As from a bear a man would run for life, / So fly I from her that would be my wife' (*Comedy of Errors,* 3.2.153–154); sometimes in earnest, as when PROSPERO describes the tormented ARIEL: 'thy groans / Did make wolves howl, and penetrate the breasts / Of everangry bears' (*Tempest* 1.2.287–289). In *The Winter's Tale* Antigonus himself uses such imagery, unconsciously and ironically anticipating his own end, when he hopes that wild animals, including 'wolves and bears' (2.3.186), will be merciful to the abandoned Perdita. This desire is pointedly hopeless, given the nature of wolves and bears. Although the bear does spare the infant, it does so only because it devours Antigonus.

Although Antigonus' death is unquestionably horrific, it also has a slightly comical note. The bear's sudden appearance is as unexpected as a punch line and charged with the awkward unreality of an actor costumed as a bear. The Clown's later description is frankly humorous. The bear's brief appearance thus offers an emotional transition from the tragic first half of the play to the pastoral comedy of Act 4.

Scholars and theatrical directors have speculated on whether Shakespeare intended the use of a live bear on stage. Some scholars have suggested that he did, as live bears attracted crowds to the bear-baiting arena a few doors from the GLOBE THEATRE, where the audience paid to see dogs attack the bears. However, there are many objections to this idea, beginning with the notoriously temperamental nature of bears (tame bears were known in 17th-century England, but they were always leashed—an inappropriate condition for a savage killer). An actor costumed as a bear was most probably what Shakespeare had in mind; a bear is much the easiest wild animal for a human being to imitate, and bear costumes are known to have been used fairly frequently in Shakespeare's day.

**Beatrice**   Character in *Much Ado About Nothing,* sharp-tongued rival in wits—and later the lover—of BENEDICK. Beatrice, who initially disparages love and Benedick, later rejects these attitudes and becomes his betrothed. She in fact loves him all along, as the audience knows; her own awareness comes only with the assurance that he loves her. Their relationship matures when they act together to defend her defamed cousin HERO at the crisis point of the play.

Beatrice bluntly disdains love, sneering, 'I had rather hear my dog bark at a crow than a man swear he loves me' (1.1.120–122), but her first words (1.1. 28–29) have already betrayed her interest in Benedick, although she covers it with a veneer of witty insults and teasing. She has suffered through an earlier unhappy romance with Benedick, as she suggests in 1.1.59 and 2.1.261–264, and her barbed wit is plainly defensive, disguising her true feelings even from herself. Her brashness is nicely contrasted with Hero's reticence in 2.1: Hero is twice prompted about her response to the expected courtship of Don PEDRO, and on both occasions Beatrice's comments against marriage prevent her reply.

Tricked into believing that Benedick loves her, Beatrice immediately discards her cynicism, saying, 'contempt, farewell, and maiden pride, adieu!' (3.1.109–110), in a lyrical 10-line outburst—almost her only verse lines in the play—that emphasises her elation. Swallowing her pride, she must accept her friends' teasing in 3.4.

When Hero is cruelly rejected on false evidence of promiscuity, Beatrice proves her essential goodness, believing in her cousin's innocence in the face of the evidence and demanding support from Benedick. The two witty lovers become involved in a serious conflict, bolstered by each other's trust. In asking for Benedick's aid, Beatrice confirms her love and acknowledges his.

Nevertheless, once Hero's problem is solved, Beatrice and Benedick briefly retreat from love in 5.4. Their strength is almost not great enough to overcome their old habits, but when their friends produce their love poems, they are forced to reaffirm their true feelings. Beatrice's quick wit cannot resist an attempt at having the last word (5.4.94–96), so Benedick silences her with a kiss.

This rather abrupt close to Beatrice's part suggests an important aspect of the playwright's attitude towards women: Beatrice, like other Shakespearean heroines, such as KATHERINA in *The Taming of the Shrew*, displays a spirited individuality, but in the end she willingly accepts a position subordinate to a man, as was conventionally expected of Elizabethan women. At first, denying that she wants or needs a husband, Beatrice asserts her independence, demonstrating the freedom of will that enlivens Shakespeare's most attractive female characters. However, when she seeks to defend Hero's innocence, she concedes that a male presence is required, saying of the vengeance she desires on her cousin's behalf, 'It is a man's office' (4.1.265). She asks Benedick to fulfil the role that she cannot, reminding us of the ultimately dependent position of women in Shakespeare's world.

Intriguingly, Beatrice shares two further character-

istics with Shakespeare's other bold young women, including the 'Dark Lady' of the SONNETS: a sharp wit and a dark complexion. It seems plausible, though altogether unprovable, that these were the traits of a woman (entirely unidentifiable) who was romantically important to Shakespeare.

Beatrice is sometimes seen as shrewish, but this is a misconception; Shakespeare plainly intended to present a delightful young woman—defensive about love but charming and candid. While her repartee can be made to seem malicious or mean-spirited in performance, it is more fittingly delivered with great mirth and gaiety; Don Pedro remarks that she is 'a pleasant-spirited lady' (2.1.320). Shakespeare took Beatrice's name from the Latin name *Beatrix*, meaning 'she who blesses'. She is thus appropriately matched with Benedict (from the Latin *Benedictus*, meaning 'blessed').

**Beaumont (1)**   Minor character in *Henry V*, a French nobleman. Beaumont is a GHOST CHARACTER; i.e., he appears but does not speak. He is named in 3.5.44 and in a stage direction in 4.2.1. His death in the battle of AGINCOURT is reported in 4.8.102. Shakespeare apparently took the name from the list of casualties in HOLINSHED's *Chronicles*, perhaps intending to develop the character further.

**Beaumont (2), Francis (c. 1584–1616)**   English dramatist best known as a collaborator with John FLETCHER (2). As a young man, Beaumont studied at the INNS OF COURT, where he began writing poetry, possibly with the encouragement of Michael DRAYTON, a family friend. He began writing plays under the influence of Ben JONSON, whose friend and protégé he became. His earliest play, a COMEDY OF HUMOURS entitled *The Woman Hater* (1606), was staged by the Children of Paul's (see CHILDREN'S COMPANIES). In 1608 his *The Knight of the Burning Pestle*, a satire on the conventions of drama and literature, flopped dismally, though modern commentators regard it as one of the most endearing Jacobean comedies. In the same year he began his brief but highly successful collaboration with Fletcher. They wrote 15 plays together—one of them, *Philaster* (1610), was among the most important works of the age (see JACOBEAN DRAMA), and in the 1630s, their plays were more popular than Shakespeare's. Their partnership ended in 1613, when Beaumont married a wealthy heiress and retired from the theatre. Beaumont's last dramatic work, written by himself, was *The Masque of the Inner Temple and Gray's Inn* (1613), a courtly MASQUE written to celebrate the marriage of Princess ELIZABETH (3). A scene from it was restaged by Fletcher in *The Two Noble Kinsmen*.

**Bedford (1), John Plantagenet, Duke of (1389–1435)**   Historical figure and character in *1 Henry VI* and *Henry V*, the younger brother of King HENRY V and uncle of HENRY VI. (The same individual appears as Prince John of LANCASTER [3], in *1* and *2 Henry IV.*) In *1 Henry VI* Bedford is a regent, ruling FRANCE (1) for the infant King Henry. Bedford opens the play memorably, mourning the deceased Henry V in portentous terms: 'Hung be the heavens with black, yield day to night!' (1.1.1). In Act 2 Bedford proves himself a capable warrior when ORLÉANS (1) is captured, but in Act 3 he is an aged invalid, confined to a chair, whom JOAN LA PUCELLE taunts as 'good grey-beard' (3.2.50). He dies happily after witnessing the English victory at ROUEN.

The historical Bedford did die in Rouen, though at the age of 45 or 46, while the city was under English rule; the battle scene in the play is fictitious. He outlived Joan of Arc by several years. In fact, he played a major role in Joan's capture and trial, but Shakespeare transferred this important aspect of his career to YORK (8) in order to lend importance to the character who was to be a leading figure in the civil wars to come.

In *Henry V* a younger Bedford is an inconsequential member of the King's entourage. The historical Bedford, however, played an important role in the English conquest of France. Although he is present at the battle of AGINCOURT in the play, he was actually in England at the time, ruling in Henry's absence. Then he won a crucial naval battle in the second of Henry's campaigns in France. This campaign is ignored by Shakespeare, although it was actually more important than Agincourt in precipitating the final French surrender depicted in 5.2.

**Bedford (2), Lucy, Countess of (1581–1627)** English literary patron. Lucy Harington was married at the age of 13 to Edward Russell, Earl of Bedford; their marriage is one of several suggested as the occasion of the first performance of *A Midsummer Night's Dream.* Lucy Bedford was the patron of many of the most important English writers of her day, including John Donne (1573–1631), Samuel DANIEL, Michael DRAYTON, John FLORIO, and Ben JONSON. She was also a person of affairs, serving on the council of the Virginia Company and, when her husband was disabled by illness, as a leader of an important political faction in the turbulent 1620s.

**Beeston, Christopher (d. 1638)** English actor and theatrical entrepreneur. Beeston began his career as an apprentice to Augustine PHILLIPS of the CHAMBERLAIN'S MEN. He may have appeared with STRANGE'S MEN in 1590, though his earliest certain role was with the Chamberlain's Men in 1598. In 1602 he joined the WORCESTER'S MEN, remaining with the company when it became the QUEEN'S MEN (2). He managed the company—ineptly and perhaps dishonestly—from 1612 until it dissolved upon the queen's death in 1619. He then joined PRINCE CHARLES' MEN as its manager and went on to run LADY ELIZABETH'S MEN (1622–1625)

and Queen Henrietta's Men (1625–1637). He had already expanded his operations: in 1617 he had built a theatre, the Phoenix, where these and other companies performed. Shortly before his death, he formed his own troupe of boy actors, the King and Queen's Young Company, popularly known as 'Beeston's Boys' (see CHILDREN'S COMPANIES).

His son, William Beeston (d. 1682), also an actor, later provided the antiquarian James Aubrey (1626–1697) with anecdotes about Shakespeare, reporting that his father had found the playwright 'a handsome, well-shaped man; very good company, and of a very ready and pleasant smooth wit . . . [who] wouldn't be debauched'. He also is the source of the report that Shakespeare had briefly been a schoolteacher as a young man.

**Beethoven, Ludwig van (1770–1827)** German composer, several of whose works were inspired in part by Shakespeare. Like many artists of the Romantic movement of the late 18th and early 19th centuries, Beethoven was deeply moved by Shakespeare and his broad presentation of life that dealt with grand themes and was written in stirring poetry. One movement of a string quartet (opus 18, no. 1; c. 1798) is thought to be based on Beethoven's response to *Romeo and Juliet,* and while his 'Overture to *Coriolanus*' (1807) was composed to accompany a contemporary Viennese imitation of Shakespeare's play, he surely considered the original as well. Beethoven's Piano Sonata no. 17 (1802) is known as *The Tempest* because he once declared that a clue to its meaning could be found by reading Shakespeare's play.

**Begger** Character in *The Taming of the Shrew.* See SLY (1).

**Belarius** Character in *Cymbeline,* the foster-father of GUIDERIUS and ARVIRAGUS. Belarius was unjustly exiled from the court of King CYMBELINE many years before the time of the play, and, in revenge, had kidnapped the king's infant sons. He has since raised them in the wilds of WALES (1). When the Roman army invades Britain, Belarius helps his foster-sons save the British army and the three are honoured by the king. However, because Guiderius has killed Prince CLOTEN, he is threatened with the death sentence prescribed for commoners who kill a prince. Belarius, to save the young man's life, reveals the truth. Though he has exposed himself to capital punishment because he had kidnapped the heir to the throne, Belarius is forgiven by the king in the play's final sequence of mercies and reconciliations. Belarius is a good man, unjustly persecuted, who only recovers his position by accident. He thus embodies an important theme of the play, that man is helpless without the aid of providence.

Belarius has taken the name Morgan, but he is designated Belarius in speech headings and stage directions. His Welsh pseudonym goes well with his comic habit of speaking in moralising clichés, for he fills the 17th-century English stereotype of the dull Welshman.

**Belch, Sir Toby** Character in *Twelfth Night*. See SIR TOBY.

**Belleforest, François de (1530–1583)** French author and translator who possibly influenced Shakespeare. An aristocratic courtier, Belleforest wrote poetry and compiled a collection of tales entitled *Histoires Tragiques* (1572), largely translations from the work of the Italian author Matteo BANDELLO. As a young man, Belleforest was a court favourite of Queen Margaret of Navarre (1492–1549), who wrote a famous book of tales, *The Heptameron* (published 1559), that doubtless inspired his own work.

Shakespeare may have taken ideas or details for several of his works—for example, *Hamlet, Titus Andronicus,* and *Twelfth Night*—from the *Histoires Tragiques,* but other sources were available to him in each instance, so we cannot be sure he knew Belleforest's tales. Nevertheless, the fact of several such coincidences suggests that he did, possibly from editions of 1576 or 1582. He may also have known the partial translation by Geoffrey FENTON (2), which was published in English in 1566, before the complete French version had appeared.

**Bellini, Vincenzo (1801–1835)** Italian composer, creator of an opera based on *Romeo and Juliet.* Bellini was one of the originators of bel canto–style opera in the early 19th century. His *I Capuleti e I Montecchi* was popular for a number of years following its premiere in 1830, but after 1847 it was not performed for almost a century. It now holds a place in modern operatic repertory, though Bellini is much better known for *La Sonnambula, Norma* (both of 1831), and *I Puritani* (1835).

**Belmont** Location in *The Merchant of Venice,* the estate of PORTIA (1). BASSANIO comes to Belmont to court Portia and succeeds in the lottery of caskets, in 3.2, before being called away by news of SHYLOCK's intended villainy. The estate is also a refuge for LORENZO and JESSICA. At the close of the play, Lorenzo and Jessica rhapsodise romantically about love and the beauties of the night, while ensconced at Belmont, where the episode of the betrothal rings is played out, and the comedy is concluded, as was proper to a 16th-century comedy, with the union of lovers.

Belmont, a fictitious place, is apparently located on the mainland near VENICE; its name means 'beautiful hill'. Shakespeare simply took the estate and its name from his source, FIORENTINO's *Il Pecorone,* but he made the place his own. Belmont, like the forest of ARDEN (1) in *As You Like It,* is an artificial world, removed from

the dreary acquisitiveness and commercialism represented by Shylock, where the conflicts that burden human affairs in the 'real' world can be resolved.

**Belott, Stephen (active 1602–1613)** Wigmaker of LONDON, plaintiff in a lawsuit in which Shakespeare testified. Belott, the son of French Huguenot immigrants, was apprenticed to Christopher MOUNTJOY, a 'tire-maker'—creator of the elaborate, ornamented headresses worn by aristocratic women. After serving his term and becoming Mountjoy's hired employee, he married his master's daughter. Shakespeare, who was a lodger in Mountjoy's house, participated in the negotiations about the marriage settlement, carrying messages between the father and the prospective bridegroom. After their marriage the Belotts established a rival business, initiating a feud with Mountjoy. After Mountjoy's wife died in 1606, the couple moved back in with him, but arguments over money soon resulted in their departure. Eventually, Belott sued Mountjoy for refusing to relinquish money agreed upon in the marriage settlement. Shakespeare testified in the case (see MOUNTJOY). Belott was eventually awarded a token settlement, though the arbitrators criticised him for debauchery. No more is known of his life.

**Benedick** Character in *Much Ado About Nothing,* rival of BEATRICE in contests of wit and later her lover. Benedick initially ridicules love, insisting that cuckoldry is the inevitable fate of married men, but he becomes a joyous bridegroom at the play's end. His playful dislike of Beatrice, which predates the beginning of the play, extends to all women, including HERO, whom his friend CLAUDIO (1) loves, but Benedick subtly reveals an underlying readiness to abandon his misogyny when he contrasts his 'custom, as being a professed tyrant to their sex' with his 'simple true judgement' (1.1.154–157). Tricked by Claudio and Don PEDRO into believing that Beatrice loves him, Benedick permits his own suppressed affection to emerge. At the play's climax, when Beatrice asks him to support the maligned Hero, he agrees, though this means turning from the comfortable companionship of Claudio and Don PEDRO. Trusting in his certainty of Beatrice's essential decency, Benedick has grown from shallow misogyny to implicit faith in his lover. His maturation, along with Beatrice's corresponding development, is the chief psychological theme of the play.

Benedick is essentially a comic figure. His friends value him for his sense of humour; Don Pedro says of him, 'from the crown of his head to the sole of his foot he is all mirth' (3.2.9). He is also sometimes a figure of fun. He crosses verbal swords with Beatrice, but she is too quick-witted for him, and he can only respond in her absence, as in the humorous speech that he delivers to Don Pedro in 2.1.223–245. Tricked into believing that Beatrice loves him, he comically imagines romantic double meanings in her derisive words. Even filled with passion, he can be funny: 'I will live in thy heart, die in thy lap, and be buried in thy eyes; and moreover, I will go with thee to thy uncle's' (5.2. 94–96).

However, Benedick is no buffoon. His essential honour is often displayed. In 2.1, although hurt and humiliated himself, he accosts Don Pedro on Claudio's behalf when it appears that the older man is stealing Hero. When he defends the falsely accused and dishonoured Hero in 5.1, Benedick manfully resigns from Don Pedro's service and challenges Claudio to a duel. At the end of the play, fully committed to marrying Beatrice, he recants his earlier misogyny with no loss of dignity whatever. He admits freely that he had been wrong and is prepared to accept any ridicule that may be attempted against him, saying, ' . . . since I do purpose to marry, I will think nothing to any purpose that the world can say against it' (5.4. 103–105). In acknowledgeing his earlier foolishness, he offers a motto that might well sum up Shakespeare's comedies: 'man is a giddy thing, and this is my conclusion' (5.4.107).

Benedick, a common name in medieval England, comes from the Latin *Benedictus,* meaning 'blessed'; he is thus appropriately matched with Beatrice (from *Beatrix,* or 'she who blesses'). Shakespeare's character has become so firmly entrenched in the imagination of generations of readers and theatre-goers that his name, sometimes spelled 'Benedict', has become a common noun meaning a newly married man who has long been a bachelor.

**Benfield, Robert (d. c. 1650)** English actor. Benfield was one of the 26 men listed in the FIRST FOLIO as the 'Principall Actors' in Shakespeare's plays. He specialised in dignified figures such as kings and old men. He was with LADY ELIZABETH'S MEN in 1613 and may have joined the KING'S MEN upon the death of William OSTLER in 1614, for he took at least one of Ostler's parts. In any case he was a member of the company by 1619 and remained with the company until its dissolution in 1642, with the opening of the Civil Wars.

**Bensley, Robert (1742–1817)** English actor. Best known for his portrayal of MALVOLIO, Bensley was a highly mannered actor who frequently played in the productions of David GARRICK. He was a major figure on the London stage of the last decades of the 18th century.

**Benson (1), Frank Robert (1858–1939)** English actor and producer. F. R. Benson formed a touring company in 1883 that pointedly de-emphasised spectacle in staging Shakespeare, in contrast to the prevailing fashion for lush productions, such as those of Henry IRVING and Herbert Beerbohm TREE. From 1888 to 1919, with few exceptions, Benson directed the annual Shakespeare Festival at STRATFORD. His own performances in leading roles were acclaimed. More important, he presented almost all the plays—only *Titus Andronicus* and *Troilus and Cressida* were omitted—in texts with few cuts or interpolations and on plain stages that focussed attention on Shakespeare's words. In 1900 he staged the complete four- to five-hour-long text of *Hamlet* in London, and at Stratford in 1908 he produced the complete HISTORY PLAYS as a single unit for the first time. In 1916 on the occasion of the tercentenary of Shakespeare's death, Benson was knighted by King George V for his services to the British Shakespearean tradition.

**Benson (2), John (d. 1667)** London publisher and bookseller, producer of the first collection of Shakespeare's poems. Benson's *Poems* contains most of the SONNETS, *A Lover's Complaint, The Phoenix and Turtle,* excerpts from *Measure for Measure* and *As You Like It, THE PASSIONATE PILGRIM* (much of which is not Shakespeare's), a few other misattributed works, and a number of poems about Shakespeare by other poets, including MILTON, JONSON, BEAUMONT (2), Leonard DIGGES (2), and William BASSE. Only six of the Sonnets (numbers 18, 19, 43, 56, 75, and 76) are missing, though the remainder are altered to make them appear to be addressed only to a woman. Although the text of Thomas THORPE's 1609 edition was employed, the Sonnets are arranged in a different order, with titles occasionally assigned to a group of two or three.

**Bentley, John (1553–1585)** English actor, a member of the QUEEN'S MEN (1). Bentley, one of the original members of the Queen's Men, is best known as the central figure in a brawl of 1583 in which a would-be gate-crasher of a Queen's Men's performance was killed. Though Richard TARLTON attempted to restrain him, Bentley pursued the fleeing miscreant, who hit him with a rock. Bentley and a companion drew their swords, and in the ensuing fight one of them killed the man. There is no record of a criminal prosecution for the killing, which occurred in 1583 during the Queen's Men's first season. As an actor, Bentley was well regarded by his contemporaries, being compared with Tarlton and William ALLEYN, acknowledged leaders of the profession.

**Benvolio** Character in *Romeo and Juliet,* friend and cousin of ROMEO. Benvolio's good sense and calm temperament are contrasted with the belligerence of Romeo's other friend, MERCUTIO. In 2.1, knowing that Romeo wishes to be alone, Benvolio draws Mercutio away. He attempts to prevent the brawl among the servants in 1.1 and the fight between Mercutio and TYBALT in 3.1; in both cases, he is ineffectual. This courteous and gentle character (whose apt name means 'good will') appropriately disappears from the play as the tragedy unfolds.

**Berkeley (1)** Minor character in *Richard III,* one of two named gentlemen among the group that accompanies Lady ANNE (2) and the corpse of HENRY VI in 1.2.

**Berkeley (2), Lord Thomas (d. 1417)** Historical figure and minor character in *Richard II,* an ally of the Duke of YORK (4). A GLOUCESTERSHIRE nobleman whose castle has assumed strategic importance in the rebellion of BOLINGBROKE (1) against King RICHARD II, Berkeley greets Bolingbroke on York's behalf.

The historical Berkeley apparently allied himself with Bolingbroke when York did, for he served on the commission of noblemen that issued the formal declaration of Richard's deposition, and he opposed the rebellion against the new king, capturing the Duke of SURREY (2) and the Earl of SALISBURY (1). He turned his prisoners over to a mob, who killed them; their deaths are reported in 5.6.8. In later years Berkeley fought for Henry IV, as Bolingbroke became known, against Owen GLENDOWER.

**Berlioz, Hector (1803–1869)** French composer, creator of several works inspired by Shakespeare's plays. Berlioz, the leading French composer of the Romantic school, wrote the 'King Lear Overture' (1831) and a 'dramatic symphony', as he called it, based on *Romeo and Juliet* (1838). A symphonic fantasy on *The Tempest* (1830) was absorbed into a later work. Two choral works, 'Death March for the Last Scene of *Hamlet*' (with sung but wordless cries of grief) and 'La Mort d'Ophelia' (with a French text after Shakespeare by Ernest Legouvé [1807–1903]), were published in 1848 but may have been written much earlier. Later in his career Berlioz wrote an opera based on *Much Ado About Nothing,* called *Béatrice et Bénédict* (1862), a work that is considered among his finest. Another opera, *Les Troyens* (1859), contains a lyrical episode inspired by the love scene in 5.1 of *The Merchant of Venice.*

Berlioz profoundly influenced 19th-century French culture with dramatic compositions that reflected the romantic spirit of the age. As a young man he abandoned medical studies for music. In 1828 he fell in love with a leading actress, Harriet SMITHSON—famous in France for her OPHELIA—and he may have written his works inspired by *Hamlet* at this time. His *Symphonie Fantastique* (1830)—intended as an expression of his passion for Smithson—established him as a leading composer. He married her in 1833, but then abandoned her for another woman, though he did return to her much later and nursed her through her final illness. His own last days were solitary and unhappy; he proposed for his epitaph MACBETH's despairing cry that life is 'a tale / Told by an idiot, full of sound and fury, / Signifying nothing' (*Macbeth,* 5.5.26–28).

**Bernardo** Character in *Hamlet.* See BARNARDO.

**Berners, John Bourchier, Lord (1467–1533)** English translator. Lord Berners' translation (1523–1525) of the 14th-century *Chroniques* of FROISSART may have influenced the composition of *Richard II,* and his English version of a 13th-century French adventure tale, *The Boke of Duke Huon of Bordeaux* (1534), may have inspired something of Shakespeare's OBERON in *A Midsummer Night's Dream.*

Lord Berners was an important political figure; as a young nobleman he supported the Earl of RICHMOND (who appears in *Richard III*) when he seized the throne as King Henry VII in 1485. He was appointed Lord Chancellor by King HENRY VIII in 1516 (though he is not the CHANCELLOR of the play *Henry VIII*), and in his later years served as Deputy of Calais, the English outpost on the coast of FRANCE (1).

**Bernhardt, Sarah (1845–1923)** French actress. Though not chiefly a Shakespearean actress, Bernhardt scored one of her first great successes as CORDELIA in a French translation of *King Lear.* She also

*Sarah Bernhardt was one of several women to play the title role in major late 19th-century productions of* Hamlet. *(Courtesy of Culver Pictures, Inc.)*

made an important contribution to the role of LADY (6) MACBETH, as the first to display an overt sensuality that has been heavily stressed by most of her 20th-century successors. In addition, she is strongly associated with HAMLET, a part she played in Paris, London, and New York in 1899 to 1901, as well as in the first FILM of *Hamlet*, a silent movie of 1900.

**Berowne (Biron)**   Character in *Love's Labour's Lost*, one of the gentlemen in the court of the KING (19) of Navarre. Berowne is the witty exponent of the play's two main points: that love is superior to the pursuit of knowledge; and that pretensions, especially verbal ones, cannot be successful. When the King demands that his courtiers follow a three-year ascetic regimen dedicated to scholarship, Berowne argues that this is unhealthy and doomed to failure, because young men will naturally succumb to love. Berowne's common sense is opposed to the affectation of scholarly devotion, and his awareness of real emotion counters the fakery of academic rhetoric.

Unlike the other lovers in *Love's Labour's Lost*, who function simply as vehicles for the conventional proposition that the emotions should take precedence over the intellect, Berowne is a humanly believable character, as well as a funny one. The gentleman mocks himself in a humorous soliloquy at the end of 3.1, confessing that he has fallen under the sway of 'this signor junior, giant-dwarf, dan Cupid' (3.1.175). He is delighted to find that the King and the other courtiers, DUMAINE and LONGAVILLE, are similarly smitten, in the comic high point of the play, a stock eavesdropping scene repeated three times to a height of absurdity (4.3). Berowne proclaims a manifesto in favour of love, using his wit and warmth in a speech that contains perhaps the best verse in the play (4.3.285–361).

The gentlemen attempt to court the ladies with a masquerade and high-flown sentiments, and they are mocked by the women they would woo. Berowne realises that their pretensions have failed them, and he eloquently advances the play's campaign against foolish rhetoric, rejecting: 'Taffeta phrases, silken terms precise, / Three-pil'd hyperboles, spruce affection, / Figures pedantical . . . / Henceforth my wooing mind shall be express'd / In russet yeas and honest kersey noes. . . .' (5.2.406–413).

During the pageant in the same scene, Berowne is merciless in his heckling, perhaps evidencing the essential immaturity of the gentlemen. As a result of his wounding wit, ROSALINE, at the play's dénouement, requires that Berowne must spend a year visiting the sick in hospitals before she will accept him. Berowne, no cardboard character as are his fellows and the King, has human faults that must be corrected, even though he is also the chief exponent of the honest emotional life promoted by the play.

Berowne's name, pronounced 'B'roon', is taken from that of a contemporary French Protestant general, the Duc de Biron, who was a principal adviser to the historical King of Navarre.

**Berri, Jean of France, Duke of (1340–1416)**   Historical figure and minor character in *Henry V*, a follower of the FRENCH KING. Berri does not speak, but he is referred to in 2.4.4 and 3.5.41. The historical Berri was the uncle of Charles VI, the French King of the play, and sometimes served as regent during Charles' bouts of insanity. He was thus an important figure in the French political conflict that resulted from the King's incapacity, although Shakespeare ignored this aspect of HENRY V's conquest. Berri is now famed for his great collection of medieval books of hours, whose beautiful illuminations inspired the costumes and sets for Laurence OLIVIER's well-known FILM of *Henry V*.

**Bertram**   Character in *All's Well That Ends Well*, a young French nobleman, the errant husband of HELENA (2). Bertram is an imperfect man whose decline from callous self-absorption to more serious sin is arrested only by Helena's forceful entrapment. That his peccadilloes make him seem unworthy of Helena's love is one of the play's most bothersome features; as Samuel JOHNSON (7) complained, Bertram is 'dismissed into happiness' that he clearly does not deserve. Moreover, his highly qualified acceptance of Helena in the play's final scene does much to dilute any sense of resolution. This is one of the aspects of *All's Well* that places it among the PROBLEM PLAYS.

Helena persuades the KING (17) to make Bertram marry her as her reward for curing the monarch. Under the influence of the foppish coward PAROLLES, Bertram defies the King and abandons Helena, an act that the other characters uniformly deplore, and he departs from her with casual cruelty in 2.5. Bertram then declines into further immorality as he attempts to seduce the virginal DIANA (1). As his mother, the COUNTESS (2), remarks, he 'cannot thrive' (3.4.26) without Helena's influence.

Our attitude towards this undeniably dubious figure must colour our sense of the play as a whole, and many commentators have felt that he is important evidence that *All's Well* is a bitter satire. However, we can see that Shakespeare took considerable pains to mitigate Bertram's failings: the playwright altered his source, a tale by BOCCACCIO, in Bertram's favour, and he emphasised his youth, by way of excuse for his misdeeds, and his virtues, by way of compensation for them. In Boccaccio, the character corresponding to Bertram goes to the wars expressly to avoid his wife, while Shakespeare's young man displays an earlier desire to leave, a noble urge to distinguish himself in battle. His unwelcome marriage makes flight all the more alluring, and Parolles encourages him in this rebellion. Parolles is himself an addition to the tale, and although Bertram's unthinking acceptance of Parolles' advice reveals his own shallowness, it is also clear that Parolles' chief function is to deflect blame from Bertram. Not only does he encourage Bertram's flight, but he is also the go-between who furthers his seduction of Diana. Other characters, particularly the First LORD (6) and the Countess, explicitly hold Parolles responsible for corrupting Bertram.

Bertram's youth, another plausible excuse for his folly, is repeatedly referred to. He is in his 'minority' (4.5.69), a ward of the King, who feels he is too young be a soldier. Lord LAFEW is asked to advise him for he is 'unseason'd' (1.1.67). When he rejects Helena, the King calls him a 'proud, scornful boy' (2.3.151), and when his mother learns of his flight, she calls him a 'rash and unbridled boy' (3.2.27). Even Parolles describes him as 'a foolish idle boy', 'a dangerous and lascivious boy', 'that lascivious young boy' (4.3.207, 212, 290). In 5.3 the Countess asks the King to forgive Bertram his 'natural rebellion done i' th' blade of youth' (5.3.6), and he himself confesses to having seduced Diana 'i' th' wanton way of youth' (5.3.210).

Not only is Bertram excused for his youth, but he is also aggrandised for his virtues. The DUKE (2) of FLORENCE appoints him a cavalry commander despite his age, and he triumphs, being reported 'high in fame' (5.3.31). (In Boccaccio, his counterpart was merely an officer.) He receives the praise of both the Countess and the King, as well as the intense approval of Helena. Even the First and Second Lords, though they deplore his morals, nonetheless recognise that 'he contrives against his own nobility' (4.3.23–24). Further, Bertram is linked with the virtues of his late father by both the Countess and the King in 1.1 and 1.2. The hope that Bertram will grow into nobility does much to enhance our acceptance of his youthful faults.

In 5.3 Bertram is exposed as a moral coward and a liar, falsely maligning Diana and retreating ignominiously before the King's interrogation. His disgrace is complete. Then suddenly he is rescued by Helena's return. Bertram's wickedness is stressed mercilessly just before he is restored to favour, in order to emphasise the power of his redemption through Helena's love. His central position in the reconciliation that closes the play elevates him to Helena's level of goodness.

However, Bertram's ignominy cannot be completely ignored, and Shakespeare acknowledges the truth of the situation by keeping Bertram in character to the end. His initial response to Helena's arrival is ambiguous: his 'O pardon!' (5.3.302) has been seen as genuine repentance but also as a self-serving effort to lessen his disgrace, for when Helena asks him to acknowledge that he is truly her husband, he does not reply to her but speaks only to the King and only with a qualification: 'If she, my liege, can make me know this clearly / I'll love her dearly, ever, ever dearly'

(5.3.309–310). We can hardly fail to doubt the prospects for Bertram and Helena's happiness; even the King, closing the play, can only venture that 'All yet seems well . . .' (5.3.327).

Shakespeare tried to merge the traditional happy ending demanded by comedy with the psychological realism of Bertram's portrayal as a callow, thoughtless youth. The attempt is generally regarded as a failure; that Bertram is all too human is part of the problematic nature of All's Well That Ends Well. However, the portrait is an absorbing effort to adapt moral mediocrity to a romantic framework; figures such as POSTHUMUS of Cymbeline and LEONTES of The Winter's Tale owe something of their development to this less successful predecessor.

**Bestrafte Brudermord, Der (Fratricide Punished)** Eighteenth-century German version of Hamlet thought to derive in part from the UR-HAMLET. This work, fully titled Tragoedia der Bestrafte Brudermord oder Prinz Hamlet aus Dännemark but conventionally referred to as BB, is known only from the 1789 publication of a manuscript said to have been dated 1710. BB is essentially a BAD QUARTO of Hamlet with additional scenes, including an allegorical PROLOGUE (1) and several episodes of slapstick comedy. English actors frequently performed in Germany in the 16th and 17th centuries (see, e.g., Robert BROWNE; John GREEN; William KEMPE), and the actors who provided the dialogue translated into German as BB knew Hamlet in both of its early forms, published as the Q1 (1603) and Q2 (1604) editions; the additional material stems largely from medieval German traditions. However, some details in BB do not come from Hamlet yet correspond to a source for the play, François BELLEFOREST's version of the story. For instance, the QUEEN (9) blames her remarriage for Hamlet's madness, and Hamlet accuses his mother of hypocritically pretending to cry during their confrontation in her bedroom. These may have been introduced by actors who had performed in the Ur-Hamlet.

**Betterton, Thomas (1635–1710)** English actor, the dominant figure in Restoration theatre. Betterton was apprenticed to a bookseller in 1660, when English theatres reopened with the restoration of the monarchy, after 18 years of Puritan government. His employer opened a theatre, and Betterton was among the actors absorbed into William DAVENANT's troupe when two companies were licensed. Betterton quickly became the leading actor in London. Best known as HAMLET, his versatility was such that his other most appreciated role was as SIR TOBY in Twelfth Night. He was also especially acclaimed as MACBETH, MERCUTIO, OTHELLO, and HENRY VIII. After Davenant's death in 1671, Betterton led the company until it merged with the other London company in 1682. In 1695 he established a rival company, with which he was successful until he retired shortly before his death.

Betterton wrote a number of dramas; he also adapted Shakespeare's *Henry IV* plays to the tastes of the period. When his version was first staged in 1682, he played HOTSPUR; it was so popular that it was revived repeatedly for 18 years, by which time he played FALSTAFF. Betterton and his wife, Mary SAUNDERSON, were much loved in the London theatre world for their ready assistance to young players, most notably Anne BRACEGIRDLE.

Betterton's talent was viewed as more than extraordinary by his contemporaries. Samuel PEPYS reported that his Hamlet was 'beyond imagination' in 1661; when the actor took the part again in 1668, Pepys described the performance as 'the best . . . that ever man acted'. At the other end of his career, Betterton inspired Colley CIBBER (1) to write that he 'was an actor as Shakespeare was an author, both without competitors, formed for the mutual assistance and illustration of each other's genius'.

**Betty, William Henry West (1791–1874)**  English actor. A famous child prodigy, Master Betty, as he was known, was the greatest sensation of the London theatrical season of 1804–1805, having previously achieved success in Ireland and Scotland. He played several of the great classical roles of English drama that winter, including ROMEO and HAMLET (he was said to have memorised the latter role in a few hours). He also was notable as ARTHUR in *King John*. For a year he was the most popular English actor by far, overshadowing such established figures as John Philip KEMBLE (3). However, his star faded rapidly. In 1808, playing RICHARD III, he was booed off the stage, and he retired long enough to graduate from Cambridge; his subsequent attempt to resume his career was unsuccessful. His father squandered the fortune his earlier success had brought him, and he lived the remainder of his long life in poverty and obscurity.

**Bevis, George**  Minor character in *2 Henry VI*, a follower of Jack CADE. Bevis discusses Cade's rebellion with his friend John HOLLAND (3) in 4.2, and the two men join the revolt. In 4.7 Bevis, here called George, serves as the guard over the captured Lord SAY. Since John Holland is known to have been a minor actor of the early 1590s, George Bevis probably was also, and his name was likely given to this character, by either Shakespeare or the keeper of a PROMPT-BOOK, as a convenience.

**Bianca (1)**  Character in *The Taming of the Shrew*, a young woman courted by three men, LUCENTIO, HORTENSIO, and GRUMIO, in the SUB-PLOT of the play. At first, Bianca seems simply a demure and dutiful foil for her shrewish older sister, the title character, KA-THERINA. Katherina's stubbornness prevents Bianca from marrying, since their father, BAPTISTA (1), has ordered that the elder must be wed first. Bianca's sweet submissiveness also seems to make her a perfect object for the stereotypical romantic rapture of Lucentio, who elopes with her at the climax of the sub-plot.

However, Bianca is more complex than she initially appears. She is catty and self-righteous when she resists Katherina's violence in 2.1, not only declaring her own virtue but also twitting her sister about her age. Furthermore, Bianca draws attention to her supposed moral superiority over Katherina, as when she admonishes her sister to 'content you in my discontent' (1.1.80). Her ambiguous sweetness may help to explain Katherina's generalised belligerence, which has presumably flowered after frequent comparison with her sister's apparent virtue.

When alone with her tutors (not yet revealed to be suitors in disguise), Bianca is decidedly wilful, insisting, 'I'll not be tied to hours nor 'pointed times, / But learn my lessons as I please myself' (3.1.19–20). She is haughtily flirtatious with Lucentio ('presume not . . . despair not' [3.1.43]), and she rejects Hortensio with curt brutality. We are not surprised to find Bianca shrewish herself in the final scene, holding Lucentio up to ridicule for believing in her wifely obedience. This revelation emphasises the ironic contrast between the two sisters' marriages. Katherina has found true love after an explicitly mercenary courtship, whereas Bianca's union with Lucentio, the product of a conventionally idyllic romance, seems likely to be unhappy.

**Bianca (2)**  Character in *Othello*, a courtesan of CYPRUS and the lover of CASSIO. IAGO calls Bianca 'A housewife that by selling her desires / Buys herself bread and clothes' (4.1.94–95), where 'housewife' is intended with the common Elizabethan meaning of 'courtesan'. However, she is not a lowly prostitute; she has her own house (and is thus a literal housewife) and has the pride to be offended by the insults of EMILIA (2) in 5.1. Moreover, her obviously genuine concern for the wounded Cassio in the same scene touchingly demonstrates that she is a fundamentally decent person. This degree of dignity makes it possible for her relationship with Cassio to function as a foil for that of OTHELLO and DESDEMONA. The comparison is emphasised when Iago makes Cassio a part of his campaign to arouse Othello's jealousy of his wife. More pointedly, Bianca is jealous of Cassio—she complains, in 3.4, that he has avoided her and, in 4.1, she rages at him when she suspects that he has another lover. Her emotion echoes Othello's with the pointed difference that it is justified: Bianca's love for Cassio cannot be based on trust for she knows that, in the nature of relations between soldiers and courtesans, he will eventually leave her. In this context her jealousy seems both entirely rational and entirely vain, thus pointing up Othello's grievous error in two different ways.

**Bible** The Christian sacred scripture. The Bible was basic reading for Shakespeare and his age, and this is evident throughout the plays. Although the Bible is mentioned by name only once (*Merry Wives*, 2.3.7; it is also referred to as 'Holy Writ' several times) and explicit references to biblical characters or tales are few, Shakespeare, like many other authors, was influenced by biblical idioms and linguistic rhythms.

Several versions of the Bible were available in England in the 16th century. The version Shakespeare knew best was the Geneva Bible, which was translated in the centre of European Calvinism by Protestant exiles during the reign of the Catholic Queen Mary I (1553–1558) and published in England in 1560. He also knew the Bishop's Bible (1568), a revision of an earlier English text that was undertaken in part to counter the influence of radical Calvinism on the Geneva version. However, the Geneva Bible was so powerful a literary text that the Bishop's Bible actually relied on it to some extent, as, later, did the creators of the King James Version (1611), which was prescribed in the Anglican Church until late in the 19th century and is still commonly used and read. Shakespeare doubtless knew it, but only after his career was nearly over. As a reader of Latin, Shakespeare could also refer to the Vulgate of St Jerome, the basic Bible for western Europe from the fifth century to the 16th, when the Reformation stimulated the use of translations.

**Bigot (Bigod), Roger (d. 1220)** Historical figure and minor character in *King John,* a rebel against King JOHN (3). Bigot is one of the noblemen who oppose the King, responding to the death of ARTHUR, and who treacherously ally themselves with the invading French. Bigot speaks in only one of the four scenes in which he appears.

The historical Bigot was one of the barons who opposed John in 1214 and forced him to sign the Magna Charta. He was a great landowner in eastern England.

**Biondello** Character in *The Taming of the Shrew,* servant of LUCENTIO. Biondello acts as servant to his fellow employee, TRANIO, who is disguised as their master. His mischievous delight in the situation lends humorous force to his only important passage, the description of PETRUCHIO (2) approaching the wedding (3.2.30–83).

**Birmingham Shakespeare Memorial Library** Major collection of Shakespeareana in Birmingham, England. Founded in 1864 on the occasion of the playwright's 300th birthday, the library, despite its destruction by fire in 1879, now houses one of the most important collections of early texts, and records of later productions of Shakespeare's plays, with a particular strength in 18th-century materials.

**Birnam Wood** See DUNSINANE.

**Biron** See BEROWNE.

*Birth of Merlin* Play formerly attributed to Shakespeare, part of the Shakespeare APOCRYPHA. The earliest known text of *The Birth of Merlin* is a QUARTO published in 1662 by Francis KIRKMAN, who ascribed the play to Shakespeare and William ROWLEY (2). *Merlin,* a lively entertainment that features dragons, visions, a comet, and a devil, is usually dated to the 1620s based on the evidence of its style and vocabulary. Thus it is too late to be Shakespeare's play. Also, the writing is inferior and it is generally dissimilar to the playwright's known work. However, most scholars believe that Rowley wrote at least part of the play, perhaps in collaboration with Thomas MIDDLETON.

**Birthplace, Shakespeare's** House in STRATFORD where the playwright was probably born. The birthplace consists of two buildings on Henley Street that were bought on separate occasions by Shakespeare's father, John SHAKESPEARE (9), and joined together. Tradition assigns Shakespeare's birth to the western half, but no actual evidence exists. John Shakespeare lived in an unspecified building on Henley Street in 1552, and in 1556 he bought the eastern half of what was to be the birthplace, but at the same time he bought another house, and it is unclear where he lived. An unrecorded purchase could have been made before the playwright's birth, but John's only other known real estate acquisitions are two houses bought in 1575, one of which may have been the western half. In any case the family was living in the western half by 1597, and the eastern half was used for business.

In 1601 Shakespeare inherited the house upon his father's death. The eastern half was leased to the keepers of an inn called the Maidenhead, and the western half continued to be inhabited by the family; the playwright's sister Joan SHAKESPEARE (8) Hart and her family were living there when Shakespeare died. He left Joan a lifetime lease on it, while leaving the building to his daughter Susanna SHAKESPEARE (14) Hall, who in turn left it to her daughter Elizabeth HALL (3). In the meantime Joan's son and grandsons continued to live there. In 1670 Elizabeth Hall bequeathed it to Joan's grandson George Hart (1636–1702), whose descendants continued to occupy it for another century.

In 1806 the Harts sold the property to one Thomas Court, under whose ownership it became a butcher shop; his widow auctioned it off in 1846, advertising it as 'the house in which the immortal Poet of Nature was born'. The house was purchased by a nonprofit organisation formed for the purpose and 10 years later was restored, using the public's contributions (among the fund-raisers was Charles DICKENS). In 1891 the Birthplace Trust was incorporated to care for the building and such other properties as NEW PLACE (acquired in 1862), Anne HATHAWAY's cottage (1891), the supposed ARDEN (2) home (1930), and Hall's Croft, the Stratford residence of Dr John HALL (4) (1949).

**Bishop (1)**   Either of two minor characters in *Richard III*, clergymen who accompany RICHARD III as he receives the MAYOR (3) in 3.7. They convey the impression that Richard has been busy with devotional concerns. In fact, this is a contrived deception, and the 'Bishops' are actually unscrupulous lower-ranking clergymen, John SHAA and Friar PENKER, whom Richard has summoned for the purpose.

**Bishop (2), Henry Rowley (1786–1855)**   English composer and conductor. Best known for writing the song 'Home, Sweet Home', Bishop also composed the music for many of Frederick REYNOLDS' operatic adaptations of Shakespeare's plays. In 1842 Bishop became the first musician to be knighted by a British monarch.

**Blackfriars Gatehouse**   House in LONDON owned by Shakespeare. In 1613 Shakespeare bought a residence that had once served as the gatehouse on the estate of the BLACKFRIARS ABBEY. This was his last investment that we know of and his only non-theatrical one in London. He bought the building for £140 from Henry WALKER (1), paying £80 in cash and immediately mortgaging the house to Walker for the remaining £60. He had three trustees who were technically co-owners with him: William JOHNSON (8), John JACKSON (2), and John HEMINGE. They put up no money and had no ownership rights; this arrangement had the effect of eliminating the rights in the property of Shakespeare's wife, Anne HATHAWAY Shakespeare—perhaps because Shakespeare intended to leave the property to his daughter Susanna SHAKESPEARE (14) Hall, which he did in fact do. The trustees surrendered their shares to her in 1618, 'in performance of the confidence and trust in them reposed by William Shakespeare', as the legal document had it.

The gatehouse was very close to the BLACKFRIARS THEATRE, the principal venue for the KING's MEN, but Shakespeare clearly did not intend to use it. He already lived in STRATFORD full-time, and the purchase was simply an investment. The location, however, suggests how the property could have come to his attention. He leased the gatehouse soon after buying it, to one John ROBINSON (1), who was still living there in 1616. The later history of the building is obscure. It was probably destroyed in the Great Fire of London (1666).

**Blackfriars Priory**   Former Dominican priory building in LONDON, a setting for a scene in *Henry VIII*. In 2.4 the Blackfriars priory houses the proceedings that lead to King HENRY VIII's divorce from Queen KATHERINE, the king having declared it 'The most convenient place [he could] think of / for such receipt of learning' (2.2.137–138). Shakespeare followed his source, HOLINSHED's *Chronicles*, in placing this meeting at the Blackfriars. After England adopted Protestantism, the priory's property was seized by the crown and sold to various private interests. By Shakespeare's time, different buildings of the old priory had become the BLACKFRIARS THEATRE and BLACKFRIARS GATEHOUSE.

**Blackfriars Theatre**   Playhouse in LONDON established by Richard BURBAGE (3), the home from 1600 to 1608 of the Children of the Chapel (see CHILDREN's COMPANIES), and later of Shakespeare's company, the KING's MEN. Burbage inherited the Blackfriars from his father, James BURBAGE (2), who died before it was ready for use. The theatre was part of the medieval BLACKFRIARS PRIORY, which had been broken up and sold to private investors at the Reformation. The theatre was rented to Henry EVANS (2) of the Children of the Chapel, but after Evans' failure, Burbage bought back the lease, in partnership with his brother Cuthbert BURBAGE (1), four King's Men—Shakespeare, Henry CONDELL, John HEMINGE, and William SLY (2)—and a relative of Evans. The King's Men used the theatre in the winter from 1609 on. (Before the Burbages' enterprise, between 1576 and 1584 there had been a smaller theatre in part of the same building, which is known as the original, or first Blackfriars Theatre.)

The Blackfriars was called a 'private' theatre, for it had a roof, unlike the King's Men's summer venue, the GLOBE THEATRE, and other public playhouses. Because admission prices were as much as five times greater than in the public theatres, the audiences were higher ranking, socially, and generally better educated. Their tastes were correspondingly different—more influenced by literature and by the courtly MASQUE whose popularity was on the rise in the first decades of the 17th century. All this, combined with the greater intimacy of the theatre itself and its novel and striking candlelit stage, produced important changes in JACOBEAN DRAMA. Shakespeare's ROMANCES and the plays of Francis BEAUMONT (2) and John FLETCHER (2), the King's Men's other main playwrights, were directly influenced by the Blackfriars Theatre.

**Blackheath**   Open land on the south bank of the Thames east of London, a traditional fairground and public meeting place and the location of several scenes in *2 Henry VI.* Blackheath was famous in Shakespeare's time, as in the period of the play's action, as an assembly point for rebellious bands marching on London, and it figures as such in 4.2–3 of the play. The army of Jack CADE, arriving from KENT, gathers here to be harangued by its leader and to fight its first skirmish before proceeding to the capital. Ironically, when the Duke of YORK (8) returns from Ireland with his army in 5.1—ostensibly to oppose Cade, but also, secretly, to foster insurrection—he also appears at Blackheath.

**Blanche (Blanch) of Spain (1188–1252)**  Historical figure and minor character in *King John,* the niece of King JOHN (3), who marries LEWIS (1), the French Dauphin, after 2.1. Blanche finds herself with mixed loyalties when hostilities break out between her uncle and her new husband. In 3.1 she unsuccessfully attempts to persuade her husband and his father, King PHILIP (2), to refrain from fighting England. She is reduced to a bewildered lament that plaintively expresses the helplessness of the noncombatant.

The historical Blanche of Castile, as she is better known, was raised in Spain. Her mother was John's sister Eleanor, and her father was the King of Castile. A treaty between John and Philip provided for the marriage of Lewis to a princess of Castile, and Queen ELEANOR travelled to Spain and selected Blanche from among several eligible sisters. Thus, at 12, Blanche was taken by her grandmother, whom she had not met before, to another country to marry a man whom she had never met. Although her initial depression in her new home was noted in a contemporary chronicle, she went on to become one of the great women in French history. After the brief reign of Lewis (Louis VIII), Blanche acted as regent for her son, Louis IX, known to history as St Louis. She put down several rebellions and completed the subjection of southern France to royal rule. St Louis spent much of his reign crusading in the Holy Land, and Blanche governed effectively in his absence.

**Blank Verse**  Metrical pattern (see METRE) composed of lines of unrhymed iambic pentameter. The typical pattern in English poetry—though neither exclusively nor originally English—blank verse is the medium of many long poems and nearly all verse dramas, including Shakespeare's, though the plays also contain prose and, more rarely, other forms of verse. Iambic pentameter is especially appropriate for drama and narrative poetry, for it more closely resembles the normal patterns of English speech than does any other sort of poetic pattern (except unmetred free verse). Its stresses imitate the natural flow of clauses and phrases, while the line endings fall at intervals that are easily followed without counting. Unlike rhymed patterns such as, say, the couplet or the limerick, which subtly suggest a point of view by the way they sound,

blank verse is neutral in tone and allows the content of the poetry to determine its emotional shading. This is both an advantage and a challenge: blank verse does not easily lend itself to the lively and varied tone that a work of any length requires.

Blank verse was first used in English poetry in the early 16th century in translations of VIRGIL by Henry Howard, Earl of SURREY (1). Surrey was inspired by similar Italian verse and, probably, the example of unrhymed verse in traditional Middle English poetry. The form became popular in England after Christopher MARLOWE (1) established the pattern, in *Tamburlaine* (c. 1587), as the standard for dramatic works. Shakespeare's poetic genius led him to vary the pattern much more freely than his predecessors had, permitting the expression of a wider range of effects, from broad comedy to lyrical ecstasy to raging anger. For the first time, the musical patterns of poetry could approximate the range and specificity of prose.

In Shakespeare's day, blank verse was a very familiar medium; he could expect at least part of his audience to recognise it when spoken, as JAQUES (1) does in *As You Like It,* upon hearing only a single line (4.1.28). Except during the late 17th and early 18th centuries, blank verse remained prominent in English poetry until recent times. It was the favoured medium of such masters of the long poem as John MILTON, William Wordsworth (1770–1850), Robert Browning (1812–1889), and T. S. ELIOT (2). In the 20th century the use of blank verse has declined, due largely to the disappearance of an audience for verse drama and the long poem. To some extent, it has come to represent conservative poetry, compared to free verse.

**Blount, Edward (1564–1632)**  English bookseller and publisher, a partner in the production of the FIRST FOLIO (1623). In 1601 Blount published LOVE'S MARTYR, including Shakespeare's *The Phoenix and Turtle.* In 1608 he registered two of Shakespeare's plays for publication—*Antony and Cleopatra* and *Pericles*—but did not produce either of them; scholars believe this reflects a 'blocking action' undertaken on behalf of the KING'S MEN to protect their plays from pirated publication. The degree of co-operation with the acting company implied by Blount's action suggests that Shakespeare may have known him personally. Blount and Isaac JAGGARD jointly held the rights to 16 plays in the First Folio—all but two of those that had not been previously published—making them leading members of the syndicate that financed its printing (the others were John SMETHWICK and William ASPLEY). Jaggard and Blount are designated co-publishers of the book on its title page.

Blount became a member of the STATIONERS' COMPANY in 1588, after 10 years of apprenticeship, and he prospered, eventually owning two bookshops and remaining active until at least 1630. He was evidently a sincere appreciator of literature, publishing prefaces praising his authors and apologising for printer's errors. He published works by Christopher MARLOWE (1) and John LYLY in addition to Shakespeare.

**Blunt (1), Sir James (d. 1493)** Historical figure and minor character in *Richard III*, a follower of RICHMOND. Richmond uses Blunt as a messenger before the battle of BOSWORTH FIELD. Blunt is the great-grandson of Sir Walter BLUNT (3), who appears in *1 Henry IV*. He may have been selected for his tiny role, from all the possible officers in Richmond's army, as a gesture towards the Blunt family, who were STRATFORD landowners of Shakespeare's day, and were related to the playwright's friends in the COMBE family.

**Blunt (2), Sir John (d. 1418)** Historical figure and minor character in *2 Henry IV*, an aide to Prince John of LANCASTER (3). Blunt appears only once and says nothing; he is assigned to guard the captive COLEVILE (4.3.73). Blunt was also mentioned in two stage directions in the QUARTO edition of the play (1600), but these references are absent in the FIRST FOLIO (1623) and have generally been omitted since. It is speculated that this alteration may reflect minor cuts made for an early production, perhaps by Shakespeare himself. The historical John Blunt was a minor courtier, the son of Walter BLUNT (3), who appears in *1 Henry IV*.

**Blunt (3), Sir Walter (d. 1403)** Historical figure and character in *1 Henry IV*, a follower of King HENRY IV. Blunt is a respected adviser and emissary, and his calm personality contrasts with that of the tormented Henry and the temperamental HOTSPUR. In 1.3 Blunt attempts to mediate the quarrel between the King and Hotspur. In 3.2.163–179 he brings the dramatic news that the rebel forces are gathering at SHREWSBURY, a report that propels PRINCE (6) HAL into action. In 4.3 Blunt acts as the King's ambassador, and he is properly short with the bellicose Hotspur. In 5.3 he is dressed as the King, in a standard medieval battlefield tactic, and is killed by DOUGLAS. The sight of his corpse causes FALSTAFF to remark ironically, 'There's honour for you!' (5.3.32).

The historical Blunt was a long-time follower of King Henry's father, John of GAUNT. He was Gaunt's executor, and he naturally became one of Henry's chief advisers. He was indeed killed at Shrewsbury, but he was not among those disguised as the King. He bore the King's standard, a position of honour that suggests a sound reputation as a military man. He was the father of Sir John BLUNT (2), who appears in *2 Henry IV*, and great-grandfather of Sir James BLUNT (1) of *Richard III*.

**Boar's Head Tavern** Inn in EASTCHEAP, in LONDON, setting for several scenes in *1* and *2 Henry IV* and possibly one in *Henry V*. The Boar's Head, run by the HOSTESS (2) and frequented by FALSTAFF, PRINCE (6) HAL, and their friends, is a haven for petty criminals whose riotous drinking and wenching is depicted with a colourful vigour unmatched until Charles Dickens in the 19th century. In addition to Falstaff's principal followers—BARDOLPH (1), PISTOL, PETO, and DOLL TEARSHEET—numerous minor characters, such as GADSHILL, FRANCIS (1), the VINTNER, the MUSICIANS (4), and the DRAWERS, add verisimilitude to this world.

In *1 Henry IV* the Boar's Head is the scene of several typical episodes in the delinquent career of Prince Hal. In 2.4 he baits Falstaff about his bungled highway robbery, and he joins the fat knight in a mirthful mockery of King HENRY IV. In 3.3 a comical dispute erupts between Falstaff and the Hostess, and the Prince deflects an attempt by a SHERIFF (4) to arrest Falstaff. In 2.1 of *2 Henry IV*, the Hostess attempts to have Falstaff arrested for debt, and a potential brawl is averted only by the timely arrival of the CHIEF JUSTICE. In 2.4 Falstaff hosts an uproarious dinner party at the tavern. Mournful meditations on Falstaff's death are offered by his companions in 2.3 of *Henry V*. This scene is traditionally located in front of the tavern, and, although the original texts provide no site designation, it seems appropriate that the Boar's Head should witness the remembrances for its most famous patron.

The Boar's Head was a famous establishment in Elizabethan London, and, although Shakespeare does not actually name it explicitly (a broad hint is made in *2 Henry IV*, 2.2.138–140), his audiences clearly recognised it, as surviving contemporary references reveal. However, the Boar's Head Tavern is not to be confused with the Boar's Head Theatre, the suburban venue of the QUEEN'S MEN (2), an early 17th-century acting company.

**Boas, Frederick S. (1862–1957)** British scholar. Boas wrote several important books on Shakespeare, including *Shakespeare and his Predecessors* (1896)—in which he introduced the term PROBLEM PLAY to Shakespeare studies—and *An Introduction to the Reading of Shakespeare* (1927). He also wrote about other figures of the age, including Thomas HEYWOOD (2), Christopher MARLOWE (1), and Sir Philip SIDNEY. He was the longtime editor of *The Year's Work in English Studies,* an annual collection of essays that summarised significant scholarly work.

**Boatswain** Minor character in *The Tempest*, a crew member of the ship that is wrecked on PROSPERO's island. In 1.1 the Boatswain curses the arrogant SEBASTIAN (5) and ANTONIO (3), who insist on interfering during the great storm that threatens the vessel. Prospero's sprite ARIEL magically preserves the ship and its crew, and in 5.1, as the play closes, the Boatswain is brought to Prospero by Ariel and reports on the ship's miraculous restoration. The Boatswain is a plain-spoken working man whose contrast with Sebastian and Antonio helps establish their villainous natures at the outset and whose reappearance at the close suggests the everyday world to which the play's characters will soon return.

**Boccaccio, Giovanni (1313–1375)**    Italian story writer and poet, a frequent source for Shakespeare. The main plots of *All's Well That Ends Well* and *Cymbeline*, as well as details in *The Winter's Tale*, all derive from Boccaccio's *Decameron* (1353), a collection of tales that Shakespeare probably knew in the translations of William PAINTER (2) (into English) and Antoine MAÇON (into French). The *Decameron* may also have provided the main plot of *The Two Gentlemen of Verona*, though this material was heavily modified by other sources. The playwright's other uses of Boccaccio's works were indirect: Geoffrey CHAUCER's *Troilus and Criseyde*, the source for *Troilus and Cressida*, was itself based on Boccaccio's poem the *Filostrato* (1338); Boccaccio's epic poem the *Teseide* (1339–1340) was the source for Chaucer's 'The Knight's Tale', which was in turn the source for both *The Two Noble Kinsmen* and parts of *A Midsummer Night's Dream*; lastly, the stories of Giovanni FIORENTINO, probably sources for *The Merchant of Venice* and *The Merry Wives of Windsor*, were modelled on tales in the *Decameron*.

Boccaccio is considered a founder of Italian RENAISSANCE literature. Among his works are the *Filostrato*, a romance in verse; the *Teseide*, the first epic poem in Italian; the *Fiammetta* (c. 1343), sometimes seen as the earliest European novel; the *Ninfale Fieselano (The Nymph of Fiesole*, c. 1345), a PASTORAL romance in verse that is considered Boccaccio's second greatest work; and the greatest, the *Decameron*. All of these works were written in Italian, but following a religious crisis, Boccaccio decided that writing in the vernacular was sinful and rejected all his works. His later writings in Latin, scholarly works on classical culture, were important to the development of European humanism.

**Bodleian Library**    Major collection of Shakespeareana, at Oxford University, England. The library was founded by the diplomat and scholar Thomas Bodley (1545–1613) in 1597 when an earlier university library, dating to 1445, was reorganised. The Bodleian Library was originally composed largely of theological materials, but in 1821, with the acquisition of the library of Edmond MALONE, it became a great Shakespearean library. It has maintained that status to the present day, with a collection that is especially noted for its early texts of Shakespeare's non-dramatic poetry.

**Boece (Boyce), Hector (c. 1465–1536)**    Scottish historian, author of a source for *Macbeth*. Boece's *Scotorum Historiae*, a history of Scotland in Latin, was the source for Raphael HOLINSHED's Scottish history in his *Chronicles of England, Scotland, and Ireland* (1577), which was Shakespeare's source for the tale of MACBETH, as well as for other materials used in the play.

Boece, a native of Dundee, was a famous professor at the University of Paris when, in 1498, he was invited back to Scotland to participate in the founding of King's College in Aberdeen. His *Scotorum Historiae* was the first work to cover all of Scotland's history (to 1488). It is heavily infused with legendary material—as is much of Macbeth's story—but it was for generations regarded as the best text on its subject. Translated into French, it became well known throughout Europe. In 1536 the King of Scotland commissioned a translation into Scots; this work, by the poet John Bellenden (c. 1500–c. 1548) is the oldest surviving work of Scots prose. In the academic fashion of the times, Boece took a Latin surname and is sometimes still referred to as Hector Boëthius, after the Roman philosopher (c. 480–c. 524).

**Bohemia**    Central European region, part of modern Czechoslovakia, the setting for part of *The Winter's Tale*. In 3.3 ANTIGONUS abandons the infant PERDITA—banished from SICILIA by her father, King LEONTES, who believes her illegitimate—on the Bohemian seacoast. She is found by the SHEPHERD (2) and his son, who raise her as a shepherdess. In Act 4, 16 years later, Prince FLORIZEL, son of the King of Bohemia, falls in love with Perdita, and she with him. The king, however, opposes their marriage, and they flee to Sicilia, where Act 5 takes place.

Bohemia is specified as the setting for the rugged seacoast of 3.3 and the pastoral world of the shepherds in Act 4, but there is nothing nationally distinctive in the text of the play. Shakespeare merely took the name from his source, *Pandosto* by Robert GREENE (2) (though there the princess was exiled from Bohemia and raised in Sicilia). In many ways Shakespeare's Bohemia is a lovingly idealised portrait of English rural life, although the rugged coast and man-eating BEAR of 3.3 add overtones of nature's harshness.

Shakespeare's attribution of a seacoast to Bohemia has inspired much comment, for that land does not in fact have one. It has been argued that the discrepancy points to the playwright's ignorance and provinciality, or to his carelessness in simply accepting the notion from *Pandosto*. The 18th-century scholar Thomas HANMER substituted Bithynia, a region of Asia Minor, for Bohemia, and many later editions of the play followed his lead. Other commentators hold that Shakespeare may legitimately have thought Bohemia bordered the Adriatic Sea, since after 1526 it was part of the Hapsburg Empire, which did so. Also, medieval Bohemia had briefly controlled a stretch of the same coast. However, the actuality of Bohemia's coast is irrelevant; *The Winter's Tale*, as one of the ROMANCES, was expected to dazzle its viewers with exotic locales. Bohemia was very little known in England during Shakespeare's lifetime, for it was small and deep within continental Europe, in an age of difficult travel and communication. Most of *The Winter's Tale*'s original audience doubtless accepted a Bohemian coastline without thinking about it; it was a satisfying image, providing a dramatic approach to a fabulous land. For those who knew the truth, probably including Shakespeare himself, the anomaly may have been mildly amusing, like modern jokes about the Swiss Navy.

**Boito, Arrigo (1842–1918)**   Italian operatic composer and librettist. Boito, who composed several operas of his own, is best known for two librettos—both adaptations of Shakespeare—that he wrote for Giuseppe VERDI: *Otello* (1887; based on *Othello*) and *Falstaff* (1893; based on *The Merry Wives of Windsor*). These are widely regarded as among the best opera librettos ever written.

**Boleyn, Anne**   See ANNE (1).

**Bolingbroke (1) (Bullingbrook), Henry (later King HENRY IV, 1366–1413)**   Historical figure and character in *Richard II,* the usurper of the throne from King RICHARD II. (The same individual appears as King HENRY IV in *1* and *2 Henry IV.*) Bolingbroke's rise to the throne balances Richard's fall, and Bolingbroke, like Richard, undergoes personal change. In 1.1 he uses elaborate rhetoric to accuse MOWBRAY (1) of murdering the Duke of GLOUCESTER (6) and to challenge him to a trial by combat. We learn in 1.2 that Gloucester's murder was Richard's doing, as Bolingbroke must have known. It is clear that Bolingbroke is hostile to Richard from the very beginning and that the King has no effective response. Bolingbroke's triumph can already be foreseen. (Shakespeare will have assumed that his audience knew that Bolingbroke was to become King in any case.) Although Bolingbroke accepts his banishment, we know that he will shortly reappear as Richard's enemy. Thus Bolingbroke seems an unscrupulous schemer from the beginning.

When he returns from exile to claim his inheritance—the estates of his father, John of GAUNT—his first actions reinforce this impression. In 2.3 he welcomes PERCY (2), ROSS (2), and WILLOUGHBY (3) as his allies with apparently frank gratitude, but, having seen his ambition we doubt his sincerity. Moreover, the playwright will probably have counted on his audience's familiarity with the fate of Percy, who later died in rebellion against Bolingbroke (as is enacted in *1 Henry IV*). Later in this scene, Bolingbroke offers an elaborate rationale for his rebellion against the crown when he is criticised by the Duke of YORK (4); it is clear that he thinks it important to maintain an appearance of justified innocence, masking his ambition with assertions of political rectitude. Further, he proclaims that he has come only to claim his inheritance, but he also proceeds to execute the alleged villains BUSHY and GREENE (1) for 'crimes' that are actually offences against Bolingbroke personally rather than against the state.

Significantly, Bolingbroke's diction changes at this point. As Richard's strikingly poetic manner of speaking becomes prominent in his emotional collapse, Bolingbroke adopts a plainer mode of speech intended to reveal his motives. His practical realism is emblematic of the new era in politics that he represents. Bolingbroke is a Machiavellian leader, prepared to take whatever measures are necessary to acquire and preserve power, whereas Richard, relying on long-standing tradition, believes in the ancient theory of divine right. The passing of the romantic medieval world represented by that tradition is a major theme of the play. Bolingbroke's easy reliance on his own strength is a new attribute of kingship, reflected in his speech and manner as soon as he begins to assert his power.

A third Bolingbroke, the generous victor, begins to assume importance in 3.1. Although he undertakes a ruthless act of state in condemning Bushy and Greene, he anticipates his later development in demonstrating his sympathy for Richard's QUEEN (13), instructing that she be treated well. Bolingbroke's magnanimity is further stressed in Act 5, when he pardons CARLISLE and AUMERLE and when he repudiates Richard's murder. The playwright is clearly paving the way for Bolingbroke's appearance as Henry IV.

The historical Bolingbroke was Richard's close contemporary, although the playwright makes the usurper younger than the deposed King (e.g., in 3.3. 204–205) to emphasise his greater vitality. Henry Bolingbroke was so called because he was born at Bolingbroke, a castle in Lincolnshire. (The alternative version of his name, Bullingbrook, first used in the Q1 edition of the play, suggests its probable pronunciation in Elizabethan English.) As a young man, Bolingbroke belonged to a political faction, led by Gloucester, that nearly dethroned Richard in 1387. However, he remained aloof from the politics of the court throughout the 1390s, spending much of his time as a Crusader in Lithuania, and he seems to have had nothing to do with the conflict of 1397 that resulted in Gloucester's death. His motivation in challenging Mowbray two years later is unclear, although the play makes it appear to be ambition for the throne. Actually, even after his invasion, Bolingbroke may have intended only to claim his inheritance; it is unclear when he decided to seize power.

Shakespeare invented several aspects of Bolingbroke's assumption of the crown. The deposition scene, in which Bolingbroke formally displaces Richard, is entirely fictitious; the triumphant usurper had no interest in providing his defeated opponent with a public platform. Similarly, his instigation of the murder of Richard by Piers EXTON is unhistorical. The episode, in which Bolingbroke vows to go on crusade to atone for Exton's crime, is intended to introduce the religious tendencies of Henry IV. Although the playwright took this incident from his chief source and certainly believed it, Bolingbroke's repudiation of Exton after the murder is Shakespeare's fiction. A similar story concerning Thomas à Becket and Henry II was one of several apocryphal anecdotes that the playwright might have used as a model; an account in PLUTARCH was another.

**Bolingbroke (2), Roger (d. 1441)**  Historical figure and minor character in *2 Henry VI*, a sorcerer who, along with John SOUTHWELL and MARGERY JOURDAIN, is hired by HUME to summon and question a spirit for the DUCHESS (1) of Gloucester, who wishes to know the prospects for a coup. Bolingbroke addresses the spirit, ASNATH. He asks it questions, provided by the duchess, about the futures of the king and nobles. They are all arrested by the dukes of YORK (8) and BUCKINGHAM (3). In 2.3 the king sentences Bolingbroke to be strangled.

The historical Bolingbroke was a priest. His execution was of a sort reserved for particularly heinous criminals: he was hanged and then publicly disembowelled and quartered.

**Bona, Lady (b. after 1447, d. 1485)**  Historical figure and character in *3 Henry VI*, the proposed French bride of EDWARD IV, whose rejection of her sparks the defection of the Earl of WARWICK (3). In 3.3 Bona, the sister-in-law of King LEWIS (3), is agreeable to the marriage, having heard good things of Edward, but Edward has instead married an English commoner. Bona adds her voice to a chorus of demands for revenge for this slight, and thus approves of the alliance among Lewis, Warwick, and MARGARET (1), aimed at deposing Edward and reinstating HENRY VI. This episode is one of many in the *Henry VI* plays in which broken oaths result in catastrophe for England—in this case, another phase of the WARS OF THE ROSES. It is analogous to the similar abandonment of a marriage agreement by King Henry in order to marry Margaret at the close of *1 Henry VI*.

The historical Lady Bona of Savoy, Louis XI's sister-in-law, was indeed proposed as a bride for Edward, but the matter never progressed very far. She subsequently married a Duke of Milan, and, after his death, she briefly ruled that duchy as regent for her son.

**Bonian, Richard (active 1598–1611)**  London publisher and bookseller. Bonian began as a printer's apprentice and flourished, becoming a member of the STATIONERS' COMPANY and owning three London bookshops. In 1609 he co-published, with Henry WALLEY, the QUARTO edition of *Troilus and Cressida*. By the time of the publication of the FIRST FOLIO, in 1623, Bonian had died. Little more is known of him.

**Booth (1), Barton (1681–1733)**  English actor. Booth was Thomas BETTERTON's successor as the leading tragic actor on the London stage. He was particularly noted for his portrayal of OTHELLO, but he also played many other Shakespearean roles, including LEAR, HOTSPUR, BRUTUS (4), TIMON, and HAMLET. A reformed alcoholic, he became a co-manager of the Drury Lane Theatre with Colley CIBBER (1) and was one of the most influential figures in the London theatre world of the early 18th century.

**Booth (2), Edwin (1833–1893)**  American actor. Booth, son of Junius Brutus BOOTH (4), was the leading American actor of his day. He first achieved acclaim when he stood in for his ailing father as RICHARD III in 1851. Among Shakespearean roles, he was best known for his portrayal of HAMLET, but he also played most of the other tragic heroes. In 1862 he became manager of a New York theatre, where he staged a number of Shakespeare's plays. In the winter of 1864–1865 he presented a production of *Hamlet* that ran for 100 performances, then a record for the play. Almost immediately thereafter, his brother John Wilkes

*Edwin Booth in the role of Hamlet. Booth's famous 100-night run in this role in 1864 was a record that stood until 1922. In 1865 Booth was forced into temporary retirement by the scandal of Lincoln's assassination at the hand of his brother John Wilkes Booth. (Courtesy of Culver Pictures, Inc.)*

BOOTH (3) assassinated Abraham Lincoln, and Booth retired temporarily. He returned to the stage in 1866. The theatre he ran burned down, and he built his own, which opened in 1869, but in four years he was bankrupt. He then toured for several years in America and abroad. In London in 1882, he and Henry IRVING alternated the parts of OTHELLO and IAGO. Returning to America, he became partners with Lawrence BARRETT and performed a variety of roles with him, Helena MODJESKA (in *Macbeth*), and Tommaso SALVINI (who played Othello to Booth's Iago). His last performance was as Hamlet in 1891.

**Booth (3), John Wilkes (1839–1865)** American actor best known for assassinating Abraham Lincoln. Booth, son of Junius Brutus BOOTH (4) and brother of Edwin BOOTH (2) and Junius Brutus BOOTH (5), Jr., was a well-known actor in 1865—the year of Lincoln's murder. He had played a variety of classical and modern roles, and was particularly noted for his portrayal of RICHARD III. Contemporary opinion varied as to his sanity when he assassinated Lincoln; he himself claimed patriotic motives in support of the Confederacy, which had just lost the Civil War, and for which he may have once been a secret agent. In any case he was at least a competent professional, though in the shadow of his great brother Edwin. He is said to have adopted his father's grandiloquent style in conscious opposition to Edwin's more restrained manner. He was killed while fleeing after the assassination.

**Booth (4), Junius Brutus (1796–1852)** English actor, father of three notable American stars, Edwin BOOTH (2), John Wilkes BOOTH (3), and Junius Brutus BOOTH (5), Jr. The elder Booth, born to a London lawyer whose republican political sentiments were reflected in his son's name, became a major rival of Edmund KEAN (2) after making his debut as RICHARD III in 1815. He was noted for his portrayals of HAMLET and SHYLOCK. Joining Kean's company in 1820, he played IAGO to Kean's OTHELLO and EDGAR to his LEAR. In 1821 he deserted his wife and son and emigrated to the United States with his lover, a London flower-seller who was to be the mother of the actors and seven other children. Booth helped popularise Shakespeare in America, playing a variety of roles in New York and on extensive tours. He made his last appearance in New Orleans, before dying on a Mississippi River steamboat.

**Booth (5), Junius Brutus, Jr. (1821–1883)** American actor. Booth, son of Junius Brutus BOOTH (4), was regarded as a lesser actor than either his father or his younger brother Edwin BOOTH (2), though he had a long and successful career in a variety of parts, mostly non-Shakespearean. He played IAGO opposite his father's OTHELLO on several occasions, and once played CASSIUS opposite his two brothers, Edwin and John Wilkes BOOTH (3), who played BRUTUS (4) and ANTONY,

respectively. He was respected as a highly competent producer and stage manager.

**Borachio** Character in *Much Ado About Nothing*, follower of Don JOHN (1). Borachio, Don John's chief lieutenant, receives 1,000 ducats from his master for devising a scheme to prevent the marriage of CLAUDIO (1), whom Don John resents and despises, to the desirable HERO. Borachio masquerades with Hero's waiting-woman, MARGARET (2), as Hero and a clandestine lover. This charade convinces Claudio and Don PEDRO that Hero is promiscuous, and she finds herself publicly humiliated as an unfaithful fiancée. However, when Borachio brags of his success to his friend CONRADE, the WATCHMEN (3) overhear him, and the plot is eventually exposed. In the general reconciliation that closes the play, Borachio repents, confessing his guilt freely and adding that he duped Margaret.

Some modern editors give the lines of BALTHASAR (4) in 2.1.92–102, where he flirts with Margaret, to Borachio. Errors in some of these speech prefixes suggest that the printers of the early editions were confused, and, since Borachio is elsewhere associated with the waiting-woman, he is sometimes given that connection here as well. Borachio's name comes from the Spanish *borracho*, meaning 'drunkard'. This rather undignified appellation reflects the petty villainy of the character, while also implying a relative innocence that makes his acknowledgement of guilt at the end of the play more believable.

**Bordeaux** City in south-west FRANCE (1), the site of a battle in *1 Henry VI*. In 4.2 TALBOT approaches the walls of Bordeaux and demands its surrender. He is spurned by a French GENERAL, who declares his confidence in the approaching French army. In 4.6 and 4.7, the battle takes place, and Talbot and his son, JOHN (6), are killed.

In reality, Talbot and his forces occupied Bordeaux, which welcomed the English, months before the fatal battle, and the fight took place 50 miles away at Castillon, where Talbot had marched to relieve a siege. The historical battle took place in 1453 and was the last major conflict of the HUNDRED YEARS WAR. Shakespeare placed it earlier in the war in order to suggest that Talbot's death was a direct consequence of the rivalry between YORK (8) and SOMERSET (3). The playwright thereby emphasised the aristocratic discord that led, in the play's sequels, *2* and *3 Henry VI* and *Richard III*, to the WARS OF THE ROSES.

**Boswell, James the younger (1778–1822)** British scholar, editor of the Third VARIORUM EDITION of Shakespeare's works. Boswell's father (1740–1795), the famed biographer of Samuel JOHNSON (7), was a close friend and colleague of the Shakespearean scholar Edmond MALONE. When Malone died in 1812 while assembling his second edition of Shakespeare's works, the younger Boswell completed the task. The 21-volume result (1821) added to Malone's many notes and essays much of George STEEVENS' and Isaac REED's 1803 Second Variorum edition. It remained the most comprehensive work of its kind for over a century, until the New Variorum of H. H. FURNESS was completed. The Third Variorum, also known as 'Boswell's Malone', is regarded as one of the most important editions of Shakespeare ever published. Its wide range of scholarship has been basic to virtually all later research on the playwright and his work.

**Bosworth Field**   Battle site in central England, the setting of the final three scenes of *Richard III*. Arguably the most famous battle in English history, Bosworth, fought in August 1485, provides the finale for Shakespeare's first TETRALOGY of HISTORY PLAYS. The army led by the Earl of RICHMOND defeats the forces of King RICHARD III, killing Richard. The WARS OF THE ROSES end, and the TUDOR dynasty is established, as Richmond claims the throne to rule as Henry VII.

Shakespeare's presentation of this event is highly elaborate and symbolic. The prelude to the battle, in 5.3, features councils of war and opposing statements of purpose, climaxed by the appearance of the spirits of Richard's victims (see GHOST [1]). This is far more significant to the narrative than the minor vignettes of combat in 5.4 and the opening action of 5.5, although these scenes encompass the death of Richard. The play is then closed by Richmond's coronation, as he proclaims an end to the wars. Historically, this prediction could not have been certain, of course, and in fact, skirmishes and minor risings were to continue for years. However, the playwright's purpose was not reportorial but dramatic, almost sacramental: the treachery and violence enacted in *Richard III* and the *Henry VI* plays are expiated in a ritual letting of blood followed by a formal reconciliation.

**Bottom, Nick**   Character in *A Midsummer Night's Dream,* a weaver of ATHENS. His comical ignorance and his tendency to mangle language make Bottom a typi-

*James Cagney as Bottom in Max Reinhardt's 1935 film of* A Midsummer Night's Dream. *Given the head of an ass by the mischievous Puck, Bottom temporarily becomes the beloved of the magically charmed Titania.* (Courtesy of Movie Star News)

cal Shakespearean CLOWN (1). He is repeatedly placed in ludicrous situations, but his supremely good opinion of himself is unshakeable. As the leading player in the amateur production of PYRAMUS AND THISBE, Bottom cuts a silly figure as a know-it-all who is unaware of his true ignorance. Given the head of an ass by the fairy PUCK, Bottom temporarily becomes the beloved of the magically charmed TITANIA, and his decorum in this extraordinary situation is ridiculous.

However, Bottom is a sympathetic figure as well. He is not pompous, and he is unfailingly civil to everyone. He is not patronising to his fellow artisans when he lectures them (preposterously) on stagecraft, and he is courteous to his fairy attendants, PEASEBLOSSOM, COBWEB, MOTH (2), and MUSTARDSEED. His self-confidence, though humorous in its fog-like density, is not entirely misplaced: he is a leader among his fellows, as they are quite aware, and we can believe he is surely an excellent craftsman. His comedy lies in the contrast between his circumstances and his lack of awareness, but he is not a victim. His courage makes him admirable as well as amusing.

It is ironic that Bottom, who remains absurdly unperturbed, is the only mortal who actually meets any of the fairies. Yet in the end, he is plainly moved by his experience. Awakening from what he calls 'a most rare vision' (4.1.203), he discovers that he cannot quite recollect it. He expresses his bafflement in comically garbled terms that reflect, among other things, St Paul's description (1 Cor. 2:7–9) of the 'hidden wisdom which God ordained before the world'. We do not need to know the source to sense the power of these words. Bottom aptly observes of his vision, 'It shall be called "Bottom's Dream", because it hath no bottom' (4.1.214–215); he has sensed that something profound has happened to him.

Bottom's name refers to a tool of his trade, the core on which a skein of yarn is wound or, figuratively, the skein itself; its suggestions of the fundamental or basic element of something are equally appropriate to this representative of the common man. To 'get to the bottom' of a subject is to find its essential quality, and Bottom displays the combination of practicality, courage, and blind confidence that underlies much human achievement. The word had no anatomical connotations in Elizabethan English.

**Boult** Minor character in *Pericles*, brothel employee responsible for training and advertising the kidnapped MARINA. The energetic Boult ('Performance shall follow' [4.2.59], he says proudly) pretends to be cruel and cynical. When he speaks of Marina's modesty, he declares that 'these blushes of hers must be quench'd with some present practice' (4.2.122–124). However, though he threatens to destroy her innocence through rape, in 4.6, she recognises that she can appeal to his inner revulsion at his profession, and

tells him his job would shame 'the pained'st fiend / Of hell' (4.6.162–163). He can only plead, 'What would you have me do? go to the wars, would you? Where a man may serve seven years for the loss of a leg, and have not money enough in the end to buy him a wooden one?' (4.6.169–172). This brief, compelling outburst demonstrates the breadth of Shakespeare's humanity: he transforms a minor character's crisis into a striking commentary on a pervasive scandal of his times; the distressing status of military veterans. Boult agrees to help Marina escape the brothel, which we later learn she does. In addition to helping Marina, Boult also contributes to the comic relief from melodrama provided by the brothel scenes.

**Bourbon (1), Jean, Duke of (1380–1434)** Historical figure and minor character in *Henry V*, a French nobleman. In 4.5, in the confusion of the French defeat at AGINCOURT, Bourbon determines to launch a counterattack. However, in 4.8 he is a prisoner of King HENRY V. Following the QUARTO edition of the play, some editions assign to Bourbon the lines of BRETAGNE in 3.5; this reflects the elimination of Bretagne's part in an early production. The Quarto also gives the lines of the DAUPHIN (3) in 3.7 to Bourbon, suggesting that the actor who played the Duke in the same early production was held in high regard.

The historical Bourbon, after being taken prisoner at Agincourt, spent the rest of his life in captivity in England. The BOURBON (2) who appears in *3 Henry VI* was his illegitimate son.

**Bourbon (2), Lewis (Louis), Lord (active 1460s)** Historical figure and minor character in *3 Henry VI*, an admiral in the service of King LEWIS (3) of FRANCE (1). In 3.3, when Lewis decides to provide soldiers for MARGARET (1) and WARWICK (3), he orders Bourbon to arrange their passage to England. The historical admiral was the illegitimate son of the Duke of BOURBON (1), who appears in *Henry V*.

**Bowdler, Thomas (1754–1825)** English editor. Bowdler published a censored version of Shakespeare's plays, his 10-volume *Family Shakespeare* (1818), in which 'those words and expressions are omitted which cannot with propriety be read aloud in a family' or 'by a gentleman to a company of ladies'. A professed admirer of the playwright, he nonetheless felt that without 'profaneness or obscenity . . . the transcendent genius of the poet would undoubtedly shine with more unclouded lustre'. He accordingly changed all expletive uses of 'God' to 'Heaven', and cut extensive passages that he deemed obscene. Some plays involved more drastic action—DOLL TEARSHEET is simply eliminated from *2 Henry IV* and *Henry V*, for instance— and sometimes he had to confess himself defeated, publishing *Measure for Measure* and *Othello* with warnings.

Bowdler's *Shakespeare* was immensely popular and was reprinted many times. It became so well known—or notorious—that it sparked a new word that is still in use: bowdlerise, meaning to censor a text by omitting vulgarities. Bowdler also produced a bowdlerised version of Gibbons' *The Decline and Fall of the Roman Empire*, published posthumously in 1826.

**Boy (1)**   Minor character in *1 Henry VI*, the son of the MASTER-GUNNER of ORLÉANS (1). In 1.4 the Boy is instructed by his father that their cannon is trained on a tower where the English leaders are known to stand watch, and he subsequently fires the shot that kills the Duke of SALISBURY (3).

**Boy (2) (Edward Plantagenet, Earl of Warwick, 1475–1499)**   Historical figure and minor character in *Richard III*, the son of CLARENCE (1). The Boy appears in 2.2, in which he refuses to believe that his uncle, RICHARD III, has killed his father. He is not seen again, but we hear of his imprisonment by Richard in 4.3.36. Crimes against children are a recurring motif in the *Henry VI* plays and *Richard III*, and this instance is clearly intended to add to the enormity of Richard's crimes. The villain has felt it unnecessary to kill the boy, despite his position as a possible claimant to the throne, only because the boy is 'foolish' (4.2.55), meaning mentally retarded. It is unclear whether or not this was so, but it is known that the historical Boy, Edward of Warwick, was in fact imprisoned not by Richard but by his successor, Henry VII, the RICHMOND of the play. In fact, although the record is obscure, it is thought that Richard may have named Warwick his successor after the death of his own son (who does not appear in the play) in 1484. Later, after a number of people attempted to impersonate the imprisoned Warwick and seize power, Henry finally had him executed.

**Boy (3)**   Character in *Henry V*, servant of BARDOLPH (1), PISTOL, and NYM. Having been employed by FALSTAFF as a page—the same figure appears in *2 Henry IV* as the PAGE (5) and in *The Merry Wives of Windsor* as ROBIN (1)—he accompanies his late master's cronies to France as part of King HENRY V's army. In 3.2.28–57 he elicits our sympathy by regretting his association with such cowardly thieves. At the battle of AGINCOURT he acts as an interpreter between Pistol and the captive FRENCH SOLDIER in 4.4, and after this sorry episode he again bemoans his continued connection with Pistol; he also reveals that Bardolph and Nym have been hung. In this speech (4.4.69–80) he remarks that only he and other boys guard the English baggage train, which would thus make a good target for the French, if only they knew the situation. With this ob-

servation the Boy grimly heralds his own death, for in 4.7.5 GOWER (2) reports the French massacre of all these youngsters.

**Boy (4)**   Minor character in *Much Ado About Nothing*, servant of BENEDICK. In 2.3 Benedick sends the Boy on an errand whose sole purpose seems to be to permit the mention that the scene is set in an orchard or garden. The Boy flippantly asserts that his speed will be such that 'I am here already, sir' (2.3.5), an effervescent pleasantry suited to the early action of the play.

**Boy (5)**   Minor character in *Troilus and Cressida*, a servant of TROILUS. In 1.2 the Boy summons PANDARUS to his master's house. The incident leaves CRESSIDA alone to soliloquise on her love for Troilus.

**Boy (6)**   Minor character in *Measure for Measure*, servant of MARIANA (2). At the opening of 4.1 the Boy sings a stanza of the SONG 'Take, O take those lips away' and is dismissed. The Boy provides the relief of a song as the plot tightens and helps, by his presence, to indicate the social status of Mariana.

**Boy (7)**   Minor character in *Antony and Cleopatra*, a singer. Some modern editions include a stage direction specifying that a Boy sings the SONG that accompanies the dance led by ENOBARBUS (2.7.111–116) because Enobarbus stipulates that 'the boy shall sing' (2.7.108), although the authoritative FIRST FOLIO text does not include a specific mention of the Boy.

**Boy (8)**   Minor character in *Coriolanus*, the son of the title character. After CORIOLANUS has been banished, he joins the VOLSCIANS and threatens ROME with destruction. His mother and wife go to beg him to desist, and they bring the Boy with them. Coriolanus addresses his son with a brief homily of the warrior's honour that he himself has lost: 'The god of soldiers . . . inform / Thy thoughts with nobleness, that thou mayst prove / To shame unvulnerable' (5.3.70–73). The Boy speaks only once. With both courage and good sense, he declares that his father 'shall not tread on me. / I'll run away till I am bigger, but then I'll fight' (5.3.127–128). Coriolanus is clearly touched and insists that he must listen no more to his family or he'll give in. Eventually—at the play's climactic turning point—he does indeed surrender to their influence, to which the Boy has added his share.

The Boy is described in 1.3.55–68 as an energetic lad who would rather play at war than go to school and who has a temper like his father's, which leads him to kill a butterfly with his teeth. This image is effectively reprised when MENENIUS describes the fearful approach of the Volscians—led by Coriolanus—who advance confidently, like 'boys pursuing summer butterflies' (4.6.95). The image contributes to the anti-war theme that runs through the play.

**Boy (9)**   Minor character in *Henry VIII*, an attendant of Bishop GARDINER (1). Identified in the stage directions opening 5.1 as the bishop's page, the Boy carries a torch for his master and in his three words confirms that it is one o'clock. He thus establishes the time of night, while also indicating by his presence the high rank of Gardiner, once the king's secretary.

**Boy (10)**   Minor character in *The Two Noble Kinsmen*, a singer at the wedding of THESEUS (2) and HIPPOLYTA (2). In 1.1.1–24 the Boy sings the SONG 'Roses, their sharp spines being gone' and strews flowers. He provides a note of decorous festivity before the ceremony is interrupted by the arrival of the three Queens (see QUEEN [1]).

**Boydell, John (1719–1804)**   British engraver and publisher. Boydell founded an art gallery devoted to depictions of scenes from Shakespeare's plays, engravings of which were published for profit. He was supported in this endeavour by Britain's leading artist, Joshua Reynolds (1723–1792), who hoped to promote an indigenous school of English history painting. The gallery was opened in 1789 with a collection of 34 paintings commissioned from a number of notable artists, including Reynolds, Joseph Wright of Derby (1734–1797), and Henry Fuseli (1741–1825). The collection eventually grew to almost 200 pieces, and many engravings were sold. Despite their popularity, however, the venture foundered economically, and Boydell's heirs were forced to sell the collection in 1805.

**Boyet**   Minor character in *Love's Labour's Lost*, a gentleman in the entourage of the PRINCESS (1) of France. Boyet is a smooth courtier, a familiar type in the Elizabethan court. We first see him flattering his mistress and being put in his place. He often serves as a messenger. He happens to overhear the plans of the King and his gentlemen to masquerade as Russians, and he warns the Princess and her ladies. BEROWNE expresses his dislike for Boyet in 5.2.315–327.

**Brabantio (Brabanzio)**   Minor character in *Othello*, DESDEMONA's father. Brabantio, a senator of VENICE, learns from IAGO of Desdemona's secret marriage to the Moorish general OTHELLO and is outraged at the thought of his daughter on 'the sooty bosom / Of such a thing as [Othello]' (1.2.70–71). He accuses Othello of having 'enchanted her . . . with foul charms . . . with drugs or minerals' (1.2.63–74) and seeks his imprisonment as a sorcerer, but he is foiled when Desdemona testifies to her love for the general. Defeated, he departs, but his final speech carries heavy irony as he

warns Othello, '. . . have a quick eye to see: / She has deceiv'd her father, [and] may do thee' (1.3.292–293). Brabantio disappears from the play at this point, though we are told in 5.2 that he has died of grief at Desdemona's marriage. He serves chiefly to establish, through his racial prejudice and enmity towards Othello, the extent to which the Moor is isolated in Venetian society.

**Bracegirdle, Anne (c. 1673–1748)**   English actress. Bracegirdle began her career as a child actress and a student of Thomas BETTERTON and Mary SAUNDERSON. She was best known for her roles in the comedies of William Congreve (1670–1729), whose wife or mistress she was (the record is unclear), but she also played many Shakespearean roles, especially CORDELIA, DESDEMONA, OPHELIA, and PORTIA.

**Bradley, Andrew Cecil (1851–1935)**   British critic and scholar. Bradley was a professor of literature at several English universities. He is best known for his book, *Shakespearean Tragedy* (1904), which centres on comprehensive analyses of the characters in *Hamlet*, *King Lear*, *Macbeth*, and *Othello*. Though criticised by modern commentators as overly dependent on the idea that the characters—who are, after all, fictions—can have genuinely human psychologies, it was nonetheless a dominant work among students of Shakespeare for almost 30 years.

**Bradock (Bradocke), Richard (active 1581–1615)**   London printer. Bradock, about whom little is known, printed several editions of *Venus and Adonis* for William LEAKE between 1599 and 1603. In 1608 Thomas PAVIER hired him to print the first edition of A YORKSHIRE TRAGEDY, a play that was falsely attributed to Shakespeare.

**Brakenbury (Brackenbury), Robert (d. 1485)**   Historical figure and character in *Richard III*, the commander of the TOWER OF LONDON and thus the chief gaoler of, first, CLARENCE (1) and, later, the young PRINCE (5) Edward and his brother, YORK (7). Some editions of the play follow the first QUARTO and assign Brakenbury the lines of the KEEPER (3) in 1.4.

The historical Brakenbury was a Constable of the Tower, but not at the time of Clarence's death. The inconsistency doubtless resulted from Shakespeare's marked compression of historical time in the early part of the play. Brakenbury was killed at the battle of BOSWORTH FIELD, as is reported in 5.5.14.

**Brandon (1)**   Minor character in *Henry VIII*, an officer who arrests the Duke of BUCKINGHAM (1) and Lord ABERGAVENNY. Brandon appears in 1.1 and instructs a SERGEANT (3) AT ARMS to arrest the two noblemen. Brandon is sorry to have this duty and civilly explains that they are alleged to be part of a conspiracy against the king. His apologetic attitude helps convey the play's point of view, that Buckingham's enemy Cardinal WOLSEY is in the wrong.

Brandon may be the same person as the Duke of SUFFOLK (1), who appears later in the play and whose name was Charles Brandon. The designation of one character by two names might indicate joint authorship of the play, or it might simply be an instance of Shakespeare's carelessness in such matters, evident throughout his plays.

**Brandon (2), Sir William (d. 1485)**   Historical figure and minor character in *Richard III*, a follower of the Earl of RICHMOND. In 5.3 Brandon is among Richmond's officers and is designated as the Earl's standard-bearer in the forthcoming battle of BOSWORTH FIELD. In 5.5 his death in the battle is reported. Historically, Brandon was the father of the Duke of SUFFOLK (1), who appears in *Henry VIII*.

**Bretagne (Britaine, Brittany), Jean, Duke of (1389–1442)**   Historical figure and minor character in *Henry V*, a follower of the FRENCH KING. In 3.5 Bretagne and other French noblemen marvel at the fighting abilities of the English. Brittany was still an independent state in the 14th century, and the historical Duke of Bretagne (Brittany) was an important ally of FRANCE (1). He was the son-in-law of Charles VI, the French King of the play.

**Bretchgirdle, John (d. 1565)**   Vicar at STRATFORD. Bretchgirdle probably christened Shakespeare, on April 26, 1564. The record does not include the name of the officiating clergyman, but it was probably Bretchgirdle, who was vicar at Stratford from 1561 until his death. A graduate of Oxford, Bretchgirdle had been a vicar and schoolmaster in Cheshire before coming to Stratford. He was a literate man who bequeathed a large library, much of it to the Stratford Grammar School where Shakespeare was educated.

**Bright, Timothy (1550–1615)**   English author of a probable source for *Hamlet*. Bright, a science writer and the inventor of shorthand notation, was a physician and clergyman. His *A Treatise of Melancholy* (1586) analysed depression and mental illness in general; numerous similarities in ideas and wording suggest that this book influenced Shakespeare's portrait of his melancholy prince HAMLET. However, Bright's *Treatise* was one of many contemporary books on mental depression, a subject that fascinated Elizabethan England, and it need not have been the only inspiration for the creation of a melancholy protagonist, as was once commonly asserted.

A successful physician as a young man, Bright became so obsessed with developing his shorthand system—a rather cumbersome one that was soon superseded—that he neglected his medical practice until he was dismissed from his post in a London hospital. He moved to the country to live as a rural clergyman, but he was dismissed from two positions there for similar reasons, and he retired.

**Bristol (Bristow)**   City in western England, a location in *Richard II*. King RICHARD II's cowardly friends BUSHY and GREENE (1) flee to Bristol when BOLINGBROKE (1) appears with an army to challenge the King. Bristol was the principal port for trade with Ireland and thus a logical place for them to meet Richard upon his return. However, Bolingbroke arrives ahead of Richard, and he captures Bushy and Greene. In 3.1 he condemns them to death before the walls of Bristol Castle.

**Britten, Benjamin (b. 1913)**   British composer, creator of an operatic version of *A Midsummer Night's Dream*. Britten began composing orchestral music as a child, and by the 1930s he was an influential modern composer. He has created many operas and choral works including *A Midsummer Night's Dream* (1960).

**Brook (1)**   Name used by the disguised FORD (1) in *The Merry Wives of Windsor*. Ford, unreasonably jealous, believes that his wife, MISTRESS (1) Ford, intends to commit adultery with FALSTAFF. He visits Falstaff posing as Brook, a would-be lover of Mistress Ford, and he encourages Falstaff to seduce his wife, pretending to hope to follow in his footsteps as Brook. He actually wants to catch his wife in her adultery with the fat knight. His assumed name figures in several jokes, as in 2.2.145–146 and 5.5.241–242.

It is thought that this alias was Shakespeare's subtle, jesting reference to an alteration in his work that had recently been forced upon him. A Puritan leader, William Brooke, Lord COBHAM—or perhaps his son Henry Brooke—had been offended by a fat, lecherous, ne'er-do-well character in *1 Henry IV* whose name, OLDCASTLE, was the same as that of one of his revered ancestors. Cobham was a powerful aristocrat, and his complaint was honoured: Oldcastle became Falstaff. However, in the first play in which the new name was used from the outset, *The Merry Wives*, Shakespeare permitted himself a mild revenge, associating the Cobham family name with a character whose foolishness might be said to resemble their own pridefulness. Since the Oldcastle furore was well known in London, the joke, if it was one, would certainly have been widely understood.

However, Shakespeare's jest was itself subject to revision. In the FIRST FOLIO edition of the play (1623), Ford uses the name Broome throughout. Since the 1602 QUARTO uses Brooke, this change must have been made between 1602 and 1623. It may be that

Henry Brooke demanded the change, although its apparent late date seems to distance the alteration from the original controversy. Several other theories have been proposed; the most convincing asserts that the name was changed for a performance at the court of King JAMES I in November 1604, 18 months after his accession. In the previous year both Henry Brooke and his brother George had attempted coups against the new King and had been convicted of treason. George was executed, and Henry was imprisoned for life. Their surname may have been removed from the play to avoid an unnecessary reminder of James' difficulties.

**Brook (2), Peter (b. 1925)** British theatrical and FILM director. Brook, an innovative director who has consciously attempted to incorporate influences from many times and cultures into his work, is one of the most important figures in contemporary world theatre, as well as in the more restricted context of Shakespearean production. His many stagings of Shakespeare have varied in style from the Watteauesque romanticism of a 1947 *Love's Labour's Lost* to a brutal 1962 *King Lear*—with Paul SCOFIELD in what is acclaimed as one of the greatest Shakespearean performances of modern times—to the dramatically avant-garde 1970 presentation of *A Midsummer Night's Dream*, which incorporated circus routines, played within a set that was a huge white box. Other famous Brook productions include *Measure for Measure* and *The Winter's Tale* in 1951, both with John GIELGUD, and *Titus Andronicus*, starring Laurence OLIVIER, in 1955.

Brook was an adviser on a 1953 TELEVISION version of *King Lear* starring Orson WELLES, and he made his own film of *Lear* in 1969 with Scofield. While filming *Lear* in Denmark, Brook corresponded about the project with Grigori KOZINTSEV, who was also filming the play in Russia. Brook's result is a bleak depiction characterised by the purposefully disconcerting use of such cinematic techniques as montage, hand-held camerawork, and silent-screen titles. It attracted both great praise and disgusted criticism.

In the 1980s Brook was largely concerned with non-Shakespearean projects, the most notable of which was probably his 1987 staging of the ancient Indian epic *The Mahabharata*. Critics sometimes find Brook's experiments pretentious or criticise a disparity between style and content, but all agree that his successes are major ones, and that his energy and daring have contributed greatly to late 20th-century theatre.

**Brooke (1), Arthur (d. 1563)** English poet, author of the principal source for *Romeo and Juliet*. Brooke's poem *The Tragicall Historye of Romeus and Juliet* (1562)—a loose translation of a French prose tale that was in turn derived from an Italian story by Matteo BANDELLO—served Shakespeare as his chief source for his version of the tale of tragic lovers. The poem also contributed details to *The Two Gentlemen of Verona* and *3 Henry VI*.

Little is known of Brooke's life, except that he drowned while still a young man on a military expedition to aid the Huguenots in the Wars of Religion of FRANCE (1). He may well have entered the military out of religious conviction, for his introductory remarks to *Romeus and Juliet* are moralistic in a Protestant vein.

**Brooke (2), C. F. Tucker (1883–1946)** American scholar. A longtime professor at Yale University, Brooke wrote several significant books on Shakespeare, including *The Shakespeare Apocrypha* (1908), *The Tudor Drama* (1911), and *Shakespeare's Sonnets* (1936). He was also a general editor of the Yale edition of Shakespeare's works, published in 40 volumes between 1917 and 1927.

**Brooke (3), William, Lord Cobham** See COBHAM.

**Broome** See BROOK (1).

**Brother (1)** Minor character in *2 Henry VI*, brother of Sir Humphrey STAFFORD (2). Accompanying Sir Humphrey on a mission to put down the revolt led by Jack CADE, the Brother supports Stafford in his undiplomatic approach to the rebels in 4.2; they are both killed in the skirmish in 4.3. It is known from historical sources that the brother's name was Sir William Stafford (d. 1450).

**Brother (2)** Either of two minor characters in *Cymbeline*, the deceased siblings of POSTHUMUS who appear to him as apparitions, in 5.4. The Brothers appear with the spirits of their father, SICILIUS LEONATUS, and their MOTHER. Led by Sicilius, the group pleads with Jupiter for mercy on Posthumus. The Brothers point out Posthumus' qualities in an elaborate poem; the First Brother speaks two stanzas and the Second Brother one. The Second Brother notes that they had both died, with their father, before Posthumus was born. This fact has been previously mentioned in 1.1. 35–36. The episode adds to the romantic strangeness of the play, and the Brothers have the eerie presence of supernatural beings.

**Brother (3)** Minor character in *The Two Noble Kinsmen*, brother of the GAOLER (4). In 4.1 the Brother accompanies the Gaoler's deranged DAUGHTER (2), who is returning home. He is a mere pawn who speaks only a few lines. He was probably created by Shakespeare's collaborator, John FLETCHER (2), who wrote this scene in the opinion of most scholars.

**Browne, Robert (active 1583–1620)** English actor and theatrical entrepreneur. Browne was a member of

WORCESTER'S MEN in 1583–1584, Derby's Men (see DERBY [3]) in 1599–1601, and a partner in the Children of the Queen's Revels (see CHILDREN'S COMPANIES) in 1610, but he is best known for his career in Europe, especially in Germany. Between 1590 and 1620 he toured Germany and the Low Countries with a series of his own acting companies. He performed chiefly English plays, at first entirely in English but increasingly in German. His was the most important of a group of English acting companies whose tours were extremely popular and are generally thought to have contributed greatly to the German theatre of the time. Another prominent figure was Browne's follower, John GREEN. Browne's company is known to have performed plays by Christopher MARLOWE (1), and he probably staged Shakespeare's plays as well, for Green is known to have done so. In 1593 while Browne was on tour, his wife and children died in a London epidemic; two years later he remarried, possibly to a sister of William SLY (2), who in 1608 bequeathed his share in the GLOBE THEATRE to a Robert Browne who is thought to be this man.

**Brutus (1), Decius**　Character in *Julius Caesar*. See DECIUS.

**Brutus (2), Junius (active 509 B.C.)**　Quasi-historical founder of the Roman Republic and minor figure in *The Rape of Lucrece*. He avenges TARQUIN's assault on LUCRECE and expels the last king of Rome, Tarquin's father. (The same figure appears in *Coriolanus*, though as a very different character. See BRUTUS [3].) Brutus appears only in the closing stanzas of *Lucrece*, beginning in line 1807. He rallies the grief-stricken husband and father of Lucrece, COLLATINE and LUCRETIUS, to pursue the villain, with the consequence, stated briefly in the last line of the poem, that Tarquin is banished. Shakespeare described this conclusion slightly more elaborately in the final sentence of the ARGUMENT: '. . . the Tarquins were all exiled, and the state government changed from kings to consuls'.

Brutus is said to have been a foolish young man, best known 'for sportive words and utt'ring foolish things' (line 1813), before finding maturity in undertaking this act of revenge and revolution. Shakespeare took this characterisation from his Latin sources, OVID and LIVY. However, these writers lived five centuries after Brutus; very little is actually known of the historical figure, if he actually existed. His name, meaning 'brutish' (like that of HAMLET), was probably an insult, originally, referring to his careless early life. However, Roman tradition revered Brutus as the leader of the revolt that established the republic in 509 B.C., though all that was recorded of him, and only recorded somewhat later, was that he was one of the first two consuls, the officers who replaced the kings and ruled jointly for a year at a time. (The association of the revolution

with a rape is entirely legendary.) Marcus BRUTUS (4), the assassin of Julius CAESAR (1), claimed descent from him, as is mentioned several times in *Julius Caesar* (e.g., in 2.1.53–54). Brutus is also mentioned in *Henry V*, 2.4.37, where his legendary mis-spent youth is compared with PRINCE (6) HAL's.

**Brutus (3), Junius**　Quasi-historical figure and character in *Coriolanus*, a tribune of ROME. Brutus shares power with Sicinius Velutus, another legendary tribune, but since they are very similar characters who always appear together (except for a brief final appearance by Sicinius in 5.4), they are both covered here. The tribunes represent the common people's share in political power, and they reject their foe, the aristocratic Roman warrior CORIOLANUS. By orchestrating mob violence—and aided by Coriolanus' foolish actions—they succeed in having him banished from Rome. They enjoy their triumph, but when the exiled Coriolanus attacks Rome, the tribunes deny their responsibility; 'Say not we brought it' (4.6.121), they retort, and insist that the aristocrats resolve the crisis. The tribunes are stereotypes of scurvy politicians and are scarcely distinguishable from each other, but Shakespeare does vary their functions somewhat, with Brutus dominant in the first half of the play.

The shortsightedness of the tribunes' campaign against Coriolanus certainly threatens the city. They are an example of the dangers that result when power is accorded to the common people (see CITIZEN [5]), an important theme of the play. At the same time, however, they are concerned with the health of the city. Their offices were created as a result of the corn riots that open the play. The riots are attributed to the arrogance of Coriolanus and the other aristocrats in the face of the common people's hunger. As Sicinius observes in the wake of Coriolanus' banishment, Rome enjoys 'peace / and quietness' as a result of their victory, while the aristocrats 'blush that the world goes well' (4.6.2–3, 5). When Coriolanus contemptuously asks Brutus, 'What do you prate of service?', the tribune replies with dignity, 'I talk of that, that know it' (3.3.84–85). Indeed, he seems to attempt more service for his people than does the foolish and treacherous warrior for his fellow aristocrats. Nevertheless, the tribunes have a chiefly negative significance in the play's political world, for in a properly run society—as Shakespeare conceived it—the common people would follow the leadership of their social superiors, and have no tribunes. However, Coriolanus' pride has promoted social disruption, of which the tribunes are a result.

The social conflict enacted in *Coriolanus*—taken by Shakespeare from his source, PLUTARCH's *Lives*—is representative of several such episodes that occured in the late 6th century B.C. as the Roman republic came into being. Though the story of Coriolanus is entirely legendary, Brutus may have been a real person. He appears as Junius BRUTUS (2) in Shakespeare's *The Rape of Lucrece,* though as a very different character. Shakespeare followed Thomas NORTH's translation of Plutarch and erroneously transcribed Sicinius' second name as Velutus, which Plutarch renders as Bellutus. In any case, Plutarch's Sicinius is otherwise unknown in Roman legend, unless he is identifiable with Lucius Sicinius Dentatus, who appears in other sources and is said to have represented the plebeians, though at a somewhat later period.

**Brutus (4), Marcus (c. 85–42 B.C.)**  Historical figure and character in *Julius Caesar,* leader of the assassins of CAESAR (1) and of the forces opposing Mark ANTONY in the subsequent civil war. Brutus, the protagonist of *Caesar,* is representative of the moral ambiguity that is the play's central theme. He seems both good and evil: a patriotic and honourable man who nonetheless brings about Rome's downfall and his own.

When Caesar's apparent ambition to rule alone begins to disturb Roman aristocrats, Brutus is drawn by

*Brutus, the protagonist of* Julius Caesar. *While trying to save Rome from Caesar's dictatorship, he becomes, ironically, like a dictator himself.* (Courtesy of Culver Pictures, Inc.)

CASSIUS to lead a plot against him. 'With himself at war' (1.2.45), Brutus debates the murder of his friend and mentor: Shall his patriotism be stronger than his love and respect? He concludes that Caesar must be killed, despite his personal virtues, to save Rome from tyranny. Brutus then approaches the assassination as a moral imperative, but Shakespeare offers much evidence that Brutus is not the wholly selfless figure he believes himself to be. Not only does his decision prove to be politically catastrophic, but it appears to be morally flawed, too, for Brutus is unconsciously in pursuit of power himself.

Brutus' self-appraisal has often been mistaken for Shakespeare's portrait of him, but the playwright, while acknowledgeing his protagonist's patriotism and honourable intentions, presents a host of opposing indications that paint another picture. Brutus is wilful and arrogant, resembling the tyrant he kills and growing more like him as the play unfolds. As leader of the conspiracy, he peremptorily opposes anyone else's initiative, refusing to share leadership with either Cassius or CICERO. His disdainful over-confidence is disastrous when he dismisses Antony as a man of little importance in 2.1.181–183. He overrules Cassius, insisting that Antony be spared and then that Antony be permitted to speak at Caesar's funeral. Both decisions prove fateful. As the battle of PHILIPPI approaches, Brutus once again demands his own way—and leads his cause to defeat. In insisting on his own way at all times, Brutus displays the dictatorial behaviour he had feared in Caesar. But, unlike Caesar, he is not a competent leader. Lacking insight into other men's motives, as he abundantly demonstrates with respect to Cassius and Antony, he is an inadequate politician. He is also an inexperienced and impatient general.

Brutus' self-delusion is startlingly apparent on several occasions. On one level he considers the assassination a high moral duty; yet, subconsciously guilty, he also needs to justify it, saying, 'Let's be sacrificers, but not butchers' (2.1.166). Further, when Caesar has been stabbed to death, Brutus improvises a cleansing ritual—the assassins bathe their hands in their victim's blood—but this act accentuates, not alleviates, the violence of the deed. Brutus does not see the gore through his own vision of rectitude.

Particularly striking is Brutus' unconscious hypocrisy in praising himself for refusing to acquire funds through graft or by accepting bribery, saying, 'I can raise no money by vile means' (4.3.71), while at the same time castigating Cassius for refusing to share with him his own ill-gotten gains. In another instance, in 4.3.180–194, he pretends to accept with great stoicism the news of the death of PORTIA (2'), when he has in fact known of it for some time. (It has been contended that Shakespeare had excised this passage from the play, it surviving only because of a printer's error; however, the ploy suits Brutus' imperiousness quite well, and the rejection of the passage seems unnecessary.) This deception may be defended as good for the morale of his underlings, but it is nevertheless quite as patronising as Caesar's feigned reluctance to accept a crown, as reported in 1.2.230–263.

A possible source of Brutus' self-deception is his repeated denial of his emotions and thus his inability to recognise his own drives. He rejects his love for Caesar, for Cassius, even for Portia, lest they contaminate the higher faculty of his reason. His errors in trusting Antony and relying on the support of the PLEBEIANS stem from his assumption that they, like he, will act rationally. Not only does he undervalue the significance and power of passion in others, he does not see its operation in himself. Thus blinded, Brutus never sees the error of his attack on Caesar. The unnecessary disaster of the civil war has resulted from his own obsession with controlling the Roman political world, but he honestly sees only his own idealistic point of view. Thus his actions are virtuous in their intent but evil in their consequences. Precisely because of this contradiction, Brutus resembles a tragic hero, attempting great things and failing through his own psychological flaws.

*Julius Caesar* is not simply the story of a man who injures his society by an illicit rebellion or of a man who murders a friend for bad reasons. Rather, the tragic grandeur of Brutus' moral imperfection lies in his effort to transcend human limitations and create a political world without the potential for evil and exploitation. Like OTHELLO or HAMLET, Brutus possesses an integrity that impels him towards a wrong course. Attempting the impossible, he can produce only chaos, and he brings about the downfall of both his world and himself. Antony's final eulogy not only acknowledges the nobility of Brutus' conscious intentions in killing Caesar but also reminds us of his weakness, observing that he was an honourable man who did not recognise the dishonour of his actions.

The historical Brutus was a rather different person than Shakespeare's patriotic but deluded idealist, and much of his career is neither enacted nor alluded to in *Julius Caesar*. Renowned in his own day as an admirable Roman nobleman—upright in his dealings and grave in demeanour—Brutus was descended from an illustrious patrician family. His mother was Caesar's mistress for many years, giving rise to the rumour that Brutus was Caesar's son (alluded to in *2 Henry VI*, 4.1.136), though the relationship probably began only after Brutus' birth. Brutus had a highly successful political career; he received profitable appointments as an administrator of Roman territories abroad. He was also a prominent player in the factional politics of the period. Prior to the time of the play, Brutus was a

follower of Pompey the Great (106–48) in his civil war against Caesar, but after Caesar's decisive victory at the battle of Pharsala (48 B.C.) he switched sides. Caesar rewarded him with appointments to high offices. However, Brutus seems to have regretted his betrayal of Pompey; he published a defence of Cato, a prominent Pompeian, and he married Portia, Cato's daughter, which his contemporaries recognised as a gesture of opposition to Caesar.

Brutus and the conspirators compared themselves to Brutus' ancestor, Junius BRUTUS (2), a legendary Roman patriot, as Shakespeare indicates in 1.2.157 and 2.1.53–54, but in fact their ends were more selfish than patriotic. They stood for the privileges and vested interests of the Roman aristocracy, threatened by Caesar's long-standing dictatorship—normally a temporary office held during a crisis. Caesar seemed to be establishing a new order, in which the nobles would be subordinated to him and to his government.

Brutus' ritual bloodbath, described above, is Shakespeare's invention, intended to emphasise both the violence of the deed and its political nature. PLUTARCH, Shakespeare's source, reports the murder in brutal imagery drawn from hunting, presenting just the sort of picture Brutus attempts, in the play, to avoid. Thus the playwright distorted his source material in order to create a telling effect.

Shakespeare greatly compressed the complicated events following Caesar's death for dramatic reasons, and Brutus' struggles to maintain a political position in Rome are ignored. After the assassination Brutus and the conspirators negotiated with Antony and other Caesarians, and for several weeks the two groups governed Rome jointly, although the citizenry frequently rioted against the assassins. Numerous intrigues, now obscure, dominated Roman politics; Brutus and Cassius attempted to recruit followers among the rural aristocrats with only modest success. In mid-April they left Rome for good. They remained in Italy throughout the summer, during which a possible alliance between Antony and Octavius began to seem threatening. Brutus then left for Macedonia, where he held a government appointment. Negotiations between the assassins and Antony continued throughout the winter, but the civil war began in the spring of 43 B.C., with Antony defeating DECIUS in northern Italy. In November, Antony and Octavius formed the Triumvirate with Lepidus, and the following summer they launched the campaign that led to Philippi.

Except for collapsing two battles into one, Shakespeare's account of Brutus' defeat and death at Philippi is accurately retold from Plutarch, although other sources indicate that Cassius did not oppose the decision to march to Philippi; the conspirators' forces were supported by the local population, while Antony and Octavius were short of supplies. One other mild distortion of Brutus' nature follows from Shakespeare's compression of events: in the twenty days between battles, Brutus most fully revealed his serious incompetence as a general, for he had only to wait for time and hunger to defeat his enemies and he could not do it.

**Bryan, George (active 1586–1613)** English actor. Bryan appears in the list of 26 'Principall Actors' who performed in Shakespeare's plays recorded in the FIRST FOLIO (1623), though he is not known to have played any specific role. He was among the English actors that visited Denmark in 1586 and was a player in STRANGE'S MEN at least from 1590–1593. He was probably still among them when they became the CHAMBERLAIN'S MEN in 1594, for he is recorded as a co-receiver of a payment to that company in 1596, implying that he was an important member of the group. However, he is not listed among the casts of particular Chamberlain's Men plays; the earliest such list dates from 1598, and scholars speculate that Bryan had retired by then. Apparently successful as a minor courtier, Bryan was recorded as a member of the Queen's household, in an unspecified capacity, in 1603 and in 1611–1613.

**Buchanan, George (1506–1582)** Scottish poet and historian, Scotland's leading Protestant humanist of the 16th century, and the author of a minor source for *Macbeth*. Buchanan's history of Scotland in Latin, *Rerum Scotiarum Historia* (1582), may have influenced Shakespeare in the development of Macbeth's character, as well as providing several political details.

The history, considered one of the great works of late Latin literature, was the crowning achievement of a long and varied career. As a student at the University of Paris, Buchanan wrote notorious satires aimed at the clerical corruption that was stimulating the Protestant Reformation. Back in Scotland c. 1528, Buchanan was imprisoned for his writings, but escaped and established himself as a professor at a college in Bordeaux, where one of his pupils was MONTAIGNE. He wrote a number of notable Latin plays at this time. In 1548 he was appointed the head of a university in Portugal, but while there he was imprisoned by the Inquisition. In prison he wrote an acclaimed Latin rendition of the Book of Psalms.

Buchanan returned to Scotland in 1560 and converted to Calvinism. Tutor to Mary, Queen of Scots, he later became her enemy, assisting in her prosecution for treason in England. Upon her imprisonment he was made tutor to her son, later King JAMES I of England. During James' childhood as ruler of Scotland, Buchanan was an important figure in the government. In his last years he wrote his major works: a treatise on government that was condemned for its

democratic tendencies and the history of Scotland that Shakespeare read.

**Buckingham (1), Edward Stafford, Duke of (1478–1521)** Historical figure and minor character in *Henry VIII*, a nobleman falsely convicted of treason and sentenced to death, a victim of Cardinal WOLSEY's intrigues. In 1.1 Buckingham's anger at Wolsey's duplicitous misuse of power establishes the cardinal as a villain. His own contrasting goodness is demonstrated as he calmly accepts his arrest for treason, even though it becomes apparent that Wolsey has bribed the duke's former SURVEYOR to commit perjury. In 2.1, on his way to be executed, Buckingham furthers the contrast by forgiving his enemies, wishing King HENRY VIII well, and humbly preparing for death. Buckingham's victimisation marks one end of the play's most important development—the growth of King Henry—for the ease with which the king is deceived by Wolsey and the Surveyor is soon replaced by increasing maturity and wisdom.

In 2.1.106–123 Buckingham compares himself to his father, also falsely executed for treason. That Duke of BUCKINGHAM (2) appears in *Richard III*, and *his* father, this duke's grandfather, is the BUCKINGHAM (3) of *2 Henry VI*.

**Buckingham (2), Henry Stafford, Duke of (1455–1483)** Historical figure and character in *Richard III*, the most important supporter of RICHARD III before he deserts the King in response to his ingratitude. Buckingham acts as a spokesman for Richard's positions, especially to the MAYOR (3) and the people of London. His style of speaking, bombastic and obscure, is typical of devious politicians, and his wily, conspiratorial nature makes him an important adviser to Richard at several junctures, notably in hatching the plot against HASTINGS (3). He prides himself on his capacity for deceit in the remarkable conversation that opens 3.5.

However, in 4.2, when Richard, now enthroned, proposes to go further and kill the young PRINCE (5) of Wales and his brother, Buckingham is somewhat reluctant, perhaps sensing that a king should be more cautious. Richard, angered, then refuses Buckingham the earldom he had promised him. Buckingham perceives that he is in danger of suffering Hastings' fate, and he decides to abandon the King. He raises an army in rebellion but is quickly captured. In 5.1 Buckingham, about to be executed, formally reflects on his circumstances, recollecting past oaths and prophecies almost in the manner of a Greek CHORUS (1). Thus, in a prelude to the approaching doom of Richard, Buckingham invokes the sense of ordained fate that is central to the play.

Shakespeare's sources offered several possible motives for Buckingham's revolt, but Shakespeare chose one that was definitely untrue, for Richard had given

Buckingham his earldom prior to his defection. The question cannot be answered with the surviving evidence; he may simply have anticipated Richard's overthrow by RICHMOND. It has been suggested that Buckingham was ambitious to rule, for he had a distant claim to the throne himself, being descended from Thomas, Duke of GLOUCESTER (6), the youngest brother of RICHARD II. Buckingham's father was the Duke of BUCKINGHAM (3) of *2 Henry VI*, and his son appears as BUCKINGHAM (1) in *Henry VIII*.

**Buckingham (3), Sir Humphrey Stafford, Duke of (d. 1455)** Historical figure and character in *2 Henry VI*, an ally of the Duke of SUFFOLK (3) against GLOUCESTER (4) and later of King HENRY VI against the Duke of YORK (8). Buckingham enters Suffolk's conspiracy cheerfully, nominating himself as a possible replacement for Gloucester as Lord Protector (1.1.177–178). When the DUCHESS (1) of Gloucester is driven from the assembled court by Queen MARGARET (1), Buckingham volunteers to follow her, remarking that the woman's anger will make her 'gallop far enough to her destruction' (1.3.151), and in the next scene, indeed, Buckingham is able to arrest the Duchess for witchcraft. When Gloucester himself is arrested, Buckingham impatiently urges on the action (3.1.186–187). In 4.4 Buckingham counsels the King during the rebellion led by Jack CADE, and, with CLIFFORD (2), he later (4.8) defuses that uprising by presenting the rebels with the King's offer of pardon. In 5.1 he acts as the King's representative to the Duke of York. Shakespeare's peremptory, sharp-spoken Buckingham rings one of the notes of individual personality among the group of fractious nobles that mark this play as an improvement over *1 Henry VI*.

The historical Buckingham died in the battle of Northampton, and his death is noted in *3 Henry VI* (1.1), though it is placed at the battle of ST. ALBANS, fought at the close of *2 Henry VI*. His son, Henry, Duke of BUCKINGHAM (2), figures in *Richard III*.

**Bullcalf, Peter** Minor character in *2 Henry IV*, one of the men whom FALSTAFF recruits for the army in 3.2. Bullcalf claims to be ill, despite the robust appearance his name suggests, but he is recruited anyway. However, his friend Ralph MOULDY secures release for them both by bribing Corporal BARDOLPLH (1). The episode satirises the notoriously corrupt practices of 16th-century recruiters.

**Bullen, Anne** Character in *Henry VIII*. See ANNE (1).

**Bullingbrook** Character in *Richard II*. See BOLINGBROKE (1).

**Bullough, Geoffrey (1901–1982)** British scholar. Bullough, long-time professor of English literature at London University, is best known for his eight-volume *Narrative and Dramatic Sources of Shakespeare* (1957–1975). This definitive work is commonly known as 'Bullough' and is considered a necessary reference for any Shakespearean scholarship. Bullough also edited a collection of the poems and plays of Fulke GREVILLE (2).

**Burbage (1), Cuthbert (c. 1566–1636)** English theatrical entrepreneur, son of James BURBAGE (2) and brother of Richard BURBAGE (3). Cuthbert, unlike his brother and father, was never an actor, but he was nevertheless an important figure in ELIZABETHAN THEATRE. Cuthbert managed the first LONDON playhouse, the THEATRE, which he inherited when his father died in early 1597, just before the expiration of the lease for the land on which the building was constructed. After fruitless negotiations over its renewal, Cuthbert simply had the building torn down and reassembled as the GLOBE THEATRE, which was owned half by himself and Richard, and half by a group of actors from the KING'S MEN, including Shakespeare. Cuthbert was also a partner in a similar arrangement for the BLACKFRIARS THEATRE.

**Burbage (2), James (c. 1530–1597)** English theatrical entrepreneur, builder of the first LONDON theatre and father of Cuthbert and Richard BURBAGE (1, 3). A poor carpenter who turned actor, Burbage was a leading member of LEICESTER'S MEN when he decided, in 1575, to construct a building devoted only to the performance of plays, in the hopes of profiting from the admissions fees. His wealthy brother-in-law John Brayne provided the capital for the venture, and Burbage took a 21-year lease on a plot of land just north of the city. On it he built the THEATRE, which was opened sometime in late 1576 or early 1577. Burbage was evidently a fiery and argumentative man, and he and Brayne, and later Brayne's widow, disputed vigorously about the distribution of the profits in court and, on one occasion, in a physical brawl in front of an arriving audience. Burbage prospered at the Theatre, and in 1596 he bought a building that he converted into the BLACKFRIARS THEATRE. At his death he left the Theatre and its ground lease to Cuthbert, and the Blackfriars Theatre to Richard.

**Burbage (3), Richard (c. 1568–1619)** English actor, son of James BURBAGE (2) and brother of Cuthbert BURBAGE (1), the leading actor of the CHAMBERLAIN'S MEN and the original portrayer of many of Shakespeare's protagonists. With William ALLEYN, Burbage is said to have been the greatest actor of the ELIZABETHAN THEATRE. Contemporary allusions establish that Burbage played HAMLET, LEAR, MALVOLIO, OTHELLO, and RICHARD III, and he probably played many more major Shakespearean roles.

*Richard Burbage, the greatest English actor of Shakespeare's time, originated the roles of Richard III, Hamlet, Othello, and Lear. He was the leading tragedian of the Chamberlain's Men.* (Courtesy of Billy Rose Theatre Collection; New York Public Library at Lincoln Center; Astor, Lenox and Tilden Foundations)

Burbage's early career is obscure. He probably appeared with the company composed of the ADMIRAL'S MEN and STRANGE'S MEN, who played at his father's playhouse, the THEATRE, in 1590–1591. He first achieved widespread recognition in *Richard III,* the play that also established Shakespeare as a playwright, around 1591. (In connection with this role, Burbage figures in the only surviving contemporary anecdote about Shakespeare; see MANNINGHAM.) He apparently did not tour with this troupe during the plague years, 1593–1594, but he was an early member of the Chamberlain's Men, as Strange's was known after 1594. He may have been with PEMBROKE'S MEN in the interim. He remained with the Chamberlain's Men, later the KING'S MEN, until his death, though the last record of a performance dates from 1610.

When James Burbage died in 1597, he left Cuthbert the theatre (which he tore down and reassembled as the GLOBE THEATRE) and Richard the BLACKFRIARS THEATRE; the brothers shared them through partnerships with each other. Burbage was also a painter. A well-known likeness of him is thought to be a self-

portrait and the CHANDOS PORTRAIT, long thought to be of Shakespeare, was traditionally attributed to him. As a painter, he collaborated with Shakespeare on an allegorical shield for the Earl of RUTLAND (2).

**Burby, Cuthbert (d. 1607)**    London publisher and bookseller. In 1594 Burby published THE TAMING OF A SHREW, probably a BAD QUARTO of Shakespeare's *The Taming of the Shrew.* He also published the first edition of *Love's Labour's Lost* (1598) and the second (Q2) of *Romeo and Juliet* (1599). In 1607, just before his death, he sold the rights to all three works to Nicholas LING. Burby was a brother-in-law of the printer Thomas SNODHAM.

**Burghley (Burleigh), Lord (William Cecil) (1520–1598)**    The leading statesman of Elizabethan England, chief minister to Queen ELIZABETH (1); sometimes said to have been a model for POLONIUS in *Hamlet.* An aristocratic courtier, Burghley was the most important member of Elizabeth's government from her accession in 1558 until his death. After the Pope excommunicated the Protestant Elizabeth and encouraged her assassination (and that of her chief minister) in 1570, Burghley set up an early variety of secret police, using espionage and torture in a ruthless and largely successful campaign to cripple the Counter-Reformation in England. Though he privately declared his dislike of these methods, he remains a symbol of unscrupulous state power. He is also remembered for his *Ten Precepts,* a pamphlet of sententious advice on gentlemanly conduct addressed to his son Robert CECIL (1), who succeeded him as the most powerful man in England.

Some scholars nominate Lord Burghley as a possible satirical model for Polonius chiefly because the character was named CORAMBIS—an obviously satirical name—in Shakespeare's source, the lost play called the UR-HAMLET, probably written by Thomas KYD. Polonius resembles Burghley in being a high government official and in delivering 'precepts' (1.3.58) to his son. Also, in 2.1 Polonius sends his servant REYNALDO to spy on his son LAERTES, who is at school in Paris, and a connection has been drawn to Burghley's espionage network and to the fact that his eldest son, Thomas CECIL (2), led a notoriously dissolute life on the continent for several years in his youth. However, if Corambis was intended as a satire on Burghley—or anyone else—it was Kyd's idea, not Shakespeare's; indeed, the name Polonius may have been intended to defuse any such reference.

Even if Kyd's Corambis is linked to Burghley, Shakespeare's Polonius is not. Burghley had been most powerful in the 1570s and 1580s—and had been dead for several years by the time *Hamlet* was written—making a satire on him by Shakespeare almost pointless. Also, Shakespeare was not given to personal satire—he had been willing to change the names of characters in *1* and *2 Henry IV* to avoid offence (see HARVEY [1]; OLDCASTLE; ROSSILL)—and the likelihood that he would have attempted to mock the father of a powerful member of the court is slim.

Other factors also weigh against the association of Burghley with Polonius. *Ten Precepts* was not published until 1637, and, although the sophisticated literary world may have known of it in 1601, most of the satire's hypothetical audience would not have. In any case, such collections of paternal wisdom were widely popular, and Polonius' version does not particularly resemble Burghley's. A father spying on his high-living son was likewise not unusual in literature, and the episode in *Hamlet* has legitimate dramatic purposes and need not be associated with anything outside the play.

**Burgundy (1), Duke of**  Minor character in *King Lear*, a suitor who rejects CORDELIA when she is disinherited by King LEAR. Burgundy appears only in 1.1; he and the King of FRANCE (2) have been summoned to determine which of them will marry Lear's youngest daughter and thus govern one-third of Britain. Burgundy's concern is with a politically and materially advantageous match, and when Cordelia is disinherited he simply loses interest in her. She dismisses his frank but polite apology cooly, saying, 'Peace be with Burgundy! / Since that respect and fortunes are his love, / I shall not be his wife' (1.1.246–248). Burgundy's conventionally greedy behaviour contrasts tellingly with the response of France, who recognises Cordelia's virtues and marries her.

The Duke's equal footing with the King of France reflects a reality of medieval Europe: the Duchy of Burgundy, though formally a client state of FRANCE (1), was an independent and wealthy country (see BURGUNDY [2]). However, this medieval context is an anachronism, for in the early period in which *King Lear* is set the Duchy of Burgundy did not yet exist.

**Burgundy (2), Philip, Duke of (1396–1467)**  Historical figure and character in *1 Henry VI* and *Henry V*, an ally of the English in the HUNDRED YEARS WAR who defects to the side of FRANCE (1). Early in *1 Henry VI* Burgundy assists the English at ORLÉANS (1) and ROUEN; then in 3.3 JOAN LA PUCELLE persuades him to align himself with France. In *Henry V*, set some years earlier, a younger Burgundy encourages HENRY V and the FRENCH KING to make peace in 5.2.23–67. He speaks at length on the horrors of war, in a passage that contributes much to the play's modern reception as an anti-war work. Burgundy then attends the French King in the final negotiations of the treaty of TROYES, which occur off stage while Henry courts KATHARINE (2). Upon returning, Burgundy jests lewdly with Henry about his forthcoming marriage.

The historical Burgundy was not an ally of France at Troyes, and he was a much more important figure than his role suggests. He was a cousin of Charles VI, the French King of the play, and he ruled the most powerful of the independent French duchies. His father, Duke John (1371–1419), was the Duke of Burgundy mentioned in *Henry V* 3.5.42 and 4.8.99; Duke John fought against Henry at AGINCOURT. He was murdered in the factional disputes over the rule of France during Charles' frequent bouts of insanity, and Philip of Burgundy, upon inheriting the duchy, sought support from outside the circle of French rivalries. He sided with England and thus assured Henry V's victory, a phenomenon that Shakespeare, focussing on the accomplishments of the English King, ignored in *Henry V*. Burgundy's subsequent alliance with England under HENRY VI was marred by many disputes over policy and by his feud with the Duke of GLOUCESTER (4); he eventually restored his family's traditional amity with France, helping to drive the English from the country in the 1450s, as is depicted in *1 Henry VI*. However, both historically and in Shakespeare's sources, Joan of Arc had nothing to do with Burgundy's defection, which took place four years after her death. This alteration serves to amplify the importance of Joan, who is Shakespeare's chief representative of the deceitful and villainous French.

**Burleigh, William Cecil, Lord**  See BURGHLEY.

**Burnaby, William (c. 1672–1706)**  Minor English playwright. Burnaby is remembered primarily because he incorporated adaptations of scenes from *Twelfth Night* into his 1703 comedy *Love Betray'd, or The Agreeable Disappointment*.

**Bury St Edmunds**  Town in the English county of Suffolk, site of a famed medieval abbey and the setting for Act 3 of *2 Henry VI*. Here, in the ancient abbey, the Duke of GLOUCESTER (4) is prosecuted and then murdered by the clique surrounding Queen MARGARET (1) and the Duke of SUFFOLK (3). Consequently, the King exiles Suffolk for life at the insistence of an outraged mob, and CARDINAL (1) BEAUFORT, one of the conspirators, dies with a bad conscience.

Bury St Edmunds was an unusually isolated location for a meeting of Parliament. Although Shakespeare does not mention it, much of his audience will have realised that this town was deep in the home territory of the Duke of Suffolk, far from Gloucester's power base in London. The mob appearing in the play to demand Suffolk's punishment is fictitious; precisely because of its location, Gloucester's arrest went unprotested. Suffolk was not in fact banished until much later, and for different reasons.

As ST EDMUNDSBURY, the town is a location in *King John*.

**Busby, John (active 1576–1619)**   London bookseller and publisher. Busby was associated with apparently pirated publications of three of Shakespeare's plays. In 1600 Busby and John MILLINGTON published the first QUARTO edition of *Henry V*. In 1602 he registered a forthcoming publication of *The Merry Wives of Windsor* with the STATIONERS' COMPANY but immediately sold his 'rights' to his long-time business partner, Arthur JOHNSON (1), whose name appared alone on the title page of the play. In 1607 he registered *King Lear* jointly with Nathaniel BUTTER, though again, when the play was published the next year, Busby's name was dropped. Each of these editions was a BAD QUARTO, that is, it was transcribed from the recollections of actors who had performed in the play. This method was used by publishers who had no access to the proper text of a play—carefully withheld by acting companies in the hope of foiling such pirates as Busby.

**Bushy (Bussy), Sir John (d. 1399)**   Historical figure and character in *Richard II*, a supporter of RICHARD II. Bushy, John BAGOT, and Henry GREENE (1) are the 'caterpillars' (2.3.165) whose influence on the King is alleged by BOLINGBROKE (1) to have been disastrous for England. Bushy attempts to comfort the distraught QUEEN (13) Isabel in 2.2; his elaborate courtier's language seems grotesque even to modern ears, unaware that it parodies 16th-century religious meditations. Later in 2.2 Bushy, Bagot, and Greene recognise that their position as favourites of the King is likely to prove dangerous if their master is defeated by Bolingbroke. The three decide to flee when Bolingbroke approaches; Bushy and Greene seek safety in BRISTOL Castle, but Bolingbroke captures them and sentences them to death.

The historical Bushy was a minor politician; he was frequently Speaker of the House of COMMONS—not an important post in his day—and was also three times Sheriff of London. Originally a supporter of the Duke of GLOUCESTER (6), he was recruited to Richard's party in the 1390s, before the murder of the Duke.

**Butcher**   Minor character in *2 Henry VI*. See DICK THE BUTCHER.

**Butter, Nathaniel (d. 1664)**   London bookseller and publisher who issued the first edition of *King Lear*. In 1607, jointly with John BUSBY, who several times pirated Shakespeare's plays, Butter registered a forthcoming edition of the play with the STATIONERS' COMPANY. However, when the QUARTO edition of the play appeared the next year it was attributed solely to Butter. It was a BAD QUARTO, an inaccurate text assembled from the recollections of actors, a frequent recourse of unauthorised publishers. Butter also published THE LONDON PRODIGAL (1605), a play that was falsely attributed to Shakespeare, and he is known to have pirated a play by Thomas HEYWOOD.

Butter, the son of a printer and bookseller, published his first book in 1604, opened a bookshop (at the sign of the 'Pied Bull') the next year, and sold books at various locations until his death. After 1622 he specialised in publishing news sheets, early predecessors of newspapers, but he did not flourish and is said to have died a pauper.

**Butts, Doctor (William Butts, d. 1545)**   Historical figure and minor character in *Henry VIII*, King HENRY VIII's physician. In 5.2 Doctor Butts leads Henry to an upper room where he can secretly view his council's meeting below, in order to thwart the councillors' attempt to imprison Thomas CRANMER, Archbishop of Canterbury. Butts informs the king that the archbishop has been humiliated by having to wait with the servants outside the meeting room, and this adds to the king's anger. Shakespeare took Butts' role in this incident from his source, FOXE's *Actes and Monumentes*. Butts was King Henry's personal physician for many years, and his death is said to have distressed the king greatly. His personal appearance has been preserved in a fine portrait by Hans Holbein the Younger (c. 1497–1543).

# C

**Cade, Jack (d. 1450)** Historical figure and character in *2 Henry VI,* the leader of a rebellion and pretender to the throne of England. Cade, whose revolt occupies most of Act 4, is presented as a buffoonish but brutal figure. He makes preposterous promises to his followers and proposes to legislate on such matters as the length of Lent. He also whimsically executes people for being literate or for being ignorant of an arbitrary change in his title. He enthusiastically seconds a follower's proposal: 'The first thing we do, let's kill all the lawyers' (4.2.73). In the case of Lord SAY, the victim's actual virtues, such as having been a benefactor of education, are used by Cade as grounds for his death. Cade orders the destruction of London Bridge, the Tower of London, and the INNS OF COURT as well. All this viciousness is explained as having been commissioned by the Duke of YORK (8) in order to give him a reason to bring an army into England and suppress the rebels.

In presenting this episode, Shakespeare took remarkable liberties with history, for not only did the historical York have nothing to do with Cade's rebellion, but the uprising itself is based in part on accounts of a different event, the Peasants' Rebellion of 1381, when there were attempts to destroy London Bridge and the Inns of Court. The proposal to kill the lawyers also dates from the earlier revolt, which was a much more anarchic and bloody affair than the one actually led by Cade.

The historical Cade was probably Irish; he had married into a minor landholding family in KENT (1), and the rebels he led were lesser gentry, artisans, and tradesmen—that is, members of the nascent middle class. Their revolt was intended to achieve well-defined ends that were expressed in a document, the 'Complaint of the Commons of Kent', which demonstrates an informed awareness of real political problems. It refers to the loss of France and subsequent Kentish business losses, and to excessive taxation and the extravagance of the royal household. It complains of the dominance of the Duke of SUFFOLK (3) among the King's councilors, for Suffolk was hated in Kent as an unreasonable and extortionate magnate.

As Cade and his men approached London, in June 1450, they ambushed a party of royal troops and killed the commander, Sir Humphrey STAFFORD (2), and his BROTHER (1), as in the play. At this point, the royal government placed Lord SAY in the Tower of London as a sop to popular sentiment, and fled to the countryside. (Say was a widely detested Kentish landowner and no model aristocrat, as Shakespeare presents him.) On July 4, the people of London welcomed the rebels into the city, and Say was taken from the Tower and executed. After several days, the Kentishmen had seemingly worn out their welcome, for the citizens, aided by the Tower guards under Lord SCALES, who appears in the play, drove them south across the Thames into SOUTHWARK. There, the King's pardon was offered to all who would disperse, and most did. Cade himself did not, and he was pursued and killed by Alexander IDEN, who was the Sheriff of Kent, and not the simple, patriotic landowner of the play.

Shakespeare thus took a real episode from the period of his play and altered its character in order to make certain points. From the prevalent Elizabethan point of view, which Shakespeare shared, Cade and others like him were traitors pure and simple, propagators of vicious and immoral doctrines that could only undermine society. Thus the playwright felt perfectly justified in depicting Cade's undertaking as a more brutal and violent event than it in fact was, for an important point addressed by the history plays is the value of political stability. The distinction between Cade's revolt and the 1381 uprising was unimportant to Shakespeare; each constituted an unacceptable subversion of a properly ordered society.

The episode of Cade, as it is presented, serves three purposes. First, it provides comic relief after the sustained political battle, ending in the murder of GLOUCESTER (4), of Acts 1–3. The buffoonery of Cade and his followers is in an old tradition of comical rusticity that Shakespeare always favoured. However, the humour quickly turns vicious, and the evil of anarchy is abundantly demonstrated, which is the second function of the action. The uncontrolled common people mirror the dissensions of the nobles and demonstrate, conversely Shakespeare's most important political point—that all social good derives from a stable monarchy. Third, the episode is associated with the rise of York and thus serves to introduce the final sequence of the drama, the ambitious advance to open rebellion by that lord. Thus aristocratic ambition is demonstrated to have directly produced tragic disorder among the common people.

**Cadwal** In *Cymbeline,* the false name under which King CYMBELINE'S son ARVIRAGUS is raised from infancy by his kidnapper and foster-father, BELARIUS.

**Caesar (1), Julius (102–44 B.C.)** Historical figure and title character of *Julius Caesar,* ancient Roman political leader assassinated by conspirators led by Marcus BRUTUS (4). Caesar's role is not a large one, but the character dominates the play even after his murder early in Act 3. He is an enigmatic figure, representative of the central theme of the play, the moral ambiguity surrounding his murder. The assassination victim is both a valuable leader and an arrogant tyrant; thus the conspiracy against him seems alternately malevolent and noble.

Caesar is undeniably imperious. When he first appears, in 1.2, surrounded by admiring followers, he is clearly accustomed to command. Irritated by the warning of the SOOTHSAYER (1) to beware the ides of March, he coolly dismisses him. Knowing the outcome, as Shakespeare assumed his audience would, we see immediately that Caesar's self-confidence is misplaced. Caesar's smug sense of power is strikingly evident in his language; he frequently refers to himself with the royal 'we', as in 3.1.8, and sometimes even in the third person, as when he declares his intention to defy bad omens and go the Senate, saying, 'Caesar should be a beast without a heart / If he should stay at home to-day for fear. / No, Caesar shall not. Danger knows full well / That Caesar is more dangerous than he' (2.2.42–45). His wife, CALPHURNIA, warns that his 'wisdom is consum'd in confidence' (2.2.49), and we clearly see that he is ripe for a fall. In the last moments of his life Caesar's arrogance extends almost to blasphemy, as he dismisses all argument with the order, 'Hence! Wilt thou lift up Olympus?' (3.1.74). The assassination, which follows immediately, seems entirely justified.

On the other hand, Caesar is also presented as 'the foremost man of all this world' (4.3.22), as Brutus calls him. He is certainly a strong leader; the only weaknesses attributed to him are physical: some deafness and mild epilepsy (1.2.210, 251) and the poor swimming and susceptibility to illness that CASSIUS complains of in 1.2.99–114, matters so patently unimportant that they tell us more about Cassius' petty envy than they do about Caesar. In 2.1.20–21 Brutus observes that Caesar has never let his emotions alter his judgement, and we learn the value of that judgement when we hear his acute portrayal of Cassius in 1.2. 189–207. The funeral orations of Brutus and ANTONY in 3.2 offer evidence of his virtues, and indeed Cae-

sar's greatness is evident in the respect that almost all the other characters show him.

It may seem odd that a figure killed before the halfway point should be the title character of a play, but it is appropriate here, for Caesar's spirit continues to dominate the action after his death. Not only does Antony's revenge for Caesar's murder provide the plot of the play's second half, but the thought of Caesar recurs repeatedly to Brutus and Cassius as well. Notably, each speaks of Caesar at his death. Moreover, Caesar's arrogance is taken up by Brutus in a subtle demonstration of the psychology of power. The survival of Caesar's spirit is made tangible by the appearance of Caesar's GHOST (2) in 4.3 and at the battle of PHILIPPI (reported by Brutus in 5.5.17–20).

Caesar's greatest importance lies in the action he stimulates, his assassination. The murder of the seemingly tyrannical Caesar triggers a civil war and—as Shakespeare and his audiences were aware—would soon lead to much greater despotism under the Empire of OCTAVIUS, later known as CAESAR (2). Thus Caesar symbolises a social good that is flawed by the potential evil of tyranny, as opposed to the social disruption created by Brutus' ideal of a political world in which no such evil exists.

Shakespeare added salient details to the Caesar he found in his source, PLUTARCH's *Lives,* humanising the leader by inventing physical defects that the historical figure did not have: deafness and poor swimming. He also ascribed to Caesar a concern with superstition in his last days, stressing an intellectual corruption produced by power, in preparation for the audience's sympathetic response to the assassins when the murder is committed. On the other hand, he did omit a number of anecdotes from Plutarch that would have portrayed Caesar too negatively, leaving less room for doubt about the killing. For instance, Caesar is said to have looted a famous temple and to have acquiesced in dishonouring an earlier wife in order to divorce her.

More significantly, Shakespeare followed Plutarch in exaggerating Caesar's real threat to the privileges of the Roman aristocracy that spurred the assassins historically. In fact, modern scholars find, Caesar's policies were surely not directed towards creating a monarchy, as the conspirators—and Plutarch—believed. They were to some extent not directed at all, being largely driven by events.

After his well-known conquests in Gaul and Britain, Caesar had, at the time of the play, recently won a civil war against another Roman political and military leader, Pompey the Great (106–48). As the head of a faction intent on admitting new members to Rome's small ruling class, Caesar had fought a group of conservatives and had more nearly represented the republican ideals later associated with Brutus—in part because of Shakespeare's presentation—than Brutus himself did. He was in no sense a revolutionary, however. In the course of his conflict with Pompey, Caesar had assumed the dictatorship, a legitimate office of the Roman government that carried extensive powers and was temporarily awarded to leading military commanders in times of crisis. Caesar had been dictator briefly in 49 B.C., but this time he had held the dictatorship for several years, using its powers to protect his gains in the civil war. In early 44 B.C. the Senate—which Caesar had greatly enlarged and filled with his followers—declared him dictator for life. This event sealed the conspirators' determination.

It was rumoured that Caesar intended to be crowned and to move the capital to Ilium, a Roman possession in the Near East. However, this was never likely—the ceremony in which he rejected the crown, as reported by CASCA in 1.2, was planned by Caesar expressly to defuse these rumours—and it seems probable that Caesar was more conservative than the nobility feared. He assumed his extraordinary powers because the forces of Pompey's son (the POMPEY [2] of *Antony and Cleopatra*) still threatened him and because he was aware of the threat of assassination. To preserve the government, newly established after years of disorder, Caesar needed dictatorial power to suppress his enemies. He did, however, protect ancient privileges to a considerable degree, resisting pressures from his more radical followers for drastic reforms.

Moreover, Caesar understood the need for a strong ruler to maintain order in a nation that had been disrupted by years of internal strife. He is said (though not by Plutarch) to have anticipated his end, observing that his assassination would produce terrible consequences for Rome; the actual result was the effective elimination of the old Roman aristocracy under the Empire. As Shakespeare felt, although he did not clearly see the underlying historical reality, Caesar's assassination unnecessarily disrupted the Roman state, already weakened by civil wars, and it only led to a much greater tyranny.

**Caesar (2), Octavius (63 B.C.–A.D. 14)** Character in *Antony and Cleopatra*, the successful rival of Mark AN-TONY for control of the government of ROME. (The same figure appears in *Julius Caesar* as OCTAVIUS.) Caesar is to some extent a foil for Antony. He is a coldly ambitious, dispassionate, and manipulative political and military leader whose triumph points up Antony's opposite traits: passion, generosity, and misjudgement. Caesar typically regrets drinking wine at a celebratory banquet, saying 'our graver business / Frowns at this levity' (2.7.118–119). In consequence he is superior to his rivals in action; in war, as CANIDIUS remarks before the battle of ACTIUM, 'this speed of Caesar's / Carries beyond belief' (3.7.74–75). Less attractively, Caesar breaks his treaty with POMPEY (2) and betrays LEPIDUS, while Antony, in contrast, magnanimously forgives ENOBARBUS for deserting. But

whatever else Caesar may be, he is successful. At the outset of *Antony and Cleopatra,* Caesar shares power with Antony and LEPIDUS in the Triumvirate, but in the course of the action he defeats each of them in separate civil wars, and before the play's climax he assumes sole power over Rome's vast territories.

However, Caesar's greatest importance comes in Act 5, after Antony's death, when he is powerfully contrasted with CLEOPATRA. His Roman dedication to power stands in opposition to her vivid appeal to passion as the justification for life. Caesar schemes to prevent Cleopatra's suicide. He treacherously assures her of his goodwill, when in fact he intends to exhibit her in a parade of triumph in Rome and subject her to the ultimate humiliation in order to demonstrate Rome's relentless power and his own strength. Though Cleopatra achieves transcendence in death, Caesar commands the stage at the close of the play and Rome's triumph is finally asserted.

However, Caesar is not simply a villain; he clearly cares for his sister OCTAVIA—though he also uses her as a political pawn when he marries her to Antony—and he is capable of appreciating Antony's virtues. In his first lines, opening 1.4, he declares his admiration for his rival, and in his final tribute to the 'pair so famous' (5.2.358) he recognises the 'strong toil of grace' (5.2.346) that Cleopatra has shown in her noble death. Nevertheless, Caesar is a ruler whose actions are not governed by his emotions; he can understand his opponents sympathetically but he makes them his victims all the same.

As the representative of the growing Roman power, Caesar has a significance that is quite independent of his personal qualities. He declares that his victory will usher in a 'time of universal peace' (4.6.5). In a stroke of dramatic irony, Caesar cannot recognise the implications of this remark, but for the playwright and his original audiences its meaning was both profound and obvious. It refers to the imminent coming of Christ, for Caesar went on to found the Roman Empire, whose establishment of political unity in the Mediterranean world—the *pax romana*—was seen in the 17th century as a manifestation of the will of God, the period of peace that ushered in the coming of the Messiah. Thus, Caesar displays a dignity and majesty that seem to reach beyond the world of the play.

Shakespeare's cold and ambitious ruler seems to correspond fairly closely to the historical Octavius Caesar—who took the title Augustus upon becoming emperor—though it is difficult to be certain as Octavius is known in history from only a few biased accounts, one of which is Shakespeare's source, PLU-TARCH's *Lives.* However, it is noteworthy that the playwright significantly altered the story he read in Plutarch. Shakespeare's Caesar has failings—particularly moral ones—but is nonetheless a singularly potent figure who personally dominates the political and military worlds of the play. However, though undeniably a great leader, Octavius Caesar was highly dependent on his subordinates. Only the most notable of these—AGRIPPA, in the military realm, and MAECENAS, as a diplomat—have even minor roles in *Antony and Cleopatra*. The triumphant warrior of the play was in fact a weak and sickly campaigner; this is alluded to by the embittered Antony in 3.11.35–40, but little is made of it. Shakespeare's aggrandisement of an already grand figure reinforces our sense of Caesar's dignity and majesty in support of the religious aspect of his significance.

**Caius (1)**    Minor character in *Titus Andronicus*. Mentioned only in stage directions, Caius does not speak. He is present for the shooting of arrows to the gods in 4.3, and he helps to capture CHIRON and DEMETRIUS (1) in 5.2.

**Caius (2), Doctor**    Character in *The Merry Wives of Windsor*, a French physician and suitor of ANNE (3) Page. Caius is descended from a traditional stock figure, the blustering, arrogant, and ineffective doctor, although his profession is not important in the play; his bad temper and aggressive nature are exemplified by his explosive reiterations of the expletive 'By gar'—e.g., in 5.5.203–207. Caius is also a stereotypical foreigner, mangling the English language and behaving with notable wrong-headedness. He challenges EVANS (3) to a duel for having attempted to assist SLENDER, a rival for Anne's hand. The duel is averted by a group of townsmen, led by the HOST (2). Caius and Evans then conspire against the Host, arranging to steal his horses. Although Caius' combativeness is generally amusing, this petty vengeance, combined with his vanity, isolates him from the generally mild temper of the play, and it is probably significant that he and Evans, a Welshman, are WINDSOR's only foreigners. Caius is also the only character to withdraw wilfully from the reconciliations in 5.5.

**Caius (3) Ligarius**    Character in *Julius Caesar*. See LIGARIUS.

**Caius (4)**    In *King Lear*, the name adopted by the Earl of KENT (2) as part of his disguise as a yeoman. This Roman name is inappropriate to the pre-Roman Britain in which the play is ostensibly set, but such anachronisms abound in *King Lear* and the playwright doubtless felt that 'Caius' was appropriately antique for the ancient world in which the work is set. However, Kent only uses his alias at the very close of the play, in 5.3.282, where it attracts little notice. Shakespeare may have thought he had used it earlier; the slip would be typical of the many small errors and inconsistencies to which he was inclined.

**Calchas**    Legendary figure and character in *Troilus and Cressida*, the father of CRESSIDA. Calchas, a Trojan priest, has foreseen the defeat of TROY in the TROJAN WAR and has deserted to the Greeks before the play begins. In 3.3.1–29 he proposes a prisoner exchange: the Greeks can repay him for his treason by trading the newly captured Trojan prince ANTENOR for his daughter. Thus Cressida is removed from her lover, TROILUS, just as their affair has begun, and she is exposed to the temptation that leads her to betray Troilus in favour of the Greek warrior DIOMEDES. Aside from triggering this development, Calchas' role in the play is insignificant.

In the *Iliad* of HOMER, Calchas is a Greek prophet who foretells the length of the war. His transformation into a Trojan occurs in the later, pro-Trojan version of the legend that was the basis for the English accounts on which Shakespeare relied.

**Caldwell, Zoë (b. 1933)**    Australian-born British actress. Caldwell was a prominent actress in Australia in her early twenties, when she went to England and played a variety of roles at STRATFORD. Her first major role was as HELENA (2) in Tyrone GUTHRIE's 1959 production of *All's Well That Ends Well*. She has been acclaimed in many other Shakespearean parts, including CORDELIA—opposite Charles LAUGHTON—OPHELIA, LADY (6) MACBETH, and, perhaps most notably, CLEOPATRA.

**Caliban**    Character in *The Tempest*, the beastlike slave of the magician PROSPERO. Before the time of the play, Prospero and his daughter MIRANDA took Caliban, the illegitimate son of a witch and a devil, into their home and taught him to speak and function as a human, but his response was to attempt to rape the girl. In the course of the play he and STEPHANO (2) attempt to murder Prospero. Though Caliban is powerless to effect his schemes, his villainous nature is an important element in *The Tempest*'s scheme of things. At the play's close a chastened Caliban declares, 'I'll be wise hereafter, / And seek for grace' (5.1.294–295) as part of the general reconciliation engineered by Prospero.

Caliban is only partly human. He is a 'monster' (2.2.66), a 'moon-calf' (2.2.107), a 'born devil' (4.1.188), and a 'thing of darkness' (5.1.275). Because his father was a devil, Caliban is supernatural like ARIEL, but unlike that airy spirit, he has no supernatural powers. He is more like a debased human than like any other supernatural creature in Shakespeare. He has intelligence enough to learn language, but he is seemingly incapable of moral sense; reminded of his attempted rape, he merely asserts his animal drive to procreate. Caliban serves as a foil for the other characters: his foolish credulity in accepting Stephano as a god contrasts with Prospero's wisdom, his viciousness with Miranda's innocence, his amorality with the honourable love of FERDINAND (2), and, most significantly, his finally regenerate state with the intransigent evil of ANTONIO (5).

Caliban's human qualities illuminate another of the play's themes and, in doing so, shed light on Shakespeare's world, which was just becoming aware of the natives of America (see EPENOW). As Prospero's 'slave' (1.2.310) Caliban is linked with America; his mother's god, Setebos, was known by Shakespeare as a South American deity; in finding Stephano divine and in responding greedily to his liquor, Caliban behaves like the American natives of early explorers' accounts.

The discovery of native American societies in the early 17th century stimulated debate on an ancient question: is 'natural man' a savage whose life is governed only by animal drives, or is he in a blessed state, unspoiled by the manifold corruptions of civilisation? Although the idealism of the latter view is reflected in GONZALO's praise of primitive society in 2.1.143–164 (drawn from remarks on America by the French essayist MONTAIGNE), Caliban's nature contradicts it. He represents 'natural man', but his very name, an anagram of 'canibal' (a legitimate 17th-century spelling of 'cannibal'), lends a negative quality to the connection.

It is precisely his naturalness that condemns Caliban. He is confined to brute slavery because he has refused to accept a civil role in Prospero's household. Prospero says that 'on [his] nature / Nurture can never stick' (4.1.188–189). In a telling comparison, Caliban's resistance to his wood-carrying chores is contrasted with Ferdinand's philosophical delight in similar labours. The young man knows that 'some kinds of baseness / Are nobly undergone; and most poor matters / Point to rich ends' (3.1.2–4). Miranda expressly judges both Ferdinand and Caliban: the first is 'a thing divine' (4.1.421), the second, 'a thing most brutish' (1.2.358).

Yet Caliban has some positive attributes, which qualify Shakespeare's condemnation of 'natural man'. Though he proclaims that his education has merely taught him 'how to curse' (1.2.366), his use of language is in fact quite impressive, and he rises to lyrical poetry—revealing an aesthetic sensibility—in describing his dreams of 'a thousand twangling instruments' (3.2.135). He can imagine a level below himself to which he does not want to descend, for he fears he and his companions will be 'turn'd to barnacles, or to apes / With foreheads villainous low' (4.1.248–249). Though he is foolish enough to follow Stephano and TRINCULO, he is more sensible than they and scorns their frivolous absorption with mere 'luggage' (4.1.231). His proposed revolt is both repulsive and ineffectual, but Caliban's dislike for his enslavement is one with which we instinctively sympathise. His initial statement of grievance is compelling; he helped Prospero and Miranda survive and is now enslaved. Only then do we learn of his crime, but even afterwards,

Caliban is permitted his say on his status: his elaborate complaint of Prospero's harassment in 2.2.1–14 casts his master in a bad light, and his comical enthusiasm for 'Freedom, high-day! high-day, freedom! freedom, high-day, freedom!' (2.2.186–187) is infectious.

For all his villainy, Caliban contributes to the general sense of regeneration with which the play closes. He recognises his folly and expresses his intention to improve himself in a religious metaphor—he will 'seek for grace' (5.1.295). His earlier behaviour certainly makes us wonder if reform is really possible, but Shakespeare pointedly elevates this beastlike character's moral stature before he exits forever. However appalling Caliban's fallen state, he offers the hope for restoration to grace that is part of Shakespeare's sense of human possibility.

**Calphurnia (Calpurnia) (active 59–44 B.C.)**  Historical figure and character in *Julius Caesar*, the wife of CAESAR (1). In 2.2 Calphurnia, alarmed by accounts of dire omens, begs Caesar not to attend the Senate session on the Ides of March. She asserts that his 'wisdom is consum'd in confidence' (2.2.49) and prevails on him to stay home. However, her work is immediately undone by DECIUS, and Caesar goes to his death. The episode demonstrates Calphurnia's devotion to her mighty husband and casts a softer light on him than we would otherwise have. Further, it reminds us that his assassination was a domestic tragedy as well as a political event, thus humanising the play's account of murderous intrigue and civil war.

Caesar married the historical Calpurnia—as her name was spelled in Latin—in 59 B.C. to cement a political alliance with her father. Although Caesar was blatantly unfaithful and came close to divorcing her a few years later in order to make another political marriage, Calpurnia was thought by contemporaries to have been a genuinely devoted wife; the tale of her entreaty, as reported in Shakespeare's source, PLUTARCH's *Lives,* is probably true. After the assassination, Calpurnia assisted Mark ANTONY's campaign against the conspirators by turning over to him Caesar's papers and a large amount of cash. Little else is known of her life.

The spelling Calphurnia, though less familiar than Calpurnia and incorrect in Latin, is increasingly used by modern editors, restoring the style of the FIRST FOLIO (1623), which is also followed by most of Shakespeare's contemporaries in other writings about Caesar. (In Shakespeare's source, NORTH's English translation of Plutarch, both forms are used.) In the 18th century, editors of Shakespeare chose to revert to the Latin form, establishing a different tradition.

**Calvert, Charles (1828–1879)**  British theatrical producer. Calvert was a follower of Samuel PHELPS in restoring Shakespeare's texts and simplifying productions. After a career as an actor, he became the manager of a theatre in Manchester, England, where he established his reputation as a producer. From 1864 to 1875 he staged many revivals of Shakespeare plays in London, focussing on works that were traditionally less frequently performed, such as *2 Henry IV* and *Henry VIII*, but also presenting popular pieces like *Richard III* and *The Merchant of Venice* (the latter in 1871 with music by Arthur SULLIVAN [1]). However, his theatre was not financially successful, and he returned to touring at the close of his career.

**Cambio**   In *The Taming of the Shrew*, the name LUCENTIO takes when disguised as a scholar of languages in order to be appointed tutor to BIANCA (1).

**Cambridge, Richard York, Earl of (1376–1415)** Historical figure and character in *Henry V*, a traitor who plans to assassinate King HENRY V but is foiled and condemned to death. In 2.2 Henry, who knows of the intended treason, asks Cambridge and his co-conspirators, Lord SCROOP (1) and Sir Thomas GREY (3), how to deal with a drunken soldier who has spoken against him. They all insist that Henry be firm against any hint of disloyalty. Then Henry reveals his knowledge of their treason and applies their own advice, denying them clemency and sentencing them to death. Cambridge, who has no distinctive personality, welcomes death with conventional remorse, as do the others, in a passage intended to emphasise Henry's godlike majesty.

The historical Cambridge benefited from Henry's benevolence, for the King had restored his older brother to the dukedom of YORK (5), despite his history of rebellion against HENRY IV, and had elevated Cambridge to his earldom. However, the Earl firmly opposed Henry IV's usurpation of the throne from RICHARD II, and he continued to rebel. In *Henry V* French gold alone motivates the traitors, although in 2.2.155–157 Cambridge observes that he wants the cash for a purpose that Shakespeare did not specify because he wished his audience to focus on Henry's enemies in France. The historical traitors, however, planned to replace Henry on the throne with Edmund MORTIMER (1), Cambridge's brother-in-law, whose father was held to have been the rightful heir to Richard II. Mortimer himself was loyal and turned in the conspirators, which Shakespeare does not mention, but his claim to the throne was revived by Cambridge's son, the Duke of YORK (8) of the *Henry VI* plays, and the WARS OF THE ROSES ensued as a result. Thus this minor scene in *Henry V* carries the germ of future English disasters, as many people in Shakespeare's original audiences will have recognised.

**Camden, William (1551–1623)**   English historian, author of a minor source for *Coriolanus*. Camden, a noted educator, scholar, and antiquarian, wrote a massive Latin work on ancient and medieval England, *Britannia* (1586). An English translation by Philemon HOLLAND (4) came out in 1610, but English excerpts had already been published in *Remaines of a greater Worke concerning Britaine* in 1605. From the *Remaines*, Shakespeare took some details for MENENIUS' famous 'belly speech' (*Coriolanus*, 1.1.95–159). The *Remaines* also contains an appreciation of Shakespeare as one of England's greatest writers.

Camden was a longtime secondary school teacher and headmaster, who taught poetry composition to Ben JONSON, among others. He remained a lifelong friend of Jonson and through him may have known Shakespeare personally. He was also a noted authority on heraldry and the chief founder of the Society of Antiquaries, an important intellectual institution of the day. In addition to *Britannia*, Camden wrote a Latin history of the reign of Queen ELIZABETH (1) and an English account of the Gunpowder Plot (see GARNET).

**Camillo**   Character in *The Winter's Tale*, an adviser of King LEONTES of SICILIA. The mad Leontes suspects his best friend, King POLIXENES of BOHEMIA, of committing adultery with his wife, and in 1.2 he orders Camillo to poison Polixenes. Instead, Camillo informs Polixenes and flees with him to Bohemia. Camillo reappears there in the second half of the play, set 16 years later. He has been a faithful adviser to Polixenes, and in 4.4 he helps the king thwart the romance between Prince FLORIZEL and a shepherd girl, PERDITA. However, he then helps the couple flee to Sicilia, where it is discovered that Perdita is the lost daughter of Leontes, and the play ends in an atmosphere of general reconciliation and love.

Camillo represents a familiar character type in the romantic literature on which *The Winter's Tale* is based: the servant who aids his master by disobeying him. As such, he is one of the good people who fight the evil that infects the play's world. Only providence, supported by the power of love, can bring the play's characters through to the happy ending, but human agency, chiefly that of Camillo and PAULINA, is an important auxiliary. Thus, Camillo supports a major theme of the play, that humanity must energetically use its capacity for good. Fittingly, he becomes engaged to Paulina, by royal command, at the play's close.

**Campeius, Cardinal Laurence (Lorenzo Campeggio, 1472–1539)**   Historical figure and minor character in *Henry VIII*, the pope's ambassador to the court of King HENRY VIII. Campeius comes to England to consider the legality of Henry's proposed divorce of Queen KATHERINE; Cardinal WOLSEY has assured the king that Campeius will rule in his favour, but in 2.4 the Roman cardinal merely postpones a decision. Irritated, Henry complains, 'These cardinals trifle with me: I abhor / This dilatory sloth and tricks of Rome' (2.4.234–235). Here—as throughout—Campeius embodies the untrustworthiness of Catholicism from the play's point of view. The episode also demonstrates Henry's growing mistrust of Wolsey, as he moves from gullibility to wisdom, a principal theme of the play. In 3.2 Campeius is said to have 'stolen away to Rome . . . / [having] left the cause o'th'king unhandled' (3.2.57–58).

The historical Campeggio—Shakespeare uses the Latin form of his name—was responsible for English affairs at the Vatican and had visited England before he arrived to adjudicate Henry's divorce in 1528. In fact, Henry had appointed him absentee Bishop of Salisbury in 1524. Unknown to Wolsey, he was under instructions to delay Henry's divorce as long as possible, for the pope did not want to offend the Holy Roman Emperor, Queen Katherine's nephew. He succeeded in postponing the trial for nine months and then, when it seemed likely that Henry would win his case, he declared an adjournment and left for Rome. Henry eventually declared himself divorced when he assumed papal powers in England as part of the Reformation, and at that time Campeggio lost his English bishopric.

**Canidius (Camidius) (Publius Canidius Crassus, d. 30 B.C.)**  Historical figure and character in *Antony and Cleopatra*, a general in ANTONY's army. Canidius appears only briefly, in 3.7 where he objects to Antony's decision to fight CAESAR (2) at sea, and in 3.10 where he declares that he will surrender his troops to Caesar after Antony has lost the battle of ACTIUM. Antony's power and authority waned due to the influence of CLEOPATRA, and his followers lost their faith in his success. The character Canidius demonstrates this.

The historical Canidius was in fact the only major figure among Antony's followers to stay with him to the bitter end. He fled after Actium and made his way back to ALEXANDRIA, where he was captured and executed upon his leader's final defeat and death. Shakespeare's source, PLUTARCH's *Lives*, was based on an anti-Antony source (see MESSALA), and modern scholars believe that Canidius' impressive record as a hardy and loyal officer makes Plutarch's interpretation of his actions unlikely.

**Canon**  An authoritative list of the works of an author. The canon of Shakespeare's plays varies slightly according to the opinions of various scholars, but it usually includes 38 titles: the 36 plays of the FIRST FOLIO, plus *Pericles* and *The Two Noble Kinsmen*. However, some scholars doubt the Folio's reliability, especially with regard to *Henry VIII*—perhaps written in part by John FLETCHER (2)—while others often. relegate *Pericles* or *The Two Noble Kinsmen*—especially the latter—to the APOCRYPHA, a list of dubious titles. Other titles are also occasionally disputed.

This book assumes that the canon consists of the 38 plays specified above; i.e., in alphabetical order: *All's Well That Ends Well, Antony and Cleopatra, As You Like It, The Comedy of Errors, Coriolanus, Cymbeline, Hamlet, 1 & 2 Henry IV, Henry V, 1, 2, & 3 Henry VI, Henry VIII, Julius Caesar, King John, King Lear, Love's Labour's Lost, Macbeth, Measure for Measure, The Merchant of Venice, The Merry Wives of Windsor, A Midsummer Night's Dream, Much Ado About Nothing, Othello, Pericles, Richard II, Richard III, Romeo and Juliet, The Taming of the Shrew, The Tempest, Timon of Athens, Titus Andronicus, Troilus and Cressida, Twelfth Night, The Two Gentlemen of Verona, The Two Noble Kinsmen,* and *The Winter's Tale.*

In Shakespeare studies, the term 'canon' often applies only to the plays. However, a broader usage, equally correct, would also include the 154 SONNETS (though a few of them are disputed), the long poems *Venus and Adonis* and *The Rape of Lucrece*, and various shorter poems, including *The Phoenix and Turtle,* some of the works in THE PASSIONATE PILGRIM, and some EPITAPHS (though other epitaphs are clearly apocryphal). Other poems are sometimes suggested for the canon, e.g., 'SHALL I DIE?'; scholars periodically nominate new discoveries for inclusion, and disputes over the correct list can last for decades without resolution.

**Canterbury (1), Henry Chichele, Archbishop of, (1362–1443)**  Historical figure and character in *Henry V* who gives King HENRY V a rationale for going to war with FRANCE (1). In 1.1 Canterbury, speaking with the Bishop of ELY (2), expresses his hope that a state of war—especially when supported by the large donation he has offered the King—will divert the introduction of legislation requiring a vast state seizure of church property. In 1.2 he presents the King with a long, legalistic argument in support of his hereditary claim to the French crown, and he joins others in encouraging a conquest of France.

Shakespeare's portrayal of Canterbury is flawed, though only because his sources were. The historical Henry Chichele did not become Archbishop until some time after the war began; until then he was Henry's ambassador to France. Shakespeare followed HALL (2) in this error. More significantly, the church was not particularly instrumental in promoting the war, and the Archbishop's motives, although Shakespeare took them from HOLINSHED, are unhistorical. In fact, although the legislation to seize church property had been proposed under King HENRY IV (as Canterbury observes in 1.1.2–3), it was not reintroduced under Henry V. Thus the church had no reason to promote the war, and, although it contributed to the King's war fund, as was customary, its donation was not exceptionally great, as it is in the play.

**Canterbury (2), Archbishop of, Thomas Cranmer** Character in *Henry VIII*. See CRANMER.

**Capell, Edward (1713–1781)** Shakespearean scholar. Capell was the first scholar to collate the old editions of Shakespeare's plays to arrive at the most accurately rendered texts possible, and he also introduced the first serious scholarly consideration of Shakespeare's sources. After 24 years of labour, his edition of the collected plays was published in 1768. His *Commentary, Notes and Various Readings to Shakespeare*, begun in 1774, was published posthumously in 1783. Though his judgements are still acclaimed today, he is very little read except by specialists, in part because of his tedious prose. As Samuel JOHNSON (7) put it, 'he doth gabble monstrously'.

**Caphis** Minor character in *Timon of Athens*, servant of a SENATOR (4). In 2.1 the Senator sends Caphis to collect a debt from TIMON, who he fears will soon be bankrupt. The servant barely speaks and serves simply as a vehicle for the Senator's greed. In 2.2 he joins other servants in asking Timon for payment on their masters' behalf.

**Capilet** See WIDOW (2).

**Captain (1)** Minor character in *Titus Andronicus*, the officer who announces the arrival of TITUS (1) Andronicus in 1.1 and praises his virtues as a general.

**Captain (2)** Minor character in *1 Henry VI*, an English officer. When TALBOT is invited to visit the Countess of AUVERGNE, in 2.2, he rightly suspects a trap and confers with the Captain. Though he is not seen in 2.3, the Captain is presumably responsible for the troop of soldiers who immediately free Talbot when the trap is sprung.

The same character (or perhaps a different Captain) challenges the cowardly FASTOLFE, who is fleeing from the battle in 3.2. And, in 4.4, a Captain precedes Sir William LUCY (2) in seeking reinforcements from the Duke of SOMERSET (3).

**Captain (3)** Character in *2 Henry VI*. Some editions, following the CONTENTION, or BAD QUARTO, assign this rank to the LIEUTENANT (1), who appears in 4.1. This small difference presumably resulted from an actor or viewer's assumption that the leader of the pirates would be called their captain. The Quarto presents a reconstruction of the play from memory, while the Lieutenant's rank in the FIRST FOLIO edition and its successors is believed to come from the original manuscript.

**Captain (4)** Minor character in *Richard II*, the Welsh commander of troops who desert the cause of RICHARD II in 2.4, after the King has not appeared for many days. The Captain tells of rumours that Richard has died and cites menacing omens that seem to substantiate them. Shakespeare may have associated the Captain with Owen GLENDOWER, who is mentioned in 3.1.43.

**Captain (5)** Minor character in *Twelfth Night*, the rescuer of VIOLA. After saving Viola from a shipwreck, the Captain offers her hope that her brother may also have been saved, thereby establishing that SEBASTIAN (2) will eventually appear. The Captain goes on to direct Viola's attention to the court of Duke ORSINO, which she determines to visit, disguised as a man. Unlike ANTONIO (4), who saves Sebastian, the Captain is not a salty mariner; oddly, he is something of a gentleman, speaking familiarly of the duke's affairs and quoting an image from OVID (1.1.15). Otherwise the Captain has no real personality; he simply introduces developments and indicates by his attitude that Viola is an attractive heroine.

**Captain (6)** Minor character in *Hamlet*, an officer in the Norwegian army of Prince FORTINBRAS. In 4.4 the Captain tells HAMLET of Fortinbras' march with 20,000 soldiers to conquer a small, valueless parcel of land in Poland. Shakespeare may take an ironical stance towards the folly of war in these brief and straightforward lines, but Hamlet seems to accept Fortinbras' goal as reasonable, responding to the Captain's account only by comparing his own scruples and hesitations with the unthinking commitment of the soldiers, who will die fighting for so small a prize. Thus the incident emphasises Hamlet's concern with his failure to avenge his father's death—the central strand of the play's plot—and reminds us of Fortinbras' strength, which will assume greater importance at the end of the play.

**Captain (7)** Character in *King Lear*. See OFFICER (5).

**Captain (8) (Sergeant)** Minor character in *Macbeth*, a wounded soldier who describes the brave MACBETH's achievements in battle against the rebels who oppose King DUNCAN. In 1.2 the Captain offers an image of Macbeth as an hero, and the shock of Macbeth's later treason is the greater because this initial image is shattered. The effect is furthered by the Captain's considerable dignity; he speaks in measured rhetorical cadences and his own suffering is bravely suppressed until he closes touchingly with, 'But I am faint, my gashes cry for help' (1.2.43). He is not seen further, however, being important only as a commentator on the opening situation.

Some modern editors note that the Captain is referred to by MALCOLM as 'the Sergeant' in 1.2.3 and designate him with that rank in the stage directions and speech headings. However, he is called 'Captain' in those places in the first edition of the play, in the FIRST FOLIO (1623), and other editors retain this designation. It is supposed that 'Sergeant' refers to the character's function as a valued but not high-ranking subordinate.

**Captain (9)**   Minor character in *Antony and Cleopatra*, an officer in ANTONY's army. In 4.4 the Captain greets Antony cheerfully on the morning of a battle, listens to his leader's parting remarks to CLEOPATRA, and leaves with him. His function is to add a note of martial bustle to the scene. In the first edition of the play, in the FIRST FOLIO, this character was designated as ALEXAS, but this reflects an error—probably Shakespeare's—for in 4.6.12–16 we learn of Alexas' earlier treason and execution. Nicholas ROWE altered the designation and assigned the Captain his rank in the 1709 edition of the plays, and all subsequent editors have accepted the change.

**Captain (10)**   Minor character in *Cymbeline*, an officer in the Roman army. In 4.2 the Captain reports to LUCIUS (4) that the army has landed in WALES (1). His six terse lines serve to convey information that moves the plot to a new stage.

**Captain (11)**   Either of two minor characters in *Cymbeline*, officers in the British army. In 5.3 after the British victory over the Romans that is described by POSTHUMUS earlier in the scene, the Captains discover Posthumus in his Roman uniform and take him prisoner. They turn him over to King CYMBELINE in a DUMB SHOW that ends the scene. With only a few lines between them, the Captains' function is to further the plot. However, they also inform the audience that in addition to the heroes BELARIUS, GUIDERIUS, and ARVIRAGUS—already described by Posthumus—there was a fourth. This leads us to guess that this man was Posthumus himself, which proves to be the case.

**Capuchius (Capucius), Lord (Eustace Chapuys, active 1530s)**   Historical figure and minor character in *Henry VIII*, ambassador to England from the Holy Roman Empire, a visitor to Queen KATHERINE. In 4.2 Capuchius bears a message from King HENRY VIII wishing good health to the dying Katherine. She observes mildly that the gesture comes too late. She asks Capuchius to take the king a letter, in which she requests that he look after their daughter—and remember her to the child—and treat her followers and servants well. She then retires to die. The episode, which Shakespeare knew from his source, HOLINSHED's *Chronicles*, offers a final demonstration of Katherine's virtue.

Following Holinshed, Shakespeare used the Latin form of the ambassador's name. Chapuys' surviving official correspondence casts light on the intrigues of the period. One letter declares that Cardinal WOLSEY had written to him recommending that the pope excommunicate King Henry and use arms to enforce Catholicism in England. In an unrelated treason trial of 1533, it was alleged that Chapuys had planned an invasion of England in support of Katherine, but that the emperor had vetoed the idea. This may not have been taken seriously, because Chapuys continued in his post and, as we have seen, was permitted to visit Katherine.

**Capulet (1)**   Character in *Romeo and Juliet*, the father of JULIET (1) and the head of the family bearing his name, rivals to the MONTAGUE (1) clan. Though short-tempered, Capulet at first seems benevolent: he resists the marriage proposal by PARIS (2) in 1.2, observing that Juliet is too young, and in 1.5 he orders TYBALT to leave the banquet rather than fight ROMEO. However, in 3.4 he suddenly decides to give Juliet, by now secretly married to Romeo, to Paris and rages furiously at his daughter when she resists; he belongs to the conventional, unfeeling world that opposes the lovers. When he impulsively moves the wedding date up by a day (4.2), Capulet becomes an agent of fate, hastening the play's tragic climax. His humorous involvement in the wedding preparations does not restore him to our affections, nor does his cursory and somewhat stilted mourning when he believes the drugged Juliet to be dead. Only at the end of the play, when his daughter's actual death impels him to seek a reconciliation with Montague, can we again find him humanly sympathetic.

The feud between the Capulets and the Montagues did not in fact occur, although Shakespeare and his sources believed it to have been real. See VERONA.

**Capulet (2), Cousin**   Minor character in *Romeo and Juliet*, an aged relative of CAPULET (1). Cousin Capulet (called 'Old Man' in some editions) speaks only two lines in a brief conversation, at the feast in 1.5, on the rapid flight of the years. This episode, occurring just as ROMEO and JULIET (1) are about to meet, is one instance of the motif of time's passage, which recurs throughout the tragedy.

**Capulet (3), Lady**   Character in *Romeo and Juliet*, mother of JULIET (1) and wife of CAPULET (1). Desiring the marriage of Juliet to PARIS (2), Lady Capulet is curt, imperious, and coldly unsympathetic to her daughter's qualms, even without knowing that they stem from her passion for Romeo; she is a representative of the conventional world that opposes the young lovers. Her grief in 4.5, when she believes the drugged Juliet is dead, elicits our sympathy, but we may remember her enraged demands for revenge on Tybalt's murderer in 3.1. She does not speak in the final scene of reconciliation.

**Cardenio** Lost play, possibly written by Shakespeare and John FLETCHER (2). In 1613 the KING'S MEN twice performed a play recorded as *Cardenno* or *Cardenna*. In 1653 the manuscript collector and publisher Humphrey MOSELEY claimed the copyright on an old play, *The History of Cardennio*, said to be by Shakespeare and Fletcher, but his copy did not survive. In 1727 Lewis THEOBALD produced a drama titled *Double Falsehood* (published 1728), which he asserted he had adapted from an unpublished play manuscript by Shakespeare. This play derives from a story in Miguel de CERVANTES' *Don Quixote*, whose hero is named Cardenio. Theobald wrote that he owned three manuscript copies of the play, but they subsequently disappeared, and when he published his edition of Shakespeare's plays in 1733, he did not include this one. Moreover, scholars agree that the play, at least in Theobald's version, is very un-Shakespearean. It is speculated that the King's Men's play of 1613 was passed on, in a corrupt form, as far as Theobald, who came to reject its authenticity.

Around 1613 Fletcher and Shakespeare collaborated on *The Two Noble Kinsmen* and possibly *Henry VIII*, so there is nothing unlikely about a third such project. Moreover, a translation of *Don Quixote* was published in 1612. Fletcher used it as a source for later plays, so that his hand in the King's Men's play of 1613 seems likely. However, the play's absence from the FIRST FOLIO (1623) suggests that its editors—King's Men themselves—felt it was not by Shakespeare, either because his part in it was too slight to merit mention or simply because he had nothing to do with it at all.

**Cardinal (1) Beaufort, Henry (1374–1447)** Historical figure and character in *2 Henry VI*, a leader of the plot against the Duke of GLOUCESTER (4) that dominates the first half of the play. The Cardinal, the illegitimate son of John of GAUNT, is a great-uncle of the King and a powerful secular lord in his own right. (The same historical person appeared in *1 Henry VI* as the Bishop of WINCHESTER (1), where his rivalry with Gloucester is developed; he is sometimes referred to in *2 Henry VI* as Winchester—as in 1.1.56.) In 1.1 the Cardinal smoothly recruits other noblemen to his cause, accusing Gloucester, the heir apparent to the throne, of self-interest, turning against him what should be to his credit—his patriotic anger at the King's foolish cession of lands in his marriage contract. The Cardinal and Gloucester agree to fight a duel in 2.1, but they are interrupted. At the end of that scene, word is brought that Gloucester's wife has been arrested for witchcraft, and the Cardinal gloats that his rival, abruptly humiliated, will not have the heart to fight.

When Gloucester himself is arrested for treason, in 3.1, the Cardinal and his confederates agree that the Duke should be murdered, and the Cardinal volunteers to hire the murderer, although SUFFOLK (3) actually performs that deed. After Gloucester's murder, word is brought to the King that the Cardinal is dying of a sudden illness. When the King and WARWICK (3) visit him in 3.3, he appears to have a bad conscience. The Cardinal's ravings are not quite specific but they nonetheless convict him.

Historically, Cardinal Beaufort, although he was in fact a rival of Gloucester, was not his murderer; in fact, Gloucester was probably not murdered at all. The Cardinal may not even have had anything to do with Gloucester's arrest by Suffolk, which led to the Duke's death, for Beaufort by this time had largely abandoned his political role and retired from public life. Shakespeare's version of the Cardinal's death is pure fiction; he actually died at home in a normal manner at the age of 73, some months after Gloucester's death. However, the playwright held the opinion, along with his sources, that 'good Duke Humphrey' had been victimised by his rivals (see WINCHESTER [1]), and he accordingly made an unscrupulous villain, or MACHIAVEL, of the Cardinal, who was actually a far more prudent and statesmanlike figure than Gloucester.

**Cardinal (2), Lord (Thomas Bourchier, c. 1404–1486)** Historical figure and minor character in *Richard III*, the Archbishop of Canterbury. In 3.1 the Cardinal is persuaded by BUCKINGHAM (2) to remove the young Duke of YORK (7) from sanctuary in a church. The historical Bourchier was a politically accommodating prelate who crowned EDWARD IV, RICHARD III, and Henry VII, the RICHMOND of the play.

In some modern editions of the play, the ARCHBISHOP (4) of York is eliminated and his lines are given to the Cardinal, following the 16th-century QUARTO editions. This change was presumably made as an economy for the acting company.

**Cardinal (3) Campeius** Character in *Henry VIII*. See CAMPEIUS.

**Cardinal (4), Pandulph** Character in *King John*. See PANDULPH.

**Cardinal (5) Wolsey** Character in *Henry VIII*. See WOLSEY.

**Carew, Richard (1555–1620)** English scholar and contemporary admirer of Shakespeare. Carew, a country gentleman and self-taught student of languages and early English history, translated poetry from Italian and Spanish and also published his own verse. His major work was a history of Cornwall (1602), but he is remembered today chiefly for a remark in a letter (1603) to William CAMDEN, in which he offered an early assessment of 'Shakespeare', declaring him the equal of Catullus as a poet. The letter was published in the second edition (1614) of Camden's *Remaines*.

**Carey (1), George, Baron Hunsdon**  See HUNSDON (1).

**Carey (2), Henry, Baron Hunsdon**  See HUNSDON (2).

**Carlisle, Thomas Merke, Bishop of (d. 1409)**  Historical figure and character in *Richard II,* a supporter of King RICHARD II. Carlisle accompanies Richard on his return from Ireland to face BOLINGBROKE (1), and he warns the King against inaction, but his speech is equivocal. His ambivalence is immediately emphasised by the Duke of AUMERLE's much more pointed statement of the same warning. Nonetheless, Carlisle is the only defender of Richard in the deposition scene, 4.1. In a formal speech he appeals to the assembled aristocrats not to violate the sanctity of a King, divinely placed on the throne—'What subject can give sentence on his king?' (4.1.121), he asks rhetorically— and he predicts disaster for England if the deposition is carried out. NORTHUMBERLAND (1) promptly arrests him for treason, and he is placed in the custody of the ABBOT of Westminster. At the close of the scene Carlisle joins the Abbot and Aumerle in a plot against Bolingbroke. At the end of the play he is brought before Bolingbroke, now King HENRY IV, who pardons him, referring to his honourable character.

The historical Carlisle was a Benedictine monk who served Richard ably as an administrator and was rewarded with his bishopric as a result. He did not protest Henry's accession; his speech is drawn from accounts of his opposition to a later proposal to try Richard on criminal charges. These accounts may have been invented, however, for they derive from an unreliable, propagandistic tract, probably written by a member of QUEEN (13) Isabel's French household, that was the source for Shakespeare's source, HOLINSHED's *Chronicles.* However, regardless of its historical reality, Carlisle's speech presents an important aspect of Tudor political dogma: the citizenry may not judge its monarch in any way. This idea is emphasised in Holinshed, and it is present throughout the HISTORY PLAYS.

Carlisle did participate in the Abbot's conspiracy, but he was not willingly pardoned by Henry. Tried and convicted, he was dismissed from his see, and his life was spared only by papal intervention.

**Carpenter**  Minor character in *Julius Caesar,* a COMMONER (1). In 1.1 the Carpenter, who speaks one line (1.1.6), is part of a crowd being dispersed by the tribunes FLAVIUS (1) and MARULLUS. He identifies himself by profession, establishing the social class of the group. In some editions the Carpenter is identified as the First Commoner.

**Carrier**  Either of two minor characters in *1 Henry IV,* freight haulers who prepare to take a cargo to LONDON from ROCHESTER in 2.1. The Carriers comically complain about conditions at the inn. They tellingly distrust the highwayman GADSHILL when he asks to borrow a lantern, but they unwittingly supply him with information, commenting that they expect gentlemen carrying valuables to accompany them on the road. At least one of the Carriers is apparently among the TRAVELLERS who are ambushed in 2.2, for he appears in London with the SHERIFF (4) in 2.4, having recognised FALSTAFF during the robbery.

**Casca, Publius Servius (d. 42 B.C.)**  Historical figure and character in *Julius Caesar,* one of the assassins of CAESAR (1). In 1.2 Casca officiously orders the festival crowds to be silent in Caesar's presence, but later he speaks contemptuously to BRUTUS (4) and CASSIUS about Caesar's rejection of the crown and his fit of epilepsy. In addition, he pokes fun at the pedantry of CICERO and his companions, who had remarked on Caesar in Greek; Casca delivers one of Shakespeare's most-quoted lines, 'It was Greek to me' (1.2.281), implying that he scorned to know a foreign language. Brutus calls him a 'blunt fellow' (1.2.292), but Cassius defends him as a bold man, useful in any difficult enterprise. Casca, who is vain, holds the same opinion, saying, 'I will set this foot of mine as far as who goes furthest' (1.3.119–120). However, earlier in the same scene he has shown himself to be cowardly, trembling at reports of dire omens, in telling contrast to Cicero's coolness. Casca is also a hypocrite; in 2.1, as the conspirators hatch their plot, he swiftly reverses his opinion of Cicero in response to Brutus' ('Let us not leave him out' [2.1.143]; 'Indeed he is not fit' [2.1.153]). In 3.1 Casca is the first of the conspirators to stab the defenseless Caesar, although he disappears from the play thereafter. (It has been speculated that Shakespeare discontinued the role at this point in order to free an actor to take the part of OCTAVIUS, who appears somewhat later.)

Little is known about the historical Casca, aside from his participation in Caesar's murder. Shakespeare's source, PLUTARCH, states that he was the first to stab Caesar and that Caesar called him 'vile' or 'vicious' (in different accounts of the assassination), and these two brief mentions are the basis of Shakespeare's fairly elaborate portrait. The playwright omitted two other episodes concerning Casca—that he almost revealed the conspiracy inadvertently and that he was responsible for the brutal killing of prisoners at PHILIPPI—but these inglorious moments doubtless contributed to the playwright's vision of Casca's unpleasant personality. Plutarch does not record Casca's suicide after the battle of Philippi, an honourable end by Roman standards and an episode that might have altered Shakespeare's characterisation.

**Cassandra** Legendary figure and character in *Troilus and Cressida,* a princess of TROY, the daughter of King PRIAM and sister to the princes HECTOR, TROILUS, and PARIS (3). Cassandra, a seer, twice foretells the fall of Troy. First, she hysterically interrupts a council of war to warn, 'Troy burns, or else let Helen go' (2.2.113), only to be dismissed as the victim of 'brain-sick raptures' (2.2.123). In 5.3, in calmer tones, she joins ANDROMACHE and Priam in trying to persuade Hector not to enter battle on a day of ill omens. Rebuffed again, she bids her brother a sad farewell. Although the other characters do not believe her, Cassandra's prophecies contribute to the play's atmosphere of fateful destiny, for they are known by the audience to be ironically correct.

In the *Iliad* of HOMER, Cassandra is a minor figure and not a seer. She first appears as a prophet in Greek literature of the 5th century B.C. According to the dramatist Aeschylus, her prophetic power was given to her by Apollo, but when she refused his love, he transformed it into a curse, causing her to be always disbelieved. This myth has been well known since ancient times, and Shakespeare could presume that his audience would recognise Apollo's curse in the Trojans' rejection of Cassandra's warnings.

**Cassio** Character in *Othello,* a Florentine officer serving under OTHELLO. IAGO is the enemy of both Othello and Cassio because Cassio has been appointed Othello's lieutenant, a post Iago had coveted for himself. Iago gets Cassio drunk and incites RODERIGO to fight him; the lieutenant disgraces himself by brawling drunkenly while on guard duty and is demoted. More important, Iago convinces Othello that his wife, DESDEMONA, is Cassio's lover, going so far as to plant on Cassio a handkerchief that Othello has given Desdemona. The enraged general commissions Iago to kill Cassio, and Iago again employs Roderigo. However, Cassio survives the attack and testifies against Iago in the play's closing moments.

The change in Othello's attitude towards Cassio is paralleled by Cassio's change towards Iago. Before his disgrace, Cassio is distant and refuses to be friendly with Iago, as we see at the beginning of 2.3. However, when Iago befriends him after he is discharged by Othello he accepts him entirely. He calls him 'honest Iago' (2.3.326) and says, 'I never knew / A Florentine more kind and honest' (3.1.40–41). He is grateful for what seems like excellent advice from Iago to ally himself with Desdemona. Though this is to have disastrous consequences, Cassio does not see through Iago until much too late, after the villain is exposed in the wake of Desdemona's murder.

Cassio's relationship with BIANCA (2), a courtesan of CYPRUS is another echo of the main plot. Though they are not married we compare them with Othello and Desdemona, partially because Iago employs the unwitting Bianca in deceiving Othello about the handkerchief, in 4.1. More pointedly, though Bianca is jealous on Cassio's account—just as Othello is on Desdemona's—Cassio disdains her, in striking contrast to Desdemona's intense love for Othello. Cassio's tawdry affair casts light on the nature of Othello's blessed but rejected marriage.

Cassio's relationship with Bianca and his account of it to Iago, in 4.1, reflect the worldliness of a professional soldier, accustomed to finding women wherever he is stationed. As a competent soldier, he is respected and valued by Othello before Iago's poison begins its work. We see this in his appointment as lieutenant, and in the general's easy conversational tone as Cassio assumes guard duty, in 2.3. The lieutenant is apparently a gentleman, and he has enough learning to be mocked by Iago for his 'bookish theoric' (1.1.24). In 2.1.61–87 he expresses his reverence for Desdemona in courtly formal rhetoric that reflects his respect for Othello as well, establishing clearly an aura of gentlemanly honour and stately virtue.

On the other hand, while Cassio's soldierly dignity helps stress the vulgarity of Iago, he is often without that dignity, being drunk in 2.3 and awkwardly humiliated most of the time after that. Though his remorse at his irresponsibility is genuine and honourable—he regrets having 'deceive[d] so good a commander, with so light, so drunken, and indiscreet an officer' (2.3. 269–271)—he is nevertheless somewhat ridiculous: he foolishly drinks wine he doesn't want and then quickly falls into Iago's next trap. His speech is often ludicrously high-flown; he declares, 'O thou invisible spirit of wine, if thou hast no name to be known by, let us call thee devil!' (2.3.273–275).

Yet Cassio 'has a daily beauty in his life' (5.1.19) that stirs Iago's envy, and his reputation and dignity are restored by the end of the play. He is given the command of Cyprus, and he shows a quiet assurance in insisting to Othello, 'Dear general, I did never give you cause' (5.2.300). At the close it is fitting that Cassio is the only person to recognise the grandeur of the suicidal general, declaring 'This did I fear, . . . For he was great of heart' (5.2.361–362).

**Cassius (Caius Cassius Longinus) (d. 42 B.C.)** Historical figure and character in *Julius Caesar,* one of the assassins of CAESAR (1) and, with BRUTUS (4), a leader of the forces opposing Mark ANTONY in the subsequent civil war. Cassius presents two quite different aspects in the course of the play. He first appears as a cynical, unscrupulous conspirator whose scheming stresses the evil side of political ambition. However, he later proves to be a courageous fighter, a sensible general, and a friend to Brutus. Cassius can thus be seen as a foil for Brutus and *his* two sides, first as a noble conspirator and then as an increasingly imperious leader; further, Cassius' two faces reinforce the play's insistence that the qualities that make up a political leader result from the continuous interaction of good and evil.

Prior to Caesar's murder, Cassius is bitterly envious of his power, and his diatribes against his leader in 1.2 and 1.3 are hysterically petty. Although it is typical of Brutus that he does not recognise Cassius for what he is, Caesar analyses him with great perceptiveness in his famous remarks on his enemy's 'lean and hungry look. . . . Such men as he be never at heart's ease / Whiles they behold a greater than themselves, / And therefore are they very dangerous' (1.2.191, 205–207).

Cassius knows that Brutus' sense of honour makes him susceptible to manipulation, and his soliloquy at the close of 1.2 reveals his intention to seduce Brutus into leading the conspiracy against Caesar. This speech presents Cassius as a MACHIAVEL, the typical political villain of ELIZABETHAN DRAMA. It also pointedly contrasts Cassius' cynical scheming with Brutus' honourable motives (though these are seriously questioned elsewhere), and it thus establishes two possible points of view towards the assassination of Caesar.

Cassius has an unstable personality. He rages over trifles like Caesar's poor swimming and susceptibility to illness (1.2.99–130). During the assassination, he loses his nerve and Brutus has to reassure him that POPILIUS does not know of their plot. In 5.1.71–89 he wavers in the face of unfavourable omens before PHILIPPI. His weakness had great consequences, for it causes him to give in to Brutus' insistence that Antony should be spared and then permitted to speak at Caesar's funeral. Later, he similarly accedes to Brutus' strategy at Philippi with equally catastrophic results. Cassius' death at Philippi, when he too hastily believes a report of defeat, reflects this character flaw; a stronger man would have resisted longer.

However, in Acts 4 and 5 Cassius is generally a finer figure than he is before the assassination. He is an experienced and sensible general, although he permits himself to be overruled, and he attracts the loyalty and admiration of his officers. He displays a touching affection for Brutus, especially when he learns of his friend's grief over the death of PORTIA (2), and he generously forgives Brutus his fatal errors. When they exchange farewells before the battle, in 5.1.116–122, their mutual affection rings true, reflecting Shakespeare's constant inclination to believe that people are not wholly bad.

The historical Cassius was noted in his own day for his violent temper and sarcastic speech, as is reflected in Shakespeare's source, PLUTARCH's Lives, and other ancient documents. Before the time of the play, Cassius had fought against Caesar in an earlier civil war, and Caesar had forgiven him. He apparently originated the plot against Caesar; his motives are unclear, though Shakespeare followed Plutarch's contention that his private dislike for Caesar stimulated his public hatred of tyranny. Shakespeare's account of Cassius' death at Philippi is also accurately retold from Plutarch. However, other sources indicate that Brutus and Cassius did not disagree on the decision to march to Philippi; their forces were supported by the local population, while Antony and OCTAVIUS were short of supplies. The loss of Cassius was decisive. Shakespeare compressed two battles of Philippi, which actually occurred 20 days apart, into one; it is thought that Cassius, a more experienced general than Brutus, would not have fought the second one, in which the forces of Caesar's assassins were finally defeated.

**Casson, Lewis (1875–1969)** British actor and producer. After a successful career as an actor, Casson turned to production and was especially known for staging ancient Greek drama and Shakespeare, usually in collaboration with his wife, the actress Sybil THORNDIKE. Particularly noteworthy was his 1938 production of Coriolanus, starring Thorndike and Laurence OLIVIER, which is widely credited for establishing the play's place in the British theatrical repertory.

**Cardinal (4) Pandulph** Character in King John. See PANDULPH.

**Castelnuovo-Tedesco, Mario (1895–1968)** Italian composer with a particular interest in Shakespeare. Castelnuovo-Tedesco wrote music in a variety of forms, and was the composer of five operas, two of them based on Shakespeare's plays—All's Well That Ends Well (1958) and The Merchant of Venice (1961). He also wrote overtures to five more of the plays and settings for all of the SONGS. After 1938 the composer lived in Hollywood, where he wrote music for numerous films.

**Castiglione, Baldassare (1478–1529)** Italian writer and diplomat, author of Il Libro del Cortegiano (The Book of the Courtier, 1528), a possible influence on Much Ado About Nothing. Castiglione, a nobleman of MANTUA, was a highly successful diplomat, serving the Montefeltro family, dukes of Urbino. When they were dispossessed of their dukedom by the pope in 1516, Castiglione returned to Mantua and served as the city's envoy to Rome. His famous book, on which he worked for 20 years, is one of the most important documents of the Italian RENAISSANCE. In it he describes an ideal courtly society, set in the ducal court of Urbino, renowned in his day as one of the most artistic and intellectually accomplished courts of Europe. Castiglione's vision of excellence included the idea—revolutionary at the time—that women have much to contribute to society. To illustrate this point, he composed a series of sprightly debates between a man and a woman that may well have inspired the battles of wit between BEA-

TRICE and BENEDICK in *Much Ado. Il Libro del Cortegiano* was translated into English by Sir Thomas HOBY (1), appearing in 1561 as *The Courtyer*. Shakespeare may have read Castiglione in Italian, however.

**Catesby, Sir William (d. 1485)** Historical figure and character in *Richard III*, a follower of King RICHARD III. Catesby is a useful underling who appears in many scenes, mostly as a messenger, and he lacks a distinct personality. The historical Catesby was a lawyer who served as estate manager for Lord HASTINGS (3). He was captured and executed after the battle of BOSWORTH FIELD.

**Catherine** See KATHARINE.

**Cathness (Caithness), Thorfin Sigurdsson, Earl of (active 1014–1065)** Historical figure and minor character in *Macbeth*, a Scottish nobleman. In 5.2 Cathness, with MENTETH, ANGUS, and LENOX, marches to join the army led by MALCOLM and MACDUFF against MACBETH. In 5.4 they prepare to march on DUNSINANE, though Cathness does not speak. This Scottish soldier helps to suggest the play's national scope, for the rebellion of which he is a part results in the restoration of good government and social stability in SCOTLAND.

The historical Earl of Caithness was in fact a Viking lord, the powerful independent ruler of the Orkney and Hebrides Islands and parts of mainland Scotland, including Caithness on the northernmost coast. Known as Thorfin the Mighty, he is also a minor figure in *King Harald's Saga*, a classic of medieval Norse literature. His daughter (or possibly his sister) later married Malcolm.

**Catling, Simon** Character in *Romeo and Juliet*. See MUSICIANS (2).

**Cato** Minor character in *Julius Caesar*, soldier in the army of BRUTUS (4). In 5.4.4, at the battle of PHILIPPI, Cato's bold battle cry declares that his father was Marcus Cato, a famous opponent of CAESAR (1). He is killed shortly afterwards. Shakespeare took this gallant but fatal exploit—a motif popular with Elizabethan audiences—from PLUTARCH'S *Lives*. Cato's sister was Brutus' wife, PORTIA (2).

**Cawdor, Thane of** In *Macbeth*, a noble title forfeited by a defeated rebel against King DUNCAN of SCOTLAND and granted, with its lands and income, to MACBETH as a reward for valour in 1.2.67. Thereafter, the title refers to Macbeth, though he does not know of this development when the WITCHES predict, in 1.3, that he will become Thane of Cawdor and then king. When he receives Cawdor's title the reinforcement of the prophecy stimulates his ambition to be king. The title thus comes to carry a reference to the aura of evil that

attends Macbeth's rise to power. The original Cawdor's repentant acceptance of his execution is reported to Duncan with the famous remark, 'Nothing in his life / Became him like the leaving it' (1.4.7–8). In this the first Cawdor contrasts with his successor, Macbeth, who struggles to preserve his life even after it has become a burden and he is 'aweary of the sun' (5.5.49). On the other hand, there is also irony in the resemblance between the two, as the rebel yields his title to a man who thereupon becomes a usurper himself.

**Caxton, William (c. 1422–1491)** English translator and printer. In 1475 Caxton produced the first book printed in English, *The Recuyell of the Historyes of Troye*, his own translation (from a French version) of Guido delle COLONNE's Latin history of the TROJAN WAR. This work, probably in its 5th edition (1596), provided Shakespeare with much of the detail for his account of the war in *Troilus and Cressida*. Caxton also translated and published, in 1484, a French tale that may have inspired the husbands' wager on their wives' obedience in 5.2 of *The Taming of the Shrew*.

Caxton, who is known as the father of English printing, began as an apprentice to a cloth merchant. A capable businessman, he became the representative of the Merchants' Guild in the busy European commercial centre at Bruges, eventually being appointed governor of the English commercial and diplomatic colony. In 1469 Caxton became an adviser to the Duchess of Burgundy; as such he had the leisure to devote to literature, and he began his translating career. He also learned printing while in the Duchess' employ, and the *Recuyell* was printed in Bruges. He returned to England in 1476 and continued publishing until his death. His publications (more than 100 titles, including many of CHAUCER's works) were extremely influential on English literature for more than a century.

**Cecil (1), Robert, Earl of Salisbury (1563–1612)** Elizabethan and Jacobean statesman, one of the most powerful men in Shakespeare's England. The son of Lord BURGHLEY, Cecil was intended for statesmanship from his youth. He was an enemy of the Earl of ESSEX (2) in the 1590s, but after Essex's attempted rebellion, Cecil intervened to save the Earl of SOUTHAMPTON (2), Essex's follower and Shakespeare's patron, from the death penalty. Cecil was acting secretary of state before he turned 30, and he held the office officially from 1596 until just before his death, thus controlling English foreign policy for almost 20 years. He helped prepare for the peaceful accession of King JAMES I in 1603, for which he was rewarded with great wealth and high rank, becoming the first Earl of Salisbury in 1605. After 1608 he effectively ran the government. He was responsible for the downfall of Sir Walter RALEIGH in 1606, but eventually his political rivals brought him down the same way, by poisoning the king's opinion of him. He fell from favour in 1611, dying not long thereafter.

Cecil spent much of his money on the patronage of art, including the creation of one of the finest Jacobean mansions, Hatfield House. His father is sometimes thought to have been a model for POLONIUS, in part because of the letters of moralistic advice he sent to the young Cecil. If so, Cecil's resemblance to the impulsive fighter LAERTES stops there, for the Earl of Salisbury was deformed and physically weak while being entirely in control of himself emotionally and intellectually.

**Cecil (2), Thomas (1542–1623)** Soldier, opponent of the Earl of ESSEX (2). The eldest son of Lord BURGHLEY, Cecil led a notoriously dissolute life in Paris and Germany before taking up a military career. He served with distinction in Scotland and the Netherlands and at sea against the Spanish Armada. In 1599 he was appointed military governor of northern England; visiting London while on leave from this post in February 1601, Cecil improvised the military opposition to Essex' abortive uprising, crushing it immediately.

**Cecil (3), William** See BURGHLEY.

**Celia** Character in *As You Like It*, ROSALIND's cousin and friend, daughter of DUKE (1) FREDERICK. Celia is a secondary but important figure. In 1.3 she defies her tyrannical father when he banishes Rosalind; her spirited loyalty and sense of morality trigger the central action of the play, the two women's flight to the Forest of ARDEN (1). Thereafter, Celia listens to the disguised Rosalind's professions of love for ORLANDO, which she cannot otherwise express while disguised as a man. Celia responds skeptically in remarks such as, '. . . the oath of a lover is no stronger than the word of a tapster' (3.4.27–28), which maintain the play's ironic stance towards romance until the climactic resolution.

When Celia herself is betrothed to OLIVER (1) in Act 5, the triumph of love is complete. The marriage of the chaste Celia to the once-villainous Oliver has been criticised as unrealistic, unfair to Celia, and unduly generous to Oliver. However, the union is largely symbolic in intent. It serves to confirm the sincerity of Oliver's repentance, and it contributes greatly to the spirit of reconciliation that closes the play.

**Censorship** Governmental regulation of plays and other works. In Shakespeare's England, plays had to be submitted to the MASTER OF REVELS, who often required revisions both large and small before granting the required licence. After 1606 his powers were extended to the publication of plays as well. As early as 1559, Queen ELIZABETH (1) prohibited the dramatic treatment of religious or political issues. It is believed that the absence of the 'deposition scene' of *Richard II* (4.1) from the first three editions of the play is a result of this law. (As late as 1680, Nahum TATE's adaptation of *Richard II* was suppressed by the government, despite his attempt to disguise the work as *The Sicilian Usurper.*) The 1606 statute—called an 'Act to Restrain Abuses of Players'—outlawed the slightest profanity, and this feature is reflected in many of Shakespeare's plays, where such expletives as 'God', which appear in the earliest published versions, are replaced with 'Jove' or 'heavens' in the FIRST FOLIO (1623).

Sometimes the texts reveal self-censorship practised by the playwright or the acting companies. While not strictly censorship, in not being imposed, the excisions might not have been made but for the possibility of trouble with the authorities. For instance, some scholars believe that a passage deleted from Q2 of *Hamlet*—2.2.335–358, mocking the CHILDREN'S COMPANIES—was removed for fear that it might offend the new king, JAMES I, who had just taken a children's company under royal protection. Another passage, on the drunkenness of Danes (1.4.17–38), does not appear in the FOLIO edition of the play, perhaps to avoid giving offence to King James' queen, Anne of Denmark.

An informal, quasi-governmental censorship sometimes operated alongside the official system, as when pressure from an offended aristocrat apparently brought about the change of a notable character's name from OLDCASTLE to FALSTAFF (see COBHAM). Such efforts were unusual, but their effectiveness was ensured by the threat of official censorship, for the government frequently used a heavy censorial hand. For instance, when a play by Thomas NASHE, *Isle of Dogs* (1597; now lost), was declared seditious, all the LONDON theatres were closed for the summer and three of the actors were given gaol sentences. In 1605 George CHAPMAN and Ben JONSON were gaoled because their play *Eastward Ho!* contained passages that offended King James. (Jonson had been one of the three *Isle of Dogs* actors.) The ultimate form of state censorship came from the STUART DYNASTY's opposition, however, when the revolutionary Puritan government outlawed the theatre at the outset of the Civil Wars in 1642. Drama of any sort (excepting 'opera', see DAVENANT) was illegal until the restoration of the monarchy in 1660.

**Ceres** Pagan goddess and minor figure in *The Tempest*, a character in the MASQUE presented by the sprite ARIEL, at PROSPERO's orders, to celebrate the engagement of MIRANDA and FERDINAND (2). Ceres, goddess of harvests, is presented by IRIS but declares she will not participate unless she can be assured that Venus and Cupid will not be present. This reminds us of Prospero's insistence on Miranda's virginity before marriage, part of the play's theme of moral discipline.

Once reassured, Ceres joins JUNO in singing a hymn of blessing, wishing 'Earth's increase, foison [abundance] plenty' (4.1.110) for the couple.

In ancient mythology Ceres—from whose name comes our word *cereal*—was a pre-Roman corn-goddess. She became identified with the Greek goddess Demeter, who governed all fruits of the earth, especially grain. According to a central myth of the classical world, Ceres' daughter was stolen by the god of the underworld; the goddess responded by withholding her bounty until a compromise was achieved: her daughter spends half the year in the underworld, during which time Ceres resumes her grief and winter rules. In *The Tempest* Ceres blames Venus and Cupid for her daughter's theft, following the account given in OVID's *Metamorphosis* (the same incident is referred to in *The Winter's Tale* 4.4.116–118).

**Cerimon, Lord** Character in *Pericles*, a nobleman and physician of EPHESUS who revives the seemingly dead THAISA. Cerimon's benevolence as well as his expertise as a scientist is conveyed in his conversation with two neighbours (see GENTLEMAN [9]), in 3.2. He assists a SERVANT (26) who has suffered the great storm of the night before—the storm during which the unconscious Thaisa was mistakenly buried at sea, in 3.1—and he speaks of his long study of 'physic, [the] secret art [of] the blest infusions / That dwells in vegetives, in metals, stones' (3.2.32–36). Today, we might call him an alchemist. He revives Thaisa by invoking the spirit of Aesculapius, the Greek god of healing, which suggests ancient medical wisdom. Cerimon guides Thaisa to the famous Temple of DIANA (2)—one of the most important ancient pagan temples—when the revived queen, certain she will never see her husband again, desires 'a vestal livery' (3.4.9). In 5.3 when Thaisa, by then a high priestess at the Temple, is reunited with PERICLES, Cerimon is there, and, as the only calm person present, is able to confirm Thaisa's story. This kind and intelligent scholar foreshadows Shakespeare's last great protagonist, the magician PROSPERO of *The Tempest*.

**Cervantes Saavedra, Miguel de (1547–1616)** Spanish novelist, author of *Don Quixote* (1605–1615), a probable influence on the lost play CARDENIO, possibly by Shakespeare and John FLETCHER (2). The first part of *Don Quixote* was translated into English by Thomas Shelton (active 1612–1620) and published in 1612. A story within it is presumed to be the source for *Cardenio,* and Fletcher used Cervantes' work as inspiration for several of his own plays.

Cervantes had an adventurous military career: he lost a hand at the battle of Lepanto (1571), was later captured, and spent five years as a slave in Algiers before returning to Spain in 1580. He was disap-pointed not to receive a lucrative appointment as a reward and was reduced to extreme poverty. He struggled through his later life as a petty government employee—he was once gaoled for irregularities in handling funds—but he nevertheless managed to write a number of plays, poems, and novels, including the only one that was successful in his own time, the masterpiece for which he is still famous. He died on the same day as Shakespeare.

**Cesario** In *Twelfth Night,* name taken by VIOLA in her disguise as a young man.

**Chamberlain (1)** Minor character in *1 Henry IV,* an inn employee who scouts for the highwayman GADSHILL. In 2.1 the Chamberlain tells Gadshill of two likely victims who are staying at his inn and who will soon be leaving for LONDON. He is promised a share in the highwayman's take. In 2.2 Gadshill, FALSTAFF, and others rob the unfortunate TRAVELLERS. In Shakespeare's day the employees of inns were generally mistrusted, and contemporary writings describe many instances of this particular arrangement among thieves.

**Chamberlain (2), Lord** Character in *Henry VIII,* an official of King HENRY VIII's household, overseer of the king's travel, entertainment, and wardrobe. In 1.4 he assists Sir Henry GUILFORD with Cardinal WOLSEY's banquet, where he introduces the king to ANNE (1) BULLEN. In 2.2 and 3.2 he appears briefly as a plotter against Wolsey with the Dukes of NORFOLK (3) and SUFFOLK (1), and in 5.2 he is a member of the royal council, though he speaks only a few lines. In 5.3 he helps prepare for the christening of Princess ELIZABETH (1). Throughout he is representative of the elaborate world of courtly entertainment. Historically, the Chamberlain was Sir William SANDS, but Shakespeare mistakenly gave that nobleman another part in the play.

**Chamberlain's Men** Acting company of the ELIZABETHAN THEATRE, troupe in which Shakespeare was a partner. Though Shakespeare may have been involved with various other acting companies (see ADMIRAL'S MEN, DERBY'S MEN, LEICESTER'S MEN, PEMBROKE'S MEN, QUEEN'S MEN [1], STRANGE'S MEN, and SUSSEX'S MEN), he is most closely associated with the Chamberlain's Men (known as the KING'S MEN after the accession of King JAMES I in 1603). He was a partner in this troupe from at least December of 1594 until his retirement almost 20 years later.

The Chamberlain's Men was created in the spring of 1594 as a reorganisation of Derby's Men—originally Strange's Men—following the death of Lord Ferdinando STRANGE, the patron of the company. A patron was legally necessary for an acting company, so

Henry Carey, Baron HUNSDON (2), agreed to place the actors under his protection. Since Lord Hunsdon was the Lord Chamberlain to Queen ELIZABETH (1), the company was known thereafter as the Chamberlain's Men. In July 1596, when the Lord Chamberlain died, his son, also Lord HUNSDON (1), became patron of the company, which was briefly known as HUNSDON'S MEN. However, Hunsdon became Chamberlain himself, in March 1597, and the troupe resumed its old name.

The earliest surviving mention of the Chamberlain's Men records an appearance at NEWINGTON BUTTS in June 1594, though it soon moved to the THEATRE, whose owner, James BURBAGE (2), had earlier been part of a provincial company patronised by Hunsdon. The original partners in the Chamberlain's Men were probably George BRYAN, Richard COWLEY, John HEMINGE (who functioned as the group's business manager), William KEMPE, Augustin PHILLIPS, Thomas POPE (2), Richard BURBAGE (3), and Shakespeare, though the last two may have joined the others later in 1594. Bryan retired sometime before 1598, and Pope did likewise around 1600. They were replaced by William SLY (2) and Henry CONDELL, both of whom had performed earlier with the company; Kempe left in 1599 (though he may have returned briefly in 1601 or 1602) and was replaced by Robert ARMIN. The makeup of the partnership did not otherwise change until after the creation of the King's Men in 1603.

The Chamberlain's Men originally played at the Theatre in summer and the CROSS KEYS INN in winter, but in 1596 the latter venue was closed by the city, and the company is thought to have moved to the SWAN THEATRE. A year later it played the CURTAIN THEATRE, and a group of the partners built their own house, the GLOBE THEATRE, in 1599; there they remained for the duration of their existence. Each year over the Christmas holidays, the troupe also performed at the court of the queen, whose invitations were a mark of success and prestige. At first their rivals, the Admiral's Men, vied closely with them for this honour, but gradually the Chamberlain's Men dominated the competition; over their nine-year lifetime, the Chamberlain's Men performed at court 32 times and the Admirals' Men only 20. The Chamberlain's Men specialised in plays by their own Shakespeare, though they also performed a number of Ben JONSON's dramas as well as occasional works by others, including Thomas DEKKER and John MARSTON. (For the history of the troupe after 1603, see KING'S MEN.)

**Chambers, Edmund Kerchever (1866–1954)** English scholar, author of several standard works on Shakespeare and the ELIZABETHAN THEATRE. Chambers was a civil servant who also wrote dramatic criticism. In the 1890s he began writing a small book on Shakespeare that eventually grew to become *The Medieval*

*Stage* (2 vol., 1903), *The Elizabethan Stage* (4 vol., 1923), and *William Shakespeare: A Study of the Facts and Problems* (2 vol., 1930). He also produced critical editions of Francis BEAUMONT (2), John Donne (1572–1631), John FLETCHER (2), John MILTON, and others. He wrote biographies of Matthew Arnold (1822–1888) and Samuel Taylor COLERIDGE, and he edited the *Shakespeare Allusion Book* (1932) (see INGLEBY).

**Chancellor** Minor character in *Henry VIII*, the highest-ranking official of King HENRY VIII's government and keeper of the Great Seal of England, used to signify royal approval of any document. In 5.2 the Chancellor chairs the meeting of the royal council at which Bishop GARDINER attacks Archbishop CRANMER. He sides with Gardiner, but when the king intervenes for Cranmer, the Chancellor declares that their intention was simply to provide the archbishop with a chance to clear his name. He typifies the malevolence that the king overcomes in the final political episode of the play.

We hear in 3.2.393–394 that Sir Thomas MORE has succeeded Cardinal WOLSEY as Chancellor, but Shakespeare's Chancellor is nameless. In fact, More held the office for only three years, and the Chancellor at the time of 4.1 and 5.2 was Sir Thomas Audley (1488–1544). However, the specific identification is immaterial; the Chancellor is present simply as a representative of the highest levels of government.

**Chandos portrait** Possible portrait of Shakespeare. The Chandos portrait—named for its long-time owners, the Dukes of Chandos—was traditionally said to have been painted by Richard BURBAGE (3) and given by the artist to Joseph TAYLOR, who in turn bequeathed it to William DAVENANT. However, modern scholars find this tradition improbable. Taylor was 20 years younger than Burbage and not connected with him professionally—he only joined the KING'S MEN after the older man had died. It is therefore unlikely that he was intimate with Burbage. Moreover, he left nothing to Davenant or anyone else, for he died intestate. Nevertheless, the Chandos portrait is a quite competent portrait, almost certainly painted from life—unlike either of the two portraits regarded as authoritative (see DROESHOUT; JANSSEN [2]). However, since it only vaguely resembles the authoritative likenesses, the identity of the sitter is questionable, at best. The Chandos portrait was widely considered to be a picture of Shakespeare until well into the 19th century, and some commentators still argue that it is possibly genuine. In 1856 it became the first possession of the fledgling British National Portrait Gallery. It was the basis for Peter SCHEEMAKER's statue of Shakespeare in WESTMINSTER (1) ABBEY, and a copy of it, painted for John DRYDEN by the renowned portraitist Sir Godfrey

Kneller (1646–1723), now hangs in the FOLGER LIBRARY.

**Chapman, George (c. 1559–1634)**   English poet and playwright, a major figure in both ELIZABETHAN and JACOBEAN DRAMA, a noted translator of HOMER, and the author of minor sources for *The Merry Wives of Windsor* and *Troilus and Cressida*. Chapman may have been the model for the character HOLOFERNES in *Love's Labour's Lost*, and he is sometimes identified with the 'rival poet' of the SONNETS. Scholars who believe that many of Shakespeare's works were written in part by other playwrights (see, e.g., FLEAY and ROBERTSON) have attributed to Chapman passages or whole scenes in a number of the plays, especially *All's Well That Ends Well, Measure for Measure,* and *Troilus and Cressida;* however, modern scholars dispute most such attributions.

Chapman was a melancholy and disputatious man who made many enemies, possibly including Shakespeare, for some scholars believe that the playwright satirised him as the pedantic Holofernes. In any case Chapman's book-length philosophical poem *The Shadow of Night* (1594) is probably alluded to several times in the obscure jests that stud *Love's Labour's Lost*, and the drama may have been conceived as an answer to *The Shadow of Night*'s denigration of pleasure and practicality in favour of a contemplative life. Shakespeare exploited Chapman in other works. NYM's comical use of the word *humour* in *The Merry Wives of Windsor* is borrowed from Chapman's highly successful COMEDY OF HUMOURS, *The Blind Beggar of Alexandria* (1596), and several passages in *Troilus and Cressida* echo Chapman's initial partial translation of Homer's *Iliad* (1598). Some scholars believe that the latter play was also intended to counter Chapman, who rejected the usual English view that favoured the Trojans in the TROJAN WAR.

Chapman's only literary friends appear to have been the equally acerbic Ben JONSON and Thomas MARSTON. His embittered bellicosity emerged in his writing, sometimes with disastrous effects. In 1605 he and Jonson were briefly gaoled when King JAMES I took offence at remarks about SCOTLAND in their play *Eastward Ho!* (1605, written with Marston). He encountered government CENSORSHIP again in 1608, over another play, and he retired from the theatre to concentrate on his translation of Homer, which was only completed in 1615. This was his masterpiece and remained the standard English version for generations, though it is full of inaccuracies and has long been superseded.

Although Chapman was more a poet than a playwright, Francis MERES classed him as a leading writer of both COMEDY and TRAGEDY. *The Blind Beggar of Alexandria* (his first play) was a great success, and his tragedy *Bussy D'Ambois* (1607) is still performed occasionally today. However, despite the appreciative opinions of his contemporaries, Chapman's works are largely ignored by modern readers. He is now probably best known for John KEATS' great sonnet, 'On First Looking into Chapman's Homer'.

**Charles**   Minor character in *As You Like It,* a wrestler. Charles is a professional performer who takes on all comers, under the patronage of the aristocratic OLIVER (1). In 1.1 Oliver's younger brother ORLANDO proposes to challenge Charles at a forthcoming festival, and Oliver falsely informs Charles that Orlando, by nature an evil man, intends to kill him. He promises Charles that he will not be punished if Orlando dies instead, and the wrestler assures Oliver that this will be the outcome. In 1.2, however, Orlando defeats Charles soundly. This scene helps to establish Orlando as an hero. Charles also introduces a major theme in 1.1, informing us—and Oliver—of the fact that DUKE (7) Senior, having been deposed and exiled by his brother, DUKE (1) Frederick, has set up a court in the Forest of ARDEN (1).

Shakespeare derived his wrestler from his source, Thomas LODGE's *Rosalynde,* but toned down the character considerably. The original, an inhumanly strong and cruel villain, takes a bribe to kill Orlando's counterpart, but Charles is led to believe he will be in the right to do so; Lodge's wrestler kills his earlier opponents outright, while Charles' survive. Lodge made much of the contrast between his hero and the gigantic, villainous wrestler; Shakespeare's Charles is a more neutral figure who is simply defeated for the good of the plot.

**Charles VI, King of France**   Character in *Henry V.* See FRENCH KING.

**Charles VII, King of France (1403–1461)**   Historical figure and character in *1 Henry VI.* The historical Charles VII became King of FRANCE (1) upon the death of his father CHARLES VI, as is recorded in 1.1. However, he is throughout the play referred to as the Dauphin (sometimes rendered as Dolphin), a title traditionally applied to the eldest son of a French monarch and not to a king. This reflects the historical English position that the treaties following the conquests of HENRY V gave the French crown to the English king. Charles' enthronement was therefore an act of rebellion, and the French subsequently drove the English from their lands.

In the play, Charles is not readily distinguishable from the other French noblemen, who are all depicted as boastful but inept, treacherous, and cowardly warriors. Charles moons lovingly over JOAN LA PUCELLE at first—for instance, in 1.2.110–117—but he is quick to turn on her at the first misadventure of their campaign (2.1.50–53). In his final scene (5.4), he takes the advice of his nobles and agrees to a peace treaty with the intention of violating it later. (Historically, the treaty referred to was a mere truce, followed by the fighting—already undergone in the play—that drove the English out of France.)

**Charmian** Character in *Antony and Cleopatra,* an attendant of CLEOPATRA. In 1.2 Charmian is pleasantly humorous as she banters with her friends ALEXAS and IRAS over the predictions of the SOOTHSAYER (2), and one can understand Cleopatra's obvious fondness for her. The queen addresses Charmian more intimately and much more often than she does her other servants. She confides in her and permits her to offer advice, even if she usually rejects it. Charmian reminisces with her mistress about fishing expeditions she took with ANTONY, in 2.5.15–18; she also boldly attempts to restrain the queen's temper when she says, 'Good madam, keep yourself within yourself' (2.5.75), and she teases her about her past affair with Julius CAESAR (1), in 1.5.67–73. Charmian is a spirited, attractive young woman of a type that Shakespeare often depicted.

In 4.13, however, it is Charmian who makes the ill-fated suggestion that Cleopatra let Antony believe she has committed suicide. This is perhaps a device whereby Shakespeare intended to remove blame from the queen, whose transition from courtesan to transcendent lover is about to take place. Charmian herself undergoes such a change along with her mistress, fulfilling the Soothsayer's prediction that she 'shall be yet far fairer' (1.2.16) than she already is. Her loyalty takes on a grandeur as she accompanies her mistress' grave poetry with cries of grief—'Dissolve, thick cloud, and rain, that I may say, / The gods themselves do weep' (5.2.298–299)—and she cries out to the queen with almost religious intensity, 'O eastern star!' (5.2.307). When Cleopatra dies, Charmian touchingly straightens her mistress' crown before she kills herself in the same way. As she dies, she proudly declares to a Roman soldier that Cleopatra's suicide 'is well done, and fitting for a princess / Descended of so many royal kings' (5.2.325–326). Her coda to Cleopatra's grand declaration of ultimate love adds an echo of ecstasy before Caesar's final triumph.

Shakespeare adapted Charmian from a mere mention in his source, PLUTARCH's *Lives,* and developed the character greatly. Plutarch states that Cleopatra was attended at her death by a serving-woman named Charmian, but this person is otherwise unknown in history.

**Chatillon (Chatillion)** Minor character in *King John,* the ambassador of King PHILIP (2) of FRANCE (1) to King JOHN (3). A haughty lord, Chatillon opens the play by delivering an ultimatum to John in terms that are obviously meant to be insulting. He reappears only briefly, bearing the news of John's invasion of France in 2.1; while belittling the English, he must

speak of their military success. Chatillon's role helps to develop a strong sense of the arrogance of power, heightening the impact of treachery in high places, one of the play's major themes.

**Chatterton, Frederick Balsir (1831–1886)** English theatrical producer. Between 1863 and 1879, F. B. Chatterton was manager of the Drury Lane Theatre in London, and he was a notable promoter of Shakespeare's plays, especially as presented by Samuel PHELPS. Unfortunately, these productions were not generally profitable, and Chatterton is remembered for a famous witticism, inspired by a production of an ephemeral play by the poet Byron: 'Shakespeare spells ruin and Byron bankruptcy'.

**Chaucer, Geoffrey (c. 1340–1400)** English poet, Shakespeare's greatest predecessor and the author of sources for several of the plays. Chaucer's *Troilus and Criseyde* was the main source for the Trojan scenes in *Troilus and Cressida.* The same work taught Shakespeare about leitmotifs—recurring images that provide a sense of aesthetic continuity in a work whose tone changes considerably—a technique that he used in *Romeo and Juliet* and elsewhere. Moreover, *Troilus and Criseyde* had influenced the *Romeus* of Arthur BROOKE (1), the chief source for *Romeo and Juliet,* and Chaucer's *Parliament of Fowles* provided material for MERCUTIO's 'Queen MAB' speech in the same play. Chaucer's 'The Knight's Tale' in *The Canterbury Tales* was the main source for *The Two Noble Kinsmen* and for parts of *A Midsummer Night's Dream.* 'The Merchant's Tale' and 'Sir Tophas' from *The Canterbury Tales* contributed further details to the *Dream.* The personality of the HOST (2) in *The Merry Wives of Windsor* was probably influenced by Chaucer's innkeeper in *The Canterbury Tales.* Lastly, various works of Chaucer provided minor details in other plays (e.g., *2 Henry VI* 3.2.115–116).

Chaucer was the son of a vintner with connections to the court of King Edward III (ruled 1327–1377), and he is first recorded as a teenaged page to the Duke of Clarence, the king's son, with whom he went to war in FRANCE (1) at the outset of the HUNDRED YEARS WAR. For the rest of his life he was an employee of the royal courts in one way or another, mostly as an official of the customs service. His greatest patron was John of GAUNT (who appears in *Richard II*), probably because he married a sister of Katherine Swynford, Gaunt's long-time mistress and eventual wife (although the identity of Chaucer's wife remains obscure). Little is known of Chaucer's private life, though passages in his works suggest that he was improvident and a bad administrator, that he had an unhappy marriage but a loving mistress (by whom he probably had a son), and that he possessed a sunny disposition. He had many friends—among them the poet John GOWER (3)—who attested to his virtues.

Chaucer, who wrote in Middle English (an early dialect), was the first great poet in English and is still considered among the finest English poets of all time. His works cannot be dated precisely as they were not published until after his death (printing did not exist in his lifetime). Nevertheless, his career can be divided into periods. Among his best-known early works is *The Book of the Duchess;* his middle period—following two trips to Italy in the 1370s, when he encountered the works of Dante and BOCCACCIO—produced *The Legend of Good Women, The Parliament of Fowles,* and *Troilus and Criseyde.* Chaucer's final period encompasses the composition of one of the masterworks of the English language, the unfinished *Canterbury Tales.* These lively, often bawdy stories are supposedly told by various pilgrims on their way to the shrine at Canterbury. Though difficult to read without practice, the *Tales* are immensely gratifying, filled with sharp character studies, sly asides on human behaviour, and inimitable descriptions. After his death, Chaucer was the first poet to be buried in what became the famous 'poet's corner' in WESTMINSTER (1) ABBEY.

**Chettle, Henry (c. 1560–c. 1607)** English printer and dramatist. As a printer, Chettle (briefly a partner of John DANTER) is best known for having published *Groatsworth of Wit* (1592) by Robert GREENE (2), which contains a denunciation of Shakespeare as an arrogant young plagiarist, the first published reference to the playwright. Chettle, who had apparently edited Greene's work, subsequently apologised for it in a pamphlet of his own, and wrote that he knew Shakespeare to be an honest man and a good writer. Chettle had turned to writing plays by 1598, when he was mentioned by Francis MERES as a fine writer of comedies, and he is known to have written or collaborated on at least 48 dramas—one of them being SIR THOMAS MORE—for the ADMIRAL'S MEN and Philip HENSLOWE.

**Chester, Robert** See LOVE'S MARTYR.

**Chichele, Henry, Archbishop of Canterbury** Character in *Henry V.* See CANTERBURY (1).

**Chief Justice, Lord** Character in *2 Henry IV,* the highest-ranking judicial officer of England. The Chief Justice chastises FALSTAFF twice. In 1.2 he observes that only Falstaff's success at the battle of SHREWSBURY has kept him from being prosecuted for the highway robbery at GAD'S HILL in *1 Henry IV,* and he warns the knight against continuing his dissolute life. In 2.1 he orders Falstaff to repay a debt to the HOSTESS (2). In both cases the Chief Justice has enough intelligence and humour to appreciate Falstaff's wit and to recog-

nise that the fat knight cannot be cajoled into an honest life, but his own sense of public morality urges him to make the attempt.

In 1.2.55–56 Falstaff's PAGE (5) calls the Chief Justice 'the nobleman that committed the Prince for striking him about Bardolph', referring to an earlier imprisonment of PRINCE (6) HAL. In 5.2, after HENRY IV's death, the Chief Justice expects to find the new King vengeful, but when he defends his action, noting that he was right to follow the law irrespective of the offender's rank, the former Prince approves entirely and confirms him in his office. The young King asserts that he will be guided by the justice, and when he rejects Falstaff in 5.5, his formal diction seems to reflect the judge's influence. The Chief Justice later implements Hal's decision to banish Falstaff.

The story of Hal's assault on the Chief Justice was part of the popular legend of 'wild Prince Hal': he is said to have been reprimanded by the justice for seeking a favourable ruling on behalf of a delinquent acquaintance, whereupon he struck the judge and was gaoled for it; as in the play, he maintained the justice in office upon becoming Henry V. However, this tale is almost surely fictitious; the earliest written reference to any such event did not appear until 1531, more than a century later, in Thomas ELYOT's *The Boke named the Gouernour.* Moreover, Elyot reports no assault, merely the Justice's reprimand, which the Prince accepted meekly. The assault and incarceration occur only in THE FAMOUS VICTORIES, a 16th-century farce that has no historical validity whatsoever. Shakespeare doubtless knew this, but the tale was too dramatic to waste. The Chief Justice of Hal's day, unnamed in the play or in any of Shakespeare's sources, was Sir William Gascoigne (c. 1350–1419), a distinguished jurist who had long served King Henry IV, having been his attorney when he was in exile as Henry BOLINGBROKE (1) (as enacted in *Richard II*). As King Henry's chief legal officer, Gascoigne had presided over the sentencing and execution of the rebels captured at GAULTREE, although Shakespeare does not associate him with this event in 4.3 of the play.

**Children** Minor characters in *The Merry Wives of Windsor* who imitate fairies and elves to torment FALSTAFF in 5.5. ANNE (3), WILLIAM (1), and other Children, disguised as diminutive supernatural beings, help to carry out MISTRESS (3) Page's plot for the final humiliation of Falstaff, devised in 4.4.28–64. When the lecherous Falstaff meets Mistress Page and MISTRESS (1) Ford in the forest, seeking double adultery, the Children appear, led by Mistress QUICKLY, PISTOL, and EVANS (3). They dance in a circle (while ceremonial references to the Order of the Garter are made—see *The Merry Wives of Windsor,* 'Text of the Play'), and they hold candles to Falstaff and pinch him, while singing a song condemning 'lust and luxury' (5.5.95).

**Children's Companies**  English acting companies in the 16th and 17th centuries composed of boys. Before the ELIZABETHAN THEATRE became well established in the 1570s, professional companies tended to be troupes of acrobats and mimes, more appropriate to a country fair than to the court of Queen ELIZABETH (1). There, entertainment was often provided by schoolboys from Eton and Westminster, and by the Chapel Royal, a boys' choir that provided schooling for the boys it recruited from church choirs around the country. These groups traditionally staged plays in Latin (the language of their education). The Chapel Royal even had its own dramatic company, known as the Children of the Chapel, as early as the 1520s. In the 1550s two more such groups were created, the Children of Paul's at the school attached to St Paul's Cathedral and the Children of Windsor at the church grammar school in WINDSOR. These groups were very popular at the queen's court: in the first 20 years of Elizabeth's reign, boys performed at court half again as often as did men. Though composed of children, these companies performed plays written for adults and featuring adult characters.

However, by the late 1570s, the adult troupes had become legitimate theatre companies. LEICESTER'S MEN became favourites at court, and one member, James BURBAGE (2), built the first LONDON playhouse, the THEATRE, in 1576. The children's companies appeared to be falling from favour, but their course also changed in 1576. The Children of Windsor and of the Chapel merged, under the direction of Richard FARRANT, who leased rooms at a former priory and created the first BLACKFRIARS THEATRE, where his boys played to the public as well as continuing to perform at court. After Farrant's death, the company was directed by William HUNNIS, but its popularity waned and play production ceased after 1584, when the landlord took back the Blackfriars building. In the final season, another children's company, patronised by the Earl of OXFORD (1), joined the troupe at Blackfriars.

From 1584 to 1600 the children's companies ceased performing plays, as the QUEEN'S MEN (1) and other professional troupes took over, though the choirs were maintained. In 1600, however, Nathaniel GILES and Henry EVANS (2) revived the Children of the Chapel as a theatre company, leasing the second Blackfriars Theatre from Richard BURBAGE (3). They were immediately popular, due in good part to the involvement of Ben JONSON, as both actor and playwright. The Children of Paul's also re-entered the theatrical arena at this time, performing at court and at the school, which had a theatre. They staged plays by George CHAPMAN, Thomas DEKKER, Thomas MIDDLETON, and John WEBSTER (2), and they too competed with the adult companies. The children's companies were fierce rivals, and their competition spilled over into the contents of the plays they staged, in the so-

called WAR OF THE THEATRES—a development alluded to in *Hamlet* 2.2.326–258.

In 1602 Giles and Evans were accused of graft and the misuse of the Chapel Royal's recruiting privileges to enroll non-singers; Evans fled the country, and Giles retired from play production. Under King JAMES I, who was crowned in 1603, Evans returned to the theatre, but his connection with the Chapel Royal was severed. Instead, he and Edward KIRKHAM formed the Children of the Queen's Revels, under the patronage of the queen. However, they lost the royal favour by staging controversial plays—especially the allegedly seditious *Eastward Ho!*, by Jonson, Chapman, and Thomas MARSTON (see CENSORSHIP)—and in 1605 they changed their name to Children of the Revels, and then, at the insistence of the crown, to Children of Blackfriars.

In 1606 a new children's company entered the field, the Children of the King's Revels, owned by a group including Michael DRAYTON and managed by Martin SLATER. (This troupe may have been the Children of Paul's, reorganised, for that company disappears from the records at this time.) They performed at a new playhouse founded for the purpose, the WHITEFRIARS THEATRE. The King's Revels company was unsuccessful, however, and died in 1609, amid rancorous litigation among the partners.

In 1608 Evans' old company, now under new direction, moved to the new theatre as the Children of Whitefriars. In 1610—under yet another management group including Robert BROWNE, Richard JONES (2), and others—they were restored to royal favour and once again were known as Children of the Queen's Revels. Their chief actor and playwright was Nathan FIELD (1). This company was absorbed into LADY ELIZABETH'S MEN in 1613. Though troupes of boys were occasionally organised as late as the 1630s, the great era of the children's companies was over.

**Chiron**  Character in *Titus Andronicus*, son of TAMORA. Chiron and his brother DEMETRIUS (1) murder BASSIANUS and then commit the horrible rape and mutilation of LAVINIA, the daughter of TITUS (1) Andronicus; they are encouraged and abetted by AARON. Titus' counter-revenge includes the killing of the two brothers, who are baked in a meat pie and served to their mother in the final scene.

**Chorus (1)**  Dramatic device, originally from ancient Greek drama, employed by Shakespeare in various forms. A chorus is a character or allegorical figure who usually does not participate in the action of the play, but rather provides a commentary on it. He does this either by offering a critique of the actions and attitudes of the other characters or by supplying missing facts or filling in the narrative where it is not actually enacted. Two such figures in Shakespeare are frankly designated as choruses—the CHORUS (2) of *Romeo and Juliet* and the CHORUS (3) of *Henry V*—while one allegorical figure and one named character are in fact choruses: TIME in *The Winter's Tale* and GOWER (3) in *Pericles*. Also, a number of plays have a figure designated the PROLOGUE (1), whose choric function is limited to the introduction of the action. RUMOUR *(2 Henry IV)* is also a prologue figure. In addition, some regular characters occasionally step aside from the action and speak about it in a choric manner—a good example is the BASTARD (1) of *King John*—and other characters are obviously commentators on the action without stepping back from it, as exemplified by *King Lear's* FOOL (2), who is often figuratively referred to as a chorus.

The use of a chorus, whether frankly or subtly employed, lets the playwright establish a point of view that the characters themselves, by and large, do not share, thus bringing the audience into the play without making it identify with some characters to the exclusion of others. The chorus also invites the audience to help ensure the success of the drama by willingly engaging its own imagination and sympathies. This is especially important if the play is an allegorical spectacle like *Pericles*, whose story Gower concedes he could not 'convey / Unless your thoughts went on my way' (4.Chorus.49–50). Or, as the Chorus of *Henry V* demands, in an appropriately military tone, we must 'Follow, follow! / Grapple [our] minds to sternage of this navy' (3.Chorus.17–18).

In the Greek theatre, the chorus was a group of actors—originally 50, later as few as 12—who sang lyrical passages of commentary and explanation while dancing; their passages are also referred to as choruses. In RENAISSANCE and later plays, a chorus is usually a single character or small group who speaks similar lyrical explanatory passages. (In a more literally accurate use of the term, a chorus is also the group of singing and dancing background figures in opera or musical theatre.) The ancient Greek use of the chorus probably evolved from singing in religious ceremonies. However, the practice was not transmitted to Roman drama, where choruses appear only in SENECA's works, which were not intended for performance. For Seneca, the chorus was a conscious archaism intended to invoke the spirit of Greece as the fountainhead of Roman culture. However, in Shakespeare's day, ancient drama was known only from Seneca's work; thus, the Renaissance delight in classicism encouraged the use of choruses in English plays, although such a ritualistic device is actually quite inappropriate to the distinctly secular ELIZABETHAN DRAMA. It was never employed in the strict sense of group recitation, let alone singing and dancing; rather, various approximations, like those of Shakespeare, came into use.

**Chorus (2)**   Minor character in *Romeo and Juliet*, the nondramatic figure who comments on the play in each PROLOGUE (1), preceding Acts 1 and 2 respectively. In the manner of an ancient Greek CHORUS (1), this character comments on the drama from outside it, displaying a knowledge that no character could have. In the Prologue to Act 1, the Chorus not only provides a terse account of the tragedy's course but suggests a response to it, pointing out that the feud between families 'makes civil hands unclean' (Prologue.4) and that the 'fearful passage' (Prologue.9) of the love affair will provide the only resolution of the conflict. Prior to Act 2, the Chorus extols the two lovers while outlining the difficulties that the feud will cause them. Each prologue takes the form of a SONNET, traditionally reserved for romantic poetry, preparing the audience (which in Shakespeare's day will have been likely to recognise the form on hearing it) for a love story. This treatment reflects the fact that a tragic love story was a novelty in the 1590s. TRAGEDY ordinarily concerned warriors and kings; lovers were expected to appear in COMEDY, where they would find a happy ending in marriage.

**Chorus (3)**   Allegorical figure in *Henry V*, speaker of the PROLOGUE (1) (where he is identified in a stage direction as the Prologue), an introduction to each act, and the EPILOGUE. The Chorus apologises for the inadequacy of the theatre to present historical events in a sufficiently grand manner, and he therefore offers a supplementary account of the events dramatised. He uses a stylised and artificial diction that is in marked contrast with the realism of the dramatic scenes, and the Chorus' grand rhetoric contributes to the epic quality so important to the play. However, if *Henry V* is considered as an acid satire on politics, then the Chorus' epic voice has an ironic quality, sardonically at odds with the cynical waging of an unnecessary war by an hypocritically religious King. In the Epilogue—a formally correct SONNET—the Chorus again remarks on the inadequacy of historical drama, and he praises the accomplishments of HENRY V anew. Then he goes on to observe that all of Henry's gains in FRANCE (1) were almost immediately lost under HENRY VI, closing with a reference to Shakespeare's well-known *Henry VI* plays, which depict this loss.

The Chorus repeatedly invokes imaginary scenes: in the Prologue he asks the audience to 'piece out our imperfections with your thoughts' (Prologue.23) and thereby to 'carry [characters] here and there, jumping o'er times' (line 29). In 3.Chorus.18 he requests, 'Grapple your minds', and later, 'Work, work your thoughts, and therein see . . .' (line 25), and lastly, 'eke out our performance with your mind' (line 35). Thus the Chorus, by insisting on the audience's part in shaping the narrative, supplying with their imaginations what cannot be provided in a theatre, helps to provide an almost cinematic sweep of time and events.

**Christopher (1) Sly** Character in *The Taming of the Shrew.* See SLY (1).

**Christopher (2) Urswick (1448–1522)** Historical figure and minor character in *Richard III,* a follower of RICHMOND. Prior to Richmond's invasion of England, Sir Christopher Urswick makes contact with Lord Thomas STANLEY (3), Richmond's stepfather, who confirms his intention to defect from RICHARD III. The historical Urswick was a priest in the employ of Margaret Beaufort, Richmond's mother and Stanley's wife.

**Cibber (1), Colley (1671–1757)** English actor, playwright, and producer. Cibber, the son of a Danish sculptor who had moved to England, began his career in 1690 as an actor in Thomas BETTERTON's company, and by 1696 he had his first play staged. He was a successful actor, portraying mostly comical fops, often in his own plays, which were fashionable comedies of sentiment, set in high society. His tragedies were generally unsuccessful, except for his adaptation of *Richard III* (1700)—more than half of which he wrote himself—which was immensely popular and became the standard version of Shakespeare's play for more than a century. As a long-time manager of the Drury Lane Theatre, Cibber staged a number of Shakespeare's plays—or rather adaptations of them—including his own *Romeo and Juliet* and *Papal Tyranny in the Reign of King John.* He played a number of Shakespearean characters, including Cardinal WOLSEY, IAGO, and JAQUES (1) (the last in LOVE IN A FOREST by Charles JOHNSON [2]). His autobiography, *Apology for the Life of Colley Cibber, Comedian* (1740), provides many interesting glimpses of 18th-century theatre life. Cibber was named Poet Laureate in 1730. Theophilus CIBBER (3) was his son.

**Cibber (2), Susannah Maria (1714–1766)** English actress. Susannah Cibber, a sister of Thomas ARNE, married Theophilus CIBBER (3) in 1734, though they only lived together briefly. Originally an opera singer, she was coached as an actress by her father-in-law, the actor and producer Colley CIBBER (1). Her husband's flight from England, to avoid creditors, exposed the scandalous *ménage à trois* they had maintained with another man, and Susannah retired from the stage for several years. She later returned to a successful career in the productions of David GARRICK. She was especially acclaimed as CONSTANCE in *King John.*

**Cibber (3), Theophilus (1703–1758)** English actor. The son of Colley CIBBER (1), Theophilus Cibber was best known for comic roles, especially PISTOL and PA-ROLLES. After the scandalous dissolution of his marriage to Susannah Maria CIBBER (2), Theophilus Cibber's stage career collapsed, and he supported himself as a hack writer. He wrote a brief biography of Shakespeare in his *The Lives of the Poets* (1753)—probably ghost-written—that is the only source for the anecdote that Shakespeare began his career as a 'horse boy', holding horses for members of the audience as they dismounted outside the theatre.

**Cicero, M. Tullius (106–43 B.C.)** Historical figure and minor character in *Julius Caesar,* a senator of ROME. Cicero appears only to dismiss CASCA's concern about omens in 1.3. Earlier Casca had described in comical terms Cicero's pedantic use of Greek ('It was Greek to me' [1.2.281]), and later BRUTUS (4) rejects the suggestion that Cicero be included in the conspiracy against CAESAR (1) as an elder statesman. Brutus says that Cicero is too independent and will 'never follow any thing that other men begin' (2.1.151–152). Cicero's execution by ANTONY and OCTAVIUS is reported in 4.3. 176–177.

Although he is an interesting background presence, Cicero is of no real importance to the play. Probably his inclusion simply reflects his immense stature as a writer. Cicero was perhaps the most influential of all classical authors. His works were highly respected in his own lifetime and throughout the period of the Roman Empire; during the Middle Ages he was revered as a master of rhetoric. In the RENAISSANCE his works were well known to all educated people, and they influenced humanistic writers on a broad range of subjects. In Shakespeare's time Cicero was certainly one of the best-known ancient Romans, and it was therefore natural for the playwright to present him on stage. Cicero was often known in the 16th century as 'Tully', from his middle name, and he is so referred to in *2 Henry VI,* 4.1.136, and *Titus Andronicus,* 4.1.14.

Cicero was also a highly successful lawyer and politician. He was among the most important men in the Roman world at the time of the play. He was a leader of the opposition to Caesar's party, although he had no part in Brutus' plot, and after the assassination he denounced Antony in a series of speeches. As is reported in the play, he was executed as a result.

**Cinna (1), Gaius Helvetius (Helvius) (d. 44 B.C.)** Historical figure and minor character in *Julius Caesar,* victim of a mob of PLEBEIANS (1). In 3.3 Cinna, a poet, is mistaken for CINNA (2), one of the assassins of CAESAR (1), and he is killed by the ferocious Roman mob incited by Mark ANTONY's funeral oration for Caesar. The historical Cinna—called Helvetius Cinna for his birth in what is now Switzerland—was a noted poet of his day. His epic poem *Zmyrna* was famous for generations as a difficult 'modernist' masterpiece, but it is now lost. Not mentioned in Shakespeare's source, PLUTARCH's *Lives*, is Cinna's political role; he was Caesar's ally, and he became a tribune when Caesar deposed FLAVIUS (1) and MARULLUS. His murder by the pro-Caesar mob was therefore all the more ironic, but the playwright did not know this.

**Cinna (2), Lucius Cornelius the Younger (active 44 B.C.)** Historical figure and minor character in *Julius Caesar*, one of the assassins of CAESAR (1). In 1.3 CASSIUS assigns Cinna to distribute anonymous letters encouraging BRUTUS (4) to join the conspiracy against Caesar. When Caesar is stabbed, Cinna cries, 'Liberty! Freedom! Tyranny is dead!' (3.1.78).

The historical Cinna—whose father (d. 84 B.C.) had been a famous radical leader under whom Caesar had served in the earlier Roman civil wars—had been appointed to high office under Caesar. Shakespeare's source, PLUTARCH, mentioned Cinna as one of the conspirators and reported that, after the assassination, he made a speech against Caesar that infuriated the crowd. It is not historically certain, however, that Cinna was actually one of Caesar's murderers; he may merely have been among those who supported the assassins after the fact. In either case, he was identified with the killing in contemporary minds; as is enacted in 3.3, a pro-Caesar mob encountered Helvetius CINNA (1) and, believing him to be L. Cornelius Cinna, beat him to death.

**Cinthio (Giovanni Battista Giraldi) (1504–1573)** Italian poet, novelist, and playwright, author of sources for *Measure for Measure* and *Othello*. The story of OTHELLO and DESDEMONA and the main plot of *Measure for Measure* came from two different tales in Cinthio's *Hecatommithi* (1565), a cycle of novellas modelled on BOCCACCIO's *Decameron*. *Measure for Measure* was also influenced by Cinthio's *Epitia*, a dramatisation of the source novella, published posthumously in 1583. The same tale was translated into English by George WHETSTONE, but Shakespeare does not appear to have used it. The *Othello* source tale was not translated into English until the 18th century, so Shakespeare must have known Cinthio's work elsewhere. He may have read it in the original Italian, or in a French translation of 1584, or there may have been an English translation that is now lost.

Giraldi (known as Cinthio in England from the name Cinzio, which he called himself in his poetry) was a famed professor of philosophy and rhetoric. As a playwright, he was noted for his efforts to reform tragic drama, based in his time on ancient models, so that it reflected tenets of Christian humanism. In his eight published plays, including *Epitia*, a CHORUS (1) commented on the action, which consisted in good part of debates on such subjects as the proper rela-

tionship between love and justice. This aspect of his work is reflected particularly in the highly moral character of ISABELLA and the political musings of the DUKE (9) in *Measure for Measure*. On the other hand, Cinthio was also the first RENAISSANCE playwright to present atrocities on stage, which perhaps indirectly influenced Shakespeare to write such noteworthy scenes of violence and gore as those in *Titus Andronicus*, *King Lear*, and *Othello*.

**Citizen (1)** One of several minor characters in *2 Henry VI*. In 4.5 one of a group of citizens reports to Lord SCALES, the commander of the Tower of LONDON, that the rebels led by Jack CADE are successfully assaulting London Bridge and that the Lord Mayor has requested Scales' assistance.

**Citizen (2)** Any of several minor characters in *Richard III*, common people of LONDON who respond to the sinister affairs surrounding the crown. In 2.3, three Citizens discuss the death of King EDWARD IV and the ambitions of RICHARD III in tones of anxious foreboding. One of them summarises their viewpoint: 'All may be well; but if God sort it so / 'Tis more than we deserve, or I expect' (2.3.36–37). In 3.7 a number of Citizens accompany the MAYOR (3) to witness Richard's charade of unwillingness to accept the crown, and their silence speaks volumes about the usurper's impropriety.

**Citizen (3)** Any of several minor characters in *Romeo and Juliet*, townspeople of VERONA who attempt to halt the street fighting between the feuding MONTAGUE (1) and CAPULET (1) families in 1.1 and 3.1. Their presence reflects the importance Shakespeare placed on civil disorder—one of his favourite themes—as an element in his tragedy of young lovers.

**Citizen (4)** Minor character in *King John*, a citizen of ANGIERS who appears on the walls of the city in 2.1 to explain to the kings PHILIP (2) of France (1) and JOHN (3) of England why the gates are closed. He declares the town's allegiance to the King of England but adds that, until it is established whether John or ARTHUR is properly holder of that office, the citizens have 'ramm'd up our gates against the world' (2.1.272). The Citizen's suspicion of his leaders illuminates the treacherous nature of royal politics, a major theme of the play.

In the FIRST FOLIO, where *King John* was first published, the Citizen departs at 2.1.282 and HUBERT acts as representative of Angiers to the forces outside after entering at line 325. However, in some modern editions, Hubert's lines in 2.1 are given to the Citizen. Conversely, in other editions, the Citizen's part in its entirety is given to Hubert.

**Citizen (5)** Any of several minor but significant characters in *Coriolanus*, residents of ROME. The Citizens are chiefly important for their fickleness, as their opinions of CORIOLANUS change repeatedly under the influence of various other characters. In this they symbolise a political doctrine that Shakespeare espoused in a number of plays: the common people, however sympathetic as individuals, are politically irresponsible as a class.

The Citizens are most distinguishable as individuals in 1.1. Amid a riot, the First Citizen introduces the play's most important motif: the excessive pride of Coriolanus. He recommends killing him, but the Second Citizen opposes this suggestion, and points out the great services that Coriolanus has performed as the military genius of Rome. He thereby introduces the counter-theme and prepares us for the tragedy that will constitute the main plot, as the noble hero falls victim to his own pride. The riot is halted as the Citizens listen to the aristocrat MENENIUS justify the powers of the aristocracy with a simplistic fable—his famed 'belly speech' (1.1.95–153)—and though the First Citizen offers sensible objections, the crowd as a whole is diverted from its original intentions. The arrival of Coriolanus cows them altogether, and they depart in an initial demonstration of their malleability.

Thereafter, the Citizens serve chiefly to further the same point. They are manipulated by the aristocrats, who influence them to vote for Coriolanus in Act 2, and by their own representatives—the tribunes BRUTUS (3) and SICINIUS—who organise them as a mob in Act 3, and bring about the banishment of Coriolanus. Lastly, in 4.6 some Citizens thank the tribunes for getting rid of their enemy, but when word arrives that the banished Coriolanus is marching on Rome with the army of the VOLSCIANS, they reappear to declare that they had had misgivings about the banishment all along. With the exception of the First Citizen in 1.1, the Citizens are not portrayed as individuals and serve only as pawns, both of the tribunes and the playwright.

**Citizen (6)** Minor character in *Coriolanus*, a resident of ANTIUM. In three brief lines the Citizen directs CORIOLANUS to the home of AUFIDIUS. He serves merely to advance the plot.

**Clarence (1), George York, Duke of (1449–1478)**
Historical figure and character in *Richard III*, the victimised brother of RICHARD III. Richard reveals in his opening soliloquy (1.1) that he has turned King EDWARD IV, his oldest brother, against Clarence, his next oldest. When Clarence is arrested, in the same scene, Richard sympathises with him and promises him assistance, but in fact, he proceeds to hire two murder-

ers to kill him. Thus Clarence is removed from the succession to the crown, leaving Richard in his place.

In 1.4 we see Clarence in his cell in the TOWER OF LONDON. He has just awakened from a terrible nightmare, in which he was drowned and went to hell. There he encountered the spirits of both the Earl of WARWICK (3), whom he had betrayed, and the one-time PRINCE (4) OF WALES, whom he had helped to murder (Both events are enacted, with Clarence appearing as GEORGE [2], in *3 Henry VI*.) Awake but still afraid, he admits that his conscience is heavy.

The murderers arrive, and Clarence learns that Richard, whom he had thought he might rely on in his distress, has hired them. He piteously bewails his fate. The SECOND MURDERER (2), who had displayed pangs of conscience earlier, is prepared to relent, but the FIRST MURDERER (2) proceeds to stab Clarence and, for good measure, seals him in a cask of wine to ensure that he won't survive.

Clarence's death scene is an emotional highlight of the play. It has tremendous impact, shocking the audience, for Richard's villainy, which has been seductively entertaining up to this point, is now seen to have serious consequences. Clarence's account of his dream reveals a soul in torment; he speaks in passionate verse, the most lyrical in the play. His spiritual suffering—his heavy-hearted loss of hope and fear of death—is intense. The scene anchors much of the action that follows: although Richard's cold-hearted machinations result only in off-stage violence, they nevertheless cannot be witnessed without recalling this chilling evidence of their real weight.

Shakespeare's account of Clarence's death has little relation to history, though the playwright certainly believed it to be true; he took it from his chief source for the HISTORY PLAYS, the account of the WARS OF THE ROSES written by Edward HALL (2). Historically, Richard actually protested against Clarence's imprisonment and execution. However, Clarence's position was irreparable, for he had persisted in involving himself in plots against King Edward. After forgiving his brother several times (one of these occasions is dramatised in *3 Henry VI*), Edward finally ordered Clarence's trial for treason, appearing in person as the prosecutor. Clarence was sentenced to death, and a few days later his death was announced, although there was no public execution, as would have been ordinary. This last detail may account for the persistence of the rumour that Richard had Clarence murdered, which was, by Shakespeare's time, accepted as fact.

**Clarence (2), Thomas, Duke of (1388–1421)** Historical figure and minor character in *2 Henry IV* and *Henry V*, son of King HENRY IV and younger brother of PRINCE (6) HAL. In *2 Henry IV* Clarence receives advice from his dying father on dealing with Hal after he succeeds to the throne. In *Henry V,* although he receives a command from the King in 5.2.84, he does not reply, nor is he named in the stage directions or the DRAMATIS PERSONAE in most editions of the play.

The historical Clarence was an important figure in the regimes of his father and brother. A young governor of Ireland in the first years of Henry IV's reign, Clarence replaced Hal on the King's council when the latter was dismissed in 1411, and he led a successful military expedition in GASCONY in 1412. Late in the reign of Henry V, Clarence was killed in battle in FRANCE (1).

**Clarke, Mary Cowden (1809–1898) and Charles Cowden (1787–1877)** British Shakespearean commentators. The Clarkes, who married in 1828, studied and wrote about Shakespeare throughout their married life. Mary Cowden Clarke prepared a concordance to Shakespeare's work (1844–1845), and wrote a best-selling three-volume collection of short fictions entitled *The Girlhood of Shakespeare's Heroines* (1851–1852). Charles Cowden Clarke published his lectures on *Shakespeare's Characters* (1863). The couple produced jointly an edition of the complete plays (1868), a popular guide to Shakespeare's language entitled *Shakespeare Key* (1879), and editions of the works of George Herbert (1593–1633) and others. Their *Recollections of Writers* (1878) is a memoir of their friendships with such 19th-century luminaries as John KEATS, Charles and Mary LAMB (1), and Charles DICKENS.

**Claudio (1)** Character in *Much Ado About Nothing,* lover of HERO. Claudio falls in love with Hero on sight, but he rejects her when the deceitful Don JOHN (1) presents him with false evidence of her infidelity. Once aware of his error, and believing that Hero has died of shame, Claudio repents and agrees to marry Hero's supposed cousin, who turns out to be Hero herself, and the couple is at last united. Claudio's apparent lack of awareness and his haste to mistrust his beloved make him seem shallow and insensitive, and modern audiences tend to find him one of the least likeable or interesting of Shakespeare's young noblemen.

However, Claudio may be considered from another point of view that more likely reflects Shakespeare's intentions. Claudio, like Hero, is a model young Elizabethan. Even before he appears, he is extolled by the MESSENGER (14) as a paragon of knightly virtues, 'doing, in the figure of a lamb, the feats of a lion' (1.1.13–14). His youth and inexperience make him a plausible target for Don John's lies; his passive wooing of Hero, dependent on Don PEDRO's assistance, emphasises his vulnerability. He is often faulted for a seemingly mercenary interest in Hero (1.1.274), but his inquiry about her inheritance is merely conven-

tional: any young man of Shakespeare's day would ask such a question of a prospective bride, and the query simply demonstrates his interest in marriage. Gullible, he believes Hero has been unfaithful, but Shakespeare takes care to make his credulousness less ridiculous by having Don Pedro seem duped as well. The viciousness of Claudio's response indicates the extent to which he has been hurt by his seeming rejection. Both Claudio and Don Pedro regret the understandable anger of Leonato and ANTONIO (3) in 5.1, and they refrain from a violent response. Their awkward jesting confirms their embarrassment over the situation. Claudio's repentance and atonement are sometimes regarded as cursory and hypocritical, but Shakespeare treats them seriously. Although the scene at Hero's supposed tomb is brief, it is solemn. In 5.4 Claudio's return to happiness is complete, and he is unquestionably accepted in LEONATO's generous and cheerful court.

This more charitable interpretation of Claudio better suits the play, which is after all a comedy. Don John, the villain, is plainly saddled with all the blame. In any case, the play revolves around BEATRICE and BENEDICK; as Claudio's conventionality suggests, he is a relatively unimportant figure whose personality need not be well developed. Significantly, after the disguised Hero is revealed, the re-united lovers do not speak, as the focus of the play immediately shifts to Beatrice and Benedick. As Claudio's usefulness as a character is spent, he recedes into the background.

**Claudio (2)** Character in *Julius Caesar.* See CLAUDIUS (1).

**Claudio (3)** Character in *Measure for Measure,* a condemned prisoner and brother of ISABELLA. Claudio has impregnated JULIET (2) out of wedlock, and has been condemned to death, under an antiquated law, by ANGELO (2), the deputy of the DUKE (9) of VIENNA. This is the basic situation from which the play's central conflict arises—Angelo's demand of sex from Isabella in exchange for Claudio's life. Claudio's intentions are clearly honourable, however; he wants only to marry Juliet. Their sexual relations would have been perfectly legal but for a delay in marriage arrangements, and his condemnation is an evil excess on Angelo's part, as all the other characters agree.

Claudio's situation is a result of the Duke's lax regime in Vienna. Despite his aristocratic upbringing, the young man is familiar with the bordello world of LUCIO, POMPEY (1), and MISTRESS (2) OVERDONE, from whom we first learn of his plight, in 1.2. We recognise the stereotype of an immature young man in bad company, and we are not surprised that his ascetic sister is disappointed in him when his fear of death overcomes his sense of nobility. The moving passage in which he begs her to accommodate Angelo begins, 'to die, and go we know not where' (3.1.117). His reaction is touchingly human and we do not share Isabella's hysterical condemnation; the episode helps us realise that she is, in her way, as extreme as Angelo. Claudio's moral character is favourably compared with Angelo's in the contrast between his loving relationship with Juliet and Angelo's desertion of MARIANA (1).

**Claudius (Claudio) (1)** Minor character in *Julius Caesar*, a soldier in the army of BRUTUS (4). Claudius and VARRO, serving as messengers, sleep through the appearance of the GHOST (2) of CAESAR (1) in Brutus' tent and are awakened by Brutus to confirm that they have seen nothing.

In the first edition of *Julius Caesar*, that in the FOLIO (1623), Claudius' name is rendered as Claudio, and some modern editors follow this practice. Others, however, use Claudius, which is correct in Latin and appears in Shakespeare's source, NORTH's translation of PLUTARCH's *Lives*.

**Claudius (2), King** Character in *Hamlet*. See KING (5).

**Cleomenes (Cleomines) and Dion** Minor characters in *The Winter's Tale*, followers of King LEONTES of SICILIA. Cleomenes and Dion are virtually indistinguishable, and they share their only significant function, so they are treated together here. Seeking support for his accusation that Queen HERMIONE is guilty of adultery, King Leontes sends them to consult the oracle of Apollo. They describe the oracle in awestruck tones, with Dion ecstatically reminiscing, 'O, the sacrifice! / How ceremonious, solemn and unearthly' (3.1.6–7), and Cleomenes declaring that 'the ear-deaf'ning voice o' th' Oracle, / Kin to Jove's thunder, so surpris'd my sense, / That I was nothing' (3.1.9–11). Their remarks stand in for the actual appearance of a god—a feature of the other ROMANCES—and introduce the climactic moment of the play's first half, the checking of Leontes' madness through the apparent intervention of Apollo. However, when the oracle's pronouncement is delivered in 3.2, Cleomenes and Dion speak only half a line, in unison, swearing that they have not read the message. They reappear briefly in 5.1, but they are merely pawns of the plot.

**Cleon** Character in *Pericles*, governor of THARSUS and husband of DIONYZA. In 1.4 Cleon bemoans the catastrophic famine that has beset Tharsus, and when PERICLES brings relief, he is very grateful. He curses anyone who may ever harm his benefactor, and includes 'our wives, our children, or ourselves' (1.4. 103). This remark proves very ironic when Dionyza attempts to murder Pericles' daughter, MARINA, who has been left in their care. Cleon disapproves of his wife's deed, but he gives in to her harangue against his

cowardice, and, as the head of the family, he eventually receives much of the blame for it. The play's spokesman, GOWER (3), tells us in the EPILOGUE that Cleon and his entire family have been massacred by the citizens of Tharsus, who were incensed when they learned of the murder. When his bravery is questioned by Dionyza, Cleon resembles MACBETH (in *Macbeth* 1.7, 2.2, and 3.4) and the Duke of ALBANY (in *King Lear* 4.2), but he is a very minor figure whose function is to depict man's weakness in the face of evil.

**Cleopatra, Queen of Egypt (68–30 B.C.)** Historical figure and title character of *Antony and Cleopatra*, the Queen of Egypt and the lover of the Roman general, Mark ANTONY. Throughout Acts 1–4 Cleopatra displays the powerful charms of an experienced and thoroughly professional courtesan. She attempts to control her lover with a strategy of alternate taunts and insults and seductive sexuality. Then in Act 5, after Antony is dead, Cleopatra acknowledges the depth of her true feelings for her lover and dedicates her suicide to their joint love. She thereby transcends her earlier nature through the power of passion.

Many commentators, who admire Cleopatra's ultimate nobility do not accept the reality of her earlier role as the exploiter of Antony's sexuality. But Shakespeare's Cleopatra is clearly representative of a familiar dramatic character type: the scheming courtesan. From her first appearance she ridicules Antony, makes outrageous demands for his exclusive affection, declares that his love is insufficient—all classic techniques of emotional domination—and is oblivious to Antony's more romantic interpretation of love. She even uses his devotion against him when she declares that his lack of affection for his wife is evidence that he will eventually desert her as well.

Cleopatra also has great charm and she richly deserves the famous tribute from ENOBARBUS, 'Age cannot wither her, nor custom stale / Her infinite variety' (2.2.235–236). She is witty even in the direst extremity. As the dying Antony is hoisted to her hide-out she can jest, in 4.15.32. In fact, some critics consider her one of the great comic figures in Shakespeare, comparable to FALSTAFF. She has a pleasing delight in mischief; Enobarbus accompanies his description of her magnificence with an account of when she put aside regal dignity and hopped gaily through the streets. Her beauty is enrapturing, and she has in abundance the intoxicating sexuality essential to the successful courtesan; as Enobarbus puts it, 'vilest things / Become themselves in her' (2.2.238–239).

She also has genuine affection for Antony, but even as she reveals her fondness for him—in his absence—she discloses her past history as a courtesan. She speaks in 1.5.18–34 of her earlier affairs with Julius CAESAR (1) and Pompey the Great (father of the play's POMPEY [2]). Her hurt and anger at the news of Antony's marriage to OCTAVIA are certainly genuine, but when she learns of Octavia's unattractive physical features her spirits are restored, for, courtesan-like, her confidence in her sexual allure assures her that she will win her lover back. She does, but when her flight from the battle of ACTIUM brings about Antony's disgrace, she once again displays her essentially selfish nature, in 3.13, when she accepts Caesar's offer of an alliance, conveyed by THIDIAS. She coolly waits out Antony's rage—'I must stay his time' (3.13.155)—and resumes the role of docile and playful lover. However, when her sailors again betray Antony and his rage drives her away, she resorts to an extremely cynical ploy, the pretended suicide that sparks Antony's real one. Falsely assumed emotion—the favourite weapon of the courtesan—remains Cleopatra's most characteristic resource.

However, in the end she is transformed through her noble response to the death of her lover. In 4.15.25–26 she first mentions the idea of suicide simply as a way to foil Caesar's potential humiliations, but after Antony's death she refers to it as a noble ideal on the model Antony himself has offered, 'the high Roman fashion' (4.15.87). In refusing to be humiliated, Cleopatra finds herself at one with Antony in the Roman ideal of honourable suicide. SELEUCUS' revelation that she has withheld treasure from Caesar is sometimes taken as evidence that Cleopatra reverts briefly to ideas of survival, though another interpretation is that she chose to deceive Caesar as to her intentions so that he would not prevent them. However, even if we suppose that she does waver, she also returns to the idea of a noble death, and her focus remains on Antony—rather than on Caesar—as she approaches the deed.

Cleopatra accepts death because it is the only end equal to her newly awakened love for Antony. It is in her ecstatic appraisal of him as 'an Emperor Antony . . .' (5.2.76–100) that she first finds the exalted note of commitment to the memory of her lover that carries her through to the end. When she cries, 'Husband, I come' (5.2.286), she completes her transformation into 'fire, and air; my other elements / I give to baser life' (5.2.288–289). When she abandons her actual, earthly relationship with Antony for an eternal union, Cleopatra transcends the mortal world of politics and courtesanship where she and Antony had come to grief.

Cleopatra's personality does not change with her final ecstasy—Shakespeare was too good a writer to exchange one sort of portrayal for another at the close of the play. Cleopatra dies, but she makes her death a luxurious and hedonistic one. She combines the splendour of grand costume—'Give me my robe, put on my crown' (5.2.279)—with an almost sexual surrender to death at the end, when she cries, 'As sweet as balm, as soft as air, as gentle. / O Antony!' (5.2.310–311). Her theatrical nature provides the gran-

deur that elevates the tragedy provoked by her earlier conduct. Thus we can see Cleopatra's moral defects—her selfishness as a lover and her practice of the courtesan's wiles—in a new light, as inextricable elements of a personality powerful enough to generate the mysterious grace that she brings to her final gesture. Through this grace and power, Cleopatra's vision of reunion with Antony after death is a triumphant affirmation of love and life. Even in seeming defeat she embodies the imagination of the individual and the value of what could have been over what worldly power has insisted on. She knows that compared to her, Caesar is 'but Fortune's knave' (5.2.3), for the conqueror, with his limited vision, can only suppose that 'her life in Rome / Would be eternal in our triumph' (5.1.65–66), but Cleopatra's death is the true triumph celebrated by the play.

The historical Cleopatra bore little resemblance to Shakespeare's character. She was not particularly beautiful—Shakespeare's source, PLUTARCH's Lives, attributes her magnetism to her conversation. Nor, in all probability, did she die for the sake of love but rather for the more practical end of avoiding a horrible captivity, and she only killed herself after she attempted to win Caesar with a promise to betray Antony. She was descended from one of the Greek successors of Alexander the Great, and was entirely of Greek ancestry and not African in any degree, despite the modern tendency to classify her among Shakespeare's black characters. Cleopatra inherited the throne of Egypt in 51 B.C., at the age of 17. Deposed by an aristocratic clique in 49 B.C., she was restored with the assistance of Julius Caesar a year later.

She became Caesar's mistress, and she later filled the same function for Pompey the Great and Antony—unlike in the play, however, she did not become Antony's mistress until after his marriage to Octavia. In all three cases her motive is clear; she needed the political support of the forces of Rome present in the eastern Mediterranean, and thus she ingratiated herself with whoever commanded them. Modern scholars think it unlikely that she influenced the policies of any of her protectors, who simply used her as a means of extracting wealth from Egypt. Antony's gifts to her of kingdoms and power that Octavius Caesar complains of in the play were merely ordinary applications of Roman policy by which administrative jurisdictions in conquered lands were consolidated under a client ruler. The arrangement inspired no mistrust at the time. Cleopatra, who was reportedly greedy for even the trappings of power, persistently requested more such titular kingdoms, but Antony refused her.

When Antony found himself at war with Caesar he naturally made use of the Egyptian kingdom that he governed through Cleopatra, but the unreliability of Egyptian forces at Actium and afterwards—as recounted in the play—cannot be attributed to her influence. It is uncertain whether Antony and Cleopatra were married, but she bore three children by him; the two boys were killed after Caesar's victory, and the girl later became a pawn of Roman politics and was married to a Numidian king.

**Clerk**   Minor character in *2 Henry VI*, a victim executed by the rebels led by Jack CADE. Cade and his men are suspicious of the clerk's literacy, which they construe as a sign of hostility towards the peasantry. They are particularly infuriated by the fact that his given name is Emmanuel, a word often used to head legal documents. Cade orders him hung 'with his pen and ink-horn about his neck' (4.2.103–104). The incident is one of several that Shakespeare uses to depict Cade's rebellion as an anarchic uprising by ignorant peasants concerned only with killing their betters, although historically this was not the case.

**Clifford (1), Lord John (c. 1435–1461)**   Character in *2* and *3 Henry VI*, the obsessed avenger of his father's death, who kills both the Duke of YORK (8) and his young son, RUTLAND (1). As Young Clifford, this character appears briefly in Act 5 of *2 Henry VI* as a supporter of King HENRY VI against the Duke of York and as a participant in the battle of ST. ALBANS. On the battlefield, he sees the dead body of his father, Thomas CLIFFORD (2), whom York has killed, and he delivers a famous speech (5.2.40–65), a rhetorical comparison of this death with the last judgement, closing with a vow of revenge that prefigures some of the most dramatic action in *3 Henry VI*.

In the later play Clifford's bloodthirsty quest for revenge reflects the bestiality that England's aristocracy has descended to as the civil war progresses. 'Patience is for poltroons', he cries (1.1.62), when King Henry tries to placate an angry earl. In 1.3, when he encounters Rutland, a child attempting to flee the battle of WAKEFIELD, he kills the boy, despite his pleas for mercy, citing his own father's death as justification. When York is captured in 1.4, Queen MARGARET (1) can only with difficulty restrain Clifford long enough to enjoy herself tormenting her enemy with an account of Rutland's murder. Finally, unable to wait any longer, Clifford kills York also. In 2.2, before the battle of TOWTON, Clifford chastises King Henry for his 'harmful pity' in a speech filled with the animal imagery that contributes to the impression of savagery that runs so strongly throughout the play. Ironically, it is another bloody deed by Clifford that costs his side the battle: when WARWICK (3) hears that Clifford has killed his brother, that seemingly defeated leader is aroused and inspires the Yorkists to rally and win the day. In 2.6 Clifford appears, wounded in this battle, to deliver a death-bed speech in which he regrets the weakness of the monarch that has brought the country to this bloody pass. He recognises that his enemies are upon

him, and he dies daring them to wreak their vengeance on him. When they recognise him, before they realise he is dead, they taunt and mock him.

Shakespeare took his account of Clifford's revenge on Rutland from HALL (2), but it is entirely unhistorical. Rutland was not a child; he was an officer in the Yorkist army. While he did die at Wakefield, it was never known who killed him. Moreover, it is not known who killed Clifford's father at St Albans either; he died in the thick of the battle, as the playwright also reports in *3 Henry VI* (in 1.1.9), in a famous instance of Shakespearean carelessness. Lastly, Clifford did not die at Towton, but in a skirmish several days earlier. He was struck in the neck by an arrow, as in the play, but was reported at the time to have died instantly.

**Clifford (2), Lord Thomas (1414–1455)**   Historical figure and character in *2 Henry VI*, a backer of King HENRY VI against the claims of the Duke of YORK (8). Clifford first appears as a representative of the King, offering a pardon to the rebel followers of Jack CADE in 4.8. Following York's declaration of rebellion in 5.1, Clifford supports the King and exchanges insults and challenges with the Earl of WARWICK (3), but in the ensuing first battle of ST. ALBANS, he is killed by York. His son, Young CLIFFORD (1), on seeing his father's corpse, vows revenge on the followers of York, anticipating events in *3 Henry VI*. In a famous instance of Shakespeare's carelessness, Clifford's death is reported in different ways in *3 Henry VI*. In 1.1.9, it is stated that Clifford was killed by common soldiers, which almost surely is historically accurate. However, in 1.3.5 and 1.3.46, his son declares that he was killed by York. The playwright was following separate accounts in his sources, making good dramatic use of the son's reported remark—probably a rhetorical one—and forgetting to omit the altogether more plausible version.

**Clitus (active 42 B.C.)**   Historical figure and minor character in *Julius Caesar*, a soldier in the army of BRUTUS (4). In 5.5 Clitus—like DARDANIUS and VOLUMNIUS—refuses to help Brutus to commit suicide after the battle of PHILIPPI, saying 'I'll rather kill myself' (5.5.7). The episode shows the fondness with which Brutus' subordinates regard him, fostering an aura of sentiment around his death. Little is known of the historical Clitus, whose role Shakespeare took from PLUTARCH's *Lives*.

**Clive, Kitty (1711–1785)**   English actress. A great comic actress, Clive spent most of her career playing opposite David GARRICK. She was especially acclaimed as CELIA in *As You Like It*, and she also played OLIVIA. She was perhaps best known for her performances in the title role of Garrick's *Catherine and Petruchio*, an adaptation of *The Taming of the Shrew*. Though she played PORTIA (to the SHYLOCK of Charles MACKLIN), OPHELIA, and HAMLET (in accordance with the 18th-century vogue for female Hamlets), her strength was in broad COMEDY, and she is said to have fought with Garrick over his reluctance to cast her in TRAGEDY. She was especially popular in the London literary world and was a good friend of Samuel JOHNSON (7) and the writer Horace Walpole (1717–1797).

**Cloten**   Character in *Cymbeline,* the uncouth son of the QUEEN (2) and the rejected suitor of IMOGEN, who then plans to rape her and kill her husband, POST-HUMUS. Cloten is a comic villain for the most part. He is a stupid and vainglorious man who inspires bemused contempt, though he has his threatening moments and reminds us of the potential for tragedy that underlies the fairy-tale ambience of much of the play. He is finally killed when he happens, entirely by chance, on the lost prince GUIDERIUS, who handily beheads him and then remarks, 'This Cloten was a fool, an empty purse' (4.2.113). His function is that of a fairy-tale villain whose fate is to be defeated by the hand of providence.

Cloten's personality and function vary considerably in the course of the play. In Acts 1–2 Cloten is quite simply a boor; a braggart who is mocked by his own companions (see LORD [15]) and by Imogen's LADY (3). Imogen tells him he is not worth the 'mean'st garment' of Posthumus (2.3.132), and complains that she is 'sprited with a fool' (2.3.138). In Act 3 Cloten takes on a different, less inane, air as he blusters patriotically and helps to commit Britain to a foolish war against ROME. Finally, in Act 4 he is the villain who schemes to kill Posthumus in front of Imogen before he rapes her, and who crassly insults Guiderius for his supposed inferiority.

Such changes make it hard to precisely characterise Cloten's function in the play, and this problem offers a hint of Shakespeare's trouble with the ROMANCES, a new genre in which *Cymbeline* was an experiment. The irregularities in Cloten's personality are similar to those of the play as a whole, and they betray the playwright's difficulty in melding the realistic characters to which he was accustomed with the ethereal figures required by the romances. Cloten seems to be a compound of several types of writing, created as Shakespeare struggled with the task of generating a new type of character, a villain who must convincingly represent evil without being so real as to intrude on a world of fantasy. Though a faulty character, Cloten foreshadows a much more successful figure of this kind, CALIBAN of *The Tempest.*

Some scholars have speculated that portions of Cloten's role may have been considerably modified by the actor who played the character, probably Robert ARMIN. Armin wrote plays and was famous for improvisation, so he was capable of creating additional dia-

logue. Moreover, in addition to his Shakespearean roles, he specialised in playing a character type of his own devising, a mentally limited CLOWN (1) who may be reflected in some of Cloten's doltishness. Cloten's speeches are in both prose and verse, and this theory suggests that the prose passages were written—or at least altered in performance, before publication—by Armin. However, though some such alteration could have contaminated the text—if it was based on a PROMPT-BOOK—this idea cannot be proven. More probably the evidence reflects the difficulties mentioned above.

**Clown** (1)   Character type often used by Shakespeare, a humorously ignorant and unsophisticated figure, usually male and often associated with rustic ways. The clown is to some extent a comic caricature of a peasant; his humour is earthy and simple, often featuring awkwardness and confusion, such as the unintentionally comic misuse of language, but there is an underlying element of shrewdness as well. Shakespeare's clowns include some of his most delightful characters, from such early creations as LAUNCE in *Two Gentlemen of Verona* and COSTARD in *Love's Labour's Lost,* through DOGBERRY in *Much Ado About Nothing* and BOTTOM in *A Midsummer Night's Dream,* to the CLOWN (8) in *The Winter's Tale.* Most common in COMEDY, the clown is usually minor in the HISTORY PLAYS (see, e.g., FEE-BLE)—though Mistress QUICKLY has something of the clown and was probably played by an actor who specialised in the type. The clown, however, often appears in TRAGEDY, where he provides comic relief. The CLOWN (2) of *Titus Andronicus* foreshadows such more developed figures as the CLOWN (7) who is the incongruous bearer of CLEOPATRA's deadly asps in *Antony and Cleopatra,* the PORTER (3) in *Macbeth,* and, perhaps most famous of Shakespeare's clowns, the GRAVE-DIG-GER in *Hamlet.*

The clown is usually distinguished from another Shakespearean character type, the FOOL (1), although the Elizabethans used the terms synonymously. (For example, FESTE, who is unquestionably a fool, being a professional jester, and who is called a 'fool' by the other characters, is identified as 'Clown' in speech headings and stage directions throughout the play.) Nevertheless, the difference between the two comic roles is unmistakable. Where the clown's comic effects are accidental results of his bumbling nature, the fool is intentionally witty. Clowns, moreover, tend to operate outside the main plots and often—especially in such early figures as Launce and LAUNCELOT (of *The Merchant of Venice*)—address the audience in somewhat elaborate asides, usually narratives. In contrast, the fool is more involved with the main characters and speaks more analytically.

Although, to some extent, these different comic figures may reflect changes in the actors Shakespeare wrote for (see ARMIN; KEMPE), the distinction is significant in itself. The fool's subtle and intellectual comedy provides a satirical edge, whereas the clown serves a different symbolic function. He is to some extent a parody of the sublimely simple rustic of PASTORAL tradition, but the mockery is not cruel. The clown is ridiculous but worthy; he retains the virtues of nature and is fundamentally sensible, as is demonstrated when Dogberry accidentally discovers the villains, or when Bottom is the only mortal to experience fairyland. To some extent, this is a reflection of his social position—because he has nothing to lose, he can speak the truth as he sees it—but the clown is also closer to nature and thus closer to the unconscious. He manifests our simplest, often 'vulgar' impulses, with the solid strength of one who is relatively uncorrupted by society. With a natural good grace, he accepts his clumsiness, like his inferior social position, as part of his destined lot. Because he is more obviously long-suffering than profound, the clown parallels on a more accessible plane the stoicism of the tragic hero.

**Clown (2)**   Minor character in *Titus Andronicus*. The clown appears in 4.3, carrying two pigeons in a basket. After some conversation, in which the Clown reveals himself to be a comically naïve rustic, a traditional dramatic type (see CLOWN [1]), TITUS (1) offers him a fee to make the pigeons an offering to the Emperor SATURNINUS. Titus includes a taunting message of his own, wrapped around a dagger. When, in 4.4, the hapless Clown delivers his birds, and Titus' message, to Saturninus, the infuriated emperor orders him killed. He is led away, exclaiming, 'Hang'd, by 'r-Lady! then I have brought up a neck to a fair end' (4.4.48–49). This insignificant addition to the play's roster of victims is one of Shakespeare's earliest Clowns, and his realistic, if dim-witted, voice provides a simple, earthy moment of relief from the savagery that dominates the play.

**Clown (3)**   Character in *Twelfth Night*. See FESTE.

**Clown (4)**   Either of two characters in *Hamlet*. See GRAVE-DIGGER; OTHER.

**Clown (5)**   Character in *All's Well That Ends Well*, court jester to the COUNTESS (2) of ROSSILLION. The Clown comments on aspects of the play, both through parody and by direct references. He professes to be a rustic (as his designation as a CLOWN [1] suggests), 'a woodland fellow' (4.5.44) who enjoys ridiculing the royal court, but he is clearly a sophisticated professional FOOL (1). His somewhat cynical worldliness adds an element of realism that counters the improbabilities of the play.

Sometimes the Clown is overtly contemptuous, as in his insults to PAROLLES in 2.4 and his disparagement

of Bertram in 3.2, but usually his function is more indirectly carried out; his concerns parallel those of the main plot, drawing our attention to it in odd ways. For instance, he expounds upon his proposed marriage to 'Isbel the woman' (1.3.16) just after we have been introduced to HELENA and BERTRAM. He goes on to equate Helena with HELEN of TROY, a digression that suggests the sexual conflict emerging in the main story line. Later, in 3.2, he rejects Isbel, apparently out of sexual exhaustion, just as the Countess is reading the letter in which Bertram tells of his rejection of Helena. The Clown's parody of courtly manners in 2.2 immediately precedes PAROLLES' assumption of gentlemanly airs in 2.3 and is itself a commentary on the vanity of social rank, a theme of the play. In his final lines, in which he asserts exuberantly that Parolles smells bad, he not only emphasises Parolles' loss of status, but the rankness of his 'similes of comfort' (5.2.24–25) seems to sum up the play's obnoxious developments to this point. At the same time, he offers some sympathy for Parolles, declaring 'I do pity his distress' (5.2.24), thus maintaining our hope of a milder outcome, which is indeed about to develop.

The Clown is an oddly melancholy jester, with his low-key parodies of theology and his claim to be in the service of 'the black prince . . . alias the devil' (4.5.39–40). He is sometimes somewhat nasty, as when he rejects Isbel, and he can be overly wordy, as LAFEW reminds us when he tells him 'Go thy ways; I begin to be aweary of thee' (4.5.53). However, the Countess clearly enjoys him, though she recognises that he is a 'shrewd knave and an unhappy' (4.5.60). He reminds her of her late husband, 'who made himself much sport out of him' (4.5.61–62). The pleasant relationship between the Countess and her jester contributes to our sense of her household as a source of generosity and kindness that helps to offset the unpleasant aspects of the play.

It is presumed that the Clown's part was intended for Robert ARMIN, the actor who specialised in jesters for the KING'S MEN. His name, Lavatch (sometimes rendered Lavache), is not mentioned until 5.2.1. The name is usually regarded as a corruption of the French *la vache* ('the cow'), though some scholars believe it represents the French *lavage* or the Italian *lavaggio* ('washing, cleansing').

**Clown (6)**   Minor character in *Othello*, a jester, or FOOL (1), in the retinue of OTHELLO. The Clown jokes lewdly with the MUSICIANS (6), in 3.1, before dismissing them with Othello's payment. In 3.4 he briefly jests with DESDEMONA before carrying a message for her. As comic relief, the Clown does not do much to interrupt the play's increasing tension; he may well have been merely a conventional figure, expected by Shakespeare's audiences and therefore supplied by the playwright.

**Clown (7)**   Minor character in *Antony and Cleopatra*, the pretended fig seller who provides CLEOPATRA with the poisonous snakes with which she kills herself. The Clown, summoned by CHARMIAN in 5.2, is a CLOWN (1) in the literary meaning of the term in Shakespeare's day. He is a conventional comic figure, the ludicrously naïve country bumpkin who had figured in COMEDY from ancient times. He comically warns Cleopatra that poisonous snakes are dangerous. Solemnly, he states, '. . . his biting is immortal: those that do die of it, do seldom or never recover' (5.2.245–247). Clowns are usually talkative, and he goes on to tell of 'a very honest woman, but something given to lie' (5.2.250–251) who has reported on her own death by snake bite. He further expounds on the tendency of women to be corrupted by the devil—another medieval comic routine—before Cleopatra can get him to leave.

With ANTONY dead and Cleopatra about to kill herself, this episode comes at an agonising point in the play's climax. The scene shatters the fascinated horror of the audience, while at the same time heightening it by the inane and excruciating postponement of the plot's development. Further, the play's sudden comic tone at this crucial moment highlights the triumphant, celebratory aspect of Cleopatra's suicide; the traditional ending of a romantic COMEDY is evoked, and the transcendence of Cleopatra's total commitment to love is emphasised.

**Clown (8)**   Character in *The Winter's Tale*, foster-brother of PERDITA. The Clown is present in 3.3 when the abandoned infant Perdita is discovered by his father, the SHEPHERD (2). In Act 4, 16 years later, the Clown is part of Perdita's pastoral world, though he has no direct contact with her. As his designation implies (see CLOWN [1]), he is an oafish rustic, a likeable and well-meaning fellow who is somewhat stupid and unconsciously comical. In 3.3 he is unwittingly funny when describing the horrible deaths of ANTIGONUS and the MARINER (1), helping to establish the comic tone of the play's second half. A gullible victim, he is robbed by AUTOLYCUS in 4.3, and in 4.4, at the shepherds' festival, his foolish pleasure in buying gifts for his girlfriend, MOPSA, adds to our enjoyment of the scene. He declares to the peddler (Autolycus in disguise), 'If I were not in love with Mopsa, thou shouldst take no money of me; but being enthralled as I am, it will also be the bondage of certain ribbons and gloves' (4.4.233–236).

Later in 4.4, when King POLIXENES, angry at Perdita's love for his son FLORIZEL, threatens the Shepherd with death, the Clown encourages his father to disclaim his adopted daughter. Autolycus offers to take them to the king for a fee, but he tricks them onto the ship carrying Perdita and Florizel to SICILIA, where Perdita's identity as King LEONTES' daughter is discovered. The Shepherd and the Clown are rewarded with

a raise in status, and in 5.2 the Clown comically brags of being 'a gentleman born . . . and [having] been so any time these four hours' (5.2.134–136). Despite his foolishness and his single act of cowardice—understandable in a shepherd facing a king's wrath—the Clown is clearly a good person. As such, he contributes to the atmosphere of human virtue that characterises the second half of the play, countering the evil of the first.

**Coat of arms, Shakespeare's**   Heraldic escutcheon signifying the social status of the family as members of the gentry, awarded in 1596 to Shakespeare's father, John SHAKESPEARE (9), by the Garter King of Arms (a government official charged with authorising such honours). This honour was said to reflect the services of an unnamed ancestor to King Henry VII, founder of the TUDOR DYNASTY, but in fact depended on the growing success of John's son as a playwright. John Shakespeare had applied for a grant of arms 20 years earlier, but his financial reversals derailed the effort. In a class-conscious society such as 16th-century England, such an award was an important symbol of a family's honourable place in society and was commonly acquired by men who had attained social prominence and wealth. As a visual emblem, the coat of arms could be displayed on one's door, on personal items, and the like. Specifically, the Shakespeare coat of arms consists of a gold shield with a diagonal black band bearing the image of a gold spear—a visual pun on the name 'Shakespeare'—with a silver head. Above the shield is a falcon holding another spear. It appears on Shakespeare's tomb in the parish church in STRATFORD.

**Cobbler**   Minor character in *Julius Caesar*, a COMMONER (1). In 1.1, as the tribunes FLAVIUS (1) and MARULLUS disperse a crowd of artisans gathered to cheer CAESAR (1), the Cobbler jests impertinently when they ask about his profession. He calls himself 'a mender of bad soles' (1.1.13) and asserts that he has joined the crowd to encourage the others to wear out their shoes and thus gain extra business. This brief bit of comedy immediately brings the audience into the reality of ancient ROME and prepares them for the contrasting spectacle of the rioting PLEBEIANS (1) in Act 3. In some editions the Cobbler is identified as the Second Commoner.

**Cobham, William Brooke, Lord (d. 1597)**   Contemporary of Shakespeare, powerful aristocrat whose pressure probably resulted in the change of the name OLDCASTLE to FALSTAFF. Cobham was descended from the historical Oldcastle and was offended by the use of the name for a gluttonous lecher and coward in *1* and *2 Henry IV*. His position as Lord Chamberlain, the official responsible for the royal entertainment budget, made him important to the acting companies, and therefore the character's name was altered.

Cobham held his office only from August 1596 until his death in March 1597. His predecessor, Lord HUNS-DON (2) had used the position to protect the theatrical profession from the London government, which was dominated by Puritans and thus opposed to public drama. However, under Cobham, the London authorities achieved a long-sought goal and banished the players from the city limits.

The power of his office and his antipathy to the theatre suggest that it was Cobham who instigated the change in Oldcastle's name, but the complainant may have been his son, Henry Brooke. In either case, the family may well have regretted the attempt to protect their ancestor's name, for their protest became a public joke, as various references in surviving letters of the time make clear. Moreover, the substitution of the name Falstaff was in itself another joke, for, in addition to its punning suggestion of sexual impotence, it referred to a notorious coward, Sir John FASTOLFE, or Falstaffe, who appears in *1 Henry VI*. Oldcastle's descendants were now associated not only with the offensive character in the *Henry IV* plays, but also with a second unpleasant character from another very popular work. In addition, in *The Merry Wives of Windsor,* when Frank FORD (1) foolishly worries that he is being cuckolded by Falstaff, he disguises himself and adopts the name BROOK (1), a probable reference to the Cobhams' family name. (Ford's pseudonym was later changed, possibly after further protest by Henry Brooke.) A number of subtle references to Oldcastle are made in *The Merry Wives* (e.g., in 4.5.5), further ensuring that the audience would not forget the increasingly comical conflict. Worst of all, from the Cobhams' point of view, the *Henry IV* plays were frequently performed using the name Oldcastle until well into the 17th century, despite Shakespeare's changes. Further, in other writings of the period the name Oldcastle is linked to the gluttonous, lascivious behaviour we call Falstaffian.

**Coburn, Charles Douville (1877–1961)** American actor and producer. With his actress wife, Ivah Wills Coburn, Coburn founded the Coburn Shakespearian Players in 1906, and they produced many of Shakespeare's plays, as well as others, with great success. In 1934 they founded one of the first summer theatre festivals at Union College in Schenectady, New York. Coburn retired upon his wife's death in 1937, returning to the stage only once more, in 1946, to play FAL-STAFF, the role for which he had been best known.

**Cobweb** Character in *A Midsummer Night's Dream,* a fairy, an attendant to the Fairy Queen TITANIA. In 3.1 Titania assigns Cobweb to the retinue of the comical rustic BOTTOM because the Queen has been magically induced to love him. Cobweb serves Bottom by hunting for honey in 4.1. His name suggests the spider's short-lived weaving; Bottom also refers to the ancient use of cobwebs to stop small cuts from bleeding (3.1.176); perhaps the name suggests that Cobweb possesses medicinal lore.

**Coleridge, Samuel Taylor (1772–1834)** English poet and literary critic. Best known as a poet, Coleridge also lectured and wrote on literature. His lectures on Shakespeare, delivered between 1802 and 1818, were not published until 1849, but they were nevertheless influential in their own time. While regarded as highly uneven in quality, they offer telling insights into the process of creating characters and letting the play evolve through that process. On certain plays—*Richard II,* for instance—Coleridge's opinions are still regarded as among the most stimulating available. He was among the first English critics to acclaim Shakespeare's poetry—as opposed to the theatrical virtues of the plays—since the 17th century, for the intervening generations had tended to ignore this aspect of the playwright's work. Inspired in part by the work of A. W. SCHLEGEL, which he had studied in Germany, Coleridge's lectures were an important stimulus to the literary criticism of the English Romantic movement.

**Colevile (Coleville) of the Dale, Sir John (d. 1405)** Historical figure and minor character in *2 Henry IV,* a rebel knight captured by FALSTAFF. After the rebels have been tricked into dispersing without a battle, Colevile peaceably surrenders to Falstaff, who makes much of his own valour as he turns his prisoner over to Prince John of LANCASTER (3). Lancaster sends Colevile to be executed. The episode provides a comical glimpse of Falstaff in the long and otherwise entirely political Act 4.

Shakespeare took Colevile's name from HOLINSHED, who lists him among the executed rebels, but it is possible that Colevile was pardoned and lived to be recorded as Sir John Colvyl, who fought in FRANCE (1) with HENRY V.

**Collatine (Tarquinius Collatinus)** Legendary husband of the Roman matron Lucretia and minor figure in *The Rape of Lucrece,* the husband of LUCRECE. After being sexually assaulted by the king's son, TARQUIN, Lucrece sends for her father and Collatine, or Collatinus, as he is occasionally called (e.g., in line 218). Collatine does not appear until line 1584, and he is mostly tongue-tied by grief for the rest of the poem, for Lucrece informs the men what has happened and kills herself after demanding vengeance. Collatinus is roused to revenge only by another witness of Lucrece's account, Junius BRUTUS (2).

The last words of the poem's introductory ARGU-

MENT observe that the vengeance that Brutus exacted upon Tarquin resulted in the fall of his father's kingdom and the establishment of the Roman Republic. Shakespeare took this conclusion from his sources, OVID and LIVY, but the association of the birth of the republic with a rape has no historical truth. All that is known of the historical Tarquinius Collatinus is that in 509 B.C. he was (with Brutus) one of the first two consuls, the executives who jointly ruled the republican government of Rome. His name suggests that he was Etruscan, like the departing royal family.

**Collier (1), Constance (1878–1955)**  English actress. Constance Collier began her long career playing PEASEBLOSSOM at the age of three. She subsequently became one of the famous Gaiety Girls but left to play in more serious dramas. A member of Beerbohm TREE's company from 1901 to 1908, she played numerous Shakespearean parts. Beginning in 1908 she divided her career between New York and London and was very popular in both cities. She played QUEEN (9) Gertrude to John BARRYMORE's HAMLET in his London production of 1925.

**Collier (2), John Payne (1789–1883)**  English scholar and forger. A one-time journalist and lawyer, Collier established himself as a Shakespeare scholar with a series of books published between 1835 and 1850. He is best known, however, for having forged a number of documents in support of his literary theories: annotations in 17th-century books; contemporary references to Shakespeare; theatrical business records; a source for *The Tempest,* etc. Collier claimed to own an annotated copy of the second FOLIO and published the notations as *Notes and Emendations to the Text of Shakespeare's Plays* (1852). The authenticity of this material was questioned by a number of scholars, and further investigation revealed both its falseness and the existence of other forgeries. Collier's forgeries still have an impact on Shakespearean scholarship, for the extent of his handiwork cannot be precisely established, and any documents to which he is known to have had access must be viewed with scepticism.

**Collins, Francis (d. 1617)**  Lawyer in STRATFORD, the drafter of Shakespeare's will. Collins, who served Shakespeare as a lawyer on a business deal in 1605, was probably also a friend, for he received a sizeable bequest in the playwright's will, though it probably included his fee for drawing it up. He also witnessed the will. Collins held various public offices in Stratford, beginning in 1600, though by 1613 he lived in Warwick. He was a close friend of John COMBE (1) and drew up his will (which contained a bequest to Shakespeare). He moved back to Stratford in 1617, when offered the post of town clerk on the condition that he do so, but he died a few months later.

**Colman, George (1732–1794)**  English playwright and theatrical entrepreneur. Colman was a close associate of David GARRICK, who produced his plays, including *The Jealous Wife* (1761), one of the most popular comedies of its time. After a dispute with Garrick over the casting of a play, however, Colman leased the Covent Garden Theatre, where, from 1767 to 1774, he produced many plays, including those of Oliver Goldsmith (1730–1774). He staged *Cymbeline,* but his most important Shakespearean production was *King Lear,* from which he dropped many of the alterations made by Nahum TATE, though he added some of his own. He later managed another theatre before retiring in 1789. Among the plays Colman produced were the early works of his son, also George Colman (1762–1836), later a notable comic dramatist.

**Colonne, Guido delle (active late 13th century)**  Sicilian writer, author of a source of *Troilus and Cressida.* Colonne translated the *Roman de Troie* by Benoit de SAINTE-MAURE, a 12th-century poem on the TROJAN WAR, into Latin prose. His version, the *Historia destructionis Troiae* (published 1270–1287) became the standard work on the subject until the rediscovery of HOMER during the RENAISSANCE. Colonne's book influenced Shakespeare through two English works. A French translation was re-translated into English by William CAXTON as *The Recuyell of the Historyes of Troye* (1471), and John LYDGATE was inspired by the *Historia* to compose a long poem entitled *Troy Book* (1420, publ. 1512, 1555). These two works provide much of the detail in the account of the war reported in *Troilus and Cressida.*

**Combe (1), John (before 1561–1614)**  Landowner and money-lender in STRATFORD, a friend of Shakespeare. Said to have been the richest citizen of Stratford in his day, Combe was noted for his charities. Though he often sued for repayment of the loans he made, several of these creditors later named him in their wills as their good friend. He died a bachelor, and in his will he left the large sum of £30 to be distributed among the poor of the town. He and his uncle William COMBE (4) sold Shakespeare 127 acres of land near WELCOMBE in 1602. His brother Thomas and his nephews Thomas and William COMBE (2, 3, 5) were also associates of Shakespeare. Combe and the playwright appear to have been close friends. He left Shakespeare £5 in his will—a quite sizeable token. His tomb in Stratford's Holy Trinity Church, like Shakespeare's tomb nearby, was designed by Gheerart JANSSEN (2). Later in the 17th century, two EPITAPHS on Combe were attributed to Shakespeare. One is simply a variant on a traditional rhyme about usurers, and the other seems un-Shakespearean sytlistically, so modern scholars tend to doubt the ascriptions.

**Combe (2), Thomas (d. 1609)** Landowner in STRAT-FORD, a business associate of Shakespeare and the brother of his friend John COMBE (1). Thomas Combe was partner with Shakespeare in a lease to collect the tithes—or church taxes—on some agricultural land near WELCOMBE (the rights to such taxes were transferable, like commodities shares). When he died, his share in the lease was passed on to his elder son, William COMBE (5), who proved a difficult business partner. His second son, another Thomas COMBE (3), was a friend of Shakespeare. According to an 18th-century tradition, Shakespeare wrote an insulting poem about this Thomas Combe, by way of a humorous EPITAPH; it was published in 1740. Modern scholars generally reject the attribution.

**Combe (3), Thomas (1589–1657)** Lawyer in STRATFORD and friend of Shakespeare, son of Thomas COMBE (2). In his will Shakespeare left Thomas Combe his sword, as a mark of esteem and friendship, but nothing more is known of their relationship. Thomas supported his brother William COMBE (5) in the controversy over the enclosure of lands at WELCOMBE, and like William, he seems to have been a violent man; Thomas GREENE (3) recorded an account of Combe 'kicking and beating' a shepherd who demanded his pay.

**Combe (4), William (1551–1610)** Landowner in WARWICKSHIRE. Combe, the uncle of Shakespeare's friend John COMBE (1), lived in the city of Warwick but owned land in and around STRATFORD and served as a lawyer for that town. In 1602 he and his nephew sold Shakespeare some land near WELCOMBE. Combe was frequently a member of parliament for Warwickshire.

**Combe (5), William (1586–1667)** Lawyer, money-lender, and landowner in STRATFORD, a business associate of Shakespeare. Combe was a son of Thomas COMBE (2) and brother of Thomas COMBE (3). From his father, he inherited a share with Shakespeare in a tithe lease—the leased right to collect the taxes on a piece of land. In 1611 Shakespeare sued him for tardiness in paying his share of the rent, leaving the lease open to seizure. This was part of a complicated series of legal actions involving a number of others, and it was settled equably between Shakespeare and Combe. Combe supported an attempt to enclose large tracts of cultivated land at WELCOMBE for sheep grazing, an episode in which he played a brutal part. At one point Julian SHAW (4), the bailiff, or mayor, of Stratford, wrote to Combes that it seemed his conscience was 'blinded . . . with a desire to make yourself rich with other men's loss'. In the 1620s he was said to be richer than his uncle John COMBE (1) had been, suggesting a considerable fortune. During the Civil Wars he fought for the Parliamentarian side, and Royalist troops sacked his house in Stratford. His fortunes declined during the decade of the wars, and in 1650 he was reported to be in considerable debt, with all his land up for sale.

**Comedy** Drama that provokes laughter at human behaviour, usually involves romantic love, and usually has a happy ending. In Shakespeare's day the conventional comedy enacted the struggle of young lovers to surmount some difficulty, usually presented by their elders, and the play ended happily in marriage or the prospect of marriage. Sometimes the struggle was to bring separated lovers or family members together, and their reunion was the happy culmination (this often involved marriage also). Shakespeare generally observed these conventions, though his inventiveness within them yielded many variations.

Eighteen plays are generally included among Shakespeare's comedies. In approximate order of composition, they are *The Comedy of Errors, The Taming of the Shrew, The Two Gentlemen of Verona, Love's Labour's Lost, A Midsummer Night's Dream, The Merchant of Venice, The Merry Wives of Windsor, Much Ado About Nothing, As You Like It, Twelfth Night, Troilus and Cressida, Measure for Measure, All's Well That Ends Well, Pericles, Cymbeline, The Winter's Tale, The Tempest*, and *The Two Noble Kinsmen*. These works are often divided into distinct subclasses reflecting the playwright's development. The first seven, all written before about 1598, are loosely classed as the 'early comedies', though they vary considerably in both quality and character. The last four of these—*Love's Labour's Lost*, the *Dream*, the *Merchant*, and the *Merry Wives*—are sometimes separated as a transitional group, or linked with the next three in a large 'middle comedies' classification. The *Merry Wives* is somewhat anomalous in any case; it represents a type of comedy—the 'city play', a speciality of such writers as Ben JONSON and Thomas DEKKER—that Shakespeare did not otherwise write. The next three plays, *Much Ado, As You Like It*, and *Twelfth Night*, are often thought to constitute Shakespeare's greatest achievement in comedy; all written around 1599–1600, they are called the romantic, or mature, comedies. The next group of three plays, called the PROBLEM PLAYS, were written in the first years of the 17th century, as Shakespeare was simultaneously creating his greatest tragedies. The final cluster, all written between about 1607 and 1613, make up the bulk of the playwright's final period. They are known as the ROMANCES. (The problem plays and romances were intended to merge TRAGEDY and comedy in TRAGICOMEDY, and they are treated separately in this book.) Many minor variations in this classification scheme are possible; indeed, the boundaries of the whole genre are not fixed, for *Timon of Athens* is often included among the comedies, and *Troilus and Cressida* is sometimes considered a tragedy.

Shakespeare's earliest comedies are similar to existing plays, reflecting his inexperience. *The Comedy of Errors*—thought by many scholars to be his first drama, though the dating of Shakespeare's early works is extremely difficult—is built on a play by the ancient Roman dramatist PLAUTUS. Characteristically, Shakespeare enriched his source, but with material from another play by Plautus. The SUB-PLOT of *The Taming of the Shrew* was taken from a popular play of a generation earlier, and the main plot was well known in folklore, though the combination was ingeniously devised. *The Two Gentlemen of Verona* likewise deals with familiar literary material, treating it in the manner of John LYLY, the most successful comedy writer when Shakespeare began his career.

However, the young playwright soon found the confidence to experiment, and in *Love's Labour's Lost,* the *Dream,* and the *Merchant,* he created a group of unusual works that surely startled Elizabethan playgoers, though pleasurably, we may presume. In the first he created his own main plot and used a distinctively English variation on COMMEDIA DELL' ARTE traditions for a sub-plot. He thus produced a splendid array of comic situations. The play's abundant topical humour was certainly appreciated by the original audiences, although today we don't always know what it is about. In any case, the major characters are charming young lovers, the minor ones are droll eccentrics, and the closing *coup de théâtre*, with which a darkening mood brings the work to a close, is a stunning innovation. Already, the eventual turn towards tragicomedy is foreshadowed. *A Midsummer Night's Dream* mingles motifs from many sources, but the story is again the playwright's own; moreover, the play's extraordinary combination of oddity and beauty was entirely unprecedented and has rarely been approximated since. *The Merchant of Venice* mixes a social theme, usury, into a conventional comedy plot to deepen the resonance of the final outcome as well as to vary the formula. Here, the threat that is finally averted is so dire as to generate an almost tragic mood, again anticipating developments later in the playwright's career.

The mastery that Shakespeare had achieved by the late 1590s is reflected in the insouciance of the titles he gave his mature comedies (*Twelfth Night*'s subtitle—'What You Will'—matches the others). That mastery is accompanied by a serious intent that is lacking in the earliest comedies. Shakespeare could not ignore the inherent poignancy in the contrast between life as it is lived and the escape from life represented by comedy. In *Much Ado*, as in *The Merchant of Venice*, a serious threat to life and happiness counters the froth of a romantic farce. Even in *As You Like It,* one of the most purely entertaining of Shakespeare's plays, the melancholy JAQUES (1) interposes his conviction that life is irredeemably corrupt. FESTE's song at the close of *Twelfth Night* gives touching expression to such sentiments, as he sends us from the theatre with the melancholy refrain, 'the rain it raineth every day' (5.1.391). We are not expected to take him too seriously, but we cannot avoid the realisation that even the life of a jester may be a sad one. The mature comedies thus further a blending of comedy and tragedy.

In the end, however, all of Shakespeare's comedies, including the later problem plays and romances, are driven by love. Love in Shakespearean comedy is stronger than the inertia of custom, the power of evil, or the fortunes of chance and time. In all of these plays but one (*Troilus and Cressida*), the obstacles presented to love are triumphantly overcome, as conflicts are resolved and errors forgiven in a general aura of reconciliation and marital bliss at the play's close. Such intransigent characters as SHYLOCK, MALVOLIO, and Don JOHN (1), who choose not to act out of love, cannot be accommodated in this scheme, and they are carefully isolated from the action before the climax.

In their resolutions Shakespeare's comedies resemble the medieval MORALITY PLAY, which centres on a sinful human who receives God's mercy. In these secular works, a human authority figure—Don PEDRO or DUKE (7) SENIOR, for instance—is symbolically divine, the opponents of love are the representatives of sin, and all of the participants in the closing vignette partake of the play's love and forgiveness. Moreover, the context of marriage—at least alluded to at the close of all but *Troilus and Cressida*—is the cap-stone of the comedic solution, for these plays not only delight and entertain, they affirm, guaranteeing the future. Marriage, with its promise of offspring, reinvigorates society and transcends the purely personal element in sexual attraction and romantic love. Tragedy's focus on the individual makes death the central fact of life, but comedy, with its insistence on the ongoing process of love and sex and birth, confirms our awareness that life transcends the individual.

## Comedy of Errors, The

### SYNOPSIS

*Act 1, Scene 1*

The DUKE (8) of EPHESUS informs EGEON, a merchant of Syracuse, that he is subject to the death penalty, prescribed for any citizen of Syracuse found in Ephesus, unless he can pay an immense ransom. Egeon tells of the long search that has brought him to Ephesus: 23 years earlier, his wife and one of their infant twin sons had been separated from him in a shipwreck. The other son had set forth, at the age of 18, in search of his lost brother. He took with him his servant, who had also been separated from a twin brother in the same shipwreck. Egeon himself had then begun to

Antipholus remarks to himself on the reputation of Ephesus as a centre for witchcraft and thievery, and he hurries back to his inn, fearing theft.

*Act 2, Scene 1*
ADRIANA, the wife of Antipholus of Ephesus, complains that her husband is late for lunch, thus triggering a disputation on marriage with her sister, LUCIANA; Luciana holds for wifely obedience in all things, while Adriana asserts her independence. Dromio of Ephesus returns to tell of the beating he has received. Adriana sends him out again to fetch Antipholus home. Adriana asserts that her husband prefers the company of other women to her own, though Luciana rebukes her for unjustified jealousy.

*Act 2, Scene 2*
Antipholus of Syracuse encounters his own servant, whom he berates for the behaviour of the other Dromio and then beats when he declares his innocence. Adriana and Luciana appear, and Adriana, thinking Antipholus of Syracuse to be her husband, chastises him for infidelity. When he responds with natural confusion, he is rebuked by Luciana. The servant also claims ignorance, and the two are jointly condemned by the women. The visitors are mystified and fear that supernatural doings are afoot. However, Antipholus decides to follow the drift of things in the hope of discovering the truth, and he permits himself to be taken to Adriana's home, where Dromio is assigned the gate-guarding duties of his namesake.

*Act 3, Scene 1*
Antipholus of Ephesus enters with his servant Dromio and two friends, ANGELO (1), a goldsmith, and BALTHASAR (1), a merchant. Antipholus invites his friends to come to his house, but they are turned away at the gate by Dromio of Syracuse, who is obeying his orders to keep out all comers. Another servant, LUCE, and finally Adriana herself, persist in keeping Antipholus out, believing him to be an imposter. The outraged husband announces that he will pay a visit to a COURTESAN he knows and that, moreover, he will give that woman the gold necklace he had commissioned from Angelo as a gift for his wife.

*Act 3, Scene 2*
Luciana is appalled that Antipholus of Syracuse, whom she believes to be her brother-in-law, Antipholus of Ephesus, has declared his love for her. She concludes that he is mad and flees, announcing her intention to tell Adriana about this turn of events. Dromio of Syracuse enters and tells of the extravagantly ugly kitchen-maid, NELL (1), who has claimed him as a husband. Antipholus sends him to prepare to depart; as he observes in a soliloquy, they must flee the witchery of the place, especially since he has fallen in love with one of the supernatural creatures—

*'Methinks you are my glass, and not my brother'* (The Comedy of Errors 5.1.417). *The two Dromios, brothers separated at birth, are reunited at the end of the play.* (Courtesy of Culver Pictures, Inc.)

roam the world for news of either son. The Duke is sympathetic to this tragic tale; he gives the prisoner the rest of the day to beg or borrow ransom money.

*Act 1, Scene 2*
A local MERCHANT (1) advises ANTIPHOLUS OF SYRACUSE, newly arrived, not to reveal his origins, telling of the fate of Egeon. Antipholus instructs his servant, DROMIO OF SYRACUSE, to return to their inn and guard their money. In a soliloquy, Antipholus tells of his search for his lost brother, and the audience realises that he is one of Egeon's sons. DROMIO OF EPHESUS enters and mistakes Antipholus for his own master, ANTIPHOLUS OF EPHESUS. Antipholus of Syracuse in turn mistakes this Dromio for his own servant. The presence in the city of the two sets of twins is now known to the audience. Dromio of Ephesus relays his mistress' demand that his master return home. Antipholus of Syracuse asks about the safety of the money, and Dromio denies knowledge of any money. Antipholus beats him, and the mystified servant runs away.

namely Luciana. Angelo appears with the gold chain commissioned by the other Antipholus and turns it over to this one, despite the latter's bewildered protests.

### Act 4, Scene 1

A Merchant demands of Angelo the repayment of a debt, and he is accompanied by an OFFICER (1) empowered to arrest debtors. Angelo says that he can satisfy the debt as soon as Antipholus pays him for the gold chain. Just then, Antipholus of Ephesus appears with his servant, whom he sends to buy a rope, with which he proposes to whip his wife for having kept him out of his house. When he sees Angelo, he protests that he has not received the chain. Confusion leads to anger, and Antipholus is arrested. At this point, Dromio of Syracuse appears. He announces that he has arranged passage on a ship and bids Antipholus go aboard. For this seeming asininity, and for not having a rope, Antipholus rebukes Dromio and promises him a future beating. The servant is then sent to Adriana for bail money.

### Act 4, Scene 2

Luciana and Adriana discuss the apparent infidelity of Antipholus. Dromio of Syracuse enters and tells of the need for bail. The women, who think he is Dromio of Ephesus, send him back with the required funds.

### Act 4, Scene 3

Antipholus of Syracuse is wearing the gold chain provided by Angelo. Dromio of Syracuse arrives with the bail money, but of course his master does not know what he is talking about. Antipholus attributes their confusion to the supernatural qualities of Ephesus. Consequently, when the Courtesan appears, asking if his gold chain is the one he has promised her, he responds by asserting that she must be an agent of the devil. When she demands the return of a ring she had given him, the two Syracusans flee. The Courtesan reflects that Antipholus must surely be mad. She determines to tell Adriana of her husband's state.

### Act 4, Scene 4

Antipholus of Ephesus, in the custody of the Officer, sees Dromio of Ephesus and thinks his bail money has arrived. This Dromio, however, has the rope he was sent to purchase. He is struck with it by the furious Antipholus and delivers an elaborate lament on being beaten. Adriana, Luciana, and the Courtesan arrive, with Doctor PINCH, whom Adriana entreats to restore Antipholus to sanity. Antipholus, becoming more and more enraged, attempts to strike Adriana, and he and Dromio are restrained and tied up by a group of passers-by. Pinch takes the two prisoners to Adriana's house for treatment. Antipholus and Dromio of Syracuse appear; the others flee, believing the two have escaped from Pinch and are bent on revenge.

### Act 5, Scene 1

Angelo and the Merchant discuss the strange behaviour of Antipholus of Ephesus. Antipholus and Dromio of Syracuse appear; Angelo charges Antipholus with dishonesty, and tempers flare. Antipholus and the Merchant draw their swords. Adriana, Luciana, and the Courtesan reappear, calling for help in capturing Antipholus and Dromio. The two Syracusans flee, taking sanctuary in the PRIORY. The Abbess of the Priory, EMILIA (1), emerges. Adriana demands the return of her husband; the Abbess refuses to permit a violation of the right to sanctuary.

Adriana determines to appeal to the Duke. The Duke appears, with a retinue including the unfortunate Egeon, who is to be beheaded. Antipholus and Dromio of Ephesus arrive, having escaped from Pinch. Antipholus, too, demands justice of the Duke. Charges and counter-charges are exchanged by Antipholus, Angelo, Adriana, and the Courtesan. The extent of the confusion overwhelms the Duke, who sends for the Abbess. Egeon claims Antipholus of Ephesus as his son, but, as it is the wrong Antipholus he addresses, he is repudiated. The Abbess reappears with Antipholus and Dromio of Syracuse. All are stunned by the presence, together for the first time, of the two sets of identical twins. The Abbess recognises Egeon and reveals that she is his long-lost wife, Emilia. The identities of the twins are quickly established, and Emilia invites all the company to a feast of celebration in the Priory.

### COMMENTARY

*The Comedy of Errors* is an early work, lacking most of the features we associate with Shakespeare's masterpieces. It contains no brilliant dialogue or poetry, no very impressive characters, and, most strikingly, its plot line is difficult to take at all seriously. Of all Shakespeare's plays, *The Comedy of Errors* most nearly resembles a FARCE, pure and simple, which the *Oxford English Dictionary* defines as 'a dramatic work (usually short) which has for its sole object to excite laughter'.

This play is both short and funny, but it is also more than that. Shakespeare's genius lies in his concern with what it is to be human and here he elevates a common farce by means of telling depictions of the human condition. He presents and resolves disruptions and anxieties that invite sympathy and stimulate compassion. In watching or reading *The Comedy of Errors*, we experience an awareness of the value to an individual of relationships to other people. Further, the play presents aspects of the situation of women in Elizabethan society, a matter Shakespeare often dealt with. The redeeming power of love, a profound theme in much of the playwright's later work, is also presented here, in an uncomplicated foreshadowing of subtler renderings.

A traditional opinion among scholars and critics,

only lately being revised, is that *The Comedy of Errors* is best regarded as an apprentice work, only marginally related to the greater plays that followed. There is some justification for this point of view. For one thing, the play is very conventional, conforming in staging and general outline to standard Elizabethan ideas, derived from what was known of ancient Roman drama, of what constituted a proper play. In staging his play, Shakespeare was content to abide by most of the ancient conventions of the form. In accordance with accepted neoclassical doctrine, the action of the play takes place in a single place and in a single day. The setting consists of three buildings—the PHOENIX, the PORCUPINE, and the PRIORY, each labelled with a sign or emblem—in imitation of Roman stagecraft as it was understood in Shakespeare's time.

Moreover, Shakespeare's play is undeniably farcical in its assembled absurdities. These are simply conventions of farce, as acceptable to a 16th-century audience as those of the Marx Brothers are acceptable today, and no different in kind. In adding the twin servants to the story he received from PLAUTUS (see 'Sources', below), Shakespeare doubled the chances for misadventure and created a set of complications that has been likened to a Bach fugue, but the principles of farce remain the same.

Another striking addition Shakespeare made, changing the character of the work in a very important way, is the sub-plot featuring Egeon. Egeon's explanation of his family's separation in 1.1 serves as a PROLOGUE (1) to the play, a classical device that Shakespeare used more formally elsewhere. More important, Egeon's pathetic circumstances serve to colour the farcical main plot: we cannot wholly forget this poor, unfortunate father to the Antipholus twins. Because this is a humorous play, we of course presume that all will end well, but we know that before it does this potential tragedy will have to be overcome somehow. Indeed, Egeon experiences a moment of extreme despair, after his seeming rejection by his long-sought son (5.1.298–322). Thus the coming reconciliation scene ends a truly important human crisis, as well as resolving the comic confusions of the central tale. Shakespeare, even as a young man at the beginning of his career, felt that a happy ending should not be divorced from an awareness of mortality and human frailty. In this he utterly transcends the genre of farce.

Some critics have charged that this device damages a play that might have been a fine farce but that, in its present form, is neither tragic nor wholly comic. However, modern opinion has generally held that the Egeon sub-plot is necessary, providing a moral ground for an otherwise unenlightening display of low comedy. In any case, this sub-plot is an early example of an important aspect of Shakespeare's art—the formulation of more than one point of view, generating different and potentially conflicting responses from the audience.

Chief among the characters involved in the central story of *The Comedy of Errors* is Adriana, one of the earliest of Shakespeare's many attractive heroines. Shakespeare developed Adriana from a stereotype of the contentious, jealous shrew, and she conforms to this image. But she is raised from a type to a real human being through the wit her creator gives her. Further, her evident loyalty to and love for her difficult husband render her quite sympathetic and admirable. She resembles such other Shakespearean women as KATHERINA, in *The Taming of the Shrew,* and BEATRICE, in *Much Ado About Nothing,* in being sharp-tongued and independent-minded, but ultimately tender and accepting. The playwright could thus present the reality of Elizabethan women whose personal strengths enabled them to temper, if not overcome, the general subservience of their gender, while at the same time confirming the legitimacy of the system, as his own conservatism inclined him to do. Adriana is contrasted with her sister, Luciana, who is a dimmer figure, demure and passive. The debate between the two women on the proper relation of man and wife (2.1.7–42) is a set-piece disputation of a sort often presented on the Elizabethan stage. Although Adriana is a much more interesting and appealing character, Luciana's attitude to marriage seems to prevail at the play's end, in keeping with the common opinion of the day, which most women and Shakespeare shared.

Many of Shakespeare's plays hinge on a basic political question, the nature of the relationships among the citizen, the ruler, and the state. In this early work, the matter is only touched upon, but in a fashion that reveals an attitude that the playwright was to hold all his life. In a brief but telling passage, the Duke of Ephesus refuses to allow any alteration in the laws (1.1.142–148). He is explicit: his personal honour requires this relationship to the state. This is a kingly ideal that is expressed repeatedly, in much greater elaboration, in later plays. That the young Shakespeare found occasion to present it here, without any compelling reason to do so, suggests its early importance for him.

For Shakespeare and his contemporaries, everyone, not just the king, took his or her identity from a relationship with society as a whole. One was not simply a conscious, individual being, but, more important, one occupied a position in the social framework. Shakespeare was to consider this matter of social identity in a number of ways in later plays; it is touched on in this early work. Antipholus of Syracuse is concerned for his lost selfhood when he regrets the loss of his family in a touching soliloquy (1.2.33–40) on his lack of contentment. Also, it is evident that the distress undergone by the four misidentified twins is caused by the loss of their sense of identity; as the people in their world fail to recognise them, they experience a painful uncertainty as to who they are themselves.

Antipholus of Syracuse, in his confusion, seeks to be remade, through love, by Luciana. The transforming power of love was always an important theme for Shakespeare; in several later plays, it is a major concern. Here, it is overwhelmed by the farce for the most part, but we see it roughly sketched out with reference to romantic love in the depiction of the marriage of Adriana and Antipholus of Ephesus, and in the wooing of Luciana by Antipholus of Syracuse. Familial love triumphs in the reunion at the close of the play. And Emilia, the Abbess, who provides the resolution when the Duke, for all his power, cannot, represents the strength of Christian grace and mercy, a transcendent form of love.

Shakespeare's interest in the inner and outer worlds of human experience is what makes him great. He writes of the web of relationships, both political and domestic, that make up a society, and his characters have inner lives that we can recognise as realistic. In *The Comedy of Errors*, although it is derivative and rather limited in range, we see his talent already beginning to produce a drama of conflict and resolution in a world of basic human concerns, using themes and materials that would recur in his mature work.

## SOURCES OF THE PLAY

Shakespeare's principal source for *The Comedy of Errors* was *The Menaechmi*, a play by the ancient Roman playwright Plautus. The first English translation of *The Menaechmi*, by William WARNER, was not published until 1595, a little later than the date when Shakespeare's play was presumably written, but the playwright may have known the translation in manuscript, as was common at that time, or he might have read it in one of several 16th-century Latin editions. Shakespeare made a number of important changes in the story, as he usually did when using sources. His boldest and best-known alteration was the addition of a second set of misidentified twins, a twist he took from another play by Plautus, *Amphitryon*. A number of other changes result in a general shift in the qualities of the play. For example, a ribald emphasis on a husband's relations with a mistress is elevated to a concern with the virtues of courtship and marriage.

The sub-plot concerning Egeon may derive from any of a number of sources; the motif of separated and reunited families had been familiar since ancient times. Shakespeare surely knew it from the medieval *Gesta Romanorum*, translated by Richard ROBINSON (3)—later a source for *The Merchant of Venice*—and the *Confessio Amantis*, by John GOWER (3)—later a source for *Pericles*. However, the hostility between cities resulting in a traveller's death penalty comes from George GASCOIGNE's *Supposes* (performed 1566, pub-

lished 1573), where the situation is invented as part of a ruse; it is used in the same way to dupe the PEDANT in *The Taming of the Shrew*.

## TEXT OF THE PLAY

*The Comedy of Errors* is sometimes said to have been the first play that Shakespeare wrote, although this cannot be proven. It was certainly one of his earliest. The play's first recorded performance was held on December 28, 1594, as part of a programme of Christmas revels at Gray's Inn (see INNS OF COURT). This private performance, the play's brevity (with fewer than 1,800 lines, it is Shakespeare's shortest), and its resemblance to ancient Roman comedy have prompted some scholars to suggest that the play was commissioned for this presentation to a particularly learned audience. However, most scholarly opinion holds that it was written at an earlier date; estimates have ranged from the late 1580s to 1594.

The play was initially published in the FIRST FOLIO, in 1623. This version is believed to have been derived from Shakespeare's FOUL PAPERS. The Folio contains the only early publication of *The Comedy of Errors,* and it has been the basis for all subsequent editions of the play.

## THEATRICAL HISTORY OF THE PLAY

The Gray's Inn performance of December 1594 and a performance at the court of King James I in the Christmas season of 1604 are the only known early productions, although various references in contemporary plays and books suggest that there were probably other 16th- and 17th-century stagings. In the 18th century and well into the 19th, all presentations of *The Comedy of Errors*, with the possible exception of a brief run in 1741, were adaptations that varied more or less grossly from the original. The brevity of the play, its esoteric relation to classical drama, and a sense that it was more an 'apprentice' piece than a mature work seem to have combined to provide justification for a long series of illegitimate productions, by Thomas HULL and others. Perhaps the strangest of these offspring was the 1819 opera produced by Frederick REYNOLDS (1), whose libretto included songs from *As You Like It, Love's Labour's Lost, King Lear,* and *Othello,* plus two of the SONNETS, and which used additional dialogue and entire scenes from various sources, only some of them Shakespearean.

Shakespeare's play was first restored to the stage in its proper form by Samuel PHELPS in 1855. It has gradually increased in popularity since then and has often been produced in recent years. Variations on the play have also continued to be produced in the 20th century; the 1938 musical comedy *The Boys from Syracuse,* by Richard Rodgers and Lorenz Hart, is an example. In 1976, Trevor NUNN made a FILM of *The Comedy of*

*Errors,* with Judi DENCH as Adriana, and the play has been made for TELEVISION several times.

**Comedy of Humours** Genre of ELIZABETHAN DRAMA, plays in which each character possesses some strong, clearly identifiable personality trait or quirk that determines his or her behaviour in any circumstances. For instance, a lecher will find all occasions appropriate for chasing women; a glutton will continually be concerned with food; a jealous husband will always look for evidence of his wife's infidelity. Among Shakespeare's plays, *The Merry Wives of Windsor* and *Twelfth Night* most nearly exemplify the genre, although he tended to combine features of several types of play. The most important practitioner of the comedy of humours was Ben JONSON.

In the late 1580s and early 1590s the term 'humour', referring to striking aspects of personality or patterns of behaviour, became prominent in Elizabethan London. It stemmed from a medieval medical theory—in its last decades of respectability and increasingly recognised as problematical—that held that human health depends on a proper balance among four 'humours', or bodily fluids: black bile, yellow bile, blood, and phlegm. When the balance was upset and one 'humour' dominated, a person was likely to become ill and/or act strangely. The word became associated with all striking behaviour, and it began to take on the association with comedy that it has today.

In the 1590s the attribution of prominent humours to dramatic characters arose as a plausible way to use the elaborate system of character types that occur in ancient Roman drama, especially in the plays of PLAUTUS. Comedies of humours were generally intended to ridicule the 'humorous' behaviour they presented. Elaborate complications involving intrigue and deceit typified their plots. Characters often bore tag names indicating their qualities, as do Shakespeare's SHALLOW and MALVOLIO.

The vogue for comedy of humours—and for using the word 'humour'—was itself a subject for comedy. For example, NYM, who appears in *The Merry Wives of Windsor* and *Henry V,* uses the word 'humour' in almost every speech he makes. He took this trait from a character in a successful play by George CHAPMAN, *The Blind Beggar of Alexandria* (1596). The comedy of humours reached its peak with Jonson's works of the early 17th century, but it remained popular for about another 100 years.

**Cominius** Legendary figure and character in *Coriolanus,* a Roman general. Cominius is the commander of the Roman troops fighting against the VOLSCIANS at CORIOLES, and his friend MARTIUS (2) (later CORIOLANUS), is a general under him. Cominius is a discreet general who contrasts with the hero. He executes a sensible withdrawal in 1.6, before he is joined by Coriolanus who goads him on to a successful counterattack. In the same scene we see Cominius as the subject of Martius' bizarre enthusiasm. Excited by the fighting, Martius embraces him with the fervour, he says, of his wedding night. The commander accepts this as normal battlefield comradeship, however, and in 1.9 he praises Martius and proposes that he take the honourable name Coriolanus. In 2.2 he nominates Coriolanus to the consulate. However, in Act 3 he cannot prevent Coriolanus' obstinate pride from bringing about his own banishment, and in 5.1 he reports that he has been unable to persuade Coriolanus—now fighting for the Volscians—from his campaign against Rome. Cominius is a representative of the ineffectual aristocracy who cannot control events.

Shakespeare took Cominius from his source, PLUTARCH's *Lives,* but added the intimacy of his relationship with Coriolanus, and thereby established him as a foil to the protagonist. As Coriolanus' friend, Cominius helps us see Coriolanus at his problematical best, early in the play. We recognise his value to his fellows while we acknowledge that he is excessive in his enthusiasm for combat.

**Commedia dell' Arte** Genre of 16th- and 17th-century Italian COMEDY, probable influence on several of Shakespeare's plays. In commedia dell' arte—which was frequently performed in England by travelling Italian companies, especially in the 1570s and 1580s—dialogue was largely improvised, as the action followed prescribed general lines familiar to both players and spectators; the plays were in any case so obvious that the troupes could find success with non-Italian-speaking audiences. The melodramatic and/or sentimental plots usually featured farcical intrigues involving love and money, though several involved a shipwreck on a magician's island, perhaps suggesting to Shakespeare the basic situation of *The Tempest.* The principal characters wore masks and were thus immediately recognisable; their personalities were understood before they said a word. They represented stock character types, some of which are thought to have influenced Shakespeare's characters.

Among the most important of these types was the pantaloon, an avaricious and lecherous old man, often a miser offering windy and moralistic advice to the young lovers. He may have contributed something to POLONIUS. At any rate, Shakespeare presumed his audiences were at least familiar with this figure, for in *As You Like It* he has JAQUES (1) cite 'the lean and slipper'd pantaloon . . . His youthful hose well sav'd' (2.7.158–160) as a symbol of old age. Another commedia figure was a lawyer, Dr Graziano or the *dottore,* also amorous but distinguished by his pretentious pedantry. HOLOFERNES, of *Love's Labour's Lost,* is quite similar to the *dottore,* and his fellow comical rustic in that play, ARMADO, resembles a third commedia figure, the *capitano,* a braggart soldier, the descendant of the ancient Roman MILES GLORIOSUS. Several other Shakespearean characters resemble the *capitano,* including most notably PAROLLES and FALSTAFF.

An important feature of the commedia dell' arte was a group of ostensibly minor comic characters called *zanni*—the root of our word *zany*—who were servants to the major figures but often dominated the action. In fact, another name for the genre is *commedia dei zanni.* They shared the characteristics of greed and shrewdness but evolved into a number of distinctive figures. Chief among them were Arlequino, a clever rascal (who survived the passing of the genre as Harlequin), and Pulcinella (Punch), a violent egotist. The *zanni* were descendants of the stock clever slaves and servants of Roman drama, which Shakespeare knew from PLAUTUS. So, although the DROMIOS of *The Comedy of Errors* and TRANIO of *The Taming of the Shrew* resemble *zanni,* Shakespeare need not have taken them from the commedia. However, the playwright's demonstrable awareness of the Italian players strongly suggests that the commedia dell' arte exercised at least some influence on Shakespeare's characters.

**Commoner (1)**   Any of several minor characters in *Julius Caesar,* working people of ROME. In 1.1 the tribunes FLAVIUS (1) and MARULLUS disperse a crowd of Commoners who have gathered to cheer CAESAR (1). Two of the Commoners speak, the CARPENTER only to identify himself, the COBBLER to bandy crude witticisms with the officers. (In some editions the speakers are identified as the First and Second Commoners.) This pleasingly vital episode comically introduces the urban mob that, as the PLEBEIANS (1), flares into riot in Act 3.

**Commoner (2)**   Any of several minor characters in *Coriolanus,* citizens of ANTIUM who first support and then turn against CORIOLANUS. In 5.6 Coriolanus has spared ROME from destruction at the hands of his Volscian troops, and he reports to the Volscian leaders at Antium accompanied by a throng of enthusiastic Commoners. In ironic contrast to his history in Rome, Coriolanus now has the support of the common people for the first time in the play. However, once AUFIDIUS accuses him of treason, they turn against their hero. 'Tear him to pieces!' (5.6.120), they cry, in an episode that parallels the fury of the populace in 3.3 that led to Coriolanus' banishment from Rome (see CITIZEN [5]). Though mostly mute—their three lines are assigned to the whole group—the Commoners' placement in the play's last moments is crucial. They stress again an important theme of the play, one that has been demonstrated repeatedly by their fellows in Rome: the common people, as a group, are susceptible to inflammatory rhetoric and are therefore unreliable participants in political life.

**Commons**   Group of extras in *2 Henry VI,* members of the parliament assembled at BURY ST EDMUNDS. These representatives of the common people gather in an unruly crowd in 3.2 to protest the murder of the Duke of GLOUCESTER (4) and demand punishment for the Duke of SUFFOLK (3). As is usual in Shakespeare, the common people en masse, as distinguished from individual characters, are presented as a thoughtless rabble, controllable only by aristocrats, here the Earls of WARWICK (3) and SALISBURY (2). Warwick refers to them as 'an angry hive of bees / That want their leader' (3.2.124–125), and Salisbury speaks for them in their address to the King. They prepare the audience for the later appearance of the rebels led by Jack CADE, as the disorder in the state intensifies.

**Complaint**   Poem intended to express unhappiness. A popular genre from the 14th through the 17th centuries, the complaint could take many forms, from meditations on the general sorrows of life to the bewailing of a particular event or situation—especially unrequited love—to humorous laments over trivial subjects, though these last were less common. Shakespeare's *The Rape of Lucrece* is often classed as a complaint—although the form was usually written in the first person—and it was written in RHYME ROYAL, the pattern that theorists prescribed for the genre. After Shakespeare's time the complaint was gradually replaced by the less expressly plaintive lament or elegy.

**Compton, Fay (1895–1978)**   English actress. Fay Compton played numerous Shakespearean parts in her long and distinguished career, most notably appearing as OPHELIA opposite the HAMLETS of both John BARRYMORE and John GIELGUD. She was the sister of the noted novelist Compton Mackenzie (1883–1972), and her own memoirs (*Rosemary,* 1926) were very popular.

**Condell, Henry (d. 1627)**   English actor and co-editor, with John HEMINGE, of the FIRST FOLIO edition of Shakespeare's plays. Listed in the Folio as one of the 26 'Principall Actors' in the plays, Condell became a partner in the CHAMBERLAIN'S MEN in 1598 and had probably acted with the company from its inception in 1594. He remained with its successor, the KING'S MEN, until his death. He acted in both tragedies and comedies, but he is not known for any particular Shakespearean role. His friendship with Shakespeare is evidenced by the playwright's small legacy to him in his will. Condell was one of the original partners in the BLACKFRIARS THEATRE, and he later acquired shares in the GLOBE THEATRE as well. He apparently invested well, for he died a wealthy man.

**Conrade (Conrad)** Character in *Much Ado About Nothing,* follower of Don JOHN (1). In 3.3 Conrade listens as his friend BORACHIO tells of the scheme to implicate the innocent HERO as a promiscuous woman. This conversation is overheard by the WATCHMEN (3), which leads ultimately to the exposure of Don John's villainy. Conrade is a simple pawn, needing no personality, but he does display a vehement temper when, irritated by Constable DOGBERRY's interrogation, he blurts out, 'You are an ass, you are an ass' (4.2.70). This triggers one of Dogberry's best comic bits, his indignant repetition of the insult.

**Conspirators** Minor characters in *Coriolanus,* followers of AUFIDIUS. In 5.6 the Conspirators affirm that they will help Aufidius take revenge on CORIOLANUS. They encourage him in his anger and point out that Coriolanus is overshadowing him. When Aufidius accuses his enemy of treason, they lead the mob in demanding Coriolanus' death, a demand they then fulfil by killing him with their swords. Though the conspirators are designated First, Second, and Third, they are indistinguishable from each other, and their speeches are divisions of a single voice. The Conspirators help to illuminate one of the play's principal themes: the common people (see COMMONER [2]) are susceptible to manipulation, and are thus an unstable and unreliable component of society. On the other hand, because they encourage—even goad—Aufidius to kill Coriolanus in such an ignominious fashion, they also help demonstrate the inadequacies of the warrior class.

**Constable of France, Charles d'Albret (Delabreth) (d. 1415)** Historical figure and character in *Henry V,* a high-ranking officer in the French army. Although the Constable recognises that King HENRY V is not the dissolute figure the DAUPHIN (3) believes him to be, he nonetheless falls prey to the over-confidence of the French prior to the battle of AGINCOURT. His death in the battle and his name are reported in 4.8. 94.

**Constance, Duchess of Brittany (d. 1201)** Historical figure and character in *King John,* mother of ARTHUR. Before the play begins, Constance has gained the support of King PHILIP (2) of FRANCE (1) in her attempt to place Arthur on the throne of England, from which King JOHN (3), his uncle, has displaced him. In 3.1 she rages furiously at the betrayal of her cause by Philip and the Archduke of AUSTRIA emphasising the theme of treachery that runs throughout the play. However, she then helps persuade Philip to another betrayal, as he turns on his new ally, King John. In 3.3 (3.4; for

citation, see *King John,* 'Synopsis'), Constance grieves hysterically over Arthur's capture by King John. She raves about making love to death (3.3.25–36), and Philip fears that she will harm herself. Her death 'in a frenzy' is reported in 4.2.122. Her agonising madness helps to stress the evil of John's usurpation.

The historical Constance was the daughter of a rebellious duke of Brittany whom King John's father, Henry II, defeated. In an effort to assure Brittany's loyalty, Henry insisted that Constance marry his son Geoffrey. After Geoffrey's death Constance ruled Brittany for Arthur, whose name may suggest her ambition to see her son rule England. Her ambition is reflected in Shakespeare's sources, but the playwright altered the details of her life freely. For instance, Constance bemoans her 'husbandless' state in 2.2.14 (3.1. 14), but in fact she married twice after Geoffrey's death. Also, in order to continue a deliberate pairing of Constance with ELEANOR, he has the the two women die at the same time, although in fact Constance died three years before.

**Contention, The** Abbreviated title of the first QUARTO edition of *2 Henry VI.* Published in 1594 by Thomas MILLINGTON, the play was originally titled, in the florid manner of the time, *The First part of the Contention betwixt the two famous Houses of Yorke and Lancaster, with the death of the good Duke Humphrey: And the banishment and death of the Duke of Suffolke, and the Tragicall end of the proud Cardinall of Winchester, with the notable Rebellion of Iacke Cade: And the Duke of Yorkes first claime unto the Crowne. The Contention,* known as the Q1 edition of *2 Henry VI,* is a shorter, inferior version of the F edition in the FIRST FOLIO, published in 1623. The Q2 edition of *2 Henry VI,* varying very little from Q1, was published by Millington in 1600, also as *The Contention.* Q3, a more heavily edited version, appeared in 1619, combined with a BAD QUARTO edition of *3 Henry VI* in one volume now known as THE WHOLE CONTENTION.

The existence of Q1 has generated a number of theories. It has been regarded as an original play, written earlier than *2 Henry VI,* probably by GREENE (2), PEELE, NASHE, MARLOWE (1), or possibly Shakespeare himself (or some combination of these in collaboration). Later, according to this theory, Shakespeare revised the play for a new production, creating the F text.

Another theory holds that *The Contention* is a 're-ported' version of *2 Henry VI,* i.e., a bad quarto that was assembled from the recollections of actors or viewers for purposes of unauthorised publication. It has even been speculated that *The Contention* may be a reported version of yet another play, a lost original. *2 Henry VI* would then be a revision of either *The Contention* or of the lost play.

All these theories can be supported in one way or another, and the truth of the matter cannot be ascertained from the existing evidence. However, modern scholarship has generally, though not unanimously, accepted the second of these propositions—that *The Contention* is a reported, or 'memorial', text of *2 Henry VI*. It was perhaps created in 1593, at the time of the bankruptcy and temporary collapse of the PEMBROKE'S MEN, the acting company that originally produced the play.

**Cooke (1), Alexander (d. 1614)**   English actor, one of the 26 men listed in the FIRST FOLIO as the 'Principall Actors' of Shakespeare's plays. Cooke apparently became a member of the KING'S MEN in 1604—having served as a hired actor earlier—and he remained with them at least into 1613. He was probably apprenticed to John HEMINGE, whom he refers to as 'my master' in his will.

Cooke may have appeared with PEMBROKE'S MEN in THE TAMING OF A SHREW, sometime between 1592 and 1594. In that BAD QUARTO of *The Taming of the Shrew* (where the text was assembled from actors' memories), one of the PLAYERS (1) is designated 'San' or 'Sander', and Sander—a common Elizabethan nickname for Alexander—is the name of the equivalent of Shakespeare's GRUMIO. Their speeches are fairly accurately reproduced in *A Shrew*, so if Cooke did play these parts, he was one of the actors who compiled the text.

**Cooke (2), George Frederick (1756–1811)**   English actor. Cooke was a rival of John Philip KEMBLE (3) in the early years of the 19th century. He was especially noted for his OTHELLO, with which he established himself as a respected actor. He played many Shakespearean roles, including RICHARD III, HENRY VIII, and FALSTAFF. He eventually moved to America and died in New York. Remarkably, Cooke played a Shakespearean role nearly 170 years after his death, when his skull—preserved by his physician upon his death and eventually given to a Philadelphia university—was employed as that of YORICK in a 1980 TELEVISION production of *Hamlet*.

**Corambis**   Name given to POLONIUS in the BAD QUARTO (Q1, 1604) of *Hamlet*. Corambis is thought to allude to a well-known Latin proverb on triteness: *Crambe bis posita mors est* ('Cabbage served twice is deadly'); this seems appropriate to the long-winded Polonius but the reason for the variation in names is uncertain. Polonius' servant, REYNALDO (1), is also renamed in Q1 as MONTANO (1), suggesting a satirical point to the names—a cabbage attended by a mountain might caricature a prominent bore and his hulking assistant—but no target is now identifiable, although some scholars nominate Lord BURGHLEY, a leading English statesman.

Q1 is a version of the play compiled from the memo-

ries of actors who played in it, and some scholars suppose that Corambis was the name of the equivalent character in an earlier play, now lost, the UR-HAMLET, and that it was inserted in Q1 by an actor who also knew the earlier work. If so, then any satirical point was intended not by Shakespeare but by the author of the *Ur-Hamlet*, probably Thomas KYD; perhaps Shakespeare changed the name in order to dissociate his character from the earlier caricature.

Corambis may be a corruption of Corambus, a form that appears in DER BESTRAFTE BRUDERMORD, a German version of *Hamlet* derived in part from Q1. Shakespeare used this form in passing in *All's Well That Ends Well* (4.3.158), which is sometimes taken as circumstantial evidence that, since he knew the name, he could perhaps have taken it from the *Ur-Hamlet*.

**Cordelia**   Character in *King Lear*, the virtuous daughter whom King LEAR mistakenly rejects. Knowing she will marry, Cordelia refuses to assert that all of her love will forever go to her father, unlike REGAN and GONERIL, her hypocritical sisters. Lear mistakes Cordelia's honesty for a lack of affection and disinherits her, though the King of FRANCE (2) recognises her innate worth and marries her anyway. She leaves Britain with him at the end of 1.1 and does not reappear until Act 4, when she arrives with an army. She intends to restore her father to his throne, for he has been humiliated and banished to the wilderness by Regan and Goneril. Lear and Cordelia are reunited, but are nonetheless defeated in battle, and the villainous EDMUND imprisons them and orders their murder, in 5.3. Although Edmund is defeated by EDGAR it is too late; the assassin has killed Cordelia, though Lear kills him. In the play's final episode Lear grieves over his daughter's corpse and dies of a broken heart.

During her long absence from the play we are not permitted to forget Cordelia, for her goodness and self-sacrifice are central to the tragedy: the FOOL (2) is said to have 'much pined away' for her, in 1.4.72; in 2.2, the loyal KENT (2) reveals that she knows of Lear's situation; Lear himself refers to her in 2.4.211; and her invasion force is mentioned several times, beginning in 3.1.30.

Many commentators believe that Shakespeare specifically intended Cordelia as an example of the Christian virtues of self-sacrifice and acceptance of God's will. Cordelia accepts her undeserved fate while she displays undiminished love for her erring father. In this view she is a Christlike figure in a pagan world who offers a suggestion of Christianity's coming redemption of humanity. Her death thus symbolises Christ's crucifixion, and the tragedy's lesson is the mysterious nature of God's will.

A non-religious interpretation of Cordelia's sacrifice is also proposed by many critics, who see her virtue as its own reward, for as a pagan she lacks the

Christian's promise of recompense in the afterlife. In this humanistic view her goodness inspires our admiration all the more for being unrewarded, and the pure light of her courage offers the most compelling sense that the play's tragedy is not utterly futile. Also, many critics hold that Shakespeare intended Lear to die believing that Cordelia is still alive, in which case his own fate is greatly eased, and we can feel more strongly the redemptive effect of her virtues. A final variation on her importance does not diminish it: some writers hold that *King Lear* reflects a despairing and pessimistic view of life that denies aid for human folly in a tragic universe. In this interpretation Cordelia's virtues, combined with the injustice of both her rejection by her father and her ultimate death, offer striking confirmation of the dire point of view attributed to the playwright.

In almost any view Cordelia's manifest virtue is a dominating element of the play, giving her an importance seemingly unjustified by her relatively few appearances on stage. In her pure honesty and unqualified love she seems almost devoid of ordinary human personality traits, and her saintly qualities are especially stressed by the GENTLEMAN (7) who reports on her in 4.3, preparing the audience for her return to the drama. In a passage rich in imagery and rhetoric he describes her mingled joy and sorrow at news of Lear, saying, for instance, '. . . she shook / The holy water from her heavenly eyes' (4.3.29–30). Later, she is described as one 'Who redeems nature from the general curse' (4.6.203). Evoked in these terms, Cordelia resembles an angel more than she does a worldly character. Her vague personality contributes to our sense of dislocation in *King Lear*. She is remote from the more active figures, even the fighters against evil, Edgar, Kent, and ALBANY, and this draws attention to the failure of human interaction in the play's tragic universe.

Cordelia may also be seen in a more human light. In fact, some writers declare that she exhibits a prideful stubbornness in Act 1, only adopting an attitude of loving generosity when she sees the damage that has been done. In this light her moral progress may be said to parallel that of her father. This is a minority view, however, for most commentators feel that Shakespeare intended her initial insistence on honesty to be an obvious virtue.

**Corin** Character in *As You Like It,* an honest, elderly shepherd. In 2.4 and in 3.5 Corin is associated with SILVIUS, a conventional shepherd who is filled with literary conceits about love; in most PASTORAL literature the countryside was an idealised setting for amorous tales of shepherds and shepherdesses, such as Silvius and his beloved, PHEBE. Corin, by contrast, is a real shepherd. He describes the economic plight of the shepherd to ROSALIND and CELIA in 2.4.73–84,

while at the same time establishing himself as a representative of traditional rural values, offering such modest hospitality as he can.

In 3.2 Corin expresses his down-to-earth relationship to his world, and he can say, 'I am a true labourer: I earn that I eat, get that I wear; owe no man hate, envy no man's happiness . . .' (3.2.71–72). TOUCHSTONE wittily derides this simple life, but he cannot upset Corin. The honest shepherd anchors the rustic life of ARDEN (1) in the real world and thus offsets the high-flown sentiment of pastoral tradition.

Corin's name was commonly applied to shepherds in late medieval and Renaissance romantic literature; it may be a masculine form of Corinna (active c. 500–470 B.C.), an ancient Greek lyric poetess. Shakespeare may have been inspired to use the name by an English play of the 1570s, published in 1599, *Syre Clyomon and Clamydes,* in which a princess disguised as a man serves a shepherd named Corin.

**Coriolanus, Martius** Legendary figure and title character of *Coriolanus,* a famed Roman warrior whose excessive pride leads him to dishonour and death. His pride is part of his sense of himself as a warrior and aristocrat, a self-image that he has acquired from a rigorous upbringing by his extraordinary mother, VOLUMNIA. When the changing political world of ROME—represented by the tribunes BRUTUS (3) and SICINIUS—demands compromises that his pride will not accept, Coriolanus is driven from Rome and joins the city's enemies, the VOLSCIANS. Finally, when his mother persuades him to spare Rome, he is killed by the Volscian leader, his archrival AUFIDIUS.

Like OTHELLO and MACBETH, Coriolanus is a successful warrior who finds himself in a situation—here, the political world of Rome—to which he is temperamentally unsuited and in which he can be manipulated by others. Politically unsophisticated and emotionally immature, he can neither strike political deals with the tribunes nor resist his mother's insistence that he do so. He is reduced to blind vengeance, but she blocks him in that direction as well. Under these pressures, his great strength can only destroy him. His fate contains the irony found in all Shakespeare's tragedies: with greatness comes great weakness. Coriolanus' pride makes him great, but it also brings about his downfall.

Coriolanus' relationship with his mother makes him one of the most psychologically interesting of Shakespeare's protagonists. He is entirely Volumnia's creation, and thus Coriolanus is psychologically dependent on her good opinion, as is demonstrated in both of their crucial scenes. In 3.2 she bullies him into political compromise as his resistance collapses under her disdain: 'Thy valiantness was mine . . . but owe thy pride thyself' (3.2.129–130). In 5.3 he cannot withstand another personal denial—'This fellow had a

Volscian to his mother' (5.3.178)—and he abandons his life rather than suffer his mother's disapproval. She can manipulate him because when she created him she deprived him of all motives but one, his pride, which depends on her continuing approval. Though he avoids the psychological trauma of her rejection and saves his honour as a Roman warrior, by giving in to her he must accept an ignominious death at the hands of his enemy Aufidius.

Nevertheless, Coriolanus is brave and ready to go beyond his duty as a soldier; he is clearly a noble figure. His name reminds us of this: he is known as MARTIUS (2) through the first eight scenes, and is re-named in honour of his military exploits at CORIOLES. The hero's nobility is made clear throughout the play, in the opinions of both the Romans—friends like MENENIUS all but worship him, and even the tribunes concede that he has 'served well for Rome' (3.3.84)—and of his enemy Aufidius, who calls him 'all-noble Martius' (4.5.107). Moreover, the play's final state-ment is that Coriolanus 'shall have a noble memory' (5.6.153). However, he lacks a genuine sense of him-self, and Volumnia's inflexible creation becomes in-creasingly dehumanized under the pressure of devel-opments. He is isolated from others—significantly, Shakespeare used the word 'alone' more often in this play than in any other. Strikingly, he characterises himself as a 'lonely dragon' (4.1.30). By the time he has joined the Volscians, he is chillingly described as 'a kind of nothing, titleless, / Till he had forg'd himself a name o'th'fire / Of burning Rome' (5.1.13–15). He wilfully sheds his connection with humanity. 'Wife, mother, child, I know not' (5.2.80), he cries. However, he cannot distance his weakness. As he anticipates his fall, he cries out, 'I melt, and am not / Of stronger earth than others' (5.3.28–29), and he attempts to find strength by imagining himself to be parentless: 'I'll . . . stand / As if a man were author of himself / And knew no other kin' (5.3.35–37).

In the final moments of the play, Shakespeare deftly reminds us of his protagonist's ultimate weakness. Coriolanus protests against being called a 'boy of tears' (5.6.101), and he cites his triumph at Corioles. 'Alone I did it' (5.6.116) he cries, and this 'Alone' only makes clearer the nature of his failure. His perverse dependence on his mother has made him unable to recognise and accept his need for involvement with others—first the people of Rome, and now the Vols-cians. The result is that his truly noble elements—his bravery and his warrior's achievements—are negated. It is because he has indeed remained a boy, emotion-ally, that he has been unable to avoid his final calamity.

Shakespeare had long been interested in Cori-olanus' tale, as we know from his use of it as a meta-phor for revenge in *Titus Andronicus* 4.4.67–68, but in *Coriolanus* the playwright made a subtle but important change in the character he found in his source, PLU-TARCH's *Lives*. The ancient historian stated that Cori-olanus' pride was the consequence of his father's early death and his resulting lack of guidance. Shakespeare, however, does not present his hero's failings as a func-tion of neglect, but rather as the product of a Roman aristocratic ideal that is applied excessively. The com-mentary on the potential harm in this situation is strongly made and is one of the play's important themes. Though both Shakespeare and Plutarch be-lieved Coriolanus' story to be historically accurate, modern historians realise that it was based on a pre-Roman fable, probably Volscian, that may have told originally of the local deity who gave his name to Corioles.

## Coriolanus

### SYNOPSIS

*Act 1, Scene 1*
Rioting Romans (see CITIZEN [5]) seek the death of MARTIUS (2), a leading aristocrat who is known for his pride. MENENIUS stalls them with a humorous fable that justifies the aristocracy. Martius arrives, and his scathing anger quiets the rioters. He reports that the rioting has resulted in a concession to the commoners: the people have been allowed to elect their own judges, called tribunes, two of whom are Sicinius and BRUTUS (3). News arrives that ROME is threatened by a neighbouring tribe, the VOLSCIANS. A municipal dele-gation—the generals COMINIUS and LARTIUS, some Senators (see SENATOR [2]), and the new tribunes—seek Martius' support in repelling the invaders. He agrees, and remarks on his desire to fight the noble Volscian general, AUFIDIUS, who is a former foe. The aristocrats all depart to prepare for war and leave the tribunes, who talk of their hatred of Martius.

*Act 1, Scene 2*
At CORIOLES, the Volscian Senators (see SENATOR [3]) meet with Aufidius to plan their campaign. Aufidius will take the field, and the Senators will defend Cori-oles.

*Act 1, Scene 3*
Martius' mother, VOLUMNIA, berates his wife, VIRGILIA, because she is not pleased that he has gone to war. She declares that her son's honourable death would bring her more joy than his birth had. She describes the wounds she hopes her son will receive, which will in-crease his honour, and she mocks Virgilia's revulsion. Virgilia's friend VALERIA appears, and they discuss the son of Martius and Virgilia, who resembles his father. Valeria brings the news that Martius and Cominius have Corioles under siege.

*Act 1, Scene 4*
At Corioles, a delegation of Volscian Senators defies the Romans, and combat begins. The Romans retreat.

Martius curses them and charges alone through the city's gates. The Romans believe he has been killed, but he emerges from Corioles, chased by Volscians, and the Romans rally to his defence.

*Act 1, Scene 5*
Corioles has been taken, and Martius insists, despite his wounds, that he join Cominius who is fighting Aufidius.

*Act 1, Scene 6*
Martius arrives as Cominius withdraws against superior forces. Full of enthusiasm for battle, Martius insists that he resume the fight and face Aufidius.

*Act 1, Scene 7*
Lartius places a LIEUTENANT (3) in charge of Corioles and goes to join Cominius and Martius.

*Act 1, Scene 8*
Martius and Aufidius fight. Several Volscians arrive to assist their general, but Martius drives them all away. Aufidius cries out that he has been shamed by their support.

*Act 1, Scene 9*
Martius modestly objects to hearing his deeds praised amidst the cheers of the soldiers. Cominius proposes that in honour of his courage at Corioles, he shall hereafter be known as CORIOLANUS.

*Act 1, Scene 10*
Aufidius rages against Martius, who has now defeated him five times. He swears that next time he will not lose even if he must resort to treachery rather than valour.

*Act 2, Scene 1*
Menenius berates Sicinius and Brutus for their animosity towards Martius, and he scorns the bad judgement of the common people they represent. Martius, now Coriolanus, returns and is formally welcomed and taken by the aristocrats to the Capitol to receive further honours. The tribunes voice their resentment of Coriolanus, who will now be nominated as consul, the highest office in Rome. However, they reflect that his pride will probably prevent him from displaying his scars to the commoners—as tradition requires—and that as the commoners' representatives, they can then oppose him and keep him from the office.

*Act 2, Scene 2*
An OFFICER (7) and his two fellows speculate that Coriolanus' pride will lead to his rejection as consul, though they believe him worthy of the office. Coriolanus is nominated for the consulate, but he asks to be excused from exhibiting himself to the common people. The tribunes refuse to accept the idea, and the aristocrats attempt to persuade Coriolanus to go through with it. Though uneasy, he agrees and goes with them to perform the ceremony.

*Act 2, Scene 3*
A group of citizens decide to support Coriolanus if he will formally ask them to. Coriolanus arrives, dressed in the traditional humble garb, and he asks groups of citizens for their support, though in a surly, begrudging manner. They agree to support him, and Menenius and the tribunes confirm his election. Coriolanus and Menenius leave, and the tribunes upbraid the citizens for supporting the proud Coriolanus. They convince them to rescind their approval before Coriolanus' formal installation as consul.

*Act 3, Scene 1*
Coriolanus hears that Aufidius has expressed a desire to fight with him, and he wishes for a war. The tribunes report that a mob has risen against Coriolanus. Despite the efforts of the aristocrats to calm him, Coriolanus angrily declares the commoners unworthy of a voice in the selection of a consul. The tribunes declare him a traitor to the laws of Rome and summon the mob. The mob follows Sicinius' lead and demands that Coriolanus be killed. Coriolanus draws his sword, but the aristocrats take him away. Brutus and Sicinius continue to raise the mob's fury, but Menenius convinces them to follow legal procedures and try Coriolanus for treason in the tribunes' court. He promises to get the general to attend it.

*Act 3, Scene 2*
Volumnia helps the other aristocrats convince Coriolanus to swallow his pride and apologise to the commoners as a matter of practical politics. After lengthy argument, he finally agrees.

*Act 3, Scene 4*
Brutus and Sicinius instruct a subordinate to prepare the crowd to support whatever line they take in the trial of Coriolanus, who they plan to provoke to anger. Coriolanus and his friends appear, and at first Coriolanus mildly makes the recantation demanded by the tribunes. When Sicinius calls him a traitor, however, he responds wrathfully and rejects the authority of the common people in insulting terms. The tribunes convict him of treasonous hostility to the people's justice and declare him banished from Rome; the mob takes up the cry. Coriolanus replies angrily that he shall be glad to leave a city controlled by such ignorant commoners, and he departs. The tribunes encourage the mob to follow him out the gates of the city.

*Act 4, Scene 1*
Coriolanus bids farewell to his family and friends and departs for exile.

*Act 4, Scene 2*
Volumnia rages furiously at the victorious tribunes.

*Act 4, Scene 3*
A ROMAN (2) gives information to a VOLSCE, telling him of Coriolanus' banishment. He recommends that the

Volscians strike against the city now that it has lost its most illustrious general.

*Act 4, Scene 4*
Coriolanus, disguised a poor man, arrives in ANTIUM and is directed to Aufidius' house.

*Act 4, Scene 5*
Coriolanus finds Aufidius and tells him bitterly of his banishment; he offers to fight for the Volscians against Rome. Aufidius is ecstatic at encountering his great enemy and agrees enthusiastically. Aufidius' servants (see SERVING-MAN [7]) marvel that their master has accepted a poor wanderer, but when one of them learns the truth they rejoice at the prospects for a successful war.

*Act 4, Scene 6*
The tribunes refuse to believe the news that the Volscians are again attacking Roman territory, led by Coriolanus. A crowd arrives, and the citizens declare that they had had misgivings about the banishment all along. The worried tribunes hope that the news will prove untrue.

*Act 4, Scene 7*
A Volscian LIEUTENANT (4) worries that Aufidius will be overshadowed by Coriolanus' growing popularity among their soldiers. Aufidius confides that he intends eventually to turn against the Roman.

*Act 5, Scene 1*
Cominius reports that Coriolanus, whose Volscian army threatens the city, has refused to meet with him. The tribunes convince Menenius to attempt to beg mercy for the city. Cominius declares that Menenius will also fail, and that their only hope lies in Coriolanus' mother and wife.

*Act 5, Scene 2*
Volscian guards declare to Menenius that Coriolanus has specifically refused entry to any Roman. When Menenius insists that he is an old friend and will be accepted, they mock him. Coriolanus appears and pointedly rejects Menenius.

*Act 5, Scene 3*
Volumnia appears, accompanied by Virgilia, Valeria, and a BOY (8)—Coriolanus' son. Coriolanus becomes increasingly upset as he hears and rejects their petitions for mercy. Finally, a long speech by Volumnia convinces him to make peace with Rome. Aufidius, in an aside, observes that he now has the means to get revenge on Coriolanus.

*Act 5, Scene 4*
Menenius and Sicinius despair for the city, but news arrives of Volumnia's success and the withdrawal of the Volscian forces.

*Act 5, Scene 5*
The Senators thankfully welcome Volumnia and the other women back to Rome.

*Act 5, Scene 6*
Aufidius consults with a group of CONSPIRATORS. They agree to support his charges of treason against Coriolanus and then to help him kill his enemy. Coriolanus appears, followed by an enthusiastic crowd of Volscians (see COMMONER [2]). Coriolanus presents his treaty with Rome as a conquest, but Aufidius accuses him of treachery. He calls him unmanly because he has given up the city in response to a woman's plea. Coriolanus angrily threatens to beat him, but Aufidius turns the crowd against him. When the mob loudly demands that Coriolanus be lynched as an enemy, the Conspirators attack him in a group and kill him. Aufidius defends the killing as motivated by patriotic rage, but he goes on to observe that Coriolanus was a great warrior and stipulates that he should have a noble funeral.

## COMMENTARY

*Coriolanus* is one of the most politically oriented of Shakespeare's plays; it depicts political confrontation between social classes. However, though *Coriolanus* opens with a civil insurrection and features the political manipulations of tribunes and aristocrats, Roman political strife is not the principal subject matter. Rather, it provides a context for the main plot, which is another sort of story. The play is first and foremost a TRAGEDY, the personal story of a great man whose greatness is accompanied by moral and psychological failings that bring about his downfall. As Coriolanus' story unfolds, Roman politics fall away, and the climactic confrontation in 5.3 does not oppose social classes or even political rivals. Rather, it presents an internal conflict within the protagonist, the clash between his pride in himself and his psychological dependence on his mother.

Coriolanus' importance to the plot is immediately established in Act 1, where he is prominently regarded as a brilliant military hero. Moreover, after the tragedy has run its course, the statement that 'he shall have a noble memory' (5.6.153) confirms this status for the protagonist. In between, his excessive pride produces catastrophe. Even before Coriolanus appears, his pride is carefully established as a major theme of the play in the remarks of the First Citizen. Then, it is flagrantly demonstrated with his first entrance. After Menenius has established a truce of sorts with the rioting commoners, Coriolanus appears and destroys it. His first three lines are a burst of anger that immediately creates a gulf between himself and the people that will never be bridged. He has the pride appropriate to a warrior, but he lacks a sense of ordinary social

*Shakespeare's Coriolanus is a great and noble warrior, but excessive pride leads to his defeat.* (Courtesy of Culver Pictures, Inc.)

intercourse, let alone of compromise. He does not consider the justice of the commoners' complaints; he is simply offended that they should question aristocratic authority at all. His response is to suggest a massacre: 'Hang 'em! . . . I'd make a quarry / With thousands of these quarter'd slaves' (1.1.189–198). From this initial outburst to his final anger at Aufidius' taunt that he is a 'boy of tears' (5.6.101), Coriolanus is incapable of flexibility. He has sense enough to see the propriety in other approaches—he understands Volumnia's Machiavellian argument in 3.2, and, too late, he courts the Volscian common people in Act 5—but his pride repeatedly overwhelms his common sense.

The influence of Volumnia is the driving power behind Coriolanus and the play. Well may she boast to her son, 'Thou art my warrior: / I holp to frame thee' (5.3.62–63), for she has bred in her son the pride that makes him believe that he and his class are incontesta-

bly superior. Yet Coriolanus is entirely incapable of dealing with the play's developments. At two crucial moments, Volumnia makes demands of her son that are inconsistent with his sense of his own superiority. After her persuasion in 3.2 he attempts to compromise with the political world, but the tribunes trigger his too-ready anger and he is banished from Rome. Thus, he loses his only honourable standing—as a Roman warrior—and he deserts to the Volscians. When his mother comes to plead that he refrain from assaulting the city, in 5.3, he is trapped. If he destroys Rome, he will destroy himself psychologically through his mother's rejection, but by giving in to her he accepts an ignominious death at the hands of Aufidius. His responses are woefully limited, and his inflexibility proves his undoing; he is fragile in his great strength. Yet it was his mother who bred in him the sternly martial pride that brought him to eminence in the first place. This ironic situation demonstrates the basic theme of all Shakespearean tragedy: great strength is inextricably interwoven with correspondingly great weakness.

The changing world of Rome provides the secondary component of the play, its political plot. The heavy political emphasis of much modern commentary on *Coriolanus* is not misplaced, for the conflicts that spark the tragic hero's downfall are representative of the social clashes that constitute much of political history. The play stresses a theme that was important to Shakespeare when he wrote his earlier English HISTORY PLAYS: the impact of immoral behaviour in the ruling class on the peace and prosperity of all of society. As Shakespeare knew from his source, PLUTARCH's *Lives*, the ancient warrior was thought of as a member of peaceful society as well as a leader in war. To maintain his honour, he was obliged to participate in society by submitting to its laws and customs just as did his non-heroic fellow citizens. Coriolanus lacks the moral discipline to honour this social contract; indeed, he would rather abandon the contract altogether and join Rome's enemies than honour it and accept Rome's common people. Not only does he imperil himself, he endangers the city's very existence. Thus, the personality defects of the protagonist have profound political consequences.

The other aristocrats are conscious of the need to compromise with the commoners, and to a certain extent they counteract Coriolanus' ill effects. However, their grudging willingness to accept the need of such an arrangement also corrupts the social contract. Menenius' 'belly speech' (1.1.95–153) is politic and mild, but it is accompanied by an undisguised disdain for the common man, the 'great toe' (1.1.154) of society. In 3.2.41–86 Volumnia recommends that Coriolanus be hypocritical with the people. This Machiavellian speech betrays a cynical disregard for 'th'ignorant' (3.2.76) that flouts the social co-opera-tion that it supposedly furthers. Coriolanus' indignant assumption that Brutus knows nothing of 'service' (3.3.83) is typical of the aristocratic rejection of social co-operation, though the tribune is obviously an in-dustrious representative of his constituency. In fact, one may conclude that Brutus provides more useful service to the commoners than the proud warrior does to his own caste. Coriolanus represents the ideal of one sort of virtue: the warrior's single-minded quest for glory as the military hero of his people. This ideal is no longer desirable in a community that acknowl-edges the demands of all its people. The emergence of the new political morality causes Coriolanus' fall; put another way, the stresses of that emergence are enacted in his catastrophe and death.

These themes are reinforced by a fascinating and bizarre motif, the confusion of normal love, sexual and maternal, with the warrior's enthusiasm for war. Coriolanus embraces a fellow warrior on the battle-field and declares that his delight equals that of his wedding night (1.6.29–32), and later, Aufidius re-sponds to him in similar fashion, in a passage (4.5. 107–127) of extraordinary sensuality. The general Cominius announces that his patriotic feelings are 'more holy and profound, than mine own life, / My dear wife's estimate, her womb's increase / And trea-sure of my loins' (3.3.113–115). When we first see Volumnia, in 1.3, she compares the thrill of giving birth to Coriolanus with that of seeing him as a soldier, and goes on to identify the beauty of a mother's breast with the sight of a head wound. She later attributes Coriolanus' fierceness in combat to her nursing of him, in 3.2.129. In her final manipulation of her son, she equates motherhood with the state in a violent image—'. . . assault thy country [and] tread / . . . on thy mother's womb' (5.3.123–124)—that reinforces our sense that she is a horrifyingly abnormal mother. In fact, when Coriolanus attempts to resist Volumnia's influence, he supposes himself outside the procreative process, 'as if a man were author of himself' (5.3.36). This recurring theme of emotional misplacement is a strong reminder that the moral world of Coriolanus and Volumnia is an unhealthy one, and that their story can only come to a tragic end.

The common people are not the cause of the city's near fall. Their objections to the rule of the aristocracy are given a fair presentation, especially in Act 1, where the First Citizen makes a sensible argument against the unfair distribution of corn that is the cause of the commoners' rebellion. Yet the cynicism of the tri-bunes, combined with the fickleness of the crowd, sup-ports the aristocratic argument that the common peo-ple are not worthy of power. The critical element in Rome's catastrophe is Coriolanus' decision to defect, not simply his banishment, and he would not have defected had he not been driven from Rome by the ungrateful people who were manipulated by the tri-bunes. Moreover, this issue is reprised in the episode of the Volscian commoners in 5.6, where Coriolanus is again abandoned by a fickle mob.

Thus, the faults of both the aristocracy and the plebeians are exposed. The combination has pro-duced a bewildering range of critical assessments, and *Coriolanus* has been declared to be the vehicle of fas-cist, conservative, moderate/pragmatic, liberal, and communist sentiments. While Shakespeare certainly displayed a conservative bias in favour of the estab-lished, hierarchical society, he was aware of, and wished to present, both sides of the political question. As a playwright, he was more interested in dramatic effect than in political science, and in this work he heightened the human foibles that lead to conflicts of the sort that he found in his sources.

The common people as a social and political class are more prominent in *Coriolanus* than in the history plays, which may reflect developments in England just before the play was written. (Also, the Roman plays, set in a remote time and place, offered Shakespeare a chance to explore more fully the fissures in society that government CENSORSHIP might well have disal-lowed in works dealing with relatively recent English history.) In *Coriolanus,* Shakespeare emphasises a corn shortage as the cause of plebeian discontent, while in Plutarch it was a relatively minor factor. Scholars con-nect this alteration with the extensive corn riots—called the Midlands Insurrection—that shook much of rural England in 1607. These demonstrations, which extended to brief losses of governmental control of some areas, raised issues of poverty and powerless-ness that had not been publicly considered in genera-tions. As a landowner and agricultural investor, Shakespeare may be presumed to have taken a particu-lar interest in the phenomenon. He may even have witnessed a riot—or at least spoken to witnesses—since disturbances erupted near STRATFORD at a time when he may have been there. Thus, the class warfare we see in *Coriolanus* may reflect events in England, which, though Shakespeare could not know it, was only a generation away from a cataclysmic civil war.

Thus, *Coriolanus* displays the political concerns of the history plays within the more grandiose framework of a tragedy. Shakespeare emphasised the stresses that result from these political concerns, rather than at-tempting to alleviate them, and *Coriolanus* is a very complex and dynamic play. Its rough, spontaneous poetic style is accompanied by structural devices in-tended to reinforce our sense of crowded conflict. Surprises in tone startle us at several important points: Volumnia's violent manner of speech in a pointedly domestic setting, in 1.3; the banished Coriolanus' un-expected appearance in Antium in 4.4; and the silence at the close of Volumnia's long, final speech. This is one of Shakespeare's most brilliant *coups de théâtre,* specified in the stage direction, 'Holds her by the hand silent' (5.3.183). All of these serve to keep the audience's attention at a peak, aware that the play's developments do not flow predictably.

The inevitability of events is nevertheless made clear through another structural device, the use of many parallel scenes and images. Menenius' 'belly speech' of 1.1 is repeatedly invoked with images of food and physiology that stud the play. In 1.3 Coriolanus' son is vividly described as like his father when he kills a butterfly with his teeth, and when Coriolanus marches on Rome with the Volscians, their advance is likened to 'boys pursuing summer butterflies' (4.6. 95). At the close of Act 3 the plebeians throng to see Coriolanus 'out at gates' (3.3.142); the warrior's banishment reminds us of his triumph in 1.4 when he was similarly repudiated by the commoners—this time, the cowardly soldiers—and alone passed through the gates of a city, Corioles. As we have seen, the Volscian Commoners re-enact the Roman mob's change of heart towards Coriolanus in the play's final episode. Aufidius' welcome to Coriolanus in 4.5 echoes the strange mixture of love and war that Coriolanus displayed to Cominius in 1.6. When he calls him a 'traitor' (5.6.85), Aufidius tempts Coriolanus into the defiance that results in his death with the same technique that Sicinius used to elicit the defiance that resulted in his banishment, in 3.3.66. Most striking, Volumnia's dramatic final plea echoes her earlier effort to move her son to submit to her instructions, in 3.2. These parallel themes are startling as they are recognised on each occasion, and are also cumulatively powerful as Coriolanus' fate inexorably unfolds. The great strength of the play is its complexity, for its similarity to both the history play and the tragedy make possible its difficult presentation of Coriolanus as a tragic hero in a real society.

## SOURCES OF THE PLAY

Shakespeare's principal source for *Coriolanus* was PLU-TARCH's *Lives,* in Thomas NORTH's translation (2nd ed., 1595). The general course of developments is taken from this account, and several important passages—e.g., Volumnia's appeal in 5.3.94–182—follow North's text very closely. Though Shakespeare invented several minor incidents—including all of Volumnia's other appearances—and developed the psychology of his hero, his fidelity to Plutarch was generally quite close in this play as compared to the other Roman plays.

Only one passage strongly reflects other sources. Menenius' comparison of politics and anatomy in 1.1. 95–159—very well-known since ancient times—was derived from several earlier renderings. In addition to North's version, which he followed fairly closely, Shakespeare also took a number of significant details from William CAMDEN's *Remaines* (1605), where the

fable is told by a medieval pope, and from another variant of the Coriolanus story found in LIVY's *Ab urbe condita,* translated by Philemon HOLLAND (4) as *The Romane Historie* (1600).

## TEXT OF THE PLAY

It is difficult to determine the date *Coriolanus* was written, and estimates range from 1603 to 1612. However, most scholars favour 1605 to 1609, for several reasons. First, the play must be later than Camden's *Remaines,* which was possibly available to Shakespeare in manuscript as early as 1603, though more probably used after its publication in 1605. Second, there is an apparent allusion to *Coriolanus* in Ben JONSON's play *Epicoene,* which was produced in late 1609 or early 1610. This implies that Shakespeare's play was written and staged somewhat earlier.

Further support, especially for the later part of this range of dates, is provided by other evidence. Applications of the VERSE TEST suggest that the play was roughly contemporary with *Antony and Cleopatra* (c. 1606), *Pericles* (c. 1607), *Cymbeline* (c. 1608–1610), and *The Winter's Tale* (c. 1610–1611). Also, some commentators find topical allusions in the text of the play. For example, 'fire on the ice' (1.1.172) may refer to the freezing over of the Thames River in the winter of 1607–1608, and Coriolanus' metaphor for treachery, 'he'll turn your current in a ditch / And make your channel his' (3.1.95–96), may have been inspired by the much-discussed failure of an English canal-building scheme in 1609. Some scholars believe that Shakespeare's treatment of relations between the aristocracy and the plebeians may have been stimulated in part by the Midlands Insurrection of 1607. This featured extensive corn riots suggestive of the similar disturbances that open the play. Further, psychoanalytically minded commentators feel that the prominence of Volumnia may reflect the death of Shakespeare's mother, Mary ARDEN (2), in 1608. Since none of these suggestions can be confirmed or denied, the date of composition of *Coriolanus* remains uncertain, with 1608 as perhaps the best estimate.

The play was initially published in the FIRST FOLIO (1623). The text was probably printed from Shakespeare's own manuscript, or FOUL PAPERS, for it contains elaborate and literary stage directions (e.g., at 1.3.1 and 5.3.183), variable speech headings *(Cor., Corio., Coriol.),* and idiosyncratic spellings (especially Sc for S in Sicinius, a form closely associated with Shakespeare [see SIR THOMAS MORE]). It also contains other irregularities that would have been omitted or corrected in a copy made by a scribe or in a PROMPT-BOOK.

## THEATRICAL HISTORY OF THE PLAY

Though no evidence of early productions of *Coriolanus* has survived, an apparent allusion to the play in Jonson's *Epicoene* implies that the work was performed c. 1609. Richard BURBAGE (3) was probably the original Coriolanus. The lack of contemporary references suggests that it was staged infrequently, and the play has never been consistently popular. Many productions have been intended primarily as political propaganda, and Shakespeare's text has been persistently altered to serve these ends.

The earliest recorded version of *Coriolanus* is the adaptation by Nahum TATE, *The Ingratitude of a Commonwealth*, which was performed in 1681–1682, an uncertain period in English politics. This version stressed the importance of respectful loyalty, and supported Coriolanus' complaints about the commoners of Rome and de-emphasised the hero's faults. Though it retained some of Shakespeare's text, it was virtually a different play, and included numerous passages of lurid violence. Despite these features, it was a commercial failure. In 1718 John RICH (2) staged a *Coriolanus* that was probably Shakespeare's, but it was immediately followed by another politically motivated adaptation, *The Invader of His Country: or, The Fatal Resentment,* by John DENNIS (2). This work—largely Dennis' text, with insertions of Shakespeare's—was directed against the 1715 invasion of Britain by the exiled STUART DYNASTY. It starred the popular Barton BOOTH (1) but nevertheless lasted only three performances.

Though Dennis' failure apparently triggered presentations of Shakespeare's play—in some form, at least—in each of the next three years, *Coriolanus* was then ignored for a generation. In 1754 Thomas SHERIDAN combined Shakespeare's play with another *Coriolanus*—an entirely independent work by James Thomson (1700–1748)—in an adaptation that was quite popular and was frequently revived for almost 15 years. In 1754 David GARRICK attempted to rival it with an abridged version of Shakespeare's text, but this production lasted only a week.

In the 19th century the play's popularity grew. Between 1789 and 1817 John Philip KEMBLE (3) staged a series of successful versions of Sheridan's adaptation that usually starred himself and his sister, Sarah SIDDONS. In 1819 W. C. MACREADY—and in 1820, Charles KEAN (1)—staged the play with abridged but otherwise genuine Shakespearean texts. Kean's version was a failure, but Macready's was popular, and he revived it frequently for almost 20 years. Samuel PHELPS—who had played Aufidius in one of Macready's productions—put on the play several times in the 1840s and '50s, but after this the play was again ignored in England for years, though Edwin FORREST scored notable successes in New York. In the 1890s Frank BENSON (1) restored the play to the English stage with several successful productions.

The 20th century's apocalyptic history has prompted a continuing interest in this most political of Shakespeare's plays. In fact, *Coriolanus* has played a small part in that history. In the winter of 1933–34 a Paris production—condemned as Fascist and briefly closed by the government—provoked pro- and anti-Fascist street demonstrations. The uproar is said to have contributed to the rallying of public support for the French government at a time when it very nearly fell to Fascist and royalist conspirators. In Nazi Germany *Coriolanus* was taught in schools. The protagonist was identified with Hitler as a model of firm leadership, and the injustice of his banishment was emphasised. After World War II the American occupation forces banned the play until 1953.

On the other hand, a 1935 Moscow production of *Coriolanus* stressed the protagonist's treachery and his aristocratic pride. It was acclaimed by Stalin's propagandists as an excellent lesson in the betrayal of the people by an individualistic leader in the Western mode. Perhaps the most notorious modern adaptation of the play is that of the Marxist German playwright Berthold Brecht (1898–1956), who prepared a text for an East German ensemble that cut all hints of approval of Coriolanus or of disapproval towards the common people. This version is a simplified text that unambiguously celebrates the revolution led by the tribunes. The West German writer Günter Grass (b. 1927) was stimulated by this work to write a play called *The Plebeians Rehearse the Uprising* (1970), in which Brecht is ironically seen rehearsing his *Coriolanus* during the 1953 anti-government riots in East Berlin. However, Brecht's play was not produced until after his death in 1963.

In England, Benson continued to produce the play through 1919, and numerous later productions have confirmed the play's popularity. The most significant of these was probably Lewis CASSON's 1938 production that starred Laurence OLIVIER and Sybil THORNDIKE. This version's success firmly established the play in the repertoire of the modern British theatre. Other notable productions include those of Glen Byam SHAW (3) (1952, with Anthony QUAYLE in the title role), Peter HALL (5) (1959, with Olivier and Edith EVANS [1], and 1984, with Ian MCKELLEN), Joseph PAPP (1965, in New York's Central Park), and Trevor NUNN (1973, with Nicol WILLIAMSON). *Coriolanus* has not been produced as a FILM, though two versions have been made for TELEVISION, and it is included in THE SPREAD OF THE EAGLE, an adaptation of all of the ROMAN PLAYS.

**Corioles (Corioli)**   Ancient Italian city of the VOLSCIANS, located about 25 miles south-east of ROME, setting for four scenes of Act 1 of *Coriolanus*. In 1.2 the Volscians make their plans to defend against the expected siege by the Romans. In 1.4–6 the Roman MARTIUS (2) displays great bravery after an initial success by the Volscians when he charges single-handed through the city gates and turns the tide of battle. In 1.7 the Roman general LARTIUS leaves a LIEUTENANT (3) in charge of the city. In 1.9 Martius is honoured for his bravery at Corioles with a new name, CORIOLANUS, by which he is known for the rest of the play.

There is nothing to distinguish Corioles from the many other besieged towns in Shakespeare—the gates and walls of a medieval city are called for in the stage directions, and nothing more is shown. Shakespeare presented the town because it was called for in his story. The ancient Volscian city has been lost, but it is believed to have been located near the modern Velletri.

**Cornelius (1)**    Minor character in *Hamlet,* ambassador to the King of Norway from the KING (5) of Denmark. In 1.2 Cornelius and VOLTEMAND are appointed to carry a message to Norway. The two ambassadors return in 2.2, and Voltemand reports Norway's reply. Cornelius barely speaks and serves only to flesh out the play's presentation of courtly diplomacy.

**Cornelius (2)**    Character in *Cymbeline,* a physician to the QUEEN (2) of Britain. In 1.6 Cornelius has provided the Queen with a poison—for experimental purposes, she says—but he informs us in an aside that he distrusts her and has substituted a sleeping potion. IMOGEN later takes this and is mistaken for dead. Later, in the play's final scene, he recounts the dying Queen's confession (5.5.31–61) and explains again about the poison (5.5.243–258). Cornelius' function is to further the plot and highlight the Queen's evilness.

**Cornell, Katharine (1898–1974)**    American actress. Though best known as a leading lady in contemporary romantic dramas, Cornell also played in classic works by Chekhov, G. B. SHAW (2), and Shakespeare. She was closely associated with the role of JULIET (1), which she played several times, perhaps most notably on a 77-city tour of the depression-era U.S. beginning in 1932.

**Cornwall, Duke of**    Character in *King Lear,* the villainous husband of King LEAR's usurping daughter REGAN. Cornwall takes a prominent part in the evil deeds that spark much of the play's action. In 2.1 he declares that EDGAR, who has been falsely accused of a murder plot against his father, GLOUCESTER (1), shall be executed, and he adopts as a follower Edgar's persecutor, EDMUND. He places Lear's loyal follower KENT in the stocks and he supports his wife and sister-in-law GONERIL in their expulsion of Lear. At his most cruel, in 3.7 he puts out Gloucester's eyes when the earl remains loyal to the outcast former king. For this offence he is killed by an appalled SERVANT (19), as is reported in 4.2 by a MESSENGER (20). His death is

proof that the triumph of villainy will not be total, but at the same time the enormity of his final deed contributes greatly to the general atmosphere of horror that so distinguishes the play.

**Costard**    Character in *Love's Labour's Lost,* a quick-witted CLOWN (1) who is at the centre of the rustic sub-plot. In 3.1 Costard is employed by Armado to send a love letter to JAQUENETTA and by BEROWNE to send another one to ROSALINE (1). He delivers each to the wrong woman, resulting in two comical outcomes: Armado's pompous rhetoric is read aloud to the amusement of the PRINCESS (1) of France and her retinue; and Berowne's love poem exposes to his fellow courtiers his own susceptibility to romance, just as he is chastising them for the same failing.

To a great degree, Costard is simply a character type derived from the Italian COMMEDIA DELL' ARTE tradition—that of the servant or rustic yokel descended from the comic slave figures of ancient ROMAN DRAMA. He engages in several bits of standard by-play—for instance, when he comes to believe that 're-muneration' means a three-farthing coin and 'guer-don' a shilling. However, he displays realistic touches of humanity that rank among the play's literary gems. A participant in the comical pageant of the Nine WORTHIES, Costard plays Pompey the Great (see POMPEY [2]), but he muffs his lines and shamefacedly apologises, in 5.2.554–555. Some twenty lines later, Costard demonstrates an appreciation for his fellows that exceeds the restricted humanity of a stock figure, when he speaks up for NATHANIEL (1) the Curate, who has been driven away by stage fright.

Costard's name is an old word meaning 'apple' or 'head', which stimulates a cluster of jokes in 3.1.

**Cottom (Cottam), John (active 1566–1581)**    STRATFORD schoolmaster, one of Shakespeare's teachers. Cottom taught at Stratford from 1579–1581 and probably supervised the last years of Shakespeare's formal education (though the records of Shakespeare's attendance have not survived). He was recruited for the job by his predecessor, to whom he paid £6 (about a third of a year's pay) for the opportunity. Cottom's younger brother, a Jesuit priest, was tried for treason in November 1581, for his active opposition to the Protestant state religion. He was executed the next spring. In December 1581 John Cotton resigned his position at Stratford, probably under pressure because of his brother's situation. He eventually inherited a country estate where he lived in retirement and practised Catholicism. His religion may have influenced Shakespeare, who seems to have been at least tolerant of Catholicism in an intolerant age, and who some scholars believe may have been a secret Catholic himself.

**Countess (1) of Auvergne**    Minor character in *1 Henry VI*, a French noblewoman who attempts to capture TALBOT by means of a ruse. She invites him to visit her castle, pretending an innocent desire to meet so valiant an hero in person. He receives the invitation in 2.2, but, suspicious, he plans a counter-ploy. In 2.3 she springs her trap, but following his plan, a troop of soldiers immediately frees him. Talbot gracefully accepts the Countess' apology.

This episode is entirely fictitious, probably derived by the playwright from similar events in the 'Robin Hood' cycle of tales. It serves to emphasise the virtues of Talbot, whose eventual loss to the English is one of the climaxes of the play. In attributing such deceit to the French, implicitly denying their military strength, the episode contributes to the play's chief point—that the successes of the French could not have occurred without dissensions among the English.

**Countess (2) of Rossillion**    Character in *All's Well That Ends Well*, the mother of BERTRAM and guardian of HELENA (2). The Countess comments on the main action of the play, overseeing from her estate at ROSSILLION the relationship between her son and her ward. Loving Helena, she promotes their marriage; loving Bertram, she rues his foolishness in abandoning his bride, and she is present to see them reconciled at the play's close. With Lord LAFEW and the KING (17), the Countess helps to create a world of kindness and generosity that counters the play's unpleasant aspects.

One of her most important functions is to guide the audience's responses to the major characters through her own, exalting Helena and forgiving Bertram. Her love for Helena is as generous as her affection for her son is natural. Her sympathy for Helena's love, based on her 'remembrances of days foregone' (1.3.129), is touching, and her collaboration with Helena serves to start the heroine on her way. She is also aware of Bertram's defects, while at the same time remaining willing to make allowances and forgive. The Countess loves her son, but, when he abandons Helena, she recognises that he is a 'rash and unbridled boy' (3.2. 27) and sends letters that she hopes will bring him to his senses. The Countess is an especially sympathetic character in a play full of moral ambiguity. George Bernard SHAW (2) called hers 'the most beautiful old woman's part ever written'.

**Countrymen**    Group of minor characters in *The Two Noble Kinsmen*, peasants. In 2.2 four Countrymen tell ARCITE of wrestling and running competitions at a country fair. The outcast nobleman subsequently distinguishes himself at the fair, coming to the attention of the court of Duke THESEUS (2), and thus meeting his beloved, EMILIA (4). Six Countrymen appear in 3.5, one of them dressed as a BAVIAN, or baboon, as part of the duke's entertainment; five of them, with NELL (2)

and her friends, perform a dance under the direction of the SCHOOLMASTER (2). Most scholars agree that neither 2.1 nor 3.5 was written by Shakespeare; thus, the Countrymen are probably the creation of John FLETCHER (2).

**Court, Alexander**    Minor character in *Henry V*, soldier who meets the incognito King HENRY V on the eve of the battle of AGINCOURT. His companions, BATES and WILLIAMS (2), converse with the king, but Court speaks only one line.

**Courtesan**    Minor character in *The Comedy of Errors*, a 'professional entertainer' visited off-stage by ANTIPHOLUS OF EPHESUS after he is mistakenly rejected by his wife, ADRIANA. The Courtesan appears later, in 4.3, to claim a necklace Antipholus promised her in exchange for her ring. She mistakenly approaches ANTIPHOLUS OF SYRACUSE, who rejects her as a sorceress or agent of the devil. She goes to Adriana and accuses her husband of lunacy and of theft of the ring, thus triggering the pursuit that results in Antipholus of Ephesus' treatment for insanity at the hands of PINCH.

**Cousin Capulet**    Character in *Romeo and Juliet*. See CAPULET (2).

**Coventry**    City in WARWICKSHIRE in central England, the setting for a scene each in *3 Henry VI* and *Richard II*. In *3 Henry VI* Coventry is the site of an encounter (5.1) between the Earl of WARWICK (3) and the Yorkist leaders, at which GEORGE (2) is brought to abandon Warwick's cause, prior to a battle in the following scenes. In *Richard II*, Coventry is the scene (1.3) of the scheduled trial by combat between BOLINGBROKE (1) and MOWBRAY (1) that RICHARD II cancels, sending the two disputants into exile instead.

**Cowley, Richard (d. 1619)**    English actor, one of the 26 men listed in the FIRST FOLIO as the 'Principall Actors' in Shakespeare's plays. Cowley is known to have performed with STRANGE'S MEN as early as 1590, and was probably with the CHAMBERLAIN'S MEN from their formation in 1594, though the earliest surviving documentation dates from 1600. He was a member of the KING'S MEN—as the Chamberlain's became—at least through 1605 and probably much later, for several associates of the King's Men witnessed his will in 1618. Speech prefixes in early texts reveal that Cowley played VERGES in *Much Ado About Nothing* and QUINCE in *A Midsummer Night's Dream;* he is thus presumed to have worked well as a straight man to the great comic actor Will KEMPE, who played DOGBERRY and BOTTOM, the respective counterparts to Cowley's roles.

**Cox, Robert (d. 1655)**    English actor, famed for his performances of DROLLS, which were brief playlets at fairs and in taverns from 1642 to 1660, when English theatres were closed by the revolutionary government, Cox performed his drolls illegally until he was arrested and imprisoned in 1653. A collection of his scripts—some of which he wrote, though most were adaptations of scenes from well-known plays—was published by Henry MARSH and Francis KIRKMAN in 1662.

**Crab**   Dog in *The Two Gentlemen of Verona*. LAUNCE's pet is the subject of his two memorable comic monologues, in 2.3 and 4.4. The name refers to the crab apple, and it suggests an animal small in size and sour in expression.

**Craig (1), Gordon (1872–1966)**   English actor, producer, and theatrical designer. The son of Ellen TERRY (1) and the famed architect and designer Edward Godwin (1833–1886), Craig was a successful child actor and in his late teens and early 20s was a member of Henry IRVING's company. He played many leading Shakespearean roles, but his fame rests on his later career as a producer, designer, and theoretician. He advocated simple productions and aspired to approximate the Elizabethan stage; he was an important influence on Harley GRANVILLE-BARKER. Among Craig's most important books are *The Art of the Theatre* (1905), *Towards a New Theatre* (1911), and *The Theatre Advancing* (1921). He also wrote books on both Terry and Irving.

**Craig (2), Hardin (1875–1968)**   American scholar, author of several important works on Shakespeare. A long-time professor at the University of Missouri, Craig believed that an understanding of the cultural and intellectual world in which Shakespeare lived was crucial to the comprehension of his poetry and plays. Craig's best-known works were *The Enchanted Glass: The Elizabethan Mind in Literature* (1935) and *New Lamps for Old: A Sequel to the Enchanted Glass* (1960).

**Crane, Ralph (active 1620s)**   Professional copyist, or scribe, whose copies of some of Shakespeare's plays were probably published in the FIRST FOLIO. Crane, a legal clerk who chiefly copied documents for lawyers, also did free-lance work copying plays—either from the playwrights' FOUL PAPERS or from a PROMPTBOOK—for private libraries (a common practice of the day). He also worked for the KING's MEN in the early 1620s. Several signed Crane transcripts survive (though none of a Shakespeare play), so his idiosyncratic style can be identified. On the basis of this style, scholars believe that he provided the copy used in printing five of the plays in the First Folio (1623)—*Measure for Measure, The Merry Wives of Windsor, The Tempest, The Two Gentlemen of Verona,* and *The Winter's Tale.*

Scholars distinguish Crane's work by his peculiar habits of punctuation—especially his use of hyphens to join adjectives and their nouns, as in 'palsied-Eld' (*Measure for Measure* 3.1.36), and his frequent use of parentheses to set off words or phrases, as in 'that same knave (Ford her husband) hath' (*Merry Wives of Windsor* 5.1.18). Scholars also point to Crane's idiosyncratic spellings, like 'sirha' for 'sirrah', and his provision of 'massed entrances', in which all of the characters in a scene are listed in a group at its opening, without regard for when they actually come on stage.

**Cranmer, Thomas (1489–1556)**   Historical figure and character in *Henry VIII,* an adviser to King HENRY VIII and later Archbishop of Canterbury. Cranmer is the central figure in 5.1–2, as Bishop GARDINER (1) and the Lord CHANCELLOR attempt to charge him with heresy at a meeting of the royal council, only to be thwarted by the king's intervention. The episode demonstrates the king's mastery of the situation—Henry's increasing wisdom is an important theme of the play. It also illustrates the triumph of the Protestant leaders—Cranmer and the king—over the pro-Catholic conspirators.

Cranmer is sometimes confused with another Archbishop of Canterbury in the play, whom the king addresses in 2.4.215–217. However, this figure—who remains mute—is Cranmer's predecessor, Archbishop William Warham (d. 1532), for Cranmer is abroad at this point. Henry wishes Cranmer were present in 2.4.236–237; his return and his appointment as Archbishop are reported in 3.2.64, 74.

At the close of the play, Cranmer's prediction of glory for the infant ELIZABETH (1) even includes praise of her successor, JAMES I, and thus extends *Henry VIII* into Shakespeare's own time. In this, the play differs from all the other HISTORY PLAYS. Cranmer, well known to 17th-century audiences as a martyred religious hero, is a suitable vehicle for such a spiritual evocation of 'the happiness of England' (5.4.56).

The historical Cranmer was a professor at Cambridge University in the 1520s who was influenced by continental Protestant doctrines, especially on papal authority. He proposed that King Henry did not need the pope's permission to divorce Queen KATHERINE if he had the approval of other authoritative clerics. Henry sent Cranmer and others to solicit opinions, some of them approving, from religious thinkers throughout England and Europe. When Cranmer was appointed archbishop in 1533, he declared the king's marriage invalid. Cranmer's greatest historical importance, however, lies in his work as the chief creator of a liturgy for the new Protestant Church of England. He supervised the production of the first two editions (1549, 1552) of a prayer book and promulgated a formal statement of doctrine in 42 articles (1552), later reduced to 39. An oath of adherence to the 39 Articles, as they were known, was required of all Anglican clergymen and became a bone of contention in English politics for generations. Cranmer also edited and wrote parts of the first book of *Homilies* (1547), intended to be used for sermons in Anglican churches. For these works and his leadership as archbishop, Cranmer is regarded as the principal founder of the Church of England. Under the Catholic Queen Mary (ruled 1553–1558), he was ousted from his archbishopric and charged with heresy. He formally recanted but was condemned anyway and burned at the stake.

**Creede, Thomas (active 1578–1617)** London printer, producer of editions of several of Shakespeare's plays. Creede printed the first editions of *2 Henry VI* (Q1, 1594, for Thomas MILLINGTON), *Henry V* (Q1, 1600, for Millington and John BUSBY), and *The Merry Wives of Windsor* (Q1, 1602, for Arthur JOHNSON [1]). He also printed second editions of *Henry V* (Q2, 1602, for Thomas PAVIER) and *Romeo and Juliet* (Q2, 1599, for Cuthbert BURBY). Creede also produced four editions of *Richard III* (Q2–Q5, 1598, 1602, 1605, 1612; the first two for Andrew WISE and the others for Matthew LAW). Creede is regarded as among the most skilful printers of the period, and he had a long and successful career. He became a member of the STATIONERS' COMPANY in 1578 and operated his own press from at least 1593. He probably died in 1617 when his partner became sole owner of his company.

**Cressida** Legendary figure and title character in *Troilus and Cressida*, lover of TROILUS. Because Cressida's betrayal of her lover in favour of the Greek DIOMEDES is the focal event of the love plot, many commentators have seen her role as that of a villain, though in fact Shakespeare did not treat her unsympathetically. Her disloyalty is a necessary element of his story, and she is representative of human or perhaps (for Shakespeare) feminine weakness, but she is certainly not a vicious breaker of hearts, nor, despite ULYSSES' mistaken assumption upon meeting her in 4.5, is she a prostitute, for she shows no hint of mercenary motives. Diomedes courts her in 5.2 with the same wiles she used on Troilus earlier—affecting disinterest and a readiness to ignore her—and she is susceptible, though she resists confusedly. She is a frankly sensual woman, as has been evident from her affair with Troilus, and now, alone in a new world, having just been removed from TROY to the Greek camp, she succumbs to her nature.

Cressida is frequently associated with HELEN (1), the worthless prize of the TROJAN WAR, in order to underscore her similar deficiency as a motive for Troilus. She is a much more alert and interesting personality than Helen, however. She is a knowledgeable flirt, able to consider the tactics of courtship, and she is scornfully aware that PANDARUS is 'a bawd' (1.2.286). Once united with Troilus in 3.2, she frankly confesses her love, but in confusion she regrets abandoning her tactical game. Tellingly, she speaks of her 'unkind self, that itself will leave / To be another's fool' (3.2.146–147). Swept up in the excitement of the moment, she deludes herself that a real romance is in the offing, but her profession of faith is couched in negative terms, allowing the prediction—recognised by the audience to be accurate in a textbook instance of dramatic irony—that the future will call 'false maids in love . . . "as false as Cressid" ' (3.2.188–194). Although she pledges her loyalty to Troilus in the enthusiasm of passion, she recognises her need for Diomedes in Troilus' absence. She admits her guilt, attributing it to her gender: 'Ah, poor our sex! . . . The error of our eye directs our mind' (5.2.108–109). Such simple awareness of guilt is unique in this play filled with hypocrisy and self-delusion.

Cressida's name stems from a character in the *Iliad* of HOMER, Briseis, a slave and concubine of first ACHILLES and then AGAMEMNON and a source of dispute between them; she had nothing to do with Troilus. The name evolved through Briseida, to Griseida, and then Criseyde—in the works of SAINTE-MAURE, BOCCACCIO, and CHAUCER respectively—before Shakespeare used the variant that is now standard.

**Créton, Jean (c. 1340–after 1400)** French writer whose poem *Histoire du Roy d'Angleterre Richard* may have influenced the writing of *Richard II*. Créton, a French nobleman, was a visitor to RICHARD II's court beginning in 1398. He accompanied Richard to Ireland and was with the King when he was captured by BOLINGBROKE (1). His account is highly favourable to Richard.

**Crier** Minor character in *Henry VIII*, petty official at the divorce trial of Queen KATHERINE. In 2.4.7 and 10, upon the orders of the SCRIBE, the Crier formally demands the presence of King HENRY VIII and the queen. In this he emphasises the pomp and ceremony with which the king is proceeding against Katherine, thereby increasing our sense of her vulnerability.

**Cromer, Sir James (d. 1450)** Historical figure mentioned in *2 Henry VI*, the son-in-law of Lord SAY. Cromer himself does not appear in the play, but the rebel Jack CADE orders him executed, along with his father-in-law, in 4.7, and the revolutionaries carry his head on a pole at the end of that scene.

**Cromwell, Thomas (c. 1485–1540)** Historical figure and character in *Henry VIII*, secretary to Cardinal WOLSEY and later to King HENRY VIII's council. In 3.2, as Wolsey's downfall becomes clear, Cromwell's demonstration of loyalty improves our image of Wolsey. He seems genuinely grieved, crying out, 'O my lord, / Must I then leave you? must I needs forgo / So good, so noble and so true a master?' (3.2.421–423). The episode also offers an opportunity for the fallen cardinal to display magnanimity—concerning himself with Cromwell's welfare amid the debacle of his own affairs and thereby demonstrating his capacity for moral regeneration in adversity, an important theme of the play. Cromwell's subsequent political rise is mentioned by the Third GENTLEMAN (14), who calls him 'A man in much esteem with th'king' (4.1.109). In 5.2 Cromwell defends Archbishop CRANMER against heresy charges and is himself accused of Protestant leanings by the orthodox Bishop GARDINER (1). The episode points up the political importance of religious rivalries in the play's world. Also, that the one-time aide to Wolsey should become the king's ally demonstrates the progress from evil to good so central to *Henry VIII.*

The historical Cromwell served as Wolsey's secretary, but Shakespeare invented his sympathetic response to the cardinal's plight. Cromwell eventually succeeded Wolsey as the king's chief minister. A vigorous administrator, he devised and oversaw the dissolution of English monasteries to enrich the crown and set up an intensive domestic intelligence service, sometimes called the first prototype of a secret police force. Eventually, however, Cromwell shared Wolsey's fate. He tried to ally England with the Protestant powers of northern Europe, and to that end arranged Henry's fourth marriage, in 1540, to the German princess, Anne of Cleves (1515–1557). The rapid failure of the marriage was the minister's downfall. He was convicted of treason and executed. (His fate is obscurely alluded to in 3.2.449.) His career was the subject of the play THOMAS LORD CROMWELL, at one time attributed to Shakespeare.

**Cross Keys Inn**   Inn in LONDON whose courtyard was used for play performances in the 16th century, and at which Shakespeare performed early in his career. From its foundation in 1594, the CHAMBERLAIN'S MEN, of which Shakespeare was a member, performed in the winter at the Cross Keys and in the summer at the THEATRE—the first true playhouse in England. Plays had been performed at the inn—in summer and winter—since at least as early as 1579. Other entertainments were also conducted there; a performing horse, for example, is recorded sometime before 1588. In 1596 the London government outlawed play performances within the city limits, and the Cross Keys Inn ceased to function as a playhouse.

**Crosse, Samuel (active c. 1604)**   English actor, a member of the CHAMBERLAIN'S MEN or KING'S MEN. Cross is listed in the FIRST FOLIO among the 'Principall Actors' in Shakespeare's plays, but he is unknown elsewhere. He may only have been with the company before it became the King's Men in 1603, for he was not among the nine members listed in the patent granted at that time. On the other hand, he may have joined soon thereafter, since the group numbered 12 in the summer of 1604. However, he was apparently not with the company in May 1605, when Augustine PHILLIPS bequeathed small legacies to twelve named members of the company; some scholars believe he died in the interim.

**Crowne, John (c. 1640–1703)**   English dramatist who adapted *2* and *3 Henry VI.* In 1680 Crowne combined the last two Acts of *2 Henry VI* with *3 Henry VI* in a play entitled *The Misery of Civil War.* This was a topical work, intended as propaganda for the early Whig political party in the disputes of the day, as was its successor, which was based on the earlier parts of *2 Henry VI,* though titled *Henry VI, the First Part* (1681).

**Cumberland, Richard (1732–1811)**   British playwright, creator of an adaptation of *Timon of Athens.* A minor politician, Cumberland also wrote a number of sentimental plays, most of which are now forgotten. His adaptation of *Timon* was unsuccessfully staged in 1771. He was caricatured as Sir Fretful Plagiary in Richard Brinsley Sheridan's play *The Critic* (1779).

**Cupid**   In *Timon of Athens* the name taken by a LADY (2) who leads the MASQUE in 1.2. Her disguise as the Roman god of love demonstrates both the fashionable neoclassicism of such aristocratic entertainments and the slightly lascivious quality that enlivened many of them.

**Curan**   Minor character in *King Lear,* a follower of the Earl of GLOUCESTER (1). In 2.1 Curan tells EDMUND of a rumour that the Dukes of CORNWALL and ALBANY—the husbands of REGAN and GONERIL, to whom King LEAR has foolishly given power—are soon to fall into civil war. This is the first hint that Lear's error, already disastrous for him personally, is also a potential catastrophe for the kingdom as a whole.

**Curio**   Minor character in *Twelfth Night,* a follower of Duke ORSINO of ILLYRIA. Curio has no personality and very few lines, serving to fill out the Duke's retinue. In 1.1.16–18 Curio achieves his greatest prominence when he provides the occasion for a pun by his master.

**Curtain Theatre, The**   Second LONDON playhouse, probably built by Henry LANEMAN in 1577. It was apparently a round or multi-sided three-storey building, located near the first playhouse, the THEATRE, in Shoreditch, a northern suburb of London. Its name refers to its neighbourhood, the Curtain Close, and not to theatre curtains, which were not in use at that time. Between 1590 and 1592 STRANGE'S MEN—perhaps including the young Shakespeare—often played at the Curtain, and in 1597–1598, the CHAMBERLAIN'S MEN, definitely Shakespeare's company, played there before moving to the new GLOBE THEATRE in the following year. It was during this period that Shakespeare wrote *Henry V,* with its mention of a circular theatre as 'this wooden O' (Prologue, 13). This is often taken as an allusion to the Globe but more probably refers to the Curtain. From 1603 until at least 1609, the QUEEN'S MEN (2) were usually tenants of the Curtain, and PRINCE CHARLES' COMPANY played there after 1621. The theatre is last mentioned in 1627.

**Curtis**   Minor character in *The Taming of the Shrew,* a servant of PETRUCHIO (2). Curtis, who has been in charge of the household in his master's absence, greets the returning GRUMIO and engages him in comical repartee at the beginning of 4.1. Later in the scene, he is one of the servants whom Petruchio abuses as part of his programme to demonstrate to KATHERINA the ugliness of shrewish behaviour. Curtis' name is thought to be that of an actor who played him, possibly Curtis GREVILLE (1).

**Cushman, Charlotte (1816–1876)**   American actress, generally considered the first great American-born actress. Cushman, who began her career as an opera singer, was particularly noted for her fierce portrayals of LADY (6) MACBETH, which she played opposite William MACREADY, Edwin FORREST, Edwin BOOTH (2), and others. She was also highly praised as DESDEMONA and *Henry VIII*'s Queen KATHERINE of Aragon. In addition, she was noted for her successes in male parts, especially ROMEO—opposite the JULIET (1) of her sister, Susan—Cardinal WOLSEY, and HAMLET.

**Cymbeline (d. c. A.D. 40)**   Historical figure and title character of *Cymbeline,* the king of Britain and father of IMOGEN. Though Cymbeline is the title character, he is not an important one. The title of the play suggests the land he rules, rather than him personally. He is a typical king of fairy-tale and romantic literature. He loses his prosperity when he follows evil advisers, and then recovers it in a traditional happy ending through the workings of a benevolent fate. Influenced by his vicious QUEEN (2) and her son CLOTEN, he proceeds unjustly against his innocent daughter and her husband, POSTHUMUS. He loses Imogen as he once lost his sons, by another unjust action, the banishment of BELARIUS twenty years earlier. Moreover, still under the influence of his wife and stepson, he commits Britain to a foolish war against ROME. However, fate intervenes, and Cymbeline is eventually freed from evil. The Romans are miraculously defeated by the king's long-lost sons, and Cymbeline recovers his family and survives to be merciful to his enemies at the play's close.

Cymbeline is a passive figure whose competence as a ruler can only be restored by a happy ending brought about by chance, rather than by himself. On the other hand, his crimes are equally not his own; he is only unintentionally cruel, and though wrongheaded, he is quite willing to admit his folly and accept the mercy of providence. He is a figure from traditional lore who is necessary to the plot but does not contribute to it. His character is not fully developed, and what we see is a feeble store of anger in early scenes, a dumbfounded confusion later on, and a mild exaltation at the end.

The historical Cymbeline, generally called Cunobelinus, was a powerful ruler among the Celtic tribes of south-east England, but Shakespeare's figure bears virtually no resemblance to him. Shakespeare's source, HOLINSHED's *Chronicles,* was rather vague and inaccurate regarding Cunobelinus' reign, but the playwright did not follow his source particularly closely in any case. The most striking difference is that Rome's invasion—a successful one that established Roman rule in Britain—came several years after Cunobelinus' death. Cunobelinus was among the most successful of England's tribal kings in terms of conquering his neighbours, but little else is known of his reign.

## *Cymbeline*

### SYNOPSIS

*Act 1, Scene 1*
One GENTLEMAN (12) tells another that King CYMBELINE's daughter IMOGEN has married a poor but worthy nobleman, POSTHUMUS LEONATUS, whose father had died—before he was born—in the king's service. However, Posthumus has been banished from Britain because the king had wanted Imogen to marry CLOTEN, the boorish son of the QUEEN (2). He adds that Imogen is the king's only child, with the exception of two sons who were kidnapped 20 years earlier and never recovered.

*Act 1, Scene 2*
The Queen affects friendship for Imogen and the departing Posthumus, but Imogen mistrusts her. The Queen warns them that the king may find them, but in an aside she declares that she will send the king their way. As they bid each other farewell, Imogen gives Posthumus a diamond ring and he gives her a bracelet. The king appears and angrily drives Posthumus away. Posthumus' servant PISANIO reports to Imogen that his master has told him to remain at court and serve her. He adds that Posthumus and Cloten have fought but that Posthumus refrained from hurting his opponent.

*Act 1, Scene 3*
Cloten boasts to a LORD (15) of his swordplay against Posthumus while a Second Lord mocks him behind his back.

*Act 1, Scene 4*
Pisanio tells the lovesick Imogen of Posthumus' departure.

*Act 1, Scene 5*
In ROME the exiled Posthumus meets IACHIMO. They speak of a duel that Posthumus had once fought over his claim that Imogen was superior to all other women, both in beauty and virtue. Iachimo declares that Imogen is not so virtuous. He offers to bet his estate against Posthumus' diamond ring that he can seduce her, and the enraged Posthumus accepts the wager.

*Act 1, Scene 6*
In Britain; the Queen assures the physician CORNELIUS (2) that the poison he has given her is intended only for experiments on small animals, to further her education in herbal lore. Pisanio arrives, and the Queen muses to herself that she will poison him since he serves Cloten's enemy. In a soliloquy, Cornelius reveals that since he mistrusts the Queen he has substituted a powerful sleeping potion for the poison; a victim will appear dead for a time but will suffer no harm. The Queen tries to recruit Pisanio to convince Imogen to marry Cloten, and as a reward she gives him the poison. She tells him it is a potent restorative.

*Act 1, Scene 7*
Iachimo arrives at court and meets Imogen. He tells her that Posthumus leads a riotous life in Rome, and that he speaks mockingly of his faithful lover at home. He encourages her to seek revenge by sleeping with him. When she angrily dismisses him, he declares that he did not mean it but had merely been testing her virtue to see if Posthumus' praise had been true. Imogen is mollified and agrees to assist Iachimo. She says she will keep a chest containing valuables that are partly owned by Posthumus safe in the most secure possible location—her own bedchamber.

*Act 2, Scene 1*
Cloten brags of his ill temper over gambling losses and is mocked behind his back by the Second Lord, who sympathises with Imogen in a soliloquy.

*Act 2, Scene 2*
In her bedchamber Imogen retires for the night. Iachimo emerges from the chest, which is being kept there as Imogen had agreed. He memorises the nature of the furnishings and decorations, takes a bracelet from the sleeping Imogen's wrist, notices a mole on her breast, and returns to the chest.

*Act 2, Scene 3*
MUSICIANS (7) hired by Cloten serenade Imogen, but she does not respond. He accosts her. She tries to turn him away politely, but when he persists she lashes out at him and declares that he is not worth the clothes Posthumus wears. She leaves, and Cloten vows revenge.

*Act 2, Scene 4*
In Rome; Iachimo has returned from Britain and claims the diamond ring Posthumus had wagered. He offers a description of Imogen's bedchamber as proof that he has slept with her. When Posthumus refuses to believe him, he displays the bracelet—which Posthumus had given Imogen—and then clinches his case when he tells of the mole on Imogen's breast. Posthumus believes him and, cursing all women, vows to seek revenge on Imogen.

*Act 3, Scene 1*
In Britain; LUCIUS (4), the ambassador from the Roman emperor, informs Cymbeline that Britain owes tribute money to the Romans. Cloten boldly insists that the tribute shall not be paid, and the king agrees. Lucius replies with a declaration of war.

*Act 3, Scene 2*
Pisanio grieves over a letter from Posthumus that orders him to murder Imogen as punishment for her adultery; he is confident that Posthumus has been tricked. Imogen arrives and Pisanio gives her a letter from Posthumus; it tells her to run away and join him at Milford Haven, a port in WALES (1). Delighted, she immediately makes plans to do so.

*Act 3, Scene 3*
BELARIUS stands outside a cave in Wales and addresses his sons GUIDERIUS and ARVIRAGUS. He praises the wilderness life they lead as infinitely superior to life at a king's court. The two young men respectfully declare that they regret the lack of an opportunity to prove themselves in the great world. Belarius argues that his own unjust banishment justifies his remarks. The sons leave to prepare for the day's hunt, and Belarius soliloguises that their enthusiasm for accomplishment reflects their royal blood. Although they believe him to be their father, they are actually royal princes, the sons of King Cymbeline, kidnapped by Belarius when he was exiled.

*Act 3, Scene 4*
Near Milford Haven, Pisanio shows Imogen the letter from Posthumus that declares her unfaithfulness and commands her murder. Grief stricken, Imogen raves madly until Pisanio proposes a plan. The deceived Posthumus must be made to believe she is dead until he can learn the truth. Pisanio will claim to Posthumus that he has killed Imogen, and news of her disappearance from court will confirm the account. In the meantime, she should disguise herself as a page boy and take service with Lucius, who is expected in Wales soon. She can then go to Rome and at least maintain contact with Posthumus. She agrees and assumes her disguise. Pisanio gives her the medicine he received

from the queen in case she falls ill while alone, and returns to the court.

*Act 3, Scene 5*
Lucius regrets the end of his friendship with Cymbeline and leaves the court for Milford Haven where he will sail for Rome. Imogen's absence is reported. Cloten encounters Pisanio and threatens to kill him if he does not tell where Imogen is. He reveals Posthumus' letter to Imogen that tells her to meet him in Wales. Cloten then orders Pisanio to bring him some of Posthumus' clothes. After a soliloquy in which he plans to kill Posthumus in front of Imogen and then rape her, all while wearing the very clothes that she had insultingly compared him with, he sets out for Wales.

*Act 3, Scene 6*
Imogen, tired and in despair, comes to Belarius' cave. Seeking rest, she calls out; she gets no answer and enters the cave.

*Act 3, Scene 7*
Belarius, Guiderius, and Arviragus return from the hunt and discover Imogen, disguised as a boy. She identifies herself as 'Fidele' and says that she is travelling to join her master at Milford. Struck by 'his' courtly manners and almost supernatural beauty, the two young men declare their brotherly love for the stranger. They invite Imogen to stay the night before travelling on.

*Act 3, Scene 8*
In Rome a SENATOR (5) issues plans for the invasion of Britain. Lucius is to command a force raised from the gentry of Rome.

*Act 4, Scene 1*
In Wales, Cloten wears Posthumus' clothes and compliments himself on his appearance. He believes he will soon find his enemy and have his revenge.

*Act 4, Scene 2*
Imogen, who is ill, takes the medicine Pisanio has given her and retires to the cave. Cloten appears; Belarius recognises him and believes he has been sent to arrest them. He and Arviragus go to scout for soldiers, and Guiderius addresses the intruder. After Cloten insults him, the two begin to fight and they skirmish their way off stage. Belarius and Arviragus reappear and meet Guiderius, who returns with Cloten's head. Belarius is afraid of the consequences, but the two young men are happily defiant. Their pleasure collapses when they discover that 'Fidele' has apparently died. They sing an elegy for 'him' and leave the body with the headless corpse of Cloten, while they go to prepare a funeral. Imogen awakes and sees a headless body in Posthumus' clothes. She believes that her lover is dead. Grief stricken, she falls insensate on the body. Lucius appears, on his way to join

the troops arriving from Rome. He sees Imogen, who identifies herself again as Fidele and says that her master has been killed by brigands. She is taken into Lucius' service, the Roman orders his men to bury the corpse, and he departs with his new page.

*Act 4, Scene 3*
Cymbeline is distracted because Imogen is missing and the Queen has been stricken with madness since Cloten is also missing. He threatens Pisanio with torture if he does not reveal Imogen's whereabouts. News arrives of the approaching Roman army, and the king goes with his lords to prepare. Pisanio, in a soliloquy, admits bewilderment, having heard nothing from either Posthumus or Imogen. He puts his hope in providence, for he can do nothing.

*Act 4, Scene 4*
At their cave, Belarius, Guiderius, and Arviragus hear the battle. Belarius wishes to retreat into the mountains, but the young men insist on fighting. They say that it would be dishonourable not to take the opportunity to prove themselves. They convince him, and the three go to join the British forces.

*Act 5, Scene 1*
Posthumus is serving as a Roman officer. He contemplates the bloody cloth Pisanio has sent him as proof of Imogen's death, and he is stricken with remorse. He wishes he had died rather than she and decides that he will disguise himself as a peasant and fight for the British until he is killed.

*Act 5, Scene 2*
The Roman army, which includes Lucius and Iachimo, skirmishes with the British army, which includes Posthumus. Iachimo is disarmed by Posthumus but is left alone as the battle shifts off-stage. He laments that he has blackened Imogen's name and supposes that his burden of guilt has made him inept in battle. The battle continues; Cymbeline is briefly captured by the Romans, but Belarius, Guiderius, and Arviragus, aided by Posthumus, rally the British troops and rescue him.

*Act 5, Scene 3*
Posthumus tells a fleeing Briton that the British, though nearly defeated, have won the battle thanks to an old man and two handsome young ones, who rallied the British troops. Posthumus regrets that he was not killed in battle and decides to resume his Roman garb and be captured by the British. He hopes that they will avenge the day's slaughter by killing their prisoners. A British CAPTAIN (11) appears and talks about the old man and his sons who saved the army, and a Second Captain adds that they were assisted by a British peasant. Posthumus accosts them and is taken prisoner.

*Act 5, Scene 4*

In gaol Posthumus prays for death. He falls asleep and has a vision. His father, SICILIUS LEONATUS, appears, accompanied by his MOTHER and brothers (see BROTHER [2]). In solemn rhymes they beseech JUPITER to have mercy on Posthumus, who has suffered enough. The god himself appears, riding an eagle, and declares that Posthumus shall recover and marry Imogen. Posthumus awakes, and a GAOLER (2) arrives to escort him to his execution. However, a summons calls Posthumus to the king.

*Act 5, Scene 5*

Cymbeline knights Belarius, Guiderius, and Arviragus as the heroes of the battle and regrets that he cannot find the peasant who fought beside them. Cornelius arrives with word of the Queen's death and reports her death-bed confession. She had planned to poison the king and place Cloten on his throne. The Roman prisoners include Lucius, Iachimo, the SOOTHSAYER (3), Posthumus, and Imogen, who is still disguised as Fidele. Lucius asks mercy for Fidele; Cymbeline is struck by 'his' appearance and offers the 'boy' a boon. Imogen demands that Iachimo explain where he got the diamond ring he wears. Iachimo tells of his wager for Posthumus' ring, and Posthumus comes forward, declares himself a gullible fool, and confesses that he had Imogen murdered. This leads to a series of explanations that reveal the play's complications to all. Cymbeline, delighted with the return of his sons, forgives Belarius for kidnapping them and then frees the Roman captives. Iachimo begs for death, as punishment for his wager, but Posthumus pardons him. Cymbeline declares that his happiness makes him desire peace, and he agrees to resume paying the Roman tribute. He commands a celebration of the renewed alliance.

## COMMENTARY

With *Cymbeline*, Shakespeare continued to develop the ROMANCES, an experiment with a new genre that began with *Pericles* and culminated in his two late masterpieces, *The Winter's Tale* and *The Tempest*. His attempt to blend the features of TRAGEDY and COMEDY with the magical fantasy of romance, a literary mode familiar from 16th-century prose and poetry, was not yet successful. The play is a veritable anthology of motifs and situations from romantic literature: a wicked stepmother, long-lost children, the discovery of bodily identification marks, a decoded riddle, the appearance of a god, and so on. These motifs appear in a profusion intended to generate a seductive fairy-tale world. However, in *Cymbeline* vestiges of earlier modes remain—from the tragedies, in particular—and the effect of the romantic features is seriously undercut. The realism in character and setting that creates our emotional involvement in the tragedies is not appro-priate to the idealisation of the new genre, and the domestic pleasantries of comedy are not yet sublimated in the unreal world of romance.

*Cymbeline* therefore exhibits a jarring set of components that distract from the play's themes. The central message of the play is that order transcends chaos and that ultimately, despite our human ineffectuality, peace and love can triumph in a grand reconciliation of disordered elements. This idea is present throughout the romances. Here, marking an advance on *Pericles,* the emphasis falls on forgiveness of others: it is necessary for humans to act with mercy, rather than justice, in keeping with the behaviour of the gods. However, the potential for catastrophe is too strongly presented in *Cymbeline,* and by the time Jupiter appears to reassure us that all will be well, a state of near chaos has steadily grown and events appear to be entirely out of control. Iachimo's scheme has succeeded; Imogen believes Posthumus has been killed by Pisanio, who is in fact her only ally; Guiderius and Arviragus remain unrecognised as princes; and Britain is locked in a foolish war against Rome. Most dire of all, perhaps, Posthumus is suicidal because he believes Imogen is dead, a situation appallingly suggestive of *Romeo and Juliet.* The generally romantic context suggests that these problems will be resolved, but the tone is almost as anarchic as that of *Macbeth.* The play's final sequence of revelations and reconciliations therefore seems confusing, if not simply arbitrary, and its message is accordingly weakened.

Nevertheless, the play has many real virtues, one of the greatest being its variety of attractive characters. Imogen's considerable charm, which we shall consider later, heads the list, of course, but several of the other characters are also quite entertaining. For instance, Cloten's offensiveness is of an intriguing sort. His vice and violence are accompanied by great foolishness—he inspires the Second Lord's mockery and is several times referred to as a fool—and he is clearly intended to be a humorous grotesque. He is a predecessor of *The Tempest*'s CALIBAN. Along with his mother, the archetypal wicked stepmother of fairy tale, Cloten manifests the other-worldliness of romance. The other comic villain of the piece, Iachimo, is a pleasing creation who also helps maintain the play's tone. He is a stock MACHIAVEL and is often downright comic—for example when he emerges from his trunk like a jack-in-the-box and compares himself vaingloriously to the truly menacing TARQUIN. His humorous aspect takes the edge off his villainy and permits us to recognise that Imogen's disgrace can have no lasting consequences in the world of romance. In 5.5 Iachimo's long confession, as boastful as it is apologetic, constitutes a plea for forgiveness and entitles him to share in the play's final reconciliation. Pisanio is another sort of figure, the loyal and clever servant of tradition who stands firmly for common sense, truth, and resourceful continuance. Finally, however, as the chaos of the plot builds, he throws up his hands and commits himself to providence. 'Fortune brings in some boats that are not steer'd' (4.3.46), he declares.

*Cymbeline* is very exciting to watch on the stage, for the complexities and improbabilities of its plot yield many splendid surprises. The role of the central figure, Imogen, shifts constantly. The plot turns from the theme of separated lovers, to that of a wager on the maiden's chastity (and two different, equally repellent, assaults on it), to the maiden's ambivalent journey—she braves the wilderness to find her lover but is actually being ambushed by him—and finally to a traditional comic ploy, the maiden disguised as a boy. In the meantime, two other plots have been introduced, either of which might be central in a more conventional play. One concerns lost princes raised in the wild, and the other offers high politics and war as Britain refuses tribute to Rome.

Particular episodes offer individual surprises as well. Iachimo's first appearance, in 1.5, is entirely unanticipated, and he later startles us again when he emerges from the trunk in Imogen's bedroom. The first presentation of Belarius' cave suddenly introduces a very different sub-plot, just as the main plot is growing increasingly complicated. We are shocked (though probably delighted) when Cloten's head is borne on-stage by Guiderius, and while we are prepared for Imogen's false death, its conjunction with Cloten's headless corpse is a pleasantly novel complication. Not least, Posthumus' supernatural vision in 5.4 is probably the most spectacular eruption of the unexpected in Shakespeare. Shakespeare's earlier works had occasionally offered surprises—the final episode in *Love's Labour's Lost* is a famous example—but a great emphasis on novelty is distinctive to the romances, and the dramatic excitement produced is strongly felt by audiences.

This emphasis on the playwright's artfulness has inspired many commentators to insist that *Cymbeline* is merely an artistic experiment undertaken for its own sake. However, the play's marked esthetic aspect generates a sense of unreality that is important to the cental theme of the romances—humanity's dependence on providence—and to their major motif—magic and the supernatural. We are notified that the play is *not* about real life, and if we permit it, a state of timeless suspension is the result.

The play's complications and surprises also serve another purpose. Tragedy and comedy each enact events that lead towards a conclusion, be it the triumph of love or of disaster. In *Cymbeline,* however, the pattern is so complicated and the turnings of fate so unpredictable that we can only rely on the final surprise of 5.4 (final to us; 5.5 offers a long series of surprises for the characters), the literal *deus ex machina* of Jupiter's appearance, to resolve the situation. Jupiter's descent is significantly climactic. It follows the battle scene that envelops all the characters, and precedes the all-too-human fumbling that is revealed in the comically complicated final scene. We are reminded of Pisanio's prediction—fortune, not steering, will bring in the boats—and that humanity is dependent on providence.

The play's seeming peculiarities reflect this message. Its variety of characters and tonalities—comic or tragic, realistic or fantastic—all are reconciled in a positive and unifying vision. The comic is never farcical, and the potentially tragic remains merely potential. The realistic does not preclude abstraction, and the elements of romance do not give way to an entirely escapist retreat from reality. *Cymbeline* thus suggests and attempts to demonstrate, in not completely effective fashion, a vision of human weakness transcended. Shakespeare more successfully accomplished this vision in less complicated and more homogeneous plays, *The Winter's Tale* and *The Tempest.* For though its themes are dramatic, *Cymbeline* is nevertheless decidedly flawed. As we have seen, it leans disconcertingly towards tragedy, as if the author's intentions had been uncertain. Similarly, several of the characters seem to reflect too many differing ideas, and are inconsistently presented. Iachimo, for instance, while a conventional comic villain, also offers glimpses of tragedy, as when he envisions infidelity in terms of passion and damnation and invokes 'all the plagues of hell' (1.7.111). Here, as when he fleetingly identifies himself with utter evil—'hell is here' (2.2.50)—he sounds more like OTHELLO or MACBETH than the play can bear. Posthumus, likewise, is presented to us as the traditional romantic hero—the 'most prais'd, most lov'd' of men (1.1.47)—but when he accepts the wager, believes Iachimo, and finally takes revenge through Pisanio, he is immature and ignoble. He resembles Othello, also, in his insecurity; he believes that Imogen would find it easy to betray him. His tirade against women with its vividly bestial image of Imogen and Iachimo strikes a horrifying note that is as unromantic as Iachimo's earlier evocations of evil. Posthumus' ultimate decision to seek death in battle is also unsuitably grim.

Imogen is subject to similar inconsistencies, and the main plot seems to have caused Shakespeare to revert to familiar modes of creation. The heroine is the traditional, idealised princess, 'more goddess-like than wife-like' (3.2.8), and the proper mate to Posthumus' glorious prince. However, in her resourcefulness and wit, Imogen is plainly a typical Shakespearean comic heroine, capable of disguising herself as a man and going in search of her lover. She sharply—and wittily—rejects the unwanted attentions of Cloten; she acknowledges—and overcomes—her feminine fear of swords. She resembles ROSALIND of *As You Like It,* BEATRICE of *Much Ado,* and VIOLA of *Twelfth Night,* rather more than she does the passive object of adoration and intrigue that is the central figure in traditional romance. Imogen is enchanting, and her transformations onstage are delightful, but while she captures our affections, the fashion in which she does so is contrary to the general direction of the play.

Further, the presence of differing character types seems similarly disjointed. Fairy-tale figures such as the queen and the lost princes coexist with more psychologically developed figures. The more peripheral characters seem more appropriate to the essentially comic optimism of romance, while the central situation has the potential for tragedy. The play is also disjointed in its setting. No fewer than four distinct worlds are evoked: classical Rome, RENAISSANCE Italy, pagan Britain, and the abstracted countryside of pastoral romance (represented by Wales). The intricate reconciliation of these venues in the final scene requires such extraordinary ingenuity that it has inspired equal measures of praise and ridicule, as perhaps no other scene in Shakespeare has. Another device, the use of comic relief, such as in 2.1 (see LORD [15]) and 5.4.152–192 (see GAOLER [2]), reflects the need to dilute a mood of growing tragedy that is counter to the play's general thrust.

In *Cymbeline* the seams of Shakespeare's construction show—they don't in *The Winter's Tale* and *The Tempest*. We should not reject the play altogether, however, for as we have seen, it has magic. Samuel JOHNSON (8) complained of the play that 'to remark the folly of the fiction, the absurdity . . . , the confusion . . . were to waste criticism upon unresisting imbecility, upon faults too evident for detection . . .'. However, these evident faults also provide, along with folly and confusion, the escapist charms of romantic literature in general and of Imogen's world in particular. They need not be apologised for but merely accepted, and *Cymbeline* may be enjoyed for itself as well as for its place as the immediate predecessor of Shakespeare's last two masterpieces.

## SOURCES OF THE PLAY

The main plot of *Cymbeline*—a man wagers on his lover's chastity and is fooled, orders her death, which a good servant prevents, and is finally reunited with her—had been popular for centuries in various forms and in several languages. Shakespeare's version drew on two sources: one, an anonymous English translation of a Dutch tale, *Frederyke of Jennen* (Antwerp, 1518; London, 1520, 1560), and, much better known, a tale in the *Decameron* (1353) of Giovanni BOCCACCIO. Although no English translation of Boccaccio's story appeared before 1620, Shakespeare may have read it in Italian (though his capacity to do so is disputed), or in a French translation such as the very popular version of Antoine LE MAÇON (1545). The same tale was to be a minor source for *The Winter's Tale*. Boccaccio's tale and *Frederyke of Jennen* (i.e., of Genoa), apparently stem

from the same medieval Italian source, which is now lost. They both tell essentially the same story, but *Cymbeline* reflects details exclusive to each.

Another source was Raphael HOLINSHED's *Chronicles of England, Scotland, and Ireland* (2nd ed., 1587), which provided an account of the historical Cymbeline's reign. However, minor details come from at least two other historical sources, Robert FABYAN's *New Chronicle of England and of France* (1516) and A MIRROR FOR MAGISTRATES (1587), a popular collection of biographies. An obscure, anonymous English play, *The Rare Triumphs of Love and Fortune* (performed in 1582, published in 1589), provided Shakespeare with most of the other important components of *Cymbeline*—Posthumus and Imogen's love, Cloten's jealousy, Posthumus' banishment, Imogen's flight to an unjustly banished courtier who lives in a cave—along with various minor details. Some scholars speculate that a nearly contemporary play, *Philaster*, by Francis BEAUMONT (2) and John FLETCHER (2), may have influenced some of the language in *Cymbeline*, but since the dates of both plays are obscure and since Beaumont and Fletcher were novice playwrights at the time, other scholars believe that the younger men imitated Shakespeare.

## TEXT OF THE PLAY

*Cymbeline* was probably written c. 1608–1610, but firm evidence is lacking. A performance was recorded in the summer of 1611, so the play cannot have been composed later than early in that year. Stylistic evidence makes clear that it was roughly contemporary with the other ROMANCES, especially *The Winter's Tale* (c. 1610–1611), and it seems to represent an advance over *Pericles* (c. 1607) in the development of the genre. Some scholars believe it was written during the plague-imposed closure of the London theatres from the summer of 1608 to December 1609.

The play was not published in Shakespeare's lifetime, and appeared first in the FIRST FOLIO (1623). This text was probably printed from a transcription of Shakespeare's FOUL PAPERS, though some scholars believe it was taken from a PROMPT-BOOK. As the only early version of the play, the Folio text has been the basis for all subsequent editions.

## THEATRICAL HISTORY OF THE PLAY

The earliest known performance of *Cymbeline*—probably at the GLOBE THEATRE—was recorded by Simon FORMAN in the summer of 1611; no other early performances are known. Thomas D'URFEY adapted the play as *The Injured Princess or the Fatal Wager* (1682), a popular version with an elaborate sub-plot in which Cloten kidnaps a daughter of Pisanio. It was revived periodically for 80 years.

Colley CIBBER (1) produced a version of Shakespeare's play in 1744, and *Cymbeline* was mildly popular for the rest of the 18th century, though only with altered texts. David GARRICK, who staged the play several times beginning in 1761, was especially noted for his Posthumus (opposite Sarah SIDDONS, in the 1780s). In 1767 the play was staged in colonial New York. The 19th century saw few productions of *Cymbeline,* but they were very elaborately staged. The most important of these were the productions of John Philip KEMBLE (3) (1806, 1827). Helen FAUCIT played the heroine a number of times up to the age of 48, with great success, and Adelaide NEILSON (1) was also associated with the role. Ellen TERRY (1), in Henry IRVING's production of 1896, was widely acclaimed as the century's greatest Imogen. This production was heavily abridged (as most have been); for example, the vision of Jupiter was cut.

*Cymbeline* has not been widely produced in the 20th century, either, though George Bernard SHAW (2) staged his own witty version of Act 5, titled *Cymbeline Refinished,* in 1937. Probably the most notable modern productions of the play have been the 1923 modern dress staging by Barry JACKSON (1)—his first such experiment—and the 1957 STRATFORD staging by Peter HALL (5), starring Peggy ASHCROFT as Imogen. Though *Cymbeline* was twice made into a silent FILM—in the United States (1913) and Germany (1925)—it has not been a movie since. The BBC produced a TELEVISION version starring Claire Bloom in 1984.

**Cyprus**  Large island in the eastern Mediterranean, now a country, the setting for much of *Othello.* Although there is nothing especially exotic—let alone specifically Cypriot—about Acts 2–5 of *Othello,* Shake-speare's placement of the action on this remote outpost of the Venetian Empire is significant. After leaving VENICE the characters are removed from the buffering effects of society. In the isolation of Cyprus IAGO's influence over OTHELLO works its poison in the absence of any social or political distractions that might direct the general's attention elsewhere, or suggest different responses. Similarly, DESDEMONA has no peers to turn to for advice or intervention.

To effect this isolation, Shakespeare invented the 'Cyprus wars' (1.1.150) of the play, which do not appear in his source, CINTHIO's tale. Moreover, although conflict between Venice and the Ottoman Turks was constant in the 15th and 16th centuries, the situation described in *Othello*—with the Turks threatening both Cyprus and Rhodes (see 1.3.14)—never arose. The Turks did not attack Cyprus until 1570, long after they controlled Rhodes. However, Shakespeare may have had this attack in mind, mistaking the details while intending to associate his hero with it, for its direct result was the naval battle of Lepanto (1571), in which an alliance led by Venice and Spain defeated the Turkish fleet. This was united Christendom's last great victory over Islam, and in Shakespeare's day and for generations thereafter it was regarded as one of the key events of European history. Its aura of epic victory doubtless influenced early audiences' sense of Othello as a grand figure. Nevertheless, Lepanto was an expensive victory and Venice, retrenching in its aftermath, ceded Cyprus to the Turks in 1573. Thus, for Shakespeare, Cyprus was associated with vulnerability as well as strength, a combination reflected in Othello's personality.

**Daly, Augustin (1838–1899)** American theatrical entrepreneur. Daly operated theatres in both London and New York. With Ada REHAN as the centre-piece of his company, he specialised in classical COMEDY (along with modern drama) and produced most of Shakespeare's comedies, usually with greatly abridged texts and spectacular scenic effects. He was also a playwright with about 100 plays to his credit (though scholars believe his brother may have written most of them, and they are virtually all adapted from earlier plays, mostly French or German). These works were all highly colourful melodramas: his first great success in the theatre was with a famous and often imitated scene of a man tied on railroad tracks in front of an oncoming train.

**Dance, James (1722–1774)** English actor and playwright, author of an adaptation of *Timon of Athens.* Dance, son of a famous architect, took the name James Love for his acting career. He was best known for his portrayals of FALSTAFF. His version of *Timon* (1768) combined Shakespeare's text with Thomas SHADWELL's earlier adaptation. It was only moderately successful. Dance also wrote a popular long poem on cricket.

**Daniel, Samuel (c. 1562–1619)** English poet and dramatist, author of sources for several of Shakespeare's plays. Daniel's epic poem *The Civil Wars between the two Houses of York and Lancaster* (1595) influenced Act 5 of *Richard II* and the minor TETRALOGY of HISTORY PLAYS in general. His *The Complaint of Rosamund* (1592), a love story in verse, inspired several passages in *Romeo and Juliet;* moreover, Shakespeare's use of it helps date the play. Daniel's TRAGEDY *Cleopatra* (1594) influenced Shakespeare's treatment of his Egyptian queen, and another Daniel play, *The Queen's Arcadia* (1605), provided minor details for *Macbeth.* Also, Daniel's immensely popular SONNET sequence *Delia* (1592) may have helped inspire Shakespeare to write his SONNETS.

A minor diplomat early in his career, Daniel was later a tutor to William Herbert, Earl of PEMBROKE (3). His connection with Pembroke has inspired speculation that he may be the 'rival poet' of Shakespeare's sonnets. By 1595 Daniel was well established as a major literary figure of the day, and after 1603 he often composed MASQUES for the court of King JAMES I. A play produced by the Children of the Revels (see CHILDREN'S COMPANIES) in 1604 got him in trouble with state CENSORSHIP, for it seemed to express sympathy for the rebellious Earl of ESSEX (2), but Daniel nevertheless continued to write for the court. He also wrote a prose *History of England* (1612) that was very influential during the political turmoil of the 1620s and 1630s, as England approached civil war. In the last years of his life he became reclusive; Shakespeare is said to have been among the few people he would accept as visitors.

**Danter, John (d. 1599)** London printer, producer of editions of two of Shakespeare's plays. In 1594 Danter printed the first QUARTO edition of *Titus Andronicus* for publishers Thomas MILLINGTON and Edward WHITE (1), and in 1597 he undertook a pirated edition, the first, of *Romeo and Juliet,* only to have his press seized by the STATIONERS' COMPANY for other such piracies before the job was finished. It was completed by Edward ALLDE. Danter was in trouble for piracy throughout his career, but he always re-established himself. However, all of his surviving work is sloppily done. He was also suspended in 1596 for printing illegal Catholic materials. He was a business partner of Henry CHETTLE from 1589 to 1591.

**Dardanius (Dardanus) (active 42 B.C.)** Historical figure and minor character in *Julius Caesar,* a soldier in the army of BRUTUS (4). At PHILIPPI, Dardanius, along with CLITUS and VOLUMNIUS, refuses to help Brutus to commit suicide, saying, 'Shall I do such a deed?' (5.5.8). The episode demonstrates that Brutus was regarded with affection by his subordinates, adding sentiment to the presentation of his death. Shakespeare mis-spelled the name of the historical figure, Dardanus. Little is known of this individual, whose role Shakespeare took from PLUTARCH's *Lives.*

**Dark Lady** See SONNETS.

**Daughter (1)** Minor character in *Pericles,* incestuous lover of her father, King ANTIOCHUS of Syria. PERICLES attempts to win the Daughter in marriage by solving

Antiochus' riddle, but when the solution reveals the incest, he withdraws in horror, repelled by the sin and fearful of Antiochus' wrath. When she appears in 1.1 the Daughter is presented as a personification of fertility, 'apparell'd like the spring' (1.1.13). However, a warning is immediately voiced by her father, who calls her 'this fair Hesperides, / With golden fruit, but dangerous to be touch'd' (1.1.28–29). She speaks only two lines and approves of her suitor, but when Pericles learns the truth, he rejects her and says 'Good sooth, I care not for you' (1.1.87). He later speaks of her and her father as 'both like serpents . . . who though they feed / On sweetest flowers, yet they poison breed' (1.1.133–134). In Act 2 THAISA and her father, SIMONIDES, are implicitly contrasted with the Daughter and Antiochus, whose deaths by divine vengeance are reported in 2.4: 'A fire from heaven came and shrivell'd up / Their bodies . . .' (2.4.9–10). The Daughter has no personality and is a convenient agent of evil in the play's melodramatic plot.

**Daughter (2)**   Character in *The Two Noble Kinsmen*, deranged lover of PALAMON and child of the GAOLER (4). Although she has already agreed to marry the WOOER, in 2.1 the Daughter falls in love with Palamon, a prisoner of war in her father's prison. After remarking to her father on the nobility of Palamon and his fellow prisoner, ARCITE, in 2.1, the Daughter appears alone for her next four scenes, all soliloquies. In 2.3 she declares that she will help Palamon escape, and in 2.5 she reports that she has done so. In 3.2 she is alone in the woods, unable to find Palamon and clearly going mad. She decides that Palamon has been eaten by wild animals and contemplates suicide. Her fourth soliloquy in 3.4 is frankly insane, as she gabbles of shipwrecks and a magic frog and sings scraps of SONG. In 3.5, wandering insanely through the countryside, she is recruited for the rustic entertainment directed by the SCHOOLMASTER. Finally, in Act 4 she returns home, where the DOCTOR (4) prescribes that the Wooer, disguised as Palamon, take her to bed. The treatment apparently works, for her father later reports that she is is 'well restored, / And to be married shortly' (5.4.27–28).

Though she resembles Shakespeare's OPHELIA—both are unlucky in love, both gather flowers by a lakeside (see 4.1.54, 78), and both sing bits of song (in 4.1.108 the Daughter names a song Ophelia sings in *Hamlet* 4.5.184)—the Daughter is a very un-Shakespearean character. Her chief function is clearly as an object of humour, for in Shakespeare's day insanity was regarded as highly amusing (see, e.g., PINCH). Her diatribes are conventional indications of madness, artificial and unconvincing, and her cure is laughable, as it was doubtless intended to be. She was almost certainly not created by Shakespeare but by his collaborator, John FLETCHER (2), who probably wrote all the scenes she appears in (though some scholars attribute

2.1 and the best of her soliloquies, 3.2, to Shakespeare).

**Dauphin (1) Charles, the**   Character in *1 Henry VI*. See Charles VII.

**Dauphin (2) Lewis, the**   Character in *King John*. See Lewis (1).

**Dauphin (3) Lewis, the (1396–1415)**   Historical figure and character in *Henry V*, son of the FRENCH KING. The Dauphin—who bore the traditional title of the eldest son of a king of FRANCE (1)—leads the French nobles in their cocky over-confidence before the battle of AGINCOURT. In 1.2 the French AMBASSADOR (1) delivers a sneering message to Henry from the Dauphin, accompanied by a shipment of tennis balls, said to be appropriate weapons for so foolish a monarch; the insult gives Henry an occasion to declare war on France. When the English invade, the Dauphin and his friends are preposterously boastful and arrogant caricatures, presented only to be put down by events. In 4.5 a hysterically suicidal Dauphin is shown in defeat; his capture is reported in 4.8.78.

Shakespeare's Dauphin, besides being a stock figure, misrepresents the historical Dauphin in several small matters of fact as well. He mocks Henry for his youth, as in 2.4.28, but he was in fact nine years younger than his foe. Nor was he present at Agincourt; too sick to fight, he died two months after the battle.

**Davenant (D'Avenant), William (1606–1668)**   English poet, playwright, and theatrical entrepreneur. Davenant, along with Thomas KILLIGREW, dominated the LONDON theatrical world during the 1660s. When the monarchy was restored in 1660, the theatres of England were reopened after their long closure by the Puritan revolutionary government, and Davenant received one of the two licences to put on plays in London. His Duke of York's Company—named for its patron, the future King James II—staged many plays by Shakespeare and others. Davenant's licence assigned him the rights to 10—later amended to 13—of Shakespeare's plays: *Hamlet,* the *Henry VI* plays (considered as one work), *Henry VIII, King Lear, Macbeth, Measure for Measure, Much Ado About Nothing, Pericles, Romeo and Juliet, The Tempest, Timon of Athens, Troilus and Cressida,* and *Twelfth Night.*

Davenant is notorious for his adaptations of the plays. He combined *Measure for Measure* and *Much Ado About Nothing* in THE LAW AGAINST LOVERS (1662), and he greatly abridged and altered the texts of the others, changing names, rewriting passages, inserting his own words—or sometimes merely inserting Shakespeare's words into his own play—and taking care to 'refine' (his word) Shakespeare's language. This process was particularly egregious in his *Macbeth*. With John DRYDEN, he adapted *The Tempest* as *The Tempest, or The*

*Enchanted Island* (1667, published 1670), adding many characters and situations from the work of the Spanish playwright Pedro Calderón (1600–1681) and retaining little of Shakespeare's text. This adaptation was hugely popular, especially in Thomas SHADWELL's operatic version (1674; Henry PURCELL provided a new score in 1690). Modern commentators condemn it, but the Davenant/Dryden *Tempest* influenced all other versions of the play for almost 200 years.

As a young man, Davenant was a playwright, composing several tragedies in the style of JACOBEAN DRAMA and a popular comedy of manners, *The Wits* (1633). He collaborated on several MASQUES with Inigo Jones, the royal architect, and when Ben JONSON died in 1637, Davenant was awarded his masque-writing duties and his pension (the equivalent of being named Poet Laureate). He fought for the royalists in the Civil Wars and was knighted for valour by King Charles I. Captured in 1650, he was imprisoned for more than a year before being freed by the poet John MILTON, who was a member of the revolutionary government. (Davenant was to repay the service upon the restoration of the monarchy in 1660, when Milton was sentenced to death.) Upon his release, Davenant wrote plays that he managed to stage despite the ban on theatres, by adding music and calling them operas. His *The Siege of Rhodes* (1656) is considered the first opera performed in England. Thus, when the restored monarchy legalised the theatre again, Davenant was already in business.

Davenant claimed to be Shakespeare's illegitimate son. His parents had run an inn on the road between STRATFORD and London, and Davenant declared that he had been conceived during a stopover. In a variation of this claim—the version reportedly varied with alcohol consumption—he took the status of godson. Neither claim is supported by any evidence.

**Davies (1), John, of Hereford (c. 1565–1618)** English poet, author of early references to Shakespeare. Davies published several volumes of poetry between 1603 and 1617, including one, *The Scourge of Folly* (c. 1610), containing a poem praising Shakespeare as 'our English TERENCE'. His *Microcosmos* (1603) and *Civil Wars of Death and Fortune* (1605) contain praises of the actors 'W.S'. and 'R.B.', presumed to be Shakespeare and Richard BURBAGE (3). Davies taught writing to the ill-fated Prince of Wales, Henry (1594–1612), son of King JAMES I.

**Davies (2), Sir John (1569–1626)** English poet and lawyer, author of a minor source for *Julius Caesar*. Davies published several volumes of poetry, including *Epigrams* (1590), *Orchestra, or a Poeme of Dauncing* (1596)—a long poem justifying the pleasures of dancing—and *Hymnes of Astraea* (1599), a collection of acrostics based on the name of Queen ELIZABETH (1).

Also published in 1599 was his *Nosce Teipsum* ('Know Thyself'), a long philosophical poem on the nature of the human soul. Several minor echoes of this text in *Julius Caesar* establish that Shakespeare was familiar with the work.

Davies was by profession a lawyer. He was disbarred from 1598 to 1601 after he assaulted a fellow attorney, but he was reinstated under King JAMES I and was highly successful. He was first solicitor general and then attorney general of Ireland from 1603–1619. He supported King Charles I in his early disputes with Parliament and in return was appointed Lord Chief Justice, the highest-ranking judicial post in England, but he died before taking office.

**Davy** Character in *2 Henry IV*, steward to Justice SHALLOW. In 5.1 Davy makes the necessary arrangements when FALSTAFF visits Shallow and conducts ordinary business—seeing to minor repairs, planting, paying the blacksmith, and so on—at the same time. As a typical resident of GLOUCESTERSHIRE, he is part of the play's delightful presentation of English country life. On behalf of his friend William VISOR, Davy asks his master for a favourable ruling in a lawsuit, offering a humorous look at small-time legal chicanery. At Shallow's drinking party in 5.3, Davy manages to function as host, guest, and servant

**Day, John (c. 1574–c. 1640)** English playwright, possible collaborator with Shakespeare. Day, a minor figure in the ELIZABETHAN THEATRE, collaborated with many playwrights, including Thomas DEKKER, Samuel ROWLEY (1), George WILKINS, and possibly Christopher MARLOWE (1). He may also have had a hand in *Timon of Athens* and/or *Pericles*, though in both cases the identity—or even existence—of collaborators is uncertain.

Day became a hack writer in LONDON after being expelled from Cambridge University for theft in 1593. Little is known of his life, except that he was chronically in debt, and that in 1599 he stabbed and killed the playwright Henry PORTER (5), apparently in self-defence. Day wrote plays for the ADMIRAL'S MEN from 1599 to 1603, usually in collaboration, though after this period he mostly wrote alone. The later plays, of which six have survived, were generally staged by the Children of the Revels (see CHILDREN'S COMPANIES). One of them, *Isle of Gulls* (1606), a satire on Anglo-Scottish relations, offended the government and resulted in the imprisonment of several of its producers. He also wrote a series of non-dramatic dialogues, *The Parliament of Bees* (1608), that is considered his masterpiece, though it is a minor work.

**Decius (Decimus) Brutus (d. 43 B.C.)** Historical figure and minor character in *Julius Caesar*, one of the assassins of CAESAR (1). In 2.2 Decius persuades Caesar to proceed with his fateful plans after CALPHURNIA has convinced him to stay at home. Caesar thus goes to the Senate and is assassinated.

The historical figure was named Decimus Brutus, not Decius; the error originated with Jacques AMYOT, who translated PLUTARCH into French. His work was retranslated into English by Sir Thomas NORTH, who transmitted the incorrect name to Shakespeare. Decimus Brutus (a cousin of Marcus BRUTUS [4]) had distinguished himself as a commander under Caesar in Gaul. Although awarded high office under Caesar, he joined the conspiracy against his leader and played the part enacted in the play. He was killed in the ensuing civil war.

**Decretas (Decretus, Dercetas, Dercetaeus, Dercetus) (active 30 B.C.)** Historical figure and minor character in *Antony and Cleopatra,* a member of ANTONY's personal guard. In 4.14 Antony stabs himself with his sword, and Decretas, seeing that his master's defeat is now complete, takes Antony's sword to CAESAR (2), where he hopes to ingratiate himself with the conqueror by being the first to tell him of his enemy's death. In 5.1.5–26 he makes his presentation to Caesar and praises Antony eloquently, after which he disappears from the play. He demonstrates, by his flight to Caesar, the collapse of loyalty around Antony, and then—somewhat incongruously—he bears witness to the nobility of the hero's end, a major theme of Act 5.

Shakespeare took the name of this minor figure— unknown in history outside this anecdote—from his source, PLUTARCH's *Lives,* and it has been variously rendered. In Plutarch and in Sir Thomas NORTH's English translation his name is Dercetaeus. Shakespeare—or someone else associated with early productions of the play—simplified this spelling, and it appears in the FIRST FOLIO (1623) as 'Decretas' (twice, plus several abbreviations beginning 'Dec') and 'Dercetus' (once). In 1725, Alexander POPE (1) compromised and introduced a new variant, 'Dercetas', and subsequent editors have chosen from among these possibilities.

**Deiphobus** Legendary figure and minor character in *Troilus and Cressida,* a Trojan warrior. Deiphobus appears in five scenes but speaks only two lines, serving merely to flesh out the Trojan aristocracy. In the *Iliad* of HOMER, Deiphobus, a son of King PRIAM, is a prominent warrior.

**Dekker, Thomas (c. 1572–c. 1632)** English dramatist. Between 1598 and 1605, Dekker wrote about 44 plays (many of them in collaboration) for the ADMIRAL's MEN and WORCESTER's MEN, but only six have survived. He is best known for two comedies, *The Shoemaker's Holiday* (1599) and *The Honest Whore* (1604, with Thomas MIDDLETON). Writing for the Children of

Paul's (see CHILDREN's COMPANIES), he participated in the WAR OF THE THEATRES, an exchange of satirical plays among rival playwrights. His *Satiromastix* (1601, with John MARSTON) was a reply to Ben JONSON's satire of him in an earlier work. Jonson struck again in *The Poetaster* (1601), calling Dekker a 'playdresser and plagiary'.

Dekker went on to write many pamphlets, including a vivid group describing a plague epidemic. In the 1620s he returned to writing plays, mostly for PRINCE CHARLES' MEN and mostly in collaboration with such dramatists as John DAY, John FORD, and Philip MASSINGER. Little is known of Dekker's life, though his works reveal him to have been a pleasant, cheerful man, with an admiration for the strengths of London's poor, of whom he was one. He was perennially in debt; he spent almost eight years in debtors' prison between 1612 and 1619 and may have returned just before his death.

**Deloney, Thomas (c. 1550–1600)** English writer, possibly the author of a poem sometimes ascribed to Shakespeare. The poem, 'Crabbed age and youth cannot live together', published as number XII in THE PASSIONATE PILGRIM (1599) where it was attributed to Shakespeare, appeared as Deloney's work in a posthumously published anthology, *Garland of Goodwill* (1631). Most modern scholars do not believe the poem was written by Shakespeare, though a minority opinion holds that it might be an early work of the playwright. If Deloney's, it is one of his best poems.

Deloney was a minor poet of the 1580s and 1590s— best known for three long ballads on the Spanish Armada—who turned to prose and wrote several socalled 'craft novels'. These were prose narratives which celebrated various urban occupations. One of them, *The Gentle Craft* (1598), about shoemakers, was the chief source for Thomas DEKKER's well-known play, *The Shoemaker's Holiday* (1599). Deloney's novels are notable for their descriptions of LONDON life, and although they were popular, Elizabethan novelists were ill-rewarded and Deloney died in poverty.

**Demetrius (1)** Character in *Titus Andronicus,* a son of TAMORA. Demetrius and his brother CHIRON murder BASSIANUS and then commit the appalling rape and mutilation of LAVINIA, the daughter of TITUS (1) Andronicus; they are encouraged and abetted by AARON. Titus' counter revenge includes the killing of the two brothers, who are baked in a meat pie and served to their mother in the final scene.

**Demetrius (2)** Character in *A Midsummer Night's Dream,* the lover of HERMIA whose affections are magically diverted to HELENA (1). Chosen by EGEUS to be Hermia's husband, Demetrius had wooed Helena earlier, before the opening of the play, but had abandoned her. In addition to fickleness, Demetrius shows an unpleasant shortness with Helena, who pursues him, but on the whole he is—like Hermia's beloved, LYSANDER—a colourless young man who exists merely to be manipulated by OBERON's spells.

**Demetrius (3)** Minor character in *Antony and Cleopatra*, a follower of ANTONY. In 1.1 Demetrius and his friend PHILO discuss Antony's neglect of his military duties while he dallies with the Queen of Egypt, CLEOPATRA. The episode establishes a disapproving Roman view of the love affair.

**Dench, Judi (b. 1934)** English actress. Dench began her Shakespearean career as OPHELIA in Michael BENTHALL's 1957 *Hamlet* and went on to a much acclaimed JULIET (2) in Franco ZEFFERELLI's 1960 staging of *Romeo and Juliet*. She has played many of Shakespeare's best female roles since, including a remarkable performance as both HERMIONE and PERDITA in *The Winter's Tale* (1969). She played LADY (6) MACBETH both in

Trevor NUNN's 1976 production at STRATFORD and in his 1979 TELEVISION version.

**Denmark** Country in northern Europe, the setting for *Hamlet*. The entire play takes place in and around the royal castle in ELSINORE, a seaport in northern Denmark. Denmark was familiar to English audiences as a rival in the Baltic Sea trade, and Shakespeare offers several glimpses of Danish ways, focussing chiefly on the Danes' reputation for excessive drinking, which HAMLET remarks on disparagingly in 1.4. 13–38. Sixteenth-century accounts confirm bits of information provided in the play, such as the popularity of Rhine wines (1.4.10) and the habit of accompanying a toast with kettledrums (1.4.11) or, more extravagantly, with cannon fire (1.2.126). Further, it is thought that the description of Danish preparations for war in 1.1.74–81 reflects news of contemporary conflicts between Denmark and Sweden.

Scholars have occasionally proposed that Shakespeare's knowledge of Denmark reflects a visit he

*Kronborg Castle in Elsinore, Denmark, is thought to be the place Shakespeare had in mind as the setting for* Hamlet. *Here a crew sets up to film a 1964 joint BBC-Danish Television Service production of the play.* (Courtesy of Culver Pictures, Inc.)

made to that country with an English acting company in 1585 or 1586, when such trips are known to have occurred (see e.g. KEMPE), but many contemporary sources provided sufficient information on the country and its customs to account for the play's descriptions. In fact, Shakespeare's extremely faulty knowledge of the geography of Denmark—a flat country with no 'cliff / That beetles o'er his base into the sea' (1.4.70–71) and that is not connected by land to Norway or Poland, as the route of FORTINBRAS' army would imply (see 2.2.75–78; 4.4.10–12)—suggests strongly that he had not been there.

**Dennis (1)** Minor character in *As You Like It*, servant of OLIVER (1). Dennis appears only to announce the arrival of the wrestler CHARLES in 1.1.88–92.

**Dennis (2), John (1657–1734)** English playwright. Dennis, a minor poet and dramatist, wrote and produced two unsuccessful adaptations of Shakespeare plays. His *The Comical Gallant* (1702) is a crude version of *The Merry Wives of Windsor*. It was unpopular and disappeared quickly; it is now remembered only for its preface, where Dennis recorded the belief that Shakespeare had written *The Merry Wives* in 14 days at the command of Queen ELIZABETH (1). Dennis' *The Invader of His Country* (1719) employed excerpts from *Coriolanus* in its political statement against FRANCE (1) for having aided the exiled STUART DYNASTY's attempted invasion of England in 1715. It was booed off the stage and closed after three performances. Dennis wrote other anti-French plays, and he amused the literary world by being egotistical enough to ask that a special clause be inserted in the Treaty of Utrecht (1713), specifically protecting him from French reprisals.

**Denny, Sir Anthony (1501–1549)** Historical figure and minor character in *Henry VIII*, a member of King HENRY VIII's court. In 5.1.80–81 Denny reports that he has brought Archbishop CRANMER to a midnight meeting with the king, as Henry has instructed. After escorting Cranmer to the king, he disappears from the play. Shakespeare took Denny's tiny role from a source, FOXE's *Actes and Monumentes*, and used it to intensify the air of intrigue surrounding the meeting, which begins the major episode of Act 5. The historical Denny was a close friend of the king.

**De Quincey, Thomas (1785–1859)** English essayist. Best known for his memoir, *Confessions of an English Opium Eater* (1822), De Quincey also wrote many miscellaneous essays in an impressionistic style reflective of the tumultuous Romantic period. These include a remarkable piece that is still widely read, 'On the Knocking on the Gate in *Macbeth*' (1823), interpreting the role of the PORTER (3) in the play. De Quincey also wrote a long article on Shakespeare for the 7th edition of the *Encyclopaedia Brittanica* (1838).

**Derby (1), Ferdinando Stanley, Earl of** Contemporary of Shakespeare. See STRANGE.

**Derby (2), Thomas Stanley, Earl of** Character in *Richard III*. See STANLEY (3).

**Derby (3), William Stanley, Earl of (1561–1642)** English theatrical patron and writer, younger brother and successor of Ferdinando, Lord STRANGE. In 1594 William Stanley succeeded Strange as Earl of Derby, and in January 1595 he married; the wedding may have been the occasion for the first performance of *A Midsummer Night's Dream*. From 1594 to 1618 Derby maintained a troupe of actors known as Derby's Men. This group is not to be confused with his brother's STRANGE'S MEN, who also briefly used that name (see DERBY'S MEN) and with whom Shakespeare may have been associated. The Derby's Men of William Stanley appeared at court in 1599–1601 under the leadership of Robert BROWNE, but they usually toured the provinces. In 1599 it was said that Derby's Men performed comedies written by Stanley; his plays have not survived, but this report has led to Derby's occasional nomination as the 'real' Shakespeare (see AUTHORSHIP CONTROVERSY).

**Derby's Men** Name used between September 25, 1593, and the spring of 1594 by the theatrical company better known as STRANGE'S MEN or the CHAMBERLAIN'S MEN. Shakespeare may have been a member of the company during this time. The LONDON theatres were closed by a plague epidemic and Strange's Men were on tour when the father of their patron, Lord STRANGE, died; Lord Strange assumed his father's title, Earl of Derby, so the company changed its name accordingly. On the following April 16, the new Earl of Derby also died, and the actors, still on tour as Derby's Men, sought a new patron. When they returned to London, where the theatres had reopened, they found one in Lord HUNSDON (2), the Lord Chamberlain, and they were known thereafter as the Chamberlain's Men. The exact date of the transition is not known, but they performed under the new name on June 5, 1594, at the theatre in NEWINGTON BUTTS. The earliest record of Shakespeare as an actor places him in the Chamberlain's Men in December 1594, but he may have been with the company earlier, when it was still Derby's Men.

Earlier, in the 1560s and 1570s, Lord Strange's father had maintained a company of players, which became known as Derby's Men after 1572, when the father had become Earl of Derby. This troupe played the provinces exclusively and is not to be confused with the later company, basically a London organisation.

**Dering Manuscript**  Early 17th-century document, the handwritten text of a play combining and abridging *1* and *2 Henry IV*. Possibly prepared for a private performance, perhaps at the court of King JAMES I, the Dering manuscript contains various revisions made by Sir Edward Dering (1598–1644), a gentleman from Kent. The manuscript is based on the Q5 edition (1613) of *1 Henry IV* and Q (1600) of *2 Henry IV;* most of the former play is represented, but much of the latter is not. The primary emphasis of Dering's version is the relationship between HENRY IV and PRINCE (6) HAL, especially at the expense of FALSTAFF. For instance, the scenes of *2 Henry IV* set in GLOUCESTERSHIRE are entirely omitted. Dering's alterations seem to incorporate some minor features from the FIRST FOLIO versions of the plays and are thus dated to 1623 or 1624.

**Desdemona**  Character in *Othello,* the wife of OTHELLO. Desdemona is unjustly suspected of adultery and murdered by her jealous husband, who has believed the lies of his villainous aide, IAGO. She is a strong, outspoken woman, unafraid to challenge the racial bias of VENICE or the opinions of her imposing husband, and she is also touching in her sorrow as Othello's love turns to hostility. Desdemona's function, however, is largely symbolic; she represents the spirit of self-sacrifice traditionally associated with the most intense and spiritual love. Indeed, in her martyr-like resignation to an entirely undeserved death, many commentators see her as symbolising Christian love and acceptance of God's will. In Desdemona, Shakespeare created an emblematic figure that was familiar to his original audiences from the medieval MORALITY PLAY, still a well-known theatrical form in the early 17th century. She resembles the angel that opposes the devil in such a play, struggling for control of the central character, who is a symbol of humanity. Like the angel, Desdemona evokes the forgiveness of God, and, as in the medieval play, the good she represents is acknowledged at the close and thus is seen to be the play's central theme.

Desdemona's role is a passive one; her only significant action—marrying Othello—has been taken before the play opens. She is the chief repository of the play's values. Othello knows this when he says, 'I do love thee, and when I love thee not, / Chaos is come again' (3.3.92–93). She alone has recognised his inner worth. She says she 'saw Othello's visage in his mind' (1.3.252), and even when his virtue is obscured she retains her vision. As she puts it, '. . . his unkindness may defeat my life, / But never taint my love' (4.2.162–163), and even as she dies, she declares her love of the inner, obscured Othello, saying, 'Commend me to my kind lord' (5.2.126).

At first, Desdemona's nobility of spirit is matched by that of her new husband. When the couple justify their elopement before the DUKE (5), in 1.3, they display a mature love that is both spiritual, in their mutual appreciation of each other's virtues, and sensual, in their excited anticipation of the physical side of married life. Desdemona's strength of character is evident in her calm resistance to her father, BRABANTIO, who holds that loving a black man is 'Against all rules of nature' (1.3.101). She firmly and courageously stands up to the prejudices of the only society she has ever known. Once committed to Othello she is steadfast; the central fact of the play is her unswerving loyalty. The suspicion that Iago induces in Othello is always seen to be completely unjustified. In 4.3 EMILIA (2) defends adultery, but Desdemona spurns this temptation in an episode that parallels Othello's failure to resist Iago. Desdemona recognises that Othello's jealousy is ignoble, but she continues to give him her love to its fullest extent, saying, '. . . my love doth so approve him, / That even his stubbornness, his checks and frowns, / . . . have grace and favour in them' (4.3.19–21). Her love is literally unconditional, standing in stark contrast to the malevolence of Iago.

**Diana (1)**  Character in *All's Well That Ends Well*, young woman of FLORENCE who assists HELENA (2) to entrap her runaway husband, BERTRAM. The lustful Bertram wishes to seduce Diana, who is respected in FLORENCE for 'a most chaste renown' (4.3.14). She, honourably determined to remain a virgin, resists his advances until in 4.2, as part of Helena's plot, she agrees to sleep with him (though Helena will in fact occupy her bed). She is demure and pliant in making this arrangement, but she expresses herself zestily after Bertram's departure, brusquely critiquing male morals and declaring, '. . . in this disguise, I think't no sin / To cozen him that would unjustly win' (4.2.75–76). In 5.3 she confronts Bertram in the presence of the KING (17) and accuses him of violating his promise to marry her. She is denounced as a whore, and then, when she claims to be a virgin although Bertram has seduced her, she is further subjected to the irritated King's threat of imprisonment before Helena appears and resolves matters. The King thereupon grants her a sumptuous dowry as part of the final reconciliation that closes the play.

Diana has little real personality, being a stereotype of the virginal maiden, but her symbolic importance is considerable. As the object of Bertram's attempts at seduction, she serves by contrast to emphasise his evil nature; as the long-suffering complainant of 5.3, she exemplifies victimisation, making the final outcome more dramatically satisfying.

**Diana (2)**    Pagan goddess and minor character in *Pericles, Prince of Tyre*. After PERICLES has been reunited with his daughter MARINA, Diana appears to him in a vision, in 5.1.238–247. She instructs him to go to her temple at EPHESUS and publicly tell of his continued separation from his wife, THAISA. In 5.3 he does so and is thereby reunited with Thaisa, for she is a priestess at the temple. The play's protagonist thus finds final relief from his suffering through supernatural intervention, and this stresses the play's most important theme: the helplessness of humanity in the face of destiny.

Diana, the ancient goddess of the moon and the hunt, was a familiar theatrical personage in Shakespeare's day. She appears in a number of 16th- and 17th-century dramatic productions, generally clad in a costume decorated in silver with emblems of the moon, and carrying a silver bow (which she mentions here, in 5.1.246). Her appearance in *Pericles*, the first of Shakespeare's ROMANCES, heralds the supernatural atmosphere and dreamlike quality that characterises these late plays.

**Dick the Butcher**    Minor character in *2 Henry VI*, a follower of the revolutionary Jack CADE. After making several small jokes at his leader's expense when the rebels are introduced in 4.2, Dick also delivers the famous line 'The first thing we do, let's kill all the lawyers' (4.2.73). Elsewhere in the depiction of Cade's uprising, Dick further displays the anarchic brutality that Shakespeare attributed to the episode.

**Dickens, Charles (1812–1870)**    English novelist. Dickens lent his prestige as a world-famous novelist to help raise funds to preserve Shakespeare's birthplace in STRATFORD, and he took a prominent part in the project. He also wrote numerous articles on the playwright. Dickens maintained a small theatre in his house where he performed in amateur productions; he was particularly noted for his portrayal of SHALLOW in a production of *The Merry Wives of Windsor* that toured northern England and Scotland to raise money for the birthplace project.

**Digges (1), Dudley (1583–1639)**    English politician, entrepreneur of colonial expeditions, and possible source of inspiration for *The Tempest*. Digges, brother of Leonard DIGGES (2) and stepson of Shakespeare's friend, Thomas RUSSELL, was probably acquainted with Shakespeare. He was closely involved in the exploration of the New World and could have been the playwright's source for the 1610 letter by William STRACHEY (2) describing a shipwreck in Bermuda. Scholars speculate that Digges edited a pamphlet that was another possible source of inspiration for the play, *A True Declaration of the state of the Colonie in Virginia* (1610), which was published by a group of investors defending the colonial enterprise.

Digges was financially and intellectually involved in numerous other foreign expeditions. He was active in the East India and Muscovy companies, as well as the proposed colony in Virginia, and he also promoted geographical exploration with only remote commercial applications. He helped finance Henry Hudson's search for the North-west Passage and wrote tracts asserting the existence of that route to China; he even advocated a purely scientific expedition to the North Pole. In 1618 he travelled to Russia on a combined scientific and diplomatic mission. Politically, he served in parliament intermittently from 1601 to 1628 and in the 1620s was a leader of the opposition to King Charles I that would eventually lead to the Civil Wars. He was twice briefly imprisoned for his opposition, but was reconciled with the king before his death.

**Digges (2), Leonard (1588–1635)**    Poet, translator, and acquaintance of Shakespeare, author of two notable poems commending the playwright. Digges knew Shakespeare through his stepfather, Thomas RUSSELL, and probably wrote the poems about the playwright in 1616 on the occasion of his death. The first was published as part of the preface to the FIRST FOLIO edition of the plays (1623); the other appeared posthumously in the 1640 edition of Shakespeare's *Poems*, published by John BENSON (2). Digges, brother of Dudley DIGGES (1), was a respected poet and a translator of several languages, especially noted for his renderings of Spanish.

**Diomedes (1)**    Legendary figure and character in *Troilus and Cressida*, a Greek warrior and seducer of CRESSIDA. Diomedes plays a very minor role in the TROJAN WAR until he is assigned to oversee the exchange of prisoners whereby Cressida is traded for ANTENOR. When he arrives among the Trojans, he expresses a sharply cynical view of HELEN (1) that makes plain his lack of the romantic idealism that has led TROILUS to deceive himself about love. Thus, when he manipulates Cressida's emotions in 5.2, using an affected disinterest—the tactic with which she herself beguiled Troilus—we recognise him as a cold-blooded seducer. When she agrees to a sexual assignation, he demands from her the love token given her by Troilus, thus climaxing her betrayal. Diomedes is coolly amoral, contributing to our sense of the corruption that infects the play's world.

In the *Iliad* of HOMER, Diomedes is the king of Argos, a Greek state owing allegiance to AGAMEMNON, and he is second only to his overlord in prestige and power. He plays a prominent part in the Trojan War, both as a warrior and strategist, and he is closely associated with Odysseus (the play's ULYSSES). He has no love life in the *Iliad* (his connection to Cressida arose only with the development of her story in the Middle Ages), though a post-Homeric tradition gave him a wife whose infidelity while he was at Troy causes him to emigrate to Italy after his return; there he founded several cities and chivalrously refused to fight the Trojan refugees who also came there. He was an object of cult worship in Italy, especially on the shores of the Adriatic, where the sea birds were believed to be the souls of his followers.

**Diomedes (2) (Diomed) (active 30 b.c.)** Historical figure and minor character in *Antony and Cleopatra,* a servant of CLEOPATRA. In 4.14 Diomedes comes to ANTONY with a message which states that his mistress is alive, despite an earlier report that she had committed suicide, but he arrives too late, for Antony has just stabbed himself. Diomedes accompanies the soldiers who carry Antony to Cleopatra and announces their arrival in 4.15. Diomedes appears by name in Shakespeare's source, PLUTARCH's *Lives,* but is otherwise unknown in history.

**Dion** Character in *The Winter's Tale.* See CLEOMENES AND DION.

**Dionyza** Character in *Pericles,* would-be murderer of MARINA. In 3.3 PERICLES leaves his daughter Marina in the care of Dionyza and her husband CLEON. However, Dionyza grows jealous of the girl as she overshadows their own daughter, and in 4.1 she forces her servant LEONINE to agree to kill Marina. Though he does not do so, he tells his mistress he has, and in 4.3 Dionyza faces Cleon's horror at her deeds—she has also poisoned Leonine to ensure secrecy. In response to his dread, she says 'I think you'll turn child again' (4.3.4) and compares his qualms to complaining that 'winter kills the flies' (4.3.50). She clearly resembles her forerunner LADY (6) MACBETH but is a much less developed character. In 1.4 we see her as she echoes her husband's distress over a famine, and her transition to evil seems unmotivated. She is merely a stereotype of the wicked stepmother, evil because the plot requires it.

**Doctor (1)** Character in *King Lear,* a physician who reports to CORDELIA on the condition of her father, King LEAR. In 4.4 he tells Cordelia that Lear's sanity can be restored through rest, saying, 'Our foster-nurse of nature is repose' (4.4.12). He assures her that he can provide drugs to sedate the mad king. Later, he oversees the touching reunion of the rested Lear with his daughter. He ends the meeting for the good of his patient, but again reassures Cordelia that 'the great rage . . . is kill'd in him' (4.7.78–79). His kindly ministrations contrast with the evil that has permeated Lear's world to this point.

**Doctor (2)** Minor character in *Macbeth,* an English physician serving King Edward the Confessor of England (ruled 1042–1066). In 4.3 the Doctor tells MALCOLM and MACDUFF of King Edward's power to miraculously cure disease by merely touching the victims. This is a reference to a well-known superstition that any English sovereign could cure scrofula, a tuberculosis of the lymph nodes that could leave its victims 'All swoln and ulcerous, pitiful to the eye' (4.3.151), as Malcolm puts it. The positive magic of the saintly king is contrasted with the evil machinations of the WITCHES who support MACBETH. The episode may also have been intended as a compliment to the new King of England, JAMES I; it suggests the sacred status of his office. Some scholars believe that the entire passage, 4.3.139–159—probably written by Shakespeare—may have been interpolated into the original text of the play on the occasion of a performance before the king.

**Doctor (3)** Minor character in *Macbeth,* a physician who attends LADY (6) MACBETH. The Doctor witnesses Lady Macbeth's hallucinations in the sleep-walking scene (5.1) and understands the allusions to the murders she has on her conscience. He observes, 'Unnatural deeds / Do breed unnatural troubles . . . More needs she the divine than the physician' (5.1.68–71). This emphasises the play's connection of evil with psychological disorders. Further, the Doctor points up the atmosphere of fear and distrust that surrounds the rule of MACBETH when he departs, saying, 'I think, but dare not speak' (5.1.76). In 5.3 at besieged DUNSINANE, the Doctor reports to Macbeth that Lady Macbeth continues to suffer from mental disturbances; he confesses that he cannot cure them and incurs the king's disdain. Again, he has a pertinent exit line: 'Were I from Dunsinane away and clear, / Profit again should hardly draw me here' (5.3.61–62), a salty reminder of Macbeth's evil influence as it was felt by ordinary citizens of SCOTLAND.

**Doctor (4)** Minor character in *The Two Noble Kinsmen,* a physician who treats the deranged DAUGHTER (2) of the GAOLER (4). The Daughter is obsessed with the nobleman PALAMON, whom she helps escape from gaol but does not see again. In 4.3 the Doctor prescribes that her WOOER humour her by pretending to be Palamon. In 5.2 he adds that the disguised Wooer should sleep with her, to which the young man readily agrees. In 5.4 the Gaoler reports that his Daughter is 'well restored, / And to be married shortly' (5.4.27–28). The comic Doctor was probably created by Shakespeare's collaborator, John FLETCHER (2), to whom scholars usually assign both 4.3 and 5.2.

**Doctor (5) of Divinity** Character in *Hamlet.* See PRIEST (3).

**Dogberry**  Character in *Much Ado About Nothing*, comical rustic constable in charge of the WATCHMEN (3). Dogberry, his second-in-command VERGES, and the Watchmen are humorously inept, but their apprehension of BORACHIO and CONRADE nonetheless exposes the nefarious plot of Don JOHN (1) against CLAUDIO (1) and HERO. However, Dogberry's officious bumbling postpones this result long enough that Claudio is deceived and Hero humiliated. The tensest moment of the play occurs when Dogberry's tediousness prevents Hero's father, LEONATO, from learning the truth before the wedding, where Hero is to be accused of promiscuity. We are exasperated by the constable's foolishness and infuriated by his preening when he is appointed to interrogate the suspects, but he is nonetheless endearingly amusing.

Although the ridiculous policeman who garbles language was an ancient theatrical character type—Shakespeare had used the figure before in Constable DULL of *Love's Labour's Lost*—Dogberry is one of Shakespeare's most impressive comic creations. A typical Shakespearean CLOWN (1), he affects a more pretentious vocabulary that he can master, misusing the language spectacularly. He is very much a distinctive personality, however. Preposterously long-winded, smugly self-assured, touchingly (though absurdly) incredulous that CONRADE could call him 'an ass' (4.2.70), Dogberry has a naïve dignity that has charmed audiences and readers for centuries.

In part, this response reflects our gratitude for the relief from melodrama that his comedy produces. Dogberry is an important element in Shakespeare's strategy to lighten Hero's plight and maintain a comic tone throughout the play. His foolish locutions and ideas provide comic relief at several points. In 3.3, just after Don John's scheme has begun to bear fruit, we first encounter Dogberry and the Watchmen; our knowledge that the villain's plot will eventually be exposed makes Hero's humiliation less painful. Dogberry's laughable confusion during the interrogation of Conrade and Borachio takes the edge off the revelation of their evil, and in 5.1 his arrival as a comical *deus ex machina* resolves the plot on a note of hilarity.

In the early texts of the play, a number of Dogberry's speech prefixes in 4.2 refer to 'Kempe' or 'Kemp'; it is accordingly believed that the actor William KEMPE first played the role. Dogberry's odd name refers to the fruit of the wild dogwood, a common English shrub. 'Berry' may also designate fish roe, a common Elizabethan usage. The anomalous reference thus produced—dog roe—seems appropriate to the constable's absurdity.

**Dolabella, Cornelius (active 30 B.C.)**  Historical figure and minor character in *Antony and Cleopatra*, a follower of Octavius CAESAR (2). Dolabella appears as a minor member of Caesar's entourage in 3.12, 4.6, and 5.1; in the third of these scenes we see him sent to ANTONY with a demand for surrender, before it is known that Antony is dead. Attention is brought to this errand later in the scene when Caesar recollects it; thus the focus is drawn to Antony once again. In 5.2, now delegated to guard CLEOPATRA, Dolabella succumbs to her charms and reveals to her that Caesar intends to humiliate her in a triumphal parade in ROME. This furthers her decision to commit suicide.

Little is known of the historical Dolabella beyond the anecdote of his brief encounter with Cleopatra, told in Shakespeare's source, PLUTARCH's *Lives*. Modern scholars believe that Caesar was actually manoeuvring Cleopatra towards suicide. He wanted her out of the way but found the execution of a woman an undignified proceeding for a Roman ruler, so Dolabella may not have been as charitable—or as charmed—as it seems in Plutarch and Shakespeare. Another Roman writer later reported that Dolabella was an intimate of the Emperor Augustus, as Octavius Caesar became known.

**Doll Tearsheet**  Character in *2 Henry IV* and *Henry V*, lover of FALSTAFF. Doll joins Falstaff at his uproarious dinner at the BOAR'S HEAD TAVERN in 2.4. She is clearly a prostitute, but her affection for Falstaff is more than commercial. Although they fight with gusto, Doll's sentimental fondness for the fat knight is evident. She invokes their long-standing friendship in a hard world: 'Come, I'll be friends with thee, Jack, thou art going to the wars, and whether I shall ever see thee again or no there is nobody cares' (2.4.64–66). He feels comfortable enough with her to admit, 'I am old, I am old', and she assures him, 'I love thee better than I love e'er a scurvy young boy of them all' (2.4.268–270). When Falstaff departs to join the troops, Doll is genuinely upset, unable to speak for tears.

In 5.4 Doll and the HOSTESS (2) are arrested for their involvement in a murder, and Doll's capacity for invective and deceit comes to the fore as she berates the BEADLE (2) while claiming a fictitious pregnancy, potentially useful in court. This episode emphasises the criminality of Falstaff's world and indicates a change in the lax moral climate that has existed in LONDON, foreshadowing the crucial scene in which PRINCE (6) HAL rejects Falstaff.

Doll was a name conventionally applied to prostitutes. Moreover, as other allusions in 16th- and 17th-century literature make clear, Doll's last name is also related to her profession, implying vigour in its practice. In *Henry V* PISTOL says that Doll is in hospital with a venereal disease (2.1.74–77), and her death is reported in 5.1.85.

**Don (1) John**  Character in *Much Ado About Nothing*. See JOHN (1).

**Don (2) Pedro**   Character in *Much Ado About Nothing.* See PEDRO.

**Donalbain (c. 1033–1099)**   Historical figure and character in *Macbeth,* the younger son of the murdered King DUNCAN of SCOTLAND. Donalbain plays a very minor part in the play; after he attends his father in three scenes of Act 1, he speaks for the first time in 2.3 after Duncan's murder. He suggests to his brother, MALCOLM, that they flee, lest suspicion fall upon them. He declares that he will go to Ireland while Malcolm goes to England. Malcolm returns to reclaim the kingdom from MACBETH, but Donalbain does not reappear in the play though he is mentioned several times, lastly in 5.2.7–8, where it is observed that he is not with Malcolm's army of invasion. However, in the play's final speech, Malcolm says that he intends 'calling home our exil'd friends abroad' (5.9.32), a remark that may remind us of Donalbain.

The historical Donalbain was a child when Macbeth seized the throne from Duncan in 1039. His name is a corruption of Donald Ban, or Donald the White, which suggests that he was flaxen-haired. For dramatic purposes, Shakespeare altered the story and increased the ages of the brothers, but they did in fact leave Scotland—taken by adults, however—for separate exiles, Donalbain going to the Hebrides Islands off Scotland's north-west coast. He may have spent some time in Ireland, but it is from the Hebrides that he re-entered history years later. Donald became the leader of the conservative Celtic nobility of north-western Scotland who opposed the European orientation that Malcolm, as king, gave the country. When Malcolm died fighting the Norman rulers of England in 1093, Donald invaded Scotland and deposed Malcolm's heir, Duncan II, with the help of one of Duncan's brothers. They ruled jointly for three years. However, another brother reconquered Scotland with the assistance of England—gained by accepting feudal subordination to the English king—and in 1099 Donald was captured, blinded, and imprisoned for the last few months of his life.

**Dorcas**   Character in *The Winter's Tale,* a shepherdess. Dorcas appears only in the shepherds' festival in 4.4. She speaks briefly, chiefly to tease her friend MOPSA about her engagement to the CLOWN (8), and she sings a SONG with Mopsa and AUTOLYCUS. She has no personality to speak of, but she contributes to the festive atmosphere of the occasion. Dorcas' name is from the Bible (see Acts 9:36–39).

**Doricles**   In *The Winter's Tale,* name taken by Prince FLORIZEL of BOHEMIA when he disguises himself to court PERDITA, a seeming shepherdess.

**Dorset, Thomas Grey, Marquis of (1451–1501)**   Historical figure and character in *Richard III,* the son of Queen ELIZABETH (2) by her first marriage. Dorset appears with his mother several times in the early scenes of the play. In 2.2 he offers her the rather cold comfort, on the occasion of the death of King EDWARD IV, that God is simply taking back the gift of royalty that He had given. In 4.1, when the Queen receives word that RICHARD III has seized the crown, Dorset is sent abroad to join RICHMOND. Following the FIRST FOLIO stage directions, many modern editions include Dorset among Richmond's followers at BOSWORTH FIELD in 5.3, although he does not speak. In actuality, the invading Earl had left Dorset in France, as a hostage to ensure the co-operation of his mother's party.

**Douglas, Archibald, Earl of (1369–1424)**   Historical figure and character in *1 Henry IV,* the leader of the Scottish army that joins the rebels against King HENRY IV. Douglas' appearance is preceded by word of his reputation for courage and military prowess. In 3.2 the King speaks of his renown by way of praising HOTSPUR, who has captured him at the battle of HOLMEDON, and FALSTAFF describes him as 'that sprightly Scot of Scots, Douglas, that runs a-horseback up a hill perpendicular . . .' (2.4.339–340). In accordance with WORCESTER's plan, Hotspur frees Douglas and recruits him for the rebellion against Henry. A bold talker ('. . . there is not such a word spoke of in Scotland as this term of fear' [4.1.84–85]) and fighter, Douglas' fiery temperament resembles Hotspur's, and both men urge the rebels into the battle of SHREWSBURY without waiting for reinforcements. During the battle, in 5.3–4, Douglas seeks out Henry, first slaying Sir Walter BLUNT (3). He nearly kills the King, but PRINCE (6) HAL drives him away. He then attacks FALSTAFF, who feigns death. In 5.5 Douglas' capture is reported, but Prince Hal declares that he shall be freed without the payment of ransom, as a tribute to his valour.

Black Douglas, as the historical figure was known, was indeed a famous warrior, although he may have been a bad commander, for he was never on the winning side in a major battle. He was not in fact released at Shrewsbury; he was only freed five years later, after the payment of a very large ransom. Shakespeare followed his source, HOLINSHED, in this error. Douglas later fought against the English for King CHARLES VII of France in the HUNDRED YEARS WAR, and he died in FRANCE (1).

**Dover**   City in south-eastern England, near which much of *King Lear* is set. The invasion of England by an army under CORDELIA and FRANCE (2) draws the play's action to this seaport on the English Channel, famous for the white chalk cliffs overlooking the sea that are vividly described by EDGAR in 4.6.11–24. Some scholars think this description may reflect Shakespeare's personal response to the natural phenomenon, for he probably visited Dover as an actor; his company—the CHAMBERLAIN'S MEN, later the KING'S MEN—performed there in 1597 and 1605.

**Dowden, Edward (1843–1913)**   Irish literary scholar. Dowden was a long-time professor of English literature at Dublin's Trinity College. He established himself as a significant Shakespearean scholar with his *Shakespeare: A Critical Study of his Mind and Art* (1875), the first book in English (but see GERVINUS) to consider the growth of the playwright through the course of his career. Though regarded by later critics as a sentimental work, too inclined to idealise its subject, Dowden's book influenced all later Shakespearean biography because of its developmental approach. Dowden also published other works on Shakespeare, editions of some of the plays, biographies of other literary figures, and editions of SPENSER and other English poets.

**Downton, Thomas (active 1593–1622)**   English actor, a leading member of the ADMIRAL'S MEN for many years. Downton was probably one of the amalgamated troupe of Admiral's Men and STRANGE'S MEN that toured England in 1593–1594 while the LONDON theatres were closed by the plague. He was a charter member of the reorganised Admiral's Men of 1594, and he was still with the company in 1615 when it was the PALSGRAVE'S MEN, though he had briefly performed for PEMBROKE'S MEN in 1597. He played a variety of roles and was involved in the business affairs of the troupe. In 1618 he married the widow of a wine merchant and took up that profession.

**Drawer**   Any of several minor characters in *2 Henry IV*, servants at the BOAR'S HEAD TAVERN. In 2.4 the Drawers, who 'draw' wine from casks for their customers, prepare for FALSTAFF's dinner party. They enjoy an anecdote in which PRINCE (6) HAL taunts Falstaff about his age, and they plan for entertainment with a musician named SNEAK. Among their number is FRANCIS (1), who also appears in *1 Henry IV*. The Drawers present one of the many glimpses of working-class life in the *Henry IV* plays.

**Drayton, Michael (1563–1631)**   English poet and dramatist. Though best known for his poetry, Drayton also wrote for the stage. In the late 1590s and early 17th century, he wrote about 20 plays for the ADMIRAL'S MEN, all in collaboration with other playwrights, including Anthony MUNDAY and Richard HATHWAY. One of their plays was SIR JOHN OLDCASTLE, later published as Shakespeare's. In 1598 Francis MERES praised Drayton as among England's best writers of tragedies. Drayton helped found the WHITEFRIARS THEATRE in 1608 and joined Martin SLATER in forming

a short-lived boy's troupe (see CHILDREN'S COMPANIES) that played there. Drayton was raised as a page in an aristocratic household near STRATFORD and visited there often later in life. He was treated by Shakespeare's son-in-law, Dr John HALL (4), and so may have known the playwright. However, there seems to be no truth in the legend that Shakespeare died after a drinking bout with Drayton and Ben JONSON, for Drayton was well known for his strict sobriety.

**Drew, John (1853–1927)**   American actor. One of the leading actors of his day, John Drew was especially noted for his PETRUCHIO in *The Taming of the Shrew*. For many years he appeared in the productions of Augustin DALY, often opposite Ada REHAN. Through his sister he was the uncle of John BARRYMORE.

**Droeshout, Martin (1601–c. 1650)**   English engraver, creator of the portrait of Shakespeare that illustrates the FIRST FOLIO edition (1623) of the plays. This is one of the two portraits of the playwright considered by scholars to reflect his actual appearance (the other is a sculpture by Gheerart JANSSEN [2]). Droeshout was a poor draftsman, and the portrait is badly flawed—for instance, the head is much too big relative to the torso, and one eye is larger and lower than the other. However, because it was acceptable to Shakespeare's friends, the Folio editors who published it and Ben JONSON who praised it, it is presumed to have provided a reasonable likeness. Scholars believe that Droeshout worked from a drawing or painting and probably never saw the playwright. For all its defects, the Droeshout portrait has been copied many times and is probably the basis for most people's sense of Shakespeare's appearance.

Droeshout was the grandson of a Protestant artist who fled from religious persecution in Brabant (in what is now Belgium) in 1566. His family were members of the same LONDON church as that of Gheerart Janssen, and it is thought that the sculptor may have helped secure the Folio commission for a fellow Netherlander. Droeshout later produced portraits of other notable figures.

**Droll**   Brief playlet, often an adaptation of scenes from full-length plays, performed in 1642–1660, when theatres were closed by the English revolutionary government. Drolls were presented at fairs and in taverns in conjunction with such licensed forms of entertainment as rope dancing. One of the best-known performers of drolls was Robert COX, a collection of whose scripts was published by Henry MARSH and Francis KIRKMAN—after the restoration of the monarchy and the reopening of the theatres—as *The Wits, or Sport upon Sport* (1662). Among the most famous of drolls were 'The Grave-diggers', from *Hamlet*, and

'The Merry conceited Humours of Bottom the Weaver', from *A Midsummer Night's Dream.* The latter was published separately in 1661, when it was described on the title page as having been performed in legitimate, public performances and '. . . lately, privately, presented by several apprentices for their harmless recreation'.

**Dromio of Ephesus and Dromio of Syracuse**  Two characters in *The Comedy of Errors,* twin servants to the twin masters ANTIPHOLUS OF EPHESUS and ANTIPHOLUS OF SYRACUSE. The Dromios were separated from each other in infancy, each with a similarly separated master, in a shipwreck. They share with their masters the confusions and errors that mistaken identities lead to. As comic buffoons, the Dromios receive numerous beatings as their masters' affairs become increasingly disordered, and they respond with quips and quibbles, in a tradition of stock humorous servants and slaves that extends back at least to the Roman drama from which Shakespeare took much of the material for the play. The Dromios also share with their masters the joyful reunion at the end of the play.

Shakespeare may have taken the name Dromio from the play *Mother Bombie* by John LYLY (published 1594), who may, in turn, have based it on the name Dromo, frequently used for slaves in the work of the Roman dramatist Terence.

**Dryden, John (1631–1700)**  English poet, playwright, and literary critic. One of the leading playwrights of the Restoration period (1660–1688), Dryden also wrote extensive assessments of English writers and was an acute appreciator of Shakespeare. However, while admiring 'the divine Shakespeare', he also felt that ELIZABETHAN DRAMA was in general crude, and that Shakespeare shared in its defects. Thus, like many others of his day, he did not hesitate to alter Shakespeare's works. He is notorious for his rewriting of *The Tempest,* in collaboration with William DAVENANT, as *The Tempest, or The Enchanted Island* (1667, published 1670). This adaptation adds whole SUB-PLOTS and retains little of Shakespeare's text. Many of the additions were taken from a Spanish playwright, Pedro Calderón (1600–1681). Although this work was hugely popular, it is deplored by modern commentators. Dryden also adapted *Troilus and Cressida,* which he described in his preface as a 'heap of rubbish', in an equally radical and unfortunate alteration known by its subtitle as *Truth Found Too Late* (1679). His own best play, *All for Love* (1677), was a version of *Antony and Cleopatra;* it has appealed to audiences ever since.

**Du Bartas, Guillaume de Sallust (1544–1590)**  French poet, author of a minor source for *Romeo and Juliet.* A poem by Du Bartas—featured in English translation in the *Ortho-epia Gallica* (1593) of John ELIOT (1)—inspired the debate on bird song between ROMEO and JULIET (1) in 3.5 of *Romeo and Juliet.*

Most of Du Bartas' work was of a more serious nature. Born a nobleman in Gascony, Du Bartas was a friend of the King of Navarre—later Henri IV of France—the leader of the Protestant faction in the civil and religious conflict that tore France apart in the late 16th century. The poet composed monumental poems on religious themes and fought on the battlefield. In 1587 Henri sent Du Bartas on a diplomatic mission to Scotland, where he became a close friend of King James, later JAMES I of England. His works were highly regarded throughout Protestant Europe, were widely translated, and greatly influenced 17th-century religious poetry, including, most notably, John MILTON's *Paradise Lost.*

**Duchess (1) of Gloucester, Eleanor Cobham, (d. 1454)**  Historical figure and character in *2 Henry VI,* the wife of Duke Humphrey of GLOUCESTER (4). The Duchess is ambitious for her husband, the heir apparent to King HENRY VI, but the Duke repudiates her desire that he be king. She therefore proceeds behind his back. In 1.2 she meets with a renegade priest, John HUME, who has hired conjurers for her so that she may see the future in order to plan a coup. Hume, however, is in the pay of Gloucester's enemy, the Duke of SUFFOLK (3), and the Duchess is arrested in 1.4, along with the sorcerers SOUTHWELL and BOLINGBROKE (2) and a witch, MARGERY JOURDAIN. These commoners are sentenced to death in 2.3, but the Duchess' punishment is limited to the humiliation of public exposure in a parade through the streets of London, followed by lifelong banishment to a castle on the Isle of Man, in the Irish Sea. Her unscrupulous attempt to harness the supernatural as an aid to treason marks the first stage in the downfall of 'good Duke Humphrey', the chief business of Acts 1–3.

The historical Eleanor Cobham was a young woman of relatively low standing, compared to the PLANTAGENET (1) lineage of her husband, and her position seemed to some degree scandalous, both to her own contemporaries and to Shakespeare's. The Duke had married her after an earlier marriage, to a Burgundian noblewoman stolen from her husband, had been annulled. The new Duchess dabbled in witchcraft, and she apparently attempted to divine the date of the King's death through the assistance of Hume and the others. However, there seems to be no evidence that she plotted against the King's life. Nor is there evidence that Gloucester's enemies plotted against her; they did not need to, for the Duchess initiated her indiscretions herself. She was tried and convicted of using sorcery, and, as in the play, she was sentenced to public humiliation—a punishment usually reserved for common prostitutes—and banishment. She died on the Isle of Man some years later, after enforced residence in several other, less remote locations.

Shakespeare's only important departure from the historical record of this incident is chronological. The Duchess' disgrace actually occurred four years prior to the arrival of Queen MARGARET (1) in England, with which the play begins, and while the incident was troublesome for her husband, it did not contribute directly to his own ultimate collapse in fortunes. However, the playwright wished to compress all the Duke's embarrassments into a brief sequence of bad luck, and to associate them with Margaret and Suffolk. In this way, the play emphasises the degree to which selfish ambition undercut the one man whose judgement and honesty, in the light of history as Shakespeare and his contemporaries understood it, might have prevented civil war.

**Duchess (2) of Gloucester, Eleanor de Bohun (1367–1399)**   Historical figure and minor character in *Richard II*, sister-in-law of John of GAUNT and widow of Duke Thomas of GLOUCESTER (6). In 1.2 the Duchess visits Gaunt to discuss her husband's murder. She blames King RICHARD II for his death and passionately entreats Gaunt to avenge it. He insists that vengeance against a king may be taken only by God, and the Duchess wrathfully expresses the hope that BOLINGBROKE (1) will kill MOWBRAY (1), whom she says murdered Gloucester at the king's order. Then she resignedly asserts that she will soon die of grief and departs for her home. Her death is reported in 2.2.97. The episode casts light on the conflicts of 1.1 and 1.3, making clear to the audience that Richard is implicated in Gloucester's murder and that Bolingbroke's accusation of Mowbray is embarrassing to the king.

Although the Duchess appears to be Gaunt's contemporary, she was actually a generation younger, being only 32 when she died, reportedly of grief at the death of her only son. Shakespeare's rendering of her as an older woman helps to heighten the pathos of the vanishing medieval world that colours his story of the king's fall.

**Duchess (3) of York, Cicely Neville (1415–1495)**
Historical figure and character in *Richard III*, the mother of RICHARD III and his brothers, EDWARD IV and CLARENCE (1). The widow of Richard, Duke of YORK (8), a major figure in the *Henry VI* plays, she was also the mother of RUTLAND, who figures briefly in *3 Henry VI*. The Duchess is a symbolic figure, whose role is to lament Richard's evil nature in a stylised manner reminiscent of a Greek CHORUS (1). Shakespeare's sources hardly mention her; it is thought that the playwright was influenced by similar characters in the plays of SENECA. The historical Cicely Neville was a daughter

of Ralph, Earl of WESTMORELAND (1), who appears in *1* and *2 Henry IV* and *Henry V*.

**Duchess (4) of York, Isabel of Castile (1355–1393)**
Historical figure and minor character in *Richard II*, mother of the Duke of AUMERLE. When her husband, the Duke of YORK (4), discovers Aumerle's part in a plot against the new king (BOLINGBROKE [1]), he insists on protecting the monarch by revealing the conspiracy, exposing his son to charges of treason. The Duchess' objections go unheeded, and in 5.3, after sending Aumerle ahead, she goes to the king herself and argues against her husband, opposing her motherly anguish to his concern for the state. She receives Bolingbroke's pardon of Aumerle with great gratitude. A powerful dramatic presentation of maternal passion, the episode also serves to stress the magnanimity of Bolingbroke in preparation for his role as King HENRY IV in *1* and *2 Henry IV*.

The incident is entirely fictitious; the real Duchess Isabel had been dead for years before the events depicted in the play took place. The Duke of York had remarried, but the second duchess, besides not being Aumerle's mother, had nothing to do with his being pardoned by King Henry.

**Duffett, Thomas (active 1673–1678)**   English dramatist, author of parodies of two adaptations of Shakespeare. Passages in Duffett's *The Empress of Morocco* (c. 1673) mocked William DAVENANT's extravagant production of *Macbeth*, and his *The Mock-Tempest, or The Enchanted Castle* (1674) was a full-scale comic imitation of Thomas SHADWELL's operatic version of *The Tempest* (1674).

Duffett was a milliner who took up playwrighting with some success. Four of his plays were staged between 1673 and 1676. Three—including the two named above—were burlesques of other works, and the fourth was a MASQUE.

**Duke (1) Frederick**   Character in *As You Like It*, younger brother and deposer of DUKE (7) Senior. Duke Frederick is the villain of the play. A cardboard character with no real personality, he is a conventional bad man, intended simply to anchor one end of the play's scale of values. He not only exiles his brother to the Forest of ARDEN (1), but he also banishes his innocent niece, ROSALIND, thus provoking the flight of his daughter, CELIA. His hostility towards Rosalind is said to be based 'upon no other argument / But that the people praise her for her virtues, / And pity her for her good father's sake' (1.3.268–271). The Duke's reported reformation, after encountering 'an old religious man' (5.4.159) while launching an army against Arden, is entirely unbelievable in human terms. However, it symbolises the play's climactic triumph of harmony and reconciliation.

**Duke (2) of Florence**  Character in *All's Well That Ends Well,* the ruler of FLORENCE. In 3.1 the Duke welcomes the French noblemen who have come to fight for him against Siena, and in 3.3 he appoints BERTRAM to command his cavalry. The Duke is merely an example of a courtly ruler, offering a contrast with the less chivalrous behaviour of Bertram and PAROLLES.

**Duke (3) of Milan**  Minor character in *The Two Gentlemen of Verona,* the father of SILVIA and the ruler of the court where the main action of the play takes place. Informed by PROTEUS that Silvia plans to elope with VALENTINE, the Duke banishes Valentine from the realm. In the final scene, the Duke appears, as ruler and as father of the future bride, to approve the final happy outcome.

**Duke (4) of Venice**  Minor character in *The Merchant of Venice,* the ruler of VENICE. The Duke presides over the trial of SHYLOCK's suit against ANTONIO (2). He is helpless to influence matters, being bound by the laws of the state, a position in which Shakespeare often places his rulers (see, e.g., the DUKE [8] of EPHESUS). In this way the Duke emphasises a principle to which the playwright was strongly committed: the importance of the law in a well-ordered society. Although the Duke is prepared to see Antonio die, as the full rigour of the law dictates, he is merciful to SHYLOCK after the case is resolved in Antonio's favour, thus highlighting another virtue Shakespeare saw in an ideal ruler.

**Duke (5) of Venice**  Character in *Othello,* the ruler of VENICE. In 1.3 the Duke meets with his advisers (see SENATOR [1]) to decide on a response to the Turkish assault on CYPRUS. Summoning OTHELLO, their chief general, they are faced with BRABANTIO's accusation that Othello has used witchcraft to marry his daughter, DESDEMONA. When Desdemona confirms that theirs is a love match, Brabantio is bitter, but the Duke offers wise proverbs on emotional moderation, such as, 'To mourn a mischief that is past and gone, / Is the next way to draw more mischief on' (1.3.204–205). He represents a social wisdom that is markedly lacking in the main plot.

**Duke (6) Orsino of Illyria**  Character in *Twelfth Night.* See ORSINO.

**Duke (7) Senior**  Character in *As You Like It,* ruler deposed by his brother, DUKE (1) Frederick, and exiled to the Forest of ARDEN (1). The father of ROSALIND, Duke Senior is a symbol of authority and wisdom with little distinctive personality. Before we meet him, we are told that he and his followers in exile 'fleet the time

carelessly as they did in the golden world' (1.1.118–119), a reference to the rustic life idealised in PASTORAL literature. In his first speech the Duke introduces the audience to Arden and firmly establishes the contrast between the woodland world and the realities of politics and power: 'Hath not old custom made this life more sweet / Than that of painted pomp? Are not these woods / More free from peril than the envious court?' (2.1.2–4). The Duke makes the best of his exile, finding 'tongues in trees, books in the running brooks, / Sermons in stones, and good in everything' (2.1.16–17). Such remarks, like the songs of AMIENS, express the ideal of an escape from the pressures of the real world.

However, the Duke is aware that Arden is no paradise. He acknowledges that he has 'seen better days' (2.7.120), and he shares some attitudes with the alienated and melancholy courtier JAQUES (1). In 2.1.22–25 he regrets having to kill deer for food shortly before an elaboration on the thought is attributed to Jaques. In 2.7.137–139 he suggests to Jaques his famous comparison of human life to the action in a drama ('All the world's a stage, / And all the men and women merely players' [2.7.139–140]). Nevertheless, the Duke also opposes this point of view: in 2.7.64–69, he chastises Jaques for wishing to satirise the world when he is himself hardly free from sin, and, in doing so, he sets a limit on the play's tolerance for Jaques' criticisms. Most important, when Duke Frederick's religious conversion and abdication are reported in 5.4, Duke Senior is immediately ready to resume his dukedom, and, as Jaques remarks, his 'patience and . . . virtue well deserve it' (5.4.186). The Duke's fondness for the pastoral life is less powerful than his sense of social responsibility, mirroring Shakespeare's own view that a ruler's duty to his position is paramount.

**Duke (8) Solinus of Ephesus**  Character in *The Comedy of Errors,* the ruler of the city of Ephesus, where the play takes place. The Duke first appears in 1.1 to condemn EGEON, a wandering merchant from Syracuse who has arrived in Ephesus, unaware of the hostilities between that city and his own, and is sentenced to either death or an immense fine, which he cannot pay. Egeon tells of his separated family and his search for them, and the Duke expresses pity for the old man but says he cannot exempt him from the law.

The sources and use of power are subjects that were important to the playwright, and they are dealt with in a number of the plays. In this early work, the Duke, regrets that he cannot act on his pity, but explains that the law explicitly limits his range of action, while at the same time it is the implicit source of his authority. His crown and his dignity are equated with his oath, a matter of law. However, the Duke will bend as far as he feels he legally can, out of pity for the aged wanderer, and he gives Egeon a day in which to find some way to raise his ransom money. This day becomes the time in which the play proper takes place.

Neither the Duke nor Egeon reappears until the final scene, when the confusions and mistaken identities that are the chief material of the play have reached a climax. When he re-enters, at 5.1.131, he is still sympathetic to Egeon's plight, although the unfortunate victim is escorted by the EXECUTIONER and seems fated soon to die. The Duke is immediately swept up in the misunderstandings of the central plot, being requested to rule against the Abbess, EMILIA (1), who has granted sanctuary in her PRIORY to ANTIPHOLUS OF SYRACUSE.

When ANTIPHOLUS OF EPHESUS appears, the true complexity of the situation becomes apparent. The Duke, the representative of secular law, is clearly baffled, so he sends for Emilia, who enters with the second Antipholus, bringing the twins together for the first time. Further, Emilia recognises Egeon as her long-lost husband, and the resolution of the play's complexities begins. The intervention of Christian grace and mercy, represented by Emilia and the Priory, has tempered the insensitive cruelties of secular justice. However, the Duke is quite evidently pleased with the outcome, in keeping with his consistently sympathetic attitude. When Emilia proposes a 'gossip feast' or celebratory party, the Duke accepts with enthusiasm and leads the company off-stage to close the play.

Shakespeare may have taken the name Solinus (which appears only in 1.1.1) from that of an ancient geographer, Gaius Julius Solinus, who described (c. 200 A.D.) the seaports of the Mediterranean. His work was published in an English translation in 1587, a few years before *The Comedy of Errors* was probably written.

**Duke (9) Vincentio of Vienna**   Character in *Measure for Measure,* the ruler of VIENNA. The Duke, who appoints the stern ANGELO (2) as his deputy and then spies on his performance, personifies a major theme of the play: the relationship of government to Christian doctrines of forgiveness and mercy. The Duke's government has been lax, as he admits to the FRIAR (1) in 1.3, but in designating Angelo to restore a strict public morality he errs to the opposite extreme. His deputy is incapable of applying the law flexibly, and the result is a harsh injustice, the death sentence for the honourable CLAUDIO (3). However, the Duke is intent on personal improvement—ESCALUS (2) says of him that he 'above all other strifes, contended especially to know himself' (3.2.226–227)—and his effort teaches him to acknowledge the need for mercy to counteract human weakness.

Significantly, the Duke's disguise as he investigates Angelo's governance is that of a friar; in adopting a religious role he manifests the God-given authority that Shakespeare and his original audiences ascribed

to all rulers. Angelo's lust for ISABELLA, Claudio's intercessor, produces a seemingly unresolvable conflict. However, the Duke, in his friar's guise, takes over the play and effects two improbable schemes: the substitution of another head for that of the supposedly executed Claudio, and of another woman, MARIANA (2), for Isabella. Having thus negated Angelo's evil intent, the Duke re-emerges, in 5.1, to bring the play to a close in a flurry of pardons and marriages.

Many commentators have found this dénouement lacking in credibility, but Shakespeare's purpose was symbolic, and realism should not be expected. The Duke controls the outcome and thus fulfils the ruler's proper role in the play's scheme of things. He offers the mercy of God to the deserving and undeserving alike. It is he who recognises in BARNARDINE, the vicious murderer, a mere 'creature unprepar'd' (4.3.66), and he forgives LUCIO his slanders, despite the insult to both his personal pride and his authority. Most important, he proves susceptible to the pleas of Mariana and Isabella for mercy towards the villainous Angelo. Finally, though he has earlier claimed immunity from 'the dribbling dart of love' (1.3.2), he proposes marriage to Isabella. In striking contrast to the negative attitudes of both Angelo and Isabella, early in the play, the Duke underscores Shakespeare's belief in the happy marriages that traditionally close a COMEDY.

**Duke Humphrey**   Possible lost play by Shakespeare. In 1660 the publisher Humphrey MOSELEY claimed the copyrights to a number of old plays, including *Duke Humphrey.* The 18th-century antiquarian John WARBURTON reported owning a copy as well, but otherwise the play is unknown, unless the title refers to *2 Henry VI,* which was originally published as 'The First part of the Contention betwixt the two famous Houses of Yorke and Lancaster, with the death of the good Duke Humphrey' (a reference to the Duke of GLOUCESTER [4]; see CONTENTION). However, since both Moseley and Warburton were mistaken in claiming other plays as Shakespeare's, scholars generally do not believe that *Duke Humphrey* was written by him.

**Duke of York's Men**   See PRINCE CHARLES' MEN.

**Dull, Anthony**   Minor character in *Love's Labour's Lost,* the slow-witted rustic constable. Dull is a character type whose name summarises his nature. Dull acts as a foil to the comical pedants ARMADO, HOLOFERNES, and NATHANIEL (1), offsetting their elaborate contortions of language by being himself. At one point, Holofernes observes, '*Via*, goodman Dull! Thou hast spoken no word all this while'. Dull replies, 'Nor understand none neither, sir' (5.1.141).

**Dumaine (Dumain)**   Character in *Love's Labour's Lost,* one of the gentlemen who fall in love and thus disrupt the ascetic academic programme of the KING (19) of Navarre. Although committed to the King's idea at the outset of the play, Dumaine falls in love with KATHARINE (1), a lady-in-waiting of the PRINCESS (1) of France. Along with the King and the other courtiers, he breaks his vows and abandons scholarship for love.

The Duc de Mayenne, well known in Shakespeare's London for his role in the French Wars of Religion, is usually thought to have provided the name Dumaine. Unlike the originals of LONGAVILLE and BEROWNE, he was not an aide to the historical King of Navarre; rather, he was a principal enemy of the insurgent monarch, but this inconsistency would probably not have bothered either the playwright or his audience. An alternative, the less notable General D'Aumont, who was an aide to the King of Navarre at the time, has been proposed.

**Dumb Show**   Scene performed in pantomime, especially as part of an Elizabethan TRAGEDY. Shakespeare employed dumb shows in several scenes of *Pericles,* a single scene in *Cymbeline,* and in *Hamlet.* A dumb show could function as a PROLOGUE (1) or CHORUS (1); it sometimes illustrated an off-stage event, presented plot elements that were not fully acted out, or enacted what was shortly to come in the main action, intimating a symbolic meaning.

In *Pericles* three dumb shows are employed in the choric narrations of GOWER (3). At 2.Chorus.16 a dumb show enacts the reception of a letter by PERICLES, followed by his hasty departure; Gower reveals that the message has warned the hero of danger and he has fled. At 3.Chorus.14 a more elaborate enactment depicts Pericles receiving another letter, read also by his new father-in-law, SIMONIDIES. The attending courtiers kneel to Pericles. He then departs with his new wife, who is pregnant. Gower explains that the letter has summoned Pericles to TYRE, where he is ruler, thus revealing his royalty and sparking another journey. Lastly, in 4.4 a dumb show presents Pericles weeping at the tomb of his supposedly dead daughter, MARINA, though the audience knows that Marina is actually alive. Thus, in *Pericles,* the dumb show is a simple device that compresses the plot by providing brief summaries of what would otherwise require complete scenes.

In *Cymbeline* a brief dumb show occurs at the close of 5.3. In it POSTHUMUS, disguised as a Roman soldier, is brought as a prisoner to CYMBELINE, who turns him over to a GAOLER (2). This may not be a dumb show proper, but rather a survival in the printed play of notes for a scene that was never actually written (see CYMBELINE, 'Text of the Play').

The PLAYERS (2) in *Hamlet* stage a dumb show before their performance of THE MURDER OF GONZAGO, the playlet that HAMLET hopes will inspire an unconscious revelation of guilt in his uncle, the KING (5), who has murdered his father. The dumb show is described in an elaborate stage direction at 3.2.133. After being affectionately embraced by his queen, a king sleeps and a man puts a poison in his ear. The queen returns and mourns the dead king, but she responds to the attentions of the poisoner, who takes her away with him as the king's body is removed. This enactment resembles the real king's crime—as Hamlet has been informed by the GHOST (3)—but the king does not respond until the spoken dialogue of the playlet later in the scene.

This delay presents one of the many small problems that have puzzled commentators on *Hamlet* for generations: have two different renderings of the playlet been accidentally preserved, when only one was intended for performance? Are we supposed to believe that the king was not paying attention or that he did not recognise his crime in the dumb show, only in the more elaborate rendering that followed? Or was he able to stand the sight of his guilty action once but not twice (the so-called 'second tooth' theory)? In Shakespeare's text the king remains inscrutable during the dumb show, perhaps to heighten the buildup of tension, but many productions present him as engaged in conversation with the QUEEN (9) thus not seeing the dumb show, or as silently but visibly aghast, recovering himself only to collapse later.

The 'second tooth' theory has been most widely accepted by scholars, but whatever theory is correct, the King's inscrutability works well on stage and the dumb show serves a definite theatrical purpose: A formal device that is not itself a part of the plot, it outlines the coming playlet, permitting the audience to concern itself with the responses of Hamlet and the King. Moreover, the playlet is never completed after the King's guilty reaction disrupts it, so its closure with the queen's acceptance of the murderer—analogous to the behaviour of Hamlet's mother, the real Queen—is known only through the dumb show.

It is likely that the dumb show originated in RENAISSANCE Italy. Probably always accompanied by music, it was intended as an elaborate and diverting spectacle, and Shakespeare assumed his audience would recognise it as having this function for the Danish court in *Hamlet,* just as it presumably did for the actual viewers of *Pericles.*

**Duncan, King of Scotland (c. 1001–1039)**   Historical figure and character in *Macbeth,* ruler of SCOTLAND who MACBETH murders for his throne. Shakespeare's Duncan is an elderly man, a respected and noble figure; as Macbeth reflects, he 'Hath borne his faculties so meek, hath been / So clear in his great office, that his virtues / Will plead like angels, trumpet-tongu'd' (1.7.17–19). Duncan's generous and trusting nature contrasts strikingly with the evil which surrounds

Macbeth. Though he appears only in Act 1, he is an important symbol of the values that are to be defeated and restored in the course of the play. His generosity and fatherly affection for Macbeth make his murder even more appalling. The unconscious irony is sharp when he greets Macbeth, who is already plotting against him, with a declaration of his *own* ingratitude, in 1.4.14–16. Duncan's faith, misplaced first in the rebellious CAWDOR and then in MACBETH, provides the audience with an introduction to the atmosphere of betrayal that exists throughout the world of the play.

The historical Duncan was a much younger man than Shakespeare's character, only a few years older than Macbeth. The playwright altered Duncan's age to stress the evil of Macbeth's crime, but in fact Macbeth did not murder Duncan; he usurped the crown through a civil war, and Duncan died in battle. The two were first cousins, both grandsons of Duncan's predecessor on the throne of Scotland, King Malcolm II (ruled 1005–1034). Duncan's claim to the throne was somewhat stronger than Macbeth's as it appears that Malcolm II had named Duncan as his heir, although the facts are obscure. However, Macbeth's action was an ordinary political manoeuvre in 11th-century Scotland; King Malcolm II took the throne previously by murdering his cousin, Kenneth III (997–1005). Shakespeare devised his version of Duncan's death from an account of an earlier royal assassination, that of Malcolm II's uncle, King Duff (d. 967), in his source, Raphael HOLINSHED's history.

**Dunsinane (Dunsinnan)**  Castle near Perth in central Scotland, the setting for Act 5 of *Macbeth.* 'Great Dunsinane' (5.2.12), whose 'strength / Will laugh a siege to scorn' (5.5.2–3), is clearly an imposing structure—one appropriate to the grim events of the play's climax. Macbeth resists the army of Prince MALCOLM, Lord MACDUFF, and the English lord, SIWARD, within its walls. A few miles away lies Birnam Wood, the royal forest featured in the WITCHES' prediction Macbeth believes ensures his safety: '. . . until / Great Birnam wood to high Dunsinane hill / Shall come against him' (4.1.92–94). When the camouflage devised by Malcolm seems to bring the wood to the castle, in 5.5, Macbeth's fate becomes apparent. The castle proves to be no hindrance to the invaders, being 'gently render'd' (5.7.24) by all its inhabitants but the doomed king.

Historically, Dunsinane was not the site of Macbeth's final defeat, though Siward did win a battle

there in 1054. Malcolm was only finally victorious—and Macbeth slain—at a battle elsewhere in Scotland, three years later. Shakespeare took the error from his source, HOLINSHED's *Chronicles,* and doubtless believed it to be correct.

**D'Urfey, Thomas (1653–1723)**  English dramatist, author of an adaptation of *Cymbeline.* D'Urfey's *The Injured Princess or the Fatal Wager* was staged and published in 1682 (though its EPILOGUE notes that it had been written nine years earlier). Shakespeare's language—including most of the names—was much altered by D'Urfey, but the plot remained fairly close to the original. It differs only in the addition of an elaborate sub-plot in which Cloten kidnaps a daughter of Pisanio, and the fact that Pisanio mistrusts Imogen as much as Posthumus does. *The Injured Princess* was quite popular and was revived periodically for almost 60 years.

Tom D'Urfey wrote plays and song lyrics; the latter were set to music by his composer friends, among them Henry PURCELL. His songs were published in six volumes entitled *Wit and Mirth, or Pills to Purge Melancholy* (1720). He also wrote 29 plays, many of which were very popular.

**Dutchman and Spaniard**  Minor characters in *Cymbeline,* non-speaking witnesses of the wager between POSTHUMUS and IACHIMO. Neither the Dutchman nor his companion the Spaniard does anything at all; they are only mentioned in the stage directions at 1.3.1. Shakespeare found both figures in one of his sources, *Frederyke of Jennen,* but scholars differ on their function in the play. Each may be a GHOST CHARACTER, considered by the playwright but then abandoned and therefore not actually employed in early productions. Alternatively, lines they spoke, probably brief explanatory ones, may have been lost. Finally, Shakespeare may have intended them as comic caricatures of their nationalities—a popular dramatic feature in his day—and perhaps he intended them to be in a drunken stupor, also popular in comedy.

**Dutton, Laurence (active 1571–1591)**  English actor. Dutton was a member of at least five different acting companies, including OXFORD'S MEN and the QUEEN'S MEN (1); his brother John worked with him in three of them. Their reputation for fickleness prompted an anonymous satirist of 1580 to refer to them as the 'chameleon' Duttons.

# E

**Eastcheap** Neighbourhood in LONDON, location of the BOAR'S HEAD TAVERN and setting for several scenes in *1* and *2 Henry IV* and *Henry V*. Eastcheap, an ancient and impoverished commercial district—'cheap' comes from an Anglo-Saxon word for 'bargain'—was noted for its butcher shops and meat markets. It was also known as a dangerous and disreputable area and was thus an appropriate locale for FALSTAFF's world of petty crime and dissipation, which PRINCE (6) HAL samples and rejects. The neighbourhood is specified as the scene of the Prince's delinquencies in Shakespeare's source, the FAMOUS VICTORIES.

**Ecclestone, William (active 1610–1623)** English actor, a member of the KING'S MEN. Ecclestone is one of the 26 men listed in the FIRST FOLIO as the 'Principall Actors' in Shakespeare's plays. He was with the King's Men from 1610 until at least 1623, except for two years (1611–1613) when he was with the newly formed LADY ELIZABETH'S MEN. He may have played a LORD (6) in *All's Well That Ends Well*, designated as 'E' in the Folio text of the play. He performed in many of the plays of Francis BEAUMONT (2) and John FLETCHER (2), and is thought to have specialised in playing spirited young men given to sword fights.

**Eden, Richard (c. 1521–1576)** English translator of a probable minor source for *The Tempest*. Eden's *History of Travaille* (1577) provided Shakespeare with several details for his play, including the name of CALIBAN's god, Setebos. The book, which was published posthumously, was composed of two translations; Shakespeare's material came from an account of the first circumnavigation of the globe, led by Ferdinand Magellan (c. 1480–1521).

As a young man, Eden was secretary to the statesman Lord BURGHLEY. He then travelled for several years before taking up a career as a scientific translator from Latin, Italian, and Spanish. He helped advance the capabilities of English seamanship with his *Arte of Navigation* (1561), from the pioneering manual by the Spaniard Martin Cortes (active 1551), and his subsequent translations of various writings on navigation and exploration increased English awareness of the New World. Eden's other books, like the *History of Travaille*, focussed on the exploration of the New World, and he is regarded as the most important predecessor of Richard HAKLUYT.

**Edgar** Character in *King Lear*, the banished son of the Earl of GLOUCESTER (1). Misled by his illegitimate son EDMUND, Gloucester formally exiles Edgar to the wilderness; this action parallels King LEAR's rejection of his daughter CORDELIA. In 2.3 under threat of execution, Edgar disguises himself as a wandering lunatic. When Lear is banished by his villainous daughters the disguised Edgar accompanies him, in 3.4 and 3.6. When Gloucester is blinded and expelled because he has remained loyal to Lear, Edgar, still disguised, becomes his father's guide, in 4.1, and saves him from suicide and a murder attempt by OSWALD, in 4.6. In Act 5 Edgar finally takes control of the play, exposing Edmund and GONERIL's plot to murder the Duke of ALBANY and defeating Edmund in a trial by combat. At the play's close Edgar is invited by Albany to share in the rule of Britain; with his final lines, he offers a possible lesson to be drawn from the play—that we must be aware of our human susceptibility to folly, as Lear was not—saying, 'The weight of this sad time we must obey' (5.3.322). (In some editions these lines are given to Albany.)

As the insane Tom O'Bedlam, Edgar embodies the play's theme of disease and misery as products and emblems of human folly. Tom blames his insanity on his sexual promiscuity, thus illustrating the morbid attitude towards sex that permeates the world of the play. Similarly, when he is again himself, Edgar attributes Gloucester's tragedy to 'The dark and vicious place' (5.3.171) where Edmund was conceived, that is, to sex outside of marriage.

On the other hand, Edgar's loving loyalty to his father parallels Cordelia's to Lear. Both present a Christlike willingness to sacrifice themselves that is often cited as a lesson in accepting the will of God. Even from a non-religious viewpoint, Edgar is an agent of redemption, preserving order and goodness where chaos and evil have threatened by acting as a guide and saviour first for Lear, then for his father, and finally for Britain as a whole. When he saves his father from suicide, in 4.6, he offers a way to renew acceptance of life. Deceiving Gloucester into believing he has jumped from a cliff and lived, Edgar declares his father's survival to be 'a miracle' (4.6.55); the blind man concludes that he should not give in to despair, but endure. Thus, Edgar illuminates a basic principle that is at the core of the tragedy: we must struggle to make the best of our lives, accepting death only when its time comes. As he says to his father, 'Men must endure / Their going hence, even as their coming hither: / Ripeness is all' (5.2.9–11).

**Edmund**    Character in *King Lear*, the unscrupulous and ambitious illegitimate son of the Earl of GLOUCES-TER (1). Edmund conspires against his legitimate brother EDGAR, who is banished into the wilderness in 2.1; he betrays his father to King LEAR's evil daughter REGAN and her husband, the Duke of CORNWALL, who put out the old man's eyes, in 3.7; and he pursues a love affair with Lear's other daughter GONERIL, with whom, in 4.2, he plots to murder her husband, the Duke of ALBANY. When Cornwall is killed the widowed Regan schemes to take Edmund from Goneril, and this unsavoury love triangle is an important part of the play's atmosphere of moral collapse.

In Act 5 Edmund leads Cornwall's army against the supporters of Lear's faithful daughter CORDELIA; victorious, he thwarts Albany's plans for mercy and imprisons Lear and Cordelia, ordering their execution. Edgar learns of the plot against Albany, charges Edmund with treason and challenges him to a trial by combat, wounding him fatally. The dying Edmund confesses his intention towards Lear, but it is too late to prevent Cordelia's death, and Lear dies of a broken heart soon thereafter.

Edmund's villainy is a central element in *King Lear*; his schemes are crisply executed and do much to provide a dramatic structure in the SUB-PLOT that the more idea-oriented main story lacks. However, Edmund is a stereotypical villain with little human complexity—his deeds are more interesting than he is himself—and his schemes are effective due to the moral weakness of others, not his compelling personality. His declaration of repentance—'some good I mean to do / Despite of mine own nature' (5.3.242–243)—is perfunctory and unconvincing. It serves to spark the final episode—Lear's fatal grief—after which Edmund is carried away to die. Albany's brusque dismissal of the news of his death demonstrates the extent of the villain's defeat; compared to the lessons to be absorbed from Lear's end, Edmund's demise is 'but a trifle here' (5.3.294).

Shakespeare identified Edmund's unscrupulous ambition with a troubling social phenomenon of his own day, the rise of the new commercially active classes—the bourgeoisie of the cities and the lesser landowners, or gentry, of the countryside. The success of these groups depended on their willingness to engage in trade and banking, as opposed to the traditional dependence on the land, and in this they were at odds with the great territorial nobles of the old aristocracy. A worldly emphasis on practical finance characterised the commercial classes, and this was regarded as unscrupulous by hostile eyes. From this point of view, Edmund represents the new man in his lack of chivalric scruples and his concern for his own advancement.

Traditionalists conventionally associated such an attitude with a new, 'modern' strain of thought, and Edmund quite plainly identifies himself with this new mode. In his first soliloquy he declares, 'Thou, Nature, art my goddess' (1.2.1), boldly stating his independence of 'the plague of custom' (1.2.3) and its man-made moral standards. Such sophisticated agnosticism arose in part from the RENAISSANCE rediscovery of classical paganism, and it was reflected in such works as the *Essays* of MONTAIGNE, which Shakespeare had read and which he admired in some respects. However, in placing these sentiments in the mouth of a self-proclaimed villain, Shakespeare declares his alliance with the old world of the aristocracy that is quite clearly represented by Lear, Gloucester, and Edgar, Edmund's enemies.

**Edward III**    An anonymous play perhaps written in part by Shakespeare but generally regarded as part of the Shakespeare APOCRYPHA. Published in 1596 by Cuthbert BURBY, *The Raigne of King Edward the third* was first ascribed to Shakespeare in 1656 by the generally unreliable William LEY. Although the 18th-century scholar Edward CAPELL supported the attribution, modern scholars are sceptical and believe that at most only parts of the play could have been written by Shakespeare. At least two writers seem to have composed the work; the principal evidence suggesting that one of them was Shakespeare is a single line—'Lilies that fester smell far worse than weeds'—that also appears in one of the SONNETS (number 94). However, Shakespeare could have remembered the image from the anonymous play, or the unknown playwright may have known the sonnet in manuscript form.

**Edward IV, King of England (1442–1483)**    Historical figure and character in *2* and *3 Henry VI* and *Richard III*. Known simply as Edward until Act 3 in *3 Henry VI*, King Edward IV receives his crown as a result of the machinations of his ambitious father, the Duke of YORK (1), and his heirs are murdered later by his brother, who succeeds him as RICHARD III.

In *2 Henry VI* Edward appears in 5.1 to support his father in his claim to the throne. Edward has only one line, which Richard immediately tops. In *3 Henry VI*, although Edward comes into his own, he continues to be overshadowed by his brother. He becomes King, but the leadership of the Yorkist cause is clearly provided by WARWICK (3), prior to that lord's defection, and by Richard. Edward displays the unscrupulous ambition that characterises the aristocrats in all the *Henry VI* plays. He baldly displays his own dishonesty, claiming that '. . . for a kingdom any oath may be broken: / I would break a thousand oaths to reign one year' (1.2.16–17). However, Edward is outclassed in criminality by his brother Richard.

Edward demonstrates a selfish disregard for the responsibilities of kingship, and his behaviour necessitates a renewal of the WARS OF THE ROSES. He ignores the benefits of an alliance with FRANCE (1) and abandons a marriage to Lady BONA in order to satisfy his lust for ELIZABETH (2). In the resulting war, he indulges in pointless bravado and permits himself to be captured in 4.3. After the final Yorkist victory, Edward casually allows Richard to murder the finally displaced King Henry, demonstrating a lack of concern for civil order that typifies England's corrupt public life. In *Richard III* Edward appears only in 2.1, on his deathbed. He learns of the death of CLARENCE (1), and his dismay, it is implied, leads to his own rapid demise. His death is reported in 2.2.

Shakespeare's treatment of the reign of Edward IV is extremely unhistorical, for the playwright wished to emphasise the disruption of English public life that the coming of the TUDOR dynasty repaired. Edward's 22-year tenure is presented as a rapid succession of quarrels and battles. In fact, though, Edward was a very competent ruler. He was judiciously merciful to most of the Lancastrians; he introduced badly needed financial reforms; he withdrew from France—at the cost of considerable personal popularity, but to the immense benefit of the country. His marriage to Elizabeth was not the chief, or even an important, cause of Warwick's rebellion. Although his lusty appetites, given much emphasis in the play, were well known to his contemporaries, they do not seem to have interfered with his public duty, although it has been suggested that over-indulgence in wine and women may have resulted in his early death.

**Edwards (Edwardes), Richard (c. 1523–1566)** English poet, musician and playwright, author of a minor source for *The Two Gentlemen of Verona* and of a song quoted in *Romeo and Juliet*. Edwards was choral director of the Children of the Chapel (see CHILDREN'S COMPANIES). Under his direction the choirboys performed two of his plays, *Damon and Pythias* (1565) and *Palamon and Arcite* (1566) two of the earliest musical dramas. The former, published in 1571, was a tale of male friendship, an ancient genre, and it provided minor details for Shakespeare's similar effort, *The Two Gentlemen*. *Palamon and Arcite*, like *The Two Noble Kinsmen*, was based on CHAUCER's *The Knight's Tale*, but it is not believed to have influenced Shakespeare and his collaborator, John FLETCHER (2). In *Romeo and Juliet*, PETER (2) sings a few lines of a well-known song, 'In

Commendation of Musique', written by Edwards and published in his posthumous *The Paradise of Dainty Devises* (1575), an anthology of his and others' works.

**Egeon (Aegeon)** Character in *The Comedy of Errors*, the condemned man who proves to be the father of the long-separated twins ANTIPHOLUS OF EPHESUS and ANTIPHOLUS OF SYRACUSE. Egeon's tale is presented only in the first and last scenes of the play, framing the principal plot. A wandering merchant from Syracuse, in Sicily, Egeon comes to EPHESUS, on the Aegean coast of Asia Minor, not knowing that hostility has arisen between that city and his home. The penalty of death or a large ransom has been imposed by each city upon any citizen of the other who enters it. Egeon has thus been sentenced to pay a thousand marks of ransom or die.

In 1.1 his situation is revealed in his conversation with Solinus, the DUKE (8) of Ephesus. Egeon elaborates on the tragedy that has enveloped his life, beginning when he was separated from his wife and one of his infant twin sons in a shipwreck 23 years before, never to see them again. The other son, at the age of 18, had insisted on setting out to search for his lost brother. Egeon himself has unsuccessfully spent the last five years looking for news of either twin. The Duke, sympathetic though stern, offers Egeon the freedom of the city for the coming day so that he can beg or borrow the money to pay his ransom. These hours become the time of the action of the play.

Egeon does not reappear until well into the final scene of the play, but the audience cannot forget his desperate plight. Although the comic misadventures and errors that follow are chiefly farcical, they are coloured by our sombre recollection of Egeon's imminent fate.

In the final scene, Egeon is escorted on stage by the Duke, accompanied by the EXECUTIONER and seemingly doomed to die. The Duke reminds us of his plight (5.1.130–132) before being sidetracked into attempting to unravel the confusions of the main plot. Amidst these complexities, Egeon, upon seeing Antipholus of Ephesus, believes him to be the other Antipholus, the son who left Syracuse five years earlier. He identifies himself to this Antipholus, only to be rejected, of course, for Antipholus of Ephesus does not know him. Egeon's stricken response is rendered in a moving passage (5.1.298–322); the Duke concludes that Egeon's 'age and dangers' have driven him mad.

As the confusion and errors are eventually resolved and the play reaches its conclusion, Egeon is a spectator, for the most part; the principals in this dénouement are the two sets of twins and EMILIA (1), Egeon's long-lost wife, whose recognition of her husband begins the resolution. Although he has good lines in both 1.1 and 5.1 and is an important figure, Egeon is not so much a fully developed character as he is a vehicle for a simple, secondary plot, an evocation of pathos intended to temper our view of the central wrangle of error and delusion.

**Egeus** Character in *A Midsummer Night's Dream,* the father of HERMIA. Egeus' angry demand for severe punishment of his daughter for refusing to marry DE-METRIUS (2) interrupts the blissful anticipation of marriage with which the play opens. Duke THESEUS hopes to persuade Egeus to abandon his intentions, but we see in 4.1, when Egeus and the Duke discover the sleeping lovers in the enchanted woods, that his attempts have not succeeded. Egeus insists that LYSAN-DER be executed for having tried to elope with Hermia. His harshness makes him no more sympathetic to the Duke than to the audience, and Theseus takes evident pleasure in announcing, 'Egeus, I will overbear your will' (4.1.178). Shakespeare apparently took the name Egeus from CHAUCER's 'The Knight's Tale' (see *A Midsummer Night's Dream,* 'Sources of the Play'), in which Egeus is Theseus' father.

**Eglamour** Minor character in *The Two Gentlemen of Verona,* the gentleman who helps SILVIA flee her father's court in search of VALENTINE in 5.1. In selecting Eglamour as her confidant and guide, Silvia acclaims him 'valiant, wise, . . . well-accomplished' (4.3.13) and is certain she can rely on his honour and courage. Yet, when Silvia is captured by the OUTLAWS, he is reported to have fled ignominiously, 'being nimble-footed' (5.3.6). This unlikely inconsistency, along with the fact that one of JULIA's suitors is also named Eglamour (1.2.9), has sparked some debate. This may simply be one of the many instances of Shakespeare's carelessness in matters of detail, or it may reflect the former existence of two versions of the play. Also, it may be that a jocularly presented instance of cowardice is intended to undercut the seriousness of the romantic ideals that the play simultaneously depends on and laughs at.

**Egyptian** Minor character in *Antony and Cleopatra,* a messenger for CLEOPATRA. The 'poor Egyptian', as he describes himself in 5.1.52, appears before Octavius CAESAR (2), who has just defeated the forces of Cleopatra and Mark ANTONY. He has been sent to learn Caesar's orders to the Egyptian queen; Caesar sends him back with a conciliatory message. This episode demonstrates Cleopatra's changed circumstances; she is no longer mistress of her own fate, a situation that she will find intolerable. The Egyptian's modest mission ushers in the final development of the play.

**Elbow** Minor character in *Measure for Measure,* a comic constable of VIENNA. Elbow brings POMPEY (1) to court, in 2.1, and attempts to prosecute FROTH for an unspecified insult to his, Elbow's, wife. However, with his comical mispronunciations and unconscious double meanings he is a stereotypical CLOWN (1), and he cannot make a sensible accusation. He is foiled by Pompey's humorous evasions, which result in the dismissal of the case. The episode serves as comic relief from the increasingly tense main plot. It also illustrates vividly the SUB-PLOT's world of petty vice and crime, standing in striking contrast with the more rigid world of the DUKE (9), ANGELO (2), and ISABELLA. In 3.2 Elbow has the satisfaction of bringing Pompey to prison, though his triumph is not so humorous as his defeat. Compared to his better-known predecessor DOGBERRY, Elbow is a less successful version of an ancient character type—the bumbling, foolish constable. His is a familiar figure in traditional English drama: in 2.1.169, ESCALUS (2) compares Elbow and Pompey to Justice and Iniquity, characters in a MORALITY PLAY.

**Eld (Elde), George (d. 1624)** London printer and publisher, producer of first editions of *Troilus and Cressida* and the SONNETS. In 1609 Eld printed the QUARTO edition of Shakespeare's play for publishers Richard BONIAN and Henry WALLEY, and Thomas THORPE's edition of the Sonnets. Eld himself sometimes published the plays he printed, including THE PURITAN (1607), which was attributed to 'W. S.', perhaps in an effort to falsely associate the work with Shakespeare. Eld, apprenticed to a printer from 1592–1600, acquired his business by marrying a woman twice the widow of earlier owners. He died in a plague epidemic, but little more is known of his life.

**Eleanor (Elinor) of Aquitaine, Queen of England (1122–1204)** Historical figure and character in *King John,* mother of King JOHN (3). Queen Eleanor is a bold and forthright character, quick to respond to possible insult to her son, whether from CHATILLON (1.1.5) or from King PHILIP (2) of FRANCE (1) (2.1.120). She is fully prepared to fight (1.1.40), but she is also a wise diplomat, equally ready to make peace when it seems profitable (2.1.468–479). It is clear that she is a very important figure in John's life, and his distraction following her death just as the French invade, in 4.2, is completely understandable.

The historical Eleanor of Aquitaine was one of the most remarkable women of the Middle Ages. The daughter of the Duke of Aquitaine, she inherited her father's duchy, a powerful independent territory in what is now the south of France, at the age of 15. Three months later, she married the Dauphin of France; one month after that, her new father-in-law died, and she became Queen of France. However, she bore no heirs to Louis VII. This fact, the great personality differences between herself and the King, and her marital infidelities, referred to in 2.1.125, resulted in their divorce in 1152. Eleanor was publicly humiliated in the process, but as Duchess of Aquitaine, the greatest heiress in Europe, she was able to avenge herself immediately by marrying Louis' greatest rival, Henry II of England. By Henry she bore four sons, among them both Richard I and John. However, her relations with her second husband were no better than with her first, and she incited her sons to rebel against him. When the revolt failed, she was imprisoned for 15 years, being released only upon Henry's death. She devoted the rest of her life to supporting her sons, and her death in 1204, at 83, must indeed have seemed a monumental loss to John, although it occurred many years before the crisis with which it is associated in the play.

**Eliot (1), John (b. 1562)**  English author and translator, creator of a minor source for *Romeo and Juliet* and several other plays. Eliot's *Ortho-Epia Gallica* (1593) was a collection of lively colloquial essays—written in French and published with Eliot's English translation on facing pages—that dealt with LONDON life, European travel, and contemporary French poetry. It contained a translation of a poem by the French poet Guillaume DU BARTAS that influenced the lovers' debate on bird song in 3.5. Other material in *Ortho-Epia* inspired minor details in other plays as well, most notably elements of PISTOL's roguish speech.

Like Shakespeare, Eliot was from WARWICKSHIRE. After he attended Oxford he became a novice monk, but he withdrew before he took his vows. Instead, he wandered in Europe and supported himself as a schoolmaster, a hack journalist, and, possibly, a spy for one (or more) of the factions in the religious and civil wars of FRANCE (1). He returned to England in 1589—apparently fleeing the aftermath of King Henri III's assassination—and settled in London as a teacher and translator of French. His *Survey or Topographical Description of France* appeared in 1592, followed by the popular *Ortho-Epia*. After this Eliot disappeared from history. Scholars presume he returned to France, possibly when King Henri IV was crowned in 1594. Eliot was probably acquainted with Shakespeare, for they are known to have had mutual friends in the London literary and theatrical worlds.

**Eliot (2), Thomas Stearns (1888–1965)**  American-British poet and critic. T. S. Eliot is best known as one of the leading poets of the 20th century, but he also wrote a great deal of literary criticism. Much of this focussed on the Elizabethan era and included critical essays on a number of Shakespeare's plays. As a Shakespearean critic he is notorious for his assessment of *Hamlet* as 'an artistic failure'. Less controversially, he observed, 'About any one so great as Shakespeare, it is probable that we can never be right; and if we can never be right, it is better that we should from time to time change our way of being wrong'.

References to Shakespearean characters occur in a number of Eliot's poems, and his 'Coriolan' (a suite of two poems: 'Triumphal March' and 'Difficulties of a Statesman') probably helped spark the tremendous increase in critical and theatrical attention given Shakespeare's *Coriolanus* in the 20th century. Eliot's enthusiasm for, and perceptive studies of, Elizabethan literature certainly did much to generate a revival of interest in the subject as a whole. Eliot also wrote several modern plays in verse, the best known of which is *Murder in the Cathedral* (1935).

**Elizabeth (1), Queen of England (1533–1603)**  Ruler of England for much of Shakespeare's life and a very minor character in *Henry VIII*, written 10 years after her death. Elizabeth appears as an infant—that is, as a prop held by an actor—in 5.4 of the play, where she is the subject of a long eulogy by Archbishop CRANMER. Queen Elizabeth was the most important patron of ELIZABETHAN THEATRE: her influence was essential in protecting the theatrical profession from Puritan-inspired prohibitions, and her court provided an

*Elizabeth I ruled while England became a world power. The works of Shakespeare are only the most prominent of many great artistic and intellectual achievements that occurred in England during her reign.* (Courtesy of Colonial Williamsburg)

important source of income and prestige for the leading LONDON acting companies. She especially favoured Shakespeare's company, the CHAMBERLAIN'S MEN, and he often performed for her.

The queen is said to have been so pleased with FALSTAFF in the *Henry IV* plays, that she commanded the playwright to produce a play in which the fat knight falls in love; the result was *The Merry Wives of Windsor*—written, according to legend, in two weeks. There may be a germ of truth to the tale, for *The Merry Wives* was probably written for a royal occasion. In any case, Elizabeth's fondness for Shakespeare's plays is testified to in Ben JONSON's accolade, printed in the FIRST FOLIO, in which he refers to the playwright's 'flights . . . That so did take Eliza . . .'.

Shakespeare rendered appropriate tribute. Twice in *A Midsummer Night's Dream*, passages subtly allude to Elizabeth, probably because she was expected to be present at the wedding celebration for which the play is believed to have been written. In 2.1.155–164 she is complimented by a lyrical description that evokes the conventional allegorical representations of the queen in popular prints of the day. In 5.1.89–105 Duke THESEUS (1) praises a monarch's benevolent reception of tongue-tied subjects, behaviour that Elizabeth is known to have prided herself on.

Cranmer's eulogy to Elizabeth in *Henry VIII*, delivered by an important English national hero, doubtless reflects the nostalgia for her reign felt by England a decade after her death. Elizabeth was the only child of King HENRY VIII and Anne Boleyn, the ANNE (1) of *Henry VIII*. After succeeding her Catholic stepsister Mary (ruled 1553–1558), she had a long and successful reign. (Only Queen Victoria [1837–1901] has since outlasted her.) Under Elizabeth, Protestantism was firmly established in England, and the nation showed its strength against its Catholic enemies with the defeat of the Spanish Armada in 1588. Elizabeth's reign also encompassed magnificent achievements in English literature. Although drama itself was not appreciated as art, the great value of the prose and poetry of Philip SIDNEY, Edmund SPENSER, Thomas NORTH, and others—including the Shakespeare of *Venus and Adonis* and *The Rape of Lucrece*—was recognised and appreciated. In the early 17th century, Elizabeth's reign was already considered—as it has been ever since—England's golden age.

**Elizabeth (2) Woodville (Woodvile), Lady Grey (later Queen, 1437–1492)** Historical figure and character in *3 Henry VI* and *Richard III*, the wife of King EDWARD IV. Her brother is Lord RIVERS in the same plays, and her father is Richard WOODVILLE in *1 Henry VI*. Known as Lady Grey until Act 4 of *3 Henry VI*, Elizabeth becomes Queen when Edward marries her after she refuses to become his mistress. Edward was already promised to Lady BONA of FRANCE (1), so the marriage

becomes a stimulus for warfare. Elizabeth is a pawn in the troubled politics of the time. However, she displays dignity in an awkward position, as in her speech at 4.1.66–73, and her instinct to protect her unborn child in 4.4 is also noteworthy. She quite properly distrusts the treacherous and violent noblemen of the disturbed nation, but she is powerless.

In *Richard III* Elizabeth is cursed in 1.3 by the former Queen, MARGARET (1), and sees her enemy's wishes come true as Edward dies and Richard murders her two sons by Edward. He also has her brother, Rivers, and a son, GREY (2), executed, while another son, DORSET, is forced into exile. However, Richard fails to exploit her family further. Elizabeth resists him in 4.4, when he attempts to win her approval of his plan to marry her daughter. She rejects his efforts to swear an oath, stifling him until he is reduced to wishing ill on himself, fatefully (4.4.397–409). Elizabeth suspends the conversation at 4.4.428–429, leaving the resolution of the matter in doubt. (Her daughter is betrothed by the victorious invader RICHMOND at the play's end.)

Historically, WARWICK's alienation from Edward was provoked by disagreements over policy and not simply by the King's marriage, as Shakespeare would have it, but among the minor causes was the behaviour of the greedy Woodvilles. Elizabeth Woodville was the first commoner to become Queen of England, and her many male relatives exploited her new position by marrying the cream of eligible heiresses. However, Elizabeth attracted supporters when, after the death of King Edward, her son inherited the crown. Edward had appointed Richard the boy's Protector, with ruling power, before he died; Elizabeth's allies attempted to circumvent this arrangement with a coup. They were defeated by Richard, as in the play, though he treated Elizabeth herself with great generosity and provided her with a distinguished place at his court.

Richard repeatedly denied rumours that he planned to marry Elizabeth's daughter. In fact, since he had in part based his claim to the throne on the charge that Edward himself was illegitimate, an attempt to marry his daughter would seem self-defeating. However, Shakespeare's sources reported the rumours, and the playwright expanded them into a powerful scene. Elizabeth herself had other plans; it appears that she secretly allied herself with Richmond (later King Henry VII) before his invasion, with the agreement that, should he succeed, he would marry the daughter, which he did. Elizabeth lived out her life as an honoured dowager at the court of her son-in-law.

**Elizabeth (3) Stuart, Queen of Bohemia (1596–1662)** Daughter of King JAMES I of England and Scotland, patron of a theatre company, LADY ELIZABETH'S MEN, and somewhat later an international figure by virtue of her ill-starred marriage to a powerful German prince, Frederick V, Elector Palatine and briefly King of BOHEMIA. Elizabeth's marriage was celebrated by a season-long series of festivities over the winter of 1612–1613, in which Shakespeare's acting company, the KING'S MEN, had a notable part. They put on 20 different plays, eight of them Shakespeare's, probably including *1* and *2 Henry IV, Julius Caesar, Much Ado About Nothing, The Winter's Tale,* and *The Tempest.* (Some scholars believe that the MASQUE in 4.1 of *The Tempest* was inserted into the play for this occasion.) Her marriage stirred nation-wide enthusiasm and was regarded as the consummation of an idyllic romance.

However, Elizabeth's destiny was tragic. After five years of comfort and pleasure at Frederick's capital in Heidelberg, the couple were swept up in the complex religious politics of the Holy Roman Empire. Frederick unwisely accepted the throne of Bohemia, a Protestant country that had rebelled against the Catholic Hapsburgs, rulers of the empire. After a brief reign—Frederick is known to history as 'the Winter King'—he was deposed by the emperor, in the first phase of the Thirty Years War. Elizabeth spent the rest of her life in exile, mostly in The Hague, attempting to recover her husband's position.

Frederick died in 1632, leaving Elizabeth unhappy and, by royal standards, poor, especially after the STUART DYNASTY was also dethroned by the English revolution. She had 13 children but quarrelled with them all; when her eldest son recovered the Palatine Electorate, he refused to provide her with a home. Finally, with the restoration of the monarchy in England, she returned to London in 1661, only to die within months. Eventually, her grandson ruled England as George I (ruled 1714–1727).

**Elizabethan Drama**   Art of writing for the theatre as practised in England during the reign of Queen ELIZABETH (1) (1558–1603). Shakespeare was undeniably the major figure of Elizabethan drama, but many other playwrights were active, and the period constitutes a Golden Age in English drama, indeed in the drama of the world.

In 1558, when Elizabeth became queen, almost no English drama was being written; Elizabethan drama came of age in the late 1570s, growing out of the competition between the CHILDREN'S COMPANIES, composed of schoolboys, and the adult companies who had come to LONDON under the protection of noble patrons, both seeking the favour of the queen and her courtiers (see ELIZABETHAN THEATRE). The children's companies performed Latin plays (both ancient Roman works and modern imitations) and English works modelled on them. These plays had greater appeal to the educated tastes of the court than did the often bawdy INTERLUDE—derived from native English roots in medieval festivals and the MORALITY PLAY—that was the stock-in-trade of the adult companies, just

beginning to perform in public theatres. The adult companies, however, sought playwrights who could appeal to court tastes as well and found them in the literary world growing up in early modern London. A tremendous wellspring of talent was tapped, and thousands of plays were produced over the next several decades.

In the 1580s Elizabethan drama was dominated by a group of playwrights known as the UNIVERSITY WITS, who brought together various influences: classical literature and its contemporary imitation in ACADEMIC DRAMA, morality plays, and contemporary RENAISSANCE literature from Italy and France. In the 1590s a broader range of playwrights emerged, including Shakespeare.

Elizabethan TRAGEDY (which was strongly influenced by the ancient dramas of SENECA) consisted of two general varieties. The REVENGE PLAY was introduced by Thomas KYD in his very popular *Spanish Tragedy* (c. 1588) and was most fully developed in *Hamlet.* John MARSTON was a later practitioner of the revenge play. Another sort of tragedy presented grandiose fantasies about the downfall of powerful rulers; this genre burst forth in the *Tamburlaine* of Christopher MARLOWE (1), in which BLANK VERSE was established as the medium for Elizabethan drama. Shakespeare brought the genre to complex new levels in such works as *Macbeth, King Lear,* and the ROMAN PLAYS.

Elizabethan COMEDY took several distinct forms. Romantic comedy, a popular genre centred on young love, reached its pinnacle in Shakespeare's comedies of the 1590s, such as *Much Ado About Nothing* and *As You Like It.* Lesser figures writing this sort of play included Robert GREENE (2) and Thomas DEKKER. Towards the end of the 1590s, a variation arose, the COMEDY OF HUMOURS, in which bold character types were employed to ridicule contemporary behaviour. Ben JONSON was the leading exponent of the comedy of humours. The so-called court comedy was written with an aristocratic audience in mind. These plays often used mythological or classical subjects and were distinguished by their emphasis on refined dialogue and prominent allusions to Renaissance learning. John LYLY was the most important writer of court comedy; his plays influenced Shakespeare's early work, especially *Love's Labour's Lost.* Another category, the chronicle or HISTORY PLAY, while it had roots in didactic, allegorical dramas akin to morality plays, was essentially developed by Shakespeare, in his enactments of the WARS OF THE ROSES.

Elizabethan drama is sometimes considered to include work from the next two reigns, those of Kings JAMES I and Charles I, until the theatres of England were closed by revolution (1603–1642). However, the more restricted sense is used here, for the subsequent period, which includes Shakespeare's late work, saw pronounced changes in taste and in theatrical techniques, making for differences in tone and subject matter (see JACOBEAN DRAMA).

**Elizabethan Theatre**   Professional presentation of dramas as practised in Shakespeare's time, especially during the reign of Queen ELIZABETH (1) (1558–1603). Elizabethan theatre was very different from today's theatre in its organisation, methods, and even in the nature of the buildings used. Before the 1570s English theatre barely existed, but in the course of Shakespeare's lifetime, a thriving centre of dramatic art evolved in LONDON.

At the outset of Elizabeth's reign in 1558, English drama consisted largely of religious enactments such as the MORALITY PLAY presented at medieval festivals, and these were generally performed by members of the trade guilds of different towns. Professional entertainers were mostly wandering acrobats, musicians, and clowns, more like circus performers than actors. They were legally classed with vagabonds and could be jailed merely for pursuing their calling. Some troupes, however, were taken into the households of aristocrats and were therefore exempt from such laws. They provided entertainment for the lord and his guests, often performing an INTERLUDE at a meal, a much more drama-like feature than the 'feats of activitie' commonly recorded. These troupes often travelled, performing for other nobles and gradually taking over the guilds' functions for the dramatic elements of seasonal festivals.

London naturally became a focus for such activities. London companies were still under the patronage of some great nobleman but were no longer closely affiliated with his household, though they might perform at his country home on special occasions. (The law required that actors be members of a noble household, and certain nobles co-operated with the actors, but the patrons generally had nothing else to do with the operations of a company.) Performances in London were usually held in large inns or taverns, most of which were within the walls of the city. However, the London government, largely controlled by Puritans, was particularly hostile to actors, so the companies began to arrange their performances in nearby areas. In 1576 the THEATRE, the first building in England intended solely for the performance of plays, was built by James BURBAGE (2), just north of the city line. Other playhouses soon followed.

In a different social world, Queen Elizabeth catered extensively to performers, and the royal court became a second centre of the nascent theatre world. In 1574 the queen proclaimed one of the acting companies, LEICESTER'S MEN, to be members of her household and thus exempt from even London's laws against performing. Also during this time students at schools, universities, and the INNS OF COURT, affected by the RENAISSANCE revival of classical literature, began to

read and perform the plays of ancient ROME and their modern imitations. These sophisticated entertainments were more to the taste of the queen and her courtiers than the interludes of the adult acting companies, so the CHILDREN'S COMPANIES were generally more featured at court. Entrepreneurs such as Burbage and Philip HENSLOWE then began to hire dramatists to produce work that would attract sophisticated patrons and gain them the prestige of association with the court. ELIZABETHAN DRAMA was born.

For almost a decade, Leicester's Men were the most important theatre company in London, but the QUEEN'S MEN, created by Elizabeth in 1583, soon eclipsed them. In the early 1590s, two other companies arose that were to dominate Elizabethan theatre thereafter: the ADMIRAL'S MEN and STRANGE'S MEN, later the CHAMBERLAIN'S MEN, Shakespeare's company. Other companies included OXFORD'S MEN, PEMBROKE'S MEN, and SUSSEX'S MEN. They played at court and at the Theatre and the other public playhouses: the CURTAIN THEATRE (built near the Theatre in 1577), the ROSE THEATRE (the first in SOUTHWARK, which became the most important theatre district), the SWAN THEATRE, the GLOBE THEATRE, and the FORTUNE THEATRE. Plays were also staged at the CROSS KEYS INN, until London outlawed the theatre in 1596, and in an outlying district, NEWINGTON BUTTS.

These theatres were generally roughly cylindrical, three-storied buildings surrounding a central, unroofed space containing the stage, built out from a section of the building that served as a backstage area. (Indoor theatres appeared somewhat later, in Shakespeare's lifetime but during the reign of King JAMES I; they are part of the story of JACOBEAN DRAMA.) The actual appearance of these theatres is obscure, since the only evidence is a single drawing—of unknown reliability—depicting the interior of the Swan Theatre and the contract for the building of the Fortune. Some spectators stood on the ground around the stage, within the 'wooden O' (*Henry V*, Prologue, 13) of the building; the 'groundlings', as they were called, paid a cheap admission price. Each floor of the building was divided into galleries, which offered a better view of the stage and were more expensive. In the most expensive galleries seating was provided, and seats were also available, at the highest price, on the stage itself. A canopy, called the 'heavens' or the 'shadow', extended over the stage from its rear wall. The stage itself probably contained one or more trapdoors, often used to represent graves or the mouth of hell. (Supernatural phenomena were popular on the Elizabethan stage, and Shakespeare often presented them [see, e.g., APPARITION, ASNATH, and GHOST].) Behind the stage, the building contained dressing rooms—the 'tiring [attiring] house'—and upper rooms for musicians and for the machinery used to hoist actors or props in spectacular ascents or descents through the 'heavens'. Atop the whole structure was a hut, or 'penthouse', from which flags were flown and trumpets sounded to announce a performance.

Plays were held outdoors (very few seem to have been cancelled by weather, suggesting a hardy audience). They usually began at two o'clock in the afternoon, and they had to be finished before nightfall, for the only illumination besides the sun were torches to provide partial relief on an overcast day or at the onset of dusk. (This limitation is often incorporated into the texture of the play. For instance, near the end of *Julius Caesar* a character witnesses the suicide of CASSIUS and observes, 'O setting sun, / As in thy red rays thou dost sink to night, / So in his red blood Cassius' day is set / The sun of Rome is set. Our day is gone' [5.3.60–63], and the audience could confirm his remarks with their own eyes.) The average duration of a performance was about two hours—the CHORUS (2) of *Romeo and Juliet* speaks of 'the two hours' traffic of our stage' (Prologue, 12)—though many plays must have taken longer. Often the play was followed by a jig—a brief, often bawdy, miniature comic opera, with wild dancing and simple lyrics set to the melodies of popular SONGS.

A performance in the Elizabethan theatre was very different from one today. The stages were simply raised areas amid the audience, with very little if any scenery. No curtain opened on a prepared scene or closed on a finished one. The actors had to enter at the beginning and immediately command the audience's attention, with the consequence that scenes tended to begin with powerful material. They also had to exit at the end to make room for the next sequence, so scenes generally did not end on a note of crisis, as is common in modern plays.

Acting styles seem to have been very different as well, according to written evidence that values a very formal and artificial style. Rhetorical flourishes and conventional poses created a distance that was felt to enhance the effect of the lines. Realistic portrayals were simply not expected, though some of Shakespeare's characters begin the evolution towards modern dramatic realism. Costumes were contemporary for the most part, regardless of the setting of the play, except for special outfits that conventionally identified figures from the classical world (a toga or a plumed helmet and armour), from the exotic Middle East (billowing trousers, a turban, and a scimitar), or supernatural beings such as gods or ghosts.

The strangest feature of the Elizabethan stage, by comparison with our own, was the absence of women. In the children's companies all the roles were taken by boys, but among the adult companies the effect was even stranger, for the boys played the women (though old, comical women, such as Mistress QUICKLY or the NURSE [3] in *Romeo and Juliet,* could be played by men). Even then boys as the heroines of romance must have

seemed somewhat comic, for playwrights often build on this peculiarity by having the heroine disguise herself as a boy. Thus, a boy plays a girl who plays a boy. A further complication was often invoked by having a woman (played by a boy) mistakenly fall in love with the disguised woman (also played by a boy). The situation is not only comical, but also suggestive of hidden depths of human sexuality. The use of boys as women was commonly attacked by Puritan critics as immoral, and many non-Puritans agreed. When the English theatres were reopened in 1660, after being closed by the Puritan revolution, only women were allowed to play women.

In Elizabethan times the boys also played the parts of boys, of course, and some of these roles, though brief, were demanding (see, e.g., BOY [3], SON [1], MOTH). A boy was sometimes apprenticed to an adult actor, who trained, educated, and supported him until he was capable of playing men's roles. The adult recovered his expenses by 'selling' the trained boy to an acting company, perhaps his own. Neither party was bound by strict contracts, as in other trades, for members of noble households—as actors formally were—were not covered by the laws on apprenticeship.

An actor's status as an aristocratic retainer was merely a legal fiction, for acting companies were actually commercial enterprises, with share-holding partners and paid employees. Some companies, including the Admiral's Men, used a performance space owned by an entrepreneur, such as Philip HENSLOWE or Francis LANGLEY, while others, typified by the Chamberlain's Men, controlled their own theatre. Five of the Chamberlain's Men, including Shakespeare, owned half of the Globe, with Cuthbert BURBAGE (1) and Richard BURBAGE (3)—himself an actor in the company—owning the other half. As owners, or 'housekeepers', these men profited from the owner's share of the theatre's receipts and paid the owner's expenses; as partners in the acting company, or 'sharers', they profited from the other side of the arrangement. The housekeepers received half the receipts from the galleries, with which they maintained the building and paid the ground rent for the land on which it stood. The sharers received the company's part of a performance's receipts: all of the income from the cheaper admissions paid by the groundlings and half of that from the more expensive galleries. They shared this as profit after meeting their own expenses. They hired their employees—extra actors, stagehands, musicians, and others—and paid for costumes and props; most important and most expensive, they commissioned dramas.

Playwrights sold plays to acting companies, who then owned the script; unless he was a member of the company, the author received no further income from his efforts. Some playwrights worked under contract, especially with Henslowe, who employed dozens of writers. Others, most notably Shakespeare, wrote only for a company in which they were sharers. A few, like Ben JONSON, free-lanced, writing for a variety of companies in succession.

Plays were performed in a repertoire that was rotated frequently; a given play was rarely staged more than once a week but might be staged frequently during a season, which might include a dozen or more plays. Popular plays, such as those of Shakespeare or Christopher MARLOWE (1), might be revived periodically over many years or rewritten to appeal to changing fashions.

New plays were in great demand and were produced at an extraordinary rate. It has been estimated that at least several thousand plays were written for London theatre companies during the years of Shakespeare's career; he himself wrote 39 (including CARDENIO), for an average of almost two a year. Thomas HEYWOOD (2) declared that he had written or collaborated on 220 plays. Once a company bought a play, they submitted it, with the necessary fee, to the MASTER OF THE REVELS, who had to approve it for performance. He might refuse or demand changes for political or religious reasons (see CENSORSHIP). The company might sell a script to a publisher, who then profited exclusively from it, but they preferred not to, for as long as they owned it, they could anticipate further profits. Thus, the vast majority of the plays that were written in Shakespeare's time were never published and are lost.

**Elsinore** Danish seaport (Helsingør in Danish), setting for *Hamlet*. The royal castle of the KING (5) of DENMARK, located in Elsinore, is the setting for every scene in the play except 5.1, which is set in a nearby graveyard; three dramatically striking early scenes (1.1, 1.4–5), are set on its fortified walls. The town is mentioned several times (e.g., in 1.2.174), but it is not described at all.

Elsinore was well known to Elizabethan England, being located on the narrow straits between Denmark and Sweden, an important trade route for English ships. It was the site of a Danish fortress, Kronborg, doubtless the castle envisioned by Shakespeare, from which tolls were collected from all ships entering or leaving the Baltic Sea. The castle is now a maritime museum where Shakespeare's plays are regularly performed. English acting companies travelled to Elsinore in 1585 and 1586—and possibly on other, unrecorded tours—and it has been speculated that Shakespeare may have been among the players who performed there, although there is no clear evidence of this, and his faulty knowledge of the physical place—Elsinore has no 'cliff / That beetles o'er his base into the sea' (1.4.70–71), for example—suggests that he never made the trip.

**Ely (1), Bishop of** Character in *Henry VIII*. See BISHOP (3).

**Ely (2), John Fordham, Bishop of (d. 1435)** Historical figure and character in *Henry V* who supports the Archbishop of CANTERBURY (1) in urging war to King HENRY V. In 1.1 Ely and Canterbury express their hope that a state of war—especially when supported by a large donation from the church—will forestall the introduction of legislation requiring a vast state seizure of church property. In 1.2 Ely, Canterbury, and others encourage Henry to invade FRANCE (1).

**Ely (3), John Morton, Bishop of (c. 1420–1500)** Historical figure and minor character in *Richard III*, a pawn in the scenario arranged by RICHARD III as he strikes at Lord HASTINGS (2) in 3.4. At a council meeting, Richard requests that the genial Ely send for some strawberries from his garden, thereby establishing a mood of cordiality that he shortly shatters with his accusations of treason. Both Hastings and the audience have been lulled into a false sense of security that is rudely smashed, in a manner symbolic of Richard's effect on the entire realm. As ineffectual as Ely seems here, he is later, at 4.3.46, said to have joined the forces of the Earl of RICHMOND, thus contributing to Richard's downfall.

The historical John Morton had been a rising young ecclesiastical lawyer when the WARS OF THE ROSES broke out. He became a firm Lancastrian, to the extent of joining Queen MARGARET (1) in exile. However, after the Yorkist victory, he submitted to the victors and resumed his clerical and legal career with great success. He was appointed Bishop of Ely in 1479, and he was the executor of the will of King EDWARD IV. But under Richard he fared less well. After the incident described above, Ely, as an adherent of the young PRINCE (5), was among those arrested. He was placed in the TOWER OF LONDON, but the Duke of BUCKINGHAM (2) took over his custody after several years and recruited him to his rebellious conspiracy. Ely joined Richmond abroad, and when that Earl was crowned as Henry VII, the Bishop became a prominent member of his government. Morton was also to become the patron of the young Thomas MORE, whose history was Shakespeare's source for the strawberry anecdote. Thus its historical accuracy seems certain.

**Ely Palace portrait** Possible portrait of Shakespeare. The Ely Palace portrait, discovered in 1845, bears an inscription stating that the anonymous sitter was 39 years old in 1603—as was Shakespeare—when it was painted. It closely resembles the DROESHOUT engraving, one of the two authoritative likenesses of the playwright, and it may be the original from which the engraver worked. However, it may also be a postdated copy of the engraving; scholars remain uncertain. The portrait at one time hung in the official residence of a 19th-century bishop of Ely and is now owned by the Shakespeare's Birthplace Trust and hangs in STRATFORD.

**Elyot, Sir Thomas (c. 1490–1546)** English author, an influence on several of Shakespeare's plays. Elyot's most famous work is *The Boke Called the Governour* (1531), an extended essay on political morality and the education of statesmen. Echoes of this work appear in a number of Shakespeare's early works, including *The Two Gentlemen of Verona* and *2 Henry IV*. Elyot covers the WARS OF THE ROSES at length, and observes that they represent a deterioration of the English nation's unity that the TUDOR dynasty had fortunately repaired. These ideas were highly important to Shakespeare when he wrote his HISTORY PLAYS. Though such doctrines were also widely available elsewhere, Shakespeare's evident familiarity with the *Governour* makes it clear that he was especially influenced by these ideas through Elyot.

Elyot was an important figure in RENAISSANCE English literature. He translated a number of Latin works, promoted the study of the classics, and compiled the first Latin-English dictionary (1538). He also published a popular health manual. He served King HENRY VIII as a diplomat, and attempted fruitlessly to gain the support of the Holy Roman Emperor for Henry's divorce of KATHERINE of Aragon.

**Emery, John (1777–1822)** English actor. An actor from childhood, Emery was typically cast as an old man even in his teens, and he became a leading character actor and comedian. He was best known for his portrayal of CALIBAN, and he was also acclaimed as DOGBERRY, the GRAVE-DIGGER in *Hamlet*, and SIR TOBY BELCH. Emery also had a career as a successful painter.

**Emilia (1) (Aemilia)** Character in *The Comedy of Errors*, the stern and peremptory Abbess of the PRIORY who is revealed to be the long-lost wife of EGEON and mother of the twins ANTIPHOLUS OF EPHESUS and ANTIPHOLUS OF SYRACUSE. She first appears in the final scene (at 5.1.37), after Antipholus and DROMIO of Syracuse take refuge in her Priory, a place of legal sanctuary. She determines that ADRIANA has been jealous of her husband and delivers a short, epigrammatic sermon on the evils of jealous womankind (5.1.69–86). Emilia further declares that the sanctuary of the Priory may not be violated by the return of the two refugees, and she exits briskly.

Later in the scene, having been sent for by the DUKE (8) of Ephesus to help resolve the confusions that have by now come to a head, Emilia returns with Antipholus of Syracuse, placing the twins on stage together for the first time (5.1.329). Ten lines later, she recognises the condemned EGEON as her lost husband. She relates how kidnappers had stolen away the infants who had survived the shipwreck that separated the family years before. The Duke deduces that these infants are now the adults Antipholus and Dromio of Ephesus. After all is revealed, she invites the company to the Priory for a 'gossip's feast' of celebration (5.1.405), to which all depart, ending the play. The term 'gossip's feast' refers to a baptismal or christening party, underlining the importance of Emilia as a symbol of Christian mercy, softening the hard authority of the Duke's laws and embodying the resolution of the play's complexities.

**Emilia (2)** Character in *Othello*, lady-in-waiting to DESDEMONA and wife of IAGO. Despite Emilia's loyalty to and fondness for Desdemona she is manipulated by Iago, who convinces OTHELLO that Desdemona is having a love affair with CASSIO. Unwittingly, Emilia aids Iago in this deception when she provides him with Desdemona's handkerchief, a love token from Othello that Iago plants on Cassio. In 5.2 after the jealous Othello has been driven to murder, Emilia fearlessly denounces him, and when Iago's involvement becomes apparent she exposes his schemes just as boldly. In reprisal Iago stabs her. Dying, she asks to be placed next to Desdemona and makes a final oath that her mistress was faithful to Othello.

Except in this final scene, Emilia serves principally as a foil to her mistress. A sharp-tongued woman whose worldly cynicism makes plausible her marriage to the ambitious and unscrupulous Iago, her nature contrasts tellingly with Desdemona's loving innocence. Though Emilia does not suspect Iago's motives, their marriage is obviously unhappy. She stoically receives his insults, but when alone with Desdemona she rails against men and marriage, declaring, in 4.3, that she would commit adultery, given the chance. Despite her unhappiness, Desdemona rejects this idea firmly, in contrast with Othello's failure to repudiate Iago's sentiments.

**Emilia (3)** Minor character in *The Winter's Tale*, a lady-in-waiting to Queen HERMIONE. In 2.2, when PAULINA attempts to visit the unjustly imprisoned Hermione, the GAOLER (3) only lets her see Emilia. She tells Paulina that the queen has given birth and returns to her mistress with Paulina's suggestion that the infant be brought to the king in a bid for mercy. Emilia's role is small, and she is an uncomplicated messenger, a simple tool of the plot without any real personality.

**Emilia (4)** Character in *The Two Noble Kinsmen*, sister of HIPPOLYTA (2) and the beloved of both PALAMON and ARCITE, the title characters. The subject of the obsession that destroys the friendship of the kinsmen, Emilia is to some extent a pawn of the plot. At first unconscious of the situation, she is inconsequential;

later, as the cousins prepare to duel for the right to marry her, she is emotionally distressed, but the focus remains on the men. However, as a virtuous and noble figure, she is a potent symbol, and she is finally, in her helplessness, an important illustration of the play's central theme, that human beings are unable to control their destiny but must strive to maintain dignity as they confront their fate.

Shakespeare introduces Emilia as an attractive, serious young woman. In 1.1 her pity and magnanimity as she responds to the pleas of the three widows (see QUEEN [1]) establish her as a noble person. In 1.3 she tenderly recalls a close childhood friendship with a girl who has died, and she is quietly confident that she will never love a man as much; later, we realise that her expectation was all too appropriate, for her part in the play's love story is tragically involuntary.

However, as a character, Emilia suffers from the defects of the play, which was written collaboratively by Shakespeare and John FLETCHER (2). Shakespeare's Emilia is a promising figure, but Fletcher, who wrote all of her scenes in Acts 2–4, did not develop her; at first she is simply another young woman of the court, interested in flowers in 2.1, when the two kinsmen fall in love with her beauty, and politely agreeable to the disguised Arcite in 3.5. Then Fletcher alters her radically, but the change is entirely artificial. She agonises over her choice of lovers in a highly rhetorical passage (4.2.1–54) that introduces the arrival of the duellists in a melodramatic manner, but reduces her to a mere illustration of hysteria. Nevertheless, the speech furthers the course of the play, for it demonstrates that she, like the kinsmen, is trapped by destiny. As she puts it, 'my reason is lost in me, / I have no choice' and 'I am sotted, / Utterly lost' (4.2.34–35, 45–46). Emilia embodies humanity's helplessness, both here and in Act 5, where she is again Shakespeare's creation and a more dignified and credible character.

In 5.1, before the duel, Emilia addresses the goddess Diana, seeking assistance in her quandary. She asks the goddess to make sure the winner is the cousin who genuinely loves her the most, adding that she would prefer to remain unmarried. In response, a rose tree with a single rose appears on the altar; supposing that its singleness means she will not have to marry either cousin, Emilia is delighted, but then the rose falls. Chagrined, Emilia remains hopeful, closing touchingly with the plea, 'Unclasp thy mystery.— I hope she's pleased; / Her signs were gracious' (5.1.172–173). In 5.3 she is too distracted to watch the duel, which is reported to her by a SERVANT (30), and we cannot help but sympathise. When she is awarded to Arcite and Palamon is sent to be executed, according to the rules for the duel, Emilia cries out, 'Is this winning? / O all you heavenly powers, where is your mercy?' (5.3.138–139). This despairing cry is the nadir of the play; however, Emilia immediately accepts her fate, rejecting suicide in the next line, because the gods' 'wills have said it must be so' (5.3.140). By the play's end Emilia can accept the final twist of fate—Arcite dies accidentally and Palamon wins her by default—with equanimity. She has learned the lesson that THESEUS (2) declaims in the final line: we must 'bear us as the time' (5.4.137).

**Emmanuel** Minor character in *2 Henry VI*. See CLERK (1).

**Enobarbus (Cnaeus Domitius Ahenobarbus) (d. 31 B.C.)** Historical figure and character in *Antony and Cleopatra*, ANTONY's chief lieutenant who later deserts him and joins Octavius CAESAR (2). Antony's closest friend and adviser through Acts 1–3, Enobarbus abandons his leader when he perceives, in 3.13, that Antony's involvement with CLEOPATRA has led to inevitable defeat. However, when he learns of Antony's sympathetic response to the betrayal, Enobarbus feels terrible pangs of guilt and declares that he will 'go seek / Some ditch, wherein to die' (4.6.37–38). In 4.9 a SENTRY (2) and his WATCHMEN (4) listen as Enobarbus praises Antony and prays for death, then they see him collapse and die. Enobarbus realises that he was wrong to permit good sense to overrule loyalty, for by being prudent he has broken his own heart. The episode foreshadows Cleopatra's final transcendence, and demonstrates that the power of love can invalidate questions of military and political success. In fact, Enobarbus' betrayal is loving, for it is clear that he leaves Antony because he cannot bear to witness his leader's slide into weak-willed failure. Enobarbus thus offers another complex angle on the play's themes of love and power.

Enobarbus is a wise and witty figure before his crisis draws him under. He frequently offers frank, sardonic comments on the other characters and fills some of the functions of a CHORUS (1). For instance, his mockery of LEPIDUS, in 3.2, satirises the dishonesty of Roman politics. On the other hand, his persistent criticism of Antony's love affair helps establish the point of view of the rigorously disciplined ROME, as opposed to the pleasure-oriented world of Cleopatra's court. Enobarbus rises to fine poetry, as in his famous description of the first meeting of Antony and Cleopatra—'The barge she sat in, like a burnish'd throne / Burn'd on the water . . .' (2.2.191 ff.), but he is more often a gruff veteran of the civil wars who jests about the conflict's ups and downs and feels comradeship with his one-time and future enemies. His soldier's humour is well developed and provides a significant portion of the play's comic spirit, an important element in Shakespeare's dramatic strategy.

The historical Domitius Ahenobarbus, as he was called, came from an important Roman political and military family. He fought for Pompey the Great (father of the character in *Antony and Cleopatra*) against Julius CAESAR (1) and was later convicted of participating in Caesar's murder in 44 B.C. He commanded a naval force for BRUTUS (4) at PHILIPPI in 42 B.C., though he does not appear in *Julius Caesar*. After Philippi, he established himself as a warlord. He controlled the Adriatic Sea with his fleet and issued coins bearing his portrait. In 40 B.C. he allied himself with Antony. He opposed Cleopatra's participation in the war against Caesar, and in 31 B.C. he changed sides, as in the play, but he did it just before the battle of ACTIUM, rather than afterwards. Shakespeare knew this from his source, PLUTARCH, but he preferred that his character be a basically loyal subordinate who only leaves when Antony's failings have made defeat inevitable. Ahenobarbus, on the other hand, deserted when his services must still have seemed valuable to his new master. However, he immediately became too sick to command troops, and he died soon after the battle.

**Epenow** Historical figure probably alluded to in *Henry VIII*, a Native American who visited LONDON. In *Henry VIII* the PORTER (4) alludes to the enthusiasm of women for a 'strange Indian with the great tool come to court' (5.3.33–34). Scholars believe this lewd reference is to Epenow, a large man of impressive courage and equanimity, whose appearance in London is recorded in several contemporary sources. He was one of a number of American natives brought to England in the first quarter of the 17th century, some under the auspices of Shakespeare's patron, the Earl of SOUTH-AMPTON (2). Their celebrity as mysterious visitors from the New World may have influenced Shakespeare's creation of CALIBAN.

Brought to England in 1611, Epenow was lionised for a time, but his hosts soon turned to exhibiting him for a fee in a travelling show. Dissatisfied, Epenow devised an escape from England. He persuaded a group of investors that he knew of a gold mine on an island off New England. A vessel was outfitted, and Epenow sailed with it as a guide, but as soon as the ship reached familiar shores, the guide dove overboard, swam ashore, and disappeared.

**Ephesus** Ancient city in Greek Asia Minor (now in Turkey), the setting for *The Comedy of Errors* and several scenes of *Pericles*. In Shakespeare's chief source for the play, *The Menaechmi*, by PLAUTUS, the setting is in another city, Epidamnum. The playwright is presumed to have made the change for two reasons. First, Ephesus was certainly better known to his audience through St Paul's Epistle to the Ephesians and other New Testament references. Second, Ephesus was notorious, through these allusions, as a centre of witchcraft and sorcery. This made it an appropriate setting for Shakespeare's tale of strangeness and confusion.

In 1.2.97–102 ANTIPHOLUS OF SYRACUSE refers to this characteristic of the city to which he has come.

One reason for this reputation was the importance of Ephesus as an ancient centre of paganism, especially due to the presence of a famous temple to DIANA (2) that figures in *Pericles*. PERICLES' wife, THAISA, is mistakenly buried at sea, near Ephesus. She recovers, but, believing that she will never see her husband again, she decides to enter a convent dedicated to Diana. In Act 5 after the goddess has appeared in a vision to Pericles, he comes to the Temple of Diana where Thaisa has become a priestess and they are reunited. Shakespeare took this episode from his source, and except for the references to the temple, the play does not evoke the actual city. However, the herbal lore with which CERIMON revives the unconscious Thaisa is appropriate to an ancient centre of magical arts.

**Epilogue** A speech at the end of a play referring to the performance that has just been completed, often asking for applause. The actor who speaks the Epilogue speaks directly to the audience and is often not in character (in which case, he may be designated as 'Epilogue', himself, in stage directions and speech headings). The device provides a sense of closure to the work and acknowledges its artificiality, returning the spectator to the real world. Eleven of Shakespeare's plays conclude with an Epilogue: *All's Well That Ends Well, As You Like It, 2 Henry IV, Henry V, Henry VIII, A Midsummer Night's Dream, Pericles, The Tempest, Troilus and Cressida, Twelfth Night,* and *The Two Noble Kinsmen*.

**Epitaph** Brief literary work memorialising a deceased person. A number of epitaphs are attributed to Shakespeare, with varying degrees of probability (see COMBE (1); JAMES; JONSON; STRANGE), including one to himself. A number of other poets wrote epitaphs to Shakespeare shortly after the playwright's death (see BASSE; DIGGES (2); HOLLAND (2); JONSON; MILTON).

Although an epitaph is by definition suitable for inscription on a grave marker, it need not be intended for that purpose and may simply be a brief expression of sentiment, ranging from elegiac to humorous, about the deceased. Shakespeare's reputed epitaph on Jonson (said to have been written jointly with Jonson himself) is a 4-line jest; Milton's on Shakespeare, on the other hand, is a 16-line masterpiece on the capacity of art—Shakespeare's plays in particular—to negate mortality.

**Eros** Character in *Antony and Cleopatra*, servant of ANTONY. Eros first appears in 3.5 where he reports to ENOBARBUS that Octavius CAESAR (2) has defeated POMPEY (2) and imprisoned LEPIDUS, news that foreshadows the conflict with Caesar that will prove fatal to

Antony. Eros appears thereafter several times—in 3.11, 4.4, 4.5, and 4.7—as an obviously devoted servant; in 4.14 the defeated Antony, believing that CLEO-PATRA has committed suicide, orders Eros to take his sword and kill him, in accordance with a promise made when Antony had freed the servant from slavery, years earlier. However, Eros cannot bring himself to do it and kills himself instead. Antony, declaring Eros 'Thrice-nobler than myself' (4.14.95), follows his example and stabs himself. This episode, a familiar dramatic exercise (compare, for example, the death of Marcus BRUTUS [4], in 5.5 of *Julius Caesar*), lends pathos to the noble death of Antony.

**Erpingham, Sir Thomas (1357–1428)** Historical figure and minor character in *Henry V*, officer in the army of King HENRY V. In 4.1, on the eve of the battle of AGINCOURT, Erpingham rejects Henry's suggestion that he is too old to sleep on the hard ground, asserting that he enjoys being able to say, 'Now lie I like a king' (4.1.17). Henry congratulates him on his spirit, thus contributing to the episode's emphasis on the high morale of the English army.

The historical Erpingham supported the King's father, Henry BOLINGBROKE (1), later King HENRY IV, when he deposed King RICHARD II (enacted in *Richard II*) and later served as his chancellor. He was one of the highest-ranking officers at Agincourt.

**Escalus (1), Prince of Verona** Character in *Romeo and Juliet*. See PRINCE (1).

**Escalus (2)** Character in *Measure for Measure*, a subordinate to the DUKE (9) of VIENNA. Escalus is a respected elder—the Duke praises the 'art and practice' of 'Old Escalus' (1.1.12, 45). He is appointed ANGELO's (2) second-in-command in the Duke's absence, and serves as his foil in the play. He consistently advocates mercy for CLAUDIO (3), in opposition to Angelo's determination to execute the young man for fornication. Though his pleas are dismissed, he continues to defend the ideal of justice tempered with mercy. On the other hand, in the comical trial scene of 2.1 Escalus represents the opposite failing of government in being too lax when he releases the pander POMPEY (1) with a warning—one for which the pimp has no respect. This produces the anomaly that a hardened promoter of prostitution goes unpunished while the honourable Claudio remains under sentence of death. Escalus contrasts with Angelo in another respect: he is true to his duty while the Duke's deputy is corrupted by his lust for ISABELLA. Though he disagrees with Angelo's severity towards Claudio, he limits his resistance to argument and makes no effort to forestall the decision of his superior officer. The Duke recognises his devotion to duty at the play's close. Escalus' chief function

is to serve as a symbol of both dutiful submission and kindness.

**Escanes** Minor character in *Pericles*, a lord of TYRE. Escanes appears with PERICLES' deputy, HELICANUS, in 1.3 and 2.4—mute in the former scene and speaking two short lines in the latter. In 4.4.13–16 he is said to be governing Tyre while Pericles and Helicanus are abroad. His presence adds dignity to Helicanus, for whom he serves as a retinue.

**Eschenburg, Johann Joachim (1743–1820)** German scholar. Eschenburg translated all of Shakespeare's plays into German prose. Based in part on the translations of C. M. WIELAND, Eschenburg's edition (1775–1782) was the first complete rendering of the plays in German. It dominated German Shakespeare studies until it was superseded by the verse versions of A. W. von SCHLEGEL in the early 19th century.

**Essex (1), Geoffrey FitzPeter (d. 1213)** Historical figure and minor character in *King John*, follower of King JOHN (3). Essex appears only in 1.1 and has only one short speech. Textual scholars speculate that Essex' lines were assigned to Lord BIGOT—perhaps in 1601, after the failed rebellion of the later Earl of ESSEX (2)—and that this alteration was overlooked in the one speech in the FIRST FOLIO text. The historical Essex, no relation to Shakespeare's contemporary, had been named an earl by John and remained a loyal follower of the King.

**Essex (2), Robert Devereux, Earl of (1566–1601)** English aristocrat, a major political figure in Elizabethan England and a close friend of Shakespeare's patron, the Earl of SOUTHAMPTON (2). Essex, long a favourite of Queen ELIZABETH (1), attempted to raise a rebellion against the queen on February 8, 1601. It failed miserably, and Essex was executed in March. The day before the scheduled uprising, Essex's followers hired Shakespeare's acting company, the CHAMBERLAIN'S MEN, to stage a performance of *Richard II*, apparently with the hope that the depiction of a sovereign's deposition might inspire backing among the citizens of LONDON. After Essex's defeat, the company had to send a representative to explain themselves, but they were exonerated and in fact performed for the queen the day before Essex's execution.

Essex succeeded his stepfather, the Earl of LEICES-TER, as the queen's closest courtier, and probably was her lover. He fought in the Netherlands in 1589–1590 alongside Philip SIDNEY, whose widow he married on his return. The queen was angry, but she eventually forgave Essex, and he was again in favour. He became involved in the factional politics of the court, emerging as the chief rival of Lord BURGHLEY. Among his

*The Earl of Essex was one of the most compelling figures of Shakespeare's time. A daring military victory at Cadiz led to his becoming a national hero and the favourite of Queen Elizabeth. But political intrigues led to his downfall. He was tried and executed for treason in 1601, with Elizabeth herself signing the death warrant.* (Courtesy of National Portrait Gallery, London)

enemies was Sir Walter RALEIGH, and it is thought that the many now-incomprehensible inside jokes that stud *Love's Labour's Lost* may have been intended as a satire on Raleigh's circle, on behalf of Essex and Southampton. In 1596 Essex achieved his greatest success, leading, with Charles HOWARD, a successful raid on the Spanish port of Cadiz. Nevertheless, his relations with the queen deteriorated to the point where his rudeness caused her to strike him, and he drew his sword in anger. Another reconciliation took place, and he was given command of a military expedition to put down a revolt in Ireland in 1599.

At this point, probably because Shakespeare's patron was Essex's close friend and political ally, the playwright alluded to Essex flatteringly in a play, one of the few times that contemporary political affairs are noticed at all in the plays. In *Henry V*, written just as Essex left for Ireland, the CHORUS (3) suggests that the audience envision HENRY V's triumphant return to England as though it were that of 'the general of our gracious empress, / . . . from Ireland coming, / Bringing rebellion broached on his sword' (5.Chorus.30–32). However, Essex failed in Ireland; apparently gripped by inertia, he was unable to conquer the re-

bels and he made a treaty that England regarded as shameful. He returned before he was ordered, in September 1599, and the angry queen arrested him. Eventually, a board of inquiry ordered him deprived of his titles. His rebellion was his last hope, so he attempted to raise the city of London against the government, but found no support, and after one day of minor skirmishing, he surrendered.

**Euphronius**    Character in *Antony and Cleopatra*. See AMBASSADOR (3).

**Evans (1), Edith (1888–1976)**    British actress. One of the most acclaimed actresses of the 20th century, Dame Edith Evans played a great range of parts in plays of all sorts. She made her stage debut in 1912 as CRESSIDA in the first recorded production of the complete text of *Troilus and Cressida*. She eventually portrayed most of Shakespeare's comedic heroines, as well as the NURSE (3) in *Romeo and Juliet*. She was also successful in tragic roles, playing such differing characters as CLEOPATRA, VOLUMNIA, and Queen KATHERINE of Aragon.

**Evans (2), Henry (active 1583–1612)**    Welsh-born LONDON theatrical entrepreneur. In 1583–1584 Evans was a partner with William HUNNIS, master of the Children of the Chapel (see CHILDREN'S COMPANIES), in productions staged at the original BLACKFRIARS THEATRE. Beginning in 1584 Evans was also associated with a boys' company patronised by the Earl of OXFORD (1). In 1600 he joined Nathaniel GILES, the new master of the Children of the Chapel, and they produced plays at the revived Blackfriars, which Evans leased from Richard BURBAGE (3). However, in 1602 Evans and Giles were accused of graft and other improprieties. Evans fled the country. He returned in 1603 after the accession of King JAMES I. He then joined Edward KIRKHAM as director of the successor to the Children of the Chapel, the Children of the Queen's Revels. They again performed at Blackfriars, which Evans continued to lease from Burbage. However, the company lost its royal patronage when it performed allegedly seditious plays, and Evans surrendered the lease of the theatre to Burbage and the KING'S MEN in 1608, though a Thomas Evans, believed to be Henry Evans' representative, retained a one-seventh interest in the proceeds of the theatre. Events of Evans' later life are unknown, though in 1611–1612 he was the subject of several lawsuits filed by his one-time partner Kirkham.

**Evans (3), Sir Hugh**    Character in *The Merry Wives of Windsor*, a Welsh clergyman and schoolmaster. A peaceable busybody, Evans is distinguished by his heavy Welsh accent—FALSTAFF says he 'makes fritters of English' (5.5.144). In 1.1 he volunteers to form a committee to settle a dispute between Falstaff and SHALLOW, and he repeatedly tries to allay the irrational jealousy of Master FORD (1). When he attempts to promote SLENDER's marriage to ANNE (3), he is challenged to a duel by Dr CAIUS (2). The clergyman is daunted by this prospect, describing himself as 'full of . . . trempling of mind' (3.1.11–12). To calm himself, he sings a popular Elizabethan love SONG (with words by Christopher MARLOWE [1]), comically borrowing a line from the Bible. The HOST (2) defuses the duel by sending the two men to different rendezvous. To preserve his honour, Evans proposes an alliance with Caius against the Host, claiming that they have been made fools of. They later are apparently responsible for the theft of the Host's horses.

Evans also figures in the famous 'Latin scene' (4.1), in which he quizzes young WILLIAM (1) on his Latin lessons. In lines that parody the standard Latin textbook of Shakespeare's day, LILY's *Latin Grammar,* Evans' accent and Mistress QUICKLY's capacity for misunderstanding join to make fritters of Latin. The scene is full of double entendres and bilingual puns, presumably intended especially for the educated audience for whom the play was originally written. The episode may also reflect Shakespeare's own memories of childhood: he learned Latin from Lily's *Grammar* at school in STRATFORD, where he probably had a teacher of Welsh ancestry, Thomas JENKINS.

Evans was popular with London theatre-goers of the late 16th century; when *The Merry Wives* was first published, in 1600, he figured in the subtitle—as 'Syr Hugh the Welch Knight'—for it was thought that his name would attract buyers. Shakespeare was plainly aware of the popular English stereotype of the Welsh as stubbornly foreign and naturally given to music and theft. Also, along with the interest in WALES (1) demonstrated in several other works, especially *1 Henry IV* and *Henry V,* the character of Evans probably indicates that Shakespeare's acting company included one or more Welshmen in the late 1590s.

**Evans (4), Maurice (1901–1989)**   Anglo-American actor, one of the leading Shakespearean performers of the 1930s and 1940s. Though born in England, Evans acted in America for much of his career and became a citizen of the United States in 1941. As a member of the armed forces, he organised entertainment for troops and toured the Pacific in an abridged version of *Hamlet* that he later staged in America as well. Having achieved great acclaim as HAMLET in 1938—in the play's first full-length staging in America, produced by himself and directed by Margaret Webster—Evans was particularly associated with the part. Other notable roles included ROMEO, opposite Katharine CORNELL, RICHARD II in the Margaret Webster production of 1937, and FALSTAFF in her 1939 *1 Henry IV.* In 1962 Evans performed with Helen Hayes in 'Shakespeare

Revisited', a programme of excerpts from the plays that was staged in 69 American cities. He also starred in TELEVISION productions of *Hamlet, Richard II,* and *Macbeth.*

**Executioner (1)**   Minor character in *The Comedy of Errors,* the ax man prepared to behead EGEON. The Executioner, who does not speak, appears in 5.1 in the entourage of DUKE (8) Solinus. His presence attests to Egeon's desperate plight.

**Executioner (2)**   Any of two or more minor characters in *King John,* HUBERT's assistants in the preparations to blind ARTHUR. Before Hubert dismisses the Executioners, one of them, the First Executioner, voices the distaste with which these hardened men view the prospect of practising their profession on a boy. His qualms heighten the pathos of the scene.

**Executioner (3)**   Minor character in *The Two Noble Kinsmen,* the ax man prepared to behead PALAMON. The executioner does not speak as he stands ready in 5.4; his presence merely serves to heighten the tension with a visible reminder of Palamon's apparent end, before a pardon arrives.

**Exeter (1), Henry Holland, Duke of (1430–1473)** Historical figure and minor character in *3 Henry VI,* a supporter of King HENRY VI and Queen MARGARET (1). Exeter acknowledges the claim to rule of the Duke of YORK (8) in 1.1, but he remains loyal to Henry. This may represent a slip by the playwright, or it may be a subtle reminder of the difficulty of the issue for the participants.

**Exeter (2), Thomas Beaufort, Duke of (1337–1427)** Historical figure and character in *1 Henry VI* and *Henry V,* illegitimate son of John of GAUNT and younger brother of the Bishop of WINCHESTER (1). In *1 Henry VI* Exeter speaks of his position as the 'special governor' (1.1.171) of the infant King HENRY VI, which reflects his historical appointment, under the will of HENRY V, as the new King's tutor. Although the historical Exeter died a few years thereafter, before most of the events of the play, Shakespeare kept him alive to function as a periodic commentator on the action, like a Greek CHORUS (1), predicting disaster for the feuding English. For instance, he closes 3.1 with a grim forecast of the WARS OF THE ROSES, hoping that his own 'days may finish ere that hapless time' (3.1.189–201).

In *Henry V,* set a decade earlier, Exeter is a valued follower of his nephew the King, but he has no distinctive personality. He bears a boldly defiant message from Henry to the FRENCH KING and the DAUPHIN (3) in 2.4, and in 4.6 he recounts the death of the Duke of YORK (5) at AGINCOURT, in tones reminiscent of courtly epic poetry. Thus Exeter's formulaic speeches help to maintain a distinctive tone in both plays.

The historical Exeter, though born a bastard, was granted princely titles and incomes even before being legitimised by his father at the age of 40. He was an important military commander under both HENRY IV and Henry V, and he was named an executor of the latter's will. As in *Henry V,* 3.3.51–54, Exeter was made Governor of HARFLEUR after its capture by Henry, though it is unclear whether or not he fought at Agincourt. He was not named Duke of Exeter until after most of the events of *Henry V;* Shakespeare took this minor inaccuracy from HOLINSHED's *Chronicles.*

**Exton, Sir Piers (Pierce)** Character in *Richard II,* the murderer of RICHARD II. Exton, an ambitious nobleman who wishes to curry favour with BOLINGBROKE (1), the new king, decides in 5.4 that he will murder the old one, believing that Bolingbroke has expressed a desire that this deed be done. In 5.5 Exton leads a gang of hired murderers against Richard in his cell at POMFRET CASTLE, and they kill the ex-king, although Exton suf-fers pangs of conscience. He presents the corpse to Bolingbroke, now HENRY IV, hoping for a reward, but the king rejects him.

Shakespeare took the account of Exton's deed from his chief source, HOLINSHED, but the anonymous French author of Holinshed's source, probably a member of QUEEN (13) Isabel's household, apparently invented the story. No other early source mentions Exton or supposes that Richard died violently; the only other contemporary chronicler asserts that Richard was starved to death, either by his gaolers or by his own will. This source, also French, has its own propagandistic bias, and Richard may well have died of natural causes. His skeleton was exhumed and examined in the 1870s, and no evidence of violence was found.

We cannot say conclusively how the ex-king died, but, in any case, Henry IV's rejection of the murderer appears to be Shakespeare's own addition to the tale, possibly in anticipation of the opening of *1 Henry IV.* A similar story concerning Thomas à Becket and Henry II was only one of several apocryphal anecdotes that might have served the playwright as a model; an account in PLUTARCH was another.

# F

**Fabian** Character in *Twelfth Night*, member of OLIVIA's household and friend of SIR TOBY and MARIA (2). Fabian joins Sir Toby, SIR ANDREW, and Maria (2) in their plot to embarrass MALVOLIO, Olivia's steward. He shares their zest for good times and, like them, represents the spirit of fun that triumphs over Malvolio's stiff ill humour. In his final speech (5.1.354–367) he distinguishes himself as a peacemaker and diplomat, elevating the tone of the comic SUB-PLOT.

As their scheme unfolds and the conspirators observe Malvolio envisioning himself as Olivia's husband, Fabian restrains an outraged Sir Toby from assaulting their victim, saying, 'Nay, patience, or we break the sinews of our plot' (2.5.75–76). He later assists Sir Toby in his practical joke against Sir Andrew, who is manoeuvred into a duel with Cesario (the disguised VIOLA) and shows himself a coward. Fabian's wit and common sense give him an ironic detachment, and in 5.1 he comes into his own, first reading Malvolio's letter (5.1.301–310) and then, more significantly, when quick-wittedly protecting Maria when her forging of Olivia's handwriting becomes evident; he blames himself and Sir Toby, whose marriage to Maria he reveals. He goes on to hope that their plotting 'may rather pluck on laughter than revenge' (5.1.365), forestalling Malvolio's aggrieved cry for vengeance and pointing to the reconciliation that follows.

Fabian's social position is unclear. He seems to be a servant when Olivia addresses him as 'sirrah' (5.1.300), yet he can refer casually to Olivia's kinsman, Sir Toby, as 'Toby' (5.1.358). Shakespeare may have pictured him as a flippant servant or as an impoverished gentleman, dependent on the charity of a wealthy relative or other connection, such as commonly lived in aristocratic households of the 16th and 17th centuries.

**Fabyan, Robert (d. 1513)** English historian, author of a source for Shakespeare's HISTORY PLAYS. Fabyan, a wealthy merchant, assembled a history book by combining miscellaneous works by earlier writers in his posthumously published *New Chronicle of England and of France* (1516). It has very little historical value, but it includes, at its close, an account of the London of his own times that is of interest to scholars of Tudor En-

gland. His chronicle was consulted by Shakespeare, particularly when he wrote *1 Henry VI*.

**Fair Copy** In textual studies, an amended manuscript of a play prepared for a printer or a theatrical company, usually by a professional scribe. No original Shakespearean manuscript exists (except, probably, three pages of SIR THOMAS MORE), but scholars can determine from what sort of copy the printers of an early edition set their type—whether from a manuscript or an earlier printing, and if from a manuscript, whether fair copy or FOUL PAPERS (the author's uncorrected manuscript). Modern editors can determine from such information how closely a given printed text represents what Shakespeare actually wrote.

If the printers used fair copy as their source, the published text is likely to contain many of the characteristic signs of a copyist's work: uniformity of proper names in speech headings and stage directions, consistent spelling, and edited colloquialisms or contractions. This last feature, editorial intervention, is often identified by a resulting metrical defect. For instance 'Before the game's afoot thou still let'st slip' (*1 Henry IV*, 1.3.272) is a pentameter line (see METRE) as it appears in the early QUARTO editions of the play; someone, however, changed 'game's' to 'game is' in the fair copy from which the FIRST FOLIO edition was printed, and the resulting line does not scan properly. This item alone would mean very little, but numerous such instances indicate that the Quarto edition of *1 Henry IV* presents Shakespeare's foul papers and the Folio the fair copy. Modern editors are therefore inclined to favour the Quarto version over the Folio text when they conflict because it was probably printed from Shakespeare's actual manuscript, rather than a copy.

**Fair Em** Anonymous play formerly attributed to Shakespeare, part of the Shakespeare APOCRYPHA. *Fair Em* is a romantic comedy set in the time of William the Conqueror. It was published in 1593 by an unknown publisher who declared that the play had been acted by STRANGE'S MEN, by whom the young Shakespeare was probably employed. Though the play was included with MUCEDORUS and THE MERRY DEVIL OF EDMONTON in King Charles II's specially assembled collection of Shakespeare's plays, the 19th-century scholar Richard SIMPSON was the chief supporter of the theory that *Fair Em* was written by Shakespeare. Simpson argued that the comedy was a retort to the 1592 attack upon the playwright by Robert GREENE (2). Modern scholars unanimously reject this idea, for aside from the convoluted quality of Simpson's argument, it fails to address the considerable difference between *Fair Em* and Shakespeare's known works. The anonymous comedy is an extremely feeble play that lacks wit or poetry of any quality and contains only the crudest of characters and two almost totally unrelated plots.

**Fairy**   Any of several minor characters in *A Midsummer Night's Dream*, attendants of TITANIA and Oberon. In 2.1 a nameless Fairy encounters PUCK, and their conversation establishes the nature of the quarrel between Titania and OBERON. In 2.2 Titania is accompanied by several Fairies, who sing her to sleep. Other Fairies in the play are COBWEB, MOTH (2), MUSTARDSEED, PEASEBLOSSOM, and Puck.

**Falconbridge (1) (Faulconbridge)**   Any of several characters in *King John*. See BASTARD (1); LADY (5); ROBERT.

**Falconbridge (2) (Fauconberg, Faulconbridge), William Neville, Lord (d. 1463)**   Historical figure mentioned in *3 Henry VI*, sometimes assigned the lines of the Marquess of MONTAGUE (3) in Act 1. Montague's assertions of kinship with EDWARD (3) would make more sense if spoken by Falconbridge, who was Edward's brother-in-law. His connection with the sea, at 1.1.216, also applies better to Falconbridge, who was at the time a military commander responsible for the English Channel defenses, as is mentioned 30 lines later. It is supposed that Falconbridge was deleted and his lines reassigned, possibly before any performances were given, as an economy measure for the production.

**False Folio**   Collection of 10 pirated or spurious plays published as Shakespeare's in 1619. William and Isaac JAGGARD and Thomas PAVIER produced a group of QUARTO editions of plays attributed to Shakespeare, though only a few were proper texts of Shakespeare's plays. (Though not in FOLIO format, they are named by analogy with the earliest legitimate collection of Shakespearean plays, the FIRST FOLIO.) Two of the False Folio's offerings, A YORKSHIRE TRAGEDY and *Part 1* of SIR JOHN OLDCASTLE, were not by Shakespeare at all, and six more were BAD QUARTOS of Shakespearean plays (*2* and *3 Henry VI* [see WHOLE CONTENTION], *Henry V*, *The Merry Wives of Windsor*, *King Lear*, and *Pericles*). The publishers held the rights to only one of the two respectable texts, that of *A Midsummer Night's*

*Dream*, which had been bought by Jaggard as part of his purchase of James ROBERTS' company in 1608. The rights to the other, *The Merchant of Venice*, were held by Laurence HEYES, who protested to the STATIONERS' COMPANY, as did the Lord Chamberlain at the time, Lord PEMBROKE (3), who spoke on behalf of the KING's MEN. The publishers responded by backdating the unprinted titles (only three had been issued) so that they could pass for the original editions. However, they were printed in a distinctive format, slightly taller than a standard quarto, on paper with the same watermark, and bibliographical scholars have no difficulty identifying these pirated editions. While the publishers seem blatantly dishonest by modern standards, in the world of 17th-century publishing, their behaviour was not particularly unscrupulous and it did not prevent the Jaggards from joining the syndicate that published the First Folio a few years later.

**Falstaff, Sir John**   Character in *1* and *2 Henry IV* and *The Merry Wives of Windsor*. Falstaff—physically huge, stunningly amoral, and outrageously funny—is generally regarded as one of the greatest characters in English literature. Lecherous, gluttonous, obese, cowardly, and a thief, he lies to the world but is honest with himself. His monumental presence, both literal and metaphoric, dominates the plays in which he appears, and he has become one of the most familiar of Shakespeare's creations, having inspired work ranging from pub signs and ceramic mugs to operas and symphonic works.

In the *Henry IV* plays Falstaff, although an entirely credible human being, also functions as a symbol of an extreme lifestyle. In *1 Henry IV* young PRINCE (6) HAL begins to come to grips with his role as the future King of England, and he is presented with strong figures who suggest modes of adulthood. Unlike Hal's father, the calculating and politically shrewd King HENRY IV, and unlike the intensely single-minded warrior HOTSPUR, Falstaff, in the free and dissolute ambience of the BOAR's HEAD TAVERN, indulges in food, drink, and adventure, whether sexual or criminal, and rejects life's demands for courage or honour. From the beginning the Prince states his intention to reject Falstaff's world, in the famous 'reformation' speech (1.2.190–212). Still, throughout the play he is clearly delighted with his friend's bold effronteries and witty lies; at its close he promises to support Falstaff's claim to have killed Hotspur. In *Part 1* Falstaff is a decided rascal, cowardly and deceitful, but his common sense and tolerance counter the values of Hotspur and King Henry.

In *2 Henry IV* the Prince is closer to his assumption of power, and he is accordingly more remote from Falstaff. Falstaff dominates this play entirely. He is still very funny—as he puts it, 'I am not only witty in myself, but the cause that wit is in other men' (1.2.8–

*Sir John Falstaff (seated on tabletop) in a scene from a modern production of* 1 Henry IV. *Shakespeare's corrupt but outrageously funny knight teaches Prince Hal things he cannot learn from more conventional role models.* (American Shakespeare Festival, Stratford, Connecticut. Photo courtesy of Billy Rose Theater Collection; New York Public Library at Lincoln Center; Astor, Lenox and Tilden Foundations)

9)—but he is presented in a significantly darker light, contributing to the play's atmosphere of disease and death. He is ill; his first words deal with a diagnosis (1.2.1), and he describes himself as sick on several occasions. He refers to his age several times, as when he doubts his attractiveness to DOLL TEARSHEET, saying, 'I am old, I am old' (2.4.268). In *Part 1* he says he is in his 50s (2.4.418–419), while in *Part 2* his acquaintance with SHALLOW is said to date from 'fifty-five year ago' (3.2.205), making him at least 70.

Most important, his misdeeds are distinctly more serious in *2 Henry IV*. In *Part 1* his extortion of bribes from draft evaders is merely reported (4.2.11–48), while we actually see it happen in *Part 2*, 3.2. Moreover, his impressed soldiers, anonymous victims in *Part 1*, take human shape in *Part 2* as such sympathetic, if minor, figures as SHADOW and FEEBLE. The recruiting scene is hilarious, but it remains on the record as evidence of Falstaff's criminality. In fact, the episode was clearly intended as a satirical condemna-

tion of a real practice that plagued the English poor in Shakespeare's time. Perhaps Falstaff's most serious offence is his selfish exploitation of his friends. He promises love but instead bleeds money from his loyal admirer the HOSTESS (2), as she herself describes in 2.1.84–101. The preposterous Shallow is a natural victim, but Falstaff's cynical rationale for fleecing him— 'If the young dace be a bait for the old pike, I see no reason in the law of nature but I may snap at him' (3.2.325–326)—is, however wittily put, morally repugnant.

Hal is distant and hostile to Falstaff when they meet in 2.4, and when the knight seeks to profit from Hal's succession to the crown, the new king forbids his presence. Hal is cold and forceful—although he mercifully provides his former friend with a generous pension— and Falstaff's fall seems abrupt, although it has been prepared for throughout both plays. The needs of the greater, political and military world of Prince Hal triumph in the end.

Still, however fully one may endorse Prince Hal's rejection of Falstaff (and many people do not accept it at all), the fat knight remains a generally sympathetic figure. If his misdeeds would be offensive in real life, they are frequently delightful on stage. He deflates pretension with the needle of his satire, and he counters excessive rigour with his entertainingly flexible morals. His combination of grandiose rhetoric, penetrating wit, and common sense shines in such virtuoso passages of comic monologue as his battlefield rejection of courage (*1 Henry IV*, 5.4.110–120)—leading to a particularly outrageous gesture, the stabbing of Hotspur's corpse—and his tribute to wine (*2 Henry IV*, 4.3.85–123), long acclaimed as one of the most delectable discourses in English literature. In the plays' tavern scenes (2.4 in each) he is uproarious and hearty. His ceaseless flow of parody and imitation evokes a wide and enjoyable range of personages from aristocrats to highwaymen.

Falstaff is a figure of immense psychological resonance; through him we can enjoy our own fantasies of life without responsibilities. When it seems he can offer no excuse for some misdeed and must surely be brought down, like the rest of us, he devises some extravagant lie or joke and escapes. His vitality seems limitless; as he puts it himself, 'banish plump Jack, and banish all the world' (*1 Henry IV*, 2.4.473–474). However, Falstaff *is* banished, for he also represents amoral disloyalty, criminal exploitation, and weak social values. Less sternly, he is often compared to springlike weather in autumn (e.g., in *1 Henry IV*, 1.1.154–155, and *2 Henry IV*, 2.2.112), a common metaphor for youthful energy in old age. The fat knight clearly reflects Shakespeare's fond appreciation of tavern life and its pleasurable delinquencies, but one of the values most important to the playwright—as is especially plain in the HISTORY PLAYS—was the maintenance of social order. Thus Falstaff is repudiated in no uncertain terms, both in the *Henry IV* plays and in *The Merry Wives*.

Part of Falstaff's humour lies in his burlesque of the chivalric values of the aristocracy, and part of his vital force in his energetic individuality. These traits lead many modern readers to think of the *Henry IV* plays as ironical satires of war and government and of Falstaff's rejection as proof that human authenticity is tragically at odds with the practice of politics. However, this ascribes to Shakespeare the views of our own age, when the worth of the individual is placed above that of traditional societal values. But in earlier times Falstaff was held to be flatly villainous. The first great Shakespearean editor, Nicholas ROWE, called him 'a Thief, Lying, Cowardly, Vainglorious, and in short every way vicious' in his 1709 edition of the plays. A little later, Samuel JOHNSON (7) wrote that Falstaff 'has nothing in him that can be esteemed'. Although Shakespeare himself was surely less critical of his creation, he certainly would have understood their point of view. In the RENAISSANCE the potential of the individual was beginning to be recognised, as Shakespeare's interest in and respect for human psychology exemplify, but the ancient, biblically sanctioned, hierarchical society of medieval Europe is persistently championed in the plays, as well as in other works of Elizabethan literature. Therefore, necessity—that national order be restored after a civil war—demands the rejection of the thoughtless pleasures and the irresponsibility that Falstaff displays.

Falstaff's popularity on the Elizabethan stage prompted Shakespeare to announce, in the EPILOGUE to *2 Henry IV*, that the fat knight would appear in another play. However, he does not appear in *Henry V*, although he may have been a character in a lost, probably unacted version of that play. A number of textual peculiarities make it clear that *Henry V* was altered after it was first written; most strikingly, PISTOL takes on Falstaffian characteristics in several passages. Following his humiliation in 5.1, he speaks of growing old and of losing Doll Tearsheet, lines that are plainly more appropriate to Falstaff. Also, Pistol's capture of the FRENCH SOLDIER parallels Falstaff's comic achievements in *1* and *2 Henry IV*. Scholars speculate that, in an original draft of the play, Falstaff was the chief comic character, that he was deleted by the playwright—for it appears that the present version of the play derives from Shakespeare's manuscript—and that much of his part was transferred to Pistol. This theory cannot be proven, but it does explain the textual evidence.

Why would Shakespeare have eliminated Falstaff? Two answers present themselves. The first supposes that the controversy surrounding Falstaff's original name, OLDCASTLE, was still current and that pressure from the son of Lord COBHAM necessitated another change, finally ending the enmity of a powerful aristocrat towards the CHAMBERLAIN'S MEN, Shakespeare's company. However, Shakespeare may simply have thought better of resurrecting his mammoth exemplar of immorality in a play that is dedicated to the English triumph at AGINCOURT. Falstaff had already been rejected on well-established grounds, and his powerful presence may have seemed too distracting from the patriotic themes of *Henry V*.

However, the fat knight's death is described in *Henry V*, 2.3, by Pistol, the Hostess, BARDOLPH (1), and NYM, and their affection for him reflects the playwright's. When Bardolph wishes he were with Falstaff 'wheresome'er he is, either in heaven or in Hell!' (2.3.7–8), the Hostess asserts that he is surely in heaven; she goes on to describe his death-bed touchingly: '. . . after I saw him fumble with the sheets and play with flowers and smile upon his fingers' end, I knew there was but one way; for his nose was as sharp as a pen, and a' babbled of green fields . . . a' cried out "God, God,

God!" three or four times . . .' (2.3.14–20). Thus Falstaff's humanly believable end summons our sympathy one last time for the knight who had 'more flesh than another man, and therefore more frailty' (*1 Henry IV*, 3.3.167–168).

*The Merry Wives of Windsor* was written before *Henry V*, probably during the creation of *2 Henry IV*, and here Falstaff is a less complex figure than the giant of the *Henry IV* plays. His function is more purely comic and stands at the centre of the play rather than in contrast to the realities of history. He is more nearly a traditional character type, the comic villain whose downfall is obvious from the outset. He is also associated with another type, the foolish and boastful would-be lady's man, although in attempting to seduce the wives to get at their husbands' money, Falstaff is not erotically inclined. However, he is thereby linked with the familiar theme of the jealous husband, and the sexual side of his story links him with the sub-plots centred on the courting of ANNE (3) Page.

The complications caused by Falstaff's greedy impulses lead him to receive a humorous retribution and then forgiveness. His personality has not changed—he is still brassy, shrewd, and amorally selfish—but the resourceful prankster and brazen reprobate of the *Henry IV* plays no longer has the initiative. He is easily tricked by the wives, not once but three times. This is sometimes regarded as an unfortunate trivialisation of a great character, but it may also be argued that Falstaff's lesser magnitude in *The Merry Wives* suits his simpler function as a comic butt. In the world of Prince Hal, Falstaff was a shrewd courtier in addition to his other roles, and he never forgot his status—indeed, several of his fantastic excuses for his misbehaviour refer to the exalted position of the Prince. In Windsor he assumes regal attitudes: he tyrannically bullies Pistol and Nym, and he attempts to lord it over the townspeople. His changed behaviour—in addition to demonstrating Shakespeare's acute perception of social relations—makes Falstaff an entirely appropriate target for a comic comeuppance.

This aspect of the character is particularly evident in Falstaff's apologetic confession following his final humiliation (5.5.122–129)—often seen, in its 'un-Falstaffian' quality as evidence of a lost source play. However, in the masquelike finale, where none of the characters present their ordinary characteristics, symbolic expression is given to the play's implicit moral—the triumph of domesticity. Here, then, Falstaff makes the formal surrender that his status as a traditional comic butt requires.

In this respect, Falstaff has been seen as a representation of an ancient fertility spirit in a tradition that in the playwright's time was still alive in remote regions of Britain and was still generally understood. As such, his figurative role was that of the sacrificial victim punished for the sins of society in ancient religious practices. This image need not be taken literally to see that the Falstaff of *The Merry Wives* is identified with common human foibles.

Indeed, Falstaff has the same function in the *Henry IV* plays as well. He moves us, in a way that Hal or Hotspur or Anne Page cannot, because, like him, we all often feel irresponsible, dishonest, selfish inclinations. We know that Falstaff is part of us, like it or not. In the *Henry IV* plays he represents a childish, self-centred universe of pleasure that adults are doomed to leave and that is defeated by a harsh and demanding political ideal, insistent on duty and order. In *The Merry Wives* Falstaff is again opposed by a triumphant principle, in this case the world of domestic security. In both cases, he embodies the need of each of us to rebel against the constraints of society and thus find our individual potential, and his defeat symbolises the need to sublimate that rebellion in light of our innate dependence on each other.

In his first appearance, Hal excuses Falstaff from even an awareness of time, 'unless hours were cups of sack, and minutes capons, and clocks the tongues of bawds, and dials the signs of leaping-houses, and the blessed sun himself a fair hot wench in flame-coloured taffeta' (*1 Henry IV*, 1.2.7–10). The essential nature of Falstaff's personality is revealed in this passage, for the thrust of his wit, and of his life, is to elaborate this fantasy and to defend it against the demands of reality. We delight in the brilliant energy of his efforts, and we mourn the impossibility of their success.

**Falstaffe (Falstaff), Sir John**    Name given to Sir John FASTOLFE in some editions of *1 Henry VI*.

*Famous Victories, The*    Abbreviated title commonly used for *The Famous Victories of Henry the Fifth*, an anonymous late 16th-century play that was an important source for *1* and *2 Henry IV* and a minor one for *Henry V*. *The Famous Victories* is a farce in two parts, the first of which concerns the adventures of PRINCE (6) HAL before he accedes to the throne and the second of which covers his reign as HENRY V.

There are numerous resemblances between the farce and Shakespeare's plays, including appearances by GADSHILL, POINS, the CHIEF JUSTICE, Princess KATHARINE (2) of France, and Sir John OLDCASTLE, which was the original name of FALSTAFF in *1* and *2 Henry IV*. Many of the incidents in *1* and *2 Henry IV* also occur in the *Famous Victories*, though they are presented very crudely by comparison. Such similarities make it clear that Shakespeare used *The Famous Victories* as a source, but he made major alterations, quite aside from his integration of its farcical material with another, more serious plot line. The Prince in the *Famous Victories* is simply a hooligan, wishing his father dead and roaring drunkenly about the stage. Shakespeare's Hal is a reflective young man who states early in *1 Henry IV* his intention to reform, and his participation in Falstaff's highway robbery is limited to stealing from the thieves. He is generally intent on affairs of state in *2 Henry IV*, his mischief extending only to disguising himself as a DRAWER in 2.4. Oldcastle is an insignificant character who bears little resemblance to his successor. And in *Henry V* King Henry's wooing of Princess Katharine in 5.2 was developed from a similar but less elaborate scene in *The Famous Victories*, which otherwise provided only a few minor details.

The only surviving version of *The Famous Victories* was published in 1598; it is clearly a 'memorial' version of the play, a BAD QUARTO assembled from the recollections of actors. It is a very poor text, commonly judged to be unactable, and it is generally presumed that Shakespeare knew a superior version, perhaps a publication recorded in 1594 that is now lost. However, some scholars hold that *The Famous Victories*, along with Shakespeare's plays, derives from an earlier play on the same subject (perhaps the one published in 1594, perhaps one that Shakespeare himself wrote earlier in his career).

**Fang**   Minor character in *2 Henry IV*, a constable who attempts to arrest FALSTAFF for debt. In 2.1 the HOSTESS (2) employs Fang and his assistant, SNARE, to arrest the fat knight, but when Falstaff and his companion, BARDOLPH (1), draw their swords, the officers are helpless. The CHIEF JUSTICE appears and resolves the situation without their assistance. Fang's name, which in Elizabethan English meant 'snare' or 'trap', is appropriate to his function, if not to his abilities.

**Farce**   A play, usually short, that has no purpose but to generate laughter in the audience. A form of COMEDY, it uses artificial situations, unrealistic plots, and physical humour rather than wit to achieve its end. Common plot components include mistaken identity, overheard information, accidental encounters, reunions of long-separated people, and extraordinary coincidences. Characterisation, meaningful plotting, or any intellectual elements are eschewed. Farce has been widely popular from ancient times to the present. None of Shakespeare's plays is properly called a farce, though *The Comedy of Errors* is very like one but contains additional elements.

**Farrant, Richard (d. 1580)**   English composer and theatrical entrepreneur, founder of the first BLACKFRIARS THEATRE. In 1564 Farrant, a court musician, became director of the Children of Windsor, a boys' choir in the service of Queen ELIZABETH (1). The boys also performed plays (see CHILDREN'S COMPANIES), and in 1576, when Farrant became the deputy of William HUNNIS, director of the similar Children of the Chapel, he was assigned responsibility for the productions of the combined companies. He accordingly leased rooms in the defunct BLACKFRIARS PRIORY and staged plays there, in what became known as the original Blackfriars Theatre. Farrant, who was also the queen's organist, composed church music, some of which is still performed, and may also have composed music for the boys' plays.

**Fastolfe, Sir John (c. 1378–1459)**   Historical figure and character in *1 Henry VI*, an English officer in the HUNDRED YEARS WAR. In the play Fastolfe is depicted as a cowardly soldier whose hasty retreats cause great losses to the English. His retreat at Patay, near ORLÉANS, was recorded in the chronicles that were Shakespeare's sources, but the playwright magnified this single event in order to create a striking contrast to the heroism of the play's most important figure, TALBOT. The defeat at Patay is reported in 1.1 by a MESSENGER (3), who says that Fastolfe has 'play'd the coward' (1.1.131). In 1.4 Talbot describes his resultant captivity, and he rails against the 'treacherous Fastolfe' (1.4.34). Fastolfe first appears on stage in 3.2; he is fleeing ignominiously during the assault on ROUEN, an entirely fictitious episode. Asked whether he is abandoning Talbot, Fastolfe replies, 'Ay, all the Talbots in the world, to save my life' (3.2.108). Finally, in 4.1, Talbot angrily tears the Order of the Garter from Fastolfe's leg, describing again the action at Patay. The king promptly banishes the coward, who departs in silence.

The historical Fastolfe had a very different career. The incident at Patay, which did not result in Talbot's captivity, is viewed by modern historians as having been chiefly due to bad generalship by Shakespeare's hero, necessitating a sensible withdrawal by Fastolfe, his fellow commander. The Duke of BEDFORD (1) seems to have been most upset by the episode; it is he, not Talbot, who stripped Fastolfe of his Garter (temporarily and probably without authority) while an investigation was conducted at Talbot's request. The investigators exonerated Fastolfe completely, and he went on to complete a distinguished career as a general and diplomat.

The only early text of *1 Henry VI*, that in the FIRST FOLIO of 1623, names this character Falstaffe. Subsequent editors, however, generally have used the historical figure's correct name, thereby avoiding confusion with Shakespeare's great comedic figure FALSTAFF.

**Father That Hath Killed His Son, The**   Minor but significant character in *3 Henry VI*, a participant in the battle of TOWTON in 2.5. The Father, a soldier, prepares to loot the corpse of an enemy he has killed, when he discovers that the body is that of his own son. He mourns for himself and for the times: 'O, pity, God, this miserable age! / What stratagems, how fell, how butcherly, / Erroneous, mutinous, and unnatural, / This deadly quarrel daily doth beget!' (2.5.88–91).

The Father's discovery and grief are witnessed by King HENRY VI, who has withdrawn from the battle to wish despairingly that he were a rustic shepherd, rather than a combatant. This incident, along with that of the SON THAT HATH KILLED HIS FATHER, is juxtaposed ironically with Henry's pastoral musings to highlight the horrors of civil war.

**Faucit, Helen (1817–1898)** British actress. Faucit played most of Shakespeare's major female roles, usually opposite W. C. MACREADY, but she was particularly associated with BEATRICE and HERMIONE. She recorded her interpretations in a book, *On Some of Shakespeare's Female Characters* (1885).

**Faulconbridge (1) (Falconbridge), Lady** Character in *King John*. See LADY (5).

**Faulconbridge (2) (Falconbridge), Philip** Character in *King John*. See BASTARD (1).

**Faulconbridge (3) (Falconbridge), Robert** Character in *King John*. See ROBERT.

**Faulconbridge (4), William Neville, Lord** Character in *3 Henry VI*. See FALCONBRIDGE (2).

**Feeble, Francis** Minor character in *2 Henry IV*, one of the men whom FALSTAFF recruits for the army in 3.2. Feeble is selected over hardier men who bribe their way out of service, and Falstaff justifies the choice by saying that Feeble will be useful in retreat, being already inclined to run. However, Feeble is willing to fight if he has to, saying, 'I will do my good will, sir, you can have no more' (3.2.155), and '. . . he that dies this year is quit for the next' (3.2.233). Feeble gives his occupation as a 'woman's tailor', which gives rise to ribaldry: 'tailor' was Elizabethan slang for the genitals, male or female.

**Fenton (1)** Character in *The Merry Wives of Windsor*, suitor of ANNE (3) Page. Fenton, a conventional young romantic lead, has little personality, although we are told that he 'kept company with the wild Prince and Poins' (3.2.66–67). Anne's father, George PAGE (12), objects to Fenton on this ground and on the related one that he is too socially high-ranking to be an appropriate husband for the bourgeois maid. Moreover, Page suspects Fenton is a treasure hunter. Fenton himself admits to Anne in 4.3.12–18 that, although he has fallen in love with her since, Page's money was his original motive for courting her. Nevertheless, he compares favourably with Anne's other suitors, SLENDER and CAIUS (2), and when Anne's parents each plot to have her abducted and married by one of these

misfits, her elopement with Fenton comes as a natural course of action. When Fenton announces their marriage in 5.5.216–227, her parents gracefully accept the situation in the spirit of reconciliation that closes the play.

**Fenton (2), Geoffrey (c. 1540–1608)** English translator, creator of a possible minor source for several of Shakespeare's plays. As a young nobleman living in Paris, Fenton wrote English versions of 13 of Matteo BANDELLO's Italian tales, working from the French translations of Pierre Boaistuau (d. 1566) and François BELLEFOREST. The resulting book, *Certaine Tragicall Discources* (1566), was very popular, and Shakespeare almost certainly knew it. He may have been influenced by it when he wrote *Hamlet, Titus Andronicus,* and *Twelfth Night,* all of which were based on tales that appear in Bandello, though which of several possible versions was used by the playwright is in each case uncertain.

Fenton translated several other French works, mostly religious in nature, including an attack on drama that was popular among English Puritans who opposed ELIZABETHAN THEATRE. He was best known in his day for his *History of the Wars of Italy* (1579), taken from French translations of the writings of the Italian political theorist Francesco Guicciardini (1483–1540). After 1580 Fenton deserted literature for a successful career as a member of the Irish colonial establishment and lived out his life in Dublin.

**Fenton (3), Richard (1746–1821)** English author. Fenton, a lawyer, wrote and published poetry and essays. In his *A Tour in Quest of Genealogy through several Parts of Wales* (1811), published anonymously, he claimed to have found a copy—in the handwriting of Anne HATHAWAY—of a journal kept by Shakespeare, from which he quotes a number of passages concerning the playwright's career. Though some contemporaries took this material seriously, most scholars, then and now, believe that Fenton's discovery was merely a mild hoax, intended humorously.

**Ferdinand (1)** Character in *Love's Labour's Lost*. See KING (19).

**Ferdinand (2)** Character in *The Tempest*, the lover of the magician PROSPERO's daughter, MIRANDA. Prospero arranges the match between Miranda and the son of his old enemy, King ALONSO of Naples, as part of the atmosphere of reconciliation and forgiveness with which he resolves his own exile. Prospero pretends to distrust Ferdinand and puts him to forced labour, but when the young man's love survives this trial, Prospero blesses the future marriage of the couple. Ferdinand's ardour is important to the play's scheme of things, for he and Miranda symbolise the healing value

of love. Ferdinand is accordingly a sterotypical romantic leading man, though his role is relatively small.

Ferdinand is tellingly compared with Prospero's
bestial slave, CALIBAN. Miranda explicitly judges the
two, in pointedly contrasting terms: Caliban is 'a thing
most brutish' (1.2.358) and Ferdinand 'a thing divine'
(4.1.421). Caliban has attempted to rape Miranda, but
Ferdinand vows to respect her virginity until they are
married. Caliban truculently resists his chore of delivering fire wood with whines and curses; Ferdinand is
assigned a similar task—carrying logs—but he rejoices
in the labour, for it is associated with his love. Ferdinand's mourning for his father, whom he believes
drowned, is also part of the play's depiction of goodness and helps (with Alonso's similarly mistaken grief
over his son) to ameliorate the king's earlier crime
against Prospero.

**Feste** Character in *Twelfth Night,* jester, or professional FOOL (1), in the household of OLIVIA. Feste
represents the play's spirit of festivity, which eventually triumphs over the steward MALVOLIO's chilly ill
humour. Outside the coils of the lovers' confusions,
Feste can take an ironic view of them and their world.
He appears in a number of settings, the better to apply
his vision to all. He frequents the courts of both Olivia
and Duke ORSINO, encounters both VIOLA and SEBAS-
TIAN (2), challenges the first appearance of Malvolio,
and takes part in the revelry of SIR TOBY and SIR AN-
DREW. He also carries the comic SUB-PLOT to its far-
thest extreme, disguising himself as a curate, Sir
TOPAS, and pretending to exorcise the imprisoned
Malvolio. As he himself observes, 'Foolery, sir, doth
walk about the orb like the sun, it shines everywhere'
(3.1.39–40).

As an officially designated fool, it is Feste's duty to
point out with jests and barbs the folly of those who
are supposed to be wise. As Viola remarks when she
meets Feste, 'This fellow is wise enough to play the
fool, / . . . For folly that he wisely shows is fit; / But
wise men, folly-fall'n, quite taint their wit' (3.1.61–69),
and Olivia tells Malvolio, 'There is no slander in an
allowed fool, though he do nothing but rail' (1.5.93–
94). Feste wittily demonstrates that Olivia is foolish to
mourn her brother's ascent to heaven, and her good
humour is immediately restored. Although his jests
are less effective against Orsino's foolish self-image as
a romantic melancholic, they make the duke's mental
disorder plain. Feste compares himself to Sir Andrew,
saying, 'Better a witty fool than a foolish wit' (1.5.36),
pointing out both Sir Andrew's limitations and his
own role. He also cares for the drunken Sir Toby,
observing bitingly, 'the fool shall look to the madman'
(1.5.138–139).

Finally, Feste's pretended exorcism of Malvolio
casts light on the steward's character. Malvolio's humourless ambition and incapacity to love are meta-

phorically alluded to in Feste's diagnosis: 'I say there
is no darkness but ignorance, in which thou are more
puzzled than the Egyptians in their fog' (4.2.43–45).
The subsequent comic dialogue deals obliquely with
Malvolio's underlying deficiency—his lack of concern
for anyone but himself. Feste declares that Malvolio
will 'remain . . . in darkness [until] thou shalt . . . fear
to kill a woodcock lest thou dispossess the soul of thy
grandam' (4.2.58–61).

In *Twelfth Night* Shakespeare deliberately undercut
the conventions of romantic comedy; one of his techniques was to establish what has long been called 'the
problem of Malvolio'; the steward's discomfiture
seems out of proportion to his offence, giving rise to
an uncertain response in the audience, which responds with both delight at Malvolio's comeuppance
and sympathy for his victimisation. Feste's final encounter with Malvolio, upon the steward's release,
contributes to this ambiguity. Here, the fool cruelly
uses Malvolio's own words against him and then observes that 'the whirligig of time brings in his re-
venges' (5.1.375–376); while 'whirligig' is funny, 're-
venges' is not.

Feste's songs are an important part of his role, illuminating different aspects of the play. In 2.3 he sings
a love song for boisterous Sir Toby and Sir Andrew,
and the audience shares the delight of the two knights,
but the lyrics have a somewhat depressing tinge, for
they advocate seizing love while one is young because
'what's to come is still unsure' (2.3.50). This observation is part of the play's disturbing undertone, as is
Feste's next song, 'Come away death' (2.4.51–66),
which is humorously suited to Orsino's affected sadness but is also strikingly melancholy in itself.

Feste's last song, which closes the play, offers a poignant moment. Left outside the happy ending the lovers enjoy, the fool sings a bitter ditty that sums up the
play's anti-romantic secondary theme. He sings of the
sorry, loveless life of a drunkard for whom, as the
chorus insists, 'the rain it raineth every day' (5.1.391
et al.). These lyrics emphasise Shakespeare's ironic
view of the limitations of comedy. However, this message is greatly offset by the music, and the gross exaggeration in the words makes them somewhat comical;
also, the song's final stanza presents a standard EPI-
LOGUE, asking for applause and promising that the
actors will 'strive to please you every day' (5.1.407).
Feste remains a generally sunny character whose
darker moments serve to make him, and the play,
more complex and humanly interesting.

**Ffarington, William (1537–1610)** Steward to Ferdinando Stanley, Lord STRANGE, and possibly a model
for MALVOLIO in *Twelfth Night* and OSWALD in *King Lear*.
Ffarington—whose personality and habits have been
recorded in his own elaborate housekeeping accounts
and elsewhere—resembled both characters to some

degree. Like Malvolio, he was noted for his severe mode of dress but was also fond of fine fabric and precious stones (see TWELFTH NIGHT, 2.5.48, 61), and he disinherited his son for refusing a financially and socially advantageous marriage, betraying an attitude suggestive of Malvolio's own matrimonial ambition. Ffarington's style of dress also is reminiscent of Oswald, castigated by KENT (2) as a vain and pretentious imitator of gentlemen in *King Lear*, 2.2.13–24. Kent also calls Oswald 'action-taking' and 'super-serviceable' (2.2.16), evoking Ffarington's noted readiness to begin a legal action and undeniable devotion to his master

Ffarington's employer was the patron of an acting company, STRANGE'S MEN, to which the young Shakespeare probably belonged. Strange's Men often visited their patron's home in Lancashire, as did other companies whose members were later Shakespeare's associates. Thus Shakespeare may have known Ffarington personally and almost certainly had at least heard of him. Ffarington was probably a singularly unpleasant figure to the travelling players, for he detested actors and the theatre, as his own accounts make clear (he commented adversely on his employer's enthusiasm). In fact, Ffarington disliked all festivities; in 1580 he attempted to suppress the local May games, a longstanding tradition.

This gentleman certainly seems a plausible target for satire. Moreover, unlike Sir Ambrose WILLOUGHBY (1) and Sir William KNOLLYS—the other chief candidates as models for Malvolio—he was not so high in the social hierarchy as to be too dangerous to satirise (both the others were valued servants of Queen ELIZABETH [1]). However, most scholars regard the true identity of the model for Shakespeare's stewards—and for most other Shakespearean characters—as ultimately unknowable.

**Fidele**  In *Cymbeline*, the name taken by IMOGEN in her disguise as a young man. Fidele is a French name, and this contributes to the multilingual confusion of the play, a characteristic feature of Shakespeare's ROMANCES.

**Field (1), Nathan (1587–1620)**  English actor and dramatist. Field was one of the 26 men listed in the FIRST FOLIO as the 'Principall Actors' in Shakespeare's plays. He joined the KING'S MEN in 1615 or 1616—scholars speculate that he replaced Shakespeare just before or after the playwright's death—after a long association with one of the CHILDREN'S COMPANIES and with the LADY ELIZABETH'S MEN. He was particularly noted in the title role of George CHAPMAN's *Bussy d'Amboise*. As a playwright he collaborated with Philip MASSINGER, John FLETCHER (2), and perhaps others, and he wrote two comedies himself, along with a defence of the stage.

Field, whose Puritan father had written fiercely against the stage before his death in 1588, was recruited from the choir of a secondary school into the Children of the Chapel (later the Children of the Queen's Revels) in 1600. As a boy actor in this company Field continued his education under the tutorship of Ben JONSON, who was later to name Field and Richard BURBAGE (3) as the finest English actors. After the Children of the Revels were absorbed by the Lady Elizabeth's Men in 1613, Field became the leader of the combined company before he joined the King's Men.

**Field (2), Richard (1561–1624)**  London printer, producer of the first several editions of *Venus and Adonis* and the first editions of *The Rape of Lucrece* and *The Phoenix and Turtle*. A native of STRATFORD whose father knew Shakespeare's father, Field is presumed to have been a friend of the playwright's. Scholars speculate that Shakespeare may have playfully referred to Field when the disguised IMOGEN claims employment with one 'Richard du Champ' (*Cymbeline* 4.2.377), i.e., 'Richard Field' in French. In 1593 Field published the young playwright's first ambitious literary undertaking, *Venus and Adonis,* in a QUARTO edition known today as Q1. He then sold the rights to this work and *Lucrece* to John HARRISON (2), who hired him to print the second, third, and fourth editions (Q2–4, 1594–1596) of *Venus and Adonis* and the first quarto (Q1, 1594) of *Lucrece*. He later printed, for publisher Edward BLOUNT, the first edition of LOVE'S MARTYR (1601), which contained *The Phoenix and Turtle.*

Field's early life in Stratford is unknown, apart from the fact that his father was a tanner. He was apprenticed to a London printer in 1579; on the death of his second master, in 1587, he took over that man's business and married the widow. He doubtless regretted the sale of the rights to *Venus and Adonis* and *Lucrece*, which became very popular, but he prospered nonetheless. Among other works, he produced the first edition of HARINGTON's translation of *Orlando Furioso*, a 1598 edition of SIDNEY's *Arcadia,* and several editions of NORTH's translation of PLUTARCH.

**Fiend**  Any of several minor characters in *1 Henry VI,* the supernatural beings that JOAN LA PUCELLE summons by means of sorcery in 5.3. Joan asks the assistance of these creatures 'cull'd / out of the powerful regions under earth' (5.3.10–11) in fighting England. However, they silently refuse, leading her to realise that all is lost. Her capture follows immediately.

**Fife**  Region in Scotland, the setting for 4.2 of *Macbeth*. When Fife's ruler, Lord MACDUFF, betrays the usurper MACBETH and joins the rebels led by Prince MALCOLM, Macbeth sends murderers (see FIRST MURDERER [3]) to Macduff's castle where they kill his wife,

LADY (7) MACDUFF, and his SON in an episode that marks the depths of Macbeth's evil. Shakespeare took the setting from his source, Raphael HOLINSHED's history, but there is nothing in the scene that particularly denotes Fife.

**Film**  Medium in which most of Shakespeare's plays have been produced. Many of the plays have been filmed more than once, in numerous languages. *Hamlet,* for example, has been filmed more than two dozen times. The earliest movie made from Shakespeare was of a single scene from Beerbohm TREE's stage production of *King John,* but the film has been lost. Oddly, many silent films of Shakespeare plays were made, perhaps because the medium sought respectability in its earliest days. Among the most notable directors and producers of Shakespearean films have been Grigori KOZINTSEV, Akira KUROSAWA, Laurence OLIVIER, Max REINHARDT, Orson WELLES, and Franco ZEFFIRELLI.

**Fiorentino, Giovanni (active 14th century)**  Italian author, writer of a collection of tales that included sources for *The Merchant of Venice* and *The Merry Wives of Windsor.* Little is known of Fiorentino, whose collection of stories, *Il Pecorone (The Simpleton),* was written in the 1370s but not published until 1558. He was a Florentine clerk, and his tales were closely modelled on the works of BOCCACCIO.

There is no known Elizabethan translation of *Il Pecorone* into English, yet Shakespeare's use of it seems extremely likely, expecially in the case of *The Merchant of Venice.* The playwright may have read the work in Italian, although his ability to do so is not certain. There may have existed an English version that has not survived, or he may have been told the relevant details by someone who had read it. In any case, his knowledge of Latin would have permitted him to struggle through the Italian, once he knew there was material there that he was interested in.

**First Clown**  Character in *Hamlet.* See GRAVE-DIGGER.

**First Commoner**  Character in *Julius Caesar.* See CARPENTER.

**First Executioner**  Character in *King John.* See EXECUTIONER (2).

**First Folio**  Earliest published collection of Shakespeare's plays, appearing in 1623. Produced in the FOLIO format, the First Folio was edited by John HEMINGE and Henry CONDELL, who had been professional associates of Shakespeare in the CHAMBERLAIN'S MEN and its successor, the KING'S MEN. The First Folio contains 36 plays, 18 of which were not otherwise published and would probably have been lost without this edition. These plays are *All's Well That Ends Well, Antony and Cleopatra, As You Like It, The Comedy of Errors, Coriolanus, Cymbeline, 3 Henry VI, Henry VIII, Julius Caesar, King John, Macbeth, Measure for Measure, The Taming of the Shrew, The Tempest, Timon of Athens, Twelfth Night, Two Gentlemen of Verona,* and *The Winter's Tale.*

The editors' intention in publishing Shakespeare's plays was also to counter the imperfect editions that did exist. Since they knew the works intimately, having worked with the playwright for most of his career, their corrections of other editions are significant to scholars, as is their selection of 36 plays. Heminge and Condell would have selected only plays they knew to have been written by Shakespeare—or at least mostly by him, in cases of collaboration. Thus, the First Folio constitutes a basic CANON of the plays. (However, the earliest part of Shakespeare's career may not have been known to them very well, and even in the case of the more mature works, while those included are almost certainly Shakespearean, the editors could have excluded plays for such reasons as defective texts, copyright problems, or CENSORSHIP.)

Besides the plays, the First Folio contains various minor elements: a title page decorated with the DROESHOUT PORTRAIT, facing a poem by Ben JONSON commending the likeness; a brief introduction by the editors, stating their purpose; a dedication to the Earls of PEMBROKE (3) and MONTGOMERY (2); verses on Shakespeare by Jonson, Hugh HOLLAND (2), Leonard DIGGES (2), and 'I.M'. (probably James MABBE); a list of 26 'Principall Actors in all these Playes'; and a table of contents. It was printed in an edition of about 1200, of which about 230 have survived. Oddly, it appears that no two copies are identical (though they have not all been collated), for proof-reading and correction went on simultaneously with printing. The process began in April 1621, but was interrupted and was not completed until December 1623.

The title page contains the information that the book was printed by Isaac JAGGARD and Edward BLOUNT. A colophon on the last page states that it was printed for William JAGGARD (Isaac's father, who died just before the book was issued), Blount, John SMETHWICK, and William ASPLEY. The members of this syndicate held copyrights to the previously published plays. Blount and Isaac Jaggard held most of them, which probably accounts for their joint listing on the title page, for Blount was not in fact a printer. Isaac Jaggard oversaw the publishing process, and Heminge and Condell may have done little more than supply Jaggard with the texts. The actual editing may have been done by Edward KNIGHT (4), the King's Men's book-keeper, who was responsible for maintaining the PROMPT-BOOK of each play.

**First Grave-digger**  Character in *Hamlet.* See GRAVE-DIGGER.

**First Lord (1)**    Character in *As You Like It.* See LORD (4).

**First Lord (2)**    Character in *All's Well That Ends Well.* See LORD (6).

**First Murderer (1)**    One of 'two or three' characters in *2 Henry VI,* the killers of the Duke of GLOUCESTER (4). Several men, two of whom speak, flee the scene of the crime at the beginning of 3.2. The First Murderer calmly accepts payment for the crime from the Duke of SUFFOLK (3), thus distinguishing himself from the SECOND MURDERER (1), who is conscience-stricken.

**First Murderer (2)**    Character in *Richard III,* one of two hired assassins employed by RICHARD III to kill his brother the Duke of CLARENCE (1). The First Murderer coolly accepts his role as a killer, whereas the SECOND MURDERER (2) has an attack of conscience as they approach their victim in 1.4. Later in this scene, when Clarence pleads for mercy and the Second Murderer seems inclined to yield, the First stabs the Duke, carries him off stage, and drowns him in a large barrel of wine.

**First Murderer (3)**    Minor character in *Macbeth,* an assassin recruited by MACBETH. In 3.1 the First Murderer and his accomplice, the Second Murderer, accept Macbeth's assignment to kill BANQUO and FLEANCE. They are virtually indistinguishable from each other. Neither speaks much, although each makes a brief complaint (3.1.107–113) about the desperation of his unfortunate life and his determination to perform any deed that may improve his lot. In 3.3 the Murderers, assisted by the THIRD MURDERER, undertake their commission. They cooly assault their targets and kill Banquo, though Fleance escapes. In 3.4 the First Murderer reports the deed succinctly to Macbeth. He takes pride in their fierceness and describes Banquo's wounds as 'twenty trenched gashes on his head; / The least a death . . .' (3.4.26–27).

In 4.2 an unspecified number of Murderers, probably the First and Second, kill the SON (1) of LADY (7) Macduff and chase her off stage where they kill her, as we learn in 4.3. Their cold-bloodedness is here particularly horrifying as one of them notes his victim's youth, calling the Son an 'egg' (4.2.82) as he kills him.

The Murderers are not distinct from each other as individuals. The First Murderer offers a pleasing description of a sunset in 3.3.5–7, but we do not imagine that he is a man of esthetic sensibility. He is merely a vessel for Shakespeare's poetic lyricism, which here helps to establish the eerie atmosphere of dusk for a scene that, in the playwright's theatre, was performed without modern stage lighting to set the mood.

**First Officer**    Character in *Twelfth Night.* See OFFICER (3).

**First Player (1)**    Character in *The Taming of the Shrew.* See PLAYERS (1).

**First Player (2)**    Character in *Hamlet,* the leading member of the PLAYERS (2), a travelling company of actors who visit ELSINORE and perform before the court of KING (5) Claudius. In 2.2 HAMLET greets the Players with enthusiasm and requests that the First Player recite a speech he remembers hearing him deliver in a play. Hamlet begins the speech, and the First Player takes it up; it is a highly dramatic account of an episode in the TROJAN WAR, the vengeful killing of King PRIAM by PYRRHUS, followed by the grief of Queen HECUBA. The First Player's fine recital is testified to by POLONIUS, who observes approvingly that he has 'turned his colour and has tears in's eyes' (2.2.515–516), effects that were conventionally associated with fine acting in a tradition extending back to Plato. The First Player receives Hamlet's instructions to stage THE MURDER OF GONZAGO before the court in 2.2.531–536, and he presumably appears as the PLAYER KING in the playlet.

**First Soldier (1)**    Character in *All's Well That Ends Well.* See SOLDIER (7).

**Fisher, Thomas (active 1600–1602)**    London publisher and bookseller, publisher of the first edition of *A Midsummer Night's Dream.* Fisher hired an unknown printer (possibly Edward ALLDE or Richard BRADOCK) to produce Q1 of Shakespeare's play, which appeared in 1600. This was Fisher's only noteworthy publication; he was a draper who joined the STATIONERS' COMPANY in 1600 and operated a bookshop for the next two years, but little more is known of him.

**Fishermen**    Three minor characters in *Pericles,* poor men of PENTAPOLIS. In 2.1 the Fishermen assist the shipwrecked PERICLES and inform him that the ruler of Pentapolis is King SIMONIDES, whose daughter, THAISA, is to marry the winner of a jousting tournament. When Pericles' armour is brought up in the Fishermen's net, he decides to use it in the king's tourney, and the Fishermen agree to guide him to Simonides' court.

This episode introduces the next scene in the play, but the Fishermen also have a greater significance, as they reflect the play's major theme. Before they encounter Pericles they speak of the shipwreck and regret their inability to help the victims 'when, well-a-day, we could scarce help ourselves' (2.1.22). They also philosophise on the ways of the world in a humorous way. They observe, for instance, that fish live 'as men do a-land: the great ones eat up the little ones'

(2.1.28–29). Thus, the Fishermen present the idea that people are at the mercy of forces outside themselves, whether natural or social. This helplessness is the central element of the play's world.

The First Fisherman is the leader of the group; he refers to the Second and Third Fishermen by their names—Pilch and Patch-breech—both humorous terms for raggedy clothes. These labels suggest the general appearance of the Fishermen, which is that of a traditional comic character, the rustic CLOWN (1).

**Fitton, Mary (1578–1647)** Maid of honour to Queen ELIZABETH (1), possibly the model for the 'Dark Lady' of the SONNETS. Mary Fitton joined the queen's court in 1595 through the influence of Sir William KNOLLYS, a friend of her father. Knollys fell in love with her—generating gossip that may have helped inspire Shakespeare's creation of MALVOLIO's courtship of OLIVIA in *Twelfth Night*—but she became the mistress of William Herbert, the Earl of PEMBROKE (3), by whom she became pregnant in 1600. She was banished from the court in disgrace, Pembroke refused to marry her (preferring a prison term instead), and the infant died shortly after it was born. Fitton went on to marry and be widowed twice.

In his 1890 edition of the Sonnets, Thomas TYLER (2) suggested that Mary Fitton was the Dark Lady—on the assumption that the poems were addressed to Pembroke—and the theory was made widely popular by Frank HARRIS (1). However, most scholars now find the hypothesis improbable, chiefly because two surviving portraits of Fitton show that she had a fair complexion, brown hair, and grey eyes.

**Fitzwater (Fitzwalter), Lord Walter (c. 1368–1407)** Historical figure and minor character in *Richard II*, a supporter of BOLINGBROKE (1). In 4.1 Fitzwater seconds BAGOT's assertion that AUMERLE had boasted of killing the Duke of GLOUCESTER (6), and he challenges Aumerle to a trial by combat. He is in turn challenged by the Duke of SURREY (3), as the scene erupts in charges and counter-charges. The episode reflects England's political chaos, for Bolingbroke has just displaced King RICHARD II. In 5.6 Fitzwater reports the defeat of a rebellion against Bolingbroke, and is promised rewards by the new king.

**Flaminius** Minor character in *Timon of Athens*, a servant of TIMON. In 2.2 Flaminius is told to ask Lord LUCULLUS for a loan to assist his master, whose extravagant generosity—to Lucullus, among others—has led him to bankruptcy. However, in 3.1 Lucullus refuses, and tries to hide his ingratitude by bribing Flaminius to say he could not be found, but the loyal servant is outraged and flings the offered coins at Lucullus. He follows this gesture with an heated condemnation that helps emphasise one of the play's major themes: the appalling ingratitude of the Athenian aristocracy. Flaminius' major function is to further the unfolding of Timon's abandonment by his friends.

**Flavius (1) (L. Caesetius Flavus) (active 44 B.C.)** Historical figure and minor character in *Julius Caesar*, a tribune of ROME and an ally of BRUTUS (4). In 1.1 Flavius, with his fellow tribune, MARULLUS, disperses a crowd (see COMMONER [1]) that has assembled to cheer CAESAR (1) upon his triumph over Pompey in a civil war. The tribunes criticise the Commoners for their disloyalty to Pompey, whom they had earlier supported. After the crowd has dispersed, Flavius and Marullus decide to strip the city's statues, which are decorated in Caesar's honour, because they fear the triumphant general will become a tyrant. In 1.2.282–283 CASCA reports that Flavius and Marullus have been 'put to silence' for this deed. The episode establishes a widespread mistrust of Caesar. Flavius also appears briefly in 5.4 as a member of the army of BRUTUS (4) at the battle of PHILIPPI.

Shakespeare followed an error of his source, PLUTARCH's *Lives*—transmitted through the translations of AMYOT and NORTH—in mis-spelling the name of the historical tribune, Flavus. Little is known of Flavus beyond the incident enacted: he and Marullus were dismissed from their positions by Caesar. Flavus' appearance at Philippi is Shakespeare's invention.

**Flavius (2)** Character in *Timon of Athens*. See STEWARD (2).

**Fleance** Minor character in *Macbeth*, the son of BANQUO and the intended murder victim of MACBETH. The WITCHES predict to Macbeth that he will be king but that Banquo's descendants will rule, rather than his own, so once Macbeth has seized the throne of SCOTLAND, he decides that he must kill Banquo and Fleance to prevent the prediction coming true. Fleance appears briefly in 2.1, simply to establish his existence, and when Banquo is killed in 3.3 Fleance escapes after an even briefer appearance. Thus, the possibility is preserved that Banquo's line will eventually replace Macbeth's, and this is Fleance's sole function in *Macbeth*. Once his survival is noted, he is not mentioned in the remainder of the play.

Banquo and Fleance are named as forefathers of the STUART dynasty in Shakespeare's source for the play, HOLINSHED's *Chronicles*. A Stuart ruled England at the time *Macbeth* was written in the person of King JAMES I, and the playwright dutifully included the information (the connection to the Stuarts is made by Banquo's GHOST [4]). However, this was simply a legend recorded as fact in Holinshed's source, the semi-legendary history by Hector BOECE. Fleance in fact never existed, although the name may well have been used by some ancient Scottish lord.

**Fleay, Frederick Gard (1831–1909)** Shakespearean scholar. F. G. Fleay, who turned to the study of ancient Egypt and Assyria after publishing several works on Shakespeare and his world, was among the early advocates of close study of the plays. He helped develop the VERSE TEST as an analytic tool and was one of the first 'disintegrators', a school of critics who believe that many of the plays attributed to Shakespeare were written by more than one person and who attempt to determine by literary analysis who wrote what. Fleay, like J. M. ROBERTSON, approached this question through a subjective comparison of styles, a procedure that is generally frowned on by more scientifically minded scholars.

**Fletcher (1), Giles (1546–1611)** English diplomat and writer, author of a possible influence on *Love's Labour's Lost*. Fletcher, after a journey to Russia to negotiate trading rights, wrote *On the Russe Common Wealth* (1591). He was highly critical of the Russians, who had treated him badly. English merchants, fearful of insult to their potential customers, attempted to have the book suppressed. However, parts of it were republished by Richard HAKLUYT and others, and the book went on to become quite popular. Scholars believe that Fletcher's book was the stimulus for the pageant of comic Russians performed at the INNS OF COURT in 1594; this performance influenced in turn Shakespeare's comical Russian masquerade in 5.2 of *Love's Labour's Lost*.

Fletcher was born into a clerical family—his brother (the father of the playwright John FLETCHER [2]) became the bishop of London—and he was a prominent lay administrator in the Church of England before becoming a diplomat. He was also noted for a volume of sonnets in the style of SPENSER, published in 1593. In 1600 he served as executor for his brother, the bishop, who had died in debt, and was almost imprisoned for that debt himself. He was saved through the influence of his friend the Earl of ESSEX (2), and when the Earl staged an unsuccessful rebellion against Queen ELIZABETH (1) the next year, Fletcher stood up for his saviour to the extent that he was imprisoned for several years and his diplomatic career was ended.

**Fletcher (2), John (1579–1625)** English playwright, collaborator with Shakespeare, and a leading figure of JACOBEAN DRAMA. Fletcher wrote parts of *The Two Noble Kinsmen* and possibly parts of both *Henry VIII* and a lost play, CARDENIO. He succeeded Shakespeare as principal dramatist for the KING'S MEN theatre company. Fletcher's earliest works, influenced by Ben JONSON'S COMEDY OF HUMOURS and written for the CHILDREN'S COMPANIES, were not very successful. In 1608 he began to collaborate with Francis BEAUMONT (2), a similarly unsuccessful young writer of COMEDY. The two enjoyed tremendous success and became the closest of friends, sharing the same lodgings—and, re-

portedly, the same mistress—while writing about 15 plays in eight years. They were the most important English dramatists in the generation that followed Shakespeare's retirement. Beaumont retired in 1613, but Fletcher wrote many more plays, all of them for the King's Men, many in collaboration with other playwrights, especially Philip MASSINGER but also Jonson, George CHAPMAN, and Thomas MIDDLETON.

Beaumont and Fletcher first achieved success with *Philaster* (1610), a TRAGICOMEDY that was hugely popular and influenced English drama for decades. They followed their success with more of the same, as well as with tragedies and romantic comedies. Among their best known works are *Cupid's Revenge* (1608), *The Maid's Tragedy* (1610), *A King and No King* (1611), and *The Scornful Lady* (1613). In the 1630s, and again in the 1660s, the popularity of Beaumont and Fletcher surpassed that of all other English dramatists, including Shakespeare.

Fletcher's own dramas are often difficult to identify, for so much of his work was collaborative. However, scholars believe that he wrote at least 16 works of his own. They included tragicomedies, such as *The Island Princess* (c. 1619–1621), which confirmed the style set by *Philaster,* and comedies of manners, like *The Wild-Goose Chase* (1621), which were to be very influential on Restoration comedy. In all his works, Fletcher's goal is simply entertainment, whether provided in high-flown rhetoric of death and love, farcical romantic entanglements, or graceful songs. His work is part of an escapist and decadent period in English drama, but in its own terms, it is undeniably successful.

**Fletcher (3), Laurence (d. 1608)** English actor active in SCOTLAND. Fletcher was recorded as an 'English player' employed by the King, later, King JAMES I of England. He was at the head of the list of members of Shakespeare's KING'S MEN when they received their licence in 1603 upon the occasion of the accession of King James to the English throne. However, since there is no other mention of Fletcher in connection with the King's Men, scholars believe that he may have been included on the licence simply because he had headed James' company in Scotland and was never actually an active member of the London company. He was a minor member of King James' household until his death. Some scholars believe that Shakespeare may have performed with Fletcher in Scotland in 1601, but no solid evidence exists to support this notion. Shakespeare may have left London in the wake of the seeming involvement of the CHAMBERLAIN'S MEN in the rebellion of the Earl of ESSEX (2).

**Flint Castle** Fortified castle in northern WALES (1), location in *Richard II*. In 3.3 BOLINGBROKE (1) takes custody of King RICHARD II at Flint while professing to be his humble subject. Historically Richard was already the prisoner of Bolingbroke's lieutenant,

NORTHUMBERLAND (1), when he was taken to Flint, a notoriously impregnable castle. It was the first of the many castles that the English built in Wales when they occupied the country in the 13th century.

**Florence**   Italian city, a location in *All's Well That Ends Well.* Various French noblemen, including BERTRAM, join the army of the DUKE (2) of Florence in his war with Siena, and HELENA (2), pursuing Bertram, follows them. Much of Acts 3 and 4 take place in Florence and vicinity. However, nothing in the play is distinctively Florentine—or even Italian—and it is clear that Shakespeare merely followed BOCCACCIO, his ultimate source, in setting part of the action there.

**Florizel**   Character in *The Winter's Tale,* son of King POLIXENES of BOHEMIA and suitor of PERDITA. Florizel defies his father's anger at his intention to marry Perdita, a shepherd girl deemed unsuitable for the heir to the kingdom, and the couple flees to SICILIA. There her identity as the daughter of King LEONTES is discovered, leading to the couple's formal engagement and the reconciliation of their fathers. Florizel is present in only three scenes—4.4, 5.1, and 5.3— and he does not speak in 5.3. Moreover, he is something of a cardboard hero, a stereotype of the chivalric young knight of traditional romantic literature—brave, handsome, and passionately loyal to his lover but with little further in the way of personality. Nevertheless, though his emotional range is restricted, Florizel is important to the play, for his cheerful adoration of Perdita is a charming and forceful manifestation of young love, and his courageous persistence in the face of Polixenes' wrath permits the pair to remain together long enough for the solution to emerge. He is thus an emblem of the power of love to withstand tyrannous opposition. His name probably comes from that of a similar hero, Florizel de Niquea, the protagonist of a chivalric romance by the 16th-century Spanish author Feliciano de Silva (c. 1492–1558).

**Flower portrait**   Portrait of Shakespeare, probably a copy of the DROESHOUT engraving. Some commentators hold that the Flower portrait—named for Sir Desmond Flower, who donated it to the Shakespeare Museum in STRATFORD in 1911—was the original from which Martin Droeshout did his engraving, which is considered an authoritative likeness. However, most scholars believe that it is a copy of the engraving, for it more closely resembles a corrected version of Droeshout's work rather than his initial effort. Moreover, the painting's inscription, 'Willm. Shakespeare, 1609', is in a script that did not come into use until somewhat later, and the paint includes a pigment not used until the 18th century. Therefore, the portrait was probably made in the 18th century, as a forgery.

**Florio, John (Giovanni) (c. 1553–1625)**   English translator whose version of the French essays of Michel de MONTAIGNE supplied minor sources for *The Tempest, Hamlet,* and *King Lear.* Florio's *Essayes on Morall, Politike, and Millitarie Discourses* (1603), his most significant work, was an eccentric elaboration of Montaigne's writing rather than a literal translation. Florio indulged in extravagant alliteration and euphuistic imagery (see LYLY), and he frequently included his own pedantic digressions and fantasies. Although a very inaccurate rendering of Montaigne's spare, crisp prose, Florio's book is a minor English masterpiece in its own right. Florio also wrote an Italian-English dictionary, *A Worlde of Wordes* (1598, 1611), and a series of textbooks for the study of Italian.

Florio taught Italian to the Earl of SOUTHAMPTON (2) and was a friend of Ben JONSON; scholars accordingly presume that Shakespeare was at least acquainted with the translator. Less probably, it is sometimes supposed that Shakespeare's comic pedant of *Love's Labour's Lost,* HOLOFERNES, was intended as a caricature of Florio. Holofernes does quote an Italian proverb found in *Second Fruits* (and elsewhere) in 4.2.93–94. Further, an anonymous sonnet in praise of Florio, published with his Italian text *Second Fruits* (1591), is sometimes attributed to Shakespeare.

Florio was born in LONDON to Italian Protestants who had fled from religious persecution. He attended Oxford, where he later taught French and Italian. Florio moved to London sometime before 1600 and became a tutor to the wife and children of King JAMES I. He was a notable member of the London literary world; besides his acquaintance with Jonson and (probably) Shakespeare, he was married to a sister of Samuel DANIEL.

**Fluellen**   Character in *Henry V,* a Welsh officer in the army of King HENRY V. Fluellen, although hot-tempered, rather humourless, and pedantic, is open, honest, and courageous as well. He is further distinguished by a comically extravagant Welsh accent. His prickly insistence on military traditions leads him to speak sharply to Captain MACMORRIS in 3.2, PISTOL in 3.6, WILLIAMS (2) in 4.8, and GOWER (2) at several points. Irked by Pistol's anti-Welsh mockery, Fluellen forces him to eat a leek, the Welsh national emblem, in 5.1. The king remarks that Fluellen is 'touch'd with choler, hot as gunpowder' (4.7.185).

Fluellen's bravery and sense of military honour mark him as a fine soldier, and his enthusiasm for Henry—especially in his humorous comparison of the king and Alexander the Great (4.7.12–55)—supports the play's presentation of the king as an epic hero. On the other hand, his fiery irrationality and suffocating self-confidence are also to be associated with the king and thus colour the alternative view that Henry is a vicious militarist and the play a satirical picture of war and political power. Shakespeare intended both aspects of the play to be felt, and Fluellen, in his small way, contributes to this effect.

Fluellen's name is a variant of the more common Welsh name Llewelyn; Shakespeare may have borrowed the surname of one William Fluellen, an associate of his father, John SHAKESPEARE (9). Fluellen's Welshness helps to demonstrate the unity of the peoples of Britain under Henry V, especially in the 'international scene' (3.2), where Wales, England, Ireland, and Scotland are represented by Fluellen, Gower, Macmorris, and JAMY respectively. Also, the emphasis on Fluellen's accent probably reflects the presence of a Welshman in Shakespeare's acting company (see WALES [1]).

**Flute**    Character in *A Midsummer Night's Dream,* a bellows-mender of ATHENS and a performer in the comical amateur production of PYRAMUS AND THISBE staged at the wedding celebration of Duke THESEUS (1) and Queen HIPPOLYTA (1). Flute plays Thisbe in the INTERLUDE, which is directed by Peter QUINCE. In 1.2 Flute resents being cast as a woman, asserting that he has 'a beard coming' (1.2.43–44). His objection makes clear that in fact he is still a beardless youth. Flute's name, like those of his fellow artisans, refers to his trade; the flute is the nozzle through which a bellows expels air. The name also suggests the high-pitched quality of the character's voice, and Shakespeare may well have selected the name, and then the occupation, to suit the player of Thisbe.

**Folger Shakespeare Library**    Major collection of Shakespeareana in Washington, D.C. The Folger Library was founded in 1930 by Henry Clay Folger (1857–1930), an oil executive whose private collection provided the core of the Library's holdings. The Library, which is administered by Amherst College, also offers Shakespearean and modern plays on an Elizabethan-style stage (see ELIZABETHAN THEATRE), and publishes books and pamphlets of general interest on Shakespeare and his world. The Library houses 79 copies of the FIRST FOLIO, over 200 QUARTO editions of the plays, and thousands of other volumes in one of the world's largest and finest collections.

**Folio**    Format for a page or a book. A folio is a sheet of paper that is folded in half to make two leaves—four pages—or a book composed of such pages. (See also QUARTO.) Since printing paper is large to begin with, a folio volume is large in size, usually about 15 inches tall. In Shakespearean studies the term Folio—capitalised—usually refers to the FIRST FOLIO, the earliest collected edition of Shakespeare's plays (1623), which was published in the folio format. Three more folio-size editions appeared in the 17th century, the Second, Third, and Fourth Folios (1632, 1663, 1685). Each was printed from the preceding edition and added its own corrections and errors. Since they have

no connection to an original manuscript or other prepublication source, they are of little scholarly interest. However, the Third Folio (copies of which are relatively rare, probably because many were lost in the fire that destroyed much of London in 1666) incorporated *Pericles* for the first time and introduced a number of plays into the Shakespeare APOCRYPHA as well.

**Follower**    Any of several minor characters in *Hamlet,* rebels led by LAERTES. Upset about the killing of his father, POLONIUS, by Prince HAMLET, Laertes has returned to DENMARK from abroad in a fury. When he arrives in 4.5, he and his Followers break down the door to get to the KING (5). However, he immediately dismisses his men, and the King persuades him to seek revenge against Hamlet rather than through revolution. The Followers speak very little and serve primarily to demonstrate the widespread effects of evil, as political rebellion and social disorder arise from the more personal conflict between Hamlet and the King.

**Fool (1)**    Character type often used by Shakespeare, a sharp-tongued comic, usually a professional jester, who wittily insults the other characters and comments on their actions. He often serves as a CHORUS (1), providing a position outside the plot with which we, the audience, can identify. Real jesters were well known in Shakespeare's day—Queen ELIZABETH (1) employed fools, for instance—and the playwright found this recognised social figure, with his well-defined traditional role, a useful embodiment of objectivity to balance the improbabilities of COMEDY.

Shakespeare did not use fools in his early work, though SPEED in *Two Gentlemen of Verona* and the BASTARD (1) in *King John* foreshadow later figures. In *A Midsummer Night's Dream,* PUCK serves as a jester to OBERON, and he demonstrates an important attribute of the fool, a cool detachment from the problems of the plot and a somewhat self-centred focus on his own notions of humour. The FALSTAFF of the *Henry IV* plays also has points in common with the jesters of later plays. Not only does he present some similar attributes—verbal dexterity, a facility for imitation, and an inventive sense of the absurd—but he also shares the fool's deeper significance as an emblem of freedom from convention. It is with the development of Shakespeare's mature comedy that we find his true jesters. FESTE in *Twelfth Night* and TOUCHSTONE in *As You Like It,* are quintessential fools. Delighted by Touchstone, JAQUES (1) describes and defines the fool's profession and purposes at length, in a striking series of speeches (2.7.12–61). The fool's critique is seen as powerful enough to 'cleanse the foul body of th'infected world' (2.7.60).

A fool can also prove useful in TRAGEDY, providing comic relief as well as his customary objectivity. The FOOL (2) who serves King LEAR, for example, develops the character type to a new level of dramatic expression. He is virtually an alter ego of the king. His jests are a foil to Lear's frenzy, and his riddles, songs, and scraps of rhyme—combined with his ridicule of the king's folly—offer a sense that somewhere outside the terrifying universe of the play, there remains a real world in which sanity still exists.

In Shakespeare's PROBLEM PLAYS, the fools are less attractive figures. In *All's Well That Ends Well*, the jester to the COUNTESS (2) of ROSSILLION—named Lavatch but designated CLOWN (5)—is a melancholy and sometimes slightly obnoxious character; rather strikingly, when PAROLLES, the comic villain of the play, is defeated, he finds recourse in becoming a professional fool, with the hope that his reputation as a hapless knave will seem entertaining. THERSITES in *Troilus and Cressida* is an abusive and rancorous bandier of insults; while funny, he is also somewhat dispiriting. In *Timon of Athens* (sometimes classed with the darker comedies), APEMANTUS, though technically not a fool—in that he is not a jester—is similar to Thersites. *Measure for Measure* has no fool, but the malicious defamation practised by LUCIO gives him something of Thersites' quality also. The fool's objectivity is not desirable in the unreal world of the ROMANCES, Shakespeare's last works, and the only fool to appear in them—TRINCULO of *The Tempest*—is, although a jester, rather more a CLOWN (1) than a fool.

The distinction between clown and fool is significant, although the Elizabethans tended to treat the terms as synonyms (Lavatch and Feste—both professional jesters—are designated 'Clowns'). The clown tends to be outside the plot's main developments, while the fool is involved with the central characters. Whereas the clown's humour is unintentional, the fool's intellectual wit and trenchant observation are deliberate. With his blunt, earthy spontaneity, the clown lacks the fool's satirical edge. Shakespeare's fools may reflect the stage manner of Robert ARMIN, who joined the playwright's troupe just before the creation of Touchstone, but the type also carries meaning: the fool's sardonic attitude towards the defects of human society adds an underlying melancholy to the essentially positive stance of comedy.

**Fool (2)**   Character in *King Lear*, the court jester or FOOL (1) to King LEAR. The Fool sees that Lear should not have rejected CORDELIA and placed himself in the power of REGAN and GONERIL, and he repeatedly reminds his master of this. He employs barbed quips, for instance, having caused Lear to observe that 'nothing can be made out of nothing', the Fool remarks, '. . . so much the rent of his land comes to' (1.4.130–132). He also utters simple truths, such as 'Thou should'st not have been old till thou hadst been wise' (1.5.41–42). He strives to use his wit to ease Lear's mind as the king goes insane, and he accompanies him into the stormy wilderness in Act 3. The Fool is last seen leaving with Lear and KENT after GLOUCESTER (1) has warned them

*Nicholas Pennell as the Fool in the 1985 Stratford (Ontario) festival production of* King Lear. (Photograph by David Cooper)

of a murder plot against the king. His last line, 'And I'll go to bed at noon' (3.6.83), suggests an early death, but his fate is not reported.

The Fool is deeply moved by Lear's plight, but he is capable of detachment from it. Lear's Fool shares with other Shakespearean jesters, such as FESTE and TOUCHSTONE, an irony that permits him to comment on the action of the play, as does a CHORUS (1). With jokes, riddles, and scraps of SONG, he clarifies the central situation by commenting on it more intelligently than the other characters. Especially pertinent is his observation, '. . . the Fool will stay, / And let the wise man fly' (2.4.79–80); with it he makes a declaration of loyalty that helps contrast a moral world with the tragic one that dominates the play. Similarly, his sanity is a foil for Lear's increasing disintegration.

The Fool is closely associated with Cordelia at two significant points. Before his first entrance in 1.4.72, he is said to have 'much pined away' for her, the first mention of Lear's daughter since her departure in 1.1. At the play's close, Lear, grieving over Cordelia's corpse, says, 'And my poor fool is hang'd' (5.3.304). 'Fool' was a common term of endearment in Shakespeare's day, and Lear may simply be referring to his lost daughter, but the playwright nevertheless takes the occasion to compare the two characters. The Fool resembles Cordelia in both his devotion to Lear and his commitment to a truthful assessment of life. He replaces her as the exponent of these virtues during her long absence from the play; in fact, some scholars suggest that the two roles may have been taken by the same actor in the original productions by the KING'S MEN. Others, however, hold that the part of the Fool was probably played by the famed comedian Robert ARMIN, whose notoriety would have made him an unlikely Cordelia.

**Fool (3)**   Minor character in *Timon of Athens,* a professional jester. This FOOL (1) accompanies APEMANTUS in 2.2 and exchanges witticisms with VARRO'S SERVANT and others. He is apparently employed by a courtesan who is the subject of two jests about venereal disease, but his circumstances and qualities are not developed. His major speech (2.2.112–118) contains a pithy condemnation of ATHENS, which furthers an important theme of the play. However, most commentators believe that he may represent a false start for the playwright, who introduced him with the intention of developing a SUB-PLOT around him and then did not do so before he abandoned this incomplete play.

*Johnston Forbes-Robertson was renowned for the power of his voice. His portrayal of Hamlet (as seen here) was said to be the greatest of his time. (Courtesy of Culver Pictures, Inc.)*

**Forbes-Robertson, Johnston (1853–1947)**   British actor. Forbes-Robertson studied acting under Samuel PHELPS. He was especially noted for his HAMLET, ROMEO, MACBETH, and OTHELLO and often starred in Henry IRVING's productions. He succeeded Irving as manager of the Lyceum Theatre in 1895 and produced several of Shakespeare's tragedies, including *Hamlet* (1897), to which he restored the closing episode following Hamlet's death, seldom enacted in the 19th century.

**Ford (1), Frank**   Character in *The Merry Wives of Windsor,* jealous husband of MISTRESS (1) Alice Ford. Ford is to some extent a character type, representing a traditional figure in European folklore and literature, the jealous husband, but he is also humanly credible. His emotional excess is not only a source of simple comedy; it also adds to our rich sense of domestic life in Windsor. Ford's jealous tendencies are established before he appears, when his wife remarks on them to her friend MISTRESS (3) Page in 2.1.97–103. Then, in a psychologically masterful manner, Shakespeare demonstrates the growth of an episode of jealousy. At first Ford disbelieves PISTOL's assertion that FALSTAFF is courting his wife, though only for a rather uncomplimentary reason— 'Why, sir, my wife is not young' (2.1.109)—but then he tersely directs himself to look into this possibility, in lines scattered within NYM's insinuations of a similar adultery to PAGE (12) and he refuses to follow Page in his dismissal of the accusations. When his wife observes that Ford appears preoccupied, he snaps at her. She remarks that he has 'some crotchets in thy head now' (2.1.148), and we are aware that mistrust and anxiety have taken control of him. When Mistress QUICKLY says that his wife 'leads an ill life with him' (2.2.85), we easily believe her.

Ford's strategy—taking the name BROOK (1) and encouraging Falstaff to approach his wife so that he can catch him at it—is a simple-minded device suitable to the jealous husband in a farce, and the wily wives make Ford foolish at the same time that they dupe Falstaff. Although we do not sympathise with Ford, his heartfelt relief when the situation is revealed to him is touching. Moved to impromptu rhetoric, he asserts to his wife, 'I rather will suspect the sun with cold than thee with wantonness' (4.4.7–8), inspiring Page to remark tellingly, 'Be not as extreme in submission as in offence' (4.4.11–12).

**Ford (2), John (1586–c. 1639)**   English dramatist, one of the last playwrights of JACOBEAN DRAMA. Ford began to write plays around 1612, collaborating with Thomas DEKKER, John WEBSTER (2), and others. Of his own works, he is chiefly remembered for several tragedies marked by bitter resignation and despair, the best known of which is *'Tis Pity She's a Whore* (c. 1632), a tale of incest between brother and sister. His historical drama *Perkin Warbeck* (1633) is also highly regarded. Ford lived much of his life in poverty and is thought to have spent his last years in seclusion.

**Ford (3), Mistress Alice**   Character in *The Merry Wives of Windsor.* See MISTRESS (1).

**Forester**   Minor character in *Love's Labour's Lost,* the guide for a royal hunt. The Forester's naïve honesty provides a foil for the wit of the PRINCESS (1) of France in 4.1.

**Forman, Simon (1552–1611)**   English astrologer and diarist. Forman recorded several early performances of Shakespeare's plays. His records—generally brief synopses—help scholars determine the dates, and in some cases the likelihood of variation from the published texts, of various plays, including three of Shakespeare's works: *Macbeth, Cymbeline,* and *The Winter's Tale.*

Astrology was a more reputable occupation then than now, but Forman may have been less than scrupulous. He was frequently gaoled for practising medicine without a licence, and because of his reputation, it was suspected, when he drowned in the Thames after predicting the date of his death, that he was a suicide.

**Forrest, Edwin (1806–1872)**   American actor. The first great American Shakespearean actor, Forrest helped create popular enthusiasm for Shakespeare in the United States, especially with his performances as OTHELLO and LEAR. He appeared in London in 1836 and 1845, and a rivalry developed between him and W. C. MACREADY. Comparisons of the two took on a nationalistic colour, especially in America, and led to the notorious Astor Place riot in New York in 1849, when a mob of Forrest fans—and opportunistic, anti-England political agitators—stormed a theatre where Macready was playing and the commotion left 22 dead. In the opinion of contemporaries and most subsequent scholars, Forrest personally instigated the affair, and the actor's popularity slowly waned after this incident. He eventually fell from favour entirely, dying an embittered failure.

**Fortinbras**   Character in *Hamlet,* Prince of Norway and enemy of DENMARK. Although he does not appear until 4.4, Fortinbras is described in 1.1.98–107 as a hot-blooded young warrior intent on recapturing lands taken from Norway after the combat in which his father, the late King of Norway, was killed by HAMLET's father, the late King of Denmark. Thus he is immediately established as a parallel figure to Hamlet, one who is also compelled to avenge his father's death. Fortinbras' brief appearance in 4.4 on his way to an invasion of neighbouring Poland energises Hamlet, who sees in this war, directed at no more than 'a little patch of ground . . . a straw . . . an eggshell' (4.4.18, 26, 53), a direct and shaming contrast to his own inaction in taking revenge against his father's murderer, KING (5) Claudius. When Hamlet, nearing death at the play's end, learns that Fortinbras is returning from Poland, he proclaims him heir to the crown of Denmark. When he arrives, Fortinbras takes command and orders a military funeral for Hamlet.

While Fortinbras' example inspires Hamlet to fierce declarations—'My thoughts be bloody or be nothing worth' (4.4.66)—Hamlet's rhetoric is an overreaction to a situation that is not in fact analogous to his own. As the play unfolds, Hamlet comes to realise that an acceptance of fate and its evils is the only way to understand human life; within this context, Fortinbras, who works his will in the world and is doubtless uninterested in such philosophical matters, is clearly a lesser figure. Still, his stalwart resolution and military valour—reminiscent of Shakespeare's HENRY V—are not only admirable but also stand in important contrast to the evil and debased intrigue of Hamlet's world.

When Fortinbras appears after Hamlet's death in 5.2, he reminds us that he comes as a hostile power, declaring that he will claim his revenge as his 'vantage doth invite' (5.2.395), and we realise that Claudius' evil has damaged his kingdom to the extent that an outsider has taken over. Thus Fortinbras symbolises a lesson in political morality that Shakespeare offered in several plays (e.g., *Titus Andronicus, Macbeth, King Lear*): personal evil in powerful members of society will weaken the state as a whole, often resulting in a surrender of sovereignty to another country.

**Fortune Theatre**   Playhouse built in a northern LONDON suburb by Philip HENSLOWE and William ALLEYN in 1600, long the home of the ADMIRAL'S MEN and its successors, PRINCE HENRY'S MEN and the PALSGRAVE'S MEN. The Fortune may have been built in response to the construction of the GLOBE THEATRE near Henslowe and Alleyn's ROSE THEATRE in SOUTHWARK, south of the city. Some scholars theorise that when Cuthbert BURBAGE (1) and the CHAMBERLAIN'S MEN moved to the Globe in 1599, Henslowe and Alleyn saw an opportunity to avoid direct competition while at the same time filling the vacuum created by the Chamberlain's departure from the CURTAIN THEATRE, to the north of London. Moreover, their lease on the ground the Rose was built on was about to expire. In any event, the Fortune was meant to rival the Globe; it was commissioned from the same builder, under a contract requiring that it be 'finished and done according to the manner and fashion of the said house called the Globe'. It took its name from a statue of the Goddess of Fortune over its entrance. When the Fortune burned down in 1621, it was described as 'the fairest playhouse' in London. It was rebuilt in 1623 and was used for surreptitious play productions after the Puritans' revolutionary government made theatre illegal in 1642, at the beginning of the Civil Wars. The building was pillaged by soldiers in 1649 and finally destroyed around 1656.

**Foul Papers**  In textual studies, a playwright's original, unpolished manuscript from which the printers of an early edition of a play might set the type. This version differs from FAIR COPY, which was used for the same purpose but was provided by a scribe, who might make various corrections to the original manuscript. A published text set from foul papers is therefore distinctively flawed by minor errors and inconsistencies taken from the source.

In the case of Shakespeare, the playwright's careless slips survived into the printed text: his spelling is often irregular, and inconsistent names occur in speech headings and stage directions. Lady CAPULET (3), for instance, is designated in the Q2 edition of *Romeo and Juliet* as *Capu. Wi, Ca. Wi, Wife, Old La., La., Mo.,* and *M.* Sometimes an actor's name will appear as a speech heading—e.g., KEMPE for DOGBERRY in 4.2 of *Much Ado About Nothing*—which is evidence that Shakespeare created the part with a particular player in mind. GHOST CHARACTERS may appear without again being mentioned, like INNOGEN in 1.1 and 2.1 of *Much Ado*. In fair copy most of these problems were corrected. Also, when a text was printed from foul papers new errors resulted from the use of a rapidly composed manuscript that was likely to be difficult to read and was further confused by handwritten amendments and marginal insertions.

Sometimes material was retained by the typesetter that the author intended to cut. For instance, Q2 of *Hamlet* preserves a line Shakespeare had rejected; two lines of similar meaning occur together, and the first one does not rhyme with any other although it is in the midst of a long passage of rhyming couplets. Clearly, the playwright rejected it in favour of the second (3.2. 162) as he was writing, but the substitution was not evident to the printer, who simply reproduced everything he saw. The error was corrected in the FIRST FOLIO edition.

Stage directions in foul papers are sometimes casually imprecise, as in 'Enter . . . others, as many as can be' (*Titus Andronicus*, 1.1.70). They may also reveal the playwright's thoughts on production in more elaborate and specific stage directions than usual, such as: 'Enter VOLUMNIA and VIRGILIA, mother and wife to MARTIUS. They set them down on two low stools and sew' (*Coriolanus*, 1.3.S.D.). These parenthetical remarks were normally abbreviated or eliminated by a copyist.

With the probable exception of three pages of SIR THOMAS MORE, no original Shakespearean manuscript exists, but by observing such features as those mentioned above, scholars can determine what sort of copy was the basis for an early edition—whether a manuscript or an earlier printing, and if a manuscript, whether fair copy or foul papers. Modern editors can determine from such information how closely a given printed text represents what Shakespeare actually wrote.

**Foxe (Fox), John (1516–1587)**  English historian of religion, author of a source for *2 Henry VI, King John,* and especially *Henry VIII.* Foxe's *Actes and Monumentes,* better known as the *Book of Martyrs,* is a history of Protestantism, focussing on the English Protestants who were persecuted during the reign of Queen Mary (ruled 1553–1558), a zealous Catholic. Passages from his account of Thomas CRANMER's life were Shakespeare's principal source for Cranmer's trial in 5.1–2 of *Henry VIII.* Other material provided details for *2 Henry VI* and *King John.*

Foxe's book was written in Latin during his exile from England during Mary's reign. He returned in 1559 and translated and published his work in 1563, enlarging it for a second edition in 1570. It immediately became immensely popular and influential—the 1570 edition was required by law to be available to worshippers in all English cathedrals and for generations it was regarded by English Protestants as a virtual supplement to the Bible. Many houses contained only those two books. The *Book of Martyrs* was republished many times in the 16th and 17th centuries; Shakespeare probably used the fourth edition (1583).

**France (1)**  Country in Europe. France, England's most powerful neighbour and perennial rival, was its enemy in the HUNDRED YEARS WAR and earlier conflicts. It thus provides settings in three of the HISTORY PLAYS and is prominent in several other plays as well.

In *1 Henry V* and *Henry VI,* Shakespeare presented the later phases of the Hundred Years War, the major struggle between England and France in the 14th and 15th centuries. King HENRY V's triumph at the battle of AGINCOURT (1415) is enacted in Act 4 of *Henry V* and followed by the negotiation of the treaty of TROYES in 5.2, completing the English conquest. King Henry V is betrothed on this occasion to Princess KATHARINE (2) of France; their child is to be King HENRY VI.

In *1 Henry VI,* English forces besiege ORLÉANS (1) and ROUEN, and the young Henry is crowned king of France in PARIS (1). However, the English conquest of France is actually being undone under the leadership of JOAN LA PUCELLE and CHARLES VII. The final battle of the war, the English loss at BORDEAUX, occupies most of Act 4, though Shakespeare salvaged a seeming victory by staging Joan's trial at ANGIERS in 5.3.

France is unimportant in the other *Henry VI* plays,

though one scene of *3 Henry VI* (3.3) is set at the court of King LEWIS (3), who offers aid to English rebels. In *King John*, set much earlier in history, King JOHN (3) also fights in France, protecting PLANTAGENET lands against the French King PHILIP (2). This war centres on Angiers, where fighting occurs in 2.1 and 3.2.

Long after the Hundred Years War, rivalry with France remained a prominent feature of English politics. Only in 1564, the year of Shakespeare's birth, did England finally renounce its last claims to French territory, and, during the playwright's lifetime, war between the two countries seemed likely on more than one occasion. Catholic France was seen by Protestant England as a potential religious enemy, for Europe was still plagued by sectarian wars. Thus, along with another rival, Spain, France loomed as large in the fears of Shakespeare's contemporaries as the Soviet Union does to many Westerners today. England and France remained hostile for centuries after Shakespeare's time; only in the 20th century has warfare between them seemed improbable.

Because Shakespeare's audiences shared an interest in France and French affairs, he also used this country and its people outside the history plays. A king of France (FRANCE [2]) finds his way into ancient British myth in *King Lear*. In *Love's Labour's Lost*, the presentation of a KING (19) of Navarre reflects the importance in contemporary French politics of the current King of Navarre, soon to become King Henri IV of France. A comical Frenchman, Dr CAIUS (2), is mocked in *The Merry Wives of Windsor*.

*All's Well That Ends Well* is set partially in France, in the province of ROSSILLION (the French Roussillon), and Shakespeare elaborates on his sources in providing a realistic political relationship between France and Italy that reflects the French military involvement in Italy throughout the first half of the 16th century.

It has been speculated that Shakespeare travelled in France, although no evidence has survived to confirm this. It is clear, though, that he knew the French language. Not only did he sometimes use French sources that had not been translated into English, but his French dialogue—e.g., in *Henry V*, 3.4, 4.4, 5.2—is only slightly flawed.

**France (2), King of**    Character in *King Lear*, the suitor and later the husband of CORDELIA, King LEAR's rejected daughter. France, as the king is called, appears only in 1.1. He recognises the honesty and virtue in Cordelia and thus emphasises Lear's moral blindness. He agrees to marry her, saying 'She is herself a dowry' (1.1.240), and takes her back to FRANCE (1). Cordelia is thus absent for most of the action as her sisters humiliate and banish their father. The Earl of KENT (1) soon knows that 'from France there comes a power' (3.1.30) to aid Lear, but France himself does not reappear; he has returned home to deal with 'something

he left imperfect in the state' (4.3.3), while a French general unsuccessfully attempts to re-establish Lear on the throne. The subject of foreign invasion was a touchy one in Shakespeare's day because Protestant England felt threatened by Catholic enemies, including France, and scholars believe that the playwright found it expedient, in view of government CENSORSHIP, to deemphasise the role of France, both man and country, in *King Lear*.

**France (3), Princess of**    Character in *Love's Labour's Lost*. See PRINCESS (1) OF FRANCE.

**France (4), Queen of**    Character in *Henry V*. See ISABEL (2).

**Francesca (Francisca)**    Character in *Measure for Measure*. See NUN.

**Francis (1)**    Minor character in *1* and *2 Henry IV*, an indentured servant at the BOAR'S HEAD TAVERN. In 2.4 of *1 Henry IV* PRINCE (6) HAL teases Francis, engaging him in conversation while POINS, by pre-arrangement, summons him. The endearingly simple-minded Francis can only reply with the well-known protest of the harried waiter, 'Anon, anon', as Hal has predicted. Hal suggests that Francis might run away from the tavern, and then he extravagantly promises Francis £1,000 for a packet of sugar. He next asks if Francis will rob the innkeeper and goes on to speak of Francis' likely future. 'Why then your brown bastard is your only drink', he says, 'for look you, Francis, your white canvas doublet will sully. In Barbary, sir, it cannot come to so much' (2.4.72–74). Francis is now hopelessly confused, and he exits hurriedly as Poins, Hal, and his boss, the VINTNER, all call him at once.

This puzzling exchange has elicited a number of explanations, the simplest of which is that Hal is merely playing a practical joke on Francis, an example of the idle tavern life that he will later reject. However, while a joke is clearly intended, the Prince is deliberately placing himself on familiar terms with an 'under-skinker' (2.4.24), continuing his exploration of the lives of the common people whom he will later rule. Thus the episode helps to demonstrate that Hal's participation in FALSTAFF's world is part of his preparation for his greater role, and not simply dissipation. He suggests as much when, asked by Poins what the point of the joke was, he replies that he is now 'of all humours' (2.4.90) and compares his good mood with HOTSPUR's mania for war. In Francis' humble life, he has seen a contentment that the warrior can never discover. Further, Hal observes that, if Francis will not be tempted by theft or flight, he must accept the low life of a servant. This may reflect, albeit in a resigned manner, Hal's attitude towards his own destiny to become a leader, rather than a participant in the easier, irresponsible world of the tavern.

In *2 Henry IV* Francis appears to have been promoted, as he organises the service for Falstaff's dinner in 2.4.

**Francis (2), Friar**  Character in *Much Ado About Nothing*. See FRIAR (2).

**Francisco (1)**  Minor character in *Hamlet*, a sentry on the walls of the castle at ELSINORE. Francisco is relieved from duty by BARNARDO at the opening of 1.1, as the scene's locale is established. He declares himself 'sick at heart' (1.1.9), suggesting immediately that something is amiss in the play's world.

**Francisco (2)**  Minor character in *The Tempest*, a follower of King ALONSO of Naples. In 2.1.109–118 Francisco attempts to reassure the king that Prince FERDINAND (2) has survived their shipwreck. This passage is an extension of GONZALO's efforts to cheer the king, and Francisco speaks only three more words, in 3.3.40, so there seems little reason for his presence in the play. In some editions, in fact, he is deleted and his lines given to Gonzalo. Some scholars have taken him and ADRIAN (2) as evidence of an earlier version of *The Tempest*, in which they played a greater part. He may have been intended for scenes that Shakespeare originally planned but then discarded in the course of composition. In any case, royal figures are conventionally endowed with unimportant attendants throughout Shakespeare's work.

**Frederick**  Character in *As You Like It*. See DUKE (1).

**French, George Russell (1803–1881)**  English architect and amateur scholar, publisher of a genealogy of Shakespeare. French's *Shakespeareana Genealogica* (1869), covered Shakespeare's ancestors, relatives, and descendants, along with genealogical notes on the characters in the HISTORY PLAYS, *Hamlet*, and *Macbeth*. His was the first work in this area, and it is still valuable to scholars. French also wrote genealogies of Admiral Horatio Nelson (1758–1805) and the Duke of Wellington (1769–1852), and he was a well-known campaigner against the drinking of alcohol.

**French King (Charles VI of France, 1368–1422)**  Historical figure and character in *Henry V*, the opponent of King HENRY V. The French King plays an inconsequential role. He presents a brief history of earlier English conquests in FRANCE (1) in 2.4.48–64; he encourages his noblemen before the battle of AGINCOURT in 3.5; and in 5.2 he accepts the terms of the treaty of TROYES, surrendering to Henry the inheritance of his crown, as well as the hand of his daughter,

Princess KATHARINE (2). The ineffectual French King complements another model of French inadequacy, the caricature of foolish bravado that is his son the DAUPHIN (3).

This perfunctory portrait omits the most important fact about the historical Charles VI: he was intermittently insane. His illness—later to surface in his grandson King HENRY VI of England—was known to Shakespeare, but the playwright, who had not touched on madness in the *Henry VI* plays either, may have disliked pointing out defects in the ancestral line of his own ruler, Queen ELIZABETH (1). Also, focussing on Henry V's greatness, he probably did not wish to elaborate on France's weakness. For in failing to mention Charles' lunacy, Shakespeare also omitted its most important consequence—a state of virtual civil war in France that made the English conquest much easier.

Two factions vied with each other for the regency of France when the King was sick. When Henry invaded, the party in power at first refused to fight him, fearing that their rivals would seize Paris in their absence. This led to the Dauphin's failure to relieve HARFLEUR, of which its GOVERNOR (1) complains in 3.3. The French pulled themselves together—note the French King's roll-call, including noblemen of both factions, in 3.5.40–45—but the victory at Agincourt saved the English. When Henry again entered France, in 1417, the same situation prevailed; as a result, the English were able to conquer Normandy and claim the French crown. (See HUNDRED YEARS WAR.)

**French Soldier**  Minor character in *Henry V*, a gentleman taken prisoner by PISTOL at AGINCOURT. In a grimly comic scene Pistol, who speaks no French, attempts to extract ransom from the Soldier, who tries to offer it but does not speak English. Finally the BOY (3) interprets, and Pistol agrees not to kill his captive.

**Frenchman**  Minor character in *Cymbeline*, a friend of the Roman gentleman PHILARIO. In 1.5 POSTHUMUS arrives in ROME. He has been exiled from Britain because he married the king's daughter, IMOGEN, and he meets the Frenchman and IACHIMO at Philario's home. The Frenchman has known Posthumus in the past, and he recollects a duel the Briton once fought over the virtues of a woman. This triggers the fateful wager between Posthumus and Iachimo over Imogen's chastity. The Frenchman is a pawn of plot development, and represents the world of gentlemanly duels inhabited by Posthumus and Iachimo.

**Friar (1)**  Character in *Measure for Measure*, helper of the DUKE (9) of VIENNA. In 1.3 the Duke asks the Friar to disguise him as another friar so that he can return to Vienna incognito and observe the administration of his deputy, ANGELO (2). In 4.5 the Duke revisits the

Friar, who assists in his plans to expose the misconduct of Angelo, and in 4.6 the Friar escorts ISABELLA
and MARIANA (2) as part of those plans. Finally, in 5.1
he introduces the two women as witnesses to Angelo's
evil doings. Though the Duke speaks of him in 1.3 as
an intimate friend, the relationship is not developed
and the Friar serves merely to further the plot.

The Friar is named Thomas in the stage direction at
the beginning of 1.3, but the name is never used elsewhere, and in a later appearance he is named Peter.
Shakespeare—who made such minor slips throughout
the plays—apparently gave the Friar a name when he
first created him, but then forgot about it before writing Act 4 where he gave him another one. The earliest
text of the play, that of the FOLIO, was printed from a
transcription of Shakespeare's manuscript, and his
original note was erroneously included.

**Friar (2) Francis** Minor character in *Much Ado About
Nothing*, clergyman who supports the slandered HERO,
restoring her father LEONATO's faith in her. The Friar
officiates at the wedding of Hero and CLAUDIO (1), only
to see the ceremony disrupted. Claudio (1), misled by
Don JOHN (1), rejects his bride, accusing her publicly
of promiscuity. Hero faints in response, and Leonato,
humiliated, curses her. However, the Friar believes
Hero is innocent, and his spiritual authority persuades
Leonato. The Friar then proposes a plan intended to
rouse Claudio's guilt and sympathy and renew his love
for Hero; Hero should be said to be dead. While this
plan has no effect on Claudio, it provides an interesting detour in the plot, during which Don John's
scheme is exposed by other means. The Friar marries
Hero to Claudio and BEATRICE to BENEDICK as the play
closes.

**Friar (3) John** Minor character in *Romeo and Juliet*, an
unsuccessful emissary between FRIAR (4) LAURENCE
and the exiled ROMEO. In 5.2 Friar John reports that
he has been unable to deliver Laurence's letter to
Romeo, having been quarantined as a suspected
plague carrier. Thus Romeo remains unaware that the
death of JULIET (1) is feigned, and the tragic dénouement is launched.

**Friar (4) Laurence (Lawrence)** Character in *Romeo
and Juliet*, the clergyman who assists ROMEO and JULIET
(1). Although presented as a respectable, well-meaning old gentleman given to platitudes, the Friar serves
as an agent of malevolent fate. In his first speech (2.3.
1–26) a sententious bouquet of rhymed observations
on plant lore, he demonstrates the conventionality of
thought that will lead him to proceed recklessly—to
the lovers' destruction—while maintaining an air of
caution. Moreover, his remarks on good and bad uses
for herbs foreshadow the role of potions and poisons

later in the play. He warns Romeo against haste in
such passages as 2.6.9–15, but nonetheless agrees to
perform the secret marriage of the young lovers. The
Friar's flimsy morality is evident when he advises the
distraught Juliet in 4.1. Accepting a bigamous marriage as an alternative, though not an ideal one, he
proposes a devious capitulation to her parents' wishes,
accompanied by the desperate expedient of the sleeping potion. In the final scene, his lack of character is
richly demonstrated as he abandons Juliet in the predicament his rash plans have brought about.

**Friend** Either of two minor characters in *The Two
Noble Kinsmen*, acquaintances of the GAOLER (4). In 4.1
the Friends assure the Gaoler that THESEUS (2), Duke
of ATHENS, has forgiven him for the fact that PALAMON
has escaped from his gaol with the assistance of his
DAUGHTER (2), and they sympathise with him when the
WOOER brings evidence that the Daughter is deranged.
The Friends, mere pawns of the plot, were probably
not Shakespeare's creations, for most scholars agree
that 4.1 was written by his collaborator, John
FLETCHER (2).

**Frogmore** Village near WINDSOR, the setting for 3.1
of *The Merry Wives of Windsor*. In this scene the curate
EVANS (3), challenged to a duel by Dr CAIUS (2), awaits
his foe in a field near Frogmore. The duel is averted,
and the enemies return to Windsor as allies. Shakespeare used the name Frogmore simply to evoke the
neighbourhood of Windsor, which was well known to
his original audience, members of the court of Queen
ELIZABETH (1).

**Froissart, Jean (1338–1410)** French chronicler
whose work may have influenced the writing of *Richard
II*, particularly in presenting a highly favourable account of John of GAUNT. Further, it is speculated that
Froissart's romantic presentation of the pomp and
pageantry of medieval ceremonies may have helped
form Shakespeare's sense of the courtly world of King
RICHARD II. The playwright will have known Froissart's
work in Lord BERNERS' translation (1523–1525).

In his *Chroniques* Froissart wrote of the contemporary HUNDRED YEARS WAR, interviewing many key participants and observing some events himself. His colourful history ends with the deposition of RICHARD II.
Froissart is considered to have been the last great
medieval writer; his vivid and exciting description of
the traditions and practices of the chivalric aristocracy
records a world that was fast vanishing in his own time.
His chronicles are still regarded as classics of European literature.

**Froth** Minor character in *Measure for Measure*, a customer of MISTRESS (2) Overdone's bordello and bar

who is arrested by the comical constable, ELBOW. In an episode of comic relief, Froth is brought to court along with Mistress Overdone's accomplice, POMPEY (1), in 2.1. Froth says very little and serves only as the subject of the humorous dispute between Elbow and Pompey. Dismissed by the judge ESCALUS (2), Froth makes his only substantial remark, a joke that seems to account for his name. He jests that he never enters a tap-room willingly, but is drawn in; a reference to the foam, or froth, 'drawn' by a tapster in the course of serving ale.

**Furness, Horace Howard (1833–1912)** American scholar, first editor of the *New Variorum* edition of Shakespeare's plays (see VARIORUM EDITION). Furness began work on this annotated collection of the plays in 1871 with *Romeo and Juliet*. In this edition he provided textual notes and excerpts from pertinent critical writings from many eras and several languages. With the assistance of his wife, Helen Kate Furness (1837–1883), and his son, H. H. Furness, Jr. (1865–1930), he had completed 18 volumes before he died. His son succeeded him as general editor of the series, which was not completed until 1953.

**Furnivall, Frederick James (1825–1910)** English scholar. Furnivall encouraged the study of Shakespeare's works as a whole—still a new pursuit in his day—in his notable introductions written for each play, in his scholarly edition of the *Works* (1876), and with the English translation of G. G. GERVINUS' *Shakespeare Commentaries* (1875). He was particularly associated with the development of the VERSE TEST as a tool for determining the chronological order of the plays. He also edited a 43-volume collection of facsimiles of the QUARTO editions of the plays (1880–1889).

Furnivall was a prolific scholar and educator with many interests besides Shakespearean studies. He founded many scholarly organisations, including the Early English Text, Chaucer, Ballad, New Shakespeare, Wyclif, Browning, and Shelley Societies; he was involved in the creation of the Oxford English Dictionary, and he produced a number of scholarly editions, most notably a collection of six texts of CHAUCER's *The Canterbury Tales* (1868).

# G

**Gad's Hill (Gadshill, Gads Hill)** Geographical feature near the city of ROCHESTER, setting for the highway robbery in 2.2 of *1 Henry IV*. Gad's Hill, on the road from Rochester to London, was a notorious site for highway robberies, both in the 16th century and in the period when the play is set. It is there that GADS-HILL, FALSTAFF, and others rob the TRAVELLERS, only to be robbed themselves by PRINCE (6) HAL and POINS.

The name of this infamous setting provided a nickname for a robber who operated there in the playwright's source, the FAMOUS VICTORIES, and Shakespeare simply adopted the name for the Gadshill of *1 Henry IV*. In old editions of the play, the site is spelled as one word, and some modern editors follow this style. Others adopt one of the two-word variants, also used in Elizabethan times, and thus ease the slight confusion that the duplication can produce. Shakespeare's double use of the name is one of many instances of the playwright's toleration for minor confusions and inconsistencies in his texts.

**Gadshill** Character in *1 Henry IV*, a highway robber and friend of FALSTAFF and PRINCE (6) HAL. In 2.1 of *1 Henry IV* Gadshill uses a well-known highwayman's tactic: an accomplice, the CHAMBERLAIN (1) of an inn, tips him off about the travel plans of rich guests. Then he and Falstaff and others rob these TRAVELLERS in 2.2, only to be robbed in their turn by the Prince and POINS. Gadshill—a professional thief, unlike Falstaff and the Prince—serves to demonstrate the depths of delinquency from which the Prince must emerge.

Gadshill is a nickname taken from Shakespeare's anonymous source, the FAMOUS VICTORIES, where it is applied to a highwayman whose favourite working locale was GAD'S HILL. No proper name is given for Shakespeare's character.

**Gallus, Caius Cornelius (c. 69–27 B.C.)** Historical figure and minor character in *Antony and Cleopatra*, a follower of Octavius CAESAR (2). In 5.1 Gallus wordlessly follows Caesar's order to accompany PROCULEIUS on his mission to offer mercy to CLEO-PATRA, and in 5.2 he arrives at the quarters of the Egyptian queen with a squad of soldiers (see GUARDS-MAN [2]). Gallus leaves immediately, but his appear-

ance—and his remark, 'You see how easily she may be surpris'd' (5.2.35)—makes clear that Cleopatra is now entirely in Caesar's control. She responds by attempting to stab herself, but she is prevented by Proculeius. Gallus reappears as part of Caesar's entourage later in the scene, but he does not speak again.

The historical Gallus was an important Roman poet, regarded as the principal inventor of the Roman love elegy, but only a fragment of a single line of his work survives. He abandoned art for war after an unsuccessful love affair and became a leading member of Caesar's military establishment; historians give him much of the credit for Antony's final defeat. After the war he became the first Roman governor of Egypt. He put down several rebellions and travelled up the Nile into what is now Sudan where he established relations between Rome and Ethiopia. However, he was a notably poor administrator, and a scandal, the details of which are lost, resulted in his dismissal. He was convicted of treason and punished with exile from Rome, to which he responded by killing himself.

**Ganymede** In *As You Like It*, name taken by ROSALIND when, banished by DUKE (1) Frederick, she travels with CELIA to the Forest of ARDEN (1) disguised as a young man. In Greek mythology Zeus, the king of the gods, became infatuated with Ganymede, a beautiful boy, and took the form of an eagle to kidnap him and carry him to Mount Olympus, where the youth became a cup-bearer to the gods. The name Ganymede thus came to suggest boyish beauty.

**Gaoler (1)** Minor character in *The Merchant of Venice*, the custodian of ANTONIO (2), who is arrested for debt, in 3.3. The Gaoler, who does not speak, represents the authority of the state, mutely showing that Antonio may not be exempted from the law. Shakespeare believed such rigour to be necessary, however undesirable the personal consequences.

**Gaoler (2)** Either of two minor characters in *Cymbeline*, keepers of the captured POSTHUMUS, who is believed to be a Roman prisoner of war. In 5.4 the First Gaoler is a CLOWN (1) who interrupts the action with humorous remarks on life and death (the Second

Gaoler speaks only half a line). He provides comic relief as the plot becomes most troubling. He offers a sardonic philosophy of death as a relief from life, a view that encapsulates Posthumus' depressed state.

The placement of this character is significant. The Gaoler (after a mute appearance in 5.3, and a brief one at the opening of 5.4) arrives to summon Posthumus to his execution, at 5.4.152. This is after Posthumus has had his vision of SICILIUS LEONATUS and JUPITER—which we recognise as the climax of the play. Thus, the Gaoler's comic approach to the tragic potential of life comes only after an assurance that the play will have a happy ending.

The Gaoler resembles such predecessors as the PORTER (3) of *Macbeth* and the GRAVE-DIGGER of *Hamlet*. Some scholars believe that the Gaoler's part was written to be performed by the same actor who played CLOTEN—probably Robert ARMIN. This hypothetical idea is based on the clownishness of the two characters and the possibility of one person playing both, since Cloten dies early in Act 4.

**Gaoler (3)**   Minor character in *The Winter's Tale*, the custodian of the imprisoned Queen HERMIONE. When Lady PAULINA visits the unjustly incarcerated queen, the Gaoler is sympathetic—calling her 'a worthy lady / And one who much I honour' (2.2.5–6)—but he sticks to his duty, only allowing her to see Hermione's lady-in-waiting, EMILIA (3), and only in his presence. When Paulina proposes to take Hermione's daughter—born in the prison—to the king, the Gaoler is reluctant, saying, 'I know not what I shall incur to pass it, / Having no warrant' (2.2.57–58), but in the face of Paulina's insistence he accedes. This weak figure provides a foil for Paulina, establishing her as the powerful presence that will dominate several later scenes; at the same time, by reminding us of the authority he represents, he contributes to our growing sense of tragedy.

**Gaoler (4)**   Character in *The Two Noble Kinsmen*, the prison-warden whose DAUGHTER (2) goes mad with unrequited love for PALAMON, a prisoner of war and one of the title characters. The Daughter helps Palamon escape, but when he returns to the aristocratic world, she loses her mind. The Gaoler first appears in 2.1, where he agrees to the WOOER's suit for the Daughter's hand, and where he is a conventional warden to his prisoners. He is unaware of his daughter's state when he reappears in 4.1, worrying that he will be blamed for Palamon's escape. Once informed of the Daughter's madness, he is helpless to ease her plight. In 5.2 he objects mildly to the DOCTOR's (4) prescription—that the Wooer disguise himself as Palamon and sleep with her—but he goes along and reports her cure in 5.4. A simple pawn of the plot, he is

believed to have been the creation of Shakespeare's collaborator, John FLETCHER (2).

**Gardener**   Minor character in *Richard II*, a worker in the household of the Duke of YORK (4). In 3.4 the Gardener and his assistants (see MAN [1]) discuss the news of the capture and likely deposition of King RICHARD II by BOLINGBROKE (1). In their conversation the garden is an extended metaphor for the state: just as a garden must be constantly tended if it is to bear flowers and fruits, so must the state be kept in order by its rulers if it is to function healthily. Thus the Gardener summarises one of the play's important moral points.

The episode also has another function. The QUEEN (13) overhears the Gardener's remarks and reacts with hysterical anger. Although she curses him, the Gardener is sympathetic to her grief, and his response neatly emphasises the human side of Richard's story. Up to this point we have been encouraged to judge the King harshly as a self-centred and unreliable ruler; here, the Gardener's pity stirs an awareness that Richard's fall, however deserved it may be, has a personal dimension. Our sympathies begin to shift, preparing us for the tragic and philosophical Richard of the second half of the play.

**Gardiner (1), Stephen (d. 1555)**   Historical figure and character in *Henry VIII*, a follower of Cardinal WOLSEY and later his successor as the play's principal villain. In 2.2 Gardiner appears as King HENRY VIII's new secretary; in an aside he assures Wolsey of his personal loyalty, and the cardinal tells CAMPEIUS that Gardiner will do as he tells him. When we next see Gardiner, in the coronation parade in 4.1, he has become a bishop, and a GENTLEMAN (14) remarks that he is the powerful enemy of the Archbishop of Canterbury, Thomas CRANMER. In 5.1 and 5.2 Gardiner leads an effort to convict Cranmer of heresy, but the king intervenes and he is stymied. In Act 5 Gardiner is the unscrupulous, pro-Catholic schemer that Wolsey was before his fall, but here the king is more than a match for the villain. This indicates Henry's growth from gullibility to wisdom, an important theme of the play.

The historical Gardiner, a bright young priest, was employed by Wolsey to represent him in ROME before becoming the cardinal's secretary. Wolsey promoted his protégé into the king's service, presumably for the reasons given in the play, and Gardiner prospered. He became the king's secretary in 1529 and Bishop of Winchester in 1531. A conservative cleric, his opposition to Cranmer centred on the archbishop's prominent role in the Reformation in England. Henry balanced one against the other, but after the king's death, Cranmer gained power and Gardiner was imprisoned. However, under the Catholic Queen Mary (ruled

1553–1558), Gardiner was restored to power and Cranmer was executed, though Gardiner died before his enemy went to the stake.

**Gardiner (2), William (1531–1597)**  Contemporary of Shakespeare, a wealthy London real-estate investor and Justice of the Peace who figured in a dispute that also involved Shakespeare. Gardiner, who bought his judgeship, seems to have been a notorious swindler; he was also imprisoned several times for abusive and violent actions and even faced charges of murder by witchcraft. In 1596 he feuded for unknown reasons with Francis LANGLEY, the proprietor of the SWAN THEATRE, and Langley sought the protection of the courts against him and his stepson William Wayte. In response, apparently, Wayte sought the same protection against Langley, Shakespeare, and two women who are otherwise unknown. Shakespeare's connection with the quarrel cannot be determined, but some scholars have inferred (though others disagree) that either he lived in BANKSIDE, which was part of Gardiner's judicial jurisdiction or that Shakespeare's acting company at the time, the CHAMBERLAIN'S MEN, played at the Swan, although there is no other evidence of this.

The noted scholar Leslie HOTSON has proposed that Shakespeare intended the comical Justice SHALLOW in *The Merry Wives of Windsor* as a satirical portrait of Gardiner, with his dim-witted relative SLENDER intended as Wayte. Shallow's coat of arms, described in *The Merry Wives*, 1.1.15–25, resembles Gardiner's, and, like Gardiner, Shallow threatens to use the law against an enemy. Moreover, Shallow intends to marry Slender to a rich young woman, a circumstance that might refer to Wayte's marriage to an heiress whom Gardiner subsequently swindled. Since *The Merry Wives* was written a few months after Wayte's complaint against Shakespeare, a literary retaliation, if one were attempted, might reasonably appear there.

However, this evidence is somewhat weak. The Elizabethan era was highly litigious, and the use of the law against one's enemies was quite ordinary. Though the coats of arms of Gardiner and Shallow both include luces, a kind of fish, the heraldic resemblance between them is not especially close (closer to Shallow's arms are those of Sir Thomas LUCY [1]). Moreover, Shallow is losing his memory and based in rural GLOUCESTERSHIRE, whereas Gardiner was a wily London businessman. Further, no slightest resemblance to Gardiner can be found in Shallow's appearance in *2 Henry IV*, written at the same time. Most significantly, although Shallow is a comic figure, his personality seems inappropriate to a scoundrel such as Gardiner appears to have been. Shakespeare's pleasant portrait of a garrulous and gullible but warm-hearted elderly country gentleman seems an unlikely weapon of vengeance.

**Gargrave, Thomas (d. 1429)**  Historical figure and minor character in *1 Henry VI*, an officer who is killed by the same cannon shot that kills the Earl of SALISBURY (3) at the siege of ORLÉANS (1) in 1.4. The historical Gargrave is a minor figure in Shakespeare's sources, a nobleman who is recorded as having been killed at the siege.

**Garnet, Henry (1555–1606)**  English Jesuit priest whose execution for treason is cryptically referred to in *Macbeth*. As the play's horror mounts, the PORTER (3), in a comical interlude, drunkenly pretends to serve as the door-keeper to Hell. He welcomes 'an equivocator, that could swear in both the scales against either scale; who committed treason enough for God's sake, yet could not equivocate to heaven' (2.3.8–11). The word 'equivocate' was highly charged in the English political world at the time that this scene was written (c. 1606), and it had particular pertinence to Garnet's treason trial, a notorious public event. Moreover, the Porter also welcomes to Hell 'a farmer, that hang'd himself' (2.3.4–5), a reference to the name 'Mr Farmer', used by Garnet as an underground alias. Shakespeare's original audiences will certainly have understood these lines as a political joke.

In 1605 England was shaken by the exposure of the Gunpowder Plot, an attempt by radical Catholics to blow up the Houses of Parliament and kill King JAMES I as part of an effort to install a Catholic monarch. Garnet, a Catholic convert, was the director of the clandestine Catholic Church in England. Though not one of the plotters, he was charged with complicity in the scheme for he had known of it ahead of time and had concealed his knowledge, itself a treasonable act under English law. He denied his foreknowledge at first, but when faced with an informer he confessed and justified his perjury with the doctrine of equivocation, a term he used repeatedly at his trial. 'Equivocation' was a Catholic theological term describing morally acceptable perjury, condoned when undertaken in the name of Catholic opposition to Protestantism. This defence was of course rejected, and Garnet was convicted of perjury as well as treason; he was sentenced to death and hanged.

**Garrick, David (1717–1779)**  British actor and producer. For 35 years, beginning in 1740, Garrick dominated the London stage. He led a revolution in acting, rejecting the tradition of formal declamation still employed by James QUIN and others in favour of naturalistic speech and actions. As the longtime manager of the Drury Lane Theatre (1747–1766), he also altered the presentation of plays, introducing realistic scenery and hidden lighting, and eliminating the presence of spectators on the stage. He did much to popularise Shakespeare, producing 24 of his plays. He often restored excised text and eliminated the additions of earlier producers such as Nahum TATE and William DAVENANT. Among the Shakespeare plays he resurrected in this way were *Macbeth, Coriolanus, Cymbeline, Antony and Cleopatra, The Tempest, Romeo and Juliet,* and *King Lear*—though he added his own passages to several of these and altered some of the other plays quite radically. He rewrote two plays as operas—*A Midsummer Night's Dream* (*The Fairies* [1755]) and *The Tempest* (1756)—and his *Catherine and Petruchio* (1754) and *Florizel and Perdita* (1756) were severely altered versions of *The Taming of the Shrew* and *The Winter's Tale,* respectively. His *Hamlet* (1772) was his most notorious adaptation, for he eliminated most of Act 5.

As an actor, Garrick played 17 different Shakespearean roles. He was best known as BENEDICK, RICHARD III (the part that established him as a major actor), HAMLET, MACBETH, and LEAR. In 1769 Garrick organised the Shakespeare Jubilee at STRATFORD, an elaborate celebration of the playwright that did much to make Stratford a mecca for Shakespearean enthusiasts. Garrick also wrote several successful plays, mostly farces, and several volumes of poetry. He was buried at WESTMINSTER (1) ABBEY.

**Garter (Garter King-at-Arms)**   Minor character in *Henry VIII,* an official of the court of HENRY VIII. The Garter, whose duties include making formal proclamations at official ceremonies, is present, though mute, at the coronation of ANNE (1), and he recites a brief prayer after the christening of the future Queen ELIZABETH (1) in 5.4.1–3. His small role adds pomp and circumstance to the picture of the court.

**Gascoigne, George (c. 1535–1577)**   English poet, author, and playwright, creator of a source for several of Shakespeare's plays. Gascoigne's *Supposes* (performed 1566, published 1575), a translation of the Italian drama *I Suppositi* (1509) by Ludovico ARIOSTO, provided the SUB-PLOT concerning BIANCA (1) in *The Taming of the Shrew,* along with many details in *The Comedy of Errors* and *The Two Gentlemen of Verona.*

Gascoigne, who wrote poetry, prose, and plays, was a literary innovator. His *Notes concerning the making of verse* (1575) is one of the earliest examples of literary criticism in English, and his TRAGEDY *Jocasta* (1566) was only the second English play to be written in BLANK VERSE. His adaptation of Ariosto helped introduce a taste for RENAISSANCE Italian literature into England.

Born into a wealthy family, Gascoigne led a dissolute life as a young man. He studied 'such lattyn as I forgat' at Cambridge, and supposedly studied law at the INNS OF COURT. He was chronically in debt and occasionally in trouble for questionable financial dealings. In 1561 he married a wealthy widow—and thus became stepfather to the noted poet Nicholas Breton

(c. 1545–c. 1626)—but in 1570 he again had money troubles and was gaoled for debt. In 1572 he joined the English volunteer soldiers aiding the Dutch rebellion against the Spanish. He was intermittently in the Low Countries for the last years of his life, although he returned to England to write and publish several works, among them a final volume—*The Glass of Government* (1575)—that recorded his moral conversion.

**Gascony**   Region in south-western FRANCE (1), an English colony from 1204 to 1453 and the location for Act 4 of *1 Henry VI.* Much of the act focusses on the battle near BORDEAUX, in which the English hero TALBOT is killed; 4.3–4 are set at English camps elsewhere in Gascony. The loss of the region following this battle, fought in 1453, effectively ended the HUNDRED YEARS WAR.

**Gaultree Forest**   Extensive woodland near YORK (2) in northern England, setting for 4.1–3 of *2 Henry IV.* Following his sources, Shakespeare recorded an encounter between the army of King HENRY IV and that of the rebels led by the ARCHBISHOP (3) of York at the ancient royal hunting grounds of Gaultree, or Galtres. Prince John of LANCASTER (3), Henry's son, offers the rebels a fair hearing of their grievances before the King if they will disband their forces. Once they do so, he has them arrested for treason and executed. He justifies this treachery by contending that all he had promised was that the King would hear their complaints, not that they would be safe from prosecution. The episode brings Lancaster to the fore—FALSTAFF delivers an amusing assessment of him in 4.3.84–123—and it offers a closer look at the rebels. The situation is discussed, especially by the Archbishop and WESTMORELAND (1) in 4.1, in terms that offer a human understanding of the rebels' position but that also condemn rebellion as an unjustifiable disruption of society, particularly when linked to religious sentiments.

Shakespeare substituted Lancaster for Westmoreland, who actually conducted the negotiations and perpetrated the betrayal, in order to emphasise the importance of Henry's family in the web of treachery and conflict that followed his usurpation of the throne (enacted in *Richard II*). Otherwise, the historical event is accurately depicted. Lancaster is presented as a cold-blooded Machiavellian, although his ruse is not explicitly disparaged; many such ploys were used in late medieval warfare, and neither the historians whom Shakespeare read nor the playwright himself seem to treat this one as particularly heinous, particularly when compared to the much greater crime of rebellion against an anointed ruler.

**Gaunt, John of (Duke of Lancaster, 1340–1399)**   Historical figure and character in *Richard II,* King

RICHARD II's uncle and father of BOLINGBROKE (1). Gaunt, though he dies in 2.1, is an important figure. He represents a grand tradition of statesmanlike patriotism and honour, encouraging Bolingbroke, in 1.1 and 1.3, towards the ideal of obedience to the King, whom he believes rules by divine right. On the same grounds, he resists the DUCHESS (2) of Gloucester's demands in 1.2 for vengeance against the King for the murder of her husband, Gaunt's brother. Yet he is aware of Richard's failings, and, before dying, he chastises the King severely for ruining the country through overtaxation and self-indulgence. Preparing himself for this final encounter with Richard, he meditates on England in a patriotic passage that has been famous since it was first performed: 'This royal throne of kings, this scept'red isle, . . . This blessed plot, this earth, this realm, this England, . . .' (2.1.40–50).

The historical Gaunt was a very different sort of man from the paragon of virtue presented in the play. Shakespeare altered the much more accurate portrait found in his principal source, HOLINSHED's *Chronicles*, in part because Queen ELIZABETH (1) traced her ancestry to Gaunt, but also in order to hold up an ideal representative of the chivalric age, whose passing is a major theme of the play. Gaunt, named for his birth in English-occupied Ghent, in Flanders, was a greedy and aggressive aristocrat, devoted to his own interests, not to the common welfare. Before the time of the play, he spent several years—and vast amounts of English wealth—fighting in Spain in an unsuccessful attempt to seize the crown of Castile for himself. He was widely detested in England, and during the great revolt of 1381 his palace in London was thoroughly sacked by gleeful crowds.

**General**  Minor character in *1 Henry VI*, a French officer on the walls of BORDEAUX. He rejects TALBOT's demand for the surrender of the city in 4.2.

**Gentleman (1)**  Either of two minor characters in *2 Henry VI*, captives of pirates in 4.1, along with the Duke of SUFFOLK (3). After the gentlemen agree to pay a ransom for their lives, Suffolk is executed by the pirates. One of the gentlemen is released to carry ransom messages to London, and he also receives Suffolk's severed head to deliver to Queen MARGARET (1).

**Gentleman (2)**  Minor character in *Richard III*. The Gentleman vainly attempts to prevent RICHARD III from interrupting the funeral procession of HENRY VI early in 1.2, and then restarts the procession, at Richard's command, later in this scene. He speaks one line on each occasion. His first line is sometimes assigned to a HALBERDIER, for the abuse the character takes from Richard is thought inappropriate for a gentleman. Villainous though he is, it is supposed that Rich-

ard would observe the formal distinctions between aristocrats and commoners.

**Gentleman (3)**  Minor character in *Hamlet*. In 4.5 the Gentleman brings QUEEN (9) Gertrude news of OPHELIA's madness, describing her erratic behaviour and confused language, 'That carry but half sense . . . [but] would make one think there might be thought . . .' (4.5.7–12). He thus prepares us to understand the meaning in Ophelia's disconnected songs and talk in the rest of the scene.

**Gentleman (4)**  Minor character in *All's Well That Ends Well*, a nobleman who helps HELENA (2). In 5.1 the Gentleman tells Helena that the KING (17) has left MARSEILLES. He takes her message to the King, appearing in 5.3 with the letter that entraps BERTRAM at the play's climax. The Gentleman is merely a stereotypical courtier and a pawn of plot development.

**Gentleman (5)**  Either of two minor characters in *Measure for Measure*, friends of LUCIO. The Gentlemen appear briefly in 1.2 where they help establish the ambience of the play's SUB-PLOT, the atmosphere of vice and degradation amid good spirits that characterises the underworld of VIENNA. They are soldiers who callously regret the prospects of peace and go on to jest about venereal disease, especially when MISTRESS (2) Overdone appears. The Gentlemen have no distinct personalities and are not distinguishable from each other. After this brief scene they disappear from the play.

**Gentleman (6)**  Any of three minor characters in *Othello*, Venetian noblemen and members of the occupation force on CYPRUS. In 2.1 two Gentlemen talk with MONTANO (2) about the dispersal of the Turkish fleet by storm, then a third appears with news of OTHELLO's arrival to take command of the island. In 2.2 one of the Gentlemen (designated as Othello's Herald in the FOLIO and some other editions) reads the general's formal proclamation declaring a holiday, and in 3.2 another accompanies Othello on an inspection of the fort, uttering a single line. These figures are representative of the Venetian military presence, serving to further the plot.

**Gentleman (7)**  Minor character in *King Lear*, a follower of LEAR. The Gentleman assists the loyal KENT (2) in his efforts to aid the wandering and insane king. Primarily a useful attendant, the Gentleman delivers two important descriptions that help form the audience's responses to the play in significant ways. In 3.1 he reports vividly to Kent on Lear's raging in the storm and prepares the audience for the wild scene to follow. In 4.3 he movingly describes CORDELIA's haunting response to the news of her wretched father. Rich in religious imagery, this passage provides a strong sense of Cordelia's saintly nature, a central image of the play.

**Gentleman (8)**   Minor character in *King Lear,* a follower of the Duke of ALBANY. In 5.3, the horrified Gentleman announces the deaths of GONERIL and REGAN. Goneril has stabbed herself after confessing that she poisoned Regan. The character adds to the increasing hysteria of the final scene.

**Gentleman (9)**   Either of two minor characters in *Pericles,* neighbours of the physician Lord CERIMON. In 3.2, after a great storm, the Gentlemen encounter Cerimon and he remarks on his medical practise and knowledge of arcane herbal treatments. This establishes the physician's credentials to the audience, in readiness for the next episode—his revival of THAISA—which the Gentlemen observe and comment on briefly. The Gentlemen serve to carry the plot forward.

**Gentleman (10)**   Either of two minor characters in *Pericles,* visitors to a bordello who are converted to virtue through their encounter with MARINA. In 4.5 the two Gentlemen discuss the young woman whose virtuous nature has shamed them. They marvel that 'divinity [has been] preach'd there' (4.5.4), and one of them declares, 'I'll do anything now that's virtuous' (4.5.8). With this very brief (nine-line) scene, Shakespeare establishes Marina's superiority to her circumstances. We have just seen her sold to the bordello by PIRATES who had kidnapped her earlier, and this scene makes it clear that good is in the process of triumphing over evil.

**Gentleman (11)**   Any of several minor characters in *Pericles,* attendants of PERICLES. In 5.1 the Gentlemen are summoned to receive LYSIMACHUS, the governor of MYTILENE, who is visiting Pericles' ship. One Gentleman acknowledges the call in four words, but otherwise these courtiers do not speak. They are extras, intended to increase the atmosphere of ceremonious formality that surrounds Pericles.

**Gentleman (12)**   Either of two minor characters in *Cymbeline,* noblemen at King CYMBELINE's court. In 1.1 the First Gentleman tells the Second Gentleman about the marriage of the king's daughter, IMOGEN, to POSTHUMUS, a poor but noble youth who has been banished from Britain because the king had wanted Imogen to marry the boorish CLOTEN. He adds that Imogen is the king's only child, other than two lost sons, kidnapped 20 years earlier and never recovered. The First Gentleman's excitement is clear in his hurried speech. This stirs interest in the audience, though his compan-

ion merely punctuates his monologue with brief questions. The episode, which fills the whole of the play's first scene, establishes the basic situation of the plot.

**Gentleman (13)**   Any of three minor characters in *The Winter's Tale,* courtiers at the court of King LEONTES of SICILIA. They report to AUTOLYCUS on the off-stage encounter of Leontes and his old friend King POLIXENES, whom he had earlier wronged, and of the discovery by Leontes of his long-lost daughter, PERDITA. The First Gentleman knows only that something extraordinary has happened, the Second knows the result, but only the Third Gentleman can describe the events as they happened, which he does at length, in 5.2.31–103. The language of all three Gentlemen is flowery and ornate, typical of the courtly idiom of the 17th century. Although they display little individual personality, they are nevertheless interesting as miniature portraits of Jacobean courtiers. (Some editors presume that the SERVANT [27] of 5.1 is another such courtier and designate him a Gentleman.) Shakespeare's presentation of crucial events through the reporting of minor characters is sometimes criticised, but here he avoids a scene that would repeat much that the audience already knows. He also provides a contrast with the play's true climax, still to come in 5.3.

**Gentleman (14)**   Any of three minor characters in *Henry VIII,* members of the court of King HENRY VIII. In 2.1 two of the Gentlemen discuss the trial and conviction of the Duke of BUCKINGHAM (1). They attribute the duke's fall to Cardinal WOLSEY, who they say is hated by the common people as much as Buckingham is loved. After witnessing Buckingham's moving farewell, they discuss Wolsey's effort to bring down Queen KATHERINE and mention the arrival of Cardinal CAMPEIUS as part of that story. Thus, they convey much important information about the plot, while stirring the audience's responses to the villain and his victims.

In 4.1 the Gentlemen reappear, this time at the coronation of Queen ANNE (1). They speak of the deposed Katherine's exile to KIMBOLTON, and as the royal procession passes by, they identify and remark on its participants. They are then joined by a Third Gentleman, who describes the actual coronation ceremony in exalted terms that foster the play's depiction of Anne as a saintly queen, rejoiced in by the country. They go on to discuss the advancement of Thomas CRANMER and Thomas CROMWELL in the wake of Wolsey's fall, and they mention the rivalry between Cranmer, now Archbishop of Canterbury, and Bishop GARDINER (1). This foreshadows the political developments of Act 5. Once again, the Gentlemen convey information while also suggesting the play's point of view.

**Gentleman (15)** Minor character in *Henry VIII*, an attendant to Queen KATHERINE. In 3.1 the Gentleman announces the arrival of 'two great cardinals' (3.1.16), WOLSEY and CAMPEIUS, thus introducing the main business of the scene.

**Gentleman (16)** Minor character in *The Two Noble Kinsmen*, a messenger from Duke THESEUS (2) of ATHENS to EMILIA (4). In 4.2 the Gentleman informs the sorrowing Emilia that ARCITE and PALAMON are prepared to duel for her love. He serves merely to translate the scene from Emilia's soliloquy to the preparations for the duel. Most scholars agree that 4.1 and the Gentleman were the work of Shakespeare's collaborator, John FLETCHER (2).

**Gentleman-poet** Character in *The Winter's Tale*. See SERVANT (27).

**Gentleman Usher** Minor character in *Henry VIII*, an attendant to Queen KATHERINE and her official escort at her divorce trial. The Gentleman Usher, accompanied by a lesser servant carrying a silver mace, walks before the Queen with great ceremony, in the stage direction opening 2.4. Later in the scene, he speaks one line, following King HENRY VIII's order that the departing queen be called back. He serves merely to emphasise the pomp of the proceedings. The same figure reappears under his proper name, GRIFFITH, in 4.2.

**Gentlewoman (1)** Minor character in *Macbeth*, an attendant to LADY (6) MACBETH. The Gentlewoman confers with the DOCTOR (3) on her mistress' somnambulism, and together they witness Lady Macbeth's hallucinatory manifestations of guilt in the famous sleep-walking scene (5.1). Before Lady Macbeth appears, the Gentlewoman refuses to tell the Doctor what she has heard—her mistress' obsession with MACBETH's murders—without a witness to back her up. This demonstrates the distrust that permeates the play's world, one of *Macbeth*'s important themes.

**Gentlewoman (2)** Minor character in *Coriolanus*, an attendant to VIRGILIA and VOLUMNIA. In 1.3 the Gentlewoman announces the arrival of VALERIA and then escorts her on stage. She speaks only a single line and serves to indicate the prestige and wealth of the ladies she serves.

**Geoffrey of Monmouth (c. 1100–1154)** English medieval writer, creator of the Arthurian cycle of tales. Geoffrey's *Historia Regum Britanniae* (c. 1140) provided much material for Raphael HOLINSHED's *Chronicles of England, Scotland, and Ireland* (1577, 1587), Shakespeare's principal source for his two plays dealing with pre-medieval Britain, *King Lear* and *Cymbeline*. Geof-

frey's book was not actually a history so much as a collection intended to appeal to the fashion for courtly tales—for example, the French stories of Charlemagne—and it immediately became very popular. It claimed to be a Latin translation of a book in Cymric, the language of WALES, that told the history of Britain up to the reign of King Arthur. It was in fact a mixture of various old chronicles, traditional stories and, probably, outright fictions. It established King Arthur as a British cultural hero, and it has been called the most important literary work of the 12th century.

Geoffrey was born into a family of clergymen and was educated at Monmouth's famed Benedictine abbey. He was probably a monk, though he was primarily a writer rather than a man of the cloth. In his old age he was made a bishop due to the influence of his aristocratic patrons—possibly including King Stephen of England—but he had to be ordained a priest for the occasion.

**George (1)** Character in *2 Henry VI*. See BEVIS.

**George (2) York, Duke of Clarence (1449–1478)** Historical figure and character in *3 Henry VI*, the untrustworthy younger brother of EDWARD IV. George returns from exile following the death of his father, the Duke of YORK (8). He supports Edward in his pursuit of the crown, becoming Duke of Clarence upon his brother's accession. However, resenting the advancement of his brother's in-laws (see ELIZABETH [2]), he joins WARWICK (3) in his rebellion, leaving Edward's court in 4.1. After helping Warwick reinstate HENRY VI, George is persuaded to defect again by his younger brother Richard (see RICHARD III) in 5.1, and he returns to Edward's cause. After fighting for Edward at BARNET and TEWKESBURY and participating in the murder of the PRINCE (4) of Wales, George is present in the final scene to pledge his rather doubtful loyalty to his elder brother. In *Richard III* the same figure appears as CLARENCE (1), and he is often so called, by himself and other characters, in *3 Henry VI*.

The historical George remained abroad in exile until Edward was crowned, at which time he was still only 12 years old. Shakespeare brings him into the action before that time, and as an adult, in order to establish him as a member of Edward's court well before he deserts it. Also, George's prominence in the play does much to emphasise the disloyalty and lack of honour that prevailed at the time of the WARS OF THE ROSES.

**German, Edward (1862–1936)** British composer, creator of incidental music for *Henry VIII*. German—whose name is pronounced with a hard 'G'—established himself as a composer for the theatre with three dances created for Henry IRVING's 1892 production of *Henry VIII*. These pieces were immediately popular and were staples of the music-hall repertoire for years, besides adorning subsequent productions of Shakespeare's play. German went on to a successful career as a composer of light opera—most notably *Merrie England* (1902)—and miscellaneous theatrical music.

**Gertrude**   Character in *Hamlet*. See QUEEN (9).

**Gervinus, Georg Gottfried (1805–1871)**   German scholar. A professor of literature at the University of Heidelberg, Gervinus published a four-volume collection of commentaries on Shakespeare's plays (1849, translated as *Shakespeare Commentaries* in 1863), which was highly influential on Shakespeare scholars in both Germany and England. He was an important advocate of the VERSE TEST, used to determine the chronology of the plays, and he is considered the first writer to study the development of the playwright's work over the course of his career.

**Ghost (1)**   Any of 11 minor but significant characters in *Richard III*, the ghosts of the victims of RICHARD III, who appear to the King and his enemy RICHMOND in 5.3, on the eve of the battle of BOSWORTH FIELD. The ghosts each deliver brief messages, insisting that Richard shall 'despair and die' and assuring Richmond of victory. The ghosts appear in the order in which they died: the ghosts of the PRINCE (4) of Wales and his father, HENRY VI, hark back to murders Richard committed in *3 Henry VI*, the preceding play in Shakespeare's TETRALOGY. Next appears the ghost of Richard's brother CLARENCE (1), followed by those of lords RIVERS, GREY (2), and VAUGHAN. The ghost of Lord William HASTINGS (3) comes forth next, succeeded by those of the two children Richard had ordered killed—another PRINCE (5) of Wales and his brother YORK (7). Richard is then faced by the ghost of his wife ANNE (2), only recently eliminated so that the King could make a politically convenient second marriage. The ghost of Richard's closest ally in his bloody rise to power, the Duke of BUCKINGHAM (2), executed only two scenes earlier, appears last. Shakespeare's source, the history by Edward HALL (2), mentions rumours that Richard had complained of nightmares before the battle, but the content of the dreams appears to be the playwright's invention.

**Ghost (2)**   Character in *Julius Caesar,* the spirit of the assassinated CAESAR (1). In 4.3, as BRUTUS rests in his tent near SARDIS, the Ghost appears to him, identifies itself as Brutus' 'evil spirit', and warns, 'thou shalt see me at Philippi' (4.3.281, 285)—that is, at the subsequent battle of PHILIPPI. In 5.5, defeated and preparing for suicide, Brutus recounts that the Ghost of Caesar has appeared to him a second time and concludes, 'I know my hour is come' (5.5.20). Shakespeare's presentation of the Ghost closely follows the account in PLUTARCH's *Lives.*

**Ghost (3)**   Character in *Hamlet,* the spirit of the murdered King of Denmark, HAMLET's late father. The Ghost, which has been silent in its appearances before the play opens and in 1.1 and 1.4, speaks to Hamlet in 1.5, revealing the secret of his death—'Murder most foul' (1.5.27) at the hands of his brother, Claudius, the present KING (5)—and insisting that Hamlet exact revenge. This demand establishes the stress that disturbs Hamlet throughout the play. The Ghost reappears in 3.4 to remind Hamlet that he has not yet accomplished his revenge, thereby increasing the pressure on the prince.

The Ghost is clearly an awesome presence, as the responses of BARNARDO, MARCELLUS, and HORATIO make clear in 1.1 and 1.4, and we are plainly meant to be impressed by Hamlet's bravery in speaking to it. At first, Hamlet cannot be sure whether it is 'a spirit of health or goblin damn'd' (1.4.40), and his doubts recur when he suspects that its message may be a lie that 'Abuses me to damn me' (2.2.599). Only Claudius' reaction to the playlet re-enacting the murder makes clear that the Ghost is to be trusted.

The Ghost pushes Hamlet to face the trauma of his father's murder and his mother's acceptance of the murderer. It keeps his anguish sharp. However, the Ghost is absent at the end of the drama. It has represented the emotional demands of Hamlet's grief and despair; when Act 5 offers the play's reconciliation of good and evil, the Ghost has no further function.

Belief in ghosts was common in Shakespeare's world—King JAMES I, who was regarded as a competent writer on religious matters, wrote a treatise on their characteristics—though many educated people regarded such beliefs as unfounded superstition. Shakespeare's own opinion cannot be known, for the only evidence is the attitudes he ascribes to his fictional characters; Hamlet certainly accepts the reality of the spirit, doubting only its purposes for a time. In any case, a ghost was a common feature of the REVENGE PLAY, a popular genre in the early 17th century, and Shakespeare took the Ghost in *Hamlet* from one such work, the UR-HAMLET.

**Ghost (4)**   Character in *Macbeth,* the spirit of the murdered BANQUO. The Ghost appears at the banquet hosted by MACBETH and LADY (6) MACBETH in 3.4. It can only be seen by Macbeth, who had ordered Banquo's murder and is the only one present who knows he is dead. It appears again in 4.1 in the company of the ghostly procession of future KINGS shown to Macbeth by the WITCHES. In both cases the Ghost is silent. In 4.1 Macbeth observes that it 'points at them [the Kings] for his' (4.1.124); this confirms the Witches' prediction that Banquo's descendants will be kings. On both occasions the Ghost appears when Macbeth names Banquo, first, when he hypocritically praises him at the banquet, in 3.4, and then when he demands to know about the prediction, in 4.1. This highlights the connection between the Ghost and Macbeth's internal state. Moreover, in 3.4, the Ghost is seen only by Macbeth, which further points up his disturbed state of mind in the aftermath of his crimes.

That no one else can see the Ghost in 3.4 is sometimes taken as evidence that the spectre does not in fact exist and is merely Macbeth's hallucination. However, it was believed by many in Shakespeare's day that ghosts and other supernatural beings could limit their visibility at will to particular individuals at particular times. (For instance, the GHOST (3) in *Hamlet* is seen by HAMLET and several other characters in Act 1, but is invisible to GERTRUDE when Hamlet sees it again in 3.4.) Banquo's Ghost thus serves as both a supernatural and a natural—that is, psychological—phenomenon, and no conclusions can be drawn as to Shakespeare's belief in ghosts. In any case, whether it is real or not, Banquo's Ghost adds to the eerie supernatural atmosphere that permeates the play and stresses the unnaturalness of Macbeth's evil.

The Ghost is usually played by the actor who has played Banquo, though some productions employ film or slide projections or some other image, like the huge mask in Orson WELLES' controversial 'voodoo' *Macbeth*. In other productions Macbeth is presented as hallucinating, and the Ghost does not actually appear.

**Ghost Character** Person mentioned in stage directions but not actually appearing in a play, having been excised or possibly simply forgotten about in the course of composition. The existence of such a character is often taken as evidence that the text in which it first appears was printed from the playwright's FOUL PAPERS, for such a superfluous figure would presumably have been deleted from any more evolved text, such as a PROMPT-BOOK. Ghost characters in Shakespeare's plays include VIOLENTA in *All's Well That Ends Well;* LAMPRIUS, RANNIUS, and LUCILLIUS in *Antony and Cleopatra;* BEAUMONT (1) in *Henry V;* INNOGEN in *Much Ado About Nothing;* PETRUCHIO (1) in *Romeo and Juliet;* and the MERCER in *Timon of Athens.*

**Gibborne, Thomas (active 1624)** English actor. Though known as a member of the PALSGRAVE'S MEN according to a document of 1624, Gibborne is thought by some scholars to have been the actor who played Shakespeare's RAMBURES in *Henry V,* because the character is designated as 'Gebon' in speech headings and stage directions of the BAD QUARTO edition of the play (1600). However, Samuel GILBURNE is generally thought a more likely nominee.

**Gide, André (1869–1951)** French author and translator of Shakespeare. Gide is best known for his novels (*The Immoralist* [1902], *The Plague* [1947], etc.), but he also translated *Hamlet* and *Antony and Cleopatra* into French and wrote prefaces to translations of several other of the plays. He was awarded the Nobel Prize for Literature in 1947.

**Gielgud, John (b. 1904)** British actor and director. Gielgud's long and distinguished career began with an appearance as the HERALD (4) in *Henry V* at the OLD VIC THEATRE in 1921. His portrayals of HAMLET and RICHARD II are especially renowned, but he has also played most of Shakespeare's other protagonists. He has produced a number of Shakespeare's plays, including *Hamlet, Macbeth,* and *Romeo and Juliet.* His 1949 production of *Much Ado About Nothing,* with himself as BENEDICK, was revived several times in the 1950s. With Laurence OLIVIER and Ralph RICHARDSON (2), Gielgud is considered one of the greatest Shakespearean actors of the 20th century.

**Gilbard, William (d. 1612)** Stratford teacher and clerk, possible inspiration for Shakespeare's character NATHANIEL (1) of *Love's Labour's Lost.* Gilbard is recorded as the assistant schoolmaster in 1561–1562 and as the acting schoolmaster on many occasions thereafter, until 1574; thus, he probably taught the young Shakespeare. By 1576 Gilbard was a curate and assisted the parish priest. His literacy enabled him to supplement his income as a clerk—he drew up many wills, for instance, including that of Anne HATHAWAY's father—and from 1603–1611 he was the parish clerk. The records he kept in this capacity contain a much higher proportion of Latin words and phrases than other clerks of the time used, which suggests that he was proud of his education. Gilbard has been suggested as a model for Nathaniel, also a curate, though there is no actual evidence to support the idea.

**Gilburne, Samuel (active 1605)** English actor. Gilburne is listed in the FIRST FOLIO as one of the 26 'Principall Actors' in Shakespeare's plays, but he is otherwise known only as a beneficiary of Augustine PHILLIPS' will (1605), where he is said to have been Phillips' apprentice, presumably as a boy. Gilburne may have played a LORD (6) in *All's Well That Ends Well*—designated as 'G' in the Folio text of the play— and *Henry V*'s RAMBURES, who is designated as 'Gebon' in the BAD QUARTO edition (1600).

**Gildon, Charles (1665–1724)** English playwright and critic. Trained as a Roman Catholic priest, Gildon abandoned his calling to become a hack writer. He published popular commentaries on English poetry and drama, including an anthology of biographical pieces (some written by him, though all unsigned) that included a brief and entirely unreliable life of Shakespeare. In 1699 he produced a play entitled *Measure for Measure, or Beauty the Best Advocate,* based loosely on Shakespeare's play—or rather on William DAVENANT's earlier adaptation, THE LAW AGAINST LOVERS. Gildon dropped much of Davenant's introduced material and replaced it, not with Shakespeare's text, but with a play within a play, an operatic MASQUE on the ancient Roman legend of Dido and AENEAS. In 1710 Gildon published *Poems* by Shakespeare, which was bound as a seventh volume of Nicholas ROWE's six-volume collection of the plays though not published by the same publisher. This piece of near-piracy earned Gildon an insulting passage in the famous literary satire, *The Dunciad* (1728), by Alexander POPE (1).

**Giles, Nathaniel (c. 1559–1634)**   Choirmaster and sometime director of the Children of the Chapel (see CHILDREN'S COMPANIES). Giles, a Protestant minister and musician, was appointed director of the Chapel Royal, the court choir of Queen ELIZABETH (1), which recruited boys from church choirs all over the country and placed them in a school at court, where they were educated while performing for the queen. In 1600 Giles joined Henry EVANS (2) in producing plays performed by the Chapel school's acting company, the Children of the Chapel, at the WHITEFRIARS THEATRE. However, in 1602 Giles and Evans were accused of misusing the Chapel Royal's recruiting power to enroll non-singers for the acting company. Evans fled the country and only returned after the queen's death; Giles continued to run the company, but in 1616 the choir's connection with Evans and the actors was severed by royal command. Giles remained as choirmaster until his death. He also was a noted composer of church music.

**Girl (Margaret Plantagenet, 1473–1541)**   Historical figure and minor character in *Richard III*, the daughter of CLARENCE (1). The Girl mourns her father's murder in 2.2 and is present but silent in 4.1. Richard is fearful that a husband of the Girl might claim the throne, her father having been the heir apparent. He remarks in 4.3.37 that he has therefore married her to a low-ranking husband, who cannot claim the crown. Historically, this manoeuvre was performed by Richard's conqueror and successor, Henry VII, the RICHMOND of the play. At the age of 68, being the last surviving PLANTAGENET, Margaret was beheaded by a paranoid HENRY VIII.

**Giulio Romano (Giulio Pippi) (1492–1546)**   Italian painter and architect, the only RENAISSANCE artist mentioned in Shakespeare. In *The Winter's Tale,* when PAULINA announces that she has a statue representing Queen HERMIONE, believed long dead, the statue is

said to be 'performed'—meaning either made or painted—'by that rare Italian master, Julio Romano, who, had he himself eternity and could put breath into his work, would beguile Nature of her custom, so perfectly he is her ape' (5.2.95–99). Since the sculpture turns out not to be a sculpture at all, its ascription to Giulio proves irrelevant; the use of the name merely lends verisimilitude to the gossip surrounding Paulina's cover story.

That Shakespeare should use Giulio's name in such a context suggests that his audience knew the artist's work, but that he should mistakenly make him a sculptor—or a mere finisher of sculptures—suggests that the playwright and presumably his audience did not know his work very well. It is of course an anachronism to name a Renaissance artist in a tale set in ancient times, but Shakespeare was tolerant of such inconsistencies, which appear throughout his plays. In any case, in Shakespeare's ROMANCES, with their welter of languages and exotic settings, a degree of confusion is probably intentional, promoting a sense of timelessness that furthers the playwright's ends.

The historical Giulio Romano (born Peppi but later named for his birthplace, ROME) was the chief pupil and assistant of Raphael (1483–1520), one of the most important Italian painters. Giulio himself became one of the leading painters and architects of his day, an innovator with a boldly pioneering style. He completed a number of Raphael's great decorative programmes at the Vatican on the master's death and then moved to MANTUA, where he was court painter and architect to Duke Federigo Gonzaga (1500–1540). His masterpiece is a ducal palace, the Palazzo del Tè, begun in 1526; both its architecture and its elaborately painted decor broke the conventions of Renaissance art to create bizarre and startling effects—an early example of the Mannerist style that dominated the second half of the 16th century. Giulio's painting, which combined elements from Raphael and Michelangelo (1475–1564), was widely influential.

**Glansdale, Sir William (fl. 1429)**   Historical figure and minor character in *1 Henry VI*, an officer present when the Earl of SALISBURY (3) is killed at the siege of ORLÉANS (1) in 1.4. The historical Glansdale is a minor figure in Shakespeare's sources as well; he was an officer who is recorded as having been present at the siege.

**Glendower, Owen (c. 1359–c. 1416)**   Historical figure and character in *1 Henry IV*, military leader from WALES (1) who joins rebellious English noblemen against King HENRY IV. In 3.1, at a rebel council of war, Glendower boasts of supernatural powers, displaying the superstitiousness traditionally associated with the Welsh, to the disgust of HOTSPUR. The clash of these two personalities almost upsets the alliance, though

Glendower, admiring his hot-headed ally, makes peace several times during the scene. In a lighter vein Glendower interprets for his daughter, LADY (8) Mortimer, who is in love with her husband, Lord MORTIMER (2), but does not speak English. Father and daughter together reveal their lyrical sentimental streak and a love of music, also traits stereotypically associated with the Welsh.

Later, in 4.4.16–18, Glendower is reported to have absented himself from the crucial battle of SHREWSBURY, 'o'er-rul'd by prophecies'. This episode adds Glendower's superstitiousness to the general weakness and incapacity that plague the rebel cause. Also, the account lends Hotspur's defeat an ominous, fated quality that is in keeping with the play's condemnation of rebellion.

Although Shakespeare's sources mention Glendower's training in law and his youthful service at the English court, he is chiefly portrayed as a barbaric and ruthless Welsh outlaw, as is reflected in the report on him by the Earl of WESTMORELAND (1) in 1.1.40–46. However, Shakespeare amplifies and softens this figure, and his Glendower is a composer and scholar whom Mortimer can describe as 'a worthy gentleman, . . . valiant as a lion, and wondrous affable, and as bountiful as mines of India' (3.1.159–163). Traditional English bias against the Welsh may account for the brute of the chronicles; the music-loving sage of the play may reflect Shakespeare's acquaintance with Welsh residents of London. Glendower's superstitiousness may also derive from the playwright's personal knowledge, for the English stereotype of the superstitious Welshman was grounded in the survival of a strong Celtic religious sensibility in Wales. Although Hotspur finds this trait ridiculous (3.1.142–158), Shakespeare himself apparently regarded it more sympathetically, as a humorous failing. Glendower is on the whole a positive figure, if a weak one. Even Hotspur's raillery against him is enjoyable rhetoric.

The historical Glendower led the last and most nearly successful Welsh rebellion against the English. In 1400, shortly after Henry IV's deposition of RICHARD II, Glendower led an uprising that grew from a quarrel with his English neighbour into a full-scale revolt. In 1403 the Welsh rebels joined with those from northern England led by Hotspur, and only Henry's decisive advance on Shrewsbury prevented their forces from combining. That Glendower's superstition led him to abandon the rebels at Shrewsbury is not reported in Shakespeare's sources; HOLINSHED, in fact, mistakenly says that Glendower was at the battle, and DANIEL, like modern historians, attributes his absence only to King Henry's superior generalship. In 1404, with most of Wales under his control, Glendower established a national government at Harlech, where a parliament elected him Prince of Wales, and

he entered into an alliance with England's enemy, FRANCE (1). In 1405, with French troops reinforcing his own, he invaded England but was defeated by Henry. This was the high-water mark of his rebellion, and by 1409 Glendower had lost even Harlech and had retreated deep into the mountains. After 1410 he disappears from history, though he is thought to have lived somewhat longer. Although only briefly successful, Glendower united Wales—a land of petty principalities before the English invaded in the 12th century—and led it to an independence it never again attained. He remains a great hero of Welsh culture.

A minor character in *Richard II*, the CAPTAIN (4), is sometimes thought to have been intended as Glendower, and the famous leader is specifically referred to in that play as Glendor (3.1.43). He is also inaccurately said to have imprisoned his son-in-law Mortimer in *2 Henry VI* (2.2.40). His death is reported (several years too early, due to an error in Holinshed) in *2 Henry IV* (3.1.103).

**Globe Theatre**  Theatre in SOUTHWARK built by Cuthbert BURBAGE (1) in 1599, the principal home of Shakespeare's acting company and the site of the first performances of many of his plays. The Globe was built for the CHAMBERLAIN'S MEN when Burbage was unable to renew the ground lease for the land on which their old home, the THEATRE, stood. He therefore had the Theatre, a timber building, taken down

*Artists' depictions such as this one, while not fully trustworthy, give us an idea of what the Globe Theatre might have looked like. (Courtesy of Culver Pictures, Inc.)*

and reassembled at a new site, in Southwark, on the south side of the Thames River, beyond the jurisdiction of the LONDON government, which was opposed to theatre. The lease for the land was jointly held, half by Burbage and his brother Richard BURBAGE (3), and half by a group of five actors—Shakespeare, John HEMINGE, Augustine PHILLIPS, Thomas POPE (2), and Will KEMPE—who put their shares in trust with William LEVESON and Thomas SAVAGE. The Globe opened in late 1599; *As You Like It* may have been written for the occasion, and when Shakespeare had JAQUES (1) say, 'All the world's a stage . . .' (2.7.139), he may have been slyly alluding to the new theatre.

The Globe was a roughly cylindrical—probably polygonal—three-storey timber building, unroofed over the stage in the centre. Each floor contained open galleries with seats. The galleries extended around much of the circle, and the stage was built out into the centre from the remaining part of the building. In the building behind the stage were dressing rooms—the 'tiring house'—perhaps galleries for musicians, and apparatus for scenery and props. Above the thatched roof rose a tower, or 'penthouse', from which flags were flown and trumpets sounded to announce a production. An 18th-century account asserted that on its facade the Globe sported a painted sign depicting Hercules supporting the planet Earth (one of his legendary tasks was to stand in for Atlas). If this was so—and scholars generally believe it was—this sign may be alluded to in *Hamlet*, where the CHILDREN'S COMPANIES, in a satirical passage on the WAR OF THE THEATRES, are said to have triumphed over both the PLAYERS (2) and 'Hercules and his load too' (2.2.358).

On June 29, 1613, the Globe's thatched roof was set on fire by a cannon fired during a performance of *Henry VIII*, as called for in the stage direction at 1.4. 49, and the building burned to the ground. It was open again within a year, rebuilt to much the same plan, but this time the roof was tiled. In 1644, two years after the theatres of England were closed by the revolutionary government, the Globe was torn down and tenements built on the lot.

The appearance of the Globe can only roughly be determined, from several drawings of its exterior (in large-scale city scenes), from the specifications in the builder's contract for the FORTUNE THEATRE (which was modelled on the Globe), and by extrapolating from the only sketch of the interior of an Elizabethan playhouse, the SWAN THEATRE. Nevertheless, two modern replicas of the Globe have been made. One opened in 1988 in Tokyo with a British production of *Henry V*, and the other is scheduled to open in 1991 in London (though at a different location from the original).

**Gloucester (1), Earl of**   Character in *King Lear,* father of EDGAR and EDMUND. Gloucester is the central figure of the play's SUB-PLOT, in which his illegitimate son

Edmund's villainy and his own error lead him to disaster and suffering from which he recovers only to die. This progression parallels the story of King LEAR in the main plot. Deceived by Edmund, who wants to inherit the earldom, Gloucester disinherits and banishes his legitimate son Edgar. Because Gloucester is faithful to the outcast and insane Lear, Edmund turns him over to Lear's enemy, the Duke of CORNWALL, who puts out Gloucester's eyes and banishes him into the wilderness. Edgar, disguised as a wandering lunatic, tends to his father. He saves him from suicide, in 4.6, and renews in him the strength to endure. Finally, however, when Gloucester learns Edgar's identity, the old man dies; 'his flaw'd heart, . . . 'Twixt two extremes of passion, joy and grief, / Burst smilingly' (5.3.195–198).

Gloucester's tale offers a significant parallel to that of Lear; like the king's, Gloucester's tragedy is self-induced, for his actual blinding is preceded by figurative blindness when he fails to see either Edgar's virtue or Edmund's villainy. Like Lear, Gloucester recognises his error—'I stumbled when I saw' (4.1.19), he confesses—when it is too late. His helpless wanderings, dependent on the aid of a seeming lunatic, suggest powerfully the similar straits of the mad king. The similarity between the two reaches a horrific climax, in 4.6, when they encounter each other on the beach at DOVER; it is one of the most touching passages in Shakespeare. The mad and the blind old men recognise each other and acknowledge their joint status as victims; their consciousness, though it is flawed by their handicaps, is clearly more acute than it was before.

Their parallel tales, and the close sympathy of Lear and Gloucester when they meet, is highly significant for our interpretation of the play's final moments. Gloucester's death immediately precedes Lear's at the close of the play, and because their parallel development has been stressed, we may read in the king's death the same 'extremes of passion' and presume that his heart, too, 'burst smilingly'. Thus, Gloucester's tragedy helps confirm the nobility of human suffering, a central message of the play.

**Gloucester (2), Eleanor Cobham, Duchess of**   Character in *2 Henry VI.* See DUCHESS (1).

**Gloucester (3), Eleanor de Bohun, Duchess of**   Character in *Richard II.* See DUCHESS (2).

**Gloucester (4), Humphrey, Duke of (1390–1447)**   Historical figure and character in *1* and *2 Henry VI, 2 Henry IV,* and *Henry V,* the youngest son of King HENRY IV and the brother of King HENRY V and the dukes of CLARENCE (2) and LANCASTER (3). He is an important figure in the aristocratic disputes of the *Henry VI* plays, presented as the chief cause of the English loss to FRANCE (1) in the HUNDRED YEARS WAR. In the later works, where he is a younger man, he is a minor character.

In the *Henry VI* plays Gloucester engages in a running dispute with his uncle the Bishop of WINCHESTER (1). He is depicted as a valorous defender of England's honour, whereas Winchester is an opportunistic politician. Their feud rages through 3.1 of *Part 1,* after which it is replaced in importance by that between YORK (8) and SOMERSET (3). In *Part 2* Gloucester's wife, the DUCHESS (1) of Gloucester, is convicted on charges of witchcraft and banished. Then, in 3.1, Gloucester himself is arrested at BURY ST. EDMUNDS, falsely charged with treason, and killed. Hired murderers flee the scene of the crime at the beginning of 3.2; the SECOND MURDERER (1) regrets the deed because the duke's death had been marked by religious penitence.

After Gloucester's death the country slides into civil war, and we are meant to see him as having been the guardian against such an event. In order to magnify the duke's virtues, two otherwise irrelevant anecdotes are inserted into the story. In 2.1 Gloucester demonstrates his perceptiveness by exposing the imposter SIMPCOX, and in 3.1 he wisely postpones a potentially explosive issue, York's appointment as regent in France, until a marginally related dispute can be resolved (see PETER [1]; HORNER). These incidents demonstrate the qualities of prudence and judgement that are shortly to be denied the country by the duke's murder.

The historical Gloucester was very different from the 'good Duke Humphrey' (*2 Henry VI,* 3.2.322) of these plays. Shakespeare, following his sources and the established opinion of his own time, was opposed to the political position of Gloucester's enemies and he thus depicted Humphrey as a patriot. Winchester headed a 'peace party' that advocated a withdrawal from a war virtually lost. Gloucester and the 'hawks' of the day, however, insisted that the war go on. In the HISTORY PLAYS Shakespeare presents the view that the French were able to drive the English from France only because of English disunity, and Gloucester's insistence on continuing the war was taken to demonstrate a patriotic faith in English arms that the 'peace party' lacked.

Gloucester was in fact selfishly ambitious, quite willing to pursue his own interests at the expense of the country's, once the restraining influence of Henry V was gone. After Henry's death Gloucester's power was restricted by a council of nobles who recognised his headstrong selfishness. He rebelled; the dispute with Winchester at the TOWER OF LONDON (*1 Henry VI,* 1.3) reflects Gloucester's actual coup attempt of 1425. A year later, he eloped with the wife of a close friend of the Duke of BURGUNDY (2), England's most important ally, and then recruited an army to support his new wife's claims. A duel with Burgundy was avoided only by the annulment of the marriage. This affair was among the grievances that Burgundy cited when he eventually defected from the English alliance against France. Later Gloucester scandalously married his mistress, Eleanor Cobham, who, as Duchess of Gloucester, was found guilty of treason and witchcraft.

No evidence has ever been offered to support the belief that Gloucester was murdered. Although he died while in Suffolk's custody, historians generally believe that his death was natural. No question of murder arose at the time, and Suffolk's banishment only occurred some years later, for different reasons.

In *2 Henry IV* and *Henry V,* set years earlier, Gloucester's role is minor. He is present at his father's deathbed in 4.4 and 4.5 of the first play, and in 5.2 he commiserates with the CHIEF JUSTICE on the treatment the jurist expects to receive from the new king, whom he believes is an enemy. In *Henry V* Gloucester is an almost anonymous member of the king's entourage.

**Gloucester (5), Richard Plantagenet, Duke of (later RICHARD III, King of England)**   Title held by RICHARD III after 2.6 of *3 Henry VI* and until he is crowned king in 4.2 of *Richard III.* Some modern editions of these plays follow 16th- and 17th-century practise and designate the character as Gloucester (Gloster) in stage directions and speech headings in Acts 3–5 of *3 Henry VI* and Acts 1–3 of *Richard III.* Other editions name him Richard, throughout.

The prior holder of Richard's dukedom had been the ill-fated Humphrey, Duke of GLOUCESTER (4), whose murder occurs off-stage in 3.2 of *2 Henry VI.* Therefore, as Shakespeare's audience will have recognised, the title bodes evil for its holder. Richard himself points this out in 2.6.107 of *3 Henry VI.* His words ironically prefigure his own fall, in a technique Shakespeare frequently used in the HISTORY PLAYS: references in the dialogue to past or future events serve to heighten dramatic tension, which is threatened by the long period of time over which the action takes place.

**Gloucester (6), Thomas of Woodstock, Duke of (1355–1397)**   Historical figure mentioned prominently in *Richard II,* brother of John of GAUNT, uncle of King RICHARD II, and husband of the DUCHESS (2) of Gloucester. Although he does not appear in the play, the Duke of Gloucester, often called Woodstock, is an important figure in Acts 1–2. His murder, which occurred six months prior to the play's opening, sparks the crises that lead to Richard's deposition.

In 1.1 BOLINGBROKE (1) accuses MOWBRAY (1) of complicity in the death of Gloucester, who died in Mowbray's custody in the prison of the English fortress at Calais. In 1.2 Gaunt and the duchess discuss Woodstock's death: they know that Mowbray did indeed kill the duke, and that he did so under the king's orders. In 4.1, just before Richard's deposition, the murder is again mentioned—Richard's favourite, the

Duke of AUMERLE, is now implicated—to reinforce our sense of Richard's guilt. Gloucester's murder is given importance as a symptom of illness in the body politic, evidence that Richard's fall has been made inevitable by his own misdeeds.

Gloucester is presented as a splendid figure of humanity. Gaunt, in his dying speech to Richard, refers to Gloucester as a 'plain, well-meaning soul' (2.1.128), alluding both to his sturdy, unfashionable dress and his frank and open mode of speech. He is several times referred to as 'noble'. The duchess loved him as a husband, and she calls him 'the model of [his father, the late King Edward III's] life' (1.2.28), thus equating him with England's greatest contemporary hero. Furthermore, the duchess points out that his royal blood should have made him sacrosanct; with his death, an important tradition has been defiled. Gloucester is thus a focus of nostalgia: he symbolises the chivalric ethic of Edward III's day, a glorious age whose passing is one of the major themes of the play.

Shakespeare's Gloucester presents an image of the man that was widely held in the 16th century and that is reflected in a number of the playwright's sources, particularly the anonymous play WOODSTOCK. However, Shakespeare's principal source for *Richard II*, HOLINSHED's *Chronicles*, depicts Gloucester as a wilfully violent man of little judgement. Modern scholarship finds Holinshed much nearer the mark. The historical Gloucester was a scheming, power-hungry aristocrat who clearly attempted to subvert the rule of his nephew.

When Edward III died, in 1377, Gloucester, though young, was markedly abler than his older brothers, and he became the power behind the throne of the pre-adolescent King Richard. As Richard matured, he attempted to assume power himself. The resulting conflict with his uncle escalated into a brief civil war in 1387. Gloucester's faction was victorious, forcing the exile or execution of several of Richard's favourites and effectively ruling the country for a time. In 1389 Richard, now 22 years old, declared that he would rule, and the coalition of nobles accepted his sovereignty. Richard was a successful king, and he cultivated his own group of supporters, including former followers of Gloucester such as Mowbray and Bolingbroke. Another rupture between the king and his uncle came in 1397. This time Richard quickly prevailed, imprisoning his opponents with little difficulty. Gloucester was placed in Mowbray's custody and died in the prison at Calais, as the play states. Whether or not he was murdered under Richard's orders cannot be confirmed, but modern scholarship seconds the contemporary popular opinion that he was.

**Gloucestershire**   County in south-western England, setting for three scenes of *2 Henry IV* and one of *Richard II*.

In 3.2 of *2 Henry IV* FALSTAFF, marching to join the army at GAULTREE FOREST, drafts several recruits from among a number of villagers assembled by the local justice of the peace, SHALLOW. The scene is chiefly a satire of corrupt Elizabethan recruiting practices, but it also presents a collection of humorous provincial portraits, both of the gentry—bluff, silly Shallow and his taciturn cousin SILENCE—and of the villagers MOULDY, SHADOW, WART, FEEBLE, and BULLCALF. A reference to the Lincolnshire market town of Stamford (3.2.38) suggests that this scene may have been intended to be set in that county, which would make much more sense in terms of Falstaff's march from London to Gaultree. However, Shallow's jurisdiction is specified as Gloucestershire in 4.3.80 and 126, as well as in the opening lines of *The Merry Wives of Windsor*. It is thought that Shakespeare changed his mind about the location while writing *2 Henry IV*—possibly while interrupting that task to write *The Merry Wives of Windsor*—and, with his typical inattention to minor contradictions, did not rewrite the earlier scene.

In 5.1 and 5.3 of *2 Henry IV* Shallow's home is the setting for another delightful sampling of rural England, where the daily tasks of a small country estate are attended to and a party honouring Falstaff is arranged and then held. Shallow reminisces windily about his hell-raising student days, while Silence turns mildly boisterous when drunk. Shallow's steward, DAVY, is introduced; he sees to the running of his master's farm and demands a court ruling in favour of a friend, in an amusing vignette of small-time corruption. Place names and family names—e.g., William VISOR of Woncot and Clement PERKES 'a'th'Hill' (5.1.35)—are used with a congenial familiarity. Although this rural ambience is somewhat comical and its inhabitants humorously limited, it is plain that Shakespeare was fond of these people, and the Gloucestershire scenes of the play contribute greatly to *2 Henry IV*'s depiction of English life.

In 2.3 of *Richard II*, Gloucestershire's location, near WALES (1) and the Irish Sea, makes it strategically important. BOLINGBROKE (1) marches there to intercept King RICHARD II as he returns from Ireland. The Earl of NORTHUMBERLAND (1) speaks of Gloucestershire's 'high wild hills and rough uneven ways' (2.3.4), referring to the Cotswold Hills. Although this region seems tame today, it was heavily forested and difficult to cross in Shakespeare's day.

**Glover, Julia (1781–1850)**   English actress. One of the most respected performers of her time, Glover, who claimed descent from Thomas BETTERTON, made her debut as a child, playing the Duke of YORK (7), young nephew of RICHARD III. Although she became quite obese, she successfully portrayed DESDEMONA, LADY (6) MACBETH, HAMLET, and other Shakespearean characters, and she was one of the few women ever to play FALSTAFF.

**Glyn, Isabel (active 1849–1867)**  English actress. Isabel Glyn was best known for her performances as CLEOPATRA. She played the role in several of the few 19th-century revivals of *Antony and Cleopatra,* most notably that of Samuel PHELPS in 1849, which reintroduced the play to the London stage. She also succeeded as QUEEN (9) Gertrude in *Hamlet.*

**Gobbo (1), Launcelot**  Character in *The Merchant of Venice.* See LAUNCELOT.

**Gobbo (2), Old**  Minor character in *The Merchant of Venice,* father of LAUNCELOT. Gobbo, nearly blind, is teased by Launcelot, who pretends to be a stranger and informs the old man that his son has died. Rewarded by his father's distress, Launcelot tells him the truth and enlists him to help approach BASSANIO about a job. After providing these few moments of incidental mirth, Gobbo disappears from the play.

**Goethe, Johann Wolfgang von (1749–1832)**  German poet, dramatist, novelist, and critic. Goethe was one of the leaders of the Romantic movement that swept Europe in the early 19th century, and he found some of his inspiration in the scale and power of Shakespeare's plays. As the foremost German writer of his day—or any other, in most opinions—his enthusiasm made Shakespeare's position in German literature permanent. His influence in this respect, as in many others, spread beyond Germany to the rest of Europe.

A lawyer, the young Goethe wrote poems and plays, including *Götz von Berlichingen* (1773), a historical drama modelled on Shakespeare's HISTORY PLAYS. His novel *The Sorrows of Young Werther* (1774), the story of an unrequited lover who commits suicide, was a sensation throughout Europe and established Goethe as a leading literary figure. In 1775 he became a government minister in Weimar, one of the many small countries of 18th-century Germany, and remained there for the rest of his life. In addition to serving as the chief aide to the ruling Duke, he also ran a small theatre that was highly influential on subsequent German drama. Oddly, however, he did not find Shakespeare's plays successful on stage, and focussed instead on their literary qualities. The only one he produced was his own radical abridgement of *Romeo and Juliet* (1812), using the translation of August von SCHLEGEL.

Goethe is still regarded as one of the giants of European literature—one of the few writers of Shakespeare's stature—and one of the great men of German history. Among his many works are the play *Iphigenia in Tauris* (1788), the epic poem *Faust* (published at intervals from 1790–1832), and the novel *Wilhelm Meister* (1796). He was also a scientist, and he published respected works on optics, anatomy, and botany.

**Goffe (Gough), Matthew (d. 1450)**  Historical figure mentioned briefly in *2 Henry VI.* In 4.5, during the battle to drive Jack CADE's rebels from London, Lord SCALES asserts that he will assign Goffe to a sector of the fighting, and, in a stage direction at the beginning of 4.7, Goffe is said to be killed in a skirmish. The historical Gough, a renowned warrior in the French wars, had shared command of the Tower of London with Scales, and he was indeed killed while fighting the rebels. His phantom presence in the play may reflect an actual appearance that was deleted in a revision.

**Golding, Arthur (c. 1536–c. 1605)**  English writer and translator. In 1567 Golding published his famous translation of OVID's *Metamorphoses,* which appears to have been one of Shakespeare's favourite books; material derived from it, as well as direct quotations, pepper the plays and poems. The work was widely popular among other Elizabethan readers as well, at least in part because Ovid's poetry is somewhat racy, though Golding was himself a staunch conservative Protestant who allegorised and moralised the ancient poet's mythological tales. He also translated selections from the classical historians and from contemporary Protestant reformers, most notably John Calvin.

**Goneril**  Character in *King Lear,* one of the villainous daughters of King LEAR. Goneril and her sister REGAN declare their great love for Lear, in 1.1, when in fact they merely want the portion of his kingdom that he has foolishly promised to whichever daughter can assure him she loves him most. They share the prize when their honest younger sister CORDELIA enrages the king with a frank admission that her love will be given in part to her future husband. Goneril takes the lead in the two sisters' villainy. She introduces the idea of humiliating Lear, in 1.1, and she orders her steward, OSWALD, to commence the practise, in 1.3. In 1.4 she starts the dispute over Lear's followers that sends the ex-king fleeing into the storm, where he descends into madness. In 4.2 Goneril's wickedness becomes more pronounced as she enters into a love affair with the ambitious EDMUND and hints at the existence of a murder plot against her husband, the virtuous but weak Duke of ALBANY. She and Regan both desire Edmund, and Goneril declares that she would rather lose the battle against the avenging forces led by Cordelia than lose Edmund to her sister. This rivalry depicts the vicious sexuality that is part of the play's general atmosphere of moral and physical unhealthiness. When Goneril and Edmund's plot against Albany is exposed, she poisons Regan and then commits suicide as the GENTLEMAN (8) reports in 5.3.225–226.

Goneril's extravagantly evil nature is so boldly and unsubtly drawn that only her greater aggression distinguishes her from her sister. Her manipulation of her husband foreshadows Shakespeare's LADY (6) MACBETH, but Goneril, a less sophisticated creation, is simply an imitation of a standard male villain, cruel and ambitious. Unlike Lady Macbeth, she cannot compare herself with conventional femininity, nor does she succumb to illness through a bad conscience, for she is a much less complex character and serves chiefly as an emblem of evil.

**Gonzalo**   Character in *The Tempest*, adviser to King ALONSO of Naples. Gonzalo is a kind and charitable, if ineffectual, figure who is a foil to the cynical villainy of ANTONIO (5), Duke of MILAN, his master's ally. Gonzalo's goodness is an important element in the play. He persistently takes a generous and optimistic point of view, as in his fantasy of an ideal society in 2.1.143–164 (see also MONTAIGNE). At the play's close, when PROSPERO's schemes result in a final reconciliation and the seemingly miraculous restoration of the king's son, FERDINAND (2), it is the ageing adviser—called by Prospero 'Holy Gonzalo, honourable man' (5.1.62)—who cries out, 'O, rejoice / Beyond a common joy!' (5.1.206–207).

In 1.1, as the king's ship sinks, Gonzalo's calm acceptance of fate contrasts with Antonio's arrogant fury and helps establish our sense of the moral polarities with which the play is concerned. In 1.2 we learn that Alonso assisted Antonio in deposing his brother, PROSPERO, and abandoning him and his infant daughter MIRANDA at sea, but that Gonzalo helped the victims by providing them with supplies. The contrast between Antonio and Gonzalo remains throughout the play. In 2.1 Gonzalo is mocked by Antonio and SEBASTIAN (3) for his attempts to cheer the king, and Antonio proposes to kill Gonzalo along with Alonso in his scheme to place Alonso's brother Sebastian on the throne of Naples. At the close Gonzalo's hearty participation in the aura of reconciliation points up Antonio's refusal to accept it.

**Good Quarto**   An early edition of a Shakespeare play, printed in QUARTO format. A Good Quarto was derived from an authoritative source, such as Shakespeare's FOUL PAPERS, and reflects what the author actually wrote, as opposed to a BAD QUARTO, which was reconstructed from memory. Fourteen early editions of Shakespeare's plays are Good Quartos. They are: Q1 of *Titus Andronicus* (1594); Q1 of *Richard II* (1597); Q1 of *Richard III* (1597); Q of *Love's Labour's Lost* (1598); Q0 of *1 Henry IV* (1598); Q2 of *Romeo and Juliet* (1599); Q of *2 Henry IV* (1600); Q1 of *The Merchant of Venice* (1600); Q1 of *A Midsummer Night's Dream* (1600); Q of *Much Ado About Nothing* (1600); Q2 of *Hamlet* (1604); Q of *Troilus and Cressida* (1609); Q1 of *Othello* (1622);

and Q of *The Two Noble Kinsmen* (1634). *Romeo and Juliet* and *Hamlet* also appeared as Bad Quartos, and Q1 of *Richard III* is sometimes classed as a Bad Quarto, for its generally sound text contains certain minor flaws that suggest that it was reconstructed from memory.

**Goslicius, Laurentius Grimalius (Wawrzyniec Goślicki) (d. 1604)**   Polish statesman and author, whose chief work was possibly a minor source for *Hamlet* and *Measure for Measure*. Goslicius (sometimes known in English as Grimaldus) is considered the greatest statesman of 16th-century Poland. He wrote in Latin a manual of advice for government officials and diplomats, *De Optimo Senatore* (Venice, 1568), that was among the most admired books of its kind for several generations. An anonymous English translation, *The Counsellor*, appeared in 1598 (2nd ed., 1604), and it is echoed in several passages in *Hamlet*. Goslicius is thought to have inspired the name POLONIUS; the title page of *The Counsellor* declared the work 'consecrated to the Polonian Empire', and it seems likely that Shakespeare whimsically appropriated the author's nationality as a name for his Danish minister. Further, Goslicius' work may have influenced the creation of both the DUKE (9) and ANGELO (2)—for it expounds on both good and bad magistrates—in *Measure for Measure*.

**Gosson (1), Henry (active 1601–1640)**   LONDON publisher and bookseller, producer of the first two editions of *Pericles*. In 1609 Gosson capitalised on the great popularity of Shakespeare's ROMANCE and had William WHITE (2) print a pirated edition of *Pericles*. Known as Q1, it is a BAD QUARTO, whose text was taken from the recollections of actors or viewers. The publication was a great success, and Gosson produced a second edition (Q2) in the same year. This made *Pericles* one of the few Shakespeare plays to appear in two Quartos in the same year.

Gosson, who inherited his business from his father, published mostly short-lived literature such as ballads, news sheets, and joke books. *Pericles* was the only play text he produced. He prospered and owned several shops in London, but little else is known of his life.

**Gosson (2), Stephen (1554–1624)**   English writer, a Puritan opponent of the professional theatre. Gosson, a poet, dramatist, and—probably—actor, changed his life in his early 20s and became a clergyman. He wrote three books (published between 1579 and 1582) that declared poetry and drama unnsavoury influences on society. The theatre—which he called a 'market of bawdry'—came in for particular abuse. He was willing to exclude only a few sober plays, including one of his own, from his general verdict that drama 'was not to be suffered in a Christian common weale'. Thomas LODGE began his literary career with a rejoinder, *De-*

*fence of Plays* (1581), and Sir Philip SIDNEY may have been inspired by him to write his great *Apology for Poetry* (1583). Several companies revived Gosson's plays, hoping to embarrass him and capitalise on the publicity the controversy had created. Despite his enmity towards his former profession, Gosson remained a lifelong friend of the great actor Edward ALLEYN.

Gosson was among the most prominent of Puritan opponents of the theatre. Although in the 16th century such opinions were merely a nuisance to the profession (see, e.g., COBHAM), they triumphed later during the Civil Wars. Beginning in 1642 the Puritan revolutionary government closed the theatres of England for almost 20 years.

**Goths**   Barbarian European tribe known to the ancient Romans. In *Titus Andronicus* Shakespeare uses the Goths as the enemies of Rome whose forces are necessary to restore order within the empire, which has been disrupted through the villainy of AARON and TAMORA. This device anticipates several later occasions, notably in *Hamlet* and *Macbeth,* when forces from outside the affected society must take charge, thereby heightening the playwright's emphasis on the catastrophic results of social disorder.

**Gough (Goughe), Robert (d. 1624)**   English actor. Gough is one of the 26 men listed in the FIRST FOLIO as the 'Principall Actors' in Shakespeare's plays, but he is not known to have performed in any particular role and was clearly a minor player. He may have played a LORD (6) in *All's Well That Ends Well,* for the character is designated as 'G' in speech headings in the Folio text of the play (but see GILBURNE). Gough was probably a member of STRANGE'S MEN by 1590—'R. Go' appears in a Strange's Men's cast list. He was probably employed by the CHAMBERLAIN'S MEN or its successor, the KING'S MEN, sometime before 1603, when Thomas POPE (2) willed him some of his costumes and stage weapons. He was married to Augustine PHILLIPS' sister in 1603, and he witnessed Phillips' will in 1605. He is recorded as a partner in the King's Men in 1619 and 1621, but no more is known of him. His son, Alexander Gough (1614–after 1655) was also an actor for the King's Men who specialised in female characters. He was with the company until the theatres were closed by the revolutionary government in 1642, after which he participated for some time in clandestine performances at private homes. He eventually became a publisher.

**Gounod, Charles François (1818–1893)**   French composer who wrote an opera based on *Romeo and Juliet.* A popular composer in his own day, Gounod is now considered a minor figure in French music history, best known for *Roméo et Juliette* (1867) and an-

other opera, his masterpiece, *Faust* (1859). Few of his other compositions are still performed.

**Governor (1) of Harfleur**   Minor character in *Henry V,* a French official. The Governor surrenders the town of HARFLEUR to HENRY V, confessing in 3.3.44–50 that, without the support of the DAUPHIN (3), the town is indefensible.

**Governor (2) of Paris**   Minor character in *1 Henry VI,* an official commanding the capital of English-occupied FRANCE (1). The Governor wordlessly takes an oath of allegiance to HENRY VI when the King is crowned monarch of France in 4.1.

**Gower (1)**   Minor character in *2 Henry IV,* a messenger. In 2.1 Gower brings the CHIEF JUSTICE a report that King HENRY IV and PRINCE (6) HAL have returned to London from fighting rebels in WALES (1), and he answers the judge's questions about military news. His knowledge suggests that he is in the army, but there is no other evidence to link him with Captain GOWER (2) in *Henry V* and he is generally regarded as a different character.

**Gower (2)**   Minor character in *Henry V,* an officer in the army of King HENRY V. Gower functions chiefly as a foil to FLUELLEN, a calm and restraining friend of—and audience for—the irascible Welshman. Gower, a stolid military man, reveals his own personality only when he voices his heartfelt disapproval of PISTOL, whom he sees as a petty thief and braggart impersonating a soldier, in 3.6.67–82, his sole substantial speech.

**Gower (3), John (c. 1330–1408)**   English poet, a historical figure and a character in *Pericles.* Gower's major work, the *Confessio Amantis* (1390), was Shakespeare's chief source for *Pericles* and a possible influence on *The Comedy of Errors* and *The Merchant of Venice.* In *Pericles* Gower acts as a CHORUS (1) who summarises off-stage action and moralises on the course of developments. He appears in brief PROLOGUE-like passages before each act, and also in 4.4 and 5.2. At the play's close he delivers a brief EPILOGUE. His manner of speaking is quaintly old-fashioned by the standards of the 17th century, which indicates his historical position as well as clarifying the remote and romantic nature of the story being enacted. Occasionally, Shakespeare's character clearly imitates the real Gower's poetic style, as in 3.Chorus. Also, two passages not spoken by the character—1.1.65–72 and 3.2.70–77—follow the real poet's verse quite closely.

Gower's *Confessio Amantis* contained 141 ancient tales from various sources, rendered in English verse. One of its stories, the Greek 'Apollonius of Tyre', dates to at least the 3rd century A.D., though Gower took it from the work of a later chronicler, Godfrey of Viterbo (c. 1120–c. 1196). A 1554 edition of Gower's *Confessio* provided Shakespeare with the general outline of events, the locations, and most of the characters of *Pericles*. The same tale may also have inspired the sub-plot concerning EGEON in *The Comedy of Errors* and the episode of the three caskets in *The Merchant of Venice*.

Gower was a minor nobleman who pursued his literary career in London, supported by rents from two small country estates. He wrote major works in Latin, French, and English, though the *Confessio* (which may have been commissioned by King RICHARD II) is by far the most important. Its 33,000 lines of eight-syllable couplets constitutes one of the greatest achievements of 14th-century English poetry. Gower was a contemporary and friend of Geoffrey CHAUCER, who dedicated his *Troilus and Criseyde* to him. However, the two poets may have become estranged, for a tribute to Chaucer in the first manuscript edition of the *Confessio* is omitted from later ones produced in Gower's lifetime.

**Grafton, Richard (d. 1572)** English chronicler and historian whose works, published between 1562 and 1571, were consulted by Shakespeare when writing his HISTORY PLAYS. They provided the playwright with a number of minor details.

**Granada, Luis de (1504–1588)** Spanish mystic and writer, author of a minor source for *Hamlet*. De Granada, a Dominican monk and theologian, wrote several works on prayer and mystical contemplation, including *Libro de la Oración y Consideración* (1554), usually translated as *Of Prayer and Meditation*, which probably influenced some of HAMLET's observations on graves and death in 5.1. This book was among the most popular religious treatises of the 16th century, and many English translations were published, beginning with the work of Richard HOPKINS in 1582. De Granada emphasised the presence of God as manifested in nature in lyrical works that are still appreciated; an anthology in English, *The Summa of Christian Life*, was published as recently as 1954.

**Grandpré** Minor character in *Henry V*, a French nobleman. Grandpré appears only once, to describe, in 4.2.38–55, the listless and dispirited English army just before the battle of AGINCOURT. The speech contributes to the presentation of French overconfidence. Grandpré's death is reported in 4.8.101. Shakespeare apparently took the name from the list of casualties in HOLINSHED's account of the battle.

**Granville, George (1667–1735)** English dramatist and politician, creator of an adaptation of *The Merchant of Venice*. After graduating from Cambridge University, Granville wrote *The Jew of Venice*, a farce based on Shakespeare's play that was produced in 1701 with Thomas BETTERTON playing BASSANIO and the popular comic Thomas Doggett (c. 1670–1721) as SHYLOCK. Though it has little literary merit, this work was popular for 40 years before it was superseded by Charles MACKLIN's revival of Shakespeare's play.

Granville was elected to Parliament in 1702, which was the beginning of his meteoric political career. He became secretary of war in 1710 and a peer in 1711, but he was imprisoned in 1715 for supporting the Jacobite invasion (see STUART DYNASTY). From 1722–1732 he lived in exile in France.

**Granville-Barker, Harley (1877–1946)** English actor, director, and Shakespearean commentator. After a successful career in the theatre, Granville-Barker wrote a series of *Prefaces to Shakespeare* (1927–1946) that covered 12 of Shakespeare's plays. He addressed questions of interpretation and staging that arise in actual production in the theatre, rather than taking a scholar's point of view. It is for these well-written and influential texts that he remains best known today.

As a director, Granville-Barker specialised in modern works, chiefly those of Ibsen and George Bernard SHAW (2). He only staged three of Shakespeare's plays—*The Winter's Tale* and *Twelfth Night* in 1912, and *A Midsummer Night's Dream* in 1914—but they were revolutionary and have greatly influenced the modern staging of ELIZABETHAN DRAMA. He used uncut texts and sped up the pace, and he also cut much traditional stage business to focus attention on the plays themselves. He extended the stage into the audience in an effort to simulate the theatre of Elizabethan times. By applying William POEL's notions of simplified staging, though he didn't go so far as to eliminate scenery altogether, Granville-Barker succeeded in making a commercial success of an idealistic approach to Shakespearean production.

As a young man, Granville-Barker acted in the productions of Poel and Ben GREET; he was especially acclaimed as RICHARD II. He also wrote plays, and his *The Voysey Inheritance* (1905), a satirical comedy in the vein of his close friend Shaw, is regarded as one of the best dramas of its period.

**Gratiano (1)** Character in *The Merchant of Venice*, friend of BASSANIO and lover of NERISSA. Gratiano is a crude and frivolous companion. As Bassanio himself puts it, 'Gratiano speaks an infinite deal of nothing' (1.1.114). He can be tactless, as in 1.1, where he is the only one of Antonio's friends who fails to see the propriety of leaving Antonio and Bassanio to confer privately. Bassanio, fearful that his friend will embarrass him before PORTIA (1), feels constrained to chastise him, 'Thou art too wild, too rude, and bold of voice . . .' (2.2.172). Gratiano's bluff heartiness turns ugly in the trial scene (4.1), when he baits the desperate SHYLOCK, and his lewd remarks, as in 3.2.216, mark him as a lesser person than the gentlemanly Bassanio. His courtship of Nerissa is simply an echo of Bassanio's wooing of Portia and seems to have no point but symmetry; such doubling was very popular among Elizabethan audiences. Gratiano's name comes from the Italian COMMEDIA DELL'ARTE tradition, where it was used for a stock character, the comical doctor

**Gratiano (2) (Graziano)**    Minor character in *Othello*, a Venetian nobleman, DESDEMONA's uncle. Gratiano is a member of the delegation from VENICE that comes to CYPRUS at the close of the play and witnesses the climax of OTHELLO's madness. He ineffectually responds to the cries of CASSIO and EMILIA (2) for assistance, in 5.1 and 5.2, respectively. In both cases he fails to prevent IAGO's wicked schemes. In this respect he is representative of the society at large, whose racial prejudice has helped make Othello vulnerable to Iago. In his most important remark, Gratiano declares that Desdemona's father, BRABANTIO, has died of grief at her marriage to Othello.

**Grave-digger (First Clown, First Grave-digger)** Minor character in *Hamlet*, the digger of OPHELIA's grave. At the opening of 5.1, the Grave-digger talks with his friend, called the OTHER, in a comical series of exchanges on suicide, the law, and the profession of grave-digging. HAMLET, meditating with HORATIO in the graveyard, speaks with the Grave-digger, who gives flip and enigmatic answers to his questions. In the course of describing the decomposition of corpses, he presents the prince with the skull of the late court jester, YORICK. This plunges Hamlet into another conversation with Horatio, and the Grave-digger does not speak again.

This scene does not further the plot; indeed, it quite distinctly delays development, providing some needed comic relief in the face of the rapidly approaching climax. The Grave-digger also serves as a subtle commentator on the main action, rather like a CHORUS (1). He frankly suggests the possibility of Ophelia's suicide, and his equally honest and humorous attitude to the world of the aristocrats and 'great folk [who] have countenance in this world to drown or hang themselves more than their even-Christen' (5.1. 27–29) reminds us of the extent to which intrigue infects Hamlet's world.

Most important, the Grave-digger's remarks and behaviour reflect the play's attitude towards death: it is the normal human fate to die. The Grave-digger's job makes this an everyday fact rather than a philosophical observation. At a crucial point in the play, his demeanour, both prosaic and comical, helps to make clear to the audience that Hamlet's meditations on death no

longer reflect the depression and grief that characterised him in Acts 1–4 but are rather the healthy recognition that death and decay are parts of life that must be accepted.

The Grave-digger is addressed by his companion as 'Goodman Delver' (5.1.14), which may be his surname preceded by the honorific 'Goodman' (roughly equivalent to 'Mister'), or it may simply refer to his occupation as a digger. In his uneducated but knowing humour, he is a good instance of a character type, the rustic CLOWN (1) and some editions, including the earliest ones, designate him accordingly in stage directions and speech headings.

**Gravelot, Hubert (1699–1773)**    French painter and engraver, illustrator of Shakespeare's plays. Gravelot worked on two illustrated editions of Shakespeare, THEOBALD's second edition (1740) and HANMER's deluxe volumes (1744), each of which contained 36 illustrations. For the first of these, Gravelot provided all of the 36 illustrations but engraved only eight of them himself; for the second, he provided only five illustrations but engraved all 36. The other images were provided by Francis HAYMAN.

During his residency in London (1732–1745), Gravelot was for English artists the most important source of the French rococo style in painting and decoration. He was more important as an illustrator than as a painter, and few of his paintings survive, but he was an important influence on painters such as his close friend William Hogarth (1697–1764) and his students Hayman and Thomas Gainsborough (1727–1788).

**Green, John (active 1606–1627)**    English actor active in Germany. Green was a member of one of Robert BROWNE's touring companies as early as 1606, and he had his own company beginning in 1615 until at least 1627. He succeeded Browne as the most important English influence on the roots of German drama, which were influenced by English touring companies between the 1590s and the middle of the 17th century. A listing of Green's repertoire in 1626 has survived; it included plays titled *Romeo and Juliet, Julius Caesar, Lear König von Engelandt,* and *Hamlet einem printzen in Dennemark,* almost certainly Shakespeare's plays or adaptations of them.

**Greene (1) (Green), Henry (d. 1399)**    Historical figure and character in *Richard II*, a supporter of King RICHARD II. Greene, John BAGOT, and John BUSHY are the 'caterpillars' (2.3.165) whose influence on the King is alleged by BOLINGBROKE (1) to have been disastrous for England. In 1.4 Greene, the least prominent of the three, advises the King that he must address the pressing problem of a rebellion in Ireland. The three favourites recognise that their closeness to the King is likely to prove dangerous if their master is defeated by Bolingbroke. In 2.2 they decide to flee when Bolingbroke appears; Bushy and Greene seek safety in BRISTOL Castle, but Bolingbroke captures them and sentences them to death.

Little is known about the historical Greene, a member of the gentry who was recruited for Richard's faction from among the supporters of the Duke of GLOUCESTER (6) some time before the Duke's murder.

**Greene (2), Robert (1558–1592)** English writer, author of the earliest literary reference to Shakespeare, as well as of the chief source for *The Winter's Tale* and a minor source for *Troilus and Cressida*. Greene was one of the UNIVERSITY WITS who revolutionised ELIZABETHAN DRAMA in the 1580s. He wrote at least 10 plays, mostly romantic comedies, the best-known of which is *Friar Bacon and Friar Bungay* (1589), still occasionally staged. He also wrote romantic novels—including *Pandosto* (1588), from which Shakespeare took the plot of *The Winter's Tale*—and numerous essays, such as those collected in *Eupheus his Censure to Philautus* (1587), which provided minor ideas and incidents for *Troilus and Cressida*.

Greene's reference to the young Shakespeare was made in *Greene's Groatsworth of Wit* (1592), one of several brief repentant but embittered autobiographies written as he approached death (he had led a dissolute life among criminals and whores after abandoning his wife and child). In this angry tract Greene advised other playwrights not to trust actors, declaring them to be uneducated, dishonest poseurs and citing the example of 'an upstart Crow . . . that with his *Tygers hart wrapt in a Players hyde* [Greene's emphasis], supposes he is as well able to bombast out a blanke verse as the best of you: and . . . is in his owne conceit the onely Shake-scene in a country'.

After Greene's death, his editor, Henry CHETTLE, issued a public apology to Shakespeare, but the power of slander survives retraction: the parody of 'O tiger's heart wrapp'd in a woman's hide' (*3 Henry VI* 1.4.137) has been offered as evidence that Greene wrote the play—or at least part of it, including that line—and that he was complaining of plagiarism, or at least usurped credit. Moreover, Shakespearean commentators who believe that much in Shakespeare's early plays was written by other playwrights (see, e.g., FLEAY and ROBERTSON) have suggested that Greene was also responsible for parts of *Titus Andronicus, 1* and *2 Henry VI, The Comedy of Errors, The Two Gentlemen of Verona,* and sometimes others. Most modern scholars discount these theories, however, and believe that the parody in *Groatsworth of Wit* was simply a mocking of Shakespeare's bold language.

**Greene (3), Thomas (c. 1578–1641)** Lawyer in STRATFORD, friend and possibly kinsman of Shakespeare. Greene, who was from nearby Warwick, became the town clerk of Stratford in 1602, shortly after becoming a lawyer. He may have known Shakespeare in LONDON when he studied at the INNS OF COURT, for he knew the playwright John MARSTON, but he was in any case close to the Shakespeare family for years in Stratford. His children were named after the playwright and his wife, Anne HATHAWAY Shakespeare, and he and his family lived at Shakespeare's NEW PLACE for a time, perhaps more than a year, while waiting on the renovation of another home. Some of his correspondence has survived, and in it he several times refers to Shakespeare as his 'cousin'. No family connection is known, and the word was used loosely in those days, but Greene may have been a blood relation of the playwright.

Greene was closely involved in the political crisis that gripped Stratford in the years just preceding Shakespeare's death (see WELCOMBE). He and Shakespeare jointly owned a contract to collect the taxes on agricultural lands that were proposed in 1614 for conversion to sheep farming—a politically unpopular process known as enclosure. Shakespeare negotiated an arrangement whereby they were protected against loss if enclosure went through and might profit. However, the town of Stratford opposed enclosure and, as town clerk, Greene worked against it successfully. It has been suggested that disagreements over this political crisis, which gripped Stratford for two years, may have led to the odd fact that Greene is not mentioned in Shakespeare's will. A year after Shakespeare's death, Greene moved to Bristol.

**Greet, Philip Barling Ben (1857–1936)** British actor and theatrical entrepreneur. As an actor, director, and producer, Ben Greet was dedicated to presenting Shakespeare's plays with fidelity to the playwright's text, after centuries of adaptation and traditional stage business had become attached to virtually all of the plays. He insisted on simple staging, in contrast to the late-19th-century fondness for extravagant spectacle, and he endeavoured to bring Shakespeare's plays to a wide audience. Between 1886 and 1914 he toured Britain and America with a repertory company that he then took to the OLD VIC THEATRE, which he helped establish as Britain's most important centre of Shakespearean production.

**Greg, Walter Wilson (1875–1959)** British scholar. Widely regarded as among the greatest of Shakespearean scholars, Greg edited the diaries and papers of Philip HENSLOWE (published 1904–1908), and assisted A. W. POLLARD in researching his ground-breaking *Shakespeare Folios and Quartos* (1909). He went on to produce many valuable studies, including *Dramatic Documents of the Elizabethan Playhouses* (1931), *The Editorial Problem in Shakespeare* (1942), *Shakespeare First Folio*

(1955), and the monumental four-volume *A Bibliography of the English Printed Drama to the Restoration* (1939–1959).

**Gregory (1)**  Minor character in *Romeo and Juliet*, a servant of the CAPULET (1) household. Gregory and his fellow servant SAMPSON brawl with servants of the MONTAGUE (1) family in 1.1, after opening the play with a pun-filled comic dialogue in which Gregory taunts his companion for being a coward. The brawl is purely verbal until TYBALT appears and the rival households come to blows. The episode illustrates the lengths to which the feud between the families has gone, with their servants pursuing the quarrel in the streets.

**Gremio**  Character in *The Taming of the Shrew*, an elderly suitor of BIANCA (1). Gremio is referred to as a 'pantaloon' (3.1.36), the humorous figure of a greedy old man in the COMMEDIA DELL'ARTE, and he is indeed simply a character type with little real personality. He is comically cowardly, fearful that the assertiveness of PETRUCHIO (2) will offend BAPTISTA, Bianca's father. His own style is offensively humble; approaching Baptista, he refers to himself as a 'poor petitioner' (2.1.72), in the obsequious language of a minor courtier. He lies about his wealth when Baptista promises his daughter to the wealthiest suitor, but to no avail. Gremio is absurdly ineffective; in fact, in his attempt to win Bianca's hand he actually introduces the successful suitor into her presence, for in 2.1 he hires the disguised LUCENTIO as a tutor for the girl, hoping to impress her father.

**Greville (1), Curtis (active 1622–1631)**  English actor who may have performed in early productions of *The Two Noble Kinsmen* and *The Taming of the Shrew*. In the first edition of *Kinsmen* (Q1, 1634), the stage direction at 4.2.70 designates the MESSENGER (32) as 'Curtis'; in the opening stage direction of 5.3, the Attendants called for—one of whom is presumably the SERVANT (30)—are named, one of them 'Curtis'. Scholars believe that these references are to Greville, indicating that he played the parts in an early production by the KING'S MEN. Greville was with the company from before 1626 until 1631, so this clue (with similar evidence concerning Thomas TUCKFIELD) suggests that Q1 was printed from a PROMPT-BOOK of the 1620s. Some scholars believe that *The Shrew*'s CURTIS similarly takes his name from Greville's portrayal.

Little is known of Greville. In 1622 he moved from LADY ELIZABETH'S MEN to the PALSGRAVE'S MEN, presumably as part of the latter company's effort to re-open the FORTUNE THEATRE, closed by fire. By 1626 Greville was with the King's Men, with whom he is known to have played several minor roles.

**Greville (2), Fulke (Lord Brooke) (1554–1628)**  English poet and author, possibly a patron of Shakespeare. Greville is best known for his biography of Philip SIDNEY, whose close friend he had been since the age of 10. However, he also wrote a considerable body of poetry, two plays, and several treatises on politics, religion, and education. He was a significant figure in RENAISSANCE English literature in other ways, as well. As a member of the 'Areopagus' group of poets—with Sidney, Edmund SPENSER, and others—he helped stimulate the use of classical METRE in English poetry. As a wealthy man he was a patron of writers, and assisted Samuel DANIEL, among others. He also served as a diplomat and economic adviser to both Queen ELIZABETH (1) and King JAMES I. The latter monarch made him a baron on his retirement from government in 1621, and he is sometimes known as Lord Brooke.

The young Shakespeare may have benefited from Greville's largesse. According to a 1665 account, Greville once described himself as worthy only because he had been 'Shakespeare and Ben JONSON's master . . . and Sir Philip Sidney's friend'. Most scholars regard this anecdote as apocryphal, but whether or not he did indeed act as an elder adviser and patron to the young playwright, the remark reflects Greville's famed modesty. His EPITAPH, composed by himself, reads 'Servant to Queen Elizabeth, Counsellor to King James, Friend to Sir Philip Sydney.'

**Grey (1), Lady**  Character in *3 Henry VI*. See ELIZABETH (2).

**Grey (2), Sir Richard (d. 1483)**  Historical figure and character in *Richard III*, a kinsman of Queen ELIZABETH (2) and a victim of RICHARD III. Grey simply functions as a pawn in Richard's game of power politics. He is executed in 3.3 solely because he is the Queen's relative. As he goes to his death, along with RIVERS and VAUGHAN, who had anticipated this event in 1.3, he recollects the curses of Queen MARGARET (1), who had anticipated this event in 1.3.

Shakespeare was apparently confused about Grey's relationship to Elizabeth, although his habitual carelessness about minor matters suggests that he probably did not concern himself about it. Historically, Grey was Elizabeth's son by her first marriage, but in the play he is implied to be her brother. However, in recalling Margaret's curse, he speaks as though he were DORSET, unquestionably a son of Elizabeth.

**Grey (3), Thomas (d. 1415)**  Historical figure and minor character in *Henry V*, a traitor who plans to assassinate King HENRY V but is captured and sentenced to death. In 2.2 Henry, who knows of their plot, asks Grey and his fellow conspirators, Lord SCROOP (1) and the Earl of CAMBRIDGE, for advice about a drunken soldier who has criticised him. They all recommend severity, insisting that Henry be firm against any hint of disloyalty. Then Henry reveals his awareness of their treason and applies their own rule against them, sentencing them to death. Grey, like the others, offers a conventionally remorseful speech, thanking God for the defeat of the conspiracy and welcoming death. Grey has no personality; the episode merely serves to emphasise Henry's godlike majesty.

The historical Grey was a landowner in Northumberland and is thought to have been allied to the Percy family, persistent rebels against King HENRY IV. The revolt led by Cambridge may have been a final spasm of the civil conflict enacted in *1* and *2 Henry IV.*

**Griffin, Bartholomew (d. 1602)**  Author of at least one and probably four of the poems attributed to Shakespeare in THE PASSIONATE PILGRIM (1599). Little is known of Griffin, who is remembered primarily because one SONNET from his 62-sonnet sequence, *Fidessa* (1596)—a conventional and undistinguished work—was published as no. 11 in William JAGGARD's spurious anthology. Three other poems in the collection (nos. 4, 6, and 9) resemble no. 11 closely enough that they are often attributed to Griffin as well. His preface to *Fidessa* suggests that Griffin may have been a gentleman and a lawyer, and it also asserted that he was writing a long pastoral poem, but, if this was completed and published, it has not survived.

**Griffith**  Minor character in *Henry VIII*, an attendant to Queen KATHERINE. Griffith is the GENTLEMAN USHER to the Queen in 2.4, but in 4.2 he has a more intimate function, as a faithful servant who continues to attend the now-deposed queen in exile at KIMBOLTON. Griffith tells Katherine that Cardinal WOLSEY repented of his evil deeds before dying. As Wolsey's victim, Katherine speaks harshly of him, but Griffith suggests a more charitable view of the cardinal, emphasising his good works. Katherine thanks Griffith for reminding her of the proper Christian attitude towards her enemy, since she is near death herself. Griffith is tender with the dying queen; along with the waiting-woman PATIENCE, he helps surround the queen's death with an atmosphere of virtuous mildness. Griffith is named in Shakespeare's sources, but only in connection with his duties as the queen's gentleman usher; the playwright invented his role in 4.2, as part of his association of Katherine with the themes of forgiveness and patience in adversity.

**Groom (1)**  Minor character in *Richard II*, a supporter of RICHARD II. The Groom visits the imprisoned Richard in 5.5, in a demonstration of allegiance that raises the ex-King's spirits. He tells Richard of the use of the horse BARBARY by BOLINGBROKE (1). This minor incident illustrates that Richard could inspire loyalty in a simple servant and thus heightens the pathos of the deposed ruler's murder, which follows immediately.

**Groom (2)**  Any of two or three minor characters in *2 Henry IV*, servants who strew the London streets with rushes in preparation for the crowds attending PRINCE (6) HAL's coronation as HENRY V. Their presence at the opening of 5.5 sets the scene. They are identified as two Grooms in the FOLIO edition of the play, and as three Strewers in the QUARTO edition; modern editions vary.

**Grumio**  Character in *The Taming of the Shrew*, servant of PETRUCHIO (2). Grumio is a distinctly English comic figure in all respects except his name. At 1.2.28, he even fails to recognise Italian. Grumio represents a long theatrical tradition—the comical servant whose nonsense masks shrewdness. His wily foolishness is a vehicle for humour when, in 1.2, he remarks sharply on the mercenary marriage that his master is pursuing. It can also be a means of manipulating others, as when he feigns incomprehension—first with KATHERINA and later with the TAILOR—in 4.3. His name comes from a character in an ancient Roman play, *The Haunted House*, by PLAUTUS.

**Guardsman (1)**  Any of several minor characters in *Antony and Cleopatra*, soldiers who serve as ANTONY's personal guards. In 4.14 three Guardsmen (designated First, Second and Third Guardsman) discover the wounded Antony who requests that they kill him as he has unsuccessfully attempted suicide. Horrified, they flee from the room. Twenty lines later, when called by DIOMEDES (2), several of them return and carry the wounded Antony to CLEOPATRA. Though dismayed and sorrowful, the Guardsmen have no real personalities; they merely reflect the demoralised state of their leader.

**Guardsman (2)**  Any of several minor characters in *Antony and Cleopatra*, soldiers in the army of Octavius CAESAR (2) assigned to guard CLEOPATRA. In 5.2 they enter with GALLUS at 5.2.34, but none of them speak until 5.2.232, when one of them announces the arrival of the CLOWN (7) who secretly delivers to Cleopatra the poisonous asps with which she will kill herself. After her death the Guardsmen enter as a group to discover the situation and call an officer, DOLABELLA. Two of them speak, and they are designated First and Second Guardsman. Their presence emphasises Cleopatra's captivity and thus helps to justify her suicide.

**Guiderius**  Character in *Cymbeline*, one of the two kidnapped sons of King CYMBELINE. Guiderius and his younger brother ARVIRAGUS have been raised as hunters in the wilderness of WALES (1) by their foster-father

BELARIUS, who kidnapped them in infancy when he was unjustly exiled by Cymbeline. Guiderius shares with his brother the desire to prove himself in war, which is evidence of his inherently regal courage. When their sister IMOGEN, disguised as a boy, appears by chance, both young men immediately love 'him', which stresses to the audience that they are siblings. When the Romans invade Britain, the brothers display their innate capacity for leadership and save the British army. They are honoured by the king and then identified and reunited with him, as part of the revelations and reconciliations at the play's close.

Guiderius, like Arviragus, is a simple fairy-tale figure—a lost prince who is restored to his rightful position—and his personality is mostly seen in courage and high spirits. However, Shakespeare takes care to distinguish the brothers from each other. As the future heir to the throne, Guiderius is more forceful and dynamic than his reflective brother Arviragus. When they discuss Imogen's virtues, Guiderius proves more practical when he mentions her cooking, while Arviragus praises her singing. When they believe her dead, Guiderius cuts short his brother's 'wench-like words' (4.2.23.) and says, 'Let us bury him, / And not protract with admiration what / Is now due debt. To th'grave!' (4.2.230–233). At his most striking, Guiderius kills CLOTEN, earlier in the same scene, with soldierly aplomb. He brandishes his victim's head while he remarks, 'This Cloten was a fool, an empty purse' (4.2.113). Later, he declares he will throw the head into the creek 'to tell the fishes he's the queen's son' (4.2.153). In 5.5 he manfully acknowledges that he has killed Cloten despite the threat of capital punishment for killing a prince (he is not yet known to be a prince himself). His 'I have spoke it, and I did it' (5.5.290) has a kingly simplicity and force. Belarius has given Guiderius the name Polydore, and this name is occasionally used in dialogue, but he is designated as Guiderius in speech headings and stage directions.

**Guildenstern** Character in *Hamlet.* See ROSENCRANTZ AND GUILDENSTERN.

**Guilford (Guildford), Sir Henry (1489–1532)** Historical figure and minor character in *Henry VIII,* a steward to Cardinal WOLSEY. In 1.4 Guilford, welcoming the guests to the cardinal's banquet, cheerfully delights in the 'good company, good wine, good welcome' (1.4.6). He speaks briefly as the scene opens and then disappears from the play, having served to establish the mood of this occasion, when King HENRY VIII meets his future bride ANNE (1) BULLEN. The historical Guilford later became a steward to King Henry and functioned as his MASTER OF THE REVELS, before that office was formally created.

**Gurney, James** Minor character in *King John,* a friend or servant of LADY (5) Faulconbridge. Gurney speaks only half of one line (1.1.231), a friendly response to his dismissal from the scene (and the play) by the BASTARD (1), Lady Faulconbridge's son. This moment illuminates the world of rural informality that the Bastard has come from.

**Guthrie, Tyrone (1900–1971)** British theatrical producer. Guthrie directed the OLD VIC THEATRE from 1933 to 1945, and he was chiefly responsible for the creation of the Shakespeare Festival in Stratford, Ontario, in 1953 and the Guthrie Theatre in Minneapolis in 1963. His daringly experimental productions sparked controversy in England and America. Particularly noted were his 1937 *Twelfth Night* and his renderings of *All's Well That Ends Well* as a farce (1953 and 1959, in Ontario and STRATFORD, England, respectively). He wrote several books, including *Theatre Prospect* (1932) and *A New Theatre* (1964).

**Gwinne (Gwinn), Matthew (c. 1558–1627)** English physician and playwright, author of a possible inspiration for *Macbeth.* Gwinne's Latin MASQUE *Tres Sibyllae* was performed on the occasion of King JAMES I's visit to Oxford in 1605. It features prophecies addressed to MACBETH and BANQUO, and alludes to the king's legendary descent from Banquo. Some scholars believe that its success with its royal auditor may have inspired Shakespeare to compose his own version of the Macbeth tale.

Gwinne was closely associated with Oxford, though he also had a medical practise in London. He was the supervisor of theatrical productions at the university in the 1590s, and he was highly respected as an academic dramatist, chiefly on the strength of two Latin plays, *Nero* (1603) and *Vertumnis* (1605). The latter work gained an unfortunate notoriety when it put the king to sleep.

**Haberdasher, The** Minor character in *The Taming of the Shrew,* an artisan whom PETRUCHIO (2) abuses. The Haberdasher, who has been commissioned to make a hat for KATHERINA, speaks only one line before being driven away by his client, who is demonstrating the ugliness of shrewish behaviour to his bride.

**Hakluyt, Richard (c. 1552–1616)** English geographer. Hakluyt (pronounced 'haklit') was a clergyman, but he devoted his career to the publication of materials concerning the exploration of the New World and the promotion of English efforts in this realm. He learned the major European languages in order to have access to all possible sources of information. In 1582 he published *Divers voyages touching the discoveries of America.* He was also employed as a diplomat and spy by the government, serving as chaplain to the British ambassador in FRANCE (1) from 1583–1589. During this period, he compiled his most important work, *The Principall Navigations, Voyages, and Discoveries of the English Nation* (1589). As revised in 1600, this work contained a well-known map, probably the 'new map with the augmentation of the Indies' referred to in *Twelfth Night* (3.2.76–77). Some of Hakluyt's material was gathered by John PORY, and the collection was further enlarged by Hakluyt's friend Samuel Purchas (c. 1575–1626), who published an account of a shipwreck by William STRACHEY (2) that influenced Shakespeare's *The Tempest.* Hakluyt's *Voyages,* as his book is known, was very influential on the course of English exploration, besides being extremely popular among lay readers. It is still in print. In 1846 the Royal Geographic Society founded the Hakluyt Society, which continues to publish historical accounts of explorations and travels, including new editions of Hakluyt's works.

**Hal, Prince** Character in *1* and *2 Henry IV.* See PRINCE (6).

**Halberdier** Minor character in *Richard III,* one of the soldiers guarding the coffin of King HENRY VI in 1.2. The Halberdier vainly attempts to prevent RICHARD III from interrupting the King's funeral procession. (A halberd, the weapon assigned this character in the stage directions, was a combination of lance and battle-ax, mounted on a long pole.)

The Halberdier's single speech is attributed to him by modern editors who feel that older editions err in giving it to the GENTLEMAN (2). A gentleman, it is argued, would neither receive nor accept the abuse that Richard heaps on the unfortunate soldier. Villainous though he is, it is supposed that Richard would observe the formal distinctions between aristocrats and commoners.

**Hall (1), Arthur (c. 1540–1604)** English writer. Hall completed the first English translation of HOMER; his version of the first 10 books of the *Iliad* was published in 1581. Shakespeare surely knew this work, and it may have influenced his treatment of Homeric materials in *The Rape of Lucrece* and *Troilus and Cressida* (although it is clear that in the latter work he relied chiefly on the translation by George CHAPMAN).

Hall, an orphan, was raised in the household of the leading Elizabethan statesman Lord BURGHLEY. As an adult, he was notorious for riotous living and was imprisoned several times; although he began his translation of the *Iliad* while in his 20s, he did not complete it for many years. Inaccurate and awkward, it was completely overshadowed by Chapman's *Iliad,* which appeared between 1598 and 1611, and has been little read ever since.

**Hall (2) (Halle), Edward (c. 1498–1547)** English historian, author of an important source for Shakespeare's HISTORY PLAYS. Hall's account of the 15th-century WARS OF THE ROSES, *The Union of the Two Noble and Illustre Families of Lancaster and York* (1548), was particularly influential on the *Henry VI* plays, though echoes of it occur throughout the eight plays (see TETRALOGY) that deal with the wars. Hall's central theme in the *Union* is that the weakness of King HENRY VI and the resulting wars were God's punishment for the sin of Henry's grandfather, HENRY IV, who altered God's intended line of kings when he usurped the throne. This notion is in turn based on the premise that history has a moral purpose, set by God. Both of these ideas are strongly evident in Shakespeare's plays. However, Hall's work was also employed by Shakespeare's most important source on British history, Raphael HOLINSHED, and it is often difficult to determine which source the playwright was using. Scholars generally feel that Hall was his major source for the history of the wars, while Holinshed was used chiefly for additional details, particularly in the *Henry VI* plays and *Richard III*.

Hall incorporated earlier histories into the *Union*, notably Sir Thomas MORE's *History of Richard III* (published in Richard GRAFTON's chronicles), and Polydore VERGIL's *Historia Anglia* (1534). Hall was in turn incorporated by later writers, including Holinshed and John STOW. Thus, his work is a central element in the 16th century's picture of the 15th. Hall was a lawyer and politician who wrote his history with the specific intention of glorifying the TUDOR dynasty, whose foundation ended the Wars of the Roses. In this, he was part of a well-established tradition of Tudor history writing that was consciously instituted by King Henry VII (see HISTORY PLAYS) as a type of propaganda. Shakespeare, though his own sensibility permeates his work and makes it more interesting and comprehensive, was also a part of this tradition.

**Hall (3), Elizabeth (1608–1670)** Shakespeare's grand-daughter, child of Susanna SHAKESPEARE (14) and John HALL (4). Elizabeth was eight when Shakespeare died, and the playwright left her most of his silver. After her mother's death she also inherited most of the rest of the Shakespeare estate, including NEW PLACE and the BIRTHPLACE. She married Thomas NASH (2) in 1626 and lived with him at New Place, though probably not until after her father's death in 1635. Nash died in 1647 and she was remarried in 1649 to John Bernard (d. 1674), with whom she moved to Northamptonshire. She had no children by either husband and was Shakespeare's last descendant. She left the Shakespeare birthplace to her cousin George Hart, grandson of Joan SHAKESPEARE (8), and the remainder of her grandfather's estate, including New Place, to Bernard, whose heirs sold it.

**Hall (4), John (1575–1635)** Shakespeare's son-in-law, the husband of Susanna SHAKESPEARE (14) and father of Elizabeth HALL (3). Hall was a notable doctor who probably treated his father-in-law and was certainly well-regarded by him, for with his wife he was executor of the playwright's will. Hall, the son of a physician from Bedfordshire, studied medicine at Cambridge University and possibly in France, though he never received a formal degree in the subject. He settled in STRATFORD around 1600 and was soon regarded as the region's leading doctor. He was reportedly a very devout Protestant, perhaps with Puritan

leanings, and it has been speculated that he did not approve of his famous father-in-law's profession. During the Civil Wars his widow sold one of his Latin medical notebooks—apparently not realising that he had written it—and it was later published as *Select Observations on English Bodies* (1657). It contains accounts of many of his patients—including his wife and Michael DRAYTON—but unfortunately begins only in 1617 and so does not treat Shakespeare.

**Hall (5), Peter (b. 1930)** British theatrical director. Hall directed the ROYAL SHAKESPEARE COMPANY in STRATFORD from 1960 to 1968 and the National Theatre Company of Britain from 1972 to 1988. Among his most notable Shakespearean productions have been *Henry V* (1960), two stagings of *Coriolanus* (1959 and 1984, starring Laurence OLIVIER and Ian MCKELLEN, respectively), and a rare uncut *Hamlet* (1975).

**Hall (6), Susanna Shakespeare** Shakespeare's daughter, wife of John HALL (4). See SHAKESPEARE (14).

**Hall (7), William (active 1577–1620)** English printer, a possible 'Mr W. H.' of the dedication to the first edition (1609) of the SONNETS. Hall was mostly a printer of business papers, and had no known connection with Shakespeare or his works. However, he has been suggested by the scholar Sidney LEE as a possible 'Mr W. H'. on the strength of the coincidence of initials and the fact that the next word in the dedication is 'all'. Lee speculated that Hall acquired for publisher Thomas THORPE the copies of the poems from which the book was published, and was thus called the 'onlie begetter' of the Sonnets. Aside from this supposition there is no evidence to associate Hall with the work.

**Halle, Edward** See HALL (2).

**Halliwell-Phillips, James Orchard (1820–1889)** British scholar. A long-time librarian at Jesus College, Cambridge, Halliwell-Phillips was one of the most important 19th-century Shakespeare scholars. He published a *Life of Shakespeare* (1848), an edition of the *Works* (1853–1861), and a collection of documentary materials on the playwright's life, *Outlines of the Life of Shakespeare* (1881). The *Outlines* is a trove of material that has been used by all later biographers. He was a founder of the original Shakespeare Society in 1840 and the first editor of the STRATFORD archives.

**Hamlet** Title character of *Hamlet*, the crown prince of DENMARK. Prince Hamlet is required by his murdered father's GHOST (3) to take vengeance on the present KING (5), his uncle, who committed the murder and then married the widow of his victim, Hamlet's mother, the QUEEN (9). Hamlet's troubled response to this situation, his disturbed relations with those around him, and his eventual acceptance of his destiny constitute the play.

Hamlet is almost universally considered one of the most remarkable characters in all of literature. His language, extraordinary even in Shakespeare's oeuvre, sweeps us up in a seemingly endless stream of brilliant impressions. He does not often use the similes and metaphors of ordinary speech, instead pouring forth fully fleshed images that convey the excitement of his thought. His psychology is stirringly genuine because it is humanly complex; he is filled with passion and contradiction, and his emotional life develops credibly through the course of the play. His personality, his attitudes and ideas, even his subconscious, have intrigued readers and theatre-goers for centuries, and copious commentary on him is still being written. Many writers have supposed that Hamlet's troubled mind reflects a traumatic development in Shakespeare's life, although there is almost no evidence of the playwright's personal life to confirm or refute this theory.

Although Hamlet foreshadows the psychologically realistic characters of modern drama, Shakespeare did not create the prince's emotional life for its own sake but rather as a vehicle for presenting a philosophical attitude. Hamlet's troubled mind demonstrates the development of an acceptance of life despite the existence of human evil, and this is the dominant theme of the play. The critical element in this development is the prince's recognition of evil in himself; in containing both good and evil, he represents the dual nature of humankind. The reconciliation of humanity with its own flawed nature is a central concern of Shakespeare's work, and in Hamlet an evolution of attitudes leading to this conclusion is displayed in a grand and powerful portrait.

Although he can deal in a practical manner with the world of intrigue that surrounds him, Hamlet is more a thinker than a doer, and he directs our attention often to his own concerns, large issues such as suicide, the virtues and defects of humankind, and the possibility of life after death. Above all, his circumstances demand that he consider the nature of evil.

We first encounter the prince as he struggles to deal with his father's death. In 1.2.76–86 he describes his mournful state; dressed in funereal black, conscious that he looks dejected and can be seen to have been weeping, he nevertheless asserts that this appearance cannot convey the depths of his grief. By focussing on the difference between appearance and reality—a difference that here is merely one of degree since his inner state is at least superficially indicated by his dress and demeanour—Hamlet betrays the confused perception that comes with great emotional trauma. In the early stages of grief, the ordinary aspects of existence seem absurdly thin and weak, inappropriate to the mourner's overwhelming sense of pain and loss.

In this state of mind, Hamlet is strongly offended by his mother's hasty and incestuous remarriage, even before he learns from the Ghost of his father's murder. He sees his father as an ideal man and a great king, an assumption supported by other opinions in the play and by the dignity and grandeur of the Ghost. He is thus appalled by his mother's willingness to accept an inferior man, a libertine and—as is soon revealed—a murderer. Hamlet comes to see his mother as evil and is devastated by the idea. Although he is the son of a godlike father, he is also the son of a mother who readily beds with 'a satyr' (1.2.140). Plunged into despondency, he rejects life, saying, 'How weary, stale, flat, and unprofitable / Seem to me all the uses of this world! . . . things rank and gross in nature / Possess it merely' (1.2.133–136). This attitude is further expressed in one of literature's most powerful evocations of mental depression, 'I have of late . . . lost all my mirth [and] this goodly frame the earth seems to me a sterile promontory, this most excellent canopy the air . . . appeareth nothing to me but a foul and pestilent congregation of vapours. What a piece of work is a man, . . . and yet, to me, what is this quintessence of dust? Man delights not me—nor woman neither . . .' (2.2.295–309).

He declares that his life is not worth 'a pin's fee' (1.4.65); indeed, he longs for death, as he declares more than once, wishing, for instance, '. . . that this too too sullied flesh would melt' (1.2.129) and declaring death '. . . a consummation / Devoutly to be wish'd' (3.1.63–64), though in both of these speeches he also rejects suicide, once because of the religious injunction against it and once out of fear of the afterlife.

His disgust with life turns, therefore, to a revulsion against sex, the mechanism of life's continuance. Not only does sex generate life, with its evils, but the attractions of sex have led his mother to adultery and incest. Though some commentators have supposed that Hamlet unconsciously desires his mother sexually, as in the Oedipus complex hypothesised by Freud, such a theory is unnecessary, for the play's world provides the prince with real, not fantasised, parental conflicts: his father is dead, and he is the enemy of his mother's lover. However, the facts of Hamlet's situation, dire as they are, are less important than the interpretation that he puts upon them. Plainly influenced by his disgust with sex, he is obsessed by the image of his mother's 'incestuous sheets' (1.2. 157); he virtually ignores the political consequences of his father's murder—the murderer's succession as King—and focusses on the sexual implications, and, most significantly, he transfers his mother's sexual guilt to OPHELIA.

Hamlet denies his love for Ophelia in 3.1.117–119,

though only after affirming it two lines earlier, and Shakespeare plainly intended us to take Hamlet's courtship of Ophelia before the play begins as having been sincere. Ophelia's shy description in 1.3.110–114, along with her regretful one in 3.1.97–99, make this clear. Moreover, Hamlet's intensity and confusion as he parts from Ophelia—in the strange behaviour she recounts in 2.1.77–100 and in his famous insistence that she enter a nunnery in 3.1.121–151—indicate his great emotional involvement. However, although he apparently loved her earlier, Hamlet does not actually respond to Ophelia as a person in the course of the play. Theirs is not a love story but rather a dramatisation of Hamlet's rejection of life, and of love, marriage, and sex. 'Why wouldst thou be a breeder of sinners?' he cries in 3.1.121–122, and he immediately goes on to identify himself with the world's evil-doers. Hamlet cannot avoid his sexual desire for Ophelia, as his obscene jesting in 3.2.108–119 demonstrates, but this episode is also a plain indication of the disgust he now feels for sex. His attitude symbolises his condemnation of life, a viewpoint that he overcomes by the end of the play.

Hamlet's delay in seeking revenge may similarly be seen as a psychological trait emphasised to make a philosophical point. The prince's procrastination is not immediately obvious, for not much time seems to pass and only one plain opportunity for revenge presents itself (in the 'prayer scene', 3.3), but Hamlet insists upon its importance, berating himself as 'a rogue and peasant slave . . . / A dull and muddy-mettled rascal' (2.2.544, 562); his assumption of guilt is clearly excessive. Though committed to the idea that revenge is his duty, Hamlet senses the evil in the obligation, sent from 'heaven and hell' (2.2.580), and he resists.

Once the King's guilt is firmly established by his response to the performance of THE MURDER OF GONZAGO, Hamlet falls victim to a pathological rage. This is first shown in his chilling resolution, ' 'Tis now the very witching time of night, / . . . Now could I drink hot blood . . .' (3.2.379–381). This state of mind persists as he demands eternal damnation for the King, not merely murderous revenge, and therefore avoids killing him at prayer in 3.3. Then in 3.4 he vents his hysterical rage at his mother and kills POLONIUS with a furious gesture in the process. This crime lacks even the justification of revenge. Whatever his faults, Polonius was innocent of Hamlet's father's murder, and, moreover, his death leads to the insanity and subsequent death of Ophelia, whose blamelessness is absolute. Hamlet's avoidance of one evil has thus involved him in another, greater one.

Hamlet's rage and his descent into evil are central to the play, both literally, occurring near its mid-point, and figuratively, for his deeds trigger its climactic de-velopment. Polonius' son, LAERTES, seeks revenge and eventually kills Hamlet, and more immediately, Polonius' death results in Hamlet's exile, during which he finds his salvation.

In Act 5 we find that Hamlet has changed. He meditates on death in the graveyard in 5.1, but now death is neither welcoming nor fearful; it is merely the normal human destiny and the prince's remarks are satirical thrusts at the living. His memories of YORICK are pleasurable appreciations of the past, as well as occasions for sardonic humour. Ophelia's funeral triggers a last explosion of emotion as Hamlet assaults Laertes, but although this resembles his fury of Act 3, here Hamlet restrains himself and departs. His outburst has been cathartic, producing two significant declarations. As he challenges Laertes, Hamlet proclaims himself 'Hamlet the Dane' (5.1.251), at last accepting his role as his father's heir—Denmark, once his 'prison' (2.2.243) is now his kingdom—and at the same time implicitly challenging the King. Perhaps given courage or awareness by this pronouncement he goes on to assert the feelings he had suppressed in his anger and depression, stating 'I lov'd Ophelia' (5.1.264). The prince is no longer in the grip of his grief.

In 5.2 Hamlet confides to HORATIO the cause of the change in his sense of himself: by impulsively rewriting his death warrant to save himself, he has realised that his hesitations and ponderings had been beside the point. He sees that 'Our indiscretion sometime serves us well / When our deep plots do pall. . . . There's a divinity that shapes our ends, / Rough-hew them how we will . . .' (5.2.8–11). He acknowledges that he cannot carry out the revenge called for by the Ghost without committing murder, the very crime he must avenge. He accepts that he must be evil in order to counter evil. He senses a basic truth: the capacity for evil exists in him because he is human.

In accepting his destiny, Hamlet also prepares for his own death. He senses his end approaching, as the King's plot takes form, but he remains composed, saying, 'There is special providence in the fall of a sparrow. If it be now, 'tis not to come; if it be not to come, it will be now; if it be not now, yet it will come. The readiness is all. Since no man, of aught he leaves, knows aught, what is't to leave betimes? Let be' (5.2.215–220). This final remark—since we know so little of the world, it is no great matter to leave it early—reflects the prince's awareness of the futility of his earlier philosophical inquiries. It is more important to live and then to die, coming to terms with one's fate.

Hamlet's salvation—his awareness of his human failings—comes only with his death. However, Horatio's prayer for him, '[May] flights of angels sing thee to thy rest' (5.2.365), offers the hope of an eternal release from the stresses the prince has undergone.

The playwright leaves us assured that his tragic hero has finally found peace.

## *Hamlet*

SYNOPSIS

### *Act 1, Scene 1*

On the castle wall in ELSINORE, a sentry, BARNARDO, replaces FRANCISCO (1) on guard and is joined by HORATIO and MARCELLUS. Barnardo and Marcellus tell of a supernatural being they have seen. The GHOST (3) of the late King of DENMARK silently appears and withdraws. The three agree that this visitation seems especially ominous in view of an impending war with Norway. The Ghost re-enters but disappears again when a cock crows. Horatio decides that they should tell Prince HAMLET of the appearance of his father's spirit.

### *Act 1, Scene 2*

Claudius, the KING (5) of Denmark, speaks of the recent death of the late king, his brother, and of his marriage to QUEEN (9) Gertrude, his brother's widow and Hamlet's mother. He also tells of an invasion threat from young Prince FORTINBRAS of Norway, who is acting without the knowledge of his uncle, the Norwegian king. The King therefore sends CORNELIUS (1) and VOLTEMAND with a letter to the King of Norway advocating restraint. LAERTES, the son of the King's adviser POLONIUS, requests permission to return to his studies in France, which the King grants. The King and Queen urge Hamlet to cease mourning his father's death. The King denies Hamlet permission to return to his own studies at Wittenberg; the Queen adds her wish that he stay in Denmark, and Hamlet agrees to do so. The monarchs and their retinue depart. Hamlet remains and muses mournfully on his mother's hasty and incestuous marriage. Horatio, Marcellus, and Barnardo appear and tell Hamlet about the Ghost. With great excitement, he arranges to meet them on the castle wall that night.

### *Act 1, Scene 3*

Laertes, leaving for France, warns his sister, OPHELIA, about Hamlet's affection for her, which he says cannot be permanent in view of the prince's royal status. Polonius arrives and gives Laertes moralising advice on his conduct abroad. Laertes departs with a last word to Ophelia about Hamlet; this triggers a diatribe from Polonius about the suspect morals of young men, and he forbids Ophelia to see the prince.

### *Act 1, Scene 4*

The Ghost appears to Hamlet, Horatio, and Marcellus, and Hamlet speaks to it. It beckons, and Hamlet follows.

### *Act 1, Scene 5*

The Ghost confirms that it is the spirit of Hamlet's father. It declares that the prince must avenge his murder: the King had poured poison in his ear. The Ghost departs, and Hamlet vows to carry out its wishes. Horatio and Marcellus appear, and Hamlet swears them to secrecy—about the Ghost and about his own intention to feign madness—as the Ghost's disembodied voice demands their oaths.

### *Act 2, Scene 1*

Polonius sends his servant REYNALDO (1) to spy on Laertes in Paris. Ophelia reports that Hamlet has come to her and behaved as if he were insane. Polonius concludes that his separation of Ophelia and Hamlet has driven the prince mad, and he decides to inform the King of this.

### *Act 2, Scene 2*

The King and Queen welcome ROSENCRANTZ AND GUILDENSTERN, fellow students of Hamlet, who have been summoned in the hope that the prince will confide in them. They agree to spy on their friend. Voltemand and Cornelius arrive to report that the King of Norway has agreed to redirect Fortinbras' invasion to Poland. Polonius then declares—with comical tediousness—that Hamlet is lovesick, producing a love letter from the prince that he has confiscated from Ophelia. He offers to arrange for the King to eavesdrop on an encounter between Ophelia and Hamlet. Hamlet appears; Polonius advises the King and Queen to leave, and he approaches the prince alone. Hamlet answers him with nonsensical remarks and absurd insults. Polonius interprets these as symptoms of madness and departs, as Rosencrantz and Guildenstern enter. Hamlet greets them with more wild talk, and he badgers them into admitting that they have been sent to observe him. PLAYERS (2) from the city arrive, and Hamlet welcomes them enthusiastically, asking the FIRST PLAYER (2) to recite a dramatic monologue describing an episode of revenge from the TROJAN WAR. Hamlet requests that the Players perform THE MURDER OF GONZAGO before the court that night, inserting lines that he will compose. He dismisses the actors and the courtiers and soliloquises on his delay in avenging the Ghost. He suspects that the spirit may have lied; he will have the Players enact a killing similar to his father's murder, and if Claudius responds guiltily, he will know that the Ghost has spoken the truth.

### *Act 3, Scene 1*

Polonius instructs Ophelia to meet Hamlet while he and the King eavesdrop. The two men hide themselves as Hamlet approaches, meditating on the value of life, and Ophelia greets him. He passionately rejects her with a wild diatribe against women. He leaves her grieving for his apparent madness. The King tells Polonius that he has decided to send Hamlet on a mission to England, accompanied by Rosencrantz and Guildenstern. Polonius suggests further surveillance in the meantime, proposing that his mother summon

Hamlet after the performance by the Players; he, Polonius, will spy on their conversation.

### Act 3, Scene 2

Hamlet lectures the Players on acting, saying that overacting and improvisation are distractions from a play's purposes. The court assembles, and the Players perform an introductory DUMB SHOW, in which a murderer kills a king by pouring poison in his ear as he sleeps. He then takes the king's crown and exits with the king's wife. The PLAYER KING and PLAYER QUEEN then speak; she asserts that she will never remarry if he dies, but he insists that she will. He then rests, falling asleep. Another Player, in the part of LUCIANUS, speaks darkly of the evil powers of poison and pours a potion in the ear of the PLAYER KING. The real King, distressed, rises and leaves in anger. Hamlet exults in the success of his plan. Rosencrantz and Guildenstern, and then Polonius, deliver the Queen's summons to Hamlet, and he agrees to go to her, but not before ridiculing them. He prepares himself to meet his mother, feeling great anger but reminding himself not to use violence against her.

### Act 3, Scene 3

Polonius tells the King that Hamlet is on his way to the Queen's chamber, where he, Polonius, will spy on their meeting. He goes, and the King soliloquises about his murder of his brother. He says that he has been unable to pray for forgiveness because he is conscious that he is still enjoying the fruits of his crime—his brother's kingdom and his widow. He tries again to pray; Hamlet enters, sees the King on his knees, and contemplates killing him on the spot. He reflects, however, that, if the King dies while at prayer, he will probably go to heaven and the revenge will be incomplete. He decides instead to wait until he finds the King engaged in some sin, however petty, and then kill him, ensuring that his soul will go to hell.

### Act 3, Scene 4

Polonius hides behind a curtain in the Queen's chamber. Hamlet arrives; he attempts to make his mother sit down, and she cries for help. Polonius cries out also, and Hamlet stabs him through the drapery, killing him. After expressing regret that his victim was not the King, Hamlet condemns his mother's behaviour. He compares the virtues of his father to the vices of his uncle; the distraught Queen's cries for mercy only enrage him more. The Ghost appears. The Queen, unaware of its presence, thinks Hamlet is mad as he speaks with the spirit. The Ghost reminds Hamlet of the vengeance he must exact, urges pity on the Queen, and departs. Less violently than before, Hamlet urges his mother to confess her sins and refuse to have sex with the King. He leaves, dragging the body of Polonius with him.

### Act 4, Scene 1

The Queen tells the King that Hamlet has killed Polonius. The King sends Rosencrantz and Guildenstern to recover the body.

### Act 4, Scene 2

Rosencrantz and Guildenstern confront Hamlet. He mocks them, refusing to tell them where the body is, but he goes with them to the King.

### Act 4, Scene 3

The King tells his LORDS (5) that Hamlet is dangerous, yet, because of the prince's popularity, his exile to England must seem routine. Rosencrantz and Guildenstern return with Hamlet under guard. Hamlet expounds humorously on corpses before revealing where he has put Polonius' body. The King tells Hamlet that he is being sent to England immediately for his own safety. The King's entourage escorts Hamlet to the boat, leaving the King alone to muse on his plot: he is sending letters to the English that threaten war unless they kill Hamlet immediately.

### Act 4, Scene 4

Hamlet, accompanied by Rosencrantz and Guildenstern, encounters a CAPTAIN (6) from Fortinbras' army, on its way to Poland. The Captain speaks of Fortinbras' war as a fight over a small, insignificant piece of territory. Hamlet compares himself, unable to avenge his father's death, with the 20,000 men who will fight and die for an inconsequential goal. He vows that in the future, he will value only bloody thoughts.

### Act 4, Scene 5

A GENTLEMAN (3) tells the Queen that Ophelia is insane, rambling wildly in senseless speeches that yet seem to convey some unhappy truth. Ophelia enters, singing a song about a dead lover. The King arrives, and Ophelia sings of seduction and betrayal. She leaves, speaking distractedly about a burial. A MESSENGER (16) appears with the news that Laertes has raised a rebellion and is approaching the castle. Laertes and several FOLLOWERS break down the door and enter. He demands vengeance for his father's death, and the King promises that he shall have it. Ophelia returns, singing about a funeral, and distributes flowers to the King, the Queen, and Laertes. She sings again, about an old man's death, and departs. The King takes Laertes away to plot revenge on Hamlet.

### Act 4, Scene 6

A SAILOR (1) brings Horatio a letter from Hamlet. It tells of his capture by pirates who have agreed to release him; Rosencrantz and Guildenstern continue to sail to England. Horatio goes with the sailor to meet Hamlet.

### Act 4, Scene 7

The King tells Laertes that he cannot act directly against Hamlet, out of consideration for the Queen and because of the prince's popularity. The King proposes a plot: they shall arrange a fencing match between Hamlet and Laertes, in which Hamlet will use a blunted sword intended for sport while Laertes shall secretly have a sharp sword. Laertes agrees and adds that he has a powerful poison that he will apply to his sword point. The King further suggests a poisoned glass of wine to be given Hamlet when the sport has made him thirsty. The Queen appears with the news that Ophelia has drowned, and Laertes collapses in tears.

*Act 5, Scene 1*
A GRAVE-DIGGER who is a CLOWN (1) speaks with his friend, the OTHER clown, about Ophelia, who has been granted Christian burial although possibly a suicide. He comically misconstrues the law on suicide and jokes about grave-digging. Hamlet and Horatio arrive, and Hamlet meditates on death's levelling of the wealthy and ambitious. He talks with the Grave-digger, who displays a skull that had belonged to YORICK, a court jester whom Hamlet had known. The prince reflects on the inevitability of death. Ophelia's funeral procession arrives, accompanied by Laertes and the King and Queen; the PRIEST (3) declares her death a suicide. When Hamlet realises whose funeral he is witnessing, he rushes forth and tries to fight Laertes, challenging his position as chief mourner. Restrained, he departs in a rage. The King assures Laertes that he will get his revenge.

*Act 5, Scene 2*
Hamlet tells Horatio how he rewrote the King's letter arrangeing his death, substituting Rosencrantz and Guildenstern's names for his own. He assumes that the two courtiers were killed, but he feels no remorse, since they were schemers. OSRIC, an obsequious and mannered courtier, arrives with the King's request that Hamlet fence with Laertes; the King has wagered that Hamlet can win. Hamlet mocks Osric before sending word that he will fight. He tells Horatio that the proposed match makes him uneasy but says that he is prepared to die. The King and Queen, a group of courtiers, and Laertes arrive for the match. The King pours wine to toast Hamlet's first successful round, and he places a pearl—a congratulatory token, he says—in Hamlet's cup. Hamlet and Laertes fence, but after his first victory Hamlet postpones refreshment and resumes the match. The Queen drinks from his cup, although the King tries to stop her. Laertes wounds Hamlet with the poisoned sword, the two fighters scuffle and accidentally exchange swords, and Hamlet wounds Laertes. The Queen falls, exclaims that she is poisoned, and dies. Laertes, himself poisoned by the exchanged sword, reveals the King's plot. Hamlet wounds the King with the sword and then forces him to drink the poisoned wine. Hamlet

and Laertes forgive each other, and Laertes dies. Horatio starts to drink the poisoned wine, but Hamlet demands that he remain alive to tell his side of the story. Osric announces the return of Fortinbras from Poland; Hamlet declares Fortinbras his successor and dies. Fortinbras arrives and takes command, ordering a stately funeral for Hamlet.

COMMENTARY

*Hamlet* is the most notoriously problematic of Shakespeare's plays, and questions about it still bedevil commentators after almost 400 years. Tremendous amounts of energy have gone into considering its possible interpretations, and the range of opinions on them is immense; as Oscar Wilde wittily put it, perhaps the greatest question raised by *Hamlet* is, 'Are the critics mad or only pretending to be so?'

*Hamlet* was classed with the PROBLEM PLAYS when that term was first applied to Shakespeare's works of the early 17th century (see BOAS). Like those dark comedies, this TRAGEDY deals with death and sex and with the psychological and social tensions arising from these basic facts of life. And like the problem plays, *Hamlet* treats these issues without providing clear-cut resolutions, thereby leaving us with complicated, highly emotional responses that cause both satisfac-

*Illustration of the grave-diggers scene in* Hamlet. *'Alas, poor Yorick. I knew him, Horatio' (5.1.178). Hamlet confronts the fact of human mortality.* (Courtesy of Culver Pictures, Inc.)

tion—at seeing basic elements of our own lives treated dramatically—and pain—at the nagging persistence of these difficulties, as in real life.

It is precisely through such ambiguity, however, that *Hamlet* offers a robust and vital assertion of human worth, for the play is essentially a moral drama whose theme is the existence of both good and evil in human nature, a central concern in Shakespeare's work as a whole. Although it anticipates modern psychological dramas in some respects, *Hamlet* is not itself such a work; the extraordinary presentation of Prince Hamlet's troubled mind is simply the vehicle—albeit a vivid one—for the development of his acceptance of humanity's flawed nature. Shakespeare's great accomplishment in *Hamlet* was to express the philosophy that underlies this realisation.

Some of the play's many puzzles are interesting but superficial, such as Horatio's status at the Danish court, the identification of Hamlet's inserted lines in *The Murder of Gonzago*, or the determination of the prince's age. These matters chiefly reflect the playwright's lack of concern for minor inconsistencies, a trait seen throughout the plays. Others are deeper matters of plotting and psychology: Is Hamlet's emotional disturbance real or feigned? What is the nature of his relationship to Ophelia? Is King Claudius an unalloyed villain? The 'problem of problems', as it has been called, is Hamlet's unnecessary delay in executing the revenge he plainly accepts as his duty.

The basic story—a young man grieves for his father while faced with the duty to avenge his death—came from Shakespeare's source, the UR-HAMLET, and its genre, the REVENGE PLAY, but Shakespeare's attitude towards vengeance is not the traditionally approving one. Hamlet's regret when he says, 'The time is out of joint. O cursed spite, / That ever I was born to set it right' (1.5.196–197), testifies to this, as does the existence of a parallel revenge plot, that of Laertes' revenge of *his* father's murder by Hamlet. The hero of one plot, Hamlet is in effect the villain of the other, casting an inescapable doubt upon his heroic role. Hamlet recognises the ambivalence of his position when he says of Polonius' death, '. . . heaven hath pleas'd it so, / To punish me with this and this with me' (3.4.175–176).

This paradox suggests the essential duality of human nature, which is both noble and wicked, and numerous comparisons throughout the drama stress this point. Several times Hamlet contrasts his murdered father and his uncle—the former an ideal ruler, just and magnanimous; the latter an unscrupulous killer and lustful adulterer. Similarly, Hamlet juxtaposes his father's virtues with his mother's sin in accepting her husband's murderer and having sex with him. Other polarities abound: the chaste Ophelia versus the incestuous Queen; the faithful Horatio ver-

sus the treacherous Rosencrantz and Guildenstern; the devious duellist Laertes versus the manly soldier Fortinbras. Each of these contrasts recalls and reinforces the play's basic opposition between good and evil.

Faced with the awareness of evil, Hamlet longs for death and is disgusted with life, especially as it is manifested in sex, which he not only sees as the drive behind his mother's sin but which he abhors as the force that inexorably produces more life and thus more evil. 'Why wouldst thou be a breeder of sinners?' (3.1.121–122), he cries to Ophelia, and his rejection of her stems from his rejection of sex. Shakespeare did not intend their relationship as a love story; instead, it is an allegory of the condemnation of life, a point of view whose ultimate rejection is central to the play.

Hamlet's notorious procrastination of his revenge has a similar function. Though he accepts the Ghost's orders, he senses the evil in this duty, sent from 'heaven and hell' (2.2.580), and he resists its fulfilment. Though psychologically true to life, Hamlet's delay serves primarily to offer opportunities to stress the duality of human nature: as revenger, Hamlet is both opposed to and involved in evil. His repeated insistence on postponing his highly ambiguous duty emphasises his ambivalence and stimulates our own. Emotionally, Hamlet's procrastination produces in him a growing rage that leads to his killing of Polonius in 3.4, an act that provokes the King and Laertes to set in motion the incidents that lead to the bloody climax and that hastens Hamlet's exile and his escape from the King's execution plot. This event, in turn, jars Hamlet from his absorption in his personal tragedy and prepares him to find the 'divinity that shapes our ends' (5.2.10).

Both Hamlet and the play undergo a sweeping change before the climax, and this change is well prepared for by the establishment of a dominant tone in the play's language that is later varied to quite dramatic effect. Through Acts 1–4, the pervasiveness of evil and its capacity to corrupt human life are conveyed by an extended use of the imagery of illness, evoking a strong sense of stress and unease. In the play's opening moments, Francisco declares himself 'sick at heart' (1.1.9), and Horatio, speaking of evil omens, refers to the moon being 'sick almost to doomsday with eclipse' (1.1.123). Hamlet equates evil with bodily disorder when he speaks of a birthmark, 'nature's livery' (1.4.32), as the 'dram of evil' (1.4.36) that makes a virtuous man seem corrupt and ignoble. He is referring figuratively to the excessive drinking of Danish courtiers, rather than to the more serious evils soon to arise, but he strikes a note of disease, death, and physical corruption that recurs throughout the play.

For instance, Hamlet speaks of the King's prayer as

'physic [that] prolongs thy sickly days' (3.3.96) and of resolution as 'sicklied o'er' (3.1.85); the King refers to those who tell Laertes of his father's death as '. . . buzzers [who] infect his ear / With pestilent speeches . . .' (4.5.90–91). Strikingly, diseases of the skin, where an inner evil is presumed to be present, are often mentioned, as in Hamlet's reference to a 'flattering unction . . . [that] will but skin and film the ulcerous place, / Whiles rank corruption . . . / Infects unseen' (3.4.146–151), or in his image for the outbreak of a pointless war: an abscess 'that inward breaks, and shows no cause without / Why the man dies' (4.4.27–29).

Planning to exile Hamlet, the King observes, 'Diseases desperate grown / By desperate appliance are reliev'd' (4.3.9–10). He refers not only to the danger he faces from an avengeing Hamlet, but he is also thinking of Hamlet's apparent insanity. Hamlet's lunacy seems at times to be real, at least in some respects, such as his hysterical rejection of sex and love, but he himself asserts that it is false on several occasions—e.g., in 3.4.142–146. The question remains one of the play's many enigmas. In any case, Hamlet's insanity, whether feigned or real, is itself a major instance of the imagery of sickness, a constant reminder that 'something is rotten in the state of Denmark' (1.5.90).

A particularly vivid example of disease imagery is the Ghost's clinical description of the action of the poison that first thinned his blood and then produced on his skin 'a vile and loathsome crust' (1.5.72) before killing him. The poisoning is enacted twice in 3.2, first in the Players' dumb show and then by the Player playing Lucianus. Further, a similar fate awaits the four major characters in 5.2.

An extension of the play's imagery of death is the repeated suggestion of suicide, although it is rejected. Hamlet's first soliloquy regrets the religious 'canon 'gainst self-slaughter' (1.2.132). Horatio worries that the Ghost may tempt Hamlet to the 'toys of desperation' (1.4.75) on a cliff overlooking the sea. In 5.1 the Grave-digger discusses the law on suicides, and Ophelia's death is declared 'doubtful' (5.1.220) by the Priest. In his last moment, Hamlet prevents Horatio from killing himself with the poisoned cup. The prince also discusses the possibility of suicide at length in the soliloquy beginning 'To be or not to be . . .' (3.1.56–88) before rejecting the idea. More important, near the crucial mid-point of the play, just before his dramatic rejection of Ophelia and love, Hamlet raises the question of the desirability of life and answers, in effect, that we have no choice but to accept our destiny and live. Thus, while suicide serves as part of the play's imagery of despair, its rejection foreshadows the ultimate acceptance of life and its evils.

Act 5 opens with Hamlet meditating on death in the graveyard, but now death, represented with ghoulish humour by the skulls dug up by the Grave-digger, is not a potential escape, nor is it the fearful introduction to a possibly malign afterlife; it is merely the destined end for all humans. The conversation with the Grave-diggers offers comic relief as the climax draws closer, and Hamlet's recollections of Yorick offer a healthy appreciation of the pleasures of the past as well as a sardonic acceptance of death: 'Now get you to my lady's chamber and tell her, . . . to this favour she must come' (5.1.186–188). The prince is no longer in the grip of his grief. Ophelia's funeral and Hamlet's encounter with Laertes bring a final catharsis, and he is able to assert the love for Ophelia that he once denied and to accept his role in life by taking the royal title 'the Dane' (5.1.251).

In the first episode of 5.2, we hear of the cause of this change as Hamlet tells of the plot he has foiled by sending Rosencrantz and Guildenstern to their deaths in his place; in impulsively acting to save himself, he has learned, 'There's a divinity that shapes our ends, / Rough-hew them how we will . . .' (5.2.10–11). Hamlet finally comes to terms with his duty to exact vengeance, even though he cannot do so without committing the very crime he avenges, murder. In realising that he must be evil in order to counter evil, Hamlet also accepts his own death; although he senses his end approaching as the King's plot takes form, he remains composed, saying, 'There is special providence in the fall of a sparrow. If it be now, 'tis not to come; if it be not to come, it will be now; if it be not now, yet it will come. The readiness is all' (5.2.215–218).

The tragic paradox at the close of *Hamlet* is that the protagonist's psychological liberation comes only with his own death, a death that inspires Horatio's lovely farewell wish to Hamlet that 'flights of angels sing thee to thy rest' (5.2.365). The attitude towards death expressed in this elegiac prayer is unlike anything earlier in the play, and its emphatic placement after the climax clearly marks it as the drama's conclusive statement, a confirmation of the benevolence of fate despite the inevitability of evil and death.

## SOURCES OF THE PLAY

Shakespeare's basic source for *Hamlet* was the UR-HAMLET (c. 1588), a play on the same subject that is known to have been popular in London in the 1580s but for which no text survives. This work, believed to have been written by Thomas KYD, was apparently derived from a tale in François BELLEFOREST's collection *Histoires Traqiques* (1580). Although Shakespeare knew Belleforest's work, he adopted a central element of *Hamlet*, the Ghost, from the *Ur-Hamlet*, and this fact, along with the theatrical success of the lost work, suggests that it was Shakespeare's chief source.

Belleforest retold a story from a 12th-century Latin work, the *Historiae Danicae*, by SAXO GRAMMATICUS, first published in 1514. Saxo provides the earliest complete account of a legendary tale—9th-century fragments are known from the Icelandic sagas—of Amleth, a Danish nobleman who took revenge after his uncle killed his father and married his mother. The name Amleth, from Old Norse, means 'dim-witted' or 'brutish', in reference to his stratagem of feigning madness after his father's murder. Many other elements of *Hamlet*—including a dramatic encounter between Amleth and his mother, during which he kills a spy; his love affair with a beautiful woman; his exile to England and his escape by replacing the order for his execution with one condemning his escorts—are present in Saxo's account.

Shakespeare doubtless found much of this in the *Ur-Hamlet*, but this work, to judge by its probable companion piece, Kyd's *The Spanish Tragedy* (1588–1589), lacked *Hamlet*'s dramatic development and thematic unity; Shakespeare may have found hints of a unified point of view in Belleforest's version. In particular, the French writer develops the contrast between the good king who is murdered and his evil, incestuous killer, a comparison that is prominent in Hamlet's thoughts.

Many scholars believe that *The Spanish Tragedy,* also a revenge play, was itself a source for numerous elements in *Hamlet.* For instance, Kyd's play has a procrastinating protagonist who berates himself for talking instead of acting and who dies as he achieves his revenge; it also features a play within a play, a heroine whose love is opposed by her family, and another woman who becomes insane and commits suicide. However, some commentators feel that Kyd took at least some of these elements from the *Ur-Hamlet,* whether he wrote it or not, and that Shakespeare could have done so as well.

Other sources contributed to *Hamlet* in minor ways. A play that provokes a confession of guilt was a well-established literary motif, but Shakespeare's company had recently staged an anonymous drama, *A Warning for Fair Women* (1599), in which it is used, so this work was probably the immediate stimulus for Hamlet's 'Mousetrap' plot. The physician Timothy BRIGHT's *A Treatise of Melancholy* (1586) may have influenced Shakespeare's portrayal of Hamlet's depression. Thomas NASHE's widely popular pamphlet, *Pierce Penniless His Supplication to the Devil* (1592), influenced several passages of the play, especially Hamlet's diatribe on drunkenness in 1.4.16–38. Some of Hamlet's remarks on graves and death in 5.1 echo a popular religious work, *Of Prayer and Meditation,* by the Spanish mystic Luis de GRANADA, which Shakespeare probably read in the translation by Richard HOPKINS. *The Counsellor* (1598), an anonymous translation of a volume on good government by the famed Polish diplomat Laurentius GOSLICIUS is echoed in several passages, most notably Hamlet's speech beginning, 'What a piece of work is man' (2.2.303).

PLUTARCH's *Lives,* always one of Shakespeare's favourite sources, mentions a Greek tyrant, famed for many cold-blooded murders, who wept at a recital of HECUBA's woes, and this may have inspired the recitation by the First Player in 2.2. However, the playwright also knew the tale of Hecuba from VIRGIL's *Aeneid,* where it first appears, and from *The Tragedy of Dido* (1594), a play by Nashe and Christopher MARLOWE (1).

Shakespeare could also have read a retelling of Plutarch's Hecuba anecdote in the *Essays* of Michel de MONTAIGNE, either in French (publ. between 1580 and 1595) or in a manuscript of John FLORIO's translation, (publ. 1603). Echoes of Montaigne occur in several key passages—e.g., both Hamlet and the French essayist liken death to a sleep and to a 'consummation' (3.1.63).

Some scholars believe that an incident of 1577 at the court of Marguerite de Valois, a French princess married to the King of Navarre, influenced Shakespeare's conception of Ophelia's death. A young woman of the court was reported to have died of love for a young nobleman; he was absent from the court at the time and learned of her death only when he accidentally encountered the funeral procession upon his return. This event was widely reported in England at the time, due to the English support of the Protestant forces, led by Navarre, in the French Wars of Religion. The same event is thought to be referred to in *Love's Labour's Lost* (see KATHARINE [1]).

A real event also inspired the murder of Hamlet's father by pouring poison in his ear. In 1538 the Duke of Urbino, one of the leading military and political figures of day, died. His barber-surgeon confessed that he had killed the duke by putting a lotion in his ears, having been hired to do so by one Luigi Gonzaga. Shakespeare gave the name of the plotter to the victim (as *Gonzago* [3.2.233]), but the combination of his name and the unusual method of poisoning point to this actual crime as the stimulus to the playwright's fictional one, although the *Ur-Hamlet* may have used it first.

### TEXT OF THE PLAY

Hamlet was probably written in late 1599 or early 1600, though possibly a year later. It followed *Julius Caesar*—performed in September 1599—for it echoes *Caesar* in 1.1.116–118 and alludes to it in 3.2.102–105, and it probably preceded John MARSTON's play *Antonio's Revenge,* staged in late 1600, which recalls *Hamlet* in many places, indicating that Shakespeare's play had been performed by no later than the autumn of 1600.

However, one passage in *Hamlet*—2.2.336–358, describing the competition of the PLAYERS (2) with a troupe of child actors—clearly refers to THE WAR OF THE THEATRES, a rivalry among acting companies that dominated the London theatre in the spring of 1601. If *Hamlet* was written in 1600, then this passage must have been inserted later. Some scholars, however, hold that *Hamlet* was written in its entirety in early 1601 and that either *Antonio's Revenge* was Shakespeare's source rather than the other way around or both Marston and Shakespeare took their common materials from the *Ur-Hamlet*.

*Hamlet* was first published in 1603 by Nicholas LING and John TRUNDELL in a QUARTO edition (known as Q1) printed by Valentine SIMMES. Q1 is a BAD QUARTO, a mangled version of the text, assembled from the memories of actors who had performed in the play. It was supplanted by Q2 (1604, with some copies dated 1605), printed by John ROBERTS and published by him and Ling. A sound text, Q2 is believed to have been printed from Shakespeare's own manuscript, or FOUL PAPERS, with occasional reference to Q1 where the manuscript was unclear. However, two substantial passages appear to have been deliberately cut from Q2: Hamlet's reflections on Denmark as a prison (2.2.239–269), perhaps thought offensive to the Danish wife of England's new king, JAMES I; and the passage on child actors mentioned above, which may have been cut because James patronised a CHILDREN'S COMPANY or perhaps simply because it was out of date by 1604. In 1607 Ling sold his rights to the play to John SMETHWICK, who published three further quartos, Q3 (1611), Q4 (1622), and Q5 (1637), each of which was printed from its predecessor.

*Hamlet* was published in the FIRST FOLIO edition of Shakespeare's plays (1623). This text, known as F, derives from Q2 but differs from it significantly. It corrects many small errors and improves on Q2's stage directions, but it also contains its own, more numerous, omissions and errors. F 'modernises' words the editors or printers thought old-fashioned, and some bits of dialogue apparently derive from actors' ad libs, such as a cry of 'Oh Vengeance!' in the middle of Hamlet's soliloquy at the end of 2.2. More important, F provides the significant passages cut from Q2. It is thought that the printers of F followed both Q2—probably a copy that had been annotated for production use—and a FAIR COPY, a transcription of Shakespeare's manuscript, with errors and alterations made by a scribe but including the missing material.

Modern editions rely on Q2 because it is plainly closest to Shakespeare's own manuscript, but they turn to F for its restored cuts and for frequent minor improvements. Rarely, Q1 provides a correction of an obvious error in the other two texts or a clarification in stage directions.

## THEATRICAL HISTORY OF THE PLAY

From the outset, Hamlet has been recognised as one of the greatest works of the English stage, and it has remained the most widely produced of Shakespeare's plays (though most productions—probably including the original one—have used an abridged text). Most leading actors—and some actresses—of every generation have played the title part. The play has also been frequently performed in other languages.

The first production was that of the CHAMBERLAIN'S MEN in 1600 or 1601, referred to in the registration of the play with the STATIONERS' COMPANY in 1602. Contemporary references, along with many echoes of the play in the work of other playwrights, testify to its early popularity. Richard BURBAGE (3) was the first Hamlet; after his death in 1619 the role was taken, to great acclaim, by Joseph TAYLOR. A tradition first recorded by Nicholas ROWE in 1709 reports that Shakespeare played the Ghost in the original production.

'The Grave-Makers', an adaptation of 5.1 of *Hamlet*, was performed as a DROLL during the period of revolutionary government in England (1642–1660), when the theatres were legally closed. After the restoration of the monarchy, *Hamlet* was revived by William DAVENANT, though with a much abridged text, in a 1661 production starring Thomas BETTERTON, who was celebrated in the role for the rest of the century.

David GARRICK played Hamlet many times between 1734 and his retirement in 1776. Susannah Maria CIBBER (2), who often played opposite him, was regarded as the best Ophelia of the day. Garrick's production of 1772 was one of the most severely altered, and is still notorious for its elimination of much of Act 5. Beginning in 1783, John Philip KEMBLE (3), regarded as one of the greatest Hamlets, played the part often, sometimes opposite his sister, Sarah SIDDONS, as Ophelia.

Siddons herself was the first of many women to play Hamlet, taking the role in 1775. Female Hamlets were most popular in the late 18th and 19th centuries; among the best known were Kitty CLIVE, Charlotte CUSHMAN, Julia GLOVER, and Sarah BERNHARDT. In the 20th century Judith ANDERSON (1) (at the age of 73) and Eva Le Gallienne, among others, have also played the prince.

Most of the major theatrical entrepreneurs of the 19th century produced *Hamlet* at least once. Among the most acclaimed Hamlets of the period were Ira ALDRIDGE, William Charles MACREADY, Edwin BOOTH (1), and Henry Irving (usually opposite Ellen TERRY [1] as Ophelia). Irving had his first great Shakespearean success with the play in 1874, later staging an extravagantly scenic and very popular version (1879). William POEL used the Q1 text in 1881.

F. R. BENSON (1) staged Shakespeare's complete text in 1900, confirming that the resulting four- to five-hour performance was feasible. Other noteworthy 20th-century *Hamlet*s have included the controversial 1925 Barry JACKSON (1) production, which introduced modern dress to the Shakespearean stage; a New York staging by Margaret WEBSTER (3), starring Maurice EVANS (4) (1939); and Joseph PAPP's productions of 1972 and 1987, starring Stacy Keach and Kevin Kline respectively. Several 20th-century actors are especially well known for their portrayals of Hamlet, including John BARRYMORE, John GIELGUD, Laurence OLIVIER, and Evans.

*Hamlet* has been acted on FILM at least 25 times—far more than any other Shakespeare play—since 1900, when Sarah Bernhardt played the prince in a silent movie. Among the best-known films are Olivier's heavily abridged version of 1948, with music by William WALTON; the Russian Grigori KOZINTSEV's epic presentation of a prose translation by Boris Pasternak (1964); and the 1969 film by Tony Richardson (b. 1928), with Nicol WILLIAMSON. *Hamlet* has also been presented on TELEVISION five times.

**Hamlett, Katherine (d. 1579)** Englishwoman whose death may be reflected in that of OPHELIA in *Hamlet*. A resident of Tippington, a village near STRATFORD, Mistress Hamlett was drowned in the Avon River while fetching water, and a coroner's jury hesitated over the possibility of suicide before declaring, two months later, that she had died a natural death. It has been speculated that the coincidental similarity between a family name he once knew and the name of his protagonist might have recalled Katherine Hamlett's death to the playwright—who was 15 when it occurred—as he described Ophelia's death by drowning, declared 'doubtful' (5.1.220) by the PRIEST (3), although the coroner 'finds it Christian burial' (5.1.4–5).

**Hands, Terry (b. 1941)** British theatrical director. Hands has been associated with the ROYAL SHAKESPEARE COMPANY in STRATFORD since 1966, serving as associate director, joint artistic director from 1978, and artistic director and chief executive since 1986. He has directed many of Shakespeare's plays, at Stratford, in the United States, and on the Continent.

**Hanmer, Thomas (1677–1746)** Early editor of Shakespeare's plays. Hanmer, a former Speaker of the House of Commons, was the fourth editor of the collected plays. His edition was published in 1744 in an elaborately bound and expensive set of six volumes. It was illustrated by Hubert GRAVELOT and Francis HAYMAN and was intended for a wealthy market. Hanmer was a disrespectful editor who inserted alterations of his own, insisted that passages he did not approve of could not have been by Shakespeare, and failed to annotate adoptions of the readings of earlier editors. In addition, he did not go back to the early texts but simply worked from the collection published by Alexander POPE (1) in 1725.

**Harcourt** Minor character in *2 Henry IV*, a messenger. In 4.4 Harcourt brings King HENRY IV news that Lord BARDOLPH (2) and the Earl of NORTHUMBERLAND (1) have been defeated, thus ending the rebellion that began in *1 Henry IV*.

**Harfleur** City on the northern coast of FRANCE (1), location in *Henry V*. Harfleur is besieged by the army of HENRY V. In 3.3 the king describes the bloody terror Harfleur can expect if it continues to resist, and the GOVERNOR (1) surrenders the city. This episode is a good instance of the play's ambiguity. Henry may be seen as merciful and statesmanlike; he spares the town, and he explicitly orders EXETER (2), 'Use mercy to them all' (3.3.54). On the other hand, his brilliant evocation of a sacked city, with vivid descriptions of rape and murder, stresses the horrors of an army gone amok, an emphasis that reinforces a reading of *Henry V* as a mordant anti-war work.

**Harington, Sir John (1561–1612)** First English translator of ARIOSTO's *Orlando Furioso*, a source for *Much Ado About Nothing*. Harington, a godson of Queen ELIZABETH (1), spent much of his life at court. It is thought that his translation of *Orlando Furioso* (1591) was made at the Queen's command, as an ironic punishment for having independently translated one of its indecent passages.

**Harpy** Supernatural creature in whose guise ARIEL appears in 3.3 in *The Tempest*. PROSPERO's sprite accuses the 'three men of sin'—ALONSO, ANTONIO (5), and SEBASTIAN (3)—and his disguise makes him more terrifying. The Harpies, three mythological monsters, sisters, were woman-headed birds. They stole things from mortals—especially food (appropriate to the banquet setting of Ariel's appearance)—and defecated vilely as they left. Apparently wind-gods in origin, these semi-divine beings may have derived in part from rumours reaching Greece of an actual creature in India, a large, fruit-eating bat noted for its excrement.

**Harris (1), Frank (James Thomas) (1856–1931)** British author and editor. Best known today for his sexually explicit autobiography, *My Life and Loves* (1927), Harris also wrote short stories, two plays, a novel, essays, biographies, and other works. Among these were *The Man Shakespeare and His Tragic Life Story* (1909), a biography laced with elaborate interpretations of the SONNETS and various plays as detailed evidence of Shakespeare's life, especially his love life. For example, Harris advocated the theory, first suggested by Thomas TYLER (2), that Mary FITTON was the 'Dark Lady' of the SONNETS, and he furthered this notion in his play *Shakespeare and His Love* (1910) and in another book, *The Women of Shakespeare* (1911). He saw Shakespeare's works as delivering a message to humanity, extolling forgiveness and love, and he equated it with Christ's. Being immensely egotistical, he identified himself with these two personages—and GOETHE—as 'God's spies' (*King Lear*, 5.3.17).

Harris was an adventurer before he became a literary figure; he ran away from his home in Scotland at 14 and worked at various jobs, including cowboy, in America and Europe, before settling in London and establishing himself as a writer of fiction. He became the editor of two of Britain's most important magazines, the *Fortnightly Review* (1886–1894) and the *Saturday Review* (1894–1898), in which he published H. G. Wells, Oscar Wilde, and George Bernard SHAW (2), among others. He later wrote biographies of Wilde and Shaw. He cultivated a scandalous reputation, aided by his persistent campaign against Victorian prudery and his pro-German sentiments during World War I. He made many enemies, and by 1920 he was neglected and impoverished. While his reputation as a writer has improved since his death and his importance in literary history is acknowledged, his scholarship—including his work on Shakespeare—is generally derided; even his autobiography has been found to be grossly inaccurate and self-serving.

**Harris (2), Henry (c. 1630–1681)**   English actor. A leading man in William DAVENANT's theatre company, Harris acted many Shakespearean parts, including Cardinal WOLSEY in *Henry VIII,* for which he was particularly noted. He also played HORATIO opposite the HAMLET of the great Thomas BETTERTON, in the first staging of *Hamlet* (1661) after the reopening of the English theatres following the Puritan revolution. In 1662 he became the first ROMEO to play opposite a female JULIET (1) (Mary SAUNDERSON), as actresses were admitted to English stages. He was felt by some contemporaries, including Samuel PEPYS, to be as fine an actor as Betterton. He joined Betterton in 1671 in the management of London's Dorset Garden Theatre, serving as the artistic director.

**Harrison (1), George Bagshawe (b. 1894)**   English scholar, author of many works on Shakespeare. An authority on the Elizabethan background of Shakespeare's life, Harrison was also the general editor of the Penguin editions of Shakespeare's works, published between 1937 and 1959. His *England in Shakespeare's Day* (1928) and *Shakespeare at Work* (1933) are general studies, and he compiled a wealth of primary material from the period 1590 to 1610 in his *Elizabethan* and *Jacobean Journals* (1928, 1933, 1941), which remain essential references for the Shakespeare scholar.

**Harrison (2), John (d. 1617)**   Highly successful London publisher and bookseller, a founding member of the STATIONERS' COMPANY. In 1594 Harrison purchased the rights to Shakespeare's narrative poems *Venus and Adonis* and *The Rape of Lucrece* from Richard FIELD (2), who had already produced the first edition of the former. Between 1594 and 1596 Harrison pub-

lished the second, third, and fourth editions (known as Q2–4, though only the first of them was a QUARTO; the others were published in an octavo format), employing Field as the printer. In 1596 he sold the rights to the poem to William LEAKE. Harrison published the first edition of *Lucrece,* printed by Field, in 1594 and the second, printed by Peter SHORT, in 1598. He passed on the rights to this work to his younger half-brother, also named John Harrison, who published Q3 and Q4 (both 1600), printed by Short, and Q5 (1607), printed by Nicholas OKES. The younger Harrison sold the rights to *Lucrece* to Roger JACKSON (3) in 1614.

**Harrison (3), William (1534–1593)**   English historian, collaborator with Raphael HOLINSHED on Holinshed's *Chronicles of England, Scotland, and Ireland* (1577), which in its second edition (1587) was an important source for Shakespeare. Harrison, a clergyman who was personal chaplain to Lord COBHAM, served as Holinshed's assistant editor and contributed greatly to the *Chronicles.* He translated Hector BOECE's Latin history of SCOTLAND and wrote descriptions of the geography of England and Scotland. After his work with Holinshed, Harrison wrote extensively on his theory that Britain had once been inhabited by giants. He left a massive history of the world unfinished at his death.

**Harsnett, Samuel (1561–1631)**   English clergyman and writer, author of a source for *King Lear.* An ambitious clerical politician, Harsnett wrote *A Declaration of Egregious Popish Impostures* (1603), a diatribe against Catholic priests who had claimed to exorcise demons from several lunatics in a famous case of 18 years earlier. Shakespeare took many details of the pretended insanity of EDGAR from this work, who, in his disguise as a wandering lunatic, claims to be pursued by demons. Early in his career Harsnett was denounced as a Catholic, but he recovered and rose to be a leading figure at Cambridge University as well as bishop of several different sees. He was famous for his harsh manner and was forced to resign from his position at Cambridge when his fellow scholars launched a formal campaign against him. However, in 1628 he was named Archbishop of YORK (2), the second-highest position in the Anglican Church.

**Hart (1), Charles (d. 1693)**   Leading actor of the Restoration period, presumed illegitimate son of William HART (3), who was the son of Shakespeare's sister Joan SHAKESPEARE (8) Hart. Shakespeare's grandnephew, Charles Hart was apprenticed to Richard ROBINSON (4) of the KING'S MEN and performed at the BLACKFRIARS THEATRE as a child, playing women's roles. During the Civil Wars, he achieved distinction in combat as an officer in the Royalist forces, and after the war he was a member of Thomas KILLIGREW's King's Company. He was particularly distinguished as OTHELLO and BRUTUS (4).

**Hart (2), Joan Shakespeare** Shakespeare's sister. See SHAKESPEARE (8).

**Hart (3), William (1600–1639)** An actor, Shakespeare's nephew, son of Joan SHAKESPEARE (8) Hart. William Hart was a member of the KING's MEN in the mid-1630s and played FALSTAFF, among other roles. He apparently died unmarried, though Charles HART (1) is believed to have been his illegitimate son.

**Harvey (1)** Original name of PETO in *1* and *2 Henry IV*. When the name Peto was substituted for Harvey, shortly after the plays were written, in 1596–1597, one instance of the original designation inadvertently remained in the early texts of *1 Henry IV*, in 1.2.158, revealing that the change had occurred. Since the 18th century this reference has also been altered in most editions. The change of name was made at the same time that OLDCASTLE became FALSTAFF—at the insistence of Lord COBHAM, a descendant of the historical Oldcastle—presumably in the hope of avoiding a similar problem with another prominent aristocrat, Sir William HERVEY (also known as Harvey).

**Harvey (2), Gabriel (c. 1545–1630)** English writer, a major literary figure of Shakespeare's day and possibly a model for the pedantic HOLOFERNES of *Love's Labour's Lost*. Harvey was a lecturer at Cambridge University and an unpopular gadfly of the academic world. He published his generally critical opinions of the literature of the day and spent much energy futilely advocating the use of Latin prosody in English poetry. Extremely vain and critical of others, he made many enemies, and his disputatious nature hindered his aspirations to higher office in the educational establishment. In the 1590s Harvey quarrelled with both Robert GREENE (2) and Thomas NASHE in a battle of pamphlets that was much talked about in LONDON. This dispute may be the subject of the obscure topical jokes that fill *Love's Labour's Lost*, and some scholars propose that Harvey was satirised as Holofernes, though the point cannot be proven with the existing evidence. Harvey annotated the margins of his books densely, and his *Marginalia* (published 1913) record his opinions of what he read, along with much else, providing scholars with a detailed glimpse of the academic and literary world of the late 16th century. Among other things, Harvey observed that 'the younger sort takes much delight in Shakespeare's *Venus and Adonis*, but his *Lucrece*, and [*Hamlet*] have it in them to please the wiser sort'.

**Harvey (3), William** See HERVEY.

**Hastings (1), Pursuivant** Minor character in *Richard III*, a petty official. In 3.2 Lord HASTINGS (3), converses briefly with his like-named acquaintance, conveying the information that his enemies, the allies of Queen ELIZABETH (2), have been imprisoned. The Lord remarks that they had last met when he himself had been under arrest and in danger of execution; the audience is aware that, ironically, he is about to be imperiled again. This curious incident, although it depicts a historical event recorded in Shakespeare's sources, seems to have little point in the drama, unless it is intended to help to emphasise the intricate workings of fate, by virtue of the coincidences of names and circumstances. However, many editions of the play have followed the FIRST FOLIO version in ignoring this character's name, referring to him only by his title, Pursuivant, which signifies a minor subordinate of a herald.

**Hastings (2), Lord Ralph (d. 1405)** Historical figure and character in *2 Henry IV*, a rebel against King HENRY IV. An ally of the ARCHBISHOP (3) of York, Hastings makes several errors of judgement, first advocating that the rebels proceed against the King despite the desertion of NORTHUMBERLAND (1) and then, when they find themselves outnumbered at GAULTREE FOREST, recommending that they accept the peace offered by Prince John of LANCASTER (3). Lancaster's offer proves treacherous, and Hastings and the other rebels are arrested and sentenced to death. The historical Hastings was a minor nobleman of northern Yorkshire.

**Hastings (3), Lord William (c. 1430–1483)** Historical figure and character in *3 Henry VI* and *Richard III*, a Yorkist supporter who becomes a victim of political murder. In *3 Henry VI* Hastings is only a minor nobleman attached to EDWARD IV, but in *Richard III* he is more prominent. He exemplifies the pettiness of English public life during the WARS OF THE ROSES. He profits from Richard's rise, as his old enemies are imprisoned and sentenced to death, but he is unwilling to aid his leader's attempt to seize the crown; he is reluctant to oppose the legal heirs. Richard accordingly turns on him, but Hastings, ignoring warnings, has too little imagination to conceive that his situation has changed. In 3.4 Richard fabricates a tale of treason, accuses Hastings, and condemns him to death in one sentence, as his victim sits speechless. In 3.7 Richard justifies Hastings' immediate execution, citing the dangers of the supposed plot.

The historical Hastings played an obscure role in the events surrounding Richard's accession. Shakespeare followed his source in having Richard fabricate Hastings' treason, but it was probably real. In June 1483 he apparently joined in an attempt to unseat Richard from his position as Protector of Edward's young heir. The plot failed, and Richard arrested Hastings and had him executed without a trial, as in the play.

**Hathaway, Anne (Anne Hathaway Shakespeare) (c. 1556–1623)** Shakespeare's wife. Anne Hathaway was the daughter of a farmer in Shottery, a village a mile from STRATFORD. (The farmhouse in which she grew up was bought by the Shakespeare BIRTHPLACE Trust, which maintains it as a showplace.) She was eight years older than her husband, with whom she had three children: Susanna SHAKESPEARE (14), born in 1583, and twins, Hamnet and Judith SHAKESPEARE (5, 10), born in 1585. Susanna was born only six months after the wedding, and it is obvious that Anne's pregnancy prompted the marriage, which was arranged in haste (see WHITGIFT; SANDELLS; RICHARDSON [1]). A number of commentators have presumed that the playwright came to regret his marriage to Anne—at 21 he found himself 'saddled' (as some see it) with three children

and a wife nearing 30, and the plays contain a number of recommendations against both pre-marital sex and the taking of older wives by young men—but these are conventional remarks by fictional characters, and there exists no actual evidence of such discontent. While Shakespeare conducted his career in LONDON— as he had to—he maintained close contact with Stratford, and he eventually returned there and again lived with Anne. In his will he notoriously left Anne only the 'second best bed', though this probably had no emotional significance, for she was by ancient custom entitled to one-third of the estate, so he knew she was provided for. The special bequest of the bed was most likely made in response to some particular association with it, of which we cannot know.

**Hathway (Hathaway), Richard (active 1598–1603)** English playwright. In 1598 Hathway was named by Francis MERES as a leading writer of comedies. He wrote plays for the ADMIRAL'S MEN, usually in collabo-

*Anne Hathaway's picturesque thatched-roof house has been restored and is now a popular tourist attraction.* (Courtesy of British Tourist Authority)

ration with other playwrights such as Michael DRAYTON and Anthony MUNDAY. Payment to Hathway for 18 such works is recorded, but the only play that has survived is SIR JOHN OLDCASTLE, a work that was later attributed to Shakespeare. Hathway, whose name was often spelled 'Hathaway', is sometimes confused with Shakespeare's brother-in-law, also Richard, but the playwright was no relation to Anne HATHAWAY.

**Hayman, Francis (1708–1776)**   English painter, illustrator of the HANMER edition of Shakespeare's plays. Hayman was a one-time scene painter at the Drury Lane Theatre. He had become a well-known painter of portraits and 'conversation pieces'—informal group portraits—when he was commissioned, along with Hubert GRAVELOT, to illustrate Shakespeare's plays. These he executed in a light rococo style. Hayman provided 31 of the 36 images for the illustrations, but Gravelot engraved all of them.

Under the influence of his master, Gravelot, Hayman was one of the artists who translated the French rococo style into an English idiom. He was an important influence on the young Thomas Gainsborough (1727–1788) and, later, a founding member of the Royal Academy.

**Hazlitt, William (1778–1830)**   English essayist and literary critic. Hazlitt, a journalist who published essays on the leading English political figures of the first decade of the 19th century, turned to literary and dramatic criticism around 1815. He wrote *Characters of Shakespeare's Plays* (1817), in which he expressed his delight in Shakespeare's poetry, an aspect of the playwright's accomplishment that was largely ignored in earlier periods. His *Lectures on the English Poets* (1818) and *Lectures on the English Comic Writers* (1819) covered English literature from the 16th century to his contemporaries. Like his close friend Charles LAMB (1), Hazlitt was an early admirer of the Romantic poets. He later turned again to political subjects in *The Spirit of the Age* (1825), with its studies of the great public figures of his times, and a massive *Life of Napoleon* (1830). He contributed to the Romantic era's idea of Shakespeare as a consummate literary artist as well as simply a great dramatist, and he helped begin the systematic study of the history of English literature.

**Headsman**   Character in *The Comedy of Errors*. See EXECUTIONER.

**Hecate (Hecat, Heccat)**   Minor character in *Macbeth*, a supernatural being allied with the WITCHES. In 3.5 Hecate appears to the Witches and chides them because they did not include her in their entrapment of MACBETH. She goes on to plan for another encounter with him and promises to devise extremely powerful spells for the occasion. Then ghostly music begins,

and Hecate is called away by invisible singers. In 4.1 she appears briefly to the Witches as they prepare for their second meeting with Macbeth. She praises their witchcraft and leaves to the accompaniment of another spectral song.

Hecate's appearance in *Macbeth* was obviously added to the play after it was originally written (c. 1606) but before it was published (1623). This can be determined because the songs were written by Thomas MIDDLETON for a play, *The Witch*, probably written sometime between 1610 and 1620, and because 3.6 has been moved from its proper chronological position (it should follow 4.1), in order to separate the two Witch scenes, 3.5 and 4.1, which would otherwise be in direct sequence. Because Middleton was associated with the KING'S MEN, the theatrical company that performed *Macbeth* in the early 17th century, and because the Hecate episodes are clearly designed to introduce Middleton's songs, it has been traditionally presumed that he wrote them. However, the Hecate passages of *Macbeth* are quite different in style from Middleton's work, and most modern scholars believe that someone else wrote these lines, possibly—though it is a minority opinion—Shakespeare himself.

Hecate was a familiar figure in classical literature and was frequently invoked, for instance, in SENECA, whose plays were well known to Shakespeare. She was a fearsome goddess of the underworld, associated with witchcraft and other ghostly and uncanny things. The ancients commonly worshipped three-faced statues of her at lonely country crossroads, where she glared down a side lane and both directions of the main trail. She remained well known throughout the Middle Ages, especially in connection with black magic, and Shakespeare was clearly familiar with her. Whether or not he employed her as a character in *Macbeth*, he had his protagonist mention her twice, in 2.1.52 and 3.2.41 (in passages that were definitely written by Shakespeare). Further, she is also invoked in *Hamlet* (3.2.252), *A Midsummer Night's Dream* (5.1.370), and *King Lear* (1.1.109). Her name is a synonym for witch in *1 Henry VI* (3.2.64), though here the name has three syllables—pronounced *heckity* rather than *heckit*—and, partly for this reason, some scholars think this passage may have been written by someone else.

**Hector**   Legendary figure and character in *Troilus and Cressida*, the crown prince of TROY, son of King PRIAM and brother of TROILUS and PARIS. Hector, the leading Trojan warrior, holds to an ideal chivalric code centred on the notion of personal honour and the possibility of glory. Thus he is a principal element of the play's sardonic presentation of the false glamour of war.

Though he is to some extent a character type—the romantic warrior-hero—Hector is made more humanly interesting through his deviations from the chivalric norm. He recognises the defects of his position when, at the Trojan council of war, he advocates returning HELEN (1) to the Greeks and ending the fighting, and he points out the evil consequences of permitting 'the hot passion of distemper'd blood [to influence] a free determination / 'Twixt right and wrong' (2.2.170–172). However, he subordinates such wisdom to his enthusiasm for personal honour and glory and agrees with Troilus that they must carry on the conflict. Like his Greek counterpart as a spokesman for sanity, ULYSSES, Hector presents an image of right behaviour that he cannot live up to himself, reinforcing the play's bitter commentary.

Hector's humanly malleable ideals play a part in his death in 5.8, which results from an ironic combination of obsessive adherence to, and temporary abandonment of, his chivalric code. Citing 'the faith of valour' (5.3.69), he ignores dire omens and refuses the pleas of his father, his wife, ANDROMACHE, and his sister, CASSANDRA, that he not fight. On the battlefield he chivalrously permits ACHILLES to recover from exhaustion in 5.6. Then, in an uncharacteristic moment of greed and vanity, Hector kills a Greek soldier in order to loot the corpse of its fine armour. While doing so, he removes his own armour, and in this vulnerable moment he is killed by the MYRMIDONS. Nevertheless, Hector remains one of the most positive figures in the play, self-deluded and weak at a critical moment but essentially honourable.

Hector's name is probably a variation of an ancient Greek word for 'holder' or 'stayer', and this leads scholars to surmise that he is an invention of HOMER or earlier Greek poets, rather than a rendering of a historical person. He has no importance in classical myth and literature outside Homer's Iliad, though he was the subject of cult worship in several places, notably at later settlements around Troy. Hector remained famous throughout medieval and RENAISSANCE times. He was one of the panoply of traditional heroes known as the Nine WORTHIES, and as such he is depicted in the comical pageant in Love's Labour's Lost (5.2.541–717).

**Hecuba** Legendary Trojan queen whose famed grief is described dramatically in Hamlet. In 2.2 the FIRST PLAYER (2), at HAMLET's insistence, delivers a monologue telling of Hecuba's response to the killing of her husband, King PRIAM, by PYRRHUS; her grief is said to have produced tears in '. . . the burning eyes of heaven / and passion in the gods' (2.2.513–514). Her distress is implicitly compared with the short-lived widowhood of Hamlet's mother, the QUEEN (9), before she married her husband's murderer, KING (5) Claudius. Thus the passage reminds Hamlet and the audience of the central focus of his life and of the play—his need to avenge his murdered father.

Hecuba was well known in Shakespeare's day as one of the great heroines of classical mythology; she appears in HOMER's Iliad, where she elaborately mourns the death of her son HECTOR (an episode alluded to in 5.10.15–21 of Troilus and Cressida), in several Greek tragedies, and in VIRGIL's Aeneid. PLUTARCH's Lives—a favourite Shakespearean source—reports that a Greek tyrant, famed for many cold-blooded murders, once wept at a recital of Hecuba's woes; this may have inspired Hamlet's request for the monologue.

The most famous classical model of the sorrowing woman, Hecuba is often referred to in Shakespeare's plays, most frequently in Troilus and Cressida, where she is actually said to be present in 1.2.1—though she does not appear on stage—but also in Titus Andronicus (4.1.20–21), Coriolanus (1.3.40–43), and Cymbeline (4.2.313). Also, in a famous passage in The Rape of Lucrece (lines 1464–1491), the woeful LUCRECE vents her emotions by acting the part of the grieving Hecuba.

**Heicroft, Henry (c. 1549–1600)** Vicar of STRATFORD, baptiser of Susanna Shakespeare (14). Heicroft was the vicar of Stratford from 1569 to 1584, when he left for a better paying position. In 1583 he baptised Shakespeare's first child. Heicroft was a graduate of Cambridge University. He married two years after his arrival in Stratford, and had five children, three of whom died before he moved to his new post. Little more is known of his life.

**Helen (1)** Legendary figure and character in Troilus and Cressida, the mistress of Prince PARIS (3) of TROY. Years before the play opens, Paris stole Helen from King MENELAUS of Sparta, thereby sparking the TROJAN WAR. Helen appears only in 3.1, where she is portrayed as a simpering lady of fashion whose vapid coquetry induces PANDARUS to sing a love song while she entirely misses her guest's transmission of a message to Paris. That the object of the conflict should be this inane society hostess illustrates the play's lessons on the false glamour of both sex and war, and these lessons are confirmed by the warriors' own opinions of Helen. She is repeatedly declared an inadequate cause of war by HECTOR, PRIAM, DIOMEDES (with particularly scathing remarks in 4.1.56–67), and even by TROILUS in 1.1.90–94, although elsewhere Troilus, arguing for the continuance of the war, calls Helen 'a pearl / Whose price hath launched a thousand ships' (2.2.82–83). (Shakespeare's alteration of this famous line by MARLOWE (1)—even better known then than it is now—is significant; Helen's price, rather than her face, as in Dr Faustus, launches the ships.)

In classical mythology, Helen is one of the offspring resulting from the rape of Leda by Zeus, who was disguised as a swan. She was accordingly born from an egg, whose shell was reputedly preserved as a relic in Sparta into historical times. This cult, and the fact that her name is not Greek, may reflect Helen's status as a 'faded' deity, a goddess in an earlier, now lost religion who survived as a mortal in Greek mythology. Helen's abduction sparks the Trojan War in the *Iliad* of HOMER, as in the play, but in Homer she becomes Paris' wife, rather than his mistress, and she is deeply disturbed by her bigamous status. A later tradition held that Paris, deceived by a friendly goddess, carried off a mere phantom of Helen to Troy. Helen thus preserved her honour, spending the war years in Egypt. After the war, she is reunited with Menelaus in all accounts.

**Helen (2)**   Character in *All's Well that Ends Well.* See HELENA (2).

**Helena (1)**   Character in *A Midsummer Night's Dream,* the lover of DEMETRIUS (2). Helena is obsessed with Demetrius, who has betrayed her, and while she realises she is shaming herself, she cannot stop pursuing him, even to the extent of betraying her friend HERMIA. That she has lost her self-respect is evident in her first words, 'Call you me fair? That fair again unsay!' (1.1. 181). When, through OBERON's magic, both men woo her, she can only construe their praise as ridicule. Her frustration leads her to insult Hermia viciously in the four-way quarrel in 3.2. Her flawed personality has nothing to do with her finally winning Demetrius, as she knows; she treats the outcome as a miracle, saying, 'I have found Demetrius like a jewel, / Mine own, and not mine own' (4.1.190–191).

**Helena (2)**   Character in *All's Well That Ends Well,* the lover of BERTRAM. Helena's pursuit of Bertram constitutes the main plot of *All's Well,* and his lack of interest, combined with her use of the vulgar 'bed trick'—substituting herself for another woman in bed and thus inducing him to father her child—help to give the work the dark and troubling quality that places it among the so-called PROBLEM PLAYS. The central figure in the play, Helena is subject to quite contradictory interpretations, depending largely on one's view of the play as a whole.

Some commentators have found Helena wholly good. Samuel Taylor COLERIDGE called her Shakespeare's 'loveliest character', and her persistent efforts to win Bertram despite his feelings have been seen as an allegorical representation of Christian grace, chiefly on the strength of a remark by the COUNTESS (2), Bertram's mother, that her son 'cannot thrive, / Unless her prayers, whom heaven delights to hear / And loves to grant, reprieve him from the wrath / Of greatest justice' (3.4.26–29). However, other critics have seen in Helena a satirical portrait of an ambitious, possessive woman, intent on marrying a man who does not love her and unscrupulous in using her body to deceive him.

In 1.1 Helena is introduced as a young woman of great energy and determination. She is first seen dressed in mourning, with the elderly Countess and LAFEW. They discuss the late Count's death and then her own father's and the seemingly terminal illness of the KING (17). Helena is especially depressed because her secret love, Bertram, is leaving, and, as she puts it, 'there is no living, none, / If Bertram be away' (1.1.82–83), and she prepares to 'sanctify his relics' (1.1.96). Then PAROLLES, the play's comic villain, appears, and his cynical banter about virginity makes Helena realise that she must fear the influence of such worldly wisdom on Bertram: 'The court's a learning-place', she reflects, 'and he is one—' (1.1.173); she suppresses the observation that Bertram is likely to be an apt pupil. More important, Parolles' vitality stimulates a similar energy in Helena. He leaves, and in the ensuing soliloquy, written in formal couplets intended to suggest her elevated mood, she firmly decides to pursue Bertram.

Thus the main plot opens with the establishment of Helena's initiative. But whether she is an admirably plucky young woman or an ambitious schemer remains a matter of interpretation. This unresolved question is often considered part of the play's larger failure to combine naturalistic elements with the scheme of reconciliation and love that COMEDY traditionally demands. To some extent, the contradictory points of view may be taken to represent different aspects of the same personality, and, as so often in Shakespeare, the resulting paradox offers us a rewarding sense of the complexity of human nature.

However, there are numerous clues that Shakespeare intended Helena as a virtuous and spunky heroine. Most significantly, the play's final resolution is accomplished only by a highly dramatic, carefully planned appearance by Helena late in the closing scene, in which she disentangles the plot's complications in a few lines, like a deus ex machina. A satirical figure used in this manner could only inspire sardonic reflections on the hypocrisy of happy endings, and nothing in the dialogue suggests any such intent on the playwright's part. Further, the fairy-tale motif of the maiden who cures the King is presented in the solemn music of rhymed couplets and mystical language that would be utterly inappropriate to a satirical purpose. Similarly, Helena has several other striking and lyrical speeches, such as her declaration of love in 1.3.186–212 and her dramatic renunciation in 3.2.99–129, whose evident sincerity tends to enforce a view of her as an admirable heroine.

In addition, Shakespeare altered the story that he took from his source, a tale by BOCCACCIO, and some of his changes were plainly designed to elevate the moral character of the heroine. For instance, he added such sympathetic characters as the elderly Countess and her friend Lord Lafew, whose chief purpose is to shape our opinions of the major characters. They convincingly inform us of Helena's virtues, as does the

King. Shakespeare also added another theme to the tale, in which Helena is clearly an heroine: the King, responding to Bertram's rejection of her as a commoner, defends her as an illustration of the value of an individual's spiritual nature regardless of his or her rank in society. In Boccaccio, the pursuer and pursued are aristocrats of equal status, and no social question is raised.

When Boccaccio's protagonist triumphs at the end, she presents her reluctant husband with twin sons. In *All's Well*, only the merest mention is made of Helena's pregnancy, in 5.3.307; Shakespeare plainly wished to de-emphasise the physical aspect of the bed trick because this ruse is clearly the most embarrassing episode of Helena's story. In another significant departure from his source, Shakespeare altered the circumstances of Helena's appearance in FLORENCE. In Boccaccio, she hears of her husband's attempt at seduction, devises the bed trick, and goes to Italy to perform it. In *All's Well*, she wanders to Florence as a pilgrim and must be informed by the WIDOW (2) of Bertram's presence. Thus the bed trick seems a product of fortunate happenstance, rather than a calculated ploy.

Shakespeare also used dramatic structure to mitigate the bed trick's bad impression and maintain Helena's heroic stature. After 3.2 Helena is much less frequently on-stage than before. She appears in only four brief scenes and has no important speeches before returning 30 lines from the end of the play. We remember her in the highly positive light in which she was presented in the first half of the play, and we are influenced by the Countess' observations on the efficacy of Helena's prayers, the similarly complimentary remarks of the two LORDS (6) in 4.3, and the loving regrets of the Countess' household when they believe her dead—even the cynical CLOWN (5) is moved to call her 'the sweet-marjoram of the sallet' (4.5.15). Shakespeare therefore establishes Helena as an heroine early in the play, and later, when her actions seem less heroic, he downplays her, permitting only brief and positive glimpses.

Thus Helena seems intended as a delightful romantic heroine. Lafew says she can 'quicken a rock, and make you dance canary / With sprightly fire and motion' (2.1.73–74)—and her infatuation with Bertram's 'arched brows, his hawking eye, his curls' (1.1.92) is no less endearing for her healthy interest in sex. In this light, she seems to be a lively, virtuous young woman to whom divine favour offers opportunity and then success. And in the second half of the play, the possibly manipulative exploiter of sex is more properly regarded as a contrite, self-sacrificing wife whom fortune has led to a happy resolution of her problems. At the play's conclusion she is received with the awe due a goddess, and her summation of the play's final statement of reconciliation suggests that she deserves this

treatment. Indeed, Helena's role is an exalted one: in the course of capturing and keeping a husband, she has saved the King's life, preserved Bertram from a life of idle sin, and brought new life, in the form of their child, into the world. The absorption in death with which the play opened has been dispelled.

**Helenus**    Legendary figure and minor character in *Troilus and Cressida*, a son of King PRIAM. In 2.2.33–36 Helenus challenges TROILUS' insistence on Trojan honour as a justification for retaining the kidnapped HELEN (1) and continuing the TROJAN WAR, but Troilus dismisses him with the remark, 'You are for dreams and slumbers, brother priest' (2.2.37), and an accusation of cowardice, and Helenus is not mentioned again. Shakespeare took this incident—which appears in two of his sources, William CAXTON's *The Recuyell of the Historyes of Troye* and John LYDGATE's *Troy Book*—to help establish Troilus' hot-blooded chivalrousness. Helenus himself is of no consequence and has no personality.

**Helicanus**    Minor character in *Pericles*, adviser to and surrogate ruler for Prince PERICLES of TYRE. In 1.2 Helicanus stands out among a group of flattering courtiers (see LORD [11]) when he makes a speech that stresses the value of honest criticism to a ruler. Impressed, Pericles leaves Helicanus in charge of Tyre when he must flee from the powerful King ANTIOCHUS of Syria. In 2.4 the Tyrian nobles desire a ruler who is in residence, and suggest that Helicanus declare himself Pericles' successor, but the faithful adviser summons Pericles home instead. In Act 5 Helicanus serves Pericles again. He acts as Pericles' spokesman when the grief-stricken prince—he has been separated from his wife and daughter—refuses to speak. He witnesses Pericles' reunions with MARINA, in 5.1, and THAISA, in 5.3. Helicanus demonstrates that loyalty and goodness do continue to exist among humans, despite the misfortunes that plague Pericles. Pericles praises Helicanus' virtues several times, and calls him 'fit counsellor and servant for a prince, / Who by thy wisdom makes a prince thy servant' (1.2.63–64), and 'a grave and noble counsellor' (5.1.182). This wise elder's presence seems appropriate to the play's conclusion in divinely wrought happiness and good fortune.

**Heminge (Heminges), John (d. 1630)**    English actor and a co-editor, with Henry CONDELL, of the FIRST FOLIO edition of Shakespeare's plays. One of the 26 'Principall Actors' listed in the First Folio, Heminge was a member of STRANGE'S MEN, of the CHAMBERLAIN'S MEN (probably from its inception in 1594), and of its successor, the KING'S MEN, until his death. Thus, most of his career was spent alongside Shakespeare. He was apparently the business manager of the company, probably beginning at least in 1596, and he seems to have stopped acting after 1611.

He served as a trustee in Shakespeare's purchase of the BLACKFRIARS GATEHOUSE, and he was executor or overseer of the wills of several of the King's Men. Shakespeare and most of the other members of the troupe left him small legacies, tokens of their friendship. Heminge was a shrewd businessman and became quite wealthy. At his death, he owned about a quarter of the shares in the GLOBE THEATRE and the BLACKFRIARS THEATRE, including the shares originally owned by his late son-in-law William OSTLER (2), which he had claimed despite a lawsuit by his daughter.

**Henderson, John (1747–1785)**  British actor. Henderson established himself as a fine classical actor in 1777 with a portrayal of SHYLOCK. During his brief career, he was acclaimed as the leading FALSTAFF of his day, and he played a variety of other Shakespearean parts, including MALVOLIO and IAGO.

**Henry (1), Prince (later King Henry III of England) (1207–1272)**  Historical figure and minor character in *King John,* the son of King JOHN (3). Henry appears only in the final scene, 5.7, in which he witnesses the death of his father and accepts the submission of the noblemen to him as the next King. He is thus a symbol of the restoration of social order after the dislocations of John's reign.

Shakespeare's Henry is a young man but definitely an adult, capable of musing on the nature of disease and death. The historical Prince was only nine years old upon his succession. He ruled England well for 56 years. His great-great-great-grandson was RICHARD II (see PLANTAGENET [1]).

**Henry (2) Frederick, Prince of Wales (1594–1612)**  Son of King JAMES I, heir-apparent to the English throne until his death, and patron of PRINCE HENRY'S MEN, formerly the ADMIRAL'S MEN. Though Prince Henry died young, he was already a significant supporter of the arts. He patronised George CHAPMAN and Ben JONSON, and he defended Walter RALEIGH. He was the first major supporter of Inigo Jones (1573–1652), later the royal architect and collaborator with Jonson (see MASQUE). Most significantly for the theatrical world, he became the patron of the Admiral's Men. Unfortunately, the young prince died of typhoid fever, just before the planned wedding of his sister, Princess ELIZABETH (3). Her husband-to-be, a German prince, took over the patronage of Henry's theatre company, which became known as the PALSGRAVE'S MEN.

*Henry I* and *Henry II*  Lost plays attributed, probably wrongly, to Shakespeare and Robert Davenport (c. 1590–1640). In 1653 the publisher Humphrey MOSELEY claimed the copyrights to a number of old plays, including 'Henry ye first, & Hen: ye 2. by Shakespeare and Davenport'. The 18th-century collector John WARBURTON reported owning a copy of *Henry I,* by 'Will. Shakespeare & Rob. Davenport'. However, none of these manuscripts has survived, and their attribution to Shakespeare, even as a collaborator, is extremely doubtful. *Henry I* was licenced for the KING'S MEN to perform in 1624—eight years after Shakespeare's death—but only in Davenport's name. Moreover, Davenport himself is first recorded only in 1620; a much younger and inferior playwright, he would have been an unlikely collaborator for Shakespeare.

**Henry IV, King of England (1366–1413)**  Historical figure and title character in *1* and *2 Henry IV.* (The same figure appears in *Richard II* as BOLINGBROKE [1].) King Henry is not the most prominent character in the plays that take his name, but he is nonetheless an important figure. The major concern of the plays is the growth of his son and successor, PRINCE (6) HAL. The question of what constitutes a good ruler is thus paramount, and as king, Henry personifies the issue. He is viewed from three distinct points of view in *Part 1:* he sees himself as a weary but effective monarch; Hotspur regards him as a dishonourable politician who first deposed a king (as is enacted in *Richard II*) and then betrayed those who helped him do so; and Falstaff considers him a cold, rigid opponent of comfort and licence. By *Part 2* Henry is almost a tragic figure. The cost of power shows itself in his illness and fatigue, while he himself suggests that his decline and death are the deserved fate of a usurper.

Henry is presented as a strong ruler: for instance, his dismissal of Hotspur and NORTHUMBERLAND (1) in 1.3.116–122 of *Part 1* makes it clear that he does not tolerate insubordination, and in 3.1 of *Part 2* he overcomes his illness and melancholy to face the rebellion squarely, saying, 'Are these things then necessities? then let us meet them like necessities' (3.1.92–93). He is also politically astute to the point of cynicism. In *Part 1* (3.2.39–59) he describes the appearance of regal splendour that he assumed during his rebellion against Richard II in order to win the hearts of the populace (Richard also describes this in *Richard II,* 1.4.23–36), and his distinctly Machiavellian deathbed advice to Hal—divert potential rebels by engaging in wars abroad—is chilling.

But, despite his strength, Henry's principal characteristic is weariness. From the first line of *Part 1* Henry presents himself as a sick and tired man who wants to embark on a crusade to the Holy Land to atone for his role in the murder of Richard II. Moreover, his disappointment over Prince Hal's dissolute life embitters him. In 3.1 of *Part 2* he comments that the terrible burden of power prevents him from sleeping; he broods, 'uneasy lies the head that wears a crown' (3.1. 31). He goes on to wish, 'Oh God, that one might read the book of fate . . .' (3.1.45), in tones that foreshadow the darkly brilliant meditations of Shakespeare's tragic heroes.

Hotspur sees Henry as a treacherous usurper who has turned against his allies. Henry himself is very much aware that he has been a rebel. In his deathbed conversation with Hal, he plainly suffers guilt for the 'by-paths and indirect crook'd ways' (*2 Henry IV*, 4.5. 184) by which he gained power, a reference to the deposition and murder of Richard II. He observes that many of his allies against Richard later resented his assumption of power. He anticipates that Hal will have an easier time when he ascends the throne, being legitimately descended from a sitting king. This indeed proves to be so, as the end of *2 Henry IV* and all of *Henry V* demonstrate. However, as Shakespeare and his contemporaries were well aware, the disputes over the royal succession that Henry's actions had triggered were settled only by the disastrous WARS OF THE ROSES, and Henry's sense of guilt is a reflection of the curse that his sinful usurpation has brought upon himself, his family (see LANCASTER [1]), and his country. Nevertheless, Henry is the established power in these plays, and Hotspur and his allies sin in rebelling against him and are repeatedly condemned as a result.

Henry's ultimate significance in the drama is as the holder of the position for which Prince Hal must equip himself. While Henry's cold, Machiavellian world of political manipulation is too rigid and inhumane for the young man to grow up in, he does in the end enter it. In 4.5, in a reprise of the king's lament over the stresses of kingship (*2 Henry IV*, 3.1.4–31), Hal rhetorically addresses Henry's crown and speaks of the burden that kingship demands. He accepts that burden for himself, emphasising his decision by placing the crown on his own head. One consequence of this decision is that he must become like Henry to some degree; he must enact in the real world the disciplinarian's role he had taken in the tavern burlesque of *Part 1*. Hal is often criticised for his icily brutal dismissal of Falstaff in 5.5; readers have thought that, in rejecting Falstaff, Hal also rejects part of his own humanity, but it may equally well be argued that he is simply adopting a different type of humanity, that of his weary, careworn father.

The history of Henry's reign is strenuously compressed in the plays, producing an impression of greater civil disorder than in fact occurred. While the various rebellions of the play did take place, they were widely spaced and relatively easily suppressed. Henry was a strong king, although he was not a competent administrator and his regime had persistent financial troubles. Two significant variations from history in the plays concern Henry personally. First, in *Part 1* Henry is committed from the very beginning (indeed, from *Richard II*, 5.6.49–50) to a crusade to ease his conscience, thus stressing sin and retribution as the ulti-mate causes of the unrest of Henry's reign. In fact, and in Shakespeare's sources, Henry did not propose a crusade until late in his reign, when it seems to have been intended to expand his influence in European diplomacy. Second, Henry's illness, which he actually developed only a year before his death, plagues him for most of his reign in the plays, dominating all his appearances in *2 Henry IV*. Shakespeare may have been influenced in this direction by Samuel DANIEL, whose *Civil Wars* stresses Henry's deathbed struggles with his bad conscience. The effect produced, a melancholy sense of impending death, makes more fateful and solemn Hal's acceptance of his kingly burden.

## *Henry IV*, PART 1

### SYNOPSIS

*Act 1, Scene 1*
King HENRY IV's plans for a crusade are upset by a report from the Earl of WESTMORELAND (1) that Welsh rebels under Owen GLENDOWER have defeated and captured Edmund MORTIMER (2). There is better news, however: young Henry Percy, nicknamed HOTSPUR, has defeated rebellious Scots under the Earl of DOUGLAS and has taken many prisoners. Henry observes that Hotspur's honourable success in war reflects badly on his own son, PRINCE (6) HAL, who leads a dissolute life in LONDON. However, he goes on to complain of Hotspur's prideful refusal to turn over his prisoners to the king, as is customary. Westmoreland attributes this stubborness to the influence of Hotspur's uncle, Thomas Percy, Earl of WORCESTER.

*Act 1, Scene 2*
Prince Hal and FALSTAFF jest about their debauched life of petty crime, drunkenness, and wenching. POINS arrives with a plan for a highway robbery. At first, the Prince does not wish to participate, but, after Falstaff leaves, Poins proposes to Hal that they play a joke on Falstaff: they will go to the scene of the crime but avoid taking part; then, after Falstaff and the others have stolen the money, Poins and the Prince can steal it from them; the cowardice of Falstaff and his friends will make this easy. Later they will have the pleasure of listening to Falstaff lie about the episode, followed by the further delight of exposing the old rogue. Hal agrees, and Poins leaves. In a soliloquy the Prince reveals his intention to eventually abandon his life of idle dissolution and become a sound ruler.

*Act 1, Scene 3*
Hotspur tells the king that he had not refused to surrender his prisoners, as Henry believes, but had merely responded in hasty anger to the arrogant courtier who had presented the king's claim. Unappeased, the king observes that Hotspur not only still holds the prisoners but also insists that Mortimer be ransomed

from the Welsh before he turns them over. Henry asserts that Mortimer, who has married Glendower's daughter, has treasonably defected to the Welsh, and he refuses to ransom him. Hotspur defends Mortimer, and the king exits angrily. Hotspur rages against Henry's ingratitude to the Percy family, which helped the king depose RICHARD II. With difficulty, Worcester calms Hotspur and proposes that Hotspur should release his Scottish prisoners and enlist them in a rebellion against the king while his father, the Earl of NORTHUMBERLAND (1), recruits the ARCHBISHOP (3) of York. Worcester himself will join Glendower when the time is ripe, and the three forces will rise simultaneously.

### Act 2, Scene 1
At an inn in ROCHESTER, TWO CARRIERS prepare to leave for London. GADSHILL, a highwayman, appears and learns from them that they will be accompanied by some gentlemen carrying valuables. The CHAMBERLAIN (1) of the inn tells Gadshill of these potential victims in more detail. Gadshill boasts of an accomplice in high places who can get them off if the theft goes wrong.

### Act 2, Scene 2
The robbers assemble at GAD'S HILL. Hal arranges an ambush, placing himself and Poins in a reserve position just down the road. The Prince and Poins leave just before the TRAVELLERS appear. The thieves rob the Travellers and bundle them off-stage; when the thieves return, they are themselves effortlessly robbed by the Prince and Poins.

### Act 2, Scene 3
Hotspur reads a letter from a nobleman who makes excuses for not joining the rebellion. LADY (10) Percy appears, and Hotspur announces his imminent departure. She speaks worriedly of his absorption in his plans—he even speaks of military matters in his sleep—and she demands to be told what they are. Hotspur playfully refuses to tell her, claiming military secrecy.

### Act 2, Scene 4
At the BOAR'S HEAD TAVERN, Prince Hal teases FRANCIS (1), a waiter, and he laughingly compares his own good humour with Hotspur's mania for war. Falstaff enters; egged on by Hal and Poins, he tells an elaborate tale of his courage in resisting the brigands who robbed him. After leading Falstaff on to ludicrous exaggerations, the Prince reveals the truth, and Falstaff comically claims to have recognised Hal at the time and to have fled so as to avoid harming the heir apparent of the realm. A message from King Henry commands Hal's presence in the morning; a rebellion, led by Hotspur, has begun. Falstaff anticipates the king's anger at Hal and suggests that the Prince rehearse his response. Falstaff pretends to be Henry and chastises Hal for the company he keeps, excepting only one commendable man called Falstaff. They change roles, and Hal, as the king, upbraids his 'son' for tolerating so bad a man as Falstaff. Falstaff, playing the Prince, defends Falstaff. He is interrupted by the approach of the SHERIFF (4). Falstaff was recognised at Gad's Hill and has been traced to the tavern. Falstaff hides; the Prince assures the Sheriff that the thief is not present and that he, the Prince, will guarantee that any stolen money will be refunded. The Sheriff leaves, and Hal discovers that Falstaff has fallen asleep in his hiding place. The Prince looks forward to the campaign against the rebels.

### Act 3, Scene 1
The rebel leaders convene to make a formal alliance, but friction between Glendower and Hotspur threatens to break up the meeting. The discussion turns to the division of the realm after King Henry has been deposed. Hotspur objects that his portion is too small, and his arrogance offends Glendower. They argue again, but the Welshman gives in and a tenuous peace is maintained. Glendower leaves, and Mortimer and Worcester chastise an unapologetic Hotspur for offending a valuable ally. Glendower returns with his daughter, LADY (8) Mortimer, and Lady Percy. Mortimer regrets that he cannot speak Welsh, his wife's only language; Glendower interprets as the couple exchange loving remarks. Lady Mortimer invites her husband to lie in her lap while she sings to him. Hotspur humorously mocks this in conversation with his wife, whom he teases affectionately. After Lady Mortimer's song, the men leave to join their troops.

### Act 3, Scene 2
Henry speaks to Prince Hal about his dissipated behaviour and doubts his son's loyalty in the coming conflict. Hal apologises for his debaucheries and assures his father that he intends to conquer Hotspur. News arrives that the rebels have assembled at SHREWSBURY, and the King devises a plan for the campaign; Hal is to command one of the armies.

### Act 3, Scene 3
At the Boar's Head, Falstaff speaks of repentance for his ways but goes on to praise bawdiness and merriment. He teases BARDOLPH (1) about his fiery complexion and banters with the HOSTESS (2). The Prince arrives, excited about the coming campaign; he tells Falstaff to meet him the next day to receive his orders. He leaves, and Falstaff turns to his meal, wishing he could conduct his part in the war from the tavern.

### Act 4, Scene 1
Hotspur, Worcester, and Douglas, encamped at Shrewsbury, receive word that Mortimer is extremely sick and cannot join them with his forces. Sir Richard VERNON (2) reports the approach of the King's armies and reveals that Glendower's troops cannot come for

another two weeks. Although the rebels are seriously outnumbered, Hotspur urges that they fight anyway.

### Act 4, Scene 2

Falstaff, marching towards Shrewsbury, soliloquises on the money he has made selling exemptions from the draft. The Prince and Westmoreland meet him and urge him to hurry, for the battle will soon begin. After they leave, Falstaff remarks to himself that he hopes to arrive just as the battle ends.

### Act 4, Scene 3

Hotspur and Douglas argue for an immediate attack on the king's forces, but Vernon and Worcester want to wait for reinforcements. Sir Walter BLUNT (3) appears with a message from King Henry offering a negotiated peace. Hotspur condemns Henry's usurpation of the throne and his ingratitude towards those who helped him carry it out. However, he agrees to have Worcester meet with the king the next day.

### Act 4, Scene 4

The Archbishop speaks of the likely defeat of the rebels at Shrewsbury, and he begins to prepare for further opposition to the king.

### Act 5, Scene 1

Worcester and Vernon arrive to negotiate with King Henry. Worcester justifies rebellion by pointing out the king's ingratitude. Prince Hal offers to fight Hotspur in single combat to settle all issues, but Henry rejects the idea, offering the rebels a last chance for surrender with amnesty: if they reject it, the two armies must fight. Worcester and Vernon depart. Falstaff asks the Prince to protect him in the battle; Hal, leaving, responds that he will have to take his chances. Falstaff muses that he will not follow an honourable course in the battle, for honour is a minor matter compared to life.

### Act 5, Scene 2

Worcester insists to Vernon that they not tell Hotspur of the king's offer of an amnesty lest he accept it; he believes that Henry cannot be trusted and that, while Hotspur may be forgiven on grounds of youth and high-spiritedness, he, Worcester, would bear the brunt of the king's wrath. Worcester accordingly reports that the king has elected to fight, and he tells of Hal's challenge. Hotspur responds by preparing for battle.

### Act 5, Scene 3

During the battle Blunt, disguised as King Henry, is killed by Douglas. Falstaff meets Prince Hal and lies about his courageous combat, but the Prince discovers a bottle of sack in Falstaff's pistol case.

### Act 5, Scene 4

During a lull in the battle the king suggests that his sons Prince Hal and Prince John of LANCASTER (3)

retire from the fighting, but they both refuse. Lancaster rejoins the fray, and Hal lauds his fighting spirit before following him. Douglas appears and fights the king, nearly killing him; the Prince returns and slays Douglas. The king comments that Hal has proved himself. Henry exits, and Hotspur arrives to exchange challenges and fight with the Prince. Falstaff watches this combat until Douglas enters to fight him; Falstaff feigns death, and Douglas moves on. The Prince kills Hotspur and eulogises his dead foe. He then sees Falstaff and, believing him dead, pronounces a more casual benediction before leaving. Falstaff rises, stabs Hotspur's corpse with his sword, and declares that he will take credit for killing him. The Prince and Lancaster return and are surprised to see Falstaff alive. Falstaff claims to have killed Hotspur and supposes that the king will reward him; out of friendship, the Prince agrees to corroborate his lie.

### Act 5, Scene 5

King Henry sentences the captured Worcester and Vernon to death, while Douglas is to be set free. The king begins to make plans to fight the remaining rebels.

### COMMENTARY

*Henry IV, Part 1,* was a highly innovative work in 1596 for precisely the reasons that make it one of the greatest of Shakespeare's HISTORY PLAYS. It marks an advance both in Shakespeare's development and in the growth of English drama, for, by repeatedly shifting its focus between affairs of state and bawdy irreverence, the play presents a composite image of a whole society, something that had never been attempted before. In addition to the quarrels and alliances among the aristocracy, the principal interest of the earlier histories, here Shakespeare offers the scruffy circle of common laborers and petty criminals who frequent the Boar's Head Tavern. Both worlds are more vivid for the contrast, and a dramatic tension is established between them. Groundbreaking in its own day, *1 Henry IV* is still impressive in ours, due to the range of people, events, and language, from the most casual ribaldry to the boldest rhetoric, realistically presented on stage.

Prince Hal belongs to both worlds; surrounding him are such boldly drawn figures as the volatile Hotspur and his charming wife, the talkative Hostess, and the many personalities evoked by Falstaff's parodies and imitations: churchmen and highwaymen, knights and knaves. The Prince's significance lies in the choice he must make between worlds, and his dilemma emphasises, as in the other history plays, the question of order in society. Both the Falstaffian delinquents of the Boar's Head Tavern and the rebels led by Hotspur have contributed to the decay of the social fabric, and King Henry believes that both groups have been sent by heaven in revenge for his own disturbance of society, the deposition of King RICHARD II (as enacted in *Richard II*). Hal's choice is indeed pivotal for the future of the realm. Of course, Shakespeare's original audiences knew that Hal went on to become the highly successful King HENRY V, so there is no suspense about the Prince's choice; the tension lies instead in the presentation of the alternatives.

Although the sub-plot concerning Falstaff is highly diverting, the major concern is Hal's decision to embrace his role as Hotspur's rival, abandoning the life of a barfly for that of a military leader. This central issue is not fully resolved until the end of *2 Henry IV*, when Hal rejects Falstaff, but *Part 1* presents an initial phase of Hal's development, his acceptance of his role as princely hero.

The play's climax is the hand-to-hand combat between Hal and Hotspur at Shrewsbury. Not only does the play build to this climax through a series of episodes depicting the progress of Hotspur's rebellion, but Hal and Hotspur are repeatedly compared, both by the king—as early as 1.1.77–90—and by Hal himself. The king regrets that his own son seems so feckless in comparison to the rebel leader. Hal assures his father that he is not the dissipated playboy he seems and that he will prove superior to Hotspur when the time is ripe. This motif—the potential readiness of the Prince—has already been established in Hal's famous 'reformation' speech (1.2.190–212). Shakespeare makes it abundantly clear that the Prince will indeed prove himself in the traditional terms of chivalry, and in the combat at Shrewsbury, an episode devised by the playwright for this purpose, Hal becomes the hero whom he has promised to be.

Hotspur's defeat attests that chivalry is not an unalloyed virtue, as does his outsised personality, which consists of impatience and an exaggerated sense of honour. Hotspur is a temperamental, driven man who is concerned only about his reputation for bravery in battle. His fixation is as excessive in its way as is Falstaff's licentiousness. This leads to his own destruction, as he cannot bring himself to postpone the battle at Shrewsbury until his side has a better chance.

Hotspur has his redeeming features as well. Hal admits that his military accomplishments are worth aspiring to, and the Prince's eulogy over Hotspur's corpse (5.4.86–100) is genuinely admiring. Moreover, while the rebellious noblemen are certainly self-serving to various degrees, Hotspur's own motive is not personal gain or power; he is driven by an ambition for honourable action that one could admire if it were in better balance in his life. Hotspur's loving marriage to the engaging Lady Percy is presented in 2.3 and 3.1, and we recognise that he is not simply a 'wasp-stung and impatient fool', as his father calls him in 1.3.233, but also a husband who credibly inspires affection. His domestic bliss does not in any way negate the problem of his flawed values, but it makes him a multi-dimensional character.

Falstaff embodies an opposite weakness to Hotspur's, that of an anarchic refusal to accept responsibility. His world of food, women, and wine has no need for 'redeeming time'—as Hal vows to do in the 'reformation' speech (1.2.190–212)—for time is of no consequence when one refuses to acknowledge any obligations. Falstaff staves off all demands and responsibilities—the stuff of history—with humour, continually devising witticisms and preposterous excuses for his behaviour. We are as delighted with his inventive comedy as Hal is in 1.2, but, like the Prince, we can see that a ruler must live a more orderly life. In addition, the fat knight displays a chilling disregard for ordinary values, in an episode that Shakespeare plainly intended as a satire on a military abuse of his own times, when he callously offers the soldiers he has recruited to be 'food for powder, food for powder' (4.2.65–66), meaning that they will be quickly consumed by gunpowder, i.e., combat. He later announces coolly that he has abandoned his troops under fire, where 'there's not three of my hundred and fifty left alive' (5.3.37). Falstaff's anarchy here has an unpleasant, faintly evil edge to it. His crimes and misdemeanours may be forgivable in a comedy—and *1 Henry IV* is somewhat comic—but they are unacceptable in the domain of history, where the hard realities of peace and war are at stake.

Just as Hotspur has an unrealistic view of the world, so does Falstaff. Falstaff lives in an immature universe where one's appetites are gratified immediately and the inevitability of age and death is denied. He has been seen as a re-creation of ancient figures of European folklore who traditionally enlivened holiday celebrations by behaving in perversely loose ways that are normally forbidden. These figures, who returned to ordinary behaviour after the festival, made a great show of eating and drinking to excess, of flouting authority, and, often, of sexual promiscuity. Thus illicit cravings were acknowledged and vicariously satisfied without disrupting the society. Such customs were prominent in pre-modern societies and were still well known, if not widely practised, in Elizabethan England. Falstaff's gluttony, his lechery, and his very fatness are easily associated with such figures.

However, Falstaff is not simply a temptation to be resisted or a negative lesson for Hal. Falstaff's world is also in itself useful for the Prince, offering him an arena in which he can test himself and come to understand the people who will be his subjects when he is king, and learn about himself as well. At the Boar's Head, Hal tries on the roles of robber, of tavern servant, even of king. The other worlds of the play—Hotspur's inflexible, honour-bound world or Henry's tense world of political calculation—do not permit the temporary attitudes and stances necessary to learning.

The world of comedy thus has virtues that the world of history cannot provide.

Just as Hotspur's happy marriage deepens his characterisation, so Falstaff is caught in a revealing moment of uneasiness about his life in 3.3, when he worries that he is wasting away and muses on his long absence from church. When his eventual death is suggested by Bardolph, the fat knight immediately reverts to his more usual comic line, but we have seen that he, too, has a soul and is subject to universal fears.

Both Hotspur and Falstaff are strong figures, and it is not wholly possible to dismiss or accept either of them; with great force of irony, we are made to sympathise with both the impatient firebrand and the irresponsible rogue, even as we recognise the faults of each. When Prince Hal comes fully into his own, it is appropriate that we see him standing between these two extremes; Falstaff lies to one side, rejecting honour by feigning death, and Hotspur lies to the other, dead because he overvalued honour.

Hal's story does not end with this play; *2 Henry IV* is a sequel. Scholars debate whether or not Shakespeare had fully evolved this relationship when he was writing *1 Henry IV*, but the evidence suggests strongly that he had. First, Hal's rejection of Falstaff in *2 Henry IV* hinted at several times in *1 Henry IV*—e.g., in his 'reformation' speech; when he portrays his father in the tavern ('I do, I will' [2.4.475]); when he dismisses Falstaff during the battle (5.3.55)—while the play closes with the fat knight at an acme of both wrongdoing and acceptance, boasting that he has killed Hotspur himself (after stabbing the corpse) and finding the Prince generous enough to let his claim stand. This situation prepares us for a continuation of Falstaff's adventures, when his death, with Hotspur's, could have closed the play effectively. Further, Shakespeare invented an important role for John of Lancaster at Shrewsbury, establishing him as a major figure in apparent anticipation of his function in *2 Henry IV*. Moreover, both the rebels and the king are preparing for further action as the play ends. Each of these points may be explained in some other way, but collectively they strongly suggest that *1 Henry IV* was written with *2 Henry IV* in mind. Nevertheless, *1 Henry IV* is a complete drama, with its own plot line that reaches fruition independently of its sequel.

Shakespeare's great achievement in *1 Henry IV* is the establishment of a sense of community between the audience and the fictional world of the play. Structurally he accomplishes this by a continual oscillation between two poles, the aristocratic and the common or the political and the hedonistic. These elements are sometimes parallel—as in 1.1 and 1.2, where preparations for war are followed by preparations for robbery—and sometimes in opposition, as in the comparison of Hal and Hotspur. Some scenes have analogues in *2 Henry IV*—e.g., Hotspur's farewell to his wife in 2.1 is comparable to Falstaff's departure from DOLL TEARSHEET in 2.4 of the sequel. Such juxtapositions enforce a comprehensive sense of a complex, lifelike fictional world, quite aside from the historical actions of the political plot.

The integration of two genres, comedy and history, permits each to influence the other. The history, presenting issues that impinge on all our lives, is made graver because it affects the lives of the comic figures. The comedy, while providing an ironic slant on social themes, is given sharpness of tone and richness of texture by its proximity to the serious aspects of life. By successfully accommodating two genres, the play—and its implicit tolerance—is made more intense: although one is made aware of human failing, one may also glory in human possibility.

## SOURCES OF THE PLAY

Shakespeare's principal source for the historical material in *1 Henry IV* was Raphael HOLINSHED's *Chronicles of England, Scotland, and Ireland* (2nd ed., 1587), but the playwright was also greatly influenced by Samuel DANIEL's epic poem *The Civil Wars Between the Two Houses of York and Lancaster* (1595). In Daniel, the streamlined narrative emphasises the relation of King Henry's troubles to his deposition of Richard II, and it climaxes with the battle of Shrewsbury, compressing the remainder of Henry's reign into a cursory account. Shakespeare's handling of historical events in *1 Henry IV* closely reflects this approach. Daniel also supplied the inspiration for the hand-to-hand encounter between Hal and Hotspur in 5.4 and for the alteration in Hotspur's age. Daniel, while stating no ages, implies that Hotspur was of Hal's generation; Shakespeare makes this explicit. Historically, however, Hotspur was older than Hal's father.

The anonymous play WOODSTOCK (c. 1592–1595) provided various details for the fictitious highway robbery in 2.2, and, more significantly, featured a story of national politics that is integrated with comical doings by a high-ranking criminal, a possible predecessor of Falstaff. Tales of Prince Hal's mis-spent youth had been part of English popular lore since his own time; Shakespeare derived his account chiefly from the anonymous play *The Famous Victories of Henry the Fifth* (see FAMOUS VICTORIES), a farce that was acted at least as early as 1588. Most of the episodes of Hal's dissipated existence in Eastcheap, and of his later rejection of it, were presented in this work, which in turn drew on several earlier accounts, including the historical works of John STOW. Shakespeare probably consulted these independently, finding there the assertion that Hal refunded the victims of his companions' robberies, along with some additional details.

Other sources, including well-known ballads about the Percy-Douglas feuds and a biography of Glendower in the popular collection A MIRROR FOR MAGIS-

TRATES (1559), may have provided incidental material. It has also been suggested that this play and *2 Henry IV* may have been derived from an earlier play by Shakespeare on the same subject, but this speculation is unprovable.

## TEXT OF THE PLAY

The date of composition of *1 Henry IV* can only be inferred, but with some precision. It seems to follow closely upon *Richard II;* not only does *1 Henry IV* come next in historical sequence, but *Richard II* contains material that seems to point to a sequel. *Richard II* is generally dated to 1595 or 1596; *1 Henry IV* was therefore composed no earlier than 1596. OLDCASTLE's name was changed to Falstaff as a consequence of protests following performances of the play, and that alteration was apparently made before or during the writing of *The Merry Wives of Windsor,* which was first staged in the spring of 1597. Thus it is likely that *1 Henry IV* was being performed during the winter of 1596–1597 and was probably written in early or mid-1596.

Two QUARTO editions of *1 Henry IV* were printed by Peter SHORT for publisher Andrew WISE in 1598. Only four sheets (1.3.199–2.2) survive from the earlier of these, known as Q0; the other, Q1, was printed from Q0 with minor emendations. Four more quartos were published before the FIRST FOLIO of 1623: Q2 (1599), Q3 (1608), Q4 (1613), Q5 (1622). Although Q2's title page claims that it was 'newly corrected by W. Shakespeare', it was in fact printed—again with minor changes—from Q1, and each subsequent quarto was derived from its predecessor. The Folio version of *1 Henry IV* was printed from Q5; it also contains many minor alterations, some of which may have come from a PROMPT BOOK. Q0 is thought to have been printed from Shakespeare's manuscript, either in the form of a FAIR COPY or his original FOUL PAPERS. Q1 is thus the basis for most modern editions.

In addition to the published texts, there is a handwritten copy of a play that combines *1* and *2 Henry IV,* the DERING MANUSCRIPT. The material it takes from *1 Henry IV* appears to derive from Q5 and the Folio text and is thus dated 1623–1624. Its variations from these texts are not thought to reflect either alterations by the playwright or the practices of early productions, and modern editions do not follow it.

## THEATRICAL HISTORY OF THE PLAY

Although no certain records of 16th-century performances of *1 Henry IV* have survived, numerous references in contemporary documents, especially to Hotspur or Falstaff, testify to its popularity. Several actors are said to have played Falstaff during the early 17th century, including John LOWIN, John HEMINGE, and Shakespeare's nephew William HART (3). During the Commonwealth, when the revolutionary Puritan gov-

ernment outlawed the theatre, *The Bouncing Knight,* an abbreviated version of *1 Henry IV,* was performed secretly, as a DROLL. After the restoration of the monarchy in 1660, *1 Henry IV* was among the first plays performed in the reopened theatres, and it remained popular: Samuel PEPYS records productions in 1660, 1661, 1667, and 1668. In 1682 Thomas BETTERTON produced an adaptation of the play in which he played Hotspur; this version was so popular that it was still being revived 18 years later, by which time the 65-year-old producer was playing Falstaff. In the 18th century the play was also frequently staged, and most of the leading actors of the day played Hotspur or Falstaff. David GARRICK, among others, played both; he was acclaimed as Hotspur, but the most successful Falstaffs were James QUIN in the first half of the century and John HENDERSON in the second. In the late 18th century producers twice experimented with a woman, once the famed Julia GLOVER, in Falstaff's part.

In the first half of the 19th century a number of productions of the play were popular. William Charles MACREADY and John Philip KEMBLE (3) were notable Hotspurs, and the latter's two brothers, Charles and Stephen KEMBLE (1,4), played Falstaff. The leading Falstaff of the time, however, was Charles BARTLEY.

*Henry IV, Part 1,* declined in popularity in the second half of the 19th century, although it was presented by Samuel PHELPS, F. R. BENSON (1), and Beerbohm TREE. However, it has often been staged in the 20th. Among the most successful productions was that of Margaret WEBSTER (3), starring Maurice EVANS (4) as Falstaff, in 1939. Laurence OLIVIER played Hotspur in 1940 and 1945; Ralph RICHARDSON's Falstaff in the latter production is considered one of his greatest successes. Orson WELLES adapted the two *Henry IV* plays in his 1965 FILM *Chimes at Midnight,* in which he starred as Falstaff. Several cycles of the history plays have presented *1 Henry IV,* notably those at STRATFORD in 1906, 1951 (with Michael REDGRAVE as Hotspur), and 1964. A number of TELEVISION productions of the play have been broadcast since the 1950s. The continuing appeal of the *Henry IV* plays was recently demonstrated by a 1987 production in London: the two plays and *Henry V* were staged on different nights of the week, and, most strikingly, theatre-goers responded with enthusiasm to marathon Saturday performances featuring all three works in succession.

## *Henry IV*, PART 2

### SYNOPSIS

*Induction*

A personification of RUMOUR announces that he has put forth a false report, following King HENRY IV's victory at the battle of SHREWSBURY—where PRINCE (6) HAL has killed the rebellious HOTSPUR—that the king and Prince were killed and the rebels were victorious. This report, Rumour says, is now reaching WARKWORTH CASTLE, home of Hotspur's father, the Earl of NORTHUMBERLAND (1).

*Act 1, Scene 1*
Lord BARDOLPH (2) brings Northumberland the false news of Hotspur's victory; however, TRAVERS appears with two reports, one corroborating Lord Bardolph's account and the other telling of Hotspur's death and the rebels' defeat. MORTON, an eyewitness, arrives to confirm the truth of the second story. In addition, he says that the victorious king has sent troops, under the Earl of WESTMORELAND (1) and Prince John of LANCASTER (3), to capture Northumberland. The earl rages madly, but his followers counsel calm; the revolt may still be alive. Morton says that the ARCHBISHOP (3) of York has raised a rebel army to avenge the death of King RICHARD II, whom Henry deposed and murdered. Northumberland begins to make plans for the renewal of the war.

*Act 1, Scene 2*
FALSTAFF jests about the comical disparity between his own huge bulk and that of his diminutive PAGE (5). He encounters the CHIEF JUSTICE, who upbraids him for having refused to answer a summons, observing that, although Falstaff's service at Shrewsbury has allowed earlier offences to be overlooked, he must behave better in the future. Falstaff wittily dismisses this warning. The justice attempts to shame the old man for his foolishness, but to no avail. The knight asks to borrow money from the justice, who leaves. Falstaff then sends the Page with letters to the Prince, Lancaster, Westmoreland, and a woman whom he says he has promised to marry. Complaining of his gout, he declares that a limp will prove useful: he will seem to have been wounded in the war and will get a bigger pension.

*Act 1, Scene 3*
The rebels, led by the Archbishop, lay their plans. Lord Bardolph advises that they postpone action until they can be sure of Northumberland's support. Lord HASTINGS (2), however, argues that the King's forces are divided, facing threats from the French and the Welsh as well as from themselves, and suggests that the rebels launch their campaign at once. The Archbishop agrees, citing the turn of public opinion against Henry, and they leave to assemble their forces.

*Act 2, Scene 1*
The HOSTESS (2) of the BOAR'S HEAD TAVERN enlists the officers FANG and SNARE to arrest Falstaff for debt, but when they try to do so, he and his friend BARDOLPH (1) draw their swords and prepare to fight. The furor brings the Chief Justice and his men. He asks the Hostess to explain her claim, and she states that Falstaff has proposed to her, in addition to owing her a great deal

of money. Falstaff says that the Hostess is insane, but the Chief Justice insists that he recompense her. Falstaff speaks to the Hostess in private, and he wheedles another loan from her, along with a promise of dinner. The Chief Justice receives word that immediate preparations for battle against the rebels are being made.

*Act 2, Scene 2*
Prince Hal jests with POINS, but when Poins twits him for not displaying sadness at his father's illness, the Prince observes bitterly that his dissipated life has left him with such a bad reputation that a show of melancholy could only be taken for hypocrisy. Bardolph and Falstaff's Page arrive with a saucy letter from the knight to Hal. The Page reports that Falstaff is dining with the Hostess and a harlot, DOLL TEARSHEET; the Prince and Poins concoct a plot to surprise him at his meal by disguising themselves as DRAWERS.

*Act 2, Scene 3*
LADY (10) Percy and LADY (9) Northumberland try to dissuade Northumberland from joining the rebel armies. He pleads his duty, but Lady Percy reminds him that he failed to assist his own son, her late husband, Hotspur, whom she eulogises. Humiliated, the Earl agrees to flee to Scotland.

*Act 2, Scene 4*
At the Boar's Head, the Hostess, Doll Tearsheet, and Falstaff banter drunkenly. PISTOL arrives and makes so much noise that Falstaff drives him away. The Prince and Poins, disguised, overhear Falstaff's assertions that they are inconsequential louts. When Hal confronts Falstaff, the fat knight says that he had disparaged the noblemen only in order to protect them from the ignominy of finding themselves admired by such wicked sorts as Doll and the Hostess. PETO appears with news that the king's army is urgently assembling. The Prince, conscience-stricken that he was indulging himself, hurries away. A further summons arrives for Falstaff, and he departs as well.

*Act 3, Scene 1*
King Henry sends a PAGE (6) with letters to the earls of SURREY (2) and WARWICK (2). He reflects on his heavy responsibilities, which keep him awake at night while his subjects sleep. Warwick and Surrey arrive and attempt to calm him, but he morosely speaks of the inevitable ravages of time and recalls the prophecy of RICHARD II (in *Richard II*, 5.1) that Northumberland would rebel. Warwick remarks that Northumberland's essentially false nature made such an outcome inevitable, and the observation restores Henry to a sense of the necessity for action. Warwick assures the king that the rebellion seems under control, for the Welsh leader GLENDOWER's death has been reported.

*Act 3, Scene 2*
The country justices SHALLOW and SILENCE leisurely await the arrival of the king's army recruiter, Falstaff,

for whom they have assembled a group of villagers. Shallow reminisces windily on his student days in London, where he knew Falstaff. Falstaff appears with Bardolph and comically interviews the potential soldiers, selecting several for enlistment before adjourning for a drink with the justices. Bardolph collects bribes from two of the recruits, and upon Falstaff's return tells him which ones are to be released from duty. Falstaff justifies his choice of the least likely recruits in a humorous parody of military standards. After promising another visit, Falstaff leaves. In a soliloquy, he asserts that on his return he shall fleece the gullible Shallow.

*Act 4, Scene 1*
In GAULTREE FOREST the Archbishop tells his fellow rebels that Northumberland has deserted. Westmoreland appears and demands an explanation for the rebellion. The Archbishop asserts that the illness of the realm requires that they take up the role of surgeons. Westmoreland states that Lancaster, the commander of the king's army, is prepared to hear their grievances during a period of truce. Mowbray is opposed to this offer, but the Archbishop states their complaints against the king, and Westmoreland leaves. Mowbray asserts that the king will always distrust them and that they should continue to pursue victory, for only then can they be safe. The Archbishop and Hastings, however, argue that Henry genuinely desires peace.

*Act 4, Scene 2*
Lancaster meets the rebels and promises to redress all their grievances if they will disband their forces. The Archbishop and Hastings agree, but Westmoreland arrests them once their forces have dispersed. Lancaster says that he had promised only that their grievances would be redressed, not that they themselves would be pardoned, and he sentences them to death.

*Act 4, Scene 3*
Falstaff encounters a rebel officer, John COLEVILE, who recognises him and surrenders. Falstaff transfers his prisoner to Lancaster, who sends Colevile to be executed. Lancaster announces that he must go to London, where his father, King Henry, is very sick. Lancaster grants Falstaff permission to return through Gloucestershire, and he leaves. Alone, Falstaff reflects that he cannot make the unconvivial Lancaster laugh because the prince does not drink. In a long, humorous soliloquy he praises strong drink, saying that it both improves the wit and warms the spirit. He asserts that Prince Hal is courageous only because the cold blood he inherited from King Henry has been heated by his drinking.

*Act 4, Scene 4*
The dying King Henry is attended by his younger sons, the dukes of GLOUCESTER (4) and CLARENCE (2), and by Warwick. Learning that Prince Hal is at his old haunts in London, the king rails against his dissipated son. Warwick defends Hal, asserting that he is merely studying the ways of evil men, the better to judge them as king. News arrives of the final defeat of the rebels, but the king suddenly feels much weaker and is taken into a bedroom.

*Act 4, Scene 5*
Prince Hal arrives and watches alone at his sleeping father's bedside. He addresses the royal crown, declaring that the cares and stress it represents have killed the king. Believing that his father has died, the Prince meditatively puts on the crown and absently wanders from the room. The king awakes and assumes that Hal has demonstrated an impatience to see him dead. When the Prince is found, weeping in another room, the king predicts dire disorder for England when he succeeds to the throne. The Prince explains why he took the crown and prays for the return of the king's health. The king, convinced, expresses his pleasure with the Prince and offers him advice. Having become king only through usurpation, Henry says he had made enemies. While the Prince, inheriting the crown, will be more widely accepted, he will still have some of the same enemies. The king recommends overseas wars to divert the would-be rebels and to provide an arena in which Hal can prove his valour and undo his sullied reputation. The others return, and the king asks to be taken back to the JERUSALEM CHAMBER, where he wishes to die.

*Act 5, Scene 1*
Shallow, with the help of his steward, DAVY, prepares to entertain Falstaff with a dinner. Before accompanying his host indoors, Falstaff belittles his intended victim.

*Act 5, Scene 2*
Warwick and the Chief Justice regret the death of the king and the accession of the delinquent Prince. The Chief Justice expects trouble, for he once gaoled the Prince. The Prince, now called HENRY V, arrives, and he suggests that the Chief Justice may regret that incident. The jurist defends his action, however, asserting the rule of law. Hal agrees and reappoints him to his post, vowing to mend his ways and become a proper king.

*Act 5, Scene 3*
After dinner Shallow, Silence, and Falstaff drink together in Shallow's orchard. Shallow is drunkenly hospitable, and Silence sings snatches of various songs. Pistol arrives from London with word that the king has died. Falstaff, assuming that Hal, now king, will provide richly for his old friends, makes haste to go to London and claim his fortune. He promises Shallow and Pistol all they desire, and he vows vengeance on the Chief Justice.

*Act 5, Scene 4*
The Hostess and Doll Tearsheet are under arrest, having apparently been involved in a murderous tavern brawl. They revile the BEADLE who arrested them, but to no avail.

*Act 5, Scene 5*
Falstaff and his entourage, including Shallow, attend the coronation parade. Falstaff boasts that the new king will welcome him, but when Hal appears, he rejects the old man, promising him a pension but requiring him to live at least 10 miles from court. Falstaff assures Shallow that the king has only put on a public front and will send for him later that night. Shallow is dubious. The Chief Justice, accompanied by Lancaster, arrives and sends the entire group to prison, pending their expulsion from London. Lancaster expresses satisfaction with Hal's kingly behaviour and predicts that the new king will lead a military expedition to France.

*Epilogue*
A speaker, identifying himself as the author, apologises for a recent unpopular play and hopes that this one has been more satisfactory. He then speaks of himself as a dancer whose performance may make up for the play's defects. He promises that another play featuring Falstaff will continue the story. In closing he observes that Falstaff does not represent the martyr OLDCASTLE.

## COMMENTARY

*Henry IV, Part 2,* is concerned with the demands of kingship, although Falstaff plays a much greater role than he did in *Part 1.* From the Induction and 1.1, with their emphasis on the disruptions of rebellion, to the close, when Prince Hal assumes the heavy mantle of kingship as Henry V, the lessons of *2 Henry IV* are political. Hal rejects Falstaff in 5.5, the final scene, and this incident symbolises the ethic of a ruler: strict justice, though tempered by mercy.

To an even greater degree than in *Part 1,* Shakespeare here presents a picture of all England—the common people who underlie history as well as the aristocrats who make it. Palace chambers and battlefields are set against dissolute EASTCHEAP and bucolic GLOUCESTERSHIRE. In addition to several familiar Eastcheap denizens from *Part 1,* Shakespeare here presents two other extraordinary figures: the Ancient Pistol and Doll Tearsheet. In Gloucestershire, rural England is represented by Justice Shallow and a number of splendid countrymen, including Davy and Silence. In assembling these citizens, *2 Henry IV* continues the unprecedented achievement of *Part 1,* the creation of a comprehensive sense of the diverse life of England in the context of key historical events.

As in *Part 1,* Prince Hal's development is central to

the history being presented, though here he becomes a statesman rather than a warrior. However, he is an unimportant character until 4.5, when he meditates on and accepts the burden of kingship. Then, having become king in Act 5, he accepts the Chief Justice, a symbol of honesty and duty, and rejects Falstaff, an emblem of irresponsibility. Hal is committed to becoming a good king, and this is the end to which the rest of the play leads as well, but the focus of the dramatic action is elsewhere, on values opposed to good government, represented by Falstaff on one hand and the rebels on the other.

Falstaff makes quite a different impression than he did in *1 Henry IV.* He is older and in bad health, as he remarks in 1.2.229–233; the prospect of his death looms, as Doll reminds him in 2.4.229–232. He is more distinctly and unpleasantly a swindler, preying on Shallow and the Hostess and sending FEEBLE and his fellows to their probable deaths; in *Part 1* his robbery victims were the anonymous—and supposedly rich and powerful—TRAVELLERS, and his soldiers remained unseen. Further, he justifies his selfishness in *Part 2* with a flagrantly cynical appropriation of 'the law of nature' (3.2.326). He thus seems singularly ripe for a downfall.

The groundwork for Falstaff's rejection by Hal in 5.5 was laid in *Part 1,* and it is anticipated throughout *Part 2.* Falstaff's awkward encounters with the Chief Justice in 1.2 and 2.1 foreshadow this end. In addition, Hal is conspicuously absent from Falstaff's early scenes; their only encounter prior to 5.5 is Hal's somewhat hostile appearance at Falstaff's tavern party in 2.4, which ends with the Prince's cursory farewell to his old friend as he leaves to help suppress the rebellion. Hal shows no interest in Falstaff's world after that point. But after the new king so coldly and firmly dismisses him, Falstaff persists in supposing that Hal is only putting up a public front, although by this time, even the gullible and unsophisticated Shallow sees the truth. Falstaff's rejection comes as no surprise to anyone but himself. His folly in leaping boldly into Hal's coronation scene only seals his fate. His lack of judgement is, of course, the fundamental reason why he is not acceptable company for a king.

It has often been contended that one's response to Hal's rejection of Falstaff reflects one's attitude towards Shakespeare's political sensibility, perhaps towards all political philosophy. According to this theory, the extent to which one sympathises with Falstaff, who represents comic licence and freedom, limits the value that one can simultaneously place on social order. This view, however, not only denies Shakespeare's breadth of vision, which encompassed both freedom and order, but, more important, it also depends on a more sentimental outlook than that of the 16th century. The playwright's plain purpose was to bring Falstaff to a reckoning and to complete the elevation of Prince Hal to his intended destiny as the just King Henry V.

Shakespeare is clearly more sympathetic to the fat scoundrel than the Prince is, for Falstaff is still intended as an essentially delightful character. His inventive humour is still appealing; as he says himself, 'I am not only witty in myself, but the cause that wit is in other men' (1.2.8–9). In his famous praise of wine (4.3.84–123), Falstaff compares himself favourably to the cold and calculating Lancaster, and we are irresistibly inclined to agree with him. At the end of 2.4 the Hostess and Doll Tearsheet touchingly show their affection for him, although they are fully aware of his nature. His ways may bar him from being close to a responsible ruler, but they do not prevent others from appreciating his high spirits. Shakespeare's fondness for Falstaff is further demonstrated by the remarkable leniency with which the new king treats him, however frostily Hal may address him. He is allowed to live as he pleases, with a comfortable pension; clearly, the playwright did not wish to deprive his remarkable creation of sack and capons. Moreover, as the Epilogue indicates, Shakespeare intended to bring him back in another play. Falstaff is very much a part of Shakespeare's England and thus of the historical context within which the play's political questions are set

The rebellion of the nobles is at the political core of *2 Henry IV*. The threat of social disorder runs through all the HISTORY PLAYS, and in *2 Henry IV* it manifests itself both in the petty crimes of Falstaff and in the more grievous offence of the rebels. Rebellion is cast in a highly negative light. Northumberland's apocalyptic rage in 1.1.153–160 demonstrates the anarchic morals of the rebel leaders, who are willing to permit society to collapse. And, to stress his worthlessness, Northumberland is presented as treacherous to his own treacherous cause in the Induction (lines 36–37) and in 2.3. Morton describes, in 1.1.200–209, the Archbishop's sacrilegious use of religion to stimulate armed revolt; Westmoreland elaborates on the Archbishop's particular guilt in 4.1.30–52. However, Shakespeare rarely settled for a single viewpoint on any subject, and the Archbishop makes a plainly sincere response to Westmoreland, in which he states the dilemma of the royalist who nevertheless is provoked into rebellion by misgovernment. Here and in 4.2.30–42, he offers to disband the rebel forces if his complaints are heard by the king, and it is precisely this that is promised when Lancaster deceives and traps the rebel leaders.

Nonetheless, the playwright thoroughly disparages the rebels, and it is striking that he does not similarly deplore Lancaster's treachery against them. Such a scheme, common enough in the histories Shakespeare read, seems acceptable, in the play's terms, because it works against the greater evil of the uprising. It may also serve as an example of the woeful state of public life amid the dynastic struggles that dominate most of the history plays. The rebellion itself is a continuing reminder of King Henry's situation: he is a usurper, under whom the nation cannot be calm. He himself observes this several times (e.g., 3.1.57–79, 4.5.183–186), and in dying he takes comfort that Hal, a legitimate heir, will not encounter the same difficulty.

The play's focus on political turmoil is sharpened by several secondary themes, the most important of which is the unreliability of human knowledge. This motif is repeatedly stressed. At the play's outset, Rumour summons a baffling array of 'surmises, jealousies, conjectures' (Ind. 16) that humanity must face. Among the false impressions that pervade the play are the king's fear that Hal will prove a disastrous heir, Falstaff's contrary assumption that he will prove a delightful one, the rebels' expectation of aid from Northumberland, and their betrayed hopes at Gaultree. The Archbishop seems entirely justified in his plaint 'What trust is in these times?' (1.3.100). Only Prince Hal is aware—from the beginning of *1 Henry IV*—that his own position will be regal. He alone is free of misunderstanding, as befits his ultimate heroic stature as Henry V.

Recurrent references to disease and death add to the atmosphere of urgent uncertainty. Both the king and his rival, Northumberland, are physically ill, and the King's fatal sickness is particularly prominent. Falstaff, as we have seen, encounters his mortality as well; Hal notices his white hairs and says that his 'grave doth gape' (5.5.48–53). Henry says of his kingdom, 'How foul it is, what rank diseases grow' (3.1.39), and the Archbishop constructs an elaborate metaphor on the diseased nation, asserting the need to 'purge th' obstructions which begin to stop our very veins of life' (4.1.65–66).

Animal imagery, a favourite device of Shakespeare's, serves to represent the brutal energy of civil disruption: the Archbishop likens the fickle public to a dog eating its own vomit in 4.1.95–100; Northumberland speaks of the civil conflict as 'a horse [that] madly hath broke loose, and bears down all before him' (1.1.10–11). And, when the king paints a hysterical picture of England under the rule of a profligate Hal, he says, 'the wild dog shall flesh his tooth on every innocent' (4.5.131–132).

Political realities prohibit any festive, comic resolution of *2 Henry IV*. Even Hal's succession to the throne, while an optimistic conclusion to the conflicts that have marred his father's reign, is not a consummation; rather, it points onwards to the wars of Henry V. The several worlds that are juxtaposed in *2 Henry IV*—fictional versus historical, aristocratic versus plebeian, urban versus rural—are each disturbed by political events. Their rich interactions yield a convincing portrait of difficult times, pertinent in the nervous Elizabethan era when fears of rebellion pervaded political thought, and no less relevant in our own troubled time.

## SOURCES OF THE PLAY

Shakespeare's chief source for the historical material in *2 Henry IV* was Raphael HOLINSHED's *Chronicles of England, Scotland, and Ireland* (2nd ed., 1587), modified by the account of Henry's reign in Samuel DANIEL's epic poem *The Civil Wars between the two Houses of York and Lancaster* (1595). In particular the playwright was influenced by Daniel's elaborate treatment of Henry's death-bed and of his guilt as a usurper. In addition, in developing the Chief Justice, who is merely mentioned in his other sources, Shakespeare drew either on John STOW's *Annales of England* (1592), where he found an account of Hal's encounters with the jurist, or on Stow's source, Thomas ELYOT's *The Boke called the Governour* (1531). Additional details seem to have come from the anonymous farce known as the FAMOUS VICTORIES (before 1588) and from the life of Owen Glendower in the popular anthology of biographies A MIRROR FOR MAGISTRATES (1559). It has been suggested that both *Henry IV* plays may have been derived from an earlier play by Shakespeare on the same subject, but this speculation is unprovable.

## TEXT OF THE PLAY

The composition of *2 Henry IV* can be dated only approximately. The play was probably begun early in 1597 and completed before the end of 1598. The revised Epilogue refers to *Henry V*, while the version used in the earliest productions does not. We may presume, therefore, that *2 Henry IV* was in performance before *Henry V* was begun, in the spring of 1599. The survival of the name Oldcastle in the QUARTO edition of the play indicates that Shakespeare had at least begun the play before this name was changed to Falstaff. This alteration followed the first production of *1 Henry IV* in the winter season of 1596–1597.

A Quarto edition of *2 Henry IV* was published in 1600 by Andrew WISE and William ASPLEY. Printed by Valentine SIMS, this edition, known as Qa, omitted 3.1. Later, the same individuals published Qb, a reprint of Qa that included the missing scene; although the large number of surviving copies of Qa suggests that it was in circulation for some time before Qb was printed, that interval is unknown. The 1600 Quarto (Q) is considered to consist of Qa plus 3.1 from Qb. Q evidently derives from Shakespeare's FOUL PAPERS; in addition to the usual imperfections of detail associated with foul papers, Q includes the strange spelling Scilens, for the character Silence, an idiosyncrasy that helps to identify the 'Hand D' pages of SIR THOMAS MORE as Shakespearean. No other edition of the play was published prior to the FIRST FOLIO of 1623, known as F.

Because it was derived from Shakespeare's manu-script, Q has been the basic text for modern editions, but it is supplemented by material available only from F. Eight Folio passages, ranging in length from 3 to 36 lines, are not found in Q. Some of these apparent cuts in Q may have been intended to shorten the performing time of the play; others may imply CENSORSHIP. The Folio editors took this material from an unknown source, possibly a PROMPT-BOOK, that itself probably derived from Q plus a now-lost manuscript, perhaps the same one that Q was originally printed from. F varies from Q in other ways: many words and phrases are different, its punctuation is greatly reworked, and its stage directions are almost entirely altered and improved.

In addition to the published texts, there exists a 17th-century handwritten copy of a play that combines *1* and *2 Henry IV*, the DERING MANUSCRIPT. With respect to *2 Henry IV*, it derives from Qb. Because it includes minor details from the Folio versions of both plays, it is dated 1623–1624. Its variations from the published texts are not thought to reflect either alterations by Shakespeare or the practices of early productions, and modern editions do not follow it.

## THEATRICAL HISTORY OF THE PLAY

The Quarto of *2 Henry IV* (1600) states that it had been 'sundrie times publikely acted' by the CHAMBERLAIN'S MEN, and several references to its characters in various writings of the early 17th century testify that it continued to be staged. The earliest known record of a specific performance is of Thomas BETTERTON's adaptation of 1700 (revived 1720), *The Sequel of Henry the Fourth.* As this title suggests, *2 Henry IV* has generally been less popular than *1 Henry IV*, which has been produced much more frequently. In the 1720 revival Colley CIBBER (1) was a great success as Shallow, a part he took in another adaptation that was staged in 1731 and 1736.

The play was relatively popular throughout the 18th century, and numerous adaptations appeared, frequently in conjunction with *Part 1*. James QUIN played Falstaff several times, and David GARRICK played Henry IV. King George II (incognito) played Henry in a public performance of 1753, to the scandal and delight of London. Theophilus CIBBER (3) played Pistol in his own adaptation, *The Humourists* (1754). The play was produced as part of George III's coronation ceremonies in 1761 (and W. C. MACREADY revived this production for the coronation of William IV in 1821). In 1804 J. P. KEMBLE (3) played the King opposite his brother Charles KEMBLE (1) as Hal; Charles took the same role in Macready's coronation production. In 1853 Samuel PHELPS revived Betterton's version of the play, appearing as both the king and Shallow, a widely acclaimed virtuoso accomplishment. Phelps revived this version again in both 1864 and 1874; in the latter production the young Johnston FORBES-ROBERTSON played Hal. Another revival of 1874, by Charles CALVERT, was scrupulously Shakespearean.

In the 20th century 2 Henry IV has been produced as part of the numerous cycles of the history plays that have been popular, notably those at STRATFORD in 1906, 1951, and 1964. Ralph RICHARDSON's performances as Falstaff in a 1945–1946 production of both Henry IV plays were particularly admired. Several history cycles on TELEVISION since the 1950s have included 2 Henry IV. A 1987 London production demonstrated the continuing popularity of the Henry IV plays; both parts, along with Henry V, were staged on different nights of the week, and, most strikingly, theatre-goers responded with enthusiasm to marathon Saturday performances featuring all three works in succession.

**Henry V, King of England (1387–1422)**  Historical figure and title character in Henry V, victorious leader of an English invasion of FRANCE (1) during the HUNDRED YEARS WAR. (The same individual appears as PRINCE [6] HAL in 1 and 2 Henry IV.) Henry may be seen in two very different ways, in accordance with the play's essential ambivalence. The play may be taken

Shakespeare's Henry V (here played by Laurence Harvey) can be seen either as a model of English heroism, or as an hypocritical adventurer indifferent to the cost of war. (Courtesy of Culver Pictures, Inc.)

either as an epic patriotic drama or as a satirical exposure of vicious hypocrisy, depending on one's interpretation of its protagonist; many episodes support both points of view. Henry has two dramatic functions: he is a hero whose exuberant leadership carries England to triumph over a traditional foe, yet he is also a coldly Machiavellian politician who is indifferent to the human costs of war.

Henry's stature as a model of kingship is evident from the outset. In 1.1 the Archbishop of CANTERBURY (1) extols Henry as a thoughtful and devout ruler, praising his understanding of religious, military, and political matters. The king's statesmanship is demonstrated in 2.1, when he solemnly warns of the grave consequences of war. Once agreed that honour requires him to invade France, his inflammatory response to the French AMBASSADOR (1) displays an invincible martial spirit. Henry's rule is secure within his realm, and he easily foils the assassination plot of CAMBRIDGE, SCROOP (1), and GREY (3) in 2.2 and sentences the conspirators to death. The skill with which he manipulates them demonstrates his ability to handle men, while his clemency to the drunken soldier, described in 2.2.39–43, mitigates his severity. On the eve of the invasion of France, we are told, 'all the youth of England are on fire . . . following the mirror of all Christian kings' (2.Chorus.1–6). Henry inspires his forces with one of the most famous patriotic speeches in English literature (3.1.1–34). His chivalric behaviour stands out especially by comparison with his boastful opponents, the vain and foolish French. His anger at the mocking delivery of tennis balls from the DAUPHIN (3) in 1.2 is proportionate to the foolishness of the gift. On the battlefield Henry's dignified refusal to avoid conflict in 3.6 is followed immediately by the prattle of the cocky French nobility.

At AGINCOURT, in Act 4, we see the King at his most heroic. Henry shares the anxieties of the common soldiers in 4.1, and his triumphant courage and high spirits are reflected in his officers, particularly after another famous morale-raiser, the 'St Crispin's Day' speech (4.3.18–67). His weeping response to the deaths of YORK (5) and SUFFOLK (2) in 4.6 belongs to an ancient tradition of vignettes in which great heroes grieve for their slain companions. Displaying the decisiveness of a great general, he reacts harshly in a moment of danger, ordering death for the French prisoners in 4.6.37, but this action is associated in the next two scenes with revenge for a French atrocity. In 4.7 Henry's righteous anger and the approval of GOWER (2) and FLUELLEN reflect the opinion of both Shakespeare's sources and 16th-century military theory that Henry's act was praiseworthy.

Following the battle, Henry is betrothed to Princess KATHARINE (2) of France. This completes the portrait of an epic hero, who, especially if he is a king, must produce offspring to carry on his line. Henry predicts that their son shall be a great Christian hero, rescuing Constantinople from the Turks. Further, by a dramatic convention of the day, the marriage signifies a happy ending: the war has been resolved, and a bright future is promised.

Most important to Henry's stature as an epic hero, God is on his side. His battle cry asserts, 'God for Harry . . .' (3.1.34), and the traitors acknowledge God's hand in their downfall (2.2.151, 158). Henry utters frequent prayers and assertions that earthly affairs are controlled by God. He is particularly concerned about his relations with heaven in view of his father's sins of usurpation and murder, as he reveals in his prayer for victory on the eve of Agincourt (4.1. 295–311). He refuses credit for the subsequent victory, saying, 'Praised be God, and not our strength, for it!' (4.7.89) and orders that psalms of thanksgiving be sung.

Henry seems a proper epic hero, but a contrary view is also suggested from the first. The sincerity of Canterbury's praise in 1.1 is dubious, for the archbishop frankly wants to win the king's support against Parliament. The sentimental 2.1 and 2.3, in which FAL-STAFF's followers regret his illness and then mourn his passing, place the king in a moral shadow, for the knight's death is expressly attributed to Henry—'The king hath killed his heart' (2.1.88), the HOSTESS (2) says, referring to Falstaff's rejection in *2 Henry IV*. For many, this act is a coldly ungrateful example of personal betrayal, however appropriate in terms of public policy; a germ of disapproval towards Henry is thus planted before he even appears.

Henry often seems sanctimonious rather than genuinely religious. He chiefly calls on God to justify his own intentions, and he turns ostensibly religious sentiment into a casual anti-French slur in 3.6.166–167. More significantly, Henry's prayer for victory in 4.1. 295–311 may be seen as a crass material bargain with God, an invoice, as it were, for the charitable works he has paid for since becoming King. Henry's prayer follows a long passage on the difficulties of kingship, during which it did not occur to him to seek divine assistance. Had Shakespeare intended his hero as a seriously religious person, that would have been a telling and touching moment to have him turn to God. This omission is not in itself very important, but it contributes to a sense that Henry does not truly possess the Christian spirit that he projects.

These suspicions of hypocrisy are supported by the impression that Henry is that most un-Christian figure, the ruthless militarist. The morality of Henry's war is sharply questioned. In 1.1 the play's only formal representatives of Christianity plot to foment a war to protect church property, and we must doubt the propriety of Henry's cause. In Henry's angry speech to the French Ambassadors he justifies himself as an in-strument of God's will, but he brandishes ugly threats that are far from Christian in spirit. His God seems to offer an all too convenient excuse to do what he already wants to do—that is, conquer France. At this point we may recall the advice that Henry received from his dying father in *2 Henry IV*—namely, to fight a foreign war to distract potential rivals at home.

The apparent dishonesty of the archbishop's justification for war, noted above, is striking; that it is the archbishop and not Henry who makes the argument is equally telling. Henry has placed the onus on the prelate, having cautioned him, in 1.2.13–28, that the making of war is a mighty responsibility that he refuses to accept himself. This evasion recurs when the soldier WILLIAMS (2) makes a similar point in 4.1. Henry responds with a lecture on the sinfulness of all the soldiers (4.1.150–192), cleverly deflecting moral responsibility away from himself.

Henry's military heroism has a negative side as well, for he repeatedly reveals a nasty viciousness. His spirited reply to the French Ambassadors is also brutally violent, threatening death to 'many a thousand' and grief for those 'yet ungotten and unborn' (1.2.284, 287) as vengeance for a petty insult. His handling of the traitors in 2.2 is effective, but it also suggests a catlike delight in cruelty as Henry toys with his prey. The king's threats to HARFLEUR, though not carried out—the town surrenders and spares him the trouble—are extreme, promising a list of horrors including 'naked infants spitted upon pikes' (3.3.38). The references to his killing of prisoners (4.6.37, 4.7.9–10, 4.7.65), while justifying the act, are all seemingly insistent on the image of the king as executioner. And lastly his cool response to BURGUNDY's plea for peace in 5.2—'. . . you must buy that peace' (5.2.70)—is quite chilling when viewed in light of Henry's demonstrated brutality on the battlefield.

In less political contexts Henry also seems unfeeling. As we have seen, the death of Falstaff raises this point in Act 2, and the fat knight's rejection is referred to again in 4.7.47–53, where it is associated with Alexander the Great's murder of a friend. Moreover, in 3.6.110 Henry lets BARDOLPH (1) die for a petty offence in the name of discipline. The king's cold, Machiavellian nature is thus illustrated several times, contributing to the portrait, alongside that of the epic hero, of a cynical politician.

Henry's aggressive courtship of Princess KATHARINE (2), while possessing a certain bluff charm, may also seem repellent. Not only is the king falsely humble, claiming to be a 'plain soldier', (5.2.153) but he is clearly aware that she is already properly his as a trophy of war. This scene harbours the crowning irony of the play: as Henry crows over the prospective greatness of his and Katharine's future child, we know that this son is to be the hopelessly ineffective HENRY VI, who will lose the conquests Henry is presently celebrating. This is bluntly stated in the EPILOGUE, ending the play on a note of resignation and loss that flatly oppose the idea of Henry as an epic hero.

Nonetheless, Henry V was undeniably a monumental figure in the eyes of Elizabethan England, universally accepted as a great king, and Shakespeare took this status as a given. The king is the major figure in the play in either interpretation, and the playwright took pains to emphasise his importance. It appears that Falstaff was removed from the play after it was written, presumably in order to avoid impinging on Henry's significance. Further, Shakespeare altered the historical reality of Henry's reign to the same purpose. The battle of Agincourt, fought in 1415, is the central event of the play and appears to lead directly to the surrender of France. But the decisive campaign in Normandy in 1417–1419, and the importance of naval warfare in its success, is not mentioned; nor is the English alliance with Burgundy, which made Henry's final victory possible five years after Agincourt. In the battle itself the king's role is overstated by the striking omission of a crucial and well-known element, the devastation wrought by the English longbowmen. This aspect of the English victory was already legendary in Shakespeare's time, but it was not suited to the playwright's focus on Henry.

Henry V must dominate the play, for the play's essential ambivalence towards power depends entirely on the extraordinary dual nature of the protagonist, who must function as two quite different figures at the same time. Henry V is in this way unparallelled in Shakespearean drama, though many characters are greater than he in other respects. Thus he brings us to a renewed awareness of the range of his creator's genius.

## Henry V

### SYNOPSIS

*Prologue*
The PROLOGUE laments that the players cannot adequately represent such great events as King HENRY V's war against FRANCE (1). But he begs the audience's indulgence and says that he will serve as CHORUS (3).

*Act 1, Scene 1*
The Archbishop of CANTERBURY (1) and the Bishop of ELY (2) discuss a movement in Parliament to appropriate huge amounts of the church's wealth. Canterbury says that the king, despite his decadent youth (as enacted in *1* and *2 Henry IV*), is likely to support the church; he marvels at length that the king has proved himself a wise statesman. He adds that he has just offered the king an immense sum of church money to support a war in France and assure his support against Parliament, but, before Henry could accept it, the arrival of an AMBASSADOR (1) from France postponed

their conversation. Canterbury and Ely leave to witness the king's reception of the Ambassadors.

*Act 1, Scene 2*
The king summons Canterbury for a conference before receiving the Ambassadors. The archbishop delivers a long and learned justification of Henry's claim to the throne of France. Ely, the Duke of EXETER (2), and the Earl of WESTMORELAND (1) second him in recommending a war to support that claim, and Henry decides to invade. He receives the Ambassadors, who bring an insulting message from the DAUPHIN (3): Henry has gone too far in claiming certain French dukedoms; he should stay home and play games, as suits his dissolute character. A barrel of tennis balls accompanies this insolence. Henry sends the Ambassadors home with a declaration of war.

*Act 2, Chorus*
The CHORUS tells of English preparations for war in highly rhetorical terms. He also states that three men intend to kill the king in SOUTHAMPTON (1) before he can sail for France. The Chorus assures the audience that the play will transport them to France—without seasickness—after first taking them to Southampton.

*Act 2, Scene 1*
Lieutenant BARDOLPH (1) encourages Corporal NYM to forgive PISTOL, who has married the HOSTESS (2), to whom Nym had been betrothed. Bardolph wishes them reconciled before they all go to fight in France, but Nym talks of violence against Pistol. Pistol and the Hostess appear, and he and Nym exchange insults and draw swords. Bardolph's threat to kill the first to use his weapon prevents immediate bloodshed. The BOY (3) arrives, summoning the Hostess to help FALSTAFF, who is very ill, and she leaves with him. Pistol and Nym quarrel further, but Bardolph effects a truce. The Hostess returns to report that Falstaff's sickness has worsened, and they all leave to visit him.

*Act 2, Scene 2*
Exeter, Westmoreland, and the Duke of BEDFORD (1) discuss King Henry's cool pretence that he does not know of the treason intended by the Earl of CAMBRIDGE, Henry SCROOP (1), and Thomas GREY (3). Henry arrives with the three traitors, and he mentions to them his intention to pardon a drunken soldier who has been arrested for speaking disloyally of him. They all recommend severity against any challenge to the king's authority. He then shows them the formal charges against themselves. They plead for mercy, but he cites their own arguments and sentences them to death. They acknowledge his justice before being taken away to be executed.

*Act 2, Scene 3*
Falstaff's friends mourn him before departing for France. The Hostess touchingly describes his death.

### Act 2, Scene 4

The FRENCH KING lays defensive plans against the English. The Dauphin belittles Henry's military potential, but the CONSTABLE and the king remember earlier English triumphs led by Henry's ancestors. Exeter arrives as Henry's ambassador, and he delivers a demand that the French King relinquish his crown or be conquered.

### Act 3, Chorus

The Chorus asks the audience to imagine the glorious English fleet sailing to France and, further, to imagine a French ambassador offering Henry a marriage to Princess KATHARINE (2), with a dowry of dukedoms, and being turned away as English cannons begin the fighting.

### Act 3, Scene 1

At the siege of HARFLEUR, Henry encourages his troops with a speech extolling the traditional courage of English soldiers, ending with a battle cry.

### Act 3, Scene 2

Bardolph enthusiastically shouts a battle cry, but Pistol, Nym, and the Boy seek safety. FLUELLEN appears and harasses the reluctant soldiers up to the front, though the Boy stays behind long enough to soliloquise on the cowardice and dishonesty of his masters, reflecting that he hopes to leave their service soon. GOWER (2), an English officer, talks with Fluellen, MACMORRIS, and JAMY, who are Welsh, Irish, and Scottish, respectively. They discuss the tactics of siege warfare in a conversation made comical by their various dialects and stereotypical temperaments.

### Act 3, Scene 3

Henry addresses the citizens of Harfleur, vividly describing the horrors of an army sacking a town. The GOVERNOR (2) of Harfleur appears and surrenders.

### Act 3, Scene 4

In French, Princess Katharine receives a comical lesson in English from her waiting-woman, ALICE, enlivened by gross mispronunciations and inadvertent sexual references.

### Act 3, Scene 5

The French leaders marvel at the fighting abilities of the English, and the French King orders a massive assault. The Constable remarks that this show of force will surely make the English offer ransom rather than fight, for their forces are sick, hungry, and greatly outnumbered.

### Act 3, Scene 6

Gower and Fluellen discuss the English success in taking a bridge. Fluellen praises Pistol's accomplishments there but is disappointed when Pistol appears and seeks his intervention to save Bardolph, who has been sentenced to death for stealing from a church. Fluellen refuses, favouring stern discipline, and Pistol curses him and leaves. Fluellen recollects that Pistol's supposed bravery at the bridge had consisted only of bold words, and Gower elaborately describes the sort of cowardly rogue who avoids fighting and then brags of his heroics in London taverns. Henry arrives, and Fluellen tells him of Bardolph's sentence; the king approves. A French herald, MONTJOY, arrives with a proposed truce if Henry will offer a large ransom. While admitting that he is at a disadvantage, Henry refuses to pay and prepares for battle.

### Act 3, Scene 7

The night before the battle, a group of the French leaders converse idly, anticipating an easy victory.

### Act 4, Chorus

The Chorus asks the audience to imagine the two opposing camps, busy in the night preparing for battle. The overconfident French play games, gambling prospective English prisoners with each other. The rueful English contemplate defeat and death. However, he says, Henry moves among his troops, raising their spirits. He adds that the actors will depict the ensuing battle of AGINCOURT, although their petty presentation will disgrace the battle's fame.

### Act 4, Scene 1

King Henry's cheerful approach to the coming battle is mirrored by an aged knight, Sir Thomas ERPINGHAM. Henry dismisses his attendants, and, incognito, encounters several soldiers in his army. The disguised king is roundly cursed by Pistol when he defends Fluellen. Henry then overhears a conversation between Fluellen and Gower and reflects that Fluellen is a good and careful officer. He next meets three English soldiers, one of whom, Michael WILLIAMS (2), asserts that, while common soldiers will be killed, the king risks only capture, after which he will be ransomed. Henry, speaking as another commoner, insists that this is not so; the king has vowed to die rather than be taken prisoner. Williams doubts that this will happen. After a brief argument, Williams agrees to fight his opponent after the battle, if they both live, and they exchange tokens of identity, so that they can recognise each other in the day time: each will wear the other's glove on his hat. The soldiers depart, and Henry, in a long soliloquy, meditates on the cares of kingship. Erpingham appears and delivers a request that the king confer with his nobles, and Henry sends him to convene a meeting at his tent. Alone again, the king prays that God will not permit his soldiers to fail as punishment for his father's deposition and murder of RICHARD II (enacted in *Richard II*), since he has reburied Richard and made other formal atonements for the crime.

*Act 4, Scene 2*
The French nobles, about to begin the battle, remark on the feeble opposition.

*Act 4, Scene 3*
The English nobles, though ready to fight, comment on the degree to which they are outnumbered. Westmoreland wishes they had reinforcements from England, but Henry observes that their triumph will be the greater because they are fewer. He would prefer that the faint-hearted depart so that the honour of the battle need be shared only by those who are worthy. He predicts that the day will be long remembered as a great one for England and that all those present will value the experience for the rest of their lives. Montjoy reappears with another offer of peace for ransom, but Henry sends him back with a proud refusal.

*Act 4, Scene 4*
Pistol captures a FRENCH SOLDIER and threatens bloody death if he is not paid a ransom, but the soldier doesn't understand English. Pistol comically, but viciously, rants at his helpless prisoner, until the Boy interprets into English the Frenchman's offer of money, and Pistol marches off with him. Alone, the Boy reflects that Pistol has avoided the fate of Bardolph and Nym—both hanged for theft—only through cowardice, having been afraid to steal. He observes that only he and other boys are with the army's baggage train, which makes it a good target for the French.

*Act 4, Scene 5*
The French nobles hysterically try to organise a counter-attack against the English, who are winning the battle.

*Act 4, Scene 6*
Exeter gives Henry a touching account of the death of the Duke of YORK (5). When it appears that French reinforcements have entered the battle, Henry orders all prisoners killed.

*Act 4, Scene 7*
Fluellen and Gower discuss the cowardly French massacre of the unarmed boys tending the baggage train. Praising Henry's response to this outrage—ordering the death of all prisoners—Fluellen presents a long and comical comparison between the king and Alexander the Great. Henry arrives and sends a messenger to tell the remaining French knights that they should prepare to fight or flee, for all French prisoners are to be killed. Montjoy reappears to ask that the fighting stop so that the French can bury their dead, and he concedes that the English have won the battle. Fluellen praises the king, noting his Welsh blood. Williams appears and tells the king of the oath that the glove on his hat represents. Henry sends him with a message to

Gower. The king then gives Fluellen a glove to wear on his hat, saying that he had captured it in the battle and that anyone who challenges it is a friend of the French and should be arrested. Fluellen, proud of his assignment, is also sent to Gower. Henry then instructs Warwick and Gloucester to follow Fluellen and prevent a fight between him and Williams.

*Act 4, Scene 8*
Williams encounters Fluellen and strikes him; Fluellen prepares to fight, as Warwick and Gloucester prevent him. The king arrives, explains the circumstances, and gives Williams a glove full of coins. Fluellen attempts to increase the reward with his own shilling, but Williams rejects it. Henry reads a long list of French noblemen killed in the battle, along with only four English knights, and he orders that religious rites of thanksgiving be observed.

*Act 5, Chorus*
The Chorus tells of Henry's triumphal return to London, of the peace negotiation between England and France, and of Henry's subsequent return to France.

*Act 5, Scene 1*
Fluellen tells Gower that Pistol has insulted the leek, symbol of WALES (1), that he wears in his hat. Pistol appears, and Fluellen cudgels him and forces him to eat the leek. The humiliated Pistol decides that he will return to England and take up a life of petty crime. He will pretend the scars from Fluellen's beating were obtained in battle.

*Act 5, Scene 2*
King Henry, the French King, and their respective entourages, meet to sign a peace treaty. The Duke of BURGUNDY (2) makes an eloquent plea for peace, and Henry replies that peace must be bought, as the treaty provides. The French King requests a final consultation on certain points, and Henry sends his noblemen to negotiate with the French. Henry is left with Princess Katharine and Alice. The king courts the princess, and their language difficulties are humorous. She is uncertain what to think, but she concedes that, if her father agrees to the marriage, she will also consent. The negotiators return, and all parties accept the marriage. Henry orders that wedding preparations begin.

*Epilogue*
The Chorus states in a SONNET that this ends the presentation of Henry's glory. Conquered France was left to the infant HENRY VI, during whose reign it was lost through English discord and mismanagement, as the actors have often depicted on stage.

## COMMENTARY

*Henry V* completes the second TETRALOGY of Shakespeare's HISTORY PLAYS, and this work restates a problem first dealt with in *Richard II:* Can sensitivity and warmth—the spiritual values that elevate human life—coexist with the ruthless strength and shrewdness that a ruler needs to govern? In *Henry V* this question can be plausibly answered in two ways that seem to be mutually exclusive. Some readers find the play a patriotic tribute to Henry, who is seen as an ideally heroic leader who takes England to new heights of power and defeats a traditional enemy; he is an hero suited to the threatening times England endured in the late 16th century, when the play was written, and the play has been popular in times of national crisis ever since. Alternatively, though, the play is a mordant commentary on politics and war, in which Henry is a Machiavellian militarist, a cold-blooded, power-hungry hypocrite who uses religion to justify the horrors of an unnecessary war. This anti-heroic view has found its audience primarily in recent decades, but the observations that war is hellish and that it is often conducted for selfish ends are not new, and Shakespeare could easily have found them suitable material for a play.

Both readings are equally valid, and they may reflect Shakespeare's own ambivalence towards the subject of power. In either interpretation, *Henry V* is a powerful dramatic work whose epic quality is plainly intended to invoke the grandeur of the ancient world, whether seriously or sardonically. For instance, the use of the Chorus, itself a direct reference to ancient Roman drama, places the action in a timeless, semi-mythical context. Such lines as the Prologue's desire for 'a Muse of fire' (Prologue.1) and the description of the night as filling 'the wide vessel of the universe' (4.Chorus.3) are unquestionably grand, and they lend a monumental air—ironic or otherwise—to the work. A sense of great moments passing into legend is often called forth in this play, as when Henry declares, 'Then call we this the field of Agincourt, fought on the day of Crispin Crispianus' (4.7.92–93).

However, Shakespeare remains committed to the great portrait of the common people of England that he began so successfully in the *Henry IV* plays. A group of new characters, led by Fluellen, provides a glimpse of Henry's army. Part of their function is to exemplify the stalwart bearing of the common soldier, lending dignity to Henry, but they also offer a frequently humorous cross-section of the British public. In 3.2, known as the 'international' scene, Gower, Macmorris, Jamy, and Fluellen represent England, Ireland, Scotland, and Wales respectively in a tribute to British unity under Henry. Jamy and Macmorris are simple stereotypes, but Fluellen and Gower have more depth. Likewise, Henry's conversation with BATES and Williams in 4.1 is humanly complex and real and stirs our feelings in preparation for his important soliloquy on the difficulties of kingship (4.1.236–290). These vignettes reveal that Henry's strength derives from his subjects, who in turn respond to him and are proud to be British.

However, the world of the BOAR'S HEAD TAVERN, familiar from *1* and *2 Henry IV*, is treated less sympathetically. Falstaff dies off-stage almost immediately, and the Hostess' role is brief, if poignant. Then Bardolph and Nym die ignominiously, and the Boy is killed in an atrocity of war. Finally, Pistol is humiliated by Fluellen in 5.1. These incidents serve both interpretations of the play, for, while they may represent a defeat for anarchy by the new order of the epic hero, at the same time they present Henry as an unforgiving, unfeeling politician who can cite principles of discipline while permitting an old friend to die.

Earlier, the account of Falstaff's death makes this point more explicitly. We hear of his illness and death in two sentimental scenes, 2.1 and 2.3, that give emotional resonance to his EASTCHEAP cronies; Pistol and Nym, in particular, are otherwise little better than mindlessly vicious. Their grief lends them a pathos that helps sustain the epic quality of the play, but, on the other hand, Falstaff's final agony is expressly attributed to Henry's cold and Machiavellian nature—'The king hath killed his heart' (2.1.88), the Hostess says, referring to Falstaff's rejection in *2 Henry IV*—and this contributes to the play's sardonic and cynical viewpoint.

Various sorts of evidence (see FALSTAFF) reflect the likelihood that Falstaff was originally the chief comic character of the play, and Shakespeare's deletion of the fat knight is indicative of his purposes. Henry's central role could only be compromised by the presence of so massive a personality; in either interpretation Falstaff's cheerful immorality would only distract from its primary focus, be it an epic vision of England's greatness or a biting assessment of Henry's calculating militarism.

Henry's invasion of France and the victory at Agincourt were already legendary peaks of English glory in Shakespeare's day, and national pride is patently evident at many points in the play; several passages—especially 3.1.1–34 and 4.3.56–67—have been standard items of patriotic rhetoric since they first appeared. However, the play is not merely rousing pageantry; the morality of Henry's war is questioned throughout. The major justification for the war is presented by the Archbishop of Canterbury in 1.2.33–95, and while this speech may be read with great solemnity, it also has a more ironic side—for example, in Canterbury's assertion that his complicated and legalistic argument makes Henry's claim to the French crown 'as clear as is the summer's sun' (1.2.86). That the archbishop and not Henry makes the argument demonstrates Henry's manipulative nature: he places the onus on the archbishop, cautioning him, in 1.2.13–28, that the justification of war is a mighty responsibility, but he refuses to accept that responsibility when Williams makes a similar point in 4.1.

More boldly, the play commingles with its sense of heroic chivalry several passages that are explicit condemnations of war, including Henry's 'conjuration' to the archbishop just mentioned. Best known is Burgundy's plea for peace in 5.2.24–67, in which the plight of a war-torn land is movingly evoked. Significantly, Henry's response is the cool insistence that France must 'buy that peace' (5.2.70).

Most important, the savagery of war is repeatedly described in vivid speeches that compellingly counter the heroic idea of warfare that they ostensibly promote, beginning subtly with the archbishop's strangely inappropriate equation of war booty with the peaceful activity of bees gathering honey and quickly escalating to Henry's inflamed response to the Dauphin's mockery in 1.2.261–296. At Harfleur the king describes in grisly detail the fate the town will undergo if his soldiers loot it (3.4.1–41). While Henry is in fact merciful to the citizens—because they do in fact surrender, sparing him the trouble of a battle—his graphic threat is a stark reminder of the horrors of war. Williams' description of a battle also illustrates the terrifying reality of warfare, in terms that are far from conventionally heroic rhetoric: '. . . all those legs and arms and heads, chopped off in a battle' (4.1.137–138).

Moreover, the only actual combat we see involves Pistol, who is systematically deplored throughout the play. He is decried at length for cowardice, vanity, and downright criminality by Gower in 3.6 and the Boy in 3.2 and 4.4. Further, Pistol makes us aware of a frequent consequence of war, the social havoc that can be wreaked by hardened and embittered soldiers returning to a civilian population. Having failed in war, he declares that he will become a professional thief on his return to London (5.1.89–95).

Thus the evils of war are abundantly demonstrated, even as the triumph of English arms is glorified. Both messages are strongly reinforced by the seemingly anticlimactic courtship scene, 5.2. First, Henry's development as an epic hero is brought to its proper climax by his marriage; he woos his bride briskly, with joyous predictions of a happy marriage and fine offspring. He is now a complete hero whose fine traits and accomplishments can be carried forward into the future. Moreover, the supremacy of England over France is again emphasised. However, Henry's aggressive wooing of Katharine may also be seen as an extension of his brutal conquest. In addition, the final bankruptcy of Henry's cause is frankly, if subtly, asserted: Henry predicts great heroism for his son, but we know that this son will become the ineffectual HENRY VI, under whom England's French conquests will be lost; this is expressly mentioned in the Epilogue. These references remind us, as they reminded Shakespeare's original audience—to whom all of these matters were much more familiar—that *Henry V* actually presents a mere interlude in the bloody and tragic tale of England's disruption by the selfish ambitions of feuding aristocrats. This heavy irony chillingly closes the play on a note of failure and resignation that does much to offset the epic nature of the story.

Some critics view the play's ambiguities as unintentional, claiming that Shakespeare intended a portrayal of heroic idealism but failed to present it convincingly, perhaps due to an unconscious revulsion against authority. Others assert that the play's emphasis on Henry's Machiavellian nature conflicts with his status as a national hero, resulting in a confused political statement. Perhaps a compromise position permits the fullest response: Shakespeare may have accepted Henry's status as a hero while also being aware of the sordidness of political life. In the TETRALOGY that closes with *Henry V*, Shakespeare developed his ideal of a King whose human sensitivity matches his capacity for ruthlessness, but in doing so, he perhaps discovered the limitations imposed on this ideal by the nature of power.

Shakespeare's instinctive response to the irreducible complexity of life was to be further reflected in the great plays of the next several years. *Julius Caesar*, another play about power and idealism, followed almost immediately; the great tragedies pose questions about the reliability of human motives, whether political or otherwise—questions that are implicit in the ambiguities of *Henry V*. The need for social order is an important issue throughout Shakespeare's work; however, so is an evident distrust of those who hold authority. We can only conclude that the playwright recognised the paradox that underlies much political thought from the late Middle Ages to the present: the only forms of power that seem fully moral—such as those outlined in Thomas MORE's *Utopia* and its successors—are impossible to achieve. Thus the ambivalence of *Henry V* reflects our most profound political ideals as well as our most disturbing fears of political power.

## SOURCES OF THE PLAY

Shakespeare's chief source for the historical material in *Henry V* was Raphael HOLINSHED's *Chronicles of England, Scotland, and Ireland* (2nd ed., 1587), supplemented by *The Union of the Two Noble and Illustre Families of Lancaster and York* (1548) by Edward HALL (2). Other historical details may have come from the chronicles of Robert FABYAN (1516) and John STOW (1592). Shakespeare may also have read several Latin biographies of King Henry, written during the monarch's lifetime or shortly thereafter: the *Henrici Quinti Angliae Regis Gesta*, written by an army chaplain who was present at Agincourt; the *Vita et Gesta Henrici Quinti,* whose anonymous author is known as Pseudo-Elmham; and the *Vita Henrici Quinti,* by Tito Livio, which was translated as *The First English Life of King Henry the Fifth* (1513).

Several fictional episodes may have been inspired by other works. The Dauphin's insulting gift of tennis balls in 1.2, Pistol's capture of the French Soldier in 4.4, and Henry's courtship of Katharine in 5.2 probably derive from similar scenes in an earlier play about Henry V, the FAMOUS VICTORIES (before 1588). Also, Katharine's language lesson in 3.4 closely resembles several scenes in 16th-century French farces, suggesting that Shakespeare had read some of these plays, although they were published only in France and never translated into English. Henry's clemency to the drunken soldier, described in 2.2. 39–43, may derive from a similar episode in PLUTARCH's *Lives of the Noble Grecians and Romans,* translated by Thomas NORTH (1579). And the Archbishop's comparison of human society to a hive of bees (1.2.187–204) was probably inspired by a passage in the *Georgics* of VIRGIL.

## TEXT OF THE PLAY

We know that *Henry V* was written in the spring or summer of 1599, for it contains a plain allusion to a contemporary event. In 5.Chorus.30–32, the CHORUS (3) refers to the military expedition of the Earl of ESSEX (2) to Ireland, hoping that he would return triumphantly. Essex left London in March 1599 and returned ignominiously in September. The reference was probably made in the spring, for it quickly became known that the expedition was destined for failure.

The play first appeared in print in a QUARTO edition of 1600, printed by Thomas CREEDE for publishers Thomas MILLINGTON and John BUSBY. This edition, known as Q1, is a BAD QUARTO—that is, it was recorded from memory by actors who had appeared in it, and its text is seriously flawed. Moreover, Q1 lacks the Prologue, Epilogue, all of the speeches of the Chorus, three other whole scenes, and long portions of six others. Q2 (1602) and Q3 (1619), both published by Thomas PAVIER, are reprinted from Q1; they differ from it only accidentally and omit the same material. Q3 was part of the notorious FALSE FOLIO and is spuriously dated 1608.

The FIRST FOLIO version of the play (1623) is the first to present the missing material, and it has been the basis of all subsequent editions. Descriptive stage directions, the presence of a GHOST CHARACTER (see BEAUMONT [1]), and idiosyncratic spellings known to have been used by Shakespeare suggest that the Folio text was printed from the playwright's FOUL PAPERS. Minor details derived from Q3 indicate that the printers also used a copy of that edition.

## THEATRICAL HISTORY OF THE PLAY

The title page of the 1600 edition of *Henry V* asserts that the play had already been 'sundry times played', but the earliest known performance was held at the court of King JAMES I on January 7, 1605. No other 17th-century production is known, and the play has been popular only intermittently since then. A 1723 adaptation eliminated the comic characters from Eastcheap. David GARRICK produced Shakespeare's text in the 1750s, playing the Chorus. John Philip KEMBLE (3) played the King in his own quite successful version of the play between 1788 and 1811. W. C. MACREADY also played Henry several times, culminating in a memorably spectacular production of 1839. Nineteenth century producers were inclined to extraordinary effects; in 1859 Charles KEAN (1) staged a triumphal march after Agincourt that employed 550 actors. Charles CALVERT presented *Henry V* in both London (1872) and New York (1875).

At about the turn of the 20th century F. R. BENSON (1) played Henry, but the play has not often been staged since. Its patriotic aspect made it successful during both world wars; *Henry V* has been performed frequently as an anti-war play in Britain and America since the 1950s, as the nuclear age and its series of small but vicious conflicts have generated strong pacifist sentiments in Western society. Among the most notable productions was that of Peter HALL (5) at STRATFORD in 1960. The play has also been produced as part of a number of cycles of the HISTORY PLAYS, notably those at Stratford in 1901, 1906, 1951, and 1977 and on British TELEVISION in 1960, one of six television versions of the play. *Henry V* has twice been made a FILM: Laurence OLIVIER's patriotic wartime version (1944; music by William WALTON) contrasts with the bleaker 1989 movie by Kenneth Branagh (b. 1961). A 1987 London stage production demonstrated the continuing public interest in the play: both *Henry IV* plays and *Henry V* were staged on different nights of the week, and, most strikingly, theatre-goers responded with enthusiasm to marathon Saturday performances featuring all three works in succession.

**Henry VI, King of England (1421–1471)** Historical figure and title character of *1, 2,* and *3 Henry VI.* Despite their titles, King Henry is not the leading figure in any of the *Henry VI* plays. In *Part 1* he is a child, and even the story of the nobles who presume upon his weakness is overshadowed by the account of the military loss of FRANCE (1) and the bravery of TALBOT. In *Part 2* Henry is merely a witness to the political developments that occupy the play: the fall of GLOUCESTER (4) and the rise of YORK (8). In *Part 3* he is more articulate but no less helpless. Pious and plaintive, he is crushed between the contending forces that his weakness has allowed to rise. He is finally killed, and his corpse appears early in *Richard III*.

Henry is a virtuous man; he is gentle, thoughtful, and governed by a sense of moral values. However, fate has placed him on a throne and he lacks the ruthless vigour required of a medieval ruler. In fact, he is a paragon of weakness—a vacuum into which disorder rushes—and the HISTORY PLAYS are about order and disorder.

In *1 Henry VI* the king is an infant at the outset and only a young man at the end. He is distressed by the rivalries he sees around him but is unable to resolve them, being entirely incompetent in worldly matters. In his most important scene in the play (4.1.134–173), Henry makes a grave error in his haste to defuse the hostility between York and SOMERSET (3), dividing the English military command between the two disputants. At the close of the play, he succumbs to the unscrupulous arguments of the Earl of SUFFOLK (3) and agrees to marry MARGARET (1), a decision that the subsequent plays demonstrate to have been disastrous for England and for Henry himself.

In *2 Henry VI* the king, although an adult, is no more in control of his kingdom than he was in his youth. His chief interest is religion, and, in the face of dangerous dissensions, his only response is to preach the virtues of unity and peace. He is thoroughly manipulated by others, first by Suffolk and then, after that lord's death, by Queen Margaret. He permits the ruin of Gloucester, although knows it to be unjust. Even when faced with the bloody rebellion led by Jack CADE, the king cannot take decisive action, but again thinks first of his religion. When York rebels, opening the WARS OF THE ROSES, Henry is again quite helpless. He realises his own unsuitability for command and regrets his position in life.

In *3 Henry VI* the king attempts to bring about an end to the growing civil war, but the leaders of the two factions, York and his son Richard (see RICHARD III) on one side and Margaret on the other, will not be appeased. Henry protests the barbarities that ensue. He is the only important character in the play who does not espouse the principle of revenge, but he cannot influence the action. His position as king is well exemplified during the dispute among the nobles in 2.2, where he twice demands to speak (at 117 and 119–120) and has no chance to say another word in the scene. In 2.5, a scene central to the play, Henry withdraws from a raging battle to meditate lyrically on the virtues of a pastoral existence that is as far removed from his reality as it imaginably could be. In stark contrast, he immediately witnesses the grief of the SON THAT HATH KILLED HIS FATHER and the FATHER THAT HATH KILLED HIS SON. He is completely dispirited after these incidents; this gentle man is finally crushed by his world. Only as he is killed does Henry again

come alive on the stage, prophesying the future crimes of his murderer, in anticipation of the next play in the cycle, *Richard III*.

The character and career of the historical Henry VI are less clearly delineated. While he was certainly not the strong, activist monarch that his father, HENRY V, had been, it is uncertain how much his courtiers manipulated him. He possessed the powers of a medieval king and could not be defied if he were to insist on something. Even in Shakespeare, when he decrees the banishment of Suffolk, the earl leaves. However, it is uncertain when and on what points he stood firm, so we cannot know how much he is to blame for the wartime policies of the 1440s (in *Part 1*), for the unrest of the following decade (in *Part 2*), or for the policies of the civil war period. It is known that, in the early 1450s, Henry was literally incompetent for a time, being beset with a mental illness that rendered him speechless and almost immobile. The playwright chose to ignore this episode (during which York ruled and the country remained stable and at peace)—perhaps because it would have aggrandised York, perhaps becuase he wished to avoid offending the dignity of a ruler.

In any case, Shakespeare was more concerned with drama than with history, and, as Henry's character develops through the plays, we can observe the young playwright learning how to devise a suitable tragic figure whose very virtues are his undoing. The germ of some of Shakespeare's great characters is here: a man who is good finds himself in a situation where his limitations generate an evil that crushes him. In *Richard II*, and later in *Hamlet* and *King Lear*, the drama can rest upon this predicament. However, in the *Henry VI* plays the playwright had not yet honed his skills so finely and Henry VI can merely speak of his woeful ineffectuality while the world sweeps him away.

## *Henry VI*, PART 1

### SYNOPSIS

*Act 1, Scene 1*

The play opens on the funeral of King HENRY V; the Duke of BEDFORD (1) notes astrological portents of disaster. The Duke of GLOUCESTER (4) and the Bishop of WINCHESTER (1) argue, disrupting the ceremony. A MESSENGER (3) arrives with news of disastrous military defeats in FRANCE (1). A second Messenger arrives, bringing news of a general rebellion of France against England, featuring the crowning of the Dauphin as King CHARLES VII, in violation of the treaty enforced by Henry V, and the rallying to his cause of several important noblemen, including the BASTARD (2) OF ORLÉANS, REIGNIER, and the Duke of ALENÇON. Another Messenger arrives to tell of the defeat of England's leading knight, TALBOT, wounded and captured due to the cowardice of another English commander, Sir John FASTOLFE. Bedford vows to lead reinforcements to France, and the Messenger relates that the army under the Earl of SALISBURY (3) is pinned down outside ORLÉANS (1).

### Act 1, Scene 2

At the siege of Orléans, Charles VII, Alençon, and Reignier exult in their recent good fortune and mock the English. An assault occurs, and the French are driven off-stage. The three French leaders re-enter, cursing the English, and decide that they will abandon the town. The Bastard of Orléans arrives. He describes a young woman, JOAN LA PUCELLE, who has been sent by a vision from heaven to aid the French forces. Joan enters and offers to demonstrate her God-given military capacities in single combat with Charles. Charles accepts the challenge and is overwhelmed. He accepts her offer of assistance. Alençon and Reignier ask about plans for Orléans, and the newly inspired Charles declares that they will fight it out.

### Act 1, Scene 3

The Duke of Gloucester and the Bishop of Winchester argue about the right to command the Tower of London. They and their men come to blows. The MAYOR (2) OF LONDON enters, with the king's order commanding public peace. The disputants separate with insults and challenges.

### Act 1, Scene 4

The MASTER-GUNNER of Orléans instructs a BOY (1) to keep watch on a tower where English soldiers come to observe the besieged city. Several Englishmen, including Salisbury and Talbot, appear on the tower. Talbot explains that he has been exchanged for a captured Frenchman. They begin to plan an attack on the city, but they are struck by a cannonball. Salisbury falls badly wounded, and another man is killed. Talbot cries out against the loss of Salisbury's heroism and leadership. A Messenger arrives with the news that Charles and Joan have arrived with an army to raise the siege.

### Act 1, Scene 5

Skirmishing, Joan pursues a group of Englishmen across the stage. Talbot and Joan fight to a draw. Joan says that Talbot's time has not yet come, and she enters the city with the successful French troops, leaving Talbot to bemoan the poor state of English morale. In another skirmish, the English are driven back into their trenches, and Talbot concedes defeat.

### Act 1, Scene 6

Joan, Charles, Reignier, and Alençon assemble on the walls of Orléans to celebrate their victory over the English.

### Act 2, Scene 1

With a group of soldiers, Talbot, Bedford, and the Duke of BURGUNDY (2), an ally of the English, assault Orléans. The French leaders are driven over the walls. The Frenchmen exchange recriminations, but Joan encourages them to think of counter-attack. However, an English SOLDIER (1) enters, shouting Talbot's name as a war cry, and the French party flees in panic.

### Act 2, Scene 2

Bedford, Burgundy, and Talbot mourn the dead Salisbury. A Messenger arrives with an invitation for Talbot from a French noblewoman, the COUNTESS (1) of AUVERGNE, who wishes to entertain the valorous conqueror. Talbot leaves with the Messenger, but he first whispers something to a CAPTAIN (2).

### Act 2, Scene 3

The Countess of Auvergne gloats over her plan to capture Talbot. He arrives, and she mocks his physique. Offended, he begins to leave, and she announces his capture. But he springs his counter-plot, blowing his horn to summon a waiting troop of soldiers, who immediately free him.

### Act 2, Scene 4

Richard Plantagenet (see YORK [8]) argues hotly with the Duke of SOMERSET (3) in the company of several other men. Richard plucks a white rose from a garden tree, and calls on those who support him to do likewise. Somerset immediately takes a red rose as his own emblem. The Earl of WARWICK (2) joins Plantagenet; Suffolk sides with Somerset. Both Plantagenet and Somerset agree that the dispute should be settled by a majority vote among the group. However, when most support Plantagenet, Somerset hints at a duel. He goes on to cast aspersions on Plantagenet, referring to the execution of his father, the Earl of CAMBRIDGE, for treason. Plantagenet counters that the execution had not been carried out legally. He threatens action against Somerset, who replies in kind and departs. Warwick assures Plantagenet that he will be reinstated as Duke of York.

### Act 2, Scene 5

In the Tower of London, Plantagenet visits a dying relative, MORTIMER (1), who is a prisoner. Plantagenet wants to know the story of his father's death. Mortimer tells of the deposition of King RICHARD II by HENRY IV, head of the Lancastrian branch of the royal family. Mortimer, of the YORK (1) branch, had been the legitimate heir to the throne, but an attempt to install him as king has resulted in his imprisonment for life while still a young man. In the reign of Henry V, Mortimer's brother-in-law, who had been Richard Plantagenet's father, had repeated the attempt to crown Mortimer and was executed for it. Mortimer names Plantagenet his successor, and he dies, after cautioning the younger man not to act against the house of LANCAS-

TER (1), which is too strong to be removed. Plantagenet vows that he will begin to seek vengeance for his family by becoming reinstalled as Duke of York at the forthcoming Parliament.

*Act 3, Scene 1*
In the Parliament House, Winchester and Gloucester and their respective supporters argue violently. King HENRY VI, still a child, pleads for peace between the factions. The Mayor enters, reporting that the followers of Gloucester and Winchester are battling in the streets. Two SERVING-MEN burst in, fighting. The king continues to plead for peace; Gloucester says he is willing. Winchester, reluctant, finally agrees, and the servingmen are dismissed. The king agrees to restore Plantagenet as Duke of York. Gloucester announces that all the preparations have been made for Henry to be crowned King of France in Paris. As the others depart, Exeter remains and, in a soliloquy, predicts disaster for the English forces.

*Act 3, Scene 2*
Outside the gates of ROUEN, Joan and four soldiers gain entrance to the city disguised as tradesmen. She signals to the French troops, who take the city. The French leaders taunt the English, who are now outside the walls. Talbot and Burgundy exchange vows to recapture the town immediately. The dying Bedford, confined to an invalid's chair, refuses to leave the scene of battle. The skirmishing begins, and Fastolfe appears, fleeing in panic. The French are defeated, and Bedford, pronouncing himself satisfied, dies in his chair. Talbot and Burgundy exult in their victory and eulogise Bedford.

*Act 3, Scene 3*
The French leaders call the Duke of Burgundy to a parley to convince him to desert the English. Joan speaks to him of the misery of his homeland and asserts that the English are not his true friends. While suggesting that he may have been bewitched by Joan, Burgundy does change sides, declaring himself an ally of France.

*Act 3, Scene 4*
Talbot is knighted by Henry in Paris, where the king has come to be crowned. VERNON (1) and BASSET engage in another round of the York-Somerset rivalry, exchanging insults and threats.

*Act 4, Scene 1*
Winchester crowns the king, and the GOVERNOR (2) of Paris kneels and accepts the oath administered by Gloucester. Fastolfe arrives with a message from Burgundy. Talbot tears off the Order of the Garter that Fastolfe wears, declaring him a coward, and the king banishes Fastolfe. Gloucester reads Burgundy's letter, in which he declares his changed allegiance. Talbot is ordered to march against Burgundy and departs spir-

itedly. Vernon and Basset appear, demanding a trial by combat. Their dispute spreads, and York challenges Somerset to a duel. Gloucester intervenes, and the king attempts to restore order. To demonstrate his even-handedness, he foolishly divides the command of the English forces, assigning the infantry to York and the cavalry to Somerset.

*Act 4, Scene 2*
Talbot appears before the walls of BORDEAUX and demands the surrender of the city. A GENERAL on the walls refuses, confident in the strength of the approaching French army. Talbot recognises danger, and he urges his troops to fight fiercely.

*Act 4, Scene 3*
York receives a Messenger, who tells of the force that is marching to attack Talbot, and he curses Somerset for not providing cavalry support. Sir William LUCY (2) arrives from Bordeaux with an urgent plea for reinforcements. He is resisted by York, who continues to accuse Somerset.

*Act 4, Scene 4*
Lucy approaches Somerset with the same plea, and Somerset refuses, criticising York for a bad plan. He refuses to send cavalry without an explicit request from York. Lucy cries out that Talbot will be defeated and killed, and he blames Somerset for feuding.

*Act 4, Scene 5*
Talbot tells his young son, JOHN (6), that he should flee the certain death to be expected in the upcoming battle. John refuses, citing the honour of the family. They debate the matter, but the boy insists that he will stay.

*Act 4, Scene 6*
In the midst of the battle, Talbot rescues his son, fighting off surrounding attackers. The father describes the fierce fighting that has occurred, and he renews his insistence that his son should flee, but John again refuses.

*Act 4, Scene 7*
Talbot, mortally wounded, mourns the death of his son, killed in the battle, and then dies also. The victorious French leaders talk of John Talbot's valour and express thanks for York and Somerset's absence. Lucy appears, under a flag of truce, to retrieve the bodies of the two Talbots.

*Act 5, Scene 1*
Gloucester tells King Henry that a peace treaty has been arranged, and that a marriage, intended to secure the peace, has been proposed between the king and the daughter of a French nobleman, the Earl of Armagnac. The King agrees to treaty and marriage, and the visiting ambassadors are summoned to receive his formal acceptance.

*Act 5, Scene 2*

The French leaders rejoice at the news that Paris has risen against the English, but they are then disturbed by further news that the English army, reunited, is approaching.

*Act 5, Scene 3*

Joan uses witchcraft to summon a group of FIENDS, but these spirits silently refuse to aid her, and she realises that all is indeed lost. After a skirmish, York defeats Burgundy and takes Joan prisoner. He leads her away as Suffolk enters with MARGARET (1) of Anjou as his prisoner. He has already fallen in love with her, and he devises a plot to make her his lover, although he is already married. He offers to marry her to King Henry and make her Queen of England if she will be his lover. She accepts, on the condition that her father, Reignier, agree. Reignier is summoned, and he does agree, provided that he be awarded his home territories, Anjou and Maine. Suffolk promises to arrange this, and he leaves Margaret with her father.

*Act 5, Scene 4*

Joan, condemned to be burned, encounters her father, a SHEPHERD (1), but she refuses to acknowledge him, claiming descent from royalty. She declares that her death will bring damnation to her executioners. She is nevertheless ordered to the stake. Next, she claims she is pregnant, but she is sent to her death, cursing England. The French leaders arrive to settle the details of the peace. Charles at first refuses to declare himself a subject of the English king, but Reignier and Alençon convince him to sign, for he can always break his word later.

*Act 5, Scene 5*

Suffolk's description of Margaret's virtues has caused the King to desire her. Gloucester objects, citing the earlier marriage agreement. However, the king orders Suffolk to return to France to arrange a marriage to Margaret. The play closes with a soliloquy by Suffolk, in which he proposes to rule the kingdom himself, through Margaret.

COMMENTARY

*1 Henry VI* is the first of Shakespeare's HISTORY PLAYS, and it shares with the later works a particular emphasis on the state. The development of individual characters is not very important, for the theme is English history. This play commences the TETRALOGY of dramas dealing with the WARS OF THE ROSES, the great crisis that formed the English nation as it was known to Shakespeare and his contemporaries. Here, the playwright deals with the earliest of the disruptions, beginning during the last phase of the HUNDRED YEARS WAR, a series of conflicts in which the French resisted English attempts to conquer them.

The action starts after the death of King HENRY V,

who had led his forces to great victories, establishing English control over large stretches of France (as Shakespeare was later to recount in *Henry V*); in the course of this play, these territories are almost all lost. However, Shakespeare's concern is not with narrative history. Rather, he amplifies the theme that England's misfortunes were the result of selfish ambitions unchecked by a weak monarch's incompetence. King Henry VI is an infant when the play begins and only a young man when it ends. Ambitious noblemen felt they had plenty of opportunity to increase their personal power, and to indulge in feuds that a more assertive monarch would have curtailed.

Shakespeare immediately sets out his themes in 1.1. The outbreak of verbal sparring between the Duke of Gloucester and the Bishop of Winchester introduces the disorder among the nobles. Moreover, the effects of this dissension are already beginning to be felt, as the Messengers arrive to tell of military losses in France, including the catastrophic capture of a great English leader, Talbot.

French successes in the war are juxtaposed with brawling disorders in England. For example, the disagreement between Gloucester and Winchester at the Tower of London in 1.3 follows the arrival of Joan of Arc to boost the morale of the French forces. Similarly, the rock-fight that spreads even into the king's deliberations in 3.1 immediately precedes Joan's successful ruse at Rouen in 3.2. The feuding of Vernon and Basset begins in 3.4, just after the defection of the Duke of Burgundy, and it continues in 4.1, providing a sorry prelude to the death of Talbot.

This disorder in the realm is reflected in the repeated instances of hypocrisy and dishonesty on the part of various characters. Mortimer advises Plantagenet to conceal his opposition to the Lancasters (2.5). The Bishop of Winchester plots to kidnap the infant king, although this strand of the plot goes undeveloped, and he pretends to be reconciled with Gloucester after the fight in Parliament (1.1, 3.1). In the Temple garden dispute (2.4), Somerset refuses to abide by the majority vote he had agreed to honour. Suffolk plots to deceive the king in Act 5, and in the final scene, even the saintly Henry is prevailed upon to go back on his agreement to marry the daughter of Armagnac. Another recurrent motif, representing the English dissension, is the interrupted ceremony. Three times, in 1.1, 3.1, and 4.1, ceremonial occasions are disrupted, each time more than once.

Shakespeare counterbalances these ominous occurrences with the character of Talbot, a model knight who symbolises the lost English supremacy under Henry V. Talbot is the only nobleman who stands out from the array of rhetorical quarrellers. He is knightly courtesy itself at the beginning of the coronation scene, and he personifies righteous indignation when he refuses to tolerate the wearing of the Garter, symbol of valour, by the coward Fastolfe. Talbot's praises are sung repeatedly by English and French alike. But his virtues cannot survive in the prevailing climate of deceit and disorder, and his courageous death in 4.7 is presented as the direct result of the York-Somerset struggle.

Historically, the episode of York and Somerset's divided command took place in Normandy during the 1440s, while Talbot's death occurred in southern France some years later. However, to increase the contrast between the brave and honourable Talbot on the one hand and the selfish, scheming factions on the other, Shakespeare provided a direct connection between the rise of the nobles and the loss of England's hero. Neither the playwright nor his audience was concerned with historical accuracy, but *1 Henry VI* is nevertheless strikingly at odds with the record as Shakespeare knew it. For instance, although the Duke of Burgundy did indeed change sides during the Hundred Years War, he did so some years after Joan's death. Moreover, this defection resulted from two decades of minor disputes and disagreements between the English and the Burgundians. For dramatic reasons, Shakespeare compressed all this into one highly charged, if entirely fictitious, scene; this enabled him to emphasise the duplicity of the French and Joan's associations with sorcery.

Similarly, the play describes, in close succession, Talbot's death, Joan's execution, and Henry's marriage: the fall of the great English hero prepares for that of the French heroine, who in turn is succeeded in the play by another Frenchwoman, the focus of a plot against Henry's power. To achieve these emotionally resonant juxtapositions, Shakespeare wilfully ignored the chronicles, which correctly record a rather different arrangement. Joan was burned in 1431, Henry was married in 1444, and Talbot died in 1453. Smaller distortions of the historical record occur throughout the play.

The playwright also invented a number of scenes for dramatic impact. Talbot's encounter with the Countess of Auvergne (2.3), for instance, points up aspects of the hero's soldierly nature and contrasts his honesty with the Countess' deceit. A more important invention is the confrontation between the future Duke of York and his rival Somerset in the Temple garden (2.4), in which they select as emblems a white and a red rose. This scene objectifies the rivalry that was to develop into civil war in the sequels to this play. Although historically it did not happen, it is so dramatically appropriate that we might wish it had.

Such inventions and obvious errors are much more evident to a reader than to an audience. The Hundred Years War and the English political scene are made real through a highly theatrical counterpoint of formal spectacle and unpredictable violence. The disrupted ceremonies noted above are obvious manifestations of this dramatic tension; the cool equanimity of the dying Bedford amid the hurly-burly of battle in 3.2 is a subtler instance. And Joan's brief dismissal of Sir William Lucy's elegiac recital of Talbot's noble titles brings us with a jolt from the formal dignity of medieval pomp to a renewed awareness of the carnage of battle (4.7. 75–76).

King Henry himself is a humanly interesting character, unlike the caricatures of 'ambitious courtiers' around him, although his personality is more developed in *2* and *3 Henry VI*. The conflict between his nature and the requirements of his situation fuels some of the development in this play and becomes highly significant in its sequels. Henry is gentle and thoughtful. He is distressed by the dissensions around him but is unable to contain them, not only on account of his youth, but also because of his innate dislike of involvement in worldly matters.

In general, however, character development is not a strength of this play, which partly explains its general unpopularity with modern audiences. The play's style is rhetorical and formal, its content is largely expository, and the poetry tends to be somewhat stilted. Another problem arises from the playwright's need to consider the play as one of a series; a certain amount of dramatically undirected material must be used in order to establish concerns that will be dealt with only in the sequels. Most glaring of these incidents is the relationship between the Earl of Suffolk and Margaret of Anjou, which seems unrelated to anything else in the play. It is certainly used to establish a major theme of the next play. However, it also provides a natural climax to this one, completing the devastation of England's position in France with the loss of Anjou and Maine. Also, Margaret becomes the strong adversarial figure that Joan had been. It is typical of Shakespeare's strategies in *1 Henry VI* that Margaret first appears just as Joan is rendered powerless.

Among the conventional stances that the play adopts are a vicious anti-French bias and a contemptuous attitude towards Joan that now seems excessive. In the 18th and 19th centuries they were cited as evidence that the play could not have been written by Shakespeare, such attitudes being thought beneath a great writer. Such virulent Francophobia was in tune with Elizabethan attitudes, however, and the picture of Joan as a whorish sorceress comes from Shakespeare's sources and he doubtless regarded it as historically sound.

On the whole, *1 Henry VI* cannot be regarded as a successful play. It lacks cohesion, being composed of scenes whose connections are more often contrasting than developmental. It is rhetorical to an extent that inhibits an audience's responses, and it does not reflect the insights into human nature that we associate with the mature Shakespeare. On the other hand, the play does present an extensive tract of complicated history, and it does so in a manner that enables us to apprehend it intellectually and also taste something of the nerve-racking reality of confused warfare. It was probably Shakespeare's first attempt at a new form, the drama of historical narrative, and he was to improve upon it in each of its sequels, before going on to the glories of the major tetralogy.

## SOURCES OF THE PLAY

Shakespeare's chief sources for *1 Henry VI,* and its sequels were the best-known English histories of his day, Raphael HOLINSHED's *The Chronicles of England, Ireland, and Scotland* (second edition, 1587) and *The Union of the Two Noble and Illustre Families of Lancastre and York,* by Edward HALL (2) (third edition, 1550). An older text, *The New Chronicle of England and of France,* by Robert FABYAN (1516), provided some supplementary material, such as an account of the stone-throwing skirmish in 3.1.

## TEXT OF THE PLAY

In the 18th and 19th centuries a distaste for the treatment of Joan of Arc in *1 Henry VI* led to a tendency to attribute the play to other writers, especially to joint authorship—usually some combination of NASHE, GREENE, (2) and MARLOWE (1)—with only certain elements (especially 2.4, 2.5, and 4.2–7) credited to Shakespeare. Modern scholarship, however, generally finds the play to be largely Shakespearean, although some authorities still assign Act 1 to Nashe.

It is impossible to date the composition of Shakespeare's early HISTORY PLAYS with absolute certainty; the evidence is sparse, complex, and contradictory. However, *1 Henry VI* contains several minor resemblances to Edmund SPENSER's *Faerie Queene,* dated December 1589, and the play was referred to by Thomas Nashe, in the summer of 1592, as already very popular. Since the theatres were closed by plague after June of that year, the play must have been performed that spring. Therefore, we do know that it was written between 1589 and 1592.

Although it is sometimes contended that *Part 1* was written *after* the other *Henry VI* plays, modern opinion tends to support common sense in supposing that the plays of the minor tetralogy, including *Richard III,* were written in the order in which they are read. *Richard III* seems to have been known to Marlowe by early 1592; therefore, it seems likely that the four plays were composed between early 1590 and late 1591, with *1 Henry VI* being written near the beginning of this period.

The only early publication of the play was in the FIRST FOLIO edition of 1623, and this text has necessarily been the basis for all subsequent editions. The Folio version's many errors and inconsistencies have provided grist for much scholarly dispute over minor points, but the text is not seriously flawed. Some char-

acteristics—the casual stage directions and the retention of flagrant contradictions that would probably have been corrected in a performance script—seem to indicate that the Folio was printed from the author's manuscript.

## THEATRICAL HISTORY OF THE PLAY

Nashe's reference to the play as an established hit just before the theatres closed in 1592 proves that it had been performed that spring. However, no other early productions are known. After Shakespeare's time, *1 Henry VI* was all but ignored for almost three centuries, being revived only in 1738 and 1899. However, elements from it were occasionally used in abridgements of the complete set of Henry VI plays. In the 20th century it has been somewhat more frequently produced, especially in cycles presenting the history plays in clusters. It has also continued to provide material for abridged combinations, on both stage and TELEVISION. It has never been a FILM, but it was made for television in 1983 and was incorporated in two BBC series: AN AGE OF KINGS (1960) and 'The Wars of the Roses' (1964), which combines the *Henry VI* plays and *Richard III.*

## *Henry VI,* PART 2

### SYNOPSIS

*Act 1, Scene 1*
The court of HENRY VI is assembled to welcome the King's new bride, MARGARET (1) of Anjou, whom the Earl of SUFFOLK (3) has brought to England. The Duke of GLOUCESTER (4) reads aloud the terms of the marriage contract, by which Anjou and Maine, French territories that England had conquered, are ceded to Margaret's father. This so upsets him that he cannot read on. CARDINAL (1) BEAUFORT continues, reading that Margaret shall pay no dowry. The king accepts the terms. He then promotes Suffolk to a dukedom and temporarily suspends the appointment of the Duke of YORK (8) as Regent of FRANCE (1). The royal newlyweds and Suffolk depart. Gloucester, backed by York, the Earl of SALISBURY (2), and the Earl of WARWICK (3), rails against the marriage contract. He leaves, prophesying the loss of France. The Cardinal suggests that Gloucester, the heir apparent to the throne, is quarrelling only because he seeks to replace the king. He observes that Gloucester is popular and thus doubly dangerous. The Duke of BUCKINGHAM (3) agrees and proposes a plot to unseat Gloucester from his position as Lord Protector. The Cardinal leaves to recruit Suffolk for the plot, and in his absence, the Duke of SOMERSET (1) contends that the Cardinal is himself ambitious to fill the Protector's office. Salisbury and Warwick speak of the good of the country and decide to back Gloucester, an honest and competent Protec-

tor. They recruit York to their cause, but when they leave, York, in a soliloquy, confides that he thinks of himself as the rightful king and of Henry as a usurper. He determines that he will ally himself with the backers of Gloucester and await a good time to seize the throne by force.

### Act 1, Scene 2
The DUCHESS (1) of Gloucester encourages Gloucester to aspire to the throne, but he rejects the idea and rebukes her for it. A MESSENGER (4) summons the duke, who leaves. Alone, the Duchess speaks of her intention to pursue the crown for her husband. She summons HUME and arranges for a séance with a witch and a sorcerer whom he has contacted on her behalf. She pays Hume and leaves, and he reveals in a soliloquy that he is also in the pay of Suffolk and the Cardinal, arrangeing a scandalous exposure of the Duchess that will bring down Gloucester as well.

### Act 1, Scene 3
PETER (1), an armourer's apprentice, reports that his master, HORNER, has heard the Duke of York express a claim to the throne. Suffolk has Peter taken into custody and Horner sent for. The new queen complains to Suffolk that the king seems merely the equal of his noblemen. Suffolk assures her that his plots will undo the noblemen, but that she must be patient. The king arrives with the nobles of the court. They discuss the regency of France; Gloucester backs York for the position. The queen attacks Gloucester, as do Suffolk, the Cardinal, Somerset, and Buckingham. Gloucester storms off, and the queen provokes a quarrel with his wife, striking her, and the Duchess leaves also. Buckingham follows her. Gloucester returns, his anger cooled, and again proposes York for the regency, but Suffolk accuses York of treason, and Horner is brought in. Horner denies having said anything about York and asserts that his apprentice is lying. Gloucester calls for a trial by combat. Peter despairs, saying he cannot fight, but the combat is scheduled.

### Act 1, Scene 4
Hume assembles the witch MARGERY JOURDAIN and the sorcerers BOLINGBROKE (2) and SOUTHWELL to call a spirit for the Duchess of Gloucester. The spirit ASNATH appears and is asked about the future of the king. He replies ambiguously. He predicts a death by water for Suffolk, and he advises that Somerset should avoid castles. The spirit is dismissed, and York and Buckingham appear, placing everyone present under arrest.

### Act 2, Scene 1
The members of the court are hunting with falcons. Gloucester and the Cardinal quarrel to the point of arranging a duel. The king opposes the dispute but cannot stop it. A Citizen of nearby ST. ALBANS approaches, proclaiming a miracle: a man blind since birth can suddenly see. Gloucester interviews the man,

one SIMPCOX, suspecting a fraud, and his clever questioning confirms his guess. Buckingham appears with news of the arrest of the Duchess of Gloucester as a user of witchcraft and leader of a conspiracy against the king. When his enemies gloat, Gloucester announces that, if his wife has indeed done these things, he will reject her and leave her to the process of the law.

### Act 2, Scene 2
York outlines his claim to the throne to Salisbury and Warwick. Convinced, they swear allegiance to him, but he cautions them that he is not king yet. They should conceal their plot, he says, and wait for Suffolk, the Cardinal, and their allies to bring down Gloucester, who is the most important Lancastrian.

### Act 2, Scene 3
King Henry sentences the conspirators who were arrested in 1.4. The commoners are sentenced to death. The Duchess of Gloucester will be paraded ignominiously through the streets of London and then exiled. The king orders Gloucester to surrender his staff of office. He does so and leaves. Horner and Peter appear for their trial by combat. Horner, expected to win the contest, is too drunk to fight and is killed by Peter. Dying, he confesses having lied and exonerates his apprentice.

### Act 2, Scene 4
The Duke of Gloucester witnesses his wife's humiliation in the streets. She forecasts that he will soon be threatened with death by Suffolk and his allies. Gloucester asserts that his unblemished loyalty and honesty will be his protection.

### Act 3, Scene 1
The queen's clique insists to the king that Gloucester is planning a coup. The king denies it. The Duke of Somerset appears to announce the loss of all the English territories in France. The king accepts this defeat as the work of God, but York is bitter. Gloucester arrives, and Suffolk accuses him of treason. Gloucester leaves under arrest, and the king, saying that he is grief-stricken, relinquishes his authority to the queen's clique and leaves. The conspirators decide that Gloucester is still too dangerous and agree to have him murdered. A Messenger arrives from Ireland with news that a revolt is in progress there. Suffolk assigns York an army and sends him to suppress the rebels. All but York depart, and the duke reveals his plans in a long soliloquy. He exults that he has an army at his disposal, and he plans a rebellion to be staged by his hired agent, Jack CADE. Then he will take advantage of the unrest and seize the throne.

### Act 3, Scene 2
Several murderers flee from Gloucester's chambers and are met by Suffolk, who promises them their pay

for the deed. The king and his court arrive, and Suffolk is sent to summon Gloucester. He returns to announce Gloucester's death. The king faints, awakening to mourn. Margaret responds with an extravagant plaint, lamenting that she will be slandered with implications of guilt and that Henry now wishes her dead. She is interrupted by Warwick and Salisbury, who arrive with a crowd of commoners. Warwick reports that the people are distressed by rumours that Gloucester has been murdered. Warwick examines the corpse and points out signs that the duke was indeed slain. He accuses Suffolk. The two agree to a duel and depart, but they return immediately, just ahead of a mob. Salisbury reports that the people demand death or banishment for Suffolk. The king formally banishes Suffolk from England and leaves with his loyal noblemen. The queen and Suffolk are left to make their farewells, revealing that they love each other. VAUX (3) enters with news that the Cardinal is dying.

### Act 3, Scene 3
The king, Warwick, and Salisbury witness the Cardinal's death. The delirious Cardinal reveals his guilt.

### Act 4, Scene 1
On a beach, members of the crew of a pirate ship assemble their three captives, recently seized from another ship. A LIEUTENANT (1) of the pirates awards the prisoners to his men, who will collect ransom from them. Suffolk is awarded to the pirate Walter (pronounced 'water' in Elizabethan English) WHITMORE. Whitmore, having lost an eye in the battle, insists on vengeance and declares that Suffolk must die. Suffolk recalls his predicted death by water. He identifies himself, and the Lieutenant speaks against him, reciting his political crimes. Whitmore takes Suffolk off to be beheaded. The Lieutenant releases one captive, a GENTLEMAN (1), to carry ransom messages to London. Whitmore returns to deposit Suffolk's head and body at the feet of the Gentleman, who vows to carry them to the king and queen.

### Act 4, Scene 2
BEVIS and HOLLAND (3) discuss the rebellion of Jack CADE and join the uprising when the rebels arrive. Cade claims to be a PLANTAGENET (1) and the proper heir to the crown. Comically, he promises his followers preposterous rewards. One rebel proposes killing all lawyers, and Cade agrees, ranting against the use of documents. The CLERK of Chatham is brought in as a prisoner, and he is sentenced to death for being literate. A Messenger arrives to warn of the approach of troops led by Sir Humphrey STAFFORD (2). Stafford insultingly demands that the rebels surrender, but they refuse.

### Act 4, Scene 3
In a skirmish, Stafford and his BROTHER (1) are slain. Cade proposes to march on London.

### Act 4, Scene 4
In the king's palace in London, Margaret, carrying Suffolk's head, mourns her lover's death, while Henry and Buckingham plan how to deal with the rebellion. A Messenger reports the approach of the rebels, and Buckingham recommends that the king retreat until the revolt is suppressed. Another Messenger reports that the rebels have reached London and that some of the citizens are rising in sympathy with them. The king and queen depart with Buckingham.

### Act 4, Scene 5
A CITIZEN (1) reports to Lord SCALES, the commander of the Tower of London, that the rebels are successfully assaulting London Bridge and that the Lord Mayor has requested Scales' assistance. Scales promises to send aid and issues orders.

### Act 4, Scene 6
Cade declares himself Lord of London and commands that the water fountain be made to flow wine for a year. He further declares that it shall be treason to address him as anything but Lord Mortimer. A SOLDIER (3) enters, calling out for Cade, unaware of the new regulation. Cade orders him set upon, and he is killed. Cade orders that London Bridge and the Tower of London be burned down.

### Act 4, Scene 7
Lord SAY is brought to Cade's camp. Cade derisively accuses him of various deeds that are usually considered praiseworthy, such as building a grammar school. Say pleads for his life, but, after several exchanges, Cade sends him off to be beheaded with his son-in-law. Some soldiers return with the two heads on poles. Cade orders these trophies paraded through the streets.

### Act 4, Scene 8
Buckingham and Lord CLIFFORD (2) offer the king's pardon to all rebels who will declare allegiance to the throne. A great roar of 'God save the king' goes up. Cade counters with a speech that evokes a similar cry in his favour. Clifford, however, seduces the fickle mob back to the king's side. Cade flees.

### Act 4, Scene 9
The king laments his fate. Buckingham and Clifford enter and announce Cade's flight. They are accompanied by many former rebels seeking the king's forgiveness, which he grants. News arrives that York has returned from Ireland with a strong army, demanding the removal of the Duke of Somerset. The king, distressed, sends Buckingham to negotiate with York and temporarily orders Somerset to the Tower.

### Act 4, Scene 10
Cade hides in the walled garden of an estate and is discovered by its owner, Alexander IDEN. After a brief quarrel, the two fight and Cade is killed.

## Act 5, Scene 1

York, at the head of an army, announces that he has returned from Ireland to claim the throne, but he observes that he must still pretend loyalty to Henry. Buckingham delivers a message from the king and informs York that Somerset is a prisoner; York accordingly dismisses his soldiers. The king arrives, and York expresses his allegiance. Iden appears with the head of Cade, which he offers to the king. The king knights him. The queen arrives with Somerset. When he sees that Somerset is not in prison, York angrily declares that he shall no longer regard Henry as king and claims the throne for himself. Somerset and Margaret challenge him. York's sons, Edward (see EDWARD IV) and Richard (see RICHARD III), enter to support him, opposing Clifford and his son, John CLIFFORD (1), whom the Queen has summoned. Warwick and Salisbury arrive and side with York. Warwick and Clifford vow to fight each other in the battle that is now necessary, and Young Clifford exchanges insults with York.

## Act 5, Scene 2

York kills Clifford on the battlefield. The younger Clifford discovers his father's body and in a lament, compares death to the Last Judgement. He asserts his intention to kill the children of the Yorkists as they have killed his aged father. York and Somerset enter fighting, and Somerset is slain. York notes that the prediction that Somerset should avoid castles has come true; he has been killed beneath a tavern sign depicting a castle. York exists, and the king and queen arrive in retreat. Henry hesitates, but Margaret insists that they must flee in order to fight again.

## Act 5, Scene 3

Near the battlefield, Salisbury proposes to York that they should pursue their fleeing enemies. York agrees, as does Warwick, who comments that the battle is likely to become famous.

## COMMENTARY

*Henry VI, Part 2* is a political play, rather than a drama of human interaction or development. It tells of England's collapse into the anarchy and civil strife of the WARS OF THE ROSES due to selfish ambitions unleashed by the weakness of a young and indecisive ruler. As part of the minor TETRALOGY of HISTORY PLAYS, this work also furthers the underlying themes of inexorable tragedy caused by the usurpation of the crown by the LANCASTER (1) family and of the eventual retribution delivered to that dynasty. In *2 Henry VI* these concerns are developed in two episodes. The first, occupying Acts 1–3, involves the political downfall and eventual murder of Duke Humphrey of Gloucester, who is presented as a just and prudent statesman whose leadership might have preserved the kingdom. The second is an account of the final steps the Duke of York takes towards his own seizure of the crown.

This episode begins with a popular rebellion led by York's agent, Jack Cade, a comical affair providing relief after the relentless unfolding of Gloucester's fate. It turns vicious, however, illustrating the evil of anarchy unloosed by the murder of 'good Duke Humphrey'. York capitalises on the uprising to advance his own claim and brings the nation to civil war at the first battle of St Albans, with which the play closes.

Shakespeare was dramatising history in the *Henry VI* plays, but he was not at all averse to altering actual events for dramatic purposes, although *Part 2* uses less such distortion than *Part 1*. The greatest misrepresentation is the depiction of York's ambition, presented as a carefully deliberated plot by a determined usurper. Historically, York, who had nothing to do with the outbreak of Cade's rebellion, made no attempt to seize the crown until very shortly before the war broke out. Prior to that time, he does not seem to have contemplated doing so; he had fiercely competed with the Duke of Somerset for power as a minister under King Henry, but he attempted to rule himself only when it became clear that Margaret's influence on Somerset's behalf was too great to be finally overcome and that Somerset planned to destroy his own power altogether. In order to emphasise the rivalry of the Lancaster and York families, and to stress the evils of aristocratic ambition, Shakespeare humanised the confused political process that had in fact uncoiled in the 1440s and 1450s by making a convincing schemer of York. Much exciting history has simply been eliminated—most notably, York's capable assumption of the regency in 1453–1454, when the king fell helplessly insane and was unable to speak.

The story of Gloucester's fate is tightened and given a melodramatic sense of inevitability by compressing many events, widely separated historically, into a swiftly flowing narrative. The tale of the Duchess of Gloucester's sorcery and exile is historical, but it occurred four years before the arrival of Queen Margaret. The two women are made contemporary, thereby involving Margaret in Gloucester's fall, and the episode is made to contribute directly to that fall, which it did not actually do. Similarly, the exile and death of Suffolk are moved back by several years and are thereby associated directly with Gloucester's death. Thus six years of aristocratic manoeuvrings are collapsed into a matter of months in order to heighten the drama of Gloucester's fall and clearly establish it as the spark for the events that follow.

Though the play's point is made by its sequence of events, Shakespeare created a number of believable, humanly distinct characters to execute them, marking a great improvement on the masses of quarrelling nobles in *1 Henry VI*. King Henry himself—enthralled by religion, well-meaning but ineffectual—is moving towards the pathetic, almost tragic figure he becomes in *3 Henry VI*. Also striking are Queen Margaret and the

Duke of Suffolk, who are convincing as scheming villains and at the same time inspire sympathy as lovers in their farewell scene (3.2). One sees that Shakespeare is developing the capacity to produce such great later characters as the villains IAGO and RICHARD III and the lovers ROMEO and JULIET.

Richard III, in fact, makes his first appearance late in this play. His role is unimportant, and he is present simply as a harbinger of the next two dramas in the tetralogy, but he is a cleanly drawn figure, sardonically epigrammatic. Another minor figure, Buckingham, sounds an aristocratic note of peremptory command, and two men who will figure prominently in the next play, Warwick and Clifford, are strongly delineated minor characters in this one.

Given this range of characters and events, the poetic style in *2 Henry VI* is necessarily varied. The speeches of Cade and his rebels are comically gross, while Margaret and Suffolk's farewells draw on the tradition of courtly love. The vicious repartee of the feuding nobles differs from the high poetry of the pirate Lieutenant. In contrast with *1 Henry VI*, Shakespeare here shows his increasing mastery of the difficult task of writing credible speech in verse.

Shakespeare's wilful manipulation of his historical sources is successful on the whole but does misfire in some instances. Most notable in this respect are two episodes taken from widely separated accounts in the sources and used to illustrate the good judgement of the Duke of Gloucester. The incident involving Horner's reported remarks about York's ambition provides an occasion for the Duke to exercise prudence. He withholds office from York pending resolution of the matter. However, the resolution never comes; the dying Horner admits that he had made the incriminating comment, but no note is made of the obvious implications concerning York's loyalty and the matter is never again referred to; the playwright has left his audience dangling. In the other incident, Gloucester cleverly exposes the impostor Simpcox. Here, the scene is dramatically complete and quite amusing, but it is too trivial to stand up to the more important events with which it is juxtaposed.

*Henry VI, Part 2*, although it marks a considerable advance on *Part 1*, is still plainly the work of a young, less than masterly, playwright. Moreover, it suffers from its position in a sequence of plays. Much of the early exposition is intended to provide a link to the action of *1 Henry VI*, and several dramatically unnecessary characters, such as Richard and Young Clifford, appear in Act 5, where they foreshadow *3 Henry VI*. Nevertheless, it is an exciting play, composed of varied and interesting scenes that generate two plausible climaxes, and it is full of the promise of greater things to come.

## SOURCES OF THE PLAY

As in the other history plays, Shakespeare adapted material from the available chronicles. For *2 Henry VI*, his chief source was *The Union of the Two Noble and Illustre Families of Lancastre and York*, by Edward HALL (2) (third edition, 1550), supplemented by Raphael HOLINSHED's *The Chronicles of England, Ireland, and Scotland* (second edition, 1587). He also used John FOXE's *Book of Martyrs* (fourth edition, 1583), from which he took the story of Simpcox's false miracle, along with other details. Various minor suggestions seem to have come from other chronicles, including those of Robert FABYAN and Richard GRAFTON, along with a popular anthology of biographies, A MIRROR FOR MAGISTRATES.

## TEXT OF THE PLAY

It is impossible to date the early history plays with certainty, but since *1* and *2 Henry VI* both contain minor resemblances to Edmund SPENSER's *Faerie Queene*, dated December 1589, these plays cannot have been written earlier than 1590. It is thought by many that the four plays of the tetralogy were written in the order in which they are read, and the last of them, *Richard III*, was apparently known to MARLOWE (1) by early 1592. Therefore, it seems likely that the four plays were composed between early 1590 and late 1591. If the second of them is assigned the second quarter of this span of time, we may date *2 Henry VI* to the latter half of 1590.

The play was first published in the form in which we know it in the FIRST FOLIO, in 1623, and that text has been the basis for all subsequent editions. However, a BAD QUARTO edition, known as THE CONTENTION, was published by Thomas MILLINGTON in 1594 and again in 1600; these editions are known as Q1 and Q2 respectively. Thomas PAVIER published another QUARTO edition (Q3) that included a bad quarto of *3 Henry VI* (see WHOLE CONTENTION), as part of the FALSE FOLIO (1619). While Q3 may have provided some details for the Folio text (notably in the genealogy recited in 2.2, adapted by Pavier from John STOW's chronicles), the quarto editions are chiefly of historical interest.

## THEATRICAL HISTORY OF THE PLAY

No specific performances of *2 Henry VI* during Shakespeare's lifetime are recorded, but it is clear that all of the *Henry VI* plays were popular, and they were doubtless performed often. In about 1612 Ben JONSON referred to them as well-known works. The architect and designer Inigo Jones drew a costume for Jack Cade at around the same time or a little later, probably reflecting an unrecorded production. However, the earliest known performances are much later, in 1681 and 1723, and both of these were heavily reworked adaptations.

The first performance of the whole play since at least the early 17th century was given in 1864. The play has been more successful in the 20th century. F. R. BENSON (1) produced it several times, beginning in 1899. It has appeared in a number of history-play cycles, notably in two BBC TELEVISION productions: AN AGE OF KINGS (1960) and 'The Wars of the Roses' (1964), which incorporates the *Henry VI* plays and *Richard III*.

## *Henry VI*, PART 3

### SYNOPSIS

#### Act 1, Scene 1

The Duke of YORK (8), his sons Edward (see EDWARD IV) and Richard (see RICHARD III), and their followers discuss the first battle of ST. ALBANS, with which *2 Henry VI* closed. Richard displays the head of the Duke of SOMERSET (1), whom he killed in the previous play. York seats himself on the throne, which is present for an anticipated meeting of the king's council. The king arrives with a retinue. He restrains his followers from seeking immediate vengeance on the Yorkists, and the two sides parley. York states his claim to rule, based on the proposition that Henry had inherited a usurped crown, taken by his grandfather, HENRY IV, from RICHARD II, whose true heir York claims to be. The king counters weakly that Richard II had voluntarily given the kingdom to Henry IV. Lords CLIFFORD (1) and WARWICK (3) escalate the argument, and Warwick summons his hidden soldiers. The king, hoping to avert further violence, agrees to name York as his heir if he be permitted to retain the throne in his own lifetime. York accepts the offer and vows to refrain from rebellion. York and his men depart, satisfied. The king's supporters leave dissatisfied, expressing their disdain for the king's act. Queen MARGARET (1) and the PRINCE (4) of Wales arrive. Margaret reviles Henry for disinheriting their son the Prince, and declares herself divorced. She and the Prince depart to continue the battle against York.

#### Act 1, Scene 2

York's sons contend that he may properly seize the crown without violating his oath. Richard makes the case that the oath is invalid because it was not made to a proper monarch but rather to a usurper. York accepts this idea with delight and begins to plan a campaign. News arrives that Margaret's army of 20,000 men is approaching. York decides to engage the queen's army immediately, although he is outnumbered four to one.

#### Act 1, Scene 3

At the battle of WAKEFIELD, York's young son RUTLAND (1) is taken by Clifford, who declares that he will kill the child in revenge for his own father's death at

York's hands. Rutland's pleas for mercy are ignored, and Clifford kills the boy.

#### Act 1, Scene 4

York appears on the battlefield and describes the courage of his sons in a losing cause. As his pursuers approach, he realises that he is doomed. Margaret and the Prince appear, accompanied by NORTHUMBERLAND (2) and Clifford. The queen mocks York for his failure. She further taunts him by giving him a handkerchief that has been dipped in Rutland's blood. As her mood grows increasingly vicious, she orders him beheaded. York responds with a long condemnation of the queen, and he weeps for the death of Rutland. Northumberland is moved to pity the captive, but the queen and Clifford stab York to death.

#### Act 2, Scene 1

Richard and Edward, wondering about their father's fate, see three suns in the sky, which they interpret as an omen of success. News arrives of York's capture and death, and Warwick arrives with more bad news: the duke's forces have been defeated by the queen's. However, he assures the brothers that they can still achieve victory and install Edward as king.

#### Act 2, Scene 2

Outside the walls of YORK (2), Margaret points out the Duke of York's head, which has been placed on the city gate; King Henry is dismayed by the sight. Clifford chastises him for being too soft, encouraging him to fight, if only for the inheritance of his son. Henry is unimpressed, arguing that evil cannot produce success. The Yorkist leaders arrive, headed by Warwick and Edward. Edward claims to be king and demands that Henry kneel to him. Margaret and Clifford respond sharply; Richard and the other lords enter the bitter argument. Henry is ignored by all. Amid a barrage of insults, the parley breaks up.

#### Act 2, Scene 3

At the battle of TOWTON, Warwick, wounded and exhausted, seeks rest. Edward and his brother GEORGE (2) enter and fear that the battle is lost. Richard arrives to report that Warwick's brother, slain by Clifford, had cried out with his last breath for Warwick to avenge his death. Warwick, reinvigorated, vows to return to the conflict and not rest again before winning or dying. Their morale restored, the brothers go back to the battle with him.

#### Act 2, Scene 4

Richard and Clifford prepare to fight hand to hand, with declarations of intended vengeance, when Warwick arrives and Clifford flees.

#### Act 2, Scene 5

King Henry, having withdrawn from the fighting, musingly wishes that he had been born a shepherd whose time passes uneventfully in the company of his flock. He watches a soldier carry a body from the field in order to loot it, only to discover that his victim had been his own father. Henry, unseen, shares the devastating grief of the SON THAT HATH KILLED HIS FATHER. Another soldier, with another body and the same intent, discovers that he carries the corpse of his own son. Henry is likewise stricken with the horror that fills the FATHER THAT HATH KILLED HIS SON. Margaret and the Prince enter in full retreat from the victorious Yorkists, and they take the king with them.

### Act 2, Scene 6
Clifford, wounded in the neck, regrets his own imminent death because he knows it spells disaster for the king's cause. He wishes that the king had been a stronger man, for the war would not have been necessary in that case. He faints just before Edward and his followers arrive, discussing their victory and wondering where Clifford is. They discover his body just as he dies; not realising that he is dead, they revile and taunt him. Once his death is apparent, Warwick orders that his head replace York's on the city gate. Next, Warwick says, Edward shall be crowned. Then he, Warwick, will go to FRANCE (1) and arrange Edward's marriage to the French king's sister-in-law, Lady BONA. Edward agrees, conferring on Warwick the authority to act as though he were king himself.

### Act 3, Scene 1
At a game park, two KEEPERS (2) come across King Henry. He is a refugee, having fled after the battle. The Keepers accost him, and, although Henry chastises them mildly for their inconstant loyalty, he goes with them to be taken into captivity.

### Act 3, Scene 2
In London, King Edward hears the plea of Lady ELIZABETH (2) Grey that her late husband's sequestered lands be returned to her. He agrees, but only on condition that she become his mistress. She refuses, and he, infatuated, declares that he will marry her. Richard, in a long soliloquy, makes a frank declaration of his intention to become king. He cynically analyses his own capacity for villainy, acknowledgeing that he will have to murder those who precede him in the order of succession.

### Act 3, Scene 3
In France, Queen Margaret explains her and her deposed husband's plight to a sympathetic King LEWIS (3). Warwick arrives with Edward's proposal of marriage to Lady Bona, and Lewis, accepting Edward as king, consents. Then Edward's marriage to Elizabeth is announced. Warwick, furious at the dishonourable position this places him in, volunteers to abandon Edward's cause and ally himself with Margaret and the Earl of OXFORD in an effort to restore Henry to the

throne. Lewis, seeking to avenge the insult to Bona, agrees to assist them, and an invasion is planned.

### Act 4, Scene 1
George and Richard oppose the ill-considered marriage, but Edward insists that his royal prerogative negates all criticism. News of the impending invasion arrives. George's dissatisfaction comes to a boil, and he declares that he will join the rebels; he leaves, along with the Duke of SOMERSET (2). Richard declares his loyalty to Edward, after an aside confirming his true interest—the pursuit of the crown.

### Act 4, Scene 2
Warwick and Oxford have landed with the invasion force. They encounter George and Somerset and accept their alliance.

### Act 4, Scene 3
Warwick's forces rout the WATCHMEN (1) in Edward's camp and capture the king, although Richard escapes. Warwick plans to march to London and reinstate Henry as king.

### Act 4, Scene 4
Queen Elizabeth, as Edward's wife is now known, knows of her husband's capture. Pregnant, she proposes to flee to the legal sanctuary of a church to protect the unborn Yorkist heir to the crown.

### Act 4, Scene 5
Richard and others help Edward escape from captivity.

### Act 4, Scene 6
Henry, released from the TOWER OF LONDON by Warwick and George, assigns his power of command to them. The young Earl of RICHMOND is present, and Henry acclaims him as a future king. Word arrives of Edward's escape, and plans are made against him. Somerset and Oxford take Richmond into exile abroad to protect him against the possibility of Edward's victory.

### Act 4, Scene 7
Edward has arrived at York to find the city gates closed by the MAYOR (5), who cites the town's allegiance to Henry. Edward contends that he claims only his position as Duke of York, and he is admitted. MONTGOMERY (1) arrives with troops to support Edward, but only if he resumes his claim to the throne. Edward agrees and makes a formal assertion of kingship.

### Act 4, Scene 8
Warwick deploys various of Henry's supporters to raise troops and meet him in COVENTRY. They all depart, leaving Henry to be captured by Edward and Richard, who suddenly appear on their way to meet Warwick in battle.

*Act 5, Scene 1*

Warwick, within the walls of Coventry, is besieged by Edward and Richard; he receives reinforcements from several noblemen. George also arrives with troops, but Richard persuades him to abandon Warwick and rejoin Edward.

*Act 5, Scene 2*

At the battle of BARNET, Warwick lies wounded, meditating on the insignificance of his former power now that he is near death. Oxford and Somerset, retreating, tell him that the battle is lost and that they are going to join Margaret, who has an army in the field. As they speak, Warwick dies.

*Act 5, Scene 3*

Edward, Richard, and George, triumphant, plan to march to TEWKESBURY and fight the queen's army.

*Act 5, Scene 4*

At Tewkesbury, Queen Margaret makes a stirring speech, and her courage inspires her followers. The Yorkist leaders arrive, and Edward and Margaret each make brief statements signalling the start of battle.

*Act 5, Scene 5*

The queen and her followers are prisoners of Edward. The Prince defies his captors, insulting Edward and his brothers, and they stab him. Richard departs for London, stating that he has important business there. Helpless, Margaret rails against the killers of her son.

*Act 5, Scene 6*

Richard accosts Henry in his cell in the Tower of London. Henry reviles Richard for his villainy, predicting the future tragedy he will cause many people and referring to the evil omens that accompanied his birth. Richard kills him and accepts, in a soliloquy, his own evil nature, proposing to use his capacity for crime to achieve the throne.

*Act 5, Scene 7*

King Edward rejoices in his resumption of power and delights in his son, the new PRINCE (5) of Wales, and in the support of his brothers. Richard's dark asides demonstrate the king's naïveté.

## COMMENTARY

Like Shakespeare's other HISTORY PLAYS, *3 Henry VI* is essentially concerned with civil disorder. As the young playwright's skills matured, his handling of the theme improved, and this third play of the minor TETRALOGY marks a notable advance. Shakespeare's ability to organise a confused mass of material is superior to that in *1* and *2 Henry VI*. Also, and more important in light of his later development, his presentation of chaos includes disorder in the individual as well as in the state; malfunctions of personality underlie those of

politics. The painter of tableaux and pageantry is becoming a tragedian.

The dissolution of the state is the major concern of the play, which describes the overthrow of King Henry VI, but this major theme is also reflected in minor keys. Just as the organisational principle of society, the state, is disrupted, so, too, the basic social bond of the family is disturbed. Henry disinherits his own son to purchase relief from York's threats of war, and the action sparks Margaret's unilateral declaration of divorce. The opposing clan, the Yorks, are no better off. George abandons his brother's cause after Edward turns his attentions to the relatives of his new bride. Richard plots the death of both his brothers. The theme of familial collapse is given spectacular exposure in 2.5, the scene involving the Son That Hath Killed His Father and the Father That Hath Killed His Son. Further, an abandonment of individual honesty characterises the world of the play. As Edward quite coolly asserts in 1.2.16–17, '. . . for a kingdom any oath may be broken: I would break a thousand oaths to reign one year'.

These themes, so suggestive of chaos, are developed within a regularly alternating cycle of changes of fortune, beginning and ending with the ascendancy of the house of York. Yorkist success at the outset is countered by the Lancastrian victory at Wakefield and York's ignominious death. However, Warwick rallies the Yorkists, who are victorious at Towton in Act 2. In Act 3 Edward's perfidy triggers the defection of Warwick and the consequent reinstatement of Henry as king. But the last swing of the pendulum produces the defeat and death of Warwick and Richard's murders of Henry and his heir. This easily perceived sequence imposes order on the turbulent events.

Dramatic unity is furthered by the persistence of images that reflect the violence of nature. Throughout the play, the characters refer to their conflicts in terms of the killing of animals by men, as in 1.4.61–62 and 2.4.13, or the taking of prey by animals, as in 2.1.14 and 5.6.7. Even more evocative are references to the power of tempests, such as Henry's striking description of the battle of Wakefield in 2.5.5–9 and Margaret's more elaborate nautical analogy at the beginning of 5.4. Our awareness of the brutality and viciousness of the play's action is constantly reinforced by this recurrent imagery.

Moreover, Shakespeare frequently has his characters refer to the past and predict the future—devices that serve to bring all the parts of the play to the repeated attention of the audience. For instance, in 1.1.130–133 Henry foretells the coming battles and his own death; the dying York, in 1.4.165–166, wishes upon Margaret a fate that comes to pass in 5.5. Clifford, in 2.6, summarises King Henry's hapless reign. Henry, before his murder in 5.6, predicts Richard's future crimes. Many such allusions, both plain and subtle, reverberate throughout the play.

More important than this clever technique, however, is Shakespeare's increasing ability to make his characters much more convincing. Henry VI in particular has grown greatly as the playwright's skill has advanced. The king's gentleness is touchingly rendered in his revulsion at the sight of York's head in 2.2, in his wish to be a simple shepherd (2.5.1–54), and in his forgiving his prison guard in 4.6. However, Henry's virtue has a negative side, causing him to become more and more dissociated from his surroundings. The consequences are both subtly recorded, as when the king demands to speak but is ignored and remains speechless in 2.2, and obvious, as upon his virtual abdication in 4.6. Henry's position involves a tragic paradox: his goodness ought to be given scope by his power, but it is precisely his power that places him in the way of historical forces that goodness cannot resist. That Henry is believably both weak and good makes this situation humanly tragic as well as politically disturbing.

Queen Margaret also displays greater dimensions than in the earlier plays. The strength that enables her to organise the resistance to York is fuelled by intemperate rage. When she has York at her mercy in 1.4, her viciousness comes to the fore, and we are faced with a fearsome shrew in one of the most powerful scenes Shakespeare had yet written. Though Margaret is undeniably bloody-minded—as in 2.2, where she encourages Henry to gloat over York's severed head— she also possesses a capacity for military leadership and strength that is not without a noble appeal. Her persistence in the face of setbacks and her readiness to resume battle when the tide turns, in 3.3, makes credible her leadership in the face of final defeat at Tewkesbury. Her inspiring speech in 5.4 rings true, for we have seen that she is a real warrior.

Edward, too, is a well-developed figure. His stature as York's heir to the throne proves illusory once he is crowned, for he shows no regard for the responsibilities of kingship. He is wilful in pursuing his lust, and his behaviour brings on further civil war. In the conflict, he indulges in pointless bravado and permits himself to be captured. In 5.5.84, after the final victory, Edward casually permits Richard to murder Henry, evincing a lack of concern for civil order that will eventually result in his own victimisation in *Richard III*.

But Shakespeare's greatest accomplishment in the play is the creation of his first great villain—Richard. Richard's extraordinary personality bursts forth in 1.1, when he abruptly throws down the head of Somerset, saying, 'Speak thou for me, and tell them what I did' (1.1.16). Richard's violence is mixed with sardonic wit throughout the play. He gloats over Clifford's corpse in 2.6, his speech darkening from morbid humour to vicious rhetoric. Later, after killing Henry, Richard raises his bloody sword and sarcastically crows, 'See how my sword weeps for the poor King's death' (5.6.63). Richard is conscious of his own character, and he shares his self-awareness with the audience, enlarging our appreciation of his villainy. In his famous soliloquy at the end of 3.2, he observes that he 'can smile, and murder whiles I smile'; he associates himself with a paragon of atheism and amorality in claiming he will 'set the murderous Machiavel to school'(see MACHIAVEL). His appreciation of his own viciousness seems very modern, as does his psychological motivation: his personality is formed in part by his physical deformity, a hunched back. In 3.2.154– 164, he attributes his own malevolence to this defect. Richard, established in *3 Henry VI* as mis-shapen and monstrously evil, will achieve heights of villainy in the following play in the sequence, which bears his name.

Shakespeare ties together his various strands in a spectacularly ironic final scene. The victorious Edward congratulates himself on his success, in pointed contrast to Richard's Judas kiss, which prepares us for the horrors of *Richard III*. In the final line, Edward carelessly rejoices in a future happiness that the audience knows very well to be doomed. The author has combined the consummation of his play's action with a foreshadowing of its sequel.

SOURCES OF THE PLAY

Shakespeare's main source for *3 Henry VI,* as for the other *Henry VI* plays, was *The Union of the Two Noble and Illustre Families of Lancastre and York,* by Edward HALL (2) (3rd ed., 1550). The playwright supplemented Hall's basic information with ideas from other sources, as was his habit. Most notably, the poem *Romeus and Juliet* (1562), by Arthur BROOKE (1), provided the germ of Queen Margaret's rousing speech at the beginning of 5.4, and Edmund SPENSER's *Faerie Queene* influenced the descriptions of the sun in 2.1. Minor elements can also be traced to A MIRROR FOR MAGISTRATES, a popular anthology of biographies, and to *The Spanish Tragedy* (1588–1589) and *Soliman and Perseda* (1590), plays by Thomas KYD.

TEXT OF THE PLAY

It is impossible to date the early history plays with certainty, but since all three *Henry VI* plays contain minor reflections of Edmund Spenser's *Faerie Queene,* published December 1589, they cannot have been written earlier than 1590. It is thought that the four plays of the minor tetralogy were written in the order in which they are read, and the last of them, *Richard III*, was apparently known to MARLOWE (1) by early 1592 (see RICHARD III, 'Text of the Play'); therefore, it seems likely that the four plays were composed between early 1590 and late 1591. If we assume the third of them to have been written in the third quarter of this span of time, we may date *3 Henry VI* to the first half of 1591.

The play was first published in the form in which we know it in the FIRST FOLIO of 1623, and that text has been the basis for all subsequent editions. However, a BAD QUARTO edition, known as THE TRUE TRAGEDY, was published by Thomas MILLINGTON in 1595 and again in 1600: these editions are known as Q1 and Q2 respectively. In 1619 a third quarto edition, Q3, was published by Thomas PAVIER in the same volume with a bad quarto of *2 Henry VI*. This edition is known as the WHOLE CONTENTION. Its text for *Part 3* is very close to that of Q1. While some minor details of the Folio text of the play may have come from the quartos, these editions are chiefly of historical interest.

Scholars believe that the Folio edition was derived largely from Shakespeare's FAIR COPY, as is indicated by the presence of elaborate stage directions, along with other minor clues. The editors of the Folio probably used a copy made by a scribe, for their text includes various small adjustments of a sort known to have been common in the work of Elizabethan scribes.

## THEATRICAL HISTORY OF THE PLAY

*Henry VI, Part 3* seems to have been popular in Shakespeare's day, although we have no documentary evidence of any particular performances. However, the title page of *The True Tragedy* informs us that the play had been performed by PEMBROKE'S MEN before they disbanded in 1593. The play's several quarto editions indicate a continuing public interest, as does the remark made by the CHORUS (1) at the end of *Henry V* that 'oft our stage hath shown' (Epilogue, 13) the events of the *Henry VI* plays. Further, Ben JONSON, writing in about 1612, referred to these works as particularly popular.

Subsequently, however, the play has not been notably well received. Favourable critical attention in the second half of the 17th century suggests that it was still read and regarded as a successful work, but the only performances known from the period were greatly altered, containing very little of Shakespeare's text (see, e.g., CROWNE). Two such productions are also known from the 18th century. A German production of *2 Henry VI* to celebrate the tercentenary of Shakespeare's birth in 1864 seems to have provided the only performances of the 19th century. The play has been produced a number of times in the 20th century, generally in cycles with the other plays of the minor tetralogy. It has been made for TELEVISION (1983) and also incorporated in two BBC series that abridge and combine the history plays: AN AGE OF KINGS (1960) and 'The Wars of the Roses' (1964), which presents the *Henry VI* plays and *Richard III*.

**Henry VIII, King of England (1491–1547)**  Historical figure and title character of *Henry VIII*. King Henry

is nominally the protagonist of the play, but he does not create the action; rather, he is placed in a series of situations and the change in the nature of his responses—as he grows from an easily influenced tool of evil men to a wise and mature ruler—illuminates the play's themes. The play's dominant moral point concerns the importance of humanity's capacity for good, which is represented in Henry's development. On another level, the play is about the establishment of England as a Protestant country, and as such it is a celebration of the TUDOR DYNASTY. Unlike Shakespeare's other English kings (see HISTORY PLAYS), Henry is not a realistic participant in political or military events, but rather a symbol for the greatness of England.

King Henry is dramatically subordinate to other figures in each of the play's episodes, though he alone appears throughout. In Acts 1 and 2 he is manipulated by Cardinal WOLSEY. First, the cardinal deceives him about the Duke of BUCKINGHAM (1), so that he sends an innocent man to death. However, Shakespeare makes certain that we do not blame Henry. Wolsey's evident villainy and Buckingham's saintly forgiveness indicate that the king's only offence is ignorance. In 1.4 the king meets and falls in love with the virtuous ANNE (1) BULLEN, who will become the mother of ELIZABETH (1) and who, as a Protestant, anticipates the English Reformation. Henry's connection to this righteous woman prepares us to sympathise with his moral qualms about his marriage to Queen KATHERINE of Aragon. He fears his sin in marrying his brother's widow has prevented him from fathering an heir to the throne of England, and this worry makes him susceptible to Wolsey's machinations. The king is again manipulated, but this time only through his own scrupulous morality. Moreover, because Katherine's fall leads to the ascendancy of Protestantism and the birth of Elizabeth, Shakespeare's audience could be expected to find the result satisfactory. When Henry rejects the 'dilatory sloth and tricks of Rome' (2.4.235) in favour of the 'well-beloved servant CRANMER' (2.4.236)—a famous Protestant leader—we see that from the play's point of view, Henry is progressing towards wisdom.

In 3.2 Wolsey is accidentally exposed as a profiteer and an opponent of Henry's marriage to Anne, and Henry responds forcefully, though he mercifully spares the cardinal's life. Wolsey then finds atonement with God, for which he thanks the king. Henry's actions are now unmistakably a force for good, even if it has taken a providential accident to spur him.

Act 4 offers a celebration of Anne—and indirectly of the Tudors generally—along with a restatement of the mercy and forgiveness that characterise the stories of Katherine and Wolsey. These themes further free Henry from blame, in a general atmosphere of blessedness. In Act 5 Henry's actions in support of good are taken on his own initiative, as he preserves

Cranmer from the wiles of Bishop GARDINER (1), Wolsey's successor as villain. Here we see the culmination of Henry's development. He is now a wise and masterful ruler, capable of foiling the evil intentions of Catholic sympathisers and preserving the Reformation's most important leader. It is at this pinnacle of maturity that Henry, in the play's finale, can pass on to the infant Elizabeth a virtuous realm and the prospect of prosperity for England.

The historical Henry VIII was far from the wise, benevolent, and virtuous ruler Shakespeare depicts. Shakespeare de-emphasised Henry's ruthlessness and altered history in order to refocus the play on the themes of forgiveness and mercy. Only a small segment of Henry's reign is dealt with. His expensive, inconclusive wars and his court's wasteful extravagance are not mentioned, and the vicious despotism of his later years is ignored. The future execution of Anne Boleyn (as Anne is known to history) is not so much as hinted at, nor is the existence of Henry's other ill-fated wives.

At the time of his accession in 1509, Henry was an intelligent and well-educated young man who was determined to be a good king. However, his egocentric desire to be a chivalric hero led him to wars and extravagance. He wasted the considerable treasury amassed by his father, the highly competent Henry VII (see RICHMOND), and left his successors with a serious debt problem. Moreover, he was a brutally tyrannical ruler, inclined to suspect treason without cause and to punish without mercy, especially as he got older. In contrast to the play, Henry probably ordered the trumped-up execution of Buckingham, for he feared that the duke, a distant relative, might try to seize the throne. Similarly, he beheaded the last PLANTAGENET (1), 68-year-old Margaret (the GIRL of *Richard III*), simply because she was a theoretical rival.

The divorce of Katherine of Aragon was also Henry's idea, and he was much less kind to his longtime wife than in the play. Katherine, however, was permitted to live out her life in peace; the king was less considerate of his later wives. Anne soon fell victim to Henry's need for a male heir. Henry was already involved with his next wife-to-be when Anne's second pregnancy ended in stillbirth. The king arranged false charges of adultery, incest (with a brother), and treason, and within weeks—less than three years after her coronation—Anne was beheaded. Henry was to marry five other wives, one of whom was also executed. His viciousness extended to others as well: he often chose execution as a punishment for failure or opposition. Thomas CROMWELL and Sir Thomas MORE were among his victims.

The king's behaviour in his later years has often been diagnosed as psychotic. Although this diagnosis is hypothetical, Henry VIII was undeniably a violent and arbitrary ruler. Shakespeare and his contemporaries, however, had a very positive image of Elizabeth's father: he was a national hero who had led England to Protestantism and freed the country from the corrupt influence of the Vatican. This view was widely disseminated by the historians of the Tudor dynasty, including Shakespeare's chief source for the play, HOLINSHED's *Chronicles*. From the playwright's point of view, the title character of *Henry VIII* is a perfectly plausible historical figure.

## Henry VIII

### SYNOPSIS

#### Prologue

The PROLOGUE (4) disclaims any attempt at humour. The play, he says, will be serious, full of important issues and unhappiness. Its noble scenes will inspire pity and also present the truth. For those who simply like a splendid show, it will prove satisfying. But it will not be a frivolous play, with foolery and fighting. The audience should prepare to be sad, for they will see great and noble people fall upon misery.

#### Act 1, Scene 1

The Duke of NORFOLK (3) tells the Duke of BUCKINGHAM (1) about the recent meeting in FRANCE (1) between King HENRY VIII and the French ruler. The two courts competed in displaying their wealth, and elaborate jousts were held. Norfolk notes that Cardinal WOLSEY arranged the meeting. Lord ABERGAVENNY joins the conversation, and the three men criticise Wolsey, especially for having seized too much power over England's affairs. They declare that the peace he negotiated with France is no good, for France is still seizing English trade goods. Norfolk, who has heard that Buckingham is feuding with Wolsey, warns him that his foe is dangerous. Wolsey himself arrives and exchanges glares with Buckingham. He speaks with his SECRETARY about a pending interview with Buckingham's SURVEYOR, or overseer, and declares that its results will cut the duke down to size. When he leaves, Buckingham rages against him, accusing him of treason. He asserts that the cardinal deliberately negotiated a weak treaty with France after being bribed by the Holy Roman Emperor, who feared a genuine peace between France and England. BRANDON (1) appears and arrests Buckingham and Abergavenny for treason; Buckingham says that his Surveyor has doubtless been bribed.

#### Act 1, Scene 2

At a meeting of his council, the king thanks Wolsey for having suppressed Buckingham's conspiracy. The queen, KATHERINE of Aragon, arrives and speaks on behalf of the people against the unjust taxes introduced by Wolsey. Norfolk adds that uprisings are occurring as a result. The king, who knows nothing of these taxes, orders Wolsey to invalidate them and pardon the rebels. In an aside the cardinal instructs his Secretary to issue these orders but to make it seem as though the relief came from him. Queen Katherine regrets the arrest of Buckingham, and King Henry suggests she hear the evidence. Buckingham's Surveyor is brought in and testifies that Buckingham had planned to become king if Henry died. Katherine doubts his testimony, but he goes on, reporting that the duke spoke of killing Wolsey and the king. Convinced, Henry rages against Buckingham.

### Act 1, Scene 3
The Lord CHAMBERLAIN (2), Lord SANDS, and Sir Thomas LOVELL (2) jest about the recent, deplorable rise of the French influence in manners and clothes. They then leave for a dinner being given by Wolsey, praising the cardinal's bountiful table.

### Act 1, Scene 4
The guests gather at Wolsey's banquet and jest bawdily with the young women there. On his arrival Wolsey encourages his guests to drink and enjoy one another. The Lord Chamberlain introduces a group of masquers (see MASQUE) who, dressed as shepherds, dance with the women. One of them is King Henry, who is clearly attracted to his partner. After the dance, the Lord Chamberlain introduces her to him as ANNE (1) BULLEN, one of the queen's ladies-in-waiting.

### Act 2, Scene 1
On a street in LONDON, a GENTLEMAN (14) meets a friend, who tells him of Buckingham's trial and conviction. Presuming that Wolsey was behind the duke's fall, the Gentlemen discuss the cardinal's political manoeuvrings. They remark that Wolsey is as hated by the common people as Buckingham is beloved. Buckingham then appears, under guard, and makes a speech, forgiving his enemies and asking for his friends' prayers. He compares himself to his father, who was also betrayed by a servant and unjustly killed as a traitor. After he leaves for his execution, the Gentlemen rue his fate. They go on to talk of a rumour that Wolsey's next victim will be Queen Katherine. The king, they say, has been incited to divorce her by Wolsey, who seeks to embarrass the Holy Roman Emperor—Katherine's nephew—who refused Wolsey an archbishopric he wanted. Another cardinal, CAMPEIUS, has come from ROME, allegedly to oversee the divorce.

### Act 2, Scene 2
The Lord Chamberlain discusses the king's possible divorce with Norfolk and the Duke of SUFFOLK (1). They, too, see the influence of Wolsey. They hope the king will come to his senses, remember the virtues of his 20-year marriage, and recognise the cardinal for the schemer he is. After the Lord Chamberlain leaves, the dukes approach the king, who is reading. He is angry at their interruption but welcomes the arrival of

Wolsey and Campeius. Norfolk and Suffolk leave, muttering curses at Wolsey. Henry then confers briefly with his secretary, GARDINER (1), and Wolsey informs Campeius that Gardiner will do whatever he, Wolsey, tells him to. Henry sends Gardiner with a message to the queen and announces that a hearing will be convened on the divorce question.

### Act 2, Scene 3
Anne Bullen, talking with an OLD LADY, pities the queen and says it would be better to be born poor than to be queen and subject to injustice and rejection. The Old Lady accuses her of hypocrisy and asserts, with bawdy quibbles, that she herself would gladly give up virginity for a crown. Anne declares that she would not. The Lord Chamberlain appears and announces the king's gift to Anne of a rich estate and title; she receives the news with great modesty, and the Chamberlain praises her in an aside. After he leaves, the Old Lady chortles over the gift, predicting that Anne will soon be a duchess. Anne, however, is offended and thinks again of the unfortunate queen.

### Act 2, Scene 4
After a grand procession and formal proclamations by a CRIER, the divorce proceedings begin. Addressing Henry, Katherine argues that she has always been a good and faithful wife. When Wolsey and Campeius object to her personal remarks, she replies that she refuses to be judged by an enemy. She demands a hearing from the pope and leaves. Henry, while praising her, also declares Wolsey innocent of any enmity towards her or any influence on himself. He asserts that he fears that his marriage is sinful because Katherine was once married to his elder brother. Though the church approved his marriage to Katherine at the time, he wants another ruling, to clear his conscience. Campeius declares an adjournment until the queen can be made to attend. In an aside Henry deplores these formalities and wishes his adviser CRANMER were present to expedite matters.

### Act 3, Scene 1
Wolsey and Campeius visit Katherine and suggest that she abandon her defence and accept the king's decision to avoid the scandal of a divorce trial. Raging at them, she decries her helplessness but finally subsides into acceptance.

### Act 3, Scene 2
Norfolk, Suffolk, Lord SURREY (5), and the Lord Chamberlain discuss Wolsey's downfall: Henry has learned that the cardinal secretly opposed the divorce (now completed) and did not wish the king to marry the virtuous Anne Bullen. But Henry has secretly done so and plans to make her queen; moreover, Wolsey's enemy, Cranmer, has been appointed Archbishop of Canterbury. Wolsey appears, seeming troubled, and muses in an aside that he intends to

see the king marry a French duchess and not Anne Bullen. The king arrives and tells the noblemen that Wolsey has mistakenly included personal financial records among state papers sent to the king. Henry is shocked at the cardinal's wealth. He approaches Wolsey and sardonically praises him for putting his duty above personal gain. After giving him a folder of papers, Henry leaves angrily with the noblemen. When Wolsey sees that the papers include his records and his letters opposing the divorce, he realises that all is lost. The noblemen return and recite a long series of formal charges against him, adding that the king has ordered all his possessions confiscated. They leave and the cardinal soliloquises on his loss of greatness, comparing it to humanity's common end in death. He now recognises the futility of his pride and riches. When his follower CROMWELL approaches him, Wolsey declares that his downfall has led him to a fresh, healthier view of life. His conscience is finally free, and he has the fortitude to withstand whatever earthly miseries may be in store. Cromwell grieves for his master's downfall, but Wolsey encourages him to serve as an adviser to the king. For himself, he regrets not having given as much energy to religion as to the state.

### Act 4, Scene 1
The two Gentlemen meet again, at the coronation parade of Queen Anne. A grand procession passes by, including Suffolk, Norfolk, and Surrey—all now high officers of the realm—as well as the new queen. A Third Gentleman, who has seen the actual coronation, describes the ceremony in great detail. The discussion turns to political gossip: Gardiner, who is now Bishop of Winchester, is an enemy of Archbishop Cranmer, but the latter has a new and powerful ally in Cromwell, who is a close adviser of the king.

### Act 4, Scene 2
At KIMBOLTON, Katherine learns of Wolsey's death from her attendant, GRIFFITH. According to Griffith, the cardinal repented before his death and died at peace with God. When Katherine speaks bitterly of Wolsey, Griffith offers a charitable view of him, describing him as an excellent public servant who, though greedy for wealth, was also generous with his ill-gotten gains—founding two colleges, for instance. Katherine, who is near death, thanks Griffith for pointing to the Christian viewpoint. She falls asleep and sees a vision, which appears on-stage: six dancing figures ceremoniously present her with garlands of bay leaves. When she awakes, her waiting-woman PATIENCE observes that she is near death. She then receives a visitor, Lord CAPUCHIUS, the ambassador to England from her nephew the emperor. She asks him to take King Henry a letter, in which she asks to be remembered to their daughter and requests that he

treat her followers and servants well. She then retires to bed, prepared to die.

### Act 5, Scene 1
Bishop Gardiner meets Lovell in the middle of the night and learns that Queen Anne is in labour and may die. Gardiner hopes she does and insists, over Lovell's objection, that for them and their allies, it would be best if Anne, Cranmer, and Cromwell were all dead. He adds that he believes he has brought the king's council to move against Archbishop Cranmer's Protestant opinions. The council will interrogate the archbishop in the morning. After Gardiner leaves, the king arrives and meets Cranmer, whom he has sent for. Though Lovell tries to eavesdrop, the king orders him away. Henry tells Cranmer that he will have enemies at the council meeting in the morning. Cranmer declares that he has nothing to fear, but Henry warns him against false witnesses. Observing that the council may try to gaol him, he gives him a ring to signify the king's protection. Cranmer leaves, and Anne's companion the Old Lady arrives to inform the king that he has a daughter. She first comically identifies the infant as a boy and then complains about the size of the tip the king gives her.

### Act 5, Scene 2
Cranmer arrives for the council meeting but, insultingly, is kept waiting outside. Doctor BUTTS brings the king to an upper room, where he can watch the proceedings. After Cranmer is admitted, the CHANCELLOR accuses him of spreading heresies; Gardiner adds that severe treatment is called for, lest civil disorders arise from the heresy, like the religious wars then raging in Germany. Although Cranmer asserts his opposition to civil disorder, Gardiner insists that he must be imprisoned. Cromwell says Gardiner is too harsh, and Gardiner accuses him of involvement in heresy himself. The Chancellor then orders Cranmer to prison, but the archbishop produces the king's ring. His enemies are dumbfounded, realising that the king has stymied them. The king then emerges from his vantage point and castigates them mercilessly. He confirms his support for Cranmer by asking him to baptise his daughter.

### Act 5, Scene 3
On the day of the christening the PORTER (4) and his MAN (3) are unable to prevent a crowd of celebrating commoners from invading the palace courtyard. They make comical remarks about the riotous celebrants.

### Act 5, Scene 4
A grand procession escorts the infant ELIZABETH (1). It is led by the GARTER, who recites a prayer for her. Cranmer addresses the assembled court, predicting a great future for the child and happiness for the coun-

try. The king thanks him and declares the day a holiday for all.

*Epilogue*
An actor asserts that people may criticise the play for various reasons, but that all must concede that it has glorified good women, and so he supposes it will get applause, for no men will withhold it when their ladies prompt them.

## COMMENTARY

*Henry VIII*, though classed with the HISTORY PLAYS, treats English history in a very different way. The play does not realistically enact a political conflict, as the other history plays do. Rather, it is a symbolic tribute to the TUDOR DYNASTY, presented in the manner of Shakespeare's other late plays, the ROMANCES. Like these plays, it uses an episodic plot line, studded with spectacles and tableaus, and closes with the promise of a new generation. Moreover, *Henry VIII* makes the same moral point as the romances—that humanity depends on divine providence, which requires that we exercise our capacity for good through a steadfast spirit, mercy, and forgiveness. The play celebrates King Henry VIII's attainment of wisdom and the country's simultaneous rejection of the authority of Catholic Rome, but Henry does not guide the play's development so much as he is simply its leading figure. A national myth is embodied in *Henry VIII*—that England is chosen by providence for Protestant freedom—and it is Henry who leads the country there. The final tableau confirms Henry's virtues in those predicted for his daughter Elizabeth, the last and greatest of Tudor monarchs. In the earlier history plays, the qualities of the characters, good and bad, generated events; here, history is driven by destiny.

As in the romantic literature on which Shakespeare's last plays were based, the rise or fall of great personages is displayed in a series of brief, almost actionless scenes that enact a pattern of loss and regeneration. Buckingham (1) is executed and Queen Katherine humiliated because of the Cardinal Wolsey's enmity; then Wolsey is exposed and discredited. Anne Bullen (better known today as Anne Boleyn) is crowned, and Cromwell and Cranmer assume high office. Finally, Cranmer's enemies—led by Wolsey's one-time underling, Bishop Gardiner—are confounded. All these events are given significance in relation to the growth of Henry. The king is easily deceived by Wolsey about Buckingham, and his moral qualms about his first marriage help Wolsey bring about the fall of Katherine. Although the intervention of chance is necessary to expose the cardinal, the king then masterfully subdues him. The king recognises good in the virtuous—and Protestant—Anne, despite Wolsey's attempts to keep her from him, and the king's maturing wisdom contributes to the rise of Cromwell and Cranmer, two fine men, the latter an important Protestant religious hero. Finally, the king saves Cranmer from Gardiner's machinations. When the monarch has thus arrived at a summit of wisdom and maturity, he brings forth a glorious successor in Elizabeth, who is rhapsodically praised by Cranmer in 5.4. Cranmer's eulogy even extends to the monarch ruling at the time the play was written, Elizabeth's successor, King JAMES I.

*Henry VIII* also resembles the romances in its use of pageantry. The play opens with a description of elaborate ceremonies and closes with the enactment of one. Between the opening and the close there are several spectacular tableaus, often with heavily descriptive stage directions that indicate their importance to the play. These episodes are more than mere entertainment, however. In the first half of the play, they demonstrate the effects of evil on the play's world; in the second, they evidence the exaltation of its recovery from evil.

In 1.1 the meeting of monarchs in France is described in terms that convey greed and corruption. One side's display resembles 'heathen gods' (1.1.19); the other then makes 'a fool and beggar' (1.1.28) of its competitor. The women 'almost sweat to bear' (1.1.24) their jewelry. Most significant, 'these fierce vanities' (1.1.54) are associated with the villainies of Wolsey; moreover, the treaty being celebrated is shown to be worthless. In 1.4 the cardinal's banquet offers an aura of decadence, especially in the risqué conversation before the king's masque, which is important to our sense of Wolsey's evil effect on the court. (On the other hand, the masque, during which Henry falls in love with Anne—a development that counters Wolsey's evil—is a lovely, ordered dance.) In 2.1 Buckingham is solemnly led to execution with 'tipstaves before him, the axe with the edge towards him, halberds on each side' (2.1.53, stage direction); the grandeur of the play's world becomes increasingly ominous. An extremely elaborate stage direction at the opening of 2.4 describes in detail the panoply of Katherine's divorce trial. Particularly gaudy is the ecclesiastical pomp of the two cardinals, clad in their scarlet robes and escorted by 'two Gentlemen bearing two great silver pillars'. However, their rich display cannot help the king, who is attempting to rectify a sin that has deprived the nation of an heir to the throne. As the scene ends, Henry rejects the 'dilatory sloth and tricks of Rome' (2.4.235) in favour of the 'well-beloved' (2.4.236) Cranmer. Here, the play's luxuriant splendour is associated with Catholicism, but the path of recovery is evident.

After Wolsey's downfall and the revelation that Anne is to become queen in Act 3, we again find spectacle in Act 4, but now the association is entirely positive. In 4.1 a complex, 10-part stage direction presents the coronation procession. The Gentlemen remark on the participants, including Anne: '. . . the sweetest face I ever look'd on . . . an angel' (4.1.43–44). The Third Gentleman then provides a description of another ritual ceremony, the actual coronation, in entirely positive terms. The splendid and spectacular are now associated with the good of England and the triumph of virtue. Although Katherine's vision in 4.2 is in a very different key, it, too, is presented in great detail; it is also entertaining on stage and distinctly linked with virtue, in this case more personal and religious. Lastly, there is another procession preceding Cranmer's speech at Elizabeth's christening. This sumptuous parade provides a fitting culmination to the play's use of ceremony and ritual as expressions of moral tone. Here, the triumph of virtue is confirmed in another formal display of religion, but this time it is a Protestant religion—a distinction immediately evident to Shakespeare's audience, through costume as well as Cranmer's presence.

Divine intervention underlies the play's developments. In the first half this is clear in the way chance brings Anne to the king's attention and exposes Wolsey. It is also evident in the forgiving attitude and acceptance of God's will of Wolsey's victims. In the second half of the play, the religious theme becomes prominent, limiting the importance of personality among the play's chief characters. Henry demonstrates the significance of personal growth—the wisdom and maturity he attains in the course of the play are necessary to its happy conclusion—but he simply displays differing outlooks, without going through a process of internal development.

More striking as personalities are the 'tragic' characters, who embody the importance of patiently accepting fate. However, they are restricted in emotional range, precisely to emphasise their thematic significance. Buckingham, Katherine, and Cardinal Wolsey appear only briefly before meeting their fates; they achieve importance only at their downfalls, when they respond to adversity with dignity and wisdom.

Upon his arrest, Buckingham's anger against Wolsey—his only trait so far—disappears, and he simply says, 'The will of heav'n / Be done . . . I obey' (1.1. 209–210). In this he is supported by his fellow victim, Abergavenny. On his way to be executed in 2.1, Buckingham forgives his enemies and accepts his downfall as a blessing. Though he reveals some bitterness in recollecting his father's similar fate, he controls it and departs with a prayer: 'I have done, and God forgive me' (2.1.136).

Queen Katherine's conduct at her trial—her dignity as she presents her case, her fire as she turns against Wolsey, and her resolute departure—is truly impressive. Even when she recognises defeat, she finds powerful poetry to express it: 'like the lily / That once was

mistress of the field and flourish'd, / I'll hang my head and perish' (3.1.152–153). (This episode is introduced with the SONG 'Orpheus with his lute' [3.1.3–14], which in its union of mysticism and music is a typical ploy of Shakespearean romances.) Perhaps most important is Katherine's joint demonstration, with Griffith, of forgiveness towards Wolsey. In her mild way, the deposed and dying queen is bitter towards her enemy, but after Griffith's recital of the cardinal's hidden virtues, she confirms that 'religious truth and modesty' require her declaration, 'peace be with him' (4.2.74, 75). She approaches her death 'meditating / On that celestial harmony I go to' (4.2.79–80). Her vision adds supernatural sanction to our impression of her virtues, as well as reinforcing the importance of divine intervention in the play's world.

Most significant, the play's only important villain, Wolsey, makes a similar demonstration of acceptance. Once his downfall is certain, in 3.2, the cardinal recognises the futility of his struggle for wealth and power, and rejects the 'Vain pomp and glory of this world' (3.2.365). Free from the temptations of intrigue and ambition, he finds 'A peace above all earthly dignities, / A still and quiet conscience' (3.2.379–380), and he thanks the king, who has overthrown him, for his newly found 'fortitude of soul' (3.2.388). He considerately advises Cromwell on both worldly advancement and spiritual health, before departing from the court with the wish that he had 'but serv'd my God with half the zeal / I serv'd my king' (3.2.455–456). In 4.2 Griffith repeats the lesson in describing the cardinal's death: 'His overthrow heap'd happiness upon him, / For then, . . . [he] found the blessedness of being little / And . . . died fearing God' (4.2.63–68). Thus, Wolsey's end, like those of Buckingham and Katherine, points to the ultimate superiority of the divine over the mundane. The eulogies Shakespeare provides for the cardinal are all the more important when we consider what a departure they were from the standard English view of his day. For most English Protestants of the 16th and 17th centuries, Wolsey was a chief villain of pre-Reformation English Catholicism; to present him as a recipient of God's mercy was to make mercy a prominent theme indeed.

Like the romances, *Henry VIII* stresses the triumph of good and the importance of patience in adversity, elevating these propositions by placing them in a schematic plot in which it is clear that God controls all. However, unlike the romances, the plan is set in an historical world, one still very well known to the play's original audience. It is not only a moral tale of suffering borne with dignity, it is a national myth. Here the regenerative pattern of the romances is employed to display the redemption of a particular country at a particular time—England as it acquired the state church—and the anti-Catholic stance—with which its people largely identified in Shakespeare's time. In the spirit of the romances, this process yields great optimism: old errors are expiated in an atmosphere of reconciliation, and the future offers the promise of a new generation. The providence that lends strength to the allegorical characters of *Pericles, Cymbeline, The Winter's Tale,* and *The Tempest* is here devoted to an entire people. *Henry VIII* is history in a romantic mode.

## SOURCES OF THE PLAY

Shakespeare's principal source for most of *Henry VIII* was Raphael HOLINSHED's *Chronicles of England, Scotland, and Ireland* (Second edition, 1587), supplemented by the account of Henry's reign in *The Union of the Two Noble and Illustre Families of Lancaster and York* (1548) by Edward HALL (2). However, for the trial of Cranmer in 5.1–2, the playwright relied on John FOXE's *Book of Martyrs* (1563).

## TEXT OF THE PLAY

Since 1850, Shakespeare's authorship of *Henry VIII* has been disputed. Some scholars have thought the play was too badly organised to be the work of a single author and have attributed much of the play to John FLETCHER (2). Some go so far as to hold that Shakespeare did not write any of it, ascribing it to Fletcher and Philip MASSINGER. The question is still argued, but increasingly scholarly opinion tends to find the play wholly Shakespearean for a variety of reasons. For one, the FIRST FOLIO editors accepted *Henry VIII* while rejecting the plays known to be Fletcher-Shakespeare collaborations (*The Two Noble Kinsmen* and CARDENIO). Moreover, the use of sources seems consistent throughout the play, and it is different from Fletcher's practise elsewhere. Finally, the 'disorganisation' of *Henry VIII* seems less significant if one compares the play with Shakespeare's contemporary romances, which are intentionally episodic, rather than with his histories, which are more narrative in structure.

*Henry VIII* was written between late 1612 and June 1613, when the GLOBE THEATRE burned down during a performance of it. (A report of this event calls the play ALL IS TRUE, apparently a subtitle.) By its style *Henry VIII* can be identified as a very late work, so it was probably written not long before this performance. It may have been composed specifically for the celebration of the marriage of the Princess ELIZABETH (3) in February 1613, as is suggested by its patriotism and its particular attention to the princess' namesake. In any case, its suitability for Elizabeth's marriage also made it an appropriate offering to the public that spring. In sum, most commentators agree that it was first performed in early 1613 and written not long before.

*Henry VIII* was first published in the First Folio (1623). The text derives from the author's FOUL PAPERS (or possibly from the FAIR COPY made by a professional scribe), for it has elaborate and literary stage directions (some taken directly from source material), which would have been abbreviated in a PROMPT-BOOK. The Folio offers the only early text and has therefore been the basis for all subsequent editions.

## THEATRICAL HISTORY OF THE PLAY

As already noted, *Henry VIII* may have been first performed as part of the festivities celebrating the marriage of Princess Elizabeth in the winter of 1612–1613. However, it is not in the list of 14 Shakespeare plays staged by the KING'S MEN during the winter's wedding festivities (though it may have been the play cancelled due to scheduling conflicts on February 16). The earliest recorded performance (but clearly not the first) was on June 29, 1613, when cannon fire—called for in the stage direction at 1.4.49—set fire to the thatched roof of the Globe and burned the theatre to the ground. A tradition first reported in 1708 held that John LOWIN was the original Henry and 'had his instructions' from Shakespeare himself, which suggests that the playwright may have directed the production. One other early staging is known: a private performance in July 1628, commissioned by King Charles I's favourite, George Villiers, Duke of Buckingham. Though no relation to the play's Buckingham, Villiers reportedly left the performance after the duke is led away to be executed in 2.1. (He was himself assassinated a few weeks later.)

After the reopening of the London theatres following 18 years of revolutionary government, *Henry VIII* was staged by William DAVENANT in 1664, with Thomas BETTERTON as King Henry and Henry HARRIS (2) as Wolsey; Samuel PEPYS saw it, but his account of a play about Henry 'with all his wives' suggests that it may have been considerably altered by Davenant. It was recorded as a 'stock play' for Davenant's company over the next few decades, though no specific performance was noted. It then disappeared for a generation.

In 1716 it was revived by Colley CIBBER (1), who produced it frequently during the next decade and added increasingly spectacular scenic effects, especially for the coronation procession in 4.1. Appropriately, Cibber presented the play at the coronation of King George II in 1727. Barton BOOTH (1) played the title role in Cibber's presentations.

The coronation procession from *Henry VIII* was often performed separately in the middle of the 18th century, as part of a programme of pantomimes or even along with other plays. David GARRICK continued the trend to spectacle—his production, revived many times between 1742 and 1768—required 140 actors in 4.1. Other elements were cut to make time for this one, most notably the vision of Queen Katherine in 4.2. Garrick played Henry opposite the Queen Katherine of Hannah PRITCHARD.

After a 20-year hiatus, J. P. KEMBLE (3) revived *Henry VIII* in 1788, with his sister Sarah SIDDONS as Queen Katherine, a role for which she was particularly acclaimed throughout her career. Kemble himself played Cromwell (to whom he assigned Griffith's part, as well). After 1803, as manager of the Covent Garden Theatre, Kemble revived the play numerous times, often playing Wolsey, and after his retirement in 1817, his younger brother Charles KEMBLE (1) continued the tradition. In 1830 Charles' daughter Fanny KEMBLE (2), though only 20-years old, was successful as Queen Katherine.

*Henry VIII* naturally appealed to the 19th-century taste for spectacle, and the next notable production, that of Charles KEAN (1) in 1855, was probably the most elaborate. His 5.4 opened with (in his words) 'the Lord Mayor and City Council proceeding to the royal ceremonial in their state barges, to give a panoramic view [on a moving backdrop] of London, as it then appeared'. He managed nonetheless to restore material often dropped from earlier productions, such as the role of Griffith and Katherine's vision (in which Ellen TERRY [1], as a small child, played an angel in a revival of 1858). Henry IRVING staged *Henry VIII* in 1892, with Terry as Katherine, Irving himself as Wolsey, and Johnston FORBES-ROBERTSON as Buckingham. Irving's production was no less sumptuous than its predecessors, and it was wildly popular.

In the 20th century, the popularity of *Henry VIII* has waned somewhat, but a number of notable productions have been staged. Beerbohm TREE presented the play in a characteristically extravagant adaptation that cut Act 5 entirely. This spectacular, starring Tree as Wolsey, was a hit in London (1910) and New York (1916). Sir Lewis CASSON produced the play with Sybil THORNDIKE as Katherine in 1925. Margaret WEBSTER (3) presented it in New York in 1946, as the inaugural production of the American Repertory Company, with Eva Le Gallienne (b. 1899) as Katherine. Tyrone GUTHRIE has staged it three times: in 1933 at SADLER'S WELLS THEATRE, with Charles LAUGHTON in the title role; in 1949 at STRATFORD, with Anthony QUAYLE as Henry; and at the OLD VIC THEATRE in 1953, in honour of the coronation of Queen Elizabeth II. Michael BENTHALL'S OLD VIC (1958) production starred John GIELGUD as Wolsey and Edith EVANS (1) as Katherine.

Tree's 1910 production of *Henry VIII* was the basis for a brief silent FILM made in 1911, but since only five scenes were filmed, over a period of only two hours including rehearsals, it is fair to say that *Henry VIII* has not yet been produced as a movie. It was made for TELEVISION in 1979, with Claire Bloom (b. 1931) as Queen Katherine.

**Henryson, Robert (c. 1430–before 1506)** Scottish poet, author of a poem known to Shakespeare as part of Geoffrey CHAUCER's long poem *Troilus and Criseyde*, a chief source for *Troilus and Cressida*. Henryson's *Testament of Cresseid* continued Chaucer's story. Although it is written in a Scots dialect, Henryson's poem, like Chaucer's, is written in RHYME ROYAL, and for centuries it was regarded as Chaucer's work. In every edition of *Troilus and Criseyde* from 1532 to 1710, it was published as part of the poem. In Henryson's sequel to the story, CRESSIDA is stricken with leprosy as a punishment for her faithlessness and TROILUS gives her alms without recognising her. This development is referred to in *Henry V* (2.1.76) and *Twelfth Night* (3.1.56), so we know that Shakespeare had read Henryson, but oddly it is not mentioned in *Troilus and Cressida*, unless Cressida's future status as a beggar is alluded to in Troilus' pained complaint that the 'orts of her love, / The fragments, scraps, the bits, and greasy relics / Of her o'er-eaten faith are given to Diomed' (5.2.157–159).

**Henslowe, Philip (d. 1616)** English theatrical entrepreneur, owner of the ROSE, FORTUNE, and HOPE THEATRES and the keeper of a record book that has survived as a principal source on ELIZABETHAN and JACOBEAN THEATRE. Henslowe, the son of a gamekeeper, was a servant to the bailiff of a nobleman in the 1570s. He married the bailiff's widow and thereby acquired the money to establish himself in business. He was first a dyer, then a pawnbroker and a dealer in real estate, mostly in SOUTHWARK, just across the Thames River from LONDON. In 1585 he leased a plot of land there, upon which he built the Rose Theatre, which opened in 1588. In 1592 his step-daughter married the great actor William ALLEYN, who became Henslowe's partner. His company, the ADMIRAL'S MEN, played at the Rose for most of the rest of the century, making theatrical history while also making Henslowe and Alleyn rich. Henslowe also had other theatrical properties. By 1594 he either owned or leased the theatre at NEWINGTON BUTTS, and he and Alleyn bought a licence to put on bull- and bear-baiting entertainments, a profitable sideline. In 1600 he and Alleyn built the FORTUNE THEATRE, to which the Admiral's Men moved, while the Rose was abandoned when its ground lease expired. In 1613 Henslowe tore down the old animal-baiting arena and built the HOPE THEATRE, where various companies played, financed by Henslowe. These arrangements resulted in a lawsuit of 1615, in the records of which Henslowe is shown to have had a reputation as a tough businessman. However, his relations with theatrical companies seem otherwise to have been mostly good.

Henslowe's *Diary*, as the collection of his papers is called—though it is actually an account book—covers the years 1592 to 1603, recording the performances at the Rose through 1597 and the revenues each earned, as well as the loans and advances that Henslowe made to acting companies (mostly the Admiral's Men) and to individual players, for he was essentially a banker to them. Henslowe bought the plays the Admiral's Men performed, as well as their costumes and props, all of which are recorded in the *Diary*. He was repaid—with great interest—from the company's share of the playhouse revenues. His papers were inherited by Alleyn, who left them in the collections at Dulwich College, where they were forgotten until Edmond MALONE discovered them in 1790.

**Herald (1)**   Minor character in *2 Henry VI*, a messenger from the king summoning the Duke of GLOUCESTER (4) to a meeting of Parliament in 2.4.70.

**Herald (2)**   Either of two minor characters in *Richard II*, petty officials at the trial by combat between BOLINGBROKE (1) and MOWBRAY (1) in 1.3. Each Herald cries out a formal statement of purpose for one contestant.

**Herald (3)**   Either of two minor characters in *King John*, the respective representatives of King JOHN (3) of England and King PHILIP (2) of FRANCE (1), to the city of ANGIERS in 2.1. Each Herald formally proclaims the victory of his King in the preceding skirmish and demands that the city declare its loyalty to that ruler and open its gates to his soldiers. The symmetrical opposition of the Heralds emphasises the difficulty in resolving competing claims to power, an important theme of the play.

**Herald (4)**   Minor character in *Henry V*, a messenger who brings King HENRY V a written account of the French fatalities at AGINCOURT. The Herald speaks only one line.

**Herald (5)**   Character in *Othello*. See GENTLEMAN (6).

**Herald (6)**   Minor character in *King Lear*, an official at the duel in which EDGAR kills EDMUND. In 5.3.110–116 the Herald announces to the troops of ALBANY, GONERIL, and REGAN that Edmund will defend himself against any challenger who dares to assert that 'he is a manifould traitor' (5.3.112), as Albany has said someone intends to do. When Edgar, disguised, appears, the Herald formally asks him to identify himself, though once Edgar replies his answer is taken up by Albany and Edmund, and the Herald is not heard from again. His small part helps create a sense of chivalrous order to the final retribution upon Edmund.

**Herald (7)**   Minor character in *Coriolanus*. In 2.1 the Herald accompanies the army's return into ROME, and formally announces that Caius MARTIUS (2) has been awarded a new name. In honour of his extraordinary bravery in taking the city of CORIOLES, he is to be

known henceforth as CORIOLANUS. The Herald speaks five grandiose lines and concludes with the cry, 'Welcome to Rome, renowned Coriolanus!' (2.1.165), that is repeated by the assembled crowd. Shakespeare provided the Herald to lend an air of pomp and circumstance to Coriolanus' reception. This heightens the dramatic irony when this same reception turns ugly later in the same act.

**Herald (8)**   Minor character in *The Two Noble Kinsmen*, an attendant to Duke THESEUS (2) of ATHENS. In 1.4, following the defeat of King Creon of THEBES, the Herald informs Theseus of the identity of two of his noble prisoners of war, ARCITE and PALAMON, the title characters of the play. The main plot is thereby begun. The Herald is an extra, whose splendid official uniform provides colour, if not authenticity, to a scene of ancient warfare.

**Herbert (1), Henry (1595–1673)**   Longtime MASTER OF REVELS for King JAMES I and King Charles I. Herbert was a minor nobleman, a cousin of the Earls of PEMBROKE (1, 2, 3) and brother of the famed poet George Herbert (1593–1633). Beginning in 1622 Herbert leased the office of Master of Revels—licenser of theatrical productions and publications—from its appointed holder, Sir John Ashley (d. 1641), a minor courtier. He paid £150 a year and collected for himself the many fees that were paid to the Master. Though Herbert was nominally the Deputy to the Master of Revels, he was formally recognised as the rightful exerciser of the Master's powers and was knighted by King JAMES I in 1623.

Upon Ashley's death Herbert became Master in name as well as fact, but in the summer of 1642, when the civil war erupted and the Puritan government of London closed the theatres, the office ceased to pay. In 1660 when the monarchy was restored, Herbert attempted to reclaim the powers of the Master of Revels, but the new, unfettered licences granted to producers William DAVENANT and Thomas KILLIGREW took precedence. After a series of unsuccessful lawsuits, Herbert retired.

A volume of Herbert's official records, known as his *Office Book*, survived into the 18th century, when it was used and recorded in part by such scholars as George CHALMERS and Edmond MALONE. It was subsequently lost, but extensive quotations from it remain and provide scholars with an important glimpse of the 17th-century English theatre.

**Herbert (2), Henry, Philip, or William, Earls of Pembroke**   See PEMBROKE (1, 2, 3).

**Herbert (3), Sir Walter (c. 1462–after 1485)**   Historical figure and minor character in *Richard III*, an officer under RICHMOND. Herbert, whose father, William of

PEMBROKE (4), has a non-speaking role in *3 Henry VI*, speaks one line in 5.2 and is present but silent in 5.3.

**Hermia** Character in *A Midsummer Night's Dream,* one of the four lovers whose adventures in the enchanted wood are the centre-piece of the play. In 1.1, when Hermia's father, EGEUS, demands that she be punished for refusing to marry DEMETRIUS (2), her civil but firm response reveals a determined nature. Her first words, a straightforward assertion of her beloved LYSANDER's virtues, indicate that she will not easily be deterred. When Lysander's love is magically diverted to HELENA (1), Hermia is prepared to fight for her man, and she drives her friend away. Several remarks indicate that Hermia is a brunette with a dark complexion, and she has often been associated with the 'Dark Lady' of Shakespeare's SONNETS, which he was writing at about the same time.

**Hermione** Character in *The Winter's Tale,* wife of King LEONTES of SICILIA and mother of PERDITA. Unjustly accused of adultery by her mad husband, Hermione gives birth in prison to Perdita, whom Leontes condemns to be abandoned in the wilderness; then her son MAMILLIUS dies just as Leontes sentences her to death. The shock of this loss kills her, according to her ally Lady PAULINA. However, Paulina keeps Hermione alive in secret, awaiting the time when Leontes shall have sufficiently repented. In 5.3, after Perdita has miraculously reappeared, Paulina offers to display a statue of Hermione, which is actually the still-living queen herself. As the others watch in awe, Hermione comes to life, and the play closes with reunion and reconciliation.

Hermione is a passive but highly important figure in the play. Her fate in the tragic first half makes her an emblem of a major theme of the play—indeed, of all Shakespeare's ROMANCES—the critical role of providence in securing human happiness in an unreliable world. Even more, she helps illustrate that the efficacy of providence depends on the moral strength of good people in the face of evil. Her dignity in the face of her undeserved fate is highly impressive. Even the steady strength of the poetry she speaks contrasts favourably with the hysterical ranting of Leontes. She puts her faith in providence, saying, 'if powers divine / Behold our human actions (as they do), / I doubt not then but innocence shall make / False accusation blush' (3.2. 28–31). Upon her reappearance she restates this attitude when she invokes a blessing on Perdita—'You gods, look down, / And from your sacred vial pour your graces / Upon my daughter's head' (5.3.121–123).

Hermione displays a loving nature that anticipates the role of Perdita in the second half of the play. Her charm is evident in 1.2, when, at Leontes' request, she

persuades King POLIXENES of BOHEMIA to extend his visit. This arouses Leontes' jealous suspicions, but it also demonstrates Hermione's fine qualities: a readiness for friendship and an intelligent appreciation of the previous affection between her husband and Polixenes. Her capacity for love is delightfully demonstrated in 2.1, where we see her playing with Mamillius. Her evident goodness makes her apparent death all the more tragic and her apparent resurrection all the more Christlike. Although Hermione's significance diminishes in the second half, in the first—and at the conclusion—she is key to *The Winter's Tale*'s presentation of humanity's capacity for good.

**Hero** Character in *Much Ado About Nothing,* daughter of LEONATO and beloved of CLAUDIO (1). Hero is a demure and pliant maid, a conventional representative of the Elizabethan ideal of docile womanhood. She accepts an arranged marriage, first to Don PEDRO and then to Claudio. She is pleasant and has enough sparkle to engage in the ploy whereby her cousin BEATRICE is tricked into accepting BENEDICK's love, but she largely lacks personality or spirit. A pawn, first proffered in marriage to Claudio and then rejected by him, she can only faint when unjustly accused of promiscuity. Beatrice, Benedick, and the FRIAR (2) stand up for her, and Constable DOGBERRY's timely exposure of the villainous Don JOHN (1) finally clears her, but she is herself inactive. Significantly, once she and Claudio are finally reunited, they barely speak, as the play's focus immediately shifts to Beatrice and Benedick.

Hero's name—which bears no relation to the common noun *hero,* though it is pronounced the same—comes from an ancient Greek tale of two lovers that was very well known in Shakespeare's day as the subject of the immensely popular poem 'Hero and Leander', by Christopher MARLOWE (1). In naming his tractable heroine after a famous romantic lover, Shakespeare may have intended a mild irony.

**Hervey (Harvey), William (c. 1565–1642)** English soldier, possible 'Mr W. H'. of the dedication to the SONNETS. Hervey was the stepfather of Shakespeare's patron, the Earl of SOUTHAMPTON (2), and some scholars believe that he provided manuscripts of the Sonnets to the publisher, Thomas THORPE, who therefore dedicated his 1609 edition to him as the 'onlie begetter' of the poems, 'begetter' being taken to mean 'procurer'.

As a young man, Hervey distinguished himself fighting against the Spanish Armada in 1588, and he was knighted for his service under the Earl of ESSEX (2) at Cadiz in 1596. He married the Countess of Southampton in 1599, and after her death in 1607 he married Cordell Annesley, whose concern for her mad father, Brian ANNESLEY, may have helped inspire *King*

*Lear.* Hervey continued soldiering, mostly in Ireland, and was rewarded with great estates by King JAMES I. He died a wealthy man.

Shakespeare probably had Hervey (also known as Harvey) in mind when he changed the name of his character HARVEY (1), in *1. Henry IV*, to PETO. Several such name changes were made (see OLDCASTLE, ROSSILL) to avoid giving offence to powerful aristocrats.

**Heyes, Thomas (d. c. 1604)** LONDON bookseller and publisher, producer of the first edition of *The Merchant of Venice*. In 1600 Heyes bought the copyright to *The Merchant* from the printer James ROBERTS. He published a QUARTO edition, known as Q1, and used Roberts as the printer. When he died, Heyes left the rights to the play to his son Laurence (d. 1637), whose protest at Thomas PAVIER's illicit publication in 1619 led to the exposure of Pavier's FALSE FOLIO.

**Heywood (1), John (c. 1497–c. 1580)** Early English dramatist. Heywood was a musician at the courts of King HENRY VIII, King Edward VI, and Queen Mary I, and wrote dramatic dialogues for the intermissions in musical entertainments (see INTERLUDE). He contributed to the evolution from the medieval MORALITY PLAY towards the secular ELIZABETHAN DRAMA. He was also famous for his ballads. Heywood's four extant interludes—probably written between 1519 and 1528—are comedies in the form of moral debates. They are pious by later standards, but they are significantly different from their predecessors. The allegorical figures of the morality plays are replaced with real characters, drawn from contemporary society. They are inclined to a boisterous and obscene humour that was startling for the day. However, although Heywood's farcelike works stimulated a broader sense of theatrical possibility, Shakespearean COMEDY has different roots.

Heywood was probably the son of a provincial coroner. He was recruited as a boy for the choir of St Paul's School (see CHILDREN'S COMPANIES) and thus began his career. An ardent Catholic and a relative by marriage of Sir Thomas MORE, Heywood feared persecution early in the reign of Queen ELIZABETH (1). Protestantism was forcefully instituted as the state religion, and he fled England for the Spanish Netherlands in 1564. In 1578 when he was in his 80s, he again faced religious persecution when he was among the Catholics expelled from Antwerp by a Protestant mob. This was a minor episode of Protestant revolt against Spanish rule. He lived out his life in nearby Louvain, a more securely Catholic city.

**Heywood (2), Thomas (1573–1641)** English actor and playwright, possible collaborator with Shakespeare. Heywood acted and wrote for the ADMIRAL'S MEN from 1596 to 1602, and with WORCESTER'S MEN (later the QUEEN'S MEN [2]) until their dissolution in 1619. He then retired from acting but continued to write plays, both by himself and collaboratively. Some scholars believe he may have written parts of *Timon of Athens.* Heywood was astoundingly prolific and claimed to have 'had either an entire hand or at the least a main finger' in 220 plays. However many there may in fact have been, only about 20 have survived, though the names of a dozen more are known. The best-known survivors are *Four Prentices of London* (1600), which was satirised in *The Knight of the Burning Pestle* by Francis BEAUMONT (2), *A Woman Killed with Kindness* (1603), and *If You Know Not Me, You Know Nobody* (1605). Heywood also wrote a prose pamphlet countering Puritan objections to the theatre, *Apology for Actors* (published 1612), which is important for the light it casts on the ELIZABETHAN THEATRE. In a digression in it, he points out that two of his poems had been published in THE PASSIONATE PILGRIM as Shakespeare's, and he objects on Shakespeare's behalf; the publisher, William JAGGARD, withdrew the ascription.

**Higgins, John (c. 1545–1602)** English poet, author of sources for both *Julius Caesar* and *King Lear*. Higgins was a classical scholar and a writer on early British history. He collaborated with Nicholas UDALL on translations from the Roman dramatist Terence (c. 185–159 B.C.) but he is best known for his contribution to A MIRROR FOR MAGISTRATES, a popular anthology of verse biography that Shakespeare knew well. Higgins edited the third and fourth editions of *A Mirror* (1574, 1578) and contributed to it 16 long poems dealing with 'the first unfortunate Princes of this lande', the quasi-mythical kings and heroes of ancient Britain. His account of 'Leire' provided Shakespeare with a number of significant details for his *King Lear*. For the fifth edition (1587) of *A Mirror*, probably the one Shakespeare used, Higgins provided another 24 poems, all but one on figures from the classical world. Among them was a life of Julius CAESAR (1) that Shakespeare used in composing his play on the Roman leader.

**Hilliard, Nicholas (1547–1619)** English painter, the foremost English artist of Shakespeare's times and the creator of a portrait formerly believed to be of Shakespeare. The 'Hilliard miniature' was reproduced in James BOSWELL's 1821 edition of Shakespeare's works. It had been brought to the editor's attention by its owner, a descendant of a Mr Somerville, and the painting is also known as the 'Somerville miniature'. Somerville allegedly was a STRATFORD friend of the retired Shakespeare and the commissioner of the portrait. However, the Hilliard miniature does not much resemble the most authoritative portraits (see DROES-

HOUT; JANSSEN [2]), and modern scholars are confident that the portrait is not of Shakespeare.

Hilliard, chiefly a painter of miniature portraits, was inspired by the work of the great German painter Hans Holbein the younger (1497–1593). Holbein had been court portraitist to King HENRY VIII, and Hilliard worked for both Queen ELIZABETH (1) and King JAMES I. His elaborately detailed renderings of jewelry and rich costumes give his portraits an exquisite, gemlike presence that is still admired.

**Hippolyta (1)**   Character in *A Midsummer Night's Dream*, Queen of the Amazons and the bride of Duke THESEUS (1) of ATHENS. Hippolyta's role is small, but she is a sympathetic figure who contributes to the play's theme of domestic love. In 1.1 her distress at the prospect of HERMIA's punishment highlights the young lovers' plight. In 5.1 she disagrees with Theseus about the lovers' accounts of their experiences in the enchanted wood. He has doubted their story, but she observes that 'all the story of the night told over / . . . grows to something of great constancy / . . . strange and admirable' (5.1.23–26). Her mythical origins as leader of the Amazons are hinted at only fleetingly, in her recollected acquaintance with Hercules and Cadmus, in 4.1. Shakespeare took her name and gentle nature from a character in CHAUCER's 'The Knight's Tale'.

**Hippolyta (2)**   Character in *The Two Noble Kinsmen*, Queen of the Amazons, fiancée and later wife of THESEUS (2), Duke of ATHENS. Hippolyta helps establish the tone of magnanimous nobility and pity that dominates Act 1, but she is unimportant thereafter. In 1.1, when her wedding to Theseus is interrupted by the pleas of the royal widows (see QUEEN [1]) who seek the duke's aid, Hippolyta speaks in their support, insisting that her anticipated marital joy must be postponed in their cause. In 1.3 she describes the friendship between Theseus and PIRITHOUS, which offers a parallel to the relationship between the title characters, PALAMON and ARCITE, and which also signifies nobility of spirit. She herself displays a serene spirit in observing without jealousy, in fact approvingly, that Theseus might be unable to choose between Pirithous and herself. In Acts 2–4, where her part is written by John FLETCHER (2), she is an ordinary aristocratic figure, graciously attending the duke at court. She is presumably married to Theseus by this time, although the rescheduled wedding is never mentioned. In Act 5 Hippolyta hardly speaks, but she makes a significant point after the duel fought by Palamon and Arcite for EMILIA (4), when she offers a tender acknowledgement that the play's developments provoke 'Infinite pity' (5.3.144–145).

**History Plays**   Shakespeare's 10 plays dealing with events in English history. In the order in which they were written, the history plays are: (a) the so-called minor TETRALOGY—consisting of *1, 2,* and *3 Henry VI* and *Richard III*—written in 1590–1591; (b) *King John* (1591, possibly 1595); (c) the major tetralogy—*Richard II, 1* and *2 Henry IV,* and *Henry V*—written between 1595 and 1599; and (d) *Henry VIII,* perhaps written in collaboration with John FLETCHER in 1612, one of Shakespeare's last works.

The minor tetralogy deals with the English defeat by FRANCE (1) in the last years of the HUNDRED YEARS WAR (enacted in *1 Henry VI*), followed by the disputes and battles of an English civil conflict, the WARS OF THE ROSES (in the other three plays). The tetralogy begins with the death of King HENRY V in 1422 and ends with the foundation of the TUDOR dynasty in 1485. *King John* presents much earlier events, a series of incidents during the reign of King JOHN (3) (1199–1216). The major tetralogy covers the deposition and murder of King RICHARD II in 1398 *(Richard II),* two unsuccessful rebellions against his usurper, King HENRY IV, and that ruler's death *(1* and *2 Henry IV),* and the invasion and defeat of France by Henry's son and successor, King Henry V, closing with the signing of the treaty of TROYES in 1420 *(Henry V).* *Henry VIII* consists of a series of tableaux that present various events in the reign of HENRY VIII, ending with the christening of Queen ELIZABETH (1) in 1533. It is very different from the other histories and is generally regarded as greatly inferior to them.

The two tetralogies are Shakespeare's major achievement in the histories. (*King John,* although a fine play, is nevertheless an isolated excursion into an earlier, almost mythic, period.) The tetralogies cover English history from 1398 to 1485. Shakespeare plunged into the disorder of a civil war in the first four plays and then, in the second, delved into the history that preceded this cataclysm, examining its causes and painting a portrait of the nation as it changed, traumatically, from medieval to modern.

The central theme of these plays is political—they deal with the gain and loss of power—but Shakespeare transcended this subject. As he wrote his histories, the playwright increasingly pursued the definition of the perfect king. After presenting two distinctly bad rulers, the ineffectual HENRY VI and the villainous RICHARD III, he turned to a consideration of kingly virtues. He began to explore the psychology of political leaders, and these plays are, at their best, as much psychological as historical.

In *Richard II* a weak king jeopardises the stability of the realm, but, although we recognise his opponent, Henry BOLINGBROKE (1), to be a superior ruler, we nonetheless sympathise with Richard, whose spiritual qualities make him more open and responsive to life.

A conflict is established between human vulnerability and cold political calculation, and the question that dominates the next three plays is whether a successful ruler can combine humane sympathy and ruthless efficiency. Such a monarch would be able to hold the country together, as Richard cannot, while staying in touch with his subjects, a connection Bolingbroke never had and does not acquire as Henry IV.

The *Henry IV* plays focus on the development of the king's son, young PRINCE (6) HAL. In *1 Henry IV* Hal is presented with two alternatives, represented by HOTSPUR and FALSTAFF respectively, and he finds his way between them, seeing both their weaknesses and their virtues. However, in *2 Henry IV* the Prince is psychologically remote, and, as he inherits the crown from his father, he seems to abandon his friends among the commoners in order to focus on his duty as a ruler. Hal's increasing coldness is evident, but the play's great question—is personal loyalty morally superior to public duty?—is left unanswered by the Prince's final rejection of Falstaff, as is shown by the debate that the episode has engendered ever since.

In *Henry V* this basic ambivalence towards Hal—now King Henry V—remains the major theme. On the one hand, he is plainly a successful king, uniting all Britain behind him in a conquest of France and displaying the combination of leadership and camaraderie typical of an epic hero. On the other, he seems a cynical manipulator of war and peace, an hypocrite who uses a religious sensibility to mask his political ends. Both points of view are legitimate in the context of the play; Shakespeare's recognition of political complexities compelled him to explore Henry's defects. His discovery of the psychological limitations of his ideal king was to influence the great tragedies (see TRAGEDY) in the next phase of his career.

Not content to deal with the nature of kingship solely from the point of view of the rulers, Shakespeare also focusses on the lives of the common people of England, especially in the major tetralogy. Sometimes fictitious minor figures, such as the GARDENER in *Richard III* or WILLIAMS (2) in *Henry V*, fulfil an important function simply by offering their own interpretation of political events and historical personalities and thus influencing our own responses. But many common people are developed as characters in their own right. Indeed, in the *Henry IV* plays, often considered the greatest of the histories, Falstaff and a number of fully sketched minor characters offer a sort of national group portrait that is contrasted with political history. The juxtaposition generates a richly stimulating set of relationships.

That secular accounts of the past, neither legendary nor religious, were presented on the stage—and were highly popular—reflects the Elizabethan era's intense interest in history. In the late 16th century, when these plays were written, England was undergoing a great crisis. As a leading Protestant state, it found itself at odds with the great Catholic powers of Counter-Reformation Europe, including its traditional enemy, France, and a new foe, Spain. The latter, at the height of its power, was a very dangerous adversary, and England felt seriously imperiled until the defeat of the Spanish Armada in 1588. This situation sparked a tremendous patriotism among all classes of English society, and with that came an increasing interest in the nation's history, an interest that the theatre was of course delighted to serve.

Written not long after the peak of nationalistic fervour in 1588, the history plays, which were extremely popular, deal with England: the Wars of the Roses were the great crisis that had formed the nation, as Shakespeare and his contemporaries knew it. Its resolution at BOSWORTH FIELD lay in the relatively recent past—closer to the author's own day than the American Civil War or the Crimean War is to ours. Thus Elizabethans were very much aware of the significance of the events depicted in these plays. Moreover, although in hindsight the reign of Queen ELIZABETH (1) seems very different from those of the troubled 15th century, this was not so clear at the time. A number of threats to the government arose—including the failed rebellion of the Earl of ESSEX (2) in 1599, when the rebels used a performance of *Richard II* as propaganda. The English of the late 16th century felt a strong fear of civil war and anarchy; for both moral and practical reasons they valued an orderly society ruled by a strong monarch. The history plays addressed this attitude by presenting a lesson in the evils of national disunity.

This view of English history was held not only by both the playwright and most of his audience, but also by the historians whose works Shakespeare consulted. When the Tudor dynasty came to power, among the policies adopted by King Henry VII (the RICHMOND of *Richard III*) was the use of scholarly propaganda to justify his seizure of the throne. He encouraged and commissioned various works of history and biography to emphasise the faults of earlier rulers and present his own accession as the nation's salvation. Among them was an official history of England by the Italian humanist Polydore VERGIL, which was to have a strong influence on subsequent historians, including Raphael HOLINSHED and Edward HALL (2), whose chronicles were Shakespeare's chief sources. Holinshed's book, the most up-to-date and authoritative work of its kind in the 1590s, provided much of the historical detail, especially in the minor tetralogy. Hall's history of the Wars of the Roses foreshadowed Shakespeare by stressing the theme that England's happiness under its last great medieval king, Edward III, Richard II's predecessor, had been lost through Richard's weakness, which necessitated Henry IV's profoundly sinful act of deposition. This guilty deed brought down God's wrath on England, plunging the country into generations of civil conflict that was ended only by the triumph of Henry VII and the founding of the Tudor dynasty.

Such writings shaped the understanding of the past that was available to Shakespeare when he wrote the history plays. He saw—and passed on—a story of inevitable progress towards the benevolent reign of the Tudors. Shakespeare's account of historical events varies considerably from that developed by later scholarship, in part because the sources available to him were highly unreliable by modern historical standards. In any case, Shakespeare was not writing history; he was concerned with dramatic values more than with historical accuracy.

The history play, a theatrical work dealing realistically with great events of the past, was a novelty in Shakespeare's day. Shakespeare himself is often credited with inventing the genre, although its origins are somewhat obscure, since the texts of most Elizabethan plays are lost. Dramatic works dealing with historical events had been staged somewhat earlier, but these works had treated their materials allegorically, like the MORALITY PLAY from which they derived. Shakespeare was probably the first playwright to depict real events in works expressly intended to illuminate the past, although some lost plays may have anticipated him in some respects.

Other Elizabethan playwrights also wrote histories, whether influenced specifically by Shakespeare or simply by the age. However, most of these works are familiar only to scholars. Shakespeare's work has survived because he was not merely exploiting a current interest; nor was he a mere purveyor of Tudor propaganda. In writing history plays, he pursued his own concerns, exploring political values and social relations. Throughout his career he was preoccupied with the value of order in society; this theme is present in such very early and apparently unlikely works as *The Comedy of Errors*, and it recurs in most of the plays. But nowhere is it as explicitly dealt with as in the histories.

What, then, do the history plays say about this subject? As we have seen, the ideal king of the history plays, Henry V, is a highly ambiguous figure. While Shakespeare's belief in the need for authority is evident in his work, so also is a distrust of those who hold authority. This paradox reflects a fundamental irony: the only rational form of rule—power that is humane yet absolute—is also impossible to achieve. Thus the history plays point up an underlying characteristic of human societies—political power inspires disturbing fears as well as profound ideals.

### Hoby (1), Sir Thomas (1530–1566)

First English translator of CASTIGLIONE's *Il Cortegiano*, thought to

have influenced *Much Ado About Nothing*. As a young man, Hoby travelled widely on the Continent. In 1552–1553, while living in Paris, he translated *Il Cortegiano*, though the resulting work, *The Courtyer*, was not published until 1561. It became immensely popular, being reissued several times before 1588. Hoby died in 1566, while serving as the English ambassador in Paris. Thomas Posthumous HOBY (2) was his son.

### Hoby (2), Sir Thomas Posthumous (1566–1640)

Contemporary of Shakespeare, Puritan landowner who may have been a model for MALVOLIO in *Twelfth Night*. Born after the death of his father, Sir Thomas HOBY (1), Hoby ran away from home as a young man to pursue a military career; then he settled down as the husband of a wealthy heiress from Yorkshire. He acted as an agent for the Protestant government in his wife's very Catholic district, and his enthusiasm for prosecuting Catholics made him highly unpopular. In 1600 he sued several of his neighbours for coming uninvited to his house, where they drank, played cards, mocked his religious practices, and threatened to rape his wife. The case was notorious (Hoby won), and some scholars believe that it may be reflected in the antagonism between Malvolio and SIR TOBY in the play. (For other possible Malvolios, see FFARINGTON; KNOLLYS; WILLOUGHBY [1].)

### Holingshed, Raphael (c. 1528–c. 1580)

English historian, compiler and author of a source for several of Shakespeare's plays. Holinshed's *Chronicles of England, Scotland, and Ireland* (probably in its second edition, 1587) was a major source for the HISTORY PLAYS and *Macbeth*, and a minor one for *Cymbeline* and *King Lear*. The *Chronicles*—along with the work of Edward HALL (2)—provided much of Shakespeare's knowledge of the WARS OF THE ROSES, which is the subject of eight of the history plays (see TETRALOGY). With the work of John FOXE, it contributed the history covered in the two others, *King John* and *Henry VIII*. For *Macbeth*, Shakespeare used the *Chronicles'* account of the medieval King MACBETH of Scotland. The ancient British kings CYMBELINE and LEAR were also treated by Holinshed, and details of his treatments are reflected in Shakespeare's plays about them.

Holinshed's *Chronicles* was the most authoritative history of Britain in Shakespeare's day, and other Elizabethan dramatists besides Shakespeare used it as a source. Its three and a half million words were not all written by Holinshed, whose principal contribution was the section dealing with England's history. In writing it, he relied on a number of earlier works, most notably that of Hall. The history of SCOTLAND was a translation by William HARRISON (3) of the Latin chronicle of Hector BOECE, and the history of Ireland was written by Edmund Campion (1540–1581). Prefatory geographical essays were provided by Harrison for England and Scotland, and Campion and Richard Stanyhurst (1545–1615) for Ireland.

The book was the remnant of a much larger project, led by Reginald Wolfe (d. 1573), a 'cosmography of the whole world [including] the histories of every known nation', for which Holinshed was a translator. Holinshed succeeded Wolfe as editor-in-chief, though only one other volume, an atlas, was published. The *Chronicles* was published in 1578 and again, in a revised and enlarged version, in 1587. Holinshed wrote nothing else—even the second edition of the *Chronicles* was brought out by others (including John STOW)—and he became a steward on a country estate, where he died.

**Holland (1), Henry, Duke of Exeter**   Character in *3 Henry VI.* See EXETER (1).

**Holland (2), Hugh (c. 1574–1633)**   Poet and antiquarian, friend of Shakespeare's. Holland wrote an EPITAPH on Shakespeare, a SONNET that was one of the introductory poems in the FIRST FOLIO (1623). Like Shakespeare, he was a good friend of Ben JONSON and a member of the group that met regularly at the MERMAID TAVERN. Holland wrote in four languages—English, Greek, Italian, and Welsh—and he was a well-known poet in his own time, noted particularly for a long poem on Owen Tudor's courtship of Queen KATHARINE (2).

**Holland (3), John**   Minor character in *2 Henry VI,* a follower of Jack CADE. Holland discusses Cade's rebellion with his friend George BEVIS in 4.2, and they join the rebels when they appear. Holland also makes several joking asides in 4.7. A John Holland is known to have been an actor with STRANGE'S MEN in the early 1590s, and it is believed that he played this part. His name was given to the character as a convenience by either Shakespeare or the keeper of a PROMPT-BOOK.

**Holland (4), Philemon (1552–1637)**   English translator of minor sources for *Othello, Coriolanus,* and possibly *The Rape of Lucrece.* Holland's version of PLINY the Elder's *Natural History* (1601) provided details for *Othello,* mostly in the hero's account of his adventures in 1.3. A passage in Holland's translation of LIVY's history of ROME, *Ab urbe condita,* published as *The Roman Historie* (1600), is echoed in certain details of MENENIUS' famous 'belly speech' in *Coriolanus* (1.1.95–159). The same passage was also influenced by Holland's translation of William CAMDEN's *Remaines* (1605), excerpts from a Latin history of Britain. Holland's Livy may also have inspired parts of *Lucrece,* whose story it tells. However, there are no literary echoes of Holland in Shakespeare's poem, so the playwright may have only used the original.

Holland, the son of a clergyman, practised medicine in COVENTRY. He was famous for his translations from the Latin; in addition to those already mentioned, he produced English versions of three other ancient works of history, published in 1606, 1609, and 1632. After 1608 Holland gave up medicine and became the headmaster of a grammar school.

**Holmedon (Homildon)**   Site of a battle between England and Scotland (1402) that is reported in 1.1.62–74 of *1 Henry IV.* Holmedon, known today as Humbleton, is near the Scottish border. An invasion by the Scots was repelled by English forces under HOTSPUR, who captured many aristocratic prisoners—usually held for ransom under medieval practices of war—including the Scottish commander, Lord DOUGLAS. Hotspur's refusal to turn these prisoners over to King Henry triggers enmity between the two, leading to the rebellion that the play depicts.

Shakespeare alters the chronology surrounding this battle in minor ways. He asserts that the battle occurred simultaneously with another, against the Welsh, in which Lord MORTIMER (2) was captured, but in fact they occurred months apart. His alteration heightens the dramatic impact of their accounts. Both are placed closer to the beginning of Henry's reign than they actually were, thus stressing the connection of the rebellion against Henry to his usurpation of the crown (enacted in *Richard II*).

**Holofernes**   Character in *Love's Labour's Lost,* a comical pedant. Named for Dr Tubal Holofernes, a tutor in Rabelais' *Gargantua,* Shakespeare's scholar is so Latinate in his speech that he can hardly be understood. Holofernes, never without his obsequious follower, NATHANIEL (1) the Curate, is the subject of much mirth on the part of the other characters. MOTH (1) says of Holofernes and his fellow grotesque, ARMADO, that 'they have been at a great feast of languages, and stolen the scraps' (5.1.35–36). Although Holofernes is consistently wrong-headed, conceited, and intolerant of those he considers his intellectual inferiors, we nevertheless feel sorry for him when he attempts to perform in the pageant of the Nine WORTHIES and is mercilessly heckled by the gentlemen. Driven from the stage, he cries, justly, 'This is not generous, not gentle, not humble' (5.2.623).

While Shakespeare's audiences will have made more of Holofernes' ranting than we can, it is nonetheless good comedy, for much of the fun lies in its near-incomprehensibility. Some of his references are clearly to topical jokes that are now hopelessly obscure. It has been speculated that Holofernes was intended as a parody of some contemporary literary figure—John FLORIO and Gabriel HARVEY (2) have been suggested—but this theory cannot be proven.

**Homer**   Ancient Greek poet, a source, through the translation of George CHAPMAN, of *Troilus and Cressida.*

Two great epics—the *Iliad,* an account of the TROJAN WAR, and the *Odyssey,* which tells of the wanderings of Odysseus, known in Latin as ULYSSES—are attributed to Homer, as they have been since remote antiquity. However, Homer may be an apocryphal figure and his works may have been written by more than one unknown author. In the absence of persuasive evidence one way or the other, the works continue to be conventionally regarded as Homer's. In the ancient world, estimates of Homer's dates ranged over many centuries, but by comparing passages in the works with the archaeological evidence, scholars generally believe that the poems were composed in the 8th or 7th century B.C.—i.e., 400–600 years after the era depicted in them. Internal evidence further suggests that the poet(s) lived in Ionia, or Greek Asia Minor.

In the Middle Ages it was believed that other accounts of the Trojan War preceded Homer's, but they were actually written much later. Only in the RENAISSANCE were Homer's works restored to the position of eminence they had held in ancient Greece and Rome. Some of the information Shakespeare used in writing *Troilus and Cressida* came from the medieval tradition, which took a Trojan rather than a Greek point of view. However, Homer entered English literature in Shakespeare's time, and the playwright certainly knew two partial translations of the *Iliad,* that of Arthur HALL (1), taken from a French version (1581), and Chapman's, from the Greek (published in part in 1598 and in full in 1612). Indeed, he could have read nine different translations—five Latin, two French, and two English. However, it is clear that he used Chapman's translation in composing the play (c. 1602), for the incidents from Homer that he used were those covered in Chapman's first edition. Chapman's *Odyssey* was completed in 1615, and numerous translations of both works have been made since, some of them masterful works of English literature in their own right.

**Hope Theatre**  Theatre near LONDON built by Philip HENSLOWE in 1613 on the site of a bear-baiting house—an arena for audiences to watch bears or bulls being attacked by dogs—which was torn down for the purpose. Henslowe held a licence for animal-baiting, a very popular entertainment, and he wished to expand this business while perhaps attracting the audiences of the GLOBE THEATRE, which had just burned down. The Hope thus had accommodations for the animals along with the usual attributes of a theatre. The smell of the animals was apparently offensive, but LADY ELIZABETH'S MEN and other companies played there in 1614–1615. However, disputes between Henslowe and the players resulted in a series of lawsuits, which continued after Henslowe's death, and his heir, William ALLEYN, could not negotiate a settlement. During this period,. few plays were produced at the Hope, and by 1619 it had reverted to animal-baiting

exclusively. This pastime was outlawed in 1642, and the Hope was eventually torn down to make way for tenements in 1656.

**Hopkins, Richard (c. 1545–c. 1594)**  English translator of the works of Luis de GRANADA. Hopkins, a Catholic, spent his life abroad in religious exile. A student in Catholic universities in the Netherlands, Spain, and France, he probably lived chiefly in Paris, although details of his life are obscure. His translation of Granada's *Of Prayer and Meditation* was published in London in 1582 and may have influenced Shakespeare's writing of *Hamlet.*

**Horatio**  Character in *Hamlet,* friend and confidant of Prince HAMLET. Horatio is the one person in Hamlet's world whom the prince values and trusts. With Horatio he can speak freely, and in doing so he demonstrates the evolution of his emotions. Further, the presence of Horatio lessens Hamlet's otherwise total alienation and permits relief—for him and for us—from the heightened tension that characterises his existence.

Horatio is a calm and stoical figure whom Hamlet admires as 'A man that Fortune's buffets and rewards / Hast ta'en with equal thanks . . . [a] man / That is not passion's slave' (3.2.67–72). He thus represents a RENAISSANCE ideal—a person with the mental discipline to resist highly emotional responses, which were seen as evidence of humanity's fall from grace. This ideal was considerably influenced by the newly rediscovered Stoic philosophy of the classical world, and Horatio rightly thinks of himself as 'more an antique Roman than a Dane' (5.2.346). His restraint makes Horatio one who 'in suff'ring all, . . . suffers nothing' (3.2.66), and Hamlet, embattled by his own suffering, envies his friend's relative peace of mind. However, it is precisely his vulnerability that gives Hamlet's emotional odyssey the grandeur that makes it worth recording. Horatio is an admirable figure, but he does not spark our imagination or sympathies.

Horatio knew Hamlet at school, as the prince makes plain in welcoming him from Wittenberg as a 'fellow student' (1.2.177), but otherwise his past is unclear. In 1.1 he seems to be an intimate of the Danish court, but at several points—most notably when he must ask if musical accompaniment to drinking toasts is 'a custom' (1.4.12)—he appears to be unfamiliar with local ways. Horatio's status in DENMARK—Danish nobleman or foreign visitor—is an example of the many problematic points in *Hamlet* that scholarship cannot resolve. Shakespeare probably simply formulated the character in different lights as he composed the drama and did not concern himself with the minor contradictions that resulted, as was apparently his habit throughout the plays.

**Horner, Thomas**   Minor character in *2 Henry VI*, an armourer who is reported to have remarked that his client the Duke of YORK (8) was 'rightful heir to the crown' (1.3.26). Horner's apprentice, PETER, informs the Duke of SUFFOLK (3) of Horner's assertion, and Suffolk brings them both before the court in an effort to embarrass York. Horner denies Peter's assertion, and a trial by combat is ordered by the Duke of GLOUCESTER (4), the Lord Protector. Thus a potentially explosive issue is postponed and diverted into what will prove a minor spectacle for the court. Also, at Gloucester's recommendation, the reappointment of York as Regent of FRANCE (1) is withheld until this question should cool off. Thus the episode serves to illustrate Gloucester's qualities of prudence and discretion—ironically not long before his downfall.

Horner, though expected to win the combat against the cowardly Peter, arrives at the contest drunk in 2.3 and is slain by his apprentice. Dying, he confesses that Peter's account had been true, and the apprentice is exonerated. Although the combat is not treated seriously by the court, it prefigures York's rebellion in the WARS OF THE ROSES, which begins later in the play.

**Hortensio**   Character in *The Taming of the Shrew*, a suitor of BIANCA (1). A bland young man who is outsmarted in his campaign to win Bianca, Hortensio is an appropriate character to enter, ludicrously pale 'for fear' (2.1.143), to report KATHERINA's assault on him with a lute, thus providing an image of the 'shrew' of the title at her worst. After losing Bianca, Hortensio turns to a WIDOW (1) who has pursued him. He visits the country house of PETRUCHIO (2) to observe that character's shrew-taming techniques, but it is unclear at the play's end whether Hortensio will be strong enough to use them when he needs them, for the Widow proves, in 5.2, to be a formidable shrew herself.

**Hortensius**   Minor character in *Timon of Athens*, the servant to a creditor of TIMON. In 3.4 Hortensius and other servants unsuccessfully dun Timon and his STEWARD (2) for payment. The servants regret their assignment, for their greedy masters have benefited from Timon's generosity. Hortensius is especially vocal, and he says, 'I know my lord hath spent of Timon's wealth, / And now ingratitude makes it worse than stealth' (3.4.27–28). He thus stresses one of the play's important themes, the callousness of the aristocracy of ATHENS.

Hortensius appears with TITUS (2), PHILOTUS, LUCIUS' SERVANT and two men who are each designated as VARRO'S SERVANT. Since the latter three are addressed as 'Lucius' and 'Varro' (3.4.2, 3), it is presumed that Shakespeare intended the names of the first three to refer to their masters as well, perhaps reflecting a casual linguistic practise of the early 17th century.

**Host (1)**   Minor character in *The Two Gentlemen of Verona*. JULIA, disguised as a boy, converses with the Host in 4.2, having arrived at court to see her lover, PROTEUS. While she observes the infidelity of PROTEUS, the Host falls asleep, subtly isolating the heroine at this crucial moment.

**Host (2)**   Character in *The Merry Wives of Windsor*, the keeper of the Garter Tavern. The bluff and ebullient Host is a peacekeeper whom EVANS (3) nominates to the committee intended to arbitrate between SHALLOW and FALSTAFF and who later leads the effort to prevent the duel between EVANS and Dr CAIUS (2). The would-be combatants, the only two foreigners in Shakespeare's WINDSOR, reward the Host's good intentions by having his horses stolen. The Host's heartiness is evident in his extravagant rhetoric. For instance, when directing a visitor to Falstaff's rooms at the inn, he says, 'There's his chamber, his house, his castle, his standing-bed, and truckle-bed; 'tis painted about with the story of the Prodigal, fresh and new. Go, knock and call; he'll speak like an Anthropophaginian unto thee; knock, I say' (4.5.5–9). His bold language encompasses an extraordinary range of epithets, from 'bully rook' (1.3.2, et al.), 'Cavaliero' (2.1.186; 2.3.70), and 'bully Hercules' (1.3.6), to such fanciful constructs as 'Bohemian-Tartar' (4.5.18) and 'Castalian-king-Urinal' (2.3.31).

**Hostess (1)**   Minor character in *The Taming of the Shrew*, the proprietor of the tavern from which Christopher SLY (1) emerges at the beginning of the INDUCTION. Sly may be referring to her, in Ind.2.21, as Marian Hacket, believed to have been a real person who lived in a hamlet near STRATFORD and whom Shakespeare presumably knew as a boy. In any case, the brief appearance of this angry but businesslike barmaid contributes to the believable rural atmosphere of the Induction.

**Hostess (2)**   Character in *1* and *2 Henry IV* and *Henry V*, the proprietress of the BOAR'S HEAD TAVERN in EASTCHEAP. The Hostess, a good-hearted woman whose affection for FALSTAFF withstands his exploitation of her purse, is comically loquacious. Aspiring to conversational brilliance, she displays a considerable vocabulary, but she unfortunately misplaces one word for another, in an ancient comedy routine, going so far, in a state of great excitement, as to confuse 'honeyseed' and 'honeysuckle' for 'homicide' and 'homicidal' (*2 Henry IV*, 2.1.49–51). She is a denizen of the quasi-criminal underworld of London (she associates with highwaymen and harlots and is arrested when a murder is said to have occurred in her tavern), but no crimes are explicitly attributed to her. Indeed, her amiable and forgiving nature contains no hint of villainy.

The Hostess' role in *1 Henry IV* is very minor. In 2.4 she is an amused spectator of the mock drama played by PRINCE (6) HAL and Falstaff, and in 3.3 she disputes with Falstaff over his debt to her. He mocks her, and his insults spark her honest indgination.

In *2 Henry IV* the Hostess is a somewhat more substantial character. She escalates her dispute with Falstaff by summoning two officers, FANG and SNARE, to arrest the fat knight for debt. She elaborates on her complaint, remembering at length (2.1.83–101) that he had promised to marry her in order to borrow money. However, Falstaff not only talks her into calling off her legal action but also into lending him more money. She weeps, but she agrees, showing the gullibility and kindness that mark her relationship with him. In 2.4, when Falstaff is called to join the armies assembling to oppose the rebels against HENRY IV, the Hostess displays her sentimental attachment to him, weeping and saying, 'Well, fare thee well. I have known thee these twenty-nine years, come peascod-time, but an honester and true-hearted man—Well, fare thee well' (2.4.379–382). Even the Hostess' credulousness does not extend to a belief in Falstaff's honesty; she is merely expressing her love with conventional sayings that come first to her mind. The Hostess' tolerance and affection for Falstaff are important in Shakespeare's presentation of the fat rogue as an humane, though flawed, person. It comes as a shock when the Hostess and her friend DOLL TEAR-SHEET are arrested in 5.4, in a demonstration of the rigorous law enforcement of the new regime, anticipating Prince Hal's rejection of Falstaff in 5.5.

In *Henry V* the Hostess (now married to PISTOL) has a small but striking role, as she describes her attendance at Falstaff's death-bed, in a speech (2.3.9–27) that is one of the masterpieces of English comic literature, being simultaneously extremely funny, even bawdy, and touchingly tender. Her efforts to comfort a dying and conscience-stricken sinner reflect Shakespeare's own forgiving humanity.

The Hostess is given the name Mistress Quickly in all three plays (e.g., in *1 Henry IV*, 3.3.90; *2 Henry IV*, 2.1.44; *Henry V*, 2.1.19), but she is plainly a different person from the Mistress QUICKLY of *The Merry Wives of Windsor*; Shakespeare simply reused the name and comical verbal habit of the Hostess with his customary disregard for questions of consistency. Some scholars hold that the correct pronunciation of Quickly should be 'quick-lie', a legitimate Elizabethan variant that carries an obvious implication that she is a prostitute. Falstaff hints that she is (e.g., in *1 Henry IV*, 3.3.128), but, although she consorts with Doll, who is a courtesan, there is no other evidence to support this. It is more probable that her name, pronounced ordinarily (as it commonly was in the 16th century), is simply intended to suggest the hustle and bustle of an innkeeper's life.

**Hostilius** Minor character in *Timon of Athens*, a visitor to ATHENS. With his companions, the First and Second STRANGERS, Hostilius witnesses the callous rejection of TIMON's request for assistance by the miserly LUCIUS (3), in 3.2. Lucius has just insisted to Hostilius that he would always help his generous former patron. Like his friends, Hostilius represents a detached judgement on the selfish citizens of Athens—the First Stranger explicitly makes the case. This is an episode of a type familiar from the medieval MORALITY PLAY that serves to fix the play's moral point of view. In some editions Hostilius, who is named in 3.2.64, is designated as the Second Stranger.

**Hotson, Leslie (b. 1897)** Canadian literary scholar. Hotson has specialised in scholarly detective work and distinguished himself with many striking discoveries, including the probable murder of Christopher MARLOWE (1), the likely first performance of *The Merry Wives of Windsor*, and Shakespeare's connections to William GARDINER (2) and Francis LANGLEY. On the other hand, many of his proposals—such as the identification of *Troilus and Cressida* as LOVE'S LABOUR'S WON—have not been generally accepted.

**Hotspur (Henry Percy, 1364–1403)** Historical figure and character in *1 Henry IV*, a rebel against King HENRY IV. Hotspur, a fiery warrior, is repeatedly contrasted with Henry's son, PRINCE (6) HAL. The Prince's dissipation in the company of FALSTAFF is compared unfavourably with Hotspur's military prowess and chivalric honour. The play's major theme is Prince Hal's decision to abandon the tavern for the field and to compete with Hotspur, whose example inspires the Prince to adopt his proper role as a military hero. At the play's climax, the two young men meet in hand-to-hand combat at SHREWSBURY, where the Prince kills his rival. The play makes clear that Hotspur's volatile temper has led to his defeat and to the failure of his rebellion: he has carried his ideal of chivalric honour to excess. In this sense, he is contrasted with Falstaff, whose self-indulgent cowardice represents an opposite extreme. Hotspur thus resembles a figure from the MORALITY PLAYS, a symbol of a value or attitude.

Even before he appears, Hotspur is associated with military honour and prowess, as well as with excessive pride, in King Henry's account (1.1.66–74, 90–91) of his capture—and arrogant possession—of DOUGLAS. Hotspur begins the play in the service of the king, but the Percy family harbours a simmering resentment over Henry's apparent ingratitude for the help they gave him when he usurped the throne (as enacted in *Richard II*). When a dispute erupts over Hotspur's failure to relinquish custody of Douglas, and the king refuses to ransom a Percy relative, Lord MORTIMER (2), the Percies decide to rebel. Hotspur's reputation for courage and his proven success in combat, make him the natural leader of the rebellion, but his older relatives—his father, the Earl of NORTHUMBERLAND (1), and his uncle, the Earl of WORCESTER—must struggle to curb the young man's temper. Ultimately, they are unable to do so, and Hotspur's rash insistence on fighting against the odds at Shrewsbury dooms the rebellion to defeat.

Hotspur's virtues are manifest; he is a fine military leader in a world that values this trait highly. King Henry's regret that his own son is not more like Hotspur is genuine, and the Prince himself, after killing his rival, acknowledges his worth in a warm eulogy (5.4.86–100). However, Hotspur represents, like Falstaff, an unbalanced attitude towards life. He lives only for battle and identifies himself entirely with his reputation for military valour. His rhetoric grows windy on the subject, as in 1.3.199–206 and 4.1.112–123. As his wife, LADY (10) Percy, tells us in 2.3.48–63, he even fights battles in his sleep. Utterly single-minded, he rejects even sex, declaring that 'this is no world to play with mammets, and to tilt with lips' (2.3.92–93).

His impetuosity makes him as much a liability as an asset to his allies. He has no control over his emotions, letting his enthusiasm for honour dominate all other considerations; his own father calls him 'a wasp-stung and impatient fool' (1.3.233). At Shrewsbury, messengers present a steady procession of reasons for caution, as the rebel fortunes grow increasingly uncertain, but Hotspur's response is almost ludicrously inappropriate: 'Come, let us take a muster speedily— / Doomsday is near; die all, die merrily' (4.1.133–134). His foolish refusal to wait for reinforcements condemns his cause to defeat; he is so overwrought at the approach of battle that he cannot even read his despatches, saying that life is too short to waste on such petty activity. Hotspur's impulsiveness is evident even in minor details of his speech—e.g., in his habit of interrupting himself, as in 1.3.155–184 and 4.1.13. Characteristically, he dies in mid-sentence. However, he is not merely a stock emblem of fiery and foolish chivalry; he displays intelligence, humour, and high spirits, and he has a loving wife whose affection emphasises his humanity.

The historical Hotspur was as celebrated—and evidently as vain and foolish—as Shakespeare's character, and the play presents his role at Shrewsbury accurately, except in two important respects. First, his death in the battle cannot definitely be attributed to Hal, or to anyone else. Second, and more significant, he was not Hal's contemporary, being in fact older than King Henry. The alteration in his age serves to make him a more satisfying foil to Prince Hal, but at the time of Shrewsbury, when Hal was 16, Hotspur was a veteran soldier of 39, having been a famous warrior on the Scottish border—where he won the nickname Hotspur—for more than 20 years. The alteration in Hotspur's age is established in *Richard II*, in which young PERCY (2), who becomes Hotspur, is introduced as a boy.

A theatrical tradition of playing Hotspur as a stutterer—an effective indication of his excitability—seems to have arisen in 19th-century Germany, where the respected translator SCHLEGEL interpreted Lady Percy's recollection of her husband's 'speaking thick' (*2 Henry IV*, 2.3.24) as 'stammering'. Shakespeare may have been referring to his Northumbrian dialect or, more likely, to his habit of speaking rapidly. In any case, there is no record concerning the historical Hotspur's speech.

Hotspur's son, another Henry Percy, was still a boy when first his father and then his grandfather were killed fighting against King Henry. Prince Hal, upon his accession as King HENRY V, pardoned young Percy and permitted him to resume the family title. As a result, he fought for Hal's son, HENRY VI; he was the Earl of Northumberland whose death in the first battle of ST. ALBANS is reported in 1.1.4–9 of *3 Henry VI*. His son and successor, Hotspur's grandson, appears as the Earl of NORTHUMBERLAND (2) later in that play.

**Howard, Charles (1536–1624)** English admiral, a leading military figure of the late 16th century and the aristocratic patron of an acting company, the ADMIRAL'S MEN. Howard was a cousin of Queen ELIZABETH (1). He was trained for the admiralty from an early age, and after a successful career as a soldier in the Low Countries and as an English diplomat, he was appointed Lord Admiral of England in 1585. He commanded the country's resistance to the Spanish Armada in 1588, and in 1596 he was a co-commander of the successful English attack on Spain at Cadiz. The latter event is alluded to in *The Merchant of Venice* (see ANDREW [1]). Under King JAMES I, Howard continued to influence naval and foreign policy until his retirement in 1619. He was renowned for his civility and honesty and has always been regarded as one of the finest public figures of the era. Beginning in 1576, Howard was the patron of an important LONDON theatre company known first as Lord Howard's Men and later as the Admiral's Men. His role consisted of permitting them to use his name—necessary under restrictive Puritan laws (see ELIZABETHAN THEATRE)—and he had nothing to do with the company's productions.

**Howard's Men or Lord Howard's Men** See ADMIRAL'S MEN.

**Hubert** Character in *King John*, a follower of King JOHN (3) and custodian of ARTHUR. Hubert first appears as a representative of the city of ANGIERS (see also CITIZEN [4]), proposing a compromise between John and King PHILIP (2) of France. His opening remarks (2.1.325–333) emphasise the balance between opposing forces that recurs throughout the play. By 3.2 (3.3) (for citation, see *King John*, 'Synopsis'), Hubert has joined King John's entourage. When Arthur is captured in battle, Hubert accepts John's implicit order to kill him. In 4.1, one of Shakespeare's most terrifying and moving scenes, Hubert, touched by the boy's innocence, hides Arthur and tells the king that he has died. Arthur's supposed death proves politically catastrophic to the king; yet when Hubert reveals that Arthur is alive, it turns out that the young prince has in the meantime died attempting to escape. Thus Hubert's career mirrors the changes in fortune and the ambiguities of good and evil that are a principal theme of the play.

Shakespeare's character bears almost no resemblance to the historical figure who provided the name. Hubert de Burgh (d. 1243), although he briefly had custody of Arthur, seems not to have been involved in his death; he may have actually tried to prevent it. In any case, he certainly was not the bourgeois opportunist depicted in the play. On the contrary, he was one of the highest-ranking aristocrats in England, being descended directly from Charlemagne, and he was an important administrator both before and during the period of the play and under John's successor, Henry III (see HENRY [1]). Furthermore, he won a great naval victory over a French fleet that was attempting to reinforce the forces of LEWIS (1) in England. Shakespeare translates this battle—the first in Britain's long tradition of naval supremacy—into a storm, reported in 5.3.9–11, rather than give credit to Hubert. The playwright may have felt that depicting Hubert as a commoner made the unscrupulous ambition that leads him to agree to kill a boy more believable, while the character's lack of commitment to the high politics of the realm could make his subsequent mercy credible.

**Hughes, Margaret (d. 1719)** The first recorded English actress. In 1660, when English theatres were reopened following the Puritan Revolution, actresses were for the first time permitted to take the female parts, previously played by boys (see ELIZABETHAN DRAMA). Margaret Hughes was the first woman to do so, playing DESDEMONA in Thomas KILLIGREW's production of *Othello*. She had a long and successful career, joining William DAVENANT's company in 1676. She was also the mistress of the king's famous cousin, the military hero Prince Rupert (1619–1682), and mother of his illegitimate daughter.

**Hull, Thomas (1728–1808)** English actor and theatrical entrepreneur, producer of adaptations of two of Shakespeare's plays. Hull produced adaptations of *Timon of Athens* (1786) and *The Comedy of Errors* (1793). The first of these was an economic failure, but his *Comedy* was restaged for many years and only disappeared from the English stage when Shakespeare's original text was restored in the second half of the 19th century. Hull was well known in his own day as a successful actor of secondary parts who spent a nearly 50-year career in one establishment, London's Covent Garden Theatre.

**Hume, John (active 1441)** Historical figure and character in *2 Henry VI*, a dishonest priest who arranges to hire a witch, MARGERY JOURDAIN, and two sorcerers, John SOUTHWELL and Roger BOLINGBROKE (2), for the DUCHESS (1) of Gloucester. The Duchess wishes to read the future so that she can prepare for a possible coup against King HENRY VI. In 1.2 Hume reveals in a soliloquy that he is also in the pay of the Duke of SUFFOLK (3), who seeks the Duchess' downfall as part of his campaign against her husband, the Duke of GLOUCESTER (4). Consequently, Hume's information leads to the arrest of the Duchess, along with that of Hume and the magicians, at a séance in 1.4. Hume's confederacy with Suffolk does him little good, for the king sentences him to death in 2.3 for his part in the plot.

Historically, Hume, whose first name was actually Thomas, was pardoned, for reasons that the chronicles do not specify; there is, however, no evidence that he was an agent of Gloucester's enemies. Shakespeare's reason for omitting Hume's pardon, seemingly appropriate to his presentation, is not apparent. Perhaps the playwright intended a subtle intimation of treachery on Suffolk's part. Or this may simply be an instance of the petty inconsistencies to which the playwright was persistently susceptible.

**Hundred Years War (1337–1453)** Fourteenth- and 15th-century conflict between England and FRANCE (1), parts of which are enacted in *1 Henry VI* and *Henry V*. The Hundred Years War, which actually lasted 116 years, consisted of three distinct phases separated by periods of peace. Shakespeare dealt only with the third stage, which began in 1415.

The war was basically a dynastic quarrel between the PLANTAGENET family and France's House of Valois. King Edward III of England claimed the French throne by inheritance through his mother. The French countered that the ancient Salic Law—disparaged by CANTERBURY (1) in *Henry V*, 1.2.33–95—excluded women from the succession. Edward declared war on France in 1337, and the English conquered large tracts of French territory to add to their already vast holdings in GASCONY. In 1360 a peace treaty ended this first phase of the war. Nine years later a revolt broke out, and the French recovered most of their lost territory. Two decades of sporadic fighting ensued before RICHARD II negotiated a peace treaty in 1396. England conceded its losses, and the second phase of the conflict came to a close.

The third phase of the war began when HENRY V invaded France in 1415, as presented in *Henry V.* In Shakespeare's play the English victory at AGINCOURT leads directly to the French surrender at TROYES, enacted in 5.2, but in fact five more years of fighting were necessary before Henry was granted the inheritance of the French crown. However, when Henry died in 1422, the French rebelled. Their subsequent success is presented in *1 Henry VI;* over the next 30 years, aided by a charismatic leader, Joan of Arc (see JOAN LA PUCELLE), they drove the English from France (except a tiny foothold at Calais, which England held for another century) in campaigns that culminated in the battle of BORDEAUX (1453). The English were soon engaged in the internal WARS OF THE ROSES, and they never attempted another conquest; the Hundred Years War was over.

The Hundred Years War was a watershed in the history of both countries. France, finally free of English colonisation, began to unify the territories that constitute the modern French nation. England, defeated on the Continent, began to develop its naval power. In military history, the war was also decisive. Medieval warfare, which depended on the mounted knight, was now obsolete; the development of tactics involving many archers and foot soldiers—plus the first use of gunpowder in Europe—spelled the beginning of more modern armies, involving masses of common troops. Moreover, the long and bloody war almost wiped out the knights, the traditional feudal nobility of both countries, permitting the monarchs to begin to ally themselves with the rising middle class, a process that was to result in the modern nation-state. This is to some extent reflected in Shakespeare in the fall of the medieval ideal of kingship represented by Richard II, although in the playwright's day this effect was not clearly perceived.

**Hunnis, William (d. 1597)**    English poet and musician, master of the Children of the Chapel (see CHILDREN'S COMPANIES). In 1566 Hunnis succeeded Richard EDWARDS as director of the choirboys. They performed numerous plays at the court of Queen ELIZABETH (1), some of which Hunnis may have written himself. In 1576 he delegated his theatrical responsibilities to his deputy, Richard FARRANT, who organised the first BLACKFRIARS THEATRE where the boys performed. Upon Farrant's death in 1580, Hunnis resumed direction of the troupe which he led until his death, though their play production ceased almost entirely after 1584.

An accomplished composer, Hunnis was a court musician for King Edward VI as early as 1550. Under Queen Mary, his ardent Protestantism led him to join a plot against the queen. For this he was imprisoned, being freed upon Elizabeth's accession in 1558 when he resumed his career. His poetry was largely religious, though he also wrote secular works, including parts of the elaborate festivities held at KENILWORTH in 1575, which may have been witnessed by the 11-year-old Shakespeare.

**Hunsdon (1), George Carey, Baron (1547–1603)**
English diplomat and theatrical patron. George Carey, the second Lord Hunsdon, was the son of Henry Carey (see HUNSDON [2]), Lord Chamberlain to Queen ELIZABETH (1). Upon his father's death in 1596, Hunsdon assumed the patronage of his theatrical company, the CHAMBERLAIN'S MEN, of which Shakespeare was a member. Because Hunsdon did not immediately succeed his father as Chamberlain (see COBHAM), the company was known for nine months as HUNSDON'S MEN. When he was appointed Chamberlain in 1597 the company resumed its old name, which it retained until the patronage was assumed by King JAMES I in 1603, shortly before Hunsdon's death.

George Carey had a successful career as a soldier and diplomat before he succeeded to his father's title. As Lord Chamberlain, he continued his father's policy of protecting the budding ELIZABETHAN THEATRE from the persecution of the puritanical London government. He provided many occasions for performances by the Chamberlain's Men, either at court or in his own home, Hunsdon House.

**Hunsdon (2), Henry Carey, Baron (1524–1596)**    English statesman and theatrical patron. Lord Hunsdon, as he was known, was Lord Chamberlain of England. In 1594 he assumed the patronage of Shakespeare's theatrical company, DERBY'S MEN, after the death of their previous patron. In recognition of Hunsdon's high office, the company was renamed the CHAMBERLAIN'S MEN. As Lord Chamberlain, Hunsdon protected the theatrical profession (see ELIZABETHAN THEATRE) from persecution by the London government, which was controlled by Puritans, an increasingly powerful religious sect that opposed public drama.

In February 1596 Hunsdon's grand-daughter was married, and scholars speculate that her wedding may have been the occasion of the first performance of *A Midsummer Night's Dream,* staged by his company. Upon his death, the company's patronage was assumed by his son George Carey, also Baron HUNSDON (1). The elder Lord Hunsdon was one of the most valued advisers of Queen ELIZABETH (1), and he held a series of high offices in her government. His mistress, Emilia LANIER, is among the women identified by commentators as the possible Dark Lady of Shakespeare's SONNETS.

**Hunsdon's Men**  Name used by Shakespeare's theatrical company, better known as the CHAMBERLAIN'S MEN, between July 22, 1596, and the following March 17. On the first date, the patron of the Chamberlain's Men, Baron HUNSDON (2), Lord Chamberlain for Queen ELIZABETH (1), died. He left his baronial title and the patronage of the company to his son, also Lord HUNSDON (1), but since the younger Lord Hunsdon did not immediately succeed his father as chamberlain, the company's name was changed to Hunsdon's Men. Nine months later, the new baron was appointed to his father's old office, after the death of the intervening holder, Lord COBHAM, and the company resumed their old name. As Hunsdon's Men, the company continued to be the leading London troupe; during this time, they introduced *Romeo and Juliet*—as is known from the title page of the play's first edition—and they rehearsed *The Merry Wives of Windsor*, which was first staged just after the second Lord Hunsdon became chamberlain.

The elder Lord Hunsdon had maintained another company as early as 1564, also known as Hunsdon's Men. They had been associated with the ADMIRAL'S MEN in the 1580s but had chiefly toured in the provinces and are not to be confused with the brief incarnation of the Chamberlain's Men. The provincial Hunsdon's Men were disbanded around 1590.

**Hunt, Simon (active 1571–1575)**  STRATFORD schoolmaster, Shakespeare's teacher. Hunt was master of the Stratford Grammar School from 1571 to 1575. Sometime during this period, Shakespeare probably advanced in school to the point where he was taught by the master. Younger pupils were taught by an assistant, called an usher, but since no usher's names have survived from the period, Hunt probably is the earliest known teacher of Shakespeare. However, it is uncertain who Hunt was. A Simon Hunt who began a career as a Catholic clergyman in 1578 and died in 1585 is recorded. If he was Shakespeare's teacher, he may conceivably have influenced the religious sensibilities of his pupil and promoted a tolerance for Catholicism. Many scholars see this tolerance in the adult Shakespeare's work, some going so far as to believe that the playwright was a secret Catholic. However, another Simon Hunt is known to have died in Stratford in 1598, and whoever the Simon Hunt of Stratford Grammar School was, he did not teach Shakespeare long before being succeeded by Thomas JENKINS.

**Huntington Library**  Major collection of Shakespeareana in San Marino, California. The Huntington Library was created by Henry E. Huntington (1850–1927), the heir to a railroad fortune. Huntington spent much of his wealth on the art museum and library that bear his name. The library contains the largest American collection of early printed books, including many QUARTO and FOLIO editions of Shakespeare's plays. It also contains other Shakespeareana and a large collection of 16th-century music.

**Huntsman (1)**  Minor character in *3 Henry VI*, a servant assigned to escort the captive EDWARD IV. Surprised by Edward's rescuers in 4.5, the Huntsman elects to travel with the escapee's party, saying, 'Better do so than tarry and be hang'd.' (4.5.26). This one-liner provides a hint of comic relief amid a grim series of political and military manoeuvrings.

**Huntsman (2)**  Either of two minor characters in the INDUCTION to *The Taming of the Shrew*, servants of a local landowner, the LORD (1). In Ind.1 the Huntsmen assist the Lord in his practical joke on Christopher SLY (1), which is the business of the introductory scenes. The Huntsmen's role in the plot could have been filled by servants of any sort, but the Lord's conversation with them on the merits of his hounds contributes to the rural atmosphere of the Induction.

**Hyman, Earle (b. 1926)**  Black American actor. Hyman has played many parts in both classical and modern plays since beginning his career in 1942 at the American Negro Theatre of Harlem. Among his noted Shakespearean portrayals have been OTHELLO and CALIBAN.

**Hymen (1)**  Minor character in *As You Like It*, the Roman god of marriage. In 5.4.107–145 Hymen is the central figure in the MASQUE that accompanies ROSALIND's appearance, undisguised, to resolve the play's complexities. Hymen, after making a formal statement of divine pleasure when earthly confusions are resolved, announces the return of Rosalind. Rosalind in turn declares her true relationship to her father, DUKE (7) Senior, to ORLANDO, and to PHEBE, all hitherto hidden by her disguise as a young man. Hymen then solemnly blesses four couples: Rosalind and Orlando, CELIA and OLIVER (1), Phebe and SILVIUS, and TOUCHSTONE and AUDREY. He then leads a 'wedlock hymn' (5.4.136), which everyone sings. This formal celebration of marriage represents the happy conclusion of the play's various courtships.

It is unclear whether Shakespeare intended Hymen as a human impersonator of a god taking part in a festive tableau arranged by Rosalind or as an actual deity appearing to mortals, as gods do in other Shakespearean plays—e.g., in *Cymbeline,* 5.4, and *The Tempest,* 4.1. In either case, Hymen's function is the same: his masque lends a gracefully solemn air to the play's climax. The part of Hymen is often assigned to AMIENS, who is a singer and who is present in this scene, according to the stage direction at 5.4.1, but who has no spoken lines in it.

**Hymen (2)**   Minor character in *The Two Noble Kinsmen,* the Roman god of marriage, as portrayed by a celebrant in the interrupted wedding of THESEUS (2) and HIPPOLYTA (2). Hymen does not speak; he is described in the opening stage direction as entering 'with a torch burning' (1.1.1). He provides a note of formal dignity to the occasion.

**Iachimo** Character in *Cymbeline,* the villain who pretends to have seduced POSTHUMUS' new wife, IMOGEN. He thus provokes the murderous jealousy in Posthumus that stimulates much of the action of the play. Motivated only by an irresponsible pleasure in mischief, Iachimo wagers that he can seduce Imogen. When he fails, he resorts to trickery. He secretes himself in her bedroom, steals her bracelet, and then poses as her lover. He flaunts his knowledge of her intimate surroundings and declares the bracelet a gift. His plan accomplished in 2.4, Iachimo pockets the diamond ring he has won from Posthumus and disappears from the play until very near its close, when he returns to Britain as a member of the Roman army. He proves unsuccessful in combat, and he supposes that his guilt for blackening Imogen's name has weakened him as a warrior. Captured, he confesses to his crime when the disguised Imogen recognises on his hand the ring he has won. In the aura of reconciliation that closes the play, he is forgiven by Posthumus.

Commentators have often compared Iachimo to Shakespeare's most extraordinary villain, IAGO, whose lies are similar in content. His name, the diminutive of Iago, suggests a similarly evil temperament, but Iachimo is a very different sort of villain. He is closer to the likeable AUTOLYCUS, the vagabond thief of *The Winter's Tale.* Iachimo is essentially a stock comic figure, the unscrupulous Italian (see ROME). He has no intention of destroying anyone's life, as Iago does; he barely has any intention at all. He is more like a con man than a rapist, though he compares himself to the genuinely fearful TARQUIN. However, he does so just as he has comically emerged like a jack-in-the-box, from a trunk, in 2.2, and such a ludicrous villain assures us that Imogen will not be permanently damaged. This aspect of Iachimo is important to the play's generally optimistic tone. We are never in doubt that the world of romance is dominant; Iachimo is merely an instrument of fate, which controls the adventures of Posthumus and Imogen. Even in the humiliation of his final exposure, Iachimo remains comic. Our awareness of his harmlessness is reinforced as he shamelessly embroiders the truth, apparently hoping to make himself seem a pleasingly audacious young gentleman. Both boastful and apologetic, he seems an entirely appropriate object of mercy—an immature fool. Unlike the other villains of the piece, the QUEEN (2) and CLOTEN, mercy is granted to him.

**Iago** Character in *Othello,* OTHELLO's villainous aide. The play centres on Iago's effort to destroy Othello's happiness. He convinces him that his wife, DESDEMONA, has been having a love affair with CASSIO, his lieutenant. One of Shakespeare's most thoroughly villainous characters, Iago has intrigued audiences for generations through his combination of realistic malice and seemingly unjustified lust for revenge, his 'motiveless malignity', in Samuel Taylor COLERIDGE's famous words. However, Shakespeare does provide his villain with stimuli that provoke his evil. In fact, if Iago's motives seem unclear it is because he is motivated in several ways, rather than not at all.

Shakespeare provides us with much evidence of Iago's motives in his soliloquies. He has been passed over for promotion in favour of Cassio, and in his first soliloquy he schemes to reverse this development and considers entangling Desdemona and the lieutenant as a step in this direction. Much later, Iago's wife, EMILIA (2), unknowingly comes close to guessing the cause of Othello's jealousy when she remarks, 'Some busy and insinuating rogue, / . . . to get some office, / [Has] devis'd this slander' (4.2.133–135).

Military ambition is commonplace, and this is an entirely credible motive, but it does not preclude the simultaneous operation of others. A second motive is sexual jealousy, the emotion which Iago transmits to Othello. Iago suspects Emilia's adultery with Othello in 1.3.385–386, and in his second soliloquy jealousy is his only stated motive. His suspicions are sometimes thought to be only a justification in his campaign against the general, but he expresses them in soliloquy, when he need not lie, and he is also jealous of Cassio (2.1.302). Emilia speaks of his suspicions, in 4.2.149, and Iago seems to have some general grounds for his jealousy, as Emilia states explicitly that she would commit adultery, given the opportunity (4.3.70). It is telling that the weapon Iago fashions to destroy Othello is precisely the one that hurts himself. The power of sexuality as a goad is further revealed in Iago's obsessive references to bestial sex (as in 1.1.88–

89), and in his vivid description of Cassio in bed with him (3.3.425–432). It is obvious that Iago's suspicions stem from his morbid imagination, but from Iago's point of view they are no less effective as inducements to action.

Both of these motives reflect an even deeper level of feeling. Iago's professional and sexual jealousies cause him to 'hate the Moor' (1.3.384), but they also stem from a greater, generalised jealous sense, an envy of those who have advantages over him that extend beyond promotions or access to his wife. He senses that the open and virtuous qualities in others may point up his own worthlessness. He cannot 'endure . . . [Othello's] constant, noble, loving nature' (2.1.283–284), and he sees in Cassio 'a daily beauty in his life, / That makes me ugly' (5.1.19–20). Like Satan—and not coincidentally, as we shall see—Iago is envious of those who are spiritually greater than he.

Iago's multiple motives make him a humanly credible character, but these are joined by an inhuman ferocity that adds a dose of terror to our perception of him. His envy and anger are so strong that they compel him to risk his life in his passionate effort to damage Othello. Though he has motives, his response outweighs the stimulus, and thus a less easily understood motive merges with the others: Iago loves evil for its own sake. He clearly delights in what he is doing. He speaks of fooling RODERIGO as 'my sport' (1.3.384); his delighted irony all but bubbles over when he exults, 'And what's he then, that says I play the villain . . .' (2.3.327); and his enjoyment is obvious when he says, 'Pleasure, and action, make the hours seem short' (2.3.369). After his triumph in the temptation scene (3.3), he cannot refrain from returning to manipulate his enemy some more. When accident brings him Desdemona's handkerchief, he comfortably contemplates the damage he may do with it, like an artist savouring a new and exciting idea—'this may do something' (3.3.329), he slyly understates. After reducing Othello to hysteria, he gloats, 'Work on, / My medicine, work' (4.1.44–45), and even in utter defeat his final refusal to talk smacks of self-satisfaction.

With his pleasure in evil Iago resembles the VICE of medieval drama. The Vice was an allegorical figure whose delight in horseplay and mischievous humour made him a popular character. Iago, however, is a realistic, rather than an abstract, embodiment of evil. Although Iago is not a comic character, he is occasionally funny. In 1.1.118, for example, he returns BRABANTIO's 'Thou art a villain' with 'You are a senator', and in his many ironic remarks on his own honesty, as in 2.3.258 and 318, the humour is unrecognised by anyone but himself and the audience. He also adopts a jocular attitude for his own purposes, as in the conventional battle of wits in 2.1.109–166 and the drinking bout of 2.3. Many commentators and theatrical directors agree with the advice of Edwin BOOTH (2),

who insisted that actors playing Iago should 'not sneer or glower' and suggested that 'the "light comedian" . . . not the "heavy man" ' should play the part.

Many people have a problem with the plot of *Othello*: the hero is unrealistically gullible, murdering his wife on the strength of a suggestion that has no serious credibility. However, Shakespeare relied on an established dramatic convention: Iago has a double role as villain to the audience but trustworthy friend to the characters in the play. He is seen as good by everyone but the audience, which fosters a high degree of suspense. For this reason, Shakespeare made Iago's villainy evident immediately in his first exchange with Roderigo in Act 1, and his evilness is repeatedly confirmed in his soliloquies. Iago is frank about his double role, saying 'I am not what I am' (1.1.65). Even his name—that of the patron saint of England's great enemy, Spain—indicated his evil nature to a 17th-century audience. Shakespeare's audiences presumed that Iago's victims would be taken in—and most modern audiences believe this as well.

Iago deceives Othello by also manipulating other people to achieve his ends. At Iago's instigation, Cassio urges Desdemona to intervene for him, thus unwittingly inflaming Othello's jealousy, and Roderigo attacks Cassio, who might expose Iago. Iago gets Desdemona's incriminating handkerchief from Emilia, and he exploits the affair of BIANCA (2) and Cassio to mislead Othello further. He describes his schemes aptly as spiderwebs, in 2.1.168. At the close of the play he fails, when his network of villainy begins to unravel. When Cassio fails to kill Roderigo, Iago does it himself—or thinks he does, though actually Roderigo lives to testify against him, as is revealed in 5.2.325–330. Only at this point, significantly, does Iago's cool self-confidence leave him, and he hastily mutters to himself, 'This is the night / That either makes me, or fordoes me quite' (5.1.127–128).

In the end the power of Iago's envy expires, and the forces of trust and love recover, though it is a bleak victory. Othello finally recognises the goodness of Desdemona, and Iago is condemned, but in the meantime Iago has demonstrated the power of evil. His power depends, however, on the weakness in Othello. In his motives, his judgements, and his single-minded savagery, Iago embodies his victim's psychological flaws. Iago can triumph only because Othello rejects his own potential for love and trust in favour of the self-centred desperation of jealousy and envy, the passions that dominate Iago.

Iago is the evil influence on Othello, in opposition to Desdemona's good. This situation closely resembles that of the medieval MORALITY PLAY, still familiar in Shakespeare's day, in which a central character must choose between an angel and a devil. Iago is associated with satanic evil at several points in the play. For example, when Othello, fainting with rage at the image of Desdemona's infidelity cries out, 'O devil!' (4.1.43), Iago, on cue, exults, 'Work on, / My medicine, work' (4.1.44–45). Iago hints at the hellish nature of his undertaking early on when he openly (to Roderigo) claims as his allies 'all the tribe of hell' (1.3.358), and in his soliloquy declares, 'Hell and night / Must bring this monstrous birth to the world's light' (1.3.401–402). Later, when he says that his 'Dangerous conceits . . . Burn like the mines of sulpher' (3.3.331–334), he reminds us of the conventional metaphor for hellfire.

Finally, at the play's close, Iago overtly identifies himself with the devil. Othello makes the connection first, after Iago's malevolence has been exposed. He looks at the villain's feet to see if they are cloven and says, 'If that thou be'st a devil, I cannot kill thee' (5.2.288), as he attempts to stab him with his sword. Iago, wounded, gloats defiantly, 'I bleed, sir, but not kill'd' (5.2.289), fully accepting the implication. It is the last thing he says before refusing to speak any further. In this final refusal Iago brazenly displays his malice, for all along his power has been in his words, talking his evil ends into existence. In making Iago's nature so strikingly evident at the play's close, Shakespeare helps assuage our horror, for we see that the villain's uncanny malevolence is even more immense than we had thought. It is as vast as hell itself, the abode of infinite evil, and we are therefore doubly glad that his career is finished, not only in relief from the play's agonising developments, but also in satisfaction at the suppression of a truly satanic menace.

**Iden, Alexander (active 1450)** Historical figure and minor character in *2 Henry VI*, a landowner who kills the rebel Jack CADE, who has hidden in his garden, in 4.10. Iden represents an ideal of the English country gentleman and small landowner. He is the very opposite of the subversive and destructive Cade, and also of the scheming noblemen whose ambitions are the chief business of the play. We see Iden before he knows of Cade's presence, enjoying his garden and rejoicing in his lot. Challenged by the desperate and angry Cade, Iden refuses to send for help. They fight, and Iden kills Cade, cursing the rebel as he does so. In 5.1 he presents King HENRY VI with Cade's head and is knighted.

Shakespeare created this paragon of the minor gentry from a bare mention of Cade's killer in the chronicles. The historical Iden was a sheriff of Kent who presumably killed Cade for the sizeable bounty that was offered for the rebel's head, which he in fact collected.

**Illyria** Region on the Adriatic coast of present-day Yugoslavia and northern Albania, setting for *Twelfth Night*. As in most of Shakespeare's plays set overseas, there is nothing specifically Illyrian about the sur-roundings in which the action occurs; Illyria was simply remote and exotic and therefore suitable to a tale of disguise, intrigue, and romance. Like such idealised locales as the Forest of ARDEN (1) in *As You Like It*, Illyria is pervaded with music and song and its inhabitants are concerned chiefly with love and revelry. However, ANTONIO (4) observes that 'these parts . . . often prove rough and unhospitable' (3.3.9–11), reflecting the unnsavoury reputation of the Illyrian coast, which was a notorious den of piracy until the 17th century. There are references to Illyrian pirates elsewhere in Shakespeare (*2 Henry VI*, 4.1.107; *Measure for Measure*, 4.3.70) and in other Elizabethan literature.

**Imogen** Character in *Cymbeline*, daughter of King CYMBELINE and wife of POSTHUMUS. Imogen, the central character of the play, loses the love of her husband through no fault of her own, is exposed to great danger and wanders in the wilderness, and then is finally restored to happiness. She embodies the play's lesson that while humanity may exhibit courage and an undefeatable spirit of love, our happiness nevertheless depends on providence. Imogen has long been among the favourite heroines in Shakespeare. The Victorian poet SWINBURNE extravagantly called her 'the woman best beloved in all the world of song and all the tide of time'. However, her great charm is also evidence of a failure on the playwright's part as he struggled with a new genre, the ROMANCES.

Imogen is subjected to a harrowing sequence of misfortunes. Her father banishes Posthumus to Italy, and she faces the unwanted courtship of both the boorish CLOTEN and the oily IACHIMO, the latter of whom malevolently convinces Posthumus that she has been unfaithful. Posthumus thereupon arranges for her murder in the wilds of WALES (1). A faithful servant, PISANIO, warns her and provides her with a disguise as a young man, but she finds herself stranded in the wilderness. After several adventurous episodes during which she comes to believe Posthumus is dead and is herself believed to be dead by others, she returns to her father's court in the guise of a Roman prisoner of war. In the final scene's sequence of reconciliations her identity is revealed, and she is reunited with both husband and father.

Though Imogen has always enchanted audiences, her resourcefulness and charm suggest one who battles against destiny rather than the helpless victim of fate. In the literature on which Shakespeare's romances were based, the traditional character type corresponding to Imogen was the fairy-tale princess who is adored for her beauty and passive calm, an object of intrigue but not a participant in it. She represents humanity's helplessness and inspires pity in her plight, rather than admiration for her pluck. Imogen is intermittently presented in terms of this ideal. To Pisanio, she is 'more goddess-like than wife-like' (3.2.8), and Iachimo compares her to 'th'Arabian bird' (1.7.17), the fabled Phoenix who cannot die. She sometimes seems to be a helpless puppet of the plot, as when she immediately accepts Iachimo's transparently false excuse for having proposed adultery with a humble 'You make amends' (1.7.168). Moreover, she adopts a purely conventional morality when she refuses to sleep with Posthumus even after they are married, presumably because she awaits her father's approval of the match.

However, Imogen has another set of qualities as well. In her spunk, her sharp wit, and her willingness to pursue her lover—as well as in her male disguise—Imogen is typical of Shakespeare's earlier comic heroines. In *Cymbeline* the playwright approached a new sort of character but could not divorce himself from habits of characterisation that he had used earlier. This happened with several of the characters in the play. Imogen is a transitional figure; Shakespeare would soon create female characters whose ethereal serenity would fulfil the romantic ideal. In Imogen he produced an uneasy conjunction of ideal womanhood—seen in HERMIONE of *The Winter's Tale* and MIRANDA of *The Tempest*, such as had enlivened ROSALIND of *As You Like It*, and VIOLA of *Twelfth Night*, among others. Imogen, for all her charming virtues, presents an image slightly contrary to the general tone of the play and thus in part contributes to its weakness.

**Induction** Dramatic device of the 16th and 17th centuries—an introductory scene or set of scenes that frankly announce the presentation of a play—that Shakespeare used at the outset of *The Taming of the Shrew*. In two successive scenes the drunken tinker Christopher SLY (1) is persuaded by the LORD (1) that he is a nobleman, by way of a practical joke, and a group of players performs a play for him; that play is *The Taming of the Shrew*.

Strictly speaking, an induction, though similar in purpose to a PROLOGUE, consists of dialogue instead of a single speech. However, the FOLIO edition of *2 Henry IV* labels the introductory speech by RUMOUR as 'Induction', and it is traditionally separated from 1.1.

An induction was generally found most appropriate in a COMEDY, for it emphasises the artificiality of the presentation to follow and prepares the audience to accept the ridiculous confusions that characterise the genre. It places the audience at a distance from the main action, which effectively becomes a play within a play.

**Ingleby, Clement Mansfield (1823–1886)** English scholar. In 1859 Ingleby helped expose the forgeries of J. P. COLLIER (2) in his *The Shakespeare Fabrications*. He followed it with *A Complete View of the Shakespeare*

*Controversy* (1861), which is still regarded as a definitive book on Collier. He wrote a number of other books on Shakespeare and assembled *Shakespeare's Centurie of Prayse* (1875), an anthology of references to the playwright in surviving documents from the period 1591–1693. It was the first of its kind, and later editors have expanded and revised Ingleby's collection, which remains at the core of *The Shakespeare Allusion Book* (1932) edited by Sir Edmund CHAMBERS.

**Innogen** GHOST CHARACTER who is mentioned in stage directions in *Much Ado About Nothing* (at the opening of 1.1 and 2.1) but does not appear, the wife of LEONATO. The existence of a ghost character, apparently reflecting an unrealised intention of the playwright, is evidence that the original published text, the QUARTO of 1600, was printed from Shakespeare's FOUL PAPERS—his unpolished manuscript—and is therefore highly authoritative.

**Inns of Court** Four law schools in LONDON, in whose buildings at least two of Shakespeare's plays were staged, and which served as a location for a scene in *1 Henry VI*. The Inns of Court—Gray's Inn Lincoln's Inn, the Middle Temple, and the Inner Temple—were so called because part of their function was to prepare young men to be gentlemen of the royal court. In addition to academic and legal studies, students learned dancing and music, and the Inns were famous for their elaborate MASQUES and other entertainments. The masque presented in 5.2 of *Love's Labour's Lost* is believed to be based on a noteworthy pageant presented at the annual Gray's Inn Christmas Revels in 1594. Shakespeare presumably saw this event, for *The Comedy of Errors* was performed by his acting company as part of the same festival (the earliest recorded performance of the play). It is thought that the 'houses' (see PHOENIX; PORCUPINE; PRIORY) described in the *Comedy's* stage directions reflect the classically influenced stage of the Inn. Also, *Twelfth Night* was performed at the Middle Temple in 1602.

In 2.4 of *1 Henry VI*, the antagonists of what will be the WARS OF THE ROSES engage in a dispute in the Temple Garden, a precinct of the Inns of Court. They bait each other by pointedly selecting emblems from two rose bushes, one red and one white. The incident, which is fictitious, is well placed, for the Inns were legally sanctuaries, where violence of any kind was strictly forbidden. Therefore, the dispute could not come to blows but rather had to be fully explicated in words and symbols.

**Interlude** Sixteenth-century term for a play—especially a short one with few characters—used more specifically to refer to elements in two of Shakespeare's plays. In *The Taming of the Shrew*, the passage 1.1.248–253 is spoken of as an interlude because it is a return to the story of Christopher SLY (1), begun in the INDUCTION. It is believed that there were originally several other interludes and an EPILOGUE, completing the tale, and that these are presented, although in altered form, in the anonymous play *THE TAMING OF A SHREW* (published 1594), thought to be a BAD QUARTO of Shakespeare's play. These passages are sometimes included in modern editions of the play, although they are missing from the original publication of *The Taming of the Shrew;* they were probably cut from an early production because of a shortage of available actors.

The term 'interlude' is also used in *A Midsummer Night's Dream*—and by writers about the play—to refer to the performance of *PYRAMUS AND THISBE* staged by the artisans of ATHENS. The term was probably old-fashioned in Shakespeare's day and may have carried a connotation of rustic quaintness.

**Inverness**   City in northern SCOTLAND, the site of MACBETH's castle and the location of several scenes in *Macbeth.* Beginning in 1.5 when LADY (6) MACBETH learns of the WITCHES' prediction that Macbeth will be king, through 2.4, when Macbeth's upcoming coronation is abruptly announced, Inverness is associated with the planning, execution, and aftermath of the assassination of King DUNCAN. In 1.6 Duncan and BANQUO describe the castle at Inverness as a lovely building, thronged with birds and characterised by a pleasant atmosphere, but its nature quickly changes as our sense of it is influenced by the evil done there. It is associated with hell in 2.3.1–21, where the PORTER (3) comically portrays a gatekeeper of hell, an ancient dramatic tradition of medieval religious drama. The description of terrible omens in 2.4 leaves us with an impression of Inverness as a castle of horrors. Productions of *Macbeth* have commonly emphasised this idea, with sets that stress darkness and Gothic detail.

Historically, the inclusion of Inverness in the play is an anachronism. Macbeth did not murder Duncan at Inverness—he didn't murder him at all—and there was no castle at Inverness until at least a century later. However, Shakespeare took this error from his source, HOLINSHED's history, and doubtless believed it was correct.

**Iras**   Character in *Antony and Cleopatra,* an attendant of CLEOPATRA. In 1.2 Iras is a pleasantly humorous young woman who jests over the predictions of the SOOTHSAYER (2), but she displays almost no personality thereafter. She is overshadowed by CHARMIAN in the queen's household, as she is on much less intimate terms with her mistress and has a much less developed role. Significantly, the Soothsayer tells Iras only that her fortune will be the same as Charmian's (1.2.52). She appears often with Cleopatra and Charmian but speaks very little. In 5.2 as Cleopatra prepares her suicide, Iras declares her loyalty and says that she will

not see the queen as a Roman prisoner, 'for I am sure my nails / Are stronger than mine eyes' (5.2.222–223), but, as elsewhere, she is a faint echo of Charmian. When Cleopatra applies the poisonous asp to herself, Iras falls dead. Perhaps she uses the snake herself, moments earlier, or perhaps she simply dies of grief. In either case, she departs wordlessly. Shakespeare's source, PLUTARCH's *Lives,* states that Cleopatra was attended at her death by a serving-woman named Iras, but she is otherwise unknown in history.

**Ireland, William Henry (1777–1835)**   English forger. In 1794 the 17-year-old Ireland, a lawyer's clerk, forged a number of documents relating to Shakespeare. These included business papers, letters (one to Anne HATHAWAY, with a lock of hair), and the playwright's profession of religious faith. He claimed they had been given by Shakespeare to a friend, a descendant of whom had disclosed them anonymously. Ireland's father, an amateur scholar, exhibited these materials in good faith and published them as *Miscellaneous Papers and Legal Instruments under the Hand and Seal of William Shakespeare* (1796). They caused a sensation, and Ireland responded by creating two Shakespearean plays. One of them, a tragedy entitled *Vortigern and Rowena,* was produced by J. P. KEMBLE (3) in April 1796, although scholars, led by Edmond MALONE, were already suspicious. The play was laughed off the stage, and the second work *(Henry II)* was never performed. Under pressure after the publication of Malone's *Inquiry into the Authenticity of Certain Miscellaneous Papers and Legal Instruments* (1796), Ireland confessed, and wrote *An Authentic Account of the Shakespearian Manuscripts* (1796), in which he described his procedures and cleared his father. He became a hack writer and produced a number of poor novels and a memoir (*Confessions of William Henry Ireland* [1805]), before he died in poverty.

**Iris**   Pagan goddess and minor figure in *The Tempest,* a character in the MASQUE presented by the sprite ARIEL to celebrate the engagement of MIRANDA and FERDINAND (2). Iris—goddess of the rainbow and messenger of the greater deities—functions as the 'presenter' of the masque, which features CERES, goddess of harvests; JUNO, queen of the gods; and a dance of Nymphs and Reapers. Iris' beautiful invocation to Ceres in 4.1.60–75 establishes a tone of serene power appropriate to divinity. Ariel subsequently declares that he 'presented Ceres' (4.1.167), indicating that he played the part of either Ceres or Iris, the presenter; most commentators believe Shakespeare intended the former, with Iris' initial speech providing time for Ariel to costume himself.

In Greek mythology Iris is a hazy figure and was never the object of a cult of worship. Originally simply associated with the rainbow, she was perhaps considered a messenger of the gods because rainbows seem to connect sky and earth. In classical literature—as distinct from mythology—Iris was particularly associated with Juno, and Shakespeare draws on this tradition when Ariel's masquer speaks of Juno as 'the queen o' th' sky, / Whose wat'ry arch and messenger am I' (4.1.70–71).

**Irving, Henry (1838–1905)**   British actor and producer. Irving was London's leading Shakespearean actor and producer for the last quarter of the 19th century. Though he played few Shakespearean parts during the first 15 years of his acting career, Irving was highly acclaimed as HAMLET in 1874, and over the next few years portrayed MACBETH, OTHELLO, and RICHARD III, establishing himself as one of the best classical actors of the day. From 1878 to 1902 he managed his own company at London's Lyceum Theatre, with himself and Ellen TERRY (1) as the featured performers. They staged many of Shakespeare's plays, including *Hamlet* (1879), *The Merchant of Venice* (1879), *Othello* (1881), *Romeo and Juliet* (1882), *Much Ado About Nothing* (1882), *Twelfth Night* (1884), *Macbeth* (1888), *Henry VIII* (1892), *King Lear* (1892), *Cymbeline* (1896), and *Coriolanus* (1901). He was famous for his extravagant productions, with many extras, elaborate sets and costumes, and special scenic effects. Irving was a tyrannical director by all accounts, 'incapable of caring for anything outside his work', in Terry's words. His business manager at the Lyceum was Bram Stoker, the author of *Dracula,* and it has been thought that Stoker's famous protagonist reflects the actor-producer's domineering personality. Irving's acting and production were not without detractors, but he was generally praised, and in 1895 he became the first actor to be knighted. In 1902 his lease on the Lyceum was not renewed, and he turned to touring. He died a few hours after a performance on the road.

**Isabel (1), Queen of England**   Character in *Richard II.* See QUEEN (13).

**Isabel (2), Queen of France (1370–1435)**   Historical figure and character in *Henry V,* the wife of the FRENCH KING. Queen Isabel appears only in 5.2, where she blesses the marriage of King HENRY V and her daughter, Princess KATHARINE (2).

The historical Queen Isabel was a Princess of Bavaria who married Charles VI, the French King of the play, at the age of 14. She was a notoriously self-indulgent, licentious, and extravagant woman. When it became evident that her husband was insane, Isabel became a leader of the factional strife that was probably most responsible for the victories of Henry V. She went so far as to declare that her second son, the successor to the DAUPHIN (3) as the heir to the throne, was illegitimate, her love life being too rich to permit

identification of the father. He nevertheless managed to claim the crown upon the death of the king, and he appears as CHARLES VII in *1 Henry VI.*

**Isabella**   Character in *Measure for Measure,* a would-be nun and the object of the illicit lust of ANGELO (2). Isabella pleads with Angelo to pardon her brother CLAUDIO (3), who has been sentenced to death for sexual immorality; in doing so, she arouses the official's desire, and he demands sex of her in exchange for the pardon. She refuses and asserts that to avoid such a sin is worth a life; she objects hysterically when Claudio begs her to give in. She is, in her strict insistence on morality, as extreme as Angelo was when he sentenced Claudio. She realises her error by the end of the play and requests mercy for Angelo when he is condemned to death by the DUKE (9). Finally, she abandons her earlier intention to become a nun and agrees to marry the Duke, thus bringing about the play's happy ending in marriage, the traditional closing of a COMEDY.

Isabella undergoes a great change of heart in the course of the play, for neither acceptance nor leniency seem part of her nature at first. Like Angelo, before he succumbs to her beauty, she is strictly insistent on virtue. Not only is she about to enter a nunnery, she regrets that its rules are not strict enough. Like Angelo, she wants to see her own ideals applied to others, 'wishing a more strict restraint / Upon the sisters stood' (1.4.4–5) and demanding that Claudio 'Take my defiance, / [and] Die, perish!' (3.1.142–143). When she seeks mercy for Claudio, she holds fast to her morals, pleading that the fault be condemned rather than the doer of it. When this fails to work, she goes on to demand that Angelo behave as God would. Her strict attitudes appeal to Angelo's obsessiveness, sparking his lust as no simple offer of a sexual bribe could. Her extremism matches his.

As with other Shakespearean heroines, Isabella's assertiveness is an attractive feature to audiences, but here it is counterproductive and brings nearer the potential tragedy of Claudio's death. This serves, of course, to further the plot, but it also emphasises an important point: mercy may not be brought about through evil means. If Claudio is to be saved it must be through the action of good, and Isabella, concerned wholly with a rigid sense of morality, cannot provide that action.

Isabella's obsession with her virginity covers her own strong sexuality, which is startingly apparent in her response to Angelo's proposition. She declares that she'd rather die under torture, saying, 'Th'impression of keen whips I'd wear as rubies, / And strip myself to death as to a bed / That longing have been sick for . . .' (2.4.101–103). The strength of her subconscious passion suggests—as does her assertiveness—that she is not a good candidate for the convent, and at the end of the play when her judgemental attitude has softened, her assent to the Duke's marriage proposal seems appropriate, a step towards fulfilment.

Resolution is only made possible by the substitution of MARIANA (2) in the 'bed trick', permitting the entrapment of the villain without compromising the heroine. Shakespeare's introduction of this device, which is not present in his sources, suggests his attitude towards Isabella. In the original story, the Angelo figure sleeps with the Isabella figure and then is forced to marry her and restore her honour. However, Angelo and Isabella have been shown in the first half of the play to be enemies, and their obsessiveness has been presented with powerful realism. Even within the play's aura of forgiveness, these two characters simply cannot be made to accept each other without losing their dramatic power. Mariana therefore replaces Isabella, and a resolution becomes possible. What is more, Isabella participates in the resolution. She makes the arrangements for the assignation with Angelo, though a message would have sufficed, and then tells Mariana of the plot, a task that could have been performed by the Duke. Shakespeare kept Isabella in the action at this point, thus making her an active force.

Most important, Isabella pleads for Angelo. As the Duke points out, 'Her brother's ghost . . . would . . . take her hence in horror' (5.1.433–434). Isabella's intercession opposes her natural feelings towards Angelo, her intended rapist and the apparent killer of her brother, but she supports Mariana's plea. She argues in rational terms for mercy, in a fashion suited to the case, rather than in the absolute terms in which she had pleaded for Claudio. Isabella is no longer a moral extremist. Perhaps she is under the influence of Mariana's example of love, or perhaps she remembers her claim, in 2.2, that she would be merciful if she had power, or, possibly, she wishes to atone for her willingness to sacrifice Claudio for a principle. Her act flies in the face of common morality with its demand for justice, just as does Christ's command in the Sermon on the Mount to love one's enemies. Isabella has arrived at the giving of a full measure in the spirit of the biblical text that inspired the play's title.

While the play's ending often seems arbitrary to modern readers, its convenient resolution of the impending tragedy was not only perfectly acceptable in Shakespeare's day, it was highly satisfying: the triumph of good, in a clear and traditional manner, gratified the sentimental feelings of audiences. While Isabella is somewhat diminished as a character by her symbolic quality in the play's dénouement, she is nonetheless sufficiently well developed to rank among Shakespeare's most interesting heroines.

**Isidore's Servant**   Minor character in *Timon of Athens*, an employee of Isidore, a creditor of TIMON. In 2.2 Isidore's Servant, with CAPHIS and VARRO'S SERVANT, solicits Timon and his STEWARD (2) for payment, but they are put off. These servants of greedy masters are pawns of plot development; Isidore's Servant speaks even less than the others.

**Italy**   European country, the setting for many of Shakespeare's plays. Though not yet a single nation in Shakespeare's day, Italy was the fountainhead of the RENAISSANCE and the cultural leader of Europe. Many of Shakespeare's sources were Italian, with the consequence that Italian cities were the locations of many of his plays, especially the comedies. Also, Italy had been the centre of the ancient Roman Empire, so Shakespeare's ROMAN PLAYS tended to feature Italian locations, especially ROME. However, there is nothing especially Italian about Shakespeare's settings, and the Italian cities ostensibly shown—such as MANTUA, MESSINA, PADUA, VENICE, and VERONA—tend to resemble Shakespeare's LONDON. The plays in which some or all of the action is set in Italy include *All's Well That Ends Well, Antony and Cleopatra, Coriolanus, Cymbeline, Julius Caesar, The Merchant of Venice, Much Ado About Nothing, Othello, Romeo and Juliet, The Taming of the Shrew, Titus Andronicus, The Two Gentlemen of Verona,* and *The Winter's Tale.*

# J

**Jackson (1), Barry (1879–1961)** British theatrical producer. Jackson was extremely influential on 20th-century Shakespearean production, especially with his modern-dress productions of *Cymbeline* (1923), *Hamlet* (1925), and *Macbeth* (1928), staged at the Birmingham Repertory Theatre, which he founded in 1913. He was director of the Shakespeare Memorial Theatre in STRATFORD from 1945 to 1948.

**Jackson (2), John (c. 1574–c. 1625)** Friend of Shakespeare in LONDON. Jackson was a partner with Shakespeare and others in the purchase of the BLACKFRIAR'S GATEHOUSE in 1613. He was probably the John Jackson, a shipping magnate from northern England, who was a regular patron of the MERMAID TAVERN and a close friend of Thomas SAVAGE.

**Jackson (3), Roger (1601–1625)** London publisher and bookseller. Jackson bought the rights to *The Rape of Lucrece* from the younger John HARRISON (2) in 1614, and he published Q6 of the poem, the first edition to bear the full title, in 1616.

**Jacobean Drama** Art of writing for the theatre as practised in England during the reign of King JAMES I (1603–1625). The drama of this period clearly evolves from ELIZABETHAN DRAMA, and that term is often taken to cover the Jacobean period as well. However, by about 1610, Jacobean drama was quite different. It is usually characterised as decadent, by comparison, in that substantive themes and fine poetry were increasingly subordinated to the titillating effects of the spectacular and bizarre. There are certainly exceptions to this indictment, most notably the late work of Shakespeare, but commentators over the centuries have generally agreed that the period is markedly inferior to its predecessor.

Early in the Jacobean period, Shakespeare manifested the continuing vitality of English TRAGEDY with *Othello, King Lear, Macbeth, Antony and Cleopatra*, and *Coriolanus*. Another major Jacobean tragedy was written early in the period, George CHAPMAN's *Bussy D'Ambois* (1604), but besides Shakespeare, the only great Jacobean writer of tragedies, in most opinions, was John WEBSTER (2), whose *The White Devil* (1612) and

*The Duchess of Malfi* (1614) are still frequently performed. He may also have written most of *The Revenger's Tragedy* (1606), though it is frequently attributed to Cyril TOURNEUR, a much lesser talent. Webster's tragedies are all REVENGE PLAYS (as is *Bussy*), a genre that continued to be popular. Thomas MIDDLETON also wrote tragedies, and late in the period another figure arose, John FORD (2).

In line with the decadence of the period, Jacobean tragedies often rely on false starts, sudden changes of motivation, and gratuitous accidents. The artificiality of these devices reflects a different emotional tone: these works largely ignore the implications of human disaster for society or for humanity as a whole, and focus instead on the pathos of the individual. Even that tends to be diminished by a predilection for cheap sensationalism and unnsavoury sexual themes, as the open bawdiness of the Elizabethans yields to a furtive indecency.

Perhaps the best-known Jacobean dramatists are Francis BEAUMONT (2) and John FLETCHER (2), who collaborated on a number of plays that typify the spirit of the era, so much so that in the 1630s they were rated well above Shakespeare by most playgoers. Their *Philaster* (1610) sparked a vogue for a characteristic TRAGICOMEDY that was widely imitated for decades. Its unrealistic protagonist, who changes his motivation repeatedly, rejects his lover on ludicrous suspicions of infidelity. By a series of absurd coincidences, lives and nations are placed at stake while he splits hairs at great length over perverse notions of honour. Only further improbable accidents bring about a final reunion of the lovers. Mysterious in their way, grand in their pretensions, and entirely escapist, *Philaster* and its successors appealed immensely to the decadent court society that made up its audience.

In COMEDY, Shakespeare's ROMANCES, written early in the period, evidence the emerging taste for spectacle, exotic locales, romantic characters, and improbable plots. However, these works are singular for their interest in the virtues of innocence and the role of providence in human affairs. The romance literature at their roots is uproariously satirised in Beaumont's *The Knight of the Burning Pestle* (c. 1608), but Jacobean comedy in general is not so genial as this work. Ben

JONSON's 'city comedies', which evolved from the earlier COMEDY OF HUMOURS, satirised 17th-century LONDON with sharp and biting acerbity. These works—most notably *Volpone* (1606), *Epicoene* (c. 1609), *The Alchemist* (1610), and *Bartholomew Fair* (1614)—are among the greatest English comedies. They represent the positive aspect of Jacobean comedy, which otherwise tended towards coarser works chiefly concerned with the pursuit of money through bald sexual intrigue. Among the other Jacobean dramatists who wrote notable comedies are Middleton, Fletcher, and Philip MASSINGER.

Jacobean drama (the term is taken from *Jacobus*, Latin for James) is often considered to cover Caroline or Carolean drama (1625–1642), that is, during the reign of Charles I until the closure of the theatres by the Civil Wars. The only important playwrights of this period were Ford and James Shirley (1596–1666). The Jacobean tendencies to decadence continued to grow, and Puritan opposition to the theatre grew with it; the result was the 18-year demise of the theatres. The Caroline period is considered the end of the RENAISSANCE in England.

**Jaggard, William (c. 1568–1623) and Isaac (1597–1627)**  London printers and publishers, father and son, producers of the FIRST FOLIO and other editions of Shakespeare's works. In 1599 William Jaggard published THE PASSIONATE PILGRIM, an anthology of poems that he claimed was by Shakespeare, though only about a quarter of them actually were. In 1612 he reissued this work, adding to it two poems by Thomas HEYWOOD (2). When Heywood publicly protested, on his own behalf and Shakespeare's, Jaggard replaced the title page with one that named no author.

Beginning in about 1613, Isaac Jaggard increasingly controlled the firm, due to his father's failing eyesight. In 1619 the Jaggards, with Thomas PAVIER, produced a group of QUARTO editions of 10 plays attributed to Shakespeare, though only a few were proper texts of Shakespeare's plays. These are known collectively as the FALSE FOLIO. Protests prompted the publishers to backdate most of these titles so that they could pass for the original editions.

Such practices were more acceptable then than now, and did not prevent the Jaggards from joining the syndicate that published the FIRST FOLIO edition of Shakespeare's works in 1623. William Jaggard was blind by this time, and Isaac headed the project; William died before it was completed.

**Jailor**  Minor character in *The Comedy of Errors*, a guard. The attendant assigned to the condemned EGEON in 1.1 speaks only one line and functions to emphasise the power of the state and the extremity of Egeon's predicament.

**James, Elias (c. 1578–1610)**  London brewer whose EPITAPH is attributed to Shakespeare. The six-line memorial to James first appeared in a manuscript collection of poems dating from the 1630s, some years after Shakespeare's death. The poem is ascribed to Shakespeare in an unknown hand, but modern scholars are inclined to accept the attribution, for James may well have been a friend or acquaintance of the playwright. James' brewery was located near the BLACKFRIARS THEATRE, and Shakespeare's friend John JACKSON (2) married the widow of James' brother and partner Jacob James.

**James I, King of England (1566–1625)**  Ruler of England during the last years of Shakespeare's life and the patron of his acting company. James and his court were enthusiastic playgoers, and their tastes were highly influential on JACOBEAN DRAMA. James had been interested in the theatre before he came to England; as James VI of SCOTLAND, he had employed English actors led by Laurence FLETCHER (3). As king of England, he took over Shakespeare's CHAMBERLAIN'S MEN, and they performed at his court—as the KING'S

*James I was an enthusiastic patron of the theatre, and he particularly enjoyed Shakespeare's works. Ben Jonson, speaking also of James' predecessor Queen Elizabeth, wrote of Shakespeare's 'flights . . . That so did take Eliza, and our James!'* (Courtesy of National Maritime Museum, Greenwich)

MEN—more than twice as often as they had for his predecessor, Queen ELIZABETH (1). Moreover, the other two leading LONDON companies came under royal patronage, as the QUEEN'S MEN (2) and PRINCE HENRY'S MEN. The family added two more troupes around 1610, PRINCE CHARLES' MEN and LADY ELIZABETH'S MEN. On the other hand, state CENSORSHIP increased under King James, whose strong religious sentiments combined with his worries as the first ruler of the STUART DYNASTY—especially after the Gunpowder Plot (see GARNET)—to demand strict controls on the public's exposure to ideas.

Twice Shakespeare alluded to James in his plays, both times in the words of characters making auspicious prophecies of Britain's future. In *Macbeth* James' purported ancestor BANQUO is a very positive figure, and eight spectral KINGS appear to MACBETH, who realises they represent Banquo's progeny and notes that some of them carry 'two-fold balls and treble sceptres' (4.1.121). To Shakespeare's original audiences, this was an easily recognised reference to James' royal regalia as the ruler of both England and Scotland. In *Henry VIII* the play reaches its climax with Archbishop CRANMER's eulogy to the infant Elizabeth, and he adds a postscript praising her heir, declaring that he 'Shall star-like rise, as great in fame as she was, / And so stand fix'd' (5.4.46–47). James was presumably flattered by these references; that he enjoyed Shakespeare's works is attested to in Ben JONSON's poem on Shakespeare (published in the FIRST FOLIO [1623]), where he speaks of the playwright's 'flights . . . that did so take . . . our James!'

James was the son of Mary, Queen of Scots (1542–1587), and in 1567, as an infant, he was made King James VI of Scotland, on his mother's forced abdication. He never saw his mother again—after losing a civil war, she fled to England and was eventually executed by her enemy, Queen Elizabeth. He was raised a Protestant by a series of regents. The cornerstone of his policy as king was to secure his succession to the childless Elizabeth, who was his cousin. In 1589 he married Princess Anne of Denmark (1574–1619), and though he was homosexual by preference, they had seven children, three of whom survived infancy, Prince HENRY (2), Prince Charles—later King Charles I (ruled 1625–1649)—and Princess ELIZABETH (3). Though James was at first well liked in England—not least because his accession had been bloodless, despite fears of civil war—soon his popularity waned. His increasingly blatant homosexuality offended many, his sale of monopolies to his favourites angered parliament, and his policy of alliance with Spain enraged the country.

Further, his tendency to preach to his subjects eventually aroused resentment. James was undeniably a pedant; John HARINGTON, meaning no compliment, called him 'schoolmaster of the realm'. He published a number of works on theology, two books asserting the divine right of kings, and a pamphlet denouncing the evils of smoking (*A Counterblaste to Tobacco* [1604]). He also wrote and translated poetry in English, Latin, and Scots, and published a manual of Scots prosody. Though James was an intelligent king who sincerely desired to be a good ruler, he was a failure. Out of touch with the English people and by nature disinclined to compromise, he was a bad politician, and his reign widened the gap between crown and parliament that led to the Civil Wars.

**Jamy**  Character in *Henry V*, a Scottish officer in the army of King HENRY V. Jamy appears only in the 'international' scene, 3.2, with the Welsh FLUELLEN, the English GOWER (2), and the Irish MACMORRIS. The episode emphasises the diversity of British subjects serving together under Henry. Although Fluellen speaks of him as a fine soldier, Jamy merely lends colour, uttering commonplaces in an almost impenetrable brogue.

**Janssen (1), Cornelius (Cornelius Johnson or Jonson) (1593–1661)**  English painter to whom a possible portrait of Shakespeare is attributed. The 'Janssen portrait', or 'Somerset portrait', as it is known (it was owned by a Duke of Somerset in the late 18th century), somewhat resembles the most authoritative portraits of Shakespeare (see DROESHOUT; JANSSEN [2]). However, it is chiefly associated with the playwright for its inscription, which indicates that the anonymous sitter was 46 years old in 1610, the date the portrait was painted, as was Shakespeare. Even so, this could easily be coincidence, and that the painting depicts Shakespeare is regarded as highly questionable by most scholars. The work is apparently a copy of another portrait from the period, also possibly by Janssen—the clothes, elaborately detailed, are exactly identical in the two paintings—with the facial features altered to resemble the known images of Shakespeare. The creation of a portrait of a well-known figure was to be done in this way in both the 17th and 18th centuries, so the altered copy could have been made then.

Janssen, whose name is often Anglicised, was born in England of Dutch parents but probably returned to Holland for his training. He was painting in London at least as early as 1617, and he maintained a thriving practise as a portraitist until he returned to Holland for good in 1643, when he fled from the English Civil Wars. He is regarded as among the leading English painters of his day.

**Janssen (2), Gheerart (Gerard Johnson) (active 1600–1623)**  English sculptor, creator of the memorial bust of Shakespeare in Holy Trinity Church at STRATFORD, one of the two portraits of the playwright considered by scholars to reflect his actual appearance (the other is an engraving by Martin DROESHOUT). Because the Janssen bust was presumably commissioned and approved by Shakespeare's family, it probably provides a satisfactory likeness, although it is a conventionally stylised image rather than a psychologically revealing portrait. Presumably, it was made from an earlier portrait, probably a drawing or painting that is now lost. Made of painted limestone, the bust depicts a well-dressed gentleman with auburn hair and a quill pen in his right hand. The bust and its elaborate frame were installed sometime between 1616 and 1622; it was whitewashed in the late 18th century, and repainted in its present colours—though they may not be those originally provided by Janssen—in 1861. In 1790 the original pen, made of lead, was replaced with a real goosefeather quill, and a new quill is provided every year on Shakespeare's birthday.

Gheerart Janssen, whose name is sometimes Anglicised, was the son of a Dutch stone carver who arrived in England in the 1560s and established a flourishing business in SOUTHWARK, near the GLOBE THEATRE. This location suggests that Janssen may have known Shakespeare, at least by sight. Janssen inherited the family business in 1611. Another of his clients was Shakespeare's friend, John COMBE (1), whose memorial which he created is also in the Stratford church.

**Jaquenetta**  Minor character in *Love's Labour's Lost*, the young dairymaid wooed by both ARMADO and COSTARD. Jaquenetta receives a love letter that BEROWNE intended for ROSALINE and turns it over to the KING (19), on the advice of HOLOFERNES. This embarrasses Berowne, who must acknowledge his susceptibility to love. In 5.2 Costard reveals that Jaquenetta is pregnant by Armado, and the Spaniard vows fidelity to her at the end of the play.

**Jaques (1)**  Character in *As You Like It*, gloomy follower of DUKE (7) Senior who provides a contrast to the play's comic values. Jaques muses on the viciousness of human hypocrisy, affects to dislike music and dancing, and praises only the satire that can expose the sins of the world. When the duke prepares to return to his dukedom at the play's close, accompanied by most of the other characters, Jaques decides to stay in the Forest of ARDEN (1) and pursue a life of contemplation.

Jaques' pessimism and self-imposed isolation place him at odds with the play's central tenet, that love is the most valued element in human life. However, he never seriously threatens this ideal; his position is consistently undercut, in part because Shakespeare envisioned Jaques to some extent as a parody of a fashionable 16th-century affectation of cynicism and melancholy. People who held this attitude doubtless felt that they appeared intellectually superior and

penetrating, but others found them amusingly pretentious.

The ineffectuality of Jaques' ideas is repeatedly pointed up by his repudiation by the other major characters. His elaborately melancholy pose is described even before we meet him, when the duke hears of his lament over a slain deer (2.1.26–66). In 2.5, in his first appearance, Jaques satirises AMIENS' song, which mirrors the duke's sentiments about the virtues of life in Arden. Then, in 2.7, having encountered the jester TOUCHSTONE, he raves about the opportunities for a FOOL (1) to 'cleanse th'infected world' (2.7.60) through satire. However, Jaques is then sternly chastised by the duke for 'chiding sin' (2.7.64) when he has been a sinner himself. Even Jaques' most spectacular speech, his cynical depiction of the seven ages of man, beginning, 'All the world's a stage, / And all the men and women merely players' (2.7.139–140), is undercut. No character bothers to respond to it, and, immediately after Jaques' harrowing description of old age, the ancient ADAM is borne on stage and treated as a respected member of the community.

Jaques is most explicitly contrasted with the lovers ROSALIND and ORLANDO. When he first meets Orlando, Jaques declares he would rather be alone, and he disparages Orlando's poetry, his wit, and his lover's name. Jaques has said that he is seeking a fool, meaning Touchstone, but Orlando invites him to look in the brook, where he will see his own reflection. Insulted, Jaques leaves.

Rosalind is similarly dismissive. In 4.1 Jaques asserts that he is melancholy, saying, 'I do love it better than laughing' (4.1.4). The heroine fiercely insists that those who are excessive in laughter *or* melancholy are 'abominable fellows, and betray themselves to every modern censure, worse than drunkards' (4.1.5–8). Further, when he says that his state of mind has been influenced by his travels, she delivers a standard Elizabethan diatribe on the foolishness of travel. Significantly, these rebukes each occur just before one of the two major courtship scenes between Rosalind and Orlando, 3.2.290–423 and 4.1.40–190. Jaques' negativism must be overcome before the lovers' affirmation can occur.

Touchstone seems to resemble Jaques at first glance; they are both given to satire, wit, and cynicism. However, Touchstone is a professional comic whose statements are usually meant only to be humorous. His comprehension of the world's ways stirs him to amusement rather than despair. Jaques, by contrast, is a philosopher of sorts, and he has a consistently dour viewpoint that opposes sociability; as he remarks, 'I am for other than for dancing measures' (5.4.192).

Jaques wishes for a pristine past, before human societies came to Arden to kill deer, before humans existed at all, perhaps. This is an extreme form of the

PASTORAL literary conventions, a target of the play's parody. Such extravagantly anti-social desires place Jaques beyond the reach of the celebration of love that closes the play. This is a recurring device that Shakespeare uses in his COMEDIES: characters whose actions are not motivated by love and whose presence would mar the harmonious resolution of the play—such as Don JOHN (1) of *Much Ado About Nothing* and MALVOLIO of *Twelfth Night*—are left out of such scenes of reconciliation.

However, Jaques is not a villain, as is Don John. Except in his encounter with Orlando in 3.2, he behaves with civility. In 2.5 he and a group of fellow courtiers listen to music. In 4.2 he sings with others in a ribald interlude celebrating the hunt with jokes about cuckold's horns and deer's antlers (quite forgetful of his distress over the slain deer of 2.1). Even his satire of Amiens' song in 2.5 is good-natured, particularly since the 'gross fools' (2.5.53) he criticises include himself. Also, although he expresses anti-social views, Jaques converses with more different people than any other character. Finally, the blessings that Jaques bestows on the duke and each of the marrying couples in 5.4.185–192 are pleasant and humorous, as well as perceptive.

In fact, Jaques' closing lines reveal that he, too, has been affected by the general awareness of love's power that surrounds him. He knows that he is not destined to be a part of it, but he certainly does not begrudge the lovers their happiness. In fact, his final remarks concern his friends and their prospects; Jaques has become humanised. He remains isolated, but he is no longer a malcontent. He does not disparage the wedding festivities; he simply opts for something else. His reason for remaining in Arden is eminently acceptable: 'There is much matter to be heard and learn'd' (5.4.184).

Jaques' final self-acceptance is in keeping with the play's spirit of conciliation, most vividly represented by the multiple marriage in 5.4. Further, his early cynicism, although inappropriate to the world of Arden and therefore countered by the other characters, sharpens the flavour of a play that might otherwise be overly sentimental. Lastly, Jaques' railing reminds us that outside the magical world of Arden, the ways of the world are all too often wicked indeed.

**Jaques (2) de Boys** Minor character in *As You Like It*, brother of OLIVER (1) and ORLANDO. Jaques is named in 1.1.5, but he does not appear until 5.4, when he suddenly arrives with the news of DUKE (1) Frederick's armed march on ARDEN (1) and later conversion to a life of religious contemplation. The episode both provides a place for the villain in the play's ultimate reconciliation, and, in its suddenness, intensifies the play's atmosphere of romantic wonder.

The duplication of names with a major character, the pessimistic courtier JAQUES (1), presents a minor difficulty. Jaques de Boys identifies himself only as 'the second son of old Sir Rowland' (5.4.151). In the FIRST FOLIO edition of the play, stage directions identify him as 'Second Brother', and some modern editions follow this practise, avoiding the issue to some extent, but the mention of his name in 1.1 suggests carelessness on Shakespeare's part. Perhaps the playwright originally intended his melancholy courtier to be Orlando and Oliver's brother, established his existence with the reference at 1.1.5, and then developed Jaques as a member of the exiled DUKE (7) Senior's court, neglecting to remove the earlier reference.

**Jeffes, Humphrey (d. 1618)** English actor. Jeffes may have played a minor role in an early production of *3 Henry VI*, for in the FIRST FOLIO text of the play a KEEPER (2) is designated 'Humfrey' in a stage direction. If this is Jeffes, he was probably a member of PEMBROKE'S MEN in 1592–1593, when they are believed to have staged the play. Jeffes is first recorded, however, as a member of the ADMIRAL'S MEN in 1597, after the Pembroke's Men collapsed in the wake of the ISLE OF DOGS scandal. He remained with his new company for almost 20 years, and finally left its successor, the PALSGRAVE'S MEN, in 1616 to take a company on tour in the provinces, though his company soon had its permit revoked for unknown reasons.

**Jenkins, Thomas (active 1566–1579)** STRATFORD schoolmaster, Shakespeare's grammar school teacher. Jenkins was master of the Stratford Grammar School from 1575–1579, the period when Shakespeare learned much of the Latin literature that was at the core of the Elizabethan grammar school curriculum. Jenkins was a well-qualified teacher of the material, as he was an Oxford-educated clergyman and an experienced teacher. The Stratford burgesses recruited him from a similar position in Warwick. His Welsh name has suggested to scholars that he may be the inspiration for Shakespeare's creation Sir Hugh EVANS (3), the Welsh schoolteacher of *The Merry Wives of Windsor*. However, Jenkins was born in London, the son of a servant. His education was presumably provided by his father's master, who was a founder of the college at Oxford where he studied. In 1579 he resigned his position at Stratford and recruited his own successor, John COTTOM. Jenkins was married—a daughter died and a son was born during his tenure at Stratford—but little more is known of his life.

**Jerusalem Chamber** Room in WESTMINSTER (1) ABBEY, the setting for 4.4 of *2 Henry IV*. The dying King HENRY IV talks there with his younger sons and other noblemen about PRINCE (6) HAL, who the king fears is dissolute and will make a bad heir to the throne. News arrives that the rebels against the king have been defeated, but the excitement causes the king to swoon and he is taken to another room. The encounter between Hal and his father in 4.5 takes place in the second chamber; the king asks the name of the first room. Told that it is the Jerusalem Chamber, he asks to be returned there, thus fulfilling a prophecy that he would die in Jerusalem.

King Henry did in fact die in the Jerusalem Chamber, but the prophecy, which Shakespeare took from HOLINSHED, is not recorded elsewhere. The same story—a prophecy of death in Jerusalem followed by death in a church or room of that name—is told of several medieval figures and is probably apocryphal in most cases, including this one. The name of the room, which was originally part of the Abbot's residence, comes from an inscription surrounding the fireplace.

**Jessica**  Character in *The Merchant of Venice*, daughter of SHYLOCK and lover of LORENZO. Jessica is an apparently demure young woman who nevertheless abandons her father and her religion willingly in eloping with Lorenzo, and she also steals Shylock's money. TUBAL reports her extravagance with these funds in 3.1. In 5.1 the romantic rhapsodies of Lorenzo and Jessica provide the play's finest lyric poetry and establish the triumph of love, a major theme of the work.

Jessica's behaviour to her father has often been criticised, and, if Shylock is viewed as a sympathetic or tragic character, his daughter can only seem immoral. Moreover, her desertion and theft seem to be related to the anti-Semitism that infects this play. Referring to Jessica's enthusiastic readiness to steal from her father, Gratiano avers that she is 'a gentle [i.e., gentile], and no Jew' (2.6.51). That is, she qualifies as a Christian by her actions against a Jew. However, the play is clearly a traditional romantic COMEDY, and Jessica's role in that context is a simple one. She flees to romantic love from the prison of her father's miserly household, which she describes as 'hell' (2.3.2). In doing so, she illustrates a bold example of the opposition between love and greed that lies at the heart of the play. Further, her theft of her father's funds reflects Shylock's traditional function as a comic villain (although Shakespeare enlarged the character considerably) and was probably received by the play's original audiences as a comeuppance to the miser, a traditional subject of comical raillery. Jessica is humorous as she steals, archly asserting that the weight of a purloined casket is 'worth the pains' and saying she will 'gild myself with moe ducats' as she leaves (2.6.33, 49–50). She is essentially a secondary character, graceful but uncomplicated. Only her relationship to Shylock inspires comment.

**Jeweller**  Minor character in *Timon of Athens*, a flatterer of TIMON. As the play opens, the Jeweller proposes to sell a jewel to Timon, confident that the nobleman will pay a good price. Later in 1.1 he flatters his potential client. The Jeweller is simply a representative greedy flatterer.

**Joan La Pucelle (Joan of Arc) (c. 1412–1431)**  Historical figure and character in *1 Henry VI*, a leader of the French forces in the HUNDRED YEARS WAR. The historical Joan of Arc was known as La Pucelle, 'the virgin', in her own lifetime, and Shakespeare takes the name from the chronicles. In Acts 1–4 Shakespeare's Joan is in some respects difficult to distinguish from the other French leaders, CHARLES VII, ALENÇON, and REIGNIER; like them, she is intended to show, by her trickery and lack of military valour, that a French victory would have been impossible without the English dissension that is the play's chief theme. Unlike her fellows, though, Joan can be a charismatic leader. In 1.2 she revives the morale of the French after a lost skirmish, and in 1.5 she leads them in breaking the English siege of ORLÉANS (1), as the historical Joan had done.

This is as much of the real Joan of Arc's life as the play reflects, however. The English capture of Orléans in 2.1 is entirely unhistorical, as is, of course, the French leaders' flight from a single English soldier. Similarly, Joan's devious tactic while taking ROUEN in 3.2, is fictitious; in fact, the actual anecdote that Shakespeare drew upon tells of an *English* strategy in a different battle. In 3.3 Joan convinces the Duke of BURGUNDY (2) to abandon the English cause; in actuality, Burgundy did not withdraw from his alliance with England until well after Joan's death.

In Act 5 the playwright recasts Joan as a villainess in an altogether more absolute manner. Joan's sorcery in 5.3, where she calls up FIENDS, is simply intended to blacken her image. (Similarly, the other characters insult Joan freely throughout the play, casting aspersions on her courage and her virginity and frequently accusing her of witchcraft.) Lastly, in Shakespeare's most glaring misrepresentation of Joan, she makes a cowardly attempt, in 5.4, to avoid execution, first by claiming royal birth and refusing to acknowledge her father, the SHEPHERD (1), and then by disavowing her virginity and claiming to be pregnant. She goes to her death cursing England and the English.

The play's uncharitable attitude towards Joan of Arc has stimulated much hostile criticism. In fact, this feature was once taken as evidence of non-Shakespearean authorship, on the grounds that no great writer would stoop to such propagandistic viciousness. However, such keen anti-French sentiments were common in Elizabethan times, as well as in the play's source material, such as the chronicles of HALL (2) and HOLINSHED, and modern authorities, whatever their opinions as to the authorship of *1 Henry VI*, do not find it odd that a playwright should have portrayed Englishmen insulting Joan in this manner.

The historical Joan, born Jeanne Darc, began, at the age of 12, to hear voices that she understood to be those of angels and of God, advising her to lead a holy life. Later the voices instructed her to help Charles VII drive the English from FRANCE (1). In 1428 she persuaded a local military commander to take her to Charles' court, where she convinced Charles to permit her to lead a small army to relieve besieged Orléans. Remarkably, her troops were victorious, and she is still known as 'the maid of Orléans'. Her continued participation in the war infused the French with the courage and confidence that turned the tide of the conflict. She was captured by Burgundian forces in 1430. Her captors sold her to the English under WARWICK (2), who arranged for a 'show trial' for heresy before a French ecclesiastical tribunal. She was convicted and burned at the stake on May 30, 1431. Her conduct at the trial was, by all accounts, dignified and honourable, entirely unlike that of the Joan of the play. In 1456 her admirers obtained a retrial, at which her innocence was pronounced. She was declared a saint by the Catholic Church in 1920.

**John (1), Don**   Character in *Much Ado About Nothing*, the villainous brother of the prince, Don PEDRO. With the help of his follower BORACHIO, Don John schemes to mortify CLAUDIO (1) by slandering his betrothed, HERO. After Borachio arranges for an incriminating impersonation of Hero, the would-be bride is humiliatingly rejected by the deluded Claudio, but by a fortuitous accident, the plot is uncovered and Don John flees from MESSINA, only to be captured and brought back. However, his flight and final comeuppance occur off-stage and are only reported (in 4.2.58 and 5.4.123–124); Don John himself is absent at the close of the play, for his vicious nature would be out of place amid the general spirit of reconciliation.

Don John resents Claudio because 'that young start-up hath all the glory of my overthrow. If I can cross him any way, I bless myself . . .' (1.3.62–64). Claudio's advancement in Don Pedro's court has come at Don John's expense, for Claudio has shone in the war that suppressed Don John's rebellion against his brother. However, this motive is relatively unimportant; Don John plots to cause as much trouble to those around him as he can, apparently out of a simply evil nature. He declares that he would 'rather be a canker in a hedge than a rose' and describes himself as 'a plain-dealing villain' (1.3.25, 30). His is a generalised, undirected discontent; he envies other people's happiness and is therefore misanthropic.

Although Borachio compares him to the devil in 3.3.145–151, Don John is a slight figure, a study for a portrait of a villain. He is neither as grandiose as RICHARD III nor as direct as MACBETH. Nor is he as threateningly mysterious as IAGO, whom he anticipates in both his ill-defined motivation and his manipulation of the conventional sexual attitudes of his victims. Most important, he lacks the human complexity of any of these larger, more fully developed characters. Don John is a simple stereotype, intended chiefly to advance the plot of a COMEDY, offering just enough evil to necessitate a triumph for happiness but not enough to evoke terror, as in a TRAGEDY.

**John (2), Friar**   Character in *Romeo and Juliet*. See FRIAR (3).

**John (3), King of England (1167–1216)**   Historical figure and title character in *King John*. John is a complicated protagonist of a complicated play. Not quite hero or villain, he espouses values of English patriotism while his selfish ambition leads the country to catastrophe. John passes from unscrupulous strength to dispirited weakness, and his own moral failings are at the heart of his collapse. He is ultimately an inadequate leader, controlled by events rather than controlling them. As the play opens, John has usurped the English throne from his nephew ARTHUR. Nevertheless, he initially appears to be a strong king: in 1.1 he boldly defies the challenge to his rule from Arthur's supporter King PHILIP (2) of FRANCE (1). However, he soon displays his weakness when, in the treaty concluded in 2.1, he surrenders a great deal of English territory in order to protect his claim to the rest. He exhibits strength again, in a context particularly significant to 16th-century Protestant England, when he refuses to obey the dictates of the pope, conveyed by PANDULPH in 3.1, and renewed war with France results. John's forces capture Arthur, and the king dishonourably orders him killed by HUBERT in 3.2 (3.3) (for citation, see *King John*, 'Synopsis'). He also commands the BASTARD (1) to loot England's religious houses to pay for the war.

Shakespeare's handling of Arthur's death, the central event of the play, illuminates John's ambiguous nature. Before learning that Hubert has not killed the boy, John expresses regret for the crime and dishonestly tries to excuse himself in 4.2.103–105 and 205–248; he rejoices when he discovers that Arthur is alive. Yet Arthur does die when he tries to escape his captors. John is thus blamed for the death anyway and suffers the political consequences.

John's fortunes deteriorate from this point on. His barons desert him; his mother, Queen ELEANOR, dies; a wandering seer, PETER (4), predicts that he will give up his crown. The Dauphin LEWIS (1) of France invades England, and several barons join his forces. In

5.1 John formally acknowledges the supremacy of the pope over England, in return for Pandulph's promise to make the French withdraw. Lewis will not abandon his successful invasion, however, and only the efforts of the BASTARD (1) keep England's defences functioning. Demoralised and sick, John withdraws to SWINSTEAD ABBEY, where a monk, enraged by the king's pillaging of the churches, poisons him. John dies in torment, just as an urgent message of fresh disaster is being delivered. His death returns peace and stability to England, as the French finally withdraw and the Bastard leads the nobles in pledging allegiance to John's successor, HENRY (1).

The sources Shakespeare used in creating his John were not very accurate, according to modern scholarship, and the playwright altered many details in any case. The historical John was not a usurper; he did not lose the support of his barons by killing an innocent boy; he was not murdered. He was indeed an unsuccessful king, though probably due more to the assets of his enemies than to his own defects. Philip Augustus of France was a powerful soldier and statesman, and Innocent III was one of the greatest of medieval popes. John did not, however, lack leadership skills himself. Many of his nobles remained loyal to him, and he never withdrew from the fight against the rebels and their French allies; he died of a sickness contracted on the battlefield. His personality is not well recorded, but he appears to have been highly temperamental, perhaps deranged; according to one account he beat Arthur to death in a drunken rage. However, Shakespeare did not attempt to delineate John's true nature; the character is a fiction designed to illustrate the nature of misused power. The king's moral weakness is central to an intellectual drama of politics, and his personality is not relevant.

**John (4) of Gaunt**    Character in *Richard II*. See GAUNT.

**John (5) Plantagenet**    Character in *1 Henry VI; 1 & 2 Henry IV; Henry V.* See BEDFORD; LANCASTER (3).

**John (6) Talbot (also known as Young Talbot, c. 1425–1453)**    Historical figure and character in *1 Henry VI,* the son of TALBOT, England's heroic general. John appears in 4.5, fighting courageously beside his father. When Talbot realises that the coming battle is a doomed one, he attempts to persuade John to flee and save his life. The young man, citing the family honour, refuses in 4.6.42–57. John does die, and, in 4.7, Talbot, dying himself, addresses his son's corpse, praising John's exploits in the battle.

Shakespeare intended the melodramatic deaths of Talbot and John to contrast with the selfishness of YORK (8) and SOMERSET (3), whose disputes denied the heroes reinforcements. To increase the poignancy of the comparison, Young Talbot is said to be his father's only son, but, in fact, several others carried on the Talbot line. Further, John appears quite young, although the historical figure was in his late twenties and had a number of children.

**Johnson (1), Arthur (d. 1631)**    LONDON bookseller and publisher, producer of the first edition of *The Merry Wives of Windsor.* Johnson published a wide range of literature, including several plays. In 1602 he brought out the BAD QUARTO (Q1) of *The Merry Wives* and in 1608 the first edition of *The Merry Devil of Edmonton,* a play that was later wrongly attributed to Shakespeare. Sometime after 1624 Johnson moved to Dublin, where he became a stationer.

**Johnson (2), Charles (1679–1748)**    English playwright. Johnson wrote 18 plays, several of them quite successful, but he is best known today for two works derived from Shakespeare. *The Cobbler of Preston* (1716), a political play that commented on the Jacobite rebellion of 1715, was embedded in a version of the Christopher SLY (1) episode of *The Taming of the Shrew.* LOVE IN A FOREST (1723) was a loose adaptation of *As You Like It.* A prominent figure in the London literary world of his day, Johnson was among the targets of the satirical *Dunciad* (1728, 1743), by Alexander POPE (1).

**Johnson (3), Cornelius**    See JANSSEN (1).

**Johnson (4), Gerard**    See JANSSEN (2).

**Johnson (5), Robert (c. 1585–c. 1634)**    English musician and composer, probable writer of music for several of Shakespeare's plays. In the *Cheerful Ayres* (c. 1660) of John WILSON (2), Johnson is credited with music for 'Where the bee sucks' and 'Full fadom five' from *The Tempest,* possibly written for the performance of the play given as part of the wedding festivities of Princess ELIZABETH (3) in 1613. Scholars believe that Johnson also composed song music for *Cymbeline* and *The Winter's Tale,* although the surviving sheet music is anonymous. Music he wrote for a MASQUE by Francis BEAUMONT (2), also performed at Princess Elizabeth's wedding, was probably also used in performances of *The Two Noble Kinsmen.* Johnson also composed songs for *The Duchess of Malfi* (1614) by John WEBSTER, *The Witch* (1615) by Thomas MIDDLETON (this music may have been used in early productions of *Macbeth,* as well), and for five plays by Beaumont and John FLETCHER (2).

As a boy, Johnson was a servant in the household of George Carey, Lord HUNSDON (1); his abilities were already recognised, for he was employed as a music teacher. It was doubtless through Hunsdon, who was the patron of the CHAMBERLAIN'S MEN, Shakespeare's acting company, that Johnson became a theatrical composer. After 1604 he was also the royal lutenist for King JAMES I and King Charles I, composing and performing music for royal masques and other entertainments.

**Johnson (6), Robert (d. 1611)**   Vintner and innkeeper of STRATFORD and Shakespeare's tenant. Johnson owned a tavern, known at different times as the White Lion and the Swan Inn, that abutted the property on which Shakespeare's birthplace stood. He rented a barn on that property from Shakespeare and presumably used it in connection with the inn. This rental is known only because the lease is mentioned in the inventory of possessions accompanying Johnson's will, recorded in October 1611 by Thomas ASPINALL. In 1670 Johnson's son still rented the barn, when it was mentioned in the will of Elizabeth HALL (3), Shakespeare's grand-daughter.

**Johnson (7), Samuel (1709–1784)**   English poet, scholar, literary critic, and lexicographer, the leading figure in English literature in the mid-18th century. Dr Johnson, as he is universally known, wrote poems, biographies, and essays on a wide range of subjects, and he compiled the first great English dictionary (1755). In 1765 he published an edition of Shakespeare's plays. While it is not regarded as significant in terms of scholarship—it was based on an inferior text and added little in the way of notes and commentary—it was nevertheless the basis for the greater edition of George STEEVENS, and it includes a preface that is regarded as one of Johnson's finest works. Johnson's intellectual and social life as a leader of his age are still accessible to us through the *Life of Samuel Johnson* (1791) by James Boswell (1740–1795), a masterpiece of English literature.

**Johnson (8), William (active 1591–1616)**   Landlord of the MERMAID TAVERN in London and a friend of Shakespeare. Johnson, with John HEMINGE and John JACKSON (2), assisted Shakespeare by serving as a trustee in his purchase of the BLACKFRIARS GATEHOUSE in 1613. While no other connection is known, this one presumes a fairly close acquaintance. Shakespeare may have been a member of the Friday Street Club, a literary gathering that met informally at the Mermaid, or he may have stayed there while visiting London after he moved back to STRATFORD.

Johnson had served an apprenticeship with the previous landlord of the Mermaid, taking over the management himself in 1603. Shortly after his involvement in Shakespeare's purchase, Johnson found himself in legal difficulties, charged with serving meat at the tavern during Lent, though the case may not have gone to court.

**Jones (1), James Earl (b. 1931)**   American actor. Jones, one of the leading black actors of the New York stage, made his Broadway debut in 1958 and soon established a reputation as a classic actor. He was especially acclaimed as the title character in a 1973 production of *King Lear* by Joseph PAPP. He was also noteworthy as OTHELLO, opposite Christopher PLUMMER's IAGO, in Nicol WILLIAMSON's 1982 staging.

**Jones (2), Richard (active 1583–1624)**   English actor. Jones was a member of WORCESTER'S MEN in 1583–1584 with the young Edward ALLEYN, and he was probably a member of Alleyn's ADMIRAL'S MEN by 1585. He travelled in Germany with a company headed by Robert BROWNE in 1592–1593, but he rejoined the Admiral's Men again in 1594. Except for a brief period in 1597, he was with them until 1602. He is known to have played PRIAM in *Troilus and Cressida*. In 1610 he was a partner, with Browne and others, in a CHILDREN'S COMPANY that performed at the WHITEFRIARS THEATRE, but by 1615 he was again in Germany, this time with John GREEN. By 1622 he was employed as a musician in a minor German court, but he returned to England the next year. He is last known from a letter of 1624 to his German employer, asking to return, since he had not found work in England.

**Jones (3), Robert (active 1590–1615)**   Composer and theatrical entrepreneur. Jones was a famed lute player and composer of settings for songs. Shakespeare apparently adapted the song 'Farewell, dear heart' (*Twelfth Night*, 2.3.102–112) from a work in Jones' *The First Book of Songes and Ayres* (1600), though the playwright may have known the song elsewhere.

**Jones (4), William (d. 1618)**   LONDON bookseller and publisher, producer of first editions of two plays of the Shakespeare APOCRYPHA. Between 1598 and 1615 Jones published the first six editions of MUCEDORUS, one of the most popular plays of the day; none of these editions attributed the play to Shakespeare. In 1602 Jones published the first edition of THOMAS LORD CROMWELL, which was credited to 'W. S.', though it is unclear whether this attribution was intended to associate the work with Shakespeare. Jones was apprenticed to a printer in 1578, was a member of the STATIONERS' COMPANY by 1587, and when he died in 1618, left a widow who was forced to sell his copyrights. Little more is known of his life.

**Jonson, Ben (1572–1637)**   English poet and playwright, a great satirist and a leading light of JACOBEAN DRAMA. Jonson's greatest achievements were works of satiric COMEDY—especially *Volpone* (1606), *Epicoene* (c. 1609), *The Alchemist* (1610), and *Bartholomew Fair* (1614)—and MASQUES written for the court of King JAMES I. Jonson's satire influenced Shakespeare's own most nearly satirical works, such as *Troilus and Cressida* and *Timon of Athens,* and the popularity of Jonson's masques helped create the theatrical world in which Shakespeare wrote his ROMANCES. He is regarded as second only to Shakespeare among the playwrights of the period. Jonson also wrote on literary theory, and his stress on clarity over personal style, on classical forms of aesthetic organisation, and on relevance to one's own times influenced English poets and dramatists for a century.

Jonson received a good secondary education at the Westminster School, where he was taught by William CAMDEN, but as the stepson of a bricklayer, he was then apprenticed to that trade. Instead, he enlisted in the army and went to the Low Countries, where he reportedly killed an enemy soldier in a man-to-man combat staged between the opposing armies. By 1592 he was back in LONDON and married, though his life for five years is otherwise unknown. In 1597 he was a member of PEMBROKE'S MEN, gaoled as a player in the 'seditious' play *Isle of Dogs* (see CENSORSHIP), which he may have helped write. A year later he was again imprisoned, this time for killing his fellow actor Gabriel SPENCER in a duel. He escaped the death penalty only through an archaic technicality: clergymen were exempt from punishment, and clergymen were defined as all those capable of reading Latin.

Jonson's first successful play, *Every Man in His Humour,* was staged by the CHAMBERLAIN'S MEN in 1598; Shakespeare may have been responsible for its acceptance by the company, and he was in the cast. One of the finest examples of the COMEDY OF HUMOURS, this work was extremely popular. Unfortunately, its sequel the next year, *Every Man out of His Humour,* was equally unsuccessful. It was one of the first shots in the WAR OF THE THEATRES, an exchange of satirical plays by Jonson on one side and John MARSTON and Thomas DEKKER on the other. Jonson's other efforts in this fray were produced by the Children of the Chapel (see CHILDREN'S COMPANIES). Jonson next worked for Philip HENSLOWE and the ADMIRAL'S MEN, writing additional material for *The Spanish Tragedy* (c. 1588) by Thomas KYD before creating his own major work, *Sejanus* (1603). This TRAGEDY, modelled on SENECA, was staged by the KING'S MEN, again with Shakespeare in the cast (this is the last record of Shakespeare as an actor).

Beginning in 1605, Jonson began his collaboration with Inigo Jones (1573–1652), the royal architect, who designed the settings and machinery for the masques that Jonson composed. Over the next quarter-century, this partnership produced brilliant spectacles that influenced both drama and theatre design for generations. However, near the beginning of this period, Jonson once again courted royal disfavour, this time as co-author with Marston and George CHAPMAN of *Eastward Ho!* (1605), a play containing political remarks

that the king declared seditious. Jonson was briefly gaoled again, before the affair blew over. In the next few years Jonson reached his peak of achievement, with *Volpone, Epicoene,* and *The Alchemist.* The first and last of these was produced by the King's Men. *Bartholomew Fair* was staged by LADY ELIZABETH'S MEN in 1614, after Jonson returned from a year's travel in Europe as the tutor to Sir Walter RALEIGH's son.

In 1616 Jonson issued a collection of his works—poetry, prose, and drama—a deed that was widely ridiculed because plays were not generally considered to have literary value at the time. In the same year the king gave Jonson a pension for life, making him effectively the first Poet Laureate, though the honour was not so named until later. He travelled in SCOTLAND, where William Drummond of Hawthornden noted his conversational remarks on himself and his contemporaries—a record that has served modern historians of the theatre. After his return his career deteriorated. Only one further play was a success, *The Staple of News* (1625), a satire on the newsletter of Nathaniel BUTTER. A bitter fight with Inigo Jones ended his creation of masques. (Characteristically, Jonson recorded the quarrel in *A Tale of a Tub* [1633], a play that flopped in London.) He also suffered from illness and lost his extraordinary library to a disastrous fire. He died with a play half-written and was buried in WESTMINSTER (1) ABBEY.

Shakespeare and Jonson were very different men, with different sensibilities and different attitudes towards life and art, yet they seem to have been friends, beginning with the production of *Every Man in His Humour.* The tradition that Shakespeare died after a drinking bout with Jonson and Michael DRAYTON is almost certainly not true, but it reflects a reality. They probably met often at the MERMAID TAVERN, and they seem to have enjoyed criticising each other. Another story, possibly apocryphal, demonstrates the tone of their friendly rivalry: Jonson and Shakespeare, 'being merry at a tavern', composed an EPITAPH for Jonson. Jonson composed the first two lines, 'Here lies Ben Jonson / that was once one', and Shakespeare devised the final two: 'Who while he lived was a slow thing, / And now, being dead, is nothing'. (Jonson's agonising slowness in writing was often jested about.)

An amateur play about the theatre world, performed at Cambridge University in 1601 (see PARNASSUS PLAYS), refers to Shakespeare's having given Jonson 'a purge' in response to criticism. This may merely express the author's preference for Shakespeare, but it may also echo some otherwise lost piece of gossip. At least once Shakespeare alluded to Jonson in his work. In *Twelfth Night* FESTE remarks that the word *element* is 'overworn' (3.1.60), a casual reference to Dekker's satire of Jonson's alleged overuse of the term. Further, Shakespeare's AJAX, JAQUES (1), and

NYM have all been suggested as possible parodies of Jonson.

For his part, Jonson frequently remarked on Shakespeare, often acknowledgeing his friend's greatness. For instance, after Shakespeare's death, Jonson wrote, 'I lov'd the man, and do honour his memory (this side idolatry) as much as any'. However, this remark followed a criticism of Shakespeare's carelessness as a writer, and most of Jonson's recorded comments on his friend are likewise combinations of praise and censure. Jonson was an arrogant man, by all accounts, including his own, and he was a fierce critic; he once declared that John Donne (1573–1631) 'deserved hanging' for writing poetry in an irregular METRE. While he could not but admire Shakespeare's virtues, he could not refrain from finding things to criticise, particularly when such 'defects' contrasted with his own traits. For instance, Jonson's famous contention (quite untrue) that Shakespeare 'never blotted' a line, implicitly praised his own laborious technique. Similarly, his notorious remark that Shakespeare had 'small Latin and less Greek' was true only by comparison to his own great erudition. Nevertheless, each derogation was coupled with praise—'There was ever more in him to be praised, than to be pardoned', he wrote—and it was Jonson who penned one of the most famous tributes to Shakespeare, in his prefatory verses to the FIRST FOLIO (1623), 'He was not of an age, but for all time!'

**Jordan, Dorothy (1761–1816)**  Irish actress. Mrs Jordan—the adopted name by which Dorothea Bland was known—made her stage debut in Dublin in 1777, playing PHEBE in *As You Like It*. After 1775 she established herself in London, where she mostly played comedic heroines. Her best-known Shakespearean roles were ROSALIND, IMOGEN, and VIOLA. She also played in William Henry IRELAND's forged Shakespearean play, *Vortigern* (1796). She was the long-time mistress of the Duke of Clarence, later King William IV (ruled 1830–1837), by whom she had 10 children.

**Joseph**  Minor character in *The Taming of the Shrew*, a servant of PETRUCHIO (2). Joseph is one of the servants whom Petruchio abuses in 4.1, as part of his demonstration to KATHERINA of the ugliness of shrewish behaviour.

**Jourdain (1), Margery**  Character in *2 Henry VI*. See MARGERY JOURDAIN.

**Jourdain (2) (Jourdan), Sylvester (c. 1580–1650)**
English colonial entrepreneur and writer, author of a probable source for *The Tempest*. Jourdain was a member of an expedition to Virginia that was shipwrecked in Bermuda in 1609. He was marooned for 10 months, and his recounting of his experiences in *The Discovery of the Barmudas* (1610) provided Shakespeare with such details for *The Tempest* as the mysterious 'supernatural' noises that CALIBAN describes in 3.2.133–138. Jourdain's account also confirmed Shakespeare's principal source, a letter by William STRACHEY (2), which stressed the miraculous nature of their survival. Shakespeare follows these accounts in emphasising the role of providence in *The Tempest*. Jourdain was a Puritan merchant from Dorsetshire who settled in LONDON after his adventures.

**Julia**  Character in *The Two Gentlemen of Verona*, the betrayed lover of PROTEUS. Julia disguises herself as a boy and follows Proteus to court, where he has fallen in love with SILVIA. Learning of his infidelity, Julia nonetheless remains true to Proteus, serving, in her disguise, as his messenger to her rival. She is present in the final scene, when VALENTINE offers Silvia to Proteus, and her quick wit tells her to swoon, interrupting the transaction. She reveals herself, her presence restores Proteus to his original loyalty, and he vows his love for her anew.

Julia is an early instance of a type of young woman Shakespeare clearly admired—independent, active, and capable of pursuing a man, even if he is unworthy of her. Other instances include HELENA (2), in *All's Well That Ends Well* and VIOLA, in *Twelfth Night*.

**Juliet (1)**  One of the title characters in *Romeo and Juliet*, the lover of ROMEO. Juliet first appears as a conventional upper-class daughter, affectionately dependent on her NURSE (3) and accepting of the marriage to PARIS (2) that is planned for her. However, when she is gripped by passion for Romeo, she displays a heroic capacity to resist her world, despite the dangers of her love. She accepts death no less readily than Romeo when destiny has destroyed their lives.

When she first meets Romeo, she shows herself to be intelligent and perceptive. She matches wits with him in improvising their joint SONNET (1.5.92–105), and she recognises in him traces of the bookish, artificial lover he has been earlier, remarking that he kisses 'by th'book' (1.5.109). While no less enraptured than her lover during the subsequent 'balcony' scene (2.2), she is nonetheless more aware than he of their danger, as in 2.2.116–120, and it is she who sees that they must commit themselves to marriage if their plight is to be overcome. Although her response to the onset of passion is mature, she does not lose her appeal as a blooming young lover. Her soliloquy at the opening of 3.2, before she learns of Romeo's banishment, is a brilliant and utterly endearing expression of the impatience of the lover looking forward to a tryst.

When faced with Romeo's banishment and the prospect of an enforced marriage to Paris, Juliet agrees to take the sleeping potion offered by FRIAR (4) LAURENCE. In 4.3.15–58, she reviews a roster of possible

terrors she faces in a frightening speech that under-
lines the courage with which she must and does proceed. She is no less resolute at the tragic climax of the
play. Waking to find that mischance has overwhelmed
her efforts, she does not hesitate to join her lover in
death rather than continue living in a world that lacks
their love.

It has often been thought that Juliet's age, 14, represents a typical marriage age for English women of
Shakespeare's day, but historians believe that the normal age was the late teens or early twenties. In any
case, Shakespeare lowered Juliet's age from that given
in his source, 16, and lines such as 1.2.8–13 suggest
that she is supposed to be thought of as quite young
for marriage, perhaps to emphasise her vulnerability.
On the other hand, Lady CAPULET (3) states explicitly
that Veronese girls younger than Juliet were mothers
(1.3.69–71). The question remains puzzling.

**Juliet (2)**  Minor character in *Measure for Measure*, the
pregnant fiancée of CLAUDIO (3). Claudio's death sentence for having illicit sex with Juliet is the central
element of the play's plot, but the young woman is
nevertheless a shadowy and undeveloped character.
She speaks in only one of the three scenes in which she
appears (2.3), and though she is touching in her combination of repentance and love, she remains a minor
figure.

The role of Juliet is small, and this has suggested to
some scholars that the play was at some point extensively revised—by Shakespeare or someone else—and
her role was awkwardly cut. However, other commentators feel that her function as a pathetic victim is fully
realised by her mere presence, and any enlargement
of her role would be distracting.

## Julius Caesar

### SYNOPSIS

#### Act 1, Scene 1
Two tribunes, FLAVIUS (1) and MARULLUS, disperse a
crowd (see COMMONER [1]) that is celebrating the return of Julius CAESAR (1) to ROME, though not before
a COBBLER makes some flippant jokes. The tribunes
rebuke the Commoners for disloyalty in welcoming
the conqueror of another Roman, Pompey, whom they
had also celebrated in the streets. The two officers
remove the decorations that have been placed on public statues.

#### Act 1, Scene 2
At the feast of Lupercalia, Caesar arranges for Mark
ANTONY, who is to participate in a fertility rite, to ritu-
ally touch CALPHURNIA, Caesar's wife. A SOOTHSAYER
(1) warns Caesar to beware the ides (the 15th day) of
March; Caesar ignores him and leads his entourage to

the festival. CASSIUS and BRUTUS (4) remain behind
and speak of Caesar's ambition to rule alone, a violation of the Roman political tradition that all aristocrats
share power equally. Cassius says that Rome looks to
Brutus for leadership in this crisis, and they hear
cheering from the festival, which, they fear, means that
Caesar is being acclaimed king by the Commoners.
Cassius observes resentfully that he does not wish to
be ruled by a man no better than himself, as another
cheer erupts. Cassius continues to speak against Caesar's rule and refers to an ancient revolt against a king
that Brutus' ancestor had led. Brutus hints that he has
contemplated a similar action. Caesar's group returns;
Caesar confides to Antony that he distrusts Cassius
and then exits. Brutus and Cassius detain CASCA and
hear an account of the festival from him. Caesar was
offered the crown three times, Casca reports, and he
refused it each time, though only with regret. Casca
and Brutus leave, and Cassius soliloquises that Brutus,
though a very important figure, is easy to manipulate,
and he plans to further influence him with letters purporting to be from angry citizens who seek action
against Caesar.

#### Act 1, Scene 3
Amid thunder and lightning, Casca meets CICERO and
tells of omens that have accompanied the storm, fore-
telling extraordinary events. Cicero dismisses this
superstitiousness and departs. Cassius appears and
recruits Casca for a plot against Caesar, naming a
meeting place for later that night. Another conspirator, CINNA (1), arrives, and Cassius directs him to leave
messages, which he provides, in places where Brutus
will receive them.

#### Act 2, Scene 1
Brutus, having been awake all night, decides at dawn
that Caesar's ambition makes it necessary to kill him.
He receives one of Cassius' anonymous letters urging
him to protect Rome, and he resolves to lead the conspirators in assassinating Caesar. Cassius and other
plotters arrive, and they lay their plans. Brutus insists
that Antony not be killed, arguing that they must not
seem bloodthirsty and that Antony will be helpless
without Caesar. DECIUS volunteers to ensure that Caesar will attend the day's Senate session, where the
assassination is to take place. The conspirators depart.
Brutus, seeing his sleeping servant, LUCIUS (2), muses
on his own sleepless life. His wife, PORTIA (2), appears
and asks why he is disturbed. He promises to tell her
later, as a last conspirator, LIGARIUS, arrives, and she
leaves. Ligarius agrees to follow Brutus in any exploit,
and they leave together for the Senate.

#### Act 2, Scene 2
Calphurnia tells Caesar of the many appalling omens
that have been seen and insists that he stay home

rather than go to the Senate. He refuses, insisting that one must face death if it comes, but then he decides to humour Calphurnia and stay at home, pleading illness. However, Decius arrives and claims that the omens are favourable and that the Senate proposes to offer Caesar a crown. Caesar changes his mind again.

### Act 2, Scene 3

ARTEMIDORUS reads aloud a message naming the conspirators and warning Caesar against them. He vows to present it to Caesar at the Senate.

### Act 2, Scene 4

Portia worries hysterically about Brutus. The Soothsayer appears, saying that he hopes to warn Caesar of impending harm, and he goes on to the Senate. Portia sends Lucius on a pointless errand to Brutus, with orders to return and tell her how he seems.

### Act 3, Scene 1

At the Senate, Caesar encounters the Soothsayer, who warns that the ides of March is not yet over. Artemidorus attempts to deliver his message, but Caesar rejects him and proceeds with Senate business. One conspirator draws Antony away from the meeting, while another presents Caesar with a petition that he has already rejected. Caesar's continued refusal is the signal: the conspirators stab him. Caesar, dismayed that his friend Brutus should be among the attackers, dies. The assassins, led by Brutus, ritually bathe their hands in Caesar's blood, declaring their devotion to political liberty. A message arrives from Antony: he is prepared to ally himself with the conspirators if they can provide a rationale for their deed. Though Cassius has reservations, Brutus approves. Antony arrives and volunteers to die with Caesar if the conspirators wish to kill him, but Brutus insists on their alliance, and he grants Antony's request to speak at Caesar's funeral. The conspirators depart, and Antony soliloquises about his intention to avenge Caesar's death by launching a civil war. News comes of OCTAVIUS' approach to Rome.

### Act 3, Scene 2

Brutus addresses the PLEBEIANS (1), assuring them that the assassination was necessary in order to preserve the Republic. They applaud him, proposing that he be crowned himself. Antony arrives with Caesar's body, and Brutus tells the crowd to listen to Antony's funeral oration. Brutus leaves, and Antony addresses the Plebeians, praising Caesar while seeming to acknowledge the honour of the assassins. Gradually, Antony generates a mood of hostility towards the conspirators while denying his intention to do so. Introducing Caesar's will, which designates a generous bequest to be distributed among the people, he sparks a riotous response to the assassination. The

Plebeians rage into the streets, intending to burn the houses of Brutus and the others. Antony exults. Learning of Octavius' presence in Rome, he goes to join him; as he leaves he hears that Brutus and Cassius have fled the city.

### Act 3, Scene 3

A mob of Plebeians encounters the poet CINNA (2) and kills him, mistaking him for the conspirator with the same name.

### Act 4, Scene 1

Antony, Octavius, and LEPIDUS decide who must be executed to protect their new power in Rome. Antony sends Lepidus on an errand, and then belittles him as an insignificant man who is not fit to rule but who will be useful for a while. Antony and Octavius begin to plan a campaign against Brutus and Cassius, who have raised an army.

### Act 4, Scene 2

At Brutus' camp, LUCILIUS returns from a visit to Cassius' troops and reports that Cassius has not displayed the warmth of earlier meetings. Brutus interprets this as a sign of waning friendship between Cassius and himself. Cassius arrives and immediately asserts that Brutus has wronged him; Brutus suggests that they enter his tent to talk privately.

### Act 4, Scene 3

Cassius charges that Brutus has ignored his arguments and punished an officer for taking bribes. He insists that they cannot be overstrict in a time of crisis, and Brutus remarks that Cassius himself is reputed to be corrupt and accuses him of withholding funds. The infuriated Cassius, declaring that he never expected such insults from his comrade, offers his dagger and suggests that Brutus kill him. Brutus gently mocks Cassius' excess but apologises for being overheated himself, and the two shake hands in reconciliation. A POET (1) arrives and chastises the two generals for their disharmony. Cassius is amused, but Brutus dismisses him abruptly. Brutus then tells Cassius that he has been short-tempered in part because he has just learned of Portia's suicide due to her fear of the immense army that Octavius and Antony are sending against her husband. MESSALA arrives with news from Rome: Octavius and Antony have executed many political enemies and are on the march. He also reports Portia's death. Brutus hides his prior knowledge and pretends to receive the news stoically, arousing Messala's admiration. Brutus then proposes marching on PHILIPPI, where their enemies have camped. Cassius argues that they should stay where they are and let Antony and Octavius use up their energy marching, but Brutus insists that his plan is superior and Cassius gives in. Brutus then retires for the night, and the others leave. The GHOST (2) of Caesar appears to

Brutus, announces that they shall meet again at Philippi, and disappears.

### Act 5, Scene 1
Octavius and Antony reflect on their good fortune that Brutus and Cassius have taken disadvantageous positions. Octavius insists on commanding the more important right wing, despite Antony's seniority. Brutus, Cassius, and their army appear, and the opposing commanders parley. They quickly begin to exchange insults, and Octavius and Antony leave. Cassius confides to Messala that he is uneasy about the forthcoming battle. Brutus and Cassius tell each other that they will commit suicide rather than be captured.

### Act 5, Scene 2
Brutus orders an attack on Octavius' forces, which he can see weakening.

### Act 5, Scene 3
TITINIUS and Cassius, hard-pressed by the enemy, see that Brutus has launched his attack too soon and left them at a disadvantage. PINDARUS arrives with news that troops are approaching their headquarters; Cassius sends Titinius to investigate and tells Pindarus to watch from a nearby hill. Pindarus reports that Titinius is captured, and Cassius, believing that his own capture is imminent, impales himself on his sword, assisted by Pindarus. Pindarus flees, as Titinius returns safely with Messala to announce that Brutus has defeated Octavius. They find Cassius' body and realise what has happened. Messala leaves to tell Brutus, who appears and mourns his comrade. He announces that they shall launch another attack before nightfall.

### Act 5, Scene 4
Brutus is forced to retreat. Lucilius pretends to be Brutus and is captured. Antony arrives, realises that the captive is not Brutus, and praises Lucilius for courageously diverting attention from his commander.

### Act 5, Scene 5
Brutus, defeated, asks several companions to help him to commit suicide, but they refuse. As enemy troops approach, he prevails upon STRATO to help him, and he dies on his sword. Antony and Octavius appear, triumphant, and find Brutus' body. They praise him and order his honourable burial.

### COMMENTARY

*Julius Caesar* is a play about moral ambiguity in a political setting and the personal tragedy that results. It resembles both the HISTORY PLAYS, written somewhat earlier, and the great TRAGEDIES, soon to come. Like the tragedies, it presents a protagonist who aspires to heroism and fails because of his own moral shortcomings. At the same time, *Julius Caesar* also reflects the

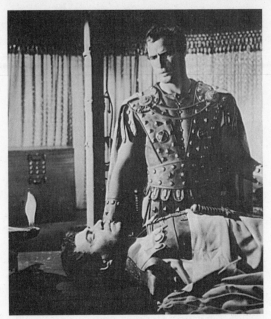

'This was the noblest Roman of them all' (Julius Caesar 5.5.68). Antony (Marlon Brando) eulogises Brutus (James Mason) in the 1953 film version. (Courtesy of Movie Star News)

political philosophy that had informed the playwright's picture of English civil war in the history plays. Because civil disorder and violence are tragic for the entire society, their avoidance is a higher moral obligation than the pursuit or control of power, even for apparently just or moral purposes. Therefore, for Shakespeare, the preservation of the political status quo is a primary good.

Brutus, the protagonist of *Julius Caesar*, is an ambivalent figure who may be seen as both good and evil—an honourable man dedicated to the good of his country, but also a destroyer of its peace. The play's central action—the murder of Caesar—may seem an act of disinterested idealism or one of inflated self-love. Twentieth-century views of the play reflect these possibilities: with the rise of fascism in the 1920s and 1930s, Brutus was aggrandised as a model of republican virtues and Caesar identified with Mussolini and Hitler. More recently, however, Caesar has been defended as a hero who is destroyed by a neurotically envious Brutus, who pursues glory without regard for the disaster he provokes.

These positions are not as mutually exclusive as they may seem; *Julius Caesar* is sometimes grouped with the PROBLEM PLAYS as a work about the uncertain outcome of human endeavours. In this light, the heart of *Julius Caesar* is the tension between Brutus' idealistic rejection of a dominating leader and the reality that human society requires the discipline that Caesar imposes. From another angle, the conflict occurs between the protagonist's obsessive demand for a perfect world and the catastrophe that follows in the real, imperfect world. Thus Brutus' actions are both virtuous and disastrous. Precisely because this ambiguity is possible, Brutus is a tragic hero who attempts the humanly impossible and fails.

At first glance, it seems odd that the play's title character is killed less than halfway through the work, but Caesar, though his part is small, dominates the whole drama. First, his assumption of power in Rome stimulates the conspiracy; later, the inescapable memory of him inspires Antony and haunts Brutus.

The telling comparisons between Brutus and Caesar demonstrate the play's most essential ambivalence: the tyrant and his opponent are not easily distinguishable. In this fashion, the morality of the assassination is questioned, and the importance of Caesar's leadership—first resented and then absent—remains evident. Both Brutus and Caesar have great leadership qualities, and, being certain of his virtues, each is susceptible to flattery and manipulation by lesser men. In murdering Caesar, Brutus follows the Caesar-like course of attempting to change society in accordance with his views. Similarly, in the war that follows the assassination, Brutus behaves as imperiously as Caesar did, enacting precisely the failings of autocratic leadership—the isolation from his followers, the presumption of sound decision-making, the potential for tyranny—that he had acted to prevent in killing Caesar. Significantly, Caesar's Ghost identifies itself as Brutus' 'evil spirit' (4.3.281).

Nevertheless, Caesar is superior to Brutus in his analysis of Cassius and in his recognition that a single leader is needed to control Rome. Moreover, Brutus persistently makes bad judgements, and he suffers the consequences, going from error to error. He refuses to share leadership of the conspiracy with Cassius or Cicero. His arrogant overconfidence is plainly demonstrated when he dismisses Antony as an inconsequential underling in 2.1.181–183. Later, he twice rejects the advice of the more experienced Cassius, resulting in the failure of his cause at Philippi. He is persistently blind to reality, following his own superficial rectitude to disaster. The patriotism he invokes is certainly a living ideal for Brutus, but it is also a cover for his vanity and his unacknowledged need to be like Caesar himself.

As Brutus deteriorates morally in the second half of the play, becoming ever more Caesar-like, so Caesar himself seems to grow in worth as Rome collapses in the leadership vacuum created by his death. This important point is made especially clear by the behaviour of the Plebeians after the murder. Ironically, they hail Brutus as an autocrat—'Let him be Caesar' (3.2.52)—just after he has murdered Caesar to prevent him from becoming one. However, the fickle mob is immediately turned against Brutus by Antony's oration, and their brutality in killing the wrong Cinna in 3.3 heralds the disorder that later prevails on a larger scale in the civil war. Brutus has unleashed a whirlwind.

Brutus' attempts to dignify the assassination by invoking the gods through ritual are pointedly undercut. Brutus wishes to make a ceremony of the killing, saying, 'Let's be sacrificers, but not butchers' (2.1.166), but he immediately goes on to reveal an unconscious awareness of public opinion: '. . . so appearing to the common eyes, / We shall be call'd purgers, not murderers' (2.1.179–180). Another attempt to ritualise the murder occurs when Brutus leads the assassins in washing their hands in Caesar's blood, an act that only accentuates the violence of the deed.

In the second half of the play, Antony, heretofore an unimportant figure, suddenly comes into his own. He dominates the conspirators, taking control of Rome by the end of 3.2. In 4.1, where he bargains the lives of his relatives with Octavius and Lepidus, and then disdains the latter as an impotent tool, we see Antony as both a cynical political operative and a strong leader, a complex figure whose ambivalent nature deepens the moral ambiguity of the play's world.

Later developments confirm that Brutus' decision to kill Caesar was wrong both politically and morally. Antony's dire prediction of the bloody course revenge will take, in 3.1.258–275, strongly invokes the conventions of the REVENGE PLAY, a popular genre of ELIZABETHAN and JACOBEAN DRAMA that Shakespeare had exploited earlier in *Titus Andronicus* and would again in *Hamlet* and *Macbeth*. In a revenge play an inexorable rule operates: a murder must be punished with another one, usually under the eye of the victim's ghost; the first murderer is doomed, regardless of politics or personality. Thus such factors as the possible benefit to Rome of Caesar's death are swept aside. Brutus' moralising has been useless; Antony will inevitably triumph. The would-be saviour of Rome has produced only a morally chaotic situation in which final victory goes, not to the high-minded assassin, nor to the hot-blooded avenger, but to the cool opportunist Octavius. This icily commanding figure takes control from Antony in 5.1.20 and disposes of matters at the play's close. Roman history was much more familiar in Shakespeare's time than in ours, and the playwright knew that his audience would immediately recognise the irony that Brutus' attempt to prevent one tyranny merely paved the way for the greater autocracy of Octavius, known to history as the first Roman emperor, Augustus CAESAR (2). (Shakespeare was to dramatise the final consolidation of Octavius' power in *Antony and Cleopatra*.)

As he did in the history plays, Shakespeare altered the historical record considerably in writing *Julius Caesar*. Following PLUTARCH, the playwright accurately presented the broad outlines of Roman history but altered many details for dramatic purposes. Notably, he compressed the chronology of events from months to a few days or hours in order to achieve a more dramatic sequence of events. For instance, Caesar's triumphant return to Rome occurred in October of 45 B.C., while the feast of Lupercalia fell in the following February. Only some weeks after this event were the tribunes Flavus (the play's Flavius) and Marullus ousted after removing public decorations that honoured Caesar. Shakespeare combined all these events into a single day, enacted in 1.1–2.

Similarly, the aftermath of the assassination covers only several hours in the play. In Plutarch the same events took months. Antony's speech followed Brutus' by several days, rather than immediately, and Brutus, whose flight is reported after the speech, did not in fact leave Rome until mid-April. Similarly, Octavius' arrival coincides with the orations in the play, but he did not actually appear in Rome until six weeks afterwards. And though Antony welcomes Octavius in the play, the two actually quarrelled to the point of warfare, and their alliance was not arranged for almost 20 months, though in the play it follows immediately.

The battle of Philippi is a dramatic example of Shakespeare's compression of events. In the play, the battle directly follows the meeting of Cassius and Brutus in 4.2–3, whereas it actually occurred more than 6 months later. In fact there were two battles at Philippi, as Plutarch reports: the first was a draw, in which Cassius killed himself; in the second, 20 days later, Brutus was defeated and also committed suicide. Shakespeare compresses the two conflicts into a single afternoon.

Other changes involve the historical figures themselves. In 1.2 Cassius refers to an estrangement between himself and Brutus, and Brutus replies that his private worries have made him distant to his friends. In fact, according to Plutarch, the hostility between the two stemmed from their rivalry for a political position. Shakespeare's version draws attention to Brutus' worries about Caesar's aspirations and also makes him seem thoughtful and conscientious, rather than politically ambitious.

Further, Shakespeare substantially elaborated Plutarch's accounts of the speeches of Brutus and Antony in 3.2 and of the riot of the Plebeians in 3.3. Plutarch merely alludes to the two orations, attaching no great importance to their styles, while Shakespeare creates antithetical deliveries—rational versus emotional—that reflect on the characters who speak them and on the very nature of politics. Similarly, while Plutarch mentions the actions of the mob, the playwright gives the crowd life and thus transforms their volatility and fickleness, even their grim sense of humour, into a significant political phenomenon.

Shakespeare had to emphasise politics in *Julius Cae-*sar, for otherwise Brutus' fate would be meaningless. Brutus himself never sees his mistake in murdering his best friend and the leader of his country. His fate is dramatically satisfactory only in light of the impact of his action on Roman society as a whole, that is, in its political consequences. His error stems from an unconscious desire for a political world in which evil is impossible. Thus his political blindness has a psychological element, reflecting Shakespeare's progress towards the psychological portraiture of the great tragedies.

## SOURCES OF THE PLAY

The primary source for *Julius Caesar* was Sir Thomas NORTH's translation of the ancient Roman biographical collection Plutarch's *Lives* in either its first or second edition (1579, 1595). Isolated passages suggest other materials that the playwright knew, including a biography of Caesar by John HIGGINS in A MIRROR FOR MAGISTRATES, the philosophical poem *Nosce Teipsum* ('Know Thyself'), by John DAVIES (2), published in 1599, and several works by CICERO. Nevertheless, three of the lives in Plutarch—those of Caesar, Brutus, and Antony—supply all of the incidents in the play. In addition, English plays about Caesar had been popular since at least the early 1580s, and this tradition must have helped stimulate the writing of *Julius Caesar*. While there is no evidence that any of these plays influenced Shakespeare directly, the famous phrase 'Et tu, Brute' (3.1.77) may have come from such a work, for it does not appear in any Latin source yet was a well-known tag line in Shakespeare's day.

## TEXT OF THE PLAY

*Julius Caesar* was probably written in early 1599. The diary of Thomas PLATTER records a performance of the play on September 21, 1599, and the play is not on the list of Shakespeare's plays published by Francis MERES in September 1598. While Meres' list does not pretend to be complete, *Caesar* was a strikingly popular work, as contemporary references indicate, and is not likely to have been omitted if it had been staged. While it might have been written during the latter part of 1598, it is fairly certain that *Much Ado About Nothing* and *Henry V* were written then, so *Julius Caesar* is thought to have followed them.

*Caesar* was not printed during Shakespeare's lifetime; the first edition is that of the FIRST FOLIO (1623). This text, known as F1, is relatively error-free—it is generally held to be the least corrupt text in the Folio—indicating that it was probably printed from a copy of Shakespeare's own manuscript, or FOUL PAPERS. This copy had probably been used as or taken from a PROMPT-BOOK, in which the playwright's characteristic mis-spellings and unnecessarily elaborate stage directions had been corrected. The later folios—and a series of late 17th-century QUARTOS—vary slightly from F1, but all are clearly based on it, as are all modern editions.

## THEATRICAL HISTORY OF THE PLAY

The earliest known performance of *Julius Caesar* was held on September 21, 1599, as recorded in Thomas Platter's diary, and many references from 1599 and the early 17th century indicate that the play was very popular with its original audience, as does the existence of a competing play about Caesar produced by Philip HENSLOWE in 1602. Leonard DIGGES wrote about *Caesar*'s enthusiastic audiences as late as the 1620s, and it was performed at the royal court at least twice, in 1613 and 1638. In the 1660s the play was included in the repertoire of Thomas KILLIGREW's company and was one of the few Shakespearean plays to be popular in the late 17th century; Charles HART (1) played Brutus for Killigrew, and later Thomas BETTERTON was successful in the part. The play was published six times between 1684 and 1691.

In the 18th century Spranger BARRY (3) was a notable Antony, while Barton BOOTH (1) and James QUIN played Brutus in several productions. The celebrated Peg WOFFINGTON appeared as Portia in the 1750s, though that small part has not generally attracted leading actresses. In the 19th century most major English actors portrayed one or more of the play's important roles, and the play was also very popular in America, where Lawrence BARRETT, Edwin FORREST, and Edwin BOOTH (2) were particularly associated with it. In 1864 Booth and his brothers Junius Brutus BOOTH (5) and John Wilkes BOOTH (3) played Brutus, Cassius, and Antony respectively, performing on the same stage for the first and only time. In London, a very popular 1895 production, presented by Beerbohm TREE, featured sets and costumes by perhaps the most famous English painter of the day, Sir Lawrence Alma-Tadema (1836–1912).

Perhaps because the rise of totalitarianism in Germany and Russia between the world wars generated a concern with political tyranny, *Julius Caesar* has often been produced in the 20th century. Particularly memorable was Orson WELLES' modern-dress rendering of 1938, in which Caesar was attired as the Italian Fascist leader Benito Mussolini. *Julius Caesar* has also yielded a number of FILMS, notably M.G.M.'s 1953 version starring Marlon Brando as Antony. The play has likewise been produced several times on TELEVISION, beginning as long ago as 1938; in 1963 the British Broadcasting Corporation presented *The Spread of the Eagle,* based on all three ROMAN PLAYS.

**Juno** Pagan goddess and minor figure in *The Tempest,* a character in the MASQUE presented by ARIEL to celebrate the engagement of MIRANDA and FERDINAND (2). After an introduction by IRIS, Juno joins CERES in singing a hymn of 'marriage-blessing' (4.1.106) to the couple. Though queen of the gods, Juno has the smallest role in the masque. However, in Shakespeare's hierarchy-conscious world, Juno's rank gave her a greater importance than she seems otherwise to have. As a queen, her presence—her 'sovereign grace' (4.1.72)—gives the masque a particularly dignified air appropriate to the betrothal of PROSPERO's daughter. If, as some scholars believe, the masque was added to the play when it was performed as part of the 1613 marriage festivities for Princess ELIZABETH (3), this feature would have had even greater import. Juno's entrance is accordingly a spectacular one. The stage direction at 4.1.72 reads 'Juno descends', indicating theatrical practise in Shakespeare's time, at least in the new BLACKFRIARS THEATRE: the goddess was lowered from the ceiling above the stage, probably seated on a throne decorated with peacocks, as mentioned by Iris in 4.1.74. (Nineteenth-century productions of *The Tempest* often featured live peacocks.)

**Jupiter** Pagan god and minor character in *Cymbeline.* Jupiter, the Roman king of the gods, appears to the desperate POSTHUMUS in a vision where he assures the spirit of Posthumus' father, SICILIUS LEONATUS, that the young man will be restored to good fortune. He then departs, and leaves a tablet with a cryptic message (5.4.138–145) that is interpreted later by the SOOTHSAYER (3) as an allegory of reunion and renewal. Posthumus does not realise that his chaotic drift towards tragedy has ended with the god's appearance, and he is still intent on death. However, the audience is aware that he shall be 'happier much by his affliction made' (5.4.108), as the god puts it. Thus, Jupiter embodies the play's moral: that humanity depends on providence for happiness.

Jupiter's style is very formal. He speaks in rhyming verse and old-fashioned language unlike anything else in the play. This signifies his supernatural nature. In performance, his lines are sometimes sung. The stage direction at his entrance reads, 'Jupiter descends in thunder and lightning, sitting upon an eagle . . .' (5.4.-92); this makes it clear that either the BLACKFRIARS THEATRE or the GLOBE, or both, were equipped with a mechanical apparatus that permitted characters to enter a scene from above by being lowered from the ceiling. As in the present case, this permitted a literal *deus ex machina,* or 'god from the machine', the phrase for a surprise appearance by a god who resolves the situation of a play. The machine was originally a crane-like device used in ancient Greek theatre to lower actors portraying deities as though they were descending from heaven.

Some scholars believe Jupiter may have been intended as an allegorical representation of King JAMES I, newly crowned as the first joint monarch of England and Scotland. In this light, the cryptic tablet reads as a tribute to the union of the two countries, a matter that was disputed in the first years of James' reign.

**Justice** Minor character in *Measure for Measure,* a magistrate of VIENNA. The Justice appears only in 2.1, speaking three lines to his superior, ESCALUS (2). This brief exchange serves to remind the audience of the condemned CLAUDIO (3) after the diversion of the long comic trial of POMPEY (1). The Justice and Escalus depart together at the close of the scene.

Some scholars believe that the Justice's absence elsewhere in the play is evidence that it was consider- ably revised. Another theory supports only a tiny re- vision, holding that the Justice's lines had originally been written for the PROVOST, but that in production they had been reassigned. Normal stage practise in Shakespeare's day frowned on an immediate re-en- trance after an exit, and since the Provost opens the next scene, he could not close this one by leaving with Escalus. So, possibly, a new character was in- vented by Shakespeare or someone else. As a matter of economy, the Justice is often cut from modern productions and his lines eliminated or given to the Provost.

**Katharina** Character in *The Taming of the Shrew*. See KATHERINA.

**Katharine (1) (Katherine; Catherine)** Character in *Love's Labour's Lost*, the beloved of DUMAINE and a lady-in-waiting to the PRINCESS (1) OF FRANCE. Although primarily a stock figure in the play's courtly tableau of lovers, she is given a flash of true human feeling. In 5.2, ROSALINE (1) teases her about a sister who was said to have died of love, and Katharine is overtaken by her memory of the occasion. 'He made her melancholy, sad, and heavy; / And so she died: had she been light, like you, / Of such a merry, nimble, stirring spirit, / She might ha' been a grandam ere she died. . . .' (5.2.14–17). This brief remark gives us not only a glimpse of a young woman's recollected grief, but we receive an impression of Rosaline's character as well.

It is thought that Shakespeare derived the story of Katharine's sister's death from a current account of a similar demise among the attendants of the historical Princess of France of the day, Marguerite of Valois, who was in fact married to the King of Navarre. The same tale may also have influenced the OPHELIA episode in *Hamlet*.

**Katharine (2) (Catherine, Katherine), Princess (1401–1438)** Historical figure and character in *Henry V*, the daughter of the FRENCH KING, later betrothed to King HENRY V. Princess Katharine is an innocent girl. She is comically instructed in English by her waiting-woman, ALICE, in 3.4, and she is the upright but somewhat baffled subject of King Henry's aggressive courtship in 5.2. Most of her lines are in French or broken English. She has little personality; she is simply the object of King Henry's affections and part of his reward for victory over FRANCE (1).

The historical Katherine of Valois was the youngest child of Charles VI, the French King of the play, and Queen ISABEL (2). She was married to Henry as part of the treaty of TROYES. After Henry's death, she married an obscure Welsh nobleman, Owen Tudor; their grandchild was to become King Henry VII of England, and he appears as the Earl of RICHMOND in *3 Henry VI* and *Richard III*.

**Katherina** Title character in *The Taming of the Shrew*, the ill-tempered young woman courted, married, and 'tamed' by PETRUCHIO (2). Katherina is sometimes thought of as a representative oppressed woman, dominated by a selfish man and trapped in a loveless marriage. But this point of view is based on modern notions of marital relations (see 'Commentary' on the play), and it obscures the real nature of the character. Katherina undergoes a positive transformation during the play: she is freed from an unhappy emotional state, and she enters a happy marriage.

In Acts 1–3 Katherina is presented as a volatile and distinctly unhappy person. She is a familiar type, a young adult who resents the rejection she receives, yet, in an effort to feel immune to the opinions of others, she simply makes herself less likeable by belligerently taking exception to everything. In addition, she has clearly been compared to her younger sister—the deceptively sweet BIANCA (1)—too often for comfort. The psychological pressure within Katherina bursts forth in violence, both threatened and actual. Not content with curtly dismissing the rudeness of HORTENSIO, for example, she goes on to express a desire to 'comb your noddle with a three-legg'd stool' (1.1.64). Corrected by a music teacher (Hortensio again, in disguise), she assaults him with a lute. Her envy and suspicion of Bianca drive her to physical abuse in 2.1. When she first encounters Petruchio, knowing only that he is a suitor, she repeatedly insults him (2.1.195–259) and she slaps him to 'try' (2.1.217) his gentlemanliness.

In Acts 4–5, however, Katherina changes, under the forceful guidance of Petruchio. His 'taming' consists of demonstrating that she need not continue to be an outcast, disliked and shunned, and that there is indeed a place in the world that she can occupy happily. His persistent references to her calm and sweetness—initially fictitious—make her realise the psychological benefits that such attributes could bring: acceptance and a sense of moral worth. His own behaviour shows her the ugliness of shrewishness. She chooses to reject her bristly defensiveness and assume the role of an ordinary wife. She will admit that the world is not hers to control; in return, she will have the emotional security of a prescribed place in it.

The submissiveness that Katherina accepts, and that troubles modern readers, was simply held to be a conventional attribute of a wife: Shakespeare and his contemporaries of both sexes believed that the Bible, as well as long-hallowed tradition, prescribed hierarchical relationships among humans: husbands ruled wives, as parents ruled children, as monarchs ruled commoners, and as God ruled all. Katherina voices this belief in her banquet speech in 5.2.

Katherina loves Petruchio. She indicates as much in the grace with which she kisses him at the end of 5.1, and her speech in 5.2 is an implicit expression of her love. At the banquet she has already demonstrated her obedience and need not do more; Petruchio merely asked her for a statement of principle, as much to aggravate the WIDOW (1) and Bianca as anything else. She goes far beyond his intent, specifically referring to her own experience and stating that she is grateful for inclusion in the system she describes. The entirely spontaneous physical act of submission that closes her speech symbolises the wifely duty demanded in this system, but it is also directed to her husband, as an expression of her gratitude. That this gesture is loving is confirmed by his affectionate response to it. Katherina has found not only comfort in an assured position in society, but happiness in a loving marriage. She is thus the vehicle for an elaboration of two of Shakespeare's persistent concerns: the virtue of an ordered, hierarchical social system and the value of marriage as a venue for love. Her psychological transformation also reflects his fascination with the mysteries of the human personality.

Katherina's is a small part, for all its importance, and, while boldly drawn, she lacks the subtlety of later Shakespearean heroines who resemble her, such as BEATRICE in *Much Ado About Nothing*. It is noteworthy that Katherina shares with several of the playwright's most lovingly developed female characters, as well as with the 'Dark Lady' of the SONNETS, a sharp temper and a dark complexion (see 2.1.248–249). It seems possible (though altogether unprovable) that these characters share the traits of a woman (entirely unidentifiable) who was romantically important to Shakespeare. The thought certainly adds resonance to his portrait of a shrew.

**Katherine (Katharine) of Aragon, Queen of England (1485–1536)** Historical figure and character in *Henry VIII*, the rejected wife of King HENRY VIII. The focus of most of Acts 2 and 3 is on Henry's finally successful effort to divorce Katherine and marry ANNE (1) BULLEN. Katherine appears first in 1.2, where she opposes the unjust taxes introduced by Cardinal WOLSEY. The episode establishes the queen as a good person and Wolsey, already designated a villain, as her enemy—and it is Wolsey's influence that leads the king to divorce her. In 2.4, at her divorce trial, Katherine spiritedly defies Wolsey, refusing to submit to his judgement and demanding an appeal to the pope. In 3.1, when she is visited by Wolsey and Cardinal CAMPEIUS, she concedes her helplessness, but refuses to co-operate in her own downfall. Finally, in 4.2, she is seen dying in exile at KIMBOLTON, after the king has married Anne and crowned her as queen. She hears of Wolsey's death, and though bitter, she accepts GRIFFITH's advice and forgives the cardinal. Throughout she is a spirited woman, insisting on the respect due a queen. Her virtues are stressed in the enactment of her dream, in which supernatural beings crown her with garlands.

Katherine's role in the play is largely symbolic. As a paragon of goodness, she makes a suitable victim for Wolsey, whose villainy dominates the first half of the play. Henry is susceptible to Wolsey's influence, but his evident affection for Katherine makes it clear that he is not himself a villain, despite the divorce. The loss of Katherine is seen as a misfortune that is compensated for by the king's later wisdom and maturity, and by the birth of ELIZABETH (1) at the play's close.

For dramatic purposes, Shakespeare places Katherine's death immediately after Wolsey's death and Anne's coronation, though she in fact lived for six years after the first event and three after the second, almost long enough to see Anne's downfall. Aside from chronology, Shakespeare's presentation of Katherine's story is fairly accurate. The daughter of King Ferdinand and Queen Isabella of Spain (ruled 1479–1516), Katherine was married to Henry's elder brother, Prince Arthur (1486–1502), the heir apparent to King Henry VII, in 1501. Prince Arthur died shortly after marrying Katherine, and she declared, then and later, that the marriage had not been sexually consummated. Henry disputed this later, when he sought an annulment and cited Katherine's marriage to his brother as having disqualified her for marriage to him. (Though traditionally called a divorce, what Henry actually obtained was a declaration that he had never been married in theological terms.) Yet when Henry had acceded to the throne in 1509, he had actually received papal approval to marry Katherine.

In marrying Katherine, Henry had wished to maintain the Spanish alliance that she represented, but he apparently loved her as well. However, when she did not produce a suitable heir to the throne—their only child was a daughter, not considered acceptable at the time—Henry considered a new marriage. Thus, on falling in love with Anne, he proceeded to dispose of his wife of 20 years. Though Katherine was badly humiliated by Henry before and after the divorce, he allowed her to live out her life in some comfort, and it was thought by contemporaries—and most modern historians agree—that his affection and respect for her never completely disappeared.

**Kean (1), Charles (1811–1868)**  British actor and producer. Charles Kean, the son of Edmund KEAN (2), was acclaimed as HAMLET, but his greatest importance was not as an actor but as the producer of Shakespeare's plays (and others) in a lavish style, incorporating elaborate spectacles that laid claim to historical accuracy. Costumes and sets were designed with scrupulous attention to archaeological detail, and immense casts of extras were used. Among his most notable productions were *Henry VIII* (1855), *The Winter's Tale* (1856), *Richard II* (1857), and *Henry V* (1859). He established a style of production that was to last into the early 20th century in the work of his followers, including Henry IRVING and Beerbohm TREE.

**Kean (2), Edmund (1787–1833)**  British actor. The abandoned son of an actress, Kean was raised in provincial touring companies, by various people—includ-ing his guardian, Moses Kean, a comic and ventriloquist who may have been his uncle, though his paternity was never clearly established. He already had many years of acting experience when he achieved a London triumph as SHYLOCK in 1814. His acting style was frenzied and active, in marked contrast to the reigning Shakespearean actor, the dignified J. P. KEMBLE (3). A contemporary, using a political metaphor, declared that Kean was 'one of the people . . . a *radical* performer', and Samuel Taylor COLERIDGE remarked of his 'rapid descents from the hyper-tragic to the infra-colloquial' that 'to see him act, is like reading Shakespeare by flashes of lightning'. His greatest successes were as villains—especially Shylock, RICHARD III, OTHELLO, and Barabas in *The Jew of Malta* by Christopher MARLOWE (1)—while his HAMLET and LEAR were sometimes criticised as unthoughtful. He was a temperamental and undisciplined man who often missed performances, and he figured in a notable sex scandal with the wife of a popular politician. Nevertheless, only Kemble and W. C. MACREADY rivalled him in popular-

*In the early 19th century, Edmund Kean (seen here as Richard III) helped replace the classical ideal of acting that had prevailed through the 18th century with a new, romantic style marked by violent emotion. The poet and critic Samuel Taylor Coleridge remarked that Kean could reveal Shakespeare through 'flashes of lightning'.* (Courtesy of Culver Pictures, Inc.)

ity. His success was so great that he has been called the theatre's first star, to whom all other features of a production were subordinated. He collapsed on-stage while playing Othello—opposite the IAGO of his son Charles KEAN (1)—and died a few weeks later.

**Keats, John (1795–1821)** English poet much influenced by Shakespeare. Generally regarded as among the greatest of all poets, Keats kept a bust of Shakespeare in his study and believed, at least sometimes, that the spirit of Shakespeare presided over his work in a supernatural way, dictating choices as he wrote his poems. In any case Shakespeare's influence on Keats' poetry—in a conventional literary sense—is very evident; his poems are steeped in Shakespearean imagery, and his letters, a literary masterpiece in themselves, abound in allusions to the playwright.

Keats had a set of small volumes of the plays (an 1814 reissue of the 1765 edition of Samuel JOHNSON [7]), which he annotated heavily. His notes have been published by Caroline SPURGEON as *Keats' Shakespeare* (1928). Some of the plays were plainly of greater interest than others: the HISTORY PLAYS, for example, were virtually ignored, while *A Midsummer Night's Dream* and *The Tempest* sparked frequent and enthusiastic commentary. Keats' remarks on Shakespeare in his letters have offered much grist for subsequent writers. In one such comment, still often cited, Keats observed that Shakespeare had the 'quality [that] went to form a Man of Achievement, especially in Literature . . . I mean *Negative Capability,* that is, when a man is capable of being in uncertainties, mysteries, doubts, without any irritable reaching after fact and reason'.

**Keeper (1)** Minor character in *1 Henry VI*, one of the guards who attends the imprisoned MORTIMER (1) in the Tower of London in 2.5.

**Keeper (2)** Either of two minor characters in *3 Henry VI*, gameskeepers who capture the refugee King HENRY VI in 3.1. Henry chastises the Keepers for their inconstant allegiance, which they once gave to him but now proclaim to be owed to King EDWARD (4). They respond with rationalisations before arresting him. This incident is another instance of changeable loyalties in the disrupted world depicted in the play.

In the FIRST FOLIO text of the play, the Keepers are designated in a stage direction as 'Sinklo' and 'Humfrey'. These are presumably the actors who played the parts in an early production, probably John SINCKLO and Humphrey JEFFES.

**Keeper (3)** Minor character in *Richard III,* the gaoler of CLARENCE (1) in the TOWER OF LONDON. The Keeper listens sympathetically to Clarence's report of a nightmare in 1.4. Some editions follow the first QUARTO and

assign the Keeper's part to BRAKENBURY. The dropping of the character doubtless reflects an economy measure by a 16th-century acting company.

**Keeper (4)** Minor character in *Richard II,* the gaoler of the deposed King RICHARD II. The Keeper brings Richard a meal in 5.5, but he refuses to taste it for poison, as had been routine, asserting that Sir Piers EXTON has forbidden him to do so. Richard strikes him in anger, and the Keeper's cries summon Exton and his murderers, who kill the prisoner.

**Keeper (5)** Minor character in *Henry VIII,* the doorman at a meeting of the king's council. In 5.2 the Keeper, following his orders, prevents CRANMER, the Archbishop of Canterbury, from entering the meeting to which he has been summoned. This is plainly an insult to a person of his rank, as King HENRY VIII realises angrily when he is informed of it by Doctor BUTTS. The incident demonstrates the enmity of Bishop GARDINER and the councillors towards Cranmer, whose support by the king is the theme of 5.1–2.

**Kemble (1), Charles (1775–1854)** British actor and producer, brother of J. P. KEMBLE (3) and Sarah SIDDONS, and father of Fanny KEMBLE (2). As an actor, Charles Kemble was best known as a player of secondary parts—such as MALCOLM, MACDUFF, MERCUTIO, and LAERTES—opposite his brother, though he was also acclaimed as BENEDICK and ORLANDO. He succeeded his brother as manager of the Covent Garden Theatre, where he presented Shakespeare's works in productions that aimed at historical accuracy in sets and costumes. Beginning with the *King John* staged by him and J. R. PLANCHÉ in 1823, his ideas influenced Shakespearean productions for the rest of the 19th century. Kemble was an unsuccessful manager and was only saved from bankruptcy by the success of his daughter, Fanny.

**Kemble (2), Fanny (1809–1893)** British actress, daughter of Charles KEMBLE (1). Fanny Kemble's stunning performances as JULIET (1) saved her father's Covent Garden Theatre from bankruptcy in 1829, and she went on to triumphs as BEATRICE and PORTIA (1). Unlike the other members of the family, she was not committed to a theatrical career, and she retired in 1834, when she married a Philadelphian. After her divorce in 1845, she returned to Britain and in the 1850s and 1860s toured both there and in America with a highly popular series of readings from Shakespeare. She finally retired in 1868 and settled in London.

**Kemble (3), John Philip (1757–1823)** British actor and producer, brother of Charles and Stephen KEM-

BLE (1, 4) and Sarah SIDDONS. J. P. Kemble played most of Shakespeare's protagonists, often opposite his sister, and was especially acclaimed for his portrayals of HAMLET, CORIOLANUS, and HENRY V. He initially established himself as Hamlet in 1783 at the Drury Lane Theatre in London, which he managed from 1788 until 1802. After that he ran the Covent Garden Theatre, finally retiring in 1817. As a producer, he continued the trend towards more realistic costumes and sets, which was begun by David GARRICK and eventually resulted in the elaborately 'historical' productions of Charles Kemble, Charles KEAN (1), and Henry IRVING. A stately and dignified actor, Kemble dominated the English stage until the rise of his only great rival, Edmund KEAN (2). The son of an actor and actress, Kemble was a child performer before training for the priesthood. He abandoned his studies and returned to the theatre in 1776, though the experience is thought to have influenced his deliberate and ascetic acting style.

**Kemble (4), Stephen (1758–1822)**  Nineteenth-century actor, brother of Charles and John Philip KEMBLE (1, 3) and Sarah SIDDONS. A child actor like his siblings, Stephen became a chemist before returning to the stage in his late twenties. Being very heavy, he often played FALSTAFF. His girth and the fact that he was quite overshadowed by John Philip led to the contemporary witticism that they were 'the big Kemble and the great Kemble'.

**Kempe (Kemp), William (d. c. 1608)**  English actor, a member of the CHAMBERLAIN'S MEN and one of the 26 men listed in the FIRST FOLIO as the 'Principall

*Will Kempe created many of the great Shakespearian comic roles. He also was famous, as shown in this contemporary illustration, for his stunt of dancing a morris along the road from London to Norwich— a distance of almost 100 miles. (Courtesy of Bodleian Library, Oxford)*

Actors' in Shakespeare's plays. Kempe's name appears in early texts of *Romeo and Juliet* (stage direction at 4.5.99) and *Much Ado About Nothing* (speech headings in 4.2), proving that he was the original portrayer of PETER (2) and DOGBERRY. As a CLOWN (1), he is also believed to have originated such other Shakespearean comic parts as BOTTOM, COSTARD, LAUNCE, LAUNCELOT, and possibly FALSTAFF, before leaving the company in 1599, when he was replaced by Robert ARMIN.

Based on the differences in such comic parts written before and after 1599, it is clear that Shakespeare wrote the earlier ones with Kempe in mind. From analysis of these characters, combined with other surviving references to Kempe, we know something of his style. He was a big man who specialised in plebeian clowns who spoke in earthy language, with seemingly ingenuous spontaneity, often addressing the audience in frank asides. Kempe's characters have a tendency to confuse and mispronounce their words, and contemporary references to his dancing and his ability to 'make a scurvy face' suggest a physical brand of humour. He was especially famous for an extraordinary publicity stunt, as it would now be called, of 1600, when he performed a morris dance along the road from LONDON to Norwich—a distance of almost 100 miles, which he covered in nine days. He then wrote a book about it, *Kemps nine daies wonder* (1600).

Kempe is first known as the jester, or FOOL (1), to the Earl of LEICESTER, with whom he travelled to the war in the Netherlands in 1585–1586. He may even have been a member of LEICESTER'S MEN at this time. During the summer of 1586 he performed with an English company in DENMARK. He was a member of STRANGE'S MEN by 1593, when he was already a noted comedian, hailed by Thomas NASHE as the successor to Richard TARLTON, another famous Elizabethan comic. Kempe is presumed to have been an original member of the Chamberlain's Men in 1594, for he was a principal partner in it the next year. In 1599 he was one of the original partners in the GLOBE THEATRE, but for reasons unknown, he left the troupe in the same year and sold his share in the theatre to Shakespeare, John HEMINGES, Augustine PHILLIPS, and Thomas POPE (2). He toured in Germany and Italy, before returning to England in 1601. He may have rejoined the Chamberlain's Men briefly, but by 1602 he was with WORCESTER'S MEN. Nothing is known of his life after 1603; he was mentioned as dead in 1608.

**Kenilworth**  Castle in WARWICKSHIRE, a location in *2 Henry VI* and the scene of an extraordinarily lavish entertainment held for Queen ELIZABETH (1) in 1575, when Shakespeare, who lived nearby, was 11 years old. It is thought that he was probably among the multitudes of commoners from the neighbourhood who were permitted to gather and view parts of the spectacle. This fabulous occasion, which lasted for three weeks, featured many MASQUES and other theatrical entertainments. Contemporary accounts of these have survived, and it is often supposed that one of them may have provided the germ of a passage in *A Midsummer Night's Dream* (2.1.148–154). In 4.9 of *2 Henry VI* King HENRY VI and Queen MARGARET (1) retreat to Kenilworth, in the remote countryside, as CADE's rebellion sweeps London.

**Kent (1)**   County in south-easternmost England, the setting of a number of scenes in *2 Henry VI*. The play reflects the position of the Duke of SUFFOLK (3) as the most powerful aristocrat in Kent. Historically, although Shakespeare does not point out the connection, Suffolk's death on a beach in Kent in 4.1 was a trigger for the rebellion led by Jack CADE, depicted in the following scenes, for Suffolk was a grasping and extortionate landlord and his power was a source of popular discontent. In the play, Cade retreats to Kent when his uprising fails, to be killed by Alexander IDEN in 4.10.

Cade's rebellion was a typically Kentish phenomenon, one of several major revolts to arise in the county between the 14th and 16th centuries. Kent, located on the coast at England's nearest point to FRANCE (1), had since prehistory been a relatively prosperous and cosmopolitan region by virtue of its trade with the Continent. In the late Middle Ages it was thus a centre of political and social discontent, as the growing merchant class combined with artisans and rising small landholders to protest against the inequities and restrictions of feudalism.

Two settings in *1 Henry IV*, ROCHESTER and GAD'S HILL, are also located in Kent.

**Kent (2), Earl of**   Character in *King Lear*, nobleman faithful to King LEAR. Kent attempts to dissuade the king from his catastrophic decision to banish CORDELIA when she honestly admits that her love will go to her husband as well as her father, but Lear banishes him as well for interfering. Kent then disguises himself and attempts to assist Lear when he is rejected by his other daughters, REGAN and GONERIL. He succeeds in keeping Lear safe from possible murder, and he reunites the king and Cordelia at DOVER. His conflict with Goneril's steward OSWALD stresses an important value in the play, the association of virtue with gentlemanly behaviour. Kent's steadfast honesty and loyalty is contrasted with the courtier's self-serving ambition. However, when Cordelia's invasion fails and she and Lear are captured by EDMUND, Kent is helpless. As he witnesses Lear's death at the play's close, he exclaims, 'Break, heart; I

prithee, break!' (5.3.311). Whether he refers to his own heart or Lear's, this forsaken cry is emblematic of the sorrowful view of humanity's plight that is an important theme of the play. Yet Kent's final declaration of his own imminent death, 'I have a journey, sir, shortly to go; / My master calls me, I must not say no' (5.3.320–321) also contributes to the play's sense of the nobility of human suffering.

Kent corresponds to a character named Perillus in Shakespeare's chief source for *Lear,* the play KING LEIR (c. 1588). Some scholars think Shakespeare may have played Perillus for the CHAMBERLAIN'S MEN in the 1590s, for a number of passages in the older play are especially closely echoed in *Lear* when Kent is onstage.

**Kesselstadt Death Mask**   Death mask formerly thought to be Shakespeare's. Discovered in 1847 at the estate sale of a Count Kesselstadt, this death mask—a cast made of the face of a dead person—was once widely believed to be Shakespeare's, chiefly because it is inscribed 'WS/1616'. However, it does not resemble either of the most authoritative portraits (see DROESHOUT; JANSSEN [2]), and the date is almost certainly false for no other non-royal death masks are known from that period. Scholars are therefore in agreement that the Kesselstadt death mask is a forgery, but it provides a good demonstration of the appeal of dramatic Shakespeareana.

**Killigrew, Thomas (1612–1683)**   English playwright and theatrical producer. Killigrew, along with William DAVENANT, dominated the London theatre world in the 1660s. Killigrew wrote several moderately successful tragicomedies (see TRAGICOMEDY) before the London theatres were closed by the Puritans in 1642, when the Civil Wars began. A royalist, he went into exile with the future King Charles II, and when the monarchy was restored in 1660, he was granted one of the two licences to produce plays in London. His King's Company was granted the rights to 20 of Shakespeare's plays, but he staged only four of them: *The Merry Wives of Windsor* (one of the first plays staged after the restoration), *1 Henry IV* (at least four times), *Julius Caesar,* and *Othello*. In Killigrew's *Othello,* on December 8, 1660, Margaret HUGHES played DESDEMONA and became the first woman to act on an English stage.

**Kimbolton Castle**   Manor house near Cambridge, England, a setting for a scene in *Henry VIII*. In 4.2 HENRY VIII's divorced and deposed queen, KATHERINE of Aragon, lives in exile at Kimbolton, accompanied by only a few attendants. When she sees a vision of herself receiving garlands from spiritlike creatures, she knows she is near death.

Kimbolton was one of several residences where the historical Katherine lived out her exile. At the time it was a fortified manor built over an ancient castle. Today, a grand neo-classical country house of the early 18th-century overlays the older establishment and is open to the public as a museum.

**King (1), Alonso of Naples** Character in *The Tempest.* See ALONSO.

**King (2) Antiochus of Syria** Character in *Pericles.* See ANTIOCHUS.

**King (3) Charles VI of France** Character in *Henry V.* See FRENCH KING.

**King (4) Charles VII of France** Character in *1 Henry VI.* See CHARLES VII.

**King (5) Claudius of Denmark** Character in *Hamlet,* murderer and royal successor of HAMLET's father and husband of his victim's widow, QUEEN (9) Gertrude, Hamlet's mother. The central issue of the play is the conflict between Hamlet's desire for vengeance against the King—to which he has been sworn by his father's GHOST (3)—and his recognition that revenge would involve him in evil himself.

The King's crime, by his own confession, 'is rank, it smells to heaven; It hath the primal eldest curse upon't' (3.3.36–37)—that is, he has followed Cain, the first criminal, in murdering his brother. Cain is referred to several times in the play—e.g., in 1.2.105 and 5.1.76—reminding us of the King's heinous offence.

Hamlet repeatedly compares his father and King Claudius. Although he is surprised when the Ghost tells him of the murder, he is not surprised, a few lines later, to learn the killer's identity, for his 'prophetic soul' (1.5.41) has already apprehended his uncle's character. Earlier, in his first soliloquy, he despises the King as an inferior successor to his father, 'so excellent a king, that was to this / [as] Hyperion [is] to a satyr' (1.2.139–140). He elaborates on this comparison when he upbraids his mother in 3.4.

In 1.1 an ideal of kingship is established in recollections of the heroic achievements of Hamlet's father and in the sense of dread occasioned by his death; the implicit contrast with Claudius persists throughout the play, as we become aware that the King's crime is the source of the evil that permeates the play's world, the 'something . . . rotten in the state of Denmark' (1.4.90). In a telling detail, the King is closely associated with excessive drinking, presented as a characteristically Danish failing. He

often proposes toasts, the rowdy behaviour of his court is noted, and Hamlet finds it likely that he would be 'distempered . . . With drink' (3.2.293–294) or 'drunk asleep' (3.3.89). Appropriately, Claudius finally falls victim to his own poisoned wine.

Despite the King's distinctly evil nature, he does have some redeeming features. In fact, some commentators believe that the playwright intended King Claudius as an admirable ruler and man and that Hamlet's contrary opinion is a result of his tragic insanity. Most critics, however, find the King's wicked nature abundantly evident; his good features exemplify Shakespeare's genius for providing fully human portraits. The King is clearly intelligent and quick-witted, particularly in 4.5.112–152, where he defuses the coup by LAERTES with smooth talk and converts the rebel into an accomplice. In 1.2, as he disposes of court business, we see that he is a reasonable man, a competent diplomat, and a generally able monarch. The King even reveals, however fleetingly, his bad conscience about his crimes when he compares his 'deed to [his] painted word' (3.1.49–54) and when he tries to pray in 3.3. However, as he recognises, 'Words without thoughts never to heaven go' (3.3.98), and, unable to repent sincerely, he continues in his evil ways.

Beginning with his recruitment of ROSENCRANTZ AND GUILDENSTERN to spy on Hamlet, the King schemes cruelly against the prince. His two death plots—to have him executed in England and to arrange a rigged fencing match—are particularly vile. The King recruits Laertes after Hamlet escapes from England, but when, at the climax, his follower repents and seeks the prince's forgiveness, the King is left as the sole focus of our sense of evil in the play. When Hamlet kills him, he cries, 'Here, thou incestuous, murd'rous, damned Dane' (5.2.330); his villainy is emphatically described and condemned. HORATIO leaves us with a final summary of the King's role when he refers to his 'carnal, bloody, and unnatural acts' (5.2.386).

Shakespeare may have named Claudius, or the name may have come from his source, the UR-HAMLET, but in either case the King was named for a Roman emperor, Claudius I (10 B.C.–54 A.D.), who was regarded in Shakespeare's day as a prime example of an evil ruler. (His modern reputation is considerably better, in part because of Robert Graves' novel *I, Claudius* [1934].) Upon his accession to the throne in 41 A.D., Claudius married his niece Agrippina, an incestuous relationship that may have influenced the choice of names. Agrippina later poisoned Claudius and was herself murdered by her son, Nero, as Hamlet recollects in 3.2.384–385.

**King (6) Cymbeline of Britain** Character in *Cymbeline.* See CYMBELINE.

**King (7) Duncan of Scotland**  Character in *Macbeth*. See DUNCAN.

**King (8) Edward IV of England**  Character in *3 Henry VI* and *Richard III*. See EDWARD IV.

**King (9) Henry IV of England**  Title character of *1* and *2 Henry IV*. See HENRY IV.

**King (10) Henry V of England**  Title character of *Henry V*. See HENRY V.

**King (11) Henry VI of England**  Title character of *1, 2,* and *3 Henry VI*. See HENRY VI.

**King (12) Henry VIII of England**  Title character of *Henry VIII*. See HENRY VIII.

**King (13) John of England**  Title character of *King John*. See JOHN (3).

**King (14) Lear of Britain**  Title character of *King Lear*. See LEAR.

**King (15) Leontes of Sicilia**  Character in *The Winter's Tale*. See LEONTES.

**King (16) Lewis (Louis XI) of France**  Character in *3 Henry VI*. See LEWIS (3).

**King (17) of France**  Character in *All's Well That Ends Well*, the ruler of FRANCE (1). The dying King recovers his health through the ministrations of HELENA (2). He rewards her with marriage to the unwilling BERTRAM. Bertram's disdain for a commoner sparks the King's most important speech, a lecture on the value of individual virtues over social rank (2.3.117–141), a trenchant summary of one of the play's important themes. In 5.3 he forgives Bertram's flight from Helena, but he then presides over the exposure of the young man's perfidy towards DIANA (1) and his justice is as stern as his forgiveness had been yielding. When Helena finally unravels the plot and the final reconciliation takes place, the King behaves with great magnanimity, granting a dowry to Diana and offering a final statement that, although qualified, insists on the traditional happy ending of COMEDY: 'All yet seems well, and if it end so meet, / The bitter past, more welcome is the sweet' (5.3.327–328).

With the COUNTESS (2) and Lord LAFEW, the King helps provide an atmosphere of generosity and wisdom that offsets the play's unpleasant aspects. His gracious welcome of Bertram in 1.2 stimulates in the audience a sense that the young man, despite his faults, is basically worthy. Similarly, his immediate appreciation of Helena in 2.1 helps to establish her virtue. The King is himself a wholly sympathetic figure, a stereotypically 'good' ruler: wise and moderate in deciding not to go to war while still permitting his young noblemen to distinguish themselves on campaign in Italy; touching in his nostalgic remembrance of Bertram's father; and generous in friendship and forgiveness to the young people.

**King (18) of France**  Character in *King Lear*. See FRANCE (2).

**King (19) Ferdinand of Navarre**  Character in *Love's Labour's Lost*, the ruler whose decision to make 'a little academe' (1.1.13) of his court leads to the action of the play. Although opposed by the sardonic humour of BEROWNE, the King bans all mirth, banqueting, and even the company of women in order to promote disinterested study. The King's humourless desire to make of his courtiers 'brave conquerors . . . / That war against your own affections / And the huge army of the world's desires' (1.1.8–10) is focussed on an abstract idea, not a love of scholarship, and is therefore vain. This self-centred seriousness is overcome by love as the play develops. The King himself succumbs to the charms of the PRINCESS (1) of France, and when, at the close of the play, she requires that he prove his love with a year of monastic life, he willingly assumes the task, asserting, 'My heart is in thy breast' (5.2.808).

**King (20) Philip Augustus of France**  Character in *King John*. See PHILIP (2).

**King (21) Polixenes of Bohemia**  Character in *The Winter's Tale*. See POLIXENES.

**King (22) Priam of Troy**  Character in *Troilus and Cressida*. See PRIAM.

**King (23) Richard II of England**  Title character of *Richard II*. See RICHARD II.

**King (24) Richard III of England**  Title character in *Richard III*. See RICHARD III.

**King (25) Simonides of Pentapolis**  Character in *Pericles*. See SIMONIDES.

**King (26), Tom (1730–1804)**  English actor, famous as TOUCHSTONE and MALVOLIO. King, one of the most popular members of the acting company run by David GARRICK, played comic roles exclusively, both in Shakespeare and 18th-century works. In the 1770s he managed the SADLER'S WELLS THEATRE. King was very successful and made a great deal of money in the theatre, but he was addicted to gambling and died in poverty.

## *King John*

### SYNOPSIS

*Note:* Act and scene numbers in *King John* vary significantly from edition to edition. Traditionally editions since THEOBALD's (1726) have altered the FOLIO's scene divisions in Acts 2 and 3; some modern editions revert to the Folio's arrangement, while others do not. In this volume citations to *King John* follow the New Arden edition, which uses the Folio designations. Where there is a difference from the traditional citation, the latter is given in parentheses.

*Act 1, Scene 1*
King JOHN (3) and his mother, Queen ELEANOR, receive a French ambassador, CHATILLON, who delivers a demand from King PHILIP (2) of FRANCE (1): John must relinquish the crown of England to his young nephew ARTHUR. John replies defiantly that he will invade France, and Chatillon departs. Eleanor supports John's decision, implying that, since his rule is illegal, it must be maintained through force. ROBERT Faulconbridge and his older brother, the BASTARD (1), enter and ask the king to judge a dispute: Robert claims their father's estate, asserting that his brother is illegitimate, having been sired by the late King Richard I. Eleanor and John recognise the strong resemblance of the Bastard to the late king, and they like his bold and saucy manner. They offer him a knighthood if he will leave the Faulconbridge estate to his brother and go to war in France with them. He accepts, and, after the others have left to prepare for the campaign, he soliloquises humorously on the manners of the courtly world he is about to enter. His mother, LADY (5) Faulconbridge, arrives, having followed her sons to court to defend her honour. However, when the Bastard tells her he has renounced his inheritance in favour of greater glories, she admits that King Richard was indeed his father. He revels in his newly discovered patrimony.

*Act 2, Scene 1*
Outside ANGIERS, an English-occupied city in France, King Philip, his son LEWIS (1), and Arthur greet the Archduke of AUSTRIA, who has agreed to fight in support of Arthur's claim to the English crown. Austria is thanked effusively by Arthur and his mother, CONSTANCE. Chatillon appears with news that an English army, led by John, is approaching. John and his entourage enter, and Philip questions John's legitimacy, noting that Arthur is the son of John's older brother and thus the proper heir. John simply denies Philip's right to judge the matter, and the two parties trade insults. A CITIZEN (4) of Angiers appears on the city walls and states that the city will admit neither ruler until it can be ascertained which one represents the true King of England. The two armies skirmish, but HUBERT, speaking for Angiers, reiterates the city's refusal to open its gates. The Bastard suggests that the two parties ally temporarily and conquer the recalcitrant town. As they prepare to do so, Hubert proposes a peaceful settlement: Lewis can marry John's niece BLANCHE of Spain, uniting the two parties. Lewis and Blanche are agreeable, and a treaty is concluded. John grants many of the English territories in France to Philip, and Philip implicitly recognises John's legitimacy in return. Arthur is to be given high rank and the rule of Angiers. Everyone enters the town to prepare for the wedding except the Bastard, who muses in a soliloquy on the dishonour that the kings have incurred, John for giving away much of his kingdom to secure the rest, Philip for having abandoned an allegedly sacred cause. He rails against 'commodity', or self-interest, but then confesses that he does so only because he has not yet had the opportunity to pursue it himself.

*Act 2, Scene 2 (Act 3, Scene 1)*
The Earl of SALISBURY (4) brings word to Constance and Arthur of the settlement between France and England. Constance rants wildly against Salisbury for bringing the news, against Philip for abandoning Arthur's cause, and against fortune for favouring King John.

*Act 3, Scene 1 (Act 3, Scene 1 continued)*
The wedding party appears, and Constance resumes her cursing. A papal legate, Cardinal PANDULPH, arrives with a demand from Rome that King John surrender to the pope's authority in a dispute over the archbishopric of Canterbury. John flatly refuses. Pandulph excommunicates him and insists that Philip abandon his new alliance with England and make war on John—or face excommunication himself. When Philip hesitates, Pandulph delivers an equivocal argument justifying the breaking of an oath. Philip rejects the alliance with John, and the two parties prepare for war.

*Act 3, Scene 2*
The armies skirmish. Resting from the battle, the Bastard displays the severed head of Austria. John arrives with the captive Arthur, whom the king turns over to Hubert, now allied with the English.

*Act 3, Scene 2 continued (Act 3, Scene 3)*
After further skirmishing, John and the Bastard enter, accompanied by Arthur, Hubert, and Eleanor. John sends the Bastard back to England with orders to loot the monasteries there. Eleanor takes Arthur aside to comfort him, while John speaks with Hubert. After flattering him and speaking of future rewards, the king

hints that he has a secret desire. Hubert offers to fulfil it, whatever it may be. John observes that Arthur is a potential problem to him, and he speaks the single word 'death'. Hubert responds that Arthur shall die, and John expresses his satisfaction.

### Act 3, Scene 3 (Act 3, Scene 4)

Philip and Lewis discuss the English victory with Pandulph. Constance appears, mad with grief at her son's capture. When she leaves, Philip follows her, fearing that she may harm herself. Pandulph tells Lewis not to lose heart and suggests a plan: John will surely kill Arthur and thus alienate his own followers, and Lewis, as Blanche's husband—she being Arthur's cousin— may claim the throne. Moreover, Pandulph urges, the Bastard's ransacking of the monasteries will also antagonise the English so that a French invasion will be welcomed by rebels in England. Pandulph and Lewis go to present this plan to King Philip.

### Act 4, Scene 1

Hubert prepares hot irons to put out Arthur's eyes. Hubert summons Arthur, who says that the only comfort he has had in his imprisonment has been the affection of Hubert. The older man, in asides, reveals his torment, but he nevertheless tells Arthur that he must put out his eyes. Arthur pleads for mercy. Hubert relents, but he insists that Arthur's death must be feigned to protect himself, Hubert, from the king's anger.

### Act 4, Scene 2

PEMBROKE (5) and Salisbury tell John that many nobles are dismayed that Arthur is kept imprisoned, and they urge him to free his nephew. He agrees, as Hubert arrives to confer with the king. The two noblemen remark that they know Hubert was assigned to kill Arthur. When John announces that Hubert has brought word of Arthur's death, they are not surprised, and they leave angrily. News arrives that the French have invaded and that Queen Eleanor has died. The Bastard appears and reports that the country is inflamed over Arthur's reported murder. John sends him to summon the disaffected nobles; in view of the invasion, he must attempt to win back their allegiance. Hubert returns and tells of superstitious fears among the populace. John blames Hubert for killing Arthur, claiming that he had not ordered him to do so. Hubert confesses that Arthur is not in fact dead, and John, relieved, tells him to carry this news to the rebellious lords.

### Act 4, Scene 3

Arthur attempts to escape by leaping off the castle wall, but he dies from the fall. Pembroke, Salisbury, and Lord BIGOT pass by, discussing their plan to join the French invaders, who have offered them an alliance. The Bastard accosts the noblemen with the king's request that they join him. They refuse. Discovering Arthur's body, they rage with increased venom, vowing revenge on John. Hubert enters, claiming that Arthur lives; when shown the body, he is shocked, but the lords do not believe him. They depart, intent on joining Lewis' army.

### Act 5, Scene 1

King John yields his crown to Pandulph and receives it back again, thus acknowledgeing the pope as the source of his authority. In return, Pandulph promises to persuade the French to leave England. The Bastard arrives with news of French successes and of Arthur's death. He rebukes the king for inaction. John explains that he has Pandulph's promise to rely on, and the Bastard is mortified, first that a papal alliance has been formed and second that no military response to France has been prepared. John tells him to make such arrangements himself.

### Act 5, Scene 2

In the French camp, the dissident nobles seal their alliance with Lewis. Salisbury weeps, lamenting the necessity to fight against his own countrymen. Pandulph appears and reports John's reconciliation with the pope, but Lewis refuses to halt his onslaught. The Bastard arrives under a flag of truce and is informed of Lewis' intransigence; he responds with a challenge to continued war. The two sides prepare for battle.

### Act 5, Scene 3

During the battle Hubert reports to King John that his armies are losing. John admits that he is sick, with fever and at heart. A message from the Bastard requests that the king leave the battlefield. John replies that he shall go to SWINSTEAD ABBEY. The MESSENGER (8) adds that French reinforcements have been lost at sea and that their army has retired to defensive positions. John is too ill to respond to this good news, and he departs for Swinstead.

### Act 5, Scene 4

A French nobleman, Lord MELUN, mortally wounded and conscience-stricken, tells the rebellious English lords of Lewis' plan to have them executed once John is defeated. Salisbury replies for the group that they will rejoin King John.

### Act 5, Scene 5

Lewis receives news of Melun's death, the disaffection of the English lords, and the wreck of his supply ships. He prepares for hard fighting the next day.

### Act 5, Scene 6

In the middle of the night Hubert encounters the Bastard and informs him that King John has been poisoned and is dying. The Bastard, whose own forces have been badly damaged by the storm, hastens to rejoin the king.

### Act 5, Scene 7

John, burning with fever and aware that he is near death, is brought to his son Prince HENRY (1). The Bastard arrives with news of the war, but the king dies as he speaks. Salisbury tells the Bastard that Lewis has made offers of peace and has already begun to return his forces to France. The nobles acknowledge Henry as the new king, and the Bastard delivers a patriotic speech, observing that, now that its internal disputes are over, England will once again be invulnerable to invasion.

### COMMENTARY

Aside from the very late and uncharacteristic play *Henry VIII*, *King John* is the only one of Shakespeare's HISTORY PLAYS that is not part of a TETRALOGY. Further, its narrative is not linked to the others, which together cover an unbroken 87-year period in English history, but rather deals with a much earlier and more obscure era. Thus *King John* has been somewhat neglected, being viewed as a minor and transitional work between the two tetralogies. However, its subject matter is basically the same—the disruption of English public life by dynastic disputes—and its moral weight is as great as that of most of the other histories. Moreover, it is especially closely linked to the contemporary concerns of the playwright's own time.

One of the issues that Shakespeare's history plays most persistently raised is the nature of good government. In *King John* the playwright impresses us with the need for a sound political ethic by presenting a near-catastrophe that stems from ethical weakness. In *Richard III* a melodramatic villain had generated the problem, and his supernaturally aided defeat at BOSWORTH FIELD had solved it. In this more intellectual work Shakespeare examines political realities and problems that require compromises, not heaven-sent intervention.

The chief political concern in the frequently disrupted monarchy of medieval and early modern England was that of the legitimacy of the ruler, and this is the play's primary focus. Shakespeare felt no compunctions about taking liberties with historical reality, and *King John* is one of his least accurate history plays. Besides using such minor anachronisms as John's threat to use cannon in 1.1.26 (gunpowder did not come into use in Europe until the HUNDRED YEARS WAR, about 150 years later), he simply rewrote the main lines of John's reign. Compressing the events of 17 years into a single brief sequence, the playwright juxtaposes conflicts that were in fact widely separated in time. John's defence of his right to rule against the partisans of Arthur occupied the first few years of his reign and was completed by 1203, when Arthur was killed. Arthur's death is the central event of the play, but it simply closed the earliest epoch of John's actual reign. In the play the death stimulates the rebellious barons to oppose John and join the invading French. But historically the barons' revolt occurred 10 years after Arthur's death and had nothing to do with it; murder was, after all, an ordinary political event in medieval times. Further, the French invasion came only after the barons' revolt had been settled by the signing of the Magna Charta in 1215 and then resumed in the following year.

The most important issue of John's reign, at the time and to Shakespeare's contemporaries, was John's dispute with Pope Innocent III. However, the playwright lessened its importance and interwove it with the other two conflicts, Arthur's claim and the barons' revolt. In fact, John's dispute with Innocent III began several years after Arthur's death, and it ended before the barons rebelled. The king surrendered to the pope—permitting Pandulph to recrown him, as in the play—precisely because he was concerned about the barons, and Pandulph was in fact John's ally against them. As depicted by Shakespeare, Pandulph's opposition to John revives Arthur's claims, which had been rejected by the marriage treaty of 2.1; the papal legate then stirs up a French invasion in anticipation of Arthur's death; and he finally proves incapable of ending the war in return for John's surrender to papal authority. All of this is flagrantly unhistorical; as always, Shakespeare was less concerned with history than with dramatic effect, and he made John's usurpation of the crown from Arthur the dominant issue in the play in support of his all-important theme, political legitimacy.

Shakespeare's John, then, is an illegitimate ruler, and illegitimacy is a recurring motif in the play. Most prominently, the Bastard raises the issue of illegitimate birth, in speech and in person; significantly, he proves nobler in his steadfast loyalty than all of the other characters, whose treachery and dishonour exemplify illegitimacy in a broader sense: illegitimate actions in terms of the courtly code that all of the aristocrats profess. The Bastard is seen as England's saving grace: he maintains the English resistance, and English honour, when John has succumbed to his moral crisis. Most important, the Bastard gives expression to the value of legitimate succession when he leads the nobles in patriotic support of Henry III in 5.7. It is clear that positive results have come from loyalty to John—that is, that this usurper has his own legitimacy.

The issue of legitimacy was not only an historical one: Queen ELIZABETH (1) faced similar political problems to a lesser degree. She was conceived outside marriage, as was well known, and Rome did not recognise her legitimacy, either in birth or as a ruler. Similarly, Innocent III had declared John an illegitimate King against whom revolt was lawful, as Pandulph affirms in 3.1.100–101 (3.1.174–175). Further, on several occasions conspiracies against Elizabeth's life were discovered, and the Earl of ESSEX (2) actually attempted rebellion towards the end of her reign. Advocates of Mary, Queen of Scots, compared her claim against Elizabeth with Arthur's claim against John; their voices were not silenced until Mary was executed. TUDOR monarchs were aware of their own dynastic roots in rebellion (as is enacted in *Richard III*), and they incorporated a new doctrine in their laws, declaring that the holder of the crown is not only in fact the wielder of power, he or she is also the proper ruler in law, despite the legitimacy of any other claim. This is the implicit principle on which the Bastard bases his loyalty to John. John makes the same claim for himself—'Doth not the crown of England prove the king?' (2.1.273)—and the play reinforces it through remarks such as Eleanor's acknowledgement that 'strong possession much more than . . . right' (1.1.40) must secure his throne, and through the analogy that the Bastard's possession of the Faulconbridge estates is sufficient evidence of right, even in the face of a legal bequest (1.1.126–133). Further, Arthur is presented as not only a tool of France, but—inaccurately—as a mere child, clearly unsuited to be king. John's legitimacy, like Elizabeth's, must be continuously reaffirmed.

Parallels between John and Elizabeth abound in the play, and Shakespeare's original audience will have recognised them immediately. Pandulph's excommunication of John (3.1.99) [3.1.173] is plainly a reference to the excommunication of Elizabeth in 1570. His promise, four lines later, of canonisation to an assassin of John was an inflammatory glance at fairly current events: in 1589 Henri III of France had been murdered by a monk who contended that the King was soft on Protestantism; the assassin's canonisation was publicly sought by Catholic groups in France, to the shock and revulsion of Protestants (and some Catholics) throughout Europe. It was widely believed in England that a similar bounty was offered in the case of Elizabeth, and Pandulph's words must have evoked patriotic horror. The conflict between Reformation and Counter-Reformation in the 16th century inspired Protestants to think of John as a predecessor who attempted to rebel against the power of Rome, and they made much of his notorious—but fictitious—poisoning at the hands of a monk. Shakespeare's Pandulph is a stereotype of the malevolent Catholic of fearful Protestant imaginations; John's insulting address to him (3.1.73–86) [3.1.147–160] is an example of 16th-century rhetoric, reflecting the attitudes of Shakespeare's England, not of John's.

Shakespeare is often regarded as sympathetic to Catholicism, and although *King John* would seem to douse that speculation thoroughly at first glance, the religious issue is nevertheless far less prominent in the play than it was in the actual historical period or in the playwright's sources. Although strong public interest would certainly have justified a strong presentation of the struggle between Rome and England, Shakespeare refrained. *King John* is primarily a play about a usurpation that did not in fact occur, rather than about the religious conflict that did. To Shakespeare, the religious question is less important than the issue of political legitimacy.

Readers today are often puzzled to find that *King John* makes no mention of what today seems the most salient feature of John's reign, the signing of the Magna Charta in 1215. However, in Shakespeare's day, when the aristocracy was definitely subordinate to the crown, John's concessions to his fractious noblemen seemed unimportant. Our own conception of the Magna Charta as the wellspring of democratic freedom from royal control was not formulated until shortly after Shakespeare's death. Opponents of King Charles I, seeking legal precedents to cite in their struggle, discovered that King John had made concessions, 400 years earlier, that could be said to establish the principle that a ruler was obliged to consult his subjects. This interpretation helped fuel a dispute that led to civil war in 1642. However, the charter signed by John was rather reactionary, restoring to the barons certain feudal rights that the central government was absorbing and would absorb again, especially under the Tudors. The political establishment of Shakespeare's day, intent on preserving its own relatively unrestricted power, certainly had no use for the Magna Charta, and Shakespeare, a supporter of a strong central government, shared this attitude.

*King John* is sometimes thought of as a failure, with an episodic, undirected plot and confused characterizations, but these seeming defects are actually purposeful techniques. The play's ambiguities and contradictions illustrate the dangers of an unreliable political world, and this is the principal point of the play. The course of the action continually varies, with the vagaries of fortune constantly before us. The characters change their natures repeatedly: John is variously a patriotic hero, resisting France and Rome; a villain, murdering Arthur; a traitor, surrendering his authority to the pope; and a simple failure, collapsing into pathetic uselessness in the face of a crisis. The Bastard first appears as a satirical baiter of aristocratic society, but he becomes the noblest of the Englishmen at the end. Hubert is first a cagey Angevin diplomat caught between big powers, then a sycophantic courtier prepared to murder a child to gain favour with the king, and finally a sorrowing penitent. Our point of view changes repeatedly, our sympathies are continually shifting, and we are drawn into the play as if into an intrigue. Such ambiguity is appropriate for a study of political confusion and uncertainty.

## SOURCES OF THE PLAY

It has traditionally been assumed that Shakespeare adapted another play, THE TROUBLESOME RAIGNE OF KING JOHN, in writing *King John*, but the proposition that the former play was derived from Shakespeare's work has gained ground in recent years. In any case, the principal source for whichever play came first was Raphael HOLINSHED's *Chronicles of England, Scotland, and Ireland* (2nd ed., 1587). Shakespeare also referred to John FOXE's *Book of Martyrs* (probably in the 4th ed., 1583), and he took various details from other sources as well. For instance, from the *Chronica Majora*, a Latin history by Matthew Paris (d. 1259), Shakespeare reworked the Bastard's account of his losses in a storm (5.6.39–42, 5.7.61–64) and elements of Salisbury's lament in 5.2. Also, Shakespeare probably knew the popular romances concerning Richard Coeur-de-Lion, from which he may have taken the erroneous identification of Austria with Limoges. His attitudes towards John and his reign may have been influenced by further reading, perhaps including the *Annals* of John STOW, in which John is taken to task as a usurper.

## TEXT OF THE PLAY

The date of *King John*'s composition is difficult to determine, if *The Troublesome Raigne of King John* was Shakespeare's source for the play. *The Troublesome Raigne* was published in 1591, and *King John* had been performed by 1598, for it appears in the list of Shakespeare's works that Francis MERES compiled then. Every year between those dates has been proposed for the writing of the play. Stylistically, it is generally thought to fall between the two major tetralogies—that is, in the first half of the 1590s.

If *The Troublesome Raigne* was derived from Shakespeare's play, however, then the date of *King John* must be 1590 or 1591: *King John* contains a reference (1.1.244) to a character in a popular play of 1590, *Soliman and Perseda* (probably by Thomas KYD). A dating of 1590 for *King John* is also supported by the play's frequent allusions to the Spanish Armada (1588)—more than in any other work by Shakespeare—suggesting that it was written soon after the attempted invasion.

*King John* was first published in the FIRST FOLIO edition of the plays (1623), and that text has been the basis of all subsequent editions. It is thought that the Folio was printed either from Shakespeare's FOUL PAPERS, probably slightly emended by the Folio editors, or from a PROMPT-BOOK, perhaps one that Shakespeare himself had revised.

## THEATRICAL HISTORY OF THE PLAY

Numerous early 17th-century references to *King John* testify to the play's popularity at that time, but no production of it is known before a revival in 1737. In 1745 Colley CIBBER (1) staged an adaptation emphasising the French invasion, attempting to capitalise on the patriotism stimulated by the defeat of the Jacobite Rebellion in that year. However, Shakespeare's play, starring David GARRICK as John, was produced at the same time, and the Cibber play folded immediately. *King John* was staged several times in colonial America, beginning with a Philadelphia production in 1768. In London in 1803, during the Napoleonic Wars, another adaptation stressing French iniquities appeared. It was wildly popular and played for years throughout Great Britain. Charles KEMBLE's 1823 production of *King John*, designed by J. R. PLANCHE, inaugurated the 19th-century Shakespearean tradition of striving for historical accuracy in costumes and stagings. Kemble's example was followed in William Charles MACREADY's successful production of 1842 and elaborate versions were staged in New York (1846) and London (1852) by Charles KEAN (1).

A great favourite in times of British national crisis, when the Bastard's patriotic speeches have proved inspiring, *King John* has been staged a number of times in the 20th century. In 1945, Peter BROOK (2) directed a striking production featuring Paul SCOFIELD as the Bastard. The play has been produced for television twice, in 1951 (with Donald Wolfit as King John) and in 1984 as part of the BBC's inclusive Shakespearean cycles. Although *King John* has not been made as a movie, excerpts from Beerbohm TREE's 1899 stage production of the play were recorded, when cinema was still experimental, in the earliest appearance of Shakespeare on film.

## *King Lear*

### SYNOPSIS

*Act 1, Scene 1*

The Earl of GLOUCESTER (1) introduces his illegitimate son EDMUND to the Earl of KENT (2) and observes that he has a legitimate son as well. King LEAR arrives with his daughters, GONERIL, REGAN, and CORDELIA, and explains his intention to abdicate and distribute Britain among his sons-in-law, the Dukes of ALBANY and CORNWALL—married to Goneril and Regan, respectively—and either the Duke of BURGUNDY (1) or the King of FRANCE (2), suitors of Cordelia. He will give the largest share of the kingdom to whichever daughter can convince him she loves him the most. Goneril and Regan declare their love effusively, but Cordelia simply states that her love is that of a daughter to a father, and that she will also love her husband when she has one. Infuriated, Lear disinherits her; Kent attempts to dissuade him, and Lear banishes him. Burgundy rejects the disinherited Cordelia, but France decides to marry her and take her back to France. Regan and Goneril confer on the need to control their obviously senile father lest he turn against them.

*Act 1, Scene 2*
Edmund bewails his illegitimacy and decides to steal his brother EDGAR's inheritance with the help of the letter he holds. Gloucester enters, and Edmund pretends to hide the letter, but his father insists upon reading it. It is supposedly from Edgar, proposing to Edmund that they murder Gloucester. Edmund pretends to believe the letter is merely a test of his morals, and he offers to arrange for Gloucester to overhear a conversation between the half brothers. Gloucester agrees and leaves; Edmund remarks on his naïveté. Edgar appears, and Edmund tells him that their father is viciously angry with him, warning him to go armed lest he be attacked.

*Act 1, Scene 3*
Goneril desires to humble her father and instructs her steward OSWALD to treat Lear and his followers disdainfully when they arrive.

*Act 1, Scene 4*
Kent, disguised, plans to rejoin the king's court at Goneril's castle. Lear arrives with his followers, and Kent is accepted among them. Oswald is surly to the king, and, to Lear's delight, Kent rails against him, knocks him down, and drives him away. Lear's FOOL (2) mocks the king for having surrendered his authority. Goneril appears and scolds Lear for the conduct of his men. She demands that he halve their number, and he declares that he will leave and go to Regan. He departs. Albany protests over Goneril's behaviour, but she silences him and sends Oswald with a letter to Regan that details her tactics with their father.

*Act 1, Scene 5*
Lear sends Kent with a letter to Regan. The Fool again taunts the king for being at the mercy of his daughters.

*Act 2, Scene 1*
Edmund encounters Edgar and advises him to flee for his life. As Gloucester approaches, Edmund tricks Edgar by saying that he must pretend to prevent Edgar's flight but that he will actually help him escape. He draws his sword and fakes a fight, hustling Edgar away. He then tells Gloucester that Edgar had assaulted him when he opposed the murder plot. Gloucester declares he will have Edgar captured and executed, and he vows to legitimate Edmund. Cornwall and Regan arrive on a visit to Gloucester; they praise Edmund and take him into their service.

*Act 2, Scene 2*
Outside Gloucester's castle, Kent insults and pummels Oswald as Edmund, Cornwall, Regan, and Gloucester appear. Asked to explain his behaviour, Kent declares that Oswald is a hypocrite. Cornwall places Kent in the stocks despite his status as messenger of the king. Gloucester protests but is ignored. When the others leave, Kent muses on a letter he has received from Cordelia, who has learned of Lear's humiliation.

*Act 2, Scene 3*
Edgar has escaped from a search party and overheard a proclamation that he is outlawed. He decides to disguise himself as a wandering lunatic, taking the name Tom O' Bedlam.

*Act 2, Scene 4*
Lear, seeking Regan, arrives at Gloucester's castle and finds Kent in the stocks. The Fool calls Kent a fool for attaching himself to a powerless master. Gloucester reports that Regan and Cornwall will not receive Lear, who begins to rage but restrains himself. Regan and Cornwall appear and Kent is freed. Regan defends Goneril against Lear's complaints as Goneril arrives. The two unite in demanding that Lear dismiss his retinue. The distressed Lear wavers between tears and anger and rages out into a storm that has arisen, followed by Gloucester and the Fool.

*Act 3, Scene 1*
Kent meets a GENTLEMAN (7) who reports that Lear is raging madly in the storm, accompanied only by the Fool. Kent asks him to report Lear's situation to Cordelia, who has arrived in DOVER with a French army.

*Act 3, Scene 2*
Lear raves in the storm, cursing his daughters. Kent appears and urges the king to take shelter in a nearby hovel. The Fool bitterly predicts disruption for England, whatever lies in store.

*Act 3, Scene 3*
Gloucester tells Edmund that Cornwall, his feudal lord, has forbidden him to take Lear in. He confides, however, that he has received a letter assuring that Lear's revenge is at hand in the form of the French invasion. Edmund decides to inform on his father so he can get his inheritance sooner.

*Act 3, Scene 4*
Lear, Kent, and the Fool approach the hovel. Lear declares that he prefers the storm to the thoughts he would have if he were sheltered, but he sends the Fool inside. He reflects on the woes of the poor and homeless, whom he had never considered when he ruled. The Fool reappears, terrified of a madman in the hovel. He is followed by Edgar, disguised as Tom O' Bedlam, who raves about being pursued by devils.

Lear sympathises with him, assuming that he too has been betrayed by his daughters. Edgar asserts that his demons are punishment for certain offences: he had been a decadent and immoral servant who slept with his mistress, among other sins. Gloucester appears and offers them shelter. He confides to Kent that Lear's daughters seek the king's death.

*Act 3, Scene 5*
Edmund has revealed Gloucester's correspondence with the French army, and Cornwall orders him to have his father arrested.

*Act 3, Scene 6*
Gloucester leaves Kent, Lear, the Fool, and Edgar in a warm room. Lear acts out a criminal trial of Goneril and Regan and finally falls asleep just as Gloucester returns and warns them to flee immediately. Kent and the Fool leave, carrying the sleeping Lear. Edgar, left behind, reflects that his own fate does not seem so bad compared with that of the mad king.

*Act 3, Scene 7*
Gloucester, under arrest, is brought before Cornwall and Regan. When he says that he will see them punished by fate, Cornwall puts out his eyes. The duke is attacked by a SERVANT (19), who cannot abide such evil. Cornwall kills the Servant, but not before being badly wounded. Regan takes him away, and the remaining Servants agree to take the blinded Gloucester to the wandering madman, who can help him safely escape.

*Act 4, Scene 1*
An OLD MAN (2) leads the blind Gloucester to Edgar, who grieves to see his father in such condition. However, still an outcast, he resumes his madman's disguise. He agrees to lead Gloucester to the cliffs of Dover.

*Act 4, Scene 2*
Oswald meets Goneril and Edmund and tells them that Albany has learned of Cordelia's invasion, which pleases him, and that Edmund has informed on Gloucester, which does not. Goneril sends Edmund with a message to Cornwall to hastily muster an army; they exchange loving farewells, accompanied by hints of a murder plot against Albany. Albany appears and berates Goneril for her evil; she replies that he is merely a coward. A MESSENGER (20) arrives with news of Cornwall's death and Gloucester's blinding. In an aside, Goneril worries that Regan has possible designs on Edmund, now that she is a widow. Albany vows privately to revenge Gloucester.

*Act 4, Scene 3*
In Dover the Gentleman tells Kent of Cordelia's tearful response to news of Lear. Kent replies that Lear is in Dover but refuses to see Cordelia, out of shame.

*Act 4, Scene 4*
Cordelia hears that Lear has been seen wandering wearing a crown of weeds and flowers, and she orders a search party. The DOCTOR (2) assures her that Lear's madness may be eased by rest, and that sedatives are available. News arrives that the armies of Albany and Cornwall are approaching.

*Act 4, Scene 5*
Oswald reports to Regan that Goneril has convinced Albany to fight against Cordelia's invasion. He also has a letter from Goneril to Edmund, which sparks Regan's jealousy; she gives Oswald a token from herself to give Edmund with Goneril's letter. She adds that if Oswald finds and kills Gloucester, he will be rewarded.

*Act 4, Scene 6*
Edgar convinces Gloucester that they have reached the top of the cliffs at Dover and then pretends to leave him. In an aside to himself he says that he must humour his father's despair in order to cure it. Gloucester leaps forward and falls to the ground. Edgar then pretends to be a passer-by at the bottom of the cliff and says that he had seen Gloucester at the top with a hideous demon. Gloucester accepts the idea that the gods have miraculously preserved him from an evil impulse, and he vows to accept his affliction in the future. Lear appears, covered with wildflowers and raving madly. A Gentleman with a search party arrives and takes Lear to Cordelia. Edgar learns from him the location of the British army. Oswald appears and attacks Gloucester, but Edgar kills him. As he dies, Oswald asks his killer to deliver his letters to Edmund. Edgar reads a letter from Goneril proposing that Edmund murder Albany and marry her.

*Act 4, Scene 7*
Cordelia greets her father, but Lear mistakes her for a spirit and only gradually realises that he is still alive. The Doctor says that he needs more rest, and he is taken indoors, leaving Kent and the Gentleman to discuss the coming battle. Kent declares that his life will end that day.

*Act 5, Scene 1*
Jealously, Regan interrogates Edmund about Goneril, and Goneril says to herself that she would rather lose the battle than see Regan get Edmund. Edgar appears in disguise, and takes Albany aside. He gives him the letter he got from Oswald. He proposes that after the battle Albany call for a challenger to prove in trial by combat that its contents are true. In a soliloquy Edmund reflects that Albany's leadership will be needed during the battle, but that he hopes Goneril will then see to killing him. He observes that Albany has proposed mercy for Lear and Cordelia, but he, Edmund, will not permit it.

*Act 5, Scene 2*

Edgar leaves Gloucester and goes to fight. Fleeing soldiers pass by, and Edgar returns, saying that Cordelia's forces have been routed and she and Lear captured. Gloucester fatalistically elects to stay, but he recovers when reminded of his resolution to endure, and the two flee together.

*Act 5, Scene 3*

Edmund sends the captured Lear and Cordelia to prison. Lear rejoices at being with Cordelia, despite the circumstances. Edmund sends an OFFICER (5) after them, telling him to carry out his written instructions mercilessly. Albany arrives with Regan and Goneril. He arrests Edmund and Goneril for treason, asserting that a challenger will appear to back the charge in trial by combat. Regan departs, suddenly sick. Edgar appears, unrecognisable in full armour, and he and Edmund fight until he wounds Edmund badly. Albany displays the letter, and Goneril departs hastily. The dying Edmund confesses his crimes. Edgar identifies himself and tells of escorting Gloucester, adding that when he finally told his father who he was the emotional shock killed the old man. An hysterical GENTLEMAN (8) reports that Goneril has confessed to poisoning Regan, and then committed suicide. Edmund reveals that he has ordered someone to kill the king and hang Cordelia in her cell, an apparent suicide. Edmund is carried away and a soldier is sent to halt the killer, but Lear appears carrying the dead Cordelia in his arms. He mourns her death, but at intervals believes she may be still alive. He sees Kent but cannot recognise or understand him; the others realise that he is mad again. Edmund's death is reported, and Albany declares that he will return Lear's kingdom to him. Lear suddenly announces that he sees Cordelia breathing, and as he does so, he dies. Albany orders funeral preparations and appoints Kent and Edgar to be his associates in rule, though Kent says that he will

*A scene from an early 20th-century* King Lear. *Lear (Robert Bruce Mantell) disinherits Cordelia, saying, 'Nothing will come of nothing'* (1.1.89). (Courtesy of Culver Pictures, Inc.)

soon die. Edgar closes the play with the assertion that such woes as Lear's shall not be seen again.

## COMMENTARY

As was his habit, Shakespeare altered his sources considerably when he wrote *King Lear,* and his most important alteration changed the nature of the story entirely. In the many versions of the tale that preceded Shakespeare's, Lear does not go mad, but recovers his throne and leaves it to Cordelia. The old story is essentially reassuring: one may make a catastrophic mistake and still survive to live a peaceful and happy life. Shakespeare plainly felt that life makes more strenuous demands than a happy ending can illustrate, and at the core of his story is human failing. Gloucester's blindness is foreshadowed in his lack of judgement about Edgar, and Lear's madness by his egotistical demand for total love. These failings are seen in conjunction with the unscrupulous ambition for power represented by Edmund, Cornwall, Goneril, and Regan, and we are repelled by crimes within families, violations of the most basic human solidarity. Our horror is compounded by the vivid depiction of villainy triumphant, which is only slightly lessened by the villains' deaths, as these are more than matched by those of Gloucester, Lear, and Cordelia. Edmund's remorse at the play's close does little to compensate for his evil, and Regan and Goneril display no final repentance at all. Our pity for Lear and Gloucester is increased by the knowledge that they brought their sufferings on themselves.

The enormity of the tragedy is unmistakable, and the play leaves us with a troubling question: How can we reconcile human dignity with human failure in the face of life's demands? This is finally unresolvable; however, several possible ways of addressing the question emerge through Shakespeare's rich presentation of human tragedy.

Perhaps most striking is the play's obvious religious interpretation, emphasised by numerous allusions to religious matters. These range from the trivial—as in the many mentions of pagan gods—to serious remarks such as Edgar's 'The Gods are just, and of our pleasant vices / Make instruments to plague us' (5.3.169–170). Also, numerous references to the end of the world are made, most strikingly in the cries of Kent, Edgar, and Albany at the horror of Cordelia's death, in 5.3.262–263. Most significantly, Cordelia, who suffers through no fault of her own and accepts her fate with uncomplaining fortitude and undiminished love, is often seen as a personification of the Christian virtues of self-sacrifice and acceptance of God's will. In fact, many commentators have found her to be a Christlike figure whose death symbolises Christ's crucifixion. This offers a positive interpretation of the play's fatal close: the tragedy is a manifestation of God's will, a reminder of the coming redemption of humanity through Christianity. On the other hand, a non-Christian interpretation of Cordelia's sacrifice is also compelling. She lacks the Christian's reward in the afterlife because she is a pagan, thus her virtue is its own reward. Her conduct is therefore all the more stirring, and our admiration of her heroic courage is increased.

The sufferings of Lear and Gloucester, which they have brought upon themselves, may be compared to punishment for sins by God. They recognise that they are at fault and are then reconciled with their children, and this development suggests God's forgiveness for those who are contrite. Their forgiveness is accompanied by death, and this points up the doctrinal importance of the Christian afterlife and its eternal mercy. However, this promise is lacking in Lear's pagan world and, as with Cordelia, a non-religious interpretation could be that Lear's endurance is heroic in itself, and his triumph lies in his recognition and acceptance of his failings before he dies. Most commentators agree, in any case, that the suffering of the characters in *Lear* is finally redemptive, for it is heroic, it leads to heightened consciousness in Lear and Gloucester, and it provides the example of Edgar and Cordelia's undiminished loyalty and love. Also, many commentators hold that Shakespeare intended Lear to die believing that Cordelia is alive, as his last words indicate, which implies a happy resolution in death akin to that of Gloucester, whose heart 'burst smilingly' (5.3.198).

Another positive conclusion can be drawn from the tragedy. Politics are as important in *King Lear* as religion. In fact, in Shakespeare's time, the references to the end of the world carried a political implication, for people commonly believed that the world's end was more or less imminent, and that one of the symptoms of approaching apocalypse would be a collapse of social structures, including political bonds. Much reassurance was found in the peaceful assession of King JAMES I—civil war was feared at the time—with its promise for the unification of England and Scotland. The threat of civil war, several times alluded to in *Lear,* raises a point that was important to Shakespeare, and which dominates the HISTORY PLAYS, the belief that personal immorality in the ruling class is a disease that spreads evil throughout society, in extreme cases causing it to fall apart. Though Lear, Gloucester, and Cordelia do not live to appreciate it, Britain at large is rescued from the evil that has overrun the highest reaches of its society; civil war in Britain is avoided, and the French invasion caused by Lear's lack of judgement is defeated by Albany. The play is thus supportive of civil authority; the catastrophe of Lear's reign might be compared, by the 17th-century playgoer, with the strength and harmony expected from that of James. It is worth noting that in 1606 *Lear* was performed at James' court on a very festive occasion, the day following Christmas.

Another point addressed in *King Lear* is that a sovereign is responsible for his subjects. Raving madly in the storm, Lear realises that he had been unaware of hunger and homelessness when he was king, and he sees that his present experience could have been valuable to him as a ruler. He says to himself: 'Take physic, Pomp; / Expose thyself to feel what wretches feel, / That thou mayst shake the superflux to them, / And show the Heavens more just' (3.4.33–36). Lear recognises that his errors are more important than others' because he is a king.

A more particular social question is also addressed in *King Lear*. In Shakespeare's day, the newly prosperous gentry and the commercially active bourgeoisie were rising in prosperity and power, largely at the expense of the old aristocracy. This conflict is plainly the cause of the extraordinary venom displayed by Kent towards Oswald in 2.2. Oswald is a caricature of a 17th-century social climber, as Kent's accusation, phrased largely in terms of social status, makes clear. Edmund also represents the new classes, with his lack of chivalric scruples and his concern for his own advancement. In his first soliloquy Edmund identifies himself with a typical modern rejection of tradition by declaring, 'Thou, Nature, art my goddess' (1.2.1), a reference to the RENAISSANCE rediscovery of classical paganism and the sophisticated agnosticism that was thought to accompany it. In placing these sentiments in the mouth of a self-declared villain, Shakespeare stresses his alliance with the old world of the aristocracy, just as he does in ridiculing Oswald through Kent.

However, though *King Lear* may lend itself to numerous interpretations, Christian or humanistic, political or moral, our response to the play is largely governed by its conclusion. Act 5 brings no relief for our anguish, despite the expectations raised by the reunion of Lear and Cordelia. The finality of death may suggest that the play reflects a morbidly depressed response to life on Shakespeare's part (without denying that other plays express other responses). Such a viewpoint has led some to compare *Lear* to the Book of Job and see the play as an explication of the power of fate, or God. However, both Edgar and Albany survive to carry on, conscious of the fragility of happiness and on guard against the errors of Lear and Gloucester, for as Edgar (Albany, in some editions) says, 'The weight of this sad time we must obey' (5.3.322).

The extraordinary woe that is at the heart of *King Lear* can make it a harrowing experience for audiences. Shakespeare maintains this atmosphere of wretched despair through a variety of subtle effects. Most striking perhaps is the repeated depiction of pain and disease, capped by Lear's madness and Gloucester's blinding, but also represented by Edmund's self-mutilation in 2.1, Edgar's feigned lunacy, and Lear's convulsion of the throat known as 'Hysteria passio' (2.4.55), among other instances. Further, painful metaphors of torment and sickness are extensively used. For instance, the Fool compares the rejected Lear to a bird that 'had it[s] head bit off' (1.4.214); Edgar speaks vividly of self-mutilation, in 2.3.14–16; and Lear speaks of his daughters' rejection as a 'mouth . . . tear[ing a] hand' (3.4.15). In a famous image, Gloucester compares humanity's relationship to the gods with that of 'flies to wanton boys . . . They kill us for their sport' (4.1.36–37).

Another aspect of the theme of disease is the play's morbid attitude towards sex. In *King Lear* sexual love is seen as evil and is only presented in the monstrous rivalry of Regan and Goneril for Edmund. It is also seen as the source of other evils. The misdeeds of Lear's daughters are firmly connected by Lear to the sexual acts from which they were conceived, and Edgar points out that Edmund was the product of illicit sex. Also, in his disguise as Tom O'Bedlam, Edgar declares that intercourse, 'the act of darkness' (3.4.85), is responsible for his painful madness. Lear goes so far as to condemn human procreation, demanding that the gods 'Crack Nature's moulds, all germens spill at once / That makes ingrateful man!' (3.2.8–9). In the extreme, the raving Lear links female sexual anatomy with evil, saying, 'there's hell, there's darkness, / There is the sulphurous pit—burning, scalding, / Stench, consumption; fie, fie, fie!' (4.6.126–128). This incrimination of a natural drive is an indication of the troubled world in *King Lear* and of the disturbed minds of its inhabitants. Happiness is only offered in the isolated and asexual world of the reunited but imprisoned Lear and Cordelia, where all other human contact is willingly forsworn; the exhausted king declares that 'Upon such sacrifices . . . / The Gods themselves throw incense' (5.3.20–21).

The play's treatment of psychological distortion is well served by its disjointed and varying tone. This is largely provided by its complex SUB-PLOT, whose differing elements include Gloucester's blinding, Edgar's exile as mad Tom, and Regan and Goneril's sexual rivalry. The intercutting of these developments with Lear's story was once much criticised; early 19th-century commentators such as Charles LAMB (1) declared that *Lear* was a bad play in theatrical terms, while acknowledgeing its power as poetry. This was long a traditionally accepted idea, influencing 20th-century critics to elaborately consider the plot's 'failings', despite the play's unquestionable success with modern audiences.

The sub-plot actually anchors the play's dramatic structure. The wanderings of Edgar and Gloucester are presented in sequential incidents, as are the machinations of Edmund and the cruel sisters. Together, they provide a well-defined structure that the main plot—Lear's foolish choice and subsequent isola-

tion—does not offer. Indeed, the principal action can hardly be called a plot at all; it is simply a progression, taking the central character from vanity and folly through deepening madness to a recovered consciousness and ultimate collapse. As we watch this progression, we do not think about the next step in the plot so much as we simply observe Lear's personal qualities and contemplate their evolution. The *events* of Lear's progress are less important and are not presented in a structured way, unlike, for example, in *Julius Caesar,* but are indicated by discrete and almost unconnected subsidiary developments.

The play also offers disconcerting suggestions of comedy that complicate our response and thus increase its emotional power. In *King Lear* Shakespeare employed a number of elements traditionally associated with comedy: a double plot; the use of a jester to comment on the action; the use of disguise; the progression of the action from royal court to country and back to court; and the counterpoint of youth and age. Moreover, Kent's ridicule of Oswald, a number of Edgar's remarks as Tom O'Bedlam, and the Fool's routines are all quite funny. These elements suggest the potential for a different sort of story altogether, not a simple tale of evil triumphant.

*King Lear* is complex also in its repeated emotional polarities. We are presented with oppositions of weeping and laughing, silence and speech, honesty and guile, madness and intelligence, delusion and clear-sightedness, love and hate. Cordelia's frankness and spirituality is contrasted with the deceit and lasciviousness of her sisters; Kent's moral firmness with Oswald's self-serving oiliness and his strength with Lear's weakness; the merciful Albany with the cruel Cornwall. Individual characters present contrasts, as well, though the playwright is careful to motivate each change so as not to dilute a character's strength as a representative figure. Kent, for instance, announces that he will 'other accents borrow / That can my speech defuse' (1.4.1–2), and he adopts a plain-spoken prose and only reverts to verse when he cannot be heard by Lear or when he expresses his love and concern for his demented master, as in 3.2.42–49, 60–67. Edgar similarly effects prose as Tom O'Bedlam but speaks poetry as himself, and the hypocritical sisters use verse to flatter their father and prose to plot against him. *Lear*'s great range of characters stimulates our strong awareness of the play as a philosophical statement about the human condition.

## SOURCES OF THE PLAY

The main plot of *King Lear* was well known in Shakespeare's day—at least 40 versions have been uncovered by scholars—but it is clear that the playwright relied chiefly on an earlier, anonymous play, KING LEIR (c. 1590). This work contains the general story of Lear's relations with his daughters, though at the

play's close King Leir is restored to his throne and Cordelia lives. Some scholars think Shakespeare may have acted in *King Leir* in the 1590s, playing a character corresponding to Kent, for a number of passages that are especially closely echoed in *Lear* are spoken when that figure is on-stage.

Shakespeare also knew the story from an account in Raphael HOLINSHED's *Chronicles of England, Scotland, and Ireland* (2nd ed., 1587), which inspired several passages. Holinshed's account of Lear is based on the work of a medieval historian, GEOFFREY of Monmouth. Details of Gloucester's attempted suicide were probably inspired by another story in Holinshed, that of a giant who was thrown to his death from the cliffs of Dover. John HIGGINS' version of the tale in A MIRROR FOR MAGISTRATES (1587) provided Shakespeare with a number of significant details, including France's praise of Cordelia's virtues. Other details can be ascribed to a variety of sources, most notably Edmund SPENSER's *The Faerie Queene* (1589), Ben JONSON's *Sejanus* (1605), Gerard LEGH's *Accedens of Armory* (1562), and, possibly, William CAMDEN's *Remaines* (1605).

Shakespeare found the sub-plot involving Gloucester, Edmund, and Edgar in a tale from Sir Philip SIDNEY's *Arcadia* (1590), about a king who is betrayed by one son and saved by another. It may also have influenced the main plot, for Sidney's tragic hero is not restored to his former glory, like King Leir, but dies of mingled joy and exhaustion, like Shakespeare's Gloucester. Also, Sidney's king is driven out into a storm, like Lear, and lives as a beggar, like Edgar. Another anecdote in *Arcadia* may have influenced Edmund's plot to disgrace Edgar, and a poem in *Arcadia* is a meditation on suicide that is echoed in several passages of the play.

Two other works contributed to the play's themes, though not to the actual plot: Samuel HARSNETT's *A Declaration of Egregious Popish Impostures* (1603), which provided the lore of demons for Edgar's assumed lunacy, and John FLORIO's English translation of the *Essays* of Michel de MONTAIGNE (1603), whose scepticism influenced Edmund's disdain for the conventional attitude towards illegitimacy, as well as his unscrupulous attitude towards morals. It is also possible that a contemporary case of insanity resembling Lear's (see Brian ANNESLEY) may have sparked Shakespeare's imagination, for in no earlier version of the tale is the king mad.

## TEXT OF THE PLAY

*King Lear* was written between the spring of 1603 and early 1606, for one of the play's sources—Samuel Harsnett's book—was published in March 1603, and a play that was influenced by *Lear*—*The Fleir,* by Edward SHARPHAM—was registered for publication in May 1606. A more precise date is difficult to determine; some passages in the play seem to offer clues, but no agreement can be reached. Similarly, relationships between *Lear* and other works published between 1603 and 1606 are generally problematic, as it is impossible to tell which is in debt to which.

The play was first published in 1608 by Nathaniel BUTTER in a QUARTO edition known as Q1. Twelve copies of Q1 exist, but they encompass 10 slightly different texts, since proof-reading and correction were carried on simultaneously with printing. Q1 is sometimes called the 'Pied Bull Quarto' because its title page refers to Butter's shop 'at the signe of the Pide Bull'. Q1 is a BAD QUARTO, assembled from the recollections of spectators or of actors who had performed in the play, but scholars differ in their conclusions about who these reporters were and whether or not they had access to a manuscript. It is a poor text with many errors, little punctuation, missing or inadequate stage directions, and many passages of verse set as prose and vice versa. A second quarto (Q2), printed from a copy of Q1, was dated 1608 and attributed to Butter, but it was actually produced in 1619 as part of the pirated FALSE FOLIO.

*King Lear* appears in the FIRST FOLIO (1623), and this version (F) is a far better text than Q1, incorporating many corrections, including amplified stage directions. Most significantly, it is a radically altered script. More than 300 lines of dialogue from Q1 are omitted in F—including a number of significant passages—and about 100 lines are added, including Lear's final lines (5.3.309–310).

It is generally believed that the omissions from Q1 reflect shortening made for performances sometime between 1608 and 1623, and that the additions are Shakespeare's, made before he retired around 1613. Scholars are divided on the form in which the printers of the Folio received the alterations, but the most widely accepted theory is that F was printed from a copy of Q1 that had been heavily annotated with amendments and references from the PROMPT-BOOK used by the KING'S MEN. However, a recently popular theory holds that the Folio text represents a re-writing of the play by Shakespeare, from which it follows that there exist two different *King Lear*s, each distinctive in tone and emphasis. One new edition of Shakespeare's works, that of Oxford University Press (1986), prints them as such, though most editors have combined the two in a single text that omits nothing of consequence while relying on F, the superior text, where the two conflict.

## THEATRICAL HISTORY

The earliest known performance of *King Lear* is recorded in the publisher's registration of the play, which asserts that it was performed at the court of King JAMES I on December 26, 1606. Scholars believe that the play was not well received in Shakespeare's day, for there are few surviving references to it in contemporary documents. However, it is known that Richard Burbage (3) was the original Lear.

After the 1660 reopening of the English theatres—they had been closed during the Puritan Revolution—*Lear* was staged only twice, in 1660 (by William DAVENANT) and 1675. It was replaced in 1681 by an adaptation, Nahum TATE's *History of King Lear.* Tate's *Lear* retained much Shakespearean dialogue, but amid vast changes in plot, including a happy ending in which Lear is restored to his throne. Thomas BETTERTON played Lear for Tate. Though modern commentators condemn this version as a travesty, it was one of the most successful plays in the history of the English theatre, continuing to be staged—with Shakespeare's text sometimes restored in varying degrees—until as late as 1843 (and occasionally in modern times as an historical curiosity).

The restoration of Shakespeare's text began with David GARRICK's production of 1742, and the process was furthered by George COLMAN (though he also added his own alterations) in 1768. In the late 18th and early 19th centuries the play was suppressed by the government, which disliked its focus on a mad monarch at a time when King George III was insane. It reappeared in 1809 in a version by John Philip KEMBLE (3) that restored most of Tate's text. Edmund KEAN (2), under the influence of the critics Charles LAMB (1) and William HAZLITT, restored Lear's death in his production of 1823, though the text was still largely Tate's. Not until 1838 were Tate's words completely removed in Charles William MACREADY's production, though Gloucester's travails were still omitted. It remained for Samuel PHELPS to produce a genuinely Shakespearean version in 1845. Edwin BOOTH (2) played Lear with Tate's text early in his career, but by 1876 he was presenting Shakespeare's play. No subsequent production reverted to Tate, but considerable editing of the original text remained common; Henry IRVING, for instance, cut more than half the play in his presentation of 1892 that starred himself and Ellen TERRY (1).

In the 20th century *King Lear* has been extremely popular. Most leading actors have played Lear; among the most notable have been Robert Bruce MANTELL early in the century; John GIELGUD and Donald WOLFIT in the 1940s; Michael REDGRAVE, Orson WELLES, and Charles LAUGHTON in the 1950s; Paul SCOFIELD, especially in a famed 1962 staging by Peter BROOK (2); and James Earl JONES (1) in Joseph PAPP's production of 1973. The role of Cordelia has similarly attracted leading actresses, among them Peggy ASHCROFT and Zoë CALDWELL. *Lear* has been presented on FILM eight times; the two most famous, by Brook and the Russian Grigori KOZINTSEV, were made simultaneously as the two directors, shooting in Denmark and Russia respectively, corresponded, comparing notes on their projects (1969). The play has been made for TELEVI-

SION five times. Also, Akira KUROSAWA's *Ran* (1985) is based on *Lear*. The play has also inspired six operas—though only one, by Aribert Reimann (1978), has entered the general operatic repertoire—and at least one well-known orchestral work, the *King Lear Overture* by Hector BERLIOZ (1831).

**King Leir**  Anonymous play of c. 1588 (publ. 1605) that influenced Shakespeare's version of the same tale, *King Lear*. The earlier play presents the general lines of the king's misjudgement of his daughters and characters who are equivalent to KENT, ALBANY, and OSWALD. Also, many minor details from it are echoed in Shakespeare's play. However, at the play's close Cordelia lives and King Leir is restored to his throne. The authorship of *King Leir* has been attributed to various playwrights, including Thomas LODGE, George PEELE, Robert GREENE (2), and Thomas KYD, but scholars remain divided on the question.

King Leir—fully titled *The True Chronicle History of King Leir and his three daughters*—is now known only in the edition of 1605, but references in the text suggest that it was written around the time an invasion of England was threatened by the Spanish Armada in 1588. It was registered with the STATIONERS' COMPANY in 1594, but if an edition was published at that time no copy has survived. Some scholars believe that Shakespeare knew the play from the stage and simply recalled the elements he employed in *Lear*. He probably knew the play before 1594, in any case, for several minor details in *Richard III* (c. 1591) can be traced to *King Leir*. In fact, Shakespeare may have acted in *King Leir*, playing the character that corresponds to KENT (2), for a number of passages in the old play that are echoed in *Lear* are spoken while that character is on-stage. It is conceivable that Shakespeare consulted the 1605 edition of *King Leir*, though it appeared only very shortly before *Lear* itself, and it is just as likely that it was republished in order to capitalise on the forthcoming appearance of a new play by Shakespeare.

**Kings**  Minor characters in *Macbeth*, eight ghostly figures who appear to MACBETH, representing future rulers. In 4.1 Macbeth seeks to learn from the WITCHES whether their earlier prediction, that BANQUO would father a line of rulers, is still true. In response, the eight spectral Kings appear in a procession led by Banquo's GHOST (4), who indicates, with a smile and a gesture, that they are indeed his descendants. Macbeth observes that some of the Kings carry 'twofold balls and treble sceptres' (4.1.121). This is a topical reference to the coronation regalia of the newly crowned ruler of England and SCOTLAND in Shakespeare's day, King JAMES I. James was of the STUART dynasty and was believed (though inaccurately) to be descended from Banquo. Moreover, the eight Kings

correspond to the eight Stuart kings, the first of whom was crowned in 1371. (Shakespeare omits the one queen in the line—Mary, Queen of Scots, James' mother—presumably because she had been the enemy of England's Queen ELIZABETH (1) and had been executed by her in 1587.) These allusions were much more obvious to Shakespeare's original audiences than they are today.

Through this episode Macbeth sees that the Witches' earlier prediction is confirmed. He realises that his ambition must remain incompletely satisfied. Thus, figuratively, Macbeth's downfall has begun. The significant message that MACDUFF has abandoned him—the first step in his actual defeat—follows immediately.

**King's Men**  Acting company in which Shakespeare was a partner, the successor to the CHAMBERLAIN'S MEN. When King JAMES I acceded to the throne of England in 1603, the Chamberlain's Men's patron, Lord HUNSDON (1), surrendered his position to the new king, an enthusiast of the stage. The number of performances at court was much higher for the troupe under James—an average of twelve times a year in Shakespeare's lifetime, versus four during the reign of Queen ELIZABETH (1)—and after 1608, the King's Men had a new winter home, the BLACKFRIARS THEATRE, with a different, more sophisticated audience. Under these influences, a new sort of play evolved and JACOBEAN DRAMA emerged, led by the King's Men.

At the time of the change of patron, the partners in the company were Shakespeare, Robert ARMIN, Richard BURBAGE (3), Henry CONDELL, Richard COWLEY, John HEMINGE, Augustine PHILLIPS, and William SLY (2). Joining them was Laurence FLETCHER (3), a member of the king's household. Fletcher had a theatrical background but seems not to have been an active participant in the King's Men. By 1605 three more members were added, probably Alexander COOKE (1), Samuel CROSSE, and John LOWIN. In 1619 the company's royal patent was renewed, and its members were named in a surviving official document. Only Burbage, Heminge, and Condell remained of the original eight; the other nine partners listed were Lowin, Nathan FIELD (1), John UNDERWOOD, Nicholas TOOLEY, William ECCLESTONE, Robert BENFIELD, Robert GOUGH, Richard ROBINSON (4), and John SHANK. Burbage died in the same month and was replaced by Joseph TAYLOR. The company's business manager was Heminge until his death in 1630, after which it was run by Lowin and Taylor.

The King's Men performed at the GLOBE THEATRE in the summer and, after 1608, at the Blackfriars in the winter. The company was universally regarded as England's best. Their many appearances at court were a measure of their prestige; especially noteworthy is the fact that they performed 20 plays—eight of them

Shakespeare's—during the weeks-long celebration of the marriage of the Princess ELIZABETH (3) in 1613. The King's Men's principal playwrights were Shakespeare and later John FLETCHER (2)—often in collaboration with Francis BEAUMONT (2)—and Philip MASSINGER. The King's Men also staged works by other dramatists, including Ben JONSON and John WEBSTER (2).

**King's Revels** See CHILDREN'S COMPANIES.

**Kirkham, Edward (active 1586–1617)** English theatrical entrepreneur. Kirkham was a subordinate to the MASTER OF THE REVELS and was therefore involved in the regulation of ELIZABETHAN THEATRE. He also invested in the profession. Between 1603 and 1608 he was a partner of Henry EVANS (2) in the productions of the Children of the Queen's Revels (see CHILDREN'S COMPANIES) at the BLACKFRIARS THEATRE, which Evans leased from Richard BURBAGE (3), Shakespeare's associate in the KING'S MEN. When the boys' company lost its royal patronage in 1608, Evans relinquished his lease on the Blackfriars to Burbage, who thereupon sold shares in the theatre to a number of people, including Shakespeare and a relative of Evans. Kirkham was effectively abandoned. He sued Evans, Burbage, and others, in unsuccessful attempts to gain from their profits. Modern scholars find in the records of these suits a number of clues as to the nature of the early 17th-century theatre, including the information that the Blackfriars was much more profitable to the King's Men than was the GLOBE THEATRE.

**Kirkman, Francis (1632–after 1674)** English writer and publisher. In 1662 Kirkman's collection of DROLLS—the brief dramas performed illicitly when the English theatres were closed in 1642–1660—was published by Henry MARSH, his business partner, as *The Wits: or Sport upon Sport*. Kirkman himself published a second edition in 1672 and a supplementary volume in 1673. He also compiled and published a *Catalogue of English Stage Plays*, which listed 690 dramas in its first edition (1661) and added 116 more in the second (1671). Kirkman also published an edition of THE BIRTH OF MERLIN (1662), which he attributed to Shakespeare and William ROWLEY (2). He translated and published romantic tales from French and Spanish and wrote several of his own, as well as at least one play.

**Kittredge, George Lyman (1860–1941)** American scholar. Kittredge, a longtime professor at Harvard University (1888–1936), was a respected authority on both Shakespeare and CHAUCER. He is best known as a teacher who influenced generations of students to a greater appreciation of English literature in general and Shakespeare's plays in particular. He also edited

an edition of Shakespeare's *Complete Works* (1936) and wrote books on Shakespeare, Chaucer, and other subjects ranging from *Sir Thomas Malory* (1925) to *Witchcraft in Old and New England* (1929).

**Knell, William (d. 1587)** English actor, a member of the QUEEN'S MEN (1). Knell is known to have played Prince Hal in THE FAMOUS VICTORIES, but his significance rests on his place in a theory about Shakespeare's early years. Knell was killed in a fight while the Queen's Men were playing in STRATFORD in June 1587, and some scholars speculate that the young Shakespeare was hired to replace him and accompanied the troupe to LONDON, thus beginning his theatrical career. This intriguing hypothesis is entirely unprovable, but Knell has nonetheless found a niche in literary history. His widow married John HEMINGE.

**Knight (1)** Minor character in *King Lear*, a follower of King LEAR. In 1.4 the Knight is sent by Lear to summon OSWALD, steward to the king's ungrateful daughter GONERIL. He returns to report that Oswald insolently refuses to come, and he goes on to remark that 'your Highness is not entertain'd with that ceremonious affection as you were wont' (1.4.56–57). This is a summary of the main plot so far: Goneril and her sister REGAN are purposefully humiliating the king. The Knight also mentions CORDELIA, the virtuous daughter whom Lear had rejected in 1.1, and reminds us that the king's plight lies in his own foolishness. Thus the Knight serves to mark the plot's development just before it intensifies with Lear's expulsion into the wilderness in the next scene.

**Knight (2)** Any of several minor characters in *Pericles*, jousters who compete with PERICLES for the hand of THAISA. In 2.2 five Knights—along with Pericles—are presented to Thaisa and her father, King SIMONIDES, and Thaisa describes their elaborate coats of arms. None of them speak. In 2.3 at the banquet that follows, one of the Knights—designated as the First Knight—offers brief courtly remarks to Pericles and the king. In 2.5 each of three Knights—First, Second, and Third—speaks a single line as they leave Simonides' court, having been told that Thaisa refuses to marry. The Knights are required for the jousting, and they add to the ceremony of Simonides' court, but they do not have individual character attributes.

**Knight (3)** Any of three minor characters in *The Two Noble Kinsmen*, companions of PALAMON. The Knights have agreed to serve as seconds to Palamon in his duel with ARCITE over the love of EMILIA (4). The rules of the combat, established by Duke THESEUS (2), require that the loser and his escorts be executed, while the winner gets Emilia. In 5.4 Palamon has lost, and his Knights prepare gallantly to die with him, uttering brave mottos such as, 'Let us bid farewell, / And with our patience anger tottering fortune' (5.4.19–20). They typify the chivalric ethos that the play depicts.

**Knight (4), Edward (active 1623–1633)** Book-keeper for the KING'S MEN. As the book-keeper for Shakespeare's theatre company, Knight was responsible for maintaining the PROMPT-BOOK of each play the company performed. He must therefore have known their repertoire quite well, and for this reason some scholars believe he may have done much of the actual editorial work on the FIRST FOLIO edition of Shakespeare's plays. Some of the correspondence he carried on with the MASTER OF THE REVELS has survived, and it sheds light on the business side of the theatrical world in Shakespeare's day.

**Knight (5), G. Wilson (1897–1985)** English literary critic. Knight boldly interpreted Shakespeare's plays as mystical poems that express their ideas through the symbolic use of imagery and themes in meaningful configurations. This view has influenced both commentary and theatrical production beginning in the 1930s. He is regarded as one of the most important 20th-century Shakespearean critics, but his emphasis on religion is not always accepted. For example, he saw *King Lear* as similar to the Book of Job and LEAR himself as symbolic of the crucified Christ. His best-known works are *The Wheel of Fire* (1930, 1949), *The Imperial Theme* (1931), *The Shakespearean Tempest* (1932), *The Crown of Life* (1947), and *The Sovereign Flower* (1958).

**Knollys, Sir William (c. 1547–1632)** High official in the court of Queen ELIZABETH (1) and possibly a satirical model for MALVOLIO in *Twelfth Night*. After a successful military career, Knollys succeeded his father, Sir Francis Knollys (c. 1514–1596), as comptroller, and later treasurer, of the royal household, a position analogous to that of steward, the office held by Malvolio in the household of OLIVIA. In the late 1590s Knollys was the subject of amused court gossip as he pursued a much younger woman, Mary FITTON, going so far as to dye his beard—a young man's fashion of the day—perhaps suggesting Malvolio's laughable courtship of Olivia. Fitton, however, had another lover, the Earl of PEMBROKE (3), by whom she became pregnant in 1600, bringing the gossip to a peak at about the time *Twelfth Night* was written. The theory linking Knollys and Malvolio was introduced by Professor Leslie HOTSON; detractors think that Shakespeare would have been unlikely to pillory a man who remained powerful at court throughout the playwright's career, particularly if *Twelfth Night* were written for a courtly occasion, as Hotson also proposed. (For other possible Malvolios, see FFARINGTON; HOBY (2); WILLOUGHBY [1].)

**Komisarjevsky, Theodore (1882–1954)** Russian director. A major figure in the theatre and opera of pre-revolutionary Russia, Komisarjevsky came to Britain in 1919. He is best known in the West for his stagings of Chekhov and for a series of avant-garde Shakespearean productions in STRATFORD in the 1930s. Especially notable were *Macbeth*, played in a severely abstract metallic set (1933), a highly praised *King Lear* (1936), and *The Comedy of Errors*, presented as a COMMEDIA DELL' ARTE play (1939).

**Kozintsev, Grigori (1903–1973)** Russian stage and FILM director. Kozintsev is best known in the West for his films of *Hamlet* (1964) and *King Lear* (1970). During the shooting of the latter, Kozintsev corresponded with Peter BROOK (2), who was simultaneously making his film of the play. Both movies are characterised by the intimacy of the acting and the epic grandeur of their landscapes, interiors, and costumes. Kozintsev also wrote an influential book, *Shakespeare: Time and Conscience* (1967).

**Kurosawa, Akira (b. 1910)** Japanese FILM director, maker of famed adaptations of *Macbeth* and *King Lear*. Kurosawa's *Throne of Blood* (1957) is based on *Macbeth*, and his *Ran* (1985) is derived from *King Lear* (*ran* means 'chaos'). These films are set in medieval Japan, and they employ many aspects of Japanese Noh drama and samurai films, unfamiliar genres in the West. Moreover, Shakespeare's tales are altered considerably (for instance, the children of Kurosawa's LEAR equivalent are male, and his LADY [6] MACBETH has a miscarriage), none of the names are the same, and the language is not at all Shakespearean, even in translation. However, these works are nonetheless powerful evocations of Shakespeare's themes, and unlike virtually all other Shakespearean adaptations, they are regarded as great works of art in their own right by nearly unanimous critical consent.

**Kyd, Thomas (1558–1594)** English playwright, author of an important influence on *Hamlet* and of minor sources for other plays. Some commentators believe that many of Shakespeare's plays were written in part by other playwrights (see, e.g., FLEAY and ROBERTSON) and have attributed passages and scenes in several plays, especially *Hamlet* and *Titus Andronicus*, to Kyd. Modern scholars, however, dispute most such attributions.

With Christopher MARLOWE (1), Kyd was the most important English playwright when Shakespeare began his career, and he was immensely influential on both the younger playwright and on ELIZABETHAN DRAMA in general. With *The Spanish Tragedy* (c. 1588), he virtually invented the REVENGE TRAGEDY, a genre that was to be immensely popular. It and its probable companion-piece, the now-lost play known as the UR-HAMLET, provided the apparent inspiration—as well as many details—for *Hamlet*. *The Spanish Tragedy* was also the source of minor elements of *Titus Andronicus, Richard III,* and *3 Henry VI;* the latter play also owes some details to Kyd's *Soliman and Perseda* (1590).

Kyd, the son of a scribe, was not university-educated, but he attended an excellent secondary school, where Edmund SPENSER was a classmate. He was at least conversant with Latin literature, for SENECA's influence on his work is great (though he would have known the Roman playwright in English translations as well). He was a close friend and probable collaborator of Marlowe, and when Marlowe was prosecuted for 'atheism and immorality' in 1593, Kyd was also arrested. Under torture, he recanted and was released, but he received no patronage thereafter and died in deep poverty.

**Lacy, John (d. 1681)** English actor and playwright, author of an adaptation of *The Taming of the Shrew.* Lacy's *Sauny the Scot* (1667) was a farcical revision in which the comical servant GRUMIO—renamed Sauny— was the principal character. The play was written in prose and set in England. Extremely popular, *Sauny* was revived periodically for a century.

Originally a dancing instructor, Lacy turned to the theatre in the 1660s and achieved fame as a comic actor in Thomas KILLIGREW's company. He was particularly noted for his FALSTAFF, and he played the title role in the original production of *Sauny.* He wrote three other comedies.

**Lady (1)** Either of two minor characters in *Richard II,* attendants of QUEEN (13) Isabel. In 3.4 the Ladies try without success to alleviate the Queen's grief at the fall of King RICHARD II.

**Lady (2)** Any of several minor characters in *Timon of Athens,* presenters of a MASQUE at TIMON's banquet. In 1.2 the Ladies, led by one who is disguised as CUPID, perform a masque and dance with Timon's guests. They present an elaborate aristocratic entertainment that suggests Timon's extravagant life-style. LUCUL-LUS' fatuous remark to Timon that the masque demonstrates 'how ample y'are belov'd' (1.2.126) suggests further that the Ladies are among the many spongers off Timon's hospitality.

**Lady (3)** Any of several minor characters in *Cymbeline,* noblewomen of King CYMBELINE's court. Attendants of IMOGEN or the QUEEN (2), the Ladies serve mostly to signify their mistresses' royal status and to swell the scene at court, though one Lady does offer an amusingly disdainful reception to the boorish Prince CLOTEN in 2.3.76–84, which helps to characterise the play's comic villain.

**Lady (4)** Any of several minor characters in *The Winter's Tale,* ladies-in-waiting to Queen HERMIONE. Two ladies, designated First Lady and Second Lady, join Hermione and her young son, MAMILLIUS, in the playful exchange that opens 2.1. Mamillius teases the ladies about their cosmetics, and they in turn tease the prince about his prospective younger sibling, pointing out that Hermione is quite pregnant. The episode provides a striking contrast with the mad brutality of King LEONTES, whose arrival interrupts these domestic pleasures. When the king appears, one of the ladies escorts Mamillius away, and the others leave with the queen when she is sent to prison. (EMILIA, who appears by name in the prison scene [2.2], is presumably one of these ladies, but here she is anonymous.) Ladies, again nameless, mutely attend Hermione at the hearing in 3.2. The courtly ladies lend a charming atmosphere to Hermione's household, contrasting with the tragic developments that surround them; at the same time they help maintain the regal atmosphere appropriate to TRAGEDY in Shakespeare's literary world.

**Lady (5) Faulconbridge (Falconbridge)** Minor character in *King John,* mother of the BASTARD (1) and ROBERT. Lady Faulconbridge follows her two sons to court, where Robert has claimed that his older brother is the illegitimate son of the late King Richard I. She hopes to preserve her reputation, but when the Bastard tells her that he has renounced his status as a Faulconbridge in favour of royal illegitimacy, she confesses that Richard was indeed his father. Her role serves merely to allow her son's spirit to manifest itself.

**Lady (6) Macbeth (c. 1005–c. 1054)** Historical figure and character in *Macbeth,* the wife of MACBETH. Lady Macbeth shares her husband's lust for power, and her fierce goading in Act 1 leads him to murder King DUNCAN in 2.2 and seize the throne of SCOTLAND. He is reluctant and fears detection. He recognises that the deed is evil, but Lady Macbeth's ferocious will inspires him with the perverse intensity necessary to overcome his scruples. However, the evils unleashed by the murder prove too much for the new queen, and she goes insane. Reduced to sleep-walking and hallucinations in 5.1, she eventually dies, as is reported in 5.5. Her death is declared a suicide in 5.9.

Lady Macbeth's principal importance lies in her ability to influence her husband early in the play when she urges him to murder the king. When she learns of

*Lady Macbeth, one of Shakespeare's grandest creations, is played here by Ellen Terry, one of the most acclaimed of all Shakespearean actresses. (Courtesy of Billy Rose Theatre Collection; New York Public Library at Lincoln Center; Astor, Lenox and Tilden Foundations)*

Duncan's approach to INVERNESS—which offers the opportunity for murder—she fervently prays, 'Come, you Spirits . . . unsex me here, / And fill me, from the crown to the toe, top-full / Of direst cruelty!' (1.5.40–43), and she asks that the milk of her breasts be changed to gall. This speech introduces an important motif: the distortion of sexuality, which is a symbol of moral disorder. She goes on to summon 'the dunnest smoke of Hell' (1.5.51) to obscure her deeds from Heaven's sight. This invocation of supernatural hor-

rors is chilling, and reminds us of the WITCHES, already established as a source of evil.

With hypocritical charm, Lady Macbeth welcomes King Duncan to Inverness in 1.6, after which she must deal with her husband's qualms. She insinuates that he is not an adequate man if he gives in to his fears. 'When you durst do it, then you were a man' (1.7.49), she taunts. This tactic is another instance of dysfunctional sexuality as a manifestation of evil. She goes on to exploit her own sexuality when she describes the experience of nursing a loving infant. She insists that she would have ruthlessly 'plucked my nipple from his boneless gums, / And dash'd the brains out' (1.7.57–58), if it had been necessary to achieve their goal. Shamed by her vigour, Macbeth agrees to proceed, but in 2.2 it is left to her to break the horror-struck trance into which he falls after he murders Duncan and to bring their plan to completion. Her ruthless intensity has brought the throne within reach, and Macbeth is crowned soon thereafter.

Lady Macbeth's viciousness has horrified generations of readers and audiences. However, her grim fervour not only makes her fascinating—the role has consistently attracted major actresses of all periods—but it also illuminates the most important element of the play: Macbeth's relationship to evil. He clearly would not have carried out the regicide, although he had already considered it, without the impetus from her. She, on the other hand, willingly commits herself to evil. The contrast makes clear the potential goodness in Macbeth that he abandons when he kills his king. Lady Macbeth thus functions as a symbol of evil until she falls victim to it herself.

However, Shakespeare's major characters are never one-dimensional, and Lady Macbeth is not a simple cartoon of villainy. She, too, is repelled by the evil inherent in murder, though only subconsciously. She can only refer to the regicide euphemistically—Duncan must be 'provided for' (1.5.66); the killing is 'this enterprise' (1.7.48) or merely 'it' (5.1.34), and she is unable to bring herself to do the deed because Duncan too closely resembles her father. When Macbeth speaks of evil just after he has killed Duncan, she prophetically declares, 'These deeds must not be thought / After these ways: so, it will make us mad' (2.2.32–33). Finally, her anguish in the sleep-walking scene demonstrates convincingly that she simply cannot tolerate her too-hastily accepted immersion in evil. Lady Macbeth's madness, along with her husband's profound emotional malaise, is essential to one of the play's strongest effects. Because we see their dreadful breakdown so vividly, we must acknowledge that they are victims of evil as well as its instruments. Indeed, Lady Macbeth finally commits suicide, as reported in 5.9.36–37.

There may also be another cause for her madness. She and Macbeth are obviously fond of each other, as we see when they first meet in 1.5. Macbeth's letter to her—read in her first speech—makes clear that they have long confided in each other, and that their ambitions are closely shared. Yet when they accomplish their long-sought goal it has an unforeseen consequence for her. Once Duncan has been killed, Lady Macbeth becomes increasingly unimportant to her husband as he begins to undergo the emotional collapse that is the play's principal development. She does not become Macbeth's 'dearest partner of greatness' (1.5.11), as both had anticipated, but is instead excluded from his confidence. He does not inform her of his plan to kill BANQUO, and after her ineffectual attempts to control him when he sees Banquo's GHOST (4), in 3.4, she disappears from the plot. The evil she was so willing to accept betrays her—as it betrays Macbeth—and produces only anguish in place of the rewards she had envisioned. Not only does she lose her husband to his increasingly dead emotional life, she also loses the access to power that had motivated her in the first place. Nothing remains to her and she goes insane. When she stimulates action, in Act 1, Lady Macbeth overflows with vitality; in 5.1 she is reduced to fear of the dark. Though she seemed much stronger than her husband, in the end she lacks the animal strength he uses to bear the aftermath of their deed to its fatal conclusion.

The intimacy between Macbeth and Lady Macbeth combined with the use of perverse sexuality as a symbol of moral disorder has led to a theatrical tradition (dating to the interpretation of Sarah BERNHARDT, in the late 19th century) that presents their relationship as highly charged sexually, and she as a bold flaunter of her sexual charms. However, the play could also suggest sublimated passions whose energies have been displaced onto political ambition. In any case, it is clear that their relationship—however construed—withers in the atmosphere of mistrust and emotional disturbance that is unleashed with Duncan's murder.

The historical Lady Macbeth, whose first name was Gruoch, was the grand-daughter of a Scottish king who was murdered in 1003 A.D., 36 years before the time the play begins. Macbeth was Gruoch's second husband. By her first, a nobleman from northern Scotland, she bore a son, Lulach, whom Shakespeare presumably had in mind when Lady Macbeth remembers nursing a child, in 1.7.54–58. When Macbeth seized the throne, his wife's royal descent doubtless supported his pretensions, though it was not necessary to his claim. There is no evidence at all that she attempted to persuade her husband to make such a claim, nor that she needed to. In fact, Gruoch is very little in evidence at any point in the history of Macbeth's reign, though after his fall her influence may be supposed. Lulach ruled briefly after Macbeth's defeat and death in 1057 before being killed by the triumphant MALCOLM. Since Lulach was known as 'the

Simple', some historians think that his mother engineered his assumption of power. Perhaps her spirit passed down to Lulach's grandson Angus, Lady Macbeth's last known descendant, who attempted unsuccessfully to seize the throne in 1120.

**Lady (7) Macduff**  Character in *Macbeth,* wife of Lord MACDUFF and a victim of MACBETH's hired Murderers (see FIRST MURDERER [3]). In 4.2 Lady Macduff is afraid that her husband's departure for England to join the rebellion against Macbeth has placed her and her children in danger. Rosse attempts to reassure her, but he can only say 'I dare not speak much further: / But cruel are the times . . .' (4.2.17–18). This exchange makes plain the extent to which evil has triumphed in Macbeth's SCOTLAND. Rosse leaves, and the Lady, in her distress, blurts out to her SON (1) that Macduff is dead. He is an intelligent lad who realises that stress has made her say it, and her loving appreciation of his childish wit shines through her distracted grief. This touching moment is interrupted by the MESSENGER (22) who warns them to flee, and the immediate appearance of the Murderers, who kill the Son and chase Lady Macduff out of the room and off the stage. Her death is reported in 4.3.

Though a minor figure, this pathetic character—created only to be unjustly killed—is a striking example of the well-crafted small role of which Shakespeare was a master. In her brief appearance she is vivid enough to contrast powerfully with LADY (6) MACBETH. As a loving mother, domestic life is more important to her than politics, and she is everything in a woman that Lady Macbeth is not. As she is the only other female character (except the WITCHES), the contrast is firmly impressed on us. She also affects us in another way, for her helpless bewilderment is another of the many instances of the nation's disorder. The terror she experiences in her last moments alive constitutes the depths of the play's horror. Her death is an important turning point, for it motivates Macduff, in 4.3, to undertake the fight against Macbeth with a stronger will than politics alone could prompt.

**Lady (8) Catherine Mortimer (active 1403–1409)**
Historical figure and character in *1 Henry IV,* daughter of GLENDOWER and wife of Lord MORTIMER (2). Lady Mortimer speaks only Welsh (with the consequence that her lines are dropped from many productions of the play) and must converse with her husband through the interpretation of her father. Glendower reports that she is upset that her husband is leaving for battle and that she is likely to cry. Through him, she asks her husband to lie in her lap while she sings to him. She sings in Welsh, to the amusement of the fiery HOTSPUR, in an episode that lends humanity to the rebel cause. It is thought that the scene may have been prompted by the presence

of actors from WALES (1) in the CHAMBERLAIN'S MEN, one of whom played Lady Mortimer.

Practically nothing is known of the historical Lady Mortimer. She is thought to have died in London after being taken prisoner when her father was defeated and her husband killed at Harlech in 1409.

**Lady (9) Northumberland (Margaret Neville, d. c. 1400)** Historical figure and character in *2 Henry IV*, the wife of the Earl of NORTHUMBERLAND (1). In 2.3 Lady Northumberland and her daughter-in-law LADY (10) Percy plead with the Earl not to join the rebels against King HENRY IV. He bows to their pressure and flees to Scotland. The incident demonstrates the weakness of Northumberland's allegiance. The historical Lady Northumberland died some time before the period of the play, but Shakespeare revived her in order to create a situation in which family loyalties oppose political ones. She was a sister of the ARCHBISHOP (3) of York, a relationship that Shakespeare ignored.

**Lady (10) Elizabeth Percy (1371–c. 1444)** Historical figure and character in *1* and *2 Henry IV*, wife, and then widow, of HOTSPUR. In 2.3 of *1 Henry IV* Lady Percy is distressed that her husband apparently intends to return to war. She playfully attempts to extract his plans from him, but he teasingly refuses to tell her. In 3.1, just before Hotspur departs for SHREWSBURY, she joins him. He affectionately teases her about her refusal to sing while LADY (8) Mortimer serenades her husband. He finds another target in her mild oath 'in good sooth' (2.3.240), and he fondly scorns her temperance. These episodes reveal that the fiery Hotspur, whose rivalry with PRINCE (6) HAL is the play's major theme, is also a loving husband who has plainly inspired affection in his wife. Hotspur's warm relationship with his wife complements the fierce fixation with battle that otherwise dominates our picture of him. Without these scenes, Hotspur might seem so one-dimensional that we could not accept the favourable opinion of him held by King HENRY IV and Hal. Lady Percy also displays a personality of her own, that of a modest, possibly somewhat stiff, but spirited and pleasant young matron.

In 2.3 of *2 Henry IV* Lady Percy makes a single appearance, joining her mother-in-law, LADY (9) Northumberland, in persuading Lord NORTHUMBERLAND (1) not to rejoin the revolt. Lady Percy bitterly observes that the elderly lord had failed to assist the rebels when Hotspur was still alive, and she goes on to eulogise her late husband glowingly.

Lady Percy's name in Shakespeare's source, HOLINSHED's *Chronicle*, is given inaccurately as Elianor, but Hotspur calls his wife Kate. Shakespeare was decidedly fond of this name—he frequently used it, perhaps most notably for KATHERINA in *The Taming of the Shrew*—and he may have regarded it as an affectionate nickname for a woman, regardless of her real name.

**Lady Elizabeth's Men** Seventeenth-century LONDON theatrical company. Founded in 1611 and named for their patron, Princess ELIZABETH (3), Lady Elizabeth's Men spent a year touring the provinces before coming to London and playing under contract to Philip HENSLOWE. Among the members were William ECCLESTONE, John RICE, and Joseph TAYLOR. They performed at the ROSE, SWAN, and WHITEFRIARS THEATRES. In 1613 they absorbed the Children of the Queen's Revels (see CHILDREN'S COMPANIES) and, with them, Nathan FIELD (1), who became their leader. After two seasons at the HOPE THEATRE, the company sued Henslowe in 1615; some of the records of the case survive and provide a glimpse of the theatre world's business side. Sometime just before or after Henslowe's death in 1616, the company formed an alliance with PRINCE CHARLES' MEN, but Field had already left and soon the company failed, though it seems to have existed in the provinces for several years. In 1622 a new company called Lady Elizabeth's Men was formed by Christopher BEESTON, and it prospered briefly, but it was stricken by plague in the epidemic of 1625 and was not founded again. Princess Elizabeth had long been gone from England, and Beeston replaced Lady Elizabeth's Men with Queen Henrietta's Men, named for the new queen.

**Laertes** Character in *Hamlet*, son of POLONIUS, who seeks vengeance against HAMLET for his father's murder. Laertes is placed in direct contrast with Hamlet by the fact that each seeks and finally achieves revenge for his father's murder, although they do so in very different ways. Laertes is distinctly unheroic. He stoops to fraud and poison with no thought for consequences or morality. Yet at the close of the play he regrets his underhandedness, offers forgiveness in place of vengeance, and is himself forgiven.

Laertes is shallow and immature, as shown by the trite moralising that inspires his insistence in 1.3 that OPHELIA distrust Hamlet's love and by his rhetorical and exaggerated responses to his sister's insanity and death in 5.1. As an avenger, he is easily manipulated in 4.5 by the KING (5), who dissuades him from his rebellion with smooth talk about the divine right of kings. He gives no thought to honour as he accepts with grim glee the King's suggestion of a rigged fencing match, adding the idea of poisoning his sword. Moreover, he is thoughtlessly bold, prepared to sacrifice the peace of the country and his own salvation— 'Conscience and grace, to the profoundest pit! / I dare damnation' (4.5.132–133), he bellows—to satisfy his rage.

Yet in the end Laertes begs to 'exchange forgiveness' (5.2.334) with Hamlet, and he admits that he is 'justly kill'd with mine own treachery' (5.2.313). 'The King—the King's to blame' (5.2.326), he cries, and, as he renounces his revenge, Laertes shifts the moral balance of the play in its last moments, leaving the King as the sole focus of evil. Laertes and Hamlet each kill his father's killer, while each forgives, and is forgiven by, his own killer. Contrasted earlier in the play—in their differing relationships with Ophelia, in Laertes' return to university while Hamlet is detained, in the contrast of a father's 'double blessing' (1.3.53) for Laertes and Hamlet's father's death and reappearance as the GHOST (3)—they come together at its close to represent the conjunction of good and evil in humanity, a fact whose acceptance is the play's major theme.

**Lafew (Lafeu), Lord** Character in *All's Well That Ends Well*, friend of the COUNTESS (2) of ROSSILLION. Lafew is an elderly gentleman who comments on the main action. He also introduces Helena to the KING (17), whom she cures, thereby winning BERTRAM as her husband. Lafew counsels Bertram, the Countess' son, to accept marriage to HELENA (2) and to reject the friendship of PAROLLES, but Bertram ignores him. Lafew is most prominent in 2.3.184–260, where he mercilessly insults Parolles, recognising that the foppish, boastful courtier lacks the nerve to fight. Lafew's temper justifies his name, the French for 'fire'. The episode clinches our recognition that Parolles is a coward and blusterer, though Bertram does not see this until later in the play. In 5.3 Lafew accepts the thoroughly defeated Parolles into his household as a FOOL (1), or jester, a generous gesture that exemplifies the play's spirit of reconciliation. Thus Lafew demonstrates the wisdom to be found in the courtly world of honour and patronage, both by exposing Parolles as a scoundrel and by sympathising with him later. Throughout the play, Lafew, with the Countess and the King, represents a world of wisdom and generosity that stands in contrast to the less pleasant major plot.

**Lamb (1), Charles (1775–1834)** English essayist, best known for his whimsical essays written under the pseudonym Elia. Lamb also wrote commentary on Shakespeare's plays, and with his sister Mary (1764–1847), he compiled prose renditions of the comedies and tragedies in *Tales from Shakespeare* (1807). Lamb's most influential critical work was his *Specimens of English Dramatic Poets who lived about the time of Shakespeare* (1808), which did much to revive interest in ELIZABETHAN DRAMA. He also wrote a notorious essay 'On the Tragedies of Shakespeare' (1811), in which he contended that the plays—especially *King Lear*—were unsuited for performance, though he also insisted that if they were staged, it should be done using Shakespeare's texts rather than adaptations. Lamb wrote essays on contemporary Romantic poetry as well; he

was one of the first critics to recognise the genius of John KEATS, and Samuel Taylor COLERIDGE and William Wordsworth (1770–1850) were close friends. He wrote poetry himself, but neither it nor his fiction is widely read today, whereas *Tales from Shakespeare* and the collected *Essays of Elia* (1823, second series 1833) have continued to be popular.

Lamb's life was stricken by personal tragedy. Mental illness ran in his family; Lamb himself was briefly hospitalised for insanity in his youth and suffered from alcoholism all his life. In 1796 his sister Mary Lamb killed their mother in a fit of temporary madness; Lamb refused to have Mary institutionalised and cared for her the rest of his life.

**Lamb (2), George (1784–1834)** British politician, playwright, and poet, author of an adaptation of *Timon of Athens*. In 1816 Lamb composed an adaptation of Shakespeare's play with the intention of restoring the original text, which was heavily altered in presentations at the time. While Lamb's *Timon* retained some features of its immediate predecessors and failed to restore some omissions, it did employ most of Shakespeare's text. Produced by Edmund KEAN (2), who also took the title role, it was only moderately successful but may have paved the way for the first staging of the complete text, by Samuel PHELPS, a generation later.

Lamb had a varied career. After briefly practising law, he shared in the management of the Drury Lane Theatre in London. He staged two of his own plays— an operetta and a farce—besides *Timon*. He was probably best known for his translation of the poems of Catullus (c. 84–c. 54 B.C.), though both it and his own poetry are generally regarded as mediocre. Introduced into politics by his brother William Lamb, Lord Melbourne (1779–1848), twice prime minister, George Lamb was a member of parliament in 1819–1820 and again from 1826 to his death. He also served briefly as undersecretary of state.

**Lambert, John (active 1587–1602)** Shakespeare's first cousin and opponent in litigation. In 1588 John SHAKESPEARE (9), acting for himself, his wife, and his son William, sued his nephew John Lambert for the return of a piece of property—a house on 56 acres of land near STRATFORD—which Lambert had inherited from his father Edmund (c. 1525–1587), Mary ARDEN (2) Shakespeare's brother-in-law. This property had been mortgaged to Edmund by John Shakespeare in 1578, in return for a loan of £40 to be repaid in two years. The money was never repaid, and Edmund still owned the land at his death. According to the Shakespeares' complaint, John Lambert had agreed to accept £20 in return for clear title to the land, but Lambert denied this and won his case. John and Mary sued again in 1597 on different grounds but again lost. Lambert sold part of the property in 1602. The naming of Shakespeare in the legal papers of 1588 is the only surviving mention of the playwright between the baptism of Hamnet and Judith SHAKESPEARE (5, 10) in Stratford in 1585 and the mocking reference by Robert GREENE (2) to the young LONDON playwright in 1592. This mention has sometimes been thought to indicate that Shakespeare was in residence in Stratford or its environs at the time, but scholars generally agree that his technical involvement in the suit has little significance.

**Lamprius**   Minor character in *Antony and Cleopatra,* an attendant of ENOBARBUS. Lamprius appears only once and does not speak; he is mentioned only in the opening stage direction of 1.2. Like RANNIUS and LUCILLIUS who accompany him, he is a GHOST CHARACTER. Some editors assume that Lamprius is the name of the SOOTHSAYER (2)—the stage direction reads '*Enter* Enobarbus, Lamprius, *a Soothsayer,* Rannius . . .'—though the Soothsayer appears to be an Egyptian in 2.3, and Lamprius is a Roman name. Shakespeare may have found the name in his source, PLUTARCH, who states that his own grandfather was named 'Lampryas'.

**Lancaster (1) Family**   Branch of the PLANTAGENET (1) dynasty, major figures in Shakespeare's HISTORY PLAYS. The Lancastrian kings were descended from John of GAUNT, Duke of Lancaster, the third son of King Edward III (d. 1377). In 1399 Gaunt's son, Henry BOLINGBROKE (1), deposed King RICHARD II and ruled as HENRY IV. He bequeathed the throne to his son, HENRY V, in 1413. These events are dealt with in the major TETRALOGY of history plays, comprising *Richard II, 1* and *2 Henry IV,* and *Henry V.* When Henry V died in 1422, his son, HENRY VI, was an infant. In the absence of a strong monarch, opposition to the illegal deposition of Richard II revived, and the YORK (1) branch of the dynasty successfully pressed its claim to the throne, overthrowing Henry VI in 1461 (he was briefly reinstated in 1470–1471). The rivalry between Lancaster and York, culminating in the WARS OF THE ROSES, is the principal subject of the minor tetralogy, consisting of *1, 2,* and *3 Henry VI* and *Richard III.* The Yorkists were finally defeated in 1485 by the last Lancastrian, the Earl of RICHMOND. This distant cousin of Henry VI, who ruled England as Henry VII, founded the TUDOR dynasty.

**Lancaster (2), John of Gaunt, Duke of**   See GAUNT.

**Lancaster (3), Prince John of (1389–1435)**   Historical figure and character in *1* and *2 Henry IV,* son of King HENRY IV and brother of PRINCE (6) HAL. (The same figure appears in *Henry V* and *1 Henry VI* as the Duke of BEDFORD [1].) In *1 Henry IV* Lancaster first appears in Act 5, at the battle of SHREWSBURY, where his energy and valour are praised by the king and

Prince Hal. He speaks only five lines, but his presence heralds his greater role in *2 Henry IV.* In that play he negotiates a truce with the rebels led by the ARCHBISHOP (3), only to seize the unsuspecting leaders once they have disbanded their troops. This treachery is followed by Lancaster's self-righteous utterance, 'God, and not we, hath safely fought today' (4.2.121). Then, in 5.5, he sanctimoniously praises Hal's rejection, as King HENRY V, of FALSTAFF.

Lancaster is portrayed as an uncompromisingly cold, calculating, humourless man. Falstaff says of him, '. . . this same young sober-blooded boy doth not love me, nor a man cannot make him laugh; but that's no marvel, he drinks no wine' (*2 Henry IV,* 4.3.85–88). He presents an extreme alternative to Falstaff's irresponsibility. But, although Falstaff is a far more attractive character, Shakespeare clearly felt that Hal's course as king must lie closer to Lancaster. Prince John's ruse at GAULTREE FOREST is not disparaged in the play. Such ploys were common in late medieval warfare, and neither Shakespeare's sources nor the playwright himself treat it as particularly heinous when compared to the much greater crime of rebellion against an anointed ruler.

Shakespeare inaccurately depicts the historical Prince John. His presence in *1 Henry IV* is fictional; he was only 13 years old at the time of Shrewsbury, and he does not appear in Shakespeare's sources until several years later. However, in addition to preparing for *2 Henry IV,* Shakespeare wished to bring the LANCASTER (1) family together at a point of crisis. Also, the 16-year-old Lancaster was not responsible for the negotiations at Gaultree; as Shakespeare knew, they were conducted by the Earl of WESTMORELAND (1). The playwright wished to attach this manoeuvre to King Henry's family, thus focussing on the web of treachery and conflict that followed Henry's usurpation of the throne (enacted in *Richard II*). John was not Duke of Lancaster—Hal bore that title, in fact—but Shakespeare's sources were confused on this point, and the playwright doubtless thought he was correct. The historical Prince John was a successful military leader who achieved distinction against the Scots and who was later, as Bedford, to help govern the kingdom when HENRY VI was a minor.

**Lance**   Character in *The Two Gentlemen of Verona.* See LAUNCE.

**Lane (1), John (1590–1640)**   Resident of STRATFORD who was sued for slander by Shakespeare's daughter, Susanna SHAKESPEARE (14) Hall. In June 1613 Lane allegedly declared that Mrs Hall had committed adultery with a local hatter, Raphael Smith (1577–1621). She promptly sued him, and when he failed to appear for the trial on July 15, she was formally declared innocent of any impropriety and he was excommunicated. Lane was apparently a difficult man; he was tried in 1619 for riot and libel after he attacked—presumably by public verbal abuse—the vicar and aldermen of Stratford, and in the same year he was declared a drunkard by the churchwardens. Stratford was a small town, and the Shakespeare and Lane families were acquainted in other contexts. Lane's uncle, Richard LANE (2), was a business partner of Shakespeare's and his first cousin, Thomas NASH (2), later married Susanna's daughter Elizabeth HALL (3).

**Lane (2), Richard (c. 1556–1613)**   Resident of STRATFORD, a business acquaintance of Shakespeare. Lane was a friend of Shakespeare's father, John SHAKESPEARE (9), who chose him in 1599 to help gather depositions in a lawsuit. In 1611 Lane joined William Shakespeare in a complicated lawsuit over tithe holdings (see COMBE [5]). In his will Lane appointed Shakespeare's son-in-law Dr John HALL (4) as trustee for his children, just a few days before Susanna SHAKESPEARE (14) Hall sued his nephew John LANE (1) for libel.

**Laneman (Lanman), Henry (1536–c. 1592)**   English theatrical entrepreneur, owner and probably the founder of the CURTAIN THEATRE. Laneman was the owner of the Curtain during the period 1585–1592, when he and James BURBAGE (2), owner of the neighbouring playhouse, THE THEATRE, agreed to pool the profits of both theatres. In 1581 he was the lessor of the land on which the Curtain stood, and so he is presumed to have built it in 1577. Nothing else is known of him.

**Langbaine, Gerard (1656–1692)**   English scholar and writer, the author of the first account of Shakespeare's sources. Langbaine's *Momus Triumphans, or the Plagiaries of the English Stage exposed* (1687) is a catalogue of the sources used by various Elizabethan and Jacobean playwrights, including Shakespeare. However, his treatment was brief and pedantic and was greatly superseded by the work of Charlotte LENNOX (2) and more modern scholars.

**Langley, Francis (1550–1601)**   Goldsmith and theatrical entrepreneur in LONDON, owner of the SWAN THEATRE. Langley's name is linked with Shakespeare's in a mysterious lawsuit. Langley bought land on the south bank of the Thames near the ROSE THEATRE in 1595 and built the Swan, despite the opposition of the London government. However, in the summer of 1597, in the theatre's second season, PEMBROKE'S MEN staged Thomas NASHE's allegedly 'seditious' play *Isle of Dogs*, with the result that the royal CENSORSHIP closed all the London theatres for four months. After that Langley kept his theatre open only with difficulty. Upon his death, the theatre was sold to another London investor.

Records show that another company played at the Swan before Pembroke's Men, and the scholar Leslie HOTSON has established a relationship between Langley and Shakespeare, which suggests that the company was probably the CHAMBERLAIN'S MEN. The owner of the Swan and the playwright were named jointly in a legal paper, though their connection is unknown (see GARDINER [2]). The most plausible relationship between the two is that of theatre-owner and representative of an acting company, so it is concluded that Shakespeare's troupe probably performed at the Swan.

**Lanier, Emilia (1570–1654)**   Mistress of theatrical patron Henry Carey, Lord HUNSDON (2), and possibly the Dark Lady of the SONNETS. Emilia Bassano was the illegitimate daughter of an Italian musician at the court of Queen ELIZABETH (1) and became the mistress of Henry Carey, Lord HUNSDON (2), when she was in her teens. In 1593 she became pregnant and was given some money and married to Alphonse Lanier, another court musician. The next year Hunsdon became the patron of Shakespeare's theatrical company, and it is possible that Emilia Lanier might have known Shakespeare through this connection. She might also have known the playwright through her husband's place in the world of court entertainment. The possibility that she was Shakespeare's Dark Lady rests chiefly on these connections, plus a description of her—by the astrologer, Simon FORMAN, with whom she may have had an affair—as a witch-like 'incuba', a characterisation thought to accord well with the poet's 'female evil . . . [who can] corrupt [a] saint to be a devil' (Sonnet 144.5–7).

Lanier's husband Alphonse was a wastrel, and they were soon impoverished. She published a book—a long poem on the women of the Bible—but it was not popular, and when Alphonse died in 1613, she was very poor. She opened a school, but it failed. Her son, Henry, a court musician to King Charles I, may have provided for her, but he died in 1633, and Lanier was left with the responsibility for his two children. She received a pension from the crown but died in near poverty.

**La Pucelle**   See JOAN LA PUCELLE.

**Lartius, Titus**   Legendary figure and minor character in *Coriolanus*, a Roman general. Lartius is a brave and capable officer who, despite earlier wounds, campaigns with MARTIUS (2) (later CORIOLANUS) against the town of CORIOLES, and leads the forces that join the heroic Martius after he has entered the city alone. After the victory, 'busied about decrees' (1.6.34), he commands the occupied town. He delivers a brief elegy when Martius is believed dead, and an even briefer compliment after the hero has triumphed. He is inconsequential thereafter, a minor member of Coriolanus' entourage who disappears entirely after 3.1. Lartius helps establish our sense of the Roman military establishment; he represents the solid virtues of the Roman aristocracy in a play where the weaknesses of the class are more often seen.

Lartius appears at Corioles in Shakespeare's source, PLUTARCH's *Lives,* but much less prominently. Shakespeare invented his praises of Coriolanus, and, perhaps to make the praiser a more vivid figure, endowed him with the crutches he uses in 1.1.241. His spirited wager with Martius in 1.4.1–7 is also an addition, probably to the same end. Thus, Lartius offers an interesting example of the playwright's manipulation of a minor figure to develop the play's world.

**Laughton, Charles (1899–1962)**  British actor. Laughton, who studied acting under Theodore KOMIS-ARJEVSKY, is probably best known for his performance in the title role of the 1933 film *The Private Lives of Henry VIII* (not based on Shakespeare's play)—for which he won an Academy Award—and other movie roles, such as Captain Bligh in *The Mutiny on the Bounty* (1935) and the *Hunchback of Notre Dame* (1939). However, in the 1930s, Laughton succeeded in a variety of Shakespearean roles at the OLD VIC THEATRE, including PROSPERO, ANGELO, and MACBETH. Also, after years in Hollywood—he became an American citizen in 1941—he returned to England in 1959 and played BOTTOM and LEAR at the Shakespeare Memorial Theatre in STRATFORD.

**Launce (Lance)**  Character in *The Two Gentlemen of Verona,* a CLOWN (1), the servant of PROTEUS. Launce is not involved with the plot of the play. However, the comparison of his jocular common sense with the absurdly rhetorical fancies of the protagonists helps to parody them, thus contributing to the play's tone. Launce's great speeches are his two prose monologues (in 2.3 and 4.4) about his dog, CRAB. In the first he bemoans the dog's lack of sympathy with his misfortune in having to leave his family to travel with Proteus. In the second, he recounts various canine offences that Crab has committed, such as urinating under the Duke's table and on SILVIA's dress. Launce himself has taken punishment for them to spare the dog. He also engages in two humorous dialogues with SPEED, one of which is preceded by Launce's soliloquy on his love life.

Launce prefigures later, more consequential Shakespearean clowns, such as LAUNCELOT Gobbo in *The Merchant of Venice,* DOGBERRY, in *Much Ado About Nothing,* and BOTTOM in *A Midsummer Night's Dream.*

**Launcelot (Lancelot) Gobbo**  Character in *The Merchant of Venice,* comical servant first of SHYLOCK, then of BASSANIO, for whom he is also a professional FOOL (1). Launcelot carries messages and announces impending arrivals, but his role in the action is otherwise unimportant. His humour is clever and resourceful, but often broad and laced with standard devices. In 2.2, when he first appears, he wittily imitates legal precision in describing the overcoming of his conscience; in he same scene he draws on the ancient comic routine of mistaken identity, teasing his blind father, Old GOBBO (2). He frequently misuses words—a regular feature of Shakespearean clowning—as when he mistakes 'reproach' for 'approach' (2.5.20) and 'impertinent' for 'pertinent' (2.2.130). He engages Lorenzo in a battle of puns and deliberate misunderstandings in 3.5, and in 5.1 he raucously imitates the blare of hunting horns. A standard stage CLOWN (1), he has no particular personality aside from his buffoonish wit.

Launcelot is called 'clown' in the stage directions of old editions, but he does not have the rustic qualities sometimes associated with that stock theatrical figure (although the terms 'clown' and 'fool' were somewhat interchangeable), and here the term may merely indicate that the part was played by the clown of the company, who specialised in broadly comic roles.

Launcelot provides evidence of Elizabethan anti-Semitism. In 2.2 he delivers a comic monologue in which he recounts a dispute between his conscience and a fiend as to whether or not he should leave Shylock's service. This passage and Launcelot's subsequent conversation with his father help to establish Shylock's reputation as a miser in virulently anti-Semitic terms. Similarly, in 3.5 he jests with JESSICA on the likelihood of her damnation as a Jew, reflecting centuries of Christian prejudice. Although plainly intended as comical, Launcelot's attitude surely indicates something of the spirit in which Shakespeare's audience received Shylock—as an obvious villain, at least in part because he is Jewish.

**Laurence, Friar**  Character in *Romeo and Juliet.* See FRIAR (4).

**Lavatch (Lavache)**  Character in *All's Well That Ends Well.* See CLOWN (5).

**Lavinia**  Character in *Titus Andronicus,* the daughter of TITUS (1) Andronicus, whose brutal rape and mutilation are the centre-piece of AARON's revenge against her father. After murdering BASSIANUS, her husband, TAMORA's sons CHIRON and DEMETRIUS (1) rape Lavinia and then cut out her tongue and cut off her hands so that she cannot testify against them. Directed by Aaron, they have improved upon OVID's tale of Philomel's rape by Tereus, who removed his victim's tongue but not her hands; she wove a tapestry that told the tale and exposed her attacker. Lavinia's plight is repeatedly compared to Philomel's. In fact, Lavinia exposes Chiron and Demetrius by inducing Titus to look in a copy of Ovid's tales and find the example. She then spells out the villains' names in the sand with a wooden staff. When Titus kills the two, Lavinia is a witness and she goes with him to cook their bodies into the meat pie that is to be presented to their mother as revenge. Her father himself stabs her to death, emulating an old legend of a man who killed his raped daughter to expunge the family's dishonour

**Law, Matthew (active 1599–1629)**  Publisher and bookseller in LONDON. Law bought the rights to three of Shakespeare's plays from Andrew WISE and then produced the third through sixth editions of *1 Henry IV* (1603, 1608, 1613, 1622), the fourth and fifth editions of *Richard II* (1608, 1615), and the fourth through sixth editions of *Richard III* (1605, 1612, 1622). Errors in the printing of each of these plays in the FIRST FOLIO (1623) point to delays in the setting of type for them; scholars attribute this delay to difficulties involved in securing Law's permission to republish them. Originally a draper, Law joined the STATIONERS' COMPANY in 1599; he had two bookshops for much of his career. He was fined several times for selling books on Sundays and for selling pirated texts.

*Law Against Lovers, The*  Play by William DAVENANT based loosely on *Measure for Measure* and *Much Ado About Nothing*. Produced in 1662, *The Law Against Lovers* had a main plot that was a much altered version of *Measure for Measure:* the SUB-PLOT and MARIANA (2) are eliminated, ANGELO (2) turns out not to be a villain, and he and ISABELLA are married at the end. This was combined with some material from the BEATRICE and BENEDICK plot of *Much Ado:* Benedick is Angelo's brother and Beatrice is his ward. Davenant also introduced many melodramatic plot developments that had nothing to do with Shakespeare's plays and preserved only some of Beatrice and Benedick's banter and part of Isabella's confrontation with the imprisoned CLAUDIO (3). Most of the dialogue is by Davenant. Davenant declared his intention to 'save' Shakespeare by making the plays palatable to a new audience, but this play was unsuccessful, receiving only a few performances and remaining unrevived thereafter. Though Samuel PEPYS liked it, an anonymous satirical poet of the day differed, saying of Davenant that '. . . only he the Art of it had / Of two good Playes to make one Bad'. *The Law Against Lovers* nevertheless inspired an imitation, Charles GILDON's *Measure for Measure, or Beauty the Best Advocate* (1699), in which much of Davenant's text was retained, but the material from *Much Ado* was replaced by an operatic MASQUE.

**Lawyer**  Minor character in *1 Henry VI*, an observer of the quarrel between the Duke of SOMERSET (3) and Richard Plantagenet (see YORK [8]). Called upon by

Somerset for an opinion, the Lawyer answers with humorous exactitude, 'Unless my study and my books be false, / The argument you held was wrong in law . . .' (2.4.57–58).

**Le Beau**  Minor character in *As You Like It,* a foppish nobleman in the court of the tyrannous DUKE (1) Frederick. ROSALIND and CELIA mock Le Beau in 1.2.86–114. He is fastidious in his diction but less so in his tastes; his description of brutal wrestling as 'good sport' (1.2.92) provokes TOUCHSTONE's quite sensible reply: 'It is the first time that ever I heard breaking of ribs was sport for ladies.' (1.2.128–129). However, Le Beau's affectations and callousness are offset when he warns ORLANDO of the Duke's evil intentions in 1.2. 251–275.

**Leake, William (d. 1633)**  London publisher of several editions of *Venus and Adonis.* After buying the rights to Shakespeare's poem from John HARRISON (2) in 1596, Leake, a prosperous bookseller and officer of the STATIONERS' COMPANY, published six editions (Q5–Q10) between 1599 and 1617.

**Lear**  Title character of *King Lear,* an ancient king of Britain. Lear rejects CORDELIA, his only honest daughter, when he mistakes her frankness for a lack of affection. He is then rejected by his other two daughters, REGAN and GONERIL, to whom he has granted his kingdom, and finds himself wandering in the wilderness, outcast and insane. His prideful wrath has blinded him to the difference between good and evil, but before the play's end he recovers his sanity in part, although too late to prevent the tragedy of Cordelia's death. However, in the course of his trials he does come to recognise his failings, which constitutes the play's most important lesson.

Lear's descent into madness, the central event of the play, illustrates the extent to which humanity can be degraded by its errors. Lear is both victim and perpetrator, for his own egocentricity has sparked the events that lead to his collapse; his ensuing suffering is a result of his inadequacy as a human being. Thus his story presents to us a powerful demonstration of humanity's frailty, and the consequent potential for tragedy in life.

Our horror at Lear's tale is alleviated somewhat by his partial recognition and acceptance of his failings. Lear's trials have been variously interpreted. They may be seen as comparable to God's punishment for sins; his recognition of his fault is followed by reconciliation with Cordelia, which is suggestive of God's forgiveness following a sinner's repentance. That the relief is accompanied by death suggests the importance of the Christian afterlife and its eternal mercy, but this promise is lacking in Lear's pagan world. In a non-religious interpretation, Lear's endurance is heroic in itself, and his triumph lies in his acceptance of his errors before he dies. These two interpretations are not, of course, mutually exclusive: Lear is heroic in both senses. Also, most commentators agree that Lear's suffering is finally redemptive, in that it leads to heightened consciousness on his part. Further, Lear's last words seem to indicate (though the question is disputed) that he dies believing that Cordelia is alive, which implies a happy resolution in death akin to that of GLOUCESTER (1), whose heart 'Burst smilingly' (5.3.198), and whose sufferings conspicuously parallel Lear's.

In the course of his wanderings, both physical and mental, the distracted Lear is able to understand his folly. He first recognises a general lack in his conduct as a ruler. Raving madly in the storm, Lear suddenly realises that he had been previously unaware of hunger and homelessness, and he sees that the knowledge would have been valuable to him as king. He tells himself 'Expose thyself to feel what wretches feel, / That thou mayst shake the superflux to them, / And show the Heavens more just' (3.4.34–36).

Lear comes to a more personal acknowledgement of fault, though his progress is fitful. At first, his guilt takes an unhealthy, morbid form, as he castigates himself for having fathered his daughters, seeing the fault in the sexual process rather than in his egotistical demands. While still on the stormy moor, he declares his torment to be 'Judicious punishment! 'twas this flesh begot / Those pelican daughters' (3.4.73–74). He elaborates on these sentiments when he equates female sexuality with the torments of hell, in 4.6.117–128. Lear's attitude towards sex—also displayed by EDGAR—is evidence of the unhealthy mental and moral state of the play's world.

However, before his lowest point, Lear learns of Cordelia's faithfulness and realises the wrong he has done her. As Kent reports, 'burning shame' (4.3.46) drives him from her camp. While wandering in the fields nearby, he encounters the blinded Gloucester and, stirred by the sight of another sufferer, acknowledges his own weakness—'they told me I was every thing', he says of his former courtly flatterers, adding sardonically, ' 'tis a lie, I am not ague-proof' (4.6.104–105). Later, as part of his remarks on patience, he declares the weakness of all humanity, firmly including himself. He is raving, but the tone of his lament is clear enough; the arrogance that informed his earlier vow of revenge is entirely gone. Finally, in Cordelia's presence, he declares himself 'a very foolish fond old man' (4.7.60) and admits that he has wronged her. He asks her to 'forget and forgive' (4.7.84), and later, as father and daughter are taken to prison, he is pleased at the prospect of perpetual atonement: 'I'll kneel down, / And ask of thee forgiveness: so we'll live . . .' (5.3.10–11).

Still, his insight is at best flawed. That a catastrophe and such a great degree of unhappiness has been necessary to elicit in Lear the acknowledgement of his faults and the existence of human ingratitude has been held against him by many readers. Shakespeare accepted no simple views on the complexities of life, and Lear is distinctly not a perfectly reformed man. Strikingly, no trace of guilt is found in his grief over Cordelia's death, and his enthusiasm for imprisonment with her is disturbingly egocentric in his lack of any sense of her life, as was his original demand for love, in 1.1. This point has been central to much recent feminist criticism of the play. However, Cordelia acquiesces and so do most audiences; the play's emphasis on forgiveness and redemption seems clear, and in this light, Lear's residual defects are perhaps best viewed as evidence of Shakespeare's honesty about human frailty. Finally, *King Lear* is a play that raises more questions than it answers, and the extent to which Lear's tragedy is illuminating to him—as opposed to us, for its potential for illumination is unquestionably clear—remains for us to contemplate.

Shakespeare doubtless believed that there was a historical king of Britain named Lear, as is recorded in his sources, but he is in fact a mythical figure. The name derives from a Celtic god of the sea, Llyr. The legendary king is reported to have founded the town of Leicester, whose name is related to his own (Lear + *castrum*, Latin for 'camp').

**Lee, Sidney (1859–1926)**  British scholar, author of a standard biography of Shakespeare. Lee, an editor and writer of the *Dictionary of National Biography*, elaborated his dictionary article on the playwright into his *Life of William Shakespeare* (1898), which remained the definitive biography for decades. He wrote other books on Shakespeare, including *Shakespeare and the Modern Stage* (1906) and *Shakespeare and the Italian Renaissance* (1915); he also edited a facsimile edition (1902) of the FIRST FOLIO.

**Legate**  Minor character in *1 Henry VI*, the papal ambassador who receives, in 5.1, the money the Bishop of WINCHESTER (1) owes the Pope for his promotion to Cardinal. The episode typifies anti-Catholic sentiment in England in Shakespeare's time.

**Legh, Gerard (d. 1563)**  English antiquarian, author of a minor source for *The Taming of the Shrew* and *King Lear*. Legh's book on heraldry, *Accedens of Armory* (1562), contains a story that probably inspired the episode of the TAILOR in 4.3 of *Shrew;* it also includes one of many versions of LEAR's story, which provided some minor details for Shakespeare's play on the subject. A prosperous draper, Legh was largely self-taught. The *Accedens*, his only work, is a compendium of miscellaneous heraldic lore in the form of a dialogue between a herald named Gerard and a knight named Legh.

**Leicester, Robert Dudley, Earl of (1532–1588)** English nobleman and theatrical patron. As patron of the acting company called LEICESTER'S MEN, Leicester was an important figure in the early history of ELIZABETHAN THEATRE, even though he merely gave the troupe the legal standing they needed and did not actively engage in the production of plays. Leicester was a favourite of Queen ELIZABETH (1) and may have been her lover, but the evidence is uncertain. Though already married, he was thought to aspire to a royal wedding; when his wife died suspiciously in 1560, rumour called it murder (historians generally disagree), so it may have been impossible for the queen to marry him even if she had wished to. She continued to demonstrate her favour in any case, giving him KENILWORTH CASTLE and making him Earl of Leicester.

Leicester became leader of an important political faction and intrigued against the queen's chief minister, Lord BURGHLEY. When he remarried in 1578, he acquired a stepson, the Earl of ESSEX (2), who came to share his hostility to Burghley. His marriage offended the queen, and Leicester was out of favour for several years, but resumed his position when given the command of English forces aiding the Dutch rebellion against Spain. The actor William KEMPE was in Leicester's retinue in the Netherlands, and some scholars speculate that the young Shakespeare may have been as well, though no confirming evidence exists. Leicester returned to England to take a high command in the army assembled to resist the Spanish Armada in 1588 and died of an illness soon after the crisis ended.

**Leicester's Men** Early English theatrical company. From at least 1559, the nobleman Robert Dudley, later Earl of LEICESTER, patronised a company of actors. Known as Dudley's Men until 1564, when their patron received his title, this troupe mostly toured the provinces. It did, however, play at the court of Queen ELIZABETH (1) several times between 1560 and 1562, perhaps because their patron was the queen's favourite, possibly her lover.

In 1572, when actors were declared vagrants unless supported by a nobleman (see ELIZABETHAN THEATRE), Leicester's Men was formally defined and its players named, including James BURBAGE (2) and Robert WILSON (4). In 1574 the queen declared Leicester's Men her own employees as well, licencing them to play anywhere in England, including LONDON. This challenged for the first time the London government's puritanical opposition to public theatre, an important watershed in the history of English drama.

For a decade Leicester's Men were the most important theatrical troupe in England, performing at Elizabeth's court and (after 1577) at Burbage's THEATRE. However, with the creation in 1583 of the QUEEN'S MEN (1), which was permitted to raid some of Leicester's best performers, their prominence diminished. In the summer of 1586, Leicester's Men played in STRATFORD, and this fact has prompted speculation that the young Shakespeare joined them at this time and returned with them to London to begin his career, although no other evidence supports this proposition. Upon Leicester's death in 1588, the company dissolved; some scholars believe that its members joined STRANGE'S MEN.

**Leigh, Vivien (1913–1967)** English actress. Leigh, the wife of Laurence OLIVIER, is best known as a movie actress, though she also performed a number of major Shakespearean roles on the stage, usually opposite her husband. Her most notable performances were as CLEOPATRA (1951) and LADY (6) MACBETH (1955).

**Le Maçon, Antoine (active c. 1550–1580)** French writer and translator. Le Maçon's translation of BOCCACCIO's *Decameron* was probably a subsidiary source for *All's Well That Ends Well* and a major source for *Cymbeline*. Shakespeare's chief source for *All's Well* was William PAINTER's translation of a tale from Boccaccio in his *The Palace of Pleasure*, but the playwright probably used Le Maçon's text also. Painter himself used it, alongside the original. The 'wager' plot of *Cymbeline* derives from a *Decameron* tale that was not translated into English before 1620, and Le Maçon's translation is one of several possible versions of the story that Shakespeare may have encountered.

Le Maçon was a courtier at the court of Princess Marguerite of Valois. His translation of Boccaccio was extremely popular throughout Europe as soon as it appeared in 1545; it was reissued 16 times during the 16th century. He also wrote a prose romance, published in 1550. Little else is known of his life.

**Lennox (1)** Character in *Macbeth*. See LENOX.

**Lennox (2), Charlotte (1720–1804)** English writer, author of the first substantial analysis of Shakespeare's sources. Lennox, who was also a novelist, wrote *Shakespear* [sic] *Illustrated; or, the Novels and Histories on which the Plays are founded* (1753), which covered more than half of Shakespeare's plays, thus improving greatly on its only predecessor, the work of Gerard LANGBAINE.

**Lenox (Lennox), Thane of** Character in *Macbeth*, a Scottish nobleman. Lenox functions as an attendant for most of the play. He is a silent companion of King DUNCAN in Act 1, and he speaks only a little when he arrives to join the king in 2.3, at the time of Duncan's murder. After MACBETH is crowned, Lenox transfers his services to the new king and attends him silently in 3.1, and with a few words in 3.4 and 4.1. Only in 3.6—a misplaced scene (in the FIRST FOLIO text) that should follow 4.1—does Lenox assume any importance. In this scene he speaks against Macbeth and makes clear the extent to which his evil is loathed in SCOTLAND. Like his fellow thanes ROSSE and ANGUS, Lenox' chief significance lies in his rebellion, which demonstrates the extremity of the nation's disorder once evil has been permitted to flourish. In Act 5 Lenox serves the cause of Prince MALCOLM. Shakespeare's use of the name Lenox may have been intended as a compliment to the new English king, JAMES I, who was descended from an Earl of Lenox.

**Leo Africanus (Joannes Leo) (active c. 1520)**  Moorish traveller and writer whose work may have influenced *Othello* and *Antony and Cleopatra*. Leo translated his writings on the regions now known as North, West and East Africa from Arabic into Italian. John PORY translated them into English in 1600 as *A Geographical History of Africa,* but they had been well known in England in Italian (and a French translation) since about 1550. Leo was among the first writers to replace ancient and medieval legends with real facts about the nations south of the Sahara (a word that Pory's translation introduced into English). His writings are still valuable for modern historians, providing a rare source of reliable information on pre-colonial sub-Saharan Africa. Pory's translation was a celebrated work in its day, and surely provided part of Shakespeare's background knowledge of North Africa, especially as reflected in 2.7 of *Antony and Cleopatra.* Moreover, Pory's preface included an account of Leo's life that is thought to have inspired OTHELLO's autobiographical remarks in 1.3.134–145. Leo's works also informed a number of other English writers, including PUTTENHAM, Richard EDEN, and Ben JONSON.

Leo Africanus, or Leo of Africa, was a North African Moor who crossed the Sahara a number of times as a free-lance soldier and scholar. He was captured c. 1520 by Christian naval forces in the Mediterranean and presented to Pope Leo X, who converted him to Christianity from Islam and gave him the baptismal name Joannes Leo.

**Leonardo**  Minor character in *The Merchant of Venice,* servant of BASSANIO. In 2.2 Leonardo speaks one line when he is instructed to arrange Bassanio's trip to BELMONT.

**Leonato**  Character in *Much Ado About Nothing,* father of HERO and uncle of BEATRICE. The governor of MESSINA, Leonato displays the formality that his position demands, but he is clearly a warm person, fond of his daughter and pleasant to all, offering avuncular advice

to Beatrice and friendship even to the villainous Don JOHN (1). He enjoys a joke and is quite willing to participate in Don PEDRO's ruse to trick BENEDICK and Beatrice into falling in love. But Leonato displays little real personality until the crisis of the play. The deluded CLAUDIO (1) rejects Hero at the altar, asserting—with the backing of the prince, Leonato's superior, Don PEDRO—that he has seen her with a lover. Leonato is so sensitive about his honour that his immediate reaction is abysmal shame for himself and furious rage at his daughter. In an hysterical passage (4.1.120–154) that foreshadows the laments of King LEAR, Leonato wishes Hero dead. FRIAR (2) Francis quickly restores his belief in her innocence, however, and he sternly proclaims that he shall have vengeance; in 5.1 he challenges Claudio to a duel. However, in 5.4, Leonato presides over the general air of reconciliation that closes the play, forgiving the errant MARGARET (2) and accepting the repentant Claudio with a practical joke, disguising Hero as a mysterious cousin whom the sinner must marry in atonement.

**Leonine**  Minor character in *Pericles,* the murderer hired by DIONYZA to kill MARINA. In 4.1 Dionyza urges Leonine to ignore his conscience, for he is reluctant to murder so fine a young woman; however, he agrees to uphold his sworn oath to do so. A civil murderer, he offers Marina time to say her prayers, and while she is doing so, he is interrupted by the coincidental arrival of marauding PIRATES, who kidnap his intended victim. Relieved to be freed from his obligation, Leonine nevertheless proposes to tell Dionyza he has in fact done the deed. As we learn in 4.3, Dionyza believed him, but she has also poisoned him to ensure secrecy. Leonine's brief appearance is thus filled with surprises, as first his conscience, then his viciousness, and finally his deceit, all prove insufficient. Such ironic changes are found throughout the play, and demonstrate that humanity is helpless before fate, an important theme for *Pericles* and Shakespeare's late plays in general.

In the *Confessio Amantis* of John GOWER (3), Shakespeare's chief source for the play, Leonine, which means lionlike, is the name of the PANDAR. The playwright presumably transferred the name to the murderer to make better use of its reference to a ferocious beast.

**Leontes**  Character in *The Winter's Tale,* the King of SICILIA, husband of HERMIONE and father of PERDITA. Leontes' insane jealousy is the disorder at the centre of the TRAGEDY that comprises the first half of the play. In 1.2, convinced that Hermione has committed adultery with King POLIXENES of BOHEMIA, Leontes orders her tried for treason. In 2.3, believing the newborn Perdita to be Polixenes' child, he condemns her to abandonment in the wilderness. Even when the oracle of Apollo declares Hermione innocent in 3.2, Leontes refuses to believe it. Finally, the death from grief of his son MAMILLIUS, taken as an act of vengeance by Apollo, convinces him, and he repents. However, Hermione is apparently dead of grief also, and the mournful Leontes 'shuts himself up' (4.1.19), emerging only in Act 5, after 16 years of 'saint-like sorrow' (5.1.2), to learn that both Perdita and Hermione have survived.

Shakespeare gives Leontes some weight as a particular person: he is about 30 in Act 1; he has inspired love in Hermione and Mamillius and demonstrates his own love for his son; he is conscious of public opinion when he sends messengers to the oracle to 'Give rest to th' minds of others' (2.1.191) and holds a trial that he may 'be clear'd / Of being tyrannous' (3.2.5). Nevertheless, his personality is not well developed, for it is not as a person that Leontes has importance. He functions as a symbol of disorder and chaos; he is not intended to be a realistic human being so much as an obstacle to happiness. He is villainous because the story calls for villainy, not from any well-established motive. His madness is as much a surprise to the other characters as it is to the audience or reader. Leontes is thus also a victim, a man rendered suddenly insane, subject to the whims of fate. It is highly significant that it takes an act of divine intervention to effect his cure. One of the lessons of the play—and of the ROMANCES in general—is that humankind depends on providence for happiness in an insecure world.

At the close of 3.2 Leontes subsides into grief, and there is a sense of calm acceptance of evil's consequences that resembles a tragedy's close. However, Leontes' repentance occurs as abruptly as the sin that made it necessary; it fails to produce any spiritual growth or any profound expressions of torment such as those offered by OTHELLO and LEAR. His repentance, like his jealousy, is archetypal. Still, though Leontes' psychology is not explored, his repentance nevertheless serves as a symbol of the gentler world in which the climactic reconciliations can occur.

**Lepidus, Marcus Aemilius (d. 13 B.C.)** Historical figure and character in *Julius Caesar* and *Antony and Cleopatra*. Lepidus is a member of the Triumvirate, the three-man governing committee that consists of Lepidus, OCTAVIUS (later Octavius CAESAR [2]), and Mark ANTONY. The Triumvirate rules Rome in the aftermath of the assassination of Julius CAESAR (1). Octavius imprisons Lepidus and then fights Antony for sole control of the Empire. In both plays Lepidus is a markedly weaker figure than his colleagues, and their casual dominance of him helps establish an impression of Roman power politics that is important in each work.

A minor character in *Julius Caesar*, Lepidus appears only once, in 4.1, when the Triumvirs decide on a list of political enemies that must be arrested and exe-

cuted as part of their campaign against BRUTUS (4) and CASSIUS. After a brief exchange, Antony sends Lepidus on an errand and then belittles him to Octavius. He calls him 'a slight unmeritable man' (4.1.12) and a 'barren-spirited fellow' (4.1.36), and says he does not deserve a position as ruler. He compares him to an ass or horse, whose usefulness is limited and who will be turned out to pasture when he has fulfilled his role. Lepidus does not reappear in the play, and Antony's opinion of him seems appropriate. This episode may deepen our impression of Antony as a cynical political manipulator, or, may justify his boldness in seizing leadership in a power vacuum. In either view, Lepidus serves as a foil to sharpen our sense of Antony.

In *Antony and Cleopatra* Lepidus is similarly weak, though he plays a more prominent role in affairs. He is dominated by Caesar as the two confer on Antony's absence, in 1.4. In 2.4 he pointlessly urges reconciliation between Antony and Caesar, who are already intent on it, and he has little to say once negotiations are underway. He is again a minor player in the talks with POMPEY (2) in 2.6, and at the subsequent banquet he is the butt of a humiliating joke as he has been pressured into drinking too much. He makes a fool of himself and finally must be carried away—in pointed contrast to Caesar, who ends the party with a complaint about the ill effects of wine. The episode is comical, but even a SERVANT (21) recognises its significance for Lepidus' position in high politics, saying, 'To be called into a huge sphere, and not to be seen to move in't, are the holes where eyes should be . . .' (2.7.14–15). Lepidus disappears from the play at this point, though his fate is later reported: Caesar has accused him of treason and imprisoned him 'till death enlarge his confine' (3.5.11–12). Once again, Lepidus provides an example of the necessity for sharp wits and hard morals in the world of power politics, though here the contrast reflects more on Caesar than on Antony.

The historical Lepidus was indeed a lesser figure than his colleagues, though Shakespeare exaggerated this to emphasise the brutal competition of Roman politics. Lepidus was from a traditionally powerful Roman family. He supported Julius Caesar in his rise to power, and in the aftermath of Caesar's assassination in 44 B.C. he naturally allied himself with Antony. By chance, he commanded troops in the vicinity of Rome at the time, and he was able to control the city. It was at this point that he probably held as much real power as he ever would. In *Julius Caesar,* events are telescoped; the Triumvirate only came together after an 18-month period, during which Lepidus was courted by Antony and Octavius, and by BRUTUS (4) and CASSIUS. Upon the formation of the Triumvirate Lepidus was given control of Italy and Gaul, but soon Caesar took over these important commands and Lepidus was shifted to Africa, also important but more remote. From this base, Lepidus assisted—though only slightly—in the defeat of Pompey's forces in Sicily by Caesar's general, AGRIPPA, in 35 B.C., soon after the events of Act 2 of *Antony and Cleopatra*. However, when Lepidus attempted to override Agrippa once the victory was assured, Caesar daringly entered Lepidus' camp, unarmed, and demanded his surrender to arrest. Lepidus' basic weakness was disliked by his own troops, and they seized him. He was forced to publicly plead for mercy, after which he was formally ousted from the Triumvirate. His treatment was better than is implied in Shakespeare, however. He was permitted to retain his post as Pontifex Maximus—the chief clergyman of the state religion—and was mercifully exiled to a comfortable retreat where he lived out his life.

**Lessing, Gotthold Ephraim (1729–1781)**   German playwright and critic, the first important appreciator of Shakespeare in Germany. In 1767–1768 Lessing wrote a series of articles on German theatre that denounced its dependence on French plays and recommended the adoption of the ancient Greek dramatists and Shakespeare as primary models. These articles were extremely influential; they helped popularise the translations of Christoph WIELAND, and the critic J. G. Herder (1744–1803), a follower of Lessing, introduced Shakespeare to GOETHE, whose writings secured the playwright's place in German literary history. Germany's great enthusiasm for Shakespeare is often said to have begun with Lessing.

Lessing studied theology, literature, and philosophy before taking up journalism to make a living while he wrote plays, poems, and essays. He was greatly celebrated in his own time as Germany's leading man of letters. His plays *Miss Sarah Sampson* (1755), *Minna von Barnheim* (1767, considered one of the finest comedies in all literature), *Emilia Galotti* (1772), and *Nathan the Wise* (1769) are still performed in Germany and elsewhere. Lessing was the greatest representative of the German Enlightenment, and the first German writer to establish an international reputation.

**Leveridge, Richard (c. 1670–1758)**   English singer and composer. Leveridge, a noted bass of his day, mostly composed SONGS, including music for several songs from Shakespeare's plays. He also wrote a burlesque of Italian opera, *The Comick Masque of Pyramus and Thisbe* (1716), that took its plot from the PYRAMUS AND THISBE episode in *A Midsummer Night's Dream*. He is one of several composers whom scholars believe may have written the incidental music for *Macbeth* traditionally attributed to Matthew LOCKE.

**Leveson, William (active 1580–1612)**   English merchant, a trustee for Shakespeare's interest in the ground lease for the GLOBE THEATRE. The lease for the land on which the Globe stood was entered into by two parties, the Burbage brothers (see BURBAGE [1, 3]) and five members of the CHAMBERLAIN'S MEN acting jointly—Shakespeare, John HEMINGE, William KEMPE, Augustine PHILLIPS, and Thomas POPE (2). To make their shares independently saleable, the actors assigned their half to two trustees—Leveson and Thomas SAVAGE—who then regranted a fifth to each.

Leveson probably got this job through Heminge, whom he knew as a fellow parishioner of a London church. Leveson was an investor in overseas expeditions, serving at different times a member of the Muscovy Company (which traded to Russia), the Virginia Company, and the North-West Passage Company. Dudley DIGGES (1), son of Shakespeare's friend Thomas RUSSELL, was Leveson's fellow investor in all of these enterprises.

**Lewis (1), the Dauphin (later King Louis VIII of France, 1187–1226)**   Historical figure and character in *King John*, son of King PHILIP (2) of FRANCE (1). Lewis joins his father in supporting ARTHUR, whose rightful inheritance of the English crown has been prevented by King JOHN (3). The French abandon Arthur's cause for a favourable peace, under whose terms Lewis marries John's niece BLANCHE. In 3.1, despite his bride's pleas, Lewis urges his father to support the pope and turn on John, and he later leads an invasion of England. He refuses to cease fighting when John makes his peace with Rome, insisting that France would be dishonoured by retreat. He withdraws only when deserted by the disaffected English lords who had been aiding him. Lewis is a superficially civil but treacherous Frenchman of a type that Shakespeare often depicted; here the stereotype not only heightens the patriotic sentiments of *King John*, but also stresses the motif of faithlessness that runs through the play.

The historical Lewis did invade England and was successful at first. However, the invasion was not prompted by the pope's quarrel with John, which had been settled earlier. In fact, it was undertaken in defiance of a papal prohibition; it was intended to place Lewis on the English throne, at the invitation of rebellious English barons. A reunited England under John's successor, HENRY (1), drove Lewis back to France. Lewis is frequently referred to as the Dauphin, or Dolphin, a title traditionally given to the eldest son of a King of France, as Prince of Wales is given to his English equivalent. However, this practise began only in 1350, so its application to Lewis is inaccurate.

**Lewis (2) The Dauphin**   Character in *Henry V*. See DAUPHIN (3).

**Lewis (3), King of France (1423–1483)**   Historical figure and minor character in *3 Henry VI*, King Louis XI of FRANCE (1). In 3.3 Lewis is insulted when King

EDWARD IV of England voids his agreement to marry the French King's sister-in-law, Lady BONA. Lewis agrees to back an effort by MARGARET (1) and WARWICK (3) to invade England and reinstate the deposed HENRY VI as king, thereby beginning another phase of the WARS OF THE ROSES.

In a gross over-simplification of years of foreign-policy manoeuvrings, Shakespeare presents a cardboard French king who simply wavers from sympathy with Margaret to alliance with Edward and back again. In reality, Louis XI, known as 'the Spider' for ruthless diplomacy, had long enjoyed good relations with Warwick. Upon Edward's accession, Warwick had backed an English alliance with France and had proposed the marriage to Bona, though nothing came of the idea. Edward, on the other hand, had opted for a connection with Louis' enemy, Burgundy. When Warwick initiated his coup in 1469, Louis discreetly provided him funds. Then, when Warwick was forced to flee England, it was Louis who initiated the alliance with Margaret in June 1470, six years after Edward's marriage to Lady Elizabeth. He financed Warwick's invasion and surely regarded the money as well spent, despite Warwick's ultimate failure, because the incident disrupted English politics significantly.

**Licio**    Name employed in *The Taming of the Shrew*. See LITIO.

**Lieutenant (1)**    Minor character in *2 Henry VI*, an officer, sometimes called a CAPTAIN (3), of a pirate ship. In 4.1 the Lieutenant distributes among his crew the prisoners his ship has taken; each crewman is entitled to extract a ransom from his prisoner. When Walter WHITMORE asserts a desire to kill his instead, the Lieutenant counsels mercy. However, upon learning that the prisoner is the Duke of SUFFOLK (3), the Lieutenant patriotically vows to see him slain, knowing that the Duke's ambitious conspiracies have harmed England. He delivers a virulent recital of Suffolk's political offences and sends him off to be executed by Whitmore.

**Lieutenant (2)**    Minor character in *3 Henry VI*, a guard in the TOWER OF LONDON. When HENRY VI is released from the Tower upon his reinstatement as King in 4.6, the Lieutenant asks and receives the monarch's pardon for having been his gaoler. Henry assures him that he appreciates the Lieutenant's civil behaviour as a guard. When Richard (see RICHARD III) comes to murder the re-imprisoned Henry in 5.6, he dismisses the Lieutenant from his guard post.

**Lieutenant (3)**    Minor character in *Coriolanus*, a Roman officer. In 1.7 the Lieutenant receives orders from LARTIUS to maintain control of CORIOLES, which the Romans have captured from the VOLSCIANS. He

speaks only half a line in reply, in an episode whose purpose is to tell that the town has been captured.

**Lieutenant (4)**    Minor character in *Coriolanus*, a follower of AUFIDIUS. In 4.7 the Lieutenant tells Aufidius that CORIOLANUS, who has deserted from the Romans, is growing in popularity among the VOLSCIANS. He regrets that Aufidius has permitted Coriolanus to command troops, because Aufidius is becoming overshadowed. The Lieutenant furthers the play's development with these remarks, for they inform us of Coriolanus' successes and spark Aufidius' hostile replies, which foreshadow the play's concluding episode.

**Ligarius, Caius (Quintus) (d. 44 B.C.)**    Historical figure and minor character in *Julius Caesar*, one of the assassins of CAESAR (1). In 2.1 Ligarius (designated Caius in the FIRST FOLIO text and some modern editions), although ill, accepts the invitation of BRUTUS (4) to engage in an honourable exploit, saying, 'By all the Gods that Romans bow before, I here discard my sickness' (2.1.320–321). Though Brutus does not specify the nature of the deed, he refers to the planned assassination of Caesar, and Ligarius is among the conspirators who accompany Caesar to the Senate in 2.2, although he does not appear in the murder scene (3.1). Ligarius represents the stoical Roman virtues in disregarding poor health to follow duty; more important, his immediate, unquestioning acceptance of Brutus' leadership also demonstrates the authority that Brutus holds among the conspirators.

In 2.1.215–216 Ligarius is said to 'bear Caesar hard, who rated him for speaking well of Pompey'. In fact, the historical Ligarius had fought long and hard for Pompey the Great (106–48 B.C.) against Caesar in an earlier civil war and had been pardoned. In Shakespeare's source, PLUTARCH's *Lives*, he is said to have joined the conspirators out of hatred for Caesar's tyranny. He died shortly after the assassination, probably of natural causes. His name was actually Quintus; the error was Plutarch's.

**Lillo, George (1693–1739)**    British dramatist, creator of a crude adaptation of *Pericles*. In his *Marina* (1738), Lillo used only the last two acts of Shakespeare's play, and he altered those almost beyond recognition. The moderate success of Lillo's version of *Pericles* does not attest to any popularity for the original play; on the contrary, it was the only production of *Pericles* (or rather, related to *Pericles*) during the 18th century.

Lillo was among the leading British playwrights of his day. His best-known work, *George Barnwell* (1731), is a melodramatic tale of a young Londoner led by passion to murder, which ends with a morally proper punishment. It is considered a good example of the 18th-century vogue for sentimental dramas set among the urban bourgeoisie.

**Lincoln, Bishop of (John Longland, 1473–1547)**
Historical figure and minor character in *Henry VIII*,
confessor to King HENRY VIII. In 2.4.209–214 Lincoln
confirms the king's statement that as his confessor, he,
Lincoln, advised Henry to pursue a divorce of Queen
KATHERINE. His small part helps justify the king's action.

Longland, Bishop of Lincoln and Henry's long-time
confessor, was later to record that the king hounded
him at length about the divorce, insisting on his consent. Although Longland did consent—and was on
one occasion stoned by a disapproving public—he
later declared a change of mind. After the establishment of the Church of England, Longland became
known for his religious intolerance and his support of
the king's supremacy in matters of religious doctrine.

**Ling, Nicholas (active 1570–1607)** Printer, publisher, and bookseller in LONDON who produced the
first two editions of *Hamlet*. In 1603 Ling and John
TRUMBELL published the QUARTO edition known as Q1.
It is a BAD QUARTO version of the play, recorded from
the memories of actors, probably for this pirated edition. James ROBERTS had registered the play earlier,
but he probably sold his rights to Ling, who also produced the first legitimate edition of *Hamlet*—employing Roberts as the printer—in 1604. In November
1607, shortly before his death, Ling sold John SMETH-
WICK the rights to *Hamlet*, along with those to *Love's
Labour's Lost, Romeo and Juliet*—which he had bought
from Cuthbert BURBY but never used—and THE TAM-
ING OF A SHREW (a Bad Quarto of *The Taming of the
Shrew*). Ling had also bought *A Shrew* from Burby, but
he produced an edition of it (Q3, 1607) before selling
the rights.

**Lily (Lilly, Lyly), William (c. 1468–1522)** English
scholar and co-author of the standard Latin textbook
of Shakespeare's day, known as *Lily's Latin Grammar*,
which is quoted several times in the plays—e.g., in 4.1
(the 'Latin' scene) of *The Merry Wives of Windsor*, 1.1.
162 of *The Taming of the Shrew*, and 4.2.20–21 of *Titus
Andronicus*. Lily's book, written in collaboration with
the famous humanist scholar John Colet, was the basic
text used at the Grammar School in STRATFORD, where
Shakespeare was educated. Lily was a close friend of
Sir Thomas MORE and the grandfather of playwright
and novelist John LYLY.

**Litio (Licio)** In *The Taming of the Shrew*, the name
HORTENSIO takes when he disguises himself as a music
teacher in order to be appointed instructor to BIANCA
(1).

**Livy (Titus Livius, 59 B.C.–17 A.D.)** Ancient Roman
author of a Latin history of ROME, a minor source for

*Coriolanus* and possibly an inspiration for *The Rape of
Lucrece*. Livy's *Ab urbe condita* was translated by Philemon HOLLAND (4) as *The Romane Historie* (1600), and a
passage from Holland's book is echoed in MENENIUS'
famous 'belly speech' in *Coriolanus*. Livy's history also
contains the story of LUCRECE and was probably consulted by Shakespeare in writing his poem on the subject, though whether it initially inspired him is unknown.

Livy was a prominent member of the literary circle
surrounding the Emperor Augustus (see CAESAR [2]).
His only major work was his immense history, covering Rome from its mythical beginnings until 9 B.C. He
began it at the age of 30 and worked on it for 40 years.
Of the 142 books that composed the work, only 35
survived into the Middle Ages, though summaries of
most of the others were compiled by other Latin authors. The book made Livy famous even before it was
completed, and it dominated the Western world's
knowledge of Roman history until the RENAISSANCE.
Modern scholars, however, give him more credit for
his fine literary style than for the accuracy of his account.

**Locke, Matthew (c. 1630–1677)** English composer
of church and theatre music, including incidental
music for John DRYDEN and William DAVENANT's 1667
version of *The Tempest*. Locke was long believed to
have written the once-famous incidental music to
Davenant's *Macbeth* (1663), on the strength of an attribution published in 1708. Modern musicologists disagree, believing on stylistic grounds that the music
was probably written by a later composer. (It is in any
case based on the much older work of Robert JOHNSON
[5] for Thomas MIDDLETON's *The Witch* [c. 1610–1620];
scholars attribute the revision to any of several composers, including Richard LEVERIDGE and Henry PUR-
CELL.) Locke had a highly successful career before his
early death. He wrote some of the music for the first
English opera, Davenant's *Siege of Rhodes* (1656), and
in 1661 he was named composer to the newly restored
King Charles II.

*Locrine* Anonymous play sometimes attributed to
Shakespeare, part of the Shakespeare APOCRYPHA. *Lo-
crine*, a melodrama of ancient kings, was published by
Thomas CREEDE in 1595 and credited to 'W. S.', possibly in the hope that the public would believe it was by
Shakespeare. In 1664 it was published in the Third
FOLIO, but modern scholars are confident that Shakespeare did not write the play, for it is very different
from Shakespeare's work in style and content. However, a positive attribution has not been agreed upon.
On stylistic grounds, Robert GREENE (2), Christopher
MARLOWE (1), and various others have been nominated, while W. W. GREG discovered a copy of the
1595 edition with early 17th-century notes that ascribe

it to one Charles Tilney (d. 1586). Tilney is otherwise unknown as a writer.

**Lodge, Thomas (c. 1557–1625)**  English writer, creator of the major source for *As You Like It.* Lodge, one of the UNIVERSITY WITS who dominated ELIZABETHAN DRAMA in the 1580s, wrote only two plays—one in collaboration with Robert GREENE (2). He was best known for his lyric poetry and a prose romance, *Rosalynde* (1590), that provided the central elements of *As You Like It.* Shakespearean scholars who believe many of Shakespeare's early plays were written collaboratively (see, e.g., FLEAY and ROBERTSON) have often cited Lodge as a possible co-author of *1 Henry VI, The Taming of the Shrew,* and others, but this theory is now generally deprecated. Lodge's very popular romantic poetry may have influenced Shakespeare in the writing of *Venus and Adonis,* though specific connections are absent.

Lodge is regarded as a minor writer whose work was chiefly derived from that of others; *Rosalynde,* for instance, is an imitation of John LYLY's novels. Son of the Lord Mayor of London, Lodge attended Oxford University and the INNS OF COURT, before commencing his literary career with a defence of poetry and drama against the attacks of Stephen GOSSON (2). He produced most of his literary work during the 1580s, after which he lived abroad and travelled—he was part of an expedition that explored South America in 1591 to 1593, for example. On his return, he practised medicine and wrote an account of his travels (now lost). A convert to Catholicism, he faced religious persecution and briefly fled the country in 1616. He died in near-poverty.

**Lodovico**  Character in *Othello,* an emissary from VENICE to CYPRUS. Lodovico appears only towards the end of the play, arriving on Cyprus just as OTHELLO's madness approaches its climax. He serves a symbolic function, representing the life of normal society from which the main characters have been isolated since Act 2. On Cyprus, IAGO's influence can work its poison free of social or political affairs that might engage Othello's attention, and DESDEMONA cannot seek advice or intervention from other Venetian aristocrats. Lodovico is unable to prevent the catastrophe of Desdemona's murder, but in the final scene after Iago's duplicity has been exposed and Othello has committed suicide, Lodovico assumes the mantle of leadership and disposes of practical matters in the wake of the tragedy.

**Lodowick**  In *Measure for Measure,* the name taken by the disguised DUKE (9) of Vienna.

**London**  Principal city of England, a location in each of Shakespeare's HISTORY PLAYS and his residence for much of his life. In Shakespeare's time London was not only the great metropolitan centre of England, home to about 300,000 people (almost 10 percent of the nation's population); it was also the third-largest city in Europe (behind Naples and Paris) and was soon to be the largest. Outside the medieval walled city were new suburban expansions; to the south, across the Thames River via London Bridge, was SOUTHWARK, where the GLOBE THEATRE and several other theatres were established during Shakespeare's residency in the city (see ELIZABETHAN THEATRE).

Shakespeare lived in a number of known locales in London. In October 1596 he was assessed for taxes as a resident of Bishopsgate. This neighbourhood was near the north-easternmost city gate, beyond which, in the suburb of Shoreditch, was the THEATRE, where his acting company, the CHAMBERLAIN'S MEN, performed. However, by November he had apparently moved to the southern suburbs, for he was subject to the jurisdiction of the county of Surrey when he was involved in litigation between Francis LANGLEY and William GARDINER (2). The move probably reflects a season spent at the SWAN THEATRE by the Chamberlain's Men in the winter of 1596–1597. Shakespeare's tax bill followed him and was forwarded in 1600 to the diocese of Winchester, which governed the Clink, a neighbourhood in Southwark near the Globe, so Shakespeare probably lived there at the close of the 16th century.

The playwright can next be located in 1604 as the tenant of Christopher MOUNTJOY in Cripplegate, at the north-west corner of the city. He was probably there as early as 1602 and may have remained for some years after 1604, though no later evidence of a London address for him exists. After 1608 his principal theatrical venue was the BLACKFRIARS THEATRE, north of the river near the western wall of the city. Shakespeare probably moved back to Stratford by about 1610. His connections with the city were still strong, however, and he visited London several times after that, possibly staying at the MERMAID TAVERN, whose manager was his friend William JOHNSON (8). In 1613 he invested in London real estate, buying the BLACKFRIARS GATEHOUSE. Both the Blackfriars Theatre and the Blackfriars Gatehouse were on the grounds of the former BLACKFRIARS ABBEY.

London's buzzing life is frequently manifested in Shakespeare's work. In the English history plays, Shakespeare was dealing with events that often occurred in London, so many scenes are set there. Numerous buildings and other landmarks familiar to his London audiences are presented, including the TOWER OF LONDON, the INNS OF COURT, PARLIAMENT HOUSE, BAYNARD CASTLE, ST. JAMES PALACE, and Blackfriars Abbey. Especially common are interiors of WESTMINSTER (4) PALACE, where the political leaders often assembled.

Some scenes in the histories are particularly note-worthy for their vivid glimpses of the London populace. In Act 4 of *2 Henry VI* Jack CADE's rebellion spreads to the city from KENT (1) and we see the citizenry rise up in support of rebellion, as they did historically, not only for Cade but on other occasions as well. Incidents of Cade's rebellion occur at BLACK-HEATH and SMITHFIELD, semi-rural areas adjacent to the city. Another aspect of civil disorder that London knew all too well was the helplessness of the common people in the face of aristocratic quarrels and civil war. This is well exemplified in 2.3 of *Richard III*, where several Londoners (see CITIZEN [2]) discuss the political situation in resigned tones. Another view of such politics is given in 5.2.1–40 of *Richard II*, where the Duke of YORK (4) describes a triumphal entrance into London, in which the assembled people hail the conqueror, BOLINGBROKE (1), and ridicule the fallen RICHARD II. Shakespeare's most famous depiction of the life of London is in the *Henry IV* plays, where much of the action is centred on the BOAR'S HEAD TAVERN in the neighbourhood of EASTCHEAP. There a colourful subsection of city life, the world of petty thieves and slumming aristocrats, is presented with infectious gusto.

Sometimes scenes in plays set elsewhere in Europe reflect the realities of life in London in a manner familiar to London audiences. For instance, the VENICE of *The Merchant of Venice* offers a satirical slant on the business world of Shakespeare's London, and the VIENNA of *Measure for Measure* includes a sort of Eastcheap underworld. The outbreak of plague in VERONA, with its 'searchers of the town' (*Romeo and Juliet* 5.2.8), reflects a disaster that was common in London. Further, the politically unruly commoners of London seem to inhabit the ROME of *Julius Caesar* and *Coriolanus* (see CARPENTER, COBBLER, COMMONER [1, 2], PLEBEIANS).

**London Prodigal, The**   Play formerly attributed to Shakespeare, part of the Shakespeare APOCRYPHA. *The London Prodigal,* a domestic comedy of a prodigal husband's reformation by his wife, was published in 1605 by Nathaniel BUTTER, who ascribed it to Shakespeare. This was probably a conscious fraud, for *The London Prodigal* is totally unlike Shakespeare's plays. Its characters are uniformly shallow, its poetry is weak, and it is of a genre unused by Shakespeare—a comedy set in contemporary London. Though the editors of the FIRST FOLIO rejected it, the play was again published as Shakespeare's in the Third and Fourth Folios (see FOLIO) and in the editions of Nicholas ROWE and Alexander POPE (1). The authorship of *The London Prodigal* remains unknown, though some scholars attribute it to Thomas MARSTON.

**Longaville (Longueville)**   Character in *Love's Labour's Lost,* one of the gentlemen who fall in love and thus disrupt the ascetic academic programme of the KING (19) of Navarre. In 1.1 Longaville is enthusiastic about the King's idea, but he falls in love with MARIA (1), one of the ladies-in-waiting to the PRINCESS (1) of France, and, along with the King and the other courtiers, he breaks his vow and abandons scholarship for love.

Longaville's name was taken from that of a French contemporary of Shakespeare, the Duc de Longueville, a well-known figure in the Wars of Religion. Longueville was an aide to Henri de Bourbon, who was the historical King of Navarre and later ruled France as Henri IV.

**Longleat Manuscript**   Single page containing the earliest known illustration from Shakespeare, a scene taken from *Titus Andronicus.* This document, in the library at Longleat, the estate of the Marquess of Bath, bears a semi-legible date, generally held to be 1594 or 1595, and is signed by Henry Peachem (c. 1576–1643), an artist and writer. The illustration, at the top of the page, depicts TAMORA on her knees before TITUS (1) Andronicus, with two bound figures behind her on the right and AARON behind them. At the left, behind Titus, are two soldiers bearing halberds. Below the picture is a text consisting of Tamora's plea for mercy when her son is to be sacrificed (1.1.104–120) and the captive Aaron's defiant proclamation of his own evil (5.1.125–144). These speeches are linked by three lines not from the play, presumably composed by Peachem. It is speculated that the Longleat manuscript may have been created for a private, amateur theatrical production.

**Longueville**   See LONGAVILLE.

**Lopez, Roderigo (d. 1594)**   Contemporary of Shakespeare, a Portuguese doctor living in England whose trial and execution for treason may have helped inspire the composition of *The Merchant of Venice.* Lopez, born Jewish but a Christian convert, fled the Portuguese Inquisition in 1579 and by 1586 was appointed physician to Queen ELIZABETH (1). In 1592 he entered into a dangerous intrigue involving a pretender to the Portuguese throne, and he appears to have antagonised the powerful Earl of ESSEX (2), who accused him of plotting to poison the Queen. Although Lopez was almost certainly innocent, some of his servants testified under torture that the charge was true, and he was hanged on June 7, 1594. His trial stimulated an outbreak of anti-Semitic feeling in London and also spurred a series of revivals of *The Jew of Malta,* by Christopher MARLOWE (1). It has often been thought that when GRATIANO (1) insultingly tells Shylock that his soul is that of 'a wolf . . . hanged for human slaughter' (4.1.134), he was punning on Lopez' name, which means 'wolf'.

**Lord (1)**  Character in *The Taming of the Shrew,* a country gentleman who appears in the INDUCTION. The Lord takes in the besotted and unconscious Christopher SLY (1) and, as a practical joke, installs the rustic tinker in his home as a gentleman. The Lord is not a three-dimensional character, but he offers a plausible picture of a country gentleman amid his pleasures.

**Lord (2)**  Minor character in *Richard II,* an accuser of the Duke of AUMERLE in 4.1. The Lord asserts that Aumerle falsely denied his complicity in an earlier murder plot, and he challenges Aumerle to a trial by combat. His accusation and challenge follow several others and lend a vivid sense of excess and confusion to the scene, thereby suggesting the potential for chaos produced by the victory of BOLINGBROKE (1) over King RICHARD II.

**Lord (3)**  Minor character in *Much Ado About Nothing,* follower of CLAUDIO (1). The Lord walks with Claudio in HERO's supposed funeral procession in 5.3; he speaks only one line.

**Lord (4)**  Any of several minor characters in *As You Like It,* noblemen in the court of the exiled DUKE (7) Senior. In 2.1 two Lords tell the duke of an encounter with JAQUES (1), and in 2.7 they attend the duke's forest banquet. They also seem likely to be the unspecified 'others' of several stage directions—e.g., at the opening of 2.5.

In addition, two other Lords, from the court of the evil DUKE (1) Frederick, tell their master in 2.2 that ROSALIND, CELIA, and TOUCHSTONE have fled his court.

**Lord (5)**  Any of several minor characters in *Hamlet,* members of the court of the KING (5) of DENMARK. In 4.3 the Lords provide an audience for the King's remarks on the danger of Prince HAMLET's madness. In 5.1 they attend the funeral of OPHELIA and help break up the fight between Hamlet and LAERTES. In 5.2 one of the Lords delivers a request from the QUEEN (9) that Hamlet make peace with Laertes before their upcoming fencing match, and the Lords are presumably among the crowd of courtiers—'all the State' in the stage direction at 5.2.220—who witness that contest. As anonymous onlookers, the Lords heighten our sense of Hamlet's isolation, and they also contribute to a sense of the stratified social world in which the prince lives.

**Lord (6)**  Either of two characters in *All's Well That Ends Well,* French noblemen. Though distinguished as the First Lord and the Second Lord, these two characters are very similar and serve the same dramatic purpose. Reappearing throughout the play, they offer a distinct viewpoint on its developments, especially on the progress of BERTRAM and PAROLLES, and they help

to mould the audience's opinions. Recognising the dishonourable cowardice of Parolles, they devise a plan to expose him to Bertram. They recognise Bertram's moral weakness, but they believe in his capacity for improvement, thereby offsetting our possible distaste for him. In addition, their fond admiration of the KING (17) in 1.2 and 2.1 stimulates our appreciation of him, which in turn influences our opinions of Bertram and HELENA (2) when the King shows affection for them. The Lords encourage our positive response to Helena when they sympathise with her abandonment by Bertram in 3.2, while at the same time they downplay Bertram's guilt by blaming Parolles for his behaviour.

The Lords are stereotypes of noble courtiers, and they lack individual personalities. Their parts differ slightly only once, when, at the end of 3.6, the First Lord assumes the job of capturing Parolles while the Second Lord leaves with Bertram for an off-stage visit to DIANA (1), thus enabling him to report on Bertram's attempted seduction when the two Lords critique the young count in 4.3.

In the FIRST FOLIO text of the play, the First and Second Lords are respectively designated 'G' and 'E' in speech headings and stage directions. These initials are presumed to refer to actors in the KING'S MEN who played the parts, probably William ECCLESTONE and Samuel GILBURNE or Robert GOUGH.

**Lord (7)**  Any of four minor characters in *All's Well That Ends Well,* young noblemen whom HELENA (2) rejects as possible husbands. In 2.3, having recovered his health through Helena's treatment, the KING (17) offers her the agreed-upon reward: her choice of a husband from among the young men of his court. She speaks to several of the Lords before choosing BERTRAM, as she had intended all along. The rejected Lords merely comprise a tableau of knightly personages; they speak only three lines among them.

**Lord (8)**  Any of several minor characters in *Macbeth,* members of MACBETH's royal court. In 3.4 several Lords are present at a banquet and witness Macbeth's distress at the appearance of the GHOST (4) of BANQUO. They accept LADY (6) MACBETH's explanation—that the king is suffering the effects of an old illness—and depart. In 3.6 a single, unidentified Lord meets with LENOX, and they observe that Prince MALCOLM has arrived in England, and that Macbeth has defected to his cause. In both scenes, the anonymous noblemen bear witness to the unravelling of Macbeth's power.

Some scholars agree with the suggestion of Samuel JOHNSON (7) that the FIRST FOLIO stage direction calling for 'Lenox and another lord' at the opening of 3.6 was an error that resulted from the misinterpretation of a manuscript abbreviation—'An'.—for ANGUS, who was actually intended as Lenox' companion. This idea cannot be proven, and in any case, as Angus is a minor character like the Lords, the effect would be identical.

**Lord (9)**   Any of several minor characters in *Coriolanus*, noblemen of ANTIUM. In 5.6 AUFIDIUS presents the Lords of the City, as they are designated in the stage directions, with his evidence that CORIOLANUS has betrayed the Volscian army, which he had joined when he was banished from ROME. Aufidius' inflammatory speech rouses the crowd (see COMMONER [2]) into a lynch mob, while various Lords—designated as First, Second, and Third Lord—attempt to keep order without effect. Like MENENIUS in Rome, the Lords are peaceable men whose efforts to control the mob are ineffective when faced with a leader who can manipulate the shifting moods of the common people. Thus, they help demonstrate an important point of the play: that the common people are unreliable participants in political life.

**Lord (10)**   Any of several minor characters in *Timon of Athens*, flatterers of TIMON. In 1.1 two Lords—designated First and Second Lords but indistinguishable from one another—are criticised by APEMANTUS as dishonest flatterers whose intent is to profit from Timon's generosity. As soon as he departs, the Lords laugh over their good fortune in knowing Timon, and it is clear that Apemantus' judgement was correct. In 1.2 a Third Lord joins them and their flattery is again mocked by Apemantus; all are rewarded with expensive gifts. In 3.6 four Lords gather to receive more bounty, even after they have given patently self-serving excuses why they cannot make loans to the newly impoverished Timon. However, Timon curses them and throws them out, and we see no more of them. The Lords have one personality trait between them—they are greedy hypocrites. They talk about their generosity, but are actually misers. Some commentators have identified these characters with Timon's faithless friends, LUCIUS (3), LUCULLUS, SEMPRONIUS, and VENTIDIUS (2).

**Lord (11)**   Any of several minor characters in *Pericles*, gentlemen of PERICLES' court. The Lords appear briefly in 1.2, flattering Pericles. HELICANES denounces them and thereby gains the confidence of Pericles, who puts him in charge when he leaves TYRE. In 2.4 a group of Lords insist that Tyre needs a resident ruler and that if Pericles does not return, Helicanes should take his place. Helicanes puts them off for a year while he sends for Pericles, who returns to Tyre and is thus separated from his wife and child. Thus, the Lords further the inexorable workings of fate.

**Lord (12)**   Minor character in *Pericles*, a gentleman of THARSUS. In 1.4 the Lord brings CLEON word that a convoy of ships approaches. Though Cleon fears invasion, the Lord observes that the ships bear flags of truce. Sent to escort the arrivals to Cleon, the Lord returns with PERICLES. The Lord is not a developed character, though his common sense presents a mild opposition to Cleon's pessimism.

**Lord (13)**   Any of several minor characters in *Pericles*, attendants of King SIMONIDES of PENTAPOLIS. At the king's jousting tournament in 2.2, three of the Lords mock PERICLES who is wearing rusty armour. This elicits Simonides' observation that 'Opinion's but a fool, that makes us scan / The outward habit by the inward man' (2.2.55–57). The Lords speak only eight lines between them and serve to introduce this single point.

**Lord (14)**   Minor character in *Pericles*, an attendant of LYSIMACHUS. In 5.1 Lysimachus confers with HELICANUS about the speechless despair of PERICLES, and a member of his retinue, the First Lord, reminds his master of the extraordinary qualities of MARINA, who may be able to 'win some words of him' (5.1.43). This timely suggestion brings about the climactic reunion of Pericles and Marina. The fact that the suggestion is made by a minor figure maintains the dignity of Lysimachus—who should not seem preoccupied with Marina—and adds to the atmosphere of courtly formality with which the play abounds.

**Lord (15)**   Any of several minor characters in *Cymbeline*, noblemen at the court of King CYMBELINE. In 1.3 and 2.1 two of the noblemen are featured as followers of the uncouth Prince CLOTEN; the First Lord is attentive and flattering, but the Second Lord mocks the obnoxious prince behind his back, which helps to characterise the play's comic villain. In Acts 3–5, the Lords play a smaller part as often-silent figures who swell the scene at Cymbeline's court. A single Lord appears in 5.3 as a soldier who has fled from the battle against the Romans. Though this could possibly be a different person, POSTHUMUS' disdain for him would be appropriate if he were one of Cloten's followers. In any case, this Lord serves to receive information as Posthumus tells him—and the audience—of the battle's outcome.

**Lord (16)**   Any of several minor characters in *The Winter's Tale*, followers of King LEONTES of SICILIA. A Lord, one of several present, objects to Leontes' brutal imprisonment of his Queen HERMIONE for adultery with King POLIXENES of BOHEMIA. When another Lord, ANTIGONUS, supports the first in his certainty that Hermione is innocent, the king goes so far as to admit that he has submitted the question to the oracle of Apollo. The Lords are present in 2.3 when the raging king sentences his infant daughter, PERDITA, to death. Again, they and Antigonus temper the king's course somewhat, although Leontes still orders the baby abandoned in the wilderness. The Lords are present at Hermione's trial in 3.2 and a Lord announces the return of King Polixenes in 5.1, but their chief function has already been filled. They help maintain a background of outraged virtue against which the madness of Leontes stands out in the first, tragic half of the play.

**Lord (17) Bardolph** Character in *2 Henry IV*. See BARDOLPH (2).

**Lord (18) Chamberlain** Character in *Henry VIII*. See CHAMBERLAIN (2).

**Lord (19) Chancellor** Character in *Henry VIII*. See CHANCELLOR.

**Lord (20) Chief Justice** Character in *2 Henry IV*. See CHIEF JUSTICE.

**Lord (21) Marshal** Character in *Richard II*. See MARSHAL (1).

**Lorenzo** Character in *The Merchant of Venice*, suitor and then husband of JESSICA. A friend of ANTONIO (2) and BASSANIO, Lorenzo is a stock theatrical figure, a stylish young aristocrat with little distinctive personality. However, the rhapsodies of Lorenzo and Jessica on moonlight and music in 5.1 provide the play's finest lyric poetry. Lorenzo's musing on the music of the spheres (5.1.55–65) presents an idea of universal harmony that is appropriate to the play's conclusion, in which the oppositions that have been its principal substance—love versus greed, justice versus mercy—are resolved.

*Love in a Forest* Play by Charles JOHNSON (2) based loosely on *As You Like It*. Produced in 1723, *Love in a Forest* was the first version of Shakespeare's play to appear for more than a century, but it was a radically changed text. It incorporated elements from several of Shakespeare's other plays—including *A Midsummer Night's Dream, Much Ado About Nothing, Twelfth Night*, and even *Richard II*—and eliminated a number of characters, among them TOUCHSTONE, AUDREY, WILLIAM (2), PHEBE, and CORIN. Colley CIBBER (1) played JAQUES (1). Popular for a time, *Love in a Forest* was superseded in the 1740s by a production of *As You Like It* itself.

**Lovell (1) (Lovel), Sir Francis (1454–1487)** Historical figure and character in *Richard III*, a supporter of RICHARD III. Lovell is willing to undertake Richard's dirty work; he assists RATCLIFFE in the execution of HASTINGS (3), bringing that lord's severed head to Richard in 3.5.

The historical Lovell was Richard's Lord Chamberlain. He escaped capture after the battle of BOSWORTH FIELD and died two years later, fighting in an uprising against RICHMOND, by then King Henry VII. He was a distant cousin of Sir Thomas LOVELL (2), who appears in *Henry VIII*.

**Lovell (2), Sir Thomas (d. 1524)** Historical figure and minor character in *Henry VIII*, a follower of Cardinal WOLSEY and later Bishop GARDINER (1). Lovell appears as a member of Cardinal Wolsey's entourage in Acts 1 and 3. In 1.3–4 his bawdy banter helps establish the decadent flavour of King HENRY VIII's court while it is under the influence of Wolsey. In 2.1 he appears briefly to escort BUCKINGHAM (1) to his execution, a fate arranged by Wolsey. Here, however, he expresses sympathy for the Duke, in an incident that provides evidence of Buckingham's virtues, in contrast to Wolsey's vices. In 5.1 Bishop Gardiner has become Wolsey's successor as villain, and Lovell's support signifies as much; a pawn of the plot, he also provides the audience with information on the new political situation. The historical Lovell was a distant cousin of Sir Francis LOVELL (1), who appears in *Richard III*.

*A Lover's Complaint* Poem accompanying the SONNETS in their first edition (1609). A 329-line poem in RHYME ROYAL, *A Lover's Complaint* has often been declared non-Shakespearean, chiefly due to its inferior poetry, but current scholarly opinion finds it likely to be an early work of Shakespeare's. The poem consists largely of a monologue delivered to an aged shepherd (who never speaks and goes unmentioned after his introduction) by a distraught young woman who has been betrayed by her lover. Her complaint is overheard by an unnamed narrator who also disappears from the poem once he has set the scene.

The woman tells of having encountered a man whom everyone loved, a paragon of male beauty and wit. She realised, however, that he repeatedly broke his vows of love and fathered many illegitimate children, and she vowed not to succumb to him. However, when he approached her, he acknowledged his reputation but insisted that only in knowing her had he experienced true love. He wept because she could not love him, and she gave in and slept with him. Now, in disgrace and apparently abandoned, she regrets having fallen prey to his wiles, while admitting that he was so attractive that she might do the same thing again.

The COMPLAINT, the genre to which the poem belongs, was very popular in the 1590s, and *A Lover's Complaint* may be, like *Venus and Adonis* and *The Rape of Lucrece*, a product of the young playwright's enforced idleness during the period when the London theatres were closed by a plague epidemic (June 1592–May 1594). If Shakespeare wrote it, it is unquestionably an immature and undeveloped work, particularly in its presentation of personality—as a result of which some have felt it may date from even earlier in Shakespeare's career—but it does contain pleasing passages, and it is in fact a quite respectable example of Elizabethan verse. On the other hand, it is an essentially trivial work—unlike the two narrative poems, most of the sonnets, and *The Phoenix and Turtle*, the acknowledged Shakespearean poems—and it contains a high percentage of words not found elsewhere in Shakespeare's works; these considerations argue against its inclusion in the Shakespearean CANON. The matter cannot be satisfactorily settled unless new evidence appears, which is unlikely, so *A Lover's Complaint* is best appreciated as a piece of good Elizabethan poetry that can suggest something of the poet's relation to the literary world of his day. If it is by Shakespeare, it is certainly among the least of his works.

## *Love's Labour's Lost*

### SYNOPSIS

#### Act 1, Scene 1

The KING (19) of Navarre proposes to dedicate himself and his courtiers to the pursuit of scholarship. He requires his three gentlemen-in-waiting to sign an oath, swearing off revelry, banqueting, and the company of women for three years. LONGAVILLE and DUMAINE sign readily, but BEROWNE argues against such rigour. He points out a problem with forbidding the company of women: the PRINCESS (1) of France is scheduled to arrive shortly. The King agrees that she will have to be an exception. DULL, a constable, appears with COSTARD, a CLOWN (1), and delivers a comically rhetorical letter from ARMADO, a visiting Spaniard whose ludicrous pedantry is well known. The letter accuses Costard of speaking with JAQUENETTA, contrary to the King's proclamation against consorting with women. The King sentences Costard to a week's diet of bran and water, to be overseen by Armado.

#### Act 1, Scene 2

Armado and his page, MOTH (1), exchange pedantries; the saucy page mocks his master, who is too slow-witted to notice. Armado confesses his love for Jaquenetta, but he feels ashamed of it because she is a common country girl. Costard, Dull, and Jaquenetta appear. Dull announces Costard's scheduled fast. Before Jaquenetta departs with Dull, Armado speaks to her of his love; she is cool. Armado angrily sends Costard away to be imprisoned, in the custody of Moth, and soliloquises ruefully on the power of love.

#### Act 2, Scene 1

The Princess of France and her entourage arrive. In light of rumours concerning the King's vow to exclude women from his court, the Princess sends her adviser BOYET ahead to announce her approach. She talks with her waiting-women about the King of Navarre's cour-

tiers, whom they have met before. MARIA (1) praises Longaville, KATHARINE (1) admires Dumaine, and ROSALINE (1) is taken with Berowne. Boyet returns and announces that the King, who is arriving with his courtiers, plans to house the visiting women in tents outside the court, in accordance with his vows. The King and his courtiers arrive. The Princess upbraids the King for his poor hospitality, and she delivers a written message from her father. The courtiers converse with the ladies. Berowne and Rosaline exchange witty remarks; she sharply parries his advances. The King apologises for the accommodations he must provide because of his oath, and he and his retinue depart. Dumaine, Longaville, and Berowne each re-enter in turn to inquire of Boyet the name of the gentlewoman he has been conversing with.

#### Act 3, Scene 1

Armado orders Moth to free Costard, who is to deliver a love letter to Jaquenetta. Moth goes, after teasing his master about his infatuation, and returns with Costard, who is given the letter. Berowne enters and commissions Costard to deliver a letter to Rosaline. Costard departs, and Berowne, in a soliloquy, despairs that he has been captured by love.

#### Act 4, Scene 1

Costard interrupts the Princess' deer-hunting party to deliver Berowne's letter to Rosaline. The Princess gleefully asks Boyet to open it and read it aloud. However, Costard has delivered the wrong letter; it is Armado's letter to Jaquenetta, and its preposterous style causes great glee.

#### Act 4, Scene 2

HOLOFERNES, a comically pedantic schoolmaster, and his follower NATHANIEL (1) discuss the deer hunt in absurdly scholastical terms, to the consternation of Dull. Jaquenetta appears with Costard, seeking a literate person to read her the letter she has received. Nathaniel reads it; it is a sonnet by Berowne, intended for Rosaline. Holofernes realises that it has been misdelivered, and he instructs Jaquenetta to take it to the King, for it may be important.

#### Act 4, Scene 3

Berowne, alone, again bemoans the fact that he is in love. He hides himself as the King approaches. The King reads a poem he has written and reveals that he, too, is in love. The King also hides when Longaville appears, and Longaville does the same thing, hiding in his turn when Dumaine appears and also reads a love poem. As Dumaine finishes, Longaville comes forth to tease him, but the King in turn chastises them both for breaking their ascetic vows. Berowne comes forth to rebuke the King for hypocrisy, and he takes a superior attitude to them all until Jaquenetta arrives with his letter to Rosaline. Admitting his love, Berowne then provides a rationale for romantic behaviour. He says that their vows are unnatural for young men, and, further, that love, superior to all else, should be their proper subject of study. The King and the other courtiers rejoice in his solution and lay plans for festive entertainments to help woo their intended lovers.

*Act 5, Scene 1*
Armado, while bragging grandiloquently of his close relations with the King, announces that he has been asked to arrange a pageant to entertain the Princess. He consults with Holofernes, who proposes a presentation of 'The Nine WORTHIES', a traditional tableau.

*Act 5, Scene 2*
The Princess and her gentlewomen mock their suitors, comparing the gifts of jewelry and poems they have received. Boyet arrives to report that he has overheard the courtiers planning to approach the ladies disguised as a delegation of Russians. The Princess devises a counter-plot: the ladies shall be masked, and shall each wear the jewelry given to another of them, so each suitor will address the wrong woman. The gentlemen enter, and the ladies teasingly refuse to dance with them. Each suitor then proceeds to take aside the wrong lady and profess his love. The women continue their ridicule, and soon the gentlemen beat a retreat. The ladies exult in their triumph. Shortly, the gentlemen return undisguised. The women tease the men further by jesting about the fools garbed as Russians that had been present earlier. The embarrassed gentlemen realise that the women had known them all along, and Berowne makes a confessional speech disavowing 'perjury'. The King, reaffirming his earlier vows of love, is perplexed when Rosaline claims to have received them, rather than the Princess. Berowne realises what has happened and rails against Boyet as a spy and teller of tales.

Costard arrives, announcing that the pageant of the Nine Worthies is about to begin. The noblemen heckle the commoners; they drive Nathaniel and then Holofernes from the stage. Costard, misunderstanding part of Armado's performance, breaks in and reveals that Jaquenetta is pregnant by the Spaniard. Armado and Costard are egged on towards a duel by the gentlemen, but MARCADE appears with news of the death of the King of France, the Princess' father.

The emotional tone of the play changes instantly. The 'Worthies' are dismissed; the Princess prepares to depart and, in a new mood of sadness, apologises to the king for the ridicule that she and her maids have used. The King, aided by Berowne, persists in courtship; the Princess responds by promising him her love only if he will adopt a severely monastic life for a year. Katharine and Maria also require a year's wait for Dumaine and Longaville. Rosaline, observing that Berowne has an excessively mocking wit, requires that he spend the same year visiting dying patients in hospi-

tals to learn a more proper seriousness. Armado returns and requests that the nobles hear the song intended to close the pageant. The assembled commoners then conclude the play with a song 'in praise of the owl and the cuckoo' (5.2.878–879).

## COMMENTARY

*Love's Labour's Lost* is a difficult play for modern readers, but it can prove to be a rewarding one. Its basic story-line, in which pretensions are deflated and love conquers all, has a universal appeal. It is well plotted and constructed, and it contains a number of attractive lyrical passages and many comical sketches. Its cheerfully unrealistic atmosphere of games and festive play yields, at the last, to a sterner but nevertheless attractive vision of achieved maturity in the real world and the promise of future happiness.

Nevertheless, the play can seem unapproachable. It is full of in-jokes for Shakespeare's contemporaries, and much of its more accessible humour concerns the use of over-elaborate language, which is of course even farther from our own English than most Elizabethan dialogue. Its characters are often types drawn from older traditions and based on social roles that no longer exist. And its four sets of lovers who barely know each other seem implausible, to say the least. However, the playwright's organisational and linguistic genius carries the audience through the development of the play's comic situation to the satisfactions of its resolution.

The reader can dispose of many of the play's difficulties by dealing with them in a fashion that makes its virtues more evident. The witticisms in *Love's Labour's Lost* are frequently baffling to the most committed scholars and may simply be ignored. It is enough to know that they refer to lost controversies that were possibly obscure even to much of the original audience. Similarly, the inflated rhetorical posturings of Armado and Holofernes are amusingly pretentious, although we may not recognise the once-fashionable manners being parodied. Indeed, the greater part of the humour of a scene such a 4.2, which introduces Holofernes and Nathaniel, lies in its incomprehensibility—to the audience no less than to Dull. Shakespeare's point—that pomposity and pretension in language are laughable—is easy to enjoy in itself, and it also is linked to the main plot.

The romance of the gentlemen and ladies provides the main interest. The play begins with the King's unnatural demand for a dry and rigorous asceticism in the name of learning. This strange proposition, counter to common sense and human instinct, is established in order that it may be refuted. Berowne begins, even in 1.1, to oppose it; his sense of reality never completely deserts him, and he is the first to shake off the fakery that the gentlemen have entangled themselves in. We see the extent to which the false ideal of ascetic scholarship has been manifested in language, and the SUB-PLOT's connection to the main plot emerges. Just as the gentlemen violate their own natures in attempting to emphasise dry learning over real living, so do the lesser characters err in reducing learning itself to foolish verbiage. In a sense, these figures may be said to be parodies of the King's gentlemen as well as of contemporary manners and mores.

The dramatic conflict between the high-flown pretensions of the King and the sensible humour of the Princess of France and her ladies is established early, and the comedy of the main plot lies in two chief manifestations of that tension: the embarrassed attempts by the gentlemen to resist and then deny love; and the practical joke played on them by the disguised ladies. The story alternates with the sub-plot, scene by scene, with very little overlap. A third component, the element of pageantry, integrates the two plots to some degree, although Shakespeare had not yet mastered the complex interwoven plots of his later, richer works.

If the characters in *Love's Labour's Lost* tend to be rather one-dimensional, this is not inappropriate to the somewhat abstract nature of the play. It is a comedy of notions, in which a blatantly false ideal is overcome by common sense and love is permitted to prevail. The humorous characters of the sub-plot derive mostly from the comical archetypes of the Italian COMMEDIA DELL'ARTE; the lords and ladies are simply courtly representatives of the warring ideals. The exception is Berowne, whose humanity provides a foil for the cold, ascetic withdrawal proposed by the King. His humorous self-mocking soliloquy in which he admits to having fallen in love (3.1.168–200) propels the play towards its lively series of climaxes, and his energy drives the comic tour de force in 4.3, when the King and his three courtiers discover that they have all succumbed to love.

Although Berowne is the most fully developed character in the play, several other figures briefly exhibit flashes of Shakespearean life. The Princess, for instance, is also humanly believable; from her first speech (2.1.13–34), she is intelligent and sensible. Rosaline's sharp wit and balanced sensibility also inspire affection. Katharine has one touching moment of reality, when she is reminded of the death of her sister (5.2.14–18). Costard, primarily a character type, a combination of CLOWN (1) and FOOL (1), also engages our sympathy in a more personal way when he shamefacedly apologises for misreading a line in the pageant of the Worthies (5.2.554–555) and when, shortly thereafter, he speaks up for Nathaniel, who is stricken with stage fright (5.2.575–579).

On the whole, however, the play does not exploit or depend on the delineation of character. It is a formal exercise, balancing the fantastic and the actual, and is as near to dance as it is to psychological realism. As

such it must be crisply organised. The alternations of verse and prose, of main plot and sub-plot, merge in the pageantry of the final scene. Acts 1–2 constitute the exposition, Acts 3–4 develop both story lines, and Act 5 creates a transcendent world of romance and festivity, enabling the audience to forget the mundane world. The unreal atmosphere of the play is finally shattered by the appearance of Marcade, a messenger from the real world.

This bold and unexpected stroke, a *coup de théâtre*, changes the tone of the play instantly. 'The scene begins to cloud', Berowne observes (5.2.714), and the final few minutes take place in a more sober atmosphere. But although the interval of festive mirth is ended, it is not repudiated. It must be found in a larger universe, the real world that includes grief and business, but it is allowed its place. A maturation that has taken place permits this, for the gentlemen have advanced from a self-absorbed withdrawal in the name of abstract ideas to a more humane involvement with others. The ladies require of the gentlemen a testing period before their loves can be consummated, but, beyond this chastening trial, the prospect of a happy conclusion is unmistakable. The reappearance of the entire company to sing the opposing songs of Winter and Spring expresses the reality of ongoing life.

## SOURCES OF THE PLAY

No written source for the plot of *Love's Labour's Lost* has ever been found, although it has been speculated that an earlier play may have been revised, as is true of other Shakespearean dramas. However, there is no actual evidence that such a predecessor existed, and most authorities conclude that the playwright invented his own stories in this play.

Nevertheless, many details may be traced to the general public knowledge of the day concerning the French Wars of Religion, then drawing to a close. English interest in that conflict was very great, largely because English troops participated in it, in 1591–1593, on the side of the Protestant rebel Henri, King of Navarre, later Henri IV of France. Thus Shakespeare and his audience were familiar with the events in France that *Love's Labour's Lost* alludes to. The central figure in the play is also the King of Navarre, and the names of his courtiers correspond to well-known political figures in Henri's world. Also, Henri did receive a delegation from France headed by a princess; although he was married to her at the time, they were on opposite sides in the war and were engaged in renegotiating her dowry, an important component of which was Aquitaine, the focus of the Princess's embassy in the play. Moreover, Henri of Navarre was one of many 16th-century rulers to found an academy based on Italian Renaissance models. All of these facts were common knowledge in England, thanks to the presence there of many Protestant refugees from the wars and through many printed accounts.

However, a prominent literary work may also have figured in the genesis of the play: it has been theorised that *Love's Labour's Lost* was written as a rejoinder to 'Shadow of Night', a long poem by George CHAPMAN that extols a life of contemplation and study, as opposed to the concerns of mundane existence. According to this theory, the playwright was involved in a literary dispute among politically hostile aristocratic cliques; references to some of the participants in this feud (see, e.g., Thomas NASHE) are certainly hidden in the now-obscure passages of by-play that baffle most modern readers, such as 3.1.81–95. An attack on Chapman, and on esoteric knowledge, was an attack on Sir Walter RALEIGH and his friends, made on behalf of a rival group led by the Earl of ESSEX (2), whose close friend, the Earl of SOUTHAMPTON (2), was Shakespeare's patron.

The Russian masquerade in 5.2 is thought to have been inserted in a revision of the play made no earlier than 1595, for it, too, can be associated with historical evidence. In 1594 the annual Christmas revels at Gray's Inn (see INNS OF COURT) included a comical pageant of Russians (probably stimulated by the publication in 1591 of a popular and influential book on Russia by Giles FLETCHER [1] an early English traveller to Moscow). We may suppose that Shakespeare knew of this event, for *The Comedy of Errors* was performed at the same festival, a production which the playwright probably acted in himself. Moreover, certain details in *Love's Labour's Lost* correspond with accounts of the Gray's Inn pageant of Russians.

## TEXT OF THE PLAY

Scholars agree, for a number of reasons, that the text of *Love's Labour's Lost* reflects two renderings of the play. Most prominently, there are several passages that are printed in two versions. Also, there is variation in the names provided for several characters in stage directions and dialogue headings, and there is an evident change in the casting of the pageant of the Nine Worthies between its planning in 5.1 and its presentation in 5.2. Further, it has been speculated that the play may originally have ended at 5.2.870, before the anticlimactic songs of Winter and Spring, and that a scene involving Armado and Moth was cut, leaving Costard's puzzling lines at 4.1.145–150. Internal evidence suggests dates for both an original version and a revision. (See 'Sources of the Play'.) The original composition of *Love's Labour's Lost* probably dates from around 1593, at the height of the literary dispute with which it is associated and while England was still involved in the French wars; the play was apparently revised after 1594.

The earliest surviving text of the play is the QUARTO edition of 1598, by William WHITE (2) for publisher Cuthbert BURBY; this is, incidentally, the earliest play text to carry Shakespeare's name on the title page. The phrase 'newly corrected and augmented' also appears on the title page, suggesting that an earlier edition, of which no copy has survived, had been printed. (However, the phrase may simply refer to the revision of the play.) The 1598 edition was very clumsily printed, with many typographical errors, but it has nevertheless served as the basis for all subsequent editions, including that in the FIRST FOLIO of 1623.

## THEATRICAL HISTORY OF THE PLAY

The title page of the Quarto edition of 1598 records that *Love's Labour's Lost* was performed at the court of Queen Elizabeth during the Christmas festivities of 1597, and it had probably been staged previously as well. The only other specifically recorded early production was also held at court, in 1604, although the Quarto of 1631 asserts that the play had been performed at the BLACKFRIARS THEATRE, where Shakespeare's works were not produced before 1608. The very existence of the second Quarto edition suggests that the play remained popular through the first decades of the 17th century. It then completely disappeared from the stage for two centuries, although its songs were occasionally adapted in other works.

First revived in 1839, *Love's Labour's Lost* was both staged and published a number of times in the 19th century. In the 20th it has received a great deal of scholarly and critical attention and is now regarded as one of Shakespeare's most important early works. As such, it has been presented in several major productions and has proven to be quite popular with theatre goers. It has not been made a FILM, but it has been presented twice on TELEVISION.

*Love's Labour's Won* Possible lost play by Shakespeare. In 1598 Francis MERES listed *Love's Labour's Won* among Shakespeare's comedies. This title was for many years identified with *The Taming of the Shrew*, the only pre-1598 Shakespearean COMEDY that Meres omitted. However, the question was raised anew in 1953, with the discovery of a 1603 bookseller's catalogue listing both *Shrew* and *Love's Labour's Won*. *Won* could still be *Shrew*, published under another title sometime before 1603 in an edition that has not survived. It could also be such an edition of one of the other comedies appearing after 1598—and so not in Meres' list—but before 1603. The most likely nominees are *All's Well That Ends Well* and *Much Ado About Nothing*, though *As You Like It* and *Troilus and Cressida* have also been suggested.

*Love's Martyr* Allegorical poem by Robert Chester, published in 1601 with a collection of shorter poems by other poets, including Shakespeare's *The Phoenix and Turtle*, in a book of the same name. Nothing is known of Chester except that he was a member of the household of Sir John SALUSBURY, whose marriage in 1586 this book so commemorates. An allegory, the poem tells of a mystical love between two birds—the turtledove (commonly called 'turtle' in Elizabethan English), a symbol of fidelity, and the mythological phoenix, an ancient emblem of immortality. The allegory is, however, interspersed with discourses on King Arthur, precious stones, natural history, and so on. Eventually, the phoenix and the turtle decide to die together, and they construct a funeral pyre and burn to death.

The love between phoenix and turtledove is also the theme of the poems later added to Chester's, including *The Phoenix and Turtle*. Salusbury was knighted in 1601, and this was probably the occasion for the poem's publication, with the addition of work by much better-known writers, several of them Salusbury's friends; *Love's Martyr* also includes contributions by George CHAPMAN, Ben JONSON, and John MARSTON, among others. Shakespeare's *Phoenix* is now the only well-known piece in the book.

*Love's Martyr* was first published in 1601 by Edward BLOUNT in a QUARTO edition printed by Richard FIELD (2). Ten years later it was republished with a new title, *The Annals of Great Britain,* but only the title-page varied from the original quarto. The 1601 edition has therefore been the basis of all subsequent editions of both Chester's poem, which was not republished until 1878, and of *The Phoenix and Turtle*.

**Lowin (Lowen), John (1576–1653)**   English actor. One of the 26 men listed in the FIRST FOLIO as the 'Principall Actors' of Shakespeare's plays, Lowin was one of the most noted members of the KING'S MEN in the early 17th century. A very large man, he was famous for his FALSTAFF, and he may have originated the part of HENRY VIII (although this report—that Lowin learned the part from Shakespeare himself—dates from 1708 and is suspect).

Lowin was apprenticed to a goldsmith as a boy, but as soon as he was free he turned to the stage. He was a member of WORCESTER'S MEN in 1602–1603, but in 1603 joined the King's Men, becoming a partner in 1604. After 1630 he was a co-manager of the company, with Joseph TAYLOR, and he remained with them until the closing of the theatres by the revolution in 1642. After retirement he owned a small tavern, but died in poverty.

**Luce**   Minor character in *The Comedy of Errors*, a servant who, with ADRIANA, refuses ANTIPHOLUS OF EPHESUS entrance to his own home in 3.1, believing him to be an imposter. Luce is often identified with NELL (1), who is referred to later in the play.

**Lucentio**   Character in *The Taming of the Shrew*, the successful suitor of BIANCA (1). Lucentio, aided by his servant TRANIO, disguises himself as a tutor of languages and thus gains access to Bianca, against the wishes of her father, BAPTISTA. Eventually, he elopes with his lover. His wealthy father, VINCENTIO (1) assures Baptista that he will provide an adequate financial settlement on the couple, and Lucentio is forgiven, only to find, in the final scene, that Bianca is not the ideally demure young bride he had anticipated.

Although the romance of Bianca and Lucentio is contrasted to the mercenary calculations of her father, Lucentio is a rather bloodless lover. He is simply a stereotype—the handsome young male romantic lead—representing a tradition as old as ancient Roman drama. However, in earlier plays, this character tended to marry for money and extend romantic love to mistresses and courtesans; Shakespeare's alteration reflects his concern with love in marriage, a major theme of *The Taming of the Shrew*.

**Lucetta**   Minor character in *The Two Gentlemen of Verona*, the waiting-woman to JULIA. Like the other servants in the play, SPEED and LAUNCE, Lucetta seems at least as alert and intelligent as her employer. She is aware of her mistress' love for Proteus before Julia is willing to admit it to herself, and she suspects Proteus of disloyalty when Julia is all too trusting.

**Lucian (c. 120–180 A.D.)**   Greek satirist, author of a probable source for *Timon of Athens*. Lucian's *Timon the Misanthrope* is a satirical dialogue that contains numerous elements of Shakespeare's plot, and clearly was known to Shakespeare in some form. Though no English translation of this work existed in Shakespeare's day, he may have known it in Latin, French, or Italian. Alternatively, he may have used another source based on Lucian, perhaps an anonymous English play known as the 'old *Timon*' (c. 1580–1610), or perhaps some work now lost, possibly a source for the 'old *Timon*' that derived from Lucian.

Lucian was originally from a Greek-speaking settlement in what is now Syria. He travelled around the Roman Empire lecturing on philosophy and rhetoric. He settled in Athens around the age of 40, and there wrote the dialogues that made him famous throughout the Mediterranean as a clever satirist of philosophical and religious ideas.

**Luciana**   Character in *The Comedy of Errors*, the sister-in-law of ANTIPHOLUS OF EPHESUS and the beloved of ANTIPHOLUS OF SYRACUSE. Luciana first appears in an argument with her sister, ADRIANA, about marital relations, in a standard disputation of the day. Luciana says that a man is properly the master of his wife and urges: 'O, know he is the bridle of your will' (2.1.13).

Luciana's demure pliancy is apparently attractive to Antipholus of Syracuse, for when he finds himself in his brother's house, not knowing himself to be mistaken for his twin, he meets Luciana, falls in love, and attempts to court the object of his affections. Luciana, believing him to be her brother-in-law, is naturally horrified by his advances and chastises him roundly (3.2.1–70). Moreover, she describes this exchange to Adriana, thereby furthering the confusion and misunderstanding at the heart of the play. Luciana's subsequent importance to the action is slight. Even when Antipholus of Syracuse observes at the play's conclusion that the re-establishment of his identity will permit him to court her in earnest, Luciana remains silent.

Luciana represents a type, rather than a fully drawn human being. She is the modest and subservient female, whose stipulated position in Elizabethan society served to perpetuate an ideal notion of the family (and, by extension, society at large) as a secure and lasting hierarchy, decreed by God and tradition and undisturbed by change or individual assertion. (Such assertion was of course present among Elizabethan womanhood, as represented by Adriana.) The two sisters together constitute an early attempt by the playwright to achieve a complex portrait of contemporary femininity. While Luciana is thus an incomplete character, she foreshadows aspects of later, more successful Shakespearean heroines, such as VIOLA, in *Twelfth Night*, and IMOGEN, in *Cymbeline*.

**Lucianus** Character in THE MURDER OF GONZAGO, the playlet presented within *Hamlet*. In 3.2 the PLAYERS (2), following HAMLET's instructions, perform before the court of KING (5) Claudius. In their play Lucianus murders the PLAYER KING by pouring poison in his ear, paralleling the murder of Hamlet's father by the real King. The play is interrupted by the King's guilty response—according to Hamlet's plan—and Lucianus does not get to complete his role, which would have involved marrying the PLAYER QUEEN. Significantly, Lucianus is the nephew of the king he kills—not the brother, as a strict analogy with Claudius' crime would require—and thus he presents to the King not only the image of himself as murderer but also that of Hamlet as avenger. Lucianus' only lines—a brief address to his poison 'of midnight weeds collected' (3.2.251)—are in a highly rhetorical style that is designed to highlight the artificiality of the play within a play.

**Lucilius (1) (active 42 B.C.)** Historical figure and minor character in *Julius Caesar*, an officer in the army of BRUTUS (4). Brutus confides in Lucilius, clearly a trusted subordinate, at SARDIS in 4.2 and 4.3 and at PHILIPPI in Act 5. In 5.4, as Brutus' army is overrun by the soldiers of Mark ANTONY, Lucilius pretends to be Brutus—daring his opponents to kill him and be acclaimed—in an effort to divert attention from his commander. He is taken prisoner, and Antony, who realises his captive is not Brutus, praises Lucilius' bravery and orders that he be treated kindly.

Lucilius' diversionary tactic was admired in ancient and medieval literature (and, presumably, in warfare) and was popular on the Elizabethan stage. Shakespeare had used it in *1 Henry IV*, where Sir Walter BLUNT (3) is killed while impersonating King HENRY IV. The playwright took Lucilius' exploit from PLUTARCH's *Lives*, where the officer is reported to have been a friend of Brutus and to have remained loyal to Antony after Philippi.

**Lucilius (2)** Minor character in *Timon of Athens*, a servant of TIMON. When an OLD ATHENIAN complains to Timon that the socially inferior Lucilius is courting his daughter, Timon promises Lucilius a fortune and thus makes him acceptable. The episode helps establish Timon's generosity and extravagance. Lucilius speaks very little and serves merely to further the plot.

**Lucillius** GHOST CHARACTER in *Antony and Cleopatra*, an attendant of ENOBARBUS. Lucillius appears only once and does not speak; he is mentioned only in the opening stage direction of 1.2, along with LAMPRIUS and RANNIUS.

**Lucio** Character in *Measure for Measure*, a dissolute gentleman who befriends the condemned CLAUDIO (3) and slanders the DUKE (9) of VIENNA. Although, as Claudio's friend, Lucio supports ISABELLA in her encounters with the obsessively strict official, ANGELO (2), he is nonetheless an unsavoury character. He maliciously defames the Duke and callously admits to having abandoned a pregnant woman; that he is forgiven his crimes in the end is an important part of the play's emphasis on the value of forgiveness.

We first see Lucio in 1.2, jesting lewdly about venereal disease with his friends (see GENTLEMAN [5]). A customer of the bordello run by MISTRESS (2) Overdone and POMPEY (1), Lucio represents the degenerate life that has flourished in Vienna because of the Duke's lax regime. He is not without good qualities, however. In standing by Isabella, in 2.2 and 2.4, he seems a positive figure, but beginning in 3.2 he takes on another aspect. He flippantly refuses to help Pompey avoid imprisonment, and Mistress Overdone declares that he has informed on her; these episodes make us realise that Lucio's Vienna is an ugly one. In 3.2 and 4.3 Lucio amuses himself by making up the libellous stories about the Duke for which he is punished in 5.1. He does not realise that the 'friar' with whom he converses is the disguised ruler himself.

While Lucio's slanderous lies are plainly malicious,

he seems funny, not evil, to modern sensibilities. But abuse of a ruler—believed to be appointed by God to maintain order in society—was a much more serious matter in Shakespeare's day than in our own, and Lucio's offence, although comical, is decidedly criminal. 17th-century audiences would not have been surprised by the severity of the Duke's proposed punishment: 'Let him be whipp'd and hang'd' (5.1.511). Nevertheless, Lucio remains wittily uncompromising at the end. This testifies to Shakespeare's sympathy with the rebellious individual, even in a play which stresses the importance of authority and the values of society at large.

**Lucius (1)** Character in *Titus Andronicus*, a son of TITUS (1) Andronicus. In 1.1 Lucius demands the ritual sacrifice of TAMORA's son, thus triggering the cycle of vengeance that drives the action. Later, he is banished from Rome and he joins the GOTHS. He returns in Act 5 at the head of the Gothic troops, and, in that capacity, he sentences the captured AARON to death. Continuing to Rome, he is present at the grisly finale, as is his son, YOUNG LUCIUS. Following the deaths of SATURNINUS and his father, he is acclaimed the new Emperor.

**Lucius (2)** Minor character in *Julius Caesar*, a young servant of BRUTUS. In 2.1 Lucius falls asleep while the conspirators plot the death of CAESAR (1), and Brutus expresses envy of the boy's carefree state. In 2.4 Lucius appears as an innocent foil to the near-hysterical worry of PORTIA (2). In 4.3, at Brutus' camp near SARDIS, Lucius plays a lute at his master's command, and Brutus shows consideration and affection for the boy in a scene that shows the zealous conspirator in an unusually soft light.

The episodes in which Lucius appears have a distinctive emotional tone. His role offers an important touch of domestic tenderness and loyalty in a work that is dominated by the darker themes of murderous politics and civil war.

**Lucius (3)** Character in *Timon of Athens*, an ungrateful friend to TIMON. In 3.2 Lucius hears that LUCULLUS has refused to assist Timon with a loan after Timon has impoverished himself by showering gifts on his friends. Like Lucullus, Lucius is also the beneficiary of Timon's excessive generosity, and he proudly declares to HOSTILIUS and two visitors (see STRANGER) that he would never turn away a friend. However, when Timon's servant SERVILIUS appears and asks for help, Lucius brazenly declares that he cannot make a loan. The hypocritical Lucius helps demonstrate—with Lucullus and SEMPRONIUS—the callousness of the Athenian aristocrats, one of the play's important themes.

**Lucius (4)** Character in *Cymbeline*, ambassador from ROME to the Britain of King CYMBELINE, later the commander of the invading Roman army and the employer of the disguised IMOGEN. In 3.1 Lucius informs Cymbeline that Rome demands tribute from Britain. When he receives the king's refusal he transmits his government's declaration of war. However, he adds that he regrets this, for he appreciates the hospitality he has received in Britain. His gentlemanly nature is again evident in 3.5, when he departs from the king's court, and we understand why PISANIO recommends that the disguised Imogen become a page for Lucius. He calls the Roman 'honourable, and . . . most holy' (3.4.178–179). In 4.2 Lucius readily offers employment and protection to Imogen. He believes that she is a young man, FIDELE, and he takes particular care of 'him' when the Romans are defeated in battle in 5.2. Finally, in 5.5 Lucius nobly faces death at the hands of the victorious Cymbeline, before he receives mercy in the play's final aura of reconciliation.

Lucius is a noble person who is unable to influence the course of events in the play. He is contrasted with assorted weak, but not evil, figures like POSTHUMUS and the king, and thus he offers a positive image of humanity's need for the intervention of providence. The ancient tradition that a soldier named Lucius was the first Roman converted to Christianity may be reflected in Shakespeare's choice of name for this positive character. Two of Shakespeare's other characters named Lucius (see LUCIUS [1, 2]) are also right-minded and in the military, so these may well be conscious references to the ancient convert, who was still fairly well known in the 17th century.

**Lucius' Servant** Minor character in *Timon of Athens*, the employee of LUCIUS (3), a former friend and creditor of TIMON. In 3.4 Lucius' Servant joins a group of colleagues who unsuccessfully dun Timon and his STEWARD (2) for repayment of loans. He and his fellows regret the necessity of serving greedy masters who once benefited from Timon's generosity. However, Lucius' Servant is somewhat more aggressive in demanding payment. He observes that Timon's has been a 'prodigal course' (3.4.12), and rejects an excuse of ill health, offered by Timon's servant, when he says, 'Methinks he should the sooner pay his debts / And make a clear way to the gods' (3.4.74–75). He thus reflects the atrocious behaviour of his master, who in 3.2 hypocritically refuses to assist the impoverished Timon after he has declared that he would help a friend in need.

**Lucrece (Lucretia)** Legendary Roman matron and central figure in *The Rape of Lucrece*, the victim of a rape by TARQUIN. Lucrece kills herself rather than accept the disgrace of having slept with someone other than her husband. The bulk of the 1,855-line poem—from her first awareness of Tarquin's menace in line 442 until her death in line 1724—is dedicated to Lucrece's responses, fearful, horrified, ashamed, and determinedly suicidal. Her great wordiness is often considered a weakness of the poem, but her meditations are nonetheless studded with brilliant passages and also reflect an aspect of Shakespeare's attitude towards women.

Sometimes seen as a victim who is further victimised, Lucrece is actually rather like the boldly assertive young women of Shakespeare's work who have charmed COMEDY audiences for generations. She is admittedly less well realised, however, and her situation is less rewarding, both for herself and for modern readers. Lucrece's values, impossibly remote from modern ones, lead her to adopt a course of great bravery against the advice of the men around her (see lines 1709–1710). She realises that only her death can repair the damage done to her self-esteem, and through her suicide she achieves heroic stature. In an aristocratic value system that gives great weight to marital loyalty—especially in women, who bear children and thus transmit the family line—Lucrece has been forcibly removed from the ranks of the pure, a status in which she has plainly taken great pride. She poignantly expresses her sense of her predicament by comparing herself to a damaged tree: '. . . the bark pill'd from the lofty pine, His leaves will wither and his sap decay; So must my soul, her bark being pill'd away' (lines 1167–1169).

In ancient heroic traditions, these situations are no more subject to rationalisation than are natural catastrophes. Lucrece's response preserves her honour, all that remains within her control. Although Lucrece's action is criticised by BRUTUS [2] (lines 1823–1827), she is nevertheless presented as an heroic figure and her actions stimulate an heroic act, the revolution against the Tarquinian kings and the establishment of the Roman Republic. Moreover, Lucrece's tale was so perfectly in accord with notions of honour and heroism that it survived through almost 2,000 years and several upheavals in European civilisation to find continued acceptance among the Elizabethans.

Shakespeare took the story of Lucrece's rape and its political consequences from his Latin sources, LIVY and OVID, but it is not historical, deriving in fact from pre-Latin traditions. Someone involved with the establishment of the republic may have had a wife named Lucretia (the Latin spelling of Lucrece), but nothing at all is known of her.

**Lucretius**  Legendary father of the Roman matron Lucretia and minor figure in *The Rape of Lucrece*, the father of LUCRECE. Lucretius appears only late in the poem. He is implicitly present from line 1583 but is not mentioned until line 1732, after Lucrece has told of TARQUIN's crime against her and killed herself. He delivers a touching, three-stanza outburst of grief (lines 1751–1771), but it is one of the other witnesses, BRUTUS (2), who rallies the mourners to exact vengeance against Tarquin, finally resulting in the fall of the monarchy. Shakespeare took Lucretius from his Latin sources, OVID and LIVY, who lived several centuries after these events supposedly took place; modern historians have found no record of Lucretius from his own time.

**Lucullus**  Character in *Timon of Athens*, an ungrateful friend of TIMON. In 1.2 Lucullus is among the guests at Timon's banquet. In 2.2 when Timon finds that his extravagant hospitality has bankrupted him, Lucullus is among those he presumes he can count on for assistance. However, when Lucullus is approached by Timon's servant FLAMINIUS for a loan, he declares that he had warned his friend. With unconscious irony, he says, 'Many a time and often I ha' din'd with him, and . . . come again to supper to him of purpose to have him spend less' (3.1.23–25). He sums up his position when he observes that 'this is no time to lend money, especially upon bare friendship, without security' (3.1. 41–43). He then tries to hide his ingratitude by bribing Flaminius to say he could not be found. Like LUCIUS (3) and SEMPRONIUS, whose similar responses occur in the next two scenes, Lucullus helps demonstrate the heartlessness of the Athenian aristocrats, one of the play's important themes.

**Lucy (1), Sir Thomas (1532–1600)**  Contemporary of Shakespeare, a WARWICKSHIRE landowner sometimes identified with Justice SHALLOW, a comic character in *2 Henry IV* and *The Merry Wives of Windsor*. According to a local tradition—first published by Nicholas ROWE in 1709—the young Shakespeare was caught poaching deer on Lucy's estate near STRATFORD; he was prosecuted for the crime and took vengeance by writing an insulting ballad about Sir Thomas. The same tradition was also recorded at about the same time by Richard DAVIES (3), testifying to its currency in the 17th century. In the 18th century several versions of the scurrilous ballad were published by various antiquarians.

Sir Thomas Lucy's heraldic emblem of three vertical white fish (luces—i.e., pike) resembles that of Shallow, as described with comic solemnity and confusion in *The Merry Wives*, 1.1.15–25, and Shallow threatens Falstaff with a lawsuit for having killed his deer. It thus appears that, if the tale of young Shakespeare and Lucy is true, the playwright could have been mocking his old enemy. However, there are a number of reasons to doubt that this is the case. No further resemblance to Lucy can be found in *The Merry Wives* or *2 Henry IV*. The heraldic luces may be found in other coats of arms—in fact, they support the argument in favour of a different identification of Shallow (see William GARDINER [2]). Further, *The Merry Wives* was first presented at the Queen's court, where it would have been foolish of Shakespeare to pillory a powerful nobleman, supposing—improbably—that his audience would have understood the allusions, and pointless if they would not. Lastly, the story itself is subject to considerable doubt. It is impossible to rely on a tale whose earliest known recounting dates from more than a century after the events it describes. Lucy may not have kept deer; he did not have the required licence to do so, although unlicensed deer parks were known in Elizabethan times, and his grandson later took out a licence for the same land. In any case, the poaching tale could well have arisen from the play, rather than vice versa, the seeming allusions to Lucy perhaps being associated with his grandson's recorded prosecution of poachers in 1610. However, perhaps significantly, Lucy himself in 1584 introduced a bill in Parliament that would have made poaching a felony. Incidentally, a separate tradition tells that the grandson, another Thomas Lucy (1585–1640), was a friend of Shakespeare after the playwright's retirement.

Sir Thomas was one of the richest landlords in Warwickshire; in 1572, when Shakespeare was eight years old, Queen ELIZABETH (1) visited his estate. He would have been a powerful enemy. A zealous Protestant, he was a local leader in the persecution of Catholics. Sir William LUCY (2), who appears in *1 Henry VI*, was his great-great-great grandfather.

**Lucy (2), Sir William**  Character in *1 Henry VI*, an officer who seeks reinforcements for TALBOT during that general's fatal battle in Act 4. Lucy approaches both YORK (8) and SOMERSET (3), but these noblemen are feuding; each blames the other for Talbot's position, and each refuses to send assistance. Lucy grieves for the loss of England's conquests in FRANCE (1), emphasising Shakespeare's point that only dissensions among the English made a French victory possible.

**Lupton, Thomas (active 1570s and 1580s)**  English writer, author of a minor source for *Measure for Measure*. Lupton's collection of political anecdotes and utopian tales, *The Second Part and knitting up of the booke entitled Too Good to be True* (1581; *Too Good to be True* appeared in 1580), contains an account of the Italian judicial scandal of 1547 that was the original source of Shakespeare's play, though the playwright also knew of this event from several other sources that were more important. From Lupton came the germ of the encounters between ANGELO (2) and ISABELLA and, perhaps, the sense of urgency conveyed by repeated, precise references to the scheduling of the imminent execution of CLAUDIO (3).

Though Lupton is today remembered chiefly for his contribution to *Measure for Measure*, he also wrote one of the last English MORALITY plays, and a number of anti-Catholic religious tracts. However, he was best known in his own time for a layman's health manual, a collection of recipes and cures entitled *A Thousand Notable Things of Sundry Sorts* (1579), which was immensely popular and was republished at intervals until 1793.

**Lychorida**  Minor character in *Pericles*, the nurse of MARINA, servant of PERICLES and THAISA. Lychorida accompanies the pregnant Thaisa and Pericles as they embark on a sea journey, shown in the DUMB SHOW in 3.Chorus. In 3.1, aboard ship, she presents the newborn Marina to Pericles and reports that Thaisa has died in childbirth. In 3.3 she carries Marina but does not speak when Pericles leaves infant and nurse in THARSUS. Marina's grief at Lychorida's death 14 years later is probably mentioned in 4.1.11, though the text is unclear. In Shakespeare's world the company of a nurse was a regular attribute of a well-born young woman. Through her service to Thaisa and then her daughter, Lychorida embodies dedicated domestic service and contributes to the play's atmosphere of ceremonious and courtly life.

**Lydgate, John (c. 1370–c. 1451)**  English poet, author of a source of *Troilus and Cressida*. Inspired by Guido delle COLONNE's *Historia destructionis Troiae* (1287), Lydgate wrote a long poem on the TROJAN WAR, entitled *Troy Book* (1420, publ. 1512, 1555), which influenced Shakespeare's play, especially in its emphasis on the chivalric aspects of the war.

Though an ordained priest, Lydgate spent much of his life staging pageants for the guilds of London. He was a friend of the great poet Geoffrey CHAUCER, and he enjoyed the patronage of Humphrey, Duke of GLOUCESTER (4), who appears in four Shakespearean plays and through whom Lydgate became the official poet of the court of King HENRY VI. Though his reputation was quite good in his own day, Lydgate is now generally regarded as a bad poet whose medieval religiosity and prosaic language are no longer of interest. However, his translation of BOCCACCIO's *The Fate of Illustrious Men* (1355–1374)—published as *Falls of Princes* (1431–1438, publ. 1494)—was an influence on the compilers of A MIRROR FOR MAGISTRATES, a prominent work in Shakespeare's day that was also a source for the playwright.

**Lyly, John (c. 1554–1606)**  English novelist and playwright, a major influence on Shakespeare's early plays. Lyly's extravagant novels and courtly comedies were quite fashionable in LONDON in the 1580s, and they evidently fascinated the young Shakespeare. In elaborate language Lyly's plays presented tales of conflicting love and friendship often involving journeys to exotic climes frequented by outlaws. Their tone, combining sentimentality and sharp wit, seems to have contributed much to Shakespeare's early comedies—especially *Love's Labour's Lost*, but also *The Comedy of Errors, The Two Gentlemen of Verona,* and *A Midsummer Night's Dream*. Literal borrowings, however, are rare and minor.

Lyly, grandson of the humanist scholar William LILY, was the oldest member of the UNIVERSITY WITS, who revolutionised ELIZABETHAN DRAMA in the 1580s. He first achieved fame as the author of a romantic novel of courtly love and genteel adventure, *Euphues, the Anatomy of Wit* (1578), whose extravagant prose style startled readers with its novelty. *Euphues* was studded with puns, repetitions, alliterations, high-flown rhetorical digressions, and fanciful references to classical mythology and natural history (often invented). So distinctive was the style that it became known (and is still known) as euphuism. It was highly fashionable for years and was much imitated. Shakespeare was as likely to mock euphuism as imitate it, and in *1 Henry IV* 2.4.393–426, FALSTAFF indulges in a delightful parody of it.

After publishing a second volume of his novel—*Euphues and his England* (1580)—Lyly turned to the theatre. He wrote numerous elegant comedies for two CHILDREN'S COMPANIES, primarily between 1584 and 1590, but also occasionally until 1602. He was also associated with Henry EVANS (2) and William HUNNIS in the first BLACKFRIARS THEATRE. He then turned to politics and the court of Queen ELIZABETH (1). He was several times a member of parliament, and for years, he unsuccessfully pursued an appointment as the queen's MASTER OF THE REVELS.

**Lysander**   Character in *A Midsummer Night's Dream,* the lover of HERMIA. When mistakenly anointed with a magical love potion, however, his affections are transferred to HELENA (1). Lysander is the least distinctive of the lovers in the play. His love interest changed from one young woman to another and back again by the magic of OBERON's herbs, Lysander is merely a pawn in Shakespeare's game of rotating lovers.

**Lysimachus**   Character in *Pericles,* the governor of MYTILENE who becomes betrothed to MARINA. In 4.6 Lysimachus visits the brothel to which the kidnapped Marina has been sold. His familiar banter with the BAWD and BOULT suggests that he is a regular customer. Once alone with Marina, he seems baffled by her refusal to acknowledge the situation, and he insists 'Come, bring me to some private place; come, come' (4.6.89–90). She counters, 'If you were born to honour, show it now' (4.6.91) and goes on to express her revulsion for the brothel. Lysimachus is impressed and shamed. He claims to have come 'with no ill intent' (4.6.109), and says that he wished only to observe Marina's already famous virtue. However, his flight is hasty, and without being funny he suggests the comic potential of the exposed hypocrite. In any case, he serves admirably as a foil for Marina's virtue, courage, and wit. The Lysimachus of Shakespeare's sources is much more plainly a lecher, and when the playwright provided him with an excuse, he certainly intended us to take it as an indication of the governor's essential decency.

In 5.1 Lysimachus witnesses the reunion of Marina and her father PERICLES. When he learns that she is a suitable bride for a ruler, he asks Pericles for her hand. In the final reconciliations and reunions of 5.3 his engagement to Marina is formally declared, and the couple is assigned the rule of TYRE, though Lysimachus does not speak. He is merely a conventional highborn figure, a suitable husband for the heroine.

**Mab** Fairy queen referred to in *Romeo and Juliet*. MER-CUTIO delivers an elaborate jesting speech (1.4.53–95) describing Queen Mab as a bringer of dreams to humans in a variety of social situations. The passage, a montage of fairy lore, country superstition, and humorous character types, has the chaotic energy that characterises both Mercutio and the violent world that opposes the private universe of the young lovers, ROMEO and JULIET (1). Parts of the speech have literary antecedents—notably in *The Parliament of Fowles*, by CHAUCER—but Queen Mab as 'midwife' (1.4.54) of dreams is known only in this passage and is probably Shakespeare's invention.

The name Mab is associated with fairies; there was a Queen Mabh in Irish fairy lore, and in the dialect of Shakespeare's native WARWICKSHIRE the word 'Mabled' was once current, meaning 'led astray by fairies or elves'. Also, Mab is expressly tiny, and the word 'mab' means 'small child' in Cymric, the language of WALES (1). Shakespeare's interest in Wales and its language at the period when *Romeo and Juliet* was written, and its importance as the origin of many elements of Warwickshire folklore, make it a possible source for the name.

**Mabbe, James (1572–1642)** English writer, possibly the author of one of the introductory poems to the FOLIO edition (1623) of Shakespeare's plays. Mabbe is best known as the translator of a major work of the Spanish RENAISSANCE, the novel *La Celestina*, by Fernando de Rojas (d. c. 1541). He was a long-time friend of Leonard DIGGES, who knew Shakespeare, and scholars generally believe he is the author of 'To the memorie of M. *W. Shake-speare'*, a poem of four rhymed couplets that is signed 'I. M'. in the Folio (but see MAYNE).

**Macbeth (c. 1005–1057)** Historical figure and title character of *Macbeth*, a Scottish nobleman who kills King DUNCAN of SCOTLAND and rules the country until he is killed in combat by Lord MACDUFF. The evil of Macbeth's deed, and its effects on him and on Scotland, are the central elements of the play. He is conscious of the evil his ambition gives rise to, but he cannot overcome temptation. This is combined with his ambition, the urging of the equally ambitious LADY

(6) MACBETH, and the encouragement given him by the WITCHES, whose supernatural powers seem certain to help him though in fact they bring him to his doom. As a man who abandons his own potential for good, Macbeth may be seen as an illustration of the fall of man, the prime Judeo-Christian example of sinful humanity's loss of God's grace. Eventually, Macbeth is destroyed by two virtuous men—Macduff and Duncan's son MALCOLM—who are his opposites in the play's balance of good and evil.

One of the play's manifestations of the power of evil is the collapse of Macbeth's personality. Macbeth commits, or causes to be committed, more than four murders: first, that of the king, which he performs himself in 2.2, and then those of Banquo, in 3.3, and of LADY (7) Macduff and her children, in 4.2. His behaviour during and after each of these events is different, and in this progression is the heart of the drama.

We hear of Macbeth before we see him. In 1.1 the Witches reveal that he is their target, and in 1.2 the king hears of his prowess on the battlefield. He appears to be a brave and loyal follower of the king, but when the Witches suggest, in 1.3, that Macbeth is to become king himself, we see that he has already entertained the possibility of usurping Duncan's crown. However, in 1.7, as he contemplates the prospect of killing King Duncan, he wavers. He still remembers his society's crude discipline, the 'even-handed Justice' (1.7.10) that dictates that if he kills the king, someone else may kill him. He further acknowledges that in simple decency he should not kill the man who is his kinsman and his guest, and who has, moreover, been notably kind to him. On another ethical level, he recognises that it is evil to deprive society of a virtuous man and a fine ruler.

Macbeth still retains the moral sensibility to declare, 'I dare do all that may become a man. / Who dares do more is none' (1.7.46–47), but Lady Macbeth encourages him to overcome his scruples, and in 2.2 he kills the king. He is immediately plagued by his conscience; he tells of how he 'could not say Amen' (2.2.28) and of the voices that foretold sleeplessness. His absorption with his bloody hands foreshadows his wife's descent into madness in 5.1. Nevertheless, he carries his plot through and is crowned between 2.4 and 3.1.

*In Orson Welles' 1948 film version of* Macbeth, *Malcolm (Roddy McDowell) prepares to lead his army against Macbeth's fortress, Dunsinane, to avenge the murder of his father, Duncan. Malcolm's trick of camouflaging his men with tree branches is instrumental in Macbeth's downfall.* (Courtesy of Culver Pictures, Inc.)

Though the influence of the Witches and of Lady Macbeth is very prominent and reflects different aspects of the ways we can fall into evil, Macbeth is basically not controlled by them. His story is one of a moral choice, and the consequences of that choice. It is clear that Lady Macbeth's influence helps him on his way, but once he has killed Duncan he withdraws from her, and she has no role in his subsequent plots; he plainly *can* get along without her. At the same time, his response to the supernatural is carefully contrasted with Banquo's suspicion of the Witches. Macbeth has every opportunity to avoid his fate: he could have ignored Lady Macbeth, or followed the lead of Banquo. However, he made a different choice, for he is a driven, self-destructive man.

Once installed as king, he considers murdering Banquo. He hopes to dispose of the Witches' prediction that Banquo's descendants will rule. He is troubled and cannot rest; he sees life as a 'fitful fever' (3.2.23), and he cries out, 'O! full of scorpions is my mind' (3.2.36). But he hires murderers (see FIRST MURDERER [3]) to dispose of Banquo and his son FLEANCE. Again, he is tormented by his conscience, especially by the sight of Banquo's GHOST (4). He returns to the

Witches a second time and is warned by the APPARITIONS against Macduff. He determines to eliminate this threat also, with the result that the murderers kill Macduff's wife and children, although Macduff has already escaped to England.

By now, however, Macbeth's qualms have disappeared, replaced by a more fundamental disorder. We next see him in 5.3 as he prepares to defend himself against the army of Malcolm and Macduff, and he has become a different person. He veers wildly between rage and despair and has lost any emotional connection to his fellow humans. He declares that he is 'sick at heart' and has 'lived long enough' (5.3.19, 22), and he realises that all that he might once have expected in his old age, 'honour, love, obedience, troops of friends' (5.3.25), is irrevocably lost. Informed of Lady Macbeth's death, he can only reflect on the meaninglessness of life. He has lost his ordinary human repertoire of responses to life and death.

Even his courage, the only virtue he has retained, has an inhuman quality: 'bear-like, I must fight the course' (5.7.2), he growls. Only when he finally understands the deceptive prophecies of the Apparitions does he succumb once again, too late, to a genuine human emotion. He feels sheer terror—'it hath cow'd my better part of man', he cries (5.8.18) when he realises that Macduff is not 'of woman born' (5.8.13). He recovers courage enough to die, and thus in death he is not wholly lost.

His basic strength is also demonstrated in his capacity to face and withstand the ugly truth about himself. He sees the evil to which he has subjected himself and his world. He recognises his own immorality, and he is not satisfied with the position he attains, but he nevertheless defends this position with continued murder. He is aware of this irrational phenomenon; one of his most fascinating features is that he is conscious of the goodness he abandons. When he first contemplates the murder of Duncan, he says its 'horrid image doth unfix my hair' (1.3.135). He recognises the 'deep damnation' to be expected and his hallucination of the dagger confirms the force of this knowledge. After he commits the murder his immediate concern is not with being discovered, but with his conscience. 'To know my deed, 'twere best not know myself' (2.2.72), he says. And at the end of the play he is tormented by the awareness that his life could have been altogether different. It is the contrast with what might have been that makes Macbeth a tragic figure. Though Malcolm understandably refers to 'this dead butcher, and his fiend-like Queen' (5.9.35), the real point of the play resides in the extent to which Macbeth is not simply a monster. He cannot accept his evil callously; he suffers for it.

The historical Macbeth did indeed seize the throne from his cousin Duncan, but Shakespeare's depiction of the man and his reign is otherwise entirely fictional.

Shakespeare took some of his errors from his source, HOLINSHED's *Chronicles*, which itself depended upon the unreliable, quasi-legendary history of Hector BOECE. However, much of the playwright's version varies from Holinshed, anyway, for he was interested in drama, not history.

Though in the play the stigma against Macbeth's action is immense, his usurpation was fairly ordinary in 11th-century Scotland. Duncan's predecessor, King Malcolm II, had taken the throne when he murdered his cousin, Kenneth III. By the standards of the day, Macbeth's claim to the throne was fairly legitimate, as Holinshed makes clear. Macbeth, like Duncan, was a grandson of Malcolm II, and thus a plausible heir. He might also have asserted a claim as the husband of Gruoch (the real Lady Macbeth), who was a granddaughter of Kenneth III. However, there is no evidence that he received—or needed—any prodding from his wife to usurp power. Tradition dictated that any male member of the royal family who could establish that he had regal qualities—usually interpreted as control of an armed force—was qualified to succeed to the crown. In principle, an election within the family settled conflicting claims, though a resort to force was ordinary.

Macbeth, however, did not murder Duncan; he launched a civil war, and Duncan died in battle. Shakespeare took from Holinshed an account of an earlier royal assassination and ascribed it to his protagonist. Further, the play shows Scotland convulsed by the usurper's crime and tormented by his tyranny, but in fact Macbeth was a benign and successful king who ruled in peace for 15 years. Holinshed reported Macbeth's virtues as a king, but Shakespeare ignored them in the interests of drama. As in the play, Macbeth's reign ended when the exiled Prince Malcolm invaded the country with English forces. Malcolm's first attempt at conquest was only partially successful. SIWARD won a victory at DUNSINANE Castle in 1054, but it was not until 1057 that Macbeth was finally defeated in a battle nowhere near Dunsinane.

## Macbeth

SYNOPSIS

*Act 1, Scene 1*
The three WITCHES meet during a storm and declare their intention to encounter MACBETH.

*Act 1, Scene 2*
The wounded CAPTAIN (8) tells King DUNCAN of SCOTLAND and his son MALCOLM of the bravery of Macbeth and BANQUO in battle against rebels led by the Thane of CAWDOR. ANGUS and ROSSE arrive and report that the battle has been won, and that Cawdor has surrendered. The King orders them to see that Cawdor is

executed and to convey the rebel's title and estates to Macbeth.

*Act 1, Scene 3*
The Witches gather and boast of their evil deeds. Macbeth and Banquo encounter them, and they address Macbeth as Thane of Cawdor and as the future king. They also declare that though Banquo will not be king, his descendants will rule. The Witches disappear despite Macbeth's pleas for more information. Rosse and Angus arrive and inform Macbeth that he is now the Thane of Cawdor. Banquo and Macbeth are stunned by this confirmation of part of the Witches' prophecy. Macbeth muses to himself on his ambition to be king, which has been strengthened by these events.

*Act 1, Scene 4*
King Duncan praises Macbeth greatly and tells him that he wishes to visit his castle at INVERNESS. Duncan also announces that when he dies, Malcolm shall inherit the throne. Macbeth volunteers to travel ahead and prepare to receive the king; he reflects to himself that his ambition to be king is hindered by Malcolm's new status.

*Act 1, Scene 5*
LADY (6) MACBETH reads a letter from her husband that tells of the Witches' prophecy and its partial fulfilment. She is delighted, but fears that Macbeth's emotional weakness will prevent him from becoming king. Word arrives of Duncan's approach, and Lady Macbeth exults in this unexpected opportunity to kill Duncan. Macbeth arrives, and he is less enthusiastic, but she declares spiritedly that she will take charge of the murder.

*Act 1, Scene 6*
Lady Macbeth greets King Duncan courteously on his arrival at Inverness.

*Act 1, Scene 7*
Macbeth worries about his fate in the afterlife if he becomes a murderer. Lady Macbeth mocks him and fiercely stirs his ambition with the fury of her own. He declares that he will go ahead with the murder.

*Act 2, Scene 1*
Banquo and Macbeth speak briefly of the Witches. Macbeth discounts their importance as Banquo warns of the temptations that might arise from their prophecies. Left alone, Macbeth sees a hallucination of a bloody dagger. He acknowledges that he is horrified at the prospect of murdering the king, but he forces himself to proceed.

*Act 2, Scene 2*
Lady Macbeth has drugged the king's guards, and she awaits Macbeth's return. He comes to report that he

has killed Duncan, but he is fearful of divine punishment because when he heard Duncan's sons Malcolm and DONALBAIN praying he could not say 'Amen' to himself. He also says he heard a voice that predicted that he would never again be able to sleep. Lady Macbeth upbraids him because he has brought the bloody daggers with him instead of leaving them in the hands of the guards, as they had planned. She goes to complete the deed, and as she returns they hear a knock at the castle entry. She insists that they must go to bed and pretend they have been asleep.

### Act 2, Scene 3

The knocking continues as a drunken PORTER (3) amuses himself with the pretence that he is the doorkeeper of hell. He finally admits MACDUFF and LENOX, and Macbeth arrives to greet them. He pretends to have been awakened by their arrival. Macduff goes to greet the king, while Lenox tells Macbeth of the night's violent and ominous storm. Macduff reappears and cries that the king has been murdered; he raises the alarm as Macbeth runs to the king's chamber. Lady Macbeth, Banquo, Malcolm, and Donalbain arrive in great confusion. Macbeth returns and reports that in his fury at the murder he has killed the guards, who he says are the murderers. As the group departs to dress and meet again, Malcolm and Donalbain confer. They fear that they will be suspected of the murder. They also fear for their lives, and they decide to flee the country.

### Act 2, Scene 4

An OLD MAN (3) tells Rosse of the strange omens that had preceded the king's death. Macduff reports that the flight of Malcolm and Donalbain has convinced everyone of their guilt and that Macbeth is to be crowned as Duncan's successor.

### Act 3, Scene 1

Banquo, alone, voices his suspicion that Macbeth killed Duncan, and he reflects on the Witches' prophecy that his own heirs will rule. Macbeth, now the king, arrives. He learns that Banquo proposes to go horseback riding with his son FLEANCE, and he insists that they return in time for the evening meal. Banquo leaves and Macbeth plans his murder, lest the Witches' prophecy come true. He sends for the FIRST MURDERER (3) and his companion and arranges for them to kill Banquo and Fleance as the victims return from riding.

### Act 3, Scene 2

Macbeth and Lady Macbeth discuss the danger Banquo presents, and Macbeth darkly hints at the plot he has set in motion.

### Act 3, Scene 3

The two Murderers, joined by a THIRD MURDERER—sent by Macbeth—attack Banquo and Fleance. Banquo is killed, but Fleance escapes.

### Act 3, Scene 4

The First Murderer reports to Macbeth during a banquet. When the king returns to his guests, the GHOST (4) of Banquo appears and sits in his chair. No one sees it but Macbeth, who reacts with horror. Lady Macbeth tells the guests that he is suffering from an old illness, and when the Ghost disappears, Macbeth recovers. But it soon reappears and evokes a strong response from Macbeth; the banquet is disrupted and the nobles leave. Macbeth tells Lady Macbeth that he will consult the Witches, to learn of all possible threats.

### Act 3, Scene 5

HECATE chastises the Witches because they have not included her in their dealings with Macbeth. She tells them that they must prepare especially potent spells to delude Macbeth when he consults them.

### Act 3, Scene 6

LENOX and another LORD (8) discuss the suspicious deaths of Duncan and Banquo, the exiled Malcolm's support from the King of England, and Macduff's defection to his cause. They hope for aid from England against Macbeth.

### Act 4, Scene 1

The Witches and Hecate cast spells, and Hecate departs as Macbeth arrives. The Witches summon three APPARITIONS to answer Macbeth's questions. The first, an armed head, warns Macbeth against Macduff; the second, a bloody child, declares that no man born of a woman can harm him; the third, a crowned child, assures him that he will not be conquered until the forest at BIRNAM marches to DUNSINANE. Macbeth concludes that he is certain of continued success. Macbeth asks if Banquo's descendants shall ever rule Scotland. A parade of eight KINGS appears, escorted by Banquo's Ghost, which smilingly indicates that these are his offspring. The apparitions and Witches disappear. Lenox brings news of Macduff's desertion, and Macbeth decides he will kill all of Macduff's family and followers, as punishment.

### Act 4, Scene 2

LADY (7) Macduff bemoans her husband's departure. She tells her SON (1) that his father is dead, but the clever boy realises this isn't true, and engages his mother in a humorous exchange. A MESSENGER (22) appears, quickly delivers a warning of their imminent danger, and flees. The Murderers appear, kill the boy, and chase his mother as she attempts to escape.

### Act 4, Scene 3

In England, Malcolm tests Macduff's loyalty to Scotland. He pretends to confess to extreme depravity, and when Macduff mourns for his country, Malcolm knows he is a true patriot. Rosse brings the news that

Macbeth has slaughtered Macduff's family. Macduff vows revenge, and he and Malcolm prepare to launch an army against Macbeth.

*Act 5, Scene 1*
Observed by a GENTLEWOMAN (1) and a DOCTOR (3), Lady Macbeth walks in her sleep and raves about the blood on her hands. She mentions the murders of Duncan, Lady Macduff, and Banquo.

*Act 5, Scene 2*
A group of Scottish rebels against Macbeth speak of the approaching English army led by Malcolm, Macduff, and SIWARD. They prepare to rendezvous at Birnam Wood, near the castle at Dunsinane where Macbeth has established his defence.

*Act 5, Scene 3*
Macbeth boasts that he does not fear the invaders because of the assurances of the Apparitions. The Doctor reports that Lady Macbeth is troubled by hallucinations, which he cannot cure. Macbeth rejects him angrily.

*Act 5, Scene 4*
Malcolm orders that each of his soldiers, assembled at Birnam Wood, shall carry a branch cut from a tree to provide camouflage and confuse the enemy as to their numbers.

*Act 5, Scene 5*
SEYTON reports to Macbeth, on the castle walls, that Lady Macbeth is dead. Macbeth laments the nature of life. His Messenger arrives and reports that, unbelievably, Birnam Wood appears to be moving towards the castle. Macbeth recognises the danger predicted in the Apparition's prophecy, but he declares himself ready to die.

*Act 5, Scene 6*
Malcolm, Siward, and Macduff approach the castle.

*Act 5, Scene 7*
Macbeth fights YOUNG SIWARD, kills him, and leaves to fight elsewhere. Macduff appears and follows him.

*Act 5, Scene 8*
Macduff finds Macbeth and they fight. Macbeth boasts that he cannot be killed by any man born of a woman, but his opponent counters with the information that he, Macduff, was taken surgically from his mother's womb before birth, and in this sense was not born of a woman. They fight, and Macduff kills Macbeth.

*Act 5, Scene 9*
Macduff appears with Macbeth's head and hails Malcolm as King of Scotland. Malcolm declares that when he is crowned his supporters shall be made Earls, in celebration of the defeat of Macbeth.

## COMMENTARY

*Macbeth* is a study of the human potential for evil; it illustrates—though not in a religious context—the Judeo-Christian concept of the Fall, humanity's loss of God's grace. We see the triumph of evil in a man with many good qualities. We are made aware that the potential for evil is frighteningly present in all of us and needs only the wrong circumstances and a relaxation of our desire for good. The good in Macbeth cries out poignantly through his feverish imagination, but his worldly ambition, the influence of Lady Macbeth (though she too has an inarticulate angel struggling against her own evil), and the instigation of a supernatural power all combine to crush his better nature. By the end of the play Macbeth has collapsed beneath the weight of his evil, and the desperate tyrant has so isolated himself from society—and from his own moral sensibility—that for him life seems 'a tale / Told by an idiot, full of sound and fury, / Signifying nothing' (5.5.26–28).

Macbeth's despair strikes a responsive chord in modern audiences and readers partly because it resembles an existentialist response to the uncertainties of modern life. However, Shakespeare was not a philosopher, and in the 17th century existentialism did not exist. Nevertheless, he understood the potential for social and emotional collapse in the absence of morality. Macbeth and his lady chill us with their monstrous perversion of principles so obviously pertinent to people in all periods.

Shakespeare's depiction of evil in *Macbeth* has two aspects, natural and supernatural. The former is the portrait of the man, Macbeth; the latter is the representation of the supernatural world. Evil exists outside the protagonist in the world of black magic, represented most strikingly by the Witches. The appearance of these embodiments of the devil in 1.1 establishes the play's tone of mysterious evil. The Witches cause Macbeth to respond in ways that are 'Against the use of nature' (1.3.137), and his mind 'is smother'd in surmise, / And nothing is, but what is not' (1.3.141–142). When Macbeth finally recognises that their predictions were not what they seemed, he denounces 'th'equivocation of the fiend, / That lies like truth' (5.5.43–44). He thus touches on their most important quality: the Witches deform the lives they interfere with because they disturb a necessary element of human society: its dependence on mutual trust.

Other emblems of the supernatural in *Macbeth* are the omens associated with the murder of Duncan. As he approaches the deed, Macbeth remarks on the ominous night: 'Nature seems dead, . . . Witchcraft celebrates . . .' (2.1.50–51). Moments later, Lady Macbeth hears an owl's hoot and the sound of crickets, both traditional omens of death. Lenox' account of the night's terrifying storm is full of ancient superstition told in explicit detail, with 'strange screams of death' (2.3.55), earthquakes, and dire prophesies by owls. In 2.4 the Old Man and Rosse intensify the motif when they discuss the day's strange darkness, the killing of a hawk by an owl, and the deadly combat among Duncan's horses. These are gross disruptions of nature that signify the presence of active evil.

The supernatural world is the most extreme example of power that is beyond human control, and it is therefore an apt symbol for the unpredictable forces of human motivation. This larger aspect of evil influences our impression of its more particular manifestation in the man Macbeth. Thus, the pervasive magic in the world of *Macbeth* supports our awareness that the behaviour of the protagonist is, in human terms, unnatural. The portrayal of the evildoer, while convincing, is not psychological in intent; instead, it emphasises the mystery of human behaviour. The play presents possibilities and influences—Macbeth's political ambition, Lady Macbeth's urging, the Witches' bald temptation—but we still wonder why Macbeth does what he does. Macbeth is revolted by himself and his self-awareness makes his descent even more appalling; it also maintains our consciousness of the power of evil. He succumbs to temptation in an almost ritualistic way. He acknowledges each evil and then proceeds, prepared to accept 'deep damnation' (1.7.-20) from the time he first recognises temptation until he is left with no alternative but death.

Macbeth's relation to evil is symbolic. Lady Macbeth, too, though she rejects her husband's scruples, is entirely aware that the proposed murder is evil. She avoids mentioning it too explicitly, and she cannot bring herself to do the deed herself. Finally, her anguished madness—presented in 5.1 and confirmed by her suicide—demonstrates her inability to absorb what she has helped unleash. Thus, she too presents the weakness of humanity in the face of evil. We recognise that they are susceptible to the mental ravages of guilt, and this keeps us from seeing either Macbeth or Lady Macbeth as simply a monstrous sociopath. In fact, much of the play's tension is created because neither of them can simply accept their evil callously. Thus, Macbeth is as much a victim of evil as its instrument, and he is doubly symbolic as a negator of the good in humanity.

Macbeth clearly sees that his evil is a perversion of human values, and the fact that he persists in the face of this awareness demonstrates a profound moral disorder. Indeed, disorder permeates his world. Disrupted sleep—commonly considered a symptom of guilt in Shakespeare's day and in our own—plagues both Macbeth and his wife. He hears a voice predict 'Macbeth shall sleep no more!' (2.2.42) as he commits the murder, and later he speaks of 'these terrible

dreams that shake us nightly' (3.2.18–19). Lady Macbeth demonstrates the disorder physically in the sleep-walking scene (5.1). Macbeth even envies the murdered Duncan, for 'After life's fitful fever he sleeps well' (3.2.23).

Emotional disorder is particularly strongly presented in a repeated emphasis on sexual dysfunction. Lady Macbeth makes sex a weapon in her efforts to spur Macbeth's ambition. She casts aspersions on his sexuality when she equates it with his fear. 'Such I account thy love' (1.7.39), she says, and adds 'When you durst do it, then you were a man' (1.7.49). In 3.4 she uses the same technique when she urges him to conquer his fear of Banquo's Ghost. She calls the bloody-handed Macbeth 'My husband!' (2.2.13) when he has just killed the king. This—the only time she calls him 'husband'—suggests that she finds him sexually impressive in his gore. She also distorts her own gender in a startling fashion when she prays, 'Spirits . . . unsex me here' (1.5.40–41), and perversely elevates and then denies her maternal instincts in a vivid description of infanticide in 1.7.54–59. In 2.3.28–35 the Porter delivers a short description of sexual dysfunction from drink just at the moment when Duncan's murder, accomplished but not yet discovered, hangs over the play's world, emphasising the motif. Macbeth's later withdrawal from his wife—he excludes her from his plans for Banquo and she takes no part in his story thereafter—suggests that their marriage has been destroyed, not strengthened, by their immersion in evil.

This motif, combined with the obvious pleasure that Macbeth and Lady Macbeth take in each other upon their first meeting in the play (1.5.54 ff.), has led most modern actors and directors to present their relationship as highly charged sexually, sometimes including sadomasochistic bouts of slapping and grappling. However, the text could also support the suggestion of an icy incapacity to express themselves sexually. In either light, sex is an issue between Macbeth and Lady Macbeth, and the normal marital relationship is pathologically distorted—one way or another—by the force of the evil to which they commit themselves.

The theme of unnatural disorder is reinforced throughout the play. When Macbeth first considers murdering the king, he acknowledges the evil of the deed with a vivid image of the disorder of the elements, 'Stars, hide your fires!' (1.4.50). His doubts are stimulated by his subconscious recognition that there is no possible way to integrate his desires with the proper order of things. Once Macbeth is fully committed to his evil course, this lack of integration is manifested in 3.4. He is horribly isolated at the banquet when only he sees Banquo's Ghost. His response, the decision to return to the Witches, illustrates nicely the widening difference between himself and other men.

The contrast is stressed in the comparison of Macbeth and Macduff, which becomes an important theme at this point in the play. In 3.6 Lenox and another Lord discuss Macduff's opposition to Macbeth in terms of holiness versus evil. Perhaps most forceful are the parallel impressions of Macduff and Macbeth in grief. Macduff's response to news of the massacre of his family is a powerful demonstration of true humanity—he must 'feel it as a man' (4.3.221). Macbeth's reaction to Lady Macbeth's death—'To-morrow, and to-morrow, and to-morrow, / Creeps in this petty pace . . .' (5.5.19–20)—is the wretched cry of a man so used to evil that he has lost his emotional reflexes. Macbeth's advanced disorder also manifests itself more violently when he alternates between despair and rage in Act 5. He now lacks the capacity for normal emotions.

The force that affects the man also affects the whole society in which he lives. The evil created by the Witches inspires mistrust throughout the world of the play. Significantly, after the Witches' 'overture' in 1.1 the play opens with the suppression of a treasonous rebellion. Duncan's 'absolute trust' (1.4.14) in the Thane of Cawdor was misplaced, and with broad irony, Shakespeare permits the king to award the defeated rebel's title to another man he should not trust. Though trust is still available to the characters, it is already misplaced. Once Duncan has been killed, doubt and confusion grow. This development is signalled by the Porter's allusions to treachery and to the doctrine of 'equivocation', a justification for lying (see GARNET). Duncan's sons feel the world is faithless. They fear that they shall themselves be murdered, and they suspect everyone, particularly one who would be most reliable in a morally sound world, their own relative, Macbeth: '. . . the near in blood / The nearer bloody' (2.3.138–139).

Rosse describes vividly the overwhelming lack of trust that afflicts the land ruled by Macbeth: '. . . cruel are the times, when we are traitors, / And do not know ourselves . . . [and] know not what we fear, / But float upon a wild and violent sea' (4.2.18–21). The subsequent quasi-comical dialogue on treachery between Lady Macduff and her Son offers another slant on the same phenomenon, as does the deliberately false nature assumed by Malcolm to test Macduff, in 4.3. At the play's climax Macbeth discovers that he has been the victim of the 'equivocation of the fiend / That lies like truth' (5.5.43–44), and thus reprises the Porter's motif. Only with Macbeth's defeat and death can honesty return. Siward is proud that his son died having 'paid his score' (5.9.18). When he hails Malcolm as the new king, Macduff wants to express what is in his mind; and Malcolm, in response, declares his wish to be 'even with' his supporters (5.9.28). The malaise

generated by Macbeth's evil is dissolved, and 'the grace of Grace' (5.9.38) has returned to the world of the play.

As Malcolm begins to conduct the business of the state, we see that the motif of mistrust has been significant for the play's secondary theme, a political one. Throughout his career, Shakespeare was concerned with the influence on society of the moral quality of its leaders—this issue dominates the HISTORY PLAYS, for instance—and in *Macbeth* he applies his ideas to a tale of ancient Scotland. Like many of the histories, *Macbeth* begins and ends with a battle (one reported, one enacted), and the fate of the country is never ignored. The travails of Scotland while governed by the evil usurper are clearly presented, especially in the conversation among Malcolm, Macduff, and Rosse in 4.3. The fate of Scotland is a parallel development to Macbeth's descent into evil. This strengthens our awareness of his decline, but also stresses the important lesson that the immoral behaviour of a society's leader is a dangerous disease, capable of producing widespread catastrophe.

The political aspect of the play also had a contemporary significance for Shakespeare's original audiences. The alliance of English and Scottish forces against Macbeth predicts the joining of the two countries under King James I in 1603, a recent event still prominent in the public eye, and James' rule is pointed to more directly in the apparition of future rulers presented in 4.1. Moreover, the enormity of regicide, combined with the Porter's allusions to the trial of Henry Garnet, will have brought forcibly to mind the recently exposed Gunpowder Plot, giving the play a thrilling relevance to the biggest political story in many years.

When he devised his drama of personal evil and public affairs, Shakespeare drew on the history of Scotland as presented in his source, HOLINSHED's *Chronicles,* but much of his version varies from Holinshed for he was interested in drama, not history. (See MACBETH, MALCOLM, et al.) These inaccuracies are of no consequence, for the play's bold art generates more power than could a dispassionate presentation of real facts. *Macbeth,* which contains some of Shakespeare's greatest poetry, offers one of literature's most striking accounts of an individual soul's descent into the darkness of evil, and its resulting isolation from society. Macbeth's rejection of morality, and its consequences—the loss of his soul and the disruption of the society that he influences—horrifies us. This is a drama that is as terrifying as the plots and wars of real usurpers and kings.

## SOURCES OF THE PLAY

The chief source for *Macbeth* was Raphael HO-LINSHED's *Chronicles of England, Scotland, and Ireland* (2nd ed., 1587), whose account of Scotland was derived from the Latin *Scotorum Historiae* (1527) of Hector BOECE. Shakespeare used Holinshed's report of Macbeth's encounter with witches and subsequent usurpation of the throne, though the playwright altered the story considerably. He also used an account in Holinshed of another Scottish regicide that provided the details of Macbeth's crime and included his wife's involvement. Other details may have come from other Scottish tales in Holinshed. Another history of Scotland, George BUCHANAN's Latin *Rerum Scotiarum Historia* (1582), may also have influenced the playwright in the development of Macbeth's character and in several political details.

Various other sources contributed to *Macbeth* in minor ways. Reginald SCOT's *Discovery of Witchcraft* (1584) contributed to the depiction of the Witches, as did a work by King James I, *Daemonologie* (1599). Another tract by James, his *Counterblast to Tobacco* (1604) provided additional details. The Latin memoirs of Erasmus, *Colloquia* (1500)—which the playwright may have read in school—provided the original version of Macbeth's remarks on dogs and men in 3.1.91–100. Lines from two contemporary plays are echoed in *Macbeth,* Samuel DANIEL's *The Queen's Arcadia* (1605) and John MARSTON's *Sophonisba* (1606). Another play, Matthew GWINNE's Latin work, *Tres Sibyllae* (1605), may have suggested the subject matter in the first place. Some scholars believe, however, that the idea may have come from a lost play on Macbeth thought to have been performed in the 1590s. Also, Shakespeare exploited the plays of SENECA in *Macbeth,* particularly in the depiction of Lady Macbeth. He also used details from three of his own earlier works, *2 Henry VI, Richard III,* and, especially, THE RAPE OF LUCRECE.

TEXT OF THE PLAY

*Macbeth* was probably written between 1603 and 1606. It is dated after King James' accession to the throne in the former year and before the publication in 1607 of THE PURITAN, a play whose author—probably Thomas MIDDLETON—had clearly seen *Macbeth.* Some critics feel that the references to James were added later and that the play was written before he came to power, perhaps as early as 1599. However, most scholars believe that the style suggests the later dates. Also, several pieces of evidence—the probable influence of Gwinne and Marston and certain allusions to the treason of Henry GARNET—suggest the summer of 1606 as a more precise date. However, these items could also have been added, and the date of composition remains uncertain.

The scenes involving HECATE in *Macbeth*—3.5 and 4.1.39–43—were obviously added. They include material that came from Thomas MIDDLETON's play *The Witch* (c. 1610–1620), and it is traditionally assumed that Middleton wrote them. However, some scholars

point out differences in style and conclude that some other writer, now unknown, was responsible. The scenes were presumably written for a KING'S MEN production sometime after Shakespeare's retirement, but before the publication of the play.

*Macbeth* was first published in the FIRST FOLIO (1623). At 2,500 lines, it is the shortest of the tragedies, and scholars generally believe that the play was cut considerably before publication and that the surviving text is the acting version of a longer original work. Other alterations are suspected—by Shakespeare or another writer—and the relationship of the published text to the playwright's original manuscript is unknown. The Folio text was probably printed from a PROMPT-BOOK, or a transcript of a prompt-book made for the purpose. As the only old text, the Folio has been the basis for all subsequent editions.

THEATRICAL HISTORY OF THE PLAY

Simon FORMAN recorded the earliest known performance of *Macbeth* in April 1611, but since the play influenced a work published in early 1607, we know it must have been performed at least as early as 1606. Richard BURBAGE (3) is thought to have created the title role. No other early stagings are recorded, but alterations evident in the Folio text (1623) imply that several productions had been mounted by that time.

The English theatres were closed for 18 years while the Puritan government was in power, and when they reopened William DAVENANT produced an adaptation of *Macbeth* (1663) that altered the play greatly. Much of Shakespeare's text was omitted or 'refined' (e.g., 'The devil damn thee black, thou cream-faced loon!' [5.3.11] became 'Now Friend, what means this change of Countenance?'), and musical numbers featuring singers and dancers were added to the Witches' scenes. These scenes were satirised in Thomas DUFFET's *The Empress of Morocco* (c. 1673). Among the actors who were noted for their portrayals of Macbeth in the adaptation were Thomas BETTERTON and James QUIN.

Davenant's version was quite popular, and it was not until David GARRICK's 1744 production that Shakespeare's *Macbeth* was partially restored. Though Garrick consulted Samuel JOHNSON (7) about the text, he still cut some 300 lines, retained many of Davenant's operatic embellishments, and added some lines of his own. Macbeth was one of Garrick's great roles, and he played it for many years. He ceased only upon the death of his longtime Lady Macbeth, Hannah PRITCHARD, in 1768. Another popular 18th-century Macbeth was Charles MACKLIN, who introduced the use of Scottish kilts and plaids in 1773. In the late 18th and early 19th centuries Sarah SIDDONS was a very popular Lady Macbeth, and frequently played opposite her brother, John Philip KEMBLE (3).

Samuel PHELPS' production of 1847 omitted Davenant's operatic elements for the first time. Edwin BOOTH (2) was an especially acclaimed Macbeth in the 19th century, and he often played opposite Helena MODJESKA. Charlotte CUSHMAN played Lady Macbeth opposite both William MACREADY and Edwin FORREST. Cushman and Siddons, in particular, were noted for the ferociousness of their interpretations, but styles changed later in the century when Ellen TERRY (1) played the character as a less assertive partner to Henry IRVING's dominating Macbeth. In the 1890s, Sarah BERNHARDT introduced an explicit sexuality to the role that has been stressed in the 20th century.

*Macbeth* remains extremely popular with modern audiences, and most leading actors and actresses aspire to the roles of Macbeth and his Lady. There have been many remarkable productions in the 20th century, and one of these was the 1928 modern-dress presentation by Barry JACKSON (1). Another was Orson WELLES' notorious 'voodoo' *Macbeth* of 1936, which was set in 18th-century Haiti and featured a gigantic mask as Banquo's Ghost, a Hecate with a 12-foot bull-whip, and a band of on-stage drummers. The 1941 New York production directed by Margaret WEBSTER (3), which starred Judith ANDERSON (2) and Maurice EVANS (4), and Trevor NUNN's 1976 staging at STRATFORD, with Ian MCKELLEN and Judi DENCH, were both memorable. Other notable Macbeths have included Robert Bruce MANTELL, Laurence OLIVIER, and John GIELGUD. Zoë CALDWELL and Sybil THORNDIKE have been acclaimed as Lady Macbeth. In 1981 a company from the University of Illinois adapted *Macbeth* to kabuki, the traditional, stylised Japanese drama, and performed in several American cities.

*Macbeth* has been made into a FILM 17 times. The earliest of these was in 1908, when the first of seven silent versions was made. The last of them, by D. W. Griffith, starred Beerbohm TREE. Orson Welles directed and starred in a movie of 1948, and Maurice Evans and Judith Anderson re-created their stage success on the screen in 1960. Probably the best-known (and by virtually unanimous critical acclaim the best) film of *Macbeth* is an adaptation, Akira KUROSAWA's *Throne of Blood* (1957). Five TELEVISION productions of the play have been broadcast, the first in 1949, though one of these simply recorded a performance of Nunn's 1976 stage production.

## Macduff, Thane of Fife (active c. 1054?)

Quasi-historical figure and character in *Macbeth,* the rival and vanquisher of MACBETH. After Macbeth murders King DUNCAN of SCOTLAND and succeeds him on the throne, Macduff joins Duncan's son MALCOLM in exile in England. There he learns that Macbeth has massacred his family, and when he and Malcolm lead an army against Macbeth, Macduff seeks out the usurper at DUNSINANE to exact personal vengeance. Macbeth relies on the supernatural assurance that no man 'of woman born'

(4.1.80, 5.8.13) can harm him, but it turns out that Macduff was 'from his mother's womb / Untimely ripp'd' (5.8.14–15)—that is, delivered by Caesarean section and thus not 'born' in the ordinary construction of the word. In the subsequent fight, Macduff kills Macbeth; he presents the usurper's severed head to Malcolm, in 5.9.

Shakespeare painstakingly builds Macduff up as the play's agent of retribution. We first notice Macduff in 2.4, when he returns to FIFE rather than attend Macbeth's coronation. In 3.4 Macbeth suspects Macduff is hostile, and in 3.6 we hear that he has fled to join Malcolm. Thus, even before he takes a prominent role, Macduff distinguishes himself because he refuses to accept Macbeth's succession to the crown. In 4.1 Macbeth is told by the APPARITIONS to 'Beware Macduff' (4.1.71), and it is evident that the Thane of Fife will be the usurper's rival though Macbeth is calmed by the Apparitions' other predictions. In 4.3 Macduff proves that he is a disinterested patriot. Malcolm fears that Macduff may be Macbeth's agent and tests him. The prince pretends to be a degenerate who would make a terrible king. Macduff despairs for Scotland, and Malcolm accordingly accepts him. Thus, the playwright places Macduff's virtue in clear opposition to the villainy of Macbeth.

As a symbol of triumphant good, Macduff is a somewhat stylised character. He rejects Macbeth, he proves himself dedicated to Scotland, he is able to overcome the magic that Macbeth relies on, and in the end he kills the villain. A multifaceted persona is not required for such a character, and generally we do not see one. However, he has one majestic moment that powerfully evokes our sympathy for him as a man. In one of Shakespeare's most moving episodes, Macduff grieves for the death of his wife, LADY (7) Macduff, and their family, at the hands of Macbeth's hired killers. At first, he can hardly believe it: 'All my pretty ones? / Did you say all?—O Hell-kite!—All?' (4.3.216–217), he cries. When Malcolm encourages him to revenge and says, 'Dispute it like a man' (4.3.220), Macduff replies with great dignity, 'I shall do so; / But I must also feel it as a man: / I cannot but remember such things were / That were most precious to me' (4.3.220–223). We are deeply moved, aware that the grieving thane is profoundly engaged with his love and sorrow. The source of Macduff's virtue is exposed: he is a complete human being who cannot sever the bonds of kinship and love. We see that Macduff's strong acceptance of his grief is the opposite of the cold inhumanity of Macbeth and LADY (6) MACBETH.

It is uncertain whether Macduff existed in history. Shakespeare found him in HOLINSHED's *Chronicles,* which was based on the quasi-legendary history of Hector BOECE, but he cannot be certainly identified with anyone recorded in 11th-century documents. Nevertheless, the name probably represents a historical ruler of Fife who was an ally of Malcolm against Macbeth. His birth by Caesarean section is even more speculative. The procedure, though known to have existed since ancient times, was certainly extremely rare in medieval Scotland, if practised at all. In premodern societies the strangeness of this mode of birth led to its being associated with the extraordinary figures of history and legend—such as Julius CAESAR (1), for whom it is named—and this doubtless accounts for the belief that Macbeth's killer entered the world in this fashion.

**Machiavel** Villainous but humorous character type of ELIZABETHAN DRAMA, a sly cynic who loves evil for its own sake. A Machiavel is characterised by a delight in evil that makes other motivation unnecessary, the habit of commenting on his own activities in humorous soliloquies, treachery to his own allies, a tendency to lewdness, and a cynical contempt for goodness and religion. By convention, the good characters never recognise the Machiavel's evil intentions until it is too late. OTHELLO's extraordinary gullibility is paradoxically explained, in part, by IAGO's obvious villainy, for its very obviousness to the audience presumes its invisibility to the characters.

Shakespeare's principal Machiavels besides Iago—who is probably the most famous of all such characters—were AARON, EDMUND, and RICHARD III. A number of other Shakespearean characters display the features of the type to a lesser degree—for example, the Bishop of WINCHESTER (1) in *1 Henry VI* and CASSIUS in *Julius Caesar*. The first famous Machiavel—who doubtless influenced Shakespeare—was Barabas, the villain of *The Jew of Malta* by Christopher MARLOWE (1). Also, a character named Machiavel speaks the PROLOGUE (1) to the play. Other dramatists of the period employed the figure as well.

The Machiavel takes his name from the Italian political philosopher Niccolo Machiavelli (1469–1527), who was (and is) popularly misunderstood to have advocated atheism, treachery, and criminality as preferable to other means of statecraft. This model was applied to an already-existing character type, the VICE, a humorous villain from the medieval MORALITY PLAY. Machiavelli added elements of intelligence, craftiness, and political ambition. Shakespeare's Richard, who identifies himself as a superior Machiavel in *3 Henry VI* 3.2.193 (probably referring to Marlowe's prologue-speaker), also describes his methods, 'Plots have I laid, inductions dangerous', and adds for good measure that he is 'subtle, false, and treacherous' (*Richard III* 1.1.33, 37).

**Macklin, Charles (c. 1700–1797)** Irish actor, a notable SHYLOCK. Macklin is best known as the actor who restored Shakespeare's Shylock after the part had for at least a generation been customarily played for laughs by crude comedians. After Macklin, the dignity and pathos of the figure never again lapsed so far, though even Macklin played him as a melodramatic villain. Macklin played many comic parts in Shakespeare, and in 1754 he delivered a series of lectures on the playwright that are the earliest ever recorded. He was also a playwright who wrote two successful comedies. He retired in 1789, at about age 90, after forgetting his lines while playing Shylock.

**Macmorris** Character in *Henry V,* an Irish officer in the army of King HENRY V. Macmorris appears only in the 'international' scene, 3.2, with the Welsh FLUELLEN, the Scottish JAMY, and the English GOWER (2). Hot-tempered, Macmorris takes offence at Fluellen's reference to the Irish, presuming he means an insult, and they nearly come to blows, though both respond professionally to the call of duty and postpone their quarrel. The episode exploits ethnic stereotypes to demonstrate the diversity of British subjects working to a common end under King Henry.

**Macready, William Charles (1793–1873)** British actor and producer. Macready, one of the great tragedians of the 19th century, played all of Shakespeare's great protagonists, as well as numerous other figures, such as HOTSPUR, IAGO, and JAQUES (1). He often played opposite Helen FAUCIT. He helped pioneer the period's return to genuine Shakespearean texts, removing the accretions of earlier centuries, especially in his productions of *King Lear, Coriolanus,* and *The Tempest.* However, Macready's versions were themselves abridgements, in part to make room for the spectacular tableaus for which he was well known, and in part to censor Shakespeare, removing, for instance, the grisly fate of GLOUCESTER (1) from *King Lear.* With Edmund KEAN (2), Macready dominated the English theatre of the 1820s and was alone its major figure in the following decade. His diaries, published in 1875, offer a lively picture of the theatre of his day. Macready played in New York in 1826 and 1848; on the latter occasion, the rivalry of Edwin FORREST led to the notorious Astor Place riots.

**Maecenas, Gaius (d. 8 B.C.)** Historical figure and minor character in *Antony and Cleopatra,* a follower of Octavius CAESAR (2). Maecenas is a courtier who serves to swell the ranks of Caesar's court. He offers some important advice in 4.1 when he encourages Caesar to advance on ANTONY and finish him off while he is distracted with rage and humiliation after the battle of ACTIUM. This remark helps signal Antony's approaching end.

The historical Maecenas was far more important to Caesar than the play indicates. He was among the future emperor's earliest allies, and he assisted Caesar's arrival in Italy to claim the inheritance of the assassinated Julius CAESAR (1) in 44 B.C. (Maecenas does not appear in Shakespeare's *Julius Caesar*, however.) Along with AGRIPPA, Maecenas was one of the most trusted friends and advisers of Caesar throughout the civil wars and in the early days of the empire, and he conducted numerous delicate diplomatic missions. He was descended from the ancient kings of Etruria, though his family's fortunes had fallen when his grandfather joined a revolt against Rome. However, Maecenas became one of the highest-ranking and richest men of the early Roman Empire. As such, he was a great patron of Roman literature, the role for which he is now best known. He befriended and supported many poets and writers, including VIRGIL.

**Malcolm (Prince Malcolm Canmore, d. 1093)** Historical figure and character in *Macbeth*, son of the murdered King DUNCAN of SCOTLAND. In 1.4 Malcolm is named his father's successor to the dismay of MACBETH, who plots to take the crown himself. However, when Duncan is murdered, Malcolm and his brother DONALBAIN fear for their lives and worry that suspicion will fall on them. They flee the country in 2.3 and leave Macbeth to occupy the throne. Malcolm seeks refuge at the court of the English king, where we find him in 4.3. MACDUFF joins him there, and they lead an army to Scotland in Act 5, and defeat and kill Macbeth. At the play's close, Malcolm makes a stately speech that thanks his supporters and announces his forthcoming coronation as King of Scotland.

Like Macduff, the young prince is a figure of goodness placed in opposition to Macbeth's evil, and as such is somewhat two-dimensional. He is clever when he devises a form of camouflage—each soldier carries a branch of a tree as the army marches on DUNSINANE—that proves significant in Macbeth's downfall. However, Malcolm is most distinctive when he tests Macduff's patriotism, in 4.3.1–139. The prospective king describes himself as an intemperate and dishonest degenerate, certain to be bad for the country. When Macduff despairs for Scotland, Malcolm reveals himself as a virtuous prince and accepts Macduff as a leader of his invasion army. This episode has two functions: most important, it stresses the atmosphere of distrust that Macbeth's evil has loosed on Scotland. It also presents Malcolm as a sensible, cautious young man who seems likely to be a successful ruler. This impression, along with our recollection of the clever camouflage, helps establish the sense of healing that comes with his triumph at the play's close. CATHNESS refers to him, appropriately, as 'the med'cine of the sickly weal' (5.2.27).

The historical Malcolm did return from exile to defeat Macbeth, but Shakespeare's treatment of his career is otherwise almost entirely altered. Malcolm was a young child when Macbeth seized the throne in 1039. Duncan was not murdered, so Malcolm did not flee to avoid suspicion. He was in fact sent to his uncle, Earl SIWARD, and he later lived at the court of King Edward the Confessor of England, as in the play. Only 15 years later, once he was a man, did Malcolm attempt an invasion of Scotland in 1054. The attack was repulsed though some territory was taken. Three years later a second attempt succeeded; Macbeth was defeated and killed, and Malcolm took the throne.

Malcolm's reign began a highly important period in Scottish history, the first European orientation for the country. Malcolm's second wife, later known as St. Margaret, was an English princess who had been raised at the cosmopolitan medieval court of the kings of Hungary. Under her influence, Scotland accepted the Roman rather than the Celtic church and the arts and culture of Europe as opposed to those of ancient Britain. Margaret had been a refugee from the Norman Conquest of England in 1066, and Malcolm engaged in periodic warfare against William the Conqueror. He died in battle in 1093, during his fifth invasion of England. His successor was Duncan II, his oldest son by his first wife (the sister or daughter of Cathness). Duncan was overthrown by his uncle, Donalbain, but eventually another of Malcolm's sons (by Margaret) ruled Scotland as King David I (ruled 1124–1153). Through him, Malcolm was an ancestor of JAMES I, the ruler of England in Shakespeare's time.

**Malone, Edmond (1741–1812)** English scholar. Malone was probably the greatest of 18th-century Shakespearean scholars, and one of the greatest of all time. His *Attempt to ascertain the Order in which the Plays of Shakespeare were written*—the first such effort—was published in George STEEVENS' 1778 edition of the plays, and he edited two volumes added in 1780 to Steevens' collection, containing the poems, the doubtful plays of the third FOLIO, and Malone's history of ELIZABETHAN THEATRE. In 1790 he brought out his own edition of the plays, incorporating a tremendous amount of scholarship, including his massive *Life* of Shakespeare, the basis for all subsequent biographies. In 1796 he led the exposure of the forgeries of William Henry IRELAND, and when he died he was at work on a new edition of the plays. This was eventually completed by James BOSWELL the Younger. Known as the 'Third Variorum' (see VARIORUM EDITION), it has been the foundation of modern Shakespeare studies.

**Malvolio** Character in *Twelfth Night*, mean-spirited steward to OLIVIA. Malvolio is the focus of the comic SUB-PLOT, in which a group of characters led by MARIA (2) and SIR TOBY conspire to embarrass him, with the result that he is incarcerated as a lunatic. This plot is clearly secondary to the main story of the lovers— VIOLA, ORSINO, SEBASTIAN (2), and Olivia—but Malvolio is such a strongly drawn character that the play sometimes seems to centre on him. In fact, several documents of the 17th century identify the play as 'Malvolio', and leading actors have always been pleased to take the role. In addition to embodying an ordinary comic villain—an obvious misfit who mistreats others and in the end is humiliated by a crude stratagem—Malvolio is also a humanly interesting victim, and he inspires sympathy as well as derision, thus contributing to Shakespeare's ironic undercutting of the conventional romantic comedy.

Malvolio rejects humour and love in favour of a stern coldness and a consuming personal ambition. His dislike of merriment and his rigorously sober dress and behaviour justify his name, an approximation of the Italian for 'ill will'. (These features also resemble the typical 16th-century—and later—stereotype of the Puritan, but Shakespeare certainly did not consider Malvolio a Puritan, as is clear in 2.3.140–146.) Malvolio opposes the frivolity of Sir Toby, SIR ANDREW, and FESTE in 2.3, inspiring Sir Toby's famous riposte, 'Dost thou think because thou art virtuous, there shall be no more cakes and ale?' (2.3.114–115). Driven away by this assault on his dignity, the angry Malvolio gratuitously threatens Maria, thereby triggering the plot that brings him down.

The steward behaves badly to Viola, who is disguised as a young man, when he brusquely delivers Olivia's ring to her in 2.2, and he is unnecessarily nasty to Feste in 1.5. His churlish behaviour quite plainly foreshadows the comeuppance that he later receives. Even more repellent is the cold ambition of his entirely loveless courtship of Olivia, undertaken in accordance with the comical instructions of Maria's letter but contemplated by him in 2.5, before he finds this missive. His musings on the power and position he hopes to gain strongly illuminate his personality, as he solemnly and pompously contemplates punishing Sir Toby. These boldly unattractive features have inspired scholarly speculations that Shakespeare intended Malvolio as a satire on a particular living person (see William FFARINGTON; Thomas Posthumous HOBY [2]; William KNOLLYS; Ambrose WILLOUGHBY [1]), but these hypotheses have never been convincingly established and they do not alter the character's function in the play.

For all his noxious characteristics, Malvolio is not a serious threat in the manner of, say, SHYLOCK; ultimately he is simply laughed off the stage. Nor does he grow or change in the course of the play; instead he is exposed for what he is by the actions of other characters. There is no question about his destiny; in a comedy such a hypocrite and would-be villain deserves his downfall, and this comes about in an entertaining manner.

Nevertheless, Malvolio's imprisonment and humiliation seem excessive relative to his offence. The 'problem of Malvolio', as this imbalance has long been called, lends the sub-plot a viciousness that contributes to Shakespeare presentation of comedy's limitations. Feste's teasing of the imprisoned Malvolio in 4.2 is undeniably humorous, but even Sir Toby concedes that this continuing torment of their victim may be going too far, remarking 'I would we were well rid of this knavery' (4.2.69–70). Then, provoking the steward's angry final departure in 5.1, Feste mocks the steward even more mercilessly. We sympathise with Malvolio's anger, which seems justifiable, and with his ugly departure and its cry for revenge 'on the whole pack of you!' (5.1.377) Despite the play's happy ending, an aftertaste of bitter feeling remains. A 19th-century critic, Charles LAMB (1), went so far as to find 'tragic interest' in 'the catastrophe of this character'. Although Malvolio lacks the grandeur of a tragic hero, Lamb's comment raises an interesting moral question: How is Malvolio's shabby treatment—or his unrepentant final response—to be reconciled with the happy ending?

While poetic justice requires that Malvolio be brought down, for his rejection of love is insane in the play's scheme of things, Shakespeare softens his actual defeat in several ways. The victim's final cry for vengeance is neutralised by FABIAN's wish that the conspirators' 'sportful malice . . . may rather pluck on laughter than revenge' (5.1.364–365). Moreover, the two leading figures of ILLYRIA offer the promise of reconciliation: Olivia, though amused at the plot against her humiliated steward, is sympathetic towards him, saying, 'Alas, poor fool, how have they baffled thee!' (5.1.368), and Orsino orders that someone follow him and 'entreat him to a peace' (5.1.379).

After Malvolio's exit, the play moves to its happy conclusion; the steward is simply too out of harmony with the joyful spirit of the ending to remain among the celebrants. Though his downfall gives an edge to the romantic comedy—we see that Illyria has its share of the sins of the real world—this point is easily abandoned in the enthusiasm of the lovers. Nevertheless, the 'problem of Malvolio' makes both the character and the play more complex and humanly interesting.

**Mamillius**  Character in *The Winter's Tale,* the son of King LEONTES of SICILIA and Queen HERMIONE, who dies of grief when his father persecutes his mother unjustly. In 1.1 Mamillius is presented as the pride of his parents and the entire kingdom; his future as a man and ruler looks brilliant. These sentiments, however, will soon seem ironic. In 1.2 and 2.1 he appears a likeable boy, especially in 2.1, when he jests with his mother's ladies-in-waiting (see LADY [4]) and tells his mother a story 'of sprites and goblins' because 'a sad tale's best for winter' (2.1.26, 25). The remark confirms our sense of coming tragedy. Mamillius dies of grief, off-stage, during his mother's trial. The shock of his death, reported in 3.2.144–145, stirs his father, too late, to recognise his own injustice. The death of

Mamillius, a completely innocent victim, demonstrates the appalling cost of Leontes' madness; it is the low point of the play's tragic development.

Shakespeare created Mamillius from the mere mention of the analogous figure in his source, the prose romance *Pandosto* by Robert GREENE (2). His name may have been derived from the title of two earlier romances by Greene, *Mamillia* (1583, 1593).

**Man (1)**    Minor character in *Richard II,* the GARDENER's assistant. The Man asks the Gardener why they should bother to tend their plants when the larger 'garden', the country as a whole, is falling into ruin due to neglect. In other words, he maintains that the state must be kept in order by its rulers, just as a garden must by its humbler caretakers.

**Man (2)**    Minor character in *Troilus and Cressida,* a servant of TROILUS. In 3.2 the Man informs PANDARUS that Troilus is waiting for him.

**Man (3)**    Minor character in *Henry VIII,* assistant to the PORTER (4). In 5.3, on the day of the christening of Princess ELIZABETH (1), the Man defends his inability to prevent a crowd of celebrating commoners from entering the courtyard of the royal palace. He comically exaggerates, in military terms, the combats he has undergone.

**Manningham, John (c. 1576–1622)**    English diarist. Manningham, a lawyer and minor official, was an avid theatre-goer who recorded the earliest known performance of *Twelfth Night,* in 1602. In the same year he also preserved the only surviving contemporary anecdote of Shakespeare's life. He had been told, he wrote in his diary, that the playwright, during a performance of *Richard III,* had overheard a message from a female admirer to its star, Richard BURBAGE (2), inviting him to a dalliance later that evening. Shakespeare, according to the story, arrived at the appointment before Burbage and was enjoying the company of the young woman when a servant brought word that 'Richard III' was at the door. Shakespeare then sent back a message that 'William the Conqueror was before Richard III'. While a student at the INNS OF COURT, Manningham knew William COMBE (5), and through him he may have been personally acquainted with Shakespeare.

**Mantell, Robert Bruce (1854–1928)**    Scottish-American actor. Mantell began his career in Ireland and went to America in 1878, joining Helena MODJESKA's company. After a brief return to Britain, Mantell remained in New York for good. A romantic leading man early in his career and a character actor as an older man, he played many Shakespearean parts.

**Mantua**    City in northern Italy, a location in *Romeo and Juliet.* Romeo flees to Mantua when banished from VERONA, and he is seen there in 5.1. Shakespeare took this incident from his source, the poem *Romeus and Iuliet,* by Arthur BROOKE (1). The same source accounts for a reference to the city in *The Two Gentlemen of Verona,* in which SILVIA asserts (mistakenly) that VALENTINE is in exile there (4.3.24). The city is also named in *The Taming of the Shrew* (4.2.77–85); it is referred to as a port, and this has often been cited as an error on Shakespeare's part. But in the 16th century Mantua, situated on the Mincio River, participated in the considerable river-and-canal trade that was prominent in northern Italy until the advent of the railroads in the 19th century.

**Marcade (Mercadé)**    Minor character in *Love's Labour's Lost,* the messenger who brings the PRINCESS (1) of France news of her father's death in 5.2, thus changing the tenor of the play in its closing minutes.

**Marcellus**    Minor character in *Hamlet.* Marcellus, with BARNARDO, has seen the GHOST (3) of HAMLET's father before the opening of the play. In 1.1 they tell HORATIO about the spirit, and in 1.2 Hamlet is informed as well. Marcellus accompanies Hamlet and Horatio when they encounter the Ghost in 1.4; he and Horatio fearfully attempt to dissuade Hamlet from following it, and in 1.5 Hamlet swears them to secrecy. Speculating on the cause of the phenomenon, Marcellus utters the famous observation 'Something is rotten in the state of Denmark' (1.4.90). Scholars believe that the BAD QUARTO of *Hamlet* (Q1, 1603) was recorded by an actor who had played Marcellus, since that role is the only one whose dialogue is very accurately rendered there.

**March, Earl of**    Historically, the hereditary title of the head of the Mortimer family. Several earls of March laid claim to the English throne by virtue of their descent from a daughter of Lionel Plantagenet, Duke of Clarence, the oldest brother of the deposed King RICHARD II. In *1 Henry VI,* this claim is transmitted to the family of the Duke of YORK (8) by Edmund MORTIMER (1), thus helping to lay the groundwork for the WARS OF THE ROSES. Due to confusion in his sources, Shakespeare gave the title, in *1 Henry IV,* to Edmund MORTIMER (2), who was historically a younger brother and thus neither an Earl of March nor in the royal line of descent.

In *3 Henry VI,* Edward of York, soon to be King EDWARD IV, is referred to as the Earl of March, at 2.1.179 and 2.1.192, in connection with his allies among the Welsh, for the Earldom's lands bordered Wales. The word 'march', meaning 'border region', had been added to the title generations earlier.

**Marcus Andronicus**  Character in *Titus Andronicus,* the brother of TITUS (1). Marcus proposes his brother as a candidate for the vacant imperial throne in 1.1, though he accedes to Titus' determination that SATURNINUS should reign. He sides with BASSIANUS and Titus' sons in the dispute over LAVINIA, but a reconciliation is soon effected. In 2.4 Marcus discovers Lavinia in her ravished state, and his seemingly incongruous response—distant and rhetorical despite the extremity of her plight—often puzzles modern readers. It is a good instance of a mode of formal discourse, intended to promote a sense of strangeness and unreality, that was highly prized in Renaissance times but is now quite unfamiliar.

In 3.2, which Shakespeare may not have written, Marcus kills a fly, provoking so manic a response in Titus that he seems unbalanced by grief. Such mania is an important theme in a REVENGE PLAY, which *Titus Andronicus* is. In the rest of the play, Marcus seconds his brother's sentiments of grief and his plans for revenge and mourns Titus at the end.

**Mardian**  Minor character in *Antony and Cleopatra,* a eunuch in the court of CLEOPATRA. Mardian is a minor member of the queen's entourage. In 4.14 he performs his only significant act when, on Cleopatra's orders, he delivers to ANTONY the false message that she has committed suicide. This triggers Antony's suicide attempt. Mardian is the closest thing to a jester, or FOOL (1), in Cleopatra's court. He is referred to as 'saucy' (4.14.25), and he is mildly amusing when he declares that he thinks on 'What Venus did with Mars' (1.5.18) when his mistress jests about his sexlessness. He appears to be the court musician, though he never performs as Cleopatra's willfulness leads her to reject his songs before she hears them. Aside from these semi-official functions, Mardian's function is to swell the ranks of Cleopatra's grand establishment.

**Margarelon**  Legendary figure and minor character in *Troilus and Cressida,* an illegitimate son of King PRIAM. In 5.7 Margarelon challenges THERSITES on the battlefield, identifying himself as 'A bastard son of Priam's' (5.7.15). Thersites declares himself 'a bastard, too . . . bastard begot, bastard instructed, bastard in mind, bastard in valour, in everything illegitimate' (5.7.16–18); he then flees. The episode serves only to display Thersites' coarse wit and cowardice. Margarelon speaks only three lines and has no personality.

In the earliest editions of the play, which reflect Shakespeare's manuscript, this character is identified merely as 'Bastard'. By a tradition dating from the 18th century, he is given the name of a bastard of Priam's that appears in a list of Trojan warriors (5.5.7). Shakespeare took the name from either William CAXTON's *The Recuyell of the Historyes of Troye* or John LYDGATE's *Troy Book,* where it is variously spelled

Margareton or Margariton. (The change from 't' to 'l' was probably a typesetter's error.) Margareton, one of Priam's many illegitimate sons, had no other importance in classical mythology.

**Margaret (1) of Anjou (1430–1482)**  Historical figure and character in *1, 2,* and *3 Henry VI* and *Richard III,* the French-born Queen, and later widow, of King HENRY VI. Taken as a single role, running through four plays, Margaret is surely the greatest female part in Shakespeare. She develops from an ingenuous young woman thrust into prominence, through a career as a scheming plotter and a courageous and persistent military leader, to a final appearance as a raging, Fury-like crier of curses against her triumphant enemies.

In *1 Henry VI* Margaret plays only a brief role as a French prisoner of war intended as a bride for King Henry by the devious SUFFOLK (3), who loves her himself. Her importance is chiefly to prepare the groundwork for the action of *2 Henry VI.* She replaces JOAN LA PUCELLE (Joan of Arc) as the symbolic Frenchwoman who plagues an England that is divided by the selfish ambitions of the aristocracy. Her appearance marks the completion of one disaster, the loss of FRANCE (1), and begins another, a civil war.

In *2 Henry VI* Margaret's flawed personality is demonstrated early on. She conspires with Suffolk to bring about the fall of Duke Humphrey of GLOUCESTER (4) because she resents Gloucester's influence over the King and her own resulting insignificance. She displays an evil temper when she abuses the PETITIONERS in 1.3; later in this scene she mocks her husband's piety. When Gloucester is forced by his wife's disgrace (see DUCHESS [1]) to leave his position as Lord Protector, Margaret exults, comparing Gloucester's relinquished sceptre of office to an amputated limb (2.3.42). We are not surprised when this bloody-minded woman proposes killing her enemy to ensure against his possible return to power. When the King mourns Gloucester's subsequent murder, Margaret dares to complain that Henry is paying too little attention to her. Henry banishes Suffolk from England for his part in the crime, and, as the Queen and the Duke bid each other farewell, they reveal their passionate love. Shakespeare, aware as always of the complexities of human nature, offsets his portrait of this villainess by evoking a glimmer of sympathy for a woman losing her lover.

In *3 Henry VI* the Queen assumes a major role in the civil war, replacing the ineffectual King at the head of his armies. Her bold and cruel nature reveals itself most fully at the battle of WAKEFIELD, when York has been captured. Margaret insists on postponing his death so that she may torment him with barbs and, most chillingly, with evidence of the murder of his child, RUTLAND (1). Before he dies, York rages at her, calling her a 'she-wolf of France' (1.4.111), an epithet that has been applied to her by writers ever since, and as a 'tiger's heart wrapp'd in a woman's hide' (1.4. 137), a line that was parodied in the earliest reference to Shakespeare that has survived (see Robert GREENE [2]).

At the crucial battle of TOWTON, Margaret is plainly the leader of the King's forces; in fact, she orders Henry to stay away from the fighting. Although the battle is lost and York's son Edward (see EDWARD IV) is enthroned in Henry's place, Margaret refuses to give up and she goes to France in search of military aid. When she is once again prepared to fight, she sends word to Edward, 'Tell him my mourning weeds are laid aside, / And I am ready to put armour on' (3.3.229–230). Despite her viciousness, this dauntless warrior does command some admiration.

The subsequent battle of TEWKESBURY results in Margaret's final defeat. Forced to witness the killing of her son, the PRINCE (4) of Wales, Margaret is reduced to lamentations and curses ironically similar to those delivered by York just three acts earlier. Richard, later RICHARD III, wishes to kill Margaret, saying, 'Why should she live to fill the world with words?' (5.5.43). He aptly predicts her role in *Richard III*.

Margaret's role in that work is limited to only two scenes, but it is a very powerful element of the play, for she represents Nemesis, the personification of retribution through fate, a theme that underlies the entire minor TETRALOGY, which *Richard III* closes. In 1.3 she heaps elaborate curses upon her victorious foes, reserving for Richard her choicest and subtlest imprecations, hoping that his punishment not come to pass until his 'sins be ripe' (1.3.219). In the formal and theatrical manner of a Greek CHORUS (1), Margaret restates past grievances and suggests future developments. She departs with the prediction that her enemies will come to regard her as 'a prophetess' (1.3. 301). Before her return, in 4.4, many of her curses will have been substantially fulfilled through Richard's murderous malignity, and Richard's own downfall is in progress. Several of Richard's victims reflect on Margaret's curses as they go to their deaths, thereby making more evident her role as Nemesis.

In 4.4 Margaret gloats over the misfortunes of Queen ELIZABETH (2), and leaves for France, content that she has stayed in England long enough to witness the fall of those who brought about her decline. As she departs, the climax of the play is about to unfold, and she has fulfilled her function. As an almost supernatural embodiment of Vengeance, she has represented an amoral world that is now to be overcome by the Christian reconciliation of RICHMOND.

Although Margaret of Anjou was a central figure in the Wars of the Roses, Shakespeare took considerable liberties with her story. He magnified the importance, and the evil, of a Queen who only naturally used her strengths to shore up the fortunes of her incompetent husband. Her foreignness and her gender made her useful as a witchlike figure at the centre of the web of treachery and violence that characterise the plays of the minor tetralogy.

For instance, Margaret's love affair with Suffolk, from its beginnings in *1 Henry VI,* is entirely fictitious. In *Part 2* Shakespeare ascribes to her an important role in English politics almost from the moment she sets foot in England in 1444. In fact, Margaret was a 14-year-old bride with no political experience, placed in an unfamiliar court and country, and she had little or no impact on English affairs for a decade. The fall of the Duchess of Gloucester, which she helps bring about in the play, occurred historically before her arrival. The Duke of Gloucester was probably not murdered, and Margaret had little to do with his political defeat in any case. In 1453 she attempted to assume the Regency of the realm during the period of her husband's insanity (ignored by Shakespeare). However, government by a Frenchwoman was unacceptable to the English aristocracy, and York was appointed Protector. His replacement by the Queen's protégé, SOMERSET (1), eventually led to the opening of the wars, with the first battle of ST. ALBANS.

The Queen was not present at that conflict, as she is in Shakespeare, but in the period immediately following it, she became an important leader of Henry's forces. However, the central incidents in the playwright's version of Margaret's role as a leader are fictitious. The Queen was not present to seize control on the occasion of Henry's concessions to York, enacted in 1.1 of *3 Henry VI;* nor was she a party to the killing of York, depicted with such extravagance in 1.4. Although she was indeed a force behind the later renewal of Lancastrian hopes, WARWICK (3) was far more important. She was in any case neither captured at Tewkesbury nor forced to witness her son's death; he was actually killed in the fighting, and she escaped to be captured a week later. She was imprisoned for several years and then ransomed by the King of France, to whose court she retired for the last six years of her life.

In *Richard III* Margaret's mere presence constitutes a final distortion of history, for she first appears on an occasion that actually took place only after her death in France. Shakespeare ignored this reality in order to use once more, in a highly symbolic manner, the strong but malign character he had developed in the course of the *Henry VI* plays.

**Margaret (2)**    Character in *Much Ado About Nothing,* attendant to HERO. Drawn into Don JOHN (1) and BORACHIO's plan to slander Hero, Margaret dresses in her mistress' clothes and meets Borachio at night, although this occurs off-stage. Hero's betrothed, CLAUDIO (1), is lured to the scene by Don John, and, believing that Hero is seeing a lover, he refuses to marry her.

When the villainy is finally exposed, however, Margaret is judged to have been an unwitting accomplice.

An impersonator of Hero is necessary to the plot, but Shakespeare wished to minimise the villainy in *Much Ado,* stressing comedy over melodrama, and he provided a number of proofs of Margaret's innocence. She is clearly a valued member of the genial circle of friends surrounding Hero; we see her only in scenes of mirthful fun, and she has a playful sense of humour—BENEDICK says her 'wit is as quick as the greyhound's mouth' (5.2.11). Moreover, Borachio's recruitment of Margaret, like the charade itself, is kept off-stage, and when Borachio confesses in 5.1, he insists that Margaret 'knew not what she did . . . but always hath been just and virtuous' (5.1.295–296). Once Hero is finally cleared, Leonato remarks, 'Margaret was in some fault for this, although against her will, as it appears' (5.4.4–5). Her participation resembles, in fact, a well-known masquerading game, recorded in accounts of 16th-century courtly pastimes, in which a woman would dress herself as a bride and thereby demand more elaborate endearments from her sweetheart. In a small but telling touch, Margaret's fondness for clothes is presented in her delighted description of an elaborate gown in 3.4.17–20.

**Margery Jourdain (d. 1441)**   Historical figure and minor character in *2 Henry VI,* a witch hired by HUME to summon a spirit for the DUCHESS (1) of Gloucester. In 1.4, at a séance, Margery summons the spirit ASNATH, and, after it has been questioned by the sorcerer BOLINGBROKE (2), she is arrested, with her fellows and the Duchess, by the dukes of YORK (8) and BUCKINGHAM (3). In 2.3 the King sentences her to be burned at the stake. The historical Jourdain claimed to have magical powers and was convicted of using them in the employ of the Duchess, and she was indeed burned at the stake.

**Maria (1)**   Character in *Love's Labour's Lost,* the beloved of LONGAVILLE and one of the ladies-in-waiting to the PRINCESS OF FRANCE. Maria, like her lover, functions simply as a figure in the courtly pageant of love that constitutes the play's main plot. She has no distinctive personality traits, although she may be said to anticipate more fully developed secondary female characters, such as NERISSA, in *The Merchant of Venice.*

**Maria (2)**   Character in *Twelfth Night,* chambermaid to OLIVIA. With SIR TOBY, SIR ANDREW, and FABIAN, Maria represents the spirit of fun that opposes the humourless severity of Olivia's steward, MALVOLIO, in the play's comic SUB-PLOT. Of the group, Maria is much the smartest. She devises the plot to embarrass the steward, and she composes the remarkably clever forged letter to Malvolio—read aloud by the victim himself in 2.5.92–159—playing on his ambitions and

his vanity to impel him to bring about his own downfall. Then in 4.2 she devises a capstone to the joke, disguising the jester FESTE as a curate, Sir TOPAS, to visit and torment Malvolio, who has been locked up as a lunatic.

In witty speeches like those in 3.2.65–80, Maria provides a commentary on Malvolio's actions that establish strongly our favourable, indeed indulgent, attitude towards a 'knavery', as Sir Toby calls it (4.2.70), that might easily turn vicious. When, at the conclusion of the play, we learn that Sir Toby has married Maria out of delight with her wit, we realise that she will be able to control her new husband successfully without repressing his high spirits. Moreover, this marriage provides a parallel to the pairings of the characters in the main plot, ORSINO with VIOLA and SEBASTIAN (2) with Olivia.

**Mariana (1)**   Minor character in *All's Well That Ends Well,* a neighbour of the WIDOW (2) Capilet, a Florentine innkeeper. In 3.5.16–28 Mariana roundly condemns PAROLLES and BERTRAM as unscrupulous womanisers, thus helping to establish the situation when HELENA (2) arrives in FLORENCE. She has no personality beyond that of a stereotypical gossip.

**Mariana (2)**   Character in *Measure for Measure,* the abandoned fiancée and eventual wife of ANGELO (2). By means of the 'bed trick' instituted by the DUKE (9), Mariana replaces ISABELLA—from whom Angelo has attempted to extort sex—in Angelo's bed. When Angelo's evil is exposed, the Duke orders Angelo to marry Mariana—thereby legitimising her action—following which he will be executed. Mariana pleads for mercy, convincing Isabella to join her, and the Duke finally relents in the atmosphere of reconciliation and forgiveness that closes the play. Aside from her rather formal melancholy as she pines for Angelo in seclusion when we first meet her, in 4.1, Mariana is not a developed character, though her plea, in 5.1, is touchingly expressive of the play's charitable point of view. She insists that 'best men are moulded out of faults, / And . . . become much more the better / For being a little bad' (5.1.437–439).

Her plea gives her special significance, for with it she triggers the sequence of pardons and forgiveness that close the play. Perhaps most important, she persuades Isabella to join her. Though Isabella's intercession goes against her natural enmity towards Angelo, she nevertheless proceeds to offer a sensible case for mercy. It is her conversion to this forgiving point of view—one quite removed from her earlier insistence on morality even if it meant the death of her brother—that is the play's climax. Mariana's plea is essentially selfish; she wishes to preserve the husband she has so long sought. But Isabella is totally objective, and it is this that makes her action impressive. Only the existence of Mariana as a proper mate for Angelo makes this possible.

No hint of Mariana is to be found in Shakespeare's sources for *Measure for Measure,* and the character has particular importance as she is an invention of the playwright that changes the nature of his story in a significant manner. In all of the sources for the play, the Angelo figure successfully extorts sex from the Isabella figure, and then, when exposed, he is forced to marry her. However, in Shakespeare's rendering of the tale, Isabella and Angelo have effectively been presented as intense figures whose opposing psychological strengths make such a union impossible to contemplate. Mariana therefore replaces Isabella. The bed trick, an ancient comedic device that Shakespeare also used in *All's Well,* accomplishes this end. Isabella is preserved as the virtuous counterpart to Angelo's corruption, and Mariana can influence her towards forgiveness as her rigidity relaxes. The device may seem arbitrary to modern readers—like a *deus ex machina,* it disposes of the impending tragedy with ease and convenience—but in Shakespeare's day this conclusion was not only perfectly acceptable, it was highly gratifying to the audience's sentimental feelings.

**Marina** Character in *Pericles,* daughter of PERICLES and THAISA. Marina appears only in Acts 4–5 (except as a newborn infant—i.e., as a stage prop—in 3.1), but she is nevertheless a major character. Along with her father, she bears the weight of the play's central lesson: the value of patience in the face of fate. Marina, like Pericles, is helpless before her destiny, which subjects her to the loss of her family and great dangers as well. Her name, which implies her birth at sea, suggests her destiny-driven life. Her spirit does not flag, however; she resists despair, as her father does not, and becomes his saviour. Finally, her moral virtues are rewarded by reunion with her parents and a prospective marriage with LYSIMACHUS.

Like Pericles, Marina suffers great misfortune—separation from her parents in infancy, a murder attempt by her foster-mother, a kidnapping and sale to a brothel—through no fault of her own and despite her extraordinary virtue. Also like her father, she is an idealised character, more important as an emblem than as a personality. She represents absolute innocence and purity; she says, 'I never spake bad word . . . never kill'd a mouse, nor hurt a fly . . . But I wept for't' (4.1.75–79). However, though she resembles 'Patience gazing on kings' graves, and smiling / Extremity out of act' (5.1.138–139), she is not without spirit. She demonstrates patience by never giving up on the world, but she is not passive like her father. Her stubborn refusal to surrender her virginity saves her, as she first talks her way out of the brothel and then becomes such a model of grace and kindness that she is called upon to cure the depression of the man who

proves to be her father. Marina is typical of Shakespeare's plucky, spirited heroines, even though she does not seek out her adventures but is cast into them by fate.

Marina's ideal virtue and the simplicity and inflexibility of her motives places her in a disturbing contrast with the social reality of the BAWD, the PANDAR, and BOULT. This contrast is often seen as a defect, but the objection ignores the playwright's allegorical purposes, which are emphasised by the contrast. Like Shakespeare's other late heroines, PERDITA and MIRANDA, Marina represents a sort of redemption, a renewal of life. Her spirit revives that of Pericles, who calls her 'Thou that beget'st him that did thee beget' (5.1.195). Through her, he can transcend the buffetings of fate and be reconciled with a life whose disillusionments have been too much to bear. Her healing nature also effects the customers of the brothel (see GENTLEMAN [10]) and even the hard-boiled Boult. Moreover, Marina has been symbolically dead: she was believed dead by Pericles and has undergone a journey through the underworld of the brothel. She thus is representative of resurrection, the play's most important motif. She is an appropriate symbol of the spirit of hope and renewal with which the play ends.

**Mariner (1)** Minor character in *The Winter's Tale,* seaman who sets ANTIGONUS ashore in BOHEMIA in 3.3 for the purpose of abandoning the infant PERDITA. The Mariner dislikes their task, which has been ordered by the mad King LEONTES, and he fears that the gods will dislike it as well. He warns Antigonus to hurry because bad weather is approaching and because the coast is famous for its wild animals. He is borne out on both points as a storm arises—he perishes in it, as is reported in 3.3.90–94—and Antigonus is eaten by a BEAR. The Mariner offers a point of view outside the story, that of the common man who pities the infant and fears the gods. Like a CHORUS (1), he provides a brief commentary on developments.

The Mariner's death has a dual significance in the play's scheme. A good man, repelled by Perdita's fate, he is himself a victim of Leontes' madness. As such he represents the human cost exacted by evil. On the other hand, as Antigonus' guide, he is Leontes' agent, albeit an unwilling one. His death is part of the necessary workings of providence, for the evil of Leontes' deeds must be thoroughly extirpated as a condition of redemption, and the Mariner, like Antigonus, embodies that evil to some degree.

**Mariner (2)** Any of several minor characters in *The Tempest,* the crew of the ship that is wrecked on PROSPERO's island. As the play opens, the Mariners receive orders from the BOATSWAIN—'Heigh, my hearts! . . . yare, yare! Take in the topsail' (1.1.5–6). A little later several of them cry out in unison, 'All lost, to prayers, to prayers! all lost!' (1.1.51), signalling the close of the scene, as the passengers prepare for death. These characters are extras, providing a sense of hysteria aboard the doomed vessel.

**Markham, Gervase (Jervis) (c. 1568–1637)** English poet and author, writer of possible minor sources for Shakespeare's plays, and perhaps a model for the boastful soldier ARMADO or the 'rival poet' of the SON-NETS. Markham was a noted soldier and horseman—he probably introduced the Arabian horse to England—who turned to hack literature after his military career. He wrote copiously on a variety of subjects, especially military tactics, falconry, fishing, housekeeping, and all aspects of owning and breeding horses. His easy, colloquial style made him popular, and he still offers readers a pleasant introduction to the Elizabethan age. Scholars believe that some of his practical information is echoed in Shakespeare's plays, for instance, in PETRUCHIO's elaborate description of falcon training in *The Taming of the Shrew* (4.1.175–198). Markham's easy assurance of infallibility suggests he may have been satirised in Shakespeare's Armado, though the point cannot be proven with existing evidence.

Markham was an extremely prolific author, who sometimes issued almost identical texts under different titles to increase sales. At one point a group of London booksellers, seeing that he was flooding his own market, persuaded him to sign an agreement not to write any more books on blacksmithing, but he soon violated the pact. He occasionally ascended to more serious literature, and because he dedicated one such work to Shakespeare's patron, the Earl of SOUTHAMP-TON (2), he has been associated with the 'rival poet', though most scholars find the identification extremely dubious.

**Marlowe (1), Christopher (1564–1593)** English playwright, Shakespeare's immediate predecessor as leading English dramatist and a considerable influence on his work. Marlowe, with Thomas KYD, virtually invented Elizabethan TRAGEDY, and Marlowe's influence on ELIZABETHAN DRAMA in general was great. In his *Tamburlaine* (1587) he successfully established BLANK VERSE as the standard medium for drama, and the grandeur of his protagonists and themes elevated his successors' aspirations.

Many passages in Shakespeare's early works are clearly modelled on Marlowe; scholars who believe that many of Shakespeare's plays were written in part by other playwrights have even attributed parts of the *Henry VI* plays, *Richard III, Titus Andronicus,* and others to Marlowe, though modern scholars mistrust most of these attributions. In *As You Like It,* PHEBE quotes a line from a Marlowe poem, ascribing it to a 'dead shepherd' (3.5.81–82), Shakespeare's only certain reference to a contemporary poet. Further quotations from

and allusions to Marlowe's work abound in the plays (e.g., *A Midsummer Night's Dream* 1.1.170, *Merry Wives of Windsor* 3.1.16–35, *Much Ado About Nothing* 5.2.29), attesting not only to Shakespeare's admiration but also to his confidence that his audiences knew and appreciated Marlowe's work. In addition, Marlowe's *The Jew of Malta* (1589) probably helped inspire Shakespeare's SHYLOCK; similarly, Marlowe's *Edward II* (1592) probably informed *Richard II*'s presentation of a flawed ruler, and his poem 'Hero and Leander' offered a model for *Venus and Adonis.* (Marlowe's poem was unfinished at his death and published posthumously—with additions by George CHAPMAN—in 1598, but Shakespeare knew it earlier, in manuscript.)

Marlowe led a violent, dissolute, and dramatic life. A notorious drinker and brawler, he flaunted his homosexuality at a time when homosexuality was a capital crime. He was a soldier in the Netherlands, from which he was deported for counterfeiting gold coins, and he was probably a spy for the government of Queen ELIZABETH (1)—both abroad and in England. In 1589 he was involved in a street fight in which a man was killed. He was one of the earliest Englishmen to publicly admit to atheism, and in 1593 he was charged with blasphemy—along with Kyd—but before he could be tried, he was stabbed to death, reportedly in a dispute over a tavern bill. Some historians believe he was murdered, silenced by a government agent; in any case, his killer, who is known to have been a fellow spy, was immediately pardoned. (Marlowe's death may be alluded to in *As You Like It* 3.3.9–12.)

The son of a shoemaker, Marlowe nevertheless received a good education, graduating from Cambridge University in 1587, in the same year that his first play, *Tamburlaine,* became the talk of LONDON. He followed it with *Tamburlaine, Part 2* (1588), *The Jew of Malta* (1589), *Dr Faustus* (1592), *Edward II* (1592)—the first English historical play—and *The Massacre at Paris* (1593). Most of his plays were probably commissioned by the ADMIRAL'S MEN and his heroic protagonists first played by Edward ALLEYN. At his death Marlowe left another play unfinished—*Dido, Queen of Carthage,* completed by Thomas NASHE and staged in 1594—along with 'Hero and Leander'. His oeuvre was completed by two other short poems (one of them, the delightful 'Passionate Shepherd to his Love', which was falsely attributed to Shakespeare in THE PASSIONATE PILGRIM). While the body of work is small, it encompasses at least three great plays—*Tamburlaine, The Jew of Malta,* and *Dr Faustus*—and a magnificent lyric poem, 'Hero and Leander'. Marlowe, who was born the same year as Shakespeare, was only 29 when he was killed.

**Marlowe (2), Julia (1865–1950)** American actress. Born in Britain, Marlowe came to America at age four, began acting with a touring company at 12, and made her New York debut at 21. She quickly established herself as a leading actress, especially in Shakespearean comedy, playing VIOLA, ROSALIND, BEATRICE, and PORTIA (1). She also excelled as JULIET (1). In 1904 Marlowe founded a Shakespearean repertory company with E. H. SOTHERN, whom she was to marry. She took on more tragic roles, including LADY (6) MACBETH. Just after her retirement in 1924, she and Sothern staged 10 Shakespearean performances whose proceeds were donated to the Shakespeare Memorial Theatre in STRATFORD.

**Marseilles**  City in southern FRANCE (1), setting for one scene in *All's Well That Ends Well*. HELENA (2) announces her intention to leave FLORENCE and find the KING (17) of France at 'Marcellus' (4.4.9)—indicating the Elizabethan pronunciation of the name—and in 5.1 she is said in the stage directions to be there, only to discover that the King has left for ROSSILLION. No characteristics of Marseilles or southern France are alluded to, but the setting is apt because Marseilles is the major city on either a land or land-and-sea route from Florence to Rossillion.

**Marsh, Henry (d. 1665)**  English publisher. Marsh published the first edition of a famous collection of DROLLS, *The Wits, or Sport upon Sport* (1662), assembled by his partner, Francis KIRKMAN. He may have been a royalist and in exile during the period of the Puritan revolutionary government (1642–1660), for he is absent from the publishing records from 1642 to 1658. When he died he left his business to Kirkman.

**Marshal (1) (Lord Marshal)**  Minor character in *Richard II*, the nobleman who presides over the trial by combat between BOLINGBROKE (1) and MOWBRAY (1) in 1.3. Historically the Marshal on this occasion was the Duke of SURREY (3), a supporter of RICHARD II and thus an enemy of Bolingbroke. Shakespeare apparently forgot this fact, which appears in his chief source, HOLINSHED's history, when he presented the Marshal as a friend of Bolingbroke in 1.3.251–252. This is one of the many minor errors and inconsistencies that appear throughout the plays.

**Marshall (2)**  Minor character in *Pericles*, an official of the court of King SIMONIDES. In 2.3 the Marshall designates a seat for PERICLES at the royal banquet; he speaks only four lines and serves merely to indicate the grandeur of the occasion.

**Marston, John (c. 1575–1634)**  English dramatist. Marston abandoned a legal education to be a writer. In 1598 he established himself in the literary world with two long poems, one erotic (*The Metamorphosis of Pygmalion's Image*) and one satiric (*The Scourge of Villainy*). In 1599 he wrote for Philip HENSLOWE and the ADMIRAL'S MEN, but in the same year he began writing for the CHILDREN'S COMPANIES, where he spent the rest of his short career. He is chiefly remembered for bitter satirical COMEDY, but he also specialised in the REVENGE PLAY. With his best-known work, *The Malcontent* (1604), he managed to combine the two genres. Writing for the Children of Paul's, Marston began the WAR OF THE THEATRES with his *Historio-Mastix* (1599), a comedy containing a satire on Ben JONSON. In reply to Jonson's responses, he added *Jack Drum's Entertainment* (1600) and *What You Will* (1601) to the fray, as well as collaborating with Thomas DEKKER on *Satiromastix* (1601). He was on good terms with Jonson by 1604, when he dedicated *The Malcontent* to his one-time rival. In that year, Marston began writing for the Children of the Queen's Revels, and in 1605 he collaborated with Jonson and George CHAPMAN on *Eastward Ho!* King JAMES I deemed the play seditious, with the result that Marston's collaborators were gaoled, though Marston fled LONDON until the affair blew over, thereby igniting Jonson's enmity anew. In 1608, however, Marston was imprisoned for offending the king again, with a play now lost, and he abandoned the theatre, leaving a final play unfinished. By 1616 he was a Protestant minister.

**Martext, Sir Oliver**  Minor character in *As You Like It*, a country priest. In 3.3 TOUCHSTONE and AUDREY meet with Martext, 'the vicar of the next village' (3.3.37), to be married. Martext speaks only two lines before the ceremony is broken up by JAQUES (1), who belittles the virtues of a marriage performed by a country bumpkin and leads the couple away.

Martext is a parodic figure with particular relevance to Shakespeare's audiences. The English Reformation—instituted about 50 years before the play was written—had produced a shortage of trained clergy, for not only did many Catholic priests refuse to transfer their allegiance to the Church of England, but the new church did not develop training programmes immediately. The quality of the lesser clergy was accordingly poor, even as late as the 17th century, and the illiteracy and ignorance of country priests were subjects of much scandal and humour, of which this scene is an example.

Martext's name not only suggests his incompetence, but it may also be a satirical reference to Martin Marprelate, the central figure in a religious controversy of the late 1580s. Marprelate—a fictitious name with anti-clerical overtones—was the supposed author of a series of anonymous tracts advocating radical Puritanism. Their publisher defied the government's CENSORSHIP for several years, before being captured and hung. Martext's name may therefore suggest that he is a radical as well as an oaf—thus doubly a target for comic insult. However, Shakespeare's humour on religious subjects is never bitter, and the playwright permits Sir Oliver a dignified response to his rejection:

once alone, Martext says, ' 'Tis no matter. Ne'er a fantastical knave of them all shall flout me out of my calling' (3.3.97–98).

**Martius (1)**   Minor character in *Titus Andronicus,* a son of TITUS (1) Andronicus. Martius, with QUINTUS, is framed by AARON for the murder of BASSIANUS in 2.3. After the two are executed, their heads are delivered to Titus, in 3.1.

**Martius (2) (Marcius)**   In *Coriolanus,* the name by which Caius Martius CORIOLANUS is known before 1.9. 64, when he receives his new name, his 'addition' (1.9.65) of honour for his military exploits in the taking of the city CORIOLES. In the ancient Roman naming system, Martius is a clan name; there is no similar system in modern Western naming. Shakespeare apparently followed tradition (and his source, Thomas NORTH's translation of PLUTARCH's *Lives*) when he used it as a family name in the sense we understand. However, the names Caius and Martius are mistakenly reversed several times in the play—including at 1.9.64—an example of the numerous minor errors to which Shakespeare was prone throughout his career.

**Marullus (Murellus), C. Epidius (active 44 B.C.)**   Historical figure and minor character in *Julius Caesar,* a tribune of ROME and an ally of BRUTUS (4). In 1.1 Marullus and his fellow tribune, FLAVIUS (1), disperse a crowd (see COMMONER [1]) that has assembled to greet the triumphant CAESAR (1). The tribunes criticise their disloyalty to Pompey, whom they had supported earlier and whom Caesar has defeated in civil war. After the crowd has gone, Flavius and Marullus destroy the public decorations that have been put up in Caesar's honour because they fear the triumphant general will become a tyrant. In 1.2.282–283 CASCA reports that Flavius and Marullus have been 'put to silence' for this deed. The episode establishes a widespread mistrust of Caesar from the outset of the play.

Little is known of the historical Marullus, but Shakespeare's source, PLUTARCH's *Lives,* reports that Caesar dismissed the two tribunes from their positions because they had made the gesture dramatised in the play. However, in Plutarch's account this occurred months after Caesar's triumph. Shakespeare compressed these events for dramatic purposes.

In the FIRST FOLIO, where the play was first published, Marullus is identified throughout as 'Murellus', and some modern editions preserve this spelling, though others follow the historically correct rendering of the name.

**Masque**   Courtly entertainment that evolved into a drama-like theatrical genre. Masques appques appear in various forms in a number of Shakespeare's plays.

Originally an amateur masquerade in which members of the court put on masks and costumes and fêted the monarch with dancing on holiday occasions, the masque evolved under King JAMES I into a theatrical presentation with extremely elaborate sets and costumes, many professional musicians and dancers in support of the aristocratic amateurs, and highly literary scripts by such writers as Francis BEAUMONT (2), Samuel DANIEL, and most notably Ben JONSON. These productions were staged on significant royal occasions, such as weddings and birthdays. (Non-royal aristocrats also staged masques on such occasions.) The masques were allegorical in nature, with mythological or emblematic characters who represented particular virtues and vices or more or less clearcut ideas, such as marriage or PASTORAL contentment. The great expense of such extravaganzas eventually became a significant political issue, and the courtly masque did not survive the revolution that began in 1642.

The 17th-century masque exerted considerable influence on JACOBEAN DRAMA. Shakespeare's last works—the ROMANCES plus *Henry VIII,* which were written for the aristocratic audiences at the BLACKFRIARS THEATRE—all contain elaborate masquelike elements. Masques also appear in several earlier Shakespeare plays: simple maskings of a social sort are enacted in *Love's Labour's Lost, Romeo and Juliet* (see MASQUERS), and *Much Ado About Nothing,* while more formal stagings, featuring named mythological characters, occur in *As You Like It* and *Timon of Athens.* In addition, there are masquelike elements in other plays, most strikingly in *A Midsummer Night's Dream.*

As in movies that contain scraps of older movies as part of the characters' experience, the appearance of masques in plays amused their audiences with enactments of familiar—or at least notorious—pleasures while also furthering the play's developments. For instance, in *The Winter's Tale,* a masquelike 'dance of twelve Satyrs' (4.4.343) is presented at a sheep-shearing festival. A delightful theatrical spectacle in itself, it demonstrates the vitality of pastoral life and at the same time, by evoking an aristocratic entertainment, expresses the hidden nobility present, for the leading shepherdess is actually the lost princess PERDITA. In *Timon of Athens,* CUPID's brief masque in 1.2 displays the aristocratic elegance of the title character's household while providing an occasion for an irascible complaint against extravagant vanity by the play's philosopher-jester, APEMANTUS. An actual royal masque of 1527 is re-enacted in 1.4 of *Henry VIII,* and the betrothal masque in 4.1 of *The Tempest* resembles contemporary (c. 1611) masques and lends grandeur to the proposed marriage of FERDINAND (2) and MIRANDA, whose status as future royalty has significance in the play's scheme of things. The masque in 3.5 of *The Two Noble Kinsmen* was in fact a scene from a real masque, Beaumont's *Masque of the Inner Temple and Gray's Inn*

(1613) (see INNS OF COURT), though this borrowing was the work of Shakespeare's collaborator, John FLETCHER (2).

The masque was known at least as far back as the 14th century, during the reign of RICHARD II. It was formalised, with prepared scenarios, under Queen ELIZABETH (1), but it only became a literary, quasi-dramatic genre under James. However, even Jacobean masques always contained large elements of dance, the original masque medium, and—at least in life, if not always on the stage—masques were normally preludes to social dancing, in which the participants joined the spectators at a ball. A masque was accordingly an occasion for coquetry and sexual intrigue, as is quite clear in Shakespeare.

Masques were influential on literature, as well as drama. Masquelike elements appear in such works as *The Faerie Queene* by Edmund SPENSER, and some late masques are significant literary works in their own right, most notably John MILTON's *Comus* (performed 1634; published 1637). The courtly masque did not reappear after the Puritan revolution; the last known script was written by William DAVENANT in 1640.

**Masquers**  Group of non-speaking characters in *Romeo and Juliet*, the men who accompany ROMEO to the banquet held by CAPULET (1). In the 16th-century courtly entertainment that evolved into the formal MASQUE, guests often costumed themselves, as Romeo and his friends do in 1.4, and were known as masquers. Arriving in groups and often dressed thematically, the masquers declared themselves to be party-crashers and demanded to dance. Uproarious flirtation was expected to follow. Named characters sometimes appear as masquers elsewhere in Shakespeare's plays (e.g., in *Much Ado About Nothing*, 2.1.78 and *Henry VIII*, 1.4.64–87).

**Massinger, Philip (1583–1640)**  English playwright, a secondary figure of JACOBEAN DRAMA. Massinger's plays are characterised by his imitation of Shakespeare's verse style, to the extent that though no known work of Massinger's can be dated before 1616, he is sometimes thought to have written the parts usually assigned to Shakespeare in his collaborations with John FLETCHER (2), *The Two Noble Kinsmen* and possibly *Henry VIII*. Most scholars, however, deem Massinger's involvement extremely unlikely, though he did collaborate with Fletcher, his close friend, on many plays. He also worked with numerous other playwrights. After Fletcher's death, Massinger became the chief playwright for the KING'S MEN.

Massinger wrote a variety of works. He is best remembered for his satirical comedies, especially *A New Way to Pay Old Debts* (1621), and *The City Madam* (1632). He also wrote tragedies. His *Duke of Milan* (1621), which is based on *Othello*, is regarded as among the better Jacobean tragedies. In the late 17th century, Massinger's *The Roman Actor* (1626) was thought to be by Shakespeare. Massinger often faced governmental CENSORSHIP, for he frequently touched on such sensitive issues as Catholicism (he was himself a Catholic convert), foreign policy, and various public figures.

**Master (1)**  Minor character in *2 Henry VI*, a petty officer on a pirate ship. In 4.1 the LIEUTENANT (1) of the ship awards to the Master the ransom of a GENTLEMAN (1), one of several captured by the pirates.

**Master (2)**  Minor character in *The Tempest*, captain of the ship that is wrecked on PROSPERO's island. The Master speaks only two lines, at the play's opening, instructing the BOATSWAIN to see that the men act swiftly, or they will go aground. In 5.1 he reappears with the Boatswain, who reports on the miraculous restoration of the vessel, but he does not speak himself. He is an extra, helping to provide a realistic depiction of a ship's company.

**Master-Gunner**  Minor character in *1 Henry VI*, a French soldier in the besieged city of ORLÉANS (1). The Master-Gunner instructs his BOY (1) in 1.4 that their cannon is trained on a certain tower where the English leaders are known to stand watch. The Boy subsequently fires the shot that kills the Duke of SALISBURY (3).

**Master of Revels**  English official of the 16th and 17th centuries who regulated the theatre. The Master headed the Revels Office, a department of the royal household that originally dealt with the annual royal entertainments during the Revels season, from All Saint's Day (November 1) to the beginning of Lent in the following spring. The position of Master of Revels was created in 1545 under King HENRY VIII. At first, the Master was simply responsible for hiring and paying entertainers, but gradually the powers of the office were expanded. By Shakespeare's time, the Revels Office consisted of the Master and four full-time subordinates, and it not only hired theatrical companies to perform at court, but provided them with scenery and costumes from its own stores. It also selected the plays they were to perform and oversaw the content of the plays. The Master thus had the authority of a censor (see CENSORSHIP), especially after the passage of the 1606 anti-blasphemy statute, 'Act to Restrain Abuses of Players', which enlarged his authority to cover the publication of plays as well.

The Master collected various fees, as he issued licences for provincial acting companies, for the performance and publication of individual plays, and for dispensations to companies who wished to perform during Lent. In addition, he was frequently bribed.

The office of Master of Revels was accordingly an extremely profitable one. The nominal salary was only £10 a year, but it is known that in 1603 the Master made about £100. Beginning in 1623 Sir Henry HERBERT (1) paid the ostensible Master £150 a year to perform the office and collect the income, which must have been considerably greater. The office of Master of Revels fell into disuse when the theatres were closed at the outset of the civil war in 1642. Herbert tried to revive it upon the restoration of the monarchy in 1660, but his attempt failed, and the office was formally eliminated.

**Mate**   Minor character in *2 Henry VI*, a sailor on a pirate ship. In 4.1 the LIEUTENANT (1) of the ship awards the Mate the ransom of a GENTLEMAN (1), one of several captured by the pirates.

**Mayne, Jasper (1604–1672)**   English writer, possibly the author of one of the introductory poems to the FIRST FOLIO edition (1623) of Shakespeare's plays. Mayne published several poems and two plays (both written c. 1638), one of which contains a scene apparently inspired by the interrogation of PAROLLES in 4.3 of *All's Well That Ends Well*. He also translated the Latin author Lucian. After 1660 he was chaplain to King Charles II. Some scholars attribute to him the poem 'To the memorie of M. *W. Shake-speare*', a poem of four rhymed couplets that is signed 'I. M'. in the Folio. However, because Mayne was quite young in 1623, James MABBE is more commonly believed to be its author.

**Mayor (1) of Coventry**   Minor character in *3 Henry VI*, a supporter of WARWICK (3) in his attempt to reinstate HENRY VI as king. The Mayor, who does not speak, appears on the walls of Coventry with Warwick in 5.1, lending local authority to the effort.

**Mayor (2) of London**   Minor character in *1 Henry VI*. In 1.3 the Mayor breaks up a brawl between the men of the Duke of GLOUCESTER (4) and those of the Bishop of WINCHESTER (1). In 3.1 he tells the king's conference of further disorders. The incidents serve to illustrate the spreading social chaos that aristocratic dissensions have engendered.

**Mayor (3) of London**   Minor character in *Richard III*, a subservient figure who is cowed by RICHARD III. The Mayor appears in several scenes in Act 3. He provides a cover of legality for Richard's actions, approving an execution and acclaiming Richard as king when he moves to seize the throne.

**Mayor (4) of St Albans**   Minor character in *2 Henry VI*. The Mayor accompanies SIMPCOX, a confidence man who is presented to the king's hawking party in 2.1.

**Mayor (5) of York**   Minor character in *3 Henry VI*, the chief officer of the city of YORK (2). In 4.7 the Mayor cites his loyalty to King HENRY VI as the reason for refusing to open the gates of the city to EDWARD IV. Lying, Edward asserts that he will make no claim on the crown but wishes only to be Duke of York. Believing him, the Mayor admits him. The incident illustrates the lack of honour among the feuding royalty during the WARS OF THE ROSES.

**McKellen, Ian (b. 1935)**   English actor. McKellen is noted for a variety of roles, having played most of Shakespeare's protagonists. He played MACBETH in Trevor NUNN's 1976 staging of *Macbeth* in STRATFORD and in the subsequent TELEVISION presentation. He also played the title role in the first known professional performance of SIR THOMAS MORE in 1964.

## *Measure for Measure*

### SYNOPSIS

*Act 1, Scene 1*
As he prepares to leave the city, the DUKE (9) of VIENNA appoints ESCALUS (2) second in command to ANGELO (2), the deputy who will exercise power in the Duke's absence. Angelo receives his orders, and the Duke praises him for his life of devotion to duty.

*Act 1, Scene 2*
MISTRESS (2) Overdone, a bordello keeper, interrupts the lewd banter of LUCIO and two GENTLEMEN (5) to tell them that CLAUDIO (3) has been sentenced to death for having made JULIET (2) pregnant. POMPEY (1) tells Mistress Overdone of a new law that orders the destruction of bordellos; he assures her that she will survive and that he will continue to work for her. The PROVOST appears and exhibits Claudio in the streets as part of his punishment. Claudio tells Lucio that he slept with Juliet in the belief that they would soon be married, but that her relatives had held up her dowry. Then, after Juliet became pregnant, Angelo began to enforce a long-neglected law making sexual immorality a capital crime. Claudio tells Lucio of his sister who is about to enter a convent, and asks Lucio to ask her to seek mercy from Angelo.

*Act 1, Scene 3*
The Duke visits the FRIAR (1) and tells him that he has placed Angelo in charge during a revival of disused morality laws. He fears that to revive these laws under his own authority might give them too great a force; this way he can see how they are received and act accordingly. He intends to secretly return to Vienna and oversee the process, disguised as a friar.

*Act 1, Scene 4*
Lucio visits Claudio's sister, ISABELLA, at the convent. He tells her of Claudio's predicament, and she agrees to plead for mercy from Angelo.

*Act 2, Scene 1*
Escalus proposes mercy for Claudio, but Angelo refuses. Constable ELBOW brings Pompey and FROTH before the officials; in comically confused speech he charges his prisoners with running a bordello for Mistress Overdone and adds that they attempted to recruit his wife. Pompey's wittily long-winded reply drives Angelo away; he leaves the case to Escalus. After further comical exchanges, Escalus releases Froth and Pompey with a warning that law enforcement is becoming stricter; Pompey leaves sassily.

*Act 2, Scene 2*
Despite the Provost's pleas, Angelo orders Claudio's execution for the next day. Isabella arrives and pleads at length for mercy. Angelo promises only to reconsider and tell her of his decision the next day. Angelo, alone, reflects distractedly that he has fallen in love with Isabella and is tempted to sin by offering a pardon for Claudio in exchange for her love.

*Act 2, Scene 3*
The Duke, disguised as a friar, ministers to the inmates of the prison. He encounters Juliet, urges her repentance, and promises that he will visit her condemned lover.

*Act 2, Scene 4*
Angelo soliloquises that he cannot pray for strength against temptation because his thoughts are filled by Isabella. Isabella arrives and renews her plea. Angelo tells her he will have mercy on Claudio only if she will become his lover. She refuses, and he swears that he will have Claudio tortured. He gives her a day to change her mind and leaves. Alone, she declares her confidence in Claudio. As a man of honour, he will agree that her avoidance of sin is more important than his rescue.

*Act 3, Scene 1*
The Duke, as a friar, counsels Claudio to prepare for death by considering the ills of life. Isabella arrives, and the 'friar' eavesdrops as she tells Claudio of Angelo's evil ultimatum. Though Claudio at first supports her refusal, he is overcome by fear of death and pleads with her to save him. Furious, she berates him hysterically and leaves. The 'friar' intercepts her and tells her he knows of Angelo's intentions. He proposes to her a plot. Angelo had once abandoned a woman he was supposed to marry named MARIANA (2) and she still loves him. If Isabella arranges to have sex with Angelo on condition that the transaction be silent and in the dark, Mariana could actually keep the appointment. Isabella agrees.

*Act 3, Scene 2*
Elbow brings Pompey to the prison; Lucio appears, and Pompey asks him for bail but is refused. Lucio

speaks with the Duke, thinking he is actually a friar. He claims to be an intimate of the Duke, gossips about him slanderously and leaves. Mistress Overdone is gaoled despite her claim that Lucio has informed on her because she keeps his illegitimate child. Before he leaves to visit Claudio, Escalus observes to the 'friar' that the absent Duke would not have been so merciless as Angelo. Alone, the Duke reflects on the virtues needed in a ruler and rails against Angelo's violation of these standards.

*Act 4, Scene 1*
The Duke, as the 'friar', visits Mariana. Isabella arrives and reports that she has agreed to meet Angelo that night in his garden. Mariana accepts her part in the plot.

*Act 4, Scene 2*
The Provost offers Pompey parole if he will serve as assistant to the executioner, ABHORSON, in the beheadings of Claudio and another man, BARNARDINE; he agrees. The disguised Duke arrives and predicts that Claudio will be pardoned. However, a MESSENGER (18) brings the order that Claudio is to be killed immediately and his head sent to Angelo. The 'friar' suggests that Barnardine's head be substituted for Claudio's. The Provost says he cannot do this because of his duty. The 'friar' confides that he knows the Duke's intentions and produces letters from him as proof.

*Act 4, Scene 3*
Pompey and Abhorson summon Barnardine to be executed, but he refuses because he has a terrible hangover. The Provost appears, and the 'friar' observes that Barnardine is so unrepentant that if he died he would surely go to hell, placing a moral burden on his executioners; the Provost remarks that another prisoner has by chance died that morning, and they agree that his head can be used as the substitute for Claudio's. Isabella arrives, and the disguised Duke decides to postpone telling her of the plot to spare Claudio. He tells her instead that Angelo has demanded and received Claudio's head. He promises her revenge; she is to take a letter to a friar who will bring her to the Duke, and Angelo's guilt will be exposed. As she leaves, Lucio arrives; he brags that he has abandoned a pregnant woman and claims to know the Duke has done the same.

*Act 4, Scene 4*
Angelo and Escalus discuss the Duke's peculiar instructions: they are to proclaim that any complaints of injustice should be made publicly and then meet him outside the city. Escalus leaves to send out this decree; alone, Angelo bemoans his guilty conscience. Not only did he deflower Isabella, he had Claudio killed for fear he would someday seek revenge. He regrets his decision and cries that one sin leads to more.

*Act 4, Scene 5*
The Duke visits the Friar again and plans his return to Vienna.

*Act 4, Scene 6*
Isabella and Mariana ready themselves to encounter Angelo and the Duke; the 'friar' has warned Isabella that she must expect to be mistreated before she triumphs. The real Friar, Friar Peter, arrives to escort them to the Duke's ceremonial return.

*Act 5, Scene 1*
The Duke returns, and Isabella demands justice. The Duke refuses to believe her tale and has her arrested; she claims that Friar Lodowick can support her. Friar Peter says that he will present the evidence of Friar Lodowick, who is sick. He calls Mariana, who reveals her role as Angelo's sexual partner. Angelo denies having seen her for years and accuses Friar Lodowick of plotting against him. The Duke sends the Provost for Friar Lodowick and orders Angelo and Escalus to handle the investigation while he leaves briefly. The Provost returns with Friar Lodowick—the Duke in his disguise—who loudly declares Angelo's guilt. The Provost and Lucio attempt to arrest the disguised Duke for slander, and in the struggle his identity is revealed. Angelo realises his guilt is known and confesses. The Duke orders him to marry Mariana immediately, and Friar Peter takes the two away to be wed. When Angelo returns with his new wife, the Duke sentences him to death for having killed Claudio. Mariana, joined by Isabella, pleads for his life, but the Duke refuses. The Provost declares that in repentance for having executed Claudio, he has left another prisoner alive. The Duke sends for that man. Barnardine appears, accompanied by Claudio, and the Duke pardons them both. He proposes marriage to Isabella and then pardons Angelo. He declares that Lucio must marry the woman he had abandoned; afterwards, he will be whipped and hung, but in the spirit of forgiveness he withdraws the punishments. He insists on the marriage of Claudio and Juliet, thanks the Provost and Escalus for their good services, and closes the play with an elaboration of his proposal to Isabella.

## COMMENTARY

*Measure for Measure* is a dark play in its focus on evil and its seemingly cynical attitude towards two basic human concerns, sex and the ordering of society. These elements place it among the PROBLEM PLAYS, and like its fellows, *Troilus and Cressida* and *All's Well That Ends Well*, it has generally been among the least popular of Shakespeare's plays during almost four centuries, though they have all increased in popularity during our troubled age. Nevertheless, although its subject matter may have more appeal in the 20th century, the play continues to dissatisfy many readers and viewers.

As in the other problem plays, the realistic characters do not readily mesh with the artificial plot or with the happy ending and marriages traditional in COMEDY.

As a TRAGICOMEDY, *Measure for Measure* purposefully combines tragic development with a comic resolution, utilising irony to distance the story line; this technique emphasises the play's symbolic significance. The play addresses its issues—questions of good government and personal morality—through teachings from the Bible, though in a highly secular context. When this is taken into consideration, *Measure for Measure* may seem the least problematic of the problem plays, for its elements then cohere in a convincing manner to justify the traditional happy ending in marriage.

The play's title refers to Christ's Sermon on the Mount, 'measure for measure' being a well-established proverbial abridgement of one of its lessons. In Matt. 7:2 and Luke 6:38 (and in Mark 4:24, in the context of a different sermon) we are taught to use a full, unstinting measure in distributing grain to others, for we shall receive measures in the same way that we distribute them. This lesson was commonly used by preachers and religious books of Shakespeare's day. On a particular Sunday, the version in Luke was by rule the subject of the sermon in all English churches. Thus, we can be sure that Shakespeare was familiar with the text that the proverbial expression referred to, and he could presume that his audience was, too. (He had, in fact, used 'measure for measure' before, in *3 Henry VI*, 2.6.55 and *King John*, 2.1.556–557.)

In Luke and Matthew the 'measure for measure' passages are closely linked to Christ's important pronouncements on the doctrine of Christian forgiveness. The proverb insists on such forgiveness, for only by practising mercy can one expect to receive it. In the play, Angelo's lack of mercy is strikingly compared with Isabella's pleas for it, especially when she seeks mercy for Angelo himself, in 5.1. The biblical passages also contain the familiar instruction not to judge others lest you incur judgement, another lesson in reciprocation. Both ideas were specifically linked with the exercise of power, as well as with personal ethics, by 16th- and 17th-century English Bible commentators. *Measure for Measure* is particularly concerned with the proper exercise of power, at least with respect to the administration of justice; a good ruler, the Duke, uncovers and punishes a bad one, Angelo.

The subject was appropriate in 1604 when Shakespeare wrote *Measure for Measure*. The duties of a Christian ruler were being widely discussed in London, for England had a new king, JAMES I, who was interested in theological matters and had raised the issue himself. In the 17th century it was believed that a ruler's authority came from God, and a good ruler was expected to attempt to be like God in justice and mercy alike. Because of this relationship, it was almost universally held, a ruler was exempted from the prohibition against vengeance and the exaction of punishment. The ruler was specifically required to use his power to punish wrongdoers, not only to preserve social order but to act as God's weapon in the fight against evil. As such, the ruler could use extraordinary methods that might in others be immoral. Thus, the Duke's disguise and other deceptions, including the bed trick, were entirely acceptable to Shakespeare's audiences. Similarly, the Duke's position justifies his attempts to circumvent the rulings of Angelo, who as a ruler's deputy is also God's appointee. This point is clearly made in the play when the Provost refuses to act against Angelo until the disguised Duke produces a letter indicating that the 'friar' acts for the supposedly absent Duke.

Christian interpretations of the play can be highly literal—some critics have found in it an allegory of divine atonement, in which Angelo is an Everyman figure and the Duke represents Christ, Lucio the Devil, and Isabella the soul. In a more general sense, many commentators have seen Isabella as a particularly Christian figure in her desire to be a nun, her adamant chastity, and her ultimate mercy. However, one need not view the play as purposeful religious doctrine, though it plainly reflects Christian sentiments. Shakespeare's other plays are distinctly *not* allegorical or sermonising, and *Measure for Measure* does not resemble traditional allegory, for most of its characters are believable human beings set in a socially realistic world. The play is easily understood as a traditional secular comedy whose themes have been drawn from a prominent Christian text.

The specifically Christian nature of the play's issues did not have to be raised; the playwright expected his audience to take these ideas for granted and go on to consider their application to the rather grim sex scandal being enacted. As a tale of official misconduct, the play evoked one aspect of the Christian lesson; through its presentation of human psychology a more personal application could be considered. *Measure for Measure* vividly offers both, and in both contexts the final lesson is the same: the power of good (in the form of Christian charity, as stressed by the title) can effect a reconciliation that untangles all plots, rights all wrongs, and leads to marital happiness, just as surely as does secular love in the traditional comedic mode.

As a play on the misuse of authority, *Measure for Measure* opposes two different sorts of bad government, an arrangement appropriate to its title. The Duke's administration of justice prior to the play has been too lax, as he himself admits, saying, '. . . Liberty plucks Justice by the nose, / The baby beats the nurse, and quite athwart / Goes all decorum. / . . . 'twas my fault to give the people scope . . .' (1.3.29–35). It is to rectify this situation that the Duke has transferred his

authority to Angelo, but the deputy proves to be the opposite sort of bad governor. He is uncompromisingly strict and cannot apply mercy where it is appropriate, that is, in Claudio's case. The Duke's lax government is also represented in the comic SUB-PLOT by Escalus' release of Pompey. Thus the long comic 'trial' scene featuring Constable Elbow results in freedom for a career pimp, while Claudio, an honourable young man who wishes only to become a husband and father, is still condemned to death. The consequences of the dramatic situation are more extreme than in Shakespeare's other comedies. Angelo's intention towards Isabella is quite simply rape (and he believes he carries it out); then he further blackens himself by going back on his word, and Claudio is very nearly killed.

The remedy begins with the Duke's idea to monitor Angelo, which he actually adopts before the play opens. Significantly, the ruler takes on a religious role. He disguises himself as a friar, thus stressing the divinity of authority. The result, in addition to the preservation of Isabella's honour and Claudio's life, is the emphasis on the Duke's mercy and forgiveness at the play's close. This dénouement might seem exaggerated to modern sensibilities but is utterly fitting to a proper ruler in the world of the play.

In terms of human psychology, the play places Angelo and Isabella in opposition. Angelo's inexcusable refusal of mercy stems from an excess of zeal for the rule of law. This position is related to his notion of himself as a virtuous public servant, one who is beyond examination because he is dutiful. In this Angelo is contrasted with the Duke, who acknowledges his failings and investigates his own government. Because Angelo has not questioned himself, he cannot see the humanity in Claudio, as Isabella points out. His stiff assumption of virtue deprives him of the capacity for honest judgement. Moreover, so confident is he in his own rightness that he is entirely incapable of resisting lust—though he wishes to—when it arises.

The heroine, like the villain, is strictly virtuous. Not only is she prepared to enter a nunnery, she regrets that its rules are not strict enough. Like Angelo, she insists that her own ideas about life be applied to others, 'wishing a more strict restraint / Upon the sisters stood' (1.4.4–5) and demanding that Claudio 'Take my defiance, [and] Die, perish!' (3.1.142–143). Her assertiveness, while attractive in its bold spirit, is uncharitable, also proving Isabella an unlikely nun. Thus, we need not be surprised when she accepts the Duke's proposal of marriage at the close; once her enthusiasm has been allied with a forgiving tolerance she can adopt a more natural destiny than seclusion from the world.

The stiff, unyielding attitudes of the two chief characters establish the play's major conflict. This quality is fittingly expressed in the play's general atmosphere, for all of Acts 2 and 3 and much of Act 4 take place within a prison or courthouse, and of the nine remaining scenes, three take place in the Friar's cell or the nunnery and one in Mariana's 'moated grange' (3.1.265), a doubly isolated place, both rustic and fortified. Four more scenes (1.1,2; 4.4,6) are in nondescript locales, but they are all distinctly anxious in tone; only the final scene of reconciliation (5.1) takes place in a setting of openness and freedom—'at the gates' (4.4.-4), the site of the Duke's ceremonious re-entry of Vienna.

The play's comic sub-plot both reinforces the claustrophobic atmosphere and relieves it. The shady world of Pompey, Lucio, and Mistress Overdone deals with similar themes as the main plot—sex and criminal justice—but contrasts with it greatly in tone, being bawdy about sex and jocularly dismissive of the courts. The tension of Claudio's fate is thus relaxed, but at the same time the sub-plot offers a dark view of Vienna's civic life that supports a sense of imminent doom. The jesting on venereal disease by Lucio and his friends in 1.2, Mistress Overdone's assertion that Lucio has betrayed her, and the association of Pompey with the executioner Abhorson all contribute to our growing recognition that these humorous figures do not represent an idyllic world of irresponsibility but rather an unpleasant one of commercialised sex and a collapse of values.

In the main story the conflict between Angelo and Isabella becomes unbearably tense. Claudio pleads with Isabella to sin and save him and she denounces him hysterically; by 3.1 it seems painfully clear that either Isabella must break or Claudio must die. The nature of the play changes at this point. No longer an enactment of psychological tension and moral extremism, it becomes a symbolic representation of the power of reconciliation to produce harmony and love where strife had been. The presence of the disguised Duke suggests such an outcome from the beginning. With a balance that is reflected in the title, the second half of the play counters the first. The Duke takes control of the plot, and Angelo, Isabella, and Claudio become much less important. The highly expressive poetry of the first half is replaced by a more mundane mixture of poetry and prose, and the aura of impending tragedy becomes ironic comedy. Through his somewhat absurd plotting, the Duke replaces punishment and death with pardons and marriages. While this development often strikes modern readers as silly, it was for Shakespeare's original audiences a recognisable variant on traditional comedy as well as on medieval MORALITY plays, which generally centred on an undeniable sinner who is forgiven. In Shakespeare's world the fact that Angelo's crime is exceptionally dreadful suggests strongly that he will be forgiven, particularly in light of the play's title.

However, the power of Shakespeare's realistic portrayals of Angelo and Isabella in the first half of the play made a significant change in his source material necessary. In all the variants of the tale the playwright saw, the Angelo figure had his way with the Isabella figure, and then, in the final resolution, was forced to marry her in order that her honour could be restored. However, given the psychological strength with which the two characters have earlier been invested, they simply cannot be made to accept each other without losing their power to move an audience, and much of the play's power also. Mariana therefore replaces Isabella through the use of the bed trick, an ancient comedic device that Shakespeare also used in *All's Well*. Here, the Duke's unquestioned authority makes it seem a less squalid device, though like a *deus ex machina,* this *coup de théâtre* disposes of the impending tragedy with an ease and convenience that is troubling to modern sensibilities. However, in Shakespeare's day this conclusion was perfectly acceptable, the triumph of good had been made explicit in a manner that was satisfying to the sentimental feelings of his audiences.

Mariana also triggers the sequence of pardons in 5.1 by pleading for Angelo's life. More important, she persuades Isabella to join her. Mariana's plea is essentially selfish—she wishes to preserve the husband she has so long sought. Isabella's intercession is, however, more objective; indeed, it goes against her natural enmity towards the man who is her intended rapist and the apparent killer of her brother. The Duke points this out when he says, 'Her brother's ghost . . . would . . . take her hence in horror' (5.1.433–434). But Isabella not only kneels in support of Mariana's plea—which is as much as Mariana asked—but goes on to make a reasoned case for mercy towards her tormentor. Her act flies in the face of common sense, just as does Christ's command in the Sermon on the Mount to love one's enemies. Whether under the influence of Mariana's example of love, or because she remembers her claim to Angelo that she would be merciful if she had his power, or, perhaps, to make up for her willingness to sacrifice Claudio for a principle, Isabella has arrived at the giving of a full measure in the spirit of the text that inspired the play's title.

Thus the play yields a satisfactory outcome on its own terms, those of Christian moral doctrine presented in the form of traditional comedy. The drama is one of ideas, rather than real life. However, Shakespeare's strengths as a dramatist actually diminish this effort, for the psychological and social realism of the play combine to smother the spiritual aura that might otherwise make the play's message more dramatically effective. In the later ROMANCES, Shakespeare more successfully combines the symbolic and the real. Like *All's Well That Ends Well*—which it resembles in many ways—*Measure for Measure* charts the playwright's evolution from a master of personal and societal portraiture towards a more ethereal, intellectual drama. While it is not a successful example of the genre, it marks a significant experiment in its development.

## SOURCES OF THE PLAY

*Measure for Measure* derives from a striking range of sources. The main plot stems originally from a real incident which took place in Italy in 1547: the extortion of sex from the wife of a condemned murderer by a judge who promised mercy and then executed the criminal anyway. The aggrieved widow went to the authorities, and the judge was forced to marry his victim and was then executed. These events were recounted in many works in several languages, and Shakespeare drew on at least one of them, Thomas LUPTON's account in *Too Good To Be True* (1581), which is echoed in the encounters of Angelo and Isabella in Act 2.

More important as a source, however, was a fictional work stimulated by the event, a novella by the Italian author CINTHIO, published in his collection *Hecatommithi* (1565). Here, the criminal's offence is less serious—the seduction of a virgin—and the pleader for mercy is his sister, rather than his wife. At the close she pleads for the life of her violator, now her husband, and a virtuous ruler grants it; a happy ending replaces revenge. Cinthio reworked his novella as a drama, *Epitia* (1583), which also influenced Shakespeare. In *Epitia* the young criminal is spared because a merciful official substitutes a dead man's head for his, as in *Measure for Measure,* and a secondary heroine is featured, a sister of the judge who joins his victim/wife in pleading for his life; she is the original of Mariana.

Miscellaneous details suggest that Shakespeare knew Cinthio's work directly, rather than through the English version of the tale by George WHETSTONE. He could have read Cinthio in the original Italian, in a French translation, or in some now-lost English translation; he certainly did one of these, for another, untranslated Cinthio tale inspired *Othello.* However, Shakespeare was definitely influenced by Whetstone's play on the same subject, *Promos and Cassandra* (1578), which has a comic sub-plot involving harlots and panders who contrast with the virtuous major characters. Also, Whetstone first presents the object of the young criminal's seduction, the model for *Measure for Measure*'s Juliet. Whetstone also elevates the seduction to a respectable act of love that merely precedes formal marriage, as in Shakespeare.

Tales of disguised princes who investigate the workings of their governments were common in 16th-century England, and derived originally from legends concerning the Roman emperor Alexander Severus (reigned 222–235 A.D.). Shakespeare was doubtless influenced by numerous accounts, including one in Whetstone's *A Mirror for Magistrates* (1584). A popular romance dealing with similar material, *The Adventures*

of *Brusanus Prince of Hungary* (1592), by Barnabe RICH (1), was probably the source for Lucio's interactions with the disguised Duke.

The political attitudes of the play, such as those expressed by the Duke in 1.1, may reflect a very popular book on kingship, *Basilicon Doron* (1603), by King James, and the Duke may have been modelled on James himself. At any rate, Shakespeare's remarks on crowd behaviour, in 1.1.67–70 and 2.4.24–30, clearly echo a tract of 1604, *The Time Triumphant,* probably by Shakespeare's fellow actor, Robert ARMIN, describing King James' arrival in London. One further source may have contributed to the political sensibility of the play, the most famous contemporary guide for statesmen, *De Optimo Senatore* (1568), by Laurentius GOSLICIUS (anonymously translated as *The Counsellor* [1598]), which develops criteria to distinguish good and bad public officials that seem reflected in the Duke's opinions on the subject.

## TEXT OF THE PLAY

*Measure for Measure* was written during the spring or summer of 1604. Angelo's remarks on the nuisance of adoring crowds echo a source published in the spring of that year, and Lucio's references to peace talks in 1.2.1–3 are thought to refer to English negotiations with Spain, resulting in a treaty signed in August. Also, Mistress Overdone mentions 'the war, . . . the sweat, . . . the gallows' (1.2.75–76), probably referring to England's continuing war with Spain, an outbreak of plague in London, and the execution of a number of the alleged co-conspirators of Sir Walter RALEIGH, all noteworthy events of early 1604.

The play was first published in the FIRST FOLIO (1623). This text was printed from a copy of the play that had been transcribed by Ralph CRANE, as distinctive punctuation and spelling reveal. Scholars dispute whether Crane's transcription was of Shakespeare's FOUL PAPERS or a later revision of the play—by Shakespeare or someone else—which may have been responsible for irregularities in several scenes, such as the divided soliloquy whose halves appear in 3.2.179–182 and 4.1.60–65. As the only early text, the Folio version has served as the basis for all subsequent editions.

## THEATRICAL HISTORY OF THE PLAY

*Measure for Measure* was performed at court on December 26, 1604, though some topical references in it suggest that it had been performed in public somewhat earlier, perhaps during the previous summer. It was apparently not very popular; the next recorded production was over a century later. It was exploited in two notorious adaptations, one, THE LAW AGAINST LOVERS (1662) by William DAVENENT, which incorporated some material from *Much Ado About Nothing,* and a second, based on the first, Charles GILDON's *Measure for Measure, or Beauty the Best Advocate* (1699), which featured a full-scale operatic MASQUE (taken from Henry PURCELL) that comprised the sub-plot. Thomas BETTERTON and Anne BRACEGIRDLE starred in the latter work.

*Measure for Measure* was popular in the 18th century. In 1720 John RICH (2) staged a version that was close to Shakespeare's play, and after more than a decade's popularity it was replaced by a version by Colley CIBBER (1). Like the adaptations, both of these versions and most of their 18th-century successors eliminated all or most of the sub-plot, which was viewed as grossly undignified. Isabella was a particularly esteemed role, and many of the leading 18th-century actresses played it, including Mary Ann YATES (1), Ann BARRY (1), and Sarah SIDDONS.

In the early 19th century John Philip KEMBLE (3) restored the sub-plot in a staging that was much more purely Shakespearean, but the play was not greatly liked nor often produced during the century. Adelaide NEILSON (1) was a noted Isabella in the 1870s. The play has been more popular in the 20th century: among the memorable productions have been those of Oscar ASCHE (1906), Peter BROOK (2) (1950, starring John GIELGUD as Angelo), and John BARTON (1) (1970). *Measure for Measure* has twice been done on FILM, once each in Italian (1942) and German (1963), and has once been broadcast on TELEVISION, in a 1979 BBC production starring Kate Nelligan. The great German composer Richard Wagner's second opera (and his first produced), *Das Liebesverbot* (1836), was based on the play.

**Melun (Melune), Giles de, Lord (d. 1216)** Historical figure and minor character in *King John.* The fatally wounded Melun, a French lord, relieves his conscience before dying by warning the rebellious English nobles who have aided the French invasion that LEWIS (1), the French leader, intends to kill them after he has defeated King JOHN (3). This information sparks the renewed loyalty of the rebels, led by the Earl of SALISBURY (4).

Shakespeare took this incident from HOLINSHED's history, but it is probably not accurate. In any case, little more is known of Melun. In the play he speaks of his English grandfather, who may have been Robert de Melun, Bishop of Hereford (d. 1164); this cannot be confirmed by known records, however.

**Menas (active, c. 40–c. 35 B.C.)** Historical figure and character in *Antony and Cleopatra,* a pirate who fights for POMPEY (2). Menas and MENECRATES are called famed buccaneers who make 'hot inroads' (1.4.50) on the coast of Italy in support of Pompey's rebellion. In 2.1 Menas confers with Pompey and predicts accurately the future disputes of ANTONY and Octavius CAESAR (2). In 2.6 he is among his leader's advisers at the signing of the Treaty of MISENUM, though he privately disapproves of it and says, 'Pompey doth this day laugh away his fortune' (2.6.103). In 2.7, during the banquet aboard Pompey's ship, Menas proves himself a true pirate and advises Pompey to cut the throats of the Roman leadership—Caesar, Antony, and LEPIDUS—and seize the state. When Pompey refuses, Menas decides to abandon him as doomed, for 'Who seeks and will not take, when once 'tis offer'd, / Shall never find it more' (2.7.82–83). This shrewdly cynical sailor reveals the mistrust and disloyalty that informs the politics of the play.

The historical Menas is well represented in the play, for he was indeed a notably cynical turncoat. He deserted Pompey at Misenum in 39 B.C. and joined Caesar. Discontented with his rewards, he deserted again and returned to Pompey in time to participate in his defence of Sicily in 36 B.C. Again, however, he disapproved of what he saw as Pompey's lethargy and indecision—an opinion shared by military historians—and he changed sides for a third time and rejoined Caesar. Little more is known of him.

**Menecrates (active c. 40 B.C.)** Historical figure and character in *Antony and Cleopatra,* a pirate who fights for POMPEY (2). Mentioned with MENAS as one of two 'famous pirates' (1.4.48) who support Pompey's rebellion against Rome with 'hot inroads' (1.4.50) on the coast of Italy, Menecrates turns out to be a mild buccaneer when he appears, in 2.1. He philosophically recommends that Pompey have patience with the slow pace of his success. He then disappears from the play. He is mentioned with the more important Menas as a 'notable pirate' in Shakespeare's source, PLUTARCH's *Lives.*

In the FIRST FOLIO text of the play, all the speeches in 2.1 except Pompey's are designated 'Mene' and seem to belong to Menecrates, though Menas is spelled Menes once elsewhere in the Folio. However, since one of these five speeches—2.1.38–41—clearly belongs to Menas, editors have restored that speech to him and often give him more. In fact, beginning with the 1765 edition of Samuel JOHNSON (7), some editors give all these lines to Menas, leaving Menecrates mute.

**Menelaus** Legendary figure and minor character in *Troilus and Cressida,* king of Sparta and a leader of the Greeks in the TROJAN WAR. Before the play opens, the theft of Menelaus' wife, HELEN (1), by Prince PARIS (3) of Troy has sparked the war. However, although he is the ostensible beneficiary of the war and the younger brother of the Greek commander AGAMEMNON, he is an inconsequential figure. He speaks more than one line in only one scene, 4.5, where in brief exchanges he is wittily mortified by both PATROCLUS and CRESSIDA. His insignificance makes the cause of the war seem all the more trivial, an important motif of the play. This theme is further supported by the frequent derisive references to Menelaus' status as a cuckold.

In the *Iliad* of HOMER, Menelaus is intermittently a major figure—defeating Paris in a duel but prevented from killing him by the goddess Aphrodite, for example—but he consciously subordinates himself to Agamemnon. In the *Odyssey* and later works he resumes a comfortable domestic life with Helen after the war.

**Menenius Agrippa**   Legendary figure and character in *Coriolanus,* friend and adviser of the title character. Menenius is an elderly aristocrat who is distinguished by his canny political sense in a time of popular discontent in ROME. In 1.1 he defuses a riot with his clever speech, and he establishes a rapport with the people's tribunes, BRUTUS (3) and SICINIUS. Nonetheless, he cannot prevent CORIOLANUS from destroying himself politically by refusing to compromise his stern aristocratic ideals. In this respect, Menenius' actions are as futile as those of all the aristocrats. Their failure to control Coriolanus is fatal to the hero himself and almost to all of Rome.

Though Menenius' capacity for compromise makes him stand out, and a CITIZEN (5) calls him 'one that hath always loved the people' (1.1.50–51), he nonetheless shares the aristocracy's disdain for the common people. He thereby contributes to the sense of a disturbed society that is one of the play's important themes. He cleverly deflects the mob with his 'belly speech' (1.1.95–153), an elaborate comparison of the body politic to the human anatomy that justifies the hierarchy of Roman society. This was an ancient political fable when it appeared in Shakespeare's source, PLUTARCH's *Lives,* and it was still current in the playwright's time. However, Menenius goes on to dismiss the intelligent remarks of the First Citizen. He calls him the 'great toe' of society (1.1.154), and he insults the tribunes as 'the herdsmen of the beastly plebeians' (2.1.94–95). Like the other aristocrats, Menenius is too proud to contribute to the welfare of the entire city, and instead he contributes to the play's disasters.

After 1.1 Menenius is merely a mildly amusing figure, in his own words a 'humorous patrician, and one that loves a cup of hot wine' (2.1.46–47) ('humorous' here meaning 'temperamental'). He idolises the much younger Coriolanus and greets him with 'A hundred thousand welcomes. I could weep, / And I could laugh, I am light and heavy. Welcome!' (2.1.182–183). He rejoices girlishly over a letter from his hero, and fumes angrily when the tribunes belittle him. However, after Coriolanus has joined the VOLSCIANS and is besieging Rome, he goes to plead with him to spare the city. His rejection yields a moment of genuine pathos and stoic dignity as the elderly gentleman, heartbroken, turns away and says 'He that hath a will to die by himself, fears it not from another' (5.2.102–103).

Menenius Agrippa speaks his 'belly speech' in Plutarch but is otherwise unimportant. Shakespeare made him a paternal friend of his protagonist to lend pathos to the story. Despite Menenius' appearance in Plutarch and other ancient histories, modern scholars recognise him to be entirely legendary.

**Menteth (Menteith), Walter Dalyell, Thane of (active 1056)**   Historical figure and minor character in *Macbeth,* a Scottish nobleman. In 5.2 Menteth, with CATHNESS, ANGUS, and LENOX, joins the army led by MALCOLM and MACDUFF against MACBETH. They are presumably among the 'many worthy fellows' (4.3. 183) reported earlier to have risen in arms against Macbeth's tyranny. In 5.4 they prepare to march on DUNSINANE. Though his character is not developed, Menteth's presence helps strengthen the political aspect of the play. The rebellion of the nobles indicates the extent of political and social disruption in SCOTLAND due to Macbeth's evil.

The historical Walter Dalyell ruled Menteith, a territory in central Scotland. Little more is known of him; Shakespeare took his name from a list of Malcolm's allies in his source, HOLINSHED's history.

**Mercadé**   See MARCADE.

**Mercer**   GHOST CHARACTER in *Timon of Athens.* The Mercer is listed in the opening stage direction of 1.1, but he does not appear. Shakespeare apparently listed a number of characters he thought he would make use of in the course of writing the scene, and then when he did not in fact employ a Mercer, he did not bother to delete the reference. Many such minor inconsistencies are found in the plays; *Timon,* as an unfinished play, is naturally subject to them.

**Merchant (1)**   Either of two minor characters in *The Comedy of Errors.* Two Merchants appear in this play (they enter first in 2.2 and 4.1 respectively), and, while Shakespeare apparently made no distinction between them by name, they are plainly different people. The first to appear is familiar with the affairs of Ephesus, offering advice to the foreigner ANTIPHOLUS OF SYRACUSE and warning him not to reveal himself as a Syracusan, lest he be sentenced to death. Having thus reminded the audience of EGEON's desperate plight, this Merchant disappears from the play. He is generally distinguished in modern editions as 'First Merchant'.

The 'Second Merchant', however, seems to be a visitor himself, for he must inquire (5.1.4) about the reputation of ANTIPHOLUS OF EPHESUS, a well-known local figure. Attempting to collect a debt owed ANGELO (1) by one Antipholus, the Merchant mistakenly challenges Antipholus of Syracuse to a duel, precipitating that twin's flight into the PRIORY, which ultimately leads to the resolution of the play.

**Merchant (2)**   Minor character in *Timon of Athens,* a flatterer of TIMON. In 1.1 the Merchant and his friend the JEWELLER discuss Timon's free-spending nature and intend to profit from it. The Merchant speaks little and serves chiefly as a sounding board for his colleague. Both of them are representative greedy flatterers.

## The Merchant of Venice

SYNOPSIS

*Act 1, Scene 1*
SALERIO and SOLANIO attempt to cheer up their friend ANTONIO (2); they are assisted by BASSANIO, LORENZO, and GRATIANO (1). Antonio denies that he is worried about his investments in far-flung trading voyages, for he is confident of their success. The friends, except Bassanio, depart. Antonio inquires about the love affair Bassanio has promised to speak of. Bassanio replies that his extravagant lifestyle, which he has supported with loans from friends, especially Antonio, may pay off if he can successfully woo and marry PORTIA (1), a rich heiress. However, he wishes to borrow more money in order to present himself as an impressive enough suitor to compete with his wealthy rivals. Antonio assures his friend that he will loan him as much as he needs. Because Antonio's funds are all invested in ships at the moment, he promises to borrow the money to support Bassanio's courtship.

*Act 1, Scene 2*
Portia discusses her late father's will with her maid, NERISSA. Under its terms, she must marry the man who selects from among three chests or caskets—one each of gold, silver, and lead—the one that contains the consent placed in it by her father. Portia worries about the sort of husband she may win in this lottery. She and Nerissa discuss and humorously dismiss a number of potential suitors, and Nerissa reveals, to the relief of her mistress, that all of them have decided not to choose among the caskets because of a penalty that Portia's father has decreed for those who pick either of the wrong ones. Nerissa reminds Portia of Bassanio, who had visited some time before, and they agree that he would make an acceptable suitor. Word comes that a new suitor, the Prince of MOROCCO, has arrived.

*Act 1, Scene 3*
Bassanio and Antonio ask the Jewish moneylender SHYLOCK for a loan. Antonio remarks that he is opposed to usury, the lending of money at interest, and Shylock defends the practise. Further, Shylock observes that Antonio has often spat on him and insulted him for being a Jew, and he asks why he should be

expected to assist his tormentor. Antonio frankly acknowledges that Shylock must regard the loan as one made to an enemy. Shylock, however, insists that he wishes to be friendly and offers to lend him the money interest-free for three months, requiring only a humorous collateral; if Antonio cannot repay the loan when it comes due, he will permit Shylock to cut from his body one pound of flesh. Although Bassanio is uneasy about this arrangement, Antonio signs a legal contract for the loan, confident that his business ventures will soon bring him nine times the amount required.

*Act 2, Scene 1*
Morocco declares his love for Portia and agrees to be bound by her father's will: if he selects the right casket, he will marry her, but he must solemnly swear that, if he chooses one of the others, he will never marry anyone.

*Act 2, Scene 2*
Shylock's clownish servant, LAUNCELOT Gobbo, soliloquises humorously on his desire to run away from his master. His blind father, Old GOBBO (2), appears. Launcelot teases his father, pretending to be a stranger, but finally speaks seriously of his plan to desert Shylock and work for Bassanio, a more liberal and generous master. Bassanio happens by, and Gobbo, with much comical prompting from his son, speaks to him about employing Launcelot. Bassanio, finding the youth amusing, agrees, and Launcelot departs to give notice to Shylock. Gratiano enters and asks to accompany Bassanio when he travels to Portia's estate. Bassanio agrees but insists that Gratiano curb his usual wild humour.

*Act 2, Scene 3*
Shylock's daughter, JESSICA, bids Launcelot farewell and gives him a letter to deliver to Lorenzo. Alone, she regrets that she is Shylock's daughter but takes heart in the prospect of marrying Lorenzo and converting to Christianity.

*Act 2, Scene 4*
Lorenzo, with Gratiano, Salerio, and Solanio, are preparing for a masque, when Launcelot arrives with the letter from Jessica. Lorenzo gives him a message for Jessica: he, Lorenzo, shall not fail her. Salerio and Solanio leave, and Lorenzo tells Gratiano that he and Jessica plan to elope that evening.

*Act 2, Scene 5*
Launcelot delivers an invitation to dinner from Bassanio to Shylock and hints to Jessica that Lorenzo is about to arrive.

*Act 2, Scene 6*
Lorenzo, accompanied by Gratiano and Salerio, takes Jessica from Shylock's house. Antonio enters and

gives Gratiano the message that Bassanio is preparing to leave for BELMONT, Portia's estate.

### Act 2, Scene 7
With Portia, Morocco reads the inscriptions on the caskets. The gold one promises 'what many men desire'; the silver offers as much as the chooser deserves; the lead warns that the chooser 'must give and hazard all he hath'. Morocco rejects the lead as a plainly foolish choice and the silver as inadequate. He selects the gold casket but finds inside it a rhyme informing him that he has lost. He departs, to Portia's relief.

### Act 2, Scene 8
Salerio and Solanio gossip about Shylock's hysterical discovery that Jessica has fled and taken much of his money. They reflect that Shylock's anger will affect Antonio if he fails to repay his debt, and they worry that a rich Venetian ship, reported lost, may be one of his.

### Act 2, Scene 9
The Prince of ARRAGON ventures to choose one of the caskets and win Portia's hand. He rejects the gold's offer of 'what many men desire' as the choice of the foolish multitudes who value outward appearance. Feeling that he is quite worthy, he elects the silver casket's promise of as much as he deserves. However, a rhyme inside the casket announces his failure, and he leaves. A MESSENGER (10) brings word that a young Venetian intends to enter the lottery of the caskets. Portia and Nerissa hope that he will prove to be Bassanio.

### Act 3, Scene 1
Solanio and Salerio discuss the rumoured loss of Antonio's ship. Shylock appears and curses Jessica; he also rails against Antonio, vowing that he will collect his pound of flesh as revenge for Antonio's anti-Semitism. Shylock observes that Jews are like Christians in bodily respects, and he will prove that their desire for revenge is also the same. A message from Antonio causes the gentlemen to depart, and Shylock's friend TUBAL arrives. Tubal reports that he has been unable to find Jessica, but he has heard of her extravagance with her father's money. Shylock is frantic about his lost wealth, but Tubal also tells his friend that Antonio has suffered further losses and is said to be bankrupt. Shylock becomes exultant.

### Act 3, Scene 2
Portia asks Bassanio to postpone choosing among the caskets, for he must leave if he fails and she has fallen in love with him. Bassanio, however, cannot tolerate the suspense, and he proceeds to his selection. He rejects the gold and silver as representing false glamour and expensive show, and he opens the lead casket. Inside he finds Portia's picture and a text confirming that he has won her hand. She gives him a ring, which

he swears to wear until he dies. Gratiano and Nerissa reveal that they have also fallen in love, and a double wedding is proposed. Salerio arrives from Venice with Lorenzo and Jessica. He tells Bassanio that Antonio has lost all his vessels and that Shylock has said that he will demand the pound of flesh. Portia offers to pay Shylock many times over.

### Act 3, Scene 3
Antonio, in the custody of a GAOLER (1), approaches Shylock, but the Jew will not speak to him; he angrily repeats his demand for the pound of flesh and departs. Antonio prepares to die; he hopes only to see Bassanio again.

### Act 3, Scene 4
Portia announces her intention to enter a religious retreat while Bassanio tries to help Antonio in Venice. She instructs her servant BALTHASAR (3) to deliver a letter to her cousin in PADUA. He is then to meet her with the documents and clothing the cousin will give him. She tells Nerissa of her plan: they shall go to Venice disguised as men.

### Act 3, Scene 5
Launcelot, in his capacity as a professional FOOL (1), impudently jests with Jessica and Lorenzo, who then banter affectionately.

### Act 4, Scene 1
The DUKE (4) of Venice convenes a court to try Shylock's claim. Shylock is asked to be merciful, but he refuses. The Duke announces that he has sent to a Paduan scholar for a legal opinion. Portia and Nerissa arrive, disguised as a lawyer and his clerk sent by the scholar. Portia interviews Shylock and Antonio. After Shylock repeatedly demands strict justice, she awards him his pound of flesh but prohibits him from drawing any blood—for blood is not mentioned in the contract—on pain of death. Realising that he is beaten, Shylock says he will accept the money, but Portia rules that he shall have only the exact justice he has demanded: he may attempt to extract his bloodless flesh, or he may withdraw his suit, but he cannot claim the money. Shylock concedes defeat and is about to leave when Portia further rules that, as a non-Venetian who has attempted to take the life of a citizen, he is subject to the death penalty—unless the Duke pardons him—and to the confiscation of all his possessions. The Duke permits him to live, and Antonio suggests that he be allowed to keep half of his earthly goods in exchange for converting to Christianity and deeding the other half to Lorenzo and Jessica. Shylock agrees to these terms. The Paduan lawyer (Portia) refuses a fee but asks Bassanio for his ring as a token of thanks. He refuses, saying that it was a sacred gift from his wife, but he repents after she leaves, accusing himself of ingratitude. He sends Gratiano to give the ring to the lawyer.

## Act 4, Scene 2

Gratiano gives the ring to Portia, who asks him to direct her clerk (Nerissa) to Shylock's house to deliver the deed that the money-lender must sign. Nerissa tells Portia that she will contrive to get Gratiano to give her his ring as well.

## Act 5, Scene 1

Lorenzo and Jessica enjoy the moonlight and music at Belmont, joyfully comparing themselves to various famous lovers. Word arrives that Portia and Nerissa are returning from the monastery, and Launcelot, comically imitating a hunting horn, heralds the approach of Bassanio. The lovers resume their contemplation, and Lorenzo reflects on the harmony of the spheres. Portia and Nerissa enter, just ahead of Bassanio, Gratiano, and Antonio. The women 'discover' that their husbands no longer have their rings, and they chastise them severely, evoking pained excuses. Finally, Portia reveals the truth, and the party moves indoors to celebrate their reunion.

## COMMENTARY

*The Merchant of Venice* is a richly complicated work in which several themes are presented in the framework of a traditional COMEDY, which calls for the triumph of young lovers over their unromantic elders. Before this end is achieved, three distinct plots are resolved: the winning of Portia by the lottery of the caskets, the settlement of Shylock's claim, and the final complication of the betrothal rings. All of these developments further the traditional romantic purpose of the play.

But before looking at Shakespeare's intentions and devices, let us consider the evidently anti-Semitic nature of the play, which is particularly repellent in light of the Holocaust (1933–1945), in which 6 million European Jews were executed in Nazi concentration camps. Great historical events unavoidably affect the thoughts and sensibilities of later generations, and this terrifying 20th-century manifestation of anti-Semitism must colour our response to *The Merchant of Venice*. Its villain is a stereotypical Jew, and his Jewishness is persistently derided by the Christians in the play. Even though Shylock has his moments of sympathetic humanity, they are rather qualified, and he is finally found deserving of treatment that is unquestionably shabby by modern Western ethical and legal standards. He is deprived of his life's earnings and coerced into renouncing his religion by avowed anti-Semites who preach justice and mercy all the while. Many have asked how Shakespeare could have depicted such behaviour in characters clearly intended to be taken as good people—Portia, Antonio, and their friends—when in the rest of his work his characterisations are so strikingly humane. One must conclude that, to at least some extent, Shakespeare shared in the anti-Semitic biases of his age.

Of course, the anti-Semitism of Shakespeare's England was rather theoretical: practising Jews had been rare there since their expulsion from the country in 1290, and active anti-Jewish bigotry was accordingly unusual. But, while 16th-century Londoners may have found Jews more exotic than malevolent, they also had a generally negative image of Judaism that was the legacy of centuries of bias. Christian tradition, from the New Testament on, stimulated anti-Semitism, and if the 16th-century English version was milder than others, it was nonetheless real. Shakespeare, very much a man of his time and place, probably harboured it to some degree; he was at least willing to accommodate his public, which had responded with great delight to *The Jew of Malta*, by Christopher MARLOWE (1), whose spectacularly villainous title character probably influenced the creation of Shylock. Also, the trial and execution of Roderigo LOPEZ in 1594, not long before Shakespeare wrote this play, generated a spate of more overt expressions of bigotry. (Elizabethan prejudices are similarly addressed in the play's negative presentations of a black man, Morocco, and a Spaniard, Arragon.) In any case, English anti-Semitism was only one expression of a widespread European phenomenon, and there is unquestionably a historical connection across the centuries between the attitudes of Shakespeare's characters and the atrocities of the Holocaust.

Anti-Semitism contributed to the development of Shylock's character simply by providing the only well-known image of a Jew. Sixteenth-century Englishmen tended to attribute to Jews only two important characteristics, both negative: first, that Jews detested Christians and gave much energy to devising evils for gentiles to undergo, and second, that Jews practised usury. The latter assumption was grounded in an old, though disappearing, reluctance on the part of Christians to lend money, due to Biblical injunctions against the practise within one's own religious community. Despite the growth of modern banking in the 16th century, it remained true in much of Europe—including Italy, the source of Shakespeare's story—that lending money at interest was confined by law to non-Christians. In England, however, Christians could and did practise usury, at a legally sanctioned rate of 10 percent. Usury's increasing importance in everyday life was a prominent and widely disliked aspect of economic development in Shakespeare's day, a phenomenon that doubtless led the playwright to adapt a tale that condemned it. That it also condemned a Jew was as much a result of actual Continental practices at the time as of Shakespeare's prejudices. His source featured a Jewish usurer as a villain, and he borrowed this character. He gave the role more life than he found in the source, as he typically did, but he did not alter its anti-Semitic overtones.

Although Shakespeare was influenced by the anti-

Semitism of his day in writing *The Merchant of Venice*, the play was not itself motivated by anti-Semitism, nor was it intended to spread anti-Semitic doctrines. Instead, *The Merchant of Venice* illustrates a theme that occupied Shakespeare in most of his comedies, the triumph of love over false and inhumane attitudes towards life.

The central plot of the play deals with Bassanio's courtship of Portia. Antonio goes to Shylock for a loan only because his friend wishes to woo Portia, and the usurer's undoing comes about through Portia's desire to help the friend of her beloved. The seemingly strange ending of the play is the culmination of Portia and Bassanio's betrothal.

The courtship is based on an ancient folk motif, that of a choice among caskets, the suitor's correct choice being rewarded with marriage to the maiden in question. Bassanio expresses his distrust of rich appearances in 3.2.73–107, as he selects the casket of lead. Such sentiments, attached to similar stories, were common in Elizabethan literature and reflected the ideal of true love. Only a true lover would value the maid for herself and choose the plainest casket, which requires him to 'give and hazard all he hath' (2.7.9). (This ideal is not sullied by Bassanio's frank assessment of Portia's wealth in 1.2.161–176, for such considerations were normal when contemplating marriage in the 16th century; Bassanio could not reasonably bring up the subject with Antonio and fail to mention Portia's wealth, particularly since he was asking to borrow money to accomplish his courtship.)

The tale of the caskets also casts light on another theme of the play, that of the misuse of wealth. The title character of any work may be supposed to represent its essential spirit, and the title character here is Antonio, who risks his wealth—and his life, as it turns out—to aid his friend Bassanio. His enemy, Shylock, is a grotesque miser who loves his ducats more than his daughter. Though his stereotypical Jewishness is essential to his personality, Shylock is more significantly related to another tradition, that of the miser whose mean-spiritedness is contrasted with, and overcome by, the power of love felt by the romantic young. However, the conflict is not simply between money and love, but rather between two different attitudes towards money. Both Antonio and Shylock engage in commerce, but only Antonio is willing to use his wealth in the service of others, resembling Bassanio in his willingness to 'hazard all' for his friends. Shylock has the same blind pride as Arragon, assuming that he deserves as much as he is capable of getting.

In Shakespeare's time, money was a particularly troubling subject. Commercial banking was a relatively new phenomenon in England, where land-based wealth had been the norm for centuries, and it inspired much distrust and resentment. Shakespeare's own position seems somewhat ambiguous: his sympa-thies with old England and his conservative social and political orientation are evident throughout his work, but he himself was a competent businessman, on good terms with the leading usurer of STRATFORD, John COMBE (1). It has been speculated that his ambivalence may have inspired him to create so three-dimensional a figure as Shylock where a conventional stage villain might have served his traditional comic aims just as well. However, Shylock's humanity gives him great weight; he forcefully represents money's great power to foster hatred and strife, and the open generosity of Antonio and Portia are more convincingly triumphant over Shylock's lust for vengeance when we can clearly see the psychology of his evil need.

As greed is set against love in *The Merchant of Venice*, so is justice placed in opposition to mercy, especially in the trial scene (4.1). The Duke, asking Shylock to excuse Antonio's penalty, asks him, 'How shalt thou hope for mercy rend'ring none?' (4.1.88); he is referring to the usurer's expectations in the afterlife. So is Shylock, when he answers, 'What judgement shall I dread doing no wrong?' (4.1.89). This exchange refers implicitly to a conventional comparison of the Old Testament and the New, in which the former is seen to emphasise strict obedience as humanity's obligation to God while the latter stresses God's mercy. Shylock stands for the strict interpretation of law, for justice in its most rigorous and unbending form. Portia argues for divine clemency, observing, 'The quality of mercy is not strained' (4.1.180), at the opening of her most famous speech.

But Shylock is not wholly evil. His position is defensible, and his demand for vengeance is made humanly understandable. He has earlier traced his own evil to a plausible source in remarking to his tormentors Salerio and Solanio that 'the villainy you teach me I will execute' (3.1.65). Further, Portia, once her battle is won, is not particularly given to mercy, depriving Shylock of any repayment of his loan and then sentencing him to death as well. Shakespeare invented Portia's invocation of a capital punishment statute; it is not in his sources. Thus he emphasised the paradoxical conclusion that Shylock's downfall results from his own insistence on strict justice.

Antonio mercifully rescinds the death penalty, but Shylock is deprived of all his support in life—as Shakespeare permits him to observe in 4.1.370–373. The main thrust of the trial scene is clear: Shylock has been given enough rope to hang himself, and then harsh justice has been tempered by the mercy of the title figure. Antonio, whose affairs have both promoted Bassanio's romantic success and produced his own woes, remains the source of the play's action.

The two primary plots demonstrate and reconcile opposing principles. We see how wealth can aid romance as well as hinder it and that justice can be merciful as well as vengeful. These themes are tied together in the seemingly gratuitous anecdote of the betrothal rings. Portia's ploy is not simply a practical joke; the rings are carefully presented as tokens first of love, then of gratitude, and finally of forgiveness. Bassanio understands the dilemma he faces when he gives his ring to the lawyer 'Balthasar'; he is not disloyal to Portia, but he recognises that he owes a debt of gratitude to the young lawyer who has saved his friend. Portia knows this, and while she effectively adopts Shylock's position, insisting on the letter of the oath with which the ring was received originally, she clearly intends to forgive Bassanio after teasing him a bit. The story of the rings—a well-known tale in Shakespeare's day—was introduced by the playwright in order to recapitulate in a lightly comic manner the lessons won from the stressful trial. The other elements of 5.1—the rhapsodic musings of Lorenzo and Jessica and the meditations on music—serve a similar purpose. Although often seen as an ill-considered aberration, this scene alleviates the mood of the preceding one. It provides an anticlimax that returns us to the lovers and their world. Without it, *The Merchant of Venice* would resemble the later PROBLEM PLAYS, which tend to deal with unpleasant social phenomena in an ambiguous way. Here, even such a grossly sentimental—and wholly implausible—event as Portia's announcement that Antonio's ships have miraculously survived (5.1.274–279) can be accepted wholeheartedly. The audience is permitted to share in the triumph of love and playfulness—the spirit of comedy—over the selfish and inhumane stinginess that Shylock represents.

Modern readers, aware of the extremes to which anti-Semitism can lead, tend to give Shylock more sympathy than his place in the play's tight structure can bear. Shakespeare and his audiences were comfortable with a formal, allegorical presentation of human truth that often seems obscure to modern sensibilities, which are far more attuned to realism. Shylock's symbolic role, that of an obvious villain opposed to characters representing generosity and love, is more important to the play's themes than is his Jewishness or his personality. Eighteenth- and 19th-century theatrical tradition humanised the character, presenting to our own century a very different figure from the one whom Shakespeare originally conceived.

*The Merchant of Venice* presents great opportunity for such varying approaches; indeed, it demands them. For example, Shylock can be sympathised with, but he may also be seen as an overdeveloped figure who interferes with a romantic comedy. On the other hand, sometimes 5.1 is seen as a defective scene that draws attention away from Shylock. Portia's strategem of leading Shylock on in his claims to justice can be seen as high-handed and the trial scene regarded as a satire on law and its cruel strictures. Some critics see the focus of the play as the relationship between Antonio

and Bassanio; the theme of friendship among men was prominent in medieval literature and was more plainly employed by Shakespeare in *The Two Gentlemen of Verona*. Some go so far as to hold that Shakespeare intended Antonio's affection to be taken as homosexual. These varied interpretations demonstrate the richness of *The Merchant of Venice:* many different views of the play can be plausibly presented. Its diverse complications are not stiffly theatrical, despite their roots in dramatic conventions and old tales. Instead, they derive from the problems and ambiguities of human experience.

SOURCES OF THE PLAY

The primary source for *The Merchant of Venice* was a story in an Italian collection, *Il Pecorone (The Simpleton),* by Giovanni FIORENTINO, published in Milan (1558). This tale presents all the components of Shakespeare's play in considerable detail, except for the lottery of the caskets and the practise of usury by Shylock (his equivalent loans money at no interest). A possible intervening source has often been proposed: a lost English play, *The Jew,* mentioned in a publication of 1579, may have been reworked by Shakespeare. However, the only reference to *The Jew* is brief and ambiguous, and such complicated plots as that of *The Merchant of Venice* were virtually unknown in the 1570s. This hypothesis is thus increasingly unpopular.

The introduction of the usury theme could have been suggested by several contemporary sources, including Anthony MUNDAY's novel *Zelauto* (1580) and a well-known ballad, 'Gernutus', both of which tell of a similarly forfeited loan, in each case to a usurer. The lottery of three caskets is an ancient motif that the playwright also may have known from a number of sources. The *Confessio Amantis,* by John GOWER (3), which Shakespeare unquestionably knew, contains a variation taken from BOCCACCIO, but the most closely corresponding version is in a translation by Richard ROBINSON (3) of the *Gesta Romanorum,* a famed medieval collection of tales, published in 1577 and 1595. The elopement and conversion of Jessica may have been suggested by similar characters in either *Zelauto* or Marlowe's *The Jew of Malta* (c. 1592). The latter's immense popularity is often thought to have sparked Shakespeare's adaptation of Fiorentino's tale (or *The Jew*) in the first place, and its title character probably influenced the creation of Shylock.

TEXT OF THE PLAY

*The Merchant of Venice* was written between the summer of 1596 and the summer of 1598. The later date is certain because the play was registered for publication in July of that year, and it is mentioned as a produced play in Francis MERES' book, published in September 1598. The earlier date, though less certain, seems probable in view of Salerio's reference in 1.1.27 to the ship ANDREW (1)—that is, the *St Andrew,* a Spanish vessel captured by the English in 1596. (Although such a reference could have been added some time after the play was written, earlier dates seem unlikely in view of the play's stylistic similarities to such later works as *1* and *2 Henry IV* and *Much Ado About Nothing.*)

*The Merchant of Venice* was first published in 1600 in a QUARTO edition known as Q1. It was printed by James ROBERTS for the publisher Thomas HEYES. Its stage directions, which contain many superfluous remarks, suggest that Q1 was printed from Shakespeare's manuscript, though whether from his FOUL PAPERS or from the FAIR COPY, is uncertain. A second edition, Q2, was a reprint of Q1, produced in 1619 by William JAGGARD for Thomas PAVIER as part of the FALSE FOLIO. The publisher, who was reprinting the play without authorisation, asserted on the title page that the edition had been printed by Roberts in 1600—that is, it was in fact Q1. Until the early 20th century, scholars believed it to be the first edition of the play. But, although taken from Q1, Q2 contains several minor alterations of the original text, as well as many new errors. Q3 (1637) and the FIRST FOLIO text of 1623 were based on Q1, and Q1 has also served as the basic text for most subsequent editions. However, the Folio edition contains improved stage directions (probably derived from a text used in early productions), and these have frequently been followed by modern editors.

## THEATRICAL HISTORY OF THE PLAY

According to the title page of the first edition of the play in 1600, *The Merchant of Venice* had been performed 'divers times' by that date, but the first performance of which a record has survived was held at the court of King JAMES I in the spring of 1605. It was so well received that the King ordered a second performance several days later, but no other 17th-century performance is known. In 1701 George GRANVILLE produced an adaptation, *The Jew of Venice,* in which Shylock was played for laughs by a popular comic. This version was still quite popular in 1741, when Charles MACKLIN restored Shakespeare's play, portraying Shylock as a melodramatic villain. The play was performed in various versions throughout the rest of the 18th century, with most of the important actors of the day playing the Jew. Shylock was apparently treated as the major figure in the play, and, following Macklin's example, he was depicted as thoroughly malignant.

The first Shylock intended to arouse sympathy was that of Edmund KEAN (2), whose Jew was scornful of his enemies and raged against their pretensions to mercy. William HAZLITT, in a famous review, said of Kean's Shylock, 'He is honest in his vices; they are hypocrites in their virtues'. Other notable 19th-century Shylocks included William Charles MACREADY,

Charles KEAN (1), and Edwin BOOTH (2). Beginning in 1879 Henry IRVING was particularly successful playing the villain in a grandly tragic manner. A somewhat later production went so far as to have Shylock commit suicide on stage following his last lines.

In the 20th century the emphasis on Shylock has been modified, and various interpretations have been offered. In a famous 1921 production the German producer Max REINHARDT presented the villain as a buffoon and the play as a farce with a notorious blue and white Cubist-style set, but most attempts have been soberer. In general it has been found that, with Shylock somewhat de-emphasised, productions have been able to assert the essential unity of the play. *The Merchant of Venice* has remained among the most popular of Shakespeare's plays, and many leading players have performed in it, including John GIELGUD and Sybil THORNDIKE. The play had been produced as a silent FILM six times by 1923 but has only once been a movie since, in an Italian version of 1952. It has, however, been presented on TELEVISION five times, including a production by Jonathan MILLER (2) (1970), starring Laurence OLIVIER and Joan PLOWRIGHT.

**Mercutio**   Character in Romeo and Juliet, ROMEO's friend who is killed by TYBALT. Mercutio, a buoyantly ribald and belligerent young gallant, serves as a foil for the maturing Romeo, who is discovering that love offers a more profound world than that of gentlemanly pleasures and enmities. Named for Mercury, the impudent god of thievery, Mercutio embodies an instability inherent in the noble society of Verona. His brilliant comedic monologue on Queen MAB (1.4.53–95) builds to a chaotic crescendo that suggests the violence that is lurking just beneath the surface of Veronese life. He is one of Shakespeare's bawdiest characters; in a mock incantation in 2.1, in which he lists the anatomical parts of Romeo's supposed beloved, ROSALINE (2), he deflates the rhetoric of romance. His unabashedly carnal approach to love contrasts with the pure devotion that Romeo learns, and his hostility is compared with Romeo's intention to make peace with Tybalt after his marriage to JULIET (1).

Mercutio ultimately belongs to the conventional world that opposes the young lovers. He blindly fulfils his role in that world by pointlessly insisting on fighting TYBALT, thereby launching the tragic complications of the play. While we can admire his wit, his loyalty to Romeo, and his courage in death, we also see that Mercutio has little business declaring 'a plague o' both your houses' (3.1.92, 108) when he has himself contributed so dramatically to the final catastrophe.

**Meres, Francis (1565–1647)**   English writer, author of a contemporary assessment of Shakespeare's early career. Meres is considered a pioneer literary critic, for in his *Palladis Tamia: Wit's Treasury,* an anthology of philosophical and literary maxims, he compares the English writers of his day with classical models. He declares that OVID's soul lives in Shakespeare, citing 'his *Venus and Adonis,* his *Lucrece,* his sugred Sonnets among his private friends'. Thus we know that by 1598, at least some of the SONNETS had been written and circulated in manuscript among Shakespeare's friends. Meres thought Sir Philip SIDNEY was the greatest English poet, but he proclaimed Shakespeare the equal of PLAUTUS in COMEDY and SENECA in TRAGEDY, and 'among the English . . . the most excellent in both kinds for the stage'. Here, he cited six comedies and six tragedies: 'his *Gentlemen of Verona,* his *Errors,* his *Loue labours lost,* his *Loue labours wonne,* his *Midsummers night dreame,* & his *Merchant of Venice* . . . his *Richard the 2, Richard the 3, Henry the 4, King John, Titus Andronicus* and his *Romeo* and *Juliet'*. This list names all of Shakespeare's plays that other evidence indicates had been written by this time, except the *Henry VI* plays and *The Taming of the Shrew* (though the latter may be the mysterious *LOVE'S LABOUR'S WON*). Meres' remarks have helped scholars date the early works and offer evidence of the great respect commanded by Shakespeare among his contemporaries, even early in his career. Meres had only a brief career in LONDON as a writer—he also wrote devotional works—before he became a rural minister and schoolmaster.

**Mermaid Tavern** Tavern in LONDON, meeting place of a literary club thought to have included Shakespeare. The Friday Street Club, named for the Mermaid's address, was a famous convivial gathering of London writers. Among its members were Francis BEAUMONT (2), John FLETCHER (2), and Ben JONSON. Shakespeare is traditionally counted a member as well, but this is not confirmed in any surviving contemporary accounts, and the club's great days came after the playwright had probably retired to STRATFORD. However, the idea is supported by Shakespeare's close connections with Jonson and Fletcher and his acquaintance at least with the innkeeper at the Mermaid, William JOHNSON (8).

**Merry Devil of Edmonton, The** Anonymous play formerly attributed to Shakespeare, part of the Shakespeare APOCRYPHA. *The Merry Devil of Edmonton* is a comedy about lovers who elope to escape the bride's parents' plans for a mercenary marriage. It was published in six 17th-century editions, beginning with that of Arthur JOHNSON (1) (1608). It was also popular on the stage, as is shown by many contemporary references to performances. It was first ascribed to Shakespeare by Francis KIRKMAN in 1661, but almost no later scholars have accepted this suggestion. Though *The Merry Devil* is one of the few apocryphal plays that commentators agree is an excellent drama, modern scholars are confident that it is not by Shakespeare. It is not like his work stylistically, and it was never associated with the playwright when it was new, despite the well-established commercial value of his name. Some scholars speculate that it was written by Michael DRAYTON or Thomas HEYWOOD (2), but its authorship remains uncertain.

### The Merry Wives of Windsor

#### SYNOPSIS

*Act 1, Scene 1*

SHALLOW, in Windsor to sue FALSTAFF, confers with his young relative SLENDER and the local parson, the Welshman EVANS (3). Shallow boasts that his noble ancestry is equal to Falstaff's, and Evans offers to arbitrate the quarrel. Slender mentions his inclination to marry, and Evans suggests ANNE (3) Page, an attractive young woman who has just inherited some money. Shallow suggests that they call on her father, George PAGE (12), whom, Evans says, Falstaff is also visiting. They knock on Page's door and speak with him briefly; Falstaff emerges with BARDOLPH (1), NYM, and PISTOL. Shallow accuses Falstaff of assaulting his men, poaching deer, and breaking into his hunting lodge. Falstaff grandly admits to these deeds and asserts that if Shallow takes the case to the king's council, he will be laughed at. Slender adds that Falstaff's companions have robbed him. They deny it. Evans insists that he, Page, and the HOST (2) of the local tavern shall form a committee to settle these disputes. MISTRESS (3) Page, Anne, and MISTRESS (1) Ford appear with refreshments, and everyone goes indoors except the nervous Slender. Shallow and Evans emerge to say that his marriage to Anne has been proposed. Anne enters to summon the men to dinner, and Shallow and Evans leave her with Slender. Slender is too embarrassed to go in with her, and he makes awkward conversation until Page comes out and insists.

*Act 1, Scene 2*

Evans sends Slender's servant, SIMPLE, to the house of Dr CAIUS (2) with a letter for his housekeeper, Mistress QUICKLY, asking her to encourage Anne Page to marry Slender.

*Act 1, Scene 3*

Falstaff persuades the tavern's Host to hire Bardolph as a tapster. He tells Pistol and Nym of his plan to get money: he will seduce both Mistress Ford and Mistress Page. He believes that each woman has found him attractive, and he knows that each controls her family's funds. He has written letters to them, and he asks his followers to deliver them. However, they spurn such a task as unworthy of soldiers, and he dismisses them, giving the letters to his page, ROBIN (1), and then leaving. Pistol and Nym decide to avenge their dismissal by telling FORD (1) and Page of Falstaff's intentions.

*Act 1, Scene 4*
Mistress Quickly tells Simple that she will assist Slender's courtship. At Dr Caius' approach, Quickly puts Simple in the closet. Caius finds him, and when he tells of his errand, the doctor rages against Evans for sending him, for he—Caius—intends to marry Anne Page himself. Caius writes a letter challenging Evans to a duel and sends Simple back with it. Caius leaves, and FENTON (1) appears. Quickly assures him that his courtship of Anne is going well. Pleased, he gives her money and asks for her continuing assistance.

*Act 2, Scene 1*
Mistress Page reads Falstaff's love letter. She feels insulted, as does Mistress Ford, who appears with a similar letter. The two women plot revenge: they will tempt Falstaff to spend his money courting them—to no avail—until he is bankrupt. Mistress Ford is particularly irritated with Falstaff because of her husband's quick jealousy. The two women withdraw to discuss their plot, and their husbands appear, accompanied by Pistol and Nym. Pistol and Nym tell the husbands that Falstaff is pursuing their wives, and they leave. The wives reappear as Mistress Quickly arrives, and they decide to employ her as their messenger to Falstaff; the three women leave together. Page and Ford talk; Page doesn't believe the stories of Pistol and Nym, but Ford is worried. The Host and Shallow enter on their way to oversee the duel between Caius and Evans. Shallow tells Page of a plan to interfere with the duel. Ford bribes the Host to introduce him to Falstaff as 'BROOK' (1). He says to himself that he will see what he can find out about Falstaff and his wife.

*Act 2, Scene 2*
Quickly delivers messages from the wives to Falstaff. Mistress Page writes of her desire for a meeting, but Mistress Ford makes an appointment for that morning. Quickly leaves, and Ford, disguised as 'Brook', arrives. 'Brook' gives Falstaff a gift of money and confesses that he has fallen in love with Ford's wife but that her marital fidelity puts him off. He therefore asks Falstaff to seduce her so that he—'Brook'—may catch her in adultery and thus justify his own advances. Falstaff accepts the bargain; he tells 'Brook' of his appointment with Mistress Ford for that very morning, and he leaves. Ford soliloquises jealously and vows revenge.

*Act 2, Scene 3*
Dr Caius awaits the arrival of Evans to start the duel. Instead, the Host, Shallow, Slender, and Page appear. All but Slender (who can only moon over Anne Page) talk with the doctor, complimenting him on his valour, while pointing out the good fortune that has kept him from having to kill Evans. The Host tells Shallow and Page to find Evans, who has been sent elsewhere to duel, and they will meet later. He then tells Caius that he will take him to visit Anne Page.

*Act 3, Scene 1*
Evans awaits the arrival of Dr Caius to start the duel. Page, Shallow, and Slender arrive, and Evans heaps insults on Dr Caius. The Host appears with Caius. The two would-be duellists argue over where they were to meet, and the Host reveals that he has misled them; he proposes that they be friends again. Evans suggests to Caius that they unite in seeking vengeance on the Host, who has made fools of them both. Caius agrees, and they become allies.

*Act 3, Scene 2*
Ford encounters Mistress Page, accompanied by Robin, who is on loan from Falstaff. He believes that the situation confirms the infidelity of both women. He proposes to himself to unmask Falstaff, disillusion Page, and punish his wife all at once. The group returning from the averted duel appears, and Ford invites them to his house, although Shallow and Slender go to call on Anne Page. Page remarks that he favours Slender as a son-in-law, while his wife prefers Caius. He rejects Fenton as a suitor, observing that the young aristocrat—too high-ranking to marry Anne—is probably a fortune-hunter, being poor despite his rank, and is notably dissolute, having been friends with PRINCE (6) HAL and POINS (of *1* and *2 Henry IV*).

*Act 3, Scene 3*
The wives lay their plan: they instruct two SERVANTS (10) to be ready to carry away a big basket of laundry and dump it in the river. Falstaff arrives and woos Mistress Ford; Mistress Page appears, and Falstaff hides behind the curtains. Mistress Page announces that an angry Ford is approaching, seeking his wife's lover. Falstaff leaps from his hiding place into the laundry basket, which the two Servants carry out as Ford enters. Ford searches the house, watched by Page, Evans, and Caius, who assert that he is foolish. Left together, the two wives exult over Falstaff's discomfiture and decide to try it again the next morning. Unable to find any lover in the house, Ford admits his error. Page invites the men to go hawking the next morning. Evans and Caius confer about their revenge on the Host.

*Act 3, Scene 4*
Anne asks Fenton to continue to try to befriend her father before they think of elopement. Quickly arrives with Shallow and Slender. Slender is bashful, but Shallow leaves him to talk with Anne. Anne asks him frankly what his intentions are, and he replies that he himself has none but that others say he should marry her. Anne's parents arrive and announce their approval of Slender's suit and disparage Fenton's presence. Page and Slender leave. Fenton appeals to Mis-

tress Page to support his loving courtship, and Anne states her dislike of both Slender and Caius. Mistress Page relents to the point of promising to consult with Anne, and the two women leave. Quickly takes credit for softening Mistress Page, and Fenton gives her some money. She soliloquises that, having promised to help all three suitors, she will do so, but she favours Fenton.

### Act 3, Scene 5

Falstaff laments having been dumped in the river. Quickly brings him an apologetic message from Mistress Ford, who extends another invitation for that morning, while her husband is hawking. Ford arrives, again disguised as 'Brook'. Falstaff tells of his escape in the laundry and of his new opportunity. He leaves, and Ford rages angrily that this time he will catch Falstaff in his house.

### Act 4, Scene 1

Evans drills young WILLIAM (1) Page in his Latin grammar, and Quickly listens with comical misunderstanding.

### Act 4, Scene 2:

Falstaff calls on Mistress Ford, and once again Mistress Page arrives, sending him into hiding. Again, she tells of Ford's angry approach. The wives disguise Falstaff as the old woman of Brainford, a reputed witch whom Ford particularly despises. Ford arrives with a group of witnesses and ransacks the laundry in search of Falstaff; then in his fury he drives the 'old woman' from the house, beating 'her' mercilessly. He begins to search the house once more, and in his absence the wives decide to tell their husbands of their campaign against Falstaff so that all four may participate in another round of imposture.

### Act 4, Scene 3

Bardolph informs the Host that the agents of a German count, soon to arrive at the king's court, wish to hire horses. The Host agrees to let them use his, proposing to overcharge them.

### Act 4, Scene 4

The Pages and Fords, with Evans, concoct a plot against Falstaff. They will arrange to have the fat knight meet the women at an ancient sacred oak in the woods at midnight, disguised as a mythological creature, Herne the Hunter, who wears stag's antlers. When he arrives at the rendezvous, he will be accosted by a group of CHILDREN disguised as fairies and elves, led by Anne. They will pinch him and ridicule him until he admits his shabby dealings. Then all the hidden adults will emerge to mock him. As they lay their plans, Ford muses to himself that he may take advantage of the occasion to spirit Anne away with Slender

and have them married. Mistress Ford plots similarly with Dr Caius in mind.

### Act 4, Scene 5

Simple has followed the old woman of Brainford to Falstaff's rooms to ask her questions of behalf of his master. Falstaff says that he has spoken with the witch, and he gives Simple trick answers when he asks about Slender's chances of winning Anne Page. Bardolph reports to the Host that the Germans have made off with the horses; Evans and then Caius arrive with warnings that the Germans are not to be trusted. Realising that he has been robbed, the Host rages and rushes off. Quickly appears with a message to Falstaff from the two wives, and he takes her to his chamber to hear their proposition in detail.

### Act 4, Scene 6

Fenton bribes the Host to help him. Anne has learned of her parents' respective schemes, and the two lovers have hatched a counterplot. The Host agrees to arrange for a minister to marry the couple that night.

### Act 5, Scene 1

Falstaff sends Quickly to prepare for his masquerade that night, just as Ford arrives, disguised as 'Brook'. Falstaff assures him that tonight all they had planned will be accomplished.

### Act 5, Scene 2

Page, Shallow, and Slender lie in wait, planning for Slender's elopement with Anne.

### Act 5, Scene 3

The wives, with Caius, lie in wait, planning for the doctor's elopement with Anne.

### Act 5, Scene 4

Evans and the Children lie in wait, planning to accost Falstaff.

### Act 5, Scene 5

Falstaff, disguised as Herne, arrives at the rendezvous and compares himself with Jupiter, who took the forms of animals for sexual purposes. The wives appear; Falstaff is jubilant, thinking that his liaison is finally to occur, but the women hear a noise and flee. Evans and the Children, with Pistol and Quickly, all disguised as fairies and elves, come out and conduct a ceremony. They then torment Falstaff, burning him with their candles and pinching him. Slender and Caius arrive, and each steals away with a different fairy; Fenton takes Anne. Page, Ford, and the wives come forward and reveal their hoax to Falstaff, who is mortified. Slender returns to complain that his intended bride has proved to be a boy; Caius appears with the same story. Fenton and Anne return and explain that they have married. The Pages make the best of it and accept Fenton as their son-in-law. In a conciliatory spirit of fellowship, Falstaff is invited to join the others in a festive celebration at the Ford household.

## COMMENTARY

*The Merry Wives of Windsor* was probably written for a ceremonial occasion (see 'Text of the Play'), and it is clearly intended primarily as an entertainment. Unlike such earlier comedies as *The Comedy of Errors* and *The Two Gentlemen of Verona*, *The Merry Wives* is not coloured by any possibility of serious unhappiness that must be forestalled. In this respect, it is the shallowest COMEDY of Shakespeare's plays, and it is therefore sometimes thought of as an unimportant diversion in Shakespeare's development, an essentially trivial work that does not warrant attention. However, the play's suc-

*In 2.1 of* The Merry Wives of Windsor, *Mistress Ford and Mistress Page discover that Falstaff is courting them both with love letters. They plot their revenge. In this 19th-century production Ada Rehan (left) stars as Mistress Ford. (Courtesy of Culver Pictures, Inc.)*

cess on the stage—historical and current—has affirmed its value, and modern commentators have increasingly found it to be a particularly interesting work.

*The Merry Wives* is a variation on a medieval moral tale, and thus it draws on the theatrical traditions of Shakespeare's day. But Shakespeare added contemporary elements; it is the only one of his works to focus exclusively on English life in his own time. Moreover, in *The Merry Wives* the playwright gave the initiative in the play's plot to the wives, rather than to male characters, as was normal in earlier comedies, including his own. This points intriguingly to the prominence of heroines in his later comedies.

As a moral tale *The Merry Wives* recounts the triumph of domestic values over the threat of corruption brought in by an outsider, Falstaff, whose amoral selfishness is contrasted with the communal solidarity of the townspeople and whose status as a courtier makes him a social alien. In an ancient tradition, known in Shakespeare's day through both Roman drama and the medieval MORALITY PLAY, satirical comedy exposed human foibles by making fun of them. The happy resolution that defines the genre usually consisted in precisely the sort of humiliation and forgiveness that befall Falstaff in the play. Thus Shakespeare applied a familiar formula, immediately understood by his audience and so self-evident in its intentions that subsequent readers and theatre-goers have responded just as instinctively.

The play also offers another sort of tale, a standard plot in Elizabethan Comedy: the triumph of young lovers—Anne Page and Fenton—over the machinations of the girl's parents and her mercenary suitors. The final comic resolution of this story buttresses that of the Falstaff plot. Moreover, the double dénouement is both forecast and supported by the sub-plot of the enmity and reconciliation of Caius and Evans, whose proposed duel is defused by the collective efforts of various townspeople. Thus the play's theme—the power of good over evil—is developed in several mutually reinforcing ways.

The contemporaneity of *The Merry Wives* is one of its strikingly novel features. In this work, as in the *Henry IV* plays, written at almost exactly the same time, Shakespeare dramatises his own world with unprecedented theatrical realism. He doubtless created the BOAR'S HEAD TAVERN in *1 Henry IV* to strengthen that play's historical themes by associating them with a more mundane aspect of English society. In *The Merry Wives,* which is concerned solely with entertainment, historical markers are almost nonexistent (although a few references are made—e.g., in 3.2.66–67—to the world of Henry IV), and the entire play is a detailed slice of Elizabethan rural life. The characters enjoy such country entertainments as greyhound racing (1.1.81–89) and hunting with small hawks (3.3.214–

215); they are familiar with stiles (3.1.32), goose-pens (3.4.40), bilberries (5.5.46), and the ways of the cuckoo (2.1.121). The specific geographical references—FROGMORE (2.3.81), Eton (4.5.63), Datchet Mead (3.3.12), Herne's oak in Windsor Forest (4.4.53)—lend great realism to the play's setting.

More sophisticated tastes are also provided for in the literary humour of William's Latin lesson (4.1) and in the inside jokes about the Count of MOMPELGARD in 4.3 and 4.5, accessible only to the highest ranks of courtly society. Also, several minor jests involve quotations from the works of SIDNEY and MARLOWE (1), requiring an educated familiarity with contemporary literature, although Shakespeare's audience will have recognised these references much more readily than modern readers can.

Despite its innovativeness, the play was also conspicuously part of the contemporary vogue for the COMEDY OF HUMOURS, in which social types are represented by boldly identifiable characters, each sporting a notable eccentricity of speech or behaviour. Most of the secondary figures in *The Merry Wives* exhibit such traits: Evans and Caius each speak with a comic foreign dialect—Welsh and French respectively. Pistol is an archetypal swaggerer, Slender a foolish bumpkin, the Host a jovial gladhander. Ford, though more humanly complex, belongs to a very ancient tradition, that of the unreasonably jealous husband. Even Falstaff takes on the role of a character type, the unsuccessful lecher, although his motive in approaching the wives is actually mercenary.

The play's many comic characters are ranged around Falstaff, who, although he is a less masterful figure than in the *Henry IV* plays, is nonetheless as brassy, zestful, and humorously rhetorical as ever, brandishing language like a torch to baffle and confuse his intended victims. The difference is that in *The Merry Wives* he does not succeed, even temporarily. He is a comic butt, destined from the outset to be defeated by the forthright and faithful wives. That the resourceful rogue of *1 Henry IV* should be so easily bested, not just once but three times, has been regretted by some, who see in Falstaff's downfall the trivialisation of a great comic figure. However, in *The Merry Wives* Falstaff's function is different. He is not placed in contrast with a historical plot involving politics and war, a circumstance that gives his wit extraordinary resonance in the *Henry IV* plays; here, he has an almost abstract, allegorical role, as the spirit of malevolence that, while comic and releasing, must be roundly crushed. The Falstaff of *The Merry Wives* has been seen as similar to the scapegoat, a sacrificial animal of pre-Christian religious traditions, who is figuratively laden with the misdeeds of the people and then released into the wilderness or killed, taking with it the sins of the community. Certainly 5.5 is suggestive of such rites, which were still remembered and understood in

Shakespeare's day, having disappeared only recently—they may, in fact, have still been alive in the remotest parts of Britain. In any case, at the close of the play, Falstaff's humiliation is mitigated by the fact that Page and his wife have also been foiled in their plans for Anne, and the fat villain is included in the final forgiveness and good cheer that embody the spirit of Shakespearean comedy.

*The Merry Wives* anticipates Shakespeare's later work in its emphasis on women. While the wives, comfortably settled in middle-aged domesticity, are not much like the bold and venturesome heroines that the playwright was soon to create—BEATRICE (*Much Ado About Nothing*), ROSALIND (*As You Like It*), VIOLA (*Twelfth Night*), and HELENA (*All's Well That Ends Well*)—they nonetheless prefigure them. They are clearly the most sensible and competent people in Shakespeare's Windsor. They know who they are, and they firmly assert themselves; we are left in no doubt that they are 'merry, and yet honest too', as Mistress Page says (4.2.96). Falstaff's greed is the first stimulus to the plot, but the wives are his target precisely because they are the important figures in their households, and the initiative in the plot's development lies squarely with them. They repeatedly lead Falstaff on—and thus, indirectly, Ford—although the men think they are imposing their wills on the world. The wives' vigour is evident not only in the execution of their plans but in their language: for instance, Mistress Page passes boldly from technological to classical to sexual imagery in condemning Falstaff's use of identical love letters (2.1.71–78), closing with the ornithological: 'I will find you twenty lascivious turtles [turtledoves] ere one chaste man'. (2.1.78). The merry wives are the defenders of domesticity against promiscuity—of order against misrule, that is—and their symbolic importance clearly indicates, for the first time in the plays, the high value Shakespeare placed on female influence in human affairs, a position that he would reassert, perhaps more strikingly, in later works.

*The Merry Wives of Windsor* is not one of Shakespeare's greatest plays; it lacks stirring poetry and monumental characters, and its concerns are not so sophisticated as the political philosophy and psychological exploration of some of the more important works. However, it is a bold reminder of the popular morality theatre of medieval England, and it also presents a delightfully picturesque view of 16th-century rural life. An expertly plotted farce that ranges from gentle charm to high hilarity, it deploys a dozen splendid comic characters in a world of solid virtue that is exemplified by its commendable though understated heroines. As such, the play has been appreciated by generations of theatre-goers, and increasing attention from scholars and critics will reinforce its continuing popularity.

## SOURCES OF THE PLAY

A number of loose ends in *The Merry Wives of Windsor*—especially Shallow's threatened and then forgotten lawsuit—have suggested to some scholars that the play is based on another one, now lost. This would have been a logical tactic for Shakespeare to use, if it is true that the play was written in two weeks at the Queen's command (see 'Text of the Play'). However, no evidence exists to link *The Merry Wives* to any earlier play, and the inconsistencies within the play may simply be evidence of hasty composition, whether in response to a royal command or not. In any case, nothing in *The Merry Wives* seems beyond the invention of a well-read and creative mind. Its incidents and characters resemble material that had long been current in European literature and folklore. Jealous husbands and lovers who triumph over adversarial parents are staples of Western storytelling, and Shakespeare could simply have thought of stories he had heard or read without referring to particular works. Also, the contemporary vogue for the comedy of humours must have influenced *The Merry Wives*, which, while transcending the genre, certainly incorporates features from it.

Nevertheless, several likely literary sources may be mentioned. A number of details of Falstaff's escapes from the jealous Ford may have been anticipated in a story from Giovanni FIORENTINO's collection *Il Pecorone (The Simpleton)*, published in Milan (1558) and a source for *The Merchant of Venice*. A comical English prose work, Robert Copland's *Gyl of Braintfords Testament* (1560) may have suggested Falstaff's disguise as the old woman of Brainford, and his departure in the laundry basket may derive from a story by Barnabe RICH (1) in his *Farewell to Militarie Profession* (1581). The personality of the Host was probably influenced by Geoffrey CHAUCER's famous innkeeper in *The Canterbury Tales*, and George CHAPMAN's *The Blind Beggar of Alexandria* (1596), a highly successful comedy of humours, contained a character whose comical overuse of the word 'humour' clearly contributed to the creation of Shakespeare's Nym. The famous 'Latin' scene, 4.1, is representative of a set piece in several contemporary French farces, which Shakespeare would have known of and may have read. Lastly, Falstaff's torment at the hands of fairy-impersonators was perhaps based on a scene in John LYLY's play *Endimion* (1588), in which a lecher is punished for his lust by fairies.

## TEXT OF THE PLAY

Although absolute proof is lacking, scholars, led by Dr Leslie HOTSON, have convincingly established that *The Merry Wives* was commissioned for a particular occasion, a feast hosted by the Queen on April 23, 1597, in honour of newly elected members of the knightly Order of the Garter. In 5.5.56–75 Quickly, in the guise of the Queen of Fairies, issues instructions to prepare Windsor Castle for the Knights of the Garter. Apparent references to the German Count of MÖMPELGARD also reflect this occasion, as does the setting of the play in Windsor, rather than in Shakespeare's native WARWICKSHIRE or some other rural location. Among the noblemen joining the Order of the Garter on this occasion was George CAREY (1), Lord Hunsdon—patron of Shakespeare's company, HUNSDON'S MEN—who had just become Elizabeth's Lord Chamberlain (the company was called the CHAMBERLAIN'S MEN from then on), and he probably commissioned the play. These circumstances appear to confirm a longstanding tradition that *The Merry Wives* was written in 14 days to fulfil a desire expressed by Queen ELIZABETH (1) to see Falstaff in love. This notion does not appear in print until 1702, but it fits well with the evident purpose of the play's composition: if a play were offered to the Queen, it is quite possible that she would specify a choice of subject. It is known that Hunsdon's Men had performed at court several times in the winter of 1596–1597, and it is likely that they presented their most recent popular success, *1 Henry IV*, in which Elizabeth would have become acquainted with Falstaff.

The play is therefore dated to early 1597. A change in the apparent home of Justice Shallow in *2 Henry IV* (see GLOUCESTERSHIRE) suggests that the composition of that play was interrupted by the writing of *The Merry Wives*, in which Shallow explicitly comes from Gloucestershire (1.1.5). *Henry IV, Part 2*, was probably begun in early 1597, thus pushing the creation of *The Merry Wives* a little closer to the beginning of rehearsals for its April presentation; this allows very little time for the job, perhaps only 14 days, although this cannot be known precisely, of course.

The play was first published in 1602 in a BAD QUARTO edition by Arthur JOHNSON (1), who bought the rights to it from John BUSBY. This edition, known as Q1, was printed by Thomas CREEDE. It was reprinted with minor alterations in 1619 by William JAGGARD, for the FALSE FOLIO of publisher Thomas PAVIER. This edition is known as Q2. The 1623 FIRST FOLIO version of *The Merry Wives* is a greatly superior text. It includes five scenes omitted in the Quartos, and it provides more comprehensible, smoother readings throughout. Scholars believe that the Folio was printed from a transcript of Shakespeare's manuscript, perhaps in a version reflecting a court performance of 1604 (see BROOK [1]); certain idiosyncracies in the text point to the hand of Ralph CRANE, a professional scribe whose work is well known. Q1 represents an already abridged version of the play, one intended for the public theatre rather than for the play's original aristocratic audience at the Queen's banquet. It omits the scenes dealing with the Order of the Garter, along with the 'Latin' scene, presumably thought inappropriate for the relatively uneducated public. The Folio was immediately recognised as the superior text, and subsequent editions have been largely based on it, with occasional alterations deriving from Q1.

## THEATRICAL HISTORY OF THE PLAY

*The Merry Wives* was enthusiastically received by its original audience. The subtitle of the 1602 edition of the play asserts that it had been performed 'divers times' both before the Queen and elsewhere, and it specifically mentions Falstaff, Evans, Shallow, Slender, Pistol, and Nym, attesting to the fame of these figures. The earliest specific performance of which a record survives was held at the court of King JAMES I in 1604. An ambiguous record of 1613 may or may not refer to *The Merry Wives,* but the play was certainly played at the court of Charles I in 1638, testifying to its ongoing popularity. After the theatres were reopened following their 20-year closure by the Puritan revolution, *The Merry Wives* was one of the first plays to be staged. Samuel PEPYS saw it in 1660, 1661, and 1667. The programme of an unsuccessful adaptation of 1702, *The Comical Gallant* by John DENNIS (2), implies that *The Merry Wives* had been produced several times in the intervening years, though no late 17th-century performances are recorded. In 1704 Shakespeare's text was staged by Thomas BETTERTON, who played Falstaff, and James QUIN duplicated the project a year later. Since the 1720s the play has been extremely popular both in Britain and America, and many major Shakespearean actors of the 18th and 19th centuries played Falstaff, Ford, or both.

*The Merry Wives* has remained a favourite in the 20th century; the many productions of the play have included those of Oscar ASCHE and Theodore KOMISARJEVSKY. It was twice a silent FILM (1910, 1917), but has not been a movie since. It has been made for TELEVISION four times, including the 1955 production of Glen Byam SHAW (3), starring Anthony QUAYLE. A number of operas have been based on the play, beginning in 1824, when Fredric REYNOLDS (1) produced an opera with music by Henry BISHOP (2). Among others have been such well-known works as Ralph VAUGHAN WILLIAMS' *Sir John in Love* (1929), and, by general consent the greatest of them, Giuseppe VERDI's *Falstaff* (1893). Another musical work inspired in part by *The Merry Wives* is the English composer Edward Elgar's symphonic study *Falstaff* (1913).

**Messala, Marcus Valerius (64 B.C.–8 A.D.)** Historical figure and minor character in *Julius Caesar,* a general under BRUTUS (4) and CASSIUS. In 4.3 Messala brings Brutus news of the death of PORTIA (2) and witnesses Brutus' feigned stoicism, to which he responds with admiration, saying 'Even so great men great losses should endure' (4.3.192). Messala appears frequently

at the battle of PHILIPPI in Act 5, but his only important moment comes when he discovers the corpse of Cassius in 5.3. In 5.5 he has been captured by OCTAVIUS and ANTONY.

The historical Messala, better known as Messala Corvinus Valerius, was offered the command of Brutus' army as it crumbled at Philippi, but he joined Octavius and Antony instead. Ten years later he fought for Octavius against Antony at ACTIUM (though he does not appear in *Antony and Cleopatra,* where that battle is enacted). Under Augustus CAESAR (2), as Octavius became known, Messala held various offices, was a patron of a group of pastoral poets, and wrote books on history and literature; his work—famous in its day—was a source for Shakespeare's source, PLUTARCH, though none of it has survived.

**Messenger (1)** Minor character in *The Comedy of Errors.* In 5.1.168–184 he brings ADRIANA a frantic account of the escape of ANTIPHOLUS OF EPHESUS from the custody of PINCH and comically describes Antipholus' revenge on that pseudo-physician. He is identified as a Servant.

**Messenger (2)** Minor character in *Titus Andronicus.* The Messenger brings TITUS (1) a grisly package—the severed heads of his two sons and the general's own severed hand—that AARON has sent in mockery. The Messenger is sympathetic, remarking on the injustice with a personal note that is rare in this play.

**Messenger (3)** Any of several minor characters in *1 Henry VI,* mostly soldiers who deliver accounts of battle situations. In the opening scenes, the repeated interruptions of HENRY V's funeral by Messengers bearing tidings of English defeats establish the theme of loss and disruption. In 4.3 a Messenger announces to the Duke of YORK (8) the commencement of the battle that will prove fatal to TALBOT. In 2.2 a French Messenger brings Talbot the deceitful invitation from the Countess of AUVERGNE.

**Messenger (4)** Any of several minor characters in *2 Henry VI,* whose announcements spark action by greater figures or provide news of events off-stage. In 1.2 a Messenger summons the Duke of GLOUCESTER (4) to a royal hawking party, leaving his wife the DUCHESS (1) alone to pursue the plot that will eventually bring them both down. In 4.4 a Messenger informs the king of the progress of Jack CADE's rebellion, and in 4.7 another man announces to Cade the capture of an important nobleman, Lord SAY. Lastly, in 4.9, a Messenger brings the king the momentous news that the Duke of YORK (8) has returned from his duty in Ireland at the head of an army, an event that heralds the coming civil war.

**Messenger (5)**   Any of several minor characters in *3 Henry VI*, soldiers bringing military reports. The Messengers simply report troop movements, except for the first of two in 2.1, who brings a detailed account of the death of the Duke of YORK (8).

In the FIRST FOLIO text of the play, believed to have been printed from Shakespeare's manuscript, the Messenger is referred to in the stage direction at 1.2.47 as 'Gabriel'. This apparently refers to the actor Gabriel SPENCER, who presumably played the part in the original production.

**Messenger (6)**   Any of several minor characters in *Richard III*, bearers of news. In 2.4 a Messenger brings word to Queen ELIZABETH (2) that her son and brother have been imprisoned, and in 3.2 a Messenger delivers to HASTINGS (3) an account of an ominous dream from STANLEY (3). In a highly dramatic use of messengers, Shakespeare brings four on stage successively in 4.4, within a few lines, to demonstrate Richard's lack of control as news floods in of rebellion against him. In 5.3 one last Messenger brings Richard word of Stanley's desertion at BOSWORTH FIELD.

**Messenger (7)**   Minor character in *The Taming of the Shrew*, the announcer, in the INDUCTION, of the performance by the PLAYERS (1) that begins the play proper. In Ind.2 he informs SLY (1) of the coming presentation and recommends viewing it as a healthy pastime. Various editions of the play have assigned his part to the LORD (1) or a SERVANT (5).

**Messenger (8)**   Minor character in *King John*. In 4.2 the Messenger brings King JOHN (3) news of both the French invasion and the death of John's mother, Queen ELEANOR, and in 5.3 he reappears with a message from the BASTARD (1), urging the king to remove himself from battle. Thus this underling marks the beginning and end of John's collapse.

**Messenger (9)**   Minor character in *King John*. In 5.5 the Messenger brings LEWIS (1) three pieces of bad news: the death of Lord MELUN, the desertion from the French forces of the English barons who had been in revolt against King JOHN (3), and the loss of French ships at sea. These tidings collectively spell doom for the French invasion of England.

**Messenger (10)**   Minor character in *The Merchant of Venice*, servant of PORTIA (1). In 2.9 the Messenger tells Portia that BASSANIO is approaching.

**Messenger (11)**   Any of several minor characters in *1 Henry IV* who bring messages to HOTSPUR. A Messenger informs Hotspur of his father's illness on the eve of the battle of SHREWSBURY in 4.1. Two more Messengers appear in 5.2, just before the battle, in an episode that heightens the excitement of the occasion. One brings letters that Hotspur, in his agitation, refuses to read, and the second brings word that King HENRY IV's army is approaching.

**Messenger (12)**   Minor character in *2 Henry IV*, a soldier. In 4.1 the Messenger brings the rebel leaders a report that the army of Prince John of LANCASTER (3) is approaching.

**Messenger (13)**   Any of several minor characters in *Henry V*, servants in the court of the FRENCH KING. In 2.4 a Messenger announces the arrival of an English ambassador. In 3.7 and 4.2 Messengers, perhaps soldiers, bring word of English troop dispositions prior to the battle of AGINCOURT.

**Messenger (14)**   Minor character in *Much Ado About Nothing*, a servant of Don PEDRO. In 1.1 the Messenger tells Leonato of Don Pedro's successes in war, citing the noble deeds of CLAUDIO (1) and BENEDICK and thus providing expository material on the play's romantic leads. The mention of Benedick subjects the Messenger to BEATRICE's sharp verbal sallies; the passage (1.1. 28–83) presents one of the play's major motifs, the witty—though prickly—independence of its heroine. In 3.5.50–51 and 5.4.123–124 the Messenger presents brief reports of off-stage action.

**Messenger (15)**   Minor character in *Julius Caesar*, a soldier in the army of OCTAVIUS and ANTONY. In 5.1 the Messenger announces the approach of the army of BRUTUS (4) and CASSIUS just before the battle of PHILIPPI.

**Messenger (16)**   Minor character in *Hamlet*. The Messenger brings the KING (5) of DENMARK news that LAERTES has raised a rebellion and is approaching. His hysteria emphasises the degree of disruption that the play's developments have produced. In a calmer mood the Messenger brings the King letters from HAMLET in 4.7.

**Messenger (17)**   Minor character in *All's Well That Ends Well*, a servant of BERTRAM. In 4.3 the Messenger tells two gentlemen (see LORD [6]) that his master will soon be returning to FRANCE (1). His single brief speech separates two elements of a long scene: the Lords' critique of Bertram's morality and Bertram's arrival for the interrogation of PAROLLES.

**Messenger (18)**   Minor character in *Measure for Measure*, servant of ANGELO (2). In 4.2 the Messenger delivers to the PROVOST Angelo's command for the execution of CLAUDIO (3), though a pardon has been expected. Angelo's employment of the Messenger makes his deed seem even more monstrous as he distances himself from it.

**Messenger (19)** Minor character in *Othello,* bearer of a dispatch from MONTANO (2) to the DUKE (5) of VENICE. In 1.3 the Messenger delivers news of the Turkish attack on CYPRUS that OTHELLO will be sent to oppose. His brief part increases the urgency of the scene.

**Messenger (20)** Minor character in *King Lear,* a servant of REGAN. In 4.2 the Messenger interrupts a dispute between GONERIL and ALBANY with the news that GLOUCESTER (1) has been blinded and CORNWALL is dead. Goneril immediately withdraws to plan her selfish response to the latter event, in contrast to her husband's shocked dismay over the former. The Messenger then adds that Gloucester had been betrayed by his son EDMUND. The episode stresses the evil that Albany realises he must oppose as the play approaches its climax.

**Messenger (21)** Minor character in *King Lear,* a follower of CORDELIA. In 4.4 the Messenger brings his mistress the news that the armies of GONERIL and REGAN are approaching. His brief announcement immediately throws the newly arrived Cordelia into the fury of battle, and thereby increases the play's pace as it reaches its climax.

**Messenger (22)** Minor character in *Macbeth,* a servant of MACBETH. In 1.5 the Messenger brings LADY (6) MACBETH the news that King DUNCAN, whose murder she has just been contemplating, approaches. Her startled response to this sudden opportunity for the crime serves to escalate the plot's tension. In 4.2 the Messenger (or, possibly, another one) betrays his master when he warns LADY (7) Macduff that Macbeth's hired killers approach (see FIRST MURDERER [3]). He is bravely willing to stand up against Macbeth's villainy and his action provides a moment of relief from the growing evil of the plot. In 5.5 the Messenger, still employed by Macbeth (unless, again, he is a different person), brings his master word that the forest appears to be moving. This message signals Macbeth's downfall, and his wrathful response emphasises his desperate position. Though they seem unimportant, all three of the Messenger's appearances mark a change in the play's emotional tone, a striking Shakespearean technique.

**Messenger (23)** Any of three minor characters in *Antony and Cleopatra,* bearers of news to ANTONY. In 1.2 the First Messenger tells that Antony's wife and brother have been defeated by Octavius CAESAR (2) in the Roman civil wars. He also tells of the conquest of Roman territory in Egypt by a renegade Roman general. A Second Messenger announces the arrival of a

Third Messenger, who brings word that Antony's wife has died. The rapid sequence of messages establishes the importance of both the political and personal situation in which Antony lives. Although he seems unnecessary, the Second Messenger, who speaks only five words, contributes to the atmosphere of crisis. One of the Messengers (or, perhaps, a fourth) reappears in 3.7 at the battle of ACTIUM with word of Caesar's troop movements.

**Messenger (24)** Either of two minor characters in *Antony and Cleopatra,* bearers of news to Octavius CAESAR (2). In 1.4 the Messengers appear, one after the other, with news of the success of POMPEY (2) and of his alliance with the pirates MENECRATES and MENAS. One of the Messengers (or, possibly, a third) appears in 4.6 with word of ANTONY's preparations for battle. The Messengers strengthen our sense of Caesar as an informed and decisive leader.

**Messenger (25)** Minor character in *Antony and Cleopatra,* a servant who brings CLEOPATRA news of ANTONY's marriage to OCTAVIA. In 2.5 Cleopatra's rage is so great when she hears of Antony's action that she beats the Messenger and threatens to kill him. He naturally flees. He is coaxed to return and repeat his message to the unwilling queen, and he flees again when she is again angry. In 3.3 he assures Cleopatra that he has seen Octavia and knows her to be an extremely unattractive woman whose defects he details. For this tactful report, Cleopatra rewards him with gold and agrees that he is a 'proper man' (3.3.37). The episode demonstrates the mercurial nature of the Egyptian queen. The Messenger represents an ancient theatrical stereotype, the comic servant.

**Messenger (26)** Character in *Antony and Cleopatra.* See ATTENDANT (1).

**Messenger (27)** Any of several minor characters in *Coriolanus,* bearers of tidings. In 1.1, 1.4, and 1.6, Messengers who are apparently military men (or perhaps the same man each time), bring reports on the advancing VOLSCIANS to CORIOLANUS or COMINIUS. In 2.1, 4.6, and 5.4, other Messengers who are apparently civilians (or, again, perhaps a single person), bring news of events in ROME to the tribunes, BRUTUS (3) and SICINIUS. The Messengers serve to announce plot developments.

**Messenger (28)** Any of several minor characters in *Timon of Athens.* In 1.1 two Messengers bring TIMON news, first of the imprisonment for debt of VENTIDIUS (2), and later of the approach of ALCIBIADES. In 5.2 a Messenger reports on Alcibiades' march on Athens. These may well be different men—servants of Ventidius, Timon, and an anonymous SENATOR (4), respectively—but they are indistinguishable and serve to inform the audience of off-stage events.

**Messenger (29)**   Minor character in *Pericles,* a servant of King ANTIOCHUS of Syria. In 1.1 the Messenger informs Antiochus that PERICLES—whom the king intends to kill—has fled the country. The Messenger, who speaks only a single line, helps heighten the melodramatic tension of the scene.

**Messenger (30)**   Minor character in *Cymbeline,* a servant of King CYMBELINE. In 2.3 the Messenger announces the arrival of an ambassador, and in 5.4 he summons POSTHUMUS from his pending execution to an audience with the king. The Messenger's function is to advance the plot.

**Messenger (31)**   Minor character in *Henry VIII,* a servant of Queen KATHERINE. In 4.2 the Messenger, announcing the arrival of Lord CAPUCHIUS, addresses the now-deposed queen as if she were a mere duchess. She instantly rebukes him and orders GRIFFITH to see that he is never sent to her again. The episode, which derives from an historical incident, offers a last demonstration of strength in the victimised and dying Katherine.

**Messenger (32)**   Any of three minor characters in *The Two Noble Kinsmen,* bearers of news. In 4.2 a Messenger reports on the arrival of ARCITE and PALAMON for their duel, describing the combatants and their supporters in elaborately courtly terms. In 5.2 another Messenger (probably played by the same actor, however) tells the GAOLER (4), the DOCTOR (4), and the WOOER about the duel in a few brief lines. Scholars generally agree that Shakespeare's collaborator John FLETCHER (2) wrote both 4.2 and 5.2, but that Shakespeare created the Messenger in 5.4, who dramatically races on-stage to halt the execution of Palamon, cry- ing 'Hold, hold, O hold, hold, hold!' (5.4.40), as PIRI- THOUS arrives with a pardon. This bold *coup de théâtre* advances the play to its final episode. In some 17th- century productions, the Messenger was probably played by Curtis GREVILLE (1).

**Messina**   City in Sicily, setting for *Much Ado About Nothing* and one scene of *Antony and Cleopatra.* Although there is nothing particularly Sicilian—let alone Messinian—about the events or locations in *Much Ado,* one of Shakespeare's sources for the play, Matteo BAN- DELLO's novella, is set in Messina, where an Aragonese army (see PEDRO) is celebrating its conquest of Sicily. Sicily was ruled by the kings of Aragon—and later Spain—from 1282 until 1713. Messina was the site of the first Aragonese victory, in 1282, against the French, who ruled the island until then. This doubt-

less accounts for Bandello's location, which Shake- speare simply adopted.

In 2.1 of *Antony and Cleopatra* POMPEY (2) confers with MENAS and MENECRATES about their war against Octavius CAESAR (2), LEPIDUS, and Mark ANTONY. Shakespeare did not indicate the locale of this confer- ence, but scholars have identified it. Beginning with Edward CAPELL in 1768, editors have generally pro- vided a stage direction that places this scene in Mes- sina. This follows Shakespeare's source, PLUTARCH's *Lives,* which locates Pompey's headquarters there. Sicily was Pompey's principal base for much of his rebellion against Rome, and his occupation of Mes- sina, which commanded the strait between the island and mainland Italy, was strategically important. His final defeat was only possible through Caesar's block- ade of Messina in 36 B.C., in a very difficult campaign that is casually referred to in 3.5.4. of the play.

**Metellus Cimber (L. Tillius Cimber) (d. c. 44 B.C.)** Historical figure and character in *Julius Caesar,* one of the assassins of CAESAR (1). In 3.1, as part of the assas- sination plot, Metellus requests that Caesar pardon his brother, who has been banished; since Caesar has re- fused this plea once, the conspirators are confident that he will do so again, and this refusal is to be the signal—and ostensible stimulus—for their attack. Metellus has no distinctive personality; he simply per- forms his role and then stabs Caesar along with the others.

The historical figure was actually named Lucius Til- lius Cimber; the error comes from Shakespeare's source, PLUTARCH's *Lives,* where Cimber is given two different names, both of them wrong. Cimber had been an associate of Caesar's but abandoned him and joined Brutus' conspiracy. He probably died in com- bat at PHILIPPI; he fought with Brutus' forces, but no further record of him has survived.

**Metre**   Regular rhythmic pattern in poetry. While some poetry lacks metre—it is called free verse—al- most all pre-modern poetry, including Shakespeare's, is metrical; the words are arranged in a definite mea- surable pattern. The term 'metre' derives from the Greek word for 'measure'. Some metres are *syllabic,* measuring simply the number of syllables in a line; some are *accentual,* measuring only the syllables that are stressed or accented when the poetry is read. *Quantitative* metres measure the duration of the sounds as they are spoken; ancient Greek, Latin, and Sanskrit verse usually follow this pattern. Most En- glish poetry, including Shakespeare's, is composed in accentual-syllabic metres; that is, both the stresses and the syllables are counted.

These patterns of stresses and syllables are gener- ally organised into elements known as *feet.* Six types of feet are most common in English poetry, though very rarely others—usually taken from quantitative systems—are used. The six feet are the *iamb*, consisting of an unstressed syllable followed by a stressed one, as in the word 'delight'; the *anapest*, consisting of two unstressed syllables followed by one stressed one, as in the word 'intervene'; the *trochee*, one stressed syllable followed by an unstressed one, as in 'hotter'; the *dactyl*, one stressed syllable followed by two unstressed ones, as in 'lovingly'; the *spondee*, two stressed syllables, as in 'amen'; and the *pyrrhic*, two unstressed syllables, as in the syllables '-es of', in the line 'I'll gild the faces of the grooms withal' (*Macbeth*, 2.2.55), where all the other feet are iambs. As this last example demonstrates, a foot does not necessarily correspond to a word or phrase; also, the same word or words may comprise a different sort of foot, depending on the feet surrounding it in the line.

Metres are named according to the number of feet in a line, using the Greek prefixes for numbers—*dimeter* for two feet, *trimeter* for three, *tetrameter* for four, *pentameter* for five, *hexameter* for six, and so on—and according to the kind of foot that dominates in the line—iambic, anapestic, trochaic, dactylic, spondaic, or pyrrhic. Variation is necessary; a poem of any length consisting solely of one sort of foot would sound intolerably mechanical. Thus an iambic pentameter line—typical of Shakespeare's poetry (see BLANK VERSE)—does not always consist only of iambs, and all the lines of an iambic pentameter poem or passage need not have five feet. However, throughout a work that is said to be written in iambic pentameter, iambs will dominate and almost all the lines will have five feet.

**Michael (1)**  Minor character in *2 Henry VI*, a follower of the rebel Jack CADE. In 4.2 Michael brings word that Sir Humphrey STAFFORD (2) is approaching with troops to put down the rebellion.

**Michael (2), Sir**  Minor character in *1 Henry IV*, friend of the ARCHBISHOP (3) of York. In 4.4 the Archbishop and Sir Michael discuss the rebels' likely defeat against King HENRY IV at SHREWSBURY. The episode introduces the Archbishop's subsequent further rebellion against the King, to be enacted in *2 Henry IV*.

No historical Michael is known among the Archbishop's associates. Sir Michael's presence in the play may reflect a lost source that the playwright consulted, or he may be Shakespeare's invention.

**Middleham Castle**  Heavily fortified and moated castle in northern England, a location in *3 Henry VI*. The grounds of Middleham Castle, home to the brother of the Duke of WARWICK (3), are the setting for 4.5, in which the Duke's captive, King EDWARD IV, is rescued by his allies.

**Middleton, Thomas (1580–1627)**  English playwright, a prolific writer of JACOBEAN DRAMA. As a young man, Middleton worked for Philip HENSLOWE, turning out plays in collaboration with Thomas DEKKER, Michael DRAYTON, and Anthony MUNDAY. He wrote comedies for various CHILDREN'S COMPANIES between 1602 and 1608; he then worked with Dekker on *The Roaring Girl* (1610), a highly successful COMEDY of the period. In the 1620s, Middleton collaborated with William ROWLEY (2), who wrote comic SUB-PLOTS, on several plays for PRINCE CHARLES' MEN. These included his greatest play, *The Changeling* (1622), a TRAGEDY of murder, madness, and obsessive love that has frequently been revived in the 20th century. Another of his best works, *Women Beware Women* (c. 1625), is also a tragedy of perverse attractions and grave moral sickness. One of Middleton's last works, *A Game at Chess* (1624), is a boldly anti-Catholic, anti-Spanish allegory that blatantly alluded to King JAMES I's pursuit of a marital alliance with the Spanish Hapsburgs. It was huge success at the GLOBE THEATRE, running for nine days—two days would have been unusual at that time (see ELIZABETHAN THEATRE)—before the government prohibited it and briefly gaoled its author.

Two SONGS from Middleton's tragedy *The Witch* (c. 1610–1620) were printed in the first edition of *Macbeth*, having been interpolated in Shakespeare's play for some early performance. Middleton may have written THE PURITAN and collaborated with William ROWLEY (2) on THE BIRTH OF MERLIN, both plays at one time ascribed to Shakespeare, and some scholars give him a role as a collaborator in Shakespeare's unfinished play *Timon of Athens*.

## *A Midsummer Night's Dream*

### SYNOPSIS

*Act 1, Scene 1*

THESEUS (1), Duke of ATHENS, discusses with HIPPOLYTA (1) their forthcoming marriage, only days away. EGEUS arrives with his daughter, HERMIA, and her two suitors, DEMETRIUS (2) and LYSANDER. Since Hermia will not marry Demetrius, whom her father prefers, but insists that she loves Lysander, Egeus wants her subjected to a law that will condemn her to death or a life as a nun for refusing to marry the groom her father has chosen. Theseus reluctantly rules that he must enforce the law, but he gives Hermia until the day of his own wedding to decide what she will do. Lysander, declaring himself the better marital prospect, reveals that Demetrius has earlier courted Hermia's friend HELENA (1) and made her fall in love with him. Theseus leaves, taking with him all but Lysander and Hermia, who decide to elope, agreeing to meet in the woods the next night. Helena appears, pining for Demetrius; Lysander and Hermia encourage her by telling of their plan and asserting that, with Hermia gone, Demetrius will be free again. The lovers leave, and the love-sick Helena, in a soliloquy, devises a plot to curry favour with Demetrius: she will tell him of the planned elopement and accompany him to the woods to intercept the pair.

*Act 1, Scene 2*
QUINCE, with his fellow artisans SNUG, FLUTE, SNOUT, STARVELING, and BOTTOM, gather to rehearse the IN-TERLUDE they are to perform at Theseus and Hippolyta's wedding. Quince, the director, announces the subject of their playlet—the tale of PYRAMUS AND THISBE—and distributes the parts among the players. Bottom, who is to play Pyramus, is so confident of his acting abilities that he wants most of the other parts as well. Quince declares that, in order to keep their spectacle a surprise, they will rehearse in secret, meeting the next night in the woods.

*Act 2, Scene 1*
PUCK and a FAIRY discuss the conflict between the King of the Fairies, OBERON, whom Puck serves, and the Fairy Queen, TITANIA, the Fairy's mistress. Titania and Oberon arrive and begin arguing. She refuses to give up a changeling boy whom Oberon covets. She leaves, and Oberon vows vengeance. He instructs Puck to gather for him a certain flower that he will apply to Titania's eyes while she sleeps and that will cause her to fall in love with the first living being she sees when she wakes. While awaiting Puck's return, Oberon overhears Demetrius and Helena, who are now in the woods, and when Demetrius persistently repulses his admirer, the Fairy King decides that he will dose him with the flower also. Puck returns with the magical herb, and Oberon takes some of it to give to Titania. He tells Puck to find the Athenian couple who are roaming in the woods and to apply the rest of the potion to Demetrius.

*Act 2, Scene 2*
Titania's retinue sings her to sleep. Oberon appears and puts juice from the plant on her eyes. He leaves, and Lysander and Hermia enter, exhausted from wandering. They sleep, though only after Hermia has insisted that they maintain a proper distance from each other. Puck arrives, sees that they are Athenians, and, presuming that their physical separation implies a lack of love, supposes that he has found his target. He administers the juice to Lysander's eyes and leaves. Demetrius appears, pursued by Helena. He shakes her off and goes on alone. Lysander awakes, and, seeing Helena, falls in love with her. She, offended by his seeming fickleness, leaves. He follows her, and Hermia wakes to find herself alone. Titania remains asleep.

*Act 3, Scene 1*
Quince, Bottom, and their colleagues rehearse in the woods. Puck happens on them and decides to make mischief; he gives Bottom an ass' head, which all but he can see. The other artisans are frightened by this transformation and flee. Bottom, unaware of it, concludes that they are attempting to scare him. To demonstrate his courage, he sings a song, thus waking Titania, who falls in love with him as a result of Oberon's magic. Claiming him, she assigns him an entourage of four fairies, PEASEBLOSSOM, COBWEB, MOTH (2), and MUSTARDSEED.

*Act 3, Scene 2*
Puck reports on Titania's ludicrous infatuation, to Oberon's delight. Demetrius and Hermia appear, arguing. She leaves angrily, and Demetrius, worn out, falls asleep. Oberon realises that the wrong man has been treated with the magical juice. He commands Puck to lure Helena, while he himself charms Demetrius with the herb. When Helena arrives, Lysander follows, pleading his love. Demetrius wakes; he falls in love with Helena and begins to praise her beauty. She concludes that the two men are mocking her, and she chastises them. Hermia enters in search of Lysander. She expresses bewilderment at her lover's new preference for Helena. Helena takes this as a deliberate insult and concludes that Hermia has joined the men in belittling her. After a series of exchanges, during which first the men and then the women almost come to blows, Lysander and Demetrius stalk off to fight a duel, Helena flees Hermia's wrath, and Hermia leaves baffled. Oberon directs Puck to summon a dense fog and then to impersonate each man to the other and lead them away from any conflict. Then he is to apply an antidote to Lysander's eyes. Puck leads the men on separate chases until each falls exhausted on an opposite side of the stage. Helena and Hermia, both lost in the woods, find spots to sleep. Puck squeezes the juice on Lysander's eyes, singing a song of reconciliation.

*Act 4, Scene 1*
Watched by Oberon, Titania leads Bottom into the clearing where the lovers sleep. Bottom is pampered by his fairy attendants, and he requests hay to eat. Titania speaks adoringly to Bottom and curls up to sleep with him. Puck appears, and Oberon confides that Titania has surrendered her changeling to him; he decides to release her from his spell. He wakes her and tells Puck to remove the ass' head from Bottom. After casting a spell of deep sleep on the mortals, the fairies leave. Theseus, Hippolyta, and Egeus enter; they are hunting with hounds. They discover the lovers and wake them. Lysander tells of his and Hermia's intended elopement, and Egeus angrily demands his execution for having attempted to prevent Hermia's marriage to Demetrius. However, Demetrius an-

nounces his intention to marry Helena. Theseus is delighted and commands that the two reunited couples shall be married that day, along with himself and Hippolyta. They all return to Athens, leaving Bottom, who awakes amazedly and muses on the strange dream that he can't quite remember.

*Act 4, Scene 2*
Quince, Flute, Snout, and Starveling wonder at Bottom's absence, and Snug arrives to tell them that the Duke's festivities are about to begin. Their distress is relieved when Bottom arrives, not quite able to recount what he has seen, but prepared to lead them on-stage.

*Act 5, Scene 1*
Theseus discounts the lovers' experiences in the woods, attributing to them a madness that also affects lunatics and poets. The newlyweds arrive, and Theseus calls for entertainment. Quince's production of *Pyramus and Thisbe* is performed, provoking amusement. Following the performance, everyone departs,

and the fairies, led by Puck, arrive to bless the marriages. They leave, and Puck delivers an EPILOGUE suggesting that, if the audience is offended by being asked to believe in fairies, they should simply pretend that they have slept and dreamed.

COMMENTARY

Scholars generally agree that *A Midsummer Night's Dream* was written to be performed at an aristocratic wedding. Everything in the play is related to the theme of marriage. Theseus and Hippolyta's nuptials are the goal towards which all the action is directed—the fairies have come to Athens to bless the occasion; the artisans' performance is intended for it; Hermia's judgement, and thus the climax of the lovers' story, is scheduled to coincide with it, and finally the young lovers are married along with the ducal couple. The very first line emphasises the importance of the forthcoming 'nuptial hour' (1.1.1), and the dénouement is a blessing of the three weddings in terms that suggest a performance within a dwelling, as Oberon orders the

*A fairy procession from the 1935 film of* A Midsummer Night's Dream *by Max Reinhardt. The Austrian-born director was famous for his lavish sets and costumes.* (Courtesy of Culver Pictures, Inc.)

fairies to distribute blessings 'through this house' (5.1. 388). (See 'Theatrical History of the Play'.)

The play suits such an occasion well, for it has the formality of a MASQUE, an entertainment often performed at noble weddings. Like many masques, this comedy presents a world of magic and metamorphosis in brilliant spectacles involving picturesque supernatural beings. It also makes much use of music and dance, and its finale is itself masquelike. It is given over to celebration, with further dancing and a comical performance *(Pyramus and Thisbe)* similar to an anti-masque—the realistic farce that was commonly part of a masque itself. Like a masque again, Acts 1–4 are very symmetrically plotted, moving from the court of Theseus to the woods and back again. In part, this reflects an archetypal plot pattern of withdrawal and return, common in the romance literature preceding Shakespeare and in his own work, but the arrangement here is particularly formal. (Compare, for example, *The Two Gentlemen of Verona* or *Cymbeline.*) There are internal symmetries also. For example, two songs are used—one to put Titania to sleep in 2.2, and the other to wake her in 3.1—and Quince and his cast appear four times, twice on either side of Bottom's adventure.

As is natural in such a formal context, the characters are stylised and unrealistic: they do not interact as people normally do. Theseus and Hipplyta are remote ideals of classical calm; Puck is a typical goblin; and Titania and Oberon are distant in their regal immortality, elemental forces of nature with the power to influence the climate and to bless marriages. Only Bottom and his fellow artisans represent ordinary people, and they are plainly character types with little personality beyond their buffoonery.

The lovers, too, are static; although Lysander and Demetrius are transformed by Oberon's magical herb, they are altered only in their stance towards another character, and in Lysander's case the change is only temporary. Demetrius is left in a position he had held before the opening of the play and thus is ultimately unchanged also. Change occurs only in the pattern of the lovers' relationships, which has often been compared to a dance: first the two men address one of the women while the other woman is alone; then one man's affection is changed, and a circular chase unfolds. Lysander woos Helena, who is still pursuing Demetrius, who continues to court Hermia, who still wants Lysander. Next, when Demetrius is put under Oberon's spell, the two men face the other woman, and the first woman is alone. Finally the only stable arrangement is achieved, with Lysander and Demetrius each returned to his original love interest.

Such intricate masquelike plotting is appropriate not only to a festive occasion but also to the world of dreamy confusion that is central to the story. Much of the action, from 2.1 into 4.1, takes place at night; the lovers assert several times that they are looking at the stars (e.g., 3.2.61, 3.2.188), thus drawing attention to the night-time setting (which was usually enacted in afternoon sunlight in an Elizabethan public theatre). The nocturnal universe of shadowy strangeness is further evoked in the play's imagery. The moon is referred to prominently, beginning in the very first few lines (1.1.3,4,9): Moonlight is mentioned three times more often in *A Midsummer Night's Dream* than in all of Shakespeare's other plays combined. In many different contexts the moon is used in figures of speech: to indicate time of day (1.1.209–210) and of month (1.1. 83); with reference to catastrophic flooding (2.1.103) and to the speed of fairies (2.1.7, 4.1.97); cuckoldry (5.1.232) and in connection with chastity (1.1.73, 2.1. 162) and opposition to chastity (3.1.191–193). 'Moonshine' is even a character in the artisans' play. The eerie quality of moonlight is reinforced by frequent evocations of the beauty of the woods at night.

Flowers are frequently mentioned as well, as in 1.1. 185 and 2.1.110, and of course the magical aphrodisiac is a flower (2.1.166). Even the doggerel of *Pyramus and Thisbe* provides a floral motif (3.1.88–89). Birds, too, are alluded to throughout the play. Afoot (5.1.380) and in flight (3.2.21), as emblems of sight (2.2.113, 3.2.142) and of sound (1.1.184, 1.2.78, 5.1. 362), they sing (5.1.384) and soar (3.2.23) in the play's highly lyrical language. Even Bottom, when he sings, brings forth a country ditty about birds (3.1.120–128).

Animals also inhabit the enchanted woods, though they lurk ominously, for the most part. Even a bee poses a threat (4.1.15–16), however slight. The image of preying carnivores is invoked by Helena to describe her desperate pursuit of Demetrius in 2.1.232–233. Dead sheep are part of Titania's vision of disordered nature (2.1.97). Theseus evokes a night-time fear that a bush may be a bear (5.1.22). Potential tragedy is presented in a humorous context only, in the artisans' INTERLUDE, but in that episode tragedy is wrought by a ravening lion. Puck, introducing the fairies' blessings with a reminder of the cruel world that they may also be associated with, remarks that 'the hungry lion roars, / And the wolf behowls the moon' (5.1.357–358).

Indeed, the dream-world of the play involves several hints of nightmare, providing a contrast to its harmonies of love. Hermia awakes from a nightmare at the end of 2.2, and the 'drooping fog, as black as Acheron' (3.2.357) summoned by Puck to deceive Lysander and Demetrius carries a hint of terror, though its purpose is benign. Shakespeare never lets the fairy world seem altogether sweet and light; Puck has a touch of malice to his personality, and he reminds the audience of the fairies' alliance to dark powers in the speech, cited above, that introduces the final ritual, the blessing of the house.

One of the functions of that blessing, indeed, is to

exorcise all potential evil at last. The interlude has just performed a similar task in rendering a lovers' tragedy as farce. In fact, Quince, Bottom, and the boys act as an earthy counterweight to the uncanny airiness of the fairies. This is like an exorcism, because the unreal world of Puck and Oberon, Titania and Peaseblossom is supremely alien and potentially dangerous. The mortals can be manipulated and never know it: the lovers, returning to Athens, believe themselves to have awakened from dreams (4.1.197–198), as does Bottom (4.1.204).

But generations of viewers and readers and critics have felt compelled to ask whether Shakespeare intends us to take the enchanted woods as dream or as reality. The title of the play—related to 'midsummer madness', proverbially a lovers' sickness—suggests that the mortals' experience in the woods is but a figment, perhaps that the whole play is. But we the audience, having witnessed it ourselves, may agree with Hippolyta that 'all the story of the night told over, . . . grows to something of great constancy' (5.1.23–26). Unlike Theseus, who sees only lunacy in the 'forms of things unknown [that] imagination bodies forth' (5.1.14–15), Hippolyta recognises the essential reality, or constancy, that 'things unknown' have, when given by the 'poet's pen . . . a local habitation and a name' (5.1.16–17). We the audience can realise even more: that the play, the poet's embodiment of imaginary things, has made the unreal real.

We must return to our starting point, the occasion for which the play was evidently written. Shakespeare's original audience, guests at a wedding, was removed from the world of reality, just as modern audiences are, and then returned to it by the ritual at its close. The exact definition of reality is not addressed by the play; indeed, the play's ambiguity on the point is deliberate. The experience is all that matters, and the experience, as Bottom knew, is a profound one. When he wakes from his experience in the woods and observes, 'The eye of man hath not heard, the ear of man hath not seen, man's hand is not able to taste, his tongue to conceive, nor his heart to report, what my dream was' (4.1.209–212). Bottom has experienced, though he is unable to express it, the depths of mystery that underlie all things, real and unreal alike. By evoking such awareness, the play fulfils its original and primary function as a celebratory hymn to the beauties of married love.

## SOURCES OF THE PLAY

*A Midsummer Night's Dream* is one of the few Shakespearean plays that seem to have been generated principally from the playwright's own imagination; no known literary work is a source for it. However, it draws on a number of diverse traditions—the courtly spectacle or pageant, the folklore of fairies, and a delight in the antics of the rustic CLOWN (1)—that were common in Shakespeare's day. And the playwright did make use of a number of ideas and images that came from literature, and *A Midsummer Night's Dream*—more, perhaps, than a work that is based firmly on another work, such as *Romeo and Juliet* or *Hamlet*—suggests the range of the author's reading.

At least a dozen works provided general ideas for and/or bits and pieces of this play. Prominent among them is one of the most famous of ancient books, well known to Shakespeare and his audience, *The Golden Ass*, by Apuleius, written in the 2nd century A.D. and translated into English by William ADLINGTON in 1566; this tale tells of a man transformed into an ass. Shakespeare also took ingredients from several works by his greatest English predecessor, Geoffrey CHAUCER, notably 'The Knight's Tale', which provided the characters Theseus and Hippolyta as Duke of Athens and Queen of the Amazons, as well as several situations in the play: the marriage of Chaucer's ducal couple is postponed by the arbitration of a dispute, for example, and Theseus uses his authority to uphold a supernatural resolution of complicated lovers' quarrels. He also interrupts a duel between rivals, as Oberon does in the play. Further, Chaucer's 'The Merchant's Tale' presents a fairy king and queen who are at odds over a human being and who intervene in mortal affairs. Also, his 'Sir Tophas', a satire of knightly romance, features a comical knight-errant who dreams of marrying an 'elf-queene'.

One of Shakespeare's favourite books, OVID's *Metamorphoses* (in the 1567 translation by Arthur GOLDING) was the source of the legend of Pyramus and Thisbe as presented in the interlude in 5.1. That the playwright also knew Ovid in the original Latin is demonstrated by his use of the name Titania, which is not in Golding, but which the Roman poet used several times in contexts relevant to the play's motifs—as another name for Diana, the moon goddess, and for Circe, who transformed men into animals.

The Fairy King, Oberon, was a well-known figure both in folklore and in medieval literature. In *Huon of Bordeaux*, a 13th-century French adventure tale translated by Lord BERNERS (1534), he resembles Shakespeare's character in presiding over a magical forest where mortals become lost and in explicitly distinguishing himself from evil spirits; in both stories he intervenes to bring about a happy ending.

The play incorporates many minor echoes of a work of Shakespeare's own time, *The Discoverie of Witchcraft* (1584) by Reginald SCOT, a tract opposing the prosecution of witches. Shakespeare used Scot's accounts of fairy lore, especially about Robin Goodfellow, or Puck, although Scot derides belief in such things as groundless superstition. Scot also tells of a magical procedure reputed to give a man the head of an ass.

Shakespeare's knowledge of other works is also reflected in the play. These works include Edmund

SPENSER'S *Shepheardes Calender* (1579), Bartholomew YONG's translation of *Diana Enamorada,* by the Portuguese author Jorge de MONTEMAYOR (a chief source of *The Two Gentlemen of Verona*), several plays by SENECA and several by John LYLY, plus novels *Euphues* (1578) and *Euphues and His England* (1580). In addition, Thomas NORTH's translation of PLUTARCH's 'Life of Theseus' (1579) provided a number of proper names; this was Shakespeare's first use of a source that would become very important to him.

## TEXT OF THE PLAY

Dating the composition of *A Midsummer Night's Dream* precisely is not possible with the existing evidence, but we can assume it was written in 1595 or early 1596. The comical worry about the possible ferocity of a theatrical lion (1.2.70–75, 3.1.26–44, 5.1.214–221) was almost certainly inspired by an account, published in London in late 1594, of a planned appearance by a lion at a christening, cancelled as possibly dangerous and certainly alarming. Further, Titania's description of the cataclysmic weather caused by her dispute with Oberon (2.1.88–114) apparently refers to a series of three extraordinarily cold, wet summers in 1594–1596. This allows us to assume that the play was written between 1595 and 1598, when it was recorded in the list of Shakespeare's works assembled by Francis MERES. However, we know that from 1596 onwards Shakespeare was working on plays—*The Merchant of Venice, 1* and *2 Henry IV,* and *The Merry Wives of Windsor*—very unlike the lyrical *Dream.* The latter work, moreover, is linked stylistically to several plays—*Love's Labour's Lost, Romeo and Juliet,* and *Richard II*—that can be dated to 1593–1595.

The first edition of the *Dream* was published as a QUARTO by Thomas FISHER in 1600. It appears to have been printed from Shakespeare's FOUL PAPERS, with irregular stage directions and other mistakes that would have been corrected in any later manuscript. This edition is known as Q1. The next edition, Q2, was printed by Thomas PAVIER and William JAGGARD in 1619, as part of the notorious FALSE FOLIO; it was dated 1600 in order not to seem a new, unauthorised publication. Q2 was simply an inaccurate reprint of Q1, with many minor errors. It nonetheless served as the basis for the FIRST FOLIO edition of 1623, though its editors also referred to a PROMPT-BOOK of the play, resulting in superior stage directions in their version. Q1, derived from Shakespeare's own manuscript, is regarded as the most authoritative text, and it has been the basis for all modern editions, except with respect to stage directions, for which the Folio text is favoured.

## THEATRICAL HISTORY OF THE PLAY

The first performance of *A Midsummer Night's Dream* was almost certainly at an aristocratic wedding of the 1590s, although no record of the event exists. The occasion may have been the marriage in February 1596 of Elizabeth Carey, grand-daughter of Henry CAREY (2) the patron of the CHAMBERLAIN'S MEN, with whom Shakespeare was associated at the time. Another possible wedding was that of the Earl of DERBY (3) a year earlier, for Derby's older brother, Lord STRANGE, had been the same company's patron before his death in 1594.

In 1600 the title page of the first Quarto edition of the play asserted that it had 'been sundry times publickely acted' by the Chamberlain's Men, but the earliest recorded performance, perhaps of an adaptation, was held at the court of King James I in 1604 under the title *A Play of Robin Goodfellow.* No other productions during the playwright's lifetime are known.

A scandal was aroused in 1631 by a Sunday performance of the *Dream* in the house of a bishop, and an excerpt from the play was performed surreptitiously between 1642 and 1660, when the theatres were closed by the revolutionary government. This abridged version was published as a DROLL—*The Merry Conceits of Bottom the Weaver*— in 1661 by Henry MARSH and Francis KIRKMAN. The diarist Samuel PEPYS attended a performance of the *Dream* in 1662 and called it 'the most insipid ridiculous play that ever I saw in my life'.

This was the last recorded performance for more than a century and a half, though many adaptations were popular throughout the period. The first and most successful of these was Henry PURCELL's opera *The Fairy Queen,* produced in 1692 by Thomas BETTERTON. Musical versions continued to be produced in the 18th century, most notably Richard LEVERIDGE's operetta *A Comic Masque of Pyramus and Thisbe* (1716, revived 1745), which satirised the current London enthusiasm for Italian opera. As its title suggests, this work included only the SUB-PLOT of *A Midsummer Night's Dream.* This material was also tapped by Charles JOHNSON (2), who incorporated the comical interlude into LOVE IN A FOREST (1723), his version of *As You Like It.* David GARRICK used the main plot of Shakespeare's play, eliminating Bottom and his friends, in *The Fairies* (1755), an opera incorporating 27 songs by various authors. Frederic REYNOLDS (1) continued the musical tradition in 1816, with an operatic medley based on the *Dream.*

The earliest restoration of Shakespeare's text occurred in 1827, in Ludwig TIECK's Berlin production of SCHLEGEL's German translation featuring the famous overture and incidental music by Felix Mendelssohn (1809–1847), composed in the previous year. Mendelssohn's music also accompanied the first English revival, in 1840. Subsequent 19th-century productions included a grandly scenic staging by Charles KEAN (1) and a more restrained version by Samuel PHELPS. The 19th-century tendency to spectacular presentations of the *Dream* reached its height in Beer-bohm TREE's 1900 production, which featured live rabbits and birds amid dense foliage.

*A Midsummer Night's Dream* has been among the most frequently performed of Shakespeare's plays in the 20th century. Harley GRANVILLE-BARKER's avant-garde rendering of 1914 (New York, 1915) employed a rigorously Shakespearean text, but it also featured stylised botanical motifs in place of realistic scenery and fairies who were painted gold and used mechanical gestures to emphasise their exotic nature. This highly controversial production was influenced by the *Ballets Russes* of Diaghilev. Max REINHARDT presented highly altered versions of Shakespeare's text on the London stage in the 1920s and in a FILM of 1935, starring James Cagney as Bottom and Mickey Rooney as Puck. More conventional productions have included those of Tyrone GUTHRIE and Peter HALL (5). In 1970 Peter BROOK (2) aroused as much controversy as Granville-Barker had a half-century earlier, with a *Dream* incorporating circus acts and costumes in a bare white set. The musical tradition has continued, with operas by Carl Orff (1895–1982) and Benjamin BRITTEN (1960). Purcell's *The Fairy Queen* was revived in 1946. *Swinging the Dream* (1939) was a jazz version featuring the Benny Goodman Sextet, with Louis Armstrong as Bottom. The play has been made as a FILM seven times (five of them silent movies). It has also been seen on TELEVISION eight times.

**Milan**   City in Italy, possibly the setting of several scenes in *The Two Gentlemen of Verona*. These scenes involve the members of the court of the DUKE (5) of Milan, but the geography of the play is confused, at best, and it is difficult to know where the characters are much of the time. The actual city of Milan is in no way depicted in any case. Elsewhere in Shakespeare's works, Milan is referred to a number of times, though it is nowhere significant. It is most prominent in *The Tempest*, where the magician PROSPERO has been deposed as Duke of Milan and in the course of the play recovers that position. However, the whole play takes place on the magic island where Prospero rules in exile, and Milan is merely mentioned.

**Miles Gloriosus**   Traditional character type, dating from ancient Roman drama, that influenced several Shakespearean character types, most notably ARMADO in *Love's Labour's Lost*. The Miles Gloriosus, a foolish, bragging soldier, was well known in Shakespeare's day through Latin texts and, more important, through the braggart captain of Italian COMMEDIA DELL' ARTE. This *capitano* was usually a Spaniard, a reflection of the Spanish role in the wars that ravaged Italy in the 16th century. His nationality was naturally adopted by Shakespeare, for hostility towards Spain was also a central element of the contemporary English world-

view. Besides Armado, the Shakespearean characters who partake of the same ancestry include AJAX and THERSITES in *Troilus and Cressida* and PAROLLES in *All's Well That Ends Well*. Although FALSTAFF is often cited in this connection, he transcends the empty vainglory of the traditional type. Maurice MORGANN—the 18th-century writer on Falstaff—observed that the Miles Gloriosus provides the fat knight with no more than a trace of flavour.

**Miller (1), James (1706–1744)**   Eighteenth-century playwright, author of *The Universal Passion* (1737), a popular adaptation combining Shakespeare's *Much Ado About Nothing* and Molière's *La Princesse d'Élide*. Miller, who became famous for a satire he wrote while he was still a student, later became a clergyman but continued to write plays—generally adaptations of French works. Several of these, including *The Universal Passion,* were successfully produced.

**Miller (2), Jonathan (b. 1934)**   British director, creator of many modern productions of Shakespeare's plays, including a powerful *Merchant of Venice* (1970), with Laurence OLIVIER as SHYLOCK. He is also noted for his numerous Shakespearean TELEVISION productions in the early 1980s, as part of the BBC's complete cycle of the plays.

**Millington, Thomas (active 1583–1603)**   Publisher and bookseller in LONDON, producer of first editions of several Shakespeare plays. In 1594 Millington joined with Edward WHITE (1) to publish the first edition of *Titus Andronicus,* a QUARTO (Q1). The same year, on his own, he published Q1 of *2 Henry VI* (known as THE CONTENTION), and in 1595 he produced Q1 of *3 Henry VI* (THE TRUE TRAGEDY). In 1600 he published a second edition of both these works and, in partnership with John BUSBY, the first edition of *Henry V.* Each of these editions was pirated, for each is a BAD QUARTO, assembled from the memories of actors and published without permission of the acting company that owned the rights.

**Milton, John (1608–1674)**   Major English poet, author of *Paradise Lost, Paradise Regained, Samson Agonistes,* and many shorter works, including a well-known EPITAPH on Shakespeare. The first of Milton's poems to be published was 'An Epitaph on the admirable Dramaticke Poet, W. Shakespeare', which appeared anonymously among the introductory verses in the second FOLIO (1632). It also appeared in the third and fourth Folios (1663, 1685). It is considered one of the poet's best short works (16 lines), an elegiac lyric reflecting on the power of Shakespeare's art to outlast his death. Milton also mentions Shakespeare, in another early work, *L'Allegro,* calling him 'Fancy's child', whose plays 'warble his native wood-notes wild'.

**Miranda** Character in *The Tempest*, daughter of the magician PROSPERO. Miranda, exiled with her father at the age of two, has lived 12 years with him on the island he rules through sorcery. It is uninhabited except for the supernatural creatures ARIEL and CALIBAN, so when Prospero's magic brings people to the island, Miranda sees her first young man, FERDINAND (2), with whom she falls in love—and he with her—in 1.2. Prospero has planned this—Ferdinand is the son of his old enemy, King ALONSO of Naples—but he pretends to oppose the couple's love to ensure that Ferdinand does not take Miranda lightly. Prospero takes the young man captive, but Miranda contrives to visit him, and they confess their love and plan to marry in 3.1; in 4.1 Prospero declares his approval. As part of Prospero's arrangements for a conclusion of forgiveness and happiness, in 5.1 Miranda and Ferdinand are revealed to King Alonso, who believed his son had drowned. Miranda's marriage plans are confirmed, and Alonso declares that she and Ferdinand will inherit the kingdom of Naples.

Miranda does not speak often or at length, but she is established as a paragon of maidenhood. She displays a touching compassion—fearing for the shipwreck victims, she says, 'O, I have suffered / With those that I saw suffer!' (1.2.5–6). She also shows a capacity for delighted wonder; on first seeing Ferdinand, she cries, 'I might call him / A thing divine; for nothing natural / I ever saw so noble' (1.2.420–422). Her angry disdain for Caliban, who once attempted to rape her, displays the moral sensibility she has learned from her father, but her innocence of society gives her a simplicity that in a less overtly fantastic context would be disconcerting. She ignores the fact that Ferdinand is the son of her father's enemy, and at the play's close she is filled with pleased admiration for all of the king's party, even though some of them are arrant villains, saying, 'How beauteous mankind is! O brave new world, / That has such people in 't!' (5.1. 183–184).

Miranda represents the compassionate, forgiving, and optimistic potential in humanity. She is the only human character in the play who does not undergo some sort of purging transformation, for she does not need to. Innocent of life's difficulties and compromises, she repudiates evil and responds to nobility and beauty. She is most pointedly contrasted with the evil Caliban. Both were raised together by Prospero, but she has become a person of moral sensibility, while he is a would-be rapist who declares that his only use for language is to curse. Their responses to the arrival of strangers on the island are also contrasting: she is filled with demure awe, he with crass fear.

Though innocent, Miranda is nonetheless mindful of sexual propriety, speaking of her 'modesty, the jewel in [her] dower' (3.1.53–54) and declaring that if Ferdinand will not marry her, she will 'die [his] maid' (3.1.84). Her virginity—stressed repeatedly by the men, as in Ferdinand's first declaration of love and in Prospero's emphatic concern about sex before marriage—link her to an ancient archetype, the fertile woman, producer of new generations. The goddesses at her betrothal MASQUE sing of 'Earth's increase' and 'plants with goodly burthen bowing' (4.1.110, 113), making it clear that the occasion concerns reproduction. They also stress Miranda's virginity, for a sure knowledge of paternity has traditionally been very important to the orderly continuation of society. This is especially true among rulers, and Miranda's future as a queen is frequently pointed up. At the play's close, after Prospero's reconciliations have been effected, GONZALO blesses the moment and delights in the prospect that Prospero's 'issue / Should become Kings of Naples' (5.1.205–206). Miranda thus helps fulfil that most ancient of necessities for human societies, continuance into the future. She and Ferdinand embody the regeneration that is the theme of the play's close.

Miranda's name—Latin for 'admirable' (literally, 'to be wondered at')—was coined by Shakespeare. It reflects not only her qualities as an example of innocent womanhood but also her own admiring nature and the extraordinary sense of wonder that the play as a whole conveys. It is punned on by Ferdinand when he calls her 'Admir'd Miranda!' (3.1.37) and, more subtly, when he exclaims 'O you wonder!' (1.2.429).

***Mirror for Magistrates, A*** English anthology of biographies in verse (published in seven versions, from 1559 to 1619) that influenced Shakespeare, especially in the writing of the HISTORY PLAYS. Originally intended as a sequel to John LYDGATE's *Falls of Princes* (1431–1438, publ. 1494)—a translation of BOCCACCIO's *The Fate of Illustrious Men* (1355–1374)—*A Mirror* reflects the RENAISSANCE interest in individual lives, along with a traditional concern for the fates of kings and other monumental figures. Most tales told of the dire fate, usually ending in violent death, of a villainous tyrant or would-be tyrant, for, as its title suggests, the book was intended to exercise a moral influence. The first edition was compiled in 1555, but was suppressed by the government of Queen Mary and not published until 1559 under ELIZABETH (1), and contained 19 such 'tragedies' (see TRAGEDY) by various authors. In 1563 a second edition appeared that featured seven more biographies and included Thomas SACKVILLE's *Induction* and his *Complaint of Buckingham*, the only material in *A Mirror* that has been considered fine literature by later ages.

The material in these first two compilations dealt chiefly with English history from RICHARD II onwards, and it provided Shakespeare with details for most of his history plays. John HIGGINS, whose interests were more antiquarian, issued the third and fourth editions of *A Mirror* (1574, 1578), to which he contributed 16 poems about heroes of ancient Britain. One of these was consulted by Shakespeare in writing *King Lear*. In 1587 a fifth edition (the one Shakespeare knew) appeared. It incorporated with the earlier material new work that included another major contribution from Higgins—an additional 24 lives, all but one from the classical world. His biography of Julius CAESAR (1) provided material for Shakespeare's *Julius Caesar*. Two later editions of *A Mirror*—in 1610 and 1619—included tales of virtue rewarded and added positive lessons to the older accounts of villainy punished.

**Misenum**   Ancient Italian town, location for two scenes in *Antony and Cleopatra*. In 2.6 the co-rulers of Rome—Octavius CAESAR (2), LEPIDUS, and Mark ANTONY—meet with POMPEY (2), whose naval forces have been pillaging Italian coastal towns, and negotiate a peace treaty. Pompey accepts the rule of Sicily and Sardinia in exchange for which he will rid 'all the sea of pirates' (2.6.36), that is, his own followers represented by MENAS and MENECRATES. In 2.7 the negotiators celebrate their agreement with a drunken banquet aboard Pompey's ship, anchored off Misenum. During the banquet, the true colours of several of the participants are revealed.

Located on the northern headland of the Bay of Naples, Misenum was the site of a meeting such as is seen in the play, and it resulted in a pact known as the Treaty of Misenum in 39 B.C. Essentially, Pompey was added to the Roman Triumvirate, but the peace did not last long. Pompey renewed his raids on the Italian coast and provoked Caesar to invade his base at MESSINA and to destroy him for good in 36 B.C., a conquest that is referred to in 3.5.4.

**Mistress (1) Alice Ford**   One of the title characters in *The Merry Wives of Windsor*, wife of Frank FORD (1). When Mistress Ford and her friend MISTRESS (3) Page receive identical love letters from FALSTAFF, they feel their honour has been insulted by a gross lecher, and they plot revenge. In their plan Mistress Ford serves as bait for Falstaff, who comes to her house, where the appearance of her jealous husband causes the lecher's humiliating flight, first in a hamper of dirty laundry and then in disguise as an old woman, pummelled by Ford. Mistress Ford suffers from her husband's neurotic jealousy, but she bears with him, and we sympathise when she quietly observes that Mistress Page's more reasonable man makes her 'the happier woman' (2.1.103). By the same token we share her delight when Ford's jealousy leads him to be made as foolish as Falstaff; 'I know not which pleases me better', she exults, 'that my husband is deceived, or Sir John' (3.3. 164–165).

**Mistress (2) Overdone**   Character in *Measure for Measure*, the keeper of a bordello in VIENNA. Mistress Over-

done's principal role is as a stereotypical member of Vienna's underworld, which stands in contrast to the world of the major characters. Her servant POMPEY (1) is the most important figure of this comic SUB-PLOT. Mistress Overdone is a familiar figure to LUCIO and his friends; her entrance inspires each GENTLEMAN (5) to jest about venereal disease, establishing the bawdy, depraved tone of the sub-plot. She also introduces a major element of the main plot when she first appears in 1.2 and tells of the prosecution of CLAUDIO (3). She is comically presented as a typical innkeeper, worried about business, though this also includes worrying about the government's attempts to fight prostitution. When she is imprisoned in 3.2 she complains that she has been informed against by Lucio. This reminds us that her world of petty vice is not truly a comic one.

A comic sub-plot featuring a bordello madam and her servant was found by Shakespeare in one of the sources for *Measure for Measure*, George WHETSTONE's *Promos and Cassandra* (1578). However, Shakespeare invented the preposterous names they bear in his play; Mistress Overdone's name reflects her status as a veteran of her profession.

**Mistress (3) Margaret Page**   One of the title characters in *The Merry Wives of Windsor*, wife of George PAGE (12) and mother of ANNE (3) and WILLIAM (1). In 2.1 Mistress Page's response to FALSTAFF's love letter establishes the position of the honest and forthright wives as enemies of Falstaff's amorality. After reviewing the insult to her wifely honour, she concludes, 'How shall I be revenged on him? For revenged I will be, as sure as his guts are made of puddings' (2.1.29–31). When MISTRESS (1) Ford receives an identical letter, the two friends join forces. Mistress Page's role is to break in on Falstaff's visits to Mistress Ford, sparking his humiliating exits, first hidden in a hamper of dirty laundry and then beaten into the streets while dressed in an old woman's clothes. In 4.4 Mistress Page devises Falstaff's final punishment, his torment by children disguised as fairies. If she seems insensitive in seeking to marry Anne to the obnoxious Dr CAIUS (2), she accepts the outcome graciously when Anne elopes with FENTON, saying, 'Master Fenton, Heaven give you many, many merry days!' (5.5.236–237), and she proposes the pleasant resolution of the play, that all the chief characters 'laugh this sport o'er by a country fire, Sir John [Falstaff] and all' (5.5.239–240).

Mistress Page's ebullient strength is well matched with her husband's milder cheerfulness. With him, she contributes a large share of the play's charm, in both her vigorous good humour and her confident assertion of traditional values.

**Mistress (4) Quickly**   Character in *The Merry Wives of Windsor*. See QUICKLY.

**Modjeska, Helena (1844–1909)**  Polish-born American actress. Born Helena Opid in Cracow, she followed her brother into the local theatre, where she got her stage name from a brief first marriage. She became a leading actress in Warsaw and then, in 1876, was forced to flee from Russian-governed Poland with her second husband, who was a Polish nationalist. They went to San Francisco, where Modjeska quickly learned English and played JULIET (1) and OPHELIA, among other parts. Immediately recognised as a superior actress, she made her New York debut the next year and for almost 30 years, despite suffering a stroke in 1897, she was among the most popular of American actresses. Among Shakespearean roles, she was best known for VIOLA, ISABELLA, and LADY (6) MACBETH, playing the latter several times in the 1880s opposite Edwin BOOTH (2).

**Mohun, Michael (c. 1625–1684)**  English actor. Mohun was a boy actor (see CHILDREN'S COMPANIES) in Christopher BEESTON's company in the 1630s. He fought with distinction for the royalists in the Civil Wars, and when the theatres were reopened upon the restoration of the monarchy in 1660, he joined the King's Company under Thomas KILLIGREW. He was among the most admired actors of the period, though he mostly played secondary roles, usually opposite Charles HART (1). He was particularly noted for his portrayals of IAGO and CASSIUS.

**Mömpelgard, Frederick, Count of (later Duke of) Württemberg (d. 1608)**  Historical figure and contemporary of Shakespeare, alluded to in *The Merry Wives of Windsor*. As part of a sequence of anti-German jokes associated with the theft of horses from the HOST (2) in Act 4, several references are made to German travellers in England and particularly to a German Duke who is *not* expected to come to Windsor (4.3. 4–5; 4.5.81–84). These obscure allusions have a particular connection both to Mömpelgard and to the occasion for which the play was written.

Frederick of Mömpelgard was heir apparent to the dukedom of Württemberg, then an independent country in what is now south-western Germany. In 1592 he visited Windsor and other English cities (those specified in 4.5.70–74) and developed an enthusiasm for the Order of the Garter. He repeatedly solicited Queen ELIZABETH (1) for membership in the knightly order; finally, after he had inherited the dukedom and achieved some importance in European affairs, she admitted him. However, in what appears to have been a calculated slight, he was not notified of his admission in time for him to attend the investment ceremonies in the spring of 1597. *The Merry Wives* was written for precisely those ceremonies, and thus the references to Mömpelgard's earlier visit, and to a German Duke who is *not* visiting, are quite evidently inside jokes intended for the play's first audience, the knights of the Garter, who will have been well aware of the Queen's action. These references appear only in the FIRST FOLIO edition of the play, which reflects the initial, private performance, and not in the 1602 QUARTO that is derived from early theatrical productions.

**Monarcho (d. before 1580)**  The nickname given to a well-known London lunatic of Shakespeare's day. Monarcho's mad claims to be ruler of the world inspired comment in contemporary documents, including a published epitaph titled 'The Phantasticall Monarke'. ARMADO, the braggart Spaniard in *Love's Labour's Lost,* is thought to have been based on this figure, for he is referred to as 'A phantasime, a Monarcho' (4.1.100). Shakespeare can never have seen Monarcho, who died when the playwright was still a teenager in STRATFORD, but he had clearly heard enough to be impressed.

**Monck, Nugent (1877–1958)**  British theatrical producer. In 1911 Monck founded an important theatrical company for the production of ELIZABETHAN DRAMA in Norwich, England. In 1921, he converted a 16th-century Norwich house into the Maddermarket Theatre, the first modern replica of an Elizabethan playhouse. There he staged many influential productions of Shakespeare's plays, in the crisp, spare manner of William POEL.

**Monmouth, Harry (Henry)**  Another name for PRINCE (6) HAL, later King HENRY V. Both as Prince and King, this character is occasionally called Harry Monmouth, after his birthplace on the Welsh border. (See, e.g., *1 Henry IV,* 5.4.58; *2 Henry IV,* 2.3.45; *Henry V,* 4.7.12–55; *1 Henry VI,* 2.5.23, 3.1.198.)

**Montague (1)**  Character in *Romeo and Juliet,* ROMEO's father and the head of the family bearing his name, rivals to the CAPULET (1) clan. Montague appears only briefly, in the three scenes in which the feud with the Capulets erupts into violence, and on each occasion he accepts in conventional terms the objections of the PRINCE (1) to the fighting. In the final scene of reconciliation (5.3), he offers to commission a golden statue of JULIET (1) as a public memorial to the love that the feud has doomed.

Although Shakespeare believed the Montague-Capulet conflict was a historical event, it in fact never occurred. See VERONA.

**Montague (2), Lady**  Minor character in *Romeo and Juliet,* mother of ROMEO and wife of MONTAGUE (1). Lady Montague appears only twice, beside her husband, and speaks only one line. In 5.3 she is said to have died of grief following Romeo's banishment.

## Montague (3), John Neville, Lord (c. 1428–1471)

Historical figure and minor character in *3 Henry VI*, a supporter of the Duke of YORK (8) and his sons who deserts their cause to join his brother, the Earl of WARWICK (3), in his revolt. Montague is a Yorkist through 4.1, when he declares his loyalty to King ED-WARD IV, although Warwick's rebellion has begun. However, when he next appears, in 4.6, he is with Warwick. His death in the battle of BARNET is reported in 5.2.

The motives of the historical Montague, omitted by Shakespeare, are interesting for the light they cast on the politics of the WARS OF THE ROSES. Upon his accession, Edward had confiscated the estates of the Earl of NORTHUMBERLAND (2) and given them to Montague. After Warwick's defection, seeking allies in the north, Edward gave them back to Northumberland's heir. Edward thought he had appeased Montague with new titles, but he was wrong. When Warwick landed in England with his invasion forces, Montague joined him and a large body of troops was placed under his command. This event is depicted in 5.1.

## Montaigne, Michael de (1533–1592)

French essayist, author of minor sources for *The Tempest* and perhaps for *Hamlet* and *King Lear*. Shakespeare knew Montainge's essays in the translation by John FLORIO, *Essayes on Morall, Politike, and Millitarie Discourses* (1603). A passage in Montaigne's essay 'Of Cannibals' is echoed in GONZALO's praise of primitive societies in *The Tempest* 2.1.143–164, and another essay, 'Of Crueltie', probably inspired PROSPERO's praise of reconciliation in 5.1.25–30. Montaigne's influence is less direct in the two tragedies. His views seem to inform some aspects of HAMLET's thought, as when he compares death to sleep and calls it a 'consummation' (*Hamlet* 3.1.63), or when he appraises man as 'this quintessence of dust' (2.2.308). In *King Lear* the villainous EDMUND's cynical notions probably reflect Montaigne's scepticism.

For the most part, however, Montaigne's sceptical, 'modern' attitudes are rejected in Shakespeare's work. Gonzalo's theory is decidedly refuted by the play as a whole, Hamlet's musings are obviously the product of despair, and the arguments of so villainous a figure as Edmund can only be disdained by a sympathetic audience. In the playwright's deployment of Montaigne's thought—as in his work in general—we can see that his allegiance lay with the old world of social hierarchy and unquestioned Christianity whose attitudes and customs Montaigne was prepared to question and often rejected. On the other hand, the two writers have in common a tolerant, accepting attitude towards humanity's foibles—reflected more in the use of Montaigne in *The Tempest* than elsewhere. That the playwright should have felt an affinity for the essayist's work is not surprising.

Montaigne was the son of a nobleman and government official of southern France. He became a lawyer in Bordeaux and frequently visited the royal court in Paris on business, once for 18 months. He pursued political ambitions at the court but was unsuccessful, and after his father's death in 1568, he retired to his estate and began writing. Literature occupied much of his time in the 1570s and again between 1586 and his death, but he also travelled, engaged in diplomacy on behalf of Henri of Navarre (later King Henri IV of FRANCE [1]), and was twice elected mayor of Bordeaux. His *Essays* were first published in 1580, with a considerably enlarged collection appearing in 1588; his last work was published posthumously. He also published a travel journal and a translation of a work by the Spanish philosopher Raimundo Sebonde (d. 1436), which sparked his longest and best-known essay, 'Apology for Raimond de Sebonde'.

Montaigne's essays record in an intimate, gossipy style his opinions on a wide range of subjects from minor domestic matters to political issues and philosophical topics. This sort of literary work was previously unknown, and Montaigne indicated the experimental nature of his writings by designating them *essais* (attempts), thus naming the genre as well as inventing it. His scepticism, curiosity, and amiable tolerance yielded essays of a philosophical ambiguity that is reflected in the wide range of critical interpretation they have inspired. Politically, Montaigne has been regarded as reactionary, liberal, and revolutionary, and in religion, as both a devout practitioner and an agnostic (in a famous remark the 19th-century critic Sainte-Beuve declared him a good Catholic but not a Christian). In any case, the *Essays* constitute a self-portrait of a reflective man whose concerns are universal and whose witty and intelligent style has charmed generations of readers. Still regarded as among the greatest works of European literature, Montaigne's essays offer one of the first examples of the individualism that was to dominate Western culture in subsequent centuries.

## Montano (1)

Name given REYNALDO (1) in the BAD QUARTO (Q1, 1604) of *Hamlet*. The name of Reynaldo's master, POLONIUS, also differs in Q1—it is CORAMBIS. The coincidence makes satire seem likely; the cabbage (Corambis) attended by a mountain (Montano) was perhaps a caricature of some noted figure, now unknown, and his assistant.

Q1 is a version of *Hamlet* compiled from the memories of actors who played in it, and some scholars suppose that Montano was the name of the equivalent character in an earlier play, now lost, the UR-HAMLET, and that it was inserted by an actor who knew that work. The fact that Shakespeare was shortly to use this uncommon name for a character in *Othello* is taken by some scholars as circumstantial evidence: the playwright presumably had encountered the name at some point in the early 17th century, perhaps while using the *Ur-Hamlet* as source material for his own play.

**Montano (2)**   Minor character in *Othello,* the governor of CYPRUS who is replaced by OTHELLO. Montano is acknowledged by the DUKE (5) of VENICE to be a competent governor, 'of most allowed sufficiency' (1.3. 224), though Othello, as a tried battle leader, is to replace him. Montano agrees with this judgement and declares his approval of the appointment as soon as he hears of it, in 2.1. He is wounded by the drunken CASSIO in 2.3, and his rank makes Cassio's offence even greater. In 5.2 he witnesses the furor following Othello's murder of DESDEMONA, and he displays soldierly alertness in chasing and capturing IAGO when he flees, but when LODOVICO arrives he takes charge, and it is clear that Montano is an inconsequential figure.

**Montemayor, Jorge de (c. 1521–1561)**   Portuguese-born author of a famous romance that was a source for several of Shakespeare's plays. Montemayor spent most of his life in Spain and wrote in Spanish. Though he was also a poet and composer, his fame rests entirely on his long prose romance, *Diana Enamorada,* which was published in Valencia c. 1559. It soon became popular throughout Europe; Bartholomew YONG translated it into English in 1582. Though this work was not published until 1598, Shakespeare knew the book in manuscript and was able to make use of it in that form. It was among the playwright's chief sources for *The Two Gentlemen of Verona* and *A Midsummer Night's Dream,* and it also probably influenced the writing of *As You Like It* and *Twelfth Night.*

**Montgomery (1) John (actually Thomas) (c. 1430–1495)**   Historical figure and minor character in *3 Henry VI,* a supporter of King EDWARD IV. In 4.7 Montgomery arrives at YORK (10) with troops with which he proposes to aid Edward, but only if Edward will attempt to regain the throne. Edward promptly declares himself king, renouncing his oath that he would not claim the crown, sworn earlier in the scene in order to gain admission to the city. The incident provides one of the many instances of broken promises in these plays.

The historical Montgomery was a loyal Yorkist, having been knighted on the field at TOWTON. He subsequently served Edward as a diplomat on many occasions. He gained great notoriety in 1475 as one of the ministers who negotiated a treaty with FRANCE (1) that aborted an English invasion attempt under terms that were widely viewed as dishonourable to England and that included an annual payment from Louis XI to each of the ministers and to King Edward.

Shakespeare seems to have confused Thomas Mont-

gomery with his father, John (d. 1449), although the BAD QUARTO edition may be the source of the error.

**Montgomery (2), Philip Herbert, Earl of (1584–1650)**   English aristocrat and co-dedicatee of the FIRST FOLIO (1623) of Shakespeare's plays. Montgomery had no connection with Shakespeare and was doubtless included in the dedication—made by John HEMINGE and Henry CONDELL—as a compliment to the other dedicatee, his brother, the Earl of PEMBROKE (3), who as lord chamberlain was responsible for the publication of plays. Also, the publishers may have anticipated Montgomery's becoming lord chamberlain himself, which he did three years later.

Montgomery was a model of the irresponsible aristocrat. He was a courtier from the age of 15, and he became a favourite of King JAMES I, who frequently had to extract him from violent quarrels and extravagant debts. He succeeded his brother as Earl of Pembroke in 1630, but he was offended that James' son, King Charles I (ruled 1625–1649), did not appreciate him sufficiently, and he retired to his country estate, nursing his hostility and eventually joining the Parliamentarian cause in the Civil Wars.

**Montjoy**   Minor character in *Henry V,* a French herald. Montjoy arrogantly delivers the FRENCH KING's challenge in 3.6.122–141 and patronisingly offers mercy on behalf of the CONSTABLE in 4.3.79–88, but he must humbly concede French defeat at AGINCOURT in 4.7.72–85. He is a dramatic pawn without personality, adding to the chivalric tableau of medieval warfare while formally presenting French attitudes to England, a more civil version of the overconfident French nobility represented by the DAUPHIN (3) and the Duke of ORLÉANS (3). Montjoy was actually the title of the chief herald of France, not his name, though 3.6.142–143 suggests that Shakespeare did not know this.

**Mopsa**   Character in *The Winter's Tale,* a shepherdess. Mopsa appears only at the shepherds' festival in 4.4, where she is a charming representative of rustic youth. She is engaged to the CLOWN (8), for which she is teased by her companion, DORCAS. She and Dorcas sing a ballad with AUTOLYCUS, and their enthusiasm is infectious, contributing to the pleasure of the occasion, which contrasts sharply with the pathos and stress of the first part of the play. Mopsa is pleasingly comical as well. When she declares that she wants the Clown to buy her some sheet music, she adds naïvely, 'I love a ballad in print . . . for then we are sure they are true' (4.4.261–262). She then supposes there is truth in a ballad about a usurer's wife who gives birth to bags of money.

The name Mopsa was conventionally rustic, used for peasant women in several 16th-century romantic works, including the greatest of them, Sir Philip SIDNEY's *Arcadia*. It may have been a feminine version of Mopsus, a name given to several mythological Greek prophets. However, Shakespeare clearly took the name directly from the play's chief source, *Pandosto* by Robert GREENE (2), where Mopsa is the foster-mother of Perdita's equivalent. Oddly, Mopsa is the only name taken from Greene, though Greene's Mopsa is the only character in *Pandosto* that does not reappear, under a different name, in Shakespeare's play.

**Morality play**   Medieval dramatic genre that features allegorical characters who face and overcome personified moral problems or temptations. Morality plays employ one-dimensional characters who represent abstract concepts from which they take their names—Charity, Everyman, Understanding, Perseverance, etc. The plays are constructed with alternating serious and comic scenes that are intended to entertain while they instruct. They use plots that depict the conflict between vice and virtue for the possession of the hero's soul, with virtue triumphant at the close. The moral lesson is uncomplicated and is presented in a direct manner. The best-known surviving Morality plays are *Mankind* (c. 1470) and *Everyman* (c. 1500). The genre arose in the 14th century as a combination of religious sermon and festive entertainment, and Morality plays were still performed in Shakespeare's day, though their popularity was rapidly fading.

In their structure, devices, and themes, Morality plays were influential upon ELIZABETHAN DRAMA. *Dr Faustus*, by Christopher MARLOWE (1), is regarded as the Elizabethan play most similar to a Morality play (though Marlowe pointedly gives the triumph to vice, rather than virtue), but the genre is reflected in a number of Shakespeare's plays, as well. For instance, a number of his villains—perhaps most notably AARON and RICHARD III—display the traits of a stock character from the genre, the VICE. The abstract personages of the genre also appear here and there—for instance, in the disguises of TAMORA and her sons as Revenge, Rape, and Murder (*Titus Andronicus*, 5.2), and in THE SON THAT HATH KILLED HIS FATHER and THE FATHER THAT HATH KILLED HIS SON (*3 Henry VI*, 2.5). More significantly, one of the major themes found in Morality plays, the social evil represented by sin, was to be explored repeatedly by Shakespeare, especially in the HISTORY PLAYS. Other plays where commentators find the particular influence of the genre include *Measure for Measure* and *Timon of Athens*.

**More, Sir Thomas (1478–1535)**   English writer, author of a source for *Richard III*. More is best known for his *Utopia* (1516)—a Latin account of an ideal country, whose name provided our word *utopia*. He also wrote a *History of King Richard the thirde* (written in 1513, it was first published, in part, in Richard GRAFTON's 1543

chronicle and published in full only in 1557). More's account was incorporated by both Edward HALL (2) and Raphael HOLINSHED in their histories, which were Shakespeare's chief sources for his HISTORY PLAYS. Thus, More's account was an important influence on the creation of Shakespeare's villainous RICHARD III. More's chief source for the history of the period was the manuscript of his friend Polydore VERGIL's *Historia Anglia* (1505–1533, published 1534), but he created his own King Richard. It was he who first established the popular image of a cynical and witty villain, a cripple who proves himself through ruthless ambition. More's ironic narrative plainly influenced Shakespeare's similar treatment.

As a youth, More was a page to Cardinal John Morton (1410–1500), who had known King Richard—he appears in *Richard III* as the Bishop of ELY (3). The son of a judge, More became a successful lawyer as a young man, but was also interested in humanism and literature, becoming the intimate friend of such RENAISSANCE luminaries as William LILY, John Colet (1466–1519), and Desiderius Erasmus (c. 1467–1536). He became an adviser to King HENRY VIII and rose quickly in the court hierarchy. In 1529 he succeeded Cardinal WOLSEY as Lord Chancellor (as is mentioned in *Henry VIII* 3.2.393–394), but he resigned the post in 1532 and retired, engaging in literary disputes over the emerging doctrines of Protestantism. Unwilling to support either King Henry's divorce from Queen KATHERINE or his assumption of the pope's authority in religious matters, More was tried for treason, convicted, and executed. He is considered a saint by the Catholic Church, having been canonised in 1935. His life was the subject of the play SIR THOMAS MORE, on which Shakespeare collaborated, and, more recently, of *A Man for All Seasons*, a popular play (1960) and movie (1966).

**Morgan (1)**   In *Cymbeline*, the name taken in exile by the banished courtier BELARIUS.

**Morgan (2), McNamara (d. 1762)**   Irish lawyer and playwright, author of an adaptation of *The Winter's Tale*. Morgan's *The Sheep-Shearing: or, Florizel and Perdita* (1754) focussed on Act 4 of Shakespeare's play, omitting the plot concerning LEONTES' jealousy. In 1761 it was produced as an operetta, with music by Thomas ARNE. Morgan was principally a Dublin barrister who wrote plays as a sideline; both *The Sheep-Shearing* and his tragedy, *Philoclea* (1754, based on part of SIDNEY's *Arcadia*), were produced by his friend Spranger BARRY (3).

**Morgann, Maurice (1726–1802)**   Eighteenth-century English civil servant and writer, author of an influential essay on FALSTAFF. In his *Essay on the Dramatic Character of Sir John Falstaff* (1777), Morgann initiated a style of impressionistic Shakespearean criticism, centred on a quasi-psychological interpretation of the characters that was popular throughout the 19th century into the 20th. Essentially Morgann ignores the actual evidence of the plays and emphasises one's emotional response to Falstaff. His essay strongly influenced the inclination—powerful ever since in many readers—to defend the fat knight as a bold and courageous character and to fault PRINCE (6) HAL for rejecting his old companion.

Although one of Morgann's purposes in writing was to refute Voltaire, who had called Falstaff a 'drunken savage', his defence of the fat knight displays the humanitarian influence of the French Enlightment, which valued sentiment as evidence of an humane sensibility and opposed the Machiavellian values of statecraft.

**Morley, Thomas (1557–1603)** English composer, possibly a friend of Shakespeare, who probably wrote music for two of the playwright's songs. Shakespeare's SONG 'It was a lover and his lass' (*As You Like It* 5.3.14–37) was published with Morley's music in the composer's *First Book of Ayres* (1600), but it is uncertain whether he set the playwright's words to music or Shakespeare wrote words to match Morley's tune. Another Morley tune, in his *First Book of Consort Lessons* (1599), bears the title of a Shakespeare song, 'O Mistress mine' (*Twelfth Night* 2.3.40–53); scholars generally believe the song in the play is meant and that this tune was used on stage. However, the composer may have adapted it from an earlier version by his one-time teacher, the notable composer William Byrd (c. 1543–1623).

Morley and Shakespeare were neighbours in 1596 and may have been acquainted. Morley was an organist for St Paul's Cathedral and a musician for the court of Queen ELIZABETH (1). He is best known as a composer of madrigals, contrapuntal songs for several voices that had been introduced into England from ITALY by Byrd. He also composed church music, solo songs with lute accompaniment, and compositions for strings and keyboard. He published five books on music, including *A Plain and Easy Introduction to Practical Music* (1597), the first work of its kind in English.

**Morocco (Morochus)** Character in *The Merchant of Venice*, an African prince and unsuccessful suitor of PORTIA (1). Faced with the choice among three caskets ordained by Portia's father, Morocco rationalises his choice in a long speech (2.7.13–60) that presents a viewpoint that the play as a whole invalidates. Morocco is attracted by the richness of the gold casket, which promises 'what many men desire' (2.7.5), but he finds within it an image of a death's head and a scroll whose message begins with the now-familiar line 'All that glisters is not gold' (2.7.65). Morocco fails be-

cause he equates appearance with inner worth and because he cannot imagine hazarding all in pursuit of happiness, unlike BASSANIO, who wins Portia by selecting the lead casket, and ANTONIO (2), who risks everything for his friend in accepting SHYLOCK's perilous loan.

Portia dislikes the prospect of marrying Morocco because he is black. She makes the conventional Elizabethan association of black skin and evil when she first learns of his approach (1.2.123–125). In 2.1 she politely assures him that she recognises his virtues as a man and a prince, but after his defeat, she is relieved. *The Merchant of Venice* is a play that acknowledges and makes use of Elizabethan prejudices; not only is it distinctly anti-Semitic, but the two unsuccessful suitors—both presented as examples of flawed values—are a black man and a political enemy of England, the Spaniard ARRAGON.

In both the QUARTO and FIRST FOLIO editions of the play, the name Morocco is rendered in Latin, Morochus, and some modern editions follow this practise.

**Mortimer (1), Sir Edmund, Earl of March (1391–1425)** Historical figure and character in *1 Henry VI*, uncle of Richard Plantagenet (see Duke of YORK [8]), to whom he bequeaths his claim to the throne. In 2.5 Plantagenet visits his aged and dying uncle in the Tower of London, where he is a prisoner. Mortimer tells of the deposition of King RICHARD II by HENRY IV, head of the Lancastrian branch of the royal family. Mortimer, of the York branch, had been the rightful heir to the throne (see LANCASTER [1]). An attempt to install him as king had resulted in his imprisonment for life while still a young man. Mortimer names Plantagenet his successor, and he dies. Mortimer's appearance in the play establishes York's claim to the throne, anticipating developments in *2* and *3 Henry VI*.

Mortimer's claim to royal descent was rather more controversial than the play suggests, for it depended on succession through a woman, a principle of inheritance often not accepted in the medieval world. In any case, the play mistakes this Mortimer for other historical personages, for Shakespeare's sources were likewise confused. By his reference to his mother (2.5.74), this Mortimer seems to be Edmund MORTIMER (2), actually his uncle and neither an earl nor in the royal line of descent. (However, Mortimer [2] appears in *1 Henry IV*, where the confusion continues and he is given this Mortimer's ancestors.) In his lifelong captivity, the character in *1 Henry VI* resembles both a historical cousin of his and a Lord Gray of Ruthven (a brother-in-law of the other Edmund Mortimer), both of whom died in prison late in life. The actual Edmund Mortimer, Earl of March, died a free man at the age of 36. His loyalty to the crown had been demonstrated. In 1415, his brother-in-law (and York's father), the Earl of CAMBRIDGE, plotted to kill King

HENRY V and place Mortimer on the throne. This was the attempt that is inaccurately described in *1 Henry VI*. In fact, Mortimer himself revealed the conspiracy when he learned of it, and Cambridge, with two others, was executed for treason. His sentencing is enacted in *Henry V*, 2.2, though Mortimer is not mentioned.

**Mortimer (2), Edmund (1376–1409)**    Historical figure and character in *1 Henry IV*, a rebel against King HENRY IV. Originally an army commander for the King, Mortimer's capture by GLENDOWER is reported in 1.1. However, the King learns that Mortimer has married Glendower's daughter, and he refuses to ransom him. This becomes a bone of contention between the King and HOTSPUR—whose wife, LADY (10) Percy, is Mortimer's sister—as the revolt begins. Mortimer appears at the rebels' council of war in 3.1, where he proves to be a moderate negotiator among more difficult personalities. He attempts to maintain amity between Hotspur and Glendower. He tries to control Hotspur's temper, and he forthrightly defends his father-in-law against the firebrand's slurs. Mortimer can only speak to his bride, now LADY (8) Mortimer, through the translations of her father, for he speaks no Welsh and she no English. Nevertheless, he sentimentally asserts his love for her in an episode that lends humanity to the rebel cause.

Following errors in his sources, Shakespeare confused Mortimer with his nephew, another Edmund MORTIMER (1), who was Earl of MARCH and thus an heir to the English throne. The rebels speak of his claim several times (e.g., in 1.3.144–157 and 4.3.93–95) in making the case for their fight against Henry. Although an explicit intention to place him on the throne if their rebellion succeeds is not mentioned, Mortimer is to receive England in the division of the kingdom comtemplated at the war council.

The historical Mortimer had supported Henry's usurpation of the crown several years earlier, which Shakespeare depicted in *Richard II*, although Mortimer does not appear in that play. The rebels of 1403, depicted in *1 Henry IV*, intended to place the younger Mortimer on the throne, and this Mortimer acted in support of his nephew, as well as for Glendower. After SHREWSBURY, Mortimer and Glendower were pursued by the King, as Henry stipulates he will do in 5.5.40, and Mortimer died in the unsuccessful defence of Glendower's capital at Harlech in 1409.

**Mortimer (3), Sir Hugh (d. 1460)**    Historical figure and minor character in *3 Henry VI*, an uncle and supporter of the Duke of YORK (8). In 1.2 Sir Hugh arrives with his brother, John MORTIMER (3), to offer aid to York before the battle of WAKEFIELD. Sir Hugh does not speak; the deaths of the brothers in the battle are reported in 1.4.2.

**Mortimer (4), Sir John (d. 1460)**    Historical figure and minor character in *3 Henry VI*, an uncle and supporter of the Duke of YORK (8). In 1.2 Sir John arrives with his brother, Hugh MORTIMER (3), to offer aid to York before the battle of WAKEFIELD. Sir John speaks one line; the deaths of the brothers in the battle is reported in 1.4.2. The historical figures appear only as names in the death list of the battle, where they are mentioned as 'bastard uncles' of York.

**Mortimer (5), Lady**    Character in *1 Henry IV*. See LADY (8).

**Mortimer's Cross**    Location in *3 Henry VI*, an English village near Wales and a battle site of the WARS OF THE ROSES. A plain near Mortimer's Cross is the setting of 2.1, although the battle itself is not referred to. However, an incident from that conflict is depicted; a transient atmospheric effect causes an apparent tripling of the sun in the sky. This omen appears to Edward (see EDWARD IV) and Richard (see RICHARD III), who take it to signify future success. This improbable but historical phenomenon, a type of high-latitude mirage, was indeed seen during the battle, and it inspired Edward to adopt a stylised sun as his emblem.

Shakespeare omitted the battle, which Edward's forces won in February 1461 (historically, Richard was not present, being only nine years old), because he wished to present here a string of Yorkist losses, to be reversed by the battle of TOWTON, which closes the act.

**Morton**    Minor character in *2 Henry IV*, follower of the Earl of NORTHUMBERLAND (1) and rebel against King HENRY IV. In 1.1 Morton arrives at WARKWORTH CASTLE with an eyewitness report—settling a distressing uncertainty—that the rebels have lost the battle of SHREWSBURY and that the Earl's son, HOTSPUR, has been killed by PRINCE (6) HAL. He then joins with Lord BARDOLPH (2) in rousing Northumberland from the despair this news causes him. In doing so, Morton announces (1.1.187–209) the plans of the ARCHBISHOP (3) of York, whose continuation of the rebellion will provide the central action of the rest of the play. Morton's account presents rebellion in terms of subverted religion that help to establish the play's disapproving attitude towards revolt (although Morton himself, as a rebel, finds it acceptable).

**Moseley, Humphrey (d. 1661)**    English bookseller and publisher. In 1653 Moseley claimed the copyrights to a number of old plays whose manuscripts he had collected, including THE MERRY DEVIL OF EDMONTON, CARDENIO, HENRY I AND HENRY 2. In 1660 he added DUKE HUMPHREY, *King Stephen*, and *Iphis and Iantha, or a marriage without a man*. Only *The Merry Devil of Edmonton* has survived, but scholars agree almost unanimously that of these works, only *Cardenio* and possibly *Duke Humphrey* are connected with Shakespeare.

Moseley was a successful publisher, becoming a high officer in the STATIONERS' COMPANY. He published the first collection of the plays of Francis BEAUMONT (2) and John FLETCHER (2), along with works by John MILTON and others.

**Moth (1) (Mote)** Character in *Love's Labour's Lost,* a page employed by the Spanish braggart ARMADO. Moth's quick wit is employed to ridicule his master, subtly to his face and blatantly behind his back. Moth appears only in scenes that function as set pieces, humorous sketches intended simply as entertainment. Moth is apparently an energetic teenager or child, small and slight of build. He is described as 'not so long by the head as *honorificabilitudinitatibus*' (5.1.39–40) (the longest word in Latin, and in Shakespeare). His name, pronounced 'mote' in Elizabethan English, suggests both the erratic flight of an insect and the elusiveness of a particle of dust. In the pageant of the Nine WORTHIES (5.2), he plays the infant Hercules. He is the vehicle for a number of the obscure topical jokes that make *Love's Labour's Lost* the most cryptic of Shakespeare's plays. He is believed to have been intended as a parody of the peppery Elizabethan pamphleteer and satirist Thomas NASHE.

**Moth (2)** Character in *A Midsummer Night's Dream,* a fairy attendant to the Fairy Queen TITANIA. In 3.1 Titania assigns Moth to the retinue of the comical rustic BOTTOM, whom the Fairy Queen has been magically induced to love. As the smallest and least important fairy in the group attending Bottom, Moth is never addressed by his temporary master and is given no particular task. His name means—and in Elizabethan English was pronounced—'mote' and suggests the tiny size of a speck of dust.

**Mother** Minor character in *Cymbeline,* the deceased parent of POSTHUMUS who appears to him as an apparition, in 5.4. The Mother appears with other ghosts: her husband, SICILIUS LEONATUS, and her two sons (see BROTHER [2]). Led by Sicilius, they plead with JUPITER for mercy on Posthumus. The Mother's part in this ritualistic solicitation is small; she points out that she died when she gave birth to Posthumus and left him an orphan; because of this, he deserves pity. She is a supernatural presence in an episode whose function is to create an air of eerie romance.

**Mouldy, Ralph** Minor character in *2 Henry IV,* a countryman enlisted by FALSTAFF in his capacity as an army recruiter in 3.2. After joking about his name, Falstaff drafts Mouldy over the man's objections. However, once recruited, Mouldy bribes Corporal BARDOLPH (1) to secure his own release from service, along with that of his friend Peter BULLCALF.

**Mountjoy, Christopher (active 1598–1613)** Wig-maker in LONDON, Shakespeare's landlord and the defendant in a lawsuit in which Shakespeare testified. In 1612 Mountjoy was sued by his son-in-law and former apprentice, Stephen BELOTT, who claimed that he had not been paid money promised him in his marriage agreement. Belott claimed that in 1604, in the course of the marriage negotiations, Shakespeare, then a lodger in the Mountjoy household, had told him on Mountjoy's behalf that his bride would receive a dowry of £60 plus household goods and that he would inherit £200 on Mountjoy's death. Shakespeare was summoned from STRATFORD in May 1612 to affirm or deny these assertions. He confirmed his residency with the Mountjoys in 1604 (he was probably there a year or two earlier, since he declared that he had first known both Mountjoy and Belott around 1602). He said that he had solicited Belott to marry Mountjoy's daughter at the request of the father, but that he did not remember the amount of the proposed dowry and that he knew nothing of a promised inheritance. The court turned the case over to the arbitration of the men's parish church, which criticised both men but awarded Belott a token payment, though Mountjoy evidently refused to pay it. The records of this episode reveal Shakespeare's London residence around 1602 to 1604 and that he had returned to Stratford by the spring of 1612, as well as offering a glimpse of the private life of the playwright at the period when he was writing *Othello, King Lear,* and the PROBLEM PLAYS.

Mountjoy was a French Huguenot refugee who was a 'tire-maker', or specialist in the elaborate bejewelled ornamental headgear worn by aristocratic women. He was a skilled craftsman in a rich and prestigious trade; he once made a tire for Queen ELIZABETH (1). His wife, Marie, also a Huguenot, was having an affair with a neighbouring cloth dealer during the period that Shakespeare was a lodger, as we know from the diary of the astrologer and physician Simon FORMAN, whom she consulted about a suspected pregnancy. The pregnancy may have been a false alarm or aborted, for she had no child. Shakespeare may have met the couple through his friend Richard FIELD (2), whose wife was also a Huguenot and who lived nearby.

After Marie's death in 1616, Mountjoy evidently took up 'a dissolute and unregulated life', as recorded by the French church. He feuded with his daughter and son-in-law, threatening them with disinheritance, thus sparking the lawsuit that involved Shakespeare.

**Mousetrap, The** See THE MURDER OF GONZAGO.

**Mowbray (1), Thomas, Duke of Norfolk (c. 1365–1400)** Historical figure and character in *Richard II,* an enemy of BOLINGBROKE (1). The play opens with Bolingbroke's accusation to King RICHARD II that Mowbray has committed treason by embezzling military payrolls, engaging in unspecified plots, and, most important, having murdered the king's uncle, Thomas, Duke of GLOUCESTER (6). Mowbray hotly denies these charges, and a trial by combat is scheduled. In their vehement, fiery rhetoric, both contestants evoke the stylised pageantry of a medieval world that was remote even in Shakespeare's day and whose passing is a basic theme of the play. Before the trial by combat begins, in 1.3, two decidedly sympathetic characters, John of GAUNT and the DUCHESS (2) of Gloucester, the widow of the murdered duke, make it clear that Mowbray had in fact killed Gloucester and that he had done so on Richard's orders. The king, presumably hoping to avoid potential embarrassment, cancels the combat and banishes both disputants from England. Mowbray's response is again highly oratorical, but it contains one particularly distinctive passage (1.3.159–173), in which he regrets his departure to non–English-speaking lands, asserting a psychological dependence on the ability to express himself through language. This attitude surely reflects Shakespeare's own. Later CARLISLE declares (4.1.91–102) that Mowbray has died in Venice after fighting bravely against the Saracens in a Crusade.

The historical Mowbray, like Bolingbroke, belonged to a faction, headed by Gloucester, that had rebelled against Richard in the late 1380s, and, with Bolingbroke, he subsequently joined the king's party. When Richard was again opposed by Gloucester, in 1397, the king arrested his uncle and placed him in the custody of Mowbray, who commanded the English fortress at Calais. Gloucester died in prison, and, while it cannot be confirmed, 14th-century rumour and modern scholarship alike agree with Shakespeare that Mowbray most likely had the duke killed at the king's command. When he was expelled from England, Mowbray went on a pilgrimage to the Holy Land, but he did not fight there; the Crusades had ended a full century earlier.

Mowbray's son, Thomas MOWBRAY (2), later rebelled against his father's foe, when Bolingbroke had become HENRY IV. He was captured and executed in 1405, as is enacted in *2 Henry IV.*

**Mowbray (2), Thomas, Lord (1386–1405)** Historical figure and character in *2 Henry IV,* a rebel against King HENRY IV. An ally of the ARCHBISHOP (3) of York and Lord HASTINGS (2), Mowbray argues against accepting the peace offered by Prince John of LANCASTER (3) at GAULTREE FOREST in 4.1, but he is ignored. When Lancaster's offer proves treacherous, in 4.2, Mowbray is arrested with the others and sentenced to death. The historical Mowbray, not yet 20 years old when he was executed, was the son of Thomas MOWBRAY (1), whose

quarrel with Henry BOLINGBROKE (1), later to become Henry IV, was enacted in *Richard II.*

***Mucedorus*** Anonymous play formerly attributed to Shakespeare, part of the Shakespeare APOCRYPHA. *Mucedorus* is a comedy that burlesques pastoral romance and tales of chivalry. It was first published in 1598 by William JONES (4). It was extremely popular and was printed more often than any other work of ELIZABETHAN or JACOBEAN DRAMA, yielding at least 17 editions by 1668. The play was sometimes ascribed to Shakespeare in the late 17th century, and it was included with *FAIR EM* and *THE MERRY DEVIL OF EDMONTON* in King Charles II's specially prepared collection of Shakespeare's plays. Apparently this ascription is made on the strength of the title pages beginning with the third edition (1610), which stated that the play had been staged by the KING'S MEN. Shakespeare therefore knew the work, and its depiction of a forest-dwelling 'wild man' may have influenced the creation of CALIBAN. However, no modern scholar believes Shakespeare wrote *Mucedorus,* for it is a crude drama that is beneath the standard of even the least of Shakespeare's work. Its authorship remains uncertain, though it is perhaps most frequently given to Thomas LODGE.

## *Much Ado About Nothing*

### SYNOPSIS

*Act 1, Scene 1*
A MESSENGER (14) tells LEONATO, governor of MESSINA, that Don PEDRO, Prince of Aragon, is approaching. He reports the prince's victories in war and tells of the knightly accomplishments of CLAUDIO (1), a young gentleman in Don Pedro's court. Leonato's niece, BEATRICE, asks about another gentleman, BENEDICK; she responds to the Messenger's good report with sharp raillery, which Leonato explains as part of an ongoing rivalry of wits between his niece and the young nobleman. Don Pedro arrives, accompanied by the two young men and his brother, DON JOHN (1). Benedick and Beatrice exchange humorous insults, each of them asserting an extreme aversion to love, particularly for the other. Leonato offers a special welcome to Don John, who has lately been reconciled with his brother. Most of the group departs, leaving Claudio and Benedick alone; Claudio confesses that he has fallen in love with Leonato's daughter, HERO, and wishes to marry her; Benedick derides marriage. Don Pedro returns, and Benedick reveals Claudio's desire. Don Pedro teases Benedick, predicting that he will fall in love one day. Then he helpfully offers to court Hero himself, disguised as Claudio at the MASQUE scheduled for that evening; once assured of Hero's response, he will approach her father on Claudio's behalf.

*Act 1, Scene 2*
Leonato's brother, ANTONIO (3), reports that a servant has overheard Don Pedro telling Claudio of his intention to marry Hero.

*Act 1, Scene 3*
Don John complains to his attendant CONRADE of his bitter melancholy. Conrade replies that he should disguise his attitude to preserve his newly restored place in Don Pedro's court. Don John asserts that he can only be himself and that he wishes to be a villain, spreading discontent. Another follower, BORACHIO, brings news of Don Pedro's plan to woo Hero on Claudio's behalf. Don John proposes to make mischief with this information, hurting Claudio, whose advancement he envies.

*Act 2, Scene 1*
Beatrice acidly compares the ferociously silent Don John to the overly talkative Benedick. Leonato asserts that her attitude towards men will prevent her from getting a husband. He then reminds Hero to respond to the prince's expected wooing, though Beatrice wittily preaches against marriage. Don Pedro and his courtiers arrive for the festivities, and all the participants put on masks. Don Pedro takes Hero aside as other couples flirt. Benedick and Beatrice, in disguise, trade insults, supposedly stating other people's opinions. Don John tells Claudio that he has heard the prince courting Hero. Claudio is shocked, believing that Don Pedro is stealing his prospective bride. He leaves embittered. When Don Pedro appears, Benedick berates him for betraying Claudio, but the prince assures him that he means well by their friend. The talk turns to Beatrice, and Benedick reveals that he is angered and hurt by her sharply expressed disdain for him. Claudio and Beatrice appear, and Benedick leaves. Don Pedro tells Claudio that he has arranged his marriage to Hero, and Claudio rejoices. Beatrice leaves, and the prince reveals a plan to Leonato and Claudio: he will trick Benedick and Beatrice into falling in love with each other.

*Act 2, Scene 2*
Borachio proposes to Don John a scheme to thwart Claudio's marriage: he, Borachio, will recruit Hero's waiting-woman, MARGARET (2), to disguise herself as Hero and admit him into Hero's window that night. If Don John, pretending concern for Claudio's honour, can get him and Don Pedro to witness this charade, they will believe that Hero has a lover and Claudio will repudiate her.

*Act 2, Scene 3*
In the garden Benedick reflects on the seductiveness of love. When Don Pedro, Claudio, and Leonato appear, he hides himself in an arbour. They see him, and, following Don Pedro's plan, they speak loudly about Beatrice's passionate love for him. They profess

to be reluctant to tell him of her ardour, knowing his hostility towards her. They leave, and Benedick observes that he has misjudged matters and that he will marry Beatrice. Beatrice appears to summon him to dinner. She says that she dislikes her errand and leaves, but Benedick comically imagines that he sees double meanings in her words that prove her love.

*Act 3, Scene 1*
URSULA, a waiting-woman, is sent to tell Beatrice that Hero and Margaret are talking about her in the garden. As expected, Beatrice eavesdrops on the two, and they speak loudly of Benedick's passion for her, praising him highly as they do so. They profess reluctance to tell her this news, fearing her mockery. They leave, and Beatrice decides that she will return Benedick's love, and she looks forward to happiness with him.

*Act 3, Scene 2*
Don Pedro and Claudio tease Benedick about his changed appearance, saying that he must be in love. He claims toothache, but he takes Leonato aside to speak privately, presumably about marrying Beatrice. Don John appears and tells Claudio and Don Pedro of Hero's infidelity, offering to prove the truth of his accusation that night.

*Act 3, Scene 3*
The rustic Constable DOGBERRY, assisted by VERGES, assembles the WATCHMEN (3) for their nightly patrol. In a comically confused passage they assert that all sorts of disorder and dereliction are proper procedures. Then Conrade and Borachio appear. Borachio describes the success of his plan to deceive Claudio and tells of Claudio's determination to disgrace Hero at the wedding. The Watchmen, though perplexed, realise that some villainy has been committed and they arrest the two men.

*Act 3, Scene 4*
Margaret and Hero tease Beatrice about her seeming love sickness.

*Act 3, Scene 5*
Leonato, late for Hero's wedding, interrupts Dogberry's comically long-winded account of Conrade and Borachio. He tells Dogberry to interrogate the prisoners and submit a written report.

*Act 4, Scene 1*
During the marriage ceremony, Claudio rejects Hero, asserting that he has witnessed her rendezvous with a lover. This report is confirmed by Don Pedro, and even Leonato believes it. Hero faints, and Claudio and Don Pedro leave. Leonato rages at her, wishing she were dead, but FRIAR (2) Francis, who had been officiating at the wedding, calms Leonato and states his belief in Hero's innocence. Beatrice and Benedick also support her, and Leonato recovers his faith in his daughter. The Friar suggests that they

pretend that Hero has died, thus silencing gossip and possibly stirring Claudio to grief and reviving his love. Then, if Hero is not exonerated, she can at least be secretly transferred to a nunnery. Leonato and the Friar leave, taking Hero into seclusion. Beatrice and Benedick reveal their feelings for each other, but Beatrice demands that Benedick prove his love by challenging Claudio to a duel in support of Hero. He agrees to do so.

*Act 4, Scene 2*
Dogberry tries to interrogate Conrade and Borachio, but his comical ineptitude spurs the SEXTON to take over. He questions the Watchmen, who tell of Don John's plot. The Sexton, knowing about the abortive wedding and aware that Don John has fled from Messina, realises that this story is true. He orders the prisoners bound and taken to Leonato, and he goes to report what he has learned. Conrade insults Dogberry, who responds with humorously pompous self-praise.

*Act 5, Scene 1*
Leonato and Antonio berate Claudio and Don Pedro, exiting just as Benedick arrives. Benedick challenges Claudio to a duel and leaves, declaring that they will fight later. Dogberry arrives with his prisoners, and Borachio confesses all. Leonato returns, having been told the truth by the Sexton, and Claudio begs his forgiveness, promising to perform any penance. Leonato states that he must publicly mourn Hero and then marry Hero's cousin. Claudio assents.

*Act 5, Scene 2*
Benedick tells Beatrice of his challenge to Claudio, and they tease each other on the subject of love. Ursula tells them that Don John's plot has been exposed.

*Act 5, Scene 3*
Claudio reads an epitaph for Hero at Leonato's family crypt, believing that she is buried in it. BALTHASAR (4) completes the rite with a mournful song. Don Pedro comes to escort Claudio to his wedding to Hero's cousin.

*Act 5, Scene 4*
Benedick receives Leonato's permission to marry Beatrice. Claudio prepares to marry the veiled cousin, who reveals herself to be Hero. Benedick and Beatrice cannot bring themselves to admit their love for each other, returning to their barbed wit, but Claudio produces a love poem that Benedick has written about Beatrice and Hero presents a similar lyric by Beatrice about Benedick. Exposed, Beatrice and Benedick agree to be married. As plans are made for a double wedding, word comes that Don John has been apprehended. Benedick promises to devise some suitable punishment, but he turns to celebration in the meantime. The assembled people dance.

## COMMENTARY

*Much Ado About Nothing* shares a theme common to Shakespearean COMEDY: a romance is disrupted, but love triumphs. However, unlike such earlier works as *The Two Gentlemen of Verona* and *A Midsummer Night's Dream,* this play is a comedy of character, rather than of situation; its major development—the defeat of the threat to romantic happiness—comes about through a psychological change on the part of the major characters, rather than through changes in their circumstances. While elaborate and melodramatic coincidences bring the play to its climax, that climax—Beatrice and Benedick's commitment to each other—is one of personal crisis and response.

The conflict between Beatrice and Benedick is the central element of the play, although it is sometimes seen as a SUB-PLOT, being humorous and lacking the villainous interference that adds suspense to the story of Hero and Claudio. The two scorners of love are unquestionably the brightest and most vital characters in the play, and their lively battle of wits engages much of our attention. It is introduced before Claudio and Hero even meet, and Claudio's feebly motivated love at first sight has none of its appeal. The comic trap that brings the former foes together holds our interest in the second half of the play; the tale of the foolish Claudio and his passively victimised lover seems most important as the stimulus for the growing trust between Beatrice and Benedick, who are much more fully developed characters.

The gulf that at first separates Beatrice and Benedick is not created by any outside interference; rather, the lovers themselves have established it. We are immediately aware that they love each other, despite their protestations to the contrary: in 1.1 Beatrice cannot refrain from asking after Benedick's fate in battle, though she affects scorn in doing so, and Benedick thinks first of Beatrice as a model with which to compare Hero (unfavourably) when he mocks Claudio's intention to marry. Beatrice and Benedick have apparently quarrelled in the past; she speaks of 'our last conflict' (1.1.59) and implies an earlier unhappy romance in 2.1.261–264. He is overly sensitive to her criticism, declaring himself unable to abide her company in 2.1.257–258. These hints lead us to believe that both parties are trying to protect themselves against a repetition of their previous unhappiness.

Thus their relationship develops in a way that makes it stirringly real. When Don Pedro's plot makes them fall in love with each other, it seems entirely appropriate and their responses are convincing. Each, once convinced of the other's love, accepts affection and reciprocates it. Their reactions are both comical and humanly touching, as they half-heartedly attempt to disguise their new feelings with transparent complaints of toothache (3.2.20) and head cold (3.4.40).

*In* Much Ado About Nothing *4.2, the comically inept constable Dogberry attempts an interrogation of Borachio and Conrade.* (Courtesy of Culver Pictures, Inc.)

When their friends tease them, we feel a pleasurable sense of escape, seeing on stage, at a safe distance, a kind of foolishness to which we ourselves might be susceptible.

The reaction of these vital and good-humoured figures to the denunciation of Hero lies at the moral heart of the play. The scene of Hero's rejection in church (4.1), which alludes to such religious concepts as 'grace' and 'damnation' (4.1.171, 172), presents a crisis of spiritual values. Beatrice acts on her faith in her cousin, and Benedick acts on his faith in Beatrice. This involvement in a serious issue brings them together utterly, completing the work of their friends' earlier ploys. This process permits them to return to the world of normal relations, where earlier they had isolated themselves from it.

Although Beatrice and Benedick dominate the play—significantly, it was long known by the title 'Beatrice and Benedick'—Claudio and Hero reinforce their lesson of love and faith. While these lovers are undeniably shallower than Benedick and Beatrice, this very fact makes them effective in their own way. Hero and Claudio are conformists who believe in the romantic norms that their more spirited friends reject. Their conventionality supports the comic tone of the play by preventing our emotional or sentimental involvement in their situation.

Hero is a typically pliant and acquiescent young Elizabethan woman. She shows no interest in Claudio until Don Pedro tells her that she is betrothed to him. She is mildly charming, and she is spirited enough to help trick Beatrice into loving Benedick, but she is mostly a docile participant in an arranged marriage. Claudio plays a more prominent role; if Benedick and Beatrice must learn that their opposition to love is a false sentiment, Claudio must also be freed from the naïve pseudo-love that he at first declares for Hero, an emotion not grounded in experience. Claudio has often been condemned as a cad, a mere cardboard figure, or both. However, he should be taken at his word when he professes love for Hero; even as he rejects her, he does so in sorrow, regretting that his love has been disappointed. His vicious attempt to humiliate Hero reflects the extent of his hurt. Moreover, as a conventional young man, Claudio is concerned about the offence to his honour—and to that of his prince, Don Pedro—caused by what he believes to be a plot to foist a promiscuous bride on him. While this consideration is almost meaningless today, it will have been appreciated by Elizabethan audiences, and thus we should recognise that, while Claudio is plainly foolish and gullible, he may reasonably plead in his own defence that he has sinned 'but in mistaking' (5.1. 269).

His repentance at Hero's supposed tomb is often criticised as cynical, too slight and superficial to be taken seriously, but the text of the scene (5.3) offers no justification for this view; it presents a solemn, if brief, ritual of grief and atonement, followed by a formal quatrain, spoken by Don Pedro (5.3.24–27), that invokes hope for the future. However, even though Claudio is properly repentant, he remains uninteresting and it is fitting that he and Hero are simply ignored at the end of the play, when attention turns to Benedick and Beatrice.

Don John is also a conventional figure, a 'plain-dealing villain' (1.3.30), for whom 'any bar, any cross, any impediment will be medicinable to me' (2.2.4–5). His true nature is hidden even from his brother, Don Pedro, even though he has recently rebelled against him. (In 16th-century melodrama, the evil of a villain often remains unknown to his victims until he is overtly exposed.) He is a plot device more than a truly complex character—a sort of anti-comic symbol who opposes the happy ending. Such a mechanical villain is necessary, because a true villain, like RICHARD III or IAGO, would destroy the comic assurance that all will be well for the crossed lovers. Significantly, Don John is not present at the final reconciliation, for his nature is utterly at odds with it.

*Much Ado*'s central plot device is the readiness of the characters to accept error and misinformation: Don John's false presentation of Hero is merely the most important incident in a series of erroneous reports and misunderstandings. While Don John maliciously misleads his intended victims, Don Pedro benevolently tricks Benedick and Beatrice. Dogberry is fully capable of confusing himself and everyone else.

Disguise, another source of error, is also a prominent motif. At the MASQUE in 2.1, Beatrice and Benedick converse in masks, and their dialogue, more vitriolic than usual, marks the extreme extent of their hostility. In the same scene Claudio is pretending to be Benedick when Don John tells him that Don Pedro loves Hero. More important, the play turns on Margaret's use of a disguise, Hero's clothes, as part of Don John's plot to slander Hero. This episode is lent further mystery by being only reported (twice—by Borachio in 3.3 and, slightly differently, by Claudio in 4.1) and not actually shown on stage.

The theme of error and confusion is also enhanced by various other dramatic devices. Prominent is the repeated importance of overhearing, an act that lends itself to misinterpretation and error. Don Pedro's plan to help Claudio woo Hero is overheard and misunderstood by Antonio's servant, as is retold by Antonio in 1.2, and it is also overheard—correctly but with malice—by Borachio, leading to Don John's first piece of villainy. Don John's scheme involves the invention of another overheard conversation, with which he deceives Claudio. Don Pedro uses overhearing benevolently to convince Beatrice and Benedick that each is loved by the other, and the Watchmen overhear Borachio's account of Don John's second villainy, leading to the eventual exposure of his plot. The frequent recurrence of this motif lends strength to the role of luck and timing in the comedy's gratifying resolution.

The very title of the play may contain a pun on this subject, for 'nothing' was probably pronounced like 'noting', which in Elizabethan English could mean 'overhearing' or 'eavesdropping'. This possibility seems to be supported by the wordplay in 1.1.150–152 and 2.3.157. The casual title serves a thematic purpose in any case, affirming the play's comic nature by implying that the lovers' trials will prove in the end to have been of no consequence.

The various plots of *Much Ado* are intricately interwoven in a fabric that both suggests and reinforces the complex confusions that are central to the play. From the beginning our attention is repeatedly transferred from one set of lovers to the other. One plot is conventionally melodramatic, while the other is a series of clever rejections of conventional romance; each of these qualities contradicts the other, preventing a single tone from dominating. The Claudio-Hero plot is written entirely in verse, whereas Beatrice and Benedick spar in particularly loose and lively prose. (An exception, Beatrice's lyrical outburst when she hears that Benedick loves her [3.1.107–116], is sometimes seen as evidence that Shakespeare adapted *Much Ado* from a lost play in verse, [see 'Sources of the Play'] though it is just as likely to have been intended as a sign of her sudden receptivity to romance.)

While the two stories are thus antithetical in some ways, they are similar in others. Both plots feature heroes who err in renouncing their lovers out of pride in both cases—Benedick's pride of overvalued independence, Claudio's pride required by a conventional sense of honour. Both men, however, are plainly going to end up married. Similarly, Beatrice and Hero are alike in destiny and opposed in personality. The two stories combine when they both come to their dissimilar climaxes in 4.1. In fact, Claudio's rejection of Hero sparks the co-operation and trust between Beatrice and Benedick.

Other features of plotting emphasise the play's confusions. Strikingly, Don John's villainy is first spent on a scheme that goes nowhere, the attempt to make

Claudio believe that Don Pedro is taking Hero for himself. This ruse makes us aware of important aspects of both the villain and his victim. Similarly, the third plot element, that of Dogberry and his Watchmen, is also full of confusion. But it is handled with a precision that makes *Much Ado* respected as among the most deftly plotted of Shakespeare's works. Dogberry's Watchmen appear exactly at the crucial moment when Don John's second, more potent villainy has been unfolded to us, though not to its victims. When the Watchmen overhear Borachio and Conrade, we are assured that Hero will be exonerated. Yet Dogberry's comical ineptitude ensures that she won't be cleared immediately, and the lovers' stories are allowed to continue to their resolutions.

Thus hints of tragedy alternate with comical reassurances. We learn the truth while the characters operate in ignorance of it; thus we laugh, preserving the comic nature of the play. Our emotions are insulated from the distress that the deluded characters would evoke in a tragedy or in real life. Nevertheless, the melodrama of Hero's unjust disgrace, shockingly brutal because it is set at her wedding, forbids escapism. Like the later PROBLEM PLAYS, *Much Ado* has the capacity to disturb, and we are morally engaged. The happiness that is finally attained is made more valuable by the difficulty with which it is achieved. At the end, though, as in *The Merchant of Venice*, these hardships are forgotten, and love and happiness prevail. The final reconciliation stems from the essential goodness of the world of Leonato's court: its denizens are cheerfully at home with each other, too witty to be sentimental and too kind to be unfeeling. While Claudio and Don Pedro prove vulnerable to Don John's manipulations, their error is rectified. Evil is undone through the redeeming power of love and faith and through the timely grace of chance. We can agree with Benedick when he says, 'man is a giddy thing, and this is my conclusion' (5.4.107), but perhaps it is Dogberry who most truly, if unwittingly, states the play's nature when he chastises Borachio, asserting, 'Thou wilt be condemned into everlasting redemption' (4.2.53–54).

## SOURCES OF THE PLAY

The main plot of *Much Ado About Nothing* is an example of an old European tradition—dating at least to late classical times—of stories in which a lover is deceived into believing that his beloved is unfaithful. Shakespeare drew on a version that first appeared in Ludovico ARIOSTO's massive poem *Orlando Furioso*, which he may have known in both an Italian edition (probably that of 1532) and the English translation by Sir John HARINGTON (1591). He also used another Italian rendering, itself an adaptation of Ariosto, a story by Matteo BANDELLO that was published in a 1554 collection. Between the two Italian texts, most of the details of Claudio's courtship of Hero, its villainous

thwarting, and the final happy reunion of the protagonists are foreshadowed. An English version of Ariosto's story, in George WHETSTONE's collection of tales *The Rocke of Regard* (1576), may have suggested Claudio's rejection of Hero at her own wedding.

Some scholars have argued that Shakespeare modified an earlier play to create *Much Ado*, but this viewpoint is highly speculative and largely unpopular, particularly since no existing text is offered as the missing source, although the mysterious LOVE'S LABOUR'S WON is sometimes suggested.

Ariosto and derivative texts account only for the Hero-Claudio plot, while it is the other plots in *Much Ado*—the romance of Benedick and Beatrice and the crucial intervention of the comical constabulary—which make the play a comedy; the older works are straight melodramas. Dogberry is certainly a Shakespearean original, in that no particular literary source provides a forerunner. However, humorous constables—characterised by confused speech and ludicrous logic—were a very old theatrical staple. Indeed, Shakespeare had already used the type in a more minor character, Constable DULL, of *Love's Labour's Lost*. Just as important as any model for Dogberry, in all probability, was Shakespeare's awareness of the on-stage personality of Will KEMPE, the actor for whom the role was written.

As witty scorners of romance, Beatrice and Benedick are also part of a tradition that was well established in the 16th century, but an important stimulus probably came from the Italian Baldassare CASTIGLIONE's *The Book of the Courtier* (1528), one of the most important and widely read works of the time. Shakespeare almost certainly read it, either in Italian or in the popular English translation by Thomas HOBY (1) (1561, three eds. by 1588). Castiglione presents an ideal of courtly life that included the revolutionary idea that women had much to contribute to it. To illustrate this point, he composed a series of sprightly debates between a man and a woman that may well have inspired the verbal sparring between Beatrice and Benedick.

## TEXT OF THE PLAY

*Much Ado About Nothing* is thought to have been written in mid- or late 1598, although this date cannot be proven. Francis MERES omits *Much Ado* from his list of Shakespearean comedies, published in the summer of 1598 (though it is sometimes maintained that the title LOVE'S LABOUR'S WON refers to *Much Ado*). Meres' omission suggests that the play did not exist when he wrote, although he may simply have omitted it. However, a late date is supported by the fact that the play was registered with the STATIONERS' COMPANY in 1600 as 'to be stayed'—that is, *not* to be published. This ploy was generally associated with new work, being an attempt to protect a currently popular play from piracy by unlicensed publishers. Still, even if *Much Ado* was a recent success in 1600, it was certainly written somewhat earlier, for Will KEMPE, for whom the role of Dogberry was written, left Shakespeare's company, the CHAMBERLAIN'S MEN, in January or February 1599.

The company apparently sold the rights to Andrew WISE and William ASPLEY, for they published a QUARTO edition of the play (known as Q) late in 1600. This text was probably printed (by Valentine SIMMES) from Shakespeare's own manuscript, or FOUL PAPERS, as is evidenced by casual stage directions, some of which name the actors who played Dogberry and Verges, and some of which name INNOGEN, a GHOST CHARACTER.

The next publication of the play was in the FIRST FOLIO of 1623, where it was printed from a copy of Q that had been partially amended, particularly with respect to stage directions. The Folio also made two brief cuts in the play, probably to avoid offending the court or violating the 1606 statute against profanity (see CENSORSHIP). The two texts remain very similar, and modern editions are based on both.

## THEATRICAL HISTORY OF THE PLAY

The 1600 edition of *Much Ado About Nothing* asserts that the play had been 'sundrie times publikely acted'. Although it was not reprinted between 1600 and 1623, it is evident that *Much Ado About Nothing* was immediately popular, for many references to it have survived from the early 17th century. When Leonard DIGGES (2) compared the popularity of the plays of Shakespeare and JONSON in 1640, he observed, 'let but Beatrice and Benedick be seen, lo, in a trice the Cockpit, Galleries, Boxes, all are full'. Several performances at the court of King JAMES I are recorded, among them a presentation at the wedding festivities of Princess ELIZABETH (3) in 1613. Later, King Charles I was sufficiently familiar with the play to amend the table of contents of his copy of the Second Folio (1632) by changing its name to 'Benedik and Betrice' (sic).

In the Restoration period William DAVENANT owned the rights to produce the play, but he merged it with *Measure for Measure* in THE LAW AGAINST LOVERS (1662). Another production of *Much Ado* itself is not recorded until 1721, when John RICH (2) revived it, restaging it several times over the next quarter-century. The play was again cannibalised in two popular adaptations of this period: *LOVE IN A FOREST* (1723) by Charles JOHNSON (2), a rendering of *As You Like It*, contained bits of *Much Ado;* and James MILLER (1) combined Shakespeare's play with one by Molière in 1737.

*Much Ado* was very popular throughout the rest of the 18th century and has remained só ever since. David GARRICK played Benedick many times between 1748 and 1776, and it was often said to be his best role. Among the notable Benedicks of the 19th century were Charles KEMBLE (1) and Henry IRVING; Beatrice was principally associated with two actresses, first Helen FAUCIT and then Ellen TERRY (2). Hector BERLIOZ wrote an opera—*Béatrice et Bénédict* (1862)—based on *Much Ado;* it omitted the Claudio-Hero plot.

Among the most notable of many 20th-century productions of *Much Ado* have been John GIELGUD's highly successful London presentation of 1949, revived in 1950, 1952, and 1955; Franco ZEFFIRELLI's production of 1965; Joseph PAPP's 1972 New York version, set in the turn-of-the-century United States, and a more conventional presentation of 1988; and the 1976 STRATFORD staging by John BARTON (1), set in British India. The play has been a film four times—once in the United States before the advent of sound (1926), once in East Germany (1963), and twice (1956, 1973) in the Soviet Union. Several recent productions have been adapted for TELEVISION, including Zeffirelli's (1967) and Papp's (1973).

**Munday, Anthony (c. 1560–1633)** English playwright, author of a possible influence on Shakespeare and a co-author of SIR THOMAS MORE. Munday, originally a printer apprenticed to John ALLDE, turned to acting but was unsuccessful—he appeared with OXFORD'S MEN in the late 1570s and early 1580s. He began a notorious career as a hack writer with a series of anti-Catholic tracts (c. 1578–1580). His first book was *Zelauto* (1580), a novel written in imitation of John LYLY's famed *Euphues.* Its treatment of usury and Jews may have influenced *The Merchant of Venice.* Between 1594 and 1602 he wrote plays for the ADMIRAL'S MEN. Three of these works have survived: *John à Kent and John à Cumber* (1594) may have suggested elements of the comic sub-plot of *A Midsummer Night's Dream,* and a pair of plays on Robin Hood (both 1598) may have influenced *As You Like It.* Francis MERES referred to Munday as one of England's leading comic dramatists. Munday also wrote numerous plays, including SIR JOHN OLDCASTLE, in collaboration with others. He was probably the principal author of *Sir Thomas More,* which contains a scene by Shakespeare.

**Murder of Gonzago, The** Playlet presented within *Hamlet.* In 3.2 Prince HAMLET arranges for the PLAYERS (2) to perform *The Murder of Gonzago* for his uncle, the KING (5). The plot of the playlet resembles the actual murder of Hamlet's father by the King, and Hamlet expects the King's response to reveal his guilt. For this reason, he refers to the brief play as *The Mousetrap* (3.2.232).

First, in a DUMB SHOW, a man pours poison in the ear of a sleeping king and then consoles his grieving queen, exiting with her. Then, in dialogue, the PLAYER KING denies the PLAYER QUEEN's assertion that she would not remarry if he died. In the next scene, LUCIANUS, said by Hamlet to be 'nephew to the King' (3.2.

239), poisons the sleeping Player King in his ear, just as the real King had poisoned Hamlet's father. The play has its intended effect at this point, as the King flees the room; the performance is never completed.

Hamlet speaks of a source for *The Murder of Gonzago*—which he calls 'the image of a murder done in Vienna' (3.2.233)—as 'extant, and written in very choice Italian' (3.2.256–257), but if such a document existed, scholars have not discovered it. However, the murder of Hamlet's father—and thus the playlet—is clearly based on a real murder, committed in Italy in 1538 (see *Hamlet*, 'Sources of the Play').

**Murderer**    See FIRST MURDERER; SECOND MURDERER; THIRD MURDERER.

**Murellus**    Character in *Julius Caesar*. See MARULLUS.

**Musicians (1)**    Minor characters in *The Two Gentlemen of Verona*, players hired by THURIO to assist him in wooing SILVIA by performing a SONG in her honour.

**Musicians (2)**    Minor characters in *Romeo and Juliet*, three players hired by PARIS (2) to provide music at his wedding to JULIET (1). However, Juliet is found apparently dead, and they are not needed. They are then accosted by the servant PETER (2), who demands free music and engages them in a comic exchange (4.5. 100–141). Their names, Simon Catling, Hugh Rebeck, and James Soundpost, indicate the instruments they play. A catling is a small, lutelike string instrument; a rebec, an early violin; a soundpost, for the singer in the group, is an internal component of a string instrument.

**Musicians (3)**    Minor characters in *The Merchant of Venice*, servants of PORTIA (1). The Musicians appear in two important episodes. In 3.2 their song 'Tell me where is Fancy bred' provides an interlude that heightens the suspense as BASSANIO contemplates his fateful choice among the three caskets, and it also makes a point about the nature of beauty. Further, it may offer Bassanio a clue as to which casket to select. In 5.1 the Musicians add to the romantic charm of BELMONT, dissipating the disturbing and anxious atmosphere of the preceding courtroom scene. Musicians were a normal feature of a wealthy household in Shakespeare's day.

**Musicians (4)**    Minor characters in *2 Henry IV*. In 2.4 the Musicians, led by SNEAK, perform for FALSTAFF at his drunken dinner with the HOSTESS (2) and DOLL TEARSHEET at the BOAR'S HEAD TAVERN.

**Musicians (5)**    Minor characters in *Much Ado About Nothing*, entertainers hired by LEONATO. In 5.3 the Musicians accompany BALTHASAR (4) when he sings the mournful SONG 'Pardon, Goddess of the night' as CLAUDIO (1) grieves at HERO's tomb, believing her dead. They may also accompany 'Sigh no more, ladies' in 2.3, though the stage direction is ambiguous. Musicians were a normal feature of a grand household in Elizabethan times, and their presence here helps to maintain the splendidly festive atmosphere of Leonato's court.

**Musicians (6)**    Minor characters in *Othello* (6), strolling players hired by CASSIO to serenade OTHELLO, with whom he is out of favour. Cassio's gesture is rejected, however, when Othello's CLOWN (6) pays them to leave, saying 'If you have any music that may not be heard, to 't again, but . . . to hear music, the general does not greatly care' (3.1.15–17). The Clown jests lewdly on the sexual symbolism of their instruments and associates them with venereal disease, suggesting a criticism of the courtly flattery their performance represents.

**Musicians (7)**    Minor characters in *Cymbeline*, players who serenade IMOGEN for CLOTEN. One of the Musicians sings the song, 'Hark, hark, the lark' (2.3.19–25), but otherwise they do not speak and leave as soon as they have completed their performance. The episode offers a musical diversion that is appropriate to a comedy. It also relieves the sense of menace from the previous scene—IACHIMO's trespass in Imogen's bedchamber—and from the approach of Cloten. Additionally, it provides time for Imogen to change her costume from nightclothes to daytime garb.

**Mustardseed**    Character in *A Midsummer Night's Dream*, a fairy attendant to the Fairy Queen, TITANIA. Titania assigns Mustardseed to the retinue of the comical rustic BOTTOM, whom the Queen has been magically induced to love. Bottom has been endowed by PUCK with the head of an ass, but he does not know of his new adornment, and Mustardseed serves him by helping to scratch his strangely itching face. The fairy's name suggests the several references to the tiny mustard seed in the Gospels (e.g., Luke 17:6).

**Mutius**    Minor character in *Titus Andronicus*, a son of TITUS (1) Andronicus. In 1.1 Mutius is killed by his father during the dispute with BASSIANUS over LAVINIA. His murder is symptomatic of a flaw in Titus, whose sense of honour can lead him to such a crime.

**Myrmidon**    Any of several minor characters in *Troilus and Cressida*, followers of the Greek warrior ACHILLES. In 5.7 Achilles orders the Myrmidons to avoid combat in order to save themselves for a confrontation with HECTOR, and when the Trojan leader is encountered without his armour on, in 5.8, the Myrmidons kill him. The episode, presenting an extreme of unchivalrous behaviour, caps the play's picture of the dishonour of war in general and of the TROJAN WAR in particular.

In the *Iliad* of HOMER, the Myrmidons were an ethnically distinct group of soldiers from Thessaly, in what is now north-eastern Greece; they were named for a legendary ancestor, Myrmidon. Like Achilles, the Myrmidons came from beyond the world of ancient Hellenic civilisation and were seen as somewhat barbaric and cruel by the more cosmopolitan Greeks. This attitude survives in Shakespeare's presentation.

**Mytilene**   City on the Greek island of Lesbos, a location for several scenes of *Pericles*. MARINA, the lost

daughter of PERICLES, is sold to a brothel in Mytilene in 4.2, and she remains there in 4.5 and 4.6. In 5.1, when she has escaped the brothel but remains in Mytilene, her father arrives there and they are reunited. Marina later marries the Governor of Mytilene, LYSIMACHUS. Shakespeare followed his sources in placing these episodes in Mytilene, and no specific attributes of the city are referred to in the text. The historical Mytilene was a minor port city of the Aegean Sea, famous chiefly as the home of the poet Sappho (active c. 590 B.C.).

**Mytilenian Sailor**   Character in *Pericles*. See TYRIAN SAILOR.

**Nash (1), Anthony (d. 1622)** Farmer in STRATFORD and friend of Shakespeare. Nash was a wealthy farmer who witnessed several business deals made by Shakespeare and managed some of his farm lands. He and his innkeeper brother John (d. 1623) were among the seven close friends to whom the playwright willed money to buy a commemorative ring. His eldest son was Thomas NASH (2), later the husband of Shakespeare's grand-daughter.

**Nash (2), Thomas (1593–1647)** First husband of Shakespeare's grand-daughter Elizabeth HALL (3). The son of Shakespeare's friend Anthony NASH (1), Thomas Nash may have been acquainted with the playwright as a child. He married Elizabeth Hall in 1626. They probably lived at first in his home, next door to the Shakespeare-Hall home at NEW PLACE. (Known as Nash's House, it is today maintained as a museum by the Shakespeare BIRTHPLACE Trust.) The couple were living in New Place, however, at the time of Nash's death. Nash was a lawyer, but he did not practise after inheriting his father's fortune. He also owned an inn in STRATFORD, inherited from an uncle. He was a committed Royalist in the Civil Wars. At their outset in 1642, he was noted as by far the greatest Stratford contributor of money to the king's cause, and in 1643 he hosted the harried Queen Henrietta Marie at New Place. At his death he willed Nash's House to his wife; he bequeathed New Place to another relative, but Elizabeth and her mother, Susanna SHAKESPEARE (14) Hall, fought the will in court and won.

**Nashe (Nash), Thomas (1567–c. 1601)** English writer, author of the earliest specific reference to a Shakespeare play and of minor sources for *Hamlet* and *All's Well That Ends Well*. In addition, he may be a model for the character MOTH (1) in *Love's Labour's Lost*. Nashe's popular satirical pamphlet *Pierce Penniless His Supplication to the Devil* (1592) influenced several passages in *Hamlet*, especially HAMLET's remarks on drunkenness in 1.4.16–38. *Pierce Penniless* also contains a reference to the popularity of TALBOT in *1 Henry VI*, the earliest surviving literary remark on a particular Shakespearean work (though Nashe does not mention either title or playwright). An episode in Nashe's novel *The Unfortunate Traveller* (1594) may have influenced the exposure of PAROLLES in 4.3 of *All's Well That Ends Well.*

As the first English picaresque novel, *The Unfortunate Traveller* is an important literary monument, but Nashe is probably best known for his biting satirical pamphlets. Nashe was also the anonymous author of several government counterblasts to the rebellious religious tracts of the pseudonymous Puritan Martin Marprelate (see MARTEXT). In the course of the Marprelate controversy, Nashe's avid anti-Puritanism earned him the enmity of Gabriel HARVEY (2), and the two pamphleteers conducted a long feud in print, which may be the subject of a number of obscure topical jokes in *Love's Labour's Lost*. Moreover, many scholars believe that the diminutive Nashe was satirised as the sharp-tongued and tiny youth Moth.

Nashe was one of the UNIVERSITY WITS, the playwrights who dominated ELIZABETHAN DRAMA in the 1580s, but he wrote only two plays of his own—a satirical MASQUE entitled *Summer's Last Will and Testament* (1592) and *The Isle of Dogs* (1597)—though he also collaborated with Robert GREENE (2) and Christopher MARLOWE (1). The *Isle of Dogs,* whose text is now lost, was among the most controversial of Elizabethan plays, a notable subject of government CENSORSHIP. The government found it 'seditious' and not only suppressed it, but closed all the LONDON theatres for several months; three of the actors in the play—Ben JONSON, Robert SHAW (5), and Gabriel SPENCER—were gaoled briefly, though Nashe fled London and escaped punishment. He only returned in 1599, to face a blanket condemnation of his works by the government. His last years are obscure, and we know of his death only through an elegy published some time later, in 1601.

**Nathaniel (1)** Character in *Love's Labour's Lost,* the obsequious companion of the comical pedant HOLOFERNES. Nathaniel emulates his friend, seconding his opinions with less Latinity but no less pretension. Although Nathaniel is no more than an object of derision for the most part, COSTARD presents him in a more human light, standing up for him in 5.2, when he has fled the pageant, stricken with stage fright.

**Nathaniel (2)**    Minor character in *The Taming of the Shrew,* a member of the household staff of PETRUCHIO (2). Nathaniel is one of the servants whom Petruchio abuses in 4.1 as part of his demonstration to KATHERINA of the ugliness of shrewish behaviour.

**Neighbour**    Any of three minor characters in *2 Henry VI,* supporters of Thomas HORNER when he appears, in 2.3, to defend himself in a trial by combat with his apprentice, PETER (1). Unfortunately for Horner, his friends ply him with liquor, by way of cheerful support, and, drunk, he is slain.

**Neilson (1), Adelaide (1846–1840)**    British actress. Neilson was best known for her dramatic adaptations of stories from the works of Sir Walter Scott (1771–1832), but she also played many Shakespearean roles, including JULIET (1), VIOLA, ISABELLA, and IMOGEN. She was noted for her great beauty.

**Neilson (2), Julia (1868–1957)**    British actress, the wife of Fred TERRY (2). A comic actress who played ROSALIND and other Shakespearean parts, Neilson is best known as the co-star and co-manager, with her husband, of a theatre company that presented a variety of plays between 1900 and 1930.

**Nell (1)**    Minor character in *The Comedy of Errors,* a servant in ADRIANA's household. DROMIO OF SYRACUSE refers to Nell in his account to his master of the 'kitchen wench' who claims him as her husband. This parallels Adriana's mistaken identification of the master, ANTIPHOLUS OF SYRACUSE. In a long, broadly comic passage (3.2.71–154), Dromio describes Nell as so grotesquely fat that her other, equally unattractive features are best equated with the continents of the globe.

Nell is described here (and in 5.1.414–416) as the kitchen-maid. LUCE, who appears in 3.1.48–64, is also identified as the kitchen-maid (at 4.4.72–73). This has produced confusion; the two are often thought to be the same character. Some editors of the play have gone so far as to rename Luce as Nell in both stage directions and text.

The different names may be the result of an error on Shakespeare's part; such inconsistencies are common throughout the plays. On the other hand, Dromio may be sarcastically using a pointedly common woman's name to refer to Luce, who is, to his mind, a very common woman. Most simply, the playwright may have expected us to conclude that Adriana had more than one kitchen-maid. If this is the case, and Luce and Nell are not identical, then Nell never actually appears in the play.

**Nell (2)**    Minor character in *The Two Noble Kinsmen,* a country lass who performs in a dance before Duke THESEUS (2). In 3.5 the five young women assemble for the dance; Nell is the only one who speaks, assuring her director, the SCHOOLMASTER (2), that they will do well. Her half-line—a scoffing 'Let us alone, sir' (3.5.31)—contributes to the scene's sense of rustic festivity. However, most scholars agree that Shakespeare did not write 3.5, so Nell is probably the creation of John FLETCHER (2).

**Nerissa**    Character in *The Merchant of Venice,* lady-in-waiting to PORTIA (1). Nerissa is a pert and lively companion to her mistress. In the early scenes involving the lottery of the three caskets, she assures the uneasy heiress that all will be well, and she seconds Portia in the practical joke of the betrothal rings in 5.1. Her courtship by GRATIANO (1) echoes that of Portia by BASSANIO; such symmetrical couples were quite popular in the Elizabethan theatre.

**Nestor**    Legendary figure and character in *Troilus and Cressida,* the oldest of the Greek leaders in the TROJAN WAR. Though respected for his great age, Shakespeare's Nestor is a faintly ludicrous old man who boasts about his longevity and is full of platitudes and long-winded speeches. For instance, agreeing with ULYSSES that another character's purpose is plain, Nestor says, 'True; the purpose is perspicuous as substance / Whose grossness little characters sum up' (1.3.324–325). He is chiefly a supporter of Ulysses' schemes to coax ACHILLES into battle and does very little otherwise.

Nestor was first presented in the *Iliad* of HOMER, where he is the same self-righteous and ineffectual old man we see in Shakespeare. In Homer he is somewhat more than 60, a very respectable age in the ancient world; in the Roman poet OVID's *Metamorphoses,* which Shakespeare read, he is an improbable 200 years old.

**New Place**    Shakespeare's home in STRATFORD from 1597 until his death, and that of his descendants until 1649. The purchase of New Place had considerable personal significance for Shakespeare, advertising to Stratford that his success as a LONDON playwright had restored the family fortune after the financial collapse suffered by his father, John SHAKESPEARE (9), some years earlier. It was the second-largest residential building in the town, built around 1490 by one of Stratford's most famous citizens, Hugh Clopton (d. 1496), a one-time lord mayor of London. Shakespeare bought it from William UNDERHILL in 1597, and despite difficulties created when Underhill was murdered by his son, took possession and began making repairs. Documents relating to the sale reveal that the house was 60 by 70 feet in area and that it had 10 fireplaces (and surely more rooms than fireplaces, as the latter were taxed as luxuries). On its property were two barns, two gardens, and two orchards. An 18th-century drawing shows a three-storied, five-gabled mansion.

Shakespeare did not live at New Place full-time until he retired from the theatre, around 1611, but his wife, Anna HATHAWAY Shakespeare, and his daughters doubtless moved in as soon as the repairs were completed, probably in 1598. Mary Arden SHAKESPEARE (11), the playwright's mother, may have lived at New Place after her husband's death in 1601. Shakespeare retired to New Place and died there in 1616.

Shakespeare left New Place to his daughter Susanna SHAKESPEARE (14) Hall, who lived there until her death in 1649. She in turn left it to her daughter, Elizabeth HALL (3), who had lived there with her first husband, Thomas NASH (2), and did so briefly with her second, John Bernard, whom she married just before her mother died. However, she soon moved to Northamptonshire with Bernard, and the house may have been vacant for some years. Elizabeth left New Place to her husband when she died in 1670, and on his death in 1674 the house was sold to one Edward Walker, whose daughter married a Clopton in 1699, so that the house returned to the family of its builder.

The Cloptons altered the house, virtually rebuilding it to a different ground-plan. In 1756 the property was sold to the Reverend Francis Gastrell, who demolished the house in 1759, reportedly because he felt its taxes were too high. Today, the site of New Place, encompassing the foundations of the house and a series of gardens, is owned by the Shakespeare BIRTHPLACE Trust and is open to the public.

**Newington Butts**   Suburb of LONDON, site of an early theatre. Little is known of the theatre, which was located near an archery practise field—archery targets were called butts—in the village of Newington (then a distant suburb, now well within London). The theatre was in existence by 1580, when it was ordered closed during a plague epidemic. At some point it was apparently bought or leased by Philip HENSLOWE, who hired troupes to play there in June 1594, including the earliest known performance by the CHAMBERLAIN'S MEN, Shakespeare's company. However, the only later record of this theatre is a 1631 reference to its former existence.

**Nicanor**   See ROMAN (2).

**Nicholas**   Minor character in *The Taming of the Shrew*, a member of the household staff of PETRUCHIO (2). Nicholas is one of the servants whom Petruchio abuses

in 4.1 as part of his demonstration to KATHERINA of the ugliness of shrewish behaviour.

**Nobleman**   Minor character in *3 Henry VI*, a messenger. In 3.2 the nameless Nobleman brings word to King EDWARD IV of the capture of HENRY VI.

**Norfolk (1), John Howard, Duke of (c. 1430–1485)** Historical figure and minor character in *Richard III*, commander of the forces of RICHARD III at the battle of BOSWORTH FIELD. A quiet follower of orders, Norfolk brings Richard a note warning of treachery in the forthcoming battle, in 5.3. His death in the fighting is noted at 5.5.13. His son, his second-in-command, is the Earl of SURREY (4). Norfolk was a grandson of Thomas MOWBRAY (1), who appears in *Richard II*.

In 1483 the historical Norfolk received his dukedom for his services in securing for Richard the office of Protector. This may account for his silent presence in the stage directions to 3.4.

**Norfolk (2), John Mowbray, Duke of (1415–1461)** Historical figure and minor character in *3 Henry VI*, a supporter of the Yorkist cause in the WAR OF THE ROSES. Norfolk's paternal grandfather was the Thomas MOWBRAY (1) of *Richard II*. His uncle was the Lord MOWBRAY (2) of *2 Henry IV*.

**Norfolk (3), Thomas Howard, Duke of (1443–1524)** Historical figure and character in *Henry VIII*, a nobleman at the court of King HENRY VIII. Through the first three acts, Norfolk is an enemy of Cardinal WOLSEY. In 1.1 he warns the Duke of BUCKINGHAM (1) against Wolsey's power, and in 1.2 he supports Queen KATHERINE's complaint against Wolsey's illicit taxes. In 2.2 he leads a group of noblemen in railing against the cardinal, and in 3.2 he delightedly levels formal treason charges against Wolsey, whose downfall has finally come to pass. Finally, in 5.2, he takes a small part in resisting the attack on Archbishop CRANMER by Bishop GARDINER (1). Though he is no longer prominent, he remains on the side of right in the play's scheme of the things.

The historical Norfolk—one of the great English military heroes of his day—died in 1524, before most of the events in the play took place. He was succeeded as Duke of Norfolk by his son, the play's Earl of SURREY (5). Shakespeare ignores Norfolk's death, perhaps through error or perhaps to keep this dignified hero as a fitting opponent of Wolsey and Gardiner.

Norfolk gained heroic stature by leading the English army to a decisive victory over SCOTLAND at the battle of Flodden Field in 1513. Earlier, however, he was an enemy of the TUDOR DYNASTY, for he fought for RICHARD III in 1485 at BOSWORTH FIELD, where Henry VII (see RICHMOND) established the Tudors as English monarchs. Norfolk appears in *Richard III* as the Earl of SURREY (4); his father, *Richard III*'s NORFOLK (1), was killed at Bosworth Field. Henry VII deprived the family of its ducal rank, but at the age of 70, this Norfolk won it back at Flodden.

**Norfolk (4), Thomas Mowbray, Duke of**    Character in *Richard II*. See MOWBRAY (1).

**North, Sir Thomas (c. 1535–c. 1601).**    English translator of PLUTARCH's *Lives*. North's *Lives of the Noble Grecians and Romans* (1579)—a retranslation of Jacques AMYOT's French rendering of Plutarch's original Greek—became Shakespeare's primary source for *Antony and Cleopatra*, *Coriolanus*, *Julius Caesar*, and *Timon of Athens* and a source for minor elements in other plays. North, a nobleman educated at Cambridge and the INNS OF COURT, translated various works from Spanish, French, and Italian, but he is chiefly known for his Plutarch, which, besides having inspired Shakespeare, also influenced several generations of English prose writers; it is regarded as one of the major works of 16th-century English literature.

**Northumberland (1), Henry Percy, Earl of (1342–1408)**    Historical figure and character in *Richard II* and *1* and *2 Henry IV*, a supporter of BOLINGBROKE against RICHARD II in the first play, and a rebel against him—after he has begun to rule as HENRY IV—in the two later works. In *Richard II* Northumberland is Bolingbroke's chief lieutenant; in 2.1 he leads others into rebellion against Richard by providing a rationale for revolt: 'The king is not himself, but basely led by flatterers . . .' (2.1.241–242). In 2.3 Northumberland himself resorts to flattering his leader unctuously, and in 3.3 he hypocritically conveys Bolingbroke's false declaration of loyalty to Richard. In 4.1 Northumberland takes on the most boldly disrespectful functions in the process of removing the king from his position, and in 5.1 he is the hard-hearted deputy who separates Richard and the grieving QUEEN (12). On that occasion he tersely states a cruel principle that aptly represents the new world of Machiavellian politics that Bolingbroke has inaugurated: replying to a request for mercy, he observes, 'That were some love, but little policy.' (5.1.84)

In the *Henry IV* plays he is a less prominent but no more likeable figure. Northumberland and his son, the fiery HOTSPUR, join in rebellion against King Henry, whom they perceive as ungrateful to the Percy family. However, the earl fails to appear with his forces at the crucial battle of SHREWSBURY, sending word that he is ill; the rebel forces are defeated there and Hotspur killed. At the outset of *2 Henry IV* the personification of RUMOUR claims that Northumberland was 'crafty-sick' (Ind. 37), and in 2.3 LADY (10) Percy, Hotspur's widow, chastises her father-in-law for having dishonorably abandoned his son; no other evidence is pre-

sented that Northumberland's illness was feigned, however. The earl then deserts the rebels again, fleeing to Scotland rather than supporting the renewed efforts of the ARCHBISHOP (3) of York. His final defeat is reported in 4.4.97–101.

The historical Northumberland did first rebel with Bolingbroke and then against him, but Shakespeare exaggerates his treachery and alters the facts of his life considerably. A man of King Henry's age in the play, Northumberland was actually a generation older; this change is part of Shakespeare's development of the rivalry between Hal and Hotspur by making them contemporaries. Northumberland, a major landowner in northern England and a distinguished warrior in the Scottish border conflicts, was a close friend and supporter of King Henry's father, John of GAUNT. Like Gaunt, he had supported Richard II against Thomas of GLOUCESTER (6), but he was alienated by Richard's seizure of Gaunt's estate, and when Bolingbroke returned from exile, the earl became one of his chief allies, as in *Richard II*. His despicable personality as Bolingbroke's lieutenant may derive from the playwright's knowledge of a famous incident that, surprisingly, he did not use. Sent by Bolingbroke to negotiate with Richard, Northumberland swore a sacred oath that Bolingbroke intended to allow Richard to remain in power if he were restored to Gaunt's title and estates. Richard was thus induced to forgo escape by sea and leave the castle in which he had taken shelter. He was promptly ambushed by Northumberland and taken to London, where he was deposed. It is not known whether or not Northumberland used this ploy under orders, but it was reported in Shakespeare's source, HOLINSHED's *Chronicles*, as a heinous betrayal.

Once Henry was in power, disputes arose between him and the Percies, eventually leading to their revolt. However, Northumberland's role in it in the *Henry IV* plays is almost wholly fictitious. According to Shakespeare, his unforeseen illness shocks the rebels, disturbs their plans, and contributes to their defeat at Shrewsbury, but in reality he had been sick for some time and his absence had been anticipated. The playwright's version is dramatically more interesting, and it allows the rashness of Hotspur and DOUGLAS to be emphasised. The earl's pretending to be ill is also unsupported by Shakespeare's sources; it is simply an appropriately nasty rumour to associate with his Machiavellian character. Further, his betrayal of the Archbishop is untrue; Northumberland was the elected leader of the renewed rebellion, and the Archbishop commenced the uprising prematurely, before Northumberland could join him. Only after the disaster at GAULTREE FOREST, when Henry marched on his headquarters at WARKWORTH CASTLE, did Northumberland flee to Scotland. Several years later, after recruiting arms and money in Flanders and FRANCE (1), he again revived the rebellion and invaded England, dying in unsuccessful but valorous combat, according to Holinshed. This account of tenacious courage did not at all suit Shakespeare's model of a contemptible rebel, and he simply ignored it.

**Northumberland (2), Henry Percy, Earl of (1421–1461)** Historical figure and minor character in *3 Henry VI*, a supporter of King HENRY VI. Northumberland is among the nobles who depart from Henry in anger, when the king agrees to bequeath the throne to YORK (8) in 1.1. He appears with Queen MARGARET (1) and Lord CLIFFORD (1) in 1.4, when the captive York is murdered; his sympathy for York, who is tormented with evidence of his young son's murder before his own, is chastised by the queen. He later dies at the battle of TOWTON.

This Northumberland was the grandson of Henry PERCY (2), known as HOTSPUR, who figures in *Richard II* and *1 Henry IV*. His father, Hotspur's son, died at the first battle of ST. ALBANS, as is described in the opening lines of *3 Henry VI*.

**Northumberland (3), Henry Percy, Earl of (1446–1489)** Historical figure mentioned in *Richard III*, an apparent follower of RICHARD III. On the eve of the battle of BOSWORTH FIELD, Richard refers to 'the melancholy Lord Northumberland' (5.3.69) as one of his officers. This is the son of the NORTHUMBERLAND (2) of *3 Henry VI*, who had died in the battle against the Yorkist King EDWARD IV (and against Richard) at TOWTON and whose lands and title had been seized by the victors. After the defection of WARWICK (3), King Edward sought new allies and he returned the Northumberland fiefdom to this Northumberland, who was accordingly with Richard at Bosworth. However, Shakespeare did not mention the dénouement of the relationship: Northumberland refused to bring his many troops into the fighting, and after the battle he immediately found favour with RICHMOND.

**Northumberland (4), Lady** Character in *2 Henry IV*. See LADY (9).

**Northumberland (5), Siward, Earl of** Character in *Macbeth*. See SIWARD.

**Nun** Minor character in *Measure for Measure*, a member of the convent that ISABELLA intends to join. The Nun appears only briefly, in 1.4, when she listens to Isabella's complaint that the restrictions imposed on the nuns seem insufficient. When she hears LUCIO's voice she asks Isabella to receive him, for she may not speak to a man except in the presence of the prioress and then only while hiding her face; if showing her face, she must be quiet. Having established these regulations for the audience, the Nun disappears from the play; except for a momentary disturbance at the approach of Lucio, she displays only the quiet of the stereotypical nun. The episode illustrates Isabella's extremism, as we see that she is determined to adopt a sterner rule of withdrawal than that required of the Nun.

The Nun is named Francisca (or Francesca) in the stage direction at the beginning of 1.4, but the name is not used thereafter. Scholars believe that Shakespeare named his character when he created her but then never used the name. Its survival in the earliest published text, the FIRST FOLIO (1623), is viewed as evidence that the printed text came from Shakespeare's manuscript.

**Nunn, Trevor (b. 1940)** British theatrical director and producer. As the artistic director of the Royal Shakespeare Company since 1968 (and its chief executive since 1978), Nunn has been responsible for numerous notable Shakespearean productions, including a cycle of the ROMAN PLAYS in 1972, a 1973 *Coriolanus* starring Nicol WILLIAMSON, a 1976 *Macbeth* with Ian MCKELLEN and Judi DENCH, and a 1981 *All's Well That Ends Well* that was successful in STRATFORD, London, and New York. In the 1980s Nunn's career centred on contemporary theatre, as he produced such trans-Atlantic hits as *Nicholas Nickleby*, *Cats*, and *Les Misérables*.

**Nurse (1)** Minor character in *Titus Andronicus*. In 4.2 the Nurse delivers to AARON his infant son by TAMORA. Aaron kills the Nurse to ensure her silence about the birth.

**Nurse (2)** Minor character in *3 Henry VI*. A nonspeaking character, the Nurse tends to the infant PRINCE (5) of Wales in the final scene.

**Nurse (3)** Character in *Romeo and Juliet*, a servant in the CAPULET (1) household, the nanny and former wetnurse of JULIET (1). The longwinded Nurse, a broadly comical figure who repeatedly resorts to the low humour of sexual innuendo, functions as a foil for Juliet's delicacy and openness; in 1.3 the anecdote she relates from Juliet's childhood illuminates the heroine's background. But as the tragedy deepens, the Nurse loses her humorous qualities and becomes a symbol of the conventional world that opposes the private realm of the lovers. Further, her crass recommendation that Juliet simply ignore her union to the banished ROMEO (3.5.212–225) serves to isolate the heroine at a crucial moment. In her last appearance the Nurse cackles mindlessly about sex as she attempts to wake the drugged Juliet, and she echoes the uncomprehending grief of the family when it appears that the girl is dead.

*Juliet's Nurse (played by Edna May Oliver in the 1936 film of* Romeo and Juliet) *is one of the most famous comedy roles in all of Shakespeare. A perfect foil for Juliet's idealism, the Nurse represents the crassness of the conventional world.* (Courtesy of Culver Pictures, Inc.)

**Nym** Character in *The Merry Wives of Windsor* and *Henry V*, a follower of FALSTAFF. In *The Merry Wives* Nym is a minor figure, being dismissed by his master early in the play for refusing to deliver love letters. But in three brief scenes he is memorably established as an eccentric character, using the word 'humour' in almost every speech, applying it in every imaginable way, to the point where it ceases to have meaning. This word was a fashionable and widely parodied term in late 16th-century London (see COMEDY OF HUMOURS); in fact, a character in a play of 1596, George CHAPMAN's *The Blinding Beggar of Alexandria,* had the same verbal habit and clearly seems to have influenced Shakespeare's creation of Nym.

In *Henry V* Nym feuds with PISTOL, who has married the HOSTESS (2), to whom Nym was engaged. BARDOLPH (1) reconciles the two. Nym is one of the companions of Falstaff who mourn his death in 2.3, but he says little. In 3.2, as part of King HENRY V's army in France, Nym is cowardly and is upbraided by FLUELLEN. The BOY (3) comments on the villainous characters of Nym, Pistol, and Bardolph in 3.2.28–56, describing them as braggarts, petty thieves, and cowards. In 4.4.72 the Boy reports that Nym has been hung, apparently for theft.

In *The Merry Wives*, Nym's function is comical, although he remains an undeveloped character. In *Henry V*, his more unnsavoury aspects are stressed; he is part of the underworld that is put down by King Henry. His very name suggests petty villainy; it meant 'steal' or 'filch' in Elizabethan English.

# O

**Oatcake, Hugh** Minor character in *Much Ado About Nothing,* one of the WATCHMEN (3). Oatcake, with SEACOAL, is nominated in 3.3.11 for the post of constable, for both are literate, but DOGBERRY appoints Seacoal. Oatcake is presumably one of the Watchmen who reappear in 4.2 and 5.1, but he is not again mentioned specifically. His comical name—which helps heighten the Watchmen's comical foolishness—is typical of a Shakespearean CLOWN (1).

**Oberon** Character in *A Midsummer Night's Dream,* the Fairy King who works the magic that ensures the triumph of love that is the focus of the play. Oberon gives an unpleasant first impression in 2.1, quarrelling with his queen, TITANIA, and resolving to 'torment' her (2.1.147) because she will not surrender to him a changeling he desires to raise. However, it is clear that he intends his revenge, a dose of a magic aphrodisiac, to be only temporary. Once he knows he will have his way, he is a gentle king, overseeing the confusions of the lovers' plot with good-natured amusement. When Titania, magically enchanted with the ass-headed BOTTOM, has surrendered the changeling, he feels sorry for her and lifts his spell, as he had said he would. For the remainder of the play, he is a benign figure, blessing the marriages and the palace of Duke THESEUS (1). Oberon was the traditional King of Fairies, and Shakespeare must have known of him from several sources, though the one most prominent in the play is a 13th-century French adventure tale, *Huon of Bordeaux.*

**Octavia (d. 11 B.C.)** Historical figure and character in *Antony and Cleopatra,* the sister of Octavius CAESAR (2) and wife of Mark ANTONY. In 2.2 Octavia's marriage is arranged as part of a treaty; she appears briefly in 2.3 and 3.2 as a dutiful wife. She accompanies Antony to ATHENS, where, in 3.4, she learns of renewed enmity between her husband and brother and volunteers to help negotiate a new truce. However, when she arrives in Rome in 3.6, she is greeted with the news that Antony has returned to CLEOPATRA. Once Antony's desertion is established Octavia disappears from the play. Her docile, peaceable nature makes her a suitable victim, while she also serves as a foil both to

Caesar, the cynical politician, and to Cleopatra, the irresistible sensualist.

The historical Octavia had a more prominent and complex role in Roman affairs than she does in the play. The most striking difference in Shakespeare's account concerns the timing of her marriage to Antony, which occurred in 40 B.C. This was before he had begun his affair with Cleopatra—he actually had another mistress at the time, in Athens. Also, Shakespeare telescopes events in his play and gives short shrift to Octavia's success as a diplomat. She in fact brought about a treaty between her husband and brother in 37 B.C., and it lasted for several years. After Antony deserted her, Octavia remained loyal to him. Even after he divorced her in 32 B.C., she continued to care for his children by two prior marriages. Her nobility and humanity won her widespread fame as a sympathetic and estimable figure, a reputation that is reflected in Shakespeare's source, PLUTARCH's *Lives* and survives in the 'beauty, wisdom, [and] modesty' (2.2.241) of the peaceable if ineffectual woman of the play.

**Octavius (Gaius Octavius Caesar; Octavian) (63 B.C.–14 A.D.)** Historical figure and character in *Julius Caesar,* ANTONY's ally against BRUTUS (4) and CASSIUS. (The same figure appears as CAESAR [2] in *Antony and Cleopatra.*) Octavius is a cool, self-possessed, and efficient leader, whether hearing out Antony's criticisms of LEPIDUS in 4.1, claiming command of the right wing—properly Antony's—before the battle of PHILIPPI in 5.1, or ordering the honourable burial of Brutus in 5.5. Though his part is small, it is boldly drawn and clearly anticipates the briskly calculating victor of the later play.

Shakespeare captures something of the personality of the historical Octavius but ignores the events of his life for the most part. In his will, Julius Caesar formally adopted Caius Octavius—the grandson of his sister—and made him the heir to his name and three-quarters of his immense fortune. (In legally accepting this inheritance after Caesar's murder, Octavius changed his name to Caius Julius Caesar Octavianus, and to English-speaking historians he is generally known as Octavian from this time until his assumption of the title Augustus in 27 B.C. However, Shakespeare was probably unaware of this distinction, and the character is called Octavius throughout *Julius Caesar.*) Octavius, who had been a physically frail child, was a 19-year-old student in Athens when Caesar died. When he returned to Italy to claim his inheritance, he immediately asserted himself politically but was not taken seriously at first. However, the name of Caesar was a powerful one, and he was soon at the head of an army of the pro-Caesar forces assembling to combat the assassins.

Unlike in *Julius Caesar,* Octavius was a rival of Antony's from the outset, and their alliance—joining with Lepidus in the Triumvirate—was sealed only after 18 months of antagonism that approached full-scale war. While his political acumen was considerable, Octavius was still inclined to illness and was not a competent military man; at Philippi he was notably unsuccessful, and the defeat of Brutus and Cassius was largely the work of Antony. However, Octavius was soon to assume the leadership of much of the Roman world—the situation with which *Antony and Cleopatra* opens—and his cool efficiency in the closing lines of *Julius Caesar* effectively foreshadows this achievement.

**Officer (1)** Minor character in *The Comedy of Errors,* an agent empowered to arrest debtors. In 4.1 a MERCHANT (1) engages the Officer to arrest ANGELO (1), who owes him money. ANTIPHOLUS OF EPHESUS owes Angelo enough to cover his debt to the Merchant, so Angelo in turn pays the Officer to arrest Antipholus. In 4.4 the Officer turns Antipholus over to PINCH.

**Officer (2)** Minor character in *The Taming of the Shrew,* a constable. The Officer is summoned in 5.1 to arrest VINCENTIO (1), who is thought to be an imposter. The matter is settled shortly after his entrance, and he does not speak.

**Officer (3)** Either of two minor characters in *Twelfth Night* who arrest and later act as custodians of ANTONIO (4). In 3.4 the Officers seize Antonio, who was an enemy of Duke ORSINO of ILLYRIA in a recent war. In 5.1.58–63 one of them describes Antonio's achievements as a naval warrior.

**Officer (4)** Either of two minor characters in *Othello,* soldiers of VENICE. In 1.2 an Officer tells BRABANTIO of the council meeting called by the DUKE (5), and in 1.3 another Officer announces the arrival of news from the Venetian fleet. They serve merely to increase the frantic activity surrounding the prospect of war.

**Officer (5)** Minor character in *King Lear,* the murderer of King LEAR's daughter CORDELIA. In 5.3 ED-

MUND orders the Officer, a captain (designated as 'Captain' in some editions), to kill the captured king and his daughter, hanging Cordelia to make her death seem a suicide. The officer is a petty representative of the evil that permeates the play. He responds to Edmund's promise of reward in a cynically mercenary spirit, saying 'I cannot draw a cart nor eat dried oats; / If it be man's work I'll do 't' (5.3.39–40). He succeeds in disposing of Cordelia, but he is killed by her father as he does so as we learn from Lear himself in 5.3.273.

**Officer (6)** Any of several minor characters in *King Lear,* followers of the Duke of ALBANY. In 5.3.109 an Officer relays Albany's order for a trumpet blast. A little later, an Officer (perhaps the same one) is sent after the fleeing GONERIL, but he does not speak. When it is learned that an assassin has been ordered to kill CORDELIA and LEAR, a different Officer (the pursuer of Goneril does not return) is sent to prevent him. He returns and confirms, in half a line (5.3.274), Lear's account of how he killed Cordelia's murderer. The Officers, whether two or three in number, function merely to swell the ranks of the victorious Albany's entourage in the busy climactic moments of the play.

**Officer (7)** Either of two minor characters in *Coriolanus,* petty officials who prepare for a meeting at which CORIOLANUS is to be honoured. They speak of Coriolanus' nomination to the post of consul, and remark on the possibility that the general may be rejected by the commoners of ROME (see CITIZEN [5]) because of his aristocratic disdain for them. As the First Officer puts it, 'he's vengeance proud, and loves not the common people' (2.2.5–6). They remark on the fickleness of the crowd and on the obstinacy of Coriolanus, but they agree that the warrior hero's long record of extraordinary service makes him more worthy of the post than the politicians who achieve the office by currying favour with the electorate.

Like a CHORUS (1), the Officers are anonymous and outside the action of the play. They interrupt the progress of the plot to provide a commentary on the merits and faults of Coriolanus and on the Roman political situation. Their interruption breaks the intensity of the political developments and thereby promotes a more objective attitude in the audience, permitting us to see both sides of the issue.

**Officer (8)** Any of several minor characters in *The Winter's Tale,* officials of the law court assembled by King LEONTES to try Queen HERMIONE for adultery. In 3.2.12–21 an Officer reads the formal indictment of Hermione, and in 3.2.124–129 he (or another) swears in CLEOMENES AND DION, who bring a message from the oracle of Apollo. He then reads the oracle's proclamation that Hermione is innocent. As extras, merely providing an official presence to a trial scene, the Officers have no personality.

**Okes, Nicholas (active 1596–1639)** Printer in LONDON, producer of two editions of works by Shakespeare. Okes printed the fifth edition of *The Rape of Lucrece* (Q5, 1607) for the publisher John HARRISON (2) and the first edition of *Othello* (Q1, 1622) for Thomas WALKLEY. In the 1620s Okes was prosecuted several times for publishing forbidden political satires.

**Old Athenian** Minor character in *Timon of Athens*, a citizen of ATHENS. In 1.1 the Old Athenian asks the wealthy nobleman TIMON to protect his daughter from the courtship of Timon's servant LUCILIUS (2), who is socially inferior to his intended bride. The magnanimous Timon solves the problem by providing Lucilius with enough money to be considered eligible. The episode helps establish Timon's extravagant generosity. The Old Athenian is a crude caricature of a social type; the snobbish minor gentleman willing to marry his daughter off for money.

**Old Clifford** Character in *2 Henry VI*. See CLIFFORD (2), THOMAS.

**Old Gobbo** Character in *The Merchant of Venice*. See GOBBO (2).

**Old Lady** Minor character in *Henry VIII*, a waiting-woman to ANNE (1) BULLEN. In 2.3 the Old Lady jests bawdily with Anne, who insists that she would not trade her virginity for a throne. The Old Lady contradicts her, declaring that for 'England / You'ld venture an emballing: I myself / Would for Carnarvonshire' (2.3.46–48). The episode exploits the spicy aspects of a courtly romance while not sullying the play's presentation of Anne as a saintly woman. Anne's tolerance of the Old Lady's sharp tongue also keeps her saintliness from seeming stiff-necked and inhumane.

In 5.1, where Anne is the wife of King HENRY VIII, the Old Lady informs the king of the birth of his and Anne's daughter. Confronted with the king's demand for news of a son, she fudges her announcement: '. . . a lovely boy: the God of heaven / Both now and ever bless her: 'tis a girl / Promises boys hereafter' (5.1.164–166). As she had anticipated, the traditional tip for the bearer of news is a small one, and she complains vigorously, 'I will have more, or scold it out of him' (5.1.173). The Old Lady gives a light and comic touch to the introduction of the play's final motif, the auspicious birth of the future Queen ELIZABETH (1).

**Old Man (1)** Character in *Romeo and Juliet*. See CAPULET (2).

**Old Man (2)** Minor character in *King Lear*, a vassal of the Earl of GLOUCESTER (1). In 4.1 the Old Man escorts the blind Gloucester who has had his eyes put out by the evil Duke of CORNWALL. The demoralised and fatalistic Gloucester orders him away, but the Old Man observes that he has been tenant to the Earl and his father for 'fourscore years' (4.1.14) and does not obey until he has turned his master over to an escort, the wandering lunatic Tom O'Bedlam (who is actually Gloucester's son, EDGAR, in disguise). The frailty of the Old Man emphasises Gloucester's weakness, while at the same time his devotion offers evidence that some good remains in the increasingly violent and evil world of the play.

**Old Man (3)** Minor character in *Macbeth*. The Old Man converses with ROSSE in 2.4 and comments on the evil omens that have accompanied the murder of King DUNCAN. This conversation, like a Greek CHORUS (1), offers a commentary on the action so far. The description of the omens—especially that of Duncan's horses eating each other—stresses an important theme of the play: Duncan's murder and its perpetrator are horribly unnatural. The Old Man states the theme explicitly when he describes the eerie darkness of the day. ' 'Tis unnatural, / Even like the deed that's done' (2.4.10–11), he says.

The Old Man presents himself as venerable but unsophisticated—'Threescore and ten I can remember well' (2.4.1), he says when he introduces himself. This, along with his distinctively rustic image of the 'mousing owl' (2.4.13) that killed the falcon, helps establish that the play's catastrophe is universal. SCOTLAND's collapse due to MACBETH's evil is a major motif of the play, and the country as a whole is represented by this ageing peasant.

The episode is a good instance of a technique that Shakespeare was fond of: the plot is interrupted by the introduction of an anonymous figure who comments on it and then disappears from the play. In *Macbeth* the PORTER (3) serves a similar function in a more elaborate manner; the GRAVE-DIGGER of *Hamlet* is another particularly well-known example.

**Old Vic Theatre** London theatre, famous for its tradition of Shakespearean productions. The Old Vic was built in south London as the Coburg Theatre in 1818. For years it was noted for extravagant melodrama and staged little or no Shakespeare. In 1833 it was renamed the Victoria Theatre after Princess Victoria (later Queen, ruled 1837–1901) attended a performance. In 1871 the Victoria, by now familiarly known as the Old Vic, became a music hall. In 1880 Emma Cone, a prominent opponent of alcohol, bought it and re-opened it as a temperance hall. Her niece, Lilian BAYLIS, joined her in 1898 and introduced to the repertoire first opera and, beginning in 1914, Shakespeare. By 1923, under the leadership of Baylis, Ben GREET, and Robert ATKINS, the entire CANON of Shakespeare's plays had been performed at the Old Vic, for the first time in any theatre. Under the direction of Atkins (1919–1925), Harcourt WILLIAMS (1) (1929–1933), and Tyrone GUTHRIE (1933–1945), most of the leading actors and actresses of pre-war Britain performed in Shakespeare's plays at the Old Vic. In 1940 a bomb destroyed the theatre. It was reopened in 1950, and between 1953 and 1958, the entire canon was again staged. In 1963 the Old Vic Drama Company was reorganised as the National Theatre, and in 1976 this company moved to the new National Theatre building. The Old Vic Theatre remains in use as a successful repertory theatre.

**Oldcastle**    Original name of FALSTAFF in *1* and *2 Henry IV*. Shakespeare called one of PRINCE (6) HAL's companions Sir John Oldcastle, following his source, *The Famous Victories of Henry the Fifth*. In the FAMOUS VICTORIES Oldcastle speaks very little and does not resemble his successor in any important way. Shakespeare simply took over the name and applied it to his own creation, the extraordinary figure we know as Falstaff. Soon after writing the plays (1596–1597), the playwright changed the name of the character, evidently in response to protests from William Brooke, Lord COBHAM, a descendant of the historical John Oldcastle. The name was changed before *1 Henry IV* was registered for publication, in early 1598, for Falstaff is referred to in its subtitle at that time. (The names HARVEY [1] and ROSSILL were also changed in this text for similar reasons.)

Several traces of the name Oldcastle survive in the plays. For example, the alteration from three syllables to two produces anomalies in the METRE at several points (e.g., in *1 Henry IV*, 2.2.103). There are more overt clues as well: in *1 Henry IV*, 1.2.41, Falstaff is called 'old lad of the castle'; in the QUARTO edition of *2 Henry IV* (1600), a single speech prefix (1.2.119), inadvertently uncorrected, retains the name Oldcastle; in *2 Henry IV*, 3.2.25, Falstaff is said to have been a page to Thomas MOWBRAY (1), which is thought to have been true of the historical Oldcastle. Moreover, the EPILOGUE to *2 Henry IV* specifically dissociates Falstaff from the historical Oldcastle. Also, another play, SIR JOHN OLDCASTLE was produced by the ADMIRAL'S MEN in 1599, clearly in response to the popularity of Falstaff. It presented the life of Oldcastle in a glowing light, and it opened with a prologue drawing an express distinction between its hero and Shakespeare's character. (Oddly, this play was published as Shakespeare's work by William JAGGARD in the FALSE FOLIO of 1619, and it later appeared in the third and fourth FOLIO editions of Shakespeare's work.)

The historical Oldcastle (c. 1375–1417) had been a friend of Prince Hal. His surname referred to a family estate on which there was a ruin, probably of a Roman fort. The extent to which Oldcastle was involved in the Prince's youthful excesses is unknown. He converted to Lollardy, a proto-Protestant religious movement, was convicted of heresy in 1413, and imprisoned. He escaped and led an unsuccessful religious rebellion against Hal, now King HENRY V, and was captured and executed in 1417. After the Reformation, Oldcastle came to be regarded as a Protestant martyr and was held in great respect by the strict English Protestants becoming known, in Shakespeare's time, as Puritans. That Shakespeare applied the name of a Lollard hero to a criminally debauched character seems to reflect his satirical disapproval of the growing Puritanism in English life.

Despite the name change, the association of Oldcastle with Shakespeare's celebrated reprobate lingered. The name Oldcastle was sometimes used in 17th-century performances of *1* and *2 Henry IV* despite Shakespeare's alteration, and in several other writings of the period the name appears as a humorous reference to the vices we associate with Falstaff.

**Oliver (1)**    Character in *As You Like It*, older brother of ORLANDO. Oliver is plainly a villain from the outset. In 1.1 he is seen to have deprived Orlando of his birthright, then he plots to have Orlando killed by the wrestler CHARLES. His malice derives from envy, as he admits when he observes that Orlando's virtues are so great that he, Oliver, is 'altogether misprised' (1.1.168–169). In 3.1 Oliver becomes a victim himself, as the tyrannous DUKE (1) Frederick seizes his estate and threatens him with banishment if he does not capture Orlando. Oliver protests, asserting that he 'never lov'd my brother in my life' (3.1.14) (to which the Duke replies concisely, 'More villain thou' [3.1.15]).

Yet in 4.3 Oliver is a reformed person, a gentleman of sufficient virtue to attract the love of CELIA, whom he marries in 5.4. This turnabout has no humanly credible motivation, nor is it meant to; Oliver is a cardboard character, intended to play a purely symbolic role. His villainy serves to heighten the malevolence from which the Forest of ARDEN (1) offers escape, and the change in him testifies to the power of love, as found in this idyllic wood, to defeat evil. However, Oliver's conversion is not simply magical; it is the result of Orlando's humane decision to forswear revenge and save his sleeping brother from the serpent and lioness, as Oliver describes in 4.3.102–131. This unselfish act, undertaken at the risk of Orlando's life, provokes Oliver's utter total repentance. Oliver decides to give his estates to Orlando, and his loving relationship with Celia, incredible though it is in realistic terms, is the ultimate symbolic confirmation of—and reward for—his sincerity.

**Oliver (2), Sir**    Character in *As You Like It*. See MAR-TEXT.

**Olivia**    Character in *Twelfth Night*, wealthy mistress of an estate in ILLYRIA, the lover of Cesario—who, although she does not know it, is VIOLA in disguise—and later the bride of SEBASTIAN (2). Olivia is the object of Duke ORSINO's unrequited romantic fantasies. Like Orsino, she impedes the drama's triumph of love; she, too, has a false view of herself that she must overcome. Olivia moves from one illusion to another, beginning with a wilful withdrawal into seclusion and denial of life and then falling headlong into a passion that is based on a mistake. Only the course of events, beginning with the appearance of Sebastian, can correct matters, for Olivia is never aware of her errors.

Mourning her late brother, Olivia adopts an exaggerated, irrational stance that is acutely described by VALENTINE (3): '. . . like a cloistress she will veiled walk, / And water once a day her chamber round / With eye-offending brine' (1.1.28–30). Ironically, her withdrawal gives her something in common with her steward, MALVOLIO, who scorns pleasure and love.

However, grief is counter to Olivia's true nature. In 1.5 the glee with which she responds to the jester FESTE's comical teasing reveals that she is unsuited to the ascetic pose she has adopted, and she has the common sense to see Malvolio for what he is, saying, 'O, you are sick of self-love, Malvolio, and taste with a distempered appetite.' (1.5.89–90). She forgets her brother once she has been smitten with the charms of Cesario, and her pent-up instinct for love plunges her into a 'most extracting frenzy' (5.1.279). However, her passion is misplaced, not only because a disguised woman is its object but also because she is excessively self-involved, using what she knows to be 'shameful cunning' (3.1.118) to win her beloved. She admits, 'There's something in me that reproves my fault: / But such a headstrong potent fault it is, / That it but mocks reproof.' (3.4.205–207). Olivia has gone from scorning love in the name of propriety to being possessed by love beyond the reach of conscience.

Once Sebastian has replaced Cesario, Olivia remains impetuous, though she still recognises the irrationality of her course. 'Blame not this haste of mine' (4.3.22), she pleads as she leads Sebastian to the altar. At the play's near-hysterical climax in 5.1, Olivia struggles to keep Cesario, though he denies their marriage, until Sebastian reappears to claim her and identify Viola. Olivia is almost silent as this occurs, for her role in the tale of tangled romances is over. She comes to herself only when she realises that she has lost track of Malvolio, now incarcerated as a lunatic. She sees to his release and elicits the truth of the comic SUB-PLOT that has been going on beyond her distracted attention. When the steward flees in rage, she is sympathetic but amused; she has become the humane lady of her establishment that the frenzy of misplaced love had prevented her from being.

**Olivier, Laurence (1907–1989)**    British actor and director. Olivier—whose career covered a wide range of roles, both classical and modern, on stage and in FILM and TELEVISION—is often regarded as the greatest actor of the 20th century. Only John GIELGUD and Ralph RICHARDSON (2) are ranked with him among the great Shakespearean actors of the age. Among Olivier's best-known Shakespearean roles are HAMLET, RICHARD III, HENRY V, SIR TOBY BELCH, and TITUS (1) ANDRONICUS, and he played many other Shakespearean characters.

At the age of nine, playing BRUTUS (4) in a schoolboy production of *Julius Caesar*, Olivier was by chance observed by Sybil THORNDIKE and Lewis CASSON, who recorded their opinion that he was clearly a great actor. Similarly, he attracted rave reviews playing KATHERINA in *The Taming of the Shrew* at 14. In 1926 he joined the Birmingham Repertory Company, under Barry JACKSON (1), where he mostly played non-Shakespearean parts. His fame as a Shakespearean actor began in 1935, when he and Gielgud alternated roles as ROMEO and MERCUTIO in a famous production of *Romeo and Juliet*. In 1936 he played ORLANDO in a movie version of *As You Like It* and then, in a remarkable 1937–1938 season at the OLD VIC THEATRE, he played Hamlet, Sir Toby, Henry V, MACBETH, and IAGO. He also played Hamlet at ELSINORE in 1937. In the late 1930s Olivier made a number of popular and critically acclaimed movies, such as *Wuthering Heights* (1939) and *Pride and Prejudice* (1940). His romance with Vivien LEIGH began in 1936—a subject of extensive gossip, since both were married to others—and they married in 1940.

In 1944 Olivier returned to the Old Vic, where he played RICHARD III to great acclaim and began directing plays. In the same year he produced, directed, and starred in a film of *Henry V*. He made two more films, *Hamlet* (1948) and *Richard III* (1955), starring in each. *Hamlet* won two Academy Awards, for best film and best actor. (Olivier's *Hamlet* was a radically abridged version of Shakespeare's play, however, eliminating almost half the text, including all of ROSENCRANTZ AND GUILDENSTERN's part.) In 1947, Olivier was knighted, and in 1948 he was awarded another Oscar for his achievement throughout his career.

Olivier starred in the *Titus Andronicus* of Peter BROOK (2) (1955), a production that is credited with creating a renewed interest in the play. In 1961, divorced from Vivien Leigh, he married Joan PLOWRIGHT. From 1963 to 1972 he was the founding director of the British National Theatre Company, producing notable stagings of *Othello* and *The Merchant of Venice*—with himself as OTHELLO and SHYLOCK—and many other plays, both Shakespearean and otherwise. Suffering from a degenerative muscle disease, Olivier gave his last stage performance in 1974, but he continued working in films and television. He won an Emmy for his performance in the 1983 television production of *King Lear*. His last role was a cameo appearance in a 1988 television show, *War Requiem*, based on a work by Benjamin BRITTEN. Olivier published an autobiography, *Confessions of an Actor* (1982), and another book, *On Acting* (1986).

**One (1)** Minor character in *2 Henry VI*, a citizen who approaches the royal hawking party in 2.1, proclaiming that a miracle has occurred: a blind man, who proves to be the imposter SIMPCOX, has recovered his sight.

**One (2)** Minor character in *Troilus and Cressida*, an anonymous Greek warrior killed by HECTOR. In 5.6 Hector spies the Greek fighter wearing a sumptuous suit of armour, and he declares he will take it from him. The Greek flees, but in 5.8 we see that Hector has killed him, and as the triumphant warrior takes off his own armour to put on his prize, he is treacherously killed by ACHILLES and the MYRMIDONS.

While stripping the dead Greek, Hector addresses the corpse as, 'Most putrefied core, so fair without' (5.8.1), contrasting the dead body with the pomp and splendour of his armour (in words reminiscent of Christ's condemnation of the Pharisees as 'whited sepulchres' [Matthew 23:27]). The symbolic significance of the One is thus clear: he sums up the hypocrisy of the warriors' pretensions throughout the play. At the same time, the episode also reveals Hector's death to be the result of his abandonment of his code of honourable combat to pursue a rich prize.

**One (3) Within** Minor character in *Henry VIII*, LONDON commoner. The One Within is part of a crowd of enthusiastic celebrants of the christening of Princess ELIZABETH (1), who invade the royal courtyard, despite the efforts of the PORTER (4). He speaks from off stage, claiming to be a worker in the court of King HENRY VIII in 5.3.4 and baiting the Porter in 5.3.27. His voice contributes to the riotousness of the occasion. The speech prefixes in the FIRST FOLIO edition of the play designate this character as 'Within'; however, most subsequent editors have prefaced this with 'One'.

**Ophelia** Character in *Hamlet*, lover of Prince HAMLET. In 1.3 Ophelia's brother, LAERTES, cautions Ophelia against believing Hamlet's professions of love, and her father, POLONIUS, forbids her to see him. A demure and obedient daughter, Ophelia returns Hamlet's letters and, under the pressures of the main plot, Hamlet turns on her with a seemingly insane revulsion against women in general and her in particular. She reports his behaviour in 2.1 and encounters it

*Unable to reconcile her love for her father, Polonius, with her love for her father's murderer, Hamlet, the innocent Ophelia is driven to madness in* Hamlet. *The actress in this early photo wears wildflowers in her hair, a standard device to suggest the disorder of Ophelia's mind.* (Courtesy of Culver Pictures, Inc.)

in even more virulent form in 3.1. After her former lover kills her father, Ophelia becomes insane, babbling about funerals and singing scraps of songs in 4.5. Her death by drowning is reported by the QUEEN (9) in 4.7, and her funeral in 5.1—abbreviated by the PRIEST (3) because the death seems a suicide—triggers an encounter between Hamlet and Laertes that foreshadows the play's climax.

Ophelia's nature is abundantly affectionate; her wounded but faithful love—both for her father and for Hamlet—makes her one of the most touching of Shakespeare's characters. As Laertes observes about Ophelia's lunacy: 'where [love] is fine / It sends some precious instance of itself / After the thing it loves' (4.5.161–163). He refers to her love for the dead Polonius, which has caused her to send herself figuratively (and later literally) after him to a world beyond life, but the remark is equally appropriate to her love for Hamlet.

However, the relationship between Hamlet and Ophelia is not a love story, for Hamlet has rejected love. He loved Ophelia before the play opens, as is attested first by her touching recollection of his gifts and the 'words of so sweet breath compos'd / As made the things more rich' (3.1.98–99) and then by his admission at her funeral in 5.1.264–266. He remains sexually attracted to her—as is shown by his obscene jesting in 3.2.108–117—but he has displaced on her much of his anger with his mother, the Queen. She has become for him simply a stimulus for his disgust with women and sex, and he no longer really sees her as an actual person. Ophelia's fate is thus an outgrowth of Hamlet's emotional collapse; not only is her life diminished—and ultimately destroyed—by his actions, but she is a measure of what he has lost through his mistaken vision of the world.

Ophelia's insanity is triggered by the crushing of her love for Hamlet and then intensified by the loss of her father to Hamlet's madness. Her pathetic ravings in 4.5 are concerned with lost loves and death, the grim realities that have broken her mind. She cannot absorb the conflict implicit in loving both her father and his murderer. Her bawdy songs reflect the lusts of the outside world, of which she has no experience but that have contributed to her plight. The flowers she obsessively alludes to, themselves symbols of innocence, are poignant emblems of her own youth and inability to deal with the harsh world of the play.

While the Queen's description of Ophelia's drowning in 4.7.165–182 permits us to view it as accidental—a tree branch broke as she fell—she also reports that the victim made no effort to save herself. In 5.1 the GRAVE-DIGGER and the Priest view her as a suicide, and her death is certainly a result of her madness. But her insanity is the consequence of the actions of others, and Ophelia is unquestionably a victim of the tragic events that beset DENMARK throughout the play.

Some scholars believe that Ophelia's name—which means 'succor' in Greek, a seemingly inappropriate designation for so victimised a character—may have been used in error instead of Aphelia, meaning 'simplicity' or 'innocence'. Both names were rare in Shakespeare's time.

**Orlando**    Character in *As You Like It,* the lover of ROSALIND. Orlando is first seen as a victim of his older brother, OLIVER (1), who has seized Orlando's rightful inheritance and plots to have him killed by the wrestler CHARLES. After defeating Charles (and meeting Rosalind) in 1.2, Orlando is warned by his faithful servant, ADAM, that Oliver still intends to harm him, and the two flee in 2.3. As they arrive in the Forest of ARDEN (1), Orlando's noble spirit is stressed as he stoops to robbery in order to find food for the feeble Adam. Fortunately, his efforts lead him to the court-in-exile of DUKE (7) Senior, where, in 2.7, he is welcomed as a gentleman. He recalls Rosalind in a juvenile and

conventionally romantic way, as he hangs love poems to her from the trees, but he encounters her only in her disguise as GANYMEDE, who scoffs at his professed love and suggests that he might be cured of it if he pretends to woo 'him' and is rebuffed. Orlando is consistent in his avowals, however, though only later does he come to a mature sense of what love means.

The growing power of love in him is demonstrated when he resists the temptation to let a lioness kill his evil brother and instead risks his own life to save him, as Oliver reports in 4.3.98–132. Orlando has become aware of his own need for love and reconciliation in all aspects of his life. His full maturation is triggered by the love that arises between CELIA and the reformed Oliver. Faced with the real thing, Orlando tells Ganymede, 'I can live no longer by thinking' (5.2.50), and Rosalind realises that she can now discard her disguise, for Orlando is unquestionably committed to her and not simply to the idea of romantic love. Though Rosalind is the spokesperson for most of the play's position on the nature of love, Orlando's development is a powerful secondary demonstration of love's link to self-knowledge.

Orlando is something of a cardboard character. As a handsome leading man without a very well-developed personality, he contributes to the play's parody of PASTORAL literary conventions. Shakespeare's original audiences will have recognised Orlando as a romantic hero immediately, for reasons that are less evident to modern readers and viewers. His name is a version of Roland, one of the greatest heroes of medieval legend and literature, and an Orlando was also the hero of the most popular and well-known of 16th-century pastoral romances, Ludovico ARIOSTO's *Orlando Furioso* (1516, translated into English by Sir John HARINGTON in 1591). Further, Shakespeare's Orlando is identified with two great heroes of classical legend, Aeneas and Hercules. In 2.7 Orlando carries the weak and starving Adam to the Duke's banquet, a tableau that, to a classically educated reader or theatre-goer, must have brought to mind the well-known image, from VIRGIL's *Aeneid,* of Aeneas carrying his father to safety during the sack of Troy. And, to an Elizabethan audience, Orlando's conquests of Charles and the lioness will have immediately suggested the myths of Hercules wrestling Antaeus—depictions of which were extremely popular throughout RENAISSANCE Europe—and his killing the Nemean lion barehanded. In addition, Shakespeare dropped a broader hint when Rosalind, says to Orlando, 'Now Hercules be thy speed, young man!' (1.2.198).

**Orléans (1)**    Location in *1 Henry VI,* a city in FRANCE (1). The English siege of Orléans, part of the HUNDRED YEARS WAR, is the subject of 1.2 and 1.4–2.2. Although JOAN LA PUCELLE (Joan of Arc) arrives among the

French and inspires them, and the English commander, the Earl of SALISBURY (3), is killed, the English, led by TALBOT, take the city in a night-time attack.

Shakespeare's treatment of the siege of Orléans was intended to expand Talbot's role and exalt his heroism, and the playwright took extraordinary liberties with the historical record. Most strikingly, the English never actually took Orléans; besieged for six months, the city withstood the English troops. The English were led by Salisbury for only the first few weeks of the siege, and Talbot was not with the army at the time. After Salisbury's death, command was assumed by the Earl of SUFFOLK (3), a much less competent general; 10 days after Joan arrived, the revived French drove his forces away. Neither CHARLES VII nor REIGNIER was present. Talbot's night-time attack was derived from accounts of another battle—the capture of Le Mans.

**Orléans (2), Bastard of**  See BASTARD (2) of Orléans.

**Orléans (3), Charles, Duke of (1391–1465)**  Historical figure and character in *Henry V*, one of the fatuously over-confident French nobles before the battle of AGINCOURT. Like his fellows, Orléans has no distinctive personality; he joins them in feeble humour and idle insults to the English. They are simply caricatures, braggarts set up to take a fall.

The historical Orléans, nephew of Charles VI, the FRENCH KING of the play, was an important figure in the complicated French politics of the time. He was married to the former English QUEEN (13) Isabel, the widow of RICHARD II. He was seriously wounded and captured at Agincourt (as is reported in 4.6.78), and he was imprisoned in England for 26 years. During his captivity, he began to write poetry, continuing to do so after his release, and he is regarded as one of the greatest French medieval poets.

**Orsino**  Character in *Twelfth Night,* the Duke of IL-LYRIA, lover first of OLIVIA and then of VIOLA. Orsino, like Olivia, presents a false view of love that must be corrected in the course of the play. Orsino is infatuated with Olivia, who has repeatedly rejected him, while Viola, who is disguised as Cesario, Orsino's page, loves the duke but cannot tell him so. Utterly involved in his self-image as a brooding, rejected lover, Orsino cannot accept the fact that his passion for Olivia is misplaced. Though he is a humorous figure, a parody of the melancholy lovers of conventional 16th-century romances, he also displays aspects of psychological disorder—as FESTE observes, he is irrationally changeable, his 'mind is a very opal' (2.4.75)—and his wrong-headedness contributes to a sense that all is not well in Illyria.

When we first see the duke, he demonstrates his amusingly distorted slant on reality. In his absurdly romantic pose, he demands music to satiate his love-sick soul, insists that a particular phrase be repeated, then immediately orders that the music be stopped, saying, ' 'Tis not so sweet now as it was before' (1.1.8). He tellingly reverses the image of Olivia as the object of a hunt, making himself the hunted. By the end of the scene, Olivia has almost no importance herself; Orsino is totally absorbed in his own fantasies. But Orsino is not in love with himself; he is in love with love. In 1.4 Viola, as Cesario, vainly tries to induce a sensible attitude in the duke. He boasts of his 'unstaid and skittish' (2.4.18) behaviour, which he associates with love. Feste amusingly sings him a dirge of a love song, 'Come away death' (2.4.51–66), but Orsino does not recognise the implicit critique of his exaggerated melancholy.

The duke resembles such earlier Shakespearean lovers as SILVIUS in *As You Like It* and VALENTINE (1) in *The Two Gentlemen of Verona.* As those figures are mocked by ROSALIND and SPEED respectively, so Orsino is taken to task, comically by Feste and ironically by Viola, but like his predecessors, Orsino is hard-headed and resistant. Only the course of events can make things right for him, for he does not even recognise that they are amiss.

At the play's climax, the disquieting side of Orsino's misplaced emotions erupts in threatened violence, as Olivia's continuing rejection precipitates a menacing demonstration of frustrated masculine dominance as he decides to kill Cesario in a romantic gesture combining love and death. Proposing to 'sacrifice the lamb that I do love, / To spite a raven's heart within a dove' (5.1.128–129), he inadvertently acknowledges his affection for Cesario. His blindness has kept him from recognising this, but his instincts have nonetheless directed him truly, and once Viola's identity is revealed, Orsino is immediately ready to love her.

At the close of the play, when he orders that someone 'pursue [MALVOLIO], and entreat him to a peace' (5.1.379), Orsino achieves something of the quality of THESEUS (1) in *A Midsummer Night's Dream,* or PROSPERO in *The Tempest* (though in a lesser key), wise rulers who understand the uses of power and mercy. He becomes the man his position requires once he is brought to a state of loving grace.

**Osric**  Minor character in Hamlet, a foppish nobleman in the court of KING (5) Claudius of DENMARK. In 5.2 Osric carries the King's request that HAMLET meet LAERTES in a fencing match adding that the King has made a wager on Hamlet. Osric's highly mannered language and behaviour inspire Hamlet's amused derision, and the prince mocks the messenger, demonstrating the ease with which the courtier can be made to agree to contradictory assertions and making fun of his high-flown language. Osric later umpires the fencing match, though no further attention is paid to him.

Osric functions as comic relief in the face of the King's rapidly unfolding plot against Hamlet, which hinges on the fencing match. Further, the distraction offered by Osric subtly suggests Hamlet's own detachment from the danger that threatens him. The prince's bemused handling of the silly fop is reminiscent of his healthy appreciation of YORICK in 5.1. He is no longer in the grip of grief, and, newly aware of the importance of providence in human affairs, Hamlet can *enjoy* Osric. Osric is an ancient Anglo-Saxon name that was still used occasionally in Shakespeare's day.

**Ostler (1)**   Minor character in *1 Henry IV*, groom at an inn. The Ostler shouts his one brief line from off stage, lending an impression of hectic activity to the inn yard depicted in 2.1.

**Ostler (2), William (c. 1588–1614)**   English actor, a member of the KING'S MEN. One of the 26 men listed in the FIRST FOLIO as the 'Principall Actors' in Shakespeare's plays, Ostler began his career as a boy actor (see CHILDREN'S COMPANIES). He and John UNDERWOOD probably became members of the King's Men at the same time, replacing William SLY (2) and Laurence FLETCHER (3) upon their deaths in 1608. John DAVIES (1) called Ostler 'sole King of Actors' in a poem (1611) that also implied that he had been involved in a brawl. In 1611 Ostler married Thomasine, daughter of John HEMINGES, and at the same time became a partner in the BLACKFRIARS THEATRE; a year later he acquired a share in the GLOBE THEATRE as well. After Ostler's early death, Heminges claimed Ostler's shares in the theatres, despite a lawsuit by Thomasine.

**Oswald**   Character in *King Lear*, the steward of King LEAR's villainous daughter GONERIL. In 1.3 Oswald coolly accepts Goneril's instructions to treat her father insolently, for she wishes to humiliate him thoroughly. In 1.4 Oswald acts upon these orders. Thus, the steward is identified with his mistress as a villain, and when Lord KENT (2) beats him and drives him away, we approve. In 2.2 Kent encounters Oswald again and berates him in a long, comical series of insults that focus on the steward's pretensions to gentlemanly status. Kent's speech is a scathing critique of the vain, self-serving 'glass-gazing, super-serviceable' (2.2.16–17) courtier that Oswald seems to be. Less prominent after these encounters, Oswald principally serves Goneril as a messenger, until, in 4.5, he delivers a letter to REGAN and accepts her implied commission to kill the outcast and blinded Earl of GLOUCESTER (1). When he encounters Gloucester in the next scene he attempts to do so, only to be killed himself by the blind man's son, EDGAR. With his dying breath he begs his

killer to make amends by delivering his letters. He thus demonstrates loyalty to his mistress—he is indeed 'super-serviceable'—while at the same time he reveals her secrets and provides for her ultimate downfall in the final scene.

Oswald represents a familiar character type found in the satirical comedy of JACOBEAN DRAMA, a caricature of an ambitious commoner attempting to climb into aristocratic social circles. The rise of the gentry and the birth of the bourgeoisie during the reigns of Queen ELIZABETH (1) and King JAMES I resulted in a crisis of confidence among the aristocracy, who attempted to distinguish themselves from the newly rich by insisting on proper manners and values. This social conflict is the subject of humour in many plays of the period (see, e.g., MALVOLIO, of *Twelfth Night*). In the clash between Kent and Oswald the advantage is given clearly to the old nobility at the expense of the rising class, reflecting Shakespeare's conservative social instincts. Some scholars have speculated that Oswald is further intended as a satire on an actual person, perhaps William FFARINGTON, the obnoxious steward of the Elizabethan theatre patron Lord STRANGE, but this cannot be proven.

**Othello**   Title character in *Othello*, the husband of DESDEMONA, whom he murders because he has been misled by the villainous IAGO. A Moorish general in the service of VENICE, Othello has just married the much younger Desdemona as the play opens. The central dynamic of the drama is his alteration from a noble lover to a raving killer under the malevolent influence of his aide, Iago, who convinces him that his wife is having a love affair with another officer, CASSIO. Unable to trust Desdemona—he lacks this basic element of love—Othello disintegrates morally. His destructiveness extends to his own suicide when his error is exposed. He suffers emotional agonies throughout this process, and we suffer with him, grieving for the destruction of his inherent nobility and the beauty that his marriage exemplifies at its outset.

Through 3.2 Othello is a grandly positive character—a leading figure in the Venetian establishment, a respected military man, and a loving husband. He carries himself with impressive dignity while frankly delighting in his young wife, whose love he values above 'the sea's worth' (1.2.28). When the couple defend their elopement, in 1.3, we see that their love is both spiritually satisfying and imbued with a healthy sexuality. However, in the second half of the play he abandons this transcendent love for a blind jealousy too strong to see reason. He loses faith not only in Desdemona but also in himself. When he rejects her love and trust, Othello also rejects his own capacity for love, in favour of a demanding but unsatisfiable self-centredness.

When he collapses in 4.1, Othello can only babble

as he falls at Iago's feet in a trance. He recovers his wits, but from this point he has only one goal: the deaths of Desdemona and Cassio. In his single-minded malice, Othello now shares Iago's malevolent spirit. Indeed, as the play progresses he even comes to resemble the villain in his speech, using staccato repetitions, broken sentences, and Iago's violent, sexual animal imagery. By 4.1 he cruelly insults his wife publicly, and in 4.2, the so-called 'brothel' scene, he indulges in a savage exaggeration of his jealousy when he says he believes Desdemona a harlot and EMILIA (2) her bawd. In the end, though he can still contemplate his love for his wife when he sees her asleep, he kills her with a coolness that stresses the power of his fixation. His reaction once Desdemona's innocence has been established is just as potent. He recognises that he is no longer noble—he calls himself 'he that was Othello' (5.2.285)—and equating himself with the heathen enemies he used to conquer, he kills himself.

Iago can effect this extraordinary response only because Othello is lacking in trust. This lack is implicit in the Moor's situation from the outset, for he cannot partake of the social solidarity that encourages and reinforces trust between humans. He is an outsider in Venice because of his profession—a mercenary soldier, unacquainted with civilian society 'even from [his] boyish days' (1.3.132)—and his race. Though Othello's military skills are valued and he is not denied the protection of a hearing on BRABANTIO's charge of witchcraft, he is nonetheless an alien in a prejudiced society. He is isolated from the world he has married into. Iago can convince him that Desdemona might have come to detest him because he is black; he lacks the support of a solid position in Desdemona's world that might temper the fear of rejection that his jealousy feeds on.

Though the evidence in the play is clear, some commentators have declared that Othello is not actually black—usually on the racist grounds that so noble a figure could not be a 'veritable negro', as Samuel Taylor COLERIDGE put it. Most frequently, a Moor is held to be of an Arab-related racial type, rather than a Negro. However, Shakespeare (like his contemporaries) drew no such distinction, and Othello is clearly a black African; decisively, RODERIGO calls Othello 'the thicklips' (1.1.66). (Significantly, Shakespeare's other notable Moor, AARON of *Titus Andronicus,* calls his child 'thick-lipp'd' and himself 'coal-black', and he refers to his 'fleece of woolly hair' [*Titus* 4.2.176, 99; 2.3.34].)

Shakespeare plainly intended Othello's race to have a great impact on his original audiences, many of whom, he knew, were as prejudiced as Brabantio. Othello is the earliest black character in English literature with a credible personality, let alone a sympathetic one. Shakespeare deliberately emphasised this, for in CINTHIO's tale, his source, Othello's race has little importance, while in the play it is frequently mentioned, especially in Act 1 where the nature of Venetian society is stressed. The obvious racist caricature offered before Othello appears is entirely in line with the standard English stereotypes of the day, but his actual bearing is strikingly noble. This is emphasised numerous times—Othello even claims royal birth in 1.2.21–22, a point that had much greater importance in Shakespeare's day than in ours—and the playwright must have been aware of the impact of this bold departure. For one thing, Desdemona's strength is greatly magnified by her willingness to courageously defy society's biases. Further, Shakespeare's sympathetic portrait of an alien figure, combined with the compassionate presentation of his repentance and suicide at the play's close, emphasises that the potential for tragic failure is universal.

Othello's race helps determine his status as an alienated outsider in Venice, and this makes him susceptible to Iago's persuasions, for he is grievously naïve about Desdemona's world. Iago assures him, 'I know our country disposition well' (3.3.205), and Othello, reminded of his own ignorance, accepts at face value the preposterous claim that adultery is the moral norm among Venetian women. Iago is absolutely correct when he says to Emilia, 'I told him . . . no more / Than what he found himself was apt and true' (5.2.177–178). Most significantly, once distracted, Othello is not capable of appreciating Desdemona; he knows enough of Venice to see its prejudice, but he does not recognise her steadfast courage in opposing it. Like CORIOLANUS and MACBETH, Othello has succeeded as a soldier and is accordingly endowed with dignity and pride but can only misunderstand the world outside the military camp.

With his suicide Othello acknowledges his fault, but his final recognition of Desdemona's goodness offers us—if not him—the consoling sense that in dying he recovers something of his former nobility. He honestly admits that he 'lov'd not wisely, but too well' and was 'perplex'd in the extreme' (5.2.345, 347). We see a vestige of pride when he refers to his former service to the state, and when he identifies his errant self with the 'malignant . . . Turk' (5.2.354) he once slew, we see that in dying he is as triumphant, in a way, as he was 'in Aleppo once' (5.2.353).

Othello has returned to sanity too late, but that he returns at all provides us with some sense of reconciliation. Othello's fate shows us that a noble person may fall to the depths of savagery, but that an essential humanity remains within the troubled soul. The tradition of the medieval MORALITY PLAY was still familiar in Shakespeare's day and certainly influenced him. Othello's striking placement between Iago and Desdemona resembles the situation of the central character in a morality play: symbolic of the human soul, he was placed between an angel and a devil who each demanded his loyalty. Though the devil succeeded for a time, and the character sinned (entertainingly), the mercy of God nevertheless prevailed, and the character was reclaimed by the angel and forgiven in the end. Similarly, *Othello* offers redemption at its close. Othello is emblematic of one aspect of human life; he incarnates the inexorable guilt and ultimate death that we recognise as the tragic element in humanity's fate, but his eventual awareness offers a redeeming catharsis.

## Othello

### SYNOPSIS

*Act 1, Scene 1*

RODERIGO, who has been courting DESDEMONA, is distressed at IAGO's news that she has eloped with OTHELLO, a Moorish general in the service of VENICE. Iago, who is Othello's aide, assures Roderigo that he also hates the Moor because Othello has denied him a promotion that went instead to CASSIO. He says that he only continues to serve the general in the hope of revenge. Iago and Roderigo awaken Desdemona's father, BRABANTIO, to inform him of the elopement.

*Act 1, Scene 2*

Iago tells Othello of Brabantio's anger, as Cassio arrives with word that the general has been summoned by the DUKE (5) to a council of war. Brabantio and Roderigo arrive. The angry father, informed of the Duke's council, plans to accuse Othello there.

*Act 1, Scene 3*

The Duke and several SENATORS (1) receive news of an immanent Turkish attack on the Venetian island of CYPRUS. Othello and Brabantio arrive and Brabantio makes his accusation. Othello replies that Desdomona loves him and has married him of her own free will. When she is summoned she supports his account. Brabantio concedes, and the meeting turns to business: Othello is ordered to leave for Cyprus. Desdemona is to live there with him, and Iago is to escort her in a later ship. Privately, Iago assures Roderigo that Desdemona will soon repent marriage to a Moor, and that if Roderigo will come to Cyprus he will continue to help him with his suit by delivering presents to Desdemona. Roderigo agrees and leaves; Iago reflects on how easy it is to get money from this fool. Saying that Othello is rumoured to have cuckolded him, he goes on to plot revenge upon both Othello and Cassio; he will make the general believe that Cassio is the lover of his new wife.

*Act 2, Scene 1*

In Cyprus the Venetian governor, MONTANO (2), and two friends discuss the great storm that may have destroyed the Turkish fleet. A third GENTLEMAN (6) brings news that Cassio has arrived with word that this has indeed happened, but that the ship carrying the new governor, Othello, has also disappeared. Iago arrives with Desdemona, his wife, EMILIA (2), and Roderigo. Iago engages the two women in a courtly exchange of witticisms while they await word about Othello. The general arrives safely and greets Desdemona with affection. The group moves indoors, except for Iago and Roderigo. Iago proposes a plot: he says that Desdemona is in love with Cassio and proposes that Roderigo pick a fight with the lieutenant while he commands the guard that night, in the hopes that fighting on duty will disgrace Cassio and remove him as potential competition for Desdemona. Roderigo agrees. Alone, Iago meditates on the course of his plans: he will abuse Cassio to Othello and get credit from the general, while at the same time making him sick with jealousy.

*Act 2, Scene 2*

A gentleman reads Othello's proclamation of a public holiday. All the soldiers are at liberty until eleven at night, when they must return to duty.

*Act 2, Scene 3*

Despite Cassio's insistence that a little wine will make him very drunk, Iago convinces him to drink for the sake of the holiday. They join some others, including Montano, and when Cassio goes to take his guard post he is drunk. Iago sends Roderigo after Cassio; he shortly reappears, pursued by the drunken lieutenant, who gets into a fight with Montano. Iago sends Roderigo to sound the alarm, and Othello appears and angrily dismisses Cassio from his post. Left alone with a dismayed Cassio, Iago convinces him that his only hope of recovering his position is to get Desdemona to present his case to Othello. Cassio agrees and leaves, and Iago exults in the success of his scheme: now Othello will witness—and jealously misconstrue—Desdemona's interest in Cassio.

*Act 3, Scene 1*

Cassio has hired MUSICIANS (6) to play before the general's quarters in the hope of influencing his mood. Iago sends Emilia to Cassio; she assures him that Desdemona favours his cause and agrees to take him where he may meet with the general's wife.

*Act 3, Scene 2*

Othello prepares to conduct an inspection of the fortifications.

*Act 3, Scene 3*

Desdemona assures Cassio she will plead his case to Othello. Cassio withdraws as Othello and Iago approach; Iago pretends to regard this suspiciously. Desdemona asks Othello to take Cassio back, and he agrees, saying that he loves her and can deny her nothing. She leaves, and Iago begins to ask seemingly innocent questions about Cassio. He pretends to be reluctant to express his suspicion, but goes on to inflame Othello with the idea of a sexual affair between Cassio and Desdemona. He suggests that if Othello delays Cassio's reappointment he can see if Desdemona supports the lieutenant to an excessive degree. Othello fears that Desdemona has been unfaithful because he is black or because he is old, but he tries to resist the thought. Desdemona and Emilia arrive to accompany him to a state banquet, and Othello disguises his distress. As they leave, Desdemona drops a handkerchief that was Othello's first gift to her. Emilia picks it up, and Iago takes it from her as she leaves. He states his intention to plant it on Cassio. Othello returns and angrily demands proof of Desdemona's infidelity. Iago asserts that Cassio has Desdemona's handkerchief. Enraged, Othello goes on his knees to formally swear vengeance, and Iago affirms his loyalty and joins him in the oath, promising to kill Cassio himself and to help Othello kill Desdemona.

### Act 3, Scene 4

Desdemona speaks of Cassio, but Othello demands his handkerchief. He says it was charmed by an Egyptian sorceress so that the woman who lost it would be damned in the eyes of her lover. Desdemona denies that it is lost. She tries to change the subject back to Cassio, and Othello leaves in a rage. Iago and Cassio appear; Desdemona remarks on Othello's strange anger, and Iago volunteers to go see the general. Emilia observes that Othello may be jealous of his wife, even though he has no reason, and Desdemona decides she must approach him again. The women leave Cassio as BIANCA (2) appears. She humorously chastises Cassio for not seeing her more often. He asks her to make him a copy of the embroidered handkerchief he has found.

### Act 4, Scene 1

Iago says that Cassio has admitted to sleeping with Desdemona. Beside himself with rage, Othello babbles incoherently and then faints. Cassio appears, and Iago tells him he has important news that he will give him once Othello has recovered and they can speak alone. Cassio leaves, and when Othello awakens Iago tells him that if he eavesdrops on the meeting he has arranged with Cassio, the general will hear Cassio speak of his affair with Desdemona. Cassio returns, and Iago speaks to him of Bianca, his lover. With amused disrespect, Cassio laughs about how she presumes to think she'll marry him, and Othello, crying out in asides, believes he is speaking of Desdemona. Bianca arrives, angry about the handkerchief, which she believes was given to Cassio by another woman. Othello now thinks that Cassio has given Desdemona's love token to a harlot. Bianca and Cassio leave, and Othello says he will kill Desdemona; Iago promises to kill Cassio that night. Desdemona appears with LODOVICO, who brings a message from Venice calling Othello back and placing Cassio in command

of Cyprus. When Desdemona is pleased, Othello hits her; enraged, he can barely speak. He orders her away and then leaves. Lodovico is surprised at this behaviour, but Iago confides that it is sometimes much worse.

### Act 4, Scene 2

Othello quizzes Emilia who says there is no reason to suspect Desdemona and Cassio. He does not believe her and sends her to summon his wife. When Desdemona appears he accuses her and ignores her denials. He leaves in a rage as Emilia reappears. When Desdemona tells Emilia of Othello's state, she fetches Iago, and the two try to reassure her. Desdemona and Emilia leave as Roderigo arrives. He complains that Iago has taken his money and jewels and done nothing for him. Iago tells him that because Cassio is to replace Othello as governor, the general is leaving and will take Desdemona with him. Iago promises to help Roderigo kill Cassio so that Othello will have to stay, and Desdemona will remain within reach.

### Act 4, Scene 3

On his way out, Othello tells Desdemona that she is to prepare for bed and dismiss Emilia. Desdemona says that she loves Othello despite his unreasonable anger, though she also has a presentiment of tragedy; she sings a song that was sung by an abandoned woman while she died. Though Desdemona is revolted by the idea of sexual infidelity, Emilia declares that men deserve it.

### Act 5, Scene 1

Iago sets Roderigo up to ambush Cassio; he hopes that Roderigo and Cassio will kill each other, for Roderigo may claim repayment from him and Cassio may disprove his story. Cassio appears and Roderigo attacks him, but is wounded by Cassio. Iago then wounds Cassio from behind and flees. Othello sees the wounded Cassio crying for help and exults in the sight. He leaves as Lodovico and GRATIANO (2) arrive. Iago returns, pretends to be enraged at the assault on Cassio, and kills Roderigo. Bianca arrives. Iago declares that she is probably involved in the attempted murder and places her under arrest.

### Act 5, Scene 2

Othello, at the bed of the sleeping Desdemona, is overcome with love for her and declares that he will not harm her beauty, but will kill her bloodlessly. She wakes, and he tells her to prepare for death. He says the handkerchief is proof of her adultery. She says that Cassio will clear her, but Othello triumphantly reports his death. She pleads for mercy, but Othello smothers her. Emilia appears, and Desdemona recovers enough to declare that she is dying in innocence. She dies, and Othello proclaims that he has murdered her because she was unfaithful. Emilia denies it, and Othello declares that Iago has proved it. She calls for help, and

Montano, Gratiano, and Iago appear. Othello speaks of Desdemona's handkerchief, and Emilia reveals the truth. Iago kills her and flees. Montano chases him, leaving Othello to his mounting grief. When Lodovico brings Iago back, Othello attacks him and wounds him before he is disarmed. Othello declares himself a fool but not a dishonourable one, stabs himself with a hidden weapon and dies.

## COMMENTARY

The most striking difference between *Othello* and Shakespeare's other tragedies is its more intimate scale. The terror of the supernatural is not invoked, as it is in *Hamlet* and *Macbeth*; extremes of psychological derangement, as in *King Lear,* are not present. Kingdoms are not at stake, and the political consequences of the action are not emphasised as they are in varying degrees in all of the other tragedies. Here, Shakespeare focusses on personal rather than public life; Othello's plunge into obsession occurs mostly in private—only he and Iago know it is happening—and he murders Desdemona in the seclusion of their bedroom. The play has been described as a domestic comedy gone wrong. Its tragedy lies in the destruction of the happy personal lives of the general and his bride by the perverse malice of a single unsatisfied man. Yet *Othello* is profoundly social, for the human quality that Iago lacks and that he destroys in Othello is trust, the cement that holds people together. Jealousy, the

*A scene from the 1965 film of* Othello *with Laurence Olivier as the Moor and Maggie Smith as Desdemona. The same great passion with which Othello loves his wife leads him to murder her when his faith turns into jealousy.* (Courtesy of Culver Pictures, Inc.)

play's central motif, is simply a particularly virulent form of interpersonal distrust. The tragedy of *Othello* is that a noble man loses faith and is reduced to a bestial frenzy. As a result, a love and a life are destroyed, and this loss inspires horror in the audience, which, combined with our pity for Desdemona, gives the play tremendous power. Significantly, *Othello* stands out as one of Shakespeare's plays that has been altered very little over the centuries by its producers, for its capacity to overwhelm audiences has always been recognised.

The central dynamic in *Othello* is the hero's change in attitude towards Desdemona. At first the couple are happily matched; when they defend their elopement, in 1.3, they establish themselves as mature lovers whose passion is both spiritual and sexual, mutually satisfying and based on self-knowledge. But Othello's weakness destroys his happiness as his trust in his wife turns to jealousy and then murderous hatred under the influence of Iago. On the other hand, his trust in his aide never flags until he is finally exposed. Othello comes to see love through Iago's eyes rather than Desdemona's. In a sense, Iago and Desdemona represent internalised features of the hero: he rejects his loving and generous self—that aspect of humanity that makes society possible—in favour of the dark passions of his self-centred ego. In the end, the forces of trust and love regain their strength as Othello finally recognises the goodness of Desdemona, and Iago is formally condemned, but in the meantime the action of the play has demonstrated the power of evil.

The motif of trust destroyed dominates the interactions of Iago and Othello on one hand and Othello and Desdemona on the other. Othello is placed between Iago—who cannot trust or love—and Desdemona—who offers an ideal, unconditional love. This situation closely resembles the traditional MORALITY PLAY, whose central character, usually symbolic of the human soul, is placed between an angel and a devil who each demand his loyalty. This dramatic form was still familiar to Shakespeare and his audience, and *Othello* reflects it in its distinctly allegorical quality. Iago is associated with the devil several times, and Desdemona—in her martyrlike acceptance of her entirely undeserved end—may be seen as a symbol of Christian love and resignation to the will of God.

In its structure *Othello* continually focusses our attention on its main theme, jealous mistrust. The relationships of Othello to Iago and Desdemona are paralleled in those between several minor characters in the play. For instance, Othello's credulousness is foreshadowed in that of Roderigo, whose victimisation by Iago is established in the opening scene, and makes clear the nature and extent of his villainy from the outset. Similarly, later in the play, Cassio's disastrous reversion from distrust to trust of the villain echoes the development of the main plot. Also, Cassio's admiring recognition of Desdemona's virtues offers the opposite image to Othello's loss of perception, while her appreciation of Cassio reflects ironically on Othello's mistaken opinion of Iago.

Perhaps most striking are the two 'marriages' paralleling that of Othello and Desdemona. Cassio is linked with Bianca, and while they are not formally married, a comparison is irresistible because Iago substitutes Bianca for Desdemona when he deceives Othello about the handkerchief, in 4.1. More pointedly, Bianca's jealousy of Cassio—expressed in her complaint that he has avoided her, in 3.4, and her anger when she thinks that he has been given Desdemona's handkerchief by another woman—echoes Othello's emotion but in a context where jealousy seems justified. Iago and Emilia's marriage, while plainly lacking affection, let alone love, is not immune from sexual jealousy. Iago remarks several times that he is suspicious of his wife's adultery with either Othello in 1.3. 385–386) or Cassio (2.1.302). His assumption that his wife's lover was Othello sounds intended only to justify his campaign against the general, but he seems to have some cause for suspicion: Emilia clearly states that she would indeed commit adultery, in 4.3.70–76, 84–103, as she believes that unfaithfulness is a woman's only weapon against a bad husband. The mutual distrust in which these two live offers another instance of the play's major motif, jealousy. All three marriages, with their stress on this emotion, demonstrate abundantly the fragility of trust between humans.

Iago's jealousy is particularly significant, as it suggests that when he misleads Othello he is simply transferring his own psychic ailment. In fact, Iago's jealousy extends beyond a purely sexual context; he is motivated in large part by envy, the jealous sense that others have advantages over him. He fears that the free and virtuous natures of the other characters, especially Desdemona, may demonstrate his own worthlessness. It is precisely Othello's 'constant, noble, loving nature' (2.1.284) that he cannot endure, and he recognises that Cassio 'has a daily beauty in his life, / That makes me ugly' (5.1.19–20). He accordingly proposes to 'out of [Desdemona's] goodness make the net / That shall enmesh 'em all' (2.3.352–353).

The parallels that reinforce the theme of jealousy illustrate the craftsmanship of the playwright, and indeed, *Othello* is a particularly well-constructed play. Most strikingly, Shakespeare introduces—and then contrives to disguise—what seems to be a serious defect of the plot, namely that Desdemona's infidelity should be utterly implausible to Othello for the simple reason that she has had absolutely no opportunity for it. Iago presents this fictional 'love affair' as though it had been going on for some time, while in fact Othello and Desdemona have only been married a few hours when they depart for Cyprus—on different ships, with

Cassio on a third—and once there, Othello passes the first night with Desdemona and kills her on the second. The haste with which the plot unfolds contributes tremendously to its almost unbearable tension, and for this reason Shakespeare chose an unrealistic time span rather than a weeks-long scenario in which an adulterous affair could evolve realistically. He carries it off by means of a clever device that critics refer to as 'double time'. While the two days' development is nonsensical, it is effectively disguised by a number of strategic references suggestive of a different time frame. For instance, Iago speaks of '. . . how oft, how long ago, and when' (4.1.85) Cassio and Desdemona have made love, and Othello later justifies her murder with the claim that this love-making had occurred 'a thousand times' (5.2.213); Emilia says that Iago has asked her 'a hundred times' (3.3.296) to steal Desdemona's handkerchief, and she suggests that Desdemona has had 'a year or two' (3.4.100) to become acquainted with Othello; Cassio is said to have been absent from Bianca for a week, with the implication of an established relationship before that; orders recalling Othello to Venice arrive, reflecting time enough for news of the situation on Cyprus to have reached Venice and the orders returned. These hints, among numerous others, serve to keep before us a convincing sense that more has transpired than could actually be the case.

However, 'double time' is unworkable for exposition, and Act 1 differs from the rest of the play in being performed in real time. Here, in Venice, we are introduced to the characters and their world under more realistic circumstances. Events are not compressed into a short time for before the main action is underway the playwright does not need to deceive us about the pace of events, and he can properly establish the nature of his characters, especially Iago. In the long interchanges between him and Roderigo in 1.1 and 1.3, in his lie that opens 1.2, and especially in his soliloquy that closes the Act, Iago's villainous nature and his enmity towards Othello are made clear, and we are primed for the developments to follow.

Act 1 also differs from the rest of the play in its setting. This is very telling, for Othello's place in the society of Venice plays an important, if subtle, role in his downfall. As Brabantio's response to Desdemona's marriage makes abundantly clear, Venice is a closed society, racist in its distrust of Othello. Also, Venice is seen to be influenced by inhumane commercial values. Iago exploits the degraded values of Roderigo, who thinks love is a commodity, and many commentators have seen a satire on mercantile society—Venetian and English, both—in Iago's repeated advice to Roderigo to 'put money in thy purse' (beginning at 1.3.342). This is a world that cannot appreciate Othello's virtues. The general is thus isolated from the world he has married into; Iago can convince him that

Desdemona might 'repent' the 'foul disproportion' (3.3.242, 237) of a mixed marriage, and Othello lacks the assurance of a respectable social position that might temper the fear of rejection that his jealousy feeds on.

The racial bias of Shakespeare's Venice is important and quite prominent, especially in Act 1. Brabantio's belief that Desdemona could not love 'the sooty bosom / Of such a thing' (1.2.70–71) is based on the racist assumption that such love would be 'against all rules of nature' (1.3.101). Iago and Roderigo have stimulated Brabantio's rage with labels, such as 'old black ram' (1.1.88), 'Barbary horse' (1.1.111), and 'lascivious Moor' (1.1.126), associating race with animals, sex, and the devil, characteristically racist ploys, even today. No one disputes Brabantio's statement that Desdemona has subjected herself to 'general mock' (1.2.69) by marrying a black man; prejudice is plainly widespread in Venice.

Othello is the earliest sympathetic black character in English literature, and the play's emphasis on prejudice must have had particular impact in Shakespeare's LONDON, which was a distinctly biased society. Though Africans were present in London in some numbers beginning around 1550—especially once the English slave trade got underway in the 1560s—little distinction was drawn between North African and sub-Saharan blacks. Africa and Africans had figured in English drama from an even earlier date; dozens of 16th-century plays made use of African settings or characters, though virtually all of them were wildly inaccurate and blatantly racist, depicting Africans in simple stereotypes as idle, lustful, and likely to be treacherous. Not surprisingly, the biases of English society as a whole was equally blatant. In 1599 and 1601 the government made an effort to deport all of the 'Negars and Blackamores which [have] crept into this realm'.

The Venice of *Othello,* like London in its greed and racism, has another aspect, however. As represented by the Duke and the Senators, the society offers a model of trust and co-operation. In 1.3 we see these figures arriving through consensus at a collective response to the Turkish threat, and in the same workmanlike spirit they insist that Othello be permitted a defence against Brabantio's charges. They recognise his innocence and accept him as their general, and Brabantio agrees entirely, accepting his society's collective judgement. On the whole, Venice is not a promising milieu for Iago's purposes; significantly, Shakespeare removes the action from Venice when the main plot is to get under way. On Cyprus the action is isolated; no social or political distractions remove Othello from Iago's influence, and Desdemona can have no recourse to advice or intervention. It is only when Venetian envoys come to Cyprus that the truth can be unfolded, though too late.

In another manipulation of time, Shakespeare tightens the tension rapidly as we approach the play's climax by subtly increasing the pace with which things seem to occur. As Iago puts it, 'Dull not device by coldness and delay' (2.3.378). For instance, when Iago first makes Othello desire revenge against Desdemona and Cassio, the general demands Cassio's death 'within these three days' (3.3.479) and Desdemona's death is not scheduled. But when the matter is next discussed, Othello insists on killing Desdemona 'this night . . . this night' (4.1.200–202) and Iago promises to kill Cassio 'by midnight' (4.1.207). This sudden acceleration creates an effect of heightened tension that reflects Othello's mental state. It also diverts attention from the illogicality of time's so-swift passage while increasing the pace.

Only once, and in a very telling manoeuvre, does Shakespeare slacken the pace of events—in the famed 'willow' scene (4.3), in which Desdemona prepares for bed and, unknowingly, for death. This lull prepares us for the final storm of Act 5's violence. Desdemona's melancholy at Othello's changed and angry manner yields a morbid fantasy that is, in effect, a slow, grand elegy of her innocence and virtue. She imagines herself dead, shrouded in her wedding sheets, and she remembers her mother's maid, who died of love, singing 'a song of "willow", / An old thing [that] express'd her fortune' (4.3.28–29). Ominously, Desdemona sings it herself, and its plaintive sadness soothes her even as it chills us with its portent of her death. Her calm and beautiful acceptance of fate is contrasted at the scene's close with Emilia's cynical speech on adultery. Our appreciation of Desdemona in this scene makes the approaching climax all the more horrible. Despite its languid tone, this brilliantly conceived interlude actually succeeds in heightening our anxiety.

Through a simple plot with minimal comic relief, Shakespeare avoids distractions that would permit the audience to recuperate temporarily from the increasing tension into which they are drawn. The few diversions from the main plot are mostly anxiety-producing disturbances. The midnight brawl of 2.3 that results from Cassio's drunkeness; Othello's cruel rudeness as he pretends to take his wife's bedroom for a bordello, in 4.2; another fight scene, in which Roderigo wounds Cassio and Iago kills Roderigo—all of these events offer the reverse of comic relief, tightening our emotional screws for the next stage of Iago's plot against Othello. Even at the play's close, the tension is similarly maintained as the eerie privacy in which the murder of Desdemona takes place is followed by the raucous tumult in which Iago kills Emilia and Othello wounds Iago and kills himself. Only in the very last lines of the play is there relief when Lodovico disposes of practical matters in the wake of the death of the Venetian commander on Cyprus.

Not only is the rule of society re-established at the close, but Iago's triumph over Othello is undercut by the hero's recognition of his error. The trust that had been violated is at least acknowledged in the end. In the world of tragedy, death and defeat are inescapable, thus mirroring the tragic aspects of human existence. Othello is not a hero through triumph, but because he is an incarnation of basic human energies, both good and bad. When he joins Desdemona in death he offers recompense for his grievous self-centredness earlier, and while this compensation is obviously useless to her, it offers *us* a cathartic sense of reconciliation with tragedy. The lives—and deaths—of Othello and Desdemona are in the end transcended by their involvement with each other. She sacrifices herself to her love and he himself to his grief that he was inadequate to it. Without the support of his love for Desdemona, Othello could only say, 'Chaos is come again' (3.3.93); with his recognition of his error, order is implicitly restored as the ethical meaning of the story is revealed.

## SOURCES OF THE PLAY

The source for *Othello* was a novella by the Italian author, CINTHIO, published in his collection *Hecatommithi* (1565). No surviving English translation of the tale was made until much later, and scholars dispute whether the playwright read Cinthio in Italian, in a French or Spanish translation, or in some now lost English translation. In any case, Shakespeare made a number of significant changes in Cinthio's tale. He accelerated the course of events to produce a tauter drama, and he altered the personalities of the major characters, making Othello and Desdemona nobler and Iago more coldly malevolent. He also added such minor characters as Roderigo, Brabantio, and the Venetian officials.

An actual murder may also have been a source for the play. In 1565 an Italian serving the French government was diverted from a diplomatic mission by false reports of his wife's infidelity, circulated by his enemies. Returning home, he accepted her denials, but, after earnestly seeking her forgiveness, strangled her anyway in the name of honour. Scholars speculate that knowledge of this historical event may have influenced Shakespeare in his choice of Cinthio's tale, though no known English source can be cited.

Other minor literary sources include LEO AFRICANUS' *A Geographical History of Africa* (translated by John PORY; publ. 1600) and the *Natural History* of PLINY the Elder (translated by Philemon HOLLAND [4]). Also, Shakespeare's odd mention of two otherwise unknown characters—'Signior Angelo' and 'Marcus Luccicos' (1.3.16, 44)—suggests the existence of some minor source material that is now lost.

## TEXT OF THE PLAY

*Othello* was probably written in 1603 or 1604, just before its earliest recorded performance. Some schol-

ars believe that the BAD QUARTO of *Hamlet* (Q1, 1603) is contaminated by recollections of lines from *Othello*, favouring an earlier date (possibly 1602) for *Othello*, though others find the evidence uncertain. On grounds of style and content, *Othello* cannot be dated earlier than 1602.

The play was first published in 1622 by Thomas WALKLEY, in a QUARTO edition, known as Q1, printed by Nicholas OKES. It was printed from a manuscript whose nature has been the subject of considerable scholarly debate. It may have been a FAIR COPY of Shakespeare's manuscript, or it may have been a transcript of either his FOUL PAPERS or of the PROMPT-BOOK kept by the KING'S MEN. The transcription may originally have been made for Walkley's publication, or for use by the King's Men, or, possibly, for an individual, a theatre enthusiast. Given the surviving evidence, none of these theories can be positively proven or disproven.

In 1623 *Othello* appeared in the FOLIO edition of plays, and this text (known as F) was probably printed from Q1, but amended according to another manuscript whose nature is also perplexing. It may have been Shakespeare's fair copy; it may have been a prompt-book; it may have reflected alterations resulting from years of productions; it may have included errors made by someone relying on their memory of performances; it may have incorporated Shakespeare's own alterations. Again, no hypothesis can be established firmly.

Whatever this manuscript was, it differed significantly from Q1. There are over a thousand variants, most of them minor, but F contains about 160 lines not present in Q1, including a few substantial passages. The longest fragment (4.3.31–52, 54–56) contains much of the 'willow' song, for instance. On the other hand, Q1 contains ten brief passages (the longest being four lines) not in F. Whether these variations represent additions to one text or cuts from the other is debated by scholars; in practise, modern editors have generally found F to be the superior text and have used it as the basis for their versions, while also using variants from Q1 in many particular instances. However, some editors reverse the priority.

## THEATRICAL HISTORY OF THE PLAY

The earliest known performance of *Othello* took place at the court of King JAMES I on November 1, 1604. Numerous other performances in various theatres and at court are recorded prior to the closure of the theatres by the civil war in 1642; and it appears to have been among the most popular of Shakespeare's plays in his own lifetime, as it has been ever since. Richard BURBAGE (3) was the first Othello, and though the original Iago was not recorded, it is known that after 1619 Joseph TAYLOR was famous in the role.

After the Restoration, *Othello* was among the first

plays to be staged in the re-opened theatres. On Dec. 8, 1660, Thomas KILLIGREW's version, in which Margaret HUGHES played Desdemona, featured the first woman to perform on an English stage. William DAVENANT's company performed the play as well, attesting to its continuing popularity. A number of anecdotes from this period tell of enthralled spectators leaping onto the stage to prevent the murder of Desdemona. Charles HART (1) played Othello, but Thomas BETTERTON was acknowledged the greatest Moor of the day. Michael MOHUN was a notable Iago.

In the 18th century *Othello* continued to be among the most often performed of Shakespeare's plays. Most leading actors undertook the title roles, with Barton BOOTH (1), James QUIN, and Spranger BARRY (3) prominent among them, while John HENDERSON and Charles MACKLIN were successful Iagos. In the early 19th century Edmund KEAN (2) was acclaimed as the greatest Othello of all time, a status that some critics believe may still apply, though his legend has doubtless been enhanced by the fact that he collapsed on-stage while playing the part (into the arms of Iago, played by his son Charles KEAN [1]) and never recovered, dying a few weeks later. Othello was a natural vehicle for Ira ALDRIDGE, the first great black Shakespearean actor. William MACREADY played both Othello and Iago at various times, as did Edwin FORREST and Edwin BOOTH (2). Forrest's performances as Othello in New York in 1826 are said to have inaugurated the popularity of Shakespearean tragedy in America. Charlotte CUSHMAN was acclaimed as Desdemona, opposite Forrest, in London in 1846. Booth alternated playing Othello and Iago with Henry IRVING in a famous London run of 1881, with Ellen TERRY (1) as Desdemona, and the soon-to-be-famous playwright Arthur Wing Pinero as Iago. Tommaso SALVINI played Othello in Italian, often with an English-speaking company, in productions that were immensely popular in both England and America throughout the 1870s and 1880s.

Among many noteworthy 20th-century stagings of *Othello,* perhaps the most renowned have been two American productions featuring extraordinary performances: that of Paul ROBESON as Othello—directed by Margaret WEBSTER (3) (1943)—and Christopher PLUMMER as Iago opposite the Othello of James Earl JONES (1) in Nicol WILLIAMSON's presentation (1982). Other 20th-century Othellos have included Oscar ASCHE, Earle HYMAN, Ralph RICHARDSON (2), and Donald WOLFIT. In 1981 an American company under a Japanese director adapted *Othello* to Kabuki, the traditional, stylised Japanese drama, and performed in several American cities. Eleven films have been made of *Othello*—seven of them silent movies. An Italian film shot in Venice in 1909 was the first attempt to film Shakespeare on location. The best-known films are those starring Orson WELLES (who also directed; 1952)

and Laurence OLIVIER (1965). *Othello* has also been made for TELEVISION three times, all in Great Britain (1946, 1955, 1981). In addition, *Othello* has inspired several operas, the most notable being Guiseppe VERDI's *Otello* (1887), with libretto by Arrigo BOITO, which is considered among the greatest of all operas.

**Other (Other Clown, Second Clown, Second Grave-digger)** Minor character in *Hamlet,* the GRAVE-DIGGER's friend. The Other is a straight man whose simple remarks and questions give rise to the ripostes of his companion in 5.1.1–60. Although theatrical tradition dating to the 17th century makes the Other—his designation in early editions of the play—a second grave-digger, some modern editors point out that he seems to belong to another, unspecified profession when he addresses the Grave-digger in 5.1.14. Like the Grave-digger, the Other is a CLOWN (1), and some editions identify him accordingly in stage directions and speech headings.

**Otway, Thomas (1652–1685)** English playwright, author of an adaptation of *Romeo and Juliet.* Otway's *History and Fall of Caius Marius* (1670) combined elements of Shakespeare's play with a drama based on a biography in PLUTARCH's *Lives.* Set in ancient ROME, *Caius Marius* tells of two lovers on opposite sides of a political conflict between patricians and plebeians. His ROMEO was Caius Marius (157–86 B.C.), an historical Roman commoner who rose to high political rank, marrying the daughter of a consul, one Julia (Otway's JULIET [1]), the aunt of Julius CAESAR (1). He later led one side in the first Roman civil war. Otway's *Marius* was so popular that *Romeo and Juliet* was not revived until well into the 1740s.

Otway was best known for two works that dominated the age of Restoration TRAGEDY: *The Orphan* (1680) and *Venice Preserved* (1682). Both are still revived occasionally. Though he was prolific, and his plays were produced by Thomas BETTERTON, Otway ended in poverty, dying quite suddenly at 33, after a short but dramatic life consumed by an unrequited love for Elizabeth BARRY (2). According to one report, he died in a pub; according to another, in a debtor's prison.

**Outlaws** Minor characters in *The Two Gentlemen of Verona.* The three Outlaws capture VALENTINE (2) and SPEED in 4.1. They are recognisable romantic types, gentlemen whose youthful hot-bloodedness has resulted in their exile. They are also comic figures to some extent, as is shown by their prompt election of Valentine as their chieftain because he is a handsome gentleman who is versed in foreign languages.

**Ovid (Publius Ovidius Naso) (43 B.C.–17 A.D.)** Roman poet, author of sources for many of Shakespeare's works. The story of Philomel, in Ovid's *Metamorphoses*, a collection of poems telling tales from Greek and Roman mythology, provided the germ of LAVINIA's fate in *Titus Andronicus*, and in fact Ovid's work is explicitly cited in 4.1.42. *The Metamorphoses* was also the source for *Venus and Adonis*, which has a couplet from Ovid's *Amores* (love poems) as an epigraph. Another work by Ovid—the *Fasti*, an almanac in verse with legends and historical anecdotes for each month—was the principal source for *The Rape of Lucrece*. In addition, many references to and quotations from Ovid are scattered throughout the plays, particularly the early ones. Shakespeare undoubtedly read Ovid in school, as his work figured largely in the Latin curriculum of the times, but he also made use of Arthur GOLDING's translation of *The Metamorphoses*. A Latin copy of *The Metamorphoses* in the BODLEIAN LIBRARY bears a note declaring that it was once owned by Shakespeare, but the accompanying Shakespearean signature is rejected as inauthentic by scholars and handwriting experts.

Ovid, a minor aristocrat who abandoned the practise of law for poetry, lived comfortably in Rome. He was respected for his poetry and patronised by the emperor Augustus CAESAR (2), until he was suddenly exiled in 8 A.D., partly for having written some erotic poems (his *Ars Amatoria*, or *Arts of Love*) that allegedly led the emperor's daughter to promiscuity and partly for some other, now obscure scandal. He spent the remainder of his life in a remote colonial outpost on the Black Sea. His boast at the close of *The Metamorphoses* that 'immortality is mine to wear' has proven justified, for that work has inspired poets and artists ever since.

**Oxford (1), Edward de Vere, Earl of (1550–1604)** English aristocrat, poet, and playwright. Oxford was a patron of poets and players (see OXFORD'S MEN) and wrote verse and plays himself. John LYLY was his secretary and wrote plays for his boys' company (see CHILDREN'S COMPANIES). Oxford's own plays are lost, but he was ranked with Shakespeare by Francis MERES as a good COMEDY writer.

Oxford was renowned as a violent and irresponsible nobleman. Orphaned at 12, he was raised in the household of Lord BURGHLEY, the chief minister of Queen ELIZABETH (1), and he married Burghley's daughter, though against her father's will. He may have killed a servant when he was 17, though the affair was hushed up, and his brawling was notorious. However, he was also an accomplished musician and

dancer, and he was a favourite courtier of the queen, until he converted to Roman Catholicism. He then made one of the queen's ladies-in-waiting pregnant, for which he was imprisoned in 1581. After his release, he brawled and duelled with the woman's family, finally leaving the country to fight for the Dutch Republic and incurring Elizabeth's wrath for doing so without seeking her permission. By 1590 he had spent his fortune, but when his wife died and he remarried—to another of the queen's ladies—the queen granted him a pension.

**Oxford (2), John de Vere, Earl of (1443–1513)** Historical figure and minor character in *3 Henry VI* and *Richard III*, a follower of Queen MARGARET (1) and King HENRY VI in the former play, and of RICHMOND in the latter. In *3 Henry VI* Oxford supports Margaret against WARWICK (3) at the French court in 3.3. When Warwick changes sides and joins Margaret, Oxford participates in the campaign to reinstate Henry. He is captured at the battle of TEWKESBURY and sentenced to imprisonment. The historical Oxford was not present at Tewkesbury, having fled the country after the earlier battle of BARNET. Several years later, he attempted another invasion but was defeated and captured, beginning the imprisonment mentioned in the play. After 10 years, he escaped and joined the Earl of RICHMOND in Paris. In *Richard III* Oxford, though historically an important general in Richmond's campaign, speaks only two lines.

**Oxford's Men** Acting company of the ELIZABETHAN THEATRE. In 1580 a troupe of players previously patronised by the Earl of Warwick—the Earl of LEICESTER's brother—transferred their allegiance to Edward de Vere, the Earl of OXFORD (1), though it is unclear whether they joined an extant company or constituted the founding members of Oxford's Men. Their best-known member was Laurence DUTTON. They do not seem to have been successful—mostly touring in the provinces and playing at the court of Queen ELIZABETH (1) only occasionally. Their history, however, is not clear, for Oxford also patronised a CHILDREN's COMPANY managed by Henry EVANS (2) and a troupe of tumblers and acrobats. In some cases the surviving records are unclear about which of Oxford's groups they refer to. In 1602 Oxford's Men—the troupe of adult actors—received a licence to join WORCESTER'S MEN and were absorbed by that company, probably in the same year.

**P**

**Padua**  City in northern Italy, setting for *The Taming of the Shrew*. Shakespeare transferred the scene of his story from Ferrara, where it is set in his source, GAS-COIGNE's play *Supposes*, for Padua was better known to his audience, enjoying a reputation as a major seat of learning. In fact, many English students of Shakespeare's day attended the university at Padua, which had been founded in the 13th century. The town's academic ambience is not important to the play—although in 1.1.1–24 LUCENTIO speaks of the desire for learning that has brought him to Padua—but a university town seems an apt setting for a tale of young love.

In *The Merchant of Venice* Padua is the home of PORTIA's cousin, a scholar known for his legal wisdom, and it thus figures (in 3.4.59 et al.) in the heroine's presentation of herself as a lawyer. It is also the home-town of BENEDICK in *Much Ado About Nothing*.

Shakespeare's apparent assumptions that Padua was a port (*Shrew*, 1.1.42, 4.2.83) and in Lombardy (1.1.3) have often been cited as serious errors, since Padua is neither on the coast nor in Lombardy. However, while the playwright's European geography is sometimes mistaken, here he may be excused: in his day the term Lombardy was often taken to refer to all of northern Italy, and Padua, while it is some 20 miles from the Adriatic, was a 16th-century canal port of some significance. An intricate canal network covered much of northern Italy in the Middle Ages and Renaissance; it operated until it was superseded by railroads in the 19th century. In fact, Padua can still be reached by water in small craft.

**Page (1)**  Minor character in *Richard III*, an attendant to RICHARD III. In 4.2 Richard asks the Page to recommend an ambitious nobleman to do a desperate deed. The youth names James TYRELL, whom Richard commissions to murder his nephews.

**Page (2)**  Minor character in *Romeo and Juliet*, a young servant of MERCUTIO. Mortally wounded in 3.1, Mercutio sends the Page, who does not speak, to summon a surgeon.

**Page (3)**  Minor character in *Romeo and Juliet*, a servant of PARIS (2). The Page accompanies his master on his

nocturnal visit to the grave of JULIET (1) in 5.3; when ROMEO arrives and fights with Paris, the Page summons the WATCHMAN and later testifies to the PRINCE (1).

**Page (4)**  Minor character in *The Taming of the Shrew*, servant of the local LORD (1), who directs him to masquerade as the wife of the deluded Christopher SLY (1) in the INDUCTION. He humorously discourages Sly's sexual advances, and his performance as a wife foreshadows the ideal of womanly obedience that the main play advocates. His instructions are to request, as a real wife would, 'What is't your honour will command, / Wherein your lady and your humble wife / May show her duty and make known her love?' (Ind.1.112–115), and he presents himself to Sly as 'your wife in all obedience' (Ind.2.108). These attitudes are precisely those prescribed for wives by the converted KATHERINA in 5.2.

**Page (5)**  Character in *2 Henry IV*, FALSTAFF's attendant. For the most part, the Page simply performs routine tasks and says little. However, in 2.2, where he bests BARDOLPH (1) in a battle of wits and is rewarded with money by PRINCE (6) HAL and POINS, the Page saucily comes into his own, in the manner of the pert young pages in the plays of John LYLY, whose works were well known to Shakespeare.

The Page's diminutive stature is frequently referred to in humorous terms by the other characters; e.g., in 1.2.1, he is a 'giant'; in 2.2.82, an 'upright rabbit'; in 5.1.55–56, 'my tall fellow'. It is thought that these references, with others in other plays, reflect the presence of a particularly small boy actor (see ELIZABETHAN THEATRE) in the CHAMBERLAIN'S MEN, for whom Shakespeare wrote the play. The same character appears in *The Merry Wives of Windsor* as ROBIN (1) and in *Henry V* as the BOY (3).

**Page (6)**  Minor character in *2 Henry IV*, a servant of King HENRY IV. The Page, who does not speak, carries messages for the King in 3.1.

**Page (7)**  Either of two minor characters in *As You Like It*, singers in the court of DUKE (7) Senior. In 5.3 the

Pages sing a parody of a love song for TOUCHSTONE and AUDREY that provides a brief interlude of pure entertainment before the play reaches its climax.

**Page (8)** Minor character in *All's Well That Ends Well*, a servant of the COUNTESS (2) of ROSSILLION. In 1.1.183 the Page summons PAROLLES for BERTRAM, then exits. He evokes the world of an aristocratic household but is otherwise of no consequence.

**Page (9)** Minor character in *Timon of Athens*, an illiterate messenger who asks APEMANTUS to read the addresses on letters he is to deliver. The Page is an employee of the same courtesan as the FOOL (3), and has no place in the play's plot. His brief appearance is sometimes taken as evidence of a non-Shakespearean hand in the composition of the play. However, the episode closely resembles that of the illiterate SERVANT (4) in *Romeo and Juliet*, and most scholars now conclude that the Page is Shakespeare's invention. He was probably part of a SUB-PLOT that remained undeveloped when the playwright abandoned this incomplete play.

**Page (10)** Character in *Henry VIII*. See BOY (9).

**Page (11), Anne** Character in *The Merry Wives of Windsor*. See ANNE (3).

**Page (12), George** Character in *The Merry Wives of Windsor,* the husband of MISTRESS (3) Margaret Page. Unlike his jealous friend FORD (1), Page believes in his wife's fidelity. He is consistently mild and cheerful, pleasant evidence of the solid virtues of the bourgeois life of Windsor. He is part of the group, led by the HOST (2), who mediate the quarrel between EVANS (3) and CAIUS (2), and he repeatedly tries to cajole Ford out of his irrational jealousy. If Page seems unpleasantly mercenary in attempting to marry his daughter ANNE (3) to the ridiculous SLENDER, we should remember that such motives were ordinary, indeed expected, in Elizabethan fathers, and we note that Page accepts Anne's elopement with FENTON with good grace. Page's solid common sense is exemplified in his dry reply to Ford's exaggerated protestations of trust in his wife once he has been proven wrong. Page suggests, ' 'Tis well, 'tis well; no more. Be not as extreme in submission as in offence' (4.4.10–12). Once FALSTAFF is properly humiliated for his deeds, in 5.5, it is Page who ends the punishment, saying, 'Yet be cheerful, knight: thou shalt eat a posset to-night at my house . . .' (5.5.171–172).

In 1.1.42 Evans gives Page the name Thomas, though he is called George by his wife in three places (2.1.143, 2.1.151, 5.5.199). While this may represent an error by Evans, it is more probably just a typical instance of Shakespeare's tolerance for minor inconsistencies.

**Page (13), Mistress Margaret** Character in *The Merry Wives of Windsor*. See MISTRESS (3).

**Page (14), William** Character in *The Merry Wives of Windsor*. See WILLIAM (1).

**Painter (1)** Minor character in *Timon of Athens*, a flatterer of TIMON. In 1.1 the Painter and his friend the POET (2) anticipate that they will profit from Timon's generosity when they present him with examples of their art. The Painter speaks much less than his friend, but shares his pride and false modesty. He agrees with the Poet that though Timon is now prosperous, this can change, and the 'quick blows of Fortune' (1.1.93) may reduce their host to poverty and friendlessness. Though the Painter is not among the disloyal friends depicted in Timon's downfall, he is not unlike them. In 5.1 he joins the Poet in an attempt to resume their approach to their one-time benefactor in the belief that his fortunes have again improved. 'Therefore', says the Painter, ' 'tis not amiss we tender our loves to him' (5.1.12–13). He is unconcerned that he has never painted anything for Timon. He imagines that a promise of future work is as 'Good as the best. Promising is the very air o' th' time . . . To promise is most courtly and fashionable' (5.1.22–27). However, Timon understands what they are up to, and drives them away. The Painter, like his friend the Poet, is a satirical emblem of the greed and hypocrisy of courtiers.

**Painter (2), William (c.1525–1590)** English translator, creator of source material for several of Shakespeare's works. Painter produced an anthology of more than 100 tales from Italian and Latin authors, including LIVY, PLUTARCH, BOCCACCIO, and CINTHIO, in his *Palace of Pleasure* (1566–1567). A Boccaccio story from Painter was the principal source for *All's Well That Ends Well*, and other tales provided material for *Romeo and Juliet*, *Timon of Athens*, and *The Rape of Lucrece*. Many other Elizabethan and Jacobean playwrights turned to Painter as well, and he may deserve credit for the abundance of Italian settings and stories in their plays. Painter was a government official in charge of military supplies at the TOWER OF LONDON.

**Palamon** One of the title characters of *The Two Noble Kinsmen*, cousin of ARCITE. As introduced in 1.2, Palamon and Arcite are young noblemen whose chief concern is with their knightly honour and whose lives revolve around their friendship with each other. However, while prisoners of war in ATHENS, they both fall in love with EMILIA (4), the beautiful sister-in-law of Duke THESEUS (2), and they argue over who saw her first. Eventually they fight a duel for Emilia, in which, following Theseus' rules, the loser is not to be killed but rather executed afterwards. Palamon loses, but just before he is to be beheaded, Arcite is killed by a runaway horse, and Palamon prepares to marry Emilia at the play's close. As stylised knightly protagonists, Palamon and Arcite resemble each other fairly closely, but Palamon can be distinguished as the generally more belligerent of the two. On the other hand, he also seems somewhat disillusioned at the close of their story, making him the more interesting character finally.

In 1.2 Palamon is a shallow fellow whom Arcite criticises for his narrow military outlook. In 2.1 he insists that their enthusiasm for the same, seemingly unapproachable woman is grounds for unsparing enmity, despite Arcite's efforts to find some other approach. Palamon escapes from prison with the help of the warden's DAUGHTER (2)—whom he immediately abandons—and in Act 3 he persistently pushes Arcite to duel, until Theseus intervenes and establishes the rules under which they finally fight.

Palamon's long prayer to Venus in 5.1 marks a turning point, for instead of the enraptured plea for Emilia's heart that we might expect, he vents a satirical recital of the ridiculous behaviour love inspires. He mocks the tyrant who weeps to a girl and the old man who is confident his young wife is faithful, and he recites all the ugly betrayals and offences a lover might commit, though he disclaims them. The pleasant aspects of love are not mentioned. He closes his prayer by apostrophising the goddess as one 'whose chase is this world / And we in herds thy game' (5.1.131–132). Such cynicism reflects the weight that the conflict has had—he wears Venus' 'yoke, . . . [that is] heavier / Than lead itself [and] stings more than nettles' (5.1. 95–97), for in the end he loses his friend. At the close, engaged to Emilia, he addresses his dead cousin with a plaint that typifies the confusion and helplessness of humanity in the hands of unpredictable fate, the play's most important theme: 'O cousin, / That we should things desire which do cost us / the loss of our desire! that naught could buy / Dear love but loss of dear love!' (5.4.109–112).

**Palsgrave's Men** Theatrical company in LONDON, previously known as PRINCE HENRY'S MEN and the ADMIRAL'S MEN. When Prince HENRY (2) died in November 1612, the patronage of his theatre company was taken over by Frederick V, Elector Palatine, the German fiancé of Princess ELIZABETH (3). The couple married early in 1613, and the actors took one of Frederick's titles. A palsgrave, literally 'palace count', was a noble of the Holy Roman Empire who ruled with imperial powers within his own territories. The new royal patent for the Palsgrave's Men listed the members of the company, including Samuel ROWLEY (1)—who also wrote plays for the company—Thomas DOWNTON, Humphrey JEFFES, and John SHANK. They continued to play at the FORTUNE THEATRE and at the royal court, but in 1621 the Fortune burned to the ground, and the company lost all its costumes and props, and even many play scripts. The company struggled along for several years, but never completely recovered. After a bad season in 1625—complicated by the combination of a plague epidemic and the death of King JAMES I—the company disbanded.

**Pandar** Minor character in *Pericles*, the keeper of a brothel who, with his wife, the BAWD, buys the kidnapped MARINA. The Pandar is somewhat less hard than his wife. He contemplates retirement from a trade whose practise puts them on 'sore terms . . . with the gods' (4.2.33). However, he does have a business to run, and when Marina's glorious innocence begins to produce moral reform among the clientele he despairs. He moans 'I had rather than twice the worth of her she had ne'er come here' (4.6.1–2). He then curses her with a contradictory pair of sexual problems: 'the pox upon her green-sickness' (4.6.13). Thus, the Pandar offers comic relief from the melodramatic romance of the main story.

**Pandarus** Legendary figure and character in *Troilus and Cressida*, uncle of CRESSIDA who encourages her love affair with TROILUS. Pandarus, though a comic character, is also a conventional representation of a procurer of prostitutes. As such, he is a symbol of the moral corruption that permeates the world of the play. (Although Pandarus promotes only a single, non-mercenary affair, in both Shakespeare's play and its sources, he was already well established in Shakespeare's day as a symbol of the profession.)

Pandarus uses a variety of humorously exaggerated dictions: the rather affected language of the court (as when he uses the word 'fair' is several ways in one sentence, composing an elaborate compliment to HELEN [1] in 3.1.42–45); babytalk ('Come, come, what need you blush? Shame's a baby' [3.2.39]); and the bold language of braggadocio—e.g., in his deprecation of the SOLDIERS (6) as 'Asses, fools, dolts, chaff and bran, chaff and bran; porridge after meat . . . crows and daws, crows and daws' (1.2.245–248). In these passages Pandarus resembles such other Shakespearean comic characters as FALSTAFF, FESTE, and the NURSE (3) of *Romeo and Juliet*. AENEAS parodies him in 4.2.56–59, emphasising both his comic aspect and his inferior social status.

Pandarus insinuates himself into other people's lives and is capable of outrageous interruptions, as in his interception of Cressida's despairing cry to Troilus, 'Have the god's envy?' with the thoughtless 'Ay, ay, ay, ay, 'tis too plain a case' (4.4.27–28), and even of physical intrusiveness ('Let me embrace, too' [4.4. 13]). As we know from the eventual result of the liaison he arranges, Pandarus is ultimately malevolent. This is strikingly conveyed by his association with venereal disease in 5.4 and 5.10.

In the EPILOGUE, Pandarus steps somewhat out of character, speaking verse for the first time, as the formality of the device demands. However, he is still comically reprehensible. His recital on the humblebee, whose 'Sweet honey and sweet notes together fail' (5.10.42–45) is a completely appropriate ending for this play of mistakes, misunderstandings, and failures. His flippant insults serve to distance the audience from the play as it closes. Because the audience is actually not composed of 'traitors and bawds . . . traders in the flesh . . . Brethren and sisters of the hold-door trade' (5.10.37, 46, 52), it need not identify with the play's discouraging ending and can feel itself superior to its corrupt world. The satirical nature of the play is confirmed, implicitly allowing for the existence of human virtues in contrast to the vices depicted on stage. Thus Pandarus provides some sense of the high-spirited resolution typical in COMEDY.

Pandarus appears in the *Iliad* of HOMER, but although he is an unpleasant character in that epic, he has nothing to do with Troilus or any other lovers (Cressida does not appear in Homer). It was in the Middle Ages that Pandarus first acquired his role as the lovers' go-between. By Shakespeare's day his name had become a common noun (and later a verb), although the spelling had changed slightly to *pander*, in which form it is still in common use.

**Pandulph (d. 1226)**   Historical figure and character in *King John,* papal legate and enemy of King JOHN (3). Pandulph appears in 3.1 to demand John's submission to the pope in the appointment of an archbishop. When John refuses, Pandulph threatens King PHILIP (2) of France with excommunication if he does not break his new alliance with England and declare war on John. Pandulph offers an elaborate and specious argument (3.1.189–223) justifying the breaking of an oath. In 3.3 he offers the Dauphin LEWIS (1) a plan whereby he may conquer England and claim the throne. Having thus launched an invasion of England, Pandulph promises John that he will call it off in exchange for his oath of submission to the pope. John agrees, and he relinquishes his crown to Pandulph, who recrowns him, thus symbolically asserting papal supremacy over the government of England. However, in 5.2 Lewis refuses to withdraw and is defeated only when his traitorous English allies return to King John's side. Pandulph's unscrupulous warmongering and his inability to fulfil a promise fit the stereotype he represents: that of the steely, hypocritical Jesuit, capable of arguing any side of a question to suit the ends of the Catholic Church.

The historical Pandulph, a native of Rome, was sent to England in 1211—long after the marriage of Lewis and BLANCHE in 1200, with which his arrival is associated in the play—to insist that the papal candidate be installed as Archbishop of Canterbury, as in the play. But Shakespeare's condensation of history has skewed Pandulph's subsequent role, for by the time of the barons' revolt he was John's ally. After receiving John's submission to the pope in 1213, Pandulph supported him against his rebellious nobles, excommunicating those of them who extracted the Magna Charta from the king. John rewarded him with the bishopric of Norwich. Pandulph attempted unsuccessfully to prevent Lewis' invasion in 1216. He remained an influential bishop in England after John's death, serving as one of the regents for the young King HENRY (1) until 1221, when Henry exiled him, apparently on personal grounds. Pandulph died in Rome, but he was buried in Norwich, at his own request.

Pandulph was never a cardinal, the rank he holds in the play. Shakespeare may have taken this error from an early 16th-century play on King John, but there is no other evidence that he knew the work. It is more likely that Pandulph was elevated in rank for a simple and sensible theatrical reason: to dress him in the boldly dramatic scarlet robes of a cardinal, an ordinary item in the wardrobes of acting companies.

**Panthino**   Minor character in *The Two Gentlemen of Verona,* the servant of ANTONIO (1). Panthino helps his master arrive at his fateful decision to send his son PROTEUS to court. Later, at the close of two successive scenes (2.2, 2.3), he furthers the action, appearing in order to hasten the departures of Proteus and LAUNCE respectively.

**Papp, Joseph (b. 1921)**   American theatrical producer. Papp's New York Shakespeare Festival—originally (1953) the Shakespeare Workshop—has produced almost all of Shakespeare's plays. Since 1962 the Festival has offered summer performances free of charge in the Delacorte Theatre in New York's Central Park. In 1986 Papp began a six-year cycle of productions encompassing the 36 plays in the FIRST FOLIO.

**Paris (1)**   Capital of FRANCE (1) and a location in several of Shakespeare's plays. In 3.4 and 4.1 of *1 Henry VI,* English forces occupy Paris, and King HENRY VI of England is crowned King of France there as part of the English diplomatic effort in the HUNDRED YEARS WAR. A number of scenes in *All's Well That Ends Well* (1.2, 2.1, 2.3, 2.4, 2.5) are located in the Paris palace of the KING (17) of France. One scene of *3 Henry VI* (3.3) is set at the court of King LEWIS (3), which is perhaps most plausibly assumed to be in Paris.

**Paris (2)**   Character in *Romeo and Juliet,* a nobleman who wishes to marry JULIET (1). Paris, who is forced on Juliet by her parents, confidently assumes that he will wed her. He is closely juxtaposed with ROMEO throughout the play. Though no villain, Paris is nonetheless an agent of the world that opposes the private universe of the lovers, and this is indicated by his staid and predictable behaviour and speech. His sentiments are those of the conventionally poetic lover, the type of lover Romeo was before he met Juliet. Lady CAPU-LET (3) even compares him to a book in 1.3.81–88. His smug exchange with Juliet in 4.1 can only stiffly approximate the brilliant poetry of her dialogue with Romeo. In his final appearance—at Juliet's tomb in 5.3—this well-meaning but vapid gentleman declares his grief in a formal sestet that is reminiscent of Romeo's word play in Act 1; the contrast is completed when the mature Romeo arrives, desperate and resolute. Paris honourably opposes the man whom he believes is desecrating Juliet's tomb, but he dies without comprehending, or even seeing, his rival's passion.

**Paris (3)**  Legendary figure and character in *Troilus and Cressida,* a prince of TROY, son of King PRIAM, and brother of TROILUS and HECTOR. Before the play opens, Paris' theft of HELEN (1), wife of the Greek leader MENELAUS, has caused the TROJAN WAR. Thus his story is one of the examples of human folly that comprise a leading theme of the play. Paris is a decadent figure; his father calls him 'besotted on your sweet delights' (2.2.144), referring to Helen, and Paris confirms this judgement when he avoids the battlefield, claiming, 'I would fain have armed today, but my Nell would not have it so' (3.1.132–133). In his other appearances, he is merely one among the Trojan warriors, remarking on the events of the war; he also aids Troilus' courtship of CRESSIDA, covering for his absence from a state dinner and sending a warning to the lovers that a diplomatic delegation is approaching in 4.1. In Act 5 Paris fights with Menelaus, provoking sardonic remarks from THERSITES on 'the cuckold and the cuckold-maker' (5.7.9).

In classical mythology, Paris was bribed by Aphrodite to select her as the most beautiful of three quarrelling goddesses. She rewarded him by helping him to kidnap Helen. Though this well-known legend was pre-Homeric, HOMER does not mention it, saying only that Paris abducted Helen because of her beauty. In the *Iliad,* Paris is an effective warrior, specialising in archery, though he flees Menelaus in a moment of cowardice. Recovering, he challenges Menelaus to a duel but is defeated and must be rescued by Aphrodite. According to a later legend, Paris was the eventual killer of ACHILLES, placing an arrow precisely in his only vulnerable spot, his heel.

**Parliament House**  Building housing the English Parliament in London, a location in one scene each of *1* and *3 Henry VI*. A part of WESTMINSTER (4) PALACE, this structure was a predecessor to the present Houses of Parliament, which were built in the 19th century. In 3.1 of *1 Henry VI,* an episode in the feud between GLOUCESTER (4) and WINCHESTER (1) occurs in the Par-

liament House, and in 1.1 of *3 Henry VI* YORK (8) claims the crown of HENRY VI there, pre-empting a meeting of Parliament called by Queen MARGARET (1).

In Shakespeare's day, as in the times he depicted in the HISTORY PLAYS, Parliament did not play the important policy-making and legislative role that we associate with the institution. Although Parliament's power to levy taxes made it a necessary nuisance to the monarch, the aristocracy largely controlled elections to the COMMONS (1), and, in any case, the actual administration of government was entirely in the hands of the royal ruler and his or her advisers. The first great advances towards modern representative government were to come in the quarter-century following the playwright's death.

**Parnassus Plays**  Group of three amateur plays containing several references to Shakespeare and the LONDON theatrical world. These anonymous works are titled *The Pilgrimage to Parnassus, The Return from Parnassus* (Part 1), and *The Return from Parnassus* (Part 2), and they are referred to as *1, 2,* and *3 Parnassus.* They were performed at Cambridge University, probably on Christmas 1598, 1599, and 1601. *1 Parnassus* is an allegory of travel to Mt Parnassus, sacred to the Muses; *2* and *3 Parnassus* are set in London. In *2 Parnassus* a lover quotes from *Venus and Adonis* and declares, 'I'le worshipp sweet Mr Shakspeare, and to honoure him will lay his Venus and Adonis under my pillowe'. In *3 Parnassus* Richard BURBAGE (3) and Will KEMPE appear as characters. Burbage auditions someone who recites the opening lines of *Richard III,* and another character praises both *Venus and Adonis* and *The Rape of Lucrece.* Most strikingly, Kempe declares of inferior playwrights that 'our fellow Shakespeare puts them all downe . . . and Ben Ionson too', adding that Ben JONSON 'is a pestilent fellow . . . but our fellow Shakespeare hath given him a purge'. The play's date, 1601, suggests a reference to the WAR OF THE THEATRES, in which Jonson figured, but except for an obscure allusion in *Twelfth Night* 3.1.60, Shakespeare took no part in this exchange of satires. No 'purge' he might have given Jonson has been identified. The remark may merely express the author's preference for Shakespeare, or it may reflect some lost piece of theatre gossip.

**Parolles (Paroles)**  Character in *All's Well That Ends Well,* a cowardly follower of BERTRAM. As his name, the French for 'words', suggests, Parolles is a blusterer who pretends to be a warrior and nobleman but whose deeds cannot match his boasts. Shallow and thoughtless, he influences Bertram to follow his worst instincts. Parolles aggravates Bertram's tendencies to self-indulgence, and he encourages him to disobey the KING (17) and run away to the wars in ITALY. After Parolles' humiliation in 2.4 by Lord LAFEW, who has seen through his pretensions to gentlemanly status, he is ready to leave the court; he sees his chance in Bertram's wish to abandon HELENA (2), whom the King has made him marry. 'A young man married is a man that's marr'd. / Therefore away' (2.3.294–295), he urges. Once in Italy, Parolles again supports Bertram's inclinations to vice, serving as a go-between in the young man's attempt to seduce the virginal DIANA (1). Bertram's friends, led by the First LORD (6), then 'capture' Parolles and expose his cowardice and treachery in 4.3.

Parolles' defects have been recognised all along by everyone around Bertram. Upon his first appearance, Helena calls him 'a notorious liar . . . a great way fool, solely a coward' (1.1.108–109), and the Lords agree with Bertram's mother, the COUNTESS (2), that her son has been corrupted by Parolles, who is a 'very tainted fellow, and full of wickedness' (3.2.87). Parolles thus serves an important dramatic function, deflecting the negative image that might otherwise be attached to Bertram, whose stature must not sink too low, lest the central element of the plot—the determination of Helena to marry him—become ludicrous.

In his evil influence on Bertram, Parolles is most nearly the play's villain.

However, after his exposure as a charlatan, Parolles shows a striking resilience. Though his self-promoted career as a noble warrior is over, he will make the most of his new situation. 'Simply the thing I am / Shall make me live' (4.3.322–323), he observes, realising that he can, 'being fool'd, by fool'ry thrive' (4.3.327). He resolves to become a jester, or FOOL (1), among the French lords, a role well suited to his nature. In a line that is richly suggestive of Shakespeare's generous vision of humanity, he declares that 'There's place and means for every man alive' (4.3.328). In becoming a fool and acknowledgeing his defects, Parolles shows himself wiser than Bertram, preceding him in self-knowledge, just as he has preceded him in delinquency. His acceptance of life on any terms demonstrates a tremendous vitality, and he is certainly the most dynamic character in the play, with the possible exception of Helena.

Significantly, Parolles sparks Helena's energy in 1.1. In this scene Helena is understandably depressed; the household is in mourning for both Bertram's father and her own, and Bertram, her secret love, is leaving. Then Parolles appears, and his broadly humorous exercise in fashionable cynicism about virginity has a two-fold effect on the heroine. First, she sees that the courtly life that Parolles represents will offer sexual opportunities for Bertram, which she fears he will accept. Second, Parolles' vitality inspires Helena to declare, 'Our remedies oft in ourselves do lie' (1.1.212), and to decide to pursue Bertram. Thus Parolles' energy pervades *All's Well*, infusing the spirits of both major characters for good and evil alike. Finally, in

becoming the jester for his old enemy Lafew at the close of the play, Parolles accepts—unconditionally, in contrast to Bertram—the reconciliation that is at the heart of Shakespearean COMEDY.

Although he has a distinct and credible personality, Parolles is descended from an ancient comic character type, the MILES GLORIOSUS of ancient Roman drama and the braggart soldier of Italian COMMEDIA DELL'ARTE; he shares his ancestry with several other Shakespearean characters, most notably FALSTAFF.

***The Passionate Pilgrim***   Collection of poems published as Shakespeare's in 1599, though only a quarter of the works in the anthology are known to have been written by him. William JAGGARD assembled this miscellany, apparently without Shakespeare's participation or knowledge, presumably to capitalise on the popularity of *Venus and Adonis* and *The Rape of Lucrece*. All of the poems deal with love; the title refers to a commonplace image of the seeker of love as a worshipper at a sacred shrine.

The first two poems in *The Passionate Pilgrim* are SONNETS by Shakespeare (Nos. 138 and 144), and Nos. 3, 5, and 16 (in the modern numbering of the *Pilgrim*'s poems) are versions of passages from *Love's Labour's Lost* (4.3.57–70; 4.2.101–114; 4.3.98–118). Most scholars believe that Shakespeare wrote none of the remaining poems (there are 21 poems in the early editions, in which one poem is broken into two, and 20 in modern editions, in which the reassembled poem is No. 14).

Several of the remaining poems are attributable, with varying degrees of certainty, to other poets. No. 19 combines four stanzas from a poem by Christopher MARLOWE (1), 'The Passionate Shepherd to his Love', with one from Walter RALEIGH's 'The Nymph's Reply to the Shepherd'; these were not published until 1600, but they circulated in manuscript, a common practise at the time. No. 11 had already been published (1598) as the work of Bartholomew GRIFFIN, and Nos. 4, 6, and 9, similar in content and style, are usually attributed to him as well. Nos. 8 and 20 had already been published as the work of Richard BARNFIELD.

Seven of the remaining eight poems are generally considered by critics and scholars to be grossly inferior, unlikely to have been written by Shakespeare, even in his earliest years; only one, No. 12, seems possibly authentic, and, although it has charm, it differs considerably from known Shakespearean poems in its simple assertiveness and unsophisticated poetic technique. In 1631, it appeared as one stanza of a Thomas DELONEY poem.

Two editions of *The Passionate Pilgrim* were published by Jaggard in 1599; they are known conventionally as Q1 and Q2, although they appeared in OCTAVO, not QUARTO, format. Q1 is known only through the existence of isolated pages, bound with pages from Q2 in a single surviving copy, and its date is uncertain. Q2 appears to have been printed from Q1, and it is dated. Modern editions follow the combined texts.

Jaggard published a third edition, Q3 (also an octavo), in 1612 with additional material—also ascribed to Shakespeare—that he had culled from a book by Thomas HEYWOOD (2), which he had published three years earlier. Heywood protested publicly, asserting that not only he, but also Shakespeare was 'much offended' by Jaggard's high-handedness. Jaggard then issued Q3 with a new title page omitting Shakespeare's name.

**Pastoral**  Popular RENAISSANCE literary genre that influenced a number of Shakespeare's works, especially *As You Like It* and *The Winter's Tale*. The term may be used as either an adjective or a noun. In general, pastoral literature encompasses all works that depict an idealised vision of rural life, usually within the context of a love story. Such works are frankly escapist, though they are occasionally vehicles for more elevated literary aims.

The pastoral originated in a genre of ancient Greek poetry that dealt with the lives of shepherds. It was continued in ancient Roman poetry that contrasted the urban and the rural in order to satirise the sophisticated life of urban courtiers, and it was rediscovered and imitated by Italian poets in the Renaissance. The pastoral romance, a long tale in verse or prose, begins with works by BOCCACCIO and was widely popular throughout Europe. In English, Sir Philip SIDNEY's *Arcadia* is among the greatest of pastorals, and Thomas LODGE's *Rosalynde,* the source of *As You Like It,* is a lesser example.

In the English pastoral dramas of Shakespeare's age, the delights of rustic life are conventionally idealised, and the amorous shepherds and shepherdesses are often portrayed as natural philosophers. Many dramatists essayed the genre in one form or another, notably Ben JONSON, John FLETCHER (2), and Samuel DANIEL. *As You Like It* gently parodies the conventions of the pastoral, but in Act 4 of *The Winter's Tale* they are treated more seriously, as a demonstration of human potentiality.

**Patch-breech**  Character in *Pericles.* See FISHERMEN.

**Pater, Walter (1839–1894)**  English essayist and novelist, author of several significant essays on Shakespeare. An apologist for the 'aesthetic' point of view represented by the phrase 'art for art's sake', which he helped introduce into the language, Pater was among the most noted writers of his day and an acknowledged master of English prose. He was best known for his *Studies in the History of the Renaissance* (1873)—the book that made him famous—and a novel, *Marius the Epicu-*

*rean* (1885). Three notable essays on Shakespeare—on *Measure for Measure* (1874), *Love's Labour's Lost* (1878), and the HISTORY PLAYS (1889)—were highly influential, contributing to a revaluation of the playwright's work during the period.

**Patience**  Minor character in *Henry VIII,* an attendant to Queen KATHERINE. In 4.2 Patience faithfully attends the deposed and dying queen in her exile at KIMBOLTON. Patience speaks very little, remarking on Katherine's ghastly appearance as she approaches death and saying, 'Heaven comfort her' (4.2.99); her mere presence—with that of GRIFFITH—tells us of the loyalty the good Katherine inspires. Her name is so striking that it is often thought Shakespeare created her for its sake. Griffith addresses her, 'Softly, gentle Patience' (4.2.82), as they watch their mistress sleep, and Katherine, approaching death, says, 'Patience, / You must not leave me yet' (4.2.165–166). The quality her name evokes is Katherine's signal trait and an important theme in the play: the virtue of patience in adversity. In gentle Patience, Shakespeare created an embodiment of the virtue itself, an allegorical figure like thsoe of the medieval MORALITY PLAY. This technique is characteristic of *Henry VIII,* which is filled with tableaus, MASQUE, and other emblematic episodes.

**Patricians**  See SENATOR (2).

**Patroclus**  Legendary figure and character in *Troilus and Cressida,* a Greek warrior in the TROJAN WAR and friend and follower of ACHILLES. While he himself is not an important figure, Patroclus' death is a key event in the plot, for it sparks Achilles to abandon his withdrawal from the combat and resume fighting, with the result that TROY loses the climactic battle. Patroclus represents Achilles in his dispute with the Greek leader, relaying his friend's statements of non-cooperation and carrying messages back to him. And, in an incidental episode that heightens the aura of decadence that surrounds the warriors, Achilles' jester, THERSITES, taunts Patroclus with a piece of malicious gossip, saying, 'Thou art said to be Achilles' male varlet . . . his masculine whore' (5.1.14, 16), though the imputation is carried no further and has no dramatic significance.

In the *Iliad* of HOMER, which contains the original version of Patroclus' story, Patroclus was somewhat older than Achilles. He was an attendant of the warrior because, as a boy, he had been taken under the protection of Achilles' father after accidentally killing someone. In Homer, Achilles' devoted friendship for Patroclus is one of the warrior's fine attributes, and there is no hint of a homosexual relationship. However, the tradition that the two were lovers was established by the 6th century B.C.

**Paulina** Character in *The Winter's Tale,* defender of Queen HERMIONE against the injustice of her husband, King LEONTES, and later the instrument of their reconciliation. Paulina boldly criticises the king for accusing Hermione of adultery, and her courage and common sense contrast tellingly with the king's jealous madness. After failing to prevent the king from exiling PERDITA, the infant daughter he believes illegitimate, Paulina enters into an amazing scheme: she stages Hermione's death and isolates her for 16 years, against the time when Leontes will have thoroughly repented. Perdita's return signals the ripeness of this plan, and Paulina reveals Hermione's existence in 5.3—in a stage-managed presentation of the long-lost queen as a statue. This revelation brings about the play's final reunion. Thus, Paulina, despite her bluff worldliness and overpowering manner, is an agent of redemption.

Paulina thinks clearly and acts decisively; she courageously takes it on herself to defend the queen as soon as she hears of her plight, and she handles the GAOLER (3) with the powerful courtesy of the *grande dame* that she is. Her criticism of the king is excoriating; he is reduced to insult—calling her a 'witch' (2.3.67), a 'callat [prostitute]' (2.3.90), and a 'gross hag' (2.3.107). When he threatens to burn her as a witch, she boldly replies, 'I care not' (2.3.113). Her boldness, however, does not always produce the envisioned results; her tactic of presenting the infant Perdita to the king merely aggravates his anger and results in the child's abandonment. Paulina alone cannot remedy the defect in the play's world—providence must see to that—but her efforts are important evidence that good has not died and may be restored.

Paulina has often been compared to King LEAR's faithful KENT (2). Like him, she offers a cure for the king's madness, declaring, 'I / Do come with words as medicinal as true' (2.3.35–36). Her therapy is a raw and intrusive one. In Act 5 she continues her powerful ministrations. She reinforces Leontes' repentance by continually reminding him of the supposedly dead Hermione and demands that he vow never to take a wife without her approval. She reveals Hermione's survival with a fine theatrical sense, raising dramatic expectations of sorcery by disclaiming 'wicked powers' (5.3.91), and she prevents Hermione from disclosing too much with a hasty 'There's time enough for that' (5.3.128). At the close, within the atmosphere of love and reconciliation, Paulina finally permits herself to lament the loss of her own husband, ANTIGONUS, which stirs the king to ordain her remarriage to CAMILLO. Her value in the world of the play is acknowledged when the king calls her one 'whose worth and honesty / Is richly noted' (5.3.144–145). The central theme of *The Winter's Tale* is that human moral energy must support divine providence, and Paulina's valiant efforts are a prime source of this ingredient.

**Pavier, Thomas (d. 1625)** English bookseller and publisher associated with the publication of several of Shakespeare's plays. Pavier is notorious for his involvement in the FALSE FOLIO of Shakespeare's works (1619), to which he contributed pirated texts of *2* and *3 Henry VI* (jointly, as the WHOLE CONTENTION), *Henry V, Pericles,* and two plays not actually by Shakespeare, SIR JOHN OLDCASTLE and A YORKSHIRE TRAGEDY. Pavier had earlier published the first editions of *Sir John Oldcastle* (1600) and *A Yorkshire Tragedy* (1608), and attributed the latter to Shakespeare at that time. In 1600 Pavier had purchased the 'rights' to a pirated edition of *Henry V* from Thomas MILLINGTON and John BUSBY, and he reissued their BAD QUARTO as Q2 of the play in 1602. Though Pavier's practices seem dubious from a modern point of view, the evolving world of 17th-century publishing was not so strict, and Pavier was an honoured member of the STATIONERS' COMPANY.

**Peaseblossom** Character in *A Midsummer Night's Dream,* a fairy attendant to the fairy Queen TITANIA. In 3.1 Titania assigns Peaseblossom to the retinue of the

*The fairy Peaseblossom in Max Reinhardt's 1935 film of* A Midsummer Night's Dream *is made an attendant to Bottom by Titania.* (Courtesy of Culver Pictures, Inc.)

comical rustic BOTTOM, whom the Queen has been magically induced to love. Bottom has been endowed by PUCK with the head of an ass, but he does not know of his new adornment, and Peaseblossom serves him in 4.1 by scratching his strangely itchy face.

**Pedant, The** Minor character in *The Taming of the Shrew* who impersonates VINCENTIO (1). The Pedant has no personality; he serves merely to fill out the plot of deception and disguise. He flees when his imposture is revealed and is not mentioned again.

**Pedro, Don** Character in *Much Ado About Nothing*, the Prince of Aragon, who attempts to promote romances on behalf of two of his followers, CLAUDIO (1) and BENEDICK. Visiting the court of LEONATO, governor of MESSINA, Don Pedro volunteers to help Claudio marry Leonato's daughter, HERO, whom he courts on the younger man's behalf. He also decides on the scheme that tricks Benedick and BEATRICE into falling in love. However, his success as a cupid is qualified at best.

The prince has just defeated an uprising led by his brother, Don JOHN (1), whom he has forgiven and who accompanies him. However, Don John remains a villain, and his plot to trick Claudio into believing that Hero is promiscuous fools Don Pedro as well. The prince is offended, as is Claudio, at the dishonour involved in having courted such a woman; he encourages Claudio's humiliating rejection of his bride and coolly accepts her apparent death from shame.

Benedick, like Beatrice, remains loyal to Hero and severs his relations with Don Pedro. The prince and Claudio seem decidedly at fault, for the audience knows that Hero is innocent. When Don John's trickery is exposed, Don Pedro is genuinely remorseful, and he leads Claudio to his penitential marriage to Hero's cousin, who proves to be Hero herself. The two couples are reunited and the play ends in a spirit of reconciliation, in which Don Pedro joins.

The original of Don Pedro in the playwright's source, Matteo BANDELLO's novella, is completely insignificant; Shakespeare elaborated the character to create an elderly, dignified figure who presides over the action, thus enhancing the courtly air that suffuses the play. Although vulnerable to Don John's machinations, being too concerned with personal honour to respond humanely when presented with apparently convincing evidence of Hero's guilt, Don Pedro is otherwise a gentle and likeable figure. His initial forgiveness of Don John after subduing his revolt testifies to his good will, and he participates prominently in the celebration of renewed harmony that closes the play. Like Claudio, he may be defended as having sinned 'not but in mistaking' (5.1.268–269). With the two young couples united, Don Pedro, somewhat poignantly, is left single himself. His awareness of this misfortune is evident a few lines from the end of the

play, when the exultant Benedick teasingly enjoins, 'Prince, thou art sad; get thee a wife, get thee a wife!' (5.4.121).

Shakespeare took Don Pedro's name from Bandello's tale, in which the King of Aragon, who has just conquered Sicily, is named Piero. The playwright used the Spanish form of the name, but there is no reason to believe that he was aware of the historical figure whose name he was borrowing. Aragon, one of several medieval kingdoms located in what is now Spain, ruled Sicily beginning in 1282, when a great rebellion arose there against the French. King Pedro III (1236–1285)—generally known in English as Peter the Great of Aragon—was invited by the rebels to assume the crown. He invaded and quickly drove out the French, beginning a period of Aragonese—and later Spanish—rule that was to last until 1713.

**Peele, George (c. 1557–1596)** English playwright, a possible collaborator with Shakespeare. Peele was one of the UNIVERSITY WITS, the group of dramatists that dominated the LONDON theatre in the 1580s. After attending Oxford, Peele pursued an impecunious and dissipated life in London, writing plays and other works. His most successful work was *The Old Wives' Tale*, a romantic play based on folk stories. Scholars such as FLEAY and ROBERTSON, who believe that many of Shakespeare's early plays were written by more than one person, have often attributed scenes and passages to Peele, especially in *1 Henry VI* and *Titus Andronicus*. However, most modern scholars dispute such propositions, and Peele is chiefly remembered as one of Shakespeare's immediate predecessors.

**Pembroke (1), Henry Herbert, Earl of (c. 1534–1601)** English aristocrat and theatrical patron. Pembroke was the patron of PEMBROKE'S MEN, with whom Shakespeare may have acted early in his career. Though willing to lend his name to the players, who performed sometimes at his estate, Pembroke took no active part in their operations. His interests were chiefly political and military. An important figure in the court of Queen ELIZABETH (1), he was president of the council of WALES (1) and spent much time in that land. He also took part in several important treason trials under Elizabeth, including that of Mary, Queen of Scots (see JAMES I). He was married to Mary Sidney, sister of Sir Philip SIDNEY, but he did not share the literary interests of that great patron of the arts. If Shakespeare was a member of the Pembroke's Men, it is possible that Pembroke was acquainted with the young playwright, though there is no specific evidence for any personal relationship. Some scholars believe that a continuing connection between Shakespeare and Pembroke may account for the pointed interest in Wales that appears in some of the plays. Also, there is a posthumous connection between the family and

Shakespeare, for Pembroke's sons, William and Philip (see PEMBROKE [3] and MONTGOMERY [2]), were co-dedicatees of the FIRST FOLIO.

**Pembroke (2), Philip Herbert, Lord**   See MONTGOMERY (2).

**Pembroke (3), William Herbert, Earl of (1580–1630)**   English aristocrat, a dedicatee of the FIRST FOLIO of Shakespeare's plays and a possible model for the young man to whom the SONNETS are addressed. Pembroke's father, also the Earl of PEMBROKE (1), may have been acquainted with Shakespeare in the 1590s; this, along with Pembroke's known rejection of possible brides in 1595 and 1597, and the match between his initials and the 'Mr W. H'. of Thomas THORPE's dedication to the Sonnets, has suggested to some commentators that he may have been the young man whose marriage is advocated in Sonnets 1–17. However, no certain connection between Shakespeare and Pembroke is known—the dedication of the Folio was made long after Shakespeare's death, by John HEMINGE and Henry CONDELL, doubtless because Pembroke was the lord chamberlain and therefore responsible for the publication of plays. In the absence of new evidence, Pembroke's association with the Sonnets must remain purely speculative.

Pembroke had other literary connections from an early age, however. His mother was the sister of Sir Philip SIDNEY and the patron of Edmund SPENSER and others. Samuel DANIEL was among his tutors, and as a young man, Pembroke wrote poetry himself. In the 1590s he was a courtier to Queen ELIZABETH (1), but he lost her favour in 1600 when he refused to marry his pregnant mistress, Mary FITTON. He was gaoled for this offence, but Elizabeth's successor returned him to favour, and he became a prominent member of the new court. Pembroke was a patron of Ben JONSON and the poet George Herbert (1593–1633), a distant cousin; he was also an active investor in colonial development. He was a long-time chancellor of Oxford University—Pembroke College there is named in his honour—and he contributed many volumes to the BODLEIAN LIBRARY (there is still a statue of him outside it).

**Pembroke (4), William Herbert, Earl of (d. 1469)**   Historical figure and minor character in *3 Henry VI*, a supporter of EDWARD IV. Pembroke, who does not speak, is present when the Yorkist leaders learn that WARWICK (3) has deserted their cause in 4.1. He is ordered, with Lord STAFFORD (1), to raise an army.

In 1469, the historical Pembroke, who received his title from Edward for his services in the civil war, was commissioned, with Stafford, to put down a local rebellion that Warwick had sponsored; because of a personal dispute, Stafford withheld his forces from a bat-

tle, and the rebels captured and beheaded Pembroke. The historical Pembroke was the father of Sir Walter HERBERT (3), who appears in *Richard III*. Through an illegitimate son, he was also the great-grandfather of Henry Herbert, Earl of PEMBROKE (1), the sponsor of PEMBROKE'S MEN, the actor's company with which Shakespeare was probably associated when he wrote this play.

**Pembroke (5), William Marshall, Earl of (c. 1146–1219)**   Historical figure and minor character in *King John*, a rebel against King JOHN (3). Pembroke, like Lord BIGOT, is merely a representative rebellious baron with no distinctive personality.

The historical William Marshall was a famous soldier who in fact remained loyal to John throughout his reign. Shakespeare confused him with his son, who did join the French invasion forces.

**Pembroke's Men**   Acting company of the ELIZABETHAN THEATRE, possible employer of the young Shakespeare. In late 1592 a troupe of actors sponsored by Henry Herbert, Earl of PEMBROKE (1), performed at the court of Queen ELIZABETH (1), and the following year, with the LONDON theatres closed by the plague, the company toured England. The tour was a financial failure, however, and in September 1593 their rival Philip HENSLOWE recorded that they were forced to sell costumes to pay their debts. A number of plays known to have been in their repertoire (see below) were published by other people in 1594, suggesting that they were forced to sell their rights in them as well.

A revived Pembroke's Men played in the provinces from 1595 to 1597, and in the latter year they began a year's engagement in London, at Francis LANGLEY's new SWAN THEATRE. However, their July production of Thomas NASHE's allegedly seditious play, *Isle of Dogs*, resulted in the brief imprisonment of three members of the company—Gabriel SPENCER, Ben JONSON, and Robert SHAW (5)—and the enforced closure of all the theatres for the summer. When they reopened in October, several actors had left Pembroke's for the ADMIRAL'S MEN. Soon the remnant of Pembroke's returned to the provinces, no longer able to compete in London. In 1600 two performances at Henslowe's ROSE THEATRE were flops, spelling the end of the company.

The repertoire of Pembroke's Men can be deduced in part. We know from the title-page of the BAD QUARTO of *3 Henry VI* (published as THE TRUE TRAGEDY in 1595) that this play—and, by implication, its companion, *2 Henry VI*—were staged by the company. As in any Bad Quarto, the actors' faulty memories have been supplemented by their recollections of performances in other plays. Thus, the other works echoed in these texts were probably part of the company's repertoire, including *1 Henry VI* as well as works by Christopher MARLOWE (1), Thomas KYD, and others. The title-pages of *Titus Andronicus* and THE TAMING OF A SHREW (1594)—a Bad Quarto of *The Taming of the Shrew*—declare that Pembroke's Men also performed these works. The association of Pembroke's Men with five of Shakespeare's early works has led scholars to presume that the young playwright was himself part of the company at some point during the mysterious beginnings of his career, leaving them before their collapse in 1593. The extremely poor quality of *The Taming of a Shrew* suggests that he was no longer with Pembroke's Men when it was prepared in the summer of 1592.

**Penker (Pynkie), Friar (active 1483)** Historical figure and minor character in *Richard III,* one of two clergymen who, disguised as BISHOPS (1), accompany RICHARD III as he receives the MAYOR (3) in 3.7. This imposture is intended to lend an air of religiosity to the would-be usurper. Penker and Doctor SHAA were summoned by Richard in 3.5.

In Thomas MORE's history, one of Shakespeare's sources for this anecdote, Penker's name is Pynkie, and he is described as a Provincial of the Augustine friars, a fairly high-ranking administrator.

**Pentapolis** Ancient Mediterranean land, the setting for most of Act 2 of *Pericles.* Pentapolis is the domain of King SIMONIDES, whose daughter THAISA marries PERICLES. At the end of the play, Pericles learns of Simonides' death and announces that he and Thaisa shall rule in Pentapolis. Pericles' encounter with three FISHERMEN in 2.1 establishes that Pentapolis has a seacoast, but the country is otherwise undistinctive and serves purely as an exotic locale.

In classical times, Pentapolis—Greek for 'five cities'—referred to any of five different locales, all of them political entities centred on five towns. None of them were independent kingdoms at the time of the play's only historical figure, ANTIOCHUS the Great, and it is impossible to be certain which of them Shakespeare had in mind. He may not have considered the matter, for he simply took the name from a source, the *Confessio Amantis* of John GOWER (3).

In an early Latin version of the tale—unknown to the playwright—the term clearly refers to the region also known as Cyrenaica, a Greek colony on the shores of North Africa in what is now eastern Libya. Since this was much the best known ancient Pentapolis, scholars generally associate it with the 'country of Greece' (2.1.64) of *Pericles.* (However, it could also be the Pentapolis of Greek Asia Minor, on the Aegean coast of what is now Turkey, rather closer to the other territories represented in the play.)

**Pepys, Samuel (1633–1703)** Seventeenth-century diarist and long-time administrator of the Royal Navy. Pepys kept his famous diary between 1660 and 1669. An inveterate theatre-goer, he recorded his impressions of many Restoration period adaptations of Shakespeare's plays.

**Percy (1), Henry** Character in *Richard II.* See NORTHUMBERLAND (1).

**Percy (2), Henry (1364–1403)** Historical figure and character in *Richard II,* a supporter of BOLINGBROKE (1), son of the Earl of NORTHUMBERLAND (1). The same historical figure appears as HOTSPUR in *1 Henry IV.* In *Richard II* Percy is a minor figure who primarily delivers information. He is plainly introduced solely in anticipation of his far greater importance in *1 Henry IV.* Presented as younger by a generation than he really was, Percy is thus made the contemporary of Bolingbroke's son, PRINCE (6) HAL, who is to be his great rival. Significantly, it is Percy who tells Bolingbroke the disreputable news of his son in 5.3.13–19. Percy's role is clear evidence that Shakespeare had already formulated the general outline of *1 Henry IV* while writing *Richard II.*

**Percy (3), Henry** Character in *3 Henry VI.* See NORTHUMBERLAND (2).

**Percy (4), Lady** Character in *1* and *2 Henry IV.* See LADY (10).

**Percy (5), Thomas** Character in *1 Henry IV.* See WORCESTER.

**Perdita** Character in *The Winter's Tale,* long-lost daughter of King LEONTES and Queen HERMIONE of SICILIA. The love of Perdita and Prince FLORIZEL of BOHEMIA is the central element in the romantic COMEDY that constitutes the second half of the play, balancing the TRAGEDY of Leontes' mad jealousy in the first. Though she is prominent only in 4.4, her virtue, beauty, and charming personality make Perdita a powerful symbolic force in the remainder of the play.

At the turning point of the play, in 3.3, the infant Perdita is abandoned in the wilderness because Leontes believes she is the offspring of Hermione's alleged adultery with King POLIXENES of Bohemia. A SHEPHERD (2) adopts Perdita, and by Act 4, 16 years later, she has become a charming young woman, the 'Mistress o' th' Feast' (4.4.68) at the shepherds' festival. Florizel's father, King Polixenes, disapproves of the love between his royal son and a peasant girl. When he attends the feast in disguise, he is charmed by Perdita, finding her 'Too noble for this place' (4.4.159), but he will not accept her as a daughter-in-law. He threatens her with death, and the couple flees to Sicilia, where Perdita's identity is discovered. This leads to their formal engagement, the reconciliation of Leontes and Polixenes, and the restoration of Queen Hermione, who has been kept in hiding. The prophecy of the oracle of Apollo—that only Perdita can restore the happiness Leontes has destroyed—is thus fulfilled. Perdita's love is essential to the workings of providence in the play's outcome, thereby supporting the play's major theme, that the moral virtue of good people is necessary for providence to function as a saviour in human affairs.

Raised as a shepherdess, Perdita is an honest, open young woman with no trace of pretension or sentimentality. She is embarrassed to be 'most goddess-like prank'd up' (4.4.10) in a fancy costume for the festival, and she is frankly worried about Polixenes' opposition to her, though more for Florizel's sake than her own. A clever lass, she briskly counters CAMILLO's flattery in 4.4.110–112 and more than holds her own in the debate with Polixenes in 4.4.79–103, in which she defends the simple ways of nature against the sophistication of art. She values a maidenly decorum in sexual matters, while acknowledgeing the physical side of love. She mentions, for example, a 'false way' of love (4.4.151) and speaks against 'scurrilous words' (4.4.215) in ballads, yet when Florizel jests that strewn with flowers he would be like a corpse, she replies, 'No, like a bank, for love to lie and play on: / Not like a corpse; or if—not to be buried, / But quick, and in mine arms' (4.4.130–132).

This lovely passage is suggestive of primordial rituals of death and rebirth. Along with her remarks on the Proserpina myth and mythological flower lore in 4.4.116–126, it links her with the ancient veneration of natural fertility, of which the shepherds' festival is a survival. As Florizel puts it, 'This your sheep-shearing / Is as a meeting of the petty gods, / And you the queen on 't' (4.4.3–5). All this reinforces Perdita's association with providence. It was the protection of providence that brought the tragic first half of the play to an end, and it is the love Perdita represents that proves instrumental in effecting the final reconciliations of the second.

**Pericles** Title character of *Pericles,* the ruler of TYRE. Through no fault of his own, Pericles undergoes tremendous misfortunes. He is driven into exile and becomes separated from both his wife and daughter, only to be finally reunited with them at the play's close. He accepts his fate passively, and thus he embodies a major theme of the play: that we cannot control our destiny, and the acceptance of suffering is humanity's only choice.

Pericles encounters love three times, but each time he loses it. In 1.1 he loves the DAUGHTER (1) of ANTIOCHUS, but when he learns of her incestuous relationship with her father, he withdraws his suit in horror. He is sullied by her sin although he is innocent, for the 'gods . . . inflame'd desire in [his] breast / To taste the fruit' (1.1.20–22). Disillusioned, he loses his youthful assurance and flees into exile, a tribulation that ends when he is shipwrecked on the coast of PENTAPOLIS, in 2.1. He finds love again when he meets and marries THAISA, but suffers a great loss when he wrongly believes that she has died in childbirth during a storm at sea. This is eased by the compensation of MARINA's birth, but he leaves Marina with CLEON and DIONYZA because he fears for her survival at sea. When he returns for her in 4.4, he learns—again wrongly—of her death. Significantly, he endures another storm at this point, but it happens off-stage and is merely mentioned, in 5.Chorus.14, for his fortunes have now begun to turn. Distraught and without hope, he succumbs to despair. He only recovers when he accidently encounters Marina. The goddess DIANA (2) then guides him to a reunion with Thaisa. Thus, in the course of his life Pericles manifests youthful illusions, the misery of incomprehensible suffering, and the ultimate happiness that follows from his patient acceptance of the will of the gods.

His passiveness makes Pericles a strange hero to modern tastes. However, this trait should not be seen as an aspect of his personality, but rather as an emblematic feature that offers an allegory of a possible human relationship to the universe. Like most of the play's characters, Pericles is more emblematic than real and does not have a complex, fully developed personality. He is wholly good and without flaws. Unlike Antiochus, he *is* 'a man on whom perfections wait' (1.1.80). He does not cause his misfortunes, nor does he resist them. He expresses his resignation clearly after the shipwreck. He addresses the tempest and says, 'earthly man / Is but a substance that must yield to you; / And I, as fits my nature, do obey you' (2.1.2–4). His marriage is not his own doing, either. Thaisa courts him more than he does her, and though he loves her, he declares that he has 'never aim'd so high to love' her (2.5.47). He is not without spunk—he responds with fiery indignation when SIMONIDES pretends to believe him a 'traitor' (2.5.54)—but in the world of the play he must suffer or prosper as fate decrees. Finally, his passiveness leads to his complete withdrawal when he believes Marina is dead. He retreats into speechlessness, a deathlike trance of despair from which only Marina can revive him. The play's theme of regeneration is embodied in part by this, Pericles' resurrection.

The play's strongest treatment of evil is its presentation of incest. Here, Pericles is pointedly contrasted with Antiochus and proves himself a vessel of goodness. The episode is confined to 1.1, but it is mentioned at several points throughout the play, and it makes the point that humanity is capable of gross unnaturalness. It is countered by the example of Simonides and Thaisa, but more dramatically, we see the father-daughter relationship reformulated in the reunion of Pericles and Marina. Pericles recognises her impact on his despair and calls Marina 'Thou that beget'st him that did thee beget' (5.1.195); thus, incest's horror is reversed. At the play's close, Pericles, unlike Antiochus, willingly surrenders Marina to a husband. He demonstrates the healthy paternal love that promotes the natural cycles of regeneration that are an important theme of the play.

In his summary of *Pericles,* Gower (3) speaks of the hero and his family in words that could refer to Pericles alone. He calls them 'Led on by heaven, and crown'd with joy at last' (Epilogue.6). Pericles is an extremely simple character, and Shakespeare, like many readers, may have found him a little too simple, for the subsequent ROMANCES were to contain a pattern of sin and remorse from which Pericles' story is exempt. Nevertheless, in this first of the late comedies the title character is a fine example of an allegorical protagonist, and is a dramatic success when viewed in the terms set by the play.

The play stems from the ancient Greek tale 'Apollonius of Tyre', and the protagonist's name remained Apollonius in Shakespeare's main sources for the play. The new name was probably suggested by Pyrocles, a hero of Sir Philip SYDNEY's *Arcadia,* one of the play's minor sources. Shakespeare's hero bears no resemblance at all to the Athenian statesman named Pericles (c. 495–429 B.C.), though the playwright undoubtedly read the Athenian's biography in PLUTARCH's *Lives.* The great stature of the historical Pericles may have made his name seem appropriately grand for a fictional ruler of Tyre.

### *Pericles, Prince of Tyre*

SYNOPSIS

*Act 1, Chorus*
The ghost of John GOWER (3) identifies himself and introduces the play as the enactment of an ancient tale. It opens in ANTIOCH, where King ANTIOCHUS practises incest with his beautiful DAUGHTER (1). He has stipulated that she may only marry the suitor who can solve a certain riddle, and that any suitor who attempts to do so and fails will be executed.

*Act 1, Scene 1*
PERICLES, Prince of TYRE, hears the riddle, and realises that its solution reveals Antiochus' incest. He declines to give his answer, but he makes it clear that he knows the secret. The king decides to humour him and grants him a 40-day respite before he must answer. Pericles realises that Antiochus will attempt to silence him, and he decides to flee. Antiochus orders THALIARD to kill Pericles, but word comes that Pericles has left Antioch. Thaliard is sent in pursuit.

*Act 1, Scene 2*
In Tyre, Pericles fears that Antiochus, who is a much more powerful ruler, will attack and devastate his country. A group of fawning courtiers appears, but among them is HELICANUS, who strongly disapproves of flattering a monarch. Pericles admires his spirit and confides his fears to him. Helicanus advises him that he should travel for a time, until Antiochus' rage has cooled. Pericles agrees and decides to go to THARSUS. He appoints Helicanus to rule in his absence.

*Act 1, Scene 3*
Thaliard has come to Tyre. He learns of Pericles' departure and leaves to inform Antiochus.

*Act 1, Scene 4*
CLEON, the Governor of Tharsus, and DIONYZA, his wife, are worried because a famine has overtaken their once-rich country. Pericles has heard of their plight, and arrives with shipments of food.

*Act 2, Chorus*
Gower tells the audience that Pericles is adored in Tharsus. In a DUMB SHOW, Pericles receives a message, which Gower tells us is from Helicanus, who warns the prince of Thaliard's evil intent and suggests further flight. Gower tells us that Pericles fled by sea and was shipwrecked.

*Act 2, Scene 1*
Shipwrecked, Pericles encounters three FISHERMEN, who inform him he is in PENTAPOLIS. They tell him that their king, SIMONIDES, is holding a tournament the next day at which knights will joust for the hand in marriage of his daughter. Pericles' armour is brought up in the Fishermen's net, and he decides to use it in the king's tournament.

*Act 2, Scene 2*
At the tournament, the king's daughter, THAISA, receives greetings from each KNIGHT (2) who will compete for her hand. Pericles' rusty armour is ridiculed by some courtiers, but cheers celebrate his victory off-stage.

*Act 2, Scene 3*
At a celebratory banquet, Pericles is welcomed by Thaisa as the victor and therefore her fiancé.

*Act 2, Scene 4*
In Tyre, Helicanus tells ESCANES that the gods have punished Antiochus and his daughter by killing them with a heavenly fire. A group of noblemen declare that they cannot be without a king any longer and ask Helicanus to declare himself king. He refuses, but agrees to do so if Pericles has not returned after another year.

*Act 2, Scene 5*
To test Pericles, Simonides pretends to be angry that the young man has falsely gained the affection of Thaisa, and he calls him a traitor. Pericles rejects the insult manfully, to Simonides' secret delight. Thaisa appears and says it would please her if Pericles loved

her. Simonides reveals his pleasure and declares that she and Pericles shall marry.

## Act 3, Chorus

Gower reveals that Thaisa, now married to Pericles, is pregnant. In a dumb show, Pericles receives another letter, which he shows to Thaisa and Simonides. Gower tells us that the letter is from Helicanus, summoning Pericles to Tyre. He goes on to report that Pericles and Thaisa leave by ship, only to be caught in a great storm.

## Act 3, Scene 1

Aboard ship, during the tempest, the nurse LYCHORIDA tells Pericles that Thaisa has died in childbirth. She shows him the infant, a daughter. A SAILOR (3) insists that Thaisa must be buried at sea or the ship is cursed, and the distracted Pericles agrees. Pericles orders the ship to stop at Tharsus where he will leave the infant. He is afraid she may not survive a longer voyage.

## Act 3, Scene 2

At EPHESUS a chest washed up by the great storm is brought to the nobleman and physician CERIMON. He opens it and finds the apparently dead Thaisa, but he recognises that she is merely unconscious and revives her with medicines.

## Act 3, Scene 3

At Tharsus Pericles leaves his daughter MARINA in the care of Cleon and Dionyza.

## Act 3, Scene 4

In Ephesus, Thaisa decides to enter a convent devoted to the goddess DIANA (2) since she will never find her husband again.

## Act 4, Chorus

Gower tells us that Marina has grown into a gracious and beautiful young woman. So fine a person is she, he says, that she overshadows Cleon and Dionyza's daughter. Dionyza has become so jealous that she decides to have Marina killed.

## Act 4, Scene 1

Dionyza reminds LEONINE of his oath to murder Marina, for he is reluctant. Marina appears and is persuaded to take a walk on the beach with Leonine. As he prepares to kill her, a boat-load of PIRATES come ashore and kidnap her. Leonine escapes and is relieved not to have to kill Marina. He plans to tell Dionyza that he has done so anyway.

## Act 4, Scene 2

In a brothel in MYTILENE the PANDAR, the BAWD, and their servant BOULT discuss the sorry state of business. They regret that they don't have more attractive young women to offer. A Pirate appears and offers to sell them Marina, and they accept. Despite Marina's pleas and objections, they make plans to offer her to their customers.

## Act 4, Scene 3

In Tharsus Cleon is distressed to learn that Dionyza has had Marina murdered. She has also poisoned Leonine to keep him quiet. She is cynically pleased with the success of her plan, and tells Cleon that they will inform Pericles that Marina died naturally.

## Act 4, Scene 4

Gower appears by Marina's gravestone in Tharsus with the information that Pericles has come to get his daughter. A dumb show presents his grief when he is shown the tomb by Cleon. Gower reads the flowery epitaph on the monument, and contrasts its flattery with Marina's unhappiness in Mytilene.

## Act 4, Scene 5

Two gentlemen of Mytilene discuss the wondrous virtue of a harlot they have encountered, and they vow to reform their lives.

## Act 4, Scene 6

The Bawd, the Pandar, and Boult despair at the damage Marina is doing to their business. LYSIMACHUS, the Governor of Mytilene, appears and is offered Marina. She implores him as an honourable man not to use her as a harlot, and he declares that his intention has merely been to test her virtue, of which he has heard. He leaves, but he refuses to give money to Boult. Boult angrily threatens to deflower Marina himself so that her virtue will not further upset the brothel's business. However, she shames him into agreeing instead to help her establish herself as a teacher of music, dance, and handicrafts to young women.

## Act 5, Chorus

Gower tells of Marina's success in Mytilenian society. He adds that the grief-stricken Pericles, who has been wandering at sea, has arrived in Mytilene.

## Act 5, Scene 1

Lysimachus boards Pericles' ship to greet the visitor, but he is informed by Helicanus that the prince has been made speechless by his grief. A Mytilenian courtier suggests that the charms of Marina could cure Pericles, and she is sent for. When she arrives she is left alone with Pericles, and he speaks because he is startled by her resemblance to Thaisa. In the course of their conversation their relationship becomes apparent and they are happily reunited. Exhausted by the excitement, Pericles is left alone to sleep and the goddess Diana appears to him in a vision. She directs him to go to her temple in Ephesus and proclaim the history of Marina's birth and their separation and reunion.

## Act 5, Scene 2

At the Temple of Diana in Ephesus, Thaisa, the High Priestess, stands by the altar. Gower appears and tells us that Lysimachus and Marina are engaged but will not marry until Pericles fulfils Diana's instructions, so the couple have accompanied Pericles to Ephesus.

*Act 5, Scene 3*
At the Temple altar, Pericles identifies himself and tells of Marina's birth and adventures. Thaisa recognises him and faints. Cerimon is present, and he reveals her identity to Pericles. When Thaisa recovers, she and Pericles are reunited, and Thaisa and Marina meet for the first time since Marina's birth. When he learns of Simonides' death, Pericles declares that he and Thaisa shall reign in Pentapolis and Lysimachus and Marina will rule in Tyre.

*Epilogue*
Gower compares the heavenly destruction of Antiochus and his daughter with the ultimate happiness of Pericles, Thaisa, and Marina. He goes on to praise Helicanus and Cerimon, and adds that the people of Tharsus were enraged when they heard of Marina's murder, and massacred Cleon and Dionyza. He then announces that the play is now over.

## COMMENTARY

*Pericles, Prince of Tyre* is the first of Shakespeare's RO-MANCES. Even though the opening acts are probably not his work (see 'Text of the Play'), Shakespeare took this opportunity to develop several ideas and techniques. These techniques—such as the melding of COMEDY and TRAGEDY, and the use of strange, elaborate plots and boldly symbolic characters—are the ones that he began to use in the PROBLEM PLAYS and continued to experiment with in works such as *Timon of Athens*. Most important is the growth of a theme that runs through all of the late plays; that humankind cannot alter its destiny in an inexplicable but finally benevolent universe. *Pericles* is flawed, in part due to collaboration, or a very faulty text, or both, but also due to the nature of its imperfectly combined elements. However, it constitutes a significant step towards the magnificent achievements of *The Winter's Tale* and *The Tempest*.

Though *Pericles* was extremely popular in the early 17th century, it has since been considered one of the least satisfying of Shakespeare's plays. Despite the flawed surviving text, it contains much good poetry, especially in the reunion of Pericles and Marina in 5.1, but the play's virtues are largely outweighed by its defects. Its major figures seem lifeless; it is episodic; its events are often described rather than enacted; and all this is presented in a nearly shapeless plot that is full of extreme improbabilities and absurd situations. For instance, why would Antiochus describe his sin in the riddle he invites the world to solve? Why does Thaisa enter a convent instead of going on to Tyre to rejoin her husband? Why does Pericles leave Marina in Tharsus for 14 years? Each question can be answered by reference to the conventions of folklore and

narrative romance, but taken together, the whole story lacks plausibility and dramatic interest.

Nevertheless, *Pericles* has increased in popularity in the 20th century. The bold extremes of characterisation and theme found in folklore and narrative romance may be more acceptable to a century familiar with abstraction. The play is more rewarding on the stage than in print, in any case, for it depends in good part on MASQUElike spectacle. It also entertains us with a wide range of human behaviour—however baldly represented—and of good and bad fortune. Its very conventionality is reassuring: we can suspend our sense that life cannot be both randomly threatening and neatly resolved and simply enjoy its bizarre episodes and its happy ending.

*Pericles* centres on the title character—and, late in the play, on Marina—but it features a number of boldly drawn minor figures. These are not, for the most part, endowed with real human personalities, but they demonstrate the nature of humanity. Antiochus is a regal villain, full of power and sin, while Dionyza represents the archetypal evil stepmother. On the other hand, Helicanus is a paragon of loyalty and strength, while Cerimon is a benevolent nobleman and a master of the far reaches of human knowledge. These figures are not realistic, but this is part of their point. They are symbols of the human potential for good and evil that is so much more complex and obscure in reality, or even in realistic drama. The Fishermen of 2.1 and the staff of the Mytilenian brothel in Act 4 not only provide comic relief, they also remind us of our own parallel universe, mirrored allegorically in the play.

The play is unified by a repeated pattern of loss and recovery. On the largest scale, Pericles loses his confident idealism and is tainted by sexual evil; he suffers as a result, and he recovers goodness and love at the end of his life. This pattern is repeated within the overall development, as Pericles encounters love and loses happiness three times, only to recover each time. The cycle is strikingly punctuated with storms. When he flees the horror represented by Antiochus' daughter, Pericles becomes a shipwrecked exile, but he finds love anew in Thaisa. Beset by another tempest, Pericles loses Thaisa, but takes comfort in the birth of Marina. Finally, though he is driven to despair by the apparent loss of Marina as well, fate changes its course and he recovers both daughter and wife. Significantly, the storm that Pericles endures at this point is merely mentioned briefly, in 5.Chorus.14, and is not given the emphasis of the first two. Like ancient festival rituals, *Pericles* offers an analogy to the eternal cycles of winter and spring, death and rebirth. This pattern is the play's plot.

Our sense of this 'plot' is reinforced by the play's most prominent motif, resurrection. First Thaisa and then Marina seem to die, only to be revived, literally in Thaisa's case and figuratively with Marina's release from the brothel (after which 'she sings like one immortal' [5.Chorus.3]). When Pericles discovers that his daughter is dead, he withdraws into himself and may be said to have suffered a mock death, from which he is revived by Marina. Once restored, he cries that Marina 'beget'st' him (5.1.195), which suggests his reborn state, and demands 'fresh garments' (5.1.213). The symbolic value of this gesture is difficult to ignore. He has been returned from death as surely as Marina and Thaisa seem to have been. Finally, at the play's close, the ritual cycle of death and birth is brought full circle, and Pericles' mourning for his daughter is forgotten in plans for her marriage. The recurring theme is touched on one last time when Simonides' death is reported. This allows Marina and Lysimachus to take their destined place—once that of the play's protagonist—as rulers of Tyre.

Another major motif of the play, incest, appears only once, but the issue is raised again at sensitive moments. In the play incest suggests the deepest evil to which humanity is susceptible. Pericles, drawn to Antiochus' daughter, is tainted by her sin although he is innocent, for the 'gods . . . inflame'd desire in [his] breast / To taste the fruit' (1.1.20–22). The episode's place at the opening of the play gives it great weight, and its point is further made by contrast when the hero encounters Thaisa and Simonides. Their healthy love is apparent when Simonides delightedly surrenders his daughter to Pericles in marriage. The theme is subtly and dramatically reworked in Pericles' cry to Marina: 'Thou . . . beget'st him that did thee beget' (5.1.195). The horrifying potential of incest—inbred offspring—is inverted. Finally Pericles, like Simonides and unlike Antiochus, can willingly separate himself from Marina as she joins her husband in a new life.

At the play's close, then, the influence of evil has been destroyed and the misfortunes of the hero have been ended, but neither he nor Marina have been responsible for the happy ending. Dramatic coincidence, good luck, and the intervention of the gods have propelled events. Marina, in resisting the brothel world, influences her fate to some degree, but only sheer accident reunites her with her father. The other characters, especially Pericles—who is extraordinarily passive throughout—simply suffer or succeed as fate decrees. The play emphasises that the characters cannot control their destiny, and that the patience to accept the misfortunes of life is the best way to survive them. The most important of the external forces that drive the action is the sea. Its impersonal violence is both the occasion and the symbol of Pericles' recurring losses. Further, help comes to famine-beset Tharsus by sea in 1.4; in 2.1 the shipwrecked Pericles' only remaining emblem of princely dignity, his inherited armour, is brought up in the Fishermen's net; and in 4.2 Marina's unlikely rescuers appear from the sea.

Not for nothing does the reunion of Pericles and Marina take place on a feast day dedicated to Neptune. This fact is emphasised by pointed repetition (5.Chorus.17; 5.1.17), and by reiteration of the word 'sea' and references to the sea throughout the scene. The spectacular appearance of Diana makes the divine influence on the play's events completely clear. It is only sensible that Gower should summarise the tale of Pericles' family by saying that they have been 'Led on by heaven' (Epilogue.6).

Another aspect of the characters' dependence on fate is the element of surprise that recurs throughout the play. In 1.1 Pericles is shockingly disillusioned about Antiochus' daughter; in 1.3 Thaliard finds his prey escaped; in 1.4, Cleon is astonished by the arrival of succor from famine, and so on. In almost every scene but Gower's narrations, which serve to anchor us amid seas of uncertainty, are instances of such startled amazement. Indeed, Marina feels that 'This world to me is as a lasting storm, / Whirring me from my friends' (4.1.19–20). The sublimely spiritual quality of the last act owes much to the appearance of a cause for the play's random surprises. As mistrust yields to confidence that the promised joy is real, we, like the characters, can believe that the irrational brutality of the world is a survivable danger; such a solace is to be valued as much as any human achievement.

## SOURCES OF THE PLAY

The original source for *Pericles, Prince of Tyre* was an ancient tale known as 'Apollonius of Tyre'. Though the earliest surviving version is a Latin text of the 5th–6th centuries, scholars recognise from its style that it is a translation of a Greek work of 300 years earlier. This tale was extremely popular throughout the Middle Ages and the RENAISSANCE, and Shakespeare (and his collaborators, if any) surely knew it in several different versions that were current in 17th-century England. However, only two of these possible sources are specifically represented in the play: the 14th-century *Confessio Amantis* of John GOWER (3) in a 1554 edition, and Laurence TWINE's *The Patterne of Painefull Adventures* (c. 1576).

Gower's version of the tale, which was derived from a history of the world in Latin verse by the medieval chronicler Godfrey of Viterbo (c. 1120–c. 1196), was most important to the play. It provided the general outline of events, the locations, and most of the characters. Moreover, a number of passages—including Antiochus' riddle (1.1.65–72), Pericles' note in Thaisa's coffin (3.2.70–77), and Gower's lines in 3.Chorus—follow Gower fairly closely.

Twine's rendering of Apollonius' adventures, which he translated from a French version of the famous *Gesta Romanorum*, a medieval collection of Latin tales, was less important. It was only used extensively in Marina's story, especially in 4.3, where Dionyza cynically defends the supposed murder of Marina (though similar arguments made by LADY (6) MACBETH and GONERIL also foreshadow this episode). Minor echoes of Twine's words occur elsewhere in the play as well.

Though Shakespeare's Gower resembles and must have been influenced by the allegorical CHORUS (3) of the playwright's own *Henry V*, the idea of using the author of a well-known source as a ghostly CHORUS (1) was probably stimulated by a contemporary play, *The Devil's Charter* (1607), by Barnabe BARNES. This play was derived from a work by the Italian historian Francesco Guicciardini (1483–1540) and featured Guicciardini as a choric narrator. Several of Gower's speeches contain echoes of the words of Barnes' Guicciardini.

Lastly, the hero's name—and thus that of the play—was probably inspired by Pyrocles, a major character in Sir Philip SIDNEY's pastoral romance, *Arcadia* (1590). Two passages in the play—Pericles' appearance in rusty armour in 2.2 and Marina's description of a storm in 4.1—reflect episodes in *Arcadia*.

### TEXT OF THE PLAY

Most scholars believe that *Pericles* is the work of more than one author; one or more who wrote Acts 1–2 and, perhaps, 5.2, and another—Shakespeare—who wrote the remainder and completed or revised the earlier version. However, some scholars believe that the faults of the first edition account for all discrepancies, and that the text is wholly Shakespeare's. In any case, if Shakespeare had a collaborator or collaborators, their identities are unknown, though they have been the subject of scholarly dispute since the 18th century. John DAY and Thomas HEYWOOD (2) are considered the likeliest nominees, but no identification has proven entirely satisfactory.

*Pericles* was probably written in 1607. The likely influence of Barnes' *The Devil's Charter* on the play suggests that *Pericles* was probably not completed before Barnes' play was staged early in 1607. It apparently had been completed, and probably performed, by May 1608, when the text was registered with the STATIONERS' COMPANY as 'A booke called *The booke of Pericles prynce of Tyre*'. This wording almost certainly refers to a theatrical PROMPT-BOOK. Also, there are no surviving references to this extremely popular play that date from before 1608, which implies that it appeared in or just before that year.

Edward BLOUNT registered the play, but he did not publish it, a manoeuvre that scholars believe was a 'stopping action', intended to prevent publishing piracy. The effort was unsuccessful, however, for *Pericles* was published the next year by Henry GOSSON (1) in a QUARTO edition printed by William WHITE (2) known as Q1 (1609). Q1 is a BAD QUARTO, an inaccurate text put together from the recollections of actors or viewers. Some scholars believe that two different recollections

were used, which produced the difference between Acts 1–2 and Acts 3–5. Based on this hypothesis, the text may be wholly Shakespeare's. Q1 was so popular that Gosson produced another edition (Q2) in the same year. (*Richard II* was the only other Shakespeare play to appear in two quartos in one year.) An unknown publisher brought out Q3 (1611), and Q4 (1619) was part of Thomas PAVIER'S FALSE FOLIO. Q5 and Q6 appeared in 1630 and 1635. *Pericles* was not published in the FIRST FOLIO (1623) for reasons that are unknown. Perhaps the editors knew that much of the play was not written by Shakespeare, or they may have found the bad quarto too poor a text to reproduce. *Pericles* does appear, along with several other non-Shakespearean works (see APOCRYPHA), in the Third FOLIO (F3; 1664). F3 was printed from Q6, and Q2–Q6 are all derived from Q1. The original quarto, therefore, despite its faults, has been the basis of all subsequent editions.

### THEATRICAL HISTORY OF THE PLAY

Undated diplomatic papers record that a performance of *Pericles* was attended by the Venetian and French ambassadors to England sometime between May 1606 (when the French delegate arrived in London) and the closure of London's theatres by a plague epidemic in July 1608. Scholars generally date the play to 1607, so the initial production probably opened during that year or early in 1608. The KING'S MEN made an unsuccessful effort to prevent the pirated publication of *Pericles* in 1608 because the play was already extremely popular. George WILKINS' 1609 novel based on the play capitalised on this popularity, which is further stressed by contemporary references. These include a 1609 remark that great crowds attended the play, and the 1619 record of an elaborate production and intermission banquet with which the government entertained visiting dignitaries. As late as 1631, Ben JONSON complained in print that *Pericles* was outdrawing his own works.

However, though *Pericles* was the first Shakespearean play revived when the theatres were reopened following the English civil war—Thomas BETTERTON was acclaimed in the title role in 1660 and 1661—the play was not popular thereafter. In fact, it was not produced again—except in a very un-Shakespearean adaptation by George LILLO (1738)—until Samuel PHELPS revived it in 1854. Phelps' version was greatly abridged; Gower was eliminated entirely, for instance. It was also sanitised; Victorian tastes could not tolerate the brothel scenes, in particular, so Phelps condensed Act 4 and 'disinfected it of its impurities', as a contemporary reviewer put it.

Only three other productions—two of them German—are known from before World War I, but since then the play has grown somewhat in popularity. Among the most notable 20th-century productions have been the first modern staging of the unaltered play by Robert ATKINS at the OLD VIC THEATRE (1921), and two productions starring Paul SCOFIELD (1947, 1950). *Pericles* has never been made into a FILM, though it has been produced once for TELEVISION, in 1983.

**Perkes, Clement**    GLOUCESTERSHIRE countryman named in *2 Henry IV*, a legal adversary of DAVY's friend William VISOR of Woncot. Davy, the steward of Justice SHALLOW, asks his master to rule in Visor's favour in his lawsuit against 'Clement Perkes a'th'Hill' (5.1.35), in a glimpse of rural corruption that is part of the play's depiction of English manners and mores. Perkes is thought to represent someone Shakespeare knew, a member of a family named Purchase or Perkis that lived near Woodmancote, the play's 'Woncot', in an area traditionally called 'the Hill'.

**Peter (1)**    Minor character in *2 Henry VI*, an apprentice to an armourer, Thomas HORNER. In 1.3 Peter reports that his master has said that the Duke of YORK (8) is 'rightful heir to the crown' (1.3.26). This bit of hearsay is seized upon by the Duke of SUFFOLK (3), who accuses York of treason and has Peter repeat his account later in the scene. Horner denies having said such a thing, and the question is referred to a trial by combat. This procedure, a judicious postponement of a potentially explosive issue, is ordered by the Lord Protector, the Duke of GLOUCESTER (4). In the meantime, at Gloucester's suggestion, York's reappointment as Regent of FRANCE (1) is postponed until the matter is resolved. Thus, as his downfall approaches, 'good Duke Humphrey' is given an opportunity to display the qualities of prudence and judgement that are shortly to be denied the country through the selfish ambitions of Suffolk and others.

Although Peter is desperately afraid to fight, Horner arrives for the contest drunk in 2.3, and Peter slays him. The dying armourer confesses the truth of Peter's report, and the apprentice is exonerated. Although the nobles do not take this clownish incident seriously, the episode prefigures York's actual treason, which sparks the WARS OF THE ROSES, later in the play.

**Peter (2)**    Minor character in *Romeo and Juliet*, a servant in the CAPULET (1) household, the assistant of the NURSE (3). Peter appears with the Nurse in 2.4 and makes a brief speech that both furthers a sexual innuendo and displays comical cowardice. His principal appearance, however, is in 4.5. When the MUSICIANS (2) hired for the wedding of JULIET (1) are dismissed because she is believed to have died, Peter accosts them. He demands free music and then engages them in a comic exchange, insulting them and playing on their names. A stage direction in the Q2 edition of the play (see *Romeo and Juliet*, 'Text of the Play') indicates that Peter was portrayed by Will KEMPE, a famous comic of the day.

**Peter (3)**    Minor character in *The Taming of the Shrew*, a servant of PETRUCHIO (2). Peter is one of several servants whom Petruchio abuses in 4.1. The servants realise that their master's oppressive behaviour is part of his strategy for taming his shrewish bride, KATHERINA, and Peter delivers a succinct analysis of it in the longer of his two lines: 'He kills her in her own humour' (4.1.167).

Peter is not named in any of the several lists of Petruchio's servants that are recited in the scene. This fact, combined with the mute appearance in 4.4 of a servant of LUCENTIO identified as Peter in a stage direction, suggests that his name may be that of an actor who took both small parts, the second of which appears to have been cut. However, no scholar has been able to identify the actor, and there is nothing inherently improbable in the existence of two Peters.

**Peter (4) of Pomfret (d. 1213)**    Historical figure and minor character in *King John*, a wandering 'prophet' whose public forecasts of the fall of King JOHN (3) are recounted by the BASTARD (1) in 4.2. Peter himself, who has been brought to the King, speaks only one line, affirming his belief that John will have surrendered his crown by the following Ascension Day. John orders him imprisoned, to be hung on Ascension Day, and he does not reappear. On Ascension Day, when John does indeed give up his crown—only to receive it again from the papal legate PANDULPH—he recalls the prophecy and observes that it has been fulfilled, in an unanticipated way. We are not informed of Peter's fate, however. The incident illustrates popular dissatisfaction with John's reign and also suggests that his fall was inevitable.

Shakespeare read of this prophecy in HOLINSHED's *Chronicles*, where Peter, a hermit 'in great reputation with the common people' for his powers of prophecy, offered himself to be executed if he proved wrong. On Ascension Day, John still being in power, he was hung, along with his son. Holinshed thought that the prophet was a fraud, but he records that Peter's death was popularly held to be an injustice in light of John's temporary surrender of his crown to Pandulph, which had occurred the day before and seemed to fulfil the prediction.

**Peter (5), Friar**    Character in *Measure for Measure*. See FRIAR (1).

**Petitioners**    Any of several minor characters in *2 Henry VI* who arrive at court in 1.3 with pleas for justice. The Petitioners, two of whom have spoken lines, join with PETER (1) in planning to address their grievances to the Duke of GLOUCESTER (4). Queen MARGARET (1) and the Duke of SUFFOLK (3) appear instead and demand to see their petitions; one is personal and the other requests protection from Suffolk himself, who has incorporated common lands into his estates. Peter's business proves useful to Suffolk, but Margaret scornfully rejects the other Petitioners, tearing up their written pleas and abusively ordering them to leave.

**Peto** Minor character in *1* and *2 Henry IV,* a follower of FALSTAFF. Peto participates in the highway robbery in 2.2 of *1 Henry IV,* and he later tells PRINCE (6) HAL how Falstaff attempted to disguise his cowardice. In 2.4 of *2 Henry IV* Peto brings the Prince news of the King's preparations against the rebellion, stirring Hal to action.

Peto was originally given the name HARVEY (1), but the name was changed after early performances, probably to avoid offending a prominent aristocrat, William HARVEY (3). (See also OLDCASTLE and ROSSILL.)

**Petruchio (1)** GHOST CHARACTER in *Romeo and Juliet,* a follower of TYBALT. Petruchio appears only in a stage direction at 3.1.34, though he is also mentioned as a guest at the CAPULET (1) banquet (1.5.130). Shakespeare presumably intended to develop Petruchio as he wrote 3.1, but did not in fact do so. Then, with his typical inattention to details, the playwright let the stage direction stand. Such a Ghost character is taken as evidence that the published text in which he first appears—in this case Q2 (1599) of *Romeo and Juliet*—was printed from Shakespeare's own manuscript, or FOUL PAPERS, and is thus especially authoritative.

**Petruchio (2)** Character in *The Taming of the Shrew,* the suitor, bridegroom, and tamer of KATHERINA, the shrew of the title. Petruchio is sometimes seen as a tyrannical male, selfishly dominating a woman who cannot escape him. However, this view reflects certain modern attitudes towards marriage and ignores both the world in which the character was created and the actual text of the play. Petruchio does not physically abuse her or humiliate Katherina, and in 'submitting' to him, she merely assumes the conventional role of a wife. At the end of the play she is quite evidently grateful for the change that he has wrought in her life. Theirs is a love story, though this is a subtle element set among the play's several comic plots.

Bluff and hearty, Petruchio is a humorous figure—seen in ludicrous clothes while indulging in spectacular tantrums, he provides laughs in an age-old fashion—but his primary role in the play is more serious. Although his attitude towards marriage is distinctly mercenary—'I come to wive it wealthily in Padua', he

says (1.2.74)—he is also attracted to Katherina. He is unafraid of her shrewishness, and he sees that the high spirits that underlie her terrible temper may be a positive character trait. His ironic response to the account of her assault on HORTENSIO (2.1.160–162) reflects a willingness to deal with such a person—he is attuned to Katherina even before he has met her. After the 'taming', when they enjoy their first loving kiss (5.1. 137–138), his sentimental reaction reflects his real affection for her. His response to her whole-hearted commitment to a wifely role, in her banquet speech in 5.2, is simple delight, better expressed in a kiss than in words.

However, Petruchio's importance is not as Katherina's lover but as her 'tamer'. He is the instrument of the personality change that is the central event of the play. He overrides her outbursts with his insistence that she is actually gentle and mild, and he behaves with all the virulence any shrew could ever summon. He perceptively senses in Katherina both her desire for appreciation and her instinctive distaste for shrewish conduct, and he induces her to assume the role of a normal Elizabethan wife. He does not simply bludgeon her into submission—as is common in the literature of shrewish wives, before and after Shakespeare's time—but rather functions as a teacher and guide. For much of his time on stage, Petruchio is explicitly playing a part—like many of Shakespeare's protagonists—and only pretends to be a comical tyrant. It is significant that his most important actions in this role occur off-stage and are described by other characters; in 3.2 BIONDELLO describes his outrageous appearance on his wedding day, and then GREMIO describes his outlandish behaviour at the ceremony; in 4.1 GRUMIO tells of his intemperate behaviour on the journey from Padua, and CURTIS recounts his ranting delivery of an immoderate lecture on moderation. This forces the audience to think about Petruchio's ploys rather than simply watch them and emphasises that Petruchio's shrew-taming is a kind of education: he teaches Katherina that her evil-tempered ways are not desirable and that another behaviour pattern is superior. He is training Katherina as he would a hawk, as he describes in 4.1.175–198, and the conceit, although comically grotesque, becomes a metaphor for the socialising process.

Petruchio carries out his functions somewhat mechanically—he states his purposes and accomplishes them, and as a lover he is simply sentimental—but he nevertheless possesses a distinct personality. A genially self-confident aristocrat, he delights in the good life. He understands the appeal of excellent food and fine clothes, and in the final banquet scene he is clearly at home amid the pleasures of merry company. Petruchio doubtless incorporates traits of Elizabethan gentlemen who had hosted the young Shakespeare.

*In this early 20th-century production of* The Taming of the Shrew, *Petruchio (Frank Benson) terrorises the servants before an unimpressed Katherina.* (Courtesy of Culver Pictures, Inc.)

**Phebe (Phoebe)**   Character in *As You Like It*, shepherdess loved by SILVIUS. Phebe is a caricature of the cruel shepherdess of the PASTORAL tradition, who rejects the love of the shepherd. In spurning Silvius, Phebe scorns romantic passion and denies that her coldness can wound her wooer. In presenting such a perfect parody of literary lovers, Shakespeare permits his hero and heroine, ROSALIND and ORLANDO, to seem relatively normal and to conduct their own courtship free from the extravagant posturing of traditional romances.

Rosalind, disguised as a young man, GANYMEDE, chastises Phebe for her attitude, pointing out that, being homely, she would do better to take Silvius than mock him. She advises Phebe, 'Sell when you can, you are not for all markets' (3.5.60). This extreme candour parodies the exaggerations of conventional sentiment. Then Phebe falls in love with Ganymede and thus assumes the same role as Silvius—that of the love-struck suitor. When Rosalind eventually discloses her true identity and holds Phebe to her promise to take Silvius if she could not have Ganymede, she points up the lesson of the parody: love is falsified by an excessive insistence on doting or rejection.

**Phelps, Samuel (1804–1878)**   British actor and producer. Phelps was among the most influential of 19th-century producers of Shakespeare's plays, restoring much of the original text to plays encumbered by two centuries of adaptations. In an age of lavishly spectacular sets and scenic effects, which often required Shakespeare's texts to be cut to allow time for them, Phelps introduced relative simplicity. His followers William POEL and Harley GRANVILLE-BARKER transmitted these ideas to the 20th century.

Originally a journalist, Phelps moved from amateur theatricals to the professional theatre. He was well established in the British provinces as a tragic actor before triumphing in London as SHYLOCK in 1837. After several years under Benjamin WEBSTER (1) and W. C. MACREADY, Phelps became manager of the SADLER'S WELLS THEATRE, where in 18 years (1844–1862) he staged most of Shakespeare's plays. In 1845 he presented the first staging of Shakespeare's text of *King Lear* in almost 200 years, finally superseding the radical adaptation of Nahum TATE, and his 1847 presentation of *Macbeth* did away with William DAVENANT's operatic additions. Similarly, he revived *Antony and Cleopatra* in 1849, and his 1851 *Timon of Athens* is believed to have been the initial staging of the play, which was apparently not produced in Shakespeare's time. Phelps was the leading player of his company, and he continued to act under various directors after he left Sadler's Wells. He portrayed most of the great tragic protagonists—OTHELLO and LEAR were thought to be his best parts—while also playing many other characters as well, such as MALVOLIO, PERICLES, and SHALLOW. He was particularly acclaimed as BOTTOM.

**Philario** Minor character in *Cymbeline*, POSTHUMUS' host in ROME. In 1.5 the gentlemanly Philario attempts to defuse the argument that leads to Posthumus' fatal wager with IACHIMO. In 2.4 when Iachimo claims to have won the bet by seducing IMOGEN, Philario tries to convince the enraged Posthumus not to believe him. He has no success in either endeavour. He thus represents human virtue, a force that promises good in the world but that proves useless in the face of evil. As such, he reinforces the play's theme that humankind is dependent on providence more than on its own efforts.

**Philemon** Minor character in *Pericles*, a servant of Lord CERIMON. Philemon, summoned by Cerimon, leaves immediately to carry out his master's orders to 'Get fire and meat' (3.2.3) for the victims of a storm. He speaks only four words and helps illustrate Cerimon's concerned care for others.

**Philip (1)** Minor character in *The Taming of the Shrew*, a member of the household staff of PETRUCHIO (2). Philip is one of the servants whom Petruchio abuses in 4.1 as part of his demonstration to KATHERINA of the ugliness of shrewish behaviour.

**Philip (2) Augustus, King of France (1165–1223)** Historical figure and character in *King John*, enemy of King JOHN (3) and supporter of ARTHUR. Philip is presented as an opportunist intent on political and military advantage over England by any means available, while mouthing graceful sentiments about honour. In 2.1 he backs Arthur's claim to the English throne, which John has usurped, but he willingly enters into a treaty by which his son LEWIS (1) marries John's niece BLANCHE, receiving in her dowry a large grant of En-

glish-held territory. Philip then breaks this alliance—under PANDULPH's threat of excommunication—and launches a war that results in Lewis' invasion of England in Acts 4–5. Philip himself disappears from the play in 3.3 (3.4), (for citation, see *King John*, 'Synopsis'), after Arthur's mother, CONSTANCE, delivers a fierce tirade against his treacherous abandonment of the boy.

The historical Philip is regarded as one of the great kings of FRANCE (1). He was a successful general who regained much of English-held France, to the north and west of Paris, seized territories from Flanders, and began the Albigensian Crusade, which was to result, under Blanche, in the accession of what is now southern France. Philip also successfully opposed the independence of the great barons of France, doing much to establish the powerful monarchy that was to bring France into early modern times. For these achievements he was known as Augustus, after the founder of the Roman Empire (see CAESAR [2]).

**Philip (3)** Character in *King John*. See BASTARD (1).

**Philippi** Ancient city in what is now northern Greece, a battle site in the Roman civil wars and a location in *Julius Caesar*. The armies of BRUTUS (4) and CASSIUS on one hand, and ANTONY and OCTAVIUS on the other, meet at Philippi in Act 5. Brutus risks all on this battle, against the advice of the more experienced Cassius, but he attacks too early and leaves Cassius without support, as TITINIUS remarks in 5.3.5. Brutus and Cassius are defeated, and both commit suicide rather than be captured. The battle of Philippi provides the climax wherein Antony avenges Brutus' murder of CAESAR (1).

Shakespeare altered the account of the battle that he found in his source, PLUTARCH's *Lives*. In 5.1 he invented the pre-battle meeting of the opposing generals, at which they trade insults and challenges. This exchange followed a well-known convention of medieval and Renaissance battle accounts, in which the credentials, as it were, of the warriors were established. More important, the playwright also compressed the events of several weeks into a single day to provide a dramatically more cohesive chain of events, as he had done in the HISTORY PLAYS.

There were in fact two battles at Philippi. In the first, fought on October 23, 42 B.C., the forces of Brutus and Cassius won a slight advantage. Antony's forces routed some of Cassius' troops and raided his headquarters, as is reported in 5.3.10; however, as Shakespeare also recounts, Brutus' premature attack was successful, and Octavius' men were defeated. Nevertheless, Cassius, believing mistakenly that all was lost, killed himself; an early account attributed the error to his defective eyesight. The loss was crucial, for Brutus was a bad general. Although Antony and

Octavius' forces were short of supplies in enemy country, Brutus could not control his impatience, and, after 20 days, he fought the second battle of Philippi, which, in the play, takes place on the same afternoon as the first, as per Brutus' order in 5.3.109–110. This second encounter, a bloody day-long battle, resulted in Brutus' defeat and suicide.

The combined battles were decisive; the civil war that followed the assassination of Julius Caesar had been won by the supporters of his style of dictatorial government. Moreover, the remnants of the old Roman aristocracy were largely wiped out in this campaign, which was particularly bloody by the standards of the day. Although more strife was to follow between the victors of Philippi (as is enacted in *Antony and Cleopatra*), the stage was set for the establishment of the Roman Empire under Octavius CAESAR (2).

**Phillips, Augustine (d. 1605)** One of the 26 men listed in the FIRST FOLIO as 'Principall Actors' in Shakespeare's plays, though not identified with any particular Shakespearean role. Phillips was in STRANGE'S MEN from about 1590 to 1593 and was probably an original member of the CHAMBERLAIN'S MEN. He was one of the original partners in the GLOBE THEATRE in 1599, and he was still with the Chamberlain's Men when it became the KING'S MEN in 1603. Thus, most of his professional life was spent with this troupe. This is reflected in his will, which has survived. The executors were John HEMINGE, Richard BURBAGE (3), and William SLY (2), all King's Men, and he left small bequests to many of his fellow actors, including Shakespeare. Also, Phillips' sister married another member, Robert GOUGH, who witnessed the will just days before Phillips died. Among the items Phillips bequeathed were several musical instruments, suggesting that he had been a musician as well as actor.

**Philo** Minor character in *Antony and Cleopatra*, a follower of ANTONY. In 1.1 Philo and his friend DEMETRIUS (3) discuss Antony's neglect of his military duty due to his infatuation with the queen of Egypt, CLEOPATRA. Philo's angry complaint opens the play with an emotional flourish. The episode establishes a disapproving Roman view of the love affair.

**Philostrate** Minor character in *A Midsummer Night's Dream*, the MASTER OF REVELS under Duke THESEUS (1). Philostrate arranges the entertainment for the wedding of Theseus and HIPPOLYTA (1) and presents the Duke with a list of prospective acts. A pompous courtier, Philostrate argues against Theseus' selection of the artisans' production of PYRAMUS AND THISBE on the grounds that it is blatantly undignified. Shakespeare apparently took the name Philostrate from CHAUCER's 'The Knight's Tale', in which one character uses it as an alias.

**Philotus** Minor character in *Timon of Athens*, the employee of a usurer who duns TIMON for payment of a loan. In 3.4 Philotus joins other servants when they approach Timon and his STEWARD (2) for repayment, but they are put off. They regret that they must solicit for their greedy masters, who have benefited from Timon's generosity but are now merciless when he is in need.

Philotus appears with HORTENSIUS, TITUS (2), LUCIUS' SERVANT and two men designated as VARRO'S SERVANT. Since the latter three are addressed as 'Lucius' and 'Varro' (3.4.2, 3), it is presumed that Shakespeare intended the names of the first three to refer to their masters, as well. This perhaps reflects a casual linguistic practise of the early 17th century.

**Phoenix** Name of a house, one of three on stage, in *The Comedy of Errors*. The Phoenix, which may be distinguished in a stage set by a sign above its door, is the home of ANTIPHOLUS OF EPHESUS and ADRIANA. The other houses that comprise the setting are the PORCUPINE and the PRIORY. This arrangement of three structures, each with an entrance onto the stage, was standard in ancient Roman stage design, as it was understood in Shakespeare's time, and it is quite appropriate to this play, which, of all Shakespeare's works, most closely resembles Roman drama.

***The Phoenix and Turtle*** Shakespeare's allegorical poem on the mystical nature of love. *The Phoenix and Turtle* consists of 13 quatrains (four-line stanzas) rhyming *abba*, followed by five triplets (stanzas of three rhyming lines) all in iambic tetrameter (see METRE). The poem tells of the funeral of two lovers: the phoenix, a mythological bird associated with immortality, and the turtledove (usually called 'turtle' in Elizabethan English), a symbol of fidelity. The two birds have burned themselves to death in order to be forever joined in love. The allegory celebrates an ideal of love in which an absolute spiritual union of the lovers, defying rationality and common sense, is chastely achieved through death, the ultimate rejection of the world.

The first five quatrains summon various birds to the funeral. The owl and other birds of prey—considered omens of evil—are refused admittance, while the crow and the swan, whose colour and song, respectively, are traditionally associated with death, are welcomed. The next eight stanzas comprise a funerary 'anthem' (line 21). The lovers are praised for having successfully achieved a total union, defying reason in the process. This defeat of worldly wisdom is celebrated in lyrical paradoxes, such as 'Two distincts, division none; Number there in love was slain' (lines 27–28) and 'Either was the other's mine' (line 36). Reason itself is constrained to cry out, 'Love hath reason, reason none' (line 47). Reason composes a funeral song, the 'threnos', which is presented in the last five stanzas, the solemn triple rhymes. The phoenix and the turtle are said to have embodied truth and beauty and, through their deaths, to have conveyed these qualities to all who 'are either true or fair' (line 66).

This allegory reflects a notion that was widespread in the RENAISSANCE: ideal love was felt to transcend reason and thus to represent a truer state of being than that of the material world. This idea, whose roots lay in the writings of Plato, is also related to the Christian concept of the state of grace that God offers to believers, and *The Phoenix and Turtle* has been interpreted as a specifically Christian allegory. More generally, it may be seen as illustrating the possibility of transcendence through love, an ideal that informs much of Shakespeare's work, particularly the COMEDIES.

*The Phoenix and Turtle* does not have a literary source, although the idea of an assembly of birds was a common one; for example, it appears in CHAUCER's *The Parliament of Fowls* and a famous mock funeral in OVID's *Amores,* to name only two great authors whom Shakespeare is known to have read and admired. The more specific motif of love between phoenix and turtledove was determined by its use in Robert Chester's LOVE'S MARTYR, a long allegorical poem celebrating the marriage of Sir John SALUSBURY and his wife; Shakespeare's poem was apparently written to be published with that work in 1601. The idea of love between these two symbolic birds was novel, originating with either Chester or his patron.

Salusbury and his wife are the likeliest subjects of any specific symbolism the phoenix and the turtledove may carry, in addition to their joint role as an emblem of ideal love. In addition, scholars have long speculated on possible hidden meanings in *Love's Martyr* and/or *The Phoenix and Turtle,* and various obscure references have been proposed. The two birds have been seen as Queen ELIZABETH (1) and the Earl of ESSEX (2) and as Essex and the Earl of SOUTHAMPTON (2), among other pairings. However, such hypotheses are not provable, and in any case the poem transcends whatever particular purposes it may have had, surviving as a mystical and powerful invocation of love.

**Phrynia and Timandra**   Minor characters in *Timon of Athens,* concubines of ALCIBIADES. In 4.3 Phrynia and her colleague Timandra are travelling with Alcibiades and encounter TIMON in the woods. They generally speak in unison, and are entirely indistinguishable from each other. In his misanthropic fury, Timon has decided to corrupt humanity by distributing the gold he has found. He gives some to the courtesans and accompanies the gift with vicious insults. They laughingly encourage his abuse so long as it is accompanied by gold. This mildly humorous passage satirises greed, and also provides a slight respite from Timon's

grim misanthropy. Both women represent a stock comic figure, the greedy whore.

**Picardy**   Region in northern FRANCE (1), location of the battle of AGINCOURT and the setting of several scenes in *Henry V.* In 3.6 and 3.7 the English and French armies, respectively, are shown in camp prior to the crucial battle, which itself occupies all of Act 4. Picardy is the historical term for an area north and east of the River Seine along the English Channel.

**'Pied Bull' Quarto**   See *KING LEAR*, 'Text of the Play'.

**Pilch**   Character in *Pericles.* See FISHERMEN.

**Pinch, Dr**   Character in *The Comedy of Errors,* a quack physician. Dr Pinch is consulted when ANTIPHOLUS OF EPHESUS, as a result of the confusion and mistaken identities that are the chief business of the play, is presumed to be insane. Antipholus later describes him as: '. . . one Pinch, a hungry lean-fac'd villain; / A mere anatomy, a mountebank, / A thread-bare juggler, and a fortune-teller, / A needy-hollow-ey'd-sharp-looking-wretch; / A living dead man. . . .' (5.1.238–242).

Pinch is not a physician in any modern sense; he is merely a man of some learning. He is identified as a 'schoolmaster' (in a stage direction in 4.4.38) and as a 'conjuror', or exorcist (4.4.45 and 5.1.243). Both references are to the fact that he can speak Latin, which was commonly believed in Shakespeare's day to be the language of spirits and ghosts.

Whatever his appearance or qualifications, Dr Pinch's prescription for a case of lunacy ('They must be bound and laid in some dark room' [4.4.92]) was widespread in the 16th and 17th centuries. Although it now seems inhumane, both insanity and this particular treatment of it were common subjects of humour on the Elizabethan stage. The same regime is meted out to MALVOLIO, in *Twelfth Night,* for instance. If Pinch seems a brutal doctor to us, no less so seems his fiery, filthy comeuppance (5.1.171–178), though we may be sure the original audience delighted in it, for such abuse was a comic staple. Shakespeare at least keeps it off-stage.

**Pindarus (active 42 B.C.)**   Historical figure and minor character in *Julius Caesar,* a captured Parthian slave belonging to CASSIUS. In 5.3, at PHILIPPI, Pindarus helps Cassius to commit suicide. Pindarus mistakenly reports the capture of TINTINIUS, and Cassius, in despair, decides that, rather than be captured himself, he will die. He gives Pindarus his freedom in exchange for holding the sword upon which he falls. Pindarus, now free, 'yet would not so have been' (5.3.47), elects to run far away and disappears from the play. Shakespeare took the episode, which fittingly ends the career of the emotional Cassius, from PLUTARCH's *Lives*, where Pindarus is reported to have beheaded Cassius before disappearing and to have been suspected by some of having murdered his master.

**Pirates**   Three minor characters in *Pericles*, buccaneers who kidnap MARINA. In 4.1 the Pirates interrupt LEONINE, who is about to murder Marina, and take her from her would-be killer. In 4.2 they sell her to a brothel in MYTILENE and disappear from the play. When they effect this melodramatic change in the heroine's fortunes, the Pirates bring about one of the play's many surprises, which helps demonstrate the human dependence upon fate, an important theme. The Pirates, who speak four short lines between them, display an abrupt vigour ('A prize! A prize!' cries the Second Pirate [4.1.93], in his only speech) but their function is mainly to further the plot.

**Pirithous**   Minor character in *The Two Noble Kinsmen*, friend of THESEUS (2), Duke of ATHENS. Pirithous attends Theseus in every scene in which the duke appears; he also provides commentary on ARCITE in 2.4 and, as a messenger, dramatically halts the execution of PALAMON in 5.4. However, he is significant only as the subject of a conversation in his absence. In 1.3 HIPPOLYTA reflects on the long friendship of Theseus and Pirithous, saying 'Their knot of love, / Tied, weaved, entangled . . . May be outworn, never undone' (1.3.41–44). This striking parallel to the tie between Palamon and Arcite helps establish the theme of male friendship that is woven through the play. Hippolyta's remarks also spark a variant on the theme, the account by EMILIA (4) of her similar childhood friendship with a girl.

**Pisanio**   Character in *Cymbeline*, the faithful servant of POSTHUMUS. When his master is exiled for having married IMOGEN, King CYMBELINE's daughter, Pisanio remains at court to serve her. He embodies a well-known figure of folklore and literature: the faithful servant who serves his master best by disobeying him. When Posthumus is deceived by IACHIMO and believes that Imogen has betrayed him, he orders Pisanio to murder her. Instead, the servant helps Imogen escape and provides her with a disguise as a page, in which she has further adventures. However, for all his steadfastness and common sense, Pisanio cannot provide further assistance. He loses contact with both Posthumus and Imogen and finds himself under suspicion at court. Fearful and confused, he resigns himself to whatever fate may bring. 'The heavens still must work' and 'Fortune brings in some boats that are not steer'd' (4.3.41, 46), he says. He thus states neatly the play's central lesson: that humanity is dependent on providence.

**Pistol**   Character in *2 Henry IV, The Merry Wives of Windsor*, and *Henry V*, a braggart soldier and follower of FALSTAFF. The comical Pistol serves as Falstaff's aide in King HENRY IV's campaign against the rebels in *2 Henry IV*. He first appears at Falstaff's dinner party at the BOAR'S HEAD TAVERN in 2.4, and he offends everyone present with grandiose insults while asserting his chivalric honour with distorted snatches of rhetoric from Elizabethan drama and literature. This vigorous mode of address is Pistol's principal attribute in all of his appearances. To some extent, Pistol satirises military pretensions, but his rhetoric is more pointedly a literary parody; Shakespeare exaggerates the florid language of MARLOWE (1) and his followers. Pistol is called an ancient; ancient, or ensign (standard-bearer), is a military rank, the equivalent of lieutenant, which BARDOLPH (1) calls Pistol in *Henry V*, 2.1.38. Pistol may actually be an ancient, or he may have simply appropriated the title, for part of his absurdity is his singular unsuitability for command.

Like the 16th-century sidearm for which he is named, Pistol is violently loud but incapable of serious damage. Also, the pistol was commonly associated, in Elizabethan humour, with the penis; much is made of this in *2 Henry IV*, 2.4.109–135. When the Quarto edition of *2 Henry IV* was published in 1600, its subtitle made particular reference to Pistol, whose appeal was already recognised, and he has been among Shakespeare's most popular characters ever since. His extravagant rhetoric makes him hilarious even to audiences for whom the original parodies are meaningless.

In *The Merry Wives* Pistol is again in Falstaff's entourage (apparently as a civilian), but he refuses to deliver his master's love letters, rejecting the task as unsoldierly, and Falstaff fires him. He and NYM seek revenge, and they inform FORD (1) and PAGE (12) that Falstaff has designs on their wives, thereby triggering the principal sub-plot of Ford's jealousy. Pistol is insignificant thereafter, although he does appear in the final MASQUE-like scene, disguised as a fairy. This may simply reflect the employment of the actor who played Pistol in another role, but Pistol's appearance in character might have been taken by 16th-century audiences as a clue to the ceremonial nature of the scene, in which personality is wiped out.

In *Henry V*, Pistol mourns the passing of Falstaff with his new wife, the HOSTESS (2), whom he has presumably dazzled with his extravagant braggadoccio. Once on campaign in France, he proves himself a coward in 3.2; following this episode, the BOY (3) remarks on the villainy of Pistol, Nym, and Bardolph. In 3.6 Pistol pleads unsuccessfully for FLUELLEN's intercession on behalf of Bardolph, who has been sentenced to death for looting; in 4.1 he is one of the soldiers whom the incognito King HENRY V encounters the night before the battle of AGINCOURT, though he has little to say, merely making a nasty remark about Fluellen.

In 4.4 Pistol captures a FRENCH SOLDIER and demands ransom of him, threatening to kill him otherwise. Since he speaks no French and the soldier no English, the scene is comical, but Pistol is unquestionably an unpleasant character, vicious and overbearing. The Boy acts as interpreter, saving the soldier's life, and he remarks afterwards of Pistol, 'I did never know so full a voice issue from so empty a heart' (4.4.69–70). Pistol is last seen in 5.1, where Fluellen forces him to eat a leek. The last survivor of Falstaff's followers, Pistol in *Henry V* serves to show that the anarchic element represented by Falstaff is finally rendered both harmless and completely disreputable. On the other hand, Pistol may also be seen as a symbolic parallel to King Henry's militarism: he satirises notions of military honour, while most of the combat actually presented involves Pistol at his most degenerate. Most strikingly, his threat to kill his prisoner in 4.4 foreshadows Henry's own order that 'every soldier kill his prisoner' (4.6.37).

It is thought that Falstaff appeared in an early, unacted version of *Henry V* and was then excised by Shakespeare, with remnants of his part going to Pistol, who displays Falstaffian characteristics in several scenes, particularly 5.1. This theory cannot be proven, but it is supported by textual evidence (see FALSTAFF).

**Planché, James Robinson (1796–1880)**  British playwright and theatrical designer. Planché wrote many successful burlesques and pantomimes, as well as a few legitimate dramas, over a period of 50 years, beginning in 1818. He was also a serious antiquarian—a founder of the British Archaeological Association—specialising in the history of costume. His *History of British Costume* (1834) was a standard work in the field for many years. In this capacity, he helped create the 19th-century enthusiasm for historically accurate productions of Shakespeare's plays. He designed the costumes for the first such staging, the *King John* staged by Charles KEMBLE (1) in 1823. He also was credited with much of the success of the 1840 *Midsummer Night's Dream* of Charles Mathews and Elizabeth VESTRIS; he designed the Athenian costumes and a famous finale featuring dozens of twinkling lights. Lastly, he designed the 1844 production by Benjamin WEBSTER (1) of *The Taming of the Shrew*, which is said to have legitimised the presentation of Shakespeare's plays in their original form.

Planché, the son of a watchmaker of Huguenot descent, had many other talents. He was a good professional musician and a respected authority on heraldry; he wrote opera librettos; and, following the unauthorised production of one of his plays, he became largely responsible for the first law granting modern copyright protection to dramatists.

**Plantagenet (1) family**  English ruling dynasty in 1154–1484, parts of whose history form the subject matter of most of Shakespeare's HISTORY PLAYS. *King John* deals with an early Plantagenet monarch, and the feuding between the YORK (1) and LANCASTER (1) branches of the family, culminating in the WARS OF THE ROSES, is the subject of two sequences of four plays each (see. TETRALOGY) that cover the reigns of the last Plantagenet rulers.

The earliest Plantagenet was a French nobleman, Geoffrey, Count of Anjou, and the family was originally known as the Angevin dynasty. Geoffrey's badge was a representation of a white flower, *planta argent*, from which the later family name derives. (The use of this name began only in the 1460s, when Richard, Duke of YORK (8), assumed it as part of his campaign to claim the throne for his branch of the family.)

In 1127 Geoffrey of Anjou married the daughter of Henry I of England, a younger son of William the Conqueror; Geoffrey's son, Henry II, became the first Plantagenet king. As in most medieval dynasties, the ancient rule of primogeniture provided that the crown was to be inherited by an eldest son or his descendants, or by a next-eldest son if the eldest had no sons or had died before the king. This eventually caused great difficulties for England, but for two centuries the Plantagenets transmitted their power peacefully.

Richard I, the Lionhearted, succeeded his father, Henry II. Dying childless, Richard was succeeded by his younger brother, JOHN (3), in 1199. Beginning with John's son Henry (see PRINCE [3]), son succeeded father through five generations, in a sequence ending with RICHARD II. The dynasty subsequently broke down.

The York and Lancaster branches of the Plantagenet family descended from two of the seven sons of Edward III, who died in 1377. The eldest of these sons died before his father did, and the crown passed to his son, Richard II. King Edward's second son, the Duke of Clarence, did not have a son; his daughter married into the Mortimer family. The third son was John of GAUNT, Duke of Lancaster, whose son, Henry BOLINGBROKE (1) deposed his cousin Richard in 1399 and ruled as HENRY IV, the first Lancastrian King. The fourth son of King Edward, Edmund Langley, Duke of YORK (4), could entertain no claim to rule under a normal succession. However, after Richard's deposition, the Mortimers attempted to claim the throne by virtue of their relation to King Edward's second son, who would have succeeded Richard under any circumstances but usurpation, and York's son, the Earl of CAMBRIDGE in *Henry V*, married a Mortimer and inherited their claim. Thus by the mid-15th century the Yorkist faction was the chief rival to the Lancastrians. The remaining sons of Edward III had no importance in the Plantagenet succession, though the murder of one of them, Thomas, Duke of GLOUCESTER (6), helped spark the fall of Richard II, which, along with the reigns of the first two Lancastrian monarchs, is dealt with in *Richard II, 1* and *2 Henry IV,* and *Henry V*.

When Henry V died in 1422, his son, HENRY VI, was an infant, and the illegality of Richard II's deposition was still a living issue that only a strong monarch could silence. The Yorkist claim was pressed, and the resulting wars are the principal subject of Shakespeare's earliest history plays, *1, 2,* and *3 Henry VI* and *Richard III*. Beginning in 1461, three members of the York family ruled England: EDWARD IV, Edward V (see PRINCE [5]), and RICHARD III. In 1485 Richard III was overthrown by a distant cousin of Henry VI, the Earl of RICHMOND, who ruled as King Henry VII, the founder of the TUDOR dynasty.

Two Plantagenets survived the Wars of the Roses, a BOY (2) and a GIRL, great-great-grandchildren of the original Duke of York. The boy, Edward, Earl of Warwick, was imprisoned for most of his brief life to prevent him from claiming the crown; Henry VII executed him in 1499, after rebels had made several attempts to impersonate him and seize the throne. His sister, Margaret, the last Plantagenet, lived until 1541, when she was beheaded, at the age of 68, by HENRY VIII, who also feared a rebellion in favour of the former dynasty.

**Plantagenet (2), Richard**  In *1 Henry VI,* the name by which the future Duke of YORK (8) is known until, at 3.1.159, he is restored to the dukedom, lost by the treason of his father, the Earl of CAMBRIDGE.

**Plantagenet (3), Richard**  In *King John* the name granted to the BASTARD (1) in acknowledgement that he is the illegitimate son of the late King Richard I. The Bastard is fictitious; King Richard did have an illegitimate son, but his name was Philip.

**Platter, Thomas (1574–1628)**  Swiss doctor from Basel who travelled widely in 1595–1600 and published an account of his journeys (in German) in 1604. He was in England in September–October 1599 and recorded a performance of *Julius Caesar* at the GLOBE THEATRE and an unnamed play at the CURTAIN THEATRE. His remarks are among the few sources of detail about the ELIZABETHAN THEATRE.

**Plautus, Titus Maccius (c. 254–184 B.C.)**  Ancient Roman dramatist, author of sources for *The Comedy of Errors* and *The Taming of the Shrew.* Plautus' *Menaechmi* was the principal source for *The Comedy of Errors,* providing the central plot of long-lost twins who are farcically mistaken for each other, and another of his works, *Amphitryon,* provided the second set of twins. Numerous details in *The Shrew,* including the names of

GRUMIO and TRANIO, came from Plautus' *Mostellaria (The Haunted House).* Minor elements in other plays also reflect Shakespeare's knowledge of Plautus.

Moreover, many other writers and dramatists had relied on Plautus' plays as sources, so elements from Plautus could have reached Shakespeare indirectly. For instance, one of the main sources for *The Shrew,* ARIOSTO's *I Suppositi* (1509), was itself based on Plautus' *The Captives.* The first English comedy, *Ralph Roister Doister* (c. 1553) by Nicholas UDALL, is based on Plautus' *Miles Gloriosus* (after whose hero the character type MILES GLORIOSUS is named). Plautus was still very well known in Shakespeare's day, and the playwright clearly assumed that his audience was familiar with his work, as when he had POLONIUS tritely observe that 'Plautus [cannot be] too light' (*Hamlet,* 2.2.396–397). Plautus continues to provide stimulation to writers of comedy; for instance, elements from several of his comedies were incorporated in the American musical *A Funny Thing Happened on the Way to the Forum* (1962).

Plautus wrote many plays, of which 21 survive, all of them comedies and all free translations of older Greek works, especially those of Menander (c. 342–292), some of whose plays are known only through their Plautine versions. Plautus' works are generally characterised by a casually cynical tone, complicated plots, and stereotyped characters (his character types helped stimulate the 17th-century COMEDY OF HUMOURS). Some works are merely farcical (see FARCE), while others have sentimental or social themes. He was highly popular in the Roman world, and his plays continued to be produced for centuries after his death. Many later plays were falsely ascribed to him—more than 100 have been reattributed by modern scholars. Plautus was ignored during the Middle Ages, and his rediscovery was an important stimulus to RENAISSANCE literature and drama throughout Europe.

**Player King**  Character in THE MURDER OF GONZAGO, the playlet presented within *Hamlet.* In 3.2 the PLAYERS (2) stage a play in which the Player King anticipates that his wife, the PLAYER QUEEN, will remarry if he dies, despite her protests to the contrary. Then he is murdered by LUCIANUS, who pours poison in his ear while he sleeps. This scenario resembles the actual murder of HAMLET's father by KING (5) Claudius—as the GHOST (3) has recounted it the prince—and the King reacts to it with great distress, fleeing from the room. Thus, as he had planned, Hamlet is presented with proof that the Ghost had told the truth.

The Player King speaks in a highly rhetorical style that distances the play within a play from the action of the play itself, emphasising its artificiality. The part of the Player King is presumably taken by the FIRST PLAYER (2), who demonstrates his dramatic gifts when the Players first arrive at ELSINORE in 2.2.

**Player Queen**  Character in THE MURDER OF GON-
ZAGO, the playlet presented within *Hamlet*. In 3.2 the
PLAYERS (2) perform before the court of KING (5)
Claudius. Following HAMLET's instructions, they stage
a play in which the Player Queen assures her husband,
the PLAYER KING, that she will never remarry if he dies
before her. He insists that she will; in the next scene
he is murdered. The play parallels the murder of
Hamlet's father by the King and the remarriage of his
mother, the QUEEN (9), so it is obvious that the Player
Queen's part would include her marriage to the killer.
However, the performance is interrupted by the
King's guilty reaction, and she never reappears.

The Player Queen is merely a symbolic character.
Her highly rhetorical diction helps to emphasise the
extreme artificiality of the play within a play.

**Players (1)**  Group of minor characters in *The Taming
of the Shrew*, a travelling company of actors. In the
INDUCTION the Players are hired by the local LORD (1),
who is amusing himself by providing gentlemanly
amenities to a drunken tinker, Christopher SLY (1).
The Players perform 'a pleasant comedy' (Ind.2.130)
for Sly; this play is *The Taming of the Shrew*.

One of the Players, identified in various editions as
'A Player', 'First Player', and 'Second Player', is designated by the name of a real Elizabethan actor in a
speech heading in the FIRST FOLIO edition of the play;
the part was played by John SINCKLO in an early production. In Ind.1.86 he speaks of a role he had played,
naming a character in a play by John FLETCHER (2) that
was written in about 1620. This is probably a late
insertion into Shakespeare's text, not long before its
publication in 1623, but it may be original and refer
to an otherwise unknown play of the 1580s or early
1590s that served Fletcher as a source.

**Players (2)**  Characters in *Hamlet*, touring actors who
are hired by Prince HAMLET to perform a play that he
hopes will shock the KING (5) into an unconscious revelation of guilt. After commissioning the Players to
perform THE MURDER OF GONZAGO, a brief drama that
enacts a crime similar to the King's killing of Hamlet's
father, the prince makes his famous remark 'The play's
the thing / Wherein I'll catch the conscience of the
King' (2.2.600–601). The playlet—featuring the
PLAYER KING, the PLAYER QUEEN, and LUCIANUS—
achieves the expected result in 3.2.

There are at least three Players, enough to play the
three parts in the playlet, with one of them doubling
as the speaker of the PROLOGUE (1) and all three participating in the DUMB SHOW that precedes the spoken
play. The elaborate stage direction at 3.2.133 calls for
extra players in the dumb show, but this requirement
may be ignored in production.

The troupe is led by the FIRST PLAYER (2), who demonstrates his art when he recites a monologue on PYR-
RHUS and HECUBA in 2.2. He presumably plays the
Player King in 3.2, where he also receives Hamlet's
opinions on acting—thought to reflect Shakespeare's
own—in 3.2.1–45.

In 3.2.330–358 ROSENCRANTZ AND GUILDENSTERN report that the Players' popularity has suffered due to
the success of a boys' acting company. This incident
reflects the WAR OF THE THEATRES, the competition
between the professional players and the CHILDREN's
COMPANIES that raged in London in 1601.

**Plebeians (1)**  Minor but significant characters in *Julius Caesar*, the citizens of ROME who react to the assassination of CAESAR (1). In 3.2 the Plebeians are addressed at Caesar's funeral, first by BRUTUS (4) and
then by ANTONY, and they respond enthusiastically to
the orations of each. First, when Brutus explains the
rationale behind the assassination (3.2.13–48), the
crowd excitedly approves his assertions. Ironically,
however, the Plebeians shout, 'Let him be Caesar'
(3.2.52), and speak of crowning Brutus, who has just
killed Caesar in order to prevent a crowning and preserve the Republic. Conversely, they can now say of
Caesar, whom earlier they had hailed, 'This Caesar
was a tyrant' (3.2.71). Moreover, their change in attitude merely foreshadows another one.

Antony's famous oration (3.2.75–254) plays on the
emotions of the Plebeians, whereas Brutus had appealed to their reason, and Antony's impact is much
greater. Before he is halfway through, the Plebeians
are calling Brutus and the conspirators '. . . traitors
. . . villains, murderers!' (3.2.155–158), and they go on
to raise a confused cry of 'Revenge! . . . Burn!—Fire!—
Kill!—Slay!' (3.2.206–207). Finally, the Plebeians run
amok, hurrying to burn the houses of the conspirators,
and Antony exults, 'Mischief, thou art afoot' (3.2.262).
Almost immediately he receives news that Brutus and
Cassius have had to flee the city.

In 3.3 the mob encounters CINNA (1), and simply
because he has the same name as one of the assassins—CINNA (2)—they beat him to death. In this brief
and grimly humorous scene, the Plebeians are almost
incoherent, asking questions of their victim without
listening to his answers and finally, realising that he is
not their proper prey, declaring, 'It is no matter, his
name's Cinna; pluck but his name out of his heart'
(3.3.33–34). Having demonstrated their irrational
power, they disappear from the play. The civil war that
Antony had hoped to foment (in 3.1.254–275) has
begun with their riot.

The term 'plebeian' was an ancient designation for
the ordinary citizens of the Roman Republic, as distinguished from the patricians, or aristocrats. Its use suggests the intense political context of the play at this
point, in contrast to the use of COMMONER (1) in 1.1.
Shakespeare valued individual humans regardless of
social standing—as is evidenced by many of his char-

acters, including, in this play, the COBBLER—but he distrusted the common people as a class. Two of the most important political points he made in *Julius Caesar* are that the masses are unreliable and that their ascendancy is a key symptom of social disorder. The Plebeians of the play, in their fickleness, brutality, and manipulability, demonstrate the dangers of a political world that includes them. In this respect they resemble the rebels led by Jack CADE in *2 Henry VI* and the rabble (see CITIZEN [5]) of *Coriolanus*.

**Plebeians (2)**  Characters in *Coriolanus*. See CITIZEN (5).

**Pliny the Elder (c. 23–79 A.D.)**  Roman author of an encyclopaedia of natural history that served as a minor source for *Othello*. Pliny's *Naturalis Historia,* translated by Philemon HOLLAND (4) as *Natural History* (1601) provided several details for OTHELLO's description of his adventures in 1.3.

Pliny's vast work assembles a tremendous body of lore, and though much of it is inaccurate, it remained an important reference into the RENAISSANCE. A career military officer and a close friend of the emperor Vespasian (ruled 69–79 A.D.), he wrote many books, mostly on military subjects, but only the *Natural History* survives. His scientific curiosity was so great that during the eruption of Vesuvius in 79 A.D., he travelled to Pompeii and was killed. His death is described by his nephew Pliny the Younger (61–c. 114) in a famous passage from his *Letters*.

**Plowright, Joan (b. 1929)**  English actress, widow of Laurence OLIVIER. Plowright often played opposite her husband, perhaps most notably as PORTIA (1) to his SHYLOCK in his 1970 London production of *The Merchant of Venice* and again in the 1974 TELEVISION version. Her most striking Shakespearean part was also on television, the double role of SEBASTIAN (2) and VIOLA in a 1969 production of *Twelfth Night.*

**Plummer, Christopher (b. 1929)**  Canadian actor. Plummer has played many Shakespearean roles in Stratford, Ontario, and elsewhere. At Stratford in 1972, he starred opposite Zoë CALDWELL in a memorable *Antony and Cleopatra*. He also won particular acclaim for his IAGO, opposite James Earl JONES (1), in Nicol WILLIAMSON's 1982 New York production of *Othello*.

**Plutarch (c. 46–c. 130 A.D.)**  Greek philosopher and biographer whose *Lives*—as translated by Sir Thomas NORTH—was Shakespeare's primary source for *Antony and Cleopatra, Coriolanus, Julius Caesar, Timon of Athens* and a source of minor elements in other plays. Plutarch, after studying in Athens, became a teacher of philosophy in Rome, where he received the patronage

of the emperors Hadrian and Trajan and wrote (in Greek) many works on ethical, religious, and political questions. Following Trajan's death, Plutarch returned to Greece, where he wrote his famous biographies of Greek and Roman heroes of history and legend. These works, intended as moral lessons in greatness and failure, have inspired many generations of readers. Among Plutarch's most important admirers, besides Shakespeare, have been Michel de MONTAIGNE, Ralph Waldo Emerson, and Napoleon Bonaparte.

**Poel, William (1852–1934)**  English theatrical producer. Beginning in 1894, with the founding of the Elizabethan Stage Society, Poel revolutionised the theatrical presentation of Shakespeare's plays with productions that attempted to replicate the experience of 16th- and 17th-century playgoers. Using a projecting stage, very little scenery, and original texts, his group staged numerous works by Shakespeare, Christopher MARLOWE (1), Francis BEAUMONT (2) and John FLETCHER (2), Ben JONSON, Thomas MIDDLETON, and others. Financial losses closed the society in 1905, but Poel continued to produce such works elsewhere, including DER BESTRAFTE BRUDERMORD in 1924 (its first English production) and ARDEN OF FEVERSHAM in 1925. His work influenced others, notably Nugent MONCK and Harley GRANVILLE-BARKER, and furthered a long-lasting trend towards scrupulously preserved texts produced in rigorously simple stagings that countered extravagant spectacles of the late 19th century. His work also influenced critical attitudes towards Shakespeare's work; for instance, he was the first director to stage all three PROBLEM PLAYS, thereby helping to stimulate their acceptance in a world that had previously spurned them (Poel had been instructed in college never to read *Measure for Measure* or *Troilus and Cressida* because of their gross impropriety). Poel also wrote several plays himself and a number of books on the theatre.

**Poet (1)**  Minor character in *Julius Caesar*, a wandering bard who accosts BRUTUS (4) and CASSIUS and advises them against discord. He is plainly a fool, and in any event he arrives (in 4.3.122) after the two generals have reconciled. While Cassius tolerates the Poet, Brutus arrogantly dismisses him, demonstrating in a small way the deterioration in his character that is a major theme of the play. Also, the brief episode provides a moment of needed comic relief between the dispute between the two leaders' and the revelation of the death of PORTIA (2).

Shakespeare took this episode from PLUTARCH's *Lives,* where the figure was not a poet but a self-declared philosopher, a seemingly lunatic imitator of the wandering ascetics known as Cynics. (Cynicism, founded by Hellenistic philosophers in the 4th century B.C., held that independence and self-control constituted the only human good, and they preached a 'natural' life-style, ostentatiously rejecting wealth, prestige, and even the comforts of ordinary life.) Cassius calls the Poet a 'cynic' in 4.3.132. In Plutarch, the would-be Cynic quotes a line from the Iliad of HOMER, which, after being transmuted through AMYOT and NORTH, appears comically in 4.3.130–131, where Shakespeare—perhaps mistakenly—attributes it to the speaker himself, who is therefore called a poet.

**Poet (2)**   Minor character in *Timon of Athens,* a flatterer of TIMON. In 1.1 the Poet and his friend the PAINTER (1) discuss Timon's generosity, which each hopes to exploit when he presents the nobleman with an example of his art. Pompously self-satisfied, the Poet congratulates himself on being a poet from whom art 'oozes' (1.1.21). He anticipates the play's truths when he tells that the poem he is writing, in which Timon is shown as a favourite of the goddess Fortune, contains the warning that when Fortune changes, her ex-favourites are abandoned by their seemingly loyal followers. Though the Poet is not mentioned in Timon's downfall, he is presumably among the deserters, for in 5.1 he and the Painter attempt to reingratiate themselves with him because they have heard that their one-time benefactor has found gold. Timon overhears him planning 'what I shall say I have provided for him' (5.1.32), though in fact he has written no poems for him. When he and the Painter fawningly assure Timon of their friendship, he mocks them and drives them away. The Poet is an emblematic character, satirically representative of the greed and hypocrisy of courtiers.

**Poetomachia**   See WAR OF THE THEATRES.

**Poins, Ned**   Character in *1* and *2 Henry IV,* friend of PRINCE (6) HAL. Poins suggests the two jokes that he and Hal play on FALSTAFF. In *1 Henry IV,* 1.2.156–185, he devises the plan to rob Falstaff of his takings in the highway robbery of 2.2, and in *2 Henry IV,* 2.2.164–165, he proposes that he and the Prince disguise themselves as DRAWERS and spy on Falstaff. He also participates in the Prince's joke on FRANCIS (1) in 2.4 of *1 Henry IV.* In 2.4 of *2 Henry IV* Falstaff, unaware of Poins' presence, describes him, insultingly but with considerable accuracy, in a hilarious presentation of a rowdy, empty-headed party boy (2.4.241–250). In 2.2.42 Poins demonstrates his blindness to Prince Hal's true character, expecting him to be pleased at the imminent death of his father, King HENRY IV. But in 2.2.61–65 he is conscious of his position as part of the world of delinquency that the Prince must reject, and he accepts his own limitations.

Poins is Shakespeare's version of a character named Ned in the FAMOUS VICTORIES, his chief source for the material on Hal's riotous early life. His last name may

refer to the lace ribbons, known as points, that were a prominent feature of a 16th-century courtier's elaborate garb.

**Polixenes**   Character in *The Winter's Tale,* the King of BOHEMIA. In 1.2 Polixenes, visiting his old friend King LEONTES of SICILIA, is persuaded by Leontes' wife, Queen HERMIONE, to extend his stay. However, Leontes goes mad and imagines adultery between Polixenes and Hermione. Warned by CAMILLO that Leontes intends to poison him, Polixenes flees to Bohemia and is not seen again until late in the play. Leontes believes his infant daughter, PERDITA, is the illegitimate child of Polixenes, and orders her abandoned in the wilderness. In Act 4, 16 years later, Polixenes' son, Prince FLORIZEL, falls in love with Perdita, who has been raised by shepherds in Bohemia. Polixenes opposes the match of a prince and a shepherdess, and the couple, pursued by the king, flees to Sicilia. There Perdita's identity is revealed, the couple becomes engaged, and Polixenes is reconciled with his old friend in 5.3, the play's final scene.

Polixenes is a rather colourless victim in 1.2—though his perspicacity in reading the situation contrasts sharply with Leontes' obtuseness—and he is mostly an observer in 5.3. In Act 4 he is more prominent, even though his role is a stereotype of the status-conscious adult who opposes young love. He is charmed by Perdita at the shepherds' festival, but after he removes his disguise, he threatens her with 'a death as cruel for thee / As thou art tender to 't' (4.4.441–442). Thus, in the romantic COMEDY of the play's second half, Polixenes takes the role of villain that Leontes had in the TRAGEDY of the first half.

**Pollard, Alfred William (1859–1944)**   British scholar, a founder of modern textual criticism. Pollard's major contributions to Shakespearean scholarship were his *Shakespeare's Folio's and Quartos 1594–1685* (1909), a groundbreaking consideration of the various texts of the plays, and *Shakespeare's Fight with the Pirates* (1917), a study of the illicit publication of play texts in Shakespeare's time. He helped establish that Shakespeare was a collaborator on SIR THOMAS MORE. He was also a major authority on Geoffrey CHAUCER.

**Polonius**   Character in *Hamlet,* a minister of the KING (5) of DENMARK. Polonius, the father of OPHELIA and LAERTES, loves intrigue and resorts to espionage whenever possible. He volunteers to spy for the King on HAMLET's conversation with his mother, the QUEEN (9), in 3.4, and when Hamlet discovers the intruder, he kills him. The prince stabs through a curtain, so he does not know who his victim is until he is dead, but he feels no remorse for the deed, remarking coolly that his victim has learned that 'to be too busy is some

*In Hamlet, Polonius is a pedantic bore and an hypocrite. These traits may derive from the comical Pantaloon of the Italian commedia dell'arte.* (Courtesy of Culver Pictures, Inc.)

danger' (3.4.33). This killing is the central event of the play, hastening Hamlet's exile to England and triggering Laertes' vengeance on the prince.

Polonius' deviousness and dishonesty exemplify the state of moral decay in Denmark. After he offers Laertes his famous advice, 'to thine own self be true . . . Thou canst not then be false to any man' (1.3.78–80), his hypocrisy reveals itself, for in 2.1 he sets a spy on Laertes, offering detailed instructions in espionage and duplicity to REYNALDO (1). He bars Ophelia from any contact with Hamlet, presuming that the prince's professions of love cannot be truthful, perhaps arguing from self-knowledge, and when it appears that he was wrong and that the prince has gone mad from frustrated love, he spies on the lovers himself.

However, Polonius' murder is not to be taken as justifiable; much of its point depends on our recognition of it as an evil act, leading us to the further awareness that Hamlet is capable of evil. Also, Polonius is not completely without good points, making his killing more reprehensible than it would appear if he were an absolute villain. For example, while his means are deplorable, Polonius clearly cares about his son, and his involvement in his welfare serves to cause Laertes to remain memorable through his long absence from the play (between 1.3 and 4.5); similarly, Polonius is a fool in his handling of Ophelia, but there is no doubt of his paternal concern, even if it can be overlaid with ulte-

rior interests at the same time. Ophelia's evident heartbreak at his death in her 'mad scene' (4.5) testifies to his adequacy as a parent.

Polonius is also a comic character at times. Speaking to the King and Queen of Hamlet's alleged madness, he begins by stating an ideal that he proceeds to demolish, asserting '. . . since brevity is the soul of wit, / And tediousness the limbs and outward flourishes, / I will be brief', and then goes on to use such verbiage as 'Mad call I it, for to define true madness, / What is't but to be nothing else but mad?' (2.2.93–94). When this amusing long-windedness is challenged by the Queen's request for 'More matter with less art', Polonius replies with unwitting candour, 'Madam, I swear I use no art at all' (2.2.95–96). The passage, in which Polonius repeatedly interrupts himself and loses his train of thought, parodies a popular tendency of the day to overelaborate rhetoric, and it softens the portrait of Hamlet's victim. In creating Polonius, Shakespeare may have been influenced by the Pantaloon, a comically windy moraliser from the Italian COMMEDIA DELL'ARTE.

Polonius appears as CORAMBIS in the Q1 edition of the play, and scholars believe that this reflects the name of the analogous character in Shakespeare's chief source, the UR-HAMLET. Shakespeare often changed the names in his sources for no particular reason, but here he may have wished to avoid using the caricature probably intended in the *Ur-Hamlet*. However, the name Polonius itself makes a clear reference to Poland, also known as Polonia in Elizabethan England. Scholars believe that the playwright probably intended an allusion to one of the play's minor sources, a well-known book on good government, *The Counsellor* (1598), an English translation from the Latin work of a Polish statesman, Laurentius GOSLICIUS.

**Polydore** In *Cymbeline*, the false name under which King CYMBELINE'S son GUIDERIUS is raised from infancy by his kidnapper and foster-father BELARIUS.

**Pomfret (Pontefract) Castle** Strong fortress in northern England, the site of a number of political murders and executions in the 14th and 15th centuries, two of which are presented in Shakespeare's HISTORY PLAYS. RICHARD II is murdered in his cell by EXTON in 5.5 of *Richard II*, and lords RIVERS, GREY (2), and VAUGHAN are led to execution in 3.3 of *Richard III*. The historical Earl of SALISBURY (2) was also executed at Pomfret. Lord Rivers refers to the castle's bloody history when he exclaims, just before his death in *Richard III*, 'O Pomfret, Pomfret! O thou bloody prison, / Fatal and ominous to noble peers!' (3.3.9–10).

**Pompey (1) Bum** Character in *Measure for Measure*, a pimp and servant of MISTRESS (2) Overdone. Pompey is a humorous petty criminal, a representative of the underworld of VIENNA, and the major figure in the comic SUB-PLOT, which contrasts with the main story and offers relief from its tensions. Tried as a procurer by ESCALUS (2), in 2.1, he outwits Constable ELBOW, who testifies for the prosecution, with long-winded evasions and subtle double entendres. He sassily asks the judge if he intends, through laws against prostitution, 'to geld and splay all the youth of the city' (2.1. 227–228). His bawdy wit makes a mockery of the court, helping to establish that the authority of the DUKE (9) has degenerated due to his lax regime. Pompey is eventually gaoled in the same prison as CLAUDIO (3), whose condemnation for illicit sex is at the centre of the main plot's conflict. As assistant to ABHORSON, the executioner—a position taken in return for a promise of parole—Pompey continues to jest, and his comedy lightens the oppressive atmosphere as Claudio's execution approaches.

As Escalus observes in 2.1.169, Pompey resembles Iniquity, a character from the medieval MORALITY PLAY. He represents a type that was well known, the clownish criminal (he is designated as a CLOWN [1] throughout the FOLIO text of the play). A comic sub-plot featuring a madam and her servant was found by Shakespeare in a principal source for *Measure for Measure*, George WHETSTONE's *Promos and Cassandra* (1578), and its appeal was surely immediate for the creator of FALSTAFF. Pompey's preposterous name was Shakespeare's invention: an ancient Roman hero, Pompey the Great (see POMPEY [2]), is provided with a surname that is slang for buttocks.

**Pompey (2), (Sextus Pompeius) (d. 35 B.C.)**  Historical figure and character in *Antony and Cleopatra*, a rebel against the co-leaders of ROME, Octavius CAESAR (2), LEPIDUS, and Mark ANTONY. Pompey's threat spurs Antony to action when he is luxuriating with CLEOPATRA in Act 1, but the rebel displays his weakness in Act 2. In 2.6 he negotiates a truce with the Roman leaders, but the remarks of his follower MENAS make clear that he is foolish not to continue his rebellion while he is in a strong position. In 2.7 he refuses Menas' suggestion that he murder his opponents during the feast that celebrates the truce. Pompey is unwilling to seem dishonourable and lets the opportunity go by. Menas observes that 'Who seeks and will not take, when once 'tis offer'd, / Shall never find it more' (2.7.82–83), and decides to abandon his alliance with this weak leader. Pompey is not seen again in the play, but we hear of his fate. After being defeated by the forces of Lepidus and Caesar he retreats to Antony's territory where he is murdered, as is reported in 3.5. Pompey's career offers a case study in the cold realities of Roman politics and war. He cannot win because he is not unscrupulous enough and he lacks good sense. No vestiges of the ancient Roman concept of honour survive,

and only a cool and unsentimental manipulator can triumph. It is in this context that we must weigh the conduct of Antony and the triumph of Caesar.

Antony surveys the rebel's strength in 1.2 and outlines Pompey's background. He is continuing a rebellion originated by his father—a famous and popular leader of an earlier generation—and he therefore commands a dedicated following. This is an accurate assessment of the historical Pompeius Sextus, whose father, Pompey the Great (106–48 B.C.), was one of the major figures of early Roman history. He was the defeated opponent of Julius CAESAR (1), as is mentioned several times in Shakespeare's *Julius Caesar*. The renown of Pompey the Great was such that Shakespeare could mention him in three non-Roman plays (*Henry V, 2 Henry VI, Love's Labour's Lost*) and name a comic character after him in *Measure for Measure* (see POMPEY (1) Bum), which presumes that audiences would still know of him after 1,700 years. Pompeius Sextus fought with his father's forces, and after their defeat—and Pompey the Great's murder—in 48 B.C., he reorganised the rebellion around a naval force, which centred first in Spain and later in Sicily. After Julius Caesar's assassination in 44 B.C., Pompey continued to fight against Caesar's successors, though as part of his policy he briefly supported Antony against Octavius Caesar not long before the period of the play. The peace of Misenum, enacted in 2.6, was negotiated in 39 B.C. but did not last long. Caesar attacked Pompey the next year and totally defeated him in 36 B.C. The loser retreated to Asia Minor and attempted to re-establish himself but was captured and killed by Antony's lieutenant, probably on Antony's orders, though Shakespeare protects his hero's honour by having EROS report his distress at the execution, in 3.5.18–19.

**Pope (1), Alexander (1688–1744)**  British poet and editor of Shakespeare. Best known as a poet, Pope also produced the second scholarly edition of Shakespeare's plays in 1725. He is regarded by modern scholars as a bad editor, however. He claimed to have corrected, by following QUARTO texts, many instances in which the playwright's words had been corrupted by the FOLIO editors; in fact, he mostly followed the 1709 edition of Nicholas ROWE (based on the Fourth Folio), though he did make numerous 'improvements' in his own words. Lewis THEOBALD, the first great Shakespearean scholar, pointed out many of Pope's errors in a 1726 essay, for which he was pilloried in Pope's famous literary satire, *The Dunciad* (1728). Pope, however, did incorporate many readings from Theobald's critique when he reissued his own collection in 1728. Moreover, Pope is credited with some scholarly accomplishments: he first established firmly the locations of many scenes, and he corrected the rhythm of many lines that had been improperly printed. He was also the first commentator to recognise that *The Troublesome Raigne of King John* was derived from Shakespeare's *King John* rather than the other way around.

A childhood disease left Pope a hunchback, and he was embittered by it, once describing his life as one long disease. His sharp wit and penchant for invective made him a close friend of the satirist Jonathan Swift (1667–1745), but his social relations tended to end in mutual hostility. His talent for recrimination against former friends earned him the epithet 'The Wicked Wasp of Twickenham' (where he lived). He was England's leading poet in the first half of the 18th century, with such works as *An Essay on Criticism* (1711), *The Rape of the Lock* (1712), translations of *The Iliad* and *The Odyssey* (1720, 1725), *Moral Essays* (1731–1735), and *An Essay on Man* (1732–1734).

**Pope (2), Thomas (d. c. 1603)**   English actor, member of the CHAMBERLAIN'S MEN. Though he is one of the 26 men listed in the FIRST FOLIO as the 'Principal Actors' in Shakespeare's plays, it is not known what roles he played. They must have been comic parts, for he was a clown and acrobat. He toured DENMARK and Germany with William KEMPE and others in 1586–1587, and he was a member of STRANGE'S MEN beginning in about 1591. He was probably an original member of the Chamberlain's Men, with whom he remained until at least 1599, when he became an original partner in the GLOBE THEATRE. He was not part of the troupe when it became the KING'S MEN in 1603, having probably retired. He died in late 1603 or early 1604. As late as 1612 he was still described as a memorable actor.

**Popilius Lena (active 44 B.C.)**   Historical figure and minor character in *Julius Caesar,* a senator of ROME. Popilius Lena, present as the assassins prepare to kill CAESAR (1) at the Senate, alarms CASSIUS by conversationally hoping his 'enterprise to-day may thrive' (3.1. 13) and then speaking to Caesar; Cassius fears the plot is known. However, it proves a false alarm. The episode, which Shakespeare took from PLUTARCH's *Lives,* heightens the tensions of the moment. Little is known of the historical Lena.

**Porcupine (Porpentine)**   Name of a house, one of three on stage, in *The Comedy of Errors.* The Porcupine, which may be distinguished in a stage set by a sign above its door, is the home of the COURTESAN. The other houses that comprise the setting are the PHOENIX and the PRIORY. This arrangement of three structures, each with an entrance onto the stage, was a standard device of ancient Roman stage design as it was understood in Shakespeare's time, and it is quite appropriate to this play, which, of all Shakespeare's works, most closely resembles Roman drama. It has

been speculated that Shakespeare called the Courtesan's house 'Porcupine' ('Porpentine' in Elizabethen English) after a well-known London brothel in an inn of that name.

**Porpentine**   See PORCUPINE.

**Porter (1)**   Minor character in *1 Henry VI,* a servant of the COUNTESS (1) of AUVERGNE who assists in her attempt to capture TALBOT in 2.3.

**Porter (2)**   Minor character in *2 Henry IV,* gatekeeper at WARKWORTH CASTLE, home of the Earl of NORTHUMBERLAND (1). The Porter admits Lord BARDOLPH (2) in 1.1. At the outset of the play, he embodies ordinary lives amid the doings of the aristocracy, an important aspect of the play.

**Porter (3)**   Minor character in *Macbeth,* a doorkeeper at the castle of MACBETH. In 2.3, immediately following Macbeth's murder of King DUNCAN, the Porter appears in response to a knocking at the gate. His humorous drunkenness contrasts strikingly with the grim murder scene, and thus he reinforces the suspenseful horror that we have just been exposed to. Also, in his drunkenness the Porter pretends to be the gatekeeper of hell, and this motif emphasises the fact that Macbeth has just lost his soul.

Shakespeare's original audiences will have recognised immediately that the Porter was imitating a familiar figure of the medieval MORALITY PLAY; the gatekeeper of hell who admits Christ to Limbo in the ancient legend of the 'Harrowing of Hell'. This gatekeeper guarded the literal mouth of hell—a familiar image from the painted backdrops of a gigantic, flaming lion's mouth (derived from Rev. xiii:2) used in the morality plays. The Porter makes it clear that we are to see Macbeth's castle as hell, and leaves no doubt whatever that the enormity of Macbeth's evil is of the greatest importance in the play. When the Porter finally opens the door and admits MACDUFF, a subtle analogy between Macduff and Christ is suggested. This foreshadows Macduff's role as the final conqueror of the evil Macbeth.

The Porter also provides comic relief. His humour is both topical, with references to a contemporary treason trial (see GARNET)—a resonant theme in a play of regicide—and simply vulgar, as in his remarks on the effects of drink, in 2.3.27–35. This vulgarity inspired high-minded commentators such as Alexander POPE [1] and Samuel Taylor COLERIDGE to declare the Porter a non-Shakespearean addition, on the grounds that a genius of literature would not stoop to such low comedy. However, modern critics recognise that the Porter is a typically humorous Shakespearean representation of unsophisticated humanity. With his comedy and his simple mind that nevertheless offers important commentary on the situation, the Porter is the nearest thing to a FOOL (1) in *Macbeth*. Also, like the OLD MAN (3) of 2.4, he serves the function of a CHORUS (1), and offers a point of view entirely outside that of all the other characters.

**Porter (4)**  Minor character in *Henry VIII*, a doorman at a royal palace in LONDON. In 5.3, on the day when Princess ELIZABETH (1) is to be christened, the Porter and his MAN (3) are unable to prevent a crowd of celebrating commoners from invading the palace courtyard. They make comical remarks about the riotous celebrants, until the Lord CHAMBERLAIN (2) announces the arrival of the royal party, and they return to their efforts to control the crowd. The incident demonstrates the enthusiasm of the common people for Elizabeth and the TUDOR DYNASTY, an important theme of the play, and it offers comic relief that separates the intrigue of 5.1–2 from the grand ceremony of 5.4, with which the play closes.

**Porter (5), Henry (d. 1599)**  English dramatist. Porter wrote at least six plays for Philip HENSLOWE and the ADMIRAL'S MEN, some of them in collaboration with Henry CHETTLE and Ben JONSON. He was praised by Francis MERES as among the best English writers of COMEDY. Only one play written solely by Porter has survived: *The Two Angry Women of Abingdon* (c. 1596), a comedy that resembles *The Merry Wives of Windsor*. Though greatly inferior, it was very popular in its day, and it may have stimulated Shakespeare's interest in writing a busy comedy of town life. Porter was perennially poor, and he died deep in debt. He was stabbed to death in a fight by fellow playwright John DAY.

**Portia (1)**  Character in *The Merchant of Venice*, lover of BASSANIO and defender of his friend ANTONIO (2). Portia, disguised as a lawyer, saves Antonio from the revenge of SHYLOCK. Initially a passive young woman at the mercy of her father's odd matchmaking device, the lottery of caskets, she emerges as a touching lover with Bassanio in 3.2 and achieves a grand maturity when she defends Antonio in 4.1. Her address to Shylock on the virtues of mercy (4.1.180–198) is renowned as one of the finest passages Shakespeare wrote; it is certainly his most effective presentation of Christian ideals. Her tactics in the trial—leading Shylock to believe he can win his case and thus eliciting from him his demands for the strictest interpretation of the law—have been deplored as high-handed, and they are certainly unethical by modern standards. But Shakespeare was composing an allegory, not a legal precedent, and Portia's strategy emphasises the instructive paradox that Shylock's rigid insistence on the letter of the law proves to be his own undoing. Portia, defending Antonio because he is the friend of her beloved, evidences the power of love itself, conquering Shylock, whose calculating usury is opposed to the generosity of the young lovers and Antonio.

Portia's final act—accepting, in the person of the young lawyer 'Balthasar', her own ring from Bassanio and then twitting him with disloyalty—has been seen as arbitrary and graceless, but the episode fittingly closes the play. It recapitulates the play's lesson that love and forgiveness are superior to self-centred greed. By invoking Shylock's attitude, insisting on the letter of Bassanio's oath, Portia reasserts a negative value that she immediately repudiates when she forgives her new husband, and the play closes on a note of loving reconciliation.

Before she appears, Portia is described by Bassanio in extravagantly poetic terms (1.1.161–172), and we envision her as an almost supernatural ideal of womanhood. However, with her opening line, '. . . my little body is aweary of this great world' (1.2.1–2), she instantly becomes human. Her simultaneously grand and companionable nature charms us throughout the play. She is an open young woman who can describe herself as 'an unlessoned girl, unschooled, unpractised' (3.2.159) and who can giggle with NERISSA over the disguises they will wear (3.4) and over the trick they will play on their husbands-to-be (4.2). At the same time, she inspires Bassanio's rhapsody and, most important, she is a resourceful and commanding figure who takes Antonio's fate in hand and delivers him. Shakespeare thus enshrines in virginal youth a gallant, courageous, and worldly woman.

However, Portia has an unattractive feature, to modern sensibilities: she clearly partakes of the 16th-century English racial prejudice and anti-Semitism that are reflected in this play. Addressing Shylock in court, in 4.1, she repeatedly calls him 'Jew', and she is frank about her distaste for MOROCCO's black complexion in 1.2.123–125 and 2.7.79. On the other hand, she is willing to marry the African prince if he wins the lottery of caskets, as she declares in 2.1.13–22, and her attitude towards Shylock's Jewishness—manifested only in the trial scene—is extremely mild, compared to that of other characters. *The Merchant of Venice* accommodates the prejudices of its original audiences, but Portia is not a significant bearer of this theme, and we are in no doubt that Shakespeare intended her as a delightful heroine.

Portia is a fine example of the frank and fearless young women who appear in many of the plays; like ROSALINE (1), BEATRICE, ROSALIND, and HELENA (2), she seems to embody an ideal of femininity that the playwright held and put forth often. Spirited and capable, she is willing to enter a man's world—in this case, that of the law—in pursuit of her aims, yet she ultimately accepts the conventional Elizabethan woman's status, that of a wife, at least theoretically subservient to her husband.

**Portia (2)** Historical figure and character in *Julius Caesar,* the wife of BRUTUS (4). In 2.1, observing her husband's great emotional distress, Portia insists on sharing his trouble. He has in fact been agonising over the assassination of CAESAR (1), and he is reluctant to reveal this grave plan. She insists that her stature as the wife of a great Roman and the daughter of another warrants her inclusion in matters of importance. She shows Brutus a wound in her thigh that she has given herself to demonstrate that she has the Roman virtue of self-control. He is impressed, saying, 'O ye gods, render me worthy of this noble wife!' (2.1.302–303), and he agrees to take her into his confidence, but then they are interrupted.

Although we do not see him tell her of the conspiracy against Caesar, he evidently has done so by the time she reappears in 2.4, where she is almost hysterical with concern. In both scenes Portia's concern for her husband's welfare is strong, giving the audience another positive viewpoint of Brutus, and her distress also raises the emotional pitch of the play as the first great climax, Caesar's murder, approaches.

In 4.3 we learn that Portia, in Rome as her husband campaigns against Caesar's successors, ANTONY and OCTAVIUS, has committed suicide, convinced that he cannot survive against the tremendous power that she knows has been sent against him. Portia is intended to exemplify the Roman virtues of courage and self-sacrifice. Her virtues were legendary by Shakespeare's time; he also used the name for the splendid heroine of *The Merchant of Venice,* PORTIA (1). There, her suitor alludes to her namesake, asserting that his love is 'nothing undervalu'd to Cato's daughter, Brutus' Portia'. (*Merchant,* 1.1.165–166).

The historical Portia was the daughter of Marcus Porcius Cato (95–46 B.C.), a tribune famous for his honesty and dedication; the CATO of the play is Portia's brother. Their father had opposed Caesar in an earlier civil war, committing suicide rather than be captured, only two years before the time of the play. Her own suicide was regarded as similarly honourable. In the play she is said to have 'swallow'd fire' (4.3.155). This reference follows Shakespeare's source, PLUTARCH'S life of Brutus, where Portia is said to have put hot coals in her mouth and kept her mouth closed until she choked to death. This seems improbable, and scholars have speculated that this report may reflect her actual death by carbon monoxide poisoning, produced by a smoky charcoal fire in a closed room.

**Portraits of Shakespeare** Only two depictions of Shakespeare—both posthumous—are believed to have been based on genuine portraits: the DROESHOUT engraving, which illustrates the title-page of the FIRST FOLIO, and the sculptural bust by Gheerart JANSSEN (2) that is part of the poet's memorial in Holy Trinity Church, in STRATFORD. However, numerous other im-

Mr. WILLIAM
SHAKESPEARES
COMEDIES,
HISTORIES, &
TRAGEDIES.

Published according to the True Originall Copies.

LONDON
Printed by Isaac Iaggard, and Ed. Blount. 1623.

*The title page of the First Folio has on it what is probably a reliable likeness of Shakespeare, an engraving by Martin Droeshout.*

ages have been thought of as portraits of Shakespeare, though modern scholars generally reject them. The most significant of these is probably the CHANDOS PORTRAIT, which was accepted as genuine for many years; it was the basis for the sculpture by Peter SCHEEMAKERS in WESTMINSTER (1) ABBEY. Other portraits of note include the ELY PALACE PORTRAIT, the FLOWER PORTRAIT, the KESSELSTADT DEATH MASK, and works by Nicholas HILLIARD and Cornelis JANSSEN (1).

**Pory, John (1572–1636)** English writer, the translator of the work of LEO AFRICANUS, a possible influence on *Othello.* Pory was an associate of Richard HAKLUYT, who suggested he translate Leo's Italian account of his African travels. The translation was published as *A Geographical History of Africa* (1600), and Pory's prefatory biography of Leo probably influenced OTHELLO's autobiographical remarks in 1.3.

Pory also produced a version of a famous early atlas,

*The Epitome of Ortelius* (1602), but until 1612 he made his living publishing newsletters, accounts of Parliamentary and court events that he sent to private subscribers, a practise that preceded the development of modern newspapers. He was a very widely travelled man. From 1612 to 1617 he travelled in Ireland and Europe as a agent for Sir George CAREW (1); from 1617 to 1619 he was employed by an English diplomat in Constantinople; and in 1619 he went to Virginia as secretary to the governor. Pory was on the governing council of the colony and served as the speaker of the initial session of the Burgesses, the first legislative assembly in the New World. He returned to England in 1623—after being shipwrecked and imprisoned in the Azores—and resumed his newsletter business, retiring a few years before his death.

**Post (1)**   Minor character in *2 Henry VI*, a messenger who brings word of an Irish rebellion in 3.1.

**Post (2)**   Either of two minor characters in *3 Henry VI*, express messengers. One Post carries messages between King EDWARD IV and the French court in 3.3, and returns with answers in 4.1. The replies are quite venomous, and the Post asks assurance that he will not be punished for the contents of his report. In 4.6 another Post carries word to Warwick of Edward's escape from captivity.

**Posthumus**   Character in *Cymbeline*, the husband of IMOGEN. Banished from Britain for secretly marrying the daughter of King CYMBELINE, Posthumus goes to ROME. There, he boasts of Imogen's virtues and wagers the diamond ring she has given him that the courtier IACHIMO cannot seduce her. Iachimo is unsuccessful, but he deceives Posthumus, who foolishly believes him and vows revenge on Imogen. By letter, he instructs his servant, PISANIO, to murder her. Once he has established the situation that faces Imogen in Acts 3–4, Posthumus disappears from the play until, near the end, he reappears, stricken with guilt over the murder he believes has been committed. He seeks death in battle and fights for Britain against ROME, but he is not killed. He then seeks death as a Roman prisoner of war, but while in captivity he dreams of his family (see SICILIUS LEONATUS) and the god JUPITER, who promises that his story shall end happily. Unaware of this when he awakes, Posthumus appears before the king as a Roman captive, but he reveals himself when Iachimo confesses his deception. Posthumus, in his turn, confesses to Imogen's murder before he discovers that she is alive and he is reunited with her. In the aura of reconciliation that closes the play, the king accepts Posthumus as a son-in-law.

In the course of the play, Posthumus' qualities vary enormously from the ideal to the seriously flawed. In this respect he offers clues to the difficulties Shakespeare faced when he wrote the ROMANCES, a new genre of plays in which *Cymbeline* was an experiment. The playwright faced the problem of integrating realistic settings and characters, which he was accustomed to creating, with the ethereal, almost abstract characters of fairy tale and traditional romantic literature on which the romances were based. Posthumus, like other characters in *Cymbeline*, demonstrates that he was not always successful.

As the play opens, Posthumus is praised by a GENTLEMAN (12) who declares, 'I do not think / so fair an outward, and such stuff within / Endows a man, but he' (1.1.22–24); here, he is simply a traditional romantic prince and a proper mate for Imogen. However, once on his own in Rome he is ludicrously immature, intent on an inflated idea of masculine honour. In 1.5, he, Iachimo, and the FRENCHMAN almost seem to offer a satire on duelling. His wholly unnecessary defence of Imogen's chastity is no less ridiculous than his readiness to disbelieve in it later, and his response is ignoble when he instructs his servant to murder Imogen in revenge. Nevertheless, he is once again the traditional princely hero when he helps the king's long-lost sons, GUIDERIUS and ARVIRAGUS, defeat the Romans, and it is certainly to his credit that he comes to regret his earlier actions and feel guilt. However, the basic problem with his character is most evident here. His elaborate attempts at suicide detract from our appreciation of his real personal distress. On one hand, it is difficult to accept Posthumus as a real figure like the victimised OTHELLO, while on the other, he does not provide a bold allegorical representation of human error, like, say, LEONTES, of *The Winter's Tale*. Shakespeare had not yet learned to permit the symbolic to dominate, and Posthumus' human reality interferes with his value as an archetype of jealousy. This makes him a somewhat ridiculous and unsympathetic figure.

The name Posthumus indicates that its owner was born after his father's death. It is so rare today that it seems intended to convey some extra meaning, perhaps comical. However, though unusual (like the phenomenon it commemorates), the name was regularly given in Shakespeare's day (see, e.g., Thomas Posthumous HOBY [2]).

**Potpan**   Character in *Romeo and Juliet*. See SERVINGMAN (2).

**Prentice**   Either of two minor characters in *2 Henry VI*, apprentices and friends of the armourer's apprentice PETER (1), who must fight his master, Thomas HORNER, in a trial by combat. The Prentices encourage Peter before the event, in 2.3.

**Preston, Thomas (1537–1598)**   Sixteenth-century playwright parodied by Shakespeare. Preston's play *Cambyses* (1569), whose full title described it as 'A lamentable Tragedie, mixed full of pleasant mirth . . .', is mocked in the comical presentation of PYRAMUS AND THISBE in *A Midsummer Night's Dream* (1.2.11–12, 5.1) and by FALSTAFF in *1 Henry IV* (2.4.382–389). *Cambyses*, though highly bombastic and melodramatic, represents a significant development from the MORALITY PLAY towards TRAGEDY. Preston was primarily an educator; he served as vice-chancellor of Cambridge University.

**Priam, King of Troy**   Legendary figure and character in *Troilus and Cressida,* the ruler of the city besieged by the Greeks in the TROJAN WAR. Despite his regal position, Priam plays an insignificant role, calling to order the war council in 2.2—but participating very little—and unsuccessfully attempting, along with ANDROMACHE and CASSANDRA, to persuade HECTOR not to fight on a day of disastrous omens in 5.3.

Priam was a well-known figure in classical mythology and is referred to in a number of Shakespeare's plays and in *The Rape of Lucrece.* His name was proverbial for someone who has experienced extremes of good and bad fortune. In the *Iliad* of HOMER, Priam is an old man, the father of 50 sons by various wives and concubines. His harem, along with his non-Greek name, suggests to scholars that he represents a folk-memory of some real Asiatic monarch of the second millennium B.C. His death at the hands of Neoptolemus (see PYRRHUS) is the most important incident of his life, both in Homer and in later literature. It is described in the dramatic monologue recited by the FIRST PLAYER (2) in 2.2.464–493 of *Hamlet.*

**Priest (1)**   Minor character in *Richard III,* a friend of Lord HASTINGS (3). Hastings engages in small talk with the Priest in 3.2, demonstrating his naïve lack of concern about the danger from Richard that he has been warned about.

**Priest (2)**   Minor character in *Twelfth Night,* a clergyman. The Priest speaks only once, in 5.1.154–161, to confirm that he has married OLIVIA and SEBASTIAN (2)—whom he and the bride have both mistaken for Cesario, the disguised VIOLA—thereby adding further confusion. At the same time, he provides comic relief from the intensifying crisis, for he is preposterously high-flown, using the most elaborate possible language to say a very simple thing; for instance, he observes, 'Since [the marriage], my watch hath told me, towards my grave / I have travell'd but two hours' (5.1.160–161).

**Priest (3)**   Minor character in *Hamlet,* the officiating clergyman at OPHELIA's funeral. In 5.1 the Priest denies Ophelia the full ceremony because her death appears to have been a suicide. He asserts that even an abbreviated service is too much—only 'great com-

mand' (5.1.221), presumably KING (5) Claudius', has made it possible—and suggests that, instead of prayers, 'shards, flints, and pebbles should be thrown on her' (5.1.224). He insists that the rites for the dead would be profaned if Ophelia received them. This ugly episode heralds the mood of gloom and anger that dominates the conclusion of the play.

In some editions of the play the Priest is called the Doctor of Divinity, based on the speech heading 'Doct.', used for both of his speeches in the Q2 edition (1604). Some scholars conjecture that this makes him a Protestant.

**Prince (1) Escalus of Verona**   Character in *Romeo and Juliet,* the ruler of VERONA, where the play is set. The Prince is a representative of civil order, an important ideal for Shakespeare. The Prince appears three times in the play. First, in 1.1, he describes the feud between MONTAGUE (1) and CAPULET (1). In 3.1 he banishes Romeo and precipitates the climax of the tragedy; rather too late, he states a principle of statecraft that has been too little observed in Verona: 'Mercy but murders, pardoning those that kill' (3.1.199). At the close he summarises the fateful resolution of the feud, accepting blame 'for winking at . . . discords' (5.3.293). This acknowledgement of the state's responsibility for order was not present in Shakespeare's sources; it reflects the playwright's interest in the civic as well as the purely personal ramifications of tragedy. This theme recurs throughout Shakespeare's work in dramas ranging from *Richard II* to *King Lear* to *The Tempest.*

In the stage direction that introduces him at 1.1.79, and nowhere else, the Prince is given a name, Escalus. This is a Latinisation of Della Scala, the name of the princely family that ruled Verona in the late Middle Ages.

**Prince (2) HAL (also Henry, later King Henry V)**
Character in *1* and *2 Henry IV.* See PRINCE (6) OF WALES, HENRY.

**Prince (3) Henry**   Character in *King John.* See HENRY (1).

**Prince (4) of Wales, Edward (1453–1471)**   Historical figure and character in *3 Henry VI,* the heir apparent to King HENRY VI. The young Prince Edward, son of Henry and Queen MARGARET (1), has inherited his mother's bold and courageous spirit, and, unlike his father, strongly opposes the efforts of YORK (8) and his sons to seize the throne. He reproaches his father for his weakness on several occasions, and he presents a consistently fiery front to the usurpers; in consequence, he is stabbed to death by Edward and the other York sons after being taken prisoner in the battle of TEWKESBURY in 5.5. The young Prince is a model of chivalry and thus rather dull, but he is intended as a symbolic figure, rather than a developed personality. He serves as a foil for his father's more complex and human weakness, and, further, as a suggestion of what might have been—an instance of the rigour and pride kingship demands. Shakespeare saw its absence in Henry VI as having been tragic for England. The GHOST (1) of the young Prince appears in *Richard III*.

The murder of the captive Prince was part of the Tudor version of the WARS OF THE ROSES, but it is apparently fictitious. Shakespeare took it from his chief source, Edward HALL (2) but according to earlier accounts, he was killed in the battle, a much more likely end.

### Prince (5) of Wales, Edward (Edward V, King of England) (1470–c. 1483)

Historical figure and character in *Richard III*, the son and heir of King EDWARD IV whom RICHARD III murders. The Prince appears only once, when he arrives in London after his father's death. Although technically king, he is never crowned and is known as the Prince throughout the play. Being taken to the TOWER OF LONDON and his eventual death, the Prince, 12 years old, impresses us with his serious concern for history. He also provides an ironic commentary on the way the story of his own death has been transmitted, officially unrecorded but nonetheless known. 'But say, my lord, it were not register'd / Methinks the truth should live from age to age . . .' (3.1.75–76). The murder—at Richard's instigation—of the Prince and his younger brother, the Duke of YORK (7), is reported in 4.3 and mourned thereafter. It is clearly intended to be taken as the most heinous of Richard's crimes.

Shakespeare had no doubt as to Richard's guilt, and posterity, greatly influenced by Shakespeare, has agreed. Modern scholarship, however, has thrown doubt on the whole question of the fate of the princes. It is known that they entered the Tower in June 1483 and never emerged, but how they died and who was responsible are not clear (see TYRELL) and may never be, except in the unlikely event that new evidence is uncovered.

In *3 Henry VI* the Prince appears in the final scene as an infant, virtually a stage property, to be displayed by his father. The baby is kissed by his uncles, as a token of loyalty to King Edward. This incident is noteworthy for the behaviour of Richard, who characterises himself in an aside as comparable to Judas, in kissing one to whom he intends harm.

### Prince (6) of Wales, Henry (Hal, later King HENRY V) (1387–1422)

Historical figure and character in *1* and *2 Henry IV*, the oldest son of King HENRY IV. The central concern of the *Henry IV* plays is Prince Hal's preparation for assuming the throne. (He appears as the king in Act 5 of *2 Henry IV* and in *Henry V.*) The Prince must find his way between two undesirable ex-

tremes—anarchy and obsessiveness—represented respectively by the irresponsible debauchery of FALSTAFF and the exaggerated sense of honour of the war-loving HOTSPUR. In neither play is the Prince the most prominent character, but Hotspur in *Part 1* and Falstaff in both plays derive their importance from their relationship to the Prince. In *Part 1* the Prince becomes a chivalric hero by conquering Hotspur, though he remains friendly with Falstaff. In *Part 2* he integrates himself more fully into the world of statecraft, assumes the crown upon his father's death, and makes the final, irrevocable break with Falstaff in his famous 'rejection' speech in 5.5.

The comparison of Hal and Hotspur is foreshadowed in *Richard II*, when Hotspur, then known as PERCY (2), tells of Hal's disreputable life among harlots in London (5.3.13–19). In *1 Henry IV* the dissolute Prince is contrasted with the valorous Hotspur. However, Hal assures Henry that 'the time will come' (3.2.144) when he will conquer Hotspur. Significantly, the Prince does not have to change his character to arrive at this resolution, for he is conscious of his destiny from the outset. As he makes clear in his famous 'reformation' speech (1.2.190–212), he intends to fulfil his inherited duties. He simply chooses to remain in EASTCHEAP until 'being wanted he may be more wonder'd at' (1.2.196). Once Hal has asserted his readiness to assume his proper position as Prince when the time comes—and of course, Shakespeare and his original audiences were very much aware of Hal's future success as Henry V—the ground is laid for the climactic hand-to-hand combat in which the Prince kills Hotspur.

Shakespeare took care to have Hal spurn some of the temptations offered by Falstaff, as when he rejects the old man's lascivious suggestions about a barmaid in 1.2.46. The playwright thus establishes that the Prince is not the reckless and vicious playboy of the well-known farce *The Famous Victories of Henry the Fifth* (see FAMOUS VICTORIES), but rather a good king in the making.

The essential question of the *Henry IV* plays is: can a ruler successfully combine cold-blooded political skills with the spiritual values that derive from social contacts and appreciation of one's fellows. Hal's development take place in the irresponsible world of Eastcheap because the Machiavellian world of King Henry cannot nurture humane values. At the BOAR'S HEAD TAVERN, however, Prince Hal learns about the lives of ordinary people, and he knows that this education has a purpose. 'When I am King of England, I shall command all the good lads in Eastcheap', he says in 2.4.13–14). At the same time, the Prince is learning about himself as well. He places himself in different contexts: highway robbery, in 2.2 of *Part 1,* and menial service in 2.4 of both plays. In the mock drama he enacts with Falstaff in 2.4 of *Part 1,* he even samples the role of king. In Eastcheap the Prince is free to make mistakes, to take positions he will later reject—in short, to learn.

In *Part 1*, although Hal plans to forsake Eastcheap life at some point, he still participates fully in it. He rejects duty in favour of pleasure, sending Falstaff to dispose of the king's messenger, and when the rebellion against his father is introduced, he boldly suggests, in the callous manner of a soldier, that a campaign brings the opportunity to 'buy maidenheads . . . by the hundreds' (2.4.358–359). His merriment in the same scene includes a disrespectful charade of his father. While he does go to SHREWSBURY and defeats Hotspur, the battle seems to be only an interval in his life with Falstaff. At the end of the fighting, he is ready to corroborate Falstaff's lie about his courage 'with the happiest terms I have' (5.4.156).

However, as his kingship draws closer, the Prince avoids Falstaff. In *Part 2* Hal returns to Eastcheap only once. The Prince arrives in London from the battlefield in 2.2, and the uproarious tavern scene (2.4) closes with his being called back to action. Falstaff's world is now an interlude for the Prince, rather than a primary focus. Moreover, his exchange with Falstaff is more hostile than friendly; he does not accept Falstaff's bantering excuses, as he has in the past, and Hal departs with only a cool 'Good night, Falstaff.' Therefore, when, as Henry V, Hal coldly spurns Falstaff in 5.5, we have no reason to be surprised.

Prince Hal's rejection of Falstaff is often considered callous and unfair, but in its historical context it may be seen as both necessary and relatively mild. Falstaff's behaviour is downright criminal in both plays—in fact, the scenes dealing with his corrupt recruitment of troops (*1 Henry IV*, 4.2; *2 Henry IV*, 3.2) were designed as incriminating satires of contemporary practises—yet Hal merely dismisses him with a pension. (The imprisonment imposed by the CHIEF JUSTICE—to an institution reserved for aristocrats—was understood by the playwright and his audience to be lenient and temporary.) While Hal can be thought to be rejecting part of his humanity in order to make himself fit for power, he is in fact simply adopting a different humanity, that of his weary father. In *Henry V* the new king will apply the capacity for fellowship he has learned in Eastcheap; first, in *2 Henry IV*, he becomes a king.

The crucial moment of Hal's development, and the climax of *2 Henry IV*, is Hal's encounter with his dying father in 4.5. Addressing the crown as it lies beside the king, Hal recognises the burden that kingship demands and he accepts that burden, emphasising his decision by placing the crown on his own head. Henry, thinking that Hal has selfishly desired his death in order to wear the crown, delivers an impassioned speech on the dangers England will face once his son is king, crying, 'The wild dog shall flesh his tooth on every innocent' (4.5.131–132) and regretting the col-

lapse of the order he has striven to preserve. This speech asserts powerfully, if negatively, the value of social discipline. After Hal has sworn loyalty to his father—and, implicitly, to the values just expressed—the king advises that Hal keep would-be opponents busy with overseas wars. This militarist solution—honourable in Shakespeare's world, though reprehensible in our own—is related to Henry's view of a ruler's basic duty, the maintenance of order and the avoidance of civil war. The Prince accepts this lesson and receives his father's wishes for a peaceful reign and a final blessing (4.5.219).

Shakespeare altered Hal's biography to suit his dramatic ends. Hal is introduced as an adult at a time when he was only 12 years old, as part of the playwright's strategy of presenting him and Hotspur as contemporaries, though Hotspur was in fact a generation older. Also, Hal did not fight Hotspur at Shrewsbury; the rebel died at the hands of an anonymous warrior. Shakespeare may have believed that the two heroes had met—his sources are ambiguous—but he would surely have had them do so in his play, even if they had not historically done so, to enhance the play's impact.

Prince Hal's wild life was evidently real, for contemporaries recorded his conversion to good behaviour upon being crowned. It was reported that the Prince was given to drunken brawling—and even gang warfare—in Eastcheap. Shakespeare and his contemporaries believed in the truth of a tradition that Hal had hit the Chief Justice and been imprisoned for it, but since this story cannot be traced earlier than 1531 (to an account that omits physical assault), its authenticity is dubious. A more reliable early account stated that Hal had robbed his own agents on the highway; a later version changed the victims to bearers of the king's money. Shakespeare omitted a striking anecdote, well known to the Elizabethans, that is probably true: Hal, perhaps in a spirit of atonement, approached his father wearing a dog collar and a strange garment with many needles sewn to it. This mystifying story has never been explained, and Shakespeare may have simply found it too distracting to use. Hal's unwise wearing of his dying father's crown came from Shakespeare's sources, but it is quite plainly apocryphal.

In any event, reports of 'wild Prince Hal' probably reflect only isolated incidents, and not a committed way of life, in the youth of a privileged and high-spirited soldier. Certainly, much of the Prince's energy was devoted to serious military training, for he fought in Wales beginning in 1400, and he was considered competent at the age of 16 to command a wing of Henry's army at Shrewsbury. He governed part of Northumberland shortly thereafter, and he served in increasingly important offices over the next eight years. In 1411 Hal was dismissed from the king's council, an event that is alluded to in *1 Henry IV*, 3.2.

32, where it is associated with the supposed assault on the Chief Justice. In fact, it appears that King Henry suspected his son of treasonous disloyalty; a reconciliation was effected a year later, not long before Henry's death, and this appears to be the germ of the reconciliation scenes in the plays.

**Prince Charles' Men**   Seventeenth-century LONDON theatrical company. Prince Charles' Men were organised in 1608 as a provincial company called the Duke of York's Men in honour of their patron, King JAMES I's younger son, later King Charles I (ruled 1625–1649). The company began staging plays at the royal court in London in 1610. Among their members were the dramatist William ROWLEY (2), who wrote most of their plays and directed the company, and Joseph TAYLOR, their leading actor. In 1612, when Charles' older brother HENRY (2) died, he became the heir-apparent and was known as the Prince of Wales; the company he patronised changed its name accordingly. Around 1614–1616 the company was briefly allied with LADY ELIZABETH'S MEN. They played at a variety of London playhouses as well as at the court. In 1619 Christopher BEESTON joined the company as its manager, and for several years they played regularly at his theatre, the Phoenix and then, after 1621, at the CURTAIN THEATRE. Taylor left for the KING'S MEN in 1619, and in 1623 Rowley followed him. The company dispersed when Prince Charles became king in 1625 and transferred his patronage to the King's Men.

**Prince Henry's Men**   Seventeenth-century LONDON theatrical company, formerly the ADMIRAL'S MEN. In 1603, after King JAMES I succeeded to the crown of England, his son Prince HENRY (2) assumed patronage of the company, which changed its name accordingly. Their new royal patent lists the members of the company, including Edward ALLEYN—their long-time leader—Thomas DOWNTON, Humphrey JEFFES, and Samuel ROWLEY (1), who also wrote plays for the company. By 1606 Alleyn had retired, though he kept a financial interest in the company and was part owner of the FORTUNE THEATRE, where they appeared, so he probably retained some influence on the company's affairs. In November 1612 Prince Henry died, and his patronage was taken up by the German fiancé of Princess ELIZABETH (3), Frederick V the Elector Palatine. When the royal couple married in early 1613, the company formally took on one of Frederick's titles and was known as the PALSGRAVE'S MEN.

**Princess (1) of France**   Character in *Love's Labour's Lost,* the head of an embassy from France to the court of the KING (19) of Navarre, who falls in love with her. When we first encounter the Princess, in 2.1, she reprimands her courtier, BOYET, for his flattery in sharp but sensible terms that immediately establish her as a straightforward woman. But, although we do have a sense of the Princess as a real person, her chief role in the play is as a participant in the courtly tableau of lovers that draws the King and his gentlemen to an awareness that their narrow world of asceticism is insufficient compared to the power of love.

In 5.2, when she learns of her father's death, the Princess prepares to leave Navarre immediately. She responds to the King's suit by requiring him to live as a hermit for a year to test the strength of his love. She recognises that the process of maturation that the gentlemen have undergone in the course of the play is not complete—a recognition that makes her the character who perhaps most clearly represents the play's point of view.

**Princess (2) Katharine of France**   Character in *Henry V.* See KATHARINE (2).

**Priory**   Name of a house, one of three on stage, in *The Comedy of Errors.* The Priory, which may be distinguished in a stage set by a cross or other sign above its door, is the religious house headed by EMILIA (1), its Abbess. ANTIPHOLUS and DROMIO OF SYRACUSE take refuge there early in 5.1. (Until well into the 17th century in England, a criminal or a defendant in a civil suit could take sanctuary from the law in a church or other sacred building.)

The other houses that comprise the setting are the PHOENIX and the PORCUPINE. This arrangement of three structures, each with an entrance onto the stage, was standard in ancient Roman stage design, as it was understood in Shakespeare's time, and it is quite appropriate to this play, which, of all Shakespeare's works, most closely resembles Roman drama.

**Pritchard, Hannah (1711–1768)**   British actress. Pritchard began her career as a fairground singer and was recruited for the stage by Theophilus CIBBER (3). She went on to achieve fame playing with David GARRICK. She played many Shakespearean roles and was acclaimed for her comedic heroines—especially ROSALIND—which she continued to play well into middle age. She also played tragic roles, and her greatest fame came as LADY (6) MACBETH, which she played opposite Garrick for many years. After her death, he never played MACBETH again.

**Problem Plays**   Three of Shakespeare's comedies—*All's Well That Ends Well, Measure for Measure,* and *Troilus and Cressida*—that are potent satires characterised by disturbingly ambiguous points of view and seemingly cynical attitudes towards sexual and social relations. The problem plays—all written around 1602–1604—are concerned with basic elements of life, sex, and death, and the psychological and social complications they give rise to. These issues are problematic, and the plays further stress this by pointedly offering no clear-cut resolutions, leaving audiences with a painful awareness of life's difficulties.

Many people find the plays difficult to enjoy because of various other disturbing qualities. All three feature a number of unpleasant characters, villainous or misanthropic or both, such as THERSITES and PANDARUS of *Troilus and Cressida*, PAROLLES and BERTRAM of *All's Well That Ends Well*, and ANGELO (2) of *Measure for Measure*. They all end unsatisfactorily to most tastes, with a bleak and inconclusive dénouement for *Troilus and Cressida*, and with arbitrary and unconvincing 'solutions' imposed on the other two. Perhaps most dismaying to modern tastes, psychologically astute characterisations clash with extremely artificial plotting in a disjunction that seems to weaken both the realism and fantasy in all three plays.

The unpleasant aspects of the problem plays have led some commentators to suggest that they reflect some corresponding unpleasantness in Shakespeare's life, and that they were written by an embittered man who had recently undergone some psychological trauma the nature of which can only be guessed at. Lack of evidence has not inhibited speculation, and a romantic crisis such as that described in the SONNETS, the execution of the Earl of ESSEX (2), and the death of Shakespeare's father in 1601 have all been suggested as causes of the playwright's presumed unhappiness. However, most scholars believe that no such personal explanation is necessary. The problem plays are not so much sad as they are scathing; each is placed in a distinctive and highly stylised social milieu, and their plots do not present realistic personal situations. In all these respects it seems more likely that their peculiar nature was generated by dramatic considerations rather than personal ones. The period saw a strong fashion for social satire, led by the biting comedies of Ben JONSON, and the problem plays are clearly part of this trend in JACOBEAN DRAMA. Moreover, the accession of JAMES I in 1603 stimulated a lot of theorising about society that is reflected in the problem plays, especially *Measure for Measure*.

The origin of the term 'problem play' lends support to the view that the plays were conceived as public discourse rather than private lament. The phrase was first applied to these plays—plus the slightly earlier TRAGEDY, *Hamlet*—by the Shakespearean scholar Frederick S. BOAS in his book *Shakespeare and his Predecessors* (1896). He took the term from the contemporary theatre of his day. In the 1890s 'problem play' was a new expression coined to deal with a new sort of drama—for example, the work of Ibsen, George Bernard SHAW (2), and others—that dealt frankly and purposefully with social problems. Thus, the term as applied to Shakespeare's plays has implications about the playwright's intentions: these works are, indeed, profoundly concerned with society and its discontents.

At the close of both *All's Well* and *Measure for Measure*, villainy is exposed, its effects are corrected, and faults are forgiven in an air of general reconciliation. The effect is one of moral instruction, and, in fact, all three plays are distinguished by a pronounced emphasis on ethical questions. In *All's Well* the native worth of an individual is valued above aristocratic social standing, and the value of forgiveness is stressed in its conclusion. *Measure for Measure* addresses the nature of good and bad governance, the evils of extreme and inflexible moral positions, and, again, the value of forgiveness. *Troilus and Cressida* offers a scathing critique of the soldierly pretensions to honour and of the dishonesties of fashionable courtship in a context that exposes the futility of war.

Less baldly satirical than Jonson's work, the problem plays were perhaps found too serious and troubling by their original audiences, for all three plays were badly received when they were new, and they continued to be decidedly unpopular for three centuries thereafter. They have only been widely accepted in recent times, perhaps because the modern era is inclined both to the analysis of human problems and to a fear that they may not be easily solved. Commentators such as Shaw and Walter PATER instituted a reappraisal of the problem plays in the 1870s and '80s, and William POEL's productions of all three, between 1895 and 1905, began a process of theatrical rediscovery that has not stopped. Since the 1930s the plays have been staged regularly, and they will doubtless continue to attract producers and audiences. Their problematic aspects seem fitted to our problematic times; Shaw, writing in 1907, said that in these works Shakespeare was 'ready and willing to start at the twentieth century if the seventeenth would only let him'.

With greater acceptance, the positive aspects of the problem plays have become more evident. Certain seeming defects have more virtue than is immediately apparent. For instance, the employment of the 'bed trick' by HELENA (2) in *All's Well* and ISABELLA in *Measure for Measure*, along with CRESSIDA's hasty abandonment of TROILUS, are often seen as ill-motivated perversions of the characters' personalities. However, these events have significant symbolic functions, though they may not make sense psychologically. In the problem plays the point is not simply personality but also situation, not merely reality but also ideas. These intellectual aspects need not inhibit theatrical pleasure, for all three plays contain inspiring parts for actors. These include some unattractive figures, such as Thersites and Parolles, and also such splendid non-villains as Isabella, Helena, and ULYSSES. Even some of the lesser parts, such as the COUNTESS (2) of *All's Well*, are notable for fine speeches and a sympathetic presence. Moreover, all three plays offer genuinely funny passages, and several roles—such as LUCIO, AJAX, Thersites, Pandarus, and Parolles—which are fine vehicles for good comic actors. Especially in performance, the plays have a comedic focus that makes them less dark than the ideas they deal with.

This bright aspect lends its emotional tone to another important factor, one that was more popular in the 17th century than it is today. Except in the case of *Troilus and Cressida,* the plays display marked religious overtones, specifically suggestive of Christian redemption. Both Helena and Isabella have been seen as intentionally symbolic of God's grace, and the title of *Measure for Measure* alludes to the Sermon on the Mount. The appallingly deficient moral character of Bertram and Angelo, the male protagonists of these two plays, is also a powerful symbol in such a context, for these undeserving cads have but one purpose: to sin and be forgiven. These characters are similar to the central figures in medieval MORALITY PLAYS, which were still a living tradition for Shakespeare and his original audiences.

Once we understand that moral issues are the plays' *raison d'être,* we can adjust to the symbolic aspects of character and the allegorical nature of some of the plotting. The extent to which moral questions are stressed makes clear their importance to Shakespeare, and his refusal to provide easy answers to them makes them particularly potent. Shakespeare recognises, as always, the complexity of life and the difficulty in making moral judgements. The capacity of these plays to disturb causes us to be more engaged in these questions; we become aware of the need to strive after ideals, to pursue and believe in virtue even though we, like the figures in the plays, may not fully achieve it.

**Proculeius, Caius (active c. 40–c. 20 B.C.)** Historical figure and character in *Antony and Cleopatra,* a follower of Octavius CAESAR (2). When he advises CLEOPATRA to surrender to Caesar, ANTONY tells her, 'None about Caesar trust but Proculeius' (4.15.48). In 5.1 Caesar sends Proculeius to the Egyptian queen with instructions to promise her anything. Caesar wishes to prevent her from committing suicide so that he can triumphantly display her in ROME. In 5.2 Proculeius prevents Cleopatra from stabbing herself. He counsels her to be temperate, and tells her she will receive good treatment from Caesar. Because he has been recommended for his trustworthiness, his lies stress the isolation of Cleopatra in defeat, which helps motivate her suicide.

The historical Proculeius, a military commander, had a reputation as a forthright and honest man. This doubtless accounts for Antony's mistaken assumption (Shakespeare took the entire incident from PLUTARCH's *Lives*), but his loyalty was entirely with Caesar. He was a close personal friend of his leader, and he

remained so for many years, though he never attained—or, apparently, aspired to—high office in the empire that Caesar was to found.

**Prologue (1)** Dramatic device in ELIZABETHAN DRAMA, a speech introducing a play. Sixteenth-century plays often opened with a prologue spoken by an allegorical figure—also called the Prologue (e.g., PROLOGUE [2])—commonly dressed in a distinctive black velvet cloak. He remarked briefly on the action to come, preparing the audience to respond appropriately. Elizabethan playwrights borrowed the prologue from Roman drama, which in turn had taken it from ancient Greek drama. Five of Shakespeare's plays begin with a Prologue: *Romeo and Juliet* (see CHORUS [2]), *Henry V, Troilus and Cressida, Pericles* (see GOWER [3]), and *The Two Noble Kinsmen;* in addition, three plays within a play present brief Prologues, those in *A Midsummer Night's Dream* (5.1.108–117), *Hamlet* (3.2.143–146), and *The Two Noble Kinsmen* (3.5.101–135).

**Prologue (2)** Allegorical figure in *Henry V,* the speaker of the PROLOGUE (1) that opens the play. Although he is designated in the opening stage direction as the Prologue, he identifies himself as the CHORUS (3) in line 32, and his rhetorical invocation of the Muses is taken up again, in remarks delivered under that designation, before each subsequent act (2–5) and in the EPILOGUE.

**Prologue (3)** Allegorical figure in *Troilus and Cressida* who speaks the PROLOGUE (1) that opens the play. The Prologue tells how the TROJAN WAR stemmed from the abduction of MENELAUS' wife, HELEN (1), by PARIS (3). He commences in the heroic style of traditional chroniclers of war, only to sum up, 'Ravished Helen, Menelaus' queen / With wanton Paris sleeps—and that's the quarrel' (Pro. 9–10). This stylistic jolt, both rhythmic and rhetorical, serves notice that this account of the ancient epic will not be conventional. He goes on to caution the audience that it may not like what the play depicts, for its contents vary with 'the chance of war' (Pro.31). In belittling his warlike costume, the Prologue further hints at the satire of soldiery that is to come. Some scholars believe that the provision for an 'arm'd' Prologue was inspired by, and perhaps was intended as an allusion to, the armoured Prologue in Ben JONSON's play *Poetaster* (1601).

**Prologue (4)** Allegorical figure in *Henry VIII,* the speaker of the PROLOGUE (1) that opens the play. The Prologue tells the audience that the play will be serious and sad, containing 'Such noble scenes as draw the eye to flow' (Prologue 4), and that it purports to tell the historical truth. It will include pleasing spectacles, but it will not be 'a merry bawdy play' (Prologue 14). (Scholars believe this last remark refers to an earlier, decidedly non-serious play about King HENRY VIII by Samuel ROWLEY [1].) The Prologue prepares the audience for the solemnity of the play to come, which was a different sort of history play than Shakespeare's audiences were accustomed to. Scholars who believe that *Henry VIII* was written by more than one author usually ascribe the play's prologue to Shakespeare's collaborator.

**Prologue (5)**    Allegorical figure in *The Two Noble Kinsmen,* the speaker of the PROLOGUE (1) that opens the play. The Prologue tells that the play derives from a famous poet, CHAUCER, and that it cannot compare with the original. He hopes, in the name of the acting company, that their production will be good enough to avoid disgrace. Scholars generally believe that the Prologue was written by Shakespeare's collaborator, probably John FLETCHER (2).

**Prompt-book**    Copy of a play used during performances by the prompter, called the book-holder in ELIZABETHAN THEATRE. A prompt-book contained notes for entrances and exits, music cues, cuts in the text made by the company during rehearsals, and so on. Because the author's manuscript, or FOUL PAPERS, was often difficult to use in this way, a prompt-book was usually a transcript made for the purpose and then annotated. Sometimes, however, if a play was already published when a prompt-book was required, a printed copy would be annotated. The prompt-book was usually the text presented to the MASTER OF REVELS for approval, before a play could be staged. Since the prompt-book was the acting company's official copy of a play—and probably the only one—its loss was too dangerous to risk by lending it to a publisher to be printed from. Thus only a few of Shakespeare's plays were first printed from a prompt-book, presumably when another version was not available. Texts printed from prompt-books are characterised by the appearance of actors' names for those of characters, the placing of stage directions a few lines before they are needed, instructions for sound effects, and warnings of upcoming requirements for stage properties.

**Prospero**    Character in *The Tempest,* the magician-ruler of a remote island. Prospero, once the Duke of MILAN, lives in exile with his daughter MIRANDA and two supernatural inhabitants of the island, ARIEL and CALIBAN. Through magic, Prospero controls this world completely, and he is the central figure of the play, simultaneously the sparker and spectator of its various SUB-PLOTS. He has freed Ariel from a magic spell, in exchange for his service as an assistant; he also befriended Caliban at first but enslaved him after he attempted to rape Miranda. Though embittered by his exile, Prospero has gained wisdom through his sorcery, and when chance places his one-time enemies in his power, he uses his magic to create an atmosphere of reconciliation and forgiveness, providing for the future in the union of Miranda with FERDINAND (2), the son of his enemy.

Having accomplished these things, Prospero sacrifices both his dominion over the island and his love of magic, choosing to return to Milan. In doing so, he restores a measure of justice to human society, for he had been unjustly deposed from authority before the play began. He also restores himself to a sound moral footing, for he had earlier placed a private concern—his study of magic—above his duty as a leader of society, with disastrous results. However, Prospero's success is not complete; he remains a melancholy figure at play's end, haunted by Caliban's enmity and his evil brother ANTONIO (5), who refuses regeneration. Thus Prospero brings out an important subtheme of *The Tempest* and of the ROMANCES in general: that life is an admixture of good and evil and that good cannot completely eradicate bad.

Prospero is a philosopher as well as a ruler. His magic is referred to as his 'Art' (1.2.1), consistently spelled with a capital A; this is a conventional allusion to Neoplatonic doctrines of the occult, familiar ideas in the 17th century. The Neoplatonic philosopher/magician attempted to elevate his soul through arcane knowledge of the divine, whether through alchemy, the reading of supernatural signs, or communication with spirits. If these efforts led to a magical manipulation of the real world, it was only as a byproduct of the search for spiritual knowledge. Prospero's original goal was to transcend nature, not control it. Nevertheless, it is clear that the pursuit of this goal was culpably selfish, for it resulted in his exile and the disruption of sound government in Milan, as he recounts in 1.2. He had insisted on studying magic rather than governing and as a result had been deposed by Antonio. Conscious of his failing, regretful at leaving Ariel and the beauties of 'rough magic [and] heavenly music' (5.1.50–52), distressed by his evident failure to educate Caliban, and, most important, frustrated by the intransigence of Antonio, Prospero returns to Milan at play's end without the satisfaction the conclusion brings to most of the other characters. Though restored to power, and though he has provided a hopeful future for others, he is a partial failure, and he knows it.

Prospero is not a pleasant character. He is a distant and uncommunicative father and a tyrannical master. His unjustified complaints that Miranda is not listening to him in 1.2 and his anguished disruption of the MASQUE in 4.1 are evidence of his temperamental nature. Only in his affection for Ariel is he a pleasant figure, but he is also capable of rounding vituperatively on the sprite —'Thou liest, malignant thing!' (1.2.257)—and threatening him—'I will . . . peg thee [to a tree] till / Thou hast howl'd away twelve winters'

(1.2.294–296). His programme of petty harassments of Caliban, recounted in 2.2.1–14, is equally repellent.

Prospero's exploitation of the island's inhabitants is a clearly established element of the play. Ariel, a free spirit by nature, is restive in his service, and Caliban even attempts a revolt. Some modern commentators go so far as to make this exploitation a central concern, and The Tempest has been presented as an allegory of colonialism and oppression. However, it is clear that Prospero's control has been employed for good, for he has undone the dominance of evil that he found on his arrival, when the villainous Caliban prevailed, and Ariel, a good spirit, was imprisoned by Caliban's mother. The inhumane treatment of Caliban and Ariel's dissatisfaction provide evidence of the inexorability of evil; good ends must often be compromised by morally unsatisfactory means.

A central theme of the play is transfiguration, as the characters undergo transformations that suggest the varying human capacity for improvement. Prospero's magic effects these alterations in the others, but he himself also undergoes a highly significant change. His transformation occurs largely before the time of the play, but evidence of it remains. His decision that 'the rarer action is / In virtue than in vengeance' (5.1. 27–28) implies a temptation from which he refrains. We recognise that he has grown: first a scholar of magic, he became a seeker of revenge through supernatural means, but finally he has transcended magic altogether. Once he could say 'my library / Was dukedom large enough' (1.2.109–110), but at play's end he returns to Milan to resume his proper position as a leader of society. In so doing, he renounces his magical powers and discards his semi-devine status as the island's omnipotent ruler. Prospero accepts his humanity and comes to terms with the prospect of his own death, to which he will devote 'every third thought' (5.1.311). He leaves the future in the hands of Ferdinand and Miranda.

Prospero's 'Art' fittingly takes the form of drama, the art practised by Prospero's creator. Assisted by Ariel, Prospero produces three distinctly theatrical illusions—the HARPY's banquet of 3.3, the betrothal masque of 4.1, and the presentation of Ferdinand and Miranda at chess in 5.1. As producer of these spectacles, Prospero comments on their nature at the close of the masque, in his famous speech beginning 'Our revels now are ended' (4.1.148). He points out the illusion involved and goes on to equate such an 'insubstantial pageant' (4.1.155) with life itself, which disappears once it is performed. 'We are such stuff / As dreams are made on', he concludes, 'and our little life / Is rounded with a sleep' (4.1.156–158). Many commentators have regarded Prospero's remarks as Shakespeare's personal valedictory to a career in the theatre. While this notion is imprecise, in that Shakespeare continued to write for the theatre after The Tempest, the passage does seem to reflect the experience of an artist whose long career has led to the belief that art's inherently illusory nature is analogous to, and probably related to, the impossibility of understanding life. Here we have a clue to the philosophy underlying a prominent feature of Shakespeare's work, his persistent attention to ambiguity.

Shakespeare may have taken Prospero's name from Prospero Adorno (active 1460–1488), a deposed duke of Genoa, of whom he could have read in William Thomas' History of Italy (1549). However, this is uncertain, for another source was nearer to hand: Ben JONSON's Every Man in His Humour (1600). This play, in which Shakespeare acted, contains a character—though not a deposed duke—originally named Prospero (the name was later changed to Wellbred, as it appears in modern editions).

**Proteus** One of the title characters in The Two Gentlemen of Verona, the villain who simultaneously betrays his lover, JULIA, and his friend, VALENTINE (2), by pursuing Valentine's lover, SILVIA. Proteus initially presents himself as wholly in love with Julia. His father, ANTONIO (1), forces him to attend the court, for such a sojourn is proper for a young gentleman, and he bids farewell to his beloved, pledging to be faithful. Once at court, however, he falls in love with Silvia, who is already secretly betrothed to Valentine. Proteus knows his love is disloyal, but he is prepared to forsake both Valentine and Julia. Proteus plots against Valentine and even attempts to rape Silvia, but Valentine thwarts and forgives him. Reunited with Julia, who has followed him, Proteus vows renewed fidelity, and the play ends with the planning of a double wedding.

Shakespeare took this character's name from HOMER's Odyssey, in which Proteus is a sea god who can change his shape at will. The Proteus of The Two Gentlemen of Verona, whose attitudes towards others change with his appetites, is thus fittingly named.

**Provost** Character in Measure for Measure, the warden of the prison in which CLAUDIO (3) is gaoled. From his first appearance—when he exposes Claudio to public humiliation at the orders of ANGELO (2) but declares, 'I do it not in evil disposition' (1.2.110)—we see the Provost to be a kind and honourable man. He pleads with Angelo to be merciful towards Claudio and clearly presents a sensible view of the young man's offence, thereby emphasising Angelo's extremism. Nevertheless, the Provost is prepared to do the duty of his office and oversee the young man's execution. In this way, he offers a contrast to the moral laxity that created the problem in the first place.

In a telling episode the Provost demonstrates Shakespeare's position that social order has a high value. This clearly sympathetic character who obviously favours mercy for Claudio nevertheless resists the attempts of the disguised DUKE (9) to find a way to save the young man until the Duke produces letters that reveal his authority. Then, supported by the knowledge that he will not be opposing the ruler—Shakespeare and his original audiences believed that rulers were appointed by God—he can enthusiastically help.

**Prynne, William (1600–1669)**   Puritan pamphleteer and opponent of the theatre. In his *Histriomastix, The Players Scourge* (1633), Prynne declared that 'popular stage-plays . . . are sinfull, heathenish, lewde, ungodly Spectacles' and called people who wrote, acted in, or attended plays 'unlawful, infamous and misbeseeming Christians'. Prynne's attack was only one example of Puritan hostility towards drama, and Puritan culture increasingly dominated English life from the 1580s on. After 1642 as the civil wars began and a revolutionary government controlled first London and later the country, the theatres of England were closed for 18 years (but see DROLLS).

Prynne's career also offers an impressive demonstration of the barbarous rigour of the law in 17th-century England. *Historiomastix* contained references to the just downfalls of monarchs, and insulted the queen for appearing in MASQUES. Because of this, Prynne was imprisoned for life, fined a huge amount of money, and had his ears cut off. He managed to publish from prison a pamphlet that attacked English bishops, and was therefore branded on both cheeks with the letters 'S. L'. (for 'seditious libeller'). With the approach of the revolution, he was freed in 1640. He was elected to Parliament, but he continued to attack various aspects of the revolution itself, and in 1650 he was again imprisoned for three years. Prynne finally mellowed somewhat and avoided further prosecution, though he did not cease his public commentaries. In the course of his career he published over 200 books and pamphlets. He supported the restoration of the monarchy in 1660, served again in Parliament, and was appointed to a clerical position at the TOWER OF LONDON, where he had once been imprisoned.

**Publius (1)**   Minor character in *Titus Andronicus,* the son of MARCUS ANDRONICUS. Publius participates in the seemingly mad TITUS (1) Andronicus' plan to shoot message-laden arrows to the gods in 4.3, and he helps capture CHIRON and DEMETRIUS (1) in 5.2.

**Publius (2)**   Minor character in *Julius Caesar,* a witness to the assassination of CAESAR (1). In 3.1 Publius accompanies Caesar to the Senate, and when the killing takes place, he watches horrified; he is the only figure on stage not in violent action. BRUTUS (4) reassures him that no harm is intended to him or any other citizen, and he is sent to pass along this message to others. He remains silent throughout the episode.

Publius is usually designated as a senator in the list of characters, but the text offers no indication of his status; the first such list only dates from ROWE's 1709 edition of the plays. The same Publius may be referred to when Antony consents to the condemnation of his nephew, Publius, in 4.1.4–6. Although no such relationship has been mentioned before, the name recalls the earlier figure and intensifies the picture of Antony as a ruthless politician. Not only does he condemn his own relative to solidify his political position, but he also undoes Brutus' explicit mercy of 3.1.

Publius, unlike the other named characters in *Julius Caesar,* does not appear in Shakespeare's source, PLUTARCH's *Lives.* Antony had no nephew named Publius, and no one of that name appears in Plutarch's account of the assassination. Having decided to present an innocent bystander in 3.1, Shakespeare simply invented an extra character and gave him a handy Latin name (one that he also used in 3.1.53 to identify the brother of METELLUS, who is also unnamed in Plutarch). His various uses of the name may simply be an instance of the minor carelessness that recurs throughout his plays.

**Pucelle, La**   See JOAN LA PUCELLE.

**Puck (Robin Goodfellow)**   Character in *A Midsummer Night's Dream,* a fairy and aide to OBERON, the Fairy

*In* A Midsummer Night's Dream, *Puck (played here by Mickey Rooney in the 1935 film) is a mischievous trickster who creates trouble by anointing Lysander with a love potion. (Courtesy of Culver Pictures, Inc.)*

King. Puck is a powerful supernatural creature, capable of circling the earth in 40 minutes (2.1.176) and of manipulating the elements—for example, he summons a fog in 3.2—but he is more mischievous than awe-inspiring. He reminds us of a small boy when he boasts of his talents as a trickster in 2.1.42–57 and when he calls out, 'I go, I go, look how I go!' (3.2.100). Like BOTTOM, he is a humorous character, but where Bottom is a CLOWN (1), intended to be laughed at, Puck more closely resembles a FOOL (1), like Shakespeare's jesters TOUCHSTONE and FESTE. He is removed from the practical world and expresses himself through an idiosyncratic sense of humour. He prefers 'things that befall prepost'rously' (3.2.121).

There is some malice in Puck's taste for pranks, and Puck reminds us that the fairy world is not all sweetness and light; this contributes to an undertone of potential evil that makes the comedy, while still benign, a more richly textured tale. He speaks in horrifying terms of the cruel and awesome world that is also the domain of the fairies (5.1.357–373), only to assure us that 'we fairies . . . / Now are frolic'. However, when his error in anointing LYSANDER causes trouble, Puck is immune to Oberon's regret that this has happened, replying only, 'Then fate o'er-rules' (3.2.92). He is coolly indifferent to human suffering.

While Puck explicitly calls himself a fairy in 5.1.369, quoted above, and elsewhere, there is some ambiguity in his relationship to the FAIRY in 2.1, and in 3.2.399 he is identified as a 'goblin'. Shakespeare did not care about such minor inconsistencies, and they do not interfere with Puck's effectiveness in the drama. They do, however, reflect the fairy lore known to Shakespeare, who combined in Puck two supernatural creatures that had earlier been thought of as separate beings: Robin Goodfellow, a name interchangeable with Puck in the 16th century, was a household spirit also associated with travellers; a 'puck' was not a fairy, but a small elf or goblin fond of playing practical jokes on mortals, especially at night. The puck was originally a Norse demon, identified in England with the devil.

**Purcell, Henry (c. 1659–1695)** English composer, creator of music for several adaptations of Shakespeare's plays. Perhaps the greatest English composer, Purcell led the creation of an English baroque style in music. He is best known today for two operas: *The Fairy Queen* (1692), with a libretto taken by Thomas BETTERTON from *A Midsummer Night's Dream*, and *Dido and Aeneas* (1689), parts of which were incorporated in Charles GILDON's 1699 adaptation of *Measure for Measure*. He also composed music for a 1690 revival of Thomas SHADWELL's *The Enchanted Island*, an operatic version of *The Tempest* (as adapted by John DRYDEN and William DAVENANT), and Shadwell's 1694 adaptation of *Timon of Athens*. However, in all these works, the only words of Shakespeare set to music by Purcell are two SONGS in *The Tempest*, 'Come unto these yellow sands' (1.2.377–389) and 'Full fadom five' (1.2.399–407).

**Puritan, The** Anonymous play formerly attributed to Shakespeare, part of the Shakespeare APOCRYPHA. *The Puritan,* sometimes called *The Puritan Widow* (its full title was *The Puritan or The Widdow of Watling-Streete*), is a farce with a pointed anti-Puritan bias. It was published by George ELD in 1607 as 'written by W. S.', possibly with the intention of associating the play with Shakespeare. It was also included among Shakespeare's plays in the Third and Fourth FOLIOS and in the editions of Nicholas ROWE and Alexander POPE (1). Scholars are confident, however, that *The Puritan* was not written by Shakespeare. Although it is a better drama than most of the apocryphal plays, it bears no resemblance to Shakespeare's known works as it is a topical satire set in contemporary London and written mostly in prose. Stylistically, it is tentatively ascribed by many scholars to John MARSTON or Thomas MIDDLETON.

**Pursuivant** Character in *Richard III*. See HASTINGS (2).

**Puttenham, George (c. 1529–1590) or Richard (c. 1520–1601)** English writer, author of a book of literary theory that is parodied in *King Lear*. *The Arte of English Poesie* (1589) appeared anonymously; William CAMDEN referred to it as the work of 'Maister Puttenham', but it is not known which brother wrote the book, so it is traditionally ascribed to 'Puttenham'. Puttenham's manual of style critiques the best-known English poets and is considered the first important work of English poetry criticism. It also analyses rhetorical and poetic devices, and advises on language usage. Puttenham inveighs against the use of archaic or foreign terms, and suggests adopting the accents of LONDON and the royal court. Several passages in Shakespeare's plays (e.g., *All's Well* 2.3.293–294) echo Puttenham's wording, and the prophecy of the FOOL (2) in *King Lear* (3.2.79–96) is a parody of some lines attributed to CHAUCER in the book. *The Arte of English Poesie* was published by Shakespeare's friend, Richard FIELD (2), and it is possible the playwright knew its author.

**Pyramus and Thisbe** Title of the play within *A Midsummer Night's Dream*, an INTERLUDE performed at the wedding of Duke THESEUS (1) and Queen HIPPOLYTA (1). The play is enacted in 5.1 by a group of artisans of ATHENS—led by Peter QUINCE—whom Shakespeare portrays as humorous English rustics. Nick BOTTOM, an excellent Shakespearean CLOWN (1), plays the romantic lead in a comic manner. Theseus generously gives a dignified reception to the preposterous production, although his bride is less tolerant, declaring the play to be ridiculous, which of course it is meant to be.

The story of Pyramus and Thisbe was familiar to Shakespeare through OVID's *Metamorphoses*, but even illiterate members of his audience will have known it, for Pyramus and Thisbe figured in several Elizabethan popular songs. The ancient Greek myth tells of the love of a boy and girl, Pyramus and Thisbe, who live in neighbouring buildings but whose parents have forbidden them to meet. Able to communicate only through a hole in the wall between their homes, the lovers agree to elope. Thisbe arrives at their rendezvous early. Frightened by a lion, she hides in a cave but loses her cloak as she flees. The lion has just eaten and has a bloody mouth; nuzzling her garment, he bloodies it. When Pyramus arrives, he sees the bloodstained cloak and lion's tracks and concludes that Thisbe has been killed by the animal. Heartsick, he kills himself with his sword. When Thisbe reappears and sees what has happened, she seizes his sword and kills herself.

This tale, although burlesqued by the artisans' production, provides an illuminating counterpart to the elopement of LYSANDER and HERMIA earlier in *A Midsummer Night's Dream*. It demonstrates, in a harmless context, the potential for tragedy that the lovers' predicament harboured. The contrast heightens our pleasure in the benevolent outcome that has actually occurred.

Shakespeare's parody is not directed at Ovid's classic version, but rather at the bombast and theatrical heroics in 16th-century drama, especially that of Thomas PRESTON. In addition, two minor modifications of Ovid's tale stand out. Quince's original casting of the interlude (1.2.56–59) includes the lovers' parents, who are merely mentioned in Ovid, and Bottom's assertion that the wall had 'parted their fathers' (5.1.338) introduces an inter-family feud that does not exist in Ovid. Both additions suggest aspects of *Romeo and Juliet*, and it is thought that Shakespeare's use of the legend in this fashion reflects his recent composition of that play.

**Pyrrhus** Legendary Greek warrior whose bloody killing of King PRIAM of TROY is recalled as an example of regicide in *Hamlet*. The FIRST PLAYER (2), at HAMLET's request, recites a dramatic monologue in which this episode from the TROJAN WAR is vividly recounted. Pyrrhus at first hesitates, as 'his sword . . . seem'd i'th' air to stick' (2.2.473–475) and he 'like a neutral to his will and matter, / Did nothing' (2.2.477–478). This inaction parallels that of Hamlet, who has so far failed to avenge his father's murder by KING (5) Claudius. But then Pyrrhus' 'aroused vengeance' (2.2.484) impels him to complete his deed, and the recital implicitly stimulates Hamlet to action.

Pyrrhus appears as Neoptolemus in HOMER and other early accounts of Priam's death, but he is Pyrrhus in VIRGIL's *Aeneid*, which was probably more familiar to Shakespeare. He was the son of ACHILLES, and he is mentioned as such in *Troilus and Cressida* (3.3.208). In one version of his myth, he founded a dynasty of kings, one of whom, also called Pyrrhus, is now much better known than he, as the general who achieved a costly, or Pyrrhic, victory.

# Q

**Quarto** Format for a book or page. A quarto is a sheet of paper that is folded in half twice, yielding four leaves or eight pages. It is also a book composed of such pages (see also FOLIO). Most of the early editions of Shakespeare's plays were produced in this format, and the term is often used to refer to these editions. Some of these came from authoritative sources that accurately reflected what Shakespeare wrote, such as his FOUL PAPERS; these are known as GOOD QUARTOS. Others, whose text was reconstructed by actors from memory, are seriously flawed in various ways and are known as BAD QUARTOS. Of the 38 plays in the CANON, 22 were initially published as Quartos. However, there are 10 Bad Quartos and 14 Good Quartos, for *Romeo and Juliet* and *Hamlet* appeared in both Good Quarto and Bad Quarto editions.

**Quayle, Anthony (1913–1989)** British actor and director. On both stage and screen Quayle played a variety of Shakespearean parts—including BOTTOM, PANDARUS, OTHELLO, and FALSTAFF—as well as other roles in both classic and modern drama. He was director of the Shakespeare Memorial Theatre at STRATFORD from 1948 to 1956. He wrote two novels—*Eight Hours from England* (1945) and *On Such a Night* (1947)—based on his wartime service as a leader of guerrilla bands behind Nazi lines in Europe. Quayle is probably most widely remembered for several non-Shakespearean movie roles, in *The Guns of Navarone* (1961), *Lawrence of Arabia* (1963), and *Anne of a Thousand Days* (1970). In the latter he played Cardinal Thomas WOLSEY.

**Queen (1)** Any of three minor characters in *The Two Noble Kinsmen,* deposed monarchs who seek the aid of THESEUS (2), Duke of ATHENS. The Queens interrupt Theseus' wedding to tell him that their husbands have been defeated and killed by King Creon of THEBES, who has refused to bury the kings' bodies, thereby exposing their souls to torment. They ask Theseus to avenge this deed by conquering Creon. The First Queen, as she is designated, implores Theseus; the Second Queen addresses his intended bride, the Amazon HIPPOLYTA (2), and the Third speaks to Hippolyta's sister, EMILIA (4). All three respond favoura-

bly, but the Queens are not satisfied with anything but instant action, and their petitions are restated. Finally, the wedding is postponed and Theseus sets out. In 1.4, the conquest completed, the Queens thank Theseus, and in 1.5 they proceed with their husbands' funerals.

The Queens are part of the ritualistic aspect of the play that links it to other Shakespeare ROMANCES. They are highly significant figures in 1.1, Shakespeare's spectacular opening scene. Their sudden appearance, all in black at a festive ceremony, is a *coup de théâtre,* with a grand effect on stage. Their repeated approaches, first to one character and then another, form a dancelike, stylised sequence, a kind of liturgy that reinforces the high seriousness of their purpose. In 1.5 they again offer an impressive tableau, as Act 1 closes in tragic triumph.

**Queen (2) of Britain** Character in *Cymbeline,* the wife of King CYMBELINE and stepmother of his daughter IMOGEN. The Queen, one of several villains in the play, is the most purely vicious of them. She had planned that Imogen marry her son, the oafish CLOTEN, but Imogen eloped with POSTHUMUS instead. Posthumus is banished, and the Queen directs her malice towards Imogen and PISANIO, Posthumus' servant who has stayed with Imogen. She is the archetypal wicked stepmother, and her villainy is clear from her initial appearance, in 1.2, when she pretends to protect Imogen but reveals her malice in an aside. Imogen is undeceived and notes the Queen's 'dissembling courtesy' (1.2.15); thus, the Queen's wickedness is immediately established. In 1.6 the Queen collects poison from the physician CORNELIUS (2) and offers it to Pisanio as a health-giving potion in the hope that he will take it and die. However, Cornelius 'will not trust one of her malice' (1.6.35), and has substituted a sleeping potion for the poison. The Queen is ultimately ineffective, but her evil intent is a prominent element of the first half of the play.

Once her nature is well established, the Queen plays a lesser role. At the play's close we learn of her death from an illness caused by her despair at Cloten's sudden disappearance. Her final confession of sins—including an intent to poison the king himself—prepares for the final sequence of reconciliations in 5.5. The Queen has only been forestalled by the whim of fortune: Cloten has been killed by a chance encounter that is the result of a long series of events that began with the exile of Posthumus. She has therein fulfilled the villain's role in this play, which is to be defeated by the intervention of providence.

**Queen (3) Anne of England** Character in *Henry VIII*. See ANNE (1).

**Queen (4) Anne of England** Character in *Richard III*. See ANNE (2).

**Queen (5) Cleopatra of Egypt** Title character of *Antony and Cleopatra*. See CLEOPATRA.

**Queen (6) Eleanor (Elinor) of England** Character in *King John*. See ELEANOR.

**Queen (7) Elizabeth of England** Contemporary of Shakespeare. See ELIZABETH (1).

**Queen (8) Elizabeth of England** Character in *3 Henry VI* and *Richard III*. See ELIZABETH (2).

**Queen (9) Gertrude of Denmark** Character in *Hamlet*, HAMLET's mother, who has married the brother, successor, and murderer of her late husband, the King of DENMARK. Hamlet is horrified by the Queen's acceptance, soon after her husband's death, of 'incestuous sheets' (1.2.157), and he is moved to conclude, 'Frailty, thy name is woman' (1.2.146). His disgust at her behaviour is heightened when he learns from the GHOST (3), in 1.5.42–52, that she had been the lover of Claudius, the new KING (5), before he had killed Hamlet's father. Hamlet's detestation of his mother's part in these evils is transformed into a revulsion against women in general and against the love—and sex—that they offer, which lead only to the creation of more humanity and thus more wickedness. His own beloved, OPHELIA, tragically comes to bear the brunt of the prince's misogyny.

Although the Queen provides an example of the evil that infects Denmark, she herself is a somewhat faceless character. She is basically evil through weakness rather than inclination. The Ghost attributes her wickedness to Claudius and tells Hamlet to exclude her from his revenge—'Leave her to heaven' (1.5.86). In her main scene, in which Hamlet repudiates her for her adultery and her acceptance of the King as a husband, she acknowledges her guilt, crying out that her soul is contaminated by '. . . such black and grained spots / As will not leave their tinct' (3.4.90–91). After Hamlet leaves and the King returns in 4.1, the Queen resumes her role as his accomplice. But in 5.2, when the Queen turns on her husband and cries out a warning to Hamlet as she dies, we may suppose that her son has had some effect on her.

**Queen (10) Hermione** Character in *The Winter's Tale*. See HERMIONE.

**Queen (11) Hippolyta of the Amazons** Character in *A Midsummer Night's Dream*. See HIPPOLYTA (1).

**Queen (12) Hippolyta** Character in *The Two Noble Kinsmen*. See HIPPOLYTA (2).

**Queen (13) Isabel of England (1389–1409)** Historical figure and character in *Richard II*, the wife of RICHARD II. The Queen is so completely different from her historical counterpart that she is virtually fictitious. Shakespeare introduces her to help provide a human context for the political events of the play. In 2.3 she glumly regrets the temporary absence of her husband—'so sweet a guest as . . . sweet Richard' (2.2.8–9)—casting the vain and headstrong King in a very different light than he has yet been seen. Later, after she overhears the GARDENER's remarks on Richard's capture and likely deposition by BOLINGBROKE (1), she responds with hysterical grief. She last appears in the famous farewell scene with Richard (5.1), which restates, on a personal level, the breach in the political fabric that Bolingbroke's usurpation has effected. (Richard refers to this in his speech beginning with the expostulation 'Doubly divorc'd!' [5.1.71].) The Queen's pleas that she be permitted to accompany her husband are rejected by the stony Earl of NORTHUMBERLAND (1), and the sorrowing couple are forcibly separated, just as Richard has been parted from his crown. The historical is presented on a human level, with a degree of poignancy far greater than any dismay we may feel for Richard's fall from worldly greatness or for the collapse of England's feudal traditions.

The historical Isabel was no happier than Shakespeare's Queen, but she was a child of 10 when these events occurred. The daughter of Charles VI, the FRENCH KING of *Henry V*, she was married to Richard when she was 7. While this couple seem to have been genuinely fond of one another, they had no opportunity to develop the mature relationship that Shakespeare depicts. Although she is banished to France in the play, she was actually detained in England for two years following Richard's deposition, virtually a prisoner, because the new government was reluctant to return her dowry. When she finally returned home, Isabel was still an eminently eligible princess, and she was married in 1404 to Prince Charles of ORLÉANS (3) (who appears in *Henry V*). She died in childbirth five years later, at the age of 20.

**Queen (14) Isabel of France** Character in *Henry V*. See ISABEL (2).

**Queen (15) Katherine of England (and of Aragon)**
Character in *Henry VIII*. See KATHERINE OF ARAGON.

**Queen (16) Margaret of England**   Character in *1, 2,*
and *3 Henry VI* and *Richard III.* See MARGARET (1).

**Queen (17), Player**   Character in *Hamlet.* See PLAYER
QUEEN.

**Queen's Men (1) (Queen Elizabeth's Men)**   Acting
company of the ELIZABETHAN THEATRE, possibly Shakespeare's first theatrical home. The Queen's Men were
created by order of Queen ELIZABETH (1) in 1583; at
the queen's command, her MASTER OF REVELS raided
other acting companies for some of their finest players. The Queen's Men consequently became the most
popular and important LONDON acting company for
almost a decade. Its original members included John
BENTLEY (who killed a man at an early Queen's Men
performance), the great comic actor Richard TARLTON,
John SINGER (another comic actor), and Robert WIL-
SON (4). The Queen's Men performed in London in
the winter, at the THEATRE and at the court, and toured
the provinces in the summer. In the summer of 1587,
they played in STRATFORD, a fact that has encouraged
speculation that Shakespeare may have gone with
them to London to begin his career (see KNELL).

After Tarlton's death in 1588, the fortunes of the
Queen's Men declined, and two newer companies, the
ADMIRAL'S MEN and STRANGE'S MEN, began to dominate
the theatrical scene. Between 1591 and 1594 the
Queen's Men performed only twice at court, a measure of their declining prestige. In the latter year, they
allied themselves with SUSSEX'S MEN, but to no avail;
unable to compete in London, they converted themselves into a full-time provincial touring company,
surviving until the queen's death in 1603.

**Queen's Men (2)**   Seventeenth-century LONDON theatrical company, successor to WORCESTER'S MEN. Upon
the accession of King JAMES I in 1603, his family assumed the patronage of the three London theatre
companies. His queen, Anne of Denmark (1574–
1619), gave her name to Worcester's Men, the least
important of the three, whose chief members were the
actor Christopher BEESTON and the playwright
Thomas HEYWOOD (2). When the company's royal patent was issued the next year, they were said to perform
regularly at an inn, where they had existed as Worcester's, and at the CURTAIN THEATRE, a new venue for
them. In 1609, when the patent was renewed, the locations named are the Curtain and the Red Bull Theatre,
a new playhouse. After 1617 they performed at the
Phoenix Theatre, owned by Beeston. Beeston
managed the company from 1612—ineptly and perhaps dishonestly, as the records of several lawsuits

reveal—until the company dissolved on the death of
Queen Anne in 1619.

**Queen's Revels**   See CHILDREN'S COMPANIES.

**Quickly, Mistress**   Character in *The Merry Wives of
Windsor,* housekeeper of Dr CAIUS (2). Mistress
Quickly is a shrewd yet comically foolish servant who
meddles in other people's affairs. She serves as a messenger between the merry wives and FALSTAFF, and she
impartially supports three different suitors in their
pursuit of ANNE (3) Page. Quickly is a traditional, humorously loquacious comic character, given to the
misuse of fancy words and the misinterpretation of
other people's speeches. For instance, in the famous
'Latin scene', 4.1, Quickly finds bawdy puns in Latin
grammatical exercises.

In 5.5 Quickly takes the part of the fairy queen in the
ceremonial taunting of Falstaff that is his final humiliation at the hands of the wives. Quickly is entirely out
of character in this scene, and her presence in the texts
of the play may merely reflect the playhouse practise
of having the actor who played Quickly also play the
anonymous fairy imitator. Alternatively, her distinctively uncharacteristic presence may have been intended by Shakespeare to suggest the MASQUElike unreality of the scene, emphasising its ritualistic quality.

Mistress Quickly bears the same name as the HOST-
ESS (2) of *1* and *2 Henry IV* and *Henry V,* and she shares
the Hostess' comical way with words, but she is nonetheless best considered as a different person, living in
a different world. She is unacquainted with Falstaff
when she encounters him in *The Merry Wives,* and she
has certainly never had anything to do with the BOAR'S
HEAD TAVERN in London. It seems likely that, in the
haste with which *The Merry Wives* was written, Shakespeare simply made use of an earlier creation in a new
way. Neither he nor his audience was distressed by the
inconsistencies this involves.

**Quin, James (1693–1766)**   British actor. The chief
rival to David GARRICK in the 1730s and 1740s, Quin
was renowned for his portrayal of FALSTAFF, though he
also played BRUTUS, OTHELLO, MACBETH, the GHOST (3)
in *Hamlet,* and other parts. He is considered the last
great representative of the formal and declamatory
school of acting that had been popular in the second
half of the 17th century but was supplanted by the
more naturalistic and active mode of Garrick. Quin
appears in Tobias Smollett's great novel *Humphrey
Clinker* (1771).

**Quince, Peter**   Character in *A Midsummer Night's
Dream,* a carpenter and the director of the comical
production of PYRAMUS AND THISBE, performed by several artisans of ATHENS. Quince organises an INTER-
LUDE to be performed at the wedding of Duke THESEUS

(1) and Queen HIPPOLYTA (1). Though overshadowed by his leading man, BOTTOM, he directs the performances of SNUG, FLUTE, SNOUT, and STARVELING, and he reads the PROLOGUE himself. Despite the supposedly Athenian setting of *A Midsummer Night's Dream*, Quince and his fellows are typical English artisans, excellent representatives of the humorous workers Shakespeare was fond of creating.

Quince comically performs several of the tasks of a real Elizabethan acting company. Not only the director, he has also written the script and is responsible for the properties and staging. He is something of a pedant, given to such high-flown locutions as 'I am to entreat you, request you, and desire you . . .' (1.2.92–93), but he is a tactful director, flattering Bottom into accepting his role in 1.2.79–82, and a resourceful reviser, prepared to create additional dialogue in 3.1. Less talented as an actor, he misreads his initial speech (5.1.108–117). (Quince's comical mispunctuation of the passage was a standard Elizabethan routine dating from the first English COMEDY, Nicholas UDALL's *Ralph Roister Doister* [c. 1553].)

The name Quince refers to certain tools of the carpentry trade, wooden wedges called 'quoins' or 'quines'. Quince is thought to have been originally played by Richard COWLEY.

**Quiney (1), Judith Shakespeare (1585–1662)** Shakespeare's daughter, wife of Thomas QUINEY (3). See SHAKESPEARE (10).

**Quiney (2), Richard (before 1557–1602)** Businessman in STRATFORD, an acquaintance of Shakespeare. Quiney was a dealer in fine cloth, a partner with his father, Adrian (d. 1607; a friend of Shakespeare's father John SHAKESPEARE [9]). He was evidently a respected businessman, for he represented the town of Stratford at the court of Queen ELIZABETH (1), on several occasions, and sought government relief for the town after the great fires of 1594 and 1595.

Quiney's surviving correspondence contains several references to Shakespeare as well as the only extant letter addressed to the playwright (though it was apparently never delivered). While in LONDON in January 1598, Quiney received a letter from another Stratford businessman suggesting that he try to interest Shakespeare in a real estate deal they were contemplating, and in October, again in London, he wrote a letter to the playwright asking for a loan to cover extra expenses resulting from an unforeseen delay. He apparently did not deliver this missive, which remained among his papers still sealed, probably because he was able to make his request in person; another letter of the same date, to a friend in Stratford, reports that Shakespeare promised assistance. Later during the same visit, Quiney received a letter from his father that mentions Shakespeare in connection with an otherwise obscure business deal. In addition to establishing Shakespeare's presence in London at these times, these letters also make clear the playwright's continuing involvement with the affairs of his home town.

Quiney opposed the attempt of a neighbouring nobleman, Sir Edward Greville, to enclose the town commons for sheep grazing. A drunken group of Greville's followers roughed him up one night in May 1602, and he died from his injuries. His widow was left with nine children under the age of 20, one of whom, Thomas QUINEY (3), became Shakespeare's son-in-law.

**Quiney (3), Thomas (1589–c. 1652)** Vintner in STRATFORD and Shakespeare's son-in-law. Quiney, the son of Richard QUINEY (2), ran a tavern and apparently had a reputation as a rake when he married Judith SHAKESPEARE (10) in February 1616. They were wed during Lent without obtaining the necessary special licence, for which he was briefly excommunicated. Within a month he was in worse trouble, for when one Margaret Wheeler died in childbirth in March, Quiney was named as the father of the child (who also died). He was ordered to appear as a penitent, wearing a white sheet, in the parish church on three successive Sundays, though he avoided this public disgrace by paying a fine. It has been speculated that this scandal may have hastened Shakespeare's death, for he died a few weeks later, after changing his will to protect Judith's inheritance from Quiney. Quiney established a wine and tobacco shop, but he was an unsuccessful businessman, and the shop was eventually run by trustees who assigned him a yearly allowance. The Quineys' three sons all died young. Quiney is thought to have died while visiting a brother in London sometime after 1652, though no record of his death has survived.

**Quintus** Minor character in *Titus Andronicus*, a son of TITUS (1) Andronicus. Quintus, with MARTIUS (1), is framed by AARON for the murder of BASSIANUS in 2.3. The two are executed, and their heads are delivered to Titus in 3.1.

# R

**Raleigh (Ralegh), Walter (c. 1552–1618)** English soldier, seaman, explorer, and writer. Raleigh, son of an obscure country gentleman, became a favourite of Queen ELIZABETH (1) through a combination of personal charm and a successful military career, including naval raids against Spanish overseas territories. During the 1580s Raleigh organised and financed several colonising expeditions to the New World—including the famous lost colony on Roanoke Island, Virginia—but no successful settlements resulted. He also explored the Orinoco River in South America, in search of El Dorado, the legendary city of gold.

In addition Raleigh was a poet, accepted as a literary equal by his friends Edmund SPENSER and Christopher MARLOWE (1). He wrote many poems that were circulated in manuscript, and those that have survived place him among the better poets of his day. (At least one of Raleigh's poems, 'The Nymph's Reply to the Shepherd', was attributed to Shakespeare in the *Poems* published by John BENSON [2] in 1640; also, one stanza of it—linked with the Marlowe poem to which it replies—was attributed to Shakespeare in THE PASSIONATE PILGRIM.)

A man of great intellectual curiosity, Raleigh dabbled in the magical doctrines and esoteric knowledge that were part of the budding science of the RENAISSANCE. These activities raised widespread suspicion that he was an atheist; combined with his arrogant disdain for other people's opinions, this made him generally unpopular. In 1597 he quarrelled with the Earl of ESSEX (2) over the conduct of the naval war against Spain, and they remained enemies thereafter. This feud aggravated Raleigh's unpopularity. Shakespeare may have subtly sided against Raleigh in the obscure jests of *Love's Labour's Lost*, where he seemingly parodies the circle of George CHAPMAN—which included Raleigh—for its interest in magic. The playwright may have taken such a position on behalf of his patron, the Earl of SOUTHAMPTON (2), a follower of Essex, but he may also have felt a personal aversion to the reputedly irreligious and arrogant Raleigh.

King JAMES I certainly felt such an aversion, and he accepted the accusations of conspiracy brought by Raleigh's enemies, especially Robert CECIL (1), and

imprisoned him. Raleigh was held in the TOWER OF LONDON from 1603 to 1616, during which time he began his *History of the World*, which is now considered, though incomplete, to be one of the best prose works of the day. He was released in order to conduct another search for El Dorado, on the king's behalf, but with the condition that he not attack the Spanish, whom James was pursuing as allies. However, while in South America, he raided a Spanish settlement, and on his return he was executed for treason.

**Rambures, Lord** Minor character in *Henry V*, a French nobleman. Rambures, who speaks only a few lines, shares in the French over-confidence prior to the battle of AGINCOURT in 3.7 and 4.2. His death is reported in 4.8.96, where he is said to have been the 'master of the cross-bows'. Shakespeare took this information—and the character's name—from the account of the battle in the *Chronicles* of HOLINSHED. In speech headings and stage directions of the BAD QUARTO edition of the play (1600), Rambures is designated 'Gebon', presumably indicating the actor who played the part. Scholars suppose he was either Thomas GIBBORNE or Samuel GILBURNE.

**Rannius** GHOST CHARACTER in *Antony and Cleopatra*, an attendant of ENOBARBUS. Rannius appears only once and does not speak. He is mentioned in the opening stage directions of 1.2, along with LAMPRIUS and LUCILLIUS.

*The Rape of Lucrece* Narrative poem by Shakespeare that retells the ancient Latin story of the sexual assault on Lucretia—Anglicised as LUCRECE—a high-ranking Roman woman, by Sextus Tarquinius, or TARQUIN, the son of the Roman king. Tarquin, tormented by an awareness of his own evil, proceeds to rape his victim nonetheless. Lucrece's distress is described at length, and her subsequent suicide is presented as a high-minded response to the dishonour of having slept with a man other than her husband. Before dying, Lucrece tells her husband and others of Tarquin's crime and elicits an oath of vengeance from them. The last stanza reports that they subsequently drove Tarquin and his father from Rome. An introductory ARGUMENT makes clear that, in expelling the royal family, the avengers, led by Junius BRUTUS (2), replaced the kingdom with the Roman Republic.

*Lucrece* complements the slightly earlier *Venus and Adonis,* and it is clearly the 'graver labour' promised in *Venus'* dedication to the Earl of SOUTHAMPTON (2). Both works deal with sexual desire, but the reluctant male of *Venus* is a comic subject, while the ravished female of *Lucrece* is tragic. In contrast to the essential frivolity of the earlier poem, *Lucrece* is an expressly moral work, offering the lesson that disaster will result from a serious moral offence. Scholars speculate that the notoriety achieved by the somewhat salacious *Venus*—a notoriety that is evident in many surviving references—encouraged Shakespeare to appease those possibly offended—including patrons of literature or the theatre—with a second effort of greater propriety. If this was indeed his intent, he succeeded: the critic Gabriel HARVEY (2) noted, 'The younger sort takes much delight in Shakespeare's *Venus and Adonis,* but his *Lucrece* and his tragedy of *Hamlet . . .* have it in them to please the wiser sort.'

The association with *Hamlet* is no accident, for *Lucrece* is an example of a genre that 16th-century theorists classed with tragedy, the COMPLAINT, a poem intended to reflect on the hardships of life or of a particular event. Samuel DANIEL's *The Complaint of Rosalind* (1592), an extremely popular poem, is thought to have influenced Shakespeare's choice of genre. RHYME ROYAL, the verse pattern in which both *Lucrece* and Daniel's work were composed, was regarded as the most appropriate vehicle for such elevated expressions of dismay.

The bold rhyme scheme, with each stanza ending in two couplets, is also appropriate to formal rhetoric, and *Lucrece* is extremely rhetorical, filled with antitheses, virtuoso digressions, and elaborate comparisons. Often a reader can feel overwhelmed by these forced effects and tire of Lucrece's seemingly endless laments. Such baroque passages as the 26-line description of Lucrece's complexion (lines 52–77) seem excessive to modern taste, for example. In general, however, the poet's techniques enhance his points, often in ingenious ways.

But the poem is clearly more than simply a clever technical exercise. Shakespeare was fascinated by the story, and references to it recur in his plays. The character of Junius Brutus is compared to that of the king in *Henry V* (2.4.37); MACBETH, contemplating his intended murder, thinks of Tarquin approaching his victim in terms quite similar to those used in lines 162–168. In a more casual way, Lucrece is cited as a model of chastity in *The Taming of the Shrew* (2.1.289).

Although *Lucrece* is tragic, it is not like the great plays that followed it. Instead, it resembles the early tragedy *Titus Andronicus*—a drama whose central

event is a rape and which contains several references to the story of Lucrece. Both works are crude and unsubtle, contrasting absolute good and absolute evil in a context of horrible violence. Nevertheless, in *Lucrece* several of the most important themes and motifs of Shakespeare's later work appeal. In writing *Macbeth* Shakespeare expanded on an interest in the psychology of evil that is presented forcefully in Tarquin's tortured self-awareness. Tarquin's inability to resist an impulse he detests also foreshadows OTHELLO's similar plight. Moreover, the same episode of the poem, in which Tarquin's emotions and motives and indecisions are intensely explored, seems likely to have established a precedent that the playwright followed in creating HAMLET. (Perhaps significantly, both Hamlet and Lucrece refer to the same symbol of despair, Hecuba—he in 2.2.552–553, she in lines 1447–1456.) As late as the writing of *Cymbeline* (1609), Shakespeare was still intrigued with Tarquin. As the subtle villain IACHIMO enters the heroine's bedchamber, he compares himself to Tarquin (2.2.12). Clearly, Shakespeare was fascinated with individuals who are willing to cut themselves off from basic morality, and his portrayal of Tarquin merits attention as an instance of that interest.

Lucrece also illustrates a type of which Shakespeare was fond, for although at first glance she may seem simply a passive victim, she is actually an interesting variation on the bold young women who star in the COMEDIES, such charmingly independent characters as BEATRICE in *Much Ado About Nothing* and PORTIA (1) in *The Merchant of Venice.* Lucrece, though she is indeed victimised, dictates the ultimate outcome of the catastrophe with a resolute will that demonstrates the same strength of character as Shakespeare's other Roman suicides, such as BRUTUS (4), 'the noblest Roman of them all' (*Julius Caesar,* 5.5.68). Her decision may disgust or perplex modern readers, but in terms of ancient Roman psychology and ethics, at least as understood by Shakespeare, she is a true heroine; her sense of honour guides her to the only response she could find correct. Realising that her despair is vain, she determines to take action (lines 1016–1029) and she lays a plan as efficiently as Portia devised hers against SHYLOCK; ignoring the opinions of the men around her (lines 1708–1710), she displays the confidence in her own sensibility that Beatrice shows when she defends her slandered cousin HERO. Like many of Shakespeare's plays, *The Rape of Lucrece* has a female lead.

Numerous touches in *Lucrece* reveal the poet's experience as a playwright. The poem begins at a point well along in the narrative provided by the Argument, reflecting a theatrical instinct to grab the reader with immediate excitement. The long digression to describe the painting of the siege of Troy (lines 1366–1561) allows time for Lucrece's messenger to perform his errand, a feature that will naturally have occurred to a playwright. Tarquin and Lucrece both question themselves in sharp exchanges that resemble the stichomythia that Shakespeare and other Elizabethan dramatists took from the plays of SENECA. And Shakespeare builds sympathy for one of his characters at the expense of the other. Lucrece's extensive pleading with Tarquin serves to further deepen his villainy when he remains untouched. The more reasonably she pleads, the more monstrous is his refusal to heed her. In a like fashion, Jack CADE is blackened by refusing mercy to Lord SAY in *2 Henry VI* (4.7); CLIFFORD (1) behaves similarly to RUTLAND in *3 Henry VI* (1.3).

Also, *Lucrece* contains many passages of considerable power. The detailing of the Trojan painting, mentioned above, is extraordinary; Tarquin's torch-lit approach to Lucrece's chamber (lines 302–371) is a vivid vignette of evil on the prowl, and Lucrece is touchingly vulnerable in the four stanzas of lines 386–413. Another four-stanza passage, in which Lucrece rhetorically addresses the mythological Philomel—another rape victim—is a fine Elizabethan poem in its own right. Thus, although the poem's antique rhetoric and great length can be frustrating, *The Rape of Lucrece* deserves closer examination than it usually gets, for in it the young Shakespeare demonstrated that much greater work was to come.

*Lucrece* was written between April 1593, when *Venus and Adonis* was registered for publication with the STATIONERS' COMPANY, and May 1594, when it was registered itself. During the period from June 1592 to May 1594, when the London theatres were closed because of a plague epidemic and the young Shakespeare's playwriting career was interrupted, the young dramatist turned to a more prestigious mode of literature. Poetry was then regarded as the only serious form of literature—the stage was still somewhat disreputable (see ELIZABETHAN DRAMA)—and poetry was potentially much more profitable under the patronage system that prevailed at the time. As was customary, Shakespeare offered his poems to a patron by formally dedicating them to him. Shakespeare chose to address both *Venus* and *Lucrece* to the Earl of Southampton, and the earl apparently accepted them, as the dedication to *Lucrece* implies, for its air of intimacy between writer and patron is unlike any other such passage in the literature of the time. Shakespeare's friendship with Southampton is accordingly regarded as a certain feature of the playwright's life, at least in the 1590s; this is one of the few biographical facts not supported by documentary evidence that almost all scholars accept without reservation.

The tale of Lucrece and Tarquin was well known to readers in Shakespeare's day, and the poet drew on a number of familiar sources. He used two Latin texts: OVID's *Fasti* and LIVY's *Ab urbe condita,* the two earliest surviving versions of the story. Shakespeare also used an English translation of Livy from *Palace of Pleasure* (1566), by William PAINTER (2), and he was also indebted to CHAUCER's *The Legend of Good Women* (c. 1386), which was itself based on both Ovid and Livy. At least one detail in the description of the siege of Troy was taken from the *Aeneid* of VIRGIL.

*The Rape of Lucrece* was first published in 1594 by John HARRISON (2) in a QUARTO edition (known today as Q1) printed by Richard FIELD (2). All subsequent early editions of *Lucrece* were published in octavo format, though they are conventionally known as Q2 and so on. Q6 (1616) was the last edition to appear in Shakespeare's lifetime. Each of these editions was simply a reprint of one of its predecessors, incorporating such minor changes as the printers saw fit to make, and, while they all contain variant readings, none is thought to reflect any changes that Shakespeare made. Q1 is therefore regarded as the only authoritative text, and it is the basis for modern editions.

**Ratcliffe, Sir Richard (d. 1485)** Historical figure and character in *Richard III,* a follower of RICHARD III. Ratcliffe is a minor underling, distinctive chiefly for his efficient executions of RIVERS, GREY (2), and VAUGHAN in 3.3 and HASTINGS (3) in 3.4. The historical Radcliffe was a long-time and trusted adviser of Richard who had fought with him at TEWKESBURY. He died at the battle of BOSWORTH FIELD.

**Ratsey, Gamaliel (d. 1605)** English highwayman and theatre-goer. Ratsey was hung for his crimes in March 1605, and later in the year an anonymous biography of him, *Ratseis Ghost,* appeared, of which a single copy survives. In one episode of it, Ratsey displays a fondness for theatre and an awareness of current LONDON enthusiasms. The highwayman reportedly hired a travelling company of actors to perform for him at an inn. He delivered a detailed critique of their profession in which he complained of actors who 'are grown so wealthy that they have expected to be knighted'—a possible reference to Shakespeare's acquisition of a COAT OF ARMS. Nevertheless, he paid his players 40 shillings, twice what they expected. However, the next day he robbed them on the highway, getting back his 40 shillings and more. Before he left them he amused himself by advising the leading actor to go to London to pursue his career. He remarked on the fame of 'one man'—meaning Richard BURBAGE (3)—as HAMLET and elaborated on the possibility of earning enough money to 'buy thee some place or lordship in the country'. He was perhaps referring to the success of Shakespeare—who had bought NEW PLACE in STRATFORD eight years earlier—or, more probably, that of

William ALLEYN, who had bought a country manor in 1603.

**Rebeck, Hugh**   Character in *Romeo and Juliet.* See MUSICIANS (2).

**Redgrave, Michael (1908–1985)**   British actor. Redgrave, the son of actors, was briefly a teacher before turning to the theatre in 1934. After World War II he divided his time between stage and FILM. His Shakespearean parts included HAMLET—on several stages, including that at ELSINORE—LEAR, MACBETH, SHYLOCK, and ANTONY. He also wrote two plays and a book on acting. He was knighted in 1959. His daughters Vanessa (b. 1937) and Lynn (b. 1943) are well-known actresses of stage and film.

**Reed, Isaac (1742–1807)**   British scholar, editor of the First VARIORUM EDITION of Shakespeare's works. Reed, the son of a London baker, became a lawyer but eventually focussed largely on literature. He published editions of old plays and wrote *Biographia Dramatica* (1782), a collection of critical biographies of English playwrights. Reed was a close friend of the Shakespearean scholar George STEEVENS, and he helped edit Steevens' 1785 edition of Shakespeare's works. As his friend's literary executor, he posthumously expanded his 1778 edition of Shakespeare into the First Variorum, and revised and augmented Steevens' already copious annotations.

**Regan**   Character in *King Lear,* one of the villainous daughters of King LEAR. In 1.1 Regan and her sister GONERIL hypocritically claim to love their father in order to share the portion of the kingdom lost by the honest CORDELIA, their younger sister, who frankly admits that her husband as well as her father will receive a share of her love. Regan follows Goneril's lead, and they humiliate Lear once he has surrendered power to them and their husbands. She is led on also by her husband, the Duke of CORNWALL, and supports him when he performs the play's most appalling act of cruelty and puts out the eyes of the Earl of GLOUCESTER (1), in 3.7. Cornwall is killed while performing this deed, and Regan sets her sights on Goneril's lover, the ambitious EDMUND, but her stronger sister poisons her. Regan is last seen as she withdraws, overcome by sickness. Only later is word of her death, and of Goneril's confession as to its cause, brought to the other characters. Regan is the least distinguished of the play's villains, being chiefly a follower of her sister and her husband, though her somewhat cool and aloof quality presents a contrast with the more energetic Goneril.

**Rehan, Ada (1860–1916)**   American actress. Born Ada Crehan (a printer's error in a playbill gave her a stage name), Rehan was for many years the leading actress in Augustin DALY's New York company. She specialised in classical comedy and played several of Shakespeare's heroines, including ROSALIND, VIOLA, and the part for which she was best known, KATHERINA in *The Taming of the Shrew.*

**Reignier, Duke of Anjou and King of Naples (1409–1480)**   Historical figure and character in *1 Henry VI,* one of the French leaders and father of MARGARET (1). Like the other French leaders, Reignier is depicted as a boastful but ineffectual warrior who demonstrates that the French could not have defeated England but for dissensions among the English. He is not himself of any importance in the play, but his presence paves the way for the appearance of his daughter in Act 5. She will marry HENRY VI and become a principal character in *2* and *3 Henry VI.*

The historical figure on whom Reignier is based is better known as René the Good, a proverbially popular ruler of Anjou and parts of Provence, who governed his territories wisely and displayed a penchant for literature and the arts. He wrote the text and may have painted the illustrations of one of the most beautiful of late medieval manuscripts, known as *King René's Book of Love.* René inherited the kingdom of Naples, including most of southern Italy, from a distant relative, but he ruled there for only four years; he was driven out in 1442 by Alfonso of Aragon, who ruled in Sicily. However, while René retained no kingly income or power (from Naples or from more remote claims to the kingdom of Hungary and the former Crusader kingdom of Jerusalem), his royal status made him an important figure in European international relations. His daughter was thus a fitting bride for a king of England.

**Reinhardt, Max (1873–1943)**   German theatrical producer. In the early 20th century, after 10 years as a notable character actor (specialising in old men), Reinhardt began his career as a leading avant-garde director of the classics, especially Shakespeare and the ancient Greek drama. To involve the spectators more closely than before, he extended the stage into the auditorium, where it was surrounded on three sides by seats, and he used rhythmic movements of crowds of players to sweep the audience into the world of the play (he is still considered the greatest master of crowd scenes). His use of a revolving stage quickened the pace and variety of scenes; he also added dramatic lighting and scenic effects.

Reinhardt worked mostly in Berlin until 1920 and in Vienna until 1933, but periodically produced plays in London and New York as well. In 1933 he fled the Nazi regime and lived in America for the rest of his life. Reinhardt's revolutionary techniques were both acclaimed and condemned. Particularly notable among his Shakespearean productions were his 1912 staging of *A Midsummer Night's Dream* (which he later made as a FILM starring James Cagney and Mickey Rooney [1935]) and his 1921 presentation of *The Merchant of Venice* in a notorious blue and white cubist set.

**Renaissance**    Period of rich development in European culture that marked the end of the Middle Ages and the beginning of the modern era. The Renaissance arose in ITALY in the 14th century and spread throughout Europe over the next 300 years, continuing its development in peripheral regions such as England through the first half of the 17th century. Characterised by humanism, which proposed a focus on human nature and individual expression in art and literature, the Renaissance was sparked by an enthusiasm for the newly rediscovered cultural worlds of classical Greece and Rome. The period saw extraordinary developments in more mundane areas as well, as secular governments emerged from the dominance of the medieval church, the modern commercial world of banks and debt-financed expansion arose, and Europe's expansion into the New World and Asia began. Printing magnified all these effects by permitting an unprecedented diffusion of ideas. The Reformation translated the age's spirit into new religious movements in many parts of northern Europe, including England, and a revitalised Counter-Reformation Catholic Church elsewhere.

In England, the Renaissance began in the early 16th century, though its greatest development was during the reign of Queen ELIZABETH (1) (1558–1603). The grandest accomplishments of the English Renaissance were in literature, especially in poetry and ELIZABETHAN DRAMA. Its leading figures in poetry were Edmund SPENSER, Philip SIDNEY, and Shakespeare and in drama, Shakespeare, Christopher MARLOWE (1), and Ben JONSON. The leading writers of prose included Thomas MORE and Francis Bacon (1561–1626). A flood of translations from Latin, Greek, and contemporary European languages enlivened England's intellectual life. John FLORIO's translation of MONTAIGNE, Arthur GOLDING's version of OVID's *Metamorphoses,* and Thomas NORTH's rendering of PLUTARCH stand out. In philosophy, *The Laws of Ecclesiastical Polity* (1593–1597) by Richard Hooker (c. 1554–1600) established a Protestant doctrine of religious government in elegant prose.

**Revenge Play**    Genre of ELIZABETHAN and JACOBEAN DRAMA, represented in Shakespeare's work by *Titus Andronicus* and *Hamlet.* A revenge play is a drama of retribution in which an evil is avenged—and often the vengeance itself repaid—in a series of bloody and horrible deeds. Often called the horror movies of their time, revenge plays were intended to be spectacular

theatrical events, and they were extremely popular. On stage they typically featured murders and physical mutilations, insanity (or feigned insanity), and supernatural visitations, all enacted in a bravura style coloured by extravagant imagery and bold rhetoric. Thomas KYD, with his *The Spanish Tragedy* (c. 1587), led English playwrights in the development of the genre, which was based largely on the works of the Roman dramatist SENECA. Other notable revenge plays include *The White Devil* (1612) and *The Duchess of Malfi* (1613–1614) by John WEBSTER (2), George CHAPMAN's *Bussy D'Ambois* (c. 1604), and the mysterious UR-HAMLET.

Of Shakespeare's two full-scale revenge plays, *Titus* is a perfect example of the genre, but *Hamlet* is somewhat restrained by a more complex attitude towards retribution. Shakespeare also included elements from the genre in other works, especially *Richard III, Julius Caesar,* and *Macbeth.*

**Reynaldo (1)**    Minor character in *Hamlet,* servant of POLONIUS. In 2.1 Reynaldo is assigned to spy on his master's son, LAERTES, who is studying in PARIS (1), to make sure he is not engaging in 'such wanton, wild, and usual slips / As are companions . . . / To youth and liberty' (3.2.22–24). Reynaldo hears out his employer's long-winded instructions and departs, disappearing from the play.

This brief episode humorously illustrates the corrupt moral tone of HAMLET's DENMARK, paralleling the later, more sinister use of spies—ROSENCRANTZ AND GUILDENSTERN—by the KING (5). It also displays the intrusiveness and love of spying that eventually bring Polonius to his death. Reynaldo is clearly more sensible than his master, hesitating at times over his orders, but he has little real personality.

In the BAD QUARTO of *Hamlet,* Reynaldo is named MONTANO and Polonius, CORAMBIS. Scholars speculate that these names may reflect a satirical intention in the creation of Polonius and Reynaldo—either in Shakespeare's original conception or in his source, the UR-HAMLET—that the playwright decided not to pursue.

**Reynaldo (2)**    Character in *All's Well That Ends Well.* See STEWARD (1).

**Reynolds (1), Frederick (1764–1841)**    English playwright and theatrical entrepreneur, producer of operatic versions of several of Shakespeare's plays. Reynolds altered Shakespeare's texts freely, cutting large sections and often combining elements from several plays. Most of the scores for these light operas were written by Henry Rowley BISHOP (2), though he sometimes employed music written for other purposes by such composers as Mozart and Thomas ARNE. Reynolds' Shakespearean productions were *A Midsummer*

*Night's Dream* (1816), *The Comedy of Errors* (1819), *Twelfth Night* (1820), *Two Gentlemen of Verona* (1821), *The Tempest* (1821), *The Merry Wives of Windsor* (1824), and *The Taming of the Shrew* (1828). As a young man, Reynolds was educated as a lawyer but turned to the theatre instead. He wrote more than 200 plays, the first of which was produced in 1785. They were mostly light comedies and melodramas; his most popular work, *The Caravan* (1803), featured a live dog that performed an on-stage rescue of a child from a tank of water.

**Reynolds (2), William (1575–1633)**  Resident of STRATFORD and friend of Shakespeare. In his will, Shakespeare left Reynolds money to buy a memorial ring, a common gesture of friendship, but no more is known of their relationship. Reynolds was a Catholic whose family sheltered a Jesuit priest in the dangerous days of the early 17th century, when anti-Catholic feeling ran high in England. He prospered, however, and died one of the principal landowners of Stratford.

**Rhyme Royal**  Verse pattern in which a stanza has seven lines, each in iambic pentameter (see METRE), rhyming *ababbcc*. Rhyme royal is used in *The Rape of Lucrece* and *The Lover's Complaint;* each of these works is a COMPLAINT, a genre for which the pattern was recommended by 16th-century treatises on poetry. This practise was doubtless inspired by CHAUCER's great use of rhyme royal, which is still sometimes called the Chaucerian stanza. Rhyme royal dominated English poetry in the 15th and 16th centuries. It went out of style entirely in the early 17th century, although it has reappeared occasionally in recent times—e.g., in long poems by John Masefield and W. H. Auden. Rhyme royal is a form of great flexibility and power, capable of carrying a sustained narrative without becoming monotonous, and its subtle rhyming is well suited to a wide range of effects, from simple description to ironic witticism.

**Rice, John (active 1607–1630)**  English actor, a member of the KING'S MEN and one of the 26 men listed in the FIRST FOLIO as the 'Principall Actors' in Shakespeare's plays. As a boy actor, Rice was the apprentice of John HEMINGE in 1607. He is thought to have been considered the best boy actor in the company, for twice, in 1607 and 1610, the King's Men paired him with their leading actor, Richard BURBAGE (3), when they provided players for ceremonial occasions. In 1611 Rice was a member of the LADY ELIZABETH'S MEN, but he rejoined the King's Men in 1619. No record of Rice as an actor has survived after 1625, but he is probably the 'John Rice, clerk of St Saviour's' mentioned by Heminge in his will (1630), so it appears that he retired from the stage and became a church official.

**Rich (1), Barnabe (Barnaby Riche) (c. 1540–1617)**  Contemporary of Shakespeare, author of the principal source of *Twelfth Night.* Rich was a soldier who retired from a career of active campaigning in Europe and Ireland and turned to literature. He wrote several tracts on military and political matters, but he is best known for a collection of romantic tales, derived mostly from Italian originals. One, entitled 'Apolonius and Silla'—taken from a tale by François BELLEFOREST, who had it from an anonymous Italian play, *Gl'Ingannati*—provided Shakespeare with the main plot of *Twelfth Night.* Another of Rich's tales may have inspired FALSTAFF's departure in a laundry basket in 3.3 of *The Merry Wives of Windsor.*

**Rich (2), John (1692–1761)**  British theatrical producer. Rich was a comic actor who popularised the COMMEDIA DELL'ARTE character Harlequin in England, but he is much better known as a theatrical entrepreneur. Rich staged a number of Shakespeare's plays with a company whose leading player was James QUIN. Rich's productions of *Measure for Measure* (1720) and *Much Ado About Nothing* (1721) were especially important, in that they restored much of Shakespeare's text after William DAVENANT's radical alterations. Rich was the founder of London's Covent Garden Theatre in 1733. In the 1750s he produced *Romeo and Juliet* with Spranger BARRY (3) as ROMEO, in rivalry with David GARRICK's presentation, in the '*Romeo and Juliet* war'.

**Richard II, King of England (1367–1400)**  Title character of *Richard II,* king deposed by Henry BOLINGBROKE (1). Richard is a self-centred man and an inept ruler; his fall seems both deserved and inevitable. Nevertheless, Shakespeare elicits strong sympathy for the fallen king as he suffers painful psychological trauma before coming to accept his fate.

It is quickly established that Richard is an incompetent king. In 1.2 we learn that Richard, before the play begins, had arranged the murder of his uncle the Duke of GLOUCESTER (6), an admired member of the royal family. Furthermore, his ordinary conduct as king is persistently disastrous. When his 'coffers, with too great a court / And liberal largess, are grown somewhat light' (1.4.43–44), he turns to extortionate abuses of the public. And he seizes the estate of John of GAUNT, rightly the inheritance of the exiled Bolingbroke. This not only stimulates Bolingbroke's rebellion, but it alarms many other nobles, who fear that their own holdings may similarly be in jeopardy. Richard's wrong-headedness is exemplified by his obstinate refusal to heed the good advice of his uncles Gaunt and the Duke of YORK (4). He delights in ceremony and the trappings of power, and his rhetoric is windy. Narcissistic and arrogant, he does not rule; he enjoys himself in the role of ruler.

Despite all his boasting, Richard cannot use the power of his position, and Bolingbroke's triumph, when it comes, is almost effortless.

However, in political decline Richard becomes a more sympathetic character. His speech is no less extravagant, but now his mannered style is plainly a manifestation of inner distress. He is a more complex person than he had seemed earlier; in his isolation, he is intensely introspective and racked with anxiety, alternating between unjustified hope and exaggerated despair. Finally, imprisoned and due to be killed, he acknowledges that his own failings have played some part in his fall: 'I wasted time, and now doth time waste me' (5.5.49). Richard, with his penchant for strong imagery and elaborate metaphor, is the first of Shakespeare's protagonists to demonstrate an extraordinary imagination and artistic sense. A complex and ambiguous personality, Richard foreshadows the great heroes of Shakespeare's later TRAGEDIES.

Richard's poetic language and love of ceremony place him in striking opposition to the prosaic and practical Bolingbroke. This powerful contrast reflects a basic human conflict between the doer and the dreamer. It also enhances Richard's strong symbolic role as the last representative of the medieval England of Edward III, in which the ethos of chivalry was still dominant. The passing of this nostalgically romantic period is a major theme of the play.

The historical Richard is for the most part ignored by Shakespeare, who focusses entirely on the last year of a 22-year reign. When Edward III died, Richard, his grandson and heir (see PLANTAGENET [1]), was only 10 years old. The young king seems to have been fond of pomp and splendour, and he had a reputation as a dilettante, but he was also courageous. At 14 he faced a murderous crowd during the great peasants' rebellion of 1381 and convinced them to disperse. However, England was governed during Richard's minority by his uncles, especially the Duke of Gloucester. When Richard attempted to assert himself 10 years later, an armed conflict ensued and Richard was nearly forced from the throne. A coalition of nobles ruled for two years, but Richard gathered supporters and successfully began to rule at the age of 22. He seems to have governed well. His reign was noted for his emphasis on peace; he concluded truces in Ireland in 1394 and, more important, in the HUNDRED YEARS WAR against FRANCE (1) in 1396. (By the latter treaty, he agreed to marry the young Princess Isabel, who was a child, not the adult QUEEN [13] of the play.) In 1397 another rupture between the king and Gloucester resulted in the duke's imprisonment and death. Modern scholarship tends to confirm the contemporary opinion that Richard was responsible for his uncle's murder, but the truth cannot be ascertained.

The political events of the play are roughly accurate—Shakespeare followed his sources, for the most part—but the emphasis on Richard's incompetence is distinctly overdrawn. His departure for Ireland, shortly after seizing Gaunt's estate and alienating the nobility, was a grave error, but even worse was his delay in returning once Bolingbroke's invasion had begun. This procrastination, as well as the dismissal of much of his force upon arrival in England, appears to have been advised by Richard's second-in-command, AUMERLE, who promptly deserted his master, an event that Shakespeare omits. Richard was given sworn oaths by NORTHUMBERLAND (1), who was speaking for Bolingbroke, that the latter did not intend usurpation and would disarm if Gaunt's titles and estates were restored to him. Richard accepted these terms and unknowingly allowed himself to be taken prisoner. Thus his final fall was due as much to treachery as to wrongdoing on his part. The deposition scene (4.1) is entirely fictitious; Bolingbroke certainly could not afford to give his enemy a platform, and he did not. Sir Piers EXTON's murder of Richard is also a fiction, although Shakespeare took it from his source and doubtless believed it. A contemporary report states that Richard died of starvation, either deprived of food by his gaolers or refusing to eat. The actual circumstances of Richard's death are not known, although his bones were exhumed in 1871 and no signs of violence were found.

### Richard II

#### SYNOPSIS

*Act 1, Scene 1*
Henry BOLINGBROKE (1) appears before his cousin King RICHARD II and accuses Thomas MOWBRAY (1) of treason for having embezzled funds, hatched unspecified plots, and murdered Thomas, Duke of GLOUCESTER (6), Bolingbroke and the king's uncle. Mowbray claims innocence and demands a trial by combat. Despite Richard's appeals seconded by Bolingbroke's father, John of GAUNT, the two noblemen insist on fighting; Richard gives in and designates a time and place for the encounter.

*Act 1, Scene 2*
The DUCHESS (2) of Gloucester, widow of Thomas, demands that Gaunt avenge her husband's murder, but he replies that, since the murder was ordered by the king, God's deputy, vengeance can be exacted only by God. The Duchess then prays that Mowbray shall be killed in the trial by combat.

*Act 1, Scene 3*
Mowbray and Bolingbroke prepare for the trial by combat, but at the last moment the king rules that the two disputants shall be banished from England—

Bolingbroke for 10 years, Mowbray for life. Before departing, Mowbray asserts that Bolingbroke's disloyalty will eventually surface, to Richard's regret. Richard, seeing Gaunt's despair at his son's banishment, reduces the sentence to six years, but Gaunt replies that he shall die before that time is up. The king, unmoved, departs. Gaunt attempts to cheer up his disheartened son, but to no avail.

### Act 1, Scene 4

The Duke of AUMERLE, who has pretended friendship with Bolingbroke, reports to the king that that nobleman has left England. Richard reveals his enmity towards Bolingbroke, on account of the latter's widespread popularity. Sir Henry GREENE (1) remarks that a rebellion in Ireland requires the king's attention, and Richard says that he will lead an army there. This expedition will be financed by selling to entrepreneurs the right to collect taxes and by forcing loans from wealthy noblemen. Sir John BUSHY brings news that John of Gaunt is very sick and has asked to see the king. Richard hopes for his immediate death so that he may confiscate his wealth for the Irish campaign.

### Act 2, Scene 1

The dying Gaunt confides to his brother the Duke of YORK (4) his desire to give good counsel to Richard before he dies, and he goes on to rage against the king's shady financial practises. The king arrives with a group of nobles. Gaunt reprimands him, and the angry Richard reminds his uncle of his power to have him killed; Gaunt dares him to do so, accusing him of the murder of Gloucester and asserting that the shame the king has brought on the family will kill him in any case. Gaunt retires to bed, asserting that he will soon die. The Earl of NORTHUMBERLAND (1) brings word that Gaunt has in fact died, and Richard immediately declares that he will confiscate his late uncle's wealth. York, horrified, chastises the king for this illegal seizure, comparing it ominously with the usurpation of a crown. He then exits. The king, ignoring this outburst, plans his departure for Ireland and appoints York to be governor of England in his absence. He leaves with his entourage. The remaining nobles—Northumberland, Lord ROSS (2), and Lord WILLOUGHBY (3)—discuss the king's abuses. They fear that the seizure of Gaunt's estate will set a precedent that threatens all aristocrats. Northumberland reveals that Bolingbroke is returning to England with an army, and the noblemen decide to join him.

### Act 2, Scene 2

The QUEEN (13) speaks to Bushy and BAGOT of her strange grief and depression, stimulated by Richard's departure for Ireland. Greene arrives with news that Bolingbroke has invaded England and been joined by several noblemen. York arrives, bewailing the difficulty of defending the realm when Richard has taken all available armed forces with him. A SERVANT (7) brings word of the death of the Duchess of Gloucester, from whom York had hoped to borrow money. York, undone by this news, wishes Richard had cut off his head so that he would not have to deal with his present dilemma: both king and invader are his kinsmen, and he feels he owes loyalty to each of them. Uncertain what to do, York leaves with the Queen. Bushy, Bagot, and Greene decide to flee, realising that trouble lies ahead for the king's favourites.

### Act 2, Scene 3

Bolingbroke and Northumberland, on the march, meet Northumberland's son Harry PERCY (2), who brings news that York and a small force are stationed nearby at Berkeley Castle. Ross and Willoughby also join the invading army. Lord BERKELEY enters. He bears York's demand that Bolingbroke explain his presence in England. York himself follows, and he castigates his nephew for disloyalty to the king. Bolingbroke insists that he has returned only to claim what is rightfully his—the estate of his father, Gaunt. Bolingbroke's supporters back him up. York continues to insist on the treasonous nature of their opposition to the king, but he declares that he will remain neutral, lacking power enough to oppose them, and he offers them the hospitality of the castle. Bolingbroke says that he must first go to BRISTOL to capture Bushy and Bagot.

### Act 2, Scene 4

A Welsh CAPTAIN (4) tells the Earl of SALISBURY (1) that his troops cannot be prevented from deserting Richard's cause, after 10 days with no word from the king. He tells of rumours that Richard is dead and cites dire omens that seem to support them. Salisbury foresees Richard's fall.

### Act 3, Scene 1

Bushy and Greene are prisoners of Bolingbroke, who condemns them to death, asserting that they have misled the king and caused bad relations between the king and his queen. Further, Bolingbroke alleges that they caused the king to banish him and that they then took his property in his absence.

### Act 3, Scene 2

Richard, having returned from Ireland, responds to news of Bolingbroke's successes with wild emotional swings, veering between confidence in divine support and dark despair. Finally, informed that York has joined Bolingbroke, he subsides into resignation and concedes defeat.

### Act 3, Scene 3

Bolingbroke, outside FLINT CASTLE, learns that the king has sequestered himself within, and he sends

Northumberland to negotiate with him, offering to submit completely to Richard provided that Gaunt's estates are restored to him and that his banishment is repealed. Richard appears with kingly pomp and arrogance, but he immediately agrees to Bolingbroke's terms. Awaiting Bolingbroke himself, Richard falls into despair, ranting about his own deposition and death. When Bolingbroke appears, Richard accepts the successful rebel's pretended submission but remarks that he has merely yielded to strength.

### Act 3, Scene 4

The disconsolate Queen hides herself in a garden, hoping to overhear political news in the conversation of the GARDENER and his assistants. The Gardener tells of the executions of Bushy and Greene and speculates that the king, having been seized by Bolingbroke, will soon be deposed. The Queen erupts in anger, demanding to know why the Gardener thinks this; he asserts that Richard's situation is common knowledge in London. The Queen, enraged and in despair, leaves for the city.

### Act 4, Scene 1

In WESTMINSTER (3) HALL Bolingbroke holds court. Bagot, who has turned informer, accuses Aumerle of having plotted to murder the Duke of Gloucester. After much argument, the debate is postponed, to be settled at a future trial by combat. York brings word of Richard's willingness to abdicate. The Bishop of CARLISLE speaks against the deposition of God's appointed ruler, predicting civil war as a consequence. He is arrested by Northumberland and placed in the custody of the ABBOT of Westminster. Richard is summoned, and he reluctantly surrenders his crown and sceptre to Bolingbroke. Looking in a mirror, he reflects on the fragility of kingly glory, and he smashes the glass to prove his point. Richard is taken away, and Bolingbroke, departing with his entourage, sets the date for his own coronation. Aumerle, the Abbot, and Carlisle are left behind, and they agree to plot against Bolingbroke's usurpation.

### Act 5, Scene 1

The Queen intercepts Richard as he is escorted to the TOWER OF LONDON and tries to raise his spirits. He recommends patient resignation. Northumberland appears with a change of plans: Richard is to be taken to POMFRET CASTLE, and the Queen is to be banished to FRANCE (1). Northumberland resists their pleas that they be permitted to remain together, and the royal couple bid each other an emotional farewell.

### Act 5, Scene 2

The Duke of York, after describing Bolingbroke's triumphant entry into London to the DUCHESS (4), asserts his adherence, however dismayed, to the new

king. He discovers that his son, Aumerle, is part of a plot against Bolingbroke, and he sets off to warn the king and, to alleviate the stain on his honour, turn in his son. The Duchess fails to persuade him against this course; she then tells Aumerle to ride at top speed and reach the King before his father can and plead for mercy.

### Act 5, Scene 3

Bolingbroke laments that his delinquent son, the PRINCE (6), spends his time with criminals and harlots, but he hopes for better behaviour in the future. Aumerle enters and extracts a promise of a pardon for an offence that he wishes to confess. York arrives and warns the king of the plot against him, recommending severity. The Duchess enters and pleads for mercy for Aumerle, and Bolingbroke grants it.

### Act 5, Scene 4

Sir Piers EXTON, reflecting on remarks made by Bolingbroke, believes that the new king wants Richard killed, and he resolves to do the deed himself.

### Act 5, Scene 5

Richard, in his prison cell, meditates on his lonely, defeated state. A former GROOM of Richard's appears, offering sympathy and raising the prisoner's spirits. However, he is ousted by the KEEPER (4), who brings Richard's meal. The Keeper refuses to taste the food for poison, as is his usual practise, citing orders from Exton. Aggravated, Richard strikes him, and the Keeper's cries summon a group of murderers, led by Exton, who assault Richard. He fights back but is killed. Exton, conscience-stricken, regrets the deed.

### Act 5, Scene 6

Bolingbroke receives word of the final defeat of resistance to his rule, including that of the Bishop of Carlisle, who is brought in as a prisoner. Bolingbroke forgives him magnanimously. Exton arrives with a coffin bearing Richard. He expects thanks, but Bolingbroke repudiates him, deploring the deed and regretting that his words had sparked it. He declares that he will lead a crusade to the Holy Land to atone for his part in Richard's death.

### COMMENTARY

Shakespeare wrote *Richard II* entirely in verse. The measured cadences of iambic pentameter lend a musical grandeur to the play's most didactic and explanatory passages, and the medium of verse is natural to its highly charged language. In this play emotions are expressed by means of heightened rhetoric. For instance, the parting of Richard and the Queen in 5.1 sparks an exchange of mechanical couplets that may seem emotionally sterile. But taken over the entire work, such language impels respect, for it is boldly apparent that the characters are in the grip of something higher and more important than their own personalities. The total dominance of poetry lends the play a pointedly aesthetic tone, in striking contrast to its ostensible subject matter, a military coup. The play depicts no battles; in fact, there is little action of any kind. A trial by combat is scheduled but does not take place; an army is assembled but does not fight. York vows to resist Bolingbroke but lacks the strength to do so, and Richard crumbles immediately. Action is systematically thwarted until Richard's murder in Act 5. Language, in the form of poetry, is paramount. The disparity between political history and poetic tone points to the existence of a second level of meaning: this play is about more than the deeds of historical figures. *Richard II* basically deals with the disturbing nature of historical change rather than the events themselves.

In addition, *Richard II* is a moving human document. Richard's personality is the most prominent feature of the play, and, in one of his most brilliant portraits, Shakespeare shows us a gallant but failing human effort to come to terms with change. Richard marks a significant stage in the development of the playwright's art, for he is the first of Shakespeare's tragic heroes whose personal flaws help to bring about his own downfall. His own inadequacies as king lead inexorably to his deposition. However, Richard's greater significance lies in his response to his fate. He does not resist his destiny but accepts it. In 5.5, stirred by the beauty of music and by the love of the Groom who visits him, the imprisoned Richard comes to terms with his humanity and the suffering that goes with it. With this acceptance, Richard—and we who respond to him—transcend the universal fate and thus triumph over death.

Furthermore, Richard is persistently contrasted with the world around him. At the most superficial level, the play depicts the fall of one king and the rise of another, and this automatically invites comparison between the two rulers. Richard's poetic diction and his assertion of transcendent values stand in marked contrast with the prosaic speech and practical concerns of Bolingbroke and York, and even of the Queen, who exhorts him to fight. The play presents a bold juxtaposition of utilitarian and artistic temperaments.

Yet the play also involves a comparison of worlds. Richard's sensibility, his poetic utterances, and his self-conscious awareness of his royal status are grounded in a world of ceremonious spectacle. The gorgeous tournament of 1.1 and Richard's brilliant rhetoric on the divine right of kings, as in 3.2.36–62, have a heavy grandeur that is reinforced by such formal speeches as the conventionally high-flown grief of the Queen in 3.4 and the elaborate metaphor constructed by the Gardener in the same scene. Richard is a medieval king, fully conscious of his divine appointment to rule; his personal weaknesses emphasise the pathos of being the last such ruler in history. Bolingbroke represents a new world, that of the Renaissance. He is a Machiavellian, ready to assume any posture required by the needs of the moment. This brings him political success, but it also makes him an unknowable personality, a symbol of faceless ambition. By contrast, Richard's emotional self-exposure is much more humanly sympathetic. The rising and falling monarchs are most strikingly opposed in 4.1, in which the mere presence of the nearly silent Bolingbroke has as powerful an effect as Richard's polemics. Each regal figure attempts to impose his own reality on the scene: Richard plays the tragically overthrown representative of God, while Bolingbroke maintains the importance of legal rights and social order.

It is profoundly ironic that the anointed ruler has subverted public order, while the blasphemous rebel upholds legality. Richard, though legitimate, has failed to lead his nation and moreover has exploited the kingdom shamelessly, while the usurper Bolingbroke acts in the name of legal redress and proves to be a strong leader who brings England into a new era. Underlying this paradox is a question that was posed by Shakespeare's portrayal of King HENRY VI and that was to be answered by that of HENRY V: can the spiritual qualities that seem to offer the greatest human rewards coexist with the practical, manipulative skills needed to govern a society? In *Richard II* a potentially successful government has been created, but only at the cost of eroding the spiritual underpinnings of society. The civil disorders to come are the direct result, as Carlisle's predictions in 4.1.136–147 and 322–323 remind us.

Both principal figures of *Richard II* achieve their potential yet remain ungratified: Richard's spiritual depths open upon an abyss, while Bolingbroke's political success is dampened by the need for suppression, beginning with Richard's murder This situation reflects a contradiction at the heart of the Elizabethan conception of power: a monarch was still considered to be ordained by God, as had been true in medieval times, but a newer notion dictated that he or she was expressly sent to serve the people. This concept, which was part of early modern Europe's emergence from feudalism, was related to political developments—in England, it was part of the TUDOR dynasty's justification of Henry VII's conquest (enacted in *Richard III*): the deposed king had failed to serve the people, and the new king had been sent by God to do so. Thus a ruler should not be deposed, but, if he were, the usurper should not be replaced either. In this conundrum rested the legitimacy of the reign of Queen ELIZABETH (1) and the established politics of Shakespeare's own day. In *Richard II* it is demonstrated in the ultimate inadequacy of both the usurped king and the successful rebel.

Possible solutions to this puzzling irony are offered by Shakespeare, but only as hints concerning the play's sequels. *Richard II* was consciously written as the first in a series of plays, and it is not intended to come to a conclusion. Bolingbroke, soon to be King HENRY IV, becomes more magnanimous as the play closes, pardoning Carlisle and Aumerle and spurning Exton. He turns to religion as well. Thus an improvement in the character of the usurper is at least tentatively proposed. However, Bolingbroke's essential cynicism in this play makes such a solution difficult to believe. More promising is the introduction of a character who does not actually appear, Bolingbroke's son, PRINCE (6) HAL. His bold ridicule of his father's success, as reported by Percy in 5.3.16–19, may seem immature and unproductive, but it is undeniably fresh and youthful; Hal, at least, is entirely outside the coils of politics. His time will come (as the audience knows)—as Henry V, he will be a successful king. Thus history generates its own solution to history's dilemma: whatever may befall a king or a world, youth is always preparing new history.

Finally, too, the invocation of the future suggests the larger framework of *Richard II* and of all the HISTORY PLAYS. *Richard II* introduces the grand theme of the entire cycle: the passage of England from prosperity lost through lack of respect for a divinely ordained order, to civil disruption and war, to a resumption of prosperity under the Tudors.

As was his custom, Shakespeare took some liberties with the history his play chronicles, tightening the pace where it is dramatically desirable—particularly in 2.1 and 4.1, where in each case the happenings of months are compressed into a single day—but the treatment of historical events is much more straightforward than is the case in the earlier histories. Bolingbroke is probably a more deliberate rebel than the playwright's sources demand, and Richard is certainly a more ineffective king, but these distortions serve an aesthetic purpose, illuminating greater issues. Shakespeare always subordinates historical details to a playwright's values, and *Richard II* is, above all, a dramatic presentation of human responses to inexorable change.

## SOURCES OF THE PLAY

Shakespeare's primary source for the historical material in *Richard II* was Raphael HOLINSHED's *Chronicles of England, Scotland, and Ireland* (2nd. ed., 1587). In addition, Act 5 was particularly influenced by an epic poem, *The Civil Wars between the two Houses of York and Lancaster,* by Samuel DANIEL, which was published in

early 1595, just as Shakespeare was working on this play. Another important source was a popular anthology of biographies in verse, A MIRROR FOR MAGISTRATES (1559), which contains lives of Richard, Northumberland, Mowbray, and the Duke of Gloucester. Shakespeare's John of Gaunt, very different from Holinshed's, was probably derived from the characterisation of the Duke of Gloucester in the anonymous play WOODSTOCK (c. 1592–1595), which provided many other small hints to Shakespeare. Another influence may have been the Gaunt presented in Jean FROISSART's *Chroniques,* a French history that Shakespeare could have known in the English translation (1523–1525) by Lord BERNERS. Two French works written in defence of Richard in his own time, an anonymous chronicle known as the TRAÏSON and a poem by Jean CRÉTON, *Histoire du Roy d'Angleterre Richard,* may have been available to Shakespeare and have been suggested by scholars as possible sources for minor elements. *Edward II* (c. 1592) by Christopher MARLOWE (1) may have influenced Shakespeare's general conception of a flawed king whose downfall is triggered by immoral behaviour.

## TEXT OF THE PLAY

Shakespeare completed the text of *Richard II* sometime before its publication in mid-1597 and after the publication of Daniel's *Civil War* in early 1595. The similarity of its lyrical tone to that of *Love's Labour's Lost, Romeo and Juliet,* and *A Midsummer Night's Dream,* all written in 1594 and 1595, suggest that *Richard II* was probably written in 1595.

The play was published by Andrew WISE in a QUARTO edition, known as Q1, in 1597. The play must have been popular, because Wise brought out two more quartos (Q2, Q3) in 1598. (*Pericles* is the only other Shakespeare play to have appeared in two quartos in the same year.) These editions were reprinted from Q1 and are inferior to it, having many more errors, although some corrections were also made. Wise sold his right to print the play to Mathew LAW in 1603, and Law produced Q4 (1608) and Q5 (1615), each drawn from its immediate predecessor. Q4 contains the first printing of the deposition scene (4.1.154–318), which had earlier been withheld, presumably due to government CENSORSHIP. It seems to have been printed from a 'memorial' version, dictated or written from memory by an actor. In 1623 the FIRST FOLIO contained a version of the play (F1) that appears to have been printed from Q3, except for its last few columns, taken from Q5. (This peculiarity is thought to reflect a damaged copy of Q3, repaired with two pages from Q5.) However, F1 contains a version of the deposition scene that is greatly superior to that in Q4 and Q5, where it is clearly corrupt. This is presumed to have come from a

PROMPT-BOOK that was also used to correct the Quarto copy.

Q1 is thought to have been printed from a transcript of Shakespeare's own manuscript, for it contains irregular stage directions and other signs of the author's informal version, along with errors that seem likely to have been made by someone who already knew the play, probably a member of the cast in an early production. Thus Q1 is the basis for most modern editions, supplemented by F1, from which is taken, in particular, 4.1.154–318.

THEATRICAL HISTORY OF THE PLAY

Its repeated publication in the 1590s and early 17th century suggests that *Richard II* was quite popular with early audiences. The earliest surviving record of a particular performance is a startling one. On February 7, 1601, the CHAMBERLAIN'S MEN were commissioned by backers of the Earl of ESSEX (2) to perform the play at the GLOBE Theatre. The Earl's abortive rebellion against Queen ELIZABETH (1) took place on the following day, and it was apparently thought that the enactment of Richard's deposition would encourage the population of London to support a latter-day usurpation. It had no such effect, and, although inquiries were made by the government, no action was taken against the acting company or Shakespeare.

The second known performance of the play is also surprising: in 1607 it was performed aboard an English ship off the coast of Africa. No other particular performances during Shakespeare's lifetime are known, although the play was staged at the Globe again in 1631.

In 1681 Nahum TATE produced an adaptation of *Richard II, The Sicilian Usurper,* that was suppressed by a nervous government, despite its changed setting. Other adaptations were produced over the next century, often with material borrowed from other plays, including *King Lear* and *Titus Andronicus.* Shakespeare's play was produced several times in the late 1730s, but the play was not generally popular again until the 19th century. In a highly successful production of 1857, Charles KEAN (1) used more than 500 extras in a spectacular rendition of Bolingbroke's triumph. Beerbohm TREE and William POEL also directed versions of the play. *Richard II* has been extremely popular in the 20th century. John GIELGUD and Maurice EVANS (4) have been particularly successful Richards. The play has been produced many times in recent years, both by itself and in cycles with other history plays, on stage and on TELEVISION.

**Richard III, King of England (1452–1485)** Character in *2* and *3 Henry VI* and title character of *Richard III.* Known simply as Richard or Gloucester (see GLOUCESTER [5]) until he is crowned in 4.2 of *Richard*

*Richard III (played here by Laurence Olivier) was Shakespeare's first great creation. A dazzlingly evil villain, he is as dramatically rich as many of the heroes of later plays.* (Courtesy of Culver Pictures, Inc.)

*III,* his ambition never ceases to drive him towards that moment. Richard is more than simply a villain; his dazzlingly evil nature, combining viciousness and wit, makes him as important and valuable to the drama, especially in *Richard III,* as any hero. He was Shakespeare's first great creation, marking a tremendous advance over earlier, more ordinary characters.

Richard makes his first appearance late in *2 Henry VI,* when he is called to support his father, the Duke of YORK (8). His role is minor; he is present chiefly as a foreshadowing of the sequels to the play. He is nevertheless a cleanly drawn figure, sardonically epigrammatic. For instance, he encourages himself in battle with the cry, 'Priests pray for enemies, but princes kill' (5.2.71). His bold and wilfully, even pridefully, cruel nature is already evident, after only a few lines.

In 1.1 of *3 Henry VI* Richard's extraordinary personality bursts forth. As the nobles recount their exploits at the battle of ST. ALBANS, Richard abruptly throws down the head of SOMERSET (1), saying, 'Speak thou for me, and tell them what I did (1.1. 16).' Richard's blood-thirstiness, not unmixed with dry humour, is evident throughout the play, pointing towards the horrors he is to commit in *Richard III.* In his famous soliloquy at the end of 3.2, he describes himself as able to '. . . smile, and murder whiles I smile'; he will 'set the murderous Machiavel to school' (3.2.182, 193). Killing the imprisoned King HENRY VI, Richard raises his bloody sword and sarcastically crows, 'See how my sword weeps for the poor king's death' (5.6.63). This bloody villain is fully conscious of his own viciousness and savours it with a cocky irony that seems very modern. At the close of the play, he even delightedly identifies himself with the arch-traitor of Christian tradition, Judas Iscariot. Richard's monstrously evil nature is thoroughly established in *3 Henry VI*, in order that it may attain fullest fruition in *Richard III*.

In *Richard III* the title character has the second-longest part in all of Shakespeare's work (only HAMLET speaks more lines). He murders his way to the throne, killing his brother, his young nephews, his wife, and a number of political opponents. He is still a spectacular villain, with a fondness for commenting humorously on his atrocities before committing them. Once he becomes king, however, his wit and resourcefulness desert him; he clumsily alienates his allies, and quite simply panics when he first learns of the approach of RICHMOND. In Act 5 he dies in battle, defeated at BOSWORTH FIELD. Richmond's triumph releases England from the violence and treachery of the WARS OF THE ROSES.

The personality of Shakespeare's Richard is formed in part by his physical deformity—a hunched back—referred to many times in the plays, often by Richard himself. At the end of *3 Henry VI*, for instance, he says, '. . . since the heavens have shap'd my body so, / Let hell make crook'd my mind to answer it' (5.6.78–79). He rationalises his rejection of human loyalties by theorising that his physical nature has placed him beyond ordinary relationships. Thus he can claim, 'I am myself alone' (5.6.83). Others agree with him: a number of characters associate Richard's deformity with his evil nature. Queen MARGARET (1), for example, asserts, 'Sin, death, and hell have set their marks on him . . .' (*Richard III*, 1.3.293), and various of his enemies identify him with a range of carnivorous animals and with such repulsive creatures as spiders, toads, and reptiles.

However, our fascination with Richard derives largely from the disturbing reality that he has undeniably attractive qualities as well. He has charisma and self-confidence, and he is plainly quite intelligent. He has great energy combined with immense self-control, and, probably most tellingly, he is extremely witty. He cracks a joke even as he plots the murder of his brother in 1.1.118–120 of *Richard III*.

Richard wins admiration even as he repels because he plays to the audience directly. Through his monologues and asides, he brings us into an almost conspiratorial intimacy with him. He sometimes tells us what is shortly going to occur, and then comments on it afterwards. In practising deceit, he also takes on different roles, much as an actor does: he plays a loyal follower of his brother King EDWARD IV, a lover opposite Lady ANNE (2), a friend to his brother CLARENCE (1), and a pious devotee of religion before the MAYOR (3) and his entourage.

With the collapse of his fortunes, Richard's personality changes. He loses his resilience and subtlety; he panics and is disorganised in the face of crisis. We learn that his sleep is troubled; such insomnia was a traditional consequence for royal usurpers, and Shakespeare's sources impute it to Richard conventionally, but the playwright makes more of it, letting both Anne and Richard himself remark on it, before presenting us with an actual nightmare vision in 5.3 of *Richard III*. At this low ebb, Richard seems almost deranged. He recognises his terrible isolation from humanity and despairs, crying out in anguish that his death will neither receive nor deserve pity from anyone. However, Richard recovers his spirit later in the scene and leads his men into battle with renewed flippancy.

Richard represents a well-known type who was a popular figure on the Elizabethan stage, the grandiose villain, first embodied in *Tamburlaine*, by Christopher MARLOWE (1), still popular when *Richard III* premiered. However, the character has a longer pedigree than that. The medieval MORALITY PLAY featured a villain figure, the VICE, whose resemblance to characters in Shakespeare and Marlowe is not coincidental; both writers must have been familiar with the Vice since childhood. But Richard also incorporates a more modern archetype, the MACHIAVEL, a calculating politician whose misdeeds are directed towards particular ends. The Vice's lewd jests and common horseplay give way to a grave assessment of political interest, although verbal wit is part of the Machiavel's character. The Machiavel is a naturalistic figure—a human being, if a depraved one—while the Vice is more allegorical in nature. Thus Richard's personality has a humanly believable quality that is lacking in the criminal-king of traditional history.

It is plain that Shakespeare's character bears very little resemblance to the actual King Richard III, who ruled only briefly. Surviving accounts of his times were written largely by his enemies, and modern scholarship has discovered that the reality of his reign bore little resemblance to the version Shakespeare received and popularised.

Richard has long been envisioned as the physically repellent hunchback of legend. Thomas MORE first wrote of Richard's physical deformity, and Shakespeare followed suit. However, at his coronation Richard was stripped to the waist for anointing, in accordance with tradition, and this exposure seems to have provoked no comment. In fact, a hunched back is nowhere evident in contemporary portraits or accounts of the man. It appears to have been a malicious fiction, although Shakespeare surely believed it to be true.

More interesting are the playwright's purposeful alterations of the historical record as he had it. As was his usual practise, Shakespeare took many liberties with his already unreliable sources. For instance, at the end of *2 Henry VI*, Richard is made to participate in a battle that occurred when he was only three years old. Richard actually lived in exile until after Edward was crowned. His part in history did not begin until the battle of BARNET, enacted in Act 5 of *3 Henry VI*. Shakespeare wrote him into the action earlier, in order to begin to approach the grand denouncement in *Richard III*, which he must have foreseen as he wrote the *Henry VI* plays. Richard also provides an interesting foil for Edward's tenderer character.

This premature introduction is magnified by giving Richard the desire to rule long before the question arises in the sources. Shakespeare's Richard begins to think, 'How sweet a thing it is to wear a crown' (*3 Henry VI*, 1.2.29), fully 23 years before he comes to put one on. Not only does this generate a long, slow rise in tension, but it also emphasises Richard's nefarious ambition early. Thus, when he is finally brought down, the resolution of England's predicament is a clear one: Richard's career has been so strikingly criminal that his death stimulates no further fighting in revenge.

The historical Richard was a very different man, innocent of most, if not all, of the crimes imputed to him. Shakespeare's sources attributed the murder of HENRY VI to Richard, and the playwright added urgency to his villain's action by inventing an impetuous journey to London for the purpose. Modern scholars hold that Edward gave the order for the ex-king's death; Richard, as Constable of England, would have been responsible for seeing the order carried out. Henry's son, the PRINCE (4) of Wales, murdered by Richard and his brothers in 5.5 of *3 Henry VI*, actually died in battle. Richard appears to have opposed the execution of Clarence, which was definitely Edward's doing, historically. Richard's wife, Lady Anne, died naturally.

That Richard did seize the throne is indisputable; that he had long plotted to that end seems unlikely. He could not have anticipated Edward's death at 40, and he seems to have been committed to a career as a ranking prince. He was clearly a trusted and reliable subordinate to his brother, governing the difficult northern provinces with marked success for 12 years. Edward had named Richard, the obvious choice, to serve as Protector after his death, ruling for his son, the PRINCE (5) of Wales. But when Edward died, Queen ELIZABETH (2) and her relatives attempted a coup, keeping the news of the king's death from his brother, assembling military forces, and arrangeing for the Prince's hasty coronation. However, Richard overcame these manoeuvres and assumed his role as Protector. He apparently had plans for Parliamentary confirmation of this arrangement, along with the boy's later coronation, when another coup was attempted. Richard crushed this plot, but he now decided to forestall a third coup by taking the crown himself. It is impossible, with the evidence that is known today, to reconstruct the events of June 1483 precisely, but, as far as history indicates, this marks the beginning of the process that Shakespeare presents as starting two decades earlier. Also, *Richard III* compresses Richard's two-year reign into a few frantic weeks. He seems to have been a quite competent king, though the shortness of his troubled reign makes judgement difficult. Shakespeare was unconcerned with the strengths or weaknesses of Richard as ruler; he simply wanted to introduce Richard's splendid crash immediately after his seeming success.

Richard may or may not have murdered Edward's two sons. Once presumed guilty—at least in good part on the strength of Shakespeare's evidence—Richard has attracted defenders in recent years. It has been observed that, once securely in power, he did not need to have them killed; that the Duke of BUCKINGHAM (2), thought to have coveted the crown himself, had a better motive; that Richmond, as Henry VII, might well have killed them, as he did a number of other possible pretenders to the crown. However, the two youths were never seen again after entering the Tower in 1483, and responsibility must lie with Richard.

This does not make him the fierce killer of the plays, of course; if he did have the princes murdered, he was simply following a fairly ordinary political convention of the day. However, what Shakespeare's rendering of Richard's career lacks in historical validity, it more than makes up for in theatrical success. Richard as a magnificent evildoer has entered our cultural consciousness, and there he remains; we can hardly wish it otherwise.

## *Richard III*

### SYNOPSIS

*Act 1, Scene 1*

RICHARD III observes in a soliloquy that the victory of the YORK (1) faction has ended England's civil strife. He says that he himself is unsuited for times of peace, being deformed and thus not able to engage in the games of love that occupy the court. Therefore, he proposes to be a villain, and he reveals that he has convinced his eldest brother, King EDWARD (IV), that his other brother, the Duke of CLARENCE (1), intends treason. Clarence appears, under arrest; Richard hypocritically sympathises with him and promises to secure his release. As Clarence is taken away, Richard reveals in another soliloquy that he intends to have him killed. He discusses with Lord HASTINGS (3) the news that the king is near death from illness. In a third soliloquy, Richard details his plans to kill Clarence and to marry Lady ANNE (2), whose late husband Richard helped to murder in *3 Henry VI*.

### Act 1, Scene 2

Lady Anne, attending the funeral procession of her father-in-law, the late King HENRY VI, who was also murdered by Richard in *3 Henry VI*, curses the murderer. Richard appears and accepts her scorn, asserting that his proper place in the world is in her bed and claiming that it was the thought of her beauty that caused him to kill her husband. She spits in his face as he asserts his love. He offers her his sword with which to kill him, but she cannot do it. He continues to talk, gradually hypnotising her with words, and she finally accepts a ring from him and agrees to meet him again. She leaves, and in a soliloquy Richard hoots at her susceptibility.

### Act 1, Scene 3

Queen ELIZABETH (2) tells her brother RIVERS and her sons DORSET and GREY (2) of her fear that, when the king dies, Richard will rule in the name of her son the PRINCE (5) of Wales. Other noblemen appear, including Richard, who argues with Elizabeth. Queen MARGARET (1), the widow of Henry VI, enters and heaps curses on her old enemies. She desires an early death for the king and the Prince of Wales, as well as for Dorset, Rivers, and HASTINGS (3). She wishes on Elizabeth her own fate—to continue living after seeing her husband and sons killed and herself deposed. She curses Richard most elaborately, and, before departing, goes on to warn BUCKINGHAM (2) against him. The others are called away, and Richard instructs two murderers whom he has hired to kill Clarence.

### Act 1, Scene 4

Clarence, in the TOWER OF LONDON, tells of a nightmare in which he was drowned and went to hell, where he encountered the spirits of men whom he had betrayed and murdered. The murderers arrive. The SECOND MURDERER (2) feels pangs of conscience; in a comic exchange, the FIRST MURDERER (2) reminds him of the money that Richard has promised them, and he recovers. Clarence pleads for mercy, and the Second Murderer begins to relent. But the First stabs Clarence and carries him off-stage to drown him in a large barrel of wine.

### Act 2, Scene 1

The ailing King Edward orders reconciliation among the peers, and vows of friendship are exchanged. Richard arrives and announces the death of Clarence, to the consternation of the king, who had cancelled the death warrant. Edward is stricken by remorse.

### Act 2, Scene 2

The son of Clarence, a BOY (2), reveals that Richard has told him that the king is responsible for his father's death. The DUCHESS (3) of York curses Richard, her son, but the Boy refuses to believe that his uncle has lied. The queen arrives with news of the king's death, and mourning becomes general. Richard arrives with other nobles, and plans are made to bring the young Prince of Wales to London to be crowned. When the others depart, Richard and Buckingham conspire to join the Prince's escort and keep him from his protecting relatives.

### Act 2, Scene 3

Three CITIZENS (2) discuss the rivalry between Richard and the queen's relatives. They conclude that there is trouble ahead for England.

### Act 2, Scene 4

The queen, the Duchess of York, and the Prince's younger brother, the Duke of YORK (7), await the arrival of the Prince. They are told that Richard has imprisoned several of the queen's allies. The queen decides that she and her son York must enter a church and claim sanctuary.

### Act 3, Scene 1

The Prince is formally welcomed. CARDINAL (2) Bourchier goes to remove his brother from his sanctuary. Richard informs the Prince that he and York will be housed in the TOWER OF LONDON, a prospect that disturbs the boy. The younger prince arrives, and the two are escorted to the Tower. Richard makes plans with Buckingham and CATESBY: if Hastings resists Richard's proposed seizure of the throne, he is to be executed. Richard promises that when he is king, he will reward Buckingham with an earldom.

### Act 3, Scene 2

Hastings receives a message from STANLEY (3) telling of an ominous dream of danger from Richard, but he dismisses it. Catesby enters and suggests Richard's enthronement; Hastings disapproves. Stanley arrives, still full of misgivings. The naïve Hastings engages in small talk, before leaving for a scheduled council meeting.

### Act 3, Scene 3

Richard RATCLIFFE leads Rivers, Grey, and VAUGHAN to execution. The victims recollect Margaret's seemingly clairvoyant curses.

### Act 3, Scene 4

The council is in session. Richard withdraws to confer with Buckingham about Hastings. He re-enters, raging about plots against himself, and, when Hastings speaks reassuringly, Richard accuses him of protecting the supposed plotters and sentences him to death.

### Act 3, Scene 5

Richard explains to the MAYOR (3) that the danger presented by Hastings' plot had made it necessary to execute him immediately, without a trial. The Mayor assures Richard of his approval and leaves. Richard instructs Buckingham to spread the rumour that the imprisoned princes are illegitimate sons of the late king's illicit liaisons.

### Act 3, Scene 6

A SCRIVENER shows a document approving the execution of Hastings. He knows that this justification was prepared long beforehand. He grieves that such deceitfulness should prevail.

### Act 3, Scene 7

Buckingham reports that the Mayor has been induced to discuss the possibility of Richard's becoming king. He recommends that Richard feign reluctance to rule. When the Mayor arrives, he is told that Richard is engaged in religious devotions and cannot be disturbed. Buckingham leads the Mayor to insist, and finally Richard appears, accompanied by clergymen. Buckingham, purporting to speak for the Mayor and people, asks Richard to take the throne. Richard refuses, and Buckingham leads the delegation away, but Richard has them called back and accepts their acclaim as king.

### Act 4, Scene 1

Queen Elizabeth and the Duchess of York, with Dorset, meet Lady Anne, now Richard's wife. They are not permitted to enter the Tower to visit the princes, by Richard's order. Stanley arrives to say that Richard has been declared king. He helps the women make plans: Dorset is sent abroad to join the Earl of RICHMOND; Anne goes to be crowned, having no choice; Elizabeth will return to sanctuary.

### Act 4, Scene 2

Buckingham shows reluctance as Richard, now king, insinuates that the princes should be murdered. Richard, angry, summons TYRELL. Richard orders a rumour started that Anne is deathly ill; he reveals his intention to marry the daughter of Queen Elizabeth. Tyrell agrees to murder the princes. Buckingham returns and wishes to claim the earldom promised him in 3.1; Richard refuses him and departs. Left alone, Buckingham plans his desertion of Richard.

### Act 4, Scene 3

Tyrell reports that he has killed the princes; Richard reflects that he has imprisoned Clarence's son and married his daughter to a commoner who cannot claim the crown, and that the princes and Anne are all dead. Knowing that Richmond thinks of marrying Queen Elizabeth's daughter, he proposes again to do so himself. News arrives that the Bishop of Ely has fled to join Richmond, and that Buckingham has raised an army against Richard.

### Act 4, Scene 4

Margaret joins Elizabeth and the Duchess of York, who are bewailing Richard's murder of the princes. Margaret thanks God for this development but goes on to call for vengeance on Richard. She gloats over Elizabeth's misfortunes and departs, just before Richard arrives, with a military entourage. Elizabeth and the Duchess confront him with his misdeeds; he orders his drummers and trumpeters to drown them out with noise. The Duchess delivers a tirade against her son before departing. Richard now proposes to Elizabeth that he marry her daughter. After an extended argument, she pretends to agree and leaves. News arrives of Richmond's invasion fleet, and Richard panics, blurting out confused orders and curses. Fearing treachery from Stanley, Richard orders him to leave his son as a hostage. More news arrives of Buckingham's growing rebellion, but then comes a message that his forces and Richmond's fleet have been dispersed by a great storm, followed by word that Buckingham has been captured. His spirits restored, Richard takes command and orders his troops to march.

### Act 4, Scene 5

Stanley meets with Sir CHRISTOPHER (2), a representative of Richmond, and says that he will have to postpone his intended defection to the invading Earl because Richard has seized his son.

### Act 5, Scene 1

Buckingham is escorted to his execution. He remembers Margaret's warning to him in 1.3.

### Act 5, Scene 2

Richmond, in England, speaks cheerfully of the coming battle with Richard's forces.

### Act 5, Scene 3

Richard arrives at BOSWORTH FIELD and has his tent pitched at one side of the stage. Richmond arrives and has his tent pitched at the other side. He sends a messenger to Stanley. Richard sends his own message to Stanley, a threat that his son will be killed if he deserts. Richard retires to his tent. Stanley comes to Richmond, promising at least to delay his troops. Richmond prays and goes to bed. Between the tents, a succession of spirits appears, each the GHOST (1) of a character murdered by Richard. Each delivers a similar set of messages: they remind Richard of his misdeeds and bid him 'despair and die'; turning to Richmond, they assure him of supernatural aid. Richard wakes and despairingly acknowledges his guilt. Richmond awakens, refreshed by the visions, and addresses his troops, asserting that Richard's soldiers will willingly lose, to escape being governed by such a villain. Richard curses his pangs of conscience and speaks to his army, heaping insults on his foes. A messenger reports that Stanley refuses to march; Richard orders the hostage killed but postpones the action, for the combat has begun.

*Act 5, Scene 4*
During the battle, Richard enters, crying out for a horse, rhetorically offering his kingdom in exchange for one.

*Act 5, Scene 5*
Richmond kills Richard in hand-to-hand combat and declares victory. Stanley offers him Richard's crown. Richmond proclaims an end to England's civil wars. He announces his intention to marry Elizabeth's daughter, thus uniting the feuding factions, and prays for continued peace.

## COMMENTARY

*Richard III* seems at first glance to be a fairly simple work in its general outlines: a drama with a striking central character whose rise and fall provide a straightforward entertainment, set within a context that lends moral weight to the tale. This description is adequate up to a point, and it suggests the playwright's interest in individual human capacities for good and evil, a characteristic concern of the RENAISSANCE. But because our experience of the play is dominated by its protagonist, we may lose an appreciation of its primary theme, which is a social one: the redemption of English public life through the coming of the TUDOR DYNASTY. Only secondarily, in the magnificence of its dazzling villain-hero, does it concern individuality.

Richard's immense capacity for crime is a final, climactic instance of the disruptive aristocratic ambitions that have spurred the action in all the plays of the minor TETRALOGY. Thus Richard exemplifies something larger than his own fascinating personality. Further, even more important than his negative relationship to peace and public order is the role of fate, which inexorably brings Richard's dominance to an end. Divine providence punishes the fractious Plantagenets, through the crimes of their own last representative, and grants England a restoration of grace with the advent of the Tudors. The workings of fate are revealed in the developments of the plot, of course, but they are also reflected in the organisation of the drama. The play is powered by subtle tensions, generated by contrasting its bold protagonist with its equally bold structural symmetry.

In *Richard III* Shakespeare twice used the potent device—a favourite of his—of two matching scenes, one early in the play and the other late. The second scene echoes the first but differs in revealing ways. In one instance, Richard's attempt in 4.4 to gain Queen Elizabeth's approval of his plan to marry her daughter recalls his courtship of Lady Anne in 1.2. This time, however, Richard is in decline; not only have we seen his downfall begin in earlier scenes, but here he is not the same wooer. He apologises for his deeds, in 4.4.291–298, whereas with Anne he had boldly attributed them to his love (1.2.125ff.). Elizabeth baffles him with rejections of his oaths, stifling his assertions until he is reduced to wishing ill on himself (4.4.397–409). Elizabeth suspends the conversation in 4.4.428–429, leaving its resolution in doubt, where Anne was told where to await Richard's later visit (1.2.214–220). We feel the difference and know that Richard will not have his way this time; in fact, as soon as Elizabeth departs, his downfall resumes with quickened speed. The repetition of motifs increases the strength with which we respond to the differences in situation; we feel that there lurks something fateful in the coincidences linking success and failure.

Similarly, the appearance of the Ghosts to the sleeping Richard in 5.3 reminds us of Clarence's dream in 1.4. Again, a situation where Richard's downfall is imminent is compared with an earlier one in which his villainy is triumphant. In using this device, Shakespeare took each later incident from his sources and invented the earlier ones, which makes his intention very clear. These links unite the different stages of the narrative.

This quality in the play is heightened by the repeated presentation of fulfilled predictions. For instance, the dreams of Clarence and Richard both deal with the dreamer's later death. Moreover, much is made of specific forecasts. Queen Margaret in particular is used by Shakespeare as 'a prophetess', as she calls herself in 1.3.301. In 1.3 she predicts a rash of deaths. As Richard's victims fall, they allude to Margaret's prophecy, and, when she reappears in 4.4, we recollect the the truth of her predictions (which she refers to, in case we don't) with some degree of awe. When she asserts that Richard nears 'his piteous and unpitied end' (4.4.74), we believe her. Similarly, characters predict the future even when they are unaware of it, as when Richard names his own fate to Elizabeth, even as he thinks he is warding it off, in 4.4.397–409.

Omens are equally evocative of a world governed by fate, and *Richard III* is rife with them. Hastings' tendency to ignore them is almost comical. A Citizen of London couches his uneasiness about the political future in terms of augury (2.3.32–35); the young Duke of York's request for Richard's dagger has a foreboding quality, as Richard's reply (3.1.111) makes clear. The strawberries so pointedly introduced in 3.4 had an emblematic association with serpents and the devil that was quite familiar to Shakespeare's audiences. Most ominous of all are the omens that had attended Richard's birth, which are mentioned several times.

All of these devices create an air of myth that is supported by the uniform tone that persists throughout the play. There is no sub-plot, nor faintest evidence of romantic interest. Aside from Richard's sardonic enthusiasm for his own villainy, there is very little humour. Even the violence takes place off-stage, for the most part. The plot and themes unfold largely through talk—however absorbing and varied—rather than action. The only exceptions are the stabbing of Clarence (though not his drowning) and Richard's death in single combat, each of which constitutes a climactic moment in the play's development. Each is fairly stylised. Such a restrained rendering, despite the many opportunities for bloody tableaux—which were as popular in Shakespeare's day as they are now— produces a pronounced solemnity. Combined with the flavour of sorcery discussed above, the play's pervasive calm contributes to a sense of ritual, of magical demonstration. This surreal aura supports the mythic dénouement: Richard and Richmond—opposing paragons of Evil and Good—face each other in a grand trial by combat.

These ideas might in lesser hands have yielded a set of sermons illustrating the inevitability of divine providence. However, *Richard III* is animated by the presence of Shakespeare's first great protagonist, Richard himself. Not only does this astonishing villain speak nearly one-third of the play's lines, but he delivers all of the major soliloquies as well. Significantly, many of his prominent speeches appear early in the play so that we become accustomed to his point of view. Thus he seems to be in control of the action, until fate intervenes. His wit, his acute political acumen, and his energy enthrall us at the same time that we are appalled by his diabolical sadism. The final defeat of this extraordinary figure makes the power of fate seem all the more awesome.

Richard was a product of a newly established 16th-century tradition of magnificent villain-heroes that stemmed from MARLOWE's *Tamburlaine.* Marlowe's works were wildly popular when *Richard III* was written, and Shakespeare was not the only playwright to exploit the example they set. Shakespeare's superior talent produced a greater character, a figure whose language is not only more credibly idiomatic but also has greater lyrical power. However, Richard's dominance of the play reminds us of the somewhat derivative character of the young playwright's work. He was later to develop the capacity to create believable characters of greatly varying types in a single play, thereby surpassing Marlowe utterly.

In fact, a number of the lesser characters in *Richard III* testify to that developing talent. Buckingham's woolly rhetoric marks him as a politician who prefers

evasiveness to clarity; if he were not malevolent, he would be funny. Clarence is a moving psychological portrait of a tormented sinner whose fear of hellfire makes him writhe in agony. The unfortunate but fatuous Hastings inspires both disdain and pity. None of these figures is fully developed, but each animates effective episodes.

*Richard III* is a very unreliable guide to the history of the period it purports to describe. As he did in all of the HISTORY PLAYS, Shakespeare took liberties with his sources, and these were themselves biassed and unreliable. The last 12 years of Edward's reign are compressed into 1.1–2.1 as a cluster of related incidents. Richard's career has been notably distorted, first by Tudor historians, especially Thomas MORE, whose account was the basis for much of the tale as Shakespeare received it, and then by the playwright himself, who was concerned not with historical accuracy but rather with the aggrandisement of his villain. At the end of the play, Richard's two-year reign is collapsed into a few frantic weeks, as the success of the usurper is immediately superseded by his fall. Thus the sequence of plays that began with *1 Henry VI* comes to its close. Where King HENRY V had just been lost to England at the beginning of the cycle, Richmond arrives to play the part of a new hero at its end. The death of TALBOT, accompanying the loss of English hopes in the first play, is balanced by Richard's death and their renewal in the last one. Patriotic history is combined in *Richard III* with grand entertainment, creating a drama that has always been popular.

## SOURCES OF THE PLAY

Shakespeare's chief source for *Richard III* was *The Union of the Two Noble and Illustre Families of Lancaster and York* by Edward HALL (2) (1548), supplemented by Raphael HOLINSHED's *Chronicles of England, Scotland, and Ireland* (1587 edition). Hall's account is itself an adaptation of Thomas MORE's *History of King Richard the thirde* (1543). More's chief source, in turn, was Polydore VERGIL's Latin *Historia Anglia.* Shakespeare also adapted various details from a number of other works, including several of the plays of SENECA, OVID's *Metamorphoses,* Thomas KYD's *The Spanish Tragedy* (1588–1589), Edmund SPENSER's *Faerie Queene* (1590), and a popular anthology of biographies, A MIRROR FOR MAGISTRATES. In addition, the influence of the plays of Christopher MARLOWE (1) was plainly felt by the young Shakespeare. An anonymous play of the 1590s, *The True Tragedie of Richard the Third,* has sometimes been thought to be a source for *Richard III.* However, most current scholarly opinion holds that the slight similarity between the two plays, if it reflects any relationship, shows an influence of Shakespeare on the other playwright.

## TEXT OF THE PLAY

It is impossible to date the early history plays exactly, but several echoes of *Richard III* in Marlowe's *Edward II* indicate that Shakespeare's play was the earlier of the two. The title-page of *Edward II* reports that it was performed by PEMBROKE'S MEN, presumably before the closing of the theatres by plague in June 1592. It cannot have been written, therefore, after early 1592, nor can *Richard III* have been written after late 1591. All three *Henry VI* plays contain minor reflections of Spenser's *Faerie Queene,* published in December 1589. Thus the composition of Shakespeare's cycle seems to span the years 1590–1591, and it is thought that the four plays were written in the order in which their events occur. *Richard III,* the last of them, would therefore have been written in late 1591.

The play was not published until 1597, when Andrew WISE published the first QUARTO edition (known as Q1). It was followed by seven subsequent quarto editions (known as Q2–Q8) over the next four decades. Each of these later editions was derived from its predecessor, adding progressively greater numbers of errors; they all derive ultimately from Q1. Q1 differs considerably from the version of the play that appeared in the FIRST FOLIO in 1623. The Folio text (F1) is much superior. Not only does it contain some 200 lines missing from Q1, but its lines are more metrical, its grammar better, and its poetry more impressive. Thus, F1 is the basis for most modern editions. But Q1 remains important, for it contains some material, both dialogue and stage directions, that F1 omits.

Close study of the texts has revealed that Q1 is a 'memorial' version of the play—that is, it consists of the lines as recollected by actors who had performed them—and thus it is sometimes classed as a BAD QUARTO. However, unlike most such editions, this is a solid, actable version of the play. It even includes elaborate and accurate stage directions that are generally superior to those of F1. It has been concluded that this version was prepared by an entire acting company, rather than by only a few players, as in the more corrupt quartos. This was probably done because the company lost its copy of the play. (Only a single copy of a play was ordinarily kept, to discourage pirate publishers.) The company that performed *Richard III* in the years just prior to 1597 was Shakespeare's own group, the CHAMBERLAIN'S MEN, and the playwright may have had a hand in reconstructing the play.

Textual study further suggests that the printers of F1 worked from a manuscript, probably Shakespeare's FOUL PAPERS, that was collated with one or more quarto copies of the play, certainly a copy of Q3 (of 1602) and possibly a copy of the then-newest edition, Q6 (1622).

## THEATRICAL HISTORY OF THE PLAY

*Richard III* has always been among the most popular of Shakespeare's plays. The very large number of editions published in the late 16th and early 17th centuries suggests immediate enthusiasm for the work, and this is confirmed by many allusions to it in surviving documents of the period. Richard BURBAGE (3) is known to have played the title role in the 1590's (see MANNINGHAM), but a 1633 performance at the court of King Charles I is the earliest performance to be mentioned explicitly. The play is presumed to have been staged until the closing of the theatres by the Puritan Revolution in 1642, and several productions are mentioned in records of the Restoration period, later in the 17th century.

In 1700 Colley CIBBER (1) introduced a radically altered version of the play, which was the basis for subsequent productions for more than 150 years. It was much shorter than Shakespeare's, and more than half its lines were written by Cibber himself. This version of Richard III, presented in New York in 1751, was the first Shakespeare play staged in America, in any form. In the 19th century, elaborate productions using scores of extras were in vogue. Shakespeare's text resumed the stage in the 1870s, though it has often been considerably cut. It has been made a FILM five times, four of them silent films, including Max REINHARDT's 1919 version. Laurence OLIVIER's notable movie of 1956 has introduced many people to the play, but it is a significantly altered version—most strikingly in its elimination of Queen Margaret's furious raging. *Richard III* has been made for TELEVISION once by itself, in 1983, and twice as part of BBC series incorporating groups of the history plays: AN AGE OF KINGS (1960) and 'The Wars of the Roses' (1964), which combines the *Henry VI* plays and *Richard III.*

**Richardson (1), John (d. 1594)** Farmer near STRATFORD, a friend of Anne HATHAWAY's family. In 1581 Richardson witnessed the will of Anne's father, Richard Hathaway, and in November 1582 he and Fulk SANDELLS posted a bond necessary for Anne's marriage to Shakespeare, who was a minor; they agreed to pay £40 to the church if the wedding proved unlawful. Nothing more is known of Richardson, except that he was a prosperous husbandman who owned £87 and 130 sheep when he died.

**Richardson (2), Ralph (1902–1983)** British actor. Richardson began his career in 1921, playing LORENZO in *The Merchant of Venice.* By 1926 he was acting under Barry JACKSON (1) in the Birmingham Repertory Theatre. In 1930 he joined the OLD VIC THEATRE, with which he was chiefly associated until 1949. Among his best-known Shakespearean roles were FALSTAFF, BOTTOM, and SIR TOBY BELCH, though he also played a wide range of other parts. He appeared as BUCKINGHAM (2) in Laurence OLIVIER's FILM of *Richard III*. With Olivier and John GIELGUD, Richardson is considered one of the greatest Shakespearean actors of the 20th century.

**Richmond, Earl of (Henry Tudor, later King HENRY VII, 1457–1509)** Historical figure and character in *3 Henry VI* and *Richard III*, the victor over King RICHARD III at the battle of BOSWORTH FIELD and his successor on the throne, as Henry VII. In *3 Henry VI* Richmond plays a very minor but significant role. In 4.6 he appears as a child before the newly reinstated King HENRY VI, who predicts that the boy will become a ruler and the salvation of England. This entirely fictitious episode, which Shakespeare took from his sources, reveals the extreme pro-TUDOR bias of Elizabethan historiography and therefore of the HISTORY PLAYS.

In *Richard III* Richmond's appearance in Act 5 is prepared for by Richard's panic in Act 4 at messages announcing his approach. Richmond himself arrives in 5.2; in 5.3 he is addressed by the spirits (see GHOST [1]) that appear to Richard on the night before the battle. In 5.5 he kills Richard in hand-to-hand combat, and in the final episode, he pronounces an end to the WARS OF THE ROSES, which had beleaguered England for a generation. He is a somewhat bloodless, if energetic, leader, pious and filled with an awareness of his own high mission. In addressing his troops, he can claim as allies, 'The prayers of holy saints and wronged souls' (5.3.242). He closes the play with a speech declaring a new era of peace and prosperity for England, ending with the sentiment, '. . . peace lives again. / That she may long live here, God say Amen.'

Richmond is plainly an instrument of heavenly providence rather than a three-dimensional human being, as indicated by his rather stiff bearing and stuffy diction. He must be taken at his symbolic, ritualistic value: he is the antithesis of the ambitious nobility, exemplified by Richard, that has plagued England throughout the reign of Henry VI. He brings redemption for the crimes and sins that have been committed in the names of YORK (1) and LANCASTER (1). In a confrontation reminiscent of a medieval MORALITY PLAY, whose traditions still lived in Shakespeare's time, Richmond represents Good, winning a classic showdown against Evil.

The historical Richmond was descended, through his maternal grandfather, from John of GAUNT, the original head of the Lancaster family, and he attracted the support of such former followers of Henry VI as the Duke of OXFORD (2). He was the last surviving Lancastrian male and therefore fled England in 1471, after the battle of TEWKESBURY, and lived in Brittany

and FRANCE (1). His mother, Margaret Beaufort, Countess of Richmond, remained in England, married Lord STANLEY (3), and conspired against the Yorkist kings. She is mentioned in 1.3.20–29 of *Richard III*. She negotiated her son's marriage, announced by him in the final speech of the play, to the daughter of ELIZABETH (2), thus uniting the York and Lancaster branches of the PLANTAGENET family.

Richmond's other grandfather was Owen Tudor, a minor Welsh nobleman who had married the widow of HENRY V, the Princess KATHARINE (2) of France who appears in Shakespeare's *Henry V*. Richmond inherited from his father his title and descent from the kings of France.

After the time of *Richard III*, Richmond was to rule as Henry VII, the first monarch of the Tudor dynasty. He was a highly capable ruler, sometimes called England's greatest. He restored order following the wars and administered soundly, eventually leaving a large financial surplus to his heir, HENRY VIII. Unhinted at in Shakespeare is the historical reality that Henry VII was every bit as ruthless as the Richard of the plays. While he adopted reconciliation as a general policy, he killed troublesome people when he saw fit. In fact, Shakespeare's Richard is saddled with several reprehensible deeds that Henry actually committed. For example, Richard says that he has imprisoned Edward of Warwick, the BOY (2) of *Richard III*, at 4.3.36. But Henry incarcerated him because he was a potential claimant to the throne. After a number of people attempted to impersonate Warwick and seize power, Henry finally executed him in 1499. Shakespeare has Richard manipulate the life of Warwick's sister as well, marrying the GIRL to a low-ranking man who cannot claim the crown. This was actually Henry's doing, too.

Henry also sought to ensure the popularity of his usurpation by blackening the reputation of his predecessor, Richard. He encouraged the writing of vicious biographies that contributed to the legend embodied in Shakespeare's character. He also commissioned an official history of England from the Italian humanist Polydore VERGIL; this work, published in 1534, helped create the understanding of the English past that was available to Shakespeare when he wrote his history plays.

**Rinaldo** Character in *All's Well That Ends Well*. See STEWARD (1).

**Rivers, Anthony Woodville, Earl of (c. 1442–1483)** Historical figure and character in *3 Henry VI* and *Richard III*, the brother of Queen ELIZABETH (2) and one of the victims of RICHARD III. He is the son of Richard WOODVILLE, who appears in *1 Henry VI*. Rivers plays a very minor role in *3 Henry VI*; in *Richard III* he is a pawn in a political game, being executed for no other offence than being the queen's brother and so a presumptive defender of her son, the PRINCE (5) of Wales, who stands in the way of RICHARD III's climb to power. As he is led to his death with GREY (2) and VAUGHAN in 3.3, Rivers functions as a sort of CHORUS (1), referring to POMFRET CASTLE, scene of many such events, and recollecting the curses of Queen MARGARET (1), who had foretold his end in 1.3.

The historical Rivers served King EDWARD IV as a viceroy, governing rebellious WALES (1) with great success. After the king's death, Richard assumed the office of Protector, ruling for the new heir, as Edward had stipulated. Rivers participated in an attempt to unseat the Protector; he was imprisoned and later, after a second coup failed, was executed.

**Robert Faulconbridge (Falconbridge)**   Minor character in *King John,* younger brother of the BASTARD (1). Robert comes to King JOHN (3) in 1.1, seeking to claim his father's estate. He asserts that his brother is illegitimate, having been fathered by the late King Richard I. When the Bastard accepts this lineage and joins the royal court, Robert is awarded the estate and disappears from the play. Content with comfortable nonentity, he is depicted as inferior to the Bastard, who seeks glory.

Much is made of Robert's extraordinarily thin face, as in 1.1.138–147. This is thought to indicate that the actor who originally played Robert was John SINCKLO, whose appearance is similarly noted in several other roles.

**Roberts, James (active 1564–1608)**   Printer and publisher in LONDON, producer of several editions of Shakespeare's plays. Roberts' play publications are complicated by unusual circumstances and have been the subject of much scholarly controversy. As a publisher, he specialised in almanacs and playbills, but otherwise mostly printed for other publishers. In his long career he only registered five (possibly nine) plays with the STATIONERS' COMPANY—all within five years and all belonging to Shakespeare's CHAMBERLAIN'S MEN. Four of them were registered as 'to be stayed' (i.e., explicitly not to be published without further authorisation); in any event he did not publish any of them. Scholars speculate that Roberts was attempting either to protect the plays from piracy on behalf of the Chamberlain's Men or to pirate them himself, though both theories are difficult to sustain. One of the five plays (two if he registered nine) was in fact pirated, so the first theory seems weak. Yet since Roberts himself didn't publish any and printed only two—both from reliable and thus presumably unpirated texts—the second idea seem misplaced. The problem is probably insoluble without further evidence.

In 1598 Roberts registered *The Merchant of Venice* to be stayed; in 1600 he transferred his rights in the play to Thomas HEYES, who then hired him to print an apparently legitimate edition of the play (Q1, 1600). Also in 1600 the printer registered two more Chamberlain's Men plays to be stayed, neither of them by Shakespeare and neither eventually printed by Roberts. (An adjoining entry names four other Chamberlain's Men plays—including *As You Like It, Henry V,* and *Much Ado About Nothing*—that may or may not have been registered by Roberts. One was immediately pirated, one legitimately published in the same year, and one remained unpublished until the FIRST FOLIO [1623].) In 1602 Roberts registered *Hamlet,* and though no staying order is recorded, he did not publish the play. A BAD QUARTO was put out by Nicholas LING in 1603, and then Roberts printed a good quarto for Ling (Q2, 1604). In 1603 Roberts registered one more Shakespeare play, *Troilus and Cressida;* it, too, was to be stayed, and it too was neither published nor printed by him.

In 1600, in a straightforward, uncontroversial arrangement that is unrelated to the others, Roberts printed the second edition of *Titus Andronicus* (Q2) for Edward WHITE (1). In 1619 Thomas PAVIER'S FALSE FOLIO erroneously ascribed a backdated edition of *A Midsummer Night's Dream* to Roberts, though he is not otherwise associated with that play. Roberts sold his business to William JAGGARD in 1608 and is not recorded thereafter.

**Robertson, John Mackinnon (1856–1933)**   English literary critic. Robertson was a leading member of the school of so-called 'disintegrators' among Shakespearean scholars. He thought that passages he considered to be of inferior quality must have been written by other, lesser authors, most frequently MARLOWE (1) or CHAPMAN. Robertson thought that only one play, *A Midsummer Night's Dream,* was entirely by Shakespeare. He expressed his views in his five-volume *The Shakespeare Canon,* published over 10 years beginning in 1922, and a smaller work, *The Genuine in Shakespeare* (1930). While Robertson's work has been valuable to later scholars, his overall thesis is generally thought to be exaggerated. Robertson was first a journalist and later a leading Member of Parliament. His enthusiasm for Shakespeare led him to scholarship.

**Robeson, Paul (1898–1976)**   Black American actor. Robeson played only one Shakespearean part, OTHELLO, but his American appearances as the Moor were significant to the history of 20th-century theatre. Robeson was already well known—both as an actor and singer and as a committed socialist and opponent of racism—when he triumphed in a 1930 London production of *Othello,* opposite Peggy ASHCROFT as DESDEMONA. However, American racism blocked a tour of the United States. Eventually, in 1942, Margaret WEB-

*Paul Robeson in the title role of the 1930 London production of* Othello. *Peggy Ashcroft is Desdemona.* (Courtesy of Billy Rose Theatre Collection; New York Public Library at Lincoln Center; Astor, Lenox and Tilden Foundations)

STER (3) directed a Robeson *Othello* in America. It played in several cities before it ran for almost 300 performances on Broadway in 1943, then an American record for a Shakespeare play. The production, which was widely publicised in *Life* magazine, sparked controversy as bigots objected to interracial casting, and it considerably advanced the cause of civil rights in the American theatre. Robeson again played the part in 1950 at STRATFORD.

**Robin (1)**   Character in *The Merry Wives of Windsor*, FALSTAFF's page. Robin is briefly loaned by Falstaff to MISTRESS (3) Page and is let in on their plot against his master, which he enters with apparent enthusiasm. His role is minor, limited to announcing entrances, with the exception of a remark in which he both displays his own spirit and casts a mocking aspersion on Falstaff's size and, possibly, arrogance. Speaking to Mistress

Page, he says, 'I had rather, forsooth, go before you like a man than follow him like a dwarf' (3.2.5–6).

The same character appears in *2 Henry IV* as the PAGE (5), and in *Henry V* as the BOY (3). Robin's small size is alluded to several times in *The Merry Wives*—e.g., in 3.3.19—where he is called an 'eyas-musket', or baby sparrow hawk. Along with similar references in the other plays, these are thought to reflect the presence of a particularly small boy actor in the CHAMBERLAIN'S MEN.

**Robin (2) Goodfellow**   Character in *A Midsummer Night's Dream.* See PUCK.

**Robinson (1), John (active 1616)**   Witness to Shakespeare's will. A number of John Robinsons appear in STRATFORD records, but no information—save that one was a 'labourer'—is provided about any of them.

Like another of the will's witnesses, Robert WHATCOTT, he may have been a servant in the household of either Shakespeare or his daughter Susanna SHAKESPEARE (14) Hall. In LONDON a John Robinson leased Shakespeare's BLACKFRIARS GATEHOUSE in 1616; possibly he was visiting his landlord when the will was signed. In any case, nothing more is known of him.

**Robinson (2), Mary ('Perdita') (1758–1800)** English actress. After a short but successful career on the stage, Mary Robinson became the mistress of the Prince Regent, later King George IV (ruled 1820–1830), in 1779. He became infatuated with her when she played PERDITA in David GARRICK's version of *The Winter's Tale,* and their love affair—he referred to himself as her FLORIZEL—was followed with delight by the public, who gave her the name by which she is still best known. After Garrick, struck by her great beauty, trained her for a 1776 debut as JULIET (1), she played several other parts, including ROSALIND, before her fateful encounter with the prince. When he deserted her after two years, she did not return to the stage for fear of public ridicule. She soon contracted rheumatic fever and lived the rest of her life in various spas, supporting herself with hack literary work.

**Robinson (3), Richard (active c. 1577–1600)** Contemporary of Shakespeare, a writer and translator. Robinson's translation of the famous *Gesta Romanorum,* a medieval collection of Latin tales, was published in 1577 and 1595 and may have been a source for *The Merchant of Venice.* Robinson was an unsuccessful and impoverished writer who composed many minor works in verse and prose, chiefly on religious subjects.

**Robinson (4), Richard (d. 1648)** English actor, member of the KING'S MEN. Robinson is one of the 26 men listed in the FIRST FOLIO as the 'Principall Actors' in Shakespeare's plays, though it is not known which Shakespearean roles he played. He was in part a comedian—though he played straight dramatic roles as well. Robinson first appeared with the King's Men in 1611 as a boy playing women's roles. He was still known as a 'lad' in 1616, when Ben JONSON praised his impersonation of a woman in what was apparently a practical joke. By 1619, however, he was old enough to be a witness to the will of Richard BURBAGE (3), and in the same year he succeeded Richard COWLEY as a partner in the King's Men. He was noted for his collection of 'pictures and other rarities'. Sometime before 1635, he married Burbage's widow.

**Roche, Walter (c. 1540–after 1604)** Schoolmaster, lawyer, and clergyman in STRATFORD. Roche was master of the Stratford grammar school between 1569 and 1571, before resigning to practise law; he was replaced by Simon HUNT. Roche almost certainly did not teach

Shakespeare, who was still one of the younger students and thus taught by an assistant, or usher, when Roche resigned. Nevertheless, Shakespeare certainly knew him in later years, for he remained in Stratford and lived near the Shakespeare household, even during his rectorship of a church in a nearby town (1574–1578). He mostly practised law (on one occasion representing a cousin of the Shakespeares). Later, when Shakespeare was a successful LONDON playwright whose Stratford home was NEW PLACE, Roche lived only three doors away.

**Rochester** City in south-eastern England, setting of 2.1 of *1 Henry IV.* In an inn in Rochester, the highwayman GADSHILL learns from two CARRIERS that rich TRAVELLERS are soon leaving for London, and he gets further details on these potential victims from an accomplice, the CHAMBERLAIN (1) of the inn. In 2.2 Gadshill, FALSTAFF, and others rob the Travellers at nearby GAD'S HILL and are then robbed themselves by PRINCE (6) HAL and POINS. Rochester was the half-way point on the pilgrims' route between London and Canterbury and was thus fruitful territory for highwaymen.

**Roderigo** Character in *Othello,* a Venetian gentleman who is duped by IAGO. Roderigo believes Iago is serving him as a go-between in his attempted seduction of OTHELLO's wife, DESDEMONA, though Iago has simply pocketed the expensive presents intended for the young woman. Iago's exploitation of Roderigo figures prominently early in the play, helping to establish him as a villain. Though he eventually serves as a pawn in Iago's scheme against Othello—he is persuaded to attempt the murder of CASSIO—Roderigo's story is subsidiary to the main plot, and he functions chiefly as a foil. His gullibility foreshadows Othello's credulous acceptance of Iago, and his crass attempt to buy Desdemona's affections contrasts with both the mature love of Othello before he is corrupted and the gentlemanly adoration of Cassio.

**Rogers (1), John (active 1605–1619)** Vicar in STRATFORD during Shakespeare's later years. Rogers came to Stratford in 1605, after serving in a church in nearby Warwick. After 1611 he lived near Shakespeare's home at NEW PLACE. He was probably the 'Jo. Rogers' who witnessed Shakespeare's contract with Arthur Mainwaring during the WELCOMBE enclosures crisis in October 1614. In 1615 the town asked Rogers to intercede with one of the enclosers, William COMBE (5), but he was unsuccessful. He probably presided at Shakespeare's funeral, though no record has survived. In 1618 the town awarded Rogers a gift of a fur-lined robe but at the same time hoped that he would 'amend his former faultes and faylinges'. This may be a reference to a scandal alluded to in Francis COLLINS' will, written in 1617, in which he declares that he and Rogers had been co-trustees of a legacy left for the poor, but that the vicar and another lawyer had looted it. On the other hand, when Rogers was removed from office in 1619, public outrage led to riots and accusations of Puritan influence.

**Rogers (2), Phillip (active 1603–1604)**   Apothecary in STRATFORD, a debtor to Shakespeare. Rogers, a neighbour of the Shakespeares, bought twenty pounds of malt from the household supply of NEW PLACE between March and May of 1604, agreeing to pay later. He also borrowed a small amount of money. The total debt came to a little over £2. He repaid only sixpence, and Shakespeare, at an unknown date, sued him to collect. At his apothecary shop, Rogers sold drugs, tobacco, and—after getting a licence in 1603—ale, for which he presumably used the playwright's malt.

**Roman (1)**   Any of three minor characters in *Coriolanus,* soldiers in the Roman army. At the opening of 1.5 each soldier—designated as the First, Second, and Third Roman—speaks one brief line about the loot they are carrying away from the battle of CORIOLES. CORIOLANUS appears and remarks sarcastically, 'See here these movers, that do prize their hours / At a crack'd drachma!' (1.5.4–5). These Romans, like the civilians of the city (see CITIZEN [5]) and some of their fellow warriors (see SOLDIER [11]), serve to demonstrate the unreliability of the common people, a primary theme of the play.

**Roman (2)**   Character in *Coriolanus,* a traitor who gives information on the affairs of ROME to a VOLSCE, whose tribe, the VOLSCIANS, is at war with the city. In 4.3 the Roman, named Nicanor, meets the Volsce, named Adrian, to whom he has transferred intelligence before. He tells of the banishment of CORIOLANUS, and he advises that the Volscians attack Rome at this moment of weakness. His cool treachery is an appropriate preparation for the next scenes, in which Coriolanus joins the Volscians against Rome.

**Roman Plays**   Shakespeare's three plays set in ancient ROME. In the order in which they were written, they are: *Julius Caesar, Antony and Cleopatra,* and *Coriolanus.* The much earlier *Titus Andronicus,* though Roman in setting, is generally excluded from this classification because it is a timeless tale that neither needs nor involves any real, historical world. Each of the Roman plays is a TRAGEDY, but they are unlike the other tragedies, which are placed in virtually imaginary historical situations. These works are complicated by the history of ancient Rome, which is reasonably accurately presented, and they are thus similar to the HISTORY PLAYS. The first two plays depict episodes of the civil wars that sundered the Roman Republic in

the first century B.C., while the third involves legendary events of the republic's first days, about 450 years earlier.

*Julius Caesar* deals with the assassination of the title character, CAESAR (1), by Marcus BRUTUS (4), and with Brutus' defeat at the battle of PHILIPPI (42 B.C.) by Caesar's followers, led by his nephew OCTAVIUS and Mark ANTONY. At the play's close the victors rule Rome and its territories. However, the play is less concerned with this development than with the moral ambivalence of Brutus, a highly righteous man whose action—the killing of his ruler and personal benefactor—is intended to produce good for Rome but yields instead the evil of civil war.

*Antony and Cleopatra,* set about a decade later, tells of Antony's love affair with CLEOPATRA, queen of Egypt; of the enmity this arouses in Antony's co-ruler, now known as Octavius CAESAR (2); of Antony's defeat at the battle of ACTIUM (31 B.C.); and of the subsequent suicides of the title characters. More clearly a tragedy, *Antony and Cleopatra* centres on the moral conflict in Antony as he is torn between the stern call of Roman duty and the irresistible compulsion of love for Cleopatra and her opulent life. At the play's climax Cleopatra's suicide transfigures both lovers as she seems to transcend the play's world by approaching death as intensely as she had lived.

*Coriolanus* enacts the rejection of a great warrior, CORIOLANUS, by the people of Rome who are provoked by his prideful arrogance. It goes on to tell of his desertion to the enemy VOLSCIANS with whom he attacks the city, and of his submission to his mother's entreaties that he spare the city, after which he is killed by the Volscians. On one hand, *Coriolanus* is the most distinctly personal tragedy of the Roman plays—from beginning to end, the psyche of the doomed warrior is the central concern. On the other, it offers a broader political canvas as background for its story, and features a sharply drawn struggle between aristocrats and plebeians, where *Julius Caesar* and *Antony and Cleopatra* deal only with the high politics of the ruling class.

When he wrote plays about ancient Rome, Shakespeare dealt with material that was highly meaningful to his age, and this fact is reflected in the works. Due to the RENAISSANCE rediscovery of classical literature and art, the Roman era in the Mediterranean world was seen as the high-water mark of western culture, and the general outlines of its history were familiar to all educated people. Thus, the politics of that world, and the lives of its illustrious personages, were viewed with great interest. The moral questions found in the careers of Coriolanus, Brutus, and Antony had particular importance as they were examples taken from the most important epoch in the development of western politics.

Rome's history also had importance to Christians because it was thought of as the period of Christianity's birth. In particular, the establishment of the empire was often perceived as evidence of God's intervention in human affairs. It provided a period during which the birth of Christ and the early growth of the religion named for him could take place in relative peace and stability. This belief is acknowledged in *Antony and Cleopatra*, 4.6.5–7. Thus, the events depicted held additional meaning for the original audiences.

In fact, it is important to the Roman plays that the Roman Republic was pre-Christian. Shakespeare's repeated allusions to suicide as an honourable alternative to defeat marks a striking difference in pre-Christian morality. The allusions were unavoidable in light of Roman history, but the playwright's emphasis on it suggests that these deaths had particular significance. They point to the most important distinction of the Roman tragedies: they lack Christianity's belief in divine providence as a final arbiter of human affairs. This was a very important aspect of ancient history as it was understood in Shakespeare's day. Without God's promised redemption, the moral questions of the classical world had to be resolved within an earth-bound universe of references. The protagonists of the Roman plays look to their relations with Rome and its history and cannot consider the more 'cosmic' viewpoint to which we are accustomed—and that we see in such other tragic figures as HAMLET, LEAR, and OTHELLO. Thus, Brutus' course of action can only be ambiguous; he cannot recognise an error and gain divine forgiveness, nor can he be confident that he is right in the face of worldly defeat. Similarly, the final transfiguration of Cleopatra does not involve the presumption of divine judgement that attends, say, Othello's conviction that he faces eternal punishment, or Hamlet's dying confidence that Horatio can justify his life. Cleopatra's achievement is especially admirable for its dependence on pure human spirit

The consequence is that Rome's conflicts are never clearly organised on lines of good and evil; each side contains elements of both. We cannot identify individual figures of pure evil, like IAGO, or of complete good, like DESDEMONA, because, from the Christian point of view shared by Shakespeare and his audiences, these categories simply could not exist prior to God's illumination of the world through Christ. VOLUMNIA, for instance, is not evil but is merely blind to the effects of her actions, and Brutus is a wholly moral man who even so cannot be seen as good, either by himself or by others. The deaths in defeat of Brutus, Antony, and Coriolanus all leave us aware of the limited spiritual possibilities they have had available to them, and Cleopatra's death offers only a partial exception. The Roman tragedies elicit sympathy for their protagonists because they cannot achieve fulfilment, as that idea is understood in the world of Shakespeare's plays as a group.

Surprisingly, the moral ambiguity found in the Roman plays makes them excellent for ethical discussion. In the absence of absolute values, comparisons must be made, and the three plays present a considerable range of political conduct. *Julius Caesar* simply and boldly presents a conflict of opinions about the government and the morality of resistance to despotism. It also offers a demonstration of the differing political techniques of Brutus and Antony. *Antony and Cleopatra* opposes the concerns of the state with the individualism of its protagonists, who insist on the value of private aspirations and satisfactions. In *Coriolanus* an individualist revolts against the demands of the state to the extent of treason, but in this pessimistic work neither the state nor the individual is strong, and a failure to achieve wholeness constitutes both the private tragedy and the public disaster.

Like the histories, the Roman plays reflect a widespread enthusiasm in Shakespeare's England for the study of the past. However, because they were set in remote times and places, they offered the playwright an opportunity to speculate broadly on political possibilities that English settings actually inhibited. *Coriolanus* is particularly noteworthy in this respect, for its picture of class conflict is more realistic and sober than are the glimpses of it that occur in the histories (see, e.g., Jack CADE). The government CENSORSHIP that loomed over Shakespeare's theatre would probably have found English class relations too sensitive a subject to discuss seriously in public. Ancient Rome, however, presented a more intellectual, and therefore discreet, context in which to contemplate an event such as the corn riots, similar to those found in *Coriolanus*, that raged in England not long before the play was written. Similarly, *Julius Caesar*'s central—and unresolved—moral debate on assassination is not found in the histories, nor is Cleopatra and Antony's sexual immorality observed among Shakespeare's English rulers—PRINCE (6) HAL's rejection of FALSTAFF's world at the end of *2 Henry IV* confirms this.

Commentators have often remarked that the Roman plays have points in common with two other Shakespearean genres; the tragedies and the history plays. In the tragedies a distinctively great person, because of some aspect of that greatness, suffers a crushing downfall. This causes us to reflect on the vulnerability of human existence. In the histories the uses and abuses of government are demonstrated in various ways. This causes us to consider the exercise of power and the value of political loyalty. The Roman plays' greatest strength lies in their combination of these themes. They raise important issues about the individual and society while they stimulate our awareness of both disturbing political questions and profound social ideals.

**Romances** Shakespeare's late comedies—*Pericles, Cymbeline, The Winter's Tale,* and *The Tempest*—considered as a group. *The Two Noble Kinsmen* is also often considered a Shakespearean romance, although it is largely the work of John FLETCHER (2) and deviates strongly from the group's general pattern. Written between about 1607 and 1613 (1611, if *The Kinsmen* is disregarded), the romances, with *Henry VIII*, are the works of the playwright's final period. Each is a TRAGI-COMEDY, in the broadest sense of the term: elements of TRAGEDY find their resolution in the traditional happy ending of COMEDY.

All of the romances share a number of themes, to greater or lesser degree. The theme of separation and reunion of family members is highly important. Daughters are parted from parents in *Pericles, Cymbeline, The Winter's Tale,* and *The Two Noble Kinsmen,* and wives from husbands in the first three; sons are also lost, to a father in *The Winter's Tale* (permanently) and *The Tempest,* and to parents of each sex in *Cymbeline.* The related idea of exile also features in the romances, with the banished characters—usually rulers or rulers-to-be—restored to their rightful homes at play's end. Another theme, jealousy, is prominent in *The Winter's Tale, Cymbeline,* and *The Two Noble Kinsmen,* and it has minor importance in *Pericles* and *The Tempest.* Most significant, the romances all speak to the need for patience in adversity and the importance of providence in human affairs. This visionary conception outweighs any given individual's fate or even the development of individual personalities.

Compared with earlier plays, realistic characterisation in the romances is weak; instead, the characters' symbolic meaning is more pronounced. The plots of these plays are episodic and offer improbable events in exotic locales. Their characters are frequently subjected to long journeys, often involving shipwrecks. Seemingly magical developments arise—with real sorcery in *The Tempest*—and supernatural beings appear. These developments are elaborately represented, and all of the romances rely heavily on spectacular scenic effects.

In all these respects, the romances are based on a tradition of romantic literature going back at least to Hellenistic Greece, in which love serves as the trigger for extraordinary adventures. In this tradition love is subjected to abnormal strains—often involving jealous intrigues and conflicts between male friendship and romantic love—and there are fantastic journeys to exotic lands, encounters with chivalric knights, and allegorical appearances of monsters, supernatural beings, and pagan deities. Absurdly improbable coincidences and mistaken identities complicate the plot, though everything is resolved in a conventional happy ending. The protagonists are also conventional, their chief distinction being their noble or royal blood. They lack believable motives and are merely vehicles for the elaborate plot, whose point is frankly escapist. Such tales were extremely popular in Shakespeare's day, especially in the increasingly decadent world of the court of King JAMES I, who succeeded Queen ELIZABETH (1) in 1603.

The genre had long influenced the stage, but its impact was particularly strong in the early 17th-century MASQUE, a form of drama that was popular at James' court. In the masque, lush and exotic settings framed strange, often magical tableaus and episodes. With the advent of JACOBEAN DRAMA, the taste for such allegorical presentations expanded beyond the court to the so-called private theatres. These differed from the 'public' playhouses, such as the GLOBE THEATRE, in being enclosed against the weather. They were smaller and more intimate, lit by candles and equipped with the mechanical apparatus necessary for elaborate scenic effects. To support all this, they charged a much higher admission price, and they attracted wealthier, better-educated, and more sophisticated audiences.

Shakespeare had made use of romance material throughout his career—*The Two Gentlemen of Verona* is based on a famous romance, for instance, and small-scale masques are performed in a number of plays, while others contain masquelike elements. He had not, however, applied it so fully and systematically before. Any personal motives the playwright may have had for turning to romance late in his career cannot be known, but adequate reasons were available in the theatrical world. Around 1608, his acting company, the KING'S MEN, took over the BLACKFRIARS THEATRE, a private playhouse, and began to produce plays in this new, more remunerative but more demanding venue. Shakespeare was a thoroughgoing theatrical professional—he made his living from the success of every aspect of the company's business, not simply from writing plays for pay—and he responded to the new situation by creating a drama to match it. The exotic locales, supernatural phenomena, and elaborate masques of the romances are clearly intended to satisfy the tastes of the time, and they succeeded. However, though the playwright considered popular demand, he also followed his own artistic sensibility. Unlike many similar works of the period, Shakespeare's plays build a meaningful symbolic world on the escapist premises of romance literature.

In the romances, Shakespeare returned to an idea that had been prominent in his earlier comedies: young lovers are united after various tribulations. Now, however, the focus is not only on the young lovers, but also encompasses the older generation, once the opponents of love. At the end of these plays, the emphasis is not on reward and punishment—with the young lovers wed and the obstructive elders corrected—but rather, on the reunion of parents and children and the hopeful prospect of new generations to come. The romances concern themselves with the lovers not for their own sake but for their effect on the whole continuum of life. The focus is on family groupings rather than on individuals or couples, and the action is spread over many years (except in *The Two Noble Kinsmen*), making this aspect especially clear. (*The Tempest* and *Cymbeline* take place over shorter periods—*The Tempest* within a single day—but narrations of pre-play events produce the same effect.) This broader canvas is enlarged even further with its many images of the supernatural—gods and goddesses, rituals and oracles, apparent resurrections—which add a sense of infinite mystery.

The prominence of resurrection as a motif in the romances points to their similarity to the ancient festivals celebrating the rebirth of spring each year. The mock death and staged resurrection so common in such rites are re-enacted in each of the romances. In *The Two Noble Kinsmen* the reference is oblique, but PALAMON, sentenced to death, is reprieved, and the Gaoler's DAUGHTER is restored to normal life from her descent into insanity, an emblematic death. In *Pericles* the prince undergoes a similar restoration from catatonia, and two reported deaths, MARINA's and THAISA's, prove false. Similarly, in *The Tempest*, Ferdinand and ALONSO each mistakenly believe the other is dead, as do IMOGEN and POSTHUMUS in *Cymbeline* (Posthumus' very name suggests resurrection). Also, PERDITA and HERMIONE are believed dead in *The Winter's Tale*, where an elaborate resurrection scene is staged by PAULINA.

Winter is represented as well as spring. Compared to the earlier comedies, increased importance is given to separation and bereavement, to error and conflict, in short to the anxieties associated with tragedy. A tone of resignation and grief prevails until a sudden reversal brings an ending of joy and renewal that had seemed impossible. PERICLES, LEONTES, CYMBELINE, and PROSPERO all suffer grievously. Each experiences a painful separation from all he holds dear (while Prospero, unlike the others, retains his daughter, he is isolated from everything else in his once-secure world). Each then undergoes a penance before the final reconciliation (except Pericles, an omission that Shakespeare may have consciously corrected in the subsequent plays). Here, too, the play encompasses the entire community, for each sufferer is also a ruler, so his welfare has great symbolic resonance. His winter of struggle gives way to the spring of resurrection—and regeneration, through the marriage of the young people who have been resurrected. As in an ancient ritual, temporary death turns to hope for the future.

The pagan religious component of these plays is quite overt, with the appearances of DIANA (2) in *Pericles* and JUPITER in *Cymbeline*, the vivid evocation of Apollo's oracle in 3.1 of *The Winter's Tale*, the goddesses enacted in the betrothal masque in *The Tempest* (4.1), and the stunning scenes of worship at the altars of Mars, Venus, and Diana in 5.1 of *The Two Noble Kinsmen*. In such an ambience, the merits of the characters are generally of less importance than the good will of the gods—or of Prospero, their surrogate (and even Prospero is dependent on 'bountiful Fortune' [1.2.178] to bring his enemies within range of his magic).

The plays insist that a patient acceptance of the accidents of fate is necessary to survive. The several shipwrecks in these plays and their imagery of the ocean's power make this point clear, for the impersonal violence of the sea is beyond humanity's influence. The characters are often passive and in any case are helpless to improve their situations. Their strength in adversity is supported by faith—not that the gods will save them but that the gods are great—and therein lies their eventual salvation. As Paulina puts it, 'It is requir'd / You do awake your faith' (*Winter's Tale*, 5.3.94–95). Only providence can bring about the destined resolution through strange turns of fate, whose very improbability stresses the irrelevance of human desires. In the unreal world of the romances, the characters—and we as spectators—must, like Pericles, make our 'senses credit . . . points that seem impossible' (*Pericles* 5.1.123–124).

However, more is also required. It is necessary for humankind to act with mercy, in emulation of the gods. Imogen accepts Posthumus despite his viciousness towards her; Hermione also forgives Leontes; and Prospero's forgiveness motivates the entire action of *The Tempest*. Even where repentance is not offered, most flagrantly in the case of ANTONIO in *The Tempest*, vengeance—even justice—is foresworn. All of the romances—like many of Shakespeare's comedies—have points in common with the medieval MORALITY PLAY, in which a sinful human receives God's mercy through no merit of his own. Although the romances are secular works (their pagan gods were presumed by Shakespeare and his audiences to be fictional), their Christian content is nonetheless clear. Our receptivity to such abstract philosophical concerns is eased by the fantasy inherent in the romance genre, for it offers a different level of imagination from which to view the complexities of life.

The romances conclude in a spirit of hope, as the main characters are reunited in an aura of reconciliation—a favourite motif throughout Shakespeare's career. Wrongs are righted and errors amended, exiles return to their homes, and even death is frustrated. The natural good in humanity is put under pressure but preserved through the action of providence. An emphasis on the cycle of regeneration—both in the traditional comedic emphasis on marriage and in the theme of reunited families—offers a guarantee that the preservation will be lasting.

**Romano, Giulio** See GIULIO ROMANO.

**Rome** Capital city of the ancient Roman Empire and the setting for much of *Julius Caesar, Antony and Cleopatra,* and *Coriolanus*—collectively called the ROMAN PLAYS—as well as all of *Titus Andronicus* and three scenes of *Cymbeline.* Especially in the Roman plays, Shakespeare places great importance on the idea that ancient Rome relied on a highly developed ethic of public duty. Conflicts between the demands of Roman government and the personal motives of individuals are central to the Roman plays. Though less dominant, the empire is significant in *Titus Andronicus* and *Cymbeline,* as well.

The early *Titus Andronicus* is not classed among the Roman plays for it does not deal with a factual Rome. However, even in this melodrama, Shakespeare deals with the clash between individual drives and public issues that Rome's significance evoked. TITUS (1) insists on pursuing what he sees as the correct moral action for a Roman, and the result is tragic chaos. Titus' unquestionable ethic has failed, and for him, Rome itself has failed. He declares that 'Rome is but a wilderness of tigers' (3.1.54), a line that has often been quoted as a condemnation of vicious power-seeking. The hero's inability to reconcile the Roman ideal with political reality drives him insane. Because the ideal is specifically Roman, an element of grandeur is added to his plight. The significance of Rome was much greater to RENAISSANCE audiences than it is today.

In *Julius Caesar,* the civil order of Rome is disturbed by BRUTUS (4), whose personal morals lead him to kill CAESAR (1). Civil war ensues; thus, society suffers because an individual is unwilling to compromise. On the other hand, it is evident that Brutus also represents a traditional model of Roman political morality. The individual is thus seen to relate to the state in an ambiguous manner. Here, too, the play's themes are given resonance by the fact that the state is Rome, an age-old symbol of authority. The city is the location for all of the scenes prior to 4.2, and actual sites in ancient Rome are evoked—the Forum, the Capitol, the Senate, etc.—though the people of Rome (see COMMONER [1]) seem comparable to the populace of Shakespeare's LONDON.

In *Antony and Cleopatra,* Rome is contrasted with another political venue, the luxurious court of CLEO-PATRA. The demanding ethic of Rome is set against the sensual indolence of Egypt. ANTONY finds himself wavering between a Roman ideal—rigorous response to 'the strong necessity of time' (1.3.42)—and an alien one, 'the love of Love, and her soft hours' (1.1.44). This conflict is seen immediately, in 1.1, as Antony rejects the call of duty—represented by messages from Rome—in favour of the irresponsible pastimes of Cleopatra. The city is less in evidence than in *Caesar,* for fewer scenes are set there—1.4, 2.2–2.4, 3.2, and 3.6—and they are located on anonymous streets or in interiors. However, the symbolic weight of Roman power and the energy and rigour of the men who wield it is omnipresent.

Another aspect of classical Rome as it was understood by 17th-century English audiences is important in *Antony and Cleopatra.* The Roman Empire was regarded as not only a great achievement in political history but as a significant phenomenon theologically as well. Christian doctrine held that God permitted Rome to rule the Mediterranean world in order that its power might provide peace for a long period, during which Christ was to be sent to humankind and the Christian church established. CAESAR (2) makes a reference to this doctrine that would have been unmistakably clear in Shakespeare's day. He observes of his imminent victory over Antony, 'The time of universal peace is near' (4.6.5). Thus, the power of Rome was considered a manifestation of God's will. This theme recurs in *Cymbeline.*

*Coriolanus* takes place in the legendary early days of the Roman Republic as the city is convulsed by the rise of the common people to political power. The conflict between aristocrats and plebeians permits a more detailed depiction of the city's people than in the other plays. In about half of the play's scenes the setting is stated to be Rome, but the physical city is left to the imagination of the reader or theatrical producer. The domestic life of the city is alluded to, as in 4.6.8–9, and the commoners (see CITIZEN [5]) are vividly present in the form of several well-drawn minor figures, but they are essentially no different from the common folk of the English HISTORY PLAYS.

The glory of Rome is much less evident in *Coriolanus.* The idea of a great power is evoked when MENENIUS says, '. . . you may as well / Strike at the heaven with your staves, as lift them / Against the Roman state . . .' (1.1.66–68), but in fact Rome does not fare well here. Its messy politics encompasses the cynicism of tribunes and aristocrats, and the thoughtless unreliability of the common people. The result is the expulsion of the city's greatest warrior, CORIOLANUS, who joins Rome's enemies, the VOLSCIANS. He brings defeat to the city and—because he refuses to destroy Rome utterly—death for himself. The tragedy of *Coriolanus* offers a sense of Rome's greatness in Coriolanus' power and pride, and its later corruption and fall in his foolish politics and ultimate fate. As he is driven from Rome, Coriolanus hurls a curse upon the city that predicts its history—which was entirely familiar to Shakespeare's audiences. He says, '. . . remain here with your uncertainty! / . . . [until you become] captives to some nation / that won you without blows!' (3.3.124–133). The fall of Rome is invoked, which increases the grandeur of the hero's tragic collapse.

Rome has less importance in *Cymbeline,* but the city nevertheless has two different and interesting historical aspects. Though we see only a domestic interior, 1.5 and 2.4 are set in Rome. We meet there the villainous IACHIMO, whose delight in deceit along with his decadent world of duels and drink were probably intended to suggest an idea commonly held by 17th-century English playgoers. The home of Machiavelli and of Reformation England's enemy, the Catholic Church, contemporary Rome was seen as a sink of duplicity and corruption. In this light, *Cymbeline*'s Rome is closer to SHYLOCK's VENICE than to the ancient imperial capital. On the other hand, we see the familiar toga-clad officials of ancient Rome in 3.8, and we also know from developments at the court of King CYMBELINE that the play's Rome is the capital of Augustus Caesar, whose name is pointedly repeated. Caesar's representative in Britain is the courtly LUCIUS (4), who is clearly a sympathetic character. Here, as in *Antony and Cleopatra*, Shakespeare invokes the Rome that was admired by Christian humanism, the powerful provider of good government and peace appropriate to the birth of Christianity. In this light, the brief war between Britain and Rome that takes place in *Cymbeline* has great symbolic significance. British patriotism is valued only by villains, the QUEEN (2) and CLOTEN, and though (unhistorically) the Britons successfully resist Rome, they finally yield anyway. Part of the play's joyful conclusion in 5.5 is the king's decision to 'submit to Caesar, / And to the Roman empire' (5.5.461–462), for Rome's peace must be accepted by Britain. Thus, here as in the other plays, Shakespeare gilds his drama with the glory of ancient Rome as understood by the Renaissance humanism of his own time.

**Romeo**   One of the title characters in *Romeo and Juliet*, the lover of JULIET (1). Romeo progresses from posing as the melancholy lover of ROSALINE (2) to a more mature stance as Juliet's devoted husband, committed to her despite the world's displeasure. Romeo's early speeches declaiming his affection for Rosaline are parodies of conventional courtship; preposterously bookish and artificial, they emphasise by contrast the depth of his later love for Juliet. And Romeo undergoes another maturation as well: from helpless hysteria in 3.3, after his banishment, he comes in 5.3 to a resolute acceptance of what he sees as his only choice, death with Juliet.

Romeo's growth is clearly brought about by his love. When he and Juliet first meet, he has not yet found a stronger mode of expression than the conventional SONNET, as she recognises when she observes, 'You kiss by th'book' (1.5.109). In their mutual ecstasy in the 'balcony' scene (2.2), it is Juliet who, though no less enraptured, is the more aware of the likely consequences of their love. Further, we recognise the impulsive boy in Romeo as he urges FRIAR (4) LAURENCE to haste in 2.3. Once married, however, Romeo begins

his transformation: in his attempt to make peace with TYBALT, he wishes all the world to love as he does, although to no avail. As he departs from Juliet into banishment, after their abbreviated wedding night, he offers hope to his despairing bride and displays a true maturity in sharing the mutual consolation necessary in their seemingly hopeless situation. At the end of the play, he has achieved the capacity to stand alone in the face of tragedy, as is demonstrated in the contrast between himself and PARIS (2). Paris contents himself with formal rhymed verses reminiscent of Romeo's speeches in Act 1, whereas Romeo himself burns brightly with desperate determination.

### Romeo and Juliet

#### SYNOPSIS

*Act 1, Prologue*
The CHORUS (2) tells, in a SONNET, that the play will concern a pair of lovers whose deaths shall end the conflict between their feuding families.

*Act 1, Scene 1*
SAMPSON and GREGORY (1), servants of the CAPULET (1) family, encounter ABRAM and BALTHASAR (2), of the MONTAGUE (1) household, in a street in VERONA. They fight; BENVOLIO appears and tries to stop them, but TYBALT enters and insists on duelling with him. Some CITIZENS (3) attempt to break up the brawl, as Capulet and Montague join in, to the dismay of their wives, Lady CAPULET (3) and Lady MONTAGUE (2). The PRINCE (1) arrives and chastises both families. He declares that any further fighting will be punished with death. The Prince and the Capulets depart, and the Montagues discuss with their nephew Benvolio the mysterious melancholy that afflicts their son ROMEO. As Romeo approaches, his parents leave Benvolio to interrogate him. Benvolio learns that Romeo is in love with a woman who is sworn to chastity and ignores him. Benvolio recommends that his cousin consider other women, but Romeo declares that his love's beauty will eclipse all others.

*Act 1, Scene 2*
PARIS (2) seeks Capulet's permission to marry his daughter JULIET (1). Capulet argues that Juliet is too young, but he says that, if Paris can win Juliet's affections at the banquet planned for the coming night, he will give his consent. He gives a SERVANT (4) a list of guests with instructions to deliver invitations, and he and Paris depart. Romeo and Benvolio pass by, and the Servant seeks their assistance, for he is illiterate. Romeo reads the list of guests, which includes the name of his beloved, ROSALINE (2). He and Benvolio decide to attend the banquet in disguise, Romeo wishing to see Rosaline and Benvolio hoping that the sight of many beautiful women will cure his friend's love-sickness.

### Act 1, Scene 3

The NURSE (3) reminisces at length about Juliet's childhood. Lady Capulet tells Juliet about her father's plans for her marriage, and Juliet coolly agrees to consider Paris out of filial duty.

### Act 1, Scene 4

Romeo, Benvolio, and MERCUTIO arrive at the banquet. Romeo asserts that he will not dance, due to his melancholy, and he is teased by Mercutio, who humorously enlarges on his probable enchantment by Queen MAB. The group proceeds to the party, although Romeo expresses darkly ominous feelings.

### Act 1, Scene 5

Four servants (see SERVING-MAN [2]) joke among themselves as they clear away the dinner. While the guests dance, Romeo first notices Juliet and is enthralled by her beauty. Tybalt recognises him and rages against his presence. Capulet orders him to be peaceful, and he leaves in disgust. Romeo addresses Juliet, and their love immediately blossoms as they kiss. Juliet is called to her mother, and Romeo learns who she is from the Nurse. He is dismayed to learn that her family is his family's rival, and she, when learning his identity from the Nurse, is similarly distressed.

### Act 2, Prologue

The Chorus recounts, in another sonnet, that Romeo and Juliet cannot easily meet, their families being enemies, but their passion enables them to find a way.

### Act 2, Scene 1

Romeo separates himself from his friends as they leave the party. Presuming he has gone in search of Rosaline, they depart.

### Act 2, Scene 2

Juliet appears at a high window and Romeo, in the garden below, admires her beauty. Believing herself to be alone, she soliloquises about her love for Romeo, regretting that he is a Montague. He reveals himself, and they speak of their love and exchange vows. Juliet is called away by the Nurse, but she returns to say that she will send a messenger to Romeo the next day, to whom he can convey a plan for them to marry. She leaves but returns once more, and they exchange loving farewells.

### Act 2, Scene 3

FRIAR (4) LAURENCE, picking herbs, muses on their capacity to kill or cure. Romeo arrives and tells him of his new love and asks his help in marrying her. The Friar agrees, hoping that their alliance will end their families' feuding.

### Act 2, Scene 4

Benvolio and Mercutio discuss Tybalt, who has challenged Romeo to a duel. Tybalt is well known for his skill with the sword, and Romeo's friends wonder whether the lovesick youth is up to the challenge. Meeting their friend, they banter with him about his love. The Nurse appears; Romeo's friends depart. Romeo gives the Nurse a message for Juliet: she is to go to Friar Laurence that afternoon, and they shall be married. He arranges for the Nurse to receive a rope-ladder for Juliet to lower for him that night.

### Act 2, Scene 5

The Nurse returns to an impatient Juliet. She teases her charge by withholding the message briefly; when she delivers it, Juliet departs at once.

### Act 2, Scene 6

Juliet comes to Romeo in Friar Laurence's cell, and they greet each other joyfully. The Friar prepares to marry them.

### Act 3, Scene 1

Benvolio and Mercutio encounter Tybalt, and Mercutio begins to pick a fight. Romeo appears and is immediately insulted by Tybalt, who wishes to challenge him to a duel. Romeo excuses himself, citing mysterious reasons why he and Tybalt should be friends, but Mercutio cannot tolerate such conciliatory behaviour and draws his sword on Tybalt. Romeo attempts to separate the combatants, and Mercutio is mortally wounded by Tybalt, who flees. Mercutio, after bravely jesting about his wound and cursing both Montagues and Capulets for their feuding, is carried away by Benvolio, who returns to report his death. Tybalt returns, and Romeo fights and kills him. At Benvolio's urging, Romeo flees. The Prince appears and interrogates Benvolio. Judging Tybalt to be guiltier than Romeo, he spares the latter the death sentence but banishes him from Verona.

### Act 3, Scene 2

Juliet longs for night, when Romeo is to come. The Nurse brings her word of Tybalt's death and Romeo's banishment. Doubly grieved, Juliet speaks of suicide, and the Nurse volunteers to bring Romeo to her.

### Act 3, Scene 3

Romeo, in hiding with Friar Laurence, learns of the Prince's edict and raves that death would be more merciful than life without Juliet. The Nurse arrives with word of Juliet's distress, and Romeo's grief reaches new heights; he too speaks of suicide. The Friar chastises him for his weakness and proposes that, after a night with Juliet, Romeo should flee to MANTUA, where he can live until his marriage becomes known, the families reconciled, and he pardoned. Romeo recovers his spirits and leaves to go to Juliet.

### Act 3, Scene 4

Capulet ordains that Juliet, whose grief he finds excessive, shall be married to Paris in three days.

*Act 3, Scene 5*
Romeo and Juliet reluctantly bid farewell, regretting that dawn is near. The Nurse warns that Lady Capulet is coming, and Romeo departs for Mantua. Her mother tells Juliet of the proposed marriage, and Juliet refuses, objecting to the hastiness of the plan. Her father enters and flies into a rage on hearing of her refusal. Her parents leave angrily, and the Nurse advises that Juliet ignore her marriage to Romeo, which no one else knows about, and marry Paris. Juliet resolves to seek aid from Friar Laurence.

*Act 4, Scene 1*
Paris confers with a reluctant Friar Laurence about his coming wedding. Juliet arrives and coolly deflects Paris' courtesies. Once alone with the Friar, she desperately craves assistance. Her talk of suicide suggests a plan to him: he will provide her with a potion that will make her seem to be dead. She will be placed in the family crypt, where Romeo will meet her so that they can flee together.

*Act 4, Scene 2*
As the Capulet household is busy with her wedding arrangements, Juliet appears and apoligises to her father, promising to obey him and marry Paris. Capulet moves the wedding up a day to the next morning.

*Act 4, Scene 3*
Juliet, alone in her bedroom, is afraid that the Friar's potion may actually kill her. She is also filled with revulsion at the prospect of awakening in the vault, perhaps to encounter the spirits of the dead and with the certain company of Tybalt's fresh corpse. But she steels herself and drinks the potion.

*Act 4, Scene 4*
The next morning, the wedding day, the Capulet household is astir with last-minute preparations. Capulet sends the Nurse to awaken Juliet.

*Act 4, Scene 5*
The Nurse, unable to rouse Juliet, raises the alarm that she is dead. Her parents and Paris—who arrives with Friar Laurence and the MUSICIANS (2) intended for the wedding festivities—grieve for her. Friar Laurence counsels acceptance of God's will and ordains her solemn interment in the family vault. PETER (2) then engages the Musicians in a bit of humorous byplay.

*Act 5, Scene 1*
Balthasar arrives at Romeo's refuge in Mantua with the news that Juliet has died. Romeo immediately plans to return to Verona and join his beloved in death; he buys a fast-acting poison from an APOTHE-CARY.

*Act 5, Scene 2*
FRIAR (3) JOHN reports to Friar Laurence that he has been unable to deliver Laurence's letter to Romeo. Laurence sends John to fetch a crow bar, planning to open the vault and take Juliet into hiding in his own cell until Romeo can be summoned.

*Act 5, Scene 3*
Paris visits Juliet's tomb at night. His PAGE (3), posted as a lookout, whistles a warning that someone is coming, and Paris hides. Romeo appears with Balthasar, whom he sends away with a letter to Montague. Balthasar leaves but hides nearby to observe. Romeo breaks into the tomb, and Paris steps forth to challenge him. They fight, as the Page leaves to call the WATCHMEN (2), and Romeo kills Paris. He addresses Juliet, whom he believes to be dead, saying that he will remain with her forever. He drinks the poison and dies. Friar Laurence arrives and views the carnage just as Juliet awakens. He tells Juliet what has happened and begs her to flee, for he can hear the Watchmen coming. She refuses and stays. She kisses her dead lover and stabs herself with his dagger, as the Watchmen appear. They arrest Balthasar and the Friar as the Prince arrives, followed by Juliet's parents and Romeo's father, all of them drawn by the news of the tragedy. The Friar gives an account of Juliet's feigned death and Romeo's misinformation. His tale is confirmed by Balthasar and by Romeo's letter to his father. The Prince points out that the feud between the two families has led to this moment, and Montague and Capulet forswear their hostility and vow to erect golden statues of the two lovers.

## COMMENTARY

*Romeo and Juliet* is justly famed for the quality of its lyric poetry, but it is no less extraordinary for its sophisticated organisational devices, which enhance its vivid evocation of a world of love and death. Shakespeare compressed the elapsed time of the story from more than nine months in his source (see 'Sources of the Play') to less than five days: Romeo and Juliet meet on a Sunday, marry the next day, and die in the predawn hours on the following Friday. The progression of the days is clearly marked by a succession of dramatic daybreaks: before he appears, Romeo is described as wandering at dawn (1.1.116–121); the next sunrise finds him below Juliet's window in the famous 'balcony' scene (2.2), and the following morning he leaves by that window after the couple's surreptitious wedding night. The Nurse finds Juliet's drugged body at sunrise on Thursday, and at the play's end, a gloomy daybreak accompanies the discovery of the tragedy by the Prince and the couple's parents. The playwright uses a virtuoso display of techniques to heighten the explosive speed of the plot development.

The many symmetries of the play strengthen the spectator's sense of exorably passing time. The Prince appears on three carefully spaced occasions: in 1.1 he describes the Montague-Capulet feud; in 3.1, the piv-

*George Cukor's 1935 film version of* Romeo and Juliet. *In 5.3 Friar Laurence arrives in the vault to find Juliet (Norma Shearer) awakening to the sight of her dead lover, Romeo (Leslie Howard).* (Courtesy of Culver Pictures, Inc.)

otal scene in which Tybalt is killed, he banishes Romeo and triggers the tragic conclusion; and in 5.3 he summarises the play's course. Other matching scenes link the events of the tragedy, as when the Nurse delivers a message to Juliet, delaying its contents each time, in 2.5 and in 3.1. The first message is a happy one: Romeo has summoned Juliet to their marriage; the second instead reveals Romeo's disastrous duel with Tybalt.

Telling juxtapositions also catch our attention, perhaps most strikingly when the fury and desolation of the duel scene is immediately followed by the lyrical brilliance of Juliet's soliloquy that opens 3.2. Moreover, the duel itself follows Romeo and Juliet's marriage; Romeo falls into the depths of the feud just as he ascends to seeming bliss. His very effort to effect a reconciliation with Juliet's kinsman leads to the death of Mercutio, which in turn requires vengeance. These connections do not occur in his source; Shakespeare added them to heighten the dramatic tension. In another such alteration, the playwright has Romeo first

encounter Juliet before his presence at the Capulet feast is discovered, rather than afterwards, as in the source. In this way, Romeo's ecstatic expression of love (1.5.43–52) itself provokes Tybalt's wrath, sparking the violent chain of events that follows.

An effective contrast in 4.4 emphasises a basic opposition between the lovers and the world, while also conveying the sense of hastening hours. In this scene the Capulet household hums with pre-nuptial excitement, completely unaware that Juliet lies in fateful slumber under the same roof. In another striking juxtaposition of scenes, Romeo, having learned of his bride's apparent death, exits with his newly purchased poison at the end of 5.1; at the beginning of 5.2 Friar John immediately enters to explain why he could not inform Romeo of the truth.

The repeated use of certain motifs also unites the events of the play. One such motif is the passage of time. Initially, time passes slowly. Romeo, lost in his infatuation with Rosaline, moans that 'sad hours seem long' (1.1.159). But the tempo quickens: Mercutio complains of wasted time as he and Romeo approach the Capulets' feast, and just before Romeo first sees Juliet, Capulet complains to an aged relative, Cousin CAPULET (2), that the years fly by too rapidly. As Romeo leaves the party, now in love, Capulet remarks with surprise that it has grown late. As Romeo spies Juliet at her window, he compares her with the sun and with 'a winged messenger of heaven' (2.2.28). However, the accelerating passage of events begins to take on an ominous tone. Juliet, after she and Romeo have first acknowledged their love, says fearfully: '. . . Although I joy in thee, / I have no joy of this contract tonight: / It is too rash, too unadvis'd, too sudden, / Too like the lightning, which doth cease to be / Ere one can say "It lightens".' (2.2.116–120) Hearing of Romeo's love for Juliet, the Friar warns, 'Too swift arrives as tardy as too slow' (2.6.15). From this point, the pressures of time only intensify: Romeo and Juliet must end their wedding night suddenly; Capulet impulsively moves the wedding date forward a day; Friar John's delay deprives Romeo of the truth about Juliet's apparent death; Friar Laurence arrives only seconds too late to prevent the fatal dénouement.

Several times feverish haste is described as resembling the flash of lightning or gunpowder, combining the image of fleeting seconds with that of light, the second major motif in the play. When Romeo first encounters Juliet, he compares her to the brilliant light of torches, and in the balcony scene he associates her with sunlight (2.2.3), starlight (2.2.15–17), daylight (2.2.20–22) and the brightness of an angel (2.2.26). Juliet proposes that Romeo, if she 'cut him out in little stars' (3.2.22), could fill the sky and cause the night to outshine the day. But light, with time, comes to work against the lovers. As dawn arrives to end their wedding night and signal the beginning of Romeo's exile, he moans, 'More light and light; more dark and dark our woes' (3.5.36).

Images of contrasting light and darkness colour the play's tragic climax. The Friar describes the action of the potion he gives the desperate Juliet as 'Like death when he shuts up the day of life' (4.1.101), but when Romeo opens the tomb he calls it a 'lantern' lit by Juliet's beauty, making 'This vault a feasting presence, full of light' (5.3.86). Finally, the Prince's closing speech in 5.3 begins with the observation that 'A glooming peace this morning with it brings; / The sun for sorrow will not show his head' (5.3.304–305).

As the prominence of darkness and light suggests, *Romeo and Juliet* is a play about extremes and oppositions: the union of the lovers versus the feud between their families; age against youth; the weight of the past versus the promise of the future. Most important, the lovers themselves stand in opposition to the rest of the world—Juliet's irritable father, her match-making mother, the bawdy Nurse, the volatile Mercutio, and the self-righteous Friar, all of whom are content to

enact the roles required by their places in society. The lovers, however, experience another, private world, in which they feel a finer degree of responsibility to each other and to their love. Their isolation gives their dying a sacrificial quality, atoning for the sins of their families and of Verona at large.

The lovers are especially distinguished from their fellow citizens by their speech. Their expressions of love are filled with the intense language of lyric poetry: striking images, exaggerated comparisons, and the use of rhetorical figures traditionally associated with love. Among these is the use of the sonnet, whose formal organisation and lyrical fervour suggest the nature of the play itself: rigorously paced and emotionally high-pitched. Acts 1 and 2 are each introduced by a sonnet, spoken by the Chorus, suggesting to the audience (which in Shakespeare's day, more than now, will have been likely to recognise the form on hearing it) that they will witness a structured presentation of emotion. Following a number of sonnet fragments (as in Romeo and Benvolio's exchange at the end of 1.2), Romeo and Juliet's first encounter takes the form of a sonnet (1.5.92–105) that they deliver jointly. Their subsequent dialogue is in blank verse, less stylised and more dramatically powerful, but the use of the sonnet form in the opening scenes suggests the poet's private recollection of emotion. This permits an exhibition of the lovers' intimate experience, inexpressible in ordinary speech. Shakespeare was writing his early SONNETS while he was composing *Romeo and Juliet;* the idea of integrating love lyrics within his romantic love story must have seemed delightful.

As a tragedy of love, ultimately derived from the prose fiction of RENAISSANCE Italy, *Romeo and Juliet* was a novelty in its day; Elizabethan audiences expected to find lovers in COMEDY, whose complicated plots led to happy endings in marriage. Although the tale of *Romeo and Juliet* was well known in prose versions (see 'Sources of the Play'), tragic destinies in the theatre were customarily reserved for ancient rulers and quasi-mythical figures, in dramas (such as Shakespeare's own *Titus Andronicus*) that imitated those of the Roman playwright SENECA. However, despite its unusual protagonists, *Romeo and Juliet* also reflects the traditional values of medieval melodramas of the Wheel of Fortune and, like them, carries catharsis with its load of woe. Fortune, to the medieval mind, brought down the mighty and thus demonstrated that humanity was subject to forces beyond its control, but this was not necessarily a pessimistic notion, for it expressed the certainty of a world of fate beyond human suffering. This ancient tradition was strongly reinforced by the Christian concept of heaven, which was still a vital force in Shakespeare's day. *Romeo and Juliet* concerned the destiny of two young people—not that of, say, an emperor—but it demonstrated the turnings of the Wheel of Fortune equally well. Thus the play was both conventional and novel.

*Romeo and Juliet* seems somewhat out of place in the line of Shakespeare's development as a writer of tragedy. Shakespeare's extraordinary later tragedies, such as *Hamlet, Othello,* and *King Lear,* are centred on magnificent but flawed individuals whose personalities lead them to attempt to control their destiny and thereby succumb to an inevitable downfall. Romeo and Juliet bear no resemblance to these mighty protagonists; although they have faults, it is not their weaknesses that bring them to their unhappy end but their 'inauspicious stars' (5.3.111). The young lovers are victims of fate. Thus the play does not belong in the continuum of works, from *Titus Andronicus* to *Macbeth,* that concern themselves with the relationship of evil and personal character. Rather, in its emphasis on fulfilment, its final reconciliation, and its celebration of the power of love, *Romeo and Juliet* anticipates the ROMANCES, Shakespeare's strange and great last plays.

## SOURCES OF THE PLAY

The tale of *Romeo and Juliet* had been popular in the literatures of England and the Continent before Shakespeare adapted it. His chief source was *The Tragicall Historye of Romeus and Iuliet,* a poem by Arthur BROOKE (1) (1562). He also knew the story from *Palace of Pleasure,* by William PAINTER (2), which appeared in several editions prior to 1580. In addition, George GASCOIGNE had made the tale the subject of a MASQUE in 1575, and Brooke mentions in his preface a play of the 1550s.

Brooke's poem is a free translation of a French prose work by Pierre Boaistuau (d. 1566), published in Paris in 1559. This in turn was derived from a story (1554) by the Italian writer Mateo BANDELLO, who had adapted the work of another Italian, Luigi Da Porto, whose version was published in 1530. Several variations of the tale existed before that (elements of the plot appear in Latin literature as early as the 3rd century A.D.), but Da Porto was the first author to name the lovers Romeo and Giulietta and to set the action in Verona in the midst of a feud between the Montagues and Capulets. He was also the first to assert that the tale was historical, a belief that persisted into modern times. Bandello, Boaistuau, and Brooke all added elements of plot and character, whereas Shakespeare simply rearranged the material, changed the pace considerably (see 'Commentary', and expanded the roles of several characters, notably Mercutio and the Nurse.

Brooke's chief contribution to the tale was to emphasise the role of fate. In this he was influenced by CHAUCER's *Troilus and Creseyde,* which was then the most famous of English love stories. Shakespeare, perhaps influenced by Brooke, was also affected by this work; he took from it the use of recurrent motifs that

is so strong an element in *Romeo and Juliet.* Also, Chaucer's *Parliament of Fowles* was the source for part of Mercutio's 'Queen Mab' speech (1.4.53–95).

Various other sources include Samuel DANIEL's *Complaint of Rosamund* (1592), from which Shakespeare derived Romeo's description of Juliet's body in the tomb (5.3.92–96), as well as several minor ideas and images. The well-known French poet Guillaume DU BARTAS, in a 1593 translation by John ELIOT (1), influenced the lovers' debate on bird-song in 3.5. It is also likely that the playwright was inspired by Sir Philip SIDNEY's great sonnet sequence *Astrophel and Stella* (1591) in seeing the lovers as maturing in isolation through awareness of the power of their love. And the setting of the 'balcony' scene (2.2) may derive from a similar situation in Sidney's work.

## TEXT OF THE PLAY

We can deduce that Shakespeare wrote *Romeo and Juliet* after 1593, when the latest of its sources was published, and before 1596, for the first edition of the play appeared in early 1597, bearing on its title-page the boast that the play was already popular on stage (see 'Theatrical History of the Play'). *A Midsummer Night's Dream* contains numerous phrases and ideas that resemble material in *Romeo and Juliet;* since these passages are scattered throughout *Romeo and Juliet* but mostly appear early in the *Dream,* it is presumed that Shakespeare began his comedy with the newly completed tragedy in mind. *A Midsummer Night's Dream* is dated to 1595 or early 1596; *Romeo and Juliet* is therefore thought to have been written in 1594 or early 1595.

The first edition of the play, the QUARTO of 1597, known as Q1, was a pirated edition produced by John DANTER and Edward ALLDE. It is a BAD QUARTO; that is, it was transcribed from the recollections of actors who had performed in it. It is thought that this text was originally prepared for an acting company's provincial tour, for which the play was shortened. Q1 was superseded in 1599 by a second edition (Q2), published by Cuthbert BURBY and printed by Thomas CREEDE. It is nearly 50 percent longer and includes numerous corrected passages. Q3 (1609) was a reprint of Q2, and Q4 (1622) reprinted Q3, although Q1 was also used in places. The FIRST FOLIO edition of 1623 was based on Q3 and Q4. A fifth Quarto edition, Q5, a reprint of Q4, appeared in 1637.

Q2 was probably printed from Shakespeare's FOUL PAPERS, as is indicated by its many inconsistent stage directions and other peculiarities. Therefore, it is generally regarded as the most authoritative text and is the basis for most modern editions, although Q1, which clearly reflects early performances, is often consulted, especially with reference to its more elaborate stage directions.

## THEATRICAL HISTORY OF THE PLAY

*Romeo and Juliet* has always been among the most popular of Shakespeare's plays. The title-page of the first Quarto edition asserted (in 1597) that the play had 'been often (with great applause) plaid publiquely' by HUNSDON'S MEN, and its frequent publication testifies to its continued popularity well into the 17th century. However, the earliest surviving record of a particular performance is from 1662, when William DAVENANT revived the play in an adaptation now lost. Later 17th-century productions altered Shakespeare's play greatly; for instance, in the 1670's an adaptation that preserved the lives of the lovers played in a London theatre on every other night, alternating with another version in which they died. Thomas OTWAY's *Caius Marius* (1680), a version that was staged regularly for 70 years, was set in ancient Rome. In the mid-18th century rival adaptations by Colley CIBBER (1) and David GARRICK, both somewhat truer to the original, were extremely popular. They played London at the same time in 1750—starring Spranger BARRY (3) and Garrick, respectively—in the notorious '*Romeo and Juliet* War'. Shakespeare's text was re-established on the stage in the 1840s, and it has continued to be performed frequently. In 1845, Charlotte CUSHMAN played Romeo opposite the Juliet of her sister, Susan. Henry IRVING's production of the 1880s, John GIELGUD's of 1935, and Franco ZEFFIRELLI's of 1960 were particularly notable. *Romeo and Juliet* has been very popular with movie-makers. At least 17 FILM versions have been made (only *Hamlet* has been more filmed), in 6 languages, including Arabic and Hindi, by directors such as Francis X. Bushman (1916), George Cukor (1936), Paul Czinner (1965), and Zeffirelli (1968). It has also been produced for TELEVISION 6 times, beginning as long ago as 1947.

Vincenzo BELLINI's *I Capuleti e I Montecchi* (1830) and Charles GOUNOD's *Roméo et Juliette* (1867), two of the several 19th-century operas derived from Shakespeare's play, remain in the opera repertory today. In addition, *West Side Story*, the popular American musical drama of stage (1958) and screen (1961), is an adaptation of *Romeo and Juliet*, set among street gangs in modern New York City. Shakespeare's play has also inspired classical composers, including Hector BERLIOZ, who created a 'dramatic symphony' with voices (1838), and P.I. TCHAIKOVSKY, who composed a symphonic fantasy (1864), both entitled *Romeo and Juliet*. The ballet (1936) by Serge Prokofiev (1891–1953) is a staple of modern classical dance.

**Rosalind**  Character in *As You Like It*, lover of ORLANDO and daughter of the exiled DUKE (7) Senior. Rosalind is the play's most important character. She symbolises the love and commitment that finally prevail when her manipulations result in the multiple marriages of 5.4. Both a counsellor and a learner about love, she presents many of the play's themes.

Although her banishment by DUKE (1) Frederick in 1.3 necessitates her masquerade as GANYMEDE, Rosalind retains the disguise in the Forest of ARDEN (1). As a young man she escapes the restrictions that were traditionally placed on women and can control her relationship with Orlando and influence that of SILVIUS and PHEBE, conventional shepherds of PASTORAL literature. Playing the parts of both a man and a woman, both an expert on love and its victim, she simultaneously mocks love and feels it, and she can test Orlando's feelings and her own. The result is both moving and comical, as she finds herself arguing against the conventions of love, saying, 'love is merely a madness' (3.3.388), even as she herself feels 'many fathoms deep . . . in love!' (4.1.196).

Rosalind is a natural and unpretentious figure who opposes affectation both in Phebe and her own Orlando. She punctures the unworthy Phebe's lofty scorn for Silvius, rebuking her in down-to-earth terms that satirise the conventions of the hard-to-get lover, telling her to '. . . sell when you can, you are not for all markets' (3.5.60). And when Orlando says he will die if Rosalind refuses him, she, speaking as Ganymede, denies it: '. . . men have died from time to time and worms have eaten them, but not for love' (4.1.101–103). Similarly, his conventional assertion that he will love Rosalind 'for ever, and a day' (4.1.137) brings her reply, 'Say a day, without the ever . . . men are April when they woo, December when they wed. Maids are May when they are maids, but the sky changes when they are wives.' (4.1.138–141). This recognition that emotions evolve through time does not deny the virtue of affection or imply a lessening of the intensity of her own love for Orlando. She is herself at a peak of loving good humour as she speaks; she simply wishes to counter the egotistic intensity of love-cults, knowing that a more human approach will yield a truer affection. Our final sense of the love between Rosalind and Orlando is enhanced by this evidence of its freedom from illusion.

Rosalind, in seeking Orlando's love, commits herself to an involvement in life that is directly opposed to the isolation of the melancholy JAQUES (1), the play's other major figure. She criticises Jaques' excessive pessimism when she lumps him with all other extremists, who are, she says, '. . . abominable fellows, . . . worse than drunkards' (4.1.5–8). Her repudiation of his negativism is emphasised by its juxtaposition to a passage of elated love talk with Orlando, which follows immediately. Similarly, Jaques' earlier rejection by Orlando is followed by Rosalind's initial encounter with her lover in Arden. Rosalind's love replaces Jaques' antisocial reserve repeatedly. Rosalind's opposition to Jaques thus comes across indirectly as well as in explicit dialogue.

When we first meet Rosalind, in 1.2, she is sad because of her father's banishment, but her spirits rise throughout the play, as first she meets Orlando at the wrestling match in the same scene and as she later tests and accepts his love. Her attitude towards love grows more mature as well. In 1.2 she treats love as a lark, saying, 'I will . . . devise sports. Let me see, what think you of falling in love?' (1.2.23–24). She is clearly ripe for love, but her attitude is naïve.

In Arden, Rosalind acquires a fuller understanding of love. She absorbs the jester TOUCHSTONE's bawdy parodies of love in his account of Jane Smile (2.4.43–53) and in his comic love poem 'If a hart do lack a hind' (3.2.99–110). As Ganymede, Rosalind acquires a growing sense of what love can be, as her responses to both Orlando and Phebe indicate. Then, when Orlando's own growth makes him impatient with his 'courtship' of Ganymede, in 5.2, Rosalind is ready to reintroduce herself undisguised and claim his love.

Rosalind's association with magic in Act 5—in claiming, as Ganymede, the ability to 'do strange things' (5.2.59) and in invoking the blessing of HYMEN in the MASQUE in which she appears in 5.4—suits the role she has played among the lovers. Disguised as Ganymede, she has been invisible in a sense and has been able to control the situation entirely, guiding the development of Orlando's love through the playful fantasy of portraying herself, bringing together Silvius and Phebe with her 'magical' change of sex, and overseeing the union of OLIVER (1) and CELIA as the latter's supposed brother. She embodies comic pleasure, and her humorous tricks and deceits result in the play's happy ending centred on marriage.

In the EPILOGUE, Rosalind speaks as a man, saying, 'If I were a woman . . .' (5.4.213), referring to the fact that the part was originally played by a boy. This offers a piquant twist to her final manipulations, for we are reminded of the equally magical theatrical illusion that has given us one of Shakespeare's most charming heroines.

**Rosaline (1)**   Character in *Love's Labour's Lost,* the beloved of BEROWNE and one of the ladies-in-waiting to the PRINCESS (1) of France. Rosaline is largely a stock figure—a witty, charming lady who takes part in the courtly pageant of love that is the main business of the play. However, at times we are made to sense her humanity. For instance, we hear a real person, a mischievous young woman, as she contemplates tormenting the lovestruck Berowne: 'How I would make him fawn, and beg, and seek, / And wait the season, and observe the times, / And spend his prodigal wits in bootless rimes, / And shape his service wholly to my hests / And make him proud to make me proud that jests! / So Pair-Taunt like would I o'ersway his state / That he should be my fool, and I his fate. . . .' (5.2.62–68).

Described as having a strikingly dark complexion, and demonstrating a provoking wit, Rosaline is presumed to have been linked, in Shakespeare's mind, to the DARK LADY of the SONNETS, although this cannot be proved. She does seem to anticipate later Shakespearean heroines who are plainly among his favourite types—attractive and assertive young women such as BEATRICE, PORTIA (1), and her near-namesake ROSALIND.

**Rosaline (2)**   Character who is mentioned but does not appear in *Romeo and Juliet,* the object of ROMEO's infatuation before he meets JULIET (1). Early in the play, Romeo asserts his love for the apparently indifferent Rosaline in immature, self-consciously poetic terms. The episode emphasises by contrast the depth of his passion for Juliet when it develops.

**Rose Theatre**   Playhouse built by Philip HENSLOWE in 1587, the first theatre south of the River Thames, in what later became the most important theatre district of LONDON. Henslowe leased a property that had formerly been a rose garden, in partnership with a grocer named Cholmley, who put up capital in exchange for the food concession at the theatre. The theatre was built by early 1588, but the earliest surviving records of the Rose date only to its repair in 1592, from which we known that it was built of timber and plaster on a brick foundation. (In February 1989 these foundations were uncovered during construction of a modern office building and have been partially preserved.)

Henslowe's *Diary* records the companies that played for him, presumably at the Rose, after 1592. STRANGE's MEN—possibly including the young Shakespeare—were there that spring and during the next winter season; *1 Henry VI* and *Titus Andronicus* probably premiered during this period. SUSSEX's MEN played there briefly during 1593, when the theatres were mostly closed by a plague epidemic, and shared the stage with the QUEEN's MEN (1) in the spring of 1594. In that season the ADMIRAL's MEN, led by Henslowe's son-in-law and partner William ALLEYN, moved to the Rose for a seven-year stay. PEMBROKE's MEN gave their final two performances at the Rose, just after the Admiral's Men departed in 1600, and WORCESTER's MEN played there in 1602–1603. The *Diary* goes no further, but it is known that Henslowe did not renew his ground lease in 1605. Authorities differ on the Rose's later history, but it was probably torn down around 1606.

**Rosencrantz and Guildenstern**   Two characters in *Hamlet,* courtiers who assist the KING (5) of DENMARK in his plots against HAMLET. Only once, and only in some editions, does one appear without the other. (In 4.3.11–15 some editors follow the FIRST FOLIO text and have Guildenstern enter four lines after Rosencrantz.)

So familiar as a couple, and so similar to each other are this pair, that they are best dealt with as a unit.

We first encounter Rosencrantz and Guildenstern as the King recruits them to spy on Hamlet in 2.2, where he refers to them as the prince's childhood friends. They respond in the smooth and unctuous language of courtiers, assenting readily and thus establishing themselves immediately as toadies. When they first encounter Hamlet, he sees them as his 'excellent good friends' (2.2.224), but they will not 'deal justly' (2.2.276) with him about their mission from the King, which he has guessed, and he realises that he in fact lacks allies, except HORATIO. This disappointment triggers his impressive monologue on depression (2.2.295–310). As foils to Horatio, the courtiers point up Hamlet's alienation. As agents of the rottenness that infects the Danish court, they help establish a polarity between the prince and the King.

Hamlet quickly ends friendly relations with the two courtiers, to their eventual doom. When they summon him to a meeting with his mother, he dismisses them by coldly using the royal 'we' for the only time in the play (3.2.324–325). He speaks of them to his mother as 'my two schoolfellows, / Whom I will trust as I will adders fang'd' (3.4.205). His distrust of them leads to his discovery of the documents ordering his execution in England and his plot to send the courtiers to this fate in his stead. Their deaths are bluntly reported in 5.2.376: 'Rosencrantz and Guildenstern are dead'.

This line was to provide the title for Tom Stoppard's 1967 comedy of existential dread. In *Rosencrantz and Guildenstern Are Dead* the two courtiers are innocent, facing death in a play they know nothing about, and the question of their innocence in *Hamlet* is often raised. Rosencrantz and Guildenstern almost certainly did not know of the King's deadly plot and may thus be seen as innocent victims of Hamlet's counterstroke. However, the two have unquestionably been the willing allies of the King; Hamlet has long recognised them as such and can say 'They are not near my conscience, their defeat / Does by their own insinuation grow' (5.2.58–59). The playwright plainly expects us to see the poetic justice in their end; the fate of Rosencrantz and Guildenstern reflects their involvement in the evil environment of the Danish court.

Guildenstern and Rosencrantz were notable Danish family names of the 16th century; it is recorded that at the Danish royal coronation of 1596, fully one-tenth of the aristocratic participants bore one name or the other. Moreover, several students of each name were enrolled in the university at Wittenberg—the *alma mater* of both Hamlet and the two courtiers—in the 1590s. Shakespeare was surely as delighted as we are by the faintly comical tone conveyed by the combination of these grand names (see, e.g., 2.2.33–34), but they also help to convey the foreignness of the play's locale.

**Roses, Wars of the**  See WARS OF THE ROSES.

**Ross (1)**  Character in *Macbeth*. See ROSSE.

**Ross (2) (Ros), William de (d. 1414)**  Historical figure and minor character in *Richard II*, a supporter of BOLINGBROKE (1). In 2.1 Ross, Lord WILLOUGHBY (3), and the Earl of NORTHUMBERLAND (1) agree to join Bolingbroke's rebellion against King RICHARD II. They fear that their own estates are endangered by such acts as Richard's illegal seizure of Bolingbroke's inheritance. In 2.3 they accompany Bolingbroke as he marches against the King. The historical Ross, a prominent landowner in northern England, went on to serve for a time as Lord Treasurer of England during Bolingbroke's reign as King HENRY IV.

**Rosse (Ross) Thane of**  Character in *Macbeth*, a Scottish nobleman. Rosse is a pawn of the plot; he often is the bearer of news. In 1.2 Rosse tells King DUNCAN of MACBETH's success in battle, and in 1.3 he conveys to Macbeth the king's thanks. In 2.4 he discusses evil omens with the OLD MAN (3) and speaks with MACDUFF of Macbeth's coronation. In 4.2 he attempts to encourage the bereft LADY (7) Macduff. In this scene he delivers a speech that stresses the play's motif of fear and mistrust. 'Cruel are the times, when we are traitors, / And do not know ourselves' (4.2.18–19), he says. In 4.3 he reports her murder to her husband and joins him in revolt against Macbeth. In 5.9 he tells SIWARD of the death of his son, YOUNG SIWARD. Rosse's greatest significance is seen in his gradual revolt against Macbeth. He represents SCOTLAND as a whole, which suffers from Macbeth's evil and then rejects him.

Historically, the Thane of Ross (the correct spelling, which has been adopted by many editors instead of the FIRST FOLIO's 'Rosse') was Macbeth himself, who had received the title years before the time of the play. Shakespeare took his error from his source, HOLINSHED's history, where the name appears in a list of Scottish noblemen who revolted against Macbeth.

**Rossill (Russell), Sir John**  Original name of BARDOLPH (1) in *1* and *2 Henry IV*. When the name Bardolph was substituted for Rossill, shortly after the plays were written in 1596–1597, several occurrences of the original name inadvertently remained in the early texts of the plays, revealing that the change had taken place. Since the 18th century these references have also been altered in most editions. The change of name was made at the same time that OLDCASTLE became FALSTAFF—at the insistence of Lord COBHAM, a descendant of the historical Oldcastle—presumably in the hope of avoiding a similar problem with another prominent aristocrat, William Russell, Earl of Bedford (c. 1558–1613). (See also PETO.)

**Rossillion (Rousillon)**   Region in south-western FRANCE (1), a location in *All's Well That Ends Well*. The castle of the COUNTESS (2) of Rossillion is the setting for many scenes in the play, but no specific characteristics of the region are mentioned; Shakespeare simply took the location from his sources, translations from BOCCACCIO. The Countess' son, BERTRAM, is the Count of Rossillion, and he is occasionally called this, as in 4.3.39.

Rossillion is an Anglicisation of the French Rousillon, a medieval state whose capital was Perpignan, the present-day capital of the province of Pyrénées-Orientales. Independent until 1172, Rousillon was then governed at various times by France and Aragon (later Spain), before finally becoming French in 1659. In Shakespeare's day it had been Aragonese since 1493. His placement of it under French rule derives from Boccaccio, but it may also have been designed to emphasise that the action takes place in a remote time and thus, perhaps, to make the play's improbable elements more plausible. Another Count of Rossillion was a familiar legendary figure, a follower of Charlemagne who appeared in the play *Orlando Furioso* (1594), by Robert GREENE (2).

**Rouen**   French city occupied by the English during the HUNDRED YEARS WAR, the site of a battle in *1 Henry VI* and a location for two interior scenes in *Henry V*. In *1 Henry VI*, the French take the city through a ruse by JOAN LA PUCELLE (Joan of Arc), and then the English, led by TALBOT, take it back by assault the same day (3.2). Historically, Rouen remained under English rule from 1419, when HENRY V conquered it, until 1449, 18 years after Joan had been burned there. The French retook it only when the English were driven from Normandy for good; Talbot was actually captured at the fall of Rouen in 1449 and was not ransomed until a year later. Although the incident in the play is wholly fictional, it includes details of other battles, which Shakespeare based on the chronicles of HALL (2) and FABYAN. The episode was created to heighten the contrast between the heroic Talbot and the cowardly FASTOLFE, and to emphasise Joan's trickery.

In 3.4 of *Henry V*, Princess KATHARINE (2) is comically instructed in the English language by ALICE (1), and in the next scene, the French leaders demonstrate over-confidence about facing the English in battle. Both of these interior scenes take place in Rouen, not long before its conquest by the English.

**Rowe, Nicholas (1674–1718)**   First critical editor of Shakespeare's works. Rowe, a successful though minor playwright, issued an edition of Shakespeare's plays in 1709; a second edition in 1714 included the poems. Working from the highly corrupt text of the Fourth FOLIO, Rowe made many emendations, and he also created lists of the *dramatis personae* and act and scene divisions, the first time these features were provided for most of the plays. While many of Rowe's textual emendations continue to be accepted, he was at times rather arbitrary and intrusive in a manner not tolerated by modern scholarship. For instance, where Shakespeare has HECTOR cite ARISTOTLE in *Troilus and Cressida* (2.2.167), Rowe—offended by the anachronism (for Aristotle lived centuries after the TROJAN WAR)—substituted the phrase 'graver sages' for the philosopher's name. Rowe introduced his collection with a brief biography, which he acknowledged was based largely on the lore collected by Thomas BETTERTON. Though filled with anecdotal information that modern scholars reject, Rowe's biography remained the standard life of the playwright until Edmond MALONE's work.

**Rowley (1), Samuel (d. c. 1630)**   English playwright, author of a possible precursor of *Henry VIII*. Rowley wrote plays for the ADMIRAL'S MEN (later PRINCE HENRY'S MEN and the PALSGRAVE'S MEN), for whom he was also an actor. He mostly worked collaboratively, with a variety of playwrights, including John DAY and Thomas DEKKER. The only play known to have been written wholly by him was *When you see me, You know me* (1605), a comic history play dealing with the reign of King HENRY VIII. Scholars believe Shakespeare may have been alluding to Rowley's play in *Henry VIII* when the PROLOGUE (4) promises the audience that they will see a serious work and not 'a merry bawdy play' (Prologue 14). The possible subtitle to *Henry VIII*—ALL IS TRUE—may have been intended to make the same comparison. Rowley may have written some of the comic prose that was added in 1602 to *Dr Faustus* by Christopher MARLOWE (1), and he may have written similar scenes in THE TAMING OF A SHREW and THE FAMOUS VICTORIES OF HENRY V.

**Rowley (2), William (c. 1585–1626)**   English actor and playwright, sometimes held to have been a collaborator with Shakespeare. Between 1607 and 1625, Rowley appeared with or wrote for the QUEEN'S MEN (2), PRINCE CHARLES' MEN, and the KING'S MEN. Rowley was best known in his own time as an actor, and playwriting seems to have been a sideline. He generally provided low comedy scenes in prose. He collaborated several times with Thomas MIDDLETON, most successfully on *The Changeling* (1622). He has been nominated as a co-author of *Pericles* and of THE TROUBLESOME RAIGNE OF KING JOHN, though most scholars dismiss both attributions. In 1662 Francis KIRKMAN published THE BIRTH OF MERLIN as the work of Shakespeare and Rowley, but the ascription to Shakespeare was false; scholars believe that the play is by Rowley alone or by Rowley and Middleton.

**Royal Shakespeare Company**  Modern British theatrical company famous for productions of Shakespeare's plays. In existence since the 1879 founding of the Shakespeare Memorial Theatre in STRATFORD, the Company assumed its present name in 1961. Led by such major Shakespearean directors as Frank BENSON (1), Barry JACKSON (1), Anthony QUAYLE, and Glen Byam SHAW (3), the Company achieved international fame, and since 1961, during the directorships of Peter HALL (5), Trevor NUNN, and Terry HANDS, it has continued to play a leading role in world theatre, with remarkable production of both Shakespeare and a wide range of classical and contemporary playwrights. It employs several theatres in both Stratford and London.

**Rugby, John**  Minor character in *The Merry Wives of Windsor*, servant of Dr CAIUS (2). Rugby, who says little, merely attends his bullying master, a court physician.

**Rumour**  Allegorical figure in *2 Henry IV*, the speaker of the INDUCTION (Ind.). Rumour serves as a CHORUS (1) and introduces the play. Rumour wears a costume 'painted full of tongues' (Ind. 1, stage direction), in a medieval tradition ultimately derived from a description in VIRGIL's *Aeneid*, written in the 1st century B.C. An unpleasant figure full of scorn for human credulity, he describes his own potential to cause disruption and states that he is now going to give the Earl of NORTHUMBERLAND (1) the false news that the rebels against King HENRY IV, led by the Earl's son, HOTSPUR, have won the battle of SHREWSBURY. Act 1 then commences with Northumberland's receipt of this news.

Rumour serves three functions. First, he recounts that Henry has won the battle and that there remain other rebels, under Northumberland, who are still active. Then, in asserting that Northumberland has missed the battle by being 'crafty-sick' (Ind. 37), he introduces the idea that treachery infects the rebel cause, part of the play's unfavourable presentation of revolt. Most significantly, Rumour, introduces the idea that uncertainty cannot be avoided, saying, 'which of you will stop the vent of hearing when loud Rumour speaks?' (Ind. 2). This pessimistic proposition reflects the play's dark mood and is an underlying element of the play's message that order must be maintained in society.

**Russell, Thomas (1570–1634)**  Landowner in WARWICKSHIRE and a friend of Shakespeare. In his will Shakespeare left Russell the sizeable token of £5 and appointed him an overseer of the will. Russell's first wife was a cousin of Henry WILLOUGHBY (2), who may thereby have known Shakespeare and thus possibly written about him in his mysterious poem 'Willobie his Avisa'. Russell may well have known Shakespeare in LONDON, where he lived in 1599. At this time, a widower, he was courting his second wife, who lived near the playwright. She was the widowed mother of Dudley and Leonard DIGGES (1, 2), whom Shakespeare almost certainly did know: the former may have provided information used in writing *The Tempest,* and the latter contributed dedicatory verses to the FIRST FOLIO edition of the plays. After marrying Mrs Digges in 1603, Russell lived with her at her estate near STRATFORD. The couple had already lived together for three years, marrying only when their lawyers could devise a way to break certain provisions in her late husband's will, intended to discourage remarriage. Dudley Digges later came to resent this and harried Russell for years with a long, acrimonious lawsuit.

**Rutland (1), Edmund York, Earl of (1443–1460)**
Historical figure and character in *3 Henry VI,* the murdered son of the Duke of YORK (8). Rutland, though only a child, is killed by the vengeful Lord CLIFFORD (1) as he attempts to flee from the battle of WAKEFIELD in 1.3, accompanied by his TUTOR. His blood, preserved on a handkerchief, is used in 1.4 to torment his father, whom Clifford kills as well. These highly dramatic encounters exemplify the barbarity of the WARS OF THE ROSES. Shakespeare took the incident from his source, Edward HALL (2), but it is entirely fictitious. Rutland was not a child, but, at 17 years old, was an adult by the standards of the time. He fought in the battle of Wakefield and was slain there, but, as is normal for 15th-century warfare, no particular combatant can be positively identified as his killer.

**Rutland (2), Francis Manners, Earl of (1578–1632)**
English aristocrat, a minor patron of Shakespeare. Rutland's records reveal payments to Shakespeare and Richard BURBAGE (3) for the preparation of a ceremonial shield that the Earl used at a tournament held on the 10th anniversary of King JAMES I's accession in 1613. This type of coat of arms bore a painted allegorical composition called an *impresa,* or emblem. It was not used in fighting, but was carried by a knight's page who recited a poetic interpretation of the emblem when the nobleman presented himself for the joust. Each KNIGHT (2) in 2.2 of *Pericles* bears such a shield, and the emblems are interpreted by THAISA. Presumably, Shakespeare wrote the poetic interpretation for Rutland's emblem, and Burbage painted the image, for which each man received 44 shillings in gold. This was a substantial sum of money in the 17th century, at least several month's wages for most workmen.

**Rynaldo**  Character in *All's Well That Ends Well.* See STEWARD (1).

S

**Sackville, Thomas (1536–1608)** English author and statesman, co-author of the first English TRAGEDY and the author of a source for Shakespeare's HISTORY PLAYS. Sackville's literary activity came early in his career. With Thomas Norton (1532–1584), the first English translator of Calvin and later a Puritan opponent of the theatre, Sackville wrote *Gorbuduc* (1562), the first tragedy written in English. He also wrote poetry and contributed two essays, the 'Induction' and 'Complaint of Buckingham', to the second edition (1563) of A MIRROR FOR MAGISTRATES, a collection of biographies from which Shakespeare derived material for several of the histories. Sackville's work was especially important for *2 Henry VI*.

Sackville was an extravagant young nobleman, and around 1563 he had to flee England to avoid imprisonment for debt. In ROME he was briefly gaoled on suspicion of espionage. He returned after inheriting a fortune. A cousin and favoured courtier of Queen ELIZABETH (1), he was granted an estate at Knole in KENT (1), which he renovated into one of the grandest of surviving English homes. As a diplomat, he represented the queen in several important matters, including her relations with Mary, Queen of Scots. He eventually became her lord treasurer, and he was kept in this position by her successor, King JAMES I. However, in 1608 he was accused of taking excessive bribes, and he died suddenly at his trial on these charges.

**Sadler, Hamnet (d. 1624) and Judith (d. 1614)** Couple in STRATFORD, probable godparents of Hamnet and Judith SHAKESPEARE (5, 10). Hamnet Sadler was a baker and a lifelong friend of Shakespeare. The Sadler's son, born in 1598, was named William. In Shakespeare's will, which Sadler witnessed, the baker was one of seven friends to whom the playwright left money to buy a commemorative ring (though his name appears to have been inserted as an afterthought, replacing that of Richard TYLER [1]). Sadler's family had been in Stratford for more than two centuries. Hamnet and Judith Staunton were married between 1578—when Hamnet inherited his bakery—and 1580. They had 14 children, of whom seven survived to adulthood. Sadler suffered severe losses in the Stratford fire of 1595, from which he never entirely recovered; several subsequent lawsuits by creditors are recorded. Sadler appears in the records as both Hamnet and Hamlet—he is named Hamlet in Shakespeare's will but he witnessed it as Hamnet—suggesting that the two names were actually variants of one. (In any case Shakespeare took the name for his great tragic hero from his sources, not from his friend or his son.)

**Sadler's Wells Theatre** London theatre, once a centre of Shakespearean productions. In 1684 an ancient medicinal spring was discovered on a plot of land in open country north of London. Its owner, one Mr Sadler, created on the site a 'pleasure garden', or private park where refreshments and light entertainment were sold. A few years later he built a theatre, where a variety of entertainment was offered. In 1765 a stone theatre was built—it was managed in the 1770s by Tom KING (26)—but it was not particularly distinguished until Samuel PHELPS leased it in 1844 and used it for 20 years to stage his famous and influential series of Shakespearean productions. After subsequent service as a part-time skating rink and boxing arena, as well as, from time to time, a legitimate stage, the theatre became a virtual ruin early in the 20th century. In 1931 Lilian BAYLIS bought and refurbished it, and Shakespearean productions were again resumed, though since 1934 it has chiefly been associated with opera and ballet.

**Sailor (1)** Any of several minor characters in *Hamlet*, bearers of a letter to HORATIO. In 4.6 a group of Sailors bring Horatio a message from Prince HAMLET. The First Sailor speaks for them all; he seems to lack sophistication because he delivers the missive and afterwards ascertains Horatio's identity. Horatio reads the message aloud, in an aside, and we realise that the Sailors are probably part of the pirate crew mentioned in it. Horatio leaves with them to find the prince. The episode announces Hamlet's return to Denmark and the approach of the play's climax.

**Sailor (2)** Minor character in *Othello*, a messenger. In 1.3 the Sailor brings news of the Turkish attack on CYPRUS and disappears from the play; he has no personality and serves only to increase the frantic activity of the scene.

**Sailor (3)** Either of two minor characters in *Pericles*, seamen aboard whose ship MARINA is born and THAISA apparently dies. In 3.1, during a raging storm, the Sailors believe that PERICLES' wife Thaisa has died, though in fact she is merely unconscious. They demand that she be buried at sea, for they believe that a corpse aboard ship will bring disaster. The distracted Pericles agrees, and Thaisa is cast overboard in a watertight coffin. Thus begins the long separation of husband and wife, a central development in the play's sequence of exiles and disconnections. The Sailors are hearty seamen, conspicuously unafraid of the storm. The First Sailor addresses it contemptuously, 'Blow, and split thyself' (3.1.44), to which the Second Sailor responds, 'But sea-room, and the brine and cloudy billow kiss the moon, I care not' (3.1.45–46). Shakespeare makes it clear that they are not evil; they are merely unknowing implements of fate.

**Sailor (4)** Character in *Pericles*. See TYRIAN SAILOR.

**St Albans** Village near London, near which several scenes of *2 Henry VI* occur. Now a city of more than 50,000 people, St Albans was in Shakespeare's day a small village whose chief attraction was a shrine to St Alban, the first British martyr. In 2.1 the imposter SIMPCOX, having staged a 'miraculous' cure at the shrine, is encountered nearby by the king's hawking party. In 5.2 and 5.3 the fields near the town are the scene of the first battle of St Albans, which began the WARS OF THE ROSES in 1455. The Duke of YORK (8), attempting to enforce his claim to the crown of King HENRY VI, defeats the forces of the king and forces him to retreat to London, closing the play. The battle is then alluded to in *3 Henry VI* (1.1). The second battle of St Albans occurred in 1461, and it is described in *3 Henry VI* (2.1).

**St Edmundsbury (Bury St Edmunds)** English town in Suffolk, the setting for 5.2 of *King John*. The French camp here is the site of the treasonous alliance between the Dauphin LEWIS (1) and several English noblemen, led by the Earl of SALISBURY (4), who are rebelling against King JOHN (3).

St Edmundsbury was the location of an assembly of John's rebellious nobles in 1214, as Shakespeare knew from HOLINSHED's history. The lords swore an oath to oppose the king—a prelude to the signing of the Magna Charta the next year; it was entirely unrelated to the French invasion of 1216. However, Shakespeare associated the two, both to compress the sequence of events in the interest of fast-moving drama, and in order to identify treason with the threat of foreign conquest.

As BURY ST EDMUNDS, the town is a location in *2 Henry VI*.

**Sainte-Maure, Benoît de (active c. 1150–1175)** French poet, author of a source of *Troilus and Cressida*. In about 1160 Sainte-Maure (also known as Sainte-More or Benoît) wrote his *Roman de Troie*, a very long poem (30,000 verses) on the history of Troy. This work, which derived from a 6th-century account by the pseudonymous Dares Phrygius (Dares the Trojan), was translated into Latin prose by Guido delle COLONNE, and, as his *Historia destructionis Troiae* (pub. 1270–1287), it became the standard work on the TROJAN WAR throughout the Middle Ages, until the rediscovery of HOMER in the RENAISSANCE restored the oldest account of the war to its current prominence. Colonne's *Historia* influenced Shakespeare's Greek and Trojan warriors through two English works—William CAXTON's *The Recuyell of the Historyes of Troye* (1471) and John LYDGATE's long poem *Troy Book* (1420, publ. 1512, 1555). Further, Sainte-Maure's poem inspired BOCCACCIO's *Filostrato* (1338), which, through CHAUCER's *Troilus and Criseyde* (c. 1482), gave the playwright the story of his ill-fated title characters. Sainte-Maure's work was the first to introduce this tale, which is not in Dares Phrygius or Homer.

Sainte-Maure is thought to have been a wandering troubadour, serving as court poet in one aristocratic household after another. He spent many years in England at the court of King Henry II (1133–1189). He probably wrote the *Roman de Troie* there, for it is dedicated to Henry's queen, ELEANOR of Aquitaine.

**Salarino** Character in *The Merchant of Venice*. See SALERIO.

**Salerio (Salarino)** Character in *The Merchant of Venice*, a friend of ANTONIO (2). Salerio, whose conversation in elegant verse reflects his position as a cultured gentleman of VENICE, is difficult to distinguish from his companion SOLANIO. They present certain facts to the audience, as when, consoling the melancholy Antonio in 1.1, they refer to his status as a wealthy and successful merchant. In 2.8 the same figures discuss SHYLOCK's despair and rage at JESSICA's elopement (which Salerio has assisted) and speculate that the Jew will vent his anger on Antonio if he can. In 3.1 they tease Shylock, eliciting from him his famous speech claiming equality with Christians. Salerio is simply a conventional figure whose role is to further the development of more significant characters.

In some editions Salerio's part, except in 3.2, is assigned to Salarino, who is thought of as a separate character. However, most modern scholarship holds that the latter name is simply a 16th-century typographical error.

**Salisbury (1), John Montague (Montacute), Earl of (c. 1350–1400)** Historical figure and minor character in *Richard II*, a supporter of King RICHARD II. In 2.4 Salisbury receives notice from the Welsh CAPTAIN (4) that his troops will no longer remain in Richard's army, and he mourns the likely downfall of the king. He himself stays loyal and is eventually killed fighting against Bolingbroke; his death is reported by the Earl of NORTHUMBERLAND (1) in 5.6.8.

The historical Salisbury was a trusted adviser to Richard for many years; in 1396 he negotiated the king's marriage to QUEEN (13) Isabel. A year after Richard's deposition, Salisbury was captured in battle, along with the Duke of SURREY (2), by Lord BERKELEY, who turned his prisoners over to a mob, which beheaded them. Salisbury's son was the Earl of SALISBURY (3) in *Henry V* and *1 Henry VI*.

**Salisbury (2), Richard Neville, Earl of (1400–1460)** Historical figure and character in *2 Henry VI*, a patriotic nobleman, distinguished from the selfishly ambitious aristocrats around him. In 1.1 Salisbury and his son, the Earl of WARWICK (3), determine to support the Duke of GLOUCESTER (4), an honest and capable minister, against his enemies. In general, Salisbury is overshadowed by Warwick, who is to be a major figure in *3 Henry VI*. For example, in 3.2 Salisbury, speaking for the enraged COMMONS, demands that SUFFOLK (3) be punished for Gloucester's murder. However, it was Warwick, a hundred lines earlier, who had established Suffolk's guilt.

Salisbury's finest moment comes in 5.1, when he announces his support of York's claim to the throne. Reminded by King HENRY VI of his oath of allegiance, Salisbury replies, 'It is great sin to swear unto a sin, / But greater sin to keep a sinful oath . . .' (5.1.182–183).

The historical Salisbury was the son of the Earl of WESTMORELAND (1), who appears in *1* and *2 Henry IV*. He was also the son-in-law, and thus successor to the title, of the SALISBURY (3) who dies at the siege of ORLÉANS in *1 Henry VI*. Shakespeare distorted Salisbury's political career considerably. Although he was not an enemy of Gloucester, he was not a notable ally of that lord either. As a great magnate of northern England, Salisbury was rather more limited in his concerns than the patriot depicted in *2 Henry VI*. His chief rivals were the Percy family, of neighbouring Northumberland, and he did not become close to York until well after most of the events in the play, York's rival, SOMERSET (1), fell into a dispute over land with Warwick. As Somerset's enemy, York became the Nevilles' friend, and the family allied itself with York in time for the beginning of the WARS OF THE ROSES. Salisbury was later captured at the battle of WAKEFIELD and executed at POMFRET CASTLE, although this is not mentioned when the battle occurs in *3 Henry VI*.

The early backing of York's cause by Warwick and Salisbury in *2 Henry VI* seems intended to show how even the apparently upright patriots among the aristocracy became caught in the web of hypocrisy and falsehood that pervades all of these plays. It also serves to foreshadow Warwick's importance as the chief Yorkist in *3 Henry VI*. It is sometimes argued on textual grounds that Salisbury originally had a small role in 1.2 of *3 Henry VI*, but that the character was eliminated, perhaps before any performance was given, as a measure of economy for the acting company, and Salisbury's lines were given to MONTAGUE (3).

**Salisbury (3), Thomas Montague (Montacute), Earl of (1388–1428)** Historical figure and minor character in *1 Henry VI* and *Henry V*, an English general. In *1 Henry VI* Salisbury appears only in 1.4, to be killed by a cannon-ball fired from the walls of ORLÉANS (1), dying in the arms of TALBOT. The incident emphasises the increasing revival of French fortunes in the HUNDRED YEARS WAR. In his even briefer appearance in *Henry V*, set 13 years earlier, Salisbury adds a note of epic valour to the victory of the badly outnumbered English at AGINCOURT, saying, just before the battle, 'If we no more meet till we meet in heaven, then, joyfully, . . . adieu!' (3.3.7–10).

The historical Salisbury chiefly served King HENRY V as a diplomat and administrator, and under HENRY VI he was one of England's most successful generals. Salisbury was indeed killed by a cannon-ball at Orléans, but he did not die immediately, lingering in pain for a week. Talbot was not present, and Salisbury's funeral in 2.2 is also fictitious, for his body was in fact brought back to England for burial.

**Salisbury (4), William Longsword, Earl of (d. 1226)** Historical figure and character in *King John*, the leader of the English noblemen who rebel against JOHN (3). Salisbury is the spokesman for the other rebels, the Earl of PEMBROKE (5) and Lord BIGOT. They desert John and join a French invasion force, believing that the king has foully murdered young Prince ARTHUR. They return to John's side when they learn from MELUN that the French leader, LEWIS (1), plans treachery against them. The rebellious barons represent an evil consequence of John's evil behaviour, and Salisbury effectively expresses their motives, both in disrupting the realm and in returning to loyalty.

The historical Salisbury was King John's half-brother, an illegitimate son of King Henry II. He was not a leader of the rebellious barons, but remained loyal to the king through the settlement that produced the Magna Charta in 1215. However, upon the resumption of civil war, Salisbury joined the alliance of the barons and the invading French, leaving it only after John's death. He was no relation to the other earls of Salisbury who appear in Shakespeare's plays.

**Salusbury (Salisbury), John (c. 1566–1612)** Contemporary of Shakespeare, minor nobleman whose marriage was the subject of an allegorical poem, LOVE'S MARTYR (1601), that was published with Shakespeare's *The Phoenix and Turtle.* Originally from Denbighshire, in WALES (1), Salusbury studied law in London and remained there in the court of Queen ELIZABETH (1). He became friends with a number of writers and dramatists, including Ben JONSON, John MARSTON, and probably Shakespeare. Salusbury was knighted by the Queen in 1601, possibly for his loyalty during the attempted rebellion by the Earl of ESSEX (2). This honour is thought to have been the occasion for the publication of *Love's Martyr,* written 15 years earlier by a member of Salusbury's household, with additional works by his more illustrious literary friends.

**Salvini, Tommaso (1829–1915)** Italian actor. Salvini was Italy's leading Shakespearean actor of the 19th century, playing most of the tragic heroes but specialising in OTHELLO. In the 1870s and 1880s Salvini, a massive man with a booming voice, achieved great success touring Britain and America as Othello (with Edwin BOOTH [2] as IAGO in 1886). Until 1880 these productions were wholly in Italian, and later he continued to perform in Italian while the rest of the company spoke English, but this did not interfere with his great popularity with English-speaking audiences, who admired his stage presence and great vocal power.

**Sampson** Minor character in *Romeo and Juliet,* a servant of the CAPULET (1) household. Sampson and GREGORY (1) brawl with servants of the MONTAGUE (1) family in 1.1, after opening the play with a pun-filled dialogue in which Sampson boasts of his bold fighting spirit, while Gregory taunts him for being a coward. They both content themselves with verbal battle until TYBALT inspires them to bring matters to blows. Shakespeare presumably gave Sampson an heroic name to add another touch of humour to his role, but the thought went undeveloped; the name is not spoken in the dialogue.

**Sandal Castle** Castle in Yorkshire, location in *3 Henry VI.* Now a total ruin, in the 15th century Sandal Castle was a fortification belonging to the Duke of YORK (8). In 1.2 York's sons persuade him to renew his claim to the crown, just as an army led by Queen MARGARET (1) approaches, intending to besiege them in the castle. A battle is fought over the next several scenes at nearby WAKEFIELD.

**Sandells, Fulk (1551–1624)** Farmer near STRATFORD, a friend of Anne HATHAWAY's family. In 1581 Sandells was made of supervisor of the will of Anne's father, Richard Hathaway, in which he was described as Hathaway's 'Trustee friend and neighbour'. He was responsible for paying Anne her inheritance 'at the day of her marriage'. In November 1582 he and John RICHARDSON (1) posted a bond guaranteeing the legality of Anne's intended marriage to Shakespeare, who was a minor; they agreed to pay £40 to the church if the wedding were not properly conducted.

**Sands, Lord (William Sands [Sandys], d. 1540)** Historical figure and minor character in *Henry VIII,* a nobleman at the court of King HENRY VIII. Sands jests with the Lord CHAMBERLAIN (2) in 1.3 and attends Cardinal WOLSEY's banquet in 1.4, where he flirts with ANNE (1) BULLEN. He helps establish the cheerfully decadent tone that characterises the king's court while still under the influence of Wolsey in the early part of the play.

Shakespeare was confused about the status of the historical Sands. At the time of the play's events, Sands was the Lord Chamberlain, though Shakespeare adds an anonymous holder of that office. Though he is designated as 'Sir Walter Sands' in the stage direction at 2.1.53, this nobleman's name was William, as Shakespeare knew from his source, HOLINSHED's *Chronicles;* the error probably resulted from a printer's misreading of an abbreviation for the name.

**Sardis** Ancient city in Greek Asia Minor, in what is now western Turkey, a location in *Julius Caesar.* A few days before the fatal battle of PHILIPPI, the rebel generals BRUTUS (4) and CASSIUS meet at Sardis, where they argue over dominance and where Brutus is visited by the GHOST (2) of Julius CAESAR (1). Historically the meeting at Sardis took place many months before Philippi, but Shakespeare compressed events for dramatic purposes.

Sardis was an important city at least as early as the 6th century B.C.; it was ruled by ROME and then the Byzantine Empire from 133 B.C. until the Turks conquered it in the late 11th century A.D. In 1402 the Mongols, under Tamurlane, destroyed the city, which has been a ruin ever since.

**Saturninus** Character in *Titus Andronicus,* the villainous Emperor. Saturninus becomes Emperor through the support of TITUS (1) Andronicus, but turns against him, fearing his popularity. He becomes a willing accessory to the plots against Titus spun by the Empress, TAMORA, and her lover, AARON. He sentences MARTIUS (1) and QUINTUS to death without a trial in 2.3, and, in a fit of temper, he has the CLOWN (2) killed in 4.4. In the final scene he kills Titus and is himself killed by LUCIUS (1). Saturninus is an early depiction by Shakespeare of an evil ruler who violates the ethics of kingship, an important issue for the playwright.

**Saunderson, Mary (d. 1712)** English actress. Wife of the leading actor of the time, Thomas BETTERTON, Mrs Saunderson, as she was known, was generally considered the leading actress. She was the first woman to play many Shakespearean parts, after the legalisation of women on stage in 1660, and was particularly notable as OPHELIA, JULIET (1), and LADY (6) MACBETH.

**Savage, Thomas (c. 1552–1611)** English businessman, a co-trustee with William LEVESON of Shakespeare's interest in the ground lease for the GLOBE THEATRE. Half of the lease for the land on which the Globe stood was entered into jointly by five actors in the CHAMBERLAIN'S MEN, Shakespeare, John HEMINGE, William KEMPE, Augustine PHILLIPS, and Thomas POPE (2). To make their shares independently saleable, the actors assigned their half to two trustees—Leveson and Savage—who then regranted a fifth of it to each of them.

Savage, a goldsmith whose principal occupation was as a minor official governing the coal trade, was Heminge's neighbour and landlord, which is probably why he was one of the trustees. He was also a close friend of Shakespeare's friend John JACKSON (1).

**Saxo Grammaticus (c. 1150–c. 1206)** Danish poet and historian, author of a remote source of *Hamlet*. Saxo Lange—known posthumously as Grammaticus for his scholarship—wrote in Latin a quasi-mythical history of the Danes, called the *Historiae Danicae*, which contains the earliest complete version of the legendary tale of Amleth, the predecessor of HAMLET, though earlier fragments appear in the Icelandic sagas. Saxo was a monk, the secretary of an archbishop who was chief minister for the king of DENMARK; little more is known of him. His history, though well known in medieval times through manuscript copies, was not published until 1514, in Paris; the Amleth material was then used by a French writer, François BELLEFOREST, in a story that subsequently influenced the author of the UR-HAMLET, Shakespeare's immediate source.

**Say, James Finnes, Lord (d. 1450)** Historical figure and character in *2 Henry VI,* Treasurer of England who is captured and killed by Jack CADE's rebels. Lord Say is presented as a noble and courageous man who volunteers to stay in London when the rebels approach in 4.4, although he knows that they particularly hate him, for unspecified reasons. He refuses to retreat with the king, lest his presence endanger the monarch. Seized by the rebels and taken before their leader in 4.7, Say is roundly insulted by Cade and accused of deeds ordinarily considered good, such as founding a school. He pleads his own virtues, but is beheaded by the rebels.

Shakespeare incorporated this merciless execution of a patently good man into his version of Cade's rebellion in order to paint it as thoroughly evil. Just as the reality of the revolt was different (see CADE), so was Say a different sort of nobleman than the one depicted here. He was a widely despised landowner in Kent, greedy and oppressive, and a close associate of the equally detested Duke of SUFFOLK (3). Moreover, as Treasurer, he was generally held responsible for the high taxes necessitated by the same misrule that had sparked the rebellion. When the rebels neared London, the King's government did not hesitate to imprison Say in the Tower as a sop to public sentiment before fleeing itself. When the rebels were welcomed into the city, one of their first acts was to execute Say, who made no defence that was recorded.

**Scales, Lord Thomas de (d. 1460)** Historical figure and minor character in *2 Henry VI,* the commander of the Tower of London during the rebellion led by Jack CADE in 4.5. Scales, whose historical role is accurately presented, helps drive the rebels from London. Scales is also mentioned in passing in *1 Henry VI* as having been captured by the French (1.1.146), as indeed he had been historically.

**Scarus** Character in *Antony and Cleopatra,* a follower of ANTONY. Scarus first appears at the battle of ACTIUM, in 3.10; he reports on the catastrophic rout of Antony's forces by the navy of Octavius CAESAR (2). Despite the defeat and the desertion of CANIDIUS, Scarus remains faithful to Antony. He fights bravely in his master's brief victory of 4.7 and makes light of his wounds—'I had a wound here that was like a T, / But now 'tis made an H' (4.7.7–8)—and Antony praises him to Cleopatra after the battle. He accompanies Antony to final defeat in 4.12, before he disappears from the play. This scarred veteran—his 'honour'd gashes' (4.8.11) are cited by Antony—illustrates the courageous conduct in Antony's followers to the last, even after the desertion of Canidius and ENOBARBUS. Antony's ability to hold such an honourable soldier allows us to see him and his fate as noble.

Scarus' name, which does not appear in Shakespeare's source, PLUTARCH's *Lives,* apparently is a pun referring to his scars, unless it was a mis-spelling of M. Aemilianus Scaurus (active c. 40–30 B.C.). He was a stepbrother of POMPEY (2) who joined Antony after his kinsman's final defeat in 36 B.C.—referred to in 3.5.4—and remained with him to the end. Scaurus was pardoned by the triumphant Caesar, and though he never held high office in the empire that Caesar established, his son did under the second emperor, Tiberius (ruled 14–37 A.D.).

**Scheemakers, Peter (1691–1770)** Flemish sculptor, creator of the statue of Shakespeare in WESTMINSTER (1) ABBEY. In 1740 Scheemakers was commissioned to sculpt Shakespeare in the Abbey's 'Poet's Corner' as part of a memorial designed by the architect William Kent (1684–1748) and financed by a public subscription. He based his depiction of the playwright on the CHANDOS PORTRAIT.

Scheemakers spent most of his career in London, where he was among the most popular sculptors of the mid-18th century. Fourteen of the other Westminster Abbey memorial sculptures are his work. His brother Henry (d. 1748) and nephew Thomas (1740–1808) were also well-known London sculptors.

**Schiller, Johann Christoph Friedrich (1759–1805)** German poet, dramatist, and philosopher, creator of an adaptation of *Macbeth*. In 1800 at GOETHE's Weimar theatre, Schiller staged his own translation of *Macbeth*. He altered the play radically, making Shakespeare's grand villain into a noble victim of the malignant WITCHES. For the sake of 'purity', the humorous monologue of the PORTER (3) was replaced by a pious hymn. For all his own dramatic genius, Schiller could not accept the complex, full-blooded world of Shakespeare. This reflected the limitations of the developing German theatre of the day.

Schiller is generally regarded as second only to Goethe among German writers. His first play, *The Robbers* (1781), is about a brave man who unsuccessfully defies tyranny. It established Schiller as a defender of liberty in a revolutionary age, and its dramatic virtues—it remains popular today—marked him as a leading literary figure. He also wrote poetry: his 'Ode to Joy' (1785) was used by BEETHOVEN in the chorale movement of his Ninth Symphony. In 1787 he settled in Weimar where he taught history and developed an aesthetic philosophy. Influenced by his friendship with Goethe and his study of the philosopher Kant, he stressed the sublime nature of creativity and was a formative influence on the Romantic movement. He continued to write plays and many of them were staged at Goethe's theatre. The most notable of these were *Mary Stuart* (1800), *Wilhelm Tell* (1804), and his greatest masterpiece, a trilogy of historical plays about a famous general, *Wallenstein* (1798–1799).

**Schlegel, August Wilhelm von (1767–1845)** German scholar and poet, the most important translator of Shakespeare into German. With his wife, Karoline Michaelis Schlegel (best known as Karoline Schelling; 1763–1809), also a notable writer, Schlegel translated 16 of Shakespeare's plays (published 1797–1801; a 17th was issued in 1810). Following the Schlegels' divorce in 1803 the remaining plays were translated by a group led by Ludwig TIECK. The complete set was published between 1823 and 1829. It immediately became the standard German Shakespeare, replacing the prose versions of J. J. ESCHENBURG. The Schlegel-Tieck Shakespeare is considered to be one of the masterpieces of German literature, and it confirmed the

stature that Shakespeare has since held among Germans as history's premier poet and dramatist.

Though best known for his Shakespeare translations, Schlegel also wrote poetry—some of it set to music by Franz SCHUBERT—and translated from Italian and Spanish. He produced the definitive German text of the plays of the great Spanish dramatist Pedro Calderón (1600–1681), as well as works by Dante Alighieri (1265–1321), Ludovico ARIOSTO, and Miguel de CERVANTES. He and his brother the philosopher Friedrich von Schlegel (1772–1829) are regarded as among the most important founders of German Romanticism, a literary and artistic movement that swept Europe in the early 19th century.

**Schoolmaster (1)** Character in *Antony and Cleopatra*. See AMBASSADOR (3).

**Schoolmaster (2)** Minor character in *The Two Noble Kinsmen*, the director of a country dance performance. In 3.5 the Schoolmaster directs a group of COUNTRYMEN and women, including NELL (2), in an entertainment presented to the court of Duke THESEUS (2). He is comically pedantic, both in instructing his charges and in his PROLOGUE (1) to the performance. Since most scholars believe that Shakespeare did not write 3.5, the Schoolmaster is probably the creation of John FLETCHER (2).

**Schröder, Friedrich Ludwig (1744–1816)** German actor and producer. In a series of productions beginning in 1776, Schröder introduced Shakespeare to the German theatre; except for an occasional flawed adaptation, such as *Der* BESTRAFTE BRUDERMORD, the playwright's works had not been performed in Germany since the early 17th century, when English touring companies may have presented some of them. However, beginning with Schröder's *Hamlet* (in which the producer played the GHOST [3]), Shakespeare became a staple of the German stage. Schröder was one of the leading lights of the German theatre, both as an actor and a producer. Born into a family of travelling players, he began his career at the age of three and eventually became a major figure in German cultural affairs of the late 18th and early 19th century.

**Schubert, Franz (1797–1828)** German composer of the Romantic movement whose many famous works include settings for three of the best-known songs from Shakespeare's plays (see SONG). In the summer of 1827 Schubert composed music for a *Standchen*, or 'Serenade', a translation of 'Hark, Hark, the Lark' (*Cymbeline*, 2.3.19–25), a *Trinklied*, or 'Drinking Song' (*Antony and Cleopatra*, 2.7.111–116), and, the most famous of the three, *An Sylvia*, or 'Who Is Silvia?' (*The Two Gentlemen of Verona*, 4.2.38–52). The first of these was translated by August Wilhelm von SCHLEGEL; the others by a friend of the composer, Edouard von Bauernfeld. According to a famous—though probably untrue—story, Schubert wrote *An Sylvia* on the back of a menu during a meal.

Schubert, a very prolific and highly influential composer, also set to music a great deal of poetry by J. W. von GOETHE, Friedrich SCHILLER, and Schlegel, as well as German translations of the work of such varied authors as Aeschylus, Petrarch, Alexander POPE (1), and Sir Walter Scott. Best known for his songs and chamber music, he also wrote important symphonic works.

**Schücking, Levin Ludwig (1878–1964)** German scholar. Schücking was a leading member of the so-called 'realist' school of Shakespearean criticism, which attempted to relate the plays to the traditions and practises of ELIZABETHAN DRAMA and ELIZABETHAN THEATRE, rather than simply analysing the characters and their actions. Schücking's most influential work, translated as *Character Problems in Shakespeare's Plays* (1922), deals with the techniques the playwright inherited from earlier drama, such as having characters comment on the play's developments in the manner of a CHORUS (1).

**Scofield, Paul (b. 1922)** British actor. Scofield is especially noted for his portrayals of LEAR, directed by Peter BROOK (2), both in the 1962 stage production and the 1970 FILM. As a young man, Scofield joined the Birmingham Repertory Theatre under Barry JACKSON (1), and he went with Jackson to the Shakespeare Memorial Theatre in STRATFORD in 1945. There, he established himself as a classical actor, playing ARMADO, FESTE, MERCUTIO, and HAMLET, among others. He has since played many classical and modern parts. He has only taken movie roles occasionally, but he is probably most widely known as Sir Thomas MORE in the film *A Man for All Seasons,* a part he had previously played on the stage and for which he won an Academy Award in 1966.

**Scot (Scott), Reginald (c. 1538–1599)** English writer, author of a source for *A Midsummer Night's Dream, Macbeth,* and *The Tempest.* Scot's *The Discovery of Witchcraft* (1584) provided Shakespeare with items of folklore about witches and fairies that he used in his plays, especially in his depictions of PUCK in the *Dream,* the WITCHES in *Macbeth,* and ARIEL in *The Tempest.* Scot himself, however, derided the information as silly superstitions.

Scot, a country gentleman and justice of the peace for KENT (1), was appalled by the persecution of 'witches'—mostly poor or retarded people—that was raging in his time, and he wrote his book against the practise, attempting to disprove the existence of witchcraft. He was a century ahead of his time, for witches continued to be persecuted in England until the early 18th century. Scot's work was attacked by 'authorities' on witchcraft, including King JAMES I. Scot also wrote a pioneering technical manual on the growing of hops, a major Kentish industry.

**Scotland** Country to the north of England, setting for most of *Macbeth.* The importance of the Scottish nation is stressed at the beginning of the play. Act 1 details the suppression of a revolution supported by foreigners from Norway and Ireland. MACBETH's murder of King DUNCAN is repeatedly associated with a catastrophic decline in Scotland's fortunes and the rebellion against him is specifically intended to restore 'a swift blessing [to the] suffering country' (3.6.47–48). The trials of the nation, especially as described in the conversations of the exiled lords in 4.3 demonstrate the growth of evil that Macbeth's deed triggers. As ROSSE puts it, Scotland under Macbeth seems no longer 'our mother, but our grave' (4.3.166). Shakespeare had a specific lesson in mind here: that immorality in the leaders of a country leads to its social and political disruption. This is a lesson that is very prominent in the HISTORY PLAYS, also.

Scotland loomed large in English political considerations in Shakespeare's day. It was traditionally allied with England's enemy, FRANCE (1), especially since Scotland's ruling family was Catholic, and Scottish plots were feared throughout the reign of Queen ELIZABETH (1). Mary, Queen of Scots, was imprisoned in England for many years and eventually executed. However, her son King James VI of Scotland was a Protestant, and he succeeded Elizabeth as JAMES I in 1603 and united the two lands under a single ruler for the first time (though a full merger was still a century away).

James' accession was probably the reason that Shakespeare wrote a play set in Scotland, and allusions to James' reign are scattered throughout *Macbeth.* Some scholars believe that the playwright may also have been inspired by a trip to Scotland as an actor. He and other members of the CHAMBERLAIN'S MEN may have fled to Scotland in the wake of their seeming involvement in the rebellion of the Earl of ESSEX (2) in February 1601. They may have performed with Laurence FLETCHER (3) in Aberdeen. John Dover WILSON (3) went so far as to propose that *Macbeth* was written in Scotland and first performed in Edinburgh. However, these theories cannot be convincingly supported with any known evidence.

**Scout** Minor character in *1 Henry VI,* the French soldier who brings news of the English army's approach in 5.2.

**Scribe** Minor character in *Henry VIII,* petty official at the divorce trial of Queen KATHERINE. In 2.4.6 and

8–9, the Scribe orders the CRIER to formally demand the presence of King HENRY VIII and the queen, thus opening the proceedings. His tiny role stresses the pomp and ceremony of the occasion, thereby pointing up Katherine's vulnerability to the king's power.

**Scrivener, The** Minor character in *Richard III*, a clerk who learns of a crime committed by RICHARD III. In 3.6 the Scrivener, whose job is to make formal written copies of documents, knows that a certain indictment he has copied is false. Supposedly the record of a proceeding justifying the hasty execution of Lord HASTINGS (3), it was actually written before Hastings had even been accused of any misdeed. The Scrivener realises that Richard has arranged for the death of an innocent man through legal means, and he grieves that the state of public affairs permits such a ploy to succeed.

This incident, like one in 2.3 (see CITIZEN [2]), serves to emphasise that corruption can never be secret. The common people become aware of such cynical machinations, and society comes closer to political chaos as its leaders seem increasingly untrustworthy. This pattern grows more evident as Richard's ambitions come to dominate public life.

**Scroop (1) (Le Scroop, Scroope, Scrope), Henry (c. 1376–1415)** Historical figure and minor character in *Henry V*, a traitor who plans to assassinate King HENRY V but fails and is sentenced to death. Scroop and his fellow conspirators, the Earl of CAMBRIDGE and Sir Thomas GREY (3), are asked by Henry to advise him on punishing a drunken soldier who has defamed him. They all recommend severity. Then the king reveals his knowledge of their plot and applies their own rule to them, refusing them mercy. They each thank God for preventing their success, in conventional speeches intended to emphasise Henry's own majesty.

Henry judges Cambridge and Grey in a few words, but he chastises Scroop at great length (2.2.93–142). Scroop's treason is deemed particularly heinous, for he has been Henry's close friend and confidant for many years. Henry goes so far as to call Scroop's offence 'another fall of man' (2.2.142). The combination of Henry's grief at his friend's betrayal and his unswerving sternness demonstrates both the humanity and the maturity of the king.

The historical Scroop was indeed close to Henry, but he was also associated with a history of rebellion against the LANCASTER (1) dynasty. Although Shakespeare does not mention it in *Henry V*, Scroop's father, Stephen SCROOP (3), had been a supporter of RICHARD II, who was deposed by Henry's father, Lord BOLINGBROKE (1), later King HENRY IV, as is enacted in *Richard II*. Further, Scroop's uncle, the ARCHBISHOP (3) of the *Henry IV* plays, led two revolts against Henry IV. Scroop and his father disassociated themselves from

the Archbishop, and Scroop was given high office under Henry V. Accordingly, his involvement in Cambridge's plot was punished with particular rigour: Grey and Cambridge were each beheaded, while Scroop was drawn and quartered.

**Scroop (2), (Scroope, Scrope) Richard** Character in *1, 2 Henry IV*. See ARCHBISHOP (3).

**Scroop (3), (Le Scroop, Scroope, Scrope) Stephen (c. 1350–1406)** Historical figure and minor character in *Richard II*, a supporter of RICHARD II. In 3.2 Scroop tells Richard of the popular acceptance of BOLINGBROKE (1), the execution of BUSHY and GREENE (1), and the defection of the Duke of YORK (4). These tidings undo the king, plunging him into near-hysterical despair, and Scroop remarks pointedly on the king's state; 'Sweet love, I see, changing his property, / Turns to the sourest and most deadly hate' (3.2.135–136).

The historical Scroop family did not accept Bolingbroke's rule. Stephen's brother, the ARCHBISHOP (3) of York, appears as a rebel in *1* and *2 Henry IV*. Stephen dissociated himself from that rebellion, but his son, Henry SCROOP (1), betrayed Bolingbroke's son, HENRY V, and is executed for treason in *Henry V*.

**Seacoal, George** Minor character in *Much Ado About Nothing*, one of the WATCHMEN (3) of MESSINA. In 3.3.11 Seacoal is recommended to DOGBERRY, the chief constable, as a likely leader of the watch because he is literate, and he is appointed to the position. He has no particular personality and cannot readily be distinguished from the other Watchmen. However, Seacoal may be presumed to be the speaker of commands—such as 'We charge you in the Prince's name, stand!' (3.3.159)—by virtue of his office.

A Francis Seacoal is mentioned by Dogberry at 3.5. 54; he is apparently the SEXTON, who appears in 4.2. The unnecessary and unlikely coincidence of surnames is best explained as one of the many minor errors in the plays. Here, the playwright hastily gave an inconsequential character a name that happened to be handy, forgetting that he had just used it for another such figure.

**Sebastian (1)** In *The Two Gentlemen of Verona*, the name JULIA takes while disguised as a boy.

**Sebastian (2)** Character in *Twelfth Night*, lover of OLIVIA and twin brother of VIOLA. Sebastian and Viola's virtually perfect resemblance to each other—a convention of romantic comedy—permits the traditional comic confusion of mistaken identities, but it also provides for two different presentations of love's restorative power. Sebastian resolves issues that his sister has raised, and his entrance stimulates the play's climax and helps both Olivia and ORSINO to fulfil their potential.

Much of Sebastian's tale is similar to his sister's: both are shipwrecked and saved by helpful seamen—ANTONIO (4), in Sebastian's case—who direct them to the court of ILLYRIA; both are pursued by Olivia; both are threatened with combat by SIR ANDREW; and both are betrothed in the play's happy ending. These parallels heighten the effect of the comic confusions that ensue when Sebastian is mistaken for Cesario, the disguised Viola, and it also emphasises the function Sebastian serves when the mistakes are cleared up in 5.1. While Viola's pose as Cesario has inspired love—hers for Orsino and Olivia's for Cesario—Sebastian's arrival is necessary for these passions to be properly directed.

The correct relationship among the play's lovers—skewed at first by Viola's disguise and Orsino's misplaced passion for Olivia—begins to take shape when Sebastian meets Olivia, who believes him to be Cesario, in 4.1. He is naturally mystified by this ardent woman, but he recognises the value of her love, even knowing that it is based on some mistake, and he boldly plays along. In the same spirit, Sebastian immediately accepts Olivia's proposal of marriage in 4.3.

Sebastian's situation in Illyria differs from Viola's in one highly significant way: while Viola is disguised as a man, Sebastian's gender is unconfused and permits him a forthrightness not available to his sister. When Sir Andrew and SIR TOBY oppose him, his response is squarely in the tradition of masculine assertiveness: he fights and drives them away, in both 4.1 and 5.1. His clear-cut sexual identity allows Sebastian to provide the missing elements in the lives of the other characters. He is the manly youth of Viola's disguise, and he is the lover whom Olivia thought she had found in the disguised Viola. He is the dominant male that Orsino should be but has lost sight of through his romantic affectations. He is also to become the aristocratic husband that MALVOLIO has inappropriately aspired to be.

Sebastian thus helps to redeem other characters, and this fact, combined with Viola's capacity for devotion and sacrifice, has suggested to some scholars a religious interpretation of the play. In any case, his role in the resolution of the play's entanglements makes him the central figure of Acts 4–5, although he says relatively little and lacks a vibrant personality. He is not one of Shakespeare's more endearing heroes, but he is certainly a powerful one.

**Sebastian (3)** Character in *The Tempest*, brother of King ALONSO of Naples. Sebastian is led by ANTONIO (5), the villainous deposer of PROSPERO, into greater crimes than he would otherwise have contemplated. In 1.1 Antonio and Sebastian arrogantly curse the seamen of their storm-wracked vessel, and after they are shipwrecked on Prospero's magical island they are equally offensive in ridiculing GONZALO's attempts to cheer Alonso, who believes his son is dead. However, Sebastian demonstrates no more than crude offensiveness until Antonio suggests that they kill the sleeping Alonso, so that he, Sebastian, may inherit the crown of Naples. Sebastian accepts the idea greedily, but Antonio's primacy in evil is demonstrated in their plan: Antonio will stab Alonso, while Sebastian takes on Gonzalo. This is Sebastian's moment of greatest involvement. Prospero's sprite ARIEL prevents the assassinations and reduces Sebastian and the others to madness. In 5.1, free from the spell, Sebastian has one more significant line. When Prospero restores Alonso's son, Sebastian cries, 'A most high miracle.' (5.1.177). In acknowledgeing the spiritual power of the moment, Sebastian contrasts with Antonio, who remains unmoved. Thus, Sebastian, like Alonso, finally comes to exemplify humanity's capacity for redemption.

**Second Clown** Character in *Hamlet*. See OTHER.

**Second Commoner** Character in *Julius Caesar*. See COBBLER.

**Second Grave-digger** Character in *Hamlet*. See OTHER.

**Second Murderer (1)** One of 'two or three' characters in *2 Henry VI*, the killers of the Duke of GLOUCESTER (4). Several men, two of whom speak, flee the scene of the crime at the beginning of 3.2. The Second Murderer regrets the deed because their victim had died religiously. (See also FIRST MURDERER [1].)

**Second Murderer (2)** Character in *Richard III*, one of the two assassins hired by RICHARD III to kill his brother the Duke of CLARENCE (1). The Second Murderer has an attack of conscience as the two approach their victim in 1.4, but the FIRST MURDERER (2) reminds him of the money they are to receive, and he recovers. Their short exchange provides the only real comic relief in the play. Later in this scene, in an entirely serious vein, the Second Murderer shows an inclination to grant Clarence the mercy he pleads for. The First Murderer thereupon finishes off the duke, and the Second declares that he is too remorseful to accept payment and leaves the reward to his colleague.

**Second Murderer (3)** Character in *Macbeth*. See FIRST MURDERER (3).

**Secretary** Minor character in *Henry VIII*, an aide to Cardinal WOLSEY. In 1.1 the Secretary speaks two half-lines, to inform the cardinal that the SURVEYOR who is to testify against the Duke of BUCKINGHAM (1) is ready to be interrogated. As part of Wolsey's businesslike retinue, the Secretary contributes to our sense of the cardinal's energy and power.

**Segar, William (d. 1633)** Contemporary of Shakespeare, a scholar of chivalric lore and heraldry. Segar's treatise *The Booke of Honour and Armes* (1590) probably influenced Shakespeare's humorous parodies of duelling in *Love's Labour's Lost* (1.2.167–170), *Romeo and Juliet* (2.4.19–26), and *As You Like It* (5.4.67–102), as well as his more serious treatment of trial by combat in *Richard II* (1.3.1–122). Segar held several important positions as a herald, including that of Garter King of Arms, the chief herald of England. As a result, he played an important part in arrangeing entertainments at the courts of Queen ELIZABETH (1) and King JAMES I and may thus have been personally acquainted with Shakespeare.

**Seleucus (active 30 B.C.)** Historical figure and minor character in *Antony and Cleopatra*, CLEOPATRA's treasurer. In 5.2 Cleopatra calls upon Seleucus to confirm the inventory of her household that she has submitted to the conqueror of Egypt, Octavius CAESAR (2). Instead, he tells Caesar that she has withheld more than she has listed. Caesar, who is amused by Cleopatra's ploy, tells Seleucus to leave as Cleopatra subjects him to a tirade of insults.

This episode has been variously interpreted. It can be seen as evidence of Cleopatra's shallow character. It continues the play's earlier portrayal of a grasping courtesan who here attempts to salvage what she can from the wreck of her and ANTONY's fortunes. On the other hand, it may actually demonstrate her cool—and, in the play's scheme of things, noble—intention to die rather than live on in humiliating defeat without Antony. Once Caesar has the idea that Cleopatra wishes only to retain a comfortable existence, he leaves her alone, free to arrange her suicide, whereas if her real intention were known, he would prevent her. Shakespeare may have intended Seleucus as the the queen's pawn in a successful effort to deceive the conqueror. The playwright's source, PLUTARCH's *Lives*, states that this was her plan, and though Shakespeare changes many of the details in Plutarch's account of the episode, he may well have included it for the same purpose.

**Sempronius (1)** Minor character in *Titus Andronicus*. Sempronius is present at the shooting of arrows to the gods (4.3), but he does not speak, though his name is mentioned by TITUS (1) in 4.3.10.

**Sempronius (2)** Minor character in *Timon of Athens*, an ungrateful friend of TIMON. Sempronius is among the friends to whom Timon sends for assistance when he faces bankruptcy after he has showered his friends—including Sempronius—with expensive gifts.

However, when Sempronius is approached by Timon's SERVANT (23), he pretends to be offended that Timon has gone to other friends first and he refuses to lend him money. 'Who bates mine honour shall not know my coin' (3.3.28), he declares. Sempronius—with LUCIUS (3) and LUCULLUS who have similarly rejected Timon's request in previous scenes—helps demonstrate the hypocrisy and cold-heartedness of the Athenian aristocracy, one of the play's important themes.

**Senator (1)** Any of several minor characters in *Othello*, lawmakers of VENICE. The Senators meet with the DUKE (5), in 1.3, to discuss the threat presented by a Turkish attack on CYPRUS. When they summon their chief general, OTHELLO, they hear BRABANTIO's complaint that Othello has stolen his daughter DESDEMONA. With the Duke, they find Othello innocent of any crime, appoint him commander of Venetian forces in Cyprus, and order him abroad. The Senators are spoken for by the First Senator (except for one brief passage by a Second Senator), who asks appropriate questions. The Senators and the Duke illustrate the pomp and power of the Venetian state; they also demonstrate a collective capacity for social co-operation and judgement by consensus, aspects of society that are notably absent when the main plot unfolds on Cyprus.

**Senator (2)** Any of several characters in *Coriolanus*, lawmakers of ROME. The Senators appear in 1.1 to summon CORIOLANUS to fight for the city against the VOLSCIANS, and in 2.2 they honour him by nominating him to be a consul. In all three scenes of Act 3 they fruitlessly attempt to calm Coriolanus in his encounter with the tribunes, SICINIUS and BRUTUS (3). After Coriolanus is banished, takes arms against Rome, and is dissuaded from destroying the city by the arguments of his wife and mother, two of the Senators welcome the women back from their successful intercession, in 5.5. These lawmakers are ineffectual aristocrats, and their presence in the play serves to illustrate the weakness of authority in a disordered society.

In the FIRST FOLIO edition of the play, the stage entrance at 2.2.36 designates the Senators as 'the Patricians', and speech headings for a Senator at 3.1.252 and 259 specify 'Patri'. 'Noble' also appears in 3.2. Shakespeare knew the terms were not interchangeable—they are used separately in 4.3.14 and 5.4.54—so this minor carelessness simply indicates his awareness that the Roman Senators were aristocrats.

**Senator (3)** Any of several minor characters in *Coriolanus*, lawmakers of the VOLSCIANS, enemies of ROME. In 1.2 the Senators confer with the general AUFIDIUS; two of them, designated First and Second Senator, do most of the talking. They agree that Aufidius should command the field army, while they govern the be-sieged CORIOLES, their capital. In 1.4 the Senators ineffectually defy the Romans. The presence of the Senators makes clear that the Volscians have a viable state, rather like that of Rome, and their role as Aufidius' nominal superiors helps establish the gen-eral's position as CORIOLANUS' opposite.

**Senator (4)**   Any of several minor characters in *Timon of Athens,* the aristocratic legislators of ATHENS. The Senators benefit from Timon's hospitality, but in 2.1 a Senator begins the process of the protagonist's downfall. He recognises that Timon is losing his wealth in reckless generosity, and he decides to dun his one-time benefactor for a debt before 'Lord Timon will be left a naked gull' (2.1.31). The Senators' cold ingratitude is made vivid by Timon's STEWARD (2), who tells that they refused aid for his master 'in a joint and corporate voice [and] . . . After distasteful looks . . . and cold-moving nods, / They froze me into si-lence' (2.2.208–217). In 3.5 this hard-heartedness is displayed in a different way when the Senators refuse to accept ALCIBIADES' argument for mercy towards an honourable veteran. Instead, they banish the pleader, who in response vows to conquer the city. In Act 5 the Senators unsuccessfully attempt to win back Timon as an ally against Alcibiades, and in 5.4 they are reduced to begging for mercy. The avenging general Al-cibiades grants them mercy in the play's closing atmo-sphere of reconciliation. Thus, the Senators' callous-ness has informed both of the play's plot lines, and helps to demonstrate a favourite lesson of Shake-speare's: that the immorality of the ruling class can produce disorder and potential ruin for the society as a whole.

**Senator (5)**   Either of two minor characters in *Cymbe-line,* Roman legislators. In 3.8 the Senators inform two TRIBUNES (3) that the emperor has ordered them to raise an army from the gentry of ROME to be sent against King CYMBELINE. The First Senator does all the speaking—apart from the Second Senator's single word in 3.8.11—and he serves to convey information to the tribunes and to the audience.

**Seneca, Lucius Annaeus (c. 4 B.C.–65 A.D.)**   Roman philosopher and playwright, an important influence on Shakespeare and ELIZABETHAN DRAMA in general. Seneca wrote nine tragedies that were widely adapted in 16th-century England. He followed ancient Greek TRAGEDY in his subject matter and his effort to produce a catharsis through pity and terror (see ARISTOTLE), but his focus on bloody incidents and his attention to ghosts and magic rather than divinity gave his works a very different tone. He did not intend his plays for performance, but rather as moral lessons to be read and·studied, but his English followers did not know

this. In 16th-century England, ancient Greek plays were almost unknown, and Seneca was taken as a model of the classical drama.

The REVENGE PLAY constitutes the purest Elizabe-than use of Seneca, for his works generally centre on vengeance taken for the murder of a parent or child and depict bloody killings and physical mutilations. A number of other Senecan devices were popular with Elizabethan playwrights, including Shakespeare: soliloquies, exaggerated rhetoric, insanity and feigned insanity, and the use of ghosts. After the 1560s Seneca's plays were staged infrequently, but Shake-speare presumed his audiences were at least familiar with their reputation and general character, for he has POLONIUS, tritely evaluating theatrical styles, remark that 'Seneca cannot be too heavy' (*Hamlet* 2.2.396).

Highly organised and formal, Seneca's plays ob-serve the classical unities—that is, the events take place within a few hours and occur in a single location. There are five acts, which progress from exposition to anti-climax in a prescribed sequence. The plays are filled with moralising and instructive passages and em-ploy formal devices such as the PROLOGUE (1) and the CHORUS (1). Seneca concentrated on the failings of the evil and powerful; as Sir Philip SIDNEY remarked of his works, 'high and excellent Tragedie . . . maketh kings fear to be tyrants'. *Titus Andronicus* is very Senecan in subject matter and tone, and Shakespeare employed Senecan elements in many other works, especially *Richard III, Hamlet,* and *Macbeth.* Later in his career, however, Seneca's influence diminished.

Seneca, the aristocratic son of a famous rhetorician and historian, also became a famous orator and writer. In 41 A.D. he was exiled by the emperor Claudius, for reasons that are not known; called back in 49, he be-came tutor to the future emperor Nero. He was proba-bly mentally ill to some extent, as the content of his plays suggests. He nevertheless wrote a number of works on law and philosophy—the plays themselves were meant as works of moral philosophy—but many have been lost. He advocated a stoic detachment and contempt for death that was later praised by Christian thinkers. As a minister under Nero, Seneca was reluc-tantly involved in the emperor's crimes. For instance, he composed a defence for Nero's murder of his own mother. Implicated in a conspiracy against Nero—probably unjustly—Seneca was sentenced to death. He was permitted to commit suicide, which he did with a serenity that became legendary.

**Senior**   Character in *As You Like It.* See DUKE (7).

**Sentry (1)**   Any of several minor characters in *1 Henry VI,* French soldiers. Posted on the walls of ORLÉANS (1) at the beginning of 2.1, the Sentries fail to warn their superiors of the English assault, which retakes the town. This episode, along with others, serves to ridicule the French, thus furthering the central point that only dissensions among the English could have resulted in the loss of France.

**Sentry (2)**   Minor character in *Antony and Cleopatra*, a soldier in the army of Octavius CAESAR (2). The Sentry and his two underlings, the WATCHMEN (4), are guards at Caesar's camp outside ALEXANDRIA. They discover the dying ENOBARBUS and bring him into the camp. The Sentry demonstrates the intelligence expected of a good non-commissioned officer when he holds the Watchmen back, at first, to discover what Enobarbus will say, in case he should reveal useful information. He helps demonstrate the high morale in Caesar's forces as they approach their final victory. In some editions of the play, the Sentry and the Watchmen are designated as the First, Second, and Third Soldiers.

**Sergeant (1)**   Minor character in *1 Henry VI*, a French soldier. In 2.1, just before the English retake the town of ORLÉANS (1), the Sergeant posts SENTRIES who then fail to warn the others of the English attack. This, with numerous other incidents, points up the military inadequacies of the French, thus helping to emphasise the importance of dissensions among the English in promoting France's victories.

**Sergeant (2)**   Character in *Macbeth*. See CAPTAIN (8).

**Sergeant (3)**   Minor character in *Henry VIII*, a soldier who formally arrests the Duke of BUCKINGHAM (1). In 1.1.198–202 the Sergeant follows the orders of BRANDON (1) and reads a formal charge of treason against Buckingham. He then disappears from the play. His small role adds a note of pomp and ceremony that stresses the great power underlying Buckingham's downfall.

**Servant (1)**   Character in *The Comedy of Errors*. See MESSENGER (1).

**Servant (2)**   Minor character in *1 Henry VI*. In 4.7 the Servant aids the mortally wounded TALBOT on the battlefield and mournfully announces the arrival of the corpse of the hero's son, JOHN (6), killed in the fighting.

**Servant (3)**   Minor character in *2 Henry VI* who accompanies the Duke of GLOUCESTER (4) in 2.4 when he watches his wife, the DUCHESS (1) paraded ignominiously through the streets of London as part of her punishment for conspiring against the king. The Servant suggests that he and his fellows could rescue the Duchess, but the duke rejects the idea.

**Servant (4)**   Minor character in *Romeo and Juliet*, a worker in the CAPULET (1) household. In 1.2 the Servant is given a list of guests to Capulet's banquet and instructed to deliver invitations. However, he is illiterate and seeks the help of ROMEO, who happens to be passing by. Thus Romeo learns of the banquet, which he will attend in search of ROSALINE (2) but where he will meet JULIET (1). At the banquet the Servant (or perhaps another one) is unable to identify Juliet in 1.5.42.

**Servant (5)**   Any of several minor characters in *The Taming of the Shrew*, workers in the home of the LORD (1) who takes in Christopher SLY (1) in the INDUCTION. On the Lord's instructions, the Servants offer Sly the pleasures of gentlemanly life, encouraging him to believe that he has been insane in believing himself a poor drunkard.

**Servant (6)**   Minor character in *The Taming of the Shrew*, a worker in the household of BAPTISTA. The Servant escorts the disguised suitors of BIANCA (1) in 2.1 and, in 3.1, brings Bianca a message about the imminent wedding of her sister, KATHERINA.

In the FIRST FOLIO text of the play, the name 'Nicke' designates the Servant in the speech heading at 3.1.80. Scholars recognise a reference to the actor who played the part, perhaps Nicholas TOOLEY.

**Servant (7)**   Minor character in *Richard II*, a messenger serving the Duke of YORK (4). In 2.2 the Servant brings news of the death of the DUCHESS (2) of Gloucester. This poignant moment emphasises the duke's helplessness in the face of onrushing events.

**Servant (8)**   Minor character in *Richard II*, the attendant of Sir Piers EXTON. The Servant supports Exton in his assumption that BOLINGBROKE (1) wants to have the deposed RICHARD II murdered.

**Servant (9)**   Minor character in *1 Henry IV*, a member of HOTSPUR's household. In 2.3 Hotspur summons the Servant to question him about the availability of a new horse. This brief episode helps quicken the pace of a scene—otherwise involving only the nobleman and his wife—that points to the forthcoming military crisis of Hotspur's rebellion.

**Servant (10)**   Either of two minor characters in *The Merry Wives of Windsor*, workers in the FORD (1) household. In 3.3 MISTRESS (1) Ford has the Servants, whom she addresses as John and Robert, carry FALSTAFF out of the house in a laundry basket and dump him in the river. In 4.2 they again carry out the basket, and they remark humorously on the great weight it contained before. The Servants contribute to the sense of bourgeois prosperity that pervades Shakespeare's WINDSOR.

**Servant (11)**   Minor character in *Julius Caesar,* messenger for CAESAR (1). In 2.2.5–6 Caesar sends the Servant to request an augury—a forecast of the future through the ritual examination of an animal's entrails—from the priests. He returns to report a disastrous outcome in 2.2.37–40: an animal was sacrificed and discovered to have had no heart. The episode reinforces the sense of mounting tension as Caesar's death approaches. However, Shakespeare's source, PLUTARCH's *Lives,* states that Caesar performed the augury himself; rather than attempt a spectacle— probably impractical to stage—that would distract the audience by providing a false climax before the assassination scene, the playwright moved the event offstage and added this character to convey its essence.

**Servant (12)**   Minor character in *Julius Caesar,* a messenger employed by Mark ANTONY. The Servant delivers a speech in his master's name to Caesar's assassins, offering them an alliance. In an eloquent passage (3.1. 125–134) that anticipates Antony's funeral oration, the Servant establishes a sense of Antony's cunning and strong personal style before he makes an important appearance himself.

**Servant (13)**   Minor character in *Julius Caesar,* a messenger for OCTAVIUS. In 3.1 the Servant tells Mark ANTONY of Octavius' approach to ROME. Arriving just after the assassination of CAESAR (1), his shock reminds us of the enormity of the deed. The Servant reappears in 3.2, after Antony's oration at Caesar's funeral, to report that Octavius has arrived. His brief appearances indicate the onset of Rome's future, in the person of the emperor-to-be, and remind us of the inexorability of the events that unfold in the wake of Caesar's murder.

**Servant (14)**   Minor character in *Twelfth Night,* an employee of OLIVIA. In 3.4, just as MALVOLIO appears to have turned lunatic, the Servant announces VIOLA's arrival, contributing to a sense of the busyness of Olivia's household at a moment of comic crisis.

**Servant (15)**   Minor character in *Hamlet.* The Servant tells HORATIO that some 'seafaring men' (4.6.2) (see FIRST SAILOR [1]) have letters for him. Beginning with the earliest productions of the play this part has often been cut.

**Servant (16)**   Minor character in *Troilus and Cressida,* an employee of Prince PARIS (3). In 3.1 PANDARUS asks the Servant about Paris; the Servant replies with saucy witticisms that go over Pandarus' head. The episode exposes Pandarus' foolish and supercilious manner.

**Servant (17)**   Minor character in *Troilus and Cressida,* follower of DIOMEDES. In 5.5 the Servant is instructed to take TROILUS' captured horse to CRESSIDA as Diomedes' testament to his superiority to her ex-lover.

**Servant (18)**   Minor character in *Measure for Measure,* an attendant to ANGELO (2). The Servant receives the PROVOST in 2.2 and announces ISABELLA's arrival in 2.4. His presence reminds us of Angelo's importance and power.

**Servant (19)**   Any of several minor characters in *King Lear,* members of the household of the Duke of CORNWALL. In 3.7, one of the Servants, designated the First Servant, attacks Cornwall in an effort to prevent him from barbarously putting out the eyes of the Earl of GLOUCESTER (1). The First Servant is killed, but he wounds the duke, who dies later. The Second and Third Servants assist the wounded Gloucester and they comment on the evil natures of the duke and his wife REGAN. The episode stresses the horror that has been loosed by King LEAR's folly in granting power to Regan and her sister GONERIL. At the same time, the Servants demonstrate that good still resides in some people, and thereby offer some relief from the increasing violence and terror of the plot.

**Servant (20)**   Any of several minor characters in *Macbeth,* workers in MACBETH's household. In 3.1 a Servant is sent to bring the Murderers (see FIRST MURDERER [3]) to Macbeth; in 3.2 LADY (6) MACBETH sends a Servant (possibly the same one) to summon her husband; and in 5.3, a Servant (again, perhaps the same one) reports to Macbeth that the woods appear to be advancing on DUNSINANE. In all three instances, the Servant's function is to effect a transition or provide information, though in the final scene, Macbeth's fury at the innocent Servant demonstrates his desperate and baleful state of mind.

**Servant (21)**   Any of several minor characters in *Antony and Cleopatra,* workers in the household of POMPEY (2). The servants are waiters at a banquet that celebrates the truce between Pompey and the Roman leaders—ANTONY, LEPIDUS, and Octavius CAESAR (2). At the opening of 2.7 two of the Servants—designated the First and Second Servants—gossip about Lepidus' drunkenness at the feast. They observe that Lepidus has weakened himself in relation to the others. Their conversation prepares us for the comic scene of Lepidus' intoxication that follows and points up the treachery that lurks in the world of high policy and warfare, also illustrated in the remainder of the scene.

**Servant (22)**   Any of several minor characters in *Antony and Cleopatra,* workers in the household of the title characters. In 3.13 a Servant announces the arrival of THIDIAS, an ambassador from Octavius CAESAR (2) to CLEOPATRA; when ANTONY discovers the ambassador kissing her hand, he summons Servants to whip him. Later, one of them brings Thidias back and declares that he has been punished. The actions of the Servants demonstrate that there is still a remnant of pomp and power available to Antony as he approaches his end.

**Servant (23)**  Any of several minor characters in *Timon of Athens*, workers in TIMON's household. In 4.2 the Servants, under the STEWARD (2), remain faithful to Timon when his false friends desert him. Though they must leave the bankrupt household to find other work, they remain 'fellows still, / Serving alike in sorrow' (4.2.18–19), as one of them puts it. In their loyalty they contrast tellingly with Timon's unfaithful aristocratic friends, and they emphasise one of the play's main themes: the callous heartlessness of ATHENS' ruling class. The Servants are mostly anonymous, though two of them, FLAMINIUS and SERVILIUS, are named in 2.2 and Act 3 and may be present in 4.2. Also, a Third Servant—as he is designated in the stage direction at 3.3.1—distinguishes himself with a scathing monologue criticising the miserly hypocrite, SEMPRONIUS, in 3.3.29–43.

**Servant (24)**  Minor character in *Timon of Athens*, worker in the household of LUCULLUS. In 3.1 the Servant greets FLAMINIUS, who has come from TIMON to borrow money from Lucullus. Lucullus ignobly refuses to make the loan. The Servant, who brings wine and speaks one line when he reappears, serves to indicate the affluent life of his miserly master.

**Servant (25)**  Minor character in *Pericles*, the victim of a storm who is aided by the physician CERIMON. In 3.2 Cerimon informs the Servant that his master will soon die, apparently making the diagnosis based on information the Servant has given him before the scene opened. The Servant then leaves, having spoken only briefly. He serves to help illustrate Cerimon's talents as a physician.

**Servant (26)**  Any of several minor characters in *Pericles*, employees of Lord CERIMON. The Servants deliver a large chest that has been washed ashore by a storm. It proves to be a coffin that contains the body of the supposedly dead THAISA. A Servant is sent to fetch the medical supplies with which Cerimon revives her. One Servant speaks briefly, but they serve mainly to bring stage properties into the scene.

**Servant (27)**  Any of several minor characters in *The Winter's Tale*, workers in the household of King LEONTES of SICILIA. In 2.3 a Servant informs the king of the progress of his son, MAMILLIUS, who is ill, thereby preparing the ground for the announcement by another Servant (or perhaps the same one) of the boy's death in 3.2. In 5.1 a Servant announces the

approach of FLORIZEL and PERDITA, describing Perdita's charms rapturously. This last Servant seems to be a GENTLEMAN (13) of the court, the king speaks with him of his poems about Queen HERMIONE. He is probably one of the Gentlemen who appear in 5.2, and many editions designate him as such. He is often referred to by commentators as the Gentleman-poet.

**Servant (28)**  Minor character in *The Winter's Tale*, the employee of the SHEPHERD (2). The Servant appears twice in 4.4, to announce the arrival of AUTOLYCUS and the presentation of a MASQUE at the shepherds' festival. His comical enthusiasm heightens our pleasure in the festivities. He comments, for instance, on Autolycus' singing 'O master! if you did but hear the pedlar at the door, you would never dance again after a tabor and pipe; no, the bagpipe could not move you' (4.4.183–185). He is a rustic CLOWN (1) whose naïveté contributes to the fun; for example, he foolishly construes Autolycus' songs as 'without bawdry', but adds that they contain 'delicate burdens [choruses] of dildoes and fadings, jump her and thump her' (4.4.195–196).

**Servant (29)**  Minor character in *Henry VIII*, a worker in the household of Cardinal WOLSEY. At the cardinal's banquet, the Servant announces the arrival of 'A noble troop of strangers' (1.4.53), who prove to be the masquers (see MASQUE) led by King HENRY VIII. The Servant lends an air of opulence to the occasion.

**Servant (30)**  Minor character in *The Two Noble Kinsmen*, a member of the household of EMILIA (4). In 5.3 the Servant reports to his mistress on the progress of the duel between ARCITE and PALAMON, who are fighting over her. In this way the audience is able to experience the duel while the actual combat is kept off-stage.

**Servilius**  Minor character in *Timon of Athens*, a servant of TIMON. In 2.2 Servilius is sent to ask Lord LUCIUS (3) to assist Timon with a loan, but in 3.2 Lucius refuses, though he has benefited from the extravagant generosity that has created Timon's money troubles. The episode serves to demonstrate the miserly ingratitude of the Athenian aristocracy, an important theme of the play. Servilius, though he appears briefly elsewhere, simply serves to further the plot.

**Serving-man (1)**  Any of several minor characters in *1 Henry VI*, feuding servants of the Bishop of WINCHESTER (1) and the Duke of GLOUCESTER (4). In 3.1 the king and his noblemen, assembled in the Parliament House to settle the feud between the bishop and the duke, learn that the large household staffs of these two are fighting in the streets. These Serving-men have been forbidden to carry arms because of earlier conflicts, but they are now pelting each other with rocks. Several Serving-men burst into the meeting, still fighting, and refuse to stop. One asserts, '. . . if we be forbidden stones, we'll fall to it with our teeth' (3.1. 89–90). The episode serves to point up the increasing disorder that has arisen in England because of rivalries among the aristocracy.

**Serving-man (2)**  Any of several minor characters in *Romeo and Juliet,* members of the staff of the CAPULET (1) household. A Serving-man summons Lady CAPU-LET (3) to dinner in 1.3. In 1.5 four Serving-men, one of whom is comically named Potpan, jestingly clear away the banquet while preparing for a backstairs party of their own. In 4.2 and 4.4 Serving-men joke with Capulet as they assist in his preparations for the wedding of JULIET (1). These mellow and humorous domestics serve to suggest an atmosphere of bour-geois solidity to the Capulet household.

**Serving-man (3)**  Minor character in *The Taming of the Shrew,* a servant of the country LORD (1) who informs his master of the arrival of the PLAYERS (1) in the IN-DUCTION.

**Serving-man (4)**  Any of several minor characters in *The Taming of the Shrew,* servants at the banquet in 5.2. The Serving-men do not speak.

**Serving-man (5)**  Minor character in *The Merchant of Venice,* servant of PORTIA (1). The Serving-man brings his mistress word that four unwanted suitors are leav-ing and that another suitor, the Prince of MOROCCO, is arriving.

**Serving-man (6)**  Minor character in *The Merchant of Venice,* servant of ANTONIO (2). In 3.1 the Serving-man tells SALERIO and SOLANIO that his master wishes to see them.

**Serving-man (7)**  Any of several minor characters in *Coriolanus,* servants of AUFIDIUS. In 4.5 when CORI-OLANUS arrives at Aufidius' home disguised as a poor man, the Serving-men—designated as First, Second, and Third—attempt to throw him out. He beats one of them, who runs out of the room before Aufidius arrives and the other two Serving-men withdraw. At the close of the scene, two of them reappear to discuss the stranger. They pretend to have recognised Cori-olanus' worth from the beginning, and, comically, they hesitate to speak before sounding each other's opinion. The Third Serving-man reappears with news of Coriolanus' identity and of his defection to the VOLSCIANS, for whom he will fight against ROME. The Serving-men are pleased with the prospect of an easy triumph and welcome the coming war. They make

humorously greedy predictions of excitement and loot.

In the opening of 4.5 the Serving-men fill an ancient role of foolish servants who emphasise the nobility of their social betters when they mishandle a situation. The episode may have seemed more humorous to its original audiences than it does today, for the beating of servants was a traditional comic routine, dating back to ROMAN DRAMA. At the close of the scene the Serving-men's comical nature is more evident. Their pleasure at the prospect of war is a sharp piece of social satire that keeps our attention on the political themes of the play.

**Servitor**  Any of several minor characters in *Antony and Cleopatra,* servants of ANTONY. In 4.2 Antony bids farewell to these attendants while they serve a banquet before his final battle against Octavius CAESAR (2). He announces that their allegiance to him may be at an end, and says 'Perchance to-morrow / You'll serve another master' (4.2.27–28). They respond with tears, and ENOBARBUS, also weeping, chastises Antony for causing 'discomfort' (4.2.34). Antony laughs and de-clares that he intends to be victorious in the next day's battle. He rousingly calls for the banquet to begin as the scene ends. The episode demonstrates the dis-turbed state of Antony's mind as the play's climax approaches. The Servitors, who speak only three words in unison, are merely extras who witness this demonstration.

**Sexton**  Minor character in *Much Ado About Nothing,* a scribe who records Constable DOGBERRY's comically inept interrogation of CONRADE and BORACHIO in 4.2. Exasperated, the Sexton assumes control of the inves-tigation and deduces that the WATCHMEN (3) have un-covered the plot by which the villainous Don JOHN (1) has slandered HERO. His common sense thus allows the exposure of wrongdoing that Dogberry's antics cannot.

The Sexton seems to be referred to in 3.5.54, where Dogberry calls him Francis Seacoal, giving him the same distinctive surname as George SEACOAL, one of the Watchmen. The minor confusion brought about by this unlikely coincidence is hardly noticeable on stage; it is probably simply one of the many minor slips that Shakespeare made throughout his career.

**Seyton**  Minor character in *Macbeth,* an attendant to MACBETH. Seyton appears briefly in 5.3, where he en-dures Macbeth's impatient abuse, and even more briefly in 5.5, where he informs Macbeth of the death of LADY (6) MACBETH. This triggers Macbeth's famous soliloquy on 'to-morrow, and to-morrow, and to-mor-row' (5.5.19). He is a patient servant who functions as a sounding board for Macbeth's increasing dementia.

The men of a Scottish family named Seyton (Seton,

Seaton) were hereditary armourers to the kings of Scotland, and Shakespeare may have intended Seyton as one of them. However, the Seytons' position did not exist until the rule of King Edgar (ruled 1097–1107), who was a son of Macbeth's foe and successor MALCOLM. Some scholars think Shakespeare may also have intended the name to be a pun on 'Satan', a reference to Macbeth's last loyal servant that stresses the king's depravity as he approaches his end.

**Shaa (Shaw), Ralph (or John) (d. 1484)**   Historical figure and minor character in *Richard III,* one of two clergymen who, disguised as BISHOPS (1), accompany RICHARD III as he receives the MAYOR (3) in 3.7. This imposture is intended to create an air of religiosity about the would-be usurper. Shaa and Friar PENKER were summoned by Richard in 3.5. The historical Shaa, sometimes thought to have been named John, was a minor clergyman. He is known to have been a brother of the Mayor.

**Shadow, Simon**   Minor character in *2 Henry IV,* one of the men whom FALSTAFF recruits for the army in 3.2. Shadow is extremely thin, and much is made of the appropriateness of his name. While hardier men bribe their way out of service, Falstaff justifies his choice of Shadow by observing that he will be as hard for a marksman to hit as 'the edge of a penknife' (3.2.262). It is thought that Shadow was originally played by John SINCKLO, an exceptionally thin actor who was among the CHAMBERLAIN'S MEN, the company for whom Shakespeare wrote the play.

**Shadwell, Thomas (1642–1692)**   English playwright and theatrical entrepreneur, producer of adaptations of *Timon of Athens* and *The Tempest.* Shadwell was a successful writer of comedies, usually modelling his work on that of Ben JONSON. He undertook to make an opera of William DAVENANT and John DRYDEN's adaptation of *The Tempest.* The result, *The Enchanted Island* (1674), employed music by several composers, including Matthew LOCKE, though in 1690 Henry PURCELL composed a new score. In this form the work remained popular for well over a century, influencing subsequent adaptations of Shakespeare's play. Shadwell also wrote a dramatic adaptation of *Timon of Athens.* His *Timon of Athens, the Man-Hater* (1678) altered the tone of Shakespeare's play considerably, chiefly by adding two lovers—one faithful, one not—for the title character. It was popular for more than 50 years.

**Shakespeare (1), Anne (1571–1579)**   Shakespeare's sister. Anne Shakespeare was born when the future playwright was seven and died when he was 14. There is evidence that her loss may have been particularly grievous to the family, for the record reveals that her funeral was unusually elaborate and costly, although the financial difficulties of John SHAKESPEARE (9) were great at the time. Nothing else is known of her.

**Shakespeare (2), Anne Hathaway**   Shakespeare's wife. See HATHAWAY.

**Shakespeare (3), Edmund (1580–1607)**   Shakespeare's brother, probably an actor in LONDON. The playwright's brother is only recorded as such at his christening, but he is thought to have been the 'Edmund Shakespeare, a player' who was buried in St Saviour's Church, SOUTHWARK, on December 31, 1607. In addition to the coincidence of name, his very expensive funeral, presumably unaffordable by the estate of an unknown actor, suggests a prosperous relative such as the playwright. Four months earlier, the burial of an illegitimate child, 'Edward, sonne of Edward Shackspeere' was recorded at a different London church; this may be Edmund, mistakenly given the boy's name (similar errors are known in this parish register). Edmund was probably named for his uncle Edmund Lambert (father of John LAMBERT).

**Shakespeare (4), Gilbert (1566–1612)**   Shakespeare's brother. Gilbert Shakespeare was recorded as a haberdasher in LONDON in 1597, but he also lived in STRATFORD, or at least had returned there by 1602, when he stood in for William by receiving a deed to land the playwright had bought from John and William COMBE (1, 4). In 1609 he was summoned to appear in a Stratford court concerning a lawsuit, though neither its subject nor Gilbert's connection to it is known, and in 1610 he witnessed a document in Stratford. He was buried there and recorded as a bachelor.

**Shakespeare (5), Hamnet (1585–1596)**   Shakespeare's son. The birth of Hamnet and his twin sister Judith SHAKESPEARE (10) around the end of January (they were christened on February 2) 1585, offers a datable association of the future playwright with STRATFORD before he left to pursue his career in LONDON, for they must have been conceived around April 1584. Their father is next known as an established actor and playwright in London in 1592. Hamnet's death at age 11 must have been shattering to his father, but there is no certain trace of it in the playwright's work (except possibly in the touching response of HUBERT to the death of Prince ARTHUR in 4.3.105–106 of *King John:* under a generally discredited but still possible hypothesis, this play could have been written as late as 1596). Hamnet was probably named for Shakespeare's friend (and the boy's likely godfather) Hamnet SADLER.

**Shakespeare (6), Henry (d. 1596)**   Shakespeare's uncle. Henry, the brother of the playwright's father, John SHAKESPEARE (9), was a tenant farmer on a manor near STRATFORD. He was sued several times over money matters—in 1587 John, as his guarantor, was sued as well, at a time when his own finances were in trouble. Henry was in trouble with the law on several occasions. He was fined for fighting in 1574 and in 1583 for improper garb in church, and he was gaoled in 1591 for trespass and in 1596 for debt—three months before his death. At this time his creditor went to his farm and confiscated a team of oxen. This may have paid the debt and secured his release, but he was fined a month later for not properly maintaining his land and the neighbouring highway, as he was required to do. However, despite such problems, he was reported to have been a prosperous man at his death, with money and a barn full of fodder.

**Shakespeare (7), Joan (b. 1558)**   Shakespeare's sister. Nothing is known of this Joan Shakespeare except her christening date, but she certainly died before the birth of the second Joan SHAKESPEARE (8) in 1569. She was probably named for her mother's sister Joan Arden Lambert (mother of John LAMBERT).

**Shakespeare (8), Joan (Joan Shakespeare Hart) (1569–1646)**   Shakespeare's sister. Joan Shakespeare was the only one of the playwright's siblings to survive him, and she was apparently the only one who married. She married a hatter, William Hart (d. 1616, a week before Shakespeare), about whom no more is known. In his will Shakespeare left his sister £20, all of his clothes, and a lifetime lease on the house in which she lived (the playwright's BIRTHPLACE, which he left to his daughter Susanna SHAKESPEARE [14] Hall). She lived there for the rest of her life, and her surviving son, Thomas Hart (1605–before 1670), lived there after her. Her descendants lived there until 1806. Joan had four children in all, the eldest of whom was the actor William HART (3). The other two died in childhood.

**Shakespeare (9), John (before 1530–1601)**   Shakespeare's father. John Shakespeare left the farm of his father, Richard SHAKESPEARE (12), and became an apprentice glover and tanner of fine leathers in STRATFORD. He prospered; he is recorded as a householder in 1552 and had bought more property by 1556 (possibly including the house that was to be the playwright's BIRTHPLACE). Between 1556 and 1558 he married Mary Arden (see SHAKESPEARE [11]), the youngest daughter of his father's landlord. He inherited his father's leasehold on the land, but he sold it to a brother-in-law of Mary, preferring his shop in Stratford. He eventually became a broker of wool and other commodities, in addition to his leather business. He was respected among his fellow citizens and was appointed and elected to a variety of increasingly important civic positions, including that of chamberlain, su-

pervising the town's finances. In 1565 the year after William's birth, he was elected an alderman—entitling his children to a free education at the Stratford Grammar School—and in 1568 he became bailiff of Stratford, the equivalent of mayor. He always signed his name with a mark, but this did not necessarily signify illiteracy (literate men of the time are known to have signed in this fashion). Given John Shakespeare's success as a town official, he was almost certainly literate, though he may have been able to read only. Around 1570 he began the process of applying for a COAT OF ARMS and establishing a position in the gentry.

In 1575 he bought two more houses in Stratford, but thereafter his fortunes declined. After 1577 he stopped attending the aldermen's meetings, at which he had regularly been present. In 1578 he was delinquent in taxes, and in the same year he mortgaged an estate Mary Shakespeare had inherited and sold other property that she owned. In 1580 he was fined the considerable amount of £40—more than his father had possessed at his death—for failure to appear in court and guarantee that he would keep the peace. The cause of this proceeding is unknown, but the size of the fine suggests the court's opinion that he was still a man of wealth. In 1586 he was finally removed from the board of aldermen because of inattention. By 1590 his real estate holdings had been reduced to the Henley Street house, and in 1592 he was fined for not attending church, with the notation that he was thought to be staying home in fear of arrest for debt. On the other hand, he was still a valued neighbour, and he was several times called on to evaluate people's estates, a position of trust.

It has been speculated that John Shakespeare succumbed to alcoholism in this period, but this cannot be confirmed. In any case the family's situation improved only after 20 years, presumably in consequence of Shakespeare's success in the theatre. In 1596 John was finally awarded his coat of arms. In 1597 John and William attempted unsuccessfully to recover Mary's mortgaged estate (see LAMBERT), but William bought NEW PLACE in the same year. Just before his death, John Shakespeare reappeared on the town council.

**Shakespeare (10), Judith (Judith Shakespeare Quiney) (1585–1662)**   Shakespeare's daughter. The birth of Judith and her twin brother Hamnet SHAKESPEARE (5) in late January, 1585, offers evidence that Shakespeare was in STRATFORD around the previous April, when they were conceived. He must soon thereafter have left to pursue a career in LONDON, but no record of him between then and 1592 has survived.

Judith married at 31, rather late by the standards of the day. She and Thomas QUINEY (3), who was four years younger, were wed in February 1616. Her father evidently disapproved of the match, for he changed his will to protect her portion from her husband (though the marriage is not mentioned in the will). Dying two months later, he left Judith £100 as a dowry, but a further £150 was held in reserve, and she received only the interest on it as long as Quiney lived. If she died, the sum would revert to Susanna SHAKESPEARE (14) and her heirs and not to Quiney, unless he had by then legally endowed his and Judith's children with land.

Judith and Thomas Quiney were married during Lent without obtaining the special licence required, and he, at least, was briefly excommunicated (the record is unclear about her). In November their first child, Shakespeare Quiney, was born, but he lived only five months. Their two subsequent children also died young, at 11 and 19, both in 1639.

**Shakespeare (11), Mary Arden (c. 1540–1608)** Shakespeare's mother. Mary Arden was the youngest of the eight daughters of Robert ARDEN (2), a gentleman farmer who owned land in several villages near STRATFORD. In 1556 she was the executor of her father's will though she was 16 and probably illiterate, suggesting her recognised capabilities. Her father left her some money, an estate that included a farmhouse and about 60 acres of land, and a share in another property, part of which was leased for farming by Richard SHAKESPEARE (12). He had also already given her other properties before he died. When she married John SHAKESPEARE (9) sometime between 1556 and 1558 (no record has survived), she moved from the Arden farm to the town of Stratford, where she lived for the remainder of her life. She had two children who died in infancy before William was born in 1564. Of five later children, four lived to adulthood (see Anne, Edmund, Gilbert, Joan, and Richard SHAKESPEARE [1, 3, 4, 8, 13]). All of her inherited property was lost in the course of her husband's financial difficulties. After John's death in 1601, she either lived with her married daughter Joan in the playwright's BIRTHPLACE, her home for more than 40 years, or at NEW PLACE with William's family. Little more is known of her life.

**Shakespeare (12), Richard (d. 1561)** Shakespeare's paternal grandfather. Richard Shakespeare was a farmer in Snitterfield, a village a few miles from STRATFORD. Nothing is known of him before 1529 (though a Richard 'Shakyspere' was resident in another village, eight miles away, in 1524). He was a tenant farmer working land on several different manors (as was common), one of which was owned by Shakespeare's maternal grandfather, Robert ARDEN (2). The records mentioning Richard Shakespeare reveal the ordinary life of an English yeoman: he was frequently fined for failure to attend a manor court held twice a year—rather than travel six miles there and back, he, like many farmers, preferred to pay the nominal fine—and for grazing too many cattle on the commons (though the vicar of Snitterfield was also fined for forcibly removing them).

He was a solid citizen who was several times called on to value the estates of his deceased neighbours, a position of trust. When he died, his property was valued at more than £38, making him a prosperous though not wealthy husbandman. Richard's wife is unknown, but with her he had at least two sons (records on two other Shakespeares of the neighbourhood are unclear), John SHAKESPEARE (9), the playwright's father, and Henry SHAKESPEARE (6), his uncle.

**Shakespeare (13), Richard (1574–1613)** Shakespeare's brother. Nothing is recorded of this younger brother of the playwright between his christening and his burial. He was presumably named for his paternal grandfather, Richard SHAKESPEARE (12). He probably lived in STRATFORD all his life and apparently did not marry.

**Shakespeare (14), Susanna (Susanna Shakespeare Hall) (1583–1649)** Shakespeare's daughter. Susanna Shakespeare was born only six months after her parents' marriage (see HATHAWAY). Her name, taken from the biblical Apocrypha, had only recently appeared in STRATFORD and was associated with strong religious sentiment, especially Puritan leanings. Twenty-four years later, she married a man of strong Puritan sentiments, Dr John HALL (4). (However, a year earlier, she was cited as absent from church on Easter, a criminal offence that was associated with Catholic dissent. The case was dropped, either because she was deemed innocent or because she had formally repented.) Susanna's only child, Elizabeth HALL (3), was born in February 1608, eight and a half months after her wedding. The Halls are only known to have lived at NEW PLACE, which Shakespeare bequeathed to Susanna, but another STRATFORD house, Hall's Croft (now owned by the Shakespeare BIRTHPLACE Trust) is traditionally regarded as the couple's first home. In 1613 Susanna successfully sued John LANE (1) for libel when he declared in public that she had committed adultery, but otherwise she appears only in business records associated with her inheritance. Shakespeare left her most of his estate: New Place (where she lived for the rest of her life), the family home on Henley Street (the 'Birthplace'), the BLACKFRIARS GATEHOUSE, and several leases on other properties. She and Hall were also residuary legatees. She survived her husband by 14 years and was buried with a gravestone declaring that she was 'witty above her sex' and attributing that quality to her father.

**Shakespeare (15), William (1564–1616)** The few available facts about Shakespeare's life are mostly mundane details, reflecting the ordinary existence of an Englishman of his day and social position. He exemplified the enterprising yeoman advancing to gentleman status, a common phenomenon in his day. Like many ambitious early modern Englishmen, he was attracted to LONDON without surrendering his roots in the countryside. In terms of day-to-day life, the only unusual feature was that he was a part of the theatrical world. In his day, actors, playwrights, and theatrical entrepreneurs were only just emerging from an era in which they were stigmatised by both law and custom (see ELIZABETHAN THEATRE). Though in the course of Shakespeare's lifetime, the courts of Queen ELIZABETH (1) and King JAMES I gave prestige to acting, and a few theatre people—including Shakespeare—got rich, protest against drama and acting was still very strong in England. The fascination with theatrical lives that resulted in memoirs and biographies in later periods did not yet exist. Nevertheless, the broad outlines of Shakespeare's life can be discerned.

Shakespeare's life falls into three main periods. His first 20 years were spent in STRATFORD, where his father was a member of the local establishment. His career as an actor and playwright in London lasted about 25 years. Finally, he retired to Stratford where for about five years before his death he was a moderately wealthy member of the local gentry. The first two periods are linked by several years about which we know absolutely nothing—the so-called dark years—and the transition between the last two was gradual and cannot be precisely dated.

Shakespeare was baptised on April 25, 1564, and since the normal lag between birth and baptism was several days, his birthday is conventionally regarded as April 23—also the date of his death 52 years later. His father, John SHAKESPEARE (9), was the son of a farmer who lived near Stratford. A member of the yeoman class, John became a tradesman and moved to the town. He prospered and became one of the leading figures of Stratford's establishment, only to encounter serious financial difficulties, for unknown reasons. These began during Shakespeare's adolescence and were only resolved 20 years later, with the money Shakespeare earned in the theatre. However, the family was evidently never impoverished, for the family home (see BIRTHPLACE) was never sold, and John's status in the community was probably not seriously diminished. Shakespeare's mother, Mary Arden SHAKESPEARE (11), was a member of the gentry, the next higher social class. Her father, Robert ARDEN (2), was an owner of inherited property that he both farmed himself and leased to other farmers. The boundary between the gentry and yeoman classes was notably permeable in the 16th century, and John Shakespeare's rise in status through marriage was quite typical.

No record of Shakespeare's education has survived, but he doubtless attended the excellent Stratford Grammar School, which was appropriate to his family's status and free of charge, since his father was an official of the town. Under the guidance of a series of schoolmasters—Simon HUNT, Thomas JENKINS (the most important in terms of time spent with Shakespeare), John COTTOM, and possibly Walter ROCHE and Alexander ASPINALL—Shakespeare studied mostly Latin literature, in Latin. Fragments of the standard textbook of the day, William LILY's *Latin Grammar,* appear in the plays, most amusingly in the famous 'Latin scene' (4.1) of *The Merry Wives of Windsor.* Also, the Latin authors he studied, such as OVID, LIVY, and VIRGIL, are echoed, quoted, and occasionally mentioned in the plays.

Shakespeare probably left school at the normal age, about 15, in 1579. It seems likely, particularly in view of his father's financial problems, that young William took a job of some sort at this point. A number of possibilities have been envisioned—based on various traditions and on references in the plays that imply familiarity with certain occupations—including assistant schoolmaster, law clerk, gardener, and, perhaps the most natural supposition, assistant to his father, who was a glover and dealer in commodities. In any case, John Shakespeare's business activities left the playwright with specialised knowledge that he was later to put to good use—for instance, when the CLOWN (8) in *The Winter's Tale* puzzles over the market price of wool in 4.3.32–34, or when a beard is described as 'round . . . like a glover's paring-knife' (*Merry Wives,* 1.4.18–19). Recollections of life in the countryside around Stratford are also frequently found in the plays (see, e.g., DAVY, HAMLETT, PERKES, VISOR), especially in the INDUCTION to the early *Taming of the Shrew* (see also SLY [1]). The town life he knew in Stratford itself is not often appropriate to his dramas, but it too is convincingly portrayed in *The Merry Wives of Windsor.*

Within a few years after leaving school, Shakespeare had an affair with Anne HATHAWAY, which led to her pregnancy and a hasty marriage, late in 1582. Anne, eight years older than her 18-year-old husband, was the daughter of a farmer in a nearby village. In May 1583 their first child, Susanna SHAKESPEARE (14), was born; twins, Hamnet and Judith SHAKESPEARE (5, 10), soon followed. The christening of the twins in February 1585 provides assurance that Shakespeare was in Stratford nine months earlier, but no record of his activities between then and 1592 has survived. That period, utterly opaque to modern investigation, constitutes the 'dark years'.

Scholarly speculation has not been wanting, of course. Most notoriously, there was a local tradition—first published in the 18th century—that Shakespeare had been caught poaching by a local nobleman, Sir Thomas LUCY (1), and had thus departed for London as a fugitive. Modern scholarship finds both story and conclusion highly dubious, and attention has instead focussed on Shakespeare's likely occupation during the dark years. In addition to the various possibilities already outlined, suggestions have included a term as a soldier—in the Netherlands under the Earl of LEICESTER or as part of the defence forces assembled against the Spanish Armada in 1588—or a job in the London publishing industry, perhaps with his fellow Stratfordian, the printer Richard FIELD (2).

A 17th-century writer established a tradition that Shakespeare had been a butcher during this period, reporting that young Will had been known to 'kill a calf' in uproarious spirits. His conclusion was based on a misunderstanding: to 'kill a calf' was Elizabethan theatrical slang for a particular comic routine, the details of which are lost. Nevertheless, the anecdote points to the only certain fact about the dark years: at some point Shakespeare became involved with a theatrical company. Many travelling companies played at Stratford, an important provincial town, during Shakespeare's youth, and LEICESTER'S MEN were there in 1586, followed by the QUEEN'S MEN (1) (who possibly had a vacancy [see KNELL]) in 1587. However, there is no evidence that such troupes ever recruited on the road, and Shakespeare probably had to go to London to begin his career.

He was probably in London no later than 1589, for he was established as an actor and playwright by 1592, when the scurrilous criticism of Robert GREENE (2) makes it clear that he was well known. The response by Henry CHETTLE makes it just as clear that he was respected and admired. Several of the plays were already popular—*3 Henry VI* is quoted from by Greene—and while the earliest plays are notoriously difficult to date, it seems likely that they included *The Comedy of Errors, Titus Andronicus,* the three *Henry VI* plays, and probably *Richard III* and *The Taming of the Shrew.* Several of these plays were performed by an acting company called PEMBROKE'S MEN, and it seems likely that early in his career Shakespeare wrote and acted for them. Similar considerations also suggest links with the ADMIRAL'S MEN, SUSSEX'S MEN, and STRANGE'S MEN. The latter seems especially likely, because the earliest sure evidence of his employment is a document of 1594, in which he is listed as a principal member of Strange's Men's successor, the CHAMBERLAIN'S MEN.

In the meantime his career was affected by a plague outbreak that closed the theatres in London for about two years beginning in 1592. Shakespeare may have toured the provinces with a company under William ALLEYN, but he may have left the theatre for a period. He turned his attention to a purely literary endeavour, the writing of book-length poems. His virtues as a writer had by now been established, and the theatre was not regarded as the best career for a serious literary artist in the 16th century. The likeliest avenue to fame and fortune was to write major works of poetry or prose. Writers offered their works as tokens of esteem to wealthy nobles, who, if they were pleased, might respond with a gift of money or even some extended financial support. It was the aristocracy that supported the literary world, for the most part, with publishing playing only a small role. A writer might live quite comfortably with a generous patron, and it is evident that Shakespeare attempted to tap this market during the long layoff due to the plague. He wrote his two long poems, *Venus and Adonis* (1593) and *The Rape of Lucrece* (1594), during this period and dedicated them to the Earl of SOUTHAMPTON (2). Some scholars believe he lived at Southampton's estate for some part of the time. The first of his dedications, in 1593, is an ordinary approach to a potential patron, conventionally flattering and self-deprecating, while the second suggests a warm friendship and makes it clear that the earl had responded positively to the young poet's work. In fact, that the two men were friends is one of the few undocumented aspects of Shakespeare's life that virtually all scholars accept.

However—whether out of concern for his independence or from love of the theatre or in view of some unknown factor—Shakespeare returned to the stage in 1594. Strange's Men were reorganised as the Chamberlain's Men in June of that year, and the playwright is presumed to have joined them then or shortly thereafter, since he was a prominent member of the company in December, when he was a representative of the troupe at court. He was to remain with this company for the rest of his career. During his first few years with them, he wrote a long string of successful plays, probably including (though dates continue to be uncertain) *Love's Labour's Lost, Romeo and Juliet, Richard II,* and *King John.* An earlier play, *Richard III,* was extremely popular as performed by the Chamberlain's Men; later tradition had it that it established both Shakespeare and its leading man, Richard BURBAGE (3), as important figures in the London theatre world. They became subjects of gossip, at least, for the only surviving personal anecdote of Shakespeare that can be certainly dated to his lifetime concerns Burbage and a female admirer, during a production of *Richard III* (see MANNINGHAM).

Tax assessments (see LONDON) and the records of an obscure lawsuit (see GARDINER [2]) reveal some of Shakespeare's residences during this period. He apparently moved across the city when the Chamberlain's Men moved from the THEATRE, in a northern suburb, to the SWAN THEATRE, in southern SOUTHWARK. Some scholars believe that his tax bill in the first of these homes was too large for a single man's dwelling, suggesting that his wife and children spent time with him in London. There is no further evidence to confirm this, however.

Shakespeare continued to turn out plays at a great rate, probably completing the following between 1596 and the death of Queen Elizabeth in 1603: *The Merchant of Venice*, the two *Henry IV* plays, *The Merry Wives of Windsor, Henry V, Much Ado About Nothing, Julius Caesar, As You Like It, Hamlet, Twelfth Night*, and *Troilus and Cressida*. In 1598 an edition of *Love's Labour's Lost* was the first publication to have Shakespeare's name on it, as booksellers realised the value of his growing fame. In the same year Francis MERES cited him as among England's best playwrights for both COMEDY and TRAGEDY and compared his poetry to the greatest of the ancients.

Throughout the 1590s, and perhaps somewhat later, Shakespeare wrote his SONNETS, a complex sequence of love poems that is one of the masterpieces of English poetry. These poems are often taken to reflect a real love for a man and a woman, but they probably represent merely Shakespeare's pursuit of a fashionable genre. In any case, if they are autobiographical they are deliberately obscure and can contribute little to our knowledge of his life; they recount no events or incidents, and they offer little concrete information about the persons depicted. Shakespeare also composed an allegorical poem, *The Phoenix and Turtle*, written for LOVE'S MARTYR, an anthology of poems (1601) celebrating an aristocratic marriage. In addition, a number of brief EPITAPHS are sometimes ascribed to Shakespeare by various scholars.

In 1596, after the first years of Shakespeare's theatrical success, John Shakespeare was awarded a COAT OF ARMS. Such tokens of gentlemanly status were nominally awarded for a family's services to the nation, but they were in fact bought, and it is presumed that the playwright paid the fees for the Shakespeare escutcheon. Such a public assertion of his family's recovery from their earlier troubles must have been satisfying to Shakespeare, especially when it was confirmed by the purchase of a grand Stratford mansion, NEW PLACE, in 1597. However, Shakespeare's triumphs were not unalloyed, for in 1596 his son Hamnet died at the age of 11. Shakespeare presumably returned to Stratford for Hamnet's burial, though his appearance went unrecorded; the earliest surviving documents indicating his presence in the town after 1584 are those recording the sale of New Place. The absence of any certain association of Shakespeare and Stratford for 13 years has sparked suggestions that the playwright had turned his back on his home, perhaps because of an unhappy marriage. However, the grant of arms, the purchase of New Place, and Shakespeare's continuing close involvement with Stratford thereafter constitute so firm a commitment to the town as to imply a strong earlier involvement as well. Later tradition recorded that he had all along returned frequently, and there is no reason to doubt it. That only the later visits can be substantiated merely points up the impact of wealth,

for it is Shakespeare's money matters that are mostly recorded. He was soon a force in Stratford, being recorded in 1598 as a leading owner of grain and figuring several times in the correspondence of Richard QUINEY (2) as a man of business. His father died in 1601, and Shakespeare inherited the birthplace, in half of which his family continued to live, while the other half—formerly his father's shop—was leased as an inn. New investments were made in Stratford in 1602 (see COMBE [1]) and land was added to the property surrounding New Place.

In London in 1599, Shakespeare became one of the partners in the new GLOBE THEATRE, a successful enterprise that furthered his prosperity. Most Elizabethan playwrights only wrote, and of the few who also acted—such as Thomas HEYWOOD (2) and Nathan FIELD (1)—Shakespeare alone was a partner in an acting company, deriving his income from the long-term success of the enterprise, rather than merely from the production of single plays. After the accession of King James in 1603, the company was part of the royal household—the number of courtly performances per year more than doubled—and in the first five years of the new regime, Shakespeare produced an astonishing sequence of major plays: *Othello, Measure for Measure, All's Well That Ends Well, King Lear, Macbeth, Coriolanus, Antony and Cleopatra*, and possibly *Pericles*, plus the unfinished *Timon of Athens*. Similarly, when in 1608, the company acquired the BLACKFRIARS THEATRE, with its unusual new scenic capabilities and its sophisticated clientele, Shakespeare responded with plays in a new genre, the ROMANCES. These, with *Henry VIII* and the lost play CARDENIO, comprise his final period.

Late in his career, Shakespeare was acquainted with the young Christopher BEESTON, whose son, retelling his father's reminiscences years later, left us one of the few glimpses we have of the living playwright. Beeston described Shakespeare as 'a handsome well shap't man—very good company, and of a very readie and pleasant smooth Witt'. Beeston also said that the playwright 'understood Latine pretty well, for he had been in his younger yeares a Schoolmaster in the Countrey' (the earliest such statement), and added that he was 'the more to be admired that he was not a company keeper [and] wouldn't be debauched'.

In late 1603 Shakespeare appeared in a play by Ben JONSON; this may have been his last appearance on stage, for he does not appear on later cast lists. His career as an actor is obscure. He certainly began as one—Robert Greene complained in 1592 that it was presumptuous of him, as an actor, to write plays—and he appears in the cast lists of several plays put on by the Chamberlain's Men. We do not, however, know of any role he played or even that he ever appeared in one of his own works (though as a member of the company he probably did). He may have played the title character in George PEELE's *Edward I* (c. 1593), for another character, referring to the king, says, 'Shake thy spears in honour of his name'. Several ambiguous contemporary references seem to associate him with kingship, and scholars have supposed that he played DUNCAN, HENRY IV, or HENRY VI (the great kingly protagonists such as RICHARD III and LEAR were played by Burbage, however). Later traditions ascribed to Shakespeare the roles of ADAM in *As You Like It* and the GHOST (3) in *Hamlet*. From all this it seems likely that he specialised in roles of older, dignified men, but that his contribution as an actor was not a great one.

Late in his career, Shakespeare wrote collaboratively (as he may also have done in the obscure early years) with at least one other playwright, John FLETCHER (2), who wrote parts of *Cardenio, The Two Noble Kinsmen,* and possibly *Henry VIII.* This almost surely reflects Shakespeare's retirement to Stratford; he was certainly in residence there by 1612 (when he visited London to testify in a lawsuit [see MOUNTJOY]), and some scholars believe he may have made the move as early as 1610, writing *The Tempest* in the country. He presumably visited the city to confer with Fletcher on the other late plays.

In 1607 his older daughter, Susanna, married a prominent Stratford physician, Dr John HALL (4), who seems to have become Shakespeare's friend if he was not already, and in 1608, the couple had a child, Elizabeth HALL (3). As the master of New Place, Shakespeare was one of the social leaders of the town; when visiting preachers came for high holy days, they stayed at Shakespeare's home. He continued to invest in Stratford real estate. In 1605 he bought a share of the tax revenues of some agricultural land (a purchasable commodity in those days), was involved in a lawsuit about it in 1611, and astutely managed the investment during the enclosure controversy of 1614 (see WELCOMBE). Also, in 1613 he bought an investment property in London, the BLACKFRIARS GATEHOUSE.

In January 1616 Shakespeare's lawyer, Francis COLLINS, prepared a draft of the playwright's last will and testament. In February his younger daughter Judith married the scandalous Thomas QUINEY (3), and Shakespeare rewrote his will to protect her portion from her husband, signing it on the 25th of March. On April 23 he died. We do not know the cause; a later tradition that he caught a chill drinking with his fellow playwrights Ben Jonson and Michael DRAYTON is almost certainly apocryphal. On April 25 he was buried—52 years to the day after his baptism—in the chancel of Holy Trinity Church. Sometime before 1622, the chancel wall received a memorial relief featuring a portrait bust by Gheerart JANSSEN (2), presumably commissioned by his family.

This bald recitation of facts is as much as we can know about Shakespeare's life, unless further evidence is uncovered. Over the centuries speculative scholars and fantasising enthusiasts have added a great variety of suppositions, extrapolating from the plays to make a more fully motivated, psychologically credible human being—or perhaps simply a more interesting person—than the simple documents allow. This is most easily done by assuming that the opinions expressed by the major characters in the plays—and by the persona of the poet in the Sonnets—are those of the author. However, efforts to interpret the works as fragments of autobiography are generally mistaken; the characters are imaginary, and because they must occupy all the niches of various fictional worlds, they naturally hold a wide range of attitudes and opinions. Even very broad interpretations are highly problematic. For instance, some critics have seen *The Winter's Tale,* in which unjust jealousy is followed by reconciliation, as an autobiographical rendering of the playwright's relationship with his wife. Though the story is in the play's source material, it is argued that Shakespeare must have been driven to choose that source by some similar experience of his own. However, in the absence of evidence, such a hypothesis remains untestable, and it certainly seems unnecessary. A writer who could produce almost two plays a year for 20 years and make real such diverse characters as, say, FALSTAFF, HAMLET, VOLUMNIA, and the NURSE (3) in *Romeo and Juliet,* can have had no serious problem finding material outside his own life. To argue that specific experiences are necessary for Shakespeare's art suggests that, on the evidence of *Hamlet,* he must have suffered from writer's block.

Nevertheless, if considered with care, Shakespeare's works can help us to a fuller comprehension of the man. Repeated motifs and concepts in the plays permit us to draw a few conclusions, however tentatively, about Shakespeare's sensibility and his general ideas on certain subjects. The HISTORY PLAYS and ROMAN PLAYS reflect a political conservatism—in the sense of resistance to changes in the existing system of social organisation—that we might expect of a man of his time and social position. The late 16th and early 17th centuries were an anxious period in England, for the newly Protestant country was at odds with the Catholic powers of continental Europe—to the point of repelling an attempted invasion—and internal strife bubbled up in such episodes as the rebellion led by the Earl of ESSEX (2). Indeed, civil war was regarded as a serious prospect during the last years of Elizabeth's reign (and after a brief respite it became reality, not long after Shakespeare's death). On a more personal level, the playwright's social position was newly achieved and, as his father's experience had demonstrated, precarious.

In these circumstances Shakespeare's politics were naturally conservative. For instance, the plays clearly demonstrate that he places a high value on the preservation of social order and distrusts the disorder that he sees in popular political assertiveness. From Jack

CADE, through the PLEBEIANS (1) who kill the wrong man in *Julius Caesar* and the shifty Junius BRUTUS (3) of *Coriolanus*, to *The Tempest*'s rebellious CALIBAN, the common man in his political aspect is generally a villain, though the playwright's fondness for the common people of England is evident in his many sympathetic characterisations, from the very early DROMIOS to the very late BOATSWAIN. Still, the violent and fickle common man is only a secondary villain. In both the history and Roman dramas popular disorder is seen as a *symptom* of moral sickness rather than a cause. The rulers of the state are the major focus, as aristocratic shortsightedness, greed, and ambition lead to usurpations and civil war. Shakespeare clearly found the greatest threat to society in disruption of the system at the top. Perhaps for this reason, he is sometimes interpreted as representing a proto-revolutionary strain of thought; however, his notions actually reflect the political orthodoxy of the TUDOR DYNASTY, which naturally feared the threat of an opposing aristocratic faction, having come to power as one itself. Shakespeare's work and life considered together do not show us a member of the rising bourgeoisie who is nervous about the crown's overweening power—the proto-revolutionary image—but rather the unmistakable lineaments of a country gentleman and a social conservative.

An interpretation of Shakespeare's life from his work that sparks great controversy is the suggestion that the Sonnets indicate Shakespeare was a homosexual. However, the love for a man expressed in the Sonnets is not sexual (as is specified in Sonnet 20), though sexuality is important in the world of the poems. Sonnet sequences were a fashionable vehicle for comments on love, and they conventionally took unrequited passion as their topic. The love triangle implicit in the Sonnets is probably such a convention—albeit more complex and involving than most (as we might expect of Shakespeare) and so more convincing. In any case it does not involve a homosexual relationship. Here, seeming biographical data have been forged from nothing, by applying modern values to pre-modern materials.

Moreover, the plays repeatedly focus on heterosexual love and its culmination in marriage. Shakespeare's heroines are frankly interested in sex. JULIET (1) longs for her wedding night and its 'amorous rites' (*Romeo and Juliet* 3.2.8); ROSALIND envisions ORLANDO, whom she has just met, as 'my child's father' (*As You Like It* 1.3.10); and PERDITA describes FLORIZEL's body as 'like a bank, for love to lie and play on' (4.4.130). Throughout the plays, Shakespeare celebrates sexuality in marriage, and he plainly sees marriage as a vehicle for the fulfilment of humanity's place in the natural order of things. Nothing that can be seen of his own marriage suggests that he regarded it in any different light, and there seem no grounds for the idea that he was not a conventional husband with a conventional sex life.

Propositions based on the work are necessarily speculative, but a few elements from the plays do seem related to what we know of Shakespeare's life. For instance, we have seen that Stratford is reflected in the early plays, and the playwright's love of country life is evident throughout his work. English rustics reappear in such unlikely settings as ATHENS (in both *A Midsummer Night's Dream* and *The Two Noble Kinsmen*), DENMARK (*Hamlet*), and BOHEMIA (*The Winter's Tale*). More personal concerns may also emerge. Looking at Shakespeare's remarkably similar doomed boys, the SON (1) of MACDUFF in *Macbeth* and MAMILLIUS in *The Winter's Tale*, both charming and intelligent lads seen in touching conversation with their mothers, it is easy to suppose that the playwright was remembering Hamnet. Also, we can surmise that Shakespeare's consciousness of his own increasing age is reflected in his remarkable sequence of tragic lovers. ROMEO and JULIET (created c. 1595, when Shakespeare was around 30) are virtually children, powerless in the face of adult society; TROILUS and CRESSIDA (1602) are young adults and have roles in their societies, but those roles are themselves oppressive and help undo their love; OTHELLO and DESDEMONA (c. 1604) are fully adult, married, and entirely in control of their positions in the world, though not of themselves; ANTONY and CLEOPATRA (c. 1608, Shakespeare was 44) are quite mature and have had adult lives full of incident and accomplishment. Shakespeare seems to have identified himself with different age groups as he grew older; this is of course natural, and in observing it, we are not learning about Shakespeare's life through the plays but rather confirming our awareness that he made his plays out of life.

**'Shall I die?'**   Ninety-line poem recently and controversially attributed to Shakespeare. 'Shall I die?' was stated to be an early Shakespearean work by Professor Gary Taylor in November 1985. Professor Taylor is co-editor of the 1986 Oxford University Press edition of the complete works of Shakespeare, where 'Shall I die?' is included under the title 'A Song', in its first publication anywhere. The poem was first designated as Shakespeare's in a manuscript anthology of poems—such as were commissioned by many wealthy patrons of the 16th and 17th centuries—dated 1630. (It is only known to appear in one other such manuscript, also of the 1630s, where it is unattributed.) Earlier scholars were aware of this attribution but felt that the source was unreliable: such manuscripts commonly contain misattributed poems and were compiled by unknown anthologists whose knowledge was often limited.

Taylor's attribution has generated much controversy: some scholars assert that not only does the poem fail to resemble any known works by Shakespeare, but it is bad poetry, filled with trite observations and feeble rhymes, too weak as verse to have been written by the author of *Romeo and Juliet,* say, with which Taylor says it is roughly contemporary. On the other hand, defenders point out that 'Shall I die?' contains a number of words that Shakespeare was fond of using, and, while contrived and artificial, it may nonetheless be seen as a virtuoso exercise in technique, employing a complicated rhyme scheme over nine stanzas, no easy feat.

However, while scholars now tend to believe that 'Shall I Die?' is not Shakespearean, a definitive verdict will probably not be reached for years. If ultimately accepted, the poem will become the first addition to the Shakespearean CANON since the 17th century.

**Shallow, Robert** Character in *2 Henry IV* and *The Merry Wives of Windsor,* a GLOUCESTERSHIRE Justice of the Peace. A garrulous old man who thinks himself sophisticated but is in fact very gullible, the Shallow of *2 Henry IV* is a perfect victim for FALSTAFF's exploitation. Given to lying about his youthful adventures with Falstaff and pluming himself on his status as a justice, he is somewhat ridiculous. As Falstaff remarks in a soliloquy at 3.2.296–322, he remembers the youthful Shallow as a laughing-stock, and he is certainly a comical figure in old age. However, he is never simply laughable, despite Falstaff's elaborate and comically uncomplimentary description. Upon their initial appearance, Shallow and his cousin SILENCE seem amusingly empty-headed as their conversation shifts from the deaths of old acquaintances to the price of livestock in 3.2.33–52, but while the exchange is a tour de force of subtle comedy, the characters are also movingly human: two old men whose minds wander as they confront mortality. Shallow's age and something more of his earlier life are mentioned in 3.2.205, where Silence remarks that it was 'fifty-five year ago' that Shallow entered Clement's Inn, a law school. Supposing him to be about 20 years old at that time, we see that he is about 75 at the time of the play. Clement's Inn, as Shakespeare's audience will have known, was an institution similar to the INNS OF COURT but less socially and intellectually elite. As his capacities in old age suggest, he was not accepted by the top law schools in youth. Such a circumstantial biography helps make Shallow a real person and not simply a comic butt.

Throughout the play, Shallow is a sympathetic character. He presents the pleasant world of the small landowner in *2 Henry IV*'s remarkable panoply of English scenes, hosting Falstaff and his men with a bountiful dinner of home-grown food. His incautious friendship is repaid when he is gaoled along with Falstaff in 5.5, when Falstaff is banished by PRINCE (6) HAL.

In *The Merry Wives,* although Shallow is more prominent and appears in far more scenes than in *2 Henry IV,* he is less strikingly drawn. He is the avuncular promoter of a marriage between his dim-witted young relative SLENDER and the desirable ANNE (3) Page. Also, seconding the HOST (2) in 2.1, 2.3, and 3.1, he helps avert the duel between EVANS and CAIUS, in a sub-plot that contributes to the play's conciliatory quality.

As *The Merry Wives* opens, Shallow—making pompous claims of aristocratic ancestry—threatens a lawsuit against Falstaff; this suit is immediately forgotten in the play, and it is sometimes thought that its purpose was solely to link the laughable country justice with some real person whom Shakespeare had disputed with and was now making fun of (see William GARDINER [2]; Thomas LUCY [1]). However, this is highly questionable, and the episode's peculiarly truncated quality probably reflects the haste with which the play was apparently written, or perhaps it survives from a lost play sometimes hypothesised as a source for *The Merry Wives.*

**Shank, John (c. 1565–1636)** English actor, a member of the KING'S MEN, one of the 26 men listed in the FIRST FOLIO as the 'Principall Actors' in Shakespeare's plays. Shank was a veteran comedian, especially noted for his antic dancing, when he joined the King's Men. Earlier, he had performed with PEMBROKE'S MEN, the QUEEN'S MEN, and PRINCE HENRY'S MEN (later the PALSGRAVE'S MEN). Though he does not appear in documents as a King's Man before 1619, he may have joined the company in 1615 upon the death of Robert ARMIN, whose roles he presumably played. He seems to have acted very little after 1629, and in 1631 he disappears from the cast lists. In 1635 he was successfully sued by several members of the company for having illegally acquired shares in the GLOBE and BLACKFRIARS THEATRES; in a countersuit, he claimed that the company was punishing him by keeping him off the stage. However, it is likely that he had simply been retired because of his age.

**Sharpham, Edward (1576–1608)** English playwright. Edward Sharpham wrote several plays, two of which have survived: *The Fleir* (1606) and *Cupid's Whirligig* (1607). The former includes a passage that echoes dialogue from *King Lear,* and this fact helps date Shakespeare's play, which had to have been written before Sharpham's work was registered with the STATIONERS' COMPANY in May, 1606.

**Shaw (1)** Character in *Richard III.* See SHAA.

**Shaw (2), George Bernard (1856–1950)** British playwright and essayist. As part of his persona as a crusty opponent of hidebound orthodoxy, Shaw adopted a disparaging tone towards the conventionally admired Shakespeare. He coined the term *bardolatry* to mock the attitude of such hero-worshippers as the poet Algernon SWINBURNE, and he delighted in such observations as, 'With the single exception of Homer, there is no eminent writer, not even Sir Walter Scott, whom I despise so entirely as I despise Shakespeare.' Moreover, he rewrote the final scene of *Cymbeline* (as *Cymbeline Refinished* [1937]), declaring that Shakespeare's version was simply too poor to be tolerated any longer.

However, Shaw could not help admiring Shakespeare; for instance, he wrote that *As You Like It*, though a 'cheap and pleasant falsehood', was 'one of the most effective samples of romantic nonsense in existence'. He purported to admire Shakespeare's poetry while deprecating his intellect. He wrote that 'Shakespeare's power lies in his enormous command of word-music, which gives fascination to his most blackguardly repartees, and sublimity to his hollowest platitudes.' Essentially, his attitude is egotistical, for in making Shakespeare seem both magnificent and ludicrous, he could claim him as an artistic equal while appearing to be his intellectual superior. This attitude is perhaps best represented in his one-act play *The Dark Lady of the Sonnets* (1910) and his puppet play *Shakes versus Shav* (1949).

While Shaw has been considered Shakespeare's equal by no one but himself, he was nevertheless a very good dramatist and a highly important writer. His criticism, mostly of drama and music, was a strong influence in late-19th- and early-20th-century Britain, helping to introduce modernism to a wide audience. A grand eccentric, he made himself as prominent as possible while advocating vegetarianism, antivivisection, a mystical religion based on evolutionary theory, and spelling reform. He was also an active socialist who promoted his political ideals in all his works, including a body of explicitly political essays. However, his most important role was as a dramatist. Shaw wrote more than 50 plays, among the best known of which are *Mrs Warren's Profession* (1898), *Caesar and Cleopatra* (1901), *Man and Superman* (1903), *Major Barbara* (1905), *Androcles and the Lion* (1912), *Pygmalion* (1913), *Heartbreak House* (1919), and *Saint Joan* (1923). Following the great Norwegian playwright Henrik Ibsen (1828–1906), Shaw dealt with such modern issues as the status of women and the problems of the poor, employing barbed wit and an elegant prose style. He was awarded the Nobel Prize for Literature in 1925.

**Shaw (3), Glen Byam (b. 1904)**   British actor and producer. Director of the Shakespeare Memorial Theatre in STRATFORD from 1952 to 1959 (with Anthony QUAYLE until 1956), Shaw mounted a number of noteworthy productions of Shakespeare's plays, including a particularly acclaimed *Antony and Cleopatra* of 1953, starring Michael REDGRAVE and Peggy ASHCROFT.

**Shaw (4), Julian (July) (1571–1629)**   Wool trader in STRATFORD, a friend of Shakespeare's and a witness to his will. Shaw's first name was recorded as July at his christening, his marriage, and his burial, though he signed himself 'July', 'Julynes', 'Julyns', and 'Julyne' (the *n*'s approximate the Latin rendering 'Julianus' or 'Julinus'). He leased a house near NEW PLACE and was thus Shakespeare's neighbour. He prospered trading wool and malt, becoming an important Stratford landowner, and he served in many public offices in the town, being bailiff, or mayor, at the time he witnessed Shakespeare's will. He was a stepson of Alexander ASPINALL.

**Shaw (5) (Shaa), Robert (d. 1603)**   English actor. Shaw was one of the three members of PEMBROKE'S MEN imprisoned for staging the allegedly seditious *Isle of Dogs* in July 1597. Upon his release he joined the ADMIRAL'S MEN, with whom he remained until 1602. He played a major role in the company's business affairs while he performed in minor parts. In 1602 he joined WORCESTER'S MEN, though in the same year he sold a play—*The Four Sons of Aymon*—to the Admiral's Men, who performed it in 1603; however, this work may have been an old text rather than Shaw's creation.

**Shepherd (1)**   Minor character in *1 Henry VI*, the father of JOAN LA PUCELLE, or Joan of Arc. This humble figure encounters his daughter after she has been captured and condemned to death, but she refuses to acknowledge him, claiming to be descended from a long line of kings. He responds by cursing her. This incident, entirely fictitious, is simply part of the play's strong anti-French bias.

**Shepherd (2)**   Character in *The Winter's Tale*, the foster-father of PERDITA. The mad King LEONTES of SICILIA, believing his infant daughter, Perdita, to be illegitimate, orders her abandoned in the wilderness. In 3.3 the Shepherd discovers her, wrapped in rich fabrics and supplied with identifying documents. He raises her as his daughter. In 4.4, 16 years later, the Shepherd hosts a country festival, at which King POLIXENES threatens him with death, for Prince FLORIZEL has fallen in love with Perdita, offending the royal dignity. The Shepherd and his son, the CLOWN (8), try to show Perdita's documents to the king, to prove that they are not related to her and should not be punished, but they are tricked by AUTOLYCUS into joining the fleeing couple and sailing to Sicilia. There, Perdita's identity is discovered and the Shepherd is amply rewarded; in 5.2 he and the Clown display their new finery, having been created gentlemen by King Leontes.

The Shepherd is one of Shakespeare's most charming minor creations, a true English rustic. He speaks in an upcountry dialect, remarking, 'Mercy on 's, a barne!' on discovering Perdita (3.3.69). In his touching reminiscence of his late wife (4.4.55–62), he conveys a strong and pleasant sense of rural domesticity. He is carefully distinguished from his buffoonish son by his gravity and sense of responsibility. Barring his understandable cowardice when threatened by a king, the Shepherd is a fine, upstanding man. As such, he helps maintain the play's insistence on the essential goodness of humanity in the face of evil.

**Sheridan, Thomas (1719–1788)**  Irish actor. Sheridan played numerous Shakespearean parts in London, beginning in 1744. He especially distinguished himself as HAMLET, and was generally regarded as second only to David GARRICK among the actors of the day. In 1754 Sheridan adapted Shakespeare's *Coriolanus* by combining it with another play of the same title—an entirely independent work by James Thomson (1700–1748)—and played the title role himself, to great acclaim. His production was quite popular and was frequently revived for almost 15 years and was later adapted by J. P. KEMBLE (3). In the 1770s Sheridan was a notable worker for educational reform.

**Sheriff (1)**  Minor character in *2 Henry VI*, an officer who is assigned the task of parading the DUCHESS (1) of Gloucester through the streets of London in 2.4 as part of her sentence for dabbling in witchcraft and conspiring against King HENRY VI.

**Sheriff (2)**  Minor character in *Richard III*, the officer who escorts the Duke of BUCKINGHAM (2) to his execution in 5.1. In the QUARTO editions, this part is assigned to RATCLIFFE, apparently reflecting an economy measure in some early productions.

**Sheriff (3)**  Minor character in *King John*, a petty official who escorts ROBERT Faulconbridge and the BASTARD (1) into the King's presence in 1.1.44. The Sheriff, who does not speak, represents the world of country gentry from which the brothers come.

**Sheriff (4)**  Minor character in *1 Henry IV*, a policeman who investigates the highway robbery committed by FALSTAFF. The Sheriff, who has a witness who knows Falstaff, accepts PRINCE (6) HAL's word that Falstaff is not present at the inn and that the Prince will guarantee the return of any stolen money; he then leaves.

**Shirley, Anthony (1565–c. 1635)**  English traveller and adventurer alluded to in *Twelfth Night*. Shirley, originally a soldier and a follower of the Earl of ESSEX (2), was famous for his unofficial embassy in 1598 to the court of the shah (or sophy) of Persia, Abbas the Great (1571–1629). Shirley made the treacherous overland voyage from the Mediterranean to Isfahan and negotiated rights for Christian merchants in Persia in exchange for assistance in building a modern army for the Sophy's government. (Shirley's brother Robert [c. 1581–1628] served the shah as a military adviser for 20 years.) Shirley conducted several unsuccessful diplomatic missions on behalf of the shah between 1599 and 1601, before moving on to other adventures, chiefly as a mercenary soldier fighting for Spain against the Turks. In the meantime, two books on his adventures in Persia were published in London in 1600 and 1601. These were extremely popular, and Shakespeare included two references to the sophy in *Twelfth Night* (2.5.181, 3.4.284).

**Short, Peter (d. 1603)**  English printer, producer of several editions of Shakespeare's plays and poems. In 1594 Short printed THE TAMING OF A SHREW—a BAD QUARTO of Shakespeare's *The Taming of the Shrew*—for Cuthbert BURBY, and in 1595 he printed the TRUE TRAGEDY—a bad quarto of *3 Henry VI*—for Thomas MILLINGTON, but in both cases the piracy was the publisher's doing, not Short's. Short also printed the first edition of *1 Henry IV* (1598) for Andrew WISE, the second through fourth editions of *The Rape of Lucrece* (1599, 1600) for John HARRISON (2) and his brother, and the third and fourth editions of *Venus and Adonis* (both 1599) for William LEAKE. He also printed the *Palladis Tamia* of Francis MERES. Little is known of his life.

**Shrewsbury**  Town in western England, site of a battle that occupies much of Acts 4–5 of *1 Henry IV*. The battle of Shrewsbury was fought between King HENRY IV and rebellious noblemen led by HOTSPUR, allied with Scotsmen under DOUGLAS. In 4.1 Hotspur receives news that his armies will not be reinforced by the troops of his father, NORTHUMBERLAND (1), nor by those of his Welsh ally GLENDOWER. However, the fiery warrior insists on fighting anyway. In 4.3 the rebels accept an offer to negotiate, and in 5.1 Hotspur's uncle, WORCESTER, meets with the King, who offers clemency. Worcester, fearful of treachery after a truce, does not convey this message to Hotspur, however, and the battle begins. In 5.3 and 5.4 several hand-to-hand combats take place, climaxing with a fight between Hotspur and King Henry's son, PRINCE (6) HAL. Hotspur's death at Hal's hands demoralises the rebels, and they flee, as is reported in 5.5.17–20.

Shakespeare followed his sources in relating the general course of the battle, and his account largely agrees with those of modern scholars, but he invented the close combat between Hal and Hotspur, along with other, less important details. Although Hotspur would not withdraw his outnumbered army, he did not start the battle; King Henry began the fight by breaking off the negotiations that preceded it. Hotspur's death did precipitate the rout; the two sides are thought to have sustained about the same number of casualties, and had their leader survived, the rebels might have won.

**Shylock** Character in *The Merchant of Venice*, Jewish money-lender who seeks to kill the title figure, AN-TONIO (2), by claiming a pound of his flesh, as provided for in their loan agreement. Shylock is a stereotypical Jew, shaped by anti-Semitic notions that were prevalent in Shakespeare's England. He accordingly possesses the two standard features ascribed to Jews at the time, a vicious hatred of Christians and the practise of usury, the latter entailing an obsessive miserliness. However, Shakespeare's portrayal of Shylock does not demonstrate his intent to promote or display anti-Semitism; he simply took the figure from his anti-Semitic source and used it for traditional comic purposes. But his genius also transformed the character into something far grander. Shylock has so fascinated generations of readers and theatre-goers

With Shylock, Shakespeare transforms a stock character from earlier literature, the miser, into a richer, more complex character. More than just a comic villain, Shylock is also a sympathetic victim. (Courtesy of Culver Pictures, Inc.)

that, although his name has become a byword for the warped personality of the unscupulous miser, few can avoid feeling sympathy for him.

The miser was a frequent comic villain in the drama and literature of the Middle Ages and early RENAISSANCE, and Shylock belongs to this lineage. He represents the killjoy against whom pleasure-loving characters unite. He is a schemer whose icy shrewdness daunts BASSANIO in 1.3. When Antonio enters in the same scene, Shylock reveals in an aside (1.3.36–47) his deep-seated hostility towards the merchant, 'for he is a Christian'. Yet his first words to Antonio are fawning compliments, and we immediately recognise the cruel usurer as a hypocrite as well. Throughout the play he is repeatedly associated with the devil (e.g., in 3.1.19–20). The famous speech in which he seemingly asserts his basic humanity—'Hath not a Jew eyes? . . .' (3.1.47–66)—is actually a baleful and chilling assertion of his intention to murder Antonio. Shylock grows more and more malevolent until, in the trial scene (4.1), he melodramatically hones on his shoe the knife with which he hopes to kill the merchant while obstinately refusing to grant mercy, even for huge sums of money.

As is true of all comic villains there is never any doubt that Shylock will be defeated in the end, and he is therefore never truly threatening. Further, Shylock is broadly comical at times; in this respect he somewhat resembles the VICE of the medieval MORALITY PLAY. His stinginess has a humorous quality of caricature to it, and he is depicted as a subject for ridicule in all but one of his scenes, even in the trial scene. In his first meeting with Antonio he justifies his usury by citing instances from the Bible, but he comically selects stories of crafty dealing (1.3.66–83) that actually cast him in a bad light. In 2.5, his dream is mocked by LAUNCELOT, and his obsessive insistence on locking his house is humorosly crotchety. In 3.1, following the renowned speech in which he asserts his thirst for revenge, a change of tone—preparing the audience for a return to BELMONT in 3.2—presents him as a farcical villain who becomes ludicrous as he oscillates hysterically between rage and delight when TUBAL tells him of JESSICA's extravagance and Antonio's misfortune. Even at the trial, Shylock repeatedly makes himself clownish, chortling over the absence of a surgeon, naïvely exulting in the pretence of PORTIA (1) that he will win his case, and hastily trying to recover his money when he finds he has lost. Only in 3.3 is Shylock purely evil, making more imperative the development of Portia's counterplot in 3.4.

As villain, Shylock embodies the negative element in several sets of opposing values whose conflicts provide the major themes of the play. First, he is the crabbed old man who opposes the expansive young lovers. His daughter flees him, saying that his 'house is hell' (2.3.2), and his contrast to Bassanio is carried forward to Portia's victory over him in the courtroom.

The final scene (5.1) rings with Shylock's absence, as young love triumphs. Further, he represents justice, as opposed to mercy, insisting on the letter of the law and refusing to accept any reduction of the terms of his contract with Antonio. Most significantly, he personifies greed, in contrast to the generosity of Antonio and Portia. In comically crying, 'My daughter! O my ducats! O my daughter!' (2.8.15), Shylock reveals that he loves money as much as, if not more than, Jessica. Among the reasons he gives for hating Antonio is a commercial one: the Merchant, in making interest-free loans, has depressed the going rate. Thus Shylock's love of money generates acrimony and strife.

It is evidence of Shakespeare's creative empathy that even an evil stereotype is developed to the extent that Shylock is. Not content with a conventional stage villain, the playwright gives Shylock's personality an extraordinary duality. Many of his speeches, even the most humorous and/or malicious, can be construed as cries of anguish: the villain is also a victim, we sense. It is easy to deride the two-faced miser who comically equates his daughter and his ducats, but it is also easy to perceive an old man, enraged by betrayal, who has begun to lose his mind. The usurer is given an opportunity to justify his practise in 1.3, and his solemn citations from the Bible have dignity and are not to be taken as only self-incriminating. He is finally subjected to a total and humiliating defeat: his oaths on his religion are nullified, and he is forced to convert. Yet our response to him remains complex. When the crushed moneylender last exits at the close of 4.1, he may be seen as an unrepentant malingerer ('I am not well . . .' [4.1.392]), as a hopeful Christian convert ('I am content' [4.1.389]), or simply as a properly beaten cur and an appropriate target for the cruel jests of GRATIANO (1). The scene may also be effectively played so as to give Shylock his pride, broken but not vanquished; this image diminishes the righteous triumph of Antonio's defenders. Most strikingly, perhaps, Shylock so vividly evokes Venetian anti-Semitism in 3.1. 47–66 that this speech is generally taken as a plea for fair and humane treatment, when it is in fact a justification for an extremely inhumane demand. Repeatedly, the playwright offers the possibility of contradictory responses (as he did, at about the same time, in creating FALSTAFF). However, it is basic to the nature of the character that, although Shylock has come to his extreme behaviour through suffering, his behaviour is nonetheless unacceptable: he is fundamentally a ruthless villain who plans to kill Antonio. Shakespeare does not ignore the process whereby Shylock has become what he is, but he is nonetheless appallingly vicious. Shylock himself says, '. . . since I am a dog, beware my fangs' (3.3.7).

This complex and powerful character dominates the play, despite his relatively small part: he appears in only five scenes and speaks fewer than 400 lines. His multi-faceted nature complicates the work substantially, and it has sometimes inspired criticism on the grounds that it upsets the graceful development proper to a romantic comedy. Shakespeare may have been aware of this problem when he disposed of his villain in Act 4; the final act affirms the triumph of the lovers without his disturbing presence.

Like many of Shakespeare's characters, Shylock lends himself to many interpretations, and he remains as compelling as ever; he anticipates the power and pathos of such later protagonists as OTHELLO and LEAR. But although we may recognise the deformed grandeur and nobility of Shylock, we must not lose our awareness of the ideal of loving community that is at the heart of the play, an ideal to which Shylock at bottom runs counter. Nevertheless, the playwright's complex and humane sensibility brought forth a villain whose downfall cannot be wholeheartedly enjoyed. We are forced to recognise the moral cost involved in his defeat, and to acknowledge that hatred is not easily overcome.

Shylock's name has puzzled scholars. Shakespeare may have derived it from *shallach*, the Hebrew word meaning 'cormorant', a term often used abusively to describe usurers, who were equated with that greedy fish-eating bird. The name has also been associated with Shiloh, a name used in Genesis 49:10 for the coming Messiah, and with Salah or Shelah, the father of Eber, from the whom the Hebrews took their name (Genesis 10:24, e.g.). Also, Shakespeare may have adapted a 16th-century English word for a contemptible idler, *shullock* or *shallock*.

**Sicilia** Latin for Sicily, the Italian island that is the setting for much of *The Winter's Tale*. Acts 1–2 and 3.1–2 are all set in Sicilia, where King LEONTES unjustly accuses his wife of adultery, leading to a tragic aftermath. Eventually, the action returns to Sicilia in Act 5, when a resolution is achieved. Sicilia is merely specified as Leontes' kingdom, and nothing Sicilian, or even Italian, about the realm is suggested in the text or stage directions. Shakespeare simply took the name from his source, *Pandosto* by Robert GREENE (2), though there Sicilia was the place of exile (not BOHEMIA, as in Shakespeare). Sicilia was suitable for use in a romantic drama (see ROMANCES) because it was on the fringe of familiar European geography and was thus appropriately exotic.

**Sicilius Leonatus** Minor character in *Cymbeline*, the deceased father of POSTHUMUS, who appears as a ghost in 5.4. The spirit of Sicilius is accompanied by those of his wife, Posthumus' MOTHER, and his two elder sons (see BROTHER [2]). Sicilius leads them as they plead to JUPITER on behalf of Posthumus. Sicilius observes that he died before Posthumus was born, a circumstance that earns pity for his son. The family demands that Jupiter show mercy and restore Post-humus to happiness, or else, Sicilius declares, they will appeal to 'th' shining synod of the rest' of the gods (5.4.89). Jupiter appears and promises mercy, Sicilius responds with awe and wonder, and all the apparitions disappear.

Sicilius' appearance is foreshadowed at the beginning of the play. In 1.1 a GENTLEMAN (12) tells of Posthumus' parentage. We learn that Sicilius Leonatus gained his surname, which means 'lionlike', for his bravery in battle, and that he died fighting for Britain against the Romans. Posthumus inherited the name and the bravery—as he demonstrates in battle in 5.2—so when Sicilius appears, we see him as an emblem of his son's virtues combined with the awesome presence of a supernatural creature. The episode contributes to the bizarre and romantic atmosphere of the play. Sicilius and the other ghosts employ a rhyming, singsong mode of speech that has encouraged some scholars to speculate that the passage may not have been written by Shakespeare, who was certainly capable of much more elegant poetry. However, the ghosts' language is ritualistic, and establishes an eerie air of the occult prior to the appearance of Jupiter.

**Sicinius**    Character in *Coriolanus*. See BRUTUS (3).

**Siddons, Sarah (1755–1831)**    British actress, sister of Charles and John Philip KEMBLE (1, 3), the leading tragic actress of the late 18th and early 19th century. Daughter of the manager of a travelling acting company, Mrs Siddons, as she was known throughout her career, was a child actress who at 18 married a member of the troupe. An early attempt at success in London failed, but in 1782, she triumphed in a non-Shakespearean play and was quickly regarded as the finest tragic actress of the day, a position she never relinquished. Her most famous Shakespearean parts were CONSTANCE, Queen KATHERINE of Aragon, DESDEMONA, OPHELIA, VOLUMNIA, and, most of all, LADY (6) MACBETH. In 1775, while still touring the provinces, Mrs Siddons became the first of many actresses to play HAMLET, initiating a vogue that has lasted 200 years. She continued to play the Prince of Denmark periodically until she was almost 50, though her evident age and increasing girth provoked some ridicule. She retired in 1812, after a farewell performance as Lady Macbeth, though she briefly returned to the stage several times—to terrible reviews—the last in 1819.

**Sidney, Philip (1554–1586)**    English poet, author, and soldier, whose works influenced several of Shakespeare's plays. Sidney's massive PASTORAL, *Arcadia* (c. 1580, published 1590), introduced romantic literature, a genre of the Italian RENAISSANCE, to England. It was widely influential and helped inspire a number of Shakespeare's works, notably *Two Gentlemen of Verona, As You Like It,* and the ROMANCES. It provided the SUB-PLOT concerning EDMUND and EDGAR, along with various details, to *King Lear,* and one of its heroes, Pyrocles, is thought to have inspired the name of Shakespeare's PERICLES. Sidney also wrote one of the most famous SONNET sequences, *Astrophel and Stella* (c. 1580–1584; published 1591), a work that inspired the great vogue for the genre in the 1590s, when Shakespeare wrote his SONNETS. *Astrophel and Stella* probably influenced *Romeo and Juliet* as well.

Sidney was widely regarded in his own day as an ideal Renaissance gentleman. Born into the aristocracy, he was one of the most admired gentlemen at the court of Queen ELIZABETH (1). Sidney went to war in the Low Countries, on the staff of his uncle the Earl of LEICESTER, and he was killed there. His death sparked general mourning in England; one result was a great poem, 'Astrophel', by his friend Edmund SPENSER.

**Silence**    Character in *2 Henry IV,* a rural justice of the peace, cousin of Justice SHALLOW. Silence, as his name suggests, says very little. In 3.2 he clearly admires his cousin's youthful career as 'lusty Shallow' (3.2.15), and he politely responds to Shallow's remarks. In 5.3, at Shallow's delightful garden party, Silence comes to life under the influence of wine: six times, he breaks into song—two of these excerpts are from known 16th-century ballads, and the others are presumed to derive from lost works—and he has to be carried to bed at the end of the evening. Although we hear of his daughter Ellen and his son William (3.2.6,8), Silence's own first name is never mentioned.

In the QUARTO edition of *2 Henry IV,* Silence's name is spelled Scilens on 18 occasions. This edition derives from Shakespeare's manuscript, and therefore the spelling is presumed to have been used by the playwright. Its only other known occurrence is in the 'Hand D' pages of the manuscript of SIR THOMAS MORE (where it is a common noun); this piece of evidence, along with others, leads scholars to conclude that Shakespeare wrote these pages.

**Silius**    Minor character in *Antony and Cleopatra,* a lieutenant of VENTIDIUS. Ventidius has just defeated a Parthian army in the name of Mark ANTONY, and in 3.1 he explains to Silius why he will not pursue the fleeing enemy. He does not want to succeed too thoroughly, lest Antony feel overshadowed and in revenge crush his military career. Silius admires Ventidius' political acumen. He has no personality and serves merely as a sounding board for his superior officer.

**Silvia**    Character in *The Two Gentlemen of Verona,* VALENTINE's lover, also loved by PROTEUS. Proteus betrays both Valentine and his own lover, JULIA, for Silvia's sake. She has the good sense to recognise the rogue in Proteus and reject him, and Julia, disguised as a page, is pleased with the sympathy Silvia expresses for Proteus' abandoned lover. After Valentine's banishment, Silvia bravely resolves to follow him. Captured by the OUTLAWS whom Valentine now leads, she is rescued first by Proteus, who attempts to rape her, and then by Valentine. However, her lover, in a rapturous gesture of forgiveness to his friend, presents her to Proteus as a gift. Julia's intervention forestalls this development, and at the play's end, Silvia is betrothed to Valentine. Silvia is chiefly a conventional figure, intended only as the focus of the actions of the two men. Nevertheless, she anticipates later, more humanly interesting Shakespearean women in her forthrightness and pluck.

**Silvius** Character in *As You Like It*, a young shepherd, lover of PHEBE. Silvius is a caricature of the ardent lover in the PASTORAL tradition that the play satirises. Silvius' courtship of Phebe is presented as 'a pageant truly played' (3.4.48), and as such it follows well-established traditions. Using a familiar gambit of the Elizabethan sonneteer, Silvius insists that, in rejecting his love, Phebe is harder on him than an executioner. ROSALIND calls him 'a tame snake' (4.3.70); his weakness, an exaggeration of the stock posture of the unrequited lover, is part of the play's mockery of literary conventions.

**Simmes, Valentine (active 1576–1622)** Printer of a number of early editions of Shakespeare's plays. Simmes, the best of the early LONDON printers of Shakespeare, printed nine of his plays in seven years. He printed the first edition of *Richard III* (Q1, 1597) and the first three editions of *Richard II* (Q1, 1597; Q2 and Q3, 1598), all for Andrew WISE. In 1600, working for the partnership of Wise and William ASPLEY, Simmes printed the first editions of *2 Henry IV* and *Much Ado About Nothing* (both Q, 1600). In the same year he printed Q2 of *2 Henry VI* (see THE CONTENTION) for Thomas MILLINGTON. In 1603 he printed the first edition of *Hamlet* (Q1) for Nicholas LING and John TRUNDELL. This was a BAD QUARTO or pirated edition, though the printer was not responsible for that. In 1604 Simmes printed the third edition (Q3) of *1 Henry IV* for Matthew LAW, and in 1607, another bad quarto for Ling, Q3 of THE TAMING OF A SHREW.

Simmes was often in trouble with the law. In 1589, only four years after completing his apprenticeship, he was arrested for assisting in the printing of the seditious 'Martin Marprelate' tracts (see MARTEXT), and in 1595 for pirating books. His press was seized and his type melted down, but he somehow got back in business, for in 1599 he was one of a group of printers expressly forbidden to print satires. In 1622 he was finally forbidden to work at all, though he received a pension from the STATIONERS' COMPANY.

**Simonides** Character in *Pericles*, king of PENTAPOLIS and father of THAISA. In 2.2 Simonides hosts a tournament, the winner of which is to have his daughter's hand in marriage. He welcomes the anonymous PERICLES to the contest despite his poor appearance in rusty armour. 'Opinion's but a fool, that makes us scan / The outward habit by the inward man' (2.2.55–56), he says. Pericles wins the tournament and Simonides is delighted. Pericles admires Simonides and compares him to his own royal father. In 2.5 Simonides tests the couple's readiness for marriage and pretends to distrust Pericles' motives. This elicits a manly denial from Pericles and a declaration of affection from Thaisa, following which Simonides announces his approval.

Simonides appears only in Act 2, but his symbolic importance is great. We are reminded of this when his death is reported in 5.3 after the perils and separation of Thaisa and Pericles are finally ended. His virtues are made clear before he appears, in the remarks of the FISHERMEN in 2.1. Most important, Simonides' healthy love permits him to be pleased with his daughter's marriage. This presents a powerful contrast to the relationship of ANTIOCHUS and his DAUGHTER (1), the incestuous love with which the play opens and which causes Pericles' exile. The hero's encounter with Simonides and Thaisa signals the beginning of the recovery of his fortunes, and this connection is confirmed at the play's end when Pericles cries, 'Heaven make a star of him!' (5.3.79).

In Shakespeare's sources for the play, the character corresponding to Simonides has another name. Why Shakespeare adopted the name Simonides is not known, but he presumably knew that the name belonged to two ancient poets, Simonides of Amorgos (active c. 660 B.C.) and Simonides of Ceos (c. 556–468 B.C.).

**Simpcox, Saunder** Minor character in *2 Henry VI*, an imposter who claims to have been blind and had his sight miraculously restored. The gullible villagers of ST. ALBANS present him to the king's hawking party and the equally credulous HENRY VI begins to congratulate him, but the Duke of GLOUCESTER (4) exposes the fraud through clever interrogation. Simpcox, who has also said he is lame, is whipped on Gloucester's orders, and he naturally runs away from the whipper, further revealing his imposture. Gloucester orders Simpcox and his WIFE to be whipped through every town until they arrive at the remote village they have claimed to come from. The incident, besides providing a bit of low comedy, was intended by Shakespeare to demonstrate the sound judgement of Gloucester.

**Simple, Peter** Minor character in *The Merry Wives of Windsor*, the servant of SLENDER. Simple reveals himself to be no smarter than his name suggests, as he carries messages and announces arrivals. In his most developed scene, 4.5.24–53, he is fooled by FALSTAFF's elementary verbal tricks.

**Simpson, Richard (1820–1876)** British scholar. Simpson was a Protestant clergyman who converted to Catholicism and became a literary scholar. He wrote *An Introduction to the Philosophy of Shakespeare's Sonnets* (1868), and he pioneered the study of the playwright's politics in *The Politics of Shakespeare's Historical Plays* (1874). He also edited a series of plays not usually attributed to Shakespeare (see APOCRYPHA) that he nonetheless felt the playwright had written, at least in part. Simpson was the first to suggest that part of SIR THOMAS MORE was Shakespeare's, an idea that is now generally accepted. On the other hand, his elaborate analysis of FAIR EM as Shakespeare's allegorical attack on Robert GREENE (2) has been universally rejected.

**Sincklo (Sinklo, Sincler), John (active 1590–1604)** English actor who originated several Shakespearean roles. The inclusion of Sincklo's name in stage directions or speech headings of various texts reveals that he played a KEEPER (2) in *3 Henry VI*, one of the PLAYERS (1) in *The Taming of the Shrew*, and a BEADLE (2) in *2 Henry IV*. The Beadle's extraordinary thinness is a source of humour in 5.4.8–30, and it has thus been concluded that Sincklo was notable for this feature and may therefore have been cast as particularly thin men. Indeed, it is possible that Shakespeare wrote extremely thin men into his plays because he knew that Sincklo would be impressive in the parts. A number of characters that he may have played include Dr PINCH in *A Comedy of Errors* ('a hungry, lean-fac'd villain . . . A needy-hollow-ey'd-sharp-looking-wretch' [5.1. 238–241]); FEEBLE, a tailor, and SHADOW, both in *2 Henry IV* (Shadow is compared to 'the edge of a pen-knife' [3.2.262], and tailors were proverbially skinny, but Sincklo could only have played one of them for they appear together); the TAILOR in *Shrew;* the APOTHECARY in *Romeo and Juliet;* STARVELING in *A Midsummer Night's Dream;* and ROBERT FAULCONBRIDGE in *King John.*

**Singer, John (d. c. 1605)** English actor, a noted CLOWN (1). A member of the QUEEN'S MEN (1) from their founding in 1583 and after 1594 a member of the ADMIRAL'S MEN, Singer was regarded by his contemporaries as the equal of such better-known theatrical clowns as Richard TARLTON and William KEMPE. He also wrote at least one play, for which the Admiral's Men paid him in 1603, but no other record of it survives.

**Sir Andrew Aguecheek** Character in *Twelfth Night,* friend of SIR TOBY. Sir Andrew carouses with his friend while they visit the home of OLIVIA, Sir Toby's rich young niece, whom Sir Andrew is courting. Sir Toby takes merciless advantage of Sir Andrew, but it is impossible to pity such a ridiculous figure. He fancies himself a wit, though he is a dolt; a ladies' man, though he is gaunt and repulsive, as his name suggests; and a fighter, though he proves a coward.

Sir Andrew's inanity is well demonstrated when he tries to imitate VIOLA's rhetoric, though he clearly has no idea of its meaning. He proudly recites, ' "Odours", "pregnant", and "vouchsafed": I'll get 'em all three all ready' (3.1.93). He is foolishly ignorant of ordinary references, as when he calls Jezebel a man in 2.5.41, and he mistakes FESTE's drinking song—'a song of good life' (2.3.36–37)—for a hymn to virtue and rejects it, saying, 'I care not for good life' (2.3.39). When Sir Toby offers to marry MARIA (2) out of delight with her plan against MALVOLIO, Sir Andrew duplicates the offer, forgetting his alleged love for Olivia, and then he seconds the next several remarks made (2.5.183–208) in a delicious example of comic slavishness.

Sir Andrew's combination of quarrelsomeness and cowardice—referred to by Maria in 1.3.30–33—typified the braggart, a character type dating to ancient ROMAN DRAMA. Traditional, too, is the come-uppance Sir Andrew receives when he assaults SEBASTIAN (2) and is pummelled in 4.1 and 5.1. When Sir Toby receives the same treatment, he lashes out at Sir Andrew, calling him, accurately if not charitably, 'an ass-head and a coxcomb and a knave, a thin-faced knave, a gull!' (5.1.204–205).

However, Sir Andrew is sufficiently developed to have a few poignant and sympathetic moments. Rejected by Maria, he despondently (though comically) despairs, 'Methinks sometimes I have no more wit than a Christian . . . I am a great eater of beef, and I believe that does harm to my wit' (1.3.82–85). When he wistfully remarks, 'I was adored once' (2.3.181), we suddenly see that he has a past, a remembered youth. We may not need to know more, but we recognise his humanity.

Like many Shakespearean buffoons, Sir Andrew is a foil for other characters. Sir Toby's underlying selfishness manifests itself in his exploitation of Sir Andrew. As a ridiculous suitor, Sir Andrew magnifies by contrast the somewhat slender virtues of ORSINO, who also pursues Olivia. And his self-image as a grand fellow is subtly similar to Malvolio's fantasies of aristocratic stature.

***Sir John Oldcastle*** Play formerly attributed to Shakespeare, part of the Shakespeare APOCRYPHA. Thomas PAVIER first published *The First Part of Sir John Oldcastle* as an anonymous play in a QUARTO edition known as Q1 (1600). Later in the same year, however, he released a second edition (Q2) in which the play was credited to Shakespeare, as it also was in Pavier's notorious FALSE FOLIO (1619). Pavier's false attribution also led to the play's inclusion in the Third and Fourth FOLIOS. The records of Philip HENSLOWE, who produced the play, reveal that its authors were Michael DRAYTON, Richard HATHWAY, Anthony MUNDAY, and Robert WILSON (4). *The Second Part of Sir John Oldcastle,* which is now lost, was written by Drayton alone.

*Sir John Oldcastle* concerns an historical figure, a proto-Protestant religious martyr. It was conceived in response to a controversy surrounding Shakespeare's great character, FALSTAFF. In *1* and *2 Henry IV*, Falstaff had originally been named OLDCASTLE. The historical Oldcastle's descendants were horrified, and their influence was such that the name was changed. Henslowe presumably saw a way to capitalise on the popularity—and notoriety—of Falstaff, and at the same time ingratiate himself with the historical Oldcastle's chief defender, Lord COBHAM. The prologue of *Sir John Oldcastle* expressly contrasts its hero with Shakespeare's 'pampered glutton', and Falstaff himself is twice mentioned in the play in disapproving terms.

**Sir Thomas More**   Play attributed in part to Shakespeare. *Sir Thomas More* presents episodes from the life of Thomas MORE, a Catholic martyr who was executed by King HENRY VIII for his refusal to accept the English Reformation. It was probably written around 1593 or 1600 (scholarly opinions differ) for the ADMIRAL'S MEN. The manuscript of *Sir Thomas More*, which was assembled around 1595 (or 1603), is mostly in the handwriting of Anthony MUNDAY, but with additions in five different hands, one of which—known as 'Hand D'—is generally accepted as Shakespeare's. If so, this is the only surviving sample of the playwright's handwriting, aside from six signatures on legal documents. For *Sir Thomas More*, he wrote three pages of script comprising one scene of 147 lines, in which More subdues a riot with a moving oration.

That this is Shakespeare's composition is demonstrated through several lines of evidence. First, the handwriting is very like that of the playwright's six known signatures. Further, peculiar spellings—such as *'scilens'* for *'silence'*—occur both in Hand D's pages and in editions of Shakespeare's plays that are known to derive from the author's FOUL PAPERS. Perhaps most tellingly, the imagery used in Hand D's text resembles Shakespeare's, especially in lines that are very similar to passages in both *Coriolanus* and *Troilus and Cressida.* Lastly, the political ideas expressed in Hand D's scene agree with what we know of Shakespeare's thinking, for they demonstrate a respect for social hierarchy combined with sympathy for the common people and stress the malleability of the commoners through oratory.

The odd manuscript of *Sir Thomas More* was the result of government CENSORSHIP; apparently, the play was originally submitted to Edmund Tilney, the MAS-TER OF THE REVELS, who refused to permit its performance without major revisions. Accordingly, several pages were torn from the original manuscript and replaced with others. Scholars believe that the six hands that recorded the text were those of the three collaborators on the original play plus two revisers and a professional scribe. It is generally held that the original text was written by Munday, Henry CHETTLE, and possibly Thomas HEYWOOD (2), while the revisions were written by Chettle, Thomas DEKKER, and Shakespeare. The revisions did not have their intended effect; Tilney was not moved, and *Sir Thomas More* was not performed until 1964, when it was staged in Nottingham, England.

**Sir Toby Belch**   Character in *Twelfth Night,* uncle of OLIVIA. The self-indulgent Sir Toby drinks and roars through life, and, with MARIA (2), SIR ANDREW, and FABIAN, he represents a jocular, festive spirit that triumphs over the cold and humourless rigidity of Olivia's steward, MALVOLIO, in the play's comic SUB-PLOT. His position is boldly presented in his first speech, when he complains of Olivia's mourning for her deceased brother, saying, 'What a plague means my niece to take the death of her brother thus? I am sure care's an enemy to life' (1.3.1–3). Sir Toby laughs and carouses mightily and counters Malvolio's insistence on order with the famous rebuke, 'Dost thou think because thou art virtuous, there shall be no more cakes and ale?' (2.3.114–115). Like another, greater drunken knight, Sir John FALSTAFF, Sir Toby enacts a variety of comic roles: he is Sir Andrew's mentor in debauchery and joins the jester, FESTE, in mockery and jokes. He is a singer of songs and a fierce master of the duelling code. He makes repeated references to dances in 1.3.113–131, 2.3.58, and 5.1.198.

However, Sir Toby has a darker side as well. His selfishness is very apparent. He exploits both his friend and his niece. He spends the foolish Sir Andrew's money while pretending to promote his mercenary marriage to Olivia, boasting that he has taken his dupe for 'some two thousand strong, or so' (3.2.52–53). His drunkenness turns belligerent and incoherent in 1.5.121–122, 129–130. His practical joking has a vicious edge: he forces two unwilling combatants to a duel in 3.4, and he also pushes Maria's plot against Malvolio to a new extreme, gloating, 'we'll have him in a dark room and bound . . . we may carry it thus for our pleasure' (3.4.136–138). This course is criticised in his own fear of reprimand in 4.2.70–74 and by the efforts of Olivia and ORSINO to mitigate Malvolio's humiliation in 5.1. Moreover, Sir Toby's final departure is ugly: he curses Sir Andrew as 'an ass-head and a coxcomb and a knave, a thin-faced knave, a gull!' (5.1.204–205) after his own scheme to humiliate his friend has resulted in both of them being beaten by SEBASTIAN (2).

Sir Toby's somewhat unpleasant traits offer a parallel in the sub-plot to the problematic elements of the main plot. As a result, some critics who view *Twelfth Night* as an ironic social satire regard Sir Toby as a vulgar parasite, a hanger-on in the household of his niece, concerned only with his debauched existence. Sir Toby's attitudes towards Sir Andrew and Olivia corroborate this theory somewhat, but it is surely too extreme. The knight is made to submit to his niece's anger at his ways—'Ungracious wretch . . . Out of my sight! Rudesby, be gone!' she shouts in 4.1.50—but on the other hand, the playwright permits him satisfaction at the defeat of Malvolio. While he is not present at the final scene of recognition and reconciliation, he marries the delightful Maria, as is reported in 5.1.363, again paralleling developments in the main plot. Sir Toby, though he has his faults, is basically a symbol of the values of humour and joyous living and is therefore a representative of the triumphant spirit of comedy.

**Siward (Sigurd the Dane), Earl of Northumberland (d. 1055)** Historical figure and minor character in *Macbeth*, English ally of MALCOLM and MACDUFF against MACBETH. Siward, a famous soldier who commands an army of 10,000 men, is provided by England's king to the exiled Prince Malcolm of SCOTLAND. As a noble and knightly figure, Siward stands for the virtues lost to the world of the play through Macbeth's evil, and as a foreigner who must be brought in to restore the country's health, he points up the extremity of Scotland's need. He appears briefly several times in Act 5 and is a direct and simple soldier. His most notable moment comes when he is informed that his son, YOUNG SIWARD, has died in combat. With noble fortitude he observes, 'Why then, God's soldier be he! / Had I as many sons as I have hairs, / I would not wish them to a fairer death.' (5.9.13–15).

The historical Siward, or Sigurd, was of Danish royal descent. His family had seized Northumberland during the Danish conquest of England a few generations earlier; in Northumberland it was traditionally said that his grandfather was a bear. Siward was a famous warrior who had fought for the English kings Hardicanute (ruled 1040–1042) and Edward the Confessor (1042–1066), and he was thus a fitting choice to command Malcolm's army of invasion, quite aside from his kinship to the prince. He was either Malcolm's brother-in-law or uncle—11th-century references differ. Shakespeare's source, HOLINSHED's history, mistakenly called him Malcolm's grandfather, for he was considerably older than Malcolm's father, King DUNCAN. The playwright made him Malcolm's uncle—perhaps thereby unknowingly correcting an error—to place him in the same generation as Duncan.

Much more than the legendary BANQUO, Siward de-served to be called 'the root and father / Of many kings' (3.1.5–6). His oldest son, Osberne, died fighting against Macbeth, as in the play. His younger son, Waltheof (d. 1075), led the last British resistance to William the Conqueror and was later canonised for it as Saint Waldeve. He had a daughter, Matilda, who married Malcolm's son, later King David I of Scotland (ruled 1124–1153). Two of their sons were kings of the Dunkeld dynasty, as were a grandson and great-grandson. A third son of Matilda and David was an ancestor of King Robert II (1371–1390) who was the founder of the Stewart (later STUART) dynasty. Thus Siward is an ancestor of Shakespeare's sovereign, King JAMES I, whose supposed descent from Banquo is celebrated in the play. All this was certainly unknown to Shakespeare, who simply followed Holinshed, and presumably to King James as well, for he seems to have enjoyed his supposed connection to Banquo.

**Slater (Slaughter), Martin (active 1594–1625)** English actor. A leading member of the ADMIRAL'S MEN from 1594–1597, Slater was then associated with Laurence FLETCHER (3) in England and Scotland, and with other provincial companies. In 1608 he was co-manager with Michael DRAYTON of a CHILDREN'S COMPANY that performed at the WHITEFRIARS THEATRE. In the records of a lawsuit that resulted from this enterprise, Slater is described as an ironmonger with eight children, which suggests that he had need of a sideline. He had returned to touring companies by 1610, and in 1616 he was cited for staging plays without a licence. He continued to perform with provincial troupes until at least 1625.

**Slender, Abraham** Character in *The Merry Wives of Windsor*, dull-witted suitor of ANNE (3) Page. For financial reasons, a marriage between Anne and Slender is supported by Anne's parents and by Slender's elderly relative Justice SHALLOW, but Slender himself, although attracted to the idea, can only sigh vacantly at the prospect—'. . . sweet Anne Page!' (3.1.38, 66, 105)—and make awkwardly embarrassed conversation. When he finally proposes, he can only blurt that it isn't his idea, 'Truly, for mine own part, I would little or nothing with you. Your father and my uncle hath made motions. . . . You may ask your father . . .' (3.4.61–64). Anne beseeches, 'Good mother, do not marry me to yond fool' (3.4.81), and the audience can only sympathise. However, MISTRESS (3) Page arranges for Slender to elope with Anne during the mock fairy ceremonies in 5.5. Fortunately, Anne and her true love, FENTON, foil the plan, and Slender has a boy foisted off on him, as he only discovers during the marriage ceremony.

Slender's name suggests both his appearance and his lack of self-reliance. Such feeble characters were stock figures in Elizabethan comedy. It has been speculated that Slender was also intended by Shakespeare as a satirical portrait of the stepson of his enemy William GARDINER (2), but this cannot be proven.

**Sly (1), Christopher**   Character in *The Taming of the Shrew*, a drunken tinker and the principal figure of the INDUCTION. In these two scenes, Sly is found asleep outside a tavern by a local landowner, the LORD (1), who decides to play a practical joke and has him installed as a gentleman in his home. Sly awakes to find himself treated like an aristocrat and told he has been insane to imagine himself a poor drunkard. As part of the joke, a troupe of PLAYERS (1) performs 'a pleasant comedy' (Ind.2.130) for Sly; this drama is *The Taming of the Shrew*. Sly is last seen dozing in an INTERLUDE (1.1.248–253).

Sly is a boldly drawn minor figure, full of drunken pretensions and country sayings, comically ready to assume his new life of ease, though insisting on his poor man's taste for ale over the gentry's wine. His succinct autobiography—'by birth a pedlar, by education a cardmaker, by transmutation a bear-herd, and now . . . a tinker' (Ind.2.18–21)—gives representation to a multitude of obscure lives among the 16th-century poor. Sly makes numerous explicit references to people and places in the STRATFORD area, and this portrait of a rustic sot clearly derives from the young Shakespeare's recollections of his old home.

Although Sly's story ends abruptly after 1.1 in the oldest edition of *The Taming of the Shrew*, in the FIRST FOLIO of 1623, it is complete in THE TAMING OF A SHREW, believed to be a BAD QUARTO of Shakespeare's play and to contain Shakespeare's original rendition of Sly's adventure: in three further interludes, Sly remarks on the play, eating and drinking all the while. In a fifth episode, he has fallen asleep and the Lord orders him returned to the spot where he had been found. In a 23-line EPILOGUE to *A Shrew*, Sly is discovered by the Tapster of the tavern, who remarks that Sly's wife will be angry with him for staying out all night. Sly replies that he need not fear his wife, for he has had a dream that has taught him how to deal with her. Sly was probably played by William SLY (2).

**Sly (2), William (d. 1608)**   English actor, member of the CHAMBERLAIN'S MEN and the KING'S MEN. Sly is one of the 26 men listed in the FIRST FOLIO as 'Principall Actors' in Shakespeare's plays. He was with either STRANGE'S MEN or the ADMIRAL'S MEN around 1590, for he appears in the combined company of that year. Between 1592 and 1594, he was probably associated with PEMBROKE'S MEN, for he apparently helped compile their text for THE TAMING OF A SHREW, a BAD QUARTO (text assembled from memory) of *The Taming of the Shrew*. Sly played—and was presumably the

namesake of—Christopher SLY (1) in *The Shrew*, and that part is fairly accurately reproduced in *A Shrew*. His next documented appearance was with the Chamberlain's Men in 1598, though he may have been a member of the company at its inception in 1594. He remained a member after it became the King's Men, until his death. He may have played OSRIC in *Hamlet*, though except for Christopher Sly, no Shakespearean role can be assigned with certainty to him. He was not an original partner in the GLOBE THEATRE, but he had acquired a share by 1605. In 1608 he was an original shareholder in the BLACKFRIARS THEATRE, but he died a week after the agreement was signed and his share was redistributed among the other partners. He left his share in the Globe to Robert BROWNE, who was probably his brother-in-law.

**Smethwick (Smithweeke), John (d. 1641)**   English bookseller and publisher, producer of several editions of Shakespeare's plays and a partner in the FIRST FOLIO. In 1607 Nicholas LING sold Smethwick the rights to *Hamlet, Romeo and Juliet, Love's Labour's Lost*, and THE TAMING OF A SHREW. Smethwick is only known to have produced editions of two of these, however: Q3 of *Romeo and Juliet* (1609) and Q3–5 of *Hamlet* (1611, 1622, 1637). He had a share in both the First and Second Folios of Shakespeare's collected plays (1623, 1632).

Smethwick finished nine years of apprenticeship and became a member of the STATIONERS' COMPANY in 1597. Early in his career, he was fined several times for pirating copyrighted books, but he presumably changed his ways, for he eventually became a high officer in the Stationers' Company.

**Smith (1) (Smith the Weaver)**   Minor character in *2 Henry VI*, a follower of the revolutionary Jack CADE. As the rebels are introduced in 4.2, Smith indulges in several joking asides at the expense of his leader, exhibiting the buffoonery that was one aspect of Shakespeare's characterisation of Cade's uprising. As 'Weaver', he gets one more such line in 4.7.

**Smith (2), Morgan (c. 1833–1882)**   African-American actor in Britain. Like Ira ALDRIDGE before him, Smith made a living in the English theatre at a time when black American actors could not surmount racial prejudice at home. Though not the major figure Aldridge was, he had a successful career as a touring performer, often reading a miscellany of speeches in lieu of a play production. A native of Philadelphia, Smith trained with a Welsh actor in Boston, but, when he was refused employment there, he emigrated. Four days after his arrival in England in 1866, never having appeared in public before, Smith performed successfully as OTHELLO. He also played RICHARD III, MACBETH, HAMLET, SHYLOCK, IAGO, and ROMEO, as well as a range of non-Shakespearean roles, until ill health compelled him to retire in about 1879.

**Smithfield**  An open field to the north of London, the location, in 4.7 of *2 Henry VI*, of a skirmish won by Jack CADE's rebels, after which they execute Lord SAY. This choice of location, not necessitated by Shakespeare's sources, was appropriate: Smithfield, which was London's great livestock market, was frequently the site of public executions.

**Smithson, Harriet (1800–1853)**  Irish actress, successful in France. Smithson was a relatively unknown London actress when she played OPHELIA in a production mounted in Paris by William Charles MACREADY in 1827. She was a great success, both in this role and others, notably DESDEMONA, and she toured Europe to continued acclaim. A leading Parisian critic of the day declared that she had introduced Shakespeare to France. She soon abandoned her career, however, to marry the composer Hector BERLIOZ in 1833. It was an unhappy marriage, and he eventually left her for another woman, though when she became an invalid in her last years, he returned and stayed with her until her death.

**Snare**  Minor character in *2 Henry IV*, subordinate to the constable FANG. In 2.1 Fang and Snare are hired by the HOSTESS (2) to arrest FALSTAFF for debt. Snare is nervous about the likelihood of armed resistance, and, indeed, when Falstaff and his companion, BARDOLPH (1), draw their swords, Fang and Snare are helpless. Snare's name, like Fang's, indicates his function, if not his capabilities.

**Sneak**  Musician referred to in *2 Henry IV*, the leader of the MUSICIANS (4) who play at FALSTAFF's dinner at the BOAR'S HEAD TAVERN. In 2.4.11 'Sneak's noise' is stipulated as the desired music, and in line 21 a DRAWER goes in search of him. Another reference to Sneak, in a play of 1613, suggests that there was an historical Sneak who enjoyed some renown in London, but nothing more is known of him.

**Snodham, Thomas (d. 1625)**  London printer. Snodham, who established his printing business in 1603, printed an edition of THOMAS LORD CROMWELL—a play spuriously attributed to Shakespeare—in 1613, and in 1616 he printed Q6 of *The Rape of Lucrece* for publisher Roger JACKSON (3). Snodham was a brother-in-law of publisher Cuthbert BURBY.

**Snout, Tom**  Character in *A Midsummer Night's Dream*, a tinker of ATHENS and a performer in the comical amateur production of PYRAMUS AND THISBE staged at the wedding of Duke THESEUS (1) and Queen HIPPOLYTA (1). Snout plays the Wall in the INTERLUDE,

which is directed by his fellow artisan Peter QUINCE. Snout's name, like that of his fellow artisans, refers to his trade; a tinker's most common task was repairing the spouts, often called snouts, of kettles and teapots.

**Snug**  Character in *A Midsummer Night's Dream*, a joiner of ATHENS and a performer in the comical amateur production of PYRAMUS AND THISBE staged at the wedding of Duke THESEUS (1) and Queen HIPPOLYTA (1). Snug plays the Lion in the INTERLUDE, which is directed by his fellow artisan Peter QUINCE. Snug presents himself as 'slow of study' (1.2.63), and he is mute during the rehearsal scene (3.1), but he carries off his role commendably at the performance in 5.1. In the woodworking trades, Snug's name means 'tightly fitting', an appropriate name for a joiner.

**Solanio**  Character in *The Merchant of Venice*, friend of ANTONIO (2). Solanio is a cultured gentleman of VENICE whose conversation in elegant verse reflects the advanced civilisation of his city. He is difficult to distinguish from his companion SALERIO. In commenting on the action, these two gentlemen present facts and ideas. For instance, consoling the melancholy Antonio in 1.1, they speak of his status as a wealthy and successful merchant, and in 2.8 they offer a picture of Shylock's despair and rage at JESSICA's elopement and speculate that the Jew will vent his anger on Antonio if he can. In 3.1 they tease Shylock, eliciting from him his famous speech claiming equality with Christians. Solanio is simply a conventional figure whose main purpose is to further the development of more significant characters.

**Soldier (1)**  Minor character in *1 Henry VI*, an English infantryman. In 2.1, during the retaking of the town of ORLÉANS (1) by the English, the Soldier, crying the name of the great English warrior TALBOT, drives the French leaders, including CHARLES VII and JOAN LA PUCELLE, from the stage. He gleefully claims the clothing they have left behind in their panic. This episode, entirely fictitious, emphasises the importance to the English cause of the noble Talbot. It also serves to ridicule the French, thus furthering the play's point that only dissensions among the English could have resulted in French victories.

**Soldier (2)**  Any of several minor characters in *1 Henry VI*. Four French Soldiers, disguised as peasants, accompany JOAN LA PUCELLE and gain entrance to the English-held city of ROUEN in 3.2. They spy out the weakest gate and signal the other French troops, who enter and capture the city. This episode emphasises the treacherous nature of the French by contrasting Joan's deceitful ruse with the unalloyed valour of the English hero, TALBOT.

**Soldier (3)** Minor character in *2 Henry VI,* a messenger who enters the camp of the rebel leader Jack CADE in 4.6, unaware that Cade has just declared it an act of treason to address him as anything but 'Lord Mortimer'. The Soldier, knowing no better, calls out for 'Cade'; the leader orders him set upon, and he is killed. This incident serves to present a vicious side of the uprising, which has earlier been treated as a focus of broad humour. Now Cade, in addition to being a buffoon, is shown to be a blood-thirsty tyrant in the making.

**Soldier (4)** Minor character in *3 Henry VI.* When EDWARD IV decides to declare his renewed claim to the crown, in 4.7, he calls on the Soldier to read his proclamation.

**Soldier (5)** Any of several minor characters in *Julius Caesar,* members of the armies of ANTONY and OCTAVIUS on one hand, and BRUTUS (4) and CASSIUS on the other, in the civil war that follows the assassination of CAESAR (1).

**Soldier (6)** Any of several minor characters in *Troilus and Cressida,* Trojan troops. In 1.2 the Soldiers, who do not speak, march in front of PANDARUS and CRESSIDA, provoking Pandarus to sneer, 'Asses, fools, dolts, chaff and bran, chaff and bran; porridge after meat . . . crows and daws, crows and daws' (1.2.245–248). This is one of the comically inhumane remarks that pepper the play.

**Soldier (7)** Any of several characters in *All's Well That Ends Well,* troops in the army of FLORENCE. The First Soldier is the pretended interpreter during the interrogation of PAROLLES. In 4.1 and 4.3 Parolles is captured by the First LORD (6), who proposes to demonstrate the foppish courtier's cowardice and treachery to his deluded friend, BERTRAM. The captors pretend to speak a foreign language so that their victim will not realise that they are French, and the First Soldier pretends to interpret between the Lord and the prisoner. Parolles treasonably discloses secrets, and the First Soldier induces him to insult the Lords and Bertram, which maintains a humorous tone to the scene. The Second Soldier is a messenger who is sent in 4.1 to tell Bertram of Parolles' capture. His submission to orders helps suggest the strength and efficiency of the military, which is contrasted with the cowardice and treason of Parolles.

**Soldier (8)** Minor character in *Antony and Cleopatra,* a member of ANTONY's army. In 3.8 the Soldier pleads with Antony not to fight the forthcoming battle against Octavius CAESAR (2) at sea, where the opponent has the advantage. However, Antony's pride demands that he accept Caesar's challenge to naval warfare, and he engages in the fatal battle of ACTIUM. The Soldier reappears in 4.5, and Antony acknowledges that he was right. The Soldier then reports that ENOBARBUS has deserted, an event that signals the utter collapse of Antony's fortunes just before what is to be his final battle. The Soldier thus serves as a measure of Antony's declining destiny.

**Soldier (9)** Any of several minor characters in *Antony and Cleopatra,* members of ANTONY's army. In 4.3 a group of Soldiers gather to perform sentry duty. They hear strange, wailing, musiclike noises—seemingly under the street—and they interpret this phenomenon as a bad omen that portends the loss of the next day's battle. Four of them speak and are designated as the First, Second, Third, and Fourth Soldiers. In 4.4 the Soldiers (or, perhaps, other soldiers) appear the next morning and march to the battle without complaint, but the earlier episode tells us that Antony's end is fast approaching.

**Soldier (10)** Minor character in *Antony and Cleopatra,* a member of the army of Octavius CAESAR (2). In 4.6 the Soldier brings a message to ENOBARBUS, who has deserted Mark ANTONY and joined Caesar; his former master has sent his belongings after him. The Soldier, though busy with his battle preparations, pauses to remark, 'Your emperor / Continues still a Jove' (4.6. 28–29). This disinterested praise from an enemy confirms the play's image of Antony as a great man while it also furthers the plot for it plunges Enobarbus into the guilt that will break his heart and kill him in 4.9.

**Soldier (11)** Any of several minor characters in *Coriolanus,* members of the Roman army. The Soldiers retreat before the VOLSCIANS at the gates of CORIOLES, and they refuse to follow MARTIUS (2)—later given the name CORIOLANUS—when he enters the city. 'Foolhardiness! Not I' (1.4.46) is the reply in the words of the First Soldier, who speaks for the group apart from one line given to a Second Soldier. However, when they observe Martius' return they are inspired to join him and fight their way into the city. Another group of Soldiers accompanies COMINIUS in 1.6, and they too are inspired by the arrival of the battle-torn Martius. The Soldiers say very little except in unison, and their chief function, much like that of the CITIZENS (5), is to demonstrate the changeable nature of the common man, an important theme of the play.

**Soldier (12)** Any of several minor characters in *Coriolanus,* members of the Volscian army. In 1.10 one of the Soldiers—designated the First Soldier—interjects four single lines into AUFIDIUS' long speech on CORIOLANUS' recent victory over the VOLSCIANS at CORIOLES. The First Soldier is merely a sounding board who provides the occasion for the audience to see his leader's vengefulness and rancour towards Coriolanus.

**Soldier (13)**   Minor character in *Timon of Athens,* a messenger for ALCIBIADES. In 5.3 the Soldier, sent with a message to TIMON, discovers Timon's grave. Unable to read the inscription on it, he decides to copy it and bring it to Alcibiades. He does this in 5.4, and thus inspires the play's final passage, in which Alcibiades translates Timon's last statement and remarks on it.

**Soliloquy**   Speech made by a character, usually when alone on the stage, revealing his or her inner thoughts. Originally a device of ancient Greek and Roman drama, the soliloquy was popular in the RENAISSANCE and was widely used in ELIZABETHAN DRAMA. Shakespeare frequently used this device to present the audience with material that could not be realistically delivered in dialogue. Sometimes the soliloquy simply provides information on the plot—as when villains such as AARON, IAGO, and RICHARD III comment on their own schemes—but more often it functions to reveal character through the expression of private emotional drives. This technique is particularly striking in *Hamlet* and *Macbeth,* whose soliloquies are among Shakespeare's greatest poetic achievements. The two uses can of course apply simultaneously, as when Iago both directs our knowledge of the central plot and displays his own tortuous nature. While Shakespeare's most famous soliloquies are given to his great tragic characters, the effect of a soliloquy can also be comic, as in those of MALVOLIO and BENEDICK.

Though artificial, the soliloquy nevertheless supports our sense of the play's truth to reality, for we recognise that a character has no motive for lying in a soliloquy and accordingly accept the passage as a legitimate revelation. In Shakespeare, a character's use of soliloquy often in itself demonstrates an introspective personality; Hamlet and Macbeth are actively molding their psychological and spiritual natures, whereas others, such as CORIOLANUS and ANTONY, do not concern themselves with these matters and seldom reveal themselves to the audience.

**Solinus**   Character in *The Comedy of Errors.* See DUKE (8).

**Somerset (1), Edmund Beaufort, Duke of (1406–1455)**   Historical figure and character in *2 Henry VI,* a Lancastrian rival of the Duke of YORK (8). (See Lancaster [1]; York [1].) Edmund, the younger brother of John Beaufort, the Duke of SOMERSET (3) in *1 Henry VI,* inherited both the rivalry and the title after John's death in 1444. The Somerset-York feud is a central feature in *1 Henry VI;* however, *2 Henry VI* focusses first on the fall of the Duke of GLOUCESTER (4) and later

on the sudden rebelliousness of York, and this Somerset is a relatively minor figure.

He is sufficiently consequential, however, that the DUCHESS (1) of Gloucester, seeking political advice from the supernatural world, questions a SPIRIT (1) about his future in 1.4. It is prophesied that Somerset should fear castles, a warning that at the time seems incomprehensible. In 1.3 Somerset is appointed the King's Regent in FRANCE (1), and he reappears in 3.1 to announce the loss of France, evidencing the harm that infighting among ambitious noblemen has done to England. When York returns from Ireland with an army, he demands Somerset's imprisonment. Somerset volunteers to go to the Tower if the king wishes, and York is placated. However, York encounters Somerset, still free, in 5.1 and takes the fact as cause for an armed rebellion. In the ensuing battle, the first of the WARS OF THE ROSES, Somerset is killed by York's son (later RICHARD III) beneath a tavern sign depicting a castle, thus fulfilling the prophecy. (In 1.1 of *3 Henry VI,* Richard displays Somerset's head as a demonstration of his prowess in battle.)

One theme of *2 Henry VI* is the death of 'good Duke Humphrey' at the hands of scheming nobles, who thereby deprived England of its only chance of avoiding the civil war that erupted during Henry's weak reign. Shakespeare desired to compress the events that led to that war, and he eclipsed Somerset's political importance in the process. Somerset was the favourite of Queen MARGARET (1) after the fall of SUFFOLK (3) in 1450. However, Somerset had been the commander under whom Normandy was lost in the late 1440s, and he was Henry's chief minister in 1453, when England was irrevocably defeated in southern France. He was therefore in extreme disfavour at the time. So, even though Margaret would have preferred Somerset to act as Regent in the summer of 1453, when King Henry succumbed to a disabling form of insanity, his unpopularity with both the aristocracy and the public inhibited her, and York was given the post. He governed well and faithfully until late in 1454, when the King recovered. At this point, Somerset was restored to office, and it was this action, probably taken at Margaret's insistence, that led York to gather an army and eventually declare himself king. Shakespeare thus omits several years of intricate political manoeuvring in order to clarify York's drive for the throne.

**Somerset (2), Duke of**   Character in *3 Henry VI*—a combination of two historical figures—who betrays King EDWARD IV to support WARWICK (3) in his rebellion. Shakespeare confused two dukes of Somerset who participated in the WARS OF THE ROSES, Henry (1436–1464) and his younger brother Edmund (c. 1438–1471), both of them sons of the Duke of SOMERSET (1) of *2 Henry VI.* In 4.1 of *3 Henry VI* Somerset leaves Edward's court with GEORGE (2) to join Warwick and fight for the reinstatement of the deposed King HENRY VI. This Somerset must be Henry, who deserted the Lancastrians and then rejoined them, at which point he is depicted here. Henry was finally captured and beheaded by the Yorkists. All of the subsequent appearances of Somerset in the play occur well after the date of Henry's execution and thus must portray Edmund, who succeeded to his brother's title. Edmund was always a firm Lancastrian, and it is he who is shown aiding the young RICHMOND in 4.6, supporting Warwick and MARGARET (1) in Act 5, and being sentenced to death after the battle of TEWKESBURY, in 5.5, as Edmund in fact was.

**Somerset (3), John Beaufort, Duke of (1403–1444)**
Historical figure and character in *1 Henry VI,* the rival of the Duke of YORK (8). Somerset selects a red rose as his emblem in response to Plantagenet's adopting a white one in the Temple garden scene (2.4). Thus, fictitiously, do the WARS OF THE ROSES begin. Somerset is depicted as dishonourable. He is unwilling to fulfil his agreement to accept the opinion of a majority in his dispute with Plantagenet, declaring that his argument was 'here in my scabbard' (2.4.60), and he goes on to taunt his rival about his father's execution some years earlier. When their quarrel erupts again at HENRY VI's coronation in Paris (4.1), the king unwisely attempts to settle it by dividing the command of the French troops between them. Then the death of TALBOT is attributed to York's and Somerset's refusal to provide him with reinforcements.

The historical Somerset quarrelled with York over the divided command in Normandy in the early 1440s, and Shakespeare uses this material in the sequence culminating in Talbot's death, which actually took place nine years after Somerset's own. Moreover, Somerset was a prisoner in FRANCE (1) in 1421–1438 and thus could not have had taken part in the quarrel with York at the king's coronation or in the Temple garden scene. Thus John Beaufort's younger brother Edmund, his successor as Duke of SOMERSET (1) and a character in *2 Henry VI,* is sometimes considered to have been a co-model for the Somerset of *1 Henry VI.* However, Edmund did not succeed to the title until 1448—later than all the events in *1 Henry VI* except the death of Talbot, which Shakespeare linked to an episode that unquestionably involved John, the divided command. Therefore, it seems best to regard John Beaufort as the Somerset of this play.

**Somerville, Sir John (d. 1492)** Historical figure and minor character in *3 Henry VI,* a supporter of WARWICK (3) in his rebellion against King EDWARD IV. Somerville reports to Warwick on troop movements in 5.1.

**Son (1)** Minor character in *Macbeth,* LADY (7) Macduff's child who is killed by MACBETH's hired Murderers (see FIRST MURDERER [3]), in 4.2. The Son sees that his mother is distressed by MACDUFF's departure to England to join the rebellion against Macbeth, and he attempts to understand the situation with pertly humorous questions and remarks. His wit and intelligence make his slaughter all the more vicious and contribute greatly to the power of the episode, which stresses the depths of evil to which Macbeth has descended. The boy's courage in death—he calls one of the Murderers a 'shag-hair'd villain' (4.2.82), and with his last breath he futilely attempts to warn his mother—contrasts tellingly with the villainy of his killers.

**Son (2) That Hath Killed His Father, The** Minor but significant character in *3 Henry VI,* a participant in the battle of TOWTON in 2.5. The Son, a soldier, begins to loot the corpse of an enemy he has killed, only to discover that the fallen foe is his own father. He bewails his fate and prays, with an allusion to the Crucifixion, 'Pardon me, God, I knew not what I did: / And pardon, Father, for I knew not thee' (2.5.69–70). He is witnessed by King HENRY VI, who has withdrawn from the battle to wish despairingly that he were a rustic shepherd, rather than a combatant. This incident, along with that of THE FATHER THAT HATH KILLED HIS SON, is juxtaposed ironically with King Henry's pastoral musings to highlight the horror of civil war.

**Song** Short poem accompanied by music, often used in Shakespeare's plays, though not always written by the playwright. Many of these songs are versions or fragments of popular songs known from other sources, a few were probably written by collaborators, and some may have been inserted into a play by someone other than the playwright, in the course of a theatrical run. However, scholars generally believe that the following songs (in approximate order of composition) were written by Shakespeare: 'Who Is Silvia?' (*Two Gentlemen of Verona*); 'When daisies pied' (*Love's Labour's Lost*); 'You spotted snakes' (*A Midsummer Night's Dream*); 'Tell me, where is fancy bred' (*The Merchant of Venice*); 'Sigh no more, ladies' and 'Pardon, goddess of the night' (*Much Ado About Nothing*); 'Under the greenwood tree', 'Blow, blow, thou winter wind', 'What shall he have that killed the deer?' and 'It was a lover and his lass' (*As You Like It*); 'O mistress mine', 'Come away, death', and 'When that I was and a little tiny boy' (*Twelfth Night*); 'Take, O take those lips away' (*Measure for Measure*); 'Hark, hark, the lark' and 'Fear no more the heat o' the sun' (*Cymbeline*); 'When daffodils begin to peer', 'Get you hence, for I must go', and 'Lawn as white as driven snow' (*The Winter's Tale*); 'Come unto these yellow sands', 'Full fadom five thy

*A 17th-century setting of Desdemona's song in* Othello. *Songs were elements in many of Shakespeare's plays, whether they were composed by the playwright himself, or, like this one, popular ballads of the day.* (Courtesy of the Trustees of the British Museum)

father lies', and 'Where the bee sucks' *(The Tempest);* 'Orpheus with his lute' *(Henry VIII);* and 'Roses, their sharp spines being gone' *(The Two Noble Kinsmen).*

Shakespeare's early songs mostly served to adorn a COMEDY and generally had little if any importance to the plot or characterisations. However, beginning with the songs of AMIENS and TOUCHSTONE in *As You Like It* (1599), the songs begin to relate to character and to the play's theme. This change probably reflects the talents of Robert ARMIN; before he joined the CHAMBERLAIN'S MEN, the availability of a good singer for a play was uncertain, so the playwright may have been reluctant to give a song much significance. Shakespearean TRAGEDY uses song dramatically—as in the songs of the FOOL (2) in *King Lear,* OPHELIA in *Hamlet,* and DESDEMONA in *Othello*—but these were popular ballads of the day, recognisable by the original audiences and thus even more potent dramatically.

In the last plays, the ROMANCES and *Henry VIII,* the influence of the MASQUE demanded songs, most of which Shakespeare wrote.

Little of the original music for Shakespeare's plays has survived. The tunes of currently popular songs were doubtless used for at least some of the songs, even among those Shakespeare wrote, but other melodies were composed by Robert JOHNSON (5), Thomas MORLEY, John WILSON (2), and possibly others. Shakespeare was plainly conscious of the composer's task, for he was careful to write lyrics with short, rhymed lines of varying lengths, and he emphasised vowel sounds rather than consonants, especially at the ends of lines. Many notable composers have subsequently set Shakespeare's songs to music (see, e.g., ARNE; SHUBERT; SULLIVAN [1]).

**Sonnet**   Verse form, a 14-line poem, usually in iambic pentameter (see METRE) and with any of several traditional rhyme schemes. The sonnet has been widely popular ever since its evolution from medieval Italian verse and is still used by poets in most European languages. Shakespeare's SONNETS are among the best known, and he also employed sonnets in several of his plays, most notably in *Romeo and Juliet* and *Love's Labour's Lost.*

A sonnet usually consists of two parts, an eight-line section (the octet) followed by a six-line section (the sestet). Three rhyme schemes are most commonly employed in English sonnets: the Shakespearean sonnet (abab cdcd efef gg), which is named for Shakespeare's use of it to the exclusion of other schemes; the Spenserian sonnet (abab bcbc cdcd ee), which was developed by Edmund SPENSER; and the Italian sonnet (abba abba cdecde; the sestet may have a different arrangement as long as it does not end with two rhyming lines, a couplet). The Italian sonnet, the oldest variety, is also called the Petrarchan sonnet, after its most famous exponent, Petrarch (1304–1374).

In the Petrarchan sonnet, the pattern of rhymes changes completely in the sestet. This arrangement encourages a two-part division of content; an important component of the Petrarchan sonnet is the *volta* (an Italian musical term), or 'turn of thought', the change of direction that often occurs in line 9. This change may be a feature of non-Petrarchan sonnets as well, as in Shakespeare's 'But thy eternal summer shall not fade' (Sonnet 18.9). However, the Spenserian and Shakespearean schemes—which are more appropriate to English, a language with fewer rhymes than Italian—offer another pattern of development: a progression through three quatrains to a concluding or summarising couplet. These two developments are not, of course, mutually exclusive. Sonnet 18, in fact, exemplifies both: its quatrains lead like stepping stones to a strong concluding couplet.

The sonnet, which developed in medieval Italy, first became known to English poets in the love poems of Dante (1265–1321) and Petrarch. Thomas WYATT introduced the form to England, but it was the Earl of SURREY (1) who popularised the English quatrains-and-couplet arrangement. Spenser's rhyme scheme compromises between the stricter Italian and the looser English. In Elizabethan England, sonnets were a fashionable pastime and sonneteers flourished (they are amiably satirised in *Love's Labour's Lost*). In Elizabethan poetry the sonnet was conventionally associated with love poetry; John Donne, in the early 17th century, expanded its range to encompass religious themes, and John MILTON continued this development, composing sonnets on various personal and public matters. In the 18th century, the form fell into disuse. Revived with the rise of romanticism, the sonnet has adapted well to the less formal modern world. Today it is often used with less rigorously prescribed rhyme and metre, for every imaginable subject.

**Sonnets**  Body of 154 poems, each a SONNET, written by Shakespeare over an unknown period of time, probably around 1592 to 1598. The Sonnets are love poems. They describe aspects of two different loves experienced by the poet, one for a young man and the other for a woman. Some of the Sonnets are great poems (Sonnets 18, 29, 55, 116, and 138 are among the most praised), while a few are poor, but it is as a sonnet sequence—a new genre at the time—that they are particularly fascinating, offering an extraordinary range of love poems. They encompass several distinct points of view on love, unified by a series of delightful observations on the power of poetry to record them.

The Sonnets comprise two groups of poems: the larger group (Sonnets 1–126) is addressed to the young man, the other (127–154) to the woman. (Although the sex of the addressee is unspecified in most of the Sonnets, all those that do address a man precede Sonnet 126, which as the only 12-line variation on sonnet form seems to close the initial group. Similarly, all of the Sonnets that explicitly address a woman fall in the second group.)

In the first group, the poet manifests his love for the young man in a variety of ways. In Sonnets 1–17 he speaks of his friend's beauty and insists that he should marry and have children in order to perpetuate that beauty beyond his eventual death. In the next group of poems (and in many of the others) the poet describes his love in brilliant variations on traditional love poetry, often referring to the poetry love stimulates. However, as the sequence progresses, the poet speaks of his disappointment that his friend has left him, or at least does not love him in return. In 40–42 it appears that the friend has even stolen the poet's (female) lover. In 78–86 the poet fears that his place

in his friend's affections (and perhaps in his literary patronage) has been taken by another, superior poet. In 110–111 the poet worries that his friend resents his public displays (probably a reference to Shakespeare's career as an actor). Gradually, however, over the course of the last several dozen poems of this group, the spirit of love returns, apparently reflecting a reconciliation between the friends. Sonnet 126 closes the series with a return to the subject of the young man's beauty and mortality.

Sonnets 127–154 address a woman of dark complexion and metaphorically dark morals (often referred to as Shakespeare's 'dark lady'), who has betrayed the poet's love by loving other men. She may be married, in which case the love she *has* given the poet also constituted betrayal. In 133–134 the poet complains that not only has she been unfaithful to him, she has done so with his friend, thereby leaving him abandoned by both of his loves. Apparently the situation in Sonnets 40–42 is seen from another angle. The 'dark lady' Sonnets bemoan the poet's plight as an unrequited lover, and they often rail against the woman and against love in general. These poems are sometimes called the 'vituperative sonnets'.

In these two sets of poems, a love triangle is compellingly, if only implicitly, portrayed. There is no actual evidence that the situation was not simply a literary creation, but many of the poems are so convincingly delighted or aggrieved with love that most readers find themselves assuming that the Sonnets are autobiographical, or at least based on personal experience, and that the young man, the 'dark lady', and the 'rival poet' are representations of real people. Despite the lack of evidence, a wide range of suppositions about Shakespeare's life have been engendered by the Sonnets.

The most contentious conclusion that has been drawn from the Sonnets is that Shakespeare was homosexual. However, the poems offer no unambiguous evidence on the subject. The poet refers to and addresses his friend as his 'lover', but in Shakespeare's day the word had many non-sexual connotations, and its meaning varied greatly with context. It could mean sexual partner, but it could also be used in the formal close of a letter—'Thy lover' was as common and as sexually neutral as 'Sincerely yours' (it is so used in *Julius Caesar* 2.3.7). Moreover, in the context of friendship, the word *lover* was synonymous with the word *friend*. Shakespeare often used it as such in the plays (e.g., in *The Merchant of Venice* 3.4.7; *2 Henry IV* 4.3.13; *Coriolanus* 3.3.213). Sexual puns and innuendos of all sorts, indiscriminate in their references to male and female genitals, are common throughout the Sonnets—as they are throughout Elizabethan secular literature in general—but they serve chiefly to promote an atmosphere of licentiousness rather than to suggest particular acts or attitudes. Sonnet 20 is frequently cited as evidence of Shakespeare's homosexuality, because in it the poet ascribes many feminine attributes to his friend, plays with clever references to his penis, and calls him 'the master mistress of my passion' (20.2). However, in this poem the poet actually disclaims a sexual relation with his friend—whose penis is 'to my purpose nothing' (20.12)—and willingly surrenders sex with him to women. While scholarly opinion remains varied, it is safe to say that the Sonnets do not clearly demonstrate homosexuality in its lovers, quite apart from the likelihood that Shakespeare, like other sonneteers of the day, wrote of an invented relationship.

In any case, the identity of the young man intrigues those who read the Sonnets as autobiographical. The assumption is generally drawn that he is identical with the mysterious 'Mr W. H'. described as the 'onlie begetter' of the Sonnets in the dedication to the first edition (see below). The two models most frequently suggested have been Henry Wriothesley (W. H. reversed), Earl of SOUTHAMPTON (2), and William Herbert, Earl of PEMBROKE (3). Each was a literary patron connected with Shakespeare: *Venus and Adonis* and *The Rape of Lucrece* are dedicated to Southampton and the FIRST FOLIO to Pembroke, who was also a son of the patron of PEMBROKE'S MEN, a theatrical company with which Shakespeare may have acted. Thus, they suit the implied references to patronage in several of the Sonnets. Also, each declined to marry a proposed bride—Southampton in 1590, Pembroke in 1595—making him suitable for the pleas of Sonnets 1–17. However, various commentators point to disqualifying attributes of each. In any case, the point cannot be proved, and so there have been many more nominees. Almost any near-contemporary of Shakespeare with the initials W. H. or H. W. has been proposed. A William Hughes—supposedly the object of a pun in Sonnet 20 but otherwise unrecorded—has been hypothesised (that he should be named William is suggested by the 'Will Sonnets' [135–136], where the word *will* appears 19 times, possibly echoing the names of the poet and his rival for the dark lady's love—the young man). Other possibilities emerge if the young man of the Sonnets is not considered identical with Mr W. H.; among the nominees have been the poet's son Hamnet SHAKESPEARE (5), the Earl of ESSEX (2), and Queen ELIZABETH (1) (heavily disguised).

Many proposals have been also made for the identity of the 'dark lady'. However, none has even the superficial credibility of Southampton and Pembroke, and scholars often simply ignore the question. The most frequently named dark ladies are Mary FITTON and Emilia LANIER. Others include Lucy Morgan (active 1579–1600), a one-time lady-in-waiting to Queen Elizabeth who became a brothel keeper; Penelope Rich (1563–1607), the sister of the Earl of Essex; and William DAVENANT's mother (chiefly because Davenant claimed to be Shakespeare's illegitimate son).

Speculation has similarly surrounded the 'rival poet' of Sonnets 78–86. Most poets of the period have been named, George CHAPMAN and Christopher MARLOWE (1) most often, with honourable mention to Barnabe BARNES and Gervase MARKHAM. However, none of these questions can be profitably pursued: not only is evidence entirely lacking, it is not even clear that Shakespeare had any real people in mind. All three figures function well as literary constructs—characters placed in a quasi-narrative, such as appear in many other sonnet sequences of the day.

The dates of the Sonnets are undetermined and are the subject of continuing scholarly debate. Though the only certainty is their existence before 1609, when they were published, a generally accepted view holds that they were probably all written between 1592 and 1598. These years saw a vogue for sonnet sequences—at least 20 were published—stimulated by Sir Philip SIDNEY's *Astrophel and Stella* (1591), and Shakespeare's poems were apparently part of this trend. In 1598 Francis MERES mentioned the Sonnets, and versions of two of them (138 and 144) were published in 1599 as part of THE PASSIONATE PILGRIM. Of course, it is not known that all of them had been written by then. Nevertheless, parallels to the Sonnets in Shakespeare's other works are most frequent in *Venus and Adonis* (1592–1593), *The Rape of Lucrece* (1593–1594), *Love's Labour's Lost* (c. 1593), *Romeo and Juliet* (1594–1595), and *Richard II* (1595), so the years of the sonnet craze seem the likeliest period of composition for the entire group of poems.

Commentators occasionally doubt the authorship of a few of the Sonnets, especially 145, which is a poor poem and the only Sonnet written in tetrameter (see METRE), as well as 153 and 154, which seemingly have little to do with the others and are the only ones that derive from a specific source (see below). However, each of these poems bears some relationship to its neighbours, and most scholars accept them as genuine.

The collected Sonnets were first published in 1609 by Thomas THORPE, in a QUARTO edition (printed by George ELD) known as Q. They were printed in the order described above, which has subsequently been considered standard (though various editors have altered it), and followed by *A Lover's Complaint*. An introductory page reads: 'TO THE ONLIE BEGETTER OF THESE INSVING SONNETS MR. W.H. ALL HAPPINESSE AND THAT ETERNITIE PROMISED BY OUR EVER-LIVING POET WISHETH THE WELL-WISHING ADVENTVRER IN SETTING FORTH.' This enigmatic message, signed 'T.T.', is unpunctuated (in that there is a period after every word), ungrammatical, and generally difficult to interpret. The term 'onlie begetter' may signify the inspirer of the Sonnets (presumably the young man of 1–126, as discussed above), or it may simply refer to the procurer of the manuscripts from which they were printed; some commentators find other, more arcane possibilities. In any case, the dedication has been subjected to great scholarly scrutiny, but in the absence of further evidence, it must remain intractably obscure.

As noted above, only Sonnets 153 and 154 have a clear source: they are variations on a well-known classical epigram dating to at least the 1st century A.D. (this epigram was variously rendered in several languages and Shakespeare's immediate source is not known). OVID's *Metamorphoses*, a favourite Shakespearean source, is echoed in wordings and conceits here and there throughout the Sonnets, but the overall scheme of the group as a whole—the accounts of the poet's two loves—has no literary source. However, that Shakespeare wrote a sequence of sonnets can be attributed to the influence of Sidney's *Astrophel and Stella*. Also, an earlier convention required that sonnets be devoted to love, and Shakespeare followed this tradition, though he approaches the subject in an unconventional manner. The love relationships of the Sonnets are reconfigurations of the courtly love usually depicted in love sonnets: the object of the poet's love is addressed in the formal terms of the tradition and is beautiful and virtuous, as expected, but he is, unconventionally, a man; the expected woman is present, but she is neither beautiful nor virtuous. Each Sonnet is concerned with love, as is the collection as a whole, but the points of view taken and the aspects of love dealt with vary greatly, sometimes even within an individual poem. Shakespeare's characteristic recognition that life is complicated and that contradictory ideas and impulses often coexist is very well demonstrated in these works. The Sonnets, like the best of Shakespeare's dramas, offer an experience that transcends both scholarly disputes and the differences between the poet's world and our own.

**Soothsayer (1)**    Minor but notable character in *Julius Caesar*. The Soothsayer bids Julius CAESAR (1), 'Beware the ides of March' (1.2.18, 23). Later, when the overconfident Caesar remarks that the ides of March have arrived without bringing harm, the Soothsayer replies ominously, 'Ay, Caesar, but not gone' (3.1.2). Seventy-five lines later Caesar is killed.

In Shakespeare's source, PLUTARCH's *Lives*, the Soothsayer is reported to have delivered his warning long before; the playwright compressed this account in order to achieve greater dramatic impact. The Soothsayer was probably not a real person; predictions such as his were commonly devised after the fact in ancient accounts of great events.

**Soothsayer (2)**    Minor character in *Antony and Cleopatra*, a seer patronised by Mark ANTONY. In 1.2 the Soothsayer predicts that Cleopatra's waiting-woman CHARMIAN shall outlive her mistress but will see a worse time in the future than in the past. He adds that he sees an identical fate for another waiting-woman, IRAS. He accompanies Antony to ROME, and in 2.3 he recommends that they return to Egypt to get away from Octavius CAESAR (2). He declares that Antony's spirit is bested by Caesar's when the two are together. Antony dismisses the Soothsayer curtly, but muses to himself on the truth of his observation. In both episodes the Soothsayer's remarks prove pertinent, and in hindsight the audience can recollect his words.

In 2.3 the Soothsayer appears to be an Egyptian whom Antony has brought to Rome. Some scholars, however, believe that he may be the otherwise unknown Roman LAMPRIUS, for the stage direction opening 1.2 reads, in part: '*Enter* Enobarbus, Lamprius, *a Soothsayer, . . .* '. Thus, the Soothsayer can be construed syntactically as being named Lamprius.

**Soothsayer (3)**    Minor character in *Cymbeline*, a priestly fortune-teller who serves the Roman army. In 4.2 the Soothsayer tells of his dream of 'Jove's bird, the Roman eagle' (4.2.348), which he interprets as an omen of victory for the forthcoming battle against King CYMBELINE's British forces. Though he is mistaken—the Britons win—this reference may be recalled by the audience when JUPITER (or Jove) appears to POSTHUMUS, in 5.4. In 5.5 the Soothsayer, who is now a prisoner of war, interprets the text that Jupiter left behind. He offers an interpretation that formulates the play's symbolic values of reunion and renewal. The Soothsayer's name, Philarmonus (5.5. 434), suggests the joyful conclusion that he foretells.

**Sothern, Edward Hugh (1859–1933)**    British-born American actor. At 20 Sothern began his career by joining his father, a comedian who was performing in America. Himself a comedian and romantic leading man, he was best known as MALVOLIO and also played HAMLET. From 1904 to 1926 he and Julia MARLOWE (2) headed a Shakespearean company; they married in 1911.

**Soundpost, James**    Character in *Romeo and Juliet*. See MUSICIANS (2).

**Southampton (1)**    Seaport in southern England, a location in *Henry V*. In 2.2, just before invading FRANCE (1), King HENRY V entraps three treacherous noblemen—the Earl of CAMBRIDGE, Lord SCROOP (1), and Sir Thomas GREY (3)—who have conspired with the enemy and plan to assassinate him. Shakespeare himself did not indicate the setting, but the historical event took place in Southampton, and modern editors have generally followed POPE (1) in placing the scene there.

**Southampton (2), Henry Wriothesley, Earl of (1573–1624)**  Contemporary of Shakespeare, a patron of the arts to whom Shakespeare dedicated *Venus and Adonis* (1593) and *The Rape of Lucrece* (1594). These two dedications are the only certain connection between Shakespeare and Southampton; they were written in the hope of patronage—financial support—from the young nobleman. The first dedication is an ordinary approach by a poet seeking backing from someone he does not know well, but the second reflects considerable friendship between patron and poet. Unlike any other dedication of the period, it is confident of the support it seeks and it radiates an air of intimacy. The poet may have spent some time during the plague years of 1592 to 1594—the period during which he wrote the poems—at Southampton's estate. An 18th-century account attributed to William DAVENANT the information that Southampton had given Shakespeare £1000, and though the amount is much too large to be believed—perhaps 10 to 20 times Shakespeare's annual income at the time—there may be a germ of truth to the story. Some scholars believe that Southampton may be the young man to whom most of the SONNETS are addressed, or the mysterious 'Mr W. H'. to whom they are dedicated by the publisher. This cannot be proven, but that the two men were friends is accepted by most scholars.

A favourite courtier of Queen ELIZABETH (1), Southampton was a patron of John FLORIO and other writers. He became a follower of the Earl of ESSEX (2) and accompanied him on his successful expeditions to Cadiz and the Azores in 1595 and 1596. Essex's cousin was his mistress, and he married her in 1598, when she became pregnant. The queen was angered at the match and briefly imprisoned him; he never recovered the favour of the monarch. In 1599 he joined Essex on his ill-fated mission to Ireland and shared in his subsequent disgrace. He helped plan Essex's rebellion and with him was condemned to death on its failure, but his sentence was commuted to life imprisonment on the intervention of Robert CECIL (1). Southampton spent the rest of Elizabeth's reign in the TOWER OF LONDON. King JAMES I released him and made him a favoured courtier. He became a promoter of colonising enterprises and was an important member of the Virginia Company. In 1624, commanding English troops against the Spanish in the Netherlands, he died of plague. His family name is pronounced 'Risley'.

**Southwark**  Southern suburb of LONDON, the location of a scene in *2 Henry VI,* and Shakespeare's residence between 1597 and sometime before 1602. In Shakespeare's day, Southwark was a raw, newly developed area, with crude roads and a nearby swamp. Beginning in 1587 several theatres—including the SWAN THEATRE, the ROSE THEATRE, and Shakespeare's GLOBE THEATRE—were built in Southwark because it was outside the jurisdiction of London, whose Puritan government was opposed to professional drama. Shakespeare probably moved there when his company, the CHAMBERLAIN'S MEN, left the THEATRE, to the north of London, and began to perform at the Swan. His exact residence in the district is unknown.

Southwark is also the setting for 4.8 of *2 Henry VI,* the depiction of an historical event that took place there in 1450. In 4.8 the rebellion led by Jack CADE has been driven from London across the Thames into Southwark, and the rebels are offered amnesty if they will disband, which most of them do, ending the uprising.

**Southwell, John (d. 1441)**  Historical figure and minor character in *2 Henry VI,* a sorcerer whom HUME employs, along with BOLINGBROKE (2) and MARGERY JOURDAIN, to summon a spirit for the DUCHESS (1) of Gloucester, who wishes to see the future to prepare for a possible coup. In a séance in 1.4 Southwell helps Bolingbroke to cast a magic spell that summons the spirit ASNATH, who answers questions about the king and certain noblemen. Southwell is arrested, along with his fellows and their client, by the dukes of YORK (8) and BUCKINGHAM (3). In 2.3 the king sentences him to be strangled. The historical Southwell was a priest. He died in prison the night before his scheduled execution.

**Spalding, William (1809–1859)**  Scottish scholar. Spalding was a professor of logic at the University of Edinburgh, but early in his career he published an essay that assigned authorship of different parts of *The Two Noble Kinsmen* to Shakespeare and John FLETCHER (2) by studying the verse techniques employed in the play. This ground-breaking study of 1833 contributed greatly to the use of the VERSE TEST in the study of Shakespeare plays.

**Spaniard**  Character in *Cymbeline.* See DUTCHMAN AND SPANIARD.

**Speed**  Character in *The Two Gentlemen of Verona.* Speed, the page of VALENTINE (2), is saucy and impertinent, teasing his master about his infatuation with SILVIA and engaging in witty exchanges with LAUNCE. He is an example of a character type frequently used by early Elizabethan dramatists, especially by John LYLY, whose comedies influenced the young Shakespeare.

**Spencer, Gabriel (d. 1598)**  English actor, a colleague of Shakespeare. Spencer was one of three members of PEMBROKE'S MEN—another was Ben JON-

SON—imprisoned briefly for staging the allegedly seditious play *Isle of Dogs* in July 1597. Upon his release he joined the ADMIRAL'S MEN as a principal actor. In September 1598 Jonson killed Spencer in a rapier duel. Little more is known of Spencer's life except that he himself had killed a man in a fight two years earlier.

Spencer is probably referred to in the FIRST FOLIO text of *3 Henry VI*, where a stage direction at 1.2.47 refers to the MESSENGER (5) as 'Gabriel', apparently meaning Spencer, who must have played the part. The title-page of the 1595 edition of the play states that it had been performed by Pembroke's Men, so we may conclude that Spencer was with them before that date. However, it is possible that the stage direction was written for a later production by the CHAMBERLAIN'S MEN, in which case Spencer may have been a member of that troupe between 1594 and 1597.

**Spenser, Edmund (c. 1552–1599)** English poet, a major figure in English literature, the first great writer to succeed CHAUCER, and the author of works that influenced Shakespeare. Spenser's monumental epic poem *The Faerie Queene* (published 1590, 1598) provided the playwright with the inspiration for many passages, especially in the earlier plays and poems. The PASTORAL poems in Spenser's *Shepheardes Calendar* (1579), and possibly his great wedding poem *Epithalamion* (1595), did the same for *A Midsummer Night's Dream*. Another of Spenser's poems, 'The Teares of the Muses' (1591), may be alluded to in the *Dream* (5.1.52–53).

The son of a LONDON merchant, Spenser attended Cambridge University, where he met Gabriel HARVEY (2), through whom he was introduced to the literary circle centred on Sir Philip SIDNEY, whose close friend he became. His *Faerie Queene* has been recognised since its first appearance as one of the greatest accomplishments of English poetry. A vast tapestry of chivalry and adventure, it is simultaneously a nationalistic epic, a mythic romance, and an allegory on the human soul. Spenser was also an important influence on the development of the English SONNET.

**Spirit** Character in *2 Henry VI*. See Asnath.

*The Spread of the Eagle* TELEVISION production based on Shakespeare's ROMAN PLAYS. The British Broadcasting Corporation presented *The Spread of the Eagle* in 1963, combining *Coriolanus, Julius Caesar*, and *Antony and Cleopatra* in a nine-segment depiction of Roman history from the 5th century B.C. to the defeat of Mark ANTONY by Octavius CAESAR (2) in 31 B.C.

**Spurgeon, Caroline (1869–1941)** British scholar. A long-time professor of English literature at the University of London, Spurgeon is best known for her book *Shakespeare's Imagery and What it Tells Us* (1935).

This groundbreaking study examines the patterns of images in certain plays and attempts to determine aspects of Shakespeare's personality by analysing the imagery he was most inclined to use. Spurgeon also edited *Keats' Shakespeare* (1928), a seven-volume edition of Shakespeare's works as annotated by the poet John KEATS.

**Stafford (1), Lord Humphrey (1439–1469)** Historical figure and minor character in *3 Henry VI*, a supporter of King EDWARD IV. Stafford, who does not speak, is present when the Yorkist leaders learn that WARWICK (3) has deserted their cause, and he is ordered, with Lord PEMBROKE (4), to raise an army. The historical Stafford, who was knighted by Edward during the battle of TOWTON, was sent with Pembroke in 1469 to subdue a local uprising that Warwick had incited. Because of a personal dispute between the two commanders, Stafford withheld his forces from a battle, with the result that Pembroke was captured and beheaded by the rebels. Stafford was declared a traitor and was hunted down and executed by the local authorities.

**Stafford (2), Sir Humphrey (d. 1450)** Historical figure and minor character in *2 Henry VI*, a nobleman sent, in 4.2, to deal with the rebellion led by Jack CADE. An arrogant aristocrat, Stafford takes the position *least* likely to defuse an uprising, addressing the mob as 'Rebellious hinds, the filth and scum of Kent . . .' (4.2.116). He and his BROTHER (1) are killed in the skirmish that follows in 4.3. Stafford was not related to the Duke of BUCKINGHAM (3), another figure in the play, although he bore the same name.

**Stafford (3), Simon (active 1596–1626)** LONDON printer who produced editions of several of Shakespeare's plays. Stafford, who mostly printed ballads and sermons, also printed the second QUARTO (Q2) of *1 Henry IV* (1599) for Andrew WISE, and Q3 of *Pericles* (1611) for an unknown publisher. He also printed the 1605 edition of KING LEIR, a possible source for *King Lear*.

**Stafford (4), Sir William (d. 1450)** Character in *2 Henry VI*. See BROTHER (1).

**Stanley (1), Ferdinando, Lord Strange** Contemporary of Shakespeare. See STRANGE.

**Stanley (2), Sir John (actually Thomas) (c. 1406–1459)** Historical figure and minor character in *2 Henry VI*, a nobleman to whose castle on the Isle of Man the DUCHESS (1) of Gloucester is banished in 2.3.-13. In 2.4 Sir John escorts the Duchess from London after she has been humiliated by being paraded through the streets. He is sympathetic to her for her husband's sake, and promises to treat her 'Like to a duchess, and Duke Humphrey's lady' (2.4.98). The Isle of Man, in the middle of the Irish Sea, is remote and isolated even now; in the 15th century it was an ideal place of exile. Sir Thomas Stanley inherited the island from his father, Sir John, with whom Shakespeare confused him. John had received it in 1406 from HENRY IV, as a reward for supporting the deposition of RICHARD II.

**Stanley (3), Sir Thomas (c. 1435–1504)** Historical figure and character in *Richard III*, a nobleman who betrays RICHARD III. Richard, suspecting a defection to the Earl of RICHMOND, requires Stanley's son as a hostage. Stanley allies himself with Richmond; at the battle of BOSWORTH FIELD, he refuses to march with his forces, to Richmond's advantage, but Richard's order to kill the hostage son is not carried out. After Richmond kills Richard in combat, Stanley places Richard's crown on the victor's head.

Shakespeare's Stanley is a judicious, if not a very bold, politician. The career of the historical Stanley was rather less honourable, if similarly successful. He held a powerful position in the north of England, but he was difficult to trust. During the WARS OF THE ROSES, he fought, and on occasion refused to fight, for both sides, as he strove to ally himself with the winning faction at any point. He accordingly ended up with high office under King EDWARD IV, and then under Richard. His wife, Richmond's mother, was implicated in the revolt of BUCKINGHAM (2), but Stanley maintained his position by turning against her, receiving custody of her estates. However, it is clear that he knew of Richmond's invasion before it happened. As a result, Richard took George Stanley hostage. George, who was an adult, not the boy spoken of in the play, was captured while attempting to escape; he saved his life by incriminating his uncle, William STANLEY (4). Thomas Stanley did indeed withhold his troops at Bosworth, as Shakespeare reports, and Richard did order George killed but was ignored. Stanley was amply rewarded with high offices under Henry VII.

In some editions, Stanley is designated Derby, for Shakespeare used that title in introducing him in 1.3. However, he is Stanley in all dialogue thereafter. The use of the title in the play is an anachronism, for Stanley only received it after the accession of Henry VII. Most editors have made the correction in the dialogue headings and stage directions.

**Stanley (4), Sir William (c. 1436–1495)** Historical figure and minor character in *3 Henry VI*, a supporter of King EDWARD IV. In 4.5 Stanley helps Edward to escape from captivity. He is mentioned in *Richard III*, in 4.5.13, as one of the supporters of the Earl of RICHMOND.

The historical Stanley was the son of Sir Thomas Stanley, misnamed by Shakespeare as John STANLEY (2) in *2 Henry VI*, and he was the younger brother of Sir Thomas STANLEY (3), a prominent figure in *Richard III*. William Stanley had been a consistent Yorkist prior to Richmond's invasion, when he joined his brother in supporting the usurper. His nephew George, Richard's hostage, betrayed him, and Richard declared him a traitor prior to the battle of BOSWORTH FIELD. Nevertheless, following a family tradition of ambivalent loyalty, he held his troops back during that fight until he saw that he could join the winning side. Then his appearance with 3,000 troops turned the tide for Richmond, who amply rewarded him after acceding to the throne as Henry VII. Ten years later, however, Stanley became associated with another attempted coup and was beheaded.

**Starveling, Robin** Character in *A Midsummer Night's Dream*, a tailor of ATHENS and a performer in the comical amateur production of PYRAMUS AND THISBE staged at the wedding of Duke THESEUS (1) and Queen HIPPOLYTA (1). Starveling plays the Moonshine in the INTERLUDE, which is directed by his fellow artisan Peter QUINCE. The least competent of the actors, Starveling can utter only two of his lines before reverting to prose to inform the audience what the rest of his verses would have said.

Starveling's name refers to the proverbially skinny nature of tailors, and Shakespeare's choice of name and occupation probably reflects the presence in the acting company of John SINCKLO, a strikingly thin actor who is presumed to have played the part.

**Stationers' Company** English guild of booksellers, publishers, and printers, an organisation licenced by the government to protect the interests of its members by policing the publishing industry (with the exception of the university presses of Oxford and Cambridge). For such offences as printing outlawed works or publishing works properly claimed by another member, the company could fine a printer or publisher, seize his press and type, suspend his right to conduct business, or even, in extreme cases, revoke it altogether (see DANTER; SIMMES). A member of the company could secure the rights to a work once it was licenced by the government—by the MASTER OF REVELS, in the case of plays—by registering it for a fee with the company. Where the publisher got his text was immaterial to the company, for the point was not to prevent piracy but to create copyright for the members. Also, it was not necessary to register a work with the company to publish it; however, an unregistered work could be freely reprinted by anyone. The Stationers' Company made no effort to protect the rights of an author, and even so far as it went it was inefficient—many violaters of the system went unpunished—but it marks the crude beginning of English copyright law.

**Steevens, George (1736–1800)**   English scholar. Steevens published the texts of 20 QUARTO editions of the plays in 1766, and his edition of the collected plays came out in 1773. This edition was based on the text published by Samuel JOHNSON (7), with the addition of his own corrections and notes. It was reprinted with revisions in 1778 and 1785, with the assistance of Isaac REED. In response to Edmond MALONE's 1790 edition, Steevens undertook a final edition of his own in 1793. His 1778 edition was the basis for the first two VARIORUM EDITIONS. To his assiduous scholarship, Steevens added a sardonic wit—inventing scholarly sources to which he attributed indecent interpretations, for instance. For this, he is known as 'the Puck of Commentators'.

**Stephano (1)**   Minor character in *The Merchant of Venice*, a servant of PORTIA (1). In 5.1 Stephano tells LORENZO and JESSICA that his mistress will be returning to BELMONT shortly.

**Stephano (2) (Stefano)**   Character in *The Tempest*, the drunken butler of King ALONSO of Naples, and the ally of CALIBAN in his plot to kill PROSPERO. Stephano is a loutish fellow who is drunk throughout his time on stage, bullies Caliban and TRINCULO, and is ludicrously ineffective in carrying out the plot. In 3.2, when Stephano accepts Caliban's suggestion that after killing Prospero he take MIRANDA for himself, we see that a supposedly civilised man is capable of villainy as deep as that of a bestial savage (for Caliban had already attempted to rape the young woman). Stephano's bluff—and drunken—courage distinguishes him from his companions, but when he is comically distracted from the assassination by the trivial vanity of fancy clothes in 4.1, he seems inferior to even the subhuman Caliban, at least in discipline. He offers an interesting sidelight on one of the play's themes, the relative merits of civilised and natural humanity; in his drunken foolishness, Stephano demonstrates the potential for evil inherent in civilisation's pleasures.

Nevertheless, Stephano is basically a comic villain, contrasting with the more seriously evil ANTONIO (5) in the play's network of comparisons. When he is finally punished, Stephano is reduced to punning on his name, Neapolitan slang for 'belly', by saying 'I am not Stephano, but a cramp.' (5.1.286). This jest has seemed to some scholars to confirm speculation that Shakespeare found inspiration for *The Tempest* in Italian COMMEDIA DELL'ARTE scenarios, while others point to the appropriate definition of 'stefano' in John FLORIO's Italian-English dictionary, *A Worlde of Wordes* (1598).

**Steward (1)**   Minor character in *All's Well That Ends Well*, the chief officer of the household of the COUNTESS (2) of ROSSILLION. The Steward twice offers information about HELENA (2). In 1.3 he reports having overheard her musing on her love for BERTRAM, stimulating the Countess to assist Helena's plan to pursue Bertram. In 3.4 he reads aloud Helena's letter to the Countess telling of her departure from Rossillion so that Bertram, now her unwilling husband, may live there in peace. This letter touchingly reveals the wretchedness of Helena's position.

The Steward's name—rendered by different editors as Rynaldo, Rinaldo, and Reynaldo—is mentioned only (in 3.4.19, 29) after his role is almost complete. Many commentators think that this offers a glimpse of Shakespeare's creative processes, for he appears to have been continually developing even this minor character as he wrote.

**Steward (2)**   Character in *Timon of Athens*, the manager of TIMON's household. The Steward cannot make Timon refrain from the extravagant generosity that finally bankrupts him, but he nevertheless remains loyal to his master when he loses all. In 4.2 the Steward leads Timon's employees (see SERVANT [23]) as they regret their master's fate, and in 4.3 and 5.1 he visits his exiled master, who has withdrawn to the woods outside ATHENS. Timon is misanthropic in his mad despair, but he must make an exception for this faithful servant. He declares, 'I do proclaim / One honest man', and adds, 'How fain would I have hated all mankind' (4.3.500–501, 503). The Steward's virtue counters Timon's absolute hatred of humankind. The Steward is thus very important to the play, for it is through this character that Shakespeare most clearly demonstrates that Timon's bleak view of humanity is not the vision of the play. Like most of *Timon*'s characters, the Steward is not a complex human being, but is rather an emblematic figure who embodies the virtues of pity and loyalty.

**Stoll, Elmer Edgar (1874–1959)**   American scholar. E. E. Stoll, as he is generally known, was a leading Shakespearean critic of the so-called 'realist' school, which focussed on the relationship of Shakespeare's plays to the playwright's times, especially to the practises of the ELIZABETHAN THEATRE. Stoll was a long-time professor at the University of Minnesota; his best-known work is *Art and Artifice in Shakespeare* (1933).

**Stow, John (c. 1525–1605)**   English historian whose works provided Shakespeare with minor details for the HISTORY PLAYS, perhaps especially influencing *King John*. Stow, a self-educated tailor, became an antiquarian under the influence of his friend William CAMDEN. He published a collection of the works of

CHAUCER and a summary of early English chronicles, but his major work was his *Annales* (1580), a history of Britain from its mythological foundations to the year of publication. This popular work was reissued five times by 1631, with new additions by other authors. Stow also helped prepare the 1587 edition of Raphael HOLINSHED's *Chronicles,* Shakespeare's most important historical source. He also wrote a book on the LONDON of his day, *Survey of London* (1598), that offers scholars many telling glimpses of Shakespeare's world.

**Strachey (1), Lytton (1880–1932)**   English biographer and critic. Strachey wrote an important work, *Shakespeare's Final Period* (1906), that helped revolutionise Shakespearean criticism in the early 20th century. He influenced subsequent commentators—such as E. E. STOLL and Levin SCHÜCKING—to consider the plays in light of the circumstances under which they were produced, rather than by focussing exclusively on the worlds of the characters. A major figure of the Bloomsbury group—along with novelist Virginia Woolf (1882–1941) and economist John Maynard Keynes (1883–1946)—Strachey is best known for his biographies, such as *Eminent Victorians* (1918), *Queen Victoria* (1921), and *Elizabeth and Essex* (1928).

**Strachey (2), William (c. 1567–c. 1634)**   English colonial entrepreneur and author, writer of sources for *The Tempest* and possibly *King Lear.* In June 1609 Strachey sailed for Virginia as part of a group of investors and adventurers involved in the newly established colony in Jamestown. One of the three ships in the expedition was wrecked in Bermuda, and Strachey, with Sylvester JOURDAIN (2), was marooned for 10 months before going on to Virginia. From Jamestown he wrote to England of his experiences. His letter was circulated among interested investors, and Shakespeare saw it, probably through Dudley DIGGES (1). It provided the playwright with details of the shipwreck in *The Tempest* 1.1 and ARIEL's description of St Elmo's fire in 1.2. 196–206. Perhaps more important, it emphasised the providential survival of the voyagers and stressed the fact that an island previously notorious for evil spirits turned out to be a pleasant and productive place (partly in consequence Bermuda was soon settled by the English and is now the oldest British colony). Both the role of providence and the sequence of deviltry succeeded by blessedness are paralleled in Shakespeare's depiction of PROSPERO's realm. Strachey's letter was eventually published in *Purchas his Pilgrimes* (1625), a famous anthology of exploration literature (see HAKLUYT).

Strachey was acquainted with Ben JONSON and wrote a laudatory poem for the preface to Jonson's *Sejanus* (1605). This poem may have influenced some of the wording in *King Lear.* Strachey's connection with *Seja-* *nus,* a work Shakespeare acted in, suggests that he may well have known the playwright personally.

Strachey returned to England in 1611 and helped write the first code of laws for Virginia. By 1613 he had completed a *Historie of Travell into Virginia Britania,* but this work, valued by modern historians, was not published until 1849.

**Strange, Ferdinando Stanley, Lord (c. 1559–1594)**   English theatrical patron, the sponsor of a theatrical company, STRANGE'S MEN, with whom Shakespeare may have been associated. Lord Strange (the name rhymes with 'sang') was a courtier and minor poet. He patronised a provincial company of acrobats and tumblers that eventually evolved into an important theatrical company, though his involvement was not an influence on its development. As his 'servants', the performers were protected from antitheatrical legislation (see ELIZABETHAN THEATRE), and he could call on the company for private performances, but the personnel and repertoire of the company were determined by its members. Strange's Men visited their patron's Lancashire home often, and Lord Strange may thus have known the young Shakespeare personally, though doubtless distantly. Some scholars believe that the visits (or accounts of them from other players) later influenced Shakespeare to create his comic stewards MALVOLIO (of *Twelfth Night*) and OSWALD (of *King Lear*), who may have been modelled on Strange's steward, William FFARINGTON.

Strange succeeded his father as Earl of Derby (and the company therefore took the name DERBY'S MEN) in 1593. Now that he was a leading nobleman, a conspirator against Queen ELIZABETH (1) approached him to suggest that he seize the crown on the strength of his mother's descent from Henry VII. Derby, as Strange was now known, denounced the traitor, who was executed. When the earl died a few months later it was rumoured that he had been killed in revenge, though modern scholars believe he died naturally. He was succeeded as earl by his younger brother, William Stanley (see DERBY [3]).

At Tong, in Shropshire, is the tomb of some of Lord Strange's relatives; on it are two epitaphs said to have been written by Shakespeare. This tradition, however, was first recorded years after Shakespeare's death and seems highly doubtful. Only one of the two epitaphs is of a literary quality that can plausibly be associated with Shakespeare, and in any case, the occupants of the tomb died either long before or long after the playwright's connection with the family, which existed only through Strange's Men. The traditional attribution of these texts is probably a product of local pride.

Strange's family had long been prominent in the English aristocracy, and Shakespeare depicted several of his ancestors in the HISTORY PLAYS. Ferdinando Stanley, Lord Strange, was the great-great-grandson of Sir Thomas STANLEY (3), who appears in *Richard III,* and thus Thomas and William STANLEY (2, 4) were also his relatives.

**Stranger**    Either of two minor characters in *Timon of Athens,* visitors to ATHENS. In 3.2 the Strangers accompany HOSTILIUS, who is also a visitor, and they witness the callousness of LUCIUS (3), who refuses to assist his former patron, TIMON. The First Stranger's appalled remarks capture the play's condemnation of the heartless greed of Timon's faithless friends. 'I never tasted Timon in my life', he says, 'Yet I protest' (3.2.79, 81). Because he is detached, he assumes the position of a judge. He protests against 'the monstrousness of man' (3.2.74), and declares 'Men must learn now with pity to dispense, / For policy sits above conscience' (3.2.88–89). The Second Stranger speaks only half a line, but its quiet condemnation—'Religion groans at it' (3.2.78)—powerfully reinforces his companion's critique. The episode resembles scenes found in medieval MORALITY PLAYS. It stresses the play's moral point of view and also helps the audience recognise that *Timon*'s characters are at least as much didactic models as they are psychological types.

The Strangers are sometimes considered to be three in number. In the FIRST FOLIO text of the play and some other editions HOSTILIUS is designated as the Second Stranger, in which case the religious remark in 3.2.78 is given to a Third Stranger.

**Strange's Men**    Acting company of the ELIZABETHAN THEATRE, possible employer of the young Shakespeare and predecessor of the CHAMBERLAIN'S MEN (later the KING'S MEN), undeniably the playwright's long-time professional home. Named for its patron, Ferdinando Stanley, Lord STRANGE (the name rhymes with 'sang'), Strange's Men was apparently a troupe of acrobats and tumblers when it first appeared in LONDON in the early 1580s, but in 1588, when its leader joined the QUEEN'S MEN (1), the company was reorganised; henceforth, it emphasised acting over acrobatics.

By 1590 Strange's Men was allied with the other major London troupe, the ADMIRAL'S MEN, performing at the THEATRE, owned by James BURBAGE (2), whose son, Richard BURBAGE (3), was to become the company's leading tragedian. Strange's and the Admiral's Men were associated off and on for several years; the former often played at the CURTAIN THEATRE, whose owner, Henry LANEMAN, was James Burbage's partner at the time. A cast list of 1591 shows that among the members of Strange's—or at least acting with them— were Richard Burbage, George BRYAN, Richard COWLEY, Thomas GOODALE, John HOLLAND (3), Augustine PHILLIPS, Thomas POPE (2), John SINCKLO, and William SLY (2). Bryan, Phillips, Pope, and Cowley are also recorded as members in 1593, and these four plus Burbage were charter members of the Chamberlain's

Men, when Strange's was reorganised under a new patron following Lord Strange's death in the spring of 1594. Less than a year earlier, Strange had become the Earl of Derby, so the company was also known briefly as DERBY'S MEN.

Scholars believe that Shakespeare was involved with Strange's Men, probably as both author and playwright. (He may, however, have been associated with other companies as well. See ADMIRAL'S MEN, LEICESTER'S MEN, PEMBROKE'S MEN, QUEEN'S MEN (1), and SUSSEX'S MEN.) The troupe produced *Titus Andronicus* and *Harey vj* (almost certainly *1 Henry VI*); the combined Strange's-Admiral's company probably staged both *2* and *3 Henry VI.* Further, though the earliest surviving documentary evidence linking Shakespeare with the company dates only from December 1594, after Strange's Men's demise, the playwright was already a leading figure in the Chamberlain's Men when first mentioned, receiving the company's fee for a performance at court, suggesting that he had already been involved with them for some time.

**Stratford**    Town in WARWICKSHIRE, England, Shakespeare's home town and his residence upon retirement from LONDON. Stratford-on-Avon, to give it its full name, was a simple market town of 1,500 to 2,000 people in Shakespeare's day. It was the centre of a rich farming area and the locus of its trade. Its population consisted largely of farmers, the artisans and craftsmen who served them, and the businessmen who ran stores and inns, retailed manufactured goods, and marketed the farmer's crops. John SHAKESPEARE (9), the playwright's father, advanced economically through all of these groups. The son of a farmer, he became a tanner of fine leathers, a maker and seller of gloves, and a trader in various commodities such as grain and wool. Stratford's principal industry in Shakespeare's day (and until this century) was the brewing of beer and ale (among the commodities John Shakespeare traded was barley, the brewer's basic raw material). At the top of the social scale were wealthy landowners, the class to which Shakespeare advanced when he returned to Stratford a rich man after his career in the theatre.

Stratford was a very ancient rural centre. Taking its name from its location where an ancient road—a *straet* in Anglo-Saxon—crossed the Avon River at a *ford,* it was first settled by bronze-age Celts. It was recognised as an independent market town in medieval times. A religious organisation, the Guild of the Holy Cross, provided its government and a variety of civil services, including its schools. The guild was abolished in 1547, after the coming of Protestantism under King HENRY VIII, and a secular government with elected officials was established in its place. During the 1560s and 1570s Shakespeare's father was among those officials. The guild's headquarters, the Guild Hall, built in

*Shakespeare's birthplace, Stratford-on-Avon.* (Courtesy of British Tourist Authority)

1417, still survives. A two-storey half-timbered structure, it was the central building of the town in Shakespeare's day, with the meeting rooms of the town government on the street floor and the Stratford grammar school above, in a single large classroom. Shakespeare must have attended the grammar school between approximately 1570 and 1580, though the records for these years have not survived.

The Shakespeares lived in a neighbourhood of prosperous tradesmen on the northern side of the town, in a house that was composed of two modest buildings joined to make a more substantial dwelling. Because the playwright was probably born in this house, it is known as the BIRTHPLACE and it has been renovated as a museum. Shakespeare's other home in Stratford, the mansion called NEW PLACE, no longer survives. It was the second-largest house in the town (the largest had once been a dormitory for the medieval guild).

At the south end of the town was Stratford's most important institution, the Church of the Holy Trinity. The most prominent building in Stratford, then and now, Holy Trinity is regarded as among the loveliest of England's small medieval churches. Its construction began around 1200 A.D., with different parts being added on over the centuries. Indeed, the prominent spire that tops its square tower was built long after Shakespeare's day. At the time of Shakespeare's birth, the rector of Holy Trinity was John BRETCHGIRDLE, who bequeathed to the grammar school much of its library. The first rector that Shakespeare could have known was Henry HEICROFT, who arrived when the future playwright was five and was still there to christen Susanna SHAKESPEARE (14) in 1583. The rector for most of the period after Shakespeare's return from London until after his death was John ROGERS (1). Another important man at Holy Trinity was its longtime curate, or assistant to the rector, William GILBARD, a possible model for NATHANIEL (1) in *Love's Labour's Lost.*

Soon after Shakespeare's death, Stratford's fame as the playwright's home became central to its existence. As early as 1630 a visitor described it as 'most remarkable for the birth of famous William Shakespeare'. In the centuries since, it has become a mecca for greater and greater numbers of Shakespeare enthusiasts. In 1847 a non-profit organisation was formed to buy and maintain the birthplace, which was then a butcher's shop. In 1891 the Shakespeare Birthplace Trust was incorporated, to care for this building and New Place. The Trust later acquired Anne HATHAWAY's cottage, the supposed ARDEN (2) home, the home of Shakespeare's son-in-law Dr John HALL (2), and other properties related to the playwright.

Stratford also became a centre for the performance of Shakespeare's plays. In 1769 David GARRICK held a 'Jubilee' of performances there, and in 1827 a series of festivals was instituted, though the financial failure of the first one killed the idea. However, as an outgrowth of the elaborate 1864 celebration of Shakespeare's 300th birthday, the Shakespeare Memorial Theatre was created, opening its own building in 1879 with a performance of *Much Ado About Nothing* starring Barry SULLIVAN (2) and Helen FAUCIT. A permanent company evolved under the leadership of Frank BENSON (1) from 1886 to 1919, and Stratford today enjoys an annual theatre season running from April to November. Reorganised in 1961 as the Royal Shakespeare Company, the troupe performs in London in the winter and sends road companies on tour as well, producing Shakespeare's works and other plays, both classical and modern.

**Strato (active 42 B.C.)** Historical figure and minor character in *Julius Caesar*, a soldier in the army of BRUTUS (4). At the battle of PHILIPPI, Strato helps Brutus to commit suicide. When OCTAVIUS' troops arrive, Strato defiantly proclaims that they are too late to capture his master. The victorious Octavius, admiring his spirit and Brutus', takes Strato into hi service. Strato represents an ideal of Roman martial virtue, confirming the sense of grim rectitude that surrounds the defeat and death of the conspirators who killed CAESAR (1). Little is known of the historical Strato, whose role Shakespeare took from PLUTARCH's *Lives*.

**Strewers** Characters in *2 Henry IV*. See GROOM (2).

**Stuart Dynasty** Ruling dynasty in England from 1603 to 1714 (except from 1649 to 1660). King JAMES I (ruled 1603–1625), the first Stuart monarch to govern England, ruled during the last 13 years of Shakespeare's life. James, already King James VI of SCOTLAND, succeeded to the English throne when his cousin Queen ELIZABETH (1), the last monarch of the TUDOR DYNASTY, died childless. Although the Scottish dynasty, which dated to the 14th century (see SIWARD), spelled their name Stewart, James VI's mother, Mary Queen of Scots (1542–1587), married a cousin whose branch of the Stewart family resided in FRANCE (1) and had adopted the French spelling Stuart.

James' ascension provided a Protestant ruler for England and offered the prospect of unity for the two kingdoms he ruled (though the formal union of England and Scotland did not come until 1707). Thus, in the early 17th century, Stuart rule was generally welcomed by the English. Shakespeare reflected this attitude in *Henry VIII*, where a prediction is made that James shall rule with 'Peace, plenty, love, truth, terror' (5.4.47, where 'terror' simply means 'awe-inspiring power').

However, after Shakespeare's time, the Stuart dynasty had a difficult history, in good part because of religious disputes. Though James was strongly Protestant, the next three kings were more sympathetic to Catholicism and all three married Catholic princesses from European countries. English Protestants, a vast and often militant majority, distrusted them. James' son Charles I (ruled 1625–1649) proved unable to prevent the Civil Wars of 1642–1651, in the course of which he was executed and a revolutionary government established in Britain. When the new government eventually collapsed, however, Charles' exiled son was called back and ruled as Charles II from 1660 to 1685. His reign was marked by strong anti-Catholic sentiment in English politics, and while generally popular, he was suspected of pro-Catholic leanings. He was thought to have secretly converted on his deathbed, and his successor, his brother James II (ruled 1685–1689), was suspected of practising Catholicism even before he acceded. James' first wife was a Protestant and their children, Mary and Anne (later to rule), were raised as Protestants, but his second wife was an Italian Catholic. Popular opinion suspected Vatican-inspired plots to impose Catholicism on the country. For this and other reasons, James was deposed and exiled in the Glorious Revolution of 1689, so-called for its bloodlessness.

The thoroughly Protestant Mary Stuart and her Dutch husband, William of Orange, were installed as Mary II and William III, known jointly as William and Mary (ruled 1589–1702). They were succeeded by Mary's sister Anne, during whose reign England and Scotland were formally united as the Kingdom of Great Britain. Anne died childless in 1714, the last Stuart monarch in Britain. However, the Catholic branch of the Stuarts had not yet disappeared. On three occasions—in 1689–1691, 1715, and 1745–1746—rebellions were launched in favour of James, his son, and his grandson, respectively. All were suppressed. Finally, with the defeat of James II's grandson 'Bonnie Prince Charlie' at the battle of Culloden (1746), all hope of restoring the dynasty was abandoned, even by its most fanatical adherents.

**Sub-plot** Sequence of developments secondary in importance to the main line of action in a drama. The sub-plot is a common feature of ELIZABETHAN and

JACOBEAN DRAMA—indeed, of virtually all pre-modern English drama—and few of Shakespeare's plays lack one. Sometimes his sub-plots offer a pointed contrast with the central material, as in *Love's Labour's Lost*, where the buffoonery of COSTARD and the other rustic characters emphasises the elegance of BEROWNE and the other courtiers. On the other hand, a sub-plot can parallel a main plot, offering different angles on the same theme, as in the sub-plot involving GLOUCESTER (1) in *King Lear*.

**Suffolk (1), Charles Brandon, Duke of (c. 1485–1545)** Historical figure and character in *Henry VIII*, a nobleman at the court of King HENRY VIII. Suffolk is among the enemies of Cardinal WOLSEY. In 2.2 he joins the Duke of NORFOLK (3) and the Lord CHAMBERLAIN (2) in hoping for the cardinal's downfall, and in 3.2 he takes part in the formal recitation of Wolsey's crimes and punishments. Suffolk is also present but unimportant in Act 5.

The historical Suffolk was the son of Henry VII's devoted follower, Sir William BRANDON (2), who dies at BOSWORTH FIELD in *Richard III*. From childhood on, Suffolk was a close friend of Henry VIII, as their friendly card game in 5.2 suggests. He married Henry's younger sister Mary, widow of the King of France, in 1515; their grand-daughter was the unfortunate Lady Jane Grey, executed in 1554 after the failure of a conspiracy to place her on the throne.

**Suffolk (2), Michael de la Pole, Earl of (1394–1415)** Historical figure mentioned in *Henry V*. This Earl of Suffolk was one of the few English noblemen killed at the battle of AGINCOURT; his death is described grandly in 4.6.7–32. He is not to be confused with his younger brother, SUFFOLK (3), who succeeded to the title and appears in *1* and *2 Henry VI*.

**Suffolk (3), William de la Pole, Earl, later Duke, of (1396–1450)** Historical figure and character in *1* and *2 Henry VI*, an ambitious nobleman. Suffolk attempts to control King HENRY VI through his influence on Queen MARGARET (1), whose marriage to Henry he engineers in *1 Henry VI*. With CARDINAL (1) BEAUFORT, Suffolk leads the plot against Duke Humphrey of GLOUCESTER (4) and personally engineers his murder. The downfall and death of 'good Duke Humphrey', presented as a man whose judgement and honesty might have saved the country from the WARS OF THE ROSES, dominates the first half of *2 Henry VI*. Suffolk is thus largely responsible for a national catastrophe, and he is accordingly treated as an arch-villain, calculatingly treacherous and unscrupulous, who will stop at nothing.

In *1 Henry VI* Suffolk emerges as a figure of importance for the first time in 5.3. He has captured MARGARET (1) of Anjou in battle and has fallen in love with her on sight. Plotting to make her his paramour, although he is already married, he decides to marry her to King Henry. He offers her a bargain; he will make her Queen of England if she will be his lover. She defers to her father, REIGNIER, who demands the cession of two territories, Anjou and Maine, before he will give his consent. Suffolk agrees to arrange it. In 5.5 Suffolk overcomes the scruples of the Duke of GLOUCESTER (4) and convinces the king to break a previous marriage agreement and wed Margaret. Suffolk closes the play with a soliloquy in which he proposes to rule the kingdom through Margaret when she is queen. Thus Suffolk's ambition lays the groundwork for the disasters of the civil strife to come.

At the outset of *2 Henry VI*, Suffolk presents Margaret to Henry, who is delighted with his bride, although the terms of the marriage contract include the cession of Anjou and Maine, to the anger and disgust of the assembled nobility. Suffolk's capacity for intrigue is immediately made evident in 1.2, when the renegade priest HUME, having agreed to recruit sorcerers for the DUCHESS (1) of Gloucester, reveals that he is being paid by Suffolk to set the Duchess up for arrest and prosecution. (The Duchess' séance produces a prediction that Suffolk will die by water.) In 1.3 Suffolk takes advantage of the minor episode of the armourer HORNER to embarrass the Duke of YORK (8), a potential rival. When Margaret complains to Suffolk of the arrogance of various nobles, he replies that his plots will conquer all her enemies. One of them, the Duchess, is banished in the next scene. In 3.1, after Gloucester has been arrested for treason, Suffolk urges that he be murdered by any means necessary, lest he be acquitted of the charge.

Suffolk hires the Murderers, and we see him arrangeing to pay them in 3.2. However, he has gone too far; King Henry, stimulated by a furious reaction from the COMMONS and his own grief at Gloucester's death, banishes Suffolk from England for life. Suffolk proceeds to vent his anger with a bloodcurdling series of imprecations on his foes (3.2.308–327).

The farewells of Suffolk and Margaret at the end of 3.2 reveal their passionate love. Shakespeare often, as here, made a point to emphasise the complexities of human character by evoking some sympathy for a villain. We can, astonishingly, forget Suffolk's viciousness for a moment as he laments the prospect of dying without Margaret.

Suffolk comes to an appropriate end. We see him for the last time, on a beach in KENT (1), as the prisoner of pirates who have captured the ship carrying him into exile. The LIEUTENANT (1) of the pirates assigns each captive to a different crewman, who can collect a ransom for each life. However, the pirate who receives Suffolk has lost an eye in the battle for the ship; he wants vengeance and proposes to kill his prisoner. He identifies himself as Walter WHITMORE, and, as Walter was pronounced 'water' by the Elizabethans, Suffolk sees that his death could fulfil the prophecy made to the Duchess of Gloucester in 1.4. The Lieutenant proves to be an English patriot who detests Suffolk for the damage his ambitions have done the English cause in France, and he recites Suffolk's political offences in virulent terms before turning him over to Whitmore for execution. Suffolk dies with an arrogant courage that can be admired.

The historical Suffolk was a grasping, ambitious, and extortionate aristocrat, but he probably did not earn the place he occupies in Shakespeare and in the chronicles that were the playwright's sources. He was an inept general and unsuccessful minister who bore some of the responsibility for the loss of France at the end of the HUNDRED YEARS WAR, and he did receive a dukedom, which he abused monstrously, for his role in arranging the marriage of Henry and Margaret. But his love affair with the queen is entirely fictitious, based on a passing remark in the chronicle of Edward HALL (2). The cession of Anjou and Maine occurred some time after the marriage, on the king's initiative; while Henry was doubtless influenced by Margaret, who was possibly supported by Suffolk, the duke did not arrange the matter himself. Suffolk was Gloucester's enemy, and he instituted his arrest at BURY ST. EDMUNDS, having called Parliament to that remote location, within his own territories, in order to do so. But Gloucester was probably not murdered, although rumour immediately and ever after laid his death to Suffolk. In any case, Suffolk was neither charged nor punished; in fact, his position grew stronger than ever after the deaths of Gloucester and Cardinal Beaufort. Not until three years later, when Normandy was finally and irrevocably lost, did Suffolk's enemies find their opportunity to undo him, and even then he was banished for only five years, not life. However, as in the play, his ship was captured by another one, whose crew took it upon themselves to execute the man they believed had slain 'good Duke Humphrey'. This murder proved to be the opening event in the revolt of Kentishmen led by Jack CADE.

**Sugarsop** Name mentioned in *The Taming of the Shrew*. Sugarsop is cited by GRUMIO as one of the servants of PETRUCHIO (2) in 4.1.80, but he never appears or is referred to again. This may reflect an abbreviated text, from which roles were cut because of a shortage of actors, but it is more probable that Grumio was being humorous; a sugarsop was a piece of bread soaked in a sweet or spiced sauce.

**Sullivan (1), Arthur Seymour (1842–1900)** English composer. Best known as the collaborator of W. S. Gilbert in their famous operettas, Sullivan first achieved renown with his incidental music for *The Tempest* (1862). For the tercentenary celebrations of Shakespeare's birth in 1864, he wrote the *Kenilworth Cantata*, which incorporates LORENZO's lovely speech on the beauties of the night (*Merchant of Venice* 5.1.53 ff). He also wrote accompaniments for several of Shakespeare's songs and composed incidental music for *Henry VIII* (1877) and *Macbeth* (1888).

**Sullivan (2), Barry (1821–1891)** Irish actor. Sullivan played in more than 300 Shakespearean productions. He was best known as HAMLET and RICHARD III. In 1879 he played BENEDICK opposite the BEATRICE of Helen FAUCIT in the premiere performance at the Shakespeare Memorial Theatre in STRATFORD.

**Surrey (1), Henry Howard, Earl of (c. 1517–1547)** English poet, important developer of the English SONNET and the introducer of BLANK VERSE into English poetry. Surrey studied the poets of the Italian RENAISSANCE, especially Petrarch (1301–1374), and shortly after his close friend Thomas WYATT introduced the sonnet into English, Surrey developed a variant more appropriate to the relatively rhyme-poor English language. This was the rhyme scheme that Shakespeare was to use in his SONNETS, the so-called English, or Shakespearean sonnet. In his partial translation of VIRGIL's *Aeneid* (published 1557), Surrey first used blank verse in English.

Surrey was a cousin of King HENRY VIII and a close friend of his illegitimate son. As a young man, he naturally became involved in the political intrigue of the court. In 1540 he helped his father—the SURREY (5) of *Henry VIII*—bring about the downfall of Thomas CROMWELL. Surrey fell victim to the increasing paranoia of King Henry, who was dying and feared that a promising young man of royal blood might want to hasten the process. Surrey was tried for treason on trumped-up charges and executed, only a few days before the king's death.

**Surrey (2), Thomas Fitz-Alan, Earl of (1381–1415)** Historical figure and minor character in *2 Henry IV*, a follower of King HENRY IV. In 3.1 Henry sends for Surrey and WARWICK (2) and tells them of his troubles. Surrey does not speak.

The historical Surrey was much more important than this slight role suggests. His father had been executed in 1397, along with Thomas of GLOUCESTER (6), by King RICHARD II in the conflict that was to trigger the events enacted in *Richard II*. Surrey, who fled to Flanders after his father's arrest, joined Henry IV, when, as BOLINGBROKE (1), he deposed Richard, and he remained a strong supporter of the king against the rebellions enacted in *1* and *2 Henry IV*. He was a friend of PRINCE (6) HAL who later, as King HENRY V, entrusted him with the command of major military expeditions.

**Surrey (3), Thomas Holland, Duke of (1374–1400)**
Historical figure and minor character in *Richard II*, a supporter of King RICHARD II. In 4.1 Surrey disputes Lord FITZWATER's account of the Duke of AUMERLE's role in the murder of the Duke of GLOUCESTER (6). Fitzwater challenges him to a trial by combat, one of many similar conflicts that erupt in this scene. The episode serves to demonstrate the widespread disorder that the illicit assumption of power by BOLING-BROKE (1) has engendered.

Although he is not seen again in the play, Surrey subsequently joins the revolt against Bolingbroke, for his execution is announced by NORTHUMBERLAND (1) in 5.6.8, where he is called Kent. Thomas Holland had been named Duke of Surrey by Richard in 1397, but Bolingbroke revoked that status at the time of the rebellion, so Northumberland refers to him by his lesser title, the Earl of Kent. Kent and the Earl of SALISBURY (1) were captured in battle by Lord BERKE-LEY (2), who turned them over to a mob, who beheaded them.

**Surrey (4), Thomas Howard, Earl of (1443–1524)**
Historical figure and minor character in *Richard III*, a general under RICHARD III at the battle of BOSWORTH FIELD. Surrey, second in command to his father, the Duke of NORFOLK (1), appears briefly in 5.3. He seems despondent just before the fighting, but, when questioned by Richard, assures the King that his heart is lighter than his looks.

The historical Surrey was restored to his father's titles by King Henry VII, the RICHMOND of the play, following a period of disgrace. He appears in *Henry VIII* as the Duke of NORFOLK (3). He was the father of another Earl of SURREY (5), who also appears in that play, and he was the grandfather of the poet Henry Howard, Earl of SURREY (1).

**Surrey (5), Thomas Howard, Earl of (1473–1554)**
Historical figure and character in *Henry VIII*, a nobleman at the court of King HENRY VIII. In 3.2 Surrey joins his father, the Duke of NORFOLK (3), in bringing down Cardinal WOLSEY; he thus avenges the death of his father-in-law, the Duke of BUCKINGHAM (1), who was earlier framed and sent to execution by Wolsey. In 2.1 the First GENTLEMAN (14) asserts that Wolsey has had Surrey assigned to a post in Ireland 'lest he should help his father[-in-law]' (2.1.44); this circumstance makes him a doubly appropriate addition to the play's roster of Wolsey's enemies. Surrey is present but inconspicuous in 5.2.

The historical Surrey was indeed sent to Ireland by Wolsey, almost certainly because the cardinal wanted an enemy out of England, but this occurred some time before Buckingham's treason trial and may not have been directly related to it. Shakespeare took Wolsey's motive from HOLINSHED's *Chronicles* and certainly believed it was true. However, the playwright gave Surrey a wrong name and rank, for by the time he appears in the play his father had died and he had become the Duke of Norfolk. However, since Norfolk remains alive in the play, Surrey must remain an earl. Surrey was an uncle of Anne Boleyn (see ANNE [1]), whose mother was his sister. He was the father of the famed poet Henry Howard, Earl of SURREY (1).

**Surrey (6)** Horse belonging to King RICHARD III in *Richard III*, his mount at the battle of BOSWORTH FIELD. In 5.3.65, Richard calls for 'white Surrey', who is reported killed in battle in 5.4, before Richard's famous cry, 'My kingdom for a horse' (5.4.13). Surrey's presence is based on several references in the chronicles to a great white charger ridden by Richard, but the name appears to be an invention of Shakespeare's.

**Surveyor** Minor character in *Henry VIII*, a treacherous steward to the Duke of BUCKINGHAM (1). The Surveyor, bribed by Cardinal WOLSEY, gives false testimony that convicts Buckingham of treason and leads to his execution. After performing his task in 1.2, the Surveyor disappears from the play. The episode emphasises the atmosphere of duplicity that surrounds Wolsey in the first half of the play. Historically, the Surveyor was one William Knyvet or Knevet, otherwise unknown, who had been fired by Buckingham in response to his tenants' complaints that he mistreated them.

**Sussex's Men** Acting company of the ELIZABETHAN THEATRE, possibly employers of Shakespeare early in his career. An acting company employed by Robert Radcliffe, Earl of Sussex (1573–1629), they performed at the court of Queen ELIZABETH (1) in 1592. In the winter of 1593–1594, Sussex's Men performed for Philip HENSLOWE, probably at the ROSE THEATRE, for a short interval when plays were permitted during the plague year. *Titus Andronicus* was in their repertoire at that time; some scholars think the young Shakespeare may have been a member of the company and may have written it expressly for them. In the spring of 1594, Sussex's Men performed jointly with the QUEEN'S MEN (1), and the two may have coalesced at this time, for Sussex's Men disappear from the record until 1602, when they reappear as a provincial touring company.

An earlier Sussex's Men had been employed by Robert's father, Thomas Radcliffe (c. 1530–1583), and they had appeared regularly at court, as well as on tour in the provinces, between 1572 and 1583. Because Thomas was Elizabeth's chamberlain after 1572, the company was sometimes called the Chamberlain's Men, but they are not to be confused with the later CHAMBERLAIN'S MEN, Shakespeare's company for many years.

**Swan Theatre** Playhouse in LONDON built by Francis LANGLEY around 1595 and depicted in the only surviving drawing of a 16th-century English theatre interior. Johannes de Witt, a Dutch traveller who visited London around 1596, made a drawing of the Swan, of which a copy has survived. Its accuracy has been questioned, but its major features are probably correct. They include a circular building with three stories of seats, each containing three rows, overlooking an unroofed central area into which a stage thrusts. The stage is half-covered by a canopy extending from its rear wall and supported by massive columns on stage; there are two doors in the back wall of the stage, with a set of box seats above these doors, behind the stage. At the top of this rear structure is a roofed hut, from which a flag flies and a man blows a trumpet, both signs that a play is scheduled. On the stage are three performers.

If de Witt was in fact in London in 1596—the record is obscure—then the performers may be members of Shakespeare's company, the CHAMBERLAIN'S MEN, who probably played at the Swan for a season that year. In 1597 the PEMBROKE'S MEN came to London and engaged the theatre for a year, but their production of an allegedly seditious play, *Isle of Dogs* by Thomas NASHE, resulted in the government's closure of all the London theatres for four months. When the theatres reopened, Langley was unable to recruit another company, and the Swan was not used regularly for theatre thereafter. After Langley's death in 1601, the theatre was sold to another London investor, who had no greater success. Only one play besides *Isle of Dogs* is known to have been staged there. Miscellaneous entertainments—a fencing match, a poetry improvisation contest—are also recorded, but in 1632, a writer declared the Swan was 'now fallen to decay'.

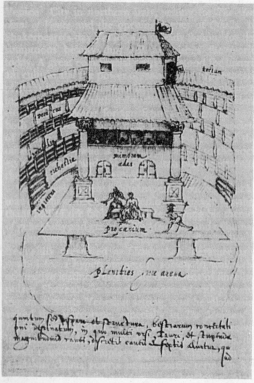

*This drawing of the Swan Theatre is the only known contemporary image of the interior of an Elizabethan theatre.*

**Swinburne, Algernon Charles (1837–1909)** English poet. Best known as a major late-Victorian poet, Swinburne also wrote literary criticism and enthusiastically encouraged a renewed interest in ELIZABETHAN DRAMA. Swinburne's Shakespearean commentary is regarded as more of a curiosity than a resource, however, for his adulation was extreme. For instance, he called *Cymbeline*'s IMOGEN 'the woman best beloved in all the world of song and all the tide of time'. Such sentimentality spurred a response led by George Bernard SHAW (2), who coined the word 'bardolatry' to mock it.

**Swinstead (Swineshead) Abbey** Religious establishment in Lincolnshire, setting for 5.6–7 of *King John,* the site of the death of King JOHN (3). Sick and dispirited, John withdraws from the fighting against the French and is poisoned by a monk. He dies the next day, and the BASTARD (1) leads the other noblemen in swearing allegiance to his successor, HENRY (1).

Swinstead Abbey, which Shakespeare misnamed following John FOXE, was not the historical site of John's death, nor was the King poisoned, although Shakespeare took the tale from HOLINSHED and Foxe. John, stricken with dysentery while battling the French-supported rebels, spent a few days at Swineshead Abbey in October 1216, but he died several days later in nearby Newark.

**Taborer** Minor character in *The Two Noble Kinsmen*, a drummer. The Taborer accompanies the COUNTRYMEN and the lasses led by NELL (2) in their dance performed before Duke THESEUS (2) in 3.5. The Taborer speaks only one line, a boisterous greeting in 3.5.24. Since most scholars agree that Shakespeare did not write 3.5, the Taborer is probably the creation of John FLETCHER (2).

**Tailor, the** Minor character in *The Taming of the Shrew*, an artisan whom PETRUCHIO (2) abuses. Commissioned by Petruchio to provide a gown for KATHERINA, the Tailor is driven away by his client. Petruchio's mistreatment of this innocent man is simply part of his demonstration to his bride of the ugliness of shrewish behaviour. Although the Tailor defends himself before being routed, he otherwise has no distinctive personality.

**Talbot, Lord John (before 1388–1453)** Historical figure and character in *1 Henry VI*, the principal English military hero in the HUNDRED YEARS WAR. In 1.1 Talbot's reported capture seems to magnify English woes. The MESSENGER (3) who brings this news describes how Talbot's actions in battle had raised English morale. Talbot's account of his captivity, related in 1.4, after he has been ransomed, further demonstrates his capacity to daunt the French enemy. The king acknowledges Talbot's virtues when he repeats his father, HENRY V's, remark, 'A stouter champion never handled sword' (3.4.19).

Talbot's fate is closely linked with that of JOAN LA PUCELLE in an alternating sequence of victories and defeats that closes with Joan's ignoble capture and death in Act 5, presented in contrast to Talbot's own glorious fall in the immediately preceding battle. The war reaches its theatrical climax in these scenes (4.2–7), in which the brave Talbot fights and dies, along with his young son, JOHN (6). He is doomed by the dispute between the dukes of YORK (8) and SOMERSET (3), which prevents reinforcements from reaching him. Sir William LUCY (2), who comes to collect his corpse, delivers a formal, elegiac recital of Talbot's feudal titles, reminding us how little removed Shakespeare was from the Middle Ages.

Throughout the play, Talbot carries the burden of destiny for the English in their struggle with the French. He is also contrasted with the selfish noblemen whose ambitions cause dissensions within the English leadership that lead to the losses to FRANCE (1). While the noblemen engage in squabbles and arguments, Talbot is consistently virtuous. Heightening the contrast, Shakespeare rearranged history so that the jealous rivalry of York and Somerset becomes a direct cause of Talbot's death.

In his *Pierce Penniless*, a book of social commentary published in 1592, Thomas NASHE remarked on the contemporary theatre's capacity to thrill its public with works depicting patriotic stories 'long buried in rusty brass and worm-eaten books'. He chose a single example as sufficient to prove his point: 'How would it have joyed brave Talbot, the terror of the French, to think that after he had lien two hundred years in his tomb he should triumph again on the stage, and have his bones new-embalmed with the tears of ten thousand spectators at least, at several times, who in the tragedian that represents his person imagine they behold him fresh bleeding.' This passage, the earliest known literary reference to *1 Henry VI*, suggests to us how successful the young Shakespeare had been when he created Talbot, a clean-cut hero for his times similar to those played by John Wayne in ours.

***The Taming of a Shrew*** Anonymous play first published in 1594, probably a BAD QUARTO of *The Taming of the Shrew* but once thought to have been the principal source of that play. *A Shrew*, as the play is conveniently known, differs most strikingly from *The Shrew* in having a simpler SUB-PLOT. *The Shrew* features a contest among three suitors for the hand of the younger of two sisters; *A Shrew* adds a third sister and matches each sister with a suitor, eliminating the rivalry. This sub-plot is equally filled with romantic intrigue, as the suitors of the younger sisters conspire to outwit the father of the girls, but it lacks the comical confusions of Shakespeare's work. The main plot is the same, and the dialogue corresponds closely throughout much of the play.

*A Shrew* is, however, a generally inferior drama, and this, combined with the difference in sub-plots, used to be taken to indicate that Shakespeare had used *A Shrew* as his chief source for *The Shrew*, unless both were derived from an earlier, subsequently lost play, designated the UR-SHREW. However, close examination of the two texts offers convincing evidence that *A Shrew* was compiled from the recollections of actors who had performed in *The Shrew*—that is, that the former is a Bad Quarto of the latter. This theory renders the Ur-Shrew hypothesis unnecessary.

Although similarities in wording occur throughout the two plays, including their sub-plots, *A Shrew*'s versions of particular passages are consistently garbled or misinterpreted renderings of the corresponding lines in *The Shrew*. Even the introductory moments of the sub-plot of *A Shrew* bear signs of its derivative nature; it appears that its complexities were not well remembered, so the compilers fell back on a more conventional love plot. Further, *A Shrew* contains echoes of other plays, especially *Tamburlaine* and *Doctor Faustus*, by Christopher MARLOWE (1). This is characteristic of reconstructed texts, reflecting faulty memories on the part of the actors. And some scenes in a Bad Quarto are invariably closer to the original text than others, indicating that the principal compilers played the characters whose roles are most accurately recollected and appeared on stage during the best-rendered scenes. It thus seems likely that much of the text of *A Shrew* was the work of the actors who had played Christopher SLY (1) and GRUMIO in *The Shrew*, probably William SLY (2) and Alexander COOKE (1), respectively. The title-page of *A Shrew* asserts that it had been performed by PEMBROKE'S MEN. This acting company toured the provinces for most of the period 1592–1594 and probably produced the text for that tour.

One of the most striking differences between the two texts is the presence in *A Shrew* of four INTERLUDES and an EPILOGUE dealing with Christopher SLY (1), whereas *The Shrew* abandons the tale after one interlude. It is presumed that the editors of the FIRST FOLIO (1623), in which *The Shrew* was first published, used a manuscript that reflected a production that cut these episodes due to a shortage of actors. Thus *A Shrew* apparently presents a version of Shakespeare's original interludes and epilogue, and this material is sometimes included in editions of *The Shrew*.

Marlowe's *Doctor Faustus* was probably written in the spring of 1592, and a compiler of *A Shrew* had acted in it, or at least seen it, so that the the text of *A Shrew* must have been assembled between the summer of 1592 and the spring of 1594, when it was registered for publication. It was published by Cuthbert BURBY, who also published QUARTO editions of several of Shakespeare's other plays. It was reissued in 1597, and Nicholas LING published a third edition in 1607.

## The Taming of the Shrew

### SYNOPSIS

*Induction, Scene 1*

Christopher SLY (1) drunkenly falls asleep on the ground. As a practical joke, the local LORD (1) decides to take the unconscious man into his home and have him awaken in the lap of luxury. He orders his servants to inform Sly that he is a gentleman who has been insane for many years, believing himself a poor drunkard. A travelling company of PLAYERS (1) arrives, and the Lord directs them to perform for Sly. He further arranges for his PAGE (4) to pose as Sly's wife.

*Induction, Scene 2*

Sly awakens in a bedroom of the Lord's house, and the servants offer him delicacies. His 'illness' is explained to him by the Lord, but Sly denies it and briefly describes his true place in the world. The Lord and his servants offer the gentlemanly pleasures they insist are properly his, including a beautiful wife, and Sly accepts their version of his life. The Page appears, dressed as a woman. Sly's lusty instincts are laid to rest by the assertion that sex will produce further delusions of poverty. The Players' performance is announced, and Sly prepares to enjoy it.

*Act 1, Scene 1*

LUCENTIO, accompanied by his servant TRANIO, has just arrived in PADUA. They observe BAPTISTA telling HORTENSIO and GREMIO that their courtship of his daughter BIANCA (1) is inappropriate, for he will not permit her to be wed until her older sister, KATHERINA, is married. The suitors state that this is an unlikely prospect, as Katherina is a notorious shrew, unacceptable to any man. Katherina's aggressive response seems to justify their remarks, while Bianca demurely accepts her father's order. Baptista asks the suitors to help him find tutors in music and poetry to keep Bianca happy, and he and his daughters depart. Hortensio and Gremio agree to try to find a husband for Katherina so that they can resume their rivalry for Bianca, and they, too, leave. Lucentio tells Tranio of his immediate and intense love for Bianca. The two devise a plan to permit him to court the girl: Lucentio shall disguise himself as a scholar and become Bianca's tutor, and Tranio shall pretend to be Lucentio. Lucentio's other servant, BIONDELLO, arrives and is told of the plan. In addition, Lucentio decides that the disguised Tranio shall declare himself a suitor to Bianca and convince Baptista to accept him. Christopher Sly, who has been dozing, is awakened by the Page and another servant, and he readies himself to watch more of the play.

*Act 1, Scene 2*

PETRUCHIO (2) arrives in Padua and calls on his old friend Hortensio. He announces that he has come in search of a wife, and Hortensio suggests Katherina, while warning that she is intolerable. Petruchio is undaunted, for he says he knows how to deal with shrews; he insists on meeting Baptista immediately. Hortensio decides to masquerade as a music teacher, to be recommended by Petruchio as Bianca's tutor. On their way to Baptista's, they encounter Gremio and Lucentio, who is dressed as a scholar. Gremio declares that he will ingratiate himself with Baptista by presenting Lucentio as a language teacher for Bianca. Tranio, disguised as Lucentio, appears and reveals, in his master's name, his intention to court Bianca.

### Act 2, Scene 1

Katherina torments Bianca until Baptista stops her, and the sisters go their separate ways. Gremio, Petruchio, and Hortensio arrive. Petruchio introduces himself as a suitor for Katherina's hand and proposes Hortensio as a music teacher to entertain his prospective bride; similarly, Gremio presents Lucentio as a language teacher, intended for Bianca. Tranio arrives, calling himself Lucentio, and declares himself a suitor of Bianca; he bears a gift of a lute and several books. Baptista distributes these to the appropriate tutors and sends the teachers to their pupils. Petruchio, saying that he is in a hurry, arranges a marriage agreement with Baptista, contingent on Katherina's acceptance. Hortensio reports that Katherina has broken the lute on his head in a fit of anger. Petruchio praises Katherina's spirit and wants to meet her. The others leave, and Petruchio reveals his plan in a soliloquy: he will assert Katherina's sweetness, no matter how shrewish her behaviour, and treat their wedding as agreed upon, whatever her protests. She appears, and he immediately takes a familiar tone, addressing her as Kate and complimenting her effusively. They engage in a bantering battle of wits, but he ignores her insults; even when she hits him he responds with moderation. She calls him a fool, but he insists that she shall marry him and he shall tame her. Baptista, Gremio, and Tranio return, and, despite Katherina's protests, Petruchio insists that she has agreed to their marriage and has been very affectionate to him. She calms down as Petruchio confirms with her father his plan to marry her on the next Sunday, and Petruchio takes her with him to get a ring. Baptista asserts that the wealthiest of Bianca's suitors shall marry his younger daughter, and they attempt to outbid each other. Tranio, speaking as Lucentio, offers far more than Gremio, citing the vast fortune of his father, VINCENTIO (1). Baptista agrees that he shall have Bianca once his parent comes to Padua and substantiates his claim. The older men leave, and Tranio plans to recruit a stand-in for Lucentio's father.

### Act 3, Scene 1

Lucentio and Hortensio refuse to leave each other alone with Bianca. Lucentio pretends to construe a passage in Latin and reveals his identity and purpose to Bianca. She is demurely wary, but she doesn't dismiss him, telling him not to despair. Hortensio gives her a love note couched as a lesson in the musical scale, but she rejects him altogether.

### Act 3, Scene 2

Petruchio, dressed in ridiculous clothes, arrives very late for his wedding to Katherina and goes in search of her. The wedding guests follow, and Tranio has a chance to tell Lucentio of his plan to find a substitute Vincentio. Gremio tells of Petruchio's obnoxious behaviour at the wedding. The rest of the wedding party appears, and Petruchio announces that he is leaving immediately with Kate, rather than staying for the banquet. Furious, Katherina resists, but he carries her off.

### Act 4, Scene 1

Petruchio's servant GRUMIO arrives at his master's house in bitter cold, having been sent ahead to arrange for the newlyweds' reception. He tells CURTIS, another servant, of the unchivalrous behaviour of Petruchio, who has allowed Katherina to lie in the mud after falling from her horse and has beaten Grumio needlessly, to his bride's horror. The couple appear. Petruchio orders dinner for Katherina, but he rails at the servants for not presenting it properly, throwing the food at them; his wife gets none. He ignores her pleas for patience and takes her off to bed. A servant reports that Petruchio continues to rant and rave, disconcerting Katherina completely. Petruchio returns, and the servants flee; in a soliloquy he describes his plan: he will continue to insist ferociously that nothing is good enough for his wife so that she will get no food, no drink, and no rest. He likens his strategy to the taming of a wild falcon.

### Act 4, Scene 2

In Padua, Hortensio brings Tranio, whom he thinks is Lucentio, to overhear Bianca's loving conversation with the real Lucentio. Tranio pretends to be affronted and joins Hortensio in criticising Bianca as frivolous and unworthy. Hortensio vows to marry a WIDOW (1) who has pursued him, and he leaves. Tranio encounters the PEDANT, a newcomer to Padua, and, after learning that he is from MANTUA, tells him that an outbreak of hostilities has resulted in a new law condemning to death any Mantuan found in Padua. He offers to protect the stranger if he will agree to pose as Vincentio. The Pedant gratefully accepts.

### Act 4, Scene 3

Petruchio brings food for Katherina, but she won't speak to him. He refuses to give it to her until she thanks him. She thanks him, but, before she can eat much, he brings in a TAILOR and a HABERDASHER to provide her with fine clothes. Petruchio rejects these garments, although Katherina likes them. He asserts that she shall have a gentlewoman's clothes only when she is gentle, and, raging, he drives the Tailor and Haberdasher away. Planning their journey to a feast at her father's house, he asserts that it is seven o'clock; when Katherina responds that it is only two, he insists that she must stop contradicting him.

### Act 4, Scene 4

Tranio and the Pedant, as Lucentio and his father, call on Baptista. The Pedant asserts his willingness to provide a dowry, and Baptista agrees to the betrothal of Bianca and Lucentio; they leave to sign a marriage contract at Lucentio's house. The real Lucentio, who is present in his role as the tutor, is sent to fetch Bianca. Biondello informs him of Tranio's plan: a priest is ready at a certain church, and Lucentio may now elope with his beloved.

### Act 4, Scene 5

On the road to Padua, Petruchio remarks that the moonlight is very bright. When Katherina observes that it is daylight, he threatens to cancel the trip if she does not stop disagreeing with him. She gives in to him, calling the sun the moon, and he says it is the sun. She concurs and states that she will agree to whatever he says. Petruchio asserts that things are now as they should be. When an elderly man approaches, Petruchio calls him a lovely maid, and Katherina, true to her promise, addresses the old gentleman as though he were a girl. Petruchio then changes his mind, and Katherina begs the man's pardon for her mistake. As they travel together, the older man identifies himself as Vincentio.

### Act 5, Scene 1

Bianca and Lucentio enter a church to be married. Petruchio, Katherina, and Vincentio arrive at Lucentio's house, where the Pedant poses as Vincentio. Petruchio and Katherina withdraw to witness this development. The clamour brings Baptista and Tranio. Tranio continues to brazen it out, and Vincentio is about to be arrested as an imposter, when Lucentio and Bianca arrive, married. Lucentio identifies himself and explains what has happened. Baptista's anger is cooled by Vincentio's assurance that he will approve Lucentio's marriage. The discussion becomes more cordial and moves indoors. Petruchio wishes to kiss Katherina before following the others inside but she is embarrassed to kiss in the street. He speaks of returning home, and she kisses him. Affectionately, they go to join the others.

### Act 5, Scene 2

A banquet celebrates the marriages of Lucentio to Bianca, Hortensio to the Widow, and, belatedly, Petruchio to Katherina. The Widow shrewishly argues with Katherina. The ladies withdraw, and the men gamble on whose wife is the most obedient. Bianca is sent for, but she sends word that she is busy and cannot come. Similarly, the Widow sends the message that, suspecting some joke, she will not come. Petruchio sends Grumio to 'command' that Katherina come, and she does. Petruchio sends her back to fetch the other women. When the women return, the Widow says she is glad not to be so compliant as Katherina, and Bianca calls Lucentio a fool for having bet on her obedience. At Petruchio's order, Katherina lectures the other women on the virtues of submissiveness. She says that the natural order of things places men in authority and that a woman's virtue and beauty are marred by revolt against nature. A husband takes risks in the world to maintain a home, whereas a woman lives in relative comfort, owing no more for her situation than obedience. She compares a woman's proper devotion to a husband with the allegiance that a subject owes a prince, and she observes that she has rebelled herself and has learned that nothing is to be gained from it. She makes a formal gesture of submission, placing her hand beneath Petruchio's foot. Petruchio, exulting in his fine wife, takes her off to bed; the others marvel at the taming of the shrew.

### COMMENTARY

*The Taming of the Shrew* is sometimes seen as an account of the tyranny of man over woman, but this is a misinterpretation stemming from our distance from the assumptions of Shakespeare's day. In Elizabethan England it was almost universally agreed that it was a God-given right, confirmed in the Bible, for a husband to dominate his wife in all things, just as a king could dictate to a citizen or a human being could control an animal. Katherina's famous speech in 5.2.137–180 expresses this belief quite plainly. However, it is a mistake to think that the story of Katherina and Petruchio is intended to make this point; rather, it takes the point for granted. Instead, the play's main plot concerns the development of character and of love in a particular sort of personality.

Shakespeare's version of the 'battle of the sexes' is a striking advance on its predecessors. In treatments of this classic theme both before and since Shakespeare, a woman is commonly beaten into submission or is tormented in some more sophisticated manner. The violence in *The Shrew*—except for conventional beatings of servants, a staple of theatrical humour dating back to Roman drama—is limited to Katherina's own assaults on Bianca and Petruchio, which demonstrate her shrewishness. Petruchio 'tames' Katherina by means of a clever strategy that startlingly resembles modern behaviour-modification therapy.

In fact, the psychology of *The Taming of the Shrew* is highly evolved, evidence that, even early in his career, Shakespeare had the capacity to delineate personalities. Acts 1–3 contain a convincingly familiar portrait of a highly defensive young woman who shields herself from criticism by attacking others first, and she is strong enough to make her father and sister regret any effort to reform her. The portrayal of the deceptively demure Bianca, who slyly taunts her sister in 2.1 and who displays her own wilfulness when she is alone with her suitors in 3.1, suggests that Katherina has been compared to her younger sister too often for her temper to tolerate. Petruchio understands this and, although he is motivated to marry for mercenary reasons, he values Katherina's high spirits. Thus he can manoeuvre her into abandoning her shrewishness, and his technique, although comically overdrawn, is psychologically sophisticated.

Petruchio persistently assures Katherina that she is a rational and loving person. On the other hand, he himself behaves terribly, throwing tantrums and flying in the face of good sense—in fact, he exaggerates the behaviour by which she has distinguished herself. She finally succumbs to him and adopts conventional wifely behaviour, represented by the humorous tests she passes in 4.5. Her transformation comes about not because Petruchio has forced her to feign acceptance of a repugnant role, but because she has seen in his antics the ugliness of her own shrewish behaviour and has also come to recognise the emotional rewards for herself in being a dutiful wife. He has understood her, and now she understands both herself and him.

That Katherina and Petruchio are in love before the play ends is sometimes disputed on the grounds that she becomes too servile to allow any relationship between them other than master and slave. However, her servility exists only in the minds of observers from another age, our own; for Shakespeare's audience, and for Katherina herself, her new position is simply a conventional one. It does not at all preclude love. Petruchio and Katherina demonstrate their growing affection, rather than declare it outright, but it is no less real. At the end of 5.1 they express affection for each other for the first time: she kisses him, and she calls him 'love'; he responds by calling her his 'sweet Kate', an epithet he has earlier used only sarcastically.

The 'submission' speech is not delivered in slavish resignation to a demand, but as a duty, carrying with it the rewards of a solid place in the world, a place described with approval in the speech itself. Petruchio has not tried to humiliate Katherina, and she is not humiliated. Instead, he has asserted her superiority to other wives and offered her a podium from which to lecture the Widow. He has not asked her to speak of her own relationship to him; it is entirely her idea to assert that her own experience of rebellion has been barren and pointless. To close the speech, she freely offers a symbolic enactment of her acceptance of the traditional wifely role. Flabbergasted, almost at a loss for words, Petruchio can only sputter, 'Why, there's a wench' (5.2.181), and kiss his bride. Shakespeare consistently gives his heroines the last word in his come-

dies, and in *The Shrew,* as always, that word confirms the triumph of love, specifically conventional married love.

It is ironic that Petruchio's frankly mercenary interest in marriage yields a love match, whereas Lucentio's rapture for Bianca lands him with a shrew. This twist reinforces the contrasts between the main plot and the SUB-PLOT. Petruchio's tactics and their happy outcome are juxtaposed with the more conventional romancing of Bianca. The sub-plot consists of an assemblage of traditional dramatic situations; youth is pitted against age; the romanticism of intrigue and disguise is compared to courtship conducted in business terms. These comparisons are familiar ones, deriving from Italian and ancient Roman models, and the participating characters are mere stereotypes, with the single exception of Bianca, who is humanly complex. Lucentio and Hortensio are stock young men of Italian romances; Tranio is part of a tradition of cunning servants that dates back to ancient Greek comedy; Baptista is a standard father-of-the-girl; and Gremio is referred to several times as a 'pantaloon', the comic old man of the COMMEDIA DELL'ARTE. These predictable characters make the eccentric individuality of Petruchio and Katherina particularly attractive.

The conventionality of the majority of the characters is just one of several features of the play that intentionally stress its artificiality. The Induction asserts that the tale is a fiction, intended for light entertainment. The final scene serves a similar function. By 5.2 the strands of the plot have all been woven together, and all that remains is a formal summation of the play's themes. The ritualistic setting of a wedding feast and the presence of most of the play's cast strengthen the element of magic in the thrice-repeated summons of the wives and their triple responses, and in the crowning gesture of Katherina's statement of proper martial relations. While it not does not do so as explicitly as the Sly plot, the ceremonial nature of this scene also emphasises the artificiality of the fantasy it closes.

*The Taming of the Shrew* relies heavily on accepted dramatic conventions, and it approaches traditional farce in many respects. It lacks the depth of Shakespeare's later comedies, but it also foreshadows them; Katherina in particular anticipates BEATRICE in *Much Ado About Nothing.* In its presentation of several psychologically resonant portraits, as well as in its strong organisation and thoughtfully developed themes, it is a remarkable early work.

## SOURCES OF THE PLAY

No specific source is known for the main plot of *The Taming of the Shrew.* Folk tales and songs about a husband disciplining a troublesome wife have been common in most cultures, and many were well known in Elizabethan England. A doggerel ballad, *A Merry Jest of a Shrewde and Curste Wyfe,* printed in 1550, is often cited as a possible source, and it resembles the play in that its shrew is the elder of two sisters; in most such works, she is the youngest of three. However, it differs from *The Shrew* in other respects. The playwright will have known many such tales and ballads, and it is unlikely that any one of them was his specific source. His own version is significantly less brutal than all of its antecedents, and it seems most likely that he simply devised a story line from his recollections of a common popular theme.

Similarly, the Induction's tale of a poor man placed in a rich man's world had widespread currency. Like the shrew theme, this was also the subject of a number of 16th-century English ballads, and a version was published in a London jest-book in 1570. The details of Christopher Sly's existence are plainly taken from the young playwright's own WARWICKSHIRE background, and it seems clear that, again, Shakespeare created his own version of a widely recognised story.

For the Bianca sub-plot, the playwright turned to the play *Supposes* (performed 1566, published 1573, 1587), by George GASCOIGNE, a translation of an Italian drama, *I Suppositi* (1509), by Ludovico ARIOSTO. Knowledgeable members of Shakespeare's audience doubtless enjoyed the coy reference to 'supposes' in 5.1.107.

Various other works have been suggested as sources of certain features. The names Grumio and Tranio appear in *The Haunted House,* by PLAUTUS. Gervase MARKHAM's writings on falconry may have contributed to Petruchio's elaborate description in 4.1.175–198. Gerard LEGH's book on heraldry, *Accedens of Armory* (1562), to which Shakespeare would refer in writing *King Lear,* contains a story similar to that of the Tailor in 4.3. In 1484 William CAXTON translated and published a French tale that might have inspired the husbands' wager in 5.2. However, such bets often appear in the folklore of marital relations. In fact, although literary sources may have provided various details, Shakespeare might just as easily have derived any of the play's minor episodes from some popular tale or ballad now lost.

## TEXT OF THE PLAY

It is difficult to determine when *The Taming of the Shrew* was written, as it is for all of Shakespeare's early plays. Estimates have ranged from the late 1580s to 1600, although the later dates reflect an assumption that Shakespeare used *The Taming of a Shrew* as a model. Most scholars now regard *A Shrew* as a BAD QUARTO of *The Shrew* and accordingly conclude that the original play must have been written before the summer of 1592, when *A Shrew* was compiled. The numerous references in the Induction to the playwright's native Warwickshire suggest that the work may have been written not long after his arrival in London, probably in 1588 or 1589. *The Taming of the Shrew* is sometimes cited as Shakespeare's earliest work, but this proposition is unprovable.

*The Shrew* was not published until it was included in the FIRST FOLIO (1623). The first QUARTO edition was published in 1631. The Folio text appears to be derived from Shakespeare's FOUL PAPERS, as transcribed by a scribe hired to make a copy for the use of an acting company. It has served as the basis for all subsequent editions, although, beginning with POPE (1) in 1723, some editors have included the interludes and the epilogue from *A Shrew* to complete the tale of Christopher Sly.

## THEATRICAL HISTORY OF THE PLAY

Little evidence of early productions of *The Taming of the Shrew* has survived. However, Shakespeare's play was certainly popular at least into the 1630s. In about 1611 *The Woman's Prize, or the Tamer Tamed* by John FLETCHER (2), offered a sequel to Shakespeare's work. This play depicts Petruchio's second marriage, following Kate's death, to a woman who applies to him the treatment he had meted out to his first wife. This could have had point only if Shakespeare's play were in vogue at the time. Moreover, the appearance of a Quarto edition of the play in 1631 implies a continuing public interest, and its title-page tells of the play's performance by the KING'S MEN at both the BLACKFRIARS and GLOBE theatres. The play was also acted at the court of King Charles I in 1633.

After a revival in 1663, no performance of Shakespeare's play was recorded for almost 180 years. *The Taming of the Shrew* was replaced by a series of adaptations, none resembling the original very closely. The first of these, John LACY's *Sauny the Scot,* appeared in 1667. A crude farce, it was extremely popular for a century. It stimulated its own spin-off—a musical entitled *A Cure for a Scold* (c. 1735)—which was itself performed until the 1760s. The episode of Christopher Sly, deleted from *Sauny,* was used in *The Cobbler of Preston* (1716), by Charles JOHNSON (2), a political play about the Jacobite Rebellion of 1715. Its popularity stimulated another, non-political, play with the same title in the same year, also based loosely on the Induction.

*Sauny* was finally replaced on the English stage by David GARRICK's *Catherine and Petruchio* (1754), an abbreviated version of Shakespeare's play, eliminating both the Induction and the Bianca sub-plot. This popular play was regularly staged for more than a century and Frederick REYNOLDS (1) made an opera of it in 1828. An even shorter version, by John Philip KEMBLE (3), competed with Garrick's production in the late 18th century and introduced a piece of stage business—Petruchio cracking a horsewhip—that became standard in subsequent productions and was probably the public's strongest image of the play into recent times.

It was not until 1844 that Shakespeare's text was revived, in a historic production by Benjamin WEBSTER (1) and J. R. PLANCHE that established the use of legitimate Shakespearean texts as a norm. By the end of the 19th century Shakespeare's version of *The Shrew* was well established on both sides of the Atlantic. Ada REHAN was particularly acclaimed as Katherina. The play has continued to be popular in the 20th century, and notable productions have included a modern-dress staging by Barry JACKSON (1) in 1928 and Joseph PAPP's 1978 presentation starring Raul Julia and Meryl Streep. *The Taming of the Shrew* has been made as a FILM eleven times, six as a silent movie. Two of the talkies are in English. The first, which featured Mary Pickford and Douglas Fairbanks, is remembered chiefly for a credit line that has become a favourite show-business joke: 'Written by William Shakespeare with additional dialogue by Sam Taylor'. Franco ZEFFIRELLI's 1966 film starring Richard Burton and Elizabeth Taylor was a box-office success. Also, the play has been produced for TELEVISION twice, most recently by Jonathan MILLER (2) in 1980.

**Tamora**  Character in *Titus Andronicus,* the villainous queen of the Goths. Tamora, her three sons, and her lover, AARON the Moor, have been captured by the Roman general TITUS (1) Andronicus before the play begins. When in 1.1, her captor permits her eldest son to be ritually sacrificed despite her eloquent plea for mercy, Tamora vows revenge and the play's bloody cycle begins. Tamora find her chance for vengeance, when the new Roman emperor, SATURNINUS, falls in love with her and marries her. Saturninus fears Titus, who is very popular, and wishes to break with him, but Tamora advises her new husband to make peace with the general until his own hold on the throne is more secure. She will see to Titus' downfall herself, she adds.

After this flamboyant introduction, Tamora recedes from the forefront of the play for a while. Her revenge is implemented largely by Aaron, though she helps him frame two of Titus' sons for a murder, and she is particularly villainous in refusing LAVINIA's plea for mercy in 2.3. Later, in 4.4, when she and Saturninus learn of an approaching army under Titus' son, her husband is stricken with fear, but she reproves him, in a well-known speech emphasising the power held by rulers (4.4.81–87). She goes on to boast that she will 'enchant the old Andronicus', that is, Titus, and prevail upon him to cancel his son's invasion.

With her sons, Tamora goes to Titus in disguise, pretending to be Revenge, a spirit from within the earth come to help the mad old man achieve his ven-

geance. In her impersonation, she anticipates later Shakespearean witches and ghosts. She believes that Titus is mad, but he is sane enough to see through her plot and pretend to be taken in. Thinking she has won, she leaves her sons with Titus, but he kills them and serves them to her at the banquet in the last scene, before killing her as well.

**Tamworth**  Village in central England, about 10 miles from BOSWORTH FIELD, setting for 5.2 of *Richard III.* As the Earl of RICHMOND approaches the forces of RICHARD III, he mentions the hamlet (in 5.2.13).

**Tarlton, Richard (d. 1588)**  English comic actor, a leading figure in ELIZABETHAN THEATRE when Shakespeare's career began. Tarlton was a member of the QUEEN's MEN (1) from its foundation in 1583 until his death. He was a particular favourite of Queen ELIZABETH (1) and served also as her personal jester or FOOL (1), though she began to dislike him when he went too far in jokes about her favourites. He also wrote plays, and his *The Seven Deadly Sins* (1585) may have been revived in the 1590s by Shakespeare's STRANGE's MEN. His greatest accomplishment, however, was the establishment of a popular style for the stage CLOWN (1)—earthy, awkward, comically confused in speech— that became standard. He was a great influence on William KEMPE, for whom Shakespeare wrote a number of parts. Tarlton was especially noted for his ability to improvise, and HAMLET's complaint about 'clowns [who] speak . . . more than is set down for them' (*Hamlet* 3.2.39) was a joke at the expense of Tarlton and his successors. The great clown became something of a cult figure after his death; taverns were named for him, and ballads and joke books about him—or allegedly by him—appeared for at least 40 years. An unproven tradition holds that Shakespeare was thinking of Tarlton when he had Hamlet reminisce fondly of the jester YORICK.

**Tarquin  (Sextus  Tarquinius)**  Semi-legendary Roman prince and figure in *The Rape of Lucrece,* the rapist who assaults LUCRECE. In the first quarter of the poem, Tarquin, though aware that his act will dishonour him forever, is gripped by sexual desire and continues, 'pawning his honour to obtain his lust' (line 156). He condemns himself at some length (lines 190–245, 260–280), but he finally commits himself to satisfying his lust. He is held between 'frozen conscience and hot burning will' (line 247), in the grip of an evil impulse 'strong past reason's weak removing' (line 243). In this respect Tarquin's story anticipates a major theme of *Macbeth,* and he is specifically referred to in that play (2.1.55).

Once Tarquin assaults Lucrece in her bedroom, the poet's attention turns to the victim (line 442), and, after committing his crime, Tarquin flees (line 740). He does not reappear, though in the last line of the poem it is reported that Lucrece's avengers, led by Junius BRUTUS (2), expel him from Rome. Earlier, in the last sentence of the ARGUMENT to the poem, Shakespeare also mentions this development, saying, '. . . the Tarquins were all exiled, and the state government changed from kings to consuls'. Thus Tarquin's crime is said to have led to the establishment of the Roman Republic.

In Shakespeare's sources, OVID and LIVY, Sextus Tarquinius is the son of the last king of the Romans, Tarquinius Superbas, and the king, deposed in favour of the Republic in 509 B.C., may have had a son who bore this name. However, the tale of Lucrece's rape has its roots in pre-Roman traditions, and Tarquin may well be totally legendary. In any case the name Tarquinius suggests that these rulers of Rome were Etruscans, whose principal city was Tarquinia.

**Tate, Nahum (1652–1715)** English poet and playwright, best known for his adaptations of Shakespeare's plays. Tate wrote a number of plays, most of them based on the works of various Elizabethan dramatists, but he is chiefly remembered for his version of *King Lear*. His *History of King Lear* (1681) retained some of Shakespeare's dialogue, but only in a drastically revised play. Tate eliminated the blinding of GLOUCESTER (1) and his suicide attempt, and he added a love affair between EDGAR and CORDELIA. He deleted the king's FOOL (2), and, most notoriously, he provided a happy ending in which LEAR is restored to his throne, abdicating in favour of Edgar and Cordelia. Though modern commentators condemn Tate's adaptation as a travesty, it was one of the most successful plays in the history of the English theatre, performed for over 150 years in successive revivals. (Shakespeare's text was restored in bits and pieces by various producers, but his ending was not again enacted until 1823, by Charles KEAN (1); and the original play as a whole was staged only in 1838, by W. C. MACREADY.)

Tate's play was not simply a tasteless avoidance of the tragic; composed in the wake of a revolution and civil war, it carried a strong moralising endorsement of civil order, which doubtless accounted in part for its original popularity. His Lear, in being both martyred and restored, recalled the recent history of the STUART DYNASTY, and assured its partisans—the establishment of the day—that disaster could be overcome. Later, its generally optimistic stance, combined with the power of Shakespeare's poetry, endeared it to generations; it continued to be staged as late as 1843.

In 1680 Tate also adapted *Richard II*, but the state CENSORSHIP was even more nervous about this story of a king's deposition than it had been in Shakespeare's day—for in the interval the reality had occurred in England. Though Tate changed the scene and characters, calling it *The Sicilian Usurper*, it was suppressed by the government. In 1681, just after his *Lear* was staged, Tate took on *Coriolanus*, again making great alterations. His *The Ingratitude of a Commonwealth* retained some of Shakespeare's text, but it was essentially a different play, most conspicuously in its passages of sensationalistic violence. It too addressed the conservative political sensibility of the day, stressing the value of respectful loyalty, supporting CORIOLANUS' complaints about rebellious commoners, and de-emphasising the hero's faults. However, unlike *The History of King Lear*, it was a commercial failure.

**Taurus, Titus Statilius (active 36–16 B.C.)** Historical figure and minor character in *Antony and Cleopatra*, a general under Octavius CAESAR (2). Taurus appears briefly at the battle of ACTIUM, and receives, in 3.8, Caesar's order to maintain his army ashore, without fighting, while the naval battle is fought. He marches wordlessly through 3.10 and avoids contact with ANTONY's forces under CANIDIUS, which stresses the inconclusive nature of the land fighting. He is a pawn of Caesar's stategy and speaks only two words.

The historical Taurus was a highly successful general, second only to AGRIPPA among Caesar's military men. His background is unknown, though his name suggests descent from the pre-Roman Lucanians of southern Italy. He is first recorded as an admiral who commanded a unit in the defeat of Sextus Pompeius—the POMPEY (2) of the play. He went on to lead numerous other campaigns and governed conquered territories in North Africa and Spain.

**Taylor, Joseph (d. 1652)** English actor, a member of the KING'S MEN. Though Taylor only joined the King's Men in 1619, he is listed among the 'Principall Actors' of Shakespeare's plays in the FIRST FOLIO of 1623. He was hired away from PRINCE CHARLES' MEN to replace Richard BURBAGE (3) within a few weeks of that star's death. He took over Burbage's most famous role, HAMLET, and was acclaimed in it. He was also noted as IAGO. In 1630 he became a partner in both the BLACKFRIARS and GLOBE THEATRES. In the same year, he became a co-manager of the company, with John LOWIN, and remained in that position until the theatres were closed down by the Puritan revolution in 1642.

**Tchaikovsky, Peter Ilyich (1840–1893)** Russian composer. One of the most popular and influential composers of the 19th century, Tchaikovsky was inspired by Shakespeare on several occasions. He wrote brief symphonic pieces for both *Hamlet* and *The Tempest*, and his symphonic fantasy *Romeo and Juliet* (1864) is one of his best-known works.

**Tearle, Godfrey (1884–1953)** British actor. The son of theatrical entrepreneurs who had staged Shakespeare at STRATFORD in the late 19th century, Tearle had a long and illustrious career on stage and screen. He was especially noted for his portrayals of HAMLET, OTHELLO, and the ANTONY of *Antony and Cleopatra.*

**Television** Medium for which all of Shakespeare's plays have been produced (except *The Two Noble Kinsmen,* which many people do not admit to the CANON of the playwright's works). Many of the plays have been produced several times. Since the earliest days of the medium, television executives have been frank about using Shakespeare to provide a veneer of high seriousness to their operations, but it is also clear that there is a widespread audience for the plays. The British Broadcasting Corporation, at the forefront of Shakespeare production for television, has broadcast the standard canon of plays more than once, including special series such as THE SPREAD OF THE EAGLE and AN AGE OF KINGS.

## The Tempest

SYNOPSIS

*Act 1, Scene 1*
On a storm-wracked ship, the BOATSWAIN exchanges curses with two arrogant passengers, ANTONIO (5) and SEBASTIAN (3), who are travelling with King ALONSO of Naples. The king's counsellor GONZALO remains calm, however, as the ship goes down.

*Act 1, Scene 2*
On a nearby island MIRANDA is upset by the shipwreck, but her father PROSPERO, a magician, assures her that the seamen will be safe. He reveals to her that he was once the Duke of MILAN. He studied magic in preference to governing and was deposed by his brother, Antonio, who was aided by King Alonso. The conspirators put Prospero and Miranda, then two years old, in a small boat and abandoned them at sea, but the kindly Gonzalo had given them supplies, including Prospero's books of magic. They then found the island and have lived there since. Through magic, Prospero has raised the storm to bring his old enemies to the island. He magically puts Miranda to sleep and summons his servant, a sprite named ARIEL. Ariel reports that he has entranced the vessel's passengers and dispersed the people around the island, taking particular care, as instructed, with FERDINAND (2), the son of King Alonso. When he complains about his tasks, the magician sternly reminds him that he must work in exchange for his rescue from magical imprisonment in a tree trunk, imposed by the now-dead witch who formerly occupied the island. Prospero promises that if his present scheme is successful, he will release the sprite. He then instructs Ariel to wear a cloak of invisibility, so that he can be seen only by Prospero, and report for further duty. After Ariel leaves, Miranda awakes and Prospero summons CALIBAN, his half-human slave, son of the late witch. Ariel returns, invisible to Miranda, and is sent away again with whispered orders. The surly Caliban reluctantly appears and complains of his slavery, but Prospero declares that he has earned it, for after being taken in and educated by the magician, he attempted to rape Miranda. Caliban is sent to gather wood. Ariel returns, leading Ferdinand by singing fairy songs. Miranda is amazed and delighted by this the first young man she has ever seen. Ferdinand is equally charmed to encounter her. Prospero observes in an aside that they are already in love, as he has planned. However, to ensure that Ferdinand will not take Miranda lightly, he adopts a stern attitude and pretends to distrust the young man. Despite Miranda's pleas, he imprisons him.

*Act 2, Scene 1*
Gonzalo attempts to cheer King Alonso with assurances that Ferdinand has survived, but he is mocked by Antonio and Sebastian. Ariel appears, invisible to the men, and puts Gonzalo and the king to sleep. Antonio suggests to Sebastian, who is the king's brother, that they should kill the sleeping men and make Sebastian king. Sebastian agrees, but as they draw their swords, Ariel reappears and awakens Gonzalo and the king. The four men go off in search of Ferdinand.

*Act 2, Scene 2*
Caliban tries to hide from TRINCULO, a FOOL (1) who has survived the shipwreck, but Trinculo sees him. Frightened by thunder, Trinculo takes refuge under Caliban's cloak. Another survivor, STEPHANO (2), appears, drunk on salvaged wine. Seeing Trinculo and Caliban, he decides they are a single, two-headed, four-legged monster. He feeds Caliban wine, hoping to tame the monster. Trinculo identifies himself, and the two friends rejoice at their reunion. Caliban is delighted with his first taste of wine and tipsily volunteers to serve the two men as though they were gods, if they will give him more. They agree and leave with him. Caliban sings drunkenly of his pleasure at leaving Prospero.

*Act 3, Scene 1*
Ferdinand, forced by Prospero to move a large pile of logs, reflects that though his princely nature rebels against such labour, the work seems joyous because he knows his master's daughter sympathises with him. Miranda appears, and they confess their love for each other, agreeing that they will marry. Prospero, overhearing them, is pleased.

*Act 3, Scene 2*
Caliban, Stephano, and Trinculo are drunk and squabble comically. Caliban proposes that Stephano

kill Prospero, stealing his magic books and taking possession of Miranda. Stephano decides to do so, envisioning himself as king of the island, with Caliban and Trinculo as viceroys. Ariel leads them away with fairy music.

### Act 3, Scene 3

Prospero causes a magical banquet to appear. Alonso, Sebastian, and Antonio step greedily forward, but the banquet disappears. Ariel, disguised as a HARPY, declares that they are evil men and that destiny has therefore stranded them on this island and taken Alonso's son. They shall be tormented until they atone and adopt a sin-free life. Alonso leaves, declaring that he will find his dead son and die beside him. Sebastian and Antonio go with him, angrily intent on fighting the spirits of the island. Gonzalo, believing that their guilt has made them crazy, follows them, to keep them from harming themselves.

### Act 4, Scene 1

Prospero consents to the engagement of Miranda and Ferdinand. He calls on Ariel to provide entertainment to celebrate the bethrothal, and several sprites impersonate the goddesses IRIS, CERES, and JUNO in a MASQUE. Prospero, recalling Caliban and Stephano's plot, sends Ariel to gather some fine clothes he has prepared, which are hung in full view. Caliban, Stephano, and Trinculo arrive, still drunk. Trinculo and Stephano, seeing the fine clothes, cannot resist trying them on, despite Caliban's warnings that Prospero will catch them. Spirits disguised as hunting dogs chase the comical villains away. Prospero reflects that his enemies are now all at his mercy. Soon his task will be complete, and Ariel can be freed.

### Act 5, Scene 1

Ariel reports that the captive Alonso, Sebastian, and Antonio are insane, while Gonzalo is grief-stricken. Ariel says he feels sorry for them, and Prospero declares that he will be merciful to them, despite the losses he has suffered at their hands. After sending Ariel to fetch them, he asserts in a soliloquy that he will renounce magic once he has cured his victims. He exchanges his magician's robes for the garments he wore as Duke of Milan, and as the victims recover their senses they recognise him. He forgives their offences, and they concede him his duchy. Alonso still mourns the loss of his son, and Prospero reveals Ferdinand and Miranda. Miranda is delighted to see so many humans, Ferdinand is reunited with his father, and the future succession of the engaged couple to the throne of Naples is proclaimed. Ariel appears with the Boatswain and MASTER (2) of the king's ship; they report that the vessel has been miraculously restored to ship-shape condition. Ariel fetches Caliban, Stephano, and Trinculo—still drunk—and Prospero sends them to restore the stolen clothes to his closet. He then invites the king and his followers indoors, to hear the story of his time on the island. He gives Ariel a last order—to prepare auspicious winds and weather for the return to Milan—and sets him free.

### COMMENTARY

With *The Tempest* Shakespeare reached new heights in a recently developed genre, the ROMANCES; indeed, some commentators find it the greatest accomplishment of his career. After progressively more successful attempts—in *Pericles, Cymbeline,* and *The Winter's Tale*—at mingling elements of TRAGEDY and COMEDY within a framework of magic and exoticism taken from literary romances, the playwright created in *The Tempest* a stunning theatrical entertainment that is also a moral allegory of great beauty and emotional power. Unlike the traditional medieval MORALITY PLAY, Shakespeare's work does not merely present symbols of already understood Christian doctrines; rather, it offers a vision as complex and ambiguous as human nature itself. Such is the inclusiveness of Shakespeare's sensibility and the power of the play's characters as emblems of humanity that *The Tempest* cannot be pinned down by any particular interpretation, but must instead be taken as the embodiment of a variety of propositions. The themes of *The Tempest* are multifarious and mingled, but nevertheless the various ele-

*A scene from* The Tempest. *A stunning mix of tragedy, comedy, and magic,* The Tempest *is considered by some to be Shakespeare's greatest accomplishment.* (Courtesy of Culver Pictures, Inc.)

ments come together in a traditional comedic happy ending of reconciliation and regeneration.

*The Tempest* has very little actual plot: the love of Ferdinand and Miranda meets only token—and feigned—opposition, and the proposed assassinations of Alonso and Prospero are never plausible, due to Prospero's overwhelming mastery of the situation. However, Shakespeare makes up for the lack of suspense with bold theatre. Bizarre characters and extravagant effects abound in a spectacular presentation that plainly reflects the influence of the courtly masque, an increasingly popular form in the early 17th century. Striking tableaus figure in almost every act: the shipwreck in 1.1, the supernatural banquet in 3.3, the formal betrothal masque and the spectral hounds in 4.1, and the sudden appearance of Ferdinand and Miranda in 5.1. These elements are almost independent of the dialogue, but their visual imagery adds meaning to the story.

Magic is a vital ingredient of *The Tempest.* The supernatural qualities of Caliban and Ariel are particularly impressive on stage—Caliban is usually costumed to resemble a sea monster and Ariel sometimes flies on cables. The text describes a number of remarkable feats of magic that add to our sense of wonder, as do Ariel's appearances with goddesses and as a harpy. Music is another strong component of the play, which incorporates many songs and several dance numbers. Indeed, music is part of Prospero's magical repertoire, as all of the visitors to the island are manipulated at some point by Ariel's tabor and pipe. The island itself seems haunted by 'sounds and sweet airs [of] a thousand twangling instruments' (3.2.134–135).

Another unifying feature of *The Tempest* is the way the conspiracies that compose the action reflect each other. Before the time of the play, Antonio stole Prospero's dukedom; on the island, that original crime is re-enacted as Antonio offers Sebastian the prospect of a kingdom if he murders Alonso and as Caliban recruits Stephano against Prospero. Each of these conspiracies is finally defused by Prospero, as order is systematically restored. Just as important, they all lead to the reconciliation with which the plays closes.

Yet another important theme is the contrast between Art and nature. Prospero rules through his magical 'Art' (1.2.1), consistently spelled with a capital A in the conventional 17th-century usage associated with the RENAISSANCE image of the magician as philosopher. Such a *mage,* as they were called, attempted to elevate his soul through arcane knowledge of the divine, whether through alchemy, the lore of supernatural signs, or communication with spirits. Although Prospero's goal was originally to transcend nature, he gains control of nature as a byproduct of his magic. This, then, provides for his control of the island.

The contrast of 'Art' and nature is furthered by the comparison of Prospero, whose learned sorcery is Art, and the 'natural' Caliban, with his lust and his beast-like resistance to education. Caliban's naturalness leads him to attempt rape—he would have 'peopled . . . this isle with Calibans' (1.2.352–353)—whereas Prospero and Ferdinand, with civilised sensibilities believe in celibacy before marriage. They understand marital happiness to depend on discipline; the satisfactions of sex are to be preceded by a formal declaration of intention, in the 'full and holy rite' (4.1.17) sanctified by tradition. Put another way, we must intelligently assert what we are doing and not simply plunge. Ferdinand, Miranda, and Prospero all exercise the self-discipline that Caliban lacks, and their success and happiness are compared with his misery. Nature is insufficient and must be built upon by civilisation.

When Prospero arrived on the island, he found it in a state of barbarity; Ariel was imprisoned and the amoral beast Caliban ran free. At the close Ariel is liberated as Caliban returns to the bondage he briefly evaded. The contrast between these two characters spans the play. Both are supernatural, and they are similar in their dislike for being under an obligation to mortals, but otherwise they are antithetical creatures—one airy and beautiful, pleasant, and allied with good; the other dank and ugly, sullen, and inclined to evil. Ariel is a spiritual being, composed of air, uninhibited by normal physical restraints, while Caliban is utterly material, confined to the earth, without the power to resist even the 'urchin-shows' (2.2.5) of Ariel's minor underlings. Explicitly non-human, Ariel and Caliban are essentially allegorical, representing human possibilities. Ariel embodies our potential spirituality, Caliban our propensity to waste that potential in materialism or sensual pleasure.

Ariel is Prospero's analogue and like him is rather isolated; except as a seeming hallucination, he has no contact with anyone but his master. Caliban, however, is pointedly compared to many other characters. He is the baseline from which all else is measured. As we have seen, his conspiracy parallels Antonio's. His inability to learn more than curses contrasts with Miranda's high moral sensibility, even though they were educated together. His response to Miranda's beauty contrasts with Ferdinand's. Caliban resists carrying wood in 1.2, while Ferdinand rejoices in his similar labour in 3.1. When Miranda judges her admirers, she finds Caliban 'a thing most brutish' (1.2.358) and Ferdinand 'a thing divine' (4.1.421).

As already suggested, the ultimate comparison is between Caliban and Prospero. The black magic of Caliban's mother Sycorax contrasts with Prospero's employment of sorcery for a good end, after which it is abjured. Caliban wishes only for 'a new master' (2.2.185) and even encourages murder to get one; Prospero pits his 'nobler reason 'gainst [his] fury', seeking 'the rarer action [that] is / In virtue' (5.1.26, 27–28).

The ineducable monster can only approach the least of humanity's capacities, while the learned magician aspires to high moral accomplishment.

Caliban represents the 'natural man' that enthralled Europeans as the New World was opened up and its natives became known. He is pointedly associated with the New World through allusions to the Patagonian god Setebos, the island of Bermuda, and such familiar anecdotes of exploration as the reception of explorers as gods and their offering liquor to the natives. With these associations, Shakespeare raised an issue that concerned thinking people throughout Europe: the relative merits of nature and civilisation. Many of Shakespeare's contemporaries viewed 'natural man' as a healthy counter to the ills of civilisation—an attitude that has survived to the present day—but the playwright disagreed. One of the chief spokesmen for the admiring view of natural man was Michel de MONTAIGNE, and Shakespeare gave his position a place in *The Tempest*—a passage from Montaigne's essay 'Of Cannibals' is echoed in Gonzalo's remarks on an ideal commonwealth in 2.1.143–164, but only as a foil to the play's point of view. The ineffectual Gonzalo envisions 'all men idle [and] women . . . innocent and pure' (2.1.150–151), but Caliban, whose name is a pointed anagram of 'cannibal', has in his idleness attempted to rape Miranda and thus represents a standing refutation of Montaigne's thesis. Caliban cannot, like Ferdinand, make the commitment of a 'patient log-man' (3.1.67), and his undisciplined lust is naturally rejected by Miranda. Similarly, Prospero's learning, the key to his power, is rejected by Caliban, and the monster is accordingly powerless. His slavery is a function of his defects as well as of Prospero's magic.

That Caliban and Ariel are non-human is part of the play's masquelike spectacle, but their supernatural quality also serves another function. The role of providence in human affairs, an important idea throughout Shakespeare's romances, is particularly emphasised by the prevalence of magic in *The Tempest*. Moreover, the references to the New World, along with the unspecific location of Prospero's island, add a sense of exotic climes in which the supernatural is to be expected. The eeriness of the play's world—'as strange a maze as e'er men trod' (5.1.242)—virtually requires divine intervention. Action by a specific divinity (provided in the other romances) is lacking here, but it is alluded to in the betrothal masque with its goddesses. They are merely portrayed—although by supernatural creatures—but their capacity to bless is evoked in striking fashion. When all has been resolved, it is natural for 'Holy Gonzalo' (5.1.62) to attribute the outcome to the gods in 5.1.201–204, and for Alonso to cry, 'I say, Amen' (5.1.204).

Prospero's magic leaves both characters and audience unclear about what is real and what is not, and the boundaries of reality constitute another important theme of the play. Mistaken beliefs abound: Ferdinand and Miranda each mistake the other for a supernatural being, and Caliban takes Trinculo and Stephano for gods. Alonso and Ferdinand each believe the other dead. Stephano thinks Caliban and Trinculo a two-headed, four-legged creature. (These three buffoons befuddle their senses with liquor and are then led astray by Ariel, so their capacity to recognise reality is doubly damaged. In a remarkable passage that encompasses both sorts of unreality, Ariel relates his supernatural effects on the trio in a delightfully naturalistic description of drunkenness.) Most strikingly, the audience shares the difficulties of Prospero's subjects. We see Ariel when the characters do not, but other illusions are designed to take us in, too. At the outset we are fooled by the supernatural storm and shipwreck. The sudden appearance of the banquet in 3.3 is obviously supernatural, but like Alonso and his party, we believe it is for eating until Ariel's Harpy makes it disappear. The king and his party, surprised to have survived the shipwreck, remain baffled throughout, until Prospero finally permits them to shed the 'subtilties o' the isle, that will not let you / Believe things certain' (5.1.124–125).

Prospero's 'subtilties' are manifested in several miniature plays, each itself a pretence of reality, reflecting Shakespeare's interest in this aspect of theatre. Prospero stages the banquet of 3.3, the masque of goddesses in 4.1, and the tableau of Ferdinand and Miranda in 5.1. After the masque he points out to his audiences—both on stage and in the theatre—that a masque is an illusion. He then adds, in one of Shakespeare's most famous passages, that reality is too; we ourselves, we are told, 'are such stuff / As dreams are made on' (4.1.156–157). The number of levels of reality exposed here is startling to contemplate: the goddesses we have just been delighting in are supernatural, but they are merely portrayed by actors presenting a masque. However, those actors are themselves supernatural, Ariel's cohorts. Yet in reminding Ferdinand of this, Prospero reminds us that these sprites are themselves actors, in *The Tempest*. Then Prospero goes on to dissolve that reality as well, along with 'the great globe itself' (4.1.153). Although we are not permitted to dwell on this proposition—Prospero immediately dismisses it as merely a 'vex'd . . . weakness' (4.1.158–159)—the point has been made, and the many veils of illusion that have been evoked remain to tantalise us.

The shifting realities of *The Tempest* are appropriate, perhaps even necessary, to its presentation of a multiplicity of themes. Comparisons of art and nature, imagination and reality, discipline and laxity, civilisation and savagery combine to yield a powerful image of the moral nature of humankind. At the same time the play's extraordinary complexity permits quite differing interpretations of what that nature is. For example, Prospero's total control over the events of the play, combined with Ariel's and Caliban's desire for freedom from his rule, has suggested political readings to many commentators, especially in the 20th century, with its concern for oppression and imperialism. Another modern interpretation, influenced by the advent of psychology, sees the characters as representing various aspects of Prospero's unconscious enacting an internal conflict. A related, less scientific idea is that the play is an allegory of Shakespeare's own life, or at least of his artistic career. A large body of interpretation has been devoted to religious readings: the play has been seen as a work of Christian mysticism or as an explication of ancient pagan mystery cults or of the cabala. Specific interpretations have ranged widely; among other things, *The Tempest* has been said to be about Neoplatonism, 16th-century French politics, Renaissance science, the creative impulse, and the discovery of America.

Obviously, not all of these interpretations can be correct—possibly none of them are—but whether psychological or political, religious or secular, all reflect an underlying quality of the play. *The Tempest* is about the inner nature of human beings revealed in circumstances of crisis and change. The characters are subject to startling personal transformations: Miranda, Alonso, and Gonzalo are magically put to sleep and awakened; for much of the play, Alonso is stricken by a grief that is based on an illusion; Ferdinand, faced with Miranda, finds that his 'spirits, as in a dream, are all bound up' (1.2.489), and he forgets his own false mourning. All of the island's visitors are subjected to a purging experience of some sort: Ferdinand is put to log-carrying, Stephano and Trinculo find themselves in a 'pickle' (5.1.282), the king and his followers are rendered 'distracted' (5.1.12). Prospero's 'insubstantial pageant' (4.1.155) is a fitting metaphor for the play's fluid, transitory world. Not for nothing does Gonzalo rejoice at the end that 'all of us [found] ourselves / When no man was his own' (5.1.212–213).

Even Prospero, the agent of transformation in others, is not immune to change, although his occurs largely before the time of the play. His decision that 'the rarer action is / In virtue than in vengeance' (5.1. 27–28) implies a temptation to avenge himself from which he has refrained. We recognise that he has undergone a series of changes: from a student of magic, he became a seeker of revenge through it, and finally he has found his way to a transcendence of it. At the end he abandons his godlike status on the island and, embracing his own humanity, returns to Milan and his proper position as duke. Like the others, he is subject to alteration in the depths of his being. These processes of transfiguration enact human possibilities; while *The Tempest* points out the clay of which we're made, it also insists on our divine potential.

Strikingly, however, one character, Antonio, is not transfigured. Shakespeare never accepted a single, simple point of view on life's complexities, and *The Tempest* does not provide a clear and unambiguous conclusion. Prospero does not entirely succeed in effecting his reconciliation, for Antonio remains silent (except for one snide witticism). The defeat of evil is not complete; perhaps Prospero's dry response to Miranda's 'O brave new world' (5.1.183)—' 'Tis new to thee' (5.1.184)—reflects his awareness of this. And while Prospero brings happiness to others, he himself remains melancholy. As in the other late plays, Shakespeare in *The Tempest* acknowledges that an evil once committed can never be entirely compensated for; there are Antonios who will refuse virtue, and Prosperos who cannot forget injustice.

Nevertheless, *The Tempest* has the traditional happy ending of comedy. Prospero is reconciled with his old enemies—he forgives Antonio despite his intransigence—and reassurance is thus offered that redemption is possible in a sinful world. The marriage of Ferdinand and Miranda is especially significant in light of this reconciliation: the daughter of the victim of an injustice marries the son of its perpetrator. The auspiciousness of the marriage is strengthened by the declaration that the couple will inherit the crown of Naples. The focus on the future suggests the rebirth of the world.

## SOURCES OF THE PLAY

The general situation in *The Tempest* may derive from the plays of the Italian COMMEDIA DELL'ARTE, several of which depict seamen shipwrecked on islands inhabited by magicians. However, Shakespeare's play is much deeper than these farcical entertainments, and the features that make it so—Ariel and Caliban, Prospero's relationship to and forgiveness of his enemies, and the importance of philosophical themes—are the playwright's inventions. Although various themes in *The Tempest* were treated in earlier works, no specific literary or theatrical sources can be associated with the central material of the play.

Nevertheless, there are various minor sources for particular elements within it. The exploration of the New World inspired Shakespeare and his contemporaries in many ways, and one event in particular probably stimulated the playwright's adoption of a remote island for his drama's setting. A shipload of Virginia-bound colonists was wrecked at Bermuda in 1609; a survivor, William STRACHEY (2), described his experience in a letter—circulated in manuscript—that Shakespeare read and exploited for *The Tempest*. The shipwreck in 1.1, Ariel's description of St Elmo's fire in 1.2.196–206, and some other details derive from this document. It was supplemented by two public accounts of the same disaster, *The Discovery of the Barmudas* (1610) by Sylvester JOURDAIN (2) and *A True Declaration of the state of the Colonie in Virginia* (1610), possibly by Dudley DIGGES (1). Besides offering historical details, these accounts all emphasise the providential survival of everyone aboard the vessel and the fact that Bermuda, previously notorious as an abode of devils and other evil spirits, turned out to be a pleasant and productive island. Both themes are paralleled in Shakespeare's depiction of Prospero's realm.

Another essay on the New World was exploited by Shakespeare, though in a different way. As already mentioned, Montaigne wrote about the native societies being discovered abroad in his essay 'Of the Cannibals', describing them as utopian societies free of the defects of civilisation. Shakespeare apparently respected Montaigne's clarity of thought, and it finds expression in Gonzalo's remarks on ideal government (2.1.143–164)—although Montaigne's ideas are rejected in general by the play. A passage in another Montaigne essay, 'Of Crueltie', probably inspired Prospero's praise of reconciliation in 5.1.25–30. In both cases Shakespeare used John FLORIO's translation of Montaigne, *Essayes on Morall, Politike, and Millitarie Discourses* (1603).

Other minor sources supplied additional material. OVID's *Metamorphoses*, either in the original Latin or as translated by Arthur GOLDING, provided much of Prospero's catalogue of supernatural beings in 5.1.33–50. Robert EDEN's *History of Travaille* (1577) also provided several details, including the name of Caliban's god, Setebos. Ferdinand's delight in the pain of worthwhile labour, in 3.1.1-14, may owe something to a similar passage in the *Confessions* of St Augustine (354–430 A.D.). MUCEDORUS (c. 1590), a comedy revived by the KING's MEN in 1610 (and later wrongly attributed to Shakespeare), features a 'wild man' (a traditional medieval figure) whose savage nature may have influenced the creation of Caliban. Caliban may also reflect Shakespeare's reading of ARISTOTLE's *Nicomachean Ethics*. Contemporary demonology and spirit lore, from common opinion as well as literary sources, are evident throughout; in particular, Reginald SCOT's *Discovery of Witchcraft* (1584) may have provided hints for Ariel's nature.

## TEXT OF THE PLAY

*The Tempest* was written in late 1610 or 1611, for several of its sources were not available until at least the late summer of 1610; a performance—not necessarily the first—occurred on November 1, 1611. Some scholars believe that *The Tempest* may be a revision of an earlier work by Shakespeare—perhaps from as early as the 1590s—but the evidence for this theory is highly tenuous, and most modern commentators assume that the play was written in a single effort.

The play was first published in the FIRST FOLIO (1623). The copy used in printing it was a transcript of either a PROMPT-BOOK or Shakespeare's FOUL PAPERS. The transcript—probably made by Ralph CRANE, whose idiosyncratic spelling and punctuation are present in the printed text—was probably made expressly for the Folio printing. As the only early version of the play, the Folio text has served as the basis for all subsequent editions.

One peculiarity of the Folio text may be suggestive of the circumstances in which the play was written: commentators have speculated that the play's elaborate stage directions may indicate that Shakespeare wrote the play in STRATFORD. Distant from the workaday world of the theatre, where the desired behaviour on stage could be established at rehearsals, Shakespeare may have felt compelled to be more specific than in earlier plays. On the other hand, these directions are like those of the courtly masque, and Shakespeare may have merely intended to stress the resemblance between masques and his play. It is also possible that the stage directions were not written by Shakespeare but were added later.

## THEATRICAL HISTORY OF THE PLAY

The earliest recorded performance of *The Tempest* was at the court of King JAMES I on November 1, 1611, and it was also staged as part of the festivities surrounding the marriage of Princess ELIZABETH (3) in February 1613. (Some scholars believe that the masque of goddesses in 4.1 may have been added to the play for this performance.) No early performances in public theatres are recorded, although John DRYDEN remarked—in the preface to his adaptation of the play—that it had been performed at the BLACKFRIARS THEATRE early in the century. It is believed that Richard BURBAGE (3) originated the role of Prospero.

Dryden's adaptation, in which William DAVENANT collaborated, was called *The Tempest, or The Enchanted Island* (1667, publ. 1670). Dryden added many characters—including siblings of the opposite sex for Miranda and Ferdinand, a female monster for Caliban, and a female spirit for Ariel—and little of Shakespeare's language was retained. Also, the additions were in good part plagiarised from the Spanish playwright, Pedro Calderón (1600–1681). Though modern commentators unanimously condemn it, *The Enchanted Island* was very popular. In 1674 Thomas SHADWELL turned it into an opera, with music by several composers, including Matthew LOCKE; this work inspired a burlesque, Thomas DUFFET's *The Mock-Tempest, or The Enchanted Castle* (1674). In 1690 Henry PURCELL composed a new score for *The Enchanted Island*. This opera remained popular for a century and continued to influence later adaptations of *The Tempest* until well into the 19th century. It was revived in London in 1959, on the tercentenary of Purcell's birth.

In 1745 a brief revival of Shakespeare's play failed, and the Dryden-Davenport version reappeared the following season. David GARRICK produced another operatic version, *The Tempest* (1756), with words by himself and Shakespeare (though very little of the original text was used) and music by John Christopher Smith (1712–1795). Immense dance numbers—one involving 60 children—were a prominent feature of this production. However, perhaps repenting, Garrick also staged Shakespeare's text in 1757, with Hannah PRITCHARD as Miranda. John Philip KEMBLE (3) revived the Dryden-Davenant version in 1789, but he included some additional Shakespearean passages and in 1806 restored much more of the original text.

In 1821 Frederic REYNOLDS (1) produced a new version of *The Enchanted Island,* with William Charles MACREADY as Prospero and with music from miscellaneous works by seven composers including Purcell, Mozart, and Rossini. The vogue for such musical pastiches of Shakespeare was past, however, and this production was not a success. Macready also played Prospero in another revival of the Dryden-Davenant *Tempest* in 1833, and then in 1838 he staged his own revival of Shakespeare's play. He cut the dialogue from 1.1 to emphasise a spectacular scenic rendering of storm and shipwreck but was otherwise reasonably faithful to the text, establishing a tradition that has not lapsed. He again played Prospero, opposite Helen FAUCIT as Miranda. Charles KEAN (1) staged a less complete but still wholly Shakespearean text in 1857, playing Prospero in a very elaborate production involving complex 'scenic appliances', as he called them, necessitating more than 140 stagehands. In the same fashion, Samuel PHELPS presented the play in 1871, with himself as Prospero, in a production featuring a proliferation of peacocks and dancers, with music by Arne and Purcell. In 1900 F. R. BENSON's *Tempest* helped introduce a more modern restraint in staging, although Beerbohm TREE continued with 19th-century extravagance in his 1904 staging, in which he played Caliban.

Among 20th-century actors, John GIELGUD has been particularly associated with *The Tempest,* playing Prospero in four noteworthy productions: two at the OLD VIC THEATRE (1930, 1940); a STRATFORD staging by Peter BROOK (2) in 1957, and a London production of 1974. James Earl JONES (1) was acclaimed as Caliban in Joseph PAPP's New York Shakespeare Festival presentation (1962). Peter HALL (5) made his directorial debut at London's National Theatre with a *Tempest* production in 1973 and ended his tenure there with another, in 1988.

In an early experiment with FILM, the opening scene of Tree's production was filmed in 1904, and the silent screen saw two full-length presentations of the play (1911, 1912). However, *The Tempest* has only once been made into a movie with sound—a purposefully bizarre version by Derek Jarman, set in an abandoned church (1970)—although a famous science-fiction film, *The Forbidden Planet* (1954), was based on it. In contrast the play has been done for TELEVISION six times, including a 1960 offering with Maurice EVANS (4) as Prospero and Richard Burton as Caliban.

Besides the operas mentioned above, *The Tempest* has inspired a number of other musical creations, including symphonic fantasies by Hector BERLIOZ (1830) and Peter Ilyich TCHAIKOVSKY (1873), and a setting by Ralph VAUGHAN WILLIAMS (1951) of Prospero's 'revels' speech and Ariel's song, 'Where the bee sucks' (4.1. 148–158; 5.1.88–94).

**Terry (1), Ellen (1848–1828)** British actress. Terry, the daughter of actors, was the leading Shakespearean actress of the last quarter of the 19th century and the first years of the 20th. She began her career at the age of eight, as MAMILLIUS in the *Winter's Tale* of Charles KEAN (1), and she retired after playing the NURSE (3) in a 1919 production of *Romeo and Juliet.* Between, she was chiefly associated with the company led by Henry IRVING, opposite whom she played many of Shakespeare's most important female roles, as well as many other parts, between 1878 and 1902. She was particularly noted as BEATRICE, IMOGEN, PORTIA (1), and LADY (6) MACBETH, but in all her roles she was acclaimed as one of the great actresses of all time. After a brief early marriage, she lived for a number of years with the famed architect and designer Edward Godwin (1833–1886), with whom she had two children, Gordon CRAIG (1) and the actress Edith Craig (1869–1947). She also had two later, childless marriages. Terry was a member of a sprawling theatrical family. Both her parents and her eight siblings—including Fred TERRY (2)—were in the theatre, and when she celebrated her fiftieth year on the stage, 24 relatives appeared with her in a special performance. John GIELGUD is her great-nephew.

**Terry (2), Fred (1863–1933)** British actor, brother of Ellen TERRY (1) and husband of Julia NEILSON (2). Terry established himself as an actor playing SEBASTIAN (2) opposite his sister's VIOLA, but he is best known as the co-star and co-manager, with his wife, of a popular theatrical company that performed in London and the British provinces between 1900 and 1930.

**Tetralogy** Either of two groupings of four HISTORY PLAYS that together deal with English dynastic history from just before the fall of King RICHARD II in 1399 until the battle of BOSWORTH FIELD on August 22, 1485, when the rule of the PLANTAGENET (1) family ended and that of the TUDOR family began. The two tetralogies are usually distinguished as the 'major' and the 'minor', one being regarded as much superior to the other, both as literature and as drama. The minor tetralogy, which was written in 1590 and 1591, consists of *1, 2,* and *3 Henry VI* and *Richard III,* and covers the later part of the historical period, from 1422 on. The major tetralogy is composed of *Richard II, 1* and

*2 Henry IV,* and *Henry V,* and it is concerned with the earlier history. It was written between 1595 and 1599.

**Tewkesbury (Tewksbury)**    Location in *3 Henry VI,* a town near Gloucester and a battle site in the WARS OF THE ROSES. The army of Queen MARGARET (1) is defeated at Tewkesbury by that of King EDWARD IV. The battle takes place between 5.4 and 5.5; the fighting itself is not staged. In the former scene, the Queen delivers a stirring speech to her followers, and in the latter they are all captives of Edward, who, with his brothers, kills Margaret's son, the PRINCE (4) of Wales. This incident is taken from the chronicle by Edward HALL (2), but earlier accounts report the Prince was killed in combat. The battle, which was fought in May 1471, three weeks after the battle of BARNET, marked the end of Lancastrian hopes and firmly secured Edward on the throne of England.

**Thaisa**    Character in *Pericles,* wife of PERICLES and mother of MARINA. The daughter of King SIMONIDES of PENTAPOLIS, Thaisa is the prize of a knightly tournament won by Pericles in 2.2. She marries him and sails with him to TYRE. En route, Marina is born, and Thaisa is mistakenly declared dead in childbirth and is buried at sea, in 3.1. She is revived by CERIMON in 3.2, but in 3.4, convinced she will never find Pericles again, she enters a convent dedicated to the goddess DIANA (2). She does not appear again until 5.3, when Diana sends Pericles to the temple where Thaisa serves and the two are reunited.

Thaisa's resurrection in 3.2 is one of the play's semi–supernatural marvels. What seems to be an ill-motivated retreat into a nunnery is merely a convention of romantic literature, as is her final reunion with her husband. However, she is not simply a cardboard figure. In Act 2 we see that she is a delightful, strong-minded young woman, like many of Shakespeare's other, more developed, heroines. She is delighted by Pericles' victory in the tournament, for though the exiled prince hides his identity, he seems to her 'like diamond to glass' (2.3.36). He is reluctant to press his right to marry her, so she pursues the matter and insists to her father that she'll marry Pericles 'or never more to view nor day nor light' (2.5.17). When Simonides pretends to be angry that Pericles has allegedly proposed to her, she declares, 'who takes offence / At that would make me glad?' (2.5.70–71). In the final scene, this strength of personality lends resonance to her speech as she recognises Pericles: 'Did you not name a tempest / A birth and death?' (5.3.33–34)

In the *Confessio Amantis* of John GOWER (3), Shakespeare's chief source for the play, Thaise is the name of Pericles' daughter, and his wife is nameless. Having selected the name Marina for his heroine, the playwright adapted the daughter's name for the mother The name is traditionally associated with the legend-ary beauty of Thais, the mistress of Alexander the Great.

**Thaliard**    Minor character in *Pericles,* assassin sent by King ANTIOCHUS of Syria to kill PERICLES. In 1.1 Thaliard accepts his assignment with cool professionalism, but in 1.3, once he has followed Pericles to TYRE, he expresses reluctance. He declares that he only contemplates committing the deed out of fear of punishment if he refuses and a sense of obligation to his oath of loyalty to Antiochus. He is relieved to learn that his quarry has fled. Thaliard, as a potential assassin, represents an unjust fate, but he is also a victim, trapped by his place in the world. He thus is a part of a major theme of the play: that humanity is helpless in the face of destiny.

**Tharsus**    Ancient river port, the present-day Turkish city Tarsus, the setting for a number of scenes in *Pericles.* Governed by CLEON, Tharsus is saved from imminent starvation when PERICLES arrives with supplies, in 1.4. In 3.3 Pericles leaves his infant daughter, MARINA, in the care of Cleon and his wife, DIONYZA, and in Act 4 Dionyza attempts to murder the child, who is now 14 years old. The location was provided by Shakespeare's sources, and the actual city is not in evidence.

The historical Tarsus was a wealthy city, the centre of a prosperous linen industry. First important as part of the Persian Empire and later a wealthy Hellenistic and Roman centre, it was a commercial centre of the Seleucid Empire at the time of the play. It straddled the Cydnus River and was the site of the first meeting of Mark ANTONY and CLEOPATRA (described in *Antony and Cleopatra,* 2.2.186 ff.), and the hometown of St Paul. It was notorious in classical literature for the luxurious life-style of its upper class, as is reflected in 1.4.21–31 of *Pericles.*

**Theatre, The**    First LONDON playhouse, built by James BURBAGE (2) in 1576. The Theatre was built on leased land in Shoreditch, a northern suburb just beyond the jurisdiction of the London city government, which was controlled by Puritans who were opposed to theatrical entertainment on moral grounds. Before the Theatre was built, plays were performed in inn yards or other buildings not intended for the purpose. No reliable image of Burbage's theatre exists, but it was apparently a polygonal, roughly cylindrical, three-story structure built around an open, unroofed central space. There were rows of galleries overlooking the centre at each level. The stage projected from one sector of the building into the centre, with the building above it reserved for backstage areas (see ELIZABE-THAN THEATRE). A number of acting companies played at the Theatre during its lifetime: LEICESTER'S MEN from 1576 to 1578, one of the groups known as OX-FORD'S MEN on occasions between 1579 and 1582, the

QUEEN'S MEN (1) between 1583 and 1589, both the ADMIRAL'S MEN and STRANGE'S MEN in 1590–1591, and the CHAMBERLAIN'S MEN after 1594. The Theatre was also used for fencing competitions and other activities. When the theatres were closed by the royal government in July 1597 after the *Isle of Dogs* scandal (see NASHE, PEMBROKE'S MEN, CENSORSHIP), the Theatre did not reopen. Burbage's ground lease had expired the previous April, just after he had died and left the Theatre and its lease to his son Cuthbert BURBAGE (1). After long negotiations, Cuthbert could not come to terms with the landowner, and in December 1598 he and a group of associates disassembled the building and used the lumber to build the GLOBE THEATRE.

**Thebes**   Ancient Greek city, setting for several scenes of *The Two Noble Kinsmen*. In 1.2 the noblemen PALA-MON and ARCITE contemplate the evils of life at the court of King Creon of Thebes and decide to leave the city. However, before they can do so, THESEUS (2), Duke of ATHENS, attacks Thebes, and the two young men are honour-bound to fight. Thus, they become prisoners of war in Athens, where most of the play takes place. In 1.4–5 Theseus permits Creon's victims to bury their dead, presumably outside the walls of the city.

There is nothing specifically Theban, or even Greek, about any of these scenes. Shakespeare took the location, along with the idea of Theban corruption, from his source, Geoffrey CHAUCER's 'The Knight's Tale'; Chaucer in turn was responding to an ancient tradition of conflict between the heroic Theseus and the villainous Creon over the latter's refusal to allow the burial of his slain foes.

**Theobald, Lewis (1688–1744)**   English scholar, the third editor of Shakespeare's collected works. A hack writer, translator, and minor producer of theatrical pantomimes, Theobald published a critique of the edition of the plays published by Alexander POPE (1)—for which he was made the protagonist of Pope's scathing satire *The Dunciad* (1728). He went on to produce his own edition in 1733. He was the first scholar to point to the importance of PLUTARCH and Raphael HO-LINSHED as sources for the plays. Though Theobald's work was superseded later in the century by such great scholars as Edward CAPELL and Edmond MALONE, his work was extremely valuable, and many of his emendations have remained standard.

**Thersites**   Legendary figure and character in *Troilus and Cressida*, the jester, or FOOL (1), to AJAX and ACHILLES. Thersites rails against everyone he encounters, and his diatribes are vicious and hateful. He is also a coward who avoids combat by unashamedly declaring himself too roguish a person to be fought by a chivalrous knight. The unhealthy aura of disgust that

distinguishes this play and contributes greatly to its satire owes much to Thersites' outbursts. Thersites is not likeable, but his language is inventive and funny, and he is capable of amusing imitations of his targets, especially when he enacts the prideful Ajax in 3.3.279–302. Further, his perception of the follies of the warriors of the TROJAN WAR is refreshingly acute, and we respect his capacity to see through the combatants' pretensions to reason and honour when they persist in fighting a sordid, irrational war.

Thersites is a composite of two ancient character types: the boastful MILES GLORIOSUS, a braggart soldier; and the scathing critic, a sort of CHORUS (1), whose usually comic commentary provides telling asides on the main action. As a court jester, he is licenced to insult his superiors, and he thus resembles, in a perverse way, other Shakespearean fools such as FESTE and the FOOL (2) in *King Lear*. However, unlike them, Thersites is 'lost in the labyrinth of [his] fury' (2.3.1–2), and his obscene jests often tell us more about his own disturbed nature than about the warriors he mocks. He displays a morbid excitement when other characters are suffering most, as when he cries out, 'Now the pledge: now, now, now!' (5.2.65), when TROILUS witnesses CRESSIDA surrendering to DIOMEDES (1) the token he had given her. Moreover, he often directs his venom at himself, declaring, for example, 'I am a rascal . . . a very filthy rogue' (5.4.28–29), and 'I am a bastard . . . I am bastard begot, bastard instructed, bastard in mind, bastard in valour, in everything illegitimate' (5.7.16–18). Thersites' pathology has dramatic value, heightening the sense of disease that the play's world conveys.

Thersites plays a similar, though much less prominent, role in the *Iliad* of HOMER, the ultimate source of the drama. In one episode, he rails at AGAMEMNON until Odysseus (Shakespeare's ULYSSES) beats him into silence. In a later tradition, Achilles kills him for insulting him while he is in mourning for an Amazon queen he has slain in combat.

**Theseus (1)**   Character in *A Midsummer Night's Dream*, the Duke of ATHENS. Theseus' wedding to Queen HIP-POLYTA (1) is the climax towards which the play moves. He is a sympathetic lover, though, as a middle-aged man, he is not given to the passions of youth. He is responsive to Hippolyta's moods, noting, for example, her distress at the plight of HERMIA in 1.1.122. Hermia's situation disturbs Theseus, too; it raises an issue that was important to Shakespeare—the relationship between authority and the law. Theseus is a model ruler who respects the laws of his domain, but he regrets the harsh consequences that they may entail for Hermia. He will attempt to help her by persuading EGEUS and DEMETRIUS (2) with 'private schooling' (1.1. 116); but if that effort fails, he is committed to carrying out the law.

Theseus is a constitutional monarch, as the TUDOR rulers of England declared themselves to be. Thus he is associated with Queen ELIZABETH (1). A closer identification of the two is implied in 5.1.89–105, in which Theseus proclaims that he responds favourably to his citizens' speeches of welcome, even when, hopelessly tongue-tied, they fail to speak at all. Elizabeth was known to take great pride in doing the same thing, and this passage is thought to embody a compliment to the sovereign and thus to suggest that she was present to receive it at the first performance of the play.

**Theseus (2)**    Character in *The Two Noble Kinsmen,* Duke of ATHENS. Theseus presides over the events of the main plot. He sets an example of noble action when he aids the royal widows (see QUEEN [1]) who petition him in 1.1; in doing so, he undertakes a war against Creon of THEBES, in the course of which he captures the title characters, ARCITE and PALAMON, creating the basic situation of the plot. In 3.6 he intervenes in the quarrel between them, overseeing their duel for EMILIA (4); and at the play's close, he sounds the note of dignified acceptance of fate that is the play's central lesson. Recognising that the fortunes of humanity are incomprehensible, and that we have no choice but to live with them, he rhetorically addresses the gods: 'O you heavenly charmers, / What things you make of us! . . . Let us be thankful / For that which is, and with you leave dispute[s] / That are above our question' (5.4.131–136). He adds, in the play's final words, 'Let's go off, / And bear us like the time' (5.4. 136–137)—that is, accept our circumstances.

Theseus is particularly dominant in Acts 1 and 5, written by Shakespeare, while in Acts 2 to 4, written by John FLETCHER (2), he is a less significant figure and his speeches are far less powerful as poetry. Theseus' importance as a model of nobility is particularly notable in Act 1, where he establishes a tone of magnanimity that would perhaps have dominated the play, had Shakespeare written it in its entirety. Throughout Shakespeare's portions of the play, Theseus' actions are quintessentially chivalrous: he aids the widowed Queens at their request; having triumphed in their cause, he offers to cover the expenses of their husbands' funerals; he demands the finest treatment for his noble prisoners of war; he orders the most opulent temple preparations for the 'noble work in hand' (5.1.6), the duel; he 'adopts' (5.4.124) Palamon's seconds at the play's close; and his concluding remarks offer an example of serene courage. On the other hand, the somewhat ignoble provision that the loser be executed was devised by Fletcher's Theseus.

With respect to aristocratic birth—a necessary component of nobility in chivalric romance—Theseus is literally of supernatural stature and can casually refer to 'Hercules our kinsman' (1.1.66). He is pointedly contrasted with the vicious Creon, to his considerable

advantage, and the Second Queen says that he was 'Born to uphold creation in that honour / First Nature styled it in' (1.1.82–83). As the highest-ranking figure in the play's world, and especially since he is presented as a strikingly noble leader, Theseus carries great moral weight; his closing remarks are thereby clearly signalled as the play's essential position.

**Thidias**    Character in *Antony and Cleopatra,* a diplomat who represents Octavius CAESAR (2). In 3.12 Caesar sends Thidias to CLEOPATRA—in the wake of her and ANTONY's defeat at the battle of ACTIUM—to promise her whatever she wishes if she will abandon Antony. In 3.13 Thidias receives from Cleopatra a lavish declaration of allegiance to Caesar, but as he kisses her hand as a formal token of this new diplomatic relationship, Antony appears. 'I am Antony yet' (3.13.93), he says furiously, and he has Thidias taken away to be whipped. A SERVANT (22) returns to report that Thidias begged for mercy during this punishment. Antony sends him back to Caesar with an angry message of defiance, and tells him that if he wants revenge he should whip one Hipparchus, a freed slave of Antony's now in Caesar's service. The episode demonstrates Antony's continuing vitality, but also the disturbed state of his mind.

In Shakespeare's source, Thomas NORTH's translation of PLUTARCH's *Lives,* Caesar's representative is named Thyreus, and many editions of the play, beginning with that of Lewis THEOBALD (1733), use this name. Presumably, Shakespeare simply misremembered the name of this minor character. (In fact, North himself was mistaken, for the ambassador in Plutarch is named Thyrsus, a figure otherwise unknown in history.)

**Thief**    Character in *Timon of Athens.* See BANDIT.

**Third Murderer**    Minor character in *Macbeth,* one of the assassins hired by MACBETH to kill BANQUO and FLEANCE. The Third Murderer joins his colleagues as they approach their targets. He was not with them when they were recruited in 3.1, and they initially distrust him, but his exact instructions convince them that he has been sent by Macbeth. His presence suggests that with the distrust typical of despots, Macbeth has felt the need to plant an agent among his hired assassins. The Third Murderer is indistinguishable from his fellows and speaks only a few brief lines.

**Thomas, Friar**    Character in *Measure for Measure.* See FRIAR (1).

**Thomas Lord Cromwell**    Anonymous play formerly attributed to Shakespeare, part of the Shakespeare APOCRYPHA. *Thomas Lord Cromwell* is a historical drama set in the time of King HENRY VIII. It was published by

William JONES (4) in 1602 as 'written by W. S.', possibly with the intention of associating the play with Shakespeare. It was also included among Shakespeare's plays in the Third and Fourth FOLIOS and in the editions of Nicholas ROWE and Alexander POPE (1). Scholars are certain, however, that Shakespeare did not write it, for it is a badly structured, poorly written drama that is clearly not as good as even the least of Shakespeare's genuine work. Its authorship remains uncertain, though Michael DRAYTON and Thomas HEYWOOD (2) are often nominated.

**Thorndike, Sybil (1882–1976)** British actress. Thorndike was noted for a number of Shakespearean roles, especially LADY (6) MACBETH, Queen KATHERINE, CONSTANCE, and VOLUMNIA. Much of her career was spent on tour, from her travels to America with Ben GREET'S company in the early days of the century to her performances in occupied Europe in 1945. She also played often with the OLD VIC THEATRE company.

**Thorpe, Thomas (active 1584–1625)** Bookseller and publisher in LONDON, producer of the first edition of Shakespeare's SONNETS. Thorpe's 1609 QUARTO edition of the *Sonnets*, known as Q, bears the obscure dedication to 'Mr. W. H.' that has baffled commentators ever since. Signed 'T. T.', this gnomic utterance seems to justify Thorpe's nickname, 'Odd'. Thorpe published a variety of other works, including John MARSTON'S *The Malcontent* (1604).

**Thurio** Minor character in *Two Gentlemen of Verona*, a suitor of SILVIA. Thurio is inveigled by PROTEUS into hiring a group of musicians to serenade Silvia, but Proteus takes credit with the lady. At the close of the play, Thurio claims Silvia's hand, but beats a cowardly retreat when challenged by VALENTINE (2).

**Thyreus** Character in *Antony and Cleopatra*. See THIDIAS.

**Tieck, Ludwig (1773–1853)** German poet, novelist, and literary critic, editor of the German translation of Shakespeare's plays begun by A. W. SCHELEGEL. The Schlegel-Tieck translation, as it is known in Germany, was not actually translated by Tieck. The 19 plays left undone by Schlegel were translated by his daughter, Dorothea Tieck, and another translator, Wolf Baudisson. They produced German texts which Tieck edited. The plays were published between 1823 and 1829. The completed collection is still regarded as a major masterpiece of German literature. Tieck was considered the leading German scholar of Shakespeare and ELIZABETHAN DRAMA, and his *Anglisches Theatre* (1811) was for many years a basic text. He was called upon to participate in productions of English plays, and in 1827 he staged *A Midsummer Night's Dream* in Schle-

gel's translation. This was the first presentation of the complete play since Shakespeare's time.

As a creative writer, Tieck was an important figure in the German Romantic movement and was especially noted for stories dealing with horror and the supernatural, as well as with the glorification of art as the only thing in life worth pursuing. He was at one time considered the equal of GOETHE, though his reputation declined before his death, and little of his work has appeal for modern readers.

**Tillyard, E. M. W. (1889–1962)** English scholar. Tillyard is best known for *The Elizabethan World Picture* (1943), an analysis of the political thought underlying the HISTORY PLAYS and Shakespeare's work in general. He argued that the plays endorse the pervasive ideas of Shakespeare's period, offering a conservative view of society and placing a high value on an orderly hierarchical system guaranteed by divine authority. More recent scholars tend to find this view too rigid in light of the rapidity of change in 16th-century England. Tillyard also wrote other influential works on both Shakespeare and John MILTON.

**Timandra** Character in *Timon of Athens*. See PHRYNIA AND TIMANDRA.

**Time** Allegorical figure who appears as a CHORUS (1) in *The Winter's Tale*. Time appears only in 4.1, where, alone on the stage, he informs us that 16 years will have passed before the play resumes in BOHEMIA. He briefly sums up the intervening years for King LEONTES and PERDITA and tells us we shall meet FLORIZEL, the son of King POLIXENES. After wishing the audience a good time, he withdraws. This isolated speech, which is virtually a PROLOGUE (1), makes it clear that we are about to witness a new drama altogether. From Time's pleasant, mildly humorous manner, we sense that the TRAGEDY of the first half of the play will be replaced by a COMEDY.

Time's stilted language, which sounded somewhat old-fashioned even in Shakespeare's day, is arranged in rhyming couplets, unlike the speech of any other character. This is appropriate to his singular role, for as a chorus, Time is outside the world of the play and should not sound like anyone in it. Time says, 'remember well / I mentioned a son o' th' king's' (4.1. 21–22), referring to earlier passages (1.2.34, 165–170) where Florizel was spoken of but not named; the use of the first person singular here has suggested to some commentators that Time represents the author of the play—Shakespeare himself. However, this is unlikely, for as a virtually abstract figure, Time is distinctly not human. He is expressly immune from the change he brings to others—'The same I am, ere ancient'st order was, / Or what is now receiv'd' (4.1.10–11)—and as he is winged, he is visually non-human as well. The reference to his having 'mentioned' simply means—with the mild humour that characterises this figure—that the mentioning occurred in the past, which is a function of time.

**Timon** Title character of *Timon of Athens*, a benevolent nobleman of ATHENS who is abandoned by his false friends when he is bankrupted by his extravagant hospitality and gift giving. He then sinks into rage and despair. He withdraws to the wilderness where he rages against humanity and dies in abject misery, an apparent suicide. He is the victim of his own excesses of both goodness and hatred.

Timon's excessive generosity is based in misplaced pride, for he attempts to embody an unrealistic ideal of friendship. When he refuses to be repaid for a debt, he says irrationally that 'there's none / Can truly say he gives, if he receives' (1.2.10–11). This absoluteness is unhealthy, for it leaves no room for a sensitive and intelligent approach to life. Timon is blind and gullible, and he ignores the sound, if unpleasantly put, advice of APEMANTUS. When he is rejected by his so-called friends he assumes an extreme degree of misanthropy, a response that is excessive even given his great provocation. Timon presumes that all of humankind is greedy and dishonest, but this is clearly contradicted by the virtues of his own household (see SERVANT [23]), especially his STEWARD (2). He refuses to accept this evidence, however, and drives himself to a death as unnecessary as his financial losses were. At the play's close, the reconciliation effected by ALCIBIADES cements our awareness that Timon has tragically wasted his life.

Nevertheless, Timon is a noble figure, for he tries to live up to an ideal conception of humanity. Before his collapse he desires the finest in human relationships, and while this has the effect of insulating him from reality, it also exalts him. It is both symbolically and psychologically appropriate that when he becomes disillusioned Timon succumbs to another excessive vision of humanity. Obsessive by nature, he can only go from one extreme to another. In both cases, the position he takes is grandiose, capable of inspiring awe along with dismay.

Like most of the characters in the play, Timon is not a fully fleshed-out human being. He is more like an allegorical figure, similar to those of the medieval MORALITY PLAY, a probable influence on Shakespeare's creation of this work. In fact, Timon assumes two such roles in the course of the play, first representing ideal friendship and then extreme despair. As a misanthrope, Timon had been a famous figure for many centuries before Shakespeare's time, but the playwright attempted to demonstrate the defects of the character both before and after his catastrophe, and thus to make a profound moral statement of the sort presented in the morality plays. Although *Timon* is an unfinished play, we can still recognise in its title character the representation of a human truth: that we are susceptible to vain and prideful extremes of behaviour.

### Timon of Athens

SYNOPSIS

*Act 1, Scene 1*
In ATHENS a POET (2), a PAINTER (1), a JEWELLER, and a MERCHANT (2) expect payment from the generous nobleman, TIMON, for their efforts to please him. Timon arrives and promises a MESSENGER (28) that he will pay the debts of VENTIDIUS (2), which will free him from prison. He promises a fortune to his servant LUCILIUS (2) so that he may marry the daughter of an aristocratic OLD ATHENIAN. The philosopher APEMANTUS appears, and the company prepares to be insulted by his heavy wit. Indulged by Timon, Apemantus denounces each of them as a dishonest flatterer. ALCIBIADES arrives, and Timon invites them all to dinner.

*Act 1, Scene 2*
At Timon's great banquet, Ventidius, whose father has left him a fortune, offers to repay Timon the money he had lent him, but Timon refuses to accept it. Apemantus criticises Timon's greedy followers who consume his banquet, but Timon praises them for the help he knows they would give if it were needed. A MASQUE is performed, and Apemantus rages against the vanity of such things. Timon offers expensive gifts to his guests. His STEWARD (2) worries that such generosity has put Timon deep in debt. Apemantus refuses to seek gifts from Timon because it would be sinful to encourage the nobleman's fondness for flattery.

*Act 2, Scene 1*
A SENATOR (4) who knows of Timon's excessive generosity decides to send his servant, CAPHIS, to collect the debt Timon owes him before it is too late.

*Act 2, Scene 2*
Caphis, VARRO'S SERVANT, and ISIDORE'S SERVANT accost Timon when they arrive to collect debts from him. He is astonished, and his Steward has to point out that he has refused to oversee his accounts despite all urging, and that now the debts caused by his generosity cannot be paid because even his lands are already mortgaged. Timon hopes to borrow money from his friends, and sends FLAMINIUS, SERVILIUS, another SERVANT (23), and the Steward to LUCIUS (3), LUCULLUS, SEMPRONIUS, and Ventidius, respectively.

*Act 3, Scene 1*
Lucullus refuses to lend money to Timon and offers to bribe Flaminius if he will say he could not find him to request the loan. Flaminius curses him.

### Act 3, Scene 2

Lucius hears of Lucullus' behaviour and swears that he would have loaned Timon the money, but when Servilius arrives to ask him for a loan, he refuses and claims to have no funds available.

### Act 3, Scene 3

Timon's Servant tells Sempronius that his master's other friends have refused to lend money, whereupon Sempronius claims to be offended that he was not asked first and therefore refuses to help.

### Act 3, Scene 4

LUCIUS' SERVANT meets the Servants of Varro, TITUS (2), HORTENSIUS, and PHILOTUS, all of whom hope to collect money from Timon. They regret the thankless-ness of their masters, who have benefited by Timon's generosity and now will not forgive him his debts. Timon appears in a rage and insists that they will have to cut up his body as payment; the servants realise they will get no money, and they leave. Timon tells the Steward to send out messages to all of his friends inviting them to an immense banquet.

### Act 3, Scene 5

Alcibiades seeks mercy from the Senators for a friend who has killed someone in a fight. They refuse, but he continues to argue, and claims that his friend should be spared because he has served as a soldier. Offended that he will not accept their decision, the Senators banish Alcibiades from Athens. He vows to take revenge on the city with his army.

### Act 3, Scene 6

Timon's friends assemble at the banquet and make excuses for not having assisted him. They hope to receive expensive gifts, as before. Timon formally curses the guests and drives them away.

### Act 4, Scene 1

As he leaves Athens, Timon maliciously wishes evil on all elements of society.

### Act 4, Scene 2

Timon's Steward and several of his former Servants part sorrowfully. The Steward soliloquises on the pointlessness of wealth and the foolishness of man. He vows to find Timon and to continue serving him.

### Act 4, Scene 3

Timon, alone in the wilderness, denounces humanity. As he digs for roots, he finds gold. He curses it as a great evil and decides to distribute it and thereby destroy society. Alcibiades appears; Timon rejects his offer of friendship but is pleased to hear of his plan to conquer Athens, and he urges him to be brutal. Alcibiades departs, and Apemantus arrives. He offers food, but Timon refuses it with curses, and Apemantus observes that Timon is as extreme in his disgust as he once was in his generosity. The two misanthropes remark on the faults of humanity and then fall into an exchange of insults. As Apemantus leaves, a group of thieves arrives. Timon sarcastically praises them for taking what they want and compares them with thieves who purport to be good citizens. He gives each BANDIT gold. They leave, as the Steward arrives. His compassion moves Timon to relent and concede that one honest man lives, but he refuses to be served by him and drives him away.

### Act 5, Scene 1

The Poet and the Painter have heard that Timon has gold, and they seek him in the woods. They intend to promise him great works so that he will give them gifts. Timon overhears their plans and pretends to trust them. He gives them gold as he denounces them and drives them away. Two Senators arrive and ask for Timon's help against Alcibiades. They offer to restore his wealth if he will return to Athens. He refuses and grimly delights in the atrocities he anticipates Alcibiades will visit on the city. He advises Athenians to hang themselves, and declares that he will leave a gravestone with further advice.

### Act 5, Scene 2

Some Senators hear of Alcibiades' approach with a large army and then of Timon's refusal of support.

### Act 5, Scene 3

As he seeks Timon with a message from Alcibiades, a SOLDIER (13) finds a bitter note that announces Timon's death. He also sees a gravestone inscribed in a language he cannot read. He makes a copy of it to take to Alcibiades.

### Act 5, Scene 4

A delegation of Senators seeks mercy from Alcibiades, and he promises that he will only take revenge on the few people who had offended him. The Soldier arrives with the gravestone text, which restates Timon's hatred of humanity. Alcibiades mourns for his friend's state of mind at death as he enters the city and vows to make a lasting peace in Athens.

### COMMENTARY

*Timon of Athens* is an experimental and ambiguous play. So much so, in fact, that this bleak picture of misanthropy is sometimes classed as a COMEDY by editors and commentators. Though its presentation of a grand figure whose downfall results from his own shortcomings is chiefly tragic, *Timon* is also like a comedy in its final statement of reconciliation and in its considerable dose of social satire. In his attempt to combine such different themes, Shakespeare was continuing a line of experiments that included the PROBLEM PLAYS and was to culminate in the ROMANCES. *Timon* is an important step in this development, though its own contradictions remain unresolved.

The play reflects a 17th-century enthusiasm for social satire. Its crass Athenian money-grubbers, who coolly resort to preposterous excuses when they refuse to return Timon's generosity, resemble the Londoners of Ben JONSON's more overtly satirical comedies. Shakespeare's Athenians are very bitterly drawn—Alcibiades illustrates the play's tone when he solemnly calls the city a 'coward and lascivious town' (5.4.1). The critique of Timon's false friends is often straightforward and uncompromising, as in the First Stranger's remarks in 3.2, but sharp comedy is nonetheless present.

In particular, Apemantus' speeches are full of crude jokes, as when he counters the insult, 'Y'are a dog' with 'Thy mother's of my generation' (1.1.200–201). Though the level of his humour is low, he is a typical ill-tempered buffoon of the 17th-century stage and is clearly intended as a comic figure. In fact, Apemantus' viciousness is often so exaggerated that it is comical in itself, which is characteristic of *Timon*, for the play's humour resides more in its situations than in its dialogue. Apemantus closely resembles Shakespeare's THERSITES, of *Troilus and Cressida*. In Act 3 the sequence of hypocritical excuses offered by Timon's supposed friends as they refuse him assistance is amusing; we appreciate these men as comic misers. Timon's story was well known in Shakespeare's time, and he knew his audience would gleefully anticipate the absurd refusals of these familiar character types. Timon's mock banquet in 3.6 is likewise comic in its use of surprises anticipated by the audience but not by the guests. The hypocrisy of his miserly friends as they make excuses to each other for being unable to help their host—though they can find time to dine with him—is broadly humorous. Even in the midst of Timon's grimly inhuman transformation in Act 4, we see humour when Phrynia and Timandra encourage gross insults about themselves, so long as those insults are accompanied by gold. This behaviour was traditionally associated with a comic stage figure, the greedy whore.

*Timon*'s humorous aspects serve a serious purpose, and Shakespeare emphasised this by fashioning the drama to resemble the medieval MORALITY PLAY, which was intended to educate by combining moral lessons with vibrant, often comical entertainment. Because of this resemblance, *Timon* would have reminded 17th-century audiences that such a lesson was being offered. Following the morality tradition closely, *Timon* presents an hero who is totally involved in the material world and only realises its deficiencies when he encounters catastrophe and is rejected by his materialistic friends. Also like a morality, the play features many allegorical characters who symbolise particular vices and virtues. Timon symbolises two: ideal friendship at first and misanthropy later. It is even thought that the most famous morality play, *Everyman*, may have partic-

ularly influenced the creation of *Timon*. However, in contrast with morality plays—a contrast much more obvious in the 17th century than it is today—*Timon* does not end with the hero's triumphant return to a proper appreciation of spiritual values, but rather with his decline into despair and a miserable death.

*Timon* can also be classed as a comedy because it culminates in a spirit of reconciliation. The traditional comedy ended in a spirit of wholesale reconciliation usually represented by a marriage, for like the morality play, it was intended to impart a sense of moral worth. Though *Timon* contains no hint of romantic love, it does nevertheless end in reconciliation and is therefore comedic in this most basic sense. With Alcibiades' ultimate rejection of vengeance when he declares he will 'use the olive with my sword, / Make war breed peace, make peace stint war' (5.4.82–83), the play offers a final contrast with Timon's story. Alcibiades' response to the cold ingratitude of Athens is to take action in the real world rather than to dwell in helpless rancour. All along, this response inspires our sympathy more than Timon's monstrous misanthropy, and Alcibiades' story culminates on a fittingly positive note. Timon's decline has ended tragically, but the playwright gives us a final statement that demonstrates the play's ultimate theme: the greater importance of mercy as opposed to justice.

Nevertheless, *Timon* is also distinctly tragic. The protagonist is elevated above his fellow Athenians by his conspicuous kindness and generosity, and comes to his downfall through the same traits. We are made aware of the fateful vulnerability of human existence, as we are in such greater tragedies as *King Lear* and *Othello*. However, unlike in *King Lear*, with which *Timon* is commonly compared, compassion is seemingly defeated, as Timon rejects the efforts of the loyal Steward to offer comfort and turns instead to brooding exile. Alcibiades' reconciliation at the play's close comes too late for Timon. Like CORIOLANUS, Timon insists on a world of moral absolutes—he prides himself first on his ideal generosity and then on his extreme bitterness—and he is unable to accept that moral absolutes are not reliable guides to social behaviour. He is isolated from the realities of the world, and his retreat into misanthropy is a psychologically plausible response to his disillusion—from one extreme, he can only leap to another. His moral sensibility is arguably noble in that it is superior to ordinary life, but this is also his tragic failing, for he cannot understand the practicality and compromise on which social behaviour rests.

Significantly, it is a Senator, one of the governors of Athens, who first decides to call in Timon's debts, in 2.1, for the role of the state in *Timon* is crucial. In 3.5 the Senators banish Alcibiades when he seeks mercy for a deserving veteran. Here they demonstrate a basic failing, a legalistic and uncharitable demand for absolute obedience. In this absoluteness they parallel Timon; also, their ingratitude to the veteran is like the ingratitude that they (and others) show to Timon. Later, their hypocrisy when they attempt to recruit Timon to help defend the city against Alcibiades reminds us of the Lords who flock to Timon's banquet in 3.6 after they have refused to help him. Thus, the evils of the play's world are summed up in the behaviour of its leaders. This is highly important, for the callousness of the Senators and the other aristocrats produces a potential civic disaster—Alcibiades' threatened sack of the city—and thus demonstrates one of Shakespeare's favourite lessons; the immorality of a ruling class leads to catastrophe for the society as a whole. This theme is central both to the comedic tale of Alcibiades' exile and return, and to the tragic story of Timon's psychological collapse.

Like the problem plays, *Timon* addresses public issues with a disconcerting combination of humour and villainy. With its tragicomic mingling of themes, combined with its seemingly old-fashioned allegorical quality and the startling bitterness of its main plot, *Timon* was definitely an experimental play. For centuries, commentators have generally felt that the experiment was a failure, despite the play's many fine moments. (However, 20th-century readers tend to find its ambiguities—often the focus of earlier criticism—more intriguing than faulty.) Because it is centred on a character whose shallowness is evident both before and after his catastrophe, the play does not achieve the grandeur of the great Shakespearean tragedies. Timon's madness is not resolved through any final self-awareness, as in the cases of the other tragic heroes. A lesser figure, Alcibiades, provides the reconciliation at the end, and though his mercy extends to the 'fault forgiven' of 'noble Timon' (5.4.79, 80), Timon himself is excluded from it. Finally, the excesses that define Timon—his belief first that humanity is worthy of ideal friendship and then that it is only capable of evil—prevent him from having any meaningful interaction with his fellow human beings, to the detriment of the play. The hero is initially aloof, and when brought low, his response is essentially withdrawal rather than opposition; such a moral and psychological progression is perhaps better illuminated in an essay or novel than on the stage.

Shakespeare presumably shared such misgivings, for it seems probable that he abandoned the play before it was complete. However, the experiment was not wasted, for *Timon* marks a stage in the evolution of the playwright's work. The romances, soon to come, treat the same themes—exile and return, the deficiency of moral absoluteness, the transcendent value of mercy—and they do so in a fashion that may reflect lessons learned from *Timon*. The inhuman response of an aggrieved protagonist is no longer the dominant element in the plot; instead, attention centres on the innocent victims of such inhumanity, who typically are driven to the exile that Timon chooses for himself. Even so, the exile is not the crucial phenomenon that it is in *Timon*. In the romances, Shakespeare expands his concerns and explores communal attitudes with a focus on many characters. The somewhat esoteric, allegorical figures of *Timon* evolve into the symbolic yet lifelike caricatures of injured innocence and vague, impersonal villainy that animate the later plays. Moreover, the effect of change on behaviour, an imperfectly developed aspect of *Timon*, becomes increasingly important, for the world of the last plays is powerfully charged with changeability.

*The Tempest* is a partial exception to some of these ideas, but it is there, in Shakespeare's final triumph, that a theme from *Timon of Athens* is displayed most spectacularly. The humane and conciliatory attitude of Alcibiades becomes the essential theme throughout, while in *Timon* its development is late and insubstantial. Thus, this flawed work retains its interest—aside from its many fine passages and strong theatrical presence—as an excellent demonstration of Shakespeare's continued growth as a playwright late in his career.

## SOURCES OF THE PLAY

Shakespeare employed several sources in writing *Timon of Athens*. Numerous elements of the plot come from a Greek comic dialogue of the 2nd century A.D., *Timon the Misanthrope*, by LUCIAN. While Shakespeare may have known this work in Latin, French, or Italian translation, no English version existed in his day. He may merely have been told of its features, for actual echoes of Lucian in the play are obscure, if present at all.

Alternatively, he may have used another source based on Lucian, the so-called 'old *Timon*', an anonymous English play of uncertain date (c. 1580–1610). This work, which has survived in manuscript, contains material that is found only in itself and Shakespeare's *Timon*—such as the mock banquet of 3.6—and thus appears to be a source. However, it may be *later* than Shakespeare's *Timon* and is in any case very different, being a farce. Scholars think that if it is earlier than Shakespeare's play, both works are based on a yet earlier work, now lost, derived from Lucian.

Shakespeare certainly knew Timon's story from the 'Life of Marcus Antonius' in Thomas NORTH's translation of PLUTARCH's *Lives* (1579), the chief source for *Antony and Cleopatra*. Mark ANTONY after losing the battle of ACTIUM is compared to the famous Athenian misanthrope, whose story is briefly recounted. Some details appear in *Timon*. Plutarch's 'Life of Alcibiades', though it contains nothing specifically reflected in Shakespeare, may have provided some ideas for that character as well. Also, many of the incongruously Latin names of *Timon*'s Athenians come from elsewhere in Plutarch. Lastly, Shakespeare may have taken minor elements from another version of Timon's story, that in *Palace of Pleasure* (1566) by William PAINTER (2).

Another possible source for some details and perhaps an overall concept is the MORALITY PLAY *Everyman* (c. 1500). This work contains passages that correspond to the introductory observations on prodigality by the Poet, in 1.1.53–90, and to the triple rejection of Timon by his friends in 3.1–3. Also, *Timon* reflects the morality play's overall theme of a representative sinner who is urged to reform by various figures that correspond to Apemantus, the Steward, and Alcibiades, with the important difference that in *Everyman* the hero does reform, while Timon dies in despair. This was perhaps intended as a purposeful contrast, for the morality play model was extremely familiar to Shakespeare's audience.

## TEXT OF THE PLAY

The many flaws of *Timon*—irregularities of verse, confusion as to the names of many minor characters, the presence of a GHOST CHARACTER, and so on—inspired the traditional hypothesis that the play was written collaboratively: either Shakespeare completed someone else's work or someone else completed his. Many possible co-authors have been suggested—including George CHAPMAN, John DAY, Thomas MIDDLETON, and George WILKINS—but scholars have generally come to the conclusion that the play is simply incomplete. Its difficulties make it clear that no one fixed up anyone else's text, for the play is not fixed. In fact, among the play's fascinations are a number of passages in which we can see Shakespeare's drafts for BLANK VERSE, with many lines still metrically irregular but carrying their information (e.g., 1.2.190–202). Shakespeare had not yet polished this work to his usual standards when he stopped working on it.

Just when he did so cannot be determined at all precisely, but scholar's assign *Timon* to c. 1606–1608. It contains no datable references to the real world, and there are no surviving references to it prior to its publication, which came after Shakespeare's death. However, its stylistic and thematic similarities with the later tragedies favour the idea that it was written around the same time as those works. The common source with *Antony and Cleopatra* (1606–1608) seems to narrow the date still further.

*Timon* was first published in the FIRST FOLIO (1623). The varied speech headings and obviously literary stage directions make it clear that the text was taken from Shakespeare's FOUL PAPERS, perhaps as transcribed for the purpose. As the only early text, the First Folio's *Timon* has been the basis for all subsequent editions.

## THEATRICAL HISTORY OF THE PLAY

No record of any early performance of *Timon* has survived, and since the play seems unfinished, it was probably never staged in Shakespeare's day. It has indeed been very infrequently performed in any period and has always been one of the least popular of Shakespeare's plays. Thomas SHADWELL presented an adaptation, *Timon of Athens the Man-Hater* (1678), that incorporated a love interest and made other great changes. This production, in which Thomas BETTERTON played Timon, was reasonably popular and was restaged several times until 1745. At different times, Barton BOOTH (1) played both Alcibiades and Timon in this version, and James QUIN was a notable Apemantus. It is believed that Shakespeare's text was staged in Dublin in 1761, though little is known of this production. Unsuccessful adaptations that combined Shadwell and Shakespeare and new material in various proportions were produced by James DANCE, Richard CUMBERLAND, and Thomas HULL, in 1768, 1771, and 1786, respectively.

Another version, close to Shakespeare's play but incorporating some of Cumberland's text, was devised by George LAMB (2) and produced in 1816 by Edmund KEAN (2), who was acclaimed in the title role. The original Shakespearean text was not finally staged until 1851—its earliest known production in England—by Samuel PHELPS, who likewise triumphed as Timon. This extremely popular presentation was revived in 1856. In 1892 F. R. BENSON (1) offered a three-act version at the SADLER'S WELLS THEATRE.

The play has continued to be unpopular, and it has been performed only rarely in the 20th century. Perhaps the best-known production starred Ralph RICHARDSON (2) as Timon at the OLD VIC THEATRE in 1956. *Timon* has never been a movie and has only been produced for TELEVISION once, by Jonathan MILLER (2) in 1981, as part of the British Broadcasting Corporation's complete cycle of Shakespeare plays.

**Titania** Character in *A Midsummer Night's Dream,* the Fairy Queen, wife of OBERON and, temporarily, the magically charmed lover of BOTTOM. Titania's infatuation with Bottom is Oberon's revenge on her for having persisted in keeping a changeling whom he wants. She asserts that she will keep the boy in memory of his mother, who died in childbirth. She is icily haughty and insists on having her way, although, since she and Oberon are elemental forces of nature, their dispute is causing bad weather, as she vividly describes in 2.1. 88–117. During her enchantment she is a vapid lover, and afterwards she merely serves a decorative role. Her chief qualities are regal pride and grand diction. She is a highly stylised character, generally magnificently costumed, who symbolises the supernatural at its most glamorous.

**Titinius (d. 42 B.C.)** Historical figure and minor character in *Julius Caesar,* friend of CASSIUS. In 5.3, during the battle of PHILIPPI, Cassius sends Titinius to determine the status of a group of approaching horsemen, and PINDARUS' mistaken report of Titinius' capture shocks Cassius. Grieving that he has sent his 'best friend' (5.3.35) to be captured, and believing that he himself is liable to be taken, Cassius kills himself. Titinius returns to find his friend and commander dead, and he kills himself also. Shakespeare took this illustration of stoic Roman military virtue from PLUTARCH's *Lives,* where Titinius is said to be one of Cassius' closest friends.

**Titus (1) Andronicus** Title character of *Titus Andronicus,* a Roman general and the central figure in the cycle of vengeance that comprises the play. Titus is initially presented as an admirable patriot whose life has been spent largely in the service of his country, but his inflexible pride and overly developed sense of honour cause him to kill one of his own sons in a dispute over loyalty to the Emperor. In 1.1 Titus permits the ritual sacrifice of the son of TAMORA, who consequently seeks revenge against him and his family. Tamora's vengeance (implemented primarily by her lover, AARON) results in the false conviction of two of Titus' sons for the murder of his son-in-law BASSIANUS and the horrible rape and mutilation of his daughter, the newly widowed LAVINIA. Further, Titus is tricked by Aaron into having one hand chopped off, and then, when his two sons have been executed, their heads are brought to him, along with his own severed hand, on a platter. His grief turns to madness, though when Tamora attempts to take advantage of his apparent lunacy, by posing as the spirit of Revenge, he shows that he has retained enough sanity to turn the tables on her. However, Titus' own revenge is anything but sane. He kills Tamora's two surviving sons, Lavinia's attackers, and bakes them into a meat pie that he serves to their mother at a banquet. First, however, he kills Lavinia herself, citing a legend in which a father kills his raped and dishonoured daughter Titus then slays Tamora and is killed himself. His only surviving son, LUCIUS (1), becomes the new Emperor.

It is thought that the name Andronicus may suggest a remote origin for the tale, although Shakespeare will not have known of it. The 12th-century Byzantine Emperor Andronicus Comnenus, famous for his cruelty, was killed by a mob after having had his right hand cut off. Perhaps the playwright's unknown source derived ultimately from medieval accounts of this ruler.

**Titus (2)** Minor character in *Timon of Athens,* the employee of a creditor of TIMON. In 3.4 Titus and other servants dun Timon and his STEWARD (2) for repayment of various loans, but they are put off. Titus introduces the theme of the episode when he observes that their masters, who solicit Timon for money, wear jewels that Timon had given them before he went bankrupt. The other servants join him, and together they regret that they must serve such greedy men, who were once the beneficiaries of Timon's generosity but are now his merciless creditors.

Titus appears with HORTENSIUS, PHILOTUS, LUCIUS' SERVANT and two men designated as VARRO'S SERVANT. Since the latter three are addressed as 'Lucius' and 'Varro' (3.4.2, 3), it is presumed that Shakespeare intended the names of the first three to refer to their masters as well. This perhaps reflects a casual linguistic practise of the early 17th century.

## *Titus Andronicus*

### SYNOPSIS

*Act 1, Scene 1*

SATURNINUS and his brother BASSIANUS both claim to succeed their father as Roman Emperor. TITUS (1) Andronicus, a vastly popular general and patriot, is expected to return shortly from a successful war against the Goths. Titus appears, mourning the loss of several sons in the campaign. A surviving son, LUCIUS (1), declares that their religion demands a human sacrifice, and he nominates ALARBUS, a son of TAMORA, the captive Queen of the Goths. Tamora's plea for mercy is ignored, and Alarbus is killed. Titus is asked to choose the new Emperor. He declares in favour of the technically legitimate successor, Saturninus, the elder of the two brothers. In gratitude, Saturninus declares that he will marry Titus' only daughter, LAVINIA. Titus then turns his prisoners over to Saturninus, who comments lyrically on Tamora's beauty. Bassianus claims Lavinia as his own betrothed, as had earlier been arranged, and Titus' sons back him. Titus accuses them of treason for opposing the will of the new Emperor. The sons and Bassianus take Lavinia away by force, and Titus kills one of his own sons in the skirmish. Saturninus, however, seizes on the chance to reject Titus, whose popularity he fears, claiming him to be associated with his family's treason. The Emperor then declares his intention to marry Tamora. Tamora purports to defend Titus, but, in an aside to Saturninus, she recommends that he take revenge later, when his throne is more secure. She assures him that she will see to it herself to avenge her son's death. Saturninus therefore pretends to forgive Titus and his family. A double wedding is proposed, and a festive hunt is planned for the next day.

*Act 2, Scene 1*

AARON, a Moor in Tamora's court, exults in his mistress' newly exalted position, from which he will profit, for he knows she loves him completely. Tamora's sons DEMETRIUS (1) and CHIRON enter, arguing over Lavinia, whom each desires. Aaron suggest that they may both have her; he proposes that they rape her during the next day's hunt.

*Act 2, Scene 2*

Titus and his sons and Saturninus and his court go festively to the hunt. The two couples, Saturninus and Tamora, and Bassianus and Lavinia, are married.

*Act 2, Scene 3*

Aaron arranges an encounter in which Demetrius and Chiron kill Bassianus and carry Lavinia off to rape her. Then, with the help of a forged letter, he frames MARTIUS (1) and QUINTUS, sons of Titus, for the murder Titus pleads for mercy, but Saturninus decrees that the sons shall be executed.

*Act 2, Scene 4*

Chiron and Demetrius taunt Lavinia, whose tongue and hands they have cut off, and abandon her. She is discovered by MARCUS ANDRONICUS, Titus' brother, who responds with elaborately rhetorical grief.

*Act 3, Scene 1*

Martius and Quintus are marched across the stage on their way to be executed. Titus describes his grief to Lucius in extravagant terms. Marcus appears with the ravished Lavinia, and more expressions of woe ensue. Aaron arrives to announce that the Emperor has declared that Titus' severed hand will be accepted as ransom for the lives of the two sons, and Titus lets Aaron cut it off and take it away. Titus' paroxysms of rhetoric are interrupted by the delivery of the two sons' heads, accompanied by his own hand, and he realises that Aaron has viciously tricked him. Titus' grief turns to a thirst for revenge; he sends Lucius to the Goths to raise an army with which to wreak vengeance.

*Act 3, Scene 2*

At dinner, Titus rants of the injuries his family has suffered. Marcus kills a fly with his knife, prompting an effusive speech against murder by Titus, but, when Marcus observes that the fly resembled Aaron, Titus seizes the knife and rhapsodises about slaying the Moor. Marcus remarks sadly that grief has unbalanced Titus.

*Act 4, Scene 1*

Mute Lavinia conveys to Titus and Marcus that she wants them to consult a book. It is Ovid's *Metamorphoses,* and she directs them to the tale of the rape of Philomel. They deduce that her case is the same, and they get her to write the names of her attackers in the sand with a wooden staff. She does so, and new vows of vengeance are sworn.

*Act 4, Scene 2*

A NURSE (1), sent by Tamora, seeks Aaron. She holds the black infant just born to Tamora, and she tells Aaron that the Empress wants him to kill it so that no one knows of her adultery with the Moor. Aaron refuses. He kills the Nurse to ensure her silence, and sends Chiron and Demetrius to buy a white baby and take it to Tamora to be passed off as the child of Saturninus. They depart, and Aaron plans to take his own child to friends among the Goths.

*Act 4, Scene 3*

Titus, seemingly mad, insists that his family shoot arrows into the sky, each bearing a message to the gods seeking justice for his wrongs. Marcus suggests that the arrows be aimed so as to land in the Emperor's courtyard. A CLOWN (2) appears, carrying two pigeons. Titus persuades the Clown, for a fee, to deliver the pigeons as an offering to the Emperor, and Titus includes with the birds a message wrapped around a dagger.

*Act 4, Scene 4*

Saturninus, who has received several of the message-arrows, asserts that Titus' madness is feigned and threatens to punish him. The Clown arrives, bearing the pigeons and Titus' message. Saturninus orders the Clown hanged and vows to execute Titus personally. AEMILIUS appears, reporting that a Gothic army under Lucius is approaching. Tamora proposes to trick Titus into halting his son's onslaught. Aemilius is sent to arrange a parley with Lucius at Titus' house.

*Act 5, Scene 1*

Aaron, who has been captured with his child, is brought before Lucius, who decrees that both be hanged. Aaron says that he will confess the truth about all his misdeeds if Lucius will spare the child. Lucius agrees, and Aaron insolently brags of his evil actions, regretting only that death will keep him from doing more. Aemilius arrives with the offer of a parley, and Lucius accepts.

*Act 5, Scene 2*

Tamora and her sons, in disguise, approach Titus' house, where she plans to delude the old man that she is Revenge, a spirit sent to aid him. Titus recognises them, but he pretends to be taken in. Tamora proposes to bring the Emperor to a banquet, where Titus can wreak his vengeance. She goes, leaving Chiron and Demetrius, whom Titus promptly has bound and gagged. He reveals his plan to cook them and serve them to Tamora at the proposed banquet. He then cuts their throats.

*Act 5, Scene 3*

Lucius, arriving at Titus' house for the parley, turns Aaron over to Marcus. Saturninus and Tamora arrive with their noble retinue, and all are seated at the banquet table. Titus welcomes them, dressed as a cook. Referring to a famous legend of a father who killed his raped daughter to remove his family's shame, he kills Lavinia before the horrified guests. He declares that she had been raped by Chiron and Demetrius. He reveals their heads baked in a meat pie that Tamora has already sampled, and then he stabs Tamora to death. Saturninus promptly kills him and is himself immediately dispatched by Lucius. The assembled nobles declare Lucius to be the new Emperor, and Titus is formally mourned. Aaron is brought forward and sentenced by Lucius to be buried to his neck and starved. He responds with a last boastful refusal to repent.

## COMMENTARY

Although *Titus Andronicus* is certainly the least satisfying Shakespearean tragedy, it was also his first attempt

*Filled with barbaric crimes and horrible slaughter,* Titus Andronicus *was the first tragedy Shakespeare wrote.* Titus *is an admirable patriot, but his overdeveloped sense of honour causes him to kill one of his own sons.* (Courtesy of Billy Rose Theatre Collection; New York Public Library at Lincoln Center; Astor, Lenox and Tilden Foundations)

at the genre, and it has features that suggest the grander achievements to come. Although it is inferior to later work, it is a fine play by the standards of 1590; the young Shakespeare was already a successful professional playwright.

The play is based on ancient Roman drama; its format and general character were taken from SENECA. The violence and degradation to which the characters are exposed stand in marked contrast to the highly decorous language in which these excesses are depicted. Also, references to classical literature, especially to OVID, abound. All this was very much in the manner of academic drama that dominated the pre-Shakespearean stage, a tradition that the playwright was soon to outgrow. At the time, still learning his trade, Shakespeare applied the tenets of Senecan drama in a polished and professional manner, using grand rhetoric and precise plotting. He was content to attempt a standard melodrama, plainly geared to box-office success, and he had two recent, immensely popular predecessors to model his work on. One was *The Jew of Malta,* by Christopher MARLOWE (1), which had created a vogue for exotic villains that the character of Aaron clearly exploits. The other was Thomas KYD's *The Spanish Tragedy,* the first great Elizabethan REVENGE PLAY, a favourite genre of the day; *Hamlet* was to be the greatest of them. In fact, *Titus* and *The Spanish Tragedy* remained the two most popular English plays for the rest of the 16th century and into the early 17th.

Glimpses of later, greater plays may be found in *Titus.* For instance, the combination of shrewdly feigned lunacy with some degree of real insanity, applied rather baldly and unconvincingly in the depiction of Titus, is a profoundly compelling trait in HAMLET. Titus also anticipates OTHELLO in being a simple man out of his depth, a successful but easily manipulated military leader. Titus also foreshadows King LEAR in that he commits crimes in the name of honour, but Titus never becomes aware of his errors, as does Lear. The villainous Aaron plainly prefigures such paragons of malevolence as IAGO and RICHARD III. Most important, *Titus* reveals Shakespeare's concern for political ethics. It opens with a question of hereditary succession to a throne, the crux of most of his later HISTORY PLAYS, and concludes with the restoration of orderly rule after disruptions caused by human frailties. Though dealt with very crudely here, these themes suggest the mature presentation to come.

However, *Titus Andronicus* in no way generates the powerful responses we associate with Shakespeare's great works. For one thing, there is no development towards a climax, but rather an assemblage of episodes, all rather similar in tone. Also, the extremely rhetorical dialogue inhibits the development of the characters, who do not reveal their feelings so much as describe them. In any case, the extremely melodramatic plot makes character development all but impossible; for one thing, more than half of the play's characters are killed, often on stage (including a prodigious three in four lines in the final scene).

This combination of academic formalism and blatant gore has appealed to few theatre-goers since the 17th century. Scholarly opinion used to deny Shakespeare's authorship of the play on the grounds that it was clearly beneath the sensibility of a great writer. However, modern scholarship has rejected this assertion and reminds us that the young Shakespeare's taste was naturally that of his time. *Titus Andronicus* may be seen as roughly equivalent to today's horror movies. As such, it was a major success; it appealed to its audience, and it established the playwright as superior to most, if not all, of his contemporaries.

SOURCES OF THE PLAY

No source for the story of *Titus Andronicus* is known, although it has been suggested that an older play, now lost, was rewritten by Shakespeare. The tale itself, although presented as historical (in accordance with a standard convention of Elizabethan TRAGEDY), is fictional, and Shakespeare may have invented it. However, scholars have noted an 18th-century chapbook, of which only one copy exists, that contains a version of the same story that seems not to be based on Shakespeare's play. It may reflect pre-Shakespearean material that the playwright knew. If so, Shakespeare made notable alterations, emphasising the political issues, especially in adding the role of Lucius and asserting the restoration of Roman authority at the conclusion.

OVID's tale of the rape and mutilation of Philomel is obviously a forerunner of Lavinia's fate in the play; this story is expressly referred to several times. *Thyestes,* by Seneca, probably influenced the general atmosphere of horror pervading *Titus Andronicus* and may have provided certain details as well. While the chapbook has a character analagous to Aaron, another source, a story by the 16th-century Italian author Matteo BANDELLO, features a Moor whose crimes are similar and whose delight in his own evil is much more like the Shakespearean character. Shakespeare may have known the Bandello tale in François BELLEFOREST's French translation or in the English of Geoffrey FENTON (2); also, the tale is known to have been rendered in a popular English ballad. Shakespeare's conception of Aaron surely owes something to Marlowe's *The Jew of Malta* (1589). Lastly, the feigned madness of Titus may derive from that of Hieronymo in Thomas Kyd's *The Spanish Tragedy* (1588–1589).

TEXT OF THE PLAY

*Titus Andronicus* has been said to be Shakespeare's first play; although this cannot be proved, it is certainly among his earliest. The precise date of composition is unknown; estimates have varied from 1588 to the year of its initial publication, 1594. The play appeared in three QUARTO editions (Q1, Q2, and Q3) before being included in the FIRST FOLIO (F1) in 1623. Q1 was printed in 1594 by John DANTER for publishers Thomas MILLINGTON and Edward WHITE (1); only one copy is known to exist. Although sloppily produced, it contains a seemingly accurate text, and it is the ultimate source for the other early texts and thus for all modern editions. Q2, printed in 1600 by James ROBERTS for White alone, was apparently taken from Q1, but from a damaged copy, for it is missing lines in a number of places. Two copies of Q2 are known. Q3, from 1611, was taken from Q2 and provides a small number of corrections to it, but with a much larger number of errors. Unfortunately, this corrupt text, printed for White by Edward ALLDE, was the basis for F1, which became the best-known Shakespeare edition for centuries. F1 contains several lines and one whole scene (3.2) that are in no other edition. These were presumably written, perhaps not by Shakespeare, after the play had been in production for some time.

Since none of the Quarto editions name a playwright, and since the crudely gory tale has often seemed to post-Elizabethan sensibilities to be beneath a great writer, some controversy has arisen over its authorship. Attributions have been made to many other Elizabethan playwrights, especially George PEELE. However, both the Folio editors, who knew Shakespeare and were members of the same theatrical company, and Francis MERES, the contemporary writer on theatre whose list of Shakespeare's works appeared in 1598, include *Titus Andronicus* among the playwright's works. Twentieth-century scholarship has generally accepted their judgement, with the proviso that the play may be Shakespeare's elaboration and expansion of a Peele work that survives chiefly in Act 1. In any case, *Titus Andronicus* securely belongs in the Shakespearean CANON.

THEATRICAL HISTORY OF THE PLAY

*Titus Andronicus* was immediately popular; the title-page of its first edition boasted that it had been performed by three different companies: DERBY'S MEN, PEMBROKE'S MEN, and SUSSEX'S MEN. For about 30 years, it remained among the most popular English dramas and was performed repeatedly. For three and a half centuries thereafter, however, it was among the most neglected of Shakespeare's plays. It was not produced at all between 1721 and 1852, nor again between 1857 and 1923; the brief revival was due to the popularity in Britain of a black American actor, Ira ALDRIDGE, who played Aaron. Several 20th-century productions—including a notable 1955 staging by Peter BROOK (2), featuring Laurence OLIVIER as Titus—have helped revive interest in the play, but it remains an oddity. It has never been made as a FILM and has only once been produced for TELEVISION, in 1985.

**Toby Belch, Sir** Character in *Twelfth Night*. See SIR TOBY.

**Tooley, Nicholas (c. 1575–1623)** English actor, member of the KING'S MEN. Tooley was one of the 26 'Principall Actors' of Shakespeare's plays listed in the FIRST FOLIO, though no important role is associated with him. He may have played the SERVANT (6) in *The Taming of the Shrew*, who is designated as 'Nicke' in a speech heading in the first edition of the play. He is known to have played a madman in a non-Shakespearean play. He was a member of the King's Men from 1605 until his death, but he had probably appeared with the company earlier, for he was apprenticed to Richard BURBAGE (3). When he died, he was lodging in the home of Cuthbert BURBAGE (1), who was executor of his will, along with Henry CONDELL.

**Topas** In *Twelfth Night*, name taken by FESTE in 4.2, when he disguises himself as a Puritan clergyman and visits MALVOLIO, who has been imprisoned as a madman. The name refers to the topaz, a semi-precious gem believed in Shakespeare's day to be capable of curing lunacy.

**Torchbearers** Group of non-speaking characters in *Romeo and Juliet*, men who accompany ROMEO and the MASQUERS to the banquet given by CAPULET (1). Romeo, mooning over ROSALINE (2), says he wishes to join the Torchbearers (1.4.11–12) because they were expected to watch from the sidelines and not participate in the dancing.

**Touchstone** Character in *As You Like It*, a professional FOOL (1) and follower of ROSALIND. Touchstone is initially in the service of DUKE (1) Frederick, but he joins Rosalind and CELIA when they flee to the Forest of ARDEN (1) after Act 1. He uses his unbridled humour to satirise all targets. In particular, Touchstone parodies the romances of the other characters, in his own courtship of the goatherd AUDREY.

A touchstone is a mineral used to test gold and silver alloys; when the alloy is rubbed with a touchstone, a discoloration, whose precise shade indicates the metal's purity, is produced. Similarly, something of the quality of the other characters is revealed through Touchstone's mockery of them. Jesting and mimicking, he tests their approaches to the worlds of PASTORAL love and country life, the themes of the play.

Unlike JAQUES (1), who also mocks the other characters, Touchstone presents no alternatives and has no clear-cut vision of the world. Also unlike Jaques, he is consistently funny; his cynicism is amused, not despairing, and his enthusiastic approach to love and rusticity stands in marked opposition to Jaques' isolation. Significantly, while Jaques withdraws from the world at the play's close, Touchstone marries and is part of the climactic festival of love and reconciliation.

The jester is a courtier, both by inclination and profession, a point he explains satirically when he says, 'I have trod a measure, I have flattered a lady, I have been politic with my friend, smooth with mine enemy, I have undone three tailors, I have had four quarrels, and like to have fought one.' (5.4.43–47). In 1.2.58–74 his first jest of the play is at the expense of knightly 'honour', and he mocks LE BEAU's callous enthusiasm for brutal sports in 1.2.127–129. In his encounter with the shepherd CORIN in 3.2.11–83 he cannot keep his arguments for the superiority of courtly wit from backfiring upon himself, so extravagant are they. His extraordinary send-up of duelling (5.4.67–102) has lost much of its point for modern readers, but it is a virtuoso satire of the handbooks of gentlemanly combat that flourished in Shakespeare's day.

Touchstone also turns his humour on the supposedly idyllic country life; when he first arrives in Arden, he exclaims, 'Ay, now am I in Arden, the more fool I; when I was at home I was in a better place . . .' (2.4.13–14). His feet hurt, and he will not let his discomfort go unnoticed. He mocks the dimness of Audrey's rustic swain, WILLIAM (2), in 5.1, and his pursuit of Audrey satirises peasant life by caricaturing an unconsidered, merely biological mating.

However, Touchstone's courtship of Audrey is most strikingly a comical contrast to the relationship of SILVIUS and PHEBE, who present the literary ideal of pastoral love. Touchstone's forthrightness and Audrey's passivity enable these lovers to achieve a very direct and uncomplicated match, whereas only Rosalind's elaborate machinations can unite the shepherd and shepherdess. Earlier, Touchstone mocks both Silvius and Rosalind, after they remark on the pathos of love, by offering the preposterous example of his own romance with 'Jane Smile' (2.4.43–53).

Touchstone's romance is also contrasted with the genuinely moving love between Rosalind and ORLANDO. In 3.2.99–110 his bawdy parody of Orlando's love poetry is intended to embarrass his mistress. She responds with an apt comparison of the jester and a soft fruit, insinuating that Touchstone will be rotten with age before his mind is ripe. The fool has the last word, however, when he says, 'You have said; but whether wisely or no, let the forest judge' (3.2.119–120). Like the forest, Touchstone's indiscriminate comedy is a force of nature, and all manner of things are 'judged' by exposure to it.

Significantly, Touchstone's initial encounter with Audrey follows immediately after Orlando's meeting with the disguised Rosalind. Orlando's promise 'by the faith of my love' (3.2.416) to demonstrate his passion for the supposedly absent Rosalind is thus juxtaposed with Touchstone's insistence on animal desire as the motive for his own romance. The jester is detached about and resigned to his role as a husband: 'As the ox hath his bow . . . so man hath his desires, and as pigeons bill, so wedlock would be nibbling' (3.3.71–73). His assumption that any wife will assuage his physical desire is the opposite extreme to Orlando's proposition that only Rosalind can possibly serve. The idealism of the latter point of view lacks the acknowledgement of instinct that Touchstone offers. As Rosalind and Orlando's relationship evolves, the play moves beyond Touchstone's simplistic position, but first it must also offer this stance as a specimen of pastoral love.

Touchstone is a professional jester, a performer who was expected to make fun of the members of an aristocratic court for their entertainment and as living proof that they did not fear criticism. His profession required a jester to seem incapable of common sense, and he was accordingly excused from ordinary social life. He developed a purposeful detachment from the real lives of the people around him in favour of a concern with the artificialities of wit. Touchstone is seen only in the light of his calling; though delightful, he is not a fully developed person. His amalgam of fast talk and brash earthiness is dazzling, but he is merely doing his job. As such, he can parody the rest of the characters, but the play is not at all dependent on him, as it is on Rosalind or Jaques. If he were absent, we would be poorer for not knowing him, but As You Like It would still make its key points.

Jesters were familiar figures in the drama and literature of the 16th century, obvious vehicles for parody and satire. It is thought that the part of Touchstone was written for Robert ARMIN, an actor who specialised in these parts and who joined the CHAMBERLAIN'S MEN at about the time when As You Like It was written. Touchstone was the first of Shakespeare's jesters, and in Jaques' speeches describing an off-stage performance by the 'motley fool' (2.7.12–61), one can almost hear the playwright exulting in the potential of this new sort of role.

**Tower of London**    Fortification and prison, a famous London landmark and a setting in several of the HISTORY PLAYS. Originally a military base built by the Norman conquerors of England, the Tower, actually a complex of several buildings, was a combination of prison, warehouse, and royal residence by the 15th century, when the plays are set. The sinister reputation of the Tower is reflected in (and to some extent inflated by) its role in Shakespeare's plays as the site of RICHARD III's notorious political murders. Richard kills HENRY VI in his Tower cell in 5.6 of 3 Henry VI. He arranges for the imprisonment of his own brother the Duke of CLARENCE (1), and then hires murderers who kill the prisoner in 1.4 of Richard III. Later in the same

play, though not on stage, a similar fate befalls Richard's young nephews the PRINCE (5) of Wales and the Duke of YORK (7). In 2.5 of 1 Henry VI, another political prisoner, Edmund MORTIMER (1), dies in the Tower, though of old age. Also, in Richard II, a later play, the deposed King RICHARD II is condemned to the Tower, although his subsequent murder occurs elsewhere.

Aside from its use as a prison, the Tower was a military storehouse and, as such, an important centre of royal power. In Shakespeare's earliest depiction of it, in 1.3 of 1 Henry VI, two feuding aristocrats dispute its control, and, during Jack CADE's rebellion, depicted in Act 4 of 2 Henry VI, the commander of the Tower, Lord SCALES, plays a leading role in driving the rebels from London in 4.5.

**Towton**    Location in 3 Henry VI, a town near YORK (10), a battle site of the WARS OF THE ROSES. The battle of Towton constitutes the action of 2.3–2.6. Although Shakespeare includes several fictitious incidents, such as the death of CLIFFORD (1) and the response of WARWICK (3) to his dying brother's call for revenge, he nonetheless accurately depicts the battle as by far the bloodiest battle of the civil war. In 2.5, a major scene, King HENRY VI withdraws from the fray and comments on its fury, its confusion, and the uncertainty of its outcome. The actual battle was fought in a raging snowstorm on the afternoon of Palm Sunday, in 1461, and, by the time it ended, hours later, about 40,000 men had been slaughtered. Its violence remained a byword in Shakespeare's time, and it was commonly asserted that soldiers had killed their own fathers or sons in the fight, a tradition that the playwright used in King Henry's moving encounters with the SON THAT HATH KILLED HIS FATHER and the FATHER THAT HATH KILLED HIS SON, also in 2.5.

**Tragedy**    Drama dealing with a noble protagonist placed in a highly stressful situation that leads to a disastrous, usually fatal conclusion. The 10 plays generally included among Shakespeare's tragedies are, in approximate order of composition, Titus Andronicus, Romeo and Juliet, Julius Caesar, Hamlet, Othello, Macbeth, King Lear, Antony and Cleopatra, Coriolanus, and Timon of Athens. A central group of four plays—Hamlet, Othello, Macbeth, and King Lear—offer Shakespeare's fullest development of tragedy, and they are sometimes collectively labelled the great or major tragedies. These plays focus on a powerful central character whose most outstanding personal quality—his tragic flaw, as it is often called—is the source of his catastrophe. He is the victim of his own strength, which will not allow accommodation with his situation, and we are appalled at this paradox and at the inexorability of his fate. These works—sometimes with the addition of Antony and Cleopatra—are often thought to constitute Shakespeare's greatest achievement as a playwright.

Naturally, Shakespeare wrote his tragedies concurrently with other plays, and the group is not isolated within his oeuvre. In fact, its boundaries are not clear cut. *Timon of Athens* is sometimes classed as a COMEDY, and the FIRST FOLIO edition of the plays (1623) listed *Cymbeline* and *Troilus and Cressida,* usually thought of as comedies, among the tragedies. Moreover, two of the HISTORY PLAYS, *Richard III* and *Richard II,* offer protagonists who have tragic aspects, though the plays themselves, with their pronounced political and social aspects, are not tragedies. Also, three of the tragedies, *Julius Caesar, Antony and Cleopatra,* and *Coriolanus,* are similarly historical in orientation and may be separately grouped as the ROMAN PLAYS.

Shakespeare's tragedies developed out of earlier 16th-century tragedies, which had antecedents in the 'tragedies' of medieval poetry—verse accounts of disaster, suffering, and death, usually of mighty rulers. The poems emphasised the fate of kings and emperors partly because of their importance in a hierarchical society, but also because, from a purely literary point of view, the contrast between their good and bad fortune was highly dramatic. These tragedies, however, did not lend themselves to the stage because they simply made a single point—that suffering and death come even to the great, without regard for merit or station—in the same fashion every time. The emotional tone remained in accord with the doctrine voiced by Aelius Donatus, a 4th-century Roman critic who was influential throughout the Middle Ages: 'The moral of tragedy is that life should be rejected.'

However, at least as early as BOCCACCIO's *The Fate of Illustrious Men* (1355–1374), RENAISSANCE authors, imbued with a sense of the value of human experience, began to alter the pattern. A wider range of subjects was assembled, and, more important, moral lessons were adduced from their lives. A good instance, and an important inspiration for Shakespeare, is the English biographical compilation A MIRROR FOR MAGISTRATES, in which the settings range from the classical and biblical worlds to quite recent history. The typical subject is a villainous tyrant whose fall is obviously and amply deserved. Retribution becomes the theme rather than simple inevitability. This material lent itself to dramatic development, as the tables were turned on the villain. It also lent itself to theatrical effect, as the villainy and the retribution alike were generally bloody. The ancient plays of SENECA were similar in subject and tone; already a part of the Renaissance fascination with the classical world, these works were exploited by 16th-century playwrights. The immediate result was the REVENGE PLAY, which offered the spectacle of the avenger being bloodily dispatched along with the original villain. Christopher MARLOWE (1) and Thomas KYD pioneered this development.

However, the emphasis on evil figures was gradually eroded by an awareness of the dramatic value of virtue, providing the moral contrasts so important to Shakespearean tragedy. The medieval heritage of the MORALITY PLAY was an important influence on this development. Sometimes the good were simply victims, as in *Titus Andronicus;* sometimes virtuous deeds resulted in death or disaster, as in the story of LUCRECE, which Shakespeare treated poetically in *The Rape of Lucrece* and which others dramatised; and sometimes the two motifs combined, in virtuous victims whose deaths are redemptive, spiritually cleansing the world of the play. *Romeo and Juliet* offers a fine example.

Shakespeare's first tragedy, *Titus Andronicus,* is a simple melodrama, frankly imitative of Seneca. With *Romeo and Juliet,* the young playwright advances considerably, developing humanly credible protagonists, virtuous young lovers who are ennobled as love triumphs over death. An essential tragic theme is established in *Romeo and Juliet:* the superiority of the human spirit to its mortal destiny. At about the same time Shakespeare takes another important step. In RICHARD III he first creates a mighty protagonist who can dominate a play by force of personality, though Richard's features are somewhat stereotyped and his tragic defect is simply a given of the plot rather than a plausibly developed personal trait. However, RICHARD II constitutes a new phenomenon, a hero who is not merely 'star-cross'd' (*Romeo,* Prologue 6) but, rather, psychologically flawed. His inner conflicts are exposed in his introspective soliloquies and self-revealing actions, and we see a complex consciousness tragically unable to deal with external circumstances. Nevertheless, Richard's fall depends chiefly on those circumstances. It is in *Julius Caesar* that Shakespeare first achieves the distinctive element of the major tragedies, a protagonist, BRUTUS (4), who is undone precisely by his own virtues, as he pursues a flawed political ideal. A paradoxical sense of the interconnectedness of good and evil permeates the play, as the hero's idealism leads to disaster for both him and his world.

Only with *Hamlet* does the hero's personal sense of that paradox become the play's central concern. In *Hamlet* and its three great successors, Shakespeare composes four variations on the overarching theme that humanity's weaknesses must be recognised as our inevitable human lot, for only by accepting our destiny can we transcend our mortality. HAMLET, unable to alter the evil around him because of his fixation on the uncertainties of moral judgement, falls into evil himself in killing POLONIUS and rejecting OPHELIA but finally recovers his humanity by recognising his ties to others. He accepts his own fate, knowing that 'readiness is all' (*Hamlet* 5.2.218). LEAR, his world in ruins of his own making, can find salvation only through madness, but in his reconciliation with CORDELIA, he too finds that destiny can be identified with, 'As if we were God's spies' (*Lear* 5.3.17). As EDGAR puts it, sounding very like Hamlet, 'Ripeness is all' (5.2.11). OTHELLO, drawn into evil by an incapacity for trust, recognises his failing and, acknowledgeing that he 'threw a pearl away' (*Othello* 5.2.348), kills himself, 'to die upon a kiss' (5.2.360). The power of love—the importance of our bonds to others—is again upheld. In *Macbeth* the same point is made negatively, as the protagonist's rejection of love and loyalty leads to an extreme human isolation, where 'Life's but a walking shadow' (5.5.24). In each of the four major tragedies, a single protagonist grows in self-awareness and knowledge of human nature, though he cannot halt his disaster. Hamlet's thoughtfulness, Lear's emotional intensity, Othello's obsessive love, MACBETH's ambition—each could be a positive feature, but each is counter to the forces of the hero's world. We find human dignity in a tragic protagonist's acceptance of a defeat made necessary by his own greatest strengths.

In the later Roman tragedies, *Antony and Cleopatra* and *Coriolanus,* we see the same pattern. Both CLEOPATRA and CORIOLANUS face their ends with equanimity. For the Egyptian queen, death is 'as sweet as balm, as soft as air, as gentle' (*Antony* 5.2.310); Coriolanus, in his more stoical way, says only, 'But let it come' (*Coriolanus* 5.3.189). However, these plays differ from their predecessors in that the central figures are placed in a complex social and political context, and the plays are strongly concerned with the relationship between the individual and society, with correspondingly less focus on the emotional development of the tragic hero. *Timon of Athens,* considered the last tragedy (though perhaps written at the same time as *Coriolanus*) is a flawed effort that Shakespeare left incomplete. Also quite socially oriented, it has a strong satirical quality that allies it as much with the comedies known as PROBLEM PLAYS as with the great tragedies. Nevertheless, as in the other tragedies, TIMON is a central figure whose decline stems from a mistaken sense of virtue. Shakespeare's attempt to integrate elements of tragedy and comedy was to be more successful in the later ROMANCES.

Shakespeare's tragedies are disturbing plays. We feel horror at the stories—a horror that is aggravated by such scenes as the blinding of GLOUCESTER (1) in *King Lear*—and we feel pity for the victims. That this pity extends to doers of evil as well—Macbeth, Othello, Lear, Coriolanus—attests to Shakespeare's power. We recognise the nobility of the human spirit, which may err catastrophically but which does so through an excess of strength, challenging its own limits. Hamlet loses his humanity before he learns to accept destiny; Lear in his madness assumes the burden of his evils and thus achieves remission. Othello, recognising the evil he has fallen to, uses his strength

to compensate in the only way remaining to him. Even Macbeth, the most explicitly villainous of the tragic protagonists, resumes his humanity at the play's close and seizes his sole virtue, courage, to face his end with vigour. The essence of these plays is that blame is not the appropriate response to evil that derives from human weakness. In a tragic universe, we are all flawed precisely because we are human, and Shakespeare's tragic heroes embody this inexorable feature of life.

**Tragicomedy** Genre of drama combining elements of TRAGEDY and COMEDY, especially when a tragic plot results in a happy ending. The genre was popular in JACOBEAN DRAMA, for its odd composition lent an ironic distance from its themes—usually a combination of sexual love and violent death in a socially significant setting—that appealed to the age's audiences. John FLETCHER (2), an accomplished practitioner of the genre, provided a neat formulation of it: 'A tragicomedy is not so called [because it combines] mirth and killing, but [because] it wants [i.e., lacks] deaths, which is enough to make it no tragedy, yet brings some [characters] near it, which is enough to make it no comedy'. Though most Jacobean tragicomedies are obsessed with grotesque rhetoric and bizarre acts of violence, in a fashion far removed from Shakespeare's work, a number of his plays may nevertheless be classed as tragicomedies in a structural sense, especially *Measure for Measure, Cymbeline,* and *The Winter's Tale.*

**Traïson** Abbreviated title of an early 15th-century French prose work that may have influenced the writing of *Richard II.* The anonymous *Chronicque de la Traïson et Mort de Richart Deux* may have been written by a member of the household of QUEEN (13) Isabel. It records the last three years of the reign of RICHARD II, closing with his murder and burial. It includes the only early account of Sir Piers EXTON, who is otherwise unknown. (Shakespeare probably took the tale from HOLINSHED, who had it from *Traïson.*) If Shakespeare did know this work, which existed only in manuscript in his day (though at least a partially complete copy is known to have circulated among his contemporaries), he took from it directly only a few minor elements; however, its positive attitude towards Richard may have helped to shape the playwright's portrait of the King.

**Tranio** Character in *The Taming of the Shrew,* a servant who impersonates his master, LUCENTIO. In 1.1 Tranio proposes that Lucentio disguise himself as a humble tutor in order to approach BIANCÀ (1), and when he is assigned to take Lucentio's place and maintain his household in PADUA, Tranio is entirely at ease in the role. He plays a smooth young nobleman with education and wit enough to cite classical authors while ingratiating himself with BAPTISTA. His initiative propels the SUB-PLOT: he launches Lucentio's courtship; in 2.1 he outbids GREMIO for Bianca's hand in his master's name; he conceives (2.1) and carries out (4.2, 4.4) the impersonation by the PEDANT of Lucentio's father, VINCENTIO (1); and he arranges for Lucentio and Bianca's elopement (4.4). And he is sufficiently bold to carry on with his plot even when the real Vincentio appears (5.1). However, for all his cleverness, he has little personality; he is a stock character, a comically deceitful servant deriving ultimately from ancient Roman drama. In fact, Shakespeare took the name Tranio from *The Haunted House,* by PLAUTUS, where it is given to a witty and resourceful slave who tells inventive lies in his master's behalf.

**Traveller**  Either of two minor characters in *1 Henry IV,* victims of highway robbery at the hands of FALSTAFF and others. The Travellers are presumably the Kentish franklin and the auditor described to GADSHILL by the CHAMBERLAIN (1) of the inn in ROCHESTER in 2.1.52–59.

**Travers**  Minor character in *2 Henry IV,* follower of the Earl of NORTHUMBERLAND (1) and a rebel against King HENRY IV. In 1.1 Travers brings Northumberland the mistaken news that the rebel forces have won the battle of SHREWSBURY, an account shortly belied by the eyewitness account of MORTON. The episode helps to develop a secondary theme of the play, the uncertainty of knowledge.

**Trebonius, Gaius (d. 43 B.C.)**  Historical figure and minor character in *Julius Caesar,* one of the plotters against CAESAR (1). In 3.1 Trebonius plays an important, if silent, role in the assassination, drawing Mark ANTONY away from the scene at the critical moment.

The historical Trebonius was a Roman aristocrat who had been an ally of Caesar in his earlier conflicts and had served as a general in Caesar's conquest of Gaul. Turning against him, he performed the part in the assassination that is enacted in the play. He died in the ensuing civil war.

**Tree, Beerbohm (1853–1917)**  British actor and producer. Born Herbert Beerbohm, Tree was a successful actor when he became manager of London's Haymarket Theatre in 1887. There, he staged several of Shakespeare's plays, including *The Merry Wives of Windsor,* in which he played FALSTAFF, and *Hamlet,* with himself in the title role. He built a new playhouse, Her (later His) Majesty's Theatre, and in 1897 he began to put on extravagant productions in the tradition of Charles KEAN (1) and Henry IRVING, with lavish sets and costumes and spectacular processions and tableaus. For *Julius Caesar* he employed elaborate scenic

*Beerbohm Tree—seen here in his role as Benedick, the confirmed bachelor who comes to marry Beatrice in* Much Ado About Nothing—*was a prominent actor and manager of the late 19th century.* (Courtesy of Culver Pictures, Inc.)

designs by the most prominent (and expensive) British artist of the day, Sir Lawrence Alma-Tadema (1836–1912). His *Midsummer Night's Dream* (1900) featured live rabbits and birds on stage, and the coronation parade in 4.1 of his *Henry VIII* (1910, 1916 in New York) was so time-consuming that he had to cut Act 5 entirely. He is the last major exponent of this characteristically 19th-century style, and it was in part rebellion against his work that inspired such modern pioneers as William POEL and Harley GRANVILLE-BARKER.

**Tressel**  Minor character in *Richard III,* one of two named gentlemen among the group accompanying Lady ANNE (2) and the corpse of HENRY VI in 1.2.

**Tribune (1)**  Either of two minor characters in *Titus Andronicus,* officials of the Roman Empire. The Tribunes are present throughout much of 1.1, largely as mute witnesses to the foolish pride of TITUS (1). In 1.1.220–222 they speak in unison, their only lines, and declare that they will honour Titus' achievements in war and permit him to choose the successor to the deceased emperor. They represent the pomp and splendour of ROME, while at the same time demonstrating the inadequacy of the society to prevent the tragedy that Titus will unleash. The tribunes of the ancient Roman government were always two in number, though neither the text nor the stage directions of *Titus Andronicus* indicate this.

**Tribune (2)** Characters in *Coriolanus*. See BRUTUS (3).

**Tribune (3)** Either of two minor characters in *Cymbeline*, Roman officials. In 3.8 the Tribunes are informed by a SENATOR (5) of the emperor's orders: They are to recruit an armed force from among the gentry of ROME that will be sent against King CYMBELINE. Only the First Tribune speaks; he asks two brief questions and tersely accepts the orders. These two figures serve as recipients of information intended principally for the audience.

**Trinculo** Character in *The Tempest*, a jester to King ALONSO of Naples and a follower of STEPHANO (2) and CALIBAN in their plot to kill PROSPERO. Trinculo is a buffoon, drunk most of the time, and alternately servile and presumptious. He is ridiculously terrified of the weather when he first appears in 2.2 and is a butt for humour when Stephano sides with Caliban against him in 3.2, especially when the invisible ARIEL imitates his voice and makes him seem argumentative when he is in fact entirely docile. In 4.1 Trinculo is comically obsequious towards Stephano, in a parody of the relationship between courtier and king. When the trio of would-be assassins is finally punished, Trinculo can only observe ruefully, 'I have been in such a pickle . . . that, I fear me, will never out of my bones' (5.1. 282–283).

Trinculo is less vicious than Stephano; he is a follower in a conspiracy he could not have conceived himself. Stephano and Trinculo are thus respectively like ANTONIO (5) and SEBASTIAN (3), within the play's various parallels and oppositions. As a professional jester, Trinculo is technically a FOOL (1), but in his buffoonery, his cowardice, and his lack of conscious irony, he more nearly resembles the rustic CLOWN (1).

**Troilus** One of the title characters of *Troilus and Cressida*, a prince of TROY, a Trojan leader in the TROJAN WAR, and the lover of CRESSIDA. As the only character to have a major part in both of the play's plot lines—a fighter for the honour of Troy in the warriors' plot and the victim of Cressida's betrayal in the ill-fated love story—Troilus contributes greatly to the play's central theme: the inadequacy of good inten-

tions in a corrupt world. Self-deluded both as a lover and a warrior, Troilus is a principal component of, and a sufferer from, the play's atmosphere of error and misdirection.

He is a typical romantic hero, but his complex and credible responses make him interesting as well. Most important, he is mistaken in his attitude towards Cressida. Although PANDARUS' lewd jests and salacious attitude make perfectly plain what sort of game is afoot, Troilus persists in pretending to himself that Cressida is 'stubborn-chaste' (1.1.97). In fact, their relationship is never more than a sexual affair that cannot be expected to last long. Subconsciously, he is aware of the truth; from the outset he is suspicious that Cressida will prove unfaithful. His language is also revealing. With romantic rhetoric, he describes Cressida as a 'pearl' (1.1.100), Pandarus as a ship, and himself as a merchant; unconsciously, he devalues his lover to the status of an object and the consummation of their love to that of a commercial transaction. When he approaches his long-sought rendezvous with Cressida, his thrill is distinctly sensual rather than emotional (as compared to, say, ROMEO). He hopes to 'wallow in the lily beds' (3.2.11) when his 'wat'ry [i.e., salivating] palate tastes . . . Love's . . . nectar' (3.2.18–19). But he does not acknowledge this, preferring to see himself as a romantic figure, 'a strange soul upon the Stygian banks' (3.2.8).

His capacity for self-deception is also important in the warriors' plot. Just as he deludes himself about Cressida, he also deludes himself about the pointless war for HELEN (1). He feels that *she* is a 'pearl' (2.2.82) and the Trojans doers of 'valiant and magnanimous deeds' (2.2.201) in defence of her. In both cases he confuses the real world with a grander, more ideal situation—like that of traditional literature and legend.

As a self-deluded warrior arguing for the continuation of the war, Troilus unconsciously presents an important theme: the unreliable nature of value judgements that are likely to change with time. In the Trojan council of 2.2 he argues that circumstances determine worth: Helen is valuable enough to fight over simply because she has been fought over already. 'What's aught but as 'tis valued?' (2.2.53), he says, but he is unaware that this argument applies to himself. Cressida will eventually value him differently, compared to the more available man, DIOMEDES (1).

When Troilus witnesses Cressida's betrayal while eavesdropping on her conversation with Diomedes in 5.2, his self-delusion becomes strikingly evident. He will not acknowledge Cressida's flighty nature, or that he was wrong about their romance. Instead, he hysterically insists that to do so would indict all womanhood, and further, that all 'beauty', all 'sanctimony . . . the gods' delight', and 'unity itself' (5.2.136, 139, 140) would be flawed. His grief and confusion are real, but his expressions of it are shallow and rhetorical. His focus is on literary images of betrayal, rather than on the particular betrayal that has just taken place. He avoids admitting that his romance was merely a sexual affair by translating it into high-flown abstractions.

His final response is just as displaced; he translates his love for Cressida into hatred for Diomedes. Significantly, when the berserk Troilus encounters Diomedes on the battlefield, he has completely forgotten why he was so enraged and demands that his foe 'pay the life thou ow'st me for my horse' (5.6.7), a line that is both funny and ironically revealing.

At the close of the play, Troilus has forgotten Cressida and is instead caught up in the death of HECTOR and Troy's loss of the climactic battle. Convinced that all is lost, he proposes to fight to the death. His despair is even more pitiful because, ironically, Troy will actually survive this immediate crisis. Just as when he refuses to fight, in 1.1, because his love seems so much more valuable than the war, Troilus attributes unwarranted grandeur to events concerning himself. In this way he demonstrates in his own person the central theme of the play.

In the *Iliad* of HOMER, Troilus was merely one of the many sons of PRIAM; he dies well before Hector does, and his role in the tale is insignificant. His connection with Cressida arose only in legends from the Middle Ages.

## Troilus and Cressida

### SYNOPSIS

*Prologue*

A PROLOGUE (3), dressed in armour, states that the scene of the play is TROY. The Greeks have invaded by sea and pitched camp outside the city. The play omits the first battles, he adds, and begins in the middle of the TROJAN WAR.

*Act 1, Scene 1*

TROILUS, a Trojan prince, is sick with love for CRESSIDA and declares he cannot join the fighting against the Greeks. He rebukes Cressida's relative, PANDARUS, who speaks of her beauty and thus aggravates his pain. Pandarus replies that he will no longer carry messages for Troilus if he is to be reprimanded, but he continues to remark on Cressida's virtues. He observes that Cressida's father has deserted to the Greeks. Troilus regrets that he must depend on Pandarus to approach Cressida. A Trojan general, AENEAS, reports that Troilus' brother PARIS (3) has been wounded by the Greek MENELAUS. This shames Troilus into returning to the battlefield.

*Act 1, Scene 2*

Cressida's servant, ALEXANDER (1), tells her that the Trojan crown prince, HECTOR, wounded by AJAX the

previous day, is raging for a fight on the battlefield. Alexander comically describes Ajax as a brute though a valiant warrior. Pandarus arrives; he and Cressida watch the Trojan warriors returning from the field while Pandarus praises Troilus. Cressida denounces Pandarus as a procurer after he leaves, but confesses that she is attracted to Troilus. She decides not to reveal her feelings, however, declaring that a man will cease desiring a woman once he knows she loves him.

*Act 1, Scene 3*

AGAMEMNON, the Greek commander-in-chief, counsels the other Greek leaders not to be discouraged by Troy's survival after seven years of warfare. The Greeks' failure to conquer, he insists, is a test imposed by Jove, who supports him. ULYSSES asserts that Troy stands only because the Greeks are weakened by disorder and faction. He sees this as a consequence of a lack of respect for rank. This is what preserves a society, he says, just as the cosmos would be weakened by insubordination of one of the planets. As an example, he points out the disrespectful behaviour of the warriors ACHILLES and PATROCLUS, who amuse themselves with insulting imitations of their superiors. NESTOR adds that Ajax and THERSITES, his jester, or FOOL (1), do the same. Aeneas arrives from Troy bearing a challenge from Hector daring any Greek to fight him in hand-to-hand combat the next day. Ulysses proposes a plot: although Hector's challenge is clearly directed at Achilles, the most renowned Greek warrior, the leaders should instead select another combatant, Ajax, through a fixed lottery. This might teach Achilles a lesson.

*Act 2, Scene 1*

Thersites subjects Ajax to witty but crude insults. He mocks him for envying Achilles' reputation. Too slow-witted to retort, Ajax beats the jester, who taunts him for it. Achilles and Patroclus appear and intervene, and Thersites insults them too, to their amusement. Achilles tells Ajax that Hector's challenge is to be met by a warrior selected by lottery.

*Act 2, Scene 2*

Hector recommends to the Trojan leaders that HELEN (1)—whose abduction by Paris from her husband Menelaus was the cause of the war—be released and the war ended. He says she is not worth further loss of life. Troilus counters that this would sully the Trojan honour. The princess CASSANDRA appears, hysterically predicts disaster for Troy unless Helen is released, and leaves. Troilus states that Cassandra should not influence them because she is insane. Paris argues for keeping Helen in the name of his honour. Hector criticises Troilus and Paris for their immaturity. He then goes on to observe that while absolute right demands that they return Menelaus' wife, he will concede that their honour is a proper issue, and concludes that they must continue fighting. He tells of the challenge he has issued to the Greeks.

### Act 2, Scene 3

Thersites, alone, rails against Ajax and Achilles and then insults Achilles and Patroclus when they arrive. When the Greek leaders and Ajax appear, Achilles enters his tent and refuses to see them. After rejecting several messages, he sends word that he refuses to fight the next day. Ajax criticises Achilles for his pride, while, in humorous asides, the other Greeks remark on Ajax' own. They then flatter him extravagantly to his face.

### Act 3, Scene 1

Pandarus calls on Paris and Helen and gives Paris a message from Troilus requesting that he make an excuse for him to King PRIAM for missing dinner that night. Paris assumes that Troilus intends to visit Cressida, but Pandarus denies it. This conversation is held in asides so that Helen does not hear it. Helen prevails on Pandarus to sing, and he delivers a song about love.

### Act 3, Scene 2

Pandarus brings Cressida to Troilus and they kiss passionately. Troilus swears undying love, and Pandarus promises the same on his niece's behalf. Cressida confesses that she has loved Troilus for a long time. He observes that although he distrusts the fidelity of women, he is himself by nature faithful; she insists that she will be also. Pandarus declares himself the formal witness to their vows and takes them to a bedroom.

### Act 3, Scene 3

Cressida's father, CALCHAS, asks the Greek leaders to reward him for having deserted to their side by exchanging Trojan prisoners for his daughter. Agamemnon agrees, and DIOMEDES (1) is told to conduct the exchange. Ulysses suggests that the Greek leaders pointedly ignore the arrogant Achilles to create an occasion for Ulysses to deliver a lecture he has prepared. They agree, and Achilles receives a lengthy talk on honour and reputation from Ulysses. A person's value can only be defined in terms of other people's applause, Ulysses says, adding that Achilles is becoming less valuable since the applause is going to Ajax. Although still relatively unknown, Ajax will now become famous through fighting Hector. Patroclus seconds the lesson, observing that Achilles' refusal to fight has diminished his reputation. Thersites arrives and comically describes Ajax' strutting pride. Achilles wishes to meet Hector and tells Patroclus to ask Ajax to arrange a meeting. Patroclus rehearses this message with Thersites playing a ludicrously inarticulate Ajax. Achilles decides to write Ajax a letter instead.

### Act 4, Scene 1

Paris escorts Diomedes and ANTENOR, the captured Trojan who is to be exchanged for Cressida, and they encounter Aeneas. Aeneas and Diomedes exchange chivalrous challenges. In asides, Paris tells Aeneas to go ahead of them and get Troilus away from Cressida's house. Talking with Paris, Diomedes denounces Helen as the cause of a pointless war.

### Act 4, Scene 2

Troilus bids farewell to Cressida at dawn; she unhappily begs him to stay. Pandarus appears and teases his niece about having lost her virginity. Aeneas arrives and tells Troilus that Cressida is to be exchanged for a prisoner and will depart immediately. Shocked and aggrieved, Troilus goes with Aeneas to meet the deputation as if by chance. The horrified Pandarus breaks the news to Cressida, who vows never to leave.

### Act 4, Scene 3

Paris sends the heartsick Troilus ahead of the deputation to bring Cressida out to be delivered to Diomedes.

### Act 4, Scene 4

Troilus assures Cressida that he will try to visit her secretly in the Greek camp. They exchange tokens of love: he gives her a sleeve, and she gives him a glove. He asks her to be faithful, and she assures him she will be, but he cautions her that the Greeks are seductive men. Diomedes arrives to accompany Cressida to the Greek camp. Troilus and Diomedes exchange rather sharp courtesies as the group leaves for the city gates. Paris and Aeneas hurry to accompany Hector to the battlefield.

### Act 4, Scene 5

Diomedes arrives with Cressida as the Greeks assemble to view the combat of Ajax and Hector. They greet her merrily, kissing her and engaging in witty repartee and sexual innuendo. After Diomedes takes her to her father, Nestor praises her wit, but Ulysses calls her sexually provocative. The Trojans arrive. Hector says he does not wish to fight to the death because Ajax, part Trojan and part Greek, is his cousin. After a brief fight he chivalrously declines to continue. Ajax introduces Hector to the Greek leaders. Achilles insults him, and the two exchange challenges and agree to a hand-to-hand combat the next day. Troilus asks Ulysses to guide him to the tent of Cressida's father.

### Act 5, Scene 1

Achilles tells Patroclus that he intends to get Hector drunk so he can defeat him more easily the next day. Thersites arrives with a letter for Achilles and engages Patroclus in an exchange of insults. Achilles announces that the letter, from his lover in Troy, has reminded him of an oath he made to her that he will not fight. He and Patroclus leave to prepare for the banquet. A number of the Greeks arrive for the banquet with Hector and Troilus. Diomedes excuses himself, and Troilus follows him accompanied by Ulysses with Thersites following them.

### Act 5, Scene 2

Diomedes meets Cressida, spied upon by Troilus and Ulysses from one direction and Thersites from another. Diomedes reminds Cressida of a promise she has made, but she tries to revoke it and beseeches him not to tempt her further. He insists on taking from her the sleeve she had been given by Troilus. She refuses to tell him who it was from, but she finally gives it to him and agrees to a later rendezvous. Thersites comments keenly on these developments; Ulysses quiets Troilus' growing anger. Diomedes leaves, and Cressida, thinking herself alone, laments her unfaithfulness to Troilus and her susceptibility to romance. After she leaves Troilus mourns the collapse of his world and swears he will kill Diomedes in the next day's fighting.

### Act 5, Scene 3

Hector's wife, ANDROMACHE, King Priam, and Cassandra attempt to persuade him not to fight on a day of terrible omens, but he insists he will. Troilus vows he will kill mercilessly. Pandarus brings Troilus a letter from Cressida, but he tears it up.

### Act 5, Scene 4

Thersites watches the fighting and describes it in disrespectful terms. Diomedes and Troilus appear, fighting, and continue off-stage. Hector challenges Thersites, but he claims he is a coward and is left alone.

### Act 5, Scene 5

Diomedes tells his SERVANT (17) to take Troilus' captured horse to Cressida. Agamemnon arrives with news of Trojan triumphs on the battlefield. Nestor appears with the corpse of Patroclus, which he sends to Achilles. Ulysses reports that Achilles, inflamed by the death of Patroclus, is arming for battle. Ajax, Diomedes, and Achilles arrive and immediately go to join the fighting.

### Act 5, Scene 6

Troilus fights Ajax and Diomedes simultaneously, as they disappear off-stage. Achilles and Hector fight; Achilles is winded, and Hector chivalrously offers him a respite, but Achilles insults him and leaves, vowing to return. Hector fights an anonymous Greek in splendid armour. He swears to capture his fine equipment.

### Act 5, Scene 7

Achilles instructs the MYRMIDONS to accompany him but to fight as little as possible. They are to save their strength for an encounter with Hector where they are to surround him and kill him. Thersites watches a running skirmish between Menelaus and Paris, cheering them on with vulgar remarks. The Trojan MARGARELON identifies himself as a bastard son of Priam and challenges Thersites to fight, but the jester flees, saying that he, too, is a bastard and a coward to boot.

### Act 5, Scene 8

Hector, having killed the Greek warrior, starts to exchange sets of armour and is thus unprotected when the Myrmidons appear. They kill Hector as Achilles looks on. As night falls, the armies separate, and Achilles announces that he will drag Hector's body behind his horse as he returns to camp.

### Act 5, Scene 9

The Greek leaders reflect that if Achilles has truly defeated Hector, then they have finally won the war.

### Act 5, Scene 10

Troilus announces Hector's death to Aeneas and other Trojans, but he insists they continue to fight the next morning. Pandarus arrives, but Troilus spurns him and leaves with the other soldiers. Pandarus delivers an EPILOGUE in which he bemoans that the fate of the procurer is to be despised. He declares that the audience are pimps too and asks their sympathy for his venereal diseases. He says that in two months he intends to draw up his will and bequeath them his ailments.

## COMMENTARY

Although *Troilus and Cressida* contains humorous material and is conventionally classed as a COMEDY, its bleak ending and its bitter picture of love and power place it among the PROBLEM PLAYS. These works are troubling and ambiguous in their treatment of society and sexuality, and they lack the clear triumph of love that is usually associated with comedy. *Troilus and Cressida* offers an extravagantly corrupt and artificial world. A venomous parody of a classic legend, it satirises the glamorous attitudes people often have towards sex and/or war. Pretensions to romantic love and to military glory are thoroughly deflated.

The basic satirical technique employed in *Troilus and Cressida* is the use of character types. The dim-witted and prideful oaf, the deluded lover, the cruel and ambitious noble, the voyeur, the coward, the abusive critic—all are presented boldly in Shakespeare's play as (respectively) Ajax, Troilus, Achilles, Pandarus, and, combining the last two, Thersites. Shakespeare makes these character types interesting, but the depiction of personality was of secondary importance as the playwright's purpose in this play was not psychological but philosophical.

Another device that helps establish the satire is the skewed presentation of familiar material. As presented by Shakespeare, the heroes of the TROJAN WAR and the figures in the famous tale of Cressida's betrayal are seen inhabiting a corrupt world. They are either agents of corruption or deluded and ineffectual victims of it. The contrast between the familiar heroic legends and Shakespeare's satire is so great that the comic intent of the work is obvious. Thirdly, the role of Thersites resembles that of the traditional CHORUS (1) and boldly emphasises the satire's critique.

The two plot lines interact very little, but they echo each other and are thematically related, for both illustrate foolish self-deception and emotional dishonesty. The human tendency to succumb to illusions about life is isolated and exaggerated by the play. The two lovers proclaim great emotional involvement, but Cressida's infidelity is hinted at from the outset, and Troilus' self-deception does not hide the true nature of their purely sexual affair. It offers no hint of the fulfilling mutual enjoyment of real love. It seems more tawdry because it is dependent on Pandarus as procurer. Though she undeniably betrays her lover, Cressida is not portrayed harshly. Rather than being a vicious breaker of hearts, she is seen as a representative of human, or perhaps feminine, weakness—'Ah, poor our sex!' (5.2.108), she cries. Troilus is the principal object of satire. His self-deception is extensively developed in both the love story and the warriors' plot, in which he is also a major figure. Just as he deludes himself about romantic love, calling Cressida a 'pearl' (1.1.100), he also deludes himself about the pointless war for Helen on the ground that *she* is a 'pearl' (2.2.82) and the Trojans doers of 'valiant and magnanimous deeds' (2.2.201) in defence of her.

The warriors talk of honour and glory, but they too are self-deluded. However, the Trojans and the Greeks are gripped by different illusions. Troilus and Hector believe the war is a chivalric game and the stakes are the personal reputations of the warriors—though in the end both succumb to other motives. Ulysses, on the other hand, believes that an orderly social hierarchy can be maintained through clever reasoning, such as he attempts to employ with Achilles. He, too, abandons his own truth and eventually argues to Achilles that the only merit is in the fleeting glory of reputation. He thus takes a position rather like Hector's, and this ironically reinforces the play's emphasis on human error. The Greek failure to observe Ulysses' ideal of social organisation leads to internal squabbling and a collective inertia that is only broken by Patroclus' death; the Trojans have a false idea of honour that leads to their utter defeat at the play's close. By the end of the play, neither honour nor reason controls the warriors; only greed, injured pride, and revenge motivate the action.

Both Troilus' violent despair and Hector's death are results of their illusions. These two idealistic, if foolish, characters represent the traditional codes of romantic love and military honour that are being deflated by the play's satire, and in the end they find themselves completely at the mercy of ugly reality. Troilus, unable to accept the reality that his romance was only a sexual encounter, takes refuge in violence, to the point of comically forgetting what he is fighting about when he demands of Diomedes 'the life thou

ow'st me for my horse' (5.6.7). Hector, who insists on the worth of chivalric honour, dies because Achilles does not observe the code. His own behaviour, however, is just as important, for he is only vulnerable to Achilles because he has abandoned his ideals long enough to pursue a rich piece of booty, the Grecian armour that he is about to don when he is attacked.

Considered alone, the warrior plot amounts to a scathing indictment of warmongers—Hector and Ulysses serving to point up the wickedness of the others—and the play is often taken as an anti-war manifesto. However, the depiction of war serves a more general purpose. War in the play has an equivalent function to that of sex—in the 17th century it was a commonly glamorised human activity—and as such is a telling venue for satire.

The delusions and misjudgements that plague the characters stem from a simple yet inexorable factor: the passage of time. The characters are aware of this, though usually unconscious of its particular effect on themselves. In 4.5, just before the warrior plot begins to build to its bloody climax, Agamemnon stresses the value of the temporary peace in terms of its impermanence: 'What's past and what's to come is strew'd with husks / And formless ruin of oblivion . . . [by contrast with] this extant moment' (4.5.165–167). This emphasis on the value of things as they are at the present moment, without respect to what they were or will be later, echoes Ulysses' claim that 'Love, friendship, charity, are subjects all / To envious and calumniating Time' (3.3.173–174).

The audience's familiarity with the legendary tales on which the play is based strengthens the irony. For instance, we are startled by a stark truth when Helen, intending only an idle pleasantry, observes that 'love will undo us all' (3.1.105). And when Pandarus unwittingly predicts the lovers' fate to become symbols of the betrayed and the betrayer (with himself the panderer), we can only hold our breath as each affirms, 'Amen' (3.2.203–205). These ironies are not only powerful theatrical moments, they also contribute to our awareness that the characters are undone by a process—time—over which they have no control.

Time also changes the value placed on things or people. Cressida observes that 'Things won are done; joy's soul lies in the doing' (1.2.292), suggesting that the value of a goal diminishes as it is achieved. Further, Ulysses proposes to Achilles that time brings the destruction of glory through forgetfulness: 'good deeds past . . . are devour'd / As fast as they are made, forgot as soon / As done' (3.3.148–150). Troilus argues that circumstances over time determine worth: once a woman becomes a man's wife, his evaluation of her must rest on that relationship, which once did not exist but is undeniable once it does (in the age before divorce). Therefore, he declares, Helen is valuable enough to fight over simply because, as 'a theme of honour and renown' (2.2.200), she has been fought over already. 'What's aught but as 'tis valued?' (2.2. 53), he says, but he doesn't apply this argument to himself: Cressida will, at another time, value him differently, placing him below the more available man.

The idea that values can change is extremely troubling because it contradicts the stabilising belief in a constant reality. The development of this difficult theme over the course of the play prepares us for the emotional tone of its chaotic culmination in Act 5. In 5.1 Achilles is reminded of his lover in Troy and decides his reputation is less important than she and refuses to fight. In 5.2 Troilus learns of Cressida's revaluation of him and is driven to berserk combat. Forecasts of disaster in 5.3 remind us of the effect time will eventually have on Troy, and the remaining scenes present brutal fighting where all is devalued. Reversing his decision of 5.1, Achilles goes to battle, the raging Troilus attaches Cressida's value to his horse, and Thersites rejects all honour. Most distressingly, perhaps, Hector is betrayed by his own chivalric values, which lead him to courteously refuse his advantage over Achilles, in 5.6, who then kills him in 5.8. Worse, Hector betrays his vision himself in chasing after loot, which leaves him vulnerable to Achilles.

The play's relativism strikes a responsive chord in modern sensibilities, and this may contribute more to its popularity in the 20th century than does its reputation as an anti-war piece. It may also account for its origins, for when it was written, England was undergoing unprecedented change as it entered the 17th century; massive revolution and civil war were only forty years away. A changing economic world generated great uneasiness (as is especially reflected in *The Merchant of Venice*). The reformation was only a few generations old, and religious tensions still pervaded society; moreover, religious beliefs placed England at odds with the two most powerful nations in Europe, FRANCE (1) and Spain. Though the Spanish Armada had been defeated in 1588, the threat of war still loomed, particularly in light of the imminent death of Queen ELIZABETH (1). Though old and in poor health, the queen refused to name a successor; the possibility of civil war or invasion by opportunistic foreign monarchs was widely discussed. This atmosphere of crisis—combined with the appearance of CHAPMAN's translation of the *Iliad*—generated a vogue for tales of Troy, and several plays on the subject were written before Shakespeare's. The English identified with the Trojans (see TROY), and the legend was regarded as a clear example of disaster. The disturbing quality of *Troilus and Cressida* is thus part of England's catharsis; the nation's uneasiness found an outlet in the re-enactment of an ancient battle.

Some critics find the play to be an assertion that life is essentially meaningless and that chaos is the inevitable outcome of humanity's futile endeavours. How-

ever, this point of view ignores what Shakespeare does in the play to undercut this. For instance, the idea that Cressida is representative of all women is introduced by Troilus, who insists that the fact of her betrayal must be denied 'for [the sake of] womanhood' (5.2. 128). However, his raving is effectively countered by its senselessness in denying what is obviously true, and by the deprecating remarks of Ulysses and Thersites. And elsewhere the tendency towards outright misanthropy is checked—the Greeks and Trojans fraternising in the peaceful 'extant moment' (4.5.167) of their truce; Ulysses evoking a world without the 'envious fever / Of pale and bloodless emulation' (1.3.133–134); Hector's commitment, however flawed, to an ideal of chivalry—such images, woven into the play's general critique of human society, collectively offer an idea of what man might be in a better world than that of the play. Ulysses and Hector, spokesmen for sanity, map out principles for such a world in their famous speeches in the war councils of the Greeks and Trojans. Ulysses advocates a social order like that of the 'heavens themselves' (1.3.85), and Hector cites the 'law in each well-order'd nation' (2.2.181). Each leader fails to institute such principles or even to be true to them himself, but they stand as ideals against which their conduct is measured by the audience. It is an essential characteristic of satire that its critique of human failings implies the possibility of improvement. Though honour and love are corruptible, they can still exist.

While it is a harshly critical work, *Troilus and Cressida* contains much humour and sympathy. For instance, the vicious anger of Thersites and the sly lewdness of Pandarus may not be likeable, but they are inventive and undeniably funny characters. Helen presents a humorous caricature of a thoughtless society hostess, and Ajax is a comical buffoon, especially as impersonated by Thersites in 3.3.279–302. Also, a number of the characters are, at times, humanly sympathetic: the lovers in their aspirations to happiness; Hector in his chivalric idealism; and Ulysses as a commonsense, reasonable man. Even the abrasive Thersites can be respected for his capacity to see through the pretensions of the Greek warriors.

The Epilogue highlights the play's essentially positive intentions. Pandarus' flippant insults make an obvious distinction between the real world of the audience—which of course is not composed of 'traitors and bawds' (5.10.37)—and the fictional world of the play. Shakespeare's comical pairing of the audience with the pander serves as a release from the bleak last moments of the play. The satire is thereby stressed a last time, contrasting the existence of human virtues—our own, at least—to the vices that have been depicted on the stage.

Thus, despite its bleak and bloody dénouement, the play shares the essential optimism of all comedy. The characters are defeated by the imperfections of themselves and their world, but most playgoers and readers care less about their fate than they do about the more general picture of human folly that the satire has so convincingly presented. *Troilus and Cressida,* like all satire, is to some extent educational, and we find ourselves more thoughtful and aware, perhaps in some sense morally elevated, through our experience of the play.

## SOURCES OF THE PLAY

Three chief sources—George CHAPMAN's translation of HOMER's *Iliad* (where the Trojan War was first recorded), and two English renderings, by William CAXTON and John LYDGATE, of a different versions—inspired Shakespeare's presentation of the war in *Troilus and Cressida.* The tale of Cressida's betrayal came from Geoffrey CHAUCER's great poem *Troilus and Criseyde.*

The incidents from Homer in *Troilus and Cressida* tend to be those covered in Chapman's translation (1598), and several verbal echoes confirm that Shakespeare used this work, though nine translations were available to him—five Latin, two French, and two English. Some scholars believe that the play may have been intended in part as a satire against Chapman, whose great admiration for the Greeks, rooted in Homer, was counter to the ordinary English reader's identification with the Trojans.

Homer was not the immediate source for English knowledge of the Trojan War. Traditionally, another work was regarded as more authoritative than the *Iliad* because it was supposedly written by a Trojan eyewitness to the war, Dares Phrygius (Dares the Trojan), himself a minor character in the *Iliad.* This Latin prose account was actually written in the 5th or 6th century A.D. It inspired a 12th-century French poem by Benoît de SAINTE-MAURE, which in turn was rendered into Latin prose by Guido delle COLONNE, a Sicilian. His *Historia destructionis Troiae* (1270–1287) was the standard work on the subject for centuries.

A French version of Colonne's *Historia* was translated by Caxton as *The Recuyell of the Historyes of Troye* (1475, 5th ed. 1596). Lydgate's long poem entitled *Troy Book* (1420, publ. 1512, 1555) was inspired directly by Colonne. Caxton provided much of the detail in Shakespeare's account of the war, while Lydgate drew attention to the chivalric aspects of the warriors' encounters.

The story of Cressida and Troilus first appeared in Saint-Maure's poem, where Diomedes and Troilus are rivals for the love of Briseis, the original of Cressida; all of them are only minor figures in Homer. BOCCACCIO's poem *Filostrato* (1338) was inspired by Saint-Maure; here Pandarus was first given prominence. *Filostrato* in turn inspired Chaucer's *Troilus and Criseyde* (c. 1482), which provided Shakespeare with his version of the story, though the playwright eliminates many incidents to achieve a fast-paced plot.

One of Shakespeare's favourite works, OVID's *Metamorphoses,* in the translation by Arthur GOLDING, probably inspired a number of passages, especially parts of Ulysses' speeches. Also, several ideas and incidents—especially in the debate among the Trojans in 2.2—may owe something to *Euphues his Censure to Philautus* (1587) by Robert GREENE (2), a work consisting of philosophical dialogues ascribed to Greek and Trojan warriors meeting during a truce.

## TEXT OF THE PLAY

*Troilus and Cressida* was registered with the STATIONERS' COMPANY by James ROBERTS in February 1603 but was not published then. Such a blocking action was commonly used to prevent piracy of a new play, so *Troilus and Cressida* was probably new in early 1603 and written in the previous year. However, the play contains considerable evidence of rewriting before publication.

It was finally published in 1609 by Richard BONIAN and Henry WALLEY, in a QUARTO edition (known as Q) printed by George ELD. Q appeared in two versions, the second of which has a different title-page and an attached 'Epistle' preceding the text of the play. These alterations were apparently made in the course of printing the edition, though sometimes the two versions are referred to as separate editions. Q is thought to have been printed from a scribal copy of Shakespeare's FOUL PAPERS, or possibly from the manuscript itself; the evidence is obscure and disputed.

In 1623 *Troilus and Cressida* was included in the FIRST FOLIO, and this text (known as F) was based on Q, but it incorporates numerous minor corrections and adds the Prologue as well as about forty other smaller passages. The manuscript used for F had probably been prepared for the KING'S MEN, the acting company that produced the play, for the Folio has many more and markedly superior stage directions.

What the manuscripts were that were used for Q and F, and how they differed, remains uncertain; subsequent editors of the play have been forced to regard both as authoritative, adopting specific readings on a case-by-case basis.

## THEATRICAL HISTORY OF THE PLAY

The early history of *Troilus and Cressida* is quite mysterious. The registration of the play in 1603 states that it had been staged by the CHAMBERLAIN's MEN (soon to become the King's Men), indicating at least one performance in 1602 or 1603. However, while the first title-page of Q (1609) observes that the play had been acted by the King's Men, the second omits this claim and the Epistle expressly denies it. These contradictions combined with the play's philosophical themes, its high-flown rhetoric, bawdy humour, and legalistic jokes, have sparked a theory that the play was commissioned for a private performance at one of the INNS OF COURT, or that an early version was altered for this purpose and Q was occasioned by this performance. In any case, the play seems to have been unpopular with 17th-century audiences, for the claim that it had not been publicly staged could not have been made if it had been widely performed. In fact, no records of any early performances of *Troilus and Cressida* have survived.

Indeed, no English production is recorded until 1907 (though it was staged in German at Munich in 1898). However, in 1679 John DRYDEN produced an abridged *Troilus and Cressida,* generally known by its subtitle, *Truth Found Too Late,* which featured a faithful Cressida and a conventionally tragic ending in which Cressida, Troilus, and Diomedes all die. This version, in which Thomas BETTERTON played Troilus, was popular for a few years, and several editions of the text were published before it disappeared from the stage.

*Troilus and Cressida* has proven popular in the 20th century; its criticisms of war and its relativistic values seem natural to modern audiences, and a number of distinctive productions have resulted. William POEL first produced an uncut text, with Edith EVANS (1) as Cressida (1912–1913). In 1938 Barry JACKSON (1) emphasised the play's anti-war message by costuming the Greeks as Nazis; similarly, Tyrone GUTHRIE's 1956 staging was set early in this century in an imaginary Central European country, and his Greeks wore the spiked helmets of 19th-century Prussian soldiers. In 1960 Peter HALL (5) produced the play on an abstract set, while John BARTON (1) used many startling properties and costumes—along with some near-nudity—in a notorious production of 1976. *Troilus and Cressida* has never been a FILM but has been produced for TELEVISION three times.

**Trojan War**    Legendary conflict between the ancient Greeks and the Trojans, often mentioned in Shakespeare's works, most notably in *Troilus and Cressida,* which enacts part of it. In classical myth and legend, beginning with the *Iliad* of HOMER, the Trojan War was fought by the city of TROY against invaders from Greece, who were attempting to avenge the abduction of a Greek queen, HELEN (1), by a Trojan prince, PARIS (3). The story was quite familiar to Shakespeare's audiences.

As the PROLOGUE (3) declares, *Troilus and Cressida* begins well into the conflict, with the Greeks continuing a seven-year-long siege of Troy, and it ends with the Trojan forces in disarray, facing apparent defeat. However, as the playwright and his audience both knew, that defeat was to be deferred until, in a later episode, Greek troops were smuggled into the city inside the famed Trojan Horse, ostensibly a gift signi-

fying the Greeks' abandonment of their siege. The subsequent sack of Troy is described in a long passage in *The Rape of Lucrece* (lines 1366–1533). Another striking use of the war occurs in *Hamlet,* where the FIRST PLAYER (2) delivers a dramatic account of the killing of King PRIAM of Troy and the grief of Queen HECUBA (2.2.448–514).

According to Greek mythology, Zeus arranged the Trojan War as a cure for overpopulation. With the assistance of Eris, goddess of discord, he sparked a dispute among three goddesses as to which was the most beautiful. Paris was appointed to decide; bribed with the promise of the world's most beautiful woman as a bride, he chose Aphrodite. She rewarded him by helping him to kidnap Helen. Though this well-known legend arose before Homer's time, he ascribes Paris' abduction of Helen to his love for her beauty, with no mention of divine aid.

**The Troublesome Raigne of King John**    Anonymous Elizabethan play published in 1591, probably derived from Shakespeare's *King John* but traditionally regarded as its source. It was long argued that *The Troublesome Raigne,* as the play is known, was adapted by Shakespeare in writing *King John,* but modern scholars—and others, beginning with Alexander POPE (1)—have challenged this assumption, noting the many respects in which the anonymous play resembles a BAD QUARTO: it contains echoes of other plays, including *3 Henry VI, Richard III,* and works by MARLOWE (1) and PEELE; its published text is riddled with errors, including ambiguous or missing stage directions; and it contains passages in which stage directions summarise and describe missing dialogue. Moreover, the 1591 title-page associates *The Troublesome Raigne* with an acting company, the QUEEN'S MEN (1), that is known to have put on a number of such derivative plays, including THE TAMING OF A SHREW.

**Troy**    Ancient city of Asia Minor, the site of the TROJAN WAR of Greek legend and the setting for *Troilus and Cressida.* In the play Troy and its people are decadent and immoral. Although they know that HELEN (1) is a worthless prize, the aristocratic warriors carry on a costly conflict simply because they wish to achieve military renown. Love in Troy is represented by the sexual encounter of CRESSIDA and Prince TROILUS as arranged by the voyeuristic PANDARUS. Once the Trojans' great hero HECTOR is killed the city is helpless, and at the play's bleak close, the Greeks are on the verge of victory.

While the Troy of the play is seen as corrupt, the leaders of Troy are distinctly less evil than the Greeks, and it is clear that the playwright felt a bias in favour of the Trojans. This may seem surprising to modern readers familiar with the pro-Greek sentiments of

Troy's first chronicler, HOMER. However, like most western Europeans at the end of the Middle Ages, the English identified with Troy, believing themselves the descendants of Trojan refugees scattered by the defeat of the city. This legend sprang from the ancient Roman belief found in the *Aeneid* of VIRGIL that Rome had been founded by AENEAS. In English tradition the British Isles were first colonised by a great-grandson of AENEAS named Brut, who was said to have founded London, naming it New Troy, and for whom Britain was believed to be named. Accordingly, the English derived the history of Troy from pro-Trojan accounts.

All histories of Troy are legendary—Homer composed his work centuries after its fall—and the historical city is known only through archaeology, principally the famous excavations by Heinrich Schliemann (1822–1890). In the north-west corner of what is now Turkey, Troy occupied a strategically important location overlooking the Dardanelles, a strait that provided access to the Black Sea and was a major route for trade. Troy's location is thought to have been the likeliest stimulus for a Greek invasion. A long succession of ancient cities stood on the same site from as early as 5,000 years ago. Each of these was a rich and heavily fortified town, presumably the capital of the surrounding territory. The seventh of these settlements is believed to have been the one besieged by the Greeks because it was destroyed by a great fire and because it existed at the right time, c. 1200 B.C. Other cities continued to occupy the site until early Christian times.

**Troyes**   City in eastern FRANCE (1), location for 5.2 of *Henry V*. In 1420 the treaty that confirmed King HENRY V's conquest of France was signed at Troyes, located in the domains of the Duke of BURGUNDY (2), England's ally. This event is presented in the play, though the principal action in the scene is Henry's courtship of Princess KATHARINE (2). The only clause of the treaty alluded to, besides the marriage of Henry and Katharine, is the declaration of Henry as the heir to the French crown, pronounced in French and Latin, in 5.2.356–360.

Historically the treaty of Troyes did not result from the English victory at AGINCOURT, as the play suggests. Simplifying his drama, and emphasising the glory of Agincourt, Shakespeare omitted the events that actually produced the treaty, several years of campaigning in Normandy and, crucially, Burgundy's alliance with England. In the play the Duke of Burgundy appears to speak for the FRENCH KING at Troyes.

*The True Tragedy*   Abbreviated title of the BAD QUARTO version of *3 Henry VI*, originally titled *The true Tragedy of Richard Duke of Yorke, and the death of good King Henrie the Sixt, with the whole contention betweene the two Houses Lancaster and Yorke, as it was sundrie times acted by the Right Honourable the Earle of Pembrooke his servants.* It was published twice by Thomas MILLINGTON, in 1595 and 1600; these are known as the Q1 and Q2 editions, respectively, of *3 Henry VI*. (Although the 1595 edition, of which only one copy has survived, was actually published in octavo format, the term *quarto* is retained for convenience.)

It was once believed that *The True Tragedy* was the text of an earlier play, by Shakespeare or someone else, that Shakespeare revised. However, it is now generally agreed that it is a 'reported' copy of *3 Henry VI*, probably recorded mostly by the actors who played WARWICK (3), CLIFFORD (1), and YORK (8). *The True Tragedy* is a good deal shorter than *3 Henry VI*, probably to reduce the playing time; the omitted sections are chiefly passages of rhetoric and poetic description that do not affect the progress of the plot. It is also possible that some passages, dealing with treason or usurpation of the crown, may have been subject to CENSORSHIP.

Q3 of *3 Henry VI*, a slightly edited version of *The True Tragedy*, was published in 1619 by Thomas PAVIER, in a volume with a 'bad quarto' version of *2 Henry VI*. This edition is known by its abbreviated title as THE WHOLE CONTENTION.

**Trundell, John (active 1603–1626)**   London publisher and bookseller. Trundell co-published the first edition (Q1) of *Hamlet* with Nicholas LING in 1603. Little else is known of him.

**Tubal**   Minor character in *The Merchant of Venice*, friend of SHYLOCK. In 3.1 Tubal tells Shylock that he has been unable to find his friend's daughter, JESSICA, who has eloped, but that he has heard reports of her extravagance with the money she has stolen from her father. Tubal also discloses that ANTONIO (2) has suffered grave commercial losses, thus putting him at the mercy of Shylock, who has loaned him money. Shylock's responses, alternating from delirious anger to exultant delight, are grimly humorous. Tubal's name occurs among the list of descendants of Noah in Genesis 10:2; Biblical scholars of Shakespeare's day thought it meant 'confusion' or 'slander', though modern scholars believe it refers to an ancient tribe.

**Tuckfeild, Thomas (active 1624)**   English actor who may have performed in early productions of *The Two Noble Kinsmen*. In the first edition of the play (Q1, 1634), the stage direction opening 5.3 names the Attendants called for; one of them is named 'T. Tucke'. Scholars believe that this refers to Tuckfeild, indicating that he played the part in an early production by the KING'S MEN. Tuckfeild was with the company in 1624, so this clue (with similar evidence concerning Curtis GREVILLE [1]) suggests that Q1 was printed from a PROMPT-BOOK of the 1620s. Tuckfeild is known from a single document, listing him among the King's Men's 'musicians and other necessary attendants'.

**Tudor Dynasty** Ruling family in England from 1485 to 1603. The first Tudor monarch was King Henry VII, who seized the throne after winning the final phase of the WARS OF THE ROSES by defeating RICHARD III at the battle of BOSWORTH FIELD. This event is the climax of the long period of conflict dealt with in Shakespeare's HISTORY PLAYS. Henry VII appears in *Richard III* as the Earl of RICHMOND. His son, King HENRY VIII, who ruled from 1509 to 1547, is depicted in *Henry VIII* as a symbol of good kingship, in a play that emphasises his part in introducing Protestantism to England. Henry's son ruled as King Edward VI from 1547 to 1553 but died at 15. His sister Mary was queen from 1553 to 1558; a Catholic, she persecuted Protestants, and it was only under her younger sister ELIZABETH (1) that English Protestantism was finally and firmly established. Queen Elizabeth, who reigned during most of Shakespeare's lifetime, was the last Tudor monarch; upon her death in 1603 the STUART DYNASTY came to the throne. The 16th century saw the country emerge from medieval economic and political practises into the early modern period. Thus, the Tudors presided over a crucial transition in the country's history.

**Tutor** Minor character in *3 Henry VI*, adult companion of the child RUTLAND (1), the son of the Duke of YORK (8). The Tutor unsuccessfully attempts to spirit the boy away from the battle of WAKEFIELD, but Lord CLIFFORD (1) captures them and, in his pursuit of vengeance against York, declares he will murder Rutland. The Tutor tries to dissuade the killer, but he is unceremoniously taken away by Clifford's soldiers and the avenger does indeed slay the child.

## *Twelfth Night*

### SYNOPSIS

*Act 1, Scene 1*

ORSINO, duke of ILLYRIA, speaks of his consuming passion for OLIVIA. His messenger, VALENTINE (3), reports that Olivia has turned him away, saying that she proposes to enter seclusion for seven years in memory of her late brother. Orsino marvels at her dedication, hoping it will someday be directed towards himself.

*Act 1, Scene 2*

VIOLA, shipwrecked but safe, is assured by the CAPTAIN (5) that her brother may have been saved also. The Captain informs her that they have landed in his home, Illyria, where the duke, Orsino, is courting a lady who has entered seclusion. Viola decides to become a follower of Orsino and pays the Captain to

help disguise her as a man and introduce her to the duke.

*Act 1, Scene 3*

SIR TOBY Belch complains of the asceticism of Olivia, his niece, with whom he is living. Olivia's chambermaid, MARIA (2), suggests that he and his visiting friend SIR ANDREW Aguecheek, who hopes to woo Olivia, lead less riotous lives, for her mistress dislikes their drunken behaviour. Sir Andrew appears and announces that he will depart, given Orsino's rivalry for Olivia's hand, but Sir Toby assures him that Olivia disdains the duke, and he decides to stay.

*Act 1, Scene 4*

Valentine assures Viola, who is disguised as a boy, Cesario, that Orsino likes 'him'. The Duke appears and sends Cesario to try to persuade Olivia to marry him. Once alone, Viola muses on her distress: she has fallen in love with the man in whose behalf she must woo.

*Act 1, Scene 5*

Maria chastises Olivia's jester, FESTE, for his absence from court. Olivia appears with her steward, MALVOLIO. She is angry with the truant Feste, but his witticisms cajole her into a friendly mood. Malvolio berates Feste, but Olivia accuses the steward of an egotistical dislike of anything contrary to his own grumpiness. Maria announces that a messenger from Orsino has arrived; she and Malvolio are sent to keep him away. Sir Toby has encountered the messenger, but he is too drunk to report on him. Malvolio returns and says that the emissary has refused to depart, describing him as more a boy than a man. Olivia decides to greet this youth, who is the disguised Viola. Cesario speaks for Orsino in poetic terms that charm Olivia. She sends him back to the duke with another refusal, but after he leaves, Olivia confesses to herself that she has fallen in love with him. She sends Malvolio after Cesario with a ring, which she asserts the duke's messenger had forced on her.

*Act 2, Scene 1*

SEBASTIAN (2) tells ANTONIO (4), who has saved him from a shipwreck, that his sister died in the same disaster. Now fully recovered, he proposes to visit Duke Orsino. He insists that Antonio not accompany him; he already owes his saviour too much, he says, and his own bad luck might prove contagious. Sebastian then leaves alone, but Antonio decides that, although he has enemies at Orsino's court, he will follow his new friend.

*Act 2, Scene 2*

Malvolio gives Olivia's ring to the disguised Viola and departs. Viola realises that Olivia has fallen in love with Cesario. She reflects on the complexity of the situation—she loves Orsino, Orsino loves Olivia, and

Olivia loves her—and she observes that time will have to undo the tangle because she certainly cannot.

### Act 2, Scene 3

Sir Toby, Sir Andrew, and Feste carouse drunkenly in Olivia's courtyard, when first Maria and then Malvolio appear to chastise them. Sir Toby mocks the steward, who departs, including Maria in his threats of reprisal as he goes. Maria proposes revenge upon Malvolio: she will write him love letters in Olivia's handwriting, and he will make a fool of himself when he responds to the supposed love of his mistress.

### Act 2, Scene 4

Orsino talks of love with the disguised Viola; Cesario speaks of his affection for someone who resembles the duke. At Orsino's request, Feste sings a sad love song. Orsino sends Cesario on another mission to Olivia.

### Act 2, Scene 5

Maria leaves a spurious love letter to be found by Malvolio. She, Sir Toby, Sir Andrew, and FABIAN, a fellow conspirator, spy on the steward, who preens himself on Olivia's love. He pictures himself married to Olivia, and he envisions a future when, as her husband, he will chastise Sir Toby; Sir Toby is furious, and his friends must restrain him. Malvolio finds the planted letter and responds as predicted; he will follow the letter's instructions, behaving oddly and wearing peculiar clothes, to signify that he has received the message. Malvolio leaves, and the conspirators rejoice in the success of their scheme.

### Act 3, Scene 1

Viola, as Cesario, bandies wit with Feste; Sir Toby and Sir Andrew take her to Olivia, whom she is visiting on behalf of Orsino. Olivia confesses her love to Cesario, who rejects her suit, and she accepts rejection as her melancholy lot.

### Act 3, Scene 2

Sir Andrew, seeing that Olivia favours Cesario, prepares to abandon his suit, but Sir Toby and Fabian reassure him, asserting that Olivia's behaviour towards the young man is intended to make Sir Andrew jealous. Sir Toby suggests that Sir Andrew challenge Cesario to a duel; Sir Andrew leaves to write a challenge to the youth. Fabian and Sir Toby chortle over the prospect of watching two cowards—Sir Andrew and Cesario—try to get out of the duel. Maria appears with word that Malvolio is ridiculously dressed, in response to the spurious love letter, and about to meet Olivia. They all run to watch.

### Act 3, Scene 3

Sebastian thanks Antonio for rejoining him; Antonio observes that, because he had once been an enemy of Duke Orsino's, he cannot afford to be seen in Illyria. He decides to seclude himself at an inn and meet Sebastian there later.

### Act 3, Scene 4

Malvolio, garishly costumed, leers and flirts with Olivia, who is mystified. When word arrives that Cesario has arrived, Olivia leaves but insists that Malvolio, obviously demented, be treated with care. Malvolio interprets her concern as evidence of her love. Sir Toby and Fabian enter, suggesting that Malvolio may be possessed by the devil; he sneers at them and leaves. The exultant plotters plan to have their victim locked up as a lunatic. Sir Andrew appears with a comical letter challenging Cesario to a duel. Sir Toby sends him to find the youth, then declares that the letter is too foolish to scare anyone, so he will deliver his own version of it directly to Cesario. The plotters withdraw as Olivia and Viola enter. Olivia repeatedly offers her love, and Cesario insists that she should grant it to Orsino. Olivia leaves, and Sir Toby ferociously challenges Cesario, allegedly on behalf of a famous swordsman; Viola, alarmed, attempts to find an excuse to leave. Sir Toby fetches Sir Andrew and tells him that Cesario has responded fiercely; he and Fabian encourage the reluctant duellists to fight. Antonio appears and draws his sword in defence of Viola, believing her to be Sebastian, but two OFFICERS (3) appear and arrest him. He asks Viola to repay an earlier loan, which he now will need, but Viola naturally denies that she knows him. As he is taken away, Antonio accuses Viola of ingratitude and calls her Sebastian. Viola realises that her brother must be alive, and she departs, ecstatic with hope. Sir Toby and Fabian point out that Cesario is a coward; Sir Andrew takes heart and sets out to resume the duel.

### Act 4, Scene 1

Feste mistakes Sebastian for Cesario and is astonished to be treated as a stranger. Sir Andrew enters, and, making the same mistake, he strikes Sebastian, who responds by beating him. Sir Toby intervenes, and he and Sebastian draw their swords, as Olivia appears. Ordering everyone else to leave, she speaks with Sebastian, whom she also believes to be Cesario. She apologises for the assault and invites him inside; mystified but delighted, he goes with her.

### Act 4, Scene 2

Feste disguises himself as Sir TOPAS, a Puritan clergyman, and visits Malvolio in prison. He insists that Malvolio is indeed mad and denies the steward's complaint that his cell is dark. Sir Toby congratulates the jester on his performance but says that it is time to end the joke, for he is in enough trouble with Olivia already. Feste again visits Malvolio, this time undisguised. Malvolio asks him for pen and paper so that he can write to Olivia about his predicament. Feste teases him before agreeing to help.

### Act 4, Scene 3

Sebastian muses happily on the bewildering fact that he is apparently loved by a beautiful noblewoman.

Olivia appears with a PRIEST (2) and suggests that she and Sebastian marry. He agrees.

### Act 5, Scene 1

Orsino calls on Olivia with Viola and other followers. Antonio appears in the custody of the Officers and is identified as the duke's enemy. He tells of Sebastian's disloyalty, referring to Viola's behaviour in 3.3. Orsino does not believe him because he knows that Cesario has been with him during the time Antonio claims to have spent with Sebastian. Olivia arrives and again rejects Orsino, who responds hysterically that he will kill Cesario, not only because he knows of Olivia's fondness for him but also because he loves the youth himself, and he seeks the pain of sacrifice. Viola declares herself willing to die for the duke, and Olivia cries out to her husband, as she believes Cesario to be. Viola denies this, and Olivia summons the Priest, who testifies to their marriage two hours earlier. As the duke berates Cesario, Sir Andrew and Sir Toby appear, wounded, claiming to have been assaulted by him. They are followed by Sebastian, whose appearance confounds everyone. Sebastian and Viola identify each other and rejoice in their reunion. The duke declares that he will marry Viola. Malvolio is summoned and shows Olivia the letter that he believes she sent him. Olivia realises that Maria has written it; Fabian defends Maria, saying that the plot was Sir Toby's idea and that Toby has married Maria. Feste teases Malvolio, who storms out vowing revenge. The duke declares that a double wedding shall soon occur, and all go indoors to celebrate, except Feste, who is left alone to sing a song of worldly resignation.

### COMMENTARY

*Twelfth Night* was the last of Shakespeare's three 'mature' COMEDIES, as it, *Much Ado About Nothing,* and *As You Like It* are called, and it was followed shortly by the first of the major TRAGEDIES, *Hamlet.* This crucial position in Shakespeare's *oeuvre* is reflected in the play's subtle complexity. It sustains the celebration of triumphant love that characterises its predecessors, yet it is distinguished by a troubling undertone that suggests the playwright's need to deal with deeper realms of the human psyche.

*Twelfth Night* may be read or seen with pleasure on the level of traditional romantic comedy alone. Shakespeare assembles some stock features—separated twins, disguises, impediments to love—and freshly arranges them in a sequence that resembles a stately dance, all accompanied by a lusty SUB-PLOT with a comic villain, Malvolio. The characters are exaggerated examples of human nature, placed in comically preposterous situations whose improbability we willingly accept as necessary for the retelling of a familiar tale. The world of the play is an undemanding one; there is always time for leisurely courtship, for

*Viola, a character in* Twelfth Night, *in a 19th-century illustration. Viola is put at the centre of the play's conflict when she poses as a young man, 'Cesario'.* (Courtesy of Culver Pictures, Inc.)

songs, and for practical jokes; Malvolio deserves his lot, because he arrogantly and egotistically refuses to enter the fun.

However, Malvolio is merely a nuisance and not a threat; the triumph of love depends on opposition—such as that offered by the villainous Don JOHN (1) in *Much Ado*—and at first glance that opposition is not present in *Twelfth Night.* It turns out to be Orsino and Olivia, two of the lovers themselves, who inhibit the fulfilment of love, assuming wholly literary self-images as romantic lover and mourning lady respectively. Their self-defeating posture suggests that something is amiss in the idyllic world of romantic comedy. The other important characters inspire a certain disquiet as well. Viola, the most clear-sighted and honest figure, is nevertheless tangled in the lie of her disguise, which prevents her from expressing her love. Sir Toby, for all his humour, is a parasite and, worse, a victimiser of the hapless Sir Andrew, as well as of Malvolio. Even the apparently frivolous Feste betrays a weary cynicism at times, as in his final song. Most significantly, Malvolio's humiliation and imprisonment seem so out of proportion to his offence that they lend the comic sub-plot a vicious air that adds to our uneasy sense that the play's comedy is darker than it seems at first.

This disturbing quality is subtly reinforced by the repeated motif of madness. Olivia asserts that Sir Toby 'speaks nothing but madman' (1.5.107), and Feste, pretending to excuse Toby's drunkenness, allows that 'he is but mad yet . . . and the fool shall look to the madman' (1.5.138–139). When Sebastian arrives in Illyria, only to be pointlessly assaulted, he cries out, 'Are all the people mad?' (4.1.26), and when Olivia mysteriously treats him as her lover, he exclaims, '[Either] I am mad, or else this is a dream' (4.1.60). Malvolio is especially associated with lunacy. His ludicrous behaviour towards Olivia—induced by Maria's letter—is received as 'midsummer madness' (3.4.55) by his mistress, and he is later imprisoned as a lunatic (the commonest treatment for mental disorder in Shakespeare's day).

These elements have led some critics to regard the play as a social commentary resembling in spirit *Troilus and Cressida* or the satirical comedies of Ben JONSON. Olivia and Orsino may be taken as comic portraits of egotists, Olivia in her extravagant withdrawal from life, and the duke in his absurd pose as a romantic lover. Most of the other Illyrians can be seen as socially ambitious and thus fit subjects for satire: In this view, Feste curries favour with Orsino because he may marry Olivia; Toby is a vulgar glutton who seeks a continued life of ease in Olivia's household; Malvolio, Sir Andrew, and Maria each seek a profitable marriage. Viola alone offers honest love in a society where affectation dominates.

Such propositions seem excessive, however, for the play lacks the acid taste of satire—although they accurately set off Viola, the drama's central figure, from the other characters. Viola is not invulnerable to love's irrationality, but, unlike the others, she recognises and acknowledges her blindness. She admits that the situation is beyond her control as soon as the three loves—hers for Orsino, Orsino's for Olivia, Olivia's for her—have become evident, saying, 'O time, thou must entangle this, not I, / It is too hard a knot for me t'untie' (2.2.39–40). She knows what she wants, however—Orsino's love—and she maintains her disguise as the duke's page and waits for a miracle. In doing so, she is a splendid example of the Shakespearean comic heroine, resourceful and aggressive in pursuit of her man.

Her effect on her fellow lovers is positive also. As the spirited Cesario, her youthful good looks and imaginative compliments to Olivia bring out the would-be recluse's capacity to love. Similarly, the irrepressible femininity beneath her disguise offers Orsino the devotion and loyalty that he subconsciously desires and to which he unwittingly responds. Thus she rescues the two leading figures of Illyria from their own illusions and paves the way for the dénouement. Moreover, Viola is the only character—aside from Feste, who is essentially an observer of the plot's intrigues—whose point of view includes a perspective on the whole action. She enters into the dramatic possibilities of her disguised state with enthusiasm, missing no opportunity for telling remarks on Orsino and Olivia or for double entendres about her ambiguous gender.

The sexual confusion implicit in Olivia's response to Cesario was of course magnified on the Elizabethan stage, where Viola and Olivia were played by boys. The humour in seeing a woman (played by a boy) respond sexually to another woman (also played by a boy) depends chiefly on the absurdity of the confusion, but it also has overtones of both male and female homosexuality. Homosexuality was rarely referred to in ELIZABETHAN DRAMA, but here it is certainly suggested implicitly. The modern use of actresses dampens our perception of this situation, but even so more complicated patterns of desire lurk beneath the surface of the conventional love comedy.

Thus, both socially and sexually, tremors of unease accompany the development of a classical comic complication that reaches its breaking point only in the final scene. Then, equally disquietingly, it generates potential violence on several fronts. Antonio is threatened with death, and Orsino hysterically threatens to 'sacrifice the lamb that I do love' (5.1.128) by killing Cesario. The crisis is heightened by the appearance of Sir Andrew and Sir Toby, both of whom have been wounded in actual violence.

The giver of these wounds follows, and he brings the play's resolution with him. Sebastian's entrance provides not only Viola's missing brother, the return of Olivia's new husband, and the correct identification of Cesario; it also makes possible the final alignment of the lovers; his first encounter with Olivia in 4.1 had begun the process, and he unhesitatingly married Olivia when she suggested it in 4.3. His sudden reappearance in 5.1, confirms his power to dissolve the network of ambiguity that has entrapped the other lovers.

Shakespeare emphasises Sebastian's sound sexual identity, a feature whose absence has heavily influenced the action thus far. In both 4.1 and 5.1 Sebastian displays the ancient warrior mystique of the wholly masculine man, overwhelming weaker males who affront his honour. More subtly, and more significantly, Sebastian represents fulfilment in the incomplete lives of the other characters. He is the figure Viola has masqueraded as and the lover Olivia subconsciously desired before Cesario awakened her. He is the dominant male whom Malvolio sought to impersonate and whom Orsino, in his romantic role-playing, has forgotten he can be. Thus Sebastian—a rather wooden traditional leading man himself—embodies the positive capacity for love that has been needed to crystallise the swirling vapours of romance that have disturbed Illyria.

Yet our earlier uneasiness is not totally dispelled. Aside from the uncanny ease with which Olivia settles for a look-alike and Orsino translates his affection for a boy into love for a wife—these are part of the improbabilities to be expected in romantic comedy, even if they have here a slight taste of the perverse—there remains the difficult resolution of the sub-plot. The 'problem of Malvolio', as it has long been termed, has attracted attention for centuries; in the 17th century the play was sometimes known as 'Malvolio', and in the 19th century Charles LAMB (1) found 'tragic interest' in 'the catastrophe of this character'. This is an overstatement, for Malvolio lacks the grandeur of a tragic hero, but it reflects the potency of the part and of the moral question the steward's unjust imprisonment raises: how is his undeniably shabby treatment—or his unrepentant final response—to be reconciled with the happy ending?

It is true that Malvolio is a comic character, the villain of a rollicking sub-plot powered by the wit of Maria and the lusty excesses of Sir Toby. He has deserved his comeuppance, and it has been delivered in a comical fashion. Nevertheless, his anger at his humiliation makes him humanly sympathetic, and his raging departure seems justified, if ugly, leaving us with an ongoing sense of disturbance. Shakespeare's purpose here is subtle but effective: our appreciation of the loving aura that closes the play is strengthened by our simultaneous sense of sadness that happiness is never pure.

Feste provides a final statement of the play's anti-romantic undertone in his bitter song (5.1.388–407), which outlines the sorry life of a drunkard. For him, the loving resolution of the main plot seems to count for nothing: 'the rain it raineth every day'. Feste's song expresses the jester's loneliness, for he remains outside the lovers' world, but it also reminds us of the limitations of comedy, which has been part of Shakespeare's message in other ways, as we have seen. Tellingly, another stanza of the same song is sung by the tragic FOOL (2) of *King Lear* (3.2.74–77).

However, the form of Feste's summation—a song—eases the burden of its message; the song is never as painful in performance as its unpleasant lyrics suggest it might be. Music's charms leave us with an echo of the happy ending's harmony. The final stanza of Feste's song also has another function: to end the play formally and send the audience on its way. Like an EPILOGUE, it makes a bid for applause and promises that the actors will 'strive to please you every day' (5.1.407).

This dénouement suggests that, although the play has unsettling aspects, the triumph of love is *Twelfth Night*'s major theme. Its subtitle, 'What You Will', obviously points to the possibility of different interpretations of the work, but its promise of that which 'you will' also hints at the dominance of a positive view. The main title itself remains mysterious. To playgoers of Shakespeare's day, the term 'Twelfth Night' designated January 6, or Epiphany, the last day in the traditional Christmas season, celebrated as the anniversary of the Magi's visit to the birthplace of Christ. In 16th-century writings, the polarity of earthly setting and heavenly signal—the manger in Bethlehem and the magical star that led the Magi—was seen as a powerful symbol of Christ's dual nature, part human and part divine. The twins Sebastian and Viola may be symbolic of this duality as well. Viola, through her patient offering of love to Orsino—expressed most vividly in her declaration 'I . . . to do you rest a thousand deaths would die' (5.1.130–131), a remark that has distinctly Christian overtones—may illustrate Christ's suffering human aspect, while Sebastian, who brings redemption within the play's schéme of things, can be taken to represent Christ's divine dimension. This interpretation may seem somewhat strained, however, given the lack of explicit religious references in the play and the fact that there is little, if any, unambiguously religious content elsewhere in the plays. *Twelfth Night*'s title, as has often been observed, may simply advertise the festive, comic quality of the work by naming a great holiday, as another title, *A Midsummer Night's Dream*, did. Also, the play was probably first performed in the autumn or early winter, as the Christmas holidays were approaching.

We have seen that the romantic comedy in *Twelfth Night* is the play's most powerful component, but the work's disturbing reverberations cannot be overlooked. In this respect the comedy points to the PROBLEM PLAYS, soon to be written. In the meantime, the play tells us that while comedy cannot dispel the pains of life, this knowledge only makes the genre a more necessary solace.

## SOURCES OF THE PLAY

Shakespeare's chief source for *Twelfth Night* was a romantic tale, 'Apolonius and Silla', in *Farewell to Militarie Profession* (1581), by Barnabe RICH (1). Shakespeare simplified this rambling narrative considerably, but it provided the essence of the relationships among Orsino, Olivia, Viola, and Sebastian (though the playwright took none of these names from his source). Rich himself took his tale from a French romance, a story in François BELLEFOREST's *Histoires Tragiques* (1570); Belleforest in turn took it from an Italian version in Matteo BANDELLO's collection of romances, *Novelle* (1554), and Bandello drew on the original source, an anonymous Italian play of the 1530s, *Gl'Ingannati* ('The Deceived Ones'). Shakespeare probably did not know the original play, and, although he did know both Bandello's and Belleforest's collections—he used them in writing other plays (notably *Hamlet* [Belleforest] and *Much Ado About Nothing* [Bandello])—they were not important for *Twelfth Night*. Only one passage—Viola's ironic evocation of a frustrated lover of Orsino (2.4.90–119)—may have been influenced by Bandello.

*Gl'Ingannati* spawned other works, including two plays by an Italian playwright, Nicolo Secchi (active c. 1550), *Gl'Inganni* and *L'Interesse*, which both contain passages resembling Viola's description of a woman whom she claims to love in her male persona (2.4.25–28). Shakespeare may have consulted these works, though some scholars believe the similarity derives simply from their exploitation of the same source.

TEXT OF THE PLAY

*Twelfth Night* was written between 1599—the publication date of the 'new map with the augmentation of the Indies' referred to in 3.2.76–77—and late 1601, in time for the earliest recorded performance in February 1602. The play may have been written for a performance on January 6, 1601, when Queen ELIZABETH (1) paid the CHAMBERLAIN'S MEN to entertain a visiting Italian nobleman named Orsino. If so, then the play must have been written in late 1600, but most scholars believe that this theory is inaccurate, although the much-talked-about visitor may have inspired Shakespeare's choice of a name for his duke, suggesting 1601 as the date of composition.

Two pieces of evidence point to the latter half of that year. First, the play's subtitle, 'What You Will', may have been Shakespeare's original title, altered when another *What You Will*, by John MARSTON, appeared in the spring of 1601. Second, Feste's remark that the word 'element' is 'overworn' (3.1.60) refers to a controversy of 1601. As part of the so-called WAR OF THE THEATRES, Thomas DEKKER's play *Satiromastix* made much fun of Ben JONSON's alleged overuse of the term. *Satiromastix* was performed by the Chamberlain's Men in the summer or fall of 1601 in answer to a Jonson play of the spring season; this suggests that Shakespeare was writing *Twelfth Night* no earlier than mid-1601.

*Twelfth Night* was first published in the FIRST FOLIO edition of 1623. The text was printed from a transcription of Shakespeare's FOUL PAPERS, made by a scribe employed by either the acting company that performed it (the Chamberlain's Men until May 1603, the KING'S MEN thereafter) or the publishers of the Folio. As the only early text of the play, it has been the basis of all subsequent editions.

THEATRICAL HISTORY OF THE PLAY

*Twelfth Night* was performed at one of the INNS OF COURT on February 2, 1602, according to the diary of John MANNINGHAM. This is the only record of a performance in Shakespeare's lifetime, though the King's Men presented the play at the court of King JAMES I in 1618 and 1623, suggesting its popularity. Robert ARMIN is believed to have created the role of Feste and Richard BURBAGE (3) that of Malvolio. During the Restoration, William DAVENANT staged the play in 1661, 1663 and 1669, though he may have altered Shakespeare's text considerably, as was his practise; Thomas BETTERTON played Sir Toby.

In 1703 William BURNABY's *Love Betray'd* incorporated several scenes from *Twelfth Night*, but the play itself was not again performed until 1741, when Charles MACKLIN staged it and played Malvolio. Somewhat later in the 18th century Richard YATES (2) was a popular Feste as a youth and played Malvolio later in his career. John HENDERSON also appeared as the steward with notable success. Dorothy JORDAN played Viola in 1790, opposite her brother as Sebastian, providing a natural similarity of looks.

In the 1810 production by J. P. KEMBLE (3), 1.1 and 1.2 were reversed, a practise that has continued intermittently to the present. Charlotte CUSHMAN was a popular Viola in 1846, Samuel PHELPS played Malvolio in his own productions of 1848 and 1857, and Henry IRVING's production of 1884 starred himself as Malvolio and Ellen TERRY (1) as Viola. Ada REHAN played Viola in Augustin DALY's production (New York, 1893; London, 1894). Nineteenth-century stagings of *Twelfth Night* tended to have elaborate sets and costumes, often based on images of aristocratic English country life, a practise that reached an extreme with Beerbohm TREE's 1901 set, featuring a terraced garden with real grass and fountains.

In 1820 Frederick REYNOLDS (1) produced a musical version incorporating, in the words of the producer, 'Songs, Glees, and Choruses . . . from the Plays, Poems, and Sonnets of Shakespeare'. Other 19th-century productions also introduced extra songs to the text; notable among these was Daly's usurpation of 'Who Is Silvia?' from *The Two Gentlemen of Verona* (4.2. 38–52), which had earlier (1827) been set to music by Franz SCHUBERT.

Among the most famous 20th-century productions of *Twelfth Night* was Harley GRANVILLE-BARKER's revolutionary rendering of 1912, which attempted to evoke the Elizabethan stage. Tyrone GUTHRIE's 1937 production featured Laurence OLIVIER as Sir Toby, and, in an experiment that was generally decried, Jessica Tandy (b. 1909) played both Sebastian and Viola, a non-speaking actor taking the former part in the reunion scene (5.1). Peggy ASHCROFT was acclaimed as Viola in 1950. Other notable productions have included John GIELGUD's (1955), starring Olivier as Malvolio and Vivien Leigh as Viola, and that of John BARTON (1) (1969), with Judi DENCH as Viola.

A silent FILM of *Twelfth Night* was made in 1910, and

Russian and German films were made in 1955 and 1963 respectively. The play has been broadcast six times on TELEVISION, beginning in 1939 with a BBC production featuring Michael REDGRAVE and Peggy Ashcroft. Another British production of 1969—with Ralph RICHARDSON (2) as Sir Toby and Joan PLOWRIGHT as both Viola and Sebastian (a feat more plausible on television than on the stage)—was also notable.

**Twine, Laurence (active 1564–1576)** English translator, creator of a source for *Pericles.* In his prose romance, *The Patterne of Painefull Adventures . . . That Befell unto Prince Apollonius,* Twine translated the tale of Apollonius of Tyre from a French version of an ancient story found in the *Gesta Romanorum,* a medieval Latin collection. Shakespeare drew from Twine's book in composing his play. *The Patterne of Painefull Adventures* was written c. 1576, but if it was published then, no copy has survived; Shakespeare probably knew it in either an undated edition of c. 1594 or a reprint of 1607.

### *The Two Gentlemen of Verona*

#### SYNOPSIS

*Act 1, Scene 1*
A young gentleman, VALENTINE (2), preparing to travel to the court of the DUKE (3) of Milan, teases his lovesick friend PROTEUS about the infatuation that keeps him home. Valentine departs, and Proteus, in a brief soliloquy, expresses his love for JULIA. Valentine's young page, SPEED, enters. Speed has carried a letter from Proteus to Julia, and he reports that she made no response to it.

*Act 1, Scene 2*
Julia asks her waiting-woman, LUCETTA, her opinion of the suitors who are wooing her. Lucetta favours Proteus, but Julia affects to disdain him. Lucetta gives her a letter from Proteus, delivered by Speed, but Julia pretends to take offence, eventually tearing the letter to pieces and sending Lucetta away. Alone, Julia berates herself and confesses that she loves Proteus.

*Act 1, Scene 3*
Proteus' father, ANTONIO (1), decides that Proteus shall join Valentine at court, as befits a gentleman's son. Proteus enters, mooning over a love letter from Julia. Antonio reveals his plan to Proteus, leaving the young man to bemoan his misfortune.

*Act 2, Scene 1*
Speed gives Valentine a glove that has been dropped by the Duke's daughter SILVIA, with whom Valentine appears to be in love. The witty Speed tauntingly diagnoses his master's condition. Valentine reports that Silvia has asked him to write a love letter to an unknown person for her. Silvia arrives, and Valentine

gives his composition to her. She promptly returns it to him; Valentine is disturbed, but Speed, in an aside, immediately sees that she loves Valentine himself. When Silvia leaves, Speed attempts to explain this, but Valentine cannot understand.

*Act 2, Scene 2*
Proteus and Julia say farewell and exchange rings. Proteus vows to be faithful while he is away.

*Act 2, Scene 3*
LAUNCE, a CLOWN (1) who is Proteus' servant, appears with his dog, CRAB, whose hard-heartedness he complains about in a comic monologue. Launce is upset because he must leave his family and go to court with his master, but Crab shows no distress.

*Act 2, Scene 4*
The Duke reports that Proteus has arrived at his court, and Valentine praises his friend warmly. Valentine tells Silvia of the love between Proteus and Julia. Proteus enters and meets Silvia, who is then called away. Valentine reveals that he and Silvia are planning to elope. Proteus confesses in a soliloquy that he has fallen madly in love with Silvia, so much so that he is willing to betray both Valentine and Julia.

*Act 2, Scene 5*
Speed welcomes Launce to court. With clownish wit, the two servants gossip about their masters' love affairs.

*Act 2, Scene 6*
In a soliloquy, Proteus plots to steal Silvia from Valentine, finding justifications for his disloyalty to his friend and Julia. He proposes to reveal the intended elopement of Valentine and Silvia, scheduled for that night, to the Duke.

*Act 2, Scene 7*
Julia plans to journey to court to see Proteus. She will travel disguised as a page. Lucetta warns that Proteus' love may have diminished, but Julia is confident he will remain faithful.

*Act 3, Scene 1*
Proteus tells the Duke of the intended elopement, exiting as Valentine approaches. The Duke 'discovers' the rope ladder hidden under Valentine's cloak, and angrily banishes Valentine from his domain. Proteus arrives with Launce and offers to help Valentine flee. The two friends depart, leaving Launce, who speaks of his own love for a milkmaid. He has a written list of her good qualities. Speed appears, and the two comic figures review this document.

*Act 3, Scene 2*
The Duke speaks with THURIO, whom he has chosen to marry his daughter. Thurio complains that Silvia loves him even less than she did before Valentine's banishment. Proteus recommends maligning Valentine to

her, and he volunteers for the job, observing that such slander will only be credible coming from someone believed to be Valentine's friend.

### Act 4, Scene 1
Valentine and Speed are captured by OUTLAWS. Learning that Valentine is an educated gentleman, as they claim to be themselves, these desperadoes elect him their captain.

### Act 4, Scene 2
Proteus soliloquises that his ongoing career of betrayal, now directed at Thurio, has only brought him Silvia's scorn. Thurio arrives with MUSICIANS (1). Also present, unknown to the others, is Julia, disguised as a page. The SONG 'Who Is Silvia?' is performed, and Julia sees that Proteus loves its subject. Thurio and the Musicians depart, and Proteus converses with Silvia, who has appeared on her balcony. He takes credit for the serenade and speaks of his love, but Silvia rebukes him, referring to his former love, Julia. He claims that Julia has died, not knowing that she is listening, and adds that he has heard that Valentine is dead as well. He asks Silvia for a picture, and she agrees to give him one in the morning.

### Act 4, Scene 3
Sir EGLAMOUR agrees to accompany Silvia on a journey to find Valentine.

### Act 4, Scene 4
In a monologue, Launce complains of Crab's doggy behaviour, for he has urinated at the Duke's dinner. Proteus agrees to employ the disguised Julia as a page, ordering 'Sebastian' to deliver a ring to Silvia, in exchange for the promised picture. Julia makes the exchange and learns that Silvia knows of and feels pity for Proteus' abandoned lover.

### Act 5, Scene 1
Eglamour and Silvia flee.

### Act 5, Scene 2
The Duke reports Silvia's flight. Thurio, Proteus, and Julia all join him in pursuit.

### Act 5, Scene 3
The Outlaws have captured Silvia and are taking her to their captain.

### Act 5, Scene 4
Valentine, alone, muses that his lonely exile is appropriate to his grief over his lost Silvia. Hearing a commotion, he hides himself, and Silvia, Proteus, and Julia enter. Proteus demands Silvia's love as a reward for having rescued her from the Outlaws; when she refuses, he attempts to rape her. Valentine comes forth and prevents him, cursing his supposed friend's disloyalty. Proteus, stricken with remorse, begs forgiveness. Valentine is so moved that he offers to yield Silvia to him; hearing this, Julia faints. Revived, she

reveals her identity, and Proteus falls in love with her again. The Outlaws arrive with the Duke and Thurio as captives, whom Valentine releases. Thurio claims Silvia, but when Valentine offers to fight him, he fearfully declines. The Duke pardons Valentine and awards him Silvia's hand.

## COMMENTARY

*The Two Gentlemen of Verona* is certainly among the most poorly received of Shakespeare's comedies. Some parts, especially the comic monologues of Launce, are accomplished, but the play as a whole is unconvincing. It is perhaps best viewed as the work of a young and inexperienced playwright who was only beginning to experiment with comedy, a genre he was to master at a later date.

In the past, some scholars have claimed that the play was simply too bad to have been written by Shakespeare, that at most he may have touched up someone else's feeble effort. Modern criticism holds that the play, while an unsuccessful early effort, is nonetheless genuinely Shakespearean. Supporters of this opinion have focussed on the young playwright's intelligent application of the literary conventions current in his day as he developed his own approach to comedy, or they have seen the play as at least in part a deliberate parody of these conventions. These two propositions are not mutually exclusive; a parodist may make use of a style for its entertainment value at the same time that he or she subverts it.

The play draws on two literary traditions: the 'friendship literature' of the Middle Ages; and romantic narrative. 'Friendship literature' told tales of manly companionship, sometimes disrupted by romance but generally restored. The account of the relationship between Valentine and Proteus is an instance of this long-popular plot line. For instance, Valentine's renunciation of Silvia (5.4.82–83), though comically abrupt in context, represents a conventional demonstration of magnanimity that was standard in this tradition.

Romantic narrative derived ultimately from classical roots and was popular throughout the Middle Ages in the form of poetry and prose dealing with courtly love and adventure. Such narratives continued to be written and widely read during the Renaissance; Sir Philip SIDNEY's *Arcadia* was the best-known English example. This tradition was already familiar in the early Elizabethan theatre. A number of plays written in the 1570s and 1580s share several of its characteristic devices: accounts of travels in several different settings; girls or women, abandoned by lovers, who assume disguises; a cynical villain; a mocking servant who comments on the romantic action; eventual reunion at the close. The audience finds in these exotic settings and stylised characters a life that seems both bolder and finer than its own, governed by values that are impossible in the real world. It is this body of conventions that Shakespeare uses in this play.

In *The Two Gentlemen of Verona,* lovers are separated through a flagrantly evil act of betrayal. After trials and rigours have been undergone, a happy ending reunites them and villainy is overcome. The promised escape has been provided. However, Shakespeare holds up the stereotype of romantic narrative to good-humoured ridicule, especially in the treatment of his hero, Valentine, who is presented throughout as a gullible and foolish young man, a comic and ridiculous hero. When we first see him, he is ridiculing love, and we know, if only from his suggestive name, that his comeuppance surely lies ahead. Valentine's ineptness as a lover is demonstrated, for instance, when he fails to comprehend Silvia's flirtatious letter-writing ploy; when Speed attempts to explain it, he proves too slow-witted to appreciate it.

Valentine's high-flown rhetoric of love, as he recounts his infatuation to Proteus in 2.4, is the voice of exuberant enthusiasm, and he presents a pleasant picture of a young man in the first blush of romance. However, his bubbling account of his planned elopement seems indiscreet at best. Later in the scene, when Proteus reveals his plan to betray his friend, we pity Valentine for the blunder he has unknowingly committed in confiding in this villain, but at the same time, we may chuckle that his effervescent 'braggardism' (2.4.159) was so untimely.

We are not surprised when Valentine steps so neatly into the Duke's trap in 3.1, for his combination of naïveté and feigned sophistication seems entirely in character. So does his helplessness once the Duke rages off; he can only bemoan his fate until Proteus bundles him out of town.

We next see Valentine in the wholly comic scene (4.1) of his capture by the Outlaws, who immediately make him the leader of their gang, in what is clearly a broad parody of romantic adventure stories. He rescues Silvia from attempted rape by Proteus, but he is so silly a hero that it does not occur to him to claim his heroine at this obvious climax. In fact, he does not even speak to her for the remainder of the play. Instead, he responds only to his former friend, who is begging forgiveness, and he goes so far as to turn Silvia over to the would-be rapist. This absurd conclusion is prevented only by the quick-witted Julia, who wants Proteus for herself, and Valentine is united with his beloved only by default.

Only two of the characters in *The Two Gentlemen of Verona* anticipate the magical figures of later works. Launce, an early clown, voices the best writing in the play in his monologues concerning his dog, Crab. The general artificiality of the play is countered to a considerable degree by the presence of this commonsensical man. However, Launce has literally nothing whatsoever to do with the plot; he simply provides intermis-

sions, as it were, in the main action. Later, Shakespeare was to integrate his comic characters more fully. Julia, whose best material is in prose, is also something of a foil to Valentine and Proteus. Her pragmatic assumption of control over events begins with her intention to overcome her enforced separation from Proteus by following him to court, and it triumphs when she abandons her disguise and reconquers his love. She clearly foreshadows such later enterprising heroines as ROSALIND, in *As You Like It,* and VIOLA, in *Twelfth Night.*

## SOURCES OF THE PLAY

The two strands that make up the plot of *The Two Gentlemen of Verona* came to the playwright from specific sources, although one derivation is not altogether clear, for Shakespeare made the material his own to a great extent. The relationships among Proteus, Valentine, and Silvia seem to be based on the story of Titus and Gisippus, a 'friendship' tale, originally found in Boccaccio's *Decameron* and very famous in Shakespeare's day. Gisippus bestows his fiancée on his friend Titus, who has fallen in love with her. This tale lacks the betrayal theme, but, as his love develops, Titus contemplates such a course, in terms remarkably similar to those Proteus uses in his soliloquy in 2.6. Also, there are English variants of this tale, and several passages that resemble lines in the play appear in one of them, published in Sir Thomas ELYOT's *The Boke named the Governour* (1531). One such passage seems to have inspired Valentine's notorious couplet of renunciation. Just how Shakespeare knew the tale, and just what he took from which source, cannot be determined.

However, the story of the betrayed love of Proteus and Julia clearly came from *Diana Enamorada,* a prose romance written in Spanish by the Portuguese author Jorge de MONTEMAYOR and first printed in 1542. Although the first English translation, by Bartholomew YONG, was not published until 1598, Shakespeare probably knew the manuscript, which had been completed 16 years earlier, for there are many echoes of it in the play.

A third source was a long poem by Arthur BROOKE (1), *The Tragical History of Romeus and Juliet,* which was also the chief source for *Romeo and Juliet.* Here, Shakespeare's only important adoption was Valentine's rope-ladder, but there are suggestions of the later play in Silvia's conspiratorial visit to a friar's cell (4.3.43–44) and in the mention of a Friar Laurence (5.2.36).

Launce was apparently a Shakespearean invention, although his character type, the rustic clown, was already well established. The early plays of John LYLY offered models for Speed; also, some details of Speed's role derive from *Damon and Pithias* a play of 1571 by Richard EDWARDS. The comical 'catalogue' scene (3.1) seems to have been suggested by a scene in Lyly's *Midas* (1588–1589). Lyly's immensely popular novel *Euphues* (1578) offered a famous instance of male friendship disturbed by sexual jealousy and, as the sensation of the age, doubtless helped form the young Shakespeare's sense of romantic atmosphere.

## TEXT OF THE PLAY

*The Two Gentlemen of Verona* is known to have been written by 1598, when it was mentioned by MERES, but features of its style suggest that it was written earlier. It has been nominated as possibly the first play Shakespeare wrote, but this cannot be proved. Proposed dates for its composition have ranged from 1590 to 1595, not counting a sometimes hypothesised rewrite of 1598. The only early publication of the play was in the FIRST FOLIO of 1623, and this text has therefore been the basis for all subsequent editions.

## THEATRICAL HISTORY OF THE PLAY

No performance of *The Two Gentlemen of Verona* is recorded before 1762, although it is presumed to have been acted in the 16th century—at least on the strength of its inclusion in the list of plays complied by Meres in 1598. The production of 1762, by David GARRICK, was of an altered text, as have been most of the scattered subsequent attempts. The play's many discrepancies have been amended to a greater or lesser extent, and additional material has often been added for Launce and Speed. The only version to achieve even a modest success with 19th-century audiences was a highly altered operatic version produced by Frederick REYNOLDS (1) in the 1820s. There have been successful 20th-century stagings—such as Joseph PAPP's musical adaptation of 1971, and a New York production of 1988 that featured a troupe of jugglers—but it remains one of the least performed of Shakespeare's plays. *Two Gentlemen of Verona* was made as a FILM in Germany (1963) and has been made for TELEVISION once, in 1983, as part of the BBC's complete cycle of Shakespeare's plays.

## *The Two Noble Kinsmen*

### SYNOPSIS

A PROLOGUE (5) declares that the play has a noble predecessor, in a work by CHAUCER, that it cannot hope to live up to.

### Act 1, Scene 1

As THESEUS (2), Duke of ATHENS, prepares to marry Queen HIPPOLYTA (2) of the Amazons, the ceremony is interrupted by a QUEEN (1) who falls on her knees before Theseus, followed by two more who address Hippolyta and her sister, EMILIA (4). The Queens tell of their husbands' deaths fighting King Creon of THEBES, who has refused to bury the kings' bodies,

thereby exposing their souls to torment. They ask Theseus to conquer Creon, insisting that any delay is dishonourable. The wedding is then postponed as Theseus prepares for war.

### Act 1, Scene 2

Two noblemen of Thebes, the cousins ARCITE and PALAMON, decide to leave the court of the villainous King Creon. VALERIUS brings word that Duke Theseus has declared war. The cousins realise that their honour requires them to stay and fight for Thebes.

### Act 1, Scene 3

Hippolyta and Emilia bid farewell to PIRITHOUS, who is about to join Theseus in Thebes. Hippolyta remarks on the long-standing friendship of Pirithous and Theseus. Emilia recalls her own, similar affection for a childhood girlfriend and declares that she will never love a man so well.

### Act 1, Scene 4

The Queens thank Theseus for his victory over Creon, and he sends them to bury their husbands. A HERALD (8) informs Theseus that Palamon and Arcite, both badly wounded, are among his prisoners of war.

### Act 1, Scene 5

The Queens lead funeral processions for their husbands.

### Act 2, Scene 1

The GAOLER (4) negotiates a marriage settlement with the WOOER of his DAUGHTER (2). The Daughter appears on her way to see the new prisoners, Palamon and Arcite, whom she admires for the spirit with which they bear their imprisonment. The three commoners leave as the two prisoners appear, reflecting on the comfort they can take in each other's company; they believe that their honourable friendship will sustain them throughout their lives. Below their windows, in a courtyard, they see Emilia conversing with a WOMAN (2). First Palamon and then Arcite fall in love with Emilia on sight. After she leaves, they quarrel over who has the right to claim her as his beloved. Each feels that his honour is offended by the other, and they vow to fight a duel if they ever have the opportunity. The Gaoler appears and takes Arcite to the duke. Palamon muses on his love for Emilia until the Gaoler returns to report that Arcite has been freed but banished from Theseus' realm, on pain of death.

### Act 2, Scene 2

Arcite, free, decides to stay in Theseus' realm and attempt to meet and woo Emilia. He encounters a group of COUNTRYMEN, who tell him of the wrestling and running competitions to be witnessed by Theseus and his court at a nearby country fair. Arcite decides to enter the competitions in order to come to the attention of the court and thus meet Emilia.

*Act 2, Scene 3*

The Gaoler's Daughter reflects on her hopeless love for Palamon. She realises that he will never love a commoner, but she decides to help him escape from prison.

*Act 2, Scene 4*

The disguised Arcite, having won the competitions, is interviewed by Theseus, who accepts him as a courtier. He is assigned to serve as an attendant to Emilia.

*Act 2, Scene 5*

The Daughter reveals in a soliloquy that she has freed Palamon, who waits in a nearby wood until she can bring him food and a file to remove his shackles. She hopes he will come to love her.

*Act 3, Scene 1*

Alone in the wood, Arcite reflects on his good fortune in having become Emilia's attendant. Overhearing this, the fugitive Palamon emerges from the trees, and they resume their argument. Though their affection for each other still stands, they agree that they must duel to uphold their respective honours. Arcite declares he will bring Palamon food and a file to remove his shackles, and then they will fight.

*Act 3, Scene 2*

The Daughter cannot find Palamon and concludes that he has been eaten by wild animals. Hysterical, she reflects that her father will be hanged for her treachery in letting Palamon escape, and she will be reduced to beggary if she does not commit suicide. She wishes she were already dead.

*Act 3, Scene 3*

Arcite returns to Palamon with food and a file. They agree not to mention Emilia but cannot refrain and fall to quarrelling again. Arcite leaves, saying he will return when Palamon has removed his shackles, and they will fight.

*Act 3, Scene 4*

Raving wildly about Palamon, her father, and other things, the Daughter sings scraps of SONG.

*Act 3, Scene 5*

A SCHOOLMASTER (2) instructs a group of peasants, one of them costumed as a BAVIAN, or baboon, on the dance they are to perform before the duke. One of the women of their group is missing, however, so they despair about being able to perform. The Daughter appears, and although they see that she is mad, the dancers recruit her for their performance. Theseus and his court appear and, after a lengthy PROLOGUE (1) from the Schoolmaster, the dance is presented.

*Act 3, Scene 6*

Palamon and Arcite meet to duel. As they put on their armour, they reminisce fondly, but they continually

renew their quarrel. They begin to fight, but Theseus and his court arrive. The cousins identify themselves, and Theseus condemns them to death: Arcite for having violated his banishment and Palamon as an escaped prisoner of war. They plead to be permitted to finish their duel, with the survivor then being executed, and Theseus agrees. However, when Hippolyta and Emilia beg for mercy for them, Theseus compromises. He decrees that the cousins shall return to Thebes and recruit seconds, come back within a month, and then duel for Emilia's hand. The duel shall not be to the death, but rather consist of a contest to force the opponent to touch a pillar erected for the purpose. The winner will marry Emilia; only the loser and his seconds will be executed. The cousins agree and depart.

*Act 4, Scene 1*

The Gaoler hears of the duel from a FRIEND and worries that he will be blamed for Palamon's escape. A Second Friend arrives and assures him that the duke, encouraged by Palamon, has pardoned the Gaoler and his Daughter. The Wooer then arrives with the news that the Daughter is mad. She appears, ranting about marrying Palamon and taking a sea voyage to meet him.

*Act 4, Scene 2*

Regretting the upcoming duel, Emilia reviews the virtues of each cousin in turn and admits that she loves them both. She is joined by Theseus and the court. Pirithous and a MESSENGER (32) have witnessed the arrival of the cousins and their seconds, and they describe the gallantly arrayed KNIGHTs (3) in detail.

*Act 4, Scene 3*

The DOCTOR (4) witnesses the Daughter's ravings and prescribes that the Wooer should dress as Palamon and court her, in the hope that the apparent fulfilment of her fantasy will shock her out of it.

*Act 5, Scene 1*

In a temple Arcite and Palamon prepare to duel. They bid each other an affectionate farewell. When Arcite and his seconds make a sacrifice to Mars, the altar resounds with thunder. Palamon and his followers make one to Venus, and the altar gives forth doves. After the knights leave for the duel, Emilia appears and makes a sacrifice to Diana. A rose tree bearing a single rose emerges, but the rose falls from it. Emilia is confused by this omen.

*Act 5, Scene 2*

The Wooer, in the guise of Palamon, reports that he has kissed the Daughter. The Doctor directs that he go on to sleep with her, and he readily agrees. The Daughter emerges from the Gaoler's house and talks of a dancing horse Palamon has given her and how another horse loves it in vain. Still pretending to be Palamon, the Wooer proposes to her, and she accepts, adding that they should go to the end of the world for the wedding. She returns indoors, and the men go to witness the duel.

*Act 5, Scene 3*
Emilia, resisting all arguments, refuses to witness the duel, so a SERVANT (30) is left with her to report. Going to and fro, he periodically recounts the action: first one cousin seems to be winning, then the other. Finally, he reports Arcite the victor. The court returns, and Arcite and Emilia are formally declared engaged. Emilia declares that only her duty to comfort Arcite, who has lost his noble kinsman, keeps her from killing herself with grief.

*Act 5, Scene 4*
Palamon and his seconds prepare to be executed. Palamon asks the Gaoler about his Daughter; he reports that she has recovered and is to be married. As Palamon is about to be beheaded by the EXECUTIONER (3), Pirithous arrives with a pardon, reporting that Arcite is dying after being crushed by a runaway horse. Theseus, Hippolyta, and Emilia appear, with Arcite in a litter. Arcite accepts Palamon's grieving farewell, bequeaths Emilia to him, receives a final kiss from her, and dies. Theseus declares a period of mourning, to be followed by the marriage of Emilia and Palamon.

*Epilogue*
An anonymous actor, pretending to have stage fright, jests about the audience's hisses and laughter. He asks for their pardon, promises a better play some other night, and bids farewell.

COMMENTARY

*The Two Noble Kinsmen* is probably the least known of Shakespeare's plays, in good part because (in the opinion of all but a few scholars) much of it was written by someone else, probably John FLETCHER (2). It has rarely been performed or even published over the centuries, though modern commentators' growing interest in Shakespeare's ROMANCES encompasses this work.

Considered separately, the parts of *The Two Noble Kinsmen* written by Shakespeare present the germ of a better and more interesting work than the play as a whole turned out to be. Shakespeare wrote Acts 1 and 5—with some exceptions—plus 3.1 and perhaps some other minor passages. With the beginning and the end of the play, he could introduce characters and themes and bring them to the climax of the action. Scenes 1.1 and 5.1 are especially strong, containing much good poetry and several spectacular theatrical effects. Shakespeare's only substantial contribution to the development between these phases is the encounter between Arcite and Palamon, when they prepare to duel

even as they recognise their profound affection for each other. A number of fine passages of verse in 3.1—especially Arcite's lyrical praise of Emilia—sharpen the audience's appreciation that the developing story is more than an assemblage of clichés about knighthood and courtly love enlivened by a comic subplot.

In Shakespeare's portions of the play, *The Two Noble Kinsmen* displays many of the characteristics of his other late works, and it is properly grouped with the romances. The playwright was clearly employing the techniques of spectacle, exotic characters and settings, and bizarre plotting with much the same intention as in other romances—to demonstrate humanity's dependence on providence in the face of inscrutable destiny and to evoke the nobility of the human spirit in the face of this knowledge.

The spectacular is less dramatic and effective in *The Two Noble Kinsmen* than in, say, *The Tempest,* but it is nonetheless present. Theseus and Hippolyta's elaborate wedding opens the play on a ceremonious note, only to be interrupted by the extraordinary sight of the three Queens, all in black and thus contrasting strikingly with the wedding party's festive finery. The Queens' manner is sternly formal, as they first address Theseus and receive his response, then do the same in turn with Hippolyta and Emilia. This ritualistic exchange makes the gravity of their plea unmistakable. The effect is augmented as the plea is repeated with variations: when they receive a promise of support, they demand instant action; when ARTESIUS is assigned to the task, they demand Theseus. The importance of this presentation becomes clear when we consider how Shakespeare has altered his source. In CHAUCER's tale (see 'Sources' below), Theseus is already married, only a single Queen pleads—and only with him—and he consents immediately. In contrast, Shakespeare delayed the process, for action is less important in *The Two Noble Kinsmen* than emotion, here manifested in an almost religious atmosphere of courtliness and mystery. It is appropriate that the first character on stage should be HYMEN (2), a god.

This religious atmosphere recurs in the funeral procession of 1.5. Throughout the play, references to rituals of various sorts, along with manifold allusions to the pagan gods, both singly and collectively, maintain our awareness of the need for harmony with the divine, a consideration that underlies the action. In 5.1 the play's evocation of religion and mystery is at its most intense. The three petitions to pagan gods and the divine responses are in themselves meaningful, as we shall see, but they are also important for the atmosphere they create. Highly elaborate, with startling sound and physical effects—doubtless devised with an eye to the increased technical capacities of the BLACK-FRIARS THEATRE—they evoke awe and wonder appropriate to the extraordinary twists of fate in the coming climax. The suppliants' prayers comprise the best poetry of the play, and the divine responses are gratifyingly spectacular. They are mysterious yet, as the baffled Emilia observes, 'gracious' (5.1.173). The exotic beauty of this scene is generally considered the high point of *The Two Noble Kinsmen*.

Such spectacle is effective simply for its own sake—Shakespeare was certainly inspired in part by the increasing popularity of the MASQUE—but it also helps further the themes of the play. As in the other late plays, the central proposition of *The Two Noble Kinsmen* is that humanity is dependent on providence. In the face of a destiny we cannot understand, we can only accept our fate and hope the gods will refrain from destroying us. This point of view is less pessimistic than it sounds when reduced to its essentials, for the nobility of humanity's continuing survival in the face of such knowledge is impressive. At least, we see the potential for such nobility in each individual.

We are repeatedly reminded of fate's importance. Even the celebratory, flower-filled opening hymn finishes with a sinister hint of fatality in its allusions to birds of ill omen. Theseus recalls the wedding day of the grieving Queen and rhetorically addresses destiny, 'O grief and time, / Fearful consumers, you will all devour!' (1.1.69–70). In 1.2 Palamon declares that Creon is corrupting Thebes by making 'heaven unfeared' (1.2.64); nevertheless, the young men seem powerless to avoid entanglement in Creon's corruption. Admitting that helplessness, Arcite entrusts their future to 'th'event, / that never-erring arbitrator' (1.2.113–114). Hippolyta hopes that Theseus, in combat, will be able 'To dure ill-dealing fortune' (1.3.5), and a defeated knight, facing execution, declares that the winners have 'Fortune, whose title is . . . momentary' (5.4.17). Even after victory Theseus speaks of 'Th'impartial gods, who from the mounted heavens / View us their mortal herd' (1.4.5). Using a different metaphor for human helplessness before fate, Pirithous describes Arcite's flagging life as 'a vessel . . . that floats but for / The surge that next approaches' (5.4.82–84). At the end, reviewing the final twist of fate, Theseus declares, 'Never fortune / Did play a subtler game' (5.4.112–113). Fortune is omnipresent in the play's world, yet it is entirely beyond human control or understanding.

Tellingly, the gods answer the eloquent prayers of 5.1, but not in a way that could have been anticipated; fortune is certain but unpredictable. Arcite prays that he may 'Be styled the lord o'th'day' (5.1.60), and he is indeed declared the winner of the duel, but he loses Emilia and his life, as the horse she gives him proves deadly. Palamon asks Venus for victory as 'true love's merit' (5.4.128), but he only gains Emilia through Arcite's accidental death. Emilia prays that the cousin who loves her best should win. This would appear to be Palamon, for he is associated with Venus rather

than Mars; moreover, since he saw her first and is more rightly her lover—as Arcite finally admits—he is more truly fighting in the cause of love, with Arcite more intent on defending his personal honour. Yet it is Arcite who wins, even though Emilia does in the end have her wish granted. As expectations are upset and then fulfilled, but fulfilled only tragically, our sense of the incomprehensibility of providence is compounded.

The play, however, counters any implicit fatalism by repeatedly stressing the importance of human nobility. The emphasis begins in the Prologue with the assertion that the story being told has in itself a 'nobleness' (Prologue, 15) that the creators of the drama are striving to uphold, and that Chaucer was its 'noble breeder' (10). The nobility of Palamon and Arcite—explicit in the play's title—is repeatedly confirmed by the other characters. Their friendship is bound up in their appreciation of each other's noble qualities, and it is itself conventionally noble in a literary tradition that was still very much alive in Shakespeare's day. From medieval times into the 17th century, intense friendship between noble young warriors, especially when disrupted by heterosexual love, was the subject of many novels, poems, and plays—including *Two Gentlemen of Verona* and some of the SONNETS. The theme of these works was the essential nobility—the spiritual superiority—of such a relationship. Arcite and Palamon had been celebrated in this light before—even before Chaucer—and Shakespeare obviously intended to do so again. The theme is paralleled in Hippolyta's description of the friendship of Theseus and Pirithous in 1.3.26–47, and in Emilia's touching account of her own childhood relationship with the deceased Lavinia in 1.3.49–82.

Emilia herself is another instance of nobility. In Act 1 she and Hippolyta demonstrate their inherent magnanimity in their response to the Queens, and in Act 5 Emilia displays a noble combination of heightened emotion and disinterested concern for honourable propriety, which is pointedly isolated by the playwright in 5.3, when the duel is held off-stage and reflected in her responses.

It is Theseus, however, who is the central figure at the play's opening and again at its end (although he is a less significant figure in Fletcher's portions of the play). His nobility is strongly emphasised. At least in Acts 1 and 5, his actions are strikingly courtly and generous at every turn: towards the Queens, towards his wounded prisoners of war, in his arrangements for the religious petitions of the duellists, and in his responses to them after the duel and its tragic aftermath. Most important, at the play's close, he adopts a pointedly serene and courageous attitude towards the buffetings of fate to which the play's world has been subjected. This stance has great moral weight, not simply because Theseus closes the play—as its highest-ranking figure, he would do that anyway in the theatrical protocol of Shakespeare's day—but because he has been established as a highly noble man.

The play's emphasis on nobility, while part of an old tradition of chivalric heroes in romance literature, also has a more immediate point: in the face of destiny, human beings are helpless, and it is necessary to accept this. In *The Two Noble Kinsmen* the nobility of the title characters lies in their unhesitating acceptance of their situation. Forced by circumstances to fight for Creon, they 'follow / the becking of our chance' (1.2. 115–116). Seized by an obsession, Arcite strives only to 'maintain [his] proceedings' and 'clear [his] own way with the mind and sword / Of a true gentleman' (3.1.53, 56–57). Palamon also accepts his fateful love, with its corollary of enmity to Arcite, 'As 'twere a wreath of roses, [though it] is heavier / Than lead itself, stings more than nettles' (5.1.96–97). The kinsmen's seemingly senseless system of honour provides them with a recourse: in the face of an inexorable destiny, nobility consists in accepting our losses and maintaining our dignity. Although Emilia can cry, 'Is this winning? / O all you heavenly powers, where is your mercy?' (5.3.138–139), she immediately concedes that if the gods' 'wills have said it must be so' (5.3.140), then she must accept it. In the play's last lines, Theseus addresses the divinities, 'O you heavenly charmers, / What things you make of us! . . . Let us be thankful / For that which is, and with you leave dispute[s] / That are above our question' (5.4.131–136). The characters in the play accept their circumstances, and therein lies their significance.

Had Shakespeare written the middle of the play as well as its introduction and close, *The Two Noble Kinsmen* might convey more of the mystery and beauty of human existence, with the power of *The Winter's Tale* or *The Tempest*. As it is, the play is greatly weakened by Fletcher's contribution. Shakespeare's resonant themes are diminished by a series of SUB-PLOTS, and his emphasis on ceremony and ritual is abandoned in favour of melodrama, comedy, and pathos. The story of the Gaoler's Daughter is weakened by the omission of any contact between her and Palamon, and her madness is an unconvincing pastiche of conventional symptoms. The Doctor's lewd prescription is at best vulgar humour; it has no function but comic relief and bears no relation to lunacy, even to the unrealistic madness depicted. The second sub-plot, the presentation of the Schoolmaster's rustic entertainment, barely deserves to be called a sub-plot, for it is merely an excuse to present a popular dance number. Pleasant but irrelevant, it lacks the vigour of the real personalities that fill Shakespeare's equivalent scenes, most notably in *The Winter's Tale*.

More important, Palamon and Arcite are much less impressive figures. In 2.1, when they fall in love with Emilia and begin to quarrel, furthering the plot and

observing the chivalric conventions, they are different men from the pair met in 1.2. Their revulsion at Thebes' corruption—their most prominent characteristic in 1.2—has been replaced by a nostalgia for 'our noble country' (2.1.61). The reliance on personal honour that permitted them to entrust themselves to the 'never-erring arbitrator' (1.2.114) is superseded by thoughts that 'fair-eyed maids shall weep our banishments' (2.1.91). Sentiment takes precedence over character. Shakespeare's maintainance of the cousins' nobility in 3.1 is utterly wasted in 3.3, a scene filled with stale jests about 'the wenches / We have known in our days!' (3.3.28–29). Only in 3.6, where they assist each other before beginning the duel and then face Theseus, do the kinsmen approach their earlier nobility. However, this scene is somewhat redundant thematically—combining the fondness and enmity already presented in 3.1—and Fletcher's poetry is distinctly more pedestrian than Shakespeare's.

*The Two Noble Kinsmen* has its virtues. It contains scattered passages of good poetry in Shakespeare's complex late style, especially in 1.1 and 5.1. The spectacles in 1.1 and 5.1, as well as the funeral procession of 1.5 and dance of 3.5, are theatrically impressive in a good production. Most important, enough of Shakespeare's premise comes through in Acts 1 and 5 that a fine performance permits an audience to experience some sense of awe at the inexorability of the human condition. However, one has only to compare this work with Shakespeare's undiluted efforts to realise how inadequate it is. It may be best seen as a business venture: Shakespeare, about to retire—possibly already living in STRATFORD—was called upon by his company, the KING'S MEN, to collaborate with its rising creative star, Fletcher, and the two produced a workmanlike job, which seems to have had at least a modicum of success. As such, it is an interesting demonstration of early 17th-century tastes, and since it incorporates what is quite possibly Shakespeare's last dramatic writing, it merits more attention than it would otherwise get.

### SOURCES OF THE PLAY

The source for the main plot of *The Two Noble Kinsmen*—the conflict between Arcite and Palamon—was taken by Shakespeare and Fletcher from Geoffrey Chaucer's 'The Knight's Tale', one of the most popular of *The Canterbury Tales* (c. 1482). Chaucer had taken the story from an epic poem by Giovanni BOCCACCIO, *Teseide* (c. 1340). The playwrights altered their source considerably, adding the interrupted wedding in 1.1 (perhaps deriving it from the similar disruption in *A Midsummer Night's Dream*, which was also altered from 'The Knight's Tale'). More significantly, they added the stipulation that the loser of the duel over Emilia must be executed. Another *Dream* source, the 'Life of

Theseus' in PLUTARCH's *Lives* (1579; translated by Thomas NORTH), provided hints for Theseus' depiction, especially in 1.1.

The tragicomic sub-plot of the Gaoler's Daughter was apparently invented for the play, probably by Fletcher, who (according to most scholarly opinion) wrote most of the scenes in which it figures. The lesser sub-plot, the Schoolmaster's presentation of a rustic entertainment, is a restaging of a scene from a popular contemporary masque by Francis BEAUMONT (2), the *Masque of the Inner Temple and Gray's Inn (1613)*.

### TEXT OF THE PLAY

Modern scholars usually believe that *The Two Noble Kinsmen* was written jointly by Shakespeare and John Fletcher, though a few hold that Shakespeare wrote none of it and a few that he wrote it all. While precise agreement is lacking on the authors' distribution of labours, it is generally thought that Shakespeare was responsible for Act 1, 3.1, and all of Act 5 except 5.2. Many variations of this arrangement are proposed, most commonly the addition of 2.1 or the Daughter's soliloquy at the beginning of 3.2, or the deletion of 1.4 and 1.5. Also, some ascribe the remaining portions not to Fletcher but to Francis Beaumont or Philip MASSINGER, or to some combination of the three.

*The Two Noble Kinsmen* was almost certainly written in 1613. The rustic entertainment in 3.5 was taken from a masque by Beaumont that was staged on February 20, 1613; the same troupe of dancers probably performed in both productions. A theatrical character named Palamon—presumably the hero of *The Two Noble Kinsmen*—is mentioned in Ben JONSON's 1614 play, *Bartholomew Fair*, suggesting that Fletcher and Shakespeare's play had already been staged by that date.

*The Two Noble Kinsmen* was the latest to be published of all Shakespeare's plays. It was omitted from the FIRST FOLIO (1623), probably because the editors knew that more than half of it was written by another playwright. The play was first published in a QUARTO edition of 1634 (known as Q1) by John WATERSON. Q1 was ascribed to Shakespeare and Fletcher on its title-page and in its registration with the STATIONERS' COMPANY. Beginning in 1679, however, *The Two Noble Kinsmen* was often published as the work of Beaumont and Fletcher, and it did not appear in a collection of Shakespeare's plays until 1841. It is frequently omitted from modern collections.

Q1 is an excellent edition, with little garbling of text and relatively few misprints. It was based on a PROMPT-BOOK, as is evident from some of the stage directions, which include instructions for the preparation of props. Two actors—'Curtis' and 'T. Tucke'—are named in place of their characters; they are probably Curtis GREVILLE (1) and Thomas TUCKFEILD, which

suggests that the prompt-book was prepared for a production of the 1620s. It may derive from the co-authors' FOUL PAPERS. Q1, as the only early text, has been the basis for all subsequent editions.

### THEATRICAL HISTORY OF THE PLAY

Jonson's 1614 reference (see 'Text of the Play') implies a performance of *The Two Noble Kinsmen* before that date, and the play was considered for performance at the royal court in 1619 (the choice made is unknown). Further, it was still in the King's Men's repertoire in the 1620s, when Q1 was printed from a prompt-book (see 'Text'). The Q1 title-page asserts that the play had been staged at the BLACKFRIARS THEATRE, but no specific record of an early performance is known.

In 1664 William DAVENANT produced his own version of the play, entitled *The Rivals*. He altered it immensely, changing all the names and locations and supplying a new beginning and a new conclusion. He replaced much of the text—including most of what is attributed to Shakespeare—with his own (which was influenced in part by passages from *Macbeth*). The only known performance is that reported by Samuel PEPYS in 1664, but since *The Rivals* was published four years later, it was probably at least somewhat popular.

*The Two Noble Kinsmen* was not seen again until 1928, when it was produced at the OLD VIC THEATRE. It has only been staged occasionally since then, and it remains among the least performed of Shakespeare's works.

**Tybalt**   Character in *Romeo and Juliet*, a cousin of JULIET (1). The belligerent Tybalt insists on fighting for the CAPULET (1) family against the MONTAGUE (1) clan on any occasion. His arrival turns the humorous verbal confrontation between servants in 1.1 into a violent brawl. When he recognises ROMEO at the feast in 1.5, he wants to duel with him on the spot. The next day he fights and kills MERCUTIO, thus inciting Romeo to slay Tybalt in revenge, the act for which he is banished. In Shakespeare's source, Tybalt is merely a name, appearing only to be killed by Romeo in a street fight. The playwright elaborates the character to generate dramatic tension in the first half of the play; Tybalt serves to emphasise the potential for violence that accompanies the developing love between hero and heroine.

**Tyler (1), Richard (1566–1636)**   Resident of STRATFORD and friend of Shakespeare. Tyler, two years younger than Shakespeare, probably knew Shakespeare at the Stratford grammar school, for his father, as an alderman, was entitled to send his children there without charge. However, his most significant connection with Shakespeare lies in his removal from the playwright's will. Though he was originally one of seven close friends given bequests of money to buy a commemorative ring, Tyler's name was scratched out and replaced with that of Hamnet SADLER. This may have been Shakespeare's response to Tyler's involvement in a scandal: as a collector of relief funds after the great Stratford fire of 1614, Tyler was charged with enriching himself. However, he apparently continued to be a friend of the family, participating in the transfer of the BLACKFRIARS GATEHOUSE to Susanna SHAKESPEARE (14) Hall in 1618.

**Tyler (2), Thomas (1826–1902)**   British scholar. Tyler was best known as a biblical scholar, but he also wrote several works on Shakespearean topics, most notably *The Philosophy of Hamlet* (1874). In his edition of the SONNETS (1890), Tyler identified Mary FITTON as Shakespeare's 'Dark Lady'. This theory was popularised by Frank HARRIS (1), but scholars now generally reject it.

**Tyre**   City of the ancient Seleucid Empire on the coast of what is now Lebanon, the setting for three scenes of *Pericles, Prince of Tyre*. The title character is the ruler of Tyre, and 1.2–3 and 2.4 are set within interiors located in the city. Shakespeare simply followed his source in placing his hero in Tyre, and the actual Mediterranean seaport is in no way present in the text of the play.

Of cities surviving today, Tyre is among the most ancient, as it has existed since prehistoric times. A famous producer of dyes—'Tyrian purple' cloth was proverbially rich and fashionable—and a significant port, Tyre was a wealthy city-state that maintained its independence while paying tribute to the succession of empires that ruled the region after its conquest by Alexander the Great in 332 B.C. At the time of Antiochus—the play's only historical figure—Tyre was actually a republic, but Shakespeare was not concerned with Middle Eastern history, and his Tyre is merely an exotic locale, appropriate to a tale of romantic adventures.

**Tyrell (Tirell), Sir James (c. 1450–1502)**   Historical figure and character in *Richard III*, an unscrupulous and ambitious nobleman who agrees to arrange the murder of the PRINCE (5) of Wales and his brother the Duke of YORK (7). RICHARD III, directed to Tyrell by a PAGE (1), commissions the killings in 4.2. At the beginning of 4.3, Tyrell returns to report that the deed has been accomplished by his hired ruffians.

The historical Tyrell was not the unknown minor aristocrat depicted by Shakespeare. He had served the Yorkist cause and been knighted at the battle of TEWKESBURY, and, at the time the princes were imprisoned, he was Richard's Master of Horse. After the accession of Henry VII, Tyrell continued to hold military posts until he was executed, on unrelated charges, in 1502. He was reported to have admitted at that time to arrangeing the murders, and Shakespeare follows Thomas MORE's account of his alleged confession. Modern scholars generally find the story unconvincing, however, and the mystery of the princes' disappearance (and probable death) remains unsolved.

**Tyrian Sailor**   Minor character in *Pericles*, a seaman on PERICLES' ship. As 5.1 opens the Tyrian Sailor tells Pericles' aide, HELICANUS, of the visit of LYSIMACHUS, the governor of MYTILENE. He then relays Helicanus' request for courtiers to greet the governor, and he finally introduces the visitor to Helicanus. This busy episode points up the formality with which Pericles is surrounded, and adds to the ceremonious atmosphere of the play.

The designation of this character as Tyrian is the consequence, first, of the QUARTO edition of the play, which provided two sailors. Later, scholars presumed that one of them was in Lysimachus' service and was thus Mytilenian; the other, Pericles' sailor, was therefore distinguished in like fashion. Editors have varied in their distribution of the episode's lines: sometimes 5.1.11–13 are given to the Mytilenian Sailor, but he is often dropped, and the Tyrian (or First) Sailor speaks all the lines. Sometimes a First and Second Sailor are provided who are both assumed to be Tyrian.

# U

**Udall, Nicholas (1504–1556)** English author and playwright, author of the earliest English COMEDY. Udall translated the Latin plays of Terence (c. 185–159 B.C.) (with John HIGGINS) and essays of the great humanist Erasmus (c. 1456–1536). He also wrote theological works, along with a number of plays, all but one of them lost. His *Ralph Roister Doister* (c. 1553, published 1566) is generally considered the earliest English comedy; only a single copy of it survived in 1825, when its importance was recognised by John Payne COLLIER (2). In boisterous rhymed dialogue, Udall borrowed elements from Terence, PLAUTUS, and crude English farces to create a distinctively original work. Among other comic touches, Udall invented a device—the mischievously mispunctuated reading of a document—that Shakespeare used in *A Midsummer Night's Dream* (5.1.108–116). Udall was discharged from his position as headmaster of Eton for homosexuality, but recovered his social standing sufficiently to find favour with Queen Mary (ruled 1553–1558), who collaborated with him in a translation, licenced him to write plays, and provided him with another headmastership, shortly before his death.

**Ulysses** Legendary figure and character in *Troilus and Cressida,* a Greek leader in the TROJAN WAR. Ulysses is a voice of sanity among the Greeks, who are fighting a dishonourable war for a pointless cause. Yet such is the corruption of the world of the play that Ulysses fails to influence his fellows and, indeed, gives up his own ideals. In both his idealism and his failure he corresponds to HECTOR among the Trojans.

However, the common sense and political wisdom of Ulysses provide a background against which to view the corrupt world of the play. He diagnoses the Greek failure in the war as due to their departure from strict adherence to a system of social hierarchy, like that of the 'heavens themselves' (1.3.85). However, in his effort to convince ACHILLES that he should return to the battle he abandons this idea and instead encourages the reluctant warrior to consider the loss of status he risks by permitting AJAX to receive the laurels he could receive himself. In giving up his ideals to promote this rivalry, Ulysses reveals himself to be a pragmatist, but the event contributes to our sense of disorder in the play's world. Moreover, his compromise fails in its purpose, for Achilles again withdraws from the battle, and only Patroclus' death finally brings his sword into play. Ulysses, though wise, is no less subject to the chances of war than anyone else.

Ulysses' judgements of the other characters, though firmly stated, are distinctly, if slightly, mistaken, adding to the play's network of self-deception and error. In 4.5, on the strength of his first impression, he declares CRESSIDA to be a prostitute; while he has perceived her sexuality, he has misread it, for she is merely a frankly sensual woman whom circumstance has placed in temptation's way. Ulysses praises DIOMEDES for a spirit that 'In aspiration lifts him from the earth' (4.5.16); he recognises an intensity of purpose, but he fails to see that Diomedes' energies are to be expended on an extremely earthly aspiration: the seduction of Cressida. Similarly, Ulysses says of Troilus that he 'gives not till judgement guide his bounty' (4.5.102), yet we know that Troilus has committed himself to Cressida without judgement. However, Troilus is an idealist in love, and Ulysses' opinion is not wrong, merely uninformed. We are made aware that wisdom and objectivity are no guarantee of knowledge in the world of the play.

Ulysses (better known by his Greek name, Odysseus) is a principal character in the *Iliad* of HOMER. He is noted for his wisdom and good sense as a strategist, and he is also a valiant warrior. He is the central figure in the *Iliad*'s successor, the *Odyssey,* which recounts his long series of adventures after the war. In Homer, Odysseus was famous for craftiness—reflected in the play in Thersites' reference to him as 'that . . . dog-fox Ulysses' (5.4.11). Although he lies fluently when he needs to he is essentially honourable. In later tradition, however, especially in the ancient Greek dramatists, he appears as a cowardly rascal. He was worshipped as a demi-god in the cults of later antiquity.

**Umfrevile, Sir John (active 1403)** Historical figure mentioned in *2 Henry IV* as an ally of the rebel Earl of NORTHUMBERLAND (1), perhaps the original speaker of some lines assigned to Lord BARDOLPH (2). In 1.1, as TRAVERS approaches WARKWORTH CASTLE with news of the battle of SHREWSBURY, Lord Bardolph tells of having encountered Travers and given him such news as he had. When he arrives, Travers reports that he met Umfrevile en route and that Umfrevile had gone ahead of him with his news, which he accordingly omits, proceeding to tell of a later encounter. The QUARTO edition of the play (1600) gives a speech prefix to Umfrevile at 1.1.161—later editors give the line to either Lord Bardolph or Travers—and in 1.3.81 Lord Bardolph reveals his ignorance of information provided in this scene. Scholars conclude that Lord Bardolph's part in 1.1 may originally have been written as Umfrevile's, and that Umfrevile's lines were later assigned to someone else in order to eliminate one character as an economy measure for an acting company.

**Underhill, William (1556–1597)**   Landowner in and around STRATFORD, the seller of NEW PLACE to Shakespeare. Underhill was a member of the gentry who held a remunerative position in the county court at Warwick and had inherited New Place and much other land at the age of 14. He sold New Place to Shakespeare in May 1597, but in July he was poisoned by his eldest son, Fulke (b. 1579), who was executed for the murder in 1599. The Underhill properties were sequestered by the state, and when the second son, Hercules (b. 1581), came of age in 1602, he had to reconfirm the sale of New Place to Shakespeare.

**Underwood, John (d. 1624)**   English actor, member of the KING'S MEN. Underwood was one of the 26 men listed in the FIRST FOLIO as 'Principall Actors' in Shakespeare's plays, though no specific Shakespearean role is associated with him. He and William OSTLER (2) probably became members of the King's Men at the same time, replacing William SLY (2) and Laurence FLETCHER (3), who died in 1608. When Underwood died, he held shares in the GLOBE, CURTAIN, and BLACK-FRIARS THEATRES. He left them to his five children, all minors, for whom his fellow actor Henry CONDELL acted as trustee.

**University Wits**   Group of English playwrights credited with the development of ELIZABETHAN DRAMA in the 1580s. Called the University Wits by modern scholars, these men were distinguished by their superior educations in a profession that had always been somewhat disreputable at best (see ELIZABETHAN THEATRE). The most notable of them were Oxford graduates Thomas LODGE, John LYLY, and George PEELE, and Cambridge alumni Robert GREENE (2), Thomas NASHE, and Christopher MARLOWE (1). These men purposefully went beyond the didactic chronicles and shapeless, knockabout farces of the existing English stage. They combined the influences of ancient Roman drama, the medieval MORALITY PLAY, ACADEMIC DRAMA, and contemporary Italian and French drama, to create plays with intelligible structure, vigorous

plotting, and vital poetry. The plays of the University Wits were very popular and helped establish the flourishing theatrical world that Shakespeare entered as a young man.

**Ur-Hamlet**   Name given to a lost Elizabethan play resembling *Hamlet* and believed to have been used by Shakespeare as a source. Several references prove that there was an earlier play involving HAMLET. In 1589 Thomas NASHE, mocking plays derived from SENECA and especially those of Thomas KYD, referred to '. . . whole Hamlets, I should say handfuls of tragical speeches'. The context of this remark leads most scholars to conclude that Kyd wrote the *Ur-Hamlet*. A performance of a play called *Hamlet* by Shakespeare's acting company, the CHAMBERLAIN'S MEN, is recorded in 1594, and a famous reference by Thomas LODGE printed two years later implies that the work was still current and provides an image from it: '. . . ghost which cried so miserably . . . *Hamlet, revenge*'.

Little more is known of the play's contents, for no text survives. However, it presumably followed the tale by François BELLEFOREST that was probably its major source. It seems it included most, if not all, of the following elements: Hamlet seeking revenge against his uncle for the murder of his father and the seduction of his mother; his feigned madness and his romantic involvement with a woman; his dramatic encounter with his mother during which he kills a spy; his exile to England and the trick whereby he arranges for the execution of his escorts instead of himself; and his killing of his uncle in a long-deferred vengeance.

Thus the *Ur-Hamlet* was plainly a REVENGE PLAY like Kyd's *The Spanish Tragedy* (1588–1589), to which it may have been a companion piece. Scholars comparing *Hamlet* and *The Spanish Tragedy* find further clues concerning the *Ur-Hamlet*: some elements of *The Spanish Tragedy*, a play that also centres on a postponed revenge, suggest themes found in Shakespeare's *Hamlet* in more developed forms, and it is thought these elements may also have been used by Kyd in the *Ur-Hamlet*. Thus, the *Ur-Hamlet* may have included a procrastinating Hamlet who dies at the play's close, an heroine whose love for Hamlet is opposed by her family and who eventually becomes insane and commits suicide, and a play within a play, all of which resemble components of *The Spanish Tragedy* yet are not present in Belleforest. Further, the sub-plot in which Hamlet kills the father of the man who kills him and of the woman who loves him is not in Belleforest and thus may have been in the *Ur-Hamlet*. However, Shakespeare may very well have devised this himself, and *The Spanish Tragedy* may simply have been an influence on *Hamlet* rather than containing the same ideas as the *Ur-Hamlet*.

One further minor source of information may exist. DER BESTRAFTE BRUDERMORD, a German version of

*Hamlet* gleaned from the recollections of English actors who toured Germany in the 17th century, offers certain minor details which do not come from *Hamlet* yet correspond to Belleforest, and it is thought these may have been remembered by actors who had also performed in the *Ur-Hamlet*.

**Ur-Shrew** Hypothetical play sometimes assumed to be the source for both *The Taming of the Shrew* and THE TAMING OF A SHREW. The *Ur-Shrew* is usually attributed to Shakespeare, but it is presumed to have been revised by the playwright in order to incorporate the SUB-PLOT involving BIANCA (1) and her suitors. The revised play, according to this theory, is *The Taming of the Shrew*, whereas *The Taming of a Shrew* is a BAD QUARTO of the *Ur-Shrew*, whose original text has been lost. The *Ur-Shrew* hypothesis exists to account for inconsistencies between *A Shrew* and *The Shrew*, especially the differences between their sub-plots. However, most recent scholarship finds that these questions can be resolved without assuming the existence of a play for which no evidence exists, and the *Ur-Shrew* theory has generally been rejected in favour of the idea that *The Shrew* is Shakespeare's original play and *A Shrew* a Bad Quarto of it.

**Ursula** Minor character in *Much Ado About Nothing*, attendant to HERO. A cheerful member of LEONATO's court, Ursula has no important function and little personality. She flirts with the aged ANTONIO (3) at the MASQUE in 2.1, and she helps her mistress fool BEATRICE into believing that BENEDICK loves her in 3.1.

**Urswick, Sir Christopher** Character in *Richard III*. See CHRISTOPHER (2).

**Usher** Minor character in *Coriolanus*, a servant of VALERIA. The Usher accompanies the lady he serves when she visits VIRGILIA and VOLUMNIA, in 1.3. He does not speak and serves merely to indicate the prestige and wealth of his mistress. He is often dropped from productions of the play. In medieval and RENAISSANCE times an usher was a servant whose function was to precede his employer and open doors, prepare seats, etc.

# V

**Valentine (1)**  Minor character in *Titus Andronicus*. Mentioned only in a stage direction, Valentine helps to capture CHIRON and DEMETRIUS (1) in 5.2.

**Valentine (2)**  One of the title characters in *The Two Gentlemen of Verona*, the lover of SILVIA, whom his disloyal friend PROTEUS attempts to steal. Valentine is both a romantic leading man and an object of fun. At first resistant to love, he then becomes an inept suitor. Once Silvia has given him her affection, he naïvely brags of it to Proteus, whose plotting quickly sends Valentine into exile. Later, after he rescues Silvia from an attempted rape by Proteus, only JULIA's intervention prevents him from inanely giving away his beloved to the man from whom he has just saved her.

**Valentine (3)**  Minor character in *Twelfth Night*, a follower of Duke ORSINO of ILLYRIA. Valentine serves as Orsino's emissary to OLIVIA before VIOLA, disguised as Cesario, takes over the job. His name is appropriate to this task, and his flowery language in 1.1.24–32 matches his master's. In this speech he introduces the audience to the play's first development, Orsino's unrequited love for Olivia, and at the opening of 1.4 he informs Cesario that Orsino is fond of him, thus introducing a major complication of the plot.

**Valeria**  Minor character in *Coriolanus*, a friend of CORIOLANUS' wife, VIRGILIA. Valeria is a cheerful, but somewhat insensitive young noblewoman who visits Virgilia in 1.3. Her bland acceptance of the Roman aristocratic ideal, combined with her charming vivacity, contrasts forcefully with the melancholy of her friend, who is distressed by the martial fervour of her mother-in-law, VOLUMNIA. Valeria describes the BOY (8), son of Coriolanus and Virgilia, in 1.3.57–65, and she is not aware that she presents a disturbing picture of the Boy killing a butterfly with his teeth. She does not speak in the three remaining scenes in which she appears, having served her function as a foil for Virgilia.

Valeria accompanies Volumnia and Virgilia on their crucial mission to dissuade Coriolanus from invading Rome, and though she does not speak, she is described in 5.3.64–67 as a particularly noble Roman woman. This allusion reflects the greater role that Valeria plays in Shakespeare's source, PLUTARCH's *Lives*, where she stirs Volumnia to action. However, the playwright preferred to have Volumnia stand alone, and Valeria's role remains minor.

**Valerius**  Minor character in *The Two Noble Kinsmen*, a gentleman of THEBES and friend of ARCITE and PALAMON. In 1.2 Valerius informs his friends of the challenge to King Creon of Thebes issued by Duke THESEUS (2) of ATHENS, who intends to conquer Thebes and avenge the king's evil behaviour in refusing burial to his defeated foes. Valerius thereby provides the link between the two title characters and Athens, where, as prisoners of war, they will enact the main plot of the drama. Having fulfilled this function, Valerius disappears from the play.

**Variorum edition**  Annotated edition of an author's work. The name comes from the Latin *cum notis variorum*, meaning 'with the notes of various [people]'. Several editions of Shakespeare's works are so designated, but in the 20th century the term usually refers to the New Variorum, edited by H. H. FURNESS and his successors, and published beginning in 1871.

The First Variorum was based on the 1778 edition of George STEEVENS' Shakespeare, which was posthumously expanded and published by Isaac REED in 1803. The collected essays and notes included in this 21-volume work offer a copious representation of 18th-century Shakespearean scholarship, though the edition omits the playwright's poems. The Second Variorum (1813) was simply a reprint of the First, but the Third Variorum incorporated the work of Edmond MALONE. James BOSWELL the younger completed Malone's second edition of Shakespeare's works after the older scholar's death in 1812 and grafted it onto Reed's work. The Third Variorum, also known as 'Boswell's Malone', was published in 1821, also in 21 volumes. It encompasses annotated texts of all the plays and the poems, Malone's life of the playwright (a basic reference for all subsequent biographers of Shakespeare), his history of the English stage, and other materials.

The New Variorum consists of one or more volumes

per play, two for the SONNETS, and one for the other poetry. Furness had produced 18 volumes before he died in 1912. The work was completed in 1953 by a series of successors, including his son H. H. Furness Jr, and J. Q. ADAMS.

**Varrius (1)**  Minor character in *Measure for Measure,* a follower of the DUKE (9) of Vienna. Varrius is addressed by the Duke in 4.5 and is mentioned in the stage direction opening 5.1, the Duke's formal entry to Vienna, but he does not speak, nor does he appear in the list of characters in the first published text of the play, in the FIRST FOLIO. Some scholars believe that this is evidence that the play had been cut before it was published. On the other hand, Varrius may be seen as a representative of the Duke's entourage whose tiny part in 4.5 prepares the audience to perceive the Duke's return in 5.1 as a ceremonious occasion.

**Varrius (2)**  Minor character in *Antony and Cleopatra,* a follower of POMPEY (2). In 2.1 Varrius brings the disquieting news to Pompey, MENAS, and MENECRATES that ANTONY has left Egypt to rejoin the coalition against Pompey. Varrius' function is to introduce a development of the plot.

**Varro (Varrus)**  Minor character in *Julius Caesar,* a soldier in the army of BRUTUS (4). In 4.3 Varro and CLAUDIUS (1) are ordered to sleep in the same tent with Brutus to be available as messengers They sleep through the visitation of the GHOST (2) of CAESAR (1), and Brutus wakes them to confirm that they have seen nothing.

In the first edition of *Julius Caesar,* that in the FIRST FOLIO, Varro's name is rendered as Varrus, and some modern editors follow the Folio in this respect. Others, however, use Varro, which is correct in Latin and appears in Shakespeare's source, NORTH's translation of PLUTARCH's *Lives.*

**Varro's Servant**  Either of two minor characters in *Timon of Athens,* employees of Varro, a creditor of TIMON. In 2.2 Varro's Servant joins two colleagues, ISIDORE'S SERVANT and CAPHIS. Together they approach Timon and his STEWARD (2), hoping for repayment of the debts Timon owes their masters, but they are put off. In 3.4 two of Varro's servants—distinguished in speech headings as First Varro's Servant and Second Varro's Servant—join LUCIUS' SERVANT, HORTENSIUS, PHILOTUS, and TITUS (2) on the same errand, again without success. In the latter scene the Servants express their reluctance to solicit for their greedy masters who have benefited in the past from Timon's generosity, but are now merciless.

**Varrus**  Character in *Julius Caesar.* See VARRO.

**Vaughan, Sir Thomas (d. 1483)**  Historical figure and minor character in *Richard III,* an ally of Queen ELIZABETH (2). Vaughan appears only to be executed by Richard (see RICHARD III) in 3.3. In going to his death, he speaks one line.

The historical Thomas Vaughan was a member of the official household of the PRINCE (5) of Wales, son of Elizabeth and King EDWARD IV. The dying king had stipulated that Richard should rule for the boy when he inherited the crown, but Vaughan participated in an attempt to unseat Richard as Protector. He was executed as a result, although the play makes his condemnation seem arbitrary.

**Vaughan Williams, Ralph (1872–1958)**  English composer. Best known for his symphonies and choral works, Vaughan Williams also wrote several operas, among them *Sir John in Love* (1929), based on *The Merry Wives of Windsor.* He often set poetry to music, including many passages from Shakespeare. Among his best known Shakespearean works is a 1951 setting for PROSPERO's famous 'revels' speech (*Tempest* 4.1. 148–148), and he declared that the last movement of his famous Sixth Symphony was based on this passage. He composed music for many of Shakespeare's songs, beginning as early as 1891 and returning to them often. In 1913, he composed incidental music for *2 Henry IV, Henry V, The Merry Wives of Windsor, Richard II,* and *Richard III,* and in 1944 wrote the score for a radio play of *Richard II.*

**Vaux (1), Sir Nicholas (d. 1523)**  Historical figure and minor character in *Henry VIII,* member of the court of King HENRY VIII. In 2.1 Vaux, with Sir Thomas LOVELL (2), escorts the Duke of BUCKINGHAM (1) to the TOWER OF LONDON. He speaks only three lines, suggesting that the prisoner should be treated in accordance with his rank, but Buckingham contradicts him, humbly accepting the loss of his duchy as his fate. Vaux's tiny part helps point up the virtues of Buckingham, which contrast with the evil of his enemy, Cardinal WOLSEY.

Vaux's father, Sir William VAUX (3), who appears in *2 Henry VI,* had lost his estates for having supported King HENRY VI in the WARS OF THE ROSES, but they had been returned to Sir Nicholas by Henry VII. Nicholas Vaux's son was the courtier-poet Thomas VAUX (2).

**Vaux (2), Sir Thomas (1509–1556)**  English poet. Vaux was a cultivated aristocrat who was a member of the courts of several English monarchs, beginning with HENRY VIII. Although his poetry was superior to that of most of his fellow courtiers, he is noteworthy today only for having written 'The aged lover renounces love', which appears, in a very garbled form, as the GRAVE-DIGGER's song in *Hamlet* (5.1.61–64, 70–73, 92–95). Vaux' poem, said to have been written on his deathbed, was still well known in Shakespeare's day as a popular song.

Vaux' father, Sir Nicholas VAUX (1), likewise a courtier, appears in *Henry VIII*, and his grandfather, Sir William VAUX (3), has a role in *2 Henry VI*.

**Vaux (3), Sir William (d. 1471)**   Minor character in *2 Henry VI*, a messenger who announces the terminal illness of CARDINAL (1) Beaufort in 3.2. Vaux gives a vivid account of the Cardinal's guilty raving about the murder of the Duke of GLOUCESTER (4). The historical Sir William Vaux was a minor member of the entourage of the Cardinal. He later died fighting for HENRY VI at the battle of TEWKESBURY. His son was the Sir Nicholas VAUX (1) who appears in *Henry VIII*, and his grandson was the poet Sir Thomas VAUX (2).

**Venice**   City in northern Italy, setting for *The Merchant of Venice* and the opening scenes of *Othello*. In Shakespeare's day Venice was already famous for the sumptuous beauty that still astonishes the world today. A great commercial centre, it stood for luxuriant culture and the power of money, and Shakespeare pictures it vividly—without describing it—by presenting his audience with its wealthy and self-confident citizens and exotic foreign figures. Significantly, in both *The Merchant* and *Othello* the prosperous society of Venice relies on an outsider—one a Jew and the other a Moor—who is not fully admitted to the society's fellowship and whose alien status is important to the drama's central conflict.

Venice was present in Shakespeare's sources, but he may also have been influenced by the image Elizabethans had of the fabled city in developing his themes of generosity and greed in *The Merchant*, and of human dignity versus envy and malice in *Othello*. Venice is frequently presented in Elizabethan literature as a symbol for a hypercommercial society in which the acquisitive instinct rules to the detriment of finer impulses. Shakespeare was not concerned with presenting an accurate Venetian setting, and he plainly invoked this stereotype, especially in *The Merchant of Venice*, where all of his Venetians express themselves in financial and commercial terms. For example, the clown LAUNCELOT employs legalistic language in 2.2; BASSANIO claims PORTIA in mercantile terms in 3.2. 139–148; and Portia can remark of her lover, 'Since you are dear bought, I will love you dear' (3.2.312). The point is less prominent in *Othello*, but the envious IAGO 'know[s his] price' (1.1.11), and RODERIGO's mode of courtship consists of conspicuous expense. Even the despairing OTHELLO compares his dead DESDEMONA to 'a pearl . . . Richer than [a] tribe' (5.2.348–349), and the saintly Desdemona says of the crucial loss of Othello's love token, 'I had rather lose my purse / Full of crusadoes' (Portuguese gold coins) (3.4.21–22).

Of course, such characteristics are not difficult to find in any cosmopolitan society. Venice was certainly a colourful and exotic locale with its commercial connections to the remote and glamorous East. It was a likely place to encounter such strange sights as a Rialto money-lender in his 'Jewish gaberdine' (*Merchant*, 1.3.107) or a Moorish general, but it surely seemed familiar in its vices to the Londoners of Shakespeare's day. In fact, Venice's success as a commercially based empire was about to be imitated on a larger scale by England. The wealthy and cultivated classes in 16th-century London regarded Venice as something of a prototype of their own developing society, and the satirical thrust of *The Merchant*'s Venice was surely not lost on its original audiences.

**Ventidius (1), Publius (c. 90–38 B.C.)**   Historical figure and minor character in *Antony and Cleopatra*, a Roman general. In 2.3 Ventidius is sent by Mark ANTONY to put down a rebellion in Parthia; in 3.1, he has accomplished his task. He appears with SILIUS, who encourages him to pursue the fleeing Parthians and conquer all of Mesopotamia. Ventidius replies with a lesson in military politics: he will not attempt to do as well against the Parthians as he might, for if he does too well, he may seem to show up his superior, Antony, who may seek vengeance and destroy his career. These remarks stress the cynicism demanded by the Roman world of politics, a cool and unemotional calculation that Antony rejects in his infatuation with CLEOPATRA.

The historical Ventidius was famous in his own day for his extraordinary rise in society amid the chronic turbulence of the time. As an infant he had been enslaved, for his family—from a pre-Roman tribe—had been involved in the last attempted revolt against Roman dominance in Italy. After serving as a Roman soldier, he became a contractor of military supplies. Like many defeated Italians, Ventidius became a backer of Julius CAESAR (1) in the Roman civil wars, and he was granted a senate seat as a reward; after Caesar's assassination he allied himself with Antony. However, despite his caution in victory—which Shakespeare took from PLUTARCH's *Lives*—his success against the Parthians ended his career. He returned to Rome where his triumph was extravagantly celebrated, but Antony discharged him amid rumours of bribes taken from a Mesopotamian ruler, and he died shortly thereafter.

**Ventidius (2)**   Minor character in *Timon of Athens*, an ungrateful recipient of TIMON's generosity. In 1.1 Timon sends the money needed to free Ventidius from debtor's prison, and in 1.2 Ventidius thanks him and offers to return the money, but Timon refuses repayment. Ventidius observes: 'A noble spirit!' (1.2. 14), and he does not speak again. However, when

Timon has bankrupted himself through extravagant generosity, he sends to several friends for help, and Ventidius—who has in the meantime inherited a fortune—is among them. Act 3 begins with Timon being repudiated by a series of his miserly friends, in the course of which it is mentioned that Ventidius has also denied assistance. Ventidius does not reappear after 1.2, and he is simply an emblem of the callous greed that permeates the aristocracy of ATHENS.

Commentators have often remarked on the oddity of Shakespeare's having so dramatically established Ventidius' indebtedness, only to omit, on-stage, his refusal to help his benefactor. In fact, this peculiarity has been offered as evidence that the authorship of the play is divided: Shakespeare may have introduced Ventidius' story and another playwright disposed of it too casually, or vice versa. However, if this is an error—and a case can be made that the anticlimax is effective because it reinforces Act 3's message—then it may simply reflect the fact that *Timon* is an incomplete work, as most scholars believe.

**Venus and Adonis**  Narrative poem by Shakespeare that tells of the goddess Venus' infatuation for a mortal human, the young hunter Adonis. In erotic and humorous passages, Venus courts the youth, attempting to persuade him to make love. Adonis resists her advances, being unmoved by what he sees as simple lust; he prefers to go hunting. The next day, at dawn, Venus discovers the body of the dead Adonis, who has been killed by a wild boar. The poem closes with her lament.

*Venus and Adonis* has less relevance for most modern readers than do Shakespeare's dramas. Conventions that largely lack meaning today contribute to the overall tone and texture of the poem, and the work is now often perceived as frigidly artificial and remote from real human experience. But although its characterisation and plotting are feeble by comparison with the plays, *Venus* boasts many charming passages. Moreover, and much more important, the poem does in fact deal with a humanly significant theme, sexual love.

Shakespeare dedicated *Venus and Adonis* to the Earl of SOUTHAMPTON (2)—a classically educated and highly sophisticated patron of the arts—thus indicating his intention that the poem be received as a fashionable exercise in delicate eroticism, deftly constructed in an artificial and elaborately rhetorical classical manner. From the literature available to Elizabethan readers, the poet turned to the best source for such a poem, the works of the Latin master of erotic poetry, OVID, which he probably knew both in Latin and in the English translation by Arthur GOLDING (1567). In Ovid's *Metamorphoses*, Adonis reciprocates Venus' love, but Shakespeare followed a variant of the tale that was also well known in England, incorporating elements from other Ovidian stories and portraying the mortal's rejection of the goddess. The epigraph to the dedication—promising a work meant for a select audience—comes from another work by Ovid, *Amores*. Classical literature was entirely familiar to 16th-century readers, and, in associating his work with Ovid's, Shakespeare was plainly declaring his intention to be similarly witty, charming, and delicately sensual. Some details, especially the episode of the stallion and the mare, were probably inspired by passages in the *Georgics* of VIRGIL, the greatest of Latin poets.

Shakespeare was probably also influenced by *Hero and Leander*, by Christopher MARLOWE (1). The date of composition of this poem is unknown—it was unfinished when the poet died in early 1593—and it was not published until 1598, but Shakespeare had probably read it in manuscript; certainly *Hero and Leander*'s unprecedented combination of wit and luxuriant sensuousness was unique before Shakespeare wrote his poem. Like *Hero and Leander*, *Venus and Adonis* was scandalously popular, to judge by the many references to it, both delighted and disapproving. It has often been speculated that the ferocity of the controversy impelled Shakespeare to follow *Venus* with a much primmer narrative poem, *The Rape of Lucrece*.

*Venus and Adonis* may be seen as simply a trivial entertainment, intended to attract the patronage of a cultured aristocrat. Or the poem may be given more weight and viewed as a scintillating example of RENAISSANCE art, an evocation of ancient ideals equivalent to, say, the paintings of Botticelli. Still, the thematic richness of the plays, which even at their weakest are intent on exploring ideas and human relations, suggest that a work by Shakespeare must have more point than simple entertainment or beauty. However, the moral to be found in *Venus and Adonis* has proven elusive, and the poem has been assessed in many different ways. Some critics feel that *Venus* is a failure, an immature effort that is confused and uncertain because the author was himself unclear about the nature of love and lust and therefore resorted to humour to patch up his undeveloped work. Others see the poem as a delightfully erotic comedy, a celebration of sexual passion. Although Adonis dies, his story is couched in humour, and his death is not a tragic one—his corpse vanishes into air and his blood becomes the goddess' nosegay. Still other readers find one of two tragic lessons in *Venus*. Accepting the erotic passages as indicative of the poet's attitude, one may see Adonis' death as the pathetic outcome of his cold and foolish aversion to love and sex. On the other hand, the horror of his death and Venus' condemnation of love at the end of the poem may be thought to condemn lust as a primal force of destruction.

All of these viewpoints offer salient truths about the poem; as is so often the case when considering Shakespeare, the most productive response combines various theories. Like *Romeo and Juliet* and *Antony and Cleo-*

*patra* in particular, *Venus* deals with perhaps the most difficult emotion to understand, love, and all three works present an essential paradox: love, an obvious manifestation of an elemental life force, is often tied to a self-destructive inclination towards death. Thus two irreconcilable attitudes about love are established, and the poem, like the plays, attempts to resolve the opposition between them.

One must start with a pervasive and obviously positive aspect of *Venus and Adonis:* the poem is unquestionably funny. Venus' overbearing seizure of Adonis, beginning in line 25, is a virtual parody of male aggressiveness; the description of the stolid Adonis as a tiny, terrified waterbird (lines 86–87) provides a droll juxtaposition; Venus' erotic characterisation of her own body as landscape (lines 229–240) is sufficiently amusing to extract a smile even from Adonis. Even at a moment of revulsion, as Venus first sees Adonis' corpse, the famous simile of the shrinking snail (lines 1033–1036) offers an irresistibly whimsical image that softens the blow; the situation is not permitted to inspire horror.

In a similar spirit, the poem boasts frequent vivid and sensual representations of country life—from such minor images as the comparison of the captive Adonis to a trapped bird (lines 67–68) or that of Venus to a 'milch doe, whose swelling dugs do ache' (line 875), to the more elaborate descriptions of the boar (lines 619–630), the boar hounds (lines 913–924), and the hunted hare (lines 679–708). Particularly impressive is the fully developed anecdote of Adonis' stallion in pursuit of a mare (lines 258–324), the last couplet of which is itself a handsome miniature landscape. Venus' repeated enthusiasm for physical love (e.g., in lines 19–24) is part of the same charming presentation of the sensual life. The poem offers an idyllic world populated by delightful plants and animals, needing only the consummated love of man and goddess—or so Venus asserts—to complete the picture.

However, a distinctly darker strain complicates matters. Venus' attraction to Adonis is not simply a delightful infatuation, but rather a fever of the soul; she tears at her beloved like a bird of prey (lines 55–58) and, when she refuses to stop kissing him, he is compared to a forcibly tamed hawk and a deer pursued to exhaustion (lines 560–561). Conversely, Adonis rejects not only Venus herself but also her idea of love, which he equates with lust, in a passage (lines 787–798) strikingly reminiscent of Sonnet 129, which decries lust as 'Th' expense of spirit in a waste of shame' (see SONNETS). For Venus, love is entirely involved with physical life, but it is only in death that Adonis can find love, as he conceives it; he says, 'I know not love . . . unless it be a boar, and then I chase it' (lines 409–410). Thus Venus and Adonis represent opposing points of view: the goddess finds fulfilment in the

delights of sensuality, while the mortal man conceives of an ideal spiritual state.

We can see that the poem often supports Adonis' position by subtly undercutting that of Venus, and vice versa. The comical sight of Venus plucking Adonis from his horse (line 30) reflects the more serious point that her powers of seduction are so inadequate that she is reduced to this undignified action. When Venus argues—as Shakespeare himself does in several of the sonnets—that love is the most appropriate human activity because it leads to reproduction (lines 163–174), she seems to represent the life force, but in the very next line all such high purpose is lost, as 'the love-sick queen began to sweat'. Even one of Venus' most delightful tactics—her somewhat lewd yet humorous description of herself in terms of landscape (lines 229–240)—results only in her further humiliation; Adonis smiles in disdain, she is reduced to helplessness by his dimples, and the poet remarks, 'being mad before, how doth she now for wits?' (line 249). However, Adonis' ideal is similarly weakened. Although he rejects the animal nature of love that Venus extols, he is himself associated with animals throughout the poem, from the early parallels between him and birds, mentioned above, through the symbolism of his runaway horse as a male lover, to his almost sexual union with the boar in mutual death. The attitude of each protagonist is therefore compromised by the manner in which it is presented.

Thus the apparently hopeless dichotomy between Venus and Adonis is resolved even as it is presented, for Shakespeare's ultimate purpose here is to present opposing views as intertwined principles. The poem opens with a paradoxical introduction of the two protagonists: in the first stanza 'rose-cheek'd Adonis' is contrasted with 'sick-thoughted Venus' (lines 3, 5). A standard romantic convention—lovesick male pursues uninterested woman—is here reversed, and this switch is at the heart of Shakespeare's strategy. Venus is a parody of a typical male suitor, while Adonis is presented in a traditionally feminine role, a sex object, especially in lines 541–564, where he is virtually raped. He is also associated with imagery suggestive of women's physical charms, as in lines 9, 50, 247–248, and, most strikingly, 1114–1116, where the boar's death blow is described in sexual terms. (Adonis' femininity is sometimes taken as evidence of a homosexual inclination in Shakespeare, but the image seems to function quite well in the poem without such a conclusion. However, it does certainly suppose the acceptability of homoerotic ideas to both the poet and his audience.) The confusion of gender anticipates the conjunction of the two points of view that is reached in the closing stanzas.

The poem simultaneously views love in contradictory ways. Though love is the noblest of imaginable states of mind, as Adonis insists, it also utterly prosaic, even ridiculous, grounded as it is in the physical desires embodied by Venus' lust. Although Adonis' death is brought about by his rejection of Venus' idea of love, it does not discredit her essentially comic approach; instead, it adds to it a tragic element, that of humanity's unachievable aspiration. Love's complicated blend of opposing qualities is asserted in the description of love in Venus' closing lament: 'Sorrow on love hereafter shall attend, [and it] shall be raging mad, and silly mild, make the young old, the old become a child. . . . It shall be merciful and too severe, and most deceiving when it seems most just' (lines 1136–1156). While Venus is 'weary of the world' (line 1189) at the tale's end, yet she also has been able to realise that, for all its pain, love may 'enrich the poor with treasures' (line 1150). This is the theme that the poem offers its readers, in as fine and showy a setting as the young Shakespeare could devise.

*Venus and Adonis* is a flawed, youthful work. The two protagonists display little credible personality; differences in tone within the poem seem to reflect indecisiveness on Shakespeare's part; in particular, Venus' final position, in which she seems to reject love in light of Adonis' death, is uncomfortably at odds with her earlier, much lighter attitude. Therefore, many readers simply accept the pleasures of the poem's numerous delightful passages and disregard an otherwise seemingly unrewarding text. However, the poem is much richer than this. Like Shakespeare's greater works, it is concerned with the human predicament, and it illuminates the young playwright's attitude towards one of his most important concerns, sexual love.

In the poem's dedication Shakespeare calls his work 'the first heir of my invention', and this is sometimes taken as evidence that *Venus and Adonis* was written before any of the plays. However, most scholars agree that it is much more likely to have been written between June 1592, when the London theatres were closed because of a plague epidemic, and April 1593, when the poem was registered with the STATIONERS' COMPANY. During this enforced break in his promising career, the young playwright turned to a mode of literature that was far more prestigious at the time. Thus the reference in the dedication is taken to allude to the poet's first effort at 'serious' writing. Not only was poetry regarded as the only important branch of literature, while the stage was still somewhat disreputable (see ELIZABETHAN DRAMA), but, under the patronage system that prevailed until long after Shakespeare's death, it was potentially much more profitable than a career in the theatre.

*Venus and Adonis* was first published in 1593 by the printer Richard FIELD (2) in a QUARTO edition (known today as Q1), of which only one copy—in Oxford's Bodleian Library—has survived. Field, who also printed *The Rape of Lucrece,* was probably a friend of Shakespeare's, and this fact, plus the great care with which both texts were printed, suggests that the narrative poems were the only works whose publication was supervised by Shakespeare himself. *Venus* was very popular, and eight more editions were published during Shakespeare's lifetime. These are known as Q2–Q9 (plus one that is unnumbered, since only a title-page has survived), though all but Q2 were actually published in an octavo format. A tenth edition, Q10, appeared shortly after Shakespeare's death. Each of these editions was simply a reprint of one of its predecessors, incorporating such minor alterations as the printers saw fit to make, and, while they all contain variant readings, none is thought to reflect any changes that Shakespeare made. Q1 is therefore regarded as the only authoritative text, and it is the basis for all modern editions.

**Verdi, Giuseppe (1813–1901)**   Italian composer of several operas inspired by Shakespeare's plays. After creating his first Shakespearean opera, *Macbeth* (1847), Verdi declared his intention of composing for all of the playwright's major works. He planned a *King Lear,* but never actually wrote it, for lack of an adequate libretto. Although his ambition was unfulfilled, his two remaining Shakespearean operas, *Otello* (1887) and *Falstaff* (1893)—the latter based on *The Merry Wives of Windsor,* with additions from the *Henry IV* plays—are great accomplishments in themselves. With libretti by Arrigo BOITO, they are the twin masterpieces of Verdi's old age and in the opinion of most commentators, two of the best operas ever written.

**Verges**   Character in *Much Ado About Nothing,* Constable DOGBERRY's second-in-command. Verges is chiefly a straight man for Dogberry to play against; his eager assistance is rejected by his superior, who prefers to do things himself. Though praised as 'an old man, . . . honest as the skin between his brows' (3.5.10–12), Verges has little personality, being rather like the other WATCHMEN (3)—and Dogberry—in his confusion and comical misuse of language.

Speech prefixes in 4.2 give Verges' lines to 'Cowley'. It is therefore assumed that the actor Richard COWLEY first played the part. Verges' name is traditionally said to be a rustic pronunciation of the word *verjuice,* meaning 'the acid juice of green or unripe fruit', but the character is not notably acid. Verges' name is more probably associated with his office, a *verge* being a rod or staff symbolising authority, usually carried by an underling or assistant to the holder of power.

**Vergil, Polydore (1470–1555)**  Italian-born English author, writer of an history of England that informed Shakespeare's sources for the HISTORY PLAYS. Vergil's *Historia Anglia*, a Latin history commissioned by King Henry VII (see RICHMOND), focussed on the WARS OF THE ROSES and emphasised the influence of divine providence in punishing HENRY IV's sin in usurping the crown from RICHARD II with the civil conflicts. Thus, he aggrandised the TUDOR DYNASTY by presenting its founder, Henry VII, as an instrument of God. This point of view was adopted by Edward HALL (2) and Raphael HOLINSHED, Shakespeare's chief sources, and so became the dominant theme of the history plays.

Vergil, born in Urbino, came to England in 1501 as a representative of the pope. Henry commissioned the *Historia Anglia* in 1505, and the Italian became an English citizen in 1510, though he returned to Urbino in 1551. He was a friend of Sir Thomas MORE, who read Vergil's history in manuscript and was influenced by it in writing his biography of RICHARD III, which was also influential on Shakespeare through Hall and Holinshed.

**Vernon (1)**  Minor character in *1 Henry VI*, a follower of Richard Plantagenet, later Duke of YORK (8). Vernon backs Plantagenet against the Duke of SOMERSET (3), in the scene (2.4) that establishes the rivalry that will eventually lead to civil war. Later, in 3.4 and 4.1, he disputes with BASSET, a backer of Somerset. By demonstrating the involvement of lesser figures, these incidents illustrate the damage to English morale caused by the dissensions among the noblemen.

**Vernon (2), Richard (d. 1403)**  Historical figure and character in *1 Henry IV*, a supporter of HOTSPUR. Vernon arrives at the rebel camp before the battle of SHREWSBURY with news that the the King's armies are approaching. He describes PRINCE (6) HAL's forces in a speech (4.1.97–110) famous for its vivid imagery. In 4.3 he advises vigorously against Hotspur's insistence on entering battle before his reinforcements arrive, and in 5.1 he participates, with WORCESTER, in the negotiations that precede the battle. Captured in the battle, he is sentenced to death by King HENRY IV in 5.5.

The historical Vernon, a powerful magnate of Cheshire, in western England, was in fact captured and beheaded at Shrewsbury, although he was not a participant in the negotiations between the two sides.

**Verona**  City in Italy, the setting for *Romeo and Juliet*. The PRINCE (1) of Verona is named Escalus, a Latinisation of Della Scala, the name of the princely family that ruled the city in the late Middle Ages, but there is nothing specifically Veronese in the play, and Shakespeare simply took the location from his source.

The feud between the MONTAGUE (1) and CAPULET (1) families was long thought to have been historical, but in fact it never occurred. The root of the error, which first appears in a story published in 1530 (see *Romeo and Juliet*, 'Sources of the Play') may be a line in Dante's *Inferno*, in which two families, the Capelleti and the Montecchi, are cited for fomenting civil disorders. However, while the Montecchi lived in Verona, the Capelletti came from Cremona, and there was no connection between them.

While the title of *The Two Gentlemen of Verona* suggests that the title characters come from that city, and several scenes (1.1–2.3 and 2.7) are presumed to take place there for the same reason, there is no textual reference to confirm these suppositions. On the other hand, at 3.1.81 and 5.4.127, it is suggested that the court of the DUKE (3) of Milan is in Verona, clearly an error. The geography of this play is confused at best, and its settings have no specificity.

Verona is mentioned in passing elsewhere in the plays. It is the home of PETRUCHIO (2) in *The Taming of the Shrew*, and several scenes take place in his nearby country house. It may also be the home of Michael CASSIO, though the reference, if it is one, is made in an apparently corrupt line (*Othello*, 2.1.26).

**Verse test**  Scholarly method used to determine the authenticity and the chronological order of Shakespeare's plays. The verse test is a statistical analysis of the playwright's use of poetic devices. At its simplest, a verse test of a work determines the relative quantities of prose and poetry, and of rhymed and unrhymed lines within the poetry, and compares the result to other plays. Additional elements that are generally noted are the number of lines with feminine endings (i.e., that do not end on a stress; see METRE), the number of speeches that end in the middle of a line; and the quantitative ratio of BLANK VERSE to rhymed verse.

Verse tests were first applied by Edmond MALONE and others in the late 18th century, but they were most important in the Shakespearean studies of the 19th century, when a body of comparisons was developed by such scholars as Frederick FURNIVALL, G. G. GERVINUS, F. G. FLEAY, and William SPALDING. In the 20th century verse tests are much less important to scholars, who apply other concepts to the same questions and find the results of verse tests to be inconclusive.

**Vestris, Elizabeth (1797–1856)**  British actress. Madame Vestris, as she was known, was born Lucia Elizabeth Bartolozzi. She kept the name of her first husband, a ballet dancer who deserted her, and became a successful comic actress, specialising in farces and burlesques. She married the actor Charles James Mathews (1803–1878). Beginning in 1839, they managed a theatrical company at the Covent Garden Theatre. They began by presenting the first performances of *Love's Labour's Lost* since the early 17th century—Madame Vestris played ROSALINE (1)—followed by *The Merry Wives of Windsor*, in which she played MISTRESS (3) PAGE and used her fine voice to sing a number of interpolated songs. In 1840 Vestris and Mathews presented *A Midsummer Night's Dream*, and though their version was abridged, it was entirely Shakespearean, again for the first time in 200 years. It was also the first English production to use the famous incidental music by Felix Mendelssohn (1809–1847). Unfortunately, these productions were not financially successful, and the couple went bankrupt. Though they never again produced Shakespeare, they continued to perform—indeed, they had to, for Madame Vestris died before their finances were restored. Mathews eventually recovered and followed a less demanding career as a minor comic actor.

**Vice, the** Conventional figure from the medieval MORALITY PLAY, an influence upon the development of both Shakespeare's villains and his comic figures. The Vice attempts to seduce the soul of the protagonist, who represents mankind, into evil ways. An hypocrite, deceit and guile are his weapons—he is able to weep at will—and he employs them with great pleasure. At the same time, the Vice is a comic figure, designed to entertain while he instructs. He typically makes lewd jokes, puns outrageously, engages in physical horseplay, and brandishes his wooden sword with comic ineffectuality (both FALSTAFF [in *1 Henry IV*, 2.4.133] and PISTOL [in *Henry V*, 4.4.73–74] are associated with this feature). Especially in the more sophisticated 16th-century morality plays, he resembles the FOOL (1). The Vice also evolved into another, more distinctly Elizabethan character type, the MACHIAVEL.

At his most striking, the Vice advertises his villainy to the audience. He revels in viciousness in extravagant, humorous asides filled with demonic laughter. It is a convention of the morality plays that his victims are the only ones who cannot see through his obvious dishonesty; thus, the Vice demonstrates the habitual blindness of the sinner. A number of Shakespeare's early villains are distinctly Vice–like. The most notable of these, perhaps, is RICHARD III, who in fact describes himself as '. . . like the formal Vice, Iniquity' (*Richard III*, 3.1.82). The character's influence is still detectable in the later Shakespearean figure IAGO.

**Vienna** City in Austria, the setting for *Measure for Measure*. Dramatic convention called for a foreign locale for Shakespeare's sensational tale, and he probably chose Vienna because it was much better known to an English audience than its neighbour, Innsbruck, where the story takes place in his chief source, CINTHIO's novella. Much of the play occurs indoors—mostly in a prison, where local colour is distinctly lacking—and no Viennese ambience is achieved or even attempted.

In fact, Shakespeare's Vienna—presented chiefly in the comic SUB-PLOT—resembles Shakespeare's London, by no coincidence, for the play's satirical edge is intended to expose the immorality and cynicism of 'modern' life of the early 17th century. The humorous catalogue of petty criminals recited by POMPEY (1), in 4.3.1–20, offers a sampling of current London stereotypes. The idle, war-loving noblemen (see GENTLEMAN [5]) who condemn peace and laugh at venereal disease are our introduction to Vienna's streets, in 1.2, and probably reflect the negotiations for peace with Spain that were held in London from May to August of 1604. During this time the citizenry were troubled with the presence of disorderly soldiers, and professional officers bemoaned the prospective interruption of their careers. Similarly, MISTRESS (2) Overdone's complaint about 'the war . . . the sweat . . . the gallows' (1.2.75–76) reflects the same situation, as well as a plague that raged in London over the winter of 1603–04, and a series of treason trials and executions that enlivened the news. Further, the proclamation for the destruction of brothels, reported by POMPEY (1) in 1.2, corresponds to a London law of 1603 ordering the razing of whole districts inhabited by 'dissolute and idle persons'—ostensibly an antiplague effort, but one that was especially directed at whorehouses and gambling dens.

**Vincentio (1)** Minor character in *The Taming of the Shrew*, the father of LUCENTIO. Vincentio, described as 'a sober ancient gentleman' (5.1.65), arrives in PADUA to find himself impersonated by the PEDANT and Lucentio by his servant TRANIO. He is understandably angry, but otherwise he has no distinctive personality traits.

**Vincentio (2)** Character in *Measure for Measure*. See DUKE (9).

**Vintner** Minor character in *1 Henry IV*, an employee of the BOAR'S HEAD TAVERN. The Vintner appears only briefly, to chasten FRANCIS (1) and announce the arrival of FALSTAFF. He contributes to the atmosphere of a busy tavern.

**Viola** Character in *Twelfth Night*, lover of Duke ORSINO of ILLYRIA and twin sister of SEBASTIAN (2). Viola is at the centre of the play's confusions. Separated from Sebastian in a shipwreck, Viola finds herself in Illyria. Disguised as a young man, Cesario, she meets and falls in love with Orsino, but her adopted persona prevents her from expressing her love for him except through service as his page. Orsino wishes her to court OLIVIA for him, placing her in a strange and difficult position that becomes worse when Olivia falls in love with Cesario. Viola, alone among the characters, knows the truth of this situation. While she is like the other Illyrians in her susceptibility to passion, she alone can honestly assess it, saying simply, 'O time, thou must untangle this, not I, / It is too hard a knot for me t'untie' (2.2.39–40).

Viola's capacity for love is extreme: when Orsino, hysterical over Olivia's continued rejection, proposes to kill Cesario in a grand gesture, she calmly acquiesces, saying to him, 'I . . . to do you rest, a thousand deaths would die' (5.1.130–131). Such self-sacrificing devotion strikes some readers as Christlike, and, along with the powers of restoration displayed by Sebastian at the play's climax, it has influenced a religious interpretation of the play by some scholars, although an entirely secular reading is probably more appropriate to the comedy and Viola's personality.

Though extravagant, Viola's attitude towards love is much more wholesome than the posturings of Orsino and Olivia, and her effect on these characters is positive. Her spirit and candour arouse love in Olivia, who has been withdrawing into grief-filled seclusion. Similarly, although Orsino is wrapped up in his self-image as a melancholy rejected lover, he responds unconsciously to Viola's devotion, conceiving a fondness for Cesario that he eventually transforms into husbandly affection for the sort of loving wife he truly needs. Viola is the heroine of the play, performing the monumental task of liberating Olivia and Orsino from their misconceived selves and thus making the play's climax possible.

In the meantime, her frank good humour keeps the audience aware of the potential realignment of the lovers. She is not afraid to make telling remarks to Olivia on her unmarried state, arguing that '. . . you do usurp yourself: for what is yours to bestow is not yours to reserve' (1.5.188–190), and she is unafraid to counter Orsino's dramatic and boastful insistence that male love is grander than female, observing (while speaking as a man herself), 'We men may say more, swear more, but indeed / Our shows are more than will: for still we prove / Much in our vows, but little in our love' (2.4.117–119). She entertains herself and the audience with ironic remarks on her own disguised state, asserting to Olivia that 'what I am, and what I would, are as secret as maidenhead' (1.5.219) and, flatly, that 'I am not what I am' (3.1. 143). Speaking as Cesario, she ironically tells Orsino that she loves someone 'of your complexion' and 'about your years, my lord' (2.4.26, 28), hiding the fact, which the audience knows, that the object of her love is Orsino himself.

However, there is also an aspect of Viola's position that contributes to *Twelfth Night*'s disturbing undertone. She cannot openly express her love, for her disguise inhibits her, and she thus embodies a disorder in the world of romantic comedy, just as Orsino and Olivia do in their self-delusion, though less blatantly. She herself laments, 'Disguise, I see thou art a wicked-ness' (2.2.26). Also, her disguise raises questions of sexual ambiguity that can be psychologically unnerving. In Shakespeare's time, Viola would of course have been played by a boy (see ELIZABETHAN THEATRE), making her situation both funnier and more troubling. The spectacle of one woman, played by a boy, mistakenly responding sexually to another one, also played by a boy, makes implicit reference to both male and female homosexuality, as well as to heterosexual love, in a way that is comical but also suggestive of hidden depths of human sexuality. While the modern use of actresses tends to obscure this point, the complexity of the situation retains some of its powerful and upsetting strength.

Nevertheless, these dark aspects do not interfere with Viola's essentially positive role. Until Sebastian arrives and resolves the play's intrigues, she alone has found an appropriate passion, and her strength and determination assure us that love will surely triumph. Whether recovering from disaster at sea, plunging into love and intrigue as Cesario, or turning to her betrothal at the play's close, Viola is one of Shakespeare's most attractive heroines—plucky, adventurous, and committed to the pursuit of love.

**Violenta**   Character named but not present in *All's Well That Ends Well*. Violenta appears in the FIRST FOLIO in the stage direction that opens 3.5. It reads, 'Enter old Widow of Florence, her daughter, Violenta, and Mariana. . .'. Violenta could be the daughter's name, set off by commas, but DIANA (1) is certainly the Widow's daughter. Shakespeare may have originally named Diana differently, or he could have intended a fourth character whom he did not in fact use, in which case Violenta is a GHOST CHARACTER. In either case, the name survived in the text through an error on the part of the printer.

**Virgil (Vergil) (70–19 B.C.)**   Ancient Roman poet, an important influence on Shakespeare's art in general—indeed, on all of English literature—whose works were also a source for details in a number of Shakespeare's plays and poems. For instance, Virgil's *Aeneid*, an epic poem on the founding of ROME, provided imagery and occasional episodes, most prominently in *The Rape of Lucrece, Hamlet,* and *The Tempest.* When the Archbishop of CANTERBURY (1) compares society to a beehive in *Henry V* (1.2.187–204), he is echoing a famous passage in Virgil's *Georgics,* a collection of hymns to the traditional rural life of Italy. Virgil's PASTORAL *Eclogues* were among the finest examples of a genre that particularly influenced *As You Like It* and *The Winter's Tale.*

However, the general impact of Virgil on the playwright's age is more important than any specific contributions. In the RENAISSANCE the works of Virgil, especially the *Aeneid,* were regarded as literature's highest achievement, and every 16th-century writer felt their impact. The stately, measured pace of Virgil's verse was an important influence on the tone of Shakespeare's poetry and that of all his contemporaries. In fact, BLANK VERSE was introduced to England in the translations of Virgil by the Earl of SURREY (1). Virgil's themes, the patriotism of the *Aeneid* and the rustic beauties of the *Eclogues* and the *Georgics*, informed Elizabethan notions of genre.

Moreover, Virgil was a great literary nationalist—not only in the *Aeneid*'s grand history, but in the local pride of place displayed in the *Eclogues* and *Georgics*. As England emerged from the Middle Ages to find itself a distinctive nation, Virgil's nationalistic vision seemed remarkably appropriate. As if to demonstrate this, more than 50 English writers translated some part of Virgil's works during the 16th and 17th centuries. Shakespeare may have read the renderings of Surrey, Thomas Phaer (c. 1510–1560), or Richard Stanyhurst (1545–1615), but he surely knew the works best in the original Latin, for he studied Virgil in school.

Virgil was born near MANTUA, the son of a prosperous peasant—a potter and beekeeper, according to some traditions. He studied rhetoric and philosophy in Milan and Rome from 55 to around 42 B.C. At this time he began writing, and he also made friends with the poet GALLUS, who introduced him to a patron, MAECENAS, the friend and adviser of Augustus CAESAR (2). Maecenas probably encouraged the publication of the *Eclogues*, which appeared around 39 B.C., and he definitely urged the poet to compose the *Georgics*, which are written in his honour, though they contain many passages eulogising Augustus. The poet read the *Georgics* to Augustus upon his return from the campaign of ACTIUM in 29 B.C. and sparked the future emperor's enthusiasm and support. Both the *Eclogues* and the *Georgics* reflect their troubled times in a nostalgia for a simpler world combined with a hopeful anticipation of better times in the peace that has been wrought by Rome's new ruler. Their patriotic tone anticipates the *Aeneid*, on which Virgil worked for the last 10 years of his life. He died with the epic still incomplete and left instructions in his will that it be burned, but the emperor overruled this stipulation and had the poem published in its unfinished state.

**Virgilia** Legendary figure and character in *Coriolanus*, the wife of CORIOLANUS. When we first see her in 1.3, Virgilia makes her strongest impression, as she worries over her husband's return to war. She can only respond feebly to the martial enthusiasm of her powerful mother-in-law, VOLUMNIA, who calls her weak because she fears for her husband's safety. Virgilia has the inner strength, however, to refuse to continue her social life. She speaks very little in the remainder of the play—Coriolanus calls her his 'gracious silence' (2.1.174)—but though her role is small, her modesty

offers a distinct and significant emotional note that contrasts with and emphasises the more strident tone of her husband and her mother-in-law.

Virgilia acts as a foil to Volumnia and makes clear that her mother-in-law's war-loving, masculine nature is not the only one possible for a Roman matron—rather, we see that Volumnia is not normal. Virgilia is also a foil to Coriolanus: in contrast with her, he seems crude. This is especially obvious when he returns from combat in 2.1 and he jokes with her about coffins and death. He is clearly not aware of her sensibilities, which we have been exposed to just a few scenes earlier.

Her presence also sheds light on her husband in a subtler fashion. He doesn't understand her or perhaps even perceive her clearly, but his recollection of their farewell kiss, 'Long as my exile, sweet as my revenge' (5.3.44–45), is touching, if also twisted. That his demure wife inspires such affection suggests to us a softer, undeveloped aspect of Coriolanus' nature. Virgilia stands for a world that might have been, and the latent presence of that world makes the dramatic reality of the tragedy more wrenching.

**Visor, William** GLOUCESTERSHIRE countryman named in *2 Henry IV,* a friend of DAVY. Davy, steward of Justice SHALLOW, wishes his master to rule in favour of his friend 'William Visor of Woncot' (5.1.34) in a lawsuit against one 'Clement PERKES a'th'Hill' (5.1. 35). Shallow observes that 'Visor is an arrant knave' (5.1.37), but Davy disingenuously asserts the greater right of a knave to favour, since, being a knave, he is likely to be denied it. He goes on to claim the privilege of a loyal servant to 'once or twice a quarter bear out a knave against an honest man' (5.1.44), and Shallow promises that Visor 'shall have no wrong' (5.1.49). We are given a humorous glimpse of small-time country corruption, one of the many vignettes of common life that the play features.

Visor is thought to represent a real person, a member of a family named Visor or Vizard, known to have lived for centuries in the village of Woodmancote, the 'Woncot' of the play. Why Shakespeare chose to present William Visor as 'an arrant knave' is not known.

**Volsce** Character in *Coriolanus*, a spy who receives information for his tribe, the VOLSCIANS, from a ROMAN (2). In 4.3 the Volsce, named Adrian, meets the Roman, named Nicanor, from whom he has gathered intelligence before. He learns of the banishment of CORIOLANUS. The episode emphasises the atmosphere of intrigue that pervades Coriolanus' world, and prepares us for his defection in the next scenes.

**Volscians** In *Coriolanus*, an Italic tribe that makes war against ROME. CORIOLANUS receives his name for his bravery when he besieges and takes the Volscian town of CORIOLES. When the Romans banish him, he joins the Volscians and leads them in a successful campaign. Under him, the Volscians almost take Rome, but the ex-Roman gives in to the pleas of his mother and spares the city. Though the resulting treaty requires large retributions from Rome, the Volscian leader AUFIDIUS has Coriolanus killed. This brings to a close the tragedy of a leader whose uncontrolled pride, combined with civil disorder, leads to catastrophe for himself and for Rome. Shakespeare employs the Volscians in this tale as he does the GOTHS in *Titus Andronicus*, FORTINBRAS in *Hamlet*, and the English in *Macbeth*—they are all foreigners who dominate a society once it succumbs to weaknesses that result from the shortcomings and misdeeds of its rulers. Thus, the Volscians are a sort of nemesis, a punishing fate that confirms the evil of selfish ambition or pride among the privileged. This was an important political point for Shakespeare throughout his career.

The historical Volscians were enemies of Rome throughout its early history. The record is obscure but many hints—including the legends surrounding Coriolanus—imply Volscian successes. They were finally defeated by the Romans during the 4th century B.C., and after 304 B.C.—about 200 years after the time of the play—they were politically incorporated into the Roman state. The Volscians were so thoroughly assimilated that almost all traces of their ancient culture had disappeared before the earliest surviving Roman accounts of them were written.

**Voltemand (Voltimand, Valtemand)**   Minor character in *Hamlet*, ambassador to the King of Norway from the KING (5) of DENMARK. In 1.2 Voltemand and CORNELIUS (1) are appointed to deliver the King's message demanding that the Norwegian king's nephew, FORTINBRAS, who is preparing an invasion of Denmark, be restrained. The two ambassadors return in 2.2, and Voltemand delivers a document of agreement that he summarises in courtly language. The episode introduces the audience to Fortinbras while demonstrating the state of national crisis in which the play takes place.

This character's name was spelled both Voltemand and Valtemand in the most authoritative early edition of the play (Q2, 1604); Voltumand and Voltemar appear in other early editions. The second FOLIO edition (1632) used Voltimand, and this became the established practise until recently, when a compromise version became popular. In any form it is a corruption of Valdemar, the name of several Danish kings.

**Volumnia**   Legendary figure and character in *Coriolanus*, the mother of the title character. Volumnia, an aristocratic Roman matron, has raised her son to be a proud warrior above all else. She dominates her son,

for she has so thoroughly bred her own values in him that he is psychologically dependent on her approval and cannot oppose her. As she claims, 'There's no man in the world / More bound to's mother' (5.3.158–159). Desiring that Coriolanus receive the consulate, ROME's highest honour, Volumnia bullies him until he agrees to sacrifice his pride and solicit the approval of the common people. This is one of Shakespeare's most Machiavellian passages—3.2.41–86. However, because Coriolanus is what Volumnia has made him, he cannot restrain his proud contempt, with the result that he is banished from Rome. When he joins the VOLSCIANS, Rome's enemy, and threatens to sack the city, Volumnia again uses her influence over him with an elaborate appeal in 5.3, a virtuoso passage that is the high point of the play, dramatically. She convinces him to withdraw his forces, though he knows this means he will be killed by the Volscians.

Volumnia controls her son by withdrawing her approval: in both 3.2 and 5.3 she disdainfully disowns him—'Thy valiantness was mine . . . but owe thy pride thyself' (3.2.129–130), and 'This fellow had a Volscian to his mother' (5.3.178). While her advice to him is sound, it is only necessary because her influence has made him incapable of functioning sensibly. Because he has only the rigorous pride she has developed in him, he goes to his destruction. He is a tragic hero precisely because his greatness is mingled with his weakness. He is incapable of being anything except what his mother has made him. The influence of Volumnia is thus central to the play.

Volumnia is correct when she boasts to Coriolanus, 'Thou art my warrior: / I holp to frame thee' (5.3.62–63). Her upbringing of him has made him both the charismatic warrior who becomes a great Roman hero and the inflexible aristocrat who sparks the hatred of the Roman people. Her rigorous martial code is revealed on her first appearance, in 1.3, where she delights in Coriolanus' return to combat. She sternly rejects the concern for his safety displayed by his wife, VIRGILIA, and rejoices in the prospect of her son's wounds, or even his death, for the sufferings of war are badges of honour to her mind.

Volumnia's moral code—and thus that of Coriolanus—is seriously flawed, and this is made clear in Shakespeare's depiction of her warped sense of maternal love. In 1.3 her thirst for glory leads her to equate her joy at Coriolanus' birth with her pleasure in his fighting, and she compares the beauty of a mother's breast to that of a head wound. This obviously pathological attitude helps demonstrate the unhealthiness of the rigorous aristocratic ideal that Volumnia upholds, and it is part of the play's critique of the aristocracy. We are not surprised when the results of Coriolanus' upbringing prove catastrophic.

Shakespeare invented all of Volumnia's appearances save that in 5.3—her dramatic appeal to save

Rome—which occurs in the play's source, PLUTARCH'S *Lives*. When he devised a powerful mother-son relationship to account for Coriolanus' submission, Shakespeare not only added psychological weight to his protagonist's sudden reversal, he found a basic component of his tragedy.

**Volumnius (active 42 B.C.)** Historical figure and minor character in *Julius Caesar,* a soldier in the army of BRUTUS (4). In 5.5 Volumnius—like CLITUS and DARDANIUS—shrinks from helping the defeated Brutus to commit suicide, saying 'That's not an office for a friend, my lord' (5.5.29). The episode illustrates the fondness with which Brutus is regarded by his subordinates, thereby contributing to the aura of sentiment surrounding his death. Little is known of the historical Volumnius, though Shakespeare's source, PLUTARCH, asserts that he had been a schoolmate of Brutus.

# W

**Wakefield** Location in *3 Henry VI*, a town in Yorkshire and a battle site during the WARS OF THE ROSES. The battle, fought in December 1460 between the army of the Duke of YORK (8) and a considerably larger force led by Queen MARGARET (1), takes place in 1.2–4. It results in the capture and death of York and a catastrophic loss for his troops. In depicting the conflict, Shakespeare took considerable liberties with the recorded accounts. York's son RUTLAND (1), who died in combat, is incorrectly depicted as a child and a brutally murdered non-combatant. York's oldest son, Edward (see EDWARD IV), whose exploits the playwright describes, was not present at the battle; he was with another armed force, one that might have relieved York had he been patient and waited for it. However, the Duke undertook to fight despite the odds, probably underestimating the leadership of Queen Margaret, and suffered the loss, which is accurately portrayed. Another son, Richard (see RICHARD III), is made to encourage the hasty decision to fight; in reality, Richard was only eight years old at the time and lived in exile in Burgundy. The playwright made these alterations for various reasons: Rutland's murder emphasises the theme of revenge; the presence of Edward and Richard tightens the succession of incidents that the play must depict; and Richard's role further reflects his importance as a major character.

**Wales (1)** Ancient kingdom to England's west, a location used in *Cymbeline* and *Richard II*, and an important subject in *1* and *2 Henry IV* and *Henry V*. A Welsh character appears in *The Merry Wives of Windsor*, and Wales is referred to occasionally in other plays as well.

In the history plays Wales is strategically important in the civil conflicts fought by King HENRY IV. In *Richard II*, when BOLINGBROKE (the future king) arrives in England with an army, intent on challenging King RICHARD II, Richard is in Ireland. Bolingbroke therefore marches to Wales to intercept him upon his return. Scenes 2.4, 3.2, and 3.3 take place in this important location, although no fighting takes place. In 2.4 Shakespeare first presents, in the person of the CAPTAIN (4), the archetypal Welshman who appears in these plays, a cautious and superstitious figure. The Captain deserts Richard's cause, and he may represent Owen GLENDOWER, a famous Welsh warrior who appears in 3.1 of *1 Henry IV*, where his superstition is a significant factor in the unfolding of the plot.

Wales became a part of Britain by conquest over the course of the 11th to 13th centuries, but periodic revolts lasted until the time of the history plays when Glendower led a rebellion that produced the last few years of Welsh independence, c. 1405–1409. In both of the *Henry IV* plays the political importance of Wales is apparent: as well as being a hotbed of rebellion, it was a fertile source of soldiers. The courage and military prowess of the Welsh were well known, as was their inclination towards feuding and personal disputes. Other characteristics of the archetypal Welshman of Shakespeare's day are embodied in Glendower and his daughter, LADY (8) MORTIMER: a sentimental streak and a love of music. Also, various peculiarities of spelling and syntax in Glendower's speeches, as they were originally published, probably reflect a Welsh accent.

Shakespeare was clearly aware of the popular English stereotype of the Welsh as distinctly foreign, but in *Henry V* Wales is specifically included in a united Britain. Shakespeare depicted HENRY V as a king of all the British peoples, especially in the so-called 'international scene' (3.2). Here the Welsh representative is Captain FLUELLEN, who is notable for his comically powerful Welsh accent. Fluellen is a hot-tempered but honest and courageous soldier; in 5.1, when PISTOL mocks him by saying he smells of leeks—the Welsh national symbol—Fluellen forces him to eat one.

Another Welsh character appears in *The Merry Wives of Windsor*, the village clergyman and schoolmaster, Sir Hugh EVANS (3). He also has a pronounced accent and a tendency towards clichés, another allegedly Welsh characteristic. Also, he is partly responsible for a theft of horses, an episode that reflects another, less attractive English stereotype of the Welsh as inveterate thieves. In the famous 'Latin scene' of *The Merry Wives* (4.1), Evans comically drills a student in the ancient language. This perhaps reflects the playwright's own experience at STRATFORD, where he may have had a schoolmaster of Welsh ancestry, Thomas JENKINS. In any case, the creation of Evans, Glendower, Lady Mortimer, and Fluellen indicates that in the late 1590s

Shakespeare's acting company, the CHAMBERLAIN'S MEN, included one or more Welshmen.

In *Cymbeline,* a much later play, Wales is the location for most of Acts 3 and 4 of the play. It is the land of exile for BELARIUS, who has been unjustly exiled from the court of King CYMBELINE, and it is also the site of a battle between the British and an invading Roman army. In addition to being a wilderness, Wales is again a military venue, as the Romans use Milford Haven, a Welsh port, as their point of invasion. However, these features are not developed in the play, and the only specifically Welsh element in *Cymbeline* is a minor one: the pseudonym, Morgan, taken by Belarius. Since Belarius/Morgan, like Evans, is given to clichés, he may also have been intended to suggest a comic Welsh stereotype.

Welsh material crops up elsewhere in the plays as well. For instance, the fairy lore of *A Midsummer Night's Dream* probably came from Wales, perhaps through the traditions of WARWICKSHIRE, Shakespeare's home, but perhaps also through the Welsh players in the Chamberlain's Men. The *Dream* was written around the same time as *Richard II,* where matters Welsh are first found in Shakespeare. In an intriguing sidelight, it is often thought that 'Ducdame, Ducdame, Ducdame' (*As You Like It,* 2.5.51), the mysterious 'nonsense' refrain in the parody song by JAQUES (1), is a version of a phrase in Cymric, the Welsh language, that means 'Come to me', and which was used in a well-known children's game. The date of *As You Like It* is uncertain, but it is thought to have been written in the same period as *The Merry Wives of Windsor, 1 Henry IV,* and *Henry V.*

**Wales (2), Prince of**   See PRINCE (4); PRINCE (5); PRINCE (6).

**Walkley, Thomas (active 1618–1649)**   London bookseller and publisher. Walkley published the first QUARTO edition of *Othello,* hiring printer Nicholas OKES. He owned two London bookstores, but little more is known of him except that he published Royalist propaganda during the civil wars.

**Walley, Henry (active 1608–1655)**   London publisher and bookseller, co-publisher of the first edition of *Troilus and Cressida.* With Richard BONIAN, Walley published the QUARTO edition of the play in 1609. When the FIRST FOLIO edition of Shakespeare's works was produced in 1623, Bonian had died and Walley alone held the rights to *Troilus and Cressida.* Textual evidence reveals that printing of the play delayed once begun, and scholars conclude that Walley drove a difficult bargain with the Folio publishers, led by Isaac JAGGARD. Walley enjoyed a long career; he entered the STATIONERS' COMPANY in 1608 and was elected its master, or chief officer, in 1655.

**Walker (1), Henry (d. 1616)**   Musician in LONDON, seller of the BLACKFRIARS GATEHOUSE to Shakespeare. Walker bought the gatehouse for £100 in 1604 and sold it to Shakespeare for £140 in 1613, issuing a short-term mortgage for £80 of it. Like Shakespeare, he had owned the house as an investment and had not lived in it. He was a musician by trade—a 'Minstrel' in the language of the deed—though he also had a shop and apprentices and was a wealthy man.

**Walker (2), William (1608–1680)**   Shakespeare's godson. Walker, the son of a prosperous cloth dealer who had served three times as bailiff, or mayor, of STRATFORD, received a cash bequest in his namesake's will. Little more is known of him, except that he too was elected bailiff, in 1649.

**Walton, William (b. 1902)**   British composer, creator of music for the FILMS of Laurence OLIVIER. Walton composed the striking scores for *Henry V* (1944), *Hamlet* (1947), and *Richard III* (1954). Walton is best known for his orchestral works; he also composed several well-known operas, including a *Troilus and Cressida,* though it is based on CHAUCER's version of the tale, rather than Shakespeare's.

**War of the Theatres**   Rivalry between playwrights—Ben JONSON versus John MARSTON and Thomas DEKKER—marked by satirical plays written and produced between 1599 and 1602. Also called the Poetomachia—Dekker's comical Greek term for 'combat of the poets'—the War of the Theatres involved seven plays produced by three acting companies. It is difficult to tell whether the rivalry was based on real animosity or was a publicity stunt. Jonson later remembered his hatred for Marston, but he was peacefully collaborating with him just a few years after this conflict, and by all accounts no one felt hostile towards the genial Dekker, either then or ever. And the contest certainly did generate publicity for the CHILDREN'S COMPANIES as they recovered their position in the public theatres in the early years of the 17th century.

The War of the Theatres began with Marston's *Histrio-mastix* (1599), staged by the Children of Paul's, which contained a humorous character modelled on Jonson. Though Marston may have meant no offence, Jonson replied by satirising his bombastic style in *Every Man out of His Humour* (1599), produced by Shakespeare's CHAMBERLAIN'S MEN (who were otherwise uninvolved in the fray). Marston countered by portraying Jonson as a cuckold in *Jack Drum's Entertainment* (1600), a Paul's play. Jonson's reply encompassed Dekker, Marston's fellow writer for Paul's, in *Cynthia's Revels* (1601) (he depicted himself in it as 'a creature of a most perfect and divine temper'); this work was staged by the Children of the Chapel. Marston immediately replied with an uncomplimentary

Jonson-figure in *What You Will* (1601), and Dekker and Marston together began to write another satire. Jonson learned of this, however, and rushed out *The Poetaster* (1601), in which Dekker is presented as a 'playdresser [i.e., reviser of other people's dramas] and plagiary' and Marston as a 'poetaster and plagiary'. This time Jonson depicted himself as the Roman poet Horace (65–8 B.C.), and in Dekker and Marston's *Satiromastix* (1601), Horace is ridiculed. The battle of plays ended at this point, as the participants moved on to other work. By 1604 Marston even dedicated a play to Jonson.

Shakespeare alluded to the War of the Theatres twice in the plays he was writing at the time. In *Hamlet* the children's companies of DENMARK are said to 'berattle the common stages', with 'much to do on both sides', and 'much throwing about of brains' (2.2. 340, 350, 356). In *Twelfth Night* FESTE's remark that the word *element* is 'overworn' (3.1.60) alludes to Dekker's satire in *Satiromastix* on Jonson's use of the word.

**Warburton, John (1682–1759)**   English antiquarian and manuscript collector. Warburton recorded his ownership of many play manuscripts, including copies of DUKE HUMPHREY (by 'Will. Shakespear') and *Henry I* (by 'Will. Shakespear and Rob. Davenport'; see HENRY I AND HENRY II). Neither manuscript survives—most of Warburton's collection was destroyed by a servant who mistook it for waste paper—but scholars doubt that either was by Shakespeare.

**Warders**   Minor characters in *1 Henry VI*, soldiers manning the Tower of London who refuse admittance to the Duke of GLOUCESTER (4) in 1.3, citing orders from the Bishop of WINCHESTER (1). The term *warder* referred to a soldier whose duty was to act as a guard, especially at the entrance to a building or fortification.

**Warkworth Castle**   Fortified dwelling in northern England, a setting in *1* and *2 Henry IV*. The principal home of the Percy family, this castle served as a headquarters for the rebellion against King HENRY IV led by HOTSPUR and his uncle WORCESTER. In 2.3 of *1 Henry IV* Hotspur here prepares for the forthcoming campaign and bids an affectionate farewell to his wife, LADY (10) Percy. In *2 Henry IV* the INDUCTION, in which RUMOUR tells of the contrary reports that the Earl of NORTHUMBERLAND (1) will soon receive, and 1.1, in which they arrive, are both set at Warkworth, as is 2.3, in which Northumberland is persuaded by LADY (9) Northumberland and Lady Percy to abandon the rebels' hopeless cause.

Warkworth Castle was built in the 12th century and remodelled in the 14th by the Earl of Northumberland of the play. A strategically important fort on England's northern border, Warkworth saw much warfare and was often besieged. In 1405 Henry IV, mopping up

the Percy rebels, damaged the castle considerably with his artillery. Today, still owned by the Percy family, it is a picturesque ruin (though still habitable in part) that is open to the public.

**Warner, William (c. 1558–1609)**   English author whose translation of *The Menaechmi* by PLAUTUS, the principal source for *The Comedy of Errors*, may have been known by Shakespeare. Although Warner's translation was not published until 1595, somewhat later than the presumed date of composition of Shakespeare's play, the playwright may have read it in manuscript, a common practise at that time. This speculation is strengthened by the fact that Warner's book was dedicated to Henry CAREY (2), Lord Hunsdon, the patron of the CHAMBERLAIN'S MEN, Shakespeare's theatrical company.

**Wars of the Roses**   English dynastic wars of 1455–1485, in which are set the first four of Shakespeare's HISTORY PLAYS: *1*, *2*, and *3 Henry VI* and *Richard III*. The wars were a struggle between two branches of the PLANTAGENET (1) family, the houses of YORK (1) and LANCASTER (1). Traditionally (though inaccurately), the Yorkists were thought to have used white roses as their emblem and the Lancastrians to have worn red ones.

In the mid-15th century a Lancastrian, HENRY VI, ruled England. A weak king, crowned while only an infant and heavily influenced by aristocratic cliques, Henry lost most of England's conquests in FRANCE (1) in the last phase of the HUNDRED YEARS WAR—the principal subject of *1 Henry VI*. These losses, along with evident corruption and extravagance at the royal court, resulted in recurring popular unrest. An opposition party of aristocrats arose, led by the Duke of YORK (8). In the political manoeuvring depicted in *2 Henry VI*, York gained ascendancy over the faction led by Queen MARGARET (1), and he ruled the country while the king was temporarily insane in 1453–1454 (Shakespeare does not mention this episode). York was excluded from power when Henry recovered, and he resorted to war, winning the battle of ST. ALBANS, with which *2 Henry VI* closes, in 1455.

York reclaimed power, but the rivalry continued, and the two sides resumed warfare in 1459. After a Yorkist victory in July 1460, the duke claimed the throne. However, this action produced resistance among the aristocracy, and York had to accept a compromise, as is enacted in 1.1 of *3 Henry VI*: Henry was permitted to continue ruling, though York would succeed him. Queen Margaret retaliated by raising an army; she won the battle of WAKEFIELD in December 1460, in which York was killed. However, her triumph was short-lived: she alarmed the aristocracy by claiming the right to dispossess her enemies of their estates, and she alienated the common people by permitting her army to loot and pillage after the battle. York's son EDWARD IV assumed his father's claim to the throne, and after a bloody victory at TOWTON in March 1461 he was crowned, ending the first phase of the Wars of the Roses.

Edward ruled England with considerable success for 22 years, though his reign was interrupted in 1470 by a Lancastrian invasion, led by Margaret and the Earl of WARWICK (3), a one-time Yorkist. They placed Henry VI back on the throne for six months, but Edward recaptured the crown in 1471 after winning the battles of BARNET and TEWKESBURY, completing the second cycle of the wars. These events occupy Acts 3–5 of *3 Henry VI.*

*Richard III* deals with the last stage of the Wars of the Roses. Edward died in April 1483. In his will he appointed his brother Richard (see RICHARD III) as Protector, ruling for the 12-year-old PRINCE (5). However, Edward's widow, Queen ELIZABETH (2), led an attempt to displace Richard, and he responded by seizing the throne in July 1483. He probably had the Prince and his younger brother murdered, although the evidence is inconclusive. In any event, his coup spurred the last, brief campaign of the Wars of the Roses: the only surviving Lancastrian claimant to the crown, the Earl of RICHMOND, invaded England and defeated Richard at the battle of BOSWORTH FIELD. Richmond took the throne as Henry VII and established the TUDOR dynasty.

The Wars of the Roses constituted an important historical watershed, bringing feudalism to an end in England. The feudal aristocracy, exhausted by the conflict, was unable to resist the establishment of a strong, centralised monarchy by the Tudors, who, under Richmond's grand-daughter Queen ELIZABETH (1), still ruled England in Shakespeare's day. One consequence of the Tudor's consolidation of power was the development of a bias in the subsequent writing of English history. Shakespeare's principal sources, the histories by HALL (2) and HOLINSHED and Thomas MORE's biography of Richard III, are fairly reliable with respect to the chronology of the wars, but they are markedly prejudiced in favour of the winning side, depicting Richmond's predecessors, especially Richard, as particularly vicious and villainous.

Shakespeare followed his sources in this respect, but he took important liberties with their account of the wars. In general he altered history in two chief ways: he compressed the time scale during which events occurred, and he exaggerated the ambitions of the Yorkists. The compression, eliminating the long stretches when the conflict was on hold, serves to maintain a high level of dramatic excitement, but it also virtually eliminates the successful reign of King Edward and thereby overstates the extent of England's disruption and over-emphasises the importance of the Tudor 'rescue' of the country. In the plays the conflict seems both horrifying and relentless, though in fact it consisted of only four campaigns, widely scattered over 30 years, and included only one episode of civil plundering, that of Margaret's army after Wakefield, and only one strikingly bloody battle, Towton.

Furthermore, Shakespeare stresses the evil of the Duke of York's attempt to rebel against an anointed king. York is shown conspiring for many years to seize the throne, when in fact his attempted usurpation was almost impulsive. Similarly, Richard III is depicted as scheming to wear the crown at a time when he was actually an infant, and his villainy, although derived from the sources, is magnified to spectacular effect. Thus sinful human greed is presented as the cause of grievous social disruption, when the actual situation, even as reported in the biased sources, was much more complex.

**Wart, Thomas**   Minor character in *2 Henry IV,* one of the men whom FALSTAFF recruits for the army in 3.2. Wart, who is dressed in rags, is initially rejected as being too poor a specimen of soldier. However, after two draftees offer bribes to Falstaff's assistant, BARDOLPH (1), they are released from service and Wart is taken. He is put through an incongruous marching exercise in 3.2.267–272. The episode satirises the notorious greed of 16th-century recruiters.

**Warwick (1), Edward Plantagenet, Earl of**   Character in *Richard III.* See BOY (2).

**Warwick (2), Richard Beauchamp, Earl of (1382–1439)**   Historical figure and character in *1 Henry VI, 2 Henry IV,* and *Henry V.* In *1 Henry VI* Warwick declares for Plantagenet (see YORK [8]) in 2.4, and in 3.1 he presents King HENRY VI with a petition in favour of Plantagenet's restoration as Duke of York. He is present but unimportant in later scenes. In *2 Henry IV* and *Henry V* we see Warwick as a younger man. In *2 Henry IV* he is an adviser to King HENRY IV. He soothes the king's melancholy and rouses him to action in 3.1, and he defends PRINCE (6) HAL in 4.5, asserting that his debauchery is instructing the young man in the ways of evil, from which he will reform himself. This passage is intended to confirm the essential nobility of the future King HENRY V. In *Henry V* Warwick speaks only one line as a member of the King's court.

The historical Warwick was much more important in the affairs of his time than the character is in the plays. As a young man, under Henry IV, he distinguished himself in the army, serving against GLENDOWER's Welsh rebellion and at the battle of SHREWSBURY. He was a highly successful general under Henry V and governed the occupied towns of Calais and ROUEN at various times. Upon the king's death, the infant Henry VI was placed in Warwick's care. In *1*

*Henry VI* Warwick is overshadowed by York, whom Shakespeare wished to emphasise, although the earl was actually a more successful and prominent figure. When he died, Warwick was governing occupied FRANCE (1) as regent for Henry VI.

Shakespeare confused Richard Beauchamp with Richard Neville, a later holder of the same title (see WARWICK [3]): in *2 Henry IV*, 3.1.66, Beauchamp is misnamed Neville, and in *2 Henry VI*, 1.1.117–120, episodes from his military career are claimed by Neville. It is sometimes thought that Neville was expressly intended as the Warwick of *1 Henry VI*, but, although the chronology of that play is hopelessly skewed, certain key features point to Beauchamp. Although Shakespeare was seemingly unaware of the distinction, it seems likely that Richard Beauchamp is the Warwick depicted.

**Warwick (3), Richard Neville, Earl of (1428–1471)**
Historical figure and character in *2* and *3 Henry VI*, the chief backer of the Duke of YORK (8) and then the leader of an effort to dethrone York's son EDWARD IV after he has become King. The Earl of WARWICK (2) in *1 Henry VI* was his father-in-law, Richard Beauchamp, and Shakespeare confused the two. Early in *2 Henry VI*, Shakespeare has Neville laying claim to certain of Beauchamp's military accomplishments (1.1.118–120).

The young nobleman of *2 Henry VI* is a bold, hot-tempered soldier, unswerving in his devotion to serving the cause of right. A proud and spirited youth, Warwick is unafraid to contradict such high-ranking lords as CARDINAL (1) BEAUFORT. Like his father, the Earl of SALISBURY (2), he seeks the good of England rather than personal advancement, in contrast to the other aristocrats. York confides in the Nevilles his intention to seize the throne, claiming descent from RICHARD II, whose crown had been usurped by HENRY VI's grandfather (see YORK [1]; LANCASTER [1]). Warwick and his father agree to support York, accepting the validity of his right to rule. In Act 5 Warwick distinguishes himself as a warrior, fighting with York's forces at the opening battle of the WARS OF THE ROSES. He closes the play exulting in their success and hoping for more to come, thus anticipating the action of *3 Henry VI*.

It is in the later play that Warwick becomes a major figure in the wars. After York is murdered by Queen MARGARET (1), Warwick becomes the leading lieutenant for the Duke's sons. He boosts their spirits, encouraging Edward to claim the throne himself, and he leads them to war against Margaret. When the battle of TOWTON is all but lost, Warwick's rousing vow to revenge the death of his brother restores Yorkist morale and the day is saved.

In consequence, Edward is crowned and Warwick seems to have accomplished his goal. He goes to FRANCE (1) and negotiates a political marriage for Edward, thus securing the Yorkist position by acquiring a strong ally. However, his arrangements are peremptorily cancelled when word arrives that Edward has married an English commoner, who becomes Queen ELIZABETH (2). Warwick, furious that his plans have been dismissed and that his promises to the French king have been dishonoured, immediately allies himself with Margaret and the displaced HENRY VI. He succeeds in capturing Edward and restoring Henry to the throne, but Edward escapes and himself captures Henry. In 5.2 Warwick is mortally wounded at the battle of BARNET. He dies musing on the insignificance of his former power and influence.

The historical Warwick, known as the 'kingmaker', was indeed the chief architect of Yorkist success, and Shakespeare's account of his drive and ambition ring true. However, in his need to compress the sequence of historical events, the playwright distorted the developments behind Warwick's defection to Margaret, which in the play seems so sudden as to be almost frivolous. Shakespeare preserved the essential features of the story, but Warwick's motives were rather more complicated and humanly interested than those of the fickle figure in the play.

Relations between the kingmaker and his former protégé became strained once Edward was in power. Although Warwick disapproved of Edward's marriage, it did not occur while he was in Paris arranging another one; nor was it the principal cause of their split, which did not occur until years later. The two fought over foreign policy, and Warwick's opinions were increasingly ignored. Moreover, when Warwick tried to arrange a marriage between his daughter and Edward's brother GEORGE (2), the king angrily rejected the idea. In 1469, eight years after Edward's coronation, George and Warwick staged a coup. Warwick ruled for nine months in Edward's name, but the king gathered loyalist supporters and drove the usurpers from the kingdom. It was at this point that Warwick, desperate, accepted the proposition of King LEWIS (3), Louis XI of France, that he ally himself with Margaret and restore Henry to the throne. Accordingly, his other daughter, ANNE (2), was betrothed to the one-time PRINCE (4) of Wales, Margaret and Henry's son. As in the play, this alliance briefly placed Henry back on the throne before losing the battle of Barnet, where Warwick did indeed die.

**Warwickshire** County in England, location of STRATFORD, Shakespeare's home, and a setting in *3 Henry VI*. In 4.2 the Duke of WARWICK (3) comes to Warwickshire, his home territory, with a French army, judging his own locality to be the safest place to commence a conquest of England on behalf of the deposed King HENRY VI. One of the chief towns of Warwickshire, COVENTRY, also figures as a location in several of the

HISTORY PLAYS. In addition, in the INDUCTION to *The Taming of the Shrew*, there are numerous references and allusions to the Stratford neighbourhood. This suggests that the play may have been written shortly after Shakespeare's arrival in LONDON.

**Watchmen (1)** Three minor characters in *3 Henry VI*, soldiers who guard the tent of King EDWARD IV. On guard in 4.3, the Watchmen remark on Edward's insistence on courting danger when he could be housed in greater safety, but they claim pridefully that they will protect their king. WARWICK (3) and his soldiers appear and capture Edward, routing the guard instantly. The episode offers an instance of Edward's immaturity, as his bravado makes difficulties for his cause. It also provides a touch of rustic humour when the Watchmen comically fly just as they proclaim their own virtues as guards.

**Watchmen (2)** Minor characters in *Romeo and Juliet*, guards who patrol the streets of VERONA at night. In 5.3 the Watchmen are summoned to the tomb of JULIET (1) by the PAGE (3), who has seen his master, PARIS (2), fighting with ROMEO. They find the bodies of Paris and the two lovers and arrest the witnesses, the FRIAR (4) and BALTHASAR (2). The Watchmen represent the general population of VERONA in opposing the bloody feuding of the MONTAGUE (1) and CAPULET (1) families.

**Watchmen (3)** Minor characters in *Much Ado About Nothing*, the police patrol of MESSINA. In 3.3 the Watchmen prepare for their night's patrol in a comical sequence in which all of the obvious duties of watchmen are denied. For instance, when their commander, DOGBERRY, orders, 'You shall also make no noise in the streets', a Watchman replies, 'We will rather sleep than talk' (3.3.34–36), and Dogberry responds to a query about 'laying hands' on a thief with the observation, '. . . by your office you may, but I think they that touch pitch will be defiled' (3.3.55–56). It has been suggested that this passage parodies a London statute of 1595 that attempted to control nighttime activity in the city.

However, for all their foolishness, these absurd lawmen play a significant role in the drama: they overhear BORACHIO speaking of the deception he has staged as part of the plot of Don JOHN (1) against HERO and CLAUDIO (1). Although still confused, they recognise villainy, and they arrest Borachio and his companion, CONRADE, and testify against them in 4.2 and 5.1, acts that lead to the exposure of the scheme and the happy resolution of the play.

Most of the Watchmen's speeches were not specifically assigned by Shakespeare to one or another of them, and they are largely indistinguishable, though Hugh OATCAKE and George SEACOAL are said to be literate and the latter is appointed the leader of the night's patrol. Scholars speculate that Shakespeare may have been inspired to create the Watchmen by a similar group in John LYLY's play *Endimion* (c. 1588, published 1591).

**Watchmen (4)** Two minor characters in *Antony and Cleopatra*, soldiers in the army of Octavius CAESAR (2). Commanded by a SENTRY (2), the Watchmen guard the perimeter of Caesar's camp outside ALEXANDRIA, in 4.9. They discover the dying ENOBARBUS and bring him into the camp. These guards, designated First and Second Watchman, are alert and active soldiers, examples of the higher morale among Caesar's forces after Antony's defeat at ACTIUM, an important development in the play. Some editions follow 18th-century editorial practise and designate the Sentry and the Watchmen as First, Second, and Third Soldiers.

**Watchmen (5)** Several minor characters in *Coriolanus*, soldiers in the Volscian army. In 5.2 the Watchmen guard the Volscian camp when it is approached by MENENIUS. He seeks to persuade CORIOLANUS, who has deserted ROME and is fighting for the VOLSCIANS, not to attack the city. Two of the Watchmen—designated First and Second Watchman—declare that Coriolanus has banned all Roman emissaries, and they mock Menenius when he claims to be an old friend who will be welcomed by the general. When Coriolanus emerges and rejects Menenius, the Watchmen redouble their taunts as the ambassador departs. This episode provides a mildly comic way to portray the depth of Coriolanus' vengeful hatred for Rome, while reserving the protagonist for the climactic scenes that follow.

**Waterson, John (active 1634)** Publisher in LONDON, producer of the first edition of *The Two Noble Kinsmen*. In 1634 Waterson published *The Two Noble Kinsmen* as a work by Shakespeare and John FLETCHER (2), in a QUARTO edition (known as Q1). Waterson is known to have been a reputable publisher who handled other plays in the repertoire of the KING'S MEN; these factors support the attribution of the play to Shakespeare and Fletcher, a point that is disputed by some scholars.

**Weaver** Minor character in *2 Henry VI*. See SMITH (1).

**Webster (1), Benjamin (1797–1882)** British actor, playwright, and producer. Webster was a successful playwright and character actor, but he is most remembered for a single production from his equally successful career as a theatre-manager In 1844, in collaboration with J. R. PLANCHÉ, he staged *The Taming of the Shrew* and made history by presenting the uncut text of Shakespeare's play. The experiment was well received by the public and the use of legitimate Shakespearean texts eventually became the norm. Webster's great-granddaughter was Margaret WEBSTER (3).

**Webster (2), John (d. 1634)**   English dramatist, a leading figure of JACOBEAN DRAMA. Webster is chiefly known for two plays that are generally considered the greatest Jacobean tragedies after Shakespeare's: *The White Devil* (1612) and *The Duchess of Malfi* (1614). These striking REVENGE PLAYS, which feature obsessed and passionate heroines, are still frequently performed. Webster's poetry, filled with leitmotifs and entrancing imagery, is more finely crafted than that of any dramatist of the period except Shakespeare. Only two other plays by Webster—lesser works—can be surely identified, but he may also have written *The Revenger's Tragedy* (1606), a gruesome and bizarre revenge play that ranks with *The White Devil* and *The Duchess of Malfi*. Published anonymously, it is sometimes attributed to Thomas MIDDLETON or, following a late-17th-century ascription, to Cyril Tourneur (d. 1626), a much lesser talent.

**Webster (3), Margaret (1905–1972)**   British actress and producer, active in the United States. The daughter of two well-known actors—and the great-granddaughter of Benjamin WEBSTER (1)—Webster made her professional debut as an actress with Sybil THORNDIKE and Lewis CASSON. She subsequently toured with Ben GREET and performed at the OLD VIC THEATRE in the early 1930s. In 1936 she moved to New York and became a leading director, especially of Shakespeare. Often employing Maurice EVANS (4) as leading man, Webster mounted many noteworthy productions, including *1 Henry IV* and *Hamlet* in 1939, *Macbeth* in 1941—with Judith ANDERSON (2) as LADY (6) MACBETH—and a controversial *Othello* starring Paul ROBESON. She also lectured widely in America and supervised the Shakespearean productions at the New York World's Fair in 1939. While she popularised Shakespeare to a great extent, she was also criticised for tampering with his texts, perhaps most notoriously when she replaced the EPILOGUE of *The Tempest* with PROSPERO's famous 'revels' speech, relocated from 4.1.148–158, in her otherwise well-received production of 1945. She wrote on her experiences as a director in *Shakespeare Without Tears* (1942).

**Weelkes, Thomas (c. 1575–1623)**   Composer of madrigals, the text to one of which was ascribed to Shakespeare in William JAGGARD's spurious anthology *The Passionate Pilgrim* (1599). 'My flocks feed not', published in Weelkes' *Madrigals to 3, 4, 5 & 6 Voices* (1597), appears as poem no. 17 in Jaggard's collection. However, since madrigalists did not usually write the lyrics to their songs, the creator of this poem remains unknown; scholars agree that it—like many of the poems in the *Pilgrim*—is definitely not Shakespearean.

Weelkes was one of the leading composers of his day, but little is known about him. He was also a noted organist, playing at Chichester Cathedral for the last two decades of his life. He published four collections of songs before 1608 but later devoted himself chiefly to church music.

**Welcombe**   Village near STRATFORD, the site of a real estate investment of Shakespeare's and the centre of a political crisis that gripped Stratford from 1614 to 1616. Shakespeare owned property near Welcome, and he also subleased tithes to lands in the village, in partnership with Thomas GREENE (3). That is, he paid a fee for the right to collect the taxes—a percentage of the profits—on specified fields, to a man who had purchased a long-term lease on these rights from the town of Stratford.

In August 1614 a proposal was made by Arthur Mainwaring, a nobleman from Shropshire who owned a large tract of land in Welcombe, to enclose the farmlands in the area and use them to raise sheep. This idea, known as enclosure, was one of the major sources of conflict in 16th- and 17th-century England. Under the traditional medieval system, agricultural lands were owned in units no larger than a few acres and generally much smaller, organised in clusters within which a given owner's or renter's holdings were scattered randomly. This system was extremely uneconomic, for such techniques as crop rotation were impractical and no one would introduce capital improvements such as irrigation when his neighbours would benefit as much or more than he. Under enclosure, these units were grouped together in larger lots that were 'enclosed' by ditches and hedges and used for grazing sheep, whose wool was sold to the burgeoning cloth industry. Though grazing was less productive per acre, it required much less labour, and when enough acres were involved, it was extremely profitable. Its eventual widespread adoption boosted England's economy into the modern world. However, the conversion of lands from agriculture to pasture was invariably fiercely resisted, for its immediate, local effects were negative. It raised the price of grain by reducing its supply, and it produced unemployment, for herding sheep required only a few shepherds for hundreds of acres.

In 1614 in Stratford, Mainwaring was joined by a local landowner, William COMBE (5), in promoting enclosure, against the opposition of the town of Stratford, protecting the majority of its citizens. Shakespeare's opinion was doubtless ambivalent, for as a tithe holder, he stood to gain if the overall productivity of the area rose, yet he might take immediate losses as arable land was converted to pasture. In any case he had the foresight to strike a deal with Mainwaring's agent, who guaranteed him and Greene against any such losses, thus forestalling their potential opposition. Greene, however, was the town clerk of Stratford and as such was opposed anyway. His correspondence on the matter has survived, and his continuing attempts to recruit Shakespeare to his side reflect the playwright's cool distance from the subject. In November 1614 he records a conversation in which Shakespeare assured him that Mainwaring's proposal would probably be dropped and need not be worried about.

However, Mainwaring and Combe proceeded, evicting tenant farmers from their lands and preparing ditches and hedges for sheep fields. They countered opposition with violence, Combe being particularly arrogant in his encounters with opponents. In March 1615 the WARWICKSHIRE court issued an injunction against the enclosure, and Mainwaring withdrew, but Combe, incensed, appealed the case and continued to persecute the tenant farmers, destroying their crops, seizing their livestock, beating them, and even briefly imprisoning some of them. He bought up lands and houses in an express attempt to depopulate Wel-

combe. The crisis dragged on for another year, before the chief justice of England ruled firmly against Combe, only refraining from punishing him because he was the sitting sheriff of Warwickshire at the time. Combe finally dropped his efforts, though he was to reinstitute the proposal several times.

**Welles, Orson (1915–1985)** American actor, director, and producer of stage and FILM. Welles is probably best remembered for his movies—especially his first, *Citizen Kane* (1940)—and his panic-inducing radio play *The War of the Worlds* (1938), but he was also a significant Shakespearean actor and director. He established himself as an actor playing MERCUTIO in Katherine CORNELL's *Romeo and Juliet* (1933). Working for the Depression-era Negro Theatre Project, Welles directed a controversial *Macbeth* (1936), with an all-black cast, that was set in 18th-century Haiti and featured a gigantic mask as BANQUO'S GHOST (4), a HECATE with a 12-foot bullwhip, and a band of on-stage drummers. In 1937 he and John Houseman (1902–1988)

*Orson Welles directed and starred in a film version of* Macbeth *and another movie,* Chimes at Midnight, *that followed the career of Falstaff through three plays. Welles brought a new, expressionistic language to Shakespeare films.* (Courtesy of Culver Pictures, Inc.)

founded the Mercury Theatre—having lost their federal financing for political reasons—and their first production was a famous, politically oriented, modern-dress *Julius Caesar* (1938), directed by Welles, who also played BRUTUS (4). The Mercury Theatre successfully presented many modern and classic plays and is regarded as a milestone in Broadway history, but Welles turned his attention to films. He went to Hollywood, where he directed several masterpieces of American cinema, including *Citizen Kane, The Magnificent Ambersons* (1941), and *Lady from Shangai* (1948). In 1948 he also filmed *Macbeth,* with himself in the title role. However, these movies were not successful at the box office, and Welles went abroad to make low-budget films, including *Othello* (1952), shot in Morocco. In 1956 he returned to the Shakespearean stage a final time, to direct and star in *King Lear.* Perhaps his finest Shakespearean film was his last one, *Chimes at Midnight* (1965; known as *Falstaff* in Europe) a combination of FALSTAFF's episodes from the *Henry IV* plays, *The Merry Wives of Windsor,* and *Henry V.*

**Westminster (1) Abbey**   London church, the location for 1.1 of *1 Henry VI* and the site of a well-known monument to Shakespeare. A masterpiece of Gothic architecture, the Abbey contains memorials to many famous English men and women, including, in the 'Poet's Corner', a monument incorporating a statue of Shakespeare by Peter SCHEEMAKERS. Westminster Abbey has been the traditional setting for British royal ceremonies since long before 1425, when the funeral of HENRY V took place there, as depicted in *1 Henry VI.*

**Westminster (2), Abbot of**   Character in *Richard II.* See ABBOT OF WESTMINSTER.

**Westminster (3) Hall**   Room in WESTMINSTER (4) PALACE, London, location in *Richard II.* King RICHARD II is forced to abdicate in Westminster Hall in 4.1. This massive chamber (70 by 240 feet) was already famous in Shakespeare's day as the site of many famous trials, including the historical deposition of Richard, although the king was not present at the actual occasion. Shortly after the play was written, the Earl of ESSEX (2) was sentenced to death in the same room. Its famous timber roof, still one of the grandest sights in London, was commissioned in 1394 by Richard himself, following flood damage. Ironically, the work was still in progress when Richard was deposed.

**Westminster (4) Palace**   Complex of buildings constituting the seat of England's royal government and the setting for many scenes in Shakespeare's HISTORY PLAYS. Often, the events depicted in Westminster Palace are of a governmental nature, whether confidential, as when the Earl of SUFFOLK (3) persuades King HENRY VI to marry the future Queen MARGARET (1) in

5.5 of *1 Henry VI,* or public, as when RICHARD III is crowned in 4.2 of *Richard III.* However, since the palace was also a royal residence in the era depicted—as it was in Shakespeare's day—some of the events set within it are private. For instance, in 2.4 of *Richard III,* Queen ELIZABETH (2) prepares to flee with her young sons into the sanctuary of a church, and in 4.5 of *2 Henry IV,* PRINCE (6) HAL encounters his father, King HENRY IV, on his death-bed.

The following scenes—some of them only specified by such stage directions as 'a room in the Queen's apartments' (*Henry VIII* 3.1.1) but some more specifically—take place in Westminster Palace: *1 Henry VI* 3.1 (in PARLIAMENT HOUSE, a separate building within the palace), 5.1, 5.5; *2 Henry VI* 1.1; *3 Henry VI* 1.1 (in Parliament House), 3.2, 4.1, 4.4, 5.7; *Richard II* 4.1 (in WESTMINSTER [3] HALL); *Richard III* 1.3, 2.1, 2.4, 4.2–4; *1 Henry IV* 1.1–2, 3.2; *2 Henry IV* 3.1, 4.5, 5.2; *Henry V* 1.1–2; and *Henry VIII* 1.1–3, 2.2–3, 3.1–2, 5.1–4.

The palace at Westminster, built by William the Conqueror (ruled 1066–1087), was added to and embellished over the centuries, gradually disappearing under the rebuilding, especially after a disastrous fire in 1298. At the time of the history plays, England's monarchs knew Westminster Palace as a warren of buildings that included offices, churches, residences, and meeting halls. Another great fire in 1834 resulted in the construction of the present-day Westminster Palace, encompassing the Houses of Parliament, one of the masterpieces of 19th-century architecture designed by Charles Barry (1795–1860) and A. W. N. Pugin (1812–1852).

**Westmoreland (1), Ralph Neville, Earl of (1364–1425)**   Historical figure and character in *1* and *2 Henry IV* and *Henry V.* In *1* and *2 Henry IV* Westmoreland is a loyal adviser to King HENRY IV, though he is rather faceless. In 1.1 of *1 Henry IV* he brings grave news of military setbacks, introducing the unrest that besets Henry's reign. He later appears briefly at the battle of SHREWSBURY. In *2 Henry IV* Westmoreland is again a solid supporter of the king, defending Henry against the rebellious noblemen's claims of mistreatment. In 4.2 he seconds Prince John of LANCASTER (3) in his fraudulent offer of a truce to the rebels at GAULTREE FOREST, and he arrests the leaders after they have unsuspectingly sent their troops home. In 4.4 he brings news of the final defeat of the rebels, closing the history of revolts against Henry.

In *Henry V* Westmoreland has a minor role and is notable only for expressing a wish for reinforcements just before the battle of AGINCOURT, provoking King HENRY V's famed 'St. Crispin's Day' speech (4.3.18–67). The historical Westmoreland was not present at Agincourt, having been placed in command of the Scottish border. His more prominent role in the *Henry IV* plays reflects his historical position more accurately, though here, too, Shakespeare altered reality. Westmoreland backed BOLINGBROKE (1), later Henry IV, in his deposition of RICHARD II, although Richard had granted him his earldom. He served the new king loyally, as the plays show. It was he who actually tricked the rebel leaders at Gaultree, not Prince John, who was a youth at the time. Shakespeare de-emphasised Westmoreland in order to keep the focus on Henry's family.

Westmoreland married twice and fathered 16 children, and several of his descendants appear in Shakespeare's plays. By his first wife he was the grandfather of the WESTMORELAND (2) who appears in *3 Henry VI*; by the second he was the father of the Earl of SALISBURY (2) of *2 Henry VI* and grandfather of the Earl of WARWICK (3), known as the 'kingmaker', of *2* and *3 Henry VI*.

**Westmoreland (2), Ralph Neville, Earl of (c. 1404–1484)** Historical figure and minor character in *3 Henry VI*, a Lancastrian nobleman (see LANCASTER [1]). Westmoreland is one of the supporters of King HENRY VI who angrily leave the monarch's presence when he agrees to bequeath the throne to YORK (8) in 1.1. Following his sources, Shakespeare erred in assigning this Westmoreland a role in the WARS OF THE ROSES. He took no part in the conflict and is thought to have been an invalid. He was the grandson of the Earl of WESTMORELAND (1) who appears in *1* and *2 Henry IV* and *Henry V*.

**Whatcott, Robert (active 1613–1616)** Witness to Shakespeare's will. In 1613 Whatcott appeared as a witness for Susanna SHAKESPEARE (14) Hall in her libel suit against John LANE (1). He may have been a servant in the Hall household.

**Whetstone, George (c. 1544–c. 1587)** English author and playwright whose works were sources for Shakespeare. Whetstone's play *Promos and Cassandra* (1578), based on a novella by the Italian writer, CINTHIO, was a principal source for *Measure for Measure*. A story in his *The Rocke of Regard* (1576) may have inspired an aspect of *Much Ado About Nothing*, the fact that HERO is rejected at her own wedding.

Whetstone, the son of a London haberdasher, was best known for *Promos and Cassandra* and for *An Heptameron of Civil Discourse*, which describes his travels in Italy in 1580 and includes a version of the Cinthio tale the play was based on. His later works, including *A Mirror for Magistrates* (1584), which also may have had some influence on *Measure for Measure*, were more didactic and sermonising as he came under the influence of Puritanism. An adventurous man, he sailed on an abortive expedition to America in 1578, and he entered the military in 1587, serving under LEICESTER in the Low Countries, where he was killed in a duel with another English officer.

**White (1), Edward (active 1577–1612)** London publisher of early editions of *Titus Andronicus*. Chiefly a publisher of ballads, White joined Thomas MILLINGTON in publishing the first edition (Q1) of *Titus* in 1594, and he published Q2 (1600) and Q3 (1611) himself. The son of a Suffolk retailer, White was a successful publisher, becoming an officer of the STATIONERS' COMPANY.

**White (2), William (active 1583–1615)** LONDON printer. White printed plays by Shakespeare and others, as well as numerous ballads. He printed first editions of *Love's Labour's Lost* (1598, for publisher Cuthbert BURBY) and *Pericles* (1609, for Henry GOSSON [1]), and later editions of *3 Henry VI* (Q2, 1600, for Thomas MILLINGTON), *Richard II* (Q4, 1608, for Matthew LAW), *Pericles* (Q2, 1609, for Gosson), and *1 Henry IV* (Q5, 1613, for Law).

**Whitefriars Theatre** Seventeenth-century LONDON playhouse. The Whitefriars Theatre, named for its site on the grounds of a former priory of the Carmelite, or White Friars, was established by Michael DRAYTON and others in 1608, as a venue for the short-lived King's Revels Company (see CHILDREN'S COMPANIES). The Queen's Revels, another boys' troupe, played there from 1609 to 1613, and an adult company, LADY ELIZABETH'S MEN, in 1613–1614, after which Drayton's lease expired. PRINCE CHARLES' MEN may have played there occasionally until at least 1621, but the later history of the theatre is obscure. It was replaced in 1629 by another theatre on the same site.

**Whitgift, John (c. 1530–1604)** English clergyman, issuer of Shakespeare's marriage licence and later a powerful leader of the Church of England. As Bishop of Worcester, the diocese that included STRATFORD, Whitgift signed the licence authorising the marriage of Shakespeare and Anne Whateley—a clerical error for Anne HATHAWAY—without the usual three banns or formal announcements of intention to marry. This dispensation was required because Advent season was beginning, during which time banns could not be declared, and a quick marriage was desired, for Anne was pregnant. Whitgift was a famously stern churchman, and that he approved the avoidance of banns indicates that it was not a shady procedure, as some have thought.

Whitgift was shortly to occupy the most powerful position in the English church. A graduate and long-time professor and administrator of Cambridge University, Whitgift forcefully opposed a strong strain of Puritanism among the faculty and students. Queen ELIZABETH (1) was pleased with his opinion on this subject, which was becoming increasingly divisive in the nation, and she appointed Whitgift Bishop of Worcester in 1577, and then Archbishop of Canterbury in 1583. As archbishop, he was most noted for his repressive campaign against Puritanism, but he was also a highly competent administrator and instituted valuable reforms. He became a close adviser to the Queen, and later officiated at the coronation of her successor, King JAMES I.

**Whitmore, Walter**  Minor character in *2 Henry VI*, a sailor on a pirate ship and the executioner of the Duke of SUFFOLK (3) in 4.1. The LIEUTENANT (1) of the vessel gives Whitmore the authority to collect a ransom from Suffolk, whom the pirates have captured from another ship. Whitmore, having lost an eye in the battle for the ship, wants revenge, not ransom, and he insists, over the Lieutenant's protests, that he will kill Suffolk. When he identifies himself by name, it is as 'Water' Whitmore, the Elizabethan pronunciation of his name, and Suffolk is reminded of the prediction made by a SPIRIT in 1.4 that he would die by water. When the Lieutenant learns who Suffolk is, he denounces the Duke's political crimes and sends him with Whitmore to be beheaded. Whitmore returns with Suffolk's head and body and gives them to a released prisoner, a GENTLEMAN (1), who is to take them to London.

**The Whole Contention**  Abbreviated title of a publication of 1619 containing BAD QUARTO texts of *2* and *3 Henry VI*. The full title of the volume is *The Whole Contention between the two Famous Houses, Lancaster and Yorke. With the Tragicall ends of the good Duke Humfrey, Richard Duke of Yorke, and King Henrie the sixt. The Whole Contention* was printed by William JAGGARD and published by Thomas PAVIER as part of the FALSE FOLIO. It consists of slightly edited earlier versions of the plays; THE CONTENTION (Q1 of *2 Henry VI*) is combined in one volume with THE TRUE TRAGEDY (Q1 of *Part 3*). *The True Tragedy* was altered only slightly by Pavier, but *The Contention* underwent many minor changes, along with the substantial addition of elaborated genealogical material, taken from the 1615 edition of John STOW's *Chronicle*.

Each of the texts in *The Whole Contention* is known as the Q3 edition of its play. For both plays, the FIRST FOLIO text is basic to all modern editions. The *Whole Contention* texts evidently had only minor influence on the composition of the Folio, except for the introduction of the new genealogical material into 2.2 of *3 Henry VI*.

**Widow (1)**  Minor character in *The Taming of the Shrew*, the bride of HORTENSIO. The Widow first appears at the banquet in 5.2. She is unwilling to obey her new husband, although he believes he is able to control her, having watched PETRUCHIO (2) handle the shrew-

ish KATHERINA. When the men bet on the obedience of their wives, the Widow flatly refuses Hortensio's mild request, and Katherina gives her a lengthy lecture on a wife's proper duties. The Widow has no developed personality; she serves simply as a foil for the newly obedient Katherina.

**Widow (2) Capilet**  Character in *All's Well That Ends Well*, a landlady of FLORENCE who befriends HELENA (2) and is the mother of DIANA (1). The Widow permits Diana to make a sexual assignation with BERTRAM, Helena's runaway husband, though Helena will occupy Diana's bed. When she first appears, in 3.5, the Widow has charm as a stereotypical gossip, and she shrewdly recognises Bertram for the cad he is, but thereafter she serves merely as a pawn of the plot.

**Wieland, Christoph Martin (1733–1813)**  German poet and translator. Wieland produced the first German translations of Shakespeare, and rendered 22 of the plays into prose between 1762 and 1766. His work inspired and was superseded by that of J. J. ESCHENBURG.

As a young man, Wieland was known for poetry that supported Pietism, a popular religious and esthetic cult of the day. He later achieved a European reputation as the creator of sophisticated, elegant, and mildly erotic verses and novels that celebrated an ideal of the Enlightenment movement, the combination of intellect and sensuality. He was regarded for a time—until the advent of GOETHE—as Germany's greatest writer. However, with the rise of Romanticism in the early 19th century, Wieland's reputation declined catastrophically, and it is only in recent years that critics have once again taken him seriously.

**Wife**  Minor character in *2 Henry VI*, the wife of the imposter SIMPCOX. In 2.1 the pair appear before the king's hawking party near ST ALBANS. She supports her husband's false story of miraculously repaired blindness, and, when the Duke of GLOUCESTER (4) unmasks their fraud, she is condemned with her husband to be whipped through every town between St Albans and the distant village they had claimed as their home.

**Wilkins, George (active 1603–1608)**  English author and dramatist. Wilkins was a hack writer who penned pamphlets, plays, and a novel; virtually nothing more is known of his life. As a playwright, he collaborated with John DAY, Thomas DEKKER, Samuel ROWLEY (1), and others, and some scholars attribute parts of *Timon of Athens* or *Pericles* to him, though these suggestions are very uncertain and much disputed. Wilkins also wrote a play on his own, *The Miseries of Enforced Marriage* (1607), which dealt with the same notorious murder that was the subject of A YORKSHIRE TRAGEDY. Wilkins' novel, *The Painful Adventures of Pericles Prince of Tyre*

(1608), was written to capitalise on the popularity of Shakespeare's *Pericles*. It is the principal reason for speculation that he wrote parts of the play, but the novel does not much resemble the parts of *Pericles* that can be attributed to a collaborator, so most scholars believe that Wilkins is unlikely to have had a hand in the play.

**William (1) Page** Character in *The Merry Wives of Windsor*, son of George PAGE (12) and MISTRESS (3) Page. William appears only in the famous 'Latin' scene (4.1), where he is quizzed by his schoolmaster, EVANS (3). Evans' Welsh accent and the confusion of an observer, Mistress QUICKLY, combine to produce a parody of the standard Latin textbook of Shakespeare's day, LILY's *Latin Grammar*. William stumbles through the interview, none too well prepared, until he is finally forced to admit, 'Forsooth, I have forgot' (4.1.-67). He is then excused from the impromptu lesson. The scene, with its bevy of double entendres and bilingual puns, was presumably intended especially for the educated audience for whom the play was written, but the episode may also reflect Shakespeare's childhood memories. He had himself learned Latin from Lily's *Grammar* at school in STRATFORD; perhaps William's name was not without sentimental significance for the playwright.

**William (2)** Minor character in *As You Like It*, a rustic swain whom TOUCHSTONE intimidates into abandoning his courtship of AUDREY. Like Audrey, William is a CLOWN (1), a comic caricature of a peasant as imagined by the London audience for whom he was created. He fancies he has 'a pretty wit' (5.1.28), but he is preposterously ill-spoken; the longest word he speaks is his own name, and his longest speech has only seven words. He has no substantial personality; he simply offers a humorous contrast to the courtly ways of the major characters. William's unsophisticated weakness parodies the conventions of love in his own way, as the attitudes of Touchstone and SILVIUS satirise them in others.

**Williams (1), Harcourt (1880–1957)** English actor and director. Williams, a successful actor who appeared mostly in modern plays—although he was the FIRST PLAYER (2) in John BARRYMORE's London presentation of *Hamlet* (1925)—was the director of the OLD VIC THEATRE from 1929 to 1934. A follower of Harley GRANVILLE-BARKER, he insisted on staging the full texts of Shakespeare's plays, with little or no scenery. He encouraged rapid speaking of Elizabethan English, both to make clear its colloquial nature in the characters' mouths and to keep the performances from flagging. In 1935 he published a memoir of his directorate, *Four Years at the Old Vic*. He resumed his acting career and returned to the Old Vic as an actor in 1946.

**Williams (2), Michael** Character in *Henry V*, a soldier who unknowingly disputes with King HENRY V, who is disguised as a common soldier, in 4.1. Henry finds that Williams doubts the virtue of the English invasion of France and asserts that, if Henry's cause is not righteous, the king must accept responsibility before God for the sin of unjustifiable killing committed by his men. Henry argues irrelevantly that the king cannot be held accountable for the soldiers' sins committed before the battle, and Williams concedes the point but doubts the king's reputed promise to fight to the death rather than be ransomed. The two men exchange gloves, to be worn on their hats as identification, and each agrees to challenge the other to a fight if he sees him after the forthcoming battle of AGINCOURT. However, when Henry, undisguised, sees Williams in 4.7, he does not acknowledge their prior meeting but sends the soldier on an errand. He then gives the glove that he holds to Fluellen and sends him to the same place as Williams, ensuring an encounter. When the two meet in 4.8, they prepare to fight; Henry appears and explains matters but demands a defence from Williams for having dared to abuse the monarch. Williams makes the obvious explanation—that he could not have known the king—and Henry returns him his glove, filled with money. Williams sharply rejects Fluellen's offer of a further gratuity.

This episode may be viewed in either of two lights, depending on one's interpretation of the play, which Shakespeare deliberately made ambiguous. If King Henry is seen as an epic hero, his encounter with Williams may be seen as evidence of the king's commendable ability to relate to the common soldiers of his army. The dispute in 4.1, from this point of view, offers the king a lesson in humility by displaying the virtues of forthright courage that may be found in all men, and it leads to the king's great soliloquy (4.1. 236–290) in which he regrets his royalty. When the king generously rewards Williams in 4.8, he recalls the magnanimity of his youth as PRINCE (6) HAL, enacted in *1* and *2 Henry IV*. On the other hand, if the play is taken as a satire on war and politics, and Henry as a hypocritical militarist, then emphasis shifts to Williams' scepticism about the morality of Henry's war. The soldier's honest doubt is shuffled off by a sophistic evasion. The business of the gloves displays Williams as a courageous commoner who is patronised by a superior who first makes a riskless challenge and then diverts it to Fluellen, seemingly for mere entertainment. Shakespeare set up a number of such ambivalent situations in this play, and Williams, a convincing British soldier—his name suggests that he may be Welsh—contributes much to the realism of this one.

**Williamson, Nicol (b. 1938)** British actor and director. Williamson has been acclaimed in a number of major Shakespearean performances, most notably perhaps as CORIOLANUS in Trevor NUNN's 1973 Royal Shakespeare Company production, as MACBETH on stage in 1974 and 1982 and on TELEVISION in 1983, and as HAMLET in London, New York, and on an American tour in 1968–1969 and in FILM in 1970. In 1982 he directed a highly successful *Othello,* with James Earl JONES (1) in the title role.

**Willoughby (1), Sir Ambrose (active 1598)** High official in the court of Queen ELIZABETH (1) and possibly a satirical model for MALVOLIO in *Twelfth Night.* Willoughby was the queen's chief sewer, the official in charge of the service of meals at court. In 1598 Willoughby had a dispute with Shakespeare's patron, the Earl of SOUTHAMPTON (2), that has been proposed as the source of Malvolio's famous encounter with SIR TOBY, SIR ANDREW, and FESTE in 2.3. After having chastised the earl and Sir Walter RALEIGH for their noisy midnight carousing in the queen's courtyard, Willoughby was physically accosted by Southampton but successfully drove the earl from the palace. The queen later publicly thanked Willoughby for the deed.

This incident's resemblance to the one in the play is the basis for the link between Willoughby and Malvolio that some scholars make. Others, however, point out that Elizabeth supported Willoughby very strongly and that the playwright was therefore unlikely to pillory him. (For other possible Malvolios, see FFARINGTON; HOBY (2); KNOLLYS.)

**Willoughby (2) (Willobie) Henry (b. c. 1575)** English poet and possibly the Mr W. H. of the SONNETS. Willoughby is believed to have been the author of the poem 'Willobie his Avisa' (1594), a long account of the attempts of various suitors, including the poet, to seduce the chaste Avisa. In an anonymous commendatory poem published with 'Willobie', Shakespeare is named as the author of *The Rape of Lucrece,* in the earliest surviving reference to him as a poet. In 'Willobie' itself, the poet, 'H. W.', tells of his conversations with his friend, the 'old player', 'W. S.', who has similarly fallen a victim to passion. Some commentators believe that Shakespeare was W. S., that the frustrating love affair of W. S. is that described in the Sonnets, and that H. W. is the Mr W. H. of Thomas THORPE's dedication to the Sonnets. Further, Avisa is sometimes held to be the 'dark lady' of the Sonnets (although it is unclear in 'Willobie' whether W. S. has loved Avisa or another woman). However, both W. S. and Avisa remain unidentified—even Willoughby is hardly known—and these speculations remain entirely unprovable. Willoughby may conceivably have known Shakespeare, however, for he was a cousin by marriage of the playwright's friend Thomas RUSSELL.

**Willoughby (3), William de (d. 1409)** Historical figure and minor character in *Richard II,* a supporter of BOLINGBROKE (1). In 2.1 Willoughby and Lord ROSS (2) join the Earl of NORTHUMBERLAND (1) in rebellion against King RICHARD II, agreeing that their status as aristocrats is imperiled by Richard's seizure of Bolingbroke's inheritance. In 2.3 they accompany Bolingbroke as he marches against the King.

The historical Willoughby, a prominent landowner in Lincolnshire, was descended from a knight in the army of William the Conqueror and thus had great prestige among the aristocracy. He later married the widow of the Duke of YORK (4), Joan of Kent—the successor to the DUCHESS (4) of the play—who went on to marry a third Shakespearean character, Henry le SCROOP (1).

**Wilson (1), Jack (c. 1585–c. 1641)** Singer and actor who may have played BALTHASAR (4) in *Much Ado About Nothing.* A stage direction in the FOLIO edition of the play (1623) refers to 'Iacke Wilson', plainly an actor who played the part—though perhaps not in the original production. Although an otherwise unknown Wilson may have been the man, Jack Wilson is known to have been an actor and singer and is thus generally favoured (but see WILSON [2]). He was the son of a travelling minstrel but was probably a lifelong resident of London himself. Little more is known of him, though he is recorded as a singer whom the city of London hired on ceremonial occasions.

**Wilson (2), John (1595–1674)** Noted composer, musician, and singer. Early in his career Wilson composed music for the stage, including settings for two Shakespearean songs, 'Take, o take those lips away' (*Measure for Measure,* 4.1.1–6) and 'Lawn as white as driven snow' (*The Winter's Tale,* 4.4.220–232). He may have been the 'Iacke Wilson' who played BALTHASAR (4), according to a stage direction in the FIRST FOLIO edition of *Much Ado About Nothing* (1623). Though he was too young to have originated the part, he could have taken the role in a later production (but see WILSON [1]). In 1635 he became a royal musician under King Charles I; in 1642, at the beginning of the Civil Wars, he fled with the king to Oxford, where he received a doctorate in music, becoming a professor of music in 1656. He published a collection of English songs, *Cheerful Ayres or Ballads* (c. 1660), which contains the pieces mentioned above, along with works by Robert JOHNSON (5) and others. Upon his death Wilson was buried in WESTMINSTER (1) ABBEY, a measure of his eminence.

**Wilson (3), John Dover (1881–1969)** English scholar. Editor of many of the plays in the New Cambridge edition of Shakespeare's plays, Dover Wilson also wrote a number of books on the playwright and his works, including *The Essential Shakespeare* (1932),

*What Happens in Hamlet* (1935), and *The Fortunes of Falstaff* (1943).

**Wilson (4), Robert (c. 1550–c. 1600)** English actor and dramatist. Wilson, associated with LEICESTER'S MEN and the QUEEN'S MEN (1), was highly respected as an actor—he was classed with the great Richard TARLTON in his ability to extemporise witty verse—and he was also noted as a playwright. He apparently retired from the stage before 1594 to concentrate exclusively on writing. He probably wrote *The Three Ladies of London* (1584), *The Three Lords and Three Ladies of London* (1590), and *The Cobbler's Prophecy* (1594), and he collaborated with others on SIR JOHN OLDCASTLE. He is also known to have written or collaborated on a number of other plays that are now lost, many of them created for the ADMIRAL'S MEN.

**Winchester (1), Henry Beaufort, Bishop of (1374–1447)** Historical figure and character in *1 Henry VI*, illegitimate son of John of GAUNT, older brother of the Duke of EXETER (2), and uncle of the dukes of SOMERSET (1, 3). The same historical figure appears in *2 Henry VI*, where he is known as CARDINAL (1) BEAUFORT. In *1 Henry VI*, 1.1, Winchester's feud with the Duke of GLOUCESTER (4) interrupts the funeral of HENRY V, introducing dissension as a major theme of the play. Winchester reveals depths of criminality by plotting to kidnap the infant king, HENRY VI, although this plan is not followed up; it seems to be presented solely as an indication of the bishop's character, although it may constitute a remnant inadvertently left in place after a revision. The bishop and Gloucester wrangle further, until their followers are battling in the streets. The king pleads for peace and, while Gloucester is willing, Winchester only reluctantly and hypocritically agrees to a truce.

The quarrel between YORK (8) and Somerset takes precedence in the rest of the play, and the bishop's role diminishes. In 5.1 he turns over to the papal LEGATE a bribe owed to the pope for his promotion to cardinal. This does not affect the course of the play, but it confirms Winchester's image as an unscrupulous villain.

Shakespeare depicts Winchester as a MACHIAVEL, unscrupulously ambitious and persistently at odds with 'good Duke Humphrey' of Gloucester. The historical Winchester led a 'peace party' that opposed Gloucester in the 1440s. To some extent, Winchester's stance was dictated by his rivalry with Gloucester; each aspired to power in the vacuum created by the king's extreme youth. On the other hand, Gloucester, as brother of HENRY V and a veteran of the battle of AGINCOURT, was committed to total victory in France and adamantly opposed any compromise. Winchester favoured an accommodation with the enemy to end the long and costly conflict. Shakespeare's position, which his sources and most of his contemporaries shared, was that England lost France as a result of internal dissension that counteracted English valour, which would otherwise have won out. Thus both the sources and the playwright favoured the 'hawk' Gloucester—in reality something of a monomaniac whose actions significantly hurt the English cause—over the 'dove' Winchester, probably the sounder statesman.

**Winchester (2), Stephen Gardiner, Bishop of** Character in *Henry VIII*. See GARDINER.

**Windsor** Town west of London, setting for *The Merry Wives of Windsor,* several scenes in *Richard II,* and one scene in *1 Henry IV*. In *The Merry Wives* the town is a typical English rural community in which the intrusion of a comical but cynical and exploitative outsider, FALSTAFF, is defeated by the homespun wiles of the title characters. *The Merry Wives* was written for a ceremonial occasion at the court of Queen ELIZABETH (1), a banquet in honour of new members of the the the Order of the Garter. The banquet was held in London, but the formal induction ceremonies were scheduled for a later date at Windsor Castle—an occasion referred to in 5.5.56–74—and this doubtless accounts for the use of Windsor as the setting.

Modern scholars have determined that the events enacted in certain scenes of the HISTORY PLAYS actually took place in Windsor Castle, a principal headquarters for British sovereigns since the days of William the Conqueror, who began its construction; thus in many modern editions the castle is designated as the setting for scenes that are not explicitly located in the original texts. These scenes are 1.1, 2.2, 5.3, 5.4, and 5.6 of *Richard II* and 1.3 of *1 Henry IV*.

## *The Winter's Tale*

### SYNOPSIS

*Act 1, Scene 1*
The courtiers CAMILLO and ARCHIDAMUS speak of their respective kings, LEONTES of SICILIA and POLIXENES of BOHEMIA, who have been friends since childhood. Polixenes has been visiting Sicilia and is about to leave. The courtiers also speak of the good qualities of Leontes' young son, MAMILLIUS, who will certainly make a fine ruler.

*Act 1, Scene 2*
Leontes tries to persuade Polixenes to extend his visit, but he insists he must return to Bohemia. Leontes then asks Queen HERMIONE to convince him. When she does, Leontes suspects that they are lovers. He sends them away and talks with Camillo, who forcefully rejects his suspicions. Insisting that he is correct, Leontes orders Camillo to poison Polixenes. Camillo

reluctantly agrees, but instead informs Polixenes, and they leave together for Bohemia.

### Act 2, Scene 1

When a LORD (16) tells Leontes of the flight of Polixenes and Camillo, the king rages about treachery. He formally accuses Hermione of adultery and treason, declaring that she is currently pregnant with Polixenes' child. She defends herself, but he sends her to prison. Although ANTIGONUS and the other lords try to dissuade the king, he insists that she is an adulteress and adds that he has sent messengers to the oracle of Apollo for confirmation of this.

### Act 2, Scene 2

Antigonus' wife, PAULINA, tries to visit Hermione in prison but is only permitted to see her attendant, EMILIA (3), who reports that the queen has given birth to a daughter. Paulina resolves to take the infant to Leontes and convince him that the child is his.

### Act 2, Scene 3

When Paulina brings the baby to Leontes, he is enraged. He sends her away and orders the baby killed. Antigonus pleads for the infant's life, and Leontes tells him to take the child—but only to abandon it in some wilderness, where it may or may not survive. Antigonus then leaves with the baby.

### Act 3, Scene 1

CLEOMENES AND DION return from the oracle and describe its awe-inspiring appearance. They bear a proclamation answering the king's inquiry.

### Act 3, Scene 2

Hermione, accompanied by Paulina, is brought to trial for adultery; she again defends herself and appeals to the oracle. Cleomenes and Dion read the oracle's judgement, which proclaims the innocence of Hermione, Polixenes, and Camillo, but Leontes refuses to believe it. Word then arrives of Mamillius' sudden death from fright at his mother's fate. Leontes interprets this event as a supernatural confirmation of the oracle and repents, but Hermione faints and must be taken away by Paulina. Just as Leontes resolves to welcome Camillo back and apologise to Polixenes, Paulina returns and reports Hermione's death. She excoriates Leontes, and he accepts her criticisms as entirely just.

### Act 3, Scene 3

In stormy weather, on a remote part of the Bohemian coast, Antigonus reports a vision in which the ghost of Hermione instructed him to take the baby there and to name her PERDITA. He is attacked and driven away by a BEAR, but a SHEPHERD (2) finds the infant. He is joined by his son, the CLOWN (8), who has seen Antigonus being eaten by the bear and his ship sinking in the storm. They discover that Perdita is wrapped in rich fabrics, which contain a supply of gold.

### Act 4, Scene 1

TIME appears and announces that 16 years have passed, that Leontes has shut himself off from the world in grief, and that the story continues in Bohemia. There, he tells us, we shall see Polixenes' son, FLORIZEL, and the 16-year-old Perdita, who lives as the Shepherd's daughter.

### Act 4, Scene 2

Camillo wishes to return to Sicilia, but Polixenes declares that he is now too important to the government to be permitted to leave. Moreover, he wants Camillo's help in preventing Prince Florizel from embarrassing the monarchy by marrying a shepherd girl.

### Act 4, Scene 3

A vagabond, AUTOLYCUS, sings merrily and brags that he is now a petty thief, although he was once a servant to Florizel. The Clown appears on his way to market to buy supplies for the upcoming shepherds' feast, and Autolycus scents prey. He lies on the ground and pretends to have been robbed; then, as the Clown helps him rise, he picks his pocket. The Clown leaves, and Autolycus decides to attend the festival, which is likely to produce further loot.

### Act 4, Scene 4

Perdita reveals her uneasiness at being courted by Florizel, for she knows that his father, the king, will oppose the match. Florizel insists he will marry her even if he has to abandon his royal status. The Shepherd and the Clown arrive for the festival, along with a group including the shepherd girls MOPSA and DORCAS, and the disguised King Polixenes and Camillo. Perdita, as hostess, distributes flowers among the guests. Mopsa and Dorcas lead a country dance, and Autolycus appears as a wandering peddler. Mopsa and Dorcas flirt with the Clown, who buys them presents, while Autolycus entertains them with SONGS; they all leave together, to continue singing and trading. At this point Polixenes reveals himself and demands that Florizel renounce Perdita. Threatening her and the Shepherd with death if she sees the prince again, he departs in a rage. The frightened Shepherd flees, and Perdita is in despair, but Florizel declares that he will not leave her. Camillo proposes that the couple should go to Sicilia, where they will be welcomed as emissaries of King Polixenes. Once there, they may eventually gain Polixenes' forgiveness. Autolycus returns, gloating over the purses he has stolen while selling his goods. Camillo makes him change clothes with Florizel, providing the prince with a disguise, and Perdita dresses as a young man. In an aside Camillo reveals that he intends to inform the king of the couple's flight and, in pursuit of them, get to Sicilia himself. When they leave, Autolycus, who has realised what is going on, plots how to profit from it. He then overhears the Shepherd and Clown planning to explain to the king that Perdita is not actually their relative, but a foundling. They have proof in the rich fabrics Perdita was found in, years before. Autolycus emerges and promises to take them to the king, for money. Privately, he plans to take them to Florizel and accept the prince's reward for keeping them from the king.

### Act 5, Scene 1
In Sicilia, Paulina insists that King Leontes should never remarry until he encounters Hermione's equal, and he agrees not to marry without Paulina's approval. Florizel and Perdita arrive, asserting that they are married. Leontes is delighted to renew relations with the son of his one-time victim, but then word arrives that Polixenes himself has come to Sicilia, to arrest his son for eloping with a shepherd's daughter. Florizel confesses that he and Perdita are not married, but he pleads with Leontes to defend their love to Polixenes, and Leontes agrees, being greatly attracted by Perdita.

### Act 5, Scene 2
Autolycus hears from a GENTLEMAN (13) and his friends that the king's missing daughter has been found, as the papers among the Shepherd's bundle of fabrics attest. The Third Gentleman describes the joy and reconciliation among the kings and their children, who are now considered engaged. He adds that the royal party has gone to Paulina's home to view a statue of Hermione. They go off to see it also, leaving Autolycus to bemoan his bad luck: he had brought the Shepherd and Clown to Florizel's ship, whereby they had come to Sicilia with their extraordinary evidence, and yet he cannot profit from it. When the Shepherd and Clown appear, dressed in new clothes and full of comical pretensions to gentlemanly status, Autolycus flatters them abjectly.

### Act 5, Scene 3
Leontes, Polixenes, Florizel, Perdita, and Camillo all accompany Paulina to see her sculpture. They marvel at its lifelike qualities, and Leontes regrets again his injustice to Hermione herself. Paulina asserts that she can make them marvel further; she tells the statue to move, and it walks down off its pedestal and takes Leontes by the hand. She then explains that the statue is Hermione herself, alive all these years but awaiting the proper moment for her return. Hermione confirms this account, identifying herself to Perdita. The king, ecstatic at being reunited with his wife, and conscious that Florizel and Perdita are soon to marry, insists that Paulina and Camillo should also wed. The three couples withdraw to savour their happiness.

### COMMENTARY

With *The Winter's Tale*, Shakespeare achieved his first great success in a new genre, the ROMANCES. After flawed endeavours in *Pericles* and *Cymbeline*, the playwright found a way to integrate the various elements of romance literature—the exotic and magical mingled with stereotypical characters and situations—with his own strengths as a realistic playwright. *The Winter's Tale* combines the grim psychopathology of Shakespearean TRAGEDY with the visionary optimism of his earlier COMEDY. It is a play with its own distinctive moral tone, balancing the divine and the human.

The most obvious way in which this conjunction is effected is structural; the play falls neatly into two halves, with the hinge at 3.3, the first scene set in Bohemia. The first half is a tragedy centred on the madness of King Leontes, whose jealousy resembles OTHELLO's and appears to have the same result, the death of his wife. The second half, however, is a traditional romantic comedy of young love triumphant and old love restored, complete with a PROLOGUE (1)—the address by Time in 4.1—and a conventional happy ending in multiple marriages. The two halves of the play present a striking opposition between the sins of the powerful and elderly and the natural goodness of youth, but the two halves also offer another, more significant contrast. The tragic first half depends for its resolution on a supernatural phenomenon, the message from the oracle, while the second relies chiefly on the fine qualities of its young lovers to carry things through to the happy conclusion. While humanity is ultimately dependent on providence—a theme that pervades the romances—here divine intervention serves chiefly to enable human virtue to exercise itself and triumph over vice.

Although Leontes' madness is cured only by Apollo, Camillo, Paulina, Hermione, and Antigonus all oppose it, and the forthright dignity of Hermione is never sullied by the abuse she undergoes. Moreover, the human opposition is much more prominent than the brief intercession of the god. Similarly, the healing process that follows remains in the characters' hands; it is accomplished through Paulina's delaying tactics, the Shepherd's kindness, Camillo's craftiness, and Florizel and Perdita's exemplary courage and devotion. In Act 4 love, charm, and humour—abetted by luck and the plotting of the wily Camillo—triumph over the injustice of Polixenes (who here re-creates in a milder key the tyranny of Leontes). The human component in the triumph of good—almost entirely absent in *Pericles* and but fitfully brought to bear in *Cymbeline*—is here given an importance that permits us to identify much more fully with the process.

Providence, however, is by no means ignored. The play is studded with overt references to the gods. Hermione's embattled confidence that 'powers divine / Behold our human actions' (3.2.28–29) is particularly striking, but it is supported by many other instances. Leontes vows daily chapel visits in 3.2.238–243, Florizel cites the love stories of the gods in 4.4.25–31, and Perdita refers to the Proserpina myth and mythological flower lore in 4.4.116–127. Paulina's mystifications as she reveals the survival of Hermione create an atmosphere of spirituality and magic in an entirely secular scene. Although theophany, or the actual appearance of a god, is avoided—in contrast to the two earlier romances (see DIANA [2], JUPITER)—the descriptions of the 'ceremonious, solemn and unearthly' rituals of Apollo (3.1.7) and 'the ear-deaf'ning voice o' th' Oracle, / Kin to Jove's thunder' (3.1.9–10) have a similar effect. The dramatic intensity of religious experience is evoked, and we are force-fully reminded of humanity's impotence before the divine.

Moreover, although the play's world is pre-Christian, some distinctly Christian ideas are alluded to, notably grace and redemption through suffering. Perdita and Hermione are associated with the words 'grace' and 'gracious' (e.g., in 1.2.233, 2.3.29, 4.1.24, and 4.4.8), as is the oracle itself (in 3.1.22). As the play ends, Hermione invokes a consummate blessing: 'You gods, look down, / And from your sacred vials pour your graces' (5.3.121–122). Leontes' story is a virtual parable of sin redeemed. He blasphemes his saintly wife and the divine oracle, and he is punished by the death of his son and (he believes) his wife. After Leontes spends years in 'saint-like sorrow' (5.1.2), Paulina (whose name is suggestive of Christianity's great preacher) effects the seemingly miraculous return of Hermione, which takes place in a 'chapel' (5.3.86). Not for nothing does Paulina assert, 'It is requir'd / You do awake your faith' (5.3.94–95). Of course, Hermione's apparent resurrection has obvious Christian overtones, and it becomes the central focus of the play's final scene, taking precedence over the more traditional conclusion of a comedy in marriage rites (though these are referred to).

Accompanying these expressly religious motifs is an implicitly sacred theme, a subtle emphasis on the cycles of nature. At the broadest level, the play is about the basic pattern of life and growth. Polixenes remembers when he and Leontes 'as twinn'd lambs did frisk i' th' sun / And bleat the one at th' other' (1.2.67–68). Later, when their dire adult drama of hatred and death is replaced by the pastoral comedy of the shepherds' festival, a cycle has been completed. The festival itself, celebrating the annual wool harvest, is an ancient marking of the passage of the seasons. (Such rustic festivals were still common in pre-industrial England, and Shakespeare could be sure that his audience would be familiar with them and at least aware of the pre-Christian religious sentiment behind them.) Perdita's enumeration of the different seasonal flowers is another potent evocation of nature's cycles. Most compelling of all is her re-enactment of the passage from winter to spring—the original resurrection—when she wishes she had spring flowers for Florizel, 'to strew him o'er and o'er!' He exclaims, 'What, like

a corpse?' and she replies, 'No, like a bank, for love to lie and play on: / Not like a corpse; or if—not to be buried, / But quick, and in mine arms' (4.4.129–132). Such references point to our primitive awareness of nature as the source of religious awe.

However, the cycle of the seasons is a natural, not a supernatural phenomenon, and its celebration is a human one. In line with this the play's religious allusions and motifs are never permitted to overshadow the central theme, the power of human virtue. The role of the oracle is critical, but it is the main characters who complete the task and achieve happiness through their virtue. It is not Paulina's magic but her foresight that leads to the 'revival' of Hermione; human intervention, not divine, produces the outcome. That Paulina's scheme seems singularly hare-brained to the rational observer is irrelevant; romances are supposed to be illogical. It is only important that a happy ending of reconciliation and love has been reached, without the need for a *deus ex machina*. Given a single assist from Apollo's oracle, the essential good in humanity defeats life's potential for disorder and unhappiness. Leontes hopes Paulina's magic will prove as 'lawful as eating' (5.3.111) and—because it is not magic after all, let alone black magic—it does. The moral drive of ordinary people is what powers *The Winter's Tale*.

Though Leontes certainly lacks such drive, he is nonetheless the central figure in the play's scheme. His sin sparks the action, and his consciousness of sin is necessary to its conclusion. That the king comes to recognise his susceptibility to error reflects Shakespeare's abiding concern for the responsibilities of rulers. Like such differing characters as RICHARD II, HENRY IV, CYMBELINE, and PROSPERO, Leontes learns about himself through the exercise of power. Especially in the romances, the lesson is that the most valuable human capacity is the capacity for mercy, for, more than justice, mercy acknowledges human equality before the divine. Like the medieval MORALITY PLAY, centred on God's mercy to humankind, Shakespeare's late works insist that the relationship between a secular ruler and subject must follow the same pattern.

Leontes moves from sin to remorse and finally finds forgiveness in the pastoral world of love represented by Perdita and Florizel. The most important moral lesson of the play is the power of love. Love is elaborately glorified and briefly threatened in 4.4—the longest scene in Shakespeare—where the pleasures of country life, a traditional romantic motif, are associated with the deep affection shared by Florizel and Perdita. As we have seen, connections are drawn to the divine, and Perdita is strongly linked to ancient emblems of fertility. The lovers acknowledge their sexuality, but recognise the spiritual side as more important. Perdita notes that love can take a 'false way' (4.4.151), and Florizel insists that his desire does not

'Burn hotter than my faith' (4.4.35). In the crisis of Polixenes' wrath against Perdita, Florizel declares that if his faithful love fails, 'let nature crush the sides o' th' earth together, / And mar the seeds within!' (4.4.480–481). The tragedy of the first half of the play results from jealousy, a gross distortion of sexual affection; the love of the second half contrasts in its purity.

The world of the lovers is a blessed one, as the play's transition from Sicilia to Bohemia makes clear, even before the powerful charm of 4.4 is exercised. In a passage that several commentators have pointed to as the pivotal moment of the play, the Shepherd, having just found Perdita and heard from the Clown of the death of Antigonus, says to his son, 'Now bless thyself: thou met'st with things dying, I with things new-born' (3.3.112–113). The old world of Leontes' despotic madness is passing away, and a new dispensation has begun. The Shepherd appreciatively declares, ' 'Tis a lucky day, boy, and we'll do good deeds on 't' (3.3.135–136). The contrast with Leontes' despairing plea, 'Come, and lead me / To these sorrows' (3.2.242–243)—spoken just moments before—could hardly be greater. A new world has been introduced, and the shepherds' festival is to be at its centre.

Autolycus, his victim the Clown, and the shepherdesses Mopsa and Dorcas, all contribute to a delightful slice of English rustic life, viewed idealistically but not entirely unrealistically. Like the Forest of ARDEN (1) and the GLOUCESTERSHIRE of *2Henry IV*, Shakespeare's Bohemia evokes nostalgia for the solid virtues of country life, and the sense of community of that world is part of the moral regeneration of the second half.

It is interesting to note the care Shakespeare took to emphasise the importance of the human element in his play by altering the story that he found in his source, *Pandosto*. In the fashion typical of 16th-century romances, *Pandosto* is full of events and schemes that are not just improbable but absolutely impossible; credibility is not an issue, any more than in a fairy tale. Shakespeare, however, changed such features enough to create a plausible tale (if only just barely to our modern sceptical minds), a tale shot through with the fabric of real life. For example, we are prepared for Mamillius' death with reports of his illness, whereas in *Pandosto* the son of the unjustly accused queen simply drops dead of dismay. In the book the infant is abandoned in an open boat at sea; her survival—let alone her arrival in the homeland of the Polixenes figure—is entirely a whim of fate. Similarly, when the aggrieved lovers—the equivalents of Perdita and Florizel—flee the king, they simply wander about, ending up in the woman's homeland purely by chance. In Shakespeare, chance is eliminated in favour of human plans; it is Antigonus who brings the infant to Bohemia and Camillo who directs the couple to Sicilia. Another telling difference is in the fate of the Leontes figure. In

*Pandosto* an angry Apollo strikes him dead, but, as we have seen, Shakespeare keeps the god at a distance and permits Leontes to survive to regret his deed.

The triumph of good in *The Winter's Tale* is accomplished only with grave difficulty, and the world of the play is shrouded with losses. The 'things dying' encountered by the Clown in 3.3 are human beings, the Mariner and Antigonus, both faultless except for their association with Leontes' sin. Their deaths seem gratuitous, but as agents of the king's wrath they embody the evils of the play's first half, and those evils must be done 'away with. Even more shocking is the death of the utterly innocent Mamillius—surely the greatest cost of Leontes' madness. Shakespeare here insists on the seriousness of sin. Other serious consequences include Paulina's widowhood and Camillo's exile (both presumably eased by their marriage at the conclusion) and the irretrievable loss of 16 potentially happy years for Leontes and Hermione. For all its joy, the final scene does not restore the unsullied world of the play's opening. The observation of wrinkles on the Hermione statue acknowledges that. The possibility of happiness is limited by evil and its consequences.

Shakespeare's picture of a moral world in *The Winter's Tale* is not, of course, a dry dissertation on faith and good works but rather an entertainment. The very title insists on the play's intention to entertain. Although the article *the* suggests a tale as harsh as the season, in Shakespeare's day the title also conjured up the festive Christmas season, for the connection of tale-telling to celebration was much stronger then than now. Both connotations are supported when the title is alluded to in the play: Mamillius announces 'A sad tale's best for winter' (2.1.25), but he does so in play with his loving mother, and the telling of his tale is plainly fun. The play as a whole also fulfils both interpretations of its title: the cold and dark of winter dominate the the tragedy of the first half, and the warmth and light of holiday festivities suffuse the comedy that follows.

Referring to the play's title in the dialogue is one of several ways in which Shakespeare insists on the artificiality of his romance. Allusions to the artfulness of the story are scattered throughout the play: Hermione, for example, compares her plight to a drama, 'devis'd / And play'd to take spectators' (3.2.36–37); dressed for the festival, Perdita muses, 'Methinks I play as I have seen them do / In Whitsun pastorals' (4.4.133–134); and the Third Gentleman speaks of news that 'is so like an old tale that the verity of it is in strong suspicion' (5.2.27–29). The naïveté of Mopsa, who declares, 'I love a ballad in print . . . for then we are sure they are true' (4.4.261–262), is a playful jab at the willing self-deception of romantic literature's audience. Moreover, there are several highly theatrical episodes set within the play: Hermione's trial, Time's prologue, the shepherds' festival, and Paulina's dramatic unveiling of the supposed statue, at which Leontes declares, rightly, 'We are mock'd with art' (5.3.68). The very structure of the play reinforces the point, as tragedy changes abruptly to comedy. In stressing the obvious, that *The Winter's Tale* is an artifact and not real life, Shakespeare adds another layer to the basic theme of the play. The very play that points out the need for goodness in human endeavours is itself a human endeavour. Art joins with virtue in challenging the threat to happiness presented by social and psychological disarray. Art, and *The Winter's Tale* in particular, orders human affairs so that we can see how they resist destruction, even the natural decay that comes with time.

## SOURCES OF THE PLAY

Shakespeare's main source for *The Winter's Tale* was a prose romance, *Pandosto* (1588) by Robert GREENE (2). The play follows *Pandosto*'s plot fairly closely and Greene's language is reproduced almost verbatim in some passages, but there is much that Shakespeare invented. Autolycus, for instance, was derived from a colourless character, and the shepherds' festival in 4.4 was sparked by a mere hint in *Pandosto*. Most significantly, Shakespeare deviated from Greene's plot in two important respects. In *Pandosto* Hermione's counterpart dies and Pandosto (Leontes) commits suicide. Shakespeare's spirit of reconciliation at the end is not paralleled in Greene's work.

Two passages probably owe their genesis to specific models. Polixenes' argument justifying art in 4.4.79–103 resembles a similar passage in PUTTENHAM's *Arte of English Poesie* (1589). Autolycus' descriptions of torture in 4.4.773–793 were adapted from a tale in Giovanni BOCCACIO's *Decameron* (1353), which Shakespeare may have read in the original Italian or in a French translation, perhaps that of Antoine LE MAÇON (1545). The same tale was the source for *Cymbeline*, written shortly before.

Other minor sources, reflected in various references and word choices, include OVID's *The Metamorphoses* (an old favourite of the playwright), other stories by Greene, passages from *The Knight of the Burning Pestle* by Francis BEAUMONT (2), and possibly two stories, themselves based on *Pandosto*, by a very minor writer, Francis Sabie (active 1595). Most of the names in the play were taken from PLUTARCH's *Lives*, another favourite source.

## TEXT OF THE PLAY

*The Winter's Tale* was probably written in 1610 or early 1611. It must have been written by May 1611, when a performance is recorded, but how much earlier it was composed cannot be precisely determined. Stylistically, it is unquestionably among the late plays, and its greater mastery of the romance genre suggests that it followed *Cymbeline* (1608–1610). Some scholars believe that Shakespeare's mention of a royal performance by the play's dancing satyrs in 4.4.337–338 is a sly reference to the presentation of Ben JONSON's *Masque of Oberon*—which has a similar scene—at the court of King JAMES I on January 1, 1611. If so, then the play may have been begun in late 1610 and completed early in 1611, in time to be staged in May. Alternatively, the play could have been completed in 1610, with the reference to *Oberon* added in the course of early performances.

The play was not published in Shakespeare's lifetime but appeared in the FIRST FOLIO (1623). It was apparently printed from a transcript of Shakespeare's FOUL PAPERS (or possibly of a PROMPT-BOOK) by Ralph CRANE, a professional copyist whose peculiar punctuation and other idiosyncrasies can be recognised in the printed text.

## THEATRICAL HISTORY OF THE PLAY

The earliest known performance of *The Winter's Tale* was at the GLOBE THEATRE on May 15, 1611, as recorded by Simon FORMAN. The play apparently was popular, for it was performed at the courts of Kings James I and Charles I at least seven times; in 1613 it was one of the plays put on by the KING'S MEN for the wedding festivities of Princess ELIZABETH (3). However, there is no record of a 17th-century performance after 1640 (though the play inspired a popular ballad, published in 1664). The next recorded production, in 1741, was advertised as the first in a century.

The 18th century saw a number of adaptations of the play that excluded or diminished Leontes and Hermione and focussed on the love story of Act 4. Among the best known was *The Sheep-Shearing: or, Florizel and Perdita* (1754) by McNamara MORGAN (2). In 1761, this was produced as an operetta with music by Thomas ARNE. Also well known was David GARRICK's *The Winter's Tale* (1756), with Garrick as Leontes and Hannah PRITCHARD as Hermione (though these parts were reduced to a few lines each). Susannah CIBBER (2) played Perdita, the central role, and Richard YATES (2) played Autolycus, whose part was greatly expanded in this and other adaptations. Garrick's version remained popular throughout the century, though Shakespeare's original text (except for some minor alterations by Thomas HULL) was staged in 1771.

In the 19th century *The Winter's Tale* was staged with spectacular sets and lavish costumes. John Philip KEMBLE (3) produced the play in 1811. His sister Sarah SIDDONS, who had played Hermione in a staging of Garrick's version, finally took on Shakespeare's much greater part in her final season. William Charles MACREADY produced the play in 1837, and Samuel PHELPS followed in 1845, using a text very close to the original. Perhaps the most memorable *Winter's Tale* of the century was that of Charles KEAN (1) in 1856. His elaborate sets and costumes, intended to reproduce ancient Sicily and Bithynia (see BOHEMIA) with archaeological exactitude, were accompanied by a lengthy set of programme notes. This production was both immensely popular and widely ridiculed, and a satirical burlesque, *Florizel and Perdita* by William Brough (1826–1870), enjoyed a successful run in a rival theatre. In Kean's play, Ellen TERRY (1), aged eight, spoke her first lines from a stage, as Mamillius. In another noteworthy production, in 1887, Mary ANDERSON (2) played both Hermione and Perdita, with Johnston FORBES-ROBERTSON as Leontes.

*The Winter's Tale* has been less popular in the 20th century, though there have been a number of notable stagings, beginning with Beerbohm TREE's 1906 effort. Still in the 19th-century vein, it starred Ellen Terry as Hermione, 50 years after her Mamillius. Harley GRANVILLE-BARKER's 1912 production featured a formally stylised, almost bare stage that scandalised traditionalists. Robert ATKINS has produced the play twice, in 1937 and 1950. The most important 20th-century production to date is probably that of Peter BROOK (2) in 1951, starring John GIELGUD as Leontes. The play was produced as a FILM three times (all silent) before 1915, but only once since, a 1960 version starring Laurence Harvey (1928–1973). It has been made for TELEVISION twice, in Great Britain (1962) and the United States (1980).

**Wise, Andrew (active 1580–1603)**   London publisher and bookseller. Wise published five of Shakespeare's plays. He produced the first three editions of *Richard III* (1597, 1598, 1602) and *Richard II* (1597, 1597, 1598), and the first two of *1 Henry IV* (1598, 1599). He sold the rights to these plays to Matthew LAW in 1603. In partnership with William ASPLEY he also published the first editions of *2 Henry IV* and *Much Ado About Nothing* (both 1600). Aspley alone held these rights when the FIRST FOLIO was published in 1623, and Wise may have been dead by that date. After nine years of apprenticeship, Wise became a member of the STATIONERS' COMPANY in 1589, but little more is known of him.

**Witches**   Group of characters in *Macbeth*, supernatural beings who encourage MACBETH in his evil inclinations. In 1.1 three Witches appear in the thunder and lightning of a storm; they say that they will meet again to encounter Macbeth. In 1.3 they boast of their evil deeds before they accost Macbeth and BANQUO. They greet the former with titles he does not possess: Thane of CAWDOR and 'King hereafter' (1.3.50)—though we already know that Macbeth has been named Thane of Cawdor—and they assure Banquo that he shall not be a king but that his descendants shall. After they make these puzzling remarks, they disappear. When Macbeth and LADY (6) MACBETH learn that he is in fact Thane of Cawdor and the Witches'

prophecy is corroborated, their ambition is sparked to murder King DUNCAN so that Macbeth can rule SCOTLAND. Then, once he is king, Macbeth worries over the Witches' pronouncement that Banquo's heirs would replace his own, and he murders him, as well. Thus, the Witches inspire the central action of the play.

In 3.5 we see the three Witches with a more powerful spirit, HECATE, who is accompanied by several more witches. (However, most scholars believe that this scene was not written by Shakespeare, and that *Macbeth*'s Witches were originally only three in number.) In 4.1 the Witches concoct a magical brew in a cauldron. They are preparing for another visit from Macbeth, who wishes to learn what he must do to assure his safety now that he is king. They summon the APPARITIONS, whose predictions seem to promise safety but actually foretell his destruction. Finally, in a passage that may be a non-Shakespearean interpolation, the Witches perform a ritual dance, after which they vanish.

Though their appearances are brief, the Witches have an important function in *Macbeth*. The play opens with their grim and stormy meeting, and this contributes greatly to its pervasive tone of mysterious evil. Moreover, they offer another important theme of the play, the psychology of evil. The Witches are an enactment of the irrational. The supernatural world is terrifying because it is beyond human control, and in the play it is therefore symbolic of the unpredictable force of human motivation. At their first appearance, the Witches state an ambiguity that rules the play until its close: 'Fair is foul, and foul is fair:' (1.1.11). Their deceptive pictures of the future—both in their initial predictions of Macbeth's rise, and in the prophecies of the Apparitions—encourage in Macbeth and Lady Macbeth a false sense of what is desirable or even possible. The magic of the Witches is thus an image of human moral disruption. Through their own uncertain nature, they demonstrate—and promote—the disruption in the world of the play. When Macbeth meets them a second time, he describes their capacity for disorder: they 'untie the winds, and let them fight / Against the Churches . . . palaces and pyramids, do slope / Their heads to their foundations . . . Even till destruction sicken' (4.1.52–60). They declare that their activity comprises 'A deed without a name' (4.1.49). Their world is without definition; similarly, Macbeth's disordered sense of the world comes to encompass the assumption that 'Life's . . . a tale / Told by an idiot, full of sound and fury, / Signifying nothing' (5.5.24–28).

Many people in Shakespeare's day believed in the reality of the supernatural world, but at the same time, a recognition that many folk beliefs had arisen as well. Shakespeare's opinion on the subject cannot be determined, for his handling of the Witches is ambiguous. Banquo asks them,

'Are ye fantastical, or that indeed which outwardly ye show?' (1.3.53–54). After they leave, he wonders if he and Macbeth have 'eaten on the insane root' (1.3.84) and have simply imagined them. Their nature is never clearly stated. Moreover, the extent to which they have powers other than those of persuasion is also uncertain, which perhaps reflects—or exploits—the generally uncertain sense of such things in the playwright's original audiences. Shakespeare may have shared his audiences' ambivalence as to the supernatural, or he may simply have played on it to devise a dramatic grouping of characters. Despite a modern disbelief in the supernatural, we can respond to its dramatic use in *Macbeth,* and find in it a symbol of obscure regions of the human psyche. In this light, the Witches can be thought of as manifestations of Macbeth's ambition and guilt. That Banquo also sees them and Lady Macbeth accepts their reality does not argue against such an interpretation of Shakespeare's intentions; it merely points up the ambivalence of 17th-century attitudes towards the supernatural (see also GHOST [4]).

It is interesting to note that Shakespeare altered the nature of the Witches considerably when he took them from his source, HOLINSHED's *Chronicles.* There, the beings who appear to Macbeth are described as 'nymphs or fairies' who could read the future through magic. A number of references connect them with the three Fates, ancient goddesses who are figures of dignity and grandeur, quite unlike the hags of British folklore. Nymphs and female fairies were traditionally beautiful, but the Witches of *Macbeth* are 'So wither'd and so wild in their attire, / That [they] look not like th'inhabitants o'th'earth' (1.3.40–41). Scholars have surmised that Shakespeare replaced Holinshed's classical spirits with his own, earthier creatures in light of King JAMES I's well-known interest in contemporary witchcraft. However, the traditionally horrifying creatures of folklore are entirely appropriate to the association in *Macbeth* of these beings with the potential evil in humankind.

**Within**  Character in *Henry VIII.* See ONE (3) WITHIN.

**Woffington, Peg (Margaret) (1714–1760)**  English actress. Born in Ireland, Woffington was a child actress who went on to become the leading comedienne of her day. She was famous for a male part, the hero of a popular contemporary comedy that she repeatedly revived to great enthusiasm, but she also played most of Shakespeare's comic heroines, including PORTIA (1), ROSALIND, VIOLA, and HELENA (2). In addition, she took some non-comic parts, such as CONSTANCE in *King John* and PORTIA (2) in *Julius Caesar.* She was David GARRICK's mistress for a number of years and had many other lovers, in a notorious life that still enthralled the public a century later, when it was the subject of a popular novel of 1853 (*Peg Woffington* by

Charles Reade [1814–1884]). She became ill in 1757, during her last performance (as Rosalind), and never recovered.

**Wolfit, Donald (1902–1968)**  British actor and director. Wolfit's long career was spent chiefly as a performer and director of Shakespeare's plays. He made his debut in 1920 as BIONDELLO and in 1929 joined the OLD VIC THEATRE company, with whom he played many major parts, including HAMLET, KING (5) CLAUDIUS, and OTHELLO. He played ANTONY in Theodore KOMISARJEVSKY's 1936 production of *Antony and Cleopatra.* In 1937 he formed a touring company and travelled in Canada and the British provinces, performing mostly Shakespeare and other 16th- and 17th-century English dramas. In 1960 he toured around the world, giving recitals of famous Shakespearean passages.

**Wolsey, Thomas Cardinal (c. 1475–1530)**  Historical figure and character in *Henry VIII,* the overpowerful chief adviser to King HENRY VIII. Wolsey is the villain of the first half of the play. He sends his enemy BUCKINGHAM (1) to execution by buying the perjured testimony of the SURVEYOR, and then, to further his foreign policy aims, he encourages the king to divorce Queen KATHERINE. Moreover, he opposes the king's marriage to the saintly ANNE (1) BULLEN. His arrogance and pride are vividly presented in such vignettes as his vicious rebuff of Buckingham in 1.1 and his later disdain for a good man he is said to have driven mad: 'He was a fool, / For he would needs be virtuous' (2.2.131–132). However, when his evils are uncovered and he is brought low, Wolsey comes to realise that his life has been wasted in the pursuit of wealth and power. He reflects that now, removed from politics and its temptations, he can rejoice in a 'still and quiet conscience' (3.2.380). Further, we learn from GRIFFITH's touching description that on his death-bed, the cardinal has 'found the blessedness of being little' (4.2.66) and made his peace with God. Good has arisen from evil, with right balancing wrong in a spiritual sense— an important theme of the play.

Wolsey's evils contribute strongly to several of the play's other themes. His victims are good people and offer important images of forgiveness and forbearance. In the play's opposition of justice and injustice, Wolsey exemplifies the latter. He also represents Catholicism, as understood by the Protestant England of Shakespeare's day. Greedy, proud, and corrupt, he is allied with ROME, in the person of Cardinal CAMPEIUS, against the virtuous—and Protestant—Anne Bullen. Perhaps most significant, early in the play the role of King Henry is defined in terms of his response to Wolsey. About Buckingham, the king is completely duped; with respect to Katherine, he finds his own approach—a blameless one, from the play's point of view—and when he finally realises Wolsey's faults, especially his opposition to Anne, he angrily drives him from office. Thus, the king's growth from immaturity to wisdom begins with his increasing awareness of the cardinal's evil influence.

Wolsey was one of the great villains for the historians inspired by the TUDOR DYNASTY, including Shakespeare's chief source for the play, Raphael HOLINSHED's *Chronicles,* and the playwright's treatment of the cardinal is particularly noteworthy in this light. The dignity the cardinal is permitted in his fall and the virtue the audience is clearly expected to find in his repentance had a great impact in the 17th century because of the contrast with the expected picture of a wholly evil figure. As in his other late plays, the ROMANCES, Shakespeare's emphasis was on the restoration of good, rather than on the evil that had prevailed earlier. His humanly forgivable Wolsey helps him present this theme in *Henry VIII.*

The historical Wolsey was the son of a prosperous, middle-class livestock dealer and wool merchant. (Wolsey's enemies habitually labelled his father a butcher—Buckingham calls the cardinal a 'butcher's cur' [1.1.120]—and this became an historical commonplace, but it was not true.) As a bright young priest, he was a tutor to the sons of the Marquess of DORSET (who appears in *Richard III*). His intelligence and drive impressed the aristocrats he met, and he was repeatedly advanced until he became Henry VII's chaplain. When Henry VIII became king in 1509, Wolsey was one of his most important advisers. He promoted Henry's invasion of FRANCE (1) in 1512, supplied the army, and negotiated the highly advantageous peace of 1514. He was rewarded with the archbishopric of York; then in 1515 the pope made him a cardinal and he became lord chancellor of England. At this point he virtually governed England for the king. He became very wealthy by accepting bribes and keeping for himself the feudal incomes from various church properties. This was perfectly normal in the 16th century, but as a non-aristocrat, Wolsey aroused great enmity by displaying his power and wealth with extravagant houses, clothes, and entertainment. He was thought, perhaps rightly, to aspire to the papal throne and to have cultivated foreign alliances to that end.

Among Wolsey's principal enemies was Buckingham, who was a leader of the aristocratic clique that had been displaced as the king's main source of advice. However, Buckingham's fate was probably ordered by Henry, who feared him as a relative of the Plantagenets and a potential claimant to the throne. Wolsey doubtless manipulated the surveyor, and he may have been pleased with the outcome, but the motivating force was the king's. Shakespeare, however, followed Holinshed in attributing the deed entirely to Wolsey.

It was the power of the emperor, which Wolsey vainly sought to harness, that finally brought about his fall. Henry ordered Wolsey to see to his divorce from Katherine—Wolsey almost certainly did not instigate this scheme; the play's intimations to that effect come from Holinshed. However, the opposition of Katherine's nephew, the Holy Roman Emperor Charles V (ruled 1519–1555), proved insuperable. Charles controlled the papacy—his troops sacked Rome in 1527, just as Henry's divorce effort began—so approval from that quarter was never possible. Wolsey probably realised this, but Henry persisted, and the cardinal's failure to achieve the impossible meant his ruin. Henry—who knew of and accepted the cardinal's other activities—could not accept frustration, and once the failure was evident, he disposed of his minister quickly in 1529. The cardinal's accidentally revealed inventory in 3.2 is an anecdote from Holinshed, but it happened to a different person, 20 years earlier; it is an excellent demonstration of Shakespeare's inventive use of his sources. In actuality, Henry simply invoked the laws defining papal interference in English affairs as treason. He dismissed Wolsey from office and confiscated most of his possessions but spared his life. The cardinal continued to communicate with Rome and the emperor, in the hope of retrieving his situation; within a year this was discovered and he was again charged with treason. He died while travelling to London for his trial.

Wolsey's contribution to history was great, though it is generally overshadowed by his role in the story of Henry's divorce. He reformed the English judiciary to establish more control for the central government, thereby contributing to England's growth into a modern nation-state, free from the dominance of feudal lords. In foreign policy he was less successful in the short term, but we see in his strategies the first experiment in balance-of-power politics in Europe, with England providing a potential counterweight to any expansion of either French or Hapsburg power. This arrangement was to characterise European international relations for centuries.

**Woman (1)**    Any of several minor characters in *Henry VIII*, attendants to Queen KATHERINE. In 3.1.3–14 one of the women sings a SONG, 'Orpheus with his lute', in an effort to cheer the despairing Katherine. The incident helps establish a melancholy atmosphere around the defeated queen.

**Woman (2)**    Minor character in *The Two Noble Kinsmen,* an attendant of EMILIA (4). In 2.1 the Woman converses with her mistress, who speaks of the maidenly virtues. They are overheard by PALAMON and ARCITE, who fall in love with Emilia. The Woman's decorous conversation simply offers openings for Emilia in an incident that furthers the plot. Since most scholars believe that 2.1 was not written by Shakespeare, the Woman is probably a creation of John FLETCHER (2).

*Woodstock (Thomas of Woodstock)*  Anonymous play, written circa 1592–1595, that was a source for *Richard II* and *1 Henry IV*. *Woodstock* deals with earlier events than does *Richard II*, focussing on the murder of Thomas of Woodstock, Duke of GLOUCESTER (6). It is sometimes referred to as *1 Richard II*; Shakespeare did not write it, but it has been speculated that he may have known a sequel to *Woodstock*—now lost, if it ever existed—on which he based his own play. The influence of *Woodstock* on *Richard II* is most evident in 2.1, which echoes the earlier work's emphasis on Richard's extravagance and extortionate financial measures. It is also thought that Shakespeare's John of GAUNT is derived from *Woodstock*'s Duke of Gloucester; both are depicted as wise elders and exemplary patriots.

*Woodstock* has a comic sub-plot involving a corrupt Chief Justice who is also a cowardly highwayman, a possible prototype of FALSTAFF. In its relationship of sub-plot to main plot, the play may also have influenced the structure of *1 Henry IV*. In any case, a number of wordings found in *Woodstock* are apparently echoed in Shakespeare's highway robbery scene, *1 Henry IV*, 2.2.

**Woodville (Woodvile), Lieutenant Richard (d. c. 1440)**  Historical figure and minor character in *1 Henry VI*, the commander of the WARDERS at the Tower of London who refuse to admit the men of the Duke of GLOUCESTER (4); Woodville cites orders from the Bishop of WINCHESTER (1). The historical Woodville became the father of ELIZABETH (2) Woodville, Lady Grey, later Queen of England, and of Lord RIVERS, both of whom appear in *3 Henry VI* and *Richard III*.

**Wooer**  Minor character in *The Two Noble Kinsmen*, the suitor of the DAUGHTER (2) of the GAOLER (4). In 2.1 the Wooer agrees with the Gaoler on a marriage contract, saying that he has the Daughter's consent to marry him. He is not seen again until Act 4, after the Daughter has gone mad with unrequited love for the nobleman PALAMON. Though unafflicted with jealousy and sympathetic to her plight, the Wooer is helpless to ease it, until in 4.3 the DOCTOR (4) prescribes that he disguise himself as Palamon and woo her, adding in 5.2 the instruction that he sleep with her, to which he readily assents. He proposes to her and is accepted, but she suggests bed before he can. The Doctor's ploy works, for the Daughter is later reported to be 'well restored, / And to be married shortly' (5.4.27–28). Slightly buffoonish, the Wooer is a gentle but undistinguished fellow, merely a necessary part of the sub-plot. He is probably the creation of Shakespeare's collaborator John FLETCHER (2), to whom the scenes he appears in are ascribed.

**Worcester, Thomas Percy, Earl of (1343–1403)**  Historical figure and character in *1 Henry IV*, HOTSPUR's uncle and a leader of the rebels against King HENRY IV. Worcester is presented as a malevolent figure who introduces the idea of rebellion against Henry, beginning in 1.3.185, and formulates its strategy later in the same scene. In 5.2, in an illustration of the evil that attends rebellion, Worcester destroys the rebels' last chance for peace on the eve of the battle of SHREWSBURY by concealing Henry's offer of amnesty, fearing that in a state of peace, the king would single him out for punishment. Although his efforts to control Hotspur's impetuosity in 4.1 and 4.3 show that Worcester well understands the likelihood of catastrophe in the coming battle, he calculatingly permits his cause to court defeat because his personal interest may be at stake. After the battle, in which he is captured, Henry sentences him to death, and he justifies himself, saying, 'What I have done my safety urg'd me to' (5.5.11).

Shakespeare followed his primary historical source, HOLINSHED, in presenting a perfidious Worcester. Modern scholarship finds the truth unclear, but, while Worcester was certainly a leader of the revolt, he was probably not its instigator. He was in fact executed after Shrewsbury, but the tale of the negotiations is probably untrue. On the day of the battle it was apparently Henry who broke off the talks and began fighting. Before the time of the play, Worcester had served ably in the government of King RICHARD II, who had made him an earl in 1397. Two years later he allied himself with BOLINGBROKE (1) when he usurped the crown and became Henry IV (as is enacted in *Richard II*; although Worcester does not appear in that play, his actions are described in 2.2.58–61 and 2.3.26–28).

**Worcester's Men**  Seventeenth-century LONDON theatrical company. Worcester's Men was originally a provincial company, sponsored by the Earl of Worcester, that toured intermittently between 1555 and 1585. They played in STRATFORD several times during Shakespeare's youth. In 1584 William ALLEYN was a teenage member of the troupe, though he soon left for London. In 1589, under a new earl, the company renewed its existence, and in 1602, they staged a play at the court of Queen ELIZABETH (1). William KEMPE and Thomas HEYWOOD (2), who wrote the play, were its leading members In the same year, Worcester's Men absorbed OXFORD's MEN, and the enlarged troupe received a licence to play before the public at an inn. Thus they became the third theatre company of London, after the ADMIRAL's MEN and Shakespeare's CHAMBERLAIN's MEN. Christopher BEESTON, the future manager of the company, joined them at this point. In February 1603 they performed a Heywood play at Philip HENSLOWE's ROSE THEATRE. Upon Queen Elizabeth's death in March 1603, Worcester's Men came under the patronage of Anne of Denmark (1574–

1619), the wife of England's new ruler, King JAMES I, and were known thereafter as the QUEEN'S MEN (2).

**Worthies, The Nine** Traditional array of medieval heroes, often presented in dramas or tableaux at fairs and festivals. The comical characters in *Love's Labour's Lost* enact such a tableau (5.2.541–717). Traditionally, the Nine Worthies were divided into three groups of three, representing Old Testament leaders, pre-Christian warriors and medieval notables. They were, respectively: Joshua, David, and Judas Maccabeus; HECTOR of Troy, Alexander the Great, and Julius CAESAR (1); and King Arthur, Charlemagne, and Godfrey of Bouillon (in England, Godfrey was sometimes replaced by Guy of Warwick). The line-up of Worthies in *Love's Labour's Lost* is quite different, which Shakespeare probably intended as a humorously ignorant error on the part of his unsophisticated characters.

**Wyatt, Thomas (c. 1503–1542)** English poet, the introducer of the SONNET into English and possibly the author of a minor source for *Twelfth Night*. Wyatt, while serving as a diplomat in Italy, translated some of the sonnets of Petrarch (1304–1374), producing the first English sonnets, around 1530. Wyatt and his friend the Earl of SURREY (1) subsequently became the first English poets to compose their own poems in this form. Wyatt also wrote in other forms and may have written the SONG sung by FESTE in *Twelfth Night* 4.2.75–80, though some scholars dispute the attribution.

Wyatt was a successful courtier who achieved high office under King HENRY VIII despite two periods of imprisonment in the TOWER OF LONDON. He was probably an early lover of the king's wife Anne Boleyn (see ANNE [1]), and his incarceration in 1536, as part of Queen Anne's trial for adultery, may have been connected with this.

# Y

**Yates (1), Mary Ann (1728–1787)** English actress, wife of Richard YATES (2). Mrs Yates, as she was known, succeeded Susannah CIBBER (2) as London's favourite tragic actress, though she also played comedic heroines, including VIOLA, ROSALIND, and ISABELLA. She was a famous LADY (6) MACBETH, and she played CLEOPATRA opposite David GARRICK in the first recorded performance of *Antony and Cleopatra* since Shakespeare's day; she was thus the first woman to play the part.

**Yates (2), Richard (c. 1706–1796)** English actor, husband of Mary Ann YATES (1). Yates, who was considered the finest comedian of his day, specialised in his version of the COMMEDIA DELL'ARTE figure Harlequin. He also played many of Shakespeare's comic characters, including TOUCHSTONE, AUTOLYCUS, FESTE, and MALVOLIO.

**Yong (Yonge, Young), Bartholomew (c. 1555–c. 1612)** English translator, creator of a work that was a source for *Two Gentlemen of Verona* and *A Midsummer Night's Dream* and may have influenced *As You Like It* and *Twelfth Night*. Yong's version of the Spanish prose romance *Diana Enamorada* by Jorge de MONTEMAYOR was not published until 1598, but it was completed in 1582 and circulated widely in manuscript. Shakespeare knew it well, as its importance to *Two Gentlemen* indicates. Yong, an alumnus of one of the INNS OF COURT, spent two years in Spain, 1577 and 1578, and became familiar with the language, though he apparently encountered Montemayor's *Diana* only after his return. His patron was Penelope Rich (1563–1607), the sister of the Earl of ESSEX (2). Yong also translated BOCCACCIO's *Fiammetta* from Italian, as *Amorous Fiammetta* (1587).

**Yorick** Figure mentioned in *Hamlet*, the deceased court jester (see FOOL [1]) whose bones are dug up by the GRAVE-DIGGER in 5.1. Yorick's skull sparks a monologue by Prince HAMLET on the inevitability of death. The prince also responds with pleasure to his recollection of Yorick in life, 'a fellow of infinite jest, of most excellent fancy' (5.1.178–179). With the Grave-

digger's earlier remarks, the passage on Yorick presents the familiar religious theme of earthly vanity: given the inevitability of death, the things of this life are inconsequential. In fact, Hamlet meditating on the skull of Yorick immediately became a popular symbol of this theme, and it has remained so.

That Hamlet can turn to this doctrine, and at the same time indulge in the healthy nostalgia of reminiscing about Yorick, a friendly figure of his youth, reflects his recovery from the racking grief that has tortured him in Acts 1–4. Thus Yorick is an emblem of the spirit of acceptance that prevails at the close of the play.

Scholars differ on the etymology of Yorick's unique name. It may be a corruption of Eric, a name appropriate to the play's setting in DENMARK; of Jörg, the Danish equivalent of George; or of Rorik, the name of Hamlet's maternal grandfather in older forms of the tale (Rorique in BELLEFOREST; Roricus in SAXO).

**York (1) Family** Branch of the PLANTAGENET (1) dynasty, major figures in Shakespeare's HISTORY PLAYS. The Yorkist kings were descended from Edmund, Duke of YORK (4), the fourth son of King Edward III (d. 1377). In the WARS OF THE ROSES the house of York fought for control of the throne with another line of the Plantagenets, the house of LANCASTER (1).

Three members of the York family ruled England: EDWARD IV, from 1461 to 1483; Edward V (see PRINCE [5]), briefly and only nominally in 1483; and RICHARD III, from 1483 to 1485. When the Earl of RICHMOND overthrew Richard III, he married Richard's niece, the daughter of Edward IV and Queen ELIZABETH (2), incorporating the York lineage into the new TUDOR dynasty.

The rivalry between York and Lancaster is the subject of Shakespeare's earliest history plays, the minor TETRALOGY, consisting of *1, 2,* and *3 Henry VI* and *Richard III*. The roots of the conflict lie farther back in history, and Shakespeare used this material in the major tetralogy—*Richard II, 1* and *2 Henry IV,* and *Henry V*. Although the Yorks are less important in this historical period, several members of the family figure in these plays as well.

**York (2)**   City in northern England, a location in *3 Henry VI* and *1* and *2 Henry IV*. Second in economic and political power only to London during the Middle Ages, York figured heavily in the history of the time and thus naturally appears in the HISTORY PLAYS.

In 2.2 of *3 Henry VI* Queen MARGARET (1) and King HENRY VI march their army to the walls of York, and the queen points out the severed head of the Duke of YORK (8), which has been placed above the city gate. In 4.7 the duke's son EDWARD (3) comes to York after the reinstatement of Henry, whom he had earlier deposed. The MAYOR (5) declares the city's loyalty to Henry, and Edward is admitted only after he swears he is not pursuing the crown. Once within the walls, he reneges on his pledge and declares himself king. The incident illustrates the treachery and dishonesty of the period's political life, an important theme of the *Henry VI* plays.

In the *Henry IV* plays York is important as the head-quarters of the ARCHBISHOP (3) of York, a leading rebel against King HENRY IV. In 4.4 of *1 Henry IV* the Archbishop, at his home in York, plans to continue the failing rebellion, thus anticipating the events of *Part 2*. In 1.3 of *2 Henry IV* the rebels hold a council of war and formulate their strategy in the same location.

**York (3), Cicely Neville, Duchess of**   Character in *Richard III*. See DUCHESS (3).

**York (4), Edmund of Langley, Duke of (1341–1402)**   Historical figure and character in *Richard II*, uncle of King RICHARD II. Like his brother John of GAUNT, York deplores the misguided rule of their nephew but believes strongly in the divine appointment of kings and is doggedly loyal to Richard. Richard, even as he is censured by York, appoints him Governor of England to rule in the king's absence, observing that 'he is just' (2.1.221). However, he is helpless to prevent the usurpation of the crown by BOLINGBROKE (1), and, once this is accomplished, he transfers his loyalty to the new king, despite his own grief at Richard's fall. He even denounces his son, the Duke of AUMERLE, as a traitor.

York is a representative of a vanishing medieval world of inviolable political and social hierarchies. In 2.3.96–105 he consciously identifies himself with that system, nostalgically recalling his comradeship with the Black Prince in the days of King Edward III. Ironically he speaks just as Bolingbroke is preparing the triumph of a more modern world of opportunistic, Machiavellian politics. York's sympathetic character is intended to heighten the pathos that colours the passing of that older world, one of the principal themes of the play.

The historical York apparently resembled Shakespeare's character. He was noted for his gentle, peace-loving nature, combined with a marked incapacity in political and military matters. He was the founder and namesake of the YORK (1) branch of the PLANTAGENET (1) family; through a younger son than Aumerle, the Earl of CAMBRIDGE, who appears in *Henry V*, York's great-grandson would eventually claim the crown and rule as King EDWARD IV.

**York (5), Edward, Duke of (c. 1373–1415)**   Historical figure and minor character in *Henry V*. (The same figure appears as the Duke of AUMERLE in *Richard II*.) In 4.3 York asks King HENRY V for permission to lead the vanguard at the battle of AGINCOURT, offering an instance of English valour. His brave death in combat is touchingly reported by the Duke of EXETER (2) in 4.6.7–32, a passage that helps to maintain the epic tone of the play's presentation of the battle.

The historical York inherited the title from his father, the YORK (4) of *Richard II*, several years after the time of that play. He was pardoned by Henry V for his rebellions against HENRY IV (one of which is enacted in *Richard II*). As he demonstrated at Agincourt, he remained loyal to the new king, but his younger brother, the Earl of CAMBRIDGE, was executed for treason, as is enacted in *Henry V*, 2.2. When York died childless, the title passed to Cambridge's son, the Duke of YORK (8) of the *Henry VI* plays. The York of *Henry V* died at Agincourt, but not in the courageous manner described in the play. Quite fat, York suffered a heart attack or some other sort of fatal seizure after falling from his horse. His heroic death is Shakespeare's invention; he may have had in mind the great popularity of his earlier description of JOHN (6) Talbot's death in battle in *1 Henry VI*, 4.7.

**York (6), Isabel of Castile, Duchess of**   Character in *Richard II*. See DUCHESS (4).

**York (7), Richard, Duke of (1473–c. 1483)**   Historical figure and character in *Richard III*, the murdered nephew of RICHARD III. The younger brother of the PRINCE (5) of Wales and his successor to the throne, York is a flippant youngster, given to ill-considered jokes about Richard's deformity. He appears with his mother, Queen ELIZABETH (2), and grandmother, the DUCHESS (3) of York, in 2.4 and with his brother and others in 3.1. In the latter scene, he jests about Richard's dagger, in an ominous foreshadowing of his fate. At the end of the scene, the two young brothers are escorted to the TOWER OF LONDON, from which they will never emerge. Although their murder is commonly attributed to Richard, modern scholarship finds the fate of the princes to be impenetrably obscure, barring the unlikely emergence of new evidence (see TYRELL).

**York (8), Richard Plantagenet, Duke of (1411–1460)**   Historical figure and character in the three *Henry VI* plays, claimant to the throne of England against the Lancastrian branch of the PLANTAGENETS (1) (see YORK [1]; LANCASTER [1]). York attempts to seize the throne at the end of *2 Henry VI*, launching the WARS OF THE ROSES. He fails, dying early in *3 Henry VI*, but his son becomes King EDWARD IV. The Yorkist cause thus succeeds, only to be brought to ruin (in *Richard III*) by the greedy machinations of York's younger son, RICHARD III, who inherits his father's ruthless ambition.

In *1 Henry VI* York's claim to the throne is established. His father, the Earl of CAMBRIDGE, has been executed for treason (as is depicted in Shakespeare's *Henry V*) for supporting the royal claims of Edmund MORTIMER (1). The dying Mortimer bequeaths his claim to York, his nephew, in 2.5 of *1 Henry VI*, thus laying the groundwork for the conflict to come. York feuds with the Duke of SOMERSET (3), even at the expense of military disaster in the HUNDRED YEARS WAR.

In *2 Henry VI* York's story is at first overshadowed by that of Humphrey, Duke of GLOUCESTER (4), whose murder is seen as making the civil war inevitable. Early in the play, York reveals his ambition to seize the throne, but this crafty planner keeps a low profile, even when his appointment as Regent in FRANCE (1) is given to another SOMERSET (1), the brother and successor to his old rival. York participates in the plot against Gloucester, but the chief conspirators are the Duke of SUFFOLK (3) and CARDINAL (1) Beaufort.

York is placed in command of an army and sent to crush a revolution in Ireland. He sees that these troops will permit him an opportunity to seize the crown. Despite the grand boldness of his scheme and his demands on himself for extraordinary courage, York's morality is sorely limited; he is prepared to expend any number of lives in the pursuit of his own ambition. He arranges for Jack CADE to foment a revolt in England, providing an excuse for him to bring in his army.

After Cade's rebellion, staged in Act 4, York returns with his army, demanding the imprisonment of Somerset. When this is not done, he announces his claim to the throne and proceeds to battle the King's troops at ST ALBANS. York's forces are victorious, but the King escapes to London. Thus the civil war has begun as the play ends.

In *3 Henry VI* York compromises: King Henry will be permitted to rule in his own lifetime but will pass the crown to York or his heirs. Richard persuades his father to seize the throne anyway, just as Queen MARGARET (1), who has herself rejected Henry's deal, arrives with an army. In the ensuing battle, York is captured; after a dramatic scene (1.4) in which Margaret mocks him viciously, the Queen and Lord CLIFFORD (1) stab him to death. In his last moments, York heaps insults on Margaret and weeps over the death of his young son RUTLAND, with whose fate the Queen had taunted him.

York generally functions more as a foil for other characters or incidents than as a well-developed figure himself. In *1 Henry VI* his ambitious rivalry with Somerset functions as a dark backdrop to the upright and patriotic career of Lord TALBOT; in *Part 2* his machinations are similarly contrasted with the fate of 'good Duke Humphrey' of Gloucester. In the latter half of *Part 2* and in *Part 3*, York simply exemplifies aristocratic ambition in a mechanical manner dependent largely on mere assertion, backed by the tableaux of the battlefield. Even his death scene serves chiefly to present Margaret in the vicious, warlike personality she assumes in that play. Only in his darkly malevolent speeches of *Part 2* is he a stimulating villain, and even then he is overshadowed by Suffolk. In any case, as an agent of evil York pales before the grand MACHIAVEL that his son Richard is to embody.

York's function as an archetype of selfish ambition is achieved at the expense of historical accuracy. The historical York actually had little role in the action of *1 Henry VI;* his presence is magnified in order to prepare for his role in *Parts 2* and *3*. The character's rise begins with the return of his dukedom to him in 3.1 of *Part 1*, but in fact, York had never been kept from that title and so could not be restored to it. York and the Duke of Somerset launch their quarrel in *Part 1*, though in reality the contest between York and Lancaster was not consequential until many years later. Further, the quarrel is made the cause of Talbot's defeat and death, but the divided command depicted by Shakespeare had occurred elsewhere and 10 years earlier. Also, York is assigned elements of the career of the Duke of BEDFORD (1). All of these fictions serve to foreshadow the conflict to come, establishing as a longstanding feud a rivalry that actually only developed some years later.

The greatest difference between the historical York and Shakespeare's character is a basic one: York's ambition is presented as a long-meditated plot to usurp the king's power. In fact, although he was undeniably a powerful figure who attempted to dominate the political world of England in the 1450s, York has nonetheless been considerably misrepresented by Shakespeare. He showed no intention to seize power until very shortly before he actually attempted to do so in 1455, the action that sparked the fighting at St Albans. He had competed fiercely with Somerset for power, but only for power as a minister under King Henry. He seems to have acted to usurp royal authority only when it became evident that his career and very possibly his life would be in great danger from Somerset and Margaret if he did not. Shakespeare has simply eliminated a great deal of intricate and fascinating politics, most notably any reference to York's capable rule in 1453–1454, when King Henry was insane and unable to speak.

It was not the playwright's concern in composing the *Henry VI* plays to render history accurately. He depicted unscrupulous aristocratic rivalry leading to civil war, thus demonstrating the importance of political stability. One of the ways in which he achieved his end was to make of the Duke of York a simple paragon of selfish ambition, and his success is demonstrated in the effectiveness of this fairly one-dimensional character in providing the impetus for a great deal of complicated action in the three *Henry VI* plays.

**York (9), Richard Scroop, Archbishop of** Character in *1* and *2 Henry IV*. See ARCHBISHOP (3).

**York (10), Thomas Rotherham, Archbishop of** Character in *Richard III*. See ARCHBISHOP (4).

*A Yorkshire Tragedy* Play formerly attributed to Shakespeare, part of the Shakespeare APOCRYPHA. *A Yorkshire Tragedy* was published by Thomas PAVIER in 1608 and again in 1619 (in the FALSE FOLIO) as a play by Shakespeare that had been performed by the KING'S MEN. It was also published in the Third and Fourth FOLIOS of Shakespeare's plays, and in the editions of Nicholas ROWE and Alexander POPE (1). However, although it is a respectable play—unlike most of the apocryphal works—scholars agree that it is not in fact by Shakespeare. This very brief play is quite dissimilar from the playwright's known works in its setting and its subject. It is set in contemporary England and concerns a sensational murder case of 1605 in which a man killed two of his children and attempted to kill his wife and a third child. Moreover, the play's poetry is distinctly inferior to Shakespeare's—especially his late work—and its only important characters, the murderer and his wife, are two-dimensional caricatures who are not even given names, and are thus entirely beneath the level of Shakespeare's characterisations. Its actual authorship remains unknown.

**Young Cato** Character in *Julius Caesar*. See CATO.

**Young Clifford** Character in *2 Henry VI*. See Lord John CLIFFORD (1).

**Young Lucius** Minor character in *Titus Andronicus*, son of LUCIUS (1) and grandson of TITUS (1). Young Lucius attends Titus in his grief and as he plans his revenge. In 4.2 he delivers to CHIRON and DEMETRIUS (1) a gift of weapons containing a cryptic message, the first of Titus' taunts to Tamora's family. He also participates in mourning Titus at the end of the play.

**Young Siward (Osberne of Northumberland, d. 1054)** Historical figure and minor character in *Macbeth*, an English soldier killed by MACBETH. Son of SIWARD, the English ally of MALCOLM and MACDUFF, Young Siward appears with the leaders in 5.4 but does not speak. In the ensuing battle he bravely challenges Macbeth to personal combat in 5.7, and dies in the encounter. The youth has no personality and serves only as a foil to Macbeth, whose evil is emphasised by the contrast with Young Siward's noble bravery, and whose malign nature is demonstrated in the otherwise unnecessary death of so fine a young man. The actual son of Siward was named Osberne. He did indeed die in combat at an early age during Malcolm's invasion of Scotland, but nothing more is known of him.

**Young Talbot** Character in *1 Henry VI*. See JOHN (6).

# Z

**Zeffirelli, Franco (b. 1923)** Modern stage and FILM director, creator of a number of noteworthy productions of Shakespeare's plays. Although he has produced many plays and operas, Zeffirelli is most widely known for his films. He produced *Romeo and Juliet* on the stage in 1960 and the screen in 1968, and his film of *The Taming of the Shrew* (1966) was extremely popular. His production of *Much Ado About Nothing* (1965) appeared on TELEVISION two years later. He is often criticised for the lavish spectacle of his productions, which are said to distract from the underlying play, but he has undeniably brought Shakespeare to a very wide audience.

# Suggested Reading

A comprehensive bibliography on Shakespeare would be many times the size of this book. The following is simply a selection of books that seem particularly interesting and appealing.

Adams, John Cranford. *The Globe Playhouse.* New York: Barnes & Noble, 1966.

Adams, Joseph Quincy. *Shakespearean Playhouses: A History of English Theatres from the Beginning to the Restoration.* Magnolia, MA: Peter Smith, 1959.

Alexander, Peter. *Shakespeare's Life and Art.* Westport, CT: Greenwood Press, 1979.

Baldwin, Thomas Whitfield. *The Organisation and Personnel of the Shakespearean Company.* Princeton: Princeton University Press, 1927.

Barber, Cesar Lombardi. *Shakespeare's Festive Comedy.* Princeton: Princeton University Press, 1972.

Bentley, Gerald Eades. *The Profession of Player in Shakespeare's Time, 1590–1642.* Princeton: Princeton University Press, 1984.

———. *Shakespeare: A Biographical Handbook.* New Haven: Yale University Press, 1974.

Boas, Frederic Samuel. *Shakespeare and His Predecessors.* Brooklyn, NY: Haskell, 1969.

Bradbrook, Muriel C. *The Artist and Society in Shakespeare's Time.* Totowa, NJ: Barnes & Noble, 1982.

———. *Elizabethan Stage Conditions.* Hamden, CT: Archon, 1962.

———. *The Rise of the Common Player.* Cambridge, Eng.: Cambridge University Press, 1979.

———. *Shakespeare and Elizabethan Poetry.* London: Chatto & Windus, 1951.

Bradley, Andrew Cecil. *Shakespearean Tragedy.* Cleveland: World, 1964.

Brown, Ivor. *How Shakespeare Spent the Day.* London: Bodley Head, 1963.

———. *Shakespeare.* Garden City, NY: Doubleday, 1949.

Brown, John Russell, and Bernard Harris, eds. *Early Shakespeare.* New York: Schocken, 1966.

Bullough, Geoffrey. *Narrative and Dramatic Sources of Shakespeare,* 8 vols. New York: Columbia University Press, 1957–1975.

Chambers, Sir Edmund Kerchever. *The Elizabethan Stage,* 4 vols. Oxford: Clarendon Press, 1961.

———. *William Shakespeare: A Study of Facts and Problems,* 2 vols. Oxford: Oxford University Press, 1989.

Chute, Marcel. *Shakespeare of London.* New York: Dutton, 1957.

Clemen, Wolfgang H. *The Development of Shakespeare's Imagery.* Cambridge, MA: Harvard University Press, 1951.

Coleridge, Samuel Taylor. *Coleridge's Criticism of Shakespeare,* ed. R. A. Foakes. Detroit: Wayne State University Press, 1989.

Colie, Rosalie. *Shakespeare's Living Art.* Princeton: Princeton University Press, 1974.

Cooper, Duff. *Sergeant Shakespeare.* New York: Haskell, 1972.

Craig, Hardin. *The Enchanted Glass: The Elizabethan Mind in Literature.* Westport, CT: Greenwood Press, 1975.

Dean, Leonard Fellows, ed. *Shakespeare: Modern Essays in Criticism.* New York: Oxford University Press, 1967.

Drakakis, John, ed. *Alternative Shakespeares.* New York: Routledge, Chapman & Hall, 1985.

Eccles, Mark. *Shakespeare in Warwickshire.* Madison: University of Wisconsin Press, 1963.

Edwards, Philip. *Shakespeare: A Writer's Progress.* Oxford: Oxford University Press, 1987.

———, ed. *Shakespeare's Styles: Essays in Honour of Kenneth Muir.* Cambridge, Eng.: Cambridge University Press, 1980.

Empson, William. *Essays on Shakespeare.* Cambridge, Eng.: Cambridge University Press, 1986.

Foakes, R. A. *Illustrations of the English Stage 1580–1642.* Stanford, CA: Stanford University Press, 1985.

Ford, Boris, ed. *The Age of Shakespeare.* New York: Penguin, 1982.

Fripp, Edgar I. *Shakespeare, Man and Artist,* 2 vols. London: Oxford University Press, 1938.

———. *Shakespeare's Stratford.* Salem, NH: Ayer, n.d., reprint of 1928 ed.

Frye, Northrop. *Fools of Time: Studies in Shakespearean Tragedy.* Toronto: University of Toronto Press, 1967.

———. *The Myth of Deliverance: Reflections on Shakespeare's Problem Comedies.* Toronto: University of Toronto Press, 1983.

Greg, Walter Wilson. *The Editorial Problem in Shakespeare.* Oxford: Clarendon Press, 1954.

———. *The Shakespeare First Folio.* Oxford: Clarendon Press, 1955.

Gurr, Andrew. *Playgoing in Shakespeare's London.* New York: Cambridge University Press, 1987.

———. *The Shakespearean Stage 1574–1642.* Cambridge, Eng.: Cambridge University Press, 1981.

Granville-Barker, Harley. *Prefaces to Shakespeare,* 2 vols. Princeton: Princeton University Press, 1978.

Greenblatt, Stephen. *Renaissance Self-Fashioning.* Chicago: University of Chicago Press, 1980.

Halliday, F. E. *Shakespeare and His Critics.* London: Duckworth, 1958.

———. *A Shakespeare Companion: 1564–1964.* Baltimore: Penguin, 1964.

———. *Shakespeare in His Age.* London: Duckworth, 1956.

Harbage, Alfred. *As They Liked It: A Study of Shakespeare's Moral Artistry.* Philadelphia: University of Pennsylvania Press, 1972.

———. *Conceptions of Shakespeare.* Cambridge, MA: Harvard University Press, 1966.

———. *Shakespeare and the Rival Traditions.* New York: Macmillan, 1952.

———. *Shakespeare's Audience.* New York: Columbia University Press, 1961.

Harrison, George Bagshawe. *Elizabethan Plays and Players.* Ann Arbour: University of Michigan Press, 1956.

———. *Shakespeare at Work.* London: Routledge, 1933.

Hartnoll, Phyllis, ed. *The Oxford Companion to the Theatre.* London: Oxford University Press, 1983.

Hill, Errol. *Shakespeare in Sable: A History of Black Shakespearean Actors.* Amherst: University of Massachusetts Press, 1986.

Hillebrand, Harold Newcomb. *The Child Actors.* Urbana: University of Illinois Press, 1926.

Hodges, Cyril W. *The Globe Restored.* New York: Somerset, 1973.

Honigmann, E. A. J. *The Stability of Shakespeare's Text.* London: Arnold, 1965.

Hotson, Leslie. *Shakespeare's Motley.* Brooklyn, NY: Haskell, 1970.

———. *Shakespeare's Sonnets Dated and Other Essays.* New York: Oxford University Press, 1949.

———. *Shakespeare's Wooden O.* London: Hart-Davis, 1959.

Hunter, George K., *Dramatic Identities and Cultural Tradition: Studies in Shakespeare and His Contemporaries.* Liverpool: Liverpool University Press, 1978.

Jones, Emrys. *The Origins of Shakespeare.* Oxford: Oxford University Press, 1977.

Jones, Ernest. *Hamlet and Oedipus.* New York: Norton, 1976.

Kirschbaum, Leo. *Shakespeare and the Stationers.* Columbus: Ohio State University Press, 1955.

Knight, George Wilson. *The Crown of Life: Essays in Interpretation of Shakespeare's Final Plays.* London: Methuen, 1947.

———. *The Wheel of Fire: Essays in Interpretation of Shakespeare's Sombre Tragedies.* New York: Routledge, Chapman & Hall, 1949.

Knights, Lionel Charles. *How Many Children Had Lady Macbeth?* New York: Haskell, 1973.

———. *Shakespeare's Politics.* London: Oxford University Press, 1957.

Lee, Sidney. *A Life of William Shakespeare.* New York: Macmillan, 1931.

————. *Shakespeare and the Modern Stage.* New York: AMS, 1974.

Leech, Clifford. *Twelfth Night and Shakespearean Comedy.* Toronto: Dalhousie University Press/University of Toronto Press, 1965.

Levin, Harry. *Shakespeare and the Revolution of the Times.* New York: Oxford University Press, 1976.

Merchant, William Moelwyn. *Shakespeare and the Artist.* London: Oxford University Press, 1959.

Miriam Joseph, Sister. *Shakespeare's Use of the Arts of Language.* New York: Columbia University Press, 1947.

Morozov, Mikhail Mikhailovich. *Shakespeare on the Soviet Stage.* London: Soviet News, 1947.

Muir, Kenneth. *Last Periods of Shakespeare, Racine, and Ibsen.* Liverpool: Liverpool University Press, 1961.

————. *Shakespeare's Sonnets.* London/Boston: Allen & Unwin, 1979.

————. *The Sources of Shakespeare's Plays.* London: Methuen, 1977.

Nagler, Alois M. *Shakespeare's Stage.* New Haven: Yale University Press, 1981.

Naylor, Edward Woodall. *Shakespeare and Music.* London: Dent, 1931.

Nevo, Ruth. *Comic Transformations in Shakespeare.* New York: Routledge, Chapman & Hall, 1981.

————. *Tragic Form in Shakespeare.* Princeton: Princeton University Press, 1972.

Noble, Richmond Samuel Howe. *Shakespeare's Biblical Knowledge.* New York: Gordon, n.d., reprint of 1935 ed.

Odell, George C. D. *Shakespeare from Betterton to Irving,* 2 vols. New York: Dover, 1966.

Onions, Charles Talbut. *A Shakespeare Glossary.* Oxford: Clarendon Press, 1986.

Orell, John. *The Quest for Shakespeare's Globe.* Cambridge, Eng.: Cambridge University Press, 1983.

Palmer, Alan, and Veronica Palmer. *Who's Who in Shakespeare's England.* New York: St Martin's, 1981.

Parker, Patricia, and Geoffrey Hartman, eds. *Shakespeare and the Question of Theory.* New York/London: Methuen, 1985.

Partridge, Eric. *Shakespeare's Bawdy.* London: Routledge & Kegan Paul, 1968.

Quennell, Peter. *Shakespeare: The Poet and His Background.* London: Weidenfeld & Nicolson, 1963.

Rabkin, Norman. *Shakespeare and the Common Understanding.* Chicago: University of Chicago Press, 1984.

————. *Shakespeare and the Problem of Meaning.* Chicago: University of Chicago Press, 1982.

Reese, Max Meredith. *Shakespeare: His World and his Work.* New York: St Martin's, 1980.

Ribner, Irving. *The English History Play in the Age of Shakespeare.* New York: Barnes & Noble, 1965.

Righter, Anne. *Shakespeare and the Idea of the Play.* Westport, CT: Greenwood Press, 1977.

Saccio, Peter. *Shakespeare's English Kings.* Oxford: Oxford University Press, 1977.

Schoenbaum, Samuel. *Shakespeare's Lives.* New York: Oxford University Press, 1970.

————. *William Shakespeare: A Compact Documentary Life.* New York: Oxford University Press, 1987.

————. *William Shakespeare: A Documentary Life.* New York: Oxford University Press, 1975.

Siegel, Paul N. *Shakespearean Tragedy and the Elizabethan Compromise: A Marxist Study.* Lanham, MD: University Press of America, 1983.

Simmons, Joseph Larry. *Shakespeare's Pagan World: The Roman Tragedies.* Charlottesville: University Press of Virginia, 1973.

Sisson, Charles Jasper. *Lost Plays of Shakespeare's Age.* Cambridge, Eng.: Cambridge University Press, 1936.

————. *The Mythical Sorrows of Shakespeare.* London: Milford, 1934.

————. *New Readings in Shakespeare.* Cambridge, Eng.: Cambridge University Press, 1956.

Smith, Hallett. *Shakespeare's Romances.* San Marino, CA: Huntington Library, 1972.

Smith, Irwin. *Shakespeare's Blackfriars Playhouse.* New York: New York University Press, 1964.

————. *Shakespeare's Globe Playhouse.* New York: Scribner's, 1956.

Smith, Logan Piersall. *On Reading Shakespeare.* New York: Somerset, n.d., reprint of 1933 ed.

Snyder, Susan. *The Comic Matrix of Shakespeare's Tragedies.* Princeton: Princeton University Press, 1979.

Speaight, Robert. *Shakespeare on the Stage: An Illustrated History of Shakespearean Performance.* Boston: Little, Brown, 1973.

Spencer, Theodore. *Shakespeare and the Nature of Man.* New York: Macmillan, 1942.

Spivack, Bernard. *Shakespeare and the Allegory of Evil.* New York: Columbia University Press, 1958.

Sprague, Arthur Colby. *Shakespeare and the Actors.* New York: Russell & Russell, 1963.

Spurgeon, Caroline. *Shakespeare's Imagery.* Cambridge, Eng.: Cambridge University Press, 1975.

Thompson, Peter W. *Shakespeare's Theatre.* London/ Boston: Routledge & Kegan Paul, 1983.

Tilley, Morris Palmer. *A Dictionary of the Proverbs in England in the Sixteenth and Seventeenth Centuries.* New York: AMS, 1982.

Tillyard, E. M. W. *The Elizabethan World Picture.* New York: Random House, 1959.

Traversi, Derek. *Shakespeare, The Last Phase.* Stanford, CA: Stanford University Press, 1955.

Trewin, John Courtenay. *Shakespeare on the English Stage 1900–1964.* London: Barrie & Rockliff, 1964.

Vickers, Brian. *The Artistry of Shakespeare's Prose.* London: Methuen, 1968.

———. *Classical Rhetoric in English Poetry.* Carbondale: Southern Illinois University Press, 1989.

Walker, Alice. *Textual Problems of the First Folio.* Cambridge, Eng.: Cambridge University Press, 1953.

Wells, Stanley, ed. *The Cambridge Companion to Shakespeare Studies.* Cambridge, Eng.: Cambridge University Press, 1986.

Welsford, Enid. *The Court Masque.* Cambridge, Eng.: Cambridge University Press, 1927.

———. *The Fool: His Social and Literary History.* Garden City, NY: Anchor, 1961.

Whitaker, Virgil Keeble. *Shakespeare's Use of Learning: An Inquiry into the Growth of His Mind and Art.* San Marino, CA: Huntington Library, 1953.

Wickham, Glynne. *Early English Stages,* 2 vols. New York: Columbia University Press, 1980.

Wilson, J. Dover *The Essential Shakespeare.* New York: Haskell, 1977.

Wright, Louis B. *Middle Class Culture in Elizabethan England.* New York: Hippocrene, 1980.

Yates, Frances. *Majesty and Magic in Shakespeare's Last Plays.* Boulder, CO: Shambhala, 1978.

# APPENDIX

## ──── Actors and Other Theatre Professionals, Composers, and Musicians ────

Plowright, Joan
Plummer, Christopher
Poel, William
Pope (2), Thomas
Prince Charles' Men
Prince Henry's Men
Pritchard, Hannah
Purcell, Henry
Quayle, Anthony
Queen's Men (1) (Queen
   Elizabeth's Men)
Queen's Men (2)
Queen's Revels (see Children's
   Companies)
Quin, James
Redgrave, Michael
Rehan, Ada
Reynolds (1), Frederick
Reinhardt, Max
Rice, John
Rich (2), John

Richardson (2), Ralph
Robeson, Paul
Robinson (2), Mary
   ('Perdita')
Robinson (4), Richard
Rowley (2), William
Royal Shakespeare
   Company
Salvini, Tommaso
Saunderson, Mary
Schroder, Friedrich Ludwig
Schubert, Franz
Scofield, Paul
Shank, John
Shaw (3), Glen Byam
Shaw (5) (Shaa), Robert
Sheridan, Thomas
Siddons, Sarah
Sincklo (Sinklo, Sincler),
   John
Singer, John

Slater (Slaughter), Martin
Sly (2), William
Smith (2), Morgan
Smithson, Harriet
Sothern, Edward Hugh
Spencer, Gabriel
Strange's Men
Sullivan (1), Arthur
   Seymour
Sullivan (2), Barry
Sussex's Men
Tarlton, Richard
Taylor, Joseph
Tchaikovsky, Peter Ilyich
Tearle, Godfrey
Terry (1), Ellen
Terry (2), Fred
Thorndike, Sybil
Tooley, Nicholas
Tree, Beerbohm
Tuckfeild, Thomas

Underwood, John
Vaughan Williams, Ralph
Vaux (1), Sir Nicholas
Verdi, Giuseppe
Vestris, Elizabeth
Walton, William
Webster (1), Benjamin
Webster (3), Margaret
Weelkes, Thomas
Welles, Orson
Williams (1), Harcourt
Williamson, Nicol
Wilson (1), Jack
Wilson (2), John
Wilson (4), Robert
Woffington, Peg (Margaret)
Wolfit, Donald
Worcester's Men
Yates (1), Mary Ann
Yates (2), Richard
Zeffirelli, Franco

## ──── Characters ────

Aaron
Abbess
Abbot of Westminister,
   William Colchester
Abergavenny, George Neville,
   Lord
Abhorson
Abram (Abraham)
Achilles
Adam
Adrian (1) (see Volsce)
Adrian (2)
Adriana
Aedile
Aegeon (see Egeon)
Aemilia (see Emilia)
Aemilius
Aeneas
Agammemnon
Agrippa, M. Vipsanius
Ajax
Alarbus
Albany, Duke of
Alcibiades
Alencon, John, Duke of
Alexander (1)
Alexas (Alexas Laodician)
Alice
Aliena (Celia)
Alonso, King of Naples
Ambassador (1)
Ambassador (2)
Ambassador (3)
Amiens
Andrew (2) Aguecheek, Sir
   (see Sir Andrew)
Andromache

Andronicus (see Marcus
   Andronichus, Titus [1])
Angelo (1)
Angelo (2)
Angus, Gilchrist, Thane of
Anne (1) Bullen (Boleyn)
Anne (2), Lady (Anne Neville)
Anne (3) Page
Another Lord (see Lord [2])
Antenor
Anthony
Antigonus
Antiochus, King of Syria
Antipholus of Ephesus;
   Antipholus of Syracuse
Antonio (1)
Antonio (2)
Antonio (3)
Antonio (4)
Antonio (5)
Antony, Mark (Marcus
   Antonius)
Apemantus
Apothecary, the
Apparitions
Archbishop (1) of Canterbury,
   Henry Chichele (see
   Canterbury [1])
Archbishop (2) of Canterbury,
   (see Cranmer)
Archbishop (3) of York,
   Richard Scroop
Archbishop (4) of York,
   Thomas Rotherham
Archidamus
Arcite
Ariel

Armado, Don Adriano de
Arragon (Aragon)
Artemidorus
Artesius
Arthur, Prince of England
Arviragus
Asnath
Attendant (1)
Attendant (2)
Audrey
Aufidius, Tullus
Aumerle, Edward York, Duke
   of
Austria Limoges (Lymoges),
   Archduke of
Autolycus
Bagot, Sir John
Balthasar (1)
Balthasar (2)
Balthasar (3)
Balthasar (4)
Bandit (Thief)
Banquo
Baptista
Bardolph (1)
Bardolph (2), Lord Thomas
Barnardine
Barnardo (Bernardo)
Bartholomew (see Page [8])
Bassanio
Basset
Bassianus
Bastard (1), Philip
   Faulconbridge, The
Bastard (2) of Orleans, Jean
   Dunois, The
Bastard (3) (see Margarelon)

Bates, John
Bavian
Bawd
Beadle (1)
Beadle (2)
Bear
Beatrice
Beaumont (1)
Bedford (1), John Platagenet,
   Duke of
Begger (see Sly [1])
Belarius
Belch, Sir Toby (see Sir Toby)
Benedick
Benvolio
Berkeley (1)
Berkeley (2), Lord Thomas
Bernardo (see Barnardo)
Berowne (Biron)
Berri, Jean of France, Duke of
Bertram
Bevis, George
Bianca (1)
Bianca (2)
Bigot (Bigod), Roger
Biondello
Biron (see Berowne)
Bishop (1)
Blanche (Blanch) of Spain
Blunt (1), Sir James
Blunt (2), Sir John
Blunt (3), Sir Walter
Boatswain
Boleyn, Anne (see Anne [1])
Bolingbroke (1)
   (Bullingbrook), Henry
Bolingbroke (2), Roger

## CHARACTERS

Bona, Lady
Borachio
Bottom, Nick
Boult
Bourbon (1), Jean, Duke of
Bourbon (2), Lewis (Louis), Lord
Boy (1)
Boy (2) (Edward Plantagenet, Earl of Warwick)
Boy (3)
Boy (4)
Boy (5)
Boy (6)
Boy (7)
Boy (8)
Boy (9)
Boy (10)
Boyet
Brabantio (Brabanzio)
Brakenbury (Brackenbury), Robert
Brandon (1)
Brandon (2), Sir William
Bretagne (Britaine, Brittany), Jean, Duke of
Brook (1)
Broome (see Brook 1)
Brother (1)
Brother (2)
Brother (3)
Brutus (1), Decius (see Decius)
Brutus (2), Junius
Brutus (3), Junius
Brutus (4), Marcus
Buckingham (1), Edward Stafford, Duke of
Buckingham (2), Henry Stafford, Duke of
Buckingham (3), Sir Humphrey Stafford, Duke of
Bullcalf, Peter
Bullen, Anne (see Anne [1])
Bullingbrook (see Bolingbroke [1])
Burgundy (1), Duke of
Burgundy (2), Philip, Duke of
Bushy (Bussy), Sir John
Butcher (see Dick the Butcher)
Butts, Doctor (William Butts)
Cade, Jack
Cadwal
Caesar (1), Julius
Caesar (2), Octavius
Caius (1)
Caius (2), Doctor
Caius (3) Ligarius
Caius (4)
Calchas
Caliban
Calphurnia (Calpurnia)
Cambio

Cambridge, Richard York, Earl of
Camillo
Campeius, Cardinal Lawrence (Lorenzo Campeggio)
Canidius (Camidius) (Publius Canidius Crassus)
Canterbury (1), Henry Chichele, Archbishop
Canterbury (2), Archbishop of, Thomas Cranmer (see Cranmer)
Caphis
Capilet (see Widow 2)
Captain (1)
Captain (2)
Captain (3)
Captain (4)
Captain (5)
Captain (6)
Captain (7) (see Officer [5])
Captain (8) (Sergeant)
Captain (9)
Captain (10)
Captain (11)
Capuchius (Capucius), Lord (Eustace Chapuys)
Capulet (1)
Capulet (2), Cousin
Capulet (3), Lady
Cardinal (1), Beaufort, Henry
Cardinal (2), Lord (Thomas Bourchier)
Cardinal (3) Campeius (see Campeius)
Cardinal (4), Pandulph (see Pandulph)
Cardinal (5) Wolsey (see Wolsey)
Carlisle, Thomas Merke, Bishop
Carpenter
Carrier
Casca, Publius Servius
Cassandra
Cassio
Cassius (Caius Cassius Longinus)
Catesby, Sir William
Catherine (see Katharine)
Cathness (Caithness), Thorfin Sigurdsson, earl of
Catling, Simon (see Musicians [2])
Cato
Cawdor, Thane of
Celia
Ceres
Cerimon, Lord
Cesario
Chamberlain (1)
Chamberlain (2), Lord

Chancellor
Charles
Charles VI, King of France (see French King)
Charles VII, King of France
Charmian
Chatillon (Chatillion)
Chief Justice, Lord
Children
Chiron
Chorus (2)
Chorus (3)
Christopher (1) (see Sly [1])
Christopher (2) Urswick
Cicero, M. Tullius
Cinna (1), Gaius Helvetius (Helvius)
Cinna (2), Lucius Cornelius the Younger
Citizen (1)
Citizen (2)
Citizen (3)
Citizen (4)
Citizen (5)
Citizen (6)
Clarence (1), George York, Duke of
Clarence (2), Thomas, Duke of
Claudio (1)
Claudio (2)
Claudio (3)
Claudius (Claudio 1)
Claudius (2), King (see King [5])
Cleomenes (Cleomines) and Dion
Cleon
Cleopatra, Queen of Egypt
Clerk
Clifford (1), Lord John
Clifford (2), Lord Thomas
Clitus
Cloten
Clown (1)
Clown (2)
Clown (3) (see Feste)
Clown (4) (see Grave-digger; Other)
Clown (5)
Clown (6)
Clown (7)
Clown (8)
Cobbler
Cobweb
Colevile (Coleville) of the Dale, Sir John
Collatine (Tarquinius Collatinus)
Cominius
Commoner (1)
Commoner (2)
Commons

Conrade (Conrad)
Conspirators
Constable of France, Charles d'Albret (Delabreth)
Constance, Duchess of Brittany
Corambis
Cordelia
Corin
Coriolanus, Martius
Cornelius (1)
Cornelius (2)
Cornwall, Duke of
Costard
Countess (1) of Auvergne
Countess (2) of Rossillion
Countrymen
Court, Alexander
Courtesan
Cousin Capulet (see Capulet [2])
Crab
Cranmer, Thomas
Cressida
Crier
Cromer, Sir James
Cromwell, Thomas
Cupid
Curan
Curio
Curtis
Cymbeline
Dardanius (Dardanus)
Daughter (1)
Daughter (2)
Dauphin (1) Charles, the (see Charles VII)
Dauphin (2) Lewis, the (see Lewis [1])
Dauphin (3) Lewis, the
Davy
Decius (Decimus) Brutus
Decretas (Decretus, Dercetas, Dercetaeus, Dercetus)
Deiphobus
Demetrius (1)
Demetrius (2)
Demetrius (3)
Dennis (1)
Denny, Sir Anthony
Derby (2), Thomas Stanley, Earl of (see Stanley)
Desdemona
Diana (1)
Diana (2)
Dick the Butcher
Diomedes (1)
Diomedes (2) (Diomed)
Dion (see Cleomenes and Dion)
Dionyza
Doctor (1)

──────────────── CHARACTERS ────────────────

Doctor (2)
Doctor (3)
Doctor (4)
Doctor (5) of Divinity (see
  Priest [3])
Dogberry
Dolabella, Cornelius
Doll Tearsheet
Don (1) John (see John)
Don (2) Pedro (see Pedro)
Donalbain
Dorcas
Doricles
Dorset, Thomas Grey,
  Marquis of
Douglas, Archibald, Earl of
Drawer
Dromio of Ephesus and
  Dromio of Syracuse
Duchess (1) of Gloucester,
  Eleanor Cobham
Duchess (2) of Gloucester,
  Eleanor de Bohun
Duchess (3) of York, Cicely
  Neville
Duchess (4) of York, Isabel of
  Castile
Duke (1) Frderick
Duke (2) of Florence
Duke (3) of Milan
Duke (4) of Venice
Duke (5) of Venice
Duke (6) Orsino of Illyria (see
  Orsino)
Duke (7) Senior
Duke (8) Solinus of Ephesus
Duke (9) Vincentio of Vienna
Dull, Anthony
Dumaine (Dumain)
Duncan, King of Scotland
Dutchman and Spaniard
Edgar
Edmund
Edward IV, King of England
Egeon (Aegeon)
Egeus
Eglamour
Egyptian
Elbow
Eleanor (Elinor) of Aquitane,
  Queen of England
Elinor, Queen (see Eleanor)
Elizabeth (1), Queen of
  England
Elizabeth (2) Woodville
  (Woodvile), Lady Grey
Ely (1) Bishop of (see Bishop
  [3])
Ely (2), John Fordham,
  Bishop of
Ely (3), John Morton, Bishop
  of
Emilia (1) (Aemilia)

Emilia (2)
Emilia (3)
Emilia (4)
Emmanuel (see Clerk)
Enobarbus (Cnaeus Domitius
  Ahenobarbus)
Epenow
Eros
Erpingham, Sir Thomas
Escalus (1), Prince of Verona
  (see Prince [1])
Escalus (2)
Escanes
Essex (1), Geoffrey FitzPeter
Euphronius (see Ambassador
  [3])
Evans (3), Sir Hugh
Executioner (1)
Executioner (2)
Executioner (3)
Exeter (1), Henry Holland,
  Duke of
Exeter (2), Thomas Beaufort,
  Duke of
Exton, Sir Piers (Pierce)
Fabian
Fairy
Falconbridge (1)
  (Faulconbridge) (see Bastard
  [1]; Lady [5]; Robert)
Falconbridge (2)
  (Faulconberg,
  Faulconbridge), William
  Neville, Lord
Falstaff, Sir John
Falstaffe (Falstaff), Sir John
  (see Fastolfe, Sir John)
Fang
Fastolfe, Sir John
Father That Hath Killed His
  Son
Faulconbridge (1)
  (Falconbridge), Lady (see
  Lady [5])
Faulconbridge (2)
  (Falconbridge), Philip (see
  Bastard [1])
Faulconbridge (3)
  (Falconbridge), Robert (see
  Robert)
Faulconbridge (4), William
  Neville, Lord (see
  Falconbridge [2])
Feeble, Francis
Fenton (1)
Ferdinand (1) (see King [19])
Ferdinand (2)
Feste
Fidele
Fiend
First Clown (see Grave-digger)
First Commoner (see
  Carpenter)

First Executioner (see
  Executioner [2])
First Lord (1) (see Lord [4])
First Lord (2) (see Lord [6])
First Murderer (1)
First Murderer (2)
First Murderer (3)
First Officer (see Officer [3])
First Player (1) (see Players
  [1])
First Player (2)
Fishermen
Fitzwater (Fitzwalter), Lord
  Walter
Flaminus
Flavius (1) (L. Caesetius
  Flavus)
Falvius (2) (see Steward [2])
Fleance
Florizel
Fluellen
Flute
Follower
Fool (1)
Fool (2)
Fool (3)
Ford (1), Frank
Ford (3), Mistress Alice (see
  Mistress [1])
Forester
Fortinbras
France (2), King of
France (3), Princess of (see
  Princess [1] of France)
France (4), Queen of (see
  Isabel [2])
Francesca (Francisca) (see
  Nun)
Francis
Francis (2), Friar (see Friar
  [2])
Francisco (1)
Francisco (2)
Frederick (see Duke [1])
French King (Charles VI of
  France)
French Soldier
Frenchman
Friar (1)
Friar (2) Francis
Friar (3) John
Friar (4) Laurence (Lawrence)
Friend
Froth
Gadshill
Gallus, Caius Cornelius
Ganymede
Gaoler (1)
Gaoler (2)
Gaoler (3)
Gaoler (4)
Gardener
Gardener (1), Stephen

Gargrave, Thomas
Garter (Garter King-at-Arms)
Gaunt, John of
General
Gentleman (1)
Gentleman (2)
Gentleman (3)
Gentleman (4)
Gentleman (5)
Gentleman (6)
Gentleman (7)
Gentleman (8)
Gentleman (9)
Gentleman (10)
Gentleman (11)
Gentleman (12)
Gentleman (13)
Gentleman (14)
Gentleman (15)
Gentleman (16)
Gentleman-poet (see Servant
  [27])
Gentleman Usher
Gentlewoman (1)
Gentlewoman (2)
George (1) (see Bevis)
George (2) York, Duke of
  Clarence
Gertrude (see Queen [9])
Ghost (1)
Ghost (2)
Ghost (3)
Ghost (4)
Girl (Margaret Plantagenet)
Glansdale, Sir William
Glendower, Owen
Gloucester (1), Earl of
Gloucester (2), Eleanor
  Cobham, Duchess of (see
  Duchess [1])
Gloucester (3), Eleanor de
  Bohun, Duchess of (see
  Duchess [2])
Gloucester (4), Humphrey,
  Duke of
Gloucester (5), Richard
  Plantagenet, Duke of
  (Richard III, King of
  England)
Gloucester (6), Thomas of
  Woodstock, Duke of
Gobbo (1), Launcelot
Gobbo (2), Old
Goffe (Gough), Matthew
Goneril
Gonzalo
Goths
Governor (1) of Harfleur
Governor (2) of Paris
Gower (1)
Gower (2)
Gower (3), John
Grandpre

## CHARACTERS

Gratiano (1)
Gratiano (2) (Graziano)
Grave-digger (First Clown, First Grave-digger)
Greene (1) (Green), Henry
Gregory (1)
Gremio
Grey (1), Lady (see Elizabeth [2])
Grey (2), Sir Richard
Grey (3), Thomas
Griffith
Groom (1)
Groom (2)
Grumio
Guardsman (1)
Guardsman (2)
Guiderius
Guildenstern (see Rosencrantz and Guildenstern)
Guilford (Guildford), Sir Henry
Gurney, James
Haberdasher, The
Hal, Prince (see Prince [6])
Halberdier
Hamlet
Harcourt
Harpy
Harvey (1)
Hastings (1), Pursuivant
Hastings (2), Lord Ralph
Hastings (3), Lord William
Headsman (see Executioner)
Hecate (Hecat, Heccat)
Hector
Hecuba
Helen (1)
Helen (2) (see Helena [2])
Helena (1)
Helena (2)
Helenus
Helicanus
Henry (1), Prince (later King Henry III)
Henry IV, King of England
Henry V, King of England
Henry VI, King of England
Henry VIII, King of England
Herald (1)
Herald (2)
Herald (3)
Herald (4)
Herald (5) (see Gentleman [6])
Herald (6)
Herald (7)
Herald (8)
Herbert (3), Sir Walter
Hermia
Hermione
Hero
Hippolyta (1)
Hippolyta (2)

Holland (1), Henry, Duke of Exeter (see Exeter [1])
Holland (3), John
Holofernes
Horatio
Horner, Thomas
Hortensio
Hortensius
Host (1)
Host (2)
Hostess (1)
Hostess (2)
Hostilius
Hotspur (Henry Percy)
Hubert
Hume, John
Huntsman (1)
Huntsman (2)
Hymen (1)
Hymen (2)
Iachimo
Iago
Iden, Alexander
Imogen
Innogen
Iras
Iris
Isabel (1), Queen of England (see Queen [3])
Isabel (2), Queen of France
Isabella
Isidore's Servant
Jailer
Jailor
Jamy
Jaquenetta
Jaques (1)
Jaques (2) de Boys
Jessica
Jeweller
Joan La Pucelle (Joan of Arc)
John (1) Don
John (2), Friar (see Friar [3])
John (3), King of England
John (4) of Gaunt (see Gaunt)
John (5) Plantagenet (see Bedford; Lancaster [3])
John (6) Talbot (Young Talbot)
Joseph
Jourdain (1), Margery (see Margery Jourdain)
Julia
Juliet (1)
Juliet (2)
Juno
Jupiter
Justice
Katharina (see Katherina)
Katharine (1), (Katherine, Catherine)
Katharine (2) (Catherine, Katherine)

Katherina
Katherine (Katharine) of Aragon, Queen of England
Keeper (1)
Keeper (2)
Keeper (3)
Keeper (4)
Keeper (5)
Kent (2), Earl of
King (1), Alonso of Naples (see Alonso)
King (2) Antiochus of Syria (see Antiochus)
King (3) Charles VI of France (see French King)
King (4) Charles VII of France (see Charles VII)
King (5) Claudius of Denmark
King (6) Cymbeline of Britain (see Cymbeline)
King (7) Duncan of Scotland (see Duncan)
King (8) Edward IV of England (see Edward IV)
King (9) Henry IV of England (see Henry IV)
King (10) Henry V of England (see Henry V)
King (11) Henry VI of England (see Henry VI)
King (12) Henry VIII of England (see Henry VIII)
King (13) John of England (see John [3])
King (14) Lear of Britain (see Lear)
King (15) Leontes of Sicilia (see Leontes)
King (16) Lewis (Louis XI) of France (see Lewis [3])
King (17) of France
King (18) of France (see France [2])
King (19) Ferdinand of Navarre
King (20) Philip Augustus of France (see Philip [2])
King (21) Polixenes of Bohemia (see Polixenes)
King (22) Priam of Troy (see Priam)
King (23) Richard II of England (see Richard II)
King (24) Richard III of England (see Richard III)
King (25) Simonides of Pentapolis (see Simonides)
Kings
Knight (1)
Knight (2)
Knight (3)
Lady (1)

Lady (2)
Lady (3)
Lady (4)
Lady (5) Faulconbridge (Falconbridge)
Lady (6) Macbeth
Lady (7) Macduff
Lady (8) Catherine Mortimer
Lady (9) Northumberland (Margaret Neville)
Lady (10) Elizabeth Percy
Laertes
Lafew (Lafeu), Lord
Lamprius
Lancaster (2), John of Gaunt, Duke of (see Gaunt)
Lancaster (3), Prince John of
Lance (see Launce)
La Pucelle (see Joan La Pucelle)
Lartius, Titus
Launce (Lance)
Launcelot (Lancelot) Gobbo
Laurence Friar (see Friar [4])
Lavatche (Lavache) (see Clown [3])
Lavinia
Lawyer
Le Beau
Lear
Legate
Lennox (1) (see Lenox)
Lenox (Lennox), Thane of
Leonardo
Leonato
Leonine
Leontes
Lepidus, Marcus Aemilius
Lewis (1), the Dauphin (later King Louis VIII)
Lewis (2), the Dauphin (see Dauphin [3])
Lewis (3), King of France
Licio (see Litio)
Lieutenant (1)
Lieutenant (2)
Lieutenant (3)
Lieutenant (4)
Ligarius, Caius (Quintus)
Lincoln, Bishop of (John Longland)
Litio (Licio)
Lodovico
Lodowick
Longaville (Longueville)
Longueville (see Longaville)
Lord (1)
Lord (2)
Lord (3)
Lord (4)
Lord (5)
Lord (6)
Lord (7)

## CHARACTERS

Lord (8)
Lord (9)
Lord (10)
Lord (11)
Lord (12)
Lord (13)
Lord (14)
Lord (15)
Lord (16)
Lord (17) Bardolph (see Bardolph)
Lord (18) Chamberlain (see Chamberlain [2])
Lord (19) Chancellor (see Chancellor)
Lord (20) Chief Justice (see Chief Justice)
Lord (21) Marshal (see Marshal [1])
Lorenzo
Lovell (1) (Lovel), Sir Francis
Lovell (2), Sir Thomas
Luce
Lucentio
Lucetta
Luciana
Lucianus
Lucilius (1)
Lucilius (2)
Lucillius
Lucio
Lucius (1)
Lucius (2)
Lucius (3)
Lucius (4)
Lucius' Servant
Lucrece (Lucretia)
Lucretius
Lucullus
Lucy (2), Sir William
Lychorida
Lysander
Lysimachus
Mab
Macbeth
Macduff, Thane of Fife
Macmorris
Maecenas, Gaius
Malcolm (Prince Malcolm Canmore)
Malvolio
Mamillius
Man (1)
Man (2)
Man (3)
Marcade (Mercade)
Marcellus
March, Earl of
Marcus Andronicus
Mardian
Margarelon
Margaret (1) of Anjou
Margaret (2)

Margery Jourdain
Maria (1)
Maria (2)
Mariana (1)
Mariana (2)
Marina
Mariner (1)
Mariner (2)
Marshall (1) (Lord Marshal)
Marshall (2)
Martext, Sir Oliver
Martius (1)
Martius (2) (Marcius)
Marullus (Murellus) C. Epidius
Masquers
Master (1)
Master (2)
Master-Gunner
Mate
Mayor (1) of Coventry
Mayor (2) of London
Mayor (3) of London
Mayor (4) of St. Albans
Mayor (5) of York
Melun (Melune), Giles de, Lord
Menas
Menecrates
Menelaus
Menenius Agrippa
Menteth (Menteith), Walter Dalyell, Thane of
Mercade (see Marcade)
Mercer
Merchant (1)
Merchant (2)
Mercutio
Messala, Marcus Valerius
Messenger (1)
Messenger (2)
Messenger (3)
Messenger (4)
Messenger (5)
Messenger (6)
Messenger (7)
Messenger (8)
Messenger (9)
Messenger (10)
Messenger (11)
Messenger (12)
Messenger (13)
Messenger (14)
Messenger (15)
Messenger (16)
Messenger (17)
Messenger (18)
Messenger (19)
Messenger (20)
Messenger (21)
Messenger (22)
Messenger (23)
Messenger (24)
Messenger (25)

Messenger (26) (see Attendant [1])
Messenger (27)
Messenger (28)
Messenger (29)
Messenger (30)
Messenger (31)
Messenger (32)
Metellus Cimber (L. Tillius Cimber)
Michael (1)
Michael (2), Sir
Miranda
Mistress (1) Alice Ford
Mistress (2) Overdone
Mistress (3) Margaret Page
Mistress (4) Quickly (see Quickly)
Montague (1)
Montague (2), Lady
Montague (3), John Neville, Lord
Montano (1)
Montano (2)
Montgomery (1) John
Morocco (Morochus)
Mortimer (1), Sir Edmund, Earl of March
Mortimer (2), Edmund
Mortimer (3), Sir Hugh
Mortimer (4), Sir John
Mortimer (5), Lady (see Lady [8])
Morton
Moth (1) (Mote)
Moth (2)
Mother
Mouldy, Ralph
Mowbray (1), Thomas, Duke of Norfolk
Mowbray (2), Thomas, Lord
Murderer (see First Murderer, Second Murderer, Third Murderer)
Murellus (see Marullus)
Musicians (1)
Musicians (2)
Musicians (3)
Musicians (4)
Musicians (5)
Musicians (6)
Musicians (7)
Mustardseed
Mutius
Myrmidon
Mytilenian Sailor (see Tyrian Sailor)
Nathaniel (1)
Nathaniel (2)
Neighbour
Nell (1)
Nell (2)
Nerissa

Nestor
Nicanor (see Roman [2])
Nicholas
Nobleman
Norfolk (1), John Howard, Duke of
Norfolk (2), John Mowbray, Duke of
Norfalk (3), Thomas Howard, Duke of
Norfolk (4), Thomas Mowbray, Duke of (see Mowbray [1])
Northumberland (1), Henry Percy, Earl of
Northumberland (2), Henry Percy, Earl of
Northumberland (3), Henry Percy, Earl of
Northumberland (4), Lady (see Lady [9])
Northumberland (5), Siward, Earl of
Nun
Nurse (1)
Nurse (2)
Nurse (3)
Nym
Oatcake, Hugh
Oberon
Octavia
Octavius (Gaius Octavius Caesar; Octavian)
Officer (1)
Officer (2)
Officer (3)
Officer (4)
Officer (5)
Officer (6)
Officer (7)
Officer (8)
Old Athenian
Old Clifford (see Clifford [2], Thomas)
Old Gobbo (see Gobbo [2])
Old Lady
Old Man (1) (see Capulet [2])
Old Man (2)
Old Man (3)
Oldcastle
Oliver (1)
Oliver (2) (see Martext)
Olivia
One (1)
One (2)
One (3) Within
Ophelia
Orlando
Orleans (2), Bastard of (see Bastard [2] of Orleans)
Orleans (3), Charles, Duke of
Orsino
Osric

## CHARACTERS

Ostler (1)
Oswald
Othello
Other (Other Clown, Second Clown, Second Gravedigger)
Outlaws
Oxford (2), John de Vere, Earl of
Page (1)
Page (2)
Page (3)
Page (4)
Page (5)
Page (6)
Page (7)
Page (8)
Page (9)
Page (10) (see Boy [9])
Page (11), Anne (see Anne [3])
Page (12), George
Page (13), Mistress Margaret (see Mistress [3])
Page (14), William (see William [1])
Painter (1)
Palamon
Pandar
Pandarus
Pandulph
Panthino
Paris (2)
Paris (3)
Parolles (Paroles)
Patch-breech (see Fishermen)
Patience
Patricians (see Senator [2])
Patroclus
Paulina
Peaseblossom
Pedant, The
Pedro, Don
Pembroke (4), William Herbert
Pembroke (5), William Marshall, Earl of
Penker (Pynkie), Friar
Percy (1), Henry (see Northumberland [1])
Percy (2), Henry
Percy (3), Henry (see Northumberland [2])
Percy (4), Lady (see Lady [10])
Perdita
Pericles
Perkes, Clement
Peter (1)
Peter (2)
Peter (3)
Peter (4) of Pomfret
Peter (5), Friar (see Friar [1])
Petitioners
Peto

Patruchio (1)
Petruchio (2)
Phebe (Phoebe)
Philario
Philemon
Philip (1)
Philip (2), Augustus, King of France
Philip (3) (see Bastard [1])
Philo
Philostrate
Philotus
Phrynia and Timandra
Pilch (see Fisherman)
Pinch, Dr.
Pindarus
Pirates
Pirithous
Pisanio
Pistol
Plantagenet (2), Richard
Plantagenet (3), Richard
Player King
Player Queen
Players (1)
Players (2)
Plebeians (1)
Plebeians (2)
Poet (1)
Poet (2)
Poins, Ned
Polixenes
Polonius
Polydore (Guiderius)
Pompey (1) Bum
Pompey (2) (Sextus Pompeius)
Popilius Lena
Porter (1)
Porter (2)
Porter (3)
Porter (4)
Portia (1)
Portia (2)
Post (1)
Post (2)
Posthumus
Potpan (see Servingman [2])
Prentice
Priam, King of Troy
Priest (1)
Priest (2)
Priest (3)
Prince (1) Escalus of Verona
Prince (2) Hal (also Henry, later King Henry V) (see Prince [6] of Wales)
Prince (3) Henry (see Henry [1])
Prince (4) of Wales, Edward
Prince (5) of Wales, Edward (Edward V, King of England)

Prince (6) of Wales, Henry (Hal, later King Henry V)
Princess (1) of France
Princess (2) Katharine of France (see Katharine [2])
Proculeius, Caius
Prologue (2)
Prologue (3)
Prologue (4)
Prologue (5)
Prospero
Proteus
Provost
Publius (1)
Publius (2)
Puck
Pursuivant (see Hastings [2])
Pyrrhus
Queen (1)
Queen (2) of Britain
Queen (3) Anne of England (see Anne [1])
Queen (4) Anne of England (see Anne [2])
Queen (5) Cleopatra of Egypt (see Cleopatra)
Queen (6) Eleanor (Elinor) of England (see Eleanor)
Queen (8) Elizabeth of England (see Elizabeth [2])
Queen (9) Gertrude of Denmark
Queen (10) Hermione (see Hermione)
Queen (11) Hippolyta of the Amazons (see Hippolyta [1])
Queen (12) Hippolyta (see Hippolyta [2])
Queen (13) Isabel of England
Queen (14) Isabel of France (see Isabel [2])
Queen (15) Katherine of England (and of Aragon) (see Katherine of Aragon)
Queen (16) Margaret of England (see Margaret [1])
Queen (17), Player (see Player Queen)
Quickly, Mistress
Quince, Peter
Quintus
Rambures, Lord
Rannius
Ratcliffe, Sir Richard
Rebeck, Hugh (see Musicians [2])
Regan
Reignier, Duke of Anjou and King of Naples
Reynaldo (1)
Reynaldo (2) (see Steward [1])
Richard II, King of England
Richard III, King of England

Richmond, Earl of (Henry Tudor, later King Henry VII)
Rinaldo (see Steward 1)
Rivers, Anthony Woddville, Earl of
Robert Faulconbridge (Falconbridge)
Robin (1)
Robin (2) Goodfellow (see Puck)
Roderigo
Roman (1)
Roman (2)
Romeo
Rosalind
Rosaline (1)
Rosaline (2)
Rosencrantz and Guildenstern
Ross (1) (see Rosse)
Ross (2) (Ros), William de
Rosse (Ross) Thane of
Rossill (Russell), Sir John
Rugby, John
Rumour
Rutland (1), Edmund York, Earl of
Rynaldo (see Steward [1])
Sailor (1)
Sailor (2)
Sailor (3)
Sailor (4) (see Tyrian Sailor)
Salarino (see Salerio)
Salerio (Salarino)
Salisbury (1), John Montague (Montacute), Earl of
Salisbury (2), Richard Neville, Earl of
Salisbury (3), Thomas Montague (Montacute), Earl of
Salisbury (4), William Longsword, Earl of
Sampson
Sands, Lord (William Sands [Sandys])
Saturninus
Say, James Finnes, Lord
Scales, Lord Thomas de
Scarus
Schoolmaster (1)
Schoolmaster (2)
Scout
Scribe
Scrivener
Scroop (1) (Le Scroop, Scroope, Scrope), Henry
Scroop (2) (Scroope, Scrope), Richard (see Archbishop [3])
Scroop (3) (Le Scroop, Scroope, Scrope), Stephen
Seacoal, George
Sebastian (1)

## CHARACTERS

Warwick (2), Richard Beauchamp, Earl of
Warwick (3), Richard Neville, Earl of
Watchmen (1)
Watchmen (2)
Watchmen (3)
Watchmen (4)
Watchmen (5)
Weaver (see Smith [1])
Westminister (2), Abbot of (see Abbot of Westminister)
Westmoreland (1), Ralph Neville, Earl of

Westmoreland (2), Ralph Neville, Earl of
Whitmore, Walter
Widow (1)
Widow (2) Capilet
Wife
William (1), Page
William (2)
Williams (2), Michael
Willoughby (3), William de
Winchester (1), Henry Beaufort, Bishop of
Winchester (2), Stephen Gardiner, Bishop of
Witches

Within
Wolsey, Thomas Cardinal
Woman (1)
Woman (2)
Woodville (Woodvile), Lieutenant Richard
Wooer
Yorick
York (3), Cicely Neville, Duchess of (see Duchess [3])
York (4), Edmund of Langley, Duke of
York (5), Edward, Duke of
York (6), Isabel of Castile, Duchess of (see Duchess [4])

York (7), Richard, Duke of
York (8), Richard Plantagenet, Duke of
York (9), Richard Scroop, Archbishop of
York (10), Thomas Rotherham, Archbishop of (see Archbishop [4])
Young Cato
Young Clifford (see Lord John Clifford [1])
Young Lucius
Young Siward (Osberne of Northumberland)
Young Talbot (see John [6])

## CONTEMPORARIES AND NEAR-CONTEMPORARIES OF SHAKESPEARE

Addenbrooke, John
Africanus, Leo (see Leo Africanus)
Allde, Edward
Alleyn, Edward
Amyot, Jacques
Annesley, Brian
Armin, Robert
Aspinall, Alexander
Aspley, William
Bandello, Matteo
Barents (Barentz), Willem
Barkstead, William
Barnes, Barnabe
Barnfield, Richard
Barton (2), Richard
Basse, William
Beaumont (2), Francis
Bedford (2), Lucy, Countess of
Beeston, Christopher
Belleforest, Francois de
Belott, Stephen
Benfield, Robert
Benson (2), John
Bentley, John
Berners, John Bouchier, Lord
Bevis, George
Blount, Edward
Bonian, Richard
Bradock (Bradocke), Richard
Bretchgirdle, John
Bright, Timothy
Brooke (1), Arthur
Brooke (3), William, Lord Cobham (see Cobham)
Browne, Robert
Bryan, George
Buchanan, George
Burbage (1), Cuthbert
Burbage, (2), James
Burbage (3), Richard
Burby, Cuthbert
Burghley (Burleigh), Lord (William Cecil)

Burleigh, William Cecil, Lord (see Burghley)
Busby, John
Butter, Nathaniel
Camden, William
Carew, Richard
Carey (1), George, Baron Hunsdon (see Hunsdon 1)
Carey (2), Henry, Baron Hunsdon (see Hunsdon 2)
Cecil (1), Robert, Earl of Salisbury
Cecil (2), Thomas
Cecil (3), William (see Burghley)
Cervantes Saavedra, Miguel de
Chapman, George
Chettle, Henry
Chester, Robert (see Love's Martyr)
Cinthio (Giovanni Battista Giraldi)
Cobham, William Brooke, Lord
Collins, Francis
Combe (1), John
Combe (2), Thomas
Combe (3), Thomas
Combe (4), William
Combe (5), William
Condell, Henry
Cooke (1), Alexander
Cottom (Cottam), John
Cowley, Richard
Cox, Robert
Crane, Ralph
Creede, Thomas
Crosse, Samuel
Daniel, Samuel
Davenant (D'Avenant), William
Davies (1), John of Hereford
Davies (2), Sir John
Day, John

Dekker, Thomas
Deloney, Thomas
Dennis (2), John
Derby (1), Fernando Stanley, Earl of (see Strange)
Derby (3), William Stanley, Earl of
Digges (1), Dudley
Digges (2), Leonard
Downton, Thomas
Drayton, Michael
Droeshout, Martin
Dryden, John
Du Bartas, Guillaume de Sallust
Dutton, Laurence
Ecclestone, William
Eden, Richard
Edwards (Edwardes), Richard
Eld (Elde), George
Eliot (1), John
Elizabeth (1), Queen of England
Elizabeth (3) Stuart, Queen of Bohemia
Essex (2), Robert Devereaux, Earl of
Evans (2), Henry
Farrant, Richard
Fenton (2) Geoffrey
Ffarington, William
Field (1), Nathan
Field (2), Richard
Fisher, Thomas
Fitton, Mary
Fletcher (1), Giles
Fletcher (2), John
Fletcher (3), Laurence
Florio, John (Giovanni)
Ford (2), John
Forman, Simon
Foxe (Fox), John
Gardiner (2), William
Garnet, Henry

Gascoigne, George
Gibborne, Thomas
Gilbard, William
Gilburne, Samuel
Giles, Nathaniel
Giulio Romano (Giulio Pippi)
Golding, Arthur
Goslicius, Laurentius Grimalius
Gosson (1), Henry
Gosson (2), Stephen
Gough (Goughe), Robert
Grafton, Richard
Granada, Luis de
Green, John
Greene (2), Robert
Greene (3), Thomas
Greville (1), Curtis
Greville (2), Fulke (Lord Brooke)
Griffin, Bartholomew
Gwinne (Gwinn), Matthew
Hakluyt, Richard
Hall, Arthur
Hall (7), William
Hamlett, Katherine
Harington, Sir John
Harris (2), Henry
Harrison (2), John
Harrison (3), William
Harsnett, Samuel
Hart (3), William
Harvey (2), Gabriel
Harvey (4), William
Hathway (Hathaway), Richard
Heicroft, Henry
Heminge (Heminges), John
Henry (2) Frederick, Prince of Wales
Henslowe, Philip
Herbert (1), Henry
Herbert (2), Henry, Philip, or William, Earls of Pembroke (see Pembroke [1, 2, 3])

## CONTEMPORARIES AND NEAR-CONTEMPORARIES OF SHAKESPEARE

Hervey (Harvey), William
Heyes, Thomas
Heywood (1), John
Heywood (2), Thomas
Higgins, John
Hilliard, Nicholas
Hoby (1), Sir Thomas
Hoby (2), Sir Thomas Posthumous
Holinshed, Raphael
Holland (2), Hugh
Holland (4), Philemon
Hopkins, Richard
Howard, Charles
Hunnis, William
Hunsdon (1), George Carey, Baron
Hunsdon (2), Henry Carey, Baron
Hunt, Simon
Jackson (2), John
Jackson (3), Roger
Jaggard, William and Isaac
James, Elias
James I, King of England
Jamy
Janssen (1), Cornelis (Cornelius Johnson)
Janssen (2), Gheerart (Gerard Johnson)
Jeffes, Humphrey
Jenkins, Thomas
Johnson (1), Arthur
Johnson (3), Cornelius (see Janssen [1])
Johnson (4), Gerard (see Janssen [2])
Johnson (5), Robert
Johnson (6), Robert
Johnson (8), William
Jones (2), Richard
Jones (3), Robert
Jones (4), William
Jonson, Ben
Jourdain (2) (Jourdan), Sylvester
Kempe (Kemp), William
Kirkham, Edward
Kirkman, Edward
Knell, William
Knight (4), Edward
Knollys, Sir William
Kyd, Thomas
Lane (1), John

Lane (2), Richard
Laneman (Lanman), Henry
Langley, Francis
Lanier, Emilia
Law, Matthew
Leake, William
Legh, Gerard
Leicester, Robert Dudley, Earl of
Le Macon, Antoine
Leo Africanus (Joannes Leo)
Leveson, William
Ling, Nicholas
Locke, Matthew
Lodge, Thomas
Lopez, Roderigo
Lowin (Lowen), John
Lucy (1), Sir Thomas
Lupton, Thomas
Lyly, John
Mabbe, James
Manningham, John
Marlowe (1), Christopher
Marsh, Henry
Marston, John
Massinger, Philip
Mayne, Jasper
Meres, Francis
Middleton, Thomas
Millington, Thomas
Milton, John
Mömpelgard, Frederick, Count of (later Duke of) Wurttemberg
Monarcho
Montaigne, Michael de
Montgomery (2), Philip Herbert, Earl of
Montjoy
Mopsa
Morgan (1) (Belarius)
Morley, Thomas
Mountjoy, Christopher
Munday, Anthony
Nash (1), Anthony
Nash (2), Thomas
Nashe (Nash), Thomas
North, Sir Thomas
Okes, Nicholas
Ostler (2), William
Oxford (1), Edward de Vere, Earl of
Painter (2), William
Pavier, Thomas

Peele, George
Pembroke (1), Henry Herbert, Earl of
Pembroke (2), Philip Herbert, Lord (see Montgomery [2])
Pembroke (3), William Herbert, Earl of
Phillips, Augustine
Platter, Thomas
Pope (2), Thomas
Porter (5), Henry
Pory, John
Preston, Thomas
Prynne, William
Puck (Robin Goodfellow)
Puttenham, George
Queen (7) Elizabeth of England
Quiney (1), Judith (see Shakespeare [10])
Quiney, (2), Richard
Quiney (3), Thomas
Raleigh, (Ralegh), Sir Walter
Ratsey, Gamaliel
Reynolds (2), William
Rice, John
Rich (1), Barnabe (Barnaby Riche)
Richardson (1), John
Roberts, James
Robinson (1), John
Robinson (3), Richard
Robinson (4), Richard
Roche, Walter
Rogers (1), John
Rogers (2), Phillip
Rowley (1), Samuel
Rowley (2), William
Russell, Thomas
Rutland (2), Francis Manners, Earl of
Sackville, Thomas
Sadler, Hamnet and Judith
Salusbury (Salisbury), John
Sandells, Fulk
Savage, Thomas
Scot (Scott), Reginald
Segar, William
Shank, John
Sharpham, Edward
Shaw (4), Julian
Shaw (5) (Shaa), Robert
Shirley, Anthony
Short, Peter

Sidney, Philip
Simmes, Valentine
Sincklo (Sinklo, Sincler), John
Singer, John
Slater (Slaughter), Martin
Sly (2), William
Smethwick (Smithweeke), John
Snodham, Thomas
Southampton (2), Henry Wriothesley, Earl of
Spencer, Gabriel
Spenser, Edmund
Stafford (3), Simon
Stanley (1), Ferdinando, Lord Strange (see Strange)
Stow, John
Strachey (2), William
Strange, Ferdinando Stanley, Lord
Tarlton, Richard
Taylor, Joseph
Thorpe, Thomas
Tooley, Nicholas
Trundell, John
Twine, Laurence
Tuckfield (Tuckfeild), Thomas
Tyler (1), Richard
Underhill, William
Underwood, John
Walker (1), Henry
Walker (2), William
Walkley, Thomas
Walley, Henry
Warner, William
Waterson, John
Webster (2), John
Weelkes, Thomas
Whatcott, Robert
Whetstone, George
White (1), Edward
White (2), William
Whitgift, John
Wilkins, George
Willoughby (1), Sir Ambrose
Willoughby (2) (Willobie) Henry
Wilson (1), Jack
Wilson (2), John
Wilson (4), Robert
Wise, Andrew
Wyatt, Thomas
Yong (Yonge, Young), Bartholomew

## DOCUMENTS AND ARTIFACTS

Chandos portrait
Coat of arms, Shakespeare's
Contention, The
Dering Manuscript

Ely Palace portrait
False Folio
First Folio

Flower portrait
Kesselstadt Death Mask
Longleat Manuscript

'Pied Bull' Quarto (see King Lear, 'Text of the Play')
Portraits of Shakespeare

## HISTORICAL REFERENCES

Andrew (1)
Hundred Years War
Lancaster (1) Family
Plantagenet (1) Family

Renaissance
Roses, Wars of the (see Wars
of the Roses)

Stuart Dynasty
Trojan War
Tudor Dynasty

Wars of the Roses
Welcombe
York (1) Family

## PLACES

Actium
Agincourt
Alexandria
Angiers
Anjou
Antioch
Antium
Arden (1), Forest of
Athens
Auvergne
Bangor
Barkloughly Castle
Barnet
Baynard Castle
Belmont
Birmingham Shakespeare
 Memorial Library
Birnam Wood (see
 Dunsinane)
Birthplace, Shakespeare's
Blackfriars Gatehouse
Blackfriars Priory
Blackfriars Theatre
Blackheath
Boar's Head Tavern
Bodleian Library
Bohemia
Bordeaux
Bosworth Field
Bristol (Bristow)
Bury St Edmunds
Corioles (Corioli)
Coventry
Cross Keys Inn

Curtain Theatre, The
Cyprus
Denmark
Dover
Dunsinane (Dunsinnan)
Eastcheap
Elsinore
Ephesus
Fife
Florence
Flint Castle
Folger Shakespeare Library
Fortune Theatre
France (1)
Frogmore
Gad's Hill (Gadshill, Gads
 Hill)
Gascony
Gaultree Forest
Globe Theatre
Gloucestershire
Harfleur
Holmedon (Homildon)
Hope Theatre
Huntington Library
Inns of Court
Inverness
Italy
Jerusalem Chamber
Kenilworth
Kent (1)
Kimbolton Castle
London
Mantua

Marseilles
Mermaid Tavern
Messina
Middleham Castle
Milan
Misenum
Mortimer's Cross
Mytilene
New Place
Newington Butts
Old Vic Theatre
Orléans (1)
Padua
Paris (1)
Parliament House
Pentapolis
Philippi
Phoenix
Picardy
Pomfret (Pontefract) Castle
Porcupine (Porpentine)
Porpentine (see Porcupine)
Priory
Rochester
Rome
Rose Theatre
Rossillion (Rousillon)
Rouen
Sadler's Wells Theatre
St Albans
St Edmundsbury (Bury St
 Edmunds)
Sandal Castle
Sardis

Scotland
Shrewsbury
Sicilia
Smithfield
Southampton (1)
Southwark
Stratford
Swan Theatre
Swinstead (Swineshead)
 Abbey
Tamworth
Tewkesbury (Tewksbury)
Tharsus (Tarsus)
Theatre, The
Thebes
Tower of London
Towton
Troy
Troyes
Tyre
Venice
Verona
Vienna
Wakefield
Wales (1)
Warkworth Castle
Warwickshire
Welcombe
Westminster (1) Abbey
Westminster (3) Hall
Westminster (4) Palace
Whitefriars Theatre
Windsor
York (2)

## THE PLAYS

All Is True (Henry VIII)
All's Well That Ends Well
Antony and Cleopatra
As You Like It
Cardenio
Comedy of Errors, The
Coriolanus
Cymbeline
Hamlet
Henry IV, Part 1
Henry IV, Part 2

Henry V
Henry VI, Part 1
Henry VI, Part 2
Henry VI, Part 3
Henry VIII
Julius Caesar
King John
King Lear
Love's Labour's Lost
Love's Labour's Won
Macbeth

Measure for Measure
Merchant of Venice, The
Merry Wives of Windsor, The
Midsummer Night's Dream, A
Much Ado About Nothing
Othello
Pericles, Prince of Tyre
Richard II
Richard III
Romeo and Juliet

Taming of the Shrew, The
Tempest, The
Timon of Athens
Titus Andronichus
Troilus and Cressida
Twelfth Night
Two Gentlemen of Verona,
 The
Two Noble Kinsmen, The
Winter's Tale, The

## The Poems

Lover's Complaint, A
Phoenix and Turtle, The

Rape of Lucrece, The

Sonnets, The

Venus and Adonis

## Related Works

Age of Kings, An
Arden of Feversham
Bestrafte Brudermord, Der
(Fratricide Punished)
Bible
Birth of Merlin, The
Contention, The
Duke Hnmphrey
Edward III
Fair Em

Famous Victories, The
Henry I and Henry II
King Leir
Law Against Lovers, The
Locrine
London Prodigal, The
Love in a Forest
Love's Martyr
Merry Devil of Edmonton, The
Mirror for Magistrates, A

Mucedorus
Passionate Pilgrim, The
Puritan, The
"Shall I Die?"
Sir John Oldcastle
Sir Thomas More
Spread of the Eagle, The
Taming of a Shrew, The
Thomas Lord Cromwell
Traïson

Troublesome Raigne of King John,
The
True Tragedy, The
Ur-Hamlet
Ur-Shrew
Whole Contention, The
Woodstock (Thomas of
Woodstock)
Yorkshire Tragedy, A

## Relatives of Shakespeare

Arden (2), Robert
Hall (3), Elizabeth
Hall (4), John
Hall (6), Susanna (see
Shakespeare[14])
Hart (2), Joan (see
Shakespeare[8])
Hart (3), William
Hathaway, Anne (Anne
Hathaway Shakespeare)

Lambert, John
Nash (2), Thomas
Quiney (1), Judith (see
Shakespeare [10])
Quiney (3), Thomas
Shakespeare (1), Anne
Shakespeare (2), Anne
Hathaway (see
Hathaway)
Shakespeare (3), Edmund

Shakespeare (4), Gilbert
Shakespeare (5), Hamnet
Shakespeare (6), Henry
Shakespeare (7), Joan
Shakespeare (8), Joan (Joan
Shakespeare Hart)
Shakespeare (9), John
Shakespeare (10), Judith
(Judith Shakespeare
Quinley)

Shakespeare (11), Mary
Arden
Shakespeare (12), Richard
Shakespeare (13), Richard
Shakespeare (14), Susanna
(Susanna Shakespeare
Hall)
Shakespeare (15),
William

## Scholars, Authors, Translators, Artists, Printers, and Publishers

Adams, Joseph Quincy
Adlington, William
Africanus, Leo (see Leo
Africanus)
Alexander (2), Peter
Allde, Edward
Amyot, Jacques
Apuleius, Lucius
Ariosto, Ludovico
Aristotle
Aspley, William
Ayscough, Samuel
Bandello, Matteo
Barkstead, William
Barnes, Barnabe
Barnfield, Richard
Basse, William
Beaumont (2) Francis
Belleforest, Francois de
Benson (2), John
Berners, John Bourchier, Lord
Blount, Edward
Boas, Frederick S.
Boccaccio, Giovanni
Boece (Boyce), Hector
Bonian, Richard
Boswell, James the younger
Bowdler, Thomas
Boydell, John
Bradley, Andrew Cecil

Bradock (Bradocke), Richard
Bright, Timothy
Brooke (1), Arthur
Brooke (2), C. F. Tucker
Buchanan, George
Bullough, Geoffrey
Burby, Cuthbert
Burnaby, William
Busby, John
Butter, Nathaniel
Camden, William
Capell, Edward
Carew, Richard
Castiglione, Baldassare
Caxton, William
Cervantes Saavedra, Miguel
de
Chambers, Edmund Kerchever
Chapman, George
Chaucer, Geoffrey
Chester, Robert
Chettle, Henry
Cibber (1), Colley
Cicero, M. Tullius
Cinthio (Giovanni Baptista
Giraldi)
Clark, Mary Cowden and
Charles Cowden
Coleridge, Samuel Taylor
Collier (2), John Payne

Colonne, Guido delle
Craig (2), Hardin
Crane, Ralph
Creede, Thomas
Créton, Jean
Crowne, John
Cumberland, Richard
Daniel, Samuel
Davies (1), John of Hereford
Davies (2), Sir John
Day, John
Dekker, Thomas
Deloney, Thomas
Dennis (2), John
De Quincey, Thomas
Derby (3), William Stanley,
Earl of
Dickens, Charles
Digges (2), Leonard
Dowden, Edward
Drayton, Michael
Droeshout, Martin
Dryden, John
Du Bartas, Guillaume de
Sallust
Duffett, Thomas
D'Urfey, Thomas
Eden, Richard
Edwards (Edwardes), Richard
Eld (Elde), George

Eliot (1), John
Eliot (2), Thomas Stearns
Elyot, Sir Thomas
Eschenburg, Johann Joachim
Fabyan, Robert
Fenton (2), Geoffrey
Fenton (3), Richard
Field (2), Richard
Fiorentino, Giovanni
Fisher, Thomas
Fleay, Frederick Gard
Fletcher (1), Giles
Fletcher (2), John
Florio, John (Giovanni)
Ford (2), John
Foxe (Fox), John
French, George Russell
Froissart, Jean
Furness, Horace Howard
Furnivall, Frederick James
Gascoigne, George
Geoffrey of Monmouth
Gervinus, Georg Gottfried
Gide, Andre
Gildon, Charles
Giulio Romano
Goethe, Johann Wolfgang von
Golding, Arthur
Goslicius, Laurentius
Grimalius

## SCHOLARS, AUTHORS, TRANSLATORS, ARTISTS, PRINTERS, AND PUBLISHERS

Gosson (1), Henry
Gosson (2), Stephen
Grafton, Richard
Granada, Luis de
Granville, George
Greene (2), Robert
Greg, Walter Wilson
Greville (2), Fulke (Lord Brooke)
Griffin, Bartholomew
Gwinne (Gwinn), Matthew
Hakluyt, Richard
Hall (1), Arthur
Hall (2) (Halle), Edward
Hall (7), William
Halle, Edward (see Hall [2])
Halliwell-Phillips, James Orchard
Hanmer, Thomas
Harington, Sir John
Harris (1), Frank (James Thomas)
Harrison (1), George Bagshawe
Harrison (2), John
Harrison (3), William
Harsnett, Samuel
Harvey (2), Gabriel
Hathway (Hathaway), Richard
Hayman, Francis
Hazlitt, William
Henryson, Robert
Heyes, Thomas
Heywood (1), John
Heywood (2), Thomas
Higgins, John
Hilliard, Nicholas
Hoby (1), Sir Thomas
Holinshed, Raphael
Holland (2), Hugh
Holland (4), Philemon
Homer
Hopkins, Richard
Hotson, Leslie
Hunnis, William
Hunnis, William
Ingleby, Clement Mansfield
Ireland, William Henry
Jackson (3), Roger
Jaggard, William and Isaac
Janssen (1), Cornelis (Cornelius Johnson)

Janssen (2), Gheerart (Gerard Johnson)
Johnson (1), Arthur
Johnson (2), Charles
Johnson (3), Cornelius (see Janssen [1])
Johnson (4) Gerard (see Janssen [2])
Johnson (7), Samuel
Jonson, Ben
Keats, John
Killigrew, Thomas
Kirkman, Francis
Kittredge, George Lyman
Knight (5), G. Wilson
Kyd, Thomas
Lacy, John
Lamb (1), Charles
Lamb (2), George
Langbaine, Gerard
Law, Matthew
Leake, William
Lee, Sidney
Legh, Gerard
Le Maçon, Antoine
Lennox (2), Charlotte
Leo Africanus (Joannes Leo)
Lessing, Gotthold Ephraim
Lillo, George
Ling, Nicholas
Lily (Lilly, Lyly), William
Livy (Titius Livius)
Lodge, Thomas
Lucian
Lupton, Thomas
Lydgate, John
Lyly, John
Mabbe, James
Malone, Edmond
Markham, Gervase
Marlowe (1), Christopher
Marsh, Henry
Marston, John
Massinger, Philip
Mayne, Jasper
Meres, Francis
Middleton, Thomas
Miller (1), James
Millington, Thomas
Milton, John
Montaigne, Michael de
Montemayer, Jorge de

More, Sir Thomas
Morgan (2) McNamara
Morgann, Maurice
Moseley, Humphrey
Munday, Anthony
Nashe (Nash), Thomas
North, Sir Thomas
Okes, Nicholas
Otway, Thomas
Ovid (Publius Ovidius Naso)
Oxford (1), Edward de Vere, Earl of
Painter (2), William
Pater, Walter
Pavier, Thomas
Peele, George
Pepys, Samuel
Planché, James Robinson
Plautus, Titus Maccius
Pliny the Elder
Plutarch
Pollard, Alfred William
Pope (1), Alexander
Porter (5), Henry
Pory, John
Preston, Thomas
Puttenham, George
Raleigh (Ralegh), Sir Walter
Reed, Isaac
Reynolds (1), Frederick
Rich (1), Barnaby (Barnabe Riche)
Roberts, James
Robertson, John Mackinnon
Robinson (3), Richard
Romano, Giulio (see Giulio Romano)
Rowe, Nicholas
Rowley (1), Samuel
Rowley (2), William
Sackville, Thomas
Sainte-Maure, Benoit de
Saxo Grammaticus
Scheemakers, Peter
Schiller, Johann Christoph Friedrich
Schlegel, August Wilhelm von
Schücking, Levin Ludwig
Scot (Scott), Reginald
Segar, William
Seneca, Lucius Annaeus
Shadwell, Thomas

Sharpham, Edward
Shaw (2), George Bernard
Short, Peter
Sidney, Philip
Simmes, Valentine
Simpson, Richard
Smethwick (Smithweeke), John
Snodham, Thomas
Spalding, William
Spenser, Edmund
Spurgeon, Caroline
Stafford (3), Simon
Stationers' Company
Steevens, George
Stoll, Elmer Edgar
Stow, John
Strachey (1), Lytton
Strachey (2), William
Surrey (1), Henry Howard, Earl of
Swinburne, Algernon Charles
Tate, Nahum
Theobold, Lewis
Thorpe, Thomas
Tieck, Ludwig
Tillyard, E. M. W.
Trundell, John
Twine, Laurence
Tyler (2), Thomas
Udall, Nicholas
University Wits
Vaux (2), Sir Thomas
Vergil, Polydore
Virgil (Vergil)
Walkley, Thomas
Walley, Henry
Warburton, John
Warner, William
Waterson, John
Webster (2), John
Whetstone, George
White (1), Edward
White (2), William
Wieland, Christoph Martin
Wilkins, George
Willoughby (2) (Willobie), Henry
Wilson (3), John Dover
Wilson (4), Robert
Wise, Andrew
Wyatt, Thomas
Yong, Bartholomew

## THEATRICAL AND LITERARY TERMS

Academic Drama
Apocrypha
Argument
Authorship controversy
Bad Quarto
Blank Verse

Canon
Censorship
Chorus (1)
Comedy
Comedy of Humors
Comedia dell' Arte

Complaint
Droll
Dumb Show
Elizabethan Drama
Elizabethan Theatre
Epilogue

Epitaph
Fair copy
Farce
Film
Folio
Foul Papers

## THEATRICAL AND LITERARY TERMS

Ghost Character
Good Quarto
History Plays
Induction
Interlude
Jacobean Drama
Machiavel
Masque
Master of Revels
Metre

Miles Gloriosus
Morality play
Parnassus plays
Pastoral
Poetomachia (see War of the
   Theatres)
Problem plays
Prologue (1)
Prompt-book
Quarto

Revenge Play
Rhyme Royal
Roman Plays
Romances
Soliloquy
Song
Sonnet
Sub-plot
Television

Tetralogy
Tragedy
Tragicomedy
University Wits
Variorum edition
Verse test
Vice, the
War of the Theatres
Worthies, The Nine